The GALE ENCYCLOPEDIA *of* MENTAL HEALTH

THIRD EDITION

The GALE ENCYCLOPEDIA of MENTAL HEALTH

THIRD EDITION

VOLUME

A–L

KRISTIN KEY, EDITOR

GALE
CENGAGE Learning

Detroit • New York • San Francisco • New Haven, Conn • Waterville, Maine • London

Gale Encyclopedia of Mental Health, Third Edition

Project Editor: Kristin Key

Editorial: Tara Atterberry, Donna Batten, Jacqueline Longe, Kristin Mallegg, Brigham Narins, Joseph Palmisano, Bob Romaniuk, Alejandro Valtierra

Product Manager: Anne Marie Sumner

Editorial Support Services: Andrea Lopeman

Indexing Services: Laurie Andriot

Rights Acquisition and Management: Margaret Chamberlain-Gaston

Composition: Evi Abou-El-Seoud

Manufacturing: Wendy Blurton

Imaging: John Watkins

Product Design: Kristine Julien

LIBRARY OF CONGRESS CATALOGING-IN-PUBLICATION DATA

The Gale encyclopedia of mental health / Kristin Key, editor. -- 3rd ed.
p. cm.
Summary: "Alphabetically arranged encyclopedia (500 entries) that covers a wide variety of disorders, treatments, tests, and therapies, focused specifically on topics in mental health"– Provided by publisher.
Includes bibliographical references and index.
ISBN 978-1-4144-9012-0 (hardback) -- ISBN 978-1-4144-9013-7 (vol. 1) – ISBN 978-1-4144-9014-4 (vol. 2)
1. Psychiatry–Encyclopedias. 2. Mental illness–Encyclopedias.
I. Key, Kristin. II. Title: Encyclopedia of mental health.
RC437.G36 2012
616.89003–dc23

2011049279

Gale
27500 Drake Rd.
Farmington Hills, MI, 48331-3535

ISBN-13: 978-1-4144-9012-0 (set) ISBN-10: 1-4144-9012-7 (set)
ISBN-13: 978-1-4144-9013-7 (vol. 1) ISBN-10: 1-4144-9013-5 (vol. 1)
ISBN-13: 978-1-4144-9014-4 (vol. 2) ISBN-10: 1-4144-9014-3 (vol. 2)

This title is also available as an e-book.
ISBN-13: 978-1-4144-9015-1 ISBN-10: 1-4144-9015-1
Contact your Gale, a part of Cengage Learning sales representative for ordering information.

Printed in China
1 2 3 4 5 6 7 16 15 14 13 12

CONTENTS

ALPHABETICAL LIST OF ENTRIES

D

E

F

G

H

Q

R

S

PLEASE READ—IMPORTANT INFORMATION

The *Gale Encyclopedia of Mental Health, Third Edition* is a health reference product designed to inform and educate readers about mental health, mental disorders, and psychiatry. Gale, Cengage Learning believes the product to be comprehensive, but not necessarily definitive. It is intended to supplement, not replace, consultation with a physician or other healthcare practitioner. While Gale, Cengage Learning has made substantial efforts to provide information that is accurate, comprehensive, and up-to-date, Gale, Cengage Learning makes no representations or warranties of any kind, including without limitation, warranties of merchantability or fitness for a particular purpose, nor does it guarantee the accuracy, comprehensiveness, or timeliness of the information contained in this product. Readers should be aware that the universe of medical knowledge is constantly growing and changing, and that differences of opinion exist among authorities. Readers are also advised to seek professional diagnosis and treatment for any medical condition, and to discuss information obtained from this book with their healthcare provider.

INTRODUCTION

The *Gale Encyclopedia of Mental Health* is a valuable source of information on mental health. The *Encyclopedia* provides in-depth coverage of specific disorders recognized by the American Psychiatric Association in its *Diagnostic and Statistical Manual of Mental Disorders* (*DSM*), as well as other mental health conditions, diagnostic procedures and techniques, therapies, psychiatric medications, alternative treatments, legal concerns, and related topics.

SCOPE

The *Gale Encyclopedia of Mental Health* includes 500 entries on disorders, drugs, tests, and treatments. The *Encyclopedia* minimizes medical jargon and uses language that any reader can understand while still providing thorough coverage, making this text useful to consumers and students alike.

Entries follow a standardized format that provides information at a glance. Categories include:

Disorders and conditions

- Definition
- Demographics
- Description
- Causes and symptoms
- Diagnosis
- Treatment
- Prognosis
- Prevention

Drugs and herbs

- Definition
- Purpose
- Description
- Recommended dosage
- Precautions
- Side effects
- Interactions

Tests and procedures

- Definition
- Purpose
- Description
- Preparation
- Aftercare
- Risks
- Results

Treatments and therapies

- Definition
- Purpose
- Demographics
- Description
- Preparation
- Aftercare
- Risks

Other areas of discussion include Origins, Benefits, Research and general acceptance, and Training and certification, when applicable.

INCLUSION CRITERIA

A preliminary list of mental disorders and related topics was compiled from a wide variety of sources, including professional medical guides and textbooks as well as consumer guides and encyclopedias. An advisory board of professionals from a variety of healthcare fields, including psychology, psychiatry, pharmacy, and social work, evaluated the topics and made suggestions for updates and inclusion. The final selections were determined by Gale editors in conjunction with the advisory board.

ABOUT THE CONTRIBUTORS

The essays in this *Encyclopedia* were written by experienced medical writers, including physicians, pharmacists, and psychologists. All essays were reviewed by advisors to ensure that they are appropriate, up-to-date, and accurate.

HOW TO USE THIS BOOK

The *Gale Encyclopedia of Mental Health* has been designed with ready reference in mind.

- Straight **alphabetical arrangement** of topics allows users to locate information quickly.
- **Bold-faced terms** within entries direct the reader to related articles.
- **Cross-references** placed throughout the *Encyclopedia* direct readers to primary entries from alternate names, drug brand names, and related topics.
- Lists of **key terms** are provided where appropriate to define unfamiliar terms or concepts. A **glossary** of key terms is also included at the back of Volume 2.
- New to this edition, **Questions to Ask Your Doctor** sidebars provide sample questions that patients can ask their physicians.
- **Biographies** of key people recognized for their important work in the field of mental health are profiled in entry sidebars.
- **Resources** at the end of every entry direct readers to additional sources of information on a topic.
- Valuable **contact information** for organizations and support groups is included with each entry and compiled in the back of Volume 2.
- A comprehensive **general index** guides readers to all topics mentioned in the text.

GRAPHICS

The *Gale Encyclopedia of Mental Health* contains 240 color photographs, illustrations, charts, and tables.

ADVISORY BOARD

Several experts in mental health have provided invaluable assistance in the formulation of this encyclopedia, from defining the scope of coverage to reviewing individual entries for accuracy and accessibility. We would like to express our sincere thanks and appreciation for all of their contributions.

Thomas E. Backer
President
Human Interaction Research Institute
Associate Clinical Professor of Medical Psychology
School of Medicine
University of California, Los Angeles
Los Angeles, CA

Debra Franko
Professor, Author
Department of Counseling and Applied Educational Psychology, Bouvé College of Health Sciences
Northeastern University
Boston, MA

Irene S. Levine, PhD
Professor, Author
New York University School of Medicine
New York, NY

Susan Mockus, PhD
Medical Writer and Editor
Pawtucket, RI

Chitra Venkatasubramanian, MD
Clinical Assistant Professor, Neurology and Neurological Sciences
Stanford University School of Medicine
Palo Alto, CA

James E. Waun, MD, MA, RPh
Adjunct Assistant Professor of Clinical Pharmacy
Ferris State University
Associate Clinical Professor
Michigan State University
Registered Pharmacist
East Lansing, MI

Eric Zehr
Vice President
Addiction & Behavioral Services
Proctor Hospital
Peoria, IL

CONTRIBUTORS

Margaret Alic, PhD
Science Writer
Eastsound, WA

William Atkins
Medical Writer
Pekin, IL

Maria Eve Basile, PhD
Medical Writer
Roselle, NJ

Rosalyn Carson-DeWitt, MD
Medical Writer
Durham, NC

Laura Jean Cataldo, RN, EdD
Medical Writer
Myersville, MD

L. Lee Culvert
Medical Writer
Alna, ME

Tish Davidson, AM
Medical Writer
Fremont, CA

L. Fleming Fallon Jr., MD, DrPH
Professor of Public Health
Bowling Green University
Bowling Green, OH

Paula Ford-Martin
Medical Writer
Warwick, RI

Rebecca J. Frey, PhD
Research and Administrative Associate
East Rock Institute
New Haven, CT

Sandra L. Friedrich, MA
Science Writer
Clinical Psychology
Chicago, IL

Gary Gilles, MA
Medical Writer
Wauconda, IL

Clare Hanrahan
Medical Writer
Asheville, NC

Kelly Karpa, RPh, PhD
Assistant Professor
Department of Pharmacology
Pennsylvania State University College of Medicine
Hershey, PA

Monique Laberge, PhD
Research Associate
Department of Biochemistry and Biophysics
McGill University
Montreal, Quebec, Canada

Judy Leaver, MA
Behavioral Health Writer and Consultant
Washington, DC

Brenda Wilmoth Lerner, RN
Medical Editor and Writer
Montrose, AL

Mark A. Mitchell, MD
Medical Writer
Seattle, WA

Teresa G. Odle
Medical Writer
Albuquerque, NM

Jack Raber, PharmD
Principal
Clinipharm Services
Seal Beach, CA

Joan Schonbeck, RN
Medical Writer
Massachusetts Department of Mental Health
Marlborough, MA

Genevieve Slomski, PhD
Medical Writer
New Britain, CT

Heidi Splete
Freelance Writer
Washington, DC

Deanna M. Swartout-Corbeil, RN
Medical Writer
Thompsons Station, TN

Samuel Uretsky, PharmD
Medical Writer
Wantagh, NY

Ken R. Wells
Freelance Writer
Laguna Hills, CA

Emily Willingham, PhD
Freelance Writer
Austin, TX

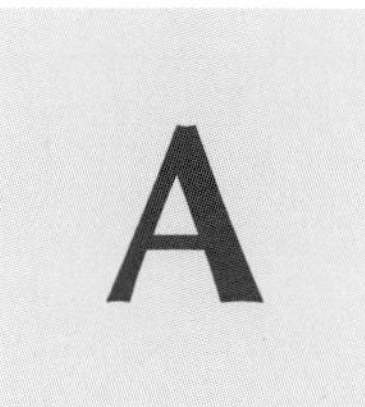

AACAP *see* **American Academy of Child & Adolescent Psychiatry**

Abnormal Involuntary Movement Scale

Definition

The Abnormal Involuntary Movement Scale (AIMS) is a rating scale that was designed in the 1970s to measure involuntary movements known as **tardive dyskinesia** (TD). TD is a disorder that sometimes develops as a side effect of long-term treatment with neuroleptic (antipsychotic) medications.

Purpose

Tardive dyskinesia, a syndrome characterized by abnormal involuntary movements of the patient's face, mouth, trunk, or limbs, affects 20% to 30% of patients who have been treated for months or years with neuroleptic medications. Patients who are older, are heavy smokers, or have diabetes mellitus are at higher risk of developing TD. The movements of the patient's limbs and trunk are sometimes described as choreathetoid, a dance-like movement that repeats itself but does not have any type of rhythm.

The AIMS is used not only to detect tardive dyskinesia but also to follow the severity of a patient's TD over time. It is a valuable tool for clinicians who are monitoring the effects of long-term treatment with neuroleptic medications and for researchers studying the effects of these drugs. The AIMS is given every three to six months to monitor the patient for the development of TD. For most patients, TD develops three months after the initiation of neuroleptic therapy; in elderly patients, however, TD can develop after as little as one month.

Description

The AIMS was designed by W. Guy in 1976 and modified by M. R. Munetz and S. Benjamin in 1988. The test is performed by trained clinicians and can be completed in about 10 minutes. The AIMS has a total of twelve items rating involuntary movements of various areas of the patient's body. These items are rated on a five-point scale of severity from 0–4. The scale is rated from lowest to highest: 0 (none), 1 (minimal), 2 (mild), 3 (moderate), and 4 (severe).

The twelve items within the AIMS are generally grouped by function or body part affected:

- four items assess facial and oral movements (muscles of facial expression, such as movement of forehead, eyebrows, and cheeks; lips and peroral [relating to the mouth] area, expressions such as pouting or puckering; jaws, such as chewing, biting, or lateral movements; and tongue, such as ability to sustain movement)
- three items assess extremity and trunk movements (upper extremity, such as wrists, finger, hands, and arms; lower extremity, such as toes, ankles, knees, and legs; and trunk, such as neck, shoulders, and hips)
- three items assess global judgments, such as severity of distress from abnormal movements, incapacitation due to abnormal movements, and patient's awareness of abnormal movements
- two items assess problems of the gums and teeth (or dentures)

The majority of items refer to the body movements themselves. The clinician or rater will ask the patient about their body movements and will also observe the patient to note firsthand any unusual movements. If the patient has noticed any unusual movements of the mouth, face, hands, or feet, the clinician will want to know if the movements annoy the patient or interfere with daily activities. The patient is then observed for any movements while sitting in a chair with feet flat on

Abnormal Involuntary Movement Scale (AIMS)

Code: 0 = None, 1 = Minimal, 2 = Mild, 3 = Moderate, 4 = Severe

Movement ratings:

Rate highest severity observed in category I, II, III.
Rate movements that occur upon activation one point less than those observed spontaneously.
Circle movements as well as code number that applies.

I. Facial & oral movements	**1. Muscles of Facial Expression:** Movements of forehead, eyebrows, periorbital area, cheeks, including frowning, blinking, smiling, grimacing	0 1 2 3 4
	2. Lips and Perioral Area: Puckering, pouting, smacking	0 1 2 3 4
	3. Jaw: Biting, clenching, chewing, mouth opening, lateral movement	0 1 2 3 4
	4. Tongue: Rate only increases in movement both in and out of mouth. NOT inability to sustain movement. Darting in and out of mouth	0 1 2 3 4
II. Extremity movements	**5. Upper (arms, wrists, hands, fingers):** Include choreic movements (rapid objectively purposeless, irregular, spontaneous), atheoid movements. DO NOT INCLUDE TREMOR (repetitive, regular, rhythmic)	0 1 2 3 4
	6. Lower (legs, knees, ankles, toes): Lateral knee movement, foot tapping, heel dropping, foot squirming, inversion and eversion of foot	0 1 2 3 4
III. Trunk movements	**7. Neck, shoulders, and hips:** Rocking, twisting, squirming, pelvic gyrations	0 1 2 3 4
IV. Global judgment	**8. Severity of abnormal movements overall**	0 1 2 3 4
	9. Incapacitation due to abnormal movements	0 1 2 3 4
	10. Patient's awareness of abnormal movements. Rate only patient's report: No awareness = 0 Aware, no distress = 1 Aware, mild distress = 2 Aware, moderate distress = 3 Aware, severe distress = 4	0 1 2 3 4
V. Dental status	**11. Current problems with teeth and/or dentures?**	YES NO
	12. Are dentures usually worn?	YES NO
	13. Endentia?	YES NO
	14. Do movements disappear with sleep?	YES NO

Scale is available in the public domain; a self-evaluation tool is also provided online by the Center for Quality Assessment and Improvement in Mental Health (CQAIMH) at http://www.cqaimh.org/tool_sideeffect.html. *(Table by PreMediaGlobal. © 2012 Cengage Learning.)*

the floor, knees separated slightly with the hands on the knees. The clinician will instruct the patient to perform specific movements—first to open his or her mouth and stick out the tongue twice, and then to tap his or her thumb with each finger very rapidly for 10 to 15 seconds, the right hand first and then the left hand. While the patient performs these actions, the clinician will observe the patient's face and legs for any abnormal movements.

After the face and hands have been tested, the patient will be asked to flex (bend) and extend one arm at a time, and then stand up so that the clinician can observe the entire body for movements. When standing, the patient will need to extend both arms in front of the body with the palms facing downward while the trunk, legs, and mouth are again observed for signs of TD. The patient must then walk a few paces, and his or her gait and hands will be observed by the clinician twice.

To assess dental care, the patient must be calm and sitting in a firm chair that does not have arms, and the patient cannot have anything in his or her mouth. The clinician will ask the patient about the condition of his or her teeth and dentures, or if he or she is having any pain or discomfort from dentures.

Preparation

Preparation for the AIMS is neither necessary nor recommended by healthcare professionals.

Aftercare

There is no patient aftercare required for the AIMS, but follow-up exams are required every three to six months to monitor the effects of long-term treatment with neuroleptic medications and/or assess the severity of and treat any signs of TD.

KEY TERMS

Choreathetoid movements—Repetitive dance-like movements that do not have any type of rhythm.

Clozapine—A newer antipsychotic medication that is often given to patients who are developing signs of tardive dyskinesia.

Neuroleptic—Another name for the older antipsychotic medications, such as haloperidol (Haldol) and chlorpromazine (Thorazine).

Syndrome—A group of symptoms that together characterize a disease or disorder.

Tardive dyskinesia—Abbreviated as TD, a condition that involves involuntary movements of the tongue, jaw, mouth, face, or other groups of skeletal muscles that usually occurs either late in antipsychotic therapy or even after the therapy is discontinued; it may be irreversible.

Results

The total AIMS score is not reported to the patient. A rating of 2 or higher on the AIMS is considered evidence of TD. If the patient has mild TD in two areas or moderate movements in one area, then he or she should be given a **diagnosis** of TD. The AIMS is extremely reliable when it is administered by trained and experienced professionals.

If the patient's score on the AIMS suggests the diagnosis of TD, the clinician must consider whether the patient still needs to be on an antipsychotic medication, as sometimes the benefits of the drug may outweigh the risks. This question should be discussed with the patient and his or her family. If the patent requires ongoing treatment with antipsychotic drugs, a lower dose may be administered to see if it relieves the TD symptoms while still performing its intended function. Another option is to place the patient on a different medication, such as **clozapine** (Clozaril) or another atypical antipsychotic. Atypical antipsychotics are a newer class of medications that produce fewer side effects than older antipsychotic drugs.

See also Medication-induced movement disorders; Schizophrenia

Resources

BOOKS

American Psychiatric Association. *Diagnostic and Statistical Manual of Mental Disorders*. 4th ed., text rev. Washington, DC: American Psychiatric Association, 2000.

Loretz, Lorraine. *Primary Care Tools for Clinicians: A Compendium of Forms, Questionnaires, and Rating Scales for Everyday Practice*. St. Louis: Elsevier Mosby, 2005.

Pavuluri, Mani N., and Philip G. Janicak. *Handbook of Psychopharmacotherapy: A Life Span Approach*. Philadelphia: Lippincott Williams & Wilkins, 2004.

Sadock, Benjamin J., Virginia A. Sadock, and Pedro Ruiz, editors. *Kaplan & Sadock's Comprehensive Textbook of Psychiatry*. Philadelphia: Wolters Kluwer Health/Lippincott Williams & Wilkins, 2009.

Smith, David S. *Field Guide to Bedside Diagnosis*. Philadelphia: Lippincott Williams & Wilkins, 2007.

Stern, Theodore A., and John B. Herman, editors. *Massachusetts General Hospital Psychiatry Update and Board Preparation*. New York City: McGraw-Hill, 2004.

OTHER

Center for Quality Assessment and Improvement in Mental Health. "STABLE [STAndards for BipoLar Excellence Project] Resource Toolkit, Side-effects Monitoring: Abnormal Involuntary Movement Scale." http://www.cqaimh.org/pdf/tool_aims.pdf (accessed October 13, 2011).

ORGANIZATIONS

National Alliance for Research on Schizophrenia and Depression, 60 Cutter Mill Road, Suite 404, Great Neck, NY, 11021, (516) 829-0091, Fax: (516) 487-6930, info@narsad.org, http://www.narsad.org.

National Institute of Mental Health, 6001 Executive Boulevard, Room 8184, Bethesda, MD, 20892-9663, (301) 443-4513, (866) 615-6464, Fax: (301) 443-4279, nimhinfo@nih.gov, http://www.nimh.nih.gov.

Susan Hobbs, M.D.
William Atkins

Abuse

Definition

Abuse refers to harmful or injurious treatment of another human being that may include physical, sexual, verbal, psychological/emotional, intellectual, or spiritual maltreatment. Abuse may coexist with **neglect**, which is defined as failure to meet a dependent person's basic physical and medical needs, emotional deprivation, and/or desertion. Neglect is sometimes described as passive abuse.

Demographics

About 1.2 per 1,000 children suffer from **sexual abuse** yearly. Girls are more likely than boys to be abused sexually. According to a conservative estimate, 38% of

Percentage of stalking and harassment victimizations reported to the police, by victim gender

	Percentage of victims					
	All		Stalking		Harassment	
	Male	Female	Male	Female	Male	Female
Reported	20.6%	32.8%	36.8%	41.0%	6.8%	13.9%
Not reported	79.4%	67.2%	63.2%	59.0%	93.2%	86.1%
Number of victims	1,941,650	3,637,570	892,340	2,528,990	1,049,320	1,108,580

Note: Table excludes 4.5% of all male victims, 4.9% of all female victims, 0.1% of female stalking victims, 8% of male harassment victims, and 14.2% of female harassment victims due to missing data.

SOURCE: Baum, Katrina et al, *Stalking Victimization in the United States* (Washington, DC: Bureau of Justice Statistics, 2009).

(Table by PreMediaGlobal. © 2012 Cengage Learning.)

girls and 16% of boys are sexually abused before their eighteenth birthday. In 2009, there were an estimated 1,770 child deaths from abuse or neglect in the United States, indicating a rate of 2.34 children for every 100,000 in the population. Of the children who survive abuse, an estimated 20% have permanent physical injury. Younger children and children with birth defects, developmental delays, or chronic illnesses are at higher risk of being abused by parents or other caregivers.

Women are more likely than men to be the targets of abuse in adult life, and one in four women will experience domestic violence in her lifetime. It is estimated that four million women in the United States are involved in abusive marriages or relationships; moreover, about 33% of female murder victims are killed by their spouses or partners rather than by strangers.

About 3.4 million people suffer from a stalking incident yearly, and about 80% of stalking cases reported to police involve men stalking women. Half of all workplace bullies are women, and the majority of workplace bullies (81%) are bosses or supervisors. Research has demonstrated that female bullies tend to bully other women, while male bullies bully both men and women.

The costs of abuse to society run into billions of dollars annually in the United States alone. They include not only the direct costs of immediate medical and psychiatric treatment of abused people but also the indirect costs of learning difficulties, interrupted education, workplace absenteeism, and long-term health problems of abuse survivors.

Description

Abuse is a complex psychosocial problem that affects large numbers of people throughout the world. Although abuse was initially defined with regard to children when it first received sustained attention in the 1950s, clinicians and researchers now recognize that adults can suffer abuse under a number of different circumstances.

Physical abuse

Physical abuse refers to striking or beating another person with the hands or an object or assaulting a person with a knife, gun, or other weapon. Physical abuse also includes such behaviors as locking someone in a closet or other small space, gagging or tying someone up, or depriving someone of sleep. Physical abuse of infants or children may include shaking them, dropping them on the floor, or throwing them against the wall or other hard object.

Sexual abuse

Sexual abuse refers to inappropriate sexual contact between a child or adult and another person. Sexual abuse may include verbal remarks, fondling or kissing, or attempted or completed intercourse. Sexual contact between a child and a biological relative is known as incest, although some therapists extend the term to cover sexual contact between a child and any trusted caregiver, including relatives by marriage.

Verbal abuse

Verbal abuse refers to regular and consistent belittling, name-calling, labeling, or ridicule of a person. It may also include spoken threats. It is one of the most difficult forms of abuse to prove because it does not leave physical scars or other evidence, but it is nonetheless hurtful. Verbal abuse may occur in schools or workplaces as well as in homes among family members.

Emotional/psychological abuse

Emotional/psychological abuse covers a variety of behaviors that hurt or injure others even though no physical contact may be involved. In fact, emotional abuse is a stronger predictor than physical abuse of the likelihood of **suicide** attempts in later life. One form of emotional abuse is emotional blackmail, which involves making another person feel guilty until he or she does what is wanted. Other behaviors in this category include giving the silent treatment, shaming or humiliating someone, or committing an act intended to cause a person emotional pain, such as destroying a valued possession.

Intellectual/spiritual abuse

Intellectual/spiritual abuse refers to such behaviors as punishing people for having different intellectual interests or religious beliefs, preventing them from attending worship services, ridiculing their opinions, and the like.

Domestic violence

Domestic violence refers to the physical, emotional, and sexual abuse of a spouse or domestic partner. Early research into the problem of wife battering focused on middle-class couples, but it has since been recognized that spousal abuse can occur within couples of any socioeconomic status or sexual orientation.

Domestic violence illustrates the tendency of abusive people to attack anyone they perceive as vulnerable: Most men who batter women also abuse their children; some battered women abuse their children; and abusive humans are frequently cruel to animals.

Elder abuse

Elder abuse has become a subject of national concern in the last two decades. As older adults live longer, many become dependent for years on adult caregivers, who may be either their own adult children or nursing home personnel. Care of the elderly can be extremely stressful, especially if the older adult has **dementia**. Elder abuse may include physical hitting or slapping; withholding food or medications; tying individuals to a chair or bed; neglecting to bathe them or help them to the toilet; taking their personal possessions, including money or property; and restricting or cutting off their contacts with friends and relatives.

Stalking

Stalking, or the repeated pursuit or surveillance of another person by physical or electronic means, is defined as a crime in all 50 states. Many cases of stalking are extensions of domestic violence, in that the stalker attempts to track down a partner who left him or her. However, stalkers may also be casual acquaintances, workplace colleagues, or even total strangers. Stalking may include a number of abusive behaviors, including forced entry into a person's home; destruction of cars or other personal property; anonymous letters to a person's friends or employer; or repeated phone calls, letters, or e-mails.

Workplace bullying

Workplace **bullying** is, like stalking, increasingly recognized as interpersonal abuse. It should not be confused with sexual harassment or racial discrimination. Workplace bullying refers to verbal abuse of other workers; interfering with their work; withholding equipment or other resources needed to do their job; or invading their personal space, including touching them in a controlling manner.

Causes and symptoms

Causes

The causes of interpersonal abuse are complex and overlapping. Some of the most important factors are:

- Early learning experiences: This factor is sometimes described as the "life cycle" of abuse. Many abusive parents were themselves abused as children and have learned to see hurtful behavior as normal childrearing. At the other end of the life cycle, some adults who abuse their elderly parent are paying back the parent for abusing them in their early years.
- Ignorance of developmental timetables: Some parents have unrealistic expectations of children in terms of the appropriate age for toilet training, feeding themselves, and similar milestones; they may attack their children for not meeting these expectations.
- Economic stress: Many caregivers cannot afford part-time day care for children or dependent elderly parents, which would relieve some of their emotional strain. Even middle-class families can be financially stressed if they find themselves responsible for the costs of caring for elderly parents before their own children are financially independent.
- Lack of social support or social resources: Caregivers who have the support of an extended family, religious group, or close friends and neighbors are less likely to lose their self-control under stress.
- Substance abuse: Alcohol and mood-altering drugs do not cause abuse directly, but they weaken or remove a person's inhibitions against violence toward others. In addition, the cost of a drug habit often gives a person with a substance addiction another reason for resenting the needs of the dependent person. A majority of workplace bullies are substance addicts.
- Mental disorders: Depression, personality disorders, dissociative disorders, and anxiety disorders can all

affect parents' ability to care for their children appropriately. A small percentage of abusive parents or spouses are psychotic.

- Belief systems: Many men still think that they have a "right" to a relationship with a woman, and many people regard parents' rights over children as absolute.
- The role of bystanders: Research in the social sciences has shown that one factor that encourages abusers to continue their hurtful behavior is discovering that people who know about or suspect the abuse are reluctant to get involved. In most cases, bystanders are afraid of possible physical, social, or legal consequences for reporting abuse. The result, however, is that many abusers come to see themselves as invulnerable.

Symptoms

PHYSICAL AND NEUROBIOLOGICAL. In addition to such direct results of **trauma** as broken bones or ruptured internal organs, physically abused children often display retarded physical growth and poor coordination. Malnutrition may slow the development of the **brain** as well as produce such dietary deficiency diseases as rickets. In both children and adults, repeated trauma produces changes in the neurochemistry of the brain that affect memory formation. Instead of memories being formed in the normal way, which allows them to be modified by later experiences and integrated into a person's ongoing life, traumatic memories are stored as chaotic fragments of emotion and sensation that are sealed off from ordinary consciousness. These traumatic memories may then erupt from time to time in the form of flashbacks. Additionally, research has shown that adults who were abused during childhood have a greater likelihood of suffering from a number of health conditions throughout their lives, including allergies, asthma, bronchitis, arthritis, ulcers, and high blood pressure.

People who have suffered abuse also demonstrate a higher risk of developing psychiatric conditions, such as **depression**, anxiety, **substance abuse**, **personality disorders**, and suicidality.

COGNITIVE AND EMOTIONAL. Abused children develop distorted patterns of cognition (knowing) due to the emotional stress of abuse. As children, their language skills and academic performance lag behind those of other children, and they often display behavioral problems in the classroom setting. As adults, they may experience cognitive distortions that make it hard for them to distinguish between normal occurrences and abnormal ones or between important matters and relatively trivial ones. They often misinterpret other people's behavior and refuse to trust them. Both children and adults with abuse histories demonstrate low self-esteem and an inability to attach or bond with others. Emotional distortions include such patterns as being unable to handle strong feelings or being unusually tolerant of behavior from others that most people would protest.

SOCIAL AND EDUCATIONAL. The cognitive and emotional aftereffects of abuse have a powerful impact on adult educational, social, and occupational functioning. Children who are abused are often in physical and emotional pain at school; they cannot concentrate on schoolwork and consequently fall behind in their grades. They often find it hard to make or keep friends, and may be victimized by bullies or become bullies themselves. In adult life, abuse survivors are at risk of repeating childhood patterns through forming relationships with abusive spouses, employers, or professionals. Even though survivors may consciously want to avoid further abuse, they are often unconsciously attracted to people who remind them of their family of origin. Abused adults are also likely to fail to complete their educations, or they accept employment that is significantly below their actual level of ability. Adults who have previously suffered abuse also have a higher risk of displaying antisocial traits.

There are higher rates of teen pregnancy, juvenile delinquency, substance abuse, adult criminal behavior, and risk taking (with increased risks of sexually transmitted diseases) among people who have been abused. Ironically and tragically, abused children often grow up to be abusive parents, perpetuating the cycle of abuse.

Treatment

Treatment of the aftereffects of abuse must be tailored to the needs of the specific individual but usually involves a variety of long-term considerations that may include legal concerns, geographical relocation, and housing or employment as well as immediate medical or psychiatric care.

Medical and psychiatric

In addition to requiring immediate treatment for physical injuries, abused children and adults often need long-term **psychotherapy** in order to recover from specific mental disorders and to learn new ways of dealing with distorted thoughts and feelings. This approach to therapy is known as cognitive restructuring. Specific mental disorders that have been linked to childhood abuse include major depression, **bulimia nervosa**, **social phobia**, Munchausen syndrome by proxy, **generalized anxiety disorder**, **post-traumatic**

KEY TERMS

Cognitive restructuring—An approach to psychotherapy that focuses on helping patients examine distorted patterns of perceiving and thinking in order to change their emotional responses to people and situations.

Dementia—A group of symptoms (syndrome) associated with a progressive loss of memory and other intellectual functions that is serious enough to interfere with a person's ability to perform the tasks of daily life. Dementia impairs memory, alters personality, leads to deterioration in personal grooming, impairs reasoning ability, and causes disorientation.

Flashback—The reemergence of a traumatic memory as a vivid recollection of sounds, images, and sensations associated with the trauma. Those having the flashbacks typically feel as if they are reliving the event.

Incest—Unlawful sexual contact between people who are biologically related. Many therapists also use the term to refer to inappropriate sexual contact between members of a family, including stepparents and stepsiblings.

Stalking—The intentional pursuit or surveillance of another person, usually with the intent of forcing that person into a dating or marriage relationship. Stalking is punishable as a crime in all 50 states.

stress disorder, **borderline personality disorder**, **dissociative amnesia**, and **dissociative identity disorder**. Abused adults may develop post-traumatic **stress** disorder, major depression, or substance abuse disorders. Research is also focused on **genetic factors** as a partial explanation of the fact that some people appear to react more intensely than others to being abused.

In cases where abuse has reached levels that result in post-traumatic stress disorder (PTSD), medications may be useful for treating the accompanying anxiety, emotional outbursts, difficulty sleeping, and nightmares. Medications that have been used in this setting include antipsychotics, **antidepressants**, anxiolytics, and the blood pressure medication called prazosin, which has shown some utility in preventing **insomnia** and nightmares.

Legal considerations

Medical professionals and, increasingly, religious professionals are required by law to report **child abuse** to law enforcement officials, usually a child protection agency. Physicians are granted immunity from lawsuits for making such reports.

Adults in abusive situations may encounter a variety of responses from law enforcement or the criminal justice system. Many communities require police officers to arrest aggressors in domestic violence situations, and a growing number of small towns as well as cities have shelters for family members fleeing violent households. All major medical, educational, and legal professional societies, as well as mainstream religious bodies, have adopted strict codes of ethics and have procedures in place for reporting cases of abuse by their members.

Prevention

Prevention of abuse requires long-term social changes in attitudes toward violence, gender roles, and the relationship of the family to other institutions. Research in the structure and function of the brain may help to develop more effective treatments for the aftereffects of abuse and possibly new approaches to help break the intergenerational cycle of abuse. As of 2011, preventive measures included protective removal of children or elders from abusive households, legal penalties for abusive spouses and professionals, and education of the public about the nature and causes of abuse.

Resources

BOOKS

American Psychiatric Association. *Diagnostic and Statistical Manual of Mental Disorders.* 4th ed., Text rev. Washington, DC: American Psychiatric Association, 2000.

Bradley, W., et al. *Neurology in Clinical Practice.* 5th ed. Philadelphia: Butterworth-Heinemann, 2008.

Stern, Theodore A., et al. *Massachusetts General Hospital Comprehensive Clinical Psychiatry.* 1st ed. Philadelphia: Mosby Elsevier, 2008.

Weiner, William J., et al. *Neurology for the Non-Neurologist (Weiner, Neurology for the Non-Neurologist).* 6th ed. Baltimore: Lippincott Williams & Wilkins, 2010.

PERIODICALS

Asnes, A.G. "Managing Child Abuse: General Principles." *Pediatric Review* 31 (February 1, 2010): 47–55.

Falk, E. "Geriatricians and Psychologists: Essential Ingredients in the Evaluation of Elder Abuse and Neglect." *Journal of Elder Abuse and Neglect* 22 (July 10, 2010): 281–90.

Shipman, K. "Mental Health Treatment of Child Abuse and Neglect: The Promise of Evidence-based Practice." *Pediatric Clinics of North America* 56 (April 1, 2009): 417–28.

WEBSITES

Child Welfare Information Gateway. "Child Abuse and Neglect Fatalities: Statistics and Interventions." Last modified February 2011. http://www.childwelfare.gov/pubs/factsheets/fatality.pdf (accessed September 16, 2011).

"Domestic Violence." MedlinePlus. Last modified September 8, 2011. http://www.nlm.nih.gov/medlineplus/domestic-violence.html (accessed September 16, 2011).

U.S. Department of Health and Human Services, Administration on Children, Youth and Families. *Child Maltreatment 2004*. http://www.acf.hhs.gov/programs/cb/pubs/cm04/cm04.pdf (accessed September 16, 2011).

ORGANIZATIONS

American Academy of Child and Adolescent Psychiatry, 3615 Wisconsin Ave. NW, Washington, DC, 20016-3007, (202) 966-7300, Fax: (202) 966-2891, http://www.aacap.org.

Kempe Foundation, Gary Pavilion at Children's Hospital Colorado, Anschutz Medical Campus, 13123 E 16th Ave., B390, Denver, CO, 80045, (303) 864-5300, http://www.kempe.org.

National Coalition Against Domestic Violence, 1120 Lincoln St., Ste. 1603, Denver, CO, 80203, (303) 839-1852; TTY: (303) 839-1681, Fax: (303) 831-9251, http://www.ncadv.org.

National Institute of Mental Health, 6001 Executive Blvd., Rm. 8184, MSC 9663, Bethesda, MD, 20892-9663, (301) 433-4513; TTY: (301) 443-8431, Fax: (301) 443-4279, Toll-free: (866) 615-6464; TTY: (866) 415-8051, nimhinfo@nih.gov, http://www.nimh.nih.gov.

Rebecca Frey, PhD
Emily Jane Willingham, PhD
Rosalyn Carson-DeWitt

Acne excoriee *see* **Dermatillomania**

Acupressure

Definition

Acupressure is a form of touch therapy that uses the principles of **acupuncture** and traditional Chinese medicine (TCM). In acupressure, the same points on the body are used as in acupuncture, but they are stimulated with finger pressure instead of with the insertion of needles. Acupressure is used to relieve a variety of symptoms and pain.

Demographics

As of 2011, the cost of acupressure massage was, on average, \$60–\$70 per hour session. A visit to a Chinese medicine physician or acupuncturist can be more expensive, comparable to a visit to an allopathic physician if the practitioner is a certified medical doctor (MD). Insurance reimbursement varies widely, and consumers should inquire as to whether their policies cover alternative treatment, acupuncture, or massage therapy.

Purpose

In Chinese medicine, disease is viewed as an imbalance of the organs and chi in the body. The goal of acupressure, and also acupuncture, is to stimulate and unblock the circulation of chi by activating very specific points, called pressure points or *acupoints*.

Acupressure is used by Chinese medicine practitioners, acupuncturists, and massage therapists. Many massage schools in the United States include acupressure techniques as part of their bodywork programs. Shiatsu massage is very closely related to acupressure, involving the same points on the body and the same general principles, although it was developed over centuries in Japan rather than in China. Reflexology is a form of bodywork based on acupressure concepts. Jin Shin Do is a bodywork technique with an increasing number of practitioners in the United States that combines acupressure and shiatsu principles with qigong, Reichian theory, and **meditation**.

Description

Origins

Acupressure and related therapies (e.g., acupuncture, shiatsu massage) have their roots in Chinese medicine. One legend has it that acupuncture and acupressure evolved as early Chinese healers studied the puncture wounds of Chinese warriors, noting that certain points on the body created interesting results when stimulated. The oldest known text specifically on acupuncture points, the *Systematic Classic of Acupuncture*, dates to about 282 A.D.

Outside of Asian American communities, Chinese medicine remained virtually unknown in the United States until the 1970s, when Richard Nixon became the first U.S. president to visit China. On Nixon's trip, journalists were amazed to observe major operations being performed on patients without the use of anesthetics. Instead, fully conscious patients were being operated on with acupuncture needles inserted into them to control pain. At that time, a famous columnist for the *New York Times*, James Reston, had to undergo surgery and elected to use acupuncture for anesthesia. Later, he wrote some convincing stories on its effectiveness. Despite being neglected by mainstream medicine and the American Medical Association (AMA), acupuncture and Chinese medicine became an option for alternative medicine practitioners in the United States. In the early 2010s, millions of patients can attest to its effectiveness, and there are nearly 9,000 practitioners dispersed across all 50 states.

Acupressure and Chinese medicine

Chinese medicine views the body as a small part of the universe, subject to the laws and principles of

KEY TERMS

Acupoint—A pressure point stimulated in acupressure.

Chi—Basic life energy.

Meridian—A channel through which chi travels in the body.

Moxibustion—An acupuncture technique that involves burning of the herb moxa or mugwort.

Shiatsu—Japanese form of acupressure massage.

Yin/yang—Universal characteristics used to describe aspects of the natural world.

harmony and balance. Chinese medicine does not make as sharp a distinction as Western medicine does between mind and body. The Chinese system asserts that emotions and mental states are every bit as influential on disease as purely physical mechanisms, meaning that factors such as work, environment, and relationships affect a person's health. Chinese medicine also uses very different symbols and ideas to discuss the body and health. While Western medicine typically describes health as mainly physical and chemical processes, the Chinese use ideas of yin and yang, chi, and the organ system to describe health and the body.

YIN AND YANG. Everything in the universe has properties of yin and yang. Yin is associated with such attributes as cold, female, passive, downward, inward, dark, and wet. Yang is the opposite—hot, male, active, upward, outward, light, dry, and so on. Nothing is either completely yin or yang. These two principles always interact and affect each other. A healthy body possesses an equal balance of both yin and yang; disease occurs when there is too much or too little of either.

CHI. Chi (pronounced *chee*, also spelled *qi* or *ki* in Japanese shiatsu) is the fundamental life energy. It is found in food, air, water, and sunlight, and it travels through the body in channels called *meridians*. There are 12 major meridians in the body that transport chi, corresponding to the 12 main organs categorized by Chinese medicine.

ORGAN SYSTEM. Chinese medicine has developed intricate systems regarding how organs are related to physical and mental symptoms, and it has devised corresponding treatments using meridian and pressure point networks that are classified and numbered. Acupressure seeks to stimulate the points on the chi meridians that pass close to the skin, as these are the easiest to unblock and manipulate with finger pressure.

Physical examination

To get a complete **diagnosis** of which organs and meridian points are out of balance, a Chinese medicine practitioner will examine a patient very thoroughly, looking at physical, mental, and emotional activity; taking the pulse, usually at the wrists; examining the tongue and complexion; and observing the patient's demeanor and attitude. When the imbalance is located, the physician recommends specific pressure points for acupuncture or acupressure. If acupressure is recommended, the patient might opt for a series of treatments from a massage therapist.

Massage therapy

In massage therapy, acupressurists evaluate a patient's symptoms and overall health, but a massage therapist's diagnostic training is not as extensive as that of a TCM physician. In a massage therapy treatment, a person usually lies on a table or mat with thin clothing on. The acupressurist gently feels and palpates the abdomen and other parts of the body to determine energy imbalances. Then, the therapist works with different meridians throughout the body, depending on which organs are imbalanced in the abdomen. The therapist uses different types of finger movements and pressure on different acupoints, depending on whether the chi needs to be increased or dispersed at different points. The therapist observes and guides the energy flow through the patient's body throughout the session. Sometimes, special herbs (*Artemesia vulgaris* or moxa) may be placed on a point to warm it, a process called *moxibustion.* A session of acupressure is generally a very pleasant experience, and some people experience great benefit immediately. For more chronic conditions, several sessions may be necessary to relieve and improve conditions.

Self-treatment

Acupressure is easy to learn, and there are many good books that illustrate the position of acupoints and meridians on the body. The procedure can also be conducted anywhere, and it is a good form of treatment for spouses and partners to give to each other and for parents to perform on children for minor conditions. As effective as acupressure may be, it should not be used to the exclusion of allopathic methods that provide more reliable relief or cure for certain diseases and disorders.

While giving self-treatment or performing acupressure on another, a mental attitude of calmness and attention is important, as one person's energy can be used to help another's. Loose, thin clothing is recommended.

There are three general techniques for stimulating a pressure point:

- Tonifying is meant to strengthen weak chi and is done by pressing the thumb or finger into an acupoint with a firm, steady pressure, holding it for up to two minutes.
- Dispersing is meant to move stagnant or blocked chi, and the finger or thumb is moved in a circular motion or slightly in and out of the point for two minutes.
- Calming the chi in a pressure point utilizes the palm to cover the point and gently stroke the area for about two minutes.

There are many pressure points that are easily found and memorized to treat common ailments.

- For headaches and pain in the upper body, the "LI4" point is recommended. It is located in the web between the thumb and index finger, on the back of the hand. Using the thumb and index finger of the other hand, a person applies a pinching pressure until the point is felt and holds it for two minutes. Pregnant women should never press this point.
- To calm the nerves, a person finds the "CV12" point that is four thumb widths above the navel in the center of the abdomen. Calm the point with the palm, using gentle stroking for several minutes.
- For headaches and tension, a person locates the "GB20" points at the base of the skull in the back of the head, just behind the bones in back of the ears and then disperses these points for two minutes with the fingers or thumbs. The individual can also find the "yintang" point, which is in the middle of the forehead between the eyebrows and disperse it with gentle pressure for two minutes to clear the mind and to relieve headaches.

Benefits

Acupressure massage performed by a therapist can be very effective both as prevention and as a treatment for many health conditions. Unlike acupuncture, which requires a visit to a professional, acupressure can be performed by anyone. Acupressure techniques are fairly easy to learn and have been used to provide quick, cost-free, and effective relief from many symptoms. Acupressure points can also be stimulated to increase energy and feelings of well-being, reduce **stress**, stimulate the immune system, and alleviate sexual dysfunction.

Precautions

Acupressure is a safe technique, but it is not meant to replace professional health care. A physician should always be consulted when there are doubts about medical conditions. If a condition is chronic, a professional should be consulted; purely symptomatic treatment can exacerbate chronic conditions. Acupressure should not be applied to open wounds or to places that are swollen or inflamed. Areas of scar tissue, blisters, boils, rashes, or varicose veins should be avoided. Finally, certain acupressure points should not be stimulated on people with high or low blood pressure or on pregnant women.

QUESTIONS TO ASK YOUR DOCTOR

- What kind of results can I expect to feel with acupressure?
- What other type of treatment do you recommend for me?
- Will acupressure therapy interfere with my current medications?
- What symptoms or behaviors are important enough that I should seek immediate treatment?

Research and general acceptance

In general, Chinese medicine has been slow to gain acceptance in the West, mainly because it rests on ideas that differ from the Western scientific model. Western scientists have trouble with the idea of chi, the invisible energy of the body, and the idea that pressing on certain points can alleviate certain conditions seems incredible.

In trying to account for the action of acupressure, Western scientists have theorized that chi is actually part of the neuroendocrine system of the body. Celebrated orthopedic surgeon Robert O. Becker, who was twice nominated for the Nobel Prize, wrote a book on the subject called *Cross Currents: The Promise of Electromedicine; The Perils of Electropollution*. By using precise electrical measuring devices, Becker and his colleagues showed that the body has a complex web of electromagnetic energy and that traditional acupressure meridians and points contain amounts of energy that non-acupressure points do not.

The mechanisms of acupuncture and acupressure remain difficult to document in terms of the biochemical processes involved. Numerous testimonials are the primary evidence supporting the effectiveness of acupressure and acupuncture. Research and **clinical trials** continue to study the effectiveness of acupressure and acupuncture techniques in treating various health problems and in controlling pain.

Training and certification

There are two methods for becoming trained in the skill of acupressure. The first is training in traditional acupuncture and Chinese medicine, for which there are many schools and certifying bodies around the United States. The majority of acupressure practitioners are trained as certified massage therapists, either as acupressure or shiatsu specialists.

Resources

BOOKS

Kolster, Bernard C., and Astrid Waskowiak. *The Acupressure Atlas*. Rochester, VT: Healing Arts Press, 2007.

Vora, Devendra. *Health in Your Hands: Acupressure and Other Natural Therapies, Vol. 2*. Mumbai, India: Navneet, 2007.

Wright, Janet. *Reflexology and Acupressure*. London: Hamlyn Press, 2008.

PERIODICALS

Agarwal, A., et al. "Acupressure for Prevention of Pre-operative Anxiety: A Prospective, Randomised, Placebo Controlled Study." *Anaesthesia* (October 2005): 978–981.

Jamigorn, Mattawan, and Vorapong Phupong. "Acupressure and Vitamin B6 to Relieve Nausea and Vomiting in Pregnancy: A Randomized Study." *Archives of Gynecology and Obstetrics* (September 2007): 245–249.

"Non-Epidural Pain Relief." *The Informed Choice Initiative (Women's Edition)* (April 2007): 91–98.

OTHER

Wisconsin Department of Health Services. "Responding to Challenging Situations: Acupressure Points for Stress Relief." http://www.dhs.wisconsin.gov/caregiver/training/pdfcaregvtrng/respAcupressure.pdf (accessed November 14, 2011).

ORGANIZATIONS

Acupressure Institute, 1533 Shattuck Ave., Berkeley, CA, 94709, (800) 442-2232, http://www.acupressureinstitute.com.

American Massage Therapy Association, 500 Davis Street, Suite 900, Evanston, IL, 60201-4695, (847) 864-0123, (877) 905-0577, Fax: (847) 864-5196, info@amtamassage.org, http://www.amtamassage.org.

American Organization for Bodywork Therapies of Asia, 1010 Haddonfield-Berlin Rd., Suite 408, Voorhees, NJ, 08043-3514, (856) 782-1616, Fax: (856) 782-1653, office@aobta.org, http://www.aobta.org.

Jin Shin Do Foundation for Bodymind Acupressure, PO Box 416, Idyllwild, CA, 92549, (951) 659-5707, http://www.jinshindo.org.

Douglas Dupler
Laura Jean Cataldo, RN, Ed.D.

Acupuncture

Definition

Acupuncture, one of the main forms of treatment in traditional Chinese medicine (TCM), involves the use of sharp, thin needles that are inserted in the skin of the body at specific points where the flow of energy is thought to be blocked. This process is believed to adjust and alter the body's energy flow into healthier patterns and is used to treat a wide variety of illnesses and health conditions. As one of the many benefits thought to accrue from its use, acupuncture is believed by many people to help relieve symptoms of mental illness. The early development of acupuncture is also deep within the medical history of Japan, Korea, Vietnam, Taiwan, and other eastern Asian regions. Today, acupuncture remains a controversial subject regarding its therapeutic effectiveness in the field of Western medicine.

Purpose

In Chinese medicine, where acupuncture seems to have originated, disease is seen as imbalance in the organ system or chi meridians, and the goal of any remedy or treatment is to assist the body in re-establishing its innate harmony. Disease can be caused by internal factors such as emotions, external factors such as the environment and weather, and other factors such as injuries, **trauma**, diet, and germs. However, infection is seen not as primarily a problem with germs and viruses but as a weakness in the energy of the body that is allowing a sickness to occur. In Chinese medicine, no two illnesses are ever the same, as each body has its own characteristics of symptoms and balance. Acupuncture is used to open or adjust the flow of chi throughout the organ system, which will strengthen the body and prompt it to physically or mentally heal itself.

Mental illnesses, or mental health disorders, are psychiatric disorders that cause atypical behaviors that alter one's feelings, moods, or thinking. Types of mental illness include **bipolar disorder**, **depression**, **obsessive-compulsive disorder**, **panic disorder**, and **schizophrenia**. Acupuncturists claim that they can use the process of acupuncture to treat the causes of such mental problems by rebalancing the internal workings of the body. Acupuncture has been widely used in the world for many centuries—dating back to the first few centuries *B.C.*—but its effectiveness for anything other than the relief of pain and nausea has not yet been established within the medical community of the United States.

Demographics

Since mental disorders affect many people without regard to age, ethnic background, religion, or income,

A recovering drug addict undergoes acupuncture treatment for withdrawal symptoms. *(© David Hoffman Photo Library/Alamy)*

they are a widespread problem in the United States and throughout the world. Consequently, acupuncture has become known as a method for treating such illnesses. The National Institutes of Health conducted a 2007 National Health Interview Survey that found about 3.1 million American adults and 150,000 children had used acupuncture in 2006. It also stated that over a six-year period, from 2002 through 2007, the frequency of acupuncture use among adults increased by about 0.3%, or approximately one million people.

As of 2011, more than 9,000 practitioners performed acupuncture within all 50 states of the United States and the District of Columbia. About 4,000 medical doctors (MDs) include it in their professional practices. Acupuncture has shown notable success in treating many conditions, and more than 15 million Americans have used it as a therapy. Acupuncture, however, remains largely unsupported by the medical establishment. The American Medical Association has been reluctant to encourage research, as the practice is based on concepts markedly unlike the Western scientific model.

Several forms of acupuncture are used in the United States. Japanese acupuncture uses extremely thin needles and does not incorporate herbal medicine in its practice. Auricular acupuncture, also called "auriculotherapy and ear acupuncture," uses acupuncture points only on the ear, which are believed to stimulate and balance internal organs. In France, where acupuncture is very popular and more widely accepted by the medical establishment, neurologist Paul Nogier (1908–1996) developed a system of acupuncture based on neuroendocrine theory rather than on traditional Chinese concepts, which has gained some use in the United States.

Description

Origins

The original text of Chinese medicine is the *Nei Ching, The Yellow Emperor's Classic of Internal Medicine*, which is estimated to be at least 2,500 years old. Thousands of books followed on the subject of Chinese healing, and its basic philosophies spread long ago to other Asian civilizations. Nearly all of the forms of Oriental medicine that are used in the West, including acupuncture, shiatsu, **acupressure** massage, and macrobiotics, are part of or have their roots in Chinese medicine. Legend has it that acupuncture developed when early Chinese physicians observed unpredicted effects of puncture wounds in Chinese warriors. The oldest known text on acupuncture, the *Systematic Classic of Acupuncture*, dates back to A.D. 282. Although acupuncture is its best-known technique, Chinese medicine traditionally uses herbal remedies, dietary therapy, lifestyle changes, and other means to treat patients.

In the early 1900s, only a few Western physicians who had visited China knew about and used acupuncture. Outside of Asian American communities, it remained virtually unknown until the 1970s, when Richard Nixon (1913–1994) became the first U.S. president to visit China. On Nixon's trip, journalists were amazed to observe major operations being performed on patients without the use of anesthetics. Instead, fully conscious patients were being operated on with only acupuncture needles inserted into them to control pain. During that time, a famous columnist for the *New York Times*, James Reston (1909–1995), had to undergo surgery in Beijing, China, and elected to use acupuncture for his post-operative pain instead of traditional pain medication. Reston later wrote some convincing stories on its effectiveness.

KEY TERMS

Acupressure—A form of massage using acupuncture points.

Auricular acupuncture—Acupuncture using only points found on the ears.

Chi—Basic life energy.

Mania—A condition of abnormally high irritability, arousal, or energy levels.

Meridian—A channel through which chi travels in the body.

Moxibustion—Acupuncture technique that involves burning the herb moxa or mugwort.

Tonification—Acupuncture technique for strengthening the body.

Yin/yang—Universal characteristics used to describe aspects of the natural world.

Basic ideas of Chinese medicine

Chinese medicine views the body as a small part of the universe, subject to universal laws and principles of harmony and balance. Chinese medicine does not draw a sharp line, as Western medicine does, between mind and body. The Chinese system believes that emotions and mental states are every bit as influential on disease as purely physical mechanisms and considers factors such as work, environment, lifestyle, and relationships as fundamental to the overall picture of a patient's health. Chinese medicine also uses very different symbols and ideas to discuss the body and health. While Western medicine typically describes health in terms of measurable physical processes made up of chemical reactions, the Chinese use the ideas of yin and yang, chi, the organ system, and the five elements to describe health and the body. To understand the ideas behind acupuncture, it is worthwhile to introduce some of these basic terms.

YIN AND YANG. According to Chinese philosophy, the universe and the body can be described by two separate but complementary principles, that of yin and yang. For example, in temperature, yin is cold and yang is hot. In gender, yin is female and yang is male. In activity, yin is passive and yang is active. In light, yin is dark and yang is bright. In direction, yin is inward and downward, and yang is outward and up. Nothing is ever completely yin or yang, but a combination of the two. These two principles are always interacting, opposing, and influencing each other. The goal of Chinese medicine is not to eliminate either yin or yang but to allow the two to balance each other and co-exist harmoniously. For instance, if a person suffers from symptoms of high blood pressure, the Chinese system would say that the heart organ might have too much yang and would recommend methods either to reduce the yang or to increase the yin of the heart, depending on the other symptoms and organs in the body. Thus, acupuncture therapies seek to either increase or reduce yang or increase or reduce yin in particular regions of the body.

CHI. Another fundamental concept of Chinese medicine is that of chi (pronounced *chee*, also spelled *qi*). According to Chinese medicine, chi is the fundamental life energy of the universe. It is invisible and is found in the environment in air, water, food, and sunlight. In the body, it is the invisible vital force that creates and animates life. Humans are all born with inherited amounts of chi, and they also acquire chi from the food they eat and the air they breathe. The level and quality of a person's chi also depends on the state of physical, mental, and emotional balance. Chi travels through the body along channels called *meridians*.

THE ORGAN SYSTEM. In the Chinese system, there are twelve main organs: the lung, large intestine, stomach, spleen, heart, small intestine, urinary bladder, kidney, liver, gallbladder, pericardium, and "triple warmer," which represents the entire torso region. Each organ has chi energy associated with it, and each organ interacts with particular emotions on the mental level. As there are twelve organs, twelve types of chi can move through the body, and these move through twelve main channels or meridians. Chinese doctors connect symptoms to organs. That is, symptoms are caused by yin/yang imbalances in one or more organs or by an unhealthy flow of chi to or from one organ to another. Each organ has a different profile of symptoms it can manifest.

THE FIVE ELEMENTS. Another basis of Chinese medicine is the belief that the world and body are made up of five main elements: wood, fire, earth, metal, and water. These elements are all interconnected, and each element either generates or controls another element. For instance, water controls fire, and earth generates metal. Each organ is associated with one of the five elements. The Chinese system uses elements and organs to describe and treat conditions. For instance, the kidney is associated with water, and the heart is associated with fire. The two organs are related as water and fire are related. If the kidney is weak, then there might be a corresponding fire problem in the heart, so treatment might be made by acupuncture or herbs to cool the heart system and/or increase energy in the kidney system.

The Chinese have developed an intricate system that describes how organs and elements are related to physical and mental symptoms, and the above example is simple. Although this system sounds suspect to Western scientists, some interesting parallels have been observed. For instance, when mental illness occurs, Chinese medicine states that an imbalance has occurred within the body—either too much or too little yin and yang. It does not, however, treat mental illness as a particular disorder. Instead, acupuncturists treat the specific symptoms within each individual patient. Consequently, different patients, each with depression but with different symptoms, will receive a unique, customized treatment based on many different acupuncture points.

A visit to the acupuncturist

Typically, an acupuncturist first gets a thorough idea of a patient's medical history and symptoms, both physical and emotional, using a questionnaire and interview. Then the acupuncturist examines the patient to find further symptoms, looking closely at the tongue, the pulse at various points in the body, the complexion, general behavior, and other signs like coughs or pains. From this examination, the practitioner can determine patterns of symptoms that indicate which organs and areas are imbalanced. Depending on the problem, the acupuncturist inserts needles to manipulate chi on one or more of the twelve organ meridians. On these twelve meridians, there are nearly 2,000 points that can be used in acupuncture, with around 200 points being most frequently used by traditional acupuncturists. During an individual treatment, one to 20 needles may be used, depending on which meridian points are chosen.

Acupuncture needles are sterilized, and acupuncture is a very safe procedure. The depth of insertion of needles varies, depending on which chi channels are being treated. Some points barely go beyond superficial layers of skin, while some acupuncture points require a depth of 1–3 in. (3–8 cm) of needle. The needles generally do not cause pain. Patients sometimes report pinching sensations and often pleasant sensations, as the body experiences healing. Depending on the problem, the acupuncturist might spin or move the needles, or even pass a slight electrical current through some of them. *Moxibustion* may sometimes be used. Moxibustion is a process in which an herbal mixture (moxa or mugwort) is burned either like incense on the acupuncture point or on the end of the needle, a process believed to stimulate chi in a particular way. Acupuncturists also sometimes use *cupping*, during which small suction cups are placed on meridian points to stimulate them.

How long the needles are inserted also varies. Some patients require only a quick in-and-out insertion to clear problems and provide *tonification* (strengthening of health), while some other conditions might require needles to remain inserted up to an hour or more. The average visit to an acupuncturist takes about 30 minutes. The number of visits to the acupuncturist varies, with some conditions improving in one or two sessions, and others requiring a series of six or more visits over the course of weeks or months.

Costs for acupuncture vary, depending on whether the practitioner is a medical physician. Initial visits with non-MD acupuncturists can run from $50–$100, with follow-up visits usually costing less. Insurance reimbursement varies widely, depending on the company and state. Regulations tend to change frequently. Some states authorize Medicaid to cover acupuncture for certain conditions, and others have mandated that general coverage pay for acupuncture. Consumers should be aware of the provisions for acupuncture in their individual policies.

Preparation

Before you use an acupuncturist, make sure they are qualified. Health care providers, physicians and other traditional medical professionals can help to find reputable personnel within the acupuncture field. In addition, national acupuncture organizations can also be used as a referral. To be assured of the qualifications of an acupuncturist, check the person's credentials. A license is required to practice acupuncture in most states. Experience and education, especially in traditional medicine, should also be considered when selecting an acupuncturist.

Risks

Acupuncture is generally a safe procedure. If individuals are in doubt about a medical condition, more than one physician should be consulted. Individuals also should feel comfortable and confident that their acupuncturist is knowledgeable and properly trained.

The National Center for Complementary and Alternative Medicine (NCCAM), the American Medical Association (AMA), and other organizations from the United States have generally agreed that acupuncture is safe to be used when under the guidance of a trained practitioner who uses sterile needles. However, as of 2011, these U.S. organizations have declined to make statements as to the efficiency of acupuncture.

Results

The World Health Organization (WHO) recommends acupuncture as an effective treatment for over 40 medical problems, along with many mental illnesses such as nervous conditions. Acupuncture has been used in the treatment of alcoholism and **substance abuse**, which are often problems associated with mental illness.

Acupuncture, as related to the treatment of mental illness, has been researched by the medical community for many decades. For instance, as early as the 1970s, medical research has been conducted around the world concerning acupuncture and the treatment of depression. American **psychologist** John Allen, from the University of Arizona (Tucson), conducted one of these studies. Allen performed a double-blind randomized study of 34 women who were depressed as per the criteria of the ***Diagnostic and Statistical Manual of Mental Disorders*** *IV* (*DSM-IV*), which is a publication by the **American Psychiatric Association** that provides standards for the classification of mental disorders.

Dr. Allen divided the subjects into three treatment groups for eight weeks of study. The first group received acupuncture treatments specifically to treat their depression, while the second group received acupuncture for general treatment, and the third group did not receive acupuncture (control group). The group that received acupuncture specifically designed to treat depression showed marked improvement in their symptoms (43%) when compared to the other two groups (22% for the general acupuncture group and 14% for the no-treatment group). At the end of the study, only half of the participants were still classified as depressed by the *DSM-IV*.

Acupuncture has also been medically studied to help relieve symptoms due to **stress**. For instance, Drs. Shu-Ming Wang, Zeev N. Kain, and Paul F. White performed a study that was published during 2008 within the journal *Anesthesia & Analgesia*, a publication of the International Anesthesia Research Society. These American researchers from Yale University showed that auricular (ear) acupuncture helped to relive post-operative anxiety

QUESTIONS TO ASK YOUR DOCTOR

- What kind of results can I expect to feel with acupuncture?
- Can acupuncture hurt or injure me?
- What other type of treatment do you recommend for me?
- Will acupuncture interfere with my current medications?
- How long will it take to see results from my acupuncture treatment?

in children. An earlier study, also from Yale University researchers, showed that mothers of children about to have surgery had lower stress levels when acupuncture was performed.

Other studies have shown that acupuncture is effective at reducing symptoms associated with other mental illnesses and psychiatric disorders, such as depressive **neurosis**, **post-traumatic stress disorder**, schizophrenia, bipolar disorder, and mania, and symptoms often associated with such conditions as mood swings and **insomnia**. However, still other medical studies do not support these contentions, and further research into these applications is needed.

Research and general acceptance

Mainstream medicine has been slow to accept acupuncture. Research continues to produce conflicting results, and although more medical doctors are using the technique, the American Medical Association does not recognize it as a specialty. The reason for this position is that the mechanism of acupuncture is difficult to understand or measure scientifically, such as the invisible energy of chi in the body. Western medicine, admitting that acupuncture works in many cases, has theorized that the energy meridians are actually part of the nervous system and that acupuncture relieves pain by releasing endorphins, or natural painkillers, into the bloodstream. Despite the ambiguity in the biochemistry involved, acupuncture continues to show effectiveness in clinical tests, from reducing pain in chronic and acute illnesses to alleviating the symptoms of mental illnesses.

Medical research in acupuncture is growing. The National Center for Complementary and Alternative Medicine of the National Institutes of Health funds research in the use of acupuncture on a number of conditions, including pain and insomnia. When acupuncture is practiced by traditional medical professionals, its effectiveness to relieve pain is primarily believed to be due to acupuncture points being able to stimulate muscles, nerves, and connective tissue, which acts to increase the production of natural painkillers found within the body, and the increased flow of blood to these targeted locations.

Healthcare team roles

Medical acupuncture has evolved in the United States in an atmosphere that focuses on traditional Western methods, such as surgical techniques and pain management, and not as part of Chinese medicine overall. In the United States, medical practitioners sometimes incorporate acupuncture methods from China, Japan, Korea, and other countries as part of their complementary and alternative medicine (CAM) program. Generally, under such Western methods, a medical doctor (MD) or an osteopathic physician (DO) performs medical acupuncture.

Certain states permit only the practice of medical acupuncture. Practitioners complete their training as part of conventional medical school programs. Since any MD can legally perform acupuncture, the *American Academy of Medical Acupuncture* (AAMA) was chartered in 1987 to support the education and correct practice of physician-trained acupuncturists. Its members must be either MDs or DOs who have completed proper study of acupuncture techniques.

Resources

BOOKS

Filshie, Jacqueline. *Introduction to Medical Acupuncture.* Oxford, England: Churchill Livingstone, 2008.

Focks, Claudia. *Atlas of Acupuncture.* Oxford, England: Churchill Livingstone, 2008.

Landgren, Kajsa. *Ear Acupuncture: A Practical Guide.* Oxford, England: Churchill Livingstone, 2008.

Maciocia, Giovanni. *The Practice of Chinese Medicine: The Treatment of Diseases with Acupuncture and Chinese Herbs.* Oxford, England: Churchill Livingstone, 2008.

PERIODICALS

Hollifield M., et al. "Acupuncture for Post-traumatic Stress Disorder: A Randomized Controlled Pilot Trial." *Journal of Nervous and Mental Diseases* (June 2007): 504–513.

Mayhew, E., and E. Ernst. "Acupuncture for Fibromyalgia: A Systematic Review of Randomized Clinical Trials." *Rheumatology* (May 2007): 801–804.

Paterson, Charlotte. "Patients' Experiences of Western-style Acupuncture: The Influence of Acupuncture 'Dose', Self-care Strategies and Integration." *Journal of Health Services Research and Policy* (April 2007): 39–45.

Tillisch, Kirsten. "Complementary and Alternative Medicine for Gastrointestinal Disorders." *Clinical Medicine, Journal of the Royal College of Physicians* (June 2007): 224–227.

Wang, Shu-Ming, Zeev N. Kain, and Paul F. White. "Acupuncture Analgesia: II. Clinical Considerations." *Anesthesia & Analgesia* 106, no. 2 (2008): 611–621. http://www.anesthesia-analgesia.org/content/106/2/611.abstract?sid=ee00e4d9-924c-4a87-876b-e40570d7aa86 (accessed June 28, 2011).

WEBSITES

Acupuncture. Mayo Clinic. (December 11, 2009). http://www.mayoclinic.com/health/acupuncture/MY00946 (accessed June 28, 2011).

Acupuncture: An Introduction. National Center for Complimentary and Alternative Medicine. (March 22, 2011). http://nccam.nih.gov/health/acupuncture/introduction.htm#ususe (accessed June 28, 2011).

ORGANIZATIONS

American Academy of Medical Acupuncture, 1970 East Grand Avenue, El Segundo, CA, 90245, (310) 364-0193, administrator@medicalacupuncture.org, http://www.medicalacupuncture.org.

American Association of Acupuncture and Oriental Medicine, PO Box 162340, Sacramento, CA, 95816, Fax: (916) 443-4766, Toll-free: (866) 455-7999, http://www.aaaomonline.org.

National Certification Commission for Acupuncture and Oriental Medicine, 76 South Laura St., Suite 1290, Jacksonville, FL, 32202, (904) 598-1005, Fax: (904) 598-5001, http://www.nccaom.org.

Douglas Dupler
Teresa G. Odle
Laura Jean Cataldo, RN, Ed.D.
William A. Atkins, B.B., B.S., M.B.A.

Acute stress disorder

Definition

Acute **stress** disorder (ASD) is an anxiety disorder characterized by a cluster of dissociative and anxiety symptoms that occur within a month of a traumatic stressor. The diagnosis was added to the fourth edition of the ***Diagnostic and Statistical Manual of Mental Disorders*** *(DSM-IV)* in 1994 to distinguish time-limited reactions to **trauma** from the longer-lasting **post-traumatic stress disorder** (PTSD). Published by the **American Psychiatric Association**, the *DSM* contains diagnostic criteria, research findings, and treatment information for mental disorders and is the primary reference for mental health professionals in the United States. A fifth edition (*DSM-5*) is expected to publish in 2013.

Demographics

Acute responses to traumatic stressors are far more widespread in the general U.S. population than was first thought in 1980, when PTSD was introduced as a diagnostic category in the *DSM-III*. The National Comorbidity Survey, a major epidemiological study conducted between 1990 and 1992, estimated that the lifetime prevalence of trauma-related stress disorders among adult Americans was 7.8%, with women (10.4%) twice as likely as men (5%) to be diagnosed. These figures represented only a small proportion of adults who had experienced at least one traumatic event—60.7% of men and 51.2% of women. More than 10% of the men and 6% of the women reported experiencing four or more types of trauma in their lives.

As of 2011, the prevalence of ASD by itself in the general U.S. population was not known. A few studies of people exposed to traumatic events found rates of ASD between 14% and 33%. According to one study, some groups are at greater risk of developing ASD or PTSD, including people living in depressed urban areas or on Native American reservations (23%) and victims of violent crimes (58%).

The U.S. Department of Veterans Affairs has provided statistics on the rates of ASD in various traumatic situations. For instance, survivors of motor vehicle accidents experienced ASD in a range of 13% to 21%, whereas survivors of industrial accidents had a rate of about 5%, victims of violent assaults had an ASD rate of 13%, and survivors of mass shootings had a rate of approximately 33%.

Reported rates for ASD are likely still inaccurate, because the majority of victims recover within two weeks of the exposure to a traumatic event, so many of these incidences are not reported. However, the rate for ASD is most likely higher than PTSD, because if ASD takes longer than four weeks to resolve, its *DSM-IV* classification becomes PTSD.

Description

ASD, like PTSD, begins with exposure to a traumatic, horrifying, or terrifying event. Such events include combat (war), personal attack (e.g., mugging), natural disasters (e.g., earthquake, hurricane), and physical sexual assault (rape). Recent events associated with symptoms of ASD among survivors include the wars in Afghanistan and Iraq; Cyclone Nargis in Myanmar on May 1, 2008; and the Haiti earthquake on January 1, 2010. In March 2011, a strong earthquake and massive tsunami near Tohoku, Japan, caused a nuclear power plant disaster at the Fukushima Daiichi nuclear complex, about 150 miles (242 km) north of Tokyo. The sequence of disasters resulted in the death of more than 15,000 people, with 5,000 more injured. Thousands were missing, and even more were exposed to radioactivity. Hundreds of thousands of buildings and homes were destroyed or damaged in the disaster. The survivors experienced many physiological and psychological disorders, including ASD.

Unlike PTSD, ASD emerges sooner and abates more quickly; it is also marked by more dissociative symptoms, such as emotional detachment, **dissociative amnesia** (memory loss due to strong psychological stress), derealization (degraded, unreal perception of the external world), or **depersonalization** (deteriorated awareness of self). If left untreated, ASD is likely to progress to PTSD. Because ASD and PTSD share many symptoms, some researchers and clinicians question the validity of maintaining separate diagnostic categories. Others explain the conditions as two phases of an extended reaction to traumatic stress.

Causes and symptoms

Causes

The immediate cause of ASD is exposure to trauma—experiencing an extreme stressor involving a threat to life or the prospect of serious injury, witnessing an event that involves the death or serious injury of another person, or learning of the violent death or serious injury of a family member or close friend. The trauma's impact is determined by its cause, scope, and extent. Natural disasters (such as floods, earthquakes, or hurricanes) or accidents (airplane crashes, workplace explosions) are considered less traumatic than intentional human acts (such as **abuse** or murder) or terrorism. Terrorist-inflicted trauma appears to produce particularly high rates of ASD and PTSD in survivors and bystanders. The terrorist attacks on the United States on September 11, 2001, with the killing and injuring of thousands of people and the destruction of the Twin Towers of the World Trade Complex in New York City and the damage to the Pentagon outside of Washington, DC, is a prime example of terrorist-inflicted trauma that develops in people who survive and witness such events.

Although most people define trauma in terms of events such as war, terrorist attacks, and other events that result in vast loss of life, the leading cause of stress-related mental disorders in the United States is motor vehicle accidents. Most Americans are involved in a traffic accident at some point in their lives, and 25% of the population are involved in accidents resulting in serious injuries. Various studies in the 2000s and 2010s found that rates of ASD from traffic/motor vehicle accidents ranged from 13% to 21%, as provided by the Department of Veterans Affairs.

Several factors influence a person's risk of developing ASD after trauma:

- Age—Older adults are less likely to develop ASD, possibly because they have had more experience coping with painful or stressful events.
- Previous exposure—People who were abused or experienced trauma as children are more likely to develop ASD (or PTSD) as adults, because these may produce long-lasting biochemical changes in the central nervous system.
- Biological vulnerability—Twin studies indicate that certain abnormalities in brain hormone levels and brain structure are inherited, and that these increase a person's susceptibility to ASD following exposure to trauma.
- Support networks—People who have a network of close friends and relatives are less likely to develop ASD.
- Perception and interpretation—People who feel inappropriate responsibility for the trauma, regard the event as punishment for personal wrongdoing, or have generally negative or pessimistic worldviews are more likely to develop ASD than those who do not personalize the trauma or are able to maintain a balanced view of life.

Symptoms

Symptoms of ASD include:

- dissociative symptoms, including psychic numbing, feeling dazed or less aware of surroundings, derealization, depersonalization, and dissociative amnesia
- trauma reexperienced in the form of recurrent dreams, images, thoughts, illusions, or flashbacks
- avoidance of people, places, objects, conversations, and other stimuli reminiscent of the trauma (for example, refusal to drive after a traffic accident)
- hyperarousal or anxiety, including sleep problems, irritability, inability to concentrate, an intense startle response, hypervigilance, and physical restlessness (pacing the floor, fidgeting)
- significantly impaired social functions and/or the inability to do necessary tasks, including seeking help
- symptoms lasting at least two days and up to a maximum of four weeks and occurring within four weeks of the traumatic event

ASD symptoms are not caused by a substance, either by taking medication or abusing a drug, nor are they caused by a physiological condition. They do not meet the criteria of a **brief psychotic disorder** and do not represent the worsening of a mental disorder that the person had before the traumatic event.

People with ASD may show symptoms of **depression**, including difficulty enjoying activities that they previously found pleasurable, difficulty concentrating, and experiencing survivor's guilt for having survived an accident or escaped serious injury when others did not. The *DSM-IV-TR* notes that people diagnosed with ASD "often perceive themselves to have greater responsibility for the consequences of the trauma than is warranted" and may feel that they will not live out their normal life span. Many symptoms of ASD are also found in patients with PTSD.

Diagnosis

ASD symptoms typically develop within a month after the traumatic event; however, why some trauma survivors develop symptoms more rapidly than others remains unknown. Delayed symptoms are often triggered by a situation that resembles the original trauma.

ASD is usually diagnosed by matching the patient's symptoms to the *DSM* criteria. The symptoms must cause the patient great distress and must be severe enough to impair the patient's daily functioning. General questionnaires are in widespread use for diagnosing ASD, as well as clinical guidelines established in the United States, the United Kingdom, and, most recently, Australia. The Australian guidelines consist of a 19-point acute stress disorder scale, which appears to be effective in diagnosing ASD but frequently makes false-positive predictions of PTSD. The authors of the scale recommend that its use should be followed by a careful clinical evaluation.

Another measure to assess ASD is the acute stress disorder interview (ASDI), which has been validated against criteria provided by the *DSM-IV-TR*. It was validated by comparing its results with diagnoses made by clinicians experienced in differentiating ASM from PTSD. In addition, the acute stress disorder scale (ASDS) has been found to correlate with results from the ASDI, along with providing reliability, validity, and internal consistency.

Treatment

Therapy for ASM requires the use of several treatment modalities, as the disorder affects interpersonal relationships and occupational functioning as well as a patient's emotional and physical well-being. Usually, a therapist asks the patient to relate what happened during the incident and to describe the emotions felt at that time and experienced thereafter. Drugs may be prescribed but are usually limited to those necessary for treating specific symptoms.

KEY TERMS

Adjustment disorder—A disorder defined by the development of significant emotional or behavioral symptoms in response to a stressful event or series of events. Symptoms may include depressed mood, anxiety, and impairment of social and occupational functioning.

Depersonalization—A dissociative symptom in which individuals feel that their body is unreal, changing, or dissolving.

Derealization—A dissociative symptom in which the external environment is perceived as unreal or dreamlike.

Dissociation—A reaction to trauma in which the mind splits off certain aspects of the traumatic event from conscious awareness. It can affect the patient's memory, sense of reality, and sense of identity.

Dissociative amnesia—A dissociative disorder characterized by loss of memory for a period or periods of time, which may occur as a result of a traumatic event.

Exposure therapy—A form of cognitive-behavioral therapy in which patients suffering from phobias are exposed to their feared objects or situations while accompanied by the therapist. The length of exposure is gradually increased until the association between the feared situation and the patient's experienced panic symptoms is no longer present.

Flashback—The reemergence of a traumatic memory as a vivid recollection of sounds, images, and sensations associated with the trauma. The person having such a memory typically feels as if he or she is reliving the event.

Hyperarousal—A symptom of traumatic stress characterized by abnormally intense reactions to stimuli. A heightened startle response is one sign of hyperarousal.

Hypervigilance—A state of abnormally intense wariness or watchfulness that is found in survivors of trauma or long-term abuse. Hypervigilance is sometimes described as the feeling of being on red alert all the time.

Personalization—The tendency to refer large-scale events or general patterns of events to the self in inappropriate ways. For example, a person who regards the loss of a loved one in an accident as punishment for having quarreled with that person before the accident is said to be personalizing the event. This tendency increases a person's risk of developing ASD or PTSD after a traumatic event.

Psychic numbing—An inability to respond emotionally with normal intensity to people or situations; this numbing affects positive as well as negative emotions.

Supportive—An approach in psychotherapy that seeks to encourage or emotionally support the patient, as distinct from insight-oriented or educational approaches to treatment.

Survivor's guilt—A psychological reaction in trauma survivors that takes the form of guilt feelings for having survived or escaped a trauma without serious injury when others did not.

Therapeutic writing—A treatment technique in which patients are asked to write an account of the traumatic event and their emotional responses to it.

Medications

Specific drugs prescribed include **clonidine** (Catapres, Kapvay, Nexiclon), for hyperarousal; **propranolol** (Inderal), **clonazepam** (Ceberclon, Klonopin, Valpax), or **alprazolam** (Niravam, Xanax), for anxiety and panic reactions; **fluoxetine** (Prozac, Rapiflux, Sarafem, Selfemra), for avoidance symptoms; and **trazodone** (Desyrel, Oleptro, Trazon, Trialodine) or topiramate (Topamax, Topiragen), for **insomnia** and nightmares. **Antidepressants** may be prescribed if ASD progresses to PTSD. These medications may include **selective serotonin reuptake inhibitors (SSRIs)**, **monoamine oxidase inhibitors (MAOIs)**, or tricyclic antidepressants.

Psychotherapy

Cognitive-behavioral therapy, exposure therapy, therapeutic writing (**journal therapy**), and supportive therapy have been found effective in treating ASD. One variant of cognitive behavioral therapy, psychoeducational therapy, appears to be three to four times as effective as supportive therapy in preventing ASD from progressing to PTSD. This treatment combines cognitive restructuring of the traumatic event with exposure to disturbing images and techniques for anxiety management. In addition, it can help patients identify and reinforce positive aspects of their experience. For example, some people discover new strengths or talents in times of crisis or discover new spiritual resources.

Group and family therapies also help reinforce effective strategies for coping with the trauma and may reduce the risk of social isolation as a reaction to the trauma. They provide opportunities for patients to describe what happened and how they responded. As patients place their experience into a coherent narrative, they integrate the trauma into their lives as a whole, and, by telling their story, they receive support from their listeners.

Critical incident **stress management** (CISM) is a comprehensive crisis-intervention system in which a team of specially trained practitioners comes to the site of a traumatic event and provides several different forms of assistance. This assistance includes one-on-one crisis support; crisis management briefing, which is a 45–75-minute **intervention** for groups affected by the traumatic event; and critical incident stress debriefing, which is a structured group discussion of the event. CISM appears to be particularly helpful in preventing burnout and ASD among emergency service personnel, rescue personnel, police, and other caregivers who are involved in treating survivors of a traumatic event.

Alternative and complementary treatments

Many mainstream practitioners recommend holistic or naturopathic approaches to recovery from ASD, including good **nutrition** with appropriate dietary supplements and regular **exercise**. **Yoga** and some forms of body work or massage therapy are helpful in treating the muscle soreness and stiffness that is often a side effect of anxiety and insomnia related to ASD. Hydrotherapy is often helpful for post-traumatic muscular aches and cramps. A skilled naturopath may also recommend peppermint or other herbal preparations to calm the patient's digestive tract. In addition, prayer, **meditation**, or counseling with a spiritual advisor have been found to be helpful in treating patients with ASD whose belief systems have been affected by the traumatic event.

ASD in children

Very little is known about the prevalence of ASD or PTSD in children, and even less is known about the effectiveness of medications and **psychotherapy** in this age group. There were as of 2011 no standardized screens or diagnostic interviews in widespread use for assessing either ASD or PTSD in children, although a Child Post-traumatic Stress Reaction Index was published in 1992. One preliminary study recommended the cautious use of low doses of **imipramine** for treating children with ASD but noted that research in this area had barely begun.

Prognosis

Untreated ASD is highly likely to progress to PTSD. One team of Australian researchers found that 80% of persons diagnosed with ASD met criteria for PTSD six months later, and 75% met criteria for PTSD two years after the traumatic event.

Clinicians in Norway compiled a list of four "early response" variables that appear to be effective predictors of ASD progressing to PTSD:

- the degree of the patient's sleep disturbance
- a strong startle reaction
- the degree of the patient's social withdrawal
- fear or phobia related to the site of the traumatic event

In addition to developing PTSD, people diagnosed with ASD are at increased risk of developing a **major depressive disorder**, particularly if their emotional responses to the trauma are marked by intense despair or hopelessness. Other possible developments are neglect of personal needs for health or safety and impulsive or needlessly risky behavior.

QUESTIONS TO ASK YOUR DOCTOR

- Do I have acute stress disorder?
- What can I do to get better?
- Do I need medication?
- Do I need counseling?
- Do you think my ASD will progress into PTSD?

Prevention

Some forms of trauma, such as natural disasters and accidents, cannot be prevented. Traumas caused by human action require major social changes to reduce their frequency and severity, but given the increasing prevalence of trauma-related stress disorders around the world, these long-term changes are worth the effort. In the short run, educating people—particularly those in the helping professions—about the signs of critical incident stress may prevent some cases of exposure to trauma from developing into ASD and progressing to PTSD.

Resources

BOOKS

American Psychiatric Association. *Diagnostic and Statistical Manual of Mental Disorders,* 4th edition, text rev. Washington, DC: American Psychiatric Association, 2000.

Beers, Mark H., ed. *The Merck Manual of Diagnosis and Therapy*. Rahway, NJ: Merck, 2006.

Friedman, Matthew. *Post-traumatic and Acute Stress Disorders: The Latest Assessment and Treatment Strategies.* Kansas City, MO: Compact Clinicals, 2006.

Mendelsohn, Michaela, et al. *The Trauma Recovery Group: A Guide for Practitioners.* New York: Guilford Press, 2011.

Van der Kolk, Bessel A., Alexander C. McFarlane, and Lars Veisaeth, eds. *Traumatic Stress: The Effects of Overwhelming Experience on Mind, Body, and Society.* New York: Guilford Press, 2007.

WEBSITES

Australian Centre for Posttraumatic Mental Health. "Australian Guidelines for the Treatment of Adults with Acute Australian Stress Disorder and Posttraumatic Stress Disorder." September 10, 2007. http://www.nhmrc.gov.au/_files_nhmrc/file/publications/synopses/mh13.pdf (accessed September 7, 2011).

Gibson, Laura E. "Acute Stress Disorder." Department of Veteran Affairs. Last modified June 16, 2010. http://www.ptsd.va.gov/professional/pages/acute-stress-disorder.asp (accessed September 7, 2011).

Phillips, Katharine E. *Report of the DSM-V Anxiety, Obsessive-Compulsive Spectrum, Posttraumatic, and Dissociative Disorders Work Group.* American Psychiatric Association. April 2009. http://www.psych.org/MainMenu/Research/DSMIV/DSMV/DSMRevisionActivities/DSM-V-Work-Group-Reports/Anxiety-Obsessive-Compulsive-Spectrum-Posttraumatic-and-Dissociative-Disorders-Work-Group-Report.aspx (accessed September 7, 2011).

ORGANIZATIONS

American Academy of Experts in Traumatic Stress, 203 Deer Rd., Ronkonkoma, NY, 11779, (631) 543-2217, Fax: (631) 543-6977, info@aaets.org, http://www.aaets.org.

Anxiety Disorders Association of America, 8730 Georgia Ave., Silver Spring, MD, 20910, (240) 485-1001, http://www.adaa.org.

International Society for Traumatic Stress Studies, 111 Deer Lake Rd., Ste. 100, Deerfield, IL, 60015, (847) 480-9028, Fax: (847) 480-9282, http://www.istss.org.

National Institute of Mental Health, 6001 Executive Blvd., Rm. 8184, MSC 9663, Bethesda, MD, 20892-9663, (301) 433-4513; TTY: (301) 443-8431, (866) 615-6464; TTY: (866) 415-8051, Fax: (301) 443-4279, nimhinfo@nih.gov, http://www.nimh.nih.gov.

Rebecca J. Frey, PhD
William A. Atkins, BB, BS, MBA

Adapin *see* **Doxepin**

Addiction

Definition

Addiction is the compulsive need to use a habit-forming substance or the irresistible urge to engage in an activity or behavior, often despite harmful consequences. Persistent use leads to dependence and ultimately tolerance, or the need to increase the amount or duration of the substance or activity in order to achieve the same effect. Discontinuation of the addiction can lead to withdrawal, the unpleasant symptoms that arise when the addicted person is prevented from using the chosen substance or engaging in the behavior.

Demographics

Addiction to substances and activities is widespread in the United States, Canada, and internationally. **Substance abuse** and addiction cost Americans about $500 billion annually in healthcare costs, lost earnings, accidents, and crime. Every year, Americans experience more than 40 million debilitating illnesses or injuries as a result of tobacco, alcohol, and other addictive drug use. Likewise, about one in ten Canadians aged 15 or older are considered addicted to alcohol or drugs. Men are more than twice as likely as women to be addicted to a substance. Gender differences are much less pronounced among adolescents, however; teenage girls are almost as likely as boys to abuse a substance. Approximately 20% of people with addictions have other mental disorders, as well.

Nicotine dependence is the most common type of addiction. It is estimated that worldwide tobacco use results in at least five million deaths annually. Cigarette smoking is the leading preventable cause of death in the United States, accounting for about one out of every five deaths, with about 40,000 additional annual deaths caused by exposure to secondhand smoke. According to the Substance Abuse and Mental Health Services Administration's *National Survey on Drug Use and Health* (NSDUH), about 27.4% of Americans aged 12 or over were considered current users of tobacco products in 2010. About 8.3% of tobacco users were between the ages of 12 and 17, with the 18–25 demographic constituting the largest usage group (40.8% of users).

Alcoholism is the most common addiction to a psychoactive substance. Alcohol addiction affects both sexes and all races and nationalities. According to the 2010 *NSDUH*, 131.3 million Americans (51.8% of the population) reported having at least one alcoholic drink in the past 30 days. In addition, 58.6 million people (23.1%) reported having five or more drinks on the same occasion (**binge drinking**), and 16.9 million (6.7%) reported having five or more drinks on at least five occasions in the past 30 days (heavy **alcohol use**). Alcohol addiction rates are highest among young adults aged 18–29 and lowest among those 65 and older.

According to the 2010 *NSDUH*, 22.6 million Americans (8.9% of the population) age 12 and older reported using illicit drugs in the preceding month. The

People can become addicted to a wide range of substances and activities. Represented in this illustration are gambling, video game, alcohol, and drug addictions. *(Illustration by Electronic Illustrators Group. © 2012 Cengage Learning.)*

most commonly abused drug was marijuana, followed by abuse of psychotherapeutic drugs (prescription pain relievers, **sedatives**, or stimulants used for nonmedical reasons).

Addictions most often first appear in adolescence. According to the survey, 10.1% of students ages 12–17 reported having used an illicit drug in the previous year. The use of illegal drugs among American teenagers declined between 2001 and 2008, thought it has risen slightly over the past few years. Cigarette smoking and alcohol use among American youth also declined significantly over the first decade of the twenty-first century.

Statistics on addictive activities (e.g., gambling, **sexual addiction**) are more difficult to obtain because these behaviors are less clearly defined than substance addiction. However, the National Council on Problem Gambling reported in 2010 that 85% of American adults have gambled at least once in their lifetimes, with 60% of the population gambling in any given year. Of these, about 1% are addicted to gambling, while another 2%–3% are considered problem gamblers. The rate of gambling addiction is related to access, with an estimated 6% of the population of Nevada being either problem or addicted gamblers. With an increase in legal gambling in the United States (only Utah and Hawaii do not have some form of legal gambling) and easy access to online gambling, the rate of gambling among teen and college-aged gamblers has increased by 600%.

Because there is no professional agreement on the definition of sexual addiction, the number of people considered to be addicted to sex is unknown. What is known is that sexual addiction is much more common in men than women. Persons addicted to sex are not necessarily sex offenders, nor are sex offenders necessarily sex addicts. Often, people addicted to sex have other mental health and impulse-control problems that contribute to their addictive behaviors.

Internet addiction is a new and growing phenomenon. The number of people addicted to the Internet is hard to pin down. One 2008 study estimated the rate at 8.2% of American Internet users. Other studies have estimated rates of 10% and 11% of Internet users in China and South Korea, respectively.

Description

Addiction most commonly refers to the compulsive use or abuse of or physical or psychological dependence on addictive substances, including:

- tobacco
- alcohol
- cocaine, including crack cocaine
- amphetamines, including methamphetamine or "crank," an extremely addictive substance
- heroin
- prescription medications

Prescription painkillers, such as the opiates Vicodin and OxyContin, have emerged as drugs of special concern because of their widespread use by high-school students.

Outside of substance use, the term "addiction" has been used to describe a wide and complex range of behaviors. These so-called process addictions are compulsive behaviors involving activities such as:

- gambling
- eating
- working
- exercising
- shopping or otherwise spending money
- sex
- Internet use

Most addictions are associated with mood modification. Initially, they make the addicted person feel better. Persons with addictions often describe a release of tension or feelings of euphoria when using the substance or engaging in the activity. Most addictions are progressive syndromes; without treatment, their severity increases over time. Furthermore, many addicts are addicted to more than one substance or activity. Addictions are characterized by frequent relapses—a return to using the abused substance or activity following a period of abstinence.

Substances can be both physically and psychologically addictive. Some substances are more addictive than others, either because they produce a rapid and intense change in mood or because they produce painful withdrawal symptoms when stopped suddenly. Drugs that are smoked or injected, giving an immediate but short-lived "high," tend to be more addictive than substances that are ingested.

The American Psychiatric Association's ***Diagnostic and Statistical Manual of Mental Disorders*** classifies substance abuse and dependence as psychological disorders that are considered major clinical syndromes (called "Axis 1"). Over time, repeated drug use changes **brain** structure and function in fundamental

KEY TERMS

Addictive personality—The concept that addiction is the result of pre-existing character defects.

Dopamine—A neurotransmitter in the brain.

Methamphetamine (meth, methadrine, "speed")—A highly addictive medication that is used to treat attention deficit hyperactivity disorder and obesity but is widely abused as a stimulant.

Neurotransmitter—One of a group of chemicals secreted by a nerve cell (neuron) to carry a chemical message to another nerve cell, often as a way of transmitting a nerve impulse. Examples of neurotransmitters include acetylcholine, dopamine, serotonin, and norepinephrine.

Process addiction—Addiction to certain mood-altering behaviors, such as eating, gambling, sexual activity, overwork, and shopping.

Relapse—A recurrence of symptoms after a period of improvement or recovery.

Tolerance—The requirement for higher doses of a substance or more frequent engagement in an activity to achieve the same effect.

Withdrawal—The unpleasant, sometimes life-threatening physiological changes that occur due to the discontinuation of some drugs after prolonged regular use.

and long-lasting ways. Evidence suggests that these long-lasting brain changes are responsible for the distortions in cognitive and emotional functioning that characterize persons with addictions, particularly the **compulsion** to use drugs. This explains why many drug users cannot stop using by force of will alone.

Risk factors

Risk factors for addiction include:

- inherited factors
- adolescence
- addictive behavior in the home or among family members or peers
- early substance use
- early aggressive behavior
- academic failure
- lack of parental supervision
- poor social skills
- other mental disorders or illnesses
- substance abuse
- substance availability
- poverty

Causes and symptoms

For much of the twentieth century, addiction was viewed as a moral failing; today, addiction is widely viewed as a disease. The disease model of alcohol and drug addiction was first introduced in the late 1940s by E. M. Jellinek and was adopted by the American Medical Association in 1956. According to the disease model, the compulsion to use alcohol and/or drugs is genetically and physiologically based and, although the disease can be treated, it is progressive, chronic, and fatal if unchecked. However, some experts argue that addiction is better understood as a learned behavior, and that the negative behavior can be unlearned and replaced by learning new positive behaviors. The causes of addiction remain the subject of ongoing research and debate.

Causes

The initial positive consequences of substance use or a potentially addictive activity can "hook" a susceptible person and turn into an addiction. Addiction comes about through an array of changes in the brain and the strengthening of new memory connections. The anterior cingulate cortex in the frontal lobe of the brain is the area responsible for the long-term craving that triggers **relapse**.

Many experts believe that addictive substances and activities affect **neurotransmitters** in the brain. The primary pathway involved in the development and persistence of addiction is the brain reward or mesolimbic pathway, which operates via a neurotransmitter called **dopamine**. Dopamine pathways may interact with those of other neurotransmitters, including opioid pathways. These neuronal pathways have been identified as underlying both substance and process addictions.

Whatever the brain chemistry involved in addiction, it usually results from the interaction of several factors:

- Social learning. This may be the most important single factor in addiction and includes patterns of substance use and activities in the addict's family or subculture, peer pressure, and advertising or media influence.
- Availability. There are marked increases in addiction rates when tobacco, alcohol, or drugs are inexpensive or readily available.
- Individual development. Before the 1980s, addiction was blamed on an "addictive personality," which was described as escapist, impulsive, dependent, devious, manipulative, and self-centered. Although individual development may play a role in addiction, many doctors now believe that these character traits develop as a result of the addiction, rather causing the addiction.
- Genetic factors. It is estimated that genetic factors account for 40%–60% of an individual's vulnerability to addiction. Twin studies have shown that addiction has a strong inherited component. Some forms of addiction seem to run in families, and some people appear to be more vulnerable to addiction because of their body chemistry.

Symptoms

The continued use of an addictive substance or engagement in an addictive activity causes the body to adjust and develop tolerance. Increasing amounts of the substance or more frequent engagement in the activity are needed to produce the same effect. Some drug users can tolerate an amount of a substance that would be lethal in someone without a tolerance, though continued dosage increase will eventually reach fatal levels. If the drug is ceased, the person may experience a withdrawal syndrome. Symptoms of withdrawal vary but may include tremor, **insomnia**, agitation, aggression, vomiting, nightmares, and sweating. Long-term substance use may result in more serious symptoms; severe symptoms of withdrawal from alcohol and some drugs may include **seizures**, hallucinatory sensations, organ damage, and **dementia**. Even for addictions that do not involve substance use, persons may experience some symptoms of withdrawal when stopping the behavior or activity.

The inability to hold a steady job and disruptions of social and familial relationships are common behavioral symptoms of all types of addiction. Other behavioral symptoms include:

- participation in activity despite danger to self or others (e.g., driving under the influence)
- continuation of activity even though it has a negative effect on personal and social life and/or physical health
- significant time spent around the substance or activity, often in place of time spent previously on hobbies or events

Danger signs that may indicate the probable onset of addiction to alcohol or drugs include:

- a frequent desire to drink or use
- increasing consumption
- memory lapses (blackouts)
- morning drinking/drug use
- hiding use from family and coworkers
- using in secret

Alcoholic psychoses are symptoms of late-stage alcohol addiction and include:

- alcohol withdrawal delirium (delirium tremens)
- hallucinations
- Korsakoff's psychosis, an irreversible brain disorder involving severe memory loss

Diagnosis

Addictions usually are diagnosed by their symptoms and by lifestyle factors, such as when the addiction interferes with a person's life, personal relationships, work, and/or health. A physician, **psychologist**, or social worker usually makes a **diagnosis** of addiction based on the following criteria:

- a pattern of frequent and compulsive substance use or engagement in an activity
- preoccupation with acquiring and using an abused substance
- tolerance or escalation of the substance use or activity
- loss of willpower
- harmful consequences
- unmanageable lifestyle
- withdrawal symptoms

Examination

A physical examination may aid in diagnosis by probing for underlying conditions, such as **depression**, emotional upset, anxiety, or **stress**. A physician may also look for signs of malnutrition or other medical problems resulting from substance abuse.

Tests

Blood and urine tests may be ordered to check for substance use or for liver or other organ damage resulting from substance abuse.

Procedures

Imaging tests may be ordered to check for organ damage resulting from substance abuse.

Treatment

Addictions are notoriously difficult to treat. Treatment often requires a combination of medical, psychological, and social approaches.

Traditional

Although addiction treatment may be provided by practicing clinicians such as psychiatrists, psychologists, and **social workers**, it is more often provided by specialized addiction treatment programs and clinics. These programs usually rely upon confrontational tactics and re-education, often employing former or recovering addicts to treat newly admitted addicts. Residential settings can be effective in helping addicted individuals to stay away from the many cues, including people and places, that form the setting for their addiction. Substance addicts may need hospital treatment to manage withdrawal symptoms.

Individual or group **psychotherapy** is often helpful for treating addictions after the substance use or addictive activity has ceased. Many of the negative behaviors and personality problems associated with addictions disappear when the substance use or activity ceases. **Family therapy** can be helpful for addressing and changing "enabling behaviors" by family members who help maintain the addiction by providing money, food, shelter, and/or emotional support.

The effectiveness of addiction treatment based on behavioral and other psychotherapeutic methods is well-documented. Specific therapies to treat addiction include:

- cognitive-behavioral approaches, which aim to prevent relapse by helping addicts recognize, avoid, and cope with situations that encourage their addictions
- motivation-enhancing strategies, which utilize positive reinforcement and incentives
- motivational interviewing, which uses strategies that promote behavior changes
- solution-oriented and other brief therapy techniques
- harm-reduction approaches

Drugs

Research continues into pharmacological treatments for easing withdrawal and treating various addictions. Some promising drugs boost the levels of neurotransmitters in the brain. Medications that are used to treat addiction include:

- nicotine-replacement therapies, including gum, patches, and inhalers
- bupropion (Zyban), an antidepressant, for tobacco addiction
- varenicline, which blocks the pleasant effects of nicotine on the brain
- disulfiram (Antabuse) and acamprosate (Campral) for treating alcoholism
- naltrexone (Depade, ReVia) for preventing relapse in alcohol and opioid addicts
- methadone, which blocks the euphoric effect of opiates
- buprenorphine (Subutex) or buprenorphine and naloxone (Suboxone) to prevent withdrawal symptoms and to treat addiction to opioids, including heroin and narcotic painkillers
- sedatives for reducing anxiety and withdrawal symptoms
- antidepressants for treating underlying problems in addicts who have been "self-medicating"

Alternative

During the past several decades, alternatives to the complete abstinence model have arisen. Controlled-use programs allow addicted individuals to reduce their use without committing to complete abstinence. This alternative is highly controversial, and the prevailing belief is that recovery is only possible by committing to complete lifelong abstinence from all substance use.

Home remedies

Many people turn to **self-help groups** such as Alcoholics Anonymous (AA) and Narcotics Anonymous (NA) to treat their addictions. The approach of one addict helping another to stay "clean," with or without additional professional help, is widely accepted in the United States and around the world.

The most frequently recommended social outpatient treatment is the 12-step program. The number of visits to 12-step self-help groups exceeds the number of visits to all mental health professionals combined. There are 12-step groups for all major substance and process addictions.

The 12 steps consist of:

- admitting powerlessness over the addiction
- believing that a power greater than oneself can restore sanity
- making a decision to turn your will and your life over to the care of your higher power
- making a searching and fearless moral inventory of yourself
- admitting to your higher power, yourself, and another human being the exact nature of your wrongs
- becoming willing to have your higher power remove all of these defects from your character
- humbly asking your higher power to remove your shortcomings
- making a list of all persons harmed by your wrongs, and becoming willing to make amends to them all
- making direct amends to such people, whenever possible, except when to do so would injure them or others
- continuing to take personal inventory, and promptly admitting any future wrongdoings
- seeking to improve contact with the higher power of your understanding through meditation and prayer
- carrying the message of spiritual awakening to others, and practicing these principles in all of your affairs

Prognosis

The prognosis for recovery from any addiction depends on the substance or process, the individual's circumstances, and the underlying personality structure. Patterns of relapse tend to be very similar regardless of the specific addiction. Two-thirds of all relapses occur within the first 90 days following treatment. Substance abusers often make repeated attempts to quit before they are successful. Physical addictions alter a person's brain chemistry in ways that make it difficult to be exposed to the addictive substance again without relapsing, and cravings may persist for years. Between 40% and 60% of drug addicts relapse following treatment. Users of more than one drug have the worst prognosis for recovery.

Substance abuse can damage organs, including the brain and liver, and can lead to serious and even fatal illness, as well as mental disorders such as dementia. Drug addiction puts the addict at risk for:

- cardiovascular disease
- stroke
- cancer
- HIV/AIDS
- hepatitis B and C

QUESTIONS TO ASK YOUR DOCTOR

- Am I addicted to this substance/activity?
- What symptoms are associated with withdrawal?
- What are the risks of continued use and/or withdrawal?
- What are my treatment options?
- Am I likely to relapse?
- What role can my family play in my treatment?

- lung disease
- obesity
- other mental disorders

Prevention

Preventive approaches are most effective when targeted at young teenagers between the ages of 11 and 13. It is during these years that most young people are likely to first experiment with drugs and alcohol. Hence, reducing experimentation during this critical period holds promise for reducing the number of adults with addictions. Effective prevention programs focus on the concerns of young people with regard to the effects of tobacco, alcohol, and drugs. Training older adolescents to help younger adolescents resist peer pressure has shown considerable effectiveness in preventing experimentation.

Preventative measures against addiction include:

- fostering self-control and positive relationships
- promoting parental monitoring and support
- promoting anti-addiction policies
- educational programs for the public
- building strong communities

The most effective form of prevention appears to be a stable family that models responsible attitudes toward mood-altering substances and behaviors.

Resources

BOOKS

American Psychiatric Association. *Diagnostic and Statistical Manual of Mental Disorders (DSM-IV-TR)*, 4th ed., text rev. Washington, DC: American Psychiatric Association, 2000.

Califano, Joseph A., Jr. *High Society: How Substance Abuse Ravages America and What to Do About It.* New York: Public Affairs Press, 2007.

DiClemente, Carlo C. *Addiction and Change: How Addictions Develop and Addicted People Recover.* New York: Guilford Press, 2006.

Erickson, Carlton K. *The Science of Addiction: From Neurobiology to Treatment.* New York: W.W. Norton, 2007.

Hoffman, John, and Susan Froemke. *Addiction: Why Can't They Just Stop?* Emmaus, PA: Rodale Books, 2007.

PERIODICALS

Grant, Jon E., Judson A. Brewer, and Marc N. Potenza. "The Neurobiology of Substance and Behavioral Addictions." *CNS Spectrums* 11 (2006): 924–930.

Johnson, Brian, et al. "Reducing the Risk of Addiction to Prescribed Medications." *Psychiatric Times* (April 15, 2007): 35.

Kushlick, Danny. "Stopping the Conveyor Belt to Addiction: Addressing the Underlying Issues of Addiction Will Help Us to Tackle It." *New Statesman* (May 21, 2007): S4–S5.

Lobo, Daniela S. S., and James L. Kennedy. "The Genetics of Gambling and Behavioral Addictions." *CNS Spectrums* 11 (2006): 931–939.

WEBSITES

National Institute on Drug Abuse. "Drugs, Brains, and Behavior—The Science of Addiction." U.S. National Institutes of Health. http://www.nida.nih.gov/scienceofaddiction (accessed October 11, 2011).

ORGANIZATIONS

Al-Anon/Alateen, 1600 Corporate Landing Parkway, Virginia Beach, VA, 23454-5617, (757) 563-1600, Fax: (757) 563-1655, wso@al-anon.org, http://www.al-anon.alateen.org.

Alcoholics Anonymous, PO Box 459, New York, NY, 10163, (212) 870-3400, http://www.aa.org.

American Academy of Child and Adolescent Psychiatry, 3615 Wisconsin Avenue NW, Washington, DC, 20016-3007, (202) 966-7300, Fax: (202) 966-2891, http://www.aacap.org.

American Psychiatric Association, 1000 Wilson Boulevard, Suite 1825, Arlington, VA, 22209-3901, (703) 907-7300, (888) 35-PSYCH (357-7924), apa@psych.org, http://www.psych.org.

Centre for Addiction and Mental Health, 33 Russell St., Toronto, Ontario, Canada, M5S 2S1, (416) 535-8501, (800) 463-6273, http://www.camh.net.

National Council on Alcoholism and Drug Dependence, Inc., 244 East 58th Street, 4th Fl., New York, NY, 10022, (212) 269-7797, (800) NCA-CALL (622-2255), Fax: (212) 269-7510, national@mcadd.org, http://www.ncadd.org.

National Institute on Alcohol Abuse and Alcoholism (NIAAA), 5635 Fishers Lane, MSC 9304, Bethesda, MD, 20892-9304, (301) 443-3860, http://www.niaaa.nih.gov.

National Institute on Drug Abuse (NIDA), 6001 Executive Boulevard, Room 5213, Bethesda, MD, 20892-9561, (301) 443-1124, information@nida.nih.gov, http://www.drugabuse.gov/NIDAHome.html.

Barbara S. Sternberg, PhD
Emily Jane Willingham, PhD
Tish Davidson, AM

ADHD *see* **Attention deficit hyperactivity disorder**

Adjustment disorders

Definition

Adjustment disorders (ADs) are a group of disorders in which a person's psychological response to a stressor elicits symptoms that warrant clinical attention. This uniting feature of the adjustment disorders can manifest as emotional distress that exceeds what is an expected norm or as notable impairment of the person's functioning in the world, whether socially, academically, and/or occupationally.

Adjustment disorders are considered subthreshold mental disorders, which means that they are less well defined and share some of their features with other diagnostic categories. This relative vagueness of definition allows for the classification of psychiatric conditions that are clinically significant but do not meet the full criteria of major syndromes. Another way of explaining adjustment disorders is that they are located on a continuum between normal **stress** reactions and specific psychiatric disorders.

Demographics

Even though adjustment disorders are commonly diagnosed, there have been few large-scale epidemiological studies of adjustment disorders. Epidemiological studies seek to understand the source and development of disease. However, adjustment disorder appears to be common in the U.S. population; it has been estimated that about 22% of adults seeking outpatient psychological treatment have one of the subtypes of this disorder. As many as 70% of children in psychiatric inpatient settings may be diagnosed with an adjustment disorder. However, this statistic may be exaggerated; in a questionnaire sent to child psychiatrists in the early 1990s, 55% of the contacted psychiatrists admitted giving children the **diagnosis** of an adjustment disorder to avoid the **stigma** associated with other disorders.

In the early 2010s, there were no studies being conducted on the differences in the frequency of adjustment disorder in different racial or ethnic groups. However, some potential exists for bias in diagnosis, particularly when the diagnostic criteria concern abnormal responses to stressors. The ***Diagnostic and Statistical Manual of Mental Disorders***, fourth edition, text revision, also known as the *DSM-IV-TR*, specifies that clinicians must take a patient's cultural background into account when evaluating his or her responses to stressors. There is some evidence that patients with average to higher-than-average incomes are more often diagnosed with an AD than patients who lack socioeconomic stability or security.

Description

Typically, a person experiences a stressful event as one that changes his or her world in some fundamental way. An adjustment disorder indicates the person's significant difficulty in adjusting to the new reality. Subsets of this disorder make up the most frequent psychiatric diagnoses among mentally ill populations, with features that include diagnosis of adjustment disorder.

As a category of disorders, adjustment disorder first appeared in the revised third edition of the *Diagnostic and Statistical Manual of Mental Disorders* (*DSM-III-R*), and the term included nine subtypes. The *DSM-IV-TR* lists six subtypes of adjustment disorder, generally based on what feature best characterizes the person's symptoms. These six subtypes are: AD with depressed mood (thought to be the most common subtype), AD with anxiety, AD with mixed anxiety and depressed mood, AD with disturbance of conduct, AD with disturbance of emotions and conduct, and AD not otherwise specified (ADNOS). This last subtype is applied when one of the other five does not fit the specific symptoms of a given patient.

The criteria for these disorders also include time parameters. One of the criteria for diagnosing an adjustment disorder is that it is an acute response to stress lasting six or fewer months. In some special cases, the response can be chronic, lasting longer than six months, usually when the stressor has lasting consequences, such as divorce or death of a family member.

The stressful events that precipitate an adjustment disorder vary widely. Stressful events include the loss of a job, the end of a romantic relationship, a life transition such as a career change or retirement, the death of a pet, or a serious accident or sickness. Some are acute one-time stressors, such as relocating to a new area, while others are chronic, such as caring for a child with mental deficits or living in a crime-ridden neighborhood.

In spite of some disagreement among professionals about the validity of the diagnosis of adjustment disorder, many consider the category useful for three reasons: (1) an adjustment disorder may be an early sign of a major mental disorder and allow for early treatment and **intervention**; (2) adjustment disorders are situational or reactive and do not imply that the patient has an underlying **brain** disease; and (3) the category does not carry the social stigma associated with such diagnostic categories as major **depression** and is less likely to affect the individual's employment or educational opportunities.

Risk factors

Risk factors for adjustment disorders include:

- more than one stressful event within a relatively short time period
- history of abusive parenting, family disruption, fetal alcohol syndrome, or frequent moves in early childhood
- concurrent mental health problems
- exposure to war or criminal violence
- poverty, homelessness, or other difficult circumstances
- social isolation or absence of a family or friendship network
- presence of chronic physical illness

Causes and symptoms

Causes are various for adjustment disorders as are the symptoms.

Causes

As of 2011, the processes leading to disruption of an individual's ability to adapt to change were not well understood. In the initial edition of the *Diagnostic and Statistical Manual of Mental Disorders,* the identifiable stressor was described as "psychosocial," a category that excludes physical illnesses and natural disasters. In the *DSM-IV-TR*, the word "psychosocial" was deleted to make the point that any stressful event can lead to an adjustment disorder. It is important to recognize, however, that while adjustment disorders are triggered by external stressors, the symptoms result from the person's interpretation of and adaptation to the stressful event or circumstances. Beliefs, perceptions, fears, and expectations influence the development and symptoms of a given individual's adjustment disorder.

Symptoms

Unlike many other disorders categorized in the *DSM-IV-TR*, adjustment disorders do not have an accompanying clearly delineated symptom profile, which has led to their being perceived as a "transitional" diagnosis, awaiting the manifestation of symptoms more clearly related to some other better-defined disorder. This ambiguity arises from the difficulty in establishing what defines a reaction within the norms of a population. The *DSM-IV-TR* states that the symptoms of an adjustment disorder must appear within three months of a stressor and that they must meet at least one of the following criteria: (1) the distress is greater than what would be expected in response to that particular stressor; or (2) the individual experiences significant impairment in social relationships or in occupational or academic settings. Moreover, the symptoms cannot represent **bereavement** as normally experienced after the death of a loved one; cannot be an exacerbation of another, pre-existing disorder; and cannot meet the criteria for another disorder.

Each of the six subtypes of adjustment disorder is characterized by its own predominant symptoms.

- With depressed mood: The chief manifestations are feelings of sadness and depression, with a sense of accompanying hopelessness. The patient may be tearful and have uncontrollable bouts of crying.
- With anxiety: Patients are troubled by feelings of apprehension, nervousness, and worry. They may also feel jittery and unable to control their thoughts of doom. Children with this subtype may express fears of separation from parents or other significant people and may refuse to go to sleep alone or attend school.
- With mixed anxiety and depressed mood: Patients have a combination of symptoms from the previous two subtypes.
- With disturbance of conduct: Patients exhibit noticeable behavioral changes such as shoplifting, truancy, reckless driving, aggressive outbursts, or sexual promiscuity. Patients disregard the rights of others or previously followed rules of conduct with little concern, guilt, or remorse.
- With mixed disturbance of emotions and conduct: Patients exhibit sudden changes in behavior combined with feelings of depression or anxiety. They may feel or express guilt about the behavior but then repeat it shortly thereafter.
- With not otherwise specified: This subtype covers patients who are adjusting poorly to stress but who do not fit into the other categories. These patients may complain of physical illness and pull away from social contact.

Adjustment disorders may lead to **suicide** or suicidal thinking. Researchers also have found that the suicidal process moves faster and evolves more rapidly in patients with adjustment disorders than in those with major depression. Adjustment disorders may complicate the

KEY TERMS

Cognitive-behavioral therapy—An approach to psychotherapy that emphasizes the correction of distorted thinking patterns and changing one's behaviors accordingly.

Decision tree—A decision support model used in medical and psychiatric diagnosis that consists of a tree-like chart or diagram, including various symptoms, tentative diagnoses, diagnostic decisions, and their possible consequences.

Group therapy—Group interaction designed to provide support, correction through feedback, constructive criticism, and a forum for consultation and reference.

Interpersonal therapy—An approach that includes psychoeducation about the sick role and emphasis on the present and improving interpersonal dynamics and relationships. Interpersonal therapy is effective in treating adjustment disorders related to physical illness.

Psychosocial—An adjective that describes the emotional and social aspects of psychological disorders.

Solution-focused therapy—A type of therapy that involves concrete goals and an emphasis on future direction rather than past experiences.

Stressor—A stimulus or event that provokes a stress response in an organism. Stressors can be categorized as acute or chronic and as external or internal to the organism.

Subthreshold—A term used in psychiatry to describe a condition that has significant clinical features but does not meet the full criteria of major disorders. Adjustment disorders are considered subthreshold disorders.

Support group—A group whose primary purpose is the provision of empathy and emotional support for its members. Support groups are less formal and less goal-directed than those groups participating in group therapy.

treatment of other diseases when, for example, a sufferer loses interest in taking medication as prescribed or adhering to diet or **exercise** regimens.

An adjustment disorder can occur at any stage of life; however, the risk of an AD appears to increase during periods typically associated with major life changes, such as late adolescence, midlife, and retirement.

Diagnosis

Adjustment disorders are usually diagnosed as the result of an interview with a **psychiatrist**. The psychiatrist will take a history, including identification of the stressor that has triggered the adjustment disorder, and evaluate the patient's responses to the stressor. The patient's primary physician may give the person a thorough physical examination to rule out a previously undiagnosed medical illness.

The **American Psychiatric Association** considers adjustment disorder to be a residual category, meaning that the diagnosis is given only when an individual does not meet the criteria for a major mental disorder. For example, if a person fits the more stringent criteria for **major depressive disorder**, the diagnosis of adjustment disorder is not given. If the patient is diagnosed with an adjustment disorder but continues to have symptoms for more than six months after the stressor and its consequences have ceased, the diagnosis is changed to another mental disorder. The one exception to this time limit is situations in which the stressor itself is chronic or has enduring consequences. In that case, the adjustment disorder is considered chronic, and the diagnosis remains applicable beyond six months.

The lack of a diagnostic checklist or decision tree for adjustment disorders distinguishes these disorders from either **post-traumatic stress disorder** or **acute stress disorder**. All three require the presence of a stressor, but the latter two define the extreme stressor and specific patterns of symptoms. With adjustment disorder, the stressor may be any event that is significant to the patient, and the disorder may take different forms in different patients.

Adjustment disorders must also be distinguished from **personality disorders**, which are caused by enduring personality traits that are inflexible and cause social, interpersonal, and occupational impairment. A personality disorder that has not yet surfaced may be made worse by a stressor and may mimic an adjustment disorder. A clinician must separate relatively stable traits in a patient's personality from passing disturbances. In some cases, however, the patient may be given both diagnoses. Again, it is important for psychiatrists to be sensitive to the role of cultural factors in the presentation of the patient's symptoms.

If the stressor is a physical illness, diagnosis is further complicated. It is important to recognize the difference between an adjustment disorder and the direct physiological effects of a medical condition (e.g., the temporary functional impairment associated with chemotherapy). This distinction can be clarified through communication with the patient's physician or education about the medical condition and its treatment. For some individuals, however, both may occur and reinforce each other.

Examination

An office physical examination of a patient with an adjustment disorder usually will not lead to any significant findings unless the patient is suffering from a concurrent physical illness or injury.

Tests

There are no laboratory or imaging tests that can be used to diagnose adjustment disorder.

Treatment

Traditional, medicinal, and alternative treatments are used to help people with adjustment disorder.

Traditional

There have been few research studies of significant scope that compared the efficacy of different treatments for adjustment disorder. The relative lack of outcome studies is partially due to the lack of specificity in the diagnosis itself. Because there is such variability in the types of stressors involved in adjustment disorders, it has proven difficult to design effective studies. As a result, there is not yet a consensus regarding the most effective treatments for adjustment disorder.

There are, however, guidelines for effective approaches in treating people with adjustment disorders. Effective treatments include stress-reduction approaches, therapies that teach coping strategies for any stressors that cannot be reduced or removed, and groups that help patients build support networks of friends, family, and people in similar circumstances. **Psychodynamic psychotherapy** may be helpful in clarifying and interpreting the meaning of the stressor for a particular patient. For example, if the person has cancer, he or she may become more dependent on others, which may be threatening for people who place a high value on self-sufficiency. By exploring those feelings, the patient can then begin to recognize all that is not lost and regain a sense of self-worth.

Therapies that encourage the patient to express the fear, anxiety, rage, helplessness, and hopelessness of dealing with the stressful situation may be helpful. These approaches include **journal therapy**, certain types of **art therapy**, and movement or **dance therapy**. **Support groups** and **group therapy** allow patients to gain perspective on the adversity and establish relationships with others who share their problem. Psychoeducation and medical crisis counseling can assist individuals and families facing stress caused by a medical illness.

Short-term therapies such as **family therapy**, **cognitive-behavioral therapy**, solution-focused therapy, and **interpersonal therapy** have all been used with some success in treating adjustment disorder.

Drugs

Clinicians do not agree on the role of drugs in treating adjustment disorders. Some argue that medications are not necessary for adjustment disorders because of their brief duration. In addition, they maintain that drugs may be counterproductive by undercutting the patient's sense of responsibility and his or her motivation to find effective solutions. At the other end of the spectrum, other clinicians maintain that medication by itself is the best form of treatment, particularly for patients with medical conditions, those who are terminally ill, and those resistant to **psychotherapy**. Others advocate a middle ground of treatment that combines medication and psychotherapy.

Alternative

Spiritual and religious counseling can be helpful, particularly for people coping with existential issues related to physical illness or with moral conflicts related to difficult personal decisions (e.g., divorce, abortion, withdrawing life support from a dying family member).

Some herbal remedies appear to be helpful to some patients with adjustment disorders. For adjustment disorder with anxiety, a randomized controlled trial

QUESTIONS TO ASK YOUR DOCTOR

- How can I tell the difference between a severe reaction to stress that is still within the normal range and an adjustment disorder?
- How many patients have you treated who were diagnosed with an adjustment disorder? What were their outcomes?
- What type of psychotherapy do you recommend for adjustment disorders?
- What is your opinion of spiritual or religious counseling?
- What is your opinion on the use of medications as part of the treatment plan?

found that the 91 patients receiving euphytose (an herbal preparation containing a combination of plant extracts, including crataegus, ballota, passiflora, valeriana, cola, and paullinia) showed significant improvement over the 91 patients taking a placebo. There have been no reported follow-up studies confirming these findings.

Prognosis

Most adults who are diagnosed with adjustment disorder have a favorable prognosis. For most people, an adjustment disorder is temporary and will either resolve by itself or respond to treatment. For some, however, the stressor remains chronic and the symptoms may worsen. In addition, patients with adjustment disorders engage in deliberate self-harm at a rate that surpasses most other mental disorders. They may also be at an increased risk for future **substance abuse** disorders. Still other patients may develop a major depressive disorder even in the absence of an additional stressor.

Some studies have been conducted to follow up on patients five years after their initial diagnosis. At that time, 71% of adults were completely well with no residual symptoms, whereas 21% had developed a major depressive disorder or alcoholism. For children aged 8–13, adjustment disorder did not predict future psychiatric disturbances. For adolescents, however, the prognosis is grimmer. After five years, 43% had developed a major psychiatric disorder, often of far greater severity. These disorders included **schizophrenia**, **schizoaffective disorder**, major depression, substance use disorders, or personality disorders. In contrast to adults, the adolescents' behavioral symptoms and the type of adjustment disorder predicted future mental disorders.

Researchers have noted that once an adjustment disorder is diagnosed, psychotherapy, medication, or both can prevent the development of a more serious mental disorder. Effective treatment is critical, as adjustment disorders are associated with an increased risk of suicide attempts, completed suicide, substance abuse, and various unexplained physical complaints. Patients with chronic stressors may require ongoing treatment for continued symptom management. While patients may not become symptom-free, treatment can halt the progression toward a more serious mental disorder by enhancing the patient's ability to cope.

Prevention

In many cases, there is little possibility of preventing the stressors that trigger adjustment disorders. One preventive strategy that is helpful to many patients, however, is learning to be proactive in managing ordinary stress and maximizing problem-solving abilities when the patients are not in crisis. In addition, the general availability of counseling following a large-scale stressful event may ameliorate some stress responses.

Resources

BOOKS

American Psychiatric Association. *Diagnostic and Statistical Manual of Mental Disorders,* 4th ed., text rev. Washington, DC: APA, 2000.

Black, Donald W., and Nancy C. Andreasen. *Introductory Textbook of Psychiatry*, 5th ed. Arlington, VA: American Psychiatric Publishing, 2011.

Heidenreich, Pascal, and Isidor Pruter, eds. *Handbook of Stress: Causes, Effects, and Control*. Hauppauge, NY: Nova Science Publishers, 2009.

PERIODICALS

Baumeister, H., and K. Kufner. "Is It Time to Adjust the Adjustment Disorder Category?" *Current Opinion in Psychiatry* 22 (July 2009): 409–12.

Casey, P. "Adjustment Disorder: Epidemiology, Diagnosis, and Treatment." *CNS Drugs* 23 (November 1, 2009): 927–38.

Kar, N. "Psychological Impact of Disasters on Children: Review of Assessment and Interventions." *World Journal of Pediatrics* 5 (February 2009): 5–11.

WEBSITES

Mayo Clinic staff. "Adjustment Disorders." MayoClinic.com. March 17, 2011. http://www.mayoclinic.com/health/adjustment-disorders/DS00584 (accessed August 13, 2011).

Benton, Tami D., and Judith A. Ifeagwu. "Adjustment Disorders." Medscape Reference. January 12, 2009. http://emedicine.medscape.com/article/292759-overview (accessed August 13, 2011).

ORGANIZATIONS

American Psychiatric Association, 1000 Wilson Blvd., Ste. 1825, Arlington, VA, 22209-3901, (703) 907-7300, (888) 35-PSYCH (357-7924), apa@psych.org, http://www.psych.org.

Mental Health America, 2000 North Beauregard St., 6th Fl., Alexandria, VA, 22311, (703) 684-7722, (800) 969-6642; TTY: (800) 433-5959, Fax: (703) 684-5968, http://www.nmha.org.

National Alliance on Mental Illness (NAMI), 3803 N. Fairfax Drive, Ste. 100, Arlington, VA, 22203, (703) 524-7600, (800) 950-NAMI (6264), Fax: (703) 524-9094, http://www.nami.org.

National Institute of Mental Health, 6001 Executive Blvd., Rm. 8184, MSC 9663, Bethesda, MD, 20892-9663, (301) 443-4513; TTY: (301) 443-8431, (866) 615-6464; TTY: (866) 415-8051, Fax: (301) 443-4279, nimhinfo@nimh.gov, http://www.nimh.nih.gov.

Holly Scherstuhl, MEd
Emily Jane Willingham, PhD
Tish Davidson, AM

Adrenaline

Definition

Adrenaline (also known as epinephrine) is a hormone and neurotransmitter that the sympathetic nervous system releases as part of the body's "fight-or-flight" response. Adrenaline increases blood and oxygen flow to the muscles, releases stored energy from the liver and fat cells, and prepares the body for quick action.

Description

Synthesis

Epinephrine is an amine hormone. It is produced and released by a region in the central part of the adrenal gland called the adrenal medulla. In a multistep process, enzymes convert the amino acid tyrosine into the chemical L-dopa, which is converted to **dopamine** and then converted to norepinephrine. Epinephrine is synthesized from norepinephrine (noradrenaline) and released into the bloodstream.

Together, epinephrine and norepinephrine are known as the catecholamines. Epinephrine makes up about 80% of the catecholamines that are released as part of the body's **stress** response.

Mechanisms of action

When the body is confronted with a dangerous or stressful situation (such as a test for which someone has not studied or an encounter with a dangerous-looking individual), the fight-or-flight response is initiated. In order to act quickly, the body diverts energy away from areas where it is not needed to those where it is most required, such as the heart and muscles.

When the body senses a threat, the hypothalamus in the **brain** releases nerve signals to the adrenal medulla to release epinephrine and norepinephrine.

When released, the epinephrine circulates around the body through the bloodstream until it reaches its target organs—the heart, blood vessels, liver, and fat cells. The hormone binds to two different types of receptors: alpha-adrenergic and beta-adrenergic receptors. Each of these receptors triggers a different action within cells. Alpha receptors initiate smooth muscle contraction and blood vessel constriction, whereas beta receptors stimulate the heart muscle.

The release of epinephrine causes the following reactions in the body:

- The heart beats faster, pumping additional blood throughout the body and especially to the muscles, in preparation for action.
- Blood vessels constrict, raising the blood pressure.
- Small tubes in the lungs called bronchioles dilate to send more oxygen throughout the body.
- Glycogen (the stored form of glucose) is broken down into glucose in the liver and released.
- Fat stores are released from adipose tissue to be used for energy.
- Blood flow slows to the digestive tract, skin, and kidneys, where it is not needed as much.

KEY TERMS

Adrenaline addiction—A drug-like response some people experience from participating in activities (such as skydiving or gambling) that trigger adrenaline release.

Beta blockers—Drugs that block beta-adrenergic receptors to reduce the actions of epinephrine, thereby lowering the heart rate and blood pressure.

Bronchioles—Tiny tubes in the lungs.

Catecholamines—A class of hormones that includes epinephrine and norepinephrine, which are involved in the fight-or-flight response.

Enzymes—Proteins that trigger chemical reactions in the body.

Glycogen—The form of glucose (sugar) that is stored in the liver and muscles.

Norepinephrine (noradrenaline)—A hormone produced by the adrenal gland, along with epinephrine, as part of the fight-or-flight response.

Tyrosine—The amino acid from which epinephrine is synthesized.

History

The first people to identify the effects of epinephrine were British physician George Oliver (1841–1915) and endocrinologist Edward Albert Sharpey-Schafer (1850–1935). In 1894, they discovered that injecting an extract from the adrenal gland into the bloodstream of an animal raised its blood pressure. Then in 1901, Japanese chemist Jokichi Takamine (1854–1922) isolated and purified epinephrine from the adrenal medulla and patented it. British pharmacologist Henry Dale (1875–1968) began using the name adrenaline for the hormone.

Medication and adrenaline

Epinephrine can be isolated from the adrenal glands of animals and used for medical purposes. It can be injected into the heart to restart the heartbeats of people who are experiencing cardiac arrest. It can open the bronchioles of the lungs in people with asthma, or in those who have had severe allergic responses to food, medications, or other substances. Drugs called **beta blockers** are often given to patients to reduce anxiety. These drugs block beta-adrenergic receptors, slowing the heart rate and lowering blood pressure.

Adrenaline addiction

Some people may experience a drug-like high from participating in behaviors that trigger the body's fight-or-flight response. They are sometimes referred to as "adrenaline junkies" or "adrenaline addicts." For example, people who seek thrills, such as skydivers, mountain climbers, and extreme skiers, experience a rush of adrenaline from the knowledge that their actions could result in severe injury or even death. Compulsive gamblers often cite the reason for their **addiction** as less the desire to win than the physical rush they get from playing. Some people who steal feel that same type of adrenaline rush from the idea that they might be apprehended. The heightened sense of awareness, increased heartbeat, and rapid breathing that occur when the adrenal medulla releases adrenaline is similar to the high that people experience when taking drugs, and it can be similarly addictive.

Resources

BOOKS

Church, Matt. *Adrenaline Junkies and Serotonin Seekers: Balance Your Brain Chemistry to Maximize Energy, Stamina, Mental Sharpness, and Emotional Well-Being.* Berkeley, CA: Ulysses Press, 2004.

Goldstein, David S. *Adrenaline and the Inner World: An Introduction to Scientific Integrative Medicine.* Baltimore, MD: Johns Hopkins University Press, 2006.

Meyer, Jerrold S., and Linda F. Quenzer. *Psychopharmacology: Drugs, the Brain and Behavior.* Sunderland, MA: Sinauer Associates, Inc., 2005.

ORGANIZATIONS

American Psychiatric Association, 1000 Wilson Boulevard, Suite 1825, Arlington, VA, 22209-3901, (703) 907-7300, apa@psych.org, http://www.psych.org.

National Alliance on Mental Illness, 3803 N Fairfax Drive, Suite 100, Arlington, VA, 22203, (703) 524-7600, http://www.nami.org.

National Institute of Mental Health, 6001 Executive Blvd., Room 8184, MSC 9663, Bethesda, MD, 20892-9663, (301) 433-4513; TTY: (301) 443-8431, Fax: (301) 443-4279, Toll-free: (866) 615-6464; TTY: (866) 415-8051, nimhinfo@nih.gov, http://www.nimh.nih.gov.

Stephanie N. Watson

Adult ADHD

Definition

Adult **attention deficit hyperactivity disorder (ADHD)** is the form of ADHD present in persons over 18 years of age. The disorder is also known as adult ADD. ADHD (or ADD) is a disorder characterized by a persistent pattern of inattention and/or hyperactivity. It is estimated that about 60% of children diagnosed with ADHD will continue to have the disorder as adults.

There are three basic types of ADHD in adults as well as children: inattentiveness, impulsiveness, and a combination of the two.

Demographics

Estimates of the prevalence of adult ADHD in North America vary from 2% to 4.4%, or about 8.5 million adults in the United States and Canada. Relatively few of these people are diagnosed, however, so it is likely that the actual rate is higher. The worldwide prevalence of ADHD in adults is estimated to be about 5%; it appears to be higher in developed countries than in poorer ones.

While childhood ADHD affects more males than females (about 2:1), the gender ratio appears to become more even in adults. Some doctors think that the reason for this shift in the ratio is that girls are more likely to fit the inattentive childhood type of the disorder (ADHD-I) and are overlooked in classroom settings, while boys are more likely to exhibit the hyperactive form (ADHD-H) and come to the attention of their teachers and other adults. Adults with ADHD, however, are more likely to be inattentive than hyperactive; thus, women in this population are as likely as men to be diagnosed. Adult ADHD is thought to be equally common in all racial and ethnic groups.

Adult ADHD imposes economic costs on the persons who suffer from it as well as on society at large. A study done in 2004 reported that adults with ADHD who graduated from high school earned $11,000 less per year than their counterparts with the same level of education, while college graduates with adult ADHD earned $4,400 less per year than their counterparts without the disorder. The study estimated that adult ADHD costs the American economy $77 billion each year. For comparison, the annual cost of drug abuse is $58 billion; for alcohol abuse, $85 billion; and for **depression**, $43 billion.

Description

Although ADHD in children has been recognized as a mental disorder since the 1840s (when it was first described by a German physician in his own son), it was not considered

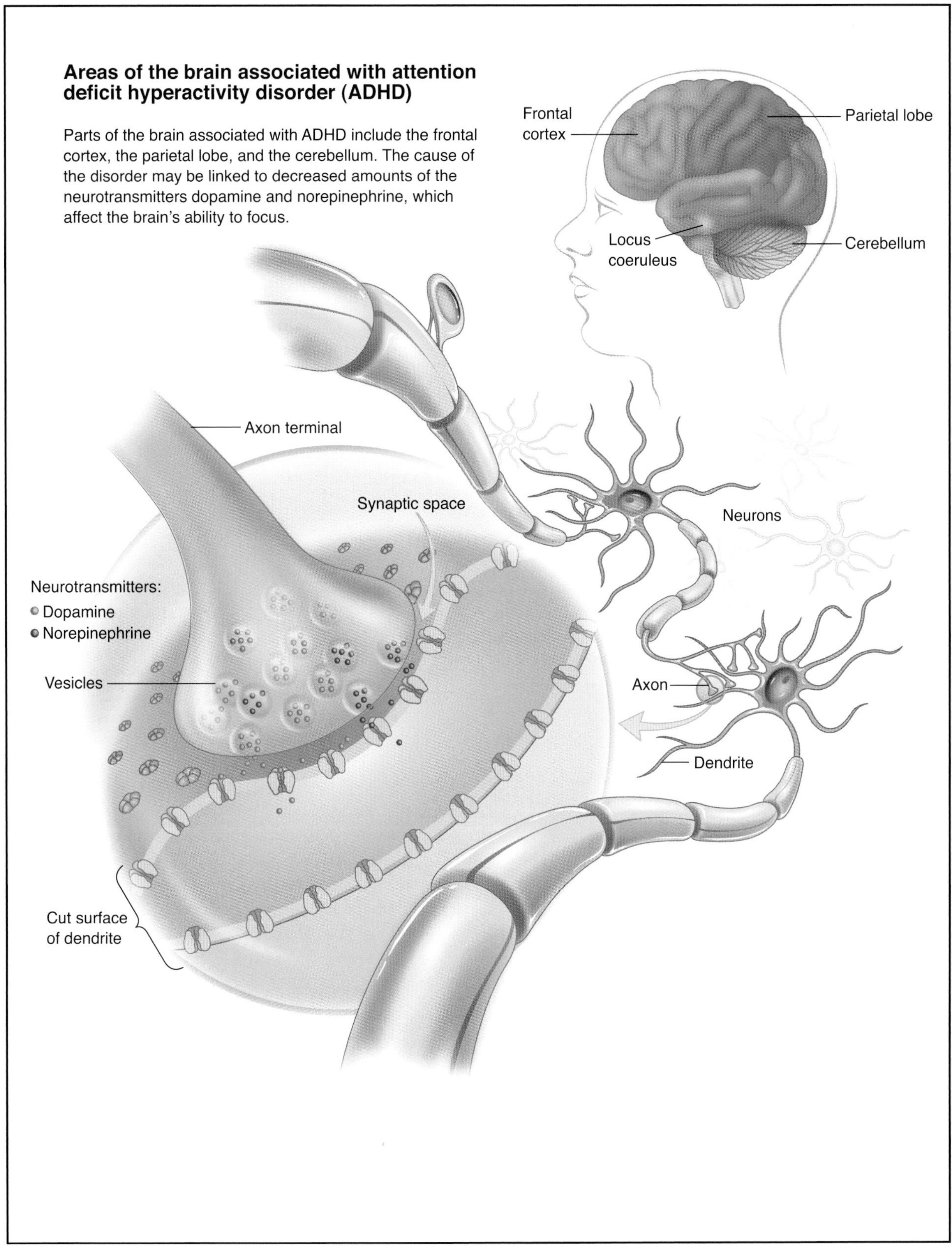

(Illustration by Electronic Illustrators Group. Reproduced by permission of Gale, a part of Cengage Learning.)

an appropriate **diagnosis** for adults until the 1970s, and formal diagnostic criteria for adult ADHD were not defined until 1987. One reason for the delay in recognizing the adult form of the disorder is that the symptoms of ADHD in adults are somewhat different from those in children; adults are less likely to display hyperactive behaviors. Adults with ADHD are more likely to say that they have trouble relaxing than feeling that they have to race around physically. Inattentiveness in an adult may take the form of forgetting meetings, work deadlines, or social get-togethers, and impulsiveness may take the form of moodiness, temper tantrums, or impatience in traffic jams. In addition, highly intelligent adults with ADHD are likely to have developed coping behaviors that mask their symptoms.

Adult ADHD can be summarized as a disorder affecting the person's executive functions, combined with difficulties in self-regulation and self-motivation. The executive functions are a set of mental abilities that control or manage other cognitive processes; they include the ability to plan ahead, to make decisions among several possible courses of action, to inhibit behaviors that are inappropriate in a specific setting, to choose appropriate behaviors, to think abstractly, and to use deductive reasoning. Adults with ADHD are likely to be seen by friends and coworkers as disorganized, unable to complete work assignments on time, easily distracted, overly emotional, or needing constant stimulation.

Risk factors

Risk factors for adult ADHD include:

- family history of the disorder
- having a mother who smoked, drank, or used drugs during pregnancy
- having a mother who was exposed to environmental toxins during pregnancy
- being born prematurely
- exposure to environmental toxins in childhood

Causes and symptoms

Causes

The causes of ADHD are not completely understood; however, studies of **brain** function using **positron emission tomography (PET)** scans indicate that the brains of children with ADHD may be structured differently from those of children without the disorder. More specifically, some researchers think that the parts of the brain that govern attentiveness do not have normal levels of **dopamine**, a chemical produced by the brain that allows nerve cells to transmit signals from one cell to another. Dopamine and another chemical called norepinephrine are **neurotransmitters** that play an important role in brain function. The uptake transporters for dopamine and norepinephrine are overly active in people with ADHD and clear these neurotransmitters from the connections between nerve cells much more rapidly than in normal individuals. The fact that medications that stimulate the release of dopamine are beneficial to patients with ADHD supports this theory.

There are also **genetic factors** involved in ADHD, though no specific causal gene has been identified as of 2011. It is known that the disorder runs in families; the parents and siblings of children with ADHD are two to eight times more likely to develop ADHD than the general population. The discovery through genome-wide association studies of a protein network implicated in adult ADHD may indicate that candidate genes for the disorder will be identified in the next few years.

Some researchers think that environmental toxins, particularly lead, and a mother's drinking or smoking during pregnancy are risk factors for ADHD. There is also some evidence that very low birth weight or premature birth may be risk factors for the disorder. It

KEY TERMS

Comorbidity—The presence of one or more disorders (or diseases) in a patient in addition to a primary disease or disorder.

Dopamine—A brain chemical that helps to regulate movement.

DSM—*Diagnostic and Statistical Manual of Mental Disorders*, a publication produced by the American Psychiatric Association and used by medical professionals in diagnosing mental disorders.

Executive functions—An umbrella term for the group of mental processes responsible for planning, abstract thinking, logical deduction, choosing appropriate behaviors and inhibiting inappropriate behaviors, and distinguishing between relevant and irrelevant sensory information.

Impairment—A physical or mental defect at the level of a major body system or organ.

Norepinephrine—Another brain chemical that affects a person's ability to pay attention.

Prevalence—The number of cases of a disease or disorder existing in a specific population at a given point in time.

Psychostimulant—A type of drug that increases the activity of the parts of the brain that produce dopamine.

is not known whether the emotional climate of a family contributes to the disorder, although some doctors think that mood or **anxiety disorders** in other family members may make a child's symptoms worse. Other theories proposing that ADHD is caused by head injuries, allergic reactions to food additives, or a diet high in sugary foods or energy drinks are considered unproven.

Symptoms

The symptoms of adult ADHD may appear in several areas of the person's life. Adults with ADHD are likely to have experienced trouble in the following areas:

- academic—underachievement in school, grade repetition, documented disciplinary infractions, incompletion of school, or frequently changed courses of study or educational institutions
- work—frequent changes of employment, history of frequent firing or poor performance reviews, difficulty moving up the employment ladder, or lower socioeconomic status
- social/legal—history of driving violations, including collisions, speeding, DUI citations, and other moving violations; use of illegal substances; heavy smoking; heavy alcohol consumption
- relationships—history of frequent breakups before marriage, repeated marriages, or frequent divorces; possible history of sexual promiscuity, unplanned pregnancy, and sexually transmitted diseases

Supervisors and coworkers may believe that the adult with ADHD does not listen to instructions, or they may resent having to finish the affected person's job assignments because he or she is easily distracted or cannot identify priorities. People related or married to an adult with ADHD often complain about having to cope with the consequences of the patient's impulsive behavior and poor decisions as well as his or her short temper, irritability, and irresponsibility.

Diagnosis

The diagnosis of adult ADHD is clinical, which means that it is based on the doctor's evaluation and judgment rather than the results of laboratory or imaging tests. Diagnosis is often complicated by the fact that between 50% and 80% of adults with ADHD have a concurrent mood or **substance abuse** disorder. In some cases, adults with ADHD consult a doctor because they are concerned about their work history, difficulties with schooling, or relationship problems; in other cases, they may seek help when they notice symptoms of ADHD in their child, or when the child is diagnosed with ADHD.

There are four major criteria for the diagnosis of adult ADHD:

- Specific symptoms. Adults with the inattentive form of ADHD may procrastinate, be indecisive, have difficulty recalling and organizing task-related materials, lose track of time, have difficulty managing time, avoid tasks or jobs that require sustained attention, have difficulty starting tasks or following through on them, and have trouble shifting attention from one task to another. Adults with the hyperactive/impulsive form of ADHD may choose only highly active, stimulating jobs; avoid uninteresting or sedentary work; moonlight at multiple jobs or work long hours; seek constant activity; become bored easily or act impatient; make impulsive decisions; frequently express irritation or lose their temper easily; and behave irresponsibly.
- Impairment in two or more areas of life (e.g., work, education, relationships, social situations). "Impairment" means that the adult's level of functioning is seriously affected by the behaviors.
- A persistent pattern of signs and symptoms beginning no later than age seven. Early recognition is essential for a later diagnosis of adult ADHD, as ADHD is not an adult-onset disorder. While it is not necessary for an adult to have been formally diagnosed with ADHD as a child, childhood symptoms of the disorder must be documented. Documentation may include school report cards; interviews with the adult's parents, if still living; or childhood symptoms self-reported by the adult.
- The symptoms cannot be better accounted for by another mental disorder. It is particularly important to evaluate the patient for mood disorders, because about 50% of adults diagnosed with ADHD have comorbid mood disorders.

Examination

A complete physical examination is important in order to rule out vision problems, hearing loss, seizure disorder, disorders of the thyroid gland, hypoglycemia (low blood sugar), or other possible physical causes of the patient's symptoms. It is also important for the doctor to be aware of any other medications that the patient may be taking for high blood pressure, diabetes, or other chronic physical disorders, as these may influence the choice of medications to treat the ADHD.

Tests

The physical examination is accompanied by a series of interviews with psychiatrists and psychologists. The patient may be given the Wechsler Adult Intelligence Scale (WAIS) or a similar test of intelligence and general knowledge in adults. The patient may also be given the **Structured Clinical Interview for DSM-IV** (SCID), which is an instrument used for the differential diagnosis of mental disorders according to *DSM-IV* categories. The SCID is useful in evaluating adult ADHD patients for comorbid mood, anxiety, or substance abuse disorders.

There are behavioral checklists and questionnaires for adult ADHD that doctors can use to narrow the diagnostic possibilities. A set of criteria called the Wender Utah Rating Scale (WURS) is commonly used to diagnose ADHD in adults:

- a history of ADHD in childhood
- hyperactivity and poor ability to focus or concentrate
- difficulty completing tasks
- mood swings
- difficulty controlling temper
- inability to handle stress
- impulsive behaviors

Another instrument that may be used in evaluating adults with ADHD is the Brown ADD Scale (BADDS) for adults. Based on Brown's model of ADHD as a disorder of executive functioning, the BADDS scale measures the patient's ability to function in six major areas:

- activation—organizing tasks and materials, estimating the time required, prioritizing tasks, and starting the work
- focus—focusing on a task and sustaining focus without being distracted
- effort—sustaining effort over long-term as well as short-term projects and remaining alert until the task is completed
- emotion—regulating and controlling emotions rather than allowing them to overwhelm thought processes and interfere with completing a task
- memory—accessing short-term memories and recalling as needed to complete a task
- action—thinking before acting impulsively, regulating the speed of work in order to complete tasks on time, and monitoring the context of interactions with other people

Procedures

In some cases, the doctor may recommend a CT scan or MRI to rule out head **trauma**, brain tumors, infections, seizure disorders, or other physical disorders that may affect the structure or functioning of the brain and produce symptoms resembling those of ADHD.

Treatment

Treatment for adults with ADHD is similar to that for children, namely, a combination of medications and **psychotherapy**. There are no surgical treatments recommended for ADHD.

Traditional

There are several different forms of psychotherapy that are reported to benefit adults diagnosed with ADHD. They include **cognitive-behavioral therapy** (CBT), which helps to correct poor self-image by encouraging the patient to look at and challenge the habits of negative thought and behavior. Relaxation training and **stress management** techniques to lower anxiety levels are also helpful. Patients who have particular difficulties with intimate relationships may be helped by **couples therapy** or **family therapy**.

Another approach to psychotherapy that is often recommended for adults with ADHD is behavioral coaching and job mentoring. The patient is taught such skills as time management; making reminder lists and keeping a calendar to organize and keep track of tasks; having one particular place in the home or office for such items as keys, bills, and other paperwork; and breaking down large or long-term tasks into smaller portions or time segments. In job mentoring, the patient is helped to gain a better understanding of workplace relationships—particularly what coworkers and supervisors reasonably should be able to expect of him or her—and ways to improve on-the-job functioning. However, coaching should not be considered a substitute for medication and formal psychotherapy.

Drugs

Medications are the mainstay of treatment for adult ADHD. The drugs most commonly prescribed are psychostimulants, which work by raising the level of dopamine and balancing the levels of other neurotransmitters in the patient's nervous system. These drugs are reported to benefit about 80% of patients. The psychostimulants most often prescribed for adults with ADHD are **methylphenidate** (Ritalin, Concerta, Daytrana, Metadate), **dextroamphetamine** (Dexedrine), **lisdexamfetamine** (Vyvanse), and dextroamphetamine-amphetamine (Adderall). Psychostimulants are available in both short-acting (about 4 hours) and long-acting (6 to 12 hours) forms; some adults with ADHD prefer the long-acting forms because they relieve concern about remembering to take another dose of medication during the day. Methylphenidate is also available in a long-acting patch form, sold under the trade name Daytrana. The patch is worn on the hip.

A newer drug that was approved by the U.S. Food and Drug Administration (FDA) in 2004 for the treatment of adult ADHD is **atomoxetine**, a

QUESTIONS TO ASK YOUR DOCTOR

- How can I tell whether I suffer from adult ADHD?
- My child has been recently diagnosed with ADHD. Does that mean that I also have the disorder?
- Have you ever treated an adult diagnosed with ADHD? Was their treatment successful?
- What is the difference between nonstimulant and psychostimulant medications?
- Can you recommend a coaching program for adults with ADHD?

nonstimulant. It was the only nonstimulant approved for this purpose as of 2011. Atomoxetine is a selective norepinephrine reuptake inhibitor sold under the trade name Strattera. Atomoxetine has a significant advantage over psychostimulants in that it is less likely to be abused, making it a good choice for patients with a history of substance abuse.

Patients with comorbid mood disorders may be prescribed antidepressant medications. The older tricyclic drugs have been found helpful in adults with ADHD, as has **venlafaxine** (Effexor), an antidepressant classified as a serotonin-norepinephrine reuptake inhibitor (SNRI). Another antidepressant found to benefit adult ADHD patients in **clinical trials** is **bupropion** (Wellbutrin), an atypical antidepressant that inhibits the reuptake of dopamine.

One important consideration for adult ADHD patients is to make sure that stimulants or other medications prescribed to treat the ADHD do not interact with other medications that the adult may be taking for chronic conditions such as high blood pressure, diabetes, anxiety disorders, and the like. In addition, adult athletes may need specialized medical therapy because many competitive sports bodies ban the use of psychostimulants.

As of mid-2011, there were 293 clinical trials of treatments for adult ADHD. Many of these are studies of the comparative effectiveness of medications already used to treat the disorder or studies of newer extended-release or long-acting formulations of these drugs. There were also several trials of investigational drugs, including **duloxetine** (Cymbalta), another norepinephrine reuptake inhibitor that was originally developed to treat major depression, and a drug identified only as PF-3654746. One study is investigating the effectiveness of massage therapy as a treatment for adult ADHD.

Alternative

Some forms of alternative medicine that have been suggested as treatments for adult ADHD include special **diets**, vitamin supplements, omega-3 fatty acids, and various herbal preparations (particularly **ginseng**, **ginkgo biloba** extract, or Chinese herbal medicines). There was no evidence as of 2011 that any of these alternative approaches was useful. There is some evidence, however, that **yoga** is a beneficial form of **exercise** for adults with ADHD, as it helps to teach focus, and the breathing exercises that are part of yoga are relaxing to many people.

Although some alternative practitioners have recommended medical marijuana as a short-term treatment for adult ADHD, most mainstream physicians disapprove its use because of the risk of substance abuse and a depressive disorder.

Prognosis

There was no cure for adult ADHD as of 2011, but the disorder usually can be managed, allowing the affected individual to improve functioning in daily life, including completing his or her education, forming stable relationships, and securing steady employment. Another benefit of treatment for ADHD is an improvement in the patient's self-esteem; perceived failures in various areas of life caused by the ADHD may cause low self-esteem and lead to mood or substance abuse disorders.

Prevention

There is no known way to prevent adult ADHD, because the causes of the disorder are still not completely understood.

Resources

BOOKS

American Psychiatric Association. *Diagnostic and Statistical Manual of Mental Disorders*. 4th ed., text rev. Washington, DC: American Psychiatric Association, 2000.

Barkley, Russell A. *Taking Charge of Adult ADHD*. New York: Guilford Press, 2010.

Brown, Thomas E. *Attention Deficit Disorder: The Unfocused Mind in Children and Adults*. New Haven, CT: Yale University Press, 2005.

Ramsay, J. Russell. *Nonmedication Treatments for Adult ADHD: Evaluating Impact on Daily Functioning and Well-Being*. Washington, DC: American Psychological Association, 2010.

Sarkis, Stephanie Moulton. *Adult ADD: A Guide for the Newly Diagnosed.* Oakland, CA: New Harbinger Publications, 2011.

Solanto, Mary V. *Cognitive-Behavioral Therapy for Adult ADHD: Targeting Executive Dysfunction*. New York: The Guilford Press, 2011.

PERIODICALS

Antshel, K.M., et al. "Advances in Understanding and Treating ADHD." *BMC Medicine* 9 (June 10, 2011): 72.

Bell, A.S. "A Critical Review of ADHD Diagnostic Criteria: What to Address in the DSM-V." *Journal of Attention Disorders* 15 (January 2011): 3–10.

Ermer, J.C., et al. "Pharmacokinetic Variability of Long-Acting Stimulants in the Treatment of Children and Adults with Attention-Deficit Hyperactivity Disorder." *CNS Drugs* 24 (December 1, 2010): 1009–25.

Haavik, J., et al. "Clinical Assessment and Diagnosis of Adults with Attention-Deficit/Hyperactivity Disorder." *Expert Review of Neurotherapeutics* 10 (October 2010): 1569–80.

Kutcher, J.S. "Treatment of Attention-Deficit Hyperactivity Disorder in Athletes." *Current Sports Medicine Reports* 10 (January–February 2011): 32–36.

Poelmans, G., et al. "Integrated Genome-wide Association Study Findings: Identification of a Neurodevelopmental Network for Attention Deficit Hyperactivity Disorder." *American Journal of Psychiatry* 168 (April 2011): 365–77.

Rösler, M., et al. "Attention Deficit Hyperactivity Disorder in Adults." *World Journal of Biological Psychiatry* 11 (August 2010): 684–98.

Rucklidge, J.J. "Gender Differences in Attention-deficit/ Hyperactivity Disorder." *Psychiatric Clinics of North America* 33 (June 2010): 357–73.

Wallis, D. "The Search for Biomarkers for Attention Deficit/ Hyperactivity Disorder." *Drug News and Perspectives* 23 (September 2010): 438–49.

WEBSITES

Adler, Lenard. "Adult ADHD" [3-1/2-minute video about ADHD in adults]. The Doctor's Channel. http://www.thedoctorschannel.com/video/2222.html?specialty=26 (accessed July 9, 2011).

"Adults Living with ADHD." National Alliance on Mental Illness (NAMI). http://www.nami.org/Template.cfm?Section=ADHD&Template=/ContentManagement/ContentDisplay.cfm&ContentID=106057 (accessed July 9, 2011).

"Attention-Deficit/Hyperactivity Disorder." U.S. Centers for Disease Control and Prevention (CDC). http://www.cdc.gov/ncbddd/adhd (accessed July 9, 2011).

Children and Adults with Attention-Deficit/Hyperactivity Disorder (CHADD). "What We Know: Diagnosis of ADHD in Adults." National Resource Center on ADHD. http://www.help4adhd.org/en/treatment/guides/WWK9 (accessed July 9, 2011).

Jaksa, Peter. "ADHD Fact Sheet." Attention Deficit Disorder Association (ADDA). http://www.add.org/?page=ADHD_Fact_Sheet (accessed July 10, 2011).

Mayo Clinic staff. "Adult ADHD (Attention-Deficit/Hyperactivity Disorder)." MayoClinic.com. http://www.mayoclinic.com/health/adult-adhd/DS01161 (accessed July 10, 2011).

National Institute of Mental Health. "Can Adults Have ADHD?" U.S. National Institutes of Health. http://www.nimh.nih.gov/health/publications/attention-deficit-hyperactivity-disorder/can-adults-have-adhd.shtml (accessed July 9, 2011).

ORGANIZATIONS

American Psychiatric Association, 1000 Wilson Boulevard, Suite 1825, Arlington, VA, 22209-3901, (703) 907-7300, apa@psych.org, http://www.psych.org.

Attention Deficit Disorder Association (ADDA), PO Box 7557, Wilmington, DE, 19803-9997, (800) 939-1019, info@add.org, http://www.add.org.

Centers for Disease Control and Prevention (CDC), 1600 Clifton Rd., Atlanta, GA, 30333, (800) 232-4636, cdcinfo@cdc.gov, http://www.cdc.gov.

Children and Adults with Attention-Deficit/Hyperactivity Disorder (CHADD), 8181 Professional Place, Suite 150, Landover, MD, 20785, (301) 306-7070, (800) 233-4050, Fax: (301) 306-7090, http://www.chadd.org.

National Alliance on Mental Illness (NAMI), 3803 N. Fairfax Dr., Suite 100, Arlington, VA, 22203, (703) 524-7600, (800) 950-NAMI, Fax: (703) 524-9094, http://www.nami.org.

National Institute of Mental Health (NIMH), 6001 Executive Boulevard, Room 8184, MSC 9663, Bethesda, MD, 20892-9663, (301) 443-4513, (866) 615-6464, Fax: (301) 443-4279, nimhinfo@nih.gov, http://www.nimh.nih.gov/index.shtml.

National Resource Center on ADHD, 8181 Professional Place, Suite 150, Landover, MD, 20785, (800) 233-4050, http://www.help4adhd.org.

Rebecca J. Frey, Ph.D.

Advance directives

Definition

An advance directive is a written document in which people clearly specify how medical decisions affecting them are to be made if they are unable to make them, or authorize a specific person to make such decisions for them. These documents are sometimes called living wills. Psychiatric advance directives serve the same purpose as general medical advance directives but are written by mental health consumers as a set of directions for others to follow prior to the onset of a period in which their decision making is impaired or an incapacitating crisis arises.

Description

Many states have passed laws related to medical advance directives and psychiatric advance directives. Advance directives usually fall into two categories: instruction directives and agent-driven directives. These two distinct documents may, in some cases, be combined into one form.

KEY TERMS

Conservator—Legal guardian.

Do Not Resuscitate order—A directive specifying that if an individual's heart stops, he or she should not receive cardiopulmonary resuscitation (CPR).

Proxy—An individual who makes decisions on behalf of another.

Instruction directives

An instruction directive is a written document that specifies the treatments individuals do and do not want, in the event that they become unable to make decisions about their care. These documents may indicate the affected individual's preferences about many aspects of treatment, including:

- people who should be contacted at a time of a medical or psychiatric crisis
- acceptable and unacceptable medications and dosages
- preferences for or against specific treatments such as tube feeding or breathing machines
- a Do Not Resuscitate order
- preferences about organ and tissue donation
- religious preferences

Agent-driven directives

An agent-driven directive may also be called a durable power of attorney. This directive is a signed, dated, and witnessed document that authorizes a designated person (usually a family member or close friend) to act as an agent or proxy. This empowers the proxy to make medical decisions for patients when they are deemed unable to make these decisions for themselves. The directive frequently includes the person's stated preferences in regard to treatment. Several states do not allow any of the following people to act as a person's proxy:

- the person's physician or other healthcare provider
- the staff of the healthcare facility(ies) providing the person's care
- guardians (often called conservators) of the person's financial affairs
- employees of federal agencies financially responsible for a person's care
- any person who serves as agent or proxy for 10 people or more

The person who is to act as the proxy should be familiar with the individual's expressed wishes about care and should understand how to work within the medical and mental health system.

Although most advance directives address situations arising from physical disability, according to Mental Health America, it has become increasingly accepted over the past 30 years for consumers of mental health services to know which treatments work best for them, and their opinions have become increasingly valued by those providing services. However, when mental health consumers become unable to make decisions or to give **informed consent** for treatments offered, others (including family, friends, judges, or care providers) make the decisions for them in crisis. In this situation, advance directives may be beneficial for people receiving care, as the legal document may protect them from unwanted treatment or **involuntary hospitalization**. In some states, the laws detail the content of psychiatric advance directives, which may include instructions about antipsychotic medication, **electroconvulsive therapy**, or hospital admission, and the naming of people who can act as surrogate decision makers if necessary.

Special concerns

In the United States, each state has specific laws about medical advance directives. How those laws apply to psychiatric advance directives can differ by state as well; a few states exclude psychiatric advance directives from their statutes altogether. The specific form the advance directive should take, the language it should use, and the number of witnesses required to make the document legal and binding vary from state to state; the document should be prepared by an attorney familiar with state advance directive requirements. In general, physicians and other healthcare professionals are expected to comply with the instructions of an advance directive, as long as those instructions are within the guidelines of accepted medical practice. It is recommended that people speak to their attorneys or physicians to ensure that their wishes are communicated in a form that is legally acceptable in their state.

In drafting an advance directive, the patient must be deemed lucid and able to communicate their wishes in order for the document to be valid. This assessment is generally done by a physician, although state laws vary, and some do not recognize this requirement.

Some other considerations associated with advance directives center on how they are implemented and whether or not a person who wants to complete one actually does so. Completing an advance directive can be difficult

QUESTIONS TO ASK YOUR DOCTOR

- Do you have an example of an advance directive from this state?
- What are some items you recommend putting into an advance directive?
- Could you explain some of the possible procedures I may wish to address in my advanced directive?
- Where should I file my advance directive?
- Can you put a copy in my file?
- Who else should I tell about my advance directive?

emotionally, and psychological, literacy, and informational barriers can exist. Various solutions have been suggested to address these problems, including a proposal for video-based advance directives in which individuals produce videotapes documenting their directives. In addition, even though as many as two-thirds of people with mental illness report that they would complete a psychiatric advance directive, only 4%–13% of outpatients receiving mental health treatment through public sector resources report having done so. A study published in the January 2011 issue of the American Psychiatric Association's journal *Psychiatric Services* found that, of more than 13,500 seniors living in nursing homes, patients with serious mental illnesses were 24% less likely to have prepared advance directives compared to residents with no mental illness. The study also noted that residents with mental illness were among the most likely groups to need advance directives, due to the high possibility of developing a disability and/or comorbid—co-occurring but unrelated—disorder. One proposal put forward to address this disconnect is the implementation of facilitated psychiatric advance directives involving a guided discussion and review of choices for completing an advance directive.

Resources

BOOKS

Kingsbury, Leigh Ann Creaney. *People Planning Ahead: A Guide to Communicating Healthcare and End of Life Wishes.* Washington, DC: American Association on Intellectual and Developmental Disabilities, 2009.

Swota, Alissa Hurwitz. *Culture, Ethics, and Advance Care Planning.* Lanham, MD: Lexington Books, 2009.

Thomas, Keri, and Ben Lobo, eds. *Advance Care Planning in End of Life Care.* Oxford: Oxford University Press, 2010.

PERIODICALS

Alfonso, Heather. "The Importance of Living Wills and Advance Directives." *Journal of Gerontological Nursing* 35, no. 10 (October 2009): 42–45.

Black, Kathy. "Promoting Advance Care Planning Through the National Healthcare Decisions Day Initiative." *Journal of Social Work in End-Of-Life and Palliative Care* 6, nos. 1–2 (January 2010): 11–26.

Pollack, Keshia M., Dan Morhaim, and Michael A. Williams. "The Public's Perspectives on Advance Directives: Implications for State Legislative and Regulatory Policy." *Health Policy* 96, no. 1 (June 2010): 57–63.

ORGANIZATIONS

American Bar Association, 321 N Clark St., Chicago, IL, 60654-7598, (800) 285-2221, http://www.americanbar.org.

American Hospital Association, 325 7th St. NW, Washington, DC, 20004-2802, (202) 638-1100, http://www.aha.org.

American Medical Association, 515 N State St., Chicago, IL, 60610, (800) 621-8335, http://www.ama-assn.org.

Joan Schonbeck, RN
Emily Jane Willingham, PhD
Tish Davidson, AM

Affect

Definition

Affect is a psychological term for an observable expression of emotion.

Description

A person's affect is the expression of emotion or feelings displayed to others through facial expressions, hand gestures, voice tone, and other emotional signs such as laughter or tears. Individual affect fluctuates according to emotional state. What is considered a normal range of affect, called the "broad affect," varies from culture to culture and even within a culture. Certain individuals may gesture prolifically while talking and display dramatic facial expressions in reaction to social situations or other stimuli. Others may show little outward response to social environments or interactions, expressing a narrow range of emotions.

There is some evidence that purposely changing affect can also bring about real changes in mood or feelings. Purposely making a face that is intended to display anger, for example, has been shown to actually increase the levels of anger and frustration. Although

KEY TERMS

Blunted affect—A lack of display of emotion or feelings, including monotone voice and expressionless face.

Labile affect—A display of frequently changing emotion or mood.

QUESTIONS TO ASK YOUR DOCTOR

- How do I know if I or my loved one is expressing a normal range of affect?
- What can I do if I feel my child is not displaying emotions normally?
- Can you recommend a psychologist or psychiatrist for an evaluation?

these changes are usually quite small, they suggest that affect is both a result of emotion and, in some cases, a cause of it.

People with psychological disorders may display variations in their affect. A "restricted" or "constricted" affect describes a mild restriction in the range or intensity of display of feelings. As the reduction in display of emotion becomes more severe, the term "blunted" affect may be applied. The absence of any exhibition of emotions is described as "flat" affect; the voice is monotone, the face expressionless, and the body immobile. "Labile" affect describes emotional instability or dramatic mood swings. When the outward display of emotion is out of context for the situation, such as laughter while describing pain or sadness, the affect is termed "inappropriate."

Resources

BOOKS

Balconi, Michela, ed. *Emotional Face Comprehension: Neuropsychological Perspectives.* New York: Nova Science, 2008.

Cole, Jonathan, and Henrietta Spalding. *The Invisible Smile: Living Without Facial Expression.* New York: Oxford University Press, 2009.

Mooney, Carla. *Mood Disorders.* San Diego, CA: Reference Point Press, 2010.

Reeve, Johnmarshall. *Understanding Motivation and Emotion,* 5th ed. Hoboken, NJ: John Wiley & Sons, 2009.

PERIODICALS

Bogaerts, Kathleen, et al. "Negative Affective Pictures Can Elicit Physical Symptoms in High Habitual Symptom Reporters." *Psychology and Health* 25, no. 6 (2010): 685–98.

Dowd, Haulie, Alex Zautra, and Michael Hogan. "Emotion, Stress, and Cardiovascular Response: An Experimental Test of Models of Positive and Negative Affect." *International Journal of Behavioral Medicine* 17, no. 3 (2010): 189–94.

ORGANIZATIONS

American Psychiatric Association, 1000 Wilson Blvd., Ste. 1825, Arlington, VA, 22209-3901, (703) 907-7300, apa@psych.org, http://www.psych.org.

American Psychological Association, 750 1st St. NE, Washington, DC, 20002-4242, (202) 336-5500; TDD/TTY: (202) 336-6123, (800) 374-2721, http://www.apa.org.

Tish Davidson, AM

Agoraphobia

Definition

Agoraphobia is an anxiety disorder characterized by intense fear related to being in situations from which escape might be difficult or embarrassing (e.g., being on a bus or train) or in which help might not be available in the event of a **panic attack** or panic symptoms. Panic is defined as extreme and unreasonable fear and anxiety.

Agoraphobia is the fear of being trapped in a place where exiting may be difficult, such as in a crowd situation.
(© bildagentur-online.com/schneider/Alamy)

Demographics

In general, phobias are the most common mental disorders in the U.S. population, affecting about 7% of adults, or 6.4 million Americans. Agoraphobia is one of the most common phobias, affecting between 2.7% and 5.8% of American adults. The onset of symptoms is most likely to occur between age 15 and age 35. The lifetime prevalence of agoraphobia is estimated at 5%–12%. Like most phobias, agoraphobia is two to four times more common in women than in men. The incidence of agoraphobia appears to be similar across racial and ethnic groups in the United States.

Description

The word "agoraphobia" comes from two Greek words that mean "marketplace" (agora) and "fear" (phobos). The anxiety associated with agoraphobia leads to avoidance of situations that involve being away from home alone, being in crowds, being on a bridge, or traveling by car or public transportation. Agoraphobia may intensify to the point that it interferes with a person's ability to take a job outside the home or to carry out such ordinary errands and activities as shopping for groceries or going out to a movie. According to the handbook used by mental health professionals to diagnose mental disorders, the ***Diagnostic and Statistical Manual of Mental Disorders***, fourth edition, text revision, also known as the *DSM-IV-TR,* individuals with agoraphobia typically are afraid of such symptoms as feeling dizzy, having an attack of diarrhea, fainting, or "going crazy."

The close association in agoraphobia between fear of being outside one's home and fear of having panic symptoms is reflected in the *DSM-IV-TR* classification of two separate disorders: **panic disorder** (PD) with agoraphobia and agoraphobia without PD. PD is characterized by sudden attacks of fear and panic. There may be no known reason for the occurrence of panic attacks; they are frequently triggered by fear-producing events or thoughts, such as driving or being in an elevator. PD is believed to be due to an abnormal activation of the body's hormonal system, causing a sudden fight-or-flight response.

People with agoraphobia appear to have two distinct types of anxiety: panic and the anticipatory anxiety related to fear of future panic attacks. The chief distinction between PD with agoraphobia and agoraphobia without PD is that individuals who are diagnosed with PD with agoraphobia meet all criteria for PD; in agoraphobia without PD, individuals are afraid of panic-like symptoms in public places, rather than full-blown panic attacks.

Proposed changes to the DSM for its fifth edition (*DSM-5*, 2013) include classifying agoraphobia as a separate and unique disorder, and removing it as a limiter for panic disorder. This revision recognizes that the two conditions may occur comorbidly, or at the same time, but considers them completely distinct.

Causes and symptoms

Causes

In the early 2010s, the causes of agoraphobia are viewed as complex and not completely understood. Research indicates several factors can contribute to the condition.

GENETIC. It has been known for some years that **anxiety disorders** tend to run in families. Recent research has confirmed earlier hypotheses that there is a genetic component to agoraphobia, and that it can be separated from susceptibility to PD. Researchers believe they have discovered a genetic locus on human chromosome 3 that governs a person's risk of developing agoraphobia. PD was found to be associated with two loci: one on human chromosome 1 and the other on chromosome 11q. Researchers concluded that agoraphobia and PD are both inheritable anxiety disorders that share some, but not all, of their genetic loci for susceptibility. If a person has a family member with agoraphobia, he or she is at higher risk of developing the disorder.

INNATE TEMPERAMENT. A number of researchers have pointed to inborn temperament as a broad vulnerability factor in the development of anxiety and mood disorders. In other words, a person's natural disposition or temperament may become a factor in developing a number of mood or anxiety disorders. Some people seem more sensitive throughout their lives to events, but upbringing and life history are also important factors in determining who will develop these disorders. Children who manifest what is known as behavioral inhibition (a group of behaviors that are displayed when the child is confronted with a new situation or unfamiliar people) in early infancy are at increased risk for developing more than one anxiety disorder in adult life, particularly if the inhibition remains over time. These behaviors include agitated movement (such as hyperextension), crying, and general irritability, followed by withdrawing, seeking comfort from a familiar person, and ceasing all action when noticing a new person or situation. Children of depressed or anxious parents are more likely to develop behavioral inhibition.

PHYSIOLOGICAL REACTIONS TO ILLNESS. Another factor in the development of PD and agoraphobia appears to be a history of respiratory disease. Some researchers have hypothesized that repeated episodes of respiratory disease can predispose a child to PD by making breathing difficult and lowering the threshold for feeling suffocated. It is also possible that respiratory diseases could generate fearful beliefs in the child's mind that would lead him or her to exaggerate the significance of respiratory symptoms.

LIFE EVENTS. About 42% of individuals diagnosed with agoraphobia report histories of real or feared separation from their parents or other caretakers in childhood. This statistic has been interpreted to mean that agoraphobia in adults is the aftermath of unresolved childhood separation anxiety. The fact that many individuals diagnosed with agoraphobia report that their first episode occurred after the death of a loved one, and the observation that other people with agoraphobia feel safe in going out as long as someone is with them, have been taken as supportive evidence of the separation anxiety hypothesis. However, there is little clinical research supporting this theory.

LEARNED BEHAVIOR. There are also theories about human learning that explain agoraphobia. It is thought that a person's initial experience of panic-like symptoms in a specific situation—for example, being alone in a subway station—may lead the person to associate physical symptoms of panic with all subway stations. Avoiding all subway stations would then reduce the level of the person's discomfort. Unfortunately, the avoidance strengthens the phobia because the person is unlikely to have the opportunity to test whether subway stations actually cause uncomfortable physical sensations. One of the most effective treatment modalities, exposure therapy, is based on the premise that phobias can be unlearned by reversing the pattern of avoidance.

SOCIAL FACTORS RELATED TO GENDER. Gender role socialization has been suggested as an explanation for the fact that the majority of individuals with agoraphobia are women. One form of this hypothesis maintains that some parents still teach girls to be fearful and timid about venturing out in public. Another version relates agoraphobia to the mother-daughter relationship, maintaining that mothers tend to give daughters mixed messages about becoming separate individuals. As a result, girls grow up with a more fragile sense of self and may stay within the physical boundaries of their home because they lack a firm sense of their internal psychological boundaries.

Symptoms

The symptoms of agoraphobia can be similar to those of specific phobia, and according to the *DSM-IV-TR,* **diagnosis** of agoraphobia "can be difficult because all of these conditions are characterized by avoidance of specific situations."

The symptoms of an episode of agoraphobia may include any or all of the following:

- trembling
- breaking out in sweat
- heart palpitations

KEY TERMS

Behavioral inhibition—A set of behaviors that appear in early infancy that are displayed when the child is confronted with a new situation or unfamiliar people. These behaviors include agitated movement, crying, and general irritability, followed by withdrawing, and seeking comfort from a familiar person. These behaviors are associated with an increased risk of social phobia and panic disorder in later life. Behavioral inhibition in children appears to be linked to anxiety and mood disorders in their parents.

Cognitive-behavioral therapy—A type of psychotherapy in which people learn to recognize and change negative and self-defeating patterns of thinking, feeling, and behavior.

Cognitive restructuring—An approach to psychotherapy that focuses on helping the individual examine distorted patterns of perceiving and thinking in order to change their emotional responses to people and situations.

Exposure therapy—A form of cognitive-behavioral therapy in which individuals with phobias are exposed to their feared objects or situations while accompanied by the therapist. The length of exposure is gradually increased until the association between the feared situation and the individual's experienced panic symptoms is no longer present.

Paresthesia—An abnormal sensation of tingling or "pins and needles." Paresthesia is a common panic-like symptom associated with agoraphobia.

Phobia—Irrational fear of places, things, or situations that lead to avoidance.

Specific phobia—A type of phobia in which the object or situation that arouses fear is clearly identifiable and limited. An older term for specific phobia is simple phobia.

- paresthesias (tingling or pins-and-needles sensations in the hands or feet)
- nausea
- fatigue
- rapid pulse or breathing rate
- a sense of impending doom

In most cases, the person with agoraphobia feels some relief from the symptoms after he or she has left the precipitating situation or returned home.

Diagnosis

The differential diagnosis of agoraphobia is described differently in *DSM-IV-TR* and in *International Classification of Diseases (ICD-10)*, the European diagnostic manual. The *DSM-IV-TR* specifies that agoraphobia must be defined in relation to PD, and that the diagnoses of **specific phobias** and social phobias must be ruled out, a condition that will hold true for *DSM-5*. The *DSM-IV-TR* also specifies that the individual's symptoms must not be related to **substance abuse**; if they are related to a general medical condition, the individual must have excessive symptoms usually associated with that condition. For example, a person with Crohn's disease has realistic concerns about an attack of diarrhea in a public place and should not be diagnosed with agoraphobia unless the fear of losing bowel control is clearly exaggerated. The *DSM-IV-TR* description does not stipulate that a person must experience agoraphobia within a set number of circumstances in order to meet the diagnostic criteria.

In contrast, the European diagnostic manual primarily distinguishes between agoraphobia and delusional or obsessive disorders and depressive episodes. In addition, *ICD-10* specifies that the individual's anxiety must be restricted to or occur primarily within two out of four specific situations: in crowds, in public places, while traveling alone, or while traveling away from home. The primary area of agreement between the American and European diagnostic manuals is that both specify avoidance of the feared situation as a diagnostic criterion.

Diagnosis of agoraphobia is usually made by a physician or mental health professional after careful exclusion of other mental disorders and physical conditions or diseases that might be related to the individual's fears. Head injury, pneumonia, and withdrawal from certain medications can produce some of the symptoms of a panic attack. In addition, the physician may ask about caffeine intake as a possible dietary factor. Currently, there are no laboratory tests or diagnostic **imaging studies** that can be used to diagnose agoraphobia.

Furthermore, there are no widely used diagnostic interviews or screening instruments specifically for agoraphobia. Dutch researchers have developed a self-report questionnaire that promises to be helpful to doctors treating people with agoraphobia. The agoraphobic self-statements questionnaire (ASQ) is intended to evaluate thinking processes in individuals with agoraphobia, as distinct from their emotional responses.

Treatment

Treatment of agoraphobia usually consists of medication plus **cognitive-behavioral therapy** (CBT). Some individuals may be advised to cut down on or give up coffee or tea, as the caffeine in these beverages can contribute to their panic symptoms.

Drugs

Drugs that have been used with individuals diagnosed with agoraphobia include the benzodiazepine tranquilizers, the MAO inhibitors (**MAOIs**), tricyclic **antidepressants** (TCAs), and the **selective serotonin reuptake inhibitors** (**SSRIs**). In the past few years, the SSRIs have come to be regarded as the first-choice medication treatment because they have fewer side effects. The **benzodiazepines** have the disadvantage of increasing the symptoms of agoraphobia when they are withdrawn, as well as interfering with CBT. Benzodiazepines can decrease mental sharpness, making it difficult for individuals taking these drugs to focus in therapy sessions. The MAOIs require individuals to follow certain dietary guidelines; for example, patients must exclude aged cheeses, red wine, and certain types of beans. MAOIs are not widely prescribed. TCAs may produce such side effects as blurred vision, constipation, dry mouth, and drowsiness.

Psychotherapy

CBT is regarded as the most effective psychotherapeutic treatment for agoraphobia. The specific CBT approach that seems to work best with agoraphobia is exposure therapy. Exposure therapy is based on undoing the association that the individual originally formed between the panic symptoms and the feared situation. By being repeatedly exposed to the feared location or situation, the individual gradually learns that he or she is not in danger, and the anxiety symptoms fade away. The therapist typically explains the procedure of exposure therapy to the individual and reassures him or her that the exposure can be stopped at any time that his or her limits of toleration have been reached. The individual is then exposed in the course of a number of

QUESTIONS TO ASK YOUR DOCTOR

- Have possible physical causes of my panic symptoms been ruled out?
- Can you recommend a psychiatrist or psychologist?
- Should I reduce my caffeine consumption?
- Do you know of any support groups for individuals with agoraphobia in this area?
- How can I best provide support for my loved one with agoraphobia?

treatment sessions to the feared situation, usually for a slightly longer period each time. A typical course of exposure therapy takes about 12 weeks.

Another approach was used by German researchers who reported good results in treating individuals with agoraphobia with individual high-density exposure therapy. The individuals were exposed to their respective feared situations for an entire day for two to three weeks. One year later, the individuals had maintained their improvement.

Exposure treatment for agoraphobia may be combined with cognitive restructuring. This form of cognitive-behavioral therapy teaches individuals to observe the thoughts that they have in the feared situation, such as "I'll die if I have to go into that railroad station," and replace these thoughts with positive statements. In this example, the individual with agoraphobia might say to him- or herself, "I'll be just fine when I go in there to buy my ticket."

Although insight-oriented therapies have generally been considered relatively ineffective in treating agoraphobia, trials of brief **psychodynamic psychotherapy** in individuals with PD with agoraphobia indicate that this form of treatment may also be beneficial. One 2001 study of 21 individuals who participated in a 24-session course of treatment (twice weekly for 12 weeks) resulted in 16 experiencing remission of their agoraphobia, with no relapses at six-month follow-up. A larger 2007 study by the same group of researchers supported these initial findings.

Alternative and complementary treatments

Individuals diagnosed with agoraphobia have reported that alternative therapies, such as **hypnotherapy** and **music therapy**, were helpful in relieving symptoms of anxiety and panic. Ayurvedic medicine, **yoga**, religious practice, and guided imagery **meditation** have also been helpful.

Prognosis

The prognosis for untreated agoraphobia is considered poor by most European as well as most American physicians. The *DSM-IV-TR* remarks that little is known about the course of agoraphobia without PD but that anecdotal evidence indicates that it may persist for years with individuals becoming increasingly impaired. The *ICD-10* describes agoraphobia as "the most incapacitating of the phobic disorders," to the point that some individuals become completely housebound. With proper treatment, however, 90% of individuals diagnosed with agoraphobia can recover and resume a normal life.

Prevention

The **genetic factors** that appear to be implicated in the development of agoraphobia cannot be prevented. However, recent recognition of the link between anxiety and mood disorders in parents and vulnerability to phobic disorders in their children may help to identify children at risk and to develop appropriate preventive strategies for them.

Resources

BOOKS

Antony, Martin M., and Murray B. Stein. *Oxford Handbook of Anxiety and Related Disorders.* New York: Oxford University Press, 2009.

Leahy, Robert L. *Anxiety Free: Unravel Your Fears Before They Unravel You.* Carlsbad, CA: Hay House, 2009.

Starcevic, Vladan. *Anxiety Disorders in Adults: A Clinical Guide,* 2nd ed. New York: Oxford University Press, 2010.

PERIODICALS

Coelho, C. M., et al. "Specific Phobias in Older Adults: Characteristics and Differential Diagnosis." *International Psychogeriatrics* 22, no. 5 (August 2010): 702–11.

King, Anna, et al. "Nomophobia: The Mobile Phone in Panic Disorder with Agoraphobia: Reducing Phobias or Worsening of Dependence?" *Cognitive and Behavioral Neurology* 23, no. 1 (March 2010): 52–54.

Milrod, Barbara, et al. "A Pilot Open Trial of Brief Psychodynamic Psychotherapy for Panic Disorder." *Journal of Psychodynamic Therapy and Research* 10 (October 2001): 239–45.

———. "A Randomized Controlled Clinical Trial of Psychoanalytic Psychotherapy for Panic Disorder." *American Journal of Psychiatry* 164 (February 2007): 265–72.

Rosellini, Anthony, et al. "The Effects of Extraverted Temperament on Agoraphobia in Panic Disorder." *Journal of Abnormal Psychology* 119, no. 2 (May 2010): 420–26.

ORGANIZATIONS

American Academy of Child and Adolescent Psychiatry, 3615 Wisconsin Ave. NW, Washington, DC, 20016-3007, (202) 966-7300, Fax: (202) 966-2891, http://www.aacap.org.

American Psychiatric Association, 1000 Wilson Blvd., Ste. 1825, Arlington, VA, 22209-3901, (703) 907-7300, (888) 357-7924, apa@psych.org, http://www.psych.org.

American Psychological Association, 750 1st St. NE, Washington, DC, 20002-4242, (202) 336-5500, (800) 374-2721, apa@psych.org, http://www.apa.org.

Mental Health America, 2000 North Beauregard St., 6th Fl., Alexandria, VA, 22311, (703) 684-7722, (800) 969-6642, Fax: (703) 684-5968, http://www.nmha.org.

National Institute of Mental Health, 6001 Executive Blvd., Rm. 8184, MSC 9663, Bethesda, MD, 20892-9663, (301) 443-4513, (866) 615-6464, Fax: (301) 443-4279, nimhinfo@nimh.gov, http://www.nimh.nih.gov.

Rebecca Frey, Ph.D.
Ruth M. Wienclaw, Ph.D.
Tish Davidson, AM

AIMS *see* **Abnormal Involuntary Movement Scale**

Akineton *see* **Biperiden**

Alcoholics Anonymous *see* **Self-help groups**

Alcohol-induced persisting amnestic disorder *see* **Wernicke-Korsakoff syndrome**

Alcohol use and related disorders

Definition

The American Medical Association (AMA) defines alcoholism or alcohol (ethanol) dependence as "a primary, chronic disease with genetic, psychosocial, and environmental factors influencing its development and manifestations." Individuals with alcoholism develop emotional and physical dependence on alcoholic beverages, increased tolerance of the effects of alcohol, and withdrawal symptoms if alcohol consumption stops.

Demographics

The World Health Organization (WHO) estimates that about two billion people worldwide consume alcoholic beverages, and alcoholism is the most common **addiction** to a psychoactive substance. Alcohol addiction affects both sexes and all races and ethnicities. According to the 2009 National Survey on Drug Use and Health, 130.6 million Americans (51.9% of the population) reported having at least one alcoholic drink in the past 30 days. In addition, 59.6 million people (23.7%) reported having five or more drinks on the same occasion (**binge drinking**) and 17.1 million (6.8%) reported having five or more drinks on at least five occasions in the past 30 days (heavy alcohol use). According

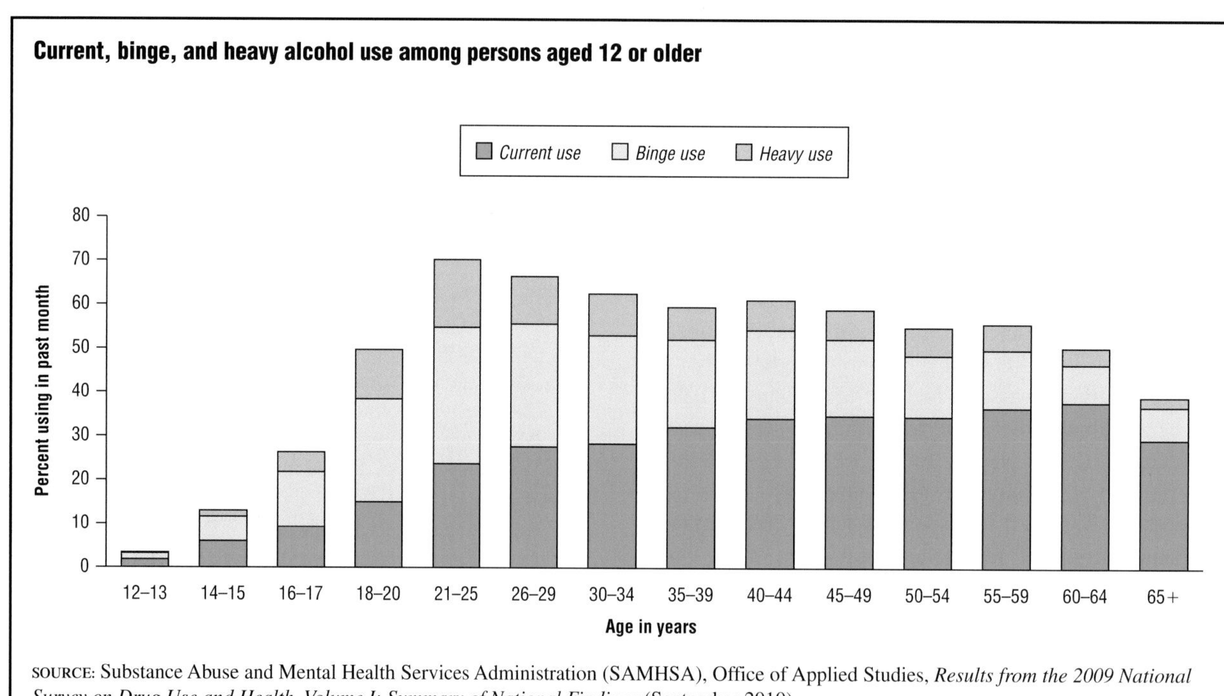

SOURCE: Substance Abuse and Mental Health Services Administration (SAMHSA), Office of Applied Studies, *Results from the 2009 National Survey on Drug Use and Health, Volume I: Summary of National Findings* (September 2010).

(Graph by PreMediaGlobal. © 2012 Cengage Learning.)

to a 2007 report from the Task Force on Community Preventive Services of the Centers for Disease Control and Prevention, excessive alcohol consumption in the United States is responsible for approximately 75,000 deaths per year, making it the third leading preventable cause of death. Alcohol addiction rates are highest among young adults aged 18–29 and lowest among those 65 and older.

Men are more than twice as likely to be alcohol dependent than women, but studies of female alcoholics indicate that women are at higher risk than men for serious health problems related to alcoholism. Because women tend to metabolize alcohol more slowly and have a lower percentage of body water and a higher percentage of body fat than men, they develop higher blood alcohol levels at a given amount of alcohol per pound of body weight. Thus, even though women typically begin to drink heavily at a later age than men, they often become dependent more rapidly. This relatively speedy progression of alcoholism in women is called telescoping. Smokers who are alcohol dependent are also much more likely to develop serious or fatal health problems associated with alcoholism.

Alcohol use by persons under age 21 is an important public health concern. In the United States, alcohol is the most commonly used and abused drug among youth. Although drinking under the age of 21 is against the law, people aged 12 to 20 years drink nearly 20% of all alcohol consumed in the United States. Much of this alcohol is consumed in the form of binge drinking.

At the other end of the age distribution, alcoholism among the elderly appears to be under-recognized. One-third of older persons with alcoholism develop the problem later in life, while the other two-thirds grow older with the medical and psychosocial consequences of early onset alcoholism. Confusion and other signs of intoxication in an elderly person are also often misinterpreted as side effects of medications. In addition, the effects of alcohol may be increased in elderly patients because of physiological changes associated with aging. The elderly are at higher risk than younger people for becoming dependent on alcohol because their bodies do not absorb alcohol as efficiently; a 90-year-old who drinks the same amount of alcohol as a 20-year-old of the same sex will have a blood alcohol level 50% higher.

Description

Alcoholism is characterized by:

- a prolonged period of frequent, heavy alcohol use
- the inability to control drinking once it has begun
- physical dependence manifested by withdrawal symptoms when the individual stops using alcohol

Risk factors for alcoholism

- **Age:** Beginning drinking at a young age increases the risk of alcohol dependence.
- **Family history:** Children of alcohol-dependent parents are at greater risk of developing alcoholism.
- **Gender:** Males are more likely to become alcohol dependent than females, but women are at an increased risk of developing complications associated with alcoholism, such as liver disease.
- **Length of use:** Regular binge drinking over an extended period of time may result in alcohol dependence.
- **Mental health:** Persons afflicted by mental health disorders such as depression may be more likely to misuse alcohol or other substances.
- **Social and cultural factors:** Being surrounded by friends who routinely drink may increase a person's level of alcohol use. Alcohol consumption in the media may also influence personal drinking habits.

SOURCE: Mayo Clinic, "Alcoholism." Available online at: http://www.mayoclinic.com/health/alcoholism/DS00340 (accessed August 17, 2010).

(Table by PreMediaGlobal. Reproduced by permission of Gale, a part of Cengage Learning.)

- tolerance, or the need to use more and more alcohol to achieve the same effects
- a variety of social and/or legal problems arising from alcohol use

The effects of alcoholism are far reaching. Alcohol affects every body system, causing a wide range of health problems. Problems include poor **nutrition**; memory disorders; difficulty with balance and walking; liver disease (including cirrhosis and hepatitis); high blood pressure; muscle weakness (including the heart); heart rhythm disturbances; anemia; clotting disorders; decreased immunity to infections; gastrointestinal inflammation and irritation; acute and chronic problems with the pancreas; low blood sugar; high cholesterol; interference with fertility; increased risk of cancer of the liver, esophagus, and breast; weakened bones; sleep disturbances; anxiety; and **depression**. About 20% of adults admitted to the hospital (for any reason) are alcohol dependent.

On a personal level, alcohol abuse may lead to difficulties in marital and other relationships, domestic violence, **child abuse** or **neglect**, difficulty finding or keeping a job, impaired school or work performance, **homelessness**, or legal problems such as driving while intoxicated (DUI).

Risk factors

The risk of developing alcoholism has a definite genetic component. Studies have demonstrated that close relatives of people with alcoholism are more likely to become alcoholics themselves. This risk exists even for children adopted away from their biological families at birth and raised in a non-alcoholic adoptive family with no knowledge of their biological family's alcohol use. However, no specific gene for alcoholism has been found, and environmental factors (e.g., **stress**) and social factors (e.g., peer behavior, socializing patterns, and the availability of alcohol) are thought to play a role in whether a person becomes alcohol dependent. People who start drinking in their teens are at a much higher risk of developing alcohol dependency problems compared to people who start drinking at age 21 or older.

Causes and symptoms

Recently, some researchers have suggested that there are two distinct types of alcoholism. According to these researchers, type 1 alcoholism develops in adulthood, often in the early twenties. It is most often associated with the desire to relieve stress and anxiety and is not associated with any criminal or antisocial behavior. Type 2 alcoholism develops earlier, usually during the teenage years. Drinking is done primarily to get intoxicated. Type 2 alcoholism is associated with violence, destructiveness, and other criminal and antisocial behavior. Those who study alcoholism do not universally accept the distinction between these two types of alcoholism. Research continues in this area.

Causes

The cause of alcoholism is related to behavioral, biological, and **genetic factors**.

Behaviorally, alcohol consumption is related to internal or external feedback. Internal feedback is the internal state a person experiences during and after alcohol consumption. External feedback is made up of the cues that other people send the person when he or she drinks. Internal states pertaining to alcohol can include shame or hangover. Alcohol-related external cues can include reprimands, criticism, or encouragement. People may drink to the point of dependence because of peer pressure, for acceptance in a peer group, or because drinking is related to specific moods (e.g., easygoing, relaxed, calm, sociable) that are related to the formation of intimate relationships.

Biologically, repeated use of alcohol can impair the **brain** levels of a "pleasure" neurotransmitter called **dopamine**. **Neurotransmitters** are chemicals in the brain that pass impulses from one nerve cell to the next. When a person is dependent on alcohol, the areas of his or her brain that produce dopamine become depleted, and the individual can no longer enjoy the pleasures of everyday life—his or her brain chemistry is rearranged to depend on alcohol for transient euphoria (state of happiness).

Genetic studies have suggested that the GABA-A receptor alpha 2 subunit gene (GABRA2) and alcohol dehydrogenase (ADH) genes increase the risk for alcohol dependence. The GABRA genes are related to a receptor for gamma-amino butyric acid (GABA), a chemical in the central nervous system that is believed to mediate some of the physiological effects of alcohol. ADH is a chemical involved in the oxidation of alcohol in the body. These genes related to alcohol abuse can be passed from parents to their children.

The symptoms of alcoholism can be broken down into two major categories: symptoms of acute alcohol use, and symptoms of long-term alcohol use.

Immediate (acute) effects of alcohol use

Alcohol exerts a depressive effect on the brain. The blood-brain barrier does not prevent alcohol from entering the brain, so the brain alcohol level will quickly become equivalent to the blood alcohol level. In the brain, alcohol interacts with various neurotransmitters to alter nerve function. Alcohol's depressive effects result in difficulty walking, poor balance, slurring of speech, and generally poor coordination (accounting in part for the increased likelihood of injury). The affected person also may have impairment of peripheral vision. At higher alcohol levels, a person's breathing and heart rates may be slowed, and vomiting may occur (with a high risk of the vomit being breathed into the lungs, potentially resulting in aspiration pneumonia.) Still higher alcohol levels may result in coma and death.

Blood alcohol concentration (BAC) produces the following symptoms of central nervous system (CNS) depression at specific levels:

- 50 mg/dL: feelings of calm or mild drowsiness
- 50–150 mg/dL: loss of physical coordination. The legal BAC for drivers in most states is 80 mg/dL.
- 150–200 mg/dL: loss of mental faculties
- 300–400 mg/dL: unconsciousness
- Over 400 mg/dL: may be fatal

Effects of long-term (chronic) alcoholism

Long-term use of alcohol affects virtually every organ system of the body:

- Nervous system. An estimated 30%–40% of all men in their teens and twenties have experienced alcoholic blackout from drinking a large quantity of alcohol.

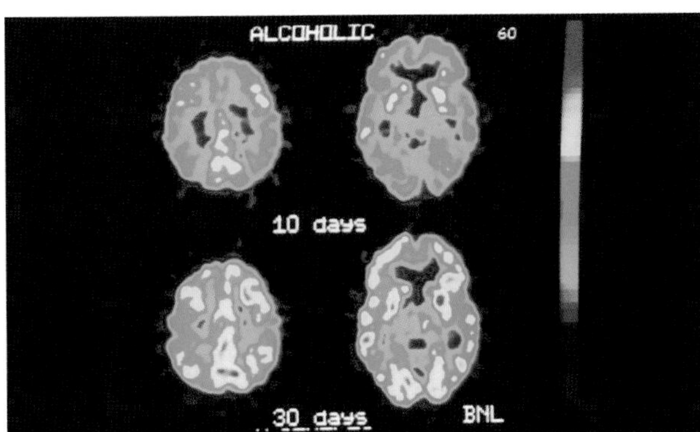

Colored positron emission tomography scans of a heavy drinker's brain during withdrawal from alcohol; the top shows brain activity after 10 days (yellow areas), and the bottom shows brain activity after 30 days without alcohol. *(© Pascal Goetgheluck/SPL/Photo Researchers, Inc.)*

This results in the loss of memory of the time surrounding the episode of drinking. Alcohol also causes sleep disturbances, so sleep quality is diminished. Numbness and tingling (paresthesia) may occur in the arms and legs. Wernicke's syndrome and Korsakoff's syndrome, which can occur together or separately, are due to the low thiamine (a B vitamin) levels found in many people with an alcohol dependence. Wernicke's syndrome results in disordered eye movements, very poor balance, and difficulty walking. Korsakoff's syndrome affects memory and prevents new learning from taking place.

- Gastrointestinal system. Alcohol-associated conditions include acid reflux, stomach ulcers, esophageal varices (enlarged blood vessels in the esophagus prone to bursting and hemorrhaging), diarrhea, pancreatitis, malnutrition, cirrhosis, and hepatitis.
- Blood. Alcohol may cause changes to all the types of blood cells. Red blood cells become abnormally large. White blood cells (important for fighting infections) decrease in number, resulting in a weakened immune system. This places alcohol-dependent individuals at increased risk for infections and may account in part for the increased risk of cancer faced by people with alcoholism. Platelets and blood clotting factors are affected, causing an increased risk of bleeding.
- Heart. Small amounts of alcohol cause a drop in blood pressure, but with increased consumption, alcohol raises blood pressure into a dangerous range (hypertension). High levels of fats circulating in the bloodstream increase the risk of heart disease. Heavy drinking results in an increase in heart size, weakening of the heart muscle, abnormal heart rhythms, a risk of blood clots forming within the chambers of the heart, and a greatly increased risk of stroke due to a blood clot entering the circulatory system and blocking a brain blood vessel.
- Reproductive system. Heavy drinking has a negative effect on fertility in both men and women. It decreases testicle and ovary size and interferes with both sperm and egg production.

People with chronic tolerance may appear to be sober (not intoxicated) even after consumption of alcohol quantities that could cause death in non-drinkers. People with alcohol dependence also develop alcohol withdrawal (a state of non-drinking) syndrome. The nervous system adapts to chronic ethanol exposure by increasing the activity of nerve-cell mechanisms that counteract alcohol's depressant effects. When drinking is abruptly reduced, the affected person develops disordered perceptions, **seizures**, and tremor (often accompanied by irritability, nausea, and vomiting). Tremor of the hands, known colloquially as "morning shakes," usually occurs in the morning due to overnight abstinence. The most serious manifestation of alcohol withdrawal syndrome is **delirium** tremens, which occurs in approximately 5% of people dependent on alcohol. Delirium tremens consists of agitation, disorientation, **insomnia**, hallucinations, **delusions**, intense sweating, fever, and increased heart rate (tachycardia). This state is a medical emergency because it can be fatal, and affected persons must be immediately hospitalized and treated with medications that control vital physiological functions.

In addition to physical symptoms, most persons with alcoholism have a history of psychiatric, occupational, financial, legal, or interpersonal problems. Alcohol misuse is the single most important predictor of violence between domestic partners as well as intergenerational violence within families. Since the early 1990s, most states have passed stricter laws against alcohol-impaired driving. These laws include such provisions as immediate license suspension for the first arrest for driving while impaired (DWI, also referred to as driving under the influence or DUI) and lowering the legal blood alcohol limit to 0.08 g/dL for adults and zero tolerance for drivers under age 21. Penalties for repeated DWI citations include prison sentences, house arrest with electronic monitoring, license plates that identify offending drivers, automobile confiscation, and putting a special ignition interlock on the offender's car. Deaths caused by a drunk driver may be punishable with prison time.

Alcoholism during pregnancy

A large body of evidence indicates that maternal alcohol consumption during pregnancy contributes adversely to a fetus's development. Abnormalities in infants and children associated with maternal alcohol consumption may include prenatal and postnatal physical retardation, neurological deficits (e.g., impaired attention control), intellectual disability, behavioral problems (e.g., impulsivity), skull or brain malformations, and facial malformations (e.g., a thin upper lip and elongated and flattened midface). These abnormalities, influenced by maternal alcohol consumption during pregnancy, are referred to as fetal alcohol effects (FAEs), or **fetal alcohol syndrome** (FAS) if a sufficient number of effects are apparent in the child.

FAS is the leading cause of intellectual disability in the United States. One to two of every 1,000 infants born in the United States are afflicted with FAS. Research studies that have followed infants with FAS and FAEs across time have found that many of these children continue to have cognitive difficulties (e.g., lower IQ scores, more learning problems, and poorer short-term memory functioning) and behavioral problems (e.g., high impulsivity and high activity level) into childhood and adolescence.

Diagnosis

The **diagnosis** of alcoholism is usually based on the patient's drinking history, a thorough physical examination, laboratory findings, and the results of psychodiagnostic assessment.

The ***Diagnostic and Statistical Manual of Mental Disorders***, 4th edition, text revision *(DSM-IV-TR)*, distinguishes between alcohol dependence and alcohol abuse largely on the basis of a compulsive element in alcohol dependence that is not present in alcohol abuse. Some psychiatrists differentiate between primary and secondary alcoholism. In primary alcoholism, the patient has no other major psychiatric diagnosis. In secondary alcoholism, the problem drinking is the patient's preferred way of medicating symptoms of another psychiatric disorder, such as depression, **schizophrenia**, **post-traumatic stress disorder**, or one of the **dissociative disorders**. Experts in other branches of medicine tend to emphasize patterns of, and attitudes toward, drinking in order to distinguish between nonproblematic use of alcohol and alcohol abuse or dependence.

The *DSM-IV-TR* requires three of the following traits to be present for a diagnosis of alcohol dependence:

- tolerance, meaning that a person becomes accustomed to consuming alcohol and must increase the amount in order to obtain the desired effect
- withdrawal, meaning that a person experiences unpleasant physical and psychological symptoms when he or she does not drink alcohol
- the tendency to drink more alcohol than one intends; being unable to avoid drinking or stop drinking once started
- devoting large blocks of time to acquiring and consuming alcohol
- unsuccessful attempts to reduce or stop alcohol use
- choosing to use alcohol at the expense of other important tasks or activities, such as work or family obligations
- drinking despite evidence of negative effects on one's physical and/or mental health

In order for a person to be diagnosed with alcohol abuse, one of the following four criteria must be met within a 12-month period. Because of drinking, a person repeatedly:

- fails to live up to his or her most important responsibilities at home, school, or work
- physically endangers himself or herself, or others (for example, by drinking and driving)
- gets into trouble with the law
- experiences difficulties in relationships or jobs

The proposed revisions for the *DSM-5* (5th edition) combine alcohol abuse and alcohol dependence and their respective diagnostic criteria into the single diagnosis of "alcohol use disorder."

Classification of alcohol use typically is based on the following five categories:

- Social drinkers. Individuals who use alcohol in minimal to moderate amounts to enhance meals or other social activities. They do not drink alone.
- Situational drinkers. These people rarely or never drink except during periods of stress. They are far more likely to drink alone than social drinkers.
- Problem drinkers. These individuals drink heavily, even when they are not under overwhelming stress. Their drinking causes some problems in their lives (e.g., DWI arrests), but they are capable of responding to warnings or advice from others.
- Binge drinkers. These drinkers uses alcohol in an out-of-control fashion at regular intervals. The binges may be planned. This pattern is a growing problem on many college campuses.
- Alcoholic drinkers. These are drinkers who have no control of any kind over their alcohol intake.

Other factors have complicated diagnosis of alcoholism in the United States, including: 1) the increasing

KEY TERMS

Acamprosate—Also called Campral, an anti-craving medication used since 1989 in Europe and since 2004 in the United States to reduce the craving for alcohol.

Alcohol Use Disorders Inventory Test (AUDIT)—A test for alcohol use developed by the World Health Organization (WHO). Its ten questions address three specific areas of drinking over a 12-month period: the amount and frequency of drinking, dependence upon alcohol, and problems that have been encountered due to drinking alcohol.

Behavioral therapy—Form of psychotherapy used to treat depression, anxiety disorders, phobias, and other forms of psychopathology.

Binge drinking—Consumption of five or more alcoholic drinks in a single, short period.

Blood-brain barrier—A network of blood vessels characterized by closely spaced cells that prevents many potentially toxic substances from penetrating the blood vessel walls to enter the brain. Alcohol is able to cross this barrier.

CAGE—A four-question assessment for the presence of alcoholism in both adults and children.

Detoxification—The phase of treatment during which a patient stops drinking and is monitored and cared for while he or she experiences withdrawal from alcohol.

Disulfiram—A medication that has been used since the late 1940s as part of a treatment plan for alcohol abuse. Disulfiram, which is sold under the trade name Antabuse, produces changes in the body's metabolism of alcohol that cause headaches, vomiting, and other unpleasant symptoms if the patient drinks even small amounts of alcohol.

Ethanol—The chemical name for beverage alcohol. It is also sometimes called ethyl alcohol or grain alcohol to distinguish it from isopropyl or rubbing alcohol.

Naltrexone—A medication originally developed to treat addiction to heroin or morphine that is also used to treat alcoholism. It works by reducing the craving for alcohol rather than by producing vomiting or other unpleasant reactions.

Neurotransmitter—One of a group of chemicals secreted by a nerve cell (neuron) to carry a chemical message to another nerve cell, often as a way of transmitting a nerve impulse. Examples of neurotransmitters include acetylcholine, dopamine, serotonin, and norepinephrine.

Relapse—A return to a disease state, after recovery appeared to be occurring. In alcoholism, relapse refers to a patient beginning to drink alcohol again after a period of avoiding alcohol.

Tolerance—A phenomenon during which a drinker becomes physically accustomed to a particular quantity of alcohol and requires ever-increasing quantities in order to obtain the same effects.

Withdrawal—Those signs and symptoms experienced by a person who has become physically dependent on a drug, experienced upon decreasing the drug's dosage or discontinuing its use.

tendency to combine alcohol with other drugs of abuse, sometimes called cross-addiction, and 2) the rising rates of alcohol abuse and dependence among children under 12 years of age.

Examination

A physician who suspects that a patient is abusing or dependent upon alcohol should perform a complete physical examination with appropriate laboratory tests, paying particular attention to liver function and the nervous system. Physical findings that suggest alcoholism include head injuries after age 18, broken bones after age 18, evidence of blackouts, frequent accidents or falls, puffy eyelids, flushed face, alcohol odor on the breath, shaky hands, slurred speech or tongue tremor, rapid involuntary eye movements (nystagmus), enlargement of the liver (hepatomegaly), hypertension, insomnia, and impotence (in males). Severe memory loss may point to advanced alcoholic damage to the central nervous system.

Tests

Several laboratory tests can be used to diagnose alcohol abuse and evaluate the presence of medical problems related to drinking. These tests include:

- Complete blood cell count (CBC). This test indicates the presence of anemia, which is common in alcoholics.
- Liver function tests. Tests for serum glutamine oxaloacetic transaminase (SGOT) and alkaline phosphatase can indicate alcohol-related injury to the liver. A high level (30 units) of gamma-glutamyltransferase (GGT) is a useful marker because it is found in 70% of heavy drinkers.

- Blood alcohol levels.
- Carbohydrate deficient transferrin (CDT) tests. This test should not be used as a screener, but it is useful in monitoring alcohol consumption in heavy drinkers (those who consume at least 60 grams of alcohol per day). When CDT is present, it indicates regular daily consumption of alcohol.

The results of these tests might not be accurate if the patient is abusing or is dependent on other substances.

Behavioral screening

Since some of the physical signs and symptoms of alcoholism can be produced by other drugs or disorders, screening tests can also help to determine the existence of a drinking problem. Several assessment instruments for alcoholism can either be self-administered or administered by a clinician. The CAGE test is a brief screening consisting of four questions:

- Have you ever felt the need to *cut down* on drinking?
- Have you ever felt *annoyed* by criticism of your drinking?
- Have you ever felt *guilty* about your drinking?
- Have you ever taken a morning *eye opener*?

One "yes" answer should raise a suspicion of alcohol abuse; two "yes" answers are considered a positive screen.

Other brief screens include the Alcohol Use Disorder Identification Test, or AUDIT, which also highlights some of the physical symptoms of alcohol abuse that doctors look for during a physical examination of the patient. The Michigan Alcoholism Screening Test, or MAST, is considered the diagnostic standard. It consists of 25 questions; a score of five or higher is considered to indicate alcohol dependency. The **Substance Abuse Subtle Screening Inventory** (SASSI), introduced in 1988, can be given in either group or individual settings in a paper-and-pencil or computerized format. The SASSI is available in an adolescent as well as an adult version from the SASSI Institute. Selection of an appropriate screen is important. Some brief screens may be inappropriate for widespread use in some subpopulations because of ethnic and gender bias.

Treatment

Traditional

Treatment of alcoholism often is a combination of inpatient and outpatient therapy, depending on the individual's alcohol history and physical condition. The person with alcoholism often resists the idea that he or she has an alcohol problem and needs to stop drinking. Treatment cannot be forced on adults unless imposed by a court of law. However, if the person is a danger to himself or herself or to others, immediate **hospitalization** may be possible without the individual's consent.

The first step in the treatment of alcoholism, called **detoxification**, involves helping the person stop drinking and ridding his or her body of the harmful (toxic) effects of alcohol. Because the person's brain and body have become accustomed to alcohol, he or she will most likely develop withdrawal symptoms and need to be supported through them. Withdrawal will be different for different individuals, depending on the severity of the alcoholism as measured by the quantity of alcohol ingested daily and the length of time the patient has been alcohol dependent.

Withdrawal symptoms can range from mild to life-threatening. Mild withdrawal symptoms include nausea, achiness, diarrhea, difficulty sleeping, sweatiness, anxiety, and trembling. This phase usually lasts no more than three to five days. More severe effects of withdrawal can include hallucinations in which a patient sees, hears, or feels something that is not actually present; seizures; an unbearable craving for more alcohol; confusion; fever; fast heart rate (tachycardia); high blood pressure (hypertension); and delirium (a fluctuating level of consciousness). Patients at the highest risk for the most severe symptoms of withdrawal are those with other medical problems, including malnutrition, liver disease, or Wernicke's syndrome. Severe withdrawal symptoms usually begin about three days after the individual's last drink and may last a variable number of days.

People going through mild withdrawal are monitored to make sure that more severe symptoms do not develop. Medications usually are unnecessary. Treatment of a patient suffering more severe effects of withdrawal may require sedative medications to relieve the discomfort of withdrawal and to avoid the potentially life-threatening complications of high blood pressure, fast heart rate, and seizures. Benzodiazepine drugs may be helpful in those patients experiencing hallucinations. If the patient vomits for an extended period, fluids may need to be given through a vein (intravenously, IV). Thiamine (a vitamin) is often included in the fluids, because thiamine levels are often very low in alcohol-dependent patients, and thiamine deficiency is responsible for the **Wernicke-Korsakoff syndrome**.

After the individual is no longer drinking and has passed through withdrawal, the next steps involve helping the individual avoid relapsing (the return to drinking). This phase of treatment is referred to as rehabilitation. It can continue for a lifetime. Many programs incorporate the family into rehabilitation therapy, because the family has likely been severely affected by the patient's drinking. Some therapists believe that family members, in an effort to deal with their loved one's drinking problem, develop patterns of behavior that unintentionally support or enable the patient's drinking. This situation is referred to as co-dependence. These patterns should be addressed in order to help successfully treat a person's alcoholism.

Sessions led by peers, in which recovering alcoholics meet regularly and provide support for each other's recoveries, are considered among the best methods of preventing a return to drinking. The best-known group following this model is Alcoholics Anonymous (AA), which uses a 12-step program and a buddy (sponsor) system to help people avoid drinking. The AA steps involve recognizing the destructive power that alcohol has held over the individual's life, looking to a higher power for help in overcoming the problem, reflecting on the ways in which the use of alcohol has hurt others and, if possible, making amends to those people. According to the **American Psychological Association** (APA), anyone, regardless of his or her religious beliefs or lack of religious beliefs, can benefit from participation in 12-step programs such as AA. The number of visits to 12-step **self-help groups** exceeds the number of visits to all mental health professionals combined.

Psychotherapy may also help affected persons to anticipate, understand, recognize, and prevent **relapse**. Along with **support groups**, behavioral therapy approaches typically include **cognitive-behavioral therapy** (CBT) and Motivated Enhancement Therapy (MET). CBT focuses on teaching alcoholics recognition and coping skills for craving states and high-risk situations that precipitate or trigger relapsing behaviors. MET can motivate patients to use their personal resources to initiate changes in behavior.

Drugs

Most drugs used to treat alcoholism fall into one of two groups: those that restrain the desire to drink by producing painful physical symptoms if the patient does drink, and those that appear to reduce the craving for alcohol directly. Several medications in the second category were originally developed to treat addiction to opioid substances (e.g., heroin and morphine). Drugs alone will not prevent relapse. They are most effective when used in conjunction with a self-help program and/or psychotherapy aimed at changing behavior.

ALCOHOL-SENSITIZING MEDICATIONS. The most commonly used alcohol-sensitizing agent is **disulfiram** (Antabuse), which has been used since the 1950s to deter alcoholics from drinking by the threat of a very unpleasant physical reaction if they do consume alcohol. The severity of the disulfiram/ethanol reaction (DER) depends on the amount of alcohol and disulfiram in the blood. A DER results when the drinker consumes alcohol because disulfiram inhibits the functioning of an enzyme called aldehyde dehydrogenase. This enzyme is needed to convert acetaldehyde, which is produced when the body begins to oxidize the alcohol. Without the aldehyde dehydrogenase, the patient's blood level of acetaldehyde rises, causing the symptoms associated with DER. The symptoms of the reaction include facial flushing, rapid heartbeat, palpitations, difficult breathing, lowered blood pressure, headaches, nausea, and vomiting. It was estimated that in 2008, 200,000 recovering alcoholics in the United States were taking disulfiram.

Another alcohol-sensitizing agent is calcium carbimide, which is marketed under the brand name Temposil. Calcium carbimide produces physiological reactions with alcohol, similar to those produced by disulfiram, but the onset of action is far more rapid, and the duration of action is much shorter.

ANTI-CRAVING MEDICATIONS. Another medication approved for the treatment of alcoholism is **naltrexone**, which appears to reduce the craving for alcohol. In addition, an injectable, long-acting form of naltrexone (**Vivitrol**) is available.

Acamprosate (Campral) is an anti-craving drug used in both the United States and Europe. It works by reducing the anxiety and insomnia that often occur when habitual drinkers become abstinent. Acamprosate has no psychotropic side effects nor any potential for abuse or dependence.

Other medications are available to treat the symptoms of alcohol withdrawal, such as shakiness, nausea, and sweating, that occur after someone with alcohol dependence stops drinking.

Clinical trial information is constantly updated by the National Institutes of Health, and the most recent information on alcoholism trials can be found at: http://clinicaltrials.gov/ct2/results?term=alcoholism

Alternative

Alternative treatments may be a helpful adjunct for the recovering alcoholic once the medical danger of withdrawal has passed. Stress is a drinking trigger for many people. Alternative therapies can help the recovering alcoholic eliminate or manage stress. These therapies include massage, **meditation**, **hypnotherapy**, **yoga**, and **acupuncture**.

Malnutrition caused by long-term alcohol use may be addressed by nutrition-oriented practitioners with careful attention to a healthy diet and the use of nutritional supplements such as vitamins A, B complex, and C, as well as certain fatty acids, amino acids, **zinc**, magnesium, and selenium.

Herbal treatments include milk thistle (*Silybum marianum*), which is thought to protect the liver against damage. Other herbs are thought to be helpful for the patient suffering through withdrawal. These include **lavender** (*Lavandula officinalis*), skullcap (*Scutellaria lateriflora*), **chamomile** (*Matricaria recutita*), peppermint (*Mentha piperita*), yarrow (*Achillea millefolium*), and **valerian** (*Valeriana officinalis*).

Prognosis

The prognosis for recovery from alcoholism varies widely. The usual course of the disorder is one of episodes of intoxication beginning in adolescence, with full-blown dependence by the mid-20s to mid-30s. The most common pattern is one of periodic attempts at abstinence alternating with relapses into uncontrolled drinking. On the other hand, it is thought that as many as 20% of persons diagnosed as alcohol dependent achieve long-term sobriety even without medical treatment.

It is difficult to compare the outcomes of the various treatment approaches to alcoholism, in part because their definitions of "success" vary. Some researchers count only total abstinence from alcohol as a successful outcome, while others regard curtailed drinking and better social adjustment as indicators of success. The role of genetic factors in the prognosis is still disputed. Available evidence suggests that such factors as the presence of a spouse, partner, or close friend in the alcoholic's life, or religious commitment can outweigh genetic vulnerability to the disorder.

Recovery from alcoholism is a lifelong process. The potential for relapse remains present and must be acknowledged and respected. Many individuals stop drinking and then relapse multiple times before attaining extended periods of sobriety. Statistics suggest that, among middle-class alcohol-dependent individuals in stable financial and family situations who have undergone treatment, 60% or more successfully stop drinking for at least one year.

Prevention

Prevention must begin at a young age, since the first instance of intoxication usually occurs during the teenage years. It is particularly important that teenagers who are at high risk for alcoholism—those with a family history of alcoholism, early or frequent use of alcohol, a tendency to drink to drunkenness, alcohol use that interferes with school work, a poor family environment, or a history of domestic violence—receive education about alcohol and its long-term effects. How this is best achieved, without alienating these young people and thus losing their attention, is the subject of continuing debate and study.

QUESTIONS TO ASK YOUR DOCTOR

- Can alcoholism be treated without medications?
- How can I best understand the factors that led to my alcoholism?
- Will I recover?
- Are lifestyle changes required?
- Are there associated conditions that also require treatment?

Resources

BOOKS

Benton, Sarah Allen. *Understanding the High-Functioning Alcoholic: Professional Views and Personal Insights.* Westport, CT: Praeger Publishers, 2009.

The Healing Project. *Voices of Alcoholism: The Healing Companion: Stories for Courage, Comfort and Strength.* Brooklyn, NY: LaChance Publishing, 2008.

Hedblom, Jack H. *Last Call: Alcoholism and Recovery.* Baltimore, MD: The Johns Hopkins University Press, 2007.

Jay, Jeff, and Debra Jay. *Love First: A Family's Guide to Intervention.* Center City, MN: Hazelden, 2008.

Maltzman, Irving. *Alcoholism: Its Treatments and Mistreatments.* Hackensack, NJ: World Scientific Publishing Co., 2008.

Tracy, Sarah W. *Alcoholism in America: From Reconstruction to Prohibition.* Baltimore, MD: The Johns Hopkins University Press, 2007.

OTHER

Substance Abuse and Mental Health Services Administration. "Faces of Change: Do I Have a Problem with Alcohol or Drugs?" U.S. Department of Health and Human Services. http://www.kap.samhsa.gov/products/brochures/pdfs/TIP35.pdf (accessed November 14, 2011).

WEBSITES

Centers for Disease Control and Prevention. "Fetal Alcohol Spectrum Disorders." http://www.cdc.gov/ncbddd/fasd/index.html (accessed November 14, 2011).

MedlinePlus. "Alcohol." U.S. National Library of Medicine, National Institutes of Health. http://www.nlm.nih.gov/medlineplus/alcohol.html (accessed November 14, 2011).

———. "Alcoholism." U.S. National Library of Medicine, National Institutes of Health. http://www.nlm.nih.gov/medlineplus/alcoholism.html (accessed November 14, 2011).

Thompson, Warren, R. Gregory Lande, and Raj K. Kalapatapu. "Alcoholism." Medscape Reference. June 9, 2011. http://emedicine.medscape.com/article/285913-overview (accessed November 14, 2011).

ORGANIZATIONS

Al-Anon/Alateen, 1600 Corporate Landing Parkway, Virginia Beach, VA, 23454-5617, (888) 4AL-ANON (425-2666), Fax: (757) 563-1655, wso@al-anon.org, http://www.al-anon.alateen.org.

Alcoholics Anonymous, http://www.aa.org, New York, NY, 10163, (212) 870-3400, http://www.aa.org.

National Council on Alcoholism and Drug Dependence, Inc., 244 East 58th Street 4th Floor, New York, NY, 10022, (212) 269-7797, 24-hour help line: (800) NCA-CALL Fax: (212) 269-7510, national@mcadd.org, http://www.ncadd.org.

National Institute on Alcohol Abuse and Alcoholism (NIAAA), 5635 Fishers Lane, MSC 9304, Bethesda, MD, 20892-9304, (301) 443-3860, http://www.niaaa.nih.gov.

Rebecca J. Frey, PhD
Joan Schonbeck, RN
Tish Davidson, AM

Alprazolam

Definition

Alprazolam is a tranquilizer. It belongs to a group of drugs called **benzodiazepines**. In the United States, alprazolam is sold under the brand name Xanax.

Purpose

The U.S. Food and Drug Administration (FDA) has approved alprazolam to treat anxiety, **panic disorder**, and anxiety associated with **depression**. Occasionally, alprazolam is used to treat alcohol withdrawal, but it is not FDA approved for this use and is not normally the first drug given when treating alcohol withdrawal symptoms.

Description

Alprazolam is classified as a benzodiazepine. Benzodiazepines are sedative-hypnotic drugs that help to relieve nervousness, tension, and other anxiety symptoms by slowing the central nervous system. To do this, they block the effects of a specific chemical involved in the transmission of nerve impulses in the **brain**, decreasing the excitement level of the nerve cells.

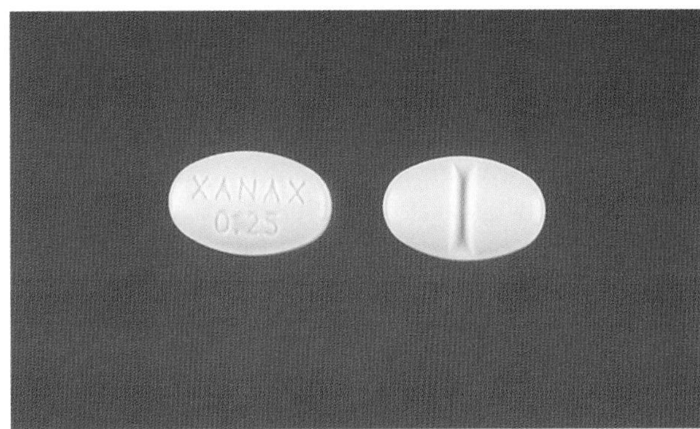

Xanax (alprazolam), 25 mg. *(U.S. Drug Enforcement Administration)*

All benzodiazepines cause sedation, including drowsiness and reduced mental alertness. However, one benefit of alprazolam is that it causes somewhat less drowsiness than many other benzodiazepine drugs.

Alprazolam comes in 0.25 mg, 0.5 mg, 1 mg and 2 mg tablets, and 1 mg/mL solution.

Recommended dosage

The recommended initial adult dose for anxiety is 0.25–0.5 mg taken three times daily. This dosage may be increased every three to four days to a maximum total of 4 mg daily. Dosage for alcohol withdrawal usually totals from 2–2.5 mg daily given in several small doses throughout the day.

The starting dose for treating panic disorder is 0.5 mg three times daily. This dosage may be increased every three to four days until the total daily dosage ranges from 2–10 mg. The total amount should be divided in at least three even daily doses. Average doses for anxiety associated with depression range from 2.5–3 mg daily, divided into even doses.

Precautions

Alprazolam should not be used by patients who are pregnant, have narrow angle glaucoma, take ketoconazole or itraconazole, or are allergic to this or any other benzodiazepine drug. The dose of alprazolam must be carefully regulated and individualized in the elderly (over age 60), people with liver or kidney disease, and those taking other medications used to treat mental disorders.

Because alprazolam is a nervous system and respiratory depressant, it should not be taken with other depressants, such as alcohol, other **sedatives**, sleeping pills, or tranquilizers. People taking this drug should not drive, operate dangerous machinery, or engage in hazardous activities that require mental alertness at least until they see how the drug affects them. Some patients taking alprazolam have engaged in "sleep driving," or operating a vehicle while sleeping, with no recollection of the event.

Alprazolam should be used under close physician supervision in patients with a history of **substance abuse**. Like other benzodiazepines, alprazolam can be habit forming. Risk and severity of dependence appears greater in patients taking doses larger than 4 mg daily. However, smaller doses may cause dependence if alprazolam is taken longer than 12 weeks. After four months, patients should be evaluated to see if they need to continue taking alprazolam.

Suddenly discontinuing alprazolam after several weeks may cause uncomfortable symptoms of withdrawal. Withdrawal symptoms in people who have taken alprazolam three months or longer may include **seizures**, anxiety, nervousness, and headache. Patients should discuss with their doctor how to gradually discontinue alprazolam use to avoid such symptoms.

Side effects

The most common side effects of alprazolam include sedation, dizziness, drowsiness, **insomnia**, and nervousness. The intensity of these side effects usually declines gradually and subsides in about eight weeks. A drop in blood pressure and an increase in heart rate may also occur in people who are taking alprazolam.

Decreased sex drive, menstrual disorders, and both weight gain and weight loss have been associated with use of alprazolam. People who experience the side effects of stomach upset, nausea, vomiting, and dry mouth should eat frequent, small meals and/or chew sugarless gum. Alprazolam has been associated with both diarrhea and constipation, as well as tremor, muscle cramps, vision disturbances, rash, and **amnesia** or memory loss.

Interactions

Alprazolam interacts with a long list of other medications. Anyone starting this drug should review the other medications they are taking with their physician and pharmacist for possible interactions. The most severe interactions occur with antifungal medications, such as ketoconazole, itraconazole, and fluconazole. These are associated with alprazolam toxicity (excessive sedation, **fatigue**, slurred speech, slowed reactions, and other types of psychomotor impairment).

Patients taking alprazolam should avoid eating grapefruit or drinking grapefruit juice due to potential adverse side effects.

Estrogens (female hormones), erythromycin (an antibiotic), **fluoxetine** (Prozac, Sarafem), cimetidine (Tagamet), isoniazid, and **disulfiram** (Antabuse) can increase the effects of alprazolam. Carbamazepine can make alprazolam less effective. When alprazolam is combined with other sedative drugs (tranquilizers, sleeping pills) or alcohol, its depressants effects are more intense. These combinations should be avoided.

KEY TERMS

Benzodiazepines—A group of central nervous system depressants used to relieve anxiety or to induce sleep.

Glaucoma—A group of eye diseases characterized by increased pressure within the eye significant enough to damage eye tissue and structures. If untreated, glaucoma results in blindness.

Resources

BOOKS

Kay, Jerald, Allan Tasman, and Jeffrey A. Lieberman. *Psychiatry: Behavioral Science and Clinical Essentials*. Philadelphia: W.B. Saunders Company, 2000.

Lacy, Charles F. *Drug Information Handbook with International Trade Names Index*. Hudson, OH: Lexi-Comp, Inc. 2011.

Pharmacia and Upjohn Company Staff. *Product Information: Xanax, Alprazolam*. Kalamazoo, MI: Pharmacia and Upjohn Company, 2011.

PERIODICALS

Yasui, N., et al. "Effects of Repeated Ingestion of Grapefruit Juice on the Single and Multiple Oral-Dose Pharmacokinetics and Pharmacodynamics of Alprazolam." *Psychopharmacology* 150, no. 2 (2000): 185–90.

WEBSITES

PubMed Health. "Alprazolam." U.S. National Library of Medicine. http://www.ncbi.nlm.nih.gov/pubmedhealth/PMH0000807 (accessed November 14, 2011).

Ajna Hamidovic, Pharm.D.

Alzheimer's disease

Definition

Alzheimer's disease (AD) is the most common form of **dementia** in those aged 65 and older. It is an irreversible and incurable progressive neurological disease caused by the degeneration and eventual death of a large number of neurons (nerve cells) in several areas of the **brain**, accompanied by diminished brain size. AD usually occurs in old age and begins with short-term memory loss. This is followed by the slow progressive loss of memory and cognitive and intellectual functions, leading to the deterioration of physical functioning and incapacitation.

Demographics

Alzheimer's disease is the most common degenerative brain disorder. It accounts for 50%–70% of all cases of dementia in the United States and for about 75% of all dementias in people over age 65. An estimated 5.1 million Americans have AD. The exact number is difficult to determine since AD is often misdiagnosed or not diagnosed until the disease is in its later stages. About 350,000 new cases of Alzheimer's disease are diagnosed each year in the United States, and approximately 65,800 people die from AD each year. It is the fourth-leading cause of death in American adults after heart disease, cancer, and **stroke**.

Alzheimer's rarely occurs before the age of 60. Early-onset AD, affecting people in their 30s, 40s, and 50s, accounts for only about 5% of total cases. About 3%–5% of men and women aged 65–74 have AD. About 20% of persons between 75 and 84 and nearly half of those over 85 have the disease. Slightly more women than men develop AD, which may be because women tend to live longer. About half of all nursing home patients in the United States have AD.

Alzheimer's disease appears to be more prevalent among African Americans, with estimates ranging from 14% to almost 100% higher than among Caucasian Americans. One study reported that the onset of AD in Hispanics occurs at an age that is, on average, five years younger than its onset in Caucasians.

The incidence of Alzheimer's in other developed countries is about the same as in the United States. In countries such as Japan that have a rapidly aging population with a higher percentage of people over 65, the incidence of AD is even higher than in the United States. In developing countries, the percentage of the

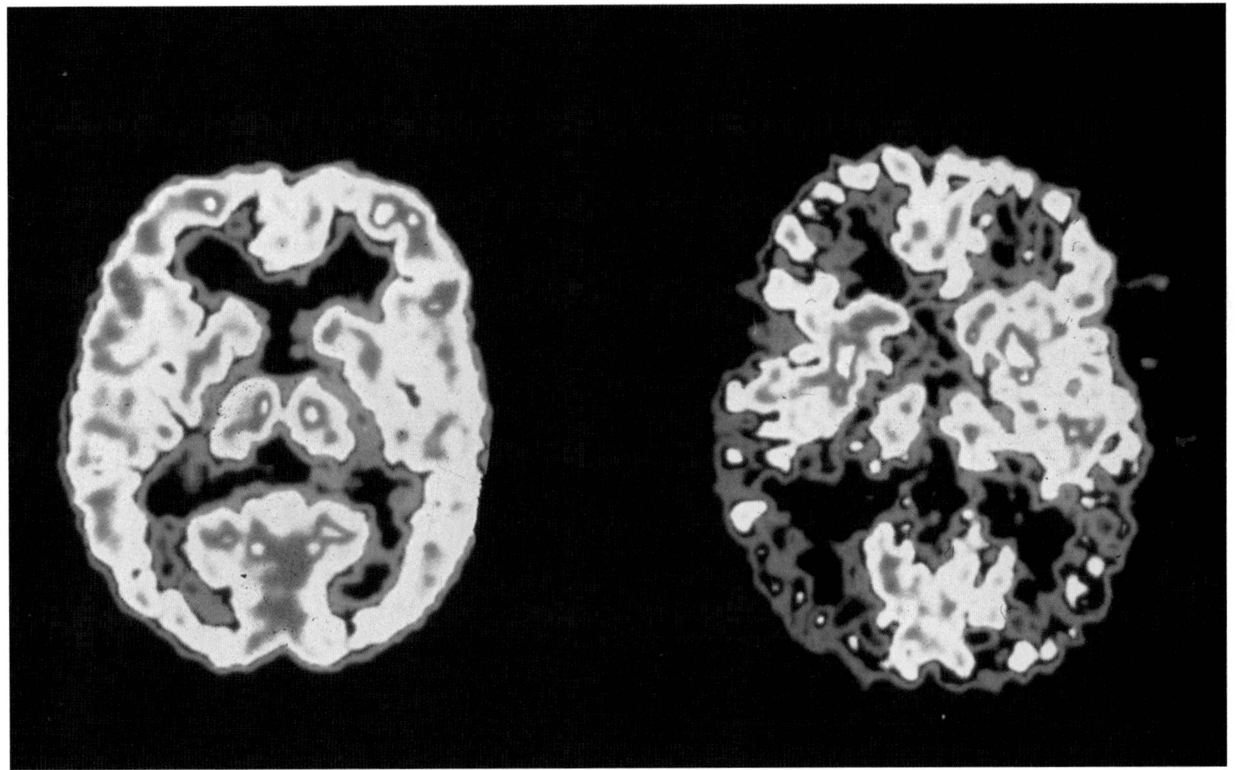

Colored positron emission tomography scans comparing a healthy brain (left) to a brain affected by Alzheimer's disease (yellow areas indicate brain activity). *(© Photo Researchers, Inc.)*

population with AD is lower because fewer people live to age 65. However, more than 50% of people with AD live in developing countries, and by 2025 this rate is expected to be above 70%.

The number of people afflicted with Alzheimer's is expected to more than triple by 2050, as the population ages and more people live longer. The number may be even higher than predicted, since recent research suggests that mild cognitive impairment observed in many elderly people may be early-stage Alzheimer's disease.

Description

In 1906 Alois Alzheimer (1864–1915), a German **psychiatrist** and neuroanatomist, was studying slides prepared from the brain of a 51-year-old woman, known as Frau D., who had died after suffering from dementia for several years. Her symptoms did not fit those of any brain disorder known at the time. Alzheimer found abnormal clumps of material—now called beta-amyloid plaques—and tangled bundles of fibers—neurofibrillary tangles—in Frau D.'s brain tissue. These plaques and tangles, found upon brain autopsy, constitute the diagnostic signature of Alzheimer's disease.

The plaques, sometimes called senile plaques, are sticky clumps or clusters of dead and dying neurons and other cellular debris surrounding insoluble deposits of beta-amyloid. The latter are fragments of a larger protein called amyloid precursor protein (APP) that was not processed properly. The plaques are located in between neurons and are believed to interfere with normal communication between neurons, eventually causing the nerve cells to die. The tangles are accumulations of twisted fragments of tau proteins inside neurons. Tau proteins normally bind and stabilize neurons. When tau proteins are damaged by the addition of phosphorus, a process called hyperphosphorylation, they form filaments that twist around each other to form neurofibrillary tangles that can no longer stabilize the neurons.

Increased beta-amyloid may cause the formation of neurofibrillary tangles. However, it is not known whether the plaques and tangles cause AD or are the result of it. Plaques and tangles occur as part of the normal aging process but are far less prevalent in normal brains than in the brains of AD patients. Because dementia had been associated with the elderly and Frau D. had been middle-aged, her disease was named presenile dementia and was thought to be a very rare disorder. It was not until the early 1950s that researchers at St. Elizabeth's Hospital in Washington, DC, came to realize that Alzheimer's disease is the single most common cause of dementia.

Scientists have since found other changes in the brains of AD patients. Connections between nerve cells are disrupted and nerve cells die in areas of the brain that are vital for memory and learning, including the hippocampus, which is a structure deep in the brain that controls short-term memory. Later, AD affects the cerebral cortex, particularly the areas responsible for language and reasoning. Eventually many areas of the brain become involved and atrophied (shrunken and dysfunctional).

The levels of the brain **neurotransmitters** norepinephrine, **serotonin**, and acetylcholine are also lower in AD. These chemicals transmit signals across the synapses, or gaps, between nerve cells. Many of the behavioral and psychiatric problems associated with AD are thought to result from low levels of these neurotransmitters. Acetylcholine and norepinephrine are important for many processes in the body, including digestion, blood vessel dilation and constriction, and regulation of heartbeat.

Public awareness of AD increased significantly when Ronald Reagan (1911–2004), the 40th president of the United States (1981–89), was diagnosed with the disease in 1994. He died from complications of AD in 2004 at the age of 93. Because of the growing numbers of people who are affected by AD, their increasing life expectancy, and the direct and indirect costs of their care, Alzheimer's disease is now considered to be a major public health concern.

Alzheimer's disease places severe emotional and financial burdens on patients and their families. In 2007, the annual cost of caring for a patient with AD was estimated at $18,400 for mild or early-stage conditions and at $36,100 for a patient with severe AD. The total annual cost of caring for AD patients in the United States was estimated to be at least $100 billion, including both direct patient costs and indirect costs, such as time lost from work by caregivers. On average, Medicare pays more than three times as much for the healthcare of a beneficiary with AD compared to a beneficiary without AD.

Risk factors

The most significant risk factor for AD is advancing age. The risk of developing AD begins to rise after age 65 and rises sharply after age 75. There are various other possible risk factors:

- About 25% of AD cases are considered to be familial Alzheimer's disease (FAD), defined as having symptoms of AD in at least three generations of a single family. About 2%–5% of all AD cases are familial early-onset FAD of one of three types (AD1, AD3, and

AD4), in which the disease develops before the age of 60—usually between the ages of 40 and 50, but sometimes as early as age 30. First-degree relatives of AD patients may have as much as a 20% lifetime risk of being affected by the disease. The risk to immediate relatives increases as more family members develop the disease. The remaining 75% of cases are sporadic Alzheimer's disease (SAD) with no clear family history.

- African American and Caribbean Hispanics who have mutations in a particular gene are at a higher than normal risk for AD, particularly if they have a family history of the disease.
- A family history of Parkinson's disease is a risk factor for AD.
- There is some evidence that neuronal damage from small strokes may be linked to AD.
- Studies have found a clear correlation between low educational and occupational attainment (employment in jobs that are not mentally challenging) and an increased risk for AD. Taking on less challenging rather than more challenging jobs as one grows older is also associated with a higher risk for AD.
- Studies on special breeds of genetically engineered (transgenic) mice have suggested high blood cholesterol levels may increase the rate of plaque deposition.
- Researchers suspect that a high-cholesterol, high-fat diet may increase the risk of AD. However, studies have not found cholesterol-lowering drugs to have any effect on AD onset.
- High systolic blood pressure combined with high blood cholesterol levels increases the risk of AD by three-to-four times.
- Obesity is a risk factor for AD.
- Mild cognitive impairment (MCI), which is characterized primarily by memory loss while other cognitive functions remain intact, increases the risk of AD. About 12% of people with MCI develop Alzheimer's disease each year. About 40% of people diagnosed with MCI have clear symptoms of AD after four years.
- High levels of an amino acid called homocysteine may be a risk factor for late-onset AD.
- Symptoms of AD may develop faster in people who have had a head trauma or hypothyroidism.
- Down syndrome patients over the age of 40 all develop the brain cell changes that are characteristic of Alzheimer's disease. Down syndrome–associated AD accounts for less than 1% of Alzheimer's cases.

Various environmental factors have been suspected of contributing to the development of AD. However, epidemiological studies have not borne out any links between AD and factors such as pollutants in drinking water, aluminum from commercial products, and metal dental fillings. Although higher-than-average levels of aluminum have been found in the brains of patients with AD, it now appears that this is a result rather than a cause of the disease.

Causes and symptoms

In most cases the cause of AD is unknown. It is most likely caused by a combination of genetic and environmental factors. Viral, immunological, and/or biochemical etiologies have also been proposed. Some studies link AD with an inability of the brain to metabolize sugar and use insulin effectively. Genetics almost certainly plays a role, even in sporadic AD. Brain inflammation and restriction of blood flow to the brain may play a role in the development of beta-amyloid plaques and neurofibrillary tangles. Highly reactive molecules called free radicals damage all types of cells through oxidative processes, especially brain cells, which have lower levels of protective antioxidants.

AD symptoms can be grouped into three categories: cognitive deficits or losses in brain function related to memory and learning, behavioral and psychiatric symptoms of dementia (BPSD), and difficulties with activities of daily life (ADL). For most of the twentieth century, studies of AD patients focused on cognitive symptoms. It was not until the 1980s and 1990s that researchers began to examine behavioral and psychiatric symptoms more closely.

There are four major cognitive deficits associated with AD:

- Amnesia (memory impairment). Patients may not be able to recall past events or form new memories, or both. A loss of the sense of time is also classified as amnesia.
- Aphasia (loss of language). Patients may not remember the names of objects and use words such as "thing" or "it" instead. They may echo what other people say or repeat a word or phrase over and over. Sometimes patients lose all language except curses.
- Apraxia (inability to perform voluntary movements). Patients with apraxia may have trouble putting on a hospital gown or brushing their teeth.
- Agnosia (inability to recognize familiar people and places). *Agnosia* comes from the Greek word meaning "to not know." Patients with agnosia may even fail to recognize their own face in a mirror.

Symptoms associated with BPSD include:

- Depression. Depression in AD is believed to result, at least in part, from lowered production of serotonin.

- Delusions (a false belief that is maintained even in the presence of evidence to the contrary). For example, AD patients may believe that someone is stealing from them when they cannot remember where they put something.
- Wandering. This behavior may result from becoming disoriented or lost, but sometimes AD patients wander for no apparent reason.
- Hallucinations (sensory experiences that seem real). Although hallucinations can affect any of the senses, most are visual or auditory. For example, AD patients may say that they see Martians in the corner of the room or hear the voices of their long-dead parents. Like delusions, hallucinations are believed to be related to the deterioration of brain tissue. However, sometimes they are caused by medications.
- Aggression (hitting, shoving, pushing, or threatening behavior)
- Agitation. Emotionally excited behavior (e.g., screaming, shouting, cursing, pacing, or fidgeting) that is disruptive or unsafe may result from brain tissue damage or be a symptom of depression. It is thought that the emotional overreactions of AD patients are related to destruction of neurons in the amygdala of the brain.

Personal-care symptoms (ADL) include difficulties with the following:

- eating, including simple cooking and washing dishes
- shopping for groceries and other necessities
- bathing, showering, or shaving
- grooming and dressing in clothing appropriate for the weather and activity
- toileting
- other aspects of personal hygiene such as teeth brushing, denture cleaning, or washing hair

Stages of AD

Although the rate of AD progression and specific symptoms vary with the individual, the general course of the progression is fairly consistent. Early-onset AD often progresses faster than the more common late-onset type. AD is generally considered to have seven stages:

- Stage 1: no decline in function yet noted. This includes individuals who may carry predictive gene mutations but have no symptoms and those who will develop AD by other mechanisms.
- Stage 2: generally normal functioning. The individual is aware of a subtle cognitive decline.
- Stage 3: early Alzheimer's disease. Patients have difficulty performing complex tasks that require cognitive skills.
- Stage 4: mild Alzheimer's disease. Patients require assistance with tasks such as paying bills or balancing a checkbook.
- Stage 5: moderate Alzheimer's disease. Patients require assistance in making everyday personal decisions such as choosing appropriate clothing or ordering from a restaurant menu.
- Stage 6: moderately severe Alzheimer's disease. Patients require assistance dressing, bathing, and using the toilet, and may have urinary and/or bowel incontinence.
- Stage 7: severe Alzheimer's disease. Vocabulary shrinks to a few words, followed by little or no verbal communication. The ability to walk is lost, followed by an inability to maintain a sitting posture in a chair. Eventually the patient experiences a profound lack of purposeful muscle control, is totally dependent for care, and cannot smile or hold up his or her head.

AD usually starts slowly with a very gradual decline that is termed "insidious." Some people are unaware of any impairment, blaming their forgetfulness on old age or "senior moments." Often the earliest symptoms are recognized only in hindsight by a friend or family member. Furthermore, since the present generation at risk for AD is the first in history to understand the implications of the disease, there are very powerful emotional reasons for attributing early signs of AD to normal aging, job **stress**, adjusting to retirement, and other less troubling factors. However, the insidious nature of AD onset is a characteristic that helps physicians to distinguish it from other causes of dementia, including **vascular dementia**.

Warning signs and symptoms

Key warning signs of early-stage AD include:

- repeatedly asking the same question
- repeatedly telling the same story, word for word
- memory loss that affects job performance
- loss of initiative
- inability to pay bills or balance a checkbook
- misplacing commonly used personal or household objects
- difficulty performing familiar tasks such as cooking, making repairs, or playing games such as cards or checkers
- poor or decreased judgment
- problems with abstract thinking
- getting lost in familiar surroundings
- relying on others to make decisions or answer questions
- disorientation of time and place

- problems with language
- mood or behavior changes
- personality changes
- neglecting personal hygiene—for example, not bathing or changing clothes regularly

The first symptoms of early-stage AD usually include forgetfulness, short-term memory loss, temporary episodes of spatial disorientation, groping for words, minor problems with arithmetic, and small errors in judgment, often accompanied by some anxiety, agitation, mild **depression**, and withdrawal. The patient may light the stove under a saucepan while forgetting to add the food or water, but most ADL are unaffected. Some patients can continue to operate a motor vehicle safely, although many people with early-stage AD voluntarily give up driving.

Everyone has occasional memory lapses that do not signify any change in cognitive function. Early-stage AD may begin with routine memory lapses—forgetting where one left the car keys—but progresses to more profound or disturbing lapses, such as forgetting that one has a car. Some AD patients are unaware that their memory is failing. Other patients are keenly aware of their memory loss and may become anxious and frustrated. Becoming lost or disoriented on a walk around the neighborhood becomes more likely as the disease progresses. Individuals with AD may forget the names of family members or forget what was said at the beginning of a sentence by the time they hear the end. Although the progression of memory loss varies, it eventually begins to interfere with daily activities.

Middle-stage Alzheimer's typically begins two to three years after the initial onset. Patients begin to lose awareness of their cognitive deficits. Memory loss, especially of recent events, becomes more severe and is accompanied by moderate spatial and temporal disorientation, loss of ability to concentrate, aphasia, and increased anxiety. Severe language problems develop. Patients cannot understand or remember the names of objects. Their speech may not flow smoothly. Because of individual variation in disease progression, some patients may still be able to carry out routine behaviors and engage in generalized conversation. However, they can no longer drive a car, cook a meal, or read a newspaper. They are unable to work, plan and execute familiar tasks, and reason and exercise judgment. They may get lost easily and find simple activities confusing. The loss of cognitive functioning becomes impossible to ignore. Mood and personality are affected. Some people become angry or violent. Behavioral and psychiatric symptoms include agitation, wandering, temper tantrums, depression, and disorientation. Patients begin to lose their basic sense of personal identity. They may be at high risk for falls and other accidents. A small number of AD patients have vision problems. Although they frequently deny that they cannot see, autopsies confirm destruction in areas of the brain that process visual images.

Eventually, spatial and temporal disorientation becomes profound and may be accompanied by **delusions**, hallucinations, and **paranoia**. Patients may not recognize a family member or may accuse a spouse of infidelity. They may become uninhibited and confrontational. Some patients exhibit inappropriate sexual behaviors. AD patients may have trouble sleeping and suffer from nighttime confusion or agitation, called sunsetting or sundowner's syndrome. Some patients repeat words, thoughts, or movements, a behavior known as perseveration. Eventually they are unable to feed, bathe, dress, or groom themselves and cannot be left unattended.

In end-stage Alzheimer's disease, patients undergo general physical decline and lose control of many physical functions. **Seizures** and hypertonicity (increased muscle movements) are common. Bladder and bowel control is lost and stiffening muscles prevent walking. Patients who can walk often wander aimlessly and must be monitored for night wandering due to altered sleep patterns. Although some patients may use a wheelchair temporarily, eventually they become completely bedridden, unable even to sit up. Many patients are unable to talk. Abnormal jerking movements may occur for no reason or in response to touch or noises. Reflexes may be exaggerated and some patients experience whole body contractions known as generalized seizures.

Once the disease affects the brain stem, the basic processes of digestion, respiration, and excretion shut down. Patients may be unable to eat or swallow, and they sleep most of the time. Their hands and feet feel cold, breathing becomes shallow, and the patient is generally unresponsive. Death often results from infection, pneumonia, or malnutrition. Otherwise, breathing simply stops. From the onset of initial symptoms, disease progression can last up to 25 years, although the typical duration is 8 to 10 years.

Genetic profile

Familial early-onset Alzheimer's disease (FAD) accounts for fewer than 10% of AD cases. It can be caused by mutations in one of three genes. It is usually an autosomal dominant trait. Autosomal means that it affects males and females with equal frequency. Dominant means that it will affect individuals even if they inherited one copy of the mutated gene from one parent and a normal copy of the gene from the other parent. Individuals who have two copies of the mutant gene will pass on the gene to all of their children. If each parent has one copy of the mutant gene, there is a 75%

KEY TERMS

Acetylcholine—A neurotransmitter with effects that are generally opposite those of the neurotransmitters dopamine and norepinephrine. Acetylcholine dilates blood vessels, lowers blood pressure, and slows heartbeat.

Agitation—Excessive restlessness or emotional disturbance that is often associated with anxiety or psychosis; common in middle-stage AD.

Agnosia—Inability to recognize familiar people, places, and objects.

Amnesia—Partial or complete loss of memory or gaps in memory.

Amygdala—An almond-shaped brain structure of the limbic system that is activated in stressful situations and triggers fear.

Antioxidant—A substance that prevents the destructive effects of oxidative chemicals in the body.

Aphasia—Loss of language abilities.

Apolipoprotein E (APOE)—A protein that transports cholesterol throughout the body. One form of this protein, APOE e4, is associated with a 60% risk of late-onset AD.

Apraxia—An inability to perform purposeful movements that is not caused by paralysis or loss of feeling.

Autosomal dominant—A gene located on a chromosome other than the X or Y sex chromosomes, whose expression is dominant over that of a second copy of the same gene.

Beta-amyloid plaques—Senile plaques; structures in the brain, composed of dead or dying nerve cells and cell debris surrounding deposits of beta-amyloid protein, that are diagnostic of AD. Beta-amyloid forms when amyloid precursor protein (APP) is not broken down properly.

Brain stem—The part of the brain that connects to the spinal cord and controls most basic bodily functions. It is the last part of the brain to be destroyed by AD.

Cholinesterase inhibitors—Drugs that may slow the progression of AD by inhibiting the enzymes that break down acetylcholine.

Computed topography (CT) scan—A scan that uses x rays and a computer to form detailed images of a part of the body.

Delirium—A disturbance of consciousness marked by confusion, inattention, delusions, hallucinations, and agitation. It is distinguished from dementia by its relatively sudden onset and variation in the severity of symptoms.

Delusion—A persistent false belief held in the face of strong contradictory evidence.

Dementia—A group of symptoms (syndrome) associated with a chronic progressive impairment of memory, reasoning ability, and other intellectual functions; personality changes; deterioration in personal grooming; and disorientation.

Donepezil hydrochloride (Aricept)—A drug that increases the levels of acetylcholine in the brain.

Down syndrome—A genetic disorder characterized by an extra chromosome 21 (trisomy 21), intellectual disabilities, and susceptibility to early-onset AD.

Free radicals—Reactive atoms or molecules with unpaired electrons that damage cells, proteins, and DNA.

that any of their children will inherit the gene. If only one parent has one copy of the gene, each of their children has a 50% of inheriting the gene.

Identification of these three genes has led to the subdivision of familial early-onset AD into three categories:

- AD1 is a genetic defect in the amyloid precursor protein (APP) gene located on chromosome 21. Mutations in the APP gene are associated with AD onset between the ages of 55 and 60.
- AD3 is a genetic defect in the presenilin 1 (PSEN1) gene located on chromosome 14. Presenilin 1 may be one of the enzymes that clips APP into beta-amyloid. It also may be important for the functioning of synaptic connections between neurons.
- AD4 is an extremely rare genetic defect in the presenilin 2 (PSEN2) gene located on chromosome 1. Presenilin 2 is also involved in processing APP.

Mutations in PSEN1 and PSEN2 are associated with AD onset between the ages of 30 and 50. These three mutations result in the production of abnormal proteins and increased amounts of beta-amyloid. Together they account for approximately 50% of early-onset FAD.

Genetic disease—A disease caused by genes inherited from one or both parents.

Ginkgo—An herb from *Ginkgo biloba*, a shade tree native to China with fan-shaped leaves and fleshy seeds with edible kernels. Some alternative practitioners recommend ginkgo extract for preventing and treating AD.

Hallucination—False sensory perceptions, such as hearing sounds or seeing people or objects that are not there. Hallucinations can also affect the senses of smell, touch, and taste.

Hippocampus—A part of the brain's limbic system that is involved in memory formation and learning.

Insidious—Progressing gradually and inconspicuously, but with serious effects.

Magnetic resonance imaging (MRI)—An imaging technique that uses electromagnetic radiation and a computer to obtain detailed images of soft tissues such as the brain.

Mild cognitive impairment (MCI)—A transitional phase of memory loss in older people that precedes dementia or AD.

Neurofibrillary tangles—Accumulations of twisted protein fragments inside nerve cells in the brain that are diagnostic of AD.

Neurotransmitters—Chemicals that carry nerve impulses from one nerve cell to another. AD causes a drop in the production of several important neurotransmitters.

Norepinephrine—A neurotransmitter and adrenal hormone and the precursor of epinephrine.

Perseveration—Continuous involuntary repetition of speech or behavior.

Polygenic—A trait or disorder that is determined by several different genes. Most human characteristics, including height, weight, and general body build, are polygenic. Schizophrenia and late-onset AD are considered polygenic disorders.

Positron emission tomography (PET)—A medical imaging method capable of displaying the metabolic activity of organs and useful for investigating brain disorders.

Presenile dementia—The original name for Alzheimer's disease.

Presenilin (PSEN)—Proteins that are involved in processing amyloid precursor protein (APP). Mutations in the genes encoding these proteins can cause early-onset AD.

Pseudodementia—Depression with symptoms resembling those of dementia. The term "dementia of depression" is now preferred.

Serotonin—A neurotransmitter found in the brain and blood. Low levels of serotonin are associated with AD.

Sunsetting—Confusion or agitation in the evening.

Systolic—Referring to the rhythmic contraction of the heart (systole) as the blood in the chambers is forced out. Systolic blood pressure is blood pressure measured during the systolic phase.

Tau protein—A protein involved in maintaining the internal structure of nerve cells. Tau protein is damaged in AD and forms neurofibrillary tangles.

Tomography—A technique for producing a focused image of the structures at a specific depth within the body, while blurring details at other depths.

Sporadic AD (SAD) is considered a polygenic disorder because it is believed to result from the effects of multiple genes combined with environmental factors. This view is supported by research involving identical twins. Only one-third of identical twins of those with AD develop AD themselves. This suggests that factors other than genetic predisposition affect the development of SAD.

Down syndrome–associated Alzheimer's is another genetically determined form of AD. Normal individuals have two copies of each of the 22 human chromosomes, one copy from each parent. People with **Down syndrome**, also called trisomy 21, have three copies of chromosome 21, which results in brain changes that are similar to those that occur in both familial and sporadic AD. This is thought to be due to the overproduction of APP from the extra chromosome 21 APP gene.

Diagnosis

An early and accurate **diagnosis** of AD is important for developing strategies for managing symptoms and helping patients and their families plan for treatment, long-term care, and financial issues while the patient can still be involved in decision making. A diagnosis of AD also may help family members to avoid unnecessary anger and feelings of helplessness when dealing with the progression of the disease.

A diagnosis of AD is based upon the finding of slowly progressive dementia, exclusion of other possible causes for dementia, and brain-imaging studies that show changes in the structure of the brain, usually in the form of shrinkage. Possible AD is diagnosed when AD is considered to be the primary cause of the symptoms, but the diagnosis is complicated by the presence of another disorder. Probable AD is diagnosed when physicians and psychiatrists have ruled out all other disorders that could produce similar symptoms.

In 2011, new diagnostic criteria were proposed that identified three distinct stages of AD progression:

- preclinical Alzheimer's disease, revealed by tests such as brain scans before actual symptoms manifest
- mild cognitive impairment (MCI) due to Alzheimer's disease, identified as the beginning of cognitive difficulties before ADL is affected
- dementia due to Alzheimer's disease, the point at which the disease has progressed to impeding everyday life

The new criteria seek to more heavily incorporate physical testing, such as brain imaging, to better supplement observation and general cognitive and neurologic assessment.

Examination

Diagnosis of Alzheimer's disease can be quite complex and require consultations with various specialists. It requires a complete physical examination and medical and family history, including family members who have had AD and their ages of onset. The results of neurological exams are generally normal in early-stage AD. A complete evaluation of **alcohol use** and prescription and over-the-counter medication history, including alternative remedies, vitamins, herbal supplements, or illicit drugs, is necessary to rule out other causes of dementia, because more than 150 drugs can cause AD-like symptoms. Diagnosis is based upon clinical findings of otherwise unexplained slowly progressing dementia. FAD is diagnosed if there is a family history of the disease. Although AD almost always develops in Down syndrome patients over age 40, it may be difficult to determine whether further impairment is due to the Down syndrome or the progression of AD.

Other types of dementia, including some that are reversible, can cause symptoms similar to those of AD. Approximately 20% of patients originally suspected of having AD turn out to have some other disorder, about half of which are treatable:

- Multi-infarct vascular dementia is caused by strokes (blood clots in the brain) that lead to stepwise destruction of mental capacities.
- Diffuse white matter disease is a form of vascular dementia that can be diagnosed by magnetic resonance imaging (MRI) that reveals the generalized death of large parts of the brain.
- Parkinson's disease is a neurodegenerative condition that causes movement and functional abnormalities. Most Parkinson's patients have tremors and rigidity in their arms and legs.
- Alcohol-associated dementia is caused by nutritional deficiencies among people who abuse alcohol, especially malnutrition and deficiencies in vitamins B1 (thiamine) and B12 (cobalamin) and niacin (nicotinic acid). It is potentially reversible.
- Chronic use of certain drugs such as tranquilizers, sedatives, and pain relievers, as well as drug interactions, can cause potentially reversible dementia.
- Endocrine abnormalities (hormone imbalances), especially thyroid dysfunction, are less common causes of dementia. They can be diagnosed by blood tests.
- Chronic infections of the central nervous system, tertiary syphilis, trauma or injury to the brain, brain tumors, psychiatric conditions such as depression (pseudodementia or dementia of depression), and genetic and degenerative disorders other than AD can also cause dementia.

Evaluations for depression and **delirium** (reduced consciousness or awareness of one's environment) are particularly important components of the diagnostic process because, although they may be symptoms of AD, they can also be mistaken for AD. Depression and memory loss are both common among the elderly and a combination of the two can lead to a mistaken diagnosis of AD. Depression can be treated with drugs, although some **antidepressants** may worsen dementia, further complicating both diagnosis and treatment.

The clinical evaluation will assess cognitive impairment other than short-term memory loss. A family member or close friend of the patient often will be questioned about the onset and duration of symptoms. A neuropsychiatric examination may be performed to determine the pattern of cognitive impairment and probe the patient's level of functioning. Patients may be asked to write a sample check, describe how they answer the telephone, interpret sample traffic signs, or pick out items on a shopping list from a display.

Tests

Blood and urine tests are used to help rule out other causes of dementia. Genetic tests are available to detect genes known to cause AD, but they do not necessarily predict the development of AD.

Several types of oral and written tests are used to help diagnose AD and track its progression, including tests of mental status, functional abilities, memory, verbal fluency, and concentration. In early-stage AD, the results of these tests are usually within the normal range. The widely used mini-mental status examination (MMSE) is one such screening test. It is not particularly sensitive for detecting cognitive impairment in well-educated individuals who have previously functioned at a high level. It may also not yield accurate results for poorly educated individuals or cultural minorities. Another test, the clock test, asks patients to draw the face of a clock, possibly including a specific time such as 3:20. Patients with AD often put the numbers out of order, put them all in one part of the clock face instead of evenly spaced, or have difficulty drawing in the clock hands.

Occasionally, the patient's cerebrospinal fluid is tested for the levels of two proteins, Tau and a specific beta-amyloid protein fragment called A beta 42. Increased Tau protein and decreased A beta 42 in the cerebrospinal fluid are indicative of AD.

Procedures

Brain neuroimaging studies such as **positron emission tomography (PET)**, MRI, **single photon emission computed tomography** (SPECT) scans, or computed topography (CT) scans may be used to detect gross cerebral cortex atrophy due to brain cell death. **PET** scans can detect the earliest changes in brain structure. MRI scans are often performed on patients who are having problems with balance or gait. MRIs can detect diffuse atrophy that is often present in the cerebrum of the brain of AD patients. PET and SPECT scans can be used to evaluate patterns of glucose (sugar) metabolism in the brain to differentiate patterns characteristic of AD from those associated with vascular dementia and Pick's disease. PET scans are more precise than SPECT scans but are more expensive. However, imaging alone cannot diagnose AD. MRI and CT scans and electroencephalographs (EEGs), which measure the electrical activity in the brain, can be useful for excluding other causes of dementia such as stroke, subdural hematoma, and brain tumors.

Although a skilled physician can diagnose probable AD with 90% accuracy, a definitive diagnosis of Alzheimer's disease comes after the patient dies. A brain autopsy and examination of the brain tissue by a histopathologist can identify AD as the cause of death. The presence of a large number of beta-amyloid plaques and intraneuronal neurofibrillary tangles are considered diagnostic of AD. Antibodies that bind to the specific amyloid proteins are tagged with a fluorescent or colorimetric molecule and visualized in a microscope. In addition, the longer the disease has progressed, the smaller the brain is at death.

Treatment

There are several treatments for AD, including counseling, providing social and emotional support, and prescribing drugs to treat the symptoms.

Traditional

Although there is no cure for Alzheimer's disease, early diagnosis and prompt **intervention** can slow its progression and enable patients to function independently for a longer period. Healthcare professionals usually assess a patient's ADL to determine what type of care is needed. The mainstay of treatment is the establishment of daily routines, good nursing care and/or home-care strategies, and providing physical and emotional support. In the initial stages, counseling by a **psychologist** or an AD support group is recommended. The patient and caregiver should establish a relationship with a primary care provider so that illnesses, such as urinary or respiratory infections, can be properly diagnosed and treated rather than being simply attributed to the inevitable decline of AD. Neurological and behavioral aspects of AD, including anxiety, agitation, defiant behavior, **insomnia**, hallucinations, and seizures are treated as needed.

Treatment of AD is a very active area of research and the National Institutes of Health (NIH) and other agencies sponsor numerous **clinical trials** of new drugs and therapies. A list of current clinical trials enrolling volunteers can be found at: http://clinicaltrials.gov/ct2/results?term=Alzheimer.

Drugs

The most common drugs prescribed for AD are inhibitors of acetylcholinesterase and butylcholinesterase, enzymes that break down the neurotransmitters acetylcholine and butylcholine, respectively. The following medications increase levels of acetylcholine in the brain, thereby improving brain function in early-stage mild-to-moderate AD:

- galantamine (Razadyne, formerly known as Reminyl)
- rivastigmine (Exelon)
- donepezil hydrochloride (Aricept)

Aricept has been approved by the FDA to treat patients through all stages of AD. This drug may improve the individual's awareness of surroundings, as well as improve memory and cognitive function, though it is not a cure for

AD. It is offered as a tablet and should be taken whole, rather than crushed or chewed. It may be taken with or without food. Aricept must be taken regularly for the patient to receive the most beneficial effects of this medication.

Memantine (Namenda) is used to treat moderate-to-severe AD; it should not be used in patients with mild AD. It acts on glutamate, another brain neurotransmitter. This drug may also improve the individual's awareness of surroundings, as well as improve memory and cognitive function, though it is not a cure for AD. It is offered as a tablet or as an oral liquid and may initially be prescribed in gradually increasing dosages as directed by the physician. It may be taken with or without food. It is used alone or in combination with **donepezil**.

These drugs can modestly increase attention span, concentration, mental acuity, and information processing and improve the ability to perform normal ADL. They slow the progression of symptoms for about six months to one year in one-third to one-half of patients with AD. All have side effects, most often mild diarrhea, nausea, vomiting, muscle cramps, dizziness, headache, **fatigue**, and sleep disturbances. **Tacrine** (Cognex), the first such drug, is no longer prescribed because of the risk of liver toxicity.

The antioxidant vitamin E may delay AD onset by protecting neurons from free-radical damage. AD patients have lower blood levels of vitamin E than other adults of the same age. The Academy of Neurology has stated that vitamin E may indeed help with some symptoms of AD. One large two-year study of moderately affected AD patients found that taking 2000 IU (international units) of vitamin E daily significantly delayed disease progression as compared with patients taking a placebo. However, high levels of vitamin E can put patients at higher risk for bleeding disorders. Vitamin E therapy, in combination with cholinesterase inhibitors, has become the standard treatment for AD.

Drugs previously used to treat AD, including selegiline (a drug for Parkinson's disease), prednisone, estrogen, and nonsteroidal anti-inflammatory drugs (NSAIDs), have been found to be ineffective.

Medications can be prescribed to manage the behavioral and psychiatric symptoms of AD, which are often very stressful for caregivers. These medications are usually prescribed for the following specific symptoms:

- typical antipsychotics, usually haloperidol (Haldol), risperidone (Risperdal), olanzapine, or quetiapine, for anxiety, aggression, delusions, or hallucinations
- short-term antianxiety drugs, usually lorazepam (Ativan) or buspirone (BuSpar), for agitation
- a selective serotonin reuptake inhibitor (SSRI), such as citalopram or sertraline, at half the adult dosage, for depression, which is common in early-stage AD

Alzheimer's disease (AD) medications

Drug name (brand/generic)	Level of AD treated	Possible side effects
Aricept (donepezil)	All stages (mild, moderate, severe)	• Bruising • Confusion • Depression or anxiety • Dizziness • Extreme fatigue • Gastrointestinal upset, including vomiting • Pain, including joint pain and muscle cramps • Personality changes • Red, scaly, itchy skin • Strange dreams • Trouble sleeping
Exelon (rivastigmine)	Mild to moderate	• Confusion • Dizziness • Excessive perspiration • Gastrointestinal upset, including vomiting • Headache • Tremor • Trouble sleeping • Weakness and fatigue
Namenda (memantine)	Moderate to severe (should not be used to treat mild AD)	• Confusion • Constipation • Coughing • Dizziness • Fatigue • Headache • Pain • Vomiting
Razadyne (galantamine)	Mild to moderate	• Depression • Dizziness • Extreme fatigue • Gastrointestinal upset, including vomiting • Headache • Pale skin • Runny nose • Tremor • Trouble sleeping

(Table by PreMediaGlobal. © 2012 Cengage Learning.)

- acetaminophen or a very low dose of codeine for pain

Patients with AD are more susceptible to the side effects of medications, especially psychoactive drugs, and are usually given lower doses than younger adults. Physicians often recommend first trying to reduce behavioral symptoms with changes to the patient's environment.

Alternative

Antioxidants have shown some degree of effectiveness in treating AD, though further studies are needed. Antioxidants, in addition to vitamin E, include:

- vitamin C
- selenium

- green tea
- ginkgo biloba extract

Derived from the leaves of the *Ginkgo biloba* tree, ginkgo also increases blood and oxygen flow to the brain and has anti-inflammatory and neuroprotective effects. It has been used for many years in China, is widely prescribed in Europe for circulatory problems, and is the most common herbal treatment for AD. However, a large-scale, well-designed 2008 study found that ginkgo extract neither prevented nor delayed AD.

Other supplements for treating AD include huperzine A, thiamine (vitamin B1), cobalamin (vitamin B12), acetyl L-carnitine, **DHEA**, and folic acid, though none of these have yet been proven successful in clinical trials.

The incidence of AD is lower in countries with **diets** that are lower in calories and fats. There have been a few reports suggesting that diets rich in fish improve mental function in patients with AD or dementia, and AD patients treated with essential fatty acids have shown greater improvement in mood and mental function than patients on placebos. Because of its disease-preventing properties, red wine in moderation may also benefit AD patients. Patients with AD should avoid environmental toxins such as tobacco smoke.

A variety of other therapies may be beneficial in the treatment of psychological symptoms of AD:

- Music therapy has been found to calm agitated AD patients and improve mood; reduce chronic pain, depression, agitation, wandering, and feelings of isolation; and enhance long-term memory. Old familiar songs can be particularly effective in improving recall.
- Light therapy in the evening can help alleviate sleep-cycle disturbances.
- Supportive therapies include touch, compliments, and displays of affection.
- Sensory stimulation through massage and aromatherapy may be beneficial.
- Socio-environmental therapies include activities related to patient, previous interests and favorite foods, as well as pleasant surroundings.
- Insight-oriented psychotherapy addresses patients' awareness of their disease.
- Dance therapy, validation therapy, reminiscence therapy, and reality-oriented therapy have also been used with AD patients.

Home care

About 70% of AD patients are cared for at home, with the remainder residing in various types of institutions. Creative strategies are necessary to help the patient stay as independent as possible. Caregivers need their own support systems to minimize anger, despair, and burnout. Becoming familiar with likely future scenarios and considering financial and legal issues early on can ease the burden on both the patient and the family.

In the early stages of AD when memory loss is minimal, it is helpful for family and friends to interact with patients as much as possible, reminding them to eat, take their medication, keep their appointments, and help sustain daily living activities. Keeping records is helpful, particularly when there are several caregivers. The household should be organized so that important items can be found easily. The patient will need help in managing finances. Providing neighbors with a house key and setting up a schedule to check in on the patient are recommended. With the help of family, neighbors, and community resources, many people with early AD are able to maintain a successful lifestyle in their home environment for months or years.

Basic safety concerns for AD patients include:

- falls
- ingestion of dangerous substances
- wandering from home and becoming lost
- injury to one's self or others with sharp objects or fire
- the inability to respond rapidly to crisis situations

Often families have to modify their homes because of safety concerns. Possible modifications include:

- installing grab bars in bathrooms, bed rails, and clutter-free passageways
- unplugging and putting away electrical appliances when not in use
- storing matches, lighters, knives, or weapons out of reach
- lowering hot water heater temperature to avoid accidental scalding
- keeping a list of emergency numbers, including the poison control center and hospital emergency room, posted by the phone

Patients who have been diagnosed with AD should never be allowed to drive because of the risk of accidents or becoming disoriented. Some local chapters of the Alzheimer's Association offer help with transportation.

A calm, structured environment with simple orientation aids such as calendars and clocks can help reduce anxiety and increase safety. Labeling cabinets and drawers can help patients focus their attention. Signs can be posted reminding patients of important phone numbers and to turn off appliances and lock doors. Scheduling meals, bathing, and other activities at regular times and places provides routine and emotional security, since unfamiliar places and activities can be disorienting.

Caregivers should develop a daily routine and take advantage of periods during the day when the patient is less confused and more cooperative. The most severe symptoms often occur at night. Sleep disturbances may be minimized by keeping the patient engaged in activities during the day. Daily supervised walks are a good general exercise for people with AD.

A loss of grooming skills—mismatched clothing, unkempt hair, and decreased interest in personal hygiene—is often one of the early symptoms of AD. Caregivers, especially spouses, may find these changes embarrassing and difficult to handle. The caregiver will increasingly assume grooming responsibilities as the disease progresses.

Feeding may require using a colored plate to focus the patient's attention on the food. Finger foods may be preferable to the use of utensils. A nutritionist can give advice on well-balanced, easily prepared meals. Eventually the caregiver may need to feed the patient. As movement and swallowing become difficult, a feeding tube may be placed into the stomach through the abdominal wall.

Incontinence presents the most difficult problem for many caregivers and is a major reason for moving people with AD to nursing home care. In the early stages, limiting fluid intake and increasing the frequency of toileting can help. Careful attention to hygiene is important to prevent skin irritation and infection from soiled clothing.

Caregiver concerns

Family members or other caregivers have a difficult and stressful job, which becomes harder still as the disease progresses. Caring for dementia patients is significantly more demanding and time-consuming than caring for patients with other illnesses. Each day may bring new challenges as the patient's ability levels decrease and new patterns of behavior develop. Many caregivers find the constant but unpredictable demands extremely difficult. The personality changes of AD can be heartbreaking for family members as a loved one deteriorates, seeming to become a different person. As the disease progresses, the patient's behavior may become increasingly erratic. It may be impossible to leave a patient unattended for even a few minutes because the patient may wander off. Neighbors should always be informed of the person's condition. However, not all AD patients develop negative behaviors: some become gentle, spending increasing amounts of time in dreamlike states.

Caregivers often develop feelings of anger, resentment, guilt, and hopelessness. Depression is common and may need to be treated. Caregivers can become susceptible to illness, especially if they do not receive adequate support from family, friends, and community. **Support groups** can help caregivers deal with stress. The location and contact numbers for AD caregiver support groups are available from the Alzheimer's Association, local social service agencies, physicians, and pharmaceutical companies that manufacture the drugs used to treat AD.

Most families eventually need outside help to care for the AD patient. Personal care assistants, either volunteer or paid, may be available through local social service agencies. Adult daycare facilities are becoming increasingly common. Meal delivery, shopping assistance, or **respite** care may also be available. Special Alzheimer's disease facilities are available for both respite daycare and permanent long-term care.

The decision to move the patient to a nursing home is often one of the most difficult for the family, who may consider that they have failed in their obligations and are abandoning their loved one. Counsulting with a physician, clergy, or other trusted adviser can ease this transition. Selecting a nursing home may require a difficult balancing of costs, services, location, and availability. Keeping the entire family involved in the decision may help prevent further stress.

Social Security Disability, Medicare, Medicaid, or Supplemental Security Income may provide financial assistance but will not usually cover nursing home care indefinitely. Long-term care insurance, if purchased prior to diagnosis; reverse mortgages; or other financial devices may be appropriate.

Prognosis

There is no cure for Alzheimer's disease, and once the symptoms develop patients do not recover. The goal is to maintain cognitive and physical function for as long as possible. Although there is considerable variation in the rate of disease progression, symptoms continue to worsen, usually over a period of years. Eventually, loss of brain cells and brain damage result in the impairment of autonomic body functions, the failure of various organ systems, coma, and death. Most AD patients die within 8 to 10 years of diagnosis, although that interval can be as short as one year or as long as 20 years. The life expectancy of AD patients is increasing because the disease is generally being diagnosed at an earlier stage.

The most common cause of death among AD patients is infection. People with AD are often in poor health and may be malnourished, which puts them at increased risk of life-threatening infections such as pneumonia. They are also susceptible to other conditions and diseases of old age. The consequences of cancer, stroke, and heart disease can be more severe in patients with AD than in otherwise healthy people.

QUESTIONS TO ASK YOUR DOCTOR

- What are the indications that my loved one may have Alzheimer's disease?
- What diagnostic tests are needed for a thorough assessment?
- What treatment options do you recommend for my loved one?
- What kind of changes can I expect to see with the medications you have prescribed for my loved one?
- What are the side effects associated with the medications you have prescribed for my loved one?
- Should my loved one see a specialist? If so, what kind of specialist should I contact?
- What tests or evaluation techniques will you perform to see if treatment has been beneficial for my loved one?
- What physical or psychological limitations do you foresee?
- How does having Alzheimer's disease put my loved one at risk for other health conditions?
- What measures can be taken to prevent the progression of symptoms?
- Are there any new or experimental treatments available?
- Is my loved one eligible for any clinical trials?
- When should my loved one stop driving?
- What symptoms or adverse effects are important enough that I should seek immediate treatment?
- Can you recommend any support groups for me and my family?

Prevention

There is no known prevention for Alzheimer's disease. Several studies have suggested that high-fat and high-calorie diets may increase the risk of developing AD. Other possible risk factors include alcohol, salt, and refined carbohydrates. Some studies have found that fish consumption reduces the incidence of AD in Europe and North America, possibly due to the omega-3 fatty acids found in fish. It is also possible that staying physically and mentally active throughout life may lower the risk of AD.

Individuals with a history of Alzheimer's disease in their families may want to consider genetic counseling to clarify possible risk factors and determine the appropriateness of available genetic tests. Possessing a certain gene, the APOE e4 gene, is a risk factor for AD, but it is not considered useful for predicting whether a person will develop the disease. The National Institute on Aging has several reasons for not recommending using the test to screen people:

- It does not predict whether an individual will develop AD.
- There are ethical implications to testing for a disease that is currently incurable.
- It may have adverse psychological consequences for individuals and their families.
- It could lead to discrimination in employment or health insurance for carriers of the gene.

Research on the prevention of AD has focused on blocking the production of amyloid protein in the brain and on breaking down beta-amyloid after it is released from cells but before it has a chance to aggregate into insoluble plaques.

Healthcare team roles

Treatment of AD is a team effort, involving primary care physicians, nurses, imaging and laboratory technicians, gerontology specialists, psychiatrists, psychologists, and caregivers. Educating patients and caregivers about the nature of the disease and its progression usually falls on nursing staff. Nurses are also the first line of access for medical care and support groups. **Social workers**, counselors, and support group facilitators may provide emotional support, practical advice, and information about community resources. Specialized Alzheimer's disease facilities may be used for either respite daycare or permanent long-term care.

Resources

BOOKS

Calo-oy, Starr, and Bob Calo-oy. *Caregiving Tips A-Z, Alzheimer's & Other Dementias.* Fremont, CA: Orchard Publications, 2008.

Chan, A. P., ed. *Alzheimer's Disease Research Trends.* Hauppauge, NY: Nova Science, 2008.

Dawbarn, David, ed. *Neurobiology of Alzheimer's Disease*, 3rd ed. New York: Oxford University Press, 2007.

Doraiswamy, P. M., et al. *The Alzheimer's Action Plan: The Experts' Guide to the Best Diagnosis and Treatment for Memory Problems.* New York: St. Martin's Press, 2008.

Lerner, Adrienne. *Alzheimer's Disease.* Farmington Hills, MI: Greenhaven Press, 2008.

Mace, Nancy L., and Peter V. Rabins. *The 36-Hour Day: A Family Guide to Caring for Persons with Alzheimer*

Disease, Other Dementias, and Memory Loss in Later Life, 4th ed. Baltimore: Johns Hopkins University Press, 2006.

McCann-Beranger, Judith. *A Caregiver's Guide to Alzheimer's & Related Diseases*. New York: Bunim & Bannigan, 2008.

Sabbagh, Marwan. *The Alzheimer's Answer: Reduce Your Risk and Keep Your Brain Healthy*. Hoboken, NJ: Wiley, 2008.

Taylor, Richard. *Alzheimer's from the Inside Out*. Baltimore: Health Professions Press, 2006.

Whitehouse, Peter J., and Daniel George. *The Myth of Alzheimer's: What You Aren't Being Told About Today's Most Dreaded Diagnosis*. New York: St. Martin's Press, 2008.

PERIODICALS

Arnst, Catherine. "Is Alzheimer's a Form of Diabetes? If So, an Insulin-Centered Treatment Could Alter the Course of the Disease." *Bloomberg Business Week* (December 6, 2007). http://www.businessweek.com/magazine/content/07_51/b4063054323389.htm (accessed July 24, 2011).

Ault, Alicia. "Debate Continues Over Early Cognition Screening: Some Argue that Obtaining a Timely Baseline Could Offset Subsequent Delays in Diagnosing Alzheimer's." *Family Practice News* (December 15, 2007): 27.

Bain, L. J., Warren Barker, David A. Loewenstein, and Ranjan Duara. "Towards an Earlier Diagnosis of Alzheimer Disease." *Alzheimer Disease and Associated Disorders* 22, no. 2 (April-June 2008): 99–110.

Christensen, Daniel D., and Peter Lin. "Practical Treatment Strategies for Patients with Alzheimer's Disease." *Journal of Family Practice* (December 2007): 17–23.

Frisoni, Giovanni B., and Jennifer L. Whitwell. "How Fast Will It Go, Doc? New Tools for an Old Question from Patients with Alzheimer Disease." *Neurology* 70, no. 23 (June 2008): 2194–95.

Grady, Denise. "Finding Alzheimer's Before a Mind Fails." *New York Times* (December 26, 2007): A1+. http://www.nytimes.com/2007/12/26/health/26alzheimers.html?pagewanted=all (accessed July 24, 2011).

Guthrie, Catherine. "Is Alzheimer's a Form of Diabetes?" *Time Health* (October 18, 2007). http://www.time.com/time/health/article/0,8599,1673236,00.html (accessed July 24, 2011).

Ji, Hong-fang, and Hong-yu Zhang. "Multipotent Natural Agents to Combat Alzheimer's Disease: Functional Spectrum and Structural Features." *Acta Pharmacologica Sinica* (February 2008): 143–51.

Kontush, Anatol, and Svetlana Schekatolina. "An Update on Using Vitamin E in Alzheimer's Disease." *Expert Opinion on Drug Discovery* (February 2008): 261–71.

Palmer, Katie, et al. "Mild Cognitive Impairment in the General Population: Occurrence and Progression to Alzheimer Disease." *American Journal of Geriatric Psychiatry* 16, no. 7 (July 2008): 603–11.

Schwab, Claudia, and Patrick L. McGeer. "Inflammatory Aspects of Alzheimer Disease and Other Neurodegenerative Disorders." *American Journal of Alzheimer's Disease & Other Dementias* 13, no. 4 (May 2008): 359–69.

WEBSITES

"Alzheimer's Disease." *American Health Assistance Foundation*. Last modified June 6, 2011. http://www.ahaf.org/alzheimers (accessed July 29, 2011).

"Alzheimer's Disease." *MedlinePlus*. Last modified July 21, 2011. http://www.nlm.nih.gov/medlineplus/alzheimersdisease.html#cat25 (accessed July 29, 2011).

"Alzheimer's Disease." *NIH Senior Health*. Last modified March 30, 2010. http://nihseniorhealth.gov/alzheimersdisease/toc.html (accessed July 29, 2011).

Alzheimer's Disease Education and Referral Center. "Alzheimer's Disease: Unraveling the Mystery." *National Institute on Aging*. Last modified January 4, 2011. http://www.nia.nih.gov/Alzheimers/Publications/Unraveling (accessed July 29, 2011).

———. "New Research Illuminates Memory Loss and Early Dementia." *Connections* (Spring 2009). http://www.nia.nih.gov/Alzheimers/ResearchInformation/Newsletter/Spring2009/feature01.htm (accessed July 29, 2011).

Mayo Clinic Staff. "Alzheimer's Disease." MayoClinic.com. http://www.mayoclinic.com/print/alzheimers-disease/DS00161/DSECTION=all&METHOD=print (accessed July 29, 2011).

ORGANIZATIONS

Alzheimer's Association, 225 N Michigan Ave., 17th Fl., Chicago, IL, 60601-7633, (312) 335-8700, (800) 272-3900, Fax: (866) 699-1246, info@alz.org, http://www.alz.org.

Alzheimer's Disease Education and Referral Center, National Institute on Aging, PO Box 8250, Silver Spring, MD, 20907-8250, (800) 438-4380, adear@nia.nih.gov, http://www.nia.nih.gov/Alzheimers.

Alzheimer's Foundation of America, 322 8th Ave., 7th Fl., New York, NY, 10001, (866) 232-8484, Fax: (646) 638-1546, info@alzfdn.org, http://www.alzfdn.org.

American Academy of Neurology, 1080 Montreal Ave., St. Paul, MN, 55116, (800) 879-1960, http://www.aan.com.

American Health Assistance Foundation, 22512 Gateway Center Dr., Clarksburg, MD, 20871, (800) 437-2423, Fax: (301) 948-4403, info@ahaf.org, http://www.ahaf.org.

American Neurological Association, 5841 Cedar Lake Rd., Ste. 204, Minneapolis, MN, 55416, (952) 545-6284, http://www.aneuroa.org.

Family Caregiver Alliance, 180 Montgomery St., Ste. 900, San Francisco, CA, 94104, (415) 434-3388, (800) 445-8106, http://www.caregiver.org.

Fisher Center for Alzheimer's Research Foundation, One Intrepid Square, W 46th St. & 12th Ave., New York, NY, 10036, (800) 259-4636, http://foundationcenter.org.

Foundation for Health in Aging, 350 5th Ave., Ste. 801, New York, NY, 10118, (212) 755-6810, http://www.healthinaging.org.

National Institutes of Health, 9000 Rockville Pike, Bethesda, MD, 20892, (301) 496-4000, http://www.nih.gov.

National Institute of Neurological Disorders and Stroke, NIH Neurological Institute, PO Box 5801, Bethesda, MD, 20824, (301) 496-5751, (800) 352-9424, http://www.ninds.nih.gov.

National Library of Medicine, 8600 Rockville Pike, Bethesda, MD, 20894, http://www.nlm.nih.gov.

U.S. Administration on Aging, 1 Massachusetts Ave. NW, Washington, DC, 20001, (202) 401-4634, http://www.aoa.gov.

Bryan Richard Cobb, PhD
Ken R. Wells
Laura Jean Cataldo, RN, EdD

Amantadine

Definition

Amantadine is a synthetic antiviral agent that also has strong antiparkinsonian properties. It is sold in the United States under the brand name Symmetrel, and is also available under its generic name.

Purpose

Amantadine is used to treat a group of side effects (called parkinsonian side effects) that includes tremors, difficulty walking, and slack muscle tone. These side effects may occur in patients who are taking antipsychotic medications used to treat mental disorders such as **schizophrenia**. An unrelated use of amantadine is in the treatment of viral infections of some strains of influenza A.

Description

Some medicines, called antipsychotic drugs, that are used to treat schizophrenia and other mental disorders can cause side effects similar to the symptoms of Parkinson's disease. The patient does not have Parkinson's disease, but may experience shaking in muscles while at rest, difficulty with voluntary movements, and poor muscle tone.

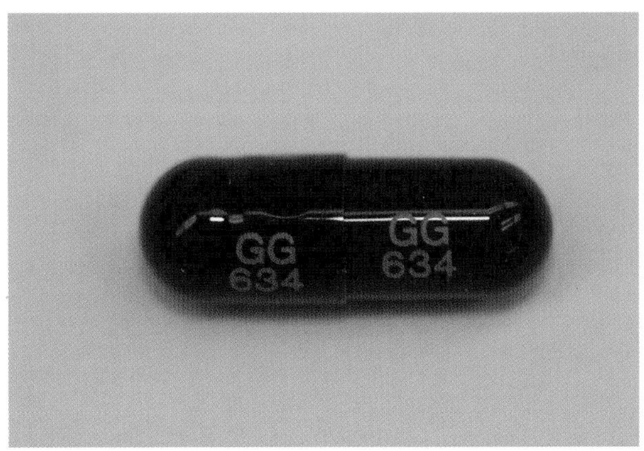

Amantadine hydrochloride, 100 mg. *(© Custom Medical Stock Photo, Inc. Reproduced by permission.)*

One way to eliminate these undesirable side effects is to stop taking the antipsychotic medicine. Unfortunately, the symptoms of the original mental disorder usually come back, so in most cases simply stopping the antipsychotic medication is not a reasonable option. Some drugs that control the symptoms of Parkinson's disease such as amantadine also control the parkinsonian side effects of antipsychotic medicines.

Amantadine works by restoring the chemical balance between **dopamine** and acetylcholine, two neurotransmitter chemicals in the **brain**. Taking amantadine along with the antipsychotic medicine helps to control symptoms of the mental disorder, while reducing parkinsonian side effects. Amantadine is in the same family of drugs (commonly known as anticholinergic drugs) as **biperiden** and **trihexyphenidyl**.

Recommended dosage

Amantadine is available in 100 mg tablets and capsules, as well as a syrup containing 50 mg of amantadine in each teaspoonful. For the treatment of drug-induced parkinsonian side effects, amantadine is usually given in a dose of 100 mg orally twice a day. Some patients may need a total daily dose as high as 300 mg. Patients who are taking other antiparkinsonian drugs at the same time may require lower daily doses of amantadine (e.g., 100 mg daily).

People with kidney disease or who are on hemodialysis must have their doses lowered. In these patients, doses may range from 100 mg daily to as little as 200 mg every seven days.

Precautions

Amantadine increases the amount of the neurotransmitter dopamine (a central nervous system stimulant) in the brain. Because of this, patients with a history of epilepsy or other seizure disorders should be carefully monitored while taking this drug. This is especially true in the elderly and in patients with kidney disease. Amantadine may cause visual disturbances and affect mental alertness and coordination. People should not operate dangerous machinery or motor vehicles while taking this drug.

Side effects

Five to ten percent of patients taking amantadine may experience the following nervous system side effects:

- dizziness or lightheadedness
- insomnia

KEY TERMS

Acetylcholine—A naturally occurring chemical in the body that transmits nerve impulses from cell to cell. It causes blood vessels to dilate, lowers blood pressure, and slows the heartbeat. Central nervous system well-being is dependent on a balance among the neurotransmitters acetylcholine, dopamine, serotonin, and norepinephrine.

Anticholinergic—Related to the ability of a drug to block the nervous system chemical acetylcholine. When acetylcholine is blocked, patients often experience dry mouth and skin, increased heart rate, blurred vision, and difficulty in urinating. In severe cases, blocking acetylcholine may cloud thinking and cause delirium.

Dopamine—A chemical in brain tissue that serves to transmit nerve impulses (is a neurotransmitter) and helps to regulate movement and emotions.

Neurotransmitter—A chemical in the brain that transmits messages between neurons, or nerve cells.

Parkinsonian—Related to symptoms associated with Parkinson's disease, a nervous system disorder characterized by abnormal muscle movement of the tongue, face, and neck; inability to walk or move quickly; walking in a shuffling manner; restlessness; and/or tremors.

- nervousness or anxiety
- impaired concentration

One to five percent of patients taking amantadine may experience the following nervous system side effects:

- irritability or agitation
- depression
- confusion
- lack of coordination
- sleepiness or nightmares
- fatigue
- headache

In addition, up to 1% of patients may experience hallucinations, euphoria (excitement), extreme forgetfulness, aggressive behavior, personality changes, or **seizures**. Seizures are the most serious of all the side effects associated with amantadine.

Gastrointestinal side effects may also occur in patients taking amantadine. Up to 10% of people taking this drug experience nausea and up to 5% have dry mouth, loss of appetite, constipation, and vomiting. In most situations, amantadine may be continued and these side effects treated symptomatically.

Between 1% and 5% of patients taking amantadine have also reported a bluish coloring of their skin (usually on the legs) that is associated with enlargement of the blood vessels (called livedo reticularis). This side effect usually appears within one month to one year of starting the drug and subsides within weeks to months after the drug is discontinued. People who think they may be experiencing this or other side effects from any medication should tell their physicians.

Interactions

Taking amantadine along with other drugs used to treat parkinsonian side effects may cause increased confusion or even hallucinations. The combination of amantadine and central nervous system stimulants (e.g., **amphetamines** or decongestants) may cause increased central nervous stimulation or increase the likelihood of seizures.

See also Medication-induced movement disorders

Resources

BOOKS

American Society of Health-System Pharmacists. *AHFS Drug Information 2008*. Bethesda, MD: American Society of Health-System Pharmacists, 2008.

PERIODICALS

Graham, Karen A., et al. "Double-Blind, Placebo-Controlled Investigation of Amantadine for Weight Loss in Subjects Who Gained Weight with Olanzapine." *American Journal of Psychiatry* 162, no. 9 (September 2005): 1744–46.

Silver, Henry, et al. "A Double-Blind, Cross-Over Comparison of the Effects of Amantadine or Placebo on Visuomotor and Cognitive Function Medicated Schizophrenia Patients." *International Clinical Psychopharmacology* 20, no. 6 (November 2005): 319–26.

Walsh, R. A., and A. E. Lang. "Multiple Impulse Control Disorders Developing in Parkinson's Disease after Initiation of Amantadine." *Movement Disorders* (September 27, 2011) [e-pub ahead of print]. http://dx.doi.org/10.1002/mds.23964 (accessed December 12, 2011).

OTHER

Enco Pharmaceuticals, Inc. "SYMMETREL (Amantadine Hydrochloride, USP) Tablets and Syrup." http://www.endo.com/PDF/symmetrel_pack_insert.pdf (accessed September 20, 2011).

Jack Raber, Pharm.D.
Ruth A. Wienclaw, PhD

Ambien *see* **Zolpidem**

American Academy of Child & Adolescent Psychiatry

Definition

The American Academy of Child and Adolescent Psychiatry (AACAP) is a 501 (c) (3) nonprofit medical organization that was founded in 1953 as an organization for practicing psychiatrists specializing in the care of youth. As of 2011, the AACAP represents over 7,500 physicians who treat the estimated 7–12 million American children and adolescents suffering from developmental or behavioral disorders. A major priority of the AACAP is expanding the workforce of specialists in adolescent and child psychiatry.

Purpose

The academy functions to establish and support ethical and professional standards in the practice of child and adolescent psychiatry; advocates for children, adolescents, and families with mental health needs; and promotes research and training to physicians and other healthcare providers. They strive to promote the healthy development of children, adolescents, and families, and to support psychiatrists working with child and adolescent populations.

Description

To qualify for membership in the academy, a person must be a doctor of medicine (MD) or a doctor of osteopathy (DO) who has completed four years of medical school; three years in an approved residency in medicine, neurology, and general psychiatry with adults; and two years of further training in psychiatric work with children, adolescents, and their families in an accredited residency in child and adolescent psychiatry. After completing these residency requirements, the candidate must then pass a certification examination in general psychiatry given by the American Board of Psychiatry and Neurology (ABPN). He or she is then eligible to take the additional certification examination in the subspecialty of child and adolescent psychiatry. Although the ABPN examinations are not required for practice, they are a further assurance of the physician's qualifications and competence.

The AACAP is governed by an elected council of 16 members; five of these members form the executive committee of the organization. Other members of the AACAP are able to join work groups, committees, and task forces (7 work groups and 60 committees were active as of 2011). Work groups and committees cover a wide variety of issues and special concerns ranging from continuing education, legal matters, religion and spirituality, and workforce issues to the special needs of adolescents (as distinct from younger children), Native American and minority youth, survivors of **trauma**, rural families, and military families. In addition to its internal committees, the academy works together with other medical professional organizations. It has a seat in the House of Delegates of the American Medical Association (AMA) and liaisons with the American Academy of Pediatrics (AAP), the **American Psychiatric Association** (APA), and the American Academy of Family Physicians (AAFP). The AACAP also sends representatives to such organizations as the National Alliance on Mental Illness (NAMI), Mental Health America, and the Federation of Families for Children's Mental Health.

Professional publications

The academy's strong commitment to furthering the understanding and treatment of children and adolescents is also reflected in the wide range of its publications, which include its official monthly, the *Journal of the American Academy of Child and Adolescent Psychiatry*, and a quarterly newsletter. The AACAP also provides information for the public in the form of *Facts for Families*, a collection of fact sheets providing frequently updated material discussing current psychiatric issues concerning children, adolescents, and their families. Topics include "Talking to Children about Terrorism and War," "Children and Video Games: Playing with Violence," "Children and Role Models," and "Psychotherapies for Children and Adolescents." The full collection is available in English and Spanish, with select translations also available in Malaysian, Polish, Icelandic, Arabic, Urdu, and Hebrew. In addition to *Facts for Families*, the academy has published two books for the general public, *Your Child* and *Your Adolescent*, and also provides online resource centers on a variety of mental health topics that affect children.

Resources

ORGANIZATIONS

American Academy of Child and Adolescent Psychiatry (AACAP), 3615 Wisconsin Avenue NW, Washington, DC, 20016-3007, (202) 966-7300, (800) 333-7636, Fax: (202) 966-2891, http://www.aacap.org.

American Academy of Family Physicians, 11400 Tomahawk Creek Pkwy., Leawood, KS, 66211-2672, (913) 906-6000, (800) 274-2237, Fax: (913) 906-6075, contactcenter@aafp.org, http://www.aafp.org.

American Academy of Pediatrics (AAP), 141 Northwest Point Boulevard, Elk Grove Village, IL, 60007, (847) 434-4000, Fax: (847) 434-8000, http://www.aap.org.

National Institute of Child Health and Human Development (NICHD), Bldg 31, Room 2A32, MSC 2425, 31 Center Drive, Bethesda, MD, 20847, (800) 370-2943; TTY: (888) 320-6942, Fax: (866) 760-5947, NICHDInformationResourceCenter@mail.nih.gov, http://www.nichd.nih.gov.

Laura Jean Cataldo, RN, Ed.D.

American Psychiatric Association

Definition

The American Psychiatric Association (APA) is a national medical society whose approximately 36,000 physician and medical student members specialize in the **diagnosis** and treatment of mental and emotional disorders. The oldest medical specialty society in the United States, the APA was begun in October 1844, when 13 physicians who specialized in the treatment of mental and emotional disorders met in Philadelphia and founded the Association of Medical Superintendents of American Institutions for the Insane. Their goals were to communicate professionally, cooperate in the collection of data, and improve the treatment of the mentally ill.

Purpose

More than one hundred and fifty years later, the APA's objectives are still designed to advance care for people with mental illnesses. Their mission is to improve treatment, rehabilitation, and care of the mentally ill and emotionally disturbed; to promote research, professional education in psychiatry and allied fields, and the prevention of psychiatric disabilities; to advance the standards of psychiatric services and facilities; to foster cooperation among those concerned with the medical, psychological, social, and legal aspects of mental health; to share psychiatric knowledge with other practitioners of medicine, scientists, and the public; and to promote the best interests of patients and others using mental health services.

Description

To be eligible to join the APA, a physician or resident must have graduated from a four-year program leading to an MD or DO degree, and have completed a residency program in psychiatry accredited by the Residency Review Committee for Psychiatry of the Accreditation Council for Graduate Medical Education (ACGME), the Royal College of Physicians and Surgeons of Canada (RCPS(C)), or the American Osteopathic Association (AOA). Applicants for membership must also provide a reference from a physician who is already a member of the APA.

The APA's annual meeting attracts more than 15,000 attendees and features hundreds of sessions and presenters. Additionally, the Association schedules more than 200 meetings each year among its councils, committees, and task forces to further advance the cause of mental health. The APA also offers a comprehensive continuing medical education program to its members.

Internal divisions of the APA include the Office of Minority and National Affairs, Early Career Psychiatrists, the Office of International Activities, women's programs, and minority and underrepresented group caucuses. The APA also operates several special interest groups and areas of study, including HIV psychiatry; disaster psychiatry; integrative medicine; and gay, lesbian, and bisexual health.

The APA has established the American Psychiatric Foundation (APF) as its philanthropic and educational arm. The Foundation seeks to educate the public about mental illness through workplace programs and other initiatives. It also supports researchers, particularly in the fields of **schizophrenia** and minority mental health, and provides fellowships for qualified APA members, including an annual fellowship for a resident in psychiatry to work in a congressional office or committee.

Professional publications

The APA supports psychiatrists and their service to patients through such publications as the *American Journal of Psychiatry*, the oldest specialty journal in the United States, and *Psychiatric News*, the Association's official newsletter. The APA also publishes numerous books, specialty journals, and reports. American Psychiatric Publishing, Inc. (APP) is a fully owned subsidiary of the APA and offers hundreds of book titles as well as six specialty journals, including eBooks and eJournals. APP has two purposes—to serve as the distributor of publications of the APA and to publish books independent of APA policies and procedures. Since its founding in 1981, APP has evolved into a full-service publishing house, with editorial, production, marketing, and business staff.

The DSM

The ***Diagnostic and Statistical Manual of Mental Disorders*** is published by the APA and is the accepted guide by medical professionals for diagnosing mental health conditions and disorders. The *DSM* provides diagnostic criteria for approximately 300 mental health disorders. The fifth edition, or *DSM-5*, is being developed and is expected to publish in 2013.

Resources

WEBSITES

American Psychiatric Publishing. http://appi.org/Pages/default.aspx (accessed December 12, 2011).

ORGANIZATIONS

American Psychiatric Association, 1000 Wilson Blvd., Ste. 1825, Arlington, VA, 22209-3901, (703) 907-7300, apa@psych.org, http://www.psych.org.

American Psychological Association

Definition

The American Psychological Association (APA) was founded in July 1892 by three dozen members. As of 2011, it had more than 154,000 members and is both the world's largest association of psychologists and the major organization representing psychology in the Unites States. Presently chartered as a corporation in the District of Columbia, the APA considers itself a scientific as well as a professional organization. The APA restricts the use of the word "psychologist" to persons who hold doctorates in the field from accredited institutions, preferring to refer to persons with master's degrees in psychology as "clinicians," "counselors," or "specialists."

Purpose

The mission of the APA is to "advance the creation, communication, and application of psychological knowledge to benefit society and improve people's lives." The organization strives to support the growth of psychology as a science and advocates for the benefits of psychology in influencing public health and well-being.

Description

The APA is governed by a president, a board of directors, a council of representatives, and various boards and committees. It oversees several programs, including four directorates in science, practice, public interest, and education. The Science Directorate promotes the exchange of ideas and research findings through conventions, conferences, publications, and traveling museum exhibits. It also helps psychologists locate and obtain research funding, and its science advocacy program works for the enhancement of federal support for psychology, research, and teaching. The Practice Directorate promotes the practice of psychology and the availability of psychological care through legislative advocacy on such issues as health care reform, regulated state licensure, and pro bono services. The Public Interest Directorate supports the application of psychology to the advancement of human welfare through program and policy development; conference planning; and support of research, training, and advocacy in such areas as minority affairs, rural health, disability issues, women's issues, and lesbian and gay health. The Education Directorate serves to advance psychology in its work with educational institutions, including precollege as well as college and graduate programs; professional agencies; continuing education for APA members; and programs and initiatives in education.

The APA is subdivided into 54 divisions, which are specialized interest groups initiated by members. Topics include developmental psychology, clinical psychology, military psychology, child and family policy and practice, and **exercise** and sport psychology, as well as societies focused on specific age groups, genders, and ethnic groups. Each division has its own officers, publications, awards, and activities, and functions within the context of the APA.

In 1953, the APA started its foundation, the American Psychology Foundation (APF), with a donation of $500. The APF began its first public initiative in 1974, a study of gifted and talented youth. This program continues to add to the field of giftedness research through its publications and by attracting younger scholars to pursue research on gifted children. In the early 1990s, the APF underwent a major expansion program in order to support graduate and postdoctoral students in psychology. A fundraising campaign in 2000 increased the APF's grant-making capacity by more than 150% in just five years. The APF focuses on enhancing the field of psychology, whether through student development in the form of scholarships or research initiatives by way of grants. Funding programs include career development and education, child and family psychology, disaster relief, gay and lesbian psychology, international efforts, mental and physical health, **stigma** and prejudice, travel grants, violence prevention, and personal awards.

Professional publications

The APA's information dissemination efforts include the publication of books, including children's books; scientific and professional journals; magazines and newsletters, including *APA Monitor*, *gradPSYCH Magazine*, and *American Psychologist*; reports and brochures; and electronic databases, including *PsychINFO*, a worldwide computer database of psychological abstracts (not full-text articles) from the 1800s to the present that has provided references in psychology and related behavioral and social sciences since the 1970s.

The APA also hosts an annual convention, considered to be the world's largest meeting of psychologists.

Resources

BOOKS

Evans, Rand B., Virginia Staudt Sexton, and Thomas C. Cadwallader, eds. *The American Psychological Association: A Historical Perspective*. Washington, DC: American Psychological Association, 1992.

ORGANIZATIONS

American Psychological Association, 750 1st St. NE, Washington, DC, 20002-4242, (202) 336-5500; TDD/ TTY: (202) 336-6123, (800) 374-2721, http://www.apa.org.

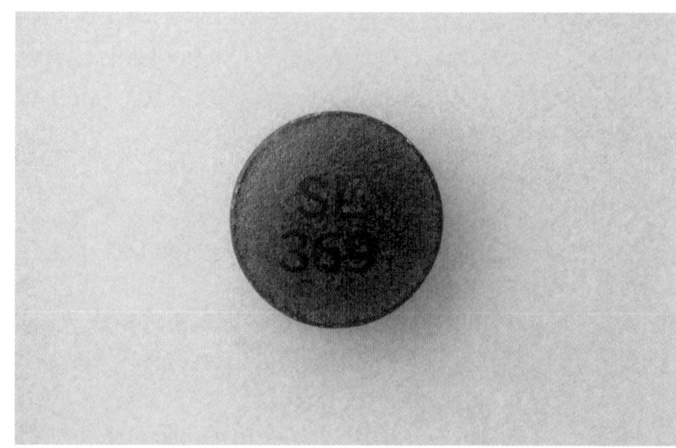

Amitriptyline, 75 mg. *(© Custom Medical Stock Photo, Inc. Reproduced by permission.)*

Amitriptyline

Definition

Amitriptyline is a medication used to treat various forms of **depression** and pain associated with the nerves (neuropathic pain), and to prevent migraine headaches. It is sold in the United States under the brand names Elavil and Endep.

Purpose

Amitriptyline helps relieve depression and pain. This medication, usually given at bedtime, also helps patients sleep better.

Description

Amitriptyline medication is one of several tricyclic **antidepressants**, so called because of the three-ring chemical structure common to these drugs. It acts to block reabsorption of **neurotransmitters** (chemicals that transmit nerve messages in the **brain**). Amitriptyline and the other tricyclic antidepressants are primarily used to treat mental depression but are increasingly being replaced by a newer and more effective group of antidepressant drugs called **selective serotonin reuptake inhibitors (SSRIs)**. Amitriptyline is sometimes prescribed to help treat pain associated with cancer. In addition, it is sometimes prescribed for various types of chronic pain. Tablets are available in 10, 25, 50, 70, and 150 mg doses.

Recommended dosage

The usual adult dose for pain management ranges from 10 mg to 150 mg at bedtime. Patients are generally started on a low dose, and the amount may be increased as needed. Side effects, such as a dry mouth and drowsiness, may make it difficult to increase the dose in older adults. Bedtime dosing helps the patient sleep. Doctors generally prescribe 75–150 mg for depression. It is given at bedtime or in divided doses during the day. It may take 30 days for the patient to feel less depressed. Pain relief is usually noticed sooner than the mood change. Teens and older adults usually receive a lower dose. If the nightly dose is missed, it should not be taken the next morning. Taking amitriptyline during waking hours could result in noticeable side effects. Patients should check with their doctors if the daily dose is missed. Those on more than one dose per day should take a missed dose as soon as it is remembered but should not take two doses at the same time. While amitriptyline is usually administered orally, injectable amitriptyline is available. It should not be used in this form long term; patients should switch to tablets as soon as possible.

Precautions

Patients should not stop taking this medication suddenly. The dose should be decreased gradually, then discontinued. If the drug is stopped abruptly, the patient may experience headache, nausea, or discomfort throughout the body, and a worsening of original symptoms. The effects of the medication last for three to seven days after it has been stopped, and older patients usually are more prone to some side effects, such as drowsiness, dizziness, mental confusion, blurry vision, dry mouth, difficulty urinating, and constipation. Taking a lower dose may help resolve these problems. Patients may need to stop this medication before surgery.

Amitriptyline should not be given to anyone with allergies to the drug or to patients recovering from a heart attack. Patients taking the **monoamine oxidase inhibitors** (MAOIs) **tranylcypromine** (Parnate) or **phenelzine** (Nardil)—different types of antidepressants—should not use amitriptyline in combination. Amitriptyline should be administered with caution to patients with glaucoma, **seizures**, urinary retention, overactive thyroid, poor liver or kidney function, alcoholism, asthma, digestive disorders, enlarged prostate, seizures, or heart disease. Pregnant women should discuss the risks and benefits of this medication with their doctors, as fetal deformities have been associated with taking this drug during pregnancy. Women should not breastfeed while using amitriptyline.

This medication should not be given to children under 12 years of age. For adolescents and adults up to age 24, amitriptyline carries an increased risk of developing suicidal thoughts while taking the drug. Patients taking amitriptyline should be monitored for signs of worsening depression or other worrisome symptoms, such as increased agitation or aggression, panic attacks, extreme irritability, or frenzied behavior. If these symptoms are experienced by the patient or observed by a caregiver, the patient's physician should be contacted.

Side effects

Common side effects include dry mouth, drowsiness, constipation, and dizziness or lightheadedness when standing. Patients can suck on ice cubes or sugarless hard candy to combat the dry mouth. Increased fiber in the diet and additional fluids may help relieve constipation. Dizziness is usually caused by a drop in blood pressure when suddenly changing position. Patients should slowly rise from a sitting or lying position if dizziness is noticed. Amitriptyline may increase the risk of falls in older adults. Patients should not drive or operate machinery or appliances while under the influence of this drug. Alcohol and other central nervous system depressants can increase drowsiness. Amitriptyline may also produce blurry vision, irregular or fast heartbeat, high or low blood pressure, palpitations, and an increase or decrease in a diabetic patient's blood sugar levels. Patients' skin may become more sensitive to the sun, and thus direct sunlight should be avoided by wearing protective clothing and applying sunscreen with a protective factor of 15 or higher.

Amitriptyline may increase appetite, cause weight gain, or produce an unpleasant taste in the mouth. It may also cause diarrhea, vomiting, or heartburn. Taking this medication with food may decrease digestive side effects. Other less likely side effects include muscle tremors, nervousness, impaired sexual function, sweating, rash, itching, hair loss, ringing in the ears, and changes in the makeup of the patient's blood, including bone marrow suppression. Patients with **schizophrenia** may develop an increase in psychiatric symptoms.

KEY TERMS

Glaucoma—A group of eye diseases characterized by increased pressure within the eye, significant enough to damage eye tissue and structures. If untreated, glaucoma results in blindness.

Methylphenidate—A mild central nervous system stimulant that is used to treat hyperactivity.

Monoamine oxidase inhibitors (MAOIs)—A group of antidepressant drugs that decrease the activity of monoamine oxidase, a neurotransmitter found in the brain that affects mood.

Urinary retention—Excessive storage of urine in the body.

Interactions

Patients should always tell all doctors and dentists that they are taking this medication. It may decrease the effectiveness of some drugs used to treat high blood pressure and should not be taken with other antidepressants, epinephrine and other adrenaline-type drugs, or **methylphenidate**. Patients should not take over-the-counter medications without checking with their doctors. For instance, amitriptyline should not be taken with Tagamet (cimetidine) or Neosynephrine. Patients taking amitriptyline should avoid the dietary supplements **St. John's wort**, belladonna, henbane, and scopolia. Black tea may decrease the absorption of this drug. Patients should ingest the drug and tea at least two hours apart.

Resources

BOOKS

Consumer Reports and American Society of Health-System Pharmacists. *Consumer Reports Complete Drug Reference, 2009 ed.* Yonkers, NY: Consumers Reports, 2009.

Ellsworth, Allan J., et al. *Mosby's Medical Drug Reference*. St. Louis, MO: Mosby, 2007.

PERIODICALS

Frese, A., et al. "Pharmacologic Treatment of Central Post-Stroke Pain." *Clinical Journal of Pain* 22, no. 3 (March-April 2006): 252–60.

Mayers, Andrew G., and David S. Baldwin. "Antidepressants and Their Effect on Sleep." *Human Psychopharmacology: Clinical and Experimental* 20, no. 8 (December 2005): 533–59.

Miyasaki, J.M., et al. "Practice Parameter: Evaluation and Treatment of Depression, Psychosis, and Dementia in Parkinson Disease (an Evidence-Based Review): Report of the Quality Standards Subcommittee of the American Academy of Neurology." *Neurology* 66, no. 7 (April 2006): 996–1002.

Sterr, Andrea, et al. "Electroencephalographic Abnormalities Associated with Antidepressant Treatment: A Comparison of Mirtazapine, Venlafaxine, Citalopram, Reboxetine, and Amitriptyline." *Journal of Clinical Psychiatry* 67, no. 2 (February 2006): 325–26.

Veldhuijzen, D. S., et al. "Acute and Subchronic Effects of Amitriptyline on Processing Capacity in Neuropathic Pain Patients Using Visual Event-Related Potentials: Preliminary Findings." *Psychopharmacology* 183, no. 4 (2006): 462–70.

Vezmar, S., et al. "Pharmacokinetics and Efficacy of Fluvoxamine and Amitriptyline in Depression." *Journal of Pharmacological Sciences* 110, no. 1 (2009): 98–104.

WEBSITES

RevolutionHealth.com. "What is Elavil? (Amitriptyline)" July 2010. http://www.revolutionhealth.com/drugs-treatments/elavil (accessed September 20, 2011).

Mark Mitchell, MD
Ruth A. Wienclaw, PhD

Amnesia

Definition

Amnesia refers to the partial or total loss of memory. The loss may be temporary or permanent. Amnestic disorders are a group of disorders that involve loss of memories previously established, loss of the ability to create new memories, or loss of the ability to learn new information.

Demographics

The overall incidence of amnestic disorders is difficult to estimate. Amnestic disorders related to head injuries may affect people in any age group. Alcohol-induced amnestic disorder is most common in people over the age of 40 with histories of prolonged heavy **alcohol use**. Amnestic disorders resulting from the abuse of drugs other than alcohol are most common in people between the ages of 20 and 40. Transient global amnesia, in which people temporarily cannot recall recent events, usually appears in people over 50 with an estimated incidence of 23.5 cases per 100,000 people per year. Only 3% of people who experience transient global amnesia have symptoms that recur within a year. About 7% of all individuals over the age of 65 have some form of **dementia** that involves some degree of amnesia, as do about 50% of all individuals over the age of 85.

Description

Memory is the ability to retain and recall information. Memory can be subdivided into short-term memory, which involves holding information for one minute or less, and long-term memory, which involves holding onto information for more than one minute. Long-term memory can be further subdivided into recent memory, which involves new learning, and remote memory, which involves old information. In general, amnestic disorders more frequently involve deficits in new learning or recent memory.

There are a number of terms that are crucial to the understanding of amnestic disorders. In order to retain information, an individual must be able to pay close enough attention to the information that is presented; this is referred to as "registration." The process whereby memories are established is referred to as "encoding" or "storage." Retaining information in the long-term memory requires passage of time during which memory is consolidated. When an individual's memory is tested, retrieval is the process whereby the individual recalls the information from memory. Working memory is the ability to manipulate information from short-term memory in order to perform some function. Amnestic disorders may affect any or all of these necessary processes.

There are two types of amnesia: retrograde and anterograde. Retrograde amnesia refers to the loss of memories made prior to the onset of amnesia. Retrograde amnesia often occurs in conjunction with head injury and results in erasure of memory of events or information from some time period (ranging from seconds to months to the whole of a person's past) prior to the head injury. Over the course of recovery and rehabilitation from a head injury, memory may be restored or the period of amnesia may eventually shorten. Anterograde amnesia refers to the inability to recall events or facts introduced since the amnesia began (i.e., the inability to retain new memories). It is more common than retrograde amnesia. Although individuals with anterograde amnesia have difficulty with the establishment of memory from that time at which the amnesia started, they may clearly recall events that happened before the amnesia began. It is possible for a single individual to have both anterograde and retrograde amnesia depending on which part of the **brain** is damaged.

The diagnostic manual used by clinicians, ***Diagnostic and Statistical Manual of Mental Disorders***, fourth

KEY TERMS

Acetylcholine—A brain chemical or neurotransmitter that carries information throughout the nervous system.

Anterograde—Memory loss for information/events occurring after the onset of the amnestic disorder.

Delirium—A condition characterized by waxing-and-waning episodes of confusion and agitation.

Dementia—A chronic condition in which thinking and memory are progressively impaired. Other symptoms may also occur, including personality changes and depression.

Electroconvulsive therapy—This type of therapy is used to treat major depression and severe mental illness that does not respond to medications. A measured dose of electricity is introduced into the brain in order to produce a convulsion. Electroconvulsive therapy is safe and effective.

Retrograde—Describes memory loss of information/events prior to the onset of the amnestic disorder.

Transient ischemic attack (TIA)—Temporary blockage of blood flow to the brain often resulting in slurred speech, vision disturbances, and loss of balance. The episode is brief and the damage is often short-term (not permanent); also called mini-stroke or warning stroke.

Wernicke-Korsakoff syndrome—A condition of the brain caused by alcohol abuse coupled with malnutrition; also called alcohol encephalopathy.

edition, text revision (*DSM-IV-TR*), lists three classifications of amnestic disorders: amnestic disorder due to a general medical condition, substance-induced persisting amnestic disorder, and amnestic disorder not otherwise specified.

Amnestic disorder due to a medical condition

The memory loss of amnestic disorder due to a general medical condition can be transient or chronic. This disorder can manifest as retrograde or anterograde loss. For **diagnosis**, individuals must experience impairment of social or occupational functioning that differs from their normal levels, and the memory loss cannot occur as part of dementia or **delirium**. The medical condition responsible must be confirmed by patient history or by physical exam or lab results.

Substance-induced persisting amnestic disorder

Substance-induced persisting amnestic disorder can occur with use of alcohol, **sedatives**, hypnotics, or anxiolytics. Methotrexate, a chemotherapy drug, can induce this condition, as can some toxins, including lead, mercury, carbon monoxide, insecticides, or industrial solvents. There are subtypes, including alcohol-induced persisting amnestic disorder. In the alcohol-induced form, the symptoms of **Wernicke-Korsakoff syndrome** may manifest as a result of the thiamine deficiency. Full recovery is not the norm with alcohol-induced amnestic disorder but is possible when caused by other drugs. The diagnostic criteria for the substance-induced form of amnestic disorder are similar to those for that induced by a general medical condition, except that the history should show exposure to the substance involved.

Amnestic disorder not otherwise specified

If the characteristics of the amnesia do not fit either of the above categories, the disorder is then classified as amnestic disorder not otherwise specified, generally because the causative agent/event is not known.

Dissociative amnesia

Dissociative amnesia is part of a different group of disorders, the **dissociative disorders**. It manifests as an inability to remember information that is personally important but possibly traumatic or stressful. It was previously called psychogenic amnesia. The memory impairment in this disorder is reversible, and memory loss can be of several types. It can be localized, in which the missing memory covers a defined period of time, or it can be selective, so that only bits and pieces of a situation are recalled. There are also three less common types: generalized (memories covering a lifetime are missing); continuous (memories are missing from a specific time period up to the present); and systematized (only memories from specific categories of information are missing, such as the names of family members). This disorder can arise in a person of any age.

Other types of amnesia

Transient global amnesia causes delirium (a period of waxing-and-waning confusion and agitation), anterograde amnesia, and retrograde amnesia for events and information from the several hours prior to the onset of the attack. It has no consistently identifiable cause, but researchers have suggested that migraine or transient ischemic attack (TIA) may be the trigger. The individual experiences sudden confusion and forgetfulness. Attacks can be as brief as 30 minutes or can last up to 24 hours. In severe attacks, an individual is completely disoriented and may also experience retrograde amnesia that extends back several years. While very frightening for the individual, transient global amnesia generally has an excellent prognosis for recovery, with no lasting memory deficit.

Childhood amnesia, a term coined by Anna Freud in the late 1940s, refers to the fact that most people cannot recall childhood experiences during the first three to five years of life. It has been suggested that this type of amnesia occurs because children and adults organize memories in different ways. The differences are based on the brain's physical development and communication among the different areas of the brain involved in developing memory. Others believe children begin remembering facts and events once they have accumulated enough experience to be able to relate experiences to each other.

Causes and symptoms

Amnesia has multiple causes. Most cases are traceable to brain injury related to physical **trauma**, disease, infection, and drug and alcohol abuse. In Wernicke-Korsakoff syndrome, for example, damage to the memory centers of the brain results from chronic use of alcohol coupled with malnutrition. Infections that damage brain tissue, such as encephalitis, also can cause amnesia, as can **stroke**. Other causes include various types of dementia (e.g., **Alzheimer's disease**), **traumatic brain injury** (e.g., concussion), accidents that involve oxygen deprivation to the brain or interruption of blood flow to the brain (e.g., ruptured aneurysms, near-drowning), tumors in the thalamus and/or hypothalamus, and **seizures**.

Sometimes procedures such as surgery or **electroconvulsive therapy** can produce amnesia. Dissociative amnesia is thought to be of psychological origin, caused by a psychological disorder or trauma.

Symptoms of amnestic disorders may include difficulty recalling remote events or information and/or difficulty learning and then recalling new information. In some cases, the individual is fully aware of the memory impairment and frustrated by it; in other cases, the individual may seem completely oblivious to the memory impairment or may even attempt to fill in the deficit in memory with confabulation. Depending on the underlying condition responsible for the amnesia, a number of other symptoms may be present as well.

Diagnosis

Diagnosis of amnestic disorders begins by establishing the level of orientation to person, place, and time. Do these individuals know who they are? Where they are? The day, date, and time? Can they recall common current events (e.g., identify the president)? Their responses may reveal information about the memory deficit. Family members or close friends may be an invaluable part of the examination, as they may provide some background information on the onset and progression of the memory loss as well as information regarding the individual's original level of functioning.

A variety of memory tests can be used to assess the ability to attend to information, utilize short-term memory, and store and retrieve information from long-term memory. Both verbal and visual memory should be tested. Verbal memory can be tested by working with an individual to memorize word lists and then testing recall after a certain amount of time has elapsed. Similarly, visual memory can be tested by asking an individual to locate several objects that were hidden in a room in the individual's presence.

Depending on what types of conditions are being considered, other tests may include blood tests, neuroimaging (CT, MRI, or **PET** scans of the brain), cerebrospinal fluid testing, and EEG testing.

Treatment

A neurologist and/or **psychiatrist** may be involved in diagnosing and treating amnestic disorders. Depending on the underlying condition responsible for the memory deficit, other specialists may be involved as well, such as occupational and speech and language therapists may be involved in rehabilitation programs for individuals who have amnestic disorders as part of their clinical picture.

Traditional

In some cases, treatment of the underlying disorder may help improve the accompanying amnesia. In mild cases of amnesia, rehabilitation may involve teaching memory techniques and encouraging the use of memory tools, such as association techniques, lists, notes, calendars, and timers. Memory exercises may be helpful. There are no specific drugs to treat amnesia. However, treatments for Alzheimer's disease and other dementias, such as **donepezil** (Aricept), are being studied to see if they may also be effective in treating amnestic disorders.

Prognosis

The prognosis is dependent on the underlying condition that has caused the memory deficit and on

QUESTIONS TO ASK YOUR DOCTOR

- What tests will you do to rule out medical conditions that might be causing or aggravating my loved one's amnestic disorder?
- How likely is it that this amnestic disorder is reversible or partially reversible?
- What kind of therapy might help my loved one regain some memories?
- Can you recommend a support group for caregivers of people with amnesia?

whether that condition has a tendency to progress or stabilize. Alzheimer's disease, for example, is relentlessly progressive, and the memory deficits that accompany this condition can be expected to worsen over time. Individuals who have memory deficits due to a brain tumor may have their symptoms improve after surgery to remove the tumor. Individuals with transient global amnesia can be expected to fully recover from their memory impairment within hours or days of its onset. In the case of some traumatic brain injuries, the amnesia may improve with time (as brain swelling decreases, for example), but some degree of amnesia for the events just prior to the moment of the injury may remain.

Prevention

Amnestic disorders are preventable in so far as brain injury can be prevented or minimized. Common sense approaches include wearing a helmet when bicycling, horseback riding, or participating in potentially dangerous sports; using automobile seat belts; and avoiding excessive alcohol or drug use. Brain infections should be treated swiftly and aggressively to minimize the damage due to swelling. Victims of strokes, brain aneurysms, and transient ischemic attacks should seek immediate medical treatment.

Resources

BOOKS

Bolzan, Scott, and Joan Bolzan. *My Life Deleted: A Memoir.* New York: HarperCollins, 2011.

Papanicolaou, Andrew C. *The Amnesias: A Clinical Textbook of Memory Disorders.* New York: Oxford University Press, 2006.

WEBSITES

"Amnesia." Mayo Clinic, October 10, 2009. http://www.mayoclinic.com/health/amnesia/DS01041 (accessed October 7, 2011).

"Memory." MedlinePlus. Last modified September 29, 2011. http://www.nlm.nih.gov/medlineplus/memory.html (accessed October 7, 2011).

Sucholeiki, Roy. "Transient Global Amnesia." Medscape Reference, June 16, 2010. http://emedicine.medscape.com/article/1160964-overview (accessed October 7, 2011).

ORGANIZATIONS

American Academy of Neurology, 1080 Montreal Ave., St. Paul, MN, 55116, (651) 695-2717, (800) 879-1960, Fax: (651) 879-2791, memberservices@aan.com, http://www.aan.com.

American Psychiatric Association, 1000 Wilson Blvd., Ste. 1825, Arlington, VA, 22209-3901, (703) 907-7300, apa@psych.org, http://www.psych.org.

National Institute of Neurological Disorders and Stroke, PO Box 5801, Bethesda, MD, 20824, (301) 496-5751; TTY: (301) 468-5981, (800) 352-9424, http://www.ninds.nih.gov.

Julia Barrett
Tish Davidson, AM

Amobarbitol *see* **Barbiturates**

Amoxapine

Definition

Amoxapine is an oral dibenzoxazepine-derivative tricyclic antidepressant. Formerly sold in the United States under the brand name Asendin, it is now manufactured and sold only under its generic name.

Purpose

Amoxapine is used primarily to treat **depression** and to treat the combination of symptoms of anxiety and depression. Like most **antidepressants** of this chemical and pharmacological class, amoxapine has also been used in limited numbers of patients to treat **panic disorder**, **obsessive-compulsive disorder**, **attention deficit hyperactivity disorder**, **enuresis** (bed-wetting), eating disorders such as **bulimia nervosa**, **cocaine addiction**, and the depressive phase of **bipolar disorder**. It has also been used to support **smoking cessation** programs.

Description

Tricyclic antidepressants act to change the balance of naturally occurring chemicals in the **brain** that regulate the transmission of nerve impulses between cells. Amoxapine acts primarily by increasing the concentration of norepinephrine and **serotonin** (chemicals that stimulate nerve cells) and, to a lesser extent, by blocking the action of another brain chemical, acetylcholine. Amoxapine shares most of the properties of other tricyclic antidepressants, such as **amitriptyline**, **clomipramine**, **desipramine**, **imipramine**, **nortriptyline**, **protriptyline**, and **trimipramine**. Studies comparing amoxapine with these other drugs have shown that amoxapine is no more or less effective than other antidepressants of its type. Its choice for treatment is as much a function of physician preference as any other factor.

The therapeutic effects of amoxapine, like other antidepressants, appear slowly. Maximum benefit is often not evident for at least two weeks after starting the drug. People taking amoxapine should be aware of this and continue taking the drug as directed, even if they do not see immediate improvement.

Recommended dosage

As with any antidepressant, amoxapine must be adjusted by the physician to produce the desired therapeutic effect. Amoxapine is available as 25 mg, 50 mg, 100 mg, and 150 mg oral tablets. Therapy is usually started at 100 to 150 mg per day and increased to 200 to 300 mg daily by the end of the first week. If no improvement is seen at this dose after two weeks, the physician may increase the dose up to 400 mg per day in outpatients, and up to 600 mg per day in hospitalized patients. Doses up to 300 mg may be given in single or divided doses. Doses of more than 300 mg per day should be divided in two or three doses daily.

Because of changes in drug metabolism of older patients, starting at about age 60, the initial dose of amoxapine should be adjusted downward to 50 to 75 mg per day and increased to 100 to 150 mg daily by the end of the first week. Some older patients may require up to 300 mg daily, but doses should never be increased beyond that.

Precautions

Like all tricyclic antidepressants, amoxapine should be used cautiously and with close physician supervision in people, especially the elderly, who have benign prostatic hypertrophy (prostate enlargement), urinary retention, and glaucoma, especially angle-closure glaucoma (the most severe form). Before starting treatment, people with these conditions should discuss the relative risks and benefits of treatment with their doctors to help determine whether amoxapine is the right antidepressant for them. Amoxapine also carries an increased risk of developing suicidal thoughts in children and adults up to age 24. All patients should be monitored for worsening depression or signs of self-harm, and physicians should be alerted to any changes in behavior.

One common problem with tricyclic antidepressants is sedation (drowsiness, lack of physical and mental alertness). This side effect is especially noticeable early in therapy. In most patients, sedation decreases or disappears entirely with time, but until then patients taking amoxapine should not perform hazardous activities requiring mental alertness or coordination. The sedative effect is increased when amoxapine is taken with other central nervous system depressants, such as alcoholic beverages, sleeping medications, other **sedatives**, or antihistamines. It may be dangerous to take amoxapine in combination with these substances. Amoxapine may increase the possibility of having **seizures**. Patients should tell their physician if they have a history of seizures, including seizures brought on by the abuse of drugs or alcohol. These people should use amoxapine only with caution and be closely monitored by their physician.

Amoxapine may increase heart rate and stress on the heart. It may be dangerous for people with cardiovascular disease, especially those who have recently had a heart attack, to take this drug or other tricyclic antidepressants. In rare cases where patients with cardiovascular disease must receive amoxapine, they should be monitored closely for cardiac rhythm disturbances and signs of cardiac stress or damage.

Side effects

Amoxapine shares side effects common to all tricyclic antidepressants. The most frequent of these are dry mouth, constipation, urinary retention, increased heart rate, sedation, irritability, dizziness, and decreased coordination. As with most side effects associated with tricyclic antidepressants, the intensity is highest at the beginning of therapy and tends to decrease with continued use.

Dry mouth, if severe to the point of causing difficulty speaking or swallowing, may be managed by dosage reduction or temporary discontinuation of the drug. Patients may also chew sugarless gum or suck on sugarless candy in order to increase the flow of saliva. Some artificial saliva products may give temporary relief.

Men with prostate enlargement who take amoxapine may be especially likely to have problems with urinary retention. Symptoms include having difficulty starting a urine flow and more difficulty than usual passing urine. In most cases, urinary retention is managed with dose reduction or by switching to another type of antidepressant. In extreme cases, patients may require treatment with bethanechol, a drug that reverses this particular side effect. People who think they may be experiencing any side effects from this or any other medication should tell their physicians.

KEY TERMS

Acetylcholine—A neurotransmitter with effects that are generally opposite those of the neurotransmitters dopamine and norepinephrine. Acetylcholine dilates blood vessels, lowers blood pressure, and slows heartbeat.

Anticholinergic—Related to the ability of a drug to block the nervous system chemical acetylcholine. When acetylcholine is blocked, patients often experience dry mouth and skin, increased heart rate, blurred vision, and difficulty urinating. In severe cases, blocking acetylcholine may cloud thinking and cause delirium.

Neurotransmitter—A naturally occurring chemical in the body that carries chemical messages to nerve cells, often by transmitting nerve impulses. Central nervous system well-being is dependent on a balance among the neurotransmitters acetylcholine, dopamine, serotonin, and norepinephrine.

Norepinephrine—A neurotransmitter in the brain that acts to constrict blood vessels and raise blood pressure. It works in combination with serotonin.

Serotonin—A widely distributed neurotransmitter that is found in blood platelets, the lining of the digestive tract, and the brain, and that works in combination with norepinephrine. It causes very powerful contractions of smooth muscle and is associated with mood, attention, emotions, and sleep. Low levels of serotonin are associated with depression.

Interactions

Dangerously high blood pressure has resulted from the combination of tricyclic antidepressants, such as amoxapine, and members of another class of antidepressants known as **monoamine oxidase inhibitors (MAOIs)**. Because of this, amoxapine should never be taken in combination with **MAOIs**. Patients taking any MAOIs, such as **phenelzine** sulfate (Nardil) or **tranylcypromine** sulfate (Parnate), should stop the MAOI and then wait at least 14 days before starting amoxapine or any other tricyclic antidepressant. The same holds true when discontinuing amoxapine and starting an MAOI.

Amoxapine may decrease the blood pressure–lowering effects of **clonidine**. Patients who take both drugs should be monitored for loss of blood pressure control, and the dose of clonidine should be increased as needed.

The sedative effects of amoxapine are increased by other central nervous system depressants, such as alcohol, sedatives, sleeping medications, or medications used for other mental disorders, such as **schizophrenia**. The anticholinergic effects of amoxapine are additive with other anticholinergic drugs, including **benztropine**, **biperiden**, **trihexyphenidyl**, and antihistamines.

Resources

BOOKS

American Society of Health-System Pharmacists. *AHFS Drug Information 2008*. Bethesda, MD: American Society of Health-System Pharmacists, 2008.

WEBSITES

PubMed Health. "Amoxapine." U.S. National Library of Medicine. http://www.ncbi.nlm.nih.gov/pubmedhealth/PMH0000609 (accessed December 12, 2011).

Jack Raber, Pharm.D.

Amphetamines

Definition

Amphetamines are a group of drugs that stimulate the central nervous system. Some of the brand names of amphetamines sold in the United States are Dexedrine, Biphetamine, Dexampex, Ferndex, Oxydess II, Spancap No. 1, Desoxyn, and Methampex. Some generic names of amphetamines include amphetamine, **dextroamphetamine**, and **methamphetamine**.

Purpose

Amphetamines stimulate the nervous system and are used in the treatment of **depression**, obesity, **attention deficit hyperactivity disorder** (ADHD), and **narcolepsy**, a disorder that causes individuals to fall asleep at inappropriate times during the day. Amphetamines are commonly abused as recreational drugs and are highly addictive.

Description

Amphetamines are usually given orally and their effects can last for hours. They produce their effects by altering chemicals that transmit nerve messages in the body. Use of amphetamines can cause considerable side effects and are especially toxic in large quantities.

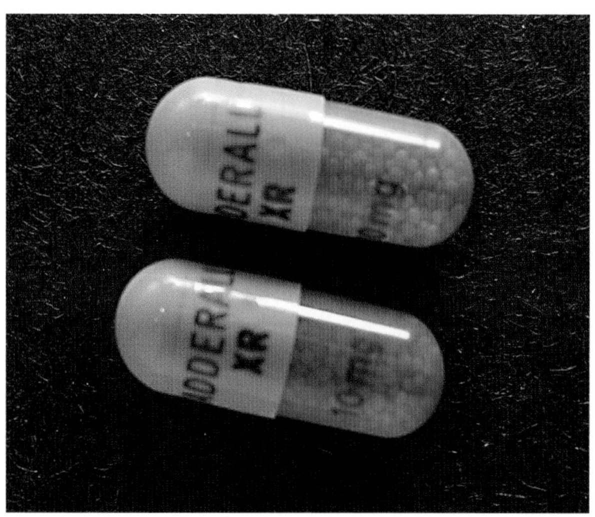

Adderall (dextroamphetamine and amphetamine), 10 mg.
(© Custom Medical Stock Photo, Inc. Reproduced by permission.)

Recommended dosage

Stimulants approved by the U.S. Food and Drug Administration (FDA) for treatment of ADHD are **methylphenidate** (sold under several trade names, including Ritalin), mixed amphetamine salts (trade name Adderall), and dextroamphetamine (trade name Dexedrine). These comparatively short-acting stimulants necessitate several doses through the day to maintain appropriate levels. Some long-acting forms are available, such as Ritalin LA and Adderall XR, and there is also a transdermal patch (trade name Daytrana) for delivery of methylphenidate through the skin.

The typical dose for amphetamines in the treatment of narcolepsy in adults ranges from 5 mg to 60 mg per day. These daily doses are usually divided into at least two small doses taken during the day. Doses usually start on the low end of the range and are increased until the desired effects occur. Children over the age of 12 years with narcolepsy receive 10 mg per day initially. Children between the ages of 6 and 12 years start with 5 mg per day. The typical dose for adults with obesity ranges from 5 mg to 30 mg per day given in divided doses. The medication is usually given about one-half hour to one hour before meals.

Precautions

Stimulant use in children with ADHD has been associated in some studies with sudden death in a small number of cases, leading to widespread concern; however, subsequent studies have found no difference in sudden death rates among children taking stimulants for ADHD and the general population using no medication. Use of these medications is not recommended for people who have known heart disease.

Another stimulant-related concern is the effects of these drugs on growth rate. Studies do indicate that while a child is taking stimulants, growth rate can slow. Some practitioners may recommend "drug holidays," in which the child stops taking the drug when circumstances require less focus or self-discipline, such as over a summer vacation. Studies indicate that the adverse effects on growth rate are eliminated by these drug holidays.

People who are taking amphetamines should not stop taking these drugs suddenly. The dose should be lowered gradually and then discontinued. Amphetamines should only be used while under the supervision of a physician. People should generally take the drug early in the day so that it does not interfere with sleep at night. Hazardous activities should be avoided until the person's condition has been stabilized with medication. The effects of amphetamines can last up to 20 hours after the medication has last been taken. Amphetamine therapy given to women for medical reasons does not present a significant risk of congenital disorders to the developing fetus. In such cases, a mild withdrawal in the newborn may occur. However, illicit use of amphetamines for nonmedical reasons presents a significant risk to the fetus and the newborn because of uncontrolled doses. Methamphetamine use during pregnancy, for example, has been associated with fetal growth retardation, premature birth, and heart and **brain** abnormalities.

Amphetamines are highly addictive and should be used only if alternative approaches have failed. They should be used with great caution in children under three years of age, anyone with a history of slightly elevated blood pressure, people with neurological tics, and individuals with Tourette syndrome. Individuals with a history of an overactive thyroid should not take amphetamines, nor should those with moderate-to-severe high blood pressure, the eye disease glaucoma, severe arteriosclerosis (hardening of the arteries), or psychotic symptoms (hallucinations and **delusions**). Individuals with a history of drug abuse, psychological agitation, or cardiovascular system disease also should not receive amphetamine therapy. In addition, patients who have taken a type of antidepressant called **monoamine oxidase inhibitors (MAOIs)** within the last 14 days should not receive amphetamines. **MAOIs** include **phenelzine** (Nardil) and **tranylcypromine** (Parnate).

Side effects

The most common side effects that are associated with amphetamines include the development of an irregular heartbeat, increased heart rate or blood pressure, dizziness, **insomnia**, restlessness, headache, shakiness, dry mouth, metallic taste, diarrhea, constipation, and weight loss. Other

KEY TERMS

Anticonvulsant drugs—Medications that relieve or prevent seizures.

Arteriosclerosis—A thickening, hardening, and loss of elasticity of the walls of the arteries.

Attention deficit hyperactivity disorder—A condition characterized by lack of concentration, impulsive or inappropriate behavior (relative to age level), and hyperactivity.

Congenital—Present at birth.

Glaucoma—A group of eye diseases characterized by increased pressure within the eye significant enough to damage eye tissue and structures. If untreated, glaucoma results in blindness.

Monoamine oxidase inhibitors (MAOIs)—A group of antidepressant drugs that decreases the activity of monoamine oxidase, a neurotransmitter in the brain that affects mood.

Tic—A sudden involuntary behavior that is difficult or impossible for the person to suppress. Tics may be either motor (related to movement) or vocal, and may become more pronounced under stress.

Tourette's syndrome—A neurological disorder characterized by multiple involuntary movements and uncontrollable vocalizations called tics that come and go over years, usually beginning in childhood and becoming chronic. Sometimes the tics include inappropriate language.

Tricyclic antidepressants—Antidepressant medications that have the common characteristic of a three-ring nucleus in their chemical structure. Imipramine and amitriptyline are examples of tricyclic antidepressants.

side effects can include changes in sexual drive, nausea, vomiting, allergic reactions, chills, depression, irritability, and other problems involving the digestive system. High doses, whether for medical purposes or illicit ones, can cause **addiction**, dependence, increased aggression, and, in some cases, psychotic episodes.

Interactions

Patients taking amphetamines should always tell their physicians and dentists that they are using this medication. Patients should consult their physicians before taking any over-the-counter medications while taking amphetamines. The interaction between over-the-counter cold medications with amphetamine is particularly dangerous, because this combination can significantly increase blood pressure. Such cold medications should be avoided when using amphetamines unless a physician has carefully analyzed the combination.

The combination of amphetamines and antacids slows down the ability of the body to eliminate the amphetamine. Furazolidone (Furoxone) combined with amphetamines can significantly increase blood pressure. Sodium bicarbonate can reduce the amount of amphetamine eliminated from the body, thereby dangerously increasing amphetamine levels in the body. Certain medications taken to control high blood pressure, including guanadrel (Hylorel) and guanethidine (Ismelin), MAOIs, and selegiline (Eldepryl) should not be used in conjunction with amphetamines. In addition, antihistamines, anticonvulsant drugs, and tricyclic **antidepressants** including **desipramine** (Norpramin) and **imipramine** (Tofranil) should not be combined with amphetamines.

Resources

BOOKS

Brunton, Laurence, Bruce Chabner, and Bjorn Knollman. *Goodman & Gilman's The Pharmacological Basis of Therapeutics*. 12th ed. New York: McGraw-Hill, 2010.

Consumer Reports and American Society of Health-System Pharmacists. *Consumer Reports Complete Drug Reference, 2009*. Yonkers, NY: Consumers Reports, 2009.

Ellsworth, Allan J., et al. *Mosby's Medical Drug Reference*. St. Louis, MO: Mosby, 2007.

Venes, Donald. *Taber's Cyclopedic Medical Dictionary*. 21st ed. Philadelphia: F.A. Davis Company, 2009.

PERIODICALS

Lopez, Frank A. "ADHD: New Pharmacological Treatments on the Horizon." *Journal of Developmental and Behavioral Pediatrics* 27, no. 5 (October 2006): 410–16.

Pliszka, Steven R. "Pharmacologic Treatment of Attention-Deficit/Hyperactivity Disorder: Efficacy, Safety, and Mechanisms of Action." *Neuropsychological Reviews* 17 (2007): 61–72. http://www.pathwayshrc.com.au/images/assets/pharmac%20adhd%20review.PDF (accessed November 9, 2011).

Sulzer, David, et al. "Mechanisms of Neurotransmitter Release by Amphetamines: A Review." *Progress in Neurobiology* 75 (2005): 406–33. http://www.sulzerlab.org/pdf_articles/Sulzer05AMPHreview.pdf (accessed November 9, 2011).

WEBSITES

Center for Substance Abuse Research. "Amphetamines." University of Maryland. http://www.cesar.umd.edu/cesar/drugs/amphetamines.asp (accessed September 29, 2011).

MedlinePlus. “Amphetamines.” U.S. National Library of Medicine, National Institutes of Health. http://www.nlm.nih.gov/nlmhome.html (accessed September 29, 2011).

Mark Mitchell, MD
Emily Jane Willingham, PhD

Amphetamines and related disorders

Definition

Amphetamines are a group of powerful and highly addictive substances that dramatically affect the central nervous system. They induce a feeling of well-being and improve alertness, attention, and performance on various cognitive and motor tasks. Closely related are the so-called substitute amphetamines, which include MDMA (**ecstasy**) and **methamphetamine**. Finally, some over-the-counter drugs used as appetite suppressants also have amphetamine-like action. Amphetamine-related disorders refer to the effects of abuse, dependence, and acute intoxication stemming from inappropriate amphetamine and amphetamine-related drug usage.

Demographics

Amphetamine dependence and abuse occur at all levels of society, most commonly among 18- to 30-year-olds. Intravenous use is more common among individuals from lower socioeconomic groups and has a male-to-female ratio of three or four to one. Among people who do not use intravenously, males and females are relatively equally divided.

Of greatest recent concern has been the rise in the use of methamphetamine, although in some areas this increase has leveled off in recent years. The lifetime prevalence of methamphetamine abuse among U.S. students in grade 12 fell from 6.2% of respondents to 4.5% over two years in one recent government survey. However, in some metropolitan areas, including Atlanta, Denver, Honolulu, and Phoenix, use has increased, and there was a 15% increase in methamphetamine treatment admissions in St. Louis from 2004 to 2005. In some parts of Texas, this drug has replaced crack as a drug of choice. Another national survey found that 10.4 million Americans age 12 or older had tried methamphetamine at least once in their lives. The problem seems to be particularly severe in Western states, although it is spreading quickly in the South and Midwest, being reported as the fastest-growing problem in metropolitan Atlanta in 2006.

Amphetamine sulfate. *(© David Hoffman/Photo Library/Alamy)*

Nonmedical use of Adderall® in the past year among full-time college students aged 18 to 22, by selected demographic characteristics, 2006 and 2007

Race/ethnicity	
White	8.6%
Black or African American	1.0%
Asian	2.1%
Two or more races	2.7%
Hispanic	2.2%
Annual family income	
Less than $20,000	8.9%
$20,000 to $49,999	3.0%
$50,000 to $74,999	4.0%
$75,000 or more	6.0%

SOURCE: Substance Abuse and Mental Health Administration, Office of Applied Studies, *The NSDUH Report: Nonmedical Use of Adderall® among Full-Time College Students*, April 7, 2009.

(Table by PreMediaGlobal.

Description

Several amphetamines are currently available in the United States, including **dextroamphetamine** (Dexedrine) and **methylphenidate** (Ritalin). These Schedule II stimulants (those that the U.S. Drug Enforcement Administration considers to have medical usefulness and a high potential for abuse), known to be highly addictive, require a triplicate prescription that cannot be refilled. Amphetamines are also known as sympathomimetics, stimulants, and psychostimulants. Methamphetamine, the most common illegally produced amphetamine, goes by the street names of “speed,” “meth,” or “chalk.” When it is smoked, it is called “ice,” “crystal,” “crank,” or “glass.” Methamphetamine is a white, odorless, bitter-tasting crystalline powder that dissolves in water or alcohol. Manufacture of methamphetamine in illegal laboratories has increased dramatically in recent years, leading to stricter laws governing the sale of products containing ephedrine or pseudoephedrine, the primary components of this drug.

The leaves of the East African bush *Catha edulis* can be chewed for their stimulant effects. This drug, cathinone, or "khat," has an effect on most of the central nervous system, in addition to providing the other properties of amphetamines. It is a stimulant drug similar in structure to amphetamines, with similar effects. The drug may be ingested by chewing the leaves, adding the leaves to food, or brewing the leaves and drinking as a tea. The stimulant effects are usually felt immediately and subside within three hours; however, they may last up to 24 hours. The potential for abuse and physical or psychological dependence is high, making this popular drug illegal in the United States.

Amphetamines intended for medical use were first used in nasal decongestants and bronchial inhalers. Early in the 1900s, they were also used to treat several medical and psychiatric conditions, including attention deficit disorders, obesity, **depression**, and **narcolepsy** (a rare condition in which individuals fall asleep at dangerous and inappropriate moments and cannot maintain normal alertness). They are still used to treat these disorders.

In the 1970s, governmental agencies initiated restrictions increasing the difficulty of obtaining amphetamines legally through prescription. During this same time period, a drug chemically related to the amphetamines began to be produced. This so-called designer drug, best known as "ecstasy" but also as MDMA, XTC, and Adam, has behavioral effects that combine amphetamine-like and hallucinogen-like properties.

The structure of amphetamines differs significantly from that of **cocaine**, even though both are stimulants with similar behavioral and physiological effects. Like cocaine, amphetamines result in an accumulation of the neurotransmitter **dopamine** in the prefrontal cortex. It is this excessive dopamine concentration that appears to produce the stimulation and feelings of euphoria experienced by the user. Cocaine is much more quickly metabolized and removed from the body, whereas amphetamines have a much longer duration of action. A large percentage of the drug remains unchanged in the body, leading to prolonged stimulant effects.

The handbook that mental health professionals use to diagnose mental disorders is the ***Diagnostic and Statistical Manual of Mental Disorders,*** also known as the *DSM*. The 2000 edition of this manual (the fourth edition, text revision, also known as *DSM-IV-TR*) describes four separate amphetamine-related disorders:

- Amphetamine dependence: Refers to chronic or episodic binges (known as "speed runs"), with brief drug-free periods of time in between use.
- Amphetamine abuse: Less severe than dependence. Individuals diagnosed with amphetamine abuse have milder, but nevertheless substantial, problems due to their drug usage.
- Amphetamine intoxication: Refers to serious maladaptive behavioral or psychological changes that develop during, or shortly after, use of an amphetamine or related substance.
- Amphetamine withdrawal: Refers to symptoms that develop within a few hours to several days after reducing or stopping heavy and prolonged amphetamine use. Withdrawal symptoms are, in general, opposite to those seen during intoxication and include fatigue, vivid and unpleasant dreams, insomnia or hypersomnia (too much sleep), increased appetite, and agitation or slowing down.

The fifth edition of the *Diagnostic and Statistical Manual of Mental Disorders,* also known as the *DSM-5* is due for publication in May 2013. Proposed changes to this edition include combining amphetamine abuse and amphetamine dependence into one condition, amphetamine use disorder.

Causes and symptoms

Causes

All amphetamines are rapidly absorbed when taken orally, and are even more rapidly absorbed when smoked, snorted, or injected. Tolerance develops with both standard and designer amphetamines, leading to the need for increasing doses.

Amphetamines produce their primary effects by causing the release of catecholamines, especially the nerve-signaling molecule or neurotransmitter dopamine, in the **brain**. These effects are particularly strong in areas of the brain associated with pleasure—specifically, the cerebral cortex and the limbic system, known as the "reward pathway." The effect on this pathway is probably responsible for the addictive quality of the amphetamines.

MDMA causes the release of the **neurotransmitters** dopamine and **serotonin** and the neurohormone norepinephrine. Serotonin is responsible for producing the hallucinogenic effects of the drug.

Symptoms

According to the *DSM-IV-TR,* symptoms of heavy, chronic, or episodic use of amphetamine, known as amphetamine dependence, can be very serious. Amphetamine dependence is characterized by compulsive drug seeking and drug use, leading to functional and molecular changes in the brain. Aggressive or violent behavior may occur, especially when high doses are ingested. Individuals may develop anxiety or paranoid ideas, or may experience terrifying psychotic episodes

KEY TERMS

Amphetamine abuse—An amphetamine problem in which the user experiences negative consequences from the use but has not reached the point of dependence.

Amphetamines—A group of powerful and highly addictive substances that stimulate the central nervous system. Amphetamines may be prescribed for various medical conditions but are often purchased illicitly and abused.

Catecholamine—A group of neurotransmitters synthesized from the amino acid tyrosine and released by the hypothalamic-pituitary-adrenal system in the brain in response to acute stress. The catecholamines include dopamine, serotonin, norepinephrine, and epinephrine.

Catha edulis—Leaves of an East African bush that can be chewed for their stimulant effect.

Dependence—A state in which a person requires a steady concentration of a particular substance to avoid experiencing withdrawal symptoms.

Designer amphetamines—Substances close in chemical structure to classic amphetamines that provide both stimulant and hallucinogenic effects.

Dopamine—A chemical in brain tissue that serves to transmit nerve impulses (i.e., a neurotransmitter) and helps to regulate movement and emotions. Large amounts of dopamine are released following ingestion of amphetamines.

Ecstasy—Best known of the so-called designer amphetamines, also known as "MDMA." It produces both stimulant and hallucinogenic effects.

Ephedrine—An amphetamine-like substance used as a nasal decongestant.

Formication—The sensation of bugs creeping on the skin.

Hyperthermia—Elevated body temperature resulting from ingestion of amphetamines.

Intoxication—The presence of significant behavioral or psychological changes following ingestion of a substance.

Methamphetamine—The most common illegally produced amphetamine.

Serotonin—A widely distributed neurotransmitter that is found in blood platelets, the lining of the digestive tract, and the brain, and that works in combination with norepinephrine. It causes very powerful contractions of smooth muscle and is associated with mood, attention, emotions, and sleep. Low levels of serotonin are associated with depression. Large amounts of serotonin are released after ingestion of MDMA.

"Speed run"—The episodic binging on amphetamines.

Withdrawal—Symptoms that occur when a drug is discontinued after prolonged regular use.

that resemble **schizophrenia**, with visual or auditory hallucinations, **delusions** such as the sensation of insects creeping on the skin (known as formication), hyperactivity, hypersexuality, confusion, and incoherence. Amphetamine-induced **psychosis** differs from true psychosis in that despite other symptoms, the disorganized thinking that is a hallmark of schizophrenia tends to be absent. Amphetamine dependence consistently affects relationships at home, school, and/or work.

Amphetamine abuse is less serious than dependence but can cause milder versions of the symptoms described above, as well as problems with family, school, and work. Legal problems may stem from aggressive behavior while using, or from obtaining drugs illegally. Individuals may continue to use despite the awareness that usage negatively impacts all areas of their lives.

Acute amphetamine intoxication begins with a "high" feeling that may be followed by feelings of euphoria. Users experience enhanced energy, becoming more outgoing and talkative, and more alert. Other symptoms include anxiety, tension, grandiosity, repetitive behavior, anger, fighting, and impaired judgment.

In both acute and chronic intoxication, individuals may experience dulled feelings, **fatigue**, sadness, and social withdrawal. These behavioral and psychological changes are accompanied by other signs and symptoms including increased or irregular heartbeat, dilation of the pupils, elevated or lowered blood pressure, heavy perspiring or chills, nausea and/or vomiting, motor agitation or retardation, muscle weakness, respiratory depression, and chest pain. Possible severe consequences include confusion, **seizures**, coma, and a variety of cardiovascular problems, including **stroke**. With amphetamine overdoses, death can result if treatment is not received immediately. Long-term abuse can lead to memory loss and contributes to increased transmission of hepatitis and HIV/AIDS, especially if users share needles. Impaired social and work functioning is another hallmark of both acute and chronic intoxication.

Following amphetamine intoxication, a "crash" occurs, characterized by symptoms of anxiety, shakiness, depressed mood, lethargy, fatigue, nightmares, headache, perspiring, muscle cramps, stomach cramps, and increased appetite. Withdrawal symptoms usually peak in two to four days and are gone within one week. The most serious withdrawal symptom is depression, which may be severe and lead to suicidal thoughts.

Use of so-called designer amphetamines, such as MDMA, leads to similar symptoms. Users also report a sense of feeling an unusual closeness with other people and enhanced personal comfort. They describe seeing an increased luminescence of objects in the environment, although these hallucinogenic effects are less than those caused by other **hallucinogens**, such as LSD. Some psychotherapists have suggested further research into the possible use of designer amphetamines in conjunction with **psychotherapy**. This idea is highly controversial.

As with other amphetamines, use of MDMA produces cardiovascular effects of increased blood pressure, heart rate, and heart oxygen consumption. People with pre-existing heart disease are at increased risk of cardiovascular catastrophe resulting from MDMA use. MDMA is not processed and removed from the body quickly and remains active for a long period of time. As a result, toxicity may rise dramatically when users take multiple doses over brief time periods, leading to harmful reactions such as dehydration, hyperthermia, and seizures.

MDMA tablets often contain other drugs, such as ephedrine, a stimulant, and dextromethorphan, a cough suppressant with PCP-like effects at high doses. These additives increase the harmful effects of MDMA. They also appear also to have toxic effects on the brain's serotonin system. In tests of learning and memory, people who use MDMA perform more poorly than people who do not use. Research with primates shows that MDMA can cause long-lasting brain damage. Exposure to MDMA during the period of pregnancy in which the fetal brain is developing is associated with learning deficits that last into adulthood.

Diagnosis

The *DSM* diagnostic criteria for amphetamine use disorder is as follows:

- use interferes with educational, occupational, or societal obligations (including home and family life)
- use causes dangerous situations (e.g., driving under the influence)
- use continues despite problems caused by the substance
- person experiences tolerance, withdrawal, and/or cravings
- substance is used in higher doses or for longer than originally intended
- use continues despite efforts to quit

QUESTIONS TO ASK YOUR DOCTOR

- What risks are associated with amphetamine abuse?
- What symptoms are associated with amphetamine dependence?
- Does amphetamine dependence and abuse put me at risk for other health conditions?
- Can you recommend any treatment and support groups for me?

- significant time is devoted to substance use
- use interferes with or replaces other activities
- use continues despite negative physical or psychological effects

At least two symptoms must occur within a 12-month period to be considered a disorder.

Treatment

According to the National Institute on Drug Abuse (NIDA), the most effective treatments for amphetamine **addiction** are cognitive-behavioral interventions. These are psychotherapeutic approaches that help individuals learn to identify and change their problematic patterns of thoughts and beliefs. As a result of changed thoughts and beliefs, feelings become more manageable and less painful. Interventions also help individuals increase their skills for coping with life's stressors. Amphetamine recovery groups and Narcotics Anonymous also appear to help.

No specific medications for amphetamine dependence are known to exist. On occasion, antidepressant medications can help combat the depressive symptoms frequently experienced by people who are newly abstinent from amphetamine use.

Overdoses of amphetamines are treated in established ways in emergency rooms. Because hyperthermia (elevated body temperature) and convulsions are common, emergency room treatment focuses on reducing body temperature and administering anticonvulsant medications.

Acute methamphetamine intoxication is often handled by observation in a safe, quiet environment. When extreme anxiety or panic is part of the reaction, treatment with antianxiety medications may be helpful. In cases of methamphetamine-induced psychoses, short-term use of antipsychotic medications is usually successful.

Prognosis

Classic amphetamines

According to the *DSM-IV-TR,* some individuals who develop abuse or dependence on amphetamines initiate use in an attempt to control their weight. Others become introduced through the illegal market. Dependence can occur very quickly when the substance is used intravenously or smoked. The few long-term data available show a tendency for people who have been dependent on amphetamines to decrease or stop using them after 8 to 10 years. This may result from the development of adverse mental and physical effects that emerge with long-term dependence. Few data are available on the long-term course of abuse.

Designer amphetamines

The NIDA reports that studies provide direct evidence that chronic use of MDMA causes brain damage in humans. Using advanced brain-imaging techniques, one study found that MDMA harms neurons that release serotonin. Serotonin plays an important role in regulating memory and other mental functions.

In a related study, researchers found that people who heavily use MDMA have memory problems that persist for at least two weeks after stopping use of the drug. Both studies strongly suggest that the extent of damage is directly related to the amount of MDMA used.

Prevention

In 1999, NIDA began a program known as the "Club Drug Initiative" in response to recent increases in abuse of MDMA and other drugs used in similar environments. This ongoing program seeks to increase awareness of the dangers of these drugs among teens, young adults, parents, and community members.

Research indicates a pervasive perception among users that MDMA is a "fun" drug with minimal risks. This myth might point to the main reason for the widespread increase in the drug's abuse. The Club Drug Initiative seeks to make the dangers of MDMA use far better known. Evidence of the program's initial success with this initiative might be seen in a growing perception by high school seniors that MDMA is a dangerous drug.

Resources

BOOKS

American Psychiatric Association. *Diagnostic and Statistical Manual of Mental Disorders.* 4th ed., text rev. Washington, DC: American Psychiatric Association, 2000.

American Psychological Association. *Publication Manual of the American Psychological Association.* 6th ed. Washington, DC: American Psychological Association, 2009.

Erickson, Carlton K, Ph.D. *Addiction Essentials: The Go-To Guide for Clinicians and Patients.* New York: W. W. Norton & Company, 2011.

PERIODICALS

Sulzer, David, et al. "Mechanisms of Neurotransmitter Release by Amphetamines: A Review." *Progress in Neurobiology* 75 (2005): 406–33.

WEBSITES

MedlinePlus. "Methamphetamine." U.S. National Library of Medicine, National Institutes of Health. http://www.nlm.nih.gov/medlineplus/methamphetamine.html (accessed November 14, 2011).

National Institute on Drug Abuse. "ClubDrugs.gov." http://www.clubdrugs.gov (accessed November 14, 2011).

———. "NIDA Infofacts: Methamphetamine." 2010. http://www.nida.nih.gov/Infofacts/methamphetamine.html (accessed November 14, 2011).

ORGANIZATIONS

American Psychological Association, 750 First Street NE, Washington, DC, 20003, (202) 336-5500, http://www.apa.org/index.aspx.

Narcotics Anonymous, PO Box 9999, Van Nuys, CA, 91409, (818) 773-9999, Fax: (818) 700-0700, http://www.na.org.

National Institute on Drug Abuse, 6001 Executive Blvd., Rm. 5213, Bethesda, MD, 20892, (301) 442-1124; Spanish: (240) 221-4007, information@nida.nih.gov, http://www.nida.nih.gov.

Substance Abuse and Mental Health Services Administration, 1 Choke Cherry Rd., Rockville, MD, 20857, (877) SAMHSA-7 (726-4727), (800) TTY: 487-4889, Fax: (240) 221-4292, SAMHSAInfo@samhsa.hhs.gov, http://www.samhsa.gov.

Barbara S. Sternberg, Ph.D.
Emily Jane Willingham, Ph.D.
Laura Jean Cataldo, RN, Ed.D.

Anafranil *see* **Clomipramine**

Anorexia nervosa

Definition

Anorexia nervosa (AN) is a psychiatric disorder characterized by an unrealistic fear of weight gain, conspicuous distortion of **body image**, and self-starvation. The individual is obsessed with becoming increasingly thinner and limits food intake to the point where health is compromised. The disorder can be fatal. The name comes from two Latin words that mean "nervous inability to eat."

The word *anorexia* alone literally means "loss of appetite" and is a symptom of several diseases. Anorexia nervosa is not a loss of appetite but the dangerous restriction of calories despite continuing hunger.

Demographics

Anorexia nervosa is a disorder of industrialized countries where food is abundant but the culture values a thin appearance. About 1% of Americans have AN, and diagnosed females outnumber males 10:1. In men, the disorder is more often diagnosed among homosexuals than heterosexuals. Some experts believe that the number of patients diagnosed represents only the most severe cases and that many more people have anorexic tendencies, but their symptoms do not rise to the level needed for a medical **diagnosis**.

Despite this belief, AN has the highest rate of death of all psychiatric disorders, based on data from a study published in the July 2011 issue of the *Archives of General Psychiatry*. In this study, which was a meta-analysis of 36 studies published between 1966 and 2010, people with AN were nearly six times more likely to die compared to healthy people. In addition, death rates among people with AN are twice as high as deaths in patients with **schizophrenia**, three times higher than patients with **bipolar disorder**, and four times higher than patients with major **depression**. When the data were broken out by age group, researchers found that individuals diagnosed with AN between ages 20 and 29 had an 18-fold risk of death compared to healthy people. By contrast, the risk of death was threefold when a diagnosis was made before the age of 15 years. The data suggest that one in five AN-related deaths is a **suicide**.

More than 95% of persons with AN are white, and about three-fourths come from households at the middle income level or above. Studies have found that the rate of AN in the United States is about double that in Europe.

Anorexia nervosa can occur in people as young as age 7 or may not develop until later in life. The most common ages of development are ages 14 and 18, which correspond with the ages of transitioning into and out of high school.

Description

Anorexia nervosa is often thought of as a modern problem, but the English physician Richard Morton first described it in 1689. AN is recognized as a psychiatric disorder in the ***Diagnostic and Statistical Manual of Mental Disorders*** (*DSM*), the handbook used by mental health professionals to diagnose mental disorders, published by the **American Psychiatric Association**.

Though most **diets** do not progress into AN, dieting is generally the starting point for future development of the disorder. As weight falls, the **obsession** with dieting increases. Affected persons may also increase physical exertion or **exercise** as weight decreases to lose even more weight. An affected person develops peculiar rules concerning exercise and eating. Patients with AN equate weight loss and avoidance of food with a sense of accomplishment and success. Weight gain is viewed as a sign of weakness ("succumbing to eating") and as failure. Eventually, the affected person becomes increasingly focused on losing weight and devotes most efforts to dieting and exercise.

Persons with AN may talk negatively about their bodies and appearance. Some are secretive about eating and will avoid eating in front of other people. They may develop abnormal eating habits such as chewing their food and then spitting it out, or they may have rigid ideas about "good" and "bad" foods (low- and high-calorie foods, respectively). AN is often concurrent with depression, **anxiety disorders**, and compulsive behavior.

There are two major subtypes of AN as classified by the *DSM*. The restrictive type involves weight loss solely through rigorously limiting the amount of calories eaten or by fasting. The person may exercise excessively or abuse drugs or herbal remedies claiming to increase the rate at which the body burns calories but does not engage in any purging behaviors. Individuals with the binge-eating/purging type eat and then purge themselves of the calories through self-induced vomiting, excessive laxative use, or abuse of diuretics or enemas. These behaviors are similar to those of **bulimia nervosa**, but patients with AN continue to restrict their diets severely when they are not binging and may fall to a very low weight, which is not common with bulimia.

Risk factors

Competitive athletes may be at risk of developing an eating disorder, especially in sports where weight is tied to performance. Jockeys, wrestlers, figure skaters, cross-country runners, and gymnasts (especially female gymnasts) have higher-than-average rates of AN. People such as actors, models, cheerleaders, and dancers (especially ballet dancers), whose performance is often tied to their appearance, are also at high risk of developing the disorder.

Other risk factors include:

- female gender
- perfectionism
- personality factors, including being eager to please other persons and having high expectations for oneself
- family history of eating disorders
- living in an industrialized society
- difficulty communicating negative emotions such as anger or fear
- difficulty resolving problems or conflict
- low self-esteem

Causes and symptoms

Causes

Anorexia nervosa is a complex disorder that does not have a single cause but appears to result from the interaction of cultural and biological factors. Research suggests that some people have a predisposition toward AN. The disorder develops after some event triggers the behavior, which then becomes self-reinforcing. The event might be a family member teasing about the person's weight, nagging about eating junk food, commenting on how clothes fit, or comparing the person unfavorably to someone else. Life events such as moving, starting a new school, breaking up with a partner, or even entering puberty can trigger anorexic behavior. Hereditary, psychological, and social factors also appear to play a role.

Research indicates that **genetic factors** play a role in more than half of AN cases. Twin studies show that if one twin has AN, the other has a greater likelihood of developing the disorder. Having a close relative, usually a mother or a sister, with AN also increases the likelihood of other (usually female) family members developing the disorder. Genetic factors can also predispose individuals to behaviors that make them susceptible to AN, such as perfectionism, **obsessive-compulsive disorder**, and anxiety.

Specialists in **family therapy** have demonstrated that dysfunctional family relationships and impaired family interaction can be associated with AN. Mothers of persons with AN tend to be intrusive, perfectionistic, overprotective, and have a fear of separation. Fathers of individuals with AN are often described as passive, withdrawn, moody, emotionally constricted, obsessive, and ineffective. Sociocultural factors include the messages given by society and the culture about women's roles and the thinness ideal for women's bodies. Developmental causes can include adolescent "acting out" or fear of adulthood transition.

Precipitating factors are often related to the developmental transitions common in adolescence. The onset of menstruation may be threatening in that it represents maturation or growing up. During this time in development, females gain weight as part of the developmental process, and this gain may cause a decrease in self-esteem. Development of AN could be a way that the adolescent retreats into childhood so as not to be burdened by maturity and physical concerns. Autonomy and independence struggles during adolescence may be acted out by developing AN. Some adolescents may develop AN because of their ambivalence about adulthood or because of feelings of loneliness, isolation, and abandonment.

There is some evidence that AN is linked to abnormal neurotransmitter activity in the part of the **brain** that controls pleasure and appetite. **Neurotransmitters** are also involved in other mental disorders such as depression.

KEY TERMS

Amenorrhea—Absence of the menses in a female who has begun to have menstrual periods.

Body dysmorphic disorder—A psychiatric disorder marked by preoccupation with an imagined physical defect.

Diuretic—A substance that removes water from the body by increasing urine production.

Electrolyte—Ions in the body that participate in metabolic reactions. The major human electrolytes are sodium (Na+), potassium (K+), calcium (Ca 2+), magnesium (Mg2+), chloride (Cl-), phosphate (HPO4 2-), bicarbonate (HCO3-), and sulfate (SO4 2-).

Hyperalimentation—A method of refeeding by infusing liquid nutrients and electrolytes directly into central veins through a catheter.

Lanugo—A soft, downy body hair that develops on the chest and arms of women with anorexia.

Neurotransmitter—One of a group of chemicals secreted by a nerve cell (neuron) to carry a chemical message to another nerve cell, often as a way of transmitting a nerve impulse. Examples of neurotransmitters are acetylcholine, dopamine, serotonin, and norepinephrine.

Purging—The use of vomiting, diuretics, or laxatives to clear the stomach and intestines after a binge.

Russell's sign—Scraped or raw areas on the patient's knuckles, caused by self-induced vomiting.

Superior mesenteric artery syndrome—A condition in which a person vomits after meals due to blockage of the blood supply to the intestine.

Research in this area is relatively new, and the findings are unclear. Also, people with AN tend to feel full sooner than other people. Some researchers believe that this is related to the fact that the stomach of people with AN tends to empty more slowly than normal; others think it may be related to the appetite control mechanism of the brain.

Although AN is still considered a disorder that largely affects women, its incidence in the male population is rising. Less is known about the causes of AN in males, but some risk factors are the same as for females. These include certain occupational goals (e.g., jockey) and increasing media emphasis on external appearance in men. Moreover, homosexual males are under pressure to conform to an ideal body weight that is less than the standard "attractive" weight for heterosexual males, which may increase the risk of dieting and weight concerns.

Symptoms

Symptoms of anorexic behavior include an overriding obsession with food and thinness that controls activities and eating patterns every hour of every day, and a refusal to admit that being severely underweight is dangerous to health.

Serious physical and psychological consequences of anorexic behavior include:

- excessive weight loss; loss of muscle
- stunted growth and delayed sexual maturation in preteens
- gastrointestinal complications, including liver damage, diarrhea, constipation, bloating, stomach pain
- cardiovascular complications, including irregular heartbeat, low pulse rate, cardiac arrest
- urinary system complications, including kidney damage, kidney failure, incontinence, urinary tract infections
- skeletal system complications, including loss of bone mass, increased risk of fractures, teeth eroded by stomach acid from repeat vomiting
- reproductive system complications in women, such as irregular menstrual periods, amenorrhea, infertility
- reproductive system complications in men, such as loss of sex drive, infertility
- fatigue, irritation, headaches, depression, anxiety, impaired judgment and thinking
- fainting, seizures, low blood sugar
- chronically cold hands and feet
- weakened immune system, swollen glands, increased susceptibility to infections
- development of fine hair called lanugo on the shoulders, back, arms, and face; head hair loss; blotchy, dry skin
- potentially life-threatening electrolyte imbalances
- coma
- increased risk of self-mutilation (cutting)
- increased risk of suicide
- death

Diagnosis

Diagnosis of AN is made when the individual meets the criteria for the disorder outlined in the *DSM*, fourth edition, text revision, also known as the *DSM-IV-TR*:

- extreme restriction of caloric intake resulting in significantly low weight (as determined after considering age, gender, level of development, and overall health)
- extreme fear of gaining weight or becoming fat, even when the individual is significantly underweight
- a distorted self-image that fuels a refusal to admit to being underweight, even when this is demonstrably true

The *DSM-IV-TR* includes in its diagnostic criteria the presence of amenorrhea, or three missed menstrual periods in a row after menstruation has been established, and a weight of less than 85% of the average weight for the patient's age and height group. These criteria have been proposed to be removed for the *DSM-5* (fifth edition, due to publish in 2013) as they are not consistent—some patients continue to have menstrual activity, and it is difficult to define low body weight with a specific numeric value.

Initial assessment usually includes a careful interview and patient history (clinical evaluation). A weight history, menstrual history, and description of daily food intake are important during initial evaluation. Risk factors and family history are also vital in suspected cases. Though patients may not admit to having AN, they may complain about related symptoms such as **fatigue**, headaches, dizziness, constipation, or frequent infections.

Tests

A physical examination begins with taking weight and blood pressure. Based on the physical exam, the physician may order laboratory tests, including a complete blood count (CBC), urinalysis, blood chemistries (to determine electrolyte levels), and liver function tests. Laboratory results can reveal anemia (low red blood cell count in the blood) and lowered white blood cells, pulse, blood pressure, and body temperature. The decreased temperature in extremities may cause a slight red-purple discoloration in limbs (acrocyanosis). The physician may also order an electrocardiogram to look for heart abnormalities. Other conditions, including metabolic disorders, brain tumors (especially hypothalamus and pituitary gland lesions), diseases of the digestive tract, and a condition called superior mesenteric artery syndrome, which can cause weight loss or vomiting after eating, may show symptoms similar to AN and need to be ruled out in medical evaluation.

The individual may be referred to a **psychiatrist** or **psychologist** for a mental status evaluation. The physician will evaluate factors such as whether the person is oriented in time and space, appearance, observable state of emotion (**affect**), attitude toward food and weight, delusional thinking, and thoughts of self-harm or suicide. This evaluation helps to distinguish between AN and other psychiatric disorders, including depression, schizophrenia, **social phobia**, obsessive-compulsive disorder, and **body dysmorphic disorder**. Three questionnaires that are often used are the Eating Attitudes Test (EAT), the Eating Disorder Examination, and the Eating Disorder Inventory (EDI). The disadvantage of these tests is that they may produce false-positive results, which means that a test result may indicate that test takers have AN when actually they do not.

Treatment

Persons affected with AN are often in **denial**, in that they do not see themselves as thin or in need of professional help. Education is important, as is engagement on the part of patients—a connection from the patients to the treatment, so that they agree to be actively involved. Engagement is a necessary but difficult task in the treatment of AN. If the affected persons' medical condition has deteriorated, **hospitalization** may be required. Initially, treatment objectives are focused on reversing behavioral abnormalities and nutritional deficiencies. Emotional support and reassurance that eating and caloric restoration will not make the person overweight are essential components during initial treatment sessions. Psychosocial (both psychological and social) issues and family dysfunction are also addressed, which may reduce the risk of relapsing behaviors or the recurrence of the disorder after a period of remission.

Traditional

Hospitalization is recommended for patients with any of the following characteristics:

- weight of 30% or more below normal, or weight loss over a three-month period of more than 30 pounds
- severely disturbed metabolism
- severe medical instability
- severe binging and purging
- signs of psychosis
- severe depression or risk of suicide
- family in crisis

Hospital inpatient care is first geared toward correcting problems that present as immediate medical crises, such as severe malnutrition, severe electrolyte imbalance, irregular heart beat, pulse below 45 beats per minute, or low body temperature. Patients are hospitalized if they are a high suicide risk, have severe clinical depression, or exhibit signs of an altered mental state. They may also need to be hospitalized to interrupt weight loss; stop the cycle of vomiting, exercising and/or laxative abuse; treat substance disorders; or for additional medical evaluation.

Day treatment or partial hospitalization, where the patient goes every day to an extensive treatment program, provides structured mealtimes, **nutrition** education, intensive therapy, medical monitoring, and supervision. If day treatment fails, the patient may need to be hospitalized or enter a full-time residential treatment facility.

Anorexia nervosa is a chronic disease and relapses are common and to be expected. Outpatient treatment provides medical supervision, **nutrition counseling**, self-help strategies, and **psychotherapy** after the patient has regained some weight and shows stability.

A nutrition consultant or dietitian is an essential part of the team needed to successfully treat AN. The first treatment concern is to get individuals medically stable by increasing calorie intake and balancing electrolytes. After that, nutritional therapy is needed to support the long process of recovery and stable weight gain. This is an intensive process involving nutrition education, meal planning, and nutrition monitoring, with the goal of developing a healthy relationship with food.

Psychotherapy

Medical **intervention** helps alleviate the immediate physical problems associated with AN, but if used alone it rarely changes behavior. Psychotherapy plays a major role in helping the patient understand and recover from AN. Several different types of psychotherapy may be used, depending on the individual's situation. Generally, the goal of psychotherapy is to help patients develop a healthy attitude toward their body and food. This may involve addressing the root causes of the anorexic behavior as well as the behavior itself.

Some types of psychotherapy have been successful in treating AN:

- Cognitive behavior therapy (CBT) is designed to change individuals' thoughts and feelings about their body and behaviors toward food, but it does not address why those thoughts or feelings exist. This therapy is relatively short-term.
- Psychodynamic therapy, also called psychoanalytic therapy, is a longer-term therapy that attempts to help individuals gain insight into the cause of the emotions that trigger anorexic behaviors.
- Interpersonal therapy is short-term therapy that helps individuals identify issues and problems in relationships. Individuals may be asked to look back at their family history to try to recognize problem areas and work toward resolving them.
- Family and couples therapy is helpful in dealing with other conflicts or disorders that may be perpetuating anorexic behavior. Family therapy is especially useful in helping parents with a child with AN or in helping parents become supportive of their child and facilitating such activities as designing a healthy eating plan for the child. Siblings of a young person with AN need support as well. Family therapy is the only therapy with strong empirical support for its effectiveness in treating AN.

A research study done at Stanford University Hospital and published in 2010 found that involving parents by putting them directly in charge of their child's

QUESTIONS TO ASK YOUR DOCTOR

- Does my loved one need to be hospitalized?
- How long do you think intensive treatment will take?
- Will my insurance pay for inpatient or outpatient treatment?
- What can we do to help?
- Can you refer us to a support group for families of persons with anorexia?

eating had a good rate of curing and preventing the redevelopment of anorexic behaviors. The program is very time intensive because the parent decides what the child must eat and then must sit at the table, sometimes for hours, until the child finishes the food. This is a departure from past practices in which parents were thought be a causative factor in the development of AN and were told not to monitor their child's eating habits.

Drugs

There is no medication that successfully treats the symptoms of AN, but a variety of medications may be prescribed to address secondary and comorbid conditions, such as physical problems caused by the eating disorder, depression, anxiety, and suicidal thoughts. The medications used vary depending on individual cases, but depression is common among persons with AN and is often treated with antidepressant drugs.

Prognosis

Anorexia nervosa is difficult to treat successfully. Medical stabilization, nutrition therapy, continued medical monitoring, and substantial psychiatric treatment give a person with AN the best chance of recovery. Estimates suggest that between 20% and 30% of people in treatment drop out too soon and have major relapses. Even those who stay in treatment **relapse** occasionally. Treating AN is often a long, slow, and expensive process. However, the longer the disorder remains untreated, the more difficult recovery is to achieve, with the consequences growing more severe. Many individuals with AN are willfully uncooperative and have difficulty being motivated to recover.

About half the people treated for AN recover completely and are able (though sometimes with difficulty) to maintain a normal weight. Of the remaining 50%, between 6% and 20% die. The most frequent causes of death associated with AN are starvation, electrolyte imbalance, heart failure, and suicide. About 20% remain dangerously underweight, and the rest remain thin. Long-term health complications are common.

Prevention

A nurturing and healthy family environment during developing years is particularly important. Recognition of the clinical signs with immediate treatment can possibly prevent disorder progression, and early diagnosis and treatment are correlated with a favorable outcome. Long-term goal setting should focus on three areas: learning new, healthy eating behaviors; learning to trust family members, friends, and health professionals who are trying to help; and learning emotional self-care so that healthy methods of coping with **stress** and pressure are exercised, rather than reverting to anorexic behavior.

Resources

BOOKS

Carleton, Pamela, and Deborah Ashin. *Take Charge of Your Child's Eating Disorder: A Physician's Step-By-Step Guide to Defeating Anorexia and Bulimia*. New York: Marlowe, 2007.

Heaton, Jeanne A., and Claudia J. Strauss. *Talking to Eating Disorders: Simple Ways to Support Someone Who Has Anorexia, Bulimia, Binge Eating or Body Image Issues*. New York, NY: New American Library, 2005.

Herzog, David B., Debra L. Franko, and Patricia Cable. *Unlocking the Mysteries of Eating Disorders*. New York: McGraw-Hill, 2007.

Liu, Aimee. *Gaining: The Truth About Life After Eating Disorders*. New York: Warner Books, 2007.

Messinger, Lisa, and Merle Goldberg. *My Thin Excuse: Understanding, Recognizing, and Overcoming Eating Disorders*. Garden City Park, NY: Square One, 2006.

Rubin, Jerome S., ed. *Eating Disorders and Weight Loss Research*. Hauppauge, NY: Nova Science, 2006.

Walsh, B. Timothy. *If Your Adolescent Has an Eating Disorder: An Essential Resource for Parents*. New York: Oxford University Press, 2005.

PERIODICALS

Arcelus, Jon, et al. "Mortality Rates in Patients With Anorexia Nervosa and Other Eating Disorders: A Meta-Analysis of 36 Studies." *Archives of General Psychiatry* 68, no. 7 (2011): 724–31. http://dx.doi.org/10.1001/archgenpsychiatry.2011.74 (accessed November 14, 2011).

Genders, R., and K. Tchanturia. "Cognitive Remediation Therapy (CRT) for Anorexia in Group Format: A Pilot Study." *Eating and Weight Disorders* 15, no. 4 (2010): e234–39.

Guillaume, S., et al. "Characteristics of Suicide Attempts in Anorexia and Bulimia Nervosa: A Case-control Study." *PLoS One* [Public Library of Science] 6, no. 8 (2011): e23578. http://dx.doi.org/10.1371/journal.pone.0023578 (accessed September 16, 2011).

Hudson, James, et al. "The Prevalence and Correlates of Eating Disorders in the National Comorbidity Survey Replication." *Biological Psychiatry* 61, no. 3 (2007): 348–58.

WEBSITES

American Psychological Association. "Eating Disorders." http://www.apa.org/helpcenter/eating.aspx (accessed September 16, 2011).

Bernstein, Bettina E. "Eating Disorder: Anorexia." Medscape Reference. October 14, 2010. http://emedicine.medscape.com/article/912187-overview (accessed September 16, 2011).

MedlinePlus. "Eating Disorders." U.S. National Library of Medicine, National Institutes of Health. March 17, 2011. http://www.nlm.nih.gov/medlineplus/eatingdisorders.html (accessed September 16, 2011).

ORGANIZATIONS

American Academy of Child and Adolescent Psychiatry, 3615 Wisconsin Ave., NW, Washington, DC, 20016-3007, (202) 966-7300, Fax: (202) 966-2891, http://aacap.org.

American Psychiatric Association, 1000 Wilson Blvd., Ste. 1825, Arlington, VA, 22209-3901, (703) 907-7300, apa@psych.org, http://www.psych.org.

American Psychological Association, 750 1st St., NE, Washington, DC, 20002-4242, (202) 336-5500; TDD/TTY: (202) 336-6123, (800) 374-2721, http://www.apa.org.

National Association of Anorexia Nervosa and Related Eating Disorders, PO Box 640, Naperville, IL, 60566, (630) 577-1330, anadhelp@anad.org, http://www.anad.org.

National Eating Disorders Association, 165 W 46th St., New York, NY, 10036, (212) 575-6200, (800) 931-2237, Fax: (212) 575-1650, info@NationalEatingDisorders.org, http://www.nationaleatingdisorders.org.

Tish Davidson, AM
Heidi Splete

Anosognosia

Definition

Anosognosia is a common but poorly understood neurological dysfunction in which a person who has suffered **brain** injury or damage is unable to recognize personal physical impairments or sensory, motor, perceptual, affective, or cognitive deficits.

Demographics

The majority of patients who suffer brain injury or damage may lack at least some degree of awareness of their physical or cognitive impairments. Reliable statistics are scarce, because often it is difficult to distinguish between anosognosia and a patients' desire to deny their illness or impairment. Nevertheless, it has been estimated that 10%–18% of **stroke** patients with partial or total paralysis on one side of their bodies (hemiparesis or hemiplegia) suffer from anosognosia. Other estimates put the incidence of anosognosia for hemiplegia (AHP) at 20%–30% of patients with one-sided paralysis following acute stroke. Furthermore, it has been estimated that about 50% of patients with **schizophrenia** and 40% of patients with **bipolar disorder** have an impaired awareness of their illness, and anosognosia is thought to be the single most important reason that such patients refuse medication. Some researchers estimate that up to 60% of individuals with mild cognitive impairment (MCI) and 81% of patients with **Alzheimer's disease** have some degree of anosognosia.

Description

Anosognosia has long been a source of fascination for cognitive scientists. In 1885, the Russian-Swiss neuropathologist Constantin von Monakow (1853–1930) described the case of a man with damage to the cerebral cortex of his brain who was unaware that he was blind. Gabriel Anton (1858–1933) wrote extensively of patients who were unaware of their severe neurological impairments. These included a man who, after damage to the right side of his brain, was unaware that he could not move his left limbs, had no feeling on his left side, and was blind in his left eye. The condition became known as Anton's syndrome. Although unawareness of blindness is sometimes referred to as Anton-Babinski syndrome, the term *anosognosia,* for the general lack of knowledge, awareness, or recognition of neurological deficits, was adopted in 1914 by the French neurologist Joseph Jules François Félix Babinski (1857–1932). The term is derived from the roots *a* (without), *noso* (illness), and *gnosia* (knowledge), meaning literally "to not know a disease." The terms *anosognosia, impaired awareness, unawareness of deficits,* and *lack of insight* are sometimes used interchangeably in the medical literature. Although **denial** of illness, in which a patient refuses to acknowledge their impairment or illness, is sometimes confused with anosognosia, the latter is caused by damage to the brain, whereas denial of illness is a psychological mechanism for managing disturbing emotions evoked by the illness or disability.

Anosognosia can be a lack of awareness of almost any type of neurological impairment or deficit that follows brain injury, including blindness, weakness or paralysis of the limbs, loss of speech or comprehension of words (aphasia), memory deficits, agnosia (the inability to recognize familiar objects or stimuli), or prosopagnosia (the inability to recognize faces). Anosognosia most often occurs in association with stroke, brain tumors, partial or total blindness or deafness arising from brain damage, Alzheimer's disease, Huntington's disease, schizophrenia, and bipolar disorder. However, anosognosia is not associated with mental confusion or other major cognitive disorders, nor is it directly related to sensory deficits.

The classic examples of anosognosia are patients who, after suffering a stroke in the right hemisphere of the brain, do not perceive that their left side is paralyzed. Such patients often insist that their left arm and leg are functioning normally, even after they fail at performing a simple task. For example, they will insist that they are raising both arms, even when they can see in a mirror that only their right arm is raised. Sometimes patients deny that a paralyzed limb belongs to them. The neurologist Oliver Sacks recounted the story of a patient who repeatedly fell out of bed from trying to throw his paralyzed leg to the floor—he thought that someone else's leg had been placed in his bed as a practical joke.

Anosognosia can be selective. A patient may be aware of one type of deficit, such as blindness in one visual field, but appear unaware of another deficit, such as paralysis of a limb. Anosognosia also can vary in degree. In its most extreme form, patients fail to recognize any impairment. In less extreme forms, patients may minimize the deficit or appear unconcerned about it, a condition referred to as anosodiaphoria.

Anosognosia is often associated with a behavioral syndrome called spatial neglect, which also can occur following brain injury. Spatial neglect refers to the inability to recognize, orient toward, or respond to stimuli, usually on the side of the body opposite the brain lesion.

Risk factors

Anosognosia is caused by injury to specific regions of the brain. Therefore, risk factors for the disorder are those associated with specific types of brain damage.

Causes and symptoms

Although the exact causes of anosognosia remain unclear, it is associated with brain damage, particularly to the right hemisphere. The frontal lobe and a part of the parietal lobe behind the frontal lobe appear to be most involved. The non-dominant parietal lobe (the right hemisphere in most people) is responsible for integrating the opposite side of the body with its environment. Thus, injury to the non-dominant lobe can lead to decreased awareness of the opposite side of the body and its environment. Some patients with anosognosia are also unable to recognize paralysis in others, suggesting that mirror neurons may be involved in such cases. Mirror neurons are brain cells that fire both when performing an action and when observing the action being performed by others.

KEY TERMS

Alzheimer's disease—A progressive, neurodegenerative disease characterized by loss of function and death of nerve cells in several areas of the brain, leading to loss of mental functions, such as memory and learning. Alzheimer's disease is the most common cause of dementia.

Aphasia—Loss of the ability to speak or understand language, due to brain injury or disease.

Bipolar disorder—A recurrent mood disorder, also known as manic-depressive disorder, in which patients have extreme mood swings from depression to mania or a mixture of both.

Cerebral cortex—The convoluted surface layer of the cerebrum or upper portion of the brain, which coordinates sensory and motor information.

Cognitive—Referring to conscious intellectual activity, including thinking, imagining, reasoning, remembering, and learning.

Confabulation—Using false or imagined details to explain physical phenomena or to fill in memory gaps.

Hemiplegia—Paralysis of one side of the body.

Lesion—An injured, diseased, or damaged area.

Mild cognitive impairment (MCI)—A transitional phase of memory loss in older people that precedes dementia or Alzheimer's disease.

Parietal lobe—The middle portion of each cerebral hemisphere of the brain; associated with bodily sensations.

Schizophrenia—A psychotic disorder characterized by loss of contact with one's environment, deterioration of everyday functioning, and personality disintegration.

Stroke—A sudden diminishing or loss of consciousness, sensation, or voluntary movement due to the rupture or obstruction of a blood vessel in the brain.

Vestibular system—The system that helps to maintain balance and orient the body.

Stroke and brain tumors affecting the right hemisphere are among the most common causes of anosognosia. Anosognosia accompanying Alzheimer's disease also may reflect impairment of the right prefrontal and/or frontal lobes and, in particular, the right inferior parietal area of the brain. Likewise, some evidence suggests that frontal lobe damage can cause anosognosia in patients with schizophrenia.

Symptoms of anosognosia not only vary among patients; they can even vary in the same patient at different times. Patients with anosognosia with hemiplegia can show varying degrees of awareness of their paralysis, ranging from anosodiaphoria—knowledge of, but indifference to, their paralysis—to complete unawareness, even in the face of confounding evidence. Patients sometimes fabricate explanations, called confabulations, for their paralyzed limbs. For example, they may claim that the paralyzed limb is far away from their body or belongs to someone else. They may even claim that someone else is lying in their bed, or may become violent toward the paralyzed limb.

Diagnosis

Examination

Anosognosia can usually be diagnosed by an interview and by the patient's behavior—for example, trying to walk despite paralysis. Patients may first be asked why they are in the hospital. If they do not acknowledge a deficit, such as paralysis, the physician may ask more specific questions about the affected body part. A patient with hemiplegia can be scored for anosognosia on a range from zero—readily acknowledging paralysis—to three, in which the patient firmly denies the problem, despite being unable to move a limb.

Anosognosia can be differentiated from denial of illness based on a patient's reaction to information about their deficit. Patients who are denying their impairment will indicate some awareness of the deficit. They will actively struggle to perform a requested task and usually become angry or resistant when confronted with information about their problem. In contrast, patients with anosognosia are unaware of their deficit, are puzzled when given information about it, and are usually indifferent or willing to try and perform a requested task. Sometimes patients with anosognosia admit to their deficit when initially confronted with information about it, but soon after they are again unaware of it. They may also confabulate. For example, patients with anosognosia with hemiplegia may explain that they are right-handed, so that their left arm is weaker, or they may claim that their paralyzed arm belongs to someone else.

QUESTIONS TO ASK YOUR DOCTOR

- Do you think that my loved one has anosognosia, or is there another cause for his/her symptoms?
- How is anosognosia diagnosed?
- What do you think caused the anosognosia?
- What is the prognosis?

Tests

Sometimes an anosognosia ratio (AR) is used to rate patients' awareness of their memory abilities. The AR compares patients' estimations of their memory abilities with objective memory scores and categorizes them as over-estimators, accurate estimators, or under-estimators. Anosognosia for memory loss is also diagnosed using the following scale:

- 1—readily admits memory loss
- 2—readily or inconsistently admits to a small degree of memory loss
- 3—is unaware of any impairment
- 4—angrily insists that there is no impairment of memory

Treatment

Traditional

Anosognosia often resolves over time. In long-term cases, cognitive therapy may be employed to train patients to cope with their impairment, although learning to cope may not relieve the anosognosia. Caloric reflex testing—stimulating the vestibular system by squirting cold water into the left ear canal—sometimes relieves anosognosia for a few hours. Although this effect is not understood, it may be that this intense stimulation of the vestibular system temporarily shifts the patient's awareness.

Drugs

Although there are no drug treatments for anosognosia, schizophrenic patients often become more aware of their illness when taking antipsychotic medications. Anosognosia in patients with bipolar disorder is even more likely to improve with medication.

Prognosis

Although anosognosia can continue indefinitely, in most cases it disappears over time. Some patients fluctuate, with increasing and decreasing periods of awareness of their deficit. However, in Alzheimer's patients, anosognosia often worsens as **dementia** progresses.

Anosognosia can have serious consequences. Patients with anosognosia usually make no attempt to compensate for their deficit, may be unwilling to participate in treatment or rehabilitation, and may suffer from increased post-stroke **depression**. Anosognosia appears to directly increase the incidence of violent behavior in patients with mental illnesses, in addition to effects attributable to medication non-adherence. Patients with severe mental illness and anosognosia may have to be coerced to take medication.

Prevention

There is no known method for preventing anosognosia. However, for patients with mental disorders, adherence to medication often relieves the condition.

Resources

BOOKS

Bayne, Tim, and Jordi Fernández. *Delusion and Self-Deception: Affective and Motivational Influences on Belief Formation.* New York: Psychological Press, 2009.

Berti, Anna, et al. "Motor Awareness and Motor Intention in Anosognosia for Hemiplegia." In *Sensorimotor Foundations of Higher Cognition,* edited by Patrick Haggard, Yves Rossetti, and Matsuo Kawato. New York: Oxford University Press, 2008.

Prigatano, George P. *The Study of Anosognosia.* New York: Oxford University Press, 2010.

Sacks, Oliver. *A Leg to Stand On.* New York: Quality Paperback Book Club, 1990.

PERIODICALS

Robbins, Matthew S., et al. "Anosognosia for Right Hemiplegia from Dominant Anterior Cerebral Artery Stroke." *Journal of the American Geriatrics Society* 57, no. 7 (July 2009): 1320–1322.

OTHER

Doty, Leilani. "Anosognosia (Unawareness of Decline or Difficulties)." AlzOnline.net. http://alzonline.phhp.ufl.edu/en/reading/Anosognosia.pdf (accessed November 19, 2010).

WEBSITES

"Anosognosia (Impaired Awareness of Illness)." Treatment Advocacy Center. http://www.treatmentadvocacycenter.org/index.php?option=com_content&task=view&id=469&Itemid=234 (accessed November 19, 2011).

ORGANIZATIONS

American Speech-Language-Hearing Association, 2200 Research Boulevard, Rockville, MD, 20850-3289, (301) 296-5700, (800) 638-8255, Fax: (301) 296-8580, actioncenter@asha.org, http://www.asha.org.

National Institute of Neurological Disorders and Stroke (NINDS), NIH Neurological Institute, PO Box 5801, Bethesda, MD, 20824, (301) 496-5751, (800) 352-9424, http://www.ninds.nih.gov/index.htm.

Treatment Advocacy Center, 200 N. Glebe Road, Suite 730, Arlington, VA, 22203, (703) 294-6001/6002, Fax: (703) 294-6010, info@treatmentadvocacycenter.org, http://www.treatmentadvocacycenter.org.

Ruvanee Pietersz Vilhauer, PhD
Margaret Alic, PhD

Antabuse *see* **Disulfiram**

Antianxiety drugs and abuse

Definition

Antianxiety drugs, or "anxiolytics," are powerful central nervous system (CNS) depressants that can slow normal **brain** function. They are often prescribed to reduce feelings of tension and anxiety and/or to bring about sleep. Antianxiety medications are among the most abused drugs in the United States, obtained both legally via prescription and illegally through the black market. These drugs are also known as **sedatives**.

Demographics

According to the Substance Abuse and Mental Health Services Administration's National Survey on Drug Use and Health, 7 million people (2.7%) aged 12 or older used prescription-type psychotherapeutic drugs in 2010. Of those, 2.4 million used psychotherapeutics nonmedically for the first time, averaging around 6,600 initiates per day. The average age for first nonmedical use of psychotherapeutics was 22, and females ages 12 to 17 were more likely than males of the same age group to be users of

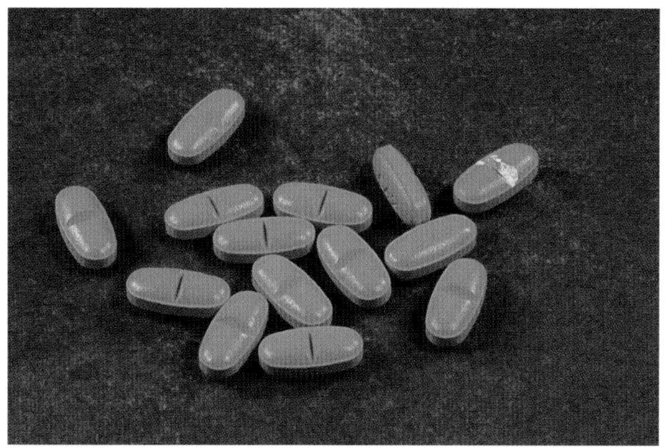

Rohypnol tablets. *(© David Hoffman Photo Library/Alamy)*

Percentage of U.S. adults (18+) reporting prescription antianxiety (anxiolytics, sedatives, and hypnotics) drug use in the past month, 1988–1994 and 2005–2008

	1988–1994	2005–2008
Total		
18 years and over, age-adjusted†	3.9	5.7
18 years and over, crude	3.6	5.8
Men		
18 years and over	2.6	4.3
18–44 years	*1.0	2.1
45–64 years	4.3	6.2
65 years and over	6.1	7.1
Women		
18 years and over	4.6	7.3
18–44 years	1.9	4.3
45–64 years	7.5	9.3
65 years and over	9.1	11.8

*Estimates are considered unreliable. Data preceded by an asterisk have a relative standard error of 20%–30%.
†Estimates are age-adjusted to the year 2000 standard population using three age groups: 18–44 years, 45–64 years, and 65 years and over.

SOURCE: Centers for Disease Control and Prevention, National Center for Health Statistics, *Health, United States, 2010*, February 2011.

(Table by PreMediaGlobal. © 2012 Cengage Learning.)

psychotherapeutics (3.7% versus 2.3%). When asked how they obtained the drugs, over one-half of the users admitted that the drugs came from a friend or relative for free. By race, American Indians or Alaska natives were the most likely to engage in this form of drug abuse, whereas African Americans were the least likely to do so.

Description

The drugs associated with this class of substance-related disorders are the **benzodiazepines** (e.g. **diazepam** [Valium], **chlordiazepoxide** [Librium], **alprazolam** [Xanax], **triazolam** [Halcion], and **estazolam** [ProSom]); the **barbiturates** (e.g., Seconal and pentobarbital [Nembutal]); and barbiturate-like substances, including Quaalude, Equanil, and Doriden. Any of these drugs is capable of producing either wakeful relief from tension or sleep, depending upon dosage. Some legal nonpsychiatric uses of antianxiety medications include medical treatment and prevention of **seizures** and use as muscle relaxants, anesthetics, and drugs to make other anesthetics work more effectively (known as adjuvants).

Although the types of central nervous system depressants work differently, they all produce a pleasant drowsy or calming effect. If used over a long period of time, tolerance develops, meaning larger doses are needed to achieve the initial effects. Continued use can lead to physical dependence and withdrawal symptoms when use is reduced or stopped. When combined with each other or other CNS depressants, such as alcohol, the effects are additive.

In addition to the drugs available in the United States by prescription, there are three other drugs that are predominantly central nervous system depressants with significant potential for abuse. These are:

- gamma hydroxybutyrate (GHB)
- flunitrazepam (Rohypnol)
- ketamine

GHB has been abused in the United States since about 1990 for its euphoric, sedative, and anabolic (bodybuilding) effects. It was widely available over the counter in health food stores until 1992. Bodybuilders used it to aid in reducing percentage of body fat and to build muscle. Street names for GHB include "Liquid ecstasy," "soap," "easy lay," and "Georgia home boy."

Rohypnol is of particular concern because of its use in date rape. When mixed with alcohol, Rohypnol can incapacitate its victims and prevent the person from resisting sexual assault. It can also lead to anterograde **amnesia**, in which individuals cannot remember what they experienced while under the influence. Rohypnol can be lethal when mixed with alcohol and/or other depressants. Rohypnol is not available by prescription in the United States, and it is illegal to import it. Even so, illegal use of Rohypnol started appearing in the United States in the early 1990s, when it became known as "rophies," "roofies," "roach," and "rope."

Ketamine is an anesthetic used predominately by veterinarians to treat animals. It can be injected or snorted. Ketamine goes by the street names of "Special K" or "Vitamin K." At certain doses, ketamine can cause dreamlike states and hallucinations. It has become particularly common in club and rave (large, all-night dance marathon) settings and has also been used as a date-rape drug. At high doses, it can cause **delirium**, amnesia, impaired motor functioning, high blood pressure, and **depression**. It can also cause potentially fatal respiratory problems.

Causes and symptoms

Causes

Antianxiety drugs can be taken orally to bring about a general calming or drowsy effect, usually experienced as pleasant. Abuse of antianxiety medication can develop with prolonged use, as tolerance grows relatively quickly. Increasing amounts of the drug are then needed to produce the initial effect. It is possible to become addicted to antianxiety drugs even when they are medically prescribed.

KEY TERMS

Abuse—A milder form of addiction than substance dependence. Generally, people who have been diagnosed with substance abuse do not experience the tolerance or withdrawal symptoms—the signs of physiological dependence—that people dependent on a substance experience.

Anxiolytic—A preparation or substance given to relieve anxiety; a tranquilizer.

Barbiturates—A class of medications (including Seconal and Nembutal) that causes sedation and drowsiness. They may be prescribed legally but may also be used as drugs of abuse.

Benzodiazepines—A group of central nervous system depressants used to relieve anxiety or to induce sleep.

Dependence—The adaptation of neurons and other physical processes to the use of a drug, followed by withdrawal symptoms when the drug is removed; physiological and/or psychological addiction.

Flunitrazepam (Rohypnol)—A central nervous system depressant that is not legal in the United States but is used as a date-rape drug.

Gamma hydroxybutyrate (GHB)—A central nervous system depressant that has been abused in the United States for euphoric, sedative, bodybuilding, and date-rape purposes.

Intoxication—The presence of significant problem behaviors or psychological changes following ingestion of a substance.

Ketamine—An anesthetic used predominately by veterinarians to treat animals that can be used as a date-rape drug.

Sedative—A medication that induces relaxation and sleep.

Tranquilizer—A medication that induces a feeling of calm and relaxation.

Withdrawal—Symptoms experienced by a person who is physically dependent on a drug when the drug use is discontinued.

A second cause of antianxiety drug abuse is their use when combined with other drugs, such as **cocaine**. It is not uncommon for a person abusing antianxiety drugs to pair the use of a stimulant, such as cocaine or **methamphetamine**, with a CNS depressant. The combination allows the user to feel alert for an extended period of time and then be able to come down from the high and even fall asleep.

Symptoms

Even when prescribed for medical reasons, an individual taking central nervous system depressants usually feels sleepy and uncoordinated during the first few days of treatment. As the body adjusts to the effects of the drug, these feelings begin to disappear. If the drug is used long term, the body develops tolerance, and increasing doses are needed to obtain the desired effect of general calming or drowsiness.

The use of antianxiety drugs can pose extreme danger when taken along with other medications that cause CNS depression, such as prescription pain medicines, some over-the-counter cold and allergy medications, and alcohol. Use of additional depressants can slow breathing and respiration and can lead to death.

Withdrawal from antianxiety medications can be dangerous if not done under medical supervision. The safest method of withdrawal involves a gradual reduction of dosage. Abrupt withdrawal from these medications can lead to seizures due to the sudden increase in brain activity.

Diagnosis

The manual used by mental health professionals to diagnose mental illnesses, the ***Diagnostic and Statistical Manual of Mental Disorders*** (*DSM*) includes specific diagnostic criteria for the four stages of substance abuse, which are:

- dependence
- abuse
- intoxication
- withdrawal

Substance dependence, the more severe form of **addiction**, is a group of cognitive, behavioral, and physiological symptoms associated with the continued use of the substance and includes both tolerance and withdrawal symptoms. Abuse is a less severe form of addiction that may also result in risky behavior, such as driving while under the influence. For example, individuals with an abuse disorder may miss work or school or get into arguments with parents or spouses about substance use. Such problems can easily escalate into full-blown dependence.

Intoxication refers to the presence of clinically significant problem behaviors or psychological changes, such as inappropriate sexual or aggressive behavior, mood swings, impaired judgment, or impaired social or work functioning, that develop during or shortly after use of an antianxiety medication. As with other CNS depressants such as alcohol, these behaviors may be accompanied by slurred speech, unsteady gait, memory or attention problems, poor coordination, and stupor or coma. Memory impairment is relatively common, especially a kind known as anterograde amnesia that resembles alcoholic blackouts.

Withdrawal is a characteristic syndrome that develops when use of the antianxiety medication is severely reduced or stopped abruptly. It is similar to abrupt cessation of heavy **alcohol use**. Symptoms may include increases in heart rate, respiratory rate, blood pressure or body temperature, sweating, hand tremor, **insomnia**, anxiety, nausea, and restlessness. Seizures may occur in perhaps as many as 20%–30% of individuals undergoing untreated withdrawal. In the more severe forms of withdrawal, hallucinations and delirium can occur. Withdrawal symptoms are generally the opposite of the acute effects experienced by first-time users of the drugs. Length of withdrawal varies depending upon the drug and may last as few as 10 hours or as long as three to four weeks. The longer the substance has been taken and the higher the dosages used, the more likely that withdrawal will be severe.

Treatment

According to the National Institute on Drug Abuse (NIDA), successful treatment for antianxiety medication addiction needs to incorporate several components. Counseling, particularly cognitive-behavioral counseling, focuses on helping addicted individuals identify and change the behaviors, attitudes, and beliefs that contributed to their drug usage. Combined with prescribed medications to make withdrawal safer and easier, counseling can help the addicted individual eventually make a full recovery. Often, it takes multiple courses of treatment before full recovery can be achieved. Various levels of care, from outpatient to residential care for up to 18 months, are available, depending upon need. Narcotics Anonymous also offers ongoing recovery support.

Prognosis

The most typical course of abuse according to the *DSM*, involves teens or young people in their early 20s who may escalate occasional use of antianxiety medications to the point at which they develop problems such as abuse or dependence. This is particularly likely for individuals who also abuse other substances. An initial pattern of use at parties can eventually lead to daily use and high degrees of tolerance.

A second course, observed somewhat less frequently, involves individuals who initially obtain medications by prescription, usually for treatment of anxiety or insomnia. Though the vast majority of people who use medications as prescribed do not go on to develop **substance abuse** problems, a small minority do. Again, tolerance develops and the need for higher dosages to reach the initial effects occurs. Individuals may justify their continued use on the basis of the original symptoms but engage in active substance seeking to ensure supply. Others at higher risk are those with alcohol dependence who might be given prescription antianxiety medications to reduce their anxiety or insomnia.

QUESTIONS TO ASK YOUR DOCTOR

- What risks are associated with antianxiety medications and antianxiety drug abuse?
- What symptoms are associated with antianxiety drug dependence?
- Does having antianxiety drug dependence and abuse put me at risk for other health conditions?
- Can you recommend any treatment and support groups for me?

Prevention

Healthcare professionals play a very important role in preventing and detecting abuse of prescription drugs. Primary care physicians, nurse practitioners, and pharmacists can all play a role.

It is estimated by the NIDA that approximately 70% of all Americans visit a healthcare provider at least once every two years. Thus, healthcare providers are in a unique position not only to prescribe medications as appropriate but also to identify **prescription drug abuse** when it exists and recommend appropriate treatment for recovery. Screening for substance abuse should be incorporated into routine history taking or when a patient currently exhibits symptoms associated with problem drug use.

Over time, providers should be alert to any increases in the amount of medication being used, which may be a sign of tolerance. They should also be aware that individuals addicted to prescription medications may engage in "doctor shopping"—that is, going from provider to provider in an effort to obtain multiple prescriptions of their abused drug.

Pharmacists can play a role in preventing prescription drug abuse as well. They should provide information and advice about the correct way to take prescribed medications and be alert to drug interactions. They can also play a role in detecting prescription fraud by noticing suspicious-looking prescription forms.

Resources

BOOKS

American Psychiatric Association. *Diagnostic and Statistical Manual of Mental Disorders.* 4th ed., Text rev. Washington, DC: American Psychiatric Association, 2000.

American Psychological Association. *Publication Manual of the American Psychological Association,* 6th ed. Washington, DC: American Psychological Association, 2009.

Erickson, Carlton K. *Addiction Essentials: The Go-To Guide for Clinicians and Patients.* New York: Norton, 2011.

PERIODICALS

Carter, Lawrence P., et al. "Relative Abuse Liability of GHB in Humans: A Comparison of Psychomotor, Subjective, and Cognitive Effects of Supratherapeutic Doses of Triazolam, Pentobarbital, and GHB." *Neuropsychopharmacology* 31, no. 11 (2006): 2537–51.

De Wit, Harriet, et al. "Evaluation of the Abuse Potential of Pagoclone, a Partial GABA-Sub(A) Agonist." *Journal of Clinical Psychopharmacology* 26, no. 3 (2006): 268–73.

McCabe, S. E., et al. "Medical Misuse of Controlled Medications Among Adolescents." *Archives of Pediatrics & Adolescent Medicine* 165, no. 8 (2011): 729–35.

Mintzer, Miriam Z., and R.R. Griffiths. "An Abuse Liability Comparison of Flunitrazepam and Triazolam in Sedative Drug Abusers." *Behavioural Pharmacology* 16, no. 7 (2005): 579–84.

WEBSITES

Smith, Melinda, Lawrence Robinson, and Jeanne Segal. "Antianxiety Medication." Helpguide.org. http://helpguide.org/mental/anxiety_medication_drugs_treatment.htm (accessed December 13, 2011).

ORGANIZATIONS

American Psychiatric Association, 1000 Wilson Blvd., Ste. 1825, Arlington, VA, 22209, (703) 907-7300, apa@psych.org, http://www.psych.org.

American Psychological Association, 750 1st St. NE, Washington, DC, 20003, (202) 336-5500, http://www.apa.org.

Anxiety Disorders Association of America, 8730 Georgia Ave., Ste. 600, Silver Spring, MD, 20910, (240) 485-1001, Fax: (240) 485-1035, http://www.adaa.org.

Mental Health America, 2000 N. Beauregard St., 6th Fl., Alexandria, VA, 22311, (703) 684-7722, (800) 969-6642, Fax: (703) 684-5968, http://www1.nmha.org.

National Alliance on Mental Illness, Colonial Place Three, 2107 Wilson Blvd., Ste. 300, Arlington, VA, 22201, (703) 524-7600, (800) 950-NAMI (6264), Fax: (703) 524-9094, http://www.nami.org.

National Institute on Drug Abuse, National Institutes of Health, 6001 Executive Blvd., Rm. 5213, Bethesda, MD, 20892, (301) 443-1124, information@nida.nih.gov, http://www.nida.nih.gov.

National Institute of Mental Health (NIMH), 6001 Executive Blvd., Rm. 8184, MSC 9663, Bethesda, MD, 20892, (301) 443-4513, (866) 615-6464, Fax: (301) 443-4279, nimhinfo@nih.gov, http://www.nimh.nih.gov.

Barbara S. Sternberg, PhD
Ruth A. Wienclaw, PhD
Laura Jean Cataldo, RN,EdD

Antidepressants

Definition

Antidepressants are medications that are used primarily to treat **depression** and depressive disorders.

Purpose

Antidepressant drugs are used to alleviate the symptoms of depression and are also sometimes used to treat other psychological disorders, including **anxiety disorders**, **seasonal affective disorder**, and some eating disorders. Because they are thought to increase the effectiveness of some pain medications, they are sometimes used in the treatment of migraine headaches. They may also be used as a component of **smoking cessation** programs and in the treatment of fibromyalgia and some types of **sleep disorders**.

Description

Depression is a serious condition that severely affects a person's quality of life. It is normal for a person to undergo brief periods of sadness or a general sense of feeling down. However, when these feelings do not subside, depression may be the cause. The three main depressive disorders include dysthymia, **major depressive disorder**, and **bipolar disorder**, which alternates between periods of "highs" (mania) and "lows" (depression). A person with major depressive disorder experiences five or more depressive symptoms for at least two weeks. These symptoms can include feelings of sadness, emptiness, guilt, or worthlessness; loss of interest in previously pleasurable activities; changes in eating and sleeping patterns; **fatigue**, lethargy, or agitation; difficulty concentrating; and suicidal thoughts. Antidepressant drugs are not the only treatment for depression; **psychotherapy** and other treatments are also independently effective in alleviating depression. Antidepressant drugs, if prescribed, are often used in combination with these other treatments.

The type of antidepressant medication prescribed depends on the particular array of symptoms a patient

Antidepressant medications (also used for anxiety disorders)

Generic name	Trade name	Drug class	FDA approved age
amitriptyline	Elavil	Tricyclic	18+
amoxapine	Asendin		18+
bupropion	Wellbutrin		18+
citalopram	Celexa	SSRI	18+
clomipramine	Anafranil	Tricyclic	10+ (for obsessive-compulsive disorder)
desipramine	Norpramin	Tricyclic	18+
desvenlafaxine	Pristiq	SNRI	18+
doxepin	Sinequan	Tricyclic	12+
duloxetine	Cymbalta	SNRI	18+
escitalopram	Lexapro	SSRI	18+; 12–17 for major depressive disorder
fluoxetine	Prozac	SSRI	8+
fluoxetine	Sarafem	SSRI	18+ (for premenstrual dysphoric disorder)
fluvoxamine	Luvox	SSRI	8+ (for obsessive-compulsive disorder)
imipramine	Tofranil	Tricyclic	6+ (for bedwetting in children)
imipramine pamoate	Tofranil-PM	Tricyclic	18+
isocarboxazid	Marplan	MAOI	18+
maprotiline	Ludiomil	Tricyclic	18+
mirtazapine	Remeron		18+
nortriptyline	Aventyl, Pamelor	Tricyclic	18+
paroxetine	Paxil	SSRI	18+
paroxetine mesylate	Pexeva	SSRI	18+
phenelzine	Nardil	MAOI	18+
protriptyline	Vivactil	Tricyclic	18+
selegiline transdermal	Emsam		18+
sertraline	Zoloft	SSRI	6+
tranylcypromine	Parnate	MAOI	18+
trazodone	Desyrel		18+
trimipramine	Surmontil	Tricyclic	18+
venlafaxine	Effexor	SNRI	18+

SOURCE: National Institute of Mental Health.

"Alphabetical List of Medications," available online at: http://www.nimh.nih.gov/health/publications/mental-health-medications/alphabetical-list-of-medications.shtml. *(Table by PreMediaGlobal. © 2012 Cengage Learning.)*

displays or reports. There are several different types of antidepressant drugs. All of them work by altering the level or activity of **neurotransmitters** in the **brain**. Neurotransmitters are chemicals that are released by neurons, or nerve cells. They attach to other neurons and activate them in various ways. Although antidepressant drugs affect communication between neurons within hours after these drugs are ingested, symptoms of depression usually improve only after a few weeks of taking the medication. Some people notice improvement in symptoms after two weeks, but most people notice a benefit only after six to eight weeks of using the medication. The reason for this delayed effect of antidepressants is not entirely clear. One theory is related to the finding that the changes in neurotransmitter activity caused by antidepressants increase the release of other chemicals, called neurotrophins, in the brain. In the normal brain, neurotrophins help neurons to grow and connect to other neurons. People with depression sometimes have shrinkage of neurons in parts of the brain. When more neurotrophins are present, neurons in these areas of the brain can grow.

The main classes of antidepressant drugs are tricyclic antidepressants, **monoamine oxidase inhibitors (MAOIs)**, **selective serotonin reuptake inhibitors (SSRIs)**, serotonin-norepinephrine reuptake inhibitors (SNRIs), and atypical antidepressants. A patient who does not improve with one type of antidepressant drug may sometimes be helped by another type of antidepressant, because different drugs work in different ways.

Tricyclic antidepressants

The first class of drugs used to treat depression was the tricyclic antidepressants. These drugs work by preventing neurons from reabsorbing the neurotransmitters **serotonin**, **dopamine**, and norepinephrine after they are released. This means that the neurotransmitters are able to remain in the gaps between neurons for a longer period of time, thus continuing to activate the neurons that receive them. Tricyclic antidepressants typically have more side effects than other types of antidepressants, because they can prevent nerve cells from functioning normally and additional neurotransmitters from working effectively. For example, they block the activity of histamine, a neurotransmitter that is involved in keeping people alert and awake. They also block the activity of acetylcholine, a neurotransmitter involved in many automatic body

Percentage of U.S. adults (18+) reporting prescription antidepressant drug use in the past month, 1988–1994 and 2005–2008

	1988–1994	2005–2008
Total		
18 years and over, age-adjusted†	2.4	11.1
18 years and over, crude	2.3	11.4
Men		
18 years and over	1.5	6.2
18–44 years	*1.0	3.6
45–64 years	*2.3	8.5
65 years and over	*2.3	10.0
Women		
18 years and over	3.1	16.2
18–44 years	2.3	11.9
45–64 years	4.6	21.9
65 years and over	3.5	17.3

*Estimates are considered unreliable. Data preceded by an asterisk have a relative standard error of 20%–30%.
†Estimates are age-adjusted to the year 2000 standard population using three age groups: 18–44 years, 45–64 years, and 65 years and over.

SOURCE: Centers for Disease Control and Prevention, National Center for Health Statistics, *Health, United States, 2010*, February 2011.

(Table by PreMediaGlobal. © 2012 Cengage Learning.)

functions. Specific tricyclic antidepressants include **imipramine** (Tofranil), **amitriptyline** (Elavil, Endep), **clomipramine** (Anafranil), **doxepin** (Sinequan, Adapin), **desipramine** (Norpramin), **nortriptyline** (Pamelor), **protriptyline** (Vivactil), and **trimipramine** (Surmontil).

MAOIs

The **monoamine oxidase inhibitors** are drugs that prevent neurotransmitters such as dopamine, serotonin, and norepinephrine from being broken down into inactive chemicals. This means that when **MAOIs** are used, more of these neurotransmitters are available to send messages in the brain. MAOIs can have potentially serious side effects, however, because they prevent the amino acid tyramine from being broken down. Tyramine is a chemical required by the body and is found in foods like aged cheese, smoked and pickled meats and fish, and raisins. If tyramine cannot be broken down, it can accumulate in the body, causing increased blood pressure and possibly **stroke**. Types of MAOIs include **isocarboxazid** (Marplan), **phenelzine** (Nardil), and **tranylcypromine** (Parnate).

SSRIs

The **selective serotonin reuptake inhibitors** work by preventing neurons from reabsorbing serotonin after it is released, so that the effect of serotonin on adjoining neurons is prolonged. The **SSRIs** include **citalopram** (Celexa), **escitalopram** (Lexapro), **fluoxetine** (Prozac), **fluvoxamine** (Luvox), **paroxetine** (Paxil), **sertraline** (Zoloft), and vilazodone (Viibryd). Vilazodone, a combination SSRI/5HT1A receptor agonist, was approved by the FDA in 2011 and may not cause some of the side effects common with other antidepressant medications, namely weight gain and sexual dysfunction.

SNRIs

Serotonin-norepinephrine reuptake inhibitors function similarly to SSRIs but block the absorption of both serotonin and norepinephrine, instead of just serotonin. Types of SNRIs include **desvenlafaxine** (Pristiq), **duloxetine** (Cymbalta), and **venlafaxine** (Effexor).

Atypical antidepressants

The atypical antidepressants are a miscellaneous collection of drugs with different chemical makeups than the other classes of antidepressants. Examples of atypical antidepressants include **bupropion** (Wellbutrin), **mirtazapine** (Remeron), and **trazodone** (Desyrel).

Recommended dosage

The dosage of antidepressants depends on the particular drug being prescribed, along with other factors such as the age of the patient, the patient's body chemistry, and the patient's body weight. Patients are usually started on a low dose to minimize side effects, and the dose is gradually increased over time to a level that is therapeutic. Newer antidepressants, however, may be started at the therapeutic dosage level.

Precautions

Use of antidepressant drugs may increase suicidal thoughts in children, adolescents, and adults through age 24. Healthcare practitioners and families of patients taking antidepressants should carefully monitor users for worsening depression, acts of self-harm, or other significant changes in behavior.

Antidepressants can precipitate mania in people who are susceptible to bipolar disorder. Healthcare practitioners typically take a detailed medical history before prescribing antidepressants. Various medical problems may affect the success or risks of antidepressants. These include—but are not limited to—angina, headaches, epilepsy, recent heart attacks or stroke, kidney disease, and diabetes. Some antidepressants may affect a fetus; pregnant women should inform their doctors about their condition before antidepressants are prescribed. Newborns of mothers who took SSRIs late in pregnancy displayed withdrawal symptoms, including tremor and respiratory problems. SSRIs may also put adults over the age of 65 at increased risk for fractures due to bone loss. Patients taking tricyclic antidepressants should carefully adhere to the dietary restrictions provided by their doctor in order to avoid potentially serious side effects. Patients who stop taking antidepressants may experience withdrawal symptoms if the drugs are abruptly discontinued.

Some medical professionals question the effectiveness of antidepressants. A 2008 review of antidepressant studies, published in *PLoS Medicine*, the journal of the Public Library of Science, concluded that for patients with mild-to-moderate depression, antidepressant drugs were not much more effective than placebos. Despite this, the number of people taking antidepressants has risen dramatically. A study published in the *Archives of General Psychiatry* revealed that use among persons aged 6 or older jumped from 5.8% of the U.S. population in 1996 to 10.1% in 2005 (27 million people). The U.S. Centers for Disease Control and Prevention estimates that 11% of adults (aged 18 or older) were prescribed antidepressants between 2005 and 2008. Because of the *PLoS* review and other studies, some feel that antidepressants may be overprescribed. Nevertheless, depression is not a condition that should be taken lightly, and patients should discuss all avenues with their physicians to find a treatment that works for them.

Side effects

People who take antidepressants may experience side effects. Though specific effects depend on the drug taken and the patient's characteristics, possible side effects include dry mouth, constipation, nausea, bladder problems, sexual problems, blurred vision, dizziness, daytime drowsiness, **insomnia**, increased heart rate, headache, nervousness, and agitation. Newer antidepressants, such as the SSRIs and SNRIs, are thought to have fewer and less troublesome side effects than the tricyclic antidepressants and the MAOIs.

Interactions

Antidepressants may result in dangerous side effects if taken in combination with other medications. There can also be dangerous side effects if different types of antidepressants are combined with each other; for instance, **serotonin syndrome** is a serious condition that can develop if there is too much serotonin in the body. Drugs that inhibit the absorption of serotonin should not be used in combination. Patients switching medications, such as from an SSRI to an MAOI (or vice versa), may need to wait a period of time before beginning the new medication. Patients should inform their doctor about all medications and herbal supplements they are taking before antidepressant drugs are prescribed and should follow dosing instructions exactly. Alcohol or other recreational drugs may decrease the effectiveness of antidepressants and should not be used in conjunction with the medication.

KEY TERMS

Acetylcholine—A neurotransmitter with effects that are generally opposite those of dopamine and norepinephrine. Acetylcholine dilates blood vessels, lowers blood pressure, and slows heartbeat.

Anxiety disorder—A type of psychological disorder characterized by unrealistic, irrational fear or intense anxiety.

Eating disorder—A type of psychological disorder characterized by disturbances in eating patterns, extreme concern about weight gain, and unhealthy efforts to control weight.

Fibromyalgia—A condition in which a person experiences chronic pain in the muscles and soft tissues around joints.

Mania—A state in which a person experiences intense excitement and euphoria.

Neurotransmitter—One of a group of chemicals secreted by a nerve cell (neuron) to carry a chemical message to another nerve cell, often as a way of transmitting a nerve impulse. Examples of neurotransmitters include acetylcholine, dopamine, serotonin, and norepinephrine.

Serotonin—5-Hydroxytryptamine; a substance that occurs throughout the body with numerous effects including neurotransmission in the brain. Inadequate amounts of serotonin are implicated in some forms of depression, obsessive-compulsive disorder, and anxiety disorders.

Stroke—A temporary loss of normal blood flow to an area of the brain, caused by blockage or rupture of a blood vessel.

See also Psychopharmacology; Star*D study

Resources

BOOKS

American Psychiatric Association. *Diagnostic and Statistical Manual of Mental Disorders*. 4th ed., text rev. Washington, DC: American Psychiatric Association, 2000.

Brenner, George M., and Craig W. Stevens. "Psychotherapeutic Drugs." Chap. 22 in *Pharmacology*. 3rd ed. Philadelphia: Saunders/Elsevier, 2010.

Diamond, Ronald, J. *Instant Psychopharmacology*. 3rd ed. New York: W.W. Norton and Company, 2009.

Dunbar, Katherine Read, ed. *Antidepressants*. Farmington Hills, MI: Greenhaven Press, 2006.

Kalat, James W. *Biological Psychology*. 10th ed. Belmont, CA: Wadsworth, 2009.

Kirsch, Irving. *The Emperor's New Drugs: Exploding the Antidepressant Myth.* New York: Basic Books, 2010.

PERIODICALS

Kirsch, Irving, et al. "Initial Severity and Antidepressant Benefits: A Meta-Analysis of Data Submitted to the Food and Drug Administration." *PLoS Medicine* 5, no. 2 (2008): e45. http://dx.doi.org/doi:10.1371/journal.pmed.0050045 (accessed September 20, 2011).

Kramer, Peter. "In Defense of Antidepressants." *New York Times*, July 9, 2011. http://www.nytimes.com/2011/07/10/opinion/sunday/10antidepressants.html?_r=1

Olfson, Mark, and Steven Marcus. "National Patterns in Antidepressant Medication Treatment." *Archives of General Psychiatry* 66, no. 8 (2009): 848–56. http://dx.doi.org/10.1001/archgenpsychiatry.2009.81 (accessed September 20, 2011).

Richards, J. Brent, et al. "Effect of Selective Serotonin Reuptake Inhibitors on the Risk of Fracture." *Archives of Internal Medicine* 167, no. 2 (2007): 188–94.

Szalavitz, Maia. "Antidepressants: Are They Effective or Just a Placebo?" *TIME*, June 3, 2010. http://www.time.com/time/health/article/0,8599,1991841,00.html (accessed September 20, 2011).

WEBSITES

MedlinePlus. "Antidepressants." U.S. National Library of Medicine, National Institutes of Health. http://www.nlm.nih.gov/medlineplus/antidepressants.html (accessed September 20, 2011).

National Institute of Mental Health. "Antidepressant Medications for Children and Adolescents: Information for Parents and Caregivers." National Institutes of Health. http://www.nimh.nih.gov/health/topics/child-and-adolescent-mental-health/antidepressant-medications-for-children-and-adolescents-information-for-parents-and-caregivers.shtml (accessed September 20, 2011).

———. "Mental Health Medications: What Medications Are Used to Treat Depression?" National Institutes of Health. http://www.nimh.nih.gov/health/publications/mental-health-medications/complete-index.shtml#pub5 (accessed September 20, 2011).

U.S. Food and Drug Administration. "Antidepressant Use in Children, Adolescents, and Adults." http://www.fda.gov/Drugs/DrugSafety/InformationbyDrugClass/UCM096273 (accessed September 20, 2011).

Ruvanee Pietersz Vilhauer, Ph.D.
James Waun

Antisocial personality disorder

Definition

Also known as psychopathy, sociopathy, dissocial personality disorder, or dyssocial personality disorder, antisocial personality disorder (APD) is a **diagnosis** applied to persons who routinely behave with little or no regard for the rights, safety, or feelings of others. This pattern of behavior is seen in children or young adolescents and can persist into adulthood.

The ***Diagnostic and Statistical Manual of Mental Disorders (DSM)***, the handbook used by medical professionals in diagnosing mental disorders, classifies APD as one of six specific types of **personality disorders**, along with **avoidant personality disorder**, **borderline personality disorder**, **narcissistic personality disorder**, **obsessive-compulsive personality disorder**, and **schizotypal personality disorder**.

Demographics

Men are three times more likely to be diagnosed with antisocial personality disorder than women, according to the World Health Organization. Mental health professionals may diagnose 3%–30% of the population in clinical settings as having the disorder. The percentages may be even higher among prison inmates or persons in treatment for **substance abuse**. By some estimates, three-quarters of the prison population may meet the diagnostic criteria for APD.

Description

Men or women diagnosed with this personality disorder demonstrate few emotions beyond contempt for other people. Their lack of empathy is often combined with an inflated sense of self-worth and a superficial charm that tends to mask an inner indifference to the needs or feelings of others. Some studies indicate that people with APD can only mimic the emotions associated with committed love relationships and friendships that most people feel naturally.

People reared by parents with antisocial personality disorder or substance abuse disorders are more likely to develop APD than members of the general population. People with the disorder may be homeless, living in poverty, suffering from a concurrent substance abuse disorder, or piling up extensive criminal records, as antisocial personality disorder is associated with low socioeconomic status and urban backgrounds. Highly intelligent individuals with APD, however, may not come to the attention of the criminal justice or mental health care systems and may be underrepresented in diagnostic statistics.

Some legal experts and mental health professionals do not think that APD should be classified as a mental disorder on the grounds that the classification appears to excuse unethical, illegal, or immoral behavior. Despite these concerns, juries in the United States have consistently demonstrated that they do not regard a diagnosis of APD as exempting a person from prosecution or punishment for crimes committed.

Furthermore, some experts disagree with the categorization by the **American Psychiatric Association** (APA) of antisocial personality disorder. The APA considers the term "psychopathy" as synonymous with APD. However, some experts make a distinction between psychopathy and APD. Dr. Robert Hare, an authority on psychopathy and the originator of the **Hare Psychopathy Checklist**, claims that all persons with psychopathy have APD but not all individuals diagnosed with APD have psychopathy. Recent reports have made this distinction even clearer, suggesting that there is an emotional deficit component of psychopathy that is not necessarily present in people with APD. One expert review comments that only 25% of people diagnosed with APD or **conduct disorder**, a related condition seen in children, will show psychopathic tendencies.

Causes and symptoms

Causes

Studies of adopted children indicate that both genetic and environmental factors influence the development of APD, with heritability estimates ranging from 44% to 72%. Both biological and adopted children of people diagnosed with the disorder have an increased risk of developing it. Children born to parents diagnosed with APD but adopted into other families resemble their biological more than their adoptive parents in this regard. The environment of the adoptive home, however, may lower the child's risk of developing APD.

Researchers have linked antisocial personality disorder to childhood physical or **sexual abuse**, neurological disorders (which are often undiagnosed), and low IQ. Some experts have recently questioned the link between psychopathy, which these experts distinguish from APD, and early environmental **trauma**. As with other personality disorders, no one has identified any specific cause of antisocial personality disorder, and multiple factors are believed to affect the risk of APD developing. Persons diagnosed with APD also have an increased incidence of **somatization disorder** and substance-related disorders.

The fourth edition of the *DSM* (*DSM-IV-TR*) states that persons who show signs of conduct disorder with accompanying **attention deficit hyperactivity disorder** before the age of 10 have a greater chance of being diagnosed with APD as adults than do other children. The manual notes that abuse or **neglect** combined with erratic parenting or inconsistent discipline appears to increase the risk that a child diagnosed with conduct disorder will develop APD as an adult.

Brain imaging studies have identified some specific characteristics in the brains of people diagnosed with APD that suggest dysfunction of structures in the frontal and temporal lobes of the brain.

Symptoms

The central characteristic of antisocial personality disorder is an extreme disregard for the rights of other people. Individuals with APD lie and cheat to gain money or power. Their disregard for authority often leads to arrest and imprisonment. Because they have little regard for others and may act impulsively, they are frequently involved in fights. They show loyalty to few if any other people and are likely to seek power over others in order to satisfy sexual desires or economic needs.

People with APD often become effective "con artists." Those with well-developed verbal abilities can often charm and fool their victims, including unsuspecting or inexperienced therapists. People with APD have no respect for what others regard as societal norms or legal constraints. They may quit jobs on short notice, move to another city, or end relationships without warning and without what others would consider good reason. Criminal activities typically include theft, selling illegal drugs, and check fraud. Because persons with antisocial personality disorder make themselves their highest priority, they are quick to exploit others. They commonly rationalize these actions by dismissing their victims as weak, stupid, or unwary.

Some work has been done on the relationship between what are called "minor physical anomalies" and the presence of various disorders, including aggression disorders and psychopathy. The presence of these features—which include low-seated ears and adherent ear lobes—is associated with developmental derailments in the fetus at the end of the third trimester of pregnancy, and they have been linked with the development of conduct disorder and violence in adulthood. Studies directly examining their association, if any, with psychopathy or APD are lacking, but birth complications are known risk factors for violent and antisocial behaviors.

Diagnosis

The diagnosis of antisocial personality disorder is usually based on a combination of a careful medical as well as psychiatric history and an interview with the patient. The doctor will look for recurrent or repetitive patterns of antisocial behavior. He or she may use a diagnostic questionnaire for APD, such as the Hare Psychopathy Checklist-Revised or the self-reporting Psychopathic Personality Inventory, if the patient's history suggests the diagnosis. A person aged 18 years or older with a childhood history of disregard for the rights of others can be diagnosed as having APD if he or she gives evidence of three of the following seven behaviors associated with disregard for others:

- Fails to conform to social norms, as indicated by frequently performing illegal acts or pursuing illegal occupations.
- Deceives and manipulates others for selfish reasons, often in order to obtain money, sex, drugs, or power. This behavior may involve repeated lying, conning, or the use of false names.
- Fails to plan ahead or displays impulsive behavior, as indicated by a long succession of short-term jobs or frequent changes of address.
- Engages in repeated fights or assaults as a consequence of irritability and aggressiveness.
- Exhibits reckless disregard for safety of self or others.
- Shows a consistent pattern of irresponsible behavior, including failure to find and keep a job for a sustained length of time and refusal to pay bills or honor debts.
- Shows no evidence of sadness, regret or remorse for actions that have hurt others.

To meet *DSM-IV-TR* criteria for APD, a person must also have had some symptoms of conduct disorder before age 15, though this qualification may be removed in the fifth edition of the *DSM*. An adult 18 years or older who does not meet all the criteria for APD may be given a diagnosis of conduct disorder.

Antisocial behavior may appear in other mental disorders as well as in APD. These conditions must be distinguished from true APD. For instance, it is not uncommon for a person with a substance abuse disorder to lie to others in order to obtain money for drugs or alcohol. But unless indications of antisocial behavior were present during the person's childhood, he or she would not be diagnosed with antisocial personality disorder. People who meet the criteria for a substance abuse disorder as well as APD would be given a dual diagnosis.

Treatment

Antisocial personality disorder is highly unresponsive to any form of treatment, in part because persons with APD rarely seek treatment voluntarily. If they do seek help, it is usually in an attempt to find relief from **depression** or other forms of emotional distress. Although there are medications that are effective in treating some of the symptoms of the disorder, noncompliance with medication regimens or abuse of the drugs prevents the widespread use of these medications. The most successful treatment programs for APD are long-term structured residential settings in which the patient systematically earns privileges as he or she modifies behavior. In other words, if a person diagnosed with APD is placed in an environment in which they cannot victimize others, their behavior may improve. It is unlikely, however, that they would maintain good behavior if they left the disciplined environment.

If some form of individual **psychotherapy** is provided along with **behavior modification** techniques, the therapist's primary task is to establish a relationship with the patient, who has usually had very few healthy relationships in his or her life and is unable to trust others. The patient should be given the opportunity to establish positive relationships with as many people as possible and be encouraged to join **self-help groups** or prosocial organizations.

Unfortunately, these approaches are rarely if ever effective. Many persons with APD use therapy sessions to learn how to turn "the system" to their advantage. Their pervasive pattern of manipulation and deceit extends to all aspects of their life, including therapy. Generally, their behavior must be controlled in a setting where they know they have no chance of getting around the rules.

Prognosis

APD can follow a chronic and unremitting course from childhood or early adolescence into adult life. The impulsiveness that characterizes the disorder often leads to a jail sentence or an early death through accident, homicide, or **suicide**. There is some evidence that the worst behaviors that define APD diminish by midlife; the more overtly aggressive symptoms of the disorder occur less frequently in older patients. This improvement is especially true of criminal behavior but may apply to other antisocial acts as well.

Prevention

Measures intended to prevent antisocial personality disorder must begin with interventions in early childhood, before youths are at risk for developing conduct

KEY TERMS

Attention deficit hyperactivity disorder—A learning and behavioral disorder characterized by difficulty in sustaining attention, impulsive behavior, and excessive activity.

Conduct disorder—A behavioral and emotional disorder of childhood and adolescence in which children display physical aggression and infringe on or violate the rights of others. Youths diagnosed with conduct disorder may set fires, exhibit cruelty toward animals or other children, sexually assault others, or lie and steal for personal gain.

Psychopathy—A psychological syndrome that includes lack of a conscience or sense of guilt, lack of empathy, egocentricity, pathological lying, repeated violations of social norms, disregard of the law, shallow emotions, and a history of victimizing others.

Somatization disorder—A long-term condition in which a person has physical symptoms that involve more than one part of the body, but no physical cause can be found. The pain and symptoms are real and not faked.

Substance abuse disorder—Disorder that is characterized by an individual's need for more of a drug or alcohol than intended, an inability to stop using by choice, and an ongoing difficulty in recovering from the effects of the substance.

disorder. Preventive strategies include education for parenthood and other programs intended to lower the incidence of **child abuse**; Big Brother/Big Sister and similar mentoring programs to provide children at risk with adult role models of responsible and prosocial behavior; and further research into the **genetic factors** involved in APD.

Resources

BOOKS

American Psychiatric Association. *Diagnostic and Statistical Manual of Mental Disorders*. 4th ed., text rev. Washington, DC: American Psychiatric Publishing, 2000.

Black, Donald, W., and C. Lindon Larson. *Bad Boys, Bad Men: Confronting Antisocial Personality Disorder*. New York: Oxford University Press, 2000.

Cleckley, Hervey. *The Mask of Sanity*. 5th ed. Augusta, GA: Emily S. Cleckley, 1988.

Hare, Robert D. *Without Conscience: The Disturbing World of the Psychopaths Among Us*. New York: Guilford Press, 1999.

Lykken, David T. *The Antisocial Personalities*. Hillsdale, NJ: Lawrence Erlbaum Associates, 1995.

Simon, Robert I. *Bad Men Do What Good Men Dream: A Forensic Psychiatrist Illuminates the Darker Side of Human Behavior*. Washington, DC: American Psychiatric Association, 1996.

PERIODICALS

Abbott, Alison. "Into the Mind of a Killer." *Nature* 410 (2001): 296–98.

WEBSITES

Hare, Robert D. "'Without Conscience': Robert Hare's Web Site Devoted to the Study of Psychopathy." http://www.hare.org (accessed September 29, 2011).

MedlinePlus. "Antisocial Personality Disorder." U.S. National Library of Medicine, National Institutes of Health. http://www.nlm.nih.gov/medlineplus/ency/article/000921.htm (accessed September 29, 2011).

Dean A. Haycock, PhD
Emily Jane Willingham, PhD

Anxiety disorders

Definition

Anxiety disorders are a group of mental disturbances characterized by anxiety as a central or core symptom. Although anxiety is a commonplace experience, not everyone who experiences it has an anxiety disorder. Anxiety is associated with a wide range of physical illnesses, medication side effects, and other psychiatric disorders.

Prior to 1980, psychiatrists classified patients on the basis of a theory that defined anxiety as the outcome of the patient's unconscious conflicts. Subsequent revisions to the ***Diagnostic and Statistical Manual of Mental Disorders*** (*DSM*), the handbook used by medical professionals in diagnosing mental disorders, introduced and refined a new classification that considered recent discoveries about the biochemical and post-traumatic origins of some types of anxiety. The present definitions are based on the external and reported symptom patterns of the disorders rather than on theories about their origins.

Demographics

Anxiety disorders vary widely in their frequency of occurrence in the general population, age of onset, family patterns, and gender distribution. **Stress** and anxiety disorders caused by medical conditions or **substance**

abuse are less age- and gender-specific. Whereas **obsessive-compulsive disorder** (OCD) affects males and females equally, **generalized anxiety disorder** (GAD), **panic disorder**, and **specific phobias** all affect women more frequently than men. GAD and panic disorders are more likely to develop in young adults, whereas phobias and OCD often begin in childhood.

Description

Stimulated by real or imagined dangers, anxiety afflicts people of all ages and social backgrounds. When the anxiety results from irrational fears, it can disrupt or disable normal life. Some researchers believe anxiety is synonymous with fear, occurring in varying degrees and in situations in which people feel threatened by some danger. Others describe anxiety as an unpleasant emotion caused by unidentifiable dangers or dangers that, in reality, pose no threat. Unlike fear, which is caused by realistic, known dangers, anxiety can be more difficult to identify and to alleviate.

Rather than attempting to formulate a strict definition of anxiety, many psychologists simply make the distinction between normal anxiety and neurotic anxiety or anxiety disorders. Normal (sometimes called objective) anxiety occurs when people react appropriately to the situation causing the anxiety. For example, many people experience stage fright—the fear of speaking in front of large groups—or feel anxious on the first day at a new job. There is little, if any, real danger posed by either situation, yet each can stimulate intense anxiety that can affect or derail a person's desires or obligations. Despite these feelings, most people carry on and eventually adapt. In contrast, anxiety that is characteristic of anxiety disorders is disproportionately intense, and the anxious feelings interfere with a person's ability to carry out normal or desired activities.

Anxiety disorders are the most common form of mental disturbance in the United States. According to the Anxiety Disorders Association of America, as many as 40 million American adults are affected by anxiety disorders. These disorders can interfere with work, schooling, and family life. They also contribute to the high rates of alcohol and substance abuse among Americans. Anxiety disorders are an additional problem for health professionals because the physical symptoms of anxiety frequently bring people to primary care doctors or emergency rooms.

The fourth edition of the *DSM* (*DSM-IV-TR*) defines 12 types of anxiety disorders in the adult population. They can be grouped under the following headings:

- Panic disorders with or without **agoraphobia**. The chief characteristic of panic disorder is the occurrence of panic attacks coupled with fear of their recurrence. In clinical settings, agoraphobia is usually not a disorder by itself but is typically associated with some form of panic disorder. Patients with agoraphobia are afraid of places or situations in which they might have a panic attack and be unable to leave or to find help. Panic disorder affects approximately 2.7% of adults.
- Specific phobias. A phobia is an intense irrational fear of a specific object or situation that compels the individual to avoid it. Some phobias concern activities or objects that involve some risk (for example, flying or driving), but many are focused on harmless animals or other objects.
- Social phobia. Social phobia involves a fear of being humiliated, judged, or scrutinized. It manifests itself as a fear of performing certain functions in the presence of others, such as public speaking or using public lavatories.
- Obsessive-compulsive disorder (OCD). This disorder is marked by unwanted, intrusive, persistent thoughts or repetitive behaviors that reflect the patient's anxiety or attempts to control it. It affects about 1% of the population. About 6% of individuals who have OCD also have panic disorders.
- Stress disorders. These include **post-traumatic stress disorder** (PTSD) and **acute stress disorder**. Stress disorders are symptomatic reactions to traumatic events in the patient's life.
- Generalized anxiety disorder (GAD). GAD is the most commonly diagnosed anxiety disorder and occurs most frequently in young adults.
- Anxiety disorders due to known physiological causes. These include general medical conditions or substance abuse.
- Anxiety disorder not otherwise specified. This last category is not a separate type of disorder but is included to cover symptoms that do not meet the specific *DSM-IV* criteria for other anxiety disorders.

All *DSM* anxiety disorder diagnoses include a criterion of severity. The anxiety must be severe enough to interfere significantly with the patient's occupational or educational functioning, social activities or close relationships, and other customary activities.

Anxiety disorders in children and adolescents

DSM-IV defines one anxiety disorder as specific to children: **separation anxiety disorder**. This disorder is defined as anxiety regarding separation from home or family that is excessive or inappropriate for the child's age. In some children, separation anxiety takes the form of school avoidance.

Children and adolescents can also be diagnosed with panic disorder, phobias, generalized anxiety disorder, and the post-traumatic stress syndromes.

DSM-5

The members of the Anxiety, Obsessive-Compulsive Spectrum, Posttraumatic, and Dissociative Disorders Work Group, who are working on the latest revision to the *DSM* (*DSM-5*, 2013) have considered several changes to the diagnostic category of anxiety disorders. Potential changes include:

- making agoraphobia a separate and codable diagnosis rather than placing it within the context of panic disorder
- providing criteria for the assessment of panic attacks
- reclassifying OCD and the stress disorders (PTSD and acute stress disorder) as obsessive-compulsive and trauma- and stressor-related disorders, respectively

Causes and symptoms

The causes of anxiety include a variety of individual and general social factors and may produce physical, cognitive, emotional, or behavioral symptoms. The patients' ethnic or cultural backgrounds may influence their vulnerability to certain forms of anxiety. **Genetic factors** that lead to biochemical abnormalities may also play a role.

Anxiety in children may be caused by having experienced abuse, as well as by the factors that cause anxiety in adults.

Diagnosis

The diagnoses of anxiety disorders are complicated by the variety of causes of anxiety and the range of disorders that may include anxiety as a symptom. Before determining the specific course of treatment, the medical professional performs a complete evaluation of the patient. Symptoms are carefully analyzed as to their cause(s). Other conditions outside the realm of anxiety disorders may be secondary or primary factors in the **diagnosis**. Further, many patients with anxiety disorders have features or symptoms of more than one disorder. Patients whose anxiety is accounted for by another mental disorder, such as **schizophrenia** or major **depression**, are not diagnosed with an anxiety disorder.

Examination

A doctor examining an anxious patient usually begins by ruling out diseases that are known to cause anxiety and then proceeds to take the patient's medication history to exclude side effects of prescription drugs. Typically, doctors ask about caffeine consumption to see if the patient's dietary habits are a factor. The patient's work and family situations will also be discussed. Often, primary care physicians exhaust resources looking for medical causes for general patient complaints, which may indicate a physical illness. The Anxiety Disorders Association of American has published guidelines to aid physicians in diagnosing and managing generalized anxiety disorder.

Tests

There are no laboratory tests that can diagnose anxiety, although the doctor may order some specific tests to rule out other diseases and conditions, such as laboratory tests for blood sugar and thyroid function. Although there is no psychiatric test that can provide definite diagnoses of anxiety disorders, there are several short-answer interviews or symptom inventories that doctors can use to evaluate the intensity of a patient's anxiety and some of its associated features. These measures include the **Hamilton Anxiety Scale** and the Anxiety Disorders Interview Schedule (ADIS).

Treatment

Generally, anxiety disorders are treated with **psychotherapy**, medication, or both. The specific treatment process is determined based on the specific problem, along with the preference of the individual.

Traditional

Before treatment is begun, the patient should inform the medical professional of any medicines and other treatments being administered currently or in the past. For relatively mild anxiety disorders, psychotherapy alone may be sufficient. In general, doctors prefer to use a combination of medications and psychotherapy with more severely anxious patients. Most patients respond better to a combination of treatment methods than to either medications or psychotherapy alone.

Drugs

Medications are prescribed by medical professionals, usually psychiatrists, who sometimes provide psychotherapy services, both individually or as a member of a team (often consisting of counselors, **social workers**, and psychologists). The medications used for anxiety disorders generally include numerous types of **antidepressants**, **antianxiety drugs**, and beta blockers. Because of the variety of medications and treatment approaches available to treat anxiety disorders, the doctor cannot predict in advance which combination will be most helpful to a specific patient. In many cases, the doctor will need to try a new medication or treatment

Antianxiety medications[1]

Generic name	Trade name	FDA approved age
alprazolam	Xanax	18+
buspirone	BuSpar	18+
chlordiazepoxide	Librium	18+
clonazepam	Klonopin	18+
clorazepate	Tranxene	18+
diazepam	Valium	18+
lorazepam	Ativan	18+
oxazepam	(generic only)	18+

[1]All of these antianxiety medications are benzodiazepines, except buspirone.

SOURCE: National Institute of Mental Health.

"Alphabetical List of Medications," available online at: http://www.nimh.nih.gov/health/publications/mental-health-medications/alphabetical-list-of-medications.shtml. *(Table by PreMediaGlobal. © 2012 Cengage Learning.)*

over a six- to eight-week period in order to assess its effectiveness. Trying a few different treatment options does not necessarily mean that the patient cannot be helped or that the doctor is incompetent. In addition, medicines used during these periods help to control the problem while psychotherapy is being initiated.

ANTIDEPRESSANTS. Antidepressants are very effective for anxiety disorders. Under normal circumstances, antidepressants take from four to six weeks to become fully effective and symptoms begin to disappear. Some of the widely used antidepressants for anxiety disorders are:

- **Selective serotonin reuptake inhibitors** (SSRIs): These relatively new types of antidepressants work by changing the concentration of serotonin, a neurotransmitter, within the brain. SSRIs are commonly started at low doses, with higher doses coming at regular intervals until a proper plateau has been reached. These have fewer side effects than older antidepressants used for anxiety disorders. Side effects include nausea, nervousness, and sexual dysfunction, which usually fade with time. Types of frequently used SSRIs include citalopram (Celexa), escitalopram (Lexapro), fluoxetine (Prozac), paroxetine (Paxil), and sertraline (Zoloft).
- Tricyclics: These older antidepressants are as effective as SSRIs for anxiety disorders, except for obsessive-compulsive disorder (OCD). Dosages usually start small and gradually increase as needed. Symptoms include dizziness, dry mouth, drowsiness, and weight gain. Commonly used tricyclics are imipramine (Tofranil) and clomipramine (Anafranil).
- **Monoamine oxidase inhibitors** (MAOIs): The oldest type of antidepressants used for anxiety disorders, MAOIs have a number of side effects with a variety of foods and beverages that contain tyramine and numerous other types of medications (such as certain pain relievers, cold and allergy medications, and others). MAOIs can also interact with SSRIs and cause serious symptoms, including seizures and blood pressure and heart irregularities. Patients ought to seek further information from the attending physician with regards to these potential adverse interactions. The most frequently used MAOIs are isocarboxazid (Marplan), phenelzine (Nardil), and tranylcypromine (Parnate).

ANTIANXIETY DRUGS. **Benzodiazepines** are effective drugs that are used to counter anxiety. They may cause drowsiness in some patients. Benzodiazepines can be habit forming and are also needed in higher doses in order to be effective. For these two reasons, benzodiazepines are usually only used for short periods. Because of their habit-forming nature, they must be slowly reduced in amount before patients completely stop taking them. **Clonazepam** (Klonopin), **lorazepam** (Ativan), and **alprazolam** (Xanax) are types of benzodiazepines often prescribed for specific anxiety disorders. **Buspirone** (Buspar), within the drug group of azapirones, is a newer type of antianxiety drug that is used to treat generalized anxiety disorder (GAD).

BETA BLOCKERS. **Beta blockers**, which are also frequently used to treat physiological problems of the heart, are sometimes used to treat anxiety disorders. Physicians often use beta blockers when people have social phobias, such as fear of talking in front of an audience, in order to reduce anxiety in such situations. **Propranolol** (Inderal) is a commonly used beta blocker.

Psychotherapy

Psychotherapy can be effective at treating anxiety disorders when administered through a well-trained and experienced mental health professional. In addition, individuals with the problem must be actively engaged in their treatment; otherwise such therapy is unlikely to work.

Psychiatrists, **psychologists**, social workers, and counselors use cognitive-behavioral therapy (CBT) to help patients learn what is causing their specific problems and how to react to the symptoms when they occur. Each patient is considered a unique case and must be treated on an individualized basis for best results. For instance, a person with a **social phobia** is shown that heart attack–like symptoms are the result of the person's fear of speaking in front of people. The individual is provided with a proactive means to minimize fears when in social situations that provoke such problems. Likewise, people with other types of anxiety disorders are helped to

KEY TERMS

Agoraphobia—Abnormal anxiety regarding public places or situations from which the patient may wish to flee or in which he or she would be helpless in the event of a panic attack.

Compulsion—A repetitive or ritualistic behavior that a person performs to reduce anxiety. Compulsions often develop as a way of controlling or undoing obsessive thoughts.

Obsession—A repetitive or persistent thought, idea, or impulse that is perceived as inappropriate and distressing.

Panic attack—A time-limited period of intense fear accompanied by physical and cognitive symptoms. It may be unexpected or triggered by specific internal or external cues.

confront their fears and to desensitize themselves to anxiety-provoking situations.

Treatment in children and adolescents

A combination of CBT and medication has been found to be the most successful form of treatment for children aged 7–17. However, antidepressants should be used with caution in children and adolescents; some drugs are not recommended for children younger than 18, and children and adults up to age 24 are at increased risk of developing suicidal thoughts and behavior. **SSRIs** are prescribed more in children than other medications, including tricyclic antidepressants. Parents should discuss all treatment options with their child's physician and watch for signs of harmful behavior or worsening depression.

Alternative

Alternative treatments for anxiety cover a variety of approaches. **Meditation** and mindfulness training are thought to be beneficial to patients with phobias and panic disorder. Hydrotherapy is useful to some anxious patients because it promotes general relaxation of the nervous system. **Yoga**, aikido, tai chi, and **dance therapy** help patients work with the physical, as well as the emotional, tensions that either promote anxiety or are created by the anxiety.

Homeopathy and traditional Chinese medicine approach anxiety as a symptom of a systemic disorder. Homeopathic practitioners select a remedy based on other associated symptoms and the patient's general constitution. Chinese medicine regards anxiety as a blockage of *qi*, or vital force, inside the patient's body that is most likely to affect the lung and large intestine meridian flow. The practitioner of Chinese medicine chooses **acupuncture** point locations and/or herbal therapy to move the *qi* and rebalance the entire system in relation to the lung and large intestine.

QUESTIONS TO ASK YOUR DOCTOR

- Do I have an anxiety disorder?
- What treatment plan is best for me?
- What medications should I use?
- Do I need counseling?

Getting help

Although anxiety disorders are not always easy to diagnose, there are several reasons why it is important for patients with severe anxiety symptoms to get help. Anxiety does not always go away by itself and can progress to panic attacks, phobias, and episodes of depression. Untreated anxiety disorders may eventually lead to a diagnosis of major depression or interfere with the patient's education or ability to keep a job. In addition, many anxious patients develop addictions to drugs or alcohol when they try to "self-medicate" their symptoms. Moreover, since children learn ways of coping with anxiety from their parents, adults who get help for anxiety disorders are in a better position to help their families cope with factors that lead to anxiety than those who remain untreated. With appropriate treatment by medical professionals, most people with anxiety disorders can return to a normal daily life.

Prognosis

The prognosis for recovery depends on the specific disorder, the severity of the patient's symptoms, the specific causes of the anxiety, and the patient's degree of control over these causes.

Prevention

Anxiety is an unavoidable feature of human existence. However, humans have some power over their reactions to anxiety-provoking events and situations. Cognitive therapy and meditation or mindfulness training appear to be beneficial in helping people lower their long-term anxiety levels.

Resources

BOOKS

American Psychiatric Association. *Diagnostic and Statistical Manual of Mental Disorders.* 4th edition, text revised. Washington, DC: American Psychiatric Association, 2000.

Challem, Jack, and Melvyn Werbach. *The Food-Mood Solution: All-Natural Ways to Banish Anxiety, Depression, Anger, Stress, Overeating, and Alcohol and Drug Problems—and Feel Good Again.* Hoboken, NJ: Wiley, 2008.

Kase, Larina, and Deborah Roth Ledley. *Anxiety Disorders.* Hoboken, NJ: John Wiley and Sons, 2007.

Otto, Michael, and Stefan Hofmann, eds. *Avoiding Treatment Failures in the Anxiety Disorders (Series in Anxiety and Related Disorders).* New York: Springer, 2009.

National Institute of Mental Health. *Anxiety Disorders.* NIH Publication No. 06-3879. Bethesda, MD: NIMH, 2006.

Pelletier, Kenneth R. "Part II: CAM Therapies for Specific Conditions: Anxiety." In *The Best Alternative Medicine.* New York: Simon & Schuster, 2007.

PERIODICALS

Hofmann, Stefan, and Jasper A. J. Smits. "Cognitive-Behavioral Therapy for Adult Anxiety Disorders: A Meta-Analysis of Randomized Placebo-Controlled Trials." *Journal of Clinical Psychiatry* 69, no. 4 (April 2008): 621–32. http://www.ncbi.nlm.nih.gov/pmc/articles/PMC2409267 (accessed September 8, 2011).

WEBSITES

"Anxiety." MedlinePlus. http://www.nlm.nih.gov/medlineplus/anxiety.html (accessed September 8, 2011).

"Anxiety Disorders." American Psychiatric Association. http://www.dsm5.org/ProposedRevision/Pages/AnxietyDisorders.aspx (accessed September 8, 2011).

"PTSD: Stress and Resilience." National Institute of Mental Health. February 25, 2010. http://www.nimh.nih.gov/media/video/tuma-short-ptsd.shtml (accessed September 8, 2011).

"Treatment of Anxiety Disorders." National Institute of Mental Health. Last reviewed July 9, 2009. http://www.nimh.nih.gov/health/publications/anxiety-disorders/treatment-of-anxiety-disorders.shtml (accessed September 8, 2011).

Xiong, Glen L. "Hypochondriasis." Medscape Reference. Updated August 3, 2011. http://emedicine.medscape.com/article/290955-overview (accessed September 8, 2011).

Yates, William R. "Anxiety Disorders." Medscape Reference. Updated August 25, 2011. http://emedicine.medscape.com/article/286227-overview (accessed September 8, 2011).

ORGANIZATIONS

American Psychiatric Association, 1000 Wilson Blvd., Ste. 1825, Arlington, VA, 22209-3901, (703) 907-7300, apa@psych.org, http://www.psych.org.

American Psychological Association, 750 1st St., NE, Washington, DC, 20002-4242, (202) 336-5500; TDD/TTY: (202) 336-6123, (800) 374-2721, http://www.apa.org.

Anxiety Disorders Association of America, 8730 Georgia Ave., Silver Spring, MD, 20910, (240) 485-1001, Fax: (240) 485-1035, http://www.adaa.org.

Mental Health America, 2000 N. Beauregard St., 6th Fl., Alexandria, VA, 22311, (703) 684-7722, (800) 969-6642, Fax: (703) 684-5968, http://www1.nmha.org.

National Alliance on Mental Illness, 2107 Wilson Blvd., Ste. 300, Arlington, VA, 22201-3042, Fax: (703) 524-9094, (800) 950-6264, http://www.nami.org.

National Institute of Mental Health, 6001 Executive Blvd., Rm. 8184, MSC 9663, Bethesda, MD, 20892-9663, (301) 433-4513; TTY: (301) 443-8431, Fax: (301) 443-4279, (866) 615-6464; TTY: (866) 415-8051, nimhinfo@nih.gov, http://www.nimh.nih.gov.

Rebecca J. Frey, PhD
Teresa G. Odle
Laura Jean Cataldo, RN, EdD
William A. Atkins, BB, BS, MBA

Anxiety reduction techniques

Definition

Anxiety reduction techniques are learned skills that can be used by individuals to help overcome anxiety and its associated mental and physical symptoms, including tension, **stress**, worry, and nervousness. These techniques include relaxation, visualization and imagery, diaphragmatic breathing, stress inoculation, **meditation**, and **cognitive-behavioral therapy**.

Relaxation or progressive relaxation

This anxiety reduction technique is based on the premise that anxiety and stress are associated with muscle tension. When one achieves deep muscle relaxation, muscle tension is reduced, and this relaxed state is incompatible with anxiety.

Visualization and imagery

This anxiety reduction technique aids individuals in making a mental image of what they want to accomplish. For example, an individual might wish to release worries or concerns or create a relaxing image to escape momentarily from a stressful event.

Diaphragmatic breathing

This technique involves breathing sufficient amounts of air to help a person's blood fill with oxygen and be purified properly. In this technique, the individual breathes deeply from the diaphragm, which is located low in the chest near the abdomen. **Yoga** class instruction often includes teaching participants how to use breathing to reduce anxiety.

Stress inoculation

Stress inoculation training is a type of therapy that teaches clients to cope with anxiety and stressful situations by learning better functional patterns of self-talk. Self-talk, or what people tell themselves about stressful situations, can be habitual. For example, a person may take an ordinary event and automatically magnify its importance. Practices that counter self-talk help individuals to deal more effectively with anxiety and other stressful situations and to react to such problems in more positive ways.

Meditation

In this anxiety reduction technique, an individual is trained to focus his or her attention on one thing at a time. Meditation techniques focus on various physical sensations or mental images to neutralize troubling emotional and mental patterns and control them.

Cognitive-behavioral therapy

Cognitive-behavioral therapy (CBT) suggests various exercises that help individuals identify thoughts and beliefs that trigger anxiety. Once these thought patterns are identified, the individual learns techniques to help change negative thought patterns into healthier ones.

Purpose

The goal of learning and implementing anxiety reduction techniques is to reduce the intensity of anxiety. These techniques are also helpful in teaching people how to relax and manage stress. Many of the techniques are used in combination with each other. For example, a person may be taught diaphragmatic breathing while also engaging in relaxation techniques, a visualization and imagery exercise, or meditation.

Relaxation or progressive relaxation

Relaxation has been used to help women during childbirth and others dealing with chronic pain. Relaxation has also been used to treat muscle tension, muscle spasms, and neck and back pain and to decrease perspiration and respiratory rates. In addition, relaxation can help with **fatigue**, **depression**, **insomnia**, irritable bowel syndrome, high blood pressure, mild phobias, and **stuttering**.

Visualization and imagery

Visualization and imagery techniques have been helpful in treating general or specific anxiety, headaches, and muscle tension and spasms. They are also useful in reducing or eliminating pain and in the recovery from illnesses and injuries. Visualization and imagery techniques have also been used by athletes who want to achieve peak performance.

Diaphragmatic breathing

Diaphragmatic breathing has been found to help people reduce anxiety, depression, irritability, muscle tension, circulation, and fatigue.

Stress inoculation

Stress inoculation has been helpful in reducing interpersonal and general anxiety. For example, these techniques may be used when a person has an upcoming job interview, speech, or test. Stress inoculation has also been used to treat phobias, fear of heights, and chronic anger problems.

Meditation

Meditation has been used to treat and prevent high blood pressure, heart disease, **stroke**, migraine headaches, immunization diseases, obsessive thinking, attention problems, anxiety, depression, and anger control problems.

Cognitive-behavioral therapy

Cognitive-behavioral therapy (CBT) focuses on thought processes and belief systems. The overall goal of the approach is to identify problematic beliefs and thought patterns, which may be irrational or unrealistic, and replace them with more rational and realistic views.

Description

Anxiety reduction techniques are often practiced and demonstrated in therapy sessions with a trained professional. In addition, the person learning the techniques practices them regularly between therapy sessions.

Relaxation or progressive relaxation

In progressive relaxation, individuals are instructed to tighten and then relax various muscles. They either lie down or sit in a chair with their head supported. Each muscle group, such as face muscles, arm muscles, or leg muscles, is tensed for 5 to 7 seconds and then relaxed for 20 to 30 seconds. This action helps individuals recognize tense and relaxed muscles. This entire procedure is repeated one to five times and usually starts with the face muscles and moves to the foot muscles. When relaxation is used with chronic pain and childbirth, the techniques focus the person's attention on breathing and relaxing muscles as a distraction from the pain.

For mastery, relaxation techniques are typically practiced every day for one to two weeks. A person may engage in these techniques anywhere from 15 minutes to one hour per session. Sometimes, individuals record and replay instructions on tightening and relaxing various muscle groups until they become familiar with the muscle groups and establish a comfortable routine.

Visualization and imagery

The basic premise of visualization and imagery is that thoughts become reality. For example, if individuals think anxious thoughts, then they will become tense. The assumption of visualization and imagery is that people can use their imagination to assist them in feeling a certain way or performing a certain desired action. Programmed, receptive, and guided visualization are the basic types.

In programmed visualization, the person creates a vivid image, including sight, taste, sound, and smell. The individual then imagines a goal he or she wants to attain or some type of healing that is desired. In the visualization, the goal is achieved or the healing occurs.

An idea underlying both receptive visualization and guided visualization is that the person is seeking an answer to a life question or resolution to an issue, and the answer or resolution is within the person but is buried or inaccessible because of fear, doubt, or anxiety. These techniques are similar to dream interpretation and free association techniques used in **psychoanalysis** or psychodynamic therapy. For example, an individual may wonder whether he or she should remain in a current job. A proponent of these techniques would maintain that below the level of conscious thought, the person knows what he or she really wants to do but is not to listening to his or her desires or to act—the message is subconsciously being blocked. The goal of these techniques is to enable the person to relax and focus enough to receive that message, so that he or she can do what needs to be done.

In receptive visualization, the individual creates a peaceful mental scene. After the image is formed, the person asks a question and waits for the answer. To continue the job scenario, the person might imagine a beach and he ask the question, "Should I leave my job?" As the person continues to relax and remain in the scene, he or she may "hear" an answer blowing in the breeze or "see" a boat sailing away, which may be symbolic of the wish to leave a job.

In guided visualization, the person creates a vivid image, as in programmed visualization, but omits some important elements. The person then waits for the subconscious to supply the missing parts. For example, a computer programmer may wonder if he or she should stay in a present job or return to school for an advanced degree. When engaging in guided visualization, the person may visualize a cubicle at work, the pictures on the desk, the feel of the desk chair, and the sounds of people working beyond the cubicle, but he or she will omit an element from the scene. In this case, the element would be the computer. The person will then wait to see what the subconscious uses to replace the computer. Within the visualization, the computer may be replaced by books, which may represent a desire to return to school.

Visualization and imagery exercises work best when a person is relaxed. Exercises are typically practiced two to three times a day for 10 to 20 minutes at a time. How quickly an individual sees results can vary. Many people report immediate symptom relief. However, the personal goals a person sets, the power of his or her imagination, and the willingness to practice can all influence how rapidly benefits are obtained. Some people find it helpful to record and replay detailed descriptions of what they want to visualize or imagine.

Diaphragmatic breathing

Diaphragmatic breathing can be learned in minutes; however, the benefits may not be recognized until after

KEY TERMS

Depression—A psychiatric disorder that causes sleeplessness, lack of energy, poor concentration, hopelessness, and other negative feelings that may lead to thoughts of suicide.

Obsessive thinking—Thoughts that overcome a person's thought processes; a compulsive way of thinking in which the same thought repeats, preventing other thoughts.

Phobia—An irrational or illogical fear or hatred of something, such as fear of heights, confined spaces, or snakes.

Yoga—A physical, mental, and meditative discipline and practice that began in India.

Zen meditation—A discipline that teaches the mind to relax, which involves sitting in prescribed positions in order to calm the body and mind, with the goal to slow heart rate and breathing to reach a reflective meditative state.

ROLLO MAY (1909–1994)

Rollo May was the second of six children and the eldest son of Earl Tuttle, a field secretary at the Young Men's Christian Association, and Matie Boughton May, a homemaker. May grew up in Michigan in a family that had "more than its share of troubles." He later described his parents as "austere disciplinarians and anti-intellectuals" and portrayed their relationship as "discordant" and the precursor for his interest in psychology and counseling. His oldest sister was diagnosed as psychotic and spent time in mental hospitals.

His lectures on counseling and personality adjustment were published as his first book, *The Art of Counseling: How to Gain and Give Mental Health* (1939), which was well regarded. May studied psychology at Columbia University in New York City. While working on his dissertation in 1942 and still counseling, May was diagnosed with tuberculosis. This confrontation with his own mortality shaped his views on existentialism. While recuperating in upstate New York for almost two years, May wrote *The Meaning of Anxiety* (1950), which he considered the "watershed" event of his career. He stressed that anxiety can be a positive, motivating force for social and personal development and that people can use their inner resources for life choices. In 1953, May published *Man's Search for Himself*, a popular and critical success that established May as a leader of existentialist thinking in the United States.

By the early 1960s, May had become a leader in challenging behaviorism and psychoanalysis. He diverted from biological determinism and stressed by contrast the unique conscious elements in individual psychology. After moving to California in 1975, he resumed his private practice as a therapist. He also served in various capacities at the Saybrook Institute of the California School of Professional Psychology. More books and ideas followed: *Power and Innocence: A Search for the Sources of Violence* (1972), *The Courage to Create* (1975), *My Quest for Beauty* (1985), and *The Cry for Myth* (1991). May wrote more than fifteen books, many of which are directly related to his own experience and development. He was the recipient of the American Psychological Association's Gold Medal for his distinguished career in psychology, Phi Beta Kappa's Ralph Waldo Emerson Award, and the Whole Life Humanitarian Award.

several months of regular practice. When breathing from the diaphragm, clients are often told to lie down on a rug or blanket with their legs slightly apart, arms to the sides not touching the body, and eyes closed. Attention is brought to the breathing by placing one hand on the chest and the other hand on the abdomen area. The client is then instructed to breathe in through the nose and exhale out the mouth. Each time the client breathes in, he or she should try to breathe deeper. This should be practiced for a minimum of five minutes once or twice a day. Over a few weeks of practice, the time period should be increased to 20 minutes, and the activity can be performed while lying down, sitting, or standing.

Stress inoculation

As people go about their daily activities, they often talk to themselves. Stress inoculation uses this self-talk in helping clients decrease their anxiety and stress. Stress inoculation therapy works to turn the client's own thought patterns into a "vaccine" against stress-induced anxiety. The first step is to develop a list of stressful situations and arrange them from least to most stressful. Once anxiety-producing situations are identified, the client is taught to curb the anxiety-provoking thoughts and replace them with more positive coping thoughts. Once these new thoughts are learned, they can be tried out in real situations. The time it takes to replace habitual thoughts with new ones varies depending on the client's amount of practice and commitment to make this change.

Meditation

There are various forms of meditation. Depending on the type used, the individual focuses his or her attention in slightly different ways. For example, Zen meditation focuses on breathing, whereas in transcendental meditation, the person makes a sound or repeats a mantra selected to keep all other images and problems from intruding on his or her thoughts. With practice, a person can reach a meditative state and obtain its benefits within a few minutes.

Benefits

Anxiety reduction techniques are coping skills, designed to help people increase their calm and confidence. Used correctly, these skills help people maximize their

QUESTIONS TO ASK YOUR DOCTOR

- Where can I find more information on anxiety reduction techniques?
- What is the best type of anxiety reduction technique for my situation?
- What local organizations and individuals provide assistance on such techniques?
- Should I take medication along with using one or more of these techniques?

abilities to meet and move through the challenges of both everyday living and stress-provoking events. Reactive and self-defeating responses to everyday stressors or crises reduce or eliminate individuals' effective and positive responses. With these techniques, people can neutralize these negative responses in order to address constructively the situations that make them anxious.

Aftercare

After a person has learned and practiced anxiety reduction techniques, he or she may need additional instruction from a trained professional. Having a trained professional review these techniques can help reinforce what the person has already learned and been practicing. Furthermore, the person may identify aspects of the techniques that he or she is doing incorrectly, areas that need more attention or focus, and alternative methods of engaging in the techniques.

Risks

There are minimal risks associated with these techniques, but some physical problems may occur. For example, precautions should be taken when doing progressive relaxation and tensing the neck and back. In some cases, excessive tightening can cause muscle or spinal damage. Additionally, tightening various muscle groups, such as the toes or feet, can cause cramps. If physical problems occur, such as difficulty taking deep breaths, unusual muscle pain, or an increased level of anxiety, the individual should stop the activity and may want to consult a physician.

Results

In general, after engaging in anxiety reduction techniques, people report an increased sense of well-being and relaxation. People have a greater sense of self-control and greater confidence in being able to cope with stressful events. They are less fearful and are less likely to avoid stressful situations.

Progressive relaxation can reduce muscle tension. Engaging in relaxation may help to improve a person's energy level; it may reduce depression and anxiety as it increases the ability to retrieve information from memory.

With meditation, people often discover that they have some control over the thoughts that rise in their minds. Many begin to recognize dysfunctional patterns of thought and perceptions that have influenced their lives. Additionally, many people report a greater ability to manage their emotions and maintain stability. When a person meditates, he or she often suppresses the activity of the sympathetic nervous system, the part of the nervous system that activates the body for emergencies. Meditation also lowers a person's metabolism, heart, and breathing rates. Additionally, meditation decreases the chemicals in the body often associated with stress, such as **adrenaline**.

Abnormal results

Once a person begins to implement these anxiety reduction techniques effectively, he or she may discover old or hidden psychological pain. The individual may feel angry, frightened, or depressed, and it may be beneficial for him or her to talk to a friend, mental health professional, or meditation teacher.

Some people have difficulty with various aspects of the different techniques. For example, an individual may feel restless when first learning how to meditate or may feel as though a thousand thoughts are running through his or her mind. However, with practice and assistance from a trained professional, these difficulties will subside. People who feel frustrated or discouraged may simply need to find ways to make the practice of these techniques more comfortable. As is the case with many other skills, effectively reducing anxiety with these techniques requires patience and practice. If an individual does not practice these techniques regularly, the benefits will probably not be obtained.

Resources

BOOKS

Bourne, Edmund J. *The Anxiety and Phobia Workbook,* 5th ed. Oakland, CA: New Harbinger Publications, 2011.

Payne, Rosemary A., and Marie Donaghy. *Payne's Handbook of Relaxation Techniques: A Practical Handbook for the Health Care Professional.* Edinburgh: Churchill Livingstone/Elsevier, 2010.

Romas, John A., and Manoj Sharma. *Practical Stress Management: A Comprehensive Workbook for Managing Change and Promoting Health,* 5th ed. San Francisco: Pearson Benjamin Cummings, 2010.

Seaward, Brian Luke. *Essentials of Managing Stress.* Sudbury, MA: Jones and Bartlett, 2011.

PERIODICALS

Arch, Joanna J., and Michelle G. Craske. "Mechanisms of Mindfulness: Emotion Regulation Following a Focused Breathing Induction." *Behaviour Research and Therapy* 44, no. 12 (December 2006): 1849–58.

Bornas, Xavier, et al. "Changes in Heart Rate Variability of Flight Phobics During a Paced Breathing Task and Exposure to Fearful Stimuli." *International Journal of Clinical and Health Psychology* 6, no. 3 (September 2006): 549–63.

Hunt, Melissa, et al. "The Role of Imagery in the Maintenance and Treatment of Snake Fear." *Journal of Behavior Therapy and Experimental Psychiatry* 37, no. 4 (December 2006): 283–98.

Lundgren, Jesper, Sven G. Carlsson, and Ulf Berggren. "Relaxation Versus Cognitive Therapies for Dental Fear—A Psychophysiological Approach." *Health Psychology* 25, no. 3 (May 2006): 267–73.

Meuret, Alicia E., Thomas Ritz, Frank H. Wilhelm, and Walton T. Roth. "Voluntary Hyperventilation in the Treatment of Panic Disorder—Functions of Hyperventilation, Their Implications for Breathing Training, and Recommendations for Standardization." *Clinical Psychology Review* 25, no. 3 (May 2005): 285–306.

Rausch, Sarah M., Sandra E. Gramling, and Stephen M. Auerbach. "Effects of a Single Session of Large-Group Meditation and Progressive Muscle Relaxation Training on Stress Reduction, Reactivity, and Recovery." *International Journal of Stress Management* 13, no. 3 (August 2006): 273–90.

Roth, Walton T. "Physiological Markers for Anxiety: Panic Disorder and Phobias." *International Journal of Psychophysiology* 58, no. 2–3 (November–December 2005): 190–98.

WEBSITES

Ajmera, Ripa. "Different Anxiety Reduction Techniques." LiveStrong.com. February 26, 2010. http://www.livestrong.com/article/87730-different-anxiety-reduction-techniques (accessed August 13, 2011).

ORGANIZATIONS

American Psychiatric Association, 1000 Wilson Blvd., Ste. 1825, Arlington, VA, 22209-3901, (703) 907-7300, (888) 35-PSYCH (357-7924), apa@psych.org, http://www.psych.org.

American Psychological Association, 750 1st St. NE, Washington, DC, 20002, (202) 336-5500, (800) 374-2721; TDD/TTY: (202) 336-6123, http://www.apa.org.

Anxiety Disorders Association of America, 8730 Georgia Ave., Silver Spring, MD, 20910, (240) 485-1001, http://www.adaa.org.

National Institute of Mental Health, 6001 Executive Blvd., Rm. 8184, Bethesda, MD, 20892-9663, (301) 443-4513, (866) 615-6464, Fax: (301) 443-4279, nimhinfo@nih.gov, http://www.nimh.nih.gov.

Keith Beard, PsyD
Ruth A. Wienclaw, PhD
William Atkins

APA *see* **American Psychiatric Association; American Psychological Association**

Apathy

Definition

Apathy can be defined as an absence or suppression of emotion, feeling, concern or passion. Apathy is an indifference to things generally found to be exciting or moving.

Description

A strong connection exists between apathy and mental disorders. Apathy is one of the hallmark symptoms of **schizophrenia**. Many people with schizophrenia express little interest in the events surrounding them. Apathy can also occur in **depression** and depressive disorders. For example, people who are depressed and have **major depressive disorder** or **dysthymic disorder** often feel numb to events occurring around them, and do not derive pleasure from experiences that they once found enjoyable.

All people may experience periods of apathy. Disappointment and dejection are elements of life, and apathy is a normal way for humans to cope with such stresses—to be able to "shrug off" disappointments enables people to move forward and try other activities and achieve new goals. When the stresses pass, the apparent apathy also disappears. A period of apathy can also be viewed as a normal and transient phase through which many people pass. Long-term apathy and detachment, however, are not normal.

Apathy syndrome is being considered for inclusion in the fifth edition of the ***Diagnostic and Statistical Manual of Mental Disorders*** (*DSM*-5, 2013). Apathy syndrome is defined as a syndrome of primary motivational loss—that is, loss of motivation not attributable to emotional distress, intellectual impairment, or diminished level of consciousness.

Treatment

Transient apathy can be overcome. Friends and professionals may be able to assist individuals to develop an interest in their surroundings. Attitude is important. Persons who desire to overcome apathy have much higher odds of succeeding than do persons lacking a positive attitude.

Other than support, no specific treatment is needed for apathy, unless other more troubling disorders are also present.

The treatment of more persistent apathy (in a depressive disorder, for example), or the apathy that is characteristic of schizophrenia, may respond to treatment for the primary disorder. For depressive disorders, a number of **antidepressants** may be effective, including tricyclic antidepressants, **monoamine oxidase inhibitors (MAOIs)**, and **selective serotonin reuptake inhibitors (SSRIs)**. The tricyclic antidepressants include **amitriptyline** (Elavil), **imipramine** (Tofranil), and **nortriptyline** (Aventyl, Pamelor). **MAOIs** include **tranylcypromine** (Parnate) and **phenelzine** (Nardil). The most commonly prescribed **SSRIs** are **fluoxetine** (Prozac), **sertraline** (Zoloft), **paroxetine** (Paxil), **fluvoxamine** (Luvox), and **citalopram** (Celexa).

SCHIZOPHRENIA. For schizophrenia, the primary goal is to treat the more prominent symptoms (**positive symptoms**) of the disorder, such as the thought disorder and hallucinations that patients experience. Atypical antipsychotics are newer medications introduced in the 1990s that have been found to be effective for the treatment of schizophrenia. These medications include **clozapine** (Clozaril), **risperidone** (Risperdal), **quetiapine** (Seroquel), **ziprasidone** (Geodon), and **olanzapine** (Zyprexa). These newer drugs are more effective in treating the **negative symptoms** of schizophrenia (such as apathy) and have fewer side effects than the older antipsychotics. Most atypical antipsychotics, however, do have weight gain as a side effect, and patients taking clozapine must have their blood monitored periodically for signs of agranulocytosis, or a drop in the number of white blood cells.

Resources

BOOKS

Gelder, Michael, Paul Harrison, and Philip Cowen. *Shorter Oxford Textbook of Psychiatry*. 5th ed. New York: Oxford University Press, 2006.

PERIODICALS

Adams, K. B. "Depressive Symptoms, Depletion, or Developmental Change? Withdrawal, Apathy, and Lack of Vigor in the Geriatric Depression Scale." *Gerontologist* 41, no. 6 (2001): 768–777.

Clarke, Diana E., et al. "Apathy and Cognitive and Functional Decline in Community-Dwelling Older Adults: Results from the Baltimore ECA Longitudinal Study." *International Psychogeriatrics* 22, no. 5 (2010): 819–29.

Kalechstein, A. D., T. F. Newton, and A. H. Leavengood. "Apathy Syndrome in Cocaine Dependence." *Psychiatry Research* 109, no. 1 (2002): 97–100.

Landes, A. M., et al. "Apathy in Alzheimer's Disease." *Journal of the American Geriatric Society* 49, no. 12 (2001): 1700–1707.

Ramirez, S. M., et al. "Relationship of Numbing to Alexithymia, Apathy, and Depression." *Psychological Reports* 88, no. 1 (2001): 189–200.

Simon, Joe J., et al. "Neural Correlates of Reward Processing in Schizophrenia—Relationship to Apathy and Depression." *Schizophrenia Research* 118, nos. 1–3 (May 2010): 154–61.

ORGANIZATIONS

American Psychiatric Association, 1000 Wilson Blvd., Ste. 1825, Arlington, VA, 22209-3901, (703) 907-7300, apa@psych.org, http://www.psych.org.

American Psychological Association, 750 1st Street NE, Washington, DC, 20002-4242, (202) 336-5500; TDD/TTY: (202) 336-6123, (800) 374-2721, http://www.apa.org.

L. Fleming Fallon, Jr., M.D., Dr.P.H.

Aprepitant

Purpose

Aprepitant (brand name Emend) is a drug used to prevent stomachaches and vomiting in persons receiving cancer treatment (chemotherapy) or who have recently taken medicines to prevent pain during surgery (anesthesia). The drug also affects substances in the part of the **brain** associated with emotions, which has led scientists to question whether aprepitant could be used to treat certain mental disorders, particularly major **depression**.

Description

Aprepitant is classified as a substance P neurokin-1 (NK-1) receptor antagonist. This means that it blocks proteins called NK-1 receptors, which sit on cells in the brain region linked to gastrointestinal problems and the body's response to **stress**, anxiety, and depression. The receptors attach or bind to a naturally occurring chemical called substance P, which is found in higher amounts in persons with depression. Blocking the NK-1 receptors causes a decrease in the normal action of substance P that would otherwise be mediated by the NK-1 receptor.

Because aprepitant affects NK-1 receptors in the brain that are associated with emotions, and because it has shown activity in several animal models of depression, scientists had theorized that aprepitant might prove to be a powerful new antidepressant. In 1998, researchers reported that more than half of patients with depression who took aprepitant had an improvement in mood. The study involved 213 people who took the drug for six weeks. The scientists also discovered that the medicine worked as well as **paroxetine** (Paxil) in reducing anxiety.

In 2001, however, a larger trial involving 700 patients with mild-to-moderate depression failed to show that aprepitant worked any better than existing antidepressant medications. Additional studies also failed. In 2003, Merck & Company, the manufacturer of aprepitant, said it would no longer pursue the drug as a treatment for depression. The decision came just a few months after aprepitant received U.S. Food and Drug Administration (FDA) approval as a preventive for chemotherapy-related stomach upset.

Some researchers still investigate aprepitant as a possible treatment for depression, but **clinical trials** have failed to show that it is more effective in treating depression than existing **antidepressants** or even a placebo. A 2010 study found that although aprepitant antagonism, or blocking of NK-1 receptors, does affect emotional processing in humans, its effects are more limited and less consistent than the effects of other antidepressants. The use of aprepitant for other conditions that involve increased NK-1 receptor activity remains under investigation.

Resources

PERIODICALS

Alvaro, G., and R. Di Fabio. "Neurokinin 1 Receptor Antagonists—Current Prospects." *Current Opinion in Drug Discovery and Development* 10, no. 5 (2007): 613–21.

Herpfer, I., and K. Lieb. "Substance P Receptor Antagonists in Psychiatry: Rationale for Development and Therapeutic Potential." *CNS Drugs* 19, no. 4 (2005): 275–93.

Keller, M., et al. "Lack of Efficacy of the Substance P (Neurokinin 1 Receptor) Antagonist Aprepitant in the Treatment of Major Depressive Disorder." *Biological Psychiatry* 59, no. 3 (2006): 216–23.

Kelli Miller Stacy
Margaret Alic, PhD

Aricept *see* **Donepezil**

Aripiprazole

Definition

Aripiprazole (Abilify) is a newer generation antipsychotic medication. It was approved by the U.S. Food & Drug Administration (FDA) in 2002 to treat **schizophrenia** symptoms. The symptoms of schizophrenia include hallucinations, **delusions**, **paranoia**, and social withdrawal. Aripiprazole is also FDA approved as a therapy for people with **bipolar disorder** who have had episodes of acute mania or mixed episodes of mania and **depression** but who have subsequently been stabilized for at least six weeks.

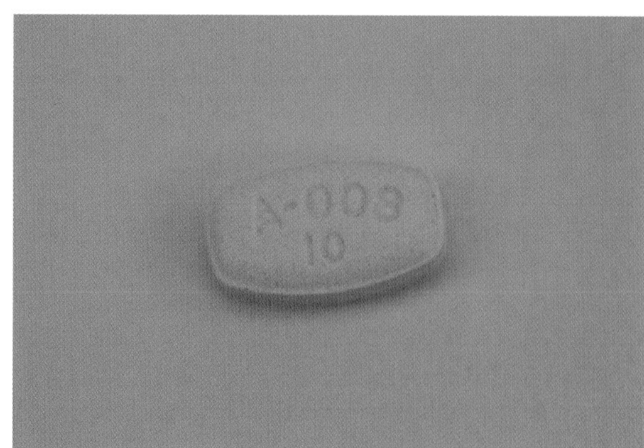

Abilify (aripiprazole), 10 mg. *(© Custom Medical Stock Photo, Inc. Reproduced by permission.)*

Purpose

Aripiprazole can be used short term to treat acute psychotic and manic states and agitation in **dementia**, as well as long term to treat chronic psychotic disorders such as schizophrenia. In the past, these conditions were typically treated with conventional antipsychotic drugs, such as phenothiazine, thioxanthene, and butyrophenone neuroleptics.

Although aripiprazole is primarily indicated for the treatment of adults, some studies suggest it also may be effective for children and adolescents with bipolar disorder. Researchers recommend a lower dose in younger patients. There is a risk of increased suicidal thoughts or actions, especially in children and adolescents taking aripiprazole and in patients with bipolar disorder.

Description

Aripiprazole is part of a class of drugs called atypical antipsychotics. Drugs in this class, which include **clozapine**, **olanzapine**, **quetiapine**, **risperidone**, and **ziprasidone**, are called "atypical" because of their relatively lower risk of certain types of adverse side effects compared to traditional antipsychotic drugs.

The exact mechanism by which aripiprazole and other atypical antipsychotic drugs work is unknown. Scientists believe that schizophrenia is caused by an imbalance of **dopamine** in the **brain**. Dopamine is a neurotransmitter that affects movement and balance. The theory is that aripiprazole acts as a partial agonist and antagonist, meaning that it binds to dopamine receptors in the brain and partially activates these receptors, while preventing dopamine from binding to and fully activating them. Conventional antipsychotic drugs, by contrast, act as full antagonists. These drugs completely block dopamine receptors and significantly interfere with dopamine transmission, which can cause severe movement side effects. Aripiprazole also affects another neurotransmitter, **serotonin**, which is involved in regulating mood and is also imbalanced in people with schizophrenia.

Although studies suggest that aripiprazole works well to treat psychotic conditions such as schizophrenia, less research has been conducted on how its effectiveness compares to that of conventional antipsychotic drugs.

Recommended dosage

Aripiprazole is only available by prescription. It is taken once a day by mouth as either a tablet or an oral solution. The oral solution is designed for older patients who have difficulty swallowing a tablet. Tablets range from 2 mg to 30 mg strengths. The oral solution is available in a 1 mg/mL solution. Aripiprazole can be taken with or without food. Some patients start on a low dose, and then their doctor increases the dose after approximately two weeks.

Precautions

Patients always need to read the accompanying medication guide before taking a prescribed drug. Aripiprazole may increase the risk for diabetes, and people who develop extreme thirst, frequent urination, or other diabetes symptoms while taking the drug should see a doctor for assessment. Because of potential interactions, people who are taking aripiprazole should tell their doctor if they have or are taking medications for any of the following conditions:

- Alzheimer's disease
- anxiety
- depression
- diabetes
- heart disease or heart failure
- high or low blood pressure
- human immunodeficiency virus (HIV)
- irritable bowel disease
- mental illness
- Parkinson's disease
- seizures
- stroke or mini-stroke
- surgery
- ulcers

Women who are pregnant, who intend to become pregnant, or who are nursing should ask their doctor before taking or discontinuing this drug. There is increased risk for extrapyramidal symptoms, a group of involuntary muscle **movement disorders**, and withdrawal symptoms in newborns whose mothers took aripiprazole during their third trimester of pregnancy. Symptoms include abnormal muscle tone, tremor, difficulty breathing and feeding, and agitation.

Because this medication may cause drowsiness and can impair judgment and motor skills, people who take it should take precautions when operating a motor vehicle or machinery. Alcohol can increase the sedative effects and is not advised for use in people who are taking aripiprazole. Also, people who take this drug should use caution when exercising, because aripiprazole can affect the body's ability to regulate temperature, potentially leading to overheating and dehydration.

This drug can increase the risk for a rare condition called **neuroleptic malignant syndrome** (NML). This condition, which is sometimes caused by drugs that interfere with the dopamine pathway, can raise body temperatures to potentially life-threatening levels.

Aripiprazole is not approved for the treatment of **psychosis** in elderly patients with dementia. The FDA in 2005 released a public health advisory warning patients and doctors against using aripiprazole and other atypical antipsychotics off-label. In studies, these drugs significantly increased the risk of death in older patients with dementia compared to placebo. Most of the deaths were associated with heart failure or infections such as pneumonia. In June 2008, the FDA required all manufacturers of antipsychotic drugs to create a warning label with information about this risk. Atypical antipsychotics also have been associated with an increased risk for **stroke** in elderly patients with dementia-related psychosis.

Aripiprazole can cause significant weight gain and the development of metabolic syndrome, the main characteristics of which are high cholesterol, increased blood pressure, insulin resistance or tolerance, or diabetes. Some practitioners use the diabetes drug metformin in patients who appear to be developing this syndrome, in an effort to avoid the development of diabetes and cardiovascular disease.

Side effects

Aripiprazole and other atypical antipsychotic drugs tend to cause fewer neurological side effects than the

KEY TERMS

Atypical antipsychotic—A class of newer-generation antipsychotic medications that are used to treat schizophrenia and other psychotic disorders.

Bipolar disorder—A brain disorder that causes extreme emotional shifts, from mania (elation or hyperactivity) to depression.

Delusions—A condition in which a person holds false beliefs despite evidence to the contrary.

Dementia—A loss of mental ability, often occurring with age, that can interfere with a person's ability to think clearly and function independently.

Dopamine—A chemical messenger in the brain that regulates movement and balance.

Extrapyramidal—Related to the motor system in the brain, the symptoms of which affect movement and coordination, including abnormal muscle movements and drooling.

Hallucinations—Seeing, hearing, feeling, smelling, or tasting things that do not exist.

Mania—A mood disorder in which a person may become impulsive or irritable and may exercise extremely poor judgment.

Neuroleptic malignant syndrome—A rare response to certain antipsychotic drugs, which can raise the body temperature to potentially life-threatening levels.

Off-label—The use of a prescription medication to treat conditions outside the indications approved by the U.S. Food and Drug Administration (FDA). It is legal for physicians to administer these drugs, but it is not legal for pharmaceutical companies to advertise drugs for off-label uses.

Paranoia—Condition in which a person has an irrational suspicion about another person or situation.

Partial agonist—A substance that partially activates a receptor in the brain while blocking the neurotransmitter for that receptor from binding to it.

Schizophrenia—A mental disorder in which a person experiences hallucinations and delusions and displays unusual behavior.

Serotonin—A chemical messenger in the brain that affects mood and emotion.

older antipsychotic drugs. In particular, they have a lower risk of extrapyramidal symptoms. However, the drug does have side effects. The most common side effects with aripiprazole are:

- anxiety
- constipation
- difficulty sleeping
- dizziness
- drowsiness
- headache
- nausea
- nervousness
- numbness
- tremor
- vomiting
- weight gain

Interactions

Aripiprazole can have potentially dangerous interactions with the following drugs:

- famotidine
- valproate
- lithium
- dextromethorphan
- warfarin
- omeprazole
- lorazepam

Patients should tell their physicians all of the drugs they are currently taking to avoid interactions.

Resources

BOOKS

Mondimore, Francis Mark. *Bipolar Disorder: A Guide for Patients and Families.* 2nd ed. Baltimore: Johns Hopkins University Press, 2006.

Stahl, Stephen M. *The Prescriber's Guide: Antipsychotics and Mood Stabilizers. Stahl's Essential Psychopharmacology.* Cambridge: Cambridge University Press, 2009.

Torrey, E. Fuller. *Surviving Schizophrenia: A Manual for Families, Patients, and Providers.* 5th ed. New York: Harper Collins, 2006.

ORGANIZATIONS

American Psychiatric Association, 1000 Wilson Blvd., Ste. 1825, Arlington, VA, 22209-3901, (703) 907-7300, apa@psych.org, http://www.psych.org.

National Alliance on Mental Illness, 2107 Wilson Blvd., Ste. 300, Arlington, VA, 22201-3042, Fax: (703) 524-9094, (800) 950-6264, http://www.nami.org.

National Institute of Mental Health, 6001 Executive Blvd., Rm. 8184, MSC 9663, Bethesda, MD, 20892-9663, (301) 433-4513; TTY: (301) 443-8431, Fax: (301) 443-4279, (866) 615-6464; TTY: (866) 415-8051, nimhinfo@nih.gov, http://www.nimh.nih.gov.

Stephanie N. Watson

Aromatherapy

Definition

Aromatherapy is the therapeutic use of plant-derived, aromatic essential oils to promote physical and psychological well-being. It is sometimes used in combination with massage and other therapeutic techniques as part of a holistic treatment approach.

Purpose

One of the basic concepts of mind/body medicine is that a positive frame of mind helps to keep people in good health. Aromatherapists maintain that essential oils derived from plants help people to slow down, relax from **stress**, and enjoy the sensory experiences of massage, warm water, and pleasant smells. Aromatherapy is thought to improve a person's mental outlook and sense of well-being by affecting the limbic system via the olfactory nerve, or the sense of smell. The limbic system is the area of the **brain** that regulates emotions. Relaxing and pleasant smells stimulate emotional responses of pleasure and relaxation. From a holistic perspective, aromatherapy is a form of preventive health care. Most aromatherapists believe that aromatherapy should be used as an adjunct to mainstream medical or psychiatric care, not as a substitute.

Aromatherapy is considered to be a useful complementary treatment for the relief of **depression**, anxiety, **insomnia**, **panic disorder**, stress-related physical disorders, menstrual cramps, and some gastrointestinal complaints. A recent Scottish study found that aromatherapy has a measurably calming effect on the symptoms of **dementia** in elderly people.

Aromatherapy can be used by itself or combined with Swedish massage, shiatsu, **acupressure**, reflexology, or **light therapy** to reinforce the positive results of these treatments.

Although there are professional aromatherapists as well as practitioners of holistic medicine who offer aromatherapy among their other services, people can also use aromatherapy at home as part of self-care. There are many guides to the various techniques of aromatherapy and the proper use of essential plant oils available in inexpensive paperback editions.

Description

Origins

Aromatic plants have been employed for their healing, preservative, and pleasurable qualities throughout recorded history in both the East and West. As early as 1500 B.C., the ancient Egyptians used waters, oils, incense, resins, and ointments scented with botanicals for their religious ceremonies.

There is evidence that the Chinese may have recognized the benefits of herbal and aromatic remedies much earlier. The oldest known herbal text, Shen Nung's *Pen Ts'ao* (c. 2700-3000 B.C.) catalogs over 200 botanicals. Ayurveda, a practice of traditional Indian medicine that dates back more than 2,500 years, also used aromatic herbs for treatment.

The Romans were well known for their use of fragrances. They bathed with botanicals and integrated them into their state and religious rituals. So did the Greeks, with a growing awareness of the medicinal properties of herbs. Greek physician and surgeon Pedanios Dioscorides, whose renown herbal text *De Materia Medica* (60 A.D.) was the standard textbook for Western medicine for 1,500 years, wrote extensively on the medicinal value of botanical aromatics. The *Medica* contained detailed information on some 500 plants and 4,740 separate medicinal uses for them, including an entire section on aromatics.

Written records of herbal distillation are found as early as the first century A.D., and around 1000 A.D., the noted Arab physician and naturalist Avicenna described the distillation of rose oil from rose petals and the medicinal properties of essential oils in his writings. However, it wasn't until 1937, when French chemist René-Maurice Gattefossé published *Aromatherapie: Les Huiles essentielles, hormones végé tales*, that aromatherapie, or aromatherapy, was introduced in Europe as a medical discipline. Gattefossé, who was employed by a French perfumeur, discovered the healing properties of **lavender** oil quite by accident when he suffered a severe burn while working and used the closest available liquid, lavender oil, to soak it.

In the late 20th century, French physician Jean Valnet used botanical aromatics as a front-line treatment for wounded soldiers in World War II. He wrote about his use of essential oils and their healing and antiseptic properties in his 1964 book *Aromatherapie, traitement des maladies par les essences des plantes*, which popularized the use of essential oils for medical and psychiatric treatment throughout France. Later, French biochemist Mauguerite Maury popularized the cosmetic benefits of essential oils, and in 1977 Robert Tisserand wrote the first English-language book on the subject, *The Art of Aromatherapy*, which introduced massage as an adjunct treatment to aromatherapy and sparked its popularity in the United Kingdom.

Types of essential oils

In aromatherapy, essential oils are carefully selected for their medicinal properties. As essential oils are absorbed into the bloodstream through application to the skin or inhalation, their active components trigger certain pharmalogical effects (e.g., pain relief).

In addition to physical benefits, aromatherapy has strong psychological benefits. The volatility of an oil, or the speed at which it evaporates in open air, is thought to be linked to its specific psychological effect. As a rule of thumb, oils that evaporate quickly are considered emotionally uplifting, while slowly-evaporating oils are thought to have a calming effect.

Some essential oils used in aromatherapy for mental health issues include:

- Roman chamomile (*Chamaemelum nobilis*). An anti-inflammatory and analgesic. Useful in treating otitis media (earache), skin conditions, menstrual pains, and depression.
- Clary sage (*Salvia sclarea*). This natural astringent is not only used to treat oily hair and skin, but is also said to be useful in regulating the menstrual cycle, improving mood, and controlling high blood pressure. Clary sage should not be used by pregnant women.
- Lavender (*Lavandula officinalis*). A popular aromatherapy oil that mixes well with most essential oils, lavender has a wide range of medicinal and cosmetic applications, including treatment of insect bites, burns, respiratory infections, intestinal discomfort, nausea, migraine, insomnia, depression, and stress.
- Neroli (bitter orange), (*Citrus aurantium*). Citrus oil extracted from bitter orange flower and peel and used to treat sore throat, insomnia, and stress- and anxiety-related conditions.
- Sweet orange (*Citrus sinensis*). An essential oil used to treat stomach complaints and known for its reported ability to lift the mood while relieving stress.

Essential oils contain active agents that can have potent physical effects. While some basic aromatherapy home treatments can be self-administered, medical aromatherapy should always be performed under the guidance of an aromatherapist, herbalist, massage therapist, nurse, or physician.

INHALATION. The most basic method of administering aromatherapy is direct or indirect inhalation of essential oils. Several drops of an essential oil can be applied to a tissue or handkerchief and gently inhaled. A small amount of essential oil can also be added to a bowl of hot water and used as a steam treatment. This technique is recommended when aromatherapy is used to treat respiratory and/or skin conditions. Aromatherapy steam devices are also available commercially. A warm bath containing essential oils can have the same effect as steam aromatherapy, with the added benefit of promoting relaxation. When used in a bath, water should be lukewarm rather than hot to slow the evaporation of the oil.

Essential oil diffusers, vaporizers, and light bulb rings can be used to disperse essential oils over a large area. These devices can be particularly effective in aromatherapy that uses essential oils to promote a healthier home environment. For example, eucalyptus and tea tree oil are known for their antiseptic qualities and are frequently used to disinfect sickrooms, and citronella and geranium can be useful in repelling insects.

DIRECT APPLICATION. Because of their potency, essential oils are diluted in a carrier oil or lotion before being applied to the skin to prevent an allergic skin reaction. The carrier oil can be a vegetable or olive based one, such as wheat germ or avocado. Light oils, such as safflower, sweet almond, grapeseed, hazelnut, apricot seed, or peach kernel, may be absorbed more easily by the skin. Standard dilutions of essential oils in carrier oils range from 2%–10%. However, some oils can be used at higher concentrations, while others should be diluted further for safe and effective use. The type of carrier oil used and the therapeutic use of the application may also influence how the essential oil is mixed. Individuals should seek guidance from a healthcare professional and/or aromatherapist when diluting essential oils.

Massage is a common therapeutic technique used in conjunction with aromatherapy to both relax the body and thoroughly administer the essential oil treatment. Essential oils can also be used in hot or cold compresses and soaks to treat muscle aches and pains (e.g., lavender and ginger). As a sore throat remedy, antiseptic and soothing essential oils (e.g., tea tree and **sage**) can be thoroughly mixed with water and used as a gargle or mouthwash.

INTERNAL USE. Some essential oils can be administered internally in tincture, infusion, or suppository form to treat certain symptoms or conditions; however, this treatment should never be self-administered. Essential oils should only be taken internally under the supervision of a qualified healthcare professional.

As nonprescription botanical preparations, the essential oils used in aromatherapy are typically not paid for by health insurance. The self-administered nature of the therapy controls costs to some degree. Aromatherapy treatment sessions from a professional aromatherapist are not covered by health insurance in most cases, although aromatherapy performed in conjunction with physical therapy, nursing, therapeutic massage, or other covered medical services may be covered. Individuals should check with their insurance provider to find out about their specific coverage.

Benefits

Aromatherapy offers diverse physical and psychological benefits, depending on the essential oil or oil combination and method of application used. Some common medicinal properties of essential oils used in aromatherapy include analgesic, antimicrobial, antiseptic, anti-inflammatory, astringent, sedative, antispasmodic, expectorant, diuretic, and sedative. Essential oils are used to treat a wide range of symptoms and conditions, including—but not limited to—gastrointestinal discomfort, skin conditions, menstrual pain and irregularities, stress-related conditions, mood disorders, circulatory problems, respiratory infections, and wounds.

Precautions

Individuals should only take essential oils internally under the guidance and close supervision of a health care professional. Some oils, such as eucalyptus, wormwood, and sage, should never be taken internally. Many essential oils are highly toxic and should not be used at all in aromatherapy. These include (but are not limited to) bitter almond, pennyroyal, mustard, sassafras, rue, and mugwort.

Citrus-based essential oils, including bitter and sweet orange, lime, lemon, grapefruit, and tangerine, are phototoxic, and exposure to direct sunlight should be avoided for at least four hours after their application.

Other essential oils, such as cinnamon leaf, black pepper, juniper, lemon, white camphor, eucalyptus blue gum, ginger, peppermint, pine needle, and thyme can be extremely irritating to the skin if applied in high enough concentration or without a carrier oil or lotion. Caution should always be exercised when applying essential oils topically. Individuals should never apply undiluted essential oils to the skin unless directed to do so by a trained healthcare professional and/or aromatherapist.

Individuals taking homeopathic remedies should avoid black pepper, camphor, eucalyptus, and peppermint essential oils. These oils may act as a remedy antidote to the homeopathic treatment.

KEY TERMS

Antiseptic—Inhibits the growth of microorganisms.

Bactericidal—An agent that destroys bacteria (e.g., *Staphylococci aureus, Streptococci pneumoniae, Escherichia coli, Salmonella enteritidis*).

Carrier oil—An oil used to dilute essential oils for use in massage and other skin care applications.

Contact dermatitis—Skin irritation as a result of contact with a foreign substance.

Enfleurage—A technique for extracting essential oils from flower petals by placing them on a layer of purified fat.

Essential oil—A volatile oil extracted from the leaves, fruit, flowers, roots, or other components of a plant and used in aromatherapy, perfumes, and foods and beverages.

Holistic—A practice of medicine that focuses on the whole patient, addressing the patient's social, emotional, and spiritual needs along with their physical treatment.

Limbic system—A group of structures in the brain that includes the amygdala, hippocampus, olfactory bulbs, and hypothalamus. The limbic system is associated with homeostasis and the regulation and arousal of emotions.

Maceration—A technique for extracting essential oils from plant leaves and stems by crushing the plant parts and soaking them in warm vegetable oil.

Olfactory nerve—The cranial nerve that regulates the sense of smell.

Phototoxic—Causes a harmful skin reaction when exposed to sunlight.

Remedy antidote—Certain foods, beverages, prescription medications, aromatic compounds, and other environmental elements that counteract the efficacy of homeopathic remedies.

Steam distillation—A process of extracting essential oils from plant products through a heating and evaporation process.

Volatile—Something that vaporizes or evaporates quickly when exposed to air.

Children should only receive aromatherapy treatment under the guidance of a trained aromatherapist or healthcare professional. Some essential oils may not be appropriate for treating children or may require additional dilution before use on children.

Certain essential oils should not be used by pregnant or nursing women or by people with specific illnesses or physical conditions. Individuals suffering from any chronic or acute health condition should inform their healthcare provider before starting treatment with any essential oil.

Asthmatic individuals should not use steam inhalation for aromatherapy, as it can aggravate their condition.

Essential oils are flammable, and should be kept away from heat sources.

Consumers should use caution when purchasing essential oils, as bargain oils are often adulterated, diluted, or synthetic. Pure essential oils can be expensive, and the cost of an oil will vary depending on its quality and availability.

Preparations

The method of extracting an essential oil varies by plant type. Common methods include water or steam distillation and cold pressing. Quality essential oils should be unadulterated and extracted from pure botanicals. Many aromatherapy oils on the market are synthetic and/or diluted, contain solvents, or are extracted from botanicals grown with pesticides or herbicides. To ensure best results, essential oils should be made from pure organic botanicals and labeled by their full botanical name. Oils should always be stored in dark bottles out of direct light.

Before using essential oils on the skin, individuals should perform a skin patch test by applying a small amount of the diluted oil behind the wrist and covering it with a bandage or cloth for up to 12 hours. If redness or irritation occurs, the oil should be diluted further and a second skin test performed, or it should be avoided altogether. Individuals should never apply undiluted essential oils to the skin unless advised to do so by a trained healthcare professional.

Risks

Side effects may occur and vary by the type of essential oil used. Citrus-based essential oils can cause heightened sensitivity to sunlight. Essential oils may also cause contact dermatitis, an allergic reaction characterized by redness and irritation. Anyone experiencing an allergic reaction to an essential oil should discontinue its use and contact their healthcare professional for further guidance. Individuals should do a small skin patch test with new essential oils before using them extensively.

Research & general acceptance

The antiseptic and bactericidal qualities of some essential oils (such as tea tree and peppermint) and their value in fighting infection has been detailed extensively in both ancient and modern medical literature.

Recent research in mainstream medical literature has also shown that aromatherapy has a positive psychological impact on patients. Several clinical studies involving both post-operative and chronically ill subjects showed that massage with essential oils can be helpful in improving emotional well-being and promoting the healing process.

Today, the use of holistic aromatherapy is widely accepted in Europe, particularly in Great Britain, where it is commonly used in conjunction with massage as both a psychological and physiological healing tool. In the United States, where aromatherapy is often misunderstood as solely a cosmetic treatment, the mainstream medical community has been slower to accept its use.

QUESTIONS TO ASK YOUR DOCTOR

- In what way do you think aromatherapy will benefit me?
- What essential oils do you recommend?
- Will aromatherapy interact with my current medications?

Training & certification

Certification or licensing is currently not required to become an aromatherapist in the United States; however, many states require that healthcare professionals who practice the "hands-on" therapies used in conjunction with aromatherapy (e.g., massage) to be licensed. There are state-licensed educational institutions that offer certificates and/or diplomas in aromatherapy training. Individuals interested in aromatherapy treatment from a professional aromatherapist may be able to obtain a referral from one of these institutions, or from their current healthcare provider.

Resources

BOOKS

Schiller, Carol, and David Schiller. *The Aromatherapy Encyclopedia: A Concise Guide to over 385 Plant Oils*. Laguna Beach, CA: Basic Health Publications, 2008.

PERIODICALS

van der Watt, G., and A. Janca. "Aromatherapy in Nursing and Mental Health Care." *Contemporary Nurse: A Journal for the Australian Nursing Profession* 30, no. 1 (2008): 69–75.

Yim, V. W., et al. "A Review on the Effects of Aromatherapy for Patients with Depressive Symptoms." *Journal of Alternative and Complementary Medicine* 15, no. 2 (2009): 187–95.

WEBSITES

National Institute of Complementary and Alternative Medicine. "Aromatherapy." National Institutes of Health. http://nccam.nih.gov/health/aromatherapy (accessed December 14, 2011).

ORGANIZATIONS

National Association of Holistic Aromatherapy, PO Box 1868, Banner Elk, NC, 28604, (828) 898-6161, Fax: (828) 898-1965, info@naha.org, http://www.naha.org.

Paula Ford-Martin
Laura Jean Cataldo, RN, Ed.D.

Artane *see* **Trihexyphenidyl**

Art therapy

Definition

Art therapy, sometimes called creative arts therapy or expressive arts therapy, encourages people to express and understand emotions through artistic outlets and the creative process.

Purpose

Art therapy provides participants with critical insight into their emotions, thoughts, and feelings. Key goals of the art therapy process include:

- Self-discovery—at its most successful, art therapy triggers an emotional catharsis, providing an outlet for otherwise internalized thoughts and feelings.
- Personal fulfillment—the creation of a tangible reward can build confidence and nurture feelings of self-worth. Personal fulfillment comes from both the creative and the analytical components of the artistic process.
- Empowerment—art therapy can help people visually express emotions and fears that they cannot express through conventional means, giving them some sense of control over these feelings.
- Relaxation and stress relief—chronic stress can be harmful to both mind and body. Stress can weaken and damage the immune system, cause insomnia and depression, and trigger circulatory problems (like high blood pressure and irregular heartbeat). When used alone or in combination with other relaxation techniques, such as guided imagery, art therapy can help relieve stress.
- Symptom relief and physical rehabilitation—art therapy can also help patients cope with pain. The therapy can promote physiological healing when patients identify and work through anger, resentment, and other emotional stressors. It is often prescribed to accompany pain control therapy for chronically and terminally ill patients.

Three men participate in an art therapy session at a center for patients with Alzheimer's disease. *(© Durand Florence/SIPA/newscom)*

Description

Art therapy, sometimes called expressive art or art psychology, encourages self-discovery and emotional growth. It is a two-part process, involving both the creation of art and the discovery of its meaning. Rooted in Sigmund Freud's and Carl Jung's theories of the subconscious and unconscious, art therapy is based on the assumption that visual symbols and images are the most accessible and natural form of communication to the human experience. Patients are encouraged to visualize and then create the thoughts and emotions that they cannot talk about. The resulting artwork is then reviewed and interpreted by the patient.

The "analysis" of the artwork produced in art therapy typically allows patients to gain some level of insight into their feelings and lets them work through these issues in a constructive manner. Art therapy is typically practiced with individual, group, or family **psychotherapy (talk therapy)**. While a therapist may provide critical guidance for these activities, a key feature of effective art therapy is that the patient/artist, not the therapist, directs the interpretation of the artwork.

Origins

Humans have expressed themselves with symbols throughout history. Masks, ritual pottery, costumes, objects used in rituals, cave drawings, Egyptian hieroglyphics, and Celtic art and symbols are all visual records of self-expression and communication through art. Art has also been associated with spiritual power, and

KEY TERMS

Catharsis—Therapeutic discharge of emotional tension after recalling past events.

Mandala—A design, usually circular, that appears in religion and art. In Buddhism and Hinduism, the mandala has religious ritual purposes and serves as a yantra (a geometric emblem or instrument of contemplation).

Organic illness—A physically, biologically based illness.

artistic forms such as the Hindu and Buddhist mandala and Native American sand painting are considered powerful healing tools.

In the late nineteenth century, French psychiatrists Ambrose Tardieu and Paul-Max Simon both published studies on the similar characteristics of and symbolism in the artwork of the mentally ill. Tardieu and Simon viewed art therapy as an effective diagnostic tool to identify specific types of mental illness or traumatic events. Later, psychologists would use this diagnostic aspect to develop psychological drawing tests (e.g., the Draw-A-Man test, the Draw-A-Person Questionnaire [DAP.Q]) and projective personality tests involving visual symbol recognition (e.g., the **Rorschach inkblot test**, the **Thematic Apperception Test** [TAT], the Holtzman Inkblot Test [HIT]).

The growing popularity of milieu therapies at psychiatric institutions in the twentieth century was an important factor in the development of art therapy in the United States. Milieu therapies (or environmental therapies) focus on putting the patient in a controlled therapeutic social setting that provides the patient with opportunities to gain self-confidence and interact with peers in a positive way. Activities that encourage self-discovery and empowerment, such as art, music, dance, and writing, are important components of this approach.

Educator and therapist Margaret Naumburg was a follower of Freud and Jung and incorporated art into psychotherapy as a means for her patients to visualize and recognize the unconscious. She founded the Walden School in 1915, where she used students' artworks in psychological counseling. She published extensively on the subject and taught seminars on the technique at New York University in the 1950s. Today, she is considered the founder of art therapy in the United States.

In the 1930s, Karl, William, and Charles Menninger introduced an art therapy program at their Kansas-based psychiatric hospital, the Menninger Clinic. The Menninger Clinic employed a number of artists in residence in the following years, and the facility was also considered a leader in the art therapy movement through the 1950s and '60s. Other noted art therapy pioneers who emerged in the '50s and '60s included Edith Kramer, Hanna Yaxa Kwiatkowska (**National Institute of Mental Health**), and Janie Rhyne.

Art therapy has traditionally centered on visual mediums, like paintings, sculptures, and drawings. Some mental healthcare providers have now broadened the definition to include music, film, dance, writing, and other types of artistic expression.

Benefits

Art therapy can be a particularly useful treatment tool for children, who frequently have limited language skills. By drawing or using other visual means to express troublesome feelings, younger patients can begin to address these issues, even if they cannot identify or label these emotions with words. Art therapy is also valuable for adolescents and adults who are unable or unwilling to talk about thoughts and feelings.

Beyond its use in mental health treatment, art therapy is also used with traditional medicine to treat organic diseases and conditions. The connection between mental and physical health is well documented, and art therapy can promote healing by relieving **stress** and allowing the patient to develop coping skills.

Art therapy is often one part of a psychiatric inpatient or outpatient treatment program, and can take place in individual or **group therapy** sessions. Group art therapy sessions often take place in hospital, clinic, shelter, and community program settings. These group therapy sessions can have the added benefits of positive social interaction, empathy, and support from peers, which helps the artist learn that others share similar concerns and issues.

Precautions

Art materials and techniques should match the age and ability of the client. People with impairments, such as **traumatic brain injury** or a neurological condition, may have difficulties with the self-discovery portion of the art therapy process, depending on their level of functioning. However, they may still benefit from the sensory stimulation provided by art therapy and the pleasure they derive from artistic creation.

While art is accessible to all (with or without a therapist to guide the process), it may be difficult to tap the full potential of the interpretive component of art therapy without a therapist to guide the process. When art therapy is chosen as a therapeutic tool to cope with a physical condition, it should be treated as a supplemental therapy and not as a substitute for conventional medical treatments.

Preparation

Before starting art therapy, the therapist may have an introductory session with the client to discuss art therapy techniques and to give the client the opportunity to ask questions about the process. The client's comfort with the artistic process is critical to successful art therapy. The therapist will ensure that appropriate materials and space are available for the client, as well as an adequate amount of time for the session. If a person is exploring art as therapy without the guidance of a trained therapist, adequate materials, space, and time are still important factors in a successful creative experience.

The supplies used in art therapy are limited only by the artist's (and/or therapist's) imagination. Some of the materials often used include paper, canvas, poster board, assorted paints, inks, markers, pencils, charcoals, chalks, fabrics, string, adhesives, clay, wood, glazes, wire, bendable metals, and natural items (like shells, leaves, etc.). Providing artists with a variety of materials in assorted colors and textures can enhance their interest in the process and may result in a richer, more diverse exploration of their emotions in the resulting artwork. Appropriate tools such as scissors, brushes, erasers, easels, supply trays, glue guns, smocks or aprons, and cleaning materials are also essential.

An appropriate workspace should be available for the creation of art. Ideally, this should be a bright, quiet, comfortable place, with large tables, counters, or other suitable surfaces. The space can be as simple as a kitchen or office table, or as fancy as a specialized artist's studio.

The artist should have adequate time to become comfortable with and explore the creative process. This is especially true for people who do not consider themselves "artists" and who may be uncomfortable with the concept. If performed in a therapy group or one-on-one session, the art therapist should be available to answer general questions about materials and/or the creative process. However, the therapist should be careful not to influence the creation or interpretation of the work.

Research and general acceptance

A wide body of literature supports the use of art therapy in a mental health capacity. In mainstream medicine, as the mind-body connection between psychological well-being and physical health is further documented by studies in the field, art therapy continues to gain greater acceptance as a therapeutic technique for organic illness.

QUESTIONS TO ASK YOUR DOCTOR

- Do I have to be artistic to participate in art therapy?
- What are the benefits of art therapy over group therapy or counseling?
- How long will I need to participate in art therapy before I begin to see results?

Resources

BOOKS

Soneff, Sharon. *Art Journals and Creative Healing: Restoring the Spirit Through Self–Expression.* Minneapolis, MN: Quarry Books, 2008.

ORGANIZATIONS

American Art Therapy Association, 225 North Fairfax Street, Alexandria, VA, 22314, info@arttherapy.org, http://www.americanarttherapyassociation.org.

Paula Anne Ford-Martin

Asenapine

Definition

Asenapine, sold under the brand name Saphris, belongs to a class of drugs known as atypical antipsychotics, which are used to treat psychiatric disorders such as **schizophrenia**. Atypical antipsychotics work by altering the levels of the **neurotransmitters serotonin** and **dopamine**, which are involved in normal **brain** function and can affect the physiological states of **psychosis** and mania. Asenapine acts to inhibit the effects of serotonin and dopamine within the brain.

Purpose

Asenapine is an antipsychotic medication used in the treatment of schizophrenia and **bipolar disorder**. For schizophrenia, asenapine may be used to treat specific episodes or as maintenance therapy. In bipolar disorder, it may be used alone or in combination with mood stabilizer drugs, but it is not usually the first choice of medication.

Description

Asenapine works by antagonizing, or blocking, the signaling of neurotransmitters in the brain by binding their corresponding neurotransmitter receptors. Since the pathology of schizophrenia involves the overactivity of neurotransmitter signaling in some areas of the brain and underactivity in others, antipsychotics such as asenapine do not completely treat the disorder. The symptoms of schizophrenia known as **positive symptoms**, such as psychosis, are best treated with asenapine. The negative and cognitive symptoms such as withdrawal and difficulty reasoning are not as well addressed with asenapine. Similarly, the mania of bipolar disorder is better treated with asenapine than the **depression**.

Recommended dosage

Asenapine is taken as a tablet and is available in both flavored and unflavored preparations. The tablets are not crushed or chewed but are placed under the tongue to dissolve and enter the bloodstream. The available dosage forms are 5 mg and 10 mg. When used during an acute episode of schizophrenia, the 5 mg dose is taken twice a day. For maintenance in schizophrenia, the dose may be increased to 10 mg twice a day after at least a week on the 5 mg dose. When asenapine is used for bipolar disorder, the 10 mg dose is used twice a day as tolerated. If side effects develop or if other drugs are used in combination, the dose may be decreased to 5 mg twice a day. Side effects impacting the immune system may make a lower dose or discontinuation of the drug necessary. Persons with some types of severe liver disease may require dosage modifications.

Precautions

Atypical antipsychotics were developed for the purpose of avoiding some of the side effects often seen with older, conventional antipsychotic medications, such as **medication-induced movement disorders**. The atypical drugs do cause far fewer **movement disorders** than traditional medications but still have the potential to produce some disturbing movement-related effects. Patients taking asenapine must be monitored for the development of movement disorders as well as **neuroleptic malignant syndrome**, a dangerous reaction characterized by stiffness, mental status changes, and increased body temperature. However, asenapine is less likely to cause these disorders than many other types of antipsychotic medications.

Patients taking asenapine must have their immune system function monitored via periodic blood tests, as the drug can cause dangerous decreases in white blood cells. High blood sugar may also develop, especially in patients at risk for diabetes. Blood sugar is measured before initiating asenapine dosing and then monitored periodically. Asenapine carries a risk of low blood pressure and possible temporary loss of consciousness, especially in older or dehydrated patients rising quickly from a lying down position. Asenapine may also alter heart rhythm, potentially producing fatal arrhythmias.

Asenapine may not be appropriate for use or may require caution in patients with **dementia**, some heart abnormalities or disease, liver dysfunction, history of **stroke** or seizure, diabetes, immune dysfunction, patients who are dehydrated, and the elderly. Asenapine should not be used by women who are pregnant or trying to become pregnant, as some infants born to mothers who used asenapine during pregnancy exhibited withdrawal symptoms and muscle tremors. Because the safety of asenapine during breastfeeding is unknown, its use is not recommended.

In June 2008, the FDA announced a requirement for manufacturers of asenapine (and other antipsychotic drugs) to issue a warning label regarding the adverse effects of using antipsychotic drugs to treat behavioral problems in older individuals with dementia-related psychosis, including death. Studies showed that older adults with dementia taking antipsychotics such as asenapine were at increased risk of having a stroke or mini-stroke during treatment and, in some cases, of dying during treatment, though the reason for the finding was unclear. The use of asenapine in treating older adults with dementia-related psychosis is not approved by the FDA.

Side effects

Atypical antipsychotics such as asenapine are known for having fewer side effects than other types of older antipsychotic medications that act on neurotransmitter receptors in different parts of the brain. This is one reason why as a general class they tend to be the drug of choice in the treatment of schizophrenia. However, as with all medication, antipsychotics such as asenapine do have side effects. Sensitivity to asenapine varies among patients, and some patients may find that lower doses are more than their body system can tolerate. Common side effects of asenapine include dizziness, dry mouth, abdominal pain, increases

KEY TERMS

Bipolar disorder—A mood disorder marked by alternating episodes of extremely low mood (depression) and exuberant highs (mania).

Cognitive—Associated with thinking, learning, perception, awareness, and judgment.

Dopamine—A type of neurotransmitter involved in regulation of concentration, impulse control, judgment, mood, attention span, psychostimulation, disease states such as addiction, and depression.

Insomnia—Disorder involving disturbance of sleep.

Mania—Physiological state of hyperactivity experienced by patients with certain psychiatric illnesses involving inappropriate elevated mood, pressured speech, poor judgment, and sometimes psychotic episodes superimposed on the state of mania.

Negative symptoms—Symptoms of schizophrenia characterized by the absence or elimination of certain behaviors, such as initiative, speech, or affect.

Neuroleptic malignant syndrome—Dangerous reaction to antipsychotic medications that involves temperature instability, muscular rigidity, and altered mental status.

Neurotransmitter—One of a group of chemicals secreted by a nerve cell (neuron) to carry a chemical message to another nerve cell, often as a way of transmitting a nerve impulse. Examples of neurotransmitters include acetylcholine, dopamine, serotonin, and norepinephrine.

Neurotransmitter receptor—A physical recipient for chemicals called neurotransmitters. Receptors sit on the surface of cells that make up body tissues, and once bound to the neurotransmitter, they initiate the chemical signaling pathway associated with neurotransmitters.

Positive symptoms—Symptoms that are characterized by the production or presence of abnormal or excessive behaviors, including hallucinations and thought-process disorder.

Psychosis—A serious mental disorder characterized by defective or lost contact with reality, often with hallucinations or delusions.

Schizophrenia—A severe mental illness in which a person has difficulty distinguishing what is real from what is not real. It is often characterized by hallucinations, delusions, and withdrawal from people and social activities.

Serotonin—A type of neurotransmitter involved in regulation of the blood vessels, brain processes, and disease states such as depression.

in appetite, weight gain, **fatigue**, **insomnia**, irritability, anxiety, depression, joint pain, toothache, restless leg syndrome, reduced sense of touch, and alterations in liver enzymes. Antipsychotics such as asenapine that block dopamine receptors may cause an increase in prolactin, the hormone that causes lactation in women and impotence in men. Low blood pressure or a drop in blood pressure upon standing may result in loss of consciousness. Rare but serious potential side effects include severe movement disorders, high blood sugar or overt diabetes, stroke, severe difficulty swallowing, dangerous changes in heart rhythm, **seizures**, and changes in blood cells, including anemia and decreased immune function.

Interactions

Patients should make their doctor aware of all medications and supplements they are taking before using asenapine. Using alcohol while taking asenapine may create toxic reactions in the body and should be avoided. Drugs that affect the liver may alter the metabolism of asenapine, resulting in too much or too little of the drug in body. This could lead to increased side effects or even toxic doses. Likewise, asenapine may affect the metabolism of other drugs, leading to greater or lower doses than therapeutically desired.

Use of asenapine in combination with a number of other drugs may adversely affect heart rhythm; such drugs include the heart medications dronedarone and amiodarone, the chemotherapeutic toremifene, the antibiotics azithromycin and ciprofloxacin, the antifungal fluconazole, the antinausea drug ondansetron, and other antipsychotics such as **pimozide**. Using asenapine with certain blood pressure medications, such as enalapril and metoprolol, may cause dangerously low blood pressure. **Sedatives** such as codeine and herbal supplements such as calendula, capsicum, kava, and lemon balm may cause severe sedation in patients using asenapine. The herbal supplement chasteberry decreases the effectiveness of asenapine.

QUESTIONS TO ASK YOUR DOCTOR

- Should I eat before taking this medication?
- Will this medication interact with any of my other prescription medications?
- Are there any over-the-counter medications I should not take with this medicine?
- Will this medicine interact with any of my herbal supplements?
- What side effects should I watch for while taking this medication?
- Can I drink alcoholic beverages in the same time frame as taking this medication?
- Can I stop taking the medication right away or do I need to stop slowly?

Resources

BOOKS

Brunton, Laurence L., et al. *Goodman and Gilman's The Pharmacological Basis of Therapeutics*. 12th ed. New York: McGraw Hill Medical, 2011.

Stargrove, Mitchell Bebel, et al. *Herb, Nutrient, and Drug Interactions: Clinical Implications and Therapeutic Strategies*. St. Louis: Mosby, 2007.

PERIODICALS

Citrome, L. "A Systematic Review of Meta-Analyses of the Efficacy of Oral Atypical Antipsychotics for the Treatment of Adult Patients with Schizophrenia." *Expert Opinion of Pharmacotherapy* (October 17, 2011) [e-pub ahead of print]. http://dx.doi.org/10.1517/14656566.2011.626769 (accessed November 3, 2011).

Gonzalez, J. M., P. M. Thompson, and T. A. Moore. "Review of the Safety, Efficacy, and Side Effect Profile of Asenapine in the Treatment of Bipolar 1 Disorder." *Patient Preference and Adherence* 5 (2011): 333–41. http://dx.doi.org/10.2147/PPA.S10968 (accessed November 3, 2011).

ORGANIZATIONS

American College of Neuropsychopharmacology, 5034-A Thoroughbred Lane, Brentwood, TN, 37027, (615) 324-2360, Fax: (615) 523-1715, acnp@acnp.org, http://www.acnp.org/default.aspx.

American Society for Clinical Pharmacology and Therapeutics, 528 N Washington St., Alexandria, VA, 22314, (703) 836-6981, info@ascpt.org, http://www.ascpt.org.

National Institute of Mental Health, 6001 Executive Blvd., Rm. 8184, MSC 9663, Bethesda, MD, 20892-9663, (301) 433-4513; TTY: (301) 443-8431, Fax: (301) 443-4279, (866) 615-6464; TTY: (866) 415-8051, nimhinfo@nih.gov, http://www.nimh.nih.gov.

U.S. Food and Drug Administration, 10903 New Hampshire Ave., Silver Spring, MD, 20993-0002, (888) INFO-FDA (463-6332), http://www.fda.gov.

Maria Eve Basile, PhD

Asendin *see* **Amoxapine**

Asperger syndrome

Definition

Asperger syndrome (AS), which is also called Asperger disorder or autistic psychopathy, belongs to a group of childhood disorders known as **pervasive developmental disorders** (PDDs) or autistic spectrum disorders. AS was first described by Hans Asperger, an Austrian **psychiatrist**, in 1944. Asperger's work was unavailable in English before the mid-1970s; as a result, AS was often unrecognized in English-speaking countries until the late 1980s. Before the fourth edition of the American Psychiatric Association's ***Diagnostic and Statistical Manual of Mental Disorders*** (*DSM-IV*, 1994), there was no official definition of AS.

Demographics

According to the National Institute of Neurological Disorders and Stroke (NINDS), the rate of occurrence of AS is not well established. Estimates range from two out of every 10,000 children to one out of every 300, with boys affected up to four times more frequently than girls. Further research is required to obtain precise AS prevalence data. In addition, little research has been done on the populations of developing countries, and no information is available about the incidence of the disorder in different racial or ethnic groups.

Description

Children with AS learn to talk at the usual age and often have above-average verbal skills. They have normal or above-normal intelligence and the ability to take care of themselves. The distinguishing features of AS are problems with social interaction, particularly reciprocating and empathizing with the feelings of others; difficulties with nonverbal communication (e.g., facial expressions); peculiar speech habits that include repeated words or phrases and a flat, emotionless vocal tone; an apparent lack of "common sense"; a fascination with obscure or limited subjects (e.g., doorknobs, railroad schedules, astronomical data, etc.), often to the exclusion of other interests; clumsy and awkward physical movements; and

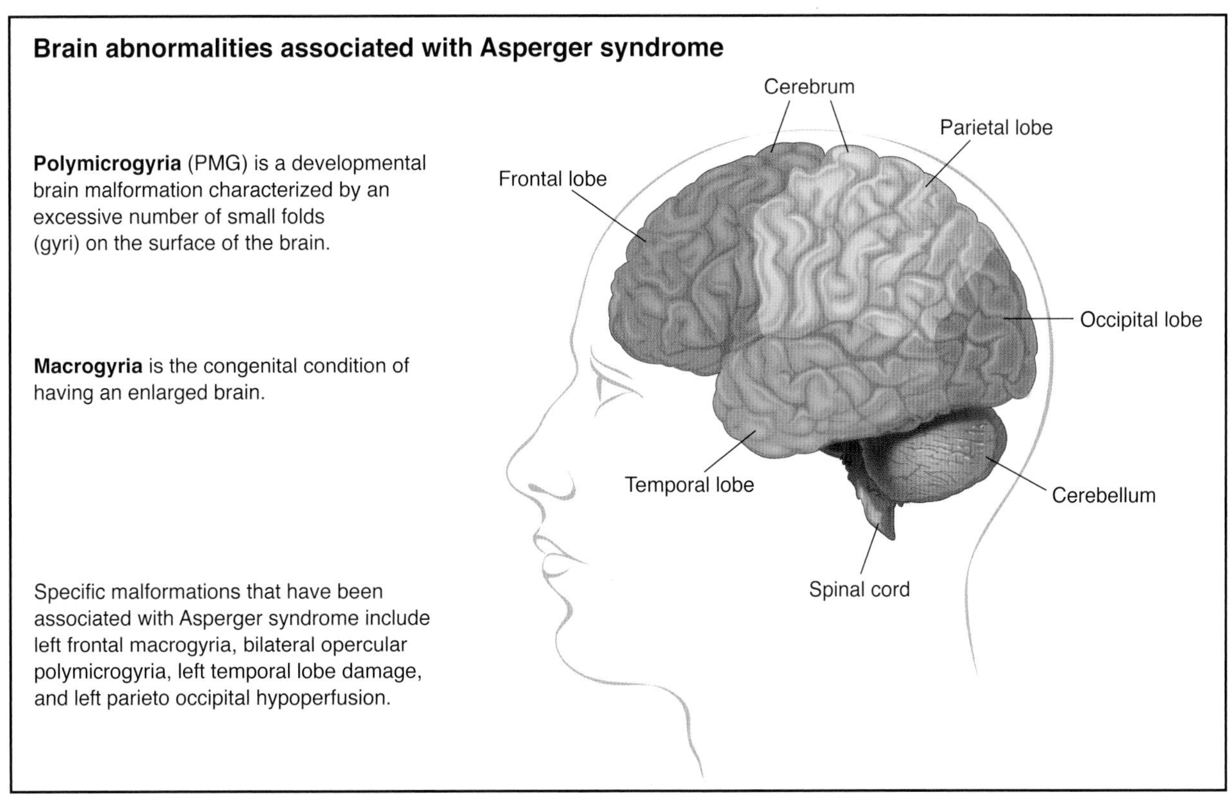

Possible brain malformations associated with Asperger syndrome. *(Illustration by Electronic Illustrators Group. Reproduced by permission of Gale, a part of Cengage Learning.)*

odd or eccentric behaviors, such as hand wringing or finger flapping, swaying or other repetitious whole-body movements, or watching spinning objects for long periods of time.

Risk factors

There is some indication that AS runs in families, particularly in families with histories of **depression** and **bipolar disorder**. Asperger noted that his initial group of patients had fathers with AS symptoms. Knowledge of the genetic profile as a risk factor continues to be limited.

Causes and symptoms

Asperger syndrome seems to run in families. **Imaging studies** have revealed differences in the structure and function of **brain** tissue. These changes appear to occur during embryonic brain development. As with **autism**, associations have been made between Asperger syndrome and a number of genes, many of which direct the formation of brain tissue and the communication between brain cells. A variety of environmental causes have also been postulated as causing Asperger syndrome, including advanced parental age, pesticides, and exposure to **valproic acid** (a seizure medication), though none of these have been proven. As with autism, although there has been popular uproar regarding a possible association between immunizations and the disorder, this association has been disproved. The research article that put forward this hypothesis has been publicly discredited, and a retraction has been printed.

In young children, the symptoms of AS typically include problems picking up social cues and understanding the basics of interacting with other children. These children may want friendships but find themselves unable to make friends. Most children with Asperger are diagnosed during the elementary school years, because the symptoms of the disorder become more apparent at this point. They include:

- poor pragmatic language skills, such as using incorrect tone or volume of voice for specific contexts or failing to understand the appropriate uses of humorous or slang expressions within social contexts
- problems with hand-eye coordination and other visual skills
- problems making eye contact with others
- learning difficulties, which may range from mild to severe
- tendency to become absorbed in a particular topic and not know when others are bored with the conversation

KEY TERMS

Autistic psychopathy—Hans Asperger's original name for Asperger syndrome. It is still used occasionally as a synonym for the disorder.

Gillberg's criteria—A six-item checklist for Asperger syndrome developed by Christopher Gillberg, a Swedish researcher. It is widely used as a diagnostic tool.

High-functioning autism (HFA)—A subcategory of autistic disorder consisting of children diagnosed with IQs of 70 or higher.

Nonverbal learning disability (NLD)—A learning disability syndrome identified in 1989 that may overlap with some of the symptoms of Asperger syndrome.

Pervasive developmental disorder (PDD)—Used by the American Psychiatric Association for individuals who meet some but not all of the criteria for autism.

- repetitive behaviors, such as counting a group of coins or marbles over and over, reciting the same song or poem several times, or buttoning and unbuttoning a jacket repeatedly

Adolescence is one of the most painful periods for young people with Asperger because social interactions are more complex in this age group and require more subtle social skills. Some boys with AS become frustrated while trying to relate to their peers and may become aggressive. Both boys and girls with the disorder are often quite naive for their age and easily manipulated by "street-wise" classmates. They are also more vulnerable than most youngsters to peer pressure.

Less research has been done regarding adults with AS. Some have serious difficulties with social and occupational functioning, but others are able to finish their schooling, join the workforce, and marry and have families.

Diagnosis

As of 2011, there were no blood tests or brain scans that could be used to diagnose AS. Until *DSM-IV* (1994), there was no "official" list of symptoms for the disorder, which made its **diagnosis** both difficult and inexact. Although most children with AS are diagnosed between five and nine years of age, many are not diagnosed until adulthood. Misdiagnoses are common; AS has been confused with such other neurological disorders as **Tourette syndrome** or with **attention deficit hyperactivity disorder (ADHD)**, **oppositional defiant disorder** (ODD), or **obsessive-compulsive disorder** (OCD). Some researchers think that AS overlaps some types of learning disability, such as the nonverbal learning disability (NLD) syndrome identified in 1989.

The inclusion of AS as a separate diagnostic category in *DSM-IV* was justified on the basis of a large international field trial of over one thousand children and adolescents. Nevertheless, the diagnosis of AS is also complicated by confusion with such other diagnostic categories as high-functioning (IQ 70) autism (HFA), and schizoid personality disorder of childhood. With regard to the latter, AS is not an unchanging set of personality traits but has a developmental dimension. AS is distinguished from HFA by the following characteristics:

- later onset of symptoms (usually around three years of age)
- early development of grammatical speech; the AS child's verbal IQ is usually higher than performance IQ (the reverse being the case in children with autism)
- less severe deficiencies in social and communication skills
- presence of intense interest in one or two topics
- physical clumsiness and lack of coordination
- family history of the disorder
- lower frequency of neurological disorders
- more positive outcome in later life

DSM-IV criteria for Asperger syndrome

DSM-IV specifies six diagnostic criteria for AS:

- The child's social interactions are impaired in at least two of the following ways: markedly limited use of nonverbal communication; lack of age-appropriate peer relationships; failure to share enjoyment, interests, or accomplishment with others; lack of reciprocity in social interactions.
- The child's behavior, interests, and activities are characterized by repetitive or rigid patterns, such as an abnormal preoccupation with one or two topics, or with parts of objects; repetitive physical movements; or rigid insistence on certain routines and rituals.
- The child's social, occupational, or educational functioning is significantly impaired.
- The child has normal age-appropriate language skills.
- The child has normal age-appropriate cognitive skills, self-help abilities, and curiosity about the environment.
- The child does not meet criteria for another specific PDD or schizophrenia.

Two 14-year-old boys with Asperger syndrome attend an afterschool program for children with the disorder. *(© AP Images/Julie Koehn)*

Other diagnostic scales and checklists

Other instruments that have been used to identify children with AS include Gillberg's criteria, a six-item list compiled by a Swedish researcher that specifies problems in social interaction, a preoccupying narrow interest, forcing routines and interests on the self or others, speech and language problems, nonverbal communication problems, and physical clumsiness; and the Australian Scale for Asperger Syndrome, a detailed multi-item questionnaire developed in 1996.

Brain imaging findings

As of 2011, only a few structural abnormalities of the brain had been linked to AS. Findings include abnormally large folds in the brain tissue in the left frontal region, abnormally small folds in the operculum (a lid-like structure composed of portions of three adjoining brain lobes), and damage to the left temporal lobe. The first single photon emission tomography (SPECT) study of a patient with AS found a lower than normal blood supply in the left parietal area of the brain. Brain imaging studies on a larger sample of patients is the next stage of research.

Diagnostic coding changes in DSM-5

The diagnosis of Asperger syndrome has been complicated by its close relationship to the symptoms found in people with autistic disorders. As a result, researchers have had a great deal of difficulty determining prevalence and incidence statistics for Asperger syndrome, and clinicians have had difficulty accessing services for their patients. After re-evaluating the diagnostic criteria for AS, autism, and other related disorders, the panel charged with creating the fifth edition of the *DSM* (*DSM-5*), due out in May 2013, is expected to combine the diagnoses of Asperger syndrome, autism, **childhood disintegrative disorder**, and pervasive developmental disorder under the rubric of autism spectrum disorders. This change in the diagnostic coding has led to some controversy and will also lead to changes in the prevalence and incidence statistics for all of the affected disorders. The new categorization, however, may have the advantage of improved diagnostic consistency, with accompanying improvement in accessibility of services.

Treatment

There is no cure for AS and no single prescribed regimen for all affected patients. Specific treatments are based on the individual's symptom pattern.

Traditional

Individuals with Asperger syndrome often benefit from **psychotherapy**, particularly during adolescence, in order to help them cope with depression and other painful feelings related to their social difficulties. Treatment aims to help patients manage the major issues associated with the condition: lack of communication skills, obsessive routines, and physical clumsiness.

Therapists who are experienced in treating children with AS have found that the child should be allowed to proceed slowly in forming an emotional bond with the therapist. Too much emotional intensity at the beginning may be more than the child can handle. Behavioral approaches seem to work best with these children. **Play therapy** can be helpful in teaching the child to recognize social cues as well as lowering the level of emotional tension.

Communication and **social skills training** groups are also often used to help children with Asperger syndrome learn and then practice skills that may benefit them in the classroom, within their families, and in their efforts to connect to their peers.

Adults with AS are most likely to benefit from individual therapy using a cognitive-behavioral approach, although many also attend **group therapy**. Some adults have been helped by working with speech therapists on their pragmatic language skills. A relatively new approach called behavioral coaching has been used to help adults with AS learn to organize and set priorities for their daily activities.

Drugs

The drugs that are recommended most often for children with AS are psychostimulants (**methylphenidate**,

pemoline), **clonidine**, or one of the tricyclic **antidepressants** (TCAs) for hyperactivity or inattention; **beta blockers**, neuroleptics, or lithium for anger, aggression, agitation, and irritability; **selective serotonin reuptake inhibitors (SSRIs)** or TCAs for rituals, repetitive behavior, depression, and preoccupations; and **SSRIs** or TCAs for anxiety and OCD-like symptoms. Low-dose **naltrexone** (a drug usually used to help alcoholics avoid drinking) has been shown to be useful in decreasing ritualistic, repetitive behaviors in people with Asperger syndrome. One alternative herbal remedy that has been tried with AS patients is **St. John's wort**.

Clinical trials

In 2011, 25 **clinical trials** for the treatment of Asperger syndrome were being sponsored by the National Institutes of Health (NIH) and other agencies.

One study (trial no. NCT00464477) was recruiting parents of children with a pervasive developmental disorder (including autism, autistic spectrum disorder, PDD-NOS, Asperger syndrome, childhood disintegrative disorder, and **Rett syndrome**) to participate in a study seeking to determine potential causes of these disorders. Other trials were evaluating drugs for treatment. For example, N-acetylcysteine was being tested for the improvement of the behavior problems often associated with autism spectrum disorders (NCT00453180). The potential beneficial effect of DMSA, an oral chelating agent that removes mercury and other metals from the body, was also being investigated (NCT00376194), as was the efficacy of **risperidone** in normalizing symptoms (NCT00352196). Other drugs being tested were **aripiprazole** (NCT00198055) and **citalopram** (NCT00086645). A **cognitive-behavioral therapy** (CBT) program was also being evaluated for treating anxiety symptoms, social problems, and adaptive behavior deficits in children with Asperger syndrome (NCT00280670).

Clinical trial information is constantly updated by NIH and the most recent information on AS trials can be found at: http://clinicaltrials.gov/ct2/results?term=Asperger+syndrome+

Prognosis

AS is a lifelong but stable condition. The prognosis for children with AS is generally good as far as intellectual development is concerned, though one challenge is equipping schools with the tools needed to meet special social needs. However, there is an increased risk of developing psychosis later in life.

QUESTIONS TO ASK YOUR DOCTOR

- Can Asperger syndrome be cured?
- What treatment options are available?
- How do they differ in terms of expected outcomes?
- Is drug therapy required?

Prevention

Effective prevention of Asperger syndrome awaits further genetic mapping together with ongoing research in the structures and functioning of the brain.

Resources

BOOKS

Attwood, T. *The Complete Guide to Asperger's Syndrome.* London: Jessica Kingsley, 2008.

Behrman R.E., et al. *Nelson Textbook of Pediatrics,* 18th ed. Philadelphia: Saunders, 2007.

Bradley, W., et al. *Neurology in Clinical Practice,* 5th ed. Philadelphia: Butterworth-Heinemann, 2008.

Carley, Michael John. *Asperger's from the Inside Out: A Supportive and Practical Guide for Anyone with Asperger's Syndrome.* New York: Perigee Trade, 2008.

Dubin, Nick, and Valerie Gaus. *Asperger Syndrome and Anxiety: A Guide to Successful Stress Management.* Philadelphia: Jessica Kingsley, 2009.

Gaus, Valerie L. *Cognitive-Behavioral Therapy for Adult Asperger Syndrome.* New York: Guilford Press, 2007.

Goetz, C.G. *Goetz's Textbook of Clinical Neurology,* 3rd ed. Philadelphia: Saunders, 2007.

Hagland, Carol. *Getting to Grips with Asperger Syndrome: Understanding Adults on the Autism Spectrum.* Philadelphia: Jessica Kingsley, 2009.

Marshack, Kathy J. *Life with a Partner or Spouse with Asperger Syndrome: Going over the Edge? Practical Steps to Saving You and Your Relationship.* Shawnee Mission, KS: Autism Asperger Publishing, 2009.

Patrick, Nancy J. *Social Skills for Teenagers and Adults with Asperger Syndrome: A Practical Guide to Day-to-day Life.* Philadelphia: Jessica Kingsley, 2008.

Robison, John Elder. *Look Me in the Eye: My Life with Asperger's.* New York: Three Rivers Press, 2008.

Silverman, Stephan M., and Rich Weinfeld. *School Success for Kids with Asperger's Syndrome: A Practical Guide for Parents and Teachers.* Waco, TX: Prufrock Press, 2007.

PERIODICALS

Bouxsein, K.J., et al. "A Comparison of General And Specific Instructions To Promote Task Engagement and Completion by a Young Man with Asperger Syndrome." *Journal of Applied Behavior Analysis* 41, no. 1 (2008): 113–16.

Fitzgerald, M. "Suicide and Asperger's Syndrome." *Crisis* 28, no. 1 (2007): 1–3.

Lopata, C., et al. "Motor and Visuomotor Skills of Children with Asperger's Disorder: Preliminary Findings." *Perceptual and Motor Skills* 104, no. 3, pt. 2 (2007): 1183–92.

Punshon, C., et al. "The Not Guilty Verdict: Psychological Reactions to a Diagnosis of Asperger Syndrome in Adulthood." *Autism* 13, no. 3 (2009): 265–83.

Rinehart, N.J., et al. "Brief Report: Inhibition of Return in Young People with Autism and Asperger's Disorder." *Autism* 12, no. 3 (2008): 249–60.

Ryburn, B., et al. "Asperger Syndrome: How Does It Relate to Non-verbal Learning Disability?" *Journal of Neuropsychology* 3, pt. 1 (2009): 107–23.

Sahlander, C., et al. "Motor Function in Adults with Asperger's Disorder: A Comparative Study." *Physiotherapy Theory and Practice* 24, no. 21 (2008): 73–81.

Senju, A., et al. "Mindblind Eyes: An Absence of Spontaneous Theory of Mind in Asperger Syndrome." *Science* 325, no. 5942 (2009): 883–85.

Tantam, D., and S. Girqis. "Recognition and Treatment of Asperger Syndrome in the Community." *British Medical Bulletin* 89 (2009): 41–62.

WEBSITES

"Asperger Syndrome." MedlinePlus. http://www.nlm.nih.gov/medlineplus/aspergerssyndrome.html (accessed October 10, 2010).

"Asperger Syndrome." National Institute of Child Health and Human Development. http://www.nichd.nih.gov/health/topics/asperger_syndrome.cfm (accessed October 10, 2010).

"Asperger Syndrome Information Page." National Institute of Neurological Disorders and Stroke. Last modified June 15, 2011. http://www.ninds.nih.gov/disorders/asperger/asperger.htm (accessed October 10, 2010).

ORGANIZATIONS

Autism Network International (ANI), PO Box 35448, Syracuse, NY, 13235-5448, http://autreat.com.

Autism Society of America, 4340 East-West Hwy., Ste. 350, Bethesda, MD, 20814, (301) 657-0881, (800) 328-8476, http://www.autism-society.org.

Global and Regional Asperger's Syndrome Partnership, 135 East 15th St., New York, NY, 10003, (646) 242-4003, info@grasp.org, http://www.grasp.org.

MAAP Services for Autism, Asperger Syndrome, and PDD, PO Box 524, Crown Point, IN, 46308, (219) 662-1311, Fax: (219) 662-0638, info@maapservices.org, http://www.maapservices.org.

National Institute of Mental Health, 6001 Executive Blvd., Rm. 8184, MSC 9663, Bethesda, MD, 20892-9663, (301) 433-4513; TTY: (301) 443-8431, Fax: (301) 443-4279, (866) 615-6464; TTY: (866) 415-8051, nimhinfo@nih.gov, http://www.nimh.nih.gov.

Rebecca J. Frey, PhD
Rosalyn Carson-DeWitt

Assertive community treatment

Definition

Assertive community treatment (ACT) is an integrative approach to treating severe mental illness, such as **schizophrenia**. Community-based, mobile teams provide patients with treatment and support services, including access to medication, counseling, education, and legal and financial support.

Purpose

ACT is aimed at older teenagers and adults with a mental illness that greatly impacts their ability to care for themselves and function at home or work. The intensive program traditionally helps patients with serious, long-term illnesses such as schizophrenia, **schizoaffective disorder**, or **bipolar disorder**, but ACT may also benefit those who have not had success with other outpatient treatment approaches or who have trouble accessing or adhering to other treatment regimens. ACT combines medication, counseling, rehabilitation, education, legal and financial support, and family assistance into one comprehensive program. Its goals aim to help people with mental illness recover in such areas as personal living (especially with regards to living independently), social interaction, relationships with friends and family members, and employment.

Description

Doctors Arnold J. Marx, Leonard I. Stein, Mary Ann Test, and additional colleagues pioneered the ACT program in the late 1960s in Madison, Wisconsin, as an alternative to admission to a psychiatric institution. While working at the Mendota State Hospital, now called the Mendota Mental Health Institute, the team noticed that patients who got better in the hospital often became sick again when reentering the community. They proposed that a round-the-clock program outside the hospital could provide the same ongoing support and therapy. In 1972, they put their theory to the test and formally launched ACT. The program is offered in many U.S. states and throughout Canada and the United Kingdom. The U.S. Department of Veterans Affairs also supports and has implemented ACT programs across the country.

Because ACT provides care outside of the doctor's office, usually in the comfort of the patient's home, the community-based program is sometimes referred to as a "hospital without walls." The cornerstone of each ACT program is a diverse team of nearly a dozen different healthcare specialists, including doctors, nurses, and counselors. Professionals involved with ACT include those with backgrounds and training in counseling, nursing, psychiatry, rehabilitation, social work, and other such relevant fields. The program provides support and care 24 hours a day, seven days a week, all year long.

Project leaders, called case managers, usually have fewer than 10 patients, which allows for highly individualized care. A patient is considered a “client” of the ACT team. ACT is different from other **community mental health** center (CMHC) services, which usually require the patient to visit a clinic for treatment. The ACT team comes to the client, and those who participate in ACT receive more personalized attention and may be in contact with the ACT team daily, as opposed to weekly or monthly. The ACT team provides all necessary care, including **substance abuse** treatment and rehabilitation. CMHC services often refer clients to an outside specialist for specific issues.

Key features

ACT has three key features: treatment, rehabilitation, and support services.

- The treatment of ACT may involve antipsychotic and antidepressant medicines, substance abuse therapy, counseling, and possible admission to a hospital for closer monitoring.
- The rehabilitation arm of the program helps the patient find volunteer work and paid employment and provides support for continuing education. Specialists teach patients new behaviors, such as how to structure schedules and perform daily activities.
- The support services advise patients on how to find legal and financial support, housing, transportation, and other services. Family members are taught how to cope with their loved one’s illness and are provided with education materials. According to the Schizophrenia Patient Outcomes Research Team (PORT) study, funded by the National Institute of Mental Health and the Agency for Health Care Policy and Research, fewer than one in ten families of persons with schizophrenia receives such education and support.

Goals

ACT is targeted to persons with very severe mental illness that has led to repeated hospital and emergency room visits, **homelessness**, or jail time. According to the National Jail Association, about 700,000 persons with mental illness are incarcerated every year. ACT programs have helped such criminal offenders meet their legal obligations while providing medical support and rehabilitation services.

The ACT program aims to:

- relieve or cure symptoms of the disorder
- reduce or prevent repeated, severe episodes associated with the disorder
- enhance the client’s quality of life
- improve functioning at work and in social settings
- encourage independence and teach necessary self-care skills
- reduce the burden of care on a patient’s family by providing education and support

Benefits

Studies have shown that ACT and similar programs greatly reduce the number of hospital stays among those with severe mental illness. One study found that ACT not only reduced overall hospital admissions but also decreased the length of the hospital stays. ACT has been shown to improve patient functioning and encourage patients to stick to their treatment routines. The benefits

KEY TERMS

Antidepressant—A drug used to treat depression.

Antipsychotic—A drug used to treat serious mental disorders that cause hallucinations or delusions.

Bipolar disorder—A mental illness marked by alternating periods of excitement and depression; also called manic-depressive disorder.

Delusion—A false belief that persists despite evidence to the contrary.

Hallucination—A false or distorted sensory experience that appears to be real to the person experiencing it, such as seeing something that is not actually there.

Schizoaffective disorder—Schizophrenic symptoms occurring concurrently with a major depressive and/or manic episode.

Schizophrenia—A severe mental illness in which a person has difficulty distinguishing what is real from what is not real. It is often characterized by hallucinations, delusions, and withdrawal from people and social activities.

Substance abuse—Overuse of a drug or alcohol, which leads to addiction.

are reported to be particularly marked among those with a coexisting mental disorder and substance abuse problem, perhaps because such patients are at higher risk of **hospitalization** and complications.

Compared to those who are admitted to an institution, ACT clients have fewer symptoms, more positive social interactions, and spend less time unemployed. Experts say anywhere between 20% and 40% of people with the most severe and persistent mental illnesses would benefit from ACT.

QUESTIONS TO ASK YOUR DOCTOR

- Does a local ACT program exist? If not, how far away is the nearest ACT program?
- Will my health insurance pay some or all of the expenses for ACT?
- Will I take medicine while going through ACT?
- What happens if ACT does not help me?

Precautions

Because there are so many specialists on an ACT team, it can be costly. Some argue that the expense is justified, particularly when compared to the cost of an extended hospital stay. According to the National Alliance on Mental Illness (NAMI), ACT costs each participant between $9,000 and $14,000 a year, while hospital costs for an extended stay can exceed $100,000.

Preparation

Preparation involves locating an ACT program. There are a limited number of ACT teams in the United States. According to NAMI, only six states (Delaware, Idaho, Missouri, Rhode Island, Texas, and Wisconsin) offer statewide programs, though 19 other states offer test, or pilot, programs in specific communities. In different states, ACT may be known by different names; it is commonly referred to as the Program of Assertive Community Treatment (PACT), and many organizations use the terms interchangeably. Other names for ACT include community support programs (CSP) and mobile treatment teams (MTT). Regardless of the title, all ACT programs abide by standards set by NAMI.

Aftercare

ACT professionals work with patients without time limits in assertive community treatment programs. As such, patients are much better prepared when their treatment ends and aftercare begins.

Risks

The risk of relapse is always present for patients with mental illness. However, assertive community treatment has been proven to help reduce that risk and is considered an effective way, both from a medical and cost standpoint, to deal with severe and persistent mental illness. According to the Center for Behavioral Health Services and Criminal Justice Research, more than 25 randomized controlled trials have been conducted on ACT. The majority of these trials found ACT to be more effective than traditional care of patients with mental illness in the areas of decreased hospitalization, increased patient satisfaction, and improvement in housing stability and general quality of life. The biggest issue with ACT is that it is considered a largely underutilized form of treatment; NAMI estimates that up to 40% of adults with mental illness could be helped by ACT if it were available in their communities.

Resources

BOOKS

Johnson, Sandra J. *Assertive Community Treatment: Evidence-based Practice or Managed Recovery.* New Brunswick, NJ: Transaction Publishers, 2011.

PERIODICALS

Marshall, Max, and Austin Lockwood. "Assertive Community Treatment for People with Severe Mental Disorders." *Cochrane Database of Systematic Reviews* 2011, no. 4 (April): CD001089.

Rosen, Alan. "Assertive Community Treatment—Issues from Scientific and Clinical Literature with Implications for Practice." *Journal of Rehabilitation Research & Development* 44, no. 6 (2007): 813–26.

OTHER

Center for Behavioral Health Services and Criminal Justice Research. "Assertive Community Treatment: Intervention Fact Sheet." http://www.cbhs-cjr.rutgers.edu/pdfs/ACT_-Fact_Sheet_2_09.pdf (accessed October 13, 2011).

WEBSITES

Assertive Community Treatment Association. "ACT History and Origins." http://www.actassociation.org/origins (accessed October 13, 2011).

Lehman, Anthony F., Donald M Steinwachs, et al. "The Schizophrenia Patient Outcomes Research Team (PORT) Treatment Recommendations—At Issue: Translating Research into Practice." Agency for Healthcare Research and Quality. http://www.ahrq.gov/clinic/schzrec.htm (accessed October 13, 2011).

National Alliance on Mental Illness. "Assertive Community Treatment (ACT)." http://www.nami.org/template.cfm?template=/contentManagement/contentDisplay.cfm&contentID=21056 (accessed October 13, 2011).

ORGANIZATIONS

Assertive Community Treatment Association, PO Box 2428, Brighton, MI, 48116, (810) 227-1859, Fax: (810) 227-5785, acta@actassociation.org, http://www.actassociation.org.

National Alliance on Mental Illness, 3803 North Fairfax Drive, Suite 100, Arlington, VA, 22203, (703) 524-7600, (800) 950-6264, Fax: (703) 524-9094, http://www.nami.org.

National Institute of Mental Health, 6001 Executive Boulevard, Room 8184, Bethesda, MD, 20892-9663, (301) 443-4513, (866) 615-6464, Fax: (301) 443-4279, nimhinfo@nih.gov, http://www.nimh.nih.gov.

Substance Abuse and Mental Health Services Administration, PO Box 2345, Bethesda, MD, 20847-2345, (877) 726-4727, Fax: (240) 221-4292, SAMHSAInfo@samhsa.hhs.gov, http://www.samhsa.org.

Kelli Miller Stacy
William Atkins

Assertiveness training

Definition

Assertiveness training is a form of behavior therapy designed to help people stand up for or empower themselves. The concept of assertiveness is a response that seeks to maintain an appropriate balance between passivity and aggression. Assertive responses promote fairness and equality in human interactions, based on a positive sense of respect for self and others. Assertiveness training may help individuals recover from daily pressures or aggravations experienced in social situations involving friends, parents, teachers, colleagues, or others.

Purpose

The purpose of assertiveness training is to teach people appropriate strategies for identifying and acting on their desires, needs, and opinions while remaining respectful of others. This form of training is tailored to the needs of specific participants and the situations they find particularly challenging. Assertiveness training is a broad approach that can be applied to many different personal, academic, healthcare, and work situations.

Description

Assertiveness training is often included within other programs, but "stand-alone" programs in self-assertion are offered in facilities like women's centers or college counseling centers. Corporate programs for new personnel sometimes offer assertiveness training as part of communication or teamwork groups, or as part of a program on sexual harassment.

Assertiveness training typically begins with an information-gathering exercise in which participants are asked to think about and list the areas in their life in which they have difficulty asserting themselves. Very often they will notice specific situations or patterns of behavior that they want to focus on during the course. The next stage in assertive training is usually "role-playing," which is designed to help participants practice clearer and more direct ways of communicating with others. The role-plays allow for practice and repetition of the new techniques, helping each person learn assertive responses by acting on them. Feedback is provided to improve the response, and the role-play is repeated. Eventually, each person is asked to practice assertive techniques in everyday life, outside the training setting. Role-plays usually incorporate specific problems for individual participants, such as difficulty speaking up to an overbearing boss, setting limits to intrusive friends, or stating a clear preference about dinner to a spouse. Role-plays often include examples of aggressive and passive responses, in addition to the assertive responses, to help participants distinguish between these extremes as they learn a new set of behaviors.

Assertiveness training promotes the use of "I" statements as a way to help individuals express their feelings and reactions to others. A commonly used model of an "I" statement is "when you _________, I feel ___________," to help the participant describe what they see the other person as doing, and how they feel about that action. "I" statements are often contrasted with "you" statements, which are usually not received well by others. For example, "When you are two hours late getting home from work, I feel both anxious and angry," is a less accusing communication than "You are a selfish and inconsiderate jerk for not telling me you would be two hours late." Prompts are often used to help participants learn new communication styles. This approach helps participants learn new ways of expressing themselves as well as how it feels to be assertive.

Learning specific techniques and perspectives such as self-observation skills, awareness of personal preferences, and assuming personal responsibility are important components of the assertiveness training process. Role-play and practice help with self-observation, while making lists can be a helpful technique for exploring personal preferences for those who may not have a good sense of their own needs and desires. Participants may be asked to list anything from their ten favorite movies or pieces of music to their favorite foods, places they would like to visit, subjects that interest them, and so on.

Origins

Assertiveness training has a decades-long history in mental health and personal growth groups, going back to the women's movement of the 1970s. The approach was introduced to encourage women to stand up for themselves appropriately in their interactions with others, particularly as they moved into graduate education and the workplace in greater numbers. The original association of assertiveness training with the women's movement in the United States grew out of the discovery of many women in the movement that they were hampered by their inability to be assertive. Today, assertiveness training is used in settings as diverse as schools, corporate boardrooms, and psychiatric hospitals, for purposes as varied as **substance abuse** treatment, **social skills training**, vocational programs, and responding to harassment. Psychological researchers at Southern Methodist University (Dallas, Texas) use a virtual-reality laboratory to teach women assertiveness skills to help prevent sexual victimization. U. S. psychologists Ernest Jouriles, Renee McDonald, and Lorelei Simpson found that women in a control group (without assertiveness training) were twice as likely to be victims of sexual victimization when compared to women who had participated in their assertiveness training.

Benefits

Learning to communicate in a clear and honest fashion helps strengthen interpersonal relationships. Specific areas of intervention and change in assertiveness training include conflict resolution, realistic goal setting, and stress management. In addition to emotional and psychological benefits, taking a more active approach to self-determination has been shown to have positive outcomes in many personal choices related to health, including being assertive in avoiding risky sexual situations, abstaining from using drugs or alcohol, and assuming responsibility for self-care if diagnosed with a chronic illness.

Precautions

There are a few precautions with assertiveness training. One potential caution would be to remain within assertive responses, rather than becoming aggressive. Some participants in assertiveness training programs who are just learning the techniques of appropriate assertiveness may "overdo" their new behaviors and come across as aggressive rather than assertive. Such overcompensation would most likely disappear with continued practice of the techniques.

One additional precaution about assertiveness training is that it should not be regarded as the equivalent of martial arts training or similar physical self-defense techniques. It is important to distinguish between contexts or situations in which verbal assertiveness is appropriate and useful, and those in which it is irrelevant. In some situations, a person's decision to leave the situation or seek help because they feel unsafe is preferable to a dangerous encounter.

Preparation

Preparation for assertiveness training varies from person to person. For some participants, prior preparation is not needed before practicing the techniques; for others, however, individual counseling or therapy may help prepare the individual for assertiveness training. For participants who may be more shy and feel uncomfortable saying "no" or speaking up for themselves, a brief course of individual therapy will help to prepare them psychologically and emotionally to use assertive techniques.

Aftercare

Aftercare can involve ongoing supportive therapy, again based on the individual's level of comfort in using the assertive techniques. For those who are comfortable using the techniques on their own, a supportive social network or occasional participation in a support group

KEY TERMS

Assertive—Confidently self-assured; able to express oneself constructively and directly.

Conflict resolution—Various methods used by psychologists and other such professionals to eliminate sources of conflict in patients.

Overcompensation—An attempt to overcome or correct a behavior by going too far in the opposite direction.

Role-playing—A technique used in assertiveness training and other forms of therapy in which participants act out roles relevant to real-life situations in order to change their attitudes and behaviors.

Stress management—A method used by medical professionals such as psychiatrists to reduce or eliminate stress (especially chronic stress) in patients' lives.

will be enough to help maintain the new behavioral patterns. The ultimate goal is for each participant to effectively self-monitor his or her use of assertive techniques on an ongoing basis.

Risks

There are minimal risks associated with assertiveness training. Personal relationships may be affected if those around the participant have difficulty accepting the changes in their friend or family member. This risk, however, is no greater than that associated with any other life change.

Another potential risk is that of overcompensating in the early stages of training by being too aggressive. With appropriate feedback, participants can usually learn to modify and improve their responses.

People who are very shy or self-conscious, or who were harshly treated as children, may experience anxiety during the training as they work toward speaking up and otherwise changing their behaviors. The anxiety may be uncomfortable but should decrease as the person becomes more comfortable with the techniques and receives encouragement from others in the program.

Results

An enhanced sense of well-being and more positive self-esteem are typical results from assertiveness training. Many participants report that they feel better about themselves and are more capable of handling the stresses of daily life. In addition, people who have participated in assertiveness training have a better sense of boundaries and are able to set appropriate and healthy limits with others. Being able to set appropriate limits (such as saying "no") helps people to avoid feeling victimized by others.

A healthy sense of self-determination and respect for others is the ultimate outcome of assertiveness training. Such a balance helps each person work better with others and make appropriate decisions for themselves.

See also Behavior modification

Resources

BOOKS

Bishop, Sue. *Develop Your Assertiveness.* London: Kogan Page, 2006.

Kemp, Jana. *NO!: How One Simple Word Can Transform Your Life.* New York: AMACOM, 2005.

Leman, Kevin. *Pleasers: Why Women Don't Have to Make Everyone Happy to be Happy.* Grand Rapids, MI: Revell, 2006.

McIntosh, Perry, and Richard A. Luecke. *Increase Your Influence at Work.* New York: American Management Association, 2011.

Newman, Susan. *The Book of No: 250 Ways to Say It—and Mean It—and Stop People-pleasing Forever.* New York: McGraw-Hill, 2006.

Townend, Anni. *Assertiveness and Diversity.* Basingstoke, UK: Palgrave Macmillan, 2007.

PERIODICALS

Hayakawa, M. "How Repeated 15-Minute Assertiveness Training Sessions Reduce Wrist Cutting in Patients with Borderline Personality Disorder." *American Journal of Psychotherapy* 63, no. 1 (2009): 41–51.

Lin, Y. R. "Evaluation of Assertiveness Training for Psychiatric Patients." *Journal of Clinical Nursing* 17, no. 21 (2008): 2875–83.

WEBSITES

Centre for Confidence and Well-Being. "Assertive Communication." http://www.centreforconfidence.co.uk/projects.php?pid=59 (accessed October 14, 2011).

Mayo Clinic staff. "Being Assertive: Reduce Stress, Communicate Better." MayoClinic.com. http://www.mayoclinic.com/health/assertive/SR00042 (accessed November 16, 2011).

Deanna Pledge, PhD
William Atkins

Assessment *see* **Psychological assessment and diagnosis**

Ativan *see* **Lorazepam**

Atomoxetine

Definition

Atomoxetine (Strattera) is a medication used to treat **attention deficit hyperactivity disorder (ADHD)**. Atomoxetine belongs to a class of drugs known as selective norepinephrine reuptake inhibitors (SNRIs), which specifically act on the neurological signaling chemical norepinephrine. Norepinephrine is a type of neurotransmitter involved in normal **brain** function and has an effect on mood and concentration.

Purpose

Atomoxetine is used to treat some of the symptoms of **ADHD** in both adults and children. It was the first nonstimulant drug approved by the U.S. Food and Drug

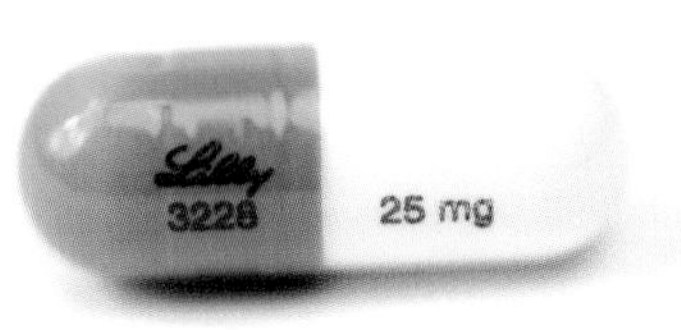

Strattera (atomoxetine), 25 mg. *(© Photo Researchers, Inc.)*

Administration for the treatment of ADHD, though the stimulants remain the mainstay of ADHD therapy. Atomoxetine is often used for patients with ADHD who develop too many side effects from stimulants or who cannot tolerate stimulants due to co-existing anxiety or **substance abuse**. Patients with Tourette syndrome may find that the stimulant medications used to treat ADHD worsen their tics; atomoxetine is useful in this scenario because it can treat the symptoms of ADHD without worsening co-existing tics. For patients with ADHD who also have co-existing **depression**, atomoxetine may have some antidepressant properties, though it has not officially been approved for use in treating depression. The decision to use atomoxetine alone or in combination with other drugs depends on the medical profile of the patient and individual health parameters.

Description

Atomoxetine has a therapeutic mechanism of action that is focused on the modulation of the natural body chemical norepinephrine. Norepinephrine is a type of neurotransmitter in the nervous system, a chemical that neurons use to signal one another in complex pathways for normal brain and body functioning. **Neurotransmitters** such as norepinephrine bind to chemical receptors on the surface of neurons (brain cells). Once bound to a receptor they affect physiological processes. The receptors activate a sequence of cellular events known as a chemical cascade or signaling pathway. Neurotransmitter signaling pathways are responsible for many regulatory processes, including neuronal signaling that affects mood and concentration.

During the signaling process, neurotransmitters such as norepinephrine travel from one neuron to the next. These chemicals need to cross a short space between the end of one neuron and the beginning of the next neuron, known as the synapse or synaptic space. Norepinephrine is released from the end of neuron one, crosses the synaptic space, and binds to a neurotransmitter-specific receptor on the surface of the next neuron (neuron two). Any extra norepinephrine that is left in the synaptic space is taken back up by neuron one in a process known as reuptake. The more neurotransmitters allowed to remain in the synaptic space, the more will eventually be allowed to bind to receptors on neuron two.

Selective norepinephrine reuptake inhibitors such as atomoxetine decrease the reuptake of the neurotransmitters by neuron one, allowing more norepinephrine to be present in the synapse. It is believed that a decrease in norepinephrine signaling contributes to disorders such as ADHD and depression. Atomoxetine mainly helps by increasing levels of norepinephrine, but it has some impact on the neurotransmitter **dopamine** in certain brain areas as well. Atomoxetine has little or no effect on the synaptic levels of other neurotransmitters such as **serotonin**.

The brain has discrete physiological areas that impact different functions of the mind and body. The area of the brain known as the prefrontal cortex affects attention span, judgment, response to external stimuli, memory, motor function, and impulse control. It is believed that increases in the available amounts of norepinephrine (and to a small degree dopamine) by drugs such as atomoxetine improve the symptoms of ADHD in the prefrontal cortex. Atomoxetine seems to function to improve the symptoms of ADHD without psychostimulation.

Recommended dosage

Atomoxetine is taken as an oral medication, usually in the morning, and often requires several weeks of therapy before ADHD symptoms improve. For adults, the dose is usually started at 40 mg for a few days, to allow the patient to adjust to the medication, and is then increased to 80 mg a day. Some patients will require the maximum dose of 100 mg a day for the best effect, but this dose should not be attempted until the patient does well on the 80 mg dose for three to four weeks. Children six years old and older and heavier than 154 lb. (70 kg) follow the same regimen but may have doses divided through the day to reduce the amount taken at any one time. Children who are older than six years and less than 70 kg are dosed based on weight. The usual starting dose is 0.5 mg per 2.2 lb. (1 kg) a day for several days, increased to 1.2 mg per kg

KEY TERMS

Bipolar disorder—Psychiatric mood disorder characterized by periods of manic behavior that may alternate with periods of depression; previously known as manic depressive disorder.

Cytochrome P450 (CYP450)—Enzymes present in the liver that metabolize drugs.

Dopamine—A type of neurotransmitter involved in regulation of concentration, impulse control, judgment, mood, attention span, psychostimulation, and disease states such as addiction, ADHD, and depression.

Glaucoma—Condition involving increased pressure within the eye that may cause damage and blindness.

Mania—Physiological state of hyperactivity experienced by patients with certain psychiatric illnesses involving inappropriate elevated mood, pressured speech, poor judgment, and sometimes psychotic episodes.

Monoamine oxidase inhibitors (MAOIs)—Type of antidepressant medication that affects various kinds of neurotransmitters, including serotonin.

Neurotransmitter—A chemical messenger that travels through the body and acts in the nervous system. Neurotransmitter signaling is responsible for a wide range of bodily processes and is often the target of medications involving the brain and cardiovascular system.

Neurotransmitter receptor—A physical recipient for chemicals called neurotransmitters. Receptors sit on the surface of cells that make up body tissues, and once bound to the neurotransmitter, they initiate the chemical signaling pathway associated with neurotransmitters.

Norepinephrine—A type of neurotransmitter involved in regulation of concentration, impulse control, judgment, mood, attention span, psychostimulation, and disease states such as ADHD and depression.

Nucleus accumbens—Area of the brain involved in psychostimulation and addiction.

Prefrontal cortex—Area of the brain involved in attention span, judgment, response to external stimuli, memory, motor function, and impulse control.

Serotonin—A type of neurotransmitter involved in regulation of the blood vessels, brain processes, and disease states such as depression.

Striatum—Area of the brain involved in psychostimulation and addiction.

Synapse—Physical space between neurons that allows the passage of neurotransmitters for chemical signaling pathways.

Tic—Involuntary movements (such as twitching or facial grimacing) or vocalizations (such as throat clearing or barking) associated with Tourette syndrome.

Tourette syndrome—An inherited neuropsychiatric disorder characterized by the development of both motor and vocal tics. The tics are preceded by a feeling of tension or urgency in the affected individual until the tic behavior is performed and relieves the perceived feeling of tension.

per day. The maximum dose in this population is 1.4 mg per kg per day.

Patients are frequently reassessed for the need for treatment, as drugs for ADHD are avoided unless absolutely necessary. The dose chosen depends on individual patient response to the medication regarding its effectiveness, and individual patient response to the medication regarding side effects. Patients are dosed at the lowest possible effective dose to avoid the development of adverse side effects. Slowly increasing the dose over time helps with minimizing side effects, and some side effects lessen with continued use. Some patients have altered metabolism of atomoxetine and require a slower pace for increasing the dose. Patients with liver impairment may not metabolize atomoxetine well and will require lower doses or may not be able to use the drug.

Precautions

Atomoxetine use is not without side effects or potential consequences. While many patients do well on atomoxetine, others are more sensitive to the medication and develop more side effects. Higher doses increase the risk of adverse effects, hence the lowest dose possible is used for treatment. Clinicians weigh the potential for benefit with atomoxetine treatment against the potential undesirable outcomes when making treatment decisions. Rare but serious reactions include very high blood pressure, glaucoma, loss of consciousness, heart arrhythmias, heart attack,

stroke, **seizures**, liver toxicity, and sudden death. Some patients develop increased aggressiveness, **psychosis**, mania, or suicidality in the first weeks of use before the intended therapeutic effects take place. Children are especially at risk for these behavioral side effects. Patients taking atomoxetine are monitored closely for behavioral changes, especially when starting treatment or after dose changes.

Atomoxetine may be contraindicated or may require caution in patients with uncontrolled hypertension, liver function impairment or liver disease, kidney function impairment, glaucoma, heart conditions or abnormalities, or seizure disorder. Kidney and liver function, as well as blood pressure, may be monitored while taking atomoxetine. Atomoxetine is discouraged from use in patients with **bipolar disorder**, as it is more likely to induce a state of mania in these individuals than in those without bipolar disorder. Atomoxetine is classified as category C for pregnancy, which means that either there are no adequate human or animal studies or that adverse fetal effects were found in animal studies, but there is no available human data. The decision whether to use category C drugs in pregnancy is generally based on weighing the critical needs of the mother against the risk to the fetus. Other lower category agents are used whenever possible. The safety of atomoxetine use during breastfeeding is unknown, so its use is not recommended.

Side effects

Atomoxetine has many negative side effects. It usually takes several weeks of medication for the treatment effect to occur, while the undesirable side effects may occur at the onset of treatment. Sensitivity to atomoxetine varies among patients, and some patients may find that even lower doses are more than their body system can tolerate. Common reactions include dry mouth, abdominal pain, nausea and vomiting, constipation, **insomnia**, **sleep disorders** and abnormal dreams, decreased appetite, changes in urination, **erectile dysfunction**, changes to the menstrual cycle, drowsiness, numbness and tingling in the extremities, dizziness, **fatigue**, hot flashes, increased blood pressure and heart rate, sweating, and palpitations.

Interactions

Patients should make their doctor aware of all medications and supplements they are taking before using atomoxetine. Using alcohol while taking atomoxetine may create toxic reactions in the body and should be avoided. Drugs that affect the liver may alter the metabolism of atomoxetine, resulting in too much or too little of the drug in the body. This could lead to increased side effects or even toxic doses. Likewise, atomoxetine may affect the metabolism of other drugs, leading to greater or lower doses than therapeutically desired.

Certain drugs may cause toxicity when used with atomoxetine, either through additive effects or through inhibition of metabolism, causing toxic levels of atomoxetine in the blood. Drugs that may cause toxicity with atomoxetine include **antidepressants** such as **bupropion** and **duloxetine**; the anti-ulcer drug cimetidine; cinacalcet, used to treat some endocrine disorders; some anticancer drugs, such as imatinib and nalotinib; caffeine; the heart drug amiodarone; certain antibiotics such as linezolid; and antipsychotics such as **haloperidol** and **thioridazine**. It is unknown which herbal supplements interact with atomoxetine.

Antidepressants called **monoamine oxidase inhibitors (MAOIs)** also increase the amounts of norepinephrine and dopamine left in the body and cannot be used concurrently with atomoxetine, as the combination may cause overstimulation of the central nervous system and toxicity. Switching drug treatment from an MAOI to atomoxetine may require a waiting period of up to two weeks between drugs. The antidepressant drug **maprotiline** may also have additive effects with atomoxetine that cause toxicity.

QUESTIONS TO ASK YOUR DOCTOR

- Can I take the full dose right away or do I need to slowly increase the dose up to the full amount?
- Can I stop taking the medication right away or do I need to slowly decrease the dose in order to go off the medication?
- When should I eat in reference to taking this medication?
- Will this medication interact with any of my other prescription medications?
- Are there any over-the-counter medications I should not take with this medicine?
- What side effects should I watch for?
- Can I drink alcoholic beverages in the same time frame as taking this medication?

Resources

BOOKS

Brunton, Laurence L., et al. *Goodman and Gilman's The Pharmacological Basis of Therapeutics.* 12th ed. New York: McGraw Hill Medical, 2011.

Stargrove, Mitchell Bebel, et al. *Herb, Nutrient, and Drug Interactions: Clinical Implications and Therapeutic Strategies.* St. Louis: Mosby, 2007.

ORGANIZATIONS

American College of Neuropsychopharmacology, 5034-A Thoroughbred Lane, Brentwood, TN, 37027, (615) 324-2360, Fax: (615) 523-1715, acnp@acnp.org, http://www.acnp.org/default.aspx

American Psychiatric Association, 1000 Wilson Blvd., Ste. 1825, Arlington, VA, 22209-3901, (703) 907-7300, apa@psych.org, http://www.psych.org

American Society for Clinical Pharmacology and Therapeutics, 528 N Washington St., Alexandria, VA, 22314, (703) 836-6981, info@ascpt.org, http://www.ascpt.org.

Mental Health America, 2000 N Beauregard St., 6th Fl., Alexandria, VA, 22311, (703) 684-7722, (800) 969-6642, Fax: (703) 684-5968, http://www.nmha.org.

Maria Eve Basile, PhD

Attachment disorder *see* **Reactive attachment disorder of infancy or early childhood**

Attention deficit hyperactivity disorder (ADHD)

Definition

Attention deficit hyperactivity disorder (ADHD) is a chronic developmental disorder characterized by attention problems, including distractibility, hyperactivity, impulsive behaviors, and the inability to remain focused on tasks or activities. Among its acronyms are AD/HD and ADD. Diagnosed in childhood, the disorder can continue into adulthood.

Demographics

ADHD is a psychiatric disorder that is generally diagnosed in children before the age of 7 years, although

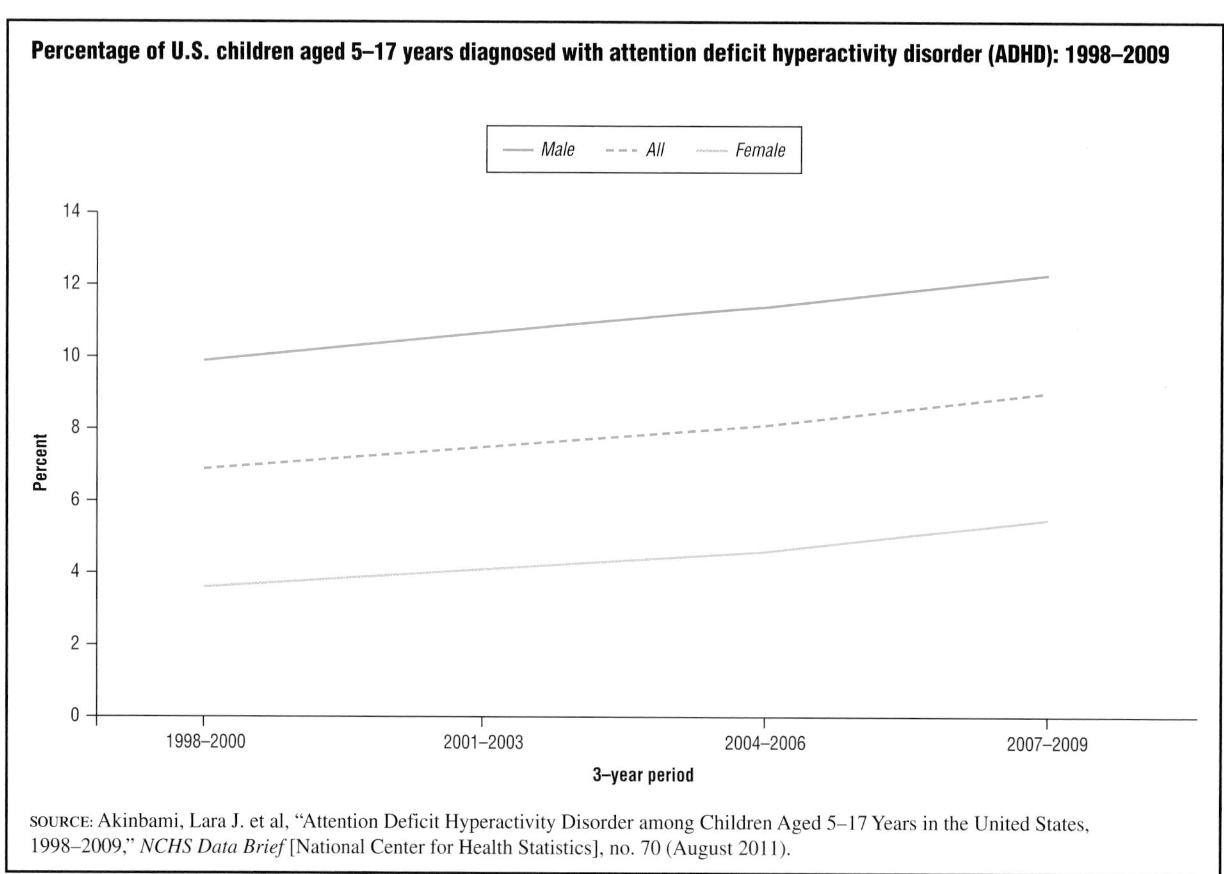

(Graph by PreMediaGlobal. © 2012 Cengage Learning.)

its symptoms can continue into adulthood. The Centers for Disease Control and Prevention (CDC) states that about 9.5% of children from 4 to 17 years of age have been diagnosed in the United States with ADHD. The disorder is more common in boys (13.2%) than in girls (5.6%). In addition, approximately 4.7% of American adults have ADHD.

In the United States, from 2007 through 2008, the average rate of ADHD varied geographically from a low of 5.6% in Nevada, in the western part of the United States, to a high of 15.6% in the east-central state of North Carolina. The CDC also reported that the **diagnosis** rate of ADHD increased by an average of 3% per year from 1997 to 2006, and from 2003 to 2007, the annual rate was 5.6%.

Worldwide, 3%–5% of children are afflicted with ADHD, with rates ranging from less than 1% in the United Kingdom (which has strict standards for diagnosis) to 12% in some countries within South America. Up to 50% of those diagnosed in childhood continue to have symptoms into adulthood.

Description

ADHD, also called hyperkinetic disorder (HKD) outside of the United States, is the most commonly diagnosed neurological disorder in children. It is frequently diagnosed by the age of seven years; however, it can be diagnosed as early as two years. Although childhood ADHD has been studied extensively, less information is available on **adult ADHD**. Studies on adults have produced a wide range of conflicting results. One reason for the wide range of findings is that the hyperactive component of the disorder often becomes less noticeable as individuals mature and develop more self-control.

Three types of ADHD are recognized by the **American Psychiatric Association** and outlined in the ***Diagnostic and Statistical Manual of Mental Disorders***, fourth edition, text revised (*DSM-IV-TR*). These are:

- predominately hyperactive type, characterized by excessive physical activity (e.g., constant fidgeting, inability to stay seated, inability to engage in quiet play) and impulsive behaviors (e.g., interrupting, difficulty waiting in line)
- predominately inattentive type, characterized by inability to pay close attention to detail, stay on task, and organize tasks; sometimes referred to as attention deficit disorder (ADD)
- combined hyperactive and inattentive type, characterized by an inappropriately high activity level with a high level of distractibility

Causes and symptoms

Causes

Although the exact causes of ADHD are not known, it is clear that specific parts of the **brain** are involved, including the frontal cortex, parietal lobe, and possibly the cerebellum. Functional **magnetic resonance imaging** (fMRI) studies comparing the brains of children with ADHD and those without the disorder show that children with ADHD have weaker brain activation of the frontal area when responding to tasks that require inhibition. Researchers believe that this is related to an imbalance in certain **neurotransmitters** (the chemicals in the brain that carry messages between nerve cells), specifically deficits in the neurotransmitters **dopamine** and norepinephrine. Drugs used to treat ADHD make dopamine and/or norepinephrine more available in the brain.

ADHD also appears to have a hereditary component. Children with a parent or sibling with ADHD are two to eight times more likely to develop the disorder. Scientists have suggested at least 20 genes that may make a person more vulnerable to ADHD or contribute to the disorder in some way. As of 2011, these genes were being studied to learn more about whether they contribute to ADHD, and, if so, to what degree.

The condition is also more likely in children whose mothers smoke tobacco products, use drugs, or have been exposed to toxins. Pregnant women who smoke tobacco products are at increased risk to giving birth to a child with ADHD. Alcohol or drug use during pregnancy may also contribute to increased risk for ADHD. Children who are exposed to toxins are more likely to acquire developmental and behavioral problems associated with ADHD when compared to children who have never been exposed to toxins. One such toxin that has been scientifically shown to produce ADHD-like symptoms is the element lead (symbol Pb), which is sometimes found in paint from old homes and buildings.

A widely publicized study conducted by Benjamin F. Feingold (1899–1982) in the early 1970s suggested that allergies to certain foods and food additives caused the characteristic hyperactivity of children with ADHD. Although some children may have adverse reactions to certain foods that can affect their behavior (for example, a rash might temporarily cause a child to be distracted from other tasks), carefully controlled follow-up studies have uncovered no link between food allergies and ADHD. Some researchers believe that artificial coloring and food preservatives may contribute to hyperactive behavior as seen in ADHD, but no link has been proven. A popularly held misconception about food and ADHD is that the consumption of sugar causes hyperactive behavior. Studies have shown no link between sugar intake and ADHD. It is important to note, however, that a nutritionally balanced diet is important for normal development in all children.

Symptoms

Children with ADHD have short attention spans, becoming easily distracted or frustrated with tasks. Although they may be quite intelligent, their lack of focus frequently results in poor grades and difficulties in school. Children with ADHD act impulsively, taking action first and thinking later. They are constantly moving, running, climbing, squirming, and fidgeting, but they often have trouble with motor skills and, as a result, may be clumsy and awkward. Their clumsiness may extend to the social arena, where they are sometimes shunned due to their impulsive and intrusive behavior. Because of these symptoms, ADHD children are often troubled by low self-esteem and may have poor relationships.

Diagnosis

There is not a single test for ADHD. Psychiatrists and other mental health professionals use the criteria listed in the *DSM-IV-TR* as a guideline for determining the presence of the disorder. A diagnosis of ADHD requires the presence of at least six of the following symptoms of inattention or six or more symptoms of hyperactivity and impulsivity combined. These symptoms must occur before the age of seven years, be present in at least two different environments (e.g., home and school) for at least six months, and not be attributable to any other developmental or mental health disorder.

Signs of inattention include:

- fails to pay close attention to detail or makes careless mistakes in schoolwork or other activities
- has difficulty sustaining attention in tasks or activities
- does not appear to listen when spoken to
- does not follow through on instructions and does not finish tasks
- has difficulty organizing tasks and activities
- avoids or dislikes tasks that require sustained mental effort (e.g., homework)
- loses things necessary for tasks (e.g., books, tools)
- is easily distracted
- is forgetful in daily activities

Signs of hyperactivity and impulsivity include:

- fidgets with hands or feet or squirms in seat
- does not remain seated or is restless when expected to sit
- runs or climbs excessively when inappropriate (in adolescents and adults, feelings of restlessness)
- has difficulty playing quietly
- blurts out answers before the question has been completed
- has difficulty waiting (e.g., to take turns, to stand in line)
- interrupts and/or intrudes on others

Additional hyperactivity/impulsivity criteria proposed for the fifth edition of the *DSM* (*DSM-5*, 2013) include:

- acts without thinking, such as starting tasks without reading instructions or speaking without considering the consequences
- is impatient and acts restless when waiting for others
- is uncomfortable doing things slowly, often rushing to complete tasks
- finds it difficult to resist temptations or opportunities, even when they involve risk

Examination

The first step in determining if a child has ADHD is to consult with a pediatrician. The pediatrician can make an initial evaluation of the child's developmental maturity compared to other children in his or her age group. The physician also can perform a comprehensive physical examination to rule out any organic causes of ADHD symptoms, such as an overactive thyroid, vision problems, or hearing problems.

If an organic problem is not found, a **psychologist**, **psychiatrist**, neurologist, neuropsychologist, or learning specialist typically is consulted to perform a comprehensive ADHD assessment. A complete medical, family, social, psychiatric, and educational history is compiled from existing medical and school records and from interviews with parents and teachers. Interviews may also be conducted with the child, depending on his or her age. Along with these interviews, several clinical inventories may also be used, such as the Conners Rating Scales (Teacher's Questionnaire and Parent's Questionnaire), Child Behavior Checklist (CBCL), and the Barkley Home Situation Questionnaire. These inventories provide valuable information on the child's behavior in different settings and situations. In addition, the Wender Utah Rating Scale has been adapted for use in diagnosing ADHD in adults. Continuous Performance Tests, which involve tasks performed on a computer, may support a diagnosis of attention-deficit type ADHD but by themselves are not diagnostic.

As many as 50% to 60% of people diagnosed with ADHD also meet the diagnostic criteria for another major psychiatric disorder such as **anxiety disorders**, **depression**, **antisocial personality disorder**, **oppositional defiant disorder**, **bipolar disorder**, **substance** abuse disorder, or **conduct disorder**. These individuals also have a high likelihood of having a learning disorder. Children with ADHD also sometimes have **Tourette syndrome**, which is a neurological disorder characterized by vocal tics or compulsive muscle spasms. A complete and comprehensive psychiatric assessment is critical to differentiate ADHD from other mood and behavioral disorders.

In the United States, public schools are required by federal law to offer free ADHD assessment upon request. A pediatrician also can provide a referral to a psychologist or pediatric psychiatrist for ADHD assessment. Parents should check with their insurance plans to see if these services are covered.

Treatment

The CDC reported that in 2007, 2.7 million children from the age of 4 to 17 years were on medication to treat ADHD. It also stated that of all the children diagnosed with ADHD, 66.3% were on medication. Concerning age, the CDC found that children from 11 to 17 years of age were more likely to take medication than children aged 4 to 10 years. In addition, boys were 2.8 times more likely to take medication than were girls. Treatment does not cure ADHD but has been found to help with its symptoms.

Therapy that addresses both psychological and social issues (called psychosocial therapy), usually combined with medications, is the treatment approach of choice to alleviate ADHD symptoms, and in younger children, therapy is preferred over medication. The combination of therapy and medication has proven to be the most effective treatment approach to ADHD. Most children who go through therapy for ADHD develop into normal functioning adults.

Drugs

Stimulant drugs, also known as psychostimulants, are considered the most effective medication for treating ADHD. These drugs generally increase the availability of neurotransmitters in the brain, which tends to reduce such symptoms as inattention, impulsivity, and hyperactivity. Drug therapy must be highly individualized with the benefits balanced against the risk of undesirable side effects. **Dextroamphetamine** (Dexedrine, Dextrostat), dextroamphetamine/amphetamine mixture (Adderall), **methylphenidate** (Concerta, Daytrana, Ritalin, Metadate), and **dexmethylphenidate** (Focalin) are common stimulant drug treatments. These drugs are available in both immediate release and extended release forms.

The use of the stimulant drug **pemoline** (Cylert) to treat ADHD was stopped in 2005 when the U.S. Food and Drug Administration (FDA) ruled that the risk of liver damage outweighed the benefits of this drug.

Attention deficit hyperactivity disorder (ADHD) medications[1]

Generic name	Trade name	FDA approved age
amphetamine	Adderall	3+
amphetamine (extended release)	Adderall XR	6+
atomoxetine	Strattera	6+
dexmethylphenidate	Focalin	6+
dexmethylphenidate (extended release)	Focalin XR	6+
dextroamphetamine	Dexedrine, Dextrostat	3+
guanfacine	Intuniv	6+
lisdexamfetamine dimesylate	Vyvanse	6+
methamphetamine	Desoxyn	6+
methylphenidate	Ritalin	6+
methylphenidate (extended release)	Metadate CD, Metadate ER, Ritalin SR	6+
methylphenidate (long-acting)	Ritalin LA, Concerta	6+
methylphenidate transdermal	Daytrana	6+
methylphenidate (oral solution and chewable tablets)	Methylin	6+

[1]All of these ADHD medications are stimulants, except atomoxetine and guanfacine.

SOURCE: National Institute of Mental Health.

"Alphabetical List of Medications," available online at: http://www.nimh.nih.gov/health/publications/mental-health-medications/alphabetical-list-of-medications.shtml. *(Table by PreMediaGlobal. © 2012 Cengage Learning.)*

Stimulant drugs may have adverse side effects in some children. These side effects include loss of appetite, **insomnia**, mood disturbance, headache, and gastrointestinal distress. Tics may also appear and should be monitored carefully. Psychotic reactions are among the more severe side effects. There is some evidence that long-term use of stimulant medication may interfere with physical growth and weight gain. Some experts feel that these effects are ameliorated by taking medication breaks (or "drug holidays") over school vacations or weekends. Increasingly, there is concern about long-term use of stimulant medications and their use of in very young children; their use is not recommended in children under age six unless absolutely necessary.

In the past, children who did not respond well to stimulant therapy were often given tricyclic **antidepressants** such as **desipramine** (Norpramin, Pertofane) and **imipramine** (Tofranil). These drugs are now rarely used, as they have a much higher risk of causing serious side effects, including cardiac arrhythmia (irregular heartbeat that can be life threatening).

Nonstimulant drugs are now the preferred choice for treating ADHD when stimulant drugs are found to be ineffective or when adverse side effects occur. Atomoxetine (Strattera) is a nonstimulant norepinephrine reuptake inhibitor. Its effect is to make norepinephrine remain in the brain longer, thus increasing the amount of norepinephrine available.

Other medications used to treat ADHD include some antidepressants (when stimulants or nonstimulants do not work or when a mood disorder is present in addition to ADHD). These include buproprion (Wellbutrin) and **venlafaxine** (Effexor), both atypical, nontricyclic antidepressants. **Clonidine** (Catapres) and **guanfacine** (Intuniv, Tenex), both systemic antihypertensive (blood pressure lowering) medications, also have been used to control aggression and hyperactivity in some ADHD children. They may also reduce symptoms such as tics or insomnia. However, these drugs can have serious side effects if taken with methylphenidate (Ritalin).

Generally, a child's response to medication will change with age and maturation, so ADHD symptoms should be monitored and prescriptions adjusted accordingly.

Therapies

It is important that drug treatment be carefully monitored and not be used exclusively in the management of ADHD. **Behavior modification** is often used in conjunction with drug therapy. Behavior modification uses a reward system to reinforce good behavior and task completion and can be implemented both in the classroom and at home. A tangible reward such as a sticker may be given to the child every time he or she completes a task or behaves in an acceptable manner. A chart system may be used to display the stickers and visually illustrate the child's progress. When a certain number of stickers are collected, the child may trade them in for a bigger reward such as a trip to the zoo or a day at the beach. The reward system stays in place until the good behavior becomes ingrained and is sustained without reward.

A variation of this technique, **cognitive-behavioral therapy**, works to decrease impulsive behavior by getting the child to recognize the connection between thoughts and behavior. Behavior is changed by altering negative thinking patterns.

Individual **psychotherapy** may help children with ADHD build self-esteem, give them a place to discuss their worries and anxieties, and help them gain insight into their behavior and feelings. **Family therapy** also may be beneficial in helping family members develop coping skills and in working through feelings of guilt or anger that the parents may be experiencing. Parenting skills training also helps parents to develop methods to better understand and deal with their children.

Social skills training can help children learn more appropriate behaviors while interacting with others. Many **support groups** are available around the country that help to provide a much needed network of information, education, and other types of support for children and their families.

Alternative treatment

A number of alternative treatments exist for ADHD. Although there is a lack of controlled studies to prove their efficacy, proponents report that they are successful in controlling symptoms in some ADHD patients. Nevertheless, none of these treatments meets the standards of safety and effectiveness required by conventional medicine. Some of the more popular alternative treatments are:

- EEG (electroencephalograph) biofeedback. By measuring brainwave activity and teaching the ADHD patient which type of brainwave is associated with attention, EEG biofeedback attempts to train patients to generate the desired brainwave activity.
- Dietary therapy. Based in part on the Feingold food allergy diet, dietary therapy focuses on a nutritional plan that is high in protein and complex carbohydrates and free of white sugar and salicylate-containing foods such as strawberries, tomatoes, and grapes. Zinc supplementation has shown positive results in alleviating symptoms of hyperactivity, impulsiveness, and social interaction problems, though additional research is needed.
- Herbal therapy. Herbal therapy uses a variety of natural remedies to address the symptoms of ADHD, such as ginkgo (*Ginkgo biloba*) for memory and mental sharpness and chamomile (*Matricaria recutita*) extract for calming. The safety of herbal remedies has not been demonstrated in controlled studies. For example, it is known that ginkgo may affect blood coagulation, but controlled studies have not yet evaluated the risk of the effect.
- Homeopathic medicine. The theory of homeopathic medicine is to treat the whole person at a core level. Constitutional homeopathic care requires consulting with a well-trained homeopath who has experience working with ADD and ADHD individuals.

Prognosis

Approximately 70% to 80% of ADHD patients treated with stimulant medication experience significant relief from symptoms, at least in the short term. Some children with ADHD seem to "outgrow" symptoms of the disorder in adolescence or early adulthood, whereas others retain some or all of their symptoms as adults. Some children diagnosed with ADHD also develop a conduct disorder. As many as 25% of adolescents with both ADHD and a conduct disorder go on to develop antisocial personality disorder and the criminal behavior, substance abuse, and high rate of **suicide** attempts that frequently accompany this psychiatric disorder.

Untreated, ADHD negatively affects a child's social and educational performance and can seriously damage his or her sense of self-esteem. Children with ADHD may have impaired relationships with their peers and be looked upon as social outcasts. They may be perceived as slow learners or troublemakers in the classroom. Siblings and even parents may develop resentful feelings toward the child.

Each child should have an individual educational plan (IEP) that outlines modifications to the regular mode of instruction that will facilitate the child's academic performance. Teachers must consider the needs of the child when giving instructions, making sure that they are well paced. They must also understand the origins of impulsive behavior—that the child is not deliberately trying to ruin a lesson or activity by acting unruly. Teachers should teach in a structured way, be comfortable with the remedial services the child may need, and be able to maintain good lines of communication with the parent.

Specialists should devise a series of compensatory strategies that will enable the child to cope with his or her attention deficit or hyperactivity. These strategies might include simple things like creating checklists of things to do before handing in assignments (name on top, check spelling, etc.), putting a clock on the child's desk to help structure time for activities, or covering the pictures on a page until the child has read the words so that he/she is not distracted.

Special assistance may not be limited to educational settings. Families frequently need help in coping with the demands and challenges of ADHD. The symptoms of inattention, shifting activities every five minutes, difficulty completing homework and household tasks, losing things, interrupting, not listening, rule breaking, constant talking, boredom, and irritability can take a toll on any family.

Parents may not understand how attention lapses or impulsivity affect daily functioning, and they might not be trained in the kind of techniques that help children with ADHD manage their behavior. Siblings may be resentful of what the child seems to "get away with" or the inordinate amount of attention he or she receives. The child with ADHD may be resentful of a younger sibling who is more accomplished at school or never seems to get in any trouble. Family interaction patterns may set up vicious cycles that become destructive and difficult to break.

Support groups for families are increasingly available through school districts and health care providers. Community colleges frequently offer courses in discipline and behavior management. Counseling services are available to complement any types of pharmacological treatment being used. There are a number of popular books available, which are informative and helpful.

KEY TERMS

Anxiety disorders—A group of psychological disorders that are all characterized by abnormal fear and/or excessive anxiety.

Bipolar disorder—A mood disorder marked by alternating episodes of extremely low mood (depression) and exuberant highs (mania).

Conduct disorder—A behavioral and emotional disorder of childhood and adolescence. Children with such a disorder act inappropriately, infringe on the rights of others, and violate societal norms.

Dopamine—A neurotransmitter that is involved in many brain activities, including movement and emotion.

Nervous tic—A repetitive, involuntary action, such as the twitching of a muscle or repeated blinking.

Neurotransmitter—One of a group of chemicals secreted by a nerve cell (neuron) to carry a chemical message to another nerve cell, often as a way of transmitting a nerve impulse. Examples of neurotransmitters are acetylcholine, dopamine, serotonin, and norepinephrine.

Norepinephrine—A type of neurotransmitter involved in regulation of concentration, impulse control, judgment, mood, attention span, and psychostimulation.

Oppositional defiant disorder—A disorder characterized by hostile, deliberately argumentative, and defiant behavior toward authority figures.

Tourette syndrome—A neurological disorder characterized by compulsive or vocal tics.

QUESTIONS TO ASK YOUR DOCTOR

- How do I know if my child has ADHD?
- What types of treatment do you recommend?
- What are the most serious side effects of medication?
- Can you refer my child to a therapist?
- Can you recommend any support groups for me and my family?

Prevention

There is no way to prevent attention deficit hyperactivity disorder. However, it is always wise for pregnant mothers to avoid the use of alcohol, drugs, and tobacco products to avoid medical problems with children later in life.

Resources

BOOKS

Alexander-Roberts, Colleen. *The AD/HD Parenting Handbook: Practical Advice for Parents From Parents*. 2nd ed. Lanham, MD: Taylor Trade, 2006.

American Psychiatric Association. *Diagnostic and Statistical Manual of Mental Disorders*. 4th ed., text rev. Washington, DC: American Psychiatric Association, 2000.

Brynie, Faith Hickman. *ADHD: Attention-Deficit Hyperactivity Disorder*. Minneapolis: Twenty-First Century Books, 2008.

Conners, Keith C. *Attention Deficit Hyperactivity Disorder in Children and Adolescents: The Latest Assessment and Treatment Strategies*. 4th ed. Kansas City, MO: Compact Clinicals, 2008.

Fitzgerald, Michael, Mark Bellgrove, and Michael Gill, eds. *Handbook of Attention-Deficit Hyperactivity Disorder*. Chichester, UK: John Wiley, 2007.

Gozal, David, and Dennis L. Molfese, eds. *Attention Deficit Hyperactivity Disorder: From Genes to Patients*. Totawa, NJ: Humana Press, 2005.

McBurnett, Keith, and Linda Pfiffner, eds. *Attention Deficit Hyperactivity Disorder: Concepts, Controversies, New Directions*. New York: Informa Healthcare, 2008.

PERIODICALS

Bálint, S., et al. "Neuropsychological Impairments in Adult Attention Deficit Hyperactivity Disorder: A Literature Review." *Psychiatric Hungary* 23, no. 5 (March 2008): 324–35.

Chen, Mandy, Carla M. Seipp, and Charlotte Johnston. "Mothers' and Fathers' Attributions and Beliefs in Families of Girls and Boys with Attention-Deficit/Hyperactivity Disorder." *Child Psychiatry and Human Development* 39, no. 1 (March 2008): 85–100.

Dennis, Tanya, et al. "Attention Deficit Hyperactivity Disorder: Parents' and Professionals' Perceptions." *Community Practitioner* 81, no. 3 (March 2008): 24–29.

Galéra, C., et al. "Early Risk Factors for Hyperactivity-Impulsivity and Inattention Trajectories from Age 17 Months to 8 Years." *Archives of General Psychiatry* 68, no. 12 (2011): 1267–75.

Sibley, Margaret H., et al. "Diagnosing ADHD in Adolescence." *Journal of Consulting and Clinical Psychology* (December 12, 2011) [e-pub ahead of print]. http://dx.doi.org/10.1037/a0026577 (accessed December 14, 2011).

WEBSITES

American Psychiatric Association. "A 10 Attention Deficit/Hyperactivity Disorder." DSM-5 Development. May 20, 2010. http://www.dsm5.org/ProposedRevisions/Pages/proposedrevision.aspx?rid=383 (accessed September 16, 2011).

Centers for Disease Control and Prevention. "Attention Deficit Hyperactivity Disorder (ADHD)." November 10, 2010. http://www.cdc.gov/ncbddd/adhd/data.html (accessed September 16, 2011).

Gordon, Selena. "New ADHD Guidelines Include Preschoolers, Older Children." HealthDay. October 16, 2011. http://www.healthfinder.gov/news/newsstory.aspx?Docid=657877 (accessed November 14, 2011).

Mayo Clinic staff. "Attention Deficit Hyperactivity Disorder (ADHD) in Children." MayoClinic.com. August 2, 2011. http://www.mayoclinic.com/health/adhd/DS00275 (accessed September 16, 2011).

MedlinePlus. "Attention Deficit Hyperactivity Disorder." U.S. National Library of Medicine, National Institutes of Health. June 23, 2011. http://www.nlm.nih.gov/medlineplus/attentiondeficithyperactivitydisorder.html (accessed September 16, 2011).

National Institute of Mental Health. "Attention Deficit Hyperactivity Disorder." July 5, 2011. http://www.nimh.nih.gov/health/publications/adhd/summary.shtml (accessed September 16, 2011).

ORGANIZATIONS

American Psychiatric Association, 1000 Wilson Blvd., Ste. 1825, Arlington, VA, 22209-3901, (703) 907-7300, apa@psych.org, http://www.psych.org.

American Psychological Association, 750 1st St. NE, Washington, DC, 20002-4242, (202) 336-5500; TDD/TTY: (202) 336-6123, (800) 374-2721, http://www.apa.org.

Attention Deficit Disorder Association, PO Box 7557, Wilmington, DE, 19803-9997, (800) 939-1019, info@add.org, http://www.add.org.

Children and Adults with Attention Deficit/Hyperactivity Disorder, 8181 Professional Place, Ste. 150, Landover, MD, 20785, (301) 306-7070, Fax: (301) 306-7090, (800) 233-4050, http://www.chadd.org.

Tish Davidson, AM
Laura Jean Cataldo, RN, EdD
William A. Atkins, BB, BS, MBA

Autism

Definition

Autism is a complex developmental disorder distinguished by difficulties with social interaction, verbal and nonverbal communication, and behavioral problems, including repetitive behaviors and narrow focus of interest.

Demographics

Estimates suggest that about 1 of every 110 children in the United States is affected by autism. Autism is almost four times more likely to be diagnosed in males. Autism is a disorder that is found worldwide, and it is not specific to any one socio-economic, ethnic, or racial group. In identical twins, if one twin has autism, there is a 60%–90% chance that the other twin will have it as well. In fraternal twins, this chance drops to 0%–24%. Previous estimates stated that parents who had one child with autism had a 5% chance of having a second child with the condition, but research published in 2011 by the journal *Pediatrics* suggested that this figure could actually be as high as 19%.

Description

Classic autism is one of several disorders categorized as autism spectrum disorders (ASD). Other ASDs include **Asperger syndrome**, **Rett syndrome**, **childhood disintegrative disorder**, and pervasive developmental disorder. As of 2011, the classification of autism and autism spectrum disorders was being re-evaluated by the **American Psychiatric Association** for revision in the fifth edition of the ***Diagnostic and Statistical Manual of Mental Disorders*** (*DSM-5*, 2013). It has been proposed that Asperger syndrome be eliminated as a separate **diagnosis**. Instead, Asperger syndrome, autism, childhood disintegrative disorder, and pervasive developmental disorder not otherwise specified (PPD-NOS) would be grouped under a single classification, termed "autism spectrum disorder." This proposal was controversial and as of 2011 remained unresolved. *DSM-5* is expected to publish in 2013.

Autism usually manifests before children are three years old, and it continues throughout their lifetime. The severity of the condition varies among individuals, ranging from the most severe (extremely unusual, repetitive, self-injurious, and aggressive behavior) to very mild. No autistic children are alike in the manifestation of their symptoms, so treatment options must be devised to treat each child individually. Autism cannot be cured but is treatable. With early diagnosis and intensive therapy, children with autism may be able to lead healthy, full lives.

Risk factors

Being a boy increases one's risk for autism; boys are 3–4 times as likely as girls to have the condition. There may be some **genetic factors** involved, as autism runs in some families. Certain **brain** conditions also increase the risk of having autism, including tuberous sclerosis, **Tourette syndrome**, epilepsy, and fragile X syndrome. Being born to a father who is older than 40 seems to increase the risk of autism. Research on mothers' ages was expected as of 2011. Despite popular concern, vaccines have not been proven to increase the risk of autism. The original research article that proposed the correlation has been discredited, and a retraction has been printed in the journal.

Causes and symptoms

Researchers know that autism is a complex brain disorder that affects the way brain tissue grows and the way brain cells communicate with each other. More than 20 genes have been identified as associated with autism. Studies have implicated several causes for the disorder, including genetic errors and possible environmental triggers (such as pesticide exposure), but more

Number of U.S. students with autism, 2000–2009

	Ages 3 to 5	Ages 6 to 11	Ages 12 to 17	Ages 18 to 21	Ages 6 to 21	Total (3–21)
2000	14,065	52,460	22,502	4,633	79,595	93,660
2002	19,039	74,707	37,260	6,702	118,669	137,708
2004	25,929	97,374	59,474	9,576	166,424	192,353
2006	35,111	125,944	85,666	12,984	224,594	259,705
2008	44,977	161,236	112,972	18,610	292,818	337,795
2009	47,204	182,446	128,345	22,443	333,234	380,438

SOURCE: Data Accountability Center, Individuals with Disabilities Education Act (IDEA).

Number of U.S. students with autism, ages 3–21, as reported to the Individuals with Disabilities Education Act (IDEA). Data captured by the Data Accountability Center and available online at http://www.ideadata.org/PartBChildCount.asp. *(Table by PreMediaGlobal. © 2012 Cengage Learning.)*

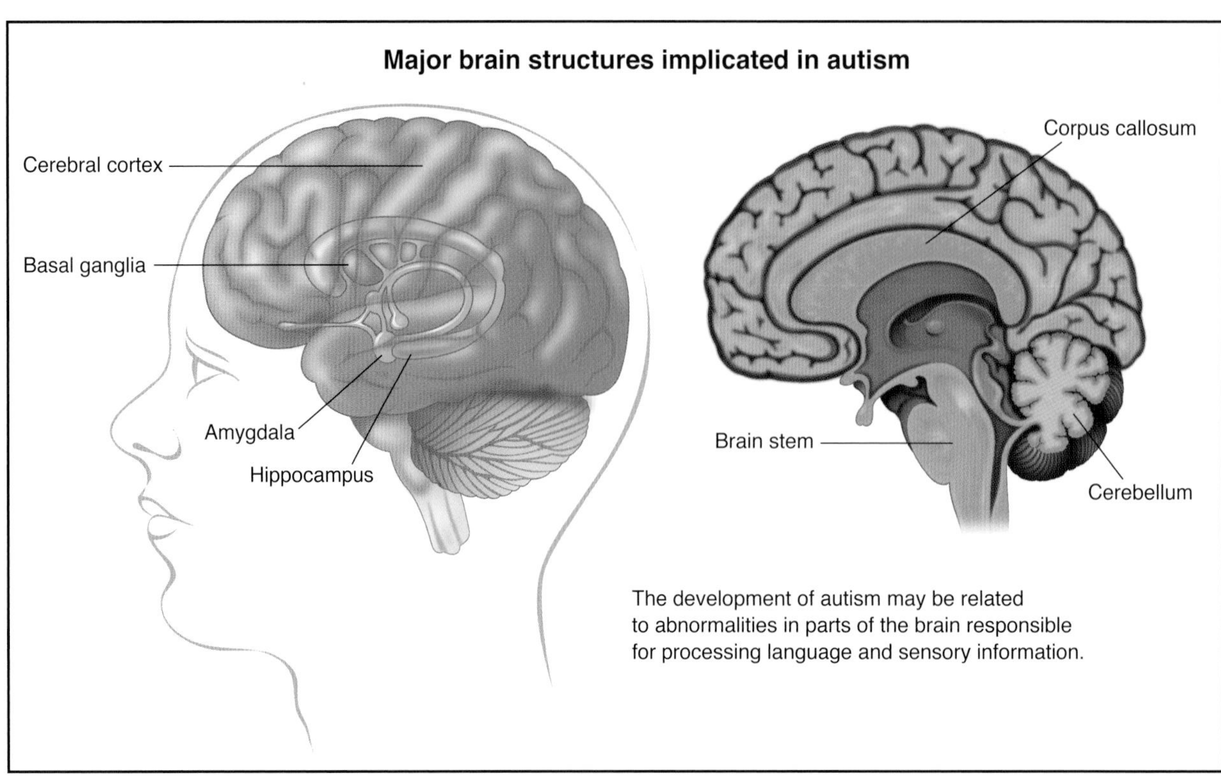

(Illustration by Electronic Illustrators Group. Reproduced by permission of Gale, a part of Cengage Learning.)

investigation is needed. Studies have found abnormalities in several parts of the brain that are believed to have occurred during fetal development. The problem may be centered in the parts of the brain responsible for processing language and information from the senses.

Profound problems with social interaction are the most common symptoms of autism and the most visible. Children with autism have different ways of learning and experiencing their environment. They often have more acute reactions to sensory stimulation such as sound and touch. This results in avoidance of eye contact, physical contact, and oftentimes an aversion to music and other sounds. It is perhaps the way children with autism experience their world that causes difficulties with social interaction, language, and nonverbal communication.

Human beings are social creatures, and social interaction is present from birth onward. Children with autism have difficulty making social connections. When infants can follow an object or person with their gaze, it is considered a developmental milestone. Children with autism tend to avoid eye contact altogether. They do not actively cuddle or hug, but rather they passively accept physical contact or they shy away from it. They may become rigid or flaccid when they are held, cry when picked up, and show little interest in human contact. Such children do not lift their arms in anticipation of being picked up. These children may appear to have formed no attachment to their parents and do not learn typical childhood games, such as peek-a-boo.

Children with autism do not readily learn social cues. They do not know when or how to react to specific social situations or exchanges. Because of this, they tend to look at and respond to different situations similarly. They do not understand that others have different perspectives and, as a result, seem to lack empathy.

Because of their problems socially and the inability to translate social interactions appropriately, children with autism seem to have uncontrolled emotional outbursts, expressing themselves in a manner that does not suit the specific social situation of the moment.

Language problems

Verbal communication problems vary greatly for autistic children. Some children do not speak at all. Some will only use one or two words at a time. Some autistic children may develop vocabulary only to lose it. Others may develop an extensive vocabulary but will have difficulty sustaining a natural, back-and-forth conversation. Children with autism tend to talk in a sing-song voice or more robotically, without emotional inflections. They do not take body language into consideration and take what is being said quite literally.

KEY TERMS

Antidepressants—A type of medication that is used to treat depression; it is also sometimes used to treat autism.

Asperger syndrome—A condition in which individuals have autistic behavior but no problems with language and no clinically significant cognitive delay.

Fragile X syndrome—A genetic condition related to the X chromosome that affects mental, physical, and sensory development.

Major tranquilizers—A group of drugs that includes the psychotropic or neuroleptic drugs, sometimes used to help people with autism. They carry significant risk of side effects, including parkinsonism and movement disorders and should be prescribed with caution.

Opiate blockers—A type of drug that blocks the effects of natural opiates in the system. This type of drug makes some people, including some people with autism, appear more responsive to their environment.

Phenylketonuria (PKU)—An enzyme deficiency present at birth that disrupts metabolism and causes brain damage. This rare inherited defect may be linked to the development of autism.

Rubella—Also known as German measles. When a woman contracts rubella during pregnancy, her developing infant may be damaged. One of the problems that may result is autism.

Stimulants—A class of drugs, including Ritalin, used to treat people with autism. They may make children calmer and better able to concentrate, but they also may limit growth or have other side effects.

Tuberous sclerosis—A genetic disease that causes skin problems, seizures, and intellectual disabilities. Autism occurs more often in individuals with tuberous sclerosis.

Because of their impinged language skills and the inability to express their needs, autistic children seem to act inappropriately to get what they need. They may grab something without asking or blurt out statements.

Restricted interests and activity

Language and social problems inhibit social play for children with autism. They do not engage in imaginative play and role playing and instead focus on repetition, some focusing on a subject of interest intensely.

Children with autism often stick to a rigid daily routine. Any variance to the routine may be upsetting to them and result in an extreme emotional response. Repetitive physical behaviors such as rocking, spinning, and arm flapping are also characteristic of autism. The repetitive behaviors are often self-soothing responses to sensory stimulation from the outside world.

Sensory problems

The sensory world poses a real problem to many autistic children, who seem overwhelmed by their own senses. Children with autism may ignore objects or become obsessed with them, continually watching the object or the movement of their fingers over it. Some children with autism may react to sounds by banging their head or flapping their fingers. Some high-functioning autistic adults who have written books about their childhood experiences report that sounds were often excruciating to them, forcing them to withdraw from their environment.

Diagnosis

There is no medical test for diagnosing autism. Diagnosis is made after careful observation and screening by parents, caregivers, and physicians. Early diagnosis is beneficial in treating the symptoms of autism. Some early warning signs are:

- avoiding eye contact
- avoiding physical contact such as hugs
- inability to play make-believe
- not pointing out interesting objects
- not responding to conversation directed at them
- practicing excessively repetitive behaviors
- repeating words or phrases
- losing skills and/or language after learning them

Once parents feel there is a problem or their pediatrician has identified developmental problems during well-baby checkups, they can seek out a developmental pediatrician for further diagnosis. There are several screening tests used. They are:

- Childhood Autism Rating Scale (CARS)—a test based on a 15-point scale where specific behaviors are observed by the physician
- Checklist for Autism in Toddlers (CHAT)—a test to detect autism in 18-month-olds that utilizes

questionnaires filled out by both the parents and the pediatrician

- Autism Screening Questionnaire—a 40-item questionnaire for diagnosing children four and older
- Screening Test for Autism in Two-Year-Olds—a direct observation of three skill areas, including play, motor imitation, and joint attention

Some children have a few of the symptoms of autism but not enough to be diagnosed with the "classical" form of the condition. Children who have autistic behavior but no problems with language may be diagnosed with Asperger syndrome by using the Autism Spectrum Screening Questionnaire, the Australian Scale for Asperger syndrome, or the Childhood Asperger Syndrome Test. Children who have no initial symptoms but who begin to show autistic behavior as they get older might be diagnosed with childhood disintegrative disorder (CDD), another autistic spectrum disorder. It is also important to rule out other problems that seem similar to autism.

Treatment

Because the symptoms of autism can vary greatly from one person to the next, there is not a single treatment that works for all individuals. A spectrum of interventions, including behavioral and educational training, diet and **nutrition**, alternative medicine and therapies, and medication, should be utilized and adjusted to treat each individual. The most strongly recommended treatment option is behavioral and educational training. Early **intervention** and treatment is key to helping autistic children grow into productive adults.

Educational and behavioral treatment

Several educational and behavioral treatments are:

- Applied Behavior Analysis (ABA)
- speech therapy
- occupational therapy, including sensory integration therapy
- social skills therapy, including play therapy

Typically, behavioral techniques are used to help the child respond and decrease symptoms. This might include positive **reinforcement** to boost language and social skills. This training includes structured, skill-oriented instruction designed to improve social and language abilities. Training needs to begin as early as possible, since early intervention appears to positively influence brain development.

Most autistic children respond to intervention at home as well as at school. Schools focus on areas in which the child may be delayed, such as in speech or socialization. As children with autism grow and move to different phases of childhood and adolescence, parents in collaboration with educators and physicians need to adapt the treatment to suit the needs of their child.

Medication

No single medication treats symptoms of autism; however, some medications have been used to combat specific needs in autistic children. Drugs can control epilepsy, which affects up to 20% of people with autism. Medication can also treat anxiety, **depression**, and hyperactivity. Medication must be individualized and adjusted as individuals develop.

Five types of drugs are sometimes prescribed to help the behavior problems of people with autism:

- stimulants, such as methylphenidate (Ritalin), can help with symptoms of hyperactivity and inattention
- antidepressants, such as fluvoxamine (Luvox), can help with symptoms of depression, anxiety, repetitive/ritualistic behaviors, and obsessive/compulsive-type symptoms
- opiate blockers, such as naltrexone (ReVia), may also improve ritualistic behaviors
- antipsychotics may be used to improve irritability and dampen aggression
- tranquilizers may be used to calm irritability and aggression and to quell anxiety

In 2010, reports were published regarding use of the drug **memantine**, traditionally used to treat Alzheimer's patients, in a study conducted by Michael Amen at Ohio State University. The study's hypothesis rested in similarities between autism and **Alzheimer's disease**, both of which involve a malfunction in the brain involving the chemical glutamate, which affects the patient's speech and interaction. While most drugs for autism only focus on lessening symptoms such as hyperactivity or repetitive actions, this study was designed to help improve communication, one of the core issues of autism. As of 2011, additional studies were ongoing.

Alternative treatment

Some parents report success with megavitamin therapy. Some studies have shown that vitamin B_6 with magnesium improves eye contact and speech and lessens tantrum behavior. Vitamin B_6 causes fewer side effects than other medications and is considered

QUESTIONS TO ASK YOUR DOCTOR

- How severe is my child's autism?
- Does my child have any associated medical problems that will need treatment along with autism?
- What sort of behaviors can I expect from my child?
- Is my child eligible for any early intervention programs available locally?
- What can I do at home to best help my child?
- What should I tell my other children/relatives/friends about this disorder?

safe when used in appropriate doses. However, not many health practitioners advocate its use in the treatment of autism, citing that the studies showing its benefit are flawed.

DMG (DIMETHYLGLYCINE). DMG (dimethylglycine), which is available in many health food stores, is legally classified as a food, not as a vitamin or drug. Some researchers claim that it improves speech in children with autism. Those who respond to this treatment will usually do so within a week. Again, many doctors do not feel that the studies are adequate to promote this treatment.

DIET. Many parents have seen beneficial effects from a gluten-free and casein-free diet. Gluten is found in the seeds of cereal plants such as wheat, barley, oats, and rye. Casein is a protein found in milk. Often people have sensitivities to these substances without realizing it. Many foods contain these substances as an ingredient; however, there are growing numbers of gluten-free and casein-free foods available for people that would like to eliminate them from their **diets**. Parents interested in using diet as a treatment should discuss with their child's doctor how to initiate an elimination diet.

EXERCISE. One researcher found that vigorous **exercise** (20 minutes or longer, three or four days a week) seems to decrease hyperactivity, aggression, self-injury, and other autistic symptoms.

Prognosis

Autism is treatable but not curable. With appropriate treatments adjusted as the patient ages, the symptoms of autism seem to improve. For the best prognosis, parents and caregivers should focus on providing the best therapies possible in order for children to develop to their highest potential. Because the incidence of autism seems to be increasing worldwide, enough so that the Centers for Disease Control and Prevention has voiced concern about its prevalence, there is more awareness of autism and more ongoing research efforts. People with autism have a normal life expectancy, and with proper intervention they can lead full lives.

Prevention

Until the cause of autism is discovered, prevention is not possible.

Resources

BOOKS

Behrman R.E., et al. *Nelson Textbook of Pediatrics.* 18th ed. Philadelphia: Saunders, 2007.

Bradley, W., et al. *Neurology in Clinical Practice.* 5th ed. Philadelphia: Butterworth-Heinemann, 2008.

Coplan, James. *Making Sense of Autistic Spectrum Disorders: Create the Brightest Future for Your Child with the Best Treatment Options.* New York: Bantam Books, 2010.

Glasberg, Beth. *Stop That Seemingly Senseless Behavior: FBA-Based Interventions for People with Autism.* Bethesda, MD: Woodbine House, 2008.

Offit, Paul A. *Autism's False Prophets: Bad Science, Risky Medicine, and the Search for a Cure.* New York: Columbia University Press, 2008.

PERIODICALS

Inglese, M. "Caring for Children with Autism Spectrum Disorder. Part I: Prevalence, Etiology, and Core Features." *Journal of Pediatric Nursing* 24 (2009): 41–48.

Ozonoff S., et al. "Recurrence Risk for Autism Spectrum Disorders: A Baby Siblings Research Consortium Study." *Pediatrics* 128, no. 3 (2011): e488–e495. http://dx.doi.org/10.1542/peds.2010-2825 (accessed October 11, 2011).

Pina-Camacho, L., et al. "Autism Spectrum Disorder: Does Neuroimaging Support the DSM-5 Proposal for a Symptom Dyad? A Systematic Review of Functional Magnetic Resonance Imaging and Diffusion Tensor Imaging Studies." *Journal of Autism and Developmental Disorders* (September 20, 2011) [e-pub ahead of print]. http://dx.doi.org/10.1007/s10803-011-1360-4 (accessed November 14, 2011).

Rice, C. "The Changing Prevalence of the Autism Spectrum Disorders." *American Family Physician* 29 (2011): 486–89.

WEBSITES

American Academy of Child and Adolescent Psychiatry. "Autism Resource Center." http://www.aacap.org/cs/Autism.ResourceCenter (accessed October 11, 2011).

Mayo Clinic staff. "Autism." MayoClinic.com. May 27, 2010. http://www.mayoclinic.com/print/autism/DS00348 (accessed October 11, 2011).

MedlinePlus. "Autism." U.S. National Library of Medicine, National Institutes of Health. April 7, 2011. http://www.nlm.nih.gov/medlineplus/autism.html (accessed October 11, 2011).

National Institute of Neurological Disorders and Stroke. "Autism Fact Sheet." U.S. National Institutes of Health. http://www.ninds.nih.gov/disorders/autism/detail_autism.htm (accessed November 14, 2011).

ORGANIZATIONS

American Academy of Child and Adolescent Psychiatry, 3615 Wisconsin Ave. NW, Washington, DC, 20016-3007, (202) 966-7300, Fax: (202) 966-2891, http://aacap.org.

American Psychiatric Association, 1000 Wilson Blvd., Ste. 1825, Arlington, VA, 22209-3901, (703) 907-7300, apa@psych.org, http://www.psych.org.

Autism Network International, PO Box 35448, Syracuse, NY, 13235-5448, http://autreat.com.

Autism Society of America, 4340 East-West Hwy., Ste. 350, Bethesda, MD, 20814, (301) 657-0881, (800) 328-8476, http://www.autism-society.org.

Autism Speaks, 1 East 33rd Street, 4th Fl., New York, NY, 10016, (212) 252-8584, Fax: (212) 252-8676, (888) AUTISM2 (288-4762), contactus@autismspeaks.org, http://www.autismspeaks.org.

Carol A. Turkington
Tish Davidson, AM
Rosalyn Carson-DeWitt

Autism spectrum disorders *see* **Asperger syndrome; Autism; Childhood disintegrative disorder; Pervasive developmental disorders**

Aventyl *see* **Nortriptyline**

Aversion therapy

Definition

Aversion therapy is a type of **cognitive-behavioral therapy** (CBT) in which an undesirable or harmful behavior is paired with an aversive or noxious stimulus in an attempt to reduce or eliminate the undesirable behavior. A form of classical conditioning, aversion therapy is based on the theory that the patient will eventually avoid the behavior because it has come to be associated with pain, unpleasantness, or unhappiness.

Purpose

The purpose of aversion therapy is to decrease or eliminate undesirable behaviors. Aversion therapy has been used since 1932 to treat alcohol and drug abuse, and this is remains its most common application. In addition to alcohol, aversion therapy is used to treat addictions to marijuana, **amphetamines** such as crystal meth, and opiates, including oxycodone and other prescription painkillers. It also is sometimes used to treat smoking, gambling **addiction**, **kleptomania** (the **compulsion** to steal), **paraphilias** (socially unacceptable sexual practices), and violent behaviors. Mild aversion therapy, followed by positive **reinforcement**, has been successfully used to treat **pica**—the compulsion to eat non-foods, such as paper or dirt, which affects 10%–32% of children between the ages of one and six, as well as some women during pregnancy. Aversion therapy is also sometimes used in conjunction with dermatologic and psychiatric treatments for dermatitis artefacta—the deliberate and conscious self-infliction of skin lesions. Aversion therapy is a common self-help treatment for such benign habits as nail biting or even writer's block.

Description

Like other behavioral therapies, aversion therapy is based on learning theory—the concept that all behaviors are learned and that, under the right circumstances, undesirable behaviors can be unlearned. Aversion therapy is an application of the branch of learning theory called classical conditioning. The best-known example of classical conditioning is Pavlov's dogs, who were conditioned to salivate in response to a bell by repeatedly pairing bell-ringing with feeding.

Unlike insight-oriented therapies, which focus on revealing unconscious motives in order to produce change, aversion therapy focuses on changing a specific behavior by matching it with an unpleasant or aversive stimulus. The unpleasant feelings or sensations eventually come to be associated with the undesirable behavior, causing the behavior to decrease in frequency or stop altogether. Aversion therapy differs from aversive procedures, which are behavioral therapies based on operant conditioning and in which the aversive stimulus, usually called a punishment, is presented after the behavior rather than together with it.

The particulars of aversion therapy depend on the behavior to be changed and the aversive stimulus. The therapy may be administered on either an inpatient or outpatient basis and either alone as a single **intervention** or as part of a multifaceted treatment program. In addition to pairing the undesirable behavior with aversive stimuli, aversion therapy sometimes pairs avoidance of the behavior with positive images, such as employment, education, or other socially appropriate activities.

Aversion therapy for alcohol or drug addiction attempts to change positive emotional associations with the substance to negative associations with the sight, smell, or taste of the abused substance. The most commonly administered aversion therapy is the use of an emetic or vomiting-producing medication to discourage alcohol consumption. **Disulfiram** (DSF) (Antabuse) is approved by the U.S. Food and Drug Administration (FDA) and has been used for alcohol-aversion therapy for more than half a century. DSF inhibits the enzyme aldehyde dehydrogenase (ALDH), which breaks down alcohol in the body. Inhibition of ALDH results in the buildup of acetaldehyde, which causes a violent noxious reaction—such as flushing, nausea, vomiting, and palpitations—when alcohol is consumed.

Various aversion therapies to help smokers to quit have been attempted with little success. The only method that has met with any success at all is rapid smoking, in which patients rapidly chain smoke cigarettes until they become sick. This method is not recommended because it is unhealthy and only occasionally successful.

Classical aversion therapy involves the administration of electric shocks. In the past, shocks were inflicted by the therapist. In the early 2010s, if electroshock aversion therapy is used, patients shock themselves using a portable battery-operated device, usually attached to their arm or leg. The shock level is uncomfortable and perhaps even painful, but not intensely painful, dangerous, or damaging. Patients shock themselves while thinking about the undesirable behavior. Sometimes pictures or other props associated with the behavior are used to reinforce the imagined behavior. Eventually the patient may become uncomfortable thinking about the behavior and the desire to engage in it may lessen or disappear.

Other aversion therapies are also self-administered. An example of a self-help aversion therapy is putting red pepper or a bitter substance on one's fingernails to discourage nail biting. Another type involves practicing a mildly painful technique, such as holding one's breath until it becomes uncomfortable, when faced with temptation or an urge for the undesirable behavior. This method has been used to treat kleptomania. Other self-help methods for minor undesirable behaviors include snapping an elastic band on the wrist when an undesirable thought or temptation is present.

A technique called **covert sensitization** or covert conditioning, developed by the American **psychologist** Joseph Cautela, is a less intrusive form of aversion therapy. Rather than using chemical aversions (such as Antabuse) or electroshock, covert sensitization utilizes imagined aversions. For example, images of an undesirable behavior, such as smoking, might be systematically paired with images of aversive stimuli, such as nausea and vomiting.

Benefits

Aversion therapy can be moderately successful for reducing or eliminating certain undesirable behaviors, especially at the outset of drug or alcohol rehabilitation. Drug and alcohol users link various environmental stimuli, such as taste, smell, sight, or surroundings, with pleasure associated with substance use. Aversive stimuli under medically supervised conditions can substitute these positive emotional associations with negative associations such as nausea and vomiting. Studies have found that aversion therapy can result in significantly improved rates of drug or alcohol abstinence. Aversion therapy has been found to be less effective for **smoking cessation**.

Covert sensitization has been used successfully to treat alcoholism, cigarette smoking, compulsive gambling, and juvenile delinquency. One study of six different cases found covert sensitization to be a fast and cost-effective treatment for a fingernail biter, a marijuana smoker, a cigarette smoker, an alcoholic, an obese patient, and a chocolate addict. All six patients eliminated their undesirable behavior and maintained abstinence throughout the follow-up period.

Precautions

Some aversion therapies, especially electroshock therapy, are potentially dangerous and should only be practiced in specialized clinics under the supervision of an experienced medical professional. Electroshock equipment should be of the highest quality, and the patient should be in control of the intensity at all times. Most importantly, aversion therapy should never be used coercively.

During the twentieth century, aversion therapy frequently involved pairing undesirable thoughts or behaviors with electric shocks of mild (faradic) but varying intensities or with potent emetics. Sometimes the consequences were disastrous, including fatalities, mental illness, and **suicide**. In some of the most egregious examples, electroshock aversion therapy was used to attempt to "cure" homosexuality. Patients were shown erotic same-sex images and if they became aroused, they received electric shocks, sometimes to the genitalia.

KEY TERMS

Antabuse—Trade name for disulfiram (DSF), a chemical used to treat alcoholism by causing a severe physiological reaction to any amount of alcohol.

Aversant—A chemical or medication with unpleasant effects that is used in aversion therapy.

Aversion—A strong feeling of unpleasantness, dislike, or disgust; stimulated in aversion therapy to reduce or eliminate an undesirable behavior.

Classical conditioning—A psychological process in which a neutral stimulus is repeatedly paired with a stimulus that produces a specific response, until the previously neutral stimulus also produces the response.

Cognitive-behavioral therapy (CBT)—A type of psychotherapy in which people learn to recognize and change negative and self-defeating patterns of thinking and behavior.

Compliance—Adherence to a treatment plan or medication regimen.

Covert sensitization or conditioning—A form of aversion therapy in which the patient imagines or views images of an undesirable behavior, followed by imagining or viewing images of an aversive consequence.

Dermatitis artefacta—A disorder characterized by the deliberate and conscious self-infliction of skin lesions.

Emetic—A medication that causes vomiting; usually used to treat poisoning but also used in aversion therapy.

Faradic—A type of discontinuous alternating electric current sometimes used in aversion therapy; named for the nineteenth-century British physicist Michael Faraday.

Operant conditioning—A psychological process in which a desired behavior or increasingly close approximations of the desired behavior are followed with positive or rewarding stimuli.

Paraphilia—Unusual or socially unacceptable sexual thoughts or behaviors.

Pica—Abnormal cravings for or eating of non-food substances, such as ashes or chalk, caused by mental illness or a nutritional deficiency.

Stimulus—An agent that directly elicits a response, such as a thought, emotion, or action, including images, smells, sounds, words, or ideas. In aversion therapy, the stimulus is typically a mild electric shock or a medication that produces unpleasant effects.

Sometimes patients could stop the shock and the image was replaced with an opposite-sex image. With another type of aversion therapy, patients were injected with a nausea-inducing drug while looking at images of homosexual activity and with a euphoria-inducing drug while viewing images of heterosexual activity. These types of aversion therapy were not only ineffectual but were later considered abusive. Both the **American Psychological Association** and the **American Psychiatric Association** declare aversion therapy for homosexuality to be a violation of professional guidelines and codes of conduct. The practice is illegal in some countries.

Although the use of electroshock is now rare, aversion therapy remains controversial. Although the foul odors, nasty tastes, and loud noises that are sometimes employed as aversive stimuli may be merely unpleasant, chemicals and medications can be physically painful and in some cases can cause severe illness. Antabuse may cause severe reactions if even a very small amount alcohol is inadvertently consumed in a sauce or vinegar within a few weeks of taking the drug. Alcohol-containing medications applied to the skin or fumes containing alcohol can also cause reactions.

There are also ethical concerns about aversion therapy. Social critics and the general public alike often consider this type of treatment to be punitive and morally objectionable. In the past, aversion therapy was sometimes used to treat mental illnesses, such as **schizophrenia**, as well as intellectual and developmental disabilities, with negative consequences. Advocates for special patient populations have called for an end to the use of all aversive stimuli, arguing that all aversive procedures are coercive and use an unnecessary degree of control or manipulation to modify behavior. These concerns have frequently been portrayed in the media. Anthony Burgess's 1962 novel *A Clockwork Orange* (and the subsequent Stanley Kubrick film) depicted a particularly brutal, and ultimately unsuccessful, form of aversion therapy for violent criminal behavior. Aversion conditioning was also explored in Aldous Huxley's 1932 novel

QUESTIONS TO ASK YOUR DOCTOR

- Would you recommend that I undergo aversion therapy? Why or why not?
- What would be involved in my aversion therapy?
- Are there unpleasant side effects to aversion therapy?
- Is aversion therapy likely to be successful?

Brave New World, in Ken Kesey's 1962 novel and the subsequent film *One Flew Over the Cuckoo's Nest*, and in the film *A Beautiful Mind*, about John Forbes Nash Jr., the Nobel Laureate in economics whose schizophrenia was treated with aversion therapy.

In addition to ethical considerations, the unpleasant effects of aversion therapy often lead to poor **compliance**, high treatment dropout rates, and potentially hostile and aggressive patients. Studies have generally shown that aversion therapy, even for **substance abuse**, is significantly less effective than positive behavioral change therapies that focus on rewards.

Preparation

In general, no particular preparation is required for aversion therapy. However, Antabuse should never be given to a patient who has consumed alcohol within at least the past 12 hours.

Aftercare

Most aversion therapies do not require aftercare. However, reactions to Antabuse can occur up to two weeks after treatment, so it is very important that patients treated with this drug avoid all contact with alcohol, including alcohol-containing fumes.

Risks

Aversion therapy with chemicals or medications has the potential to worsen heart, lung, or gastrointestinal problems. Some patients undergoing aversion therapy, especially treatment with powerful chemical or pharmacological aversive stimuli, have become negative, hostile, or aggressive. Electroshock aversion therapy may increase anxiety and anxiety-related symptoms that can interfere with the conditioning process, leading to decreased acceptance of the treatment. Finally, aversion therapy has great potential for patient abuse.

Research and general acceptance

Although aversion therapy has some adherents, especially for treating substance abuse, there is widespread opposition to the practice, both among clinicians and the general public. In addition to ethical objections, there are very few studies indicating its effectiveness. In general, operant conditioning with positive rewards is considered more effective and less intrusive than aversion therapy. However, covert sensitization may be moderately effective, is nonintrusive, and does not carry the same risks as other types of aversion therapy.

Resources

BOOKS

Spiegler, Michael D., and David C. Guevremont. *Contemporary Behavior Therapy*. Belmont, CA: Wadsworth, Cengage Learning, 2010. See esp. chap. 7, "Deceleration Behavior Therapy: Differential Reinforcement, Punishment, and Aversion Therapy."

PERIODICALS

"Smoking Cessation Interventions and Strategies." *Australian Nursing Journal* 16, no. 6 (December 2008/January 2009): 29–32.

Witkiewitz, Katie, and G. Alan Marlatt. "Behavioral Therapy Across the Spectrum." *Alcohol Research & Health* 33, no. 4 (2011): 313–19. http://pubs.niaaa.nih.gov/publications/arh334/313-319.htm (accessed December 15, 2011).

WEBSITES

"Aversion Therapy Treatment." Schick Shadel Hospital. http://schickshadel.com/programs/aversion_therapy_treatment.php (accessed September 8, 2011).

ORGANIZATIONS

American Psychological Association, 750 1st St., NE, Washington, DC, 20002-4242, (202) 336-5500; TDD/TTY: (202) 336-6123, (800) 374-2721, http://www.apa.org.

Mental Health America, 2000 N Beauregard St., 6th Fl., Alexandria, VA, 22311, (703) 684-7722, (800) 969-6642, Fax: (703) 684-5968, http://www.nmha.org.

John Garrison, PhD
Emily Jane Willingham, PhD
Margaret Alic, PhD

Avoidant personality disorder

Definition

Avoidant personality disorder (AvPD), also referred to as anxious personality disorder or anxious (avoidant) personality disorder, is characterized by hypersensitivity to rejection and criticism, desire for uncritical acceptance by others, social withdrawal despite a desire for affection and acceptance, and low self-esteem. The behavior patterns associated with avoidant personality disorder are persistent and severe, impairing a person's ability to work with others or maintain social relationships.

Demographics

Avoidant personality disorder appears to be as frequent in males as in females. It affects between 0.5% and 1.0% of adults in the general North American population, but it has been diagnosed in approximately 10% of clinical outpatients.

Description

People who are diagnosed with avoidant personality disorder desire to be in relationships with others but lack the skills and confidence needed to engage in social interactions. In order to protect themselves from anticipated criticism or ridicule, they withdraw from other people. This avoidance of interaction tends to isolate them from meaningful relationships and serves to reinforce their feelings of nervousness and awkwardness in social situations.

The behavior of people with avoidant personality disorder is characterized by social withdrawal, **shyness**, distrustfulness, and emotional distance. People with AvPD tend to be very cautious when they speak, and they convey a general impression of awkwardness in their manner. Most are highly self-conscious and self-critical about their problems relating to others.

There are varying levels of avoidant personality disorder. Some persons may be shy or social phobic and avoid forming relationships entirely. Others may be able to form relationships but have difficulty sustaining them in the long term. If a person with AvPD can manage long-term relationships, he or she may be unable to sever them when needed (e.g., moving out of his or her parent's house).

Causes and symptoms

Causes

The cause of avoidant personality disorder is not clearly defined and may be influenced by a combination of social, genetic, and biological factors. Avoidant personality traits typically appear in childhood, with signs of excessive shyness and fear when the child confronts new people and situations. These characteristics are developmentally appropriate emotions for children, however, and do not necessarily mean that a pattern of avoidant personality disorder will continue into adulthood. When shyness, unfounded fear of rejection, hypersensitivity to criticism, and a pattern of social avoidance persist and intensify through adolescence and young adulthood, a **diagnosis** of avoidant personality disorder is often indicated.

Many persons diagnosed with avoidant personality disorder have had painful early experiences of chronic parental criticism and rejection. The need to bond with the rejecting parent makes the avoidant person hungry for relationships but their longing gradually develops into a defensive shell of self-protection against repeated parental criticisms. Ridicule or rejection by peers further reinforces the young person's pattern of social withdrawal and contributes to their fear of social contact.

Symptoms

The ***Diagnostic and Statistical Manual of Mental Disorders,*** (fourth edition, text revision or *DSM-IV-TR*) specifies seven diagnostic criteria for avoidant personality disorder:

- The person avoids occupational activities that require significant interpersonal contact. Job interviews or promotions may be turned down because the person's own perceptions of his or her abilities do not match the job description.
- The person is reluctant to participate in social involvement without clear assurance that he or she will be accepted. People with this disorder assume other people are not safe to trust until proven otherwise. Others must offer repeated support and encouragement in order to persuade them to participate in a social event.
- The person fears being shamed or ridiculed in close relationships. As a result, people with this disorder become overly alert to behavioral cues that may indicate disapproval or rejection. They will flee a situation in which they believe that others might turn against them.
- The person is preoccupied with being criticized or rejected. Much mental and physical energy is spent brooding about and avoiding situations perceived as "dangerous."
- The person is inhibited in unfamiliar social situations due to feelings of inadequacy. Low self-esteem undermines his or her confidence in meeting and conversing with new acquaintances.
- The person regards him- or herself as socially inept. This self-disparagement is especially apparent when the person must make social contacts with strangers. People with avoidant personality disorder perceive themselves as unappealing or inferior to others.

- The person is reluctant to take social risks, in order to avoid possible humiliation. Persons with AvPD seek interactions that promise the greatest amount of acceptance while minimizing the likelihood of embarrassment or rejection. They might go to a school dance, for example, but remain in one corner chatting with close friends rather than going out on the dance floor with someone they do not know well.

Diagnosis

Many individuals exhibit some avoidant behaviors at one point or another in their lives. Occasional feelings of self-doubt and fear in new and unfamiliar social or personal relationships are not unusual, nor are they unhealthy, as these situations may trigger feelings of inadequacy and the wish to hide from social contact in even the most self-confident individuals. An example would be the anxious hesitancy of a new immigrant in a country with a different language and customs. Avoidant characteristics are regarded as meeting the diagnostic criteria for a personality disorder only when they begin to have a long-term negative impact on the affected person; they lead to functional impairment by significantly altering occupational choice or lifestyle, or otherwise impinging on quality of life; and they cause significant emotional distress.

Avoidant personality disorder can occur in conjunction with other social phobias, mood and **anxiety disorders**, and **personality disorders**. The diagnosis may be complicated by the fact that avoidant personality disorder may be either the cause or result of other mood and anxiety disorders. For example, individuals who have **major depressive disorder** may begin to withdraw from social situations and experience feelings of worthlessness, symptoms that are also prominent features of avoidant personality disorder. On the other hand, the insecurity and isolation that are symptoms of avoidant personality disorder can trigger feelings of **depression**.

The characteristics of avoidant personality disorder may resemble those found in both schizoid and schizotypal personality disorders. Persons with these disorders are prone to social isolation. Those diagnosed with avoidant personality disorder, however, differ from those with schizoid or schizotypal disorder, because they want to have relationships with others but are prevented by their social insecurities. Persons diagnosed with schizoid and schizotypal personality disorders, on the other hand, usually prefer social isolation.

Personality disorders are usually diagnosed following a complete medical history and an interview with the patient. Although there are no laboratory tests for personality disorders, the doctor may give the patient a physical examination to rule out the possibility that a general medical condition is affecting the patient's behavior. For example, people with disorders of the digestive tract may avoid social occasions for fear of a sudden attack of diarrhea or the need to vomit. If the interview with the patient suggests a diagnosis of avoidant personality disorder, the doctor may administer a diagnostic questionnaire or another type of assessment tool.

Assessment tools helpful in diagnosing avoidant personality disorder include:

- **Minnesota Multiphasic Personality Inventory** (MMPI)
- Millon Clinical Multiaxial Inventory (MCMI)
- Rorschach Psychodiagnostic Test
- **Thematic Apperception Test** (TAT)

In diagnosis, it is important to distinguish between the fear of rejection that characterizes avoidant personality disorder from the inability to form relationships that characterizes schizoid patients. Similarly, it is important to distinguish between the fear of relationships characteristic of AvPD and a healthy, natural desire to be alone.

Proposed changes for the fifth edition of the *DSM* (*DSM-5*, 2013) include reorganizing the category of personality disorders (other disorders include **antisocial personality disorder**, **borderline personality disorder**, **narcissistic personality disorder**, **obsessive-compulsive personality disorder**, and **schizotypal personality disorder**). The specific diagnostic criteria for avoidant personality disorder will change but will still center on the same core symptoms—impairments in identity, self-direction, empathy, and intimacy, along with the traits of withdrawal, avoidance, absence of enjoyment in life, and anxiety.

Treatment

The general goal of treatment in avoidant personality disorder is improvement of self-esteem and confidence. As the patient's self-confidence and social skills improve, he or she will become more resilient to potential or real criticism by others.

Psychodynamically oriented therapies

These approaches are usually supportive; the therapist empathizes with the patient's strong sense of shame and inadequacy in order to create a relationship of trust. Therapy usually moves slowly at first, because persons with avoidant personality disorder are mistrustful of others. Treatment that probes into their emotional state too quickly may result in more protective withdrawal by the patient. As trust is established and the patient feels safer discussing details of his or her situation, the patient may be able to draw important connections between his or her deeply felt sense of shame and the resultant behavior in social situations.

Cognitive-behavioral therapy

Cognitive-behavioral therapy (CBT) may be helpful in treating individuals with avoidant personality disorder. This approach assumes that faulty thinking patterns underlie the personality disorder, and therefore focuses on changing distorted cognitive patterns by examining the validity of the assumptions behind them. If a patient feels inferior to his or her peers, a cognitive therapist would test the reality of these assumptions by asking the patient to name friends and family who enjoy his or her company, or to describe past social encounters that were fulfilling. By showing the patient that others value his or her company and that social situations can be enjoyable, the irrationality of the patient's social fears and insecurities are exposed. This process is known as cognitive restructuring.

Group therapy

Group therapy helps provide patients with social experiences that expose them to feedback from others in a safe, controlled environment. Persons with avoidant personality disorder may, however, be reluctant to enter group therapy due to their fear of social rejection. The empathetic environment of the group setting can help each member overcome his or her social anxieties. **Social skills training** can also be incorporated into group therapy to enhance social awareness and feedback.

Family and marital therapy

Family or couple therapy can be helpful for a patient who wants to break out of a family pattern that reinforces the avoidant behavior. The focus of marital therapy would include attempting to break the cycle of rejection, criticism or ridicule that typically characterizes most avoidant marriages. Other strategies include helping the couple to develop constructive ways of relating to one another without shame.

Medications

The use of **monoamine oxidase inhibitors (MAOIs)** has proven useful in helping patients with avoidant personality disorder to control symptoms of social unease and experience initial success. The major drawback of these medications is limitations on the patient's diet. People taking **MAOIs** must avoid foods containing a substance known as tyramine, which is found in most cheeses, liver, red wines, sherry, vermouth, beans with broad pods, soy sauce, sauerkraut, and meat extracts.

KEY TERMS

Cognitive restructuring—An approach to psychotherapy that focuses on helping patients examine distorted patterns of perception and thought in order to change their emotional responses to people and situations.

Monoamine oxidase inhibitors (MAOIs)—A group of antidepressant drugs that decreases the activity of monoamine oxidase, a neurotransmitter found in the brain that affects mood. MAOIs are also used in the treatment of avoidant personality disorder.

Supportive—An approach to psychotherapy that seeks to encourage the patient or offer emotional support to him or her, as distinct from insight-oriented or educational approaches to treatment.

Prognosis

Higher-functioning persons with avoidant personality disorder can generally be expected to improve their social awareness and improve their social skills to some degree. Because of the significant social fear and deep-seated feelings of inferiority, these patterns usually do not change dramatically. Lower-functioning persons are likely to drop out of treatment if they become too anxious.

Prevention

Since avoidant personality disorder usually originates in the patient's family of origin, the only known preventive measure is a nurturing, emotionally stimulating, and expressive family environment.

Resources

BOOKS

American Psychiatric Association. *Diagnostic and Statistical Manual of Mental Disorders*. 4th ed., text rev. Washington, DC: American Psychiatric Publishing, 2000.

Kantor, Martin. *Distancing: Avoidant Personality Disorder,* Revised and expanded. Westport, CT: Praeger, 2003.

Newman, Cory F., and Randy Fingerhut. "Psychotherapy for Avoidant Personality Disorder." In *Oxford Textbook of Psychotherapy,* edited by Glen O. Gabbard, Judith S. Beck, and Jeremy Holmes. Oxford, UK: Oxford University Press, 2005.

Pretzer, James , Barbara Fleming, and Karen M. Simon. *Clinical Applications of Cognitive Therapy*. 2nd ed. New York: Springer, 2004.

Rasmussen, Paul R. *The Personality-Guided Cognitive-Behavioral Therapy*. Washington, DC: American Psychological Association, 2005.

Silverstein, Marshall L. *Disorders of the Self: A Personality-Guided Approach*. Washington, DC: American Psychological Association, 2007.

PERIODICALS

Carter, S. A., and K. D. Wu. "Relations among Symptoms of Social Phobia Subtypes, Avoidant Personality Disorder, Panic, and Depression." *Behavior Therapy* 41, no. 1 (2010): 2–13.

Emmelkamp, Paul M., et al. "Comparison of Brief Dynamic and Cognitive-Behavioural Therapies in Avoidant Personality Disorder." *British Journal of Psychiatry* 189, no. 1 (July 2006): 60–64.

Hopwood, C. J., et al. "Hierarchical Relationships Between Borderline, Schizotypal, Avoidant and Obsessive-Compulsive Personality Disorders." *Acta Psychiatrica Scandinavica* 113, no. 5 (May 2006): 430–39.

Huprich, Steven K. "Differentiating Avoidant and Depressive Personality Disorders." *Journal of Personality Disorders* 19, no. 6 (December 2005): 659–73.

Huprich, Steven K., Mark Zimmerman, and Iwona Chelminski. "Disentangling Depressive Personality Disorder from Avoidant, Borderline, and Obsessive-Compulsive Personality Disorders." *Comprehensive Psychiatry* 47, no. 4 (July–August 2006): 298–306.

Olssøn, Ingrid, and Alv A. Dahl. "Avoidant Personality Problems—Their Association with Somatic and Mental Health, Lifestyle, and Social Network. A Community-Based Study." *Comprehensive Psychiatry* (December 5, 2011) [e-pub ahead of print]. http://dx.doi.org/10.1016/j.comppsych.2011.10.007 (accessed December 15, 2011).

Ralevski, E., et al. "Avoidant Personality Disorder and Social Phobia: Distinct Enough to Be Separate Disorders?" *Acta Psychiatrica Scandinavica* 112, no. 3 (September 2005): 208–14.

Reich, James. "Avoidant Personality Disorder and its Relationship to Social Phobia." *Current Psychiatry Reports* 11, no. 1 (2009): 89–93. http://dx.doi.org/10.1007/s11920-009-0014-0 (accessed December 14, 2011).

Ripoll, L. H., J. Triebwasser, and L.J. Siever. "Evidence-Based Pharmacotherapy for Personality Disorders." *International Journal of Neuropsychopharmacology* 14, no. 9 (2011): 1257–88.

ORGANIZATIONS

American Psychiatric Association, 1000 Wilson Blvd., Ste. 1825, Arlington, VA, 22209-3901, (703) 907-7300, apa@psych.org, http://www.psych.org.

Gary Gilles, MA
Paula Ford-Martin, MA
Ruth A. Wienclaw, PhD

B

Barbiturates

Definition

Barbiturates are a large class of drugs used primarily for sedation, general anesthesia, and as a treatment for some types of epilepsy. In the past, barbiturates were used to sedate people with anxiety and similar disorders, but they have been largely replaced by **benzodiazepines**. The most drugs within the barbiturate family are the generics of amobarbital, aprobarbital, butabarbital, butalbital, mephobarbital, methohexital, pentobarbital, phenobarbital, and secobarbital.

Purpose

Barbiturates have been used to sedate patients prior to surgery as well as to produce general anesthesia, to induce sleep in patients with **insomnia**, to sedate patients with **anxiety disorders**, and to treat some forms of epilepsy. These drugs are highly addictive and are often abused as recreational drugs. Although still commercially available, barbiturates such as amobarbital, pentobarbital, and secobarbital are no longer routinely recommended for insomnia because of their ability to cause dependence, tolerance, and withdrawal. In general, barbiturates lose their efficacy when they are used to treat insomnia on a daily basis for more than two weeks. These drugs also have significant side effects when taken in large doses and can cause respiratory failure and death. Because of the high potential for abuse and adverse side effects, newer medicines, primarily benzodiazepines, have largely replaced barbiturates. Barbiturates still in use include butabarbital and secobarbital to treat insomnia and phenobarbital to treat **seizures**.

Description

The therapeutic effects of barbiturates as a class of drugs are all related to their ability to depress the central nervous system, producing sedation. At high enough doses and with certain preparations, they can induce sleep. Barbiturates were commonly prescribed in the 1960s and 1970s for treating anxiety and insomnia but were largely abused. Because the prescription of barbiturates has declined with the advent of safer drugs, rates of abuse have declined as well; however, a study presented at the American Association for Geriatric Psychiatry annual meeting in 2010 revealed that barbiturates are the primary drug used in geriatric suicides.

Some generic barbiturates (and their brand names) are:

- amobarbital (Amytal Sodium)
- amobarbital/secobarbital combination (Tuinal)
- aprobarbital (Alurate)
- butabarbital (Busodium, Butisol Sodium)
- butalbital (Fiorinal), hexobarbital (Sombulex)
- mephobarbital (Mebaral)
- methohexital (Brevital)
- pentobarbital (Nembutal)
- phenobarbital (Luminal)
- secobarbital (Seconal)
- talbutal (Lotusate)
- thiobarbital (Ibition)

Recommended dosage

Butabarbital is taken before bed if used to treat insomnia or may be taken up to four times a day to treat anxiety. Secobarbital is also taken for insomnia. For both conditions, usage should be evaluated after 7–10 days; if symptoms have not improved within two weeks, it is not likely that the condition will improve by continued use of the drug. Phenobarbital may be taken up to three times a day to treat uncontrolled seizures. Patients should never take more than the prescribed dose, nor should they take the drugs for longer than the intended time.

Precautions

Barbiturate abuse can occur when taking these drugs for a long period of time, in higher than prescribed doses, or without a prescription. Long-term barbiturate use should be avoided unless there is a strong medical need, such as uncontrolled seizures. Abuse of barbiturates can lead to **addiction**, along with serious impairment and distress to both mind and body. Women addicted to barbiturates while pregnant can give birth to addicted babies who may suffer withdrawal symptoms after birth. Symptoms of withdrawal in babies and adults include tremor, insomnia, and general agitation. Severe withdrawal in adults may progress to hallucinations and **psychosis**. Because of the severe risks associated with barbiturate use, it is against U.S. law to use these drugs without a prescription from a medical professional, and when a condition requires long-term drug use, alternative medications should be prescribed whenever possible.

Children who are hyperactive should not receive phenobarbital or other barbiturates. Paradoxically, some children become stimulated and hyperactive after receiving barbiturates.

The use of barbiturates in the elderly (over age 65 years) should be watched closely. Elderly patients must be carefully monitored for confusion, agitation, **delirium**, and excitement if they take barbiturates. Barbiturates should be avoided in elderly patients who are receiving drugs for other mental disorders such as **schizophrenia** or **depression**.

Women should be aware that barbiturate use can make hormonal birth control pills containing estrogen less effective. Women should not use barbiturates during pregnancy unless absolutely necessary. In these cases, they should take the minimum amount required to control the problem. Barbiturate use by pregnant women has been associated with increased risk of fetal damage, newborn bleeding problems, bleeding during childbirth, and, if occurring in the final three months of gestation, dependency in the newborn with attendant withdrawal effects after birth. One study has found a potential link between barbiturate use during pregnancy and **brain** tumors in the infant. Women who are breastfeeding should not take barbiturates because these drugs enter the breast milk and may cause serious side effects in the nursing baby.

People should not drive, operate heavy equipment, or perform other activities requiring mental alertness while taking barbiturates. Some patients taking butabarbital or secobarbital for insomnia have engaged in sleep-related behaviors, including eating, talking, and even driving while asleep, with no recollection of the events. If barbiturates are being used to treat insomnia, they should only be taken when the patient is able to have a full night's sleep (seven to eight hours).

KEY TERMS

Benzene—A colorless toxic liquid with a chemical formula of C_6H_6, where C stands for carbon and H for hydrogen.

Benzodiazepines—A group of drugs used to induce sleep, relieve anxiety, produce sedation, and prevent seizures; generally, such drugs are used as hypnotics in high doses, anxiolytics in medium does, and sedatives in low doses.

Diazepine—A seven-membered unsaturated heterocyclic compound with two nitrogen atoms and three double bonds.

Dependence—A state in which a person requires a steady concentration of a particular substance to avoid experiencing withdrawal symptoms.

Epilepsy—A medical condition involving episodes of irregular electrical discharge within the brain that causes impairment or loss of consciousness, followed by convulsions.

Recreational drugs—The use of a drug with the intention of creating a psychoactive (heightened) mental experience; for the most part, such use is illegal.

Tolerance—The requirement for higher doses of a substance or more frequent engagement in an activity to achieve the same effect.

Side effects

The most common side effect of barbiturate use is drowsiness. Less common side effects include agitation, confusion, breathing difficulties, abnormally low blood pressure, nausea, vomiting, constipation, lowered body temperature, decreased heart rate, movement difficulty, nightmares, anxiety, nervousness, mental depression, and dizziness. Rare but reported side effects include fever, headache, anemia, allergic reactions, and liver damage.

Interactions

Patients should always tell their doctor and dentist when they are taking barbiturates. Barbiturates should generally not be taken with other drugs used to treat mental disorders. In addition, patients should inform their healthcare providers about any health or medical problems, especially a history of alcohol or drug abuse or problems with anemia, asthma, diabetes, hyperthyroid, or kidney or liver disease, among others.

QUESTIONS TO ASK YOUR DOCTOR

- Why are you prescribing this medication?
- What alternative medications are available?
- What are the possible side effects?
- How long will I need to take the medication?

There are a number of drugs that barbiturates should not be combined with, because the barbiturates may increase the rate of breakdown of these drugs, thus reducing their availability to the body. These drugs include oral corticosteroids such as predisolone, methylprednisolone, prednisone, or dexamethasone; estrogen and oral contraceptives; blood-thinning medications such as warfarin (Coumadin); the antibiotic doxycycline (Vibramycin); and anticonvulsants such as phenytoin (Dilantin). Barbiturates may also lower the amount of absorption of vitamins D and K.

Because barbiturates work on the central nervous system, they may add to the effects of alcohol and other drugs that slow the central nervous system, such as antihistamines, cold medicine, allergy medicine, sleep aids, medicine for seizures, tranquilizers, some pain relievers, and muscle relaxants. They may also add to the effects of anesthetics, including those used for dental procedures. The combined effects of barbiturates and alcohol or other CNS depressants (drugs that slow the central nervous system) can be very dangerous, leading to unconsciousness and even death. Individuals who are taking barbiturates should not drink alcohol and should check with their physician before taking any medicines classified as CNS depressants.

Taking an overdose of barbiturates or combining barbiturates with alcohol or other central nervous system depressants can cause unconsciousness and even death. Anyone who shows signs of an overdose or a reaction to combining barbiturates with alcohol or other drugs should get emergency medical help immediately. Signs include:

- severe drowsiness
- breathing problems
- slurred speech
- staggering
- slow heartbeat
- excessive confusion
- severe weakness

Resources

BOOKS

Goodman, Louis S., et al. *Goodman & Gilman's The Pharmacological Basis of Therapeutics,* 12th ed. New York: McGraw-Hill Medical, 2011.

Henn, Debra, and Deborah de Eugenio, eds. *Barbiturates.* New York: Chelsea House, 2007.

Karch, A. M. *Lippincott's Nursing Drug Guide.* Springhouse, PA: Lippincott Williams & Wilkins, 2007.

Liska, Ken. *Drugs and the Human Body: With Implications for Society.* Upper Saddle River, NJ: Pearson Prentice Hall, 2009.

Preston, J., et al. *Handbook of Clinical Psychopharmacology for Therapists.* Oakland, CA: New Harbinger, 2008.

WEBSITES

"Barbiturate Abuse." Drugs.com. http://www.drugs.com/cg/barbiturate-abuse.html (accessed October 7, 2011).

"Barbiturate Intoxication and Overdose, Systemic." MedlinePlus. http://www.nlm.nih.gov/medlineplus/ency/article/000951.htm (accessed October 7, 2011).

Cooper, Jeffrey S. "Toxicity, Sedative-Hypnotics." Medscape Reference. http://www.emedicine.com/emerg/topic525.htm (accessed October 7, 2011).

Harrison, Pam. "Barbiturates Still Drugs of Choice in Geriatric Suicide." Medscape News, March 11, 2010. http://www.medscape.com/viewarticle/718354 (accessed October 7, 2011).

ORGANIZATIONS

American Psychiatric Association, 1000 Wilson Blvd., Ste. 1825, Arlington, VA, 22209-3901, (703) 907-7300, apa@psych.org, http://www.psych.org.

Anxiety Disorders Association of America, 8730 Georgia Ave., Silver Spring, MD, 20910, (240) 485-1001, Fax: (240) 485-1035, http://www.adaa.org.

Mental Health America, 2000 N. Beauregard St., 6th Fl., Alexandria, VA, 22311, (703) 684-7722, (800) 969-6642, Fax: (703) 684-5968, http://www1.nmha.org.

National Alliance on Mental Illness, 3803 N Fairfax Dr., Ste. 100, Arlington, VA, 22203, (703) 524-7600, http://www.nami.org.

National Institute of Mental Health, 6001 Executive Blvd., Rm. 8184, MSC 9663, Bethesda, MD, 20892-9663, (301) 443-4513; TTY: (301) 443-8431, Fax: (301) 443-4279, (866) 615-6464; TTY: (866) 415-8051, nimhinfo@nih.gov, http://www.nimh.nih.gov.

Mark Mitchell, MD
Emily Jane Willingham, PhD
William A. Atkins, BB, BS, MBA

BDI, BDI-II *see* **Beck Depression Inventory**

Beck Depression Inventory

Definition

The Beck Depression Inventory (BDI) is a series of 21 multiple-choice questions developed to measure the intensity, severity, and depth of depressive symptoms in patients aged 13 to 80 years. The questionnaire can be filled out by the patient as a self-reported test or administered verbally by a trained professional. The BDI also helps measure symptoms related to depression such as **fatigue**, irritability, guilt, weight loss, and **apathy**. A shorter form is also available; it is composed of seven questions and is designed for administration by primary care providers.

KEY TERMS

Cognitive therapy—A psychiatric treatment that focuses on changing cognitive beliefs and thinking patterns to produce behavioral change.

Depression—A mental condition in which a person feels extremely sad and loses interest in life; symptoms may include sleep problems, loss of appetite, loss of concentration, and, in severe cases, attempts at self-harm or suicide.

Dysthymia—A less severe but chronic (ongoing) form of depression.

Purpose

The BDI was first developed by American **psychiatrist** Aaron T. Beck—from the Beck Institute for Cognitive Therapy and Research and the Department of Psychiatry at the University of Pennsylvania (Philadelphia)—who is considered a pioneer in cognitive therapy. The purpose of the BDI is to detect, assess, and monitor changes in depressive symptoms among people in a mental health care setting. Its primary goal is to determine the primary cause of **depression** in patients.

Description

The BDI was first developed and published in 1961. It was adapted in the 1970s and copyrighted in 1978 (BDI-1A). A second (and latest) version of the inventory (BDI-II) was developed and published in 1996 to reflect changes in the fourth (IV) edition, text revised (TR) version of the ***Diagnostic and Statistical Manual of Mental Disorders*** (*DSM-IV-TR*), a handbook that mental health professionals use to diagnose mental disorders. (The fifth edition [*DSM-5*] is being developed for publication in May 2013.) Beck, along with Doctors Robert A. Steer and Gregory K. Brown, authored the BDI-II.

The long form of the BDI is composed of 21 questions or items, each with four possible responses. Each response is assigned a score ranging from zero to three, indicating the severity of the symptom that the patient has experienced over the past two weeks. A version designed for use by primary care providers (BDI-PC) is composed of seven self-reported items.

The BDI is divided into two subscales. The affective subscale consists of eight items that measure psychological, or mood, symptoms. The eight characteristics contained within this subscale address negative thoughts involving:

- failure
- pessimism
- guilt
- self-punishment
- self-dislike (self-dissatisfaction)
- self-criticism
- suicide
- worthlessness

The remaining 13 characteristics focus on somatic, or physical, symptoms. They consist of negative feelings representing:

- agitation
- irritability
- sadness
- crying/tearfulness
- loss of pleasure
- loss of interest (social withdrawal)
- loss of interest in sex (loss of libido)
- tiredness/fatigue
- loss of energy
- trouble concentrating
- indecisiveness
- change in appetite (especially weight loss)
- change in sleep patterns (especially insomnia)

The BDI is also used to detect depressive symptoms in a primary care setting. The BDI usually takes between five and ten minutes to complete as part of a psychological or medical examination.

Preparation

Preparation for the Beck Depression Inventory test is not necessary nor recommended by the medical community.

Aftercare

Depending on the results of the BDI, aftercare will involve treating the depression or depressive disorder.

Precautions

The BDI is designed for use by trained professionals. In order to achieve accurate results, it should be administered by a knowledgeable mental health professional who is trained in its use and interpretation. Like other tests that measure depression using inputs from patients, there is a risk of patients understating or exaggerating their symptoms.

Results

The sum of all BDI item scores indicates the severity of depression. The test is scored differently for the general population and for individuals who have been clinically diagnosed with depression. For the general population, a score of 21 or over represents depression. For people who have been clinically diagnosed, BDI-II scores from 0 to 13 represent minimal depressive symptoms, scores of 14 to 19 indicate mild depression, scores of 20 to 28 indicate moderate depression, and scores of 29 to 63 indicate severe depression. (BDI-II scores differ from those of the original BDI.) The BDI can distinguish between different subtypes of depressive disorders, such as major depression and dysthymia (a less severe form of depression).

The BDI has been extensively tested for content validity, concurrent validity, and construct validity. The BDI has content validity—the extent to which items of a test are representative of that which is to be measured—because it was constructed from a consensus among clinicians about depressive symptoms displayed by psychiatric patients. Concurrent validity is a measure of the extent to which a test concurs with already existing standards; at least 35 studies have shown concurrent validity between the BDI and such measures of depression as the **Hamilton Depression Scale** and the **Minnesota Multiphasic Personality Inventory**-D. Tests for construct validity—the degree to which a test measures an internal construct or variable—have shown the BDI to be related to medical symptoms, anxiety, **stress**, loneliness, sleep patterns, alcoholism, suicidal behaviors, and adjustment among youth.

QUESTIONS TO ASK YOUR DOCTOR

- How will the Beck Depression Inventory help me solve my depression?
- How does the BDI work?
- Is the BDI able to diagnose severe or minor cases of depression?

Factor analysis, a statistical method used to determine underlying relationships between variables, has also supported the validity of the BDI. The BDI can be interpreted as one syndrome (depression) composed of three factors: negative attitudes toward self, performance impairment, and somatic (bodily) disturbance.

The BDI has also been extensively tested for reliability, following established standards for psychological tests first published in 1985. Internal consistency has been estimated successfully by over 25 studies in many populations. The BDI has been shown to be valid and reliable, with results corresponding to clinician ratings of depression in more than 90% of all cases.

Higher BDI scores have been shown in a few studies to be inversely related to educational attainment; the BDI, however, does not consistently correlate with gender, race, or age.

The BDI is one of the most widely used assessment tests by medical professionals and researchers for measuring depressive symptoms.

See also Cognitive-behavioral therapy

Resources

BOOKS

American Psychiatric Association. *Diagnostic and Statistical Manual of Mental Disorders*. 4th ed., text rev. Washington, DC: American Psychiatric Association, 2000.

Beck, Aaron T., and Brad A. Alford. *Depression: Causes and Treatments*. Philadelphia: University of Pennsylvania Press, 2009.

Clark, David A., and Aaron T. Beck. *Cognitive Therapy of Anxiety Disorders: Science and Practice*. New York: Guilford Press, 2010.

Clark, David A., Aaron T. Beck, and Brad A. Alford. *Scientific Foundations of Cognitive Theory and Therapy of Depression*. New York City: John Wiley & Sons, 2003.

Nezu, Arthur, George F. Ronan, and Elizabeth A. Meadows, editors. *Practitioner's Guide to Empirically Based*

Measures of Depression. New York City: Springer Publishing Company, 2006.

PERIODICALS

Konstantinidis, A., et al. "A Comparison of the Major Depression Inventory (MDI) and the Beck Depression Inventory (BDI) in Severely Depressed Patients." *International Journal of Psychiatry in Clinical Practice* 15, no. 1 (2011): 56–61.

Mehl, Matthias R. "The Lay Assessment of Subclinical Depression in Daily Life." *Psychological Assessment* 18, no. 3 (September 2006): 340–45.

Quilty, L. C., K. A. Zhang, and R. M. Bagby. "The Latent Symptom Structure of the Beck Depression Inventory-II in Outpatients with Major Depression." *Psychological Assessment* 22, no. 3 (2010): 603–8.

Snijders, A. H., M. M. Robertson, and M. Orth. "Beck Depression Inventory is a Useful Screening Tool for Major Depressive Disorder in Gilles de la Tourette Syndrome." *Journal of Neurology, Neurosurgery & Psychiatry* 77, no. 6 (June 2006): 787–89.

Stulz, N, and P. Crits-Christoph. "Distinguishing Anxiety and Depression in Self-Report: Purification of the Beck Anxiety Inventory and Beck Depression Inventory-II." *Journal of Clinical Psychiatry* 66, no. 9 (2010): 927–40.

WEBSITES

Pearson Assessments. "Beck Depression Inventory®—II (BDI®—II)." http://www.pearsonassessments.com/HAIWEB/Cultures/en-us/Productdetail.htm?Pid=015-8018-370 (accessed November 16, 2010).

University of Pennsylvania, Perelman School of Medicine, Department of Psychiatry. "Aaron T. Beck, M.D." http://www.med.upenn.edu/suicide/beck/index.html (accessed October 14, 2011).

ORGANIZATIONS

American Psychiatric Association, 1000 Wilson Boulevard, Suite 1825, Arlington, VA, 22209-3901, (703) 907-7300, apa@psych.org, http://www.psych.org.

American Psychological Association, 750 First Street NE, Washington, DC, 20002, (202) 336-5500, (800) 374-2721, http://www.apa.org.

Depression and Bipolar Support Alliance, 730 North Franklin Street, Suite 501, Chicago, IL, 60654-7225, (800) 826-3632, Fax: (312) 642-7243, http://www.dbsalliance.org.

National Alliance on Mental Illness, 3803 North Fairfax Drive, Suite 100, Arlington, VA, 22203, (703) 524-7600, (800) 950-6264, Fax: (703) 524-9094, http://www.nami.org.

National Institute of Mental Health, 6001 Executive Boulevard, Room 8184, MSC 9663, Bethesda, MD, 20892-9663, (301) 443-4513, (866) 615-6464, Fax: (301) 443-4279, nimhinfo@nih.gov, http://www.nimh.nih.gov.

Michael Polgar, PhD
Ruth A. Wienclaw, PhD
William Atkins

Bed-wetting *see* **Enuresis**

Behavioral addiction *see* **Process addiction**

Behavioral neurology *see* **Neuropsychiatry**

Behavioral self-control training *see* **Self-control strategies**

Behavior modification

Definition

Behavior modification is an empirically based psychological treatment approach founded on the principles of operant conditioning. The goal is to replace undesirable behaviors with more desirable ones through positive or negative **reinforcement** of adaptive behavior. During behavior modification, various methods may be used to produce positive change. Such methods include **aversion therapy**, desensitization, and **biofeedback**, which may include such features as physical and mental persuasion (coercion), positive reinforcement (rewards), negative reinforcement (punishment), medication use, **psychotherapy**, and others.

Purpose

Behavior modification is used to treat a variety of problems in both adults and children. It was developed so that educational and treatment techniques could be used on an individualized basis while still conforming to a standard format. The process of behavior modification includes five key steps:

- Decision: Decide what the patient should do to eliminate the problem.
- Program: Devise a program to weaken or eliminate undesirable behavior and strengthen desirable behavior.
- Treatment: Carry out a treatment program according to established principles and guidelines.
- Record: Keep detailed and objective records.
- Alteration: Alter any part of the program if further progress can be made.

Behavior modification has been successfully used to treat **obsessive-compulsive disorder** (OCD), **attention deficit hyperactivity disorder (ADHD)**, phobias, **enuresis** (bed-wetting), anxiety disorder, and **separation anxiety disorder**, among others.

Description

Behavior modification is based on the principles of operant conditioning, which were developed by American behaviorist B. F. Skinner (1904–90). Skinner formulated the concept of operant conditioning, through which behavior could be shaped by reinforcement (or the lack of it). Skinner considered his concept applicable to a wide range of both human and animal behaviors and introduced operant conditioning to the general public in his 1938 book, *The Behavior of Organisms*. Behavior modification is distinguished by a focus on behavior and its consequences. Other related forms of therapy, such as **cognitive-behavioral therapy**, may take into account internal motivation and feelings as well.

Key concepts of behavior modification are:

- attribution
- biases
- self-perception
- cognitive dissonance
- learned helpfulness
- motivation
- stress reduction or tolerance

Techniques

Techniques used in behavior modification include:

- Systematic desensitization, which treats disturbances that have identifiable sources, such as a paralyzing fear of closed spaces; usually involves training the individual to relax in the presence of fear-producing stimuli.
- Aversion therapy, which treats bad habits by breaking (stopping) them with various techniques—such as applying electric shock when the bad habit appears—so as to change the habit from being perceived as positive to negative.
- Biofeedback, which treats disturbed behavior that has physical symptoms—for instance, monitoring blood pressure or heartbeat rate and rewarding the individual when positive change occurs, such as decrease in heartbeat rate.

One widely used behavior modification technique is positive reinforcement, which encourages certain behaviors through a system of rewards. In behavior therapy, it is common for the therapist to draw up a contract with the client establishing the terms of the reward system. The system can consist of goals, rewards, and consequences. In addition to being practiced either consciously or unconsciously by educators and parents, this system also has come in to widespread use as a way to address behaviors in children with attention deficit hyperactivity disorder (ADHD).

KEY TERMS

Anxiety—Worry or tension in response to real or imagined stress, danger, or dreaded situations. Physical reactions such as fast pulse, sweating, trembling, fatigue, and weakness may accompany anxiety.

Attention deficit hyperactivity disorder (ADHD)—A learning and behavioral disorder characterized by difficulty in sustaining attention, impulsive behavior, and excessive activity.

Cognitive dissonance—A conflict of anxiety resulting from the difference in one's beliefs and one's actions.

Conduct disorder—A behavioral and emotional disorder of childhood and adolescence in which children display physical aggression and infringe on or violate the rights of others. Youths diagnosed with conduct disorder may set fires, exhibit cruelty toward animals or other children, sexually assault others, or lie and steal for personal gain.

Enuresis—Involuntary urination.

Obsessive-compulsive disorder (OCD)—An anxiety disorder in which individuals cannot prevent themselves from dwelling on unwanted thoughts, acting on urges, or performing repetitious rituals, such as washing their hands or checking to make sure they turned off the lights.

Behavior modification also can discourage unwanted behavior through either negative reinforcement or punishment. Negative reinforcement refers to an undesirable response that stops only when the desired behavior is performed. Punishment is the application of an aversive or unpleasant stimulus in reaction to a particular behavior. For example, for children, this could be the removal of television privileges when they disobey a parent or teacher.

The removal of reinforcement altogether is called extinction. Extinction eliminates the incentive for unwanted behavior by withholding the expected response. A widespread parenting technique based on extinction is the time-out, in which children are separated from the group when they misbehave. This technique removes the expected reward of adult attention.

Attention deficit hyperactivity disorder

Behavior modification is important when treating children and adolescents with attention deficit hyperactivity disorder (ADHD), which is a developmental

B. F. SKINNER (1904–90)

American behavioral psychologist Burrhus Frederic (B. F.) Skinner was born in Susquehanna, Pennsylvania. Skinner became interested in behaviorist psychology after reading the works of John Watson and Ivan Pavlov. He entered Harvard University (Cambridge, Massachusetts) as a graduate student in psychology in 1928 and received his degree three years later. While at Harvard, he laid the foundation for a new system of behavioral analysis through his research in the field of animal learning, using unique experimental equipment of his own design.

Skinner's most successful and well-known apparatus, the Skinner Box, was a cage in which a laboratory rat could, by pressing on a bar, activate a mechanism that would drop a food pellet into the cage. Another device recorded each press of the bar, producing a permanent record of experimental results without the presence of a tester. Skinner analyzed the rats' bar-pressing behavior by varying his patterns of reinforcement (feeding) to learn their responses to different schedules, including random ones.

Using this box to study how rats "operated on" their environment led Skinner to formulate the principle of operant conditioning through which an experimenter can gradually shape the behavior of a subject by manipulating its responses through reinforcement or lack of it. In contrast to Pavlovian, or response, conditioning, which depends on an outside stimulus, Skinner's operant conditioning depends on the subject's responses themselves. Skinner introduced the concept of operant conditioning in his first book, *The Behavior of Organisms* (1938). His ideas eventually became so influential that the American Psychological Association created a separate division of studies related to them (Division 25: The Experimental Analysis of Behavior), and four journals of behaviorist research were established.

Skinner's work also was influential in the clinical treatment of mental and emotional disorders. In the late 1940s, he began to develop the behavior modification method in which subjects receive a series of small rewards for desired behavior. Considered a useful technique for psychologists and psychiatrists with deeply disturbed patients, behavior modification has also been widely used by the general population in overcoming obesity, shyness, speech problems, addiction to smoking, and other problems.

Extending his ideas to the realm of philosophy, Skinner concluded that all behavior was the result of either positive or negative reinforcement, meaning that the existence of free will was merely an illusion. To explore the social ramifications of his behaviorist principles, he wrote the novel *Walden Two* (1948), which depicted a utopian society in which all reinforcement was positive. While detractors of this controversial work regarded its vision of social control through strict positive reinforcement as totalitarian, the 1967 founding of the Twin Oaks Community in Virginia was inspired by Skinner's ideas. Skinner elaborated further on his ideas about positive social control in his book *Beyond Freedom and Dignity* (1971), which critiques the notion of human autonomy, arguing that many actions ascribed to free will are performed due to necessity.

disorder that is characterized by attention problems and hyperactivity often occurring before the age of seven years. Medical professionals often combine medication with behavior modification techniques to manage ADHD. Such techniques may involve child-behavior training by parents, behavior modification by academics within the classroom, and placement in special education classes and situations. Positive reinforcement may be used to encourage good behavior, while negative reinforcement is often used to discourage bad behavior.

Anxiety

Anxiety disorders can be effectively controlled by a variety of behavior modification techniques. Such disorders include **generalized anxiety disorder** (GAD), **panic disorder** (and panic disorder with **agoraphobia**), phobias (such as social anxiety disorder), obsessive-compulsive disorder (OCD), **post-traumatic stress disorder** (PTSD), separation anxiety disorder, and childhood anxiety disorder.

Eating disorders

Eating disorders such as **anorexia nervosa**, **binge eating disorder**, and **bulimia nervosa** have been successfully treated with behavior modification. Obesity has also been shown to respond well to behavior modification, and structured behavioral programs have been established for the treatment of both obesity and eating disorders. Medical research is ongoing to study behavior modification techniques with respect to the systematic manipulation of all factors relating to eating and exercise. Many studies have shown that undergoing behavior modification treatment for an average of 18 weeks is as effective as losing a modest amount of weight safely through diet and exercise, and most of the time the weight is kept off without **relapse**.

Conduct disorders

Treatment of **conduct disorder** (CD) among children has been shown to be effective when behavioral parent training programs are implemented. Children with CD do not understand the difference between right and wrong, and behavioral modification programs help them to develop and understand that distinction. Such programs are frequently performed at home under the guidance of medical professionals. The problem areas of the child, such as aggression, deceitfulness, and inappropriate behavior, are targeted.

Benefits

Behavior modification works to address and correct negative behaviors, thus helping to improve the quality of individuals' lives and their success in society, at work, and in school.

Precautions

It is important to use a credentialed and licensed therapist. A therapist who has not had the proper training can force the client to move through the process too quickly or not provide adequate treatment. Clients should have a comfortable and trusting relationship with their therapist.

Preparation

Searching for a therapist may take time and effort, just as it does when looking for any healthcare professional. Both the National Association of Cognitive-Behavioral Therapists and the Association for Behavioral and Cognitive Therapies have information on their websites on how to find a behavior modification therapist.

Aftercare

Behavior modification techniques are often continued by parents or other caregivers after therapy has ended. Such at-home care is necessary in order to reinforce the lessons learned.

QUESTIONS TO ASK YOUR DOCTOR

- Can you refer me to a good behavior modification therapist?
- Do you believe that behavior modification therapy will help my type of problem?
- How long can I expect to be in therapy?

Risks

Behavior modification has been proven effective. However, some criticize its methods for its (sometimes) overuse of punishment. Rather than changing behavior, behavior modification is sometimes thought to instill in children the sense of avoiding being punished rather than actually modifying behavior. Consequently, behavior modification is sometimes thought to be a form of control; that is, a person is punished if behaviors are not improved. Many psychologists, therapists, and **social workers** who administer behavior modification attempt to use positive reinforcement five times more frequently than negative reinforcement, what is called a 5:1 ratio of positive to negative responses. A harsher criticism of behavior modification comes from some people who believe it is not ethical to deliberately change behavior in others. Whether such criticism is valid or not, it does exist in some realms of psychology.

Controversy also surrounds the use of electroshock treatment as negative reinforcement. Electroshock therapy was used in the 1980s as a treatment for **autism** and other developmental disorders but was soon replaced by less invasive treatments. Though it is not common, the practice still exists and may be used when other treatments prove unsuccessful. Proponents of the treatment claim that the therapy is given when the patients pose a danger to themselves or others and that it is chosen to avoid serious self-harm. Such patients may suffer from **intellectual disability** disorders and may not know the extent or consequences of their actions. Opponents of the treatment raise the ethical question of whether such practice is a form of torture. Electroshock therapy is not a preferred form of behavior modification.

Resources

BOOKS

Gaus, Valerie L. *Cognitive-Behavioral Therapy for Adult Asperger Syndrome.* New York: Guilford Press, 2007.

Kaiser, Barbara, and Judy Sklar Rasminsky. *Challenging Behavior in Young Children: Understanding, Preventing, and Responding Effectively*. Upper Saddle River, NJ: Pearson, 2012.

Martin, G., and J. Pear. *Behavior Modification: What It Is and How to Do It,* 8th ed. Upper Saddle River, NJ: Pearson Prentice Hall, 2007.

Miltenberger, Raymond G. *Behavior Modification: Principles and Procedures,* 4th ed. Belmont, CA: Thomson Wadsworth, 2008.

PERIODICALS

Leaf, Justin B., et al. "A Program Description of a Community-Based Intensive Behavioral Intervention Program for Individuals with Autism Spectrum Disorders." *Education & Treatment of Children* 34, no. 2 (2011): 259–85.

Pilkington, Ed. "Shock Tactics: Treatment or Torture?" *The Guardian*, March 12, 2011. http://www.guardian.co.uk/society/2011/mar/12/electric-shock-school-matthew-israel (accessed September 8, 2011).

OTHER

Ahern, Laurie, and Eric Rosenthal. *Torture not Treatment: Electric Shock and Long-Term Restraint in the United States on Children and Adults with Disabilities at the Judge Rotenberg Center.* Washington, DC: Mental Disability Rights International, 2010. http://www.mdri.org/PDFs/USReportandUrgentAppeal.pdf (accessed September 8 2011).

WEBSITES

"Cognitive-Behavioral Therapy." National Alliance on Mental Health, June 2003. http://www.nami.org/Template.cfm?Section=About_Treatments_and_Supports&template=/ContentManagement/ContentDisplay.cfm&ContentID=7952 (accessed September 8, 2011).

"Strategies for Teaching Students with Behavioral Disorders." West Virginia University. Last updated April 20, 2007. http://www.as.wvu.edu/~scidis/behavior.html (accessed September 8, 2011).

ORGANIZATIONS

American Psychiatric Association, 1000 Wilson Blvd., Ste. 1825, Arlington, VA, 22209-3901, (703) 907-7300, apa@psych.org, http://www.psych.org.

Association for Behavioral and Cognitive Therapies, 305 7th Ave., 16th Fl., New York, NY, 10001, (212) 647-1890, Fax: (212) 647-1865, (866) 615-6464, http://www.abct.org.

National Association of Cognitive-Behavioral Therapists, PO Box 2195, Weirton, WV, 26062, (304) 723-3982, (800) 853-1135, nacbt@nacbt.org, http://www.nacbt.org.

National Institute of Mental Health, 6001 Executive Blvd., Rm. 8184, MSC 9663, Bethesda, MD, 20892-9663, (301) 433-4513; TTY: (301) 443-8431, Fax: (301) 443-4279, (866) 615-6464; TTY: (866) 415-8051, nimhinfo@nih.gov, http://www.nimh.nih.gov.

Emily Jane Willingham, PhD
Tish Davidson, AM
Brenda Lerner
William Atkins, BB, BS, MBA

Behavior therapy *see* **Cognitive-behavioral therapy**

Benadryl *see* **Diphenhydramine**

Bender Gestalt Test

Definition

The Bender Gestalt Test (BGT), or the Bender Visual Motor Gestalt Test, is a **psychological assessment** instrument used to evaluate visual-motor functioning and visual perception skills in both children and adults. The format of the test consists of the reproduction (copying) by the participant of simple line drawings (geometric designs). Scores on the test are used to identify possible organic **brain** damage and the degree of maturation of the nervous system. The Bender Gestalt was developed by American **psychiatrist** and child neuropsychiatrist Lauretta Bender (1897–1987) in the late nineteenth century.

Bender published the monograph "A Visual Motor Gestalt and Its Clinical Use" in 1935. Concentrating within the psychological and psychiatric field of child neurology, she included the psychological test within the publication. At that time, it consisted of figures drawn on three-inch by five-inch cards, which were derived from the work of Czech-born American **psychologist** Max Wertheimer (1880–1943). Test takers were asked to copy each figure onto a blank piece of paper and to reproduce each figure as well as they could. The results of the test, which normally took from seven to ten minutes, were based on accuracy of the resultant figures and other such relevant factors. The American Orthopsychiatric Association originally published the BGT. In the 1990s, the Riverside Publishing Company acquired the test.

The revised Bender Gestalt Test—the Bender Visual-Motor Gestalt Test, Second Edition (Bender-Gestalt II)—was first published in 2003. Drs. Scott L. Decker and Gary G. Brannigan authored the latest revision based on a sample of over 4,000 individuals, from 4 years of age to over 85 years of age, representing the population of the United States as it stood in the 2000 U.S. census. The revised psychological test battery features an expanded age range and a more comprehensive assessment of visual-motor skills.

Purpose

The Bender Gestalt Test is a widely used assessment tool, both in the United States and internationally, for measuring cognitive abilities and to assess brain dysfunction.

It remains a popular psychological test because it is simple to use, is brief to administer, and has proven effective for a wide range of ages (from three to over 85 years). It is also frequently used within inpatient psychiatric locations because of its ability to differentiate between serious mental disorders and brain impairment. The Bender-Gestalt II is also beneficial for recognizing cognitive decline in older adults.

The Bender Gestalt Test is used to evaluate visual-motor maturity and integration skills, style of responding, reaction to frustration, ability to correct mistakes, planning and organizational skills, and motivation. Copying figures requires fine motor skills, the ability to discriminate between varying elements of visual stimuli, the capacity to integrate visual skills with motor skills, and the ability to shift attention from the original design to what is being drawn.

The Bender-Gestalt II is used to assess the maturation of visuomotor perceptions of children and adults. It is used to offer perspective into many psychological conditions such as **Alzheimer's disease** (AD), **attention deficit hyperactivity disorder (ADHD)**, **autism**, giftedness, learning disabilities, and intellectual disabilities. Its primary purposes are to:

- furnish information to help clarify the development and neuropsychological functioning of the test taker
- disclose level of competence of visual-motor perceptions, which is related to language and intelligence functions
- provide information on the participant including the ability to take the test, attitude while completing it, physical ability and aptitude during the test, and drawing ability and technique
- impart early (screening) recognition as to psychological and neuropsychological impairment

Description

The Bender Gestalt Test is an individually administered pencil-and-paper test used to make a **diagnosis** of brain injury. The original Bender Gestalt Test contains nine geometric figures drawn in black. These figures, sometimes called stimulus cards, are presented to the examinee one at a time; then, the examinee is asked to copy the unique figure onto a blank sheet of paper with the card still in sight. Examinees are allowed to erase but may not use any mechanical aids (such as rulers). The popularity of this test among clinicians is most likely due to the short amount of time it takes to administer and score. The average amount of time to complete the test is five to ten minutes.

The Bender Gestalt Test lends itself to several variations in administration. One method requires the examinee to view each card for five seconds, after which the card is removed. Then, the examinee draws the figure from memory. Another variation involves having the examinee draw the figures by following the standard procedure. The examinee is then given a clean sheet of paper and asked to draw as many figures as he or she can recall. In a third variation, the test is given to a group, rather than to an individual. Note that these variations were not part of the original test. In addition, one of the most popular scoring systems used with the BGT is the Bender-Gestalt Test for Young Children, which was developed by American clinical child psychologist and school psychologist Elizabeth Munsterberg Koppitz (1919–1983).

The Bender-Gestalt Test II contains 16 figures and is designed to be given to people from 3 years of age to over 85 years, a small extension of the age range from the previous edition. In addition, it has a new recall procedure for visual-motor (visuomotor) memory that assures a more comprehensive assessment of such skills. It also includes new supplemental tests of simple motor and perceptual ability to help identify motor-visual deficits. An optional timed component of the test allows the administrator to time each drawing. In addition, the revised test contains new norms for copy and recall procedures. Overall, it is considered a quick way to adequately measure both visual-motor development and psychological functioning. The main test takes between five and ten minutes to administer. A period of five minutes is usually needed to complete each of the supplemental visual and motor tests. The revised scoring system for the BGT-II was developed based on research conducted on several other scoring systems, including the Global Scoring System.

The Koppitz Developmental Scoring System (Koppitz-II), authored by Dr. Cecil Reynolds, is also available to be used with the Bender-Gestalt II. The Koppitz-II has been expanded in the scope of its scoring, along with a better reliability in its scoring system for all age levels. The scoring system has been normed based on a nationally stratified representative sample (as based on the U.S. census) of children and adults (a total of 3,600 people) from all parts of the United States, determined by community size, ethnicity, geographic region, socioeconomic condition, and other important factors.

Precautions

The Bender Gestalt Test and the revised test should not be administered to an individual with severe visual impairment unless his or her vision has been adequately corrected with eyeglasses or contact lenses. Additionally, the test should not be given to an examinee with a severe motor impairment, as the impairment would affect his or her ability to draw the geometric figures correctly. The test scores might thereby be distorted.

KEY TERMS

Alzheimer's disease—A degenerative medical disorder that adversely affects the brain and causes dementia within the later years of life.

Attention deficit hyperactivity disorder—A condition involving hyperactivity in children, characterized by an inability to concentrate and inappropriate or impulsive behaviors.

Autism—A neuropsychological problem that usually begins before the age of three years and develops with respect to disorders involving speech and language, interpretation of the world, social interactions and the formation of relationships, and reaction to stimuli. Repetitive behaviors are often seen within the condition.

Visuomotor—Pertaining to visual and motor processes.

The Bender Gestalt Test has been criticized for being used to assess problems with organic factors in the brain. This criticism stems from the lack of specific signs on the Bender Gestalt Test that are definitively associated with brain injury or the diagnosis of brain injury. As such, the Bender Gestalt Test should never be used in isolation. When making a diagnosis, results from the Bender Gestalt Test should be used in conjunction with other medical, developmental, educational, psychological, and neuropsychological information.

Finally, psychometric testing requires administration and evaluation by a clinically trained examiner. If a scoring system is used, the examiner should carefully evaluate its reliability and validity, as well as the normative sample being used. A normative sample is a group within a population who take a test and represent the larger population. This group's scores on a test are then used to create "norms" with which the scores of test takers are compared.

Results

A scoring system does not have to be used to interpret performance on either form of the Bender Gestalt Test, though there are several reliable and valid scoring systems available. Many of the available scoring systems focus on specific-type difficulties experienced by the test taker. The following difficulties may indicate poor visual-motor abilities in the test taker:

- angular difficulty—increasing, decreasing, distorting, or omitting an angle in a figure
- bizarre doodling—adding peculiar components to the drawing that have no relationship to the original Bender Gestalt figure
- closure difficulty—difficulty closing open spaces on a figure, or connecting various parts of the figure, resulting in a gap in the copied figure
- cohesion—drawing a part of a figure larger or smaller than shown on the original figure and out of proportion with the rest of the figure; may also include drawing a figure or part of a figure significantly out of proportion with other figures
- collision—crowding the designs or allowing the end of one design to overlap or touch a part of another design
- contamination—occurs when a previous figure, or part of a figure, influences the examinee's completion of the current figure; for example, combining two different Bender Gestalt figures
- fragmentation—destroying part of the figure by not completing it, or breaking up the figures in ways that entirely lose the original design
- impotence—occurs when the examinee draws a figure inaccurately but seems to recognize the error, then makes several unsuccessful attempts to improve the drawing
- irregular line quality or lack of motor coordination—drawing rough lines, particularly when the examinee shows a tremor motion
- line extension—adding or extending a part of the copied figure that was not on the original figure
- omission—failing to connect the parts of a figure adequately or reproducing only parts of a figure
- overlapping difficulty—problems in drawing portions of figures that overlap, simplifying the drawing at the point that it overlaps, sketching or redrawing the overlapping portions, or otherwise distorting the figure at the point where it overlaps
- perseveration—increasing, prolonging, or continuing the number of units in a figure; for example, drawing significantly more dots or circles than shown on the original figure
- retrogression—substituting more primitive figures for the original design; for example, substituting solid lines or loops for circles, dashes for dots, dots for circles, or circles for dots, or filling in circles
- rotation—rotating a figure or part of a figure by 45° or more; also includes when the examinee rotates the stimulus card that is being copied.
- scribbling—drawing primitive lines that have no relationship to the original Bender Gestalt figure
- simplification—replacing a part of the figure with a more simplified figure, not due to maturation (Drawings that are primitive in terms of maturation would be categorized under "retrogression.")

QUESTIONS TO ASK YOUR DOCTOR

- Is the Bender Gestalt Test an appropriate assessment test for me? My children?
- Should other psychological tests be used in combination with the Bender Gestalt Test?
- What is the next step after taking the test?
- Is the test reliable?
- Does the Bender Gestalt Test help to evaluate mental decline in older adults?

- superimposition of design—drawing one or more of the figures on top of each other
- workover—reinforcing, increasing pressure, or overworking a line or lines in a whole or partial figure

Additionally, observing the examinee's behavior while drawing the figures can provide the examiner with an informal evaluation and data that can supplement the formal evaluation of the examinee's visual and perceptual functioning. For example, if an examinee takes a large amount of time to complete the geometric figures, it may suggest a slow, methodical approach to tasks, compulsive tendencies, or depressive symptoms. If an examinee rapidly completes the test, this could indicate an impulsive style.

Resources

BOOKS

Brannigan, Gary G., and Scott L. Decker. *Bender Visual-Motor Gestalt Test.* Itasca, IL: Riverside Publishing, 2003.

Hutt, M. L. *The Hutt Adaptation of the Bender Gestalt Test.* New York: Grune and Stratton, 1985.

Kaufman, Alan, S., and Elizabeth O. Lichtenberger. *Assessing Adolescent and Adult Intelligence.* Hoboken, NJ: John Wiley, 2006.

Koppitz, E. M. *The Bender Gestalt Test for Young Children.* Vol. 2. New York: Grune and Stratton, 1975.

Pascal, G. R., and B. J. Suttell. *The Bender Gestalt Test: Quantification and Validation for Adults.* New York: Grune and Stratton, 1951.

Sattler, Jerome M. "Assessment of Visual-Motor Perception and Motor Proficiency." In *Assessment of Children: Behavioral and Clinical Applications.* 4th ed. San Diego: Jerome M. Sattler, Publisher, Inc., 2002.

Watkins, E. O. *The Watkins Bender Gestalt Scoring System.* Novato, CA: Academic Therapy, 1976.

WEBSITES

"Bender Visual-Motor Gestalt Test, Second Edition (Bender-Gestalt II." Pearson. http://www.pearsonassessments.com/HAIWEB/Cultures/en-us/Productdetail.htm?Pid=015-8064-127&Mode=summary (May 19, 2011).

"Bender Visual-Motor Gestalt Test, Second Edition (Bender Gestalt II)." Western Psychological Services. http://portal.wpspublish.com/portal/page?_pageid=53,126639&_dad=portal&_schema=PORTAL (May 19, 2011).

"KOPPITZ-2: Koppitz Developmental Scoring System for the Bender Gestalt Test—Second Ed." Pro-Ed Inc. http://www.proedinc.com/customer/productView.aspx?ID=3724 (May 20, 2011).

"Koppitz Developmental Scoring System for the Bender Gestalt Test, Second Edition (KOPPITZ-2)." Riverside Publishing. http://www.riversidepublishing.com/koppitz2 (May 20, 2011).

ORGANIZATIONS

American Geriatrics Society, 40 Fulton St., 18th Fl., New York, NY, 10038, (212) 308-1414, Fax: (212) 832-8646, info@americangeriatrics.org, http://www.americangeriatrics.org.

American Psychiatric Association, 1000 Wilson Boulevard, Suite 1825, Arlington, VA, 22209, (888) 357-7924, apa@psych.org, http://www.psych.org.

National Institute on Aging, Building 31, Room 5C27, 31 Center Drive, MSC 2292, Bethesda, MD, 20892, (301) 496-1752, (800) 222-4225 (TTY), Fax: (301) 496-1072, http://www.nia.nih.gov.

National Institute of Mental Health, 6001 Executive Boulevard, Room 8184, MSC 9663, Bethesda, MD, 20892-9663, (301) 443-4513, (866) 615-6464, Fax: (301) 443-4279, nimhinfo@nih.gov, http://www.nimh.nih.gov.

National Institute of Neurological Disorders and Stroke, PO Box 5801, Bethesda, MD, 20824, (301) 496-5751. TTY: (301) 468-5981, (800) 352-9424, http://www.ninds.nih.gov.

Keith Beard, Psy.D.
William Atkins

Benzodiazepines

Definition

Benzodiazepines are medicines that help relieve nervousness, tension, and other symptoms by slowing the central nervous system.

Purpose

Benzodiazepines are a class of **antianxiety drugs**. While anxiety is a normal response to stressful situations, some people have unusually high levels of anxiety that can interfere with everyday life. Benzodiazepines help bring anxious feelings under control and also relieve other troubling symptoms of anxiety, such as pounding heartbeat, breathing problems, irritability, nausea, and faintness.

Physicians may sometimes prescribe benzodiazepines for other conditions, such as muscle spasms, epilepsy and other seizure disorders, phobias, **panic disorder**, withdrawal from alcohol, and sleeping problems. However, this medicine should not be used every day for sleep problems that last more than a few days. If used this way, the drug loses its effectiveness within a few weeks.

Description

The family of antianxiety drugs known as benzodiazepines includes **alprazolam** (Xanax), **chlordiazepoxide** (Librium), **diazepam** (Valium), and **lorazepam** (Ativan). These medicines take effect fairly quickly, starting to work within an hour after they are taken. Benzodiazepines are available only with a physician's prescription and are available in tablet, capsule, liquid, or injectable forms.

Recommended dosage

The recommended dosage depends on the type of benzodiazepine, its strength, and the condition for which it is being taken. Doses may be different for different people. Check with the physician who prescribed the drug or the pharmacist who filled the prescription for the correct dosage.

Always take benzodiazepines exactly as directed. Never take larger or more frequent doses, and do not take the drug for longer than directed. If the medicine does not seem to be working, check with the physician who prescribed it. Do not increase the dose or stop taking the medicine unless the physician says to do so. Stopping the drug suddenly may cause withdrawal symptoms, especially if it has been taken in large doses or over a long period. People who are taking the medicine for seizure disorders may have **seizures** if they stop taking it suddenly. If it is necessary to stop taking the medicine, check with a physician for directions on how to stop. The physician may recommend tapering down gradually to reduce the chance of withdrawal symptoms or other problems.

KEY TERMS

Anxiety—Worry or tension in response to real or imagined stress, danger, or dreaded situations. Physical reactions, such as fast pulse, sweating, trembling, fatigue, and weakness may accompany anxiety.

Central nervous system—The brain and spinal cord.

Dependence—A state in which a person requires a steady concentration of a particular substance to avoid experiencing withdrawal symptoms.

Epilepsy—A brain disorder with symptoms that include seizures.

Glaucoma—A condition in which pressure in the eye is abnormally high. If not treated, glaucoma may lead to blindness.

Myasthenia gravis—A chronic disease with symptoms that include muscle weakness and sometimes paralysis.

Panic disorder—A disorder in which people have sudden and intense attacks of anxiety in certain situations. Symptoms such as shortness of breath, sweating, dizziness, chest pain, and extreme fear often accompany the attacks.

Phobia—An intense, abnormal, or illogical fear of something specific, such as heights or open spaces.

Seizure—A sudden attack, spasm, or convulsion.

Sleep apnea—A condition in which a person temporarily stops breathing during sleep.

Tolerance—The requirement for higher doses of a substance or more frequent engagement in an activity to achieve the same effect.

Withdrawal symptoms—A group of physical or mental symptoms that may occur when a person suddenly stops using a drug to which he or she has become dependent.

Precautions

Seeing a physician regularly while taking benzodiazepines is important, especially during the first few months of treatment. The physician will check to make sure the medicine is working as it should and will note any unwanted side effects. People who take benzodiazepines to relieve nervousness, tension, or symptoms of panic disorder should check with their physicians every two to three months to make sure they still need to keep taking the medicine. Benzodiazepines do have some addictive potential, and long-term use of benzodiazepines may result in dependence and tolerance, so it is important that therapy is monitored.

Patients who are taking benzodiazepines for sleep problems should check with their physicians if their symptoms do not improve after seven to ten days. Sleep problems that last longer than this may be a sign of another medical problem. If the medication works successfully and is stopped, patients may have trouble sleeping for the first few nights, but this effect should only be temporary.

Some people feel drowsy, dizzy, light-headed, or less alert when using benzodiazepines. The drugs may also cause clumsiness or unsteadiness. When the medicine is taken at bedtime, these effects may even occur the next morning, producing a "hangover" effect. Persons should not drive, use machines, or participate in any other hazardous activity after taking benzodiazepines until they know how the drugs affect them. In general, older people and children are more sensitive to the effects of benzodiazepines, which may increase the chance of side effects.

Benzodiazepines may cause behavior changes in some people, similar to those seen in people who act differently when they drink alcohol. More extreme changes, such as confusion, agitation, and hallucinations, also are possible. If a person starts having strange or unusual thoughts or exhibiting strange behavior while taking this medicine, he or she should contact the prescribing physician.

Some benzodiazepines increase the likelihood of birth defects. Using these medicines during pregnancy may also cause the baby to become dependent on them, resulting in withdrawal symptoms after birth. When taken late in pregnancy or around the time of labor and delivery, these drugs can cause other problems in the newborn baby, such as weakness, breathing problems, slow heartbeat, and body temperature problems. Women who are breast-feeding their babies should also not use this medicine without checking with their physicians, as benzodiazepines may pass into breast milk.

Because benzodiazepines work on the central nervous system, they may add to the effects of alcohol and other drugs that slow down the central nervous system (CNS depressants). Such drugs include antihistamines, cold medicine, allergy medicine, sleep aids, medicine for seizures, tranquilizers, some pain relievers, and muscle relaxants. They may also add to the effects of anesthetics, including those used for dental procedures. These effects may last several days after the treatment with benzodiazepines ends. The combined effects of benzodiazepines and alcohol or other CNS depressants can be very dangerous, leading to unconsciousness or even death. Anyone taking benzodiazepines should not drink alcohol and should check with his or her physician before using any CNS depressants. Anyone who shows signs of an overdose or of the effects of combining benzodiazepines with alcohol or other drugs should get immediate emergency help. Warning signs include slurred speech or confusion, severe drowsiness, staggering, and profound weakness.

People with certain medical conditions or who are taking certain other medicines can have problems if they take benzodiazepines. Patients should let their doctors know if they have any of these conditions:

- current or past drug or alcohol abuse
- depression
- severe mental illness
- epilepsy or other seizure disorders
- swallowing problems
- chronic lung disease such as emphysema, asthma, or chronic bronchitis
- kidney disease
- liver disease
- brain disease
- glaucoma
- hyperactivity
- myasthenia gravis
- porphyria
- sleep apnea
- allergies

Side effects

The most common side effects are dizziness, lightheadedness, drowsiness, clumsiness, unsteadiness, and slurred speech. These problems usually go away as the body adjusts to the drug and do not require medical treatment unless they persist or they interfere with normal activities.

More serious side effects are not common but may occur. If any of the following side effects occur, patients should check with the physician who prescribed the medicine as soon as possible:

- behavior changes
- memory problems
- difficulty concentrating
- confusion
- depression
- seizures (convulsions)
- hallucinations
- sleep problems
- increased nervousness, excitability, or irritability
- involuntary movements of the body, including the eyes
- low blood pressure
- unusual weakness or tiredness
- skin rash or itching
- unusual bleeding or bruising
- yellow skin or eyes
- sore throat
- sores in the mouth or throat

• fever and chills

Patients who take benzodiazepines for a long time or at high doses may notice side effects for several weeks after they stop taking the drug. They should check with their physicians if these or other troublesome symptoms occur:

• irritability
• nervousness
• sleep problems

Other rare side effects may occur. Patients who experience unusual symptoms during or after treatment with benzodiazepines should contact their physician.

Interactions

Benzodiazepines may interact with a variety of other medicines. When this happens, the effects of one or both of the drugs may change or the risk of side effects may be greater. Persons taking benzodiazepines should let their physician know all other medicines they are currently taking. Among the drugs that may interact with benzodiazepines are:

• CNS depressants, such as medicine for allergies, colds, hay fever, and asthma
• sedatives
• tranquilizers
• prescription pain medicines
• muscle relaxants
• seizure medications
• sleep aids
• barbiturates
• anesthetics

Other medications may interact with benzodiazepines. Patients should check with their physician or pharmacist before combining benzodiazepines with any other prescription or nonprescription (over-the-counter) medicines.

Resources

BOOKS

American Psychiatric Association. *Diagnostic and Statistical Manual of Mental Disorders*. 4th ed., text rev. Washington, DC: American Psychiatric Publishing, 2000.

Brunton, Laurence, Bruce Chabner, and Bjorn Knollman. *Goodman & Gilman's The Pharmacological Basis of Therapeutics* 12th ed. New York: McGraw-Hill, 2010.

Doble, Adam, Ian Martin, and David J. Nutt. *Calming the Brain: Benzodiazepines and Related Drugs from Laboratory to Clinic*. London: Informa Healthcare, 2003.

PERIODICALS

Lader, Malcolm. "Benzodiazepines Revisited—Will We Ever Learn?" *Addiction* 106, no. 12 (2011): 2086–109. http://dx.doi.org/10.1111/j.1360-0443.2011.03563.x (accessed December 15, 2011).

Mugunthan, K., T. McGuire, and P. Glasziou. "Minimal Interventions to Decrease Long-Term use of Benzodiazepines in Primary Care: A Systematic Review and Meta-Analysis." *British Journal of General Practice* 61, no. 590 (2011): 573–80.

ORGANIZATIONS

U.S. Food and Drug Administration, 10903 New Hampshire Ave., Silver Spring, MD, 20993-0002, (888) INFO-FDA (463-6332), http://www.fda.gov.

Nancy Ross-Flanigan

Benztropine

Definition

Benztropine is classified as an antiparkinsonian agent. It is sold in the United States under the brand name Cogentin and is also available under its generic name.

Purpose

Benztropine is used to treat a group of side effects (called parkinsonian side effects) that includes tremors, difficulty walking, and slack muscle tone. These side effects may occur in patients who are taking antipsychotic medications used to treat mental disorders such as **schizophrenia**.

Description

Some medicines used to treat schizophrenia and other mental disorders, called antipsychotic drugs, can cause side effects that are similar to the symptoms of Parkinson's disease. Patients do not have Parkinson's disease but experience similar symptoms, such as shaking in muscles while at rest, difficulty with voluntary movements, and poor muscle tone.

One way to eliminate these undesirable side effects is to stop taking the antipsychotic medicine. Unfortunately, the symptoms of the original mental disorder usually come back, so simply stopping the antipsychotic medication is not a reasonable option in most cases. Some drugs that control the symptoms of Parkinson's disease, such as benztropine, also control the parkinsonian side effects of antipsychotic medicines.

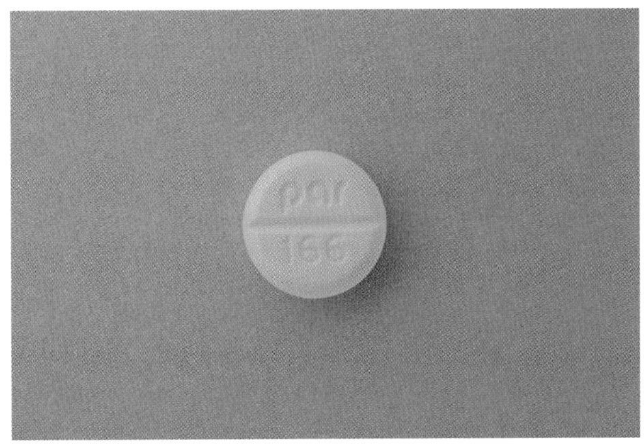

Cogentin (benztropine), 2 mg. *(© Custom Medical Stock Photo, Inc. Reproduced by permission.)*

Benztropine works by restoring the chemical balance between **dopamine** and acetylcholine, two neurotransmitter chemicals in the **brain**. Taking benztropine along with the antipsychotic medicine helps to control symptoms of the mental disorder, while reducing parkinsonian side effects. Benztropine is in the same family of drugs (commonly known as anticholinergic drugs) as **biperiden** and **trihexyphenidyl**.

Recommended dosage

Benztropine is available in 0.5, 1.0, and 2.0 mg tablets and in an injectable form containing 2 mg in each 2 mL glass container. For the treatment of tremors, poor muscle tone, and similar side effects, benztropine should be started at a dose of 1 to 2 mg orally. In cases of severe side effects, benztropine can be given as an intramuscular injection two to three times daily or as needed. Parkinson-like side effects caused by antipsychotic drugs may come and go, so benztropine may not be needed on a regular basis. Benztropine may also be prescribed to prevent these side effects before they actually occur. This is called a prophylactic (preventative) therapy.

Precautions

Benztropine should never be used in children under age three. It should be used cautiously and with close physician supervision in older children and in the elderly. Like all anticholinergic drugs, benztropine decreases the body's ability to sweat and cool itself. People who are unaccustomed to being outside in hot weather should take care to stay as cool as possible and drink extra fluids. People who are chronically ill, have a central nervous system disease, or who work outside during hot weather may need to avoid taking benztropine.

People who have the following medical problems may experience increased negative side effects when taking benztropine. Those who have these problems should discuss their conditions with their physician before starting the drug:

- glaucoma, especially closed-angle glaucoma
- intestinal obstruction
- prostate enlargement
- urinary bladder obstruction

Although rare, some patients experience euphoria while taking benztropine and may abuse it for this reason. Euphoria can occur at doses only two to four times the normal daily dose. Patients with a history of drug abuse should be observed carefully for benztropine abuse.

Side effects

Although benztropine helps to control the side effects of antipsychotic drugs, it can produce side effects of its own. A person taking benztropine may have some of the following reactions, which may vary in intensity:

- dry mouth
- dry skin
- blurred vision
- nausea or vomiting
- constipation
- disorientation
- drowsiness
- irritability
- increased heart rate
- urinary retention

Dry mouth, if severe to the point of causing difficulty speaking or swallowing, may be managed by reducing or temporarily discontinuing benztropine. Chewing sugarless gum or sucking on sugarless candy may also help to increase the flow of saliva. Some artificial saliva products may give temporary relief.

Men with prostate enlargement may be especially prone to urinary retention. Symptoms of this problem include having difficulty starting a urine flow and more difficulty passing urine than usual. This side effect may be severe and require discontinuation of the drug. Urinary retention may require catheterization. People who think they may be experiencing any side effects from this or any other medication should tell their physicians.

Patients who take an overdose of benztropine are treated with forced vomiting, removal of stomach contents and stomach washing, activated charcoal, and respiratory support if needed. They are also given physostigmine, an antidote for anticholinergic drug poisoning.

KEY TERMS

Acetylcholine—A naturally occurring chemical in the body that transmits nerve impulses from cell to cell. It causes blood vessels to dilate, lowers blood pressure, and slows the heartbeat. Central nervous system well-being is dependent on a balance among the neurotransmitters acetylcholine, dopamine, serotonin, and norepinephrine.

Anticholinergic—Related to the ability of a drug to block the nervous system chemical acetylcholine. When acetylcholine is blocked, patients often experience dry mouth and skin, increased heart rate, blurred vision, and difficulty urinating. In severe cases, blocking acetylcholine may cloud thinking and cause delirium.

Catheterization—Placing a tube in the bladder so that it can be emptied of urine.

Dopamine—A chemical in brain tissue that serves to transmit nerve impulses (is a neurotransmitter) and helps to regulate movement and emotions.

Neurotransmitter—A chemical in the brain that transmits messages between neurons, or nerve cells.

Parkinsonian—Related to symptoms associated with Parkinson's disease, a nervous system disorder characterized by abnormal muscle movement of the tongue, face, and neck; inability to walk or move quickly; walking in a shuffling manner; restlessness; and/or tremors.

Interactions

When drugs such as benztropine are taken with **antidepressants** such as **amitriptyline**, **imipramine**, **trimipramine**, **desipramine**, **nortriptyline**, **protriptyline**, **amoxapine**, and **doxepin**, or with many antihistamines that also have anticholinergic properties, the effects and side effects of benztropine are usually intensified.

Drugs such as benztropine decrease the speed with which food moves through the stomach and intestines. Because of this, the absorption of other drugs being taken may be enhanced by benztropine. Patients receiving benztropine should be alerted to unusual responses to other drugs they might be taking and report any changes to their physicians.

Resources

BOOKS

American Society of Health-System Pharmacists. *AHFS Drug Information 2008*. Bethesda, MD: American Society of Health-System Pharmacists, 2008.

Preston, John D., John H. O'Neal, and Mary C. Talaga. *Handbook of Clinical Psychopharmacology for Therapists*. 5th ed. Oakland, CA: New Harbinger Publications, 2008.

PERIODICALS

de Leon, Jose. "Letter to the Editor: Benztropine Equivalents for Antimuscarinic Medication." *American Journal of Psychiatry*. 162, no. 3 (March 2005): 627.

WEBSITES

MedlinePlus. "Benztropine Mesylate Oral." U.S. National Library of Medicine, National Institutes of Health. http://www.nlm.nih.gov/medlineplus/druginfo/meds/a682155.html (accessed December 15, 2011).

Jack Raber, Pharm.D.
Ruth A. Wienclaw, PhD

Bereavement

Definition

Bereavement is the emotional state caused by any major loss, such as the death of a loved one.

Demographics

Almost everyone experiences bereavement at some point in their lives. Many people undergo multiple bereavements. Although it is a normal part of life, some people suffer major complications of bereavement. Between 17% and 27% of people experience depressive illness during their first year of bereavement. One study found that 10% of bereaved people met the criteria for complicated **grief** disorder. Another study found that 9% of bereaved people met the criteria for **major depressive disorder** four months after their loss and 5.7% met the criteria for **post-traumatic stress disorder** (PTSD).

Description

The English word *bereavement* comes from an ancient Germanic root meaning "to rob" or "to seize by violence." *Mourning* refers to the public rituals or symbols of bereavement, including funeral services and the wearing of black. *Grief* refers to the personal experience of loss, including physical and emotional symptoms. Whereas public expressions of mourning are usually short-lived, grief caused by bereavement is a process that can last months or even years.

Bereavement is a complex experience and no two people respond in exactly the same way. Reactions to death are influenced by many factors, including ethnic and religious traditions, relationships with the deceased, personal beliefs about an afterlife, the cause of death and whether it was sudden or expected, and the deceased's age. Furthermore, the death of a loved one inevitably confronts adults and older adolescents with their own mortality. Because of this emotional complexity and variety of responses, most physicians and counselors advise bereaved people to trust their own feelings and grieve in ways that seem most helpful to them.

Grief counselors recognize that bereavement has two dimensions—the actual loss and symbolic losses. For example, parents who lose a child suffer a series of symbolic losses in addition to the child's death, such as the knowledge that their child will never graduate from high school, marry, or have children.

There are several generally recognized stages or phases of uncomplicated bereavement and grief, although for most people, bereavement feels like an emotional roller coaster rather than a sequence of stages. People may experience none, some, or all of the phases in any order, or they may vacillate between them.

- Avoidance, shocked disbelief, or denial usually lasts for about two weeks after the initial bereavement. Symptoms may include emotional numbness, deep sighing, breathlessness, choking, and loss of appetite and strength.
- As awareness of the loss develops, the bereaved may enter a confrontational phase, which typically lasts several months and includes pain and suffering, deep sadness, weeping, guilt, panic, confusion, anger, despair, blaming others, a sense of helplessness, and physical symptoms of stress.
- The bargaining phase is an attempt to somehow reverse the loss.
- Depression often sets in at about six months after the initial bereavement. Survivors may lose interest in life and become socially isolated.
- In the resolution, accommodation, or acceptance phase, which usually occurs within one to two years, people adjust to their loss and to life without the loved one, learn to cope with new roles and responsibilities, and possibly even redefine their identity.

Not all feelings and experiences associated with bereavement are negative. If the deceased was suffering from illness, some bereaved people may feel relief that the deceased's suffering has ended. Some people find that bereavement, though difficult, is a time of personal growth. They may develop a new appreciation of life and increased self-esteem as they master new tasks and adjust to the experience of carrying on independently.

Although bereavement is a normal part of life and not a psychiatric disorder, it is one of life's most stressful experiences. Bereavement is associated with a high risk for psychological distress, social isolation, physical illness, and death. The fourth edition of the ***Diagnostic and Statistical Manual of Mental Disorders*** (*DSM-IV*) classifies bereavement as a condition that may require clinical attention, since it can lead to major depressive disorder or PTSD. Since the early 1990s, thanatologists—specialists in issues related to death and dying—have identified two types of bereavement grief that do not resolve normally with the passage of time: complicated and traumatic grief. Complicated grief disorder is also referred to as atypical or abnormal grief, pathologic grief, or pathologic mourning. Outside sources have proposed that complicated grief disorder be included in the *DSM-5*, and the **American Psychiatric Association** has adapted the suggestion under the name bereavement related disorder in the proposed additions to the appendix for further study. Traumatic grief is a type of complicated grief that occurs following a loved one's death from an accident, **suicide**, homicide, disaster, or war.

Risk factors

Reactions to bereavement are influenced by many factors, including the personality of the bereaved, their relationship to the deceased, the manner of death, and cultural background. There are considerable differences among cultural groups in the ways that bereavement is expressed and in the duration of normal bereavement.

Risk factors for complicated or traumatic grief include:

- being unprepared for an untimely loss
- physical or mental suffering of the victim
- excessive dependence on the deceased
- difficulties with personal attachments or lack of emotional support
- media intrusiveness or frustration with the justice system in cases of traumatic bereavement
- lack of closure when a person is missing and/or presumed dead
- guilt, shame, and/or anger after a suicide
- disenfranchised grief over a loss that cannot be openly acknowledged, such as a secret relationship
- guilt or shame over grief for an animal

Causes and symptoms

Although the loss of a spouse or beloved friend or relative is the most common cause of bereavement, other losses—such as permanent injury, divorce, or the death of a pet—can also cause bereavement. Bereavements such as miscarriage or abortion or a loved one's **diagnosis** of **Alzheimer's disease** are referred to as "silent losses."

Mental symptoms of bereavement may include:

- sadness, anxiety, irritability, apathy, anger, fear, and mood swings
- feelings of helplessness and low self-esteem
- flashbacks and hallucinations of the deceased
- confusion and preoccupation with the deceased, resulting in poor judgment or lack of insight
- suicidal thoughts, which occur in as many as 54% of survivors up to six months after their loss
- homicidal thoughts

Physical symptoms of bereavement may include:

- poor personal hygiene and grooming
- changes in appetite and weight
- dehydration
- low energy
- fatigue
- loss of interest in sex
- sleep disturbances
- chest or throat pain
- palpitations
- headache
- hair loss
- nausea and vomiting
- gastrointestinal distress
- aches and pains
- lowered immunity

Bereavement in children

Children experience bereavement differently than adolescents and adults. Preschool children do not usually understand the finality and irreversibility of death. They may talk or act as if the deceased family member or pet will wake up or return. Children between the ages of five and nine are better able to understand the finality of death, but they tend to assume it will not affect them and are shocked by a death in their immediate family. In addition to physical symptoms of bereavement, children may regress to an earlier stage—for example, acting like an infant, with baby talk or wanting to drink from a baby bottle.

Complicated or traumatic grief

Complicated grief is an abnormally intense and prolonged response to bereavement. Whereas most people move through a period of bereavement, those with complicated grief remain in chronic mourning and are unable to function normally, accept their loss, or make the necessary adjustments for living effectively without their loved one. They cannot stop longing for the deceased and may feel that a part of them died along with the loved one. They experience persistent distressing thoughts about the deceased and may feel bitter and agitated. Although these reactions are normal during the initial months of bereavement, persistence of such symptoms beyond six months may be indicative of a pathological condition. People with complicated grief may start to behave like the deceased, mimic symptoms of their illness, act recklessly, or talk about joining their loved one in death. Although complicated grief can coexist with clinical **depression**, it is a distinct disorder.

Traumatic grief results from a sudden event involving violence, suffering, mutilation, or multiple deaths that appears to be random or preventable. Symptoms of traumatic grief are similar to those of PTSD and can include muscle tension, an exaggerated startle response, hallucinations, flashbacks, avoidance of certain situations, marked irritability, and interference with sleep and concentration.

Bereavement related disorder

Bereavement related disorder is another name for complicated grief disorder, but the *DSM-5* diagnostic criteria require that symptoms extend beyond 12 months after the death. Persons experiencing bereavement related disorder struggle with social interaction and have yet to establish or maintain a self-identity without the deceased present. They may find it difficult to make any type of plans, avoid places or people that remind them of the deceased, and continue to experience extreme and persistent longing. Traumatic grief is classified as traumatic bereavement.

Diagnosis

Abnormal bereavement can be identified through examination and tests.

Examination

Bereavement is a normal response to a death or other loss. Although in the initial months people often have symptoms that are characteristic of clinical depression or major depressive disorder, medical diagnosis is usually not necessary unless the symptoms last for more than two

KEY TERMS

Bibliotherapy—The use of books (usually self-help or problem-solving) to improve one's understanding of personal problems and/or to heal painful feelings.

Biofield healing—A general term for alternative therapies that are based on the belief that the human body is surrounded by an energy field (aura) that reflects the condition of the body and spirit. Rebalancing or repairing the energy field is thought to bring about healing in mind and body. Reiki, therapeutic touch, polarity balancing, SHEN therapy, and certain forms of color therapy are considered types of biofield healing.

Complicated grief—An abnormal response to bereavement that includes unrelieved yearning for the deceased, the total loss of positive beliefs or worldview, and general dysfunction.

Disenfranchised grief—Grief that is not openly expressed because the bereavement cannot be publicly acknowledged.

Mourning—The public expression of bereavement, including funerals and other rituals, special clothing, and symbolic gestures.

Post-traumatic stress disorder (PTSD)—A psychological reaction that continues long after a highly stressful event and is characterized by depression, anxiety, flashbacks, and nightmares.

Thanatologist—A specialist in the study of death and psychological mechanisms for coping with death.

Traumatic grief—Grief resulting from bereavement under traumatic circumstances, such as natural or transportation disasters, acts of terrorism, and murder.

months and the person experiences persistent feelings of guilt, thoughts of death, or feelings of unworthiness, or is unable to perform normal activities.

Tests

Various psychological inventories and questionnaires can be used to diagnose PTSD, major depression, or **acute stress disorder**. There are also specific questionnaires for diagnosing complicated grief.

Treatment

Abnormal bereavement can be treated with psychological therapy and with prescribed medications.

Traditional

Normal bereavement does not usually require formal treatment. However, many people choose to participate in bereavement or grief **support groups**. These are particularly helpful for guiding people through common but painful problems, such as disposing of the deceased's possessions, celebrating holidays, and coping with anniversaries. Individual and group **psychotherapy**, as well as support groups, are used to treat patients with complicated or traumatic grief or PTSD.

Drugs

Recent research suggests that antidepressant medication can help with bereavement. Complicated or traumatic grief and PTSD are also treated with antianxiety and sleep-inducing medications.

Alternative

Various alternative therapies are used to treat sleep disturbances and other symptoms of bereavement:

- meditation
- movement therapies, such as yoga and tai chi
- therapeutic touch, Reiki, and other forms of biofield healing
- bibliotherapy and journaling
- music and art therapy
- hydrotherapy
- massage therapy

Home remedies

The single most important factor in healing from bereavement is the support of others. Bereaved people are advised to face and express their feelings. Focusing on positive aspects of life and trying to find meaning in the loss are helpful coping strategies. Bereaved people often continue some form of relationship with the deceased, such as attachment to physical reminders, prayer, sensing the presence of the deceased in one's life, or commemorative festivals and rituals, such as the Day of the Dead celebration in Mexico.

Bereaved children should be reassured of their safety and the safety of their loved ones. They should be encouraged to express their feelings. Adults should ensure that bereaved children do not have any

QUESTIONS TO ASK YOUR DOCTOR

- Are my feelings and physical symptoms a normal response to bereavement?
- How long should I expect these symptoms to continue?
- Are there medications that might help me?
- Is there a bereavement support group that you can recommend?

misconceptions concerning their loss, but children should not be overloaded with facts or exposed to disturbing television images. Their daily routines should remain as normal as possible.

Prognosis

Most people progress through the stages of grieving within a few months to two years, without clinical **intervention**. Painful emotions diminish in intensity over time, eventually becoming episodic. Feelings of bereavement may reemerge with anniversaries and holidays or poignant memories. Nevertheless, bereavement can induce permanent personal changes, both positive and negative. Complicated or traumatic grief may take three or more years to resolve, even with appropriate treatment.

Prevention

Bereavement is a normal response to loss, and loss is a universal human experience. Normal grieving following bereavement should be allowed to run its course. Most bereavement counselors maintain that attempting to stifle or shorten the grief process is more likely to cause emotional difficulties in the long run. However, it is important to maintain one's physical health during bereavement.

Resources

BOOKS

American Psychiatric Association. *Diagnostic and Statistical Manual of Mental Disorders,* 4th ed., text rev. Washington, DC: American Psychiatric Association, 2000.

Bonanno, George A. *The Other Side of Sadness: What the New Science of Bereavement Tells Us About Life After Loss.* New York: Basic Books, 2009.

Hood, Ann. *Comfort: A Journey Through Grief.* New York: Norton, 2008.

Okun, Barbara, and Joseph Nowkinski. *Saying Goodbye: How Families Can Find Renewal Through Loss.* New York: Berkley, 2011.

Schechter, Harold. *The Whole Death Catalog: A Lively Guide to the Bitter End.* New York: Ballantine, 2009.

Stroebe, Margaret S., ed. *Handbook of Bereavement Research and Practice: Advances in Theory and Intervention.* Washington, DC: American Psychological Association, 2008.

PERIODICALS

Brent, David, et al. "The Incidence and Course of Depression in Bereaved Youth 21 Months After the Loss of a Parent to Suicide, Accident, or Sudden Natural Death." *American Journal of Psychiatry* 166, no. 7 (July 2009): 786–94.

Mahon, Margaret M. "Taking It to the Street... and the Hospital, the School, and the Workplace: Bereavement Research in the 21st Century." *Gerontologist* 29, no. 2 (April 2009): 285–91.

Shear, M. K., et al. "Complicated Grief and Related Bereavement Issues for DSM-5." *Depression and Anxiety* 28 (February 2011): 103–117.

Van der Houwen, Karolijne, et al. "Risk Factors for Bereavement Outcome: A Multivariate Approach." *Death Studies* 34, no. 3 (March 2010): 195–220.

OTHER

Harper, Linda R. "Healing After the Loss of Your Pet." Best Friends Animal Society. http://www.bestfriends.org/theanimals/pdfs/allpets/PetLossHarper.pdf (accessed September 8, 2011).

WEBSITES

American Academy of Child and Adolescent Psychiatry. "Children and Grief." *Facts for Families.* Last updated March 2011. http://www.aacap.org/cs/root/facts_for_families/children_and_grief (accessed September 8, 2011).

American Academy of Child and Adolescent Psychiatry. "When a Pet Dies." *Facts for Families.* Last updated March 2011. http://www.aacap.org/cs/root/facts_for_families/when_a_pet_dies (accessed September 8, 2011).

Burnett, Lynn Barkley. "Grief and Bereavement." eMedicine Health.com. http://www.emedicinehealth.com/grief_and_bereavement/article_em.htm (accessed September 8, 2011).

Lubit, Roy, H. "Acute Treatment of Disaster Survivors." Medscape Reference. Last updated April 25, 2011. http://emedicine.medscape.com/article/295003-overview (accessed September 8, 2011).

National Organization for Victim Assistance. "Survivors of Homicide Victims." National Organization of Parents of Murdered Children. http://www.pomc.com/survivor.cfm (accessed September 8, 2011).

Smith, Melinda, Ellen Jaffe-Gill, and Jeanne Segal. "Coping with Grief and Loss: Support for Grieving and Bereavement." Helpguide.org. Last updated March 2011. http://

www.helpguide.org/mental/grief_loss.htm (accessed September 8, 2011).

ORGANIZATIONS

American Academy of Child and Adolescent Psychiatry, 3615 Wisconsin Ave., NW, Washington, DC, 20016-3007, (202) 966-7300, Fax: (202) 966-2891, http://www.aacap.org.

American Hospice Foundation, 2120 L St., NW, Ste. 200, Washington, DC, 20037, (202) 223-0204, (800) 347-1413, Fax: (202) 223-0208, http://www.americanhospice.org.

American Psychiatric Association, 1000 Wilson Blvd., Ste. 1825, Arlington, VA, 22209-3901, (703) 907-7300, apa@psych.org, http://www.psych.org.

Compassionate Friends, PO Box 3696, Oak Brook, IL, 60522, (630) 990-0010, (877) 969-0010, Fax: (630) 990-0246, http://www.compassionatefriends.org.

Dougy Center, PO Box 86852, Portland, OR, 97286, (503) 775-5683, (866) 775-5683, help@dougy.org, http://www.grievingchild.org.

Mental Health America, 2000 N. Beauregard St., 6th Fl., Alexandria, VA, 22311, (703) 684-7722, (800) 969-6642, Fax: (703) 684-5968, info@mentalhealthamerica.net, http://www.mentalhealthamerica.net.

National Institute of Mental Health, 6001 Executive Blvd., Rm. 8184, MSC 9663, Bethesda, MD, 20892-9663, (301) 433-4513; TTY: (301) 443-8431, Fax: (301) 443-4279, (866) 615-6464; TTY: (866) 415-8051, nimhinfo@nih.gov, http://www.nimh.nih.gov.

Tragedy Assistance Program for Survivors, 1777 F St., NW, Ste. 600, Washington, DC, 20006, (202) 588-TAPS (8277), (800) 959-TAPS (8277), Fax: (202) 509-8282, info@taps.org, http://www.taps.org.

Rebecca Frey, PhD
Ruvanee Pietersz Vilhauer, PhD
Margaret Alic, PhD

Beta blockers

Definition

Beta blockers, also known as beta antagonists, are a class of drugs that were first developed for the treatment of certain heart conditions and hypertension. Beta blockers were later found to be useful in treating glaucoma, migraine headaches, and some psychiatric disorders such as performance anxiety, tremors secondary to lithium, and **medication-induced movement disorders** that are caused by some antipsychotic drugs. There are a number of beta blockers approved for use in the United States, including acebutolol, bisoprolol, nadolol, **propranolol**, and metoprolol, which have various trade names. Propranolol is the most commonly used in psychiatric practice.

Purpose

Beta blockers are proven effective in the treatment of performance anxiety, lithium-induced tremors, and neuroleptic-induced akathisia (a physical condition caused by certain antipsychotic drugs). Beta blockers have sometimes been used with **benzodiazepines** in treating alcohol withdrawal.

Description

Beta blockers act on that part of the central nervous system that controls mental alertness, lung function, heart rate, and blood vessels. Although there is more than one mechanism by which beta blockers work in anxiety states, the most beneficial result probably arises from the fact that beta blockers slow the heart to a normal rate and rhythm. Persons with performance anxiety, for example, would not experience the usual chest tightness and rapid heart rate that is associated with such acts as public speaking or acting.

Certain antipsychotic medications known as neuroleptics can cause an unwanted effect called akathisia, which is the inability to sit, stand still, or remain inactive. Patients are restless, and in severe cases may pace constantly and forcefully and repeatedly stomp their feet. Beta blockers can sometimes treat this condition with a lower incidence of side effects than other drugs.

Recommended dosage

Propranolol is available in several different forms. Tablets are available, as are an oral solution and an injectable form. Dosage varies considerably depending on the reason for taking the drug and the age of the person. A physician will determine the appropriate dosage, although some examples include:

- For one-time usage to treat performance anxiety, a single dose ranging from 10–40 mg taken a half hour before the performance (e.g., public speaking) is typical.
- For lithium-induced tremors that cannot be controlled by reducing caffeine intake or administering the dosage of lithium at bedtime, propranolol at a dose of 20–160 mg daily may be given in two or three evenly divided doses.
- For akathisia caused by antipsychotic medications, propranolol can be administered at doses of 10–30 mg three times daily.

Precautions

Because of their ability to narrow airways, beta blockers, especially propranolol, should not be taken by

KEY TERMS

Akathisia—Agitated or restless movement, usually affecting the legs. Movement is accompanied by a sense of discomfort and an inability to sit, stand still, or remain inactive for periods of time. Akathisia is a common side effect of some neuroleptic (antipsychotic) medications.

Benzodiazepines—A group of central nervous system depressants used to relieve anxiety or to induce sleep.

Tremor—Involuntary shaking of the hands and arms.

people with asthma and chronic obstructive pulmonary disease (COPD). If there is an urgent need to use beta blockers in persons with respiratory problems, atenolol or metoprolol are the beta blockers of choice, as they are less likely to have this side effect. However, even these drugs should be used with caution. Patients with congestive heart failure, or certain cardiac conduction abnormalities such as a heart block, should also use beta blockers with caution.

Beta blockers should be used with close physician monitoring in people with diabetes, since the symptoms of low blood sugar (increased heart rate, light-headedness, and abnormal perspiration) may be not be recognized by patients.

Side effects

Beta blockers can cause undesired decreases in blood pressure and are typically not given if blood pressure is 90/60 mm Hg or less. Beta blockers can also cause an undesired drop in heart rate. People whose resting heart rate is less than 55 beats per minute should not take beta blockers.

Occasionally, beta blockers can cause rash, weakness, nausea, vomiting, and stomach discomfort.

Interactions

Each medication in the class of beta blockers has the potential to interact with a multitude of other medications. Anyone starting beta-blocker therapy should review the other medications they are taking with their physician and pharmacist for possible interactions. Patients should always inform all of their healthcare providers, including dentists, that they are taking beta blockers.

Resources

PERIODICALS

Huh, J., D. Goebert, J. Takeshita, B. Y. Lu, and M. Kang. "Treatment of Generalized Anxiety Disorder: A Comprehensive Review of the Literature for Psychopharmacologic Alternatives to Newer Antidepressants and Benzodiazepines." *The Primary Care Companion to CNS Disorders* 13, no. 2 (2011).

WEBSITES

National Institute of Mental Health. "What Medications are Used to Treat Anxiety Disorders?" U.S. National Institutes of Health. http://www.nimh.nih.gov/health/publications/mental-health-medications/what-medications-are-used-to-treat-anxiety-disorders.shtml (accessed October 31, 2011).

Ajna Hamidovic, Pharm.D.
Emily Jane Willingham, PhD

Bibliotherapy

Definition

Bibliotherapy is a form of therapy in which structured readings are used as an adjunct to **psychotherapy**. Such readings can be used to reinforce learning or insights gained in the therapeutic session or to give individuals additional professional resources to help in personal growth and development.

Purpose

The goal of bibliotherapy is to broaden and deepen the patient's understanding of the particular problem that requires treatment. The written materials may educate the patient about the disorder itself or be used to increase the patient's acceptance of a proposed treatment. Many people find that the opportunity to read about their problem outside the therapist's office facilitates active participation in their treatment and promotes a stronger sense of personal responsibility for recovery. In addition, many are relieved to find that others have had the same disorder or problem and have coped successfully with or recovered from it. From the therapist's standpoint, providing patients with specific information or assignments to be completed outside regular in-office sessions speeds the progress of therapy.

The goals of bibliotherapy include the following:

- provide information or insight
- stimulate discussion about problems
- communicate new values or attitudes
- create awareness of the existence of the problem in the wider population
- provide potential solutions to problems

Bibliotherapy has been applied in a variety of settings to many kinds of people with psychological problems. Practitioners have reported successful use of bibliotherapy in treating people with eating disorders, anxiety and mood disorders, **agoraphobia**, alcohol and **substance abuse**, and stress-related physical disorders.

KEY TERMS

Adjunct—A form of treatment that is not strictly necessary but is helpful to a therapy regimen.

Cognitive-behavioral therapy—An approach to psychotherapy that emphasizes the correction of distorted thinking patterns and changing one's behaviors accordingly.

Dyslexia—A type of reading disorder.

Regimen—A regulated course of treatment for a medical or mental disorder.

Description

In most settings, bibliotherapy is used as an adjunct to more traditional forms of psychotherapy. Practitioners of cognitive-behavioral therapies are among the most enthusiastic supporters of bibliotherapy, particularly in the development of individualized treatment protocols, including workbooks, for specific disorders. For example, patients with eating disorders, especially **bulimia nervosa**, often benefit from receiving educational information appropriate to their stage of recovery, such as books or articles about cultural biases regarding weight, attractiveness, and dieting. This information helps patients better understand the rationale for their treatment and to work on new skills or behavioral changes more effectively.

Benefits

For many people, additional information or workbooks can be used in private to reinforce their commitment to getting better. People who lack the time or finances to attend regular psychotherapy sessions at a practitioner's office often find that bibliotherapy can bridge the gap between infrequent appointments. Further, the nature of the disorder itself may sometimes preclude in-office treatment, such as for people suffering from agoraphobia. Current research indicates that a bibliotherapeutic approach can be highly effective in helping people with agoraphobia better understand and cope with their symptoms.

Precautions

Bibliotherapy is an adjunct to psychotherapy. It is not intended as a replacement for psychotherapy or as a self-help treatment. In addition, bibliotherapy is not likely to be useful with patients who have thought disorders, psychoses, limited intellectual ability, dyslexia, or active resistance to treatment. As with any form of treatment, bibliotherapy is effective only if it actively engages the patient's desire for and belief in recovery.

Aftercare

Unlike many standard forms of psychotherapy, bibliotherapeutic approaches often include specific examples of ways to deal with relapses or setbacks. As long as the patients keep these materials, they have easy access to resources for getting back on track.

Risks

People who use self-help manuals without professional guidance run the risk of misapplying techniques or misdiagnosing their problems.

Results

As with any form of treatment, bibliotherapy is effective only if it actively engages the client's desire for and belief in recovery. For many people, additional information or workbooks can be used in private to reinforce their commitment to getting better. People who lack the time or finances to attend regular psychotherapy sessions at a practitioner's office often find that bibliotherapy can bridge the gap between infrequent appointments. Further, the nature of the disorder itself may sometimes preclude in-office treatment, such as for people suffering from agoraphobia. Current research indicates that a bibliotherapeutic approach can be highly effective in helping people with agoraphobia better understand and cope with their symptoms.

Resources

BOOKS

Hipsky, Shellie Jacobs. *The Drama Discovery Curriculum: Bibliotherapy and Theater Games for Students with Emotional and Behavioral Challenges*. Lancaster, PA: Proactive Publications, 2006.

VandenBos, Gary R. ed. *APA Dictionary of Psychology*. Washington, DC: American Psychological Association, 2006.

White, John R., and Arthur S. Freeman, eds. "Introduction." In *Cognitive-Behavioral Group Therapy for Specific Problems and Populations*, edited by John R. White and Arthur S. Freeman. Washington, DC: American Psychological Association, 2000.

PERIODICALS

Carlbring, Per, et al. "An Open Study of Internet-Based Bibliotherapy with Minimal Therapist Contact via Email for Social Phobia." *Clinical Psychologist* 10, no. 1 (March 2006): 30–38.

Febbraro, Greg A. R. "An Investigation Into the Effectiveness of Bibliotherapy and Minimal Contact Interventions in the Treatment of Panic Attacks." *Journal of Clinical Psychology* 61, no. 6 (June 2005): 763–79.

Floyd, Mark, et al. "Two-Year Follow-Up of Bibliotherapy and Individual Cognitive Therapy for Depressed Older Adults." *Behavior Modification* 30, no. 3 (May 2006): 281–94.

Foster, Tom. "Read All About It: Guided Bibliotherapy for Depression in Adults." *Irish Journal of Psychological Medicine* 23, no. 3 (September 2006): 111–13.

Heath, Melissa Allen, et al. "Bibliotherapy: A Resource to Facilitate Emotional Healing and Growth." *School Psychology International* 26 no. 5 (December 2005): 563–80.

Norcross, John C. "Integrating Self-Help Into Psychotherapy: 16 Practical Suggestions." *Professional Psychology: Research and Practice* 37, no. 6 (December 2006): 683–93.

Pehrsson, Dale E., and P. A. McMillen. "Bibliotherapy Evaluation Tool: Grounding Counselors in the Therapeutic Use of Literature." *Arts in Psychotherapy* 32, no. 1 (2005): 47–59.

Rapee, Ronald M., Maree J. Abbott, and Heidi J. Lyneham. "Bibliotherapy for Children With Anxiety Disorders Using Written Materials for Parents: A Randomized Controlled Trial." *Journal of Consulting and Clinical Psychology* 74, no. 3 (June 2006): 436–44.

Reeves, T., and J. M. Stace. "Improving Patient Access and Choice: Assisted Bibliotherapy for Mild to Moderate Stress/Anxiety in Primary Care." *Journal of Psychiatric and Mental Health Nursing* 12, no. 3 (June 2005): 341–46.

Thomas, S. P. "Bibliotherapy: New Evidence of Effectiveness." *Issues in Mental Health Nursing* 32, no. 4 (2011): 191.

Jane A. Fitzgerald, PhD
Ruth A. Wienclaw, PhD

Binge drinking

Definition

Binge drinking is the rapid consumption of alcohol with the goal of intoxication. In the past, binge drinking was usually considered to be heavy, out-of-control drinking, usually alone, for periods of up to several days. Binge drinking is now more often defined by the quantity of alcohol consumed on a single occasion. The National Advisory Council of the National Institute on Alcohol Abuse and Alcoholism (NIAAA) defines binge drinking as reaching a blood alcohol concentration (BAC) of at least 0.08 grams per deciliter, which generally corresponds to five drinks within about two hours for adult males and four drinks for adult females.

Demographics

Binge drinking is common in most parts of the world, and alcohol consumption, including binge drinking, is a major cause of death. Every year, more than

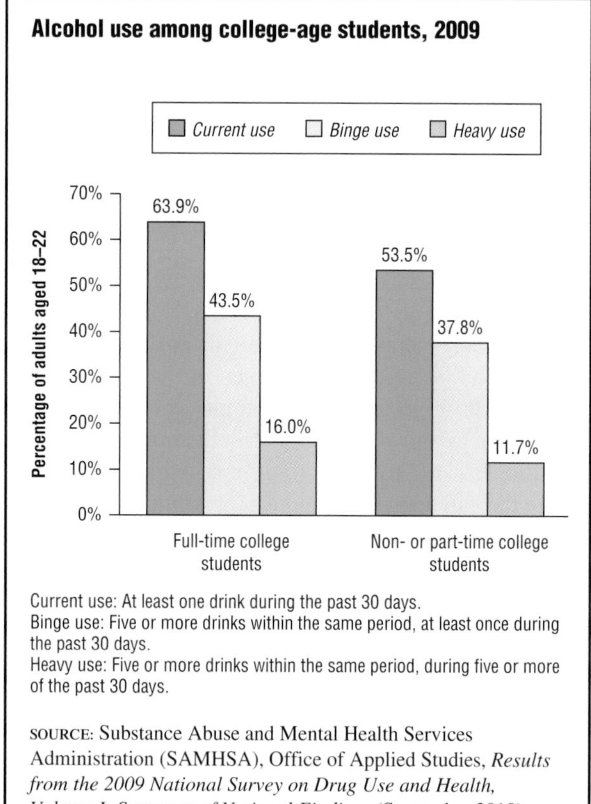

(Graph by PreMediaGlobal. © 2012 Cengage Learning.)

A group of young adults buys alcohol. Consuming five or more drinks (or four for women) within a short time period is considered binge drinking. *(© Photopqr/Ouest France/ Marc Ollivier/newscom)*

33 million adult Americans binge drink. According to national surveys released in 2010 and reported by the U.S. Centers for Disease Control and Prevention, 75% of the alcohol consumed by U.S. adults is consumed by binge drinking. Among Americans who drink, almost one in three adults and two out of three high school students binge drink. Among American adults who drink to excess, approximately 92% report binge drinking at least once in a 30-day period. Binge drinking is more prevalent in males (21% vs. 10% of females). Among non-Hispanic whites, 16% binge drink, compared with 10% of non-Hispanic blacks. Binge drinking varies greatly from state to state, with estimates of binge drinking by adults ranging from 6.8% in Tennessee to 23.9% in Wisconsin. Binge drinkers are 14 times more likely than other drinkers to drive while alcohol impaired.

Although 70% of binge-drinking episodes in the United States involve adults aged 26 and older, binge drinking by high school and college students is of particular concern. Binge drinking accounts for approximately 90% of all alcohol consumed by Americans under the age of 21, and 51% of 18–20-year-olds who drink alcohol binge drink, the highest proportion for any age group.

Although binge drinking among young people appears to be increasing in many countries, binge drinking by U.S. college students has remained stable over time. Rates vary with the individual school, from 1% to more than 70% of students. Overall, more than 40% of U.S. college students of all ages report binge drinking at least once during an average two-week period. Every year, an estimated 30,000 American college students require medical treatment for alcohol overdose. Among students who drive at least once a week, 13% report driving after having at least five drinks, and within all age groups, persons who binge drink are 14 times more likely to drive while under the influence.

Description

Binge drinking is generally recognized as a harmful—and potentially life-threatening—practice, but there is no universally accepted definition of what constitutes binge drinking. Some U.S. researchers prefer the phrase "episodic heavy drinking," referring to at least five consecutive drinks for men and at least four for women on at least one occasion in a two-week period. Three or more such episodes within two weeks constitute heavy binge drinking. In many European countries, however, binge drinking is defined by significantly more than four or five drinks. There is also considerable variation in the definition of a standard drink. Furthermore, alcohol is metabolized at different rates. A person's BAC is affected by body weight, the duration of time in which alcohol is consumed, and concurrent food intake. To account for these factors, the NIAAA has redefined binge drinking as a pattern of consumption that brings the BAC to 0.08 gram percent or above. However, all definitions of binge drinking include drinking to the point of intoxication.

One standard drink is generally defined as:

- 12 fluid ounces (fl oz) of regular beer
- 8–9 fl oz of malt liquor
- 5 fl oz of table wine
- 3–4 fl oz of fortified wine, such as sherry or port
- 2–3 fl oz of cordial, liqueur, or aperitif
- 1.5 fl oz (one jigger or shot) of brandy or 80-proof spirits (hard liquor)

The acceptability of binge drinking varies in different cultures. In some societies, binge drinking and intoxication are considered normal. In most cultures that tolerate drinking, binge drinking is more acceptable for males than for females and may even be considered a male rite of passage. Binge drinking may also be acceptable on certain occasions, such as wedding celebrations, wakes, or sports tournaments.

Binge drinking is associated with numerous social problems. It increases the likelihood of high-risk behaviors, such as driving under the influence; engaging in unplanned, unsafe, unprotected, or nonconsensual sex; accidents or injuries due to loss of physical coordination; and aggression or violence. People that binge drink are more likely to miss school or work and to perform less productively because of hangovers. They may engage in inappropriate interpersonal behaviors that negatively affect their relationships. Schools with high rates of binge drinking have higher rates of property damage and verbal, physical, and sexual violence.

Binge drinking is associated with a variety of adverse health effects, including cardiovascular problems such as atrial fibrillation. Binge drinking by pregnant women can directly harm their unborn babies and cause **fetal alcohol syndrome** or another fetal alcohol spectrum disorder. Binge drinking is also associated with liver disease, neurological damage, sexual dysfunction, and poor control of diabetes. Finally, binge drinking can cause potentially fatal alcohol poisoning.

Risk factors

Risk factors for binge drinking include **stress**, **sexual abuse**, and mental illness. Additional risk factors for college students include having engaged in binge drinking in high school and residing in a sorority or fraternity. Low-priced, easily available alcohol is strongly correlated with binge drinking by college students. Binge drinking rates among college students correlate with those of adults living in the same state—36% in the ten states with the lowest rates of adult binge drinking compared with 53% in the ten highest adult–binge drinking states.

Causes and symptoms

The causes of binge drinking can be psychological or social. Many people binge drink to escape stress or personal problems. Other binge drinkers, especially young people, report that they engage in the practice because of peer pressure, for social status, or to fit in with a drinking culture. Bars, liquor stores, and advertising promote drinking as an attractive activity.

The rise in popularity of inexpensive alcoholic energy drinks, which contain caffeine and other stimulants in addition to high alcohol levels, led to a frightening increase in binge drinking in the late 2000s, especially among college students. These products appear to be designed to support binge drinking, as the stimulants enable drinkers to stay awake and consume more alcohol, rather than passing out. Numerous hospitalizations and several deaths led some colleges and states to ban the drinks, and because the safety of such supplements in combination with alcohol had not been approved by the U.S. Food and Drug Administration (FDA), manufacturers were required by the FDA to remove caffeine from the beverages.

Although binge drinkers are not necessarily alcohol dependent, three out of five frequent binge drinkers may meet the criteria for alcohol abuse and one in five may be alcohol dependent. Some studies indicate that people who have three or more binge-drinking episodes within a two-week period display some symptoms of alcoholism.

Alcohol poisoning can be a potentially life-threatening consequence of binge drinking. Alcohol poisoning affects involuntary reflexes, including breathing and the gag reflex. An impaired gag reflex can cause drinkers to choke on their own vomit. Other signs of alcohol poisoning include:

- extreme confusion
- seizures
- unconsciousness
- slow or irregular breathing
- lowered body temperature
- pale or bluish skin

KEY TERMS

Alcoholic energy drink—Caffeinated alcoholic beverages; malt liquors which, in addition to high alcohol content, have added caffeine and sometimes other stimulants.

Alcohol poisoning—A potentially life-threatening condition caused by consuming large amounts of alcohol over a short period, negatively affecting heart rate, breathing, and the gag reflex.

Atrial fibrillation—A condition in which the upper chamber of the heart quivers instead of pumping in an organized way.

Blood alcohol concentration or content (BAC)—A measure of the amount of alcohol in the body; in most states, legal alcohol intoxication is defined as a BAC of at least 0.08 grams per deciliter of blood.

Cognitive-behavioral therapy (CBT)—A type of psychotherapy in which people learn to recognize and change negative and self-defeating patterns of thinking and behavior.

Fetal alcohol spectrum disorders—A range of birth defects, including intellectual disability, poor growth, nervous system dysfunctions, and malformations, that result from heavy maternal alcohol consumption during pregnancy.

Tolerance—The body's adjustment to a drug such as alcohol, requiring increasingly higher quantities to produce the same effects.

Withdrawal—The unpleasant, sometimes life-threatening, physiological changes that can occur due to the discontinuation of alcohol or drugs after prolonged regular use.

Diagnosis

Examination

Although people usually recover from binge drinking by "sleeping it off," alcohol poisoning is a medical emergency that requires immediate attention. The physician will check for signs and symptoms of alcohol poisoning. It is important that medical personnel be informed as to the amount and type of alcohol consumed over a specific period of time.

Tests

Blood tests are used to determine blood alcohol levels and other signs of alcohol toxicity, such as low blood sugar. A urine test may help to confirm a **diagnosis** of alcohol poisoning.

Treatment

The most important treatment for binge drinking is to stop drinking. Binge drinkers should never be allowed to drive. If alcohol poisoning is suspected, it is important to stay with the person and try to keep them conscious until medical help arrives. If they are vomiting, they should be kept in a sitting position if possible, or, if lying down, have their head turned to one side to prevent choking. Patients with alcohol poisoning must be carefully monitored to prevent breathing and gagging problems. Oxygen therapy may be required, as well as intravenous fluids to prevent dehydration.

Traditional

Patients who are physically dependent on alcohol may require medical treatment for managing symptoms of alcohol withdrawal. Counseling may be required to address the underlying reasons for alcohol abuse. Groups such as Alcoholics Anonymous (AA) have a proven track record of helping people with drinking problems. Alcoholism is also treated with **cognitive-behavioral therapy** (CBT) or interactional group **psychotherapy** based on a 12-step program. Severe cases may require **hospitalization** or treatment in a substance-abuse rehabilitation facility.

Drugs

Anxiolytic drugs are sometimes prescribed to control anxiety symptoms that accompany alcohol withdrawal. The FDA has approved three medications for the treatment of alcoholism:

- disulfiram (Antabuse) causes illness if alcohol is consumed
- naltrexone (Depade, ReVia) acts on the brain to reduce the craving for alcohol
- acamprosate (Canpral) reduces withdrawal symptoms

Prognosis

Binge drinking is particularly dangerous for young people whose brains are still developing. Young people are more likely than adults to engage in risky behaviors when binge drinking, leading to automobile accidents, violence, sexually transmitted diseases, and unplanned pregnancies. Binge drinking disrupts sleep patterns, making it harder to concentrate in school, and binge drinkers are more likely to drop out of school. Studies have shown that teens who binge drink throughout high school are more likely to be overweight and have high blood pressure by the age of 24. Binge drinking can cause people to become angry or moody and socially isolated. Frequent binge drinking can induce tolerance, so that more alcohol is required to achieve a particular level of intoxication. Over time, binge drinking can cause liver disease, heart disease, and other chronic conditions, as well as **stroke** and certain cancers. Binge drinking by pregnant women can cause fetal alcohol spectrum disorders and other harm to their babies. Severe alcohol poisoning can lead to irreversible **brain** damage or death. Finally, binge drinking may be a precursor to alcohol dependence.

Prevention

Evidence demonstrates that parental influence and family values are very powerful determinants of drinking behavior. School- and community-based educational programs, starting in middle school if not before, teach alcohol awareness and stress the dangers of binge drinking. Many colleges and universities have alcohol awareness and prevention programs, beginning with freshman orientation. Peer-to-peer counseling and interactive programs can be particularly effective. Alcohol awareness programs can also be directed toward workplaces and promoted in the mainstream media. Healthcare providers and social service workers should educate their patients and clients.

Social norms approaches teach that activities such as binge drinking are not socially acceptable. Social norming has been shown to be especially effective in reducing binge drinking among young people. For example, many young people believe that binge drinking is much more prevalent than it actually is, and correcting this misconception can discourage the practice.

One study found that in seven states that had at least four laws targeting high-volume alcohol sales, campus binge-drinking rates were lower—33% compared to 48% in states without such laws. States with other alcohol-control policies also had lower rates of college binge drinking. Other interventions that have been shown to help prevent binge drinking in college students include:

- increasing the cost of alcoholic beverages through taxation

QUESTIONS TO ASK YOUR DOCTOR

- Does my pattern of alcohol consumption qualify as binge drinking?
- What is a safe level of alcohol consumption?
- Is there a program or group that could help me control my binge drinking?

- limiting the number of retail alcohol outlets within a given area
- consistently enforcing laws against underage drinking and drunk driving
- screening and counseling students for alcohol abuse

Bars and restaurants can also play a role in reducing binge drinking. Atmosphere, such as lighting and music, can affect how much and how fast patrons drink. Serving alcohol at a slower rate, offering food and nonalcoholic drinks, and especially refusing to serve intoxicated customers and preventing them from driving are business practices that help discourage binge drinking.

Resources

BOOKS

Bakewell, Lisa. *Alcohol Information for Teens*. 2nd ed. Detroit: Omnigraphics, 2009.

Dowdall, George W. *College Drinking: Reframing a Social Problem*. Westport, CT: Praeger, 2009.

Marczinski, Cecile A., Estee C. Grant, and Vincent J. Grant. *Binge Drinking in Adolescents and College Students*. Hauppauge, NY: Nova Science, 2009.

Roloff, Tamara L. *Alcoholism*. Detroit: Greenhaven, 2010.

Young, Amy M., et al. "Drinking Like a Guy: Frequent Binge Drinking among Undergraduate Women." In: *The American Drug Scene: An Anthology*, edited by James A. Inciardi and Karen McElrath. 5th ed. New York: Oxford University Press, 2008.

PERIODICALS

Howland, Jonathan, et al. "The Effects of Binge Drinking on College Students' Next-Day Academic Test-Taking Performance and Mood State." *Addiction* 105, no. 4 (April 2010): 655–665.

Reinberg, Steven. "Binge Drinking, Hypertension a Deadly Combo." *U.S. News & World Report*, August 19, 2010. http://health.usnews.com/health-news/family-health/heart/articles/2010/08/19/binge-drinking-hypertension-a-deadly-combo (accessed October 14, 2011).

Roy-Bornstein, Carolyn. "Underage Drinking." *Pediatrics for Parents* 26 (March/April 2010): 11–12.

WEBSITES

Center for Science in the Public Interest. "Binge Drinking on College Campuses." http://www.cspinet.org/booze/collfact1.htm (accessed December 11, 2010).

Nemours Foundation. "Binge Drinking." TeensHealth.org. http://kidshealth.org/teen/drug_alcohol/alcohol/binge_drink.html (accessed December 1, 2011).

U.S. Centers for Disease Control and Prevention. "Alcohol and Public Health Fact Sheets: Binge Drinking." http://www.cdc.gov/alcohol/fact-sheets/binge-drinking.htm (accessed December 1, 2011).

———. "CDC Vital Signs: Binge Drinking." http://www.cdc.gov/vitalsigns/BingeDrinking/index.html (accessed October 14, 2011).

———. "1 in 4 High School Students and Young Adults Report Binge Drinking." http://www.cdc.gov/media/pressrel/2010/r101005.html (accessed December 1, 2011).

U.S. Food and Drug Administration. "Caffeinated Alcoholic Beverages." U.S. Department of Health and Human Services. http://www.fda.gov/Food/FoodIngredientsPackaging/ucm190366.htm (accessed December 2, 2011).

ORGANIZATIONS

International Center for Alcohol Policies, 1519 New Hampshire Avenue NW, Washington, DC, 20036, (202) 986-1159, Fax: (202) 986-2080, info@icap.org, http://www.icap.org.

National Institute on Alcohol Abuse and Alcoholism (NIAAA), 5635 Fishers Lane, MSC 9304, Bethesda, MD, 20892-9304, (301) 443-3860, http://www.niaaa.nih.gov.

Substance Abuse and Mental Health Services Administration, 1 Choke Cherry Road, Rockville, MD, 20857, (877) SAMHSA-7 (726-4727), Fax: (240) 221-4292, SAMHSAInfo@samhsa.hhs.gov, http://www.samhsa.gov.

U.S. Centers for Disease Control and Prevention, 1600 Clifton Road, Atlanta, GA, 30333, (800) CDC-INFO (232-4636), cdcinfo@cdc.gov, http://www.cdc.gov.

Jill U. Adams
Margaret Alic, PhD

Binge eating disorder

Definition

Binge eating disorder (BED) is a serious eating disorder characterized by frequent consumption of a large amount of food over a limited period of time, such as one or two hours. BED is also known as compulsive overeating.

Demographics

Binge eating disorder is the most commonly diagnosed eating disorder, affecting 3.5% of women and 2% of men at some point in their adult lives.

Although it often begins in late adolescence or early twenties, BED is also common during middle age. As many as one-half of people attending weight-loss clinics are binge eaters. Although BED affects blacks and whites equally, there has been little research on binge eating by other racial or ethnic groups.

Data from a 2011 study conducted by the National Institutes of Mental Health showed that the lifetime prevalence of binge eating disorder in teens is 1.6% (approximately 300,000 teens). The study was based on interviews with more than 10,000 adolescents aged 13 to 18 years. The study data also showed that rates of binge eating disorder, as well as bulimia, have approximately doubled since 1990, while the rates of anorexia have remained fairly stable. More girls were affected by binge eating disorder than boys, and approximately 15% of any teens with binge eating disorder had attempted **suicide**.

Description

Although most people overeat on occasion, BED is a pattern of frequently recurring abnormal overeating, which is different from continuous snacking and often occurs in the absence of hunger. Although the duration of each binge may vary significantly, binge eating is characterized by the inability to stop eating during each episode and a feeling of being out of control. A binge typically ends only when all of the desirable binge foods have been consumed or when the person feels too full to continue. Binge eaters generally eat very fast and alone—usually out of embarrassment—and suffer strong negative feelings such as guilt, shame, or **depression** following the binge.

Many eating disorder specialists define BED as overeating that occurs at least twice a week for at least three months and that has a negative effect on an individual's health, relationships, and/or daily activities. However, BED is a relatively new area of research, and many aspects of the disorder remain unclear.

In the revised fourth edition of the ***Diagnostic and Statistical Manual of Mental Disorders*** (*DSM-IV-TR*), the **American Psychiatric Association** (APA) defines the better known—but less common—eating disorders, **anorexia nervosa** and **bulimia nervosa**, as psychiatric disorders with formal diagnostic criteria. BED is classified as an eating disorder not otherwise specified (EDNOS) and has no diagnostic criteria. It has been proposed that BED be included as a specific disorder in the fifth edition of the *DSM*, *DSM-5* (2013). This is important because the classification can affect both recommended therapies and health insurance coverage for treatment. However, the proposal has proved controversial.

The proposed diagnostic criteria state that individuals must experience binge eating episodes at least once a week for three months to be diagnosed with binge eating disorder.

Some experts believe that binge eating should be classified as an obesity-related behavior. However, not all binge eaters are obese and not all obese people are binge eaters. Furthermore, binge eaters are far more likely to report significant mood problems, especially depression, and greater dissatisfaction with their weight and shape, as compared to persons with obesity.

Other experts believe that binge eating is a subtype of bulimia. Bulimia is characterized by episodes of binge eating followed by self-induced purging through vomiting; abuse of laxatives, diuretics, or enemas; fasting; or **compulsive exercise**. Although persons with BED often attempt to diet between binges, they do not purge extra calories. They also do not exhibit anorexic or self-starving behaviors, which may occur in persons with bulimia.

Risk factors

Risk factors for binge eating are similar to risk factors for other eating disorders. These include:

- a family history of eating disorders
- frequent dieting, especially rigorous diets or frequently gaining and losing large amounts of weight (weight cycling)
- preoccupation with weight and body image
- impulsiveness or poor impulse control
- low self-esteem and negative self-talk
- difficulty expressing feelings appropriately and managing anger
- a history of sexual abuse
- depression, which can be both a risk factor for binge eating and a result of binge eating

Causes and symptoms

Like other eating disorders, BED has multiple causes. Some people appear to be genetically predisposed to binge eating. Researchers believe that this may be related to abnormalities in **brain neurotransmitters** that help regulate appetite. Binge-eating episodes may occur in response to strong negative emotions, such as depression or anxiety, or to less defined feelings of distress or tension. People who binge eat are far more likely than others to describe themselves as experiencing personal and work problems and as being hypersensitive to the opinions of others. Like with bulimia, persons with BED are more likely than others to be diagnosed with major depression, substance-related disorders, and **personality disorders**. Binge eating is often triggered by stress—sometimes the **stress** is caused by very restrictive **diets**, but often the stress is caused by social and cultural factors, such as family conflicts or dysfunctional relationships. Pressure felt by cultural and media messages that promote being thin as desirable can also result in binge eating, which is used as a coping mechanism. Some patients report that their binges are related to the ingestion of certain "trigger foods," usually carbohydrates.

Whatever the cause, bingeing appears to temporarily alleviate uncomfortable or painful feelings. While bingeing, patients typically describe themselves as "numb" or "spaced out." Their relief is short-lived, leading to repeated bingeing. The out-of-control eating is a frightening experience for most people, and they usually feel embarrassed and ashamed about their bingeing. In the aftermath of a binge, many people experience overwhelming feelings of guilt, self-disgust, anxiety, and depression. They vow never to binge again but are unable to prevent it.

Symptoms of binge eating can be difficult to detect. The eating often occurs in private, and the eater tends to be secretive about food. Specific symptoms of binge eating include:

- feeling out of control and unable to stop eating
- continuing to eat despite feeling full or even painfully uncomfortable
- eating abnormally large amounts of food at one sitting, sometimes as many as 3,000–10,000 calories in a short period
- eating abnormally fast
- eating alone or in secret
- hoarding food and hiding empty food containers
- constant dieting without weight loss
- obsessive concern with weight
- depression
- anxiety
- substance abuse

KEY TERMS

Anorexia nervosa—A serious eating disorder that primarily affects young women in their teens and early twenties and is characterized by a pathological fear of gaining weight. Anorexia causes disturbed eating behavior and can lead to severe weight loss and malnutrition.

Bulimia nervosa—A serious eating disorder that primarily affects young women and is characterized by compulsive overeating followed by purging, usually self-induced vomiting or the use of laxatives or diuretics.

Cognitive-behavioral therapy (CBT)—A type of psychotherapy in which people learn to recognize and change negative and self-defeating patterns of thinking and behavior.

Electrolytes—Ions—such as sodium, potassium, calcium, magnesium, chloride, phosphate, bicarbonate, and sulfate—that are dissolved in bodily fluids such as blood and regulate or affect most metabolic processes.

Neurotransmitters—Chemicals that carry impulses between nerve cells (neurons), including acetylcholine, dopamine, serotonin, and norepinephrine.

Selective serotonin reuptake inhibitors (SSRIs)—A class of antidepressants that works by blocking the reabsorption of serotonin by brain cells, raising the level of the chemical in the brain.

Serotonin—5-Hydroxytryptamine; a neurotransmitter present throughout the body, especially in the brain. Inadequate amounts of serotonin have been implicated in numerous disorders, including depression and obsessive-compulsive disorder.

Triglycerides—A type of fat in the blood. High levels of triglycerides can increase the risk of coronary artery disease.

Weight cycling—Repeatedly gaining and losing weight.

Diagnosis

Diagnosis requires examination, tests, and compiling relevant personal information.

Examination

Diagnosis should include a physical examination and medical history, although binge eating disorder is often diagnosed and treated by a **psychiatrist** or **psychologist**. Diagnosis can be difficult. Binge eaters often go to extremes to hide how much they eat. They may, for example, buy snack food at the grocery store and eat it in the car before they get home or buy food in secret and hoard it. Although diagnosis usually begins with a personal and family history, including eating habits and **exercise**, binge eaters may lie about their eating.

Tests

Physicians usually order standard laboratory tests, including a complete blood count (CBC), urinalysis, and blood tests to check levels of cholesterol, triglycerides, and electrolytes. Additional tests, such as thyroid function, may be ordered to rule out other disorders. If the patient is obese, tests may be performed for obesity-related conditions, such as diabetes, cardiovascular disease, and sleep apnea.

Procedures

The assessment process may include a questionnaire, such as the Eating Disorder Examination Questionnaire. There are several clinical inventories or scales that are used to assess depressive symptoms, including the **Hamilton Depression Scale** (HAM-D) and the **Beck Depression Inventory** (BDI). These tests are usually administered in an office setting.

Treatment

There are various approaches in treating BED; however, for the best results, patients must want to stop binge eating.

Traditional

BED is usually treated most effectively by a combination of **psychotherapy** and **group therapy**. However, physicians are more likely to concentrate on weight-control issues, using drugs, diet, and **nutrition counseling** to reduce the health risks of obesity-related diseases. Although **nutrition** counseling and meal planning may help control weight, they do not address the impulse to binge eat. Psychologists are more likely to treat behavior and thought patterns that cause abnormal eating, since obesity may be easier to treat once bingeing behavior is controlled.

Several types of psychotherapy may be effective for treating BED. **Cognitive-behavioral therapy** (CBT) is a relatively short-term therapy designed to confront and change thoughts and feelings about one's body and behaviors toward food. It does not address the origins of those thoughts and feelings, but rather explores **self-control strategies** and the development of skills for coping with emotional distress. **Interpersonal therapy** is short-term therapy to help identify and resolve specific relationship issues and problems and has been shown to be successful in the treatment of BED. Dialectical behavior therapy (DBT) utilizes structured private and group sessions for reducing behaviors that interfere with quality of life, finding alternate solutions to current problem situations, and learning to regulate emotions. **Family therapy** is helpful for treating children who binge eat. It teaches strategies for reducing conflict, disorder, and stress that can trigger binge eating.

Drugs

There are no drugs specifically approved by the U.S. Food and Drug Administration (FDA) for treating binge eating. However, the FDA has approved **antidepressants** called **selective serotonin reuptake inhibitors (SSRIs)**, such as **fluoxetine** (Prozac) and **sertraline** (Zoloft), for the treatment of bulimia, which involves binge-eating behavior. These medications increase **serotonin** levels in the brain and are thought to affect the body's sense of fullness. **SSRIs** are often prescribed for BED, regardless of whether there are signs of depression. Tricyclic antidepressants (TCAs) and appetitive suppressants may be prescribed for BED, but their use is rare. The anticonvulsant topiramate (Topamax), which is normally used to control **seizures**, has been found to reduce binge-eating episodes, but this drug can have serious side effects.

Alternative

Alternative treatments for binge eating often focus on curbing concurrent depression. Herbal remedies that may ease symptoms of depression include **5-HTP**, **DHEA**, **saffron**, and **St. John's wort**; kava-kava root may reduce symptoms of anxiety. Relaxation exercises and techniques that may help reduce binge-eating episodes triggered by stress or depression include **music therapy**, **yoga**, and other forms of relaxation.

Home remedies

Although weight-loss programs are helpful for some people with BED, they generally are not recommended until after BED treatment, since low-calorie diets can trigger binge eating. Weight-loss programs generally do not address binge-eating triggers to the same extent as psychotherapy. Weight loss should be medically supervised.

Self-help programs, including books and manuals, videos, and **support groups**, can be helpful for treating BED. A 2010 study of patients with at least one binge-eating episode per week found that 64% of patients who attended eight therapy sessions utilizing a six-step self-help program were binge free after one year. This compared with 45% of patients who were given only basic healthy eating information and informed of available services.

Self-help programs are cost-effective as well. In another 2010 study of 123 patients with binge eating disorder, a guided self-help program was significantly more cost effective than simply providing patients with options for treatment. The cost to society in terms of binge-free days and workplace productivity was significantly reduced in the **intervention** group, with a savings of more than $26,000 per quality of life year.

Home remedies for binge eating include eating breakfast, avoiding diets, getting appropriate essential nutrients, and keeping less food in the home. Binge eaters are also advised to exercise and seek support from friends and family members.

QUESTIONS TO ASK YOUR DOCTOR

- Should I be concerned about binge eating if I am not overweight?
- What are the health consequences of binge eating?
- Will I need both medication and psychotherapy?
- Can you recommend a therapist?
- Is there anything my friends and family can do to help me overcome my binge eating?
- Can you refer me to a support group for binge eating?
- Will my insurance cover my medical and psychological treatment?

Prognosis

Overall rates of recovery are higher for BED than for bulimia. Some people find that simply the act of seeking help or taking a placebo improves their control over binge eating. This is one reason why some medical professionals do not accept binge eating as a genuine disorder. In any case, binge-eating relapses are common in response to stressful life events.

Prevention

Binge eating is difficult to prevent, since its causes are unclear, and it can be difficult to detect. Prevention strategies include:

- eating small meals every three or four hours to avoid hunger
- tracking food intake
- avoiding eating alone
- avoiding using food for comfort in times of stress
- monitoring negative self-talk and practicing positive self-talk
- spending time doing something enjoyable every day
- staying busy without becoming frantic or stressed
- being aware of situations that invite bingeing and looking for ways to avoid or defuse such situations
- avoiding extreme diets
- teaching children to have healthy attitudes toward their weight, appearance, and diet
- avoiding comparisons or teasing about body size and shape
- loving and accepting family members for who they are
- being alert for signs of low self-esteem, anxiety, depression, and drug or alcohol abuse, and seeking help if signs appear

Resources

BOOKS

Agras, W. Stewart. *Overcoming Eating Disorders: A Cognitive-Behavioral Therapy Approach for Bulimia Nervosa and Binge-Eating Disorder,* 2nd ed. New York: Oxford University Press, 2008.

American Psychiatric Association. *Diagnostic and Statistical Manual of Mental Disorders (DSM-IV-TR),* 4th ed., text rev. Washington, DC: American Psychiatric Association, 2000.

Bulik, Cynthia M. *Crave: Why You Binge Eat and How to Stop.* New York: Walker, 2009.

Favor, Lesli J. *Food as Foe: Nutrition and Eating Disorders.* New York: Marshall Cavendish Benchmark, 2008.

Herzog, David B., Debra L. Franko, and Patricia Cable. *Unlocking the Mysteries of Eating Disorders.* New York: McGraw-Hill, 2007.

Lawton, Sandra Augustyne. *Eating Disorders Information for Teens,* 2nd ed. Detroit: Omnigraphics, 2009.

Mitchell, James E. *Binge-Eating Disorder: Clinical Foundations and Treatment.* New York: Guilford, 2008.

Schulherr, Susan. *Eating Disorders for Dummies.* Hoboken, NJ: Wiley, 2008.

Seles, Monica. *Getting a Grip: On My Body, My Mind, My Self.* New York: Avery, 2009.

Silverstein, Alvin, Virginia B. Silverstein, and Laura Silverstein Nunn. *The Eating Disorders Update: Understanding Anorexia, Bulimia, and Binge Eating.* Berkeley Heights, NJ: Enslow, 2009.

PERIODICALS

Ellin, Abby. "Redefining an Eating Disorder." *New York Times* (January 19, 2010): D5.

Hellmich, Nanci. "Treatment for Binge Eating Need Not Be Extensive or Expensive Study: 64% Stopped with Six-Step Plan." *USA Today* (April 6, 2010): D4.

Lynch, Frances, et al. "Cost-effectiveness of Guided Self-help Treatment for Recurrent Binge Eating." *Journal of Consulting and Clinical Psychology* 78, no. 3 (June 2010): 322–33.

Mond, Jonathan M., Carol B. Peterson, and Phillipa J. Hay. "Prior Use of Extreme Weight-Control Behaviors in a Community Sample of Women with Binge Eating Disorder or Subthreshold Binge Eating Disorder: A Descriptive Study." *International Journal of Eating Disorders* 43, no. 5 (July 2010): 440–46.

Moon, Kenneth T. "Comparison of Psychological Treatments for Binge Eating Disorder." *American Family Physician* 82, no. 5 (September 1, 2010): 534.

Roberto, Christina A., et al. "Binge Eating, Purging, or Both: Eating Disorder Psychopathology Findings from an Internet Community Survey." *International Journal of Eating Disorders* 43, no. 8 (December 2010): 724–31.

Treasure, Janet, Angélica M. Claudino, and Nancy Zucker. "Eating Disorders." *Lancet* 375, no. 9714 (February 13–19, 2010): 583–93.

WEBSITES

"Binge-Eating Disorder." MayoClinic.com. October 9, 2010. http://www.mayoclinic.com/health/binge-eating-disorder/DS00608 (accessed September 16, 2011).

Doheny, Kathleen. "Study: Eating Disorders in Teens Are Common." WebMD. March 7, 2011. http://www.webmd.com/mental-health/anorexia-nervosa/news/20110307/study-eating-disorders-in-teens-are-common (accessed September 16, 2011).

"Eating Disorders." MedlinePlus. November 30, 2010. http://www.nlm.nih.gov/medlineplus/eatingdisorders.html (accessed September 16, 2011).

ORGANIZATIONS

American Psychological Association, 750 1st St. NE, Washington, DC, 20002-4242, (202) 336-5500, (800) 374-2721, http://www.apa.org.

National Association of Anorexia Nervosa and Associated Disorders, PO Box 640, Naperville, IL, 60566, (630) 577-1330, anadhelp@anad.org, http://www.anad.org.

National Eating Disorders Association, 165 W 46th St., New York, NY, 10036, (212) 575-6200, (800) 931-2237, Fax: (212) 575-1650, info@NationalEatingDisorders.org, http://www.nationaleatingdisorders.org.

Overeaters Anonymous, PO Box 44020, Rio Rancho, NM, 87174-4020, (505) 891-2664, Fax: (505) 891-4320, http://www.oa.org.

Weight-control Information Network, 1 WIN Way, Bethesda, MD, 20892-3665, (202) 828-1025, (877) 946-4627, Fax: (202) 828-1028, win@info.niddk.nih.gov, http://win.niddk.nih.gov/index.htm.

Tish Davidson, AM
Margaret Alic, PhD
Heidi Splete

Biofeedback

Definition

Biofeedback, or applied psychophysiological feedback, is a patient-guided treatment that teaches an individual to control muscle tension, pain, body temperature, **brain** waves, and other bodily functions and processes through relaxation, visualization, and other cognitive control techniques. Biological signals such as heart rate, skin temperature, or brain activity are measured and "fed back," or returned, to the patient in order for the patient to develop techniques for manipulating them.

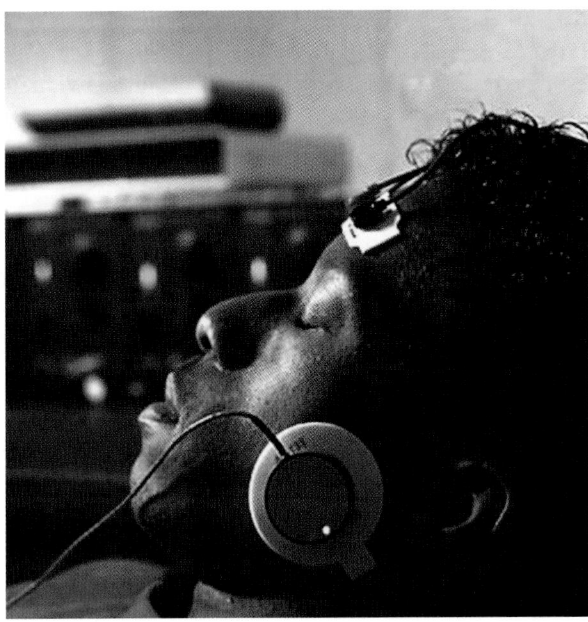

A patient undergoes biofeedback. *(© Will & Deni McIntyre/ Photo Researchers, Inc.)*

Purpose

The purpose of biofeedback is to enhance an individual's awareness of physical reactions to physical, emotional, or psychological **stress**, and their ability to influence their own physiological responses. The overall purpose is to develop self-regulation skills that play a role in improving health and well-being.

Description

Biofeedback is an important part of understanding the relationship between physical state and thoughts, feelings, and behaviors. Prior to beginning any biofeedback training, individuals may need a comprehensive psychological, educational, and/or medical assessment. Biofeedback can be used in conjunction with nonmedical treatments, such as **psychotherapy**, **cognitive-behavioral therapy**, and behavioral treatment strategies.

Biofeedback has been used as a part of a comprehensive treatment approach with a number of conditions, including chronic pain, irritable bowel syndrome (IBS), temporomandibular joint disorder (TMJ), Raynaud's syndrome, epilepsy, **attention deficit hyperactivity disorder** (ADHD), anxiety, migraine headaches, **depression**, **traumatic brain injury**, and **sleep disorders**.

Conditions related to stress are also treated using biofeedback, such as certain types of headaches, high blood pressure, bruxism (teeth grinding), **post-traumatic stress disorder** (PTSD), eating disorders, **substance abuse**, and some **anxiety disorders**. In treatment of stress-related conditions, biofeedback is often used in combination with relaxation training. Sometimes, biofeedback is used to help individuals learn how to experience deeper relaxation, such as in childbirth education or general **stress management** programs. Such training is referred to as biofeedback-assisted relaxation training. Even for individuals who can achieve relaxation through other strategies such as **meditation** or relaxation, biofeedback can be a valuable added technique. Biofeedback offers special advantages, such as allowing the clinician to track closely the places where an individual tenses up and helping the individual learn what thoughts and feelings are associated with the tension.

Origins

In 1961, Neal Miller, an experimental **psychologist**, suggested that autonomic nervous system responses (for instance, heart rate, blood pressure, gastrointestinal activity, regional blood flow) could be under voluntary control. The results of his experiments showed that such autonomic processes were controllable. This work led to the creation of biofeedback therapy. Miller's work was expanded by other researchers. In the 1970s, UCLA researcher Barry Sterman established that both cats and monkeys could be trained to control their brain wave patterns. Sterman used his techniques on human patients with epilepsy and was able to reduce **seizures** by 60% with the use of biofeedback. Other researchers published reports of their use of biofeedback in the treatment of cardiac arrhythmias, headaches, Raynaud's syndrome, and excess stomach acid, and as a tool for teaching deep relaxation. Since the early work of Miller and Sterman, biofeedback has developed into a front-line behavioral treatment for an even wider range of disorders and symptoms.

How biofeedback works

Biofeedback utilizes electronic sensors, or electrodes, attached to various parts of the body to detect changes in physical responses. Visual or auditory signals, such as a light display or a series of beeps, then inform the individual of these changes. While the individual views or listens to feedback, he or she begins to recognize thoughts, feelings, and mental images that influence his or her physical reactions. By monitoring this mind-body connection, the individual can use the same thoughts, feelings, and mental images as cues or reminders to become more relaxed or to change heartbeat, brain wave patterns, body temperature, and other body functions. The individual uses trial-and-error to change the signals in the desired direction. For example, individuals trying to control their blood pressure levels may see a light flash whenever the pressure drops below a certain level. They may then try to remember what their thoughts and feelings were at the moment and deliberately maintain them to keep the blood pressure level low.

Three stages of biofeedback training

- Awareness of the problematic physical response: Individuals may complete a psychophysiological stress profile (PSP) to identify how their bodies respond to a variety of stressors and determine their ability to overcome undesired physical reactions. Doing so involves a period of rest, stress, and recovery. For example, various sensors are attached to various parts of the body, and a baseline measurement lasting from two to four minutes records physical responses. The individual then goes through a standard set of stressors (such as rapid math calculations or running in place), each lasting from two to four minutes. This activity is followed by another relaxation period to determine the length of the recovery period.
- Using signals from the biofeedback equipment to control physical responses: The individual is assisted in reaching certain goals related to managing a specific physical response.
- Transferring control from biofeedback equipment or the healthcare professional: Individuals learn to identify triggers that alert them to implement their new-found self-regulation skills.

Types of biofeedback equipment

- Electromyograph (EMG): Sensors (or electrodes) placed on the skin on pertinent parts of the body monitor electrical activity in muscles, specifically tension. This is the most frequently used biofeedback method in the treatment of various neurologic disorders such as stroke, cerebral palsy, traumatic brain injury, and multiple sclerosis. In children and adolescents, EMG may be used to treat tension headaches, enuresis, and encopresis. In treating TMJ or bruxism, EMG sensors are placed on jaw muscles. Chronic stress is treated by monitoring muscle tension in various places on the body.
- Galvanic skin response (GSR): Sensors on the fingers monitor perspiration. This is also referred to as obtaining a skin conductance level (SCL). GSR may be used in the treatment of anxiety, phobias, stress, and sleep problems.
- Temperature or thermal sensors: Sensors monitor body temperature and changes in blood flow. Changes in hand temperature, for example, can indicate relaxation when there is increased blood flow to the skin. Temperature biofeedback may be useful for treating

migraine headache, Raynaud's disorder, and anxiety disorders.

- Heart rate sensors: A pulse monitor placed on the fingertip monitors pulse rate. Increases in heart rate are associated with emotional arousal, such as being angry or fearful. Decreases in heart rate are associated with relaxation.
- Capnometry (CAP): Respiratory sensors monitor oxygen intake and carbon dioxide output. This differentiates correct breathing from problematic breathing practices. Breath control training may be used to treat panic attacks, asthma, and a variety of stress-related conditions.
- Electroencephalographs (EEG) or neurofeedback: Sensors attached to the scalp monitor brain wave activity in different parts of the brain. It may be used to treat conditions with proven or suspected impact on brain wave patterns such as seizure disorders or epilepsy, ADHD, learning disabilities, migraine headaches, traumatic brain injury, and sleep disorders.

Biofeedback is geared toward whatever a person finds most appealing and understandable and is provided in several formats such as auditory, visual, or multimedia. Audio feedback, which may take the form of changes in tone and pitch, is useful because visual attention is not necessary. Visual feedback can be provided in various forms such as bar or line graphs on a computer screen. Initially, it was thought that over time computer signals could become boring or visually unappealing. In response to this suspicion, Barry Bittman developed Mindscope in 1992, which displays video scenes with realistic sounds on a high-definition television set connected to a computer. Physical responses detected by the biofeedback equipment control an engaging audiovisual environment of beautiful and realistic scenes. Clarity, perspective, motion, and sounds improve as individuals deepen their relaxation. For children and adolescents, this may be described as a video game for the body. Visual displays for EMG biofeedback may include sports such as basketball, baseball, and golf, where the individual plays against the computer.

The setting in which biofeedback training takes place can vary. Sometimes the clinician, client, and equipment are in the same room. Sometimes the client sits in a comfortable chair in a semi-dark, quiet room while the clinician is in another room with the equipment. In this arrangement, the clinician and client may communicate using an intercom.

In some cases, children and adolescents may reach the desired level of control in three to five sessions. Depending on the condition, biofeedback training may require a series of sessions for several days or weeks. In general, it takes 10–15 sessions at the lower end and 40–50 sessions at the higher end.

KEY TERMS

Anxiety—Experienced as a troubled feeling, a sense of dread, fear of the future, or distress over a possible threat to a person's physical or mental well-being.

Attention deficit hyperactivity disorder (ADHD)—A developmental disorder characterized by distractibility, hyperactivity, impulsive behaviors, and the inability to remain focused on tasks or activities.

Cognitive-behavioral therapy—Psychotherapy technique designed to help people change their attitudes, perceptions, and patterns of thinking.

Benefits

Through biofeedback training, individuals learn to control targeted physical responses (such as increased heart rate) and, over time, are able to recognize what is required to reduce problematic symptoms. Eventually, the external biofeedback becomes unnecessary as the individual learns to perceive internal physical responses and make the desired changes. The individual then has a powerful, portable, and self-administered treatment tool to deal with problematic symptoms that arise in response to anxiety, depression, stress, or other conditions.

Sometimes, biofeedback is used to help individuals learn how to experience deeper relaxation, such as in childbirth education or general stress management programs. Such training is referred to as biofeedback-assisted relaxation training. Even for individuals who can achieve relaxation through other strategies such as meditation or relaxation, biofeedback offers special advantages, such as allowing the clinician to track closely the places where an individual tenses up and helping the individual learn what thoughts and feelings are associated with the tension.

Precautions

Biofeedback depends on the motivation and active participation of participants. Thus, it may not be suitable for individuals with low motivation who are not willing to take a highly active role in treatment, such as those who have depression. Also, since biofeedback focuses on initiating behavioral changes, individuals inclined to examine their past to alleviate problems and symptoms may benefit more from other treatment types, such as psychotherapy. Individuals with cognitive impairment may be unable to remain engaged in the treatment, depending on their level of functioning. Also, individuals with a pacemaker or other implanted electrical devices should inform their health-care professional before entering biofeedback training, as certain types of biofeedback sensors may interfere with the devices. Patients with specific pain symptoms in which the cause is unknown should have a thorough medical examination to rule out underlying diseases or conditions before starting biofeedback training. Biofeedback can be used in combination with conventional therapies; however, while it can be used in combination with conventional medical treatment for illnesses such as cancer and diabetes, it should not replace those treatments.

The use of biofeedback techniques to treat an array of disorders has been extensively described in the medical literature. Controlled studies for some applications are limited, such as for the treatment of menopausal symptoms and premenstrual disorder (PMS). There is also some debate over the effectiveness of biofeedback in ADHD treatment. While many therapists, counselors, and mental health professionals have reported great success in treating patients with ADHD by using neurofeedback techniques, some critics attribute this positive therapeutic impact to a placebo effect.

There is also some debate among mental health professionals as to whether biofeedback should be considered a first-line treatment for some mental illnesses and to what degree other treatments, such as medication, should be employed as an adjunct therapy.

Research on the success of biofeedback in treating certain conditions is inconclusive or needs to be validated. Some research studies use a small number of participants, which makes it difficult to generalize the results for a larger population. Also, many conditions have different subtypes with a variety of psychological, social, and physical causes. This fact, combined with research design concerns, makes it difficult to compare research studies. For example, while most studies have reported positive outcomes in the treatment of alcohol abuse and dependence, problems with methods and statistical analyses have called study results into question. Also, its effectiveness in treating opiate abuse or dependence has not been consistently shown, as with its use in treating menopausal hot flashes, and there are limitations in studies relating to its use in cancer treatment. Continued research is needed to further evaluate and improve different biofeedback techniques for various conditions.

QUESTIONS TO ASK YOUR DOCTOR

- What are the indications that biofeedback would be a useful treatment approach for my condition?
- What kind of results can be determined with biofeedback treatment?
- How long will biofeedback treatment take?
- Will insurance cover biofeedback treatment?

Preparation

Biofeedback is most successful when individuals are motivated to learn. It is useful for people who have difficulty relaxing, even when they make efforts to do so. A receptive and open attitude, or "passive volition," is important for attaining desired responses rather than actively focusing on attaining them. It is important that individuals are willing to practice regularly at home to apply the skill to everyday life. Establishing a foundation of trust and confidence in the health care professional is an important component of biofeedback training.

Before beginning biofeedback training, an initial consultation is conducted to record medical history, treatment background, and biofeedback goals. The procedure is explained to provide a clear understanding of how and why the training can be helpful. The individual may be shown the equipment and told where the electrodes will be placed and how they work.

Before electrodes are placed on the body, the skin surface must be adequately prepared by using alcohol preparation pads to remove oils, makeup, and dead skin cells that may interfere with the biofeedback signal. An electrode paste is then applied to the sensor, or a small adhesive pad may be used to attach the sensor to the skin. Heart rate, temperature, and GSR monitors may be placed on the fingertip with a Velcro or elastic band. With CAP, the tip of a small, flexible, plastic tube is positioned in the nostril using tape. An individual may be taught several forms of biofeedback initially, and then the training may be tailored to the individual's preference.

The biofeedback trainer must have technical skill, an understanding of basic anatomy and physiology, knowledge of various conditions, and familiarity with computer hardware and software. The **American Psychological Association** views biofeedback as a proficiency area—master's and doctoral level training programs are available through a variety of sources, and certification is available through the Biofeedback Certification Institute of America.

Aftercare

There is no aftercare for biofeedback. Individuals apply what they learn during the sessions, and in this way, they help control their responses to stressors.

Risks

There are no known side effects with properly administered biofeedback.

Resources

BOOKS

Cade, Maxwell C., and Nona Coxhead. *The Awakened Mind: Biofeedback and the Development of Higher States of Awareness.* New York: Element Books, 2011.

Coben, Robert, and James R. Evans, eds. *Neurofeedback and Neuromodulation Techniques and Applications.* San Diego, CA: Academic Press, 2010.

Kotsirilos, Vicki, et al. *A Guide to Evidence-based Integrative and Complementary Medicine.* New York: Churchill Livingstone, 2011.

Miller, Eric B. *Bio-Guided Music Therapy: A Practitioner's Guide to the Clinical Integration of Music and Biofeedback.* Philadelphia: Jessica Kingsley, 2011.

Robbins, Jim. *A Symphony in the Brain: The Evolution of the New Brain Wave Biofeedback.* New York: Grove Press, 2008.

Swingle, Paul G. *Biofeedback for the Brain: How Neurotherapy Effectively Treats Depression, ADHD, Autism, and More.* Piscataway, NJ: Rutgers University Press, 2008.

ORGANIZATIONS

Association for Applied Psychotherapy and Biofeedback, 10200 W 44th Ave., Ste. 304, Wheat Ridge, CO, 80033, (303) 422-8436, (800) 477-8892, aapb@resourcecenter.com, http://www.aapb.org.

Biofeedback Certification International Alliance, 10200 W 44th Ave., Ste. 310, Wheat Ridge, CO, 80033, (303) 420-2902, (866) 908-8713, Fax: (303) 422-8894, info@bcia.org, http://www.bcia.org.

Joneis Thomas, PhD
Laura Jean Cataldo, RN, EdD

Biperiden

Definition

Biperiden is classified as an antiparkinsonian agent. It is sold in the United States under the brand name of Akineton.

Purpose

Biperiden is used to treat a group of side effects (called parkinsonian side effects) that includes tremors, difficulty walking, and slack muscle tone. These side effects may occur in patients who are taking antipsychotic medications used to treat mental disorders such as **schizophrenia**.

Description

Some medicines used to treat schizophrenia and other mental disorders, called antipsychotic drugs, can cause side effects that are similar to the symptoms of Parkinson's disease. The patient does not have Parkinson's disease may experience similar symptoms, including shaking in muscles while at rest, difficulty with voluntary movements, and poor muscle tone.

One way to eliminate these undesirable side effects is to stop taking the antipsychotic medicine. Unfortunately, the symptoms of the original mental disorder usually come back, so in most cases simply stopping the antipsychotic medication is not a reasonable option. Some drugs such as biperiden that control the symptoms of Parkinson's disease also control the parkinsonian side effects of antipsychotic medicines.

Biperiden works by restoring the chemical balance between **dopamine** and acetylcholine, two neurotransmitter chemicals in the **brain**. Taking biperiden along with the antipsychotic medicine helps to control symptoms of the mental disorder, while reducing parkinsonian side effects. Biperiden is in the same family of drugs (commonly known as anticholinergic drugs) as **benztropine**, **amantadine**, and **trihexyphenidyl**.

Recommended dosage

Biperiden is available in 2 mg tablets. For the treatment of tremor, poor muscle tone, and other parkinsonian side effects, the dose of biperiden is 2 mg orally taken one to three times daily. The side effects caused by antipsychotic drugs may come and go, so biperiden may not be needed on a regular basis. Biperiden may also be prescribed to prevent these side effects before they actually occur. This is called as prophylactic (preventative) therapy.

Precautions

Biperiden should never be used in children under age three. It should be used cautiously and with close physician supervision in older children and in the elderly. Biperiden, like all anticholinergic drugs, decreases sweating and the body's ability to cool itself. People who are unaccustomed to being outside in hot weather should take care to stay as cool as possible and drink extra fluids. People who are chronically ill, have a central nervous system disease, or who work outside during hot weather may need to avoid taking biperiden.

People who have the following medical problems may experience increased negative side effects when taking biperiden. Anyone with these problems should discuss their condition with their physician before starting the drug:

- glaucoma, especially closed-angle glaucoma
- intestinal obstruction
- prostate enlargement
- urinary bladder obstruction

Although rare, some patients experience euphoria while taking biperiden and may abuse it for this reason. Euphoria can occur at doses only two to four times the normal daily dose. Patients with a history of drug abuse should be observed carefully for biperiden abuse.

Side effects

Although biperiden helps control the side effects of antipsychotic drugs, it can produce side effects of its own. A person taking biperiden may have some of the following side effects, which may vary in intensity:

- dry mouth
- dry skin
- blurred vision
- nausea or vomiting
- constipation
- disorientation
- drowsiness
- irritability
- increased heart rate
- urinary retention

Dry mouth, if severe to the point of causing difficulty in speaking or swallowing, may be managed by dosage reduction or temporary discontinuation of the drug. Chewing sugarless gum or sucking on sugarless candy may also help to increase the flow of saliva. Some artificial saliva products may give temporary relief.

Men with prostate enlargement may be especially prone to urinary retention. Symptoms of this problem include having difficulty starting a urine flow and more difficulty passing urine than usual. This side effect may be severe and require discontinuation of the drug. Urinary retention may require catheterization. People who think they may be experiencing any side effects from this or any other medication should tell their physicians.

KEY TERMS

Acetylcholine—A naturally occurring chemical in the body that transmits nerve impulses from cell to cell. It causes blood vessels to dilate, lowers blood pressure, and slows the heartbeat. Central nervous system well-being is dependent on a balance among the neurotransmitters acetylcholine, dopamine, serotonin, and norepinephrine.

Anticholinergic—Related to the ability of a drug to block the nervous system chemical acetylcholine. When acetylcholine is blocked, patients often experience dry mouth and skin, increased heart rate, blurred vision, and difficulty urinating. In severe cases, blocking acetylcholine may cloud thinking and cause delirium.

Catheterization—Placing a tube in the bladder so that it can be emptied of urine.

Dopamine—A chemical in brain tissue that serves to transmit nerve impulses (a neurotransmitter) and helps to regulate movement and emotions.

Neurotransmitter—A chemical in the brain that transmits messages between neurons, or nerve cells.

Parkinsonian—Related to symptoms associated with Parkinson's disease, a nervous system disorder characterized by abnormal muscle movement of the tongue, face, and neck; inability to walk or move quickly; walking in a shuffling manner; restlessness; and/or tremors.

Patients who take an overdose of biperiden are treated with forced vomiting, removal of stomach contents and stomach washing, activated charcoal, and respiratory support if needed. They are also given physostigmine, an antidote for anticholinergic drug poisoning.

Interactions

When drugs such as biperiden are taken with **antidepressants** such as **amitriptyline**, **imipramine**, **trimipramine**, **desipramine**, **nortriptyline**, **protriptyline**, **amoxapine**, and **doxepin**, as well as with many antihistamines that also have anticholinergic properties, the effects of biperiden are usually intensified.

Drugs such as biperiden decrease the speed with which food moves through the stomach and intestines. Because of this, it is possible that the absorption of some drugs may be enhanced by biperiden. Patients receiving biperiden should be observed for unusual responses to other drugs they might be taking.

Resources

BOOKS

American Society of Health-System Pharmacists. *AHFS Drug Information 2008*. Bethesda, MD: American Society of Health-System Pharmacists, 2008.

DeVane, C. Lindsay, Pharm.D. "Drug Therapy for Mood Disorders." In *Fundamentals of Monitoring Psychoactive Drug Therapy*. Baltimore: Williams and Wilkins, 1990.

Jack Raber, Pharm.D.

Biphetamine *see* **Amphetamines**

Bipolar disorder

Definition

Bipolar disorder, formerly known as manic **depression**, is a psychiatric disorder characterized by severe and unusual changes in energy level, mood, and interactions with others. The mood swings associated with bipolar disorder are unpredictable and range from mania (elevated or irritable mood) to depression (a mood characterized by loss of interest and sadness). Bipolar disorder causes significant impairment in social, occupational, and general functioning.

Demographics

According to the National Institutes of Mental Health (NIMH), in 2008 the lifetime prevalence rate of bipolar disorder in the United States was 1%–1.6%. Other statistics suggest that 1.0% of the population has bipolar disorder type I, and 1.1% of the population has bipolar disorder type II. About another 2.4%–4.7% of the population has subthreshold bipolar disorder, meaning that these individuals show characteristics of the disorder but do not rise to the level of formal **diagnosis**. Internationally, the lifetime prevalence of reported bipolar disorder ranges from 0.3%–1.5%.

No racial differences in distribution exist. While bipolar type I occurs equally in both sexes, bipolar II and rapid-cycling bipolar disorder are more common in females than in males. The average age of onset of bipolar disorder is 25; however, about 1% of adolescents and 0.2%–0.4% of children have been diagnosed with the bipolar disorder. Controversy exists about diagnosing the disorder in these groups. Because of the complexity of the disorder, a correct diagnosis can be delayed, and between 20%–30% of adults with bipolar disorder report having had undiagnosed symptoms in childhood or adolescence.

Description

Bipolar disorder is characterized by alternating manic episodes, in which the individual feels abnormally euphoric, optimistic, and energetic, and depressive periods, in which the individual feels sad, hopeless, guilty, and sometimes suicidal. Manic or depressive periods may last for days, weeks, or months and run the spectrum from mild to severe. These episodes may be separated by periods of emotional stability during which the individual functions normally.

Bipolar I disorder is characterized by at least one **manic episode** without a major depressive episode. Manic episodes are the "high" of the manic-depressive cycle. A person experiencing a manic episode often has feelings of self-importance, elation, talkativeness, increased sociability, and a desire to embark on goal-oriented activities, coupled with the characteristics of irritability, impatience, impulsiveness, hyperactivity, and a decreased need for sleep. Usually this manic period is followed by a period of severe depression, although a few individuals may not experience a major depressive episode. Mixed states, where both manic or hypomanic symptoms and depressive symptoms occur at the same time, also may occur (e.g., the racing thoughts of mania with the listlessness of depression). Dysphoric mania, characterized by anger and irritability, is common, particularly in adolescents.

Bipolar II disorder is characterized by major depressive episodes alternating with episodes of **hypomania**, a milder form of mania. A bipolar depressive episode may be difficult to distinguish from a unipolar major depressive episode. Patients with bipolar depression tend to have extremely low energy, slowed mental and physical processes, and more profound **fatigue** (for example, **hypersomnia**, a sleep disorder marked by a need for excessive sleep or sleepiness when awake) than people with unipolar depression.

Cyclothymia refers to the cycling of hypomanic episodes with less severe depression that does not reach major depressive proportions. Some people with cyclothymia develop bipolar I or II disorder later in life.

A phenomenon known as rapid cycling occurs in up to 20% of bipolar individuals. In rapid cycling, at least four manic and depressive moods swings must occur within 12 months. In some cases of ultra-rapid cycling, the individual may bounce between manic and depressive states several times within a 24-hour period. This condition is very hard to distinguish from mixed states.

Risk factors

According to the Mayo Clinic, 60% of bipolar cases have a family history of the disease. The Child and

Adolescent Bipolar Foundation (CABF) reports that the risk for a child of one bipolar parent to develop the disorder is 15%–30%. If both parents have bipolar disorder, the risk for each child increases to 50%–75%. The risk in siblings and fraternal twins is 15%–25%. The risk in identical twins, who share the same genes, is approximately 70%. Research in identical twins indicates that both genes and other factors play a role in developing bipolar disorder.

Women who have given birth may also be at increased risk of developing subsequent episodes in the immediate period after giving birth.

Causes and symptoms

Causes

Although the source of bipolar disorder has not been clearly identified, a number of genetic and environmental factors appear to be involved in triggering episodes. Bipolar disorder has an inherited component, as children who have at least one parent with bipolar disorder are more likely to develop the disorder. Several studies have uncovered possible genetic connections to the predisposition for bipolar disorder. A large study done in Sweden reported in 2009 that **schizophrenia** and bipolar disorder appeared to share similar genetic causes.

No specific gene mutations have been identified that consistently show up in bipolar patients. However, there appears to be a potential genetic correlation between bipolar disorder and mutations in specific regions of chromosomes 13, 18, and 21. The building blocks of genes, called nucleotides, are normally arranged in a specific order and quantity. If these nucleotides are repeated in a redundant fashion, a genetic abnormality often results. Some evidence exists for an abnormal type of nucleotide sequence (CAG/CTG repeats) on chromosome 18 in patients with bipolar II disorder. However, not all bipolar patients have this mutation, and the presence of this sequence does not worsen the disorder or change the age of onset.

People with bipolar disorder tend to have other psychiatric disorders. **Oppositional defiant disorder** (ODD) and **attention deficit hyperactivity disorder** (ADHD) are among the most common. Over half of patients diagnosed with bipolar disorder have a history of **substance abuse**. A high rate of association exists between **cocaine** abuse and bipolar disorder. The emotional and physical highs and lows of cocaine use correspond to the manic depression cycle of the bipolar patient, making the disorder difficult to diagnose.

For some bipolar patients, manic and depressive episodes coincide with seasonal changes. Depressive episodes are typical during winter and fall, and manic episodes are more probable in the spring and summer months.

Brain imaging studies suggest that there are physical changes in the brains of people with bipolar disorder. It is hypothesized that **dopamine** and other **neurotransmitters** involved in mood may be involved. The possible role of hormonal imbalances in bipolar disorder is another area of investigation. Further research is needed to determine which genes are involved in bipolar disorder. It is likely that both genetic and environmental factors contribute to the disease.

Symptoms

Bipolar disorder causes recurrent dramatic mood swings that range from manic highs to depressive lows. There are often periods of normal mood in between episodes of mania and depression. Severe changes in energy and behavior accompany the swings in mood.

Manic episode symptoms include:

- increased energy, activity, and restlessness
- excessively high, euphoric mood
- extreme irritability and reactivity
- racing thoughts and fast speech that jump from one topic to another, known as a flight of ideas
- distractibility due to unimportant events and the inability to concentrate
- low perceived need for sleep
- unrealistic beliefs in personal abilities, powers, or importance
- poor judgment and impulsive behaviors
- increased sexual drive
- provocative, intrusive, or aggressive behavior
- denial that anything is wrong

Depressive episode symptoms include:

- persistent sad, anxious, or empty mood
- feelings of irritability, hopelessness, or negative mood
- feelings of guilt, worthlessness, or helplessness
- inability to take pleasure in activities
- fatigue
- inability to concentrate
- poor judgment
- extreme sleep patterns
- extreme appetite changes that result in weight change
- chronic pain or physical discomfort in the absence of physical illness or injury
- thoughts or attempts of suicide

Some people with bipolar II disorder have depressive episodes concurrent with mood reactivity and can switch from depression to hypomania. Hypomania is characterized by a mild or moderate level of mania. Because hypomania is less severe, it may be associated with increased functioning and enhanced productivity. However, hypomania is not a normal state of mind. Without proper treatment, hypomania may eventually progress into severe mania or switch into depression. Severe episodes of mania or depression may also include symptoms of **psychosis**. Psychotic symptoms include visual or auditory hallucinations and **delusions** (illogical and false but strongly held beliefs). Psychotic symptoms in bipolar disorder tend to reflect the current extreme mood episode. During mania, psychotic delusions may include grandiosity, such as believing one has special powers of flight or extreme financial wealth or power. During depressive episodes, delusions may include paranoid fears of being poisoned or the belief that one has committed a terrible crime. Because of these psychotic symptoms, bipolar disorder is sometimes mistaken for schizophrenia.

Some people with bipolar disorder display a mixed state of symptoms. A mixed bipolar state is characterized by symptoms of agitation, sleeplessness, appetite changes, psychosis, and suicidal tendencies. A depressed and hopeless mood may occur in conjunction with extreme energy. Signs of bipolar disorder may also be demonstrated outside of mental illness symptoms in behaviors such as alcohol or drug abuse, poor work performance, strained interpersonal relationships, or excessive promiscuity. Symptoms of bipolar disorder with postpartum onset usually occur within four weeks following childbirth. Bipolar disorder with a seasonal pattern displays symptoms related to seasonal change and latitude. The prevalence of the season-specific bipolar symptoms increases with higher latitudes and winter months.

Bipolar symptoms often present differently in children and adolescents. Manic episodes in these age groups are typically characterized by more psychotic features than in adults, which may lead to a misdiagnosis of schizophrenia. Children and adolescents also tend toward irritability and aggressiveness instead of elation. Further, symptoms tend to be chronic (ongoing) rather than acute (episodic). Bipolar children are easily distracted, impulsive, and hyperactive, which can lead to a misdiagnosis of ADHD. Furthermore, their aggression often leads to violence, which may be misdiagnosed as a **conduct disorder**. Complicating the picture is the fact that ADHD and conduct disorders are often present concurrently in children with bipolar disorder.

School problems are frequently encountered in children and adolescents with bipolar disorder. Teachers, **social workers**, and counselors who are knowledgeable about bipolar disorder and familiar with its symptoms can be helpful in describing behaviors seen in the classroom to parents and clinicians so that appropriate evaluation, diagnosis, and **intervention** may be determined. Modifications in portions of the daily schedule and some academic accommodations for this population may be helpful in the school environment.

KEY TERMS

Cyclothymia—A milder form of bipolar disorder characterized by alternating hypomania and less severe depressive episodes.

Dopamine—A neurotransmitter and the precursor of norepinephrine.

Neuroprotective—Conveying some form of protection to the nervous system from injury.

Neurotransmitter—One of a group of chemicals secreted by a nerve cell (neuron) to carry a chemical message to another nerve cell, often as a way of transmitting a nerve impulse. Examples of neurotransmitters include acetylcholine, dopamine, serotonin, and norepinephrine.

Nucleotides—Building blocks of genes, which are arranged in specific order and quantity.

Off-label use—The use of a prescription medication to treat conditions outside the indications approved by the U.S. Food and Drug Administration (FDA). It is legal for physicians to administer these drugs, but it is not legal for pharmaceutical companies to advertise drugs for off-label uses.

Rapid cycling—Four or more manic, hypomanic, mixed, or depressive episodes within a 12-month period.

Schizophrenia—A severe mental disorder in which a person loses touch with reality and has illogical thoughts, delusions, hallucinations, behavioral problems, and other disturbances.

Selective serotonin reuptake inhibitors (SSRIs)—A class of antidepressants that works by blocking the reabsorption of serotonin in brain cells, raising the level of the chemical in the brain. SSRIs include fluoxetine (Prozac) and sertraline hydrochloride (Zoloft).

Diagnosis

Bipolar disorder usually is diagnosed and treated by a **psychiatrist** and/or a **psychologist** with medical assistance. In addition to an interview, several clinical inventories or scales may be used to assess the patient's mental status and determine the presence of bipolar symptoms. These include the Millon Clinical Multiaxial Inventory III (MCMI-III), **Minnesota Multiphasic Personality Inventory** II (MMPI-2), the Internal State Scale (ISS), the Self-Report Manic Inventory (SRMI), and the Young Mania Rating Scale (YMRS). The tests are verbal and/or written and are administered in both hospital and outpatient settings. Taking a detailed family history is also important in making the diagnosis of bipolar disorder because it often runs in families. Laboratory tests for drug and **alcohol use** may be done to rule out other causes of the behavior.

Psychologists and psychiatrists typically use the criteria listed in the ***Diagnostic and Statistical Manual of Mental Disorders*** (*DSM*) published by the **American Psychiatric Association** to definitively diagnose bipolar disorder. The *DSM* describes a manic episode as an abnormally elevated (or elevated and irritable mood) lasting a period of at least one week that is distinguished by at least three of the mania symptoms. If the mood of the patient is irritable and not elevated, four of the symptoms are required.

Although some clinicians find the criteria too rigid, a hypomanic diagnosis requires a duration of at least four days with at least three of the symptoms indicated for manic episodes (four if mood is irritable and not elevated). The *DSM* notes that unlike manic episodes, hypomanic episodes do not cause a marked impairment in social or occupational functioning, do not require **hospitalization**, and do not have psychotic features. In addition, because hypomanic episodes are characterized by high energy and goal-directed activities, often resulting in a positive outcome and perceived in a positive manner by the patient (e.g., as a time of heightened creativity or work output), bipolar II disorder can go undiagnosed.

Substance abuse, thyroid disease, and use of prescription or over-the-counter medication can mask or mimic the presence of bipolar disorder. In cases of substance abuse, the patient must undergo a period of **detoxification** and abstinence before a mood disorder is diagnosed and treatment begins.

Treatment

Treatment for bipolar disorder relies primarily on prescribed drugs, though psychotherapy and other treatments may be administered in conjunction with medication.

Drugs

Medication is the most effective treatment for bipolar disorder. A combination of mood-stabilizing agents, **antidepressants**, antipsychotics, and anticonvulsants may be used for long-term regulation of manic and depressive episodes. In the acute phase, the choice of medication for bipolar disorder is dependent on the stage or type of current episode. Many drugs are used to treat an acute manic episode, primarily the antipsychotics and **benzodiazepines** (e.g., **lorazepam**, **clonazepam**). In the presence of psychotic symptoms, atypical antipsychotics may be used to treat psychotic symptoms and acute mania and contribute to mood stabilization. For depressive episodes, antidepressants may be used. Medications may be added temporarily to treat episodes of mania or depression that break through despite mood-stabilizer treatment.

Mood-stabilizing drugs dampen the extremes of manic and depressive episodes. Lithium (Cibalith-S, Eskalith, Lithane, Lithobid, Lithonate, Lithotabs) was the first mood stabilizer approved by the U.S. Food and Drug Administration (FDA) for the treatment of mania and the prevention of both manic and depressive episodes. Lithium is a first-line medication used in the long-term preventative treatment of extreme mood episodes in bipolar disorder. It has been demonstrated to play a neuroprotective role in brain function. Because lithium takes up to ten days to reach a therapeutic level in the bloodstream, it sometimes is prescribed in conjunction with neuroleptics and/or benzodiazepines to provide more immediate relief of a manic episode. Lithium also has been shown to be effective in regulating bipolar depression, but it is not recommended for mixed mania. Lithium may not be an effective long-term treatment option for rapid cyclers, who typically develop a tolerance for it or may not respond to it. Possible side effects of the drug include weight gain, thirst, nausea, and hand tremors. Prolonged lithium use also may cause hyperthyroidism (a disorder in which the thyroid is overactive, which may cause heart palpitations, nervousness, the presence of goiter, sweating, and a wide array of other symptoms) and abnormalities in liver function.

In addition to lithium, the following drugs are commonly used to treat bipolar disorders:

- Carbamazepine (Tegretol, Atretol) is an anticonvulsant drug often prescribed in conjunction with other mood-stabilizing agents. The drug may be used to treat bipolar patients who have not responded well to lithium therapy. Blurred vision and abnormal eye movement are two possible side effects of carbamazepine therapy.
- Divalproex sodium (Depakote) is one of the few drugs available that has been proven effective in treating

rapid cycling bipolar and mixed states patients. Valproate, an anticonvulsant, is prescribed alone or in combination with carbamazepine and/or lithium. Stomach cramps, indigestion, diarrhea, hair loss, appetite loss, nausea, and unusual weight loss or gain are some of the common side effects of valproate.

- Risperidone (Risperdal) may be used for short-term (usually no more than three weeks) treatment of acute mania associated with bipolar disorder. It may be given in conjunction with lithium or valproate. Side effects include weight gain, sedation, and abnormally low blood pressure upon rising from lying down (orthostatic hypotension).
- Quetiapine (Seroquel) is a newer antipsychotic that acts on neurotransmitters in the brain. It appears to have fewer side effects than some of the older antipsychotics.
- Olanzapine (Zyprexa, Zydis) may be used to treat acute manic episodes in individuals with bipolar I. Its mechanism of action is not clear. Side effects include orthostatic hypotension (low blood pressure when rising to a standing position).
- Symbyax, a combination of olanzapine and fluoxetine, was the first drug approved by the FDA specifically to treat bipolar disorder.

Because antidepressants may stimulate manic episodes in some bipolar patients, their use in bipolar disorder is controversial. Typically used as short-term treatment, antidepressants are not specifically approved for treating depression associated with bipolar disorder but may be prescribed off-label. **Selective serotonin reuptake inhibitors (SSRIs)** or, less often, **monoamine oxidase inhibitors** (MAO inhibitors) may be prescribed for episodes of bipolar depression. Tricyclic antidepressants used to treat unipolar depression may trigger rapid cycling in bipolar patients and are, therefore, not a preferred treatment option for bipolar depression.

Antidepressants commonly prescribed for bipolar disorder include:

- SSRIs such as fluoxetine (Prozac), sertraline (Zoloft), and paroxetine (Paxil). SSRIs treat depression by regulating levels of serotonin, a neurotransmitter. Anxiety, diarrhea, drowsiness, headache, sweating, nausea, sexual problems, and insomnia are all possible side effects of SSRIs.
- MAOIs such as tranylcypromine (Parnate) and phenelzine (Nardil). MAOIs block the action of monoamine oxidase (MAO), an enzyme in the central nervous system. Patients taking MAOIs must eliminate foods high in tyramine (found in aged cheeses and meats) from their diet to avoid hypotensive side effects.
- Bupropion (Wellbutrin), a heterocyclic antidepressant. The exact neurochemical mechanism of the drug is not known, but it has been effective in regulating bipolar depression in some patients. Side effects of bupropion include agitation, anxiety, confusion, tremor, dry mouth, fast or irregular heartbeat, headache, and insomnia.

Other drugs may be used in conjunction with a long-term pharmaceutical treatment plan:

- Long-acting benzodiazepines such as clonazepam (Klonopin) and alprazolam (Xanax) may be used for rapid treatment of manic symptoms to calm and sedate patients until mania or hypomania have waned and mood-stabilizing agents can take effect. Sedation is a common effect, and clumsiness, lightheadedness, and slurred speech are other possible side effects of benzodiazepines.
- Neuroleptics such as chlorpromazine (Thorazine) and haloperidol (Haldol) also may be used to control mania while a mood stabilizer such as lithium or valproate takes effect. Because neuroleptic side effects can be severe (difficulty in speaking or swallowing, paralysis of the eyes, loss of balance control, muscle spasms, severe restlessness, stiffness of arms and legs, tremors in fingers and hands, twisting movements of body, and weakness of arms and legs), benzodiazepines are generally preferred over neuroleptics.

Clozapine (Clozaril) is an atypical antipsychotic medication used to control manic episodes in patients who have not responded to typical mood stabilizing agents. The drug has also been a useful prophylactic, or preventative treatment, in some bipolar patients. Common side effects of clozapine are tachycardia (rapid heart rate), hypotension, constipation, and weight gain. Agranulocytosis, a potentially serious but reversible condition in which the white blood cells that typically fight infection in the body are destroyed, is a possible side effect of clozapine. Patients treated with the drug should undergo weekly blood tests to monitor white blood cell counts.

Many individuals suffer from **sleep deprivation** during the manic portion of bipolar disorder. When this occurs, chemical activity in the brain is altered, lowering the production of melatonin (a naturally occurring hormone important for stimulating sleep). Research is ongoing to look at the effects of melatonin in regulating the sleep-wake cycle for persons with bipolar disorder.

Treatment for children with bipolar disorder generally includes **psychotherapy** (including behavioral therapy and family-inclusive therapy) as well as medication therapy. Children may respond to psychiatric medication differently than adults do, so clinicians may choose to limit the dosage and duration of medication during which the child is monitored closely for medication benefits and side effects. Parents are often encouraged to note changes in behavior, mood, and sleep patterns of their child to aid in evaluation of medications and psychotherapy. In addition, psychologists and psychiatrists generally work closely with parents and the child to educate them about the illness.

Electroconvulsive therapy

Electroconvulsive therapy (ECT) has been successful in treating both unipolar and bipolar depression and mania. However, ECT usually is employed after all pharmaceutical treatment options have been explored in patients with severe depression and suicidal thoughts. ECT is given under anesthesia, and patients are given a muscle relaxant medication to prevent convulsions. The treatment consists of a series of electrical pulses that move into the brain through electrodes on the patient's head. Although the exact mechanisms behind the success of ECT therapy are not known, it is believed that this electrical current alters the electrochemical processes of the brain, consequently relieving depression. Headaches, muscle soreness, nausea, and confusion are possible side effects immediately following an ECT procedure. Temporary memory loss has also been reported in ECT patients. In bipolar patients, ECT is often used in conjunction with drug therapy.

Psychosocial interventions

Psychosocial interventions include both patient education and psychotherapy. It is important for patients to receive social support and illness management skills. Family and friends must be aware of the high rates of social dysfunction and marital discord. Involvement in national **support groups** is advisable (e.g., Depression and Bipolar Support Alliance, National Alliance on Mental Illness).

Psychoeducation usually focuses on all of the following:

- assessment of parameters that will have an impact on the outcome of patient's disease
- implementation of boundaries and requirements of treatment
- implementation of a personal cost-benefit analysis concerning specific treatment directions
- implementation of a follow-up program
- implementation of future directions, which may include adjustment or change interventions

Genetic counseling should be included in **family education** programs since the predisposition for this disorder has been genetically proven to increase among first-degree relatives.

Alternative and complementary treatment

Alternative treatments for bipolar disorder generally are used as complementary treatments to conventional therapies. General recommendations for controlling bipolar symptoms include maintaining a calm environment, avoiding over stimulation, getting plenty of rest and regular **exercise**, and eating a healthy diet.

Chinese herbs may help to soften mood swings. Traditional Chinese medicine (TCM) remedies are prescribed based on the patient's overall constitution and the presentation of symptoms. These remedies can help to stabilize moods, not just treat swings in mood. A TCM practitioner might recommend a mixture called the Iron Filings Combination, which includes the Chinese herbs asparagus, ophiopogon, fritillaria, arisaema, orange peel, polygala, acorus, forsythia, hoelen, fu-shen, scrophularia, uncaria stem, salvia, and iron filings to treat certain types of mania in the bipolar patient. There are other formulas for depression. A trained practitioner should guide all of these remedies.

Acupuncture can be used to help maintain a more even temperament.

Biofeedback is effective in helping some patients control such symptoms as irritability, poor self control, racing thoughts, and sleep problems.

A diet low in vanadium, a mineral found in meats and other foods, and high in vitamin C may be helpful in reducing depression.

Individuals using herbal remedies in addition to traditional pharmaceuticals should tell their physician, as some herbal remedies interact with conventional drugs, either heightening or depressing their effect. Recommended herbal remedies to ease depressive episodes may include damania (*Turnera diffusa*), **ginseng** (*Panax ginseng*), kola (*Cola nitida*), lady's slipper (*Cypripedium calceolus*), **lavender** (*Lavandula angustifolia*), lime blossom (*Tilia x vulgaris*), oats (*Avena sativa*), rosemary (*Rosmarinus officinalis*), skullcap (*Scutellaria laterifolia*), **St. John's wort** (*Hypericum perforatum*), **valerian** (*Valeriana officinalis*), and vervain (*Verbena officinalis*).

Prognosis

While most patients show some positive response to treatment, response varies widely, from full recovery to a complete lack of response to all drug and/or ECT therapy. Drug therapies frequently need adjustment to achieve the maximum benefit for the patient. Bipolar disorder is a chronic, recurrent illness in over 90% of

QUESTIONS TO ASK YOUR DOCTOR

- How will the prescribed medications help me?
- When should I take the medications? Should I take them with food?
- What if I miss a dose?
- What are the possible side effects of these medications and what can be done about them?
- How long before the medications take effect and what types of improvement should I expect?
- Are there specific risks to these medications?
- Can I choose to discontinue the medications?
- Are there foods, other medications, supplements, or activities that I should avoid?
- How will my other medical conditions affect the treatment?
- Are there dietary, physical activity, or lifestyle changes that might help with my bipolar episodes?
- Are there alternative treatments for bipolar disorder?
- What type of psychotherapy might useful?
- Are there support groups available for bipolar disorder?

people with the disorder. The disorder requires lifelong observation and treatment after diagnosis. According to the World Health Organization, bipolar disorder is the sixth-leading cause of disability worldwide.

Suicide is the major complication of bipolar disorder and is related to the duration of the depressive episode. Some 25%–50% of individuals with bipolar disorder attempt suicide, and 11% complete the suicide attempt. The longer the depressive episode lasts, the higher the risk of suicidal tendencies. Alcoholics and patients with other chronic medical diseases are particularly prone to planning and implementing a suicide attempt.

The groups of individuals most likely to carry out a suicide attempt are:

- individuals overwhelmed by life problems (attempts in this group tend to be related to aggression and impulsive behaviors, not depressive episodes)
- individuals attempting to control others
- individuals with a chronic medical illness
- individuals with other severe types of psychotic illness, delusions, or paranoia
- individuals with a concurrent substance abuse problem

Prevention

The ongoing medical management of bipolar disorder is critical to preventing **relapse**, or recurrence, of manic episodes. Even in carefully controlled treatment programs, bipolar patients may experience recurring episodes of the disorder. Patient education in the form of psychotherapy or **self-help groups** is crucial for training bipolar patients to recognize signs of mania and depression and to take an active part in their treatment program.

Resources

BOOKS

American Psychiatric Association. *Diagnostic and Statistical Manual of Mental Disorders.* 4th ed., text rev. Washington, DC: American Psychiatric Association, 2000.

American Psychological Association. *Publication Manual of the American Psychological Association,* 6th ed. Washington, DC: American Psychological Association, 2009.

Fast, Julie A. *Loving Someone with Bipolar Disorder: Understanding and Helping Your Partner,* 2nd ed. Oakland, CA: New Harbinger, 2012.

Haycock, Dean. *The Everything Health Guide to Adult Bipolar Disorder,* 2nd ed. Avon, MA: Adams Media, 2010.

Mondimore, Francis M. *Bipolar Disorder: A Guide for Patients and Families,* 2nd ed. Baltimore: Johns Hopkins University Press, 2006.

Otto, Michael, et al. *Living with Bipolar Disorder.* New York: Oxford University Press, 2011.

WEBSITES

"Bipolar Disorder." *MedlinePlus.* Last updated September 23, 2011. http://www.nlm.nih.gov/medlineplus/bipolardisorder.html (accessed October 3, 2011).

"Bipolar Disorder." *National Institute of Mental Health.* http://www.nimh.nih.gov/health/topics/bipolar-disorder/index.shtml (accessed October 3, 2011).

ORGANIZATIONS

American Academy of Child and Adolescent Psychiatry, 3615 Wisconsin Ave. NW, Washington, DC, 20016-3007, (202) 966-7300, Fax: (202) 966-2891, http://aacap.org.

American Psychiatric Association, 1000 Wilson Blvd., Ste. 1825, Arlington, VA, 22209-3901, (703) 907-7300, apa@psych.org, http://www.psych.org.

American Psychological Association, 750 1st St., NE, Washington, DC, 20002-4242, (202) 336-5500; TDD/TTY: (202) 336-6123, (800) 374-2721, http://www.apa.org.

Child & Adolescent Bipolar Foundation, 820 Davis St., Suite 520, Evanston, IL, 60201, info@thebalancedmind.org, http://www.thebalancedmind.org.

Depression and Bipolar Support Alliance, 730 N Franklin St., Ste. 501, Chicago, IL, 60654-7225, (800) 826-3632, Fax: (312) 642-7243, http://www.dbsalliance.org.

Mental Health America, 2000 N Beauregard St., 6th Fl., Alexandria, VA, 22311, (703) 684-7722, (800) 969-6642, Fax: (703) 684-5968, http://www.nmha.org.

National Alliance on Mental Illness, 3803 N Fairfax Dr., Ste. 100, Arlington, VA, 22203, (703) 524-7600, http://www.nami.org.

National Institute of Mental Health, 6001 Executive Blvd., Rm. 8184, MSC 9663, Bethesda, MD, 20892-9663, (301) 433-4513; TTY: (301) 443-8431, Fax: (301) 443-4279, (866) 615-6464; TTY: (866) 415-8051, nimhinfo@nih.gov, http://www.nimh.nih.gov.

National Institutes of Health, 9000 Rockville Pike, Bethesda, MD, 20892, (301) 496-4000; TTY: (301) 402-9612, http://www.nih.gov.

Maria Basile, PhD
Laura Jean Cataldo, RN, EdD

Body dysmorphic disorder

Definition

Body dysmorphic disorder (BDD) is defined by the **American Psychiatric Association** in its ***Diagnostic and Statistical Manual of Mental Disorders*** *(DSM)* as a condition marked by excessive preoccupation with an imaginary or minor defect in a facial feature or localized part of the body. The diagnostic criteria specify that the condition must be sufficiently severe to cause a decline in the patient's social, occupational, or educational functioning. The most common cause of this decline is the time lost to obsessing about the "defect." Proposed changes for the fifth edition of the *DSM* (*DSM-5*, 2013) include moving BDD to the category of obsessive-compulsive and related disorders. Previously, BDD was classified as a somatoform disorder—disorders characterized by physical complaints that appear to be medical in origin but that cannot be explained in terms of a physical disease, the results of **substance abuse**, or by another mental disorder.

Although cases of BDD have been reported in the psychiatric literature from a number of different countries for over a century, the disorder was first defined as a formal diagnostic category by the *DSM-III-R* in 1987. The word "dysmorphic" comes from two Greek words: *dys*, which means "bad" or "ugly," and *morphos*, which means "shape" or "form." BDD was previously known as dysmorphophobia.

Demographics

BDD is thought to affect 1%–2% of the population in the United States and Canada, although some doctors think that it is underdiagnosed because it coexists so often with **depression** and other disorders. In addition, individuals are often ashamed of grooming rituals and other behaviors associated with BDD and may avoid telling their doctor about them.

The usual age of onset of BDD is late childhood or early adolescence; the average age of individuals diagnosed with the disorder is 17, although the disorder may develop in older individuals who become preoccupied with the physical effects of aging. The disorder affects men and women equally, but there are no reliable data regarding racial or ethnic differences in the incidence of the disorder. BDD has a high rate of comorbidity, which means that people diagnosed with the disorder are likely to be diagnosed with another psychiatric disorder, most commonly major depression, **social phobia**, or **obsessive-compulsive disorder** (OCD). About half of all men (but not women) diagnosed with BDD also have a substance abuse disorder. About 29% of individuals with BDD eventually try to commit **suicide**.

Description

BDD is characterized by an unusually exaggerated degree of worry or concern about a specific part of the face or body (such as the nose or breasts), rather than the general size or shape of the body. It is distinguished from **anorexia nervosa** and **bulimia nervosa**, where patients are preoccupied with their overall weight and body shape. Studies have found that between 40% and 76% of people with BDD seek nonpsychiatric treatments such as cosmetic surgery or dermatological treatments, and the rates of people with BDD among all cosmetic surgery patients range from 7% to 15%; rates are similar in dermatology practices.

Since the first publication of *DSM-IV* in 1994, some psychiatrists have suggested that a subtype of BDD exists, which they termed muscle dysmorphia. Muscle dysmorphia is marked by excessive concern with one's muscularity and/or fitness. Persons with muscle dysmorphia spend unusual amounts of time working out in gyms or exercising rather than obsessing about a feature such as the skin or nose. Muscle dysmorphia is more prevalent among males. To accommodate muscle dysmorphia as a classification, the *DSM-IV-TR* has added references regarding body build and excessive weightlifting to DSM-IV's description of BDD, and the proposed changes for *DSM-5* include muscle dysmorphia as a specifier in the diagnostic criteria for BDD. The muscle dysmorphia version of BDD is associated with higher suicide rates and higher rates of substance abuse.

BDD and muscle dysmorphia can both be described as disorders resulting from the patient's distorted **body image**. Body image refers to the mental picture individuals have of their outward appearance, including size, shape, and form. It has two major components: how people perceive their physical appearance and how they feel about their body. Significant distortions in self-perception can lead to intense body dissatisfaction and dysfunctional behaviors aimed at improving appearance. Some patients with BDD are aware that their concerns are excessive; others do not have this degree of insight. About 50% of patients diagnosed with BDD also meet the criteria for a **delusional disorder**, which is characterized by beliefs that are not based in reality. The *DSM-5* revised description of body dysmorphic disorder emphasizes that the individual performs repetitive behaviors such as mirror checking, skin picking, or comparing themselves to others. Learning to control these repetitive behaviors can be crucial to a BDD treatment plan.

Causes and symptoms

Causes

The causes of BDD fall into two major categories, neurobiological and psychosocial.

NEUROBIOLOGICAL CAUSES. Research indicates that patients diagnosed with BDD have **serotonin** levels that are lower than normal. Serotonin is a neurotransmitter—a chemical produced by the **brain** that helps to transmit nerve impulses across the junctions between nerve cells. Low serotonin levels are associated with depression and other mood disorders. However, because these studies are conducted after the person has been diagnosed with BDD, it is not possible to know whether the low serotonin levels cause the BDD or are an effect of the disorder.

PSYCHOSOCIAL CAUSES. A young person's family of origin has a powerful influence on his or her vulnerability to BDD. Children whose parents are themselves obsessed with appearance, dieting, and/or bodybuilding, or who are highly critical of their children's looks, are at greater risk of developing BDD.

An additional factor in some young people is a history of childhood **trauma** or abuse. Buried feelings about the abuse or traumatic incident emerge in the form of **obsession** about a part of the face or body. This "reassignment" of emotions from the unacknowledged true cause to another issue is called displacement. For example, an adolescent who frequently felt overwhelmed in childhood by physically abusive parents may develop a preoccupation with muscular strength and power.

Another important factor in the development of BDD is the influence of the mass media in developed countries, particularly the role of advertising in spreading images of supposedly physically perfect men and women. Impressionable children and adolescents absorb the message that anything short of physical perfection is unacceptable. They may then develop distorted perceptions of their own faces and bodies.

Symptoms

The central symptom of BDD is excessive concern with a specific facial feature or body part. The parts of the body most frequently involved are the skin, hair, nose, teeth, breasts, eyes, and even eyebrows, but any feature can be a focus of the obsession.

Other symptoms of body dysmorphic disorder include:

- Ritualistic behavior. Ritualistic behavior refers to actions that the patient performs to manage anxiety and that take up excessive amounts of his or her time. Patients are typically upset if someone or something interferes with or interrupts their ritual. In the context of BDD, ritualistic behaviors may include exercise or makeup routines, assuming specific poses or postures in front of a mirror, or skin picking (dermatillomania).
- Camouflaging the "problem" feature or body part with makeup, hats, or clothing. Camouflaging appears to be the single most common symptom among persons with BDD, occurring in 94% of patients.
- Abnormal behavior around mirrors, car bumpers, large windows, or other reflective surfaces. A majority of patients diagnosed with BDD frequently check their appearance in mirrors or spend long periods of time doing so. A minority, however, react in the opposite fashion and avoid mirrors whenever possible.
- Frequently requesting reassurance from others (related to appearance).
- Frequently comparing one's appearance to others.
- Avoiding activities outside the home, including school and social events.

BDD patients have high rates of self-destructive behavior, including performing surgery on themselves at home (liposuction followed by skin stapling, sawing down teeth, and removing facial scars with sandpaper) and attempted or completed suicide. Many are unable to remain in school, form healthy relationships, or keep steady jobs. In one group of 100 patients diagnosed with BDD, 48% had been hospitalized for psychiatric reasons, and 30% had made at least one suicide attempt.

The loss of functioning resulting from BDD can have serious consequences for the patient's future. Adolescents with BDD often cut school and may be reluctant to participate in sports, join church- or civic-sponsored youth groups, or hold part-time or summer jobs. One study found that 32% of participants had missed work for at least a week in the previous month because of their BDD, while 32% of those still in school had missed classes for a week. Adults with muscle dysmorphia have been known to turn down job promotions to have more time to work out in their gym or fitness center. The economic consequences of BDD also include overspending on cosmetics, clothing, or plastic surgery.

Diagnosis

The **diagnosis** of BDD in children and adolescents is often made by physicians in family practice, as they are more likely to have developed long-term relationships of trust with the patient. With adults, it is often specialists in dermatology, cosmetic dentistry, or plastic surgery who may suspect that the patient has BDD because of frequent requests for repeated or unnecessary procedures. The diagnosis is made on the basis of the patient's history together with the physician's observations of the patient's overall mood and conversation patterns. People with BDD often come across to others as generally anxious and worried. In addition, the patient's dress or clothing styles, if attempting to hide the "problem" feature, may suggest a diagnosis of BDD.

Several questionnaires are used for assessing the presence of BDD. Researchers sometimes use a semi-structured interview called the BDD Data Form to collect information about the disorder from patients. This form includes demographic information, information about body areas of concern and the history and course of the illness, and the patient's history of **hospitalization** or suicide attempts, if any. Another diagnostic questionnaire frequently used to identify BDD patients is the Structured Clinical Interview for DSM-III-R Disorders, or SCID-II. Other questionnaires used in assessments include the Yale-Brown Obsessive Compulsive Scale Modified for Body Dysmorphic Disorder and the Body Dysmorphic Disorder Examination.

There are no brain **imaging studies** or laboratory tests used to diagnose BDD. Some studies using brain imaging have identified some characteristics similar to those seen in obsessive-compulsive disorder, although studies are not in complete agreement on whether these findings are diagnostic of BDD.

Treatment

The standard treatment regimen for body dysmorphic disorder is a combination of medications and **psychotherapy**. Surgical, dental, or dermatologic treatments have been found ineffective and in some cases may exacerbate symptoms. In one study, cosmetic surgeons reported that 40% of their patients with BDD had made legal or physical threats against them.

Medications

The medications most frequently prescribed for patients with BDD are the **selective serotonin reuptake inhibitors (SSRIs)**, most commonly **fluoxetine** (Prozac) or **sertraline** (Zoloft). Other **SSRIs** that have been used with this group of patients include **fluvoxamine** (Luvox) and **paroxetine** (Paxil). Only fluoxetine is approved by the FDA for use in children; another SSRI, **escitalopram** (Lexapro), is approved for use in adolescents aged 12 and up.

The relatively high rate of positive responses to SSRIs among BDD patients led to the hypothesis that the disorder has a neurobiological component related to serotonin levels in the body. An associated finding is that patients with BDD require higher dosages of SSRI medications to be effective than patients who are being treated for depression with these drugs.

According to experts at the Mayo Clinic in Rochester, Minnesota, it is important for BDD patients to continue to take their medications even when they are feeling better, because symptoms may suddenly recur. It is also important to attend psychotherapy sessions consistently.

Psychotherapy

The most effective approach to psychotherapy with BDD patients is **cognitive-behavioral therapy**, of which cognitive restructuring is one component. Because the disorder is related to **delusions** about one's appearance, cognitive-oriented therapy that challenges inaccurate self-perceptions is more effective than purely supportive approaches. Relaxation techniques also work well with BDD patients when they are combined with cognitive restructuring.

Prognosis

The *DSM-IV-TR* notes that the disorder "has a fairly continuous course, with few symptom-free intervals, although the intensity of symptoms may wax and wane over time."

Prevention

Given the pervasive influence of the mass media in contemporary Western societies, the best preventive strategy involves challenging those afflicted with the disorder and who consequently have unrealistic images of attractive people. Parents, teachers, primary healthcare professionals, and other adults who work with young people can point out and discuss the pitfalls of trying to look "perfect." In addition, parents or other adults can educate themselves about BDD and its symptoms, and should pay attention to any warning signs in their children's dress or behavior. They also can modulate their own behaviors of pointing out or highlighting physical "imperfections" in themselves or in their children, because there is a link between parents with such concerns and children with BDD.

Resources

BOOKS

American Psychiatric Association. *Diagnostic and Statistical Manual of Mental Disorders.* 4th ed., Text rev. Washington, DC: American Psychiatric Association, 2000.

PERIODICALS

Carey, Paul, et al. "SPECT Imaging of Body Dysmorphic Disorder." *Journal of Neuropsychiatry Clinical Neuroscience* 16 (2004): 357–59.

Crerand, Canice E., et al. "Nonpsychiatric Medical Treatment of Body Dysmorphic Disorder." *Psychosomatics* 46 (2005): 549–55.

Hunt, T. J., O. Thienhaus, and A. Ellwood. "The Mirror Lies: Body Dysmorphic Disorder." *American Family Physician* 78, no. 2 (2008: 217–22.

Leone, James E., Edward J. Sedory, and Kimberly A. Gray. "Recognition and Treatment of Muscle Dysmorphia and Related Body Image Disorders." *Journal of Athletic Training* 40 (2005): 352–59.

Phillips, Katharine A., et al. "Demographic Characteristics, Phenomenology, Comorbidity, and Family History in 200 Individuals with Body Dysmorphic Disorder." *Psychosomatics* 46 (2005): 317–26.

Phillips, Katharine A., and S.L. McElroy. "Personality Disorders and Traits in Patients with Body Dysmorphic Disorder." *Comparative Psychiatry* 41 (2000): 229–36.

Pope, Courtney G., et al. "Clinical Features of Muscle Dysmorphia Among Males with Body Dysmorphic Disorder." *Body Image* 2 (2005): 395–400.

WEBSITES

Mayo Clinic staff. "Body Dysmorphic Disorder." MayoClinic.com. http://www.mayoclinic.com/health/body-dysmorphic-disorder/DS00559 (accessed December 16, 2011).

ORGANIZATIONS

American Academy of Child and Adolescent Psychiatry, 3615 Wisconsin Ave., NW, Washington, DC, 20016-3007, (202) 966-7300, Fax: (202) 966-2891, http://aacap.org.

American Psychological Association, 750 1st St., NE, Washington, DC, 20002-4242, (202) 336-5500; TDD/TTY: (202) 336-6123, (800) 374-2721, http://www.apa.org.

Rebecca Frey, PhD
Emily Jane Willingham, PhD
Heidi Splete

Body image

Definition

Body image is a mental opinion or description that individuals have of their own physical appearance. It is a subjective concept, based on comparisons to socially constructed standards or ideals. Perception of body image among people can range from very negative to very positive. Depending on age and other factors, the degree of concern with body image can also vary widely among individuals.

Individuals who have a poor body image perceive their body as unattractive to others, whereas those with a good body image view their body as attractive to others. Their views may or may not accurately reflect the person's actual appearance or parallel how others judge a person's body—for instance, people may consider an individual attractive, when at the same time that individual views him- or herself as unattractive.

Description

Scientists have found that body image is first formed as an infant during contact or lack of contact with people such as parents and family members. Physical contact in the form of hugs, kisses, and other forms of affection can help develop an early positive body image. Lack of loving contact can have the opposite effect, forming an early negative body image.

Negative body image

Body image, especially among individuals as they go through puberty (a stage of physical and mental development that allows for sexual reproduction and causes transformation in the physical body shape), can become a problem under certain circumstances. For example, parents who are overly concerned with their children's weight and appearance may cause their children to develop negative concepts of their body. Other parents who are preoccupied with their own weight and appearance can indirectly lead their children toward being critical of their bodies. A child's peers can exert pressure, urging each other to attain a certain ideal figure or criticizing individuals who somehow do not measure up to their expectations. Media depictions of models and actors and popular discussion of celebrities in terms of their physical appearance also shape young people's perceptions about ideal body type. Body image is also closely associated with self-esteem, which is defined as the amount of value or personal worth individuals subjectively feel they have.

As puberty nears, children become increasingly focused on their physical appearance. An adolescent may mature more quickly or slowly than his or her peers. Any deviation from the perceived "ideal" can result in a negative body image, and adolescents may diet, **exercise**, or use **steroids**, stimulants, or laxatives to counter their own negative self-concept and achieve the body image they desire. Some teenage girls are even having plastic surgery (with parental permission) to "correct" what they perceive as flaws in their appearance.

Distorted body images in adolescence can lead to a number of disorders, such as **anorexia nervosa**, **bulimia nervosa**, or **body dysmorphic disorder**, a severe, clinically recognized condition characterized by an obsession with illusory body image. The behaviors that accompany these psychological disorders can be life threatening if taken to the extreme. Body image disorders are often accompanied by additional psychological problems such as **depression** or anxiety and thoughts of **suicide**. For some individuals, body image eventually becomes an all-consuming preoccupation.

Teens are especially concerned about how other people view them, and they can be more sensitive to aspects of body image and vulnerable to external pressures as they experience physiological changes. Males may be overly concerned with height when they see females of their same age who are growing taller, and females may feel sensitive about their height and weight as their bodies develop.

According to the National Eating Disorders Association, 91% of young college women report having been on at least one diet. Seventy percent of young college men report being unhappy with their body image, with 32% of all college men stating that they have dieted once or more than once. Other studies show similar percentages among young adults, which help to support the contention that young people are concerned with body image and that they generally aspire to be slim.

Differences among men and women

Concern with body image is generally more important to women than it is to men. Women usually are more critical of their overall body and individual parts of their body than are men. However, the gap between the two genders has been narrowing over recent years as men become more concerned with their body image.

Poor body image is often affected by feelings of being overweight, especially with women. Men, by contrast, often desire more muscle mass when considering their body image. Their desire to be more masculine is connected to a desire to add muscle mass and improve muscle definition. Poor body image can lead to fad dieting, obesity, and eating disorders, along with low self-esteem, depression, anxiety, and general emotional distress. However, for the most part, people with good exercise habits, positive personal and sexual lives, and excellent emotional and mental states have better and more accurate perceptions of their body image than people without those characteristics and experiences.

Causes and symptoms

Causes of negative body image

Body image can be affected by outside influences. Media sources, such as television, the Internet, and magazines, often portray people closer to the commonly accepted ideal body type than the average body type in order to sell their products and services. Consequently, people—especially older children and young adults—are overly influenced and swayed by such depictions of body image. According to the Association of Body Image and Disordered Eating (ABIDE), the average U.S. citizen is exposed to about 5,000 advertising messages every day. Studies of network television commercials have shown that attractiveness is a desirable trait that advertisers regularly use to convince viewers to purchase their products.

Family life can also affect a person's perception of body image. Parents who criticize their children about the way they look, talk, or act may have a negative effect on the development of self-esteem in their offspring.

Young people may also be affected by the comments of peers when it comes to their body image. Teasing conveys negative values about a person. Racial, sexual, and other types of teasing can have a negative impact on body image and self-esteem. Children may urge their peers to conform to trends in clothing, language, and other cultural aspects, all of which can potentially hurt a person's body image.

Symptoms of negative body image

Exaggerated and distorted concerns with body image have been linked in medical studies with decreases in self-esteem and increases in dieting and eating disorders, including anorexia nervosa, **binge eating disorder**, and bulimia. Bulimia is an eating disorder marked by episodes of binge eating followed by one or more behaviors to control weight, most commonly self-induced vomiting, laxative abuse, fasting, or excessive exercise. The disorder is rare in children under age 14. It is estimated to occur in between 1%–3% of high school– and college-aged women in the United States.

People with extreme body image problems may have body dysmorphic disorder (BDD), which involves a distorted body image without any eating disorders. Body dysmorphic disorder was recognized as a psychiatric disorder in 1997, although its symptoms have been exhibited in patients for more than 100 years. The disorder involves **obsession** and complete preoccupation with an imagined or mild physical flaw. It is known to occur in 1%–2% of Americans, but it is thought to be underdiagnosed because it often occurs in conjunction with other psychiatric disorders such as major depression and **obsessive-compulsive disorder**. Excessive preoccupation with body image and an obsession with positive body image has also been associated with the personality disorder narcissism (self-admiration or an overestimation about one's appearance).

Diagnosis

Within the field of **psychoanalysis**, a person's body image is often measured by asking individuals to rate parts of their body (such as face, stomach, and buttocks) with respect to a series of pictures representing an ideal body image. The difference in the rating between an individual's current body image and a perceived ideal body image is generally considered the amount that individuals are dissatisfied with their body.

Prevention

Without a healthy regard for one's self, people can often become very self-conscious of their body image. Feelings of depression, anxiety, and isolation may occur. With low self-esteem and body image problems, some people use alcohol or drugs to offset those negative feelings. Others turn away from their regular activities and their usual friends, becoming withdrawn and showing lack of interest in themselves and the world around them.

A person may recover from negative body image by attempting to accept things that cannot be changed and working on things that realistically could be improved. In some cases, outside help is needed in the form of a guidance counselor, parent, coach, religious leader, or someone else that is trusted and accepting of personal feelings. Crisis hotlines are also available to help with such problems.

Resources

BOOKS

Knoblich, Gunther, et al., eds. *Human Body Perception from the Inside Out.* Oxford, UK: Oxford University Press, 2005.

Messinger, Lisa, and Merle Goldberg. *My Thin Excuse: Understanding, Recognizing, and Overcoming Eating Disorders.* Garden City Park, NY: Square One Publishers, 2006.

Preester, Helena, and Veroniek Knockaert, eds. *Body Image and Body Schema: Interdisciplinary Perspectives.* Philadelphia: John Benjamins Publishing Co., 2005.

Wilhelm, Sabine. *Feeling Good About the Way You Look: A Program for Overcoming Body Image Problems.* New York: Guilford Publications, Inc., 2006.

Wykes, Maggie, and Barrie Gunter. *The Media and Body Image: If Looks Could Kill.* Thousand Oaks, CA: Sage Publications Ltd., 2005.

WEBSITES

Ahmed, Iqbal, et al. "Psychiatric Manifestations of Body Dysmorphic Disorder." Medscape Reference. http://www.emedicine.com/med/topic3124.htm (accessed September 30, 2011).

MedlinePlus. "Anorexia Nervosa." U.S. National Library of Medicine, National Institutes of Health. http://www.nlm.nih.gov/medlineplus/ency/article/000362.htm (accessed September 30, 2011).

———. "Bulimia." U.S. National Library of Medicine, National Institutes of Health. http://www.nlm.nih.gov/medlineplus/ency/article/000341.htm (accessed September 30, 2011).

ORGANIZATIONS

Academy for Eating Disorders, 111 Deer Lake Rd., Suite 100, Deerfield, IL, 60015, (847) 498-4274, Fax: (847) 480-9282, info@aedweb.org, http://www.aedweb.org.

National Association of Anorexia Nervosa and Associated Disorders, Inc, PO Box 640, Naperville, IL, 60566, (630) 577-1333, anadhelp@anad.org, http://www.anad.org.

National Eating Disorders Association, 165 West 46th Street, New York, NY, 10036, (1-800) 931-2237, info@NationalEatingDisorders.org, http://www.nationaleatingdisorders.org.

National Institute of Mental Health, 6001 Executive Blvd., Room 8184, MSC 9663, Bethesda, MD, 20892-9663, (301) 443-4513, (866) 615-6464, Fax: (301)443-4279, nimhinfo@nih.gov, http://www.nimh.nih.gov.

Tish Davidson, AM
Laura Jean Cataldo, RN, EdD

Body integrity identity disorder

Definition

Body integrity identity disorder (BIID) is a condition in which a person who is not psychotic seeks the elective amputation of one or more limbs (or body parts). In most cases the limb or body part is healthy, not malformed, and

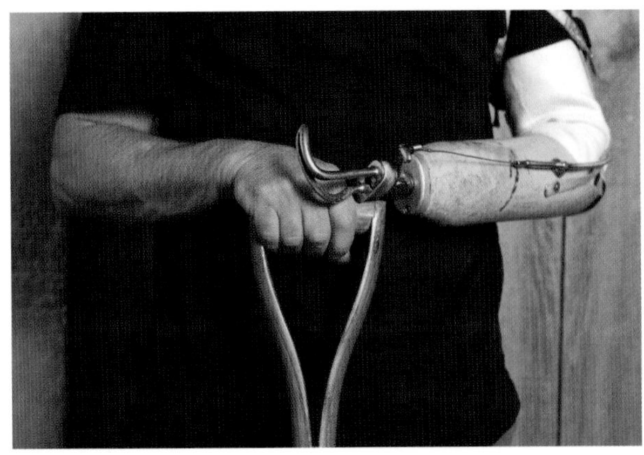

Persons with body integrity identity disorder experience an intense desire to have one (or more) limbs amputated. *(© iStockPhoto.com/Michael Courtney)*

functioning normally. People with BIID have an idealized image of themselves as amputees and wish to have their actual body altered to conform to this image.

Demographics

Most psychiatrists consider BIID a very rare disorder; a book published in 2000 by **psychologist** Gregg Furth (1945–) identified about 200 people with BIID, and a case study published in 2005 by **psychiatrist** Michael First (1956–) estimated a few thousand people worldwide. Internet sources claim that there are at least several thousand persons in Canada and the United States alone who have the disorder, but these estimates are not substantiated. Exact statistics and demographics are difficult to obtain. The majority of persons with BIID in early medical studies appear to be middle-aged Caucasian males with above-average levels of education; women accounted for only 4 of the 52 subjects profiled in First's case study. The mean age in the study was 48 years, with the youngest person 23 years old and the oldest 77.

Although no one has compiled an exhaustive survey of the body parts most likely to be chosen for amputation by persons with BIID, First's preliminary work indicates that the left leg above the knee is the most common choice, followed by fingers or toes. In his work, First maintains that people with BIID are very specific about the disability they desire or the number of limbs they want to have amputated, and the point at which they want the limb(s) removed.

Description

BIID was originally called *apotemnophilia*, a term coined by psychologist John Money (1921–2006) in 1977. The word comes from three Greek terms meaning "away from," "to cut," and "love of." Money maintained that persons with apotemnophilia had a sexual motivation for desiring amputation and considered the disorder a paraphilia, or sexual desire for unusual or extreme (and in some cases illegal) objects or situations. Since most persons with BIID do not report sexual feelings associated with their desire for amputation, apotemnophilia is now used only to refer to a condition in which a person cannot be aroused or sexually satisfied unless they obtain the desired procedure. Furth, who co-authored the 1977 article with Money, suggested supplementing apotemnophilia with *amputee identity disorder* in order to distinguish between persons who do report a sexual interest in amputation and those who do not. Furth considers himself to have amputee identity disorder and made headlines in 1999 when he went to Scotland to consult a surgeon who had already performed two amputations on healthy persons.

The term *body integrity identity disorder* was introduced by First, who served as the editor of the ***Diagnostic and Statistical Manual of Mental Disorders***, fourth edition, text revised (*DSM-IV-TR*) and who has been involved in the development of the fifth edition (*DSM-5*, 2013). BIID is not yet recognized by the *DSM*, but First supports the addition. He maintains that BIID is a more accurate name for the disorder because the condition (in his opinion) includes people who feel a need for blindness, deafness, or other disability, or paralysis or other impairment of a limb rather than amputation.

It is important to distinguish BIID from **body dysmorphic disorder** (BDD), a condition with which it is often confused because of the similarity of the names. Another reason for the confusion is that some psychiatrists initially favored adding BIID to *DSM-5* as a subtype of body dysmorphic disorder. Other researchers, however, have noted a core distinction between the two conditions. People diagnosed with BDD are excessively concerned about supposed defects in their body shape, facial features, or other aspects of their physical appearance and want to improve the features they find distressing, whereas people with BIID do not perceive the body part that they want amputated as defective or embarrassing. BIID is more nearly like **gender identity disorder** in that the person with BIID perceives their limb as incongruent with their sense of self, similar to the way in which a person with gender identity disorder perceives their biological sex as alien to their sense of self.

BIID is difficult to describe because most people—including those who have had to have a limb amputated because of traumatic injury or complications of diabetes—think of amputation as a frightening and upsetting experience. The notion that someone would consider the removal of a limb as a necessary expression of their sense of self seems absurd to the general majority. It also sounds paradoxical when a person with BIID claims that they need to have a limb (or sensory ability) removed in order to feel "complete." Moreover, many amputees report feelings of anger toward people with BIID because they feel that those with BIID are minimizing the suffering of someone who had no choice about amputation.

Another source of difficulty in describing and understanding BIID is that it has developed its own vocabulary for people who have the disorder or are attracted to someone who does. "Devotees" are people who are sexually attracted to amputees or disabled people, although some people in this group prefer to call themselves "admirers." "Wannabes" are people who have an obsessional need for amputation or impairment but have not yet had a procedure to bring it about, whereas "realized wannabes" are those who finally achieved the amputation or impairment they desired. "Pretenders" are people with BIID who use crutches, eye patches, wheel chairs, or similar devices or props in public in order to feel disabled. There is reportedly a considerable overlap among these groups, with many devotees also being pretenders or wannabes.

People with BIID frequently report having the desire for amputation from an early age. One of First's subjects reported having a desire to amputate his leg at age three or four; another man stated that his desire for amputation began in kindergarten, when he had a schoolmate who was missing his left hand and became curious about what it might be like to lose his own hand. Others with BIID maintain that they first became aware of their interest in amputation in early adolescence. There are relatively few who maintain that they were adults when they first experienced an interest in amputation or disability.

Risk factors

There were three suggested risk factors for BIID as of 2011: exposure to an amputee at an early age (three to four years), male sex, and abnormality or malfunction of the parietal lobe of the cerebral cortex.

Causes and symptoms

Causes

There is little agreement among medical professionals about the cause(s) of BIID. Some of the theories that have been proposed include:

- Imprinting. This term refers to the theory that some susceptible children who encounter an amputee at an early age are imprinted with amputation as part of their own mental picture of an ideal body.
- An unloving or dysfunctional home life. This theory holds that people with BIID feel unloved or ignored as children and come to think that amputation or disability will secure them the love they need.
- A defect in the parietal lobe of the cerebral cortex. Some preliminary studies carried out in the early 2000s at the Center for Brain and Cognition of the University of California, San Diego, suggest that people with BIID may have a neurological disorder involving proprioception, which is the body's internal sense of its position in space and of the location of various parts of the body in relation to one another. The parietal lobe of the cerebral cortex is thought to govern the brain's inner body mapping function. If the neurological theory is correct, an abnormality in the parietal lobe would mean that the person with BIID's brain fails to include the limb that he or she wants amputated in its mapping of the person's physical form.
- Conditions in the general culture at a specific point in time. This viewpoint is associated with the work of Ian Hacking, a historian of science who coined the phrase "looping effect" to explain how the classification of a mental disorder affects the behavior of people who decide that they fit that category. In other words, the definition of a new diagnostic category allows some people to reinterpret their past or present experiences in the light of that category, and then to think about actions they would not have considered earlier—such as requesting amputation.
- An extension of extreme body modification. Body modification comprises such practices as body piercing, tattoos, breast implants, and other surgical alterations of the body for aesthetic purposes. Some psychiatrists think that BIID may simply represent extreme body modification carried one step further; however, most persons who identify themselves as having BIID reject this explanation.

There was no evidence as of 2011 that BIID runs in families or that it has a genetic basis.

Symptoms

There is no universally accepted list of BIID symptoms, and not all persons who maintain that they have BIID will experience every symptom. However, some of the signs and symptoms most frequently identified as characteristic of BIID include:

- a feeling of incompleteness as an able-bodied individual, coupled with a feeling of certainty that one will feel "whole" or "complete" after obtaining the needed amputation or other impairment

KEY TERMS

Anecdotal—Based on personal experience or reported individual observations unverified by controlled experiments.

Apotemnophilia—A word coined by John Money in 1977 to describe the condition now known as body integrity identity disorder. Money originally thought that BIID had a sexual component, hence the Greek root *philia* at the end of the word.

Body dysmorphic disorder (BDD)—A psychiatric disorder in which the affected person is excessively preoccupied with a perceived defect in his or her physical appearance.

Cerebral cortex—The outer layer of the cerebrum (forebrain), composed of gray matter and containing sensory, motor, and association areas.

Devotee—Someone who is sexually attracted to amputees or disabled persons.

Ethics—The branch of philosophy that deals with questions of morality (good and evil, right and wrong).

Paraphilia—The medical term for a condition in which a person is sexually aroused by nonhuman objects, animals, corpses, children and other nonconsenting partners, or specific individuals or situations that are not part of normative stimulation.

Pretender—A person with BIID who uses assistive devices or other props in public in order to appear disabled.

Proprioception—A person's normal sense of posture, balance, direction of movement, and location in space.

Transabled—A word coined by people with BIID to express their need to be disabled.

Wannabe—A person with BIID who feels a need for an amputation or impairment.

- a very specific notion of the amputation or disability required
- feelings of intense envy when encountering another person with the needed disability or amputation
- feelings of intense shame regarding the need for the amputation or disability, due to the belief that no one else could possibly understand the condition
- repeated episodes of depression and possibly suicidal thoughts
- rehearsal for the needed amputation or disability by pretending (imitating the desired disability)
- failure of psychotherapy or medications to alleviate the feelings
- in some cases, plotting to injure oneself in order to achieve the needed amputation or other impairment

Diagnosis

There were no formal diagnostic criteria for BIID as of 2011, though the disorder is recognized by the medical community. There are also no psychological tests or inventories to screen for the disorder. Given the fact that many people with BIID are afraid to discuss their feelings, most cases seem to come to the attention of therapists only when the patient brings up the subject.

Treatment

Treatment of BIID is highly controversial. Most patients with the disorder maintain that **psychotherapy** and medications do not help, although some observe that psychotherapy has been beneficial in helping them deal more effectively with other problems in their lives. A few wannabes report that pretending helps them cope to some extent with their BIID.

Surgery

Most persons with BIID maintain that surgery is the only effective treatment for their condition. In fact, BIID first came to the attention of the general public in 2000 with media reports of Robert Smith, a surgeon in Scotland who agreed to amputate the healthy legs of two patients with BIID. Smith maintained that he performed the operations to head off the possibility that the patients would otherwise resort to self-amputation or other dangerous measures. There had been several highly publicized cases of such behavior in the late 1990s, including a man who lost his life from a botched amputation performed by a surgeon who had lost his license twenty years previously, and a man in Wisconsin who had constructed a homemade guillotine in 1999 to amputate his left arm. Other persons with BIID have packed their limbs in dry ice in order to require a surgeon to amputate them, or have blown off the unwanted limb with shotguns. Smith was forced to give up performing amputations for BIID because of the public fury that resulted from his operations.

Surgery as therapy for BIID raises a number of ethical questions. One is whether people have an absolute right to do anything they wish to their own bodies, and whether surgeons should be obligated to carry out their wishes. Moreover, unlike plastic surgery to improve a person's appearance, surgical removal of a limb or other body part may decrease the amputee's ability to work or otherwise function in society. Should taxpayers be expected to support those who intentionally seek amputation because of a psychological disorder? In addition, given the increasing scarcity of healthcare resources, should surgeons be asked to divert time and attention from patients with life-threatening emergencies in order to perform elective amputations? Last, amputation is irreversible, which concerns many surgeons who are afraid of lawsuits if the BIID patient regrets the procedure afterward. Although Smith's two patients and others who succeeded in achieving the amputation or disability they sought maintain that they are finally at peace with themselves, therapists who have studied BIID still recommend medications and psychotherapy as the first line of treatment.

There were no **clinical trials** of psychotherapy, medications, or other treatments for BIID as of 2011.

Prognosis

As no large-scale research studies of BIID had been conducted as of 2011, information about its prognosis is purely anecdotal (individual reports unverified by formal controlled experiments). One website for people with BIID maintains that the disorder becomes worse as people grow older and their need for amputation intensifies.

Prevention

There is no known way to prevent BIID, because the condition is still not understood.

Resources

BOOKS

Furth, Gregg M., and Robert Smith. *Amputee Identity Disorder: Information, Questions, Answers, and Recomendations about Self-Demand Amputation*. Bloomington, IN: AuthorHouse, 2000.

Hacking, Ian. *Mad Travelers: Reflections on the Reality of Transient Mental Illnesses*. Charlottesville, VA: University Press of Virginia, 1998.

Smith, Stephen W., and Ronan Deazley, eds. *The Legal, Medical and Cultural Regulation of the Body: Transformation and Transgression*. Burlington, VT: Ashgate, 2009.

PERIODICALS

Elliott, Carl. "A New Way to Be Mad." *The Atlantic*, December 2000. http://www.theatlantic.com/magazine/archive/2000/12/a-new-way-to-be-mad/4671 (accessed August 4, 2011).

Ellison, Jesse. "Cutting Desire." *Newsweek*, May 28, 2008. http://www.newsweek.com/2008/05/28/cutting-desire.html (accessed August 4, 2011).

First, M.B. "Desire for Amputation of a Limb: Paraphilia, Psychosis, or a New Type of Identity Disorder?" *Psychological Medicine* 35 (June 2005): 919–928.

Henig, Robin M. "At War with Their Bodies, They Seek to Sever Limbs." *New York Times*, March 22, 2005. http://query.nytimes.com/gst/fullpage.html?res=9C0CE4-D61E3CF931A15750C0A9639C8B63&pagewanted=all (accessed August 4, 2011).

Müller, S. "Body Integrity Identity Disorder (BIID)—Is the Amputation of Healthy Limbs Ethically Justified?" *American Journal of Bioethics* 9 (January 2009): 36–43.

Patrone, D. "Disfigured Anatomies and Imperfect Analogies: Body Integrity Identity Disorder and the Supposed Right to Self-demanded Amputation of Healthy Body Parts." *Journal of Medical Ethics* 35 (September 2009): 541–545.

Phillips, K.A., et al. "Body Dysmorphic Disorder: Some Key Issues for DSM-V." *Depression and Anxiety* 27 (June 2010): 573–591.

WEBSITES

Dotinga, Randy. "Out on a Limb" [account of Gregg Furth's search for a surgeon to amputate his right leg]. Salon.com. August 29, 2000. http://www.salon.com/health/feature/2000/08/29/amputation (accessed July 14, 2011).

Mulvihill, Karen, and Karlie Pouliot. "Determined to Amputate: One Man's Struggle with Body Integrity Identity Disorder." FOXNews.com. May 20, 2009. http://www.foxnews.com/story/0,2933,520811,00.html (accessed July 14, 2011).

O'Connor, Sean. *Transabled.org* (blog). http://transabled.org (accessed August 2, 2011).

"Whole: A Documentary" [2003 documentary film about BIID]. http://www.whole-documentary.com (accessed July 15, 2011).

ORGANIZATIONS

American Psychiatric Association, 1000 Wilson Boulevard, Suite 1825, Arlington, VA, 22209-3901, (703) 907-7300, apa@psych.org, http://www.psych.org.

Center for Brain and Cognition, University of California, San Diego, 109 Mandler Hall, 9500 Gilman Drive, La Jolla, CA, 92093-0109, (858) 534-6240, Fax: (858) 534-7190, ramalab@ucsd.edu, http://cbc.ucsd.edu/index.html.

Rebecca J. Frey, Ph.D.

Bodywork therapies

Definition

Bodywork therapies comprise body-based approaches to treatment that emphasize manipulation and realignment of the body's structure in order to improve its function as well as the client's mental outlook. These therapies typically combine a relatively passive phase, in which the client receives deep-tissue bodywork or postural correction from an experienced instructor or practitioner, and a more active period of movement education, in which the client practices sitting, standing, and moving about with better alignment of the body and greater ease of motion.

Bodywork should not be equated only with massage. Massage therapy is one form of bodywork, but in massage therapy, practitioners use oil or lotion to reduce the friction between their hands and the client's skin. In most forms of bodywork, little if any lubrication is used, as the goal of this type of hands-on treatment is to warm, relax, and stretch the fascia (a band or sheath of connective tissue that covers, supports, or connects the muscles and the internal organs) and underlying layers of tissue.

Purpose

The purpose of bodywork therapy is the correction of problems in the client's overall posture, connective tissue, and/or musculature in order to bring about greater ease of movement, less discomfort, and a higher level of energy in daily activity. Some forms of bodywork have as a secondary purpose the healing or prevention of repetitive stress injuries, particularly for people whose occupations require intensive use of specific parts of the body (e.g., dancers, musicians, professional athletes, and opera singers). Bodywork may also heal or prevent specific musculoskeletal problems, such as lower back pain or neck pain.

Bodywork therapies are holistic in that they stress increased self-awareness and intelligent use of one's body as one of the goals of treatment. Some of these therapies use verbal discussion, visualization, or **guided imagery** along with movement education to help clients break old patterns of moving and feeling. Although most bodywork therapists do not address mental disorders directly in their work with clients, they are often knowledgeable about the applications of bodywork to such specific emotions as **depression**, anger, or fear.

Although some bodywork therapies, such as Rolfing or Hellerwork, offer programs structured around a specific number or sequence of lessons, all therapies emphasize individualized treatment and respect for the uniqueness of each individual's body. Bodywork instructors or practitioners typically work with clients on a one-to-one basis, as distinct from a group or classroom approach.

Demographics

Massage therapy, under which many forms of bodywork are often counted, was estimated be a $16–20 billion industry in 2008. Bodywork therapies have become increasingly mainstream since the 1980s, and the industry is estimated to still be growing at a rapid pace.

Description

The following are brief descriptions of some popular bodywork therapies.

Alexander technique

The Alexander technique was developed by the Australian actor F. Matthias Alexander (1869–1955), who had voice problems that were not helped by available medical treatments. Alexander decided to set up a number of mirrors so that he could watch himself during a performance from different angles. He found that he was holding his head and neck too far forward and that these unconscious patterns were the source of the tension in his body that was harming his voice. He then developed a method for teaching others to observe the patterns of tension and stress in their posture and movement and to correct these patterns with a combination of hands-on guidance and visualization exercises. The Alexander technique is included in the curricula of the Juilliard School of Music and many other drama and music schools around the world, because performing artists are particularly vulnerable to repetitive stress injuries if they hold or move their bodies incorrectly.

In an Alexander technique session, the client works one-on-one with an instructor who uses verbal explanations as well as guided movement. Often referred to as "explorations," the sessions last about 30 minutes. Although most clients see positive changes after only two or three sessions, teachers of the technique recommend a course of 20–30 sessions so that new movement skills can be learned and changes maintained.

Rolfing

Rolfing, which is also called Rolf therapy or structural integration, is a holistic system of bodywork that uses deep manipulation of the body's soft tissue to realign and balance the body's myofascial (muscular and connective tissue) structure. It was developed by Ida Rolf (1896–1979), a biochemist who became interested in the structure of the human body after an accident damaged her health. Rolf studied with an osteopath as well as with practitioners of other forms of alternative medicine and developed her own technique of body movement, which she called structural integration. Rolfing is an approach that seeks to counteract the effects of gravity, which tends to pull the body out of alignment over time and cause the connective tissues to stiffen and contract.

Rolfing treatment begins with the "Basic Ten," a series of ten sessions each lasting 60–90 minutes, spaced a week or more apart. After a period of integration, the client may undertake advanced treatment sessions. "Tune-up" sessions are recommended every six months. In Rolfing sessions, practitioners use their fingers, hands, knuckles, or elbows to rework the connective tissue over the client's entire body. The deep tissues are worked until they become pliable, which allows the muscles to lengthen and return to their proper alignment. Rolfing treatments are done on a massage table, with the client wearing only undergarments.

Hellerwork

Hellerwork is a bodywork therapy developed by Joseph Heller, a former NASA engineer who became a certified Rolfer in 1972 and started his own version of structural integration, called Hellerwork, in 1979. Heller describes his program as "a powerful system of somatic education and structural bodywork" delivered in a series of eleven sessions. Hellerwork is similar to Rolfing in that it begins with manipulation of the deep tissues of the body. Heller, however, decided that physical realignment of the body by itself is insufficient, so he extended his system to include movement education and guided dialogue to promote self-awareness.

The bodywork aspect of Hellerwork is intended to release the tension that exists in the fascia, which is the sheath or layer of connective tissue that covers, supports, or connects the muscles and internal organs of the body. Fascia is flexible and moist in its normal state, but the effects of gravity and ongoing physical stresses lead to misalignments that cause the fascia to become rigid. The first hour of a Hellerwork session is devoted to deep connective tissue bodywork in which the Hellerwork practitioner uses his or her hands to release tension in the client's fascia. The bodywork is followed by movement education, which includes the use of video feedback to help clients learn movement patterns that will help to keep their bodies in proper alignment. The third component of Hellerwork is dialogue, which is intended to help clients become more aware of the relationships between their emotions and attitudes and their body.

Tragerwork

Trager psychophysical integration, which is often called simply Tragerwork, was developed by Milton Trager (1908–1977), who was born with a spinal deformity and earned a medical degree in his middle age after working out an approach to healing chronic pain. Tragerwork is based on the theory that many illnesses are caused by tension patterns that are held in the unconscious mind as much as in the tissues of the body; clients are advised to think of Tragerwork sessions as "learning experiences" rather than "treatments." Tragerwork sessions are divided into bodywork, which is referred to as tablework, and an **exercise** period. Trager practitioners use their hands during tablework to perform a variety of gentle motions—rocking, shaking, vibrating, and gentle stretching—intended to help the client release patterns of tension by experiencing how it feels to move freely and effortlessly on one's own. Following the tablework, clients are taught how to perform simple dance-like exercises called "Mentastics," for practice at home. Tragerwork sessions take between 60–90 minutes, and clients are advised to spend 10–15 minutes three times a day doing the Mentastics exercises.

Feldenkrais method

The Feldenkrais method, like Hellerwork, refers to its approach as "somatic education." Developed by Moshe Feldenkrais (1904–1984), a scientist and engineer who was also a judo instructor, the Feldenkrais method consists of two major applications: awareness through movement (ATM) lessons, a set of verbally directed exercise lessons intended to engage the client's intelligence as well as physical perception, and functional integration (FI), in which a Feldenkrais practitioner works with the client one-on-one, guiding the client through a series of movements that alter habitual patterns and convey new learning directly to the neuromuscular system. Functional integration is done with the client fully clothed, lying or sitting on a low padded table.

Perhaps the most distinctive feature of the Feldenkrais method is its emphasis on new patterns of thinking, attention, cognition, and imagination as byproducts of new patterns of physical movement. It is the most intellectually oriented of the various bodywork therapies and has been described as a combination of motor development, biomechanics, psychology, and martial arts. The Feldenkrais method is the form of bodywork that has been most extensively studied by mainstream medical researchers.

Trigger point therapy

Trigger point therapy, which is sometimes called myotherapy, is a treatment for pain relief in the musculoskeletal system based on the application of pressure to trigger points in the client's body. Trigger points are defined as hypersensitive spots or areas in the muscles that cause pain when subjected to stress, whether the cause is an occupational injury, a disease, or emotional stress. Trigger points are not necessarily in the same location where the client feels pain.

Myotherapy is a two-step process. In the first step, the therapist locates the client's trigger points and applies pressure to them. This step relieves pain and also relaxes the muscles associated with it. In the second part of the therapy session, the client learns a series of exercises that progressively stretch the muscles that have been relaxed by the therapist's pressure. Most clients need fewer than 10 sessions to benefit from myotherapy. One distinctive feature of trigger point therapy is that clients are asked to bring a relative or trusted friend to learn the pressure technique and the client's personal trigger points. This so-called buddy system helps the client to maintain the benefits of the therapy in the event of a **relapse**.

Shiatsu

Shiatsu is the oldest form of bodywork therapy, having been practiced for centuries in Japan as part of traditional medical treatment. It is also the type of bodywork most commonly requested by clients in Western countries as well as in East Asia. The word *shiatsu* itself is a combination of two Japanese words that mean "pressure" and "finger." Shiatsu resembles **acupuncture** in its use of the basic concepts of *ki,* the vital energy that flows throughout the body, and the meridians, or 12 major pathways that channel ki to the various organs of the body. In Asian terms, shiatsu works by unblocking and rebalancing the distribution of ki in the body. In the categories of Western medicine, shiatsu may stimulate the release of endorphins, which are chemical compounds that block the receptors in the **brain** that perceive pain.

A shiatsu treatment begins with the practitioner's assessment of the client's basic state of health, including posture, vocal tone, complexion color, and condition of hair. This evaluation is used together with ongoing information about the client's energy level gained through the actual bodywork. The shiatsu practitioner works with the client lying fully clothed on a futon. The practitioner seeks out the meridians in the client's body through finger pressure and stimulates points along the meridians known as *tsubos.* The tsubos are centers of high energy where the ki tends to collect. Pressure on the tsubos results in a release of energy that rebalances the energy level throughout the body.

Craniosacral therapy

Craniosacral therapy, or CST, is a form of treatment that originated with William Sutherland, an American osteopath of the 1930s who theorized that the manipulative techniques that osteopaths were taught could be applied to the skull. Sutherland knew from his medical training that the skull is not a single piece of bone but consists of several bones that meet at seams and that the cerebrospinal fluid that bathes the brain and spinal cord has a natural rise-and-fall rhythm. Sutherland experimented with gentle manipulation of the skull in order to correct imbalances in the distribution of the cerebrospinal fluid. Contemporary craniosacral therapists practice manipulation not only of the skull but also of the meningeal membranes that cover the brain and spinal cord and sometimes of the facial bones. Many practitioners of CST are also osteopaths.

In CST, the patient lies on a massage table while the therapist gently palpates, or presses, the skull and spine. If the practitioner is also an osteopath, he or she will take a complete medical history as well. The therapist also "listens" to the cranial rhythmic impulse or rhythmic pulsation of the cerebrospinal fluid with his or her hands. Interruptions of the normal flow by abnormalities caused by tension or injury are diagnostic clues to the practitioner. Once he or she has identified the cause of the abnormal rhythm, the skull and spinal column are gently manipulated to restore the natural rhythm of the cranial impulse. Craniosacral therapy appears to be particularly useful in treating physical disorders of the head, including migraine headaches, ringing in the ears, sinus problems, and injuries of the head, neck, and spine. In addition, patients rarely require extended periods of CST treatments.

Benefits

Benefits from bodywork include deep relaxation, improved posture, greater ease and spontaneity of movement, greater range of motion for certain joints, greater understanding of the structures and functions of the body and their relationship to emotions, and release of negative emotions.

Many persons also report healing or improvement of specific conditions, including migraine headaches, repetitive stress injuries, osteoarthritis, **insomnia**, sprains and bruises, sports injuries, stress-related illnesses, sciatica, post-pregnancy problems, menstrual cramps, temporomandibular joint disorders, lower back pain, whiplash injuries, disorders of the immune system, asthma, depression, digestive problems, chronic **fatigue**, and painful scar tissue. The Alexander technique has been reported to ease the process of childbirth by improving the mother's postural alignment prior to delivery.

Some studies of the Feldenkrais method have found that its positive effects on subjects' self-esteem, mood, and anxiety symptoms are more significant than its effects on body function.

Precautions

Persons who are seriously ill, acutely feverish, or suffering from a contagious infection should wait until

KEY TERMS

Bodywork—Any technique involving hands-on massage or manipulation of the body.

Endorphins—A group of peptide compounds released by the body in response to stress or traumatic injury. Endorphins react with opiate receptors in the brain to reduce or relieve pain sensations. Shiatsu is thought to work by stimulating the release of endorphins.

Fascia (plural, fasciae)—A band or sheath of connective tissue that covers, supports, or connects the muscles and the internal organs.

Ki—The Japanese spelling of *qi,* the traditional Chinese term for vital energy or the life force.

Meridians—In traditional Chinese medicine, a network of pathways or channels that convey *ki* through the body.

Movement education—The active phase of bodywork, in which clients learn to move with greater freedom and to maintain the proper alignment of their bodies.

Osteopathy—A system of medical practice that believes that the human body can make its own remedies to heal infection. It originally used manipulative techniques but also added surgical, hygienic, and medicinal methods when needed. Doctors of osteopathy are referred to as osteopaths or DOs.

Repetitive stress injury (RSI)—A type of injury to the musculoskeletal and nervous systems associated with occupational strain or overuse of a specific part of the body. Bodywork therapies are often recommended to people suffering from RSIs.

Somatic education—Used in both Hellerwork and the Feldenkrais method to describe the integration of bodywork with self-awareness, intelligence, and imagination.

Structural integration—The term used to describe the method and philosophy of life associated with Rolfing. Its fundamental concept is the vertical line.

Tsubo—In shiatsu, a center of high energy located along one of the body's meridians. Stimulation of the *tsubos* during a shiatsu treatment is thought to rebalance the flow of vital energy in the body.

they have recovered before beginning a course of bodywork. As a rule, types of bodywork that involve intensive manipulation or stretching of the deeper layers of body tissue are not suitable for persons who have undergone recent surgery or have recently suffered severe injury. In the case of Tragerwork, shiatsu, and trigger point therapy, clients should inform the therapist of any open wounds, bruises, or fractures so that the affected part of the body can be avoided during treatment. Craniosacral therapy, the Feldenkrais method, and the Alexander technique involve gentle touch and do not require any special precautions.

Individuals recovering from **abuse** or receiving treatment for any post-traumatic syndrome or dissociative disorder should consult their therapist before undertaking bodywork. Although bodywork is frequently recommended as an adjunctive treatment for these disorders, it can also trigger flashbacks if the bodywork therapist touches a part of the patient's body associated with the abuse or **trauma**. Many bodywork therapists, however, are well informed about post-traumatic symptoms and disorders and are able to adjust their treatments accordingly.

Preparation

Bodywork usually requires little preparation on the client's or patient's part, except for partial undressing for Rolfing, trigger point therapy, and Hellerwork.

Aftercare

Aftercare for shiatsu, trigger point therapy, and craniosacral therapy consists of a brief period of rest after the treatment.

Some bodywork approaches involve various types of long-term aftercare. Rolfing clients return for advanced treatments or tune-ups after a period of integrating the changes in their bodies resulting from the Basic Ten sessions. Tragerwork clients are taught Mentastics exercises to be done at home. The Alexander technique and the Feldenkrais approach assume that clients will continue to practice their movement and postural changes for the rest of their lives. Trigger point therapy clients are asked to involve friends or relatives who can help them maintain the benefits of the therapy after the treatment sessions are over.

Risks

The deep tissue massage and manipulation in Rolfing and Hellerwork are uncomfortable for many people, particularly during the first few sessions. There are, however, no serious risks of physical injury from any form of bodywork that is administered by a trained practitioner of the specific treatment. As mentioned,

QUESTIONS TO ASK YOUR DOCTOR

- Is bodywork therapy right for me?
- What type of bodywork therapy would you recommend?
- Do I have any injuries that would preclude bodywork therapy?
- Are there any local practitioners whom you recommend?
- Have any of your other patients tried this type of bodywork therapy? What were their experiences?
- Is bodywork therapy covered by my insurance?

however, bodywork therapies that involve intensive manipulation or stretching of the deeper layers of body tissue are not suitable for persons who have undergone recent surgery or have recently suffered severe injury.

Research and general acceptance

There is very little peer-reviewed scientific research on the effectiveness of bodywork therapies. Some studies have suggested that massage may be effective in alleviating a variety of symptoms when used in conjunction with more traditional treatments. Additional rigorous scientific study is needed to determine if bodywork therapies are more or less effective than traditional massage therapy and to discover what mechanisms underlie this effectiveness.

Training and certification

The training and certification requirements for bodywork therapy differ substantially depending on the type of therapy. Many therapies have professional associations that provide training and certification to their members. Individuals looking for a practitioner of bodywork therapy should find out if there is a professional organization for that type of therapy and what kinds of certifications are available. Responsible therapists should always be willing to provide and explain their professional credentials.

Resources

BOOKS

Benjamin, Patricia J. *Pearson's Massage Therapy: Blending Art with Science.* Upper Saddle River, NJ: Pearson, 2011.

King, Hollis H., Michael M. Patterson, and Wilfrid Janig, eds. *The Science and Clinical Application of Manual Therapy.* Edinburgh: Churchill Livingstone/Elsevier, 2010.

Stager, Leslie. *Nurturing Massage for Pregnancy: A Practical Guide to Bodywork for the Perinatal Cycle.* Baltimore: Lippincott Williams & Wilkins, 2010.

PERIODICALS

Chaitow, Leon. "Has Osteopathy a Role to Play in the Treatment of Flu?" *Journal of Bodywork & Movement Therapies* 14, no. 1 (January 2010): 1–2.

Field, Tiffany, et al. "Benefits of Combining Massage Therapy with Group Interpersonal Psychotherapy in Prenatally Depressed Women." *Journal of Bodywork & Movement Therapies* 13, no. 4 (October 2009): 297–303.

Fries, Christopher J. "Classification of Complementary and Alternative Medical Practices: Family Physicans' Ratings of Effectiveness." *Canadian Family Physician* 54, no. 11 (November 2008): 1570–71.

ORGANIZATIONS

American Massage Therapy Association, 500 Davis St., Evanston, IL, 60201, (877) 905-2700, http://www.amtamassage.org.

Associated Bodywork & Massage Professionals, 25188 Genesee Trail Rd., Golden, CO, 80401, (800) 458-2267, Fax: (800) 667-8260, http://www.abmp.com.

Rebecca Frey
Rosalyn Carson-DeWitt, MD
Tish Davidson, AM

Borderline personality disorder

Definition

Borderline personality disorder (BPD) is a serious mental illness characterized by an inability to regulate emotional responses and moods, impacting self-image and interpersonal relationships. BPD can result in impulsive, self-harming, and suicidal behaviors; **substance abuse**; eating disorders; and the disruption of family life.

Demographics

BPD accounts for 30%–60% of all diagnosed **personality disorders**. According to the National Institutes of Mental Health, approximately 2% of Americans suffer from BPD. About 20% of all psychiatric hospitalizations are due to BPD. The disorder usually becomes evident in early adulthood, with a typical age of onset of 18 years. BPD is rarely initially diagnosed in people over age 40. Though as many as 80% of patients treated for

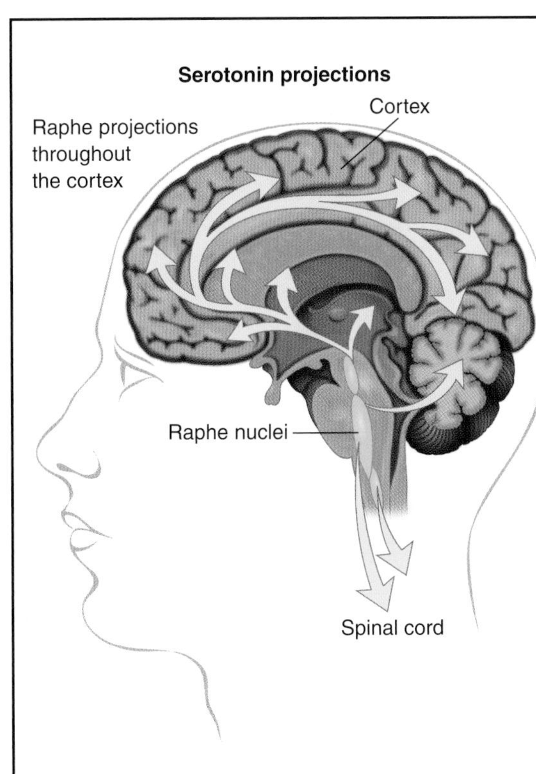

Borderline personality disorder

Diagnostic criteria for borderline personality disorder

Affective (mood-related) symptoms
1. Unstable mood caused by brief but intense episodes of depression, irritability, or anxiety
2. Chronic feelings of emptiness
3. Inappropriate and intense anger or difficulty controlling anger

Impulsive symptoms
4. Impulsive behavior in at least two areas (e.g., spending money, substance abuse, binge eating)
5. Recurrent suicidal behavior, gestures, or threats, or recurring acts of self-mutilation
6. Pattern of unstable and intense interpersonal relationships

Interpersonal symptoms
7. Extreme, persistently unstable perception of self
8. Frantic efforts to avoid abandonment

Cognitive symptoms
9. Stress-related paranoia and/or feeling disconnected from oneself

The Diagnostic and Statistical Manual of Mental Disorders states that the presence of five or more symptoms is necessary to diagnose BPD.

Diagnostic criteria for borderline personality disorder according to the *Diagnostic and Statistical Manual of Mental Disorders* (*DSM-IV-TR*). *(Illustration by Electronic Illustrators Group. Reproduced by permission of Gale, a part of Cengage Learning.)*

BPD are female, this gender bias is less obvious in samples from community populations, suggesting that women may be more likely than men to seek treatment. BPD appears to be equally common among all races and ethnicities. Although the suicidal thinking and **suicide** attempts that are characteristic of BPD are less common in traditional societies, they are becoming increasingly common both in modern societies and in traditional societies that are undergoing rapid change.

Description

The term "borderline" in BPD is now considered a misnomer. It was originally used by the **psychologist** Adolf Stern in the 1930s to describe patients with neuroses that bordered on **psychosis**. Today the term more often refers to borderline states of consciousness that BPD patients may feel when they are experiencing dissociative symptoms—feelings of disconnection from oneself. People with BPD and other personality disorders often utilize coping strategies or defense mechanisms to deny responsibility for their emotions and behaviors.

BPD is a complex disorder with many manifestations. One major feature of BPD is a defense mechanism called "splitting," in which patients alternate between idealizing the significant people in their lives as flawless and devaluing them as unfair and uncaring. Their unrealistic expectations of others inevitably lead to disappointment and unstable interpersonal relationships. Another defense mechanism is referred to as "projective identification," in which patients attribute their own feelings to others and behave in ways that reinforce those attributes. When BPD patients' hostilities are reciprocated, they do not realize that it is due to their own hostility.

BPD results in a high degree of interpersonal conflict, estrangement of family and friends, and divorce. It is also linked to substance abuse, eating disorders, and a history of physical, sexual, or emotional abuse. Self-injury and suicide attempts are common among BPD patients.

Risk factors

Abuse or other childhood **trauma**, such as separation, **neglect**, or abandonment, is a major risk factor for BPD. According to the **National Institute of Mental Health**, studies have found that between 40% and 71% of patients diagnosed with BPD report having been sexually abused as children, most often by someone who was not their primary caregiver. However, most abused children do not develop BPD, and many BPD patients

KEY TERMS

Attention deficit hyperactivity disorder (ADHD)—Conditions characterized by age-inappropriate attention span, hyperactivity, and impulsive behavior.

Bipolar disorder—A recurrent mood disorder, also known as manic-depressive disorder, in which patients have extreme mood swings from depression to mania or a mixture of both.

Cognitive—Conscious intellectual activity, including thinking, imagining, reasoning, remembering, and learning.

Cognitive-behavioral therapy (CBT)—A type of psychotherapy in which people learn to recognize and change negative and self-defeating patterns of thinking and behavior.

Depression—A mental condition in which a person feels extremely sad and loses interest in life. A depressed person may have problems with appetite, sleep, concentration, and daily functioning. Severe depression can lead to suicide attempts.

Dialectical behavior therapy (DBT)—A type of cognitive-behavioral therapy designed specifically to treat borderline personality disorder.

Dissociative—Disconnection from oneself.

Eating disorder—A condition characterized by an abnormal attitude towards food, altered appetite control, and unhealthy eating habits.

Neurotransmitters—Chemicals that transmits nerve impulses from one nerve cell to another.

Opioids—A group of endogenous polypeptides in the brain that bind to opiate receptors.

Post-traumatic stress disorder (PTSD)—A psychological response to a highly stressful event; typically characterized by depression, anxiety, flashbacks, nightmares, and avoidance of reminders of the traumatic experience.

Psychodynamic—Mental, emotional, or motivational forces or processes that affect mental state and behavior, especially unconscious processes that develop in early childhood.

Psychosis—A serious mental disorder, such as schizophrenia, characterized by loss of contact with reality.

Schizophrenia—A psychotic disorder characterized by loss of contact with one's environment, deterioration of everyday functioning, and personality disintegration.

Serotonin—A neurotransmitter located primarily in the brain, blood serum, and stomach membrane.

were not abused as children. Rather, abuse appears to act as a trigger in people who are genetically predisposed to BPD. Studies of twins suggest that at least some features of BPD, especially mood instability and impulsivity, are highly heritable.

Causes and symptoms

The biological basis of BPD is an area of active research. Recent studies suggest that BPD may involve differences in the functioning of the brain's endogenous opioid system, which helps regulate emotions. BPD may also involve disruptions in signaling pathways in the **brain**, involving the **neurotransmitters serotonin**, norepinephrine, and acetylcholine, which help regulate emotions such as anxiety, sadness, irritability, and anger. Feelings of inadequacy and self-loathing arising from childhood abuse or neglect appear to contribute to the development of BPD. It has been theorized that the idealized demands that adults with BPD make on themselves and others are attempts to compensate for care and nurturing denied in childhood.

BPD was first defined as a disorder in the third edition of the American Psychiatric Association's ***Diagnostic and Statistical Manual of Mental Disorders*** (*DSM-III*), published in 1980 and revised in subsequent editions. The revised fourth edition, *DSM-IV-TR,* requires that at least five symptoms be present for a **diagnosis** of BPD. However some clinicians suggest that a diagnosis should require symptoms from each of the three following dimensions or groupings:

- The affective dimension includes mood-related symptoms, such as brief—but intense—episodes of depression, irritability, anxiety, and, especially, inappropriate outbursts of sarcasm, anger, and/or physical violence. The level of mood instability can be a strong predictor of suicide attempts. Other affective symptoms include chronic feelings of emptiness.
- The impulsive dimension includes impulsive behaviors in at least two areas, such as spending money, sex, substance abuse, reckless driving, or binge eating. Impulsive symptoms also include recurrent suicidal threats, gestures, or behaviors, as well as recurring acts of self-mutilation, such as cutting or burning, which

result from a combination of impulsivity and rapid and intense mood swings. These latter self-harming behaviors are not generally considered suicidal, but rather serve a personal purpose, such as providing relief from an extreme emotional state.

- The interpersonal dimension includes a pattern of intense but unstable interpersonal relationships, characterized by alternating idealization and devaluation or "love-hate." It also includes a persistently unstable self-image or sense of self and frantic efforts to avoid real or perceived abandonment.

There are also cognitive criteria for diagnosis of BPD that include stress-related, short-lived **paranoia** and/or severe dissociative symptoms—feeling disconnected from oneself, as if observing one's actions from the outside. Symptoms tend to be exacerbated by feelings of isolation and lack of social support. Patients may frantically try to avoid being alone. These symptoms can lead to frequent changes in relationships, jobs, long-term goals, or gender identity. Studies have found that as many as 40% of patients with BPD report having semi-psychotic thoughts and short delusional periods, and that the presence of psychotic symptoms can be a predictor of self-harming behaviors.

Although BPD symptoms can be similar to symptoms of the better known—but less common—schizophrenic and bipolar disorders, the intense episodes of anxiety, **depression**, or anger with BPD usually last only hours, rather than days or weeks. However, these episodes may be associated with impulsive aggression, substance abuse, or self-injury. Although patients with BPD may experience auditory hallucinations, they are aware that they are hallucinating, unlike patients with **schizophrenia**.

BPD is sometimes difficult to diagnose in adolescence, since symptoms such as impulsive and experimental behaviors, insecurity, and mood swings are common in teenagers. Some researchers have further suggested that BPD is not a defined pathological condition but rather overlapping symptoms of other personality disorders.

Diagnosis

Clinicians diagnose BPD on the basis of interviews with the patient and a complete personality assessment. With the patient's permission, family members and friends also may be interviewed. The clinician may require that symptoms that have been consistently present over time match at least five of the nine criteria in the *DSM-IV-TR*. The clinician should rule out chronic substance abuse and/or medical conditions, especially central nervous system disorders, which can cause similar symptoms. The clinician will attempt to identify problems that often occur in conjunction with BPD, including mood disorders such as depression or anxiety, **post-traumatic stress disorder** (PTSD), eating disorders, or **attention deficit hyperactivity disorder** (ADHD).

Treatment

Traditional

Individuals with BPD seek psychiatric help and **hospitalization** at a much higher rate than people with other personality disorders, perhaps because of their fear of abandonment and their search for idealized interpersonal relationships. **Psychotherapy** is the treatment of choice for BPD, and patients often require long-term services. Dialectical behavior therapy (DBT), a type of **cognitive-behavioral therapy** (CBT), has emerged as an effective therapy for individuals with suicidal tendencies. This treatment focuses on decreasing self-harming behaviors and building self-confidence and coping skills through a combination of **social skills training**, mood awareness, meditative exercises, and education about the disorder. **Group therapy** is a component of DBT and is an option for some BPD patients, although patients may feel threatened by the idea of "sharing" their therapist with others.

The nature of BPD makes it a challenging disorder to treat effectively. The therapist-patient relationship is subject to the same inappropriate and unrealistic demands that individuals with BPD place on all of their significant personal relationships. Individuals with BPD are often chronic treatment seekers, who become easily frustrated when they feel that the therapist is not providing adequate attention or empathy. Symptomatic anger, impulsivity, and self-destructive behaviors can further impede the therapist-patient relationship. In addition, some BPD patients may resent any progress in therapy because of their fear of abandonment or of ending the therapist relationship. Addressing the high incidence of suicidal thoughts and tendencies in BPD patients is also a major therapeutic challenge.

Drugs

Medications are often used in conjunction with psychotherapy to treat symptoms of BPD. **Antidepressants**, especially those that enhance the activity of the neurotransmitter serotonin, can improve emotional symptoms. Mood-stabilizing drugs that enhance the activity of gamma-aminobutyric acid (GABA), the primary inhibitory neurotransmitter in the brain, may help with BPD mood swings. In severe cases, antipsychotic drugs may be prescribed. Some patients take several different medications, each designed to address a different manifestation of BPD. However, drugs are rarely effective without individual and group or **family therapy**.

QUESTIONS TO ASK YOUR DOCTOR

- What type of psychotherapy might be appropriate for my condition?
- Are there community resources that might be of help to me?
- What medications might help manage my symptoms?
- Are there resources available for my family and friends?
- Is there a hotline or other number I can call if I am having suicidal thoughts?
- Do you know a therapist who is trained in DBT?

Alternative

Several new psychotherapies have been developed for treating BPD; however, little research on their efficacy has been conducted. Schema therapy combines CBT with techniques from psychodynamic therapies to examine repetitive life patterns or schemas. Mentalization therapy is geared toward helping patients perceive the minds of others as distinct from their own, thereby enabling them to reassess their perceptions of reality. Transference-focused psychotherapy (TFP) is a psychodynamic treatment that attempts to correct patients' perceptions of their therapist and other important people in their lives.

Home remedies

BPD is a serious disorder that requires extensive mental health services and possibly medications. However, because symptoms of the illness are usually focused on interpersonal relationships, family members may need support and therapy as well.

Prognosis

Treatments for BPD have improved in recent years, and many patients are eventually able to lead productive lives. Symptoms of the disorder usually peak in young adulthood and frequently stabilize after age 30, with symptoms improving in later adulthood, especially by about age 40. However, individuals with BPD are at very high risk for suicide attempts. Although estimates vary widely, some studies have found that as many as 80% of those with BPD attempt suicide at least once, and as many as 10% complete suicide. Although suicidal behavior usually peaks when patients are in their mid-20s, most completed suicides occur among patients over 30 and most often involve those who have experienced no improvement after numerous attempts at treatment. BPD patients with a diagnosed depressive disorder have a much higher risk of suicide and require swift diagnosis and appropriate **intervention**. Adults with BPD also are at higher risk for becoming victims of violence, including rape. This may be due to poor judgment and impulsive behaviors that result in patients choosing inappropriate partners and dangerous lifestyles and environments.

Prevention

BPD is thought to result from a complex of causes, and there is no known prevention, other than ensuring a safe and nurturing childhood environment for those at risk for the disorder. Prompt, appropriate treatment for BPD is crucial for preventing the worsening of symptoms and suicidal behaviors.

Resources

BOOKS

American Psychiatric Association. *Diagnostic and Statistical Manual of Mental Disorders (DSM-IV-TR)*, 4th ed., text rev. Washington, DC: American Psychiatric Association, 2000.

Elliot, Charles H., and Laura L. Smith. *Borderline Personality Disorder for Dummies.* Hoboken, NJ: Wiley, 2009.

Krawitz, Roy, and Wendy Jackson. *Borderline Personality Disorder.* New York: Oxford University Press, 2008.

Mason, Paul T., and Randi Kreger. *Stop Walking on Eggshells: Taking Your Life Back When Someone You Care About Has Borderline Personality Disorder,* 2nd ed. Oakland, CA: New Harbinger, 2010.

Porr, Valerie. *Overcoming Borderline Personality Disorder: A Family Guide for Healing and Change.* New York: Oxford University Press, 2010.

PERIODICALS

Bandelow, Borwin, et al. "Borderline Personality Disorder: A Dysregulation of the Endogenous Opioid System?" *Psychological Review* 117, no. 2 (April 2010): 623–636.

Buckner, Randy A., et al. "Early Family Environment, Borderline Personality Symptoms, and Somatic Preoccupation Among Internal Medicine Outpatients." *Comprehensive Psychiatry* (May–June 2009), 221–225.

Eichelman, Burr. "Borderline Personality Disorder, PTSD, and Suicide." *American Journal of Psychiatry* 167, no. 10 (October 2010): 1152–1154.

Neacsiu, Andrada D., Shireen L. Rizvi, and Marsha M. Linehan. "Dialectical Behavior Therapy Skills Use as a Mediator and Outcome of Treatment for Borderline Personality Disorder." *Behaviour Research and Therapy* 48, no. 9 (September 2010): 832–839.

Prossin, Alan R., et al. "Dysregulation of Regional Endogenous Opioid Function in Borderline Personality Disorder." *American Journal of Psychiatry* 167, no. 8 (August 2010): 925–934.

Raven, Christopher. "Borderline Personality Disorder: Still a Diagnosis of Exclusion?" *Mental Health Today* (June 2009): 26–31.

Samuel, D. B., et al. "Conceptual Changes to the Definition of Borderline Personality Disorder Proposed for DSM-5." *Journal of Abnormal Psychology* (August 29, 2011) [e-pub ahead of print].

WEBSITES

"Borderline Personality Disorder." Mental Health America. http://www.mentalhealthamerica.net/go/information/get-info/borderline-personality-disporder (accessed November 29, 2010).

"Borderline Personality Disorder." National Institute of Mental Health. August 24, 2010. http://www.nimh.nih.gov/health/publications/borderline-personality-disorder-fact-sheet/index.shtml (accessed November 29, 2010).

"Frequently Asked Questions." BPDCentral. http://www.bpdcentral.com/faqs.shtml (accessed November 29, 2010).

"Treatment of Borderline Personality Disorder." Facing the Facts/BPDFamily.com. August 3, 2010. http://www.bpdfamily.com/bpdresources/nk_a107.htm (accessed November 30, 2010).

ORGANIZATIONS

American Psychiatric Association, 1000 Wilson Blvd., Ste. 1825, Arlington, VA, 22209-3901, (703) 907-7300, apa@psych.org, http://www.psych.org.

Mental Health America, 2000 N. Beauregard St., 6th Fl., Alexandria, VA, 22311, (703) 684-7722, (800) 969-6642, Fax: (703) 684-5968, http://www.nmha.org.

National Education Alliance for Borderline Personality Disorder, PO Box 974, Rye, NY, 10580.info@neabpd.com, http://www.borderlinepersonalitydisorder.com.

National Institute of Mental Health, 6001 Executive Blvd., Room 8184, MSC 9663, Bethesda, MD, 20892-9663, (301) 443-4513, (866) 615-6464, Fax: (301) 443-4279, nimhinfo@nih.gov, http://www.nimh.nih.gov.

Personality Disorders Awareness Network, 490 Sun Valley Dr., Ste. 205, Roswell, GA, 30076, (770) 642-4236 x61, Fax: (770) 642-4239, info@pdan.org, http://www.pdan.org.

Treatment and Research Advancements National Association for Personality Disorder, 23 Greene St., New York, NY, 10013, (212) 966-6514, (888) 4-TARA-APD, http://www.tara4bpd.org.

Laith Farid Guilli, MD
Margaret Alic, PhD

Brain

Definition

The brain is the part of the central nervous system (CNS) located inside the skull. It is made up of nerve cells (neurons) and supporting glial cells. Along with the spinal cord and network of nerves, the brain controls information flow throughout the body; voluntary actions such as walking, reading, and talking; involuntary (autonomic) reactions such as breathing and digestion; and cognitive functions such as thinking, learning, and memory.

Description

The human brain is a soft, shiny, grayish-white, mushroom-shaped structure. The gray matter of the brain consists primarily of nerve cell bodies, and the white matter consists primarily of long nerve cell processes called axons that are covered with myelin sheaths. Neurons carry information in the brain and throughout the nervous system in the form of brief electrical impulses. When an impulse reaches the end of an axon, **neurotransmitters** are released at junctions called synapses. These chemicals bind to receptors on the receiving neurons, triggering the continuation of the impulse.

During embryonic development, the gray matter grows faster than the white and folds in on itself, giving rise to convoluted ridges, called gyri, and grooves or valleys, called sulci, thereby creating a large surface area. At birth, the average infant's brain weighs 13.7 oz (390 g); by age 15, it has nearly reached its full adult size of about 3 lb (1.4 kg).

The brain is protected by the skull and three layers of membrane called the meninges, which also cover and protect the spinal cord. The major divisions of the brain are the brain stem, cerebellum, diencephalon, and cerebrum. The latter consists of two large, paired cerebral hemispheres.

Brain stem

The brain stem sits at the base of the brain and connects the brain with the spinal cord. The spinal cord conducts sensory and motor nerve impulses between the brain and the peripheral nervous system. Ascending nerve pathways carry the information through the brain stem to the rest of the brain, and descending nerve pathways carry information from higher brain regions to peripheral nerves to coordinate motor function. In addition, twelve pairs of cranial nerves originate in the underside of the brain, primarily in the brain stem, and exit the skull through openings. These nerves carry information to and from the sensory organs and muscles of the head and neck and the organs of the chest and upper gastrointestinal tract. The brain stem consists of the medulla oblongata, pons, and midbrain.

MEDULLA OBLONGATA. The medulla oblongata is closest to the spinal cord. It is vaguely scoop-shaped, with longitudinal grooves corresponding to numerous nerve tracts. Every nerve transmission between the brain and spinal cord passes through the medulla. The fibers on

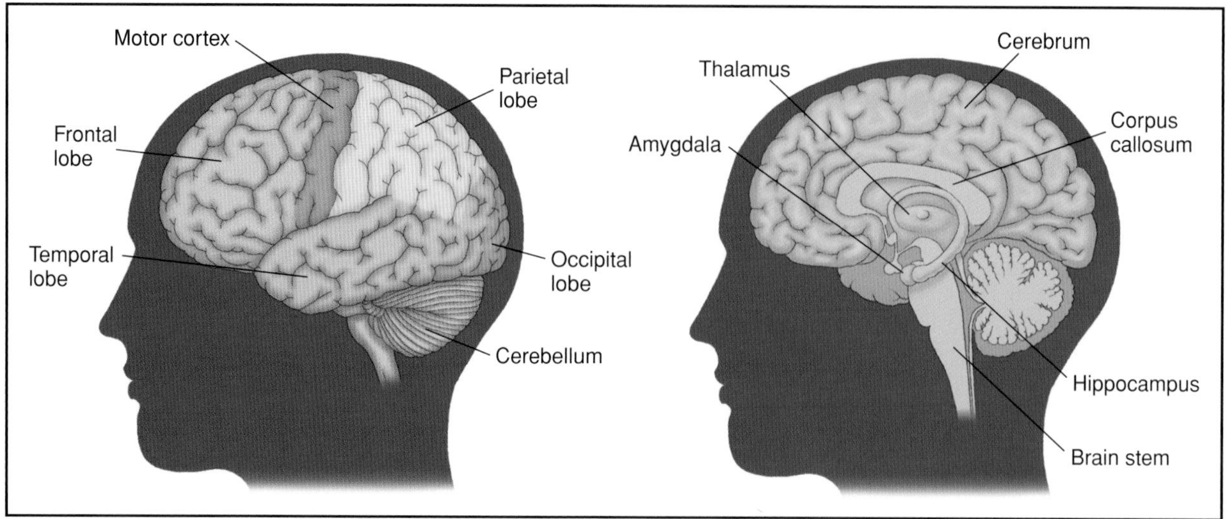

Diagram showing the exterior (left) and interior (right) anatomy of the human brain. *(Illustration by Frank Forney. Reproduced by permission of Cengage Learning.)*

the right side of the medulla cross to the left and those on the left cross to the right. Thus, each side of the brain controls the opposite side of the body. The medulla regulates vital body functions, such as heartbeat, breathing rate, and dilation of blood vessels, and helps coordinate swallowing, vomiting, hiccupping, coughing, and sneezing.

PONS. The pons, Latin for "bridge," conducts messages between the spinal cord and the rest of the brain and between different parts of the brain. It is involved in motor control, sensory analysis, and consciousness levels and sleep. Some structures within the pons are linked to the cerebellum and are involved in movement and posture.

MIDBRAIN. The midbrain or mesencephalon is the smallest and most anterior portion of the brain stem. It conveys impulses between the cerebral cortex, pons, and spinal cord, and has visual and audio reflex centers that are involved in eye and head movements. The anterior portion of the midbrain includes the cerebral peduncle, a large bundle of axons extending from the cerebral cortex through the brain stem that are important for voluntary motor function.

Diencephalon

The diencephalon, or "between brain," lies between the midbrain and the cerebral hemispheres and connects the cerebral hemispheres to the limbic system. It consists of the thalamus and hypothalamus.

The thalamus is a large body of gray matter at the top of the diencephalon, positioned deep within the forebrain. Axons from every sensory system except olfaction (smell) enter the thalamus and relay sensory information to the cerebral cortex. The thalamus also has some motor functions and regulates some emotions and memory.

The hypothalamus controls a number of body functions and helps regulate the endocrine or hormonal system through control of the pituitary gland. The hypothalamus controls the autonomic nervous system, including body temperature, heartbeat, and digestion; emotional responses including anger and aggression; thirst and hunger; and circadian rhythms including sleep.

Cerebrum

Constituting nearly 90% of the brain's weight, the cerebrum is formed by the cerebral hemispheres, which are connected by a bundle of white matter called the corpus callosum.

Each cerebral hemisphere has a somewhat different function. The left hemisphere works mainly in speech and language comprehension, logic, writing, and arithmetic. The right hemisphere is more involved with spatial relations, symbolism, art, and imagination. Because damage to the left hemisphere is more likely to cause language deficits, it is commonly referred to as the dominant hemisphere. Nearly all right-handed people and most left-handed people have a left-dominant brain, though some people have a right-dominant brain or language function that is more equally distributed between the hemispheres.

The basal ganglia are four masses of gray matter located deep within each of the cerebral hemispheres. They modulate the output of the frontal cortex involving motor function, as well as cognition and motivation. The corpus striatum is the major point of entry into the basal ganglia circuitry, receiving input from almost all cortical areas. The corpus striatum is subdivided into the caudate nucleus, putamen, and globus pallidus.

The hemispheres are covered by the gray matter of the cerebral cortex. The cortex accounts for about 40% of the brain's total mass, with a surface area of over 1 sq yd. (about 1 sq m). It is the site of the highest level of neural functioning, including higher motor functions, perception, language, cognition, emotion, and memory.

The cerebral cortex is divided into four major lobes. The frontal lobe contains the primary motor cortex and premotor area, involved in voluntary movement; Broca's area, involved in writing and speech; and the prefrontal cortex, involved in personality, insight, and foresight. The parietal lobe contains the primary somatosensory cortex, which is involved in tactile and positioning information, as well as areas affecting spatial orientation and language comprehension. The temporal lobe contains the primary auditory cortex; Wernicke's area, involved in language comprehension and meaning; and areas involved in the higher processing of visual input, along with the aspects of learning and memory associated with the limbic system. The occipital lobe contains the primary visual cortex and the visual association cortex.

Cerebellum

The cerebellum is located below the cerebrum and behind the brain stem. It is butterfly shaped, with the "wings" forming the two cerebellar hemispheres; the two halves are connected by the vermis. The cerebellum coordinates many neuromuscular functions, such as balance, movement, and posture. Disorders of or damage to the cerebellum often result in ataxia (problems with coordination), dysarthria (unclear speech due to lack of muscle control), and nystagmus (uncontrollable jerking of the eyeballs).

Limbic system

The limbic system is sometimes referred to as the "emotional brain." It is involved in drive-related behavior, memory, and emotional responses, including feeding, defense, and sexuality. The limbic system includes the limbic lobe, which is buried within the cerebrum and includes portions of the frontal, parietal, and temporal lobes. It also includes the amygdalae—one of the four basal ganglia of each hemisphere—which are involved in memory, emotion, and fear. The amygdalae lie beneath the surface of the temporal lobes where they cause a bulge called the uncus. The other structures of the limbic system are the hippocampi of the cerebral hemispheres and the thalamus and hypothalamus of the diencephalon.

The hippocampus, referred to as the "gateway to memory," is involved in learning and memory functions. It converts short-term memory into more permanent memory and is involved in the storage and retrieval of long-term memory and recall of learned spatial associations. The hippocampus is a curved sheet of cortex folded into the basal medial portion of the temporal lobe. It is divided into three multilayered sections, the dentate gyrus, hippocampus proper, and subiculum, with the latter situated as a transitional zone between the other two. The dentate gyrus receives input from the cortex and sends output to the hippocampus proper, which then sends output to the subiculum.

Nervous tracts

Tracts are groups or bundles of nerve fibers that constitute an anatomical and functional unit. Commissural tracts, such as the corpus callosum, connect the cerebral hemispheres. Association tracts make connections within the same hemisphere. Projection tracts connect the brain with the spinal cord. Sensory tracts project upward from the spinal cord into regions of the brain. Motor tracts project down from the brain into the spinal cord, bringing motor output information to the periphery. The internal capsule is the major structure carrying ascending and descending nerve projection fibers to and from the cerebral cortex.

Meninges and ventricular systems

The meninges are membranes that cover and protect the central nervous system (CNS), enclosing the cerebrospinal fluid (CSF) that buoys up the brain. The three membranes of the meninges are the thick external dura mater, which supplies mechanical strength; the middle web-like, delicate arachnoid mater, which forms a protective barrier and space for CSF circulation, and the internal pia mater, which is continuous with all the contours of the brain and forms CSF. The dura mater contains six major venous sinuses that drain the cerebral veins and several smaller sinuses.

Dural venous sinuses are formed in spaces where the two layers of the dura mater separate. The superior sagittal sinus, straight sinus, and right and left transverse sinuses meet in a structure called the confluence of the sinuses. Venous blood circulation follows a pathway through the superior sagittal and straight sinuses into the confluence and then through the transverse sinuses. Each transverse sinus carries venous blood along an S-shaped course until it empties into the internal jugular vein. The major dural sinuses also connect with several smaller sinuses.

The arachnoid mater follows the general shape of the brain. The space between the arachnoid mater and pia

KEY TERMS

Amygdala—One of the four basal ganglia in each cerebral hemisphere, consisting of a mass of gray matter in the roof of the lateral ventricle; part of the limbic system.

Anterior—Situated toward the head or front.

Axon—The long process that conducts impulses away from the nerve cell body.

Brain stem—The part of the brain that connects the forebrain and cerebrum to the spinal cord; consisting of the midbrain, pons, and medulla oblongata.

Central nervous system (CNS)—The brain and spinal cord.

Cerebellum—The part of the brain between the brain stem and back of the cerebrum, consisting of two lateral lobes and a median lobe, and involved especially in muscle coordination and maintenance of bodily equilibrium.

Cerebral cortex—The convoluted surface gray matter of the cerebrum that coordinates motor and sensory information and cognitive function.

Cerebrospinal fluid (CSF)—The fluid that circulates through the central nervous system to maintain uniform pressure on the brain and spinal cord.

Cerebrum—The enlarged, forward portion overlying the rest of the brain, consisting of the two cerebral hemispheres and connecting structures, and responsible for conscious mental processes.

Cognition—Conscious intellectual activity, including thinking, imagining, reasoning, remembering, and learning.

Corpus callosum—(plural, corpora callosa) A thick bundle of nerve fibers lying deep in the brain that connects the two cerebral hemispheres and coordinates their functions.

Diencephalon—The "between brain" or "interbrain" beneath the cerebral hemispheres and consisting of the thalamus and hypothalamus.

Glial cells—The support cells of nervous tissue, especially in the brain, spinal cord, and ganglia, interspersed between signal-transmitting neurons. There are three main types of neuroglia: astrocytes, oligodendrocytes, and microglia.

Gyri—Convoluted ridges between the sulci or grooves on the surface of the brain.

Hippocampus—A part of the limbic system that extends over the floor of the descending horn of each lateral ventricle and is important for forming, storing, and processing memory.

Hypothalamus—Part of the diencephalon beneath the thalamus that controls the autonomic nervous system and regulates hormone production by the adjacent pituitary gland.

Limbic system—Brain structures, including the hypothalamus, hippocampi, and amygdalae, that are involved in emotion and motivation.

Meninges—The three membranes that enclose the brain and spinal cord, consisting of the dura mater, arachnoid mater, and pia mater.

Myelin—A white, fatty substance that covers and protects nerves.

Neuron—Cells that transmit and receive nerve impulses; consisting of a cell body and multiple projections called dendrites or solitary axons that conduct impulses to and from the cell body.

Neurotransmitter—A chemical, such as dopamine, norepinephrine, or serotonin, that transmits nerve impulses across synapses.

Peripheral nerve—A nerve in a distant location from the brain that receives information in the form of an impulse from the brain and spinal cord.

Pituitary gland—A small endocrine organ in the brain that is associated with various hormones that control and regulate other endocrine organs. The pituitary affects most basic bodily functions, including growth and development.

Sulci—The furrows or grooves on the surface of the brain between convolutions.

Synapse—The space at which a nerve impulse passes from one neuron to the next.

Thalamus—The largest portion of the diencephalon, which relays impulses, especially sensory impulses, to and from the cerebral cortex.

Ventricular system—The system of small cavities in the brain that forms, circulates, and drains the cerebrospinal fluid.

mater is called the subarachnoid space and contains CSF. CSF enters venous circulation through small protrusions into the venous sinus called arachnoid villi. The pia mater forms part of the choroid plexus, a highly convoluted and vascular membranous material that lies within the ventricular system of the brain and is responsible for most CSF production.

The brain contains four ventricles. Each cerebral hemisphere contains a long, C-shaped lateral ventricle that communicates with the narrow, slit-shaped third ventricle of the diencephalon. The third ventricle communicates with the tent-shaped fourth ventricle of the pons and medulla, which protrudes into the cerebellum. CSF flows in a specific pattern that allows newly formed CSF to replace the old several times daily. The CSF is formed in the lateral ventricles, flows into the third and then the fourth ventricle, into basal cisterns, up and over the cerebral hemispheres, and into the arachnoid villi, where it is drained into a venous sinus for return to the venous system. Some CSF is diverted from the basal cisterns into the subarachnoid space of the spinal cord.

Studying the brain

Neurons carry information through the nervous system in the form of brief electrical impulses called action potentials. When an impulse reaches the end of an axon, neurotransmitters are released at junctions called synapses. The neurotransmitters are chemicals that bind to receptors on the receiving neurons, triggering the continuation of the impulse. Fifty different neurotransmitters have been discovered since the first was identified in 1920. By studying the chemical effects of neurotransmitters in the brain, scientists have developed treatments for mental disorders and are learning more about how drugs affect the brain.

Electroencephalogram

Technology provides useful tools for researching the brain and helping patients with brain disorders. An electroencephalogram (EEG) records brain waves, which are produced by electrical activity in the brain. It is obtained by positioning electrodes on the head and amplifying the waves with an electroencephalograph. EEGs are valuable in diagnosing brain diseases such as epilepsy and tumors.

Magnetic resonance imaging (MRI)

Using a magnetic field to display the living brain at various depths, **magnetic resonance imaging** can produce very clear and detailed pictures of brain structures. These images, which often appear as cross-sectional slices, are obtained by altering the main magnetic field of a specific brain area. MRI is particularly valuable in diagnosing damage to soft tissues, such as areas affected by head **trauma**. MRI also reveals tumors and other types of brain lesions.

Positron emission tomography (PET)

During a **positron emission tomography** scan, a technician injects the patient with a small amount of a substance, such as glucose, that is marked with a radioactive tag. By tracking the radioactive substance as it travels to the brain, physicians can see almost immediately where glucose is consumed in the brain. This indicates brain activity, an important factor in diagnosing epilepsy, **Alzheimer's disease**, or Parkinson's disease. **PET** is also valuable in locating tumors and brain areas that have been affected by a **stroke** or blood clot.

Researchers have developed a molecule, abbreviated FDDNP, that binds to the plaques and protein tangles that characterize Alzheimer's disease in the brain. This molecule also is fluorescent, and after injection of a solution of FDDNP into a patient, clinicians can use PET to capture an image of the brain showing where it has bound and is fluorescing. In this way, they can distinguish a brain even with mild cognitive impairment when compared to a brain with no cognitive impairment and also can distinguish mild impairment from Alzheimer's disease.

Magnetoencephalography (MEG)

Magnetoencephalography measures the electromagnetic fields created between neurons as electrochemical information is passed along. Of all brain-scanning methods, MEG provides the most accurate indicator of nerve cell activity, which can be measured in milliseconds. By combining an MRI with MEG, clinicians can get a noninvasive look at the brain that is especially useful in diagnosing epilepsy or migraines. MEG also helps identify specific brain areas involved with different tasks. Any movement by the patient—wiggling the toes, for example—appears on the computer screen immediately as concentric colored rings. This pinpoints brain signals even before the toes are actually wiggled. Researchers foresee that these techniques could someday help paralysis victims move by supplying information on how to stimulate their muscles or indicating the signals needed to control an artificial limb.

Computed axial tomography scan (CT or CAT)

Computed tomography scans use x rays to produce a picture of the targeted area of the body in cross sections. Clinicians may use a dye that creates a contrast between tissues to highlight a specific area of interest for the scan. In the brain, this type of scan can be used to identify an area of stroke or hemorrhage, causes of headache, and causes of lost sensory or motor function. This test may also be used in the **diagnosis** of other disorders involving the brain, including **delirium**, **dementia**, and **schizophrenia**.

Resources

BOOKS

Ashwell, Ken W. S. *Anatomica: The Complete Home Medical Reference*. Richmond Hill, Ontario: Firefly, 2010.

Carter, Rita, et al. *The Human Brain Book*. New York: DK Pub., 2009.

PERIODICALS

Brenninkmeijer, Jonna. "Taking Care of One's Brain: How Manipulating the Brain Changes People's Selves." *History of the Human Sciences* 23, no. 1 (February 2010): 107–26.

Dekosky, Steven T., Milos D. Ikonomovic, and Sam Gandy. "Traumatic Brain Injury—Football, Warfare, and Long-Term Effects." *New England Journal of Medicine* 363, no. 14 (September 30, 2010): 1293–96.

Ogilvie, Megan. "Genesis: The Life of the Brain." *Toronto Star*, (July 10, 2010): IN.1.

Raichle, Marcus E. "The Brain's (Dark Energy)." *Scientific American* 201, no. 3 (March 2010): 44.

Small, Gary W., et al. "PET of Brain Amyloid and Tau in Mild Cognitive Impairment." *The New England Journal of Medicine* 355 (2006): 2652–63.

WEBSITES

Chudler, Eric H. "Brain Facts and Figures." Neuroscience for Kids. http://faculty.washington.edu/chudler/facts.html (accessed September 30, 2011).

MedlinePlus. "Brain Diseases." U.S. National Library of Medicine, National Institutes of Health. http://www.nlm.nih.gov/medlineplus/braindiseases.html (accessed September 30, 2011).

U.S. National Institute of Mental Health. "Neuroimaging and Mental Illness: A Window Into the Brain." http://www.nimh.nih.gov/health/publications/neuroimaging-and-mental-illness-a-window-into-the-brain/neuroimaging-and-mental-illness-a-window-into-the-brain.shtml (accessed September 30, 2011).

U.S. National Institute of Neurological Disorders and Stroke. "Brain Basics: Know Your Brain." http://www.ninds.nih.gov/disorders/brain_basics/know_your_brain.htm (accessed September 30, 2011).

ZERO TO THREE: National Center for Infants, Toddlers and Families. "Early Experiences Matter." http://main.zerotothree.org/site/PageServer?pagename=ter_key_brainFAQ (accessed September 30, 2011).

ORGANIZATIONS

National Institute of Mental Health, 6001 Executive Blvd., Room 8184, MSC 9663, Bethesda, MD, 20892-9663, (301) 433-4513; TTY: (301) 443-8431, (866) 615-6464; TTY: (866) 415-8051, Fax: (301) 443-4279, nimhinfo@nih.gov, http://www.nimh.nih.gov.

National Institute of Neurological Disorders and Stroke, PO Box 5801, Bethesda, MD, 20824, (301) 496-5751; TTY: (301) 468-5981, (800) 352-9424, http://www.ninds.nih.gov.

Breathing-related sleep disorder

Definition

Breathing-related sleep disorder is marked by sleep disruption from abnormal breathing during sleep. The most common complaint of individuals with breathing-related sleep disorder is excessive daytime sleepiness, brought on by frequent interruptions of nocturnal, or nighttime, sleep. A less frequent complaint is **insomnia** or inability to sleep. About two-thirds of people with this disorder experience daytime sleepiness, and one-third experience an inability to sleep.

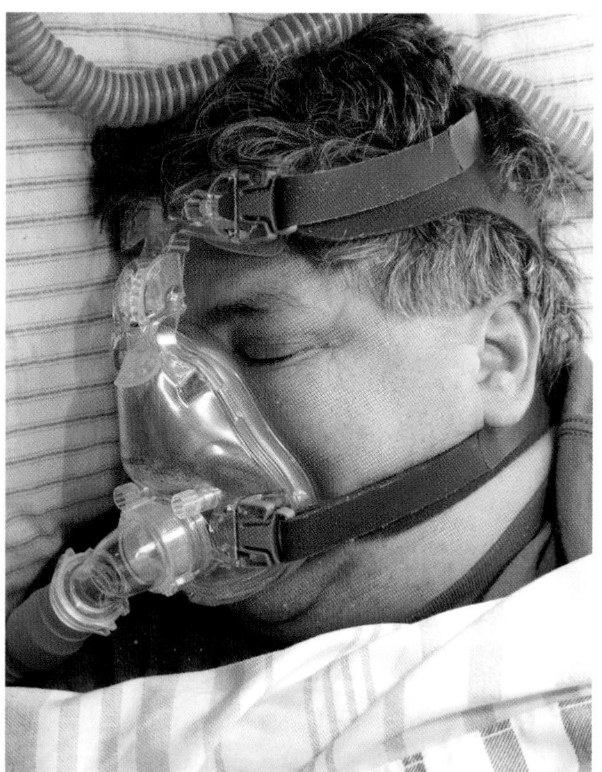

An individual undergoes the continuous positive airway pressure (CPAP) test for sleep apnea. *(© Custom Medical Stock Photo, Inc. Reproduced by permission.)*

Mental health professionals use the ***Diagnostic and Statistical Manual of Mental Disorders***, also known as the *DSM* to diagnose mental disorders. In the fourth edition, text revision *(DSM-IV-TR)*, breathing-related sleep disorder is listed as one of several different primary **sleep disorders**. Within the category of primary sleep disorders, it is classified as one of the dyssomnias, which are characterized by irregularities in the quality, timing, and amount of sleep.

The *DSM-IV-TR* lists three types of breathing-related sleep disorder: obstructive sleep apnea syndrome (the most common type), central sleep apnea syndrome, and central alveolar hypoventilation syndrome.

The fifth edition of the *DSM* (*DSM-5*, 2013) proposes placing breathing-related sleep disorder under wake-sleep disorders and dividing it into obstructive sleep apnea hypopnea syndrome, primary central sleep apnea, and primary alveolar hypoventilation.

Demographics

The National Center on Sleep Disorder Research estimates that between 40 and 70 million Americans experience chronic or intermittent sleep-related disorders. The majority of patients with the obstructive sleep apnea type of breathing-related sleep disorder are overweight, middle-aged males. Four percent of middle-aged men and 2% of middle-aged women meet the criteria for obstructive sleep apnea. Among children, the male-to-female ratio is 1:1. Prevalence of breathing-related sleep disorder among children peaks between two and eight years of age.

Description

The most common feature of any breathing-related sleep disorder is interruption of the person's sleep, leading to excessive daytime sleepiness. When the regular nighttime sleep of individuals is frequently interrupted, sleepiness at other times of the day is the usual result. People with breathing-related sleep disorder often find that they feel sleepy during relaxing activities such as reading or watching a movie. With extreme cases, those with this condition may feel so sleepy that they fall asleep during activities that require alertness, such as talking, walking, or driving.

Other people with breathing-related sleep disorder report having insomnia, or the inability to sleep. Patients also find that their sleep does not refresh them; they may awaken frequently during sleep, or have difficulty breathing while sleeping or lying down.

The two sleep apnea syndromes that are listed as subtypes of breathing-related sleep disorder are characterized by episodes of airway blockage or breathing cessation during sleep. Sleep apnea is potentially deadly. Central alveolar hypoventilation syndrome is distinguished from the other two subtypes of breathing-related sleep disorder by the fact that shallow breathing causes reduced oxygen content of the blood. The alveoli, which are the tiny air sacs in the lung tissue, cannot oxygenate the blood efficiently because those with this disorder are not breathing deeply enough. Shallow breathing often occurs when people are awake and is common in severely overweight individuals.

Causes and symptoms

Causes

Many people with the obstructive sleep apnea syndrome subtype of breathing-related sleep disorder are overweight. The symptoms often grow worse as their weight increases. People who have obstructive sleep apnea and are not overweight often have breathing passages that are narrowed by swollen tonsils, abnormally large adenoids, or other abnormalities of the various structures of the mouth and throat. The fundamental underlying cause appears to be a narrow or collapsible airway with a loss of muscle tone in the airway during sleep.

Central sleep apnea syndrome is often associated with cardiac or neurological conditions affecting airflow regulation. It is a disorder that occurs most frequently in elderly patients.

Patients diagnosed with central alveolar hypoventilation syndrome experience a breathing impairment related to abnormally low arterial oxygen levels.

Symptoms

Obstructive sleep apnea syndrome, which is the most common type of breathing-related sleep disorder, is marked by frequent episodes of upper airway obstruction during sleep. Patients with this syndrome alternate between loud snores or gasps and silent periods that usually last for 20–30 seconds. The snoring is caused by the partial blockage of the airway. The silent periods are caused by complete obstruction of the airway, which makes the patient's breathing stop. These periods of breathing cessation can last between 10 seconds and one minute.

Obstructive sleep apnea syndrome is also common in children with enlarged tonsils. The symptoms of any breathing-related sleep disorder in children are often subtle and more difficult to diagnose. Children under five years are more likely to demonstrate nighttime symptoms such as apnea and breathing difficulties. Children over five years are more likely to demonstrate daytime symptoms such as sleepiness and attention difficulties.

People with central sleep apnea syndrome experience periods when the oxygenation of blood in the lungs temporarily stops during sleep, but they do not suffer airway obstruction. Although these patients may snore, their snoring is usually mild and not a major complaint.

Central alveolar hypoventilation syndrome is characterized by excessive sleepiness and insomnia.

Diagnosis

A **diagnosis** of breathing-related sleep disorder usually requires a thorough physical examination of the patient. The patient may be referred to an otorhinolaryngologist (a doctor who specializes in disorders of the ear, nose, and throat) for a detailed evaluation of the upper respiratory tract. The physical examination is followed by observation of the patient in a sleep clinic or laboratory. Breathing patterns, including episodes of snoring and apnea, are evaluated when the patient is connected to a device called a polysomnogram. The polysomnogram uses a set of electrodes to measure several different body functions associated with sleep, including heart rate, eye movements, **brain** waves, muscle activity, breathing, changes in blood oxygen concentration, and body position. Interviews are also conducted with the patients and their partners.

To meet criteria for the diagnosis of breathing-related sleep disorder, patients must experience interruptions of sleep leading to insomnia or excessive sleepiness that have been determined to result from one of the following sleep-related breathing conditions: obstructive sleep apnea syndrome, central sleep apnea syndrome, or central alveolar hypoventilation syndrome.

The disturbance in sleep must also not be attributed to another mental disorder, to a general medical condition not related to breathing, or to the direct effects on the body of a prescription medication or drug of abuse.

Treatment

Weight loss is key to effective treatment of overweight people with breathing-related sleep disorder. It is often considered the first step in treating any disorder involving sleep apnea. Increased **exercise** and reduced-calorie **diets** are the most important components of an effective weight loss regimen.

Another approach to addressing sleep apnea is a postural change during sleep, called "positional therapy." The U.S. Food and Drug Administration (FDA) has approved a pillow that is supposed to aid in preventing the sleeper from assuming a supine (on the back) position, which may worsen sleep apnea. Postural alarms are being marketed to warn the sleeper, but many people try home-based approaches to ensure that they do not flip onto their backs during sleep. One study found that sleeping on the back with the torso elevated may result in reduced apneas but recommended that patients trying this option use foam pillows rather than soft pillows, which can push the chin onto the chest and worsen apnea.

Oral appliances may be effective for people who have mild apnea. The most common of these is the mandibular advancement device (also called MAD), which pushes the lower jaw forward, keeping the airway open.

Continuous positive airway pressure therapy, also known as CPAP therapy, is a popular form of treatment for the obstructive sleep apnea subtype of breathing-related sleep disorder. CPAP therapy, which has been in use since 1981, involves the use of a high-pressure blower that delivers continuous air flow to a mask worn by the patient during sleep. The airflow from the CPAP blower is often very effective in reducing or eliminating sleep apnea episodes. CPAP treatment is, however, inconvenient and somewhat noisy for anyone who must share a bedroom with the patient. Patients do not always comply with this form of treatment because they may find it to be too constrictive and cumbersome. In addition, they may experience mask discomfort, nasal congestion, and nose and throat dryness. Proper mask fitting and a humidifier can help to alleviate some side effects. A couple of alternative forms of CPAP may improve **compliance** by improving comfort, including bi-level positive airway pressure, which has two sets of air pressures that it delivers, one for exhalation and one for inhalation, to make using the device more comfortable. Another product is the C-Flex, which provides flexible positive airway pressure, alternating pressures for inhalation and exhalation on a breath-by-breath basis. The company that produces the C-Flex received FDA permission to market its product in 2004. CPAPs, as medical devices, must be obtained through a doctor's prescription.

There are no medications that directly target sleep apnea.

Surgery to relieve airway obstruction may be performed in some cases. If the airway obstruction is related to anatomical structures that narrow the airway, surgical reshaping of the soft palate and uvula (a small, conical-shaped piece of tissue attached to the middle of the soft palate) may be performed. Another surgical procedure that is sometimes conducted on very obese patients with obstructive sleep apnea is a tracheostomy, or an artificial opening made in the windpipe. This operation has a number of unpleasant side effects, however, and so is usually reserved for patients whose breathing-related disorder is life threatening.

KEY TERMS

Alveolar—Pertaining to alveoli, which are tiny air sacs at the ends of the small air passages in the lungs.

Apnea—A brief suspension or interruption of breathing.

Dyssomnia—A type of sleep disorder characterized by a problem with the amount, quality, or timing of the patient's sleep.

Hypoventilation—An abnormally low level of blood oxygenation in the lungs.

Polysomnogram—A machine that is used to diagnose sleep disorders by measuring and recording a variety of body functions related to sleep, including heart rate, eye movements, brain waves, muscle activity, breathing, changes in blood oxygen concentration, and body position.

Syndrome—A group of symptoms that together characterize a disease or disorder.

Tracheostomy—A surgical procedure in which an artificial opening is made in the patient's windpipe to relieve airway obstruction.

Patients with sleep apnea are advised to abstain from alcohol and sedative medications, which are often given to patients who display any type of sleeping irregularities. Alcohol and **sedatives** often increase the likelihood of upper airway problems during sleep.

Prognosis

Breathing-related sleep disorder often has a gradual long-term progression and a chronic course. For this reason, many people have the disorder for years before seeking treatment. For many, symptoms worsen during middle age, causing people to seek treatment at that point.

Successful treatment of other conditions, such as obesity, common cardiovascular and cerebrovascular comorbidities, or enlarged tonsils in children, often aids in the treatment of breathing-related sleep disorder. Weight loss often leads to spontaneous resolution of the disorder. Because **depression** has been found at high rates among people with sleep apnea (as high as 64% in some studies), any assessments should evaluate for the presence of depression to aid in improving the prognosis.

Prevention

Because overweight people are more likely to develop the more common obstructive sleep apnea type of breathing-related sleep disorder, a good preventive measure is effective weight management. Good general health and treatment of related physiological conditions are also effective in preventing the disorder.

Resources

BOOKS

American Psychiatric Association. *Diagnostic and Statistical Manual of Mental Disorders*. 4th ed., text rev. Washington, DC: American Psychiatric Publishing, 2000.

Buysse, Daniel J., Charles M. Morin, and Charles F. Reynolds III. "Sleep Disorders." In *Treatments of Psychiatric Disorders*, edited by Glen O. Gabbard. Washington, DC: American Psychiatric Publishing, 2010.

Buysse, Daniel J. *Sleep Disorders and Psychiatry*. Washington, DC: American Psychiatric Publishing, 2010.

Pollak, Charles P., Michael Thorpy, and Jan Yager. *The Encyclopedia of Sleep and Sleep Disorders*. New York: Facts on File, 2009.

PERIODICALS

Aloia, Mark S., et al. "Treatment Adherence and Outcomes in Flexible vs. Standard Continuous Positive Airway Pressure Therapy." *Chest* 127 (2005): 2085–93.

Dauvilliers, Yves, and A. Buguet. "Hypersomnia." *Dialogues in Clinical Neuroscience* 7, no. 4 (2005): 347–56.

Haba-Rubio, José. "Psychiatric Aspects of Organic Sleep Disorders." *Dialogues in Clinical Neuroscience* 7, no. 4 (2005): 335–46.

Lloberes, Patricia, et al. "Predictive Factors of Quality-of-life Improvement and Continuous Positive Airway Pressure Use in Patients with Sleep Apnea-Hypopnea Syndrome: Study at 1 Year." *Chest* 126, no. 4 (October 2004): 1241–47.

WEBSITES

Cataletto, Mary E., et al. "Breathing-Related Sleep Disorder." Medscape Reference. http://emedicine.medscape.com/article/291807-overview (accessed September 30, 2011).

U.S. National Heart Lung and Blood Institute. "What is Sleep Apnea?" http://www.nhlbi.nih.gov/health/dci/Diseases/SleepApnea/SleepApnea_WhatIs.html (accessed September 30, 2011).

ORGANIZATIONS

American Sleep Apnea Association, 6856 Eastern Ave. NW, Ste. 203, Washington, DC, (202) 293-3650, Fax: (202) 293-3656, http://www.sleepapnea.org.

American Sleep Disorders Association, 6301 Bandel Rd. NW, Ste. 101, Rochester, MN, 55901, http://www.asda.org.

National Center on Sleep Disorders Research, 6701 Rockledge Drive, Bethesda, MD, (301) 435-0199, Fax: (301) 480-3451, http://www.nhlbi.nih.gov.

National Sleep Foundation, 1010 N Glebe Rd., Ste. 310, Arlington, VA, 22201, (703) 243-1697, nsf@sleepfoundation.org, http://www.sleepfoundation.org.

Ali Fahmy, PhD
Emily Jane Willingham, PhD

Brief psychotic disorder

Definition

Brief psychotic disorder is a short-term **psychosis** lasting between one day and one month, with complete recovery following the episode. It is characterized by at least one symptom of psychosis, such as **delusions**, hallucinations, incoherence, severely disorganized thinking or behavior, or catatonic behavior.

Demographics

Although the incidence of brief psychotic disorder is not known, it is relatively rare in the United States and other developed countries. One study of 221 patients admitted to U.S. hospitals for a first-time psychotic episode found that only 9% were experiencing brief psychoses. Although mental disorders with psychotic symptoms lasting longer than one month, such as **schizophrenia**, are more prevalent in developed nations, the incidence of brief psychotic reactions and disorders appears to be up to ten-fold higher in the developing world. Some clinicians believe that brief psychotic disorder is more common among those of lower socioeconomic status, as well as among immigrants. An international epidemiological study found that brief psychotic disorder was twice as common in women as in men. In the United States, the incidence in women is more than two-fold higher than in men. Brief psychotic disorder is more common in adolescents and young adults in their twenties and thirties than in older adults. Stress-induced brief psychotic disorder most often affects adults in their twenties through their forties.

Description

Brief psychotic disorder is a **diagnosis** that is more common and better studied in Scandinavia and other parts of Western Europe than in the United States. It is defined as one or more temporary symptoms of psychosis that are not attributable to a physical disease, a clinical diagnosis of mental illness, a reaction to medication, or intoxication with drugs or alcohol. In contrast to **schizophreniform disorder**, which lasts at least one month but less than six months, and schizophrenia, which lasts longer than six months, brief psychotic disorder lasts from one day to one month. Patients may or may not be aware of their psychoses. As with all psychotic disorders, brief psychotic disorder can be severely disruptive and can potentially lead to violence or **suicide**.

There are several types of brief psychotic disorder:

- Stress-induced psychosis, also called brief psychotic disorder with obvious stressor or brief reactive psychosis, is by far the most common type. It occurs under circumstances of severe stress or trauma, such as divorce, bereavement, combat, natural disaster, an accident, or violent assault. Normal functioning generally returns once the stress is relieved, support becomes available, or the patient develops coping skills.
- Defense mechanism in personality disorder is a brief psychotic disorder that sometimes develops when individuals with personality disorders face severe stress.
- Brief psychotic disorder without obvious stressor occurs in the absence of an apparent stress or trauma.
- Postpartum psychosis occurs in women, usually within four weeks of giving birth, and is thought to be associated with dramatic hormonal changes that occur with childbirth and in the immediate postpartum period. Postpartum psychosis is often misdiagnosed and treated inappropriately. In severe cases, it can result in infanticide or suicide.
- Early-stage schizophrenia is often misdiagnosed as brief psychotic disorder.

Culture not only influences the form of a psychotic reaction, but it also determines what is considered to be psychotic. Behaviors that are viewed as psychotic or bizarre in one culture may be acceptable in another. A diagnosis of brief psychotic disorder requires that the symptoms or behaviors are not an acceptable manifestation of culture or religion and are not part of a religious practice or **meditation**. Individuals within a community or culture may exhibit behavior that is attributable to a particular cause or stimulus, such as cabin fever, witchcraft, or spiritual possession, or that may be the result of a culturally specific phobia, such as fear of sinning in a religious community or fear of being cold in tropical climates. These are known as culture-bound syndromes or culturally defined disorders. Another example is *koro,* which occurs in some parts of Asia and is a delusional **obsession** with the possibility that the genitals will retract or shrink into the body. Unrecognizable speech patterns or "speaking in tongues," which sometimes occurs as part of a religious experience, is also an example of a culture-bound syndrome.

Risk factors

A preexisting personality disorder—antisocial, paranoid, narcissistic, borderline, or schizotypal—appears to be a major risk factor for brief psychotic disorder in response to stressful situations. There is some evidence that brief psychotic disorder is more common in families with a history of mood disorders, such as **depression** or **bipolar disorder**.

Causes and symptoms

The precise causes of brief psychotic disorder are unclear. The majority of cases are triggered by an extremely stressful or traumatic event, and there is some evidence that susceptibility has a genetic basis. It also has been suggested that people with **personality disorders** may be physiologically or psychologically vulnerable to the development of psychotic symptoms. Psychodynamic theories suggest that the disorder may be caused by poor coping skills, particularly in individuals with personality disorders. Coping skills are defense mechanisms that can protect a person from dangerous fantasies and can act as an escape in overwhelmingly stressful situations. These circumstances can include family- or work-associated conflicts, accidents, severe illness, loss of a loved one, immigration difficulties, or traumatic events. Postpartum psychosis is thought to be caused by rapid hormonal changes immediately following childbirth, coupled with **stress**.

The ***Diagnostic and Statistical Manual of Mental Disorders*** (DSM) provides three major criteria for brief psychotic disorder:

- At least one positive symptom of psychosis, from the following symptoms: delusions; hallucinations; disorganized speech that is strange, peculiar, or difficult to comprehend; disorganized (bizarre or childlike) behavior; or catatonic behavior.
- Limited duration, with psychotic symptoms occurring for at least one day but less than one month and with eventual return to normal level of functioning.
- Symptoms that are not biologically influenced or attributable to another disorder—that is, symptoms not occurring as part of a mood disorder, schizoaffective disorder, or schizophrenia; not due to intoxication with drugs or alcohol; not due to an adverse reaction to a medication; and not due to a physical injury or medical illness.

Delusions are a classic feature of psychosis. Delusions are strongly held irrational or unrealistic beliefs that are extremely difficult to change, even in the face of contradictory evidence. Delusions can be paranoid or persecutory, wherein the delusional person is excessively suspicious or believes that he or she is the victim of a conspiracy. Delusions can also be unjustified grandiose beliefs that exaggerate one's importance, such as believing oneself to be a famous person or hold an enviable position. Grandiose delusions often have religious overtones, such as believing one's self to be the Virgin Mary. Delusions also can involve elaborate love fantasies (called erotomanic delusions) or extreme and irrational jealousy. Somatic delusions, from *soma,* the Greek word for body, are erroneous but strongly held beliefs about the characteristics or functioning of one's body; for example, refusing to eat because of the conviction that one's throat muscles are completely paralyzed and that only liquids can be swallowed.

Hallucinations are false perceptions. They can occur in various forms that parallel the human senses. Auditory hallucinations—usually hearing voices—are the most common hallucinations. Auditory-visual hallucinations involve both hearing and seeing what is not present. Visual hallucinations can also occur alone. Somatic hallucinations are bodily sensations, such as smelling nonexistent odors or feeling something on or under one's skin.

Incoherence or disorganized speech is distorted speech that is peculiar or difficult to comprehend. It may involve mixing words together in no coherent order, responses that are irrelevant or strange in the context of a conversation, or echolalia (repeating another person's exact words either immediately or after a delay of minutes or hours).

Disorganized or bizarre thought patterns and behaviors can range from childlike behaviors, such as skipping, singing, or hopping in inappropriate circumstances, to unusual practices, such as **hoarding** food or wrapping one's head and clothing with aluminum foil. Catatonic behaviors can be either strange bodily movements or lack of movement. Catalepsy is motionless **catatonia**, in which the patient may remain in the same position for hours. Rapid or persistently repeated movements, frequent grimacing and strange facial expressions, and unusual gestures are the opposite symptom.

Brief psychotic disorder is often accompanied by severe agitation, fear, or anger, and agitated patients are more likely to harm themselves or others. Other symptoms that may be associated with brief psychotic behavior include:

- changes in weight, energy level, or eating or sleeping habits
- indecision
- rapid mood changes and emotional volatility
- uncooperativeness
- disorientation or confusion
- impaired concentration and attention
- poor insight or judgment
- bizarre dress
- screaming or muteness

KEY TERMS

Bipolar disorder—A recurrent mood disorder, in which patients have extreme mood swings from depression to mania or a mixture of both.

Catatonia—Psychomotor disturbances that can include stupor, rigidity, muteness, or purposeless and bizarre movements.

Delusion—A persistent false belief held in the face of strong contradictory evidence.

Echolalia—A pathological repetition of what others say.

Hallucination—False sensory perceptions; hearing sounds or seeing people or objects that are not present. Hallucinations can also affect the senses of smell, touch, and taste.

Koro—A culture-specific syndrome involving a belief that one's external genitalia are shrinking or retracting and may disappear, occurring primarily in Southeast Asia.

Personality disorder—A psychopathological condition in which a person's patterns and behaviors are considered deviant or nonadaptive, but without neurosis or psychosis.

Psychodynamic—Mental, emotional, or motivational forces or processes that affect mental state and behavior, especially unconscious processes that develop in early childhood.

Psychosis—A serious mental disorder, such as schizophrenia, characterized by loss of contact with reality.

Schizophrenia—A psychotic disorder characterized by loss of contact with one's environment, deterioration of everyday functioning, and personality disintegration.

Schizophreniform disorder—A psychosis resembling schizophrenia, but lasting only between one and six months.

- memory impairment
- physical or verbal aggression
- suicidal or homicidal thoughts or behaviors

Diagnosis

The cause of the symptoms helps to determine whether the person is described as having brief psychotic disorder. If the psychotic symptoms appear as a result of a physical disease, a reaction to medication, or intoxication with drugs or alcohol, then the unusual behaviors are not classified as brief psychotic disorder.

Examination

If a physical examination reveals no biological basis for the symptoms, the patient may be referred to a **psychiatrist**. Brief psychotic disorder is usually diagnosed by interviewing the patient and possibly family members. The diagnostician usually performs a semi-structured interview called a **mental status examination**, which evaluates the patient's ability to concentrate, remember, realistically understand the situation, and think logically. Past history and/or the identification of a specific stressful event, particularly in patients with personality disorders, further suggests a diagnosis of brief psychotic disorder. Psychotic symptoms that persist for longer than one month require a different diagnosis.

Tests

Laboratory tests may be used to distinguish brief psychotic disorder from various other medical conditions. Blood alcohol levels and urine drug screening may be used to rule out substance-induced causes.

Procedures

In some cases, **imaging studies** such as x rays, **computed tomography** (CT) scans, or **magnetic resonance imaging** (MRI) may be necessary to rule out physical causes for the symptoms. An electroencephalogram (EEG) to measure **brain** waves may be performed.

Treatment

Various treatments are used for brief psychotic disorder.

Traditional

Although brief psychotic disorder is usually treated with drugs, supportive therapy or **psychotherapy** may be helpful in reducing anxiety and educating the patient about psychiatric illness. **Talk therapy** may also help the patient cope with the stress that precipitated the psychosis. Patients with acute psychosis may require **hospitalization**, both for evaluation and safety concerns. Aggressive patients may require brief seclusion or restraint. Once the psychosis has passed, individual, family, or **group therapy** may help the patient cope with stress and conflict and improve self-confidence and self-esteem.

Drugs

Antipsychotic medications are very effective at decreasing or ending brief psychotic episodes.

Haloperidol (Haldol) is commonly used for psychotic symptoms that are accompanied by agitation. It is often administered by injection. However, injected **ziprasidone** (Geodon) may be more effective and better tolerated than haloperidol. Other conventional antipsychotics that may be prescribed are **thiothixene** (Navane), thorazine, **fluphenazine** (Prolixin), **trifluoperazine** (Stelazine), **perphenazine** (Trilafon), and **thioridazine** (Mellaril). Newer-generation atypical antipsychotics are generally taken daily as tablets, capsules, or liquid by patients who are not agitated. These antipsychotics include **olanzapine** (Zyprexa), **quetiapine** (Seroquel), **paliperidone** (Invega), **risperidone** (Risperdal), and **clozapine** (Clozaril). Although these drugs can be taken for a longer period than haloperidol, they should not be used for more than one month. In addition to antipsychotics, drugs to decrease anxiety, such as **lorazepam** (Ativan) or **diazepam** (Valium), or to slow activity, such as **diphenhydramine** (Benadryl), may be prescribed. Hormones may be prescribed for postpartum psychosis.

Alternative

Symptoms of brief psychotic disorder that may be part of a culture-bound syndrome are usually most effectively treated by societal norms. For example, bathing in a sacred river might be the usual method of curing a psychotic-like state in a particular culture.

Home remedies

In cases in which the symptoms of brief psychotic disorder only minimally interfere with a patient's functioning and the specific trigger is known, elimination of the stressor may be sufficient treatment.

Prognosis

By definition, brief psychotic disorder resolves within a month. If the disorder was triggered by major stress or a traumatic experience and the patient had no previous psychiatric problems, the prognosis is good, and the disorder is unlikely to recur. European studies have found that 50%–80% of patients with brief psychotic disorder do not suffer major psychiatric problems in the future. However, the prognosis is poor in cases in which a triggering event cannot be identified, if the patient suffers from a personality disorder, or if the episode proves to be a prelude to schizophrenia or bipolar disorder. Patients with personality disorders may suffer from intermittent brief psychotic disorder throughout their lives.

Prevention

Early diagnosis and treatment of brief psychotic disorder can minimize disruptions to the patient's life. In the case of severe stressors, such as natural disasters or terrorist attacks, strong social support and immediate post-crisis counseling may prevent the development of brief psychotic disorder in susceptible people. Women who experience postpartum psychosis may choose to not have additional children or may be prescribed preventative antipsychotic medication during future postpartum periods.

QUESTIONS TO ASK YOUR DOCTOR

- Why do you believe that my symptoms constitute brief psychotic disorder?
- What medication will you prescribe?
- How long before the medication takes effect?
- Do you recommend therapy as well as medication?
- Is the psychotic disorder likely to recur?

Resources

BOOKS

American Psychiatric Association. *Diagnostic and Statistical Manual of Mental Disorders (DSM-IV-TR)*, 4th ed., text rev. Washington, DC: American Psychiatric Association, 2000.

Dziegielewski, Sophia F. *DSM-IV-TR in Action*, 2nd ed. Hoboken, NJ: John Wiley & Sons, 2010.

PERIODICALS

Correll, C. U., et al. "Predictors of Remission, Schizophrenia, and Bipolar Disorder in Adolescents with Brief Psychotic Disorder or Psychotic Disorder not Otherwise Specified Considered at Very High Risk for Schizophrenia." *Journal of Child and Adolescent Psychopharmacology* 18, no. 5 (2008): 475–90.

WEBSITES

MedlinePlus. "Brief Reactive Psychosis." U.S. Library of Medicine, National Institutes of Health. February 7, 2010. http://www.nlm.nih.gov/medlineplus/ency/article/001529.htm (accessed July 24, 2011).

———. "Haloperidol." U.S. Library of Medicine, National Institutes of Health. May 16, 2011. http://www.nlm.nih.gov/medlineplus/druginfo/meds/a682180.html (accessed July 24, 2011).

Memon, Mohammed A., and Michael Larson. "Brief Psychotic Disorder." Medscape Reference. May 15, 2009. http://emedicine.medscape.com/article/294416-overview (accessed July 24, 2011).

ORGANIZATIONS

AGS Foundation for Health in Aging, Empire State Bldg., 350 5th Ave., Ste. 801, New York, NY, 10018, (212) 755-

6810, (800) 563-4916, Fax: (212) 832-8646, http://www.healthinaging.org.

American Psychological Association, 750 1st St. NE, Washington, DC, 20002-4242, (202) 336-5500, (800) 374-2721, http://www.apa.org.

Mental Health America, 2000 N Beauregard St., 6th Fl., Alexandria, VA, 22311, (703) 684-7722, (800) 969-6642, Fax: (703) 684-5968, http://www.nmha.org.

National Alliance on Mental Illness, 3803 N Fairfax Dr., Ste. 100, Arlington, VA, 22203, (703) 524-7600, (800) 950-6264, Fax: (703) 524-9094, http://www.nami.org.

Deborah Rosch Eifert, PhD
Ruth A. Wienclaw, PhD
Margaret Alic, PhD

Bulimia nervosa

Definition

Bulimia nervosa is an eating disorder characterized by binge eating and engaging in inappropriate ways of counteracting the bingeing (using laxatives, for example) to prevent weight gain. The word "bulimia" is the Latin form of the Greek word *boulimia*, which means "extreme hunger." A binge is consuming a larger amount of food within a limited period of time than most people would eat in similar circumstances. Most people with bulimia report feelings of loss of control associated with bingeing, and some have mildly dissociative experiences in the course of a binge, which means that they feel disconnected from themselves and from reality when they binge.

The handbook mental health professionals use to aid in **diagnosis** is the ***Diagnostic and Statistical Manual of Mental Disorders***. The fourth edition, text revision, also known as the *DSM-IV-TR,* categorizes bulimia nervosa as an eating disorder, along with **anorexia nervosa**.

Demographics

Bulimia nervosa affects between 1% and 3% of women in developed countries; its prevalence is thought to have increased markedly since 1970. The rates are similar across cultures in the United States, Japan, the United Kingdom, Australia, South Africa, Canada, France, Germany, and Israel. About 80% to 90% of patients with bulimia are female. The average age at onset among women with bulimia is 14 and among men, 18. Homosexual men appear to be as vulnerable to developing bulimia as heterosexual women, while lesbians are less vulnerable.

Bulimia was previously thought to primarily affect Caucasian women in the United States, but recent studies indicate that this is no longer the case; the rates among African American and Hispanic women have risen faster than the rate of bulimia for the female population as a whole. One report indicates that the chief difference between African American and Caucasian women with bulimia is that African American patients are less likely to eat restricted **diets** between episodes of binge eating.

Description

Bulimia nervosa is classified into two subtypes according to the methods used to prevent weight gain after a binge. The purging subtype of bulimia is characterized by the use of self-induced vomiting, laxatives, enemas, or diuretics (pills that induce urination); in the nonpurging subtype, fasting or overexercising is used to compensate for binge eating.

The onset of bulimia nervosa is most common in late adolescence or early adult life. Dieting efforts and body dissatisfaction, however, often occur in the teenage years. For these reasons, bulimia is often described as a developmental disorder. Genetic researchers have identified specific genes linked to susceptibility to eating disorders, and the environmental primary factor in the development of bulimia nervosa is **stress** related to the onset of puberty. Girls who have strongly negative feelings about their bodies in response to puberty are at high risk for developing bulimia.

The binge eating associated with bulimia begins most often after a period of strict dieting. Most people with bulimia develop purging behaviors in response to the bingeing. Vomiting is used by 80%–90% of patients diagnosed with bulimia. The personal accounts of recovered bulimics suggest that most "discover" vomiting independently as a way of ridding themselves of the food rather than learning about it from other adolescents. Vomiting is often done to relieve an uncomfortable sensation of fullness in the stomach following a binge as well as to prevent absorption of the calories in the food. Vomiting is frequently induced by stimulating the gag reflex at the back of the throat by touching the area with the fingers or a toothbrush, but a minority of patients use syrup of ipecac to induce vomiting. Regular use of syrup of ipecac has severe medical consequences, including dehydration, muscle weakness, diarrhea, and serious heart problems that can lead to death. About one-third of bulimics use laxatives after binge eating to empty the digestive tract, and a minority use diuretics or enemas. Purging behaviors lead to a series of digestive and metabolic disturbances that then reinforce the behaviors.

A small proportion of bulimics **exercise** excessively (**compulsive exercise**) or fast after a binge instead of purging.

Patients with bulimia may come to the attention of a **psychiatrist** or **psychologist** because they develop medical or dental complications due to the eating disorder. In some cases, the patient's dentist is the "case finder," because the sulfuric acid that comes up from the stomach during vomiting wears away at tooth enamel. Many times, however, the person with bulimia seeks help, although often not until years after the disorder develops.

Causes and symptoms

Causes

The primary etiological model for bulimia, proposed by psychologist Eric Stice, cites the following factors as the main predictors of bulimia:

- pressure to be thin, whether from society and the media at large or from peers
- an internalization of the belief that thin is the ideal body type
- body dissatisfaction based on this belief
- dieting or other restrictive actions in an attempt to lose weight
- negative affect, based on the initial body dissatisfaction

Because the motivation for weight loss is tied to a desire to meet a fictional ideal and not an actual medical need to lose weight, results are unsatisfactory, as they are not addressing the actual problem. Both dieting and negative affect increase the risk for eating disorder behaviors, particularly bulimic symptoms such as binge eating and compensatory behaviors. Along with sociocultural pressures, familial and **genetic factors** may contribute to the desire to be thin and the development of an eating disorder.

SOCIOCULTURAL CAUSES. Emphasis in the mass media on slenderness in women as the primary criterion of beauty and desirability is commonly noted in studies of bulimia. Historians of fashion have remarked that the standard of female attractiveness has changed over the past half century in the direction of increased thinness; some have commented that actress Marilyn Monroe would have been considered "fat" by contemporary standards. The ideal female figure is not only unattainable by the vast majority of women but is lighter than the standards associated with good health by insurance companies. In 1965, the average model weighed 8% less than the average American woman; by 2001, she weighed 25% less. Recent news reports have focused on this **obsession** with thinness in the fashion industry because of the deaths of several models from eating disorders. One major fashion group in Spain went so far as to set a minimum body mass index for models on its catwalks in 2006 after a model died during a show in South America of causes apparently related to an eating disorder.

Nutrition experts have pointed to the easy availability of foods high in processed carbohydrates in developed countries as a social factor that contributes to the incidence of bulimia. One study found that subjects who were given two slices of standard mass-produced white bread with some jelly had their levels of **serotonin** increased temporarily by 450%. This finding suggests that bulimics who binge on ice cream, bread, cookies, pizza, and fast food items that are high in processed carbohydrates are simply manipulating their neurochemistry in a highly efficient manner. The incidence of bulimia may be lower in developing countries because diets that are high in vegetables and whole-grain products but low in processed carbohydrates do not affect serotonin levels in the **brain** as rapidly or as effectively.

Some overweight or obese individuals who are starting a new diet may develop bulimia as a coping strategy. In addition, individuals who are perfectionists and struggle with the cultural focus on thinness are at greater risk, as are persons involved in sports or occupations that require strict weight control, such as gymnastics, figure skating, horse jockeying, wrestling, ballet, or modeling.

FAMILIAL FACTORS. A number of recent studies point to the interpersonal relationships in the family of origin (the patient's family while growing up) as a factor in the later development of bulimia. People with bulimia are more likely than people with anorexia to have been sexually abused in childhood; studies have found that abnormalities in blood levels of serotonin (a neurotransmitter associated with mood disorders) and cortisol (the primary stress hormone in humans) in bulimic patients with a history of childhood **sexual abuse** resemble those in patients with **post-traumatic stress disorder** (PTSD). Post-traumatic stress disorder is a mental disorder that can develop after someone has experienced a traumatic event (sexual assault, for example) and is unable to process and move beyond that event. The disorder is characterized by disturbingly realistic flashbacks of the traumatic event.

A history of eating conflicts and struggles over food in the family of origin is also a risk factor for the development of bulimia nervosa, whether the parents or siblings were overweight or obese or had an eating disorder. Personal accounts by recovered bulimics frequently describe parents who were preoccupied with food or dieting. Fathers appear to be as influential as mothers in this regard. A recent study focusing on girls suggests that the influence of the father may be related to the father's own concerns and body preoccupations and that this influence may be stronger as a child gets older. Other risk factors identified in a 2007 study, which followed the children from birth, were a low activity level in early childhood and rapid eating in later childhood. In addition, and not surprisingly, peer and parental teasing about body weight or shape also increase risk, as does having a familial history of **substance abuse**.

GENETICS. Several studies have obtained results pointing to a genetic understructure for eating disorders, including bulimia. Studies investigating the relationship between characteristics of bulimia in families and their correlation with patterns of gene expression have linked bulimia to genes on human chromosome 10.

Symptoms

The *DSM-IV-TR* specifies that bingeing and the inappropriate attempts to compensate for it must occur twice a week for three months on average to meet the diagnostic criteria for bulimia nervosa. However, recent studies have shown that individuals who reported these behaviors once a week were clinically similar to those who reported such behaviors twice a week. A revision for the upcoming *DSM-5* (fifth edition, 2013) proposes changing the minimum frequency of these activities to once a week to meet the criteria for bulimia nervosa.

A second criterion of bulimia nervosa is exaggerated concern with body shape and weight. Bulimia can be distinguished from **body dysmorphic disorder** (BDD) by the fact that people with BDD usually focus on a specific physical feature—most commonly a facial feature—rather than overall shape and weight. Bulimics do, however, resemble patients with BDD in that they have distorted body images.

Bulimia is associated with a number of physical symptoms. Binge eating by itself rarely causes serious medical complications, but it is associated with nausea, abdominal distension and cramping, slowed digestion, and weight gain.

Self-induced vomiting, by contrast, may have serious medical consequences, including the following:

- Erosion of tooth enamel, particularly on the molars and maxillary incisors. Loss of tooth enamel is irreversible.
- Enlargement of the salivary glands.
- Scars and calloused areas on the knuckles from contact with the teeth.
- Irritation of the throat and esophagus from contact with stomach acid.
- Tearing of mucous membranes in the upper gastrointestinal tract or perforation of the esophagus and stomach wall. Perforation of part of the digestive tract is a rare complication of bulimia and is potentially fatal.
- Electrolyte imbalances. The loss of fluids from repeated vomiting and laxative abuse can deplete the body's stores of hydrogen chloride, potassium, sodium, and magnesium. Hypokalemia (abnormally low levels of potassium in the blood) is a potential medical emergency that can lead to muscle cramps, seizures, and heart arrhythmias.

Other physical symptoms associated with bulimia include irregular menstrual periods or amenorrhea; petechiae (pinhead-sized bruises from capillaries ruptured by increased pressure due to vomiting) in the skin around the eyes, and rectal prolapse (the lowering of the rectum from its usual position).

Diagnosis

The diagnosis of bulimia nervosa is made on the basis of a physical examination, a psychiatric assessment, the patient's eating history, and the findings of laboratory tests. Patients who do not meet the full criteria for bulimia nervosa may be given the diagnosis of subsyndromal bulimia or of an eating disorder not otherwise specified (EDNOS).

Physical examination

Patients suspected of having bulimia nervosa should be given a complete physical examination because the disorder has so many potential medical complications. In addition, most bulimics are close to normal weight or only slightly overweight, and so the presence of the disorder is not outwardly apparent. The examination should include not only vital signs and an assessment of the patient's height and weight relative to age, but also a check for such signs of bulimia as general hair loss, abdominal soreness, swelling of the parotid glands, telltale scars on the back of the hand, petechiae, edema, and teeth that look ragged or "moth-eaten."

Psychiatric assessment

Psychiatric assessment of patients with bulimia usually includes four components:

- a thorough history of body weight, eating patterns, diets, typical daily food intake, methods of purging (if used), and concept of ideal weight
- a history of the patient's significant relationships with parents, siblings, and peers, including any present or past physical, emotional, or sexual abuse

- a history of previous psychiatric treatment (if any) and assessment of any comorbid (occurring at the same time as the bulimia) mood, anxiety, substance abuse, or personality disorders
- administration of standardized instruments that measure attitudes toward eating, body size, and weight (e.g., the Eating Disorder Examination, the Eating Disorder Inventory, the Eating Attitude Test [EAT], the Kids' Eating Disorder Survey [KEDS])

Laboratory findings

Laboratory tests ordered for patients suspected of having bulimia usually include a complete blood cell count, blood serum chemistry, thyroid tests, and urinalysis. If necessary, the doctor may also order a chest x ray and an electrocardiogram (EKG). Typical findings in patients with bulimia include low levels of chloride and potassium in the blood and higher than normal levels of amylase, a digestive enzyme found in saliva.

Treatment

Treatment for bulimia nervosa typically involves several therapy approaches. However, bulimia treatment is complicated by several factors.

First, patients diagnosed with bulimia nervosa frequently have coexisting psychiatric disorders, such as major **depression**, **dysthymic disorder**, **anxiety disorders**, substance abuse disorders, or **personality disorders**. In the case of depression, the mood disorder may either precede or follow the onset of bulimia; with bulimia, the prevalence of depression is 40%–70%. With regard to substance abuse, about 30% of patients diagnosed with bulimia nervosa abuse either alcohol or stimulants over the course of the eating disorder. The personality disorders most often diagnosed in patients with bulimia are borderline, narcissistic, histrionic, and antisocial. **Borderline personality disorder** is a disorder characterized by stormy interpersonal relationships, unstable self-image, and impulsive behavior. People with **narcissistic personality disorder** believe that they are extremely important and are unable to have empathy for others. Individuals with **histrionic personality disorder** seek attention almost constantly and are very emotional. **Antisocial personality disorder** is characterized by a disregard for others' rights—people with this disorder often deceive and manipulate others. Although patients may have both bulimia nervosa and anorexia nervosa, a number of clinicians have noted that patients with predominate bulimia tend to develop impulsive and unstable personality disturbances, whereas patients with predominate anorexia tend to be more obsessional and perfectionistic. Estimates of the prevalence of personality disorders among patients with bulimia range between 2% and 50%. The clinician must then decide whether to treat the eating disorder and the comorbid conditions concurrently or sequentially. It is generally agreed, however, that a substance abuse disorder, if present, must be treated before the bulimia can be effectively managed. It is also generally agreed that mood disorders and bulimia can be treated concurrently, often using antidepressant medication along with therapy.

Second, the limitations on treatment imposed by **managed care** complicate the treatment of bulimia nervosa. When the disorder first received attention in the 1970s, patients with bulimia were often hospitalized until the most significant physical symptoms of the disorder could be treated. Few patients with bulimia are hospitalized today, with the exception of medical emergencies related to electrolyte imbalances and gastrointestinal injuries associated with the eating disorder. Most treatment protocols for bulimia nervosa now reflect cost-containment measures.

Medications

The most common medications given to patients are **antidepressants**, because bulimia is so closely associated with depression. Short-term medication trials of tricyclic antidepressants (particularly **desipramine**, **imipramine**, and **amitriptyline**) have shown promise in reducing episodes of binge eating and vomiting, but these medications are rarely used. The **monoamine oxidase inhibitors** are not recommended as initial medications for patients diagnosed with bulimia because of their side effects. The most promising results have been obtained with the **selective serotonin reuptake inhibitors**, or **SSRIs**. **Fluoxetine** (Prozac) was approved in 1998 by the U.S. Food and Drug Administration (FDA) for the treatment of bulimia nervosa. Effective dosages of fluoxetine are higher for the treatment of bulimia than they are for the treatment of depression. Although a combination of medication and **cognitive-behavioral therapy** is more effective in treating most patients with bulimia than medication alone, one team of researchers reported success with fluoxetine by itself in treating some patients who had not responded to **psychotherapy**.

Ondansetron (Zofran), a drug that was originally developed to control nausea from chemotherapy and radiation therapy for cancer, blocks serotonin reuptake and also works to inhibit vomiting. It has shown some patients in ameliorating symptoms of bulimia nervosa.

In addition to antidepressant or antinausea medications, such acid-reducing medications as cimetidine and ranitidine may be given to patients with bulimia to relieve discomfort in the digestive tract associated with irritation caused by stomach acid.

Psychotherapy

Cognitive-behavioral therapy (CBT) is regarded as the most successful psychotherapeutic approach to bulimia nervosa. CBT is intended to interrupt the faulty thinking processes associated with bulimia, such as preoccupations with food and weight, black-and-white thinking ("all or nothing" thinking, or thinking thoughts only at extreme ends of a spectrum), and low self-esteem, as well as such behaviors as the binge-purge cycle. Patients are first helped to regain control over their food intake by keeping food diaries and receiving feedback about their meal plans, symptom triggers, and nutritional balance, as well as learning the associations between thoughts, feelings, and behaviors. They are then taught to challenge rigid thought patterns through cognitive restructuring techniques and by receiving **assertiveness training** and practice in identifying and expressing their feelings in words rather than through distorted eating patterns. About 50% of patients treated with CBT are able to stop bingeing and purging. Of the remaining half, some show partial improvement and a small minority do not respond at all. Part of CBT involves setting goals to focus on at home. These goals for patients include taking things one day at a time, not blaming themselves, and spending time with supportive friends and family members.

Family therapy is sometimes recommended as an additional mode of treatment for patients with bulimia who come from severely troubled or food-obsessed families, which can increase their risk of relapsing. Family therapy can also be helpful for adolescents with bulimia nervosa as a first-line approach to addressing the disorder.

Other mainstream therapies

Medical nutrition therapy (MNT) is a recognized component of the treatment of eating disorders. Effective MNT for patients with bulimia involves an understanding of cognitive-behavioral therapy as well as the registered dietitian's usual role of assisting the physician with monitoring the patient's physical symptoms, laboratory values, and vital signs. In the treatment of bulimia, the dietitian's specialized knowledge of nutrition may be quite helpful in dealing with the myths about food and fad diets that many bulimic patients believe. The dietitian's most important task, however, is helping patients to normalize their eating patterns to break the deprivation/bingeing cycle that is characteristic of bulimia nervosa. Calorie intake is usually based on retaining the patients' weight to prevent hunger, because hunger increases susceptibility to bingeing.

Alternative and complementary treatments

Alternative therapies that have been shown to be helpful for some patients in relieving the anxiety and muscular soreness associated with bulimia nervosa are **acupuncture**, massage therapy, hydrotherapy, and shiatsu. However, it should be noted that there is no empirical evidence for the effectiveness of these treatments.

Herbal remedies that have been used to calm digestive upsets in patients with bulimia include teas made from **chamomile** or peppermint. Peppermint helps to soothe the intestines by slowing down the rate of smooth muscle contractions (peristalsis). Chamomile has been used to help expel gas from the digestive tract, a common complaint of persons with bulimia. Both herbs have a wide margin of safety.

Some patients with bulimia have responded well to **yoga** because its emphasis on focused breathing and **meditation** calls attention to and challenges the distorted thought patterns that characterize bulimia. In addition, the stretching and bending movements that are part of a yoga practice help to displace negative thoughts focused on the body's outward appearance with positive appreciation of its strength and agility. Last, because yoga is noncompetitive, it allows participants to explore the uniqueness of their bodies rather than constantly comparing themselves to other people.

Prognosis

The prognosis of bulimia depends on several factors, including age at onset, types of purging behaviors used (if any), and the presence of other psychiatric conditions or disorders. As with any eating disorder, bulimia can be treated most effectively if it is identified as soon as possible. In many cases, the disorder becomes a chronic (long-term) condition; 20%–50% of patients have symptoms for at least five years in spite of treatment. The usual pattern is an alternation between periods of remission and new episodes of bingeing. Patients whose periods of remission last for a year or longer have a better prognosis; patients diagnosed with major depression or personality disorders have a less favorable prognosis. Overall, however, the prognosis for full recovery from bulimia nervosa is considered relatively poor compared to other eating disorders.

Bulimia nervosa appears to produce changes in the functioning of the serotonin system in the brain. Researchers at the University of Pittsburgh who compared brain images taken by **positron emission**

tomography (PET) from women with bulimia who had been in remission for a year or longer with brain images from healthy women found that the women with bulimia did not have a normal age-related decline in serotonin binding. Because serotonin helps to regulate mood, appetite, and impulse control, the study may help to explain why some women may be more susceptible to developing bulimia than others.

In addition, data from one study suggest that bulimia and other eating disorders can have a negative impact on infertility. In a review of surveys from more than 11,000 pregnant women, those with past or current eating disorders were more than twice as likely to have undergone some type of infertility treatment to help them become pregnant. The study was published in August 2011 in the *British Journal of Obstetrics and Gynecology.*

Prevention

Although a genetic link to bulimia has been identified, there are currently no gene-based preventive measures. With regard to family influences, the overwhelming majority of studies have found that the most important preventive measure that can be taken is the establishment of healthful eating patterns and attitudes toward food in the family of origin.

Resources

BOOKS

American Psychiatric Association. *Diagnostic and Statistical Manual of Mental Disorders.* 4th ed., Text rev. Washington, DC: American Psychiatric Association, 2000.

Herzog, David B., et al. *Unlocking the Mysteries of Eating Disorders.* New York: McGraw-Hill, 2007.

PERIODICALS

Agras, Stewart W., et al. "Childhood Risk Factors for Thin Body Preoccupation and Social Pressure to Be Thin." *Journal of the American Academy of Child and Adolescent Psychiatry* 46 (2007): 171–78.

Bulik, Cynthia M. "Exploring the Gene: Environment Nexus in Eating Disorders." *Journal of Psychiatry and Neuroscience* 30 (2005): 335–39.

Crow, S. J., et al. "Increased Mortality in Bulimia Nervosa and Other Eating Disorders." *American Journal of Psychiatry* 166 (December 2009): 1342–46.

Engler, P.A. "Predicting Eating Disorder Group Membership: An Examination and Extension of the Sociocultural Model." *Behavior Therapy* 37, no. 1 (2006): 69–79.

Hudson, James I., Eva Hiripi Jr., Harrison G. Pope, and Ronald C. Kessler. "The Prevalence and Correlates of Eating Disorders in the National Comorbidity Survey Replication." *Biological Psychiatry* 61, no. 3 (2007): 348–358.

Little, J.W. "Eating Disorders: Dental Implications." *Oral Surgery, Oral Medicine, Oral Pathology, Oral Radiology, and Endodontics* 93 (February 2002): 138–43.

Schmidt, U., et al. "A Randomized Controlled Trial of Family Therapy and Cognitive Behavior Therapy Guided Self-Care for Adolescents with Bulimia Nervosa and Related Disorders." *American Journal of Psychiatry* 164, no. 4 (2007): 591–98.

Steinhausen, Hans-Christoph, and Sandy Weber. "The Outcome of Bulimia Nervosa: Findings From One-Quarter Century of Research." *American Journal of Psychiatry* 166, no. 12 (2009): 1331–41. http://dx.doi.org/10.1176/appi.ajp.2009.09040582 (accessed September 16, 2011).

Van den Eyndea, Frederique, and Ulrike Schmidta. "Treatment of Bulimia Nervosa and Binge Eating Disorder." *Psychiatry* 7, no. 4 (2008): 161–66.

WEBSITES

Mayo Clinic staff. "Bulimia Nervosa." MayoClinic.com. February 23, 2010. http://www.mayoclinic.com/health/bulimia/DS00607 (accessed November 14, 2011).

National Alliance on Mental Illness. "Bulimia Nervosa." http://www.nami.org/Template.cfm?Section=by_illness&template=/ContentManagement/ContentDisplay.cfm&ContentID=102972 (accessed November 14, 2011).

WomensHealth.gov. "Bulimia Nervosa Fact Sheet." U.S. Department of Health and Human Services. http://www.womenshealth.gov/publications/our-publications/fact-sheet/bulimia-nervosa.cfm (accessed November 14, 2011).

ORGANIZATIONS

American Academy of Child and Adolescent Psychiatry, 3615 Wisconsin Ave., NW, Washington, DC, 20016-3007, (202) 966-7300, Fax: (202) 966-2891, http://aacap.org.

Center for the Study of Anorexia and Bulimia, 1841 Broadway, 4th Fl., New York, NY, 10023, (212) 333-3444, Fax: (212) 333-5444, casb@icpnyc.org, http://www.csabnyc.org.

National Association of Anorexia Nervosa and Related Eating Disorders, PO Box 640, Naperville, IL, 60566, (630) 577-1330, anadhelp@anad.org, http://www.anad.org.

National Eating Disorders Association, 165 W 46th St., New York, NY, 10036, (212) 575-6200, (800) 931-2237, Fax: (212) 575-1650, info@NationalEatingDisorders.org, http://www.nationaleatingdisorders.org.

Rebecca Frey, PhD
Emily Jane Willingham, PhD
Heidi Splete

Bullying

Definition

Bullying is a persistent pattern of threatening, harassing, or aggressive behavior directed toward another person or persons who are perceived as smaller, weaker, or less powerful. Although often thought of as a childhood phenomenon, bullying can occur wherever people interact,

Child victims of bullying, during the past 12 months and in their lifetime, by gender, age, and type of bullying, 2008*

	Past 12 months	Lifetime
Physical bullying	**13.2**	**21.6**
Females	12.8	22.4
Males	16.7	25.9
2–5 yrs.	19.1	20.4
6–9 yrs.	21.5	28.0
10–13 yrs.	10.7	19.9
14–17 yrs.	8.0	28.5
Psychological bullying (e.g., teasing)	**19.7**	**29.5**
Females	23.5	35.5
Males	20.6	30.6
2–5 yrs.	13.5	14.6
6–9 yrs.	30.4	38.4
10–13 yrs.	27.8	39.6
14–17 yrs.	15.8	38.4
Internet bullying	**1.8**	**2.5**
Females	3.4	4.5
Males	1.6	2.3
2–5 yrs.	0.0	0.0
6–9 yrs.	0.0	0.0
10–13 yrs.	2.6	3.2
14–17 yrs.	5.6	7.9

*Data given as percentage of children surveyed; 4,549 total (2,276 female and 2,273 male).

SOURCE: Finkelhor, D., H. Turner, S. Ormrod, and S.L. Hamby. "Violence, Abuse, and Crime Exposure in a National Sample of Children and Youth." *Pediatrics* 124, no. 5 (2009): 1411–23.

(Table by PreMediaGlobal. © 2012 Cengage Learning.)

most often observable in the workplace and in the home in adults. Bullying is also called harassment.

Demographics

Bullying in children

Bullying among children is a persistent and substantial problem that requires serious attention. According to a study published in 2001 by the Kaiser Family Foundation and Nickelodeon Television, 55% of 8–11-year-olds and 68% of 12–15-year-olds said that bullying is a "big problem" for people their age. Seventy-four percent of the 8–11-year-olds and 86% of the 12–15-year-olds also reported that children were bullied or teased at their school. These statistics were essentially unchanged in 2011. Children at greatest risk of being bullied are those who are perceived as social isolates or outcasts by their peers, have a history of changing schools, have poor social skills or a desire to fit in "at any cost," are defenseless, or are viewed by their peers as being different.

A study of more than 16,000 children in the sixth through tenth grades conducted for the National Institute of Child Health and Human Development found that nearly 60% of the children responding had been victims of rumors. More than 50% of the children reported that they had been the victims of sexual harassment. A Canadian study reported in 2010 that cyberbullying is also a common problem, with 49% of children in a sample of 2,200 students reporting being bullied on the Internet and 34% admitting to bullying others online.

The National Center for Education Statistics (NCES) of the U.S. Department of Education found that white, non-Hispanic children were more likely to report being the victims of bullying than black or other non-Hispanic children. Younger children were more likely to report being bullied than older children, and children attending schools with gangs were more likely to report being bullied than children in schools without a major gang presence. No differences were found in these patterns between public and private schools. Fewer children reported bullying in schools that were supervised by police officers, security officers, or staff hallway monitors. Victims of bullying were more likely to be criminally victimized at school than were other children. Victims of bullying were more afraid of being attacked both at school and elsewhere and more likely to avoid certain areas of school (for example, the cafeteria, hallways or stairs, or restrooms) or activities where bullying was more likely to take place. Significantly, victims of bullies were more likely to report that they carried weapons to school for protection.

Children who are identified as bullies by the time they are eight years of age are six times more likely than other children to have a criminal conviction by the time they are 24 years old. Bullying behavior may also be accompanied by other inappropriate behavior, including criminal, delinquent, or gang behavior.

Bullying in the workplace

Although research has been conducted on workplace bullying in Europe for some time, the topic has only recently become of interest in the United States. The nonprofit Workplace Bullying Institute conducted two surveys in 2010 with over 6,000 respondents. It defined workplace bullying as "repeated mistreatment: sabotage by others that prevented work from getting done, verbal **abuse**, threatening conduct, intimidation and humiliation" and compared statistics to its 2007 survey. The 2010 survey found that 35% of workers have experienced bullying first hand (37% in 2007); 62% of bullies are men and 58% of targets are women; women bullies target women in 80% of cases; and the majority (68%) of bullying is same-gender harassment.

Prevalence and characteristics of U.S. workplace bullying, 2007 and 2010

	Prevalence (%)		18–29 yrs.		30–49 yrs.		50–54 yrs.		Hispanic		African American		Caucasian		Asian American	
Bullying characteristics	**2007**	**2010**	**2007**	**2010**	**2007**	**2010**	**2007**	**2010**	**2007**	**2010**	**2007**	**2010**	**2007**	**2010**	**2007**	**2010**
Currently bullied or bullied in the past year	12.6	8.8	18.5	27.0	16.8	50.0	9.9	23.0		12.7		11.0		7.9		8.8
Not currently bullied but bullied in the past (more than one year ago)	24.2	25.7		22.0		47.0		30.0		23.5		27.6		25.7		9.7
Witnessed only	12.3	15.5		29.0		49.0		22.0	14.0	12.3	21.1	7.9	10.8	16.8	8.5	37.6
Male targets of bullying	43.3	42.0														
Female targets of bullying	56.7	58.0														
Male bullies	60.0	62.0														
Female bullies	40.0	38.0														
Female bullies targeting women	71.0	80.0														
Female bullies targeting men	28.7	20.0														
Male bullies targeting women	46.5	45.5														
Male bullies targeting men	53.5	55.5														

SOURCE: Workplace Bullying Institute, *The WBI U.S. Workplace Bullying Survey*, 2010.

(Table by PreMediaGlobal. © 2012 Cengage Learning.)

Description

There are many forms of bullying in both children and adults. Bullies may intimidate or harass their victims physically through hitting, pushing, or other physical violence; verbally through such actions as threats or name calling; or psychologically through spreading rumors (both live and online), making sexual comments or gestures, or excluding the victim from desired activities.

There are many reasons to stop bullying. Bullying interferes with school performance, and children who are afraid of being bullied are more likely to miss school or drop out. Bullied children frequently experience developmental harm and fail to reach their full physiological, social, and academic potentials. Children who are bullied grow increasingly insecure and anxious and have persistently decreased self-esteem and greater **depression** than their peers, often even as adults. Children and adolescents have even been known to commit **suicide** as a result of being bullied; this tragic outcome has been referred to by some writers as "bullycide."

People who are bullies as children often become bullies as adults. Bullying behavior in the home is called "child abuse" or "spousal abuse." Bullying also occurs in prisons, churches, summer camps, college or boarding school dormitories, and other social groups or group living situations.

Recently, attention has been turned to the topic of bullying in the workplace, defined as occurring when bosses and organizational peers bully those whom they perceive as weaker or inferior. Those bullied at work often become perceived as ineffective, thus abrogating their career success and influencing their earning potential. Victims of workplace bullying often change jobs in search of a less hostile environment because organizations are frequently not sensitive to the issue of workplace bullying or are not equipped to deal with it adequately or justly.

Cyberbullying

Bullying does not need to occur in person: cyberbullying is a persistent pattern of threatening, harassing, or aggressive behavior carried out online. The widespread popularity of cell phones and other mobile devices means that cyberbullying can be carried out anonymously without the need for a computer. Cyberbullying can take a number of different forms:

- sending hurtful or threatening messages directly to the victim via e-mail or phone texting
- spreading rumors about the victim to others via e-mail or other forms of messaging
- setting up websites, posting videos, or creating pages on social media to hurt or humiliate the victim

Cyberbullying is increasingly considered a particularly damaging form of bullying because it can be carried on 24/7, can be shared with a wide number of people (an example would be a video that "goes viral" on YouTube), and is hard to undo due to a number of online services that archive Internet sites.

Some researchers maintain that cyberbullies fall into several different categories and do not necessarily resemble the classic schoolyard bully. While some cyberbullies are power-hungry or vengeful, others may just be bored and looking for something to do for online entertainment. Another common type of cyberbully is the inadvertent bully, typically an adolescent who doesn't think before sending a message or who is so invested in online role-playing that he or she fails to understand that the recipient of such a message may take it seriously.

Another reason for concern about cyberbullying is that electronic communication itself has the potential to intensify situations that are already touchy, because the absence of face-to-face contact makes it harder for the cyberbully to "see" the humanity of the victim. E-mail messages and texting lack vocal tone, making it easier to increase the hostility and aggressiveness of text messages. There have been several notable cases of electronic messaging escalating into real-world violence, such as the "Facebook murder" that occurred in Florida in April 2011, in which a 15-year-old boy was lured into an ambush by his former girlfriend via text messages.

Risk factors

Warning signs and factors that may indicate risk for being or becoming a bully include:

- lack of impulse control (frequent loss of temper, extreme impulsiveness, easily becoming frustrated, extreme mood swings)
- family factors (physical abuse or violence within the family, substance or alcohol abuse within the family, overly permissive parenting, lack of clear limits, inadequate parental supervision, harsh/corporal punishment, child abuse, inconsistent parenting)
- behavioral symptoms (gang affiliation, name calling or abusive language, carrying a weapon, hurting animals, abusing alcohol or drugs, making serious threats, vandalizing or damaging property, frequent physical fighting)

Causes and symptoms

There is no evidence to support the theory that there is a genetic component to bullying behavior. Particularly in children, bullying appears to result from the bully's copying the actions of role models who bully others. According to the Centers for Disease Control and Prevention (CDC), this pattern frequently occurs when bullies come from a home in which one parent bullies another or one or both parents bully the children. When such behavior is modeled for children with such personality traits as lack of impulse control or aggression, they are particularly prone to bullying behavior, which often continues into adulthood.

Bullying in children

According to the U.S. Department of Health and Human Services, children with dominant personalities and who are more impulsive and active are more prone to becoming bullies than children without these traits. Bullies also often have a history of emotional or behavioral problems. Victims of bullying, on the other hand, tend to be more anxious, insecure, and socially isolated than their peers and often lack age-appropriate social skills. The probability of victimization can be compounded when the victim has low self-esteem due to physical characteristics (for example, the victim believes her/himself to be unattractive, is disfigured in some way, or is outside the normal range for height or weight) or personal problems (for example, health problems or physical or mental disability).

Symptoms or indications that a child may be being bullied include:

- social withdrawal or isolation (few or no friends; feeling isolated, sad, and alone; feeling picked on or persecuted; feeling rejected or not liked; having poor social skills)
- somatic complaints (frequent complaints about illness; displaying victim body language, including hanging head, hunching shoulders, and avoiding eye contact)
- avoidant behavior (not wanting to go to school, skipping classes or school)
- affective reactions (crying easily; having mood swings; talking about hopelessness, running away, or suicide)
- physical clues (bringing home damaged possessions or reporting that belongings were "lost")
- behavior changes (changes in eating or sleeping patterns)
- aggressive behavior (threatening violence to self or others, taking or attempting to take a weapon to school)

Each child will react to bullying in a different manner, and some children will react with only a few of these symptoms. These differences, however, do not mean that bullying is not severe or that **intervention** is not needed.

Bullying in the workplace

Bullying in the workplace is usually motivated by political rather than personal reasons. Workers may compete for promotions, raises, and other honors. In an attempt to climb the ladder of success, some individuals do what they can to not only present themselves in a good light to their superiors, but also to make one or more coworkers seem unworthy or inept. Bullying bosses demonstrate poor leadership styles and poor motivational skills, frequently attempting to further either their own or the company's agenda through harassment, belittling, or other negative behaviors.

Common tactics used by workplace bullies include:

- discounting/belittling the victim in public (making statements such as "that's silly" in response to the victim's ideas, disregarding evidence of satisfactory or superlative work done by victim, taking credit for victim's work)
- making false accusations (rumors about victim, lies about victim's performance)
- harassing the victim (verbal putdowns based on gender, race, disability)
- isolating the victim (encouraging others to turn against victim, socially or physically isolating the victim from others)
- nonverbal aggression (staring, glaring, silent treatment)
- sabotaging the victim's work
- unequal treatment (retaliating against victim who files a complaint, making up arbitrary rules for victim to follow, assigning undesirable work as a punishment, making unreasonable/unreachable goals or deadlines for victim, performing a constructive discharge of duties)

Diagnosis

Bullying, in itself, is not a mental disorder, although aggressive or harassing behavior may be symptomatic of a number of disorders, particularly **antisocial personality disorder**. There are, however, a number of criteria to help determine whether someone is a bully. First, to qualify as bullying, the bully's behavior must be intended to cause physical or psychological harm to the other person. Second, bullying behavior is not an isolated incident but results in a consistent pattern of such behavior over time. Third, bullying occurs where there is an imbalance of power whereby the bully has more physical or psychological power than the victim. Harassing behavior is not considered to be bullying if it occurs between individuals of equal strength and status or if it is a one-time event.

Bullying behavior in children can include any of the following behaviors:

- dominance (enjoying feeling powerful and in control, seeking to dominate or manipulate others, being a poor winner or loser)
- lack of empathy (deriving satisfaction from the fears, pain, or discomfort of others; enjoying conflict between others; displaying intolerance of or prejudice toward others)

KEY TERMS

Bullycide—Suicide attributed to the victim's having been bullied.

Cyberbullying—The use of electronic devices, including computers, cell phones, and other mobile devices, to bully by means of hurtful messages, spreading rumors, or misusing social media.

- negative emotions or violence (displaying uncontrolled anger or a pattern of impulsive and chronic hitting, intimidating, or aggressive behavior)
- lack of responsibility (blaming others for his/her problems)
- other behaviors (using drugs or alcohol, hiding bullying behavior from adults, having a history of discipline problems)

Victims of bullying, whether children or adults, may need to be assessed and treated if they need help responding to, or recovering from, bullying.

Treatment

If bullying behavior is symptomatic of an underlying mental disorder such as **conduct disorder** or antisocial personality disorder, treatment should first address the underlying disorder. For situations in which bullying behavior is not part of a pattern associated with an underlying mental disorder, treatment and establishing organizational or familial processes for dealing with it are required.

Bullying in children

If parent(s) suspect that their child is a bully, help can be sought from mental health professionals and school counselors. Taking the child to a child **psychologist** and participating in **family therapy** as appropriate can help teach a bully better interpersonal skills. Contacting the school counselor or a child psychologist is also an appropriate step in helping the victims of bullies.

If parents suspect that their child may be being bullied, they should make sure that he or she understands that the problem is not his or her fault and that he or she does not have to face the situation alone. Parents can discuss ways to deal with bullies, including walking away, being assertive, and getting help. Parents should also encourage the child to report bullying behavior to a

QUESTIONS TO ASK YOUR DOCTOR

- I didn't grow up with cell phones and social media. What should I tell my children to help them protect themselves against cyberbullying?
- Have you ever treated a child or teenager who developed a physical or mental disorder because of bullying? What was the outcome?
- Have you ever treated or referred an adult who was suffering from workplace bullying?

teacher, counselor, or other trusted adult. However, parents should not try to resolve the situation themselves but should contact the school to report the behavior and to seek recommendations for further assistance.

Dealing with cyberbullying

Cyberbullying requires some different approaches than face-to-face bullying because of the nature of electronic messages and also because cyberbullying can involve legal penalties for the bully. Some practical tips for dealing with cyberbullying include:

- Save evidence of harassing e-mails and other forms of cyberbullying. These can be forwarded to a parent or trusted friend, or saved on a flash drive.
- Report cyberbullying to the service provider. Many social networking sites as well as phone companies and e-mail providers take reports of cyberbullying seriously and will block the bully's account.
- Use the block setting on cell phones or other mobile devices to stop the cyberbully from sending messages.
- Use passwords to protect online e-mail accounts and cell phones, and change the passwords frequently.

Bullying in the workplace

Bullying in the workplace can be minimized if the organization develops and enforces antiharassment policies and procedures. These should include a stated definition on what constitutes harassment, creating and implementing a disciplinary system to punish the bully rather than the victim, and instituting a formal grievance system to report workplace bullying. Other measures that can be taken include inclusiveness and harassment training, awareness training to educate employees on how to spot bullying behavior, and offering courses in conflict resolution, anger management, or **assertiveness training**.

Bullies are not the only ones needing help. The intention of a bully is to harm the other person; victims, therefore, may experience a number of negative consequences from being the victim of a bully. If the behavior associated with being a victim persists after the bullying situation has been resolved, or if the situation continues without just resolution, victims should be assessed for depression and/or an anxiety disorder (if their symptoms warrant) and should receive the appropriate treatment.

Prevention

To help keep a child from becoming a bully, it is important to be a role model for nonviolent behavior. Parents should also clearly communicate to the child that bullying behavior is not acceptable—clear limits should be established for acceptable behavior, and consequences for ignoring the limits should be defined. Teaching good social skills, including efficacious conflict-resolution skills and anger management skills, can also help potential bullies learn alternative socially acceptable behaviors.

Recent attention in the media to student suicides related to bullying as well as school shootings and similar acts of violence has prompted a search for new approaches to the problem. One approach involves making it easier for students to break the "code of silence" that makes them reluctant to inform on their peers. Safe2Tell is an anonymous 24/7 hotline that some communities have set up that allows students to report bullying, plans to attack the school, and other forms of violent behavior.

A more comprehensive approach is the Olweus (pronounced ohl-VAY-us) Bullying Prevention Program (OBBP), a systems-change approach designed by a Norwegian educator named Dan Olweus in 1983 and tested in both Norway and the United States for over 25 years. The program is designed to improve peer relations and make schools safer, more positive places for students to learn and develop. Goals of the program include reducing existing bullying problems among students, preventing new bullying problems, and achieving better peer relations at school. As of 2011, the OBBP approach had been used with over 40,000 students in both countries and was reported to reduce bullying rates by up to 50%. Designed for long-term use in elementary, middle, and junior high schools, the program includes a questionnaire about bullying for students to answer as well as training for teachers, school administrators, parents, and community leaders.

The program does not utilize conflict-resolution or peer-mediation techniques, because it believes that these approaches assume that the parties involved are equal in power or status, whereas bullying is based on power imbalances. According to proponents of the Olweus program, it reduces vandalism as well as bullying and other forms of antisocial behavior in the schools where it has been tried. It has also been successfully used in summer camps, sports teams, and other organizations for children and adolescents.

Resources

BOOKS

Hamilton, Jill, ed. *Bullying and Hazing*. Detroit, MI: Greenhaven Press, 2008.

Monks, Claire P., and Iain Coyne, eds. *Bullying in Different Contexts*. New York: Cambridge University Press, 2011.

Olweus, Dan, et al. *Olweus Bullying Prevention Program: Schoolwide Guide*. Center City, MN: Hazelden, 2007.

Pennsylvania Bar Institute. *Surviving the Schoolyard Battlefield*. Mechanicsburg, PA: PBI, 2008.

Spivet, Bonnie. *Stopping Cyberbullying*. New York: PowerKids Press, 2012.

PERIODICALS

Blosnich, J., and R. Bossarte. "Low-level Violence in Schools: Is There an Association between School Safety Measures and Peer Victimization?" *Journal of School Health* 81 (February 2011): 107–113.

Centers for Disease Control and Prevention (CDC). "Bullying among Middle School and High School Students—Massachusetts, 2009." *Morbidity and Mortality Weekly Report* 60 (April 22, 2011): 465–471.

Johnson, S.L. "An Ecological Model of Workplace Bullying: A Guide for Intervention and Research." *Nursing Forum* 46 (April 2011): 55–63.

Meloni, M., and M. Austin. "Implementation and Outcomes of a Zero Tolerance of Bullying and Harassment Program." *Australian Health Review* 35 (February 2011): 92–94.

Mishna, F., et al. "Cyber Bullying Behaviors among Middle and High School Students." *American Journal of Orthopsychiatry* 80 (July 2010): 362–374.

Olweus, D., and S.P. Limber. "Bullying in School: Evaluation and Dissemination of the Olweus Bullying Prevention Program." *American Journal of Orthopsychiatry* 80 (January 2010): 124–134.

Payne, S.R., and D.S. Elliott. "Safe2Tell(®) : An Anonymous, 24/7 Reporting System for Preventing School Violence." *New Directions for Youth Development* 129 (March 2011): 103–111.

Stagg, S.J., and D. Sheridan. "Effectiveness of Bullying and Violence Prevention Programs." *Journal of the American Association of Occupational Health Nurses* 58 (October 2010): 419–424.

Waasdorp, T.E., et al. "A Multilevel Perspective on the Climate of Bullying: Discrepancies Among Students, School Staff, and Parents." *Journal of School Violence* 10 (January 1, 2011): 115–132.

Wang, J., et al. "Cyber and Traditional Bullying: Differential Association with Depression." *Journal of Adolescent Health* 48 (April 2011): 415–417.

WEBSITES

ABC News. "Teen Triangle and Facebook Feud Lead to Murder of 15-Year-Old Florida Boy." http://abcnews.go.com/US/teen-triangle-leads-vicious-murder-15-year-florida/story?id=13422887 (accessed May 24, 2011).

American Academy of Child and Adolescent Psychiatry (AACAP) Facts for Families. "Bullying." http://www.aacap.org/cs/root/facts_for_families/bullying (accessed May 23, 2011).

Hazelden Foundation. "An Overview of the Olweus Bullying Prevention Program" (10-minute video). http://www.youtube.com/watch?v=P9C5wJ6uAk0 (accessed May 23, 2011).

Olweus Bullying Prevention Program. "What Is Bullying?" http://www.olweus.org/public/bullying.page (accessed May 22, 2011).

StopBullying.gov Home Page. http://www.stopbullying.gov (accessed May 21, 2011).

STOP Cyberbullying. "What Methods Work with the Different Kinds of Cyberbullies?" http://www.stopcyberbullying.org/parents/howdoyouhandleacyberbully.html (accessed May 22, 2011).

TeensHealth. "Cyberbullying." http://kidshealth.org/teen/school_jobs/bullying/cyberbullying.html (accessed May 22, 2011).

TeensHealth. "Dealing with Bullying." http://kidshealth.org/teen/your_mind/problems/bullies.html (accessed May 22, 2011).

Workplace Bullying Institute Home Page. http://www.workplacebullying.org (accessed May 22, 2011).

ORGANIZATIONS

Act Against Bullying, PO Box 57962, London, United Kingdom W4 2TG, (44) 208 995 9500, info@actagainstbullying.org, http://www.actagainstbullying.org/index.htm.

American Academy of Child and Adolescent Psychiatry (AACAP), 3615 Wisconsin Avenue, NW, Washington, DC, United States, 20016-3007, (202) 966-7300, Fax: (202) 966-2891, http://www.aacap.org.

Hazelden Foundation, PO Box 11, Center City, MN, United States, 55012-0011, (651) 213-4200, (800) 257-7810, info@hazelden.org, http://www.hazelden.org.

Olweus Bullying Prevention Program, (800) 328-9000, olweusinfo@hazelden.org, http://www.olweus.org/public/index.page.

STOP Cyberbullying, (201) 463-8663, parry@aftab.com, http://www.stopcyberbullying.org/index2.html.

Workplace Bullying Institute (WBI), PO Box 29915, Bellingham, WA, United States, 98228 http://www.workplacebullying.org.

Ruth A. Wienclaw, Ph.D.
Rebecca J. Frey, Ph.D.

Bupropion

Definition

Bupropion is an antidepressant drug used to elevate mood and promote recovery of a normal range of emotions in patients with depressive disorders. In addition, bupropion is used to as an aid in **smoking cessation** treatment. In the United States, bupropion is sold as an antidepressant under the brand name Wellbutrin. As a smoking cessation treatment, the drug is marketed under the brand name Zyban.

Purpose

Bupropion is approved by the U.S. Food and Drug Administration (FDA) to treat **depression** and **seasonal affective disorder** and to aid in smoking cessation. It may have therapeutic uses in **panic disorder** and **attention deficit hyperactivity disorder (ADHD)** but as of 2011 was not FDA approved for those indications.

Description

Bupropion is a nontricyclic antidepressant drug. Until the 1980s, tricyclic **antidepressants** were the mainstay of the pharmacological treatment of depression, but they had unwanted side effects, including sedation, dizziness, fainting, and weight gain. Bupropion was one of the first antidepressants to be developed by pharmaceutical researchers seeking drugs effective in treating depression but without the unwanted actions of the tricyclic antidepressants.

The exact way that bupropion works in the **brain** is not understood. Its mechanism of action appears to be different from that of most other antidepressant drugs, although bupropion does act on some of the same **neurotransmitters** and neurotransmission pathways. Neurotransmitters are naturally occurring chemicals that regulate the transmission of nerve impulses from one cell to another. Mental well-being is partially dependent on maintaining the proper balance among the various neurotransmitters in the brain. Bupropion may restore normal emotional feelings by counteracting abnormalities of neurotransmission that occur in depressive disorders.

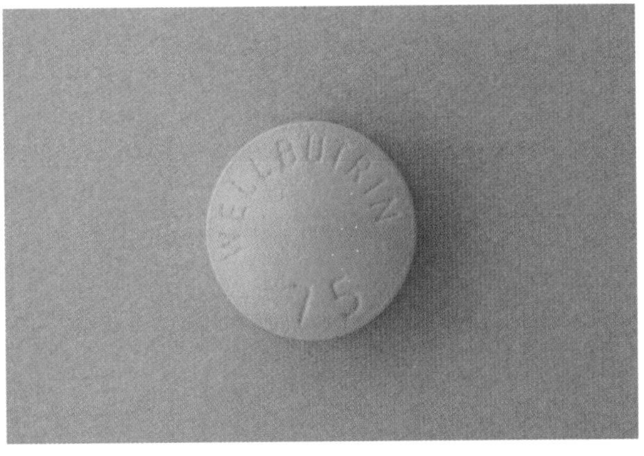

Wellbutrin (bupropion), 75 mg. *(© Custom Medical Stock Photo, Inc. Reproduced by permission.)*

Bupropion is less likely to cause weight gain and adverse effects on blood pressure and the heart, compared to other antidepressants. However, it is more likely to trigger epileptic **seizures**.

Recommended dosage

The usual adult dose of bupropion (Wellbutrin) is 100 mg, taken three times per day, with at least six hours between doses. The sustained-release form of the drug (Wellbutrin SR) is taken as 150 mg twice a day with at least eight hours between doses. An extended-release, once-daily dose (Wellbutrin XL) is also available and is usually taken in the morning. For smoking cessation, bupropion (Zyban) is taken as 150 mg sustained-release tablets twice a day, with at least eight hours between doses. Bupropion treatment should be started at a lower dose, then gradually increased to a therapeutic dosage as directed by the physician. Generally, the total dosage should not exceed 300 mg per day, except as directed by the physician.

The therapeutic effects of bupropion, like other antidepressants, appear slowly. Maximum benefit is often not evident for several weeks after starting the drug. People taking bupropion should be aware of this and continue taking the drug as directed even if they do not see immediate improvement in mood.

Since higher doses of bupropion increase the risk of seizures, no more than 150 mg should be given at any one time, and the total daily dosage should not be increased by more than 100 mg every three days. Increasing the dosage gradually also minimizes any agitation, restlessness, and **insomnia** that may occur.

Healthy elderly patients do not appear to be more sensitive to side effects of bupropion than younger adults and do not require reduced doses. Certain medical conditions, especially liver and kidney disease, may necessitate dose reduction. Although bupropion has been taken by children and adolescents under age 18, it has not yet been systematically studied in these age groups.

Precautions

Bupropion is more likely to trigger epileptic seizures than other antidepressants. The drug should not be given

KEY TERMS

Anxiety—An emotion that can be experienced as a troubled feeling, sense of dread, fear of the future, or distress over a perceived threat to a person's physical or mental well-being.

Attention deficit hyperactivity disorder (ADHD)—A developmental disorder characterized by distractibility, hyperactivity, impulsive behaviors, and the inability to remain focused on tasks or activities.

Depression—A mental state characterized by feelings of sadness, despair, discouragement, and low energy, sometimes accompanied by oversleeping and/or overeating.

Insomnia—Having difficulty falling asleep and/or staying asleep.

Seizure—A convulsion or uncontrolled discharge of nerve cells that may spread to other cells throughout the brain.

to patients who have a history of epilepsy, take other medication to help control seizures, or have some other condition associated with seizures, such as head **trauma** or alcoholism. Nevertheless, less than 1% of healthy people taking bupropion at the recommended dose have seizures. The possibility of seizures is increased at higher doses and following a sudden increase in dose. Patients should minimize alcohol intake while taking bupropion, since alcohol consumption increases the chance of seizures.

Because of the possibility of overdose, potentially suicidal patients should be given only small quantities of the drug at one time. Increases in blood pressure have occurred in patients taking bupropion along with **nicotine** treatment for smoking cessation. Monitoring blood pressure is recommended in such cases. Excessive stimulation, agitation, insomnia, and anxiety have been troublesome side effects for some patients, especially when treatment is first begun or when the dose is increased. Such adverse effects may be less intense and less frequent when the dose is increased gradually.

When taken for smoking cessation, some patients have developed severe neuropsychiatric symptoms, including aggression, depression, mania, panic attacks, and suicidal thoughts and actions. As with other antidepressants, children and adults up to 24 years of age are at increased risk for developing suicidal thoughts and actions. It is generally not advised for children under the age of 18 to take bupropion, but in some cases it may be the best treatment available. Patients should consult with their doctor and read the medication guide before starting treatment with bupropion.

It has not been determined whether bupropion is safe to take during pregnancy. Pregnant women should take bupropion only if necessary. The drug is secreted in breast milk. Women taking bupropion should consult their physicians about risks associated with breast-feeding.

Side effects

Bupropion is a very mild stimulant and may cause insomnia, agitation, confusion, restlessness, and anxiety. These effects may be more pronounced at the beginning of therapy and after dose increases. Headache, dizziness, and tremor may occur. Despite its stimulating effects, bupropion may also cause sedation.

Weight loss is more common with bupropion than weight gain, but both have been reported. Other negative side effects include:

- excessive sweating
- dry mouth
- sore throat
- nausea
- vomiting
- decreased appetite
- constipation
- blurred vision
- rapid heart rate

Interactions

Bupropion should not be administered along with other medications that lower the seizure threshold, such as **steroids** and the asthma medication theophylline. Many psychiatric medications also lower the seizure threshold. **Monoamine oxidase inhibitors (MAOIs)**, another type of antidepressant medication, should not be taken with bupropion or two weeks before starting the drug. Adverse effects may increase in patients taking levodopa and other medications for Parkinson's disease along with bupropion. Patients should inform their doctors about all other medications they are taking before starting this drug.

Nicotine patch therapy may be administered concurrently with bupropion in smoking cessation treatment. If this is done, blood pressure must be monitored, since increased blood pressure has been reported with this combination of medications.

Certain drugs, especially those eliminated by the liver, may interfere with the elimination of bupropion from the

QUESTIONS TO ASK YOUR DOCTOR

- What kind of changes can I expect to see or feel with this medication?
- Does it matter what time of day I take this medication? If so, what is the recommendation?
- Should I take this medication with or without food?
- What are the side effects associated with this medication?
- Will this medication interact or interfere with other medications I am currently taking?
- What symptoms or adverse effects are important enough that I should seek immediate treatment?

body, causing higher blood levels and increased side effects. Conversely, bupropion may delay the elimination of other medicines, including many antidepressants, antipsychotic drugs, and heart medications, resulting in higher blood levels and potentially increased side effects.

Resources

BOOKS

Albers, Lawrence J., Rhoda K. Hahn, and Christopher Reist. *Handbook of Psychiatric Drugs, 2011 Edition.* Laguna Hills, CA: Current Clinical Strategies, 2010.

American Society of Health-System Pharmacists. *AHFS Drug Information 2011.* Bethesda, MD: ASHP, 2011.

Baldwin, Robert C. *Depression in Later Life.* New York: Oxford University Press, 2010.

Graham, George. *The Disordered Mind: An Introduction to Philosophy of Mind and Mental Illness.* New York: Routledge, 2010.

Holland, Leland Norman, and Michael Patrick Adams. *Core Concepts in Pharmacology.* 3rd ed. New York: Prentice Hall, 2011.

North, Carol, and Sean Yutzy. *Goodwin and Guze's Psychiatric Diagnosis.* New York: Oxford University Press, 2010.

O'Connor, Richard. *Undoing Depression: What Therapy Doesn't Teach You and Medication Can't Give You.* 2nd ed. New York: Little, Brown, 2010.

Preston, John D., John H. O'Neal, and Mary C. Talaga. *Handbook of Clinical Psychopharmacology for Therapists.* 6th ed. Oakland, CA: New Harbinger, 2010.

PERIODICALS

Lader, M. "Foreword. A Comprehensive Review of Bupropion." *Clinical Drug Investigation* 19, no. 31, supplement 1 (2011): 1–3.

Little, John T., et al. "Bupropion and Venlafaxine Responders Differ in Pretreatment Regional Cerebral Metabolism in Unipolar Depression." *Biological Psychiatry* 57, no. 3 (February 2005): 220–28.

Thase, Michael E., et al. "Remission Rates Following Antidepressant Therapy with Bupropion or Selective Serotonin Reuptake Inhibitors: A Meta-Analysis of Original Data From 7 Randomized Controlled Trials." *Journal of Clinical Psychiatry* 66, no. 8 (August 2005): 974–81.

ORGANIZATIONS

American Academy of Clinical Toxicology, 6728 Old McLean Village Dr., McLean, VA, 22101, (703) 556-9222, Fax: (703) 556-8729, admin@clintox.org, http://www.clintox.org.

American Psychiatric Association, 1000 Wilson Blvd., Ste. 1825, Arlington, VA, 22209-3901, (703) 907-7300, apa@psych.org, http://www.psych.org.

American Society for Clinical Pharmacology and Therapeutics, 528 N Washington St., Alexandria, VA, 22314, (703) 836-6981, info@ascpt.org, http://www.ascpt.org.

American Society for Pharmacology and Experimental Therapeutics, 9650 Rockville Pike, Bethesda, MD, 20814-3995, (301) 634-7060, http://www.aspet.org.

Depression and Bipolar Support Alliance, 730 N Franklin St., Ste. 501, Chicago, IL, 60654, (800) 826-3632, Fax: (312) 642-7243, http://www.dbsalliance.org.

National Alliance on Mental Illness, 2107 Wilson Blvd., Ste. 300, Arlington, VA, 22201-3042, Fax: (703) 524-9094, (800) 950-6264, http://www.nami.org.

National Institute of Mental Health, 6001 Executive Blvd., Rm. 8184, MSC 9663, Bethesda, MD, 20892-9663, (301) 433-4513; TTY: (301) 443-8431, Fax: (301) 443-4279, (866) 615-6464; TTY: (866) 415-8051, nimhinfo@nih.gov

Richard Kapit, MD
Ruth A. Wienclaw, PhD
Laura Jean Cataldo, RN, EdD

BuSpar *see* **Buspirone**

Buspirone

Definition

Buspirone is an antianxiety (anxiolytic) drug sold in the United States under the brand name BuSpar. It is also available under its generic name.

Purpose

Buspirone is used for the treatment of generalized **anxiety disorders** and for short-term relief of symptoms of anxiety.

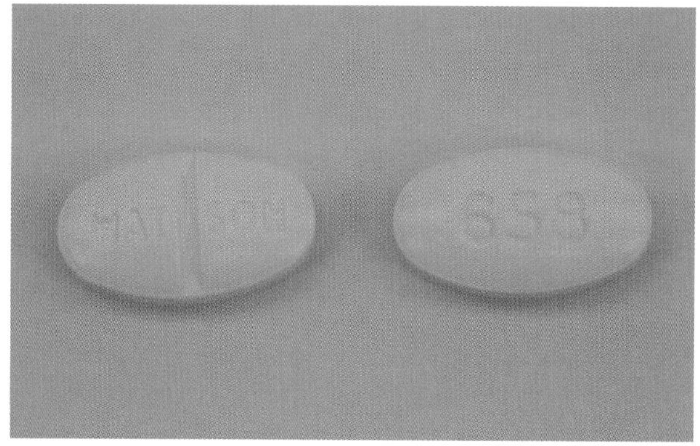

Buspirone, 10 mg. *(© Custom Medical Stock Photo, Inc. Reproduced by permission.)*

Description

Buspirone's mechanism of action is unclear but probably involves actions on such central nervous system chemicals as **dopamine**, **serotonin**, acetylcholine, and norepinephrine. These chemicals are called **neurotransmitters** and are involved in the transmission of nervous impulses from cell to cell. Mental well-being is partially dependent on maintaining a balance among different neurotransmitters.

Buspirone's actions are different from the common class of **sedatives** called **benzodiazepines**. The primary actions of benzodiazepines are to reduce anxiety, relax skeletal muscles, and induce sleep. The earliest drugs in this class were **chlordiazepoxide** (Librium) and **diazepam** (Valium). The mechanism of buspirone's action is also different from **barbiturates** such as phenobarbital. Unlike benzodiazepines, buspirone has no anticonvulsant or muscle-relaxant properties, and unlike benzodiazepines or barbiturates it does not have strong sedative properties. If **insomnia** is a component of the patient's anxiety disorder, a sedative/hypnotic drug may be taken along with buspirone at bedtime. Buspirone also diminishes anger and hostility for most people. Unlike benzodiazepines, which may aggravate anger and hostility in some patients (especially older patients), buspirone may help patients with anxiety who also have a history of aggression.

The benefits of buspirone take a long time to become evident. Unlike benzodiazepines, with which the onset of action and time to maximum benefit are short, patients must take buspirone for three to four weeks before feeling the maximum benefit of the drug. In some cases, four to six weeks of treatment may be required. Patients should be aware of this and continue to take the drug as prescribed even if they think they are not seeing any improvement.

Buspirone is available in 5, 10, 15, and 30 mg tablets.

KEY TERMS

Anxiety—An emotion that can be experienced as a troubled feeling, sense of dread, fear of the future, or distress over a possible threat to a person's physical or mental well-being.

Depression—A mental state characterized by feelings of sadness, despair, and discouragement.

Insomnia—Having difficulty falling asleep or remaining asleep.

Neurotransmitter—A chemical that aids or alters the transmission of impulses between the points that connect nerves.

Serotonin—A chemical messenger in the brain thought to play a role in mood regulation.

Recommended dosage

The usual starting dose of this drug is 10 to 15 mg per day. This total amount is divided into two or three doses. For example, a dose of 5 mg may be given two or three times per day to make a total dose of 10 to 15 mg per day. The dose may be increased in increments of 5 mg daily every two to four days. Most patients respond to a dose of 15 to 30 mg daily. Patients should not take a total dose of more than 60 mg daily. When patients are receiving certain other drugs in addition to buspirone, starting doses of buspirone may need to be lowered (e.g., 2.5 mg twice daily), and any dosage increase should be done with caution and under close physician supervision. Dosages may need to be reduced in patients with kidney or liver problems.

Precautions

Buspirone is less sedating (it causes less drowsiness and mental sluggishness) than other **antianxiety drugs**. However, some patients may still experience drowsiness and mental impairment. Because it is impossible to predict which patients may experience sedation with buspirone, those starting this drug should not drive or operate machinery until they know how the drug will affect them.

Patients who have been taking benzodiazepines for a long time should be gradually withdrawn from them while they are being switched over to buspirone. They should also be observed for symptoms of benzodiazepine withdrawal.

Patients with kidney damage should take buspirone with caution in close consultation with their physician. They may require a lower dosage of buspirone to prevent buildup of the drug in the body. Patients with severe

QUESTIONS TO ASK YOUR DOCTOR

- What kind of changes can I expect to see or feel with this medication?
- Does it matter what time of day I take this medication? If so, what is the recommendation?
- Should I take this medication with or without food?
- What are the side effects associated with this medication?
- Will this medication interact or interfere with other medications I am currently taking?
- What symptoms or adverse effects are important enough that I should seek immediate treatment?

kidney disease should not take buspirone. Patients with liver damage should likewise be monitored for a buildup of buspirone and have their doses lowered if necessary.

Side effects

The most common side effects associated with buspirone involve the nervous system. Ten percent of patients may experience dizziness, drowsiness, and headache, and another 5% may experience **fatigue**, nervousness, insomnia, and light-headedness. Patients may also experience:

- excitement
- depression
- anger
- hostility
- confusion
- nightmares or other sleep disorders
- lack of coordination
- tremor
- numbness of the extremities

Although buspirone is considered nonsedating, some patients experience drowsiness and lack of mental alertness at higher doses, especially early in therapy. In most patients, these side effects decrease with time.

The following side effects have also been associated with buspirone:

- nausea (up to 8% of patients)
- dry mouth, abdominal distress, gastric distress, diarrhea, and constipation (up to 5% of patients)
- rapid heart rate and palpitations (up to 2% of patients)
- blurred vision (up to 2% of patients)
- increased or decreased appetite
- flatulence
- nonspecific chest pain
- rash
- irregular menstrual periods and/or breakthrough bleeding

Interactions

Patients should avoid drinking grapefruit juice while on buspirone, as it inhibits the metabolism of the drug, resulting in potentially toxic amounts of the substance in the bloodstream.

Dangerously high blood pressure has resulted from the combination of buspirone and members of another class of **antidepressants** known as **monoamine oxidase inhibitors (MAOIs)**. Because of this, buspirone should never be taken in combination with MAOIs. Patients taking any MAOIs, such as **phenelzine** sulfate (Nardil) or **tranylcypromine** sulfate (Parnate), should stop the MAOIs and wait at least 14 days before starting buspirone. The same holds true when discontinuing buspirone and starting any MAOIs.

Certain drugs that affect the liver may alter the metabolism of buspirone. Examples of such drugs are erythromycin, a broad-spectrum antibiotic; itraconazole, an oral antifungal agent; and **nefazodone**, an antidepressant. When these drugs are combined with buspirone, buspirone concentrations may increase to the point of toxicity (poisoning). These combinations should either be avoided or doses of buspirone decreased to compensate for this interaction.

Resources

BOOKS

Albers, Lawrence J., Rhoda K. Hahn, and Christopher Reist. *Handbook of Psychiatric Drugs.* Laguna Hills, CA: Current Clinical Strategies, 2010.

American Society of Health-System Pharmacists. *AHFS Drug Information 2011.* Bethesda, MD: ASHP, 2011.

Graham, George. *The Disordered Mind: An Introduction to Philosophy of Mind and Mental Illness.* New York: Routledge, 2010.

Holland, Leland Norman, and Michael Patrick Adams. *Core Concepts in Pharmacology.* 3rd ed. New York: Prentice Hall, 2011.

North, Carol, and Sean Yutzy. *Goodwin and Guze's Psychiatric Diagnosis.* New York: Oxford University Press, 2010.

Preston, John D., John H. O'Neal, and Mary C. Talaga. *Handbook of Clinical Psychopharmacology for Therapists.* 6th ed. Oakland, CA: New Harbinger, 2010.

PERIODICALS

Baldwin, David S., and Claire Polkinghorn. "Evidence-based Pharmacotherapy of Generalized Anxiety Disorder." *International Journal of Neuropsychopharmacology* 8, no. 2 (June 2005): 293–302.

Buydens-Branchey, Laure, Marc Branchey, and Christine Reel-Brander. "Efficacy of Buspirone in the Treatment of Opioid Withdrawal." *Journal of Clinical Psychopharmacology* 25, no. 3 (June 2005): 230–36.

Helvink, Badalin, and Suzanne Holroyd. "Buspirone for Stereotypic Movements in Elderly with Cognitive Impairment." *Journal of Neuropsychiatry and Clinical Neurosciences* 18, no. 2 (Spring 2006): 242–44.

McRae, Aimee L., Kathleen T. Brady, and Rickey E. Carter. "Buspirone for Treatment of Marijuana Dependence: A Pilot Study." *American Journal on Addictions* 15, no. 5 (September/October 2006): 404.

Quitkin, Frederick, et al. "Medication Augmentation after the Failure of SSRIs for Depression." *New England Journal of Medicine* 354, no. 12 (March 2006): 1243–52.

Verster, Joris C., Dieuwke S. Veldhuijzen, and Edmund R Volkerts. "Is It Safe to Drive a Car When Treated with Anxiolytics? Evidence from On-the-Road Driving Studies During Normal Traffic." *Current Psychiatry Reviews* 1, no. 2 (June 2005): 215–25.

WEBSITES

PubMed Health. "Buspirone." U.S. National Library of Medicine. http://www.ncbi.nlm.nih.gov/pubmedhealth/PMH0000876 (accessed December 17, 2011).

ORGANIZATIONS

American Academy of Clinical Toxicology, 6728 Old McLean Village Dr., McLean, VA, 22101, (703) 556-9222 Fax: (703) 556-8729, admin@clintox.org, http://www.clintox.org.

American Academy of Family Physicians, 11400 Tomahawk Creek Pkwy., Leawood, KS, 66211-2672, (913) 906-6000, (800) 274-2237, Fax: (913) 906-6075, contactcenter@aafp.org, http://www.aafp.org.

American Psychiatric Association, 1000 Wilson Blvd., Ste. 1825, Arlington, VA, 22209-3901, (703) 907-7300, apa@psych.org, http://www.psych.org.

American Society for Clinical Pharmacology and Therapeutics, 528 N Washington St., Alexandria, VA, 22314, (703) 836-6981, info@ascpt.org, http://www.ascpt.org.

Anxiety Disorders Association of America, 8730 Georgia Ave., Silver Spring, MD, 20910, (240) 485-1001, Fax: (240) 485-1035, http://www.adaa.org.

National Alliance on Mental Illness, 2107 Wilson Blvd., Ste. 300, Arlington, VA, 22201-3042, Fax: (703) 524-9094, (800) 950-6264, http://www.nami.org.

National Institute of Mental Health, 6001 Executive Blvd., Rm. 8184, MSC 9663, Bethesda, MD, 20892-9663, (301) 433-4513; TTY: (301) 443-8431, Fax: (301) 443-4279, (866) 615-6464; TTY: (866) 415-8051, nimhinfo@nih.gov, http://www.nimh.nih.gov.

Jack Raber, PharmD
Ruth A. Wienclaw, PhD
Laura Jean Cataldo, RN, EdD

Caffeine-related disorders

Definition

Caffeine is a white, bitter crystalline alkaloid derived from coffee or tea. It belongs to a class of compounds called xanthines, its chemical formula being 1,3,7-trimethylxanthine. Caffeine is classified together with **cocaine** and **amphetamines** as an analeptic, or central nervous system stimulant. Coffee is the most abundant source of caffeine, although caffeine is also found in tea, cocoa, and cola beverages as well as in over-the-counter and prescription medications for pain relief.

In the clinician's handbook for diagnosing mental disorders (the ***Diagnostic and Statistical Manual of Mental Disorders***, known as the *DSM-IV-TR*), caffeine-related disorders are classified under the rubric of substance-related disorders. *DSM-IV-TR* specifies four caffeine-related disorders: caffeine intoxication, caffeine-induced anxiety disorder, caffeine-induced sleep disorder, and caffeine-related disorder not otherwise specified. A fifth disorder, caffeine withdrawal, was listed as being considered for further study in the *DSM-IV* and is proposed to be included as a **diagnosis** in the fifth edition (*DSM-5*, 2013).

Many different products contain caffeine, including coffee, tea, colas, and energy drinks. *(© Martyn F. Chillmaid/Photo Researchers, Inc.)*

Demographics

The general population of the United States has a high level of caffeine consumption, with an average intake of 200 mg per day. About 85% of the population uses caffeine in any given year. Among adults in the United States, about 30% consume 500 mg or more of caffeine each day. These figures are lower, however, than the figures for Sweden, the United Kingdom, and other parts of Europe, where the average daily consumption of caffeine among all adults is 400 mg or higher. In developing countries, the average consumption of caffeine is much lower, about 50 mg per day.

In the United States, levels of caffeine consumption among all races and ethnic groups are related to age, with usage beginning in the late teens and rising until the early 30s. Caffeine consumption tapers off in adults over 40 and decreases in adults over 65. Caffeine intake is higher among males than among females in North America.

Description

Caffeine-related disorders are often unrecognized for a number of reasons, including caffeine's "low profile" as a drug of abuse. Consumption of drinks containing caffeine is unregulated by law and is nearly universal in the United States; one well-known textbook of pharmacology refers to caffeine as "the most widely used psychoactive drug in the world." In many countries, coffee is a social lubricant as well as a stimulant; the "coffee break" is a common office ritual, and many people find it difficult to imagine eating a meal in a fine restaurant without having coffee at some point during the meal. It is estimated that 10–12 billion lb. (4–5 billion kg) of coffee are consumed worldwide each year.

People often underestimate the amount of caffeine they consume on a daily basis because they think of caffeine only in connection with coffee; however, tea, cocoa, and

Approximate amounts of caffeine in popular products

	Size	Amount of caffeine
Sprite, Fanta, 7 UP	12 oz (355 mL)	0 mg
Tea, decaffeinated	8 oz (240 mL)	1–4 mg
Coffee, decaffeinated, brewed	8 oz (240 mL)	2–12 mg
Hershey's Milk Chocolate	1.55 oz (43 g)	9 mg
Tea, green, brewed	8 oz (240 mL)	15 mg
Barq's Root Beer	12 oz (355 mL)	23 mg
Hershey's Special Dark Chocolate	1.45 oz (41 g)	31 mg
Coca-Cola Classic	12 oz (355 mL)	35 mg
Pepsi	12 oz (355 mL)	36–38 mg
Tea, black, brewed	8 oz (240 mL)	40–120 mg
Sunkist Orange, regular or diet	12 oz (355 mL)	41 mg
Dr Pepper	12 oz (355 mL)	42–44 mg
Diet Coke	12 oz (355 mL)	47 mg
Mountain Dew	12 oz (355 mL)	54 mg
Coffee, espresso	1 oz (30 mL)	58–75 mg
Excedrin® extra-strength headache	1 tablet	65 mg
Red Bull energy drink	8.3 oz (245 mL)	76 mg
SoBe No Fear energy drink	8 oz (240 mL)	83 mg
Coffee, brewed	8 oz (240 mL)	95–200 mg
5-hour ENERGY® drink	2 oz (59 mL)	138 mg
Monster Energy drink	16 oz (473 mL)	160 mg
NO-DOZ® maximum-strength caffeine	1 tablet	200 mg

(Table by PreMediaGlobal. © 2012 Cengage Learning.)

some types of soft drinks (such as colas) also contain significant amounts of caffeine. In one British case study, a teenager who was hospitalized with muscle weakness, nausea, vomiting, diarrhea, and weight loss was found to have caffeine intoxication caused by drinking about 2 gal. (8 L) of cola on a daily basis for the two years. She had been consuming over a gram of caffeine per day. Chocolate bars and coffee-flavored yogurt or ice cream are additional sources of measurable amounts of caffeine.

Caffeine has some legitimate medical uses in athletic training and in the relief of tension-type headaches. It is available in over-the-counter (OTC) preparations containing aspirin or acetaminophen for pain relief as well as in such OTC stimulants as NoDoz and Vivarin. It is also available in energy drinks and supplements and more recently in alcoholic beverages, though the latter is considered unsafe by the U.S. Food and Drug Administration (FDA), who in 2010 ordered several manufacturers of caffeinated alcoholic beverages to cease production. Some beverages are still available, but the effects of caffeine and alcohol have not been sufficiently tested, and the full extent of possible adverse effects is not yet known.

In comparison to other drugs of abuse, caffeine is less likely to produce the same degree of physical or psychological dependence. Few coffee or tea drinkers report loss of control over caffeine intake, or significant difficulty in reducing or stopping consumption of beverages and food items containing caffeine. Still, a research team at Johns Hopkins regards caffeine as a model drug for understanding **substance abuse** and dependence. The team maintains that 9%–30% of caffeine consumers in the United States may be caffeine-dependent, according to *DSM* criteria for substance dependency.

Pharmacological aspects of caffeine

An outline of the effects of caffeine on the central nervous system (CNS) and other organ systems of the body may be helpful in understanding its potential for physical dependence. When a person drinks a beverage (or eats food) containing caffeine, the caffeine is absorbed from the digestive tract without being broken down. It is rapidly distributed throughout the tissues of the body by means of the bloodstream. If a pregnant woman drinks a cup of coffee or tea, the caffeine in the drink will cross the placental barrier and enter the baby's bloodstream.

When the caffeine reaches the **brain**, it increases the secretion of norepinephrine, a neurotransmitter that is associated with the so-called "fight or flight" **stress** response. The rise in norepinephrine levels and the increased activity of the neurons, or nerve cells, in many other areas of the brain helps to explain why the symptoms of caffeine intoxication resemble the symptoms of a **panic attack**.

The effects of caffeine are thought to occur as a result of competitive antagonism at adenosine receptors. Adenosine is a water-soluble compound of adenine and ribose; it functions to modulate the activities of nerve cells and produces a mild sedative effect when it activates certain types of adenosine receptors. Caffeine competes with adenosine to bind at these receptors and counteracts the sedative effects of the adenosine. If the person stops drinking coffee, the adenosine has no competition for activating its usual receptors and may produce a sedative effect that is experienced as **fatigue** or drowsiness.

Caffeine can produce a range of physical symptoms following ingestion of as little as 100 mg, although amounts of 250 mg or higher are usually needed to produce symptoms that meet the criteria of caffeine intoxication.

Causes and symptoms

Causes

The immediate cause of caffeine intoxication and other caffeine-related disorders is consumption of an amount of caffeine sufficient to produce the symptoms specified by the *DSM* as criteria for the disorder. The precise amount of caffeine necessary to produce symptoms varies from person to person depending on body size and degree of tolerance to caffeine. Tolerance of the stimulating effects of caffeine builds up rapidly in humans; mild withdrawal symptoms have been reported in persons who were drinking as little as one to two cups of coffee per day.

Some people may find it easier than others to consume large doses of caffeine because they are insensitive to its taste. Caffeine tastes bitter to most adults, which may serve to limit their consumption of coffee and other caffeinated beverages. Slightly more than 30% of the American population, however, has an inherited inability to taste caffeine.

Symptoms

CAFFEINE INTOXICATION. The symptoms of caffeine intoxication are similar to those of an anxiety disorder and include:

- restlessness
- nervousness
- excitement
- insomnia
- flushed face
- diuresis (increased urinary output)
- gastrointestinal disturbance
- muscle twitching
- talking or thinking in a rambling manner
- tachycardia (rapid heartbeat) or disturbances of heart rhythm (arrhythmias)
- periods of inexhaustibility
- psychomotor agitation

Some people have experienced ringing in the ears or seeing flashes of light at doses of caffeine above 250 mg. Profuse sweating and diarrhea are also possible symptoms. High short-term consumption of caffeine can produce or worsen gastrointestinal problems, occasionally leading to peptic ulcers or hematemesis (vomiting blood). Doses of caffeine higher than 10 g may produce respiratory failure, **seizures**, and eventually death.

In addition to the symptoms produced by high short-term doses, long-term consumption of caffeine has been associated with fertility problems and with bone loss in women leading to osteoporosis in old age. Some studies have found that pregnant women who consume more than 150 mg per day of caffeine have an increased risk of miscarriage and low birth weight babies, but the findings are complicated by the fact that most women who drink large amounts of coffee during pregnancy are also heavy smokers. Some researchers believe that long-term consumption of caffeine is implicated in cardiovascular diseases but acknowledge that further research is required.

On the other hand, moderate doses of caffeine improve athletic performance as well as alertness. Caffeine in small doses can relieve tension headaches, and one study found that a combination of ibuprofen and caffeine was more effective in relieving tension headaches than either ibuprofen alone or a placebo. Coffee consumption also appears to lower the risk of alcoholic and nonalcoholic cirrhosis of the liver.

CAFFEINE WITHDRAWAL. Symptoms of caffeine withdrawal include:

- headache
- fatigue
- depression or irritable mood
- lack of concentration
- nausea or vomiting, or general aches and pains

DRUG INTERACTIONS. Caffeine is often combined with aspirin or acetaminophen in over-the-counter and prescription analgesics (pain relievers). It can also be combined with ibuprofen. On the other hand, certain groups of drugs should not be combined with caffeine or taken with beverages containing caffeine. Oral contraceptives, cimetidine (Tagamet), mexiletine (Mexitil), and **disulfiram** (Antabuse) interfere with the breakdown of caffeine in the body. Caffeine interferes with the body's absorption of iron, and with drugs that regulate heart rhythm, including quinidine and **propranolol** (Inderal). Caffeine may produce serious side effects when taken together with **monoamine oxidase inhibitors (MAOIs)** or with certain decongestant medications.

Combinations of ephedra and caffeine have been used in weight-loss programs because they produce greater weight loss than can be achieved by caloric restriction alone. However, side effects of supplements containing ephedra and caffeine include **insomnia**, high blood pressure (hypertension), anxiety, irritability, and, if used in the long-term, chronic fatigue. The combination may be linked to more serious side effects, including death due to altered heart rhythm, but further research is needed to determine whether the combination alone is actually causal in such adverse events.

Practitioners of homeopathy have traditionally advised patients not to drink beverages containing caffeine in the belief that caffeine "antidotes" homeopathic remedies. Contemporary homeopaths disagree on the antidoting effects of caffeine, observing that homeopathy is used widely and effectively in Europe and that Europeans tend to drink strong espresso coffee more frequently than Americans.

Diagnosis

Diagnosis of a caffeine-related disorder is usually based on the patient's recent history, a physical examination, or laboratory analysis of body fluids. In addition to medical evidence, the examiner will rule out other mental disorders, particularly manic episodes, **generalized anxiety disorder**, **panic disorder**, amphetamine intoxication, or withdrawal from **sedatives**, tranquilizers, sleep medications, or **nicotine**. All of these disorders or syndromes may produce symptoms resembling those of caffeine intoxication. In most cases, the temporal relationship of the symptoms to high levels of caffeine intake establishes the diagnosis. The examiner may consider the possibility of **depression** during the differential diagnosis, as many people with depression and eating disorders self-medicate with caffeine.

Caffeine intoxication

To meet the *DSM* criteria for caffeine intoxication, a person must develop five or more of the twelve symptoms identified; the symptoms must cause significant distress or impair the person's social or occupational functioning; and the symptoms must not be caused by a medical disorder, an anxiety disorder, or another mental disorder. Because people develop tolerance to caffeine fairly quickly with habitual use, caffeine intoxication is most likely to occur in those who consume caffeine infrequently or who have recently increased their intake significantly.

Caffeine-induced anxiety and sleep disorders

DSM criteria for caffeine-induced anxiety and **sleep disorders** specify that the symptoms of anxiety and insomnia respectively must be more severe than the symptoms associated with caffeine intoxication. In addition, the anxiety or insomnia must be severe enough to require separate clinical attention.

Caffeine withdrawal

The *DSM-5* diagnostic criteria for caffeine withdrawal is met if a person drinks caffeine daily over an extended period of time and experiences at least three of the symptoms of caffeine withdrawal once consumption is ceased (within 24 hours). As with caffeine intoxication, the symptoms must cause significant distress or impair the person's social or occupational function and must not be caused by another disorder, including physical or mental disorders.

Treatment

Treatment of caffeine-related disorders involves lowering consumption levels or abstaining from beverages containing caffeine. If withdrawal symptoms are experienced, they usually resolve quickly as the body adjusts to the absence of caffeine.

Caffeine consumption has the advantage of having relatively weak (compared to alcohol or cigarettes) social **reinforcement**, in the sense that one can easily choose a noncaffeinated or decaffeinated beverage in a restaurant or at a party without attracting comment. Thus, physical dependence on caffeine is less complicated by the social factors that reinforce nicotine and other drug habits.

Prognosis

With the exception of acute episodes of caffeinism, most people recover from caffeine intoxication without great difficulty.

Prevention

Prevention of caffeine-related disorders requires awareness of the caffeine content of caffeinated beverages, OTC drugs, and other sources of caffeine; monitoring daily intake; and substituting caffeinated coffee, tea, or soft drinks for the decaffeinated versions of these beverages.

Resources

BOOKS

American Psychiatric Association. *Diagnostic and Statistical Manual of Mental Disorders*. 4th ed., text rev. Washington, DC: American Psychiatric Publishing, 2000.

"Anxiety Due to a Physical Disorder or a Substance." In *The Merck Manual of Diagnosis and Therapy*, edited by Robert S. Porter and Justin L. Kaplan. Whitehouse Station, NJ: Merck Sharp & Dohme, 2011.

Murray, Michael, and Joseph Pizzorno. *Encyclopedia of Natural Medicine*. New York: Three Rivers Press, 1997.

O'Brien, Charles P. "Drug Addiction and Drug Abuse." In *Goodman & Gilman's The Pharmacological Basis of Therapeutics,* edited by Laurence Brunton, Bruce Chabner, and Bjornn Knollman, 12th ed. New York: McGraw-Hill, 2010.

Pelletier, Kenneth R. "Naturopathic Medicine: 'Do No Harm'." In *The Best Alternative Medicine*. New York: Touchstone, 2002.

PERIODICALS

Corrao, G., et al. "Coffee, Caffeine, and the Risk of Liver Cirrhosis." *Annals of Epidemiology* 11 (October 2001): 458–465.

De Valck, E., and R. Cluydts. "Slow-Release Caffeine as a Countermeasure to Driver Sleepiness Induced by Partial Sleep Deprivation." *Journal of Sleep Research* 10, no. 3 (September 2001): 203–209.

Diamond, S., T.K. Balm, and F.G. Freitag. "Ibuprofen Plus Caffeine in the Treatment of Tension-Type Headache." *Clinical Pharmacology and Therapeutics* 68, no. 3 (2000): 312–319.

Griffiths, R.R., and A.L. Chausmer. "Caffeine as a Model Drug of Dependence: Recent Developments in Understanding Caffeine Withdrawal, the Caffeine Dependence Syndrome, and Caffeine Negative Reinforcement." *Japanese Journal of Psychopharmacology* 20, no. 5 (November 2000): 223–231.

MacFadyen, L., D. Eadie, and T. McGowan. "Community Pharmacists' Experience of Over-the-Counter Medicine Misuse in Scotland." *Perspectives in Public Health* 121, no. 3 (September 2001): 185–192.

Preboth, Monica. "Effect of Caffeine on Exercise Performance." *American Family Physician* 61 (May 1, 2000): 628.

Rapurl, P.B., et al. "Caffeine Intake Increases the Rate of Bone Loss in Elderly Women and Interacts with Vitamin D Receptor Genotypes." *American Journal of Clinical Nutrition* 74, no. 5 (November 2001): 694–700.

Rumpler, William, et al. "Oolong Tea Increases Metabolic Rate and Fat Oxidation in Men." *Journal of Nutrition* 131, no. 11 (November 1, 2001): 2848–2852.

Sardao, V. A., P. J. Oliveira, and A. J. Moreno. "Caffeine Enhances the Calcium-Dependent Cardiac Mitochondrial Permeability Transition: Relevance for Caffeine Toxicity." *Toxicology and Applied Pharmacology* 179, no. 1 (February 2002): 50–56.

ORGANIZATIONS

American College of Sports Medicine, PO Box 1440, Indianapolis, IN, 46206-1440, (317) 637-9200, Fax: (317) 634-7817, http://www.acsm.org.

American Dietetic Association, 120 South Riverside Plz., Ste. 2000, Chicago, IL, 60606, (312) 899-0040, (800) 877-1600, http://www.eatright.org.

Center for Science in the Public Interest, 1220 L St. NW, Ste. 300, Washington, DC, 20005, (202) 332-9110, Fax: (202) 265-4954, http://www.cspinet.org.

U.S. Food and Drug Administration, 10903 New Hampshire Ave., Silver Spring, MD, 20993-0002, (888) INFO-FDA (463-6332), http://www.fda.gov.

Rebecca J. Frey, PhD

Cannabis and related disorders

Definition

Cannabis, more commonly called marijuana, refers to the several varieties of *Cannabis sativa*, or Indian hemp plant, that contain the psychoactive drug delta-9-tetrahydrocannabinol (THC). Cannabis-related disorders refer to problems associated with the use of substances derived from this plant.

Demographics

Marijuana is the most commonly used illicit drug in the United States. As with most other illicit drugs, cannabis use disorders appear more often in males and are most common among people between the ages of 18 and 30 years.

Statistics from 2010, published in the *National Survey on Drug Use and Health*, revealed that 17.4 million Americans over the age of 12 had used marijuana a minimum of one time in the previous month. The percentage of persons using marijuana has increased consistently since 2007, and approximately 60% of illicit drug users only smoke marijuana.

Experts are particularly concerned by the increase in daily or near daily use (defined as using marijuana at least 20 times in the previous 30 day period) among students in eighth, tenth, and twelfth grade. The National Institute of Drug Abuse conducts an annual nationwide study of eighth-, tenth-, and twelfth-grade students and young adults, known as the *Monitoring the Future Study*. The results track back to the 1970s, when marijuana use was at an all-time high. After a drastic dip, use started to climb again from 1992 to 1998. In 2010, roughly 15% of eighth graders, 27% of tenth graders, and 35% of twelfth graders had used marijuana in the past 12 months, with all three usage rates on a pattern of gradual incline (at rates of 1%, 3%, and 6%, respectively).

The Drug Abuse Warning Network, operated by the **Substance Abuse and Mental Health Services Administration** (SAMHSA), tracks data on emergency room admissions related to substance use, including cannabis. An estimated 376,467 people were admitted to U.S. emergency departments in 2009 as a result of marijuana use, with almost a third of patients under the age of 21

Cannabis (marijuana). *(U.S. Drug Enforcement Administration)*

Consequences of marijuana abuse

Acute (present during intoxication)

- Impairs short-term memory
- Impairs attention, judgment, and other cognitive functions
- Impairs coordination and balance
- Increases heart rate
- Psychotic episodes

Persistent (lasting longer than intoxication, but may not be permanent)

- Impairs memory and learning skills
- Sleep impairment

Long-term (cumulative effects of chronic abuse)

- Can lead to addiction
- Increases risk of chronic cough, bronchitis
- Increases risk of schizophrenia in vulnerable individuals
- May increase risk of anxiety, depression, and amotivational syndrome*

*These are often reported co-occurring symptoms/disorders with chronic marijuana use. However, research has not yet determined whether marijuana is causal or just associated with these mental problems.

SOURCE: U.S. Department of Health and Human Services, National Institute on Drug Abuse, "Marijuana Abuse," *Research Report Series*, September 2010.

(Table by PreMediaGlobal. Reproduced by permission of Gale, a part of Cengage Learning.)

(109,967). (However, it should be noted that amounts may include the use of marijuana with another drug.)

Description

Cannabis—in the form of marijuana, hashish (a dried resinous material that seeps from cannabis leaves and is more potent than marijuana), or other cannabinoids—is considered the most commonly used illegal substance in the world. Its effects have been known for thousands of years and were described as early as the fifth century B.C., when the Greek historian Herodotus told of a tribe of nomads who, after inhaling the smoke of roasted hemp seeds, emerged from their tent excited and shouting for joy.

Cannabis is a short form of the Latin name for the hemp plant, *Cannabis sativa.* All parts of the plant contain psychoactive substances, with THC making up the highest percentage. The most potent parts are the flowering tops and the dried, blackish-brown residue that comes from the leaves known as "hashish" or "hash."

There are more than 200 slang terms for marijuana, including "pot," "herb," "weed," "Mary Jane," "grass," "tea," and "ganja." It is usually chopped and/or shredded and rolled into a cigarette or "joint," or is placed in a pipe or a water pipe and smoked. One alternative method of using marijuana involves adding it to foods and eating it, such as baking it into brownies. It can also be brewed as a tea. Marijuana is also used in "blunts"—cigarettes emptied of their tobacco content and filled with a combination of marijuana and another drug such as crack **cocaine**.

Between 1840 and 1900, European and American medical journals published numerous articles on the therapeutic uses of marijuana. It was recommended as an appetite stimulant, muscle relaxant, painkiller, sedative, and anticonvulsant. As late as 1913, Sir William Osler recommended it highly for treatment of migraine. Public opinion changed, however, as alternative medications such as aspirin, opiates, and **barbiturates** became available. In 1937, the United States passed the Marijuana Tax Act, which made the drug essentially impossible to obtain for medical purposes.

The debate over the use of marijuana as a medicine continues today. THC is known to successfully treat nausea caused by cancer treatment drugs, stimulate the appetites of persons diagnosed with acquired immune deficiency syndrome (AIDS), and possibly assist in the treatment of glaucoma. Its use as a medicinal agent is still, however, highly controversial. As of 2011, medical marijuana was legally available in sixteen states: Alaska, Arizona, California, Colorado, District of Columbia, Delaware, Hawaii, Maine, Michigan, Montana, Nevada, New Jersey, New Mexico, Oregon, Rhode Island, Vermont, and Washington. Possession limits and ability to cultivate at home vary by state.

Cannabis use is generally perceived as benign, but a number of concerning research studies suggest that it has some potentially serious side effects. In addition to the known side effect of amotivational syndrome, some studies have shown an increased risk of psychotic disorders among cannabis users. While these associations have been demonstrated, causality is still unclear. The question remains as to whether individuals with these disorders are more likely to use cannabis, or whether individuals who use cannabis have a potentially higher risk of developing these disorders.

Cannabis-related disorders reflect the problematic use of cannabis products to varying degrees. These disorders include:

- Cannabis dependence—the compulsive need to use the drug, coupled with problems associated with chronic drug use.
- Cannabis abuse—periodic use that may cause legal problems; problems at work, home, or school; or danger when driving.
- Cannabis intoxication—the direct effects of acute cannabis use and reactions that accompany it, such as feeling "high," euphoria, sleepiness, lethargy, impairment in

short-term memory, stimulated appetite, impaired judgment, distorted sensory perceptions, impaired motor performance, and other symptoms.

Causes and symptoms

Causes

Cannabis-related disorders share many of the same root causes with disorders related to other addictive substances. The initial desire for a "high," combined with the widely held perception that cannabis use is not dangerous, often leads to experimentation in the teen years. It is believed that the greater availability, higher potency, and lower price of cannabis in recent years have all contributed to the increase in cannabis-related disorders.

Symptoms

CANNABIS DEPENDENCE AND ABUSE. The handbook used by mental health professionals to diagnose mental disorders is the ***Diagnostic and Statistical Manual of Mental Disorders***, also known as the *DSM-IV-TR*. This manual states that the central features of cannabis dependence are compulsive use, tolerance of its effects, and withdrawal symptoms. Use may interfere with family, school, and work, and may cause legal problems.

Regular cannabis smokers may show many of the same respiratory symptoms as tobacco smokers. These include daily cough and phlegm, chronic bronchitis, and more frequent chest colds. Marijuana smoke is known to contain 50%–70% more carcinogens than tobacco smoke. Continued use can lead to abnormal functioning of the lung tissue, which may be injured or destroyed by the cannabis smoke.

Recent research indicates that smoking marijuana has the potential to cause severe increases in heart rate and blood pressure, particularly if combined with cocaine use. Even with marijuana use alone, however, during one study the heart rate of subjects increased an average of 29 beats per minute when smoking marijuana. Additionally, heart attack risk is increased fourfold within the first hour of smoking marijuana.

A study of heavy marijuana users has shown that critical skills related to attention, memory, and learning can be impaired, even after use is discontinued for at least 24 hours. Compared to light users, heavy users made more errors on tasks and had more difficulty sustaining attention and shifting attention when required. They also had more difficulty registering, processing, and using information. These findings suggest that the greater impairment in mental functioning among heavy users is most likely due to an alteration of **brain** activity directly produced by the marijuana use.

Recent studies have found that babies born to mothers who used marijuana during pregnancy were smaller than those born to non-using mothers. Smaller babies are more likely to develop health problems. Additionally, nursing mothers who use marijuana pass some of the THC to the babies in their breast milk. Research shows that use of marijuana during the first month of breast-feeding can impair an infant's motor development.

Cannabis abuse is characterized by less frequent use and less severe problems. However, as with cannabis dependence, abuse can interfere with performance at school or work, cause legal problems, and interfere with motor activities such as driving or operating machinery; fatal traffic accidents are more common among individuals testing positive for cannabis use.

CANNABIS INTOXICATION. Cannabis intoxication refers to the occurrence of problematic behaviors or psychological changes that develop during, or shortly after, cannabis use. Intoxication usually starts with a "high" feeling followed by euphoria, inappropriate laughter, and feelings of grandiosity. Other symptoms include sedation, lethargy, impaired short-term memory, difficulty with motor tasks, impaired judgment, distorted sensory perceptions, and the feeling that time is passing unusually slowly. Sometimes severe anxiety, feelings of **depression**, or social withdrawal may occur. Along with these symptoms, common signs of cannabis intoxication include red eyes, increased appetite, dry mouth, and increased heart rate. Sometimes continued use is associated with weight gain as a result of increased appetite.

CANNABIS WITHDRAWAL. Recent research challenges the notion that cannabis use is not physically addictive. In fact, "cannabis withdrawal disorder" is a proposed addition for the fifth edition of the *DSM* (*DSM-5*, 2013). According to the NIDA, daily cannabis users experience withdrawal symptoms including irritability, stomach pain, aggression, and anxiety. Many frequent cannabis users are believed to continue using in order to avoid these unpleasant symptoms. Long-term use may lead to changes in the brain similar to those seen with long-term use of other addictive substances.

Diagnosis

Diagnosis of cannabis-related disorders is made in a number of ways. Intoxication is easiest to diagnose because of clinically observable signs, including reddened eye membranes, increased appetite, dry mouth, and increased heart rate. It is also diagnosed by the presence of problematic behavioral or psychological changes, such as impaired motor coordination, judgment, anxiety, euphoria, and social withdrawal. Occasionally, panic attacks may occur, and there may be impairment of short-term memory. Lowered immune system resistance, lowered testosterone levels in males, and chromosomal damage may also occur. Psychologically, chronic use of marijuana has been associated with a loss of ambition known as "amotivational syndrome."

Cannabis use is often paired with the use of other addictive substances, especially **nicotine**, alcohol, and cocaine. Marijuana may be mixed and smoked with opiates, phencyclidine (PCP or angel dust), or hallucinogenic drugs. Individuals who regularly use cannabis often report physical and mental lethargy and an inability to experience pleasure when not intoxicated (known as anhedonia). If taken in sufficiently high dosages, cannabinoids have psychoactive effects similar to **hallucinogens** such as lysergic acid diethylamide (LSD), and individuals using high doses may experience adverse effects that resemble hallucinogen-induced "bad trips." Paranoid ideation is another possible effect of heavy use, and, occasionally, hallucinations and **delusions** occur. Highly intoxicated individuals may feel as if they are outside their body (**depersonalization**) or as if what they are experiencing isn't real (derealization).

Urine tests can usually identify metabolites of cannabinoids. Because cannabinoids are fat soluble, they remain in the body for extended periods. Individuals who have used cannabis may show positive urine tests for as long as two to four weeks after using. Tests that analyze strands of hair can detect past marijuana use over an even longer period, up to three months. Examination of the nasopharynx and bronchial lining may also show clinical changes due to cannabis use.

Treatment

Treatment options for individuals with cannabis-related disorders are identical to those available for people with alcohol and other **substance abuse** disorders. The goal of treatment is abstinence. Treatment approaches range from inpatient **hospitalization**, drug and alcohol rehabilitation facilities, and various outpatient programs. Twelve-step programs such as Narcotics Anonymous are also treatment options. For heavy users experiencing withdrawal symptoms, treatment with antianxiety and/or antidepressant medications may assist in the treatment process.

Prognosis

According to the *DSM-IV-TR*, cannabis dependence and abuse tend to develop over a period of time. They may, however, develop more rapidly among young people with other emotional problems. Most people who become dependent begin using regularly. Over time, both frequency and amount increase. With chronic use, there can be a decrease in, or loss of, the pleasurable effects of the substance, along with increased feelings of anxiety and/or depression. As with alcohol and nicotine, cannabis use tends to begin early in the course of substance abuse, and many people later go on to develop dependence on other illicit substances. Because of this, cannabis has been referred to as a "gateway" drug, although this view is highly controversial, as not all cannabis users advance to other drugs. There is much that remains unknown about the social, psychological, and neurochemical basis of drug-use progression, and it is unclear whether marijuana use actually causes individuals to go on to use other illicit substances.

One of the long-term effects of chronic use has been termed "amotivational syndrome." This refers to the observation that many heavy, chronic users seem unambitious in relation to school and/or career. More serious consequences of cannabis use involve the acute or chronic development of psychotic or mood disorders. Some studies have suggested an association between cannabis use and sudden-onset **psychosis**, **schizophrenia**, or **bipolar disorder**, or an increased chance of **relapse** of an already-established psychiatric disorder. While a causative link has not been proven, there is some concern that cannabis use could either unmask a genetic predisposition for these psychiatric disorders or precipitate a relapse in vulnerable individuals.

Prevention

Many drug-education programs focus strongly on discouraging marijuana experimentation among young teenagers. A study reported by the NIDA indicated that high-sensation seekers—individuals who seek out new, emotionally intense experiences and are willing to take risks to obtain these experiences—are at greater risk for using marijuana and other drugs, and for using them at an earlier age. To counter this risk, the NIDA developed a series of dramatic public service announcements (PSAs) for national television that aired during programs that would appeal to high-sensation seekers, such as action-oriented television shows. The PSAs were aired in a limited television area, and the results were monitored. Marijuana use declined substantially among teens in these areas during the PSA campaigns, and long-term effects were shown for several months afterwards. In one county, marijuana use decreased by 38%, and in another, by 26.7%.

Other initiatives in prevention include drug-education programs like the D.A.R.E. (Drug Awareness and

Resistance Education) program, which targets fifth graders. D.A.R.E. and other antidrug programs focus on peer pressure resistance and the use of older teens who oppose drug use as models of a drug-free lifestyle. These programs show mixed results.

Resources

BOOKS

American Psychiatric Association. *Diagnostic and Statistical Manual of Mental Disorders*. 4th ed., text rev. Washington, DC: American Psychiatric Association, 2000.

Emmett, David, and Graeme Nice. *What You Need to Know about Cannabis: Understanding the Facts*. London; Philadelphia: Jessica Kingsley Publishers, 2009.

Maisto, Stephen A., Mark Galizio, and Gerard J. Connors. *Drug Use and Abuse*. 6th ed. Belmont, CA: Wadsworth, Cengage Learning, 2011. See esp. chap. 11, "Marijuana."

Schuckit, Marc A. *Drug and Alcohol Abuse: A Clinical Guide to Diagnosis and Treatment*. 6th ed. New York: Springer, 2010.

PERIODICALS

"Adverse Effects of Cannabis." *Prescrire International* 20, no. 112 (January 2011): 18–23.

Allsop, D.J., et al. "The Cannabis Withdrawal Scale Development: Patterns and Predictors of Cannabis Withdrawal and Distress." *Drug and Alcohol Dependence* (July 2, 2011) [e-pub ahead of print].

Copeland, J., and W. Swift. "Cannabis Use Disorder: Epidemiology and Management." *International Review of Psychiatry* 21 (April 1, 2009): 96–103.

Fernández-Artamendi S., et al. "Cannabis and Mental Health." *Actas Españolas de Psiquiatría* 39, no. 3 (2011): 180–90.

McLaren, J., et al. "Assessing Evidence for a Causal Link between Cannabis and Psychosis: A Review of Cohort Studies." *International Journal of Drug Policy* 21, no. 1 (2010): 10–19.

WEBSITES

National Cannabis Prevention and Information Centre. "Cannabis Research" [monthly bibliography of resesarch articles related to cannabis]. http://ncpic.org.au/ncpic/publications/cannabis-research (accessed September 7, 2011).

Substance Abuse and Mental Health Services Administration (SAMHSA). "Drug Abuse Warning Network (DAWN)." http://dawninfo.samhsa.gov (accessed September 7, 2011).

University of Michigan. "Monitoring the Future: A Continuing Study of American Youth." http://monitoringthefuture.org (accessed September 7, 2011).

ORGANIZATIONS

American Council for Drug Education, 50 Jay St., Brooklyn, NY, 11201, (646) 505-2061, acde@phoenixhouse.org, http://www.acde.org.

Narcotics Anonymous, PO Box 9999, Van Nuys, CA, 91409, (818) 773-9999, Fax: (818) 700-0700, http://www.na.org.

National Cannabis Prevention and Information Centre (NCPIC), PO Box 684, Randwick NSW 2031, Australia +61 2 9385 0208, info@ncpic.org.au, http://ncpic.org.au.

National Institute on Drug Abuse, 6001 Executive Blvd., Rm. 5213, Bethesda, MD, 20892, (301) 442-1124; Spanish: (240) 221-4007, information@nida.nih.gov, http://www.nida.nih.gov.

National Organization for the Reform of Marijuana Laws (NORML), 1600 K St. NW, Washington, DC, 20006, (202) 483-5500, Fax: (202) 483-0057, norml@norml.org, http://norml.org.

Substance Abuse and Mental Health Services Administration, 1 Choke Cherry Rd., Rockville, MD, 20857, (877) SAMHSA-7 (726-4727), (800) 487-4889 (TTY), Fax: (240) 221-4292, SAMHSAInfo@samhsa.hhs.gov, http://www.samhsa.gov.

Barbara S. Sternberg, PhD
Rosalyn Carson-DeWitt, MD

Capgras syndrome

Definition

Capgras syndrome (CS) is a relatively rare delusion of negative identification in which the patient believes that an individual or individuals well-known to him or her is an almost identical physiological double. CS is also known as the "illusion of doubles" and the "illusion of false recognition."

Demographics

Reported cases of CS have focused on adults, although a few cases have been reported with younger adults. It was once thought that CS is a disorder occurring only in women. However, cases have also been reported in men.

CS is related to numerous underlying causes including central nervous system disorders, **dementia**, and **psychosis**. The demographics of CS vary with the underlying cause.

Description

Capgras syndrome was named for the French **psychiatrist** Jean Capgras in 1923. In CS, the object of the delusion is typically a person with whom the patient is either particularly familiar or has an emotional tie, however, cases have been reported of the delusion being extended to pets and even inanimate objects, such as letters or a teacup. The term "syndrome"—a group of symptoms characterizing a disorder—as applied to CS is misleading; CS is more accurately described as a symptom associated with multiple physiological and psychological disorders.

Causes and symptoms

The literature is divided as to whether CS is psychological or physiological in nature. Historically, CS was thought to be a purely psychological condition. More recently, however, the focus has shifted, and CS is now considered by many clinicians to be a disorder of the central nervous system. It is estimated that between 21% and 40% of CS cases stem from physiological disorders including dementia, head **trauma**, epilepsy, and cerebrovascular disease. Neuroimaging data suggest a link between CS and abnormalities of the right hemisphere of the **brain**. In fact, the literature supports the conclusion that CS can be a symptom of virtually any central nervous system disorder.

CS has been observed in association with various systemic illnesses including vitamin B12 deficiency, chicken encephalitis, and diseases of the thyroid, parathyroid, and liver. CS has also been found associated with the use of various drugs, including morphine and **diazepam** (Valium). CS has been observed following transient physiological disturbances such as pneumocystis pneumonia in an HIV-positive patient, migraine headache, overdose of a bronchial dilator containing **adrenaline** and adropinemethonitrate, and interictal psychosis of epilepsy.

Diagnosis

Most clinicians regard CS as a symptom associated with numerous underlying causes rather than a syndrome in the classical sense of the term. **Diagnosis** should be based on psychological and personality testing as well as neuroradiological testing to determine the underlying cause rather than relying purely on behavioral descriptions.

CS can occur at any time during a psychosis and is not currently considered to be an essential element of any psychological disorder. It is impossible to predict the occurrence of CS based on the course of the overall psychopathology.

Treatment

CS is typically treated with a combination of antipsychotic medication and supportive psychological therapy in which stronger areas of mental and behavioral processes are used to overcome weaker areas of functioning. Patients presenting with CS stemming from psychosis have been found to improve on **pimozide** even when nonresponsive to **haloperidol**. CS stemming from physiological causes is best treated by treating the underlying disorder.

KEY TERMS

Central nervous system—The brain and spinal cord.

Delusion—A false idea held despite all evidence to the contrary.

Dementia—Deterioration of intellect, reasoning ability, memory, and will resulting from organic brain disease.

Interictal—Occurring between seizures.

Psychosis—A mental illness that markedly interferes with the patient's ability to deal with the demands of everyday life. Psychosis is characterized by loss of contact with reality, often accompanied by delusions and hallucinations.

Prognosis

The symptoms of CS have been found in most, but not all, cases to clear shortly after the remission of the psychosis. In the case of **depression**, however, the symptoms of CS persist longer than those of other syndromes of doubles (syndrome of Frégoli, syndrome of intermetamorphosis, syndrome of subjective doubles). The symptoms of CS invariably recur when there is a **relapse** of the basic psychotic condition with which they were associated.

Prevention

CS is an uncommon occurrence associated with a range of disorders both psychological and physiological in nature. Prevention of CS is actually a question of preventing the underlying disorder resulting in CS. There are no investigations under way concerning the prevention of CS.

Resources

BOOKS

Fewtrell, David, and Kieron O'Connor. "Capgras Syndrome and Delusions of Misidentification." in *Clinical Phenomenology and Cognitive Psychology*. New York: Routledge, 1995.

PERIODICALS

Devavrat, Joshi, et al. "Capgras Syndrome in Postictal Delirium." *Psychiatry* 7, no. 3 (March 2010) 37–39.

Ruth A. Wienclaw, PhD

Carbamazepine

Definition

Carbamazepine is an anticonvulsant that is structurally related to tricyclic **antidepressants** such as **amitriptyline** and **imipramine**. In the United States, carbamazepine is sold under the trade names Tegretol and Carbatrol.

Purpose

Carbamazepine is effective in the treatment of psychomotor and grand mal **seizures** and a type of facial pain called trigeminal neuralgia and, in combination with other drugs, for psychiatric disorders such as mania and extreme aggression. Carbamazepine is also occasionally used to control pain in persons with cancer.

Description

Carbamazepine was first marketed as an antiseizure medication and as a first-line treatment for trigeminal neuralgia. Because it was later noted to be effective in patients with certain psychiatric disorders, psychiatrists began combining it with other drugs such as lithium and major tranquilizers in severe cases of bipolar disease and aggressive behavior that could not be managed with single-drug therapy.

Carbamazepine is available in 100 mg chewable tablets, 200 mg capsules, and a suspension at 100 mg per 5 mL of liquid.

Recommended dosage

When used to treat seizure disorders or psychiatric disease, the recommended initial dosage of carbamazepine is 200 mg two times each day. The effectiveness of carbamazepine may decline with time, so if needed, the daily dosage may be increased by 200 mg once each week. Total daily dosages should not exceed 1,000 mg in children between the ages of 12 and 15 years. Total daily dosages for adults should not exceed 1,200 mg. Carbamazepine doses should be taken with meals.

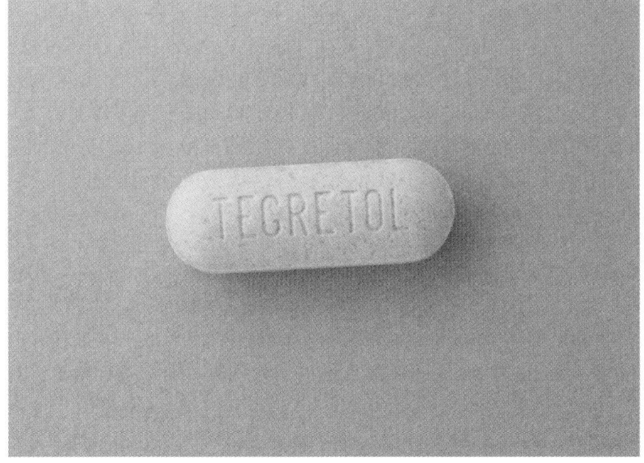

Carbamazepine, 200 mg. *(© Custom Medical Stock Photo, Inc. Reproduced by permission.)*

Precautions

Because carbamazepine may affect mental alertness, especially early in therapy, patients receiving this drug should be cautioned about operating dangerous machinery or driving a car until the drug's effects can be fully evaluated.

Carbamazepine should be used with caution in persons who also experience other types of seizure disorders such as atypical absence seizures. Among such individuals, carbamazepine usage has been associated with an increased risk of initiating, rather than controlling, generalized convulsions.

Carbamazepine should never be discontinued abruptly unless another treatment for seizures is initiated at the same time. If this does not happen, acute withdrawal of carbamazepine may result in seizures.

Carbamazepine has been reported to cause aplastic anemia, which generally does not respond to treatment. The bone marrow of persons with aplastic anemia does not produce adequate amounts of red blood cells, white blood cells, and platelets. Blood counts should be monitored in individuals using this drug. Some people with previously diagnosed **depression** of the bone marrow should not take carbamazepine. Patients should also be alert for signs and symptoms of bone marrow toxicity such as fever, sore throat, infection, mouth sores, easy bruising, or bleeding which occurs just under the skin.

Carbamazepine may cause birth defects and should be avoided by women who are pregnant. An effective contraceptive method should be used by sexually active women who are taking carbamazepine. It is important to note that this medication may decrease the effectiveness of oral contraceptives. The drug can cross into breast milk and should be avoided by women who are breast-feeding.

Side effects

The most commonly reported adverse reactions to carbamazepine are dizziness, drowsiness, unsteadiness, nausea, and vomiting. These are more common when therapy is just beginning. Carbamazepine may also cause a skin rash or sensitivity to the sun as well as blurred vision.

Interactions

Blood levels of carbamazepine may be reduced when it is used in combination with other drugs such as phenobarbital, phenytoin, or primidone. This means that inadequate amounts of carbamazepine are available to the body, limiting the ability of the drug to control seizure activity or treat psychiatric disease. Carbamazepine also causes reductions in the blood levels of the following drugs when they are used simultaneously: phenytoin, warfarin, doxycycline, **haloperidol**, **valproic acid**, and theophylline.

The simultaneous administration of carbamazepine with erythromycin, cimetidine, propoxyohene, isoniacid, **fluoxetine** and calcium channel blockers such as nifedipine and verapamil may increase the blood level of carbamazepine to a toxic range.

The simultaneous use of carbamazepine and oral contraceptives may increase the possibility that the oral contraceptive will not be effective in preventing pregnancy. Some physicians recommend that a different method of contraception be used while carbamazepine is being taken.

People taking carbamazepine should not drink grapefruit juice. Grapefruit juice slows the breakdown of carbamazepine, increasing the concentration of carbamazepine in the bloodstream.

Due to the potential of many interactions with other drugs, individuals should consult with a physician or pharmacist prior to starting any new medications either bought over the counter or initiated by another physician.

Resources

BOOKS

El-Mallakh, Rif S. "Lithium and Antiepileptic Drugs in Bipolar Depression." In *Bipolar Depression: A Comprehensive Guide*. Washington, DC: American Psychiatric Publishing, 2006.

Foreman, John C., and Torben Johansen. *Textbook of Receptor Pharmacology*. 2nd ed. Boca Raton, FL: CRC Press, 2002.

Page, Clive P., et al. *Integrated Pharmacology*. 3rd ed. St. Louis, MO: Elsevier, 2006.

Preston, John D., John H. O'Neal, and Mary C. Talaga. *Handbook of Clinical Psychopharmacology for Therapists*. 5th ed. Oakland, CA: New Harbinger Publications, 2008.

PERIODICALS

Bowden, Charles L., and Nancy U. Karren. "Anticonvulsants in Bipolar Disorder." *Australian and New Zealand Journal of Psychiatry* 40, no. 5 (May 2006): 386–93.

Cepeda, M. Soledad, and John T. Farrar. "Economic Evaluation of Oral Treatments for Neuropathic Pain." *Journal of Pain* 7, no. 2 (February 2006): 119–28.

DeBattista, Charles, and Alan F. Schatzberg. "Psychotropic Dosing and Monitoring Guidelines." *Primary Psychiatry* 13, no. 6 (June 2006): 61–81.

El-Mallakh, Rif, et al. "Bipolar II Disorder: Current and Future Treatment Options." *Annals of Clinical Psychiatry* 18, no. 4 (October–December. 2006): 259–66.

Gamble, C., et al. "A Meta-Analysis of Individual Patient Responses to Lamotrigine or Carbamazepine Monotherapy." *Neurology* 66, no. 9 (May 9, 2006): 1310–17.

Gayatri, N. A., and J. H. Livingston. "Aggravation of Epilepsy by Anti-Epileptic Drugs." *Developmental Medicine and Child Neurology* 48, no. 5 (May 2006): 394–98.

Ginsberg, Lawrence D. "Carbamazepine Extended-Release Capsules Use in Bipolar Disorder: Efficacy and Safety in Adult Patients." *Annals of Clinical Psychiatry* 18 (Suppl. 1) (May 2006): 9–14.

———. "Outcomes and Length of Treatment with Carbamazepine Extended-Release Capsules in Bipolar Disorder." *Annals of Clinical Psychiatry* 18 (Suppl. 1) (May 2006): 15–18.

———. "Predictors of Response to Carbamazepine Extended-Release Capsules Treatment in Bipolar Disorder." *Annals of Clinical Psychiatry* 18 (Suppl. 1) (May 2006): 23–26.

———. "Safety of Carbamazepine Extended-Release Capsules in Bipolar Disorder Polypharmacy." *Annals of Clinical Psychiatry* 18 (Suppl. 1) (May 2006): 19–22.

Nasrallah, Henry A., Terence A. Ketter, and Amir H. Kalali. "Carbamazepine and Valproate for The treatment of Bipolar Disorder: A Review of the Literature." *Journal of Affective Disorders* 95, no. 1 (October 2006): 69–78.

Zhang, Zhang-Jin, et al. "Adjunctive Herbal Medicine with Carbamazepine for Bipolar Disorders: A Double-Blind, Randomized, Placebo-Controlled Study." *Journal of Psychiatric Research* 41, no. 3–4 (April–June 2007): 360–69.

ORGANIZATIONS

American Academy of Clinical Toxicology, 6728 Old McLean Village Dr., McLean, VA, 22101, (703) 556-9222, Fax: (703) 556-8729, admin@clintox.org, http://www.clintox.org.

American Psychiatric Association, 1000 Wilson Blvd., Ste. 1825, Arlington, VA, 22209-3901, (703) 907-7300, apa@psych.org, http://www.psych.org.

American Society for Clinical Pharmacology and Therapeutics, 528 N Washington St., Alexandria, VA, 22314, (703) 836-6981, info@ascpt.org, http://www.ascpt.org.

U.S. Food and Drug Administration, 10903 New Hampshire Ave., Silver Spring, MD, 20993-0002, (888) INFO-FDA (463-6332), http://www.fda.gov.

L. Fleming Fallon, Jr., MD, DrPH
Ruth A. Wienclaw, PhD

Carbatrol *see* **Carbamazepine**

CASE *see* **Clinical Assessment Scales for the Elderly**

Case management

Definition

Case management is a system for managing and delivering health care with the goal of improving the quality and continuity of care and decreasing cost. Case management includes coordinating all necessary medical and mental health care as well as any associated support services.

Purpose

Case management tries to enhance access to care and improve the continuity and efficiency of services. Depending on the specific setting and locale, case managers are responsible for a variety of tasks, ranging from linking clients to services to actually providing intensive clinical or rehabilitative programs. Case management consists of four specific functions, including assessment of need, care planning, implementation, and regular review, after which the cycle begins again. Other core functions include outreach to engage clients in services, assessing individual needs, arranging requisite support services (such as housing, benefit programs, job training, etc.), monitoring medication and use of services, and advocating for client rights and entitlements.

Case management is not a time-limited service, but is intended to be ongoing. Wrap-around case management refers to efforts that are made prior to hospital admission, throughout **hospitalization**, and continuing after discharge, providing support within all dimensions of the patient's life.

In particular, case management in mental health is intended to decrease the need for hospitalization or readmission after hospitalization; to help people reintegrate into the community after hospitalization; to improve **compliance** to complicated medical regimens, particularly among psychiatric patients; and to help with socialization and daily functioning. Providing these types of case management services to the chronically mentally ill is believed to be less taxing on the economy than repeated or lengthy hospitalizations, and ongoing research is exploring this premise.

Description

Over the past 50 years, there have been fundamental changes in the system of mental health care in the United States. In the 1950s, mental health care for people with severe and persistent mental illnesses (like **schizophrenia**, **bipolar disorder**, severe **depression**, and **schizoaffective disorder**) was provided almost exclusively by large public mental hospitals. Created as part of a reform movement, these state hospitals provided a wide range of basic life supports in addition to mental health treatment, including housing, meals, clothing, and laundry services, and varying degrees of social and **vocational rehabilitation**.

During the latter half of the same decade, the introduction of neuroleptic medication provided symptomatic management of seriously disabling psychoses. This breakthrough, along with other subsequent reforms in mental health policy (including the introduction of Medicare and Medicaid in 1965 and the Supplemental Security Income [SSI] program in 1974), provided incentives for policy makers to discharge patients to the community and transfer state mental health expenditures to the federal government.

These advances—coupled with new procedural safeguards for involuntary patients, court decisions establishing the right to treatment in the least restrictive setting, and changed philosophies of care—led to widespread **deinstitutionalization**.

As a result of deinstitutionalization policies, the number of patients discharged from hospitals has risen, and the average length of stay for newly admitted patients has decreased. An increasing number of patients are never admitted at all, but are diverted to a more complex and decentralized system of community-based care. Case management was designed to remedy the confusion created by multiple care providers in different settings, and to assure accessibility, continuity of care, and accountability for individuals with long-term disabling mental illnesses. In addition, legislation has mandated that patients be managed in the "least restrictive environment" (that is, within a community setting). This is believed to be both therapeutically and economically preferable.

Models of case management

The two models of case management mentioned most often in mental health literature are **assertive community treatment** (ACT) and intensive case management. A third model, clinical case management, refers to a program where the case manager assigned to a client also functions as their primary therapist.

ASSERTIVE COMMUNITY TREATMENT. The ACT model (referred to in other locations as PACT, or Program of Assertive Community Treatment) originated in an inpatient research unit at Mendota State Hospital in Madison, Wisconsin, in the late 1960s. The program's architects, Arnold Marx, MD, Leonard Stein, MD, and Mary Ann Test, PhD, sought to create a "hospital without walls." In this model, teams of 10–12 professionals—including case managers, a **psychiatrist**, nurses, **social workers**, and vocational specialists—are assigned ongoing responsibility 24 hours a day, 7 days a week, 365 days a year, for a caseload of approximately 10 clients with severe and persistent mental illnesses.

ACT uses multidisciplinary teams with low client-to-staff ratios, practices assertive outreach, provides in-vivo services (in the client's own setting) and **crisis intervention** (as necessary), emphasizes assisting clients in managing their illness, assists with activities of daily living (ADL) skills, and promotes relationship building, emotional support, and an orientation, whenever possible, toward providing clients with services rather than linking them to other providers.

Compared to other psychosocial interventions, the ACT program has a remarkably strong evidence base. Twenty-five randomized controlled **clinical trials** have demonstrated that these programs reduce hospitalization, **homelessness**, and inappropriate hospitalization; increase housing stability; control psychiatric symptoms; and improve quality of life, especially among individuals who are high users of mental health services. However, despite ACT's widespread acceptance and proven success, statewide programs had only been implemented in six states as of 2011.

INTENSIVE CASE MANAGEMENT. Intensive case management practices are typically targeted to individuals with the greatest service needs, including individuals with a history of multiple hospitalizations, people dually diagnosed with **substance abuse** problems, individuals with mental illness who have been involved with the criminal justice system, and individuals who are both homeless and severely mentally ill.

In 2000, Richard Schaedle and Irwin Epstein conducted a survey of 22 experts and found that although intensive case management shares many critical ingredients with ACT programs, its elements are not as clearly articulated. Another distinction between intensive case management and ACT appears to be that the latter relies more heavily on a team versus individual approach. In addition, intensive case managers are more likely to "broker" treatment and rehabilitation services rather than provide them directly. Finally, intensive case management programs are more likely to focus on client strengths, empowering clients to fully participate in all treatment decisions.

CLINICAL CASE MANAGEMENT. A meta-analytic study comparing ACT and clinical case management found that although the generic approach resulted in increased hospital admissions, it significantly decreased the length of stay. This suggests that the overall impact of clinical case management is positive. Consistent with prior research, the study concluded that both ACT and high-quality clinical case management should be essential features of any mental health service system. One of the greatest tragedies of deinstitutionalization has been that most families often become de facto case managers for their family members, without any training or support. In recent years, many case management programs have expanded their teams to successfully utilize consumers as peer counselors and family members as outreach workers. The programs have also been adapted to serve older individuals with severe and persistent mental illnesses. While the ACT model offers the strongest evidential base for its effectiveness, research into the clinical and service system outcomes of this and other models of case management is ongoing.

Case management for children and adolescents

Case management is also used to coordinate care for children with serious emotional disturbances—diagnosed mental health problems that substantially disrupt a child's ability to function socially, academically, and emotionally. Although not a formal **diagnosis** in the ***Diagnostic and Statistical Manual of Mental Disorders*** (*DSM*), the handbook published by the **American Psychiatric Association** and used by mental health professionals to diagnose mental disorders, the term "serious emotional disturbance" is commonly used by states and the federal government to identify children with the greatest service needs. Although the limited research on case management for children and youth with serious emotional disturbances has been primarily focused on service use rather than clinical outcomes, there is growing evidence that case management is an effective **intervention** for this population.

Case management models used for children vary considerably. One model, called "wraparound," helps families develop a plan to address the child's individual needs across multiple life domains (home and school, for example). Research on the effectiveness of this model is still in an early stage. Another model, known as the children and youth intensive case management or expanded broker model, had been evaluated in two controlled studies. Findings suggest that this broker/advocacy model results in behavioral improvements and fewer days in hospital settings.

Funding

The effectiveness of any case management program depends upon the availability of high-quality treatment and support services in a given community, the structure

KEY TERMS

Bipolar disorder—A mood disorder marked by alternating episodes of extremely low mood (depression) and exuberant highs (mania). Also known as manic–depression disorder.

De facto—Acting as; fulfilling a role, even though the occupation of the role is not legally recognized.

Schizophrenia—A severe mental illness in which a person has difficulty distinguishing what is real from what is not real. It is often characterized by hallucinations, delusions, and withdrawal from people and social activities.

and coordination of the service system, and on the ability of an individual or family to pay for care either through private insurance or (more often) through public benefit and entitlement programs. Though the Centers for Medicaid and Medicare Services previously permitted the use of Medicaid funds for ACT, the program has since changed its policies regarding all of the types of services that have fallen under the title of "case management." Medicaid has limited its definition of reimbursable services to exclude direct service provision. Reimbursable services are restricted to assessment, planning, referrals, and monitoring of service delivery. This backlash has extended to the types of case management referred to as "community support." These types of services are also excluded for payment under Medicaid, due to an inability to exercise sufficient cost containment or verification. As a result, some community programs continue to operate under various time-limited grants, but their funding is constantly threatened. Ongoing research is attempting to prove both therapeutic efficacy and financial economy of these types of programs, in an effort to secure more stable support for the expansion and support. Possible financial benefits include the savings realized from keeping patients out of jails, hospitals, and emergency rooms. Compared to traditional outpatient programs, case management also offers a level of care that is far more comprehensive and humane for treating persons with mental illness.

Resources

BOOKS

Lloyd, Chris, Robert King, Frank Deane, and Kevin Gournay, eds. *Clinical Management in Mental Health Services.* Oxford, UK: Wiley-Blackwell, 2009.

Longhofer, Jeffrey, Paul M. Kubek, and Jerry Floersch. *On Being and Having a Case Manager*. New York: Columbia University Press, 2010.

Rapp, Charles A., and Richard J. Goscha. *The Strength Model: Case Management and People with Psychiatric Disabilities* New York: Oxford University Press, 2006.

PERIODICALS

Angell, Beth, and Colleen Mahoney. "Reconceptualizing the Case Management Relationship in Intensive Treatment: A Study of Staff Perceptions and Experiences." *Adminstration and Policy in Mental Health and Mental Health Services Research* 34, no. 2 (2007): 172–88.

Rosenthal, David A., et al. "A Survey of Current Disability Management Practice: Emerging Trends and Implications for Certification." *Rehabilitation Counseling Bulletin* 50, no. 2 (2007): 76–86.

Shattell M. "Assertive Community Treatment and the Physical Health Needs of Persons with Severe Mental Illness: Issues around Integration of Mental Health and Physical Health." *Journal of American Psychiatric Nurses Association* 34, no. 2 (2011): 57–63.

Wright-Berryman, J. "A Review of Consumer-provided Services on Assertive Community Treatment and Intensive Case Management Teams: Implications for Future Research and Practice." *Journal of American Psychiatric Nurses Association* 17 (2011): 37–44.

WEBSITES

National Alliance on Mental Illness. "Assertive Community Treatment (ACT)." http://www.nami.org/about/pact.htm (accessed September 7, 2011).

ORGANIZATIONS

Assertive Community Treatment Association, PO Box 2428, Brighton, MI, 48116, (810) 227-1859, Fax: (810) 227-5785, acta@actassociation.org, http://www.actassociation.org.

Irene S. Levine, PhD
Ruth A. Wienclaw, PhD
Rosalyn Carson-DeWitt

CAT *see* **Children's Apperception Test**

Catapres *see* **Clonidine**

Catatonia

Definition

Associated with a large number of serious mental and physical illnesses, catatonia is a condition marked by changes in muscle tone or activity. Two distinct sets of symptoms are characteristic of this condition. In catatonic stupor, the individual experiences a deficit of motor (movement) activity that can render him/her motionless.

KEY TERMS

Barbiturates—A group of medicines that slow breathing and lower the body temperature and blood pressure. They can be habit forming and are now used chiefly for anesthesia.

Benzodiazepines—A group of medicines that help reduce anxiety (especially before surgery) and to help people sleep.

Electroconvulsive therapy—A therapy used to treat major depression and severe mental illness that does not respond to medications. A measured dose of electricity is introduced into the brain in order to produce a convulsion. Electroconvulsive therapy is safe and effective.

Mutism—The inability or refusal to speak.

Negativism—Behavior characterized by resistance, opposition, and refusal to cooperate with requests, even the most reasonable ones.

Neuroleptic drugs—Antipsychotic drugs, including major tranquilizers, used in the treatment of psychoses such as schizophrenia.

Catatonic excitement, or excessive movement, is associated with violent behavior directed toward oneself or others.

Demographics

According to the ***Diagnostic and Statistical Manual of Mental Disorders***, fourth edition, text revision (*DSM-IV-TR*) between 5% and 9% of all psychiatric inpatients show some catatonic symptoms. Of these, 25–50% are associated with mood disorders, 10–15% are associated with **schizophrenia**, and the remainder are associated with other mental disorders.

Description

Catatonia is described in the *DSM-IV-TR,* as having what may seem like contradictory symptoms. In catatonic stupor, motor activity may be reduced to zero. Patients diagnosed with a catatonic disorder may maintain their body position for hours, days, weeks, or even months at a time. Individuals avoid bathing and grooming, make little or no eye contact with others, may be mute and rigid, and initiate no social behaviors. In catatonic excitement, the individual is extremely hyperactive, although the activity seems to have no purpose. Violence toward him/herself or others may be seen.

Catatonia can be categorized as intrinsic or extrinsic. If the condition has an identifiable cause, it is designated as extrinsic. If no cause can be determined following physical examination, laboratory testing, and history taking, the illness is considered to be intrinsic.

Features of catatonia may also be seen in **neuroleptic malignant syndrome** (NMS), which is an uncommon (but potentially lethal) reaction to some medications used to treat major mental illnesses, specifically antipsychotic drugs such as **haloperidol** (Haldol). NMS is considered a medical emergency since 25% of untreated cases result in death. Catatonia can also be present in individuals who may have a number of other physical and emotional conditions such as drug intoxication, **depression**, and schizophrenia. It is most commonly associated with mood disorders.

Depression with catatonic features

Individuals who are severely depressed may show disturbances of motor behavior; they may be essentially immobile or exhibit excessive but seemingly random motor activity. Extreme negativism, elective mutism (choosing not to speak), peculiar movements, mimicking words or phrases, or mimicking movements may also be part of the picture. In their most extreme forms, catatonic stupor and catatonic excitement may necessitate supervision so that the individual does not hurt him- or herself or others. Catatonic behaviors may also be seen in persons with other mood disorders, such as manic or mixed-mood states; these are also known as bipolar I and bipolar II disorders.

Catatonic schizophrenia

The catatonic type of schizophrenia is characterized by severe psychomotor disturbance. Individuals with this disorder show extreme immobility. They may stay in the same position for hours, days, weeks, or longer. The position they assume may be unusual and appear uncomfortable to the observer. If another person moves part of the catatonic individual's body, such as a limb, he or she may maintain the position into which they are placed, a condition known as "waxy flexibility." Sometimes catatonia presents itself as excessive motor activity, but the activity seems purposeless and does not appear to fit with what is happening in the environment. In its most severe forms, whether stupor or excitement, the individual may need close supervision to keep from injuring him- or herself or others.

Catatonic disorder due to general medical condition

Individuals with catatonia due to a medical condition may show symptoms similar to persons with catatonic schizophrenia and catatonic depression. However, the cause is believed to be physiological. Certain infectious, metabolic, or neurological diseases, such as encephalitis, may cause catatonic symptoms that can be either temporary or permanent. They may also appear as side effects of various medications, including several drugs of abuse.

Causes and symptoms

The causes of catatonia are largely unknown, although research indicates that **brain** structure and function are altered in this condition. While this and other information point to a physical cause, none had been proven as of 2011. A variety of medical conditions also may lead to catatonia, including head **trauma**, cerebrovascular disease, encephalitis, and certain metabolic disorders. NMS is an adverse side effect of certain antipsychotic drugs.

A variety of symptoms are associated with catatonia. Among the more common are echopraxia (imitation of the gestures of others) and echolalia (parrot-like repetition of words spoken by others). Other signs and symptoms include violence directed toward one's self, the assumption of inappropriate posture, **selective mutism**, negativism, facial grimaces, and animal-like noises.

Catatonic stupor is marked by immobility and a behavior known as *cerea flexibilitas* (waxy flexibility), in which the individual can be made to assume bizarre (and sometimes painful) postures that they will maintain for extended periods. The individual may become dehydrated and malnourished because food and liquids are refused. In extreme situations such individuals must be fed through a tube. Catatonic excitement is characterized by hyperactivity and violence; the individual may harm him- or herself or others. On rare occasions, isolation or restraint may be needed to ensure the individual's safety and the safety of others.

Diagnosis

Recognition of catatonia is made on the basis of specific movement symptoms. These include odd ways of walking such as walking on tiptoes or ritualistic pacing and, rarely, hopping and skipping. Repetitive odd movements of the fingers or hands, as well as imitating the speech or movements of others also may indicate that catatonia is present. There are no laboratory or other tests that can be used to positively diagnose this condition, but medical and neurological tests are necessary to rule out underlying lesions or disorders that may be causing the observed symptoms.

Treatment

Treatment of catatonia includes medications such as **benzodiazepines** (which are the preferred treatment) and rarely **barbiturates**. Antipsychotic drugs may be appropriate in some cases but often cause catatonia to worsen. **Electroconvulsive therapy** may prove beneficial for clients who do not respond to medication. If these approaches are unsuccessful, treatment may be redirected to attempts to control the signs and symptoms of the illness.

QUESTIONS TO ASK YOUR DOCTOR

- What kinds of tests will you do to rule out an underlying medical reason for my loved one's catatonia?
- What precautions can I take to make sure my loved one does not injure himself or herself?
- Does my loved one need inpatient treatment?
- What are the side effects of the drugs you are prescribing for my loved one?
- How soon can I expect to see improvement?

Prognosis

Catatonia usually responds quickly to medication interventions.

Prevention

There is no known way to prevent catatonia, because the cause has not yet been identified. Research efforts continue to explore possible origins. Avoiding excessive use of neuroleptic drugs can help minimize the risk of developing catatonic-like symptoms.

Resources

BOOKS

American Psychiatric Association. *Diagnostic and Statistical Manual of Mental Disorders,* 4th ed., text rev. Washington, DC: American Psychiatric Association, 2000.

Black, Donald W., and Nancy C. Andreasen. *Introductory Textbook of Psychiatry,* 5th ed. Arlington, VA: American Psychiatric Publishing, 2011.

Fink, Max, and Michael Alan Taylor. *A Clinician's Guide to Diagnosis and Treatment.* New York: Cambridge University Press, 2003.

Frisch, Noreen Cavan, and Lawrence E. Frisch. *Psychiatric Mental Health Nursing,* 4th ed. Clifton Park, NY: Delmar Publishers, 2011.

WEBSITES

Brasic, James R. "Catatonia." Medscape Reference. October 8, 2010. http://emedicine.medscape.com/article/1154851-overview (accessed July 29, 2011).

ORGANIZATIONS

American Psychiatric Association, 1000 Wilson Blvd., Ste. 1825, Arlington, VA, 22209-3901, (703)907-7300, (888) 357-7924, apa@psych.org, http://www.psych.org.

Mental Health America, 2000 N Beauregard St., 6th Fl., Alexandria, VA, 22311, (703) 684-7722, (800) 969-6642, Fax: (703) 684-5968, http://www.nmha.org.

National Alliance on Mental Illness, 3803 N Fairfax Dr., Ste. 100, Arlington, VA, 22203, (703) 524-7600, (800) 950-6264, Fax: (703) 524-9094, http://www.nami.org.

National Institute of Mental Health, 6001 Executive Blvd., Rm. 8184, MSC 9663, Bethesda, MD, 20892-9663, (301) 443-4513, (866) 615-6464, Fax: (301) 443-4279, nimhinfo@nimh.gov, http://www.nimh.nih.gov.

Donald G. Barstow, RN
Tish Davidson, AM

Catatonic disorders

Definition

Catatonic disorders are a group of symptoms characterized by disturbances in motor (muscular movement) behavior that may have either a psychological or a physiological basis. The condition itself is called **catatonia**.

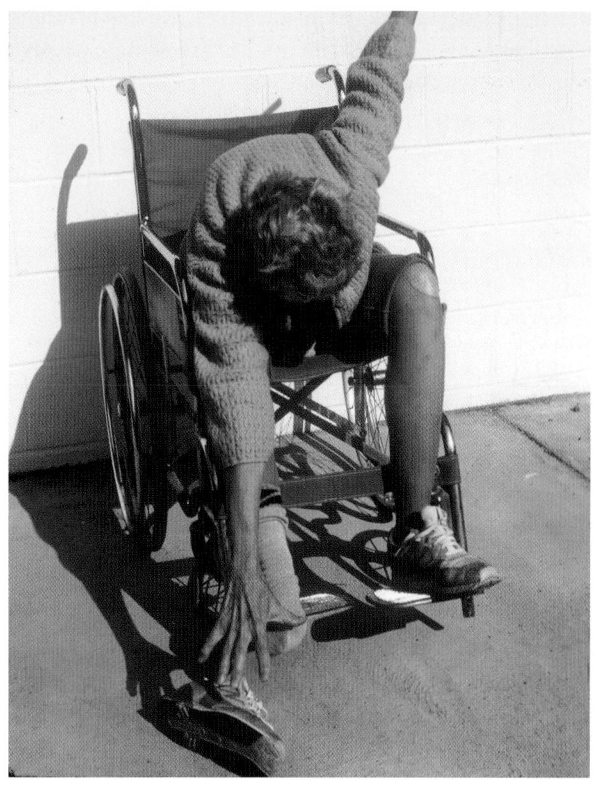

A patient with catatonic schizophrenia. *(© Photo Researchers, Inc.)*

Demographics

According to the ***Diagnostic and Statistical Manual of Mental Disorders***, fourth edition, text revision (*DSM-IV-TR*), between 5% and 9% of all psychiatric inpatients show some catatonic symptoms. Of these, 25%–50% are associated with mood disorders, 10%–15% are associated with **schizophrenia**, and the remainder are associated with other mental disorders. Catatonic symptoms also can occur in a wide variety of general medical conditions, including infectious, metabolic, and neurological disorders. They may also appear as side effects of various medications, including several drugs of abuse.

Description

The **psychiatrist** Karl Ludwig Kahlbaum first described catatonic symptoms in 1874. Kahlbaum described catatonia as a disorder characterized by unusual motor symptoms. His description of individuals with catatonic behaviors remains accurate to this day. Kahlbaum carefully documented the symptoms and the course of the illness, providing a natural history of this unusual disorder.

The *DSM-IV-TR* describes catatonia as having what may seem like contradictory symptoms. Catatonic stupor is characterized by slowed motor activity, often to the point of being motionless and appearing unaware of surroundings. Persons affected may hold their body in a single rigid position for hours, days, weeks, or even months at a time. People in semi-immobile catatonic states may allow a postural change and then “freeze” in the new posture, or may resist attempts at change. Patients may exhibit negativism, which means that they resist all attempts to be moved, or all instructions or requests to move, without any apparent motivation. In less severe situations, individuals may avoid bathing and grooming, make little or no eye contact with others, may be mute and rigid, and initiate no social behaviors. They may display a complete lack of verbalization, or echolalia (repeating or echoing heard phrases or sentences). In catatonic excitement, the condition can manifest as excessive movement and hyperactivity, such as frantic running up and down a flight of stairs or repetitive pacing. Individuals in the excited state may even try to harm themselves or others.

This range in symptoms may have its root in the fact that catatonia has a variety of causes. Because of this, catatonia is considered a condition, not a **diagnosis**. Some experts argue that, rather than being a discrete and describable classification, catatonia may instead be a collection of various illnesses without common specificities. Catatonia has been associated with a laundry list of disorders, including psychotic disorders, depressive disorders, dementias, and reactive disorders. In the *DSM*, catatonia is recognized as a symptom of schizophrenia, **schizophreniform disorder**, **schizoaffective disorder**, **psychosis**, **bipolar disorder**, depressive disorders, and general medical conditions.

DSM-IV types of catatonic disorder

CATATONIC SCHIZOPHRENIA. A characteristic of the disorders associated with schizophrenia is severe disturbance in motor behavior. Individuals with catatonic schizophrenia often show extreme immobility. They may stay in the same position for hours, days, weeks, or longer. The position they assume may be unusual and appear uncomfortable to the observer; for example, a person with catatonic schizophrenia may stand on one leg like a stork or hold one arm outstretched for a long time. If an observer moves a hand or limb of the catatonic person's body, he or she may maintain the new position. This condition is known as *cerea flexibilitas*, or waxy flexibility. In other situations, a person with catatonic schizophrenia may be extremely active, but the activity appears bizarre, purposeless, and unconnected to the situation or surroundings.

DEPRESSION WITH CATATONIC FEATURES. People who are severely depressed may show disturbances of motor behavior resembling those of patients diagnosed with catatonic schizophrenia. These people with **depression** may remain virtually motionless or move around in an extremely vigorous, but apparently random, fashion. Other parts of the symptomatic picture may include extreme negativism, elective mutism (choosing not to speak), peculiar movements, and echolalia or echopraxia (imitating another person's movements). These behaviors may require caregivers to supervise patients to ensure they do not harm themselves or others.

MOOD DISORDERS AND CATATONIA. Catatonic behaviors also may occur in people with other mood disorders. People experiencing manic or mixed mood states (a simultaneous combination of manic and depressive symptoms) may at times exhibit either the immobility or agitated random activity seen in catatonia.

CATATONIC DISORDER DUE TO A GENERAL MEDICAL CONDITION. People with catatonic disorder due to a medical condition show symptoms similar to those of catatonic schizophrenia and catatonic depression, except that the cause is believed to be related to an underlying medical condition. Neurological diseases such as encephalitis may cause catatonic symptoms that can be temporary or lasting. Overall, at least 35 distinct medical and neurological illnesses have been associated with catatonia. In addition to encephalitis, other common causative agents include structural damage to the central nervous system, metabolic disturbances, **seizures**, and exposure to some drugs.

DSM-5

Proposed changes for the fifth edition of the DSM (DSM-5, 2013) classify catatonia as a specifier for other conditions, including schizophrenia and mood disorders, rather than as its own diagnosis. The catatonia may also be of unknown origin or be related to **substance abuse** (such as in **substance-induced psychotic disorder**).

Causes and symptoms

Causes

The causes of catatonia are largely unknown, although research indicates that the brain's structure and function are altered in this condition. While this and other information point to a physical cause, none has yet been proven. Although the initiating factors of catatonia can vary greatly, research has hypothesized some common underlying mechanisms. There may be imbalances or problems in regulating signaling among nerves in the central nervous system, involving **neurotransmitters** (nerve signaling molecules) such as **dopamine** and **serotonin**. In addition, some **brain imaging studies** have found an enlarged cerebral cortex and reduced cerebellum in some people with catatonia, although this is not a consistent finding. People who have emerged from catatonic states report having had intense emotions, including uncontrollable anxiety and paralyzing fear. Others also report having experienced depression, euphoria, or aggression while in the catatonic state.

Symptoms

CATATONIC SCHIZOPHRENIA. Catatonic schizophrenia manifests with prominent motor symptoms and abnormalities. These symptoms, as given in the *DSM-IV-TR*, include:

- catalepsy, or motionlessness maintained over a long period of time
- catatonic excitement, marked by agitation and seemingly pointless movement
- catatonic stupor, with markedly slowed motor activity, often to the point of immobility and seeming unawareness of the environment
- catatonic rigidity, in which a rigid position is assumed and held against all outside efforts to change it
- catatonic posturing, in which a bizarre or inappropriate posture is assumed and maintained over a long period of time

KEY TERMS

Dopamine—A neurochemical made in the brain that is involved in many brain activities, including movement and emotion.

Neurotransmitter—One of a group of chemicals secreted by a nerve cell (neuron) to carry a chemical message to another nerve cell, often as a way of transmitting a nerve impulse. Examples of neurotransmitters include acetylcholine, dopamine, serotonin, and norepinephrine.

Serotonin—5-Hydroxytryptamine; a substance that occurs throughout the body with numerous effects including neurotransmission. Low serotonin levels are associated with mood disorders, particularly depression and obsessive-compulsive disorder.

- waxy flexibility, in which a limb or other body part of a catatonic person can be moved into another position that is then maintained (the body part is said to feel as if it were made of wax)
- akinesia, or absence of physical movement

DEPRESSION WITH CATATONIC FEATURES. Within the category of mood disorders, catatonic symptoms are most commonly associated with bipolar I disorder. Bipolar I disorder is a mood disorder involving periods of mania interspersed with depressive episodes. Symptoms of catatonic excitement, such as random activity unrelated to the environment or the repetition of words, phrases, and movements may occur during manic phases. Catatonic immobility may appear during the most severe phase of the depressive cycle. The actual catatonic symptoms are indistinguishable from those seen in catatonic schizophrenia. It is also possible for catatonic symptoms to occur in conjunction with other mood disorders, including bipolar II disorder (involving a milder form of mania called **hypomania**), mixed disorders (involving simultaneous mania and depression), and major depressive disorders.

CATATONIC DISORDER DUE TO GENERAL MEDICAL CONDITION. Symptoms of catatonic disorder caused by medical conditions are indistinguishable from those that occur in schizophrenia and mood disorders. Unlike individuals with schizophrenia, however, those with catatonic symptoms due to a medical condition demonstrate greater insight and awareness into their illness and symptoms. They have periods of clear thinking, and their **affect** (emotional response) is generally appropriate to the circumstances. Neither of these conditions is true of patients with schizophrenia or severe depression.

Diagnosis

Recognition of catatonia is made on the basis of specific movement symptoms. These include odd ways of walking, such as walking on tiptoes or ritualistic pacing, or, rarely, hopping and skipping. Repetitive odd movements of the fingers or hands or imitating the speech or movements of others also may indicate that catatonia is present. There are no laboratory or other tests that can be used to positively diagnose this condition, but medical and neurological tests are necessary to rule out underlying lesions or disorders that may be causing the observed symptoms.

Catatonic schizophrenia may be diagnosed when the patient's other symptoms include thought disorder, inappropriate affect, and a history of peculiar behavior and dysfunctional relationships. Catatonic symptoms associated with a mood disorder may be diagnosed when patients have a prior history of mood disorder or after careful psychiatric evaluation.

Treatment

Drugs

Treatment for catatonic symptoms can rely on drug-based approaches or on **electroconvulsive therapy** (ECT). **Benzodiazepines** (e.g., **lorazepam**) have often been the first-line treatment approach, although response to this therapy varies a great deal. One study has found that use of lorazepam was not effective in treating chronic catatonia, and there are other concerns about using benzodiazepines, including the fact that withdrawal from these drugs has itself been associated with inducing catatonia.

Other drugs that have been applied in cases of catatonia include antipsychotics. As with benzodiazepines, there are some concerns that the attempted cure could also be causative; these drugs have also been associated with precipitating catatonic episodes. However, the perceived reduction in rates of catatonic schizophrenia has accompanied the introduction and increasing use of these drugs.

Electroconvulsive therapy

ECT, or electroconvulsive therapy, elicits negative reactions from many people, as it involves the administration of an electric shock to the brain to precipitate a seizure. However, some psychiatrists maintain that it is a safe and effective approach and is an appropriate treatment for catatonia, especially if patients fail to respond adequately to drug therapy.

Prognosis

The prognosis for a person with catatonia varies with the cause underlying the disorder. With disorders such as

QUESTIONS TO ASK YOUR DOCTOR

- What kinds of tests will you do to rule out an underlying medical reason for my loved one's catatonia?
- What precautions can I take to make sure my loved one does not injure him/herself?
- Does my loved one need inpatient treatment?
- What are the side effects of the drugs you are prescribing?
- How soon can I expect to see improvement?

alcohol abuse disorder or affective disorder, the prognosis for resolution is relatively good; however, when catatonia accompanies schizophrenia, there is an association with earlier and higher levels of mortality. In one systematic review, the authors ranked associated catatonic disorders with their relative prognoses from best to worst, as follows: depression with catatonia, periodic catatonia, cycloid psychoses with catatonia, bipolar disorder with catatonia, catatonic schizophrenia, and non-catatonic schizophrenia. The choice of treatment also can influence prognosis.

Prevention

There are no specific preventive measures for most causes of catatonia. Infectious disease can sometimes be prevented. Catatonic symptoms caused by medications or drugs of abuse usually can be reversed by suspending use of the drug.

Resources

BOOKS

American Psychiatric Association. *Diagnostic and Statistical Manual of Mental Disorders*. 4th ed., text rev. Washington, DC: American Psychiatric Publishing, 2000.

Black, Donald W., and Nancy C. Andreasen. *Introductory Textbook of Psychiatry*. 5th ed. Arlington, VA: American Psychiatric Publishing, 2011.

Fink, Max, and Michael Alan Taylor. *A Clinician's Guide to Diagnosis and Treatment*. New York: Cambridge University Press, 2006.

Frisch, Noreen Cavan, and Lawrence E. Frisch. *Psychiatric Mental Health Nursing*. 4th ed. Farmington Hills, MI: Cengage Learning, 2011.

WEBSITES

Brasic, James R. "Catatonia." Medscape Reference. http://emedicine.medscape.com/article/1154851-overview (accessed October 1, 2011).

ORGANIZATIONS

American Psychiatric Association, 1000 Wilson Blvd., Ste. 1825, Arlington, VA, 22209-3901, (703) 907-7300, (888) 35-PSYCH (357-7924), apa@psych.org, http://www.psych.org.

Mental Health America, 2000 N Beauregard St., 6th Fl., Alexandria, VA, 22311, (703) 684-7722, (800) 969-6642, Fax: (703) 684-5968, http://www.nmha.org.

National Alliance on Mental Illness, 3803 N Fairfax Dr., Ste. 100, Arlington, VA, 22203, (703) 524-7600, (800) 950-NAMI (6264), Fax: (703) 524-9094, http://www.nami.org.

National Institute of Mental Health, 6001 Executive Blvd., Rm. 8184, MSC 9663, Bethesda, MD, 20892-9663, (301) 433-4513; TTY: (301) 443-8431, (866) 615-6464; TTY: (866) 415-8051, Fax: (301) 443-4279, nimhinfo@nih.gov, http://www.nimh.nih.gov.

Barbara Sternberg, PhD
Emily Jane Willingham, PhD
Tish Davidson, AM

CATIE

Definition

The Clinical Antipsychotic Trials of Intervention Effectiveness (CATIE) **Schizophrenia** Study was a set of **clinical trials** funded by the **National Institute of Mental Health** (NIMH) and coordinated by the University of North Carolina at Chapel Hill. The main CATIE trials were conducted between December 2000 and December 2004. According to the description of the study posted at ClinicalTrials.gov, the study was to consist of three phases: Phase I, subdivided into a Phase IA and Phase IB, to last up to 18 months; Phase II, to last 6 months; and Phase III, for patients who discontinue Phase II, no time limit specified.

Several ancillary studies, most notably the CATIE-Alzheimer's Disease (CATIE-AD) clinical trials, were conducted during the later phases of the main CATIE trials. The other studies include: a comparison of different antipsychotics for patients with schizophrenia at increased risk of cardiovascular disease; a study of the optimal medications for patients with schizophrenia; and a pilot study of metformin (a drug developed to treat type 2 diabetes) as a treatment for patients with schizophrenia who had gained weight while taking antipsychotic drugs. These studies were conducted between 2007 and 2010.

Purpose

The purpose of the early CATIE studies was to evaluate the effectiveness and side effects of newer antipsychotic drugs (sometimes called "atypical antipsychotics"), which have fewer side effects, but are more expensive, in comparison to conventional antipsychotic drugs in the treatment of schizophrenia. One of the purposes of the study was to help doctors maximize the benefits of antipsychotic drugs while minimizing their negative side effects.

Demographics

The CATIE study was open to participants from 18 to 65 years of age who had been diagnosed with schizophrenia using the ***Diagnostic and Statistical Manual of Mental Disorders***, Fourth Edition, Text Revision (*DSM-IV-TR*), and who were able to use oral medications. The initial estimated enrollment was 1,600 patients. Of the 1,460 patients who were actually enrolled in the CATIE study, 74% were male, 40% were nonwhite, and 12% were Hispanic. The mean (average) age of CATIE participants was 40.6 years. The average length of time participants had had schizophrenic episodes was 14.4 years. Participants in the study were treated at 54 different clinical sites across the country and reflected the range of people in the United States suffering from schizophrenia.

People who were intolerant of the drugs used in the trials, pregnant or breastfeeding, having their first schizophrenic episode, or diagnosed with **dementia** or intellectual disability rather than schizophrenia were excluded from the study.

Description

The primary CATIE study was designed for people with schizophrenia who might benefit from a change in their antipsychotic medication. Atypical antipsychotic medications frequently have fewer serious adverse side effects than conventional antipsychotics but are considerably more expensive. The CATIE study was an attempt to investigate scientifically the effectiveness of the newer drugs in comparison with the conventional antipsychotic drug **perphenazine** (Trilafon). All drugs used in the CATIE study had been previously approved by the U.S. Food and Drug Administration (FDA). The atypical antipsychotic drugs under investigation in the study were:

- clozapine (Clozaril)
- olanzapine (Zyprexa)
- quetiapine (Seroquel)
- risperidone (Risperdal)
- ziprasidone (Geodon)

Aripiprazole (Abilify), another atypical antipsychotic drug, was not approved by the FDA in time to be included in the study. No placebos were used in the study.

All drugs evaluated in the CATIE study had already undergone clinical trials by the representative pharmaceutical companies in order to get FDA approval to market each drug. Although these studies were appropriately rigorous to earn FDA approval, they typically had a limited number of participants, tested only two or three drugs per study, and lasted only four to eight weeks.

As compared to the clinical trials previously conducted by the pharmaceutical companies, the CATIE study lasted for 18 months and enrolled over 1,400 participants. This longer in-depth study allowed researchers to study drug actions and side effects in more detail and to examine longer-term effects of their use. Although the pharmaceutical companies donated the medications for the study and advised the researchers of optimal dosages, they had no other input into the design, implementation, analysis, or interpretation of the study results.

Study participants were randomly assigned to the experimental treatments in a double-blind study. "Double-blind" means that the doctors administering the drugs were not able to choose which medication their patients received, and that none of the researchers, administering physicians, or patients knew which treatment the patients were receiving. This study design helped ensure that preconceived expectations about the effectiveness of any of the drugs did not affect the outcome of the study. Patients were randomly assigned to either of the atypical antipsychotics or the control conventional antipsychotic. Patients continued on the assigned drug for 18 months or until the drug failed to continue to control their symptoms or produced intolerable side effects, or the patients decided to stop the medication or withdraw from the study.

Previous research has shown that patients taking antipsychotic medication are better off than those not doing so, and that staying on antipsychotic medication is critical to controlling the symptoms of schizophrenia and preventing a **relapse**. Therefore, one of the primary measures of success in the CATIE study was how long patients benefited from the medication to which they were assigned and how long before they decided it needed to be changed. When patients decided that the medication was not effective, researchers recorded the reasons the medication was stopped (for example, because the medication no longer controlled the symptoms, or the side effects were intolerable). Other data collected included the effects of the medications on the symptoms of schizophrenia and level of the patient's functioning on the medication.

Results

The study found that the conventional antipsychotic generally was equally effective and tolerated as well as the newer and more expensive atypical antipsychotic medications. Of the atypical antipsychotics, **olanzapine** performed somewhat better than the other drugs in the study. Patients on this drug were less likely to be hospitalized for psychotic relapse and tended to stay on their medication longer than patients taking other antipsychotic drugs in the study. However, patients on olanzapine also tended to gain significant amounts of weight and experienced other metabolic changes associated with diabetes, compared to patients taking the other drugs in the study.

Nearly 75% of the patients in the CATIE study switched to a different medication during the course of the study. Participants who stopped taking the medication for any reason were given the opportunity to continue in the study in one of two ways. In the so-called efficacy pathway, patients who discontinued an atypical antipsychotic because it was not sufficiently effective were randomly assigned to receive another atypical antipsychotic to help determine what treatment should be chosen for such patients. In the tolerability pathway, patients who discontinued their medication because of side effects were allowed to receive another medication in order to help determine the next best choice for patients who experience adverse side effects with an atypical antipsychotic. The conventional antipsychotic (perphenazine) was not included in this second phase of the study, because researchers had not expected the conventional medication to work as well as the newer drugs when they designed the study.

Most of the participants in the Phase II efficacy pathway study had not benefited from their first antipsychotic medication and had worse symptoms than they did at the beginning of the study. These participants also tended to have worse symptoms than those participants in the tolerability pathway study. **Clozapine** was very effective for this group and worked significantly better than the other atypical antipsychotics. Forty-four percent of participants in this part of the study were able to stay on their medication for the remainder of the study. Participants on the efficacy pathway stayed on their medication for an average of 10 months as compared to three months for those taking the other atypical antipsychotics. In addition, most of these participants had greater symptom relief than participants taking the other medications.

As in Phase I of the study, in the tolerability pathway of the Phase II study, a high rate (74%) of patients stopped taking their medication. However, 35% of the Phase II participants in the tolerability study who took olanzapine or **risperidone** continued taking their medication until the end of the study. Only 23% of participants taking **ziprasidone** and 16% of participants taking **quetiapine** in the Phase I study were able to continue throughout the entire 18 months.

The results of the Phase II study show that the choice of a different medication for patients who stop taking an antipsychotic medication depends on their reason for stopping the first medication. Participants who stopped taking their antipsychotic medication in Phase I because it was not adequately controlling their symptoms were more likely to stay on their medication if they were switched to olanzapine or risperidone rather than quetiapine or ziprasidone. There was no difference among the four medications tested in Phase II, however, for participants who had stopped taking their Phase I medication because they experienced adverse side effects.

The CATIE study has several major implications. First, the results of Phase I of the study show that it is worthwhile to start patients on less-expensive conventional antipsychotic medications before trying the atypicals. Specifically, physicians and patients should consider perphenazine as an alterative to atypical antipsychotics because of its similar effectiveness and its lower price.

The CATIE study results can also be used to help select a different antipsychotic medication for those patients who were not successfully treated on another antipsychotic. The results of the Phase II study show that the reason for stopping the first medication should be considered when choosing another medication.

The study results also show that clozapine is often a good choice of medication for patients who do not respond well to other antipsychotic medications. In Phase II of the study, clozapine was more effective in controlling symptoms than the other atypical antipsychotics under evaluation. For patients whose symptoms are not well controlled on clozapine, olanzapine and risperidone tend to be more effective than ziprasidone or quetiapine. However, the side effects of these drugs must be taken into account.

The CATIE study did not reveal a clear path of next treatment for those patients who had discontinued use of an antipsychotic due to adverse side effects. In such cases, it is important to balance the degree of symptom control from the drug with the nature of its side effects. For example, olanzapine tended to result in considerable weight gain and metabolic problems, whereas ziprasidone consistently resulted in weight loss and improvement of metabolic disorders. Of the drugs tested, risperidone had the fewest adverse side effects.

KEY TERMS

Ancillary—Subordinate or secondary.

C-reactive protein (CRP)—A protein whose levels in blood rise rapidly in response to inflammation. It can be measured to test for the presence of inflammation and response to treatment; it is also used as a rough indication of a patient's risk of heart disease.

Double-blind study—A study in which neither the individual subjects nor the researchers know who is in the control group and the experimental group.

Herpes simplex virus type 1 (HSV-1)—A virus that causes cold sores. Infection with HSV-1 appears to be correlated with an increased risk of cognitive deficits in schizophrenia patients.

Insulin resistance—A condition in which a person's natural insulin becomes less effective in lowering the blood sugar level.

Metformin—A drug developed to treat type 2 diabetes that has been used experimentally to treat weight gain in patients with schizophrenia.

Off-label—Referring to the use of a prescription medication for an unapproved reason to use it, an unapproved age group, or an unapproved dosage level.

Placebo—An inert substance or sham treatment given to a control group in a clinical trial to test the effectiveness of the real medication or treatment.

Tardive dyskinesia—A disorder characterized by involuntary and repetitive body movements that sometimes develops after long-term use of antipsychotic medications.

CATIE phase III results

CATIE subjects who had discontinued taking antipsychotics in phases I and II of the CATIE study were eligible to participate in phase III. They were offered a choice of nine antipsychotic regimens with assistance from their study doctor. The options included eight single-medication regimens (oral aripiprazole, clozapine, olanzapine, perphenazine, quetiapine, risperidone, ziprasidone, or long-acting injectable **fluphenazine** decanoate) or a combination of any two drugs on the list.

The phase III study enrolled 270 subjects out of 410 who were eligible. Only a small number selected either fluphenazine or perphenazine. The remaining seven options were chosen by 30 to 40 patients each. The researchers reported that the patients who chose clozapine or combination antipsychotic treatment were the most symptomatic, while those who selected aripiprazole and ziprasidone had the highest body mass index. The researchers concluded that combination antipsychotic therapy warrants further study. The phase III study was also the first CATIE report regarding aripiprazole, which was not available when the study began and was not included in previous phases of the study.

NIMH reconsiderations (2006)

In December 2006, the *American Journal of Psychiatry* published an article written by the CATIE researchers on the cost-effectiveness of the older antipsychotic drugs in comparison to the more expensive atypical antipsychotics. According to the NIMH, the article raised a number of questions regarding reimbursement policies for antipsychotic medications. At the time the article was published, antipsychotics were the fourth largest group of medications prescribed in the United States, with an annual cost of $10 billion. The atypical antipsychotics represented 90% of that sum, costing 10 times as much as the older drugs. About 80% of the cost for these drugs was borne by the public sector. The NIMH wished to clarify some of the implications of the cost-effectiveness data:

- People's responses to antipsychotic drugs are highly individual; therefore, the most effective drug for a given patient is the best choice whether it is the least expensive or not. The CATIE study showed that a "one-size-fits-all" approach to the treatment of schizophrenia is unworkable.
- One of the purposes of the CATIE study was to expand the range of medication choices available to patients by examining whether the older antipsychotics are still useful, rather than restricting access to any antipsychotic drug.
- The CATIE study lasted only 18 months, which is not long enough to determine whether patients are at increased risk of tardive dyskinesia, diabetes, or other long-term effects of some of the older antipsychotic drugs.

The CATIE-Alzheimer's Disease (CATIE-AD) Study

The CATIE-Alzheimer's Disease (CATIE-AD) study, funded by the NIMH, was a placebo-controlled clinical trial of three atypical antipsychotics. The study evaluated the effectiveness of antipsychotic medications in treating patients diagnosed with **Alzheimer's disease** (AD), as these drugs had been used off-label in managing the symptoms of AD and other dementias. Their safety as well their efficacy in treating AD was not clear, however. The CATIE-AD study was carried out at 42 sites around the United States. The 421 patients who participated were recruited between 2000 and December 2003 and had to manifest one or more of four symptoms of AD: hallucinations, agitation, aggressive behavior, or **delusions**. The three drugs that were tested in the CATIE-AD study were three atypical antipsychotics: risperidone (Risperdal), olanzapine (Zyprexa), and quetiapine (Seroquel). Patients who chose to discontinue the antipsychotic they were given in phase I of the AD trial could choose a different antipsychotic or **citalopram** (an antidepressant) in phase II.

The study was completed in 2005 and released its first reports in 2006. While some Alzheimer's patients appeared to benefit from the antipsychotic medications, others discontinued them because of their side effects. On the whole, the researchers concluded that the atypical antipsychotics were no more effective than a placebo in treating AD when side effects were taken into consideration. In addition, a follow-up study published in 2009 reported that the patients gained weight, particularly those who had taken olanzapine or quetiapine, and showed an increase in blood cholesterol levels. The researchers stated that patients with AD given any atypical antipsychotic to manage behavioral problems should be closely monitored for metabolic changes.

Later ancillary studies conducted by CATIE investigators

There were three ancillary studies conducted between 2007 and 2010 by researchers who had participated in the primary CATIE study:

- The METS study. This was a 16-week clinical trial of metformin, a drug prescribed for patients with diabetes to increase insulin sensitivity, as a possible treatment for weight gain related to taking antipsychotic medications.
- The Comparison of Antipsychotics for Metabolic Problems (CAMP) study. This study sought to find whether individuals with schizophrenia taking atypical antipsychotics at increased risk of heart disease (measured by body mass index and blood cholesterol levels) would benefit by switching to antidepressant therapy.
- Comparison of optimal treatments for schizophrenia. This was a clinical trial of three different antipsychotics (olanzapine, perphenazine, and aripiprazole) in combination with other drugs to reduce the side effects of the antipsychotic medications.

QUESTIONS TO ASK YOUR DOCTOR

- What is your opinion of participation in clinical trials?
- What is your opinion of the CATIE study?
- Have you ever treated a patient diagnosed with schizophrenia? If so, what medications did they take, and did they stay on them?
- Do you think antipsychotic medications are effective as a treatment for Alzheimer's?

Research and general acceptance

The CATIE study continues to stimulate questions regarding the long-term side effects of antipsychotic drugs as well as their comparative effectiveness. Researchers studying the effects of antipsychotic medications on certain biomarkers associated with an increased risk of cardiovascular disorders reported in 2009 that C-reactive protein (CRP) emerged as a useful marker of increased risk in schizophrenia patients, and that olanzapine had the most noticeable effect in raising the patients' CRP levels. A report published in 2010 noted the contribution of the CATIE study to the issue of metabolic disorders in schizophrenia patients taking antipsychotics, particularly the high rate of insulin resistance in these patients.

A 2011 report noted that some of the drugs tested in the CATIE study were superior to others in relieving symptoms of **depression** in patients with schizophrenia who suffered a major depressive episode. A study of **tardive dyskinesia** in schizophrenia patients that was also published in 2011 made use of CATIE data to show that the presence or course of tardive dyskinesia in patients diagnosed with it was not correlated with any specific antipsychotic drug nor with the length of time between the patient's beginning to take the drug and discontinuing its use. Last, a third 2011 study reported a correlation between evidence of herpes simplex virus type 1 (HSV-1) infection and neurocognitive deficits in the patients in the original CATIE study. The patient sample included all 1,308 patients for whom baseline blood samples were still available.

Resources

BOOKS

American Psychiatric Association. *Diagnostic and Statistical Manual of Mental Disorders.* 4th ed., Text rev. Washington, DC: American Psychiatric Association, 2000.

Meyer, Jonathan M., and Henry A. Nasrallah, eds. *Medical Illness and Schizophrenia*, 2nd ed. Washington, DC : American Psychiatric Pub., 2009.

Stroup, T. Scott, and Jeffrey A. Lieberman, eds. *Antipsychotic Trials in Schizophrenia: The CATIE Project*. New York: Cambridge University Press, 2010.

VandenBos, Gary R., ed. *APA Dictionary of Psychology*. Washington, DC: American Psychological Association, 2007.

PERIODICALS

Addington, D.E., et al. "Impact of Second-generation Antipsychotics and Perphenazine on Depressive Symptoms in a Randomized Trial of Treatment for Chronic Schizophrenia." *Journal of Clinical Psychiatry* 72 (January 2011): 75–80.

Caroff, S.N., et al. "Treatment Outcomes of Patients with Tardive Dyskinesia and Chronic Schizophrenia." *Journal of Clinical Psychiatry* 72 (March 2011): 295–303.

Hermes, E., et al. "The Association between Weight Change and Symptom Reduction in the CATIE Schizophrenia Trial." *Schizophrenia Research* 128 (May 2011): 166–170.

Khan, A.Y., et al. "The Adjunctive Use of Metformin to Treat or Prevent Atypical Antipsychotic-induced Weight Gain: A Review." *Psychiatric Practice* 16 (September 2010): 289–296.

Meyer, J.M. "Antipsychotics and Metabolics in the Post-CATIE Era." *Current Topics in Behavioral Neurosciences* 4 (2010): 23–42.

Meyer, J.M., et al. "Inflammatory Markers in Schizophrenia: Comparing Antipsychotic Effects in Phase 1 of the Clinical Antipsychotic Trials of Intervention Effectiveness Study." *Biological Psychiatry* 66 (December 1, 2009): 1013–1022.

Miller, E.A., et al. "Assessing the Relationship between Health Utilities, Quality of life, and Health Care Costs in Alzheimer's Disease: The CATIE-AD Study." *Current Alzheimer Research* 7 (June 2010): 348–357.

Rosenheck, R. A., et al. "Cost-Effectiveness of Second-Generation Antipsychotics and Perphenazine in a Randomized Trial of Treatment for Chronic Schizophrenia." *American Journal of Psychiatry* 163 (December 2006): 2080–2089.

Stroup, T.S., et al. "Results of Phase 3 of the CATIE Schizophrenia Trial." *Schizophrenia Research* 107 (January 2009): 1–12.

Swanson, J.W., et al. "Alternative Pathways to Violence in Persons with Schizophrenia: The Role of Childhood Antisocial Behavior Problems." *Law and Human Behavior* 32 (June 2008): 228–240.

Yolken, R.H., et al. "Serological Evidence of Exposure to Herpes Simplex Virus type 1 Is Associated with Cognitive Deficits in the CATIE Schizophrenia Sample." *Schizophrenia Research* 128 (May 2011): 61–65.

Zheng, L., et al. "Metabolic Changes Associated with Second-generation Antipsychotic Use in Alzheimer's Disease Patients: The CATIE-AD Study." *American Journal of Psychiatry* 166 (May 2009): 583–590.

WEBSITES

CATIE Home Page, University of North Carolina School of Medicine. http://www.catie.unc.edu/index.html (accessed May 15, 2011).

ClinicalTrials.gov. "CATIE–Schizophrenia Trial." July 2, 2007. http://www.clinicaltrials.gov/ct/show/NCT00014001?order=1 (accessed May 12, 2011).

ClinicalTrials.gov. "Comparison of Antipsychotics for Metabolic Problems in the Treatment of People With Schizophrenia or Schizoaffective Disorder (CAMP)." November 12, 2010. http://www.clinicaltrials.gov/show/NCT00423878 (accessed May 16, 2011).

ClinicalTrials.gov. "Comparison of Optimal Antipsychotic Treatments for Schizophrenia." July 2, 2007. http://www.clinicaltrials. gov/ct2/show/NCT00802100 (accessed May 16, 2011).

ClinicalTrials.gov. "The Use of Metformin in the Treatment of Antipsychotic-Induced Weight Gain in Schizophrenia (The METS Study)." November 12, 2010. http://www.clinicaltrials.gov/show/NCT00816907 (accessed May 16, 2011).

National Institute of Mental Health (NIMH). "Clinical Antipsychotic Trials of Intervention Effectiveness (CATIE)." December 7, 2011. http://www.nimh.nih.gov/trials/practical/catie/index.shtml (accessed May 12, 2011).

National Institute of Mental Health (NIMH) Health Topics. "Schizophrenia." http://www.nimh.nih.gov/health/topics/schizophrenia/index.shtml (accessed May 12, 2011).

ORGANIZATIONS

Alzheimer's Disease Education and Referral Center of the National Institute on Aging (ADEAR), PO Box 8250, Silver Spring, MD, 20907, Fax: (301) 495-3334, (800) 438-4380, http://www.nia.nih.gov/Alzheimers/ContactUs.htm, http://www.nia.nih.gov/Alzheimers.

National Institute of Mental Health (NIMH), 6001 Executive Boulevard, Room 8184, MSC 9663, Bethesda, MD, 20892-9663, (301) 443-4513, Fax: (301) 443-4279, (866) 615-6464, nimhinfo@nih.gov, http://www.nimh.nih.gov/index.shtml.

University of North Carolina School of Medicine, Department of Psychiatry, 110 Conner Drive, Suite 4, Chapel Hill, NC, 27514, (919) 929-7449, http://www.psychiatry.unc.edu.

Ruth A. Wienclaw, PhD
Rebecca J. Frey, PhD

CAT scan *see* **Computed tomography**

Causes of mental illness *see* **Origin of mental illnesses**

Celexa *see* **Citalopram**

Chamomile

Definition

Since about 3000 BCE in Ancient Egypt, chamomile has been grown and used in various healing applications, including as a medicine to ease **depression** and anxiety.

Dried chamomile flowers. *(© iStockPhoto.com/Magdalena Kucova)*

The plant is related to the daisy family; it has strongly scented foliage and flowers with white petals and yellow centers. The name *chamomile* is derived from two Greek words that mean "ground" and "apple," because chamomile leaves smell somewhat like apples and because the plant grows close to the ground. Chamomile is used as a homeopathic remedy for certain mental health conditions.

Purpose

The traditional German description of chamomile is *alles zutraut*, which means that the plant "is good for everything." Chamomile has been used internally for a wide variety of complaints, such as a treatment for parasitic worms (anthelmintic), to prevent or expel gas (carminative), to reduce inflammation (anti-inflammatory), and to control infection (antiseptic). Chamomile has also been used internally as an antispasmodic, to relieve intestinal cramping, digestive disorders, menstrual cramps, **premenstrual syndrome** (PMS), headache, and other stress-related disorders; and as a sedative, often in the form of tea, to treat anxiety and insomnia.

External uses (as **aromatherapy**) of chamomile for mental health conditions include blending its essential oil with **lavender** or rose for scenting perfumes, candles, creams, or other aromatherapy products intended to calm or relax the user's mind and body and reduce anxiety.

Description

There are two varieties of chamomile commonly used in herbal preparations for internal use and for aromatherapy (external use). One is called Roman chamomile (*Anthemis nobilis*), with contemporary sources in Belgium and southern England. Roman chamomile grows to a height of 9 in. (23 cm) or less and is frequently used as a ground cover along garden paths because of its pleasant apple scent. It is also called English chamomile, ground apple, whig plant, and common chamomile.

German chamomile (*Matricaria recutita*) is grown extensively in Germany, Hungary, and parts of the former Soviet Union. It is also sometimes medically called *Matricaria chamomilla,* along with common names such as Hungarian chamomile, wild chamomile, sweet false chamomile, and others. German chamomile grows to a height of about 3 ft. (1 m) and is the variety most commonly cultivated in the United States, where it is used medicinally.

Even though they are very different species of plant, the Roman and German versions of chamomile seem to have similar calming properties, which may help alleviate anxiety and **stress**, produce mild sedation, and reduce restlessness and irritability.

The chamomile flowers are harvested for both internal and external use. Chamomile flowers can be dried and used directly in teas and homemade topical preparations, but they are also available commercially in prepackaged tea bags and in capsule form. The essential oil of chamomile is pressed from the leaves as well as the flowers; it costs about $22–$35 for 5 mL. Chamomile is also available as a liquid extract.

The chemically active components of chamomile are alpha bisabobol, chamozulene, polyines, tannin, coumarin, flavonoids, and apigenin. However, no single component has been credited with all the major healing properties of whole chamomile; it is assumed that the various components work together to produce the plant's beneficial effects.

Chamomile seems to have a calming effect on people with such problems as anxiety, depression, and stress. Anxiety such as is found in generalized anxiety syndrome is a common mental health disorder that, according to the **National Institute of Mental Health**, affects about 40 million adults in the United States each year. These people often become fearful or stressed in situations that most people find normal.

Research

A study published in the *Journal of Clinical Psychopharmacology* (August 2009) showed that chamomile capsules may help to reduce symptoms of anxiety, particularly those caused by **generalized anxiety disorder** (GAD). Researchers from the University of Pennsylvania conducted a randomized, double-blind, placebo-controlled study to see if chamomile extract helped reduce symptoms in 57 participants with mild to moderate GAD. The eight-week study divided the patients into two groups: one receiving chamomile capsules containing 220 mg of pharmaceutical-grade extract from German chamomile, and the other receiving placebo capsules that were scented to smell like chamomile. Doses of the chamomile capsules were adjusted upward during the study for some participants, based on their scores on the Hamilton Anxiety Rating (HAMA) and similar tests. The researchers found that the HAMA scores for the people taking the chamomile capsules were lower than for those in the control group, meaning their anxiety had been reduced. The study concluded that the difference between the two groups was "clinically meaningful and statistically significant." The study was the first controlled clinical trial of chamomile extract for GAD, so additional studies are needed to support its findings.

Recommended dosage

No standard dosage has been made for chamomile within the medical or homeopathic community. The following are approximate guidelines. Children may be given 1–2 mL of a glycerin preparation of German chamomile three times a day; or 2–4 oz. (57–100 g) of tea, one to three times a day, depending on the child's weight. It is often used to calm a baby unwilling to fall asleep. Chamomile may also be applied to bath water or as massage oil for a baby. In addition, it may be sprayed into the air of a baby's room by diluting 12 drops of it per ounce of distilled water. In all cases, the smell of chamomile helps to calm the baby. Most importantly, though, parents should not give chamomile or any other herbal or health supplement to a child without first consulting with the child's doctor or other medical professional.

Adults may take a tea made from 0.7–1 oz. (2–3 g) of dried chamomile steeped in a cup of boiling water for five to ten minutes, three to four times daily. Alternately, adults may take 5 mL of 1:5 dilution of chamomile tincture three times daily.

Precautions

Despite its multitude of uses, chamomile has not been proven clinically effective in treating any conditions, such as those involving mental illness. Studies are ongoing; however, few studies have been conducted on the relationship between chamomile and its calming effect on people with such problems as anxiety and stress.

Because chamomile is related botanically to the ragweed plant, persons who are highly allergic to ragweed should use chamomile with caution. People who are allergic to such flowers as aster, chrysanthemum, marigold, daisy, or sunflower should avoid chamomile. Some plants such as celery also can produce adverse reactions when taken with chamomile. In addition, people with asthma should avoid chamomile because it can increase asthmatic symptoms. People who want to use chamomile need to discuss doing so with a doctor.

Chamomile is generally safe to drink when prepared using the recommended quantity of dried flowers. Highly concentrated tea made from Roman chamomile has been reported to cause nausea; this reaction is caused by a compound found in Roman chamomile called anthemic acid.

Women who are pregnant or could become pregnant should not use chamomile, according to medical persons at the University of Maryland Medical Center, because its use may increase the risk of miscarriage. In addition, mothers who are breastfeeding their newborn infant should not use chamomile because it could harm the baby.

Chamomile contains a small amount of warfarin so it produces mild blood thinning effects. Therefore, persons taking warfarin (Coumadin) or similar blood-thinning medications such as ardeparin (Normiflo), dalteparin (Fragmin), danaparoid (Orgaran), or enoxaparin (Lovenox) should use chamomile only after consulting their physician, as it may intensify the effects of anticoagulant drugs. Persons on blood-thinning medications may not be able to take chamomile or may require monitoring by a physician. These individuals need to talk with a doctor before using chamomile.

The U.S. Food and Drug Administration (FDA) does not evaluate chamomile with regards to its effectiveness, purity, or safety. In addition, regulation of the manufacturing process for chamomile products is not conducted in the United States. Users need to purchase chamomile from only reliable sources to minimize dangers within such products.

Side effects

Generally, chamomile is considered safe. However, it can cause side effects such as allergic reactions in people who are sensitive to ragweed and other substances. A doctor should be contacted immediately if an allergic reaction to chamomile occurs such as tightness in the chest, hives, rash, itching, skin irritation, vomiting, and wheezing. The side effects of chamomile over the

KEY TERMS

Allergic reaction—A physiological reaction to certain substances, such as ragweed or grass, that occurs when a susceptible person comes into close proximity with the substance.

Antispasmodic—A preparation given to relieve intestinal cramping and relax the smooth muscles of the internal organs; to relieve digestive disorders, menstrual cramps, premenstrual syndrome (PMS), headache, and other stress-related disorders.

Warfarin—A blood-thinning drug. People taking blood thinners should not take chamomile.

long term has not been determined by the medical community.

Interactions

Chamomile can increase the effects of anticoagulant medications. In addition, its tannin content may interfere with iron absorption. Chamomile may also add to the effects of **benzodiazepines**, including **diazepam** (Valium), **lorazepam** (Ativan, Temesta), and midazolam (Dormicum, Hypnovel, Versed). It could also adversely interact with **sedatives**, antiplatelet drugs, aspirin, nonsteroidal anti-inflammatory drugs (NSAIDs, such as ibuprofen and naproxen), and other drugs. Chamomile could also interact with supplements such as **ginkgo biloba**, garlic, saw palmetto, **St. John's wort**, and **valerian**.

Further, chamomile should not be taken two weeks before or after surgery. When considering whether to use chamomile, it is always advisable to seek the help of a primary healthcare professional such as the family doctor. In addition, advice from an expert in herbal/ health supplements can also be useful.

Resources

BOOKS

Arrowsmith, Nancy. *Essential Herbal Wisdom: A Complete Exploration of 50 Remarkable Herbs.* Woodbury, MN: Llewellyn, 2009.

Mayo Clinic Book of Alternative Medicine. New York: Time Home Entertainment, 2007.

McGilvery, Carole, and Jimi Reed. *The Illustrated Practical Handbook of Aromatherapy: The Power of Essential Aromatic Oils to Relax Your Body and Mind and Relieve Common Ailments.* London: Lorenz, 2007.

PDR for Herbal Medicines. 4th ed. Montvale, NJ: Thomson, 2007.

PERIODICALS

Amsterdam, J.D., et al. "A Randomized, Double-blind, Placebo-controlled Trial of Oral Matricaria Recutita (Chamomile) Extract Therapy for Generalized Anxiety Disorder." *Journal of Clinical Psychopharmacology* 29, no. 4 (August 2009): 378–82.

WEBSITES

"Chamomile." *Network of Care for Behavioral Health.* October 26, 2010. http://cuyahoga.oh.networkofcare.org/mh/library/hwdetail.cfm?hwid=ug1993spec (accessed August 24, 2011).

Griffin, R. Morgan. "Chamomile." *WebMD.* http://www.webmd.com/vitamins-and-supplements/lifestyle-guide-11/supplement-guide-chamomile (accessed August 24, 2011).

Keville, Kathy. "Aromatherapy: Chamomile." *Discovery.* http://health.howstuffworks.com/wellness/natural-medicine/aromatherapy/aromatherapy-chamomile.htm (accessed August 24, 2011).

Miller, Alicia. "Anxiety & Chamomile." *LiveStrong.com.* http://www.livestrong.com/article/240729-anxiety-chamomile (accessed August 24, 2011).

"Study Shows Chamomile Capsules Ease Anxiety Symptoms." *National Institutes of Health.* http://nccam.nih.gov/news/newsletter/2010_may/chamomileanxiety.htm (accessed August 24, 2011).

ORGANIZATIONS

American Botanical Council, 6200 Manor Rd., Austin, TX, 78723, (512) 926-4900, Fax: (512) 926-2345, abc@herbalgram.org, http://www.herbalgram.org.

American Psychiatric Association, 1000 Wilson Blvd., Ste. 1825, Arlington, VA, 22209-3901, (703) 907-7300, apa@psych.org, http://www.psych.org.

American Psychological Association, 750 1st St., NE, Washington, DC, 20002-4242, (202) 336-5500; TDD/TTY: (202) 336-6123, (800) 374-2721, http://www.apa.org.

National Association for Holistic Aromatherapy, PO Box 1868, Banner Elk, NC, 28604, (828) 898-6161, Fax: (828) 898-1965, info@naha.org, http://www.naha.org.

Rebecca J. Frey, PhD
William A. Atkins, BB, BS, MBA

Child abuse

Definition

Child abuse, sometimes called child maltreatment, describes four types of actions toward children: physical abuse, **sexual abuse**, psychological abuse, and **neglect**. In many cases, the same child experiences more than one type of **abuse**. The abusers can be parents or other family members, caregivers such as

Child abuse victims with a reported disability or mental health problem, 2009

Type of disability	Number of children abused	Percentage of total child abuse victims	Number of states reporting
Behavior problem	14,202	2.9	36
Emotional disturbance	9,928	2.1	43
Learning disability	5,011	1.0	38
Intellectual disability	2,100	0.4	41
Physical disability	3,273	0.7	27
Visual or hearing impairment	1,938	0.4	37
Other medical conditions	17,062	3.5	41
Total number of child abuse victims with a disabilty	**53,514**	**11.1**	**42**
Total number of child abuse victims	**484,076**		**42**

SOURCE: U.S. Department of Health and Human Services, Administration for Children and Families, Administration on Children, Youth and Families, Children's Bureau, *Child Maltreatment* 2009 (2010).

Report available online at http://www.acf.hhs.gov/programs/cb/pubs/cm09/cm09.pdf. *(Table by PreMediaGlobal. © 2012 Cengage Learning.)*

teachers or babysitters, acquaintances (including other children), and, in very rare instances, strangers.

Demographics

Child abuse was once viewed as a minor social problem in the United States. However, in the late twentieth century, issues of child welfare came under scrutiny by the media, law enforcement, and healthcare professionals. This increase in awareness led to a sharp rise in the number of reported cases of child abuse. Today, child abuse is recognized as a problem that occurs among households of all racial, ethnic, and income levels, although the incidence of reported cases is higher in low-income households where adult caregivers experience greater **financial stress** and social difficulties, have less education and less understanding of child development, and may have less access to social services. In addition, children of parents who are substance abusers are more likely to experience abuse than children living in households where there is no **substance abuse**. Many child abusers were themselves abused as children.

Statistically, it is difficult to find reliable national figures for cases of child abuse because each state keeps its own records and has its own definitions of what constitutes abuse. Child abuse almost always occurs in private, and because abuse often is hidden from view and its victims may be too young or too frightened to speak out, experts suggest that its true prevalence is probably greater than official data indicates. The majority of children are abused by their parents, so the child may feel that they have no advocate for their well being. However, based on information reported by states to the U.S. Department of Health and Human Services Administration for Children and Families, in 2009, approximately 702,000 children were victims of child abuse. Of those, 78% were victims of neglect, 18% were physically abused, 10% suffered sexual abuse, 8% were psychologically or emotionally maltreated, 2% experienced medical neglect, and 10% suffered other types of abuse, including congenital drug **addiction** (existing at birth). An estimated 1,770 children died as a result of abuse or neglect.

Description

There are four types of child abuse: physical (intentional infliction of injury or pain), sexual (any sexual activity, even if there is no physical contact), psychological (verbal or emotional abuse), and neglect (failure to provide for the child's basic needs).

Physical abuse

Physical abuse is the nonaccidental infliction of physical injury to a child. Legal definitions of physical child abuse vary from state to state, but injuries requiring medical attention typically are regarded as abusive. Physical abuse takes many forms, including cuts, bruises, burns, broken bones, poisoning, and internal injuries. Nonetheless, difficulties associated with defining the line between discipline and abuse are well known. Many states explicitly note that spanking "when administered in a reasonable manner" does not constitute abuse. Thus, how severely parents can inflict physical punishment upon their children without it being considered abusive remains subject to interpretation.

The physical abuser is usually a family member or other caregiver and is likely to be male. The injuries can be inflicted by such actions as punching, kicking, biting, burning, or beating, or by use of a weapon such as a baseball bat or knife. A rare form of physical abuse is Munchausen syndrome by proxy, in which a caregiver (most often the mother) seeks attention by intentionally making the child sick or appear to be sick.

Sexual abuse

Children are sexually abused when they experience contact that is for the sexual gratification of an adult or a significantly older or dominant child when they are younger than the legal age of consent or at a stage of development at which they do not possess sufficient maturity to understand the nature of the acts and therefore to provide **informed consent**. Abusers may use coercion or deceptive manipulation, but often physical force is not necessary since the perpetrator is likely to be someone with whom the child has a trusting relationship and who is in a position of authority over the child. In many states, sexual activity is automatically assumed to be abuse when a defined age difference exists between the older abuser and the younger (minor) victim independent of any consent the victim may have given.

Sexual behaviors can include touching the breasts, genitals, and buttocks while the victim is either dressed or undressed. Sexually abusive behavior also includes cunnilingus, fellatio, or penetration of the vagina or anus with sexual organs or objects. However, sexual abuse does not have to involve any actual touching. Children can be coerced into disrobing and exposing themselves or watching adults disrobe or engage in sexual activity. Pornographic photography or videography also are forms of sexual abuse of children.

Sexual abuse victims can be either boys or girls, though most, but not all, perpetrators are male. Despite publicity surrounding cases where a child is sexually assaulted by a stranger, almost all sexual abuse against children is perpetrated by a family member (e.g. father, stepfather, aunt, uncle, sibling, cousin) or family intimate (e.g., live-in partner or friend of the parent). Perpetrators go to great lengths to conceal sexual abuse. Children who have been sexually abused may not report the behavior due to threats, shame, or to a lack of understanding of what has happened.

Rape is the most violent form of sexual abuse. An act of sexual intercourse is considered rape when

- will is overcome by force or fear, whether from threats, use of weapons, violence, or use of drugs;
- mental impairment renders the victim incapable of rational judgment; or
- the victim is below the legal age established for consent.

Psychological abuse

Abuse of children is not limited to the physical body. Psychological abuse encompasses rejecting, ignoring, criticizing, belittling, humiliating, threatening with violence, or otherwise terrorizing the child, all of which have the effect of eroding the child's self-esteem and sense of security. This type of abuse can also include isolating the child from friends or other family members or destroying the child's property.

Psychological abuse may be the result of actions not directed specifically at the child. The prevalence of domestic violence exposes children to intimidating and frightening scenes every day. Many children live in homes where domestic violence is an ongoing problem that they witness regularly, often as a result of being "caught in the middle" of a parental altercation. Children who observe violence react with many of the same psychological symptoms as children who have experienced it directly.

Psychological abuse often accompanies other types of abuse. It is difficult to prove and rarely is reported.

Neglect

Neglect is the failure to satisfy a child's basic needs and can assume many forms. Physical neglect is the failure (beyond the constraints imposed by poverty) to provide adequate food, clothing, shelter, or supervision. Children may live in filthy conditions or situations where food is not provided, or where they develop infections or other medical conditions that go untreated. Failure to send children to school or otherwise provide for their education may also be considered neglect. Psychological neglect is the failure to satisfy a child's normal psychological needs and/or behavior that damages a child's normal psychological development (e.g., permitting drug abuse in the home, having the child witness domestic violence).

Risk factors

The greatest risk factor for abuse is being young; the most child fatalities due to abuse or neglect are in children younger than age four. Children who are disabled and those who are nonrhythmic (have unpredictable eating and sleeping patterns) are also more likely to be abused. Similarly, children who are distractible, impulsive, or who have high activity levels are more likely to experience physical abuse.

Causes and symptoms

Causes

SOCIOCULTURAL FACTORS. Poverty is the sociocultural factor most strongly linked to abuse. Although

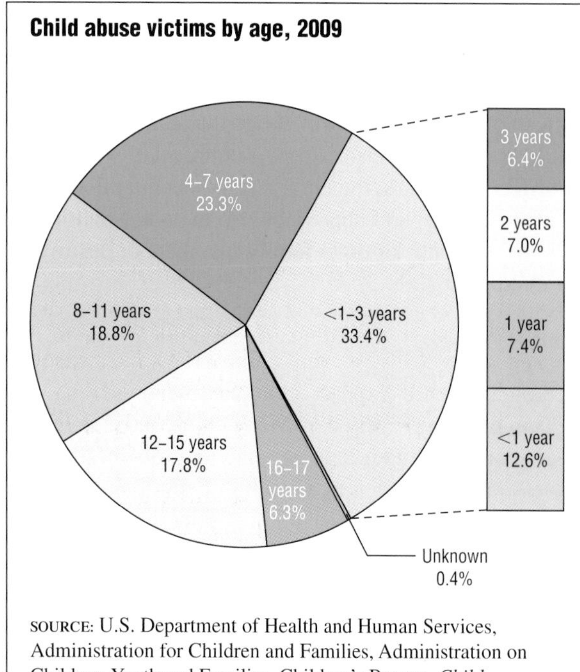

Report available online at http://www.acf.hhs.gov/programs/cb/pubs/cm09/cm09.pdf. *(Chart by PreMediaGlobal. © 2012 Cengage Learning.)*

physical abuse occurs at all income levels, it happens more often in very poor families. It is possible that abuse in middle- and upper-class families is less likely to be reported or recognized by an outside source, such as a family physician, than abuse in poorer families, where the abuse may be realized when the victim is treated in an emergency room or public clinic setting. Even with such reporting bias, however, poverty seems strongly linked to abuse, possibly due to the frustrating effects of poverty on the parents. Physical crowding is also associated with abuse, a condition more likely to occur in poverty. If too many people share a small living space, severe punishment of children as a means of maintaining control is more likely.

Job loss and dissatisfaction are other factors often associated with child abuse. Higher rates of abuse exist in military compared to non-military families. It is generally felt that the link between these environmental stressors and abuse is strengthened by the absence of social support networks that might otherwise buffer the family against adversity. Having no one to assist with child care or no one to question the use of severe discipline increases the chance that a parent may injure a child.

Perpetrators of sexual abuse in children, or pedophiles, exist in all economic and cultural groups. Psychologically, however, they share certain traits. Pedophiles often have a history of being abused themselves, and abusing other children seems to be triggered by increased life stressors such as marital problems, job layoffs, or abuse of drugs.

CAREGIVER FACTORS. Parents who abuse their children are likely to be younger than the average parent and are more likely to be single parents. Having a mental illness, such as **depression**, or abusing drugs or alcohol also makes a parent more likely to abuse his or her child. Parents who were themselves abused as children are more likely to abuse their own children, though not every parent who was abused becomes an abuser; some parents go to great lengths to ensure that they never harm their children.

Abusive parents socialize differently from nonabusive parents. Nonabusive parents tend to use ignoring or time-out procedures, whereas abusive parents tend to shout, threaten, and spank. Some forms of child abuse escalate over time, with the parent spanking harder and more frequently to get the same effect or resorting to abuse to get results. Female caregivers inflict more soft tissue injuries, broken bones, and internal injuries than male caregivers. Severe injuries from a single, explosive incident in which the child is shaken, thrown, or struck are more likely to involve male caregivers.

Abusive parents often expect their children to perform behaviors that they are not yet capable of performing. Parents who abuse young children expect them to be able to control their impulses, recall and obey complex parental rules, and perform mature chains of behavior such as getting up, washing, and getting dressed by themselves. Nonabusive parents recognize that toddlers and preschool children are incapable of such behaviors. Understanding the limitations of a young child's memory, ability to follow instructions, impulse control, and attention span is essential to developing reasonable expectations for the child. Parents who expect behavior a child cannot deliver are apt to progressively increase their control techniques in order to get the child to comply.

Abusive discipline is often the result of the belief that the young child is deliberately misbehaving to cause the parent difficulty. Parents who adopt this belief make claims such as that their 18-month-old could stay clean if she wanted to but dirties her clothing just to make more work for the mother. Abusive parents who believe a child has chosen to misbehave inflict more punishment on their children than parents who accurately recognize when a child's behavior is not intentional. Such abusive parents believe that effective parenting involves maintaining tight control over the child, which is often linked to the application of force.

Another belief abusive parents often hold is that their children should engage in reciprocal parenting. They believe that if they sometimes comfort, wait on, and take care of the child, the child should do the same for them. Such beliefs stem from the abusive parents' lack of awareness of children's developmental capabilities and possibly the parents' own immaturity or lack of support from other adults. Regardless of the source, when such expectations are not met by the child, the parent often responds with anger and hostility.

EMOTIONAL FACTORS. Anger is the most frequent trigger for parental abuse. Abusive parents appear to have a lower threshold for childish behaviors than average parents. Thus, child behaviors that are merely irritating to average parents are infuriating to abusive parents. Finally, abusive parents may have less control over their anger than nonabusive parents, either because they are unaware of their level of anger, because they are chronically angry, or because they lack anger management skills.

When considering how emotion influences child abuse, it seems important to consider positive emotions as well. Abusive parents consider their children less rewarding than nonabusive parents. In observation, abusive parents touch their children less, cuddle them less, less frequently call the affectionate names ("honey," "sweetheart"), and smile less at their children. Nonabusive parents respond flexibly to their children, letting the child lead the play interaction. Even in play, abusive parents have expectations that their children seem unable or unwilling to fulfill, making play a disagreeable chore rather than a rewarding endeavor. Abusive parents seem trapped by their own lack of skills, limited developmental understanding, inappropriate expectations, high negative emotion, and low enjoyment of the child.

Symptoms

Although these signs do not necessarily indicate that a child has been abused, they may help adults recognize that something is wrong. The possibility of abuse should be investigated if a child shows a number of these symptoms, or any of them to a marked degree.

Physical abuse:

- unexplained recurrent injuries or burns
- improbable excuses or refusal to explain injuries
- wearing clothes to cover injuries, even in hot weather
- refusal to undress for gym
- bald patches
- chronic running away
- fear of medical help or examination
- self-destructive tendencies
- aggression toward others
- fear of physical contact; shrinking back if touched
- admitting excessive punishment (such as a child being beaten every night to make him/her study)
- fear of suspected abuser being contacted

Sexual abuse:

- overly affectionate or knowledgeable in a sexual way inappropriate to the child's age
- medical problems such as chronic itching, pain in the genitals, venereal diseases
- development of depression, self-mutilation, suicide attempts, overdoses, anorexia, or other severe actions
- attempts at running away
- personality changes such as becoming insecure or clingy
- regressing to younger behavior patterns such as thumb-sucking or bringing out discarded cuddly toys
- sudden loss of appetite or engaging in compulsive eating
- social isolation or withdrawal
- inability to concentrate
- lack of trust or fear for someone they know well, such as not wanting to be alone with a babysitter or specific family member
- anxiety about clothing being removed
- wetting the bed or having nightmares
- drawing sexually explicit pictures
- trying to be "ultra-good" or perfect; overreacting to criticism

Psychological abuse:

- physical, mental, and psychological developmental lags
- sudden speech disorders
- continual self-depreciation (e.g.,"I'm stupid, ugly, worthless," etc.)
- overreaction to mistakes
- extreme fear of any new situation
- inappropriate response to pain (e.g., "I deserve this")
- neurotic behavior (e.g., rocking, hair twisting, self-mutilation)
- extremes of passivity or aggression

Neglect:

- constant hunger
- poor personal hygiene

- no social relationships
- constant tiredness
- poor state of clothing
- compulsive scavenging
- emaciation
- untreated medical problems
- destructive tendencies

A child may be subjected to a combination of different kinds of abuse. It is also possible that a child may show no outward signs and hide what is happening from everyone.

Diagnosis

Doctors and many other professionals who work with children are required by law to report suspected abuse to their state's Child Protective Services (CPS) agency. Abuse investigations often are a group effort involving medical personnel, **social workers**, police officers, and others. Some hospitals and communities maintain child protection teams that respond to cases of possible abuse. Careful questioning of the parents is crucial, as is interviewing the child (if he or she is capable of being interviewed). Trained investigators must ensure, however, that their questioning does not further traumatize the child and also that their style of questioning does not prompt the child to give the answers the child thinks the questioner wants rather than accurate answers. A physical examination for signs of physical or sexual abuse or of neglect is necessary and may include x rays, blood tests, and other procedures.

Treatment

Notification of the appropriate authorities, treatment of the child's injuries, and protecting the child from further harm are the immediate priorities in abuse cases. If the child does not require hospital treatment, protection often involves placing him or her with relatives, in a group home, or in foster care. Once the immediate concerns are dealt with, it becomes essential to determine how the child's long-term medical, psychological, educational, and other needs can best be met. This process involves evaluating not only the child's needs but also the needs of the family (e.g., drug abuse counseling, parental skills training, anger management training). The authorities also must determine whether other children living in the same household have been abused. On investigation, signs of physical abuse are discovered in about 20% of other children living in the abused child's household.

Prognosis

Child abuse often has lifelong consequences. Research shows that abused children and adolescents are more likely to do poorly in school and experience depression, extreme anger, antisocial personality traits, and other psychiatric problems. They also are more likely to become promiscuous, abuse drugs and alcohol, run away, and attempt **suicide**. As adults, they often have trouble establishing intimate relationships.

Most children who have been abused experience some symptoms of **post-traumatic stress disorder** (PTSD). PTSD in children and adolescents may be acute or delayed, meaning that the child may experience symptoms immediately or not until after a period of time has passed, perhaps when the child feels safe. Symptoms may include re-experiencing the abusive episodes at some level, feeling emotionally numb, or feeling the physiological effects of fear (elevated heart rate, abnormal breathing patterns, and so forth). Children may experience disassociation and appear to "space out" when reminded of the abuse or perpetrator. They may become enraged or feel guilt at having provoked the episodes or survived them. They may have invasive memories, repeated behaviors, or fears related to the abusive situations. They may act out some of their issues in play—punishing the bad guy or victimizing another character when playing with dolls or action figures. In severe cases of chronic **trauma**, the child may develop serious or prolonged disassociation or depression. Severe and chronic abuse has also been implicated in cases of multiple personality disorder.

Once the abuse has stopped, some of these symptoms can be treated with some form of counseling or therapy, but full recovery may be a lifelong task. Adults who have been abused as children may have to face issues long after the abuse has stopped, such as when they enter into sexual relationships or when they raise their own children. Long-term therapy by a professional trained in working with abused children and adults offers the best chance of overcoming childhood abuse.

Prevention

There are many barriers to changing abusive parental behavior. Most abusive parents' own histories suggest that strong physical discipline is the preferred model of parenting, and most abusive parents live in families and neighborhoods in which violence is not only condoned but viewed as a necessary vehicle for interpersonal influence. The stressors that are omnipresent in abusive parents' lives contribute to high levels of anger and depression, which prevent the parent from experiencing enjoyment of the child. Further, when a parent responds with strong physical discipline, the child's misbehavior typically stops, at least for that moment, reinforcing the parent's behavior.

It may be preferable to prevent the development of abusive parenting by instituting early interventions to provide parental skills, alter developmental knowledge, change unreasonable parenting expectations, and block the steady build-up of anger and extinguishing of affection for the child. Prevention programs now target teenagers before pregnancy as well as young mothers to try to break the cycle of abuse.

Government efforts to prevent abuse include home-visitor programs aimed at high-risk families and school-based efforts to teach children how to respond to attempted sexual abuse. Psychological abuse prevention has been promoted through the media.

When children reach age three, parents should begin teaching them about "bad touches" and about confiding in a suitable adult if they are touched or treated in a way that makes them uneasy. Parents also need to exercise caution in hiring babysitters and other caregivers. Anyone who suspects abuse should report those suspicions to the police or his or her local CPS agency. Prevent Child Abuse America (listed in references) is an excellent source of information on the many **support groups** and other organizations that help abused and at-risk children and their families. One of these organizations, Parents Anonymous, sponsors local **self-help groups** throughout the United States, Canada, and Europe.

Resources

WEBSITES

MedlinePlus. "Child Abuse." U.S. National Library of Medicine, National Institutes of Health. May 19, 2011. http://www.nlm.nih.gov/medlineplus/childabuse.html (accessed October 1, 2011).

U.S. Department of Health and Human Services. "Child Welfare Information Gateway." http://www.childwelfare.gov (accessed October 1, 2011).

ORGANIZATIONS

Childhelp National Child Abuse Hotline, (800) 4-A-CHILD (422-4453), TDD: (800) 2-A-CHILD (222-4453).

Parents Anonymous, Inc, 675 West Foothill Blvd., Suite 220, Claremont, CA, 91711-3475, (909) 621-6184, Fax: (909) 625-6304, Parentsanonymous@parentsanonymous.org, http://www.parentsanonymous.org.

Prevent Child Abuse America, 228 South Wabash Ave., 10th Floor, Chicago, IL, 60604, (312) 663-3520, Fax: (312) 939-8962, mailbox@preventchildabuse.org, http://www.preventchildabuse.org.

Rape, Abuse and Incest National Network (RAINN), (800) 656-HOPE (4673), http://www.rainn.org/get-help/national-sexual-assault-online-hotline.

Tish Davidson, AM

Childhood bipolar disorder *see* **Juvenile bipolar disorder**

Childhood depression *see* **Juvenile depression**

Childhood disintegrative disorder

Definition

Childhood disintegrative disorder (CDD) is a developmental disorder that resembles severe **autism**. Children with CDD undergo normal development for at least two years, followed by permanent loss of their previously acquired language, motor, adaptive, and social skills. CDD is also known as Heller (or Heller's) syndrome, **dementia** infantilis, and disintegrative **psychosis**.

Demographics

CDD is very rare, affecting only 1–2 out of every 100,000 children. In contrast, autism affects about 20 children per 10,000, and pervasive developmental disorder not otherwise specified (PDD-NOS) affects 30 per 10,000. However, CDD may be underdiagnosed because of its similarities to other developmental disorders. Although CDD is about four times more common in boys than in girls, it was long thought be equally common in both genders, because girls with **Rett syndrome** were often misdiagnosed with CDD. The average age of CDD **diagnosis** is 3.9 years.

Description

Childhood disintegrative disorder was first described by Thomas Heller, an Austrian educator, in 1908. It is a complex and poorly understood condition that affects many different areas of development. Children with CDD develop normally in all areas—language comprehension and speech, nonverbal communication, gross- and fine-motor skills, social relationships, play, and self-care—for at least their first two years. At some point before the age of ten, but usually between three and four years, they begin to lose their previously acquired skills. The losses may be gradual, occurring over a period of six to nine months or longer. Losses can also occur very rapidly, over days or weeks.

CDD is classified as a pervasive developmental disorder (PDD), along with autism, **Asperger syndrome**, Rett syndrome, and PDD-NOS. These conditions may also be collectively referred to as autism spectrum

KEY TERMS

Adaptive behavior—A person's ability to accomplish tasks and adapt to and function in an environment.

Amyloid—A waxy material, made up primarily of protein, that accumulates in organs and tissues with conditions such as Alzheimer's disease.

Asperger syndrome—A developmental disorder that is similar to mild autism. It is characterized by impaired social interaction, repetitive patterns of behavior, and restricted interests, but with normal language and cognitive development and often above-average abilities in a narrow field.

Autism—A variable developmental disorder that includes an impaired ability to communicate and form normal social relationships.

Autism spectrum disorder (ASD)—A range of disorders that includes classic autism, with Asperger syndrome at the mild end of the spectrum and childhood disintegrative disorder at the severe end.

Autoimmune disease—Disorders caused when the immune system's antibodies or T cells attack the body's own molecules, cells, or tissues.

Catatonia—Psychomotor disturbances that can include stupor, rigidity, muteness, or purposeless and bizarre movements.

Epilepsy—A chronic nervous system disorder that typically causes temporary behavior changes, uncontrolled shaking, loss of attention, or unconsciousness.

Fine motor skills—Control of the smaller muscles of the body, especially in the hands, feet, and head, for activities such as writing and crafts.

Gross motor skills—Control of the large muscles of the body, including the arms, legs, back, abdomen, and torso, for activities such as sitting, crawling, walking, and running.

Pervasive developmental disorder (PDD)—A group of five disorders—including Asperger syndrome, autism, Rett disorder, childhood disintegrative disorder (CDD), and pervasive developmental disorder not otherwise specified (PDD-NOS)—that are characterized by developmental delays or impairments.

Rett syndrome—An inherited progressive neurodevelopmental disorder that affects females, usually beginning in infancy, and is characterized by cognitive and motor deterioration, slow brain growth, and intellectual disability.

Schizophrenia—A psychotic disorder characterized by loss of contact with one's environment, deterioration of everyday functioning, and personality disintegration.

disorders (ASD), and CDD is sometimes classified as the severest form of ASD. However, the onset of CDD is usually somewhat later than the onset of autism (classical ASD), and autism does not usually involve the dramatic developmental regression that is characteristic of CDD.

CDD was listed as a separate diagnosis in the fourth edition of the ***Diagnostic and Statistical Manual of Mental Disorders***, text revised (*DSM-IV-TR*), the handbook used by medical professionals in diagnosing mental disorders. Proposed changes for the fifth edition (*DSM-5, 2013*) subsume CDD into the criteria for autism spectrum disorder. The decision came after a review of existing cases of CDD, which failed to provide enough evidence to support CDD as a distinct diagnosis from regressive autism. Still, the proposal to subsume CDD and the other **pervasive developmental disorders** into one category has been met with controversy.

Risk factors

Risk factors for CDD appear to be both genetic and environmental. Genetic risk factors may include a family history of autism, Asperger syndrome, or rolandic epilepsy. Environmental risk factors may include exposure to viruses, especially prenatal exposure to rubella, cytomegalovirus, or herpes simplex, or other infections such as toxoplasmosis. Exposure to toxins, premature birth, and birth **trauma** may also be potential risk factors.

Causes and symptoms

The cause of CDD is unknown. It may result from a combination of genetic susceptibility, possibly involving autoimmunity, and prenatal or postnatal **stress**, including infection, exposure to toxins, or birth trauma. Autoimmune responses occur when the immune system attacks the body's own components. CDD appears to involve deposition of amyloid in the **brain** and disruption of nerve transmission in the brain. It also may involve the immune system chemical interleukin-1 or the brain chemical beta-endorphin.

CDD often occurs in conjunction with other conditions, such as tuberous sclerosis, which causes noncancerous brain tumors; lipid storage diseases, in which excess fats build up in the brain and nervous system; and subacute sclerosing panencephalitis, a chronic brain infection. Other conditions commonly associated with CDD include autoimmune disorders, allergies, asthma, food sensitivities, and gastrointestinal disorders. CDD is sometimes associated with **seizures** and occasionally with brain disorders such as leukodystrophy or Schilder's disease.

CDD may begin with unexplained changes in behavior, such as anxiety, agitation, or unprovoked anger. Behavioral changes are followed by loss of communication, social, and motor skills. Children may stop speaking and communicating nonverbally or revert to single or repeated words. Some 90% of children with CDD lose the ability to feed and wash themselves, lose bowel and/or bladder control, and develop nonspecific overactivity. Essentially all children with CDD lose social skills. They may reject all social interaction and withdraw into themselves. Aggressiveness and tantrums are common. Children may withdraw from physical contact and lose the ability to be consoled. They may perform strange repetitive behaviors known as motor stereotypes or mannerisms, such as head bobbing, rocking, or spinning. They may fixate on certain objects or activities and have trouble with any changes in routine and in transitioning from one activity to another. They also may have difficulty transitioning from wakefulness to sleep and develop **insomnia**. Many children with CDD develop catatonia—a fixed posture or body position. Although the regression eventually stops, children do not usually regain their lost skills.

Diagnosis

A diagnosis of CDD requires that a child regresses dramatically in at least two of the following areas, although most children regress in multiple areas:

- receptive language skills (nonverbal and verbal comprehension)
- expressive language skills (spoken language)
- social or self-help skills, known as adaptive behavior
- imaginary play and playing with peers
- motor skills, including a decline in the ability to walk or grasp objects
- bowel or bladder control, if previously established

Examination

The first signs of CDD may be detected by a pediatrician performing a developmental screening during a routine well-child visit. Developmental screenings utilize parent reports, as well as the physician's observations of the child's language, motor, social, play, and self-help skills. More often, however, parents consult their pediatrician because of suspected developmental delay or the child's loss of previously acquired skills.

The physician will conduct a physical examination to check for conditions such as epilepsy. If a developmental disorder is suspected, the child is usually referred to a team of childhood development specialists for in-depth testing to differentiate CDD from other PDDs, as well as from **schizophrenia**. The team may include a child **psychologist** or **psychiatrist**, a neurologist, a pediatrician specializing in behavior and development, a hearing specialist or audiologist, a speech therapist, a physical therapist, and an occupational therapist.

Because CDD follows at least two years of normal development, medical records, parents' reports, baby books, photo albums, and home videos are important for documenting previous developmental milestones. A family medical history may also be relevant.

Tests

Blood tests will include a complete blood cell count (CBC), genetic tests for chromosome abnormalities and inherited diseases or conditions, and screens for heavy metal poisoning, such as mercury, arsenic, and especially lead, which can cause nervous system damage, developmental delays, behavior problems, and hearing loss. Blood tests will also measure thyroid, kidney, and liver function. Glucose tolerance and HIV testing will be performed. Urine testing may also be involved.

The child will undergo vision and hearing tests. Detailed communication and language tests will evaluate the child's verbal and nonverbal communications skills, including speech rhythms and tone, comprehension, facial expressions, body language, gestures, and social clues. A behavior inventory may utilize any of various rating scales and checklists to evaluate social interactions; play skills; responses to visual, auditory, and touch stimuli in the environment; and diagnostic behaviors such as repetitive movements.

Developmental tests determine a child's developmental age by measuring:

- gross motor skills, including walking, running, jumping, climbing, and throwing
- fine motor skills, including use of hands and fingers to manipulate objects such as pencils, scissors, and buttons
- sensory skills, including responses to sights, sounds, taste, touch, and smell
- play skills, including playing with other children and adults, as well as toys and other objects, and whether play is imaginative, goal-oriented, or purposeful

- self-care skills, including feeding, dressing, toileting, and toothbrushing
- cognitive skills, including attention, concentration, following directions, thinking, and problem solving

Specific tests may include:

- Children's Autism Rating Scale (CARS)
- Kaufman Assessment Battery for Children (KABC), an intelligence and mental processing evaluation
- other intelligence tests
- Vineland Adaptive Behavior Scale
- PDD Behavior Inventory to assess responses to intervention
- occupational therapy evaluation to determine tactile sensitivity, such as responses to touching and hugging, and to assess motor delays
- educational and achievement testing, including verbal and nonverbal communication

Procedures

Imaging procedures, such as x rays, **magnetic resonance imaging** (MRI), **positron emission tomography (PET)**, or **computed tomography** (CT) scans, will rule out brain tumors, head trauma, or anatomical abnormalities. Electrical activity in the brain is measured with an electroencephalogram (EEG), including a sleep EEG. About 50% of children with CDD have abnormal EEGs. EEGs can also help rule out seizure disorders.

Treatment

Traditional

Treatment for CDD is very similar to treatment for autism, with early and intense educational interventions that are highly structured and behavior-based. Behavior therapies require a consistent approach by psychologists; speech, physical, and occupational therapists; teachers; parents; and caregivers to help the child learn or relearn sensory integration and language, social, and self-care skills. Behavior therapy uses rewards to reinforce desirable behaviors and discourage problem behaviors. Family supportive therapy is also usually required.

Drugs

Various medications may be used to treat CDD. Atypical antipsychotics and drugs for anxiety or **depression**, such as selective **serotonin** or norepinephrine reuptake inhibitors (**SSRIs**, SNRIs), have been widely used to treat behavior and mood problems in children with CDD and can sometimes control severe problems, such as repetitive movements or aggression. Anticonvulsants may help control seizures. Sometimes very low-dose and carefully monitored treatment with stimulants or non-stimulants, such as **methylphenidate** or **atomoxetine**, can improve severely impaired attention. **Haloperidol** and **risperidone** are approved by the U.S. Food and Drug Administration (FDA) for treating irritability in childhood autism and may also help with aggression and hyperactivity. Many children and especially adolescents with CDD have impaired sleep-wake cycles and chronic **sleep deprivation** can aggravate aggressive behaviors. Sleep cycles can sometimes be improved by a melatonin agonist such as agomelatine. However, many of these drugs can have potentially serious side effects in children with CDD. Preliminary studies have suggested that corticosteroids may improve language and slow the progression of CDD. Other recent studies have indicated that **memantine**, a drug for treating **Alzheimer's disease** symptoms, may be useful for CDD.

Alternative

Various complementary therapies used for ASD may be applicable to CDD. These include art and **music therapy** and sensory integration—a technique used by occupational therapists to help normalize sensory experiences. Special **diets** and vitamin and mineral supplements are also commonly used with autistic children. However, there is no evidence that alternative treatments such as cranial manipulation or dietary therapies are useful for CDD or any other ASD. Parents who decide to try a special diet for their child should consult with a nutritionist before and after, to prevent or reverse diet-induced vitamin, mineral, or caloric changes. It is particularly important that children with CDD receive adequate **nutrition** to prevent growth retardation.

Home remedies

CDD is a devastating disorder that places tremendous burden and stress on families and caregivers. Parents must be educated in supporting their child's treatments. They must learn and practice set routines that help prevent emotional outbursts and temper tantrums. Families require regular **respite** care to provide time away from the child and the stress of CDD. However, finding appropriate service providers for children with CDD can be difficult, especially outside of large cities. **Support groups** for families can help reduce isolation and frustration, and autism support groups and organizations include CDD families in their services.

Prognosis

Children with CDD have a very poor prognosis. By the age of ten, most children have impairments similar to

QUESTIONS TO ASK YOUR DOCTOR

- What are the possible causes of my child's symptoms?
- What tests will be performed?
- Should we see a specialist?
- What treatments do you recommend?
- What is my child's prognosis?

severe autism, and lost skills are not usually regained. Only about 20% of children with CDD regain their ability to speak in sentences. The risk of seizures increases with age, peaking during adolescence. Most adults with CDD remain dependent on full-time caregivers or are institutionalized.

Prevention

There is no known prevention for CDD. Some experts believe that enriching experiences during critical stages of brain development might potentially overcome genetic predispositions. Disruption of psychosocial development at earlier stages may result in even more severe impairment.

Resources

BOOKS

Hegde, M. N. *Hegde's PocketGuide to Communication Disorders*. Clifton Park, NY: Thomson Delmar Learning, 2008.

Pierangelo, Roger, and George A. Giuliani. *Teaching Students with Autism Spectrum Disorders*.Thousand Oaks, CA: Corwin Press, 2008.

Woliver, Robbie. *Alphabet Kids from ADD to Zellweger Syndrome: A Guide to Developmental, Neurobiological and Psychological Disorders for Parents and Professionals*. Philadelphia: Jessica Kingsley, 2009.

PERIODICALS

Homan, K.J., M. W. Mellon, D. Houlihan, and M. Z. Katusic. "Brief Report: Childhood Disintegrative Disorder: A Brief Examination of Eight Case Studies." *Journal of Autism and Developmental Disorders* 41, no. 4 (2011): 497–504.

Mordekar, S. R., et al. "Corticosteroid Treatment of Behaviour, Language and Motor Regression in Childhood Disintegrative Disorder." *European Journal of Paediatric Neurology* 13, no. 4 (July 2009): 367–69.

Palomo, R., et al. "A Case Study of Childhood Disintegrative Disorder using Systematic Analysis of Family Home Movies." *Journal of Autism and Developmental Disorders* 38, no. 10 (November 2008): 1853–1858.

WEBSITES

Bernstein, Bettina E. "Childhood Disintegrative Disorder." Medscape Reference. http://emedicine.medscape.com/article/916515-overview (accessed December 9, 2011).

Mayo Clinic Staff. "Childhood Disintegrative Disorder." MayoClinic.com. September 16, 2010. http://www.mayoclinic.com/print/childhood-disintegrative-disorder/DS00801 (accessed December 9, 2011).

MedlinePlus. "Childhood Disintegrative Disorder." U.S. National Library of Medicine, National Institutes of Health. http://www.nlm.nih.gov/medlineplus/ency/article/001535.htm (accessed December 9, 2011).

ORGANIZATIONS

Autism Society, 4340 East-West Hwy., Ste. 350, Bethesda, MD, 20814, (301) 657-0881, (800) 3-AUTISM (328-8476), http://www.autism-society.org.

National Institute of Child Health and Human Development Information Resource Center, PO Box 3006, Rockville, MD, 20847, (800) 370-2943, Fax: (866) 760-5947, NICHDInformationResourceCenter@mail.nih.gov, http://www.nichd.nih.gov.

National Institute of Neurological Disorders and Stroke, NIH Neurological Institute, PO Box 5801, Bethesda, MD, 20824, (301) 496-5751, (800) 352-9424, http://www.ninds.nih.gov/index.htm.

Tish Davidson, AM
Margaret Alic, PhD

Childhood onset fluency disorder
see **Stuttering**

Children's Apperception Test (CAT)

Definition

The Children's Apperception Test (CAT) is a widely used projective thematic personality test for children aged three through ten, which analyzes the stories that children tell about pictures.

Purpose

The primary purpose of the CAT is to assess a child's personality, self-image, and view of the world, by analyzing responses to standardized pictorial stimuli. The CAT is most often used to identify and diagnose personality and emotional disorders in children. It is rarely used as the sole basis of a clinical **psychological assessment**. Rather, it is usually one of a battery of tests, including other projective tests, that supplement information obtained from interviews with the child and parents. The CAT is designed to reveal information about children's perceptions and imaginations, to help psychologists and psychiatrists understand their conscious and unconscious needs, motives, attitudes, emotions, and conflicts.

The CAT was originally developed to examine so-called psychosexual conflicts that arise at different stages of child development, including relationship issues, sibling rivalry, and aggression. However, in recent years, the CAT has come into widespread use as a general method for describing personality and assessing maturity, as well as measuring psychological health. The CAT is used in clinical, educational, and research settings. Because pictures form the content of the CAT, it is used throughout the world.

The CAT is used to reveal and assess:

- personality traits
- maturity
- life stresses
- perceptions of reality
- defenses
- aggressive tendencies
- self-control
- judgment
- degree of autonomy or independence
- psychodynamic processes

Description

The CAT is a type of personality assessment called a projective test, similar to Rorschach inkblots and the popular **Thematic Apperception Test** (TAT). Projection, a concept that originated with Sigmund Freud, is a psychological mechanism by which humans' unconscious needs, motives, and emotions are projected onto the external world and control behavior. People come to believe that these feelings are actually being expressed by the external environment and are directed back at them. Whereas cognitive tests utilize intellectual measures of a person's knowledge of the world, projective storytelling techniques, like the CAT, are open ended and encourage the free expression of thoughts and feelings that reveal personality traits.

The CAT is always administered to individual children by a trained professional, usually a **psychiatrist**, **psychologist**, social worker, or specially trained pediatrician or teacher. It may be administered as a component of therapy or as a play technique. It is not timed, but usually takes 20–45 minutes. The test must be administered in a quiet room, free of distractions.

First, the examiner establishes a rapport with the child. The child is then shown ten black-and-white picture cards, one at a time in a particular sequence, and asked to describe each situation and make up a story about the picture, with a beginning, middle, and end. For example, the child may be asked to describe what preceded the scene in the picture, how the characters in the picture are feeling, and what might happen next. The pictures have been chosen to encourage storytelling related to situations such as family life, school, illness, injury, competition, and **body image**. The examiner may choose to use only selected pictures. The child's stories are expected to reveal information about relationships with family and peers, feelings about school, and self-confidence and self-esteem. The stories may also reveal a child's anxieties and fears and psychological defenses in a variety of contexts, including school, play, and body image.

The original CAT, now referred to as the CAT-A for animals or simply the CAT, was designed specifically for younger children, who, it was thought, would more readily identify with drawings of animals. The CAT-A pictures are designed to appeal to a child's imagination and encourage storytelling. The animals are pictured within human social settings. Most involve animals interacting with their environment and are meant to represent needs that a child can identify. Pictures include:

- baby chicks seated around a table with an adult chicken in the background
- a baby bear and a large bear playing tug-of-war
- a mouse peering through a peephole at a lion seated on a throne
- a mother kangaroo with one baby kangaroo in her pouch and an older baby kangaroo beside her
- two baby bears sleeping in a small bed in front of a larger bed with two bulges in it
- a baby bear lying next to two large bears in a cave
- a ferocious tiger leaping at a monkey climbing a tree
- two adult monkeys sitting on a sofa and another adult monkey talking to a baby monkey
- a rabbit sitting on a child's bed, as seen through a doorway
- a puppy being spanked by an adult dog in front of a bathroom

Using the example of the ferocious tiger and the monkey, one child might tell a story about them playing a game. However, another child might talk about the heroic monkey escaping from the evil tiger. This could represent the child's fear of aggression or need to escape punishment.

A supplement, the CAT-S, was first published in 1952 and was designed to elicit more specific responses from children. It includes pictures of children in family situations, such as birth, death, prolonged illness, or separation from parents.

KEY TERMS

Apperception—The process of understanding something in terms of previous experience.

Cognitive—Conscious intellectual activity, including thinking, imagining, reasoning, remembering, and learning.

Defense—An unconscious mental process that protects the conscious mind from unacceptable or painful thoughts, impulses, or desires. Examples of defenses include denial, rationalization, projection, and repression. Some defenses are considered to represent lower levels of maturation than others; thus identifying a child's defenses may be helpful in evaluating his or her level of psychological maturity.

Ego—In Freudian psychology, the conscious, rational part of the mind that experiences and reacts to the outside world.

Personality test—Various standardized tasks that are used to determine aspects of personality or emotional status.

Projective test—A psychological test for assessing thinking patterns, observational abilities, attitudes, and feelings, based on open-ended responses to ambiguous stimuli; often used to evaluate personality disorders.

Psychodynamic—Mental, emotional, or motivational forces or processes that affect mental state and behavior, especially unconscious processes that develop in early childhood.

Psychosexual conflicts—In Freudian categories, internal conflicts related to problems at a particular stage of childhood development. Freud associated each developmental stage with a particular part of the human body, such as the mouth or the phallus.

Reliability—The ability of a test to yield consistent, repeatable results.

Rorschach test—A popular projective psychological test, in which a subject's interpretation of a series of ten standard inkblots are used to assess personality and emotional traits and diagnose disorders.

Sibling rivalry—Competition among brothers and sisters in a nuclear family. It is considered to be an important influence in shaping the personalities of children who grow up in middle-class Western societies but less relevant in traditional African and Asian cultures.

Superego—According to Freud, the part of the mind that represents traditional parental and societal values. The superego is the source of guilt feelings.

Thematic Apperception Test (TAT)—A clinical psychology projective test for diagnostic, psychodynamic, and personality assessments, based on responses to black and white pictures.

Validity—The ability of a test to measure accurately what it claims to measure.

The CAT-H was first published in 1965. It consists of ten pictures of human children and adults in the same common social situations that are depicted with animals in the original CAT. It is used with children who identify more readily with people than with animals, especially seven-to-ten-year-olds who view the animal pictures as childish. The CAT-H is also commonly used for research purposes. An important difference between the CAT-A and the CAT-H is that gender identity is more ambiguous in the animal pictures, enabling children to relate to all of the young animals rather than just those of their own gender, as in the CAT-H.

The complete CAT kit includes the CAT-A, CAT-H, and CAT-S picture cards and manuals, recording and analysis banks, and the "Haworth Schedule of Adaptive Mechanisms in CAT Responses." The latter is a checklist developed by Mary Haworth to aid in the qualitative analysis of CAT stories and to help formulate rough quantitative measures.

Origins

The CAT was originally developed in 1949 by the psychiatrist, psychoanalyst, and psychologist Leopold Bellak and his then-wife, Sonya Baychok Sorel Bellak. It was designed as a downward extension of the TAT for children aged three through ten. The TAT had been developed in the 1930s by the psychologists Henry A. Murray and Christiana D. Morgan. Murray believed that people's needs affect the ways in which they interact with their environment. Like the CAT, the TAT utilizes a picture interpretation technique to reveal aspects of personality and interpersonal relationships. In particular, the TAT was designed to reveal the strengths of people's needs and drives—especially their need for achievement and recognition—as well as emotions, conflicts, complexes, and unconscious fantasies. The TAT is used with adults and children aged ten and older. It consists of a series of 31 pictures portraying people in common—but ambiguous—situations, in order to elicit oral or written stories about relationships and social situations.

Preparation

The CAT should be administered, scored, and interpreted only by a trained and experienced mental health professional who is knowledgeable in the psychological theories behind the test. It is recommended that the examiner obtain a child's personal, psychological, educational, and medical histories before administering the CAT. This ensures that the examiner has a context for interpreting the child's responses. For example, stories of loss or **grief** might be considered abnormal responses or a cause for concern unless the examiner knows that the child's pet has just died.

Risks

Although many decades of experience with the CAT have indicated that it can provide accurate and useful information about personality traits, emotions, and needs, many experts remain critical of it and other projective tests, questioning their reliability, validity, and usefulness as diagnostic tools. The CAT, in particular, has been criticized for its lack of objective scoring, its reliance on the examiner's methods and bias, and results that may be inconsistent. Critics have also questioned its validity or effectiveness at measuring the traits it purports to assess, such as needs, conflicts, and motivations.

Interpretations of CAT responses are very subjective. A child's stories or the examiner's interpretations of the stories can lead to an improper **diagnosis**. Some critics also maintain that cultural and language differences between the examiner and the child can affect CAT results. Studies have found that the gender, race, and socioeconomic class of the examiner and of the child affect both the child's stories and the examiner's interpretations. For these reasons, the CAT is often referred to as an assessment tool rather than a test, and is normally used only in conjunction with other psychological assessments designed for children. It is very important that parents seek a second opinion or have their child assessed by other methods before reaching decisions based on the CAT. In addition to all of these concerns, many parents have reported that the CAT did not provide any new information about their child.

Results

The CAT is not quantitatively scored, because, as with other projective tests, there are a wide range of responses. The basic stories that a child tells are recorded, and the occurrence or lack of various thematic elements is noted on a form. Each story is analyzed in depth to reveal the child's needs, attitudes, emotions, conflicts, and response patterns. The examiner summarizes personality traits and attitudes and conflicts that are revealed by each story.

The important story components that are analyzed include the:

- main theme and conflicts
- main character or protagonist
- protagonist's primary needs or motivations
- protagonist's anxieties, fears, and conflicts
- relationship of the protagonist to his or her immediate environment
- child's perceptions of the external world, as revealed by the characters in the stories
- child's ego integration, or perception of and adaptation to reality
- functioning of the child's superego, or semi-conscious system of morality or conscience

Like other projective tests, the CAT does not have a standardized method of administration or norms for interpretation. Although the CAT is designed to be interpreted according to psychoanalytical theories, the examiner has a great deal of flexibility, and interpretation is often influenced by the examiner's preferred theories or biases.

QUESTIONS TO ASK YOUR DOCTOR

- Should my child be given the CAT or other projective psychological tests?
- Who will administer the CAT?
- Will I be informed of my child's responses on the CAT?
- How will my child's CAT responses be interpreted?
- What other psychological and diagnostic tests should my child have?

Resources

BOOKS

Bellak, Leopold, and David M. Abrams. *The Thematic Apperception Test, the Children's Apperception Test, and the Senior Apperception Technique in Clinical Use*. 6th ed. Boston: Allyn and Bacon, 1997.

Bellak, Leopold, and Sonya Sorel Bellak. *Children's Apperception Test (C.A.T.)*. Oxford, England: C.P.S., 1949.

Bellak, Leopold. *The Thematic Apperception Test and the Children's Apperception Test in Clinical Use*. Oxford, England: Grune & Stratton, 1954.

Chandler, Louis A. "The Need-Threat Analysis: A Scoring System for the Children's Apperception Test." In *A Handbook of Clinical Scoring Systems for Thematic Apperceptive Techniques,* edited by Sharon Rae Jenkins. New York: Routledge, 2007.

Teglasi, Hedwig. *Essentials of TAT and Other Storytelling Assessments*. 2nd ed. Hoboken, NJ: John Wiley & Sons, 2010.

PERIODICALS

Berant, Ety, Mario Mikulincer, and Phillip R. Shaver. "Mothers' Attachment Style, Their Mental Health, and Their Children's Emotional Vulnerabilities: A 7-Year Study of Children With Congenital Heart Disease." *Journal of Personality* 76, no. 1 (February 2008): 31–66.

Lis, A. "The Children's Apperception Test Evaluation Form: Initial Data." *Psychological Reports* 96, no. 3, Pt. 1 (June 2005): 755–68.

WEBSITES

Center for Psychological Studies, Nova Southeastern University. "Children's Apperception Test." http://www.cps.nova.edu/~cpphelp/CAT.html (accessed October 1, 2011).

ORGANIZATIONS

American Psychological Association, 750 1st St. NE, Washington, DC, 20002-4242, (202) 336-5500; TDD/TTY: (202) 336-6123, (800) 374-2721, http://www.apa.org.

Center for Psychological Studies, Nova Southeastern University, 3301 College Ave., Fort Lauderdale-Davie, FL, 33314-7796, (800) 541-6682, ext. 25700, http://www.cps.nova.edu.

Margaret Alic, PhD

Children's Depression Inventory

Definition

The Children's Depression Inventory (CDI) is a symptom-oriented instrument for assessing cognitive (thoughts), affective (emotions), and behavioral (psychological) signs of depression in children between the ages of seven and 17 years. The CDI differentiates between **major depressive disorder** (a severe case of depression) and **dysthymic disorder** (a less severe form of depression) in children. The basic CDI consists of 27 items, but a 10-item short form (CDI-S) is also available for use as a screener (a test for screening patients). The 27-item test analyzes depressive symptoms such as depressed mood, lack of hedonic (pleasure) capacity, and interpersonal behaviors. The reading level for the CDI is first grade.

The updated version of the CDI, the Children's Depression Inventory 2 (CDI-2), is based on the original CDI—retaining many of its best features—but adds several important improvements to its predecessor that were based on reports taken from parents, children and adolescents, and teachers. For instance, the CDI-2 includes new items that concentrate on the fundamental aspects of childhood depression. It also includes measurement scales that are considered more reliable and valid. The norms established by the CDI-2 are also updated, taken from a more recent sample of the U.S. population. This sample is said to be more representative of the U.S. population than the previous version. In addition, the revised CDI contains normative samples of the Parent and Teacher forms.

Purpose

First developed in 1992 by Maria Kovacs, professor of psychiatry at the University of Pittsburgh School of Medicine, the CDI was intended to assist in the difficult **diagnosis** of depression in young children. One complication was that depression was regarded as an adult disorder until the 1970s. It was thought that children's nervous systems were not sufficiently mature to manifest the neurochemical changes in **brain** function associated with depression.

The **National Institute of Mental Health** (NIMH) estimated that as many as 2.5% of children and 8.3% of adolescents under the age of 18 years in the United States have depression. A study sponsored by the NIMH of 9- to 17-year-olds found that 6.0% developed depression in a six-month period, with 4.9% diagnosed as having major depression. Research also indicates that children and adolescents experience the onset of depression at earlier ages than previous generations, are more likely to experience recurrences, and are more likely to experience severe depression as adults.

The CDI is intended to be used by clinicians and counselors in order to detect and evaluate the symptoms of a major depressive disorder or dysthymic disorder in children or adolescents and to distinguish between children with those disorders and children with other psychiatric conditions. Such professionals also use it to support diagnoses and treatment planning. The CDI can be administered repeatedly in order to measure changes in the depression over time and to evaluate the results of treatment for depressive disorders. It is regarded as adequate for assessing the severity of the depressive symptoms.

The CDI has also been used in research studies of the epidemiology of depression in children as well as studies of dissociative symptoms and post-traumatic syndromes in children. It has been rated as having adequate to excellent psychometric properties by research psychologists.

Kovacs authored the CDI-2 as well. The CDI-2 measures affective, cognitive, and behavioral symptoms of depression in school-aged children and adolescents.

Description

CDI

The CDI is self-rated, which means that the children or adolescents being evaluated record their answers to the questions on the test sheet, as distinct from giving verbal answers to questions that are then analyzed and recorded by the examiner. The basic CDI takes approximately 15 minutes to complete, while the CDI-S (the short form) takes about five minutes. Other self-rated instruments for assessing depression in children are the **Beck Depression Inventory** (BDI) and the Weinberg Screening Affective Scale (WSAS).

The CDI was standardized with the help of 1,266 children from various U.S. public schools in Florida. In all, 592 males (from the ages of seven to 15 years) and 674 females (from the ages of seven to 16 years) participated in the standardization process from grade levels of two through eight. Approximately 77% of the participants were Caucasian-Americans, and about 23% were African Americans, American Indians, and Hispanics. In addition, most of the children were from middle-class socioeconomic backgrounds, and about 20% of them came from single-parent homes. The children were divided into two age groups (7–11 years, and 12–17 years) and separated by gender (sex).

The original CDI is divided into five subscales that measure different symptom groups of depression. These subscales are:

- negative mood (anger and/or irritability)
- interpersonal difficulties (problems making and keeping social relationships)
- negative self-esteem (feelings of inadequacy in performing normal daily activities)
- ineffectiveness (lack of or reduced motivation in completing tasks)
- anhedonia (absence or decreased presence of pleasure and joy)

Each question on the CDI consists of three possible responses; the children or adolescents being evaluated select the response that most closely describes themselves over the preceding two weeks. The CDI is designed to make quantitative measurements of the following symptoms of depression: mood disturbances; capacity for enjoyment; depressed self-evaluation; disturbances in behavior toward other people; and vegetative symptoms, which include **fatigue**, oversleeping, having difficulty with activities requiring effort, and other symptoms of passivity or inactivity. The CDI is designed to assess children at numerous locations such as schools, guidance clinics, physician offices, and psychiatric offices.

CDI-2

The age range for the revised test, CDI-2, is also seven to 17 years, with an administration time of 5–15 minutes. The CDI-2 is teacher-completed, parent-completed, or youth-completed. In addition, online, software, and paper-and-pencil versions are available, with the first two versions computer-scored and the last one hand-scored. All versions are scored using the Multi-Health Systems (MHS) QuikScore™ format. Within the paper-and-pencil version, the administrator writes an evaluation on external layers of the form, which is later transferred to a hidden grid within internal layers. The internal layers are used to tabulate the results. With the other two versions, Response/E-Paper forms are available.

The CDI-2 can be completed on the Web and can be scored there, too. Administrators are linked via the Internet to an organization sponsoring the test taker, and correspondence can be sent to a website requested by each recipient. Once the test is completed, the organization can download the score through an E-Paper form.

A software program can be acquired for use with the CDI-2. The test-taker first completes a paper-and-pencil version of the test, and then the responses are transferred onto the software program, which performs the scoring procedure.

The scales for the CDI-2 include: emotional problems and functional problems. Subscales include: negative mood, negative self-esteem, ineffectiveness, and interpersonal problems. Three reports are also available: the Assessment Report, the Progress Report, and the Comparative Report. The Assessment Report provides results from one administrator, whereas the Progress Report gives an overview of changes that have occurred over time from the administration of up to four administrators. The Comparative Report provides an overview of symptoms from the test-taker taken from the responses of up to five administrators.

The various inventory forms for reporting of the results from the CDI-2 include: the Self Report (which is a full-length version of the CDI-2), the Self Report (Short), the Teacher Report, and the Parent Report. Each assesses the presence and severity of depression and its symptoms. The full-length Self Report version is used when a more descriptive assessment is needed to determine depressive symptoms. It contains 28 items, and includes both scales and all four subscales. It normally takes less than 15 minutes to complete.

The short form Self Report contains only 12 items, takes about half the time to complete when compared to the full form, and takes 5–10 minutes to administer. It is used when less of an assessment is needed. Both forms of the Self Report require only a first-grade reading level. In addition, both have test-takers make a mark for each specific statement that best describes their feelings or behavior over the past two weeks.

The Teacher and Parents forms are comparable with the short form, but its instructions are altered for its specific administrator (teacher or parent). The strength of the results for both forms is that they maximize the administrator's ability to observe depressive symptoms. For the Parent form, the mother, father, or caregiver is asked to rate the child on factors relating to the environment around the home and with the family itself over the past two weeks. For the Teacher form, the child's teacher concentrates on the academic, emotional behavior, and social characteristics of the child while in the classroom over the previous two weeks. Both forms provide a Total Score and two scale scores: Emotional Problems and Functional Problems.

The CDI-2 was normalized from a sample of 1,100 children ranging from ages of seven to 17 years, who lived in 26 states in the United States (with a similar number of states in each of the four major geographical regions of the country). The sample size was evenly distributed according to age and gender. Fifty males and 50 females filled each of the 11 age categories. In addition, the U.S. census for 2000 was used to find a representative sample of people based on race and ethnicity. Data from 319 children diagnosed with **attention deficit hyperactivity disorder (ADHD)**, **conduct disorder** (CD), **generalized anxiety disorder** (GAD), major depressive disorder (MDD), or **oppositional defiant disorder** (ODD) were also included.

Preparation

Preparation for the CDI is neither necessary nor recommended by the medical community.

KEY TERMS

Attention deficit hyperactivity disorder—A condition involving hyperactivity in children, often causing the inability to concentrate and inappropriate or impulsive behaviors.

Conduct disorder—A psychiatric disorder characterized by a distinct pattern of repetitious behavior, which is considered abnormal in everyday society and often derogatory to others.

Depression—A psychiatric disorder involving feelings of hopelessness and symptoms of fatigue, sleeplessness, suicidal tendencies, and poor concentration.

Dysthymia—A form of depression with persistent symptoms such as fatigue, insomnia, loss of appetite, and problems with self-esteem, but considered not severe enough to be classified as a psychosis (psychiatric disorder involving loss of contact with reality).

Generalized anxiety disorder—An anxiety disorder characterized by daily irrational worry that is often also excessive and uncontrolled.

Oppositional defiant disorder—A psychiatric disorder characterized by an ongoing pattern of excessively hostile, angry, and disobedient behavior that is directed toward authority figures.

Aftercare

The Child Depression Inventory, both its original form and the revised form, is one way that the medical community can accurately identify depression in children and adolescents. Once depression is identified it is much easier to treat such patients.

Risks

The CDI and CDI-2 share certain drawbacks with other self-report measures used in children, namely that children do not have the same level of ability as adults to understand and report strong internal emotions. However, children have the same ability as adults to modify their answers on the CDI/CDI-2 and similar tests to reflect what they think are the desired answers rather than what they actually feel. This phenomenon is variously known as "faking good" or "faking bad," depending on the bias of the modified answers. Some researchers have also observed that children who do not have age-appropriate reading skills may receive an inaccurate diagnosis on the basis of their CDI/CDI-2 score.

QUESTIONS TO ASK YOUR DOCTOR

- How will the Children's Depression Inventory 2 help me solve my child's depression?
- How does the CDI-2 work?
- Is the CDI-2 able to diagnose severe or minor cases of depression?
- Will the results the CDI-2 help inform what treatment to use?
- What other tests are well suited to supplement this test?

Precautions

Because depressive symptoms fluctuate somewhat in children as well as in adults, the author of the test recommends retesting children who score positive on the CDI/CDI-2, with a two- to four-week interval between the test and the retest. A child who screens positive on the CDI/CDI-2 should receive a comprehensive diagnostic evaluation by a licensed mental health professional. The evaluation should include interviews with the child or adolescent; the parents or other caregivers; and, when possible, such other observers as teachers, social service personnel, or the child's primary care physician.

Results

For each item within the CDI, the administrator scores according to the following: 0 equals an absence of symptoms; 1 equals mild symptoms; and 2 equals definite symptoms. Scoring consists of a total score and five sub-scores, which are determined by age and gender. The total score has a minimum possible score of 0 and a maximum possible value of 54. The sub-scores are named: negative mood, interpersonal difficulties, negative self-esteem, ineffectiveness, and anhedonia. The test administrator totals the responses and plots them onto a profile form. A score that falls below a cutoff point, or is 1.0–2.0 standard deviations above the mean, is considered to be positive for depression. The administrator can use a QuickScore™ Form as a help in scoring.

The results of the CDI should be evaluated only by a trained professional **psychologist** or **psychiatrist**, and not by a parent, teacher, school nurse, or other such untrained persons.

Parental Concerns

The CDI and the CDI 2 are both short and easy assessment tests to administer. They can be administered to one child or many children. The CDI/CDI-2 test is considered to possess excellent psychometric properties; that is, it is able to accurately and reliably measure depression when administered by a trained professional. Many research studies have supported these conclusions in the assessment of depression in children and adolescents.

Resources

BOOKS

American Psychiatric Association. *Diagnostic and Statistical Manual of Mental Disorders.* 4th ed., Text rev. Washington, DC: American Psychiatric Association, 2000.

Beers, Mark H., et al. *The Merck Manual of Diagnosis and Therapy.* Whitehouse Station, NJ: Merck Research Laboratories, 2006.

Clark, David A., and Aaron T. Beck. *Cognitive Therapy of Anxiety Disorders: Science and Practice.* New York: Guilford Press, 2010.

Clark, David A., Aaron T. Beck, and Brad A. Alford. *Scientific Foundations of Cognitive Theory and Therapy of Depression.* New York: John Wiley & Sons, 2003.

Nezu, Arthur, George F. Ronan, and Elizabeth A. Meadows, eds. *Practitioner's Guide to Empirically Based Measures of Depression.* New York: Springer, 2006.

VandenBos, Gary R., ed. *APA Dictionary of Psychology.* Washington, DC: American Psychological Association, 2007.

WEBSITES

"Children's Depression Inventory (CDI)." Nova Southeastern University. http://www.cps.nova.edu/~cpphelp/CDI.html (accessed October 7, 2011).

"Children's Depression Inventory (CDI)." Pearson Assessments. http://psychcorp.pearsonassessments.com/haiweb/cultures/en-us/productdetail.htm?pid=015-8044-762&Community =CA_Psych_Settings_Military (accessed October 7, 2011).

"Children's Depression Inventory 2." Mental Health Systems (MHS). http://www.mhs.com/product.aspx?gr=edu&prod=cdi2&id=overview#top (accessed May 20, 2011).

"Children's Depression Inventory 2 (CDI-2)." Pearson. http://www.pearsonpsychcorp.com.au/productdetails/448 (accessed October 7, 2011).

"Children's Depression Inventory 2 (CDI-2)." Western Psychological Services. http://portal.wpspublish.com/portal/page?_ pageid=53,272957&_dad=portal&_schema=PORTAL (accessed October 7, 2011).

"Depression." National Institute of Mental Health. http://www.nimh.nih.gov/health/publications/depression/complete-index.shtml (accessed October 7, 2011).

"Newsmaker: Maria Kovacs." *Pittsburgh Tribune-Review,* July 16, 2010. http://www.pittsburghlive.com/x/pittsburghtrib/news/cityregion/s_690591.html (accessed May 20, 2011).

ORGANIZATIONS

American Academy of Child and Adolescent Psychiatry, 3615 Wisconsin Ave. NW, Washington, DC, 20016-3007, (202) 966-7300, Fax: (202) 966-2891, http://aacap.org.

American Psychiatric Association, 1000 Wilson Blvd., Ste. 1825, Arlington, VA, 22209-3901, (703) 907-7300, apa@psych.org, http://www.psych.org.

American Psychological Association, 750 1st St. NE, Washington, DC, 20002-4242, (202) 336-5500; TDD/TTY: (202) 336-6123, (800) 374-2721, http://www.apa.org.

Depression and Bipolar Support Alliance, 730 N Franklin St., Ste. 501, Chicago, IL, 60654, (800) 826-3632, Fax: (312) 642-7243, http://www.dbsalliance.org.

National Institute of Mental Health, 6001 Executive Blvd., Rm. 8184, MSC 9663, Bethesda, MD, 20892-9663, (301) 433-4513; TTY: (301) 443-8431, Fax: (301) 443-4279, (866) 615-6464; TTY: (866) 415-8051, nimhinfo@nih.gov, http://www.nimh.nih.gov.

Rebecca J. Frey, PhD
William A. Atkins

Chloral hydrate

Definition

Chloral hydrate is a drug used to help sedate persons before and after surgery, to help relieve anxiety or tension, and to promote sleep in individuals with **insomnia**. It is sold in the United States under the brand names Aquachloral, Aquachloral Supprettes, and Noctec, as well as its generic name. In the United States, chloral hydrate has largely been replaced by other medications.

Purpose

Chloral hydrate is considered a controlled substance in the United States and is only available with a prescription. Because of a potential for **addiction** with long-term use, chloral hydrate is given only occasionally to help sedate persons before and after surgery, primarily children. Historically, it has been used to treat insomnia and anxiety but has since been replaced by other drugs.

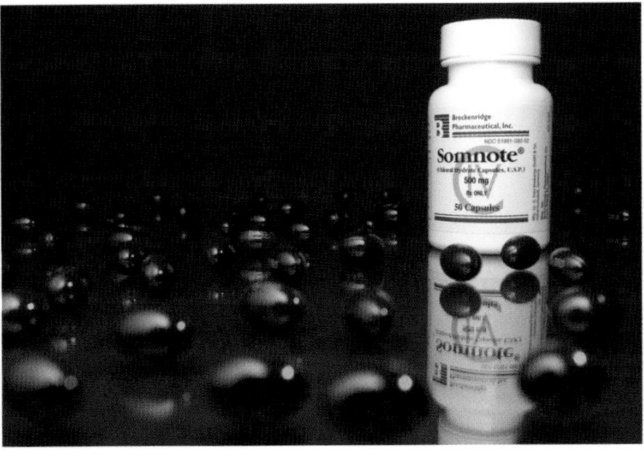

Somnote (chloral hydrate). *(© Bloomberg/Getty Images)*

Description

Chloral hydrate is classified as a sedative-hypnotic drug. The mechanism by which this drug works is not completely understood. It is believed that a chemical produced by chloral hydrate, called trichloroethanol, causes a mild depressive effect on the **brain**.

Recommended dosage

Chloral hydrate is available in oral and suppository forms. The oral form includes both capsules and syrup. Adults usually receive 500–1,000 mg taken 15–30 minutes before bedtime or surgery. These dosages are for hypnotic effects. For sedative effects, 250 mg is usually taken three times daily after meals. Total daily dosage should not be more than 2 g (2,000 mg). The hypnotic dose for children is usually 50 mg for every kilogram of body weight. The maximum amount per single dose is 1 g. Daily dosage is usually divided into several smaller doses and taken throughout the day. The sedative dose is typically one-half of the hypnotic dose. The syrup form should be combined with a half glass of fruit juice or water. The capsules should be taken with a full glass of water or juice to help prevent stomach upset.

The typical dose using suppositories is 500 to 1,000 mg at bedtime for adults to address trouble sleeping, and 325 mg three times a day for daytime sedation in adults. When given to children in preparation for a medical procedure, the dose is calculated based on body weight, usually at 50 mg per kilogram. If used to calm children before a nonsurgical procedure, such as **electroencephalography**, the dose is usually reduced to 25 mg per kilogram of body weight.

Precautions

Patients taking this drug for more than a few days should be monitored by a physician to ensure that significant side effects are not developing. Patients should not stop taking chloral hydrate suddenly. Instead, the dosage should be gradually decreased over time. Chloral hydrate should not be combined with other central nervous depressants, such as alcohol, antihistamines, and tranquilizers, as the effects will be increased.

Chloral hydrate should be used with great caution only where necessary in persons with a history of heart disease, severe kidney disease, or severe liver disease; people with gastrointestinal problems or porphyria; persons with a history of drug abuse; and in the elderly.

It should be used with caution in pregnant women and in women who are nursing. Chloral hydrate, like most drugs, can be taken in excess to the point of overdose. Signs of overdose include difficulty in swallowing, extreme weakness, confusion, **seizures**, extreme drowsiness, low body temperature, staggering, changes in heart rate, and breathing problems.

Side effects

Uncommon but serious side effects of chloral hydrate use include skin rash or hives, confusion, **hallucination**, and excessive excitement. The development of any of these side effects should be promptly reported to a doctor.

Less serious but more common side effects of chloral hydrate use include nausea, stomach pain, and vomiting. Other less common side effects include diarrhea, light-headedness, dizziness, drowsiness, and clumsiness.

Interactions

Because of additive depressant effects on the central nervous system, this drug should not be combined with alcohol. Likewise, chloral hydrate should not be combined with tricyclic **antidepressants** or with the blood-thinning drug warfarin (Coumadin). The prescribing physician should be made aware of any other drugs or medications the patient is taking to avoid complications.

Resources

BOOKS

Brunton, Laurence, Bruce Chabner, and Bjorn Knollman. *Goodman & Gilman's The Pharmacological Basis of Therapeutics*. 12th ed. New York: McGraw-Hill, 2010.

Consumer Reports and American Society of Health-System Pharmacists. *Consumer Reports Complete Drug Reference*. Yonkers, NY: Consumers Reports, 2009.

Ellsworth, Allan J., et al. *Mosby's Medical Drug Reference*. St. Louis, MO: Mosby, 2007.

Venes, Donald. *Taber's Cyclopedic Medical Dictionary*. 21st ed. Philadelphia: F.A. Davis Company, 2009.

WEBSITES

3-RX.com. "Chloral Hydrate." http://www.3-rx.com/drugs/detailed/chloral-hydrate/default.php (accessed October 1, 2011).

MedlinePlus. "Chloral Hydrate (Systemic)." U.S. National Library of Medicine. National Institutes of Health. http://www.nlm.nih.gov/medlineplus/druginfo/medmaster/a682201.html (accessed October 1, 2011).

Mark Mitchell, MD
Emily Jane Willingham, PhD

Chlordiazepoxide

Definition

Chlordiazepoxide is used to treat anxiety and also to control agitation brought on by alcohol withdrawal. It is a member of the benzodiazepine family of compounds, which slow the central nervous system to ease tension or nervousness. In the United States, it is sold under the trade names of Librium and Librax, and as Limbitrol when in combination with another drug, **amitriptyline**.

Purpose

Chlordiazepoxide is used for the short-term relief of symptoms of anxiety and the management of **anxiety disorders**. It is also used for treating symptoms of withdrawal from acute alcoholism and alcoholic intoxication. When combined with amitriptyline, it is used to treat **depression** that accompanies anxiety or tension.

Description

Chlordiazepoxide is useful when treating anxiety for short periods of time. It has sedative properties that are effective for these brief periods of use. In addition, it is occasionally used to stimulate appetites and is a weak analgesic. Its precise mechanism of action is unknown, and several hours are needed for peak levels of the drug to be achieved. Chlordiazepoxide is available in 5, 10, and 25 mg capsules.

Recommended dosage

The recommended dosage varies with **diagnosis**. The lowest possible dosage that provides relief from symptoms should be used as the drug has a high potential for causing physiological and psychological dependence. When used in adults for the treatment of moderate anxiety, the usual oral dosage is 5–10 mg three or four

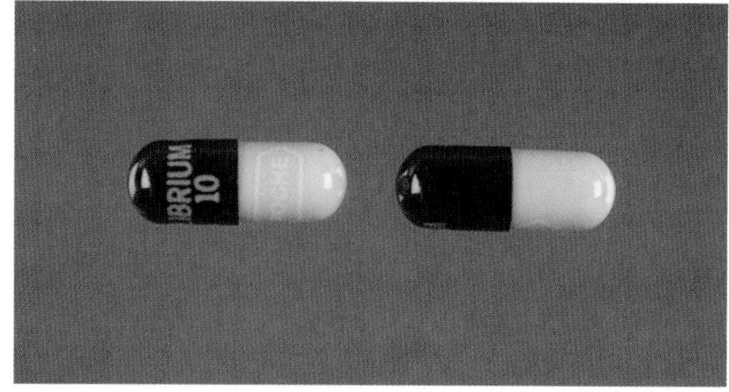

Librium (chlordiazepoxide), 10 mg. *(U.S. Drug Enforcement Administration)*

KEY TERMS

Anterograde amnesia—The inability to form new memories.

Anxiety—An emotion that can be experienced as a troubled feeling, sense of dread, fear of the future, or distress over a possible threat to a person's physical or mental well-being.

Depression—A mental state characterized by feelings of sadness, despair, discouragement, and low energy, sometimes accompanied by over-sleeping and/or overeating.

times per day. When used for the treatment of more severe anxiety and anxiety disorders, the usual oral dosage is 20–25 mg three or four times per day. When used by older persons, or to relieve symptoms of preoperative apprehension or anxiety, the usual oral dosage is 5 mg two to four times per day. If used as a preoperative medication, the usual dosage is 50–100 mg via intramuscular (IM) injection. When used to treat symptoms of acute alcoholism, the usual initial oral dosage is 50–100 mg, repeated as needed until agitation is adequately controlled. The recommended maximum dosage is 300 mg per day. The usual dosage for children is 5 mg two to four times per day.

Precautions

Persons with suicidal tendencies should be closely monitored, as chlordiazepoxide may lower the threshold for action in attempting **suicide**. Children and adolescents up to 24 years of age are especially at risk when taking the chlordiazepoxide/amitriptyline combination, as are individuals with a history or family history of **bipolar disorder**. The drug has a high potential for causing physiological or psychological dependence.

Benzodiazepines, including chlordiazepoxide, carry the risk of inducing anterograde **amnesia** (the loss of the ability to make new memories). Chlordiazepoxide is slow to metabolize and is not generally advised for use in the elderly, as the slow elimination rate can lead to accumulation in the body, producing prolonged effects. This is especially dangerous to elderly patients, who are at risk for falls.

In the early 2000s, there were cases in which pills originating overseas but sold over the counter in the United States contained chlordiazepoxide. A case from 2001 involved ingredients shipped from Asia for pill manufacture in California, and another case from 2006 involved pills from Brazil. Both resulted in warnings to consumers by the U.S. Food and Drug Administration (FDA). In the case involving Brazil, the products—marketed as dietary/weight loss supplements under the names Emagrece Sim and Herbathin—were available for sale over the Internet and imported and distributed by a Florida company. Because of the serious possibility of interactions with medication and vitamins and the lack of quality control, taking these pills was considered dangerous. The FDA advised consumers who had these products to return them to the distributor.

Side effects

Other than physiological and psychological dependence, few adverse effects have been reported. The most commonly reported include drowsiness, confusion, and movement difficulties. These are most common among older persons. Occasionally, transient loss of consciousness has been reported.

Other adverse effects include:

- edema (abnormal accumulation of fluid in bodily tissues)
- minor menstrual irregularities
- nausea
- constipation
- changes in libido (sex drive)

Also, chlordiazepoxide may impair mental or physical skills needed to perform complex motor tasks. For this reason, persons using this drug are advised not to drive automobiles or operate machinery.

This drug is known to increase the risk of birth defects in the fetus when taken by a woman during the first three months of pregnancy, and it also can cause dependency in the developing baby that can result in withdrawal symptoms following birth. Chlordiazepoxide passes into the breast milk and can cause breathing trouble and slow heartbeat in babies.

Interactions

Chlordiazepoxide may increase the effect of alcohol or other substances that depress central nervous system functions. For this reason, they should not be used at the same time. A small number of reports of interaction with oral anticoagulants have been received, and it may exacerbate porphyria, which is a group of inherited disorders in which there is abnormally increased production of substances called porphyrins. Any medications, prescribed or over the counter, should be brought to the attention of a doctor or pharmacist by individuals considering taking chlordiazepoxide.

QUESTIONS TO ASK YOUR DOCTOR

- What kind of changes can I expect to see or feel with this medication?
- Does it matter what time of day I take this medication? If so, what is the recommendation?
- Should I take this medication with or without food?
- What are the side effects associated with this medication?
- Will this medication interact or interfere with other medications I am currently taking?
- What symptoms or adverse effects are important enough that I should seek immediate treatment?

Resources

BOOKS

Albers, Lawrence J., Rhoda K. Hahn, and Christopher Reist. *Handbook of Psychiatric Drugs.* Laguna Hills, CA: Current Clinical Strategies, 2010.

American Society of Health-System Pharmacists. *AHFS Drug Information 2011.* Bethesda, MD: ASHP, 2011.

Graham, George. *The Disordered Mind: An Introduction to Philosophy of Mind and Mental Illness.* New York: Routledge, 2010.

Holland, Leland Norman, and Michael Patrick Adams. *Core Concepts in Pharmacology.* 3rd ed. New York: Prentice Hall, 2011.

North, Carol, and Sean Yutzy. *Goodwin and Guze's Psychiatric Diagnosis.* New York: Oxford University Press, 2010.

Preston, John D., John H. O'Neal, and Mary C. Talaga. *Handbook of Clinical Psychopharmacology for Therapists.* 6th ed. Oakland, CA: New Harbinger, 2010.

PERIODICALS

Alexopoulou A., A. Michael, and S.P. Dourakis. "Acute Thrombocytopenic Purpura in a Patient Treated with Chlordiazepoxide and Clidinium." *Archives of Internal Medicine* 161, no. 14 (2001): 1778–79.

ORGANIZATIONS

American Academy of Clinical Toxicology, 6728 Old McLean Village Dr., McLean, VA, 22101, (703) 556-9222, Fax: (703) 556-8729, admin@clintox.org, http://www.clintox.org.

American Academy of Family Physicians, 11400 Tomahawk Creek Pkwy., Leawood, KS, 66211-2672, (913) 906-6000, (800) 274-2237, Fax: (913) 906-6075, contactcenter@aafp.org, http://www.aafp.org.

American Medical Association, 515 N State St., Chicago, IL, 60610, (312) 464-5000, (800) 621-8335, http://www.ama-assn.org.

American Psychiatric Association, 1000 Wilson Blvd., Ste. 1825, Arlington, VA, 22209-3901, (703) 907-7300, apa@psych.org, http://www.psych.org.

American Society for Clinical Pharmacology and Therapeutics, 528 N Washington St., Alexandria, VA, 22314, (703) 836-6981, info@ascpt.org, http://www.ascpt.org.

Anxiety Disorders Association of America, 8730 Georgia Ave., Silver Spring, MD, 20910, (240) 485-1001, Fax: (240) 485-1035, http://www.adaa.org.

Mental Health America, 2000 N. Beauregard St., 6th Fl., Alexandria, VA, 22311, (703) 684-7722, (800) 969-6642, Fax: (703) 684-5968, http://www1.nmha.org.

National Alliance on Mental Illness, 2107 Wilson Blvd., Ste. 300, Arlington, VA, 22201-3042, Fax: (703) 524-9094, (800) 950-6264, http://www.nami.org.

National Institute of Mental Health, 6001 Executive Blvd., Rm. 8184, MSC 9663, Bethesda, MD, 20892-9663, (301) 433-4513; TTY: (301) 443-8431, Fax: (301) 443-4279, (866) 615-6464; TTY: (866) 415-8051, nimhinfo@nih.gov, http://www.nimh.nih.gov.

L. Fleming Fallon, Jr., MD, DrPH
Emily Jane Willingham, PhD
Laura Jean Cataldo, RN, EdD

Chlorpromazine

Definition

Chlorpromazine is an antipsychotic drug. It is a member of the phenothiazine family of compounds and is used to alleviate the symptoms and signs of **psychosis**. Psychosis is a form of severe mental illness characterized by hallucinations, **delusions**, agitation, unusual behavior, and loss of contact with reality. In the United States,

Chlorpromazine, 50 mg. *(© Custom Medical Stock Photo, Inc. Reproduced by permission.)*

HEINZ EDGAR LEHMANN (1911–1999)

Heinz Edgar Lehmann was a German-born Canadian psychiatrist best known for his use of chlorpromazine for the treatment of schizophrenia in the 1950s. Born in Berlin, Germany, he was educated at the University of Freiburg, the University of Marburg, the University of Vienna, and the University of Berlin. He emigrated to Canada in 1937. In 1947, he was appointed clinical director of Montreal's Douglas Hospital. From 1971 to 1975, he was the chairman of the McGill University Department of Psychiatry. In 1976, he was made an Officer of the Order of Canada. In 1970, he was made a fellow of the Royal Society of Canada. He was inducted into the Canadian Medical Hall of Fame in 1998. In 1999, the Canadian College of Neuropsychopharmacology established the Heinz Lehmann award in his honor, given in recognition of outstanding contributions to research in neuropsychopharmacology in Canada.

chlorpromazine is also sold under the brand name Thorazine.

Purpose

Chlorpromazine is principally used to reduce the signs and symptoms of psychosis. For this purpose, the drug is used in **schizophrenia** and the manic phase of bipolar (formerly manic-depressive) disorder. The drug is also used in the management of severe behavioral disorders with aggression, combativeness, or excessive excitability. Chlorpromazine may sometimes be used as a sedative in nonpsychotic patients with excessive anxiety and agitation. In addition, the drug has been used to relieve nausea, vomiting, and persistent hiccups.

Description

Chlorpromazine was the first antipsychotic drug. It is not an exaggeration to say that the development of this medication began a revolution in the treatment of severe mental illness, which continues in the twenty-first century. Patients with schizophrenia and other psychoses, who once would have been considered hopelessly untreatable and relegated to the back wards of state institutions, are often able, as a result of treatment with chlorpromazine or similar medications, to live in the community and lead fuller lives.

The discovery of chlorpromazine resulted from efforts of pharmaceutical researchers in the first half of the twentieth century to develop sedative medications. Several drugs of a chemical class known as phenothiazines were investigated and shown to be effective **sedatives**, but they had little effect on agitated patients with psychosis. A new phenothiazine drug, chlorpromazine, was synthesized in France in 1950 and was tested on such patients. In 1952, two French psychiatrists, Jean Delay and Pierre Deniker, announced that the drug exerted a specific effect in diminishing the symptoms and signs of psychosis in patients with severe mental illnesses.

The mechanism of action of chlorpromazine occurs primarily through its interactions with proteins on the cells that take messages from **dopamine**, a nerve signaling molecule, and send them to other cells.

Chlorpromazine, when sold under the name Thorazine, is available in many forms: tablets of 10, 25, 50, 100, and 200 mg; spansules (sustained release capsules) of 30, 75, and 150 mg; ampules for injection of 25 and 50 mg; a multidose vial of 10 mL of 25 mg/mL; syrup 10mg/5mL, 4 fl oz.; and suppositories of 25 and 100 mg. Generic chlorpromazine manufacturers may supply a somewhat different set of dosages and products.

Recommended dosage

For acutely disturbed adult patients diagnosed with a psychosis, such as schizophrenia or mania, the usual daily dosage ranges from 100 mg to 1,000 mg per day. Some patients may require a higher dosage. There is great variation in individual dosage requirements for chlorpromazine and for other antipsychotic medications. It is usually advisable to begin with a lower dosage and increase the dosage until sufficient reduction of symptoms is achieved. Maximum reduction of symptoms may take many weeks of continued treatment. Because of the possibility of side effects, which may be severe, lower dosages should be used in outpatients, children, the elderly, and patients with serious health problems. For nonpsychotic patients with excessive anxiety or agitation, amounts used are generally less than 200 mg per day, divided into two or three doses.

Precautions

Elderly patients (those over age 65), especially women, and patients receiving long-term antipsychotic treatment are prone to develop **tardive dyskinesia**. This syndrome consists of involuntary, uncoordinated movements that may not disappear or may only partially improve after the drug is stopped. Tardive dyskinesia involves involuntary movements of the tongue, jaw,

KEY TERMS

Anxiety—An emotion that can be experienced as a troubled feeling, sense of dread, fear of the future, or distress over a possible threat to a person's physical or mental well-being.

Bipolar disorder—A mood disorder marked by alternating episodes of extremely low mood (depression) and exuberant highs (mania), also known as manic-depressive disorder.

Delusions—Irrational beliefs that defy normal reasoning and remain firm even when overwhelming proof is presented to dispute them. Delusions are distinct from culturally or religiously based beliefs that may be seen as untrue by outsiders.

Epilepsy—A disorder associated with disturbed electrical discharges in the central nervous system that cause seizures.

Extrapyramidal symptoms—A group of side effects associated with antipsychotic medications and characterized by involuntary muscle movements, including contraction and tremor.

Schizophrenia—A major mental illness marked by psychotic symptoms, including hallucinations, delusions, and severe disruptions in thinking.

Seizure—A convulsion, or uncontrolled discharge of nerve cells that may spread to other cells throughout the brain.

mouth, or face or other groups of skeletal muscles and may also appear after chlorpromazine use has stopped. There is no known effective treatment for tardive dyskinesia, although gradual (but rarely complete) improvement may occur over a long period. The need for long-term antipsychotic medication should be weighed against the risk of developing tardive dyskinesia, which increases with duration of treatment.

Neuroleptic malignant syndrome (NMS), a dangerous condition with high fever, muscular rigidity, rapid pulse, sweating, and altered mental state, may occur with antipsychotic medication. NMS requires immediate medical treatment.

Phenothiazine drugs, such as chlorpromazine, may cause sedation and may interfere with driving and other tasks requiring alertness. They may increase the effects of alcohol and sedatives. The adverse effects of chlorpromazine may be increased in people with diseases of the heart, liver, or kidney, or other debilitating illnesses. Phenothiazines may lower the seizure threshold, making it more likely that a seizure will occur in people who have a history of **seizures**. People with epilepsy may require adjustment of their antiseizure medications. Chlorpromazine may cause acute muscle spasms, particularly of the head and neck, and sudden decreases of blood pressure. Patients may need to be hospitalized during the initial phase of treatment, particularly when receiving high doses or treatment by injection.

Chlorpromazine reduces the body's ability to sweat, thus interfering with the regulation of body temperature. This may be a problem for some people in very hot weather. The problem most commonly occurs in elderly people in hot buildings without air conditioning. Body temperature may reach fatal levels. People taking chlorpromazine should be aware of the possibility of developing hyperthermia (high body temperature) in very hot weather. They should seek cool places in hot weather.

Children may be especially susceptible to neurologic reactions to phenothiazines, such as muscle spasms. Elderly patients may be particularly sensitive to sedation, low blood pressure, and other side effects. These patients should start with lower doses and increase their dosage gradually under physician supervision. Chlorpromazine may decrease salivation in older patients, predisposing them to tooth decay, gum disease, and mouth infections. Candy and other sugary foods should be limited, and oral hygiene should be maintained.

Chlorpromazine, like all phenothiazines, should not be taken by pregnant women because these drugs harm the developing fetus. Babies born to mothers who took chlorpromazine during pregnancy may develop extrapyramidal symptoms (EPS) and withdrawal symptoms, including agitation, trouble breathing, and difficulty feeding. Breastfeeding is not recommended while a woman is taking the drug. Phenothiazines are secreted in breast milk and may cause harm to nursing infants.

Chlorpromazine is associated with an increased risk of death when used in elderly patients with **dementia**. In June 2008, the U.S. Food and Drug Administration (FDA) announced a requirement for manufacturers of chlorpromazine (and other antipsychotic drugs) to add a warning label to their packaging stating this risk. The reason for the increase was unclear in studies, but most deaths were found to be related either to cardiovascular complications or complications associated with infection. Chlorpromazine is not approved by the FDA for the treatment of behavior problems in older adults with dementia, and patients in this category (or caregivers of patients in this category) should discuss the risks of taking chlorpromazine with their physician.

Chlorpromazine also carries the risk of potentially fatal heart arrhythmias.

QUESTIONS TO ASK YOUR DOCTOR

- What kind of changes can I expect to see or feel with this medication?
- Does it matter what time of day I take this medication? If so, what is the recommendation?
- Should I take this medication with or without food?
- What are the side effects associated with this medication?
- Will this medication interact or interfere with other medications I am currently taking?
- What symptoms or adverse effects are important enough that I should seek immediate treatment?

Side effects

Chlorpromazine and other phenothiazines may cause many side effects. The following more common side effects are grouped by the body system affected:

- cardiovascular: decreases of blood pressure, especially on arising, which may cause dizziness or fainting; rapid heart rate and changes in heart rhythm and electrocardiogram
- nervous system: sedation, muscle spasms of the head and neck, muscle rigidity, restlessness, tremors, slowed movement, shuffling gait, increased seizure tendency
- digestive system: dry mouth, nausea, constipation, abnormal liver tests
- autonomic: blurred vision, nasal congestion, reduced sweating, difficulty urinating, problems with ejaculation, impotence
- hormonal: lactation, breast enlargement
- skin: rashes, sensitivity to sunlight
- body as a whole: weight gain

Interactions

Chlorpromazine interacts with a long list of other medications. Individuals who are starting this drug should review the other medications they are taking with their physician and pharmacist for possible interactions. Chlorpromazine and other phenothiazines may intensify the effects of drugs causing sedation, including alcohol, **barbiturates**, narcotic pain medications, minor tranquilizers, and antihistamines. Similarly, chlorpromazine may cause excessive reductions of blood pressure in patients taking other medicines that lower blood pressure. Chlorpromazine may also intensify side effects of drugs that cause blurred vision, dry mouth, diminished sweating in hot weather, and constipation. Many other antipsychotics and **antidepressants** cause such effects.

Chlorpromazine may enhance the effects of medications that lower the seizure threshold, such as steroid drugs, the asthma medication theophylline, and many other psychiatric drugs. Patients with epilepsy may require dosage adjustments of their antiseizure medications. The effectiveness of medications for Parkinson's disease may be reduced by chlorpromazine and other antipsychotics. The likelihood of changes in heart rhythm may be increased when the drug is taken with other medications that have the same effect, including other antipsychotic drugs, antidepressants, certain heart medicines, and erythromycin.

Certain drugs that are eliminated by the liver may interfere with the elimination of chlorpromazine from the body, causing higher blood levels and increased side effects. Chlorpromazine may delay the elimination of other medicines, including many antidepressants, antipsychotic drugs, and heart medications, resulting in higher levels of these other medications and possibly increased side effects.

Resources

BOOKS

Albers, Lawrence J., Rhoda K. Hahn, and Christopher Reist. *Handbook of Psychiatric Drugs.* Laguna Hills, CA: Current Clinical Strategies, 2010.

American Society of Health-System Pharmacists. *AHFS Drug Information 2011.* Bethesda, MD: ASHP, 2011.

Graham, George. *The Disordered Mind: An Introduction to Philosophy of Mind and Mental Illness.* New York: Routledge, 2010.

Holland, Leland Norman, and Michael Patrick Adams. *Core Concepts in Pharmacology.* 3rd ed. New York: Prentice Hall, 2011.

Miklowitz, David J. *Bipolar Disorder: A Family-Focused Treatment Approach.* 2nd ed. New York: Guilford Press, 2010.

North, Carol, and Sean Yutzy. *Goodwin and Guze's Psychiatric Diagnosis.* New York: Oxford University Press, 2010.

Preston, John D., John H. O'Neal, and Mary C. Talaga. *Handbook of Clinical Psychopharmacology for Therapists.* 6th ed. Oakland, CA: New Harbinger, 2010.

PERIODICALS

Rosenbloom, Michael. "Chlorpromazine and the Psychopharmacologic Revolution." *Journal of the American Medical Association* 287 (2002): 1860–61. Available online at http://jama.ama-assn.org/cgi/content/full/287/14/1860 (accessed August 25, 2011).

ORGANIZATIONS

American Academy of Clinical Toxicology, 6728 Old McLean Village Dr., McLean, VA, 22101, (703) 556-9222, Fax: (703) 556-8729, admin@clintox.org, http://www.clintox.org.

American Academy of Family Physicians, 11400 Tomahawk Creek Pkwy., Leawood, KS, 66211-2672, (913) 906-6000, (800) 274-2237, Fax: (913) 906-6075, contactcenter@aafp.org, http://www.aafp.org.

American Medical Association, 515 N State St., Chicago, IL, 60610, (312) 464-5000, (800) 621-8335, http://www.ama-assn.org.

American Psychiatric Association, 1000 Wilson Blvd., Ste. 1825, Arlington, VA, 22209-3901, (703) 907-7300, apa@psych.org, http://www.psych.org.

American Psychological Association, 750 1st St., NE, Washington, DC, 20002-4242, (202) 336-5500; TDD/TTY: (202) 336-6123, (800) 374-2721, http://www.apa.org.

American Society for Clinical Pharmacology and Therapeutics, 528 N Washington St., Alexandria, VA, 22314, (703) 836-6981, info@ascpt.org, http://www.ascpt.org.

Anxiety Disorders Association of America, 8730 Georgia Ave., Silver Spring, MD, 20910, (240) 485-1001, Fax: (240) 485-1035, http://www.adaa.org.

Depression and Bipolar Support Alliance, 730 N Franklin St., Ste. 501, Chicago, IL, 60654, (800) 826-3632, Fax: (312) 642-7243, http://www.dbsalliance.org.

Mental Health America, 2000 N Beauregard St., 6th Fl., Alexandria, VA, 22311, (703) 684-7722, (800) 969-6642, Fax: (703) 684-5968, http://www1.nmha.org.

National Alliance on Mental Illness, 2107 Wilson Blvd., Ste. 300, Arlington, VA, 22201-3042, Fax: (703) 524-9094, (800) 950-6264, http://www.nami.org.

National Institute of Mental Health, 6001 Executive Blvd., Rm. 8184, MSC 9663, Bethesda, MD, 20892-9663, (301) 433-4513; TTY: (301) 443-8431, Fax: (301) 443-4279, (866) 615-6464; TTY: (866) 415-8051, nimhinfo@nih.gov, http://www.nimh.nih.gov.

U.S. National Library of Medicine, 8600 Rockville Pike, Bethesda, MD, 20894, (301) 594-5983, (888) 346-3656; TDD: (800) 735-2258, Fax: (301) 402-1384, http://www.nlm.nih.gov.

Richard Kapit, MD
Ruth A. Wienclaw, PhD
Laura Jean Cataldo, RN, EdD

Chronic motor or vocal tic disorder *see* **Tic disorders**

Chronic pain *see* **Pain disorder**

Cigarettes *see* **Nicotine and related disorders**

Circadian rhythm sleep disorder

Definition

Circadian rhythm sleep disorder (CRSD) is any of several persistent or recurring patterns of sleep disruption that result from an altered circadian rhythm or sleep-wake cycle. CRSD leads to **insomnia** or excessive sleepiness during waking hours, resulting in impaired functioning.

Demographics

More than 70 million Americans are estimated to have some form of sleep disorder. Among CRSDs, delayed sleep phase usually begins during adolescence, affecting up to 7% of teens. Without treatment, delayed sleep phase may continue and is believed to affect up to 4% of adults. Jet-lag and shift-work CRSDs usually cause the most severe symptoms in late-middle-aged and elderly people. An estimated 14% of Americans perform shift work and up to 60% of night-shift workers have CRSD. Non-24-hour sleep-wake syndrome is probably the rarest CRSD, most often affecting people who are totally blind.

Description

There are more than 80 recognized **sleep disorders**, usually classified into seven primary groups, including CRSD, insomnia, sleep-related breathing problems, and **hypersomnia**. CRSD is a dyssomnia (having irregularities in the quality, timing, and amount of sleep) caused by alterations in circadian rhythms or a mismatch between natural circadian rhythms and external signals or demands.

Circadian rhythms are physiological, mental, and behavioral changes that occur over a period of approximately 24 hours. "Circadian" is Latin for "around a day." Most circadian rhythms are controlled by the body's master biological clock, the suprachiasmatic nucleus (SCN), located in the hypothalamus of the **brain**. Light hitting the retina of the eye sends signals through the optic nerve to the SCN. In response to light, the SCN signals the pineal gland to stop producing the hormone melatonin. After dark, melatonin levels rise and cause drowsiness. The SCN synchronizes other bodily functions, such as temperature, hormone secretion, urine production, and blood pressure, with the sleep-wake cycle. Although most people actually have a 25-hour biological clock, sunlight or other bright light normally resets the SCN to follow the sun's 24-hour cycle. To some extent, circadian rhythms can also be affected by external time cues, such as an alarm clock or meals.

Although classifications of CRSDs vary, the major types are:

- delayed sleep phase
- jet lag
- shift-work-induced
- non-24-hour sleep-wake syndrome
- medical-condition-induced
- drug- or substance-induced
- other unspecified

CRSDs cause insomnia and/or excessive drowsiness and interfere with occupational, social, and other functioning. Shift-work CRSD is of particular concern because workplace accidents tend to increase in number and severity during the night shift. Mistakes by fatigued night-shift workers can contribute to medical errors and to major industrial accidents.

The ***Diagnostic and Statistical Manual of Mental Disorders***, a handbook used by mental health professionals to diagnose mental disorders, defines circadian rhythm sleep disorder as one of several primary sleep-wake disorders.

Risk factors

Stress is a risk factor for various types of CRSD. CRSD also is common in people with **dementia**, who often sleep erratically and in snatches. Delayed sleep phase sometimes runs in families. Risk factors for jet lag include frequent flying, crossing multiple time zones, and flying east, thereby "losing" time. Night-shift workers, especially those who switch to a normal sleep schedule on days off and those who work rotating shifts, are especially at risk for CSRD. Having a more erratic biological clock may be a risk factor for substance-induced CRSD.

Causes and symptoms

Sometimes the cause of a CRSD is apparent, as with jet lag, shift work, and non-24-hour sleep-wake syndrome in the blind. In other cases the cause of CRSD is less obvious. Delayed sleep phase is often caused by stress. Various medical conditions can cause CRSD. Dementia can weaken circadian rhythms. Liver disease can also cause delayed sleep phase due to toxin buildup in the blood.

Many drugs and other substances, including alcohol, can cause CRSD. Some drugs cause early sleep, resulting in earlier awakening and an advanced sleep rhythm. The same medication may cause sleepiness in one person and insomnia in another. Herbs; vitamins and minerals; supplements such as tryptophan; antihistamines; allergy, cold, and flu remedies; sleeping pills; muscle relaxants; pain medications; some **antidepressants**; antianxiety and antipsychotic medications; drugs for Parkinson's disease: seizure medications; blood pressure, cholesterol, and heart medications; and chemotherapy can all cause drug-induced CRSD. Caffeine can cause delayed sleep phase or an irregular sleep-wake rhythm. Other stimulants, weight-control medications, **steroids**, and some asthma medications also can cause delayed sleep phase.

Symptoms of CRSD take different forms:

- Delayed sleep phase disorder causes falling asleep late, such as in the early morning, and awakening late, a cycle that is very difficult to change.
- Advanced sleep phase disorder causes falling asleep early and awakening early each day.
- Irregular sleep-wake rhythm is characterized by sleeping off and on over a 24-hour period.
- Jet lag can involve insomnia, daytime fatigue or sleepiness, early waking, general malaise, and various other symptoms. It occurs within one or two days of crossing at least two time zones, especially when traveling in an easterly direction.

KEY TERMS

Chronotherapy—A sleep disorder treatment that involves adjusting sleep and wake times to reset one's biological clock.

Circadian rhythm—An approximately 24-hour cycle of physiological and behavioral activity.

Dementia—A group of symptoms (syndrome) associated with chronic progressive impairment of memory, reasoning ability, and other intellectual functions; personality changes; deterioration in personal grooming; and disorientation.

Dyssomnia—Irregularities in the timing, length, and quality of sleep.

Insomnia—Prolonged or abnormal inability to obtain adequate sleep.

Melatonin—A hormone involved in regulation of the sleep-wake cycle and other circadian rhythms.

Pineal gland—A small endocrine gland in the brain that produces melatonin.

Sleep hygiene—Beneficial behavior and environmental choices that precede sleep and tend to help produce a good night's sleep.

Suprachiasmatic nucleus (SCN)—A pair of nerve clusters in the hypothalamus in the brain that receives light input from the retina via the optic nerve and regulates circadian rhythms.

- Shift workers are more likely to experience both insomnia and daytime sleepiness. They may have impaired performance, relationship problems, irritability, and depression, and are at increased risk for heart, digestive, mental, and emotional problems. They have almost twice the risk of falling asleep while driving.
- Free-running (non-entrained) CRSD is a non-24-hour sleep-wake syndrome, in which sleep occurs somewhat later each day. Blind people whose retinas cannot detect light often have lifelong CRSD, since their circadian rhythms follow their innate 25-hour clock, pushing sleep and wake times further back each day.
- Unspecified CRSD can cause daytime and evening sleepiness or insomnia. People with irregular sleep patterns have difficulty knowing when they will fall asleep and wake up.

Diagnosis

A **diagnosis** of CRSD requires that the sleep disturbance not be related to normal adjustments in response to a schedule change. It also must be persistent or recurring and result in family, social, or occupational problems.

Examination

The physician will perform a physical exam, including a neurological exam, and take a medical history, including past and present drug, alcohol, and medication use. Patients usually keep a sleep diary of their sleep and wake-up times for a period of several weeks, as well as the timing of any medications or other substances they take. They may use the Epworth Sleepiness Scale to rate their sleep. Patients with constant jet lag or other serious CRSDs may choose to consult a sleep specialist.

Tests

Blood tests may be performed if the physician suspects a neurological condition or other medical problem. Drug tests may be performed if substance-induced CRSD is suspected. Body temperature and melatonin levels may be measured.

Procedures

Computed tomography (CT) scans or **magnetic resonance imaging** (MRI) may be performed to detect medical conditions underlying CRSD. Some patients wear an actigraph on their wrists for one to two weeks. This device records active and inactive periods throughout the 24-hour day. In severe cases, patients may undergo direct observation in a sleep lab. However, overnight sleep studies are not usually required to diagnose CRSD unless the patient is at risk for another sleep disorder. A polysomnogram charts brain waves, heart beat, muscle activity, breathing, and arm and leg movements during sleep in the laboratory.

Treatment

Various treatments are used for DRSD, chosen in light of the specific causes of the problem.

Traditional

Treatment of CRSD depends on the type and cause. Education about good sleep hygiene and behavior counseling can be helpful. Mild cases of delayed sleep phase often resolve simply by following strict sleep and wake times. More severe cases may require incremental changes, for example, going to sleep 15–30 minutes earlier each day until an appropriate pattern is achieved. Sometimes a night of **sleep deprivation** is prescribed to reset the biological clock. Chronotherapy may include delaying sleep for three hours each night until the sleep-wake cycle has rotated around the clock. Drug-induced CRSD may involve changing or stopping a medication. Detailed sleep logs are often used to monitor progress during treatment.

Drugs

Melatonin is often used to treat jet lag and other CRSDs. Timing of the medication depends on symptoms, but generally melatonin is taken 20–60 minutes before the desired sleep time. Although some studies have found higher doses to be better at promoting sleep, doses as small as 0.5 mg may be as effective as doses of 5 mg or more. Tasimelteon, which acts like melatonin, is also used to treat CRSD. Other drugs for preventing or treating jet lag and other CRSDs include nonbenzodiazepines—such as **zolpidem** (Ambien), eszopiclone (Lunesta), and **zaleplon** (Sonata)—and **benzodiazepines**, such as **triazolam** (Halcion).

Alternative

Melatonin is available as a nutritional supplement for jet lag, shift work, and delayed sleep phase, and to improve night-time sleep in the blind. However, most melatonin supplements are high-dosage, and melatonin can build up in the body with unknown effects. Therefore, most experts discourage non-medically supervised use of melatonin supplements.

There are various other alternative treatments for jet lag. Although some frequent fliers use **aromatherapy** or homeopathy, **light therapy**, which involves exposing the eyes to light for a specific amount of time, is especially useful for jet-lagged travelers who are indoors out of the sunlight in a different time zone. There are various types of light therapy, including an artificial bright light, a light box or desk lamp, a full-spectrum lamp that simulates sunlight, or a light visor worn on the head. A dawn simulator that gradually brightens to simulate sunrise can help with waking up. Exposure to a special, very bright light close to the desired wake-up time can help reset the biological clock to a new time zone.

Home remedies

Sunlight is the best way to reset one's biological clock and maintain a regular sleep-wake cycle. Online jet-lag calculators can help determine the best time for light exposure. For example, after flying from New York to Paris, travelers are advised to obtain light exposure between 11:20 A.M. and 2 P.M. on the first day and between 8:20 A.M. and 11 A.M. on the second day. Light should be avoided between 9 A.M. and 11:20 A.M. on the first day and between 6 A.M. and 8:20 A.M. on the second day. A sleep mask or sleeping with the blinds or drapes closed can help. Dark glasses can block out light during the day. By the third or fourth day, one's biological clock should be reset to local time, especially if combined with **exercise** such as walking or jogging. Caffeine can help counter daytime sleepiness but can also make it more difficult to sleep if consumed within six hours of bedtime. If staying for a week or more in the new time zone, travelers should sleep during appropriate times for that zone.

Jet-lag **diets** are effective for some people. These often involve alternating days of feasting and fasting and high-protein and low-protein meals. Eating more high-protein foods during waking hours and more carbohydrates before sleep may also be effective.

Shift workers benefit the most from a regular work schedule. If schedule rotations cannot be avoided, it is preferable to rotate forward, with shifts becoming progressively later. Sleeping environments should be free of daytime light and noise.

Prognosis

Patients with delayed sleep phase often have great difficulty changing their sleep patterns or maintaining a preferred pattern. Jet-lag and shift-work symptoms disappear with a return to one's usual schedule and environment or adjustment to the new schedule. It is estimated that it takes about one day per time zone to recover from jet lag. Some research suggests that the human body never completely adapts to shift work, especially when there is a reversion to a normal sleep schedule on days off.

Prevention

Good sleep behavior (called sleep hygiene) is important for maintaining sleep-wake cycles.

QUESTIONS TO ASK YOUR DOCTOR

- Do you think I have a circadian rhythm sleep disorder or some other type?
- What do you think is causing my sleep disorder?
- Do you recommend melatonin supplements?
- What measures can I take to reset my biological clock?
- What is my prognosis?

Maintaining a regular sleep-wake cycle can help prevent problems even in people who are susceptible to altered circadian rhythms. Stresses such as long-distance travel, shift work, and sleep-disrupting lifestyles should be avoided if possible.

Methods for preventing or reducing jet lag include:

- getting plenty of rest before traveling
- gradually adjusting sleeping and eating schedules before leaving home—to earlier if traveling east and to later if traveling west
- arriving at one's destination a few days early to adjust to the change
- adjusting light exposure appropriately
- following the local sleeping schedule
- drinking plenty of water to prevent dehydration and avoiding caffeine and alcohol
- sleeping on airplanes if arriving at night and staying awake if arriving in the daytime

Methods for reducing CRSD in shift workers include:

- nap-friendly workplace policies
- brightly lit workplaces
- avoiding shift changes and rotations
- wearing dark glasses to block sunlight after work
- keeping the same sleep-wake schedule on days off
- using an eye mask and ear plugs to eliminate light and noise when sleeping
- avoiding caffeine near bedtime
- avoiding alcohol

Resources

BOOKS

Foldvary-Schaefer, Nancy. *The Cleveland Clinic Guide to Sleep Disorders.* New York: Kaplan, 2009.

Lee-Chiong, Teofilo L., ed. *Sleep Medicine Essentials.* Hoboken, NJ: Wiley-Blackwell, 2009.

Wright, Kenneth P., ed. *Circadian Rhythm Sleep Disorders*. Philadelphia: Saunders, 2009.

PERIODICALS

Chang, Anne-Marie, et al. "Sleep Timing and Circadian Phase in Delayed Sleep Phase Syndrome." *Journal of Biological Rhythms* 24, no. 4 (August 2009): 313–21.

Rajaratnam, Shantha M. W., et al. "Melatonin Agonist Tasimelteon (VEC-162) for Transient Insomnia after Sleep-Time Shift: Two Randomised Controlled Multi-centre Trials." *Lancet* 373, no. 9662 (February 7–13, 2009): 482–91.

Sack, Robert L. "Jet Lag." *New England Journal of Medicine* 362 (February 4, 2010): 440–47.

WEBSITES

Mayo Clinic Staff. "Jet Lag Disorder." MayoClinic.com. July 10, 2010. http://www.mayoclinic.com/health/jet-lag/DS01085 (accessed July 25, 2011).

National Institute of General Medical Sciences. "Circadian Rhythms Fact Sheet." April 23, 2011. http://www.nigms.nih.gov/Publications/Factsheet_CircadianRhythms.htm (accessed July 25, 2011).

National Institute of Neurological Disorders and Stroke. "Brain Basics: Understanding Sleep." May 21, 2007. http://www.ninds.nih.gov/disorders/brain_basics/understanding_ sleep.htm#circadian_rhythms (accessed July 25, 2011).

"Shift Work and Sleep." National Sleep Foundation. http://www.sleepfoundation.org/article/sleep-topics/shift-work-and-sleep (accessed July 25, 2011).

ORGANIZATIONS

American Academy of Sleep Medicine, 2510 N Frontage Rd., Darien, IL, 60561, (630) 737-9700, Fax: (630) 737-9790, inquiries@aasmnet.org, http://www.aasmnet.org.

National Heart, Lung, and Blood Institute, NHLBI Health Information Center, PO Box 30105, Bethesda, MD, 20824-0105, (301) 592-8573, Fax: (240) 629-3246, nhlbiinfo@nhlbi.nih.gov, http://www.nhlbi.nih.gov.

National Sleep Foundation, 1010 N. Glebe Road, Ste. 310, Arlington, VA, 22201, (703) 243-1697, nsf@sleepfoundation.org, http://www.sleepfoundation.org.

Ali Fahmy, PhD
Margaret Alic, PhD

Citalopram

Definition

Citalopram is a selective **serotonin** reuptake inhibitor (SSRI) antidepressant drug that is sold in the United States under brand name Celexa.

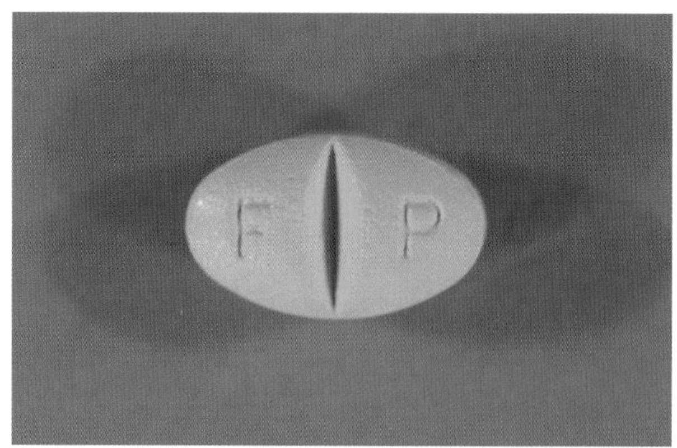

Citalopram, 20 mg. *(© Custom Medical Stock Photo, Inc. Reproduced by permission.)*

Purpose

Citalopram is approved by the U.S. Food and Drug Administration (FDA) for the treatment of **depression**. Possible off-label uses include the treatment of **panic disorder**, **obsessive-compulsive disorder**, alcoholism, **social phobia**, **post-traumatic stress disorder**, eating disorders, and **premenstrual dysphoric disorder**; however, these uses are not approved by the FDA.

Description

Serotonin is a **brain** chemical that carries nerve impulses from one nerve cell to another. Researchers think that depression and certain other mental disorders may be caused, in part, because there is not enough serotonin being released and transmitted in the brain. Like the other SSRI **antidepressants**, **fluoxetine** (Prozac), **sertraline** (Zoloft), and **paroxetine** (Paxil), citalopram increases the level of brain serotonin (also known as 5-HT). Increased serotonin levels in the brain may be beneficial in patients with obsessive-compulsive disorder, alcoholism, certain types of headaches, post-traumatic stress disorder (PTSD), premenstrual tension and mood swings, and panic disorder.

Citalopram is available in 20 mg, 40 mg, and 60 mg tablets.

Recommended dosage

The daily dosage of citalopram for depression is 20–60 mg. The initial dosage is usually 20 mg per day. This dosage may then be increased to 40 mg per day at an interval of no less than one week. Most patients experience relief from depression at this dosage and do not require more than 40 mg per day. The dosage is taken once daily, either in the morning or in the evening.

Patients who are being treated for panic disorder receive doses ranging from 20–60 mg daily. A dosage of

KEY TERMS

Anxiety—An emotion that can be experienced as a troubled feeling, sense of dread, fear of the future, or distress over a possible threat to a person's physical or mental well-being.

Depression—A mental state characterized by feelings of sadness, despair, discouragement, and low energy, sometimes with oversleeping and/or overeating.

Insomnia—The inability to fall asleep or remain asleep.

Off-label use—Drugs approved by the Food and Drug Administration (FDA) for specific uses, legally prescribed by physicians for other "off-label" uses. It is not legal for pharmaceutical companies to advertise drugs for off-label uses.

20–30 mg daily appears to be optimal for the treatment of many patients with panic disorders.

Precautions

Patients who are allergic to citalopram, any other SSRI drug, or any component of the preparation should not take citalopram.

Patients with liver problems and elderly patients (over age 65) need to take smaller amounts of the drug. Dosage for these patients should start at 20 mg but can be increased to 40 mg daily if needed. Patients with kidney problems do not need dosage adjustments. Patients with history of mania, **suicide** attempts, or seizure disorders should start citalopram with caution and only under close physician supervision. Children and young people up to age 24 are at higher risk of developing suicidal thoughts and actions, and, in general, children under 18 are not advised to take citalopram.

Side effects

More than 15% of patients develop **insomnia** while taking citalopram. Nausea and dry mouth occur in about 20% patients being treated with citalopram. Patients also experience tremor, anxiety, agitation, yawning, headaches, dizziness, restlessness, and sedation with citalopram therapy. These side effects usually diminish or disappear with continued use of the drug, although it may take up to four weeks for this to occur.

A drop in blood pressure and increased heart rate have been associated with citalopram use. In general, patients do not experience weight gain or loss after starting citalopram.

Sexual dysfunction, which includes decreased sex drive in women and difficulty ejaculating in men, is associated with the use of citalopram. In some patients, it may take up to 12 weeks for these side effects to disappear. In some patients these sexual side effects never resolve. If sexual side effects continue, the dose of citalopram may be reduced. Patients can also have drug holidays when the weekend dose is either decreased or skipped, or they can discuss with their physician the risks and benefits of switching to another antidepressant.

Interactions

Citalopram interacts with many other medications. Individuals who are starting this drug should review the other medications they are taking with their physician and pharmacist for possible interactions. Patients should always inform all their healthcare providers, including dentists, that they are taking citalopram.

Certain antifungal medications such as itraconazole, fluconazole, ketoconazole, as well as the antibiotic erythromycin, can increase the levels of citalopram in the body. This can cause increased side effects. Levomethadyl, a medication used to treat opioid dependence, may cause toxicity to the heart if used together with citalopram.

Serious side effects called **serotonin syndrome** have resulted from the combination of antidepressants such as citalopram and members of another class of antidepressants known as **monoamine oxidase inhibitors (MAOIs)**. Serotonin syndrome usually consists of at least three of the following symptoms: diarrhea, fever, sweatiness, mood or behavior changes, overactive reflexes, fast heart rate, restlessness, and shivering or shaking. Because of this syndrome, citalopram should never be taken in combination with **MAOIs**. MAOIs include **isocarboxazid**, nialamide, pargyline, selegiline, **phenelzine**, procarbazine, iproniazid, and clorgyline. Patients taking any MAOIs, should stop the MAOI then wait at least 14 days before starting citalopram or any other antidepressant. The same holds true when discontinuing citalopram and starting an MAOI.

Buspirone, an antianxiety medication, should not be used together with citalopram. Ginkgo and **St. John's wort**, herbal supplements that are common in the United States, should not be taken together with citalopram.

Use of citalopram, as with other **SSRIs**, may increase the risk of gastrointestinal bleeding. Patients should inform their doctors if they are taking anticoagulants (blood thinners).

QUESTIONS TO ASK YOUR DOCTOR

- What kind of changes can I expect to see or feel with this medication?
- Does it matter what time of day I take this medication? If so, what is the recommendation?
- Should I take this medication with or without food?
- What are the side effects associated with this medication?
- Will this medication interact or interfere with other medications I am currently taking?
- What symptoms or adverse effects are important enough that I should seek immediate treatment?

Resources

BOOKS

Albers, Lawrence J., Rhoda K. Hahn, and Christopher Reist. *Handbook of Psychiatric Drugs.* Laguna Hills, CA: Current Clinical Strategies, 2010.

American Society of Health-System Pharmacists. *AHFS Drug Information 2011.* Bethesda, MD: ASHP, 2011.

Baldwin, Robert C. *Depression in Later Life.* New York: Oxford University Press, 2010.

Graham, George. *The Disordered Mind: An Introduction to Philosophy of Mind and Mental Illness.* New York: Routledge, 2010.

Holland, Leland Norman, and Michael Patrick Adams. *Core Concepts in Pharmacology.* 3rd ed. New York: Prentice Hall, 2011.

North, Carol, and Sean Yutzy. *Goodwin and Guze's Psychiatric Diagnosis.* New York: Oxford University Press, 2010.

O'Connor, Richard. *Undoing Depression: What Therapy Doesn't Teach You and Medication Can't Give You.* 2nd ed. New York: Little, Brown, 2010.

Preston, John D., John H. O'Neal, and Mary C. Talaga. *Handbook of Clinical Psychopharmacology for Therapists.* 6th ed. Oakland, CA: New Harbinger, 2010.

ORGANIZATIONS

American Academy of Clinical Toxicology, 6728 Old McLean Village Dr., McLean, VA, 22101, (703) 556-9222, Fax: (703) 556-8729, admin@clintox.org, http://www.clintox.org.

American Academy of Family Physicians, 11400 Tomahawk Creek Pkwy., Leawood, KS, 66211-2672, (913) 906-6000, (800) 274-2237, Fax: (913) 906-6075, contactcenter@aafp.org, http://www.aafp.org.

American Medical Association, 515 N State St., Chicago, IL, 60610, (312) 464-5000, (800) 621-8335, http://www.ama-assn.org.

American Psychiatric Association, 1000 Wilson Blvd., Ste. 1825, Arlington, VA, 22209-3901, (703) 907-7300, apa@psych.org, http://www.psych.org.

American Psychological Association, 750 1st St., NE, Washington, DC, 20002-4242, (202) 336-5500; TDD/TTY: (202) 336-6123, (800) 374-2721, http://www.apa.org.

American Society for Clinical Pharmacology and Therapeutics, 528 N Washington St., Alexandria, VA, 22314, (703) 836-6981, info@ascpt.org, http://www.ascpt.org.

Anxiety Disorders Association of America, 8730 Georgia Ave., Silver Spring, MD, 20910, (240) 485-1001, Fax: (240) 485-1035, http://www.adaa.org.

Depression and Bipolar Support Alliance, 730 N Franklin St., Ste. 501, Chicago, IL, 60654, (800) 826-3632, Fax: (312) 642-7243, http://www.dbsalliance.org.

Mental Health America, 2000 N Beauregard St., 6th Fl., Alexandria, VA, 22311, (703) 684-7722, (800) 969-6642, Fax: (703) 684-5968, http://www1.nmha.org.

National Alliance on Mental Illness, 2107 Wilson Blvd., Ste. 300, Arlington, VA, 22201-3042, Fax: (703) 524-9094, (800) 950-6264, http://www.nami.org.

National Institute of Mental Health, 6001 Executive Blvd., Rm. 8184, MSC 9663, Bethesda, MD, 20892-9663, (301) 433-4513; TTY: (301) 443-8431, Fax: (301) 443-4279, (866) 615-6464; TTY: (866) 415-8051, nimhinfo@nih.gov, http://www.nimh.nih.gov.

U.S. National Library of Medicine, 8600 Rockville Pike, Bethesda, MD, 20894, (301) 594-5983, (888) 346-3656; TDD: (800) 735-2258, Fax: (301) 402-1384, http://www.nlm.nih.gov.

Ajna Hamidovic, PharmD
Laura Jean Cataldo, RN, EdD

Client-centered therapy *see* **Person-centered therapy**

Clinical Antipsychotic Trials of Intervention Effectiveness *see* **CATIE**

Clinical Assessment Scales for the Elderly

Definition

The Clinical Assessment Scales for the Elderly, often abbreviated as CASE, is a comprehensive diagnostic tool used to determine and measure the presence of acute mental disorders and other psychopathologic conditions in elderly adults. It is published by PAR, Inc. (Lutz, Florida, United States).

Purpose

The CASE is used to determine the presence of mental disorders in an elderly person as defined by the ***Diagnostic and Statistical Manual of Mental Disorders***. (*DSM*) The *DSM* is the basic reference work consulted by mental health professionals when making a **diagnosis**. The CASE, which is used with adults between the ages of 55 and 90, consists of a self-report form (labeled Form S) in which the person answers questions about himself or herself related to various scales. The test can be administered to an individual or to a group. If the elderly adult is unable to complete the form because of cognitive or physical deficiencies, an other-rating form (labeled Form R) is provided for use by a knowledgeable caregiver, such as a spouse, child, sibling, or healthcare worker. The person elected to take the test should be able to complete it within 40 minutes.

The CASE is not always used specifically for diagnosing mental disorders. It may be administered simply as a general assessment tool to gain insight about an elderly person. It may serve as a neurological screening tool to rule out other problems. The test makers also claim that it can be used as an early screening tool for **dementia**, opening the door for elderly adults to receive medications to slow the progress of **Alzheimer's disease**.

Description

The Clinical Assessment Scales for the Elderly were developed and written by American psychologists Cecil R. Reynolds (1952–) and Erin D. Bigler. The most recent version of the test was published in 2001. It is designed based on the fourth (IV) edition, text revision (TR) of the *DSM* (*DSM-IV-TR*). (The fifth edition [*DSM-5*] will be published in May 2013.) The CASE was normalized using a sample of approximately 2,000 adults in the United States from the ages of 55 to 90 (taken from the U.S. census). One thousand participants were used for each of the two test forms.

The CASE consists of 10 clinical scales that assess the following: Anxiety (ANX); Cognitive Competence (COG); **Depression** (DEP); Fear of Aging (FOA); Obsessive-Compulsiveness (OCD); **Paranoia** (PAR); Psychoticism (PSY); Somatization (SOM); Mania (MAN); and **Substance Abuse** (SUB). These scales were developed to eliminate (or, at least, minimize) any biases associated with gender and ethnicity. The degree to which an elderly person exhibits symptoms in these areas can help a mental health professional with the process of differential diagnosis for a mental disorder.

The CASE also includes three validity scales: L scale (measures positive/negative dissimulation and distortion); F scale (measures infrequently endorsed items); and V scale (measures random responses, failure to comprehend items, and lack of cooperation by patients). Generally, these scales are helpful in evaluating the consistency/inconsistency of a person's responses and whether the person is faking his or her answers.

The person who is completing the CASE, whether using the self-rating form or the other-rating form, responds to the test's written items. The test usually takes 20 to 40 minutes to finish, but it is not timed. People are generally given as much time as they need to complete it. The scoring of the CASE takes approximately 10 minutes.

A shorter version of the test, called the Clinical Assessment Scales for the Elderly-Short Form (CASE-SF), is also available when a faster assessment is needed. In addition, the Short Form is sometimes used as a preliminary assessment to determine whether a more comprehensive or other type of evaluation is needed. The CASE-SF, administered either individually or within a group, takes 10 to 20 minutes to complete and includes all ten of the clinical scales. It also includes two of the CASE validity scales: F and V scales.

Preparation

Preparation for the Clinical Assessment Scales for the Elderly is neither necessary nor recommended by the medical community.

Aftercare

The Clinical Assessment Scales for the Elderly is one way that the medical community can accurately identify the presence of mental disorders within elderly patients. Once

KEY TERMS

Depression—A psychiatric disorder involving feelings of hopelessness and symptoms of fatigue, sleeplessness, suicidal tendencies, and poor concentration.

Diagnostic and Statistical Manual of Mental Disorders—A handbook that mental health professionals use to diagnose mental disorders. The current edition is the fourth edition, text revision (*DSM-IV-TR*); the fifth edition (*DSM-5*) is being developed and is expected to be published in May 2013.

Psychopathology—The study of the causes and development of psychiatric disorders in humans.

QUESTIONS TO ASK YOUR DOCTOR

- How will the Clinical Assessment Scales for the Elderly help?
- How does the CASE work?
- How will the CASE help if we find out that mental illness is not present?
- Will the CASE be able to provide any further insight into the problem?
- Will it be able to rule out other problems?

the CASE is completed, it is much easier to treat such patients.

Benefits

The CASE has been shown to be nearly free of any ethnic and gender biases. In fact, studies of gender and ethnic biases have shown that the test is basically free of such biases for the following three ethnic groups: Caucasians, African Americans, and Hispanics. The test also contains three validity scales to identify feigning (the act of test-takers trying to hide their disorder) and for use in forensic assessments (the analysis of results for the purposes relating to crime or litigation). The test has been shown to have good reliability and validity. Construct validity for the Form S of the CASE was performed using correlations from the **Minnesota Multiphasic Personality Inventory** 2 (MMPI-2), the Back Depression Inventory (BDI), the Beck Hopelessness Scale (BHS), and both the State and Trait scales of the State-Trait Anxiety Inventory (STAI).

Results

Scoring for the CASE is relatively simple. Scores are calculated for each scale and it is then compared to age-appropriate scores to determine the presence or severity of symptoms. For example, if a person scores high on the Depression scale, this information could be used as part of an overall diagnosis for a *DSM-IV-TR* depressive disorder. A person scoring high on the Psychoticism scale may have a psychotic disorder. For any specific *DSM-IV-TR* diagnosis to be made, however, all of the required criteria for that disorder must be met. The results from the CASE may satisfy only some of the requirements.

The Fear of Aging scale assesses the person's degree of apprehension or concern about the aging process. It is not necessarily related to a particular *DSM-IV-TR* disorder. Information about a person's fear of aging, however, may be helpful during the diagnostic process. It may also be useful information for a psychotherapist or other counselor, to understand the patient's concerns or to measure progress in therapy.

See also Figure drawings; House-Tree-Person Test

Resources

BOOKS

American Psychiatric Association. *Diagnostic and Statistical Manual of Mental Disorders.* 4th edition, Text revision. Washington, DC: American Psychiatric Association, 2000.

Reynolds, Cecil R., and Erin D. Bigler. *Clinical Assessment Scales for the Elderly.* San Antonio, TX: The Psychological Corporation, 2001.

WEBSITES

"Cecil Reynolds." Texas A & M University. http://directory.cehd.tamu.edu/view.epl?nid=c-reynolds (accessed November 19, 2010).

"Clinical Assessment Scales for the Elderly™ (CASE™)." PAR, Inc. http://www4.parinc.com/Products/Product.aspx?ProductID=CASE (accessed November 19, 2010).

"Clinical Assessment Scales for the Elderly™ Short Form (CASE-SF™)." PAR, Inc. http://www4.parinc.com/Products/Product.aspx?ProductID=CASE-SF (accessed November 19, 2010).

"Erin David Bigler." Brigham Young University. http://psychology.byu.edu/Faculty/EBigler/Home.dhtml (accessed November 19, 2010).

ORGANIZATIONS

American Psychiatric Association, 1000 Wilson Blvd., Ste. 1825, Arlington, VA, 22209-3901, (703) 907-7300, apa@psych.org, http://www.psych.org.

American Psychological Association, 750 1st St., NE, Washington, DC, 20002, (202) 336-5500, (800) 374-2721, http://www.apa.org.

Depression and Bipolar Support Alliance, 730 N Franklin St., Ste. 501, Chicago, IL, 60654-7225, (800) 826-3632, Fax: (312) 642-7243, http://www.dbsalliance.org.

National Institute of Mental Health, 6001 Executive Boulevard, Room 8184, MSC 9663, Bethesda, MD, 20892-9663, (301) 443-4513, (866) 615-6464, Fax: (301) 443-4279, nimhinfo@nih.gov, http://www.nimh.nih.gov.

Ali Fahmy, PhD
Emily Jane Willingham, PhD
William Atkins

Clinical trials

Definition

A clinical trial is a controlled scientific experiment designed to determine the effectiveness of a treatment in curing or lessening the symptoms of a disease or disorder.

Description

Clinical trials typically are used to assess the effectiveness of a new treatment in comparison with the current standard of care or an existing treatment for a disease or disorder. For example, before a new drug is approved by the U.S. Food and Drug Administration (FDA) for release and use in the United States, the drug must first undergo rigorous testing to determine (a) whether or not it is effective in treating the disorder, and (b) what side effects may result from the drug use that make it inadvisable or dangerous to some or all potential patients.

Clinical trials are research studies designed according to professional standards using scientific methods. In clinical trials, as many variables as possible are controlled to determine the effects of the drug or treatment option. For example, a simple experiment to test the effectiveness of a new drug for epilepsy might include the following steps. First, researchers typically randomly divide the research subjects into two groups: one group that receives the new drug, and the other group that receives the conventional drug or treatment. The group receiving the new drug is called the experimental group, and the group receiving no treatment or conventional treatment is called the control group. Researchers then collect baseline data on the symptoms of the subjects prior to treatment, such as number and frequency of **seizures**. This phase of the experiment is called the pretest. After the pretest data are collected, the researchers give the new drug (the independent variable) to the experimental group while not changing the treatment of the control group. After an appropriate amount of time for the drug to take effect, the subjects are tested again using the same criteria as were used for the pretest to determine any difference between the two groups as a result of the drug (dependent variable). When all the data are collected, they are statistically analyzed to determine whether there is a reasonable basis to say that the effects of the new drug are significantly different from the effects of the old treatment (or no treatment) and not due to chance variations. This basic research design can be made more complicated to simultaneously answer multiple research questions, such as what dose of the new medication is most effective, whether increasing dosage levels of the medication results in more side effects, whether the drug is effective for some demographic groups but not others (e.g., only works well on adult females but not on adult males), or to compare several treatments at once.

There are several general types of clinical trials:

- treatment trials that test the relative effectiveness of new drugs or treatments or combinations of drugs and/ or treatments
- prevention trials that investigate ways to prevent a disease in individuals who have not previously had it or to prevent its return in individuals who have
- diagnostic trials that seek to find better ways to diagnose a disorder or illness
- screening trials to determine the best way to detect a disease or disorder
- quality-of-life trials that investigate how to make life easier or more normal for those with a chronic illness

Clinical trials typically have four phases. In Phase I, the experimental drug or treatment is tested on a small group of people to investigate its safety, determine a recommended dosage or range, and identify potential side effects. In Phase II, the experimental drug or treatment is tested on a larger group of people to further determine its effectiveness and safety. Phase III clinical trials examine the drug or treatment from an even wider perspective. The experimental drug or treatment is given to large groups of people to confirm the findings of the previous studies on a larger population. Phase III clinical trials are also often used to compare the relative effectiveness of treatments and gather safety information. Finally, Phase IV clinical trials are run after a drug has been marketed. At that time, a drug may undergo further studies to examine its risks, benefits, and optimal use.

KEY TERMS

Bias—When a point of view prevents impartial judgment on issues relating to the subject of that point of view.

Clinical—Pertaining to or founded on observation and treatment of participants, as distinguished from theoretical or basic science.

Food and Drug Administration (FDA)—The U.S. Department of Health and Human Services agency responsible for ensuring the safety and effectiveness of all drugs, biologics, vaccines, and medical devices. The FDA also works with the blood banking industry to safeguard the nation's blood supply.

Placebo—An inactive pill, liquid, or powder that has no treatment value.

Randomization—A method based on chance by which study participants are assigned to a treatment group.

Recruiting—Period during which a trial is attempting to identify and enroll participants.

Considerations before entering a clinical trial as a subject

Clinical trials are necessary to help ensure the safety and effectiveness of a drug or treatment before it is put into general use. In addition, joining a clinical trial as a research subject may be of potential benefit to patients who have exhausted available treatment options without success. Clinical trials give patients the opportunity to try a new drug or treatment that may help their condition when conventional methods have failed. However, certain things must be considered before joining a clinical trial as a subject.

First, there is no guarantee that subjects in clinical trials will receive the new drug or treatment. They may be randomly placed in the control group where they receive a placebo or conventional treatment rather than the new drug or treatment. There is no way to tell whether one will be in the experimental group or the control group. Frequently, even researchers or people administrating the treatment do not know which group the subject is in (this is called a double-blind study) so that their expectations will not unintentionally bias the results. Therefore, all other available treatment options should typically be tried before joining a clinical trial as a subject.

In addition, there is always the possibility of encountering unknown negative side effects from the new drug or treatment. For this reason, subjects in clinical trials are required to read, understand, and sign **informed consent** documents. The decision to join a clinical trial as a subject should always be made in conjunction with one's health care provider in order to reduce the risk of negative side effects from the treatment.

Individuals should be well informed and have a good understanding of the following prior to making a decision about participating:

- the purpose of the study
- their role in the study
- any risks, discomforts, or potential inconveniences involved
- potential conflicts of interest
- the time involved, the number of visits required, and the length of the study
- any ethical issues relating to personal information, privacy, photography, tape recording, use of information, and confidentiality

Availability of participation with NIH.gov

The research hospital of the National Institutes of Health (NIH) is located at the NIH Clinical Center in Bethesda, Maryland. New or improved medical treatments, medications, and therapies, are actualized through ongoing clinical research performed at this center. One key component in attaining information and scientific discovery is participation in the many clinical trials by volunteers. Recruitment is ongoing for sick or healthy participants. To find out more about medical research studies, various clinical trials, and availability in participating in a clinical trial with NIH, contact the Patient Recruitment and Public Liaison Office at 1-800-411-1222 or visit their website: http://www.cc.nih.gov/participate.shtml.

Resources

BOOKS

American Society of Health-System Pharmacists. *AHFS Drug Information 2011.* Bethesda, MD: American Society of Health-System Pharmacists, 2011.

Holland, Leland Norman, and Michael Patrick Adams. *Core Concepts in Pharmacology,* 3rd ed. New York: Prentice Hall, 2011.

WEBSITES

ClinicalTrials.gov. http://www.clinicaltrials.gov/ct/action/GetStudy.

ORGANIZATIONS

National Institutes of Health (NIH), 9000 Rockville Pike, Bethesda, MD, 20892, (301) 496-4000, http://www.nih.gov/index.html.

U.S. National Library of Medicine, 8600 Rockville Pike, Bethesda, MD, 20894, http://www.nlm.nih.gov/medlineplus/medlineplus.html.

Ruth A. Wienclaw, PhD
Laura Jean Cataldo, RN, EdD

Clomipramine

Definition

Clomipramine is an antidepressant drug used primarily to alleviate obsessions and compulsions in patients with **obsessive-compulsive disorder**. Clomipramine is also used in the treatment of depressive disorders and in a number of other psychiatric and medical conditions. In the United States, the drug has also been known by the brand name Anafranil.

Purpose

Clomipramine is principally used in the treatment of the obsessions and compulsions of obsessive-compulsive disorder (OCD), when these symptoms greatly disrupt patients' daily activities. Obsessions are repetitive

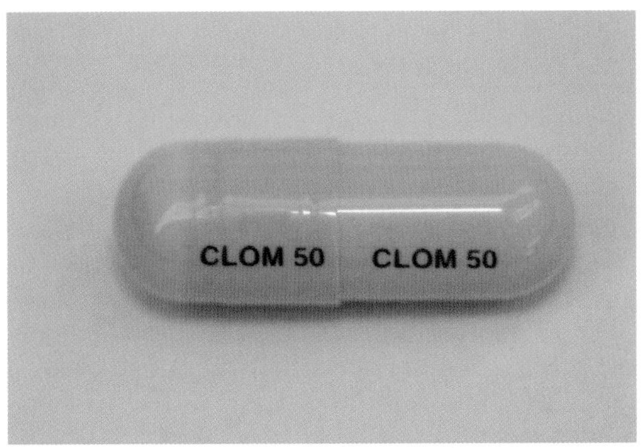

Clomipramine, 50 mg. *(© Custom Medical Stock Photo, Inc. Reproduced by permission.)*

thoughts and impulses, and compulsions are repetitive behaviors. Patients with OCD find these experiences inappropriate, distressing, and time-consuming.

Clomipramine may also be used in the treatment of depressive disorders, especially when associated with obsessions and compulsions, and in **panic disorder**, pain management, sleep attacks (**narcolepsy** and cataplexy), and **anorexia nervosa**. The drug may help to reduce compulsive behaviors in a variety of disorders with such symptoms, including **trichotillomania** (hair pulling), onychophagia (nail biting), **Tourette syndrome** (tics and vocalizations), and childhood **autism**.

Description

Clomipramine is one of the tricyclic **antidepressants**, so-called because of the three-ring chemical structure common to these drugs. In the 1940s and 1950s, pharmaceutical researchers synthesized a number of new compounds for possible medical use as antihistamines and **sedatives**. After testing in animal experiments, a few of these substances were selected for human study. One potential drug, the tricyclic compound **imipramine**, was not useful in calming agitation, but it had a striking effect in improving the mood of certain patients with **depression**.

Since the discovery of imipramine, many other tricyclic antidepressants have been developed with somewhat different pharmacological activities and side effect profiles. Within this group of drugs, clomipramine is exceptionally potent in affecting levels of **serotonin** in the **brain**. In this action, it is similar to serotonin-selective antidepressant drugs, such as **fluoxetine** (Prozac), which act specifically on serotonin levels and are effective in OCD. Serotonin is a messenger chemical (neurotransmitter) involved in transmitting signals between nerve cells. Clomipramine reduces the effects on serotonin transmission in depression and OCD symptoms.

Recommended dosage

For adults, clomipramine is administered in dosages up to a maximum of 250 mg per day. Starting with a dose of 25 mg, the dosage is increased during the first two weeks to 100 mg per day. If needed, it is further increased gradually over the next several weeks. The initial dose is low to avoid side effects, and it is increased slowly to permit the patient to develop tolerance or adapt to side effects that may occur.

Older patients (over age 65), children, and adolescents are more sensitive to the side effects and toxicities of tricyclic antidepressants such as clomipramine. The maximum daily dose is usually lower for elderly patients than for younger adults. For children and adolescents, the maximum recommended daily dose is the lesser of 100 mg or 3 mg per kg of body weight.

Precautions

Seizures are the most important risk associated with clomipramine. Among patients taking the drug for six months or more, more than 1% may experience seizures. The risk of seizure increases with larger doses, and seizures have been reported to occur following abrupt discontinuation of the medication. Caution and physician supervision are required if the patient has a history of epilepsy or some other condition associated with seizures, such as brain damage or alcoholism.

Clomipramine and other tricyclic antidepressants often cause drowsiness. Activities requiring alertness, such as driving, should be avoided until patients understand how the drug affects them. Dizziness or lightheadedness may occur on arising from a seated position, due to sudden decreases in blood pressure. Fainting may also occur. Patients with glaucoma may find their condition worsened. Persons with heart disease should use tricyclic antidepressants with caution due to a possibility of adverse effects on heart rhythm.

Studies have found that some antidepressant drugs, including clomipramine, may increase the chances of suicidal thoughts in children and adults up to age 24. Patients taking clomipramine should be monitored, regardless of age, for worsening depression or other adverse changes in behavior.

It has not been determined whether clomipramine is safe to take during pregnancy, and the patient's need for this medicine should be balanced against the possibility of harm to the fetus. Tricyclic antidepressants may be secreted in breast milk and may cause sedation and depress the breathing of a nursing infant.

Side effects

Clomipramine may cause many side effects. Initially, the side effects of tricyclic drugs may be more pronounced, but sensitivity often decreases with continued treatment. Some of the more common side effects are:

- headache
- confusion
- nervousness
- restlessness
- sleep difficulties
- numbness
- tingling sensations
- tremors
- twitches
- nausea
- loss of appetite
- indigestion
- constipation
- blurred vision
- increased sweating
- difficulty urinating (especially in men with prostate enlargement)
- menstrual pain
- ejaculatory difficulty
- impotence
- decreased sex drive
- fatigue
- weight gain

Sensitivity to ultraviolet light may increase, and sunburns may occur more easily. Patients may also develop dry mouth due to decreased saliva, possibly contributing to the development of tooth decay, gum disease, and mouth infections. Patients should avoid sweets, sugary beverages, and chewing gum containing sugar.

Less commonly, tricyclic drugs may cause adverse effects on almost any organ or system of the body, particularly the blood, hormones, kidney, and liver. Patients should consult their physicians if symptoms develop or bodily changes appear.

Interactions

Tricyclic antidepressants such as clomipramine may interact with many other drugs. Patients should inform their physicians about all other drugs they are taking before starting treatment.

Clomipramine may intensify the effects of other drugs that act on serotonin levels, possibly producing **serotonin syndrome**, a rare but dangerous condition with fever, sweating, tremors, and changes in mental state. Drugs that may interact this way include other antidepressants, especially **selective serotonin reuptake inhibitors (SSRIs)** and **monoamine oxidase inhibitors (MAOIs)**. These drugs should not be taken within two weeks of taking clomipramine. Other drugs to avoid are lithium, **alprazolam** (Xanax), fenfluramine (Pondimin), amphetamine, dextromethorphan (used in cough suppressants), meperidine (Demerol), and tramadol (Ultram).

KEY TERMS

Autonomic—The part of the nervous system that governs the heart, involuntary muscles, and glands.

Cataplexy—A symptom of narcolepsy marked by a sudden episode of muscle weakness triggered by strong emotions. The muscle weakness may cause the person's knees to buckle, or the head to drop. In severe cases, the patient may become paralyzed for a few seconds or minutes.

Epilepsy—A neurological disorder characterized by the onset of seizures. Seizures are caused by a disturbance in the electrical activity in the brain and can cause loss of consciousness, muscle spasms, rhythmic movements, abnormal sensory experiences, or altered mental states.

Kilogram—A metric unit of weight. It equals 2.2 lb.

Monoamine oxidase inhibitors (MAOIs)—A group of antidepressant drugs that decreases the activity of monoamine oxidase, a neurotransmitter found in the brain that affects mood.

Neurotransmitter—A chemical in the brain that transmits messages between neurons, or nerve cells.

Serotonin—A widely distributed neurotransmitter that is found in blood platelets, the lining of the digestive tract, and the brain, and that works in combination with norepinephrine. It causes very powerful contractions of smooth muscle, and is associated with mood, attention, emotions, and sleep. Low levels of serotonin are associated with depression.

Tricyclic drugs may intensify the effects of other drugs causing sedation, including alcohol, **barbiturates**, narcotic pain medications, minor tranquilizers, and antihistamines. Tricyclics may cause excessive reductions of blood pressure in patients taking blood pressure medicine, especially upon standing from a sitting or reclined position. Conversely, these drugs may interfere with the pressure-reducing effects of certain other blood pressure medicines and may necessitate an adjustment in dosage. Tricyclics may interact with thyroid medications to produce abnormalities of heart rhythm. Concurrent use of tricyclic antidepressants with other psychiatric medicines may result in intensification of certain side effects.

Certain drugs may interfere with the elimination of tricyclic antidepressants from the body, causing higher blood levels and increased side effects. This effect may occur with cimetidine (Tagamet), other antidepressants, **methylphenidate** (Ritalin, Concerta), and some antipsychotic medications.

Resources

BOOKS

Maina, Giuseppe, Umberto Albert, and Filippo Bogetto. "Obsessive-Compulsive Disorder Resistant to Pharmacological Treatment." In *Obsessive-Compulsive Disorder Research,* edited by B.E. Ling. Hauppauge, NY: Nova Science Publishers, 2005, 171–99.

Preston, John D., John H. O'Neal, and Mary C. Talaga. *Handbook of Clinical Psychopharmacology for Therapists.* 5th ed. Oakland, CA: New Harbinger Publications, 2008.

Simpson, H. Blair, and Michael R. Liebowitz. "Combining Pharmacotherapy and Cognitive-Behavioral Therapy in the Treatment of OCD." In *Concepts and Controversies in Obsessive-Compulsive Disorder,* by Jonathan Abramowitz and Arthur C. Houts. New York: Springer Science, 2005, 359–76.

PERIODICALS

Anderson, Shawanda W., and Marvin B. Booker. "Cognitive Behavioral Therapy Versus Psychosurgery for Refractory Obsessive-Compulsive Disorder." Letter in *Journal of Neuropsychiatry and Clinical Neurosciences* 18, no. 1 (February 2006): 129.

Fineberg, Naomi A., and Tim M. Gale. "Evidence-Based Pharmacotherapy of Obsessive-Compulsive Disorder." *International Journal of Neuropsychopharmacology* 8, no. 1 (March 2005): 107–29.

Foa, Edna B., et al. "Randomized, Placebo-Controlled Trial of Exposure and Ritual Prevention, Clomipramine, and Their Combination in the Treatment of Obsessive-Compulsive Disorder." *American Journal of Psychiatry* 162, no. 1 (January 2005): 151–61.

Shavitt, Roseli G., et al. "Clinical Features Associated with Treatment Response in Obsessive-Compulsive Disorder." *Comprehensive Psychiatry* 474 (2006): 276–81.

Simpson, Helen Blair, et al. "Response Versus Remission in Obsessive-Compulsive Disorder." *Journal of Clinical Psychiatry* 67, no. 2 (February 2006): 269–76.

ORGANIZATIONS

American Academy of Child and Adolescent Psychiatry, 3615 Wisconsin Ave. NW, Washington, DC, 20016-3007, (202) 966-7300, Fax: (202) 966-2891, http://aacap.org.

American Academy of Clinical Toxicology, 6728 Old McLean Village Dr., McLean, VA, 22101, (703) 556-9222, Fax: (703) 556-8729, admin@clintox.org, http://www.clintox.org.

American College of Neuropsychopharmacology, 5034-A Thoroughbred Ln., Brentwood, TN, 37027, (615) 324-2360, Fax: (615) 523-1715, acnp@acnp.org, http://www.acnp.org/default.aspx.

American Psychiatric Association, 1000 Wilson Blvd., Ste. 1825, Arlington, VA, 22209-3901, (703) 907-7300, apa@psych.org, http://www.psych.org.

Richard Kapit, MD
Ruth A. Wienclaw, PhD

Clonazepam

Definition

Clonazepam belongs to a group of drugs called benzodiazepines. **Benzodiazepines** are medications that help relieve nervousness, tension, symptoms of anxiety, and some types of **seizures** by slowing the central nervous system. In the United States, clonazepam is sold under brand name Klonopin.

Klonopin (clonazepam), 1 mg. *(U.S. Drug Enforcement Administration)*

Purpose

Clonazepam is approved by the U.S. Food and Drug Administration (FDA) for the treatment of **panic disorder** and some types of epilepsy. It may also be used off-label to treat **social phobia**, mania, **post-traumatic stress disorder** (PTSD), and **medication-induced movement disorders**, a side effect of some antipsychotic drugs. It is legal for physicians to administer drugs for off-label uses, but these uses are not approved by the FDA.

Description

Clonazepam belongs to a group of drugs called benzodiazepines. Benzodiazepines are sedative-hypnotic drugs that help to relieve nervousness, tension, anxiety symptoms, and seizures by slowing the central nervous system. To do this, they block the effects of a specific chemical involved in the transmission of nerve impulses in the **brain**, decreasing the excitement level of the nerve cells.

When clonazepam is used to treat panic disorder, it is more sedating than **alprazolam**, another benzodiazepine drug used to treat panic disorder. However, unlike alprazolam, clonazepam may trigger depressive episodes in patients with a previous history of **depression**. In people who experience social phobia, treatment with clonazepam reduces the rate of depression. The use of clonazepam for social phobia is considered an off-label use—a use that is legal when prescribed by a physician but that is not approved by the FDA.

Clonazepam comes in 0.5 mg, 1.0 mg, and 2.0 mg tablets.

Recommended dosage

For panic disorder, the initial recommended dose is 0.25 mg twice daily. This dose can be increased every three days in increments of 0.125–0.25 mg twice daily. The target dose for panic disorder is 1.0 mg per day, although some people benefit from doses up to a maximum of 4.0 mg per day. When a person stops taking clonazepam, the drug should be gradually discontinued by decreasing the dose by 0.125 mg twice daily every three days.

Although clonazepam is not FDA approved for the treatment of PTSD, doses in the range of 0.25–3.0 mg daily appear to help treat symptoms of this disorder. Daily dosages for the treatment of social phobia range from 1.0–2.5 mg, while the dosage to control mania may be as high as 10.0 mg daily.

Precautions

Women who are pregnant should not use clonazepam, because it may harm the developing fetus. Clonazepam should never be taken by people who have had an allergic reaction to it or another benzodiazepine drug such as **diazepam** (Valium). People with narrow-angle glaucoma or severe liver disease should not take clonazepam. People who have kidney disease may need to take a reduced dosage of the drug. Saliva production may increase while taking clonazepam. Because of this, people with respiratory disease or an impaired gag reflex should use clonazepam with close physician supervision.

Because clonazepam is a nervous system depressant, it should not be taken with other such depressants, such as alcohol, other **sedatives**, sleeping pills, or tranquilizers. People taking clonazepam may feel unusually drowsy and mentally sluggish when they first start taking the drug. They should not drive, operate machinery, or engage in activities that require mental alertness until they see how clonazepam affects them. Because of a loss of coordination, elderly patients are at risk for falls. This excessive sedation usually goes away after a short time on the drug.

People who have underlying depression should be closely monitored while taking clonazepam, especially if they are at risk for attempting **suicide**. Clonazepam treatment should not be stopped abruptly, as patients may experience withdrawal symptoms including tremor, **insomnia**, anxiety, and seizures. Clonazepam can be habit-forming.

Side effects

The main side effects of clonazepam are sedation, dizziness, impaired coordination, depression, and **fatigue**. Some people experience decreased sex drive while taking clonazepam. The drug may also cause short-term memory loss or **amnesia**.

A small number of people develop sinus problems and upper respiratory tract infections while taking clonazepam. One of the side effects of clonazepam may be increased salivation. This may cause some people to start coughing while taking clonazepam. Clonazepam may also cause anorexia and dry mouth. It may cause either constipation or diarrhea. There are a few reports of clonazepam causing menstrual irregularities or blurred vision.

Interactions

Clonazepam may increase the sedative effects of other drugs that depress the central nervous system such as certain strong pain medicines (opiates such as codeine, oxycodone, hydromorphone) and antihistamines (found in many cold and allergy medications).

KEY TERMS

Anorexia—Loss of appetite or unwillingness to eat. Can be caused by medications, depression, and/or many other factors.

Benzodiazepines—A group of central nervous system depressants used to relieve anxiety or to induce sleep.

Glaucoma—A group of eye diseases characterized by increased pressure within the eye, significant enough to damage eye tissue and structures. If untreated, glaucoma results in blindness.

The sedative effect is also increased if clonazepam is taken with alcohol.

Disulfiram (Antabuse), a medication used to treat alcohol dependence, increases the effect of clonazepam. Medications that make clonazepam ineffective include phenobarbital, phenytoin, **carbamazepine**, theophylline, rifampin, and rifabutin.

Resources

BOOKS

Lacy, Charles F., Leonard L. Lance, and Laura L. Armstrong. *Lexi-Comp's Drug Information Handbook*. Hudson, OH: Lexi-Comp, 2010.

Preston, John D., John H. O'Neal, and Mary C. Talaga. *Handbook of Clinical Psychopharmacology for Therapists*. 5th ed. Oakland, CA: New Harbinger Publications, 2008.

PERIODICALS

Nardi, Antonio E., and Giampaolo Perna. "Clonazepam in the Treatment of Psychiatric Disorders: An Update." *International Clinical Psychopharmacology* 21, no. 3 (May 2006): 131–42.

Paparrigopoulos, Thomas J. "REM Sleep Behaviour Disorder: Clinical Profiles and Pathophysiology." *International Review of Psychiatry* 17, no. 4 (August 2005): 293–300.

ORGANIZATIONS

American Academy of Child and Adolescent Psychiatry, 3615 Wisconsin Ave. NW, Washington, DC, 20016-3007, (202) 966-7300, Fax: (202) 966-2891, http://aacap.org.

American Academy of Clinical Toxicology, 6728 Old McLean Village Dr., McLean, VA, 22101, (703) 556-9222, Fax: (703) 556-8729, admin@clintox.org, http://www.clintox.org.

American College of Neuropsychopharmacology, 5034-A Thoroughbred Ln., Brentwood, TN, 37027, (615) 324-2360, Fax: (615) 523-1715, acnp@acnp.org, http://www.acnp.org/default.aspx.

American Psychiatric Association, 1000 Wilson Blvd., Ste. 1825, Arlington, VA, 22209-3901, (703) 907-7300, apa@psych.org, http://www.psych.org.

Ajna Hamidovic, PharmD
Ruth A. Wienclaw, PhD

Clonidine

Definition

Clonidine belongs to a class of drugs called central alpha-adrenergic agonists. In the United States, clonidine tablets are sold under the brand name Catapres and clonidine skin patches are sold under the brand name Catapres-TTS. The tablets are also available generically. There is an injectable form that is administered directly into the spinal cord for the treatment of postoperative pain.

Purpose

Clonidine tablets and patches are approved by the U.S. Food and Drug Administration (FDA) for the treatment of high blood pressure. In addition, clonidine has been found to be useful in the treatment of alcohol, opiate, and **nicotine** withdrawal syndromes, **attention deficit hyperactivity disorder (ADHD)**, and **Tourette syndrome**, which is one of the **tic disorders**.

Clonidine is also useful in treating neuropathic pain, which is usually characterized as a sensation of tingling, burning, or shooting pain in the limbs that may come and go quickly and erratically. Clonidine gel used topically (on the skin) provides analgesia to the affected painful

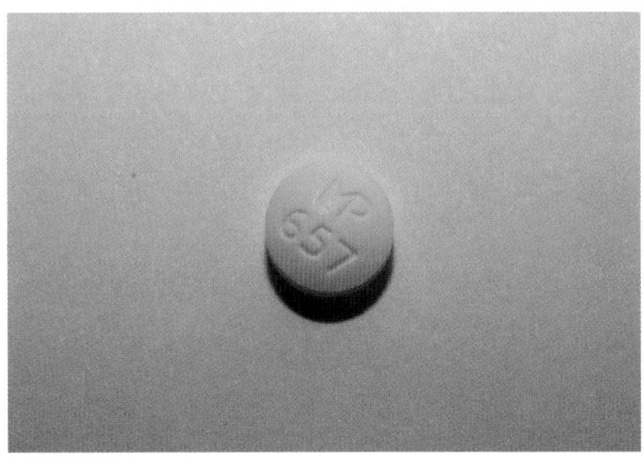

Clonidine, 0.1 mg. *(© Custom Medical Stock Photo, Inc. Reproduced by permission.)*

nerves, and though the mechanism of action is not well known, it is thought that the drug may decrease a local release of norepinephrine at the site of the nerve fibers, which stops the sensitized nerve fibers from causing pain.

Other indications

Other uses of clonidine are:

- treatment of dysmenorrhea (painful cramps during menstrual period)
- hypertensive crisis
- hot flashes associated with menopause
- as a diagnostic tool in the diagnosis of pheochromocytoma (a tumor of the adrenal glands that may be accompanied by high blood pressure, a fast heart rate, and changes in the endocrine system)

Other indications and benefits in the use of clonidine may be identified by further research. **Clinical trials** in the use of this drug for pain, anxiety, hypertension, and other conditions are ongoing.

Description

Clonidine was synthesized in the 1960s and was initially tested as a nasal decongestant. In the United States, clonidine was first used to treat hypertension, although it has also been investigated for treatment of different neuropsychiatric disorders. Clonidine works on specific nerve cells in the **brain** that are responsible for lowering blood pressure, slowing heart rate, and decreasing the body's reaction to the withdrawal of chemicals such as alcohol, opiates, and nicotine. Because of this, clonidine is often used to treat the symptoms of drug, alcohol, and nicotine withdrawal.

Clonidine is beneficial in opiate withdrawal because it treats symptoms commonly associated with that condition (watery eyes and nose, diarrhea, irritability). For this condition, clonidine is often used alone. For the treatment of alcohol withdrawal, clonidine is usually combined with benzodiazepine tranquilizers such as Librium, Valium, Xanax, or Ativan.

Several studies of treatment for **smoking cessation** showed patients treated with clonidine had decreased nicotine craving. Clonidine skin patches appear to be more effective than tablets for this condition. Both dermal patches and tablets are effective in the treatment of Tourette syndrome and **ADHD**.

Clonidine tablets are available in 0.1 mg, 0.2 mg, and 0.3 mg strengths. Clonidine skin patches are available in 0.1 mg, 0.2 mg, and 0.3 mg per day patches. Each patch lasts seven days.

KEY TERMS

Attention deficit hyperactivity disorder (ADHD)— A developmental disorder characterized by distractibility, hyperactivity, impulsive behaviors, and the inability to remain focused on tasks or activities.

Tourette syndrome—An abnormal condition that causes uncontrollable facial grimaces and tics and arm and shoulder movements. Tourette syndrome is perhaps best known for uncontrollable vocal tics that include grunts, shouts, and use of obscene language (coprolalia).

Recommended dosage

Dosages of 0.4–0.6 mg have been used for the treatment of alcohol withdrawal. Total daily dosage for the treatment of opiate withdrawal range between 0.5 and 1.4 mg, depending on the stage as well as the severity of withdrawal symptoms. If the clonidine patch is used to treat nicotine withdrawal symptoms, dosages that deliver 0.1–0.2 mg daily are used. For oral therapy (tablets), a total dosage of 0.2–0.4 mg daily is taken in divided doses.

Pediatric doses of clonidine are calculated based on the child's body weight. Clonidine dosage for ADHD in children is 5 micrograms per kilogram of body weight per day orally in four divided doses. Children who require a daily dosage of 0.2 mg usually can use the 0.3 mg dermal patch. If ADHD is associated with sleep disturbances, low to moderate doses of clonidine can be taken at bedtime. Oral doses in children with Tourette syndrome range from 3–6 micrograms per kilogram of body weight per day divided into two-to-four even doses.

Precautions

Clonidine should not be used by people who have a known allergy to this drug. If a person has underlying **depression**, clonidine should be used with caution and under close physician supervision.

Clonidine should not be abruptly withdrawn, but rather slowly decreased over several days to avoid withdrawal symptoms. Withdrawal symptoms include an increase in blood pressure, irritability, nervousness, **insomnia**, and headache. Because of the possibility of withdrawal, clonidine should not be used in patients who are unwilling or unable to follow the prescribing information.

Clonidine should be used only with caution and close physician supervision in patients with chronic renal

QUESTIONS TO ASK YOUR DOCTOR

- What kind of changes can I expect to see or feel with this medication?
- Does it matter what time of day I take this medication? If so, what is the recommendation?
- Should I take this medication with or without food?
- What are the side effects associated with this medication?
- Will this medication interact or interfere with other medications I am currently taking?
- What symptoms or adverse effects are important enough that I should seek immediate treatment?

failure, coronary artery disease, and in patients with preexisting eye problems. People with kidney disease may need to take a reduced dosage. Clonidine should not be used by pregnant women, except in the rare case where the benefits of taking clonidine outweigh the risks to the developing fetus.

Side effects

The most common side effect associated with clonidine is dizziness accompanying sudden changes in position such as standing up rapidly. In order to avoid this, patients should stand up slowly. People using the dermal patch may develop rash, hair loss, a burning sensation on the skin, or other skin irritations where the patch is applied. Switching to tablets may not completely eliminate these skin problems.

Clonidine can cause dry mouth, constipation, nausea, daytime sleepiness, weakness, and lethargy. These side effects may take several weeks to disappear. In some cases, these side effects can be eliminated with dosage readjustment. In addition, clonidine may cause eye dryness, loss of sex drive, and decreased sexual activity.

If patients experience weight gain in the beginning of therapy, they can expect this side effect to decline over a period of several days to weeks.

Interactions

Clonidine's blood pressure–lowering effects may be enhanced by other drugs that also lower blood pressure. Conversely, the blood pressure–lowering effects of clonidine may be negated by many **antidepressants**.

Resources

BOOKS

American Society of Health-System Pharmacists. *AHFS Drug Information 2011*. Bethesda, MD: ASHP, 2011.

Holland, Leland Norman, and Michael Patrick Adams. *Core Concepts in Pharmacology*. 3rd ed. New York: Prentice Hall, 2011.

Preston, John D., John H. O'Neal, and Mary C. Talaga. *Handbook of Clinical Psychopharmacology for Therapists*. 6th ed. Oakland, CA: New Harbinger, 2010.

PERIODICALS

Favrat, B., et al. "Opioid Antagonist Detoxification under Anaesthesia Versus Traditional Clonidine Detoxification Combined with an Additional Week of Psychosocial Support: A Randomized Clinical Trial." *Drug and Alcohol Dependence* 81, no. 2 (February 2006): 109–16.

Friemoth, Jerry. "What Is the Most Effective Treatment for ADHD in Children?" *Journal of Family Practice* 54, no. 2 (February 2005): 166–68.

Marsch, Lisa A., et al. "Comparison of Pharmacological Treatments for Opioid-Dependent Adolescents: A Randomized Controlled Trial." *Archives of General Psychiatry* 62, no. 10 (October 2005): 1157–64.

Ponizovsky, Alexander M., et al. "Well-Being, Psychosocial Factors, and Side-Effects Among Heroin-Dependent Inpatients after Detoxification Using Buprenorphine Versus Clonidine." *Addictive Behaviors* 31, no. 11 (November 2006): 2002–13.

Schnoes, Connie J., et al. "Pediatric Prescribing Practices for Clonidine and Other Pharmacologic Agents for Children with Sleep Disturbance." *Clinical Pediatrics* 45, no. 3 (April 2006): 229–38.

ORGANIZATIONS

American Academy of Clinical Toxicology, 6728 Old McLean Village Dr., McLean, VA, 22101, (703) 556-9222, Fax: (703) 556-8729, admin@clintox.org, http://www.clintox.org.

American Academy of Family Physicians, 11400 Tomahawk Creek Pkwy., Leawood, KS, 66211-2672, (913) 906-6000, (800) 274-2237, Fax: (913) 906-6075, contactcenter@aafp.org, http://www.aafp.org.

American Psychiatric Association, 1000 Wilson Blvd., Ste. 1825, Arlington, VA, 22209-3901, (703) 907-7300, apa@psych.org, http://www.psych.org.

National Institutes of Health, 9000 Rockville Pike, Bethesda, MD, 20892, (301) 496-4000; TTY: (301) 402-9612, http://www.nih.gov.

U.S. National Library of Medicine, 8600 Rockville Pike, Bethesda, MD, 20894, (301) 594-5983, (888) 346-3656; TDD: (800) 735-2258, Fax: (301) 402-1384, http://www.nlm.nih.gov.

Ajna Hamidovic, PharmD
Ruth A. Wienclaw, PhD
Laura Jean Cataldo, RN, EdD

Clorazepate

Definition

Clorazepate is a medication that belongs to a family of drugs called benzodiazepines—a group of pharmacologically active compounds used to produce a calming effect by relieving anxiety and tension. In the United States, clorazepate is sold under brand names Tranxene and Gen-XENE.

Purpose

Clorazepate is used for the treatment of anxiety and alcohol withdrawal. Clorazepate is also an adjunct in the management of partial **seizures**.

Description

Clorazepate binds to different sites in the **brain**, causing them to shift into a state that is less excitable. The drug is very effective in treating anxiety and **anxiety disorders**. Moreover, anxiety associated with undergoing surgical procedures is controlled with clorazepate. Clorazepate alone is not effective in treating seizures; however, if used along with other standard seizure medications, such as phenobarbital, primidone, phenytoin, **carbamazepine**, and **valproic acid**, better seizure control may be achieved. Convulsions and anxiety associated with alcohol withdrawal are controlled with clorazepate.

Clorazepate is available in two formulations. Clorazepate tablets come in 3.75 mg, 7.5 mg, and 15.0 mg doses, while slow-release tablets, administered once daily, are available in 11.25 mg and 22.5 mg strengths. Capsules are available in 3.75 mg, 7.5 mg, and 15.0 mg strengths.

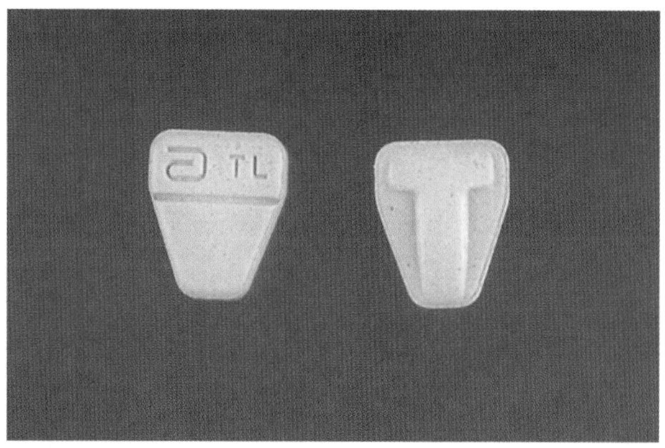

Tranxene (clorazepate), 75 mg. *(U.S. Drug Enforcement Administration)*

Recommended dosage

If used for anxiety, the dose of clorazepate usually is 15–60 mg daily in divided dose intervals. Usually, however, the average dose is 30 mg daily given in two to four doses. If slow-release formulation is used, the dose of either 11.25 mg or 22.5 mg is usually administered at bedtime. Slow-release products should not be used to initiate therapy. Doses may be lower in elderly patients and patients with liver or kidney problems.

Doses of clorazepate for the management of seizures differ in adult and pediatric populations. Patients 9–12 years of age should be started on 3.75–7.5 mg twice daily. This dose should be increased by no more than 3.75 mg weekly. The maximum dose per day is 60 mg administered in two to three divided doses. Children older than 12 and adults should receive 7.5 mg two to three times daily. This can be increased to a higher dose by adding 7.5 mg at weekly intervals. The total daily dose should not exceed 90 mg daily administered in 2–3 doses. In patients undergoing alcohol withdrawal, the first dose is 30 mg. Treatment is continued with 15 mg two to four times daily for the maximum dose of 90 mg in one day. Once maximum dose is achieved, the dose is gradually decreased over subsequent days.

Precautions

Pregnant women should not take clorazepate. Patients who have narrow-angle glaucoma should not take clorazepate, as this may worsen their condition. Clorazepate should not be used in patients younger than nine years of age.

If **depression** coexists with anxiety, clorazepate should be used with caution as it can worsen existing depression and increase the risk of **suicide**. Patients should be cautioned against engaging in activities requiring mental alertness, such as driving or operating machinery, since clorazepate causes drowsiness and dizziness. Clorazepate is a long-acting drug and it may take time for its effects to diminish. Some cases of "sleep driving," or operating a vehicle while asleep, have been reported. Elderly patients are also at increased risk for falls, due to loss of coordination.

Abrupt discontinuation of clorazepate has been associated with withdrawal symptoms and seizures. Hence, doses of clorazepate should be slowly decreased in patients who have been taking clorazepate continuously over several weeks. Other withdrawal symptoms may include nervousness, **insomnia**, irritability, diarrhea, and muscle aches.

Side effects

The most common side effects include drowsiness, dizziness, and confusion. There are a few reports about behavioral changes associated with the use of clorazepate and they include rage, depression, irritability, and aggression.

Other side effects include vision disturbances—such as blurred and double vision—decreased libido, nausea, vomiting, either decreased or increased appetite, and diarrhea or constipation. Clorazepate may also cause short-term memory loss or **amnesia**. In a few cases, clorazepate has been associated with liver toxicity where patients developed jaundice or fever. It is also known to cause a rash.

Interactions

Simultaneous use of clorazepate and dong quai, a Chinese herb, has been associated with excessive muscle relaxation and central nervous system depression. Other herbs that should not be used with clorazepate are **ginkgo biloba** and **kava kava**.

Omeprazole, a medication used to treat heartburn, should not be used together with clorazepate. **Valerian**, an herb used as a sleep aid, binds to the same receptors in the brain as clorazepate; thus, the desired effects of clorazepate may not be seen in patients taking it and valerian at the same time.

Clorazepate may increase the effects of other drugs that cause drowsiness. These drugs include antihistamines (such as Benadryl), **sedatives** (usually used to treat insomnia), pain relievers, anxiety and seizure medicines, and muscle relaxants. Alcohol combined with clorazepate also causes excessive drowsiness and should not be used. Grapefruit and grapefruit juice should also be avoided, as it may slow the metabolism of the drug in the body, prolonging the effects and potentially causing overdose if the drug is continually taken.

Resources

BOOKS

Preston, John D., John H. O'Neal, and Mary C. Talaga. *Handbook of Clinical Psychopharmacology for Therapists*. 5th ed. Oakland, CA: New Harbinger Publications, 2008.

PERIODICALS

Lelong-Boulouard, Véronique, et al. "Interactions of Buprenorphine and Dipotassium Clorazepate on Anxiety and Memory Functions in the Mouse." *Drug and Alcohol Dependence* 85, no. 2 (November 8, 2006): 103–13.

Millan, Mark J., et al. "Anxiolytic Properties of Agomelatine, an Antidepressant with Melatoninergic and Serotonergic Properties: Role of 5-HT2C Receptor Blockade." *Psychopharmacology* 177, no. 4 (February 2005): 448–58.

Quentin, Thomas, et al. "Clorazepate Affects Cell Surface Regulation of Delta and Kappa Opioid Receptors, Thereby Altering Buprenorphine-Induced Adaptation in the Rat Brain." *Brain Research* 1063, no. 1 (November 2005): 84–95.

Rowlett, James K., et al. "Anti-Conflict Effects of Benzodiazepines in Rhesus Monkeys: Relationship with Therapeutic Doses in Humans and Role of GABA-Sub(A) Receptors." *Psychopharmacology* 184, no. 2 (January 2006): 201–11.

ORGANIZATIONS

American Academy of Child and Adolescent Psychiatry, 3615 Wisconsin Ave. NW, Washington, DC, 20016-3007, (202) 966-7300, Fax: (202) 966-2891, http://aacap.org.

American Academy of Clinical Toxicology, 6728 Old McLean Village Dr., McLean, VA, 22101, (703) 556-9222, Fax: (703) 556-8729, admin@clintox.org, http://www.clintox.org.

American College of Neuropsychopharmacology, 5034-A Thoroughbred Ln., Brentwood, TN, 37027, (615) 324-2360, Fax: (615) 523-1715, acnp@acnp.org, http://www.acnp.org/default.aspx.

American Psychiatric Association, 1000 Wilson Blvd., Ste. 1825, Arlington, VA, 22209-3901, (703) 907-7300, apa@psych.org, http://www.psych.org.

Ajna Hamidovic, PharmD
Ruth A. Wienclaw, PhD

Clozapine

Definition

Clozapine is an antipsychotic drug used to alleviate the symptoms and signs of schizophrenia—a form of severe mental illness—that is characterized by hallucinations, **delusions**, unusual behavior, and loss of contact

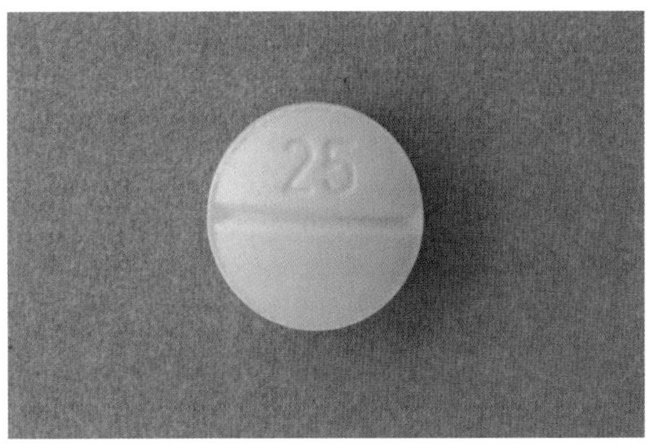

Clozaril (clozapine), 25 mg. *(© Custom Medical Stock Photo, Inc. Reproduced by permission.)*

with reality. In the United States, the drug is also known by the brand name Clozaril.

Purpose

Clozapine is principally used to reduce the signs and symptoms of severe schizophrenic illness. The drug is intended for use in patients with severe **schizophrenia** who have not responded to any other antipsychotic drug. Clozapine is also used in patients with severe schizophrenia when other antipsychotic medications have caused intolerable side effects.

Description

Clozapine is considered an atypical antipsychotic drug. Atypical antipsychotics differ from typical antipsychotics in their effectiveness in schizophrenia and their profile of side effects. Clozapine may reduce the signs and symptoms of schizophrenia in a large proportion of patients with treatment-resistant schizophrenia who do not respond to typical antipsychotics. Moreover, the drug is less likely than typical antipsychotics to cause **tardive dyskinesia** and other extrapyramidal (pertaining to a neural network in the **brain**) side effects. Tardive dyskinesia is a syndrome of involuntary, uncoordinated movements that may not disappear or may only partially improve after the drug is stopped. Tardive dyskinesia involves involuntary movements of the tongue, jaw, mouth or face, or other groups of skeletal muscles. The incidence of tardive dyskinesia increases with increasing age and with increasing dosage. It may also appear after the use of the antipsychotic has stopped. Women are at greater risk than men for developing tardive dyskinesia. There is no known effective treatment for this syndrome, although gradual (but rarely complete) improvement may occur over a long period.

Clozapine was the first atypical antipsychotic drug to be developed. In the late 1980s, clozapine was tested in severely ill patients with schizophrenia who had been treated with a typical antipsychotic drug but had not shown much improvement. A significant proportion of these patients improved as a result of treatment with clozapine.

The superiority of clozapine in patients resistant to treatment is considered an important advance, but the drug is not without problems. Clozapine is generally considered the most toxic of the antipsychotic drugs. It causes agranulocytosis, a life-threatening depletion of white blood cells, in 1%–2% of patients. It also causes epileptic **seizures** and adverse effects on the heart and blood pressure more frequently than other antipsychotic medicines. Clozapine is usually reserved for the most severely ill patients with schizophrenia who have not responded to other treatments. Other atypical antipsychotic drugs were developed subsequently and are considered safer to use than clozapine.

The mechanisms of action of antipsychotic drugs are not completely understood. The effect of clozapine is believed to be related to its actions in blocking neurotransmission due to the **neurotransmitters dopamine** and **serotonin** in a region of the brain called the limbic system, which is involved with emotions and motivation. The actions of clozapine may target the limbic system more specifically than those of typical antipsychotic drugs.

In 2005, the effectiveness of clozapine was evaluated in the Clinical Antipsychotic Trials of Intervention Effectiveness (**CATIE**) Schizophrenia Study. This study evaluated the effectiveness and side effects of atypical antipsychotics, including clozapine, in comparison to a conventional antipsychotic drug in the treatment of schizophrenia. Phase I of the study found that the newer antipsychotics were not significantly more effective than the less expensive, conventional antipsychotic medications. In Phase II of the study, it was found that participants who had not benefited from their first antipsychotic medication tended to be effectively treated by clozapine. For those patients, clozapine worked significantly better than other atypical antipsychotics; the conventional antipsychotic, however, was not included in this phase of the study.

The study results also showed that clozapine is often a good choice of medication for patients who do not respond well to other antipsychotic medications. Clozapine was more effective in controlling symptoms than the other atypical antipsychotics under evaluation. For patients whose symptoms were not well-controlled on clozapine, **olanzapine** and **risperidone** tended to be more effective than **ziprasidone** or **quetiapine**.

As many as 20%–60% of patients have schizophrenia that is treatment resistant, making the management of schizophrenia a challenge for clinicians. Whereas inadequate response to clozapine treatment is frequently encountered in practice, augmentation strategies are sometimes employed. Drug augmentation studies have been ongoing to study and evaluate the effect of adding additional antipsychotic drugs to a patient's regimen of treatment with clozapine. In the early 2000s, the results of drug augmentation studies showed only marginal therapeutic benefit.

Augmenting clozapine with other drugs such as risperidone may minimize some symptoms associated with schizophrenia; however, the effectiveness of augmentation therapy overall remains inconclusive. Continued studies were considered needed to research

KEY TERMS

Delusions—Irrational beliefs that defy normal reasoning and remain firm even when overwhelming proof is presented to dispute them. Delusions are distinct from culturally or religiously based beliefs that may be seen as untrue by outsiders.

Epilepsy—A disorder associated with disturbed electrical discharges in the central nervous system that cause seizures.

Extrapyramidal symptoms—A group of side effects associated with antipsychotic medications and characterized by involuntary muscle movements, including contraction and tremor.

Off-label use—Drugs in the United States, approved by the Food and Drug Administration (FDA) for specific uses based on the results of clinical trials, and then legally prescribed by physicians for other "off-label" uses. It is not legal for pharmaceutical companies to advertise drugs for off-label uses.

Schizophrenia—A major mental illness marked by psychotic symptoms, including hallucinations, delusions, and severe disruptions in thinking.

Seizure—A convulsion or uncontrolled discharge of nerve cells that may spread to other cells throughout the brain.

and demonstrate the effects of augmenting clozapine with other drugs aimed at diminishing the symptoms of schizophrenia.

Recommended dosage

Clozapine is available as 25 mg and 100 mg tablets. The usual dosage of clozapine is 300–600 mg per day; however, some patients may require daily dosages of up to 900 mg. To minimize side effects, the initial dose of clozapine is 12.5 mg (one-half tablet) twice a day, and the dose is increased by 25–50 mg each day, until the dose reaches 300–450 mg per day. The daily dosage of the drug is then determined based on the individual patient's response, but increases should not exceed 100 mg once or twice a week.

Precautions

Clozapine may cause agranulocytosis, a life-threatening depletion of white blood cells. The blood cells affected by clozapine defend the body against infections by bacteria and other microorganisms, and patients with agranulocytosis are subject to severe infections. Clozapine treatment is reserved for the most severely ill patients with schizophrenia who have not responded to other treatments. Clozapine is available only through a distribution system that assures close monitoring of white blood cells. Patients must have white blood cell counts determined before starting treatment, then once every week for the first six months, once every other week after that, and once a week for the first month after clozapine treatment is stopped.

Clozapine may cause epileptic seizures in about 5% of patients. The frequency of seizures goes up as the dose of the drug is increased. Usually, patients who experience seizures on clozapine discontinue the drug or reduce the dose. **Neuroleptic malignant syndrome** (NMS), a dangerous condition with high fever, muscular rigidity, rapid pulse, sweating, and altered mental state, may occur with all antipsychotic medications, including clozapine. NMS requires immediate medical treatment.

Clozapine frequently causes sedation and may interfere with driving and other tasks requiring alertness. The drug may increase the effects of alcohol and **sedatives**. Clozapine may cause low blood pressure and sudden drops in blood pressure on standing up, which may cause dizziness or fainting. Elevated heart rate may occur in 25% of patients; this effect may be a serious risk for patients with heart disease. Clozapine-induced fever, unrelated to any illness, may occur. The fever usually subsides within a few days, but it may require discontinuing the drug.

Clozapine may cause myocarditis (heart inflammation). Symptoms may be similar to the flu and include chest pain, **fatigue**, fever, joint pain, and leg swelling. If any of these or other unusual side effects develop, patients should contact their physician immediately.

Clozapine and other antipsychotic drugs are associated with an increased risk of death when used in elderly patients with **dementia**. In June 2008, the U.S. Food and Drug Administration (FDA) announced a requirement for manufacturers of clozapine (and other antipsychotic drugs) to add a warning label to their packaging stating this risk. The reason for the increase was unclear in studies, but most deaths were found to be related to either cardiovascular complications or complications associated with infection. Clozapine is not approved by the FDA for the treatment of behavior problems in older adults with dementia, and patients in this category (or caregivers of patients in this category) should discuss the risks of taking clozapine with their physician. Elderly patients may also be particularly sensitive to sedation, low blood pressure, and other side effects.

Clozapine should be used in pregnant women only when strictly necessary. Babies born to mothers who took clozapine during their pregnancy may be at risk for extrapyramidal symptoms (EPS) and symptoms of withdrawal, including agitation, trouble breathing, and difficulty feeding. Clozapine may be secreted in breast milk, and breastfeeding may not be advisable. Clozapine has a higher risk of adverse side effects in children and adolescents but may be necessary if other treatments are not effective.

Side effects

Clozapine may cause many side effects. The following side effects are grouped by the body system affected:

- cardiovascular: decreases of blood pressure, especially on arising from a seated or lying position, which may cause dizziness or fainting; rapid heart rate; changes in heart rhythm; and electrocardiogram
- nervous system: sedation, increased seizure tendency
- digestive system: increased appetite, excessive salivation, nausea, constipation, abnormal liver tests, elevated blood sugar
- autonomic: blurred vision, exacerbation of glaucoma, dry mouth, nasal congestion, decreased sweating, difficulty urinating, particularly in men with enlarged prostate
- skin: rashes
- body as a whole: weight gain, fever

Interactions

Clozapine may interact with many other drugs. Patients (or their caregivers) should inform the physician in charge about all other drugs the patient is taking before the patient starts treatment. Because of the risk of agranulocytosis, clozapine should not be given along with medications that suppress production of blood cells.

Clozapine may intensify the effects of drugs causing sedation, including alcohol, **barbiturates**, narcotic pain medications, minor tranquilizers, and antihistamines. Similarly, clozapine may cause excessive reductions of blood pressure in patients taking other medicines that lower blood pressure. Clozapine may also intensify side effects of drugs that cause blurred vision, dry mouth, diminished sweating in hot weather, and constipation. Many other antipsychotics and **antidepressants** cause such side effects.

Clozapine may increase the effects of other medications that also lower seizure threshold (make it more likely to have seizures), such as steroid drugs, the asthma medication theophylline, and many other psychiatric drugs. Patients with epilepsy may require adjustment in their dosage of antiseizure medications. Lithium may increase the risk of seizures and other nervous system adverse effects when given with clozapine.

Certain drugs that are eliminated by the liver may interfere with the elimination of clozapine from the body, causing higher blood levels and increased side effects. Conversely, clozapine may interfere with the elimination of other drugs that are eliminated by the liver. Antidepressants that affect brain serotonin levels may increase blood levels of clozapine, possibly causing increased side effects.

QUESTIONS TO ASK YOUR DOCTOR

- What kind of changes can I expect to see or feel with this medication?
- Does it matter what time of day I take this medication? If so, what is the recommendation?
- Should I take this medication with or without food?
- What are the side effects associated with this medication?
- Will this medication interact or interfere with other medications I am currently taking?
- What symptoms or adverse effects are important enough that I should seek immediate treatment?

Resources

BOOKS

Albers, Lawrence J., Rhoda K. Hahn, and Christopher Reist. *Handbook of Psychiatric Drugs.* Laguna Hills, CA: Current Clinical Strategies, 2010.

American Society of Health-System Pharmacists. *AHFS Drug Information 2011.* Bethesda, MD: ASHP, 2011.

Graham, George. *The Disordered Mind: An Introduction to Philosophy of Mind and Mental Illness.* New York: Routledge, 2010.

Holland, Leland Norman, and Michael Patrick Adams. *Core Concepts in Pharmacology.* 3rd ed. New York: Prentice Hall, 2011.

Preston, John D., John H. O'Neal, and Mary C. Talaga. *Handbook of Clinical Psychopharmacology for Therapists.* 6th ed. Oakland, CA: New Harbinger, 2010.

PERIODICALS

Brunette, Mary F., et al. "Clozapine Use and Relapses of Substance Use Disorder Among Patients with Co-occurring Schizophrenia and Substance Use Disorders." *Schizophrenia Bulletin* 32, no. 4 (October 2006): 637–43.

Essock, S.M., et al. "Effectiveness of Switching Antipsychotic Medications." *American Journal of Psychiatry* 163, no. 12 (December 2006): 2090–95.

Gogtay, N., and J. Rapoport. "Clozapine Use in Children and Adolescents." *Expert Opinion on Pharmacotherapy* 9, no. 3 (February 2008): 459–65.

Lamberti, J. Steven, et al. "Prevalence of the Metabolic Syndrome Among Patients Receiving Clozapine." *American Journal of Psychiatry* 163, no. 7 (July 2006): 1273–76.

Lieberman, J.A., et al. "Effectiveness of Antipsychotic Drugs in Patients with Chronic Schizophrenia." *New England Journal of Medicine* 353, no. 12 (September 22, 2005): 1209–23.

Luchins, Daniel J. "In the Aftermath of CATIE: How Should Administrators Value Atypical Antipsychotic Medications?" *Administration and Policy in Mental Health and Mental Health Services Research* 33, no. 5 (September 2006): 541–43.

McEvoy, J.P., et al. "Effectiveness of Clozapine versus Olanzapine, Quetiapine, and Risperidone in Patients with Chronic Schizophrenia Who Did Not Respond to Prior Atypical Antipsychotic Treatment." *American Journal of Psychiatry* 163, no. 4 (April 2006): 600–610.

Miodownik, Chanoch, et al. "The Effect of Sudden Clozapine Discontinuation on Management of Schizophrenic Patients: A Retrospective Controlled Study." *Journal of Clinical Psychiatry* 67, no. 8 (August 2006): 1204–1208.

Rocha, Fábio Lopes, and Cláudia Hara. "Benefits of Combining Aripiprazole to Clozapine: Three Case Reports." *Progress in Neuropsychopharmacology and Biological Psychiatry* 30, no. 6 (July 2006): 1167–69.

Shaw, Philip, and Judith L. Rapoport. "Decision Making about Children with Psychotic Symptoms: Using the Best Evidence in Choosing a Treatment." *Journal of the American Academy of Child and Adolescent Psychiatry* 45, no. 11 (November 2006): 1381–86.

Shaw, Philip, et al. "Childhood-Onset Schizophrenia: A Double-Blind, Randomized Clozapine-Olanzapine Comparison." *Archives of General Psychiatry* 63, no. 7 (July 2006): 721–30.

ORGANIZATIONS

American Academy of Clinical Toxicology, 6728 Old McLean Village Dr., McLean, VA, 22101, (703) 556-9222, Fax: (703) 556-8729, admin@clintox.org, http://www.clintox.org.

American Academy of Family Physicians, 11400 Tomahawk Creek Pkwy., Leawood, KS, 66211-2672, (913) 906-6000, (800) 274-2237, Fax: (913) 906-6075, contactcenter@aafp.org, http://www.aafp.org.

American Medical Association, 515 N State St., Chicago, IL, 60610, (312) 464-5000, (800) 621-8335, http://www.ama-assn.org.

American Psychiatric Association, 1000 Wilson Blvd., Ste. 1825, Arlington, VA, 22209-3901, (703) 907-7300, apa@psych.org, http://www.psych.org.

American Psychological Association, 750 1st St., NE, Washington, DC, 20002-4242, (202) 336-5500; TDD/TTY: (202) 336-6123, (800) 374-2721, http://www.apa.org.

American Society for Clinical Pharmacology and Therapeutics, 528 N Washington St., Alexandria, VA, 22314, (703) 836-6981, info@ascpt.org, http://www.ascpt.org.

Anxiety Disorders Association of America, 8730 Georgia Ave., Silver Spring, MD, 20910, (240) 485-1001, Fax: (240) 485-1035, http://www.adaa.org.

Depression and Bipolar Support Alliance, 730 N Franklin St., Ste. 501, Chicago, IL, 60654, (800) 826-3632, Fax: (312) 642-7243, http://www.dbsalliance.org.

Mental Health America, 2000 N. Beauregard St., 6th Fl., Alexandria, VA, 22311, (703) 684-7722, (800) 969-6642, Fax: (703) 684-5968, http://www1.nmha.org.

National Alliance on Mental Illness, 2107 Wilson Blvd., Ste. 300, Arlington, VA, 22201-3042, Fax: (703) 524-9094, (800) 950-6264, http://www.nami.org.

National Institute of Mental Health, 6001 Executive Blvd., Rm. 8184, MSC 9663, Bethesda, MD, 20892-9663, (301) 433-4513; TTY: (301) 443-8431, Fax: (301) 443-4279, (866) 615-6464; TTY: (866) 415-8051, nimhinfo@nih.gov, http://www.nimh.nih.gov.

National Institutes of Health, 9000 Rockville Pike, Bethesda, MD, 20892, (301) 496-4000; TTY: (301) 402-9612, http://www.nih.gov.

U.S. National Library of Medicine, 8600 Rockville Pike, Bethesda, MD, 20894, (301) 594-5983, (888) 346-3656; TDD: (800) 735-2258, Fax: (301) 402-1384, http://www.nlm.nih.gov.

Richard Kapit, MD
Ruth A. Wienclaw, PhD
Laura Jean Cataldo, RN, EdD

Clozaril *see* **Clozapine**

Cocaine and related disorders

Definition

Cocaine is extracted from the coca plant, which grows in Central and South America. The substance is processed into many forms for use as an illegal drug of abuse. Cocaine is dangerously addictive, and users of the drug experience a "high"—a feeling of euphoria or intense happiness, along with hypervigilance, increased sensitivity, irritability or anger, impaired judgment, and anxiety.

Forms of the drug

In its most common form, cocaine is a whitish crystalline powder that produces feelings of euphoria when ingested. In powder form, cocaine is known by such street names as "coke," "blow," "C," "flake," "snow" and "toot." It is most commonly inhaled or snorted. It may also be dissolved in water and injected.

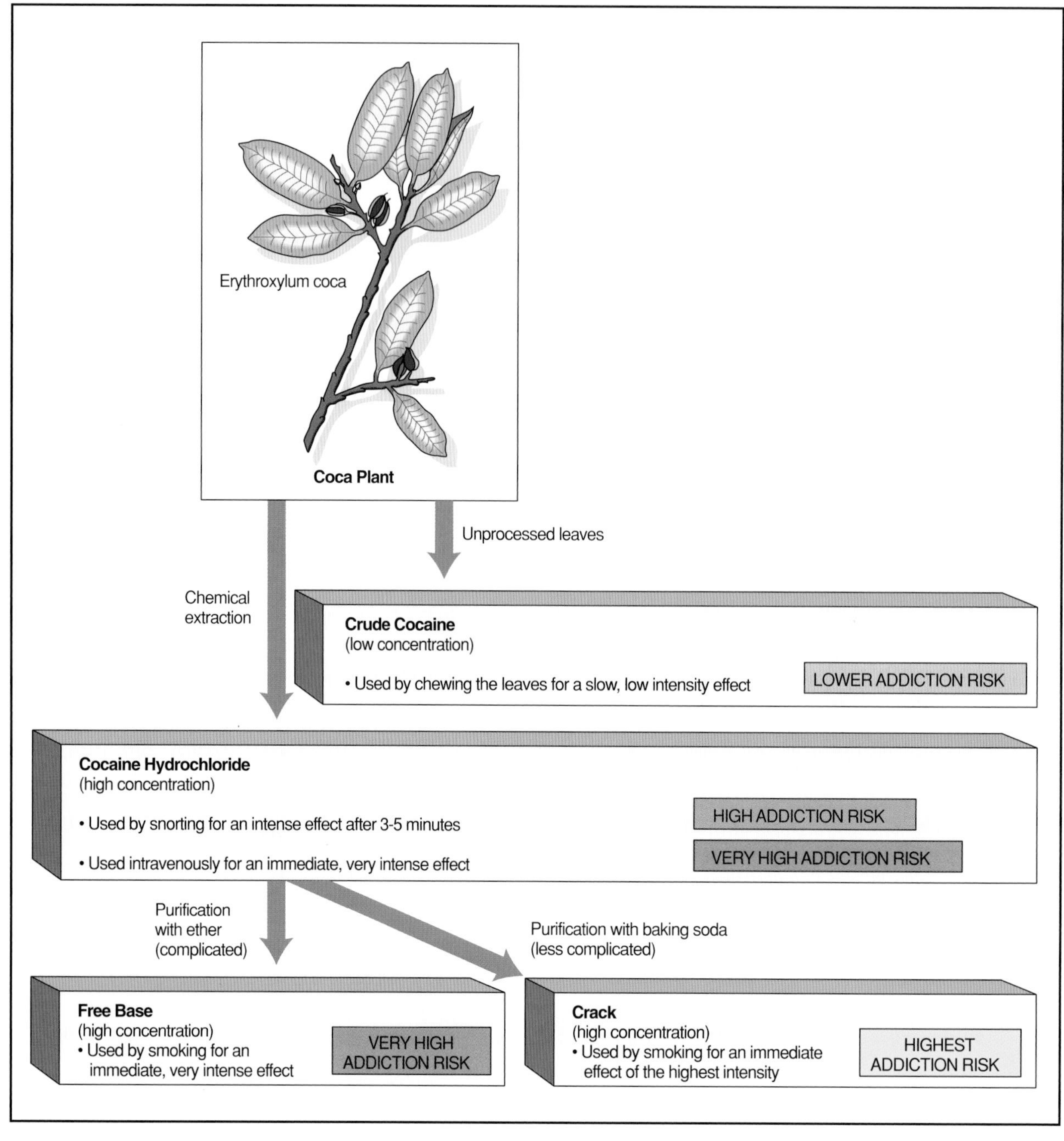

Various forms of cocaine (including the coca plant) and the addiction risks associated with them. *(Illustration by Hans & Cassady.)*

Crack is a form of cocaine that can be smoked and that produces an immediate, more intense, and more short-lived high. It comes in off-white chunks or chips called "rocks."

In addition to their stand-alone use, both cocaine and crack are often mixed with other substances. Cocaine may be mixed with methcathinone to create a "wildcat." Cigars may be hollowed out and filled with a mixture of crack and marijuana. Either cocaine or crack used in conjunction with heroin is called a "speedball." Cocaine used together with alcohol represents the most common fatal two-drug combination.

Demographics

The patterns of cocaine abuse in the United States have changed much over the past thirty years. They have been changing in other parts of the world as well, including South America and Western

Europe. In the United States, several studies have attempted to track drug abuse in many different populations. The studies include: the Monitoring the Future Study (MTF); the National Household Survey on Drug Abuse (NHSDA); the Drug Abuse Warning Network (DAWN), which gets reports from emergency rooms and medical examiners' offices on drug-related cases and deaths; and Arrestee Drug Abuse Monitoring (ADAM), which gets information on urine samples obtained from people who have been arrested.

In the annual MTF study, cocaine use among high-school seniors had declined from 13.1% in 1985 to 3.1% in 1992—the lowest it had been since 1975, when the survey was first implemented. The rate of cocaine use began to rise again and peaked at 5.5% in 1997. The NHSDA found that the levels of cocaine use declined over the same time period. The decline in the rates has been thought to be due in part to education about the risks of cocaine abuse.

The incidence of new crack cocaine users has also decreased. There was a minimal decline in the numbers of excessive cocaine users between the years 1985 and 1997. The Epidemiologic Catchment Area (ECA) studies done in the early 1980s combined cocaine dependence with cocaine abuse and found that one-month to six-month prevalence rates for cocaine abuse and dependence were low or could not be measured. The lifetime rate of cocaine abuse was 0.2%.

A 1997 study from The National Institute on Drug Abuse indicates that among outpatients who abuse substances, 55% abuse cocaine.

Cocaine abuse affects both genders and many different populations across the United States. Males are one-and-a-half to two times more likely to abuse cocaine than females. Cocaine began as a drug of the upper classes in the 1970s; now the socioeconomic status of cocaine users has shifted. Cocaine is more likely to be abused by the economically disadvantaged because it is easy for them to get, and it is inexpensive ($10 for a small bag of crack cocaine). These factors have led to increased violence (people who are cocaine dependent may become involved in illegal activity, such as drug dealing, in order to acquire funds for their habit) and higher rates of acquired immune deficiency (AIDS) among disadvantaged populations.

A National Survey on Drug Use and Health (NSDUH) survey reports that in 2009, 4.8 million Americans age 12 and older had abused cocaine in any form. Adults 18 to 25 years of age have a higher rate of cocaine use than any other age group.

Description

Cocaine-related disorders form a very broad topic. According to the mental health clinician's handbook, ***Diagnostic and Statistical Manual of Mental Disorders***, fourth edition, text revised (also known as the *DSM-IV-TR*), the broad category of cocaine-related disorders can be subdivided into two categories: cocaine use disorders and cocaine-induced disorders. Cocaine use disorders include cocaine dependence and cocaine abuse. Cocaine-induced disorders include:

- cocaine intoxication
- cocaine withdrawal
- cocaine intoxication delirium
- cocaine-induced psychotic disorder, with delusions
- cocaine-induced psychotic disorder, with hallucinations
- cocaine-induced mood disorder
- cocaine-induced anxiety disorder
- cocaine-induced sexual dysfunction
- cocaine-induced sleep disorder
- cocaine-related disorder not otherwise specified

The fifth edition of the *DSM,* also known as the *DSM-5* is due for publication in 2013. This edition may include proposed changes and revisions to some current diagnostic criteria for psychiatric diagnoses, including combining "Substance Abuse," and "Dependence," into a single disorder, thus modifying "Cocaine Abuse," and "Cocaine Dependence," to a title of "Cocaine Use Disorder."

Cocaine use disorders

COCAINE ABUSE. For the cocaine abuser, the use of the substance leads to maladaptive behavior over a 12-month period. The person may fail to meet responsibilities at school, work, or home. The cocaine abuse impairs the affected person's judgment, and he or she puts himself or herself in physical danger to use the substance. For example, the individual may use cocaine in an unsafe environment. The person who abuses cocaine may be arrested or charged with possession of the substance, yet continue to use cocaine despite all of the personal and legal problems that may result.

COCAINE DEPENDENCE. Cocaine dependence is even more serious than cocaine abuse. Dependence is a maladaptive behavior that, over a three-month period, has caused the affected individual to experience tolerance for, and withdrawal symptoms from, cocaine. Tolerance is the need to increase the amount of cocaine intake to achieve the same desired effect. In other words, someone who is dependent on cocaine needs more cocaine to produce the same "high" that a lesser amount produced in the past. The dependent person also experiences cocaine withdrawal. Withdrawal symptoms develop within hours or days after cocaine use that has been heavy and prolonged and then abruptly stopped. The symptoms include irritable mood and two or more of the following symptoms: **fatigue**, nightmares, difficulty sleeping or too much sleep, elevated appetite, agitation (restlessness), or slowed physical movements. The onset of withdrawal symptoms can cause a person to use more cocaine to avoid these painful and uncomfortable symptoms. The dependent person uses larger amounts of cocaine for longer periods of time than intended. He or she cannot cut back on the use of the substance, often has a difficult time resisting cocaine when it is available, and may abandon work or school to spend more time acquiring and planning to acquire more cocaine. The individual continues to use cocaine despite the negative effects it has on family life, work, and school.

Cocaine-induced disorders

COCAINE INTOXICATION. Cocaine intoxication occurs after recent cocaine use. The person experiences a feeling of intense happiness, hypervigilance, increased sensitivity, irritability or anger, with impaired judgement, and anxiety. The intoxication impairs the person's ability to function at work or school or in social situations. Two or more of the following symptoms are present immediately after the use of cocaine:

- enlarged pupils
- elevated heart rate
- elevated or lowered blood pressure
- chills and increased sweating
- nausea or vomiting
- weight loss
- agitation or slowed movements
- weak muscles
- chest pain
- coma
- confusion
- irregular heartbeat
- depressed respiration
- seizures
- odd postures
- odd movements

COCAINE WITHDRAWAL. Withdrawal symptoms develop within hours or days after cocaine use that has been heavy and prolonged and then abruptly stopped. The symptoms include irritable mood and two or more of the following symptoms: fatigue, nightmares, difficulty sleeping or too much sleep, elevated appetite, agitation (restlessness), or slowed physical movements.

COCAINE-INDUCED DELIRIUM. According to the *DSM-IV-TR*, several criteria must be met in order for a health care professional to establish the **diagnosis** of cocaine-induced **delirium**. Patients have a disturbance of their level of consciousness or awareness, evidenced by drowsiness or an inability to concentrate or pay attention. Patients also experience a change in their cognition (ability to think) evidenced by a deficit in their language or their memory. For example, these patients may forget where they have placed an item, or their speech may be confusing. These symptoms have rapid onset within hours or days of using cocaine, and the symptoms fluctuate throughout the course of the day. These findings cannot be explained by **dementia** (state of impaired thought processes and memory that can be caused by various diseases and conditions), and the doctor must not be able to recognize a physical reason that can account for the symptoms other than cocaine intoxication.

COCAINE-INDUCED PSYCHOTIC DISORDER, WITH DELUSIONS. The person with this disorder has experienced intoxication or withdrawal from cocaine within a month from the time he or she begins to experience **delusions** (beliefs that the person continues to maintain, despite evidence to the contrary). In order for this state to be considered cocaine-induced psychotic disorder, these symptoms cannot be due to another condition or substance.

COCAINE-INDUCED PSYCHOTIC DISORDER, WITH HALLUCINATIONS. This condition is the same as cocaine-induced psychotic disorder with delusions, except that this affected individual experiences hallucinations instead of delusions. Hallucinations can be described as hearing and seeing things that are not real.

COCAINE-INDUCED MOOD DISORDER. The person with this disorder has experienced intoxication or withdrawal from cocaine within a month from the time he or she begins to experience depressed, elevated, or irritable mood with **apathy** (lack of empathy for others, and lack of showing a broad range of appropriate emotions).

COCAINE-INDUCED ANXIETY DISORDER. The person with this disorder has experienced intoxication or withdrawal from cocaine within a month from the time he or she begins to experience anxiety, panic attacks, obsessions, or compulsions. Panic attacks are discrete episodes of intense anxiety. Persons affected with panic attacks may experience accelerated heart rate, shaking or trembling, sweating, shortness of breath, or fear of going crazy or losing control, as well as other symptoms. An

obsession is an unwelcome, uncontrollable, persistent idea, thought, image, or emotion that a person cannot help thinking even though it creates significant distress or anxiety. A **compulsion** is a repetitive, excessive, meaningless activity or mental exercise which a person performs in an attempt to avoid distress or worry.

COCAINE-INDUCED SEXUAL DYSFUNCTION. The person with this disorder has experienced intoxication or withdrawal from cocaine within a month from the time he or she begins to experience sexual difficulties, and these difficulties are deemed by the clinician to be due directly to the cocaine use. Substance-induced sexual difficulties can range from impaired desire, impaired arousal, impaired orgasm, or sexual pain.

COCAINE-INDUCED SLEEP DISORDER. This disorder is characterized by difficulty sleeping (**insomnia**) during intoxication or increased sleep duration when patients are in withdrawal.

COCAINE-RELATED DISORDER NOT OTHERWISE SPECIFIED. This classification is reserved for clinicians to use when a cocaine disorder that the clinician sees does not fit into any of the above categories.

KEY TERMS

Anxiety—Can be experienced as a troubled feeling, a sense of dread, fear of the future, or distress over a possible threat to a person's physical or mental well-being.

Depression—A mental state characterized by feelings of sadness, despair, and discouragement.

Dopamine—A chemical in brain tissue that serves to transmit nerve impulses and helps to regulate movement and emotions.

Hallucinations—To hear, see, or otherwise sense things that are not real. Hallucinations can result from nervous system abnormalities, mental disorders, or the use of certain drugs.

Panic attack—A period of intense fear or discomfort with a feeling of doom and a desire to escape. The person may shake, sweat, be short of breath, and experience chest pain.

Causes and symptoms

Causes

BIOCHEMICAL/PHYSIOLOGICAL CAUSES. Twin studies have demonstrated that there is a higher rate of cocaine abuse in identical twins as compared to fraternal twins. This indicates that **genetic factors** contribute to the development of cocaine abuse. This finding also indicates, however, that unique environmental factors contribute to the development of cocaine abuse as well. (If genes alone determined who would develop cocaine dependence, 100% of the identical twins with the predisposing genes would develop the disorder. However, because the results show only a relationship, or a correlation, between genetics and cocaine use among twins, these results indicate that other factors must be at work as well.) Studies have also shown that disorders like **attention deficit hyperactivity disorder** (ADHD), **conduct disorder**, and **antisocial personality disorder** all have genetic components, and since patients who abuse cocaine have a high incidence of these diagnoses, they may also be genetically predisposed to abusing cocaine.

REINFORCEMENT. Learning and conditioning also play a unique role in the perpetuation of cocaine abuse. Each inhalation and injection of cocaine causes pleasurable feelings that reinforce the drug-taking procedure. In addition, the patient's environment plays a role in cueing and reinforcing the experience in the patient's mind. The association between cocaine and environment is so strong that many people recovering from cocaine **addiction** report that being in an area where they used drugs brings back memories of the experience and makes them crave drugs. Specific areas of the **brain** are thought to be involved in cocaine craving, including the amygdala (a part of the brain that controls aggression and emotional reactivity) and the prefrontal cortex (a part of the brain that regulates anger, aggression, and the brain's assessment of fear, threats, and danger).

Symptoms

The following list is a summary of the acute (short-term) physical and psychological effects of cocaine on the body:

- blood vessels constrict
- elevated heart rate
- elevated blood pressure
- a feeling of intense happiness
- elevated energy level
- a state of increased alertness and sensory sensitivity
- elevated anxiety
- panic attacks
- elevated self-esteem
- diminished appetite
- spontaneous ejaculation and heightened sexual arousal
- psychosis (loss of contact with reality)

The following list is a summary of the chronic (long-term) physical and psychological effects of cocaine on the body:

- depressed mood
- irritability
- physical agitation
- decreased motivation
- difficulty sleeping
- hypervigilance
- elevated anxiety
- panic attacks
- hallucinations
- psychosis

Diagnosis

If a mental health clinician suspects cocaine use, he or she may ask the patient specifically about swallowing, injecting, or smoking the substance. Urine and blood testing will also be conducted to determine the presence of the substance. Doctors may talk to friends or relatives concerning the patient's drug use, especially for cases in which the physician suspects that the patient is not being entirely honest about substance use. The clinician may also investigate a patient's legal history for drug arrests that may give clues to periods of **substance abuse** to which the patient will not admit.

Differential diagnosis

Differential diagnosis is the process of distinguishing one condition from other, similar conditions. The cocaine abuse disorder is easily confused with other substance abuse disorders and various forms of mental illness.

The symptoms of cocaine intoxication, such as increased talkativeness, poor sleep, and the intense feelings of happiness, are similar to the symptoms for **bipolar disorder**, so the urine toxification screening test may play a key role in the diagnosis. Patients with cocaine intoxication with hallucinations and delusions can be mistaken for schizophrenic patients instead, further emphasizing the importance of the urine and blood screens. As part of establishing the diagnosis, the physician must also rule out PCP (phencyclidine) intoxication and Cushing's disease (an endocrine disorder of excessive cortisol production). Withdrawal symptoms are similar to those of the patient with major **depression**. For this reason, the clinician may ask the patient about his or her mood during times of abstinence from drug use to discern whether any true mood disorders are present. If cocaine use is causing depression, the depression should resolve within a couple of weeks of stopping drug use.

Laboratory testing

The breakdown products of cocaine remain in the urine. The length of time that they remain depends on the dose of cocaine, but most doses would not remain in the urine longer than a few days. Cocaine can also be found in other bodily fluids such as blood, saliva, sweat, and hair, and these provide better estimates as to recent cocaine use. The hair can hold evidence that a patient has been using drugs for weeks to months. **Positron emission tomography (PET)** and single-photon emission **computed tomography** (SPECT) are different kinds of **imaging studies**. Both kinds of scans look at the amount of blood that is flowing to the brain. When these images are taken of the brains of people who abuse cocaine, the resulting scans can reveal abnormalities in certain sections of the brain. The brains of people addicted to cocaine shrink, or atrophy.

Neuropsychological assessment

Neuropsychological testing is also an important tool for examining the effects of toxic substances on brain functioning. Some physicians may use neuropsychological assessments to reveal patients' cognitive and physical impairment after cocaine use. Neuropsychological testing assesses brain functioning through structured and systematic behavioral observation. Neuropsychological tests are designed to examine a variety of cognitive abilities, including speed of information processing, attention, memory, and language. An example of a task that a physician might ask the patient to complete as part of a neuropsychological examination is to name as many words beginning with a particular letter as the patient can in one minute. Patients who abuse cocaine often have difficulty completing tasks, such as the one described, that require concentration and memory.

Treatment

Psychological and social interventions

TREATMENT SETTINGS. Not all patients who abuse cocaine need to resort to long-term treatment. Treatment length varies with the degree that a person is dependent on the substance. If the patient has other psychiatric conditions, such as major depression or **schizophrenia**, or has significant medical complications of cocaine abuse, then he or she is more likely to require higher-intensity treatment. Residential programs or therapeutic communities may be helpful, particularly in more severe cases. Patients typically spend six to 12 months in such programs, which may also include vocational training and other features. The availability of such treatment, as well as medical insurance's ability to cover treatment, are all issues that affect the patient's access to treatment.

PSYCHOTHERAPY. A wide range of behavioral interventions have been successfully used to treat cocaine addiction. The approach used must be tailored to the specific needs of each individual patient, however.

Contingency management rewards drug abstinence (confirmed by urine testing) with points or vouchers that patients can exchange for such things as an evening out or membership in a gym. **Cognitive-behavioral therapy** helps users learn to recognize and avoid situations most likely to lead to cocaine use and to develop healthier ways to cope with stressful situations.

Supportive therapy helps patients to modify their behavior by preventing **relapse** by taking actions such as staying away from drug-using friends and from neighborhoods or situations where cocaine is abundant.

Self-help groups like Narcotics Anonymous (NA) or Cocaine Anonymous (CA) are helpful for many recovering substance abusers. CA is a twelve-step program for cocaine abusers, modeled after Alcoholics Anonymous (AA). **Support groups** and **group therapy** led by a therapist can be helpful because other addicts can share coping and relapse-prevention strategies. The group's support can help patients face devastating changes and life issues. Some experts recommend that patients be cocaine-free for at least two weeks before participating in a group, but other experts argue that a two-week waiting period is unnecessary and counterproductive. Group counseling sessions led by drug counselors who are in recovery themselves are also useful for some people overcoming their addictions. These group counseling sessions differ from group therapy in that the people in a counseling group are constantly changing.

The National Institute of Drug Abuse conducted a study comparing different forms of **psychotherapy**: patients who had both group drug counseling and individual drug counseling had improved outcomes. Patients who had cognitive-behavioral therapy stayed in treatment longer.

Medications

Many medications—greater than twenty—have been tested, but none has been found to reduce the intensity of withdrawal. **Dopamine** agonists like **amantadine** and bromocriptine and tricyclic **antidepressants** such as **desipramine** have failed in studies to help treat symptoms of cocaine withdrawal or intoxication.

QUESTIONS TO ASK YOUR DOCTOR

- What risks are associated with cocaine abuse?
- What symptoms are associated with cocaine dependence?
- Does having cocaine dependence and abuse put me at risk for other health conditions?
- Can you recommend any treatment and support groups for me?

Alternative therapy

Alternative techniques, such as **acupuncture**, EEG **biofeedback**, and visualization, may be useful in treating addiction when combined with conventional treatment approaches.

Prognosis

Not all cocaine abusers become dependent on the drug. However, even someone who only uses occasionally can experience the harmful effects (interpersonal relationship conflicts, work or school difficulties) of using cocaine, and even occasional use is enough to addict. In the course of a person's battle with cocaine abuse, he or she may vary the forms of the drug that he or she uses. A person may use the inhaled form at one time and the injected form at another, for example.

Many studies of short-term outpatient treatment over a six-month to two-year period indicate that people addicted to cocaine have a better chance of recovering than people who are addicted to heroin. A study of veterans who participated in an inpatient or day hospital treatment program that lasted 28 days revealed that about 60% of people who were abstinent at four months were able to maintain their abstinence at seven months.

Having a good social support network greatly improves the prognosis for recovery from cocaine abuse and dependence.

Prevention

Efforts to prevent cocaine abuse, as well as any substance abuse, begin with prevention programs that are based in schools or in the workplace, heath care clinics, criminal justice systems, and public housing. Programs such as Students Taught Awareness (STAR) are cost-effective and have reduced the rates of substance abuse in the schools. These school-based programs also foster parental involvement and education about substance abuse issues. The juvenile justice system also implements drug-prevention programs. Even many workplaces provide drug screening and treatment and counseling for those who test positive. Employers may also provide workshops on substance abuse prevention. The United States Department of Housing and Urban Development (HUD) also sponsors drug-prevention programs.

Resources

BOOKS

American Psychiatric Association. *Diagnostic and Statistical Manual of Mental Disorders.* 4th ed., Text rev. Washington, DC: American Psychiatric Association, 2000.

American Psychological Association. *Publication Manual of the American Psychological Association,* 6th ed. Washington, DC: American Psychological Association, 2009.

Erickson, Carlton K. *Addiction Essentials: The Go-To Guide for Clinicians and Patients.* New York: W. W. Norton & Company, 2011.

Sadock, Benjamin J., Virginia Alcott Sadock, and Pedro Ruiz, eds. *Kaplan and Sadock's Comprehensive Textbook of Psychiatry,* 2nd ed. New York: Lippincott Williams & Wilkins, 2009.

PERIODICALS

Adinoff, Byron, et al. "Limbic Response to Procaine in Cocaine Addicted Subjects." *American Journal of Psychiatry* (March 2001): 390-398.

Held, Gale A. "Linkages Between Substance Abuse Prevention and Other Human Services Literature Review." National Institute on Drug Abuse (NIDA) (June 1998).

Jacobsen, Leslie K., et al. "Quantitative Morphology of the Caudate and Putamen in Patients With Cocaine Dependence." *American Journal of Psychiatry* (March 2000): 486-489.

Kampman, Kyle M., et al. "Amantadine in the Treatment of Cocaine-Dependent Patients With Severe Withdrawal Symptoms." *American Journal of Psychiatry* (December 2000): 2052-2054.

WEBSITES

Leshner, Alan. "Cocaine Abuse and Addiction." *National Institute on Drug Abuse Research Report Series.* NIH Publication Number 99-4342. Washington, D.C: U.S. Government Printing Offices, 1999, revised September 2010. http://www.drugabuse.gov/ResearchReports/Cocaine/Cocaine.html (accessed December 19, 2011).

ORGANIZATIONS

American Academy of Addiction Psychiatry (AAAP), 400 Massasoiti Ave., Ste. 307, 2nd Fl., East Providence, RI, 02914, (401) 524-3076, Fax: (401) 272-0922, http://www.aaap.org.

American Psychiatric Association, 1000 Wilson Blvd., Ste. 1825, Arlington, VA, 22209, (703) 907-7300, apa@psych.org, http://www.psych.org.

American Psychological Association, 750 First Street NE, Washington, DC, 20003, (202) 336-5500, http://www.apa.org/index.aspx.

Cocaine Anonymous World Services (CAWS), 21720 S Wilmington Ave., Ste. 304, Long Beach, CA, 90810, (301) 559-5833, http://www.ca.org.

National Institute on Drug Abuse, 6001 Executive Blvd., Rm. 5213, Bethesda, MD, 20892, (301) 442-1124; Spanish: (240) 221-4007, information@nida.nih.gov, http://www.nida.nih.gov.

Substance Abuse and Mental Health Services Administration, 1 Choke Cherry Rd., Rockville, MD, 20857, (877) SAMHSA-7 (726-4727), (800) TTY: 487-4889, Fax: (240) 221-4292, SAMHSAInfo@samhsa.hhs.gov, http://www.samhsa.gov.

Susan Hobbs, MD
Peter Gregutt
Laura Jean Cataldo, RN, EdD

Cogentin *see* **Benztropine**

Cognex *see* **Tacrine**

Cognistat

Definition

The Cognistat is a standardized neurobehavioral screening test. It is a test that examines neurological (**brain** and central nervous system) health in relation to a person's behavior.

Purpose

As a screening test, the Cognistat may be administered to identify basic strengths and weaknesses so that further tests (if necessary) can be selected, and the data provided by the Cognistat can then be used as preliminary data against which scores from other tests given may be compared. Cognistat results have been used in a number of arenas, most notably in behavioral medicine. For example, Cognistat results may be useful to track cognitive decline (decreased thinking and reasoning abilities) in patients with organic brain disorders, to develop helpful strategies for cognitive problems associated with **schizophrenia**, and to help distinguish among terminally ill cancer patients those with **depression** and anxiety versus those with cognitive impairment.

Description

The Cognistat usually takes less than 45 minutes to complete, and the test explores, quantifies, and describes performance in central areas of brain-behavior relations: level of consciousness, orientation, attention, language, constructional ability, memory, calculations and reasoning. The subareas of language are spontaneous speech, comprehension, repetition, and naming. The subareas of reasoning are similarities and judgment. Exploration occurs through interactive behavioral tasks that rely on perception, cognitive processing, and motor skills. The test is more quickly administered to higher than lower functioning individuals by providing a difficult screening item at the beginning of each section. Only when a screening item is missed are the metric, or more remedial, items applied, usually from easiest to most difficult within that section.

The test begins with the examiner asking general questions of the test taker (name, address, age, etc.), and while these questions are being answered, the examiner is subjectively assessing the test taker's level of consciousness. The examiner then asks general questions to confirm the test taker's level of orientation, meaning that the test taker is correctly oriented to place and time—he or she knows what day it is and where he or she is. To test the examinee's attention and memory, the test taker will be asked to repeat a series of digits and the first part of a verbal memory task will be given. (This task will be asked about again later in the test.)

The language section begins with a sample of spontaneous speech derived by asking for a description of a detailed line drawing. The language comprehension section requires responses to simple commands that involve manipulation of common objects placed before the examinee. In the language repetition subtest, the test taker is asked to repeat short phrases and simple sentences. In naming, the last of the language subtests, the screening item differs in form from the metric (easier) items. In the screening item, the examiner holds up an object and asks the test taker to name its four major parts, as the examiner points to them one after another. If the test taker fails, he or she is asked to name eight separate objects, one after another represented by line drawings.

In the next section, constructional ability, the screening item is a visual memory task wherein a stimulus sheet is presented for ten seconds, and the examinee is asked to draw the stimuli from memory. The test taker is then asked to assemble plastic tiles into designs, one after another, as each is shown on a card. Faster completion yields greater points. After the constructional items, the test taker is asked to recall the verbal memory items presented earlier. For items he or she cannot recall, the examiner provides prompts, or clues.

The calculations section is composed of simple verbal mathematics, and is followed by the reasoning section, which includes two subtests. The first consists of associative thinking items known as similarities. In similarities items, the examinee is asked to explain how two concepts are alike. Greater points are awarded if their concept is abstract rather than concrete. The final subtest on the Cognistat is the judgment subtest of the reasoning section. In the judgment subtest, the examinee is asked to answer questions that demonstrate practical judgment in solving basic problem scenarios. Scores for this subtest are weighted based on their appropriateness. There is only one fully appropriate response to each item.

The test booklet provides space for listing medications, and for noting comments about any physical deficits and the examinee's impression of his or her own performance.

KEY TERMS

Screening test—A test given as a preliminary tool, that helps to later target a more thorough analysis.

Standardized test—A test that follows a regimented structure, and each individual's scores may be compared with those of groups of people. In the case of the Cognistat, test taker's scores can be compared to groups of young adults, middle-aged adults, the geriatric, and people who have undergone neurosurgery.

Risks

The Cognistat is more sensitive than many similar tests, but considers a limited sample of behavior at a brief point in time. Thus, its results are not generalizable and should not be viewed as conclusive indicators of the areas being assessed. It is important that the examiner be properly trained in the use of the test. Test takers may be affected by test-related discomfort or performance anxiety. This may be particularly true when prior to testing, the examinee was not fully aware of his or her deficits, especially deficits that become more apparent as testing progresses. The test's reliability has not been fully documented. Further research and standardization data is needed.

Results

When test administration is complete, the examiner tallies the points earned in each section, and plots them on the cognitive status profile located on the front of the test booklet. On the profile, numerical scores are described to fall within the normal or impaired range. The impaired range is broken down into mild, moderate and severe. An individual's scores can also be compared to standardization group data, and his or her profile may be compared to five case study profiles presented in the test guide. The few items that do not allow for quantitative analysis—the sample of spontaneous speech, for example—are factored into the interpretation of results by the examiner. There is no mechanism for transforming raw scores into percentiles or standard scores, and the test is not designed to generate one main score.

Resources

BOOKS

Northern California Neurobehavioral Group, Inc. *2011 Cognistat and Cognistat Assessment System Manual*. Fairfax, CA: 2011.

PERIODICALS

Nazem, Sarra, et al. "Montreal Cognitive Assessment Performance in Patients with Parkinson's Disease with 'Normal' Global Cognition According to Mini-Mental State Examination Score." *Journal of the American Geriatric Society* 57, no. 2 (February 2009) 304–308.

WEBSITES

Cognistat.com. http://www.cognistat.com (accessed October 30, 2011).

Geoffrey G. Grimm, PhD, LPC

Cognitive-behavioral therapy

Definition

Cognitive-behavioral therapy (CBT) is an action-oriented form of psychosocial therapy that assumes that maladaptive, or faulty, thinking patterns cause maladaptive behavior and negative emotions. (Maladaptive behavior is behavior that is counter-productive or interferes with everyday living.) The treatment focuses on changing individuals' thoughts (cognitive patterns) in order to change their behavior and emotional state. CBT can be employed with both adults and children.

Purpose

Theoretically, cognitive-behavioral therapy can be employed in any situation in which there is a pattern of unwanted behavior accompanied by distress and impairment. CBT differs from other traditional forms of supportive **psychotherapy** in that it is time-limited and does not attempt to understand the etiology of the disorder. Instead, it works to change dysfunctional, ingrained thought patterns that lead to dysfunctional behaviors. The entire process is often accomplished in 6–20 one-hour sessions.

CBT is a recommended treatment option for a number of mental disorders, including affective (mood) disorders, **personality disorders**, **social phobia**, **obsessive-compulsive disorder** (OCD), eating disorders, **substance abuse**, anxiety or **panic disorder**, **agoraphobia**, **post-traumatic stress disorder** (PTSD), and **attention deficit hyperactivity disorder (ADHD)**. Newer applications include treating **stuttering**. It is also frequently used as a tool for dealing with chronic pain for patients with illnesses such as rheumatoid arthritis, back problems, and cancer. Patients with **sleep disorders** may also find cognitive-behavioral therapy a useful treatment for **insomnia**. Some research has shown CBT alone to have better efficacy than medication alone in the treatment of these disorders; other research shows that a combination of CBT and medication offers the greatest benefit. Research supports the use of CBT (without medication) as a first-line treatment for a number of disorders, including binge eating, insomnia, and some **anxiety disorders**.

Precautions

CBT may not be suitable for some patients. Those who do not have a specific behavioral issue they wish to address and whose goals for therapy are to gain insight into the past may be better served by psychodynamic therapy. Patients must also be willing to take an active role in the treatment process.

Cognitive-behavioral **intervention** may be inappropriate for some severely psychotic patients and for cognitively impaired patients (for example, patients with organic **brain** disease or a **traumatic brain injury**), depending on their level of functioning. Some research has refuted the use of CBT in **schizophrenia** and **bipolar disorder**, although there has also been research that suggests that CBT can be useful in improving the negative and **positive symptoms** of schizophrenia, decreasing hospitalizations, and improving **compliance** with the medical regimens of both schizophrenia and bipolar disorder.

Description

CBT combines the individual goals of cognitive therapy and behavioral therapy.

Pioneered by psychologists Aaron Beck and Albert Ellis in the 1960s, cognitive therapy assumes that maladaptive behaviors and disturbed mood or emotions are the result of inappropriate or irrational thinking patterns, called automatic thoughts. Instead of reacting to the reality of a situation, individuals react to their own distorted viewpoint of the situation. For example, a person may conclude that he is "worthless" simply because he failed an exam or did not get a date. Cognitive therapists attempt to make their patients aware of these distorted thinking patterns, or cognitive distortions, and change them (a process termed cognitive restructuring).

Behavioral therapy, or **behavior modification**, trains individuals to replace undesirable behaviors with healthier behavioral patterns. Unlike psychodynamic therapies, it does not focus on uncovering or understanding the unconscious motivations that may be behind the maladaptive behavior. In other words, strictly behavioral therapists do not try to find out why their patients behave the way they do, they just teach them to change the behavior.

CBT integrates the cognitive restructuring approach of cognitive therapy with the behavioral modification techniques of behavioral therapy. The therapist works with the patient to identify both the thoughts and the behaviors that are causing distress and to change those thoughts in order to readjust the behavior. In some cases, the patient may have certain fundamental core beliefs, called schemas, which are flawed and require modification. For example, a patient with **depression** may be avoiding social contact with others and experiencing considerable emotional distress because of his or her isolation. When questioned why, the patient may reveal that he or she is afraid of rejection or of what others may do or say. Upon further exploration, the patient and therapist may discover that the patient's real fear is not rejection, but the belief that he or she is uninteresting and unlovable. The therapist might test the reality of that assertion by having the patient name friends and family who love him or her and enjoy the patient's company. By showing the patient that others value him or her, the therapist both exposes the irrationality of the patient's beliefs and provides him or her with a new model of thought to change old behavior patterns. In this case, the person learns to think, "I am an interesting and lovable person; therefore, I should not have difficulty making new friends in social situations." If enough "irrational cognitions" are changed, the patient may experience considerable relief from his depression.

A number of different techniques may be employed in CBT to help patients uncover and examine their thoughts and change their behaviors. They include:

- Behavioral homework assignments. Cognitive-behavioral therapists frequently request that their patients complete homework assignments between therapy sessions. These may consist of real-life "behavioral experiments" where patients are encouraged to try out new responses to situations discussed in therapy sessions.
- Cognitive rehearsal. The patient imagines a difficult situation and the therapist guides him through the step-by-step process of facing and successfully dealing with it. The patient then works on practicing, or rehearsing, these steps mentally. Ideally, when the situation arises in real life, the patient will draw on the rehearsed behavior to address it.
- Journal. Patients are asked to keep a detailed diary recounting their thoughts, feelings, and actions when specific situations arise. The journal helps to make patients aware of their maladaptive thoughts and to show their consequences on behavior. In later stages of therapy, it may serve to demonstrate and reinforce positive behaviors.
- Modeling. The therapist and patient engage in role-playing exercises in which the therapist acts out appropriate behaviors or responses to situations.
- Conditioning. The therapist uses reinforcement to encourage a particular behavior. For example, a child with ADHD gets a gold star every time he stays focused on tasks and accomplishes certain daily chores. The gold star reinforces and increases the desired behavior by identifying it with something positive. Reinforcement can also be used to extinguish unwanted behaviors by imposing negative consequences.
- Systematic desensitization. Patients imagine a situation they fear, while the therapist employs techniques to help them relax, helping them cope with their fear reaction and eventually eliminate the anxiety altogether. For example, patients in treatment for agoraphobia, or fear of open or public places, will relax and then picture themselves on the sidewalk outside of their house. In their next session, they may relax and then imagine a visit to a crowded shopping mall. The imagery of the anxiety-producing situations gets progressively more intense until, eventually, the therapist and patient approach the anxiety-causing situation in real-life (a "graded exposure"), perhaps by visiting a mall. Exposure may be increased to the point of "flooding," providing maximum exposure to the real situation. By repeatedly pairing a desired response (relaxation) with a fear-producing situation (open, public spaces), patients gradually become desensitized to the old response of fear and learns to react with feelings of relaxation.
- Validity testing. Patients are asked to test the validity of the automatic thoughts and schemas they encounter. The therapist may ask patients to defend or produce evidence that a schema is true. If the patients are unable to meet the challenge, the faulty nature of the schema is exposed.

- Aversive conditioning. This technique employs the principles of classical conditioning to lessen the appeal of a behavior that is difficult to change because it is either habitual or temporarily rewarding. Patients are exposed to an unpleasant stimulus while engaged in or thinking about the behavior in question. Eventually the behavior itself becomes associated with unpleasant rather than pleasant feelings. One treatment method used with alcoholics is the administration of a nausea-inducing drug together with an alcoholic beverage to produce an aversion to the taste and smell of alcohol by having it become associated with nausea. Studies investigating use of these aversive conditioning approaches have not identified a high level of therapeutic effectiveness. According to the American Psychiatric Association, aversion therapy should be practiced only in specialized centers. In counterconditioning, a maladaptive response is weakened by the strengthening of a response that is incompatible with it. A well-known type of counterconditioning is systematic desensitization, which counteracts the anxiety connected with a particular behavior or situation by inducing a relaxed response to it instead. This method is often used in the treatment of people who are afraid of flying.

Initial treatment sessions are typically spent explaining the basic tenets of CBT to patients and establishing a positive working relationship between therapist and patient. CBT is a collaborative, action-oriented therapy effort. As such, it empowers patients by giving them an active role in the therapy process and discourages any overdependence on the therapist that may occur in other therapeutic relationships. Therapy is typically administered in an outpatient setting in either an individual or group session. Therapists include psychologists, clinical **social workers**, counselors, or psychiatrists. Treatment is relatively short in comparison to some other forms of psychotherapy, usually lasting no longer than 16 weeks. Many insurance plans provide reimbursement for cognitive-behavioral therapy services. Because coverage is dependent on the disorder or illness the therapy is treating, patients should check with their individual plans.

Rational-emotive behavior therapy

Rational-emotive behavior therapy (REBT) is a popular variation of cognitive-behavioral therapy developed in 1955 by **psychologist** Albert Ellis. REBT is based on the belief that individuals' past experiences shape their belief system and thinking patterns. People form illogical, irrational thinking patterns that become the cause of both their negative emotions and of further irrational ideas. REBT focuses on helping patients discover these irrational beliefs that guide their behavior and replace them with rational beliefs and thoughts in order to relieve their emotional distress.

There are ten basic irrational assumptions that trigger maladaptive emotions and behaviors:

- It is a necessity for an adult to be loved and approved of by almost everyone for virtually everything.
- A person must be thoroughly competent, adequate, and successful in all respects.
- Certain people are bad, wicked, or villainous and should be punished for their sins.
- It is catastrophic when things are not going the way one would like.
- Human unhappiness is externally caused. People have little or no ability to control their sorrows or to rid themselves of negative feelings.
- It is right to be terribly preoccupied with and upset about something that may be dangerous or fearsome.

KEY TERMS

Automatic thoughts—Thoughts that automatically come to mind when a particular situation occurs. Cognitive-behavioral therapy seeks to challenge automatic thoughts.

Cognitive restructuring—The process of replacing maladaptive thought patterns with constructive thoughts and beliefs.

Maladaptive—Unsuitable or counterproductive; for example, maladaptive behavior is inappropriate to a given situation.

Psychodynamic therapy—A therapeutic approach that assumes dysfunctional or unwanted behavior is caused by unconscious, internal conflicts and focuses on gaining insight into these motivations.

Relaxation technique—A technique used to relieve stress. Exercise, biofeedback, hypnosis, and meditation are all effective relaxation tools. Relaxation techniques are used in cognitive-behavioral therapy to teach patients new ways of coping with stressful situations.

Schemas—Fundamental core beliefs or assumptions that are part of the perceptual filter people use to view the world. Cognitive-behavioral therapy seeks to change maladaptive schemas.

- It is easier to avoid facing many of life's difficulties and responsibilities than it is to undertake more rewarding forms of self-discipline.
- The past is all-important. Because something once strongly affected someone's life, it should continue to do so indefinitely.
- People and things should be different from the way they are. It is catastrophic if perfect solutions to the grim realities of life are not immediately found.
- Maximal human happiness can be achieved by inertia and inaction or by living passively and without commitment.

QUESTIONS TO ASK YOUR DOCTOR

- What kind of therapy is right for me?
- Does insurance usually cover this kind of treatment?
- How often should I attend therapy?
- How long will my treatment last before I see results?

Meichenbaum's self-instructional approach

Psychologist Donald Meichenbaum pioneered the self-instructional, or "self-talk," approach to CBT in the 1970s. This approach focuses on changing what people say to themselves, both internally and out loud. It is based on the belief that an individual's actions follow directly from this self-talk. This type of therapy emphasizes teaching patients coping skills that they can use in a variety of situations to help themselves. The technique used to accomplish this is self-instructional inner dialogue, a method of talking through a problem or situation as it occurs.

Preparation

Patients may seek therapy independently or be referred for treatment by a primary physician, psychologist, or **psychiatrist**. Because the patient and therapist work closely together to achieve specific therapeutic objectives, it is important that their working relationship is comfortable and their goals are compatible. Prior to beginning treatment, the patient and therapist should meet for a consultation session, or mutual interview. The consultation gives the therapist the opportunity to make an initial assessment of the patient and recommend a course of treatment and goals for therapy. It also gives the patient an opportunity to find out important details about the therapist's approach to treatment, professional credentials, and any other issues of interest.

In some managed-care clinical settings, an intake interview or evaluation is required before a patient begins therapy. The intake interview is used to evaluate the patient and assign the person to a therapist. It may be conducted by a psychiatric nurse, counselor, or social worker.

Results

Many patients who undergo CBT successfully learn how to replace their maladaptive thoughts and behaviors with positive ones that facilitate individual growth and happiness. CBT may be used in conjunction with pharmaceutical and other treatment interventions, so overall success rates are difficult to gauge. However, success rates of 65% or more have been reported with CBT alone as a treatment for panic attacks and agoraphobia. Although many of the conditions that are responsive to CBT may **relapse**, follow-up sessions can be effective, even on an as-needed basis, and often require fewer sessions than the initial round of treatment.

Resources

BOOKS

Beck, Judith S. *Cognitive Behavior Therapy: Basics and Beyond*. 2nd ed. New York: Guilford Press, 2011.

Craske, Michelle G. *Cognitive-Behavioral Therapy*. Washington, DC: American Psychological Association, 2010.

PERIODICALS

Freedman S. "Cognitive Behavior Therapy for Panic Disorder." *Israeli Journal Psychiatry and Related Sciences* 46 (2009): 251–56.

Manicavasgar V. "Mindfulness-based Cognitive Therapy vs. Cognitive Behaviour Therapy as a Treatment for Non-melancholic Depression." *Journal of Affective Disorders* 130 (2011): 138–44.

McManus F. "A Demonstration of the Efficacy of Two of the Components of Cognitive Therapy for Social Phobia." *Journal of Anxiety Disorders* 23 (2009): 496–503.

WEBSITES

"Psychotherapies." National Institutes of Health. August 16, 2010. http://www.nimh.nih.gov/health/topics/psychotherapies/index.shtml (accessed October 11, 2011).

ORGANIZATIONS

Albert Ellis Institute, 45 East 65th St., New York, NY, 10021, (212) 535-0822, (800) 323-4738, Fax: (212) 249-3582, info@albertellis.org, http://www.rebt.org.

Association for Behavioral and Cognitive Therapies, 305 7th Ave., 16th Fl., New York, NY, 10001, (212) 647-1890, Fax: (212) 647-1865, (866) 615-6464, http://www.abct.org.

Beck Institute for Cognitive Behavior Therapy, 1 Belmont Ave., Ste. 700, Bala Cynwyd, PA, 19004, (610) 664-3020, Fax: (610) 709-5336, info@beckinstitute.org, http://www.beckinstitute.org.

Paula Anne Ford-Martin
Brenda W. Lerner

Cognitive problem-solving skills training

Definition

Cognitive problem-solving skills training (CPSST) is a behavioral treatment that attempts to decrease or eliminate inappropriate or disruptive behaviors in children. The training emphasizes teaching children coping mechanisms so that they can react to situations in calm and rational ways. Using both cognitive and behavioral techniques and focusing on the child more than on the parents or the family unit, CPSST helps the child gain the ability to self-manage thoughts and feelings and interact appropriately with others by developing new perspectives and solutions. The basis of the treatment is the underlying principle that children lacking constructive ways to address the environment have problematic behaviors; teaching children positive problem solving and challenging dysfunctional thoughts improves functioning.

Purpose

The goal of CPSST is to reduce or terminate inappropriate, dysfunctional behaviors in children by expanding their "behavioral repertoire," including ways of cognitive processing. The behavioral repertoire is the range of ways of behaving that an individual possesses. With certain disorders, such as **conduct disorder**, **intermittent explosive disorder**, **oppositional defiant disorder**, antisocial behaviors, aggressive acting out, or **attention deficit hyperactivity disorder** with disruptive behavior, the number of ways of interpreting reality and responding to the world are limited and involve primarily negative responses. Although CPSST originally focused on children with problem behaviors or poor relationships with others, it has generalized its focus to a variety of different disorders in children and adults (though most of the treatment research is focused on children).

Description

The therapist conducts individual CPSST sessions with the child, usually once a week for 45 minutes to an hour, typically for several months to a year. The cognitive portion of the treatment involves changing false views of daily situations, confronting irrational interpretations of others' actions, challenging the unhelpful assumptions that typically underlie the individual's problem behaviors, and generating alternative solutions to problems. For example, if meeting with a child who has received a school suspension for becoming physically enraged at a teacher, the therapist will start by exploring the situation with the child, asking what thoughts and feelings were experienced. The child might state, "My teacher hates me. I'm always getting sent to the principal and she yells at me all the time." The therapist will try to help the child explore the supporting evidence for the "my teacher hates me" notion based on things seen or heard in the classroom. The ultimate goal is to help the child shift his or her perceptions so that, instead of seeing the student-teacher negative interactions as something external to the self, the child comes to see his or her part in the problem. This discussion also helps the child to see that he or she can help influence the outcome of the student/teacher interactions. When the child makes a global, stable, and negative attribution about why the interactions with the teacher are negative—where the attitude of the teacher is the cause of the problems—the child loses the sense of having any efficacy and is liable to show poorer behavior. By changing the child's perceptions and examining different options for the child's responses, the child recognizes that changing his or her own behavior can produce positive outcomes.

The behavioral aspect of CPSST involves **modeling** positive behaviors, role-playing challenging situations, and rewarding improvement in behavior, as well as providing corrective feedback on alternative and more appropriate ways of handling situations. In each session, the child is coached on problem-solving techniques, including brainstorming a number of possible solutions to difficulties, evaluating solutions, and planning the steps involved in gaining a desired goal (also called "means-end thinking"). For instance, when discussing a conflict, the therapist might help the child come up with some techniques for handling future situations, such as visualizing a calming scene, using a mediator to work out the issue, or avoiding problematic behaviors. The options generated would be discussed and evaluated as to how practical they are and how to implement them.

After a session, the child is given therapy homework, which might include implementing these newer ways of thinking and behaving in specific types of problematic situations, such as in school, with peers, or at home. The child might be asked to keep track of negative, externalizing thoughts by maintaining a written record of them for several days. The therapist may ask the child to try one of the new options and compare the results against past experiences. Typically, the between-sessions work begins with the conditions that appear the easiest in which to implement new behaviors, gradually progressing to more complex or challenging circumstances.

Although the bulk of the sessions involve the individual child and the therapist, the parents are brought into the therapy for a portion of the work. The parents observe the therapist and the child as they practice the new skills and are educated on how to assist the child outside of the sessions. Parents learn how to correctly remind the child to use the CPSST techniques for problem solving in daily living and assist the child with the steps involved in applying these skills. Parents are also coached on how to promote the positive behaviors by rewarding their occurrence with praise, extra attention, points toward obtaining a reward desired by the child, stickers or other small indicators of positive behavior, additional privileges, or hugs and other affectionate gestures. The scientific term for the rewarding of desired behavior is "positive reinforcement," referring to consequences that cause the desired target behavior to increase.

In research studies of outcomes, CPSST has been found to be effective in changing children's behavior. Changes in behavior have been shown to persist long term (one year) after completion of treatment. Success in altering undesirable behaviors is enhanced when CPSST is combined with **parent management training**. Parent management training is the in-depth education of parents or other primary caretakers in applying behavioral techniques such as positive **reinforcement** in their parenting.

Preparation

Parents and older children can prepare for cognitive problem-solving skills training by researching the topic before attending sessions. In addition, parents can practice positive behavior as a supplement to CPSST. Such behaviors will often help children learn how to deal with situations in more appropriate ways.

KEY TERMS

Attention deficit hyperactivity disorder (ADHD)—A persistent pattern of inattention, hyperactivity and/or impulsiveness, typically found in children.

Conduct disorder—A behavioral and emotional disorder of childhood and adolescence, characterized by socially inappropriate behaviors.

Dysfunctional—Degraded ability or inability to function emotionally.

Intermittent explosive disorder—A disorder characterized by uncontrolled anger and rage, especially when the situation is not seen as appropriate for such behaviors by normally acting persons.

Modeling—A behavioral therapy technique in which a patient first observes and then imitates a desired behavior.

Oppositional defiant disorder—A consistent public pattern of actions that display defiance and hostility toward authorities.

Precautions

The CPSST is considered to be a good way to minimize or eliminate inappropriate or disruptive behaviors in children when administered by a trained professional. Parents should seek therapists with solid credentials and experience. CPSST may not work the first time and may need to be repeated, along with additional counseling. If parent management training was not included initially, it may likely be included in repeat sessions of CPSST.

Results

While individual results vary, problematic behaviors are reduced or eliminated in many children.

See also Behavior modification; Token economy system

Resources

BOOKS

Beauchaine, Theodore P., and Stephen P. Hinshaw, eds. *Child and Adolescent Psychopathology*. Hoboken, NJ: John Wiley and Sons, 2008.

D'Zurilla, Thomas J., and Arthur M. Nezu. *Problem-Solving Therapy: A Positive Approach to Clinical Intervention*. New York: Springer, 2007.

Macdonald, Alasdair J. *Solution-Focused Therapy: Theory, Research and Practice*. Los Angeles: SAGE, 2007.

Murphy, John J. *Solution-Focused Counseling in Schools.* Alexandria, VA: American Counseling Association, 2008.

Nelson, Thorana S., and Frank N. Thomas, eds. *Handbook of Solution-Focused Brief Therapy: Clinical Applications.* New York: Haworth Press, 2007.

Weisz, John R., and Alan E. Kazdin, eds. *Evidence-Based Psychotherapies for Children and Adolescents.* New York: The Guilford Press, 2010.

PERIODICALS

Thomas, Christopher R. "Evidence-Based Practice for Conduct Disorder Symptoms." *Journal of the American Academy of Child and Adolescent Psychiatry* 45 (2006): 109–14.

ORGANIZATIONS

Association for Behavioral and Cognitive Therapies, 305 7th Avenue, 16th Floor, New York, NY, 10001, (212) 647-1890, Fax: (212) 647-1865, http://www.abct.org.

Deborah RoschEifert, PhD
Emily Jane Willingham, PhD

Cognitive remediation

Definition

Cognitive remediation is a teaching process that targets areas of neuropsychological functioning involved in learning and basic day-to-day functioning. This terminology can be confusing because some researchers use the phrase "cognitive remediation" to refer to environmental adjustments meant to ease cognitive requirements.

Cognitive remediation as a behavioral treatment is an approach designed to address cognitive deficits through neural rehabilitation. This approach relies on the idea, demonstrated in many recent studies of humans and primates, that the **brain** can circumvent damage or loss through repetition of the same activity. Through repetition, neurocognitive abilities, such as working memory, attention, problem solving, and cognitive flexibility and functioning, can be improved. Cognitive remediation usually uses computers to provide exercises to improve patients' neuropsychological skills.

Cognitive remediation (CR) is also different from the similarly sounding cognitive remediation therapy (CRT). Cognitive remediation focuses on improving the underlying neuropsychological functions that provide for memory, attention, abstract thinking, and other such concepts. In cognitive remediation therapy, the focus is on applying more effective patterns of thinking to behaviors or emotional problems.

Purpose

The primary purpose of cognitive remediation is to minimize cognitive deficits. The main goals of cognitive remediation are to bolster specific cognitive capacities that are weak. It is distinguished from a compensatory approach that seeks to get around a cognitive deficit by use of compensating strategies, such as using a notebook as a memory support in memory loss. Cognitive remediation has been applied in those who have had a **traumatic brain injury** (a **stroke**, tumor, or head injury); in those who have learning disabilities; and in people who have **schizophrenia**, **depression**, and **bipolar disorder**. For example, people with schizophrenia and other psychotic disorders often have trouble maintaining an attentive state, along with memory and problem-solving problems. Cognitive remediation can help to solve such problems. It has also been successful in treating people with **anorexia nervosa**, an eating disorder. Cognitive remediation can also be used for the treatment of alcohol and **substance abuse** disorders.

For people with brain injury, remediation typically targets the following neuropsychological functions: attention and concentration, memory, planning, monitoring one's work or behavior, and making adjustments based on feedback. For instance, individuals with a brain injury may repeat a series of letters, showing that with practice they are able to repeat longer lists. Remediation is also used to help children and adults cope with learning disabilities. Learning disabilities can interfere with progress in reading; in understanding and communicating through spoken language; in writing; in arithmetic; in understanding such nonverbal information as telling time or understanding visual information; and in comprehending social interactions and cues. Difficulties with concentration, problem solving, organization, identifying errors, and using feedback effectively are also areas that can be treated with cognitive remediation. People with schizophrenia sometimes exhibit cognitive impairment, and cognitive remediation therapy has shown promise in addressing these losses.

Description

People with cognitive problems (or deficits) have difficulties with such routine activities as remembering the appointments for the day or where they have placed their wallet or purse. They may also have problems organizing their personal life and professional lives, along with their living space. Because of such disorganization, they often misplace belongings.

Cognitive deficits occur in many forms and situations. Individuals who have had a traumatic brain injury may work with a remediator using computer programs that target one area at a time, such as attention. The individual is then helped to generalize what is learned from the program to real life. This **intervention** is usually done at a hospital, although it is not limited to clinical settings. Remediation for this group of people is considered helpful but not curative. It is typically practiced by a neuropsychologist.

Remediation for individuals with learning disabilities aims to bolster a particular area of learning or adaptation, such as in academics or socialization. Although the intervention varies according to the disability and the individual's profile of strengths and weaknesses, the remediator will make use of the person's stronger capacities to bolster the weaker ones. For example, individuals might need help with written language because they frequently omit words from their sentences. Once it has been determined that their oral language (both receptive and expressive) is adequate and that the motor aspect of writing is intact, the remediator has an idea of the individuals' strengths and weaknesses in the area of writing. In this case, the remediator makes use of their stronger auditory (hearing-related) skills to build up the capacity to translate spoken language into written (visual) language. Specifically, the remediator might read aloud a sentence written by the person (with omissions) and ask the person to identify the mistakes the person hears. The omission is identified by hearing it and then the individual is shown on paper the place where the word is missing. In this way, individuals with these deficits can learn to identify errors visually that they can already identify through the auditory modality of listening. This particular exercise fosters visual awareness of errors, which is a symptom or outcome of the deeper problem of translating language from oral to visual form.

This process can also be achieved with computer-assisted tasks. These methods focus on gradually increasing the difficulty level and complexity of the cognitive functions being applied.

The process continues with diminishing degrees of assistance. Specifically, after individuals become more skillful in matching visual omissions with the auditory ones read by the remediator, they begin to read the sentences aloud and identify the words that are missing from the sentences on the page. In the next step, they begin to read their work silently with the same kind of scrutiny as in the previous exercise. In this manner, remediation fosters both learning and internalizing a cognitive capacity.

Cognitive remediation sessions for learning disabilities usually take place twice a week. This type of intervention is practiced by psychologists, neuropsychologists, special educators, and learning specialists.

KEY TERMS

Anorexia nervosa—An eating disorder characterized by denial of a healthy body weight, a distorted image of appearance, and steadfast refusal to eat much food for a fear of gaining weight.

Bipolar disorder—A mood disorder characterized by abnormally high energy levels and moodiness, usually without depression.

Depression—A psychiatric disorder involving feelings of hopelessness and symptoms of fatigue, sleeplessness, suicidal tendencies, and poor concentration.

Schizophrenia—A serious mental disorder involving degraded thinking and emotions, often associated with hallucinations or sensory awareness of stimuli that are not present, as in hearing voices that are not there.

Stimulant abuse disorders—Also called stimulant use disorders, any disorder that involves the abuse of stimulants that affect the central nervous system.

The depth and breadth of the intervention varies according to the remediator's professional training and particular area of expertise. Some professionals specialize in working with certain types of learning disabilities; some, like psychologists, may incorporate their understanding of emotional difficulties within their work as a cognitive remediator.

Cognitive remediation can also take a strategy-oriented approach, in which the patient practices tasks that require strategizing (to plan or decide on a plan of action).

Cognitive deficits can be pinpointed by various assessment tests administered by psychological professionals. One such assessment is the Brief Assessment of Cognition in Schizophrenia (BACS). Another one is the MATRICS Consensus Cognitive Battery (MCCB). Both can identify an individual's cognitive problems and also can pinpoint what areas (conditions) need to be improved.

Schizophrenia

A study ("A Meta-Analysis of Cognitive Remediation in Schizophrenia") published in the *American Journal of Psychiatry* in December 2007, evaluated whether cognitive remediation was beneficial for improving the symptoms, cognitive abilities, and psychosocial functioning of 1,151 patients with schizophrenia. The meta-analytical study of 26 randomized, controlled trials concluded that cognitive remediation did produce "significant improvement" for all three factors. In addition, when adjunctive psychiatric rehabilitation with used with cognitive remediation with respect to psychosocial functioning, the researchers saw that the effects were much stronger than when cognitive remediation was used alone.

They concluded that, "Cognitive remediation produces moderate improvements in cognitive performance and, when combined with psychiatric rehabilitation, also improves functional outcomes."

Anorexia nervosa

Studies done by British **psychologist** Kate Tchanturia and others have focused on the use of cognitive remediation therapy in treating anorexia nervosa. In studies, patients generally received ten 45-minute sessions, with assessments before and after therapy. Tchanturia reported that preliminary results suggested that cognitive remediation may be especially successful in patients who have not had results with other forms of therapies, largely because CRT focuses on cognitive tasks and not food or related emotions. The patients found the tasks enjoyable and thus were more likely to participate, and they had a sense of achievement in applying their new thinking strategies to their behaviors, such as eating patterns.

Benefits

When remediation is targeting the problem area accurately and individuals are actively engaging in the process, then progress should be evident in the skill area targeted, in the participants' awareness of their area of difficulty, and in their awareness of some techniques and strategies that are helpful.

Cognitive remediation programs can help to improve impaired cognitive skills that interfere with daily activities. Cognitive deficits may not be eliminated, but they can be controlled and minimized with effective strategies. These are best accomplished with the help of trained professionals.

Precautions

Cognitive remediation is not suitable as a substitute for medical treatments or for the various types of **psychotherapy**. Instead, it is to be used as a complement treatment for mental disorders such as **attention deficit hyperactivity disorder** (ADHD) in children, brain injuries, early-stage **dementia** in older people, schizophrenia, and depression.

QUESTIONS TO ASK YOUR DOCTOR

- How effective is cognitive remediation in cases like mine?
- Are there any underlying medical or psychological concerns that need to be corrected before we proceed with CR?
- Should I take any assessment tests?
- Will I need CR for a short or long time? What will happen if I stop CR?

When cognitive remediation is used, the medical professional administering it must make sure the patient is clinically stable. During the process, the patient must be actively involved in the treatment process. A clinically unstable person may not be able to concentrate for twenty minutes or more, which is essential for successfully conducting cognitive remediation.

Preparation

Before remediation can begin, individuals being treated must receive a neuropsychological or in-depth psychological evaluation in order to identify the underlying neuropsychological capacities (i.e., language, memory, attention, visual perception, visual spatial abilities, motor abilities) that are interfering with their acquiring the needed skills. The evaluation is also intended to rule out emotional difficulties as the primary cause of learning problems. Children with learning disabilities frequently experience feelings of inadequacy and low self-esteem that need to be addressed. If psychological difficulties, however, are the main reason for their academic struggles, individuals should be treated with psychotherapy rather than cognitive remediation.

Aftercare

A plan of aftercare is sometimes necessary in order to return individuals to a community living style. Aftercare is normally monitored by a healthcare professional so that progress can be observed and modifications to the aftercare plan can be easily implemented, if needed. Aftercare may continue until skills are satisfactorily improved and maintained in real life situations.

Risks

Cognitive remediation may not succeed in all cases. The amount of success depends in part on the severity of the problem, along with the **diagnosis**, the specific illness, and various socio-environmental concerns. Medical studies have confirmed that improvements delivered by cognitive remediation may be temporary.

Resources

BOOKS

Evers, Rebecca B. *Planning Effective Instruction for Students with Learning and Behavior Problems.* Upper Saddle River, NJ: Pearson, 2011.

Tchanturia, Kate, and James Lock. "Cognitive Remediation Therapy for Eating Disorders: Development, Refinement and Future Directions." In *Current Topics in Behavioral Neurosciences.* Vol. 6 of *Behavioral Neurobiology of Eating Disorders.* New York: Springer, 2011.

Wilson, Mike, ed. *Disabilities Affecting Learning.* Farmington Hills, MI: Greenhaven Press, 2010.

PERIODICALS

Hylton, Hilary. "A Drug to End Drug Addiction." *Time Magazine* (January 9, 2008). http://www.time.com/time/health/article/0,8599,1701864,00.html (accessed September 16, 2011).

Keefe, R.S., et al. "The Relationship of the Brief Assessment of Cognition in Schizophrenia (BACS) to Functional Capacity and Real-world Functional Outcome." *Journal of Clinical and Experimental Neuropsychology* 2 (February 28, 2006): 260–69. http://www.ncbi.nlm.nih.gov/pubmed/16484097 (accessed September 16, 2011).

Lindenmayer, Jean-Pierre. "A Randomized Controlled Trial of Cognitive Remediation Among Inpatients With Persistent Mental Illness." *Psychiatric Services* 59 (March 2008): 241–47. http://dx.doi.org/10.1176/appi.ps.59.3.241 (accessed September 9, 2011).

McGurk, Susan R., et al. "A Meta-Analysis of Cognitive Remediation in Schizophrenia." *American Journal of Psychiatry* 164, no. 12 (December 2009): 1791–1802. http://dx.doi.org/10.1176/appi.ajp.2007.07060906 (accessed September 9, 2011).

Medalia, Alice. "Cognitive Remediation for Psychiatric Patients." *Psychiatric Times, UBM Medica* (March 9, 2009). http://www.psychiatrictimes.com/display/article/10168/1386195 (accessed September 16, 2011).

Tchanturia, Kate, Helen Davies, and Iain C. Campbell. "Cognitive Remediation Therapy for Patients with Anorexia Nervosa: Preliminary Findings." *Annals of General Psychiatry* 6, no. 14 (2007). http://dx.doi.org/10.1186/1744-859X-6-14 (accessed September 9, 2011).

WEBSITES

"Learning Disabilities Online." LDonline.com. http://www.ldonline.org (accessed September 16, 2011).

Medalia, Alice. "Question: What Is Cognitive Remediation and for Whom Is It Helpful?" Columbia Psychiatry. http://asp.cumc.columbia.edu/psych/asktheexperts/ask_the_experts_inquiry.asp?SI=300 (accessed September 16, 2011).

Vocci, Frank. *Cognitive Remediation in the Treatment of Stimulant Abuse Disorders: A Research Agenda.* APA PsycNET Direct. (December 2008). http://psycnet.apa.org/?fa=main.doiLanding&doi=10.1037/a0014101 (accessed September 16, 2011).

ORGANIZATIONS

American Psychiatric Association, 1000 Wilson Blvd., Ste. 1825, Arlington, VA, 22209-3901, (703) 907-7300, apa@psych.org, http://www.psych.org.

American Psychological Association, 750 1st St., NE, Washington, DC, 20002-4242, (202) 336-5500; TDD/TTY: (202) 336-6123, (800) 374-2721, http://www.apa.org.

Susan Fine, PsyD
Emily Jane Willingham, PhD
William Atkins, BB, BS, MBA

Cognitive retraining

Definition

Cognitive retraining is a therapeutic strategy that seeks to improve or restore a person's cognitive skills. These skills include paying attention, remembering, organizing, reasoning and understanding, problem solving, decision making, and higher level cognitive (thinking) abilities. These skills are all interrelated. Cognitive retraining is one aspect of cognitive rehabilitation, a comprehensive approach to restoring such skills after a **traumatic brain injury** or other disability.

Purpose

The purpose of cognitive retraining is the reduction of cognitive problems associated with **brain** injury, other disabilities or disorders, and aging. Cognitive retraining aims to decrease the everyday problems faced by individuals with cognitive difficulties, thereby improving the quality of their lives.

Description

The techniques of cognitive retraining are best known for their use with persons who have suffered a brain injury. However, cognitive retraining has also been used in patients with **dementia** (including **Alzheimer's disease**), **schizophrenia**, **attention deficit hyperactivity disorder (ADHD)**, **learning disorders**, **obsessive-compulsive disorder** (OCD), and cognitive changes associated with aging. Professionals from a variety of fields, such as psychology, psychiatry, occupational therapy, and **speech-language pathology**, may be involved in cognitive retraining.

There are generally two parts in the process of cognitive retraining: restoring the cognitive skill that was lost or degraded, and learning to use alternative strategies to compensate for the degraded skill. In the first part, repetitive exercises are used to strengthen skills that have been degraded or lost, such as concentration, memory, judgment, or problem solving. In the second part, strategies are taught to the patient in order to cope (or compensate) with weakened cognitive skills. In some cases, the degraded skills are restored to their normal level.

Cognitive retraining includes a considerable amount of repetitive practice that targets the skills of interest. In fact, repetition is essential for the newly retrained skills to become automatic. Regular feedback is another important element of cognitive retraining, as is the use of rewards. Retraining usually begins with simpler skills and proceeds to more complicated ones. The therapist may address cognitive skills while the person is practicing real-life tasks, in an effort to improve their performance of these tasks. In fact, practicing skills in the ways and settings they will be used in real life is critical to the success of retraining efforts. The length of time for cognitive training varies according to the type and extent of the injury and the type of retraining skills used. For example, retraining memory may take months or years. In contrast, it may take only a few days or weeks to retrain someone to organize his or her home or workplace.

The use of computerization for cognitive retraining has become an increasingly common practice. In particular, researchers have focused on developing a "mixed-reality" system, producing a virtual reality environment for the person undergoing rehabilitation. This system, called in one study a "Human Experience Modeler," places the patient in a context similar to reality—such as home or work—except that the stimuli can be controlled and the patient's experiences captured with automated feedback provided. These approaches have shown some promising success in pilot studies.

Types of cognitive retraining

Types of cognitive retraining include:

- Attention and concentration retraining. This type of cognitive retraining aims to improve several abilities, including focusing attention, dividing attention, maintaining attention while reducing the effects of boredom and fatigue, and resisting distraction. Attention has been considered the foundation of other more complicated cognitive skills and is an important skill for cognitive retraining. This area of cognitive retraining has been widely researched and has been shown to improve patients' abilities in various tasks related to attention.
- Memory retraining. Memory retraining involves teaching the patient several strategies that can be used to recall certain types of information. For example, rhymes may be used as a memory aid. A series of numbers, such as a phone number with an area code, may be broken down into smaller groups. A person may be taught to go through each letter of the alphabet until he or she remembers someone's name. Both memory and organization problems are common and often disabling after head injury.
- Organizational skills retraining. This approach is used when the person has difficulty keeping track of or finding items, doing tasks in a set order, and/or doing something in a timely manner. Strategies may include having one identified place for an item. In addition, the person can be taught to keep the items that are used most frequently closer to him or her (the front or the lower shelves of a cabinet, drawer, closet, or desk, for example). Items that are often used together (such as comb and brush, toothbrush and toothpaste) are placed beside each other. Items may be put into categories (allocating decorations to a specific holiday, such as the Fourth of July or Thanksgiving). These strategies help individuals function better in their home or work environment.
- Reasoning. Reasoning refers to the ability to connect and organize information in a logical, rational way. Reasoning retraining techniques include listing the facts or reality of a situation; excluding irrelevant facts or details; putting the steps to solve a problem in a logical order; and avoiding irrational thinking, such as jumping to conclusions based on incomplete information, or focusing on the negative aspects of the situation and ignoring the positive. When the person can connect relevant information in a logical way, they are better able to understand or comprehend it.

KEY TERMS

Attention deficit hyperactivity disorder (ADHD)—A condition found mostly in children with primary symptoms of an inability to concentrate, inappropriate behaviors, and impulsiveness.

Cognitive—Related to the acquisition of knowledge (learning).

Depression—A psychiatric disorder involving feelings of hopelessness and symptoms of fatigue, sleeplessness, suicidal tendencies, and poor concentration.

Obsessive-compulsive disorder (OCD)—A disorder that involves excess anxiety; emotions of fear, worry, and apprehension; and repetitious behaviors and obsessions.

Schizophrenia—A mental disorder involving degraded thinking and emotions.

- Problem solving. Problem-solving retraining aims to help people define a problem, come up with possible solutions to it, discuss the solution(s) with others and listen to their advice, review the various possible solutions from many perspectives, and evaluate whether the problem was solved after going through these steps. This sequence may be repeated several times until the problem is solved. This process is referred to as "SOLVE," from the first letter of the name of each step: Specify, Options, Listen, Vary, and Evaluate. The "SOLVE" technique is more appropriate for use with individuals at a higher level of functioning.
- Decision making. Decision-making retraining is used when a person must choose from a number of options. The goal of this retraining is to help him or her consider the decision thoroughly before taking any action. The considerations may range from such practical matters as money, people, and rules and policies to personality issues.
- Executive skills. Executive skills retraining refers to teaching individuals how to monitor themselves, control their thinking and actions, think in advance, set goals, manage time, act in socially acceptable ways, and transfer skills to new situations. These are higher-level cognitive skills. Charts and videotapes may be used to monitor behavior, and a variety of questions, tasks, and games may be used in retraining these skills.

Preparation

Cognitive retraining usually takes place in a quiet room without distractions. It is important for the person to feel relaxed and calm while they are being retrained in cognitive skills. Engaging in cognitive retraining is not recommended when someone is emotional distressed—e.g., after the recent loss of a loved one. The therapist usually evaluates the patient's level of cognitive skills and the extent of their cognitive problems before retraining begins. This evaluation provides a way to monitor improvement by comparing the patient's skill levels during and after retraining to his or her skill levels before retraining. Cognitive retraining requires patience and persistence on the part of everyone involved.

Aftercare

The therapist will try to promote the transfer of skills learned using cognitive retraining techniques to the settings of the patient's everyday life. Training may be continued until the patient's skills are improved, transferred to, and maintained in real world activities.

QUESTIONS TO ASK YOUR DOCTOR

- Will cognitive retraining help me (or my loved one) to recover fully?
- If I don't recover completely, how can I cope with my condition?
- How long will it take to go through cognitive retraining?
- Can you advise me on the best type of cognitive retraining in my particular case?
- Will my health insurance pay for cognitive retraining?

Precautions

The extent to which a person with a brain injury can recover from or compensate for cognitive problems varies with the person and their injury. Therapy must be tailored to each individual's needs and abilities. Some cognitive retraining techniques require higher levels of skill and, therefore, they would be more suitable for persons who have made some progress in their recovery. In addition, a person's moods and emotions have an effect on their cognitive skills. Someone who is depressed, for example, may need **psychotherapy** and/or medication before he or she can engage in and benefit from cognitive retraining. Some persons with brain injuries may find it difficult to transfer a skill learned in one setting, such as a clinic, to another setting, such as their home. Although a specific individual may show some improvement on training tasks, his or her cognitive skills may not be considered improved or restored unless there is some evidence that the skills have been transferred to everyday settings and can be maintained over time. It is important for the therapist, patient, and the patient's friends or family members not to assume that improvement on training exercises and tests automatically leads to transfer of the skills to real-life settings.

Results

Cognitive retraining may be considered successful if performance on a behavior related to a particular cognitive skill has improved. It is ultimately successful if it helps the injured person improve his or her functioning and meet his or her needs in real-life situations and settings.

Positive results are more likely obtained when caregivers are trained and educated as part of the patient's therapy. The strategies used for cognitive retraining should be familiar to caregivers, and they should encourage such strategies for the overall improvement of the patient. Improvement may take time, and it helps when the patient has an understanding support system in place.

Resources

BOOKS

Parenté, Rick, and Douglas Herrmann. *Retraining Cognition: Techniques and Applications*. Austin, TX: PRO-ED, 2010.

Schutz, Larry E. *Head Injury Recovery in Real Life*. San Diego, CA: Plural, 2010.

Silver, Jonathan M., Thomas W. McAllister, and Stuart C. Yudofsky, eds. *Textbook of Traumatic Brain Injury*. Washington, DC: American Psychiatric Association, 2011.

PERIODICALS

Buhlmann, Ulrike, et al. "Cognitive Retraining for Organizational Impairment in Obsessive-Compulsive Disorder." *Psychiatry Research* 144 (2006): 109–16.

Fidopiastis, C. M., et al. "Human Experience Modeler: Context-Driven Cognitive Retraining to Facilitate Transfer of Learning." *CyberPsychology and Behavior* 9 (2006): 183–87.

WEBSITES

American Brain Tumor Association. "Cognitive Retraining." http://www.abta.org/Becoming_Well_Again_Through../Cognitive_Retraining/199 (accessed November 21, 2011).

Joneis Thomas, PhD
Emily Jane Willingham, PhD

Cognitive self-regulation *see* **Self-control strategies**

Cognitive therapy *see* **Cognitive-behavioral therapy**

Communication disorders *see* **Expressive language disorder; Mixed receptive-expressive language disorder; Phonological disorder; Social communication disorder; Stuttering**

Community mental health

Definition

Community mental health is an approach to providing access to professional mental health care in local communities. It includes services offered through public mental health programs, public health departments, community mental health centers, private programs, medical clinics, hospitals, religious organizations, colleges and other educational institutions, and neighborhood centers. Community mental health assessment has evolved into a field of research called "psychiatric epidemiology," which determines the prevalence of various mental disorders in specific communities, with the goal of developing appropriate community mental health programs and evaluating their effectiveness.

Purpose

The primary purpose of community mental health is to decrease the need for inpatient and hospital-based mental health services as well as to supplement those services, and to help patients become successfully reintegrated into society. Community mental health services are generally dispersed among a variety of local facilities and programs, rather than isolating patients from their communities by segregating them in centralized hospitals. The goal of community mental health programs is to be more responsive to local needs and more accessible to more people. They also help alleviate "psychiatric boarding," in which patients with mental illnesses are confined in overcrowded hospital emergency departments. Community mental health centers (CMHCs) provide valuable services to people who may otherwise not have access to mental health care, especially low-income youth and families in urban and rural areas throughout the United States.

Community mental health can address a wide range of problems. Many programs, including residential, day, and outpatient treatment, are involved in transitioning patients from institutions or from parents' homes to independent or semi-independent living situations. Some programs provide diagnostic and treatment services for a wide variety of mental disorders. Others refer clients to psychologists or psychiatrists. Community mental health may provide emergency care for suicidal patients, for patients with acute **panic disorder**, or for victims and witnesses of natural disasters and other violent or traumatic events. Some community mental health programs provide **substance abuse** treatment. However, the high demand for community mental health services and the lack of adequate funding have meant that patients might not have timely access to the community-based care that they require.

Demographics

There is a tremendous need for community mental health services throughout the United States. This need skyrockets in times of **economic stress** and recession. In most states, the primary clients of community mental health services are Medicaid recipients. However, it has been estimated that as many as two-thirds of American children and teens—more than six million children—do not receive the mental health services that they need. A survey of juvenile detention facilities found that two-thirds were holding children who were awaiting community mental health services. Some of these children were as young as seven. Over a six-month period, almost 15,000 young people were being held in detention until community mental health services became available, at a very high cost to American taxpayers. These detention facilities are generally not equipped to provide care for mentally ill youth, some of whom may pose a danger to themselves or others.

Community mental health, particularly when it is integrated into other community-based organizations, can be particularly relevant for racial and ethnic minorities in the United States. African Americans are much more likely to turn to family or to their religious or social communities for emotional support than to seek professional help. African Americans also generally have less access to mental health care, even though they are disproportionately more likely to experience circumstances that increase the risk of developing a mental illness. These circumstances include **homelessness**, exposure to violence, and children in foster care or otherwise in the child welfare system.

Asian Americans and Pacific Islanders have higher rates of depressive symptoms than white Americans but have the lowest rates of utilization of mental health services. Southeast Asians, especially refugees, have particularly high rates of **depression** and **post-traumatic stress disorder** (PTSD). Their need for outpatient mental health services is twice that of the general Asian American population.

Latinos are also at higher risk for depression, anxiety, and substance abuse. American-born Latinos and long-term residents have significantly higher rates of psychiatric disorders, especially substance abuse, compared with recent immigrants. Like African Americans, Latinos are far less likely than others to seek mental health services, especially from specialized mental health facilities. In part, this appears to be related to the severe shortage of Latino and Spanish-speaking mental health care providers.

Description

The services included in community mental health programs depend on the state and local area. The focus of community mental health is on preventing psychiatric **hospitalization** and in assisting in the transition out of inpatient care. Some states offer only very limited community mental health services. Others offer a wide range of services for children, adults, and families. These may include mental health screening and assessment, psychological testing, psychiatric evaluations, individual **psychotherapy**, group psychotherapy, psychiatric medications, family and **couples therapy**, family psychological and educational counseling, peer support programs, **respite** care, **case management**, jail diversion, integrated treatment for co-existing disorders, and crisis interventions. Some community mental health programs provide supportive housing, supported employment, and even longer-term and inpatient care. A 24-hour crisis hotline or emergency psychiatric services are important components of community mental health. These may be provided in conjunction with a local hospital.

Community mental health services may be available for severely emotionally disturbed youth or for those who have been traumatized by **sexual abuse** or violence and require specialized interventions. Juveniles suspected of mental illness may be referred to community mental health programs by the courts. Community mental health also may include multidisciplinary assessments of parents with mental illness who are suspected of, or have been accused of, child maltreatment. Some programs include victims' services for child and adult crime victims and their families.

Some community mental health programs include intensive case management services for ending chronic homelessness and substance abuse. These services may include job and life-skills training, employment referrals, housing options, meals, substance abuse treatment, and other rehabilitation services. Special services may also be available for older adults, including adult day respite, home-meal delivery, housekeeping, and emergency home response, as well as screenings for nursing home placement or veterans' services, and assistance in transitions from nursing homes to independent- or assisted-living arrangements.

Programs may include the training of community mental health professionals. In addition to these specialists, community mental health may involve psychiatrists, including child and geriatric psychiatrists, clinical psychologists, clinical **social workers**, nurse practitioners, psychiatric nurses, counselors, clergy, recreational and occupational therapists, and **assertive community treatment** (ACT) teams. ACT is a community-based treatment approach for assisting in the recovery and rehabilitation of patients with severe and persistent mental illnesses.

Although some community mental health programs are based in stand-alone CMHCs, programs located within community groups or churches can reach populations that might not otherwise seek mental health services. They also can increase awareness of mental health issues and resources and reduce stigmas associated with mental disorders. Some community mental health programs are school-based, linking mental health providers with teachers and family advocates for treating children with disruptive behavior disorders. Community mental health can also be associated with:

- outpatient psychiatric clinics
- community rehabilitation programs
- community support programs
- adult daycare centers
- day treatment centers
- home health agencies
- club programs
- foster care programs
- sheltered workshops
- group and private homes

Eligibility for community mental health services varies by state and local area. In general, people in crises and children and adults with severe mental illnesses are given first priority. During times of budgetary restraint, the first to be cut from community mental health services are often those who are not enrolled in Medicaid, so as to preserve federal Medicaid matching funds. Approximately 2% of public mental health funding comes from Medicare, which, in addition to senior citizens, serves younger people with disabilities. Unlike Medicaid, Medicare does not cover many community-based services and requires co-payments for outpatient mental health treatment. In addition to Medicaid and Medicare, community mental health services may accept private insurance or offer a sliding fee scale based on ability to pay. The State Children's Health Insurance Program (SCHIP) may or may not provide the same range of mental health services as Medicaid, depending on the state. Some county and municipal local governments administer and partially fund community mental health for their residents.

Origins

During the 1960s, in response to the increased availability of psychiatric medications and an outcry over involuntary commitments, public psychiatric hospitals began reducing their populations or closing completely. Mentally ill patients were released into the community to live independently. The Community Mental Health Centers Act of 1963 aimed to create a comprehensive community mental health system to serve this population, providing prevention, early treatment, and continuity of care within larger communities and promoting the social integration of people with mental health needs. However, the programs were never adequately funded, and many planned community mental health services never materialized.

KEY TERMS

Assertive community treatment (ACT)—A service-delivery model for providing comprehensive, highly individualized, locally based treatment directly to patients with serious, persistent mental illnesses.

Community Mental Health Clinic (CMHC)—A community-based provider of limited or comprehensive mental health services; usually at least partially publicly funded.

Epidemiology—A field of medical science dealing with the incidence, distribution, and control of disease in a population.

Medicaid—A joint state and federal program for providing medical care for low-income children and families.

Medicare—The U.S. government healthcare system for those aged 65 and over.

Post-traumatic stress disorder (PTSD)—A psychological response to a highly stressful event; typically characterized by depression, anxiety, flashbacks, nightmares, and avoidance of reminders of the traumatic experience.

Psychiatric boarding—The practice of holding mentally ill patients in emergency department corridors and waiting areas, because of the lack of hospital beds or other facilities.

Respite care—Temporary care of a patient to provide caregivers with a period of physical, mental, and emotional rest.

State Children's Health Insurance Program; SCHIP; CHIP—A state-administered health insurance program for lower- and middle-income children who are without private health insurance and whose family incomes are above the Medicaid eligibility limits.

Initially, CMHCs provided outpatient care to people with less severe, episodic, or acute mental health problems. Soon they were also caring for the deinstitutionalized chronically mentally ill. With the repeal of the Mental Health Systems Act and with federal funding for CMHCs replaced by block grants to the states in the early 1980s, the system deteriorated further. Subsequent programs to provide for community mental health were relatively short-lived and impacted only a few urban centers. As a result, vast numbers of persons with mental illness have become homeless or are incarcerated in prisons.

QUESTIONS TO ASK YOUR DOCTOR

- Would community mental health services be helpful for me?
- What type of community mental health services should I pursue?
- What community mental health services are available in my area?
- Am I eligible for community mental health?
- What type of community mental health provider will I be able to see?

As of the early twenty-first century, the U.S. **Substance Abuse and Mental Health Services Administration** was continuing to fund the Comprehensive Community Mental Health Services for Children and Their Families Program. This community mental health program provides youth (from birth through age 21) and their families with cultural- and language-appropriate evidence-based mental health services and support. The National Council for Community Behavioral Healthcare advocates for improved public policies in mental and behavioral health, and offers state-of-the-science education and practice improvement resources for the personnel of community mental health programs. It has also pioneered the implantation of Mental Health First Aid USA to educate the public about the signs and symptoms of mental disorders.

Common problems

In the early 2010s, states and the federal government were attempting to deal with economic problems and massive budget deficits in part by further slashing community mental health funding and restricting eligibility for services. At the same time, the demand for mental health services was rising dramatically. Increasingly, law enforcement agencies were forced to provide emergency services for the mentally ill—services that had previously been provided by community mental health programs. In addition, managed behavioral health care and the strict use of medical management techniques decreased access to community care, resulting in more patients in crisis and increased utilization of hospital emergency departments. Low reimbursement rates under Medicaid and Medicare further reduced community mental health services. Coverage for antipsychotic drugs was reduced or eliminated. Some experts warned that the entire mental health system in the United States was on the verge of collapse.

Resources

BOOKS

Altman, Neil. *The Analyst in the Inner City: Race, Class, and Culture Through a Psychoanalytic Lens,* 2nd ed. New York: Routledge, 2010.

Fernando, Suman, and Frank Keating. *Mental Health in a Multi-Ethnic Society: A Multidisciplinary Handbook,* 2nd ed. New York: Routledge, 2009.

Kay, Jerald, and Victor Schwartz. *Mental Health Care in the College Community.* Hoboken, NJ: Wiley-Blackwell, 2010.

Moritsugu, John, Frank Y. Wong, and Karen Grover Duffy. *Community Psychology,* 4th ed. Boston: Allyn & Bacon, 2010.

Nelson, Geoffrey B., and Isaac Prilleltensky. *Community Psychology: In Pursuit of Liberation and Well-Being,* 2nd ed. New York: Palgrave Macmillan, 2010.

Roberts, Albert R., and Kenneth Yeager. *Pocket Guide to Crisis Intervention.* New York: Oxford University Press, 2009.

Schinke, Steven Paul. *Behavioral Methods in Social Welfare: Helping Children, Adults, and Families in Community Settings.* New Brunswick: Aldine Transaction, 2009.

PERIODICALS

Alakeson, Vidhya, Nalini Pande, and Michael Ludwig. "A Plan to Reduce Emergency Room 'Boarding' of Psychiatric Patients." *Health Affairs* 29, no. 9 (September 2010): 1637–1642.

Bloom, Joseph D. "'The Incarceration Revolution': The Abandonment of the Seriously Mentally Ill to Our Jails and Prisons." *Journal of Law, Medicine & Ethics* 38, no. 4 (Winter 2010): 727–734.

Duncan, Tracey M., Maureen Davey, and Adam Davey. "Transporting Functional Family Therapy to Community-Based Programs." *Family Journal* 19, no. 1 (January 2011): 41–46.

Saylers, Michelle P., et al. "Integrating Assertive Community Treatment and Illness Management and Recovery for Consumers with Severe Mental Illness." *Community Mental Health Journal* 46, no. 4 (August 2010): 319–329.

Zezima, Katie. "State Cuts Put Officers on Front Lines of Mental Care." *New York Times* (December 5, 2010): A32.

OTHER

NAMI State Advocacy. "Public Mental Health Service Funding: An Overview." National Alliance on Mental Illness. January 2010. http://www.nami.org/Content/NavigationMenu/State_Advocacy/About_the_Issue/Funding.pdf (accessed January 11, 2011).

WEBSITES

"African American Community Mental Health Fact Sheet." National Alliance on Mental Illness. http://www.nami.org/Template.cfm?Section=Fact_Sheets1&Template=/

ContentManagement/ContentDisplay.cfm&ContentID=53812 (accessed January 11, 2011).

Kortrijk, H. E., et al. "Treatment Outcome in Patients Receiving Assertive Community Treatment." *Community Mental Health Journal* 46, no. 4 (August 2010). http://www.springerlink.com/content/510q277x50364725/full text.html (accessed January 12, 2011).

National Alliance on Mental Illness. "Assertive Community Treatment (ACT)." About Treatments & Supports. http://www.nami.org/Template.cfm?Section=About_Treatments_and_Supports&template=/ContentManagement/ContentDisplay.cfm&ContentID=8075 (accessed January 12, 2011).

ORGANIZATIONS

American Psychiatric Association, 1000 Wilson Blvd., Ste. 1825, Arlington, VA, 22209-3901, (703) 907-7300, apa@psych.org, http://www.psych.org.

National Alliance on Mental Illness, 3803 N. Fairfax Dr., Ste. 100, Arlington, VA, 22203, (703) 524-7600, (800) 950-NAMI (6264), Fax: (703) 524-9094, http://www.nami.org.

National Council for Community Behavioral Healthcare, 1701 K St. NW, Ste. 400, Washington, DC, 20006, (202) 684-7457, Fax: (202) 386-9391, communications@thenationalcouncil.org, http://www.TheNationalCouncil.org.

National Institute of Mental Health, 6001 Executive Blvd., Room 8184, MSC 9663, Bethesda, MD, 20892-9663, (301) 443-4513, (866) 615-6464, Fax: (301)443-4279, nimhinfo@nih.gov, http://www.nimh.nih.gov.

Substance Abuse and Mental Health Services Administration, 1 Choke Cherry Rd., Rockville, MD, 20857, (877) SAMHSA-7 (726-4727), Fax: (240) 221-4292, SAMHSAInfo@samhsa.hhs.gov, http://www.samhsa.gov.

Michael Polgar, PhD
Emily Jane Willingham, PhD
Margaret Alic, PhD

Compliance

Definition

Compliance with appropriate, recommended, and prescribed mental health treatments simply means that a person is following a doctor's orders. Compliance is more likely when there is agreement and confidence regarding the medical **diagnosis** and prognosis. Compliance is complicated by uncertainty about the nature of an illness and/or the effects of certain treatments, particularly medications. Some practitioners argue that the concept of "compliance" is paternalistic and does not include the patient enough in the decision-making process. Many recent studies have focused more on the concept of shared decision making with a strong relationship between the patient and practitioner. Either way, the nature of this relationship can be a strong determinant of how well a patient adheres to an agreed-upon course.

In everyday usage, the term compliance means deference and obedience, elevating the authority of medical expertise. Alternatively, adherence to medical advice refers to a somewhat more informed and equitable decision by a patient to stick with appropriate medical treatment. In any case, a mental health treatment cannot be effective or even evaluated if a patient does not follow a doctor's orders. A mental health treatment that is effective for one disorder may not be beneficial for other disorders, and diagnoses may evolve over time, complicating the issue of compliance.

Description

From a health provider's viewpoint, for medical treatments to have their desired effects, complying or conforming to treatments is absolutely necessary. The concept of medication management reflects this idea that the provider is responsible and in control, while the patient is a docile body who is incapacitated by disease or condition. From the perspective of health patients, adherence to medical treatment is enhanced when there is a good healthcare relationship and when patients openly share their health beliefs and experience of illness with their provider.

Problems with compliance

In mental health care, uncertainty about compliance is a challenging source of variation in the effectiveness of treatments. Noncompliance can represent a significant risk and cost to the medical system. For providers, partial compliance or discontinuation of medications represents the difficulty of maintaining treatment successes over time. Problems with compliance are often attributed to the patient, but may also reflect the appropriateness of a medication or treatment.

Compliance rates

Rates of compliance with mental health appointments are the greatest challenge (estimated in one hospital at 91%), while medication noncompliance is the second most challenging problem in the treatment of persons with mental illness. Mental health medication compliance can be determined by questioning patients, counting pills or prescriptions, and through drug monitoring with urine, blood, or other test measures. Overall, recent research estimates compliance to be 58%. Patients who report lower rates are often considered unreliable indicators of compliance, while physicians report higher rates. Compliance with antidepressant medications is higher, on average (65%). Mental health medication compliance rates are only somewhat lower than medication compliance in other types of health care, which have been estimated at 76%.

Explaining variation in compliance

Research in psychiatry, psychology, and sociology provides many explanations for variations in compliance. In psychiatry, clinical problems such as drug or alcohol abuse are sometimes used to explain noncompliance. Patients may also discontinue taking medications because of unwanted side effects. Health beliefs and patient-provider relationships are also recognized. In psychology and sociology, health beliefs and behaviors (in context of family, work, etc.) may enhance or limit compliance. If an individual's family member supports medication compliance, and the individual believes in the medicine's benefits, compliance may be enhanced (similar to a placebo effect). If an individual feels that a medicine makes him or her drowsy and affects work, compliance may be reduced. People who have limited access to or trust in doctors or medical science, and people whose faith precludes them from certain types of medical care, are less likely to comply with treatment recommendations.

To a large extent, patient compliance is a direct reflection of the quality of the doctor-patient relationship. When health-care provider and patient achieve a successful treatment alliance, as is advocated as part of the shared decision-making approach, and when the treatment is practical and beneficial for both the provider and the patient, cooperation reduces concerns about treatment for both parties. When patients are empowered and motivated to improve their health with the help of a doctor, compliance or adherence to treatment is higher. When there is distrust, disagreement, or misunderstanding involved, as when mental health status is uncertain or treatment side effects are unwelcome, compliance is lower. One British study found that patients with mental disorders were likely to prefer the form of treatment recommended by psychiatrists with whom they had good relationships, even if the treatment itself was painful. Some patients preferred **electroconvulsive therapy** (ECT) to tranquilizers for **depression** because they had built up trusting relationships with the doctors who used ECT, and perceived the doctors who recommended medications as bullying and condescending. Because noncompliant patients are less likely to continue in care, they are also less likely to find helpful providers or successful treatments. Thus, noncompliance with treatment may become a self-fulfilling cycle.

Compliance is higher when treatments, including medications, help patients feel better, when a family supports the treatment, and when taking medication prevents **relapse** of symptoms. However, people may be distressed by potential side effects of any medication, including those psychiatric medications that limit functioning. Limited functioning through drowsiness, also a problem of the older generation of antihistamines, is the best example. It is an effect of many medicines, particularly those for mental disorders. Other unwelcome side effects of various psychiatric medications include weight gain, involuntary movements such as muscle twitching, and impaired coordination. Patients may feel embarrassed about taking medication, especially medications for illnesses that have a strong social **stigma** associated with them; may have difficulty getting a prescription for medication; and may have financial problems paying for treatment or medication. In some cases, when a patient is noncompliant or perceived to be at odds with treatment recommendations, they may risk losing autonomy over medical decisions. When at risk to self or others, people who are medication noncompliant may be pressured or forced to take medication at the risk of being involuntarily hospitalized.

Multiple challenges in mental health care

Compliance rates reflect the proportion of individuals in treatment who have the highest possibility of successful treatment. Noncompliance rates reflect those individuals who have either discontinued or avoided treatment, and thus have lower probabilities of treatment success. Sometimes patients do not want to get rid of their symptoms (mania, for example), or patients may not consider their experiences (symptoms) to be indicative of a disorder. In addition, successful mental health care is hampered by the fact that many people with mental health problems either do not use or lack access to mental health care.

The **Substance Abuse** and Mental Health Services Administration's National Survey on Drug Use and Health found in 2008 that just over half (58.7%) of adults in the United States with a serious mental illness received treatment for a mental health problem. Therefore, compliance with treatment is part of a larger national challenge to provide quality mental health care and to use it well.

Resources

BOOKS

Horwitz, Allan. *Creating Mental Illness.* Chicago: University of Chicago Press, 2002.

Pescosolido, Bernice, and Carol Boyer. "How Do People Come to Use Mental Health Services?" In *A Handbook of the Sociology of Mental Health: Social Contexts, Theories, and Systems,* by Allan Horwitz. Cambridge: Cambridge University Press, 1999.

Pescosolido, Bernice, Carol Boyer, and Keri Lubell. "The Social Dynamics of Responding to Mental Health Problems." In *The Sociology of Mental Illness.* by Jane D. McLeod and Eric R. Wright. New York: Oxford University Press. 2009.

PERIODICALS

Adams, Jared R., and Robert E. Drake. "Shared Decision-Making and Evidence-Based Practice." *Community Mental Health Journal* 42, no. 1 (February 2006): 87–105.

Bebbington, P. E. "The Content and Context of Compliance." *International Clinical Psychopharmacology* 9, no. 5 (Suppl. 1995): 41–50.

Centorrino, Franca, et al. "Factors Associated with Noncompliance with Psychiatric Outpatient Visits." *Psychiatric Services* 52 (March 2001): 378–80.

Day, J.C., et al. "Attitudes Toward Antipsychotic Medication." *Archives of General Psychiatry* 62, no. 7 (July 2005) 717–24.

Helbling, Josef, et al. "Attitudes to Antipsychotic Drugs and their Side Effects: A Comparison Between General Practitioners and the General Population." *BioMed Central Psychiatry* 6 (2006): 42.

Wang, Philip, Olga Demler, and Ronald Kessler. "Adequacy of Treatment for Serious Mental Illness in the United States." *American Journal of Public Health* 92, no. 1 (2002): 92–98.

ORGANIZATIONS

American Psychiatric Association, 1000 Wilson Blvd., Ste. 1825, Arlington, VA, 22209-3901, (703) 907-7300, apa@psych.org, http://www.psych.org.

American Sociological Association, 1430 K Street, NW, Ste. 600, Washington, DC, 20005, http://www.asanet.org.

National Institute of Mental Health, 6001 Executive Blvd., Room 8184, MSC 9663, Bethesda, MD, 20892-9663, (301) 433-4513; TTY: (301) 443-8431, Fax: (301) 443-4279, (866) 615-6464; TTY: (866) 415-8051, nimhinfo@nih.gov, http://www.nimh.nih.gov.

Substance Abuse and Mental Health Services Administration Referral Resource, 1 Choke Cherry Rd., Rockville, MD, 20857, (877) SAMHSA-7 (726-4727), (800) TTY: 487-4889, Fax: (240) 221-4292, SAMHSAInfo@samhsa.hhs.gov, http://www.samhsa.gov.

Michael Polgar, PhD
Emily Jane Willingham, PhD

Compulsion

Definition

A compulsion is a behavior or mental act performed to help reduce anxiety or distress.

Description

Compulsions are not voluntary activities and are not performed for pleasure. Instead, a person with a compulsion feels the need to engage in a particular behavior to relieve the **stress** and discomfort which would become overwhelming if the activity were not performed in a specific, repeated manner. Examples of compulsive motor activities are washing hands until raw, repeatedly checking the security of a locked door, and arranging and rearranging items in a set order. Some examples of compulsory mental acts are counting or silently repeating specific words. If a person troubled by compulsions is unable to perform such activities, stress and discomfort increase. The performance of the acts relieves distress, but only temporarily.

Often, compulsions are not acts that could logically be expected to relieve or prevent the fears that inspire them. For example, a person might feel compelled to count numbers in a certain order to "undo" the perceived damage or threat that follows a thought or behavior, or might check to make sure a door is locked every few minutes. Compulsions, in some cases, are attempts to undo obsessions and are usually not successful.

Resources

BOOKS

VandenBos, Gary R. ed. *APA Dictionary of Psychology.* Washington, DC: American Psychological Association, 2006.

Dean A. Haycock, PhD
Ruth A. Wienclaw, PhD

Compulsive exercise

Definition

Compulsive exercise is a disorder marked by excessively long and frequent athletic workouts as a form of weight control or excellence in sports. It is frequently associated with such eating disorders as **anorexia nervosa** and **bulimia nervosa**. Compulsive exercise is also known as hypergymnasia and anorexia athletica, and some researchers refer to it as exercise abuse, exercise bulimia, or exercise addiction. It is not recognized as a disorder in the ***Diagnostic and Statistical Manual of Mental Disorders*** *(DSM)* but is included as a symptom of bulimia nervosa.

Demographics

Compulsive exercising is most common in adolescents and young adults in North America, and more common in young women than in young men. It is more common among competitive athletes at the high-school and college levels than other youth. Among adult males, it is estimated that about 10% of competitive runners and 10% of bodybuilders are exercise addicts. Exact statistics for any age group are difficult to obtain, however, because of disagreements among doctors as to whether compulsive exercising is always associated with other disorders or whether it should be identified as a primary disorder.

Description

Compulsive exercise or exercise **addiction** is characterized by a need to work out physically longer than is needed to maintain fitness or is recommended by a coach or trainer. Although there is no exact length of time specified as a criterion for exercise addiction, some experts consider two hours or longer to be a starting point for evaluating student athletes. In addition to excessive time spent working out, often to the detriment of relationships and school or work obligations, the person who is exercising compulsively feels depressed or anxious when he or she cannot exercise, and exercises in spite of injury, illness, extreme weather, or medical advice in order to relieve the negative feelings.

Compulsive exercise has been associated with eating disorders, particularly bulimia nervosa and anorexia nervosa in women, and with **body dysmorphic disorder** in men. It has also been associated with distortions of **body image** and **obsessive-compulsive disorder** (OCD). More recently, however, researchers have identified persons in whom the compulsive exercising is primary—that is, the **compulsion** exists by itself rather than being secondary to poor body image, disordered eating, or another mental disorder. There are documented cases of persons who exercise excessively for the sake of feeling a temporary euphoria that is sometimes called "runner's high." The "high" results from the release of endorphins, which are chemicals produced by the pituitary gland and hypothalamus that function as natural analgesics (pain relievers) and produce a general sense of well-being.

Risk factors

Risk factors for compulsive exercise include:

- pre-existing anorexia or bulimia nervosa
- pressure from parents or coaches to excel in a sport
- participation in a sport or dance program that requires or encourages weight control or classifies athletes by weight (e.g., classical ballet, gymnastics, figure skating, wrestling, horse racing, rowing, or running)
- female sex among adolescents or male sex among adults
- existing compulsive behavior problems (e.g., shopping, gambling, Internet addiction)
- general attitude of perfectionism or a need to be the best in all aspects of life
- a strong need to feel in control
- having parents who are obsessed with their own appearance or figure flaws
- having parents who frequently criticize the weight or body shape of other family members

Causes and symptoms

Causes

Compulsive exercising is thought to be a multifactorial disorder; that is, it is the end result of a number of different factors in most people who have the disorder rather than having a single cause. The causes that have been identified include:

- the influence of mass media images of "perfect" bodies and advanced athletic performances; the omnipresence of television, social media, Internet videos, and sports- or fitness-related magazines makes these images hard to avoid
- pressures within the child's family or school athletic program to do well in competitive athletic activities
- in some families, obsession with physical fitness coupled with fear of obesity
- history of anxiety or depression in the family
- personal history of low self-esteem

There was no indication as of 2011 that compulsive exercise is inherited or has genetic causes.

Symptoms

The symptoms of compulsive exercise include the following:

- The person does not enjoy the exercise but feels a sense of obligation instead; he or she feels driven to exercise in spite of illness, injury, or bad weather conditions (including extreme heat), or in spite of the impact of long periods of exercise on school, work, or relationships.
- The exercise has a compulsive or ritualistic quality—the person's workout becomes a way to deal with feelings of stress or anxiety. If the person misses a workout one day, he or she might perform two workouts the following day.
- The exercise functions as a purging behavior—as compensation or punishment for eating "too much."

- The person develops symptoms of withdrawal—insomnia, changes in appetite, moodiness, or difficulty concentrating on schoolwork or other work—if the exercise is reduced or stopped.
- The person has recently lost a significant amount of weight or is underweight for his or her height; in females, amenorrhea (cessation of normal menstrual periods) may occur.
- The person bases his or her self-esteem on the length and number of workouts completed and is frequently dissatisfied with his or her athletic accomplishments.
- The person exercises alone in order to hide the length of the workout or to avoid having their routine disturbed.

Compulsive exercise may also produce physical symptoms, particularly if the person is combining it with a weight-reduction diet or the use of laxatives and self-induced vomiting. One common physical disorder is overtraining, which develops when an athlete does not allow enough time for rest and recovery between hard training sessions. Under normal circumstances, improvements in strength, endurance, and overall fitness take place after the rest period. This process of improvement may take days to complete. If the athlete returns to hard training with inadequate rest, his or her performance will hit a plateau and eventually decline. This decline will occur much more rapidly if the athlete is also suffering from jet lag, an infectious illness, menstruation, or poor **nutrition**.

The symptoms of overtraining have been variously ascribed to microtrauma to muscle tissue, protein deficiency, breakdown of muscle tissue due to reduced calorie intake, stress on the nervous system, and elevated levels of cortisol (a hormone associated with stress) in the body for long periods of time. Some specific symptoms of overtraining include:

- persistent muscle soreness
- unusual and long-lasting fatigue
- an elevated resting heart rate
- increased incidence of injuries
- increased susceptibility to illness
- increased irritability and moodiness

Female dancers and athletes are at risk for a gender-specific disorder known as "female athlete triad." The triad is a group of three disorders often found together in female athletes, consisting of disordered eating leading to low energy availability, amenorrhea, and low bone density leading to osteoporosis. Girls and women with the triad are at increased risk of stress fractures and overuse injuries as well as **depression**, anxiety, and a weakened immune system.

KEY TERMS

Amenorrhea—Absence of menstrual periods in a woman of reproductive age. Excessive exercise can lead to amenorrhea in females.

Body dysmorphic disorder—A mental disorder marked by obsession with real (but minor) or imagined flaws in the shape or appearance of one's body. It is sometimes referred to as "imagined ugliness."

Body image—In medicine, the sum of a person's perceptions of, beliefs about, and emotional attitudes toward his or her body.

Cortisol—A steroid hormone produced by the adrenal gland that is released in response to stress. Cortisol suppresses the immune system and slows down bone formation.

Endorphins—Neurotransmitters produced by the pituitary gland that can relieve pain and produce a feeling of well-being.

Female athlete triad—A group of three disorders often found together in female athletes, consisting of disordered eating, amenorrhea, and osteoporosis.

Runner's high—A feeling of exhilaration that occurs when a period of strenuous exercise activates the release of endorphins. While typically associated with long-distance runners, the experience of such a high has been reported by dancers and athletes in other sports.

Diagnosis

There are no formal diagnostic criteria for compulsive exercise. **Diagnosis** depends on the person's level of awareness of the problem; observations by parents, coaches, teachers, or other family members; and the primary physician's knowledge of the warning signs of compulsive exercise. In many cases, the patient's history will provide clues, particularly amenorrhea in women or a history of sudden weight loss, frequent infections, and sports-related injuries in both sexes.

Examination

The doctor will check the patient's weight, heart rate, and blood pressure as part of a standard office examination. He or she may also check for soft-tissue or joint injuries if compulsive exercise is suspected. If the examination and patient history suggest compulsive exercising, the doctor may ask the patient directly about the frequency and length of workouts and average daily calorie intake.

Tests

The doctor may order imaging tests to check for stress fractures or blood and urine tests to rule out other causes of **fatigue** and weight loss.

Although there are no criteria for compulsive exercise in the *DSM*, there are a few questionnaires that have been devised since the 1990s to screen people for exercise addiction. One tool is the Exercise Addiction Inventory (EAI), short form (1996), which consists of six questions:

1. Exercise is the most important thing in my life.
2. There have been conflicts between me and my partner (or other family members) over my exercise.
3. I use exercise to change my moods.
4. Over time, I have increased the amount of exercise I do each day.
5. I feel moody and irritable if I miss an exercise session.
6. If I cut down on the amount of exercise and then start again, I always end up exercising as often as I did before.

The person is instructed to rate each item on a five-point scale, with 1 representing "Disagree Strongly," and 5 representing "Agree Strongly." A score of 24 or higher indicates that the person is at high risk for exercise addiction.

Another self-administered questionnaire is the Exercise Dependence Scale (EDS), a 21-item questionnaire designed in 2001 for persons 18 and older. It takes about five minutes to complete. The subject is instructed to rate each item on a six-point scale, with 1 indicating "Never," and 6 indicating "Always." The EDS was modeled on the criteria for substance dependency as set forth in *DSM-IV*. The lower the person's score, the greater the likelihood of exercise dependency.

Treatment

Treatment of compulsive exercise is usually carried out by a team that includes a physical therapist, nutritionist, the person's coach or trainer, and a psychotherapist, as well as the person's primary care doctor. Psychotherapy—particularly cognitive-behavioral therapy—has been found helpful in providing patients with a more balanced perspective on physical exercise. The nutritionist can help the person plan a balanced diet, while the physical therapist and trainer can assist the person in designing a workout schedule that will keep him or her fit without feeding the compulsion.

Patients who are diagnosed with an eating disorder as well as compulsive exercise may also be treated with **antidepressants**, most commonly the class of drugs known as **selective serotonin reuptake inhibitors (SSRIs)**.

QUESTIONS TO ASK YOUR DOCTOR

- How can I tell whether I am at risk for compulsive exercising?
- How much exercising is too much? When does it become a disorder?
- How can I tell whether my child is beginning to work out compulsively?
- Have you ever treated a patient for compulsive exercising? If so, was the treatment effective?
- What is your opinion of inventories and questionnaires for compulsive exercise?
- Do you think that compulsive exercise should be considered a distinctive disorder?

Prognosis

The prognosis for compulsive exercise depends on the person's age and whether the condition is primary or secondary. In most cases, recovery from compulsive exercise is a process that takes several months to several years. In general, compulsive exercise that is a primary disorder has a better prognosis than compulsive exercise associated with an eating disorder.

Prevention

Parents are the first line of preventing compulsive exercise in children. Specific suggestions include:

- Setting a good example of self-acceptance; don't obsess over appearance and perceived flaws.
- Avoid criticizing the weight or body shape of other family members. Even teasing remarks can hurt a teenager who may be struggling with other issues.
- Don't pressure children to excel in sports; accept that different children have different levels of athletic ability, and reassure them that it is perfectly acceptable to participate in a sport without being a star.
- Choose forms of exercise that the whole family can enjoy together (e.g., hiking, swimming, cycling, beach

volleyball), to reduce the temptation for one member to exercise alone.

- When appropriate, remind children that the images of "perfect" bodies on television or the Internet are often altered by various photographic techniques and are unrealistic ideals for most people.

Resources

BOOKS

Currie-McGhee, Leanne. *Exercise Addiction*. Detroit, MI: Lucent Books, 2011.

Morgan, John F. *The Invisible Man: A Self-Help Guide for Men with Eating Disorders, Compulsive Exercise and Bigorexia*. New York: Routledge, 2008.

Szabo, Attila. *Addiction to Exercise: A Symptom or a Disorder?* New York: Nova Science, 2010.

PERIODICALS

Bewell-Weiss, C.V., and J.C. Carter. "Predictors of Excessive Exercise in Anorexia Nervosa." *Comprehensive Psychiatry* 51 (November–December 2010): 566–571.

Boecker, H., et al. "The Runner's High: Opioidergic Mechanisms in the Human Brain." *Cerebral Cortex* 18 (November 2008): 2523–2531.

Dalle Grave, R. "Features and Management of Compulsive Exercising in Eating Disorders." *The Physician and Sports Medicine* 37 (October 2009): 20–28.

Goodwin, H., et al. "Psychometric Evaluation of the Compulsive Exercise Test (CET) in an Adolescent Population: Links with Eating Psychopathology." *European Eating Disorders Review* 19 (May–June 2011): 269–279.

Homan, K. "Athletic-ideal and Thin-Ideal Internalization as Prospective Predictors of Body Dissatisfaction, Dieting, and Compulsive Exercise." *Body Image* 7 (June 2010): 240–245.

Meyer, C., et al. "Compulsive Exercise and Eating Disorders." *European Eating Disorders Review* 19 (May–June 2011): 174–189.

Smith, A.M., and A.A. Link. "Sport Psychology and the Adolescent Athlete." *Pediatric Annals* 39 (May 2010): 310–316.

Villella, C., et al. "Behavioural Addictions in Adolescents and Young Adults: Results from a Prevalence Study." *Journal of Gambling Studies* 27 (June 2011): 203–214.

White, J., and E. Hallowell. "Examination of a Sociocultural Model of Excessive Exercise among Male and Female Adolescents." *Body Image* 7 (June 2010): 227–233.

WEBSITES

American Running Association (ARA). "Know the Signs of Unhealthy Exercise Addiction." Active.com. http://www.active.com/running/Articles/Know_the_signs_of_unhealthy_exercise_addiction.htm (accessed July 24, 2011).

Female Athlete Triad Coalition. http://www.femaleathletetriad.org (accessed July 23, 2011).

Nemours. "Compulsive Exercise." KidsHealth.org. http://kidshealth.org/parent/emotions/behavior/compulsive_exercise.html (accessed July 22, 2011).

ORGANIZATIONS

American College of Sports Medicine (ACSM), PO Box 1440, Indianapolis, IN, 46206-1440, (317) 637-9200, Fax: (317) 634-7817, http://www.acsm.org/AM/Template.cfm?Section=Home.

American Council on Exercise (ACE), 4851 Paramount Dr., San Diego, CA, 92123, (858) 576-6500, Fax: (858) 576-6564, (888) 825-3636, http://www.acefitness.org/default.aspx.

American Psychiatric Association, 1000 Wilson Blvd., Ste. 1825, Arlington, VA, 22209-3901, (703) 907-7300, apa@psych.org, http://www.psych.org.

American Running Association (ARA), 4405 East-West Hwy., Ste. 405, Bethesda, MD, 20814, Fax: (301) 913-9520, (800) 776-2732 x 13, http://www.americanrunning.org/m/contact/, http://www.americanrun ning.org.

National Eating Disorders Association (NEDA), 165 W 46th St., New York, NY, 10036, (212) 575-6200, Fax: (212) 575-1650, (800) 931-2237, info@NationalEatingDisorders.org, http://www.nationaleatingdisorders.org.

National Institute of Mental Health (NIMH), 6001 Executive Blvd., Rm. 8184, MSC 9663, Bethesda, MD, 20892-9663, (301) 443-4513, Fax: (301) 443-4279, (866) 615-6464, nimhinfo@nih.gov, http://www.nimh.nih.gov/index.shtml.

Rebecca J. Frey, PhD

Compulsive gambling *see* **Gambling disorder**

Computed tomography

Definition

Computed tomography (CT) scanning, also called x-ray computed tomography scanning and computerized axial tomography (CAT) scanning, is a diagnostic tool that provides views (images) of internal body structures using x rays. In 1980, about three million CT scans were performed in the United States. That number increased to over 70 million in 2007. In the field of mental health, a CT scan may be used when a patient seeks help for symptoms that could possibly be attributed to a medical (physiologic, as opposed to psychologic) cause.

Purpose

CT scans are used to image bone, soft tissues, fluids, and air. Since the 1990s, CT equipment has become more affordable and available. CT scans have become the imaging examination of choice for the diagnoses of most

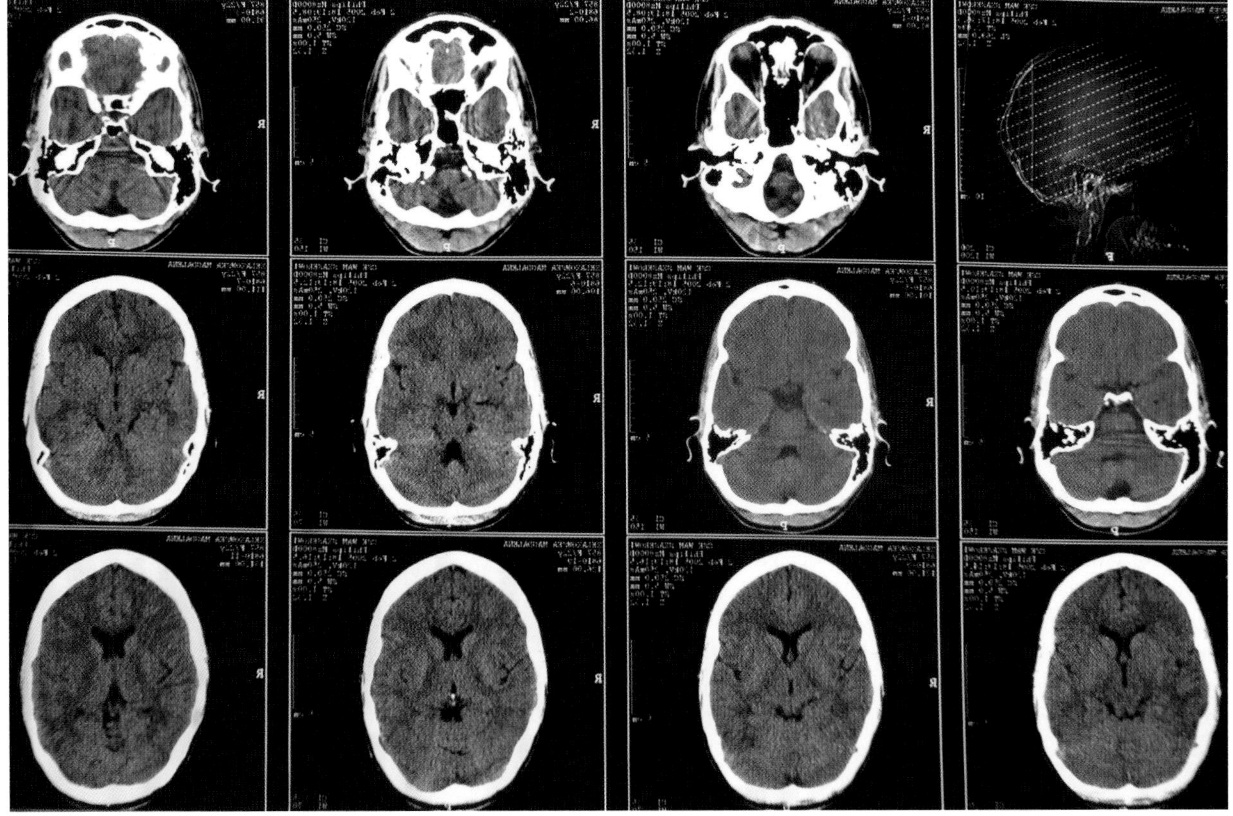

Computed tomography (CT) scan of a human brain. *(© Konrad Zelazowski/Alamy)*

solid tumors. Because the computerized image is sharp, focused, and three-dimensional, many structures can be better differentiated (visualized) when compared with standard x rays. About one-half of all diagnostic CT scans performed on adults are on the body (including the chest, abdomen, spine, and extremities), with another one-third on the head. Approximately three out of four scans are performed in the hospital, with one out of four within a single-specialty practice environment.

Common indications for CT scans include:

- Sinus. The CT scan can show details of sinusitis, bone fractures, and the presence of bony tumor involvement. Physicians may order a CT scan of the sinuses to provide an accurate map for surgery.
- Brain. Brain CT scans can detect hematomas (blood clotted mass), tumors, strokes, aneurysms (a blood vessel that ruptures), and degenerative or infected brain tissue. The introduction of CT scanning, especially spiral CT, has helped reduce the need for more invasive procedures such as cerebral angiography (inserting a wire through an artery to where it will reach brain vessels for visualization in real time).
- Body. CT scans of the chest, abdomen, spine, and extremities can detect the presence of tumors, enlarged lymph nodes, abnormal collection of fluid, and vertebral disc disease. These scans can also be helpful in evaluating the extent of bone breakdown in osteoporosis.
- Heart and aorta. CT scans can focus on the thoracic (chest) or abdominal aorta to locate aneurysms and other possible aortic diseases.
- Chest. CT scans of the chest are useful in distinguishing tumors and in detailing accumulation of fluid in chest infections.

It is important to note that CT scans alone are not used to diagnose mental disorders. Their primary function in this role is ensuring that psychological symptoms cannot be attributed to physical causes (such as a **brain** tumor) or as a supplement to a psychiatric exam. Mental health diagnoses are largely symptom based, despite physical changes in the brain.

Description

Computed tomography is the combination of focused x-ray beams and the computerized production of an image. CT applies the more general process of tomography, which is any type of imaging procedure that uses any type of electromagnetic radiation to generate sections of an object. Thus, by generating a series of two-dimensional x-ray images taken around a single-axis of rotation, a three-dimensional image of an object, such as a portion of the human body, is produced. Introduced in the early 1970s, CT has advanced rapidly and is now widely used, sometimes in the place of standard x rays.

CT procedure

A CT scan may be performed in a hospital or outpatient imaging center. Although the equipment looks large and intimidating, it is very sophisticated and fairly comfortable. The patient is asked to lie on a gantry, or narrow table, that slides into the center of the scanner. The scanner looks like a doughnut and is round in the middle, which allows the x-ray beam to rotate around the patient. The scanner section may also be tilted slightly to allow for certain cross-sectional angles.

The gantry moves very slightly as the precise adjustments for each sectional image are made. A technologist watches the procedure from a window and views the images on a computer screen. Generally, patients are alone during the procedure, though exceptions are sometimes made for pediatric patients. Communication is possible via an intercom system.

It is essential that the patient lie very still during the procedure to prevent motion blurring. In some studies, such as chest CTs, the patient will be asked to hold his or her breath during image capture.

Following the procedure, films of the images are usually printed for the radiologist and referring physician to review. A radiologist can also interpret CT examinations on the computer screen. The procedure time will vary in length depending on the area being imaged. Average study times are from 30 to 60 minutes. Some patients may be concerned about claustrophobia (a feeling of being “closed in”), but the width of the “doughnut” portion of the scanner is wide enough to ease many patients’ fears. Doctors may consider giving **sedatives** to patients who have severe claustrophobia or difficulty lying still (such as small children).

The CT image

While traditional x-ray machines image organs in two dimensions, often resulting in organs in the front of the body being superimposed over those in the back, CT scans allow for a more three-dimensional effect. CT images can be likened to slices in a loaf of bread. Precise sections of the body can be located and imaged as cross-sectional views. The screen before the technologist shows a computer’s analysis of each section detected by the x-ray beam, so various densities of tissue can be easily distinguished.

Contrast agents

Contrast agents are often used in CT exams and in other radiology procedures to illuminate certain details of anatomy more clearly. Some contrasts are natural, such as air or water. A water-based contrast agent is sometimes administered for specific diagnostic purposes. Barium sulfate is commonly used in gastroenterology procedures. The patient may drink this contrast or receive it in an enema. Oral or rectal contrast is usually given when examining the abdomen or cells, but not when scanning the brain or chest. Iodine is the most widely used intravenous contrast agent and is given through an intravenous needle.

If contrast agents are used in the CT exam, these will be administered several minutes before the study begins. Patients undergoing abdominal CT may be asked to drink a contrast medium. Some patients may experience a salty taste, flushing of the face, warmth or slight nausea, or hives from an intravenous contrast injection. Technologists and radiologists have the equipment and training to help patients through these minor reactions and to handle more severe reactions. Severe reactions to contrast are rare but do occur.

Types of CT scans

SPIRAL CT SCANS. The spiral CT scan is advantageous over traditional CT because it allows for the continuous re-creation of images. While traditional CT allows the technologist to take slices at very small and precise intervals one after the other, spiral CT stays in motion and allows for a continuous flow of images, without stopping the scanner to move to the next image slice. A major advantage of spiral CT is the ability to reconstruct images anywhere along the length of the study area. Because the procedure is faster, patients are required to lie still for shorter periods of time. The ability to image contrast more rapidly after it is injected, when it is at its highest level, is another advantage of spiral CT’s high speed.

ELECTRON BEAM TOMOGRAPHY. Electron beam CT scans are another type of CT technology that can be used to detect calcium buildup in arteries. These calcium deposits are potential risk factors for coronary artery disease. Electron beam CT scans take pictures more quickly than conventional CTs, and are therefore better able to produce clear images of the heart as it pumps blood.

Some facilities have spiral, electron, and conventional CT available. Although spiral is more advantageous for many applications, conventional CT is still a precise method for imaging many tissues and structures. The physician will evaluate which type of CT works best for the specific exam purpose.

SINGLE PHOTON EMISSION CT SCANS. Single photon emission computerized tomography (SPECT) scans are used in research and may assist in diagnosing brain disorders such as **Alzheimer's disease** and Parkinson's disease. SPECT scans use gamma-ray emitting radioisotopes (radioactive isotopes) as the method for producing images of active regions of the brain. The process begins by injecting the brain with a radioactive tracer. Because the tracer remains concentrated—it does not spread out in the brain—it lasts up to one minute. This advantage means that such a scan can be performed quickly. It is especially useful for scanning the brains of epileptic patients, because the scan can be produced after an epileptic seizure has passed.

New technologies

A new generation of CT scanning equipment was developed in the late 2000s and is expected to dramatically increase the quality and safety of CT scans. One example, the Siemens CT machine or "Somatom Definition Flash" dual-source computed tomography scanner, is able to scan a patient more than twice as fast as conventional equipment. A single scan can be completed within 43 cm/s with a temporal resolution of 75 ms. A complete scan can be performed in about 250 ms. This new technology does not require the patient to hold their breath during the scan and is especially useful in **trauma** cases when quick analysis is needed.

The first system to be installed in a medical center within the United Sates occurred at the Mayo Clinic in Rochester, Minnesota, in 2009. In addition, the dose of radiation impinging on a patient's heart is much lower than current systems. Traditional systems output from 8 to 40 mSv (units of radiation), while the new Siemens instrument produces only 1 mSv.

Precautions

Pregnant women or those who could possibly be pregnant should not have a CT scan, particularly a full body or abdominal scan, unless the diagnostic benefits outweigh the risks. If the exam is necessary for obstetric purposes, technologists are instructed not to repeat films if there are errors. Pregnant patients receiving a CT scan or any x-ray exam away from the abdominal area may be protected by a lead apron; most radiation, known as scatter, travels through the body, however, and is not totally blocked by the apron.

Contrast agents are often used in CT exams, though some types of tumors are better seen without it. Patients should discuss the use of contrast agents with their doctor, and should be asked to sign a consent form prior to the administration of contrast. One of the common contrast agents, iodine, can cause allergic reactions. Patients who are known to be allergic to iodine or shellfish should inform the physician prior to the CT scan; a combination of medications can be given to such patients before the scan to prevent or minimize the reaction. Contrast agents may also put patients with diabetes at risk of kidney failure, particularly those taking the medication metformin (Fortamet, Glucophage, Glumetza, Riomet), an oral antidiabetic drug.

Radiation exposure from a CT scan is similar to, though higher than, that of a conventional x ray. Although there is risk to pregnant women, the risk to other adults is minimal and it should produce no effects. Severe contrast reactions are rare, but they are still a risk of CT procedures.

Though some hospitals offer full-body CT scans as a preventative measure in screening disease, it is not recommended in healthy individuals. The U.S. Food and Drug Administration (FDA) advises individuals to consider both the risks and benefits of full-body screening and to discuss the procedure thoroughly with their physician.

Preparation

If a contrast medium is administered, the patient may be asked to fast for about four to six hours prior to the procedure. Patients will usually be given a gown (like a typical hospital gown) to be worn during the procedure.

KEY TERMS

Electromagnetic radiation—Radiation including gamma rays, x rays, ultraviolet light, visible light, infrared radiation, microwaves, and radio waves.

Tomography—A scanning technique that uses electromagnetic radiation (such as gamma rays or x rays) or ultrasound to produce a three-dimensional image of the structure.

Tumor—An abnormal growth of body cells, which may be malignant (harmful) or benign (harmless).

X ray—A type of electromagnetic radiation, between gamma rays and ultraviolet, with a wavelength of between 0.01 and 10 nm.

QUESTIONS TO ASK YOUR DOCTOR

- Will I need to have someone with me during the imaging scan? Will this person need to drive me home?
- What special precautions should be taken with a child?
- Should I especially be concerned with scans to my brain? How about other organs of my body?
- Should I expect any side effects?
- How many CT scans is it safe to undergo in any one year? How far apart should they be spaced?
- How will this scan help in the diagnosis of my disorder?

All metal and jewelry should be removed to avoid artifacts on the film. Depending on the type of study, patients may also be required to remove dentures.

Aftercare

Generally, no aftercare is required following a CT scan. Immediately following the exam, the technologist will continue to watch the patient for possible adverse contrast reactions. Patients are instructed to advise the technologist of any symptoms, particularly respiratory difficulty. The site of contrast injection will be bandaged and may feel tender following the exam.

Results

Normal findings on a CT exam show bone, the most dense tissue, as white areas. Tissues and fat will show as various shades of gray, and fluids will be gray or black. Air will also look black. Intravenous, oral, and rectal contrasts appear as white areas. The radiologist can determine if tissues and organs appear normal by the sensitivity of the gray shadows. Abnormal results may show different characteristics of tissues within organs. Accumulations of blood or other fluids where they do not belong may be detected. Radiologists can differentiate among types of tumors throughout the body by viewing details of their makeup.

Brain studies

The precise differences in density allowed by CT scan can clearly show tumors, strokes, or lesions in the brain area as altered densities. These lighter or darker areas on the image may indicate a tumor or hematoma within the brain and skull area. Different types of tumors can be identified by the presence of edema (fluid), by the tissue's density, or by studying blood vessel location and activity. The speed and convenience of CT often allows for detection of hemorrhage (bleeding) before symptoms even occur.

Resources

BOOKS

Armstrong, Peter, Martin L. Wastie, and Andrea G. Rockall. *Diagnostic Imaging*. Chichester, UK: Wiley-Blackwell, 2009.

Birkfellner, Wolfgang. *Applied Medical Image Processing: A Basic Course*. Boca Raton, FL: Taylor & Francis, 2011.

Frank, Eugene D. *Merrill's Atlas of Radiographic Positioning & Procedures*. St. Louis: Elsevier/Mosby, 2012.

Romans, Lois E. *Computed Tomography for Technologists: A Comprehensive Text*. Baltimore: Wolters Kluwer Health/ Lippincott Williams & Wilkins, 2011.

Seeram, Euclid. *Computed Tomography: Physical Principles, Clinical Applications and Quality Control*. St. Louis: Saunders/Elsevier, 2009.

PERIODICALS

Brenner, David J., and Eric J. Hall. "Computed Tomography—An Increasing Source of Radiation Exposure." *The New England Journal of Medicine* 357 (November 29, 2007): 2277–84. http://www.nejm.org/doi/full/10.1056/NEJMra072149 (accessed October 31, 2011).

WEBSITES

Mayo Clinic staff. "CT Scan." MayoClinic.com. January 12, 2011. http://www.mayoclinic.com/health/ct-scan/MY00309 (accessed October 31, 2011).

MedlinePlus. "Cranial CT Scan." U.S. National Library of Medicine. November 22, 2010. http://www.nlm.nih.gov/medlineplus/ency/article/003786.htm (accessed October 31, 2011).

U.S. Food and Drug Administration. "Computed Tomography." U.S. Department of Health and Human Services. http://www.fda.gov/Radiation-EmittingProducts/RadiationEmittingProductsandProcedures/MedicalImaging/MedicalX-Rays/ucm115317.htm (accessed October 31, 2011).

———. "Full-Body CT Scans: What you Need to Know." April 6, 2010. http://www.fda.gov/Radiation-EmittingProducts/RadiationEmittingProductsandProcedures/MedicalImaging/MedicalX-Rays/ucm115340.htm (accessed October 31, 2011).

ORGANIZATIONS

American College of Radiology, 1891 Preston White Drive, Reston, VA, 22091, (703) 648-8900, http://www.acr.org.

Laith Farid Gulli, MD
Teresa G. Norris, RN
William A. Atkins, BB, BS, MBA

Conduct disorder

Definition

Conduct disorder (CD), also sometimes called disruptive behavior disorder, is a childhood and adolescent behavior disorder characterized by aggressive and destructive activities (for example, fighting, **bullying**, lying, and stealing) that cause serious disruptions in the child's natural environments such as home, school, church, or neighborhood. The overriding feature of conduct disorder is the repetitive and persistent pattern of defiant or impulsive behaviors that violate societal norms and the rights of other people. Such long-term behavior and personality problems often lead to problems later in life, such as illegal drug use, further antisocial behaviors, criminal activities and legal problems.

Demographics

Studies of conduct disorder worldwide have found that overall rates are 4.6% of boys and 4.5% of girls. In the United States, it is one of the most prevalent categories of mental health problems of children, with rates estimated at 5% of children, with about 9% for males and 2% for females. According to the U.S. **Substance Abuse and Mental Health Services Administration**, in 2009, 1%–4% of 9- to 17-year-old children were affected by CD. Because of a discrepancy among mental health experts as to the exact definition of conduct disorder, estimates from other sources vary from as low as 2% to as high as 16% of children in the United States, with most of the cases developing in children in their late childhood or early teenage years. Statistics suggest the disorder is more likely to affect boys than girls. In addition, children are at more risk of CD when **child abuse** is part of their past, drug or alcohol **addiction** is found among their parents and caregivers, family conflicts are frequent, genetic defects are present within the family, and poverty is part of their experience.

Description

The specific behaviors used to produce a **diagnosis** of conduct disorder are often categorized into four groups: aggressive conduct that causes or threatens physical harm to other people or animals, nonaggressive behavior that causes property damage or loss, deceitfulness or theft, and serious violations of rules. In addition, two subtypes of conduct disorder can be delineated based on the age at which symptoms first appear. Childhood-onset type is appropriate for children showing at least one of the behaviors in question before the age of ten years. Adolescent onset type is defined by the absence of any conduct disorder criteria before the age of ten years. Severity may be described as mild, moderate, or severe, depending on the number of problems exhibited and their impact on other people.

Youngsters who show symptoms (most often aggression) before the age of ten years may also exhibit oppositional behavior and peer relationship problems. When they also show persistent conduct disorder and then develop adult **antisocial personality disorder**, they should be distinguished from individuals who had no symptoms of conduct disorder before age ten. The childhood type is more highly associated with heightened aggression, male gender, **oppositional defiant disorder**, and a family history of antisocial behavior.

The individual behaviors that can be observed when conduct disorder is diagnosed may be problematic and chronic. They tend to occur frequently and are distressingly consistent across time, settings, and families. Not surprisingly, these children function poorly in a variety of places. In fact, the behaviors clustered within the term "conduct disorder" account for a majority of clinical referrals, classroom detentions or other sanctions, being asked to stop participating in numerous activities, and can be extremely difficult (even impossible) for parents to manage.

The negative consequences of conduct disorder, particularly childhood onset, may include illicit drug use, dropping out of school, violent behavior, severe family conflict, and frequent delinquent acts. Such behaviors often result in the child's eventual placement out of the home, in special education, and/or the juvenile justice system. There is evidence that the rates of disruptive behavior disorders may be as high as 50% in youth in public sectors of care such as juvenile justice, alcohol and drug services, schools for youths with serious emotional disturbances, child welfare, and mental health.

Other mental problems are also frequently associated with conduct disorder, such as **attention deficit hyperactivity disorder** (ADHD), antisocial personality disorder (APD), **major depressive disorder** (MDD), **learning disorders**, thought disorders, **substance abuse**, mood disorders, **post-traumatic stress disorder** (PTSD), and **bipolar disorder** (BD).

The financial costs of crime and correction for repeated juvenile offenses by youth with conduct disorder are extensive. The social costs include citizens' fear of such behaviors, loss of a sense of safety, and disruptions in classrooms that interfere with other children's opportunity to learn. The costs to the child and the child's family are enormous in terms of the emotional and other resources needed to address the consequences of the constellation of symptoms that define conduct disorder.

Causes and symptoms

Various determinants tend to be present in children with conduct disorder, and it is possible there may be a genetic predisposition to this disorder. Symptoms recur among children exhibiting this disorder.

Causes

There is no known direct cause for conduct disorder. However, many determinants are proposed to explain how conduct disorder becomes present within children. These determinants include various types of factors:

- biological: such as problems during pregnancy, injuries to the brain early in life, or other mental illnesses such as anxiety disorders that contribute to CD
- environmental: factors such as a dysfunctional family life, lack of discipline in school or home, physical or mental abuse, or traumatic experiences
- genetics: often times other family members have mental illnesses or are substance or alcohol abusers
- social: poor parenting of a child can lead to conduct disorder, along with poverty or low socioeconomic status and being seen as an outcast by other students or peers

The frustrating behavior of youngsters with conduct disorder frequently leads to blaming, labeling, and other unproductive activities. Children who are "acting out" do not inspire sympathy or the benefit of the doubt. Further, other children often ostracize them. Parents of such children are often blamed as poor disciplinarians or bad parents. As a result, parents of children with conduct disorder may be reluctant to engage with schools or other authorities. At the same time, there is a strong correlation between children diagnosed with conduct disorder and a significant level of family dysfunction, poor parenting practices, an overemphasis on coercion and hostile communication patterns, verbal and physical aggression, and a history of maltreatment.

A possible genetic component may exist as a factor in conduct disorder, which has been traditionally viewed as a behavioral disorder. One study with adopted children in the mid-1990s looked at the relationship between birth parents with antisocial personality disorder and adverse adoptive home environments. When both of these adverse conditions occurred, there was significantly increased aggressiveness and conduct disorder in the adopted children. That was not the case if there was no indication of antisocial personality disorder in the birth parents. This finding, which has been supported in studies in the 2000s and 2010s, has important implications for prevention and **intervention** of conduct disorders and its associated conditions of substance abuse and aggressiveness.

Symptoms

Conduct disorder has many varied symptoms among children who have this mental disorder. Symptoms are commonly divided into four general groups: destructive behavior, aggressive behavior, violation of rules, and deceitful behavior. Some of the more common activities (which may fall into more than one of these groups) that are seen within people with CD are:

- destroying or vandalizing property such as intentionally setting a building on fire (arson)
- doing physical harm to others, such as fighting, bullying
- using dangerous weapons such as guns and knives
- being cruel to people or animals
- forcing others to have sex or having sex at an early age
- stealing, shoplifting, or breaking into cars or homes
- having wide mood swings
- running away
- getting into trouble repeatedly
- skipping school, truancy
- playing pranks on people
- lying to get something desired or to avoid doing something
- abusing alcohol or illegal drugs
- having few friends
- having little remorse (without guilt feelings) for bad behaviors

Diagnosis

Testing does not help diagnose conduct disorder. Such a diagnosis is solely based on the child's history. A comprehensive evaluation should be undertaken to find out if co-existing conditions exist, such as anxiety, mood disorders, learning problems, PTSD, ADHD, and others. Further, behavior that represents conduct disorder is more serious than simple adolescent exuberance, rebellion, or immaturity. The fourth edition, text revised, of the ***Diagnostic and Statistical Manual of Mental Disorders*** (*DSM-IV-TR*) indicates that for conduct disorder to be diagnosed, the patient must be shown to have repeatedly violated rules, age-appropriate social norms, and the rights of others for a period of at least twelve months. This is shown by three or more of the following behaviors, with at least one having taken place in the previous six months: aggression to people or animals, property destruction, lying or theft, and serious rule violations.

Aggression to people or animals includes:

- engaging in frequent bullying or threatening behavior
- often starting fights
- using a weapon that could cause serious injury (gun, knife, club, broken glass)
- showing physical cruelty to people
- showing physical cruelty to animals
- engaging in theft with confrontation (armed robbery, extortion, mugging, purse snatching)
- forcing sex upon someone

Property destruction includes deliberately setting fires to cause serious damage and/or deliberately destroying the property of others by means other than fire setting.

Lying or theft includes:

- breaking into a building, car, or house belonging to someone else
- frequently lying or breaking promises for gain or to avoid obligations (called "conning")
- stealing valuables without confrontation (burglary, forgery, shop lifting)

Serious rule violations include:

- beginning before the age of 13 years, frequently staying out at night against parents' wishes
- running away from parents overnight twice or more or once for an extended period
- engaging in frequent truancy beginning before the age of 13 years

Mild severity means there are few problems with conduct beyond those needed to make a diagnosis and all of the problems cause little harm to other people. Moderate severity means the number and effect of the conduct problems is between the extremes of mild and severe. Severe is indicated if there are many more conduct symptoms than are needed to make the diagnosis (more than three in the previous twelve months or more than one in the previous six months), or the behaviors cause other people considerable harm.

It is generally diagnosed when somebody, often a child in school, comes to the attention of authorities (school, law enforcement, and others) most often because of behavior. The person might then be referred to a **psychiatrist** or **psychologist** for assessment and diagnosis. It is unlikely that any sort of specific test is given; rather, the individual would have to meet the criteria as defined by the *DSM-IV-TR*. Usually there is a history of acting out in school, neighborhood, home, and other social settings. Court-ordered treatment would likely occur if the person comes to the attention of the police and if a crime is committed. A judge might order treatment as an alternative to jail or before a sentence is served.

Treatment

Treatment is much more successful when the child's parents or caregivers are actively involved in the process. When such members are participating, parents or caregivers at home can carry out CD techniques started by the medical professional. However, when the family is part of the problem, the child is often taken away from the disruptive environment and placed in a more stable and healthy one. Many places are available that provide such stable environments while at the same time providing behavioral modification treatment. Two of these are wilderness programs and boot camps. Medication may also be a part of the treatment.

Earlier treatments of youth with conduct disorder relied on legal processes to declare a child in need of supervision or treatment and thus able to be placed in residential settings established for this purpose. While residential placements may still be used, recent treatment models have relied less on such restrictive procedures. The increased visibility and sophistication of the consumer movement, comprising families of children and youth with mental health disorders, has brought pressure to bear on treatment providers. Such action helps to stop blaming families, to stop removing children from their families for services, to focus instead on strengths and assets in both the child and the child's family, and to use community-based interventions in several domains in which the child and family live.

Community-based interventions, sometimes called wrap-around services, attempt to handle the child within the child's natural environment in a comprehensive and flexible way. The idea is to target a range of child, parent, family, and social system factors associated with a child's behavioral problems. This approach has been successful in modifying antisocial behavior, reducing rates of restrictive placement, and lowering the cost of services.

For the most part, conduct disorder is treated based on the age of the child, the disorder's severity, and the ability of the child to deal with it on a daily basis. Treatment is usually complicated for both the patient and the administrator, especially if the patient is unwilling to cooperate due to mistrust or fear of authority figures.

The treatment process usually includes **psychotherapy**, which is used to help the child express problems and control feelings in socially acceptable ways. Specific types of psychotherapy used to treat CD are **cognitive-behavioral therapy**, which helps to improve the thinking processes and problem-solving abilities within the patient, along with anger management and impulse control, and **family therapy**, which helps to improve interactions among family members. Treatment may also include special education classes for those children having learning problems. The attending medical professional may instruct the parents or caretakers as to special educational and management programs that need to be used at home and in school. Medication is sometimes used and may be effective in controlling aggression. Most drugs used for it are also used to treat the symptoms of other mental illnesses such as **depression** and ADHD.

One treatment program that has been used with some success is child cognitive behavioral treatment and skills training, which trains children with conduct disorder in anger-coping, peer coping, and problem-solving skills.

Parent management training and family therapy are also used to treat conduct disorder. Parents learn to apply behavioral principles effectively, how to play with their children, and how to teach them new skills.

Generally, a variety of treatment modes are used to address such a complex disorder. Severe antisocial behavior on the part of the child and adverse parenting practices on the part of parents and caregivers may cause the family to stop treatment before it can be effective or before meaningful change can be achieved. Treatment takes quite long because new attitudes and behaviors must be ingrained in the child. The earlier treatment begins and the longer it is applied, the more successful the results tend to be for the child.

Prognosis

Early identification and appropriate, innovative, and comprehensive treatment will improve the course of conduct disorder and possibly prevent a host of negative outcomes that are associated with it. Unfortunately, the **stigma** of treatment and the undiagnosed problems of many parents prevent many families from seeking treatment. Instead their children come into contact with the juvenile and criminal justice system.

In addition, children with more severe symptoms or other mental problems or other illnesses (such as drug abuse) have the lowest chance of improving from conduct disorder. They may be unable to adapt to the complexities of being an adult and may have persistent problems in various aspects of their life.

Prevention

Prognosis may best be improved by prevention of conduct disorder before it becomes so resistant to treatment. Research indicates that early intervention holds the greatest promise. It incorporates several components such as child tutoring, classroom intervention, peer training, social-cognitive skills training, parent training, and family problem solving.

Other studies have included early parent or family interventions, school based interventions, and community interventions. Again, these include a variety of elements, including parent training that includes education about normal child development, child problem solving, and family communication skills training. Research is still needed to determine where and when to target specific preventive interventions.

For the most part, improving the condition of the child helps to prevent the occurrence of CD, such as making sure the child is in a positive environment that emphasizes good behaviors and minimizes bad behaviors.

KEY TERMS

Antisocial personality disorder—A condition characterized by pervasive disregard for the rights of others that begins in childhood and often continues into adulthood.

Attention deficit hyperactivity disorder—A condition characterized by lack of concentration, impulsive or inappropriate age-related behavior, and hyperactivity.

Bipolar disorder—A condition characterized by extreme mood swings, from euphoria to depression.

Learning disorder—A condition characterized by difficulty in learning that has an unknown cause.

Major depressive disorder—A condition characterized by low mood, low self-esteem, and loss of pleasure or interest in everyday activities.

Mood disorders—A group of conditions characterized by pronounced disturbances in the state of mind.

Post-traumatic stress disorder—A condition resulting from severe emotional trauma (such as from war or natural disaster) and characterized by flashbacks, low energy, anxiety, depression, and sleep disturbances.

Substance abuse—The excessive consumption of an illegal drug or other substance that has a pronounced effect on the mind or body but without any therapeutic application.

Thought disorder—A condition characterized by incomprehensible language, either written or spoken.

QUESTIONS TO ASK YOUR DOCTOR

- Does my child have conduct disorder?
- What treatment plan is best?
- What medications should be used?
- Does my child need counseling?
- Will you be able to help my child?
- Is there support available for parents?

Resources

BOOKS

American Psychiatric Association. *Diagnostic and Statistical Manual of Mental Disorders,* 4th ed., text rev. Washington, DC: American Psychiatric Association, 2000.

Leeming, David A., Kathryn Madden, and Stanton Marlan, eds. *Encyclopedia of Psychology and Religion*. New York: Springer, 2010.

Morrison, James. *DSM-IV Made Easy: The Clinician's Guide to Diagnosis.* New York: Guilford Press, 2006.

WEBSITES

"Conduct Disorder." American Academy of Child and Adolescent Psychology. Last updated July 2004. http://aacap.org/page.ww?name=Conduct+Disorder§ion= Facts+for+Families (accessed September 8, 2011).

"Conduct Disorder." MedlinePlus. Last updated February 28, 2011. http://www.nlm.nih.gov/medlineplus/ency/article/000919.htm (accessed September 8, 2011).

"Helping Children and Youth with Conduct Disorder and Oppositional Defiant Disorder: Systems of Care." U.S. Substance Abuse and Mental Health Services Administration, January 2006. http://store.samhsa.gov/product/Helping-Children-and-Youth-With-Conduct-Disorder-and-Oppositional-Defiant-Disorder-Systems-of-Care/SMA06-4200 (accessed September 8, 2011).

"Mental Health and Conduct Disorder." WebMD. http://www.webmd.com/mental-health/mental-health-conduct-disorder (accessed September 8, 2011).

ORGANIZATIONS

American Academy of Child and Adolescent Psychiatry, 3615 Wisconsin Ave., NW, Washington, DC, 20016-3007, (202) 966-7300, Fax: (202) 966-2891, http://aacap.org.

American Psychiatric Association, 1000 Wilson Blvd., Ste. 1825, Arlington, VA, 22209-3901, (703) 907-7300, apa@psych.org, http://www.psych.org.

Federation of Families for Children's Mental Health, 9605 Medical Center Dr., Rockville, MD, 20850, (240) 403-1901, Fax: (240) 403-1909, ffcmh@ffcmh.org, http://ffcmh.org.

Mental Health America, 2000 N. Beauregard St., 6th Fl., Alexandria, VA, 22311, (703) 684-7722, (800) 969-6642, Fax: (703) 684-5968, http://www1.nmha.org.

National Alliance on Mental Illness, 2107 Wilson Blvd., Ste. 300, Arlington, VA, 22201-3042, Fax: (703) 524-9094, (800) 950-6264, http://www.nami.org.

National Institute of Mental Health, 6001 Executive Blvd., Rm. 8184, MSC 9663, Bethesda, MD, 20892-9663, (301) 433-4513; TTY: (301) 443-8431, Fax: (301) 443-4279, (866) 615-6464; TTY: (866) 415-8051, nimhinfo@nih.gov, http://www.nimh.nih.gov.

Judy Leaver, MA
William Atkins, BB, BS, MBA

Conners' Rating Scales

Definition

Developed by Dr. C. Keith Conners, PhD, the latest version of the Conners' Rating Scales (CRS) is the Conners' Rating Scales–Third Edition, or Conners 3. The Conners 3 is a set of paper and pencil screening questionnaires designed to be completed by parents, teachers, and students to assist in evaluating children and teenagers for **attention deficit hyperactivity disorder (ADHD)** and related behavioral, emotional, and learning problems.

Purpose

The Conners 3 is used as part of a comprehensive examination and is designed to be easily administered and scored. Both the long and short versions serve as tools to assist in determining whether children or teenagers between the ages of 6 and 18 years might have **ADHD** or another disorder, such as **oppositional defiant disorder** or **conduct disorder**. In addition, a self-report form is used to assess children or teenagers between the ages of 8 and 18 years.

Description

The Conners 3 is available in long and short versions for parents (or caregivers) and teachers, along with a self-report version that is completed by the student. The long version takes approximately 20 minutes to complete, while the short version usually takes about 10 minutes. The ADHD Index is completed in less than five minutes. The Conners 3 is normalized based on gender-specific, age-stratified norms from a large, nationally representative sample of the U.S. population. Specifically, it was normalized using ratings from approximately 1,200 parents, 1,200 teachers, and 1,000 children and adolescent reports. The normative data was taken over a one-year period based on the age of the children and adolescents and was separated by gender. The standardization sample of the U.S. population was based on ethnicity, gender, parent education, and race.

The Conners 3 has been improved over the previous edition, the CRS-Revised (CRS-R), with respect to the following:

- updated normative data
- unlimited use when computer scoring is selected
- better focus on ADHD
- modified age range (6–18 years, as opposed to 6–17 years for previous versions)
- expanded number of scales, including two additional *DSM-IV-TR* symptom scales (*Diagnostic and Statistical Manual of Mental Disorders*, fourth edition, text revision)
- new screener items to identify any possible anxiety or depression
- availability of impairment items, which measure the problem's impact
- use of critical items that identify children who need immediate attention
- guidance in planning and monitoring interventions

Conners 3 includes six empirical scales concerning hyperactivity/impulsivity, executive functioning, learning difficulties, aggression, peer relations, and family relations. The *DSM-IV-TR* symptom scales assess the possibility of various disorders, including three types of ADHD (hyperactive/impulsive, inattentive, or combined), oppositional defiant disorder, and conduct disorder, the later two of which are new to the third edition. The Conners 3 also comprises three validity scales, also new to the third edition, and a rational scale, which assesses inattention.

The short form includes the strongest items from the long form, which are hyperactivity/impulsivity, inattention, executive functioning, learning problems, aggression, peer relations, and positive and negative impressions.

The Conners 3 also includes two indexes, the global index and the ADHD index. Each is composed of ten items. The global index measures general psychopathology, whereas the ADHD index aims to help distinguish children with ADHD from those without the condition. It is also a recommended test for the screening of large numbers of children or teenagers and is a good way to measure the effectiveness of treatment or the response to **intervention** in such children and teens.

KEY TERMS

Attention deficit hyperactivity disorder (ADHD)—A persistent pattern of inattention, hyperactivity and/or impulsiveness; the pattern is more frequent and severe than is typically observed in people at a similar level of development.

Diagnostic and Statistical Manual of Mental Disorders—The handbook that mental health professionals use to diagnose mental disorders.

Executive function—The cognitive processes that facilitate mental control, such as planning, problem solving, ability to change, prioritization, and self control.

The long version for parents contains 110 items, while the long version for teachers contains 115 items. The parents' short version contains 43 items, and the teachers' short version has 39. The self-report scale contains 59 items in the long form and 39 items in the short form. The forms span multiple pages, and numbers circled on the front or back page are automatically transferred to a middle section for use by a clinician. The clinician transfers the circled scores into appropriate scales on the middle form and totals each scale at the bottom of the page. The parent and teacher scales are written at the equivalent of a fourth-to-fifth grade reading level. The self-report scale for children is written at the third-grade reading level.

Preparation

The long form is recommended for an initial evaluation, because it more thoroughly assesses the *DSM* diagnostic criteria and may better identify specific needs of a child as compared to the short form. However, the short form is beneficial when an evaluation needs to be done on a timely basis or when many tests will be performed over a specific period (such as when the professional administrator wishes to monitor progress).

Precautions

As with all psychological evaluation instruments, the Conners 3 is not perfect. There is a risk of obtaining false positives (incorrectly diagnosing the disorder) or false negatives (failing to identify the disorder). Therefore, the information obtained from completed forms should not be used in isolation, but should be one piece of a complex evaluation that includes a clinical interview with the

QUESTIONS TO ASK YOUR DOCTOR

- What should I do next if the CRS finds that my child has ADHD?
- What qualifications should I look for in a professional administering the CRS?
- What other tests are available for diagnosing ADHD?

child, other diagnostic measures such as a computerized continuous performance test, and patient self-reports—for those old enough and with sufficient reading ability to do so. Although the Conners 3 can be readily administered and scored by a nonprofessional, a professional, such as a **psychologist** or counselor, who is familiar with the scales should facilitate the test to ensure accurate results.

Previous versions of the Conners' scales (earlier than CRS-R, which preceded Conners 3) were criticized by those claiming disparity between results obtained in different ethnic groups. This version, along with CRS-R, should dispel this concern, since it was "normed" using data from thousands of subjects crossing all cultural and ethnic boundaries. The technical manual for CRS-R even contains separate normative information for specific ethnic groups. However, there are generally no or statistically insignificant differences between age and gender groups.

Results

After transferring the raw scores to the various scales and totaling them, the total of each scale is transferred to another form designed to graphically portray the results. The clinician must be careful to transpose the raw scores to the correct age group column within each major scale. Each of these column scores can then be converted to a T-score. T-scores are standardized scores with a mean of 50 and a standard deviation of 10. These can be further converted to percentile scores as needed.

As a rule, T-scores above 60 are cause for concern and have interpretive value. Interpretable scores range from a low T-score of 61 (mildly atypical) to above 70 (markedly atypical). However, again, this information should not be used in isolation to make a **diagnosis**.

The Conners 3 can be hand scored or computer scored. A Hand-Scored Kit and a Software Kit are both available. The Software Kit provides for unlimited computer scoring with Web links to the *DSM-IV-TR* diagnostic criteria, along with an Assessment Report (total score and symptom count score), Feedback Report (assessment summary), and Progress Report (result comparison when administered more than once).

Resources

BOOKS

Austin, Vance L., and Daniel T. Sciarra. *Children and Adolescents with Emotional and Behavior Disorders*. Boston: Merrill, 2010.

Hammerness, Paul Graves. *ADHD*. Westport, CT: Greenwood Press, 2008.

McLeod, Jane D, and Eric R. Wright, editors. *The Sociology of Mental Illness: A Comprehensive Reader*. New York: Oxford University Press, 2010.

Shepherd, Terry L. *Working with Students with Emotional and Behavior Disorders: Characteristics and Teaching Strategies*. Upper Saddle River, NJ: Merrill, 2010.

WEBSITES

Pearson. "C. Keith Conners [biography]." PsychCorp.co.uk. http://www.psychcorp.co.uk/Psychology/ChildMental-Health/ChildADDADHDBehaviour/ConnersEarlyChild-hood(ConnersEC)/Authors/CKeithConners.aspx (accessed November 23, 2011).

Pearson Assessments. "Conners Third Edition (Conners 3) [product page]." http://www.pearsonassessments.com/HAIWEB/Cultures/en-us/Productdetail.htm?Pid=Conners_3 (accessed November 23, 2011).

ORGANIZATIONS

Children and Adults with Attention Deficit/Hyperactivity Disorder, 8181 Professional Place, Ste. 150, Landover, MD, 20785, (301) 306-7070, Fax: (301) 306-7090, http://www.chadd.org.

Substance Abuse and Mental Health Services Administration Referral Resource, 1 Choke Cherry Rd., Rockville, MD, 20857, (877) SAMHSA-7 (726-4727), (800) TTY: 487-4889, Fax: (240) 221-4292, SAMHSAInfo@samhsa.hhs.gov, http://www.samhsa.gov.

Jack H. Booth, PsyD
William A. Atkins

Conversion disorder

Definition

Conversion disorder is defined by the ***Diagnostic and Statistical Manual of Mental Disorders***, fourth edition, text revision, also known as the *DSM-IV-TR*, as a mental disorder whose central feature is the appearance of symptoms affecting the patient's senses or voluntary movements that suggest a neurological or general medical disease or condition. Other terms that have sometimes been used for conversion disorder include pseudoneurologic syndrome, hysterical **neurosis**, and psychogenic disorder. The *Diagnostic and Statistical Manual of Mental Disorders (DSM-5*, 2013) proposes changing the name of conversion disorder to functional neurological symptoms.

Demographics

The lifetime prevalence rates of conversion disorder in the general population are estimated to fall between 2.5 and 500 per 100,000 people. Differences among estimates reflect differences in the method of **diagnosis** as well as regional population differences. In terms of clinical populations, conversion disorder is diagnosed in 5–14% of general hospital patients; 1–3% of outpatient referrals to psychiatrists; and 5–25% of psychiatric outpatients. The frequency among clinical populations overall is reported between 20 and 120 per 100,000 patients.

Among adults, women diagnosed with conversion disorder outnumber men by a 2:1 to 10:1 ratio; among children, however, the gender ratio is closer to 1:1. Less-educated people and those of lower socioeconomic status are more likely to develop conversion disorder; race by itself does not appear to be a factor. There is, however, a major difference between the populations of developing and developed countries. In developing countries, the prevalence of conversion disorder may run as high as 31%.

Conversion disorder is a major reason for visits to primary care practitioners. One study of health care utilization estimated that 25–72% of office visits to primary care doctors involved psychological distress that takes the form of somatic (physical) symptoms. Another study estimated that at least 10% of all medical treatments and diagnostic services were ordered for patients with no evidence of organic disease. Conversion disorder carries a high economic price tag. Patients who convert their emotional problems into physical symptoms spend nine times as much for health care as people who do not somatosize; and 82% of adults with conversion disorder stop working because of their symptoms. The annual bill for conversion disorder in the United States comes to $20 billion, not counting absenteeism from work and disability payments.

Description

The *DSM-IV-TR* classifies conversion disorder as one of the **somatoform disorders**, first classified as a group of mental disorders by the *DSM III* in 1980. Somatoform disorders are marked by persistent physical symptoms that cannot be fully explained by a medical condition, **substance abuse**, or other mental disorder, but rather seem to stem from psychological issues or conflicts.

Conversion disorder has a complicated history that helps to explain the number of different names for it. Two eminent neurologists of the nineteenth century, Jean-Martin Charcot in Paris, France, and Josef Breuer in Vienna, Austria, were investigating what was then called hysteria, a disorder primarily affecting women (the term "hysteria" comes from the Greek word for uterus or womb). Women diagnosed with hysteria had frequent emotional outbursts and a variety of neurologic symptoms, including paralysis, fainting spells, convulsions, and temporary loss of sight or hearing. Pierre Janet (one of Charcot's students), and Breuer independently came to the same conclusion about the cause of hysteria—that it resulted from psychological **trauma**. Janet, in fact, coined the term "dissociation" to describe the altered state of consciousness experienced by many patients who were diagnosed with hysteria.

The next stage in the study of conversion disorder was research into the causes of "combat neurosis" in World War I (1914–1918) and World War II (1939–1945). Many of the symptoms observed in "shell-shocked" soldiers were identical to those of "hysterical" women. Two of the techniques still used in the treatment of conversion disorder, hypnosis and narcotherapy, were introduced as therapies for combat veterans. The various terms used by successive editions of the *DSM* and the *ICD* (the European equivalent of *DSM*) for conversion disorder reflect its association with hysteria and dissociation. The first edition of the *DSM* (1952) used the term "conversion reaction." The *DSM-II* (1968) called the disorder "hysterical neurosis (conversion type)," and the *DSM-III* (1980), *DSM-III-R* (1987), and *DSM-IV* (1994) have all used the term "conversion disorder." *ICD-10* refers to it as "dissociative (conversion) disorder."

DSM-IV-TR (2000) specifies six criteria for the diagnosis of conversion disorder. They are:

- The patient has one or more symptoms or deficits affecting the senses or voluntary movement that suggest a neurological or general medical disorder.
- The onset or worsening of the symptoms was preceded by conflicts or stressors in the patient's life.
- The symptom is not faked or produced intentionally.
- The symptom cannot be fully explained as the result of a general medical disorder, substance intake, or a behavior related to the patient's culture.

- The symptom is severe enough to interfere with the patient's schooling, employment, or social relationships, or is serious enough to require a medical evaluation.
- The symptom is not limited to pain or sexual dysfunction, does not occur only in the context of somatization disorder, and is not better accounted for by another mental disorder.

The *DSM-IV-TR* lists four subtypes of conversion disorder: conversion disorder with motor symptom or deficit; with sensory symptom or deficit; with **seizures** or convulsions; and with mixed presentation.

Although conversion disorder is most commonly found in individuals, it sometimes occurs in groups. One such instance occurred in 1997 in a group of three young men and six adolescent women of the Embera, an indigenous tribe in Colombia. The young people believed that they had been put under a spell or curse and developed dissociative symptoms that were not helped by antipsychotic medications or traditional herbal remedies. They were cured when shamans from their ethnic group came to visit them. The episode was attributed to psychological **stress** resulting from rapid cultural change.

Another example of group conversion disorder occurred in Iran in 1992. Ten girls out of a classroom of 26 became unable to walk or move normally following tetanus inoculations. Although the local physicians were able to treat the girls successfully, public health programs to immunize people against tetanus suffered an immediate negative impact. One explanation of group conversion disorder is that an individual who is susceptible to the disorder is typically more affected by suggestion and easier to hypnotize than the average person.

Causes and symptoms

Causes

The immediate cause of conversion disorder is a stressful event or situation that leads the patient to develop bodily symptoms as symbolic expressions of a long-standing psychological conflict or problem.

Two terms that are used in connection with the causes of conversion disorder are primary gain and secondary gain. Primary gain refers to the lessening of the anxiety and communication of the unconscious wish that the patient derives from the symptom(s). Secondary gain refers to the interference with daily tasks, removal from the uncomfortable situation, or increased attention from significant others that the patient obtains as a result of the symptom(s).

Physical, emotional, or **sexual abuse** can be a contributing cause of conversion disorder in both adults and children. In a study of 34 children who developed pseudoseizures, 32% had a history of **depression** or sexual abuse, and 44% had recently experienced a parental divorce, death, or violent quarrel. At least one study, however, has found no consistent association between dissociation and sexual or physical abuse. In the adult population, conversion disorder may be associated with mobbing, a term that originated among European psychiatrists and industrial psychologists to describe psychological abuse in the workplace. One American woman who quit her job because of mobbing was unable to walk for several months. Adult males sometimes develop conversion disorder during military basic training. Conversion disorder may also develop in adults as a long-delayed after effect of childhood abuse. A team of surgeons reported on the case of a patient who went into a psychogenic coma following a throat operation. The surgeons found that she had been repeatedly raped as a child by her father, who stifled her cries by smothering her with a pillow.

Symptoms

In general, symptoms of conversion disorder are not under the patient's conscious control, and are frequently mysterious and frightening to the patient. The symptoms usually have an acute onset, but sometimes worsen gradually.

The most frequent forms of conversion disorder in Western countries include:

- Pseudoparalysis. In pseudoparalysis, the patient loses the use of half of his/her body or of a single limb. The weakness does not follow anatomical patterns and is often inconsistent upon repeat examination.
- Pseudosensory syndromes. Patients with these syndromes often complain of numbness or lack of sensation in various parts of their bodies. The loss of sensation typically follows the patient's notion of their anatomy, rather than known characteristics of the human nervous system.
- Pseudoseizures. These are the most difficult symptoms of conversion disorder to distinguish from their organic equivalents. Between 5% and 35% of patients with pseudoseizures also have epilepsy. Electroencephalograms (EEGs) and the measurement of serum prolactin levels are useful in distinguishing pseudoseizures from epileptic seizures.
- Pseudocoma. Pseudocoma is also difficult to diagnose. Because true coma may indicate a life-threatening

condition, patients must be given standard treatments for coma until the diagnosis can be established.

- Psychogenic movement disorders. These can mimic myoclonus, parkinsonism, dystonia, dyskinesia, and tremor. Doctors sometimes give patients with suspected psychogenic movement disorders a placebo medication to determine whether the movements are psychogenic or the result of an organic disorder.
- Pseudoblindness. Pseudoblindness is one of the most common forms of conversion disorder related to vision. Placing a mirror in front of the patient and tilting it from side to side can often be used to determine pseudoblindness, because humans tend to follow the reflection of their eyes.
- Pseudodiplopia. Pseudodiplopia, or seeing double, can usually be diagnosed by examining the patient's eyes.
- Pseudoptosis. Ptosis, or drooping of the upper eyelid, is a common symptom of myasthenia gravis and a few other disorders. Some people can cause their eyelids to droop voluntarily with practice. The diagnosis can be made on the basis of the eyebrow; in true ptosis, the eyebrows are lifted, whereas in pseudoptosis they are lowered.
- Hysterical aphonia. Aphonia refers to loss of the ability to produce sounds. In hysterical aphonia, the patient's cough and whisper are normal, and examination of the throat reveals normal movement of the vocal cords.

Psychiatrists working in various parts of the Middle East and Asia report that the symptoms of conversion disorder as listed by the *DSM-IV* and the *ICD-10* do not fit well with the symptoms of the disorder most frequently encountered in their patient populations.

Diagnosis

Conversion disorder is one of the few mental disorders that appears to be overdiagnosed, particularly in emergency departments. There are numerous instances of serious neurologic illness that were initially misdiagnosed as conversion disorder. Newer techniques of diagnostic imaging have helped to lower the rate of medical errors. In addition, functional **magnetic resonance imaging** (MRI) has identified specific areas of the **brain** that show differential activation in cases of conversion disorder, and imaging findings may eventually be useful in distinguishing conversion disorder.

Diagnostic issues

Diagnosis of conversion disorder is complicated by its coexistence with physical illness in as many as 60% of patients. Alternatively explained, a diagnosis of conversion disorder does not exclude the possibility of a concurrent organic disease. The examining doctor will usually order a mental health evaluation when conversion disorder is suspected, as well as x rays, other **imaging studies** that may be useful, and appropriate laboratory tests. The doctor will also take a thorough patient history that will include the presence of recent stressors in the patient's life, as well as a history of abuse. Children and adolescents are usually asked about their school experiences, one question they are asked is whether a recent change of school or an experience related to school may have intensified academic pressure.

In addition, there are a number of bedside tests that doctors can use to distinguish between symptoms of conversion disorder and symptoms caused by physical diseases. These may include the drop test, in which a "paralyzed" arm is dropped over the patient's face. In conversion disorder, the arm will not strike the face. Other tests include applying a mildly painful stimulus to a "weak" or "numb" part of the body. The patient's pulse rate will typically rise in cases of conversion disorder, and he or she will usually pull back the limb that is being touched.

Factors suggesting a diagnosis of conversion disorder

The doctor can use a list of factors known to be associated with conversion disorder to assess the likelihood that a specific patient may have the disorder:

- Age. Conversion disorder is rarely seen in children younger than six years or adults over 35 years.
- Sex. The female:male ratio for the disorder ranges between 2:1 and 10:1. It is thought that higher rates of conversion disorder in women may reflect the greater vulnerability of females to abuse.
- Residence. People who live in rural areas are more likely to develop conversion disorder than those who live in cities.
- Level of education. Conversion disorder occurs less often among sophisticated or highly educated people.
- Family history. Children sometimes develop conversion disorder from observing their parents' reactions to stressors. This process is known as social modeling.
- A recent stressful change or event in the patient's life.

An additional feature suggesting conversion disorder is the presence of *la belle indifférence*. The French phrase refers to an attitude of relative unconcern on the patient's part about the symptoms or their implications. La belle indifférence is, however, much more common in adults

KEY TERMS

Aphonia—Inability to speak caused by a functional disturbance of the voice box or vocal cords.

(la) Belle indifférence—A psychiatric symptom sometimes found in patients with conversion disorder, in which the patient shows a surprising lack of concern about the nature or implications of his/her physical symptom(s).

Conversion—In psychiatry, a process in which a repressed feeling, impulse, thought, or memory emerges in the form of a bodily symptom.

Diplopia—A disorder of vision in which a single object appears double. Diplopia is sometimes called double vision.

Dyskinesia—Difficulty in performing voluntary muscular movements.

Dystonia—A neurological disorder characterized by involuntary muscle spasms. The spasms can cause a painful twisting of the body and difficulty walking or moving.

Electroencephalogram (EEG)—A test that measures the electrical activity of the brain by means of electrodes placed on the scalp or in the brain itself.

Factitious disorder—A type of mental disturbance in which patients intentionally act physically or mentally ill without obvious benefits. It is distinguished from malingering by the absence of an obvious motive, and from conversion disorder by intentional production of symptoms.

Hysteria—In nineteenth-century psychiatric use, a neurotic disorder characterized by violent emotional outbursts and disturbances of the sensory and motor (movement-related) functions. The term "hysterical neurosis" is still used by some psychiatrists as a synonym for conversion disorder.

Malingering—Knowingly pretending to be physically or mentally ill to avoid some unpleasant duty or responsibility, or for economic benefit.

Myoclonus—An abrupt spasm or twitching in a muscle or group of muscles.

Narcotherapy—A form of psychotherapy that involves the administration of a drug that makes the patient drowsy.

Primary gain—In psychiatry, the principal psychological reason for the development of a patient's symptoms. In conversion disorder, the primary gain from the symptom is the reduction of anxiety and the exclusion of an inner conflict from conscious awareness.

Pseudoseizure—A fit that resembles an epileptic seizure but is not associated with abnormal electrical discharges in the patient's brain.

Psychogenic—Originating in the mind, or in a mental process or condition. The term "psychogenic" is sometimes used as a synonym for "conversion."

Ptosis—Drooping of the upper eyelid.

Secondary gain—A term that refers to other benefits that a patient obtains from a conversion symptom. For example, a patient's loss of function in an arm might require other family members to do the patient's share of household chores; or they might give the patient more attention and sympathy than he or she usually receives.

Shaman—In certain indigenous tribes or groups, a person who acts as an intermediary between the natural and supernatural worlds. Shamans are regarded as having the power or ability to cure illnesses.

Social modeling—A process of learning behavioral and emotional-response patterns from observing one's parents or other adults. Some researchers think that social modeling plays a part in the development of conversion disorder in children.

Somatoform disorders—A group of psychiatric disorders in the *DSM-IV-TR* classification that are characterized by external physical symptoms or complaints that are related to psychological problems rather than organic illness. Conversion disorder is classified as a somatoform disorder.

Stressor—A stimulus or event that provokes a stress response in an organism. Stressors can be categorized as acute or chronic, and as external or internal to the organism.

with conversion disorder than in children or adolescents. Patients in these younger age groups are much more likely to react to their symptoms with fear or hopelessness. A recent review of the published reports of la belle indifférence found that this feature was not useful in discriminating conversion disorder from physically based disease because of muddy definitions and application of it in diagnosis.

Medical conditions that mimic conversion symptoms

It is important for the doctor to rule out serious medical disorders in patients who appear to have conversion symptoms. At least one study has found an approximately 4% rate of misdiagnosis of an actual physical problem as a conversion disorder. The following disorders must be considered in the differential diagnosis:

- multiple sclerosis (blindness resulting from optic neuritis)
- myasthenia gravis (muscle weakness)
- periodic paralysis (muscle weakness)
- myopathies (muscle weakness)
- polymyositis (muscle weakness)
- Guillain-Barré syndrome (motor and sensory symptoms)

Treatment

Patients diagnosed with conversion disorder frequently benefit from a team approach to treatment and from a combination of treatment modalities. A team approach is particularly beneficial if the patient has a history of abuse, or if he or she is being treated for a concurrent physical condition or illness.

Medications

While there are no drugs for the direct treatment of conversion disorder, medications are sometimes given to patients to treat the anxiety or depression that may be associated with conversion disorder.

Psychotherapy

Psychodynamic psychotherapy is sometimes used with children and adolescents to help them gain insight into their symptoms. Cognitive-behavioral approaches have also been tried, with good results. **Family therapy** is often recommended for younger patients whose symptoms may be related to family dysfunction. **Group therapy** appears to be particularly useful in helping adolescents to learn social skills and coping strategies, and to decrease their dependency on their families.

Inpatient treatment

Hospitalization is sometimes recommended for children with conversion disorders who are not helped by outpatient treatment. Inpatient treatment also allows for a more complete assessment of possible coexisting organic disorders, and for the child to improve his or her level of functioning outside of an abusive or otherwise dysfunctional home environment.

Alternative and complementary therapies

Alternative and complementary therapies that have been shown to be helpful in the treatment of conversion disorder include hypnosis, relaxation techniques, visualization, and **biofeedback**.

Prognosis

The prognosis for recovery from conversion disorder is highly favorable. Patients who have clearly identifiable stressors in their lives, acute onset of symptoms, and a short interval between symptom onset and treatment have the best prognosis. Of patients hospitalized for the disorder, over half recover within two weeks. Between 20% and 25% will **relapse** within a year. The individual symptoms of conversion disorder are usually self-limited and do not lead to lasting disabilities; however, patients with hysterical aphonia, paralysis, or visual disturbances, have better prognoses for full recovery than those with tremor or pseudoseizures.

Prevention

The incidence of conversion disorder in adults is likely to continue to decline with rising levels of formal education and the spread of basic information about human psychology. Prevention of conversion disorder in children and adolescents depends on better strategies for preventing abuse.

Resources

BOOKS

American Psychiatric Association. *Diagnostic and Statistical Manual of Mental Disorders*. 4th ed., text rev. Washington, DC: American Psychiatric Publishing, 2000.

"Conversion Disorder." In *The Merck Manual of Diagnosis and Therapy*, edited by Robert S. Porter and Justin L. Kaplan. Whitehouse Station, NJ: Merck Sharp & Dohme Corp., 2011.

Davenport, Noa, Ruth D. Schwartz, and Gail P. Elliott. *Mobbing: Emotional Abuse in the American Workplace*. Ames, IA: Civil Society Publishing, 1999.

Dorland's Pocket Medical Dictionary. Philadelphia: Elsevier Health Sciences, 2012.

Herman, Judith. *Trauma and Recovery: The Aftermath of Violence—from Domestic Abuse to Political Terror*. 14th printing. New York: Basic Books, 1997.

Pelletier, Kenneth R. "Sound Mind, Sound Body: MindBody Medicine Comes of Age." In *The Best Alternative Medicine*. New York: Touchstone, 2002.

World Health Organization (WHO). *The ICD-10 Classification of Mental and Behavioural Disorders*. Geneva: WHO, 1993.

PERIODICALS

Al-Sharbati, Marwan M., et al. "A Case of Bilateral Ptosis with Unsteady Gait: Suggestibility and Culture in Conversion Disorder." *International Journal of Psychiatry in Medicine* 31, no. 2 (2001): 225–32.

Campo, John V. "Case Study: Negative Reinforcement and Behavioral Management of Conversion Disorder." *Journal of the American Academy of Child and Adolescent Psychiatry* 39, no. 6 (June 2000): 787–90.

Glick, T.H., T.P. Workman, and S. V. Gaufberg. "Suspected Conversion Disorder: Foreseeable Risks and Avoidable Errors." *Academy of Emergency Medicine* 7, no. 11 (November 2000): 1272–77.

Haghighi, S.S., and S. Meyer. "Psychogenic Paraplegia in a Patient with Normal Electrophysiologic Findings." *Spinal Cord* 39, no. 12 (December 2001): 664–67.

Isaac, Mohan, and Prabhat K. Chand. "Dissociative and Conversion Disorders: Defining Boundaries." *Current Opinion in Psychiatry* 19, no. 1 (January 2006): 61–66.

Meyers, Timothy J., Bruce W. Jafek, and Arlen D. Meyers. "Recurrent Psychogenic Coma Following Tracheal Stenosis Repair." *Archives of Otolaryngology—Head & Neck Surgery* 125, no. 11 (November 1999): 1267–69.

Moene, F. C., et al. "Organic Syndromes Diagnosed as Conversion Disorder: Identification and Frequency in a Study of 85 Patients." *Journal of Psychosomatic Research* 49, no. 1 (July 2000): 7–12.

Mori, S., et al. "Psychogenic Hearing Loss with Panic Anxiety Attack After the Onset of Acute Inner Ear Disorder." *ORL Journal of Otorhinolaryngology and Related Specialties* 64, no. 1 (January–February 2002): 41–44.

Pineros, Marion, Diego Rosselli, Claudia Calderon. "An Epidemic of Collective Conversion and Dissociation Disorder in an Indigenous Group of Colombia: Its Relation to Cultural Change." *Social Science & Medicine* 46, no. 11 (January 1998): 1425–28.

Shaibani, Aziz, and Marwan N. Sabbagh. "Pseudoneurologic Syndromes: Recognition and Diagnoses." *American Family Physician* 57, no. 10 (May 15, 1998): 2485–94.

Stone, Jon, et al. "Systematic Review of Misdiagnosis of Conversion Symptom and 'Hysteria'" *British Medical Journal* 331 (2005): 989.

Stone, Jon, Roger Smyth, Alan Carson, Charles Warlow, and Michael Sharpe. "La Belle Indifference in Conversion Symptoms and Hysteria." *British Journal of Psychiatry* 188 (2006): 204–209.

Syed, E.U., et al. "Conversion Disorder: Difficulties in Diagnosis Using DSM-IV/ICD-10." *Journal of the Pakistan Medical Association* 51, no. 4 (April 2001): 143–45.

Wyllie, Elaine, et al. "Psychiatric Features of Children and Adults with Pseudoseizures." *Archives of Pediatrics & Adolescent Medicine* 153 (March 1999): 244–48.

Yasamy, M.T., A. Bahramnezhad, H. Ziaaddini. "Post-Vaccination Mass Psychogenic Illness in an Iranian Rural School." *Eastern Mediterranean Health Journal* 5 (July 1999): 710–16.

ORGANIZATIONS

American Academy of Child and Adolescent Psychiatry, 3615 Wisconsin Ave. NW, Washington, DC, 20016-3007, (202) 966-7300, Fax: (202) 966-2891, http://aacap.org.

National Institute of Mental Health, 6001 Executive Blvd., Room 8184, MSC 9663, Bethesda, MD, 20892-9663, (301) 433-4513; TTY: (301) 443-8431, Fax: (301) 443-4279, (866) 615-6464; TTY: (866) 415-8051, nimhinfo@nih.gov, http://www.nimh.nih.gov.

Rebecca J. Frey, PhD
Emily Jane Willingham, PhD

Co-occurring disorders

Definition

Co-occurring disorders are sets of mental illnesses that appear together in a single individual. They include a **substance abuse** disorder with at least one other Axis I or Axis II mental illness. The five Axes are standard diagnostic categories established by the **American Psychiatric Association** (APA). In co-occurring disorders, an Axis I substance abuse disorder is always present simultaneously with at least one other mental health disorder from Axis I or II. Another name for co-occurring disorders is dual **diagnosis**, although this may include more than two diagnoses. Dual diagnosis, in this case, means "more than one." Yet another name given this condition is co-morbidity, with morbidity meaning "illness."

Demographics

Children of alcoholics and of drug-addicted individuals are more likely to have co-occurring disorders than America's general population. In addition, patients with **depression** are more at risk for substance abuse and alcohol abuse disorders than people having no mental illness. In addition, the U.S. Department of Health and Human Services has found that people who have received public assistance under welfare-reform programs experienced an average of three or four severe mental disorders (SMDs) in addition to substance abuse, without receiving adequate treatment. The affected homeless population suffers similar circumstances, while youth and the aged are also affected by co-occurring disorders.

Among youth, disruptive behavior disorders occur more frequently with than without substance abuse disorders. Older adults with depression or anxiety are at higher risk for substance and alcohol abuse than middle-aged adults. Seniors may be grieving losses of family, friends, and employment. They may drink or misuse drugs to rid themselves of pain and the complications of poverty. Co-occurring disorders complicate the management of any memory problems they may have, slowing metabolism, arthritis, hypertension, diabetes, **Alzheimer's disease** and other dementias, and various additional health problems. Further, because women generally outlive men, co-occurring disorders and related physical problems are more prevalently becoming the maladies of older women. However, they also affect veterans and people with eating disorders.

Description

The term substance abuse includes substance-use disorders on a continuum from experimentation, to regular use, to drug dependence and **addiction**. Substances include prescription drugs, over-the-counter medications, marijuana, **cocaine**, heroin, mescaline (peyote), glues (sniffing), spray-can aerosols (huffing), and other categories. Substance abuse is the usual co-occurring disorder among adults with SMDs such as **bipolar disorder**, other psychoses, and depression.

Causes and symptoms

Depression itself is the most common mental illness coexisting with physical disorders. Further, depression often occurs among patients with substance abuse, whereas substance abuse can coexist with anxiety, **post-traumatic stress disorder** (PTSD), **personality disorders**, and eating disorders. Co-occurring disorders result in serious problems, such as higher rates of illness **relapse** than in cases of only one mental illness; increased numbers of hospitalizations; and higher risks for violence, incarceration, **homelessness**, **suicide**, and exposure to major infections such as HIV and hepatitis.

Substance or alcohol abuse may co-occur with eating disorders, because such patients self-medicate feelings of shame, anxiety, extreme hunger, and self-hate commonly experienced in eating disorders. This further complicates their recovery. Finally, many military veterans experience anxiety, depression, and/or post-traumatic **stress** disorder (PTSD) at the same time they have a history of substance abuse or alcoholism. Unfortunately, assessment, treatment, and prevention services for veterans have been inadequate.

According to statistics compiled by the U.S. **Substance Abuse and Mental Health Services Administration** (SAMHSA), 10 million Americans or more will develop at least one mental illness together with a substance abuse disorder in any one-year period. The APA has learned that 7% of the American population, or 21 million people, have a full-blown **psychosis** at any given time. Co-occurring disorders affect a full 50% of all individuals who have severe mental disorders such as psychoses. Kessler et al. recently found in a controlled study that 55% of the general population may experience one mental illness, 22% from two, and 23% from three co-occurring disorders. This translates to 69 million Americans having three co-occurring disorders.

SAMSHA has found that the prevalence of co-occurring disorders has increased during the last three decades. Named in the early 1980s, dual diagnoses considered most likely to occur among either youth and young adults with **schizophrenia** or people with bipolar disorder, all of whom showed a history of drug abuse and/or alcohol abuse. The medical opinion was that a person's entrance into the drug culture was the cause of another mental illness. Currently, it is thought that one or more mental disorders occur first, followed by drugs or alcohol used in self-medicating behavior used to cover unwanted mental symptoms.

Diagnosis

Careful assessment by a licensed professional and therapeutic team is necessary to plan effective treatment

KEY TERMS

Axis—One of five diagnostic categories of the American Psychiatric Association that are used for mental health diagnoses. Axis I describes the clinical syndrome or major diagnosis; Axis II lists developmental disorders or intellectual disability and personality disorders; Axis III lists physical disorders; Axis IV includes the severity of psychosocial stressors for the individual; and Axis V describes an individual's highest level of functioning currently and in the past 12 months.

Intervention—A confrontation of a substance abuser by a group of interested people who propose immediate medical treatment. An intervention is also a method of treatment used in therapy.

Substance abuse—Illicit, inaccurate, or recreational use of either prescription or illegal drugs. Alcohol can also be abused as a substance but has its own category, alcohol abuse.

Welfare-to-Work—Several American public reforms of the late 1990s and early 2000s, designed to move individuals from public assistance to paying jobs.

strategies. This begins with a detailed medical history and clinical interviews of the patient and family members to establish related health and behavioral patterns and substance or alcohol abuse history. Because **denial** is an inherent aspect of the problem, a battery of psychiatric tests can uncover mental illnesses. These tests include the **Minnesota Multiphasic Personality Inventory** (MMPI), Rorschach and other inkblot tests, other personality and projective tests, and the **Wechsler intelligence scales**. A number of substance abuse checklists can help determine substance- and alcohol-related disorders.

Treatment

Despite evidence of the high prevalence of dual diagnoses, the U.S. mental health and substance abuse systems have run separate programs, causing confusion. Failure to combine services for coordinated treatment means prolonged suffering and expense for patients, families, insurance companies, the U.S. health care system, and public assistance and disability programs. In light of welfare reform and health care improvements, the 1990s provided many programs for these patients, often more holistic and supported by federal funding for targeting ex-offenders and welfare-to-work populations.

The key factors in an integrated treatment program are (1) treatment must be approached in stages; (2) assertive outreach leads to higher client-retention rates; (3) motivational interventions accompanied by education, counseling, and social support; (4) viewing recovery as a long-term, community-based process; (5) effecting a comprehensive strategy; and (6) cultural sensitivity and cultural competence.

For many dual diagnosis patients, the criminal justice system is their last stop. Many jailed youth fail to be diagnosed. Their behavior mandated their incarceration, and mental health assessment was not considered. The juvenile and adult justice systems have become the treatment providers, but treatment is not always an option. Two-thirds (67%) of incarcerated youth with substance abuse disorders have one or more additional mental illnesses. The coexistence of a **conduct disorder** and/or attention deficit–type disorders with substance abuse results in a serious disability. However, a dual-diagnosis patient in the criminal justice system may never receive psychiatric evaluation or treatment.

One specific problem with treatments for dual diagnoses is that most mental health treatments are designed, tested, and validated through controlled studies of individuals who have only one mental diagnosis. These treatments might not be as effective when there are two or more mental disorders. However, individually prescribed treatment plans have been successful in using these specific components:

- Planned therapeutic interventions: The client is engaged and persuaded to participate in rehabilitation. In planned group and individual therapies, the patients are given coping skills and support toward managing their illnesses.
- Psychological counseling: This includes both cognitive (thinking) and behavioral skills to change negative thinking patterns and unwanted behaviors. It can include role-playing and homework.
- Social counseling: This includes support groups, group therapy, and family therapy facilitated by professionals. It includes diversity and sensitivity training and cultural competency instruction.
- Health-related education: This helps clients commit to managing their illnesses. It requires an acceptance of, and commitment to, a long-term supervised recovery process.
- Aggressive follow-up: A treatment team provides intensive, frequent patient follow-up with meetings in the patient's workplace and home as well as in the case manager's office.
- Comprehensive treatment: This holistic treatment targets education, health, employment, personal behavior patterns, stress management, peer networks, family, housing, financial skills, spiritual life, and other aspects.

Additional considerations

Alcoholics Anonymous, Al-Anon, Narcotics Anonymous, and similar 12-step programs frequently supplement treatment for substance abuse and co-occurring disorders. However, their success cannot be quantitatively validated, because they are anonymous. Further, the direct confrontation of an engagement **intervention** and that of ongoing 12-step programs can be too threatening for mental health patients. The primary care physician or therapist must decide the most appropriate strategies for each patient.

The use of psychiatric drugs to alter mood or behavior is understandably controversial in substance abuse recovery, so treatments such as **support groups** for co-occurring disorders can be more effective than drug therapies.

Prognosis

The prognosis for co-occurring disorders depends on the prognosis of the separate disorders occurring in a specific patient, along with the combined effects of those

QUESTIONS TO ASK YOUR DOCTOR

- What risks are associated with co-occurring disorders?
- What symptoms are associated with co-occurring disorders?
- Does having co-occurring disorders put me at risk for other health conditions?
- Can you recommend any treatments or support groups?

disorders. Dual diagnoses usually present a worse overall health outlook than a single mental illness.

New studies and additional research are ongoing to learn more about co-occurring disorders. **Clinical trials** surrounding the use of various pharmacological and non-pharmacological treatment therapies are ongoing. Individuals who wish to participate can find a list of clinical trials currently enrolling volunteers at http://clinicaltrials.gov. There is no cost to the patient to participate in a clinical trial.

Prevention

Early preventative education, screening, assessment, diagnosis, and treatment are vital to the health of a person experiencing or at risk for co-occurring disorders. Appropriate health-promotion education is useful and necessary in alerting the general populations to the risks and signs of co-occurring disorders and in helping themselves maintain good mental hygiene.

Resources

BOOKS

American Psychiatric Association. *Diagnostic and Statistical Manual of Mental Disorders,* 4th ed., Text rev. Washington, DC: American Psychiatric Association, 2000.

American Psychological Association. *Publication Manual of the American Psychological Association,* 6th ed. Washington, DC: American Psychological Association, 2009.

Erickson, Carlton K, Ph.D. *Addiction Essentials: The Go-To Guide for Clinicians and Patients.* New York: W. W. Norton & Company, 2011.

PERIODICALS

Kessler, Ronald C., et al. "Prevalence, Severity, and Comorbidity of 12-month DSM-IV Disorders in the National Comorbidity Survey Replication." *Archive of General Psychiatry* 62 (2005): 617–627.

Roszak, Dennis J. "Mental Illness Starts Early in Life, but Treatment Often Begins Decades Later." *Hospitals & Health Networks* 79, no. 7 (2005): 130.

Saxena, Shekhar, and Jose Manoel Bertolote. "Co-occurring Depression & Physical Disorders: Need for an Adequate Response from the Health Care System." *Indian Journal of Medical Research.* 122, no. 4 (2005): 273–276.

Watkins, Katherine E., et al. "Prevalence and Characteristics of Clients with Co-occurring Disorders in Outpatient Substance Abuse Treatment." *American Journal of Drug and Alcohol Abuse* 30, no. 4 (2004): 749–764.

WEBSITES

ClinicalTrials.gov. http://www.clinicaltrials.gov/ct/action/GetStudy.

ORGANIZATIONS

American Psychiatric Association, 1000 Wilson Boulevard, Suite 1825, Arlington, VA, 22209, (703) 907-7300, apa@psych.org, http://www.psych.org.

Dual Recovery Anonymous, PO Box 8107, Prairie Village, KS, 66208, (913) 991-2703, http://www.draonline.org/index.html.

Mental Health America, 2000 N. Beauregard Street, 6th Floor, Alexandria, VA, 22311, (703) 684-7722, (800) 969-6642, Fax: (703) 684-5968, http://www1.nmha.org.

National Alliance on Mental Illness (NAMI), Colonial Place Three, 2107 Wilson Blvd., Suite 300, Arlington, VA, 22201, (703) 524-7600, (800) 950-NAMI (6264) Fax: (703) 524-9094, http://www.nami.org.

National Institute of Mental Health (NIMH), 6001 Executive Boulevard, Room 8184, MSC 9663, Bethesda, MD, 20892, (301) 443-4513, (866) 615-6464, Fax: (301) 443-4279, nimhinfo@nih.gov, http://www.nimh.nih.gov/index.shtml.

Patty Inglish, MS
Laura Jean Cataldo, RN, EdD

Couples therapy

Definition

Couples therapy is psychological treatment for couples dealing with relationship problems and issues.

Purpose

The purpose of couples therapy is to improve a relationship and overcome problems and distress within the relationship. Couples therapy can address a wide range of problems between partners, including incompatibility, poor communication, lack of intimacy, and sexual difficulties. It may also address psychological disorders affecting one or both partners, such as **depression**, anxiety, **schizophrenia**, alcoholism, or domestic violence. Couples therapy identifies the causes of dissatisfaction and distress in a relationship and devises and implements a treatment plan for improving or alleviating symptoms and establishing a healthier level of functioning within the relationship.

Description

Couples therapy works to resolve issues affecting a couple's relationship. Couples therapy is available from psychologists, psychiatrists, and psychotherapists, many of whom specialize in treating intimate relationships. There are also proprietary commercial couples therapy programs and organized groups, as well as do-it-yourself couples therapy programs available on the Internet or as smartphone applications.

Types of couples therapy include:

- traditional behavioral
- integrative behavioral
- cognitive-behavioral
- emotionally or emotion focused
- psychoanalytic or psychodynamic
- object relations
- ego analytical
- structural strategic
- systemic
- Gottman method
- educational and preventative

Behavioral therapy models are based on rewarding and reinforcing desired behaviors. Traditional behavioral couples therapy (TBCT or BCT) assumes a link between relationship distress and aversive behaviors or lack of positive **reinforcement** and attempts to decrease negative or punishing interactions and increase positive exchanges. Behavioral therapy models focus on environmental influences, the influences of individual and couple histories, and relationship behaviors. A cornerstone of BCT is helping partners identify, address, and attempt to change problematic patterns of interaction. BCT also emphasizes listening to one's partner, expressing needs without accusation, asking for behavior changes, and developing problem-solving skills.

Integrative behavioral couples therapy (IBCT) was developed in the 1990s by psychologists Andrew Christensen and Neil Jacobson, based on their observations that some couples are unable or unwilling to change or make changes that are short-lived or emotionally unsatisfying for one partner. IBCT aims to increase emotional acceptance and understanding by each partner and to change those patterns that are bothersome to both partners, while building on BCT models of improving behavior, communication, and problem solving. IBCT tends to be more flexible and individualized for specific problems than BCT. In particular, IBCT focuses on repetitious interactions and problems that are causing relationship distress, such as the "demand-withdraw" pattern of interaction identified by Christensen. In this pattern, one partner (more often the woman) identifies a problem and nags the other about it, while the other partner (more often the man) withdraws or avoids the issue. This pattern of behavior has become a major focus of couples therapy, since it correlates directly with relationship dissatisfaction. IBCT also examines larger relationship patterns and how past issues, including those stemming from childhood, affect those patterns.

KEY TERMS

Behavioral couples therapy (BCT)—Traditional behavioral couples therapy (TBCT); relationship therapy based on behavioral psychology models.

Cognition—Conscious intellectual activity, including thinking, imagining, reasoning, remembering, and learning.

Cognitive-behavioral therapy (CBT)—A type of psychotherapy in which people learn to recognize and change negative and self-defeating patterns of thinking and behavior.

Emotionally focused therapy for couples (EFT-C)—A widely used, evidence-based system of therapy, developed in the 1980s by Leslie Greenberg and Susan Johnson, that emphasizes the individual emotions of each partner.

Integrative behavioral couples therapy (IBCT)—A widely used and more flexible and individualized form of behavioral couples therapy, developed by Andrew Christensen and Neil Jacobson in the 1990s.

Introjection—The unconscious incorporation of ideas or attitudes into one's personality or the turning toward oneself of the love or hostility felt for another.

Psychoanalytic—Understanding human motivations, emotions, and mental processes according to theories and concepts originally developed by Sigmund Freud.

Psychodynamic—Mental, emotional, or motivational forces or processes that affect mental state and behavior, especially unconscious processes that develop in early childhood.

Cognitive-behavioral couples therapy, also based on the BCT model, assumes that emotional and behavioral dysfunction in relationships is related to inappropriate information processing, such as "jumping to conclusions" and negative cognitive appraisals. Therefore, it focuses on increasing awareness of perceptions, assumptions, attributions, and/or standards in relationship interactions and on uncovering negative thought forms that drive negative behaviors.

Emotionally or emotion focused therapy for couples (EFT-C) was developed by Leslie Greenberg and Susan Johnson in the 1980s. It has been widely adopted by family therapists as well as couples therapists. EFT-C views emotion and cognition (thinking) as interdependent, with emotion as a primary driver of interpersonal expression. In the EFT-C model, distress stems from the unexpressed and unacknowledged emotional needs of each partner, leading to negative interactions and dysfunction. EFT-C helps couples acknowledge, assess, and express emotions related to their distress. It emphasizes each partner's anger, sadness, shame, and fear, as well as positive emotions, including love and compassion, rather than focusing on interactional processes. EFT-C emphasizes responsiveness to the emotional needs of each partner when discussing and resolving conflicts and recognizing and appreciating interdependence and the need for attachment between partners. Greenberg further argues that conflict results from breakdowns in both the ability to soothe one's self and to soothe one's partner and that the abilities to self-soothe and to regulate one's emotional responses are essential for disrupting negative relationship patterns and beginning to experience the relationship in new ways. Partners who can regulate their own distress are less likely to attack or withdraw.

Psychoanalytic or psychodynamic couples therapy is based on the model that early childhood experiences determine, in part, relationship behaviors. Thus, it attempts to reveal unresolved childhood conflicts with parental figures and connect these with relationship interactions. At the core of this model are the processes of introjection and childhood separation and individuation from maternal interaction. One of the goals of psychoanalytic couples therapy is to separate present feelings from those of one's childhood.

Object relations couples therapy creates a neutral, impartial environment for understanding the distortions and internalized conflicts that each partner brings to the relationship in the form of dysfunctional behaviors. This model proposes that an unconscious desire for a "mothering figure" is the central motivation for selection and attachment to a mate and that this induces further repression of poorly developed aspects of personality or "lost parts."

Ego analytic couples therapy proposes that dysfunction originates in an inability to recognize intolerance, invalidation of sensitivities, and relationship problems themselves. It further proposes that relationship problems fall into two major categories—dysfunctions brought to the relationship from early childhood experiences and **trauma** and feelings of disentitlement on the part of one partner, often due to shame or guilt. Ego analytic therapy uses methods that foster the communication of important feelings.

Structural strategic couples therapy views relationships as progressing through developmental stages. Problems reflect difficulty coping with life changes, either external or personal, and resisting change in the relationship despite dissatisfaction, preferring instead to attempt to maintain status quo baseline functioning. This therapy challenges negative perceptions, encourages positive perceptions through role playing, and presents alternative possibilities and behaviors.

Systemic couples therapy examines the rules and roles adopted by the couple, especially those that have become dysfunctional. The goal is to understand how those patterns shape the relationship and how they can be changed.

The Gottman method, developed by psychologists John and Julie Gottman, is based on the observation that happy couples behave like good friends and handle conflicts in positive ways. The goal of Gottman therapy is to learn more positive means of expression when confronting the inevitable conflicts in a relationship.

Educational and preventative couples therapy attempts to establish good communication early in a relationship. There are several evidence-based programs that focus on open communication, listening skills, and relationship training. The Prevention and Relationship Enhancement Program (PREP) program has been in use since 1989 and is practiced by mental health professionals, lay people, and clergy in 28 countries. The Couples Communication Program involves an "awareness wheel" and a "listening wheel" to help couples trace their issues and learn to listen to one another. The Practical Application of Intimate Relationship Skills (PAIRS) program explores couples' past emotional issues and how these shape their current interactions, with a focus on listening and tackling problems.

Benefits

Couples therapy can help relieve symptomatic behaviors that are causing problems and distress. Therapy can lead to healthier and more appropriate interactions and behaviors. Couples may increase their awareness and develop new relationship skills, particularly when both partners have a reasonable and sincere willingness to confront problems in a positive manner and change patterns of behavior.

Precautions

Couples should seek out a mental health professional who specializes in couples therapy and with whom both partners feel comfortable and able to develop a trusting relationship. A sincere desire to improve relationship patterns, change behaviors, and work with the process is essential for successful couples therapy. Both partners must be honest and cooperative, forthcoming with all necessary information, and willing to keep all appointments.

Preparation

In preparing for couples therapy, both partners must understand that cooperation, honesty, and emotional openness are essential, and both partners should have the desire to modify or change dysfunctional behaviors. Partners should also understand that positive results cannot be guaranteed. During the initial session, the therapist typically performs an extensive assessment that includes in-depth information gathering about the primary problem or problems. The assessment also includes information about occupations, schooling, employment, childhood development, parental history, **substance abuse**, and religion, and the medical, legal, and psychological histories of both partners. Further psychological tests and measurements may be indicated for either or both partners. Following the assessment, the therapist typically suggests a course of treatment.

Aftercare

Couples therapy usually lasts several months or longer, until the relationship is functioning at a level that is satisfactory to both partners and adequate skills have been developed for dealing with conflict. The couple should be alert for a return of old behavior patterns. Relapse-prevention techniques can be employed, and couples are advised to return to therapy if symptoms of **relapse** appear. Sometimes follow-up visits or long-term therapy are required.

Risks

Couples therapy rarely makes a relationship worse. The major risk is that the relationship fails to improve or that dysfunctional patterns return. These circumstances tend to develop when there is a breakdown in the new skills developed during therapy or if one of the partners is resistant to long-term change or cannot overcome self-defeating behaviors.

QUESTIONS TO ASK YOUR DOCTOR

- What type of couples therapy do you recommend?
- What are the advantages of this type of couples therapy?
- What is typically involved in couples therapy?
- How long do you anticipate our couples therapy will last?
- What outcomes have you experienced with couples therapy?

Research and general acceptance

There has been a great deal of research on different types of couples therapy. A 2010 study conducted by Christensen and colleagues, which compared TBCT and IBCT with chronically and severely distressed couples, found that both types yielded a high rate of satisfaction immediately after treatment. Two years after treatment, about 70% of the IBCT-treated couples reported relationship satisfaction, a very high success rate compared with other types of couples therapy. After five years, about one-half of the couples had maintained significantly improved relationships, about one-fourth of the relationships were as distressed as before treatment, and about one-fourth of the couples had separated or divorced. The study did not include follow-up sessions that would normally occur during a crisis or relapse. The U.S. Department of Veterans Affairs has chosen IBCT as its evidence-based **psychotherapy** for couples **intervention**. Christensen intends to make IBCT strategies available to couples as a free online program.

Resources

BOOKS

Abraham, Laurie. *The Husbands and Wives Club: A Year in the Life of a Couples Therapy Group.* New York: Simon & Schuster, 2010.

Baucom, Donald H., Kurt Hahlweg, and Mariann Grawe-Gerber, eds. *Enhancing Couples: The Shape of Couple Therapy to Come.* Cambridge, MA: Hogrefe, 2010.

Greenberg, Leslie S., and Rhonda N. Goldman. *Emotion-Focused Couples Therapy: The Dynamics of Emotion, Love, and Power.* Washington, DC: American Psychological Association, 2008.

Hoistad, Jan. *Romance Rehab: 10 Steps to Rescue Your Relationship.* New York: Sterling, 2010.

Knudson-Martin, Carmen, and Anne Rankin Mahoney. *Couples, Gender, and Power: Creating Change in Intimate Relationships.* New York: Springer, 2009.

O'Leary, K. Daniel, and Erica M. Woodin. *Psychological and Physical Aggression in Couples: Causes and Interventions.* Washington, DC: American Psychological Association, 2009.

Rastogi, Mudita, and Volker K. Thomas. *Multicultural Couple Therapy.* Los Angeles: Sage, 2009.

Schulz, Marc S., ed. *Strengthening Couple Relationships for Optimal Child Development: Lessons from Research and Intervention.* Washington, DC: American Psychological Association, 2010.

PERIODICALS

Christensen, Andrew, et al. "Marital Status and Satisfaction Five Years Following a Randomized Clinical Trial Comparing Traditional Versus Integrative Behavioral Couple Therapy." *Journal of Consulting and Clinical Psychology* 78, no. 2 (April 2010): 225–35.

DeAngelis, Tori. "The Couples Doctor." *Monitor on Psychology* 42, no. 1 (January 2011): 46. http://www.apa.org/monitor/2011/01/christensen.aspx (accessed July 25, 2011).

Garfield, Robert. "Male Emotional Intimacy: How Therapeutic Men's Groups Can Enhance Couples Therapy." *Family Process* 49, no. 1 (March 2010): 109–22.

Greenberg, Leslie, Serine Warwar, and Wanda Malcolm. "Emotion-Focused Couples Therapy and the Facilitation of Forgiveness." *Journal of Marital and Family Therapy* 36, no. 1 (January 2010): 28–42.

Johnson, Susan, and Dino Zuccarini. "Integrating Sex and Attachment in Emotionally Focused Couple Therapy." *Journal of Marital and Family Therapy* 36, no. 4 (October 2010): 431–45.

Luscombe, Belinda. "Honey, Can You Hear Me Now?" *Time* 176, no. 21 (November 22, 2010). http://www.time.com/time/magazine/article/0,9171,2030914,00.html (accessed July 25, 2011).

Tambling, Rachel B., and Lee N. Johnson. "Client Expectations About Couple Therapy." *American Journal of Family Therapy* 38, no. 4 (July 2010): 322–33.

ORGANIZATIONS

American Association for Marriage and Family Therapy, 112 S Alfred St., Alexandria, VA, 22314, (703) 838-9808, Fax: (703) 838-9805, http://www.aamft.org.

American Psychological Association, 750 1st St. NE, Washington, DC, 20002-4242, (202) 336-5500, (800) 374-2721, http://www.apa.org.

Interpersonal Communication Programs, 30772 Southview Dr., no. 200, Evergreen, CO, 80439, (303) 674-2051, (800) 328-5099, Fax: (303) 674-4283, icp@comskills.com, http://www.couplecommunication.com.

PAIRS Foundation, 1675 Market St., Ste. 207, Weston, FL, 33326, (877) PAIRS-4U, info@pairs.com, http://www.pairs.com.

Laith Farid Gulli, MD
Kathleen Berrisford, MSCSW, CAC
Emily Jane Willingham, PhD
Margaret Alic, PhD

Covert sensitization

Definition

Covert sensitization is a form of behavior therapy in which an undesirable behavior is paired with an unpleasant image in order to eliminate that behavior.

Purpose

As with other **behavior modification** therapies, covert sensitization is a treatment grounded in learning theory—one of the basic tenets being that all behavior is learned and that undesirable behaviors can be unlearned under the right circumstances. Covert sensitization is one of a group of behavior therapy procedures classified as covert conditioning, in which an aversive stimulus in the form of a nausea- or anxiety-producing image is paired with an undesirable behavior to change that behavior. It is best understood as a mixture of both the classical and the operant conditioning categories of learning. Based on research begun in the 1960s, psychologists Joseph Cautela and Albert Kearney published the 1986 classic *The Covert Conditioning Handbook*, which remains a definitive treatise on the subject.

The goal of covert sensitization is to directly eliminate the undesirable behavior itself, unlike insight-oriented psychotherapies that focus on uncovering unconscious motives in order to produce change. The behaviors targeted for modification are often referred to as "maladaptive approach behaviors," which includes behaviors such as alcohol abuse, drug abuse, and smoking; pathological gambling; overeating; sexual deviations, and sexually based nuisance behaviors such as obscene phone calling. The type of behavior to be changed and the characteristics of the aversive imagery to be used influence the treatment, which is usually administered in an outpatient setting either by itself or as a component of a multimodal program. Self-administered homework assignments are almost always part of the treatment package. Some therapists incorporate covert sensitization with hypnosis in the belief that outcome is enhanced.

Description

The patient being treated with covert sensitization can expect a fairly standard set of procedures. The therapist begins by assessing the problem behavior, and will most likely measure frequency, severity, and the environment in which it occurs. Depending upon the type of behavior to be changed, some therapists may also take treatment measures before, during, and after physiological arousal (such as heart rate) to better

KEY TERMS

Covert—Concealed, hidden, or disguised.

Operant—Conditioning in which the desired response is reinforced by an introduced stimulus.

Sensitization—To make sensitive or susceptible.

assess treatment impact. Although the therapeutic relationship is not the focus of treatment, the behavior therapist believes that good rapport will facilitate a more successful outcome and strives to establish positive but realistic expectations. Also, a positive relationship is necessary to establish patient confidence in the rationale for exposure to the discomfort of unpleasant images.

The therapist will explain the treatment rationale and protocol. Patient understanding and consent are important, since, by intention, he or she will be asked to experience images that arouse unpleasant and uncomfortable physical and psychological associations. The therapist and patient collaborate in creating a list of aversive images uniquely meaningful to the patient that will be applied in the treatment. Standard aversive images include vomiting, snakes, spiders, vermin, and embarrassing social consequences. An aversive image is then selected appropriate to the target problem behavior. Usually, the image with the most powerful aversive response is chosen. The patient is instructed on how to relax—an important precursor to generating intense imagery. The patient is then asked to relax and imagine approaching the situation where the undesirable behavior occurs (for example, purchasing donuts prior to overeating).

If the patient has a difficult time imagining the scene, the image may be presented verbally by the therapist. As the patient imagines getting closer to the situation (donut store), he or she is asked to clearly imagine an unpleasant consequence (such as vomiting) just before indulging in the undesirable behavior (purchasing donuts and overeating). The scene must be imagined with sufficient vividness that a sense of physiological discomfort or high anxiety is actually experienced. Then the patient imagines leaving the situation and experiencing considerable relief. The patient learns to associate unpleasant sensations (nausea and vomiting) with the undesirable behavior, leading to decreased desire and avoidance of the situation in the future. An alternative behavior incompatible with the problem behavior may be recommended (eat fruit when hungry for a donut).

The patient is given the behavioral homework assignment to practice self-administering the treatment. The patient is told to alternate the aversive scenes with scenes of self-controlled restraint in which he or she rejects the undesirable behavior before indulging in it, thus avoiding the aversive stimulus. The procedure is practiced several times with the therapist in the office, and the patient practices the procedure 10 to 20 times during each home session between office sessions. The patient is then asked to practice in the actual situation, imagining the aversive consequences and avoiding the situation. With much variation, and depending upon the nature of the behavior targeted for change, the patient may see the therapist anywhere from 5 to 20 sessions over a period of a few weeks to several months. The treatment goal is to eliminate the undesirable behavior altogether.

Aftercare

Patients completing covert sensitization treatment are likely to be asked by the therapist to return periodically over the following six to twelve months or longer, for booster sessions to prevent **relapse**.

Risks

Covert sensitization is comparatively risk-free. This is in contrast to the medical and ethical concerns raised by some other aversive procedures such as **aversion therapy**, in which potent chemical and pharmacological stimulants may be used as aversants.

Results

Depending upon the objectives established at the beginning of treatment, patients successfully completing covert sensitization might expect to stop the undesirable behavior. If they practice **relapse prevention** techniques, they can expect to maintain the improvement. Although this treatment may appear to be relatively simple, it has been found to be quite effective for treating many circumscribed problem behaviors.

Resources

BOOKS

Cautela, Joseph, and Albert Kearney. *The Covert Conditioning Handbook*. New York: Brooks/Cole Publishing Co., 1993.

Kaplan, Harold, and Benjamin Sadock, eds. *Synopsis of Psychiatry*. 10th ed. Baltimore: Lippincott Williams & Wilkins, 2007.

Plaud, Joseph, and Georg Eifert, eds. *From Behavior Theory to Behavior Therapy*. Boston: Allyn and Bacon, 1998.

ORGANIZATIONS

Association for Behavioral and Cognitive Therapies, 305 Seventh Ave., 16th Floor, New York, NY, 10001-6008, (212) 647-1890, Fax: (212) 647-1865, http://www.abct.org.

John Garrison, PhD

Creative therapies *see* **Art therapy; Dance therapy; Journal therapy; Music therapy**

Creutzfeldt-Jakob disease *see* **Dementia**

KEY TERMS

Bipolar disorder—A mood disorder characterized by abnormally high energy levels and moodiness, usually without depression.

Depression—A psychiatric disorder involving feelings of hopelessness and symptoms of fatigue, sleeplessness, suicidal tendencies, and poor concentration.

Schizophrenia—A mental disorder involving degraded thinking and emotions.

Crisis housing

Definition

Crisis housing (or sometimes also called crisis residential services) consists of supervised short-term residential alternatives to **hospitalization** for adults with serious mental illnesses or children with serious emotional or behavioral disturbances. Treatment for such crisis services consists of unlocked, non-hospital facilities in a round-the-clock setting.

Purpose

The purpose of crisis housing is to avoid hospitalization and to stabilize the patient. During this time, a determination is made as to the next steps to take for the recovery of the patient. The course of most serious mental illness (such as **schizophrenia**, **bipolar disorder**, severe **depression**, and **borderline personality disorder**) is cyclical, typically characterized by periods of relative well-being, interrupted by periods of deterioration or **relapse**. When relapse occurs, the individual generally exhibits florid symptoms that require immediate psychiatric attention and treatment. More often than not, relapse is caused by the individual's failure to comply with a prescribed medication regimen (not taking medication regularly, not taking the amount or dose prescribed, or not taking it all). Relapse can also be triggered during periods of great **stress** or can even occur spontaneously, without any marked changes in lifestyle or medication regimen. When these crises recur, the goal of treatment is to stabilize the individual as soon as possible, since research suggests that relapsing patients are also more likely to attempt **suicide**.

Description

Over the past 40 years, crisis housing programs have evolved as short-term, less costly, and less restrictive residential alternatives to hospitalization. Intended to divert individuals from emergency rooms, jails, and hospitals into community-based treatment settings, they offer intensive crisis support to individuals and their families. Services include **diagnosis**, assessment, and treatment (including medication stabilization); rehabilitation; and links to community-based services. These programs are intended to stabilize the individual as rapidly as possible—usually between 8 and 60 days—so they can return to their home or residence in the community.

Some of the earliest crisis housing programs include Soteria House and La Posada, which began in northern California in the 1970s, and the START (short-term acute residential treatment) program, which began in San Diego, California, in 1980. While programs vary from location to location, most offer acute services 24 hours a day, seven days a week, in a small noninstitutional residential setting. Adequate structure and supervision is provided by an interdisciplinary team of professionals and other trained workers.

Beginning the day they arrive, residents help develop their own plans for recovery and continued care in the community. Patients receive state-of-the art psychopharmacological treatment and other cognitive-behavioral interventions. Residents are encouraged to play an active role in the operation of the household, including meal preparation. The home-like environment is helpful in lessening the **stigma** and sense of failure that often occurs when someone needs to return to an inpatient psychiatric unit.

Similarly, in the case of seriously emotionally disturbed children and adolescents, the goal of crisis housing is to avert visits to the emergency room or hospitalization by stabilizing the individual in as normal a setting as possible. Compared to these services for adults, there is typically greater emphasis placed on involving families and schools in planning for community-based care after discharge.

Evaluations of several of these programs suggest that they may provide high-quality treatment and care at a lower cost than hospitals. In 2008, a study published by the *American Journal of Community Psychology* found that people with serious psychiatric conditions got better faster and paid less money when at a facility using a "consumer-managed residential program" (CRP), as opposed to staying at a traditional psychiatric hospital. Crisis housing is not currently available in all communities, although it is becoming more widely available.

Preparation

A wide variety of crisis housing programs exist in the United States. Some patients go into crisis housing after being directly released from psychiatric emergency rooms at hospitals or other such medical facilities. Other patients use crisis housing after being briefly admitted into a hospital, in what is considered a "step down" program that slowly treats such patients with a number of steps designed to return their lives to normalcy. Still others admit themselves directly, or do so with the help of a trusted medical professional, while bypassing such medical facilities all together. Physicians and other medical professionals, such as psychologists, help to monitor these patients. In addition, in some of the more difficult cases, treatment is over a longer period of time (around 30 to 60 days), while in other simpler cases the period is much shorter (less than 12 days).

Aftercare

Once the short-term crisis housing care has been completed, the patient has become more stable and is now ready for further help based on their stay at such crisis housing facilities.

Risks

There are always risks when interacting with people with serious mental illnesses or chronic emotional or behavioral disturbances. However, the crisis housing setting has been shown to be an effective way to treat such people in the short-term.

Results

Medical studies have shown over the past forty years that crisis housing produces outcomes that are equal to or better than inpatient services (such as psychiatric hospitals). In addition, these studies have found that the costs of such crisis housing programs are also less expensive than with inpatient facilities; in fact, such research has shown that costs can be 25%–75% less. Recent publications involving such comparisons show that even the most difficult cases can be successfully treated at crisis housing facilities.

QUESTIONS TO ASK YOUR DOCTOR

- How long will I need to stay at crisis housing?
- Could you explain further what is meant by crisis housing?
- Will my health insurance pay for such services?
- Will I be able to leave crisis housing if I wish?
- Will you be able to see me while I'm in crisis housing?

See also Bipolar disorder; Borderline personality disorder; Crisis intervention; Schizophrenia

Resources

BOOKS

Beck, Aaron T., and Brad A. Alford. *Depression: Causes and Treatments.* Philadelphia: University of Pennsylvania Press, 2009.

Clark, David A., and Aaron T. Beck. *Cognitive Therapy of Anxiety Disorders: Science and Practice.* New York: Guilford Press, 2010.

Clark, David A., Aaron T. Beck, and Brad A. Alford. *Scientific Foundations of Cognitive Theory and Therapy of Depression.* New York: John Wiley & Sons, 2003.

Johnson, Sandra J. *Assertive Community Treatment: Evidence-based Practice or Managed Recovery.* New Brunswick, NJ: Transaction, 2011.

Nezu, Arthur, George F. Ronan, and Elizabeth A. Meadows, editors. *Practitioner's Guide to Empirically Based Measures of Depression.* New York: Springer Publishing Company, 2006.

Tolman, Anton O. *Depression In Adults: The Latest Assessment And Treatment Strategies.* Kansas City, MO: Compact Clinicals, 2005.

Torrey, E. Fuller. *Surviving Schizophrenia: A Manual for Families, Consumers and Providers,* 5th ed. New York: Collins, 2006.

VandenBos, Gary R., editor. *APA Dictionary of Psychology.* Washington, DC: American Psychological Association, 2007.

PERIODICALS

Hawthorne, W.B., et al. "A Randomized Trial of Short-Term Acute Residential Treatment for Veterans." *Psychiatric Services* 56 (2005): 1379–86.

OTHERS

"Crisis Residential Facilities Healthier Than Psychiatric Hospitals?—Study Finds More Mental Health Improvements At Consumer-Managed Program." Medical News Today. August 19, 2008. http://www.medicalnewstoday.com/articles/118619.php (accessed November 23, 2010).

Crisis Residential Programs. California Institute for Mental Health. http://www.cimh.org/downloads/handouts/November%2016%202005%20Crisis%20Residential%20Services1.doc (accessed November 24, 2010).

ORGANIZATIONS

American Psychiatric Association, 1000 Wilson Blvd., Ste. 1825, Arlington, VA, 22209-3901, (703) 907-7300, apa@psych.org, http://www.psych.org.

American Psychological Association, 750 lst St., NE, Washington, DC, 20002, (202) 336-5500, (800) 374-2721, http://www.apa.org.

Depression and Bipolar Support Alliance, 730 North Franklin St., Ste. 501, Chicago, IL, 60654-7225, (800) 826-3632, Fax: (312) 642-7243, http://www.dbsalliance.org.

National Alliance on Mental Illness, 3803 North Fairfax Dr., Ste. 100, Arlington, VA, 22203, (703) 524-7600, (800) 950-6264, Fax: (703) 524-9094, http://www.nami.org.

National Institute of Mental Health, 6001 Executive Blvd., Rm 8184, MSC 9663, Bethesda, MD, 20892-9663, (301) 443-4513, (866) 615-6464, Fax: (301) 443-4279, nimhinfo@nih.gov, http://www.nimh.nih.gov.

Irene S. Levine, PhD
Emily Jane Willingham, PhD

Crisis intervention

Definition

Crisis **intervention** refers to methods used to offer immediate, short-term help to individuals who experience an event that produces emotional, mental, physical, and behavioral distress or problems. A crisis can be any situation in which an individual perceives a sudden loss of ability to use effective problem-solving and coping skills. Any number of events or circumstances can be considered crises, including life-threatening situations such as natural disasters (e.g., earthquakes, tornadoes, hurricanes), sexual assault or other criminal victimization, medical illness, mental illness, thoughts of **suicide** or homicide, or loss of or drastic changes in relationships (e.g., death of a loved one or divorce).

Purpose

Crisis intervention has several purposes. It aims to reduce the intensity of an individual's emotional, mental, physical, and behavioral reactions to a crisis. Another purpose is to help individuals return to their level of functioning before the crisis. Functioning may be improved above and beyond this by developing new coping skills and eliminating ineffective ways of coping, such as withdrawal, isolation, and **substance abuse**. In this way, individuals are better equipped to cope with future difficulties. Through talking about what happened, and the feelings about what happened, while developing ways to cope and solve problems, crisis intervention aims to assist individuals in recovering from crises and to prevent serious long-term problems from developing. Research documents positive outcomes for crisis intervention, such as decreased distress and improved problem solving.

Description

Individuals are more open to receiving help during crises. A person may have experienced the crisis within the last 24 hours or within a few weeks before seeking help. Crisis intervention is conducted in a supportive manner. The length of time for crisis intervention may range from one session to several weeks, with the average being four weeks. Crisis intervention is not sufficient for individuals with long-standing problems. Session length may range from 20 minutes to two or more hours. Crisis intervention is appropriate for children, adolescents, and younger and older adults. It can take place in a range of settings, such as hospital emergency rooms, crisis centers, counseling centers, mental health clinics, schools, correctional facilities, and other social service agencies. Local and national telephone hotlines are available to address crises related to suicide, domestic violence, sexual assault, and other concerns. They are usually available 24 hours a day, seven days a week.

Responses to crisis

A typical crisis intervention progresses through several phases. It begins with an assessment of what happened during the crisis and the individual's responses to it. There are certain common patterns of response to most crises. An individual's reaction to a crisis can include emotional reactions (e.g., fear, anger, guilt, **grief**), mental reactions (e.g., difficulty concentrating, confusion, nightmares), physical reactions (e.g., headaches, dizziness, **fatigue**, stomach problems), and behavioral reactions (e.g., sleep and appetite problems, isolation, restlessness). Assessment of the individual's potential for suicide and/or homicide is also conducted. Information about the individual's strengths, coping skills, and social support networks is obtained as well.

Education

There is an educational component to crisis intervention. It is critical for individuals to be informed about various responses to crises and informed that they are having normal reactions to an abnormal situation.

Individuals will also be told that the responses are temporary. Although there is not a specific time that people can expect to recover from crises, individuals can help recovery by engaging in coping and problem-solving skills.

Coping and problem solving

Other elements of crisis intervention include helping individuals understand the crisis and their response to it as well as becoming aware of and expressing feelings, such as anger and guilt. Exploring coping strategies is a major focus of crisis intervention. Strategies that the individuals previously used, but that have not been used to deal with the current crisis, may be enhanced or bolstered. Also, new coping skills may be developed. Coping skills may include relaxation techniques and **exercise** to reduce body tension and **stress** as well as putting thoughts and feelings on paper through journal writing instead of keeping them inside. In addition, options for social support or spending time with people who provide a feeling of comfort and caring are addressed. Another central focus of crisis intervention is problem solving. This process involves thoroughly understanding the problem and the desired changes, considering alternatives for solving the problem, discussing the pros and cons of alternative solutions, selecting a solution and developing a plan to try it out, and evaluating the outcome. Cognitive therapy, which is based on the notion that thoughts can influence feelings and behavior, can be used in crisis intervention.

In the final phase of crisis intervention, the professional will review changes the individual made in order to point out that it is possible to cope with difficult life events. Continued use of the effective coping strategies that reduced distress will be encouraged. Assistance will be provided in making realistic plans for the future, particularly in terms of dealing with potential future crises. Signs that the individual's condition is worsening or "red flags" will be discussed. Information will be provided about resources for additional help should the need arise. A telephone follow-up may be arranged for some agreed-upon time.

Preparation

There are many ways to prepare and intervene in a crisis, with results that can vary widely, depending on the severity of the crisis and other such related factors. Some of these ways to deal with the crisis include (1) suicide intervention, (2) critical incident stress debriefing and management, and (3) medical crisis counseling.

Suicide intervention

PURPOSE. Suicidal behavior is the most frequent mental health emergency. The goal of crisis intervention in that case is to keep the individual alive so that a stable state can be reached, and alternatives to suicide can be explored. In other words, the goal is to help the individual reduce distress and survive the crisis.

ASSESSMENT. Suicide intervention begins with an assessment of how likely it is that the individual will attempt suicide in the immediate future. This assessment has various components. The professional will evaluate whether or not the individual has a plan for how the act would be attempted, how deadly the method is (e.g., shooting, overdosing), whether means are available (e.g., access to weapons), and whether the plan is detailed and specific versus vague. The professional will also assess the individual's emotions, such as **depression**, hopelessness, hostility, and anxiety. Past suicide attempts as well as completed suicides among family and friends will be assessed. The nature of any current crisis event or circumstance will be evaluated, such as loss of physical abilities because of illness or accident, unemployment, and loss of an important relationship.

TREATMENT PLAN. A written safekeeping contract may be obtained. This is a statement indicating that individuals will not commit suicide and that they agree to various actions, such as notifying their clinician, family, friends, or emergency personnel, should thoughts of committing suicide again arise. The contract may also include coping strategies that the individuals agree to engage in to reduce distress. If the individuals state that they are not able to do this, then it may be determined that medical assistance is required and voluntary, or involuntary psychiatric **hospitalization** may be implemented. Most individuals with thoughts of suicide do not require hospitalization and respond well to outpatient treatment. Educating family and friends and seeking their support are important aspects of suicide intervention. Individual therapy, **family therapy**, substance abuse treatment, and/or psychiatric medication may be recommended.

KEY TERMS

Coping—In psychology, a term that refers to a person's patterns of response to stress.

Critical incident—Also known as a "crisis event." An event that is stressful enough to overwhelm the coping skills of a person or group.

Stress—A physical and psychological response that results from being exposed to a demand or pressure.

Stressor—A stimulus or event that provokes a stress response in an organism. Stressors can be categorized as acute or chronic, and as external or internal to the organism.

Critical incident stress debriefing and management

DEFINITION. Critical incident stress debriefing (CISD) uses a structured, small-group format to discuss a distressing crisis event. It is the best-known and most widely used debriefing model. Critical incident **stress management** (CISM) refers to a system of interventions that includes CISD as well as other interventions, such as one-on-one crisis intervention, **support groups** for family and significant others, stress-management education programs, and follow-up programs. Originally designed to be used with high-risk professional groups, such as emergency services, public safety, disaster response, and military personnel, it can be used with any population, including children. A trained personnel team conducts this intervention. The team usually includes professional support personnel, such as mental health professionals and clergy. In some settings, peer support personnel, such as emergency services workers, will be part of the debriefing team. It is recommended that a debriefing occur after the first 24 hours following a crisis event, but before 72 hours have passed since the incident.

PURPOSE. This process aims to prevent excessive emotional, mental, physical, and behavioral reactions and **post-traumatic stress disorder** (PTSD) from developing in response to a crisis. Its goal is to help individuals recover as quickly as possible from the stress associated with a crisis.

PHASES OF CISD. There are seven phases to a formal CISD:

1. Introductory remarks: The team sets the tone and rules for the discussion, and encourages participant cooperation.
2. Fact phase: Participants describe what happened during the incident.
3. Thought phase: Participants state the first or main thoughts while going through the incident.
4. Reaction phase: Participants discuss the elements of the situation that were worst.
5. Symptom phase: Participants describe the symptoms of distress experienced during or after the incident.
6. Teaching phase: The team provides information and suggestions that can be used to reduce the impact of stress.
7. Re-entry phase: The team answers participants' questions and makes summary comments.

PRECAUTIONS. Some concern has been expressed in the research literature about the effectiveness of CISD. It has been thought that as long as the provider(s) of CISD have been properly trained, the process should be helpful to individuals in distress. If untrained personnel conduct CISD, then it may result in harm to the participants. CISD is neither **psychotherapy** nor a substitute for it. It is not designed to solve all problems presented during the meeting. In some cases, a referral for follow-up assessment and/or treatment is recommended to individuals after a debriefing.

QUESTIONS TO ASK YOUR DOCTOR

- What is crisis intervention?
- How will it help me? Why do I need it?
- How long will I need crisis intervention?
- Will my health insurance pay for such services?
- Will I be able to stop crisis intervention at any time if I wish?
- How will I know when I am no longer in need of crisis intervention?

Medical crisis counseling

Medical crisis counseling is a brief intervention used to address psychological (anxiety, fear, and depression) and social (family conflicts) problems related to chronic illness in the health care setting. It uses coping techniques and builds social support to help patients manage the stress of being newly diagnosed with a chronic illness or suffering a worsening of a medical condition. It aims to help patients understand their reactions as normal responses to a stressful circumstance and to help them function better. Preliminary studies of medical crisis counseling indicate that one to four sessions may be needed. Research is also promising in terms of its effectiveness at decreasing patients' levels of distress and improving their functioning.

Aftercare

After the short-term crisis has subsided, and crisis intervention is completed, the patient has become more stable and is now ready for further professional assistance based on help provided during this critical time in their lives.

Risks

There are always risks when interacting with people with serious mental illnesses or chronic emotional or behavioral disturbances. However, crisis intervention has been shown to be an effective way to help such people in the short term.

Results

As with any type of interaction with individuals going through an emotional, mental, physical, or behavioral crisis, risks can and do occur. However, with the proper professional help, along with use of established and proven procedures, success is likely achieved during crisis intervention.

Resources

BOOKS

Echterling, Lennis G., Jack Presbury, and J. Edson McKee. *Crisis Intervention: Promoting Resilience and Resolution in Troubled Times.* Upper Saddle River, NJ: Prentice Hall, 2004.

Hendricks, James E., Jerome B. McKean, and Cindy Gillespie Hendricks. *Crisis Intervention: Contemporary Issues for On-Site Interveners.* 3rd ed. Springfield, IL: Charles C. Thomas Publisher, 2003.

Jackson-Cherry, Lisa R, and Bradley T. Erford. *Crisis Intervention and Prevention.* Upper Saddle River, NJ: Pearson, 2010.

James, Richard K. *Crisis Intervention Strategies.* Belmont, CA: Thomson Brooks/Cole, 2008.

Roberts, Albert R. *Crisis Intervention Handbook: Assessment, Treatment, and Research.* New York: Oxford University Press, 2005.

Stone, Howard W. *Crisis Counseling.* Minneapolis: Fortress Press, 2009.

Thyer, Bruce A. "'Tis a Consummation Devoutly to Be Wished." *Foundations of Evidence-Based Social Work Practice,* Albert R. Roberts, and Kenneth R. Yeager, eds. New York: Oxford University Press, 2006.

Wiger, Donald E., and Kathy J. Harowski. *Essentials of Crisis Counseling and Intervention.* New York: John Wiley & Sons, 2003.

PERIODICALS

Allen, Andrea, and others. "An Empirically Informed Intervention for Children Following Exposure to Severe Hurricanes." *The Behavior Therapist* 29, no. 6 (Sept. 2006): 118–24.

Basoglu, Metin, Ebru Salcioglu, and Maria Livanou. "A Randomized Controlled Study of Single-Session Behavioural Treatment of Earthquake-Related Post-Traumatic Stress Disorder Using an Earthquake Simulator." *Psychological Medicine* 37, no. 2 (Feb. 2007): 203–13.

Bruffaerts, Ronny, Marc Sabbe, and Koen Demyttenaere. "Who Visits the Psychiatric Emergency Room for the First Time?" *Social Psychiatry and Psychiatric Epidemiology* 41, no. 7 (July 2006): 580–86.

Everly, George S., Jr., and others. "Introduction to and Overview of Group Psychological First Aid." *Brief Treatment and Crisis Intervention* 6, no. 2 (May 2006): 130–36.

Gard, Betsy A., and Josef I. Ruzek. "Community Mental Health Response to Crisis." *Journal of Clinical Psychology* 62, no. 8 (Aug. 2006): 1029–41.

Roberts, Albert R. "Applying Roberts' Triple ABCD Model in the Aftermath of Crisis-Inducing and Trauma-Inducing Community Disasters." *International Journal of Emergency Mental Health* 8, no. 3 (Summer 2006): 175–82.

Roberts, Albert R. "Juvenile Offender Suicide: Prevalence, Risk Factors, Assessment, and Crisis Intervention Protocols." *International Journal of Emergency Mental Health* 8, no. 4 (Fall 2006): 255–66.

Singer, Jonathan B. "Making Stone Soup: Evidence-Based Practice for a Suicidal Youth With Comorbid Attention Deficit/Hyperactivity Disorder and Major Depressive Disorder." *Brief Treatment and Crisis Intervention* 6, no. 3 (Aug. 2006): 234–47.

Stapleton, Amy B., et al. "Effects of Medical Crisis Intervention on Anxiety, Depression, and Posttraumatic Stress Symptoms: A Meta-Analysis." *Psychiatric Quarterly* 77, no. 3 (Sept. 2006): 231–38.

Vingilis, Evelyn, et al. "Process and Outcome Evaluation of an Emergency Department Intervention for Persons with Mental Health Concerns Using a Population Health Approach." *Administration and Policy in Mental Health and Mental Health Services Research* 34, no. 2 (Mar. 2007): 160–71.

WEBSITES

American Psychiatric Association. "Disaster Psychiatry Tools." http://www.psych.org/Resources/DisasterPsychiatry.aspx (accessed November 14, 2011).

Mentor Research Institute. "What Is Crisis Counseling?" CrisisCounseling.org. October 10, 2006. http://www.crisiscounseling.org/Handouts/Whatiscrisiscounseling.htm (accessed November 24, 2011).

ORGANIZATIONS

Disaster Psychiatry Outreach, PO Box 1228, One Gustave L. Levy Place, New York, NY, 10029-6574, (646) 233-1215, info@disasterpsych.org, http://www.disasterpsych.org.

Substance Abuse and Mental Health Services Administration, 1 Choke Cherry Rd., Rockville, MD, 20857, (877) 726-4727, http://www.samhsa.gov.

Joneis Thomas, PhD
Ruth A. Wienclaw, PhD

Cyclothymic disorder

Definition

Cyclothymic disorder, also known as cyclothymia, is a relatively mild form of bipolar II disorder characterized by mood swings that may appear to be almost within the normal range of emotions. These mood swings range from mild **depression** (dysthymia) to mania of low intensity (**hypomania**).

Demographics

Patients with cyclothymic disorder are estimated to constitute 3%–10% of all psychiatric outpatients. They may be particularly well represented among those with complaints about marital and interpersonal difficulties. In the general population, the lifetime chance of developing cyclothymic disorder is about 1%. The actual percentage of the general population with cyclothymia is probably somewhat higher, however, as many patients may not be aware that they have a treatable disease or seek treatment if they do.

Cyclothymic disorder frequently coexists with **diagnosis** of cyclothymic disorder. The female-to-male ratio in cyclothymic disorder is approximately 3:2. It is estimated that 50%–75% of all patients develop the disorder between the ages of 15 and 25.

Description

Cyclothymic disorder, a symptomatically mild form of bipolar II disorder, involves mood swings ranging from mild depression to mild mania. It is possible for cyclothymia to go undiagnosed, and for individuals with the disorder to be unaware that they have a treatable disease. Individuals with cyclothymia may experience episodes of low-level depression, known as dysthymia; or periods of intense energy, creativity, and/or irritability, known as hypomania; or they may alternate between both mood states. Like other bipolar disorders, cyclothymia is a chronic illness characterized by mood swings that can occur as often as every day and last for several days, weeks, or months. Individuals with this disorder are never free of symptoms of either hypomania or mild depression for more than two months at a time.

Persons with cyclothymic disorder differ in the relative proportion of depressive versus hypomanic episodes that they experience. Some individuals have more frequent depressive episodes, whereas others are more likely to feel hypomanic. Most individuals who seek help for the disorder alternate between feelings of mild depression and intense irritability. Those who feel energized and creative when they are hypomanic and find their emotionally low periods tolerable may never seek treatment.

Causes and symptoms

Causes

Controversy exists over whether cyclothymic disorder is truly a mood disorder in either biological or psychological terms, or whether it belongs in the class of disorders known as **personality disorders**. Despite this controversy, most of the evidence from biological and genetic research supports the placement of cyclothymia within the mood disorder category.

Genetic data provide strong support that cyclothymia is indeed a mood disorder. About 30% of all patients with cyclothymia have family histories of bipolar I disorder, which involves full-blown manic episodes alternating with periods of relative emotional stability. Full-blown depressive episodes are frequently, but not always, part of the picture in bipolar I disorder. Reviews of the family histories of bipolar I patients show a tendency toward illnesses that alternate across generations: bipolar I in one generation, followed by cyclothymia in the next, followed again by bipolar I in the third generation. The general prevalence of cyclothymia in families with bipolar I diagnoses is much higher than in families with other mental disorders or in the general population. It has been reported that about one-third of patients with cyclothymic disorder subsequently develop a major mood disorder.

Most psychodynamic theorists believe that the psychosocial origins of cyclothymia lie in early traumas and unmet needs dating back to the earliest stages of childhood development. Hypomania has been described as a deficiency of self-criticism and an absence of inhibitions. The patient is believed to use **denial** to avoid external problems and internal feelings of depression. Hypomania is also believed to be frequently triggered by profound interpersonal loss. The false feeling of euphoria (giddy or intense happiness) that arises in such instances serves as a protection against painful feelings of sadness, and even possibly anger against the lost loved one.

Symptoms

The symptoms of cyclothymic disorder are identical to those of bipolar I disorder except that they are usually less severe. It is possible, however, for the symptoms of cyclothymia to be as intense as those of bipolar I, but of shorter duration. About one-half of all patients with cyclothymic disorder have depression as their major symptom. These persons are most likely to seek help for their symptoms, especially during their depressed episodes. Other patients with cyclothymic disorder experience primarily hypomanic symptoms. They are less likely to seek help than those who suffer primarily from depression. Almost all patients with cyclothymic disorder have periods of mixed symptoms (both depression and hypomania together) during which time they are highly irritable.

Cyclothymic disorder usually causes disruption in all areas of the person's life. Most individuals with this disorder are unable to succeed in their professional or personal lives as a result of their symptoms. However, a few who primarily display hypomanic episodes are high achievers who work long hours and require little sleep. A person's ability to manage the symptoms of the disorder depends upon a number of personal, social, and cultural factors.

The lives of most people diagnosed with cyclothymic disorder are difficult. The cycles of the disorder tend to be much shorter than in bipolar I. In cyclothymic disorder, mood changes are irregular and abrupt, and can occur within hours. While there are occasional periods of normal mood, the unpredictability of the patient's feelings and behavior creates great **stress** not only for the patient but for those who must live or work with him/her. Patients often feel that their moods are out of control. During mixed periods, when they are highly irritable, they may become involved in unprovoked arguments with family, friends, and coworkers, causing stress to all around them.

It is common for cyclothymic disorder patients to abuse alcohol and/or other drugs as a means of self-medicating. It is estimated that about 5%–10% of all patients with cyclothymic disorder also have substance dependence.

Diagnosis

Since the symptoms tend to be mild, a diagnosis of cyclothymic disorder is usually not made until a person with the disorder is sufficiently disturbed by the symptoms or their consequences to seek help. While there currently are no laboratory tests or **imaging studies** that can detect the disorder, the patient will usually undergo a general physical examination to rule out general medical conditions that are often associated with depressed mood. The patient will also be given a **psychological assessment** to evaluate his/her symptoms, mental state, behaviors, and other relevant data. If the patient's history or other aspects of his or her behavior during the assessment suggest the diagnosis of cyclothymic disorder, friends or family members of the patient may be interviewed to gather additional data.

The manual used by mental health professionals to diagnose mental illnesses is called the ***Diagnostic and Statistical Manual of Mental Disorders***, also known as the *DSM*. The *DSM* specifies six criteria that must be met for a diagnosis of cyclothymic disorder. They are:

- Numerous episodes of hypomania and depression that are not severe enough to be considered major depression. These episodes must have occurred for at least two years in adults or one year in children and adolescents.
- During this period, the individual has not been free from either hypomania or mild depression for more than two months at a time.
- Neither major depression nor mania has been present during the first two years of the disorder. (After the two years, manic or depressive episodes may surface.)
- The individual does not have another disorder such as schizophrenia, schizoaffective disorder, or delusional disorder.
- The symptoms are not due to the direct effects of substance use (such as a drug of abuse or a prescribed medication) or to a medical condition.
- The symptoms cause significant impairment in the patient's social, occupational, family, or other important areas of life functioning.

The *DSM-5* (2013) proposed criteria has added specifiers to account for cyclothymic disorder with mixed features (formerly mixed episodes, or symptoms of mania and major depression concurrently), rapid cycling, anxiety, **suicide** risk, seasonal pattern, and postpartum onset.

Treatment

Traditional

Psychotherapy with individuals diagnosed with cyclothymic disorder is best directed toward increasing the patients' awareness of their condition and helping them develop effective coping strategies for mood swings. Often, considerable work is needed to improve the patient's relationships with family members and workplace colleagues because of damage done to these relationships during hypomanic episodes. Because cyclothymic disorder is a lifelong condition, psychotherapy is also a long-term commitment. Working with families of cyclothymic patients, whether individually or in **family therapy** sessions, can help them adjust more effectively to the patients' mood swings as well. Other forms of therapy include **cognitive-behavioral therapy**, which focuses on identifying triggers and changing behaviors, and **group therapy**, where patients with cyclothymic disorder can relate their experiences.

Drugs

Medication is an important component of treatment for cyclothymic disorder. A class of drugs known as antimanic medications, or mood stabilizers, is usually the first line of treatment for these patients. Lithium (Eskalith, Lithobid) is considered a first-line treatment for hypomanic episodes; other drugs include **carbamazepine** (Tegretol) and sodium valproate (Depakene). **Valproic acid** (Depakene), **divalproex sodium** (Depakote), and **lamotrigine** (Lamictal), all anticonvulsant or antiseizure medications, may be given to help prevent mood swings. Antidepressant medications are generally not recommended for treating cyclothymic disorder and

KEY TERMS

Bipolar I disorder—A major mood disorder characterized by full-blown manic episodes, often interspersed with episodes of major depression.

Bipolar II disorder—Disorder with major depressive episodes and mild manic episodes known as hypomania.

Borderline personality disorder—A severe and usually life-long mental disorder characterized by violent mood swings and severe difficulties in sustaining interpersonal relationships.

Cyclothymia—An alternate name for cyclothymic disorder.

Denial—A psychological defense mechanism that reduces anxiety by excluding recognition of an addiction or similar problem from the conscious mind.

Dysthymia—Depression of low intensity.

Hypomania—A milder form of mania that is characteristic of bipolar II disorder.

Psychodynamic theorists—Therapists who believe that the origins of mental problems lie in a person's internal conflicts and complexes.

Psychosocial—A term that refers to the emotional and social aspects of psychological disorders.

should be used with caution, as the use of **antidepressants** may induce hypomanic or full-blown manic episodes. An estimated 40%–50% of all patients with cyclothymic disorder treated with antidepressants experience such episodes.

Quetiapine (Seroquel), a member of a class of drugs known as atypical antipsychotics, was approved by the U.S. Food and Drug Administration (FDA) in 2008 to treat the depressive and manic episodes of **bipolar disorder** and may have some application for treating cyclothymic disorder.

Prognosis

While some patients later diagnosed with cyclothymic disorder were considered sensitive, hyperactive, or moody as children, the onset of cyclothymic disorder usually occurs gradually during the patient's late teens or early twenties. Often school performance becomes a problem along with difficulty establishing peer relationships. Approximately one-third of all patients with cyclothymic disorder develop a major mood disorder during their lifetime, usually bipolar II disorder.

Prevention

Cyclothymic disorder appears to have a strong genetic component. It is far more common among the first-degree biological relatives of persons with bipolar I disorder than among the general population. At this time, there are no known effective preventive measures that can reduce the risk of developing cyclothymic disorder. Genetic counseling, which assists a couple in understanding their risk of producing a child with the disorder, may be of some help.

Resources

BOOKS

American Psychiatric Association. *Diagnostic and Statistical Manual of Mental Disorders.* 4th ed., text rev. Washington, DC: American Psychiatric Publishing, 2000.

Drevets, Wayne C., and Richard D. Todd. "Depression, Mania, and Related Disorders." In *Adult Psychiatry,* edited by Eugene H. Rubin and Charles F. Zorumski. 2nd ed. Malden, MA: Blackwell Publishing, 2005.

PERIODICALS

Andlin-Sobocki, Patrik, and Hans-Ulrich Wittchen. "Cost of Affective Disorders in Europe." *European Journal of Neurology* 12, Supplement (June 2005): 34–38.

Bisol, Luísa W., and Diogo R. Lara. "Low-dose Quetiapine for Patients with Dysregulation of Hyperthymic and Cyclothymic Temperaments." *Journal of Psychopharmacology* 24, no. 3 (March 2010): 421–24. http://dx.doi.org/10.1177/0269881108097715 (accessed September 1, 2011).

ORGANIZATIONS

American Psychiatric Association, 1000 Wilson Blvd., Ste. 1825, Arlington, VA, 22209-3901, (703) 907-7300, apa@psych.org, http://www.psych.org.

Mental Health Foundation, PO Box 322, Albany, NY, 12201. info@mentalhealthfoundation.net, http://www.mentalhealthfoundation.net.

Barbara S. Sternberg, PhD
Ruth A. Wienclaw, PhD

Cylert *see* **Pemoline**

Cymbalta *see* **Duloxetine**

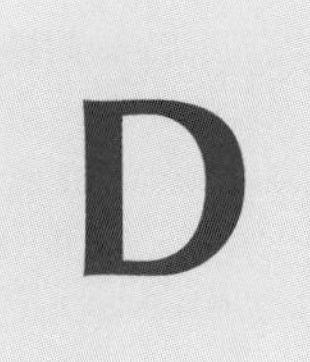

Dalmane *see* **Flurazepam**

Dance therapy

Definition

Dance therapy is a type of **psychotherapy** that uses movement to further the social, cognitive, emotional, and physical development of the individual. Dance therapists work with people who have many kinds of emotional problems, intellectual deficits, and life-threatening illnesses. They are employed in psychiatric hospitals, daycare centers, mental health centers, prisons, special schools, and private practice. They work with people of all ages in both group and individual therapy. Some dance therapists also engage in research.

Dance therapists try to help people develop communication skills, a positive self-image, and emotional stability.

Origins

Dance therapy began as a profession in the 1940s with the work of Marian Chace (1896–1970). A modern dancer, Chace began teaching dance after ending her career with the Denishawn Dance Company in 1930. In her classes, she noticed that some of her students were more interested in the emotions they expressed while dancing (loneliness, **shyness**, fear) than the mechanics of the moves. She encouraged them by emphasizing freedom of movement more than technique.

In time, doctors in the community started sending her patients. They included antisocial children, people with movement problems, and those with psychiatric illnesses. Eventually, Chace became part of the staff of St. Elizabeth's Hospital in Washington, DC. She was the first dance therapist employed in a formal position by the federal government. Chace worked with the emotionally troubled patients at St. Elizabeth's and tried to get them to reach out to others through dance. Some of them had **schizophrenia**, and others were former servicemen suffering from **post-traumatic stress disorder**. Success for these patients meant being able to participate with their class in moving to rhythmic music. Chace is quoted as having said, "This rhythmic action in unison with others results in a feeling of well-being, relaxation, and good fellowship."

Marian Chace eventually studied at the Washington School of Psychiatry and began making treatment decisions about her patients along with other members of the St. Elizabeth's medical team. Her work attracted many followers and the first dance therapy interns began learning and teaching dance therapy at St. Elizabeth's in the 1950s.

Other dancers, such as Trudi Schoop and Mary Whitehouse, began using dance therapy in the 1940s to help people feel more comfortable with themselves and their bodies. Whitehouse later became a Jungian analyst and an influential member of the dance therapy community. She developed a process called "movement in-depth," an extension of her understanding of dance, movement, and depth psychology. She helped found the contemporary movement practice called authentic movement. In this type of movement, founded on the principles of Jungian analysis, patients dance out their feelings about an internal image, often one that can help them understand their past or their current struggles. Whitehead's student, Janet Alder furthered Whitehead's work in authentic movement by establishing the Mary Starks Whitehouse Institute in 1981.

In 1966, dance therapy was formally recognized when the American Dance Therapy Association (ADTA) was formed.

Description

There are more than 1,200 dance therapists in the United Sates and in many foreign countries. Like other mental health professionals, they use a wide range of techniques to help their patients. Some of the major schools

A patient and a nurse dance during a tango therapy session at a neuropsychiatric hospital in Argentina. *(© Daniel Garcia/AFP/Getty Images)*

of thought in dance therapy are the Freudian approach, Jungian technique, and object relations orientation. Many therapists, however, do not adhere to just one school but use techniques from various types of dance therapy.

The authentic movement technique is derived from the Jungian method of analysis, in which people work with recurring images in their thoughts or dreams to derive meaning from their life. Instead of asking the patient to dance out certain emotions, the therapist instructs the patient to move when he or she feels the inner impulse. The moves are directed by the patient, and the therapist is a noncritical witness to the movement. The moves are supposed to emerge from the patient's subconscious. Similarly, in Freudian technique, dance therapists work with patients to uncover feelings hidden deep in the subconscious by expressing those feelings through dance.

In object relations technique, the therapist often helps the patient examine personal problems by considering the primary initial relationship with the patient's parents. Emotions are expressed in a physical way. For instance, a patient might work out his fears of abandonment by repeatedly coming close to and dancing at a distance from the therapist.

Dance therapists sometimes use other types of therapy along with dance, such as visual art or drama. Therapists also discuss what happens during a dancing session by spending time in **talk therapy**. Dance therapists use visualizations during sessions, too. For example, the therapist might instruct patients to imagine they are on a beautiful, peaceful beach as they dance.

In one frequently used technique, the therapist mirrors the movements of the patient as he or she expresses important emotions. This is especially powerful in one-on-one therapy. It is thought that this device provides a sense of safety and validates the patient's emotions.

The underlying premise of dance therapy is that when people dance, they are expressing highly significant emotions. A fist thrust out in anger into the air or a head bent in shame has deep significance to a dance therapist. Through dance therapy, the theory is, patients are able to more easily express painful, frightening emotions and can move past them. After experiencing dance therapy, they can talk about their feelings more freely and remove barriers they have erected between themselves and other people. The hope is that eventually they can go on to live psychologically healthy lives.

Benefits

Dance therapy can be helpful to a wide range of patients—from psychiatric patients to those with cancer to lonely elderly people. Dance therapy is often an easy way for individuals to express emotions, even when their experience is so traumatic they cannot talk about it. It is frequently used with rape victims and survivors of other forms of **sexual abuse** and incest. It can also help people with physical deficits improve their self-esteem and learn balance and coordination.

Dance therapists also work with people who have chronic health problems and life-threatening diseases to help them deal with pain, fear of death, and changes in their body. Many people with such illnesses find dance therapy classes to be a way to relax, get away from their pain and emotional difficulties for a while, and express feelings about taboo subjects (such as impending death).

Dance therapy is suitable for people who are not accomplished dancers and may even be good for those who are clumsy on the dance floor. The emphasis in dance therapy is on free movement, not restrictive steps, and expressing one's true emotions. Children who cannot master difficult dances or cannot sit still for traditional psychotherapy often benefit from free-flowing dance therapy. Even older people who cannot move well or are confined to wheelchairs can participate in dance therapy. All they need to do is move in some way to the rhythm of the music.

Dance therapy can be useful in a one-on-one situation, in which the therapist works with only one patient to provide a safe place to express emotions. Classes can help provide emotional support, enhanced communication skills, and appropriate physical boundaries (a skill that is vital for sexual abuse victims).

Preparations

People who want to use dance therapy should find a qualified therapist. The ADTA provides lists of qualified therapists. Individuals who try dance therapy benefit especially if they have an open mind and a willingness to participate.

KEY TERMS

Authentic movement—A type of movement that is influenced heavily by Jungian analysis and works by analyzing the internal images of the patient. Patients are also urged to dance only when they feel the impulse to move.

Freudian analysis—A psychological treatment based on the theories developed by Sigmund Freud, in which the therapist seeks to help the patient resolve conflicts and traumas buried in the subconscious.

Jungian analysis—A psychological treatment based on the theories of Carl Jung, in which the patient strives to understand the internal, often mythic images in thoughts and dreams.

Psychotherapy—A psychological treatment that seeks to resolve traumas and emotional conflicts, often by discussing them and emotionally reliving difficult past events.

Test anxiety—A name for the stress and intensity of emotional upset that students experience before they take exams.

Precautions

Qualified dance therapists should have completed a graduate program in dance therapy approved by the ADTA and should be registered with the ADTA. They should be able to dance, and they should have extensive training in psychology.

Side effects

There are no known side effects from dance therapy.

Research & general acceptance

Dance therapy was once dismissed as an ineffective, feel good treatment, but it is now more respected. Many research studies have proven that dance therapy can be an effective tool to help people overcome psychological problems.

In one study, older people with cognitive deficits showed that dance therapy could significantly increase their functional abilities. Patients improved their balance, rhythmic discrimination, mood, and social interaction.

In 1999, a pilot study of 21 university students showed that those who took a series of four or five group dance therapy sessions in a period of two weeks

QUESTIONS TO ASK YOUR DOCTOR

- Do I have any physical limitations that would prohibit my undertaking dance therapy?
- What kind of changes can I expect to see or feel with dance therapy?
- Will dance therapy interfere with my current medications?
- Can you recommend any support groups for me and my family?

significantly reduced their test anxiety as measured by the Test Anxiety Inventory. Afterwards, the subjects reported that their dance movement experience was positive and provided them with psychological insight. The researchers concluded that dance therapy could be a viable method of treatment for students who suffer from overwhelming test anxiety and should be researched further.

In another study presented at the ADTA national conference, dance therapist Donna Newman-Bluestein reported success in using techniques of dance therapy with cardiac patients. In a **stress reduction** class, health professionals used dance therapy methods to teach body awareness, relaxation, self-expression, creativity, and empathy. According to Newman-Bluestein, the dance therapy techniques helped the patients deal with such stressful emotions as anger, increased their self-awareness, made them more relaxed, and helped them adjust emotionally to having heart disease.

Training & certification

Dance therapists should have dance experience and a liberal arts background with coursework in psychology in their undergraduate degree. Professional dance therapy training takes place on the graduate level. A qualified dance therapist has received a graduate degree from a school approved by the ADTA or has a master's degree in dance or psychology and has taken additional dance therapy credits.

After graduation, dance therapists can become registered with the ADTA, meaning that they are qualified to practice. After two years they may receive an additional recognition when they become a registered Academy of Dance therapist. They can then teach dance therapy and can supervise interns.

Dance therapists can also obtain psychological credentials by taking a test and becoming registered by the National Board for Certified Counselors.

Resources

BOOKS

Brooke, Stephanie L., ed. *The Use of the Creative Therapies With Autism Spectrum Disorders*. Springfield, IL: Charles C. Thomas Publisher, 2009.

Chaiklin, Sharon, and Hilda Wengrower, eds. *The Art and Science of Dance/Movement Therapy: Life is Dance*. New York: Routledge, 2009.

Rennie, Jeanette, ed. *Learning Disability: Physical Therapy Treatment and Management, A Collaborative Approach*. West Sussex, England: John Wiley & Sons, 2009.

PERIODICALS

Brody, Jane. "Dancing Shoes Replace the Therapist's Couch." *The New York Times* (18 October 1995): C13.

Erwin-Grabner, Tracy, et al. "Effectiveness of Dance/Movement Therapy on Reducing Test Anxiety." *American Journal of Dance Therapy* 21, no. 1 (Spring/Summer 1999) 19–34.

Gold, D.T., et al. "Factors Associated with Persistence with Teriparatide Therapy: Results from the DANCE Observational Study." *Journal of Osteoporosis* 2011: 314970.

ORGANIZATIONS

American Dance Therapy Association, 10632 Little Patuxent Parkway, Ste. 108, Columbia, MD, 21044, (410) 997-4040, Fax: (410) 997-4048, http://www.adta.org.

Barbara Boughton
Laura Jean Cataldo, RN, EdD

Deinstitutionalization

Definition

Deinstitutionalization is a long-term trend wherein fewer people reside as patients in mental hospitals and fewer mental health treatments are delivered in public hospitals. This trend is directly due to the process of closing public hospitals and the ensuing transfers of patients to community-based mental health services in the late twentieth century. It represents the dissipation of patients over a wider variety of healthcare settings and geographic areas. Deinstitutionalization also illustrates evolution in the structure, practice, experiences, and purposes of mental health care in the United States.

Demographics

The trend called deinstitutionalization forces some individuals who have previously been housed within mental institutions, for such problems as **bipolar disorder**, **depression**, and **schizophrenia**, to take care of themselves without professional help or to rely on other means than such institutions. In most cases, these individuals receive comparable help within local community settings, such as shelters or nursing homes. However, in a few circumstances, these individuals become homeless. Sometimes, without proper preparation for life in society, they break the law and end up in jail or prison. In other cases, they become victims of criminals. The more fortunate ones seek refuge with family and friends who provide them support.

Description

History

In the United States in the nineteenth century, hospitals were built to house and care for people with chronic illness, and mental health care was a local responsibility. As with most chronic illness, **hospitalization** did not always provide a cure. Individual states assumed primary responsibilities for mental hospitals beginning in 1890. In the first part of the twentieth century, while mental health treatments had very limited efficacy, many patients received custodial care in state hospitals. Custodial care refers to care in which the patient is watched and protected, but a cure is not sought.

After the founding of the National Institutes of Mental Health (NIMH), new psychiatric medications were developed and introduced into state mental hospitals beginning in 1955. These new medicines brought new hope, and helped address some of the symptoms of mental disorders.

President John F. Kennedy's 1963 **Community Mental Health** Centers Act accelerated the trend toward deinstitutionalization with the establishment of a network of community mental health centers. In the 1960s, with the introduction of Medicare and Medicaid, the federal government assumed an increasing share of responsibility for the costs of mental health care. That trend continued into the 1970s with the implementation of the Supplemental Security Income program in 1974. State governments helped accelerate deinstitutionalization, especially of elderly people. In the 1960s and 1970s, state and national policies championed the need for comprehensive community mental health care, though this ideal was slowly and only partially realized.

Beginning in the 1980s, **managed care** systems began to review systematically the use of inpatient hospital care for mental health. Both public concerns and private health insurance policies generated financial incentives to admit fewer people to hospitals and discharge inpatients more rapidly, limit the length of patient stays, or to transfer responsibility to less costly forms of care.

Indicators and trends

Many statistical indicators show the amount of inpatient hospital care for persons with mental illness decreased during the latter half of the twentieth century, while the total volume of mental health care increased.

A patient care episode is a specific measure of the volume of care provided by an organization or system. It begins when a person visits a healthcare facility for treatment and ends when the person leaves the facility. In 1955 77% of all patient care episodes in mental health organizations took place in 24-hour hospitals. By 1994, although the numbers of patient care episodes increased by more than 500%, only 26% of mental health treatment episodes were in these hospitals. The timing of this trend varied across different states and regions, but it was consistent across a variety of indicators.

The number of inpatient beds available to each group of 100,000 civilians decreased from over 200 beds in 1970 to less than 50 in 1992. The average number of patients in psychiatric hospitals decreased from over 2,000 in 1958 to about 500 in 1978. While adjusted per-capita spending on mental health rose from $16.53 in 1969 to $19.33 in 1994, the portion of funds spent on state and county mental hospitals fell from $9.11 to $4.56.

In 2009, according to the U.S. Centers for Disease Control and Prevention (CDC), 3.2% of adults in the United States, who were not living within mental institutions, had serious psychological distress. The CDC also stated that 67% of residents in nursing homes had mental disorders, approximately 996,000 people within the country.

Transinstitutionalization

Trends toward deinstitutionalization also reflect shifting demographics and boundaries of care. For example, decreases in inpatient mental health care can be complemented by increases in outpatient mental health care. Decreases in inpatient mental health care can also be paired with increases in other forms of care, such as social welfare, criminal justice, or nursing home care. Thus, deinstitutionalization is part of a process sometimes called transinstitutionalization, the transfer of institutional populations from hospitals to jails, nursing homes, and shelters.

Causes and consequences

Causes

Deinstitutionalization, originally and idealistically portrayed by advocates and consumers as a liberating, humane policy alternative to restrictive care, may also be

KEY TERMS

Bipolar disorder—A mood disorder characterized by abnormally high energy levels and moodiness, usually without depression.

Depression—A psychiatric disorder involving feelings of hopelessness and symptoms of fatigue, sleeplessness, suicidal tendencies, and poor concentration.

Mental disorder—A psychiatric disorder of mental faculties.

Schizophrenia—A mental disorder involving degraded thinking and emotions.

interpreted as a series of health policy reforms that are associated with the gradual demise of mental health care dependent on large, state-supported hospitals. Deinstitutionalization is often attributed to decreased need for hospital care and to the advent of new psychiatric medicines.

Consequences

Ideally, deinstitutionalization represents more humane and liberal treatment of mental illness in community-based settings. Pragmatically, it represents a change in the scope of mental health care from longer, custodial inpatient care to shorter outpatient care.

The process of deinstitutionalization, combined with the scarcity of community-based care, is also associated with the visible problems of **homelessness**. Between 30% and 50% of homeless people in the United States are people with mental illness, and people with mental illness are disproportionate among the homeless.

Diagnosis

Deinstitutionalization also describes the adjustment process whereby people with illness are removed from the effects of life within institutions. Since people may become socialized to highly structured institutional environments, they often adapt their social behavior to institutional conditions. Therefore, adjusting to life outside of an institution may be difficult.

Treatment

Defined experientially, deinstitutionalization allows individuals to regain freedom and empower themselves through responsible choices and actions. With the assistance of **social workers** and through psychiatric rehabilitation, former inpatients can adjust to everyday life outside of institutional rules and expectations. This aspect of deinstitutionalization promotes hope and recovery, ongoing debates over the best structure and process of mental health service delivery notwithstanding.

Prognosis

Differing views exist among mental health professionals, advocacy groups, citizens, public officials, family members, and others as to what is best for individuals with intellectual disabilities. Discussions continue as to the most efficient and beneficial ways to deal with these individuals.

In 2007, Dr. Benedetto Saraceno, as the director of Mental Health and **Substance Abuse** within the World Health Organization (WHO), commented on the effectiveness of community based health services. Dr. Saraceno stated, "Not only are community mental health services more accessible to people living with severe mental disabilities, these are also more effective in taking care of their needs compared to mental hospitals. Community mental health services are also likely to have less possibilities for **neglect** and violations of human rights, which are too often encountered in mental hospitals."

However, in too many cases an effective network of these community mental health services are not available to help people with severe mental disabilities. Dr. Saraceno urged all countries to provide such networks for the nearly 54 million people with severe mental disorders around the world.

In whatever manner the United States and other countries proceed with regards to handling mental illness—through deinstitutionalization or other such means—mental illness has been proven to be a significant negative component on the health and productivity of people throughout the world. For instance, a comprehensive 2004 study (updated in 2008) called the Global Burden of Disease (GBD), conducted by WHO, the World Bank, and Harvard University, found that mental illness contributes about 15% to all diseases within economies of developed countries.

Prevention

The problem of mental health, especially homelessness, is partially addressed through prevention programs, which are generally considered less costly and more effective than previous programs. Although deinstitutionalization programs have helped with regards to mental illness, there is still much to do and much still wrong with the system. Barriers, such as lack of knowledge and prejudices, still exist concerning mentally ill people. Community based services such as those provided from day-care centers, schools, and community centers continue to improve on the mental health issue in the United States and around the world. These institutions help to enhance the ongoing process of deinstitutionalization.

Resources

BOOKS

Johnson, Sandra J. *Assertive Community Treatment: Evidence-based Practice or Managed Recovery.* New Brunswick, NJ: Transaction, 2011.

McLeod, Jane D., and Eric R. Wright, editors. *The Sociology of Mental Illness: A Comprehensive Reader.* New York City: Oxford University Press, 2010.

Moritsugu, John, Frank Y. Wong, and Karen Grover Duffy. *Community Psychology.* Boston: Allyn & Bacon, 2010.

Scheid, Teresa L., and Tony N. Brown, eds. *A Handbook for the Study of Mental Health: Social Contexts, Theories, and Systems.* Cambridge: Cambridge University Press, 2010.

Torrey, E. Fuller. *The Insanity Offense: How America's Failure to Treat the Seriously Mentally Ill Endangers its Citizens.* New York City, W.W. Norton, 2008.

VandenBos, Gary R., editor. *APA Dictionary of Psychology.* Washington, DC: American Psychological Association, 2007.

WEBSITES

Centers for Disease Control and Prevention. "Mental Health." http://www.cdc.gov/nchs/fastats/mental.htm (accessed December 2, 2011).

National Institutes of Mental Health. "Mental Health Topics: Statistics." August 6, 2009. http://www.nimh.nih.gov/health/topics/statistics/index.shtml (accessed December 2, 2011).

World Health Organization. "Community Mental Health Services will Lessen Social Exclusion, says WHO." June 1, 2007. http://www.who.int/mediacentre/news/notes/2007/np25/en/index.html (accessed December 2, 2011).

——— "Global Burden of Disease." October 27, 2010. http://www.who.int/topics/global_burden_of_disease/en (accessed December 2, 2011).

ORGANIZATIONS

American Psychiatric Association, 1000 Wilson Blvd., Ste. 1825, Arlington, VA, 22209-3901, (703) 907-7300, apa@psych.org, http://www.psych.org.

American Psychological Association, 750 1st St. NE, Washington, DC, 20002-4242, (202) 336-5500; TDD/TTY: (202) 336-6123, (800) 374-2721, http://www.apa.org.

American Sociological Association, 1430 K St. NW, Ste. 600, Washington, DC, 20005, (202) 383-9005, Fax: (202) 638-0882, http://www.asanet.org.

National Institute of Mental Health, 6001 Executive Blvd., Rm. 8184, MSC 9663, Bethesda, MD, 20892-9663, (301) 433-4513; TTY: (301) 443-8431, Fax: (301) 443-4279, (866) 615-6464; TTY: (866) 415-8051, nimhinfo@nih.gov, http://www.nimh.nih.gov.

Substance Abuse and Mental Health Services Administration Referral Resource, 1 Choke Cherry Rd., Rockville, MD, 20857, (877) SAMHSA-7 (726-4727), (800) TTY: 487-4889, Fax: (240) 221-4292, SAMHSAInfo@samhsa.hhs.gov, http://www.samhsa.gov.

Michael Polgar, PhD

Delirium

Definition

Delirium is a medical condition characterized by a general disorientation accompanied by cognitive impairment, mood shift, self-awareness, and inability to focus and maintain attention. The change occurs over a short period of time—hours to days—and the disturbance in consciousness fluctuates throughout the day.

Demographics

Children, possibly because of their immature **brain** development and physiological differences from adults, can be particularly susceptible to delirium. This susceptibility is most common in association with fevers or some kinds of medications (such as anticholinergics, medications used for motor control problems). A child in a state of delirium may exhibit behavior that can be mistaken for willful lack of cooperation.

The elderly are also particularly sensitivity to delirium, also probably because of differences in physiology as the body ages. Being male and elderly enhances this risk.

Description

The word delirium comes from the Latin *delirare*. In its Latin form, the word means to become crazy or to rave. A phrase often used to describe delirium is "clouding of consciousness," meaning the person has a diminished awareness of their surroundings. In the ***Diagnostic and Statistical Manual of Mental Disorders***, fourth edition, text revision (*DSM-IV-TR*), delirium is categorized based on its assumed causes; for example, "Substance-Induced Delirium." Disorders involving delirium are listed in the same section as those involving **dementia**, but the two conditions differ in several characteristics. Dementia, for example, may exhibit a longer developmental process and is typically accompanied by multiple cognitive deficits.

While the delirium is active, the person tends to fade in and out of lucidity, meaning that he or she will sometimes appear to know what's going on, but at other times may show disorientation to time, place, person, or situation. The longer the delirium goes untreated, the more progressive the disorientation becomes. It usually begins with disorientation to time, during which a patient will declare it to be morning, even though it may be late at night. Later, the person may state that he or she is in a different place rather than at home or in a hospital bed. Still later, the patient may not recognize loved ones, close friends, or relatives, or may insist that a visitor is someone else altogether. Finally, the patient may not recognize the reason for his or her **hospitalization**. This waxing and waning of consciousness is often worse at the end of a day, a phenomenon known as "sundowning."

A delirious patient has a difficult time with most mental operations, including understanding, judgement, and inference. Because the patient cannot maintain awareness of his or her environment, disorientation can result. Nevertheless, disorientation and memory loss are not essential to the **diagnosis** of delirium; the inability to focus and maintain attention, however, is essential to rendering a correct diagnosis. Left unchecked, delirium tends to transition from inattention to increased levels of lethargy, leading to torpor, stupor, and coma. In its other form, delirious patients become agitated and almost hypervigilant, with a dramatically altered sleep-wake cycle that fluctuates between great guardedness and **hypersomnia** (excessive drowsiness) during the day and wakefulness during the night. Delirious patients may also experience hallucinations of the visual, auditory, or tactile type. In such cases, the patient will see things others cannot see, hear things others cannot hear, and/or feel things that others cannot feel, such as feeling as though his or her skin is crawling. In short, the extremes of delirium range from the appearance of simple confusion and **apathy** to anxiety, agitation, and hyperactivity, with some patients experiencing both ends of the spectrum during a single episode. If delirium is suspected, it is imperative that an evaluation occurs quickly, because if left untreated, the condition can progress to death.

Causes and symptoms

Causes

While the symptoms of delirium are numerous and varied, the causes of delirium fall into four basic categories: medical, chemical, surgical, or neurological. The *DSM* attributes the causes of delirium to either a general (or multiple) medical condition or to substance use or withdrawal, which includes delirium as a side effect of medication. Delirium is often associated with factors that result in a disturbance of the normal sleep-wake cycle.

METABOLIC CAUSES. Many metabolic disorders, such as hypothyroidism, hyperthyroidism, hypokalemia, and anoxia, can cause delirium. For example, hypothyroidism (the thyroid gland emits reduced levels of thyroid hormones) brings about a change in emotional responsiveness, which can appear similar to depressive symptoms and cause a state of delirium. Other metabolic sources of delirium involve the dysfunction of the pituitary gland, pancreas, adrenal glands, and parathyroid glands. It should be noted that when a metabolic imbalance goes unattended, the brain may suffer irreparable damage.

DELIRIUM AND MEDICATION. One of the most frequent causes of delirium in the elderly is overmedication. The use of medications such as tricyclic **antidepressants** and antiparkinsonian medications can bring about an anticholinergic toxicity and subsequent delirium. In addition to the anticholinergic drugs, other drugs that can be the source of a delirium are:

- anticonvulsants, used to treat epilepsy
- antihypertensives, used to treat high blood pressure
- cardiac glycosides, such as Digoxin, used to treat heart failure
- cimetidine, used to reduce the production of stomach acid
- disulfiram, used in the treatment of alcoholism
- insulin, used to treat diabetes
- opiates, used to treat pain
- phencyclidine (PCP), used originally as an anesthetic but later removed from the market; now only produced and used illicitly
- salicylates, found in aspirin
- steroids, sometimes used to prevent muscle wasting in bedridden or other immobile patients

Additionally, systemic poisoning by chemicals or compounds such as carbon monoxide, lead, mercury, or other industrial chemicals can cause delirium.

DELIRIUM AND OTHER SUBSTANCES. Alcohol is the most widely used and most well known of the drugs whose withdrawal symptoms include delirium. Delirium onset from the abstinence of alcohol in a chronic user can begin within three days of cessation of drinking. The term *delirium tremens* is used to describe this form of delirium. The resulting symptoms of this delirium are similar in nature to other delirious states but may be preceded by clear-headed auditory hallucinations. In other words, the delirium has not begun, but the patient may experience auditory hallucinations. Delirium tremens may develop soon after and can have ominous consequences, with as many as 15% of those affected dying.

OTHER CAUSES OF DELIRIUM. Some of the structural causes of delirium include vascular blockage, subdural hematoma, and brain tumors. Any of these can damage the brain and cause delirium, whether as a direct result of the condition or by way of a secondary complication, such as oxygen deprivation. Some patients become delirious following surgery. This can be due to any of several factors, such as effects of anesthesia, infections, or a metabolic imbalance.

Infectious diseases can also cause delirium. Commonly diagnosed diseases such as urinary tract infections, pneumonia, or fever from a viral infection can induce delirium. Additionally, diseases of the liver, kidney, lungs, and cardiovascular system can cause delirium, as can infections specific to the brain. Even a deficiency of thiamine (vitamin B_1) can be a trigger for delirium.

Symptoms

Symptoms of delirium are often those associated with the disturbed sleep-wake cycle and include a confused state of mind accompanied by poor attention, impaired recent memory, irritability, inappropriate behavior (e.g., use of vulgar language with lack of a history of such behavior), and anxiety and fearfulness. In some cases, the person can appear to be psychotic, fostering illusions, **delusions**, hallucinations, and/or **paranoia**. In other cases, the patient may simply appear to be withdrawn and apathetic. In still other cases, the patient may become agitated and restless, be unable to remain in bed, and feel a strong need to pace the floor. This restlessness and hyperactivity can alternate with periods of apparent stupor.

Diagnosis

The diagnosis of delirium relies on a distinction of its occurrence from dementia. It should be determined not to arise from previously existing dementia. Other features include identifying it as a loss of clarity about the environment (inattention), sudden changes in cognition (e.g., disorientation), and a relatively sudden onset (compared to dementia).

Diagnosis of some cases of delirium may not occur at all; whether or not delirium is diagnosed in a patient depends on how it is manifested. If the person is an elderly, postoperative patient who appears quiet and apathetic, the condition may go undiagnosed. However, if the patient presents with the agitated, uncooperative type of delirium, it will certainly be noticed. In any case, where there is sudden onset of a confused state accompanied by a behavioral change, delirium should be considered, though this is not intended to imply that such a diagnosis will be made easily.

The psychotic features of delirium may be mistaken for another primary mental illness such as **schizophrenia** or a **manic episode**, such as that associated with **bipolar disorder**. However, there are major differences between these diagnoses and delirium. In people who have schizophrenia, their odd behavior, stereotyped motor activity, or abnormal speech persists in the absence of disorientation like that seen with delirium. The schizophrenic appears alert, and although delusions and/or hallucinations persist, he or she could be formally tested. In contrast, the delirious patient appears hapless and disoriented between episodes of lucidity. The delirious patient may not be testable. A manic episode could be misconstrued for agitated delirium, but consistency of elevated mood would contrast sharply to the less consistent mood of the delirious patient. Delirium should always be considered when there is a rapid onset and especially when the patient fluctuates between an aware state and a confused state.

Because delirium can be superimposed into a preexisting dementia, the most often posed question when diagnosing delirium is whether the person might have dementia instead. Both cause disturbances of memory, but a person with dementia does not reflect the disturbance of consciousness present in someone with delirium. Expert history taking is a must in differentiating dementia from delirium. Dementia is insidious in nature and progresses slowly, while delirium begins with a sudden onset and acute symptoms. A person with dementia may appear clear-headed but can harbor delusions not elicited during an interview. There is not the typical fluctuation of consciousness in dementia that manifests itself in delirium. It has been stated that, as a general rule, delirium comes and goes, but dementia comes and stays. Delirium rarely lasts more than a month. The clinician must be prepared to rule out **factitious disorder** and **malingering** as possible causes for the delirium, as well.

Frequent mental status examinations conducted at various times throughout the day may be required to render a diagnosis of delirium. This assessment is generally done using the **Mini-Mental State Examination** (MMSE). This abbreviated form of **mental status examination** assesses the patient's orientation, registration, attention and concentration, recall, language, and spatial perception. Another tool for use in diagnosing delirium is the Delirium Rating Scale-Revised-98, although studies regarding its ability to differentiate different types of delirium have not been undertaken. Yet another diagnostic tool is the Memorial Delirium Assessment Scale, or MDAS. One tool that does not require patient participation is the Confusion Assessment Method, or CAM.

When a state of delirium is confirmed, the clinician is faced with the task of making the diagnosis in appropriate context to its cause. If the delirium is caused by a general medical condition, the clinician must identify the source of the delirium within the diagnosis. For example, if the delirium is caused by liver dysfunction, in which the liver cannot rid the system of toxins and allows them to enter the system and thus the brain, the diagnosis would be delirium due to hepatic encephalopathy. Delirium may also be caused by a substance such as alcohol. To render a diagnosis of alcohol intoxication delirium, the cognitive symptoms would be more exaggerated than those found in intoxication syndrome. If the delirium is caused by withdrawal from alcohol, the diagnosis would be alcohol withdrawal delirium (delirium tremens could be a feature of this diagnosis).

There may be instances in which delirium has multiple causes, such as when a patient has a head **trauma** and liver failure, or viral encephalitis and alcohol withdrawal. When delirium comes from multiple sources, a diagnosis of delirium precedes each medical condition that contributes.

Treatment

Treating delirium means treating the underlying illness that is its basis. This could include correcting any chemical disparities within the body, such as electrolyte imbalances; treating an infection; reducing a fever; or removing or discontinuing a medication or toxin. A review of anticholinergic effects of medications administered to the patient should take place. It is suggested that **sedatives** and hypnotic-type medications not be used; however, despite the fact that they can sometimes contribute to delirium, in cases of agitated delirium, the benefits may outweigh the risks. Medications that are often used to treat agitated delirium include **haloperidol**, **thioridazine**, and **risperidone**. These can reduce the psychotic features and curb some of the volatility of the patient, but they only treat the symptoms of the delirium, not the source. **Benzodiazepines** (medications that slow the central nervous system to relax the patient) can assist in controlling agitated patients, but, since they can contribute to delirium, should be used in the lowest therapeutic doses possible. The reduction and discontinuance of all psychotropic drugs should be the goal of treatment and occur as soon as possible to permit recovery and viable assessment of the patient.

Prognosis

If a quick diagnosis and treatment of delirium occur, the condition is frequently reversible. However, if the condition goes unchecked or is treated too late, there is a high incidence of mortality or permanent brain damage. The underlying illness may respond quickly to a treatment regimen, but improvement in mental functioning may lag behind, especially in the elderly. Moreover, one study disclosed that one group of elderly survivors of

KEY TERMS

Anoxia—Lack of oxygen.

Anticholinergic toxicity—A poisonous effect brought about by ingestion of medications or other toxins that block acetylcholine receptors. When these receptors are blocked, the person taking the medication may find that he or she gets overheated, has dry mouth, has blurry vision, and retains urine.

Coma—Unconsciousness.

Factitious disorder—A false or exaggerated disorder in which the physical or psychological symptoms are controlled or produced by the patient.

Hyperthyroidism—Condition resulting from the thyroid glands secreting excessive thyroid hormone, causing an increased basal metabolic rate and an increased need for food to meet the demand of the metabolic activity; generally, however, weight loss results.

Hypervigilant—Extreme attention and focus to both internal and external stimuli.

Hypokalemia—Abnormally low levels of potassium in the blood. Hypokalemia is a potential medical emergency, as it can lead to disturbances in of the heart rhythm.

Stupor—A trance-like state that causes a person to appear numb to their environment.

Subdural hematoma—Active bleeding or a blood clot inside the dura (leathery covering of the brain). This bleeding or clot causes swelling of the brain and if left untreated can cause death.

Torpor—Sluggishness or inactivity.

Tricyclic antidepressants—Antidepressant medications that have the common characteristic of a three-ring nucleus in their chemical structure. Imipramine and amitriptyline are examples of tricyclic antidepressants.

Vascular—Pertaining to the bloodstream (arteries, veins, and blood vessels).

delirium, at three years following hospital discharge, had a 33% higher rate of death than other patients. Delirium is a medical emergency that requires prompt attention to avoid the potential for permanent brain damage and death.

Resources

BOOKS

American Psychiatric Association. *Diagnostic and Statistical Manual of Mental Disorders*. 4th ed., text rev. Washington, DC: American Psychiatric Publishing, 2000.

First, Michael B., and Allan Tasman. *Clinical Guide to the Diagnosis and Treatment of Mental Disorders*. 2nd ed. Hoboken, NJ: Wiley, 2010.

Kaplan, Harold, and Benjamin Sadock, eds. *Synopsis of Psychiatry*. 10th ed. Baltimore: Lippincott Williams & Wilkins, 2007.

Miller, Bruce L., and Bradley F. Boeve, eds. *The Behavioral Neurology of Dementia*. New York: Cambridge University Press, 2009.

Porter, Robert S., and Justin L. Kaplan, eds. *The Merck Manual of Diagnosis and Therapy*. 19th ed. Whitehouse Station, NJ: Merck Research Laboratories, 2011.

PERIODICALS

de Rooij, S.E., et al. "Clinical Subtypes of Delirium and Their Relevance for Daily Clinical Practice." *International Journal of Geriatric Psychiatry* 20, no. 7 (July 2005): 609–615.

Han, J.H., et al. "Delirium in Older Emergency Department Patients: Recognition, Risk Factors, and Psychomotor Subtypes." *Academic Emergency Medicine* 16, no. 3 (March 2009) 193–200.

Katz, Ira R., et al. "Validating the Diagnosis of Delirium and Evaluating its Association With Deterioration Over a One-Year Period." *American Journal of Geriatric Psychiatry* 9 (Spring 2001): 148–159.

Mayo-Smith, Michael F., et al. "Management of Alcohol Withdrawal Delirium." *Archives of Internal Medicine* 164, no. 13 (July 12, 2004). http://archinte.ama-assn.org/cgi/content/full/164/13/1405 (accessed October 3, 2011).

Trzepacz, Paula T., et al. "Validation of The Delirium Rating Scale-Revised-98: Comparison with the Delirium Rating Scale and the Cognitive Test for Delirium." *Journal of Neuropsychiatry and Clinical Neuroscience* 13 (May 2001): 229–242.

Webster, Robert, and Suzanne Holroyd. "Prevalence of Psychotic Symptoms in Delirium." *Psychosomatics* 41 (December 2000): 519–522.

WEBSITES

U.S. National Cancer Institute. "Cognitive Disorders and Delirium (PDQ)." http://www.cancer.gov/cancertopics/pdq/supportivecare/delirium/healthprofessional/allpages (accessed October 3, 2011).

Jack H. Booth, PsyD

Delusional disorder

Definition

Delusional disorder is a psychotic condition characterized by recurrent or persistent non-bizarre **delusions**, without other obvious symptoms of mental illness. Delusions are false beliefs, based on a mistaken interpretation of reality. The beliefs are held with strong conviction, even in the face of contradictory proof. Non-bizarre delusions are plausible, in that there is a small possibility that they could be true under other circumstances.

Demographics

Delusional disorder is rare, with a lifetime risk of less than one in 1,000. The estimated prevalence in adults is 0.03%. In contrast, the prevalence of **schizophrenia** is estimated at 1%. However, delusional disorder may account for 1%–2% of psychiatric hospital admissions. The age at onset ranges from 18–90 years, with a mean age of 40 years. Delusional disorder, especially late-onset, is more prevalent in females than in males.

Description

Individuals with delusional disorder typically do not appear abnormal, unless they are discussing aspects of their lives that are affected by delusions. They may realize that their beliefs are unusual and, therefore, often choose not to discuss them with others. However, they may make unusual day-to-day choices based on their delusions. For example, people who are under the delusion that the government is spying on them might refuse to use a telephone or credit card. Although they may find their delusional reality distressing, they are not necessarily aware that there is anything abnormal about their thought processes or functioning. They usually attribute any problems or obstacles, such as having trouble getting a job or maintaining a romantic relationship, to their delusional reality. Using the government example, people may believe that there is nothing wrong except for government interference in their lives and that, if that ceased, their other problems would disappear.

People with delusional disorder do not usually have major mood or emotional problems. They rarely, if ever, hallucinate. When hallucinations do occur, they are components of the delusional belief. For example, people who believe that their internal organs are rotting may hallucinate smells or sensations related to that delusion.

There are various forms of delusional disorder:

- Paranoid or persecutory delusional disorder is the most common type. People believe that others are plotting against them and want to harm them or their loved ones. Persecutory delusions go far beyond symptoms of a paranoid personality. They often involve elaborate plots for spying, poisoning, or murder. People with paranoid delusions may even seek legal redress against their imagined enemies.
- Jealous delusions usually involve imagined infidelity on the part of a spouse or romantic partner, based on minimal or even contrary evidence. A person with delusional jealousy may try to restrict a partner's activities. This type of delusional disorder is most likely to be associated with violent behavior.
- Erotomanic delusions involve the belief that someone, usually a celebrity or person of higher status, is secretly in love with the deluded person. Erotomanic delusions are more common in women than in men. They can lead to stalking or even violence against the other person or against a perceived romantic rival.
- Grandiose delusions are an unjustified conviction in one's own importance or uniqueness. Grandiose delusions can take many forms, such as believing that one holds an exalted position, has connections to a famous person or deity, is very wealthy or knowledgeable, or has extraordinary powers or abilities.
- Somatic delusions involve excessive, irrational concerns about bodily functioning, such as an imagined physical deformity or illness, infestation with parasites or insects, or the conviction that one is emitting a foul stench. People with somatic delusions often avoid others and seek medical treatment for their imagined afflictions.
- Mixed-type delusions involve more than one of the above types.
- Unspecified delusions do not fit any of the above categories.

Unless their delusions result in illegal behavior or affect work or daily activities, people may adapt well enough to navigate life effectively without coming to clinical attention. The decision to seek medical help may result from a desire to reduce feelings of **depression**, anxiety, fear, or rage caused by the delusions, rather than from recognition that the beliefs are delusional. Persons with delusional disorder may be perceived as being angry and threatening. Rarely, they may become violent, usually toward someone who plays a part in the delusion, most often a spouse or sexual partner.

Although delusions can be a component of various psychotic disorders, in conditions such as schizophrenia, the delusions are usually bizarre or impossible, such as believing oneself to be controlled by an external force or having strange thoughts inserted into one's **brain**. Therefore, some researchers contend that delusional disorder is not a psychotic disorder, but rather a type of depression that may respond better to **antidepressants** or therapies for treating depression. Accepted cultural or religious beliefs are not delusions, regardless of how bizarre or delusional they may appear to nonbelievers. Because so many different disorders can cause delusions and because a **diagnosis** of delusional disorder is relatively subjective, some clinicians believe that the focus should be on treating the delusional thinking rather than on diagnosis.

Risk factors

Having close family members with delusional disorder or paranoid personality traits appears to be a risk factor for delusional disorder. Family members with other types of mental illness, such as schizophrenia or schizoaffective or mood disorders, do not seem to increase the risk of delusional disorder.

Causes and symptoms

The cause of delusional disorder is unknown. Its increased incidence among closely related individuals suggests that there is an inherited or genetic component to the disorder. A number of studies have found differences in the functioning of certain brain regions in individuals with delusional disorder. Patients with delusional disorder tend to have neurological activity consistent with continually threatening conditions, whereas non-delusional people exhibit such patterns only under conditions that could truly be interpreted as threatening.

It has been suggested that delusional disorder results from dysfunctional cognitive processing or thought patterns. Delusions may arise from distorted perceptions or understandings of one's environment, particularly with regard to other people and to the causes of unusual or negative events. Studies have found that delusional individuals make inferences and formulate theories about reality based on less information than would normally be required. This "jumping to conclusions" can lead to delusional interpretations of ordinary events and a tendency to view life as a series of threatening events. For example, developing flu-like symptoms during a week when new people move into the neighborhood might lead a delusional person to the conclusion that the new neighbors are the source of the infection. The patient might not consider alternative explanations, such as a family member with the flu or co-workers recently out with the flu. Other research has found that those who are

KEY TERMS

Agitation—Excessive restlessness or emotional disturbance that is often associated with anxiety or psychosis.

Cognition—Conscious intellectual activity, including thinking, imagining, reasoning, remembering, and learning.

Delusion—A persistent false belief held in the face of strong contradictory evidence.

Dementia—A group of symptoms (syndrome) associated with chronic progressive impairment of memory, reasoning ability, and other intellectual functions; personality changes; deterioration in personal grooming; disorientation; and sometimes delusions.

Erotomania—The false belief that one is the object of another's love or sexual desire.

Hallucination—False sensory perceptions; hearing sounds or seeing people or objects that are not there. Hallucinations can also affect the senses of smell, touch, and taste.

Psychotic—Pertaining to a serious mental disorder, such as schizophrenia, characterized by loss of contact with reality.

Schizoaffective disorder—Having symptoms of both schizophrenia and bipolar disorder.

Schizophrenia—A psychotic disorder characterized by loss of contact with one's environment, deterioration of everyday functioning, and personality disintegration.

prone to delusions interpret other people differently. Their interpretations of how others view them tend to be distorted.

There may also be motivations or defense mechanisms underlying delusions. Delusional disorder in susceptible people occasionally appears to be precipitated by difficulties in coping with life or maintaining high self-esteem. In order to maintain a positive self-image, people sometimes regard others as the cause of their personal difficulties. Over time, this can become an established pattern of thought, leading to delusional disorder.

The primary symptom of delusional disorder is persistent delusions or fixed beliefs about other people, situations, or conditions, which are plausible but false. The American Psychiatric Association's ***Diagnostic and Statistical Manual of Mental Disorders***, fourth edition, text revision (*DSM-IV-TR*), specifies the criteria for delusional disorder as non-bizarre delusions that:

- persist for at least one month and are resistant to change
- are not part of a cultural or religious belief
- occur in the absence of obvious peculiar or bizarre behavior
- occur without hallucinations or with rare hallucinations that relate directly to the delusion
- occur without concurrent mood episodes or episodes that are brief relative to the duration of the delusion
- occur in the absence of memory loss; medical illness; or drug-, alcohol-, or medication-related effects that are associated with the delusions

Diagnosis

Delusions are common symptoms of many other psychiatric illnesses, such as schizophrenia and **schizoaffective disorder**. **Dementia** caused by the deterioration of brain tissue, such as **Alzheimer's disease**, can result in delusions. Delusions can also occur as a result of brain tumors or injury or drug or alcohol reactions. Therefore, diagnosis of delusional disorder involves, in part, the elimination of other causes for the delusions. For example, the absence of persistent hallucinations may rule out schizophrenia or schizoaffective disorder and the absence of memory loss can rule out dementia.

Because delusions occur in many different disorders, some clinician-researchers have argued that there is little usefulness in focusing on what diagnosis the person has been given. Those who ascribe to this view believe it is more important to focus on the symptom of delusional thinking and find ways to have an effect on delusions, whether they occur in delusional disorder or schizophrenia or schizoaffective disorder. Many **psychotherapy** techniques used in delusional disorder come from symptom-focused (as opposed to diagnosis-focused) researcher-practitioners.

Examination

The clinician will perform a physical examination and obtain a medical history. The patient interview focuses on current situations and past history. With the patient's permission, family members or friends may be interviewed. A semi-structured interview, called a **mental status examination**, may be used to assess the patient's concentration, memory, understanding, and logical thinking. The mental status examination is intended to reveal peculiar thought processes. However, delusional people often conceal their thoughts because they know they are unusual. They may resist diagnosis and treatment because they are convinced of the reality of their delusions.

Tests

Various tests may be performed to rule out other physical or mental disorders. The Peters Delusion Inventory (PDI) is a psychological test for identifying and understanding delusional thinking, although it is more commonly used in research than in clinical practice.

Procedures

An electroencephalogram (EEG) may be taken to record brain activity. **Imaging studies** such as **magnetic resonance imaging** (MRI) or **computed tomography** (CT) scans may be performed if an underlying medical or neurological problem is suspected.

Treatment

Treatment of delusional disorder can be difficult, especially if the delusions are long-lasting. Patients may not believe that they have a mental disorder and may be resistant to treatment. **Hospitalization** is usually counterproductive, since it will reinforce paranoid delusions, but sometimes partial hospitalization or day-treatment programs are required.

Traditional

Psychotherapy, especially cognitive therapy, is usually the most effective treatment for delusional disorder, especially when it focuses on symptoms. **Family therapy** may also be beneficial. The therapist usually begins by concentrating on concrete life problems and goals and reinforcing positive outcomes to improve the patient's self-confidence and self-esteem. Therapies that stress social skills and behavior- and solution-oriented goals are usually more effective than therapies that focus on self-knowledge and insight or that directly challenge the delusions. Once a supportive and trusting relationship is established, the therapist takes gentle advantage of any doubts the patient has about the delusions, beginning with the least-significant aspects. Only then can the therapist begin to draw attention to differences between the delusions and reality. Using empathy and hypothetical questions, the therapist helps the patient generate alternative, evidence-based explanations and reach logical conclusions. If the patient is unwilling to relinquish even the smallest delusional belief, the therapy will probably be very long-term. In any case, therapy is likely to last at least six to 12 months.

Drugs

Antipsychotic medications, particularly in conjunction with psychotherapy, can be helpful for delusional disorder, though patients who do not acknowledge having a disorder may be unwilling to begin or maintain treatment with antipsychotics. Atypical, also called novel or newer-generation, antipsychotic medications, such as **risperidone** (Risperdal), **quetiapine** (Seroquel), and **olanzapine** (Zyprexa), can be effective with some patients. These are generally taken orally on a daily basis for a relatively long term. Response to antipsychotics for delusional disorder appears to follow the "rule of thirds"—about one-third of patients respond somewhat positively, one-third show little change, and one-third worsen or are unable to comply with the drug regimen.

Antipsychotics can be particularly useful for ending episodes of acute agitation. Agitation is a state of frantic activity, accompanied by anger or exaggerated fearfulness, which increases the risk that patients will harm themselves or others. Agitation is a typical response to severe or harsh confrontation about delusions. Agitation can also result from preventing patients from performing inappropriate acts that they view as urgent in light of their delusional realities. In emergency situations, patients may be given an injection of **haloperidol** (Haldol), usually in combination with other medications to decrease anxiety and slow activity, such as **lorazepam** (Ativan).

Alternative

Self-help or **support groups** or nonprofessional interventions are not generally appropriate for patients with delusional disorder. Delusional people are usually suspicious and mistrustful of others and their motivations. This attitude makes group dynamics difficult and possibly counterproductive.

Prognosis

The prognosis for delusional disorder varies. Sometimes the delusions disappear in a short time. In other cases, delusions persist for months or years, perhaps varying in intensity and significance. In general, about 33%–50% of cases resolve completely; about 10% show some improvement of symptoms, although irrational beliefs continue; and about 30%–40% of cases persist with no improvement. The prognosis depends largely on the level of conviction with regard to the delusions and openness to information that contradicts the delusions. Reluctance to accept treatment worsens the prognosis. However, some people with ongoing delusional disorder continue to function reasonably well over the long term.

QUESTIONS TO ASK YOUR DOCTOR

- Do you think I have delusional disorder? Why?
- What type of psychotherapy do you recommend?
- Do I need to take antipsychotic medications?
- What are the possible side effects of these medications?
- What is my prognosis?

Prevention

There are no known preventions for delusional disorder.

Resources

BOOKS

American Psychiatric Association. *Diagnostic and Statistical Manual of Mental Disorders (DSM-IV-TR)*, 4th ed., text rev. Washington, DC: American Psychiatric Association, 2000.

Freeman, Daniel, Richard P. Bentall, and Philippa A. Garety. *Persecutory Delusions: Assessment, Theory, and Treatment.* New York: Oxford University Press, 2008.

Kantor, Martin. *Understanding Paranoia: A Guide for Professionals, Families, and Sufferers.* Westport, CT: Praeger, 2008.

PERIODICALS

Dimopoulos, N. P., C. I. Mitsonis, and V. V. Psarra. "Delusional Disorder, Somatic Type Treated with Aripiprazole-Mirtazapine Combination." *Journal of Psychopharmacology* 22, no. 7 (September 2008): 812–14.

Easton, Judith A., Todd K. Shackelford, and Lucas D. Schipper. "Delusional Disorder—Jealous Type: How Inclusive are the *DSM-IV* Diagnostic Criteria?" *Journal of Clinical Psychology* 64, no. 3 (March 2008): 264–75.

WEBSITES

"Delusional Disorder." October 27, 2009. Aetna InteliHealth. http://www.intelihealth.com/IH/ihtPrint/WSIHW000/24479/31787.html?hide=t&k=basePrint (accessed July 25, 2011).

"Delusional Disorder." PsychCentral. June 1, 2010. http://psychcentral.com/disorders/sx11.htm (accessed July 25, 2011).

National Institute of Mental Health. "Delusional (Paranoid) Disorder." Associates in Counseling and Child Guidance. http://accg.net/delusional_paranoid_disorder.htm (accessed July 25, 2011).

ORGANIZATIONS

American Psychiatric Association, 1000 Wilson Blvd., Ste. 1825, Arlington, VA, 22209-3901, (703) 907-7300, apa@psych.org, http://www.psych.org.

American Psychological Association, 750 1st St. NE, Washington, DC, 20002-4242, (202) 336-5500, (800) 374-2721, http://www.apa.org.

Mental Health America, 2000 N. Beauregard St., 6th Fl., Alexandria, VA, 22311, (703) 684-7722, (800) 969-6642, Fax: (703) 684-5968, http://www.nmha.org.

National Alliance on Mental Illness, 3803 N Fairfax Dr., Ste. 100, Arlington, VA, 22203, (703) 524-7600, (800) 950-6264, Fax: (703) 524-9094, http://www.nami.org.

National Institute of Mental Health, 6001 Executive Blvd., Rm. 8184, MSC 9663, Bethesda, MD, 20892-9663, (301) 443-4513, (866) 615-6464, Fax: (301)443-4279, nimhinfo@nih.gov, http://www.nimh.nih.gov.

Deborah Rosch Eifert, PhD
Margaret Alic, PhD

Delusions

Definition

Delusions are unshakeable false beliefs. They are irrational, defy normal reasoning, and remain firm even in the face of overwhelming proof to the contrary. Delusions are psychotic symptoms that are often accompanied by hallucinations and/or feelings of **paranoia**, which act to strengthen the delusions.

Demographics

Delusions can be symptoms of many physical and mental disorders, as well as reactions to some medications. The prevalence of **schizophrenia**, which usually includes delusions, is estimated at 1% of the population, with delusions and hallucinations in males usually beginning between the ages of 16 and 30. Women tend to develop schizophrenia later, with 25% of cases appearing after age 45. Schizophrenia affects men and women equally and the incidence is similar in various racial and ethnic groups around the world.

Other common disorders that may involve delusions include **bipolar disorder**, **depression**, **dementia**, and some types of alcohol and drug abuse. Most people with **Alzheimer's disease** eventually develop delusions.

Other disorders that cause delusions are quite rare. The estimated prevalence of delusional disorder—in which delusions are the only or the primary symptom—is 0.025%–0.03% in adults. **Shared psychotic disorder** usually occurs only in long-term relationships in which a dominant partner with a psychotic disorder induces delusions in the more submissive partner. It also can occur among groups of people closely involved with a psychotic person. Postpartum **psychosis** occurs following approximately 0.01% of births, usually within the first four weeks.

Description

Delusions are most often symptoms of psychotic disorders, in which the patient has a diminished or distorted sense of reality. Neurological and physical illnesses and some medications can also cause delusions. Delusions are distinct from acceptable cultural- or religious-based beliefs, regardless of how irrational these may seem to outsiders. Delusions are unrelated to individual intelligence levels.

Delusions sometimes are difficult to distinguish from overvalued or unreasonable ideas. Overvalued ideas may be present in **anorexia nervosa**, **obsessive-compulsive disorder**, **body dysmorphic disorder**, and **hypochondriasis**. However, with overvalued or unreasonable ideas, people usually have at least some level of doubt as to the validity of their ideas. People with delusions are absolutely convinced that their delusions are real.

Most people with schizophrenia have delusions and delusions are the primary symptom of **delusional disorder**. Delusions also may occur with:

- schizoaffective disorder
- schizophreniform disorder
- brief psychotic disorder
- substance-induced psychotic disorder
- shared psychotic disorder
- postpartum psychosis
- bipolar disorder or mania
- major depressive disorder with psychotic features or delusional depression
- personality disorders, including schizotypal, paranoid, and sometimes borderline
- delirium
- Alzheimer's disease and other dementias
- Parkinson's disease, Huntington's disease, and certain chromosomal disorders
- HIV and other brain infections
- some types of epilepsy
- stroke
- brain tumors or cysts
- traumatic brain injury

Delusions are categorized as either bizarre or non-bizarre and mood-congruent or mood-incongruent. Bizarre delusions are completely implausible, with no association with reality, such as the belief that aliens have removed one's **brain**. Non-bizarre delusions are false beliefs that would be possible under some circumstances, such as the mistaken belief that one is under constant police surveillance. Delusional disorder always involves non-bizarre delusions. A mood-congruent delusion is consistent with either a depressive or manic state. For example, a depressed person may believe that the world is coming to an end. Someone in a manic state might believe that he is a famous person or has special talents or abilities. A mood-incongruent delusion is inconsistent with both depression or mania or is mood-neutral, such as a depressed person who believes that thoughts are being inserted into her mind by some outside force, person, or group ("thought insertion").

Delusions can fall into various categories:

- Paranoid or persecutory delusions—the belief that others are plotting against the individual or are out to cause harm—are the most common type of delusion. Sometimes persecutory delusions are isolated and fragmented. Often they are well-organized belief systems, called systematized delusions, that involve elaborate plots for ruining one's reputation or spying on, poisoning, drugging, or murdering the victim. Systematized delusions can be so broad and complex as to explain every aspect of one's life.
- Jealous delusions usually involve imagined infidelity on the part of a spouse or romantic partner. A person with delusional jealousy may try to restrict a partner's activities. This type of delusion is most likely to be associated with violent behavior.
- Erotomanic delusions involve the belief that someone, usually a celebrity, famous person, or person perceived as having a higher status, is secretly in love with the deluded person. These delusions can lead to stalking or even violence against the other person or a perceived romantic rival.
- Grandiose delusions are an unjustified conviction in one's own importance and uniqueness. These can take many forms, such as believing that one holds an exalted position, has connections to a famous person or deity, is very wealthy or knowledgeable, has extraordinary powers or abilities, or has a special mission in life. People may believe that they are rock stars or Jesus Christ. More often, people believe that they have great but under-recognized accomplishments.
- Somatic delusions involve excessive and irrational concerns about bodily functioning, such as an imagined illness, physical deformity, infestation with parasites or insects, or a conviction that one is emitting a foul stench.

- Mixed type delusions have characteristics of more than one type.
- Unspecified delusions do not fit any of the above categories.

Delusions are also categorized by theme. A monothematic delusion is a single delusional belief or a few false beliefs that all relate to one theme. People with polythematic delusions have a variety of unrelated delusional beliefs. Delusions can have any theme, but there are certain common themes:

- A delusion of control is the belief that another person, group, or external force controls one's thoughts, feelings, impulses, or behavior. People may believe that aliens are controlling their bodily movements. Thought broadcasting (the belief that one's thoughts are being heard aloud), thought insertion, and thought withdrawal (the belief that an outside force, person, or group is removing or extracting a one's thoughts) are other examples of control delusions.
- A mind-reading delusion is the belief that other people are aware of one's thoughts.
- Nihilistic delusions involve the absence or nonexistence of self, parts of oneself, others, or the world. Nihilistic delusions sometimes involve the end of the world.
- A delusion of guilt, sin, or self-accusation is intense false remorse. People may believe that they have committed a horrible crime and should be punished severely or are convinced that they are responsible for a natural disaster, such as fire, flood, or earthquake.
- A delusion of reference is the false belief that insignificant remarks, events, or objects have personal meaning or significance. For example, people may believe that they are receiving special messages from their television. Although the messages are usually negative, they also can be grandiose.
- Religious delusions have a religious or spiritual content. They may be combined with other delusions, such as grandiose delusions (for example, the belief that one has been chosen by God), delusions of control, or delusions of guilt. Beliefs that are acceptable within a person's religious or cultural background are not delusions.
- The Capgras delusion is the belief that an imposter has been substituted for a close relation, such as a spouse, sibling, parent, or child.

Risk factors

Risk factors for delusions depend on the underlying cause. A family history is an important risk factor for many psychotic disorders. **Stress** and low self-esteem also are risk factors for delusions. Shared psychotic disorder most often occurs in couples who are reclusive or socially isolated.

Causes and symptoms

Although delusions are usually caused by an underlying disorder, illness, or drug reaction, the precise causes are unknown. Genetics, neurological or brain chemistry abnormalities, and psychological mechanisms may all play a role.

Delusions suggest an abnormality in thought content, patterns, or processes. They may result from distorted perceptions and understanding of one's environment, particularly with regard to other people and the causes of unusual or negative events. Studies have found that individuals with delusions make inferences and formulate theories about reality based on less information than would normally be required. This "jumping to conclusions" can lead to delusional interpretations of ordinary events. In some cases, delusions may be caused by poor coping skills. **Brief psychotic disorder** in susceptible individuals is usually triggered by an extremely stressful or traumatic event. It is sometimes argued that psychiatric delusions develop through normal cognitive processes for understanding unusual or difficult experiences.

There may be motivations or defense mechanisms underlying some delusions. It is often assumed that paranoid delusions are caused by low self-esteem. In order to maintain a positive self-image, people sometimes regard others as the cause of their personal difficulties. Over time, this can become an established pattern of thought.

Some studies have indicated that delusions may be generated by abnormalities in the limbic system, the portion of the brain on the inner edge of the cerebral cortex that helps regulate emotions. People with schizophrenia have imbalances in **serotonin** and dopamine—neurotransmitters in the brain—that affect reactions to stimuli, which can lead to delusions. Patients with delusional disorder tend to have neurological activity consistent with continually threatening conditions.

Delusions can be caused by drugs such as **amphetamines**, **cocaine**, and phencyclidine (PCP). Delusions can occur both during use and withdrawal from drugs or alcohol. Some prescription drugs, including stimulants, **steroids**, and medications for Parkinson's disease, can cause delusions.

Symptoms depend on the type of delusion. Paranoid delusions are very common in older adults with schizophrenia or dementia. People who believe that they are being poisoned may develop strange eating habits or try to avoid food completely, which can lead to malnutrition. People who believe that their possessions are being stolen may hide things. People who are overly suspicious or believe they are being persecuted may isolate themselves from others. Patients with delusional depression may have somatic delusions or delusions of

KEY TERMS

Alzheimer's disease—A progressive, neurodegenerative disease characterized by loss of function and death of nerve cells in several areas of the brain, leading to loss of mental functions, such as memory and learning. Alzheimer's disease is the most common cause of dementia.

Bipolar disorder—A recurrent mood disorder, also known as manic-depressive disorder, in which patients have extreme mood swings from depression to mania or a mixture of both.

Cognitive—Conscious intellectual activity, including thinking, imagining, reasoning, remembering, and learning.

Dementia—A group of symptoms (syndrome) associated with chronic progressive impairment of memory, reasoning ability, and other intellectual functions; personality changes; deterioration in personal grooming; disorientation; and sometimes delusions.

Hallucinations—False sensory perceptions; hearing sounds or seeing people or objects that are not there. Hallucinations can also affect the senses of smell, touch, and taste.

Limbic system—The brain structures involved in memory, emotion, and motivation, including the hippocampus and hypothalamus.

Mania—Psychotic excitement, hyperactivity, disorganized behavior, and/or elevated mood; the manic phase of bipolar disorder.

Neurotransmitters—Chemicals that carry impulses between nerve cells (neurons), including acetylcholine, dopamine, serotonin, and norepinephrine.

Paranoia—An unfounded or exaggerated distrust of others.

Personality disorder—A psychopathological condition in which a person's patterns and behaviors are considered deviant or non-adaptive, but without neurosis or psychosis.

Psychosis—A serious mental disorder, such as schizophrenia, characterized by loss of contact with reality.

Schizoaffective disorder—Having symptoms of both schizophrenia and bipolar disorder.

Schizophrenia—A psychotic disorder characterized by loss of contact with one's environment, deterioration of everyday functioning, and personality disintegration.

Schizophreniform disorder—A psychosis resembling schizophrenia, but lasting only between one and six months.

Shared psychotic disorder—Also known as folie à deux, shared psychotic disorder is a rare condition in which an otherwise healthy person, or secondary case, shares delusions with a primary case—a person with schizophrenia or another psychotic disorder who has well-established delusions.

guilt. Patients with psychotic depression may pose a danger to themselves or others.

People with delusions often resist **diagnosis** and treatment. Because of their firm convictions in their delusions, they do not believe that there is anything abnormal about their thoughts or behaviors. In many cases of shared psychotic disorder, only one partner will seek treatment.

Diagnosis

Examination

Diagnosis usually involves identifying the underlying cause of the delusions. This includes a complete physical examination and medical history. A mental health professional, usually a **psychiatrist** or **psychologist**, uses specially designed interviews and assessments to evaluate mental status and diagnose psychotic disorders. Family members or friends also may be interviewed.

Tests

Clinical inventories and other tests are used to evaluate mental status. Specific tests for underlying physical illnesses or drug reactions may be conducted.

Procedures

Imaging procedures may be used to detect brain tumors or abnormalities. An electroencephalogram (EEG) may be used to measure brain activity.

Treatment

Traditional

Treatment depends on the underlying cause of the delusions. **Psychotherapy**, cognitive therapy, and **family therapy** may be options. Treatment for shared psychotic disorder includes separating the secondary case from the primary partner. **Hospitalization** may be necessary for severe delusions. The healthcare provider may need to hear the person express delusional thoughts before ordering **involuntary hospitalization**. Sometimes **electroconvulsive therapy** (ECT) is used to treat delusions, especially conditions that fail to respond to drug treatment or psychotherapy. ECT can be especially effective for psychotic depression.

Drugs

Both conventional and new-generation or atypical antipsychotics can effectively treat delusions, although side effects are common. Antipsychotics include **thioridazine** (Mellaril), **haloperidol** (Haldol), **chlorpromazine** (Thorazine), **clozapine** (Clozaril), **risperidone** (Risperdal), **olanzapine** (Zyprexa), **quetiapine** (Seroquel), and **fluphenazine** (Prolixin Decanoate). Some of these drugs block both serotonin and **dopamine**. Antipsychotics are usually started at low dosages and are gradually increased every few days. Sometimes patients need to try several different drugs to maximize effectiveness and minimize side effects. Older adults who **relapse** after initial treatment may have to continue on antipsychotics indefinitely. Tranquilizers or **sedatives**, such as **lorazepam** (Ativan) or **diazepam** (Valium), may be used to treat anxiety, agitation, or **insomnia** accompanying delusions.

Home care

People with delusions must be treated with finesse. Trust is very important. Rather than directly confronting or arguing about the impossibility of a delusion, family members and friends should acknowledge distresses caused by the delusion, reassure the patient, respond to his or her feelings, and attempt to distract the patient with other topics or activities.

Prognosis

The prognosis for delusions depends on the underlying cause. Delusions caused by schizophrenia usually disappear within a few weeks of treatment with antipsychotics, and the shorter the duration of delusions and hallucinations, the better the long-term prognosis. Although psychotic depression is a very serious and potentially dangerous condition, depressive symptoms other than delusions are more likely to continue or return following treatment. With appropriate treatment, delusional disorder can be relieved in up to 50% of patients. However, because of their strong belief in the reality of their delusions and a lack of insight into their condition, individuals with this disorder may never seek treatment. With shared psychotic disorder, the induced delusions in the secondary partner usually disappear when the individuals are separated.

QUESTIONS TO ASK YOUR DOCTOR

- What do you think is causing my delusions?
- What types of physical and psychiatric diagnostic tests do I need?
- What are my treatment options?
- What are the expected effects of my prescribed medications?
- What are the side effects associated with these medications?

Prevention

There are no known means for preventing delusions. However, early diagnosis and treatment can help minimize disruptions and long-term effects.

Resources

BOOKS

DeLisi, Lynn E. *100 Questions & Answers About Schizophrenia: Painful Minds*, 2nd ed. Sudbury, MA: Jones & Bartlett, 2009.

Graham, George. *The Disordered Mind: An Introduction to Philosophy of Mind and Mental Illness.* New York: Routledge, 2010.

Wootton, Tom, et al. *Bipolar In Order: Looking At Depression, Mania, Hallucination, and Delusion from the Other Side.* Tiburon, CA: Bipolar Advantage, 2010.

PERIODICALS

Coltheart, Max, Robyn Langdon, and Ryan McKay. "Delusional Belief." *Annual Review of Psychology* 62 (2011): 271–298.

Lincoln, Tania M., et al. "Is Fear of Others Linked to an Uncertain Sense of Self? The Relevance of Self-Worth, Interpersonal Self-Concepts, and Dysfunctional Beliefs to Paranoia." *Behavior Therapy* 41, no. 2 (June 2010): 187–197.

Rhodes, John, and Simon Jakes. "Perspectives on the Onset of Delusions." *Clinical Psychology and Psychotherapy* 17, no. 2 (March/April 2010): 136–146.

OTHER

Duckworth, Ken. "Understanding Schizophrenia and Recovery." National Alliance on Mental Illness. http://www.nami.org/Content/Microsites316/NAMI_PA,_Cumberland_and_Perry_Cos_/Discussion_Groups559/No_Active_Discussion_Groups_for_this_Site/NAMI_Schizophrenia_Aug08.pdf (accessed December 18, 2010).

WEBSITES

Cleveland Clinic. "Shared Psychotic Disorder." June 8, 2009. http://my.clevelandclinic.org/disorders/psychotic_disorder/hic_shared_psychotic_disorder.aspx (accessed December 19, 2010).

"Delusional Disorder." October 27, 2009. Aetna InteliHealth. http://www.intelihealth.com/IH/ihtPrint/WSIHW000/24479/31787.html?hide=t&k=basePrint (accessed December 16, 2010).

Mental Health America. "Paranoia and Paranoid Disorders." http://www.nmha.org/go/paranoia (accessed December 18, 2010).

———. "Schizophrenia: What You Need to Know." http://www.mentalhealthamerica.net/go/information/get-info/schizophrenia/schizophrenia-what-you-need-to-know (accessed December 18, 2010).

National Institute of Mental Health. "Schizophrenia." http://www.nimh.nih.gov/health/publications/schizophrenia/complete-index.shtml (accessed December 19, 2010).

ORGANIZATIONS

American Psychiatric Association, 1000 Wilson Blvd., Ste. 1825, Arlington, VA, 22209, (703) 907-7300, apa@psych.org, http://www.psych.org.

Mental Health America, 2000 N. Beauregard St., 6th Fl., Alexandria, VA, 22311, (703) 684-7722, (800) 969-6642, Fax: (703) 684-5968, http://www.nmha.org.

National Alliance on Mental Illness, 3803 N. Fairfax Dr., Ste. 100, Arlington, VA, 22203, (703) 524-7600, (800) 950-NAMI (6264), Fax: (703) 524-9094, http://www.nami.org.

National Institute of Mental Health, 6001 Executive Blvd., Rm. 8184, MSC 9663, Bethesda, MD, 20892, (301) 443-4513, (866) 615-6464, Fax: (301) 443-4279, nimhinfo@nih.gov, http://www.nimh.nih.gov.

Paula Anne Ford-Martin
Laura Jean Cataldo, RN, EdD
Jennifer Hahn, PhD
Margaret Brantley
Margaret Alic, PhD

Dementia

Definition

Dementia is a condition characterized by a progressive, irreversible decline in mental ability, accompanied by changes in behavior, personality, and, in the late stage, motor functions. There is commonly a loss of memory and the skills required to carry out activities of daily living. The changes are severe enough to seriously impair the person's ability to function or to interact socially and include changes due to diseases (e.g., Alzheimer's and Creutzfeldt-Jakob diseases), changes due to **stroke** (**vascular dementia**) or repeated blows to the head (dementia pugilistica, as experienced by boxers), and damage due to long-term alcohol abuse. There are over 70 different types of dementia, but **Alzheimer's disease** (AD) is considered the form that causes the most complications.

Demographics

The demographic distribution of dementia varies somewhat according to its cause. Recent research indicates that dementia in many individuals has overlapping causes, so it is not always easy to assess the true rates of occurrence of the different types. For example, Alzheimer's disease and multi-infarct dementia are found together in about 15%–20% of cases.

Alzheimer's disease

According to the Alzheimer's Association (AA), AD is the sixth-leading cause of death in the United States and the fifth-leading cause of death for persons 65 years of age or older. Data collected between 2000 and 2008 showed a decline in the death rates of most major diseases; however, the death rate for AD increased by 66% over this same time frame.

The prevalence of dementia increases rapidly with age. It affects about 1% of people from the age of 60 to 64 years and approximately doubles every five years after age 60, affecting 30% to 50% of adults by age 85. In total, AD afflicts approximately 5.4 million individuals in the United States, two-thirds of whom are women. Researchers do not know yet whether the sex ratio simply reflects the fact that women tend to live longer than men or whether female gender is itself a risk factor for AD. Some studies suggest that the risk for dementia is higher among African Americans and Hispanic Americans than it is for Caucasians. More than half of all nursing home admissions occur because of dementia. Surveys have found that dementia is the condition most feared by older adults in the United States.

Multi-infarct dementia

Multi-infarct dementia (MID), also called vascular dementia, is responsible for 15%–20% of cases of dementia (not counting cases in which it coexists with AD). Unlike AD, MID is more common in men than in women. Diabetes, high blood pressure, a history of smoking, and heart disease are all risk factors for MID. Researchers in Sweden have suggested that MID is underdiagnosed and may coexist with other dementias more frequently than is presently recognized.

Dementia with Lewy bodies

Dementia with Lewy bodies (DLB), also called by various other names such as Lewy body dementia, is now thought to be the second most common form of dementia after Alzheimer's disease. However, because researchers do not completely understand the relationship between Lewy bodies, AD, and Parkinson's disease, the demographic distribution is unclear.

Other dementias

Frontal lobe dementia (FLD), Pick's disease (also called Pick's dementia), Huntington disease, Parkinson's disease, human immunodeficiency virus (HIV) infection, alcoholism, head **trauma**, and other causes of dementia account for about 10% of all cases. In FLD and Pick's disease, women appear to be affected slightly more often than men. Dementia pugilistic, a dementia typically occurring in boxers that develops due to repeated head injury, is thought to affect at least 15% of boxers and has been increasingly found in other contact sports, such as football.

Description

The definition of dementia has become more inclusive over the past several decades. Whereas earlier descriptions of dementia emphasized memory loss, the current ***Diagnostic and Statistical Manual of Mental Disorders*** (*DSM-IV-TR*, fourth edition, text revised) of the **American Psychiatric Association** (APA) defines dementia as an overall decline in intellectual function, including difficulties with language, simple calculations, planning and judgment, and abstract reasoning, as well as loss of memory. Dementia is not caused simply by aging, although it is quite common in older people. Many researchers regard it as resulting from injuries, infections, **brain** diseases, tumors, biochemical changes within the brain, or other disorders. Most recently, researchers have found a possible connection between dementia and **attention deficit hyperactivity disorder (ADHD)**. Argentine researchers reported in 2010 that adults with symptoms of **ADHD** are more than three times more likely than other adults to develop Lewy body dementia later in life, though further research is needed.

Risk factors

Genetic factors play a role in several types of dementia, but the importance of these factors in the development of the dementia varies considerably. AD is known, for example, to have an autosomal (non–sex related) dominant pattern in most early-onset cases as well as in some late-onset cases, and to show different degrees of penetrance (frequency of expression) in late-life cases. Researchers have not yet discovered how the genes associated with dementia interact with other risk factors to produce or trigger the dementia. One nongenetic risk factor under investigation in 2011 was exposure to toxic substances in the environment.

Causes and symptoms

Causes

Dementia can be caused by as many as 80 different diseases and conditions, ranging from dietary deficiencies and metabolic disorders to head injuries and inherited diseases. Types of dementia and their causes include:

- Primary dementia. These dementias are characterized by damage to or wasting away of the brain tissue itself. They include AD, Pick's disease, and frontal lobe dementia.
- Multi-infarct dementia. Also called vascular dementia, this type is caused by blood clots in the small blood vessels of the brain. When the clots cut off the blood supply to the brain tissue, the brain cells are damaged and may die.
- Lewy body dementia. Lewy bodies are areas of injury found on damaged nerve cells in certain parts of the brain. They are associated with AD and Parkinson's disease, but researchers do not yet know whether dementia with Lewy bodies is a distinct type of dementia or a variation of AD or Parkinson's disease.
- Dementia related to alcoholism or exposure to heavy metals (e.g., arsenic, antimony, bismuth, mercury).
- Dementia related to infectious diseases. These infections may be caused by viruses (e.g., HIV, viral encephalitis), spirochetes (e.g., Lyme disease, syphilis), or prions (e.g., Creutzfeldt-Jakob disease).
- Dementia related to abnormalities in the structure of the brain. These may include a buildup of spinal fluid in the brain (hydrocephalus), tumors, or blood collecting beneath the membrane that covers the brain (subdural hematoma).
- Dementia caused by injury. These include dementia pugilistica, also called chronic traumatic encephalopathy, which results from repeated head injury, or post-traumatic dementia, which results from one severe traumatic brain injury. Symptoms may not appear until years after the injury.

Dementia may also be associated with **depression**, low levels of thyroid hormone, niacin, or vitamin (B_{12}) deficiency. Dementia related to these conditions is often reversible.

EARLY-ONSET ALZHEIMER'S DISEASE. In early-onset AD, which accounts for 2%–7% of cases of AD, the symptoms develop before age 60 years. Early-onset AD usually is caused by an inherited genetic mutation and is prevalent in persons with **Down syndrome**.

LATE-ONSET ALZHEIMER'S DISEASE. Research indicates that late-onset AD, also called sporadic AD, is a polygenic disorder; that is, its development is influenced by more than one gene. As of 2011, at least seven genes were associated with the development of AD. Finding genetic risk factors like these helps scientists better understand how AD develops and identify possible treatments to study. Specifically, the National Institute on Aging supports several major genetics research programs, including the Alzheimer's Disease Genetics Study, the Alzheimer's Disease Genetics Consortium, the Dominantly Inherited Alzheimer Network (DIAN), and the National Cell Repository for Alzheimer' Disease (NCRAD). The Alzheimer's Disease Genetics Constortium helps to collect and conduct GWAS for tens of thousands of samples from people who have late-onset AD.

MULTI-INFARCT DEMENTIA. While the chief risk factors for MID are high blood pressure (hypertension), advanced age, smoking, diabetes mellitus (diabetes), hypercholesterolemia (high cholesterol), and cardiovascular and cerebrovascular disease, there is an inherited form of MID called CADASIL, which stands for cerebral autosomal dominant arteriopathy with subcortical infarcts and leukoencephalopathy. CADASIL can cause psychiatric disturbances and severe headaches as well as dementia.

Several studies have documented a link between elevated levels of an amino acid called homocysteine in the blood and the risk of developing dementia, primarily vascular dementia. As homocysteine concentration can be modified by diet, the finding proposes the theory that at least one risk factor for dementia may be controllable.

FRONTAL LOBE DEMENTIAS. Researchers think that between 25% and 50% of cases of FLD involve genetic factors. Pick's disease appears to have a much smaller genetic component than FLD. It is not yet known what other risk factors combine with inherited traits to influence the development of frontal lobe dementias.

FAMILIAL BRITISH DEMENTIA. Familial British dementia (FBD) is a rare autosomal dominant disorder that was first reported in the 1940s in a large British family extending over nine generations. FBD resembles AD in that the individual develops a progressive dementia related to amyloid deposits in the brain. In 1999, a mutated gene that produces the amyloid responsible for FBD was discovered on human chromosome. It was reported in 2009 that this mutation results in the production of an amyloidogenic fragment called amyloid-Bri (ABri). Studies of this mutation are yielding further clues as to the development of both FBD and AD.

CREUTZFELDT-JAKOB DISEASE. Although Creutzfeldt-Jakob disease (CJD) is caused by the random mutations in prion proteins, researchers think that 5%–15% of cases may have a genetic component, where the mutations are inherited. The genetic (hereditary) component of its cause is called familial CJD, or fCJD.

Symptoms

Dementia is marked by a gradual impoverishment of thought and other mental activities, regardless of its cause. Losses eventually affect virtually every aspect of mental functioning. Specific symptoms may vary depending on the type of dementia.

ALZHEIMER'S DISEASE. Dementia related to AD often progresses slowly; it may be accompanied by irritability, wide mood swings, and personality changes in the early stage. In second-stage AD, the individual typically gets lost easily, is completely disoriented with regard to time and space, and may become angry, uncooperative, or aggressive. In final-stage AD, the individual is completely bedridden, has lost control over bowel and bladder functions, and may be unable to swallow or eat. The risk of **seizures** increases as the individual progresses from early to end-stage AD. Death usually results from an infection or malnutrition.

MULTI-INFARCT DEMENTIA. In MID, symptoms are more likely to occur after age 70. In the early stages, the individual retains his or her personality more fully than an individual with AD. Another distinctive feature of this type of dementia is that it often progresses in a stepwise fashion; that is, the individual shows rapid changes in functioning but then remains at a plateau for a while rather than showing a continuous decline. The symptoms of MID may also have a "patchy" quality; that is, some of the individual's mental functions may be severely affected while others remain relatively undamaged. Specific symptoms of MID include exaggerated reflexes, an abnormal gait (manner of walking), loss of bladder or bowel control, and inappropriate laughing or crying.

DEMENTIA WITH LEWY BODIES. This type of dementia may combine some features of AD, such as severe memory loss and confusion, with certain symptoms associated with Parkinson's disease, such as stiff muscles, a shuffling gait, and trembling or shaking of the hands. Visual hallucinations may be one of the first symptoms of dementia with Lewy bodies.

FRONTAL LOBE DEMENTIAS. The frontal lobe dementias are gradual in onset. Pick's disease is most likely to develop in persons between the ages of 40 and

60, while FLD typically begins before age 65. The first symptoms of FLD often include socially inappropriate behavior (e.g., rude remarks, sexual gestures, lack of personal hygiene). Individuals often are obsessed with eating and may put non-food items in their mouths, as well as make frequent sucking or smacking noises. In the later stages of FLD or Pick's disease, the individual may develop muscle weakness, twitching, and **delusions** or hallucinations.

CREUTZFELDT-JAKOB DISEASE. The dementia associated with CJD occurs most often in persons between ages 40 and 60. It is typically preceded by a period of several weeks in which the individual complains of unusual tiredness, anxiety, loss of appetite, or difficulty concentrating. The first sign that a person may have CJD is rapidly advancing dementia, which leads to memory loss, hallucinations, and personality changes. These symptoms are followed with irregular movements of the body, seizures, rigid posture, speech problems, and balance/coordination dysfunction. This type of dementia usually progresses much more rapidly than other dementias, usually over a span of a few months.

Diagnosis

In some cases, a patient's primary physician may be able to diagnose dementia; in many instances, however, the patient will be referred to a neurologist or a specialist in geriatric medicine. The differential **diagnosis** of dementia is complicated because of the number of possible causes, because more than one cause may be present, and because dementia can coexist with other conditions such as depression and **delirium**. Delirium is a temporary disturbance of consciousness marked by confusion, restlessness, inability to focus attention, hallucinations, or delusions. In elderly people, delirium is frequently a side effect of surgery, medications, infectious illnesses, or dehydration. Delirium can be distinguished from dementia by the fact that delirium usually comes on suddenly (in a few hours or days) and may vary in severity—it is often worse at night. Dementia develops much more slowly, over a period of months or years, and the patient's symptoms are relatively stable. It is possible for a person to have delirium and dementia at the same time.

Another significant diagnostic distinction in elderly patients is the distinction between dementia and age-associated memory impairment (AAMI). Older people with AAMI have a mild degree of memory loss; they do not learn new information as quickly as younger people, and they may take longer to recall a certain fact or to balance their checkbook, but they do not have the degree of memory impairment that characterizes dementia and do not get progressively worse. Other problems that may be mistakenly labeled as dementia include delirium, **psychosis**, depression, and the side effects of various medications.

The *DSM-IV-TR* specifies that certain criteria must be met for an individual to be diagnosed with dementia. One criterion is significant weakening of the individual's memory with regard to learning new information as well as recalling previously learned information. In addition, the individual must be found to have one or more of the following disturbances:

- Loss of language function (aphasia). People with dementia may use vague words like "it" or "thing," often because they cannot recall the exact name of an object. They also may echo what other people say, or repeat a word or phrase over and over. People in the later stages of dementia may stop speaking completely.
- Loss of the ability to perform intentional movements even though the person is not paralyzed, has not lost their sense of touch, and knows what they are trying to do (apraxia). For example, an individual with apraxia may stop brushing their teeth or have trouble tying their shoelaces.
- Loss of the ability to recognize objects even though the person's sight and sense of touch are normal (agnosia). People with severe agnosia may fail to recognize family members or their own face reflected in a mirror.
- Problems with abstract thinking and complex behavior. This criterion refers to the loss of the ability to make plans, carry out the steps of a task in the proper order, make appropriate decisions, evaluate situations, show good judgment, etc. For example, a person with dementia might light a stove burner under a saucepan before putting food or water in the pan or be unable to record checks and balance his or her checkbook.

The *DSM-IV-TR* also specifies that these disturbances must be severe enough to cause problems in the person's daily life, and these disturbances they must represent a decline from a previously higher level of functioning.

A new edition of the *DSM* (*DSM-5*) is expected to publish in May 2013. Proposed changes for the fifth edition include replacing the diagnosis of dementia (and all related forms) with the diagnosis of major neurocognitive disorder, which will be further broken down by various causes (e.g., major neurocognitive disorder associated with Alzheimer's disease, vascular disease, etc.). A condition is considered to be a major cognitive disorder if a person exhibits great cognitive deficits in at least one (but typically in two or more) of the following areas:

- complex attention
- executive ability
- learning and memory
- language
- visual construction and perception
- social cognition

Examination

PATIENT HISTORY. The doctor will begin by taking a full history, including the patient's occupation and educational level as well as medical history. The occupational and educational history allows the examiner to make a more accurate assessment of the extent of the patient's memory loss and other evidence of intellectual decline. In some cases, the occupational history may indicate exposure to heavy metals or other toxins. A complete medical history allows the doctor to assess possibilities such as delirium, depression, alcohol-related dementia, dementia related to head injury, or dementia caused by infection. It is particularly important for the doctor to have a list of all the patient's medications, including over-the-counter preparations, because of the possibility that the patient's symptoms are related to side effects.

MENTAL STATUS EXAMINATION. A **mental status examination** (MSE) evaluates the patient's ability to communicate, follow instructions, recall information, and perform simple tasks involving movement and coordination, as well as his or her emotional state and general sense of space and time. The MSE includes the doctor's informal evaluation of the patient's appearance, vocal tone, facial expressions, posture, and gait, as well as formal questions or instructions. A common form that has been used since 1975 is the Folstein Mini-Mental Status Examination, or MMSE. Questions that are relevant to diagnosing dementia include asking the patient to count backward from 100 by 7s, to make change, to name the current president, to repeat a short phrase after the examiner, to draw a clock face or geometric figure, and to follow a set of instructions involving movement (e.g., throwing a ball or folding paper). The examiner may test the patient's abstract reasoning ability by asking him or her to explain a familiar proverb or may test the patient's judgment by asking about a problem with a common-sense solution, such as what a person should do when a prescription runs out.

NEUROLOGICAL EXAMINATION. A neurological examination includes an evaluation of the patient's cranial nerves and reflexes. The cranial nerves govern the ability to speak as well as to see, hear, taste, and smell. The patient may be asked to stick out the tongue, follow the examiner's finger with the eyes, raise the eyebrows, etc. The patient is also asked to perform certain actions that test coordination and spatial orientation, such as touching the nose with the eyes closed. The doctor will usually touch or tap certain areas of the body, such as the knee or the sole of the foot, to test the patient's reflexes. Failure to respond to the touch or tap may indicate damage to certain parts of the brain.

Tests

LABORATORY TESTS. Blood and urine samples are collected in order to rule out such conditions as thyroid deficiency, niacin (vitamin B_{12}) deficiency, heavy metal poisoning, liver disease, HIV infection, syphilis, anemia, medication reactions, or kidney failure. A lumbar puncture (spinal tap) may be done to rule out neurosyphilis.

DIAGNOSTIC IMAGING. The patient may be given a CT (**computed tomography**) scan or MRI (**magnetic resonance imaging**) scan to detect evidence of strokes, disintegration of the brain tissue in certain areas, blood clots or tumors, a buildup of spinal fluid, or bleeding into the brain tissue. **PET** (**positron emission tomography**) or SPECT (**single photon emission computed tomography**) imaging is not used routinely to diagnose dementia, but may be used to rule out AD or frontal lobe degeneration if a patient's CT or MRI scan is inconclusive.

Treatment

Traditional

Traditional methods for treating dementia are proven to be effective at slowing some of the symptoms associated with dementia. In some cases, cognitive function can be improved but not corrected. Some types of dementia respond better to treatment than others. In all cases, proper care and support for the individual afflicted with dementia is helpful, whether it is provided at home or in an institution.

REVERSIBLE AND RESPONSIVE DEMENTIAS. Some types of dementia are reversible, and a few types respond to specific treatments related to their causes. Dementia related to dietary deficiencies or metabolic disorders is treated with the appropriate vitamins or thyroid medication. Dementia related to HIV infection often responds well to zidovudine (Retrovir), a drug given to prevent the AIDS (acquired immune deficiency syndrome) virus from replicating. MID is usually treated by controlling the patient's blood pressure and/or diabetes; while treatments for these disorders cannot undo damage already caused to brain tissue, they can slow the progress of the dementia. Patients with alcohol-related dementia often improve over the long term if they are able to stop drinking. Dementias related to head injuries, hydrocephalus, and tumors are treated by surgery.

It is important to evaluate and treat elderly patients for depression, because the symptoms of depression in older people often mimic dementia. This condition is sometimes called pseudodementia. In addition, patients with both depression and dementia often show some improvement in intellectual functioning when the depression is treated.

IRREVERSIBLE DEMENTIAS. There are no medications or surgical techniques that can cure AD, the frontal lobe dementias, multi-infarct dementia, or dementia with Lewy bodies. There are also no treatments that reverse or stop the progression of these dementias.

Early **intervention** may help to minimize complications and allow the patient to compensate for the alterations in functioning, resulting in an improved quality of life. It may also allow the patient and family to plan for the future and to identify resources.

BEHAVIORAL TREATMENT. Behavioral approaches may be used to reduce the frequency or severity of problem behaviors such as aggression or socially inappropriate conduct. Problem behavior may be a reaction to frustration or over-stimulation. Understanding and modifying the situations that trigger problem behaviors can be effective; strategies may include breaking down complex tasks such as dressing or feeding into simpler steps, or reducing the amount of activity in the environment to avoid confusion and agitation. Pleasurable activities such as crafts, games, and music can provide therapeutic stimulation and improve mood.

HOME MODIFICATION. Modifying the environment can increase safety and comfort while decreasing agitation. Home modifications for safety include removal or lock-up of hazards such as sharp knives, dangerous chemicals, and tools. Childproof latches may be used to limit access as well. Bed rails and bathroom safety rails can be important safety measures. Confusion may be reduced with the use of simpler decorative schemes and the presence of familiar objects. Covering or disguising doors may reduce the tendency to wander. Positioning the bed in view of the bathroom can decrease incontinence.

LONG-TERM CARE. Long-term institutional care may be required for persons with dementia, as profound cognitive losses often precede death by a number of years. Early planning for the financial burden of nursing home care is critical. Useful information about financial planning for long-term care is available through the Alzheimer's Association.

Family members or others caring for a person with dementia are often subject to extreme **stress** and may develop feelings of anger, resentment, guilt, and hopelessness, in addition to the sorrow they feel for their loved one and for themselves. Depression is an extremely common consequence of being a full-time caregiver for a person with dementia. **Support groups** can be an important way to deal with the stress of caregiving. Contact numbers are available from the Alzheimer's Association; they may also be available through a local social service agency.

The primary goals of treatment for progressive dementias are to preserve as much functioning and independence as possible and to maintain quality of life as long as possible. Caring for a person with dementia can be difficult and complex. The patient must cope with functional and cognitive limitations, while family members or other caregivers must assume increasing responsibility for the person's physical needs. The patient and family should be educated early on in the disease progression to help them anticipate and plan for inevitable changes.

Drugs

Periodically, new drugs are studied for the treatment of dementia. The only drugs approved by the U.S. Food and Drug Administration (FDA) as of 2011 for the symptomatic treatment of AD were **tacrine** (Cognex), **donepezil** (Aricept), **rivastigmine** (Exelon), **galantamine** (Lycoremine, Nivalin, Razadyne, Razadyne ER, Reminyl), and **memantine** (Namenda). The first four are called cholinesterase inhibitors (which prevents the breakdown of acetylcholine, a chemical in the brain that is thought to help with memory and thinking), while the last one is classified as an uncompetitive low-to-moderate affinity N-methyl-D-aspartate (NMDA) receptor antagonist. The cholinesterase inhibitor drugs may provide temporary improvement in cognitive functioning for a fairly large percentage of patients with mild-to-moderate AD. Memantine is prescribed for moderate-to-severe AD only. Doctors sometimes prescribe both types of drugs for their patients. However, drug therapy can be complicated by forgetfulness, especially if the drug must be taken several times a day. New treatments for AD continue to be researched through **clinical trials**; as of August 2011, there were more than 100 active clinical trials for AD and other dementias.

Psychotic symptoms, including **paranoia**, delusions, and hallucinations, may be treated with antipsychotic drugs such as **haloperidol**, **chlorpromazine**, **risperidone**, and **clozapine**. Side effects of these drugs can be

KEY TERMS

Agnosia—Loss of the ability to recognize objects by use of the physical senses.

Amyloid—A waxy translucent substance, composed mostly of protein, that forms plaques (abnormal deposits) in the brain.

Aphasia—Loss of previously acquired ability to speak, or to understand written or spoken language.

Apraxia—Impairment of the ability to make purposeful movements, but not paralysis or loss of sensation.

Creutzfeldt-Jakob disease—A degenerative disease of the central nervous system caused by a prion, or "slow virus."

Delirium—A disturbance of consciousness marked by confusion, difficulty paying attention, delusions, hallucinations, or restlessness. It can be distinguished from dementia by its relatively sudden onset and variation in the severity of the symptoms.

Dementia pugilistica—A delayed-onset form of dementia caused by repeated head injury; often occurs in boxers.

Hematoma—An accumulation of blood, often clotted, in a body tissue or organ, usually caused by a break or tear in a blood vessel.

Huntington disease—A midlife-onset inherited disorder characterized by progressive dementia and loss of control over voluntary movements. It is sometimes called Huntington's chorea.

Hydrocephalus—The excess accumulation of cerebrospinal fluid around the brain, often causing enlargement of the head.

Lewy bodies—Areas of injury found on damaged nerve cells in certain parts of the brain associated with dementia.

Multi-infarct dementia—Dementia caused by damage to brain tissue resulting from a series of blood clots or clogs in the blood vessels. It is also called vascular dementia.

Parkinson's disease—A disease of the nervous system most common in people over 60, characterized by a shuffling gait, trembling of the fingers and hands, and muscle stiffness. It may be related in some way to Lewy body dementia.

Pick's disease—A rare type of primary dementia that affects the frontal lobes of the brain. It is characterized by a progressive loss of social skills, language, and memory, leading to personality changes and sometimes loss of moral judgment.

Pseudodementia—A term for a depression with symptoms resembling those of dementia. The term dementia of depression is now preferred.

significant. **Antianxiety drugs** such as **diazepam** (Valium) may improve behavioral symptoms, especially agitation and anxiety, although **buspirone** (BuSpar) has fewer side effects. The anticonvulsant **carbamazepine** (Tegretol) is sometimes prescribed for agitation. Depression is treated with **antidepressants**, usually beginning with **selective serotonin reuptake inhibitors (SSRIs)** such as **fluoxetine** (Prozac) or **paroxetine** (Paxil). In general, medications are administered cautiously in the lowest possible effective doses to individuals with dementia in order to minimize side effects. Supervision of taking medications is generally required.

Research is ongoing on how the brain and AD are intertwined and how studies of the brain are leading to advances in the diagnosis and treatment of AD and other dementias. Swiss researchers reported in 2011 in the *Journal of Neuroscience* that new technologies, such as digital holographic microscopy (DHM), allow researchers to more thoroughly observe neuron activity in the brain, allowing for better testing of the effects of AD drugs.

Alternative therapies

No alternative therapies have been found to conclusively prevent, reverse, or slow dementias except for those caused by nutrient deficiencies. However, some alternative therapies may help treat the specific symptoms associated with dementia. **Aromatherapy** and **music therapy** have shown promise for relieving symptoms of agitation and promoting calm in patients with dementia. **Sage** and **ginkgo biloba** have also shown some effectiveness in clinical trials with treating symptoms of AD and dementia, respectively. Though past studies touted the success of ginkgo biloba, new research released in 2009 found the herb to make little difference in the cognitive health of participants of a large-scale study. Further research is needed to test the efficacy of herbal and nutritional supplements in treating symptoms of dementia.

Prognosis

The prognosis for reversible dementia related to nutritional or thyroid problems is usually good once the

QUESTIONS TO ASK YOUR DOCTOR

- What type of dementia does my loved one have?
- How far advanced is the dementia?
- What, if anything, can be done to slow the dementia or treat accompanying symptoms?
- How long can I expect my loved one to be able to remain at home?
- What can I do to make my home safe for my loved one?
- Can you refer me to a support group for caregivers of people with dementia?
- Do you know of any adult daycare programs available for people with dementia?

cause has been identified and treated. The prognoses for dementias related to alcoholism or HIV infection depend on the patient's age and the severity of the underlying disorder.

For those with irreversible progressive dementia, the outlook often includes slow deterioration in mental and physical capacities ending in death. Eventually, help is often required when swallowing, walking, and even sitting become difficult. Aid can consist of preparing special **diets** that can be more easily consumed and making surroundings safe in case of falls. Lift assists in areas such as the bathroom can also be useful. On average, people with AD live eight years past their diagnosis, with a range from 1–20 years. Patients with frontal lobe dementia or Pick's disease live on average between five and ten years after diagnosis. The course of Creutzfeldt-Jakob disease is much more rapid, with patients living between 5 and 12 months after diagnosis. Vascular dementia is usually progressive, with death resulting from stroke, infection, or heart disease.

Prevention

Dementia caused by repeated blows to the head can be prevented by avoiding sports where head trauma is common. Alcohol abuse–related dementia can be prevented by avoiding excessive alcohol consumption or minimized by receiving early treatment for alcoholism. Good **nutrition** can prevent nutrient-deficiency dementia. Unfortunately, most forms of dementia cannot be prevented.

Resources

BOOKS

American Psychiatric Association. *Diagnostic and Statistical Manual of Mental Disorders*. 4th ed., text rev. Washington, DC: American Psychiatric Association, 2000.

Dziegielewski, Sophia F. *DSM-IV-TR in Action*. Hoboken, NJ: John Wiley & Sons, 2010.

Hardman, Lizabeth. *Dementia*. Detroit: Lucent, 2009.

Mendelson, Scott D. *Beyond Alzheimer's: How to Avoid the Modern Epidemic of Dementia*. Lanham, MD: M. Evans, 2009.

Miller, Bruce, and Bradley F. Boeve, editors. *The Behavioral Neurology of Dementia*. Cambridge, UK: Cambridge University Press, 2009.

Schulte-Markwort, Michael, Kathrin Marutt, and Peter Riedesser, eds. *Cross-walks ICD-10-DSM IV-TR: A Synopsis of Classifications of Mental Disorders*. Cambridge, MA: Hogrefe & Huber, 2003.

Steele, Cynthia. *Dementia Care*. New York: McGraw-Hill Medical, 2010.

Stoppe, Gabriela, ed. *Competence Assessment in Dementia*. Germany: Springer, 2008.

PERIODICALS

Jourdain, Pascal, et al. "Determination of Transmembrane Water Fluxes in Neurons Elicited by Glutamate Ionotropic Receptors and by the Cotransporters KCC2 and NKCC1: A Digital Holographic Microscopy Study." *The Journal of Neuroscience* 31, no. 33 (2011): 11846–54.

Snitz, Beth E., et al. "Ginkgo Biloba for Preventing Cognitive Decline in Older Adults: A Randomized Trial." *Journal of the American Medical Association* 302, no. 24 (2009): 2663–70. http://dx.doi.org/10.1001/jama.2009.1913 (accessed November 1, 2011).

WEBSITES

Alzheimer's Association. "Alzheimer's Facts and Figures." 2011. http://www.alz.org/alzheimers_disease_facts_and_figures.asp (accessed August 24, 2011).

———. "Medications for Memory Loss." November 16, 2011. http://www.alz.org/alzheimers_disease_standard_prescriptions.asp (accessed December 12, 2011).

Delacourte, André. "Familial British dementia." Alzheimer Europe. October 9, 2009. http://www.alzheimer-europe.org/Dementia/Other-forms-of-dementia/Neuro-Degenerative-Diseases/Familial-British-dementia (accessed August 23, 2011).

Mayo Clinic staff. "Dementia." MayoClinic.com. April 16, 2011. http://www.mayoclinic.com/health/dementia/DS01131 (accessed August 26, 2011).

MedlinePlus. "Dementia." U.S. National Library of Medicine, National Institutes of Health. http://www.nlm.nih.gov/medlineplus/dementia.html (accessed August 26, 2011).

U.S. National Institute of Aging. "Alzheimer's Disease Genetics Fact Sheet." U.S. National Institutes of Health. June 2011. http://www.nia.nih.gov/Alzheimers/Publications/geneticsfs.htm (accessed August 23, 2011).

ORGANIZATIONS

Alzheimer Europe, 145, route de Thionville, LuxembourgL-2611, 35229 79 70, Fax: 35229 79 72, info@alzheimer-europe.org, http://www.alzheimer-europe.org.

Alzheimer's Association, 225 North Michigan Avenue, Floor 17, Chicago, IL, 10118, (313) 335-8700, Fax: (313) 699-1246, info@alz.org, http://www.alz.org.

American Geriatrics Society, 40 Fulton St., 18th Fl., New York, NY, 10038, (212) 308-1414, Fax: (212) 832-8646, info@americangeriatrics.org, http://www.americangeriatrics.org.

Center for the Study of Traumatic Encephalopathy, (617) 638-6143, cbaugh@bu.edu, http://www.bu.edu/cste.

National Institute on Aging, Building 31, Room 5C27, 31 Center Drive, MSC 2292, Bethesda, MD, 20892, (301) 496-1752, Fax: (301) 496-1072, (800) 222-4225, http://www.nia.nih.gov.

National Institute of Mental Health, 6001 Executive Boulevard, Room 8184, MSC 9663, Bethesda, MD, 20892-9663, (301) 443-4513, Fax: (301) 443-4279, (866) 615-6464, nimhinfo@nih.gov, http://www.nimh.nih.gov.

National Institute of Neurological Disorders and Stroke, PO Box 5801, Bethesda, MD, 20824, (301) 496-5751, (800) 352-9424, http://www.ninds.nih.gov.

Deanna M. Swartout-Corbeil, RN
Tish Davidson, AM
William Atkins, BB, BS, MBA

Dementia of the Alzheimer's type *see* **Alzheimer's disease**

Denial

Definition

Denial is refusal to acknowledge the existence or severity of unpleasant external realities or internal thoughts and feelings.

Description

Theory of denial

In psychology, denial is a concept originating with the psychodynamic theories of Sigmund Freud (1856-1939), founder of the discipline of **psychoanalysis**. According to Freud, three mental dynamics, or motivating forces, influence human behavior: the id, ego, and superego. The id consists of basic survival instincts and what Freud believed to be the two dominant human drives: sex and aggression. If the id were the only influence on behavior, humans would exclusively seek to increase pleasure, decrease pain, and achieve immediate gratification of desires. The ego consists of logical and rational thinking. It enables humans to analyze the realistic risks and benefits of a situation, to tolerate some pain for future profit, and to consider alternatives to the impulse-driven behavior of the id. The superego consists of moralistic standards and forms the basis of the conscience. Although the superego is essential to a sense of right and wrong, it can also include extreme, unrealistic ideas about what one should and should not do.

These three forces all have different goals (id, pleasure; ego, reality; superego, morality) and continually strive for dominance, resulting in internal conflict. This conflict produces anxiety. The ego, which functions as a mediator between the two extremes of the id and the superego, attempts to reduce this anxiety by using defense mechanisms. Defense mechanisms are indirect ways of dealing or coping with anxiety, such as explaining problems away or blaming others for problems. Denial is one of many defense mechanisms. It entails ignoring or refusing to believe an unpleasant reality. Defense mechanisms protect one's psychological well-being in traumatic situations, or in any situation that produces anxiety or conflict. However, they do not resolve the anxiety-producing situation and, if overused, can lead to psychological disorders. Although Freud's model of the id, ego, and superego is not emphasized by most psychologists today, defense mechanisms are still regarded as potentially maladaptive behavioral patterns that may lead to psychological disorders.

Examples of denial

Death is a common occasion for denial. When someone learns of the sudden, unexpected death of a loved one, at first he or she may not be able to accept the reality of this loss. The initial denial protects that person from the emotional shock and intense **grief** that often accompanies news of death. Chronic or terminal illnesses also encourage denial. People with such illnesses may think, "It's not so bad; I'll get over it," and refuse to make any lifestyle changes.

Denial can also apply to internal thoughts and feelings. For instance, some children are taught that anger is wrong in any situation. As adults, if these individuals experience feelings of anger, they are likely to deny their feelings to others. Cultural standards and expectations can encourage denial of subjective experience. Men who belong to cultures with extreme notions of masculinity may view fear as a sign of weakness and deny internal feelings of fear. Some cultures are thought to discourage the acknowledgment of mental illness, resulting in individuals denying their psychological symptoms and often developing physical symptoms instead.

Certain **personality disorders** tend to be characterized by denial more than others. For example, those with **narcissistic personality disorder** deny information that suggests they are not perfect. Antisocial behavior is characterized by denial of the harm done to others (such as with sexual offenders or substance abusers).

Denial can also be exhibited on a large scale—among groups, cultures, or even nations. Lucy Bregman gives an example of national denial of imminent mortality in the 1950s: school children participated in drills where they hid under desks in preparation for atomic attacks. Another example of large-scale denial is the recent assertion by some that the World War II Holocaust never occurred.

TREATMENT OF DENIAL. Denial is treated differently in different types of therapy. In psychoanalytic therapy, denial is regarded as an obstacle to progress that must eventually be confronted and interpreted. Timing is important, however. Psychoanalytic therapists wait until clients appear emotionally ready or have some degree of insight into their problems before confronting them. In the humanistic and existential therapies, denial is considered the framework by which clients understand their world. Not directly confronting denial, therapists assist clients in exploring their world view and considering alternative ways of being. In cognitive-behavioral therapies, denial is not regarded as an important phenomenon. Rather, denial would suggest that an individual has not learned the appropriate behaviors to cope with a stressful situation. Therapists assist individuals in examining their current thoughts and behaviors and devising strategic ways to make changes.

Traditional treatment programs for **substance abuse** and other addictions view denial as a central theme. Such programs teach that in order to overcome addiction, one must admit to being an alcoholic or addict. Those who are unable to accept such labels are informed they are in denial. Even when the labels are accepted, individuals are still considered to be in denial if they do not acknowledge the severity of their addictions. From this perspective, progress cannot be made until individuals recognize the extent of their denial and work toward acceptance. There is much controversy in the field of addictions regarding the role of denial and how it should be addressed. Traditional programs such as these stress direct confrontation. Other professionals do not insist on the acceptance of labels. They believe that denial should be worked through more subtly, empathically focusing on the personal reasons surrounding denial and seeking to strengthen the desire to change. This subtle form of addressing denial is known as motivational enhancement therapy, and can be used with other types of disorders as well.

KEY TERMS

Antisocial behavior—Behavior characterized by high levels of anger, aggression, manipulation, or violence.

Cognitive-behavioral therapies—An approach to psychotherapy that emphasizes the correction of distorted thinking patterns and changing one's behaviors accordingly.

Defense mechanisms—Indirect strategies used to reduce anxiety rather than directly facing the issues causing the anxiety.

Dependent personality disorder—Personality disorder characterized by a constant, unhealthy need to be liked and appreciated by others at all costs.

Ego—In Freudian psychology, the conscious, rational part of the mind that experiences and reacts to the outside world.

Humanistic and existential therapies—Therapies that focus on achieving one's full potential, guided by subjective experience.

Id—A construct in Freudian psychodynamic theory that represents the irrational, self-centered aspects of human thought.

Motivational enhancement therapy—Therapy that focuses on increasing motivation for change by empathically comparing and contrasting the consequences and benefits of changing or not changing.

Narcissistic personality disorder—Personality characterized by continually exaggerating one's own positive qualities and refusing to recognize personal defects or flaws.

Psychoanalytic therapy—Therapy based on the psychodynamic theory of Sigmund Freud.

Psychodynamic—Referring to the motivational forces, unconscious as well as conscious, that form human attitudes and behavior.

Superego—According to Freud, the part of the mind that represents traditional parental and societal values. The superego is the source of guilt feelings.

Resources

BOOKS

Bregman, Lucy. *Beyond Silence and Denial: Death and Dying Reconsidered.* Louisville, Kentucky: Westminster John Knox Press, 1999.

Millon, Theodore, et al. *Personality Disorders in Modern Life.* 2nd ed. New York: John Wiley and Sons, 2004.

PERIODICALS

Cramer, Phebe, and Melissa A. Brilliant. "Defense Use and Defense Understanding in Children." *Journal of Personality* 69, no. 2 (2001): 291–321.

Parker, Gordon, Gemma Gladstone, and Kuan Tsee Chee. "Depression in the Planet's Largest Ethnic Group: The Chinese." *American Journal Of Psychiatry* 158, no. 6 (June 2001): 857–864.

Schneider, Sandra L., and Robert C. Wright. "The FoSOD: A Measurement Tool for Reconceptualizing the Role of Denial in Child Molesters." *Journal of Interpersonal Violence* 16, no. 6 (2001): 545–564.

ORGANIZATIONS

American Psychoanalytic Association, 309 East 49th Street, New York, NY, 10017-1601, (212) 752-0450, Fax: (212) 593-0571, info@apsa.org, http://www.apsa.org.

Sandra L. Friedrich, MA

Depacon *see* **Divalproex sodium**

Depakene *see* **Divalproex sodium; Valproic acid**

Depakote *see* **Divalproex sodium**

Dependent personality disorder

Definition

Dependent personality disorder (DPD) is characterized by an excessive need to be taken care of or to depend upon others. Persons with this disorder are typically submissive and display clinging behavior toward those from whom they fear separation.

Dependent personality disorder is one of several **personality disorders** listed in the standard reference guide for mental disorders, the ***Diagnostic and Statistical Manual of Mental Disorders,*** the fourth edition, text revision (*DSM-IV-TR*). Changes for the fifth edition of the *DSM* (*DSM-5*, 2013) propose that DPD be represented and diagnosed by a combination of core impairment in personality functioning and specific pathological personality traits, rather than as a specific type.

Demographics

DPD is rarely, if ever, diagnosed in children or adolescents because of their inherent dependence on others resulting from their age and developmental limitations.

DPD is one of the most frequently diagnosed personality disorders. It occurs equally in men and women, and usually appears in early- to middle-age adulthood.

Description

Persons with DPD are docile, passive, and nonassertive. They exert a great deal of energy to please others, are self-sacrificing, and constantly attempt to elicit the approval of others. They are reluctant to express disagreement with others and are often willing to go to abnormal lengths to win the approval of those on whom they rely. They are readily influenced and can be taken advantage of easily. This **compliance** and reliance upon others leads to a subtle message that someone should assume responsibility for significant areas of the patient's life. This is often displayed as helplessness, even for completion of seemingly simple tasks.

Patients with DPD have a low level of confidence in their own intelligence and abilities. They often have difficulty making decisions and undertaking projects on their own. They are prone to be pessimistic and self-doubting, and to belittle their own accomplishments. They shy away from responsibility in occupational settings.

Affected individuals are uneasy being alone and are preoccupied with the fear of being abandoned or rejected by others. Their moods are characterized by frequent bouts of anxiety or fearfulness; generally, their demeanor is sad. Their style of thinking is naïve and uncritical, and lacks discretion.

Causes and symptoms

Causes

It is commonly thought that the development of dependency in people with dependent personality disorder is a result of over-involvement and intrusive behavior by their primary caretakers. Caretakers may foster dependence in the child to meet their own dependency needs and may reward extreme loyalty but reject attempts the child makes towards independence. Families of those with DPD often do not express their emotions, are controlling, and demonstrate poorly defined relational roles within the family unit.

Individuals with DPD often have been socially humiliated by others in their developmental years. They may carry significant doubts about their abilities to perform tasks, to take on new responsibilities, and generally to function independently of others. This reinforces their suspicions that they are incapable of living autonomously. In response to these feelings, they portray helplessness in order to elicit caregiving behavior from some people in their lives.

Symptoms

The *DSM-IV-TR* specifies eight diagnostic criteria for DPD. Individuals with this disorder:

- Have difficulty making common decisions. They typically need an excessive amount of advice and reassurance before they can make even simple decisions, such as the clothing to wear on a given day.
- Need others to assume responsibility for them. Because they view themselves as incapable of being autonomous, they withdraw from adult responsibilities by acting passive and helpless. They allow others to take the initiative for many areas of their life. Adults with this disorder typically depend on a parent or spouse to make major decisions for them, such as where to work or live, or with whom to be friends.
- Have difficulty expressing disagreement with others. Disagreeing with others is often viewed as too risky. It might sever the support or approval of those they upon whom they depend. They are often overly agreeable because they fear alienating other people.
- Have difficulty initiating or doing things on their own. They lack self-confidence and believe they need help to begin or sustain tasks. They often present themselves as inept and unable to understand or accomplish the task at hand.
- Go to excessive lengths to obtain support or nurturing from others. They may even volunteer to do unpleasant tasks if they believe that doing so will evoke a positive response from others. They may subject themselves to great personal sacrifice or tolerate physical, verbal, or sexual abuse in their quest to get what they believe they need from others.
- Feel helpless when alone. Because they feel incapable of caring for themselves, they experience significant anxiety when alone. To avoid being alone, they may spend time with people with whom they have little interest.
- Quickly seek a new relationship when a previous one ends. When a marriage, dating, or other close relationship ends, there is typically an urgency to find a new relationship that will provide the support of the former relationship.
- Are preoccupied with fears of being left to take care of themselves. Their greatest fear is to be left alone and to be responsible for themselves. Even as adults, their dependence upon others may appear childlike.

Diagnosis

Age and cultural factors should be considered in diagnosing DPD. Certain cultural norms suggest a submissive, polite, or dependent posture in relating to the opposite sex or authority figures. DPD should only be diagnosed when it meets the specific criteria and is clearly outside one's cultural norms.

The **diagnosis** of DPD is based on a clinical interview to assess symptomatic behavior. Other assessment tools helpful in confirming the diagnosis include:

- The Dependent Personality Questionnaire
- Minnesota Multiphasic Personality Inventory (MMPI-2)
- Millon Clinical Multi-axial Inventory (MCMI-II)
- Rorschach Psychodiagnostic Test
- Thematic Apperception Test (TAT)

For a person to be diagnosed with DPD, at least five of the eight symptoms described must be the present, and these symptoms must begin by early adulthood and be evident in a variety of contexts.

The diagnosis of dependent personality disorder must be distinguished from **borderline personality disorder**, since there are common characteristics. Borderline personality disorder is characterized by fear of abandonment, as well, but with feelings of emptiness and rage. In contrast, the dependent personality responds to this fear of abandonment with submissiveness and searches for a replacement relationship to maintain dependency.

Likewise, persons with **histrionic personality disorder** have a strong need for reassurance and approval and may appear childlike in their clinging behavior. Histrionics are characterized by a gregarious demeanor and make active demands for attention, while dependents respond with docile and self-deprecating behavior.

Avoidant personality disorder can also be confused with DPD. Both are characterized by feelings of inadequacy, oversensitivity to criticism, and a frequent need for assurance. However, these patients typically have such an intense fear of rejection that they instinctively withdraw until they are certain of acceptance. Dependents, in contrast, actually seek out contact with others because they need the approval of others.

Treatment

The general goal of treatment is to increase the individual's sense of autonomy and ability to function independently.

Psychodynamically oriented therapies

A long-term approach to psychodynamic treatment can be successful, but may lead to heightened dependencies and difficult separation in the therapeutic relationship over time. The preferred approach is a time-limited treatment plan consisting of a predetermined number of sessions. This has been proved to facilitate the exploration process of dependency issues more effectively than long-term therapy in most patients.

Cognitive-behavioral therapy

Cognitive-behavioral approaches attempt to increase the affected person's ability to act independently of others, improve their self-esteem, and enhance the quality of their interpersonal relationships. Often, patients play an active role in setting goals. Methods often used in **cognitive-behavioral therapy** (CBT) include assertiveness and **social skills training** to help reduce reliance on others, including the therapist.

Interpersonal therapy

Treatment using an interpersonal approach can be useful because the individual is usually receptive to treatment and seeks help with interpersonal relationships. The therapist can help the patient explore their long-standing patterns of interacting with others, and understand how these have contributed to dependency issues. The goal is to show the patient the high price they pay for this dependency, and to help them develop healthier alternatives. **Assertiveness training** and learning to identify feelings is often used to heighten improve interpersonal behavior.

Group therapy

When a person is highly motivated to see growth, a more interactive therapeutic group can be successful in helping to explore passive-dependent behavior. If the individual is socially reluctant or impaired in assertiveness, decision making, or negotiation, a supportive decision-making group is more appropriate. Time-limited assertiveness-training groups with clearly defined goals have been proven to be effective.

Family and marital therapy

Individuals with DPD are usually brought to therapy by their parents. They are often young adults who are struggling with neurotic or psychotic symptoms. The goal of **family therapy** is often to untangle the enmeshed family relationships, which usually elicits considerable resistance by most family members unless all are in therapy.

Marital therapy can be productive in helping couples reduce the anxiety of both partners, who have dependency needs that arise in the relationship.

Medications

Individuals with DPD can experience anxiety and depressive disorders as well. In these cases, it may prove useful to use **antidepressants** or **antianxiety drugs**. Unless the anxiety or **depression** is severe enough to warrant a primary diagnosis, medications are generally not recommended for treatment. Persons with DPD may become overly dependent on any medication used.

KEY TERMS

Millon Clinical Multiaxial Inventory (MCMI-II)—A self-report instrument designed to help the clinician assess *DSM-IV*-related personality disorders and clinical syndromes. It provides insight into 14 personality disorders and 10 clinical syndromes.

Minnesota Multiphasic Personality Inventory (MMPI-2)—A comprehensive assessment tool widely used to diagnosed personality disorders.

Rorschach Psychodiagnostic Test—This series of 10 "ink blot" images allows the patient to project their interpretations, which can be used to diagnose particular disorders.

Thematic Apperception Test (TAT)—A projective test using stories and descriptions of pictures to reveal some of the dominant drives, emotions, sentiments, conflicts, and complexes of a personality.

Prognosis

The general prognosis for individuals with DPD is good. Persons who enter treatment can learn to become more autonomous, and improved functioning can be expected.

Prevention

Although prevention of the disorder might not be possible, treatment of DPD can sometimes allow a person who is prone to this disorder to learn more productive ways of dealing with situations.

Resources

BOOKS

American Psychiatric Association. *Diagnostic and Statistical Manual of Mental Disorders*. 4th ed., text rev. Washington, DC: American Psychiatric Publishing, 2000.

Millon, Theodore, and Roger Davis. *Disorders of Personality: DSM IV and Beyond*. New York: John Wiley and Sons, 1996.

Porter, Robert S., and Justin L. Kaplan, eds. *The Merck Manual of Diagnosis and Therapy*. 19th ed. Whitehouse Station, NJ: Merck Research Laboratories, 2011.

Sperry, Len. *Handbook of Diagnosis and Treatment of DSM-IV Personality Disorders*. 2nd ed. New York: Routledge, 2003.

PERIODICALS

Tyrer, P., J. Morgan, and D. Cicchetti. "The Dependent Personalilty Questionnaire (DPQ): A Screening Instrument for Dependent Personality." *International Journal of Social Psychiatry* 50, no. 1 (March 2004): 10–17.

WEBSITES

MedlinePlus. "Dependent Personality Disorder." U.S. National Library of Medicine, National Institutes of Health. http://medlineplus.nlm.nih.gov/medlineplus/ency/article/000941.htm (accessed October 3, 2011).

ORGANIZATIONS

American Psychiatric Association, 1000 Wilson Blvd., Suite 1825, Arlington, VA, 22209-3901, (703) 907-7300, apa@psych.org, http://www.psych.org.

International Society for the Study of Personality Disorders, University of Michigan Health System, Psychiatry MCHC-6, Box 5295, 1500 East Medical Center Drive, Ann Arbor, MI, 48109-5295, (734) 936-8316, Fax: (734) 936-9761, http://www.isspd.com.

National Institute of Mental Health, 6001 Executive Blvd., Room 8184, MSC 9663, Bethesda, MD, 20892-9663, (301) 433-4513; TTY: (301) 443-8431, (866) 615-6464; TTY: (866) 415-8051, Fax: (301) 443-4279, nimhinfo@nih.gov, http://www.nimh.nih.gov.

Gary Gilles, MA
Emily Jane Willingham, PhD

Depersonalization and depersonalization disorder

Definition

Depersonalization disorder (sometimes called "depersonalization neurosis") is a dissociative disorder marked by persistent or repeated feelings of disconnect or detachment from one' body. Depersonalization is a state in which the individual ceases to perceive the reality of the self or the environment. The patient feels that his or her body is unreal, is changing, or is dissolving; or that he or she is outside of the body.

Demographics

The lifetime prevalence of depersonalization disorder in the general population is unknown, possibly because many people are made anxious by episodes of depersonalization and are afraid to discuss them with a primary care physician. One survey done by the National Institutes of Mental Health (NIMH) indicates that about half of the adults in the United States have had one or two brief episodes of depersonalization in their lifetimes, usually resulting from severe **stress**. About a third of people exposed to life-threatening dangers develop brief periods of depersonalization, as do 40% of psychiatric inpatients. Estimates of the prevalence of depersonalization disorder in the general population range from 2.4% to 20%.

Depersonalization disorder is diagnosed about twice as often in women as in men. It is not known whether this sex ratio indicates that women are at greater risk for the disorder or if they are more likely to seek help for its symptoms, or both. Little information is available about the incidence of the disorder in different racial or ethnic groups.

Description

Depersonalization disorder is classified by the ***Diagnostic and Statistical Manual of Mental Disorders***, fourth edition, text revision, also known as the *DSM-IV-TR*, as one of the **dissociative disorders**. These are mental disorders in which the normally well-integrated functions of memory, identity, perception, and consciousness are separated (dissociated). The dissociative disorders are usually connected to recent or past **trauma**, or with an intense internal conflict that forces the mind to separate incompatible or unacceptable knowledge, information, or feelings. In depersonalization disorder, the patient's self-perception is disrupted. Patients feel as if they are external observers of their own lives, or that they are detached from their own bodies.

Depersonalization as a symptom may occur in the **diagnosis** of depersonalization disorder if the episodes of depersonalization occur only during panic attacks or following a traumatic stressor.

A person with depersonalization disorder experiences subjective symptoms of unreality that make him or her uneasy and anxious. "Subjective" is a word that refers to the thoughts and perceptions inside an individual's mind, as distinct from the objects of those thoughts and perceptions outside the mind. Because depersonalization is a subjective experience, many people who have chronic or recurrent episodes of depersonalization are afraid others will not understand if they try to describe what they are feeling, or will think they are "crazy." As a result, depersonalization disorder may be underdiagnosed because the symptom of depersonalization is underreported.

The symptom of depersonalization can also occur in normal individuals under circumstances such as **sleep deprivation**, the use of certain anesthetics, experimental conditions in a laboratory (experiments involving weightlessness, for example), and emotionally stressful situations (such as taking an important academic examination or being in a traffic accident). One such example involves some of the rescue personnel from the September 11, 2001, terrorist attacks on the World Trade Center and the Pentagon. These individuals experienced episodes of depersonalization after a day and a half without sleep. A more commonplace example is the use of nitrous oxide, or "laughing gas," as an anesthetic during oral surgery. Many dental patients report a sense of unreality or feeling of being outside their bodies during nitrous oxide administration.

To further complicate the matter, depersonalization may be experienced in different ways by different individuals. Common descriptions include a feeling of being outside one's body; "floating on the ceiling looking down at myself;" feeling as if one's body is dissolving or changing; feeling as if one is a machine or robot; an "unreal" feeling that one is in a dream or that one "is on automatic pilot." Most patients report a sense of emotional detachment or uninvolvement, or a sense of emotional numbing. Depersonalization is distinct from a dissociative symptom called derealization, in which people perceive the external world as unreal, dreamlike, or changing. The various ways that people experience depersonalization are related to their bodies or their sense of self.

Depersonalization is a common experience in the general adult population. However, when a patient's symptoms of depersonalization are severe enough to cause significant emotional distress, or interfere with normal functioning, the criteria of the *DSM-IV-TR* for depersonalization disorder are met.

Causes and symptoms

Causes

Depersonalization disorder, like dissociative disorders in general, has been regarded as the result of severe **abuse** in childhood. This can be of a physical, emotional, and/or sexual nature.

Trauma and emotional abuse in particular are strong predictors of depersonalization disorder in adult life, as well as of depersonalization as a symptom in other mental disorders. Analysis of one study of 49 patients diagnosed with depersonalization disorder indicated much higher scores than the control subjects for the total amount of emotional abuse endured and for the maximum severity of this type of abuse. The researchers concluded that emotional abuse has been relatively neglected by psychiatrists compared to other forms of childhood trauma.

It is thought that abuse in childhood or trauma in adult life may account for the distinctive cognitive (knowledge-related) profile of patients with depersonalization disorder. These patients have significant difficulties in focusing their attention, with spatial reasoning, and with short-term visual and verbal memory. However, they have intact reality testing. (Reality testing refers to a person's ability to distinguish between their internal experiences and the objective reality of persons and objects in the outside world.) Otherwise stated, a patient with depersonalization disorder may experience his/her body as unreal, but knows that "feelings aren't facts." The *DSM-IV-TR* specifies intact reality testing as a diagnostic criterion for depersonalization disorder.

The causes of depersonalization disorder are not completely understood. Recent advances in **brain** imaging and other forms of neurological testing, however, have confirmed that depersonalization disorder is a distinct diagnostic entity and should not be considered a subtype of **post-traumatic stress disorder** (PTSD). A recent study using brain-imaging techniques found that patients with depersonalization disorder do not process emotional information in the same way as healthy controls, and their differences on brain imaging reflect their reported reduced or absent emotional response to verbal material that normally would elicit strong emotion, such as "There is a bomb inside the parcel."

NEUROBIOLOGICAL. In the past few years, several features of depersonalization disorder have been traced to differences in brain functioning. A group of British researchers found that the emotional detachment that characterizes depersonalization is associated with a lower level of nerve-cell responses in regions of the brain that are responsible for emotional feeling; and an increased level of nerve-cell responses was found in regions of the brain related to emotional regulation.

A group of American researchers concluded that patients with depersonalization disorder had different patterns of response to tests of the hypothalamic-pituitary-adrenal axis (HPA; the part of the brain involved in the "fight-or-flight" reaction to stress) than did patients with PTSD. Other tests by the same research team showed that patients with depersonalization disorder can be clearly distinguished from patients with major **depression** by tests of the functioning of the HPA axis.

Other neurobiological studies involving **positron emission tomography (PET)** measurements of glucose (sugar) metabolism in different areas of the brain found that patients with depersonalization disorder appear to have abnormal functioning of the sensory cortex. The sensory cortex is the part of the brain that governs the senses of sight, hearing, and perceptions of the location of one's body in space. These studies indicate that depersonalization is a symptom that involves differences in sensory perception and subjective experiences. In the study of patients and their processing of emotional information, it was found that patients showed a similar response in the visual cortex to emotional and neutral verbal information. They did not appear to distinguish these two classes of material, which could either be because they have an overall reduced emotional response or because their response to neutral material is enhanced.

HISTORICAL. Depersonalization disorder may be a reflection of changes in people's sense of self or personal identity within Western cultures since the eighteenth century. Historians of psychiatry have noted that whereas some mental disorders, such as depression, have been reported since the beginnings of Western medicine, no instances of the dissociative disorders were recorded before the 1780s. It seems that changes in social institutions and the structure of the family since the mid-eighteenth century may have produced a psychological structure in Westerners that makes individuals increasingly vulnerable to self disorders—as they are now called. Experiences of the unreality of one's body or one's self, such as those that characterize depersonalization disorder, presuppose a certain notion of how the self is presumed to feel. The emphasis on individualism and detachment from one's family is a mark of adult maturity in contemporary Western societies that appears to be a contributing factor to the frequency of dissociative symptoms and disorders.

Symptoms

Although the *DSM-IV-TR* does not specify a list of primary symptoms of depersonalization, clinicians generally consider the triad of emotional numbing, changes in visual perception, and altered experience of one's body to be important core symptoms of depersonalization disorder.

The *DSM-IV-TR* notes that patients with depersonalization disorder frequently score high on measurements of hypnotizability.

Diagnosis

The diagnosis of depersonalization disorder is usually a diagnosis of exclusion. The doctor will take a detailed medical history, give the patient a physical examination, and order blood and urine tests in order to rule out depersonalization resulting from epilepsy, **substance abuse**, medication side effects, or recent periods of sleep deprivation.

There are several standard diagnostic questionnaires that may be given to evaluate the presence of a dissociative disorder. The Dissociative Experiences Scale (DES) is a frequently administered self-report screener for dissociation. The **Structured Clinical Interview for DSM-IV** Dissociative Disorders, or SCID-D, can be used to make the diagnosis of depersonalization disorder distinct from the other dissociative disorders defined by *DSM-IV*. The SCID-D is a semistructured interview, which means that the examiner's questions are open-ended and allow the patient to describe experiences of depersonalization in some detail—distinct from simple yes-or-no answers.

In addition to these instruments, a six-item Depersonalization Severity Scale, or DSS, has been developed to discriminate between depersonalization disorder and other dissociative or post-traumatic disorders, and to measure the effects of treatment in patients.

Treatment

Depersonalization disorder sometimes resolves on its own without treatment. Specialized treatment is recommended only if the symptoms are persistent, recurrent, or upsetting to the patient. Insight-oriented **psychodynamic psychotherapy**, cognitive-behavior therapy, and hypnosis have been demonstrated to be effective with some patients. There is, however, no single form of **psychotherapy** that is effective in treating all patients diagnosed with depersonalization disorder.

Medications that have been helpful to patients with depersonalization disorder include the benzodiazepine tranquilizers, such as **lorazepam** (Ativan), **clorazepate** (Tranxene), and **alprazolam** (Xanax), and the tricyclic **antidepressants**, such as **amitriptyline** (Elavil), **doxepin** (Sinequan), and **desipramine** (Norpramin).

KEY TERMS

Abuse—Physical, emotional, or sexual harm.

Depersonalization neurosis—Another name for depersonalization disorder.

Derealization—A dissociative symptom in which the external environment is perceived as unreal or dreamlike.

Dissociation—A reaction to trauma in which the mind splits off certain aspects of the traumatic event from conscious awareness. Dissociation can affect the patient's memory, sense of reality, and sense of identity.

Dissociative disorders—A group of disorders marked by the separation (dissociation) of perception, memory, personal identity, and consciousness. Depersonalization disorder is one of five dissociative disorders defined by *DSM-IV-TR.*

Hypothalamic-pituitary-adrenal (HPA) system—A part of the brain involved in the human stress response. The HPA system releases cortisol, the primary human stress hormone, and neurotransmitters that activate other brain structures associated with the fight-or-flight reaction. The HPA system appears to function in abnormal ways in patients diagnosed with depersonalization disorder. It is sometimes called the HPA axis.

Reality testing—A phrase that refers to a person's ability to distinguish between subjective feelings and objective reality. A person who knows that their body is real even though they may be experiencing it as unreal, for example, is said to have intact reality testing. Intact reality testing is a *DSM-IV-TR* criterion for depersonalization disorder.

Selective serotonin reuptake inhibitors (SSRIs)—Commonly prescribed drugs for treating depression. SSRIs affect the chemicals that nerves in the brain use to send messages to one another.

Serotonin—A widely distributed neurotransmitter that is found in blood platelets, the lining of the digestive tract, and in the brain where it works in combination with norepinephrine. It causes very powerful contractions of smooth muscle, and is associated with mood, attention, emotions, and sleep. Low levels of serotonin are associated with depression.

Stress—A physical and psychological response that results from being exposed to a demand or pressure.

Stressor—A stimulus or event that provokes a stress response in an organism. Stressors can be categorized as acute or chronic, and as external or internal to the organism.

Subjective—Referring to a person's unique internal thoughts and feelings, as distinct from the objects of those thoughts and feelings in the external world.

Tricyclic antidepressants (TCAs)—Antidepressant medications that have the common characteristic of a three-ring nucleus in their chemical structure. Imipramine and amitriptyline are examples of tricyclic antidepressants.

Selective serotonin reuptake inhibitors (SSRIs), which include **fluoxetine** (Prozac), **sertraline** (Zoloft), and **paroxetine** (Paxil), may also be effective. **SSRIs** affect levels of the brain chemicals that nerve cells use to send messages to each another. These chemical messengers, called (**neurotransmitters**), are released by one nerve cell and taken up by others. If the receiving cell does not take up the chemical, the sending cell will take it up, a process called "reuptake." SSRIs work by preventing the reuptake of **serotonin**, leaving more serotonin for nerve signaling. Serotonin signaling is associated with feelings of well-being.

Unfortunately, there have been very few well-designed studies comparing different medications for depersonalization disorder. Because depersonalization disorder is frequently associated with trauma, effective treatment must include other stress-related symptoms, as well.

Relaxation techniques have been reported to be a beneficial adjunctive treatment for persons diagnosed with depersonalization disorder, particularly for those who are worried about their sanity.

Prognosis

The prognosis for recovery from depersonalization disorder is good. Most patients recover completely, particularly those who developed the disorder in connection with traumas that can be explored and resolved in treatment. A few patients develop a chronic form of the disorder; this is characterized by periodic episodes of depersonalization in connection with stressful events in their lives.

Prevention

Some clinicians think that depersonalization disorder has an undetected onset in childhood, even though most patients first appear for treatment as adolescents or young adults. Preventive strategies could include the development of screening techniques for identifying children at risk, as well as further research into the effects of emotional abuse on children.

Further neurobiological research may lead to the development of medications or other treatment modalities for preventing, as well as treating, depersonalization.

Resources

BOOKS

American Psychiatric Association. *Diagnostic and Statistical Manual of Mental Disorders*. 4th ed., text rev. Washington, DC: American Psychiatric Publishing, 2000.

"Depersonalization Disorder." In *The Merck Manual of Diagnosis and Therapy*, edited by Robert S. Porter. Whitehouse Station, NJ: Merck Sharp & Dohme, 2011.

Ellenberger, Henri. *The Discovery of the Unconscious: The History and Evolution of Dynamic Psychiatry*. New York: Basic Books, 1981.

Herman, Judith. *Trauma and Recovery*. 14th printing. New York: Basic Books, 1997.

Physicians' Desk Reference 2011. 66th ed. Montvale, NJ: PDR Network, 2011.

Stout, Martha. *The Myth of Sanity: Tales of Multiple Personality in Everyday Life*. New York: Penguin Books, 2002.

PERIODICALS

Berrios, G. E., and M. Sierra. "Depersonalization: A Conceptual History." *Historical Psychiatry* 8, no. 30 Pt 2 (June 1997): 213–29.

Guralnik, O., J. Schmeidler, and D. Simeon. "Feeling Unreal: Cognitive Processes in Depersonalization." *American Journal of Psychiatry* 157 (January 2000): 103–109.

Lambert, M. V., et al. "Visual Imagery and Depersonalisation." *Psychopathology* 34, no. 5 (Sept.–Oct. 2001): 259–64.

Medford, Nicholas, et al. "Emotional Memory in Depersonalization Disorder: A Functional MRI Study." *Psychiatry Research* 148 (December 1, 2006): 93–102.

Phillips, M.L., et al. "Depersonalization Disorder: Thinking Without Feeling." *Psychiatry Research* 108, no. 3 (December 30, 2001): 145–60.

Sierra, M., and G.E. Berrios. "The Phenomenological Stability of Depersonalization: Comparing the Old with the New." *Journal of Nervous and Mental Disease* 189, no. 9 (September 2001): 629–36.

Sierra, M., et al. "Lamotrigine in the Treatment of Depersonalization Disorder." Letter to the editor in *Journal of Clinical Psychiatry* 62 (October 2001): 826–27.

Simeon, D., D.J. Stein, and E. Hollander. "Treatment of Depersonalization Disorder with Clomipramine." *Biological Psychiatry* 44, no. 4 (August 15, 1998): 302–303.

Simeon, D., et al. "Feeling Unreal: A PET Study of Depersonalization Disorder." *American Journal of Psychiatry* 157 (November 2000): 1782–88.

Simeon, D., et al. "Hypothalamic-Pituitary-Adrenal Axis Dysregulation in Depersonalization Disorder." *Neuropsychopharmacology* 25, no. 5 (November 2001): 793–95.

Simeon, D., et al. "Personality Factors Associated with Dissociation: Temperament, Defenses, and Cognitive Schemata." *American Journal of Psychiatry* 159 (March 2002): 489–91.

Simeon, D., et al. "The Role of Childhood Interpersonal Trauma in Depersonalization Disorder." *American Journal of Psychiatry* 158 (July 2001): 1027–33.

Simeon, D., O. Guralnik, and J. Schmeidler. "Development of a Depersonalization Severity Scale." *Journal of Traumatic Stress* 14, no. 2 (April 2001): 341–49.

Spitzer, Carsten, et al. "Recent Developments in the Theory of Dissociation." *World Psychiatry* 5, no. 2 (June 2006): 82–86.

Stanton, B.R., et al. "Basal Activity of the Hypothalamic-Pituitary-Adrenal Axis in Patients with Depersonalization Disorder." *Psychiatry Research* 104, no. 1 (October 10, 2001): 85–89.

Zanarini, M.C., et al. "The Dissociative Experiences of Borderline Patients." *Comprehensive Psychiatry* 41, no. 3 (May–June 2000): 223–27.

WEBSITES

Mayo Clinic staff. "Dissociative Disorders." MayoClinic.com. March 3, 2011. http://www.mayoclinic.com/health/dissociative-disorders/DS00574/DSECTION=5 (accessed October 3, 2011).

ORGANIZATIONS

International Society for the Study of Trauma and Dissociation, 8400 Westpark Dr., 2nd Fl., McLean, VA, 22102, (703) 610-9037, Fax: (703) 610-0234, http://www.isst-d.org.

International Society for Traumatic Stress Studies, 111 Deer Lake Rd., Ste. 100, Deerfield, IL, 60015, (847) 480-9028, Fax: (847) 480-9282, http://www.istss.org.

National Institute of Mental Health, 6001 Executive Blvd., Room 8184, MSC 9663, Bethesda, MD, 20892-9663, (301) 433-4513; TTY: (301) 443-8431, Fax: (301) 443-4279, (866) 615-6464; TTY: (866) 415-8051, nimhinfo@nih.gov, http://www.nimh.nih.gov.

National Organization for Rare Disorders, 55 Kenosia Ave., PO Box 1968, Danbury, CT, 06813-1968, (203) 744-0100, Fax: (203) 798-2291, (800) 999-6673, http://www.rarediseases.org.

Rebecca J. Frey, PhD
Emily Jane Willingham, PhD

Depression

Definition

Depression is the general name for a family of illnesses known as depressive disorders. As an illness, depression can affect not only the personal mood and internal thoughts of a person, but also the outwardly physical functions of affected individuals. In a depressive state, an individual may have diminished feelings, behaviors, or thoughts, along with a general lack of mental and physical health. Depression can include one or all of the following feelings: anxiety, emptiness, hopelessness, guilt, irritability, restlessness, or sadness. In addition, depressive disorders usually result from a combination of genetic, environmental, and psychological factors.

The American Psychiatric Association's *Diagnostic and Statistical Manual of Mental Disorders (DSM)* provides descriptions and standards for mental disorders. The *DSM* defines a major depressive episode (MDE) as a period of two weeks or longer during which there is either depressed mood or loss of interest or pleasure and at least four other symptoms that reflect a change in functioning, such as problems with sleep, eating, energy, concentration, and self-image.

Demographics

Depression is one of the leading causes of disability in the United States. According to the U.S. **National Institute of Mental Health** (NIMH), approximately 9.5% of adult Americans (those aged 18 years or older, about 18.8 million adults as of 2010) have some type of depressive disorder. In all, the National Institutes of Health (NIH) declares that about 20 million people in the United States are depressed. For young people in college, one out of every four students in the country has some type of diagnosable mental illness. Even small children in elementary schools have been diagnosed with depressive symptoms.

Depressive disorders

Diagnosis	Symptoms	Treatment
Sadness	Transient, normal depressive response or mood change due to stress.	Emotional support
Bereavement	Sadness related to a major loss that persists for less than two months after the loss. Thoughts of death and morbid preoccupation with worthlessness are also present.	Emotional support, counseling
Sadness problem	Sadness or irritability that begins to resemble major depressive disorder, but lower in severity and more transient.	Support, counseling, medication possible
Adjustment disorder with depressed mood	Symptoms include depressed mood, tearfulness, and hopelessness, and occur within three months of an identifiable stressor. Symptoms resolve in six months.	Psychotherapy, medication
Major depressive disorder	A depressed or irritable mood or diminished pleasure as well as three to seven of the following criteria almost daily for two weeks. The criteria include: recurrent thoughts of death and suicidal ideation, weight loss or gain, fatigue or energy loss, feelings of worthlessness, diminished ability to concentrate, insomnia or hypersomnia, and feeling hyper and jittery or abnormally slow.	Psychotherapy, medication
Dysthymic disorder	Depressed mood for most of the day, for more days than not, for one year, including the presence of two of the following symptoms: poor appetite or overeating, insomnia/hypersomnia, low energy/fatigue, poor concentration, and feelings of hopelessness. Symptoms are less severe than those of a major depressive episode but are more persistent.	Psychotherapy, medication
Bipolar I disorder, most recent episode depressed	Current major depressive episode with a history of one manic or mixed episode. (Manic episode is longer than four days and causes significant impairment in normal functioning.) Moods are not accounted for by another psychiatric disorder.	Psychotherapy, medication
Bipolar II disorder, recurrent major depressive episodes with hypomanic episodes	Presence or history of one major depressive episode and one hypomanic episode (similar to manic episode but shorter and less severe). Symptoms are not accounted for by another psychiatric disorder and cause clinically significant impairment in functioning.	Psychotherapy, medication

SOURCE: Academy of American Family Physicians, http://www.aafp.org.

Types of depressive disorders. *(Table by PreMediaGlobal. Reproduced by permission of Gale, a part of Cengage Learning.)*

The U.S. Centers for Disease Control and Prevention (CDC) states that at the end of 2010, 4.1% of American adults met the criteria for major depression. Geographically, depression is more prevalent in the southeastern states than in any other region of the United States. The CDC also states that depression is more likely to occur in people 45 to 64 years of age, women, African Americans, Hispanics, and non-Hispanic persons of other races or multiple races. People with less than a high-school education are also at greater risk of being depressed, as are persons who have undergone a divorce. In addition, individuals who are unable to work or unemployed are more likely to be depressed, along with those without health insurance.

Depression within the United States is increasing on an annual basis. Internationally, depression is estimated to become the second most common health problem in the world by 2020. According to the NIMH, many people have more than one mental disorder at any given time. Nearly half of those with any mental disorder meet criteria for two or more disorders.

That women experience depression at a rate of almost twice that of men may be partially explained by the greater willingness of women to seek psychological treatment, but this does not explain the entire discrepancy. Many physical events specific to women, such as menstruation, pregnancy, miscarriage, the postpartum period, and menopause are recognized as factors contributing to depression in women. Women in the United States may face environmental stresses with a higher frequency than do men. For instance, most single-parent households are headed by women; women still provide the majority of child and elder care, even in two-income families; and women are generally paid less than men, so financial concerns may be greater.

Particular demographic problems associated with depression include depression in the elderly (**late-life depression**) and depression in children and adolescents (**juvenile depression**). One common belief is that depression is normal in elderly people. This is not the case, although increasing age and the absence of interpersonal relationships are associated with depression. Because of this misconception, depressive disorders in the elderly population often go undiagnosed and untreated. Similarly, many parents often ignore the symptoms of a depressive disorder in their children, assuming that these symptoms are merely a phase that the child will later outgrow.

Description

Everyone feels sadness, **grief**, or despair at some point in their lives. However, unlike these normal, transient emotional states, a depressive disorder is not a temporary bout of "feeling down," but rather a serious disease that should be recognized and treated as a medical condition. Without treatment, a depressive disorder can persist, and its symptoms can go on for weeks, months, or even years.

Depression is quite widespread and one of the leading causes of disability in the world. Commonly recognized symptoms of all types of depressive disorders are recurring feelings of sadness and guilt; changes in sleeping patterns, such as **insomnia** or oversleeping; changes in appetite; decreased mental and physical energy; unusual irritability; the inability to enjoy once-favored activities; difficulty working; and thoughts of death or **suicide**. If only these "down" symptoms are experienced, the individual may have a unipolar depressive disorder such as dysthymia or major depression. If the depressed periods alternate with extreme "up" periods, the individual may have a **bipolar disorder**.

Dysthymia

Dysthymia is a relatively mild depressive disorder that is characterized by the presence of two or more of the symptoms listed above. The symptoms are not severe enough to disable the affected individual but are long-term (chronic) and may last for several years. *Dysthymia* is a compound word originating in Greek that means ill or bad (*dys-*) soul, mind, or spirit (*thymia*). Individuals affected with dysthymia often also experience episodes of major depression at some point in their lives.

Major depression

In major depression, the affected individual has five or more symptoms and experiences one or more prolonged episodes of depression that last longer than two weeks. These episodes disrupt the ability of the affected individual to the point that the person is unable to function. Individuals experiencing an episode of major depression often entertain suicidal thoughts, the presence of which contributes to this disorder being quite serious. Major depression should not be confused with a grief reaction such as that associated with the death of a loved one. Some individuals affected by major depression may experience only a single bout of disabling depression in their lifetimes. More commonly, affected individuals experience recurrent disabling episodes throughout their lives.

Other depressive disorders

The fifth edition of the *DSM* (*DSM-5*, 2013) proposes to include the following depressive disorders:

- disruptive mood dysregulation disorder
- major depressive disorder, single episode
- major depressive disorder, recurrent

- chronic depressive disorder (dysthymia)
- premenstrual dysphoric disorder
- mixed anxiety/depression
- substance-induced depressive disorder
- depressive disorder associated with a known general medical condition
- other specified depressive disorder
- unspecified depressive disorder

Previously, depressive disorders and bipolar disorder, a condition that alternates between periods of extreme excitement (mania) and periods of depression, were both classified as mood disorders. The proposed *DSM-5* changes divide the two into new categories, depressive disorders and bipolar and related disorders.

Causes and symptoms

Causes

Depressive disorders are believed to be related to genetic imbalances in **brain** chemistry, particularly in relation to the chemicals that carry signals between brain cells (**neurotransmitters**), as well as the hormones released by parts of the brain. **Serotonin** and norepinephrine are two important neurotransmitters. Disruption of the brain's circuits in areas involved with emotions, appetite, sexual drive, and sleep is a likely cause of the dysfunctions associated with depressive disorders. Thus, some of the newest treatments for depression are drugs that are known to affect brain chemistry.

There are also many non-genetic factors that cause depression, including stressful environments or situations, certain illnesses, and precipitating conditions, such as the loss of a close relationship. Alcohol abuse and the use of **sedatives**, **barbiturates**, narcotics, or other drugs can cause depression due to their effect on brain chemistry.

Symptoms

Individuals affected with depressive disorders display a wide range of symptoms. These symptoms vary in severity from person to person and vary over time in a single affected individual.

Symptoms that characterize a depressive state include:

- feelings of hopelessness
- feelings of guilt
- feelings of worthlessness
- a persistently sad or anxious mood
- restlessness or irritability
- a loss of interest in activities that were once considered pleasurable
- difficulty concentrating, remembering, or making decisions
- sleep disorders, including insomnia, early-morning awakening, and/or oversleeping

KEY TERMS

Bipolar disorder—Formerly called "manic depression," this psychological disorder is characterized by periods of mania followed by periods of depression.

Cognitive/behavioral therapies—Psychological counseling that focuses on changing the behavior of the patient.

Dysthymia—A psychological condition of chronic depression that is not disabling but prevents the individual from functioning at his or her full capacity.

Electroconvulsive therapy—A psychological treatment in which a series of controlled electrical impulses are delivered to the brain in order to induce a seizure.

Grief reaction—The normal depression felt after a traumatic major life occurrence, such as the loss of a loved one.

Interpersonal therapies—Also called "talking therapy," this type of psychological counseling is focused on determining how dysfunctional interpersonal relationships of the affected individual may be causing or influencing symptoms of depression.

Major depression—A psychological condition in which the patient experiences one or more disabling attacks of depression lasting two or more weeks.

Polygenic—A trait, characteristic, or condition that depends on the activity of more than one gene for its emergence or expression.

Psychodynamic therapies—A form of psychological counseling that seeks to determine and resolve the internal conflicts that may be causing an individual to experience the symptoms of depression.

Psychotherapy—Psychological counseling that seeks to determine the underlying causes of a patient's depression. The form of this counseling may be cognitive/behavioral, interpersonal, or psychodynamic.

- constant fatigue
- eating disorders, including weight loss or overeating
- suicidal thoughts and/or tendencies
- recurrent physical symptoms that do not respond to the normal treatments of these symptoms, such as headaches, digestive problems, and chronic pain

Diagnosis

Depression is notoriously difficult to diagnose because its symptoms are not readily apparent to the medical professional unless the patient first recognizes and admits to them. Once the individual seeks help for his or her symptoms, the first step in the **diagnosis** of a depressive disorder is a complete physical examination to rule out any medical conditions, viral infections, or currently used medications that may produce effects similar to those seen in depression. Alcohol or other drug abuse as a possible cause of the observed symptoms should also be investigated. Once a physical basis for these symptoms is eliminated, a complete psychological exam should be undertaken. This examination consists of a **mental status examination**, a complete history of both current and previously experienced symptoms, and a family history.

The mental status examination is used to determine whether a more severe psychotic condition is evident. This mental status examination will also determine whether the depressive disorder has caused changes in speech, thought patterns, or memory, which may indicate the presence of a depressive disorder. The complete psychological exam also includes a complete history of the symptoms being experienced by the affected individual. This history includes the onset of the symptoms, their duration, and whether the affected individual has had similar symptoms in the past. In the case of past symptoms, a treatment history should be completed to assess whether these symptoms previously responded to treatment, and if so, which treatments were effective. The final component of the complete psychological exam is the family history. In cases where the affected individual has similarly affected family members, a treatment history should also be completed, as thoroughly as possible, for these family members.

The diagnostic criteria for a major depressive episode (MDE) according to the DSM are:

- At least five of the following symptoms present during the same two-week period, nearly every day, and representing a change from previous functioning. At least one of the symptoms is either depressed mood or loss of interest or pleasure; the remaining four include
  1. depressed mood (alternatively, irritable mood in children and adolescents)
  2. markedly diminished interest or pleasure in all, or almost all, activities
  3. significant weight loss when not dieting, or weight gain or decrease or increase in appetite
  4. insomnia or hypersomnia
  5. psychomotor agitation or retardation
  6. fatigue or loss of energy
  7. feelings of worthlessness or excessive or inappropriate guilt
  8. diminished ability to think or concentrate, or indecisiveness
  9. recurrent thoughts of death (not just fear of dying), recurrent suicidal thoughts without a specific plan, or a suicide attempt or a specific plan for committing suicide
- The symptoms significantly disturb functions of daily life, such as social and occupational activities, and are not attributed to another medical condition (mental or physical).
- The symptoms are not a side effect of a substance (drug or prescribed medication) nor caused by an antidepressant treatment (e.g., electroshock therapy).

The *DSM-IV-TR* (fourth edition, text revised) accounts for periods of **bereavement** in what is referred to as the "grief exclusion." Feelings of grief after the loss of a loved one are similar to symptoms of depression, but a normal period of bereavement is not considered an acceptable basis for a diagnosis of depression. The *DSM-5* proposed changes eliminate the grief exclusion, the rationale being that there is not enough evidence to support the loss of a loved one as unique from other serious stressors experienced in life, such as rape, divorce, or cancer; all of these situations are likely to produce depressive symptoms, at least temporarily. This proposal is controversial, as supporters of the grief exclusion believe that its removal stigmatizes bereavement by allowing it to be diagnosed as an MDE.

Dysthymia

A diagnosis of dysthymia, or chronic depressive disorder, requires that the depression occur consistently for at least two years, or at least one year of irritability in children. Depression must be accompanied by two or more symptoms:

- loss of appetite or overeating
- insomnia or hypersomnia
- fatigue
- low self-esteem
- loss of concentration or reduced ability to make decisions
- sense of hopelessness

The symptoms cannot have more than a two-month lapse during the two-year period, cannot be caused by another psychotic or medical disorder, cannot be the result of a substance (drug or medication), and must significantly impair daily functioning.

Mixed anxiety/depression

Mixed anxiety/depression requires that the patient experience three or four symptoms of an MDE (including depressed mood), accompanied by distressing anxiety. Anxious distress requires two or more of the following: irrational worries, constant unpleasant worries, inability to relax, motor tension, and the consistent fear that something terrible will happen.

Treatment

Treatment of depression is on a case-by-case basis that is largely dependent on the outcome of the psychological examination. Some mildly affected individuals respond fully to **psychotherapy** and do not require medication. Some individuals affected with moderate or severe depression benefit from antidepressant medication. Most affected individuals respond best to a combination of antidepressant medication and psychotherapy—the medication to provide relatively rapid relief from the symptoms of depression and the psychotherapy to learn effective ways to manage and cope with problems and issues that may cause the continuation of symptoms or the onset of new symptoms of depression.

Various types of antidepressant medications are available for the treatment of depressive disorders. Many individuals affected by depression will go through a variety of **antidepressants**, or antidepressant combinations, before the best medication and dosage for them is identified. Almost all antidepressant medications must be taken regularly for at least two months before the full therapeutic effects are realized. A full course of medication is generally no shorter than six to nine months to prevent recurrence of the symptoms. In individuals affected with bipolar disorder or chronic major depression, medication may have to be continued throughout the remainder of their lives. These time-related conditions often pose problems in the management of individuals affected with depressive disorder. Many individuals who have a depressive disorder discontinue their medications before the fully prescribed course, for a variety of reasons. Some affected individuals feel side effects of the medications prior to feeling any benefits; others do not feel that the medication is helping, because of the delay between the initiation of the treatment and the feelings of symptom relief; and, many feel better prior to the full course and so cease taking the medication.

The three most commonly prescribed antidepressant drug classes consist of the older tricyclics (TCAs) and the two relatively new drug classes: the **selective serotonin reuptake inhibitors (SSRIs)** and the **monoamine oxidase inhibitors (MAOIs)**. The most common TCAs are: **amitriptyline** (Elavil), **clomipramine** (Anafranil), **desipramine** (Norpramin, Pertofrane), **doxepin** (Sinequan, Adapin), **imipramine** (Tofranil, Janimine), **nortriptyline** (Pamelor, Aventyl), **protriptyline** (Vivactil), and **trimipramine** (Surmontil). The most common **SSRIs** are: **citalopram** (Celexa), **fluoxetine** (Prozac), **fluvoxamine** (Luvox), **paroxetine** (Paxil), and **sertraline** (Zoloft). The most common **MAOIs** are: **phenelzine** (Nardil) and **tranylcypromine** (Parnate).

Many antidepressant medications cause side effects, such as agitation, bladder problems, blurred vision, constipation, drowsiness, dry mouth, headache, insomnia, nausea, nervousness, or sexual problems. Most of these side effects wear off as the treatment course progresses. The tricyclics cause more severe side effects than the newer SSRIs or MAOIs.

In the most severely affected individuals, or where antidepressant medications either have not worked or cannot be taken, **electroconvulsive therapy** (ECT) may be considered. In the ECT procedure, electrodes are placed on specific locations on the head to deliver electrical stimulation to the brain. Electrical stimulation is designed to trigger a brief seizure. These **seizures** generally last approximately 30 seconds. The patient does not consciously feel the stimulations. ECT has been much improved in recent years; specifically, it is no longer the electroshock treatment of nightmares, and its deleterious effects on long-term memory have been reduced. ECT treatments are generally administered several times a week as necessary to control the symptoms being experienced.

Several short-term (10- to 20-week) psychotherapies have also been demonstrated to be effective in the treatment of depressive disorders. These include interpersonal and **cognitive-behavioral therapy**. Interpersonal therapies focus on the interpersonal relationships of the affected individual that may both cause and heighten the depression. Cognitive-behavioral therapy focuses on how the affected individual may be able to change his or her patterns of thinking or behaving that may lead to episodes of depression. Psychodynamic therapies, which generally are not short-term psychotherapies, seek to treat the individual with a depressive disorder through a resolution of internal conflicts. Psychodynamic therapies are generally not initiated during major depressive episodes or until the symptoms of depression are significantly improved by medication or one of the short-term psychotherapies.

Alternative

St. John's wort (Hypericum perforatum) is used throughout Europe to treat depressive symptoms. Unlike traditional prescription antidepressants, this herbal antidepressant has few reported side effects. Results on the success of St. John's wort are conflicting: a review of 37 **clinical trials** comparing St. John's wort to antidepressants discovered that St. John's wort is most beneficial to persons with mild depression. The herb provided minimal effects similar to a placebo in those with major depression. However, later studies have found more positive results in using St. John' wort to treat major depression. Because supplements are not regulated by the FDA in the same way as conventional medications, care should be taken when selecting herbal treatments.

5-hydroxytryptophan (5-HT, **5-HTP**) is a precursor to serotonin and is available as a supplement. Most of the commercially available 5-HTP is extracted from the plant Griffonia simplicifolia. In several small studies, treatment with 5-HTP significantly improved depression in more than half of the patients. However, some users of 5-HTP have developed eosinophilia-myalgia syndrome (EMS), a serious medical condition characterized by myalgia and blood abnormalities. It is unclear whether the EMS was caused by the use of 5-HTP, a contaminant discovered in some 5-HTP products, or an external factor. Until more research is done, the U.S. National Library of Medicine's and National Institutes of Health's MedlinePlus service advises against using 5-HTP.

Clinical trials

In May 2011, the NIH ClinicalTrials.gov website showed 2,260 clinical trials for depression—classified as ongoing (recruiting volunteers or active but not recruiting), completed, or unknown status—along with 2,243 trials for depressive disorders and 912 clinical trials for major depressive disorders. NIH constantly updates clinical trial information. The most recent information on depression trials can be found at: http://clinicaltrials.gov/search/open/condition=%22Depression%22.

Prognosis

Over 80% of individuals affected with a depressive disorder have demonstrated improvement after receiving the appropriate combination of treatments. One significant tragedy associated with depression is the failure of many affected individuals to realize that they have a treatable medical condition. Some affected individuals who do not receive treatment may recover completely on their own (without professional medical assistance), but most will suffer needlessly. A small number of individuals with depressive disorder do not respond to treatment.

QUESTIONS TO ASK YOUR DOCTOR

- What is causing my depression?
- How severe is my depression?
- Could my depression be caused by another condition or underlying disease?
- How safe are antidepressants? Are there side effects from them? What about long-term side effects?
- How long will it take before the antidepressants begin to work?
- Are antidepressant medicines addictive?
- Can I be treated for depression without medicines?
- Is depression hereditary? Should I be concerned that I will pass depression to my children?

Prevention

Depression is not always preventable. However, persons can minimize depression's impact on their lives by recognizing the symptoms of depression and seeking help right away from a medical professional. **Stress** is an early warning sign that depression may occur. It is important to control stresses encountered in life. A social support network in the form of friends and family can help to control stress. Maintain interactions with people, whether professionally or personally. Isolation from the outside world adds to the risk of depression.

Depression is treatable, but the key to alleviating the worse forms of depression is to discuss symptoms openly with a family doctor or other trusted medical practitioner. Treating physical or mental issues is also likely to help reduce the occurrence of depression. Maintaining a high level of self-esteem will help to reduce the risk of depression or help to counter bouts of depression.

Besides seeking professional help, depression can be lessened in risk by enjoying life, eating a well-balanced and healthy diet, getting plenty of **exercise**, sleeping a sufficient number of hours each night, balancing work and personal life, and adhering to a healthy lifestyle. If feeling generally overwhelmed or stressed, seek help from self-help books, relaxation techniques (such as **yoga**, **meditation**, or tai chi), or **support groups**. A medical professional, such as a **psychologist**, can help in locating such resources. Stress can often be alleviated by eliminating unnecessary to-dos and by adding structure to daily activities (such as maintaining a list of activities and tasks to be accomplished).

Resources

BOOKS

Aguirre, Blaise A. *Depression.* Westport, CT: Greenwood Press, 2008.

Bjornlund, Lydia. *Depression.* Detroit: Lucent Books, 2010.

Gordon, James S. *Unstuck: Your Guide to the Seven-Stage Journey Out of Depression.* New York: Penguin Press, 2008.

Karp, David A. *Is It Me or My Meds?: Living with Antidepressants.* Cambridge: Harvard University Press, 2007.

Katon, Wayne, et al. *The Depression Helpbook.* Boulder, CO: Bull, 2008.

Knaus, William J. *The Cognitive Behavioral Workbook for Depression: A Step-by-step Program.* Oakland, CA: New Harbinger Publications, 2006.

Luciani, Joseph J. *Self-Coaching: The Powerful Program to Beat Anxiety and Depression,* 2nd edition, New York: Wiley, 2006.

Williams, Mark, et al. *The Mindful Way through Depression: Freeing Yourself from Chronic Unhappiness.* New York: The Guilford Press, 2007.

PERIODICALS

Adamek, M. E., and G. Y. Slater. "Depression and Anxiety." *Journal of Gerontological Social Work* 50, suppl. 1 (2008): 153–189.

American College of Physicians. "Summaries for patients. Use of drugs to treat depression: guidelines from the American College of Physicians." *Annals of Internal Medicine* 149, no. 10 (November 2008): I56.

"Check your vitamin D intake to avoid multiple health consequences. Three 2008 studies link low vitamin D levels to depression, hip fractures, and increased risk of death." *Health News* 14, no. 11 (November 2008): 9–10.

Gartlehner, G., et al., "Comparative benefits and harms of second-generation antidepressants: background paper for the American College of Physicians." *Annals of Internal Medicine* 149, no. 10 (November 2008): 734–750.

Kozasa, E. H., et al. "Evaluation of Siddha Samadhi Yoga for anxiety and depression symptoms: a preliminary study." *Psychological Reports* 103, no. 1 (August 2008): 271–274.

Krishnan, V., and E. J. Nestler. "The molecular neurobiology of depression." *Nature* 455, no. 7215 (October 2008): 894–902.

Luijendijk, H. J., et al. "Incidence and recurrence of late-life depression." *Archives of General Psychiatry* 65, no. 12 (December 2008): 1394–1401.

Mouchet-Mages, S., and F. J. Bayle. "Sadness as an integral part of depression." *Dialogues in Clinical Neuroscience* 10, no. 3 (2008): 321–327.

Paykel, E. S. "Basic concepts of depression." *Dialogues in Clinical Neuroscience* 10, no. 3 (2008): 279–289.

OTHER

Kendler, Kenneth S. [No title listed; article explains rationale behind removal of the grief exclusion criterion.] http://www.dsm5.org/about/Documents/grief%20exclusion_Kendler.pdf (accessed July 28, 2011).

WEBSITES

Centers for Disease Control and Prevention. "An Estimated 1 in 10 U.S. Adults Report Depression." March 31, 2011. http://www.cdc.gov/Features/dsDepression (accessed May 11, 2011).

First, Michael B., Ronald W. Pies, and Sidney Zisook. "Depression or Bereavement? Defining the Distinction." Medscape News. http://www.medscape.com/viewarticle/740333 (accessed July 28, 2011).

MedlinePlus. "Depression." U.S. Library of Medicine, National Institutes of Health. May 8, 2011. http://www.nlm.nih.gov/medlineplus/depression.html (accessed May 12, 2011).

National Institute of Mental Health. "Depression." http://www.nimh.nih.gov/health/publications/depression/complete-index.shtml (accessed May 11, 2011).

———. "Women and Depression: Discovering Hope." August 31, 2010. http://www.nimh.nih.gov/health/publications/depression-what-every-woman-should-know/summary.shtml (accessed May 12, 2011).

WomensHealth.gov. "Depression." March 17, 2010. http://womenshealth.gov/faq/depression.cfm (accessed May 12, 2011).

ORGANIZATIONS

American Psychiatric Association (APA), 1000 Wilson Boulevard, Suite 1825, Arlington, VA, 22209, (888) 357-7924, apa@psych.org, http://www.psych.org.

Depression and Bipolar Support Alliance, 730 N. Franklin Street, Suite 501, Chicago, IL, 60654-7225, (800) 826-3632, Fax: (312) 642-7243, info@dbsalliance.org, http://www.dbsalliance.org.

Mental Health America, 2000 N. Beauregard Street, 6th Floor, Alexandria, VA, 22311, (703) 684-7722, (800) 969-6642, Fax: (703) 684-5968, http://www.nmha.org.

National Institute of Mental Health (NIMH), 6001 Executive Boulevard, Bethesda, MD, 20892-9663, (301) 443-4513, (866) 615-6464, Fax: (301) 443-4279, nimhinfor@nih.gov, http://www.nimh.nih.gov.

Substance Abuse and Mental Health Services Administration, 1 Choke Cherry Road, Rockville, MD, 20857, (877) 726-4727, http://www.samhsa.gov.

Paul A. Johnson
Monique Laberge, PhD
William Atkins

Dermatillomania

Definition

Dermatillomania, also called psychogenic excoriation (skin removal), neurotic excoriation, acne excoriée, pathological skin picking (PSP), and compulsive skin picking, is characterized by excessive picking, scratching, or squeezing of skin. Dermatillomania is hypothesized to be an impulse control disorder related to **obsessive-compulsive disorder** (OCD), **body dysmorphic disorder** (BDD), and/or **depression**. Dermatillomania can, therefore, be distinguished from other dermatological diseases that are influenced by psychological factors (e.g., psoriasis or alopecia) because it is a dermatological manifestation of a psychiatric syndrome.

Demographics

Dermatillomania is probably underdiagnosed in the general population, partly because persons with the disorder can often hide its visible evidence under clothing or makeup, and partly because most are embarrassed to report the disorder to their doctors. In addition, children with the disorder may not think of their skin picking as abnormal. Estimates range from 1% to 5.4% of the general population in Canada and the United States, with women more likely to develop the disorder than men. The female/male ratio is variously given as 1.2:1 to 9:1. About 2% of patients seen in U.S. dermatology clinics are diagnosed with compulsive skin picking.

Estimates differ about the age range of patients with dermatillomania. Some researchers report that older children and adolescents are the most susceptible age group, whereas other observers report that the mean age at onset of the disorder is 30 to 45 years of age.

Humans are not the only species in which skin picking behavior has been reported. It has also been observed in horses, birds, cats, and dogs, and in laboratory rats given **amphetamines**.

Description

Behaviors associated with dermatillomania include excessive excoriation of skin at multiple sites that are easily reachable. Excoriation may be triggered by and occur at sites of skin lesions (e.g., acne, scabs, insect bites) or in response to such skin sensations as dryness, tingling, or pain. In some cases the skin picking is associated with **cocaine** or **methamphetamine addiction**, in that the abuse of these drugs sometimes results in a sensation known as formication, or the feeling that insects are crawling on or under the skin. Prescription drugs known to cause formication include **methylphenidate** (Ritalin) and eszopiclone (Lunesta).

The face is the most common site of excoriation that is usually performed with the fingers or fingernails but may involve the teeth or such other instruments as tweezers, pins, or blades. Other parts of the body that are commonly affected include the gums, lips, upper back, shoulders, scalp, abdomen, chest, and the fingernails, cuticles, and toenails. Excoriation may occur in brief bouts (less than 5 minutes) or for extended periods of time as long as 12 hours and is usually worse in the evening.

Impulse control disorders in general are characterized by irresistible impulses to commit acts that may be harmful to the self or others. Feelings of tension or anxiety may precede these acts that may then be followed by pleasure or gratification following the performance of the act. Guilt or regret may or may not be felt subsequent to the act. A person experiencing dermatillomania is likely to be under substantial distress and may feel embarrassed about the excoriating behavior. Social functioning may be severely affected, especially sports participation and other functions in which skin lesions will be exposed. Excoriation may result in varied medical complications, including bleeding, ulcers, infections, and temporary or permanent disfigurement.

Risk factors

Risk factors for dermatillomania include:

- female sex
- age between 8 and 40
- history of childhood abuse
- present abuse of cocaine, methamphetamine, or other stimulant drugs
- high stress level in the family, school, or workplace
- being diagnosed with a mood or anxiety disorder; between 48% and 79% of patients who pick their skin meet the criteria for a mood disorder, and 65% meet the criteria for an anxiety disorder
- being diagnosed with BDD; one study reported that 27% of patients with BDD pick at their skin
- having certain internal disorders that affect the skin, such as diabetes, lymphoma, hyperthyroidism, liver disease, anemia, or uremia

As far as is known, race or ethnicity is not a risk factor for dermatillomania.

Causes and symptoms

Causes

The causes of dermatillomania are still debated and discussed by dermatologists as well as psychiatrists, as is the disorder's relationship to mood, anxiety, impulse control, and **substance abuse** disorders. In some cases

KEY TERMS

Dermatologist—A physician who specializes in the diagnosis and treatment of disorders of the skin, scalp, hair, and nails.

Excoriation—The medical term for abrasion of the upper layer of skin caused by mechanical means, most often scratching or picking.

Formication—The medical term for the sensation of insects crawling on or under the skin. The English word is taken from *formica,* the Latin word for "ant."

Lesion—Any abnormality in or injury to a body tissue. It is derived from the Latin word for "injury."

Scabies—A contagious skin infection in humans and other animals caused by a tiny parasite that burrows under the skin and causes intense itching.

Unna sleeve—A dressing made of gauze impregnated with glycerin, zinc oxide, and calamine that can be used to protect skin injured by compulsive picking from further injury. It is named for the German dermatologist who invented it.

the onset of the disorder is triggered by an insect bite, itchy rash, acne, or other skin disorder, but in other cases there is no underlying skin disease or blemish when the patient first begins to pick at the skin. In some cases the skin picking is associated with emotional **stress**, but in others it is an unconscious process. Some patients report that their skin picking has a ritualistic quality, whereas others report being in a dissociated state during their skin picking episodes.

There was no evidence as of 2011 that **brain** abnormalities or **genetic factors** were involved in the disorder.

Symptoms

The most noticeable external symptom of dermatillomania is the appearance of scratches, scabs, open sores, and/or bruises on areas of the skin that are pulled, squeezed, or picked at. Some of the lesions may appear to be partially healed and reopened. There may or may not be visible bleeding.

Diagnosis

The **diagnosis** is made on the basis of a combination of patient history, office examination of the skin lesions, and direct questioning about skin picking. The patient may or may not volunteer information about the self-injurious behavior. There are a few online self-tests about skin picking, and the patient may seek help after taking the test. The doctor will ask about stress levels, drug use, a history of skin disorders (if any), and a history of mood, anxiety, or impulse control disorders as part of the history-taking.

Dermatillomania was not formally included in ***Diagnostic and Statistical Manual of Mental Disorders***, fourth edition, text revision (*DSM-IV-TR*), although it is proposed for inclusion under the name "Skin picking disorder" in *DSM-5*, due for publication in 2013. The editors of *DSM-5* have proposed the following diagnostic criteria for skin picking disorder:

- There is recurrent skin picking resulting in the appearance of skin lesions.
- The skin picking or pulling "causes clinically significant distress or impairment in social, occupational, or other important areas of functioning."
- The skin picking is not due directly to the physiological effects of a substance or a general medical condition that affects the skin.
- The skin picking is not restricted to the symptoms of another psychiatric disorder, such as BDD or delusional disorder.

As of 2011, the *DSM-5* development group was debating adding a fifth criterion to address the actual urges to engage in skin picking or failed attempts at resisting skin picking.

Examination

The patient's primary care physician may be able to identify lesions created by skin picking but may also refer the patient to a dermatologist for an office examination, particularly if the patient also has acne, eczema, or another skin disorder. The dermatologist can usually distinguish skin excoriations caused by compulsive skin picking from other skin disorders because the lesions are typically clean and linear with irregular borders. They are similar in size and shape to one another and occur on parts of the body that the patient can easily scratch. They are generally distributed on both sides of the body in a symmetrical pattern.

Tests

In some cases the dermatologist may take a small sample of skin to rule out scabies, a fungal infection, or other organic skin disorder. The doctor may also order a complete blood cell count, fasting blood glucose level, or urine test to rule out diabetes, anemia, or other systemic disorders. Imaging tests are not useful in diagnosing dermatillomania.

Treatment

Treatment for compulsive skin picking is usually multimodal, involving a combination of medications and **psychotherapy**.

Drugs

Case reports and small trials have examined the efficacy of various types of drugs for dermatillomania: **antidepressants**, including the **selective serotonin reuptake inhibitors** (**SSRIs**, such as **fluvoxamine**) and the tricyclics (**doxepin** and **clomipramine**), opiate antagonists (**naltrexone**), typical antipsychotics (**pimozide**), and atypical antipsychotics (**olanzapine**, **aripiprazole**). Some patients are reportedly helped by **gabapentin**, a drug originally developed to treat epilepsy that is also used to relieve neuropathic pain.

Another approach that works well for some patients is the use of an Unna sleeve or Unna boot to protect the affected part of the body while the patient is receiving psychotherapy and medications for the compulsive skin picking. Named for the German dermatologist Paul Unna (1850–1929), the Unna sleeve (or boot) is a gauze wrapping impregnated with a mixture of glycerin, **zinc** oxide, and calamine to promote healing. It has been used in the treatment of burns and venous ulcers as well as neurotic excoriation.

Psychotherapy

Behavioral treatments, including psychotherapy and hypnosis, have been examined for effectiveness in dermatillomania. Small-scale studies or case reports have suggested that habit reversal therapy (HRT), a form of **cognitive-behavioral therapy** in which a program of self-monitoring is paired with practicing a competing response, is effective. In HRT, the patient is taught first to be mindful of the situations or events that trigger the skin-picking episodes and then to practice alternative behaviors when the triggers are present. Other forms of psychotherapy, in which behavioral and emotional as well as topical therapies are practiced, can also be effective, as is **group therapy** for the disorder.

Alternative

Some patients with compulsive skin picking are helped by mindfulness **meditation** as an adjunct to HRT. Others report that the relaxation response, breathing exercises, and other **stress reduction** techniques are helpful.

QUESTIONS TO ASK YOUR DOCTOR

- Have you ever treated a patient with dermatillomania?
- What is your opinion of habit reversal training as a treatment for the disorder?
- What do you think causes the disorder?
- Why do you think women are at increased risk of dermatillomania?

Prognosis

Dermatillomania is often a long-term psychiatric problem—the mean duration of symptoms is between 5 and 21 years—but is not known to be fatal. It is, however, not well researched. One team of researchers in Minnesota reported in late 2010 that patients with dermatillomania are on average more severely impaired than patients with **trichotillomania**. There were only eight **clinical trials** of treatments for dermatillomania as of 2011; five were trials of various drugs (**escitalopram**, dronabinol, **lamotrigine**, and n-acetyl cysteine), and three trials were testing the effectiveness of cognitive behavioral interventions.

Large-scale outcome studies of dermatillomania are lacking, although some researchers suggest that visiting a dermatologist prior to experiencing symptoms for one year results in a better prognosis. Permanent scarring and complications from infection of the tissues injured by skin picking are possible. In addition, the chronic rebuilding of the injured tissues has been suggested to be a potential causative factor for skin cancer.

Prevention

There is no known way to prevent dermatillomania because its underlying causes or triggers are not well understood.

Resources

BOOKS

Aboujaoude, Elias, and Lorrin M. Koran. *Impulse Control Disorders*. New York: Cambridge University Press, 2010.

Grant, Jon E., ed. *Trichotillomania, Skin Picking, and Other Body-focused Repetitive Behaviors*. Washington, DC: American Psychiatric Publishing, 2012.

PERIODICALS

Grant, J.E., et al. "A Double-blind, Placebo-controlled Trial of Lamotrigine for Pathological Skin Picking: Treatment Efficacy and Neurocognitive Predictors of Response."

Journal of Clinical Psychopharmacology 30 (2010): 396–403.

Harris, S.S., et al. "Pathologic Grooming Behavior: Facial Dermatillomania." *Cutis* 87 (2011): 14–18.

Odlaug, Bryan L., and Jon E. Grant. "Pathologic Skin Picking." *American Journal of Drug and Alcohol Abuse* 36 (2010): 296–303.

Odlaug, Bryan L., and Jon E. Grant. "Quality of Life and Clinical Severity in Pathological Skin Picking and Trichotillomania." *Journal of Anxiety Disorders* 24, no. 8 (2010): 823–29.

Paley, K., et al. "Unna Sleeve for Neurotic Excoriations." *Cutis* 85 (2010): 149–52.

Schuck, K., et al. "The Effects of Brief Cognitive-behaviour Therapy for Pathological Skin Picking: A Randomized Comparison to Wait-list Control." *Behaviour Research and Therapy* 49 (2011): 11–17.

Snorrason, I., et al. "Motor Inhibition, Reflection Impulsivity, and Trait Impulsivity in Pathological Skin Picking." *Behavior Therapy* 42 (2011): 521–32.

Turner, B.T., et al. "The Skin Picking Impact Project: Phenomenology, Interference, and Treatment Utilization of Pathological Skin Picking in a Population-based Sample." *Journal of Anxiety Disorders* 25 (2011): 88–95.

OTHER

Hayden, Lisa. "Scars of Shame" [three-minute trailer for a documentary about dermatillomania produced by the National Film Board of Canada]. http://www.youtube.com/watch?v=UGjhx7OGcGU (accessed October 14, 2011).

WEBSITES

"Body Dysmorphic Disorder." Mayo Clinic. November 5, 2010. http://www.mayoclinic.com/health/body-dysmorphic-disorder/DS00559 (accessed October 14, 2011).

"Compulsive Skin Picking." DermNetNZ. Last updated June 28, 2011. http://dermnetnz.org/systemic/skin-picking.html (accessed October 14, 2011).

"Compulsive Skin Picking." OCD Center of Los Angeles. http://www.ocdla.com/compulsiveskinpicking.html (accessed October 14, 2011).

"Dermatillomania/Compulsive Skin Picking Test." OCD Center of Los Angeles. http://www.ocdla.com/dermatillomania-compulsive-skin-picking-test.html (accessed October 14, 2011).

"F 04 Skin Picking Disorder." American Psychiatric Association. DSM-5 Development. May 19, 2010. http://www.dsm5.org/ProposedRevision/Pages/proposedrevision.aspx?rid=401 (accessed October 14, 2011).

Scheinfeld, Noah S. "Neurotic Excoriations." Medscape. August 3, 2011. http://emedicine.medscape.com/article/1122042-overview (accessed October 14, 2011).

ORGANIZATIONS

American Academy of Dermatology, PO Box 4014, Schaumburg, IL, 60168, (847) 240-1280, Fax: (847) 240-1859, (866) 503-SKIN, http://www.aad.org.

American Psychiatric Association, 1000 Wilson Blvd., Ste. 1825, Arlington, VA, 22209-3901, (703) 907-7300, apa@psych.org, http://www.psych.org.

American Psychological Association, 750 1st St. NE, Washington, DC, 20002-4242, (202) 336-5500; TDD/TTY: (202) 336-6123, (800) 374-2721, http://www.apa.org.

National Institute of Mental Health, 6001 Executive Blvd., Rm. 8184, MSC 9663, Bethesda, MD, 20892-9663, (301) 433-4513; TTY: (301) 443-8431, Fax: (301) 443-4279, (866) 615-6464; TTY: (866) 415-8051, nimhinfo@nih.gov, http://www.nimh.nih.gov.

OCD Center of Los Angeles, 11620 Wilshire Blvd., Ste. 890, Los Angeles, CA, 90025, (310) 824-5200, http://www.ocdla.com/contactus.html, http://www.ocdla.com/index.html.

Andrew J. Bean, PhD
Rebecca J. Frey, PhD

Desensitization *see* **Systematic desensitization**

Desipramine

Definition

Desipramine is an antidepressant drug used to elevate mood and promote recovery of a normal range of emotions in patients with depressive disorders. In addition, desipramine has uses in a number of other psychiatric and medical conditions. In the United States, the drug is also known by its brand name, Norpramin.

Purpose

Desipramine is known principally as an antidepressant drug used to promote recovery of depressed patients. It also

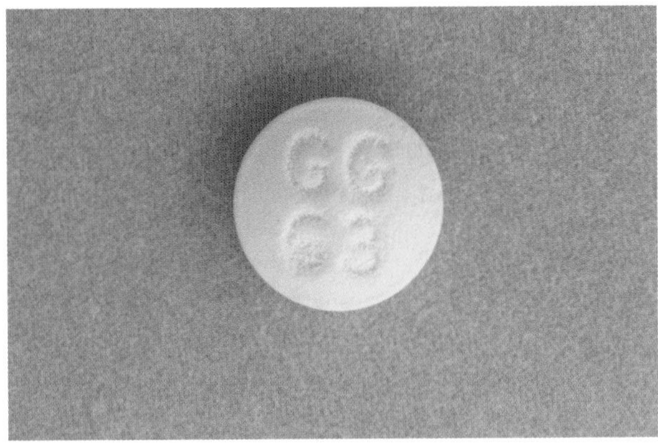

Desipramine. *(© Custom Medical Stock Photo, Inc. Reproduced by permission.)*

has therapeutic uses in **panic disorder**, pain management, **attention deficit hyperactivity disorder (ADHD)**, sleep attacks (**narcolepsy** and cataplexy), binge eating, and for **cocaine** craving in the treatment of **addiction**.

Description

Desipramine is one of the tricyclic **antidepressants**, so-called because of the three-ring chemical structure common to these drugs. Until the late 1980s, desipramine and other tricyclic antidepressants, such as **imipramine**, formed the mainstay of the pharmacological treatment of depressive disorders.

The therapeutic action of antidepressants is not completely understood. It is known that these drugs boost the levels of certain messenger chemicals, called **neurotransmitters**, which are involved in transmitting signals between nerve cells in the **brain**. This action may help to restore normal emotional feelings by counteracting abnormalities of nerve signal transmission that occur in depressive disorders.

Desipramine is one of a large number of tricyclic antidepressant compounds. Each was developed for somewhat differing pharmacological effects and side-effect profiles. The effects of desipramine are similar to those of other tricyclics, although some patients may find one drug of this group more effective or more tolerable than another. It is available as Norpramin in 10, 25, 50, 75, 100, and 150 mg tablets, although generic manufacturers may supply a somewhat different set of dosages.

Recommended dosage

For adults, desipramine is usually administered in dosages of 100–200 mg per day. Doses ranging from 75 mg to 300 mg per day are sometimes prescribed. The initial daily dose is usually low to avoid side effects, and it is usually increased, as necessary, until a therapeutic effect is achieved. Desipramine may be administered in divided doses or a single daily dose.

Geriatric patients, children, and adolescents are more sensitive to the side effects and toxicities of tricyclic antidepressants than other people. For geriatric patients, the dose may range from 25 mg to 100 mg per day. For children 6–12 years old, the recommended dose ranges from 10 mg to 30 mg per day in divided doses. For adolescents, daily dosages range from 25 mg to 50 mg but may be increased up to 100 mg, if needed.

Precautions

Because desipramine and other tricyclic antidepressants may cause drowsiness, activities requiring alertness, such as driving, may be impaired. Patients should avoid such activities until they understand how the drug affects them. Dizziness or lightheadedness may occur when standing due to sudden decreases in blood pressure. Fainting may also occur. Patients with glaucoma may find their condition aggravated. Among patients with epilepsy, **seizures** may become more frequent. Persons with heart disease should use tricyclic antidepressants with caution due to a possibility of adverse effects on heart rhythm.

Studies have found that some antidepressant drugs, including desipramine, may increase the chances of suicidal thoughts in children and adults up to age 24. Patients taking desipramine should be monitored, regardless of age, for worsening **depression** or other adverse changes in behavior.

It has not been determined whether desipramine is safe to take during pregnancy, and the patient's need for this medicine should be balanced against the possibility of harm to the fetus. Tricyclic antidepressants may be secreted in breast milk and may cause sedation and depressed breathing in a nursing infant.

Side effects

Desipramine may cause many side effects. Initially, the side effects of tricyclic drugs may be more pronounced, but sensitivity may decrease with continued treatment. Some of the more common side effects include **fatigue**, confusion, nervousness, restlessness, sleep difficulties, numbness, tingling sensations, tremors, blurred vision, difficulty urinating (especially in men with prostate enlargement), constipation, rashes, and weight gain. Sensitivity to ultraviolet light may be increased, and sunburns may occur more easily. Sweating may be reduced, causing sensitivity to heat and hot weather. Patients may also develop dry mouth due to decreased saliva, possibly contributing to the development of tooth decay, gum disease, and mouth infections. Patients should avoid sweets, sugary beverages, and chewing gum containing sugar.

Less commonly, tricyclic drugs may cause adverse effects on almost any organ or system of the body, particularly the blood, hormones, kidney, and liver. Patients should consult their physicians if symptoms develop or bodily changes occur.

Interactions

Tricyclic antidepressants such as desipramine may interact with many other drugs. Patients should inform their physicians about all other drugs they are taking. Tricyclic drugs may intensify the effects of drugs causing

KEY TERMS

Autonomic—The part of the nervous system that governs the heart, involuntary muscles, and glands.

Cataplexy—A symptom of narcolepsy marked by a sudden episode of muscle weakness triggered by strong emotions. The muscle weakness may cause the person's knees to buckle, or the head to drop. In severe cases, the patient may become paralyzed for a few seconds or minutes.

Epilepsy—A neurological disorder characterized by the onset of seizures. Seizures are caused by a disturbance in the electrical activity in the brain and can cause loss of consciousness, muscle spasms, rhythmic movements, abnormal sensory experiences, or altered mental states.

Glaucoma—A group of eye diseases characterized by increased pressure within the eye significant enough to damage eye tissue and structures. If untreated, glaucoma results in blindness.

Neurotransmitter—A chemical in the brain that transmits messages between neurons, or nerve cells.

sedation, including alcohol, **barbiturates**, narcotic pain medications, minor tranquilizers, and antihistamines. Tricyclics may cause excessive drops in blood pressure in patients taking blood-pressure medicine, especially upon sitting up or standing. Conversely, these drugs may interfere with the pressure-reducing effects of certain other blood pressure medicines. Tricyclics may interact with thyroid medications to produce heart rhythm abnormalities. Also, they may increase seizure tendency in patients with epilepsy, requiring adjustment of anti-epileptic medication. Concurrent use of tricyclic antidepressants with other antidepressants or other psychiatric medicines may result in intensification of certain side effects.

Certain drugs may interfere with the elimination of tricyclic antidepressants from the body causing higher blood levels and increased side effects. This effect may occur with cimetidine (Tagamet), other antidepressants, **methylphenidate** (Ritalin, Concerta), and some antipsychotic medications. Patients taking **monoamine oxidase inhibitors (MAOIs)** should tell their physicians before starting desipramine (or vice-versa). They will likely need to wait a period of at least 14 days after their last MAOI dosage before beginning treatment with desipramine.

Resources

BOOKS

Preston, John D., John H. O'Neal, and Mary C. Talaga. *Handbook of Clinical Psychopharmacology for Therapists*. 5th ed. Oakland, CA: New Harbinger Publications, 2008.

PERIODICALS

Amitai, Yona, and Henri Frischer. "Excess Fatality from Desipramine in Children and Adolescents." *Journal of the American Academy of Child and Adolescent Psychiatry* 45, no. 1 (January 2006): 54–60.

DeRubeis, Robert J., et al. "Cognitive Therapy vs Medications in the Treatment of Moderate to Severe Depression." *Archives of General Psychiatry* 62, no. 4 (April 2005): 409–16.

Mayers, Andrew G., and David S. Baldwin. "Antidepressants and Their Effect on Sleep." *Human Psychopharmacology: Clinical and Experimental* 20, no. 8 (December 2005): 533–59.

McDowell, David, et al. "Desipramine Treatment of Cocaine-Dependent Patients with Depression: A Placebo-Controlled Trial." *Drug and Alcohol Dependence* 80, no. 2 (November 2005): 209–21.

Musselman, Dominique L., et al. "Double-Blind, Multicenter, Parallel-Group Study of Paroxetine, Desipramine, or Placebo in Breast Cancer Patients (stages I, II, III, and IV) with Major Depression." *Journal of Clinical Psychiatry* 67, no. 2 (February 2006): 288–96.

Rains, Adrienne, L. Scahill, and V. Hamrin. "Nonstimulant Medications for the Treatment of ADHD." *Journal of Child and Adolescent Psychiatric Nursing* 19, no. 1 (February 2006): 44–47.

Walsh, B. Timothy, Robyn Sysko, and Michael K. Parides. "Early Response to Desipramine Among Women with Bulimia Nervosa." *International Journal of Eating Disorders* 39, no. 1 (January 2006): 72–75.

Wilens, Timothy E., et al. "Blood Pressure Changes Associated with Medication Treatment of Adults with Attention-Deficit/Hyperactivity Disorder." *Journal of Clinical Psychiatry* 66, no. 2 (February 2005): 253–59.

ORGANIZATIONS

American Academy of Child and Adolescent Psychiatry, 3615 Wisconsin Ave. NW, Washington, DC, 20016-3007, (202) 966-7300, Fax: (202) 966-2891, http://aacap.org.

American Academy of Clinical Toxicology, 6728 Old McLean Village Dr., McLean, VA, 22101, (703) 556-9222, Fax: (703) 556-8729, admin@clintox.org, http://www.clintox.org.

American College of Neuropsychopharmacology, 5034-A Thoroughbred Lane, Brentwood, TN, 37027, (615) 324-2360, Fax: (615) 523-1715, acnp@acnp.org, http://www.acnp.org.

American Psychiatric Association, 1000 Wilson Blvd., Ste. 1825, Arlington, VA, 22209-3901, (703) 907-7300, apa@psych.org, http://www.psych.org.

Richard Kapit, MD
Ruth A. Wienclaw, PhD

Desoxyn *see* **Amphetamines**

Desvenlafaxine

Definition

Desvenlafaxine, sold under the brand name Pristiq, is a medication used to treat **depression**. This medication belongs to a class of drugs known as selective **serotonin** norepinephrine reuptake inhibitors (SNRIs), which affect the **neurotransmitters** serotonin and norepinephrine. These chemicals are involved in normal **brain** function and are associated with clinical depression.

Purpose

Desvenlafaxine is approved for the treatment of clinical depression, though other potential uses were being explored as of 2011. Desvenlafaxine is the synthetic form of a metabolite of the antidepressant **venlafaxine**. It was developed based on the theory that a significant portion of the therapeutical benefits of venlafaxine may have come from this metabolite. Desvenlafaxine is expected to have fewer interactions with other medications than venlafaxine due to differences in how it is metabolized. Whether there is an advantage in taking desvenlafaxine instead of venlafaxine is debated.

Description

Desvenlafaxine works by acting on the neurotransmitters serotonin and norepinephrine, chemicals in the body that help regulate normal brain and body functioning. Neurotransmitters such as serotonin and norepinephrine bind to chemical receptors on the surface of the brain. Once bound to their designated receptor, they begin to affect physiological processes. It is believed that a decrease in serotonin and norepinephrine contributes to illnesses such as depression and **anxiety disorders**; SNRIs help counteract this by increasing the actions of the neurotransmitters, though desvenlafaxine has a larger impact on serotonin than norepinephrine.

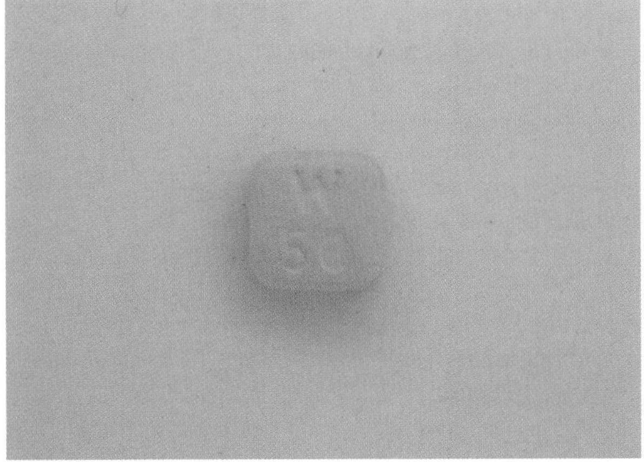

Desvenlafaxine (Pristiq), 50 mg. *(© Custom Medical Stock Photo, Inc. Reproduced by permission.)*

Whether a patient is going to benefit from taking an SNRI medication may have a genetic component. Individual response to each SNRI varies greatly. The initial trial of an SNRI can be difficult, because adverse side effects may occur before the patient begins to see the benefits of the medication, which may be frustrating to the patient. A drug that works best for one patient may not work for another patient, and having no success with one SNRI does not mean that a patient will have the same results with another SNRI. Finding which SNRI is going to work for a patient may require a trial of multiple drugs until an effective agent is identified. Generally, a drug is used for 4–6 weeks before a decision is made regarding its effectiveness. If the drug has shown some benefit but the healthcare provider thinks that it could be improved, the dose may be increased if the patient is able to tolerate it.

Recommended dosage

Desvenlafaxine is taken as an oral medication. The dosage used may vary depending on how an individual patient responds. If side effects develop that are not tolerable, the patient may require a lower dose. Desvenlafaxine is usually dosed at 50 mg daily. Higher doses rarely result in better therapeutic effects and increase the risk of adverse side effects. Elderly patients tend to develop side effects more easily and may be more sensitive to the effects of the medication; these populations may require dosing every other day. Patients with impaired liver or kidney function impacting metabolism require lower doses or less frequent dosing to avoid toxicity. Slowly increasing the dose may help minimize side effects, and some side effects may abate with continued use. Patients are periodically reassessed to determine whether there is need for continued treatment with desvenlafaxine. SNRIs, including desvenlafaxine, need to be slowly tapered off if discontinued to avoid withdrawal symptoms.

Precautions

Antidepressant drugs, including desvenlafaxine, have been associated with an increased risk of suicidal thoughts and behaviors in children and adults up to age 24. Any

KEY TERMS

Bipolar disorder—A mood disorder marked by alternating episodes of extremely low mood (depression) and exuberant highs (mania).

Glaucoma—Condition involving increased pressure within the eye that may cause damage and blindness.

Mania—Physiological state of hyperactivity experienced by patients with certain psychiatric illnesses involving inappropriate elevated mood, pressured speech, poor judgment, and sometimes psychotic episodes superimposed on the state of mania.

Metabolite—Chemical compound that occurs as a result of a parent drug being broken down and metabolized in the body. A metabolite may be a medically active or inactive compound, depending on the drug in question.

Monoamine oxidase inhibitors (MAOIs)—Type of antidepressant medication that affects various kinds of neurotransmitters including serotonin.

Neurotransmitter—One of a group of chemicals secreted by a nerve cell (neuron) to carry a chemical message to another nerve cell, often as a way of transmitting a nerve impulse. Examples of neurotransmitters include acetylcholine, dopamine, serotonin, and norepinephrine.

Neurotransmitter receptor—A physical recipient for chemicals called neurotransmitters. Receptors sit on the surface of cells that make up body tissues, and once bound to the neurotransmitter, they initiate the chemical signaling pathway associated with neurotransmitters.

Selective serotonin norepinephrine reuptake inhibitors (SNRIs)—Drug class that acts to specifically inhibit the reuptake of serotonin and norepinephrine in the neuronal synapse with little effect on other types of neurotransmitters, thereby decreasing side effects associated with broader acting drugs.

Selective serotonin reuptake inhibitors (SSRIs)—Drug class that acts to specifically inhibit the reuptake of serotonin only in the neuronal synapse with little effect on other types of neurotransmitters, thereby decreasing side effects associated with broader acting drugs.

Serotonin—A type of neurotransmitter involved in regulation of the blood vessels, brain processes, and disease states such as depression.

Serotonin syndrome—A potentially life threatening drug reaction involving an excess of the neurotransmitter serotonin, usually occurring when too many medications that increase serotonin are taken together, such as antimigraine triptans and certain antidepressants.

Synapse—Physical space between neurons that allows the passage of neurotransmitters for chemical signaling pathways.

patient taking an antidepressant drug should be monitored for changes in behavior and worsening depression. If treatment with desvenlafaxine is ceased, it should be slowly discontinued to avoid the development of SNRI discontinuation syndrome. Such withdrawal symptoms include flu-like symptoms, anxiety, agitation, vivid or bizarre dreams, **insomnia**, nausea, vomiting, diarrhea, sense of imbalance, chills, **fatigue**, dizziness, headache, numbness and tingling of the extremities, and other sensory disturbances. Discontinuation syndrome may be avoided if the dose is properly reduced over time.

SNRI overdose may result in a condition known as **serotonin syndrome**. Serotonin overdose may be caused by taking multiple drugs that increase the amount of serotonin signaling in the body. Symptoms of serotonin overdose range from mild to life-threatening, depending on the individual situation. Symptoms may include high blood pressure, high fever, nausea, diarrhea, headache, sweating, increased heart rate, tremor, muscle twitching, **delirium**, shock, coma, and death.

Desvenlafaxine may be contraindicated or may require caution in use in patients with uncontrolled hypertension, liver function impairment or liver disease, kidney function impairment, seizure disorder, bleeding disorders, glaucoma, dehydration, history of alcohol abuse, and in patients younger than 25 years of age or the elderly. Kidney and liver function, as well as blood pressure and behavioral changes, may be monitored while patients are taking desvenlafaxine. SNRIs such as desvenlafaxine are discouraged for use in patients with **bipolar disorder**, as the drugs can induce a state of mania in these individuals. There are selective conditions under which a doctor may prescribe an SNRI such as desvenlafaxine to a bipolar patient, but only for a short period and under careful monitoring. Desvenlafaxine is classified as category C for pregnancy, which means that either there are no adequate human or animal studies or that adverse fetal effects were found in animal studies, but there is no available human data. The decision whether or not to use category C drugs in pregnancy is generally based on weighing the critical needs of the mother against the risk to the fetus. Other lower category agents are used whenever possible. The safety of desvenlafaxine use during breast-feeding is unknown and, therefore, its use is not recommended.

Side effects

SNRIs tend to have fewer side effects than other types of older antidepressant medications, but side effects may still occur. Common side effects of desvenlafaxine include nausea and vomiting, headache, dizziness, fatigue, constipation or diarrhea, sexual dysfunction, sweating, dry mouth, shakiness, tremor, palpitations, loss of appetite, weight changes, hot flashes, chills, elevated blood pressure, vision changes, ringing in the ears, anxiety, abnormal dreams, and insomnia. Rare but serious potential side effects include mania, worsened depression and suicidality, **seizures**, serotonin syndrome, discontinuation syndrome, electrolyte imbalances, lung damage or disease, urinary retention, skin reactions, abnormal bleeding, liver damage, and glaucoma.

Interactions

Patients should make their doctor aware of all medications and supplements they are taking before using desvenlafaxine. Using alcohol while taking desvenlafaxine may create toxic reactions and should be avoided. Drugs that affect the liver may alter the metabolism of desvenlafaxine and may result in too much or to little of the drug in the body, though this possibility is less of a concern than with other drugs.

SNRIs should not be used with other drugs that inhibit the absorption of serotonin, such as **selective serotonin reuptake inhibitors (SSRIs)**. **Antidepressants** called **monoamine oxidase inhibitors (MAOIs)** also increase the amount of serotonin should not be used concurrently with desvenlafaxine. Patients taking **MAOIs** should stop and wait at least 14 days before starting treatment with desvenlafaxine; switching from desvenlafaxine to an MAOI may require a waiting period of up to five weeks.

Other drugs that increase serotonin in the body include sumatriptan (Imitrex), used to treat migraine headaches; the antipsychotics **chlorpromazine** and **fluphenazine**; and the herbal supplements yohimbe and **St. John's wort**. Diuretics (water pills) such as hydrochlorothiazide, diet pills such as sibutramine (Meridia), caffeine, certain diabetes drugs such as sulfonylureas, mood stabilizers such as **valproic acid**, and antipsychotics such as **haloperidol** and **clozapine** should not be used with desvenlafaxine to avoid potentially toxic effects. There is increased risk of internal bleeding when desvenlafaxine is used with anticoagulant drugs such as aspirin, warfarin, or large doses of the herbal supplements red clover, dong quai, **ginkgo biloba**, feverfew, or concentrated green tea.

QUESTIONS TO ASK YOUR DOCTOR

- Can I take the full dose right away or do I need to slowly increase the dose up to the full amount?
- Can I stop taking the medication right away or do I need to stop slowly?
- Should I eat before taking this medication?
- Will this medication interact with any of my other prescription medications? Over-the-counter medications? Herbal supplements?
- What side effects should I watch for while taking this medication?
- Can I drink alcoholic beverages in the same time frame as taking this medication?

Resources

BOOKS

Brunton, Laurence L., et al. *Goodman and Gilman's The Pharmacological Basis of Therapeutics*. 12th ed. New York: McGraw Hill Medical, 2011.

Stargrove, Mitchell Bebel, et al. *Herb, Nutrient, and Drug Interactions: Clinical Implications and Therapeutic Strategies*. St. Louis: Mosby, 2007.

PERIODICALS

Tourian, K. A., et al. "A 10-Month, Open-Label Evaluation of Desvenlafaxine in Outpatients with Major Depressive Disorder." *Primary Care Companion to CNS Disorders* 13, no. 2 (2011): e1–e10.

WEBSITES

PubMed Health. "Desvenlafaxine." U.S. National Library of Medicine. http://www.ncbi.nlm.nih.gov/pubmedhealth/PMH0000449 (accessed November 3, 2011).

ORGANIZATIONS

American College of Neuropsychopharmacology, 5034-A Thoroughbred Lane, Brentwood, TN, 37027, (615) 324-2360, Fax: (615) 523-1715, acnp@acnp.org, http://www.acnp.org/default.aspx.

American Society for Clinical Pharmacology and Therapeutics, 528 N Washington St., Alexandria, VA, 22314, (703) 836-6981, info@ascpt.org, http://www.ascpt.org.

Mental Health America, 2000 N Beauregard St., 6th Fl., Alexandria, VA, 22311, (703) 684-7722, (800) 969-6642, Fax: (703) 684-5968, http://www.nmha.org.

U.S. Food and Drug Administration, 10903 New Hampshire Ave., Silver Spring, MD, 20993-0002, (888) INFO-FDA (463-6332), http://www.fda.gov.

Maria Eve Basile, PhD

Desyrel *see* **Trazodone**

Detoxification

Definition

Detoxification is a process in which the body is allowed to free itself of a drug. During this period, the symptoms of withdrawal are also treated. Detoxification is the primary step in any drug treatment program and is used as the initial phase in treating alcohol, heroin, inhalant, sedative, and hypnotic addictions.

Purpose

Detoxification is only the first step in the long-term recovery of alcoholics and drug addicts. The immediate purposes of detoxification are to clear the toxins out of the body and help the patient achieve a substance-free condition. Detoxification treatment also aims to relieve the physical symptoms of withdrawal and treat any comorbid medical or psychiatric disorders. For the recovering person to stay abstinent on a long-term basis, detoxification needs to lead into long-term community residential program treatment or outpatient drug treatment lasting three to six months.

Demographics

Alcohol and **substance abuse** are common disorders in the general adult population in North America. The lifetime prevalence of alcoholism in American adults is estimated to be between 13.7% and 23.5%. At any one time, approximately 15.2 million Americans aged 12 and older are alcohol-dependent. There are 1.2 million hospital admissions for problems related to alcohol abuse each year in the United States. Estimates of drug dependence are more difficult to compile because the abuse of specific drugs fluctuates over time and is affected by social trends. It was thought that 3.9 million Americans were dependent on illicit drugs as of early 2010.

There is a considerable gap between the number of people who need treatment for alcohol and substance abuse and the number who actually receive it. The NIH estimates that in 2007, 23.2 million Americans aged 12 or older needed treatment for an illicit drug or **alcohol use** problem, but only 3.9 million received treatment at a specialized substance abuse facility.

The number of people undergoing detoxification is also difficult to estimate because the process has a "revolving-door" quality; that is, many persons with alcohol or drug addictions do not go on to the second phase of recovery from substance abuse. They do not maintain sobriety or freedom from drugs for more than a few days or weeks, and may require detoxification several times within a calendar year. Risk factors for repeated episodes of detoxification include:

- homelessness
- underlying mental illness
- personality disorder
- lack of support from family, friends, or other support community
- unemployment
- low level of education
- involvement with the criminal justice system
- multiple addictions
- male sex

Description

The body, when allowed to be free from drugs, detoxifies itself through its normal metabolic processes. Withdrawal symptoms are treated during this process so that the patient will be comfortable while the body detoxifies itself.

The process of substance addiction

Before discussing detoxification, it may be useful to understand how the body becomes addicted and why withdrawal symptoms are experienced. In physical **addiction** or dependence, as a person uses a substance or chemical over a long period of time, his or her body chemistry changes. Once a substance enters the body through drinking, smoking, injecting, or inhaling, it travels through the bloodstream to the **brain**. The brain has a complex reward system built in; when people engage in activities that are important for survival (such as eating), special nerve cells in the brain release chemicals (**neurotransmitters**, including **dopamine**) that induce feelings of pleasure. Because of this reward system in the brain, humans are programmed to want to repeat actions that elicit those pleasant sensations. In other words, feelings of pleasure reinforce certain activities or behaviors. Addictive substances interfere with this reward system. Some drugs mimic the effects of a natural chemical, some block the communication between nerve cells, and some substances trigger a larger-than-normal release of neurotransmitters like dopamine. The result of this interference is that dependent drug users physically need the drug to feel pleasure. As they become more dependent, their bodies become less responsive to the substance and need more of it to get the desired response—a phenomenon called tolerance. Also as a result of the interference with the brain's system, when the dependent user does not have the drug in his or her system, feelings of **depression** or unpleasant withdrawal symptoms may be experienced. These consequences also reinforce the substance use. People dependent on substances resort to using more drugs to avoid the depression or the withdrawal symptoms.

Withdrawal symptoms

The symptoms and severity of these symptoms vary from one substance to another.

ALCOHOL. After a person who has used alcohol heavily for a long time stops drinking, he or she may experience increased heart rate, shaking, difficulty sleeping, nausea, restlessness, anxiety, and even **seizures**. The affected person may also experience hallucinations (seeing, hearing, or feeling something that is not actually present). In some cases, **delirium** tremens (DTs) may occur as part of the withdrawal. Delirium tremens is a violent delirium (fading in and out of consciousness) with tremors, increased motor activity, visual hallucinations, disorientation, confusion, and fever that happens 48–96 hours after the alcohol-dependent person has had his or her last drink. These symptoms can last anywhere from three to 10 days. This state is a medical emergency because it could be fatal.

HEROIN AND OTHER OPIATES. Heroin is part of a family of drugs called opiates or **opioids**, which are made up of drugs that come from the seeds of the Asian poppy (e.g., heroin, opium, and morphine) and also manufactured drugs that act like the natural drugs (meperidine or Demerol). Symptoms of opiate withdrawal include restlessness, **insomnia**, anxiety, irritability, loss of appetite, diarrhea, abdominal cramps, nausea, sweating, chills, and runny eyes and nose.

SEDATIVES AND HYPNOTICS. **Sedatives** and hypnotics are drug families that are often considered in one group called the sedative-hypnotics. These drugs depress or slow down the body's functions, and can be used to calm anxiety or to induce sleep. When taken in high doses or when abused, these drugs can cause unconsciousness or death. These drugs include **barbiturates** and **benzodiazepines**. Some barbiturates are amobarbital (Amytal), pentobarbital (Nembutal), and secobarbital (Seconal). Some benzodiazepines include **diazepam** (Valium), **chlordiazepoxide** (Librium), and **lorazepam** (Ativan). When a person dependent on these drugs stops taking them suddenly, he or she might experience restlessness, muscle cramps, anxiety, insomnia, irritability, paranoid behavior, and even seizures or death.

Alcohol detoxification

Patients being detoxified from alcohol can safely be treated with rest, **nutrition**, vitamins, and thiamin (a B vitamin whose absorption is affected by alcohol abuse). Detoxification can be completed in an inpatient setting, or patients may participate in intensive outpatient (day hospital) treatment. People with mild or moderate withdrawal symptoms undergo detoxification over a five-day period and receive a benzodiazepine or phenobarbital to help ease the withdrawal symptoms. Delirium tremens can be treated with very high-dose benzodiazepines (such as chlordiazepoxide or diazepam) or with antipsychotic medications such as Haldol (**haloperidol**). The patient usually receives medication at doses high enough to give 60 mg or more of the medication over a 24- to 36-hour period, and the doses of these medications are gradually decreased by 20% each day. Patients who have liver disease, **dementia**, or patients who are over the age of 65 or with significant medical problems may receive lorazepam for the withdrawal symptoms.

Heroin detoxification

Patients with heroin dependence may receive help with their detoxification in one of two forms. Opioid agonists are drugs that act like heroin in the patient's body but do not provide the same "high," and are given in gradually decreasing doses. Because these medications "act" like heroin, the person does not experience withdrawal symptoms. Some examples of this kind of medication are **methadone** and levo-alpha-acetylmethadol (LAAM); buprenorphine is a partial opioid agonist, which means that it acts like heroin or methadone, but it limits the effects of opioids so that higher doses produce no greater effects. It is available as a monotherapy (meaning it is the only drug taken) or in combination with another drug, naloxone, as therapy for heroin detoxification. Some studies have found that buprenoporphine shows promise in treating pregnant women for opiate addiction; however, the current standard of care remains methadone replacement for pregnant women. The second form of help for patients undergoing heroin detoxification is the use of a drug, such as **clonidine** (Catapres), that blocks some of the withdrawal symptoms. There is also a controversial method of heroin detoxification called ultra-rapid opioid detoxification under anesthesia/sedation, and there is an experimental method using a medication called lofexidine.

METHADONE SUBSTITUTION. Methadone substitution can occur in outpatient or inpatient settings, and is a method of detoxification that involves helping patients off substances such as heroin by substituting these substances with methadone to ease the withdrawal symptoms, and gradually decreasing the dose until no methadone is needed for the symptoms. Patients may begin with a dose of methadone that is between 20 mg and 40 mg per day. The initial dose may be adjusted so that the most beneficial dose can be discovered, based on the patient's withdrawal symptoms. The dose is then gradually decreased over the next several days. The decrease in methadone dosage is called tapering. If the detoxification is being completed in an inpatient setting, the methadone dose can be tapered more quickly, because medical staff can closely monitor patients for withdrawal, and detoxification can be achieved in about five to 10 days. However, in the case of outpatient detoxification, the taper has to be done much more slowly to assure that the patient does not have an adverse reaction or **relapse** (use the drug of abuse again) to treat their withdrawal symptoms. The dose may be decreased about 10% per week initially until a dose of 20 mg is reached. Then the dose can be decreased by 3% per week for the rest of the time that the patient needs to be detoxified. Patients are usually comfortable with the slow decrease of the medication until the dose gets below 20 mg/day. At that point, patients tend to become fearful of being off opioids and having symptoms of withdrawal.

Clonidine is used much more frequently than methadone in detoxification. Methadone is used frequently as long-term maintenance treatment for heroin addiction.

BUPRENORPHINE. Buprenorphine is another medication that is used during opioid detoxification. Because it also acts like heroin in the body, the patient does not experience the withdrawal symptoms as the heroin is being eliminated from the body. It is given as an intramuscular injection or intravenously. It begins to work within 15 minutes and its effects last six hours. It is given as part of three phases of detoxification: induction, stabilization, and maintenance. Induction is the initiation of buprenoporphine therapy, which is administered once the patient has not used opiates for 12 to 24 hours. During stabilization, the dose may be adjusted as the patient stops having cravings or experiences fewer side effects. The length of the maintenance phase varies depending on the needs of the individual, and ends with medically supervised withdrawal. This drug has shown greater effectiveness than other replacement therapies in treating opiate withdrawal.

CLONIDINE. Clonidine is a medication that decreases many of the symptoms of opioid withdrawal. Patients may require nonsteroidal anti-inflammatory drugs (NSAIDS, such as ibuprofen) for the treatment of muscle aches. Clonidine's major side effects include sedation and hypotension (low blood pressure) because it is used to treat high blood pressure. Patients undergoing detoxification using clonidine will have their blood pressure and pulse checked regularly. The starting dose of clonidine is 0.1–0.3 mg every four to six hours—the maximum amount that can be given in one day is 1 mg. During days two through four of the detoxification, the dose of clonidine is adjusted to control the withdrawal symptoms. Again, however, the dose cannot exceed the maximum dose. On the fifth day of detoxification, the dose may be slowly tapered.

The clonidine patch is a transdermal patch, allowing the drug to be delivered through the skin and exposing the patient to a constant amount of the drug over a seven-day period. It also allows the person to experience a more comfortable heroin detoxification. It comes in three doses: 0.1 mg, 0.2 mg, and 0.3 mg. Patients who use the clonidine patch need to have both the patch on and take oral clonidine during the first two days of the detoxification, because it takes the patch two days to reach a steady state and be effective. The patient takes oral clonidine 0.2 mg three times a day, and the weight of the patient determines the dose of the patch. On day two, the amount of clonidine that the patient takes by mouth is reduced by half and then it is completely stopped after day three. After seven days, the patch is removed and replaced with a patch that is half the amount of the original dose. The patch is continued for as long as the patient continues to have symptoms of withdrawal. Blood pressure is monitored for the patient using the patch, as well. The detoxification process in general takes about seven days using clonidine.

CLONIDINE-NALTREXONE ULTRA-RAPID DETOXIFICATION. Clonidine-naltrexone ultra-rapid detoxification has been attempted as a faster means of detoxification than using clonidine alone, and a similar "ultra-fast" method in combination with anesthesia has also been tested. These approaches remain quite controversial, and published clinical data supporting their efficacy are lacking, as are controlled trials. Anesthesia-assisted detoxification may even have adverse effects, especially in patients with co-occurring disorders.

LOFEXIDINE. Lofexidine is used experimentally in the United Kingdom for opioid detoxification. It appears to cause less sedation and fewer cases of low blood pressure than clonidine. In the United States, the National Institute of Drug Abuse (NIDA) is conducting studies on treatments using this drug in combination with **naltrexone**.

Mixed substance abuse

Mixed substance abuse (also called polysubstance abuse) occurs when individuals abuse more than one substance. Many doctors prefer to use phenobarbital to detoxify patients with polysubstance abuse problems. Patients receiving phenobarbital may receive a test dose, and then based on his or her tolerance and symptoms, the dose will be adjusted. Patients cannot receive more than 600 mg of phenobarbital a day. After two to three days, once the patient is doing well, the dose can be reduced by 30–60 mg. Whether detoxification for polysubstance abusers will be completed on an inpatient or outpatient status depends on the drugs the patient abuses.

Benzodiazepines

These medications are often used to help patients during detoxification, but these substances themselves can be abused and addictive. Patients who have taken a prescribed benzodiazepine for two weeks, even in a therapeutic dose, need to be safely detoxified with a slow taper. The amount of drug the person takes is dropped by 10%–25% every week if the patient has minimal withdrawal symptoms. If the patient has taken very high doses for long periods of time, he or she is at increased risk for addiction. If the person has been taking a benzodiazepine medication for years, it can take months before he or she can get off the drug. Anticonvulsant medications like **carbamazepine** (Tegretol) and **divalproex sodium** (Depakote) can be used to make the detoxification process faster and more comfortable for the patient.

Benefits

All approaches to detoxification benefit patients by treating the physical symptoms of withdrawal from alcohol or drugs and by preparing patients for the later phases of recovery from substance abuse.

Specific benefits of inpatient detoxification programs include:

- Ongoing medical supervision of withdrawal symptoms.
- Separation from substance-abusing companions and environments.
- Prevention of easy access to alcohol or drugs.

Specific benefits of outpatient detoxification programs include:

- Lower expense.
- Less time-consuming.
- Patient can maintain normal employment and family routines.
- Patient can often enter second-phase rehabilitation in the same facility as first-phase detoxification.

Precautions

When individuals are physically dependent on a substance, they experience withdrawal symptoms when they abstain from the drug. Withdrawal symptoms vary with each drug of abuse, but can be severe, and even dangerous. Patients who want to overcome their dependence need help managing the withdrawal symptoms. The patient's medical team strives to get the patient off a substance on which he or she is physically dependent, while treating the withdrawal symptoms.

Pregnant women cannot be detoxified from opiates (also called narcotics, including morphine, heroin, and similar drugs) because strict detoxification can increase the risk of spontaneous abortion or premature birth. These women can be treated with methadone as an alternative. Methadone acts as a replacement for the heroin in the woman's body, but the methadone does not provide the "high" that the heroin provides. In addition, methadone is safer for the fetus than heroin.

To be an effective first step of treatment, detoxification must be an individualized process because patients have varying needs. Aspects used in determining treatment options include the type of substance(s) the person is abusing, whether more than one substance is involved, the severity of the withdrawal syndrome; and whether inpatient or outpatient detoxification is preferable for the particular patient. Outpatient detoxification is not safe for patients who:

- have delirium tremens or other potentially life-threatening complications of withdrawal
- have such serious associated medical conditions as cirrhosis, inflammation of the pancreas, or gastrointestinal bleeding
- are judged to be suicidal or homicidal
- are in difficult family or employment situations
- cannot travel to the treatment facility on a daily basis

Preparation

The first step in any detoxification, regardless of the substance, is a physical exam and history taken by a physician. This information gathering and examination will help the treatment team assess the patient's overall health. In general, the healthier the patient is, the better the chances are that the patient will experience a detoxification without serious or life-threatening complications. Patients also need to give urine and blood samples to test for drugs and alcohol.

Aftercare

After the patient has completed detoxification, he or she needs further treatment either at an outpatient, inpatient, residential, or day hospital program in order to remain drug-free for the long term. Patients are treated by trained health care professionals, and some patients are also counseled by people who are recovering from addiction themselves. Many patients benefit from 12-step programs or **self-help groups**, such as Alcoholics Anonymous (AA) or Narcotics Anonymous (NA).

Most opioid users are treated with ambulatory or outpatient detoxification or residential treatment followed by outpatient counseling. Some people who have abused opioids and have undergone detoxification and counseling are able to remain drug-free. Many, however, relapse, even after receiving **psychotherapy**. People recovering from opioid addiction can receive methadone or LAAM as maintenance therapy to prevent relapse. Similar to the aid these medications can give patients during detoxification, when taken daily as a therapy they continue to "act" as heroin, keeping the withdrawal symptoms from appearing. Methadone maintenance therapy can be provided through either residential or therapeutic communities and outpatient drug-free programs. Methadone maintenance treatment therapy is controversial, however, because it does not cure the person's addiction—it replaces it with another substance. Proponents of methadone maintenance therapy argue that people receiving methadone are able to function much better in society than people addicted to heroin. Because their drug-seeking behavior is reduced, these patients can become productive at work and their interpersonal relations improve.

People recovering from alcoholism can also benefit from counseling and support after detoxification, and a maintenance therapy is available to them, as well. **Disulfiram** (Antabuse) is a medication that interferes with the body's breakdown and processing of alcohol. When alcohol is consumed while a patient is taking disulfiram, the medication makes the effects of the alcohol much worse than the patient would normally experience; facial flushing, headache, nausea, and vomiting occurs, even if alcohol is consumed in a small amount. In order for disulfiram to be effective, the patient must want this kind of **reinforcement** to maintain abstinence and must be committed to it. Patients also must note that any form of alcohol can trigger the undesired effects, including cooking wine or mouthwash with alcohol. This drug, when used in combination with buprenorphine, also appears to be effective in treating **cocaine** addiction in people who also are addicted to heroin.

Risks

When benzodiazepines are the drug of addiction, they must be discontinued and cannot be given on an outpatient basis because of their potential for abuse. For all patients undergoing detoxification, benzodiazepine use must be monitored carefully because of the potential for new addiction. Elderly patients undergoing detoxification and receiving benzodiazepines must be monitored closely because they are more sensitive to the sedating effects of these drugs and are also more prone to falls while receiving these drugs. If benzodiazepines are not discontinued gradually, patients can have withdrawal symptoms such as irritability, poor sleep, agitation and seizures. Ultrarapid opioid detoxification under anesthesia/sedation is a serious procedure. Patients have died undergoing this procedure, and it remains controversial.

It should also be noted that many substances used in detoxification can themselves cause addiction. An example of this risk has already been given with benzodiazepines—these medications ease withdrawal symptoms during detoxification, but patients can become addicted to these medications, as well.

Results

Normal results for a well-managed detoxification would include freedom from the drug of addiction and ability to enter long-term treatment.

Success rates vary among people recovering from substance abuse. As might be expected, patients who successfully complete a full treatment program after detoxification (that includes counseling, psychotherapy, **family therapy**, and/or **group therapy** or some combination of those therapy types) achieve higher rates of success at remaining drug-free. Patients who were addicted for shorter periods of time and patients who spend longer periods in treatment are generally more successful at remaining abstinent from drugs over the long term.

Studies indicate that people who abuse alcohol and who want to stop have a higher chance of success if they undergo inpatient detoxification versus outpatient detoxification.

One abnormal result that may occur is that patients who received nasogastric or tracheal tubes for opioid detoxification under anesthesia may experience adverse effects or complications. These patients are at risk for: **trauma** to their lips, vocal cords, larynx, and teeth; nosebleeds; high blood pressure; elevated heart rate; irregular heartbeat; and vomiting, which can lead to aspiration pneumonia.

KEY TERMS

Agonist—A chemical that reproduces the mechanism of action of a neurotransmitter.

Antagonist—A substance whose actions counteract the effects of or work in the opposite way from another chemical or drug.

Buprenorphine—A medication that blocks some of the withdrawal effects during heroin detoxification.

Detoxification—A process in which the body is allowed to free itself of a drug while the symptoms of withdrawal are treated. It is the primary step in any treatment program for drug or alcohol abuse.

Disulfiram—A medication that helps reinforce abstinence in people who are recovering from alcohol abuse. If a person taking disulfiram drinks even a small amount of alcohol, he or she experiences facial flushing, headache, nausea, and vomiting.

Lofexidine—A medication approved for use in Great Britain to aid the opioid detoxification process.

Methadone—A drug often prescribed legally as a replacement for heroin. It induces a slight high but blocks heroin from producing a more powerful euphoric effect. It may be used in heroin detoxification to ease the process, or it may be used daily after detoxification as maintenance therapy. Methadone maintenance therapy is controversial.

Withdrawal—Symptoms experienced by a person who has become physically dependent on a drug, experienced when the drug use is discontinued.

An additional abnormal result would be a new addiction as a consequence of the detoxification.

After the detoxification is completed, a patient may relapse. Support is critical for the patient to continue long-term therapy and successfully overcome addiction.

See also Addiction; Disease concept of chemical dependency

Resources

BOOKS

Fisher, Gary L., and Nancy A. Roget, eds. *Encyclopedia of Substance Abuse Prevention, Treatment, and Recovery*. Los Angeles: Sage, 2008.

Galanter, Marc, and Herbert D. Kleber, eds. *The American Psychiatric Publishing Textbook of Substance Abuse Treatment*. 4th ed. Washington, DC: American Psychiatric Publishing, 2008.

Jaffe, Jerome H., et al. "Substance-Related Disorders." In *Comprehensive Textbook of Psychiatry*, edited by Benjamin J. Sadock and Virginia A. Sadock. 7th ed. Philadelphia: Lippincott Williams and Wilkins, 2000.

Matthews, John. "Substance-Related Disorders: Cocaine and Narcotics." In *Psychiatry Update and Board Preparation* edited by Thomas A. Stern and John B. Herman. New York: McGraw Hill, 2000.

Porter, Robert S., and Justin L. Kaplan, eds. *The Merck Manual of Diagnosis and Therapy*. 19th ed. Whitehouse Station, NJ: Merck Research Laboratories, 2011.

PERIODICALS

Frydrych, L.M., et al. "Self-help Program Components and Linkage to Aftercare Following Inpatient Detoxification." *Journal of Addictive Diseases* 28, no. 1 (January 2009): 21–27.

Fuller, Richard K., and Susanne Hiller-Sturmhofel. "Alcoholism Treatment in the United States: An Overview." *Alcohol Research and Health* 23 (Spring 1999): 69–77.

Khantzian, Edward J. "Methadone Treatment for Opioid Dependence." *American Journal of Psychiatry* 157 (November 2000): 1895–96.

Preuss, U.W., et al. "Personality Disorders in Alcohol-dependent Individuals: Relationship with Alcohol Dependence Severity." *European Addiction Research* 15, no. 4 (April 2009): 188–95.

Shreeram, S.S., Timothy McDonald, and Sylvia Dennison. "Psychosis After Ultrarapid Opiate Detoxification." *American Journal of Psychiatry* 158 (June 2001): 970.

WEBSITES

Buprenorphine Information Center, Center for Substance Abuse Treatment. "Buprenorphine." U.S. Substance Abuse and Mental Health Services Administration. http://buprenorphine.samhsa.gov/about.html (accessed October 3, 2011.)

Center for Substance Abuse Treatment. "Detoxification and Substance Abuse Treatment." U.S. Substance Abuse and Mental Health Services Administration. Treatment Improvement Protocol (TIP) Series 45. DHHS Publication No. (SMA) 06-4131, 2006. http://store.samhsa.gov/product/Detoxification-and-Substance-Abuse-Treatment/SMA06-4226 (accessed October 3, 2011).

Mathias, Robert. "Alcohol-Treatment Medication May Reduce Cocaine Abuse Among Heroin Treatment Patients." U.S. National Institute on Drug Abuse. NIDA Notes (16). 2005. http://archives.drugabuse.gov/NIDA_Notes/NNVol16N1/Alcohol.html (accessed October 3, 2011).

MedlinePlus. "Opiate Withdrawal." U.S. National Library of Medicine. National Institutes of Health. September 28, 2011. http://www.nlm.nih.gov/medlineplus/ency/article/000949.htm (accessed October 3, 2011).

Trachtenberg, Alan I., and Michael F. Fleming. "Diagnosis and Treatment of Drug Abuse in Family Practice." U.S. National Institute on Drug Abuse. NIDA Research Monograph. 2005. http://archives.drugabuse.gov/diagnosis-treatment/diagnosis.html (accessed October 3, 2011).

U.S. National Institute of Drug Abuse. "Effectiveness of Lofexidine to Prevent Stress-Related Opiate Relapse

During Naltrexone Treatment." http://clinicaltrials.gov/ct/gui/show/NCT00142909;jsessionid=0B14CF2553B3CC2A2D16FE2652613D76?order=48 (accessed October 3, 2011).

ORGANIZATIONS

Alcoholics Anonymous (AA) World Services, Inc, PO Box 459, New York, NY, 10163, (212) 870-3400, http://www.aa.org.

American Council on Alcoholism, http://www.aca-usa.org.

American Society of Addiction Medicine, 4601 N. Park Ave., Upper Arcade #101, Chevy Chase, MD, 20815, (301) 656-3920, Fax: (301) 656-3815, email@asam.org, http://www.asam.org.

Hazelden Foundation, PO Box 11, Center City, MN, 55012-0011, info@hazelden.org, http://www.hazelden.org.

National Institute on Alcohol Abuse and Alcoholism, 5635 Fishers Lane, MSC 9304, Bethesda, MD, 20892-9304, http://www.niaaa.nih.gov.

National Institute on Drug Abuse, 6001 Executive Blvd., Room 5213, Bethesda, MD, 20892-9561, http://www.nida.nih.gov.

Susan Hobbs, MD
Emily Jane Willingham, PhD

Developmental coordination disorder

Definition

Developmental coordination disorder is diagnosed when children do not develop normal motor coordination (coordination of movements involving the voluntary muscles).

Demographics

It is estimated that as many as 6% of children between the ages of five and 11 have developmental coordination disorder. Males and females are thought to be equally likely to have this disorder, although males may be more likely to be diagnosed. Developmental coordination disorder and speech-language disorders seem to be closely linked, although it is not clear why this is the case. Children with one disorder are more likely to have the other as well.

Description

Developmental coordination disorder has been known by many other names, some of which are still used today. It has been called clumsy child syndrome, clumsiness, developmental disorder of motor function, and congenital maladroitness. Developmental coordination disorder is usually first recognized when a child fails to reach such normal developmental milestones as walking or beginning to dress him- or herself.

Children with developmental coordination disorder often have difficulty performing tasks that involve both large and small muscles, including forming letters when they write, throwing or catching balls, and buttoning buttons. Children who have developmental coordination disorder generally have developed normally in all other ways. The disorder can, however, lead to social or academic problems for children. Because of their underdeveloped coordination, they may choose not to participate in activities on the playground. This avoidance can lead to conflicts with or rejection by their peers. Also, children who have problems forming letters when they write by hand, or drawing pictures, may become discouraged and give up academic or artistic pursuits even though they have normal intelligence.

Causes and symptoms

The symptoms of developmental coordination disorder vary greatly from child to child. The general characteristic is that the child has abnormal development of one or more types of motor skills when the child's age and intelligence quotient (IQ) are taken into account. In some children these coordination deficiencies manifest as an inability to tie shoes or catch a ball, while in other children they appear as an inability to draw objects or properly form printed letters.

Some investigators believe that there are different subtypes of developmental coordination disorder. While there is disagreement over how to define these different subtypes, they can provide a useful framework for the categorization of symptoms. There are six general groups of symptoms. These include:

- general unsteadiness and slight shaking
- an at-rest muscle tone that is below normal
- muscle tone that is consistently above normal
- inability to move smoothly because of problems putting together the subunits of the whole movement
- inability to produce written symbols
- visual perception problems related to development of the eye muscles

Children can have one or more of these types of motor difficulties.

Developmental coordination disorder usually becomes apparent when children fail to meet normal developmental milestones. Some children with developmental coordination disorder do not learn large motor skills such as walking, running, and climbing until a much later point in time than their peers. Others have problems with such small muscle skills as learning to fasten buttons, close or open zippers, or tie shoes. Some children have problems learning how to handle silverware properly. In others the disorder does not appear until they are expected to learn how to write in school. Some children just look clumsy and often walk into objects or drop things.

There are no known causes of developmental coordination disorder. There are, however, various theories about its possible causes. Some theories attribute the disorder to biological causes. Some of the possible biological causes include such prenatal complications as fetal malnutrition. Low birth weight or prematurity are thought to be possible causes, but there is no hard evidence supporting these claims.

Diagnosis

The **diagnosis** of developmental coordination disorder is most commonly made when a child's parents or teachers notice that he or she is lagging behind peers in learning motor skills, is having learning problems in school, or has frequent injuries from falls and other accidents resulting from clumsiness. In most cases, the child's pediatrician will perform a physical examination in order to rule out problems with eyesight or hearing that interfere with muscular coordination, and to rule out disorders of the nervous system. In addition to a medical examination, a learning specialist or child **psychiatrist** may be consulted to rule out other types of learning disabilities.

The types of motor impairment that lead to a diagnosis of developmental coordination disorder are somewhat vague, as the disorder has different symptoms in different children. There are many ways in which this kind of motor coordination problem can manifest itself, all of which may serve as criteria for a diagnosis of developmental coordination disorder. The core of the diagnosis rests on the child's being abnormally clumsy. To make this determination, the child's motor coordination must be compared to that of other children of a similar age and intelligence level.

The difference between a child who has developmental coordination disorder and one who is simply clumsy and awkward can be hard to determine. For a child to be diagnosed with developmental coordination disorder there must be significant negative consequences for the child's clumsiness. The negative effects may be seen in the child's performance in school, activities at play, or other activities that are necessary on a day-to-day basis. Also, for developmental coordination disorder to be diagnosed, the child's problems with motor coordination cannot result from such general medical conditions as muscular dystrophy, and cannot result directly from an intellectual disability. Some criteria require that the child have an IQ of at least 70 to be diagnosed with developmental coordination disorder.

Treatment

No treatments are known to work for all cases of developmental coordination disorder. Experts recommend that a specialized course of treatment, possibly involving work with an occupational therapist, be drawn up to address the needs of each child. Many children can be effectively helped in special education settings to work more intensively on such academic problems as letter formation. For other children, physical education classes designed to improve general motor coordination, with emphasis on skills the child can use in playing with peers, can be very successful. Any kind of physical training that allows the child to safely practice motor skills and motor control may be helpful.

It is important for children who have developmental coordination disorder to receive individualized therapy, because for many children the secondary problems that result from extreme clumsiness can be very distressing. Children who have developmental coordination disorder often have problems playing with their peers because of an inability to perform the physical movements involved in many games and sports. Unpopularity with peers or exclusion from their activities can lead to low self-esteem and poor self-image. Children may go to great lengths to avoid physical education classes and similar situations in which their motor coordination deficiencies might be noticeable. Treatments that focus on skills that are useful on the playground or in the gymnasium can help to alleviate or prevent these problems.

Children with developmental coordination disorder also frequently have problems writing letters and doing sums, or performing other motor activities required in the classroom—including coloring pictures, tracing designs, or making figures from modeling clay. These children may become frustrated by their inability to master tasks that their classmates find easy and may stop trying or become disruptive. Individualized programs designed to help children master writing or skills related to arts and crafts may help them regain confidence and interest in classroom activities.

Prognosis

For many people, developmental coordination disorder lasts into adulthood. Through specialized attention and teaching techniques it is possible over time for many children to develop the motor skills that they lack. Some

KEY TERMS

Maladroitness—Another word for awkwardness or clumsiness.

Motor skills—Skills pertaining to or involving muscular movement.

children, however, never fully develop the skills they need. Although many children improve their motor skills significantly, in most cases their motor skills will never match those of their peers at any given age.

Prevention

There is no known way to prevent developmental coordination disorder, although a healthy diet throughout pregnancy and regular prenatal care may help, as they help to prevent many childhood problems.

Resources

BOOKS

American Psychiatric Association. *Diagnostic and Statistical Manual of Mental Disorders*. 4th ed., text rev. Washington, DC: American Psychiatric Publishing, 2000.

Sadock, Benjamin J., and Virginia A. Sadock, eds. *Comprehensive Textbook of Psychiatry*. Vol. 2. 7th ed. Philadelphia: Lippincott Williams and Wilkins, 2000.

PERIODICALS

Rasmussen, Peder, and Christopher Gillberg. "Natural Outcome of ADHD with Developmental Coordination Disorder at Age 22 Years: A Controlled, Longitudinal, Community-Based Study." *Journal of the American Academy of Child and Adolescent Psychiatry* 39, no. 11 (November 2000): 1424–31.

Smyth, Mary M., Heather I. Anderson, and A. Churchill. "Visual Information and the Control of Reaching in Children: A Comparison Between Children With and Without Developmental Coordination Disorder." *Journal of Motor Behavior* 33, no. 3 (September 2001): 306–320.

WEBSITES

MedlinePlus. "Developmental Coordination Disorder." U.S. National Library of Medicine, National Institutes of Health. http://www.nlm.nih.gov/medlineplus/ency/article/001533.htm (accessed October 4, 2011).

ORGANIZATIONS

American Academy of Pediatrics, 141 Northwest Point Blvd., Elk Grove Village, IL, 60007-1098, (847) 434-4000, Fax: (847) 434-4000, http://www.aap.org.

Tish Davidson, AM
Emily Jane Willingham, PhD

Developmental disorders *see* **Pervasive developmental disorders**

Developmental reading disorder *see* **Reading disorder**

Deviance *see* **Paraphilias**

Dexedrine *see* **Amphetamines; Dextroamphetamine**

Dexmethylphenidate

Definition

Dexmethylphenidate (Focalin) is a medication used to treat **attention deficit hyperactivity disorder (ADHD)**. It belongs to the class of drugs known as central nervous system (CNS) stimulants and acts on the neurological signaling chemicals norepinephrine and **dopamine**. Norepinephrine and dopamine are types of neurotransmitter involved in normal **brain** function and have an effect on mood, concentration, and impulse control.

Purpose

Dexmethylphenidate is used to treat some of the symptoms of **ADHD** in both adults and children six years old and older. It is a CNS stimulant that improves memory, concentration, and impulse control and belongs to the category of drug that remains the mainstay of ADHD therapy. The first drug chosen for ADHD is often **methylphenidate** (Ritalin), but patients that do not do well on methylphenidate are usually given

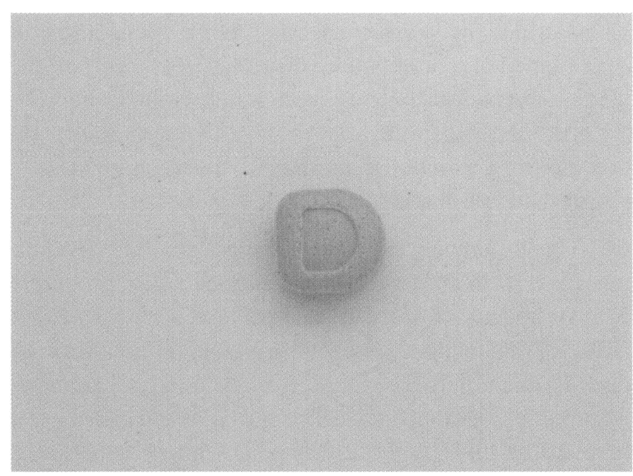

Focalin (dexmethylphenidate), 2.5 mg. *(© Custom Medical Stock Photo, Inc. Reproduced by permission.)*

dexmethylphenidate as a second-line drug. Dexmethylphenidate is available as an extended release medication, which reduces the need for re-dosing through the school or work day. It is used for patients in whom this is a priority. Because the capsules can be opened and the drug sprinkled on meals, it can be used in patients who have trouble swallowing pills. For patients with ADHD who also have co-existing **depression**, dexmethylphenidate may have some antidepressant properties and may be useful for patients who have both ADHD and depression at the same time. However, dexmethylphenidate has not officially been approved for use in treating depression.

Description

Dexmethylphenidate has a therapeutic mechanism of action that is focused on the modulation of the natural body chemicals norepinephrine and dopamine. Norepinephrine and dopamine are types of **neurotransmitters** in the nervous system, chemicals that neurons use to signal one another in complex pathways for normal brain and body functioning. Neurotransmitters bind to chemical receptors on the surface of neurons (brain cells). Once bound to a receptor they affect physiological processes. The receptors activate a sequence of cellular events known as a chemical cascade or signaling pathway.

Neurotransmitter signaling pathways are responsible for many regulatory processes, including neuronal signaling that affects mood, concentration, and impulse control. During the signaling process, neurotransmitters such as norepinephrine and dopamine travel from one neuron to the next. These chemicals need to cross a short space between the end of one neuron and the beginning of the next neuron known as the synapse or synaptic space. For example, norepinephrine is released from the end of neuron one, crosses the synaptic space, and binds to a neurotransmitter-specific receptor on the surface of the next neuron (neuron two). Any extra norepinephrine that is left in the synaptic space is taken back up by neuron one in a process known as reuptake. The more neurotransmitter allowed to remain in the synaptic space, the more will eventually be allowed to bind to receptors on neuron two and participate in the signaling process.

Neurotransmitter reuptake inhibitors such as dexmethylphenidate decrease the reuptake of norepinephrine and dopamine by neuron one, allowing more neurotransmitter to be present in the synapse and, therefore, more neurotransmitter signaling to occur. It is believed that a decrease in norepinephrine signaling contributes to disorders such as ADHD and depression. It is thought that dexmethylphenidate increases signaling of norepinephrine and dopamine by both inhibiting reuptake from the synapse and by increasing the amount released into the synapse. This has an impact on areas of the brain that involve attention span, judgment, response to external stimuli, memory, motor function, mental focus, and impulse control.

Recommended dosage

Dexmethylphenidate is given as an oral medication in pill form, but it may be sprinkled on food as well. Doses are taken early in the day with a full glass of water; doses are not taken in the evening. Patients are frequently reassessed for the need for treatment, as drugs for ADHD are avoided unless absolutely necessary. The dose chosen depends on individual patient response to the medication regarding its effectiveness, and individual patient response to the medication regarding side effects. Patients are dosed at the lowest possible effective dose to avoid the development of adverse side effects. Slowly increasing the dose over time helps with minimizing side effects.

The dose of dexmethylphenidate in both adults and children six years old and greater is started at 2.5 mg taken twice a day. The dose is increased by 5 mg or 10 mg increments every week for a maximum of 20 mg a day. The extended release formulation of dexmethylphenidate is given orally once a day at a dose of 10–30 mg. The dose is started low at 5 mg once a day taken in the morning and increased in increments of 5 mg a day over seven days to the desired dose. The maximum dose for the extended release form is 30 mg per day. Dosing of both the regular and extended release form is altered if the patient was previously taking methylphenidate and is switching to dexmethylphenidate. In this scenario the patient starts taking dexmethylphenidate at 50% of the current methylphenidate daily dose and is increased as needed from there. Doses are given at least four hours apart. Doses are lowered if side effects become intolerable.

Precautions

Dexmethylphenidate is a potentially habit-forming medication and should not be used for longer periods or at higher doses than prescribed. Patients are often given "drug holidays"—for example, when school is over for the summer—during which they forgo medication to avoid the development of adverse effects. Caution is used in patients with a history of **substance abuse**.

There is an association between ADHD and **Tourette syndrome**. Patients with Tourette syndrome often have involuntary movements or vocalizations known as tics. Patients who have Tourette syndrome and ADHD may find that the stimulant medications used to treat ADHD worsen their tics. Caution must be used in treating patients with motor tics, Tourette syndrome, or a family history of the disorder. Dexmethylphenidate may not be appropriate for use in these patients.

KEY TERMS

Bipolar disorder—Psychiatric mood disorder characterized by periods of manic behavior that may alternate with periods of depression, also known as manic depressive disorder.

Cytochrome P450 (CYP450)—Enzymes present in the liver that metabolize drugs.

Dopamine—A type of neurotransmitter involved in regulation of concentration, impulse control, judgment, mood, attention span, psychostimulation, and disease states such as addiction, ADHD, and depression.

Glaucoma—Condition involving increased pressure within the eye that may cause damage and blindness.

Mania—Physiological state of hyperactivity experienced by patients with certain psychiatric illnesses involving inappropriate elevated mood, pressured speech, poor judgment, and sometimes psychotic episodes superimposed on the state of mania.

Monoamine oxidase inhibitors (MAOIs)—Type of antidepressant medication that affects various kinds of neurotransmitters including serotonin.

Neurotransmitter—A chemical messenger that travels through the body and acts in the nervous system. Neurotransmitter signaling is responsible for a wide range of bodily processes and is often the target of medications involving the brain and cardiovascular system.

Neurotransmitter receptor—A physical recipient for chemicals called neurotransmitters. Receptors sit on the surface of cells that make up body tissues, and once bound to the neurotransmitter, they initiate the chemical signaling pathway associated with neurotransmitters.

Norepinephrine—A type of neurotransmitter involved in regulation of concentration, impulse control, judgment, mood, attention span, psychostimulation, and disease states such as ADHD and depression.

Synapse—Physical space between neurons that allows the passage of neurotransmitters for chemical signaling pathways.

Tic—Involuntary movements (such as twitching or facial grimacing) or vocalizations (such as throat clearing or barking) associated with Tourette syndrome.

Tourette syndrome—An inherited neuropsychiatric disorder characterized by the development of both motor and vocal tics. The tics are preceded by a feeling of tension or urgency in the affected individual until the tic behavior is performed and relieves the perceived feeling of tension.

Some patients taking dexmethylphenidate develop increased aggressiveness, **psychosis**, mania, or suicidal behavior in the first weeks of use. Children are especially at risk for these behavioral side effects. Patients taking dexmethylphenidate should be monitored closely for behavioral changes, especially when starting treatment or after dose changes. Dexmethylphenidate is discouraged from use in patients with **bipolar disorder**, as it is more likely to induce a state of mania in these individuals than in those without bipolar disorder.

Dexmethylphenidate may lower seizure threshold in some patients and may not be appropriate for use in patients with seizure disorder. Dexmethylphenidate may be contraindicated or may require caution in use in patients with hyperthyroidism, high blood pressure, liver function impairment or liver disease, kidney function impairment, heart conditions or abnormalities, and glaucoma. Cardiac function, heart rate, and blood pressure may be monitored while taking dexmethylphenidate. Blood cell parameters and growth progression (in pediatric patients) may need to be monitored with prolonged use, as growth retardation may occur with prolonged use.

Dexmethylphenidate is classified as category C for pregnancy, which means that either there are no adequate human or animal studies or that adverse fetal effects were found in animal studies, but there is no available human data. The decision whether to use category C drugs in pregnancy is generally based on weighing the critical needs of the mother against the risk to the fetus. Other lower category agents are used whenever possible. The safety of dexmethylphenidate use during breastfeeding is listed as probably safe, but data are limited and caution is advised.

Side effects

Dexmethylphenidate has many negative side effects. Sensitivity to dexmethylphenidate varies among patients, and some patients may find even lower doses are more than their body system can tolerate. Common reactions include abdominal discomfort or pain, dizziness,

insomnia, anxiety, headache, decreased appetite, changes in blood pressure and heart rate, weight loss, and visual disturbances. Dry mouth and throat pain are especially likely with the extended release formulation.

Rare but serious reactions include toxic skin reactions, blood disorders, heart arrhythmias, heart attack, **stroke**, **seizures**, and sudden death.

Interactions

Patients should make their doctor aware of all medications and supplements they are taking before using dexmethylphenidate. Using alcohol while taking dexmethylphenidate may create toxic reactions in the body and should be avoided. Dexmethylphenidate is metabolized by a set of liver enzymes known as cytochrome P450 (CYP450). There are many subtypes of CYP450 enzymes and dexmethylphenidate interacts with multiple subtypes. Drugs that induce or activate these enzymes may increase the metabolism of dexmethylphenidate. This results in lower levels of therapeutic medication, thereby negatively affecting treatment. Drugs that act to inhibit the action of CYP450 may cause undesired increased levels of dexmethylphenidate in the body. This could lead to increased side effects or even toxic doses. Likewise dexmethylphenidate may affect the metabolism of other drugs, leading to greater or lower doses than therapeutically desired. For example, dexmethylphenidate may inhibit the metabolism of the anticonvulsant medication phenytoin and the anticoagulant medication warfarin, causing increased levels of these drugs in the blood and toxicity. The anticonvulsant medication **carbamazepine** may lower levels of dexmethylphenidate present in the blood by inducing its metabolism, causing lower levels of dexmethylphenidate than therapeutically desired.

Certain drugs may cause toxicity when used with dexmethylphenidate, either through additive effects that cause serious side effects or through inhibition of dexmethylphenidate metabolism that cause toxic levels of dexmethylphenidate in the blood. Caffeine may cause toxicity with dexmethylphenidate by increasing the risk of heart rhythm abnormalities and excess nervous system stimulation. There have been rare reports of sudden cardiac death when dexmethylphenidate was used with the blood pressure drug **clonidine**. Use of the antipsychotic **pimozide** with dexmethylphenidate increases the risk of motor tics as a side effect of medication. Many **antidepressants** interact with dexmethylphenidate. The antidepressant **bupropion** increases risk of seizures when used with dexmethylphenidate. The antidepressant **venlafaxine** may cause greater than expected weight loss when used with dexmethylphenidate. Antidepressants called **monoamine oxidase inhibitors (MAOIs)** also increase the amount of norepinephrine and dopamine released into the synapse and cannot be used with dexmethylphenidate as it may cause overstimulation of the central nervous system and toxicity. Switching drug treatment for an individual patient from an MAOI to dexmethylphenidate may require a waiting period of up to two weeks between drugs. The antibiotic linezolid also impacts **MAOIs** and requires the same caution. Many diet drugs such as sibutramine may have additive effects with dexmethylphenidate that cause toxicity. It is unknown which herbal supplements interact with dexmethylphenidate.

QUESTIONS TO ASK YOUR DOCTOR

- Can I take the full dose right away or do I need to slowly increase the dose?
- Can I stop taking the medication right away or do I need to slowly decrease the dose?
- When should I eat in reference to taking this medication?
- What time of day should I take this medication?
- How long should I take this medication before I am reassessed?
- Will this medication interact with any of my other prescription medications?
- Are there any over-the-counter medications I should not take with this medicine?
- What are the side effects I should watch for?
- Can I drink alcoholic beverages in the same time frame as taking this medication?

Resources

BOOKS

Brunton, Laurence L., et al. *Goodman and Gilman's The Pharmacological Basis of Therapeutics.* 12th ed. New York: McGraw Hill Medical, 2011.

Stargrove, Mitchell Bebel, et al. *Herb, Nutrient, and Drug Interactions: Clinical Implications and Therapeutic Strategies.* St. Louis: Mosby, 2007.

ORGANIZATIONS

American College of Neuropsychopharmacology, 5034-A Thoroughbred Lane, Brentwood, TN, 37027, (615) 324-2360, Fax: (615) 523-1715, acnp@acnp.org, http://www.acnp.org/default.aspx.

American Psychiatric Association, 1000 Wilson Blvd., Ste. 1825, Arlington, VA, 22209-3901, (703) 907-7300, apa@psych.org, http://www.psych.org.

American Society for Clinical Pharmacology and Therapeutics, 528 N Washington St., Alexandria, VA, 22314, (703) 836-6981, info@ascpt.org, http://www.ascpt.org.

Mental Health America, 2000 N Beauregard St., 6th Fl., Alexandria, VA, 22311, (703) 684-7722, (800) 969-6642, Fax: (703) 684-5968, http://www.nmha.org.

Maria Eve Basile, PhD

Dextroamphetamine

Definition

Dextroamphetamine, sold under the brand name Dexedrine, is a medication used to treat **attention deficit hyperactivity disorder (ADHD)** and the sleep disorder **narcolepsy**. It belongs to the class of drugs known as central nervous system (CNS) stimulants and works by altering levels of the **neurotransmitters** norepinephrine and **dopamine**. Norepinephrine and dopamine are types of neurotransmitters involved in normal **brain** function and have an effect on mood, energy level, concentration, appetite, and impulse control.

Purpose

Dextroamphetamine is used to treat some of the symptoms of **ADHD** in both adults and children. This CNS stimulant improves memory, concentration, and impulse control, and belongs to the category of drug that remains the mainstay of ADHD therapy. For patients with ADHD who also have co-existing **depression**, dextroamphetamine may have some antidepressant properties, though it has not been approved by the U.S. Food and Drug Administration for this purpose. Dextroamphetamine has been approved for use in treating narcolepsy, a condition where patients experience uncontrollable sleep attacks during the day, and is one of the main treatments for this disorder. Dextroamphetamine is available as an extended release medication, which reduces the need for re-dosing throughout the school or work day. It is also available combined with the drug amphetamine in a combination pill (Adderall). The choice of using dextroamphetamine alone or in combination with other drugs depends on the medical profile of the patient.

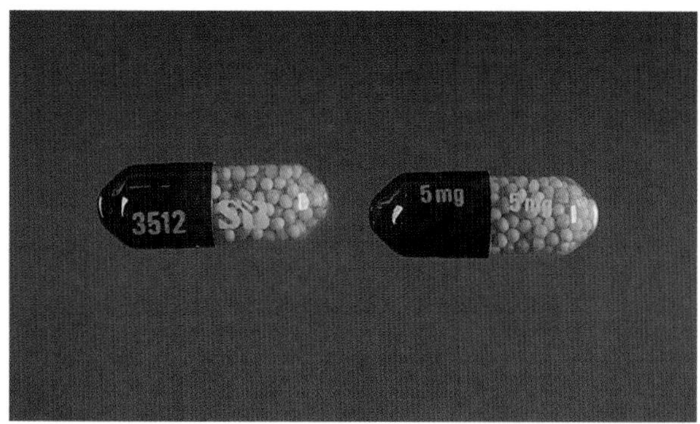

Dexedrine (dextroamphetamine), 5 mg. *(U.S. Drug Enforcement Administration)*

Description

Dextroamphetamine works by affecting the neurotransmitters norepinephrine and dopamine. Neurotransmitters are chemicals that neurons (brain cells) use to communicate with one another. It is believed that lower levels of norepinephrine and dopamine contribute to disorders such as ADHD and depression, so dextroamphetamine helps prevent the absorption of these neurotransmitters. The increase in norepinephrine and dopamine has an impact on areas of the brain that involve attention span, judgment, response to external stimuli, memory, motor function, mental focus, and impulse control.

Recommended dosage

Dextroamphetamine is given as an oral medication in pill form. Doses are taken early in the day with a full glass of water; doses are not taken in the evening. Patients are frequently reassessed for the need for treatment, as stimulant medications like dextroamphetamine are generally avoided unless absolutely necessary. The dose chosen depends on individual patient response to the medication regarding its effectiveness, and individual patient response to the medication regarding side effects. Patients are dosed at the lowest possible effective dose to avoid adverse side effects, and slowly increasing the dose may help with minimizing side effects.

The dose of dextroamphetamine for treating ADHD in both adults and children six years old and older is started at 5 mg taken once or twice a day. The dose is increased slowly after the first week as needed up to 40 mg per day, divided throughout the day. The maximum allowable dose is 60 mg per day. Similar doses are used to treat narcolepsy in adults and children greater than six years of age. Children three to five years of age being treated for ADHD are given lower doses of dextroamphetamine, beginning from 2.5 mg and slowly working up to 40 mg per day as needed. If multiple doses are used during a day, they should be taken at least four hours apart. If adverse side effects occur, doses may be lowered.

Precautions

Dextroamphetamine is a potentially habit forming medication and should never be used for longer periods or at higher doses than prescribed. Patients are often given drug "holidays"—for example, when school is over for the summer—during which they forgo medication to help avoid developing a dependence on the drug. Because of its addictive potential, caution is used in patients with a history of **substance abuse**. Dextroamphetamine causes a withdrawal syndrome when stopped abruptly; when discontinuing use, the medication should be tapered off gradually.

There is an association between ADHD and **Tourette syndrome**. Patients with Tourette syndrome often have involuntary movements or vocalizations known as tics. Patients who have Tourette syndrome with ADHD may find that the stimulant medications used to treat ADHD worsen their tics. Caution must be used in treating patients with motor tics, Tourette syndrome, or a family history of the disorder. Dextroamphetamine may not be appropriate for use in these patients.

Rare but serious reactions include severe elevations in blood pressure, heart arrhythmias, heart attack, **stroke**, **seizures**, and sudden death. Some patients develop increased aggressiveness, **psychosis**, mania, or suicidality in the first weeks of use. Children are especially at risk for these behavioral side effects. Patients taking dextroamphetamine are monitored closely for behavioral changes, especially when starting treatment or after dose changes. Growth retardation may occur with prolonged use.

Dextroamphetamine may be contraindicated or may require caution in use in patients with high blood pressure, blood vessel disease, heart rhythm abnormalities, heart conditions or structural abnormalities, certain thyroid disorders, liver function impairment or liver disease, kidney function impairment, or glaucoma. Dextroamphetamine may lower seizure threshold in some patients and may not be appropriate for use in patients with seizure disorder. Cardiac function, heart rate, and blood pressure may be monitored while taking dextroamphetamine. Dextroamphetamine is discouraged from use in patients with **bipolar disorder**, as it is more likely to induce a state of mania in these individuals than in those without bipolar disorder.

Dextroamphetamine is classified as a category C drug for pregnancy, which means either that there are no adequate human or animal studies or that adverse fetal effects were found in animal studies, but there is no available human data. The decision of whether to use category C drugs in pregnancy is generally based on weighing the critical needs of the mother against the risk to the fetus. Other lower category agents are used whenever possible. Some data suggest that dextroamphetamine may be unsafe for use during breast-feeding, and its use is not recommended.

KEY TERMS

Dopamine—A type of neurotransmitter involved in regulation of concentration, impulse control, judgment, mood, attention span, psychostimulation, and disease states such as addiction, ADHD, and depression.

Glaucoma—Condition involving increased pressure within the eye that may cause damage and blindness.

Mania—Physiological state of hyperactivity experienced by patients with certain psychiatric illnesses involving inappropriate elevated mood, pressured speech, poor judgment, and sometimes psychotic episodes superimposed on the state of mania.

Monoamine oxidase inhibitors (MAOIs)—Type of antidepressant medication that affects various kinds of neurotransmitters including serotonin.

Narcolepsy—Condition involving increased daytime sleepiness in the form of uncontrollable sleep attacks that interfere with normal functioning.

Neurotransmitter—One of a group of chemicals secreted by a nerve cell (neuron) to carry a chemical message to another nerve cell, often as a way of transmitting a nerve impulse. Examples of neurotransmitters include acetylcholine, dopamine, serotonin, and norepinephrine.

Norepinephrine—A type of neurotransmitter involved in regulation of concentration, impulse control, judgment, mood, attention span, psychostimulation, and disease states such as ADHD and depression.

Tic—Involuntary movements (such as twitching or facial grimacing) or vocalizations (such as throat clearing or barking) associated with Tourette syndrome.

Tourette syndrome—An inherited neuropsychiatric disorder characterized by the development of both motor and vocal tics. The tics are preceded by a feeling of tension or urgency in the affected individual until the tic behavior is performed and relieves the perceived feeling of tension.

Side effects

Sensitivity to dextroamphetamine varies between patients, and some patients may find that even lower doses are more than their body system can tolerate. Common reactions include dizziness, **insomnia**, anxiety, restlessness, euphoria, headache, decreased appetite, weight loss, changes in blood pressure and heart rate, palpitations, tremor, dry mouth, unpleasant taste, diarrhea or constipation, tic exacerbation, impotence, sexual dysfunction, and visual disturbances.

> **QUESTIONS TO ASK YOUR DOCTOR**
>
> - Can I take the full dose right away or do I need to slowly increase the dose?
> - Can I stop taking the medication right away or do I need to slowly decrease the dose?
> - Should I eat before taking this medication?
> - What time of day should I take this medication?
> - How long should I take this medication before I am reassessed?
> - Will this medication interact with any of my other prescription medications?
> - Are there any over-the-counter medications I should not take with this medicine?
> - What side effects should I watch for?
> - Can I drink alcoholic beverages in the same time frame as taking this medication?

Interactions

Patients should make their doctor aware of all medications and supplements they are taking before using dextroamphetamine. Using alcohol while taking dextroamphetamine may create toxic reactions in the body and should be avoided. Drugs that affect the liver may alter the metabolism of dextroamphetamine, resulting in too much or too little of dextroamphetamine in the body. This could lead to increased side effects or even toxic doses. Likewise, dextroamphetamine may affect the metabolism of other drugs, leading to greater or lower doses than therapeutically desired.

Certain drugs used in combination with dextroamphetamine may cause serious heart rhythm abnormalities, excess nervous system stimulation, or blood pressure changes. Such substances include caffeine, marijuana derivatives, the obesity drug sibutramine, some migraine medications such as ergotamines, and decongestants such as phenylephrine. Use of the antipsychotic **pimozide** with dextroamphetamine increases the risk of motor tics as a side effect of medication. Use of certain other antipsychotics such as **fluphenazine** increases risk of psychosis. Antacids and the glaucoma and diuretic drug acetazolamide decrease the excretion of dextroamphetamine from the body and may cause toxic levels to accumulate.

Many **antidepressants** interact with dextroamphetamine. The antidepressant **bupropion** increases risk of seizures when used with dextroamphetamine. **Venlafaxine** may cause greater than expected weight loss when used with dextroamphetamine. Antidepressants called **monoamine oxidase inhibitors (MAOIs)** also increase the levels of norepinephrine and dopamine in the brain and should not be used with dextroamphetamine, as the combination may cause overstimulation of the central nervous system and toxicity. Patients taking **MAOIs** will need to stop taking the MAOI for at least 14 days before starting treatment with dextroamphetamine (or vice versa). Many herbal supplements may also interact with dextroamphetamine and cause toxicity, including green tea and **ginseng**.

Resources

BOOKS

Brunton, Laurence L., et al. *Goodman and Gilman's The Pharmacological Basis of Therapeutics*. 12th ed. New York: McGraw Hill Medical, 2011.

Stargrove, Mitchell Bebel, et al. *Herb, Nutrient, and Drug Interactions: Clinical Implications and Therapeutic Strategies*. St. Louis: Mosby, 2007.

ORGANIZATIONS

American Society for Clinical Pharmacology and Therapeutics, 528 N Washington St., Alexandria, VA, 22314, (703) 836-6981, info@ascpt.org, http://www.ascpt.org.

Mental Health America, 2000 N Beauregard St., 6th Fl., Alexandria, VA, 22311, (703) 684-7722, (800) 969-6642, Fax: (703) 684-5968, http://www.nmha.org.

National Institute of Mental Health, 6001 Executive Blvd., Rm. 8184, MSC 9663, Bethesda, MD, 20892-9663, (301) 433-4513; TTY: (301) 443-8431, Fax: (301) 443-4279, (866) 615-6464; TTY: (866) 415-8051, nimhinfo@nih.gov, http://www.nimh.nih.gov.

U.S. Food and Drug Administration, 10903 New Hampshire Ave., Silver Spring, MD, 20993-0002, (888) INFO-FDA (463-6332), http://www.fda.gov.

Maria Eve Basile, PhD

DextroStat *see* **Dextroamphetamine**

DHEA

Definition

Dehydroepiandrosterone (DHEA) is a precursor (prohormone) of the sex hormones estrogen and testosterone. It is a steroid produced naturally by the adrenal glands and is also sold as a dietary supplement.

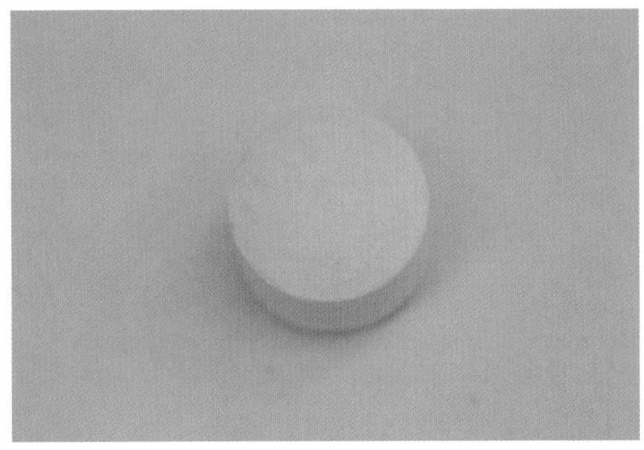

DHEA supplement. *(© Custom Medical Stock Photo, Inc. Reproduced by permission.)*

Purpose

Many claims have been made for DHEA, including that it fights aging, burns fat, increases muscle mass, boosts the immune system, eliminates symptoms of menopause, prevents **Alzheimer's disease**, and can treat everything from inflammatory bowel syndrome to **cocaine** withdrawal. There is little or highly questionable evidence to support most of these claims. DHEA does have medical uses in treating adrenal insufficiency (Addison's disease) and systemic lupus erythematosus (SLE).

Description

DHEA is a supplement with a long history of controversy. In the 1980s, it was promoted by supplement makers as a so-called miracle product that could improve athletic performance, build muscle, burn fat, restore sexual potency, and prevent aging. Many of these claims are still made by supplement makers today. In 1985, the U.S. Food and Drug Administration (FDA) banned DHEA for sale in the United States because of its potential for abuse and the high risk of serious side effects. DHEA was also banned by several sports organizations, including the International Olympic Committee and the National Football League. In 1994, the U.S. Congress passed the Dietary Supplement Health and Education Act (DSHEA). Under this law, DHEA met the definition of a dietary supplement and could once again be sold without a prescription in the United States.

DSHEA regulates supplements such as DHEA in the same way that food is regulated. Like food manufacturers, manufacturers of dietary supplements do not have to prove that their product is either safe or effective before it can be sold to the public. Manufacturers of conventional pharmaceutical drugs, must prove both safety and effectiveness in humans before a new drug is approved for use. With dietary supplements, the burden of proof falls on the FDA to show that the supplement is either unsafe or ineffective before it can be restricted or banned. Information about a supplement's safety and effectiveness is normally gathered only after people using the product develop health problems or complain that the product does not work. In the mid-2000s, there was pressure to reclassify DHEA as a hormone and ban its over-the-counter sale, but dietary supplement manufacturers have fought this move. Federal law requires that all manufacturers of dietary supplements and over-the-counter drugs report consumer complaints of adverse events (negative side effects) to the FDA. This requirement makes accumulating information on the safety of DHEA faster and easier.

DHEA is produced mainly in the adrenal glands. These are small, compact hormone-producing tissues located just above each kidney. The adrenal glands convert cholesterol into DHEA and release it into the bloodstream. DHEA is also produced in smaller amounts by the testes, liver, and possibly the **brain**.

DHEA is a prohormone, meaning that the body can convert it into several different hormones, including the female hormone estrogen and the male hormone testosterone. During development, the fetal adrenal glands produce large amounts of DHEA. After birth, production drops and remains low during childhood. As adulthood approaches, the rate of DHEA production increases, reaching a peak between ages 25 and 30. From age 30 on, the level of DHEA declines steadily until age 80; elderly men have only about 10% as much DHEA in their blood as they did at age 25.

Some researchers, observing the relationship between aging and decreased levels of DHEA, hypothesized the decrease in DHEA caused age-related problems such as cardiovascular disease, decreased sexual function, and **dementia**. They theorized that aging could be delayed by using dietary supplements to restore DHEA levels to those of a younger person. This hypothesis has not been tested, yet DHEA has been promoted as a supplement that can increase longevity and ward off a number of age-related changes.

Researchers tend to be much more cautious. For one thing, humans and other primates (apes, monkeys) produce substantial amounts of DHEA, but common laboratory animals such as rats and mice produce almost none. Therefore, it is unclear whether results of testing DHEA in lab animals can be applied to humans. Some researchers have spoken out against supplement makers, complaining that their research has been taken out of context, misrepresented, or just plain altered to support the claims of manufacturers selling DHEA, especially those selling over the Internet.

DHEA remains of great interest to researchers. **Clinical trials** are underway to determine safety and effectiveness of DHEA in a variety of situations.

DHEA's role in health care

DHEA has two uses accepted by practitioners of conventional medicine. Under supervision of a physician, DHEA has been used to successfully treat Addison's disease. Addison's disease is the result of adrenal insufficiency. The adrenal glands do not produce enough hormones. DHEA supplements simply replace what the body should be making.

DHEA has also been used by physicians to treat symptoms of systemic lupus erythematosus (SLE). SLE is a complicated autoimmune disease in which the body attacks and damages its own tissues. It is not clear why DHEA improves SLE symptoms such as joint pain and inflammation of the tissue surrounding the heart, but the majority of clinical trials in humans support this use.

There is mixed evidence to support two other claims for DHEA—that it helps with weight loss and that it relieves **depression** symptoms. A rigorous study led by researchers at the Mayo Clinic and published in 2006, found no anti-aging effects in elderly participants who took DHEA for two years. There were no measurable improvements in muscle strength, body fat, physical performance, insulin sensitivity, or quality of life.

Dietary supplement manufacturers continue to use unsubstantiated claims about DHEA that appeal to individuals searching for the fountain of youth. These include claims that DHEA improves memory, eliminates or improves symptoms of Alzheimer's disease, prevents cardiovascular disease, increases bone density, treats chronic **fatigue** syndrome, treats cocaine withdrawal, improves symptoms of Crohn's disease and inflammatory bowel syndrome, slows the development of AIDS, restores fertility, cures **erectile dysfunction**, treats symptoms of menopause such as hot flashes, helps manage **schizophrenia**, increases muscle strength and athletic performance, stimulates the immune system, prevents skin aging, and treats the symptoms of fibromyalgia. There are no independent, controlled, rigorous studies to support any of these uses. The National Center for Complementary and Alternative Medicine (NCCAM) does not recommend the use of DHEA supplements as a means to improve any health problems. The National Institute for Aging (NIA) advises against the use of DHEA supplements due to the lack of evidence proving any form of anti-aging benefit.

KEY TERMS

Depression—A mental state characterized by feelings of sadness, despair, and discouragement.

Insomnia—Waking in the middle of the night and having difficulty returning to sleep or waking too early in the morning.

Schizophrenia—A major mental illness marked by psychotic symptoms, including hallucinations, delusions, and severe disruptions in thinking.

Use of DHEA in mental health

DHEA has been determined as "possibly effective" for treatment in schizophrenia by the *Natural Medicines Comprehensive Database,* which rates effectiveness based on scientific evidence, noting that DHEA may be more effective in women than men who have schizophrenia. Additionally, the organization has given DHEA a rating of "insufficient evidence to rate effectiveness" for treatment in depression, noting that there is some (insufficient) evidence that DHEA may improve mood and help lessen symptoms associated with depression. More evidence is needed to rate DHEA for these uses.

Clinical trials regarding the effect of DHEA on depression and for anxiety symptoms of schizophrenia suggest that DHEA may be of some benefit for use in these conditions; however, further study is needed before a firm conclusion can be drawn. The long-term effects of taking DHEA are not known.

Certain drugs used in mental health, including **chlorpromazine** (Thorazine), **quetiapine** (Seroquel), and **alprazolam** (Xanax), may increase or decrease DHEA levels in the body. Further research is needed to determine the effects of DHEA administration if used by individuals taking psychiatric medication.

Clinical trials have looked at levels of naturally occurring DHEA in the body in individuals with anxiety disorder, schizophrenia, or **schizoaffective disorder**. Current information regarding participation in a clinical trial is available at the website of the NIH Clinical center (http://www.cc.nih.gov/participate).

Recommended dosage

DHEA is sold as a dietary supplement in the form of tablets, capsules, and a liquid injection. Dosage range is 25–250 mg per day. An independent study of DHEA supplements found that many supplements contained amounts of DHEA ranging from none to one and a half times the amount described on the label.

Administration and dosage of DHEA for Addison's disease or SLE is determined by a physician, who will also obtain ongoing blood tests to monitor levels of hormones in the body. The typical dosage of DHEA for Addison's disease is 25–50 mg daily and for SLE, 200 mg daily.

Precautions

People under age 40 should not take DHEA supplements.

DHEA should never be given to children. Parents should keep this and all drugs and supplements stored safely out of reach of children to prevent accidental poisoning.

Pregnant women should not take DHEA. There is some evidence that it can induce early labor. The effect on the developing fetus is unknown.

Breastfeeding women should avoid DHEA supplementation because DHEA passes into breast milk and may affect development of the infant.

People who have a high risk of developing estrogen- or testosterone-sensitive cancers, such as breast cancer or prostate cancer, should not take DHEA supplements. DHEA is converted into estrogen or testosterone. These hormones appear to stimulate the growth of certain cancers.

Athletes should be aware that some athletic governing bodies ban DHEA supplement use and test for abnormally high levels of DHEA as part of routine drug testing.

Side effects

DHEA supplementation in healthy people can cause major side effects. Many of these come about because of the conversion of DHEA into high levels of testosterone and estrogen. These include:

- masculinization of women, including deepening voice and increased body hair
- menstrual irregularities in women
- feminization of men, including, enlarged breasts and shrunken testicles
- decreased HDL ("good") cholesterol
- high blood pressure (hypertension)
- liver damage

Less serious side effects include acne, increased sweating, breast tenderness, **insomnia**, nausea, and abdominal pain.

QUESTIONS TO ASK YOUR DOCTOR

- What kind of changes can I expect to see or feel when taking DHEA?
- Does it matter what time of day I take DHEA? If so, what is the recommendation?
- Should I take DHEA with or without food?
- What are the side effects associated with DHEA?
- Will DHEA interact or interfere with other medications I am currently taking?
- What symptoms or adverse effects are important enough that I should seek immediate treatment?

Interactions

High levels of DHEA may interfere with the way the liver processes certain drugs. As a result, these drugs may accumulate in the body in high levels and cause adverse effects or be more rapidly deactivated and not produce a therapeutic response. Drugs that may be affected by high levels of DHEA are anticonvulsants, antipsychotics, corticosteroids, oral contraceptives, hormone replacement therapy drugs, insulin, and drugs to treat insomnia.

Resources

BOOKS

Ahmed, Nessar. *Clinical Biochemistry.* New York: Oxford University Press, 2011.

Ritsner, Michael S, ed. *Handbook of Schizophrenia Spectrum Disorders.* New York: Springer, 2011.

Sharon, Michael. *Nutrient A-Z: A User's Guide to Foods, Herbs, Vitamins, Minerals & Supplements*, 4th ed. New York: Carlton, 2009.

Watson, Ronald Ross, ed. *DHEA in Human Health and Aging.* Boca Raton, FL: CRC Press, 2011.

PERIODICALS

Arlt, Wiebke. "Androgen Therapy in Women." *European Journal of Endocrinology* 154, no. 1 (2006): 1–11. Available at http://eje-online.org/cgi/content/full/154/1/1 (accessed October 3, 2011).

Arnold, Julia T., and Marc R. Blackman. "Does DHEA Exert Direct Effects on Androgen and Estrogen Receptors, and Does It Promote or Prevent Prostate Cancer?" *Endocrinology* 146, no. 11 (2005): 4565–67. Available at http://endo.endojournals.org/cgi/content/full/146/11/4565 (accessed October 3, 2011).

WEBSITES

Boyles, Salynn. "Anti-Aging Hormone a Bust, Study Shows." WebMd.com. October 18, 2006. http://www.webmd.com/healthy-aging/news/20061018/antiaging-hormone-bust-study-shows (accessed October 3, 2011).

"DHEA." *MayoClinic.com*. Mayo Clinic. Last modified August 1, 2011. http://www.mayoclinic.com/health/dhea/NS_patient-dhea (accessed October 3, 2011).

"DHEA." Medline Plus. Last updated July 8, 2011. http://www.nlm.nih.gov/medlineplus/druginfo/natural/patient-dhea.html (accessed October 3, 2011).

"Dehydroepiandrosterone: Overview." University of Maryland Medical Center, April 4, 2002. http://www.umm.edu/altmed/articles/dehydroepiandrosterone-000299.htm (accessed October 3, 2011).

"Menopausal Symptoms and CAM." National Center for Complementary and Alternative Medicine, January 2008. http://nccam.nih.gov/health/menopause/menopausesymptoms.htm (accessed October 3, 2011).

ORGANIZATIONS

National Center for Complementary and Alternative Medicine, 9000 Rockville Pike, Bethesda, MD, 20892, (888) 644-6226, http://nccam.nih.gov.

National Institute on Aging, Bldg. 31, Rm. 5C27, 31 Center Drive, MSC 2292, Bethesda, MD, 20892, (301) 496-1752, (888) TTY: (800) 222-4225, Fax: (301) 496-1072, http://www.nia.nih.gov.

Office of Dietary Supplements, National Institutes of Health, 6100 Executive Blvd., Rm. 3B01, MSC 7517, Bethesda, MD, 20892-7517, (301) 435-2920, Fax: (301) 480-1845, ods@nih.gov, http://dietary-supplements.info.nih.gov.

Tish Davidson, AM
Laura Jean Cataldo, RN, EdD

Diagnosis

Definition

Diagnosis can be defined as the identification and labeling of a disease based on its signs and symptoms. Mental health clinicians (psychiatrists, psychologists, and psychiatric nurse practitioners) diagnose mental disorders using the criteria listed in the ***Diagnostic and Statistical Manual of Mental Disorders***, also known as the *DSM*, published by the **American Psychiatric Association** (APA). The *DSM* is a reference work consulted by psychiatrists, psychologists, physicians in clinical practice, **social workers**, medical and nursing students, pastoral counselors, and other professionals in health care and social services. The version of the *DSM* used as of 2012 is the fourth edition, text revision (*DSM-IV-TR*); a fifth edition of the *DSM* (*DSM-5*) is scheduled for publication in 2013.

According to the *DSM*, the term "mental disorder" is unfortunate because it implies that a mental disorder is separate from a physical illness, when actually, according to the APA, researchers and scientists now know that the distinction is not clear. The APA argues that "there is much 'physical' in 'mental disorders' and much 'mental' in 'physical disorders,'" but continues to use the term "mental disorders" because a better term has not yet been found. The APA defines a mental disorder as "a clinically significant behavioral or psychological syndrome or pattern that occurs in an individual and that is associated with present distress or disability or with a significantly increased risk of suffering death, pain, disability, or an important loss of freedom" (though this definition is being revised for the *DSM-5*).

Purpose

One of the main purposes of psychiatric diagnosis is to guide treatment planning. If doctors know that a particular disorder has been treated effectively with a specific drug or therapy, then the best practice can be applied to future diagnoses. Diagnosis also helps to establish a prognosis for the patient and his or her family, and it helps enable communication among healthcare professionals (including insurers) involved in the patient's care. Additionally, a formal diagnosis, as recognized by the *DSM*, may be necessary in order for insurers to pay for medical services. (The APA maintains, however, that the *DSM* diagnostic categories should not be used in courtroom proceedings for the purpose of establishing a defendant's legal guilt or innocence.)

Description

The process of psychiatric diagnosis varies according to the patient's overall health condition, behavioral problems (if any), and the setting of the examination. For example, a patient being examined in an emergency room with obvious signs of drug or alcohol intoxication and related injuries will require a physical work-up first, whereas a patient voluntarily consulting a **psychiatrist** about recent changes in mood or problems with memory can usually be evaluated in a series of clinical interviews. The APA's published *Practice Guideline for the Psychiatric Evaluation of Adults*, second edition (2010), outlines the basic parts of a psychiatric interview:

- reason for the evaluation (given by the patient and/or concerned others)
- history of the present illness (symptoms, severity, length of time involved)
- past psychiatric history
- history of alcohol or substance abuse

- general medical history
- developmental, psychosocial, and educational history (includes sexual orientation, marital status, children, religious or spiritual beliefs, educational level, family and social support network)
- military and occupational history
- legal history
- family history
- review of systems (ROS) (a checklist of physical symptoms related to the various organ systems in the body—ear, nose, and throat; respiratory; cardiovascular; gastrointestinal; genitourinary; musculoskeletal; skin and hair; neurological; serves to identify problems that may have a physical rather than psychiatric origin)
- physical examination

The second part of the psychiatric examination consists of a **mental status examination** (MSE), an assessment of the patient's general level of functioning, and any psychiatric tests that the examiner thinks may be necessary to establish or rule out a specific diagnosis. These tests may include a structured interview like the SCID (Structured Clinical Interview for Diagnoses) or one or more inventories for the patient to complete in the office.

In some cases the interviewer will need to consult others (bystanders, first responders, family members) to obtain necessary information about the patient's present condition and past history.

Precautions

The act of labeling a mental disorder may have unintended effects for the person with the disorder. Although the *DSM* states that its diagnoses do not label people, in reality, many people who have received diagnoses of mental disorders may feel affected by the label their disorder has been given. People diagnosed with mental disorders may feel stigmatized, and that others' perceptions of them, as well as their self-perceptions, have changed as a result of their diagnosis.

Patients who are considered a threat to their own safety and that of others may require medication (usually benzodiazepine tranquilizers or antipsychotic drugs) or (as a last resort) physical restraints before a psychiatric evaluation can be completed. Patients who are judged to be dangerous to themselves or others can be hospitalized against their will, and law enforcement notified.

Risks

The primary risk of psychiatric diagnosis is the possibility of misdiagnosis by an inexperienced interviewer or by the lack of time needed for a thorough evaluation.

KEY TERMS

Mental status examination (MSE)—A clinical evaluation in which the doctor assesses the patient's external appearance, attitude, behavior, mood and affect, speech, thought processes, thought content, perception, cognition, insight (or lack thereof), and judgment.

Review of systems (ROS)—A systematic checklist of the various organ systems in the human body—ear, nose, and throat; respiratory; cardiovascular; gastrointestinal; genitourinary; musculoskeletal; skin and hair; neurological—used to ensure that all relevant physical signs and symptoms have been taken into account during a medical or psychiatric evaluation.

Stigma—Any personal attribute that causes a person to be socially shamed, avoided, or discredited. Mental disorders are a common cause of stigma.

Resources

BOOKS

American Psychiatric Association. *Diagnostic and Statistical Manual of Mental Disorders*. 4th ed., text rev. Washington, DC: American Psychiatric Publishing, 2000.

———. *Practice Guideline for the Psychiatric Evaluation of Adults*. 2nd ed. Washington, DC: American Psychiatric Association, 2010.

Freeman, Hugh, ed. *A Century of Psychiatry*. London: Mosby, 1999.

North, Carol, and Sean Yutzy. *Goodwin and Guze's Psychiatric Diagnosis*. New York: Oxford University Press, 2010.

Regier, Darrel A., et al., eds. *The Conceptual Evolution of DSM-5*. Washington, DC: American Psychiatric Publishing, 2010.

PERIODICALS

Broome, M., and L. Bortolotti. "What's Wrong with 'Mental' Disorders? A Commentary on 'What Is a Mental/Psychiatric Disorder? From DSM-IV to DSM-V' by Stein et al. (2010)." *Psychological Medicine* 40, no. 11 (November 2010): 1783–1785.

Ronningstam, E. "Narcissistic Personality Disorder in DSM-V—In Support of Retaining a Significant Diagnosis." *Journal of Personality Disorders* 25, no. 2 (April 2011): 248–259.

Shear, M.K., et al. "Complicated Grief and Related Bereavement Issues for DSM-5." *Depression and Anxiety* 28, no. 2 (February 2011): 103–117.

Stein, D.J., et al. "What Is a Mental/Psychiatric Disorder? From DSM-IV to DSM-V." *Psychological Medicine* 40, no. 11 (November 2010): 1759–1765.

van Emmerich, Arnold A.P., and J.H. Kamphuis. "Testing a DSM-5 Reformulation of Posttraumatic Stress Disorder: Impact on Prevalence and Comorbidity Among Treatment-seeking Civilian Trauma Survivors." *Journal of Traumatic Stress* 24, no. 2 (April 2011): 213–217.

Verhoeff, B., and G. Glas. "The Search for Dysfunctions. A Commentary on 'What Is a Mental/Psychiatric Disorder? From DSM-IV to DSM-V' by Stein et al (2010)." *Psychological Medicine* 40, no. 11 (November 2010): 1787–1788.

Woods, S.W., et al. "DSM-5 and the 'Psychosis Risk Syndrome': The DSM-5 Proposal Is Better Than DSM-IV." *Psychosis* 2, no. 3 (October 2010): 187–190.

WEBSITES

American Psychiatric Association. "Definition of a Mental Disorder." DSM-5 Development. http://www.dsm5.org/ProposedRevisions/Pages/proposedrevision.aspx?rid=465 (accessed October 4, 2011).

Merck Manual for Healthcare Professionals. "Behavioral Emergencies." The Merck Manuals Online Medical Library. June 2008. http://www.merckmanuals.com/professional/sec15/ch195/ch195d.html (accessed October 4, 2011).

———. "Routine Psychiatric Assessment." http://www.merckmanuals.com/professional/sec15/ch195/ch195b.html (accessed October 4, 2011).

ORGANIZATIONS

American Psychiatric Association (APA), 1000 Wilson Boulevard, Suite 1825, Arlington, VA, 22209-3901, (703) 907-7300, apa@psych.org, http://www.psych.org.

National Institute of Mental Health (NIMH), 6001 Executive Boulevard, Room 8184, MSC 9663, Bethesda, MD, 20892-9663, (301) 443-4513, Fax: (301) 443-4279, (866) 615-6464, nimhinfo@nih.gov, http://www.nimh.nih.gov/index.shtml.

Rebecca J. Frey, PhD

Diagnostic and Statistical Manual of Mental Disorders

Definition

The *Diagnostic and Statistical Manual of Mental Disorders* (*DSM*), published by the **American Psychiatric Association**, is a reference work used by psychiatrists, psychologists, physicians, clinical researchers, regulatory agencies, health insurance companies, and other professionals to diagnose and access standard classification codes for a comprehensive list of mental disorders. Its use is varied, from promoting effective **diagnosis**, treatment, and quality of care to facilitating medical recordkeeping. The *DSM* is divided into three major parts: diagnostic classification, diagnostic criteria sets, and descriptive text.

Purpose

The stated purpose of the *DSM* is threefold: to provide "a helpful guide to clinical practice," to "facilitate research and improve communication among clinicians and researchers," and to serve as "an educational tool for teaching psychopathology."

Description

As of 2012, the version of the *DSM* most commonly in use was the fourth edition, text revised (*DSM-IV-TR*). A fifth edition was planned for release in 2013 (*DSM-5*). The changes of the *DSM*, over its five editions, can be summarized as follows:

- a move away from defining mental disorders by their causes toward defining them as clusters of symptoms
- coordination with the World Health Organization (WHO)'s *International Classification of Diseases* (ICD)
- increased use of field trials and statistical analysis in evaluating the adequacy of diagnostic terms and criteria

Origins of the DSM

The concept of the *DSM* dates back to the 1840s, when the U.S. Census Bureau attempted for the first time to count the numbers of patients confined in mental hospitals. American **psychologist** Isaac Ray (1807–81), superintendent of the Butler Hospital in Rhode Island, presented a paper at the 1849 meeting of the Association of Medical Superintendents of American Institutions for the Insane (the forerunner of the present American Psychiatric Association), in which he called for a uniform system of naming, classifying, and recording cases of mental illness. The same plea was made in 1913 by Dr. James May to the same organization, which by then had renamed itself the American Medico-Psychological Association. In 1933, the New York Academy of Medicine and the Medico-Psychological Association compiled the first edition of the *Statistical Manual for Mental Diseases*, which was also adopted by the American Neurological Association. The *Statistical Manual* went through several editions between 1933 and 1952, when the first edition of the *Diagnostic and Statistical Manual of Mental Disorders* appeared. The task of compiling mental hospital statistics was turned over to the then-newly formed **National Institute of Mental Health** (NIMH) in 1949.

DSM-I and *DSM-II*

The *DSM-I*, which appeared in 1952, maintained the coding system of earlier American manuals. Many of the disorders in this edition were termed "reactions," a term borrowed from Swiss **psychiatrist** Adolf Meyer (1866–1950). Meyer viewed mental disorders as reactions of an individual's personality to a combination of psychological, social, and biological factors. *DSM-I* also incorporated the nomenclature for disorders developed by the U.S. Army and modified by the Veterans Administration (VA) to treat the postwar mental health problems of service personnel and veterans. The VA classification system grouped mental problems into three large categories: psychophysiological, personality, and acute disorders.

DSM-II, which was published in 1968, represented the first attempt to coordinate the *DSM* with the *ICD*. *DSM-II* appeared before the ninth edition of the *ICD*, or *ICD-9*, which was published in 1975. *DSM-II* continued the *DSM-I*'s psychoanalytical approach to the etiology of the nonorganic mental disorders and **personality disorders**.

DSM-III, DSM-III-R and *DSM-IV*

DSM-III, which was published in 1980 after six years of preparatory work, represented a major break with the first two editions of the *DSM*. *DSM-III* introduced the present descriptive symptom-based approach to mental disorders, added lists of explicit diagnostic criteria, removed references to the etiology of disorders, did away with the term "neurosis," and established the present multi-axial system of symptom evaluation. This sweeping change originated in an effort begun in the early 1970s by a group of psychiatrists at the medical school of Washington University in St. Louis, Missouri, to improve the state of research in American psychiatry. The St. Louis group began by drawing up a list of "research diagnostic criteria" for **schizophrenia**, a disorder that can manifest itself in a variety of ways. The group was concerned primarily with the identification of markers for schizophrenia that would allow the disease to be studied at other research sites without introducing errors by using different types of patients in different centers.

What happened with *DSM-III*, *DSM-III-R*, and *DSM-IV* was that a tool for scholarly investigation of a few mental disorders was transformed into a diagnostic method applied to all mental disorders without further distinction. The leaders of this transformation were biological psychiatrists who wanted to empty the diagnostic manual of terms and theories associated with hypothetical or explanatory concepts. The transition from an explanatory approach to mental disorders to a descriptive or phenomenological one in the period between *DSM-II* and *DSM-III* is sometimes called the "neo-Kraepelinian revolution"; another term that has been applied to the orientation represented in *DSM-III* and its successors is *empirical*, which denotes reliance on experience or experiment alone, without recourse to theories or hypotheses. The word occurs repeatedly in the description of "The DSM-IV Revision Process" in the Introduction to *DSM-IV-TR.*

DSM-IV built upon the research generated by the empirical orientation of *DSM-III.* By the early 1990s, most psychiatric diagnoses had an accumulated body of published studies or data sets. Publications up through 1992 were reviewed for *DSM-IV*, which was published in 1994. Conflicting reports or lack of evidence were handled by data re-analyses and field trials. The NIMH sponsored 12 *DSM-IV* field trials together with the National Institute on Drug Abuse (NIDA) and the National Institute on Alcohol Abuse and Alcoholism (NIAAA). The field trials compared the diagnostic criteria sets of *DSM-III*, *DSM-III-R*, *ICD-10* (which had been published in 1992), and the proposed criteria sets for *DSM-IV*. The field trials recruited subjects from a variety of ethnic and cultural backgrounds, in keeping with a new concern for cross-cultural applicability of diagnostic standards. In addition to its inclusion of culture-specific syndromes and disorders, *DSM-IV* represented much closer cooperation and coordination with the World Health Organization experts who had worked on *ICD-10*. A modification of *ICD-10* for clinical practitioners, the *ICD-10-CM*, was introduced in the United States in 2004.

Multi-axial and biopsychosocial approach

The *DSM-III* introduced a system of five axes or dimensions for assessing all aspects of a patient's mental and emotional health. The multi-axial system was designed to provide a more comprehensive picture of complex or concurrent mental disorders. According to the *DSM-IV-TR*, the system was also intended to "promote the application of the biopsychosocial model in clinical, educational, and research settings." The reference to the biopsychosocial model is significant, because it indicates that the *DSM-IV-TR* does not reflect the view of any specific "school" or tradition within psychiatry regarding the cause or origin (etiology) of mental disorders. In other words, the *DSM-IV-TR* is theoretical in its approach to diagnosis and classification—the axes and categories do not represent any overarching theory about the sources or fundamental nature of mental disorders.

The biopsychosocial approach was originally proposed by American psychiatrist George L. Engel (1913–1999) in 1977 as a way around the disputes between psychoanalytically and biologically oriented psychiatrists who were splitting the field in the 1970s. The introduction to *DSM-IV-TR* is explicit about the manual's intentions to be "applicable in a wide variety of contexts" and "used by clinicians and researchers of many different orientations (e.g., biological, psychodynamic, cognitive, behavioral, interpersonal, family/systems)."

The atheoretical stance of the *DSM-IV-TR* is also significant in that it underlies the manual's approach to the legal implications of mental illness. *DSM* notes the existence of an "imperfect fit between questions of ultimate concern to the law and the information contained in a clinical diagnosis." What is meant here is that the *DSM-IV-TR* diagnostic categories do not meet forensic standards for defining a "mental defect," "mental disability," or similar terms. Because *DSM-IV-TR* states that "inclusion of a disorder in the classification ... does not require that there be knowledge about its etiology," it advises legal professionals against basing decisions about a person's criminal responsibility, competence, or degree of behavioral control on *DSM* diagnostic categories.

The five diagnostic axes specified by *DSM-IV-TR* are:

- Axis I: clinical disorders, including anxiety disorders, mood disorders, schizophrenia, and other psychotic disorders
- Axis II: personality disorders and intellectual disability, including notations about problematic aspects of the patient's personality that fall short of the criteria for a personality disorder
- Axis III: general medical conditions, including diseases or disorders that may be related physiologically to the mental disorder; that are sufficiently severe to affect the patient's mood or functioning; or that influence the choice of medications for treating the mental disorder
- Axis IV: psychosocial and environmental problems, including conditions or situations that influence the diagnosis, treatment, or prognosis of the patient's mental disorder, such as family or relationship problems, social problems, educational or occupational problems, housing problems, financial problems, problems with access to health care, legal problems, and other problems (war, disasters, etc.)
- Axis V: global assessment of functioning

Rating the patient's general level of functioning is intended to help the doctor draw up a treatment plan and evaluate treatment progress. The primary scale for Axis V is the global assessment of functioning (GAF) scale, which measures a patient's level of functioning on a scale of 1–100. *DSM-IV-TR* includes three specialized global scales in its appendices: the social and occupational functioning assessment scale (SOFAS), the defensive functioning scale (DFS), and the global assessment of relational functioning (GARF) scale. For instance, the GARF is a measurement of the maturity and stability of the relationships within a family or between a couple.

Diagnostic categories

DSM-IV-TR. The Axis I clinical disorders of the *DSM-IV-TR* are divided among 15 categories: disorders usually first diagnosed in infancy, childhood, or adolescence; **delirium**, **dementia**, amnestic, and other cognitive disorders; medical disorders due to a general medical condition; substance-related disorders; schizophrenia and other psychotic disorders; mood disorders; **anxiety disorders**; **somatoform disorders**; factitious disorders; **dissociative disorders**; sexual and gender identity disorders; eating disorders; **sleep disorders**; **impulse control disorders** not elsewhere classified; and **adjustment disorders**.

The diagnostic categories of *DSM-IV-TR* are essentially symptom-based, or, as the manual puts it, based "on criteria sets with defining features." Another term that is sometimes used to describe this method of classification is phenomenological. A phenomenological approach to classification is one that emphasizes externally observable phenomena rather than their underlying nature or origin.

DSM-5. Proposed changes for the *DSM-5* include revised diagnostic categories, increasing the total to 20: neurodevelopmental disorders; schizophrenia spectrum and other psychotic disorders; bipolar and related disorders; depressive disorders; anxiety disorders; obsessive-compulsive and related disorders; trauma- and stressor-related disorders; dissociative disorders; somatic symptom disorders; feeding and eating disorders; elimination disorders; sleep-wake disorders; **sexual dysfunctions**; gender dysphoria; disruptive, impulse control, and conduct disorders; substance use and addictive disorders; neurocognitive disorders; personality disorders; **paraphilias**; and other disorders.

Medical model of mental disorders

Another important characteristic of the *DSM-IV-TR* classification system is its dependence on the medical model of mental disorders. Such terms as "psychopathology," "mental illness," "differential diagnosis," and "prognosis" are all borrowed from medical practice. The medical model as it came to dominate psychiatry can be traced back to the work of Emil Kraepelin (1856–1926), a German psychiatrist whose *Handbuch der Psychiatrie* ("Handbook of Psychiatry") was the first basic textbook in the field and introduced the first nosology, or systematic classification, of mental disorders. Prior to its adoption, mental illness was attributed to supernatural or moral causes (desire to engage in bad behavior). By the early 1890s, Kraepelin's handbook was being used in medical schools across Europe. He updated and revised it periodically to accommodate new findings, including a disease (**Alzheimer's disease**) that he named after one of his clinical assistants, Aloysius (Alois) Alzheimer (1864–1915). The 1907 edition of Kraepelin's handbook included 15 categories, most of which were still used over a century later. Kraepelin's work was also significant because it represented a biologically based view of mental disorders, as opposed to the psychoanalytical approach of Sigmund Freud. Kraepelin thought that mental disorders could ultimately be traced to organic diseases of the **brain** rather than disordered emotions or psychological processes. The controversy between these two perspectives dominated psychiatric research and practice until well after World War II (1939–45).

Textual revisions in DSM-IV-TR

The text-revised edition of the *DSM-IV*, published in 2000, does not represent either a fundamental change in the basic classification structure of *DSM-IV* or the addition of new diagnostic entities. The textual revisions that were made to the 1994 edition of *DSM-IV* included:

- correction of factual errors
- review of currency of information
- changes to reflect research published after 1992, which was the last year included in the literature review prior to the publication of *DSM-IV*
- improvements to enhance the educational value of *DSM-IV*
- updated *ICD* diagnostic codes, some of which were changed in 1996

Criticisms of DSM-IV *and* DSM-IV-TR

One reason for a new edition of the *DSM* (*DSM-5*) is the number of criticisms of the fourth edition of the manual, such as:

- The medical model underlying the empirical orientation of *DSM-IV* reduces human beings to "one-dimensional" sources of data; it does not encourage practitioners to treat the whole person.
- The medical model perpetuates the social stigma attached to mental disorders.
- The symptom-based criteria sets have led to an endless multiplication of mental conditions and disorders. The unwieldy size of *DSM-IV* is a common complaint of doctors in clinical practice—a volume that was only 119 pages long in its second (1968) edition has swollen to 886 pages in less than thirty years.
- The symptom-based approach has also made it easier to politicize the process of defining new disorders for inclusion in *DSM* or dropping older ones. The inclusion of post-traumatic stress disorder (PTSD) and the deletion of homosexuality as a disorder are often cited as examples of this concern for political correctness.
- The criteria sets of *DSM-IV* incorporate implicit (implied but not expressly stated) notions of human psychological well-being that do not allow for ordinary diversity among people. Some of the diagnostic categories of *DSM-IV* come close to defining various temperamental and personality differences as mental disorders.
- The *DSM-IV* criteria do not distinguish adequately between poor adaptation to ordinary problems of living and true psychopathology. One by-product of this inadequacy is the suspiciously high rates of prevalence reported for some mental disorders. One observer remarked that "it is doubtful that 28% or 29% of the population would be judged [by managed care plans] to need mental health treatment in a year."
- The diagnostic classes defined by *DSM-IV* hinder efforts to recognize disorders that run across classes. For example, PTSD has more in common with respect to etiology and treatment with the dissociative disorders than it does with the anxiety disorders with which it is grouped. Another example is body dysmorphic disorder, which resembles the obsessive-compulsive disorders more than it does the somatoform disorders.
- The current classification is deficient in acknowledging disorders of uncontrolled anger, hostility, and aggression. Even though inappropriate expressions of anger and aggression lie at the roots of major social problems, only one *DSM-IV* disorder (intermittent explosive disorder) is explicitly concerned with them. In contrast, entire classes of disorders are devoted to depression and anxiety.
- The emphasis of *DSM-IV* on biological psychiatry has contributed to the widespread popular notion that most problems of human life can be solved by taking pills.
- The current approach to diagnosing mental disorders takes a categorical, rather than dimensional (continuum), perspective on symptoms of mental illness.

Alternative nosologies

A number of different nosologies or schemes of classification have been proposed to replace the current descriptive model of mental disorders.

THE DIMENSIONAL MODEL. Dimensional alternatives to *DSM-IV* would replace the categorical classification now in use with a recognition that mental disorders lie on a continuum with both mildly disturbed and normal behavior, rather than being qualitatively distinct. For example, the personality disorders of Axis II are increasingly regarded as extreme variants of common personality characteristics. In the dimensional model, patients would be identified in terms of their position on a specific dimension of cognitive or affective capacity rather than placed in a categorical "box."

THE HOLISTIC MODEL. The holistic approach to mental disorders places equal emphasis on social and spiritual as well as pharmacological treatments. A biochemist that was diagnosed with schizophrenia and eventually recovered compared the reductionism of the biological model of his disorder with the empowering qualities of holistic approaches. He stressed the healing potential in treating patients as whole persons rather than as isolated collections of nervous tissue with chemical imbalances, stating that "the major task in recovering from mental illness is to regain social roles and identities. This entails focusing on the individual and building a sense of responsibility and self-determination."

THE ESSENTIAL OR PERSPECTIVAL MODEL. The third and most complex alternative model is associated with the medical school of Johns Hopkins University (Baltimore, Maryland), where it is taught as part of the medical curriculum. This model identifies four broad perspectives that can be used to identify the distinctive characteristics of mental disorders, which are often obscured by the present categorical classifications.

The four perspectives are:

- Disease. This perspective works with categories and accounts for physical diseases or damage to the brain that produces psychiatric symptoms. It accounts for such disorders as Alzheimer's disease or schizophrenia.
- Dimensions. This perspective addresses disorders that arise from the combination of a cognitive or emotional weakness in the patient's constitution and a life experience that challenges the individual's vulnerability.
- Behaviors. This perspective is concerned with disorders associated with something that the patient is doing (alcoholism, drug addiction, eating disorders, etc.) that has become a dysfunctional way of life.
- Life story. This perspective focuses on disorders related to what the patient has encountered in life, such as events that have injured the person's hopes and aspirations.

In the Johns Hopkins model, each perspective has its own approach to treatment: the disease perspective seeks to cure or prevent disorders rooted in biological disease processes; the dimensional perspective attempts to strengthen constitutional weaknesses; the behavioral perspective seeks to interrupt the problematic behaviors and assist patients in overcoming their appeal; and the life story perspective offers help in "rescripting" a person's life narrative, usually through cognitive behavioral treatment.

DSM-5

The fifth edition of the *DSM* is slated for publication in May 2013. Aside from changes to specific sets of diagnostic criteria, the *DSM-5* is set to undergo a major organizational revision. Other changes are being made to correct perceived errors within criteria sets identified in the *DSM-IV*, and several diagnostic codes are being updated to coincide with updates to the *ICD-9-CM* coding system.

One of the most recognizable changes involves the title—the use of Roman numerals in previous editions is being abandoned, so the fifth edition will be the first to use Arabic numerals. Other considerations include whether to abandon the previous axis framework and consolidate the first three axes into a single axis that covers all psychiatric and medical diagnoses. This would be done in order to parallel the way the *ICD-10* is organized. Simultaneously, Axis IV (psychosocial issues such as housing or economic issues) is being reviewed in order to bring it into line with the *ICD*.

Other notable changes include collapsing a number of currently separate disorders (**Asperger syndrome**, **childhood disintegrative disorder**, and pervasive developmental disorder) under the rubric of **autism** spectrum disorder; creating a single "addiction and related disorders" category to replace **substance abuse** and dependence; including a behavioral addictions category to describe gambling; the inclusion of new **suicide** scales; the creation of risk syndromes that will help improve early recognition of evolving disorders; finer distinctions between childhood **bipolar disorder**, childhood **oppositional defiant disorder**, and newer diagnoses, such as **disruptive mood dysregulation disorder**; and honing of the criteria for eating disorders, as well as including **binge eating disorder**. The exclusion of diagnoses present in prior editions and the addition of several new disorders is already prompting controversy.

While feedback has been solicited in response to the proposed changes, controversy continues to cloud the new edition's development. Concerns about transparency of the task force has plagued the *DSM-5*'s development, and various interest groups are vocal in their support or opposition to changes to the diagnostic criteria. Interested users can follow the development of the *DSM-5* on its website: http://www.dsm5.org.

KEY TERMS

Amnestic—Having to do with, or related to, amnesia.

Biological psychiatry—An approach to psychiatry that emphasizes the biological and biochemical factors in mental illness; it tends to favor drug treatments for mental disorders rather than psychotherapy.

Biopsychosocial model—An approach to human health that holds that a combination of biological, psychological, and social factors should be taken into account when evaluating a patient rather than physical factors alone.

Delirium—A temporary mental problem characterized by confusion, restlessness, and (sometimes) hallucinations, which can be caused by a brain injury, fever, or other such accidents or maladies.

Dementia—A deterioration of cognitive/intellectual abilities, including memory, while other brain activities, such as bodily movements and senses, appear to be normal; sometimes also called senility.

Depression—A psychiatric disorder involving feelings of hopelessness and symptoms of fatigue, sleeplessness, suicidal tendencies, and poor concentration.

Empirical—Based on information gathered by scientific observation or experiments, as distinct from pure theory.

Forensic—Pertaining to legal matters or courtroom proceedings.

Medical model of mental illness—An approach to psychiatric diagnosis and treatment patterned on the process of diagnosis and treatment of physical disease.

Mental disorder—A psychiatric disorder of mental faculties.

Schizophrenia—A severe mental illness in which a person has difficulty distinguishing what is real from what is not real. It is often characterized by hallucinations, delusions, language and communication disturbances, and withdrawal from people and social activities.

Resources

BOOKS

American Psychiatric Association. *Diagnostic and Statistical Manual of Mental Disorders*. 4th ed., text rev. Washington, DC: American Psychiatric Association, 2000.

Borch-Jacobsen, Mikkel. *Making Minds and Madness: From Hysteria to Depression*. Cambridge, UK: Cambridge University Press, 2009.

Peterson, David B. *Psychological Aspects of Functioning, Disability, and Health*. New York: Springer, 2011.

Regier, Darrel A., et al., eds. *The Conceptual Evolution of DSM-5*. Washington, DC: American Psychiatric Publishing, 2011.

PERIODICALS

First, Michael B. "DSM-5 Proposals for Mood Disorders: A Cost-Benefit Analysis." *Current Opinions in Psychiatry* 29 (December 12, 2010): 1–9.

Happ, F. "Criteria, Categories, and Continua: Autism and Related Disorders in DSM-5." *Journal of the American Academy of Child and Adolescent Psychiatry* 50 (June 2011): 540–42.

Woods, Scott W. "The Case for Including Attenuated Psychotic Symptoms Syndrome in DSM-5 as a Psychosis Risk Syndrome." *Schizophrenia Research* 123, no. 2–3 (November 2010): 199–207.

WEBSITES

American Psychiatric Association. "DSM-5 Development: Frequently Asked Questions." http://www.dsm5.org/about/Pages/faq.aspx (accessed September 16, 2011).

World Health Organization. "International Classification of Diseases (ICD)." http://www.who.int/classifications/icd/en (accessed September 16, 2011).

ORGANIZATIONS

American Psychiatric Association, 1000 Wilson Blvd., Ste. 1825, Arlington, VA, 22209-3901, (703) 907-7300, apa@psych.org, http://www.psych.org.

Rebecca J. Frey, PhD
William A. Atkins, PhD

Diastat AcuDial *see* **Diazepam**

Diazepam

Definition

Diazepam is a mild tranquilizer in the class of drugs known as **benzodiazepines**. It is most commonly sold in the United States under the brand name Valium. The generic form of this drug is also available.

Purpose

Diazepam is used on a short-term basis to treat patients with mild to moderate anxiety. It is also used to treat some types of **seizures** (epilepsy), muscle spasms, nervous tension, and symptoms relating to alcohol withdrawal.

Valium (diazepam), 10 mg. *(U.S. Drug Enforcement Administration)*

KEY TERMS

Anterograde amnesia—The inability to form new memories.

Anxiety—An emotion that can be experienced as a troubled feeling, sense of dread, fear of the future, or distress over a possible threat to a person's physical or mental well-being.

Epilepsy—A disorder associated with disturbed electrical discharges in the central nervous system that cause seizures.

Seizure—A convulsion or uncontrolled discharge of nerve cells that may spread to other cells throughout the brain.

Description

Diazepam is one of many chemically related tranquilizers in the class of drugs called benzodiazepines. Benzodiazepines are sedative-hypnotic drugs that help to relieve nervousness, tension, and other anxiety symptoms by slowing the central nervous system. To do this, they block the effects of a specific chemical involved in the transmission of nerve impulses in the **brain**, decreasing the excitement level of the nerve cells. All benzodiazepines, including diazepam, cause sedation, drowsiness, and reduced mental and physical alertness.

Recommended dosage

The typical dose of diazepam used to treat anxiety or seizures in healthy adults ranges from a total of 6 mg to 40 mg per day given in three or four doses. People over age 60 are usually given lower doses in the range of 4–10 mg per day to treat anxiety or nervous tension. For acute treatment of seizures, a higher dose of diazepam is given intravenously (directly into the vein) only in a controlled medical setting such as a hospital or emergency room. For alcohol withdrawal, the typical dose is a total of 30–40 mg per day given in three or four doses.

The typical dose for a child over age six months with anxiety or seizures is a total of 3–10 mg per day divided into several doses. In general, children receive lower doses of diazepam even when they have a body weight equivalent to a small adult. Diazepam is usually taken as a pill, but an injectable form is sometimes used when a serious seizure is in progress or when muscle spasms are severe. There is a liquid oral form of the drug available, and diazepam is also available as a rectal gel, marketed as Diastat AcuDial.

Precautions

The elderly, children, and those with significant health problems need to be carefully evaluated before receiving diazepam. Children under the age of six months should not take diazepam. In addition, people with a history of liver disease, kidney disease, or those with low levels of a protein in the blood called albumin need to be carefully assessed before starting this drug.

The sedative effects of diazepam are cumulative and long lasting. People taking diazepam should not drive, operate dangerous machinery, or engage in hazardous activities that require mental alertness, because diazepam can cause drowsiness. Alcohol and any drugs that treat mental illness should not be used when taking this medication. People who have previously had an allergic reaction to any dosage level of diazepam or any other benzodiazepine drug should not take diazepam. People with acute narrow-angle glaucoma should not take diazepam.

The prescribing physician should be consulted regularly if diazepam is taken consistently for more than two weeks. Diazepam and other drugs in this class can be habit-forming. Diazepam can become a drug of abuse and should be used with caution in patients with a history of **substance abuse**. People taking diazepam should not stop taking the drug abruptly. Doing so can lead to withdrawal effects such as shaking, stomach cramps, nervousness, and irritability.

Diazepam may carry the risk of anterograde **amnesia**.

Individuals using diazepam in the form of rectal gel (Diastat AcuDial), should check the prefilled syringe applicator tip (without removing the cap) for cracks. The U.S. Food and Drug Administration (FDA) issued an alert in 2006 addressing this concern; cracks in the

QUESTIONS TO ASK YOUR DOCTOR

- What kind of changes can I expect to see or feel with this medication?
- Does it matter what time of day I take this medication? If so, what is the recommendation?
- Should I take this medication with or without food?
- What are the side effects associated with this medication?
- Will this medication interact or interfere with other medications I am currently taking?
- What symptoms or adverse effects are important enough that I should seek immediate treatment?

applicator tip have been known to occur, allowing medication to leak out and compromising the amount of medication in the syringe. This situation could result in the syringe not containing enough medication to treat a seizure. Cracks can occur over time so it is important to check syringes on a regular basis to ensure they are acceptable for use.

Side effects

Anxiety, irregular heartbeat, forgetfulness, mental **depression**, and confusion are side effects that could require prompt medical attention. However, these side effects are not common when taking diazepam. Even more unusual but serious events are behavior changes, low blood pressure, muscle weakness, and jaundice (yellowing of the eyes or skin). More common but less serious side effects include drowsiness, clumsiness, slurred speech, and dizziness. Rare among these less serious side effects are stomach cramps, headache, muscle spasm, nausea, vomiting, and dry mouth.

Once a person stops taking diazepam, the following side effects could occur from withdrawal: sleeping difficulties, nervousness, and irritability. Less common side effects from withdrawal include:

- confusion
- abdominal cramps
- mental depression
- sensitivity to light
- nausea
- shaking
- increased sweating

Rarely seen side effects include seizures, hallucinations, and feelings of distrust in the patient.

Interactions

Diazepam interacts with a long list of other medications. Individuals who are starting this drug should review the other medications they are taking with their physician and pharmacist for possible interactions. Patients should always inform all their healthcare providers, including dentists, that they are taking diazepam. Diazepam can add to the depressive effects of other central nervous system depressant drugs (for example, alcohol, other tranquilizers, or sleeping pills) when taken together. In severe cases, this effect can result in death.

Several drugs reduce the ability of diazepam to be broken down and cleared from the body, which results in higher levels of the drug in the blood and increases the probability that side effects will occur. These drugs include several antibiotics, such as erythromycin; anti-stomach acid drugs, such as cimetidine (Tagamet); and antifungal drugs, such as fluconazole. Alcohol should not be used when taking diazepam and other benzodiazepine drugs. There may also be an interaction between this drug and grapefruit juice. Other drugs that are used to treat mental disorders should not be combined with diazepam unless the patient is under the careful supervision and monitoring of a doctor.

Those who rely on urine tests to monitor blood sugar should know that this drug can produce false results with tests using Clinistix and Diastix and that they should instead use TesTape for urine testing of sugar.

Resources

BOOKS

Albers, Lawrence J., Rhoda K. Hahn, and Christopher Reist. *Handbook of Psychiatric Drugs.* Laguna Hills, CA: Current Clinical Strategies, 2010.

American Society of Health-System Pharmacists. *AHFS Drug Information 2011.* Bethesda, MD: ASHP, 2011.

Aminoff, Michael J., ed. *Neurology and General Medicine.* 4th ed. New York: Churchill Livingstone, 2007.

Devinsky, Orrin. *Epilepsy: Patient and Family Guide.* 3rd ed. New York: Demos Medical, 2007.

Holland, Leland Norman, and Michael Patrick Adams. *Core Concepts in Pharmacology.* 3rd ed. New York: Prentice Hall, 2011.

Kuzniecky, Ruben, ed. *Epilepsy 101: The Ultimate Guide for Patients and Families.* Leona, NJ: Medicus Press, 2009.

Panayiotopoulos, C.P. *Antiepileptic Drugs, Pharmacopoeia.* New York: Springer, 2010.

Patsalos, Philip N., and Blaise F.D. Bourgeois. *The Epilepsy Prescriber's Guide to Antiepileptic Drugs.* New York: Cambridge University Press, 2010.

Preston, John D., John H. O'Neal, and Mary C. Talaga. *Handbook of Clinical Psychopharmacology for Therapists.* 6th ed. Oakland, CA: New Harbinger, 2010.

Shorvon, Simon. *Handbook of Epilepsy Treatment.* 3rd ed. New York: Wiley-Blackwell, 2010.

Tatum, William O., Peter W. Kaplan, and Pierre Jallon. *Epilepsy A to Z: A Concise Encyclopedia.* 2nd ed. New York: Demos Medical, 2009.

ORGANIZATIONS

American Academy of Clinical Toxicology, 6728 Old McLean Village Dr., McLean, VA, 22101, (703) 556-9222, Fax: (703) 556-8729, admin@clintox.org, http://www.clintox.org.

American Academy of Family Physicians, 11400 Tomahawk Creek Pkwy., Leawood, KS, 66211-2672, (913) 906-6000, (800) 274-2237, Fax: (913) 906-6075, contactcenter@aafp.org, http://www.aafp.org.

American Medical Association, 515 N State St., Chicago, IL, 60610, (312) 464-5000, (800) 621-8335, http://www.ama-assn.org.

American Psychiatric Association, 1000 Wilson Blvd., Ste. 1825, Arlington, VA, 22209-3901, (703) 907-7300, apa@psych.org, http://www.psych.org.

American Psychological Association, 750 1st St., NE, Washington, DC, 20002-4242, (202) 336-5500; TDD/TTY: (202) 336-6123, (800) 374-2721, http://www.apa.org.

American Society for Clinical Pharmacology and Therapeutics, 528 N Washington St., Alexandria, VA, 22314, (703) 836-6981, info@ascpt.org, http://www.ascpt.org.

Anxiety Disorders Association of America, 8730 Georgia Ave., Silver Spring, MD, 20910, (240) 485-1001, Fax: (240) 485-1035, http://www.adaa.org.

Depression and Bipolar Support Alliance, 730 N Franklin St., Ste. 501, Chicago, IL, 60654, (800) 826-3632, Fax: (312) 642-7243, http://www.dbsalliance.org.

Mental Health America, 2000 N. Beauregard St., 6th Fl., Alexandria, VA, 22311, (703) 684-7722, (800) 969-6642, Fax: (703) 684-5968, http://www1.nmha.org.

National Alliance on Mental Illness, 2107 Wilson Blvd., Ste. 300, Arlington, VA, 22201-3042, Fax: (703) 524-9094, (800) 950-6264, http://www.nami.org.

National Institute of Mental Health, 6001 Executive Blvd., Rm. 8184, MSC 9663, Bethesda, MD, 20892-9663, (301) 433-4513; TTY: (301) 443-8431, Fax: (301) 443-4279, (866) 615-6464; TTY: (866) 415-8051, nimhinfo@nih.gov, http://www.nimh.nih.gov.

National Institutes of Health, 9000 Rockville Pike, Bethesda, MD, 20892, (301) 496-4000; TTY: (301) 402-9612, http://www.nih.gov.

U.S. National Library of Medicine, 8600 Rockville Pike, Bethesda, MD, 20894, (301) 594-5983, (888) 346-3656; TDD: (800) 735-2258, Fax: (301) 402-1384, http://www.nlm.nih.gov.

Mark Mitchell, MD
Emily Jane Willingham, PhD
Laura Jean Cataldo, RN, EdD

Diets

Definition

Special diets are designed to help individuals make changes in their usual eating habits or food selection. Some special diets involve changes in the overall diet, such as diets for people needing to gain or lose weight or eat more healthfully. Other special diets are designed to help individuals limit or avoid certain foods or dietary components that could interfere with the activity of a medication. Still other special diets are designed to counter nutritional effects of certain medications.

Purpose

Special diets are used in the treatment of people with certain mental disorders for the following reasons:

- identify and correct disordered eating patterns
- prevent or correct nutritional deficiencies or excesses
- prevent interactions between foods or nutrients and medications

Description

Special types of diets or changes in eating habits have been suggested for people with certain mental disorders. In some disorders, such as eating disorders or **substance abuse**, dietary changes are an integral part of therapy. In other disorders, such as attention deficit hyperactivity disorder, various proposed diets have questionable therapeutic value.

Many medications for mental disorders can affect appetite or nutrition-related functions such as saliva production, ability to swallow, bowel function, and activity level. Changes in diet or food choices may be required to help prevent negative effects of medications.

Finally, interactions can occur between some medications used to treat people with mental disorders and certain foods or nutritional components of the diet. For example, grapefruit and apple juice can interact with some specific psychotropic drugs (medications taken for psychiatric conditions) and should be avoided by individuals taking those medicines. Tyramine, a natural substance found in aged or fermented foods, can interfere with the functioning of **monoamine oxidase inhibitors (MAOIs)** and must be restricted in individuals using these types of medications. A person's preexisting medical condition and nutritional needs should be taken into account when designing any special diet.

KEY TERMS

Attention deficit hyperactivity disorder (ADHD)—A developmental disorder characterized by distractibility, hyperactivity, impulsive behaviors, and the inability to remain focused on tasks or activities.

Depression—A mental state characterized by feelings of sadness, despair, and discouragement.

Food allergy—An abnormal reaction to a food eaten or touched. A food allergy is related to the immune system.

Special diets for specific disorders

Eating disorders

The two main types of eating disorders are **anorexia nervosa** and **bulimia nervosa**. Individuals with anorexia nervosa starve themselves, whereas individuals with bulimia nervosa usually have normal or slightly above normal body weight but engage in binge eating followed by purging with laxatives, vomiting, or **exercise**.

Special diets for individuals with eating disorders focus on restoration of normal body weight and control of bingeing and purging. These diets are usually carried out under the supervision of a multidisciplinary team, including a physician, **psychologist**, and dietitian.

The overall dietary goal for individuals with anorexia nervosa is to restore a healthy body weight. An initial goal might be to stop weight loss and improve food choices. Energy intake is then increased gradually until normal weight is restored. Because individuals with anorexia nervosa have an intense fear of gaining weight and becoming fat, quantities of foods eaten are increased very slowly so that the patient will continue treatments and therapy.

The overall dietary goal for individuals with bulimia nervosa is to gain control over eating behavior and to achieve a healthy body weight. An initial goal is to stabilize weight and eating patterns to help individuals gain control over the binge-purge cycle. Meals and snacks are eaten at regular intervals to lessen the possibility that hunger and fasting will trigger a binge. Once eating behaviors have been stabilized, energy intake can be gradually adjusted to allow individuals to reach a normal body weight healthfully.

For individuals with either anorexia nervosa or bulimia, continued follow-up and support are required after normal weight and eating behaviors are restored, particularly since the rate of **relapse** is high. In addition to dietary changes, **psychotherapy** is an essential part of the treatment of eating disorders and helps individuals deal with fears and misconceptions about body weight and eating behavior.

Attention deficit hyperactivity disorder

Attention deficit hyperactivity disorder (ADHD) accounts for a substantial portion of referrals to child mental health services. Children with **ADHD** are inappropriately active, easily frustrated or distracted, impulsive, and have difficulty sustaining concentration. Usual treatment of ADHD involves medication, behavioral management, and education.

Many dietary factors have been proposed as causes of ADHD, including sugar, food additives, and food allergies. In the 1970s the Feingold diet became popular for treatment of ADHD. The Feingold diet excludes artificial colorings and flavorings, natural sources of chemicals called salicylates (found in fruits), and preservatives called BHT and BHA. Although scientific evidence does not support the effectiveness of the Feingold diet, a modified Feingold diet, including fruits, has been shown to be nutritionally balanced and should not be harmful as long as the child continues to receive conventional ADHD treatment also.

A high intake of sugar and sugary foods has also been implicated as a cause of ADHD. Although carefully controlled studies have shown no association between sugar and ADHD, diets high in sugar should be discouraged because they are often low in other nutrients and can contribute to dental problems.

Food allergies have also been implicated as a cause of ADHD, and some groups have suggested using elimination diets to treat ADHD. Elimination diets omit foods that most commonly cause allergies in children, such as eggs, milk, peanuts, or shellfish. Although research does not support the value of elimination diets for all children with ADHD, children with specific food allergies can become irritable and restless. Children with a suspected food allergy should be evaluated by an allergist.

Stimulant medications used to treat ADHD, such as **methylphenidate** (Ritalin), can cause appetite loss (anorexia) and retard growth, although some research suggests that a child's ultimate height appears not to be affected by stimulant medications. As a precaution, children on such medicines should receive close monitoring of growth patterns, and parents should carefully observe their child's appetite and interest in meals and snacks. Providing regular meals and snacks, even when the child is not hungry, can help to assure adequate growth.

Mood disorders

Mood disorders include both **depression** (unipolar disorder) and episodes of mania followed by depression (**bipolar disorder**). Both types of disorders can affect appetite and eating behavior.

Although some individuals with depression eat more than usual and gain weight, depression more often causes loss of appetite and weight loss. As individuals with depression lose interest in eating and social relationships, they often skip meals and ignore feelings of hunger. Unintentional weight losses of up to 15% of body mass can occur.

Treatment with antidepressant medications often reverses weight loss and restores appetite and interest in eating. If individuals have lost a significant amount of weight, they may need to follow a high-calorie diet to restore weight to normal levels and replaced nutritional deficiencies. High-calorie diets usually include three balanced meals from all the food groups and several smaller snacks throughout the day. A protein/calorie supplement may also be necessary for some individuals.

Depression is sometimes treated with **MAOIs**. Individuals on these medications need to follow a tyramine-restricted diet.

Individuals with mania are often treated with lithium. Sodium and caffeine intake can affect lithium levels in the blood, and intake of these should not suddenly be increased or decreased. Weight gain can occur in response to some antidepressant medications and lithium.

Schizophrenia

Individuals with **schizophrenia** can have hallucinations, delusional thinking, and bizarre behavior. These distorted behaviors and thought processes can also be extended to **delusions** and hallucinations about food and diet, making people with schizophrenia at risk for poor **nutrition**.

Individuals with schizophrenia may believe that certain foods are poisonous or have special properties. They may think they hear voices telling them not to eat. Some may eat huge quantities of food thinking that it gives them special powers. Individuals with untreated schizophrenia may lose a significant amount of weight. Delusional beliefs and thinking about food and eating usually improve once individuals are started on medication to treat schizophrenia.

Substance abuse

Substance abuse can include abuse of alcohol, cigarettes, marijuana, **cocaine**, or other drugs. Individuals abusing any of these substances are at risk for nutritional problems. Many of these substances can reduce appetite, decrease absorption of nutrients into the body, and cause individuals to make poor food choices.

Special diets used for withdrawal from substance abuse are designed to correct any nutritional deficiencies that have developed, aid in the withdrawal of the substance, and prevent the individual from making unhealthy food substitutions as the addictive substance is withdrawn. For example, some individuals may compulsively overeat when they stop smoking, leading to weight gain. Others may substitute caffeine-containing beverages such as soda or coffee for an addictive drug. Such harmful substitutions should be discouraged, emphasizing well-balanced eating combined with adequate rest, **stress management**, and regular exercise. Small, frequent meals and snacks that are rich in vitamins and minerals from healthful foods should be provided. Fluid intake should be generous, but caffeine-containing beverages should be limited.

Individuals withdrawing from alcohol may need extra thiamin supplementation, either intravenously or through a multivitamin supplement because alcohol metabolism in the body requires extra thiamin. Individuals taking drugs to help them avoid alcohol will need to avoid foods with even small amounts of alcohol.

Common withdrawal symptoms and dietary suggestions for coping with these symptoms include:

- Appetite loss: Eat small, frequent meals and snacks; limit caffeine; and use nutritional supplements if necessary.
- Appetite increase: Eat regular meals; eat a variety of foods; and limit sweets and caffeine.
- Diarrhea: Eat moderate amounts of fresh fruits, vegetables, concentrated sugars, juices, and milk and increase intake of cereal fiber.
- Constipation: Drink plenty of fluids; increase fiber in the diet; and increase physical activity.
- Fatigue: Eat regular meals; limit sweets and caffeine; and drink plenty of fluid.

Dietary considerations and medications

Medications that affect body weight

Many medications used to treat mental disorders promote weight gain. These include:

- anticonvulsants (divalproex)

- certain types of antidepressants (amitriptyline)
- antipsychotic medications (clozapine, olanzapine, quetiapine, and risperidone)

Dietary treatments for individuals taking these medications should focus on a balanced, low-fat diet coupled with an increase in physical activity to counter the side effects of these medications. Nutrient-rich foods such as fruits, vegetables, and whole grain products should be emphasized in the diet, whereas sweets, fats, and other foods high in energy but low in nutrients should be limited. Regular physical activity can help limit weight gain caused by these medications.

Some medications can cause loss of appetite, restlessness, and weight loss. Individuals on such medications should eat three balanced meals and several smaller snacks of protein and calorie-rich foods throughout the day. Eating on a regular schedule rather than depending on appetite can help prevent weight loss associated with loss of appetite.

Medications that affect gastrointestinal function

Many psychiatric medications can affect gastrointestinal functioning. Some drugs can cause dry mouth, difficulty swallowing, constipation, altered taste, heartburn, diarrhea, or nausea. Consuming frequent smaller meals, drinking adequate fluids, modifying texture of foods if necessary, and increasing fiber content of foods can help counter gastrointestinal effects of medications.

Monoamine oxidase inhibitors

Individuals being treated with MAOIs such as **tranylcypromine**, **phenelzine**, and **isocarboxazid**, must carefully follow a tyramine-restricted diet. Tyramine, a nitrogen-containing substance normally present in certain foods, is usually broken down in the body by oxidase. However, in individuals taking MAOIs, tyramine is not adequately broken down and builds up in the blood, causing the blood vessels to constrict and increasing blood pressure.

Tyramine is normally found in many foods, especially protein-rich foods that have been aged or fermented, pickled, or bacterially contaminated. Cheese is especially high in tyramine. A tyramine intake of less than 5 mg daily is recommended. A diet that includes even just 6 mg of tyramine can increase blood pressure; a diet that provides 25 mg of tyramine can cause life-threatening increases in blood pressure.

TYRAMINE-RESTRICTED DIET. Tyramine is found in aged, fermented, and spoiled food products. The tyramine content of a specific food can vary greatly depending on storage conditions, ripeness, or contamination. Reaction to tyramine-containing foods in individuals taking MAOIs can also vary greatly depending on what other foods are eaten with the tyramine-containing food, the length of time between MAOI dose and eating the food, and individual characteristics such as weight or age.

Foods to avoid on a tyramine-controlled diet include:

- all aged and mature cheeses or cheese spreads, including foods made with these cheeses, such as salad dressings, casseroles, or certain breads
- any outdated or nonpasteurized dairy products
- dry fermented sausages such as summer sausage, pepperoni, salami, or pastrami
- smoked or pickled fish
- nonfresh meat or poultry
- leftover foods containing meat or poultry
- tofu and soy products
- overripe, spoiled, or fermented fruits or vegetables
- sauerkraut
- fava or broad beans
- soups containing meat extracts or cheese
- gravies containing meat extracts or nonfresh meats
- tap beer
- nonalcoholic beer
- yeast extracts
- soy sauce
- liquid powdered protein supplements

Perishable refrigerated items such as milk, meat, or fruit should be eaten within 48 hours of purchase. Any spoiled food and food stored in questionable conditions should not be eaten.

Lithium

Lithium is often used to treat individuals with mania. Lithium can cause nausea, vomiting, anorexia, diarrhea, and weight gain. Almost one-half of individuals taking lithium gain weight.

Individuals taking lithium should maintain a fairly constant intake of sodium (found in table salt and other food additives) and caffeine in their diet. If an individual restricts sodium intake, less lithium is excreted in the urine and blood lithium levels rise. If an individual increases caffeine intake, more lithium is excreted in the urine and blood levels of lithium fall.

Anticonvulsant medications

Sodium caseinate and calcium caseinate can interfere with the action and effectiveness of some anticonvulsants. Individuals taking these drugs should read labels carefully to avoid foods containing these additives.

Psychotropic medications

Some psychotropic medications, such as **amitriptyline**, can decrease absorption of the vitamin riboflavin from food. Good food sources of riboflavin include milk and milk products, liver, red meat, poultry, fish, whole grain, and enriched breads and cereals. Riboflavin supplements may also be needed.

Other psychotropic drugs, such as **fluvoxamine**, **sertraline**, **nefazodone**, **alprazolam**, **triazolam**, midazolam, **carbamazepine**, and **clonazepam**, interact with grapefruit juice, so individuals taking these drugs must take care to avoid grapefruit juice. In some cases, apple juice must be avoided as well. Patients should discuss potential drug interactions with their doctors or pharmacists.

Caffeine-restricted diet

Caffeine is a stimulant and can interfere with the actions of certain medications. People taking lithium and people recovering from addictions may be asked by their treatment team to monitor (and, in the case of addictions, restrict) their caffeine intake. Foods and beverages high in caffeine include:

- chocolate
- cocoa mix and powder
- chocolate ice cream, milk, and pudding
- coffee
- cola beverages
- tea

Alcohol-restricted diet

Alcohol interacts with some medications used to treat mental disorders. In the case of alcoholism recovery, the negative interaction resulting from the combination of one medication (**disulfiram** or Antabuse) and alcohol consumption is actually part of treatment for some people. (The medication causes an extremely unpleasant reaction when any alcohol is consumed, reinforcing or rewarding the avoidance of alcohol.)

When individuals are taking medication that requires that they avoid alcohol, foods containing alcohol must be avoided as well as beverage alcohol. The following foods contain small amounts of alcohol:

- flavor extracts, such as vanilla, almond, or rum
- cooking wines
- candies or cakes prepared or filled with liqueur
- apple cider
- cider and wine vinegar
- commercial eggnog
- béarnaise or bordelaise sauces
- desserts such as crepes suzette or cherries jubilee
- teriyaki sauce
- fondues

QUESTIONS TO ASK YOUR DOCTOR

- How can I tell if I am getting the right nutrients?
- What types of diagnostic tests do I need?
- What dietary changes, if any, would you recommend for me?
- What changes in my eating regimen would you recommend?
- What kind of changes can I expect to see with the medications you have prescribed for me?
- What tests or evaluation techniques can you perform to see if my nutritional choices promote a healthy condition?
- What symptoms are important enough that I should seek immediate treatment?

Resources

BOOKS

Bean, Dianne. *Nutrition Ambition: Reaching Your Wellness Goals, Ages 8–12,* 2nd ed. Winter Park, FL: Baux, 2009.

Bender, David A. *A Dictionary of Food and Nutrition.* New York: Oxford University Press, 2009.

Cousens, Gabriel. *Conscious Eating,* 2nd ed. Berkley, CA: North Atlantic Books, 2009.

Plant, Jane, and Gill Tidey. *Eating for Better Health.* New York: Virgin Books, 2010.

Robertson, Cathie. *Safety, Nutrition and Health in Early Education,* 4th ed. Florence, KY: Wadsworth, 2009.

Shils, Maurice E. *Modern Nutrition in Health and Disease,* 11th ed. New York: Lippincott Williams & Wilkins, 2012.

Virani, Adil S., et al., eds. *Clinical Handbook of Psychotropic Drugs,* 19th ed. Cambridge, MA: Hogrefe, 2011.

PERIODICALS

Daubenmier, Jennifer J., et al. "The Contribution of Changes in Diet, Exercise, and Stress Management to Changes in Coronary Risk in Women and Men in the Multisite Cardiac Lifestyle Intervention Program." *Annals of Behavioral Medicine* 33, no. 1 (2007): 57–68.

Groesz, Lisa M., and Eric Stice. "An Experimental Test of the Effects of Dieting on Bulimic Symptoms: The Impact of Eating Episode Frequency." *Behaviour Research and Therapy* 45, no. 1 (2007): 49–62.

Hagler, Athena S., et al. "Psychosocial Correlates of Dietary Intake Among Overweight and Obese Men." *American Journal of Health Behavior* 31, no. 1 (2007): 3–12.

Jabs, Jennifer, and Carol M. Devine. "Time Scarcity and Food Choices: An Overview." *Appetite* 47, no. 2 (2006): 196–204.

Leung, Newman, and Emma Price. "Core Beliefs in Dieters and Eating Disordered Women." *Eating Behaviors* 8, no. 1 (2007): 65–72.

Mobbs, Charles V., et al. "Low-Carbohydrate Diets Cause Obesity, Low-Carbohydrate Diets Reverse Obesity: A Metabolic Mechanism Resolving the Paradox." *Appetite* 48, no. 2 (2007): 135–38.

Payne, Martha E., et al. "Vascular Nutritional Correlates of Late-Life Depression." *American Journal of Geriatric Psychiatry* 14, no. 9 (2006): 787–95.

ORGANIZATIONS

American Academy of Family Physicians, 11400 Tomahawk Creek Pkwy., Leawood, KS, 66211-2672, (913) 906-6000, (800) 274-2237, Fax: (913) 906-6075, contactcenter@aafp.org, http://www.aafp.org.

American Dietetic Association, 120 South Riverside Plaza, Ste. 2000, Chicago, IL, 60606, (312) 899-0040, (800) 877-1600, http://www.eatright.org.

American Psychiatric Association, 1000 Wilson Blvd., Ste. 1825, Arlington, VA, 22209-3901, (703) 907-7300, apa@psych.org, http://www.psych.org.

American Psychological Association, 750 1st St. NE, Washington, DC, 20002-4242, (202) 336-5500; TDD/TTY: (202) 336-6123, (800) 374-2721, http://www.apa.org.

National Eating Disorders Association, 165 W 46th St., New York, NY, 10036, (212) 575-6200, Fax: (212) 575-1650, (800) 931-2237, http://www.nationaleatingdisorders.org.

Nancy Gustafson, MS, RD, FADA, ELS
Ruth A. Wienclaw, PhD
Laura Jean Cataldo, RN, EdD

Diphenhydramine

Definition

Diphenhydramine is an antihistamine used in psychiatric medicine to treat **medication-induced movement disorders**, such as may be caused by antipsychotic drugs. When used for this purpose, diphenhydramine is prescribed in the generic form. It is used in general medicine to treat allergies and allergic reactions (sold over-the-counter as Benadryl), motion sickness, **insomnia**, cough, and nausea.

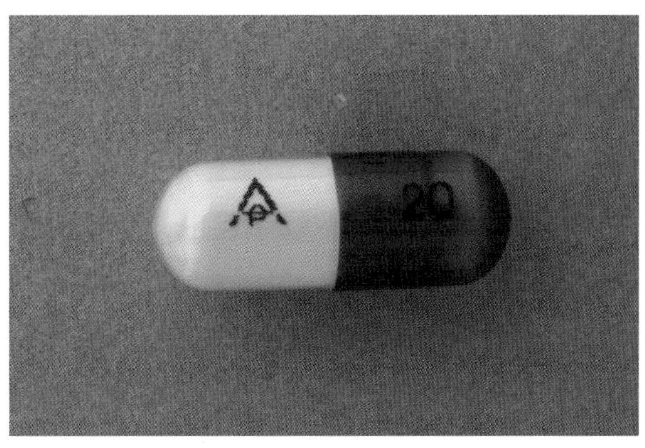

Benadryl (diphenhydramine). *(© Custom Medical Stock Photo, Inc. Reproduced by permission.)*

Purpose

Phenothiazines are sometimes used to treat psychotic disorders such as **schizophrenia**. As a side effect, these drugs may cause tremors and abnormal involuntary movements of the muscles, referred to as extrapyramidal neurologic **movement disorders**. Diphenhydramine is used to control these symptoms. It is may be used to treat the stiffness and tremor of Parkinson's disease and may induce sleep.

Description

Diphenhydramine is easily absorbed when taken by mouth and is readily distributed throughout the body. Maximal effect occurs approximately one hour after swallowing the drug and continues for four to six hours. Diphenhydramine seems to compete with the chemical histamine for specific receptor sites on cells in the **brain** and central nervous system. This means that it achieves its therapeutic effect by taking the place of the neurotransmitter histamine on these cells.

Recommended dosage

The dosage of diphenhydramine must be adjusted according to the needs of individuals and their responses. Adults are generally given 25–50 mg orally, three to four times daily. Diphenhydramine may be administered through a vein or injected deep within a muscle. The usual dosage is 10–50 mg per injection, although some people may require 100 mg. The total daily dosage should not exceed 400 mg. People who forget to take a dose of this drug should skip the dose and take the next one at the regularly scheduled time. They should not double up subsequent doses if one is missed.

People should not take diphenhydramine if they are taking other preparations that contain antihistamines unless specifically directed to do so by a physician.

Precautions

People with peptic ulcer disease, bowel obstructions, an enlarged prostate, angle closure glaucoma, or difficulty urinating due to a blockage in the bladder should not use diphenhydramine without close physician supervision and monitoring. People with asthma, heart disease, high blood pressure, or an overactive thyroid should use this drug with caution. Before taking diphenhydramine, people with these conditions should discuss the risks and benefits of this drug with their doctor. Individuals should not take diphenhydramine for several days before an allergy test, as it will interfere with the results.

Elderly people are more sensitive to the sedating effects of diphenhydramine. The drug may also lower blood pressure, which can cause dizziness and lightheadedness when switching from a seated to a standing position. Older patients should move slowly when rising to a standing position to prevent fainting.

Drowsiness commonly occurs after taking diphenhydramine. This effect may be more pronounced if alcohol or any other central nervous system depressant, such as a tranquilizer or pain medication, is also taken. People taking the drug should not drive, operate machinery, or perform tasks requiring mental alertness until the effects of the medication have worn off.

Side effects

Diphenhydramine may cause dizziness, difficulties with coordination, confusion, restlessness, nervousness, difficulty sleeping, blurry or double vision, ringing in the ears, headache, or convulsions. Stomach distress is a relatively common side effect of diphenhydramine. Some people may develop poor appetites, nausea, vomiting, diarrhea, or constipation. Individuals also may experience low blood pressure, heart palpitations, rapid or irregular heartbeats, frequent urination, or difficulty urinating. Urine may be retained in the bladder. Thickened lung secretions are common among older persons. Other side effects include hives, a rash, sensitivity to the sun, and a dry mouth and nose.

Interactions

Alcohol, pain medications, sleeping pills, tranquilizers, and **antidepressants** may make the drowsiness associated with diphenhydramine more severe. Diphenhydramine should not be used by persons taking hay-fever medicines, **sedatives**, narcotics, anesthetics, **barbiturates**, or muscle relaxants.

KEY TERMS

Anticholinergic—Related to the ability of a drug to block the nervous system chemical acetylcholine. When acetylcholine is blocked, patients often experience dry mouth and skin, increased heart rate, blurred vision, and difficulty in urinating. In severe cases, blocking acetylcholine may cloud thinking and cause delirium.

Antihistamine—A medication used to alleviate allergy or cold symptoms such as runny nose, itching, hives, watering eyes, or sneezing.

Extrapyramidal movement disorders—Involuntary movements that occur as a side effect of some psychiatric medications.

Histamine—Substance released during allergic reactions.

Hypokinesia—A condition of abnormally diminished motor activity.

Parkinson's disease—A disease of the nervous system most common in people over 60, characterized by a shuffling gait, trembling of the fingers and hands, and muscle stiffness.

Parkinsonism—A condition caused by the destruction of the brain cells that produce dopamine (a neurotransmitter); characterized by tremors of the fingers and hands, a shuffling gait, and muscular rigidity.

Phenothiazine—A class of drugs widely used in the treatment of psychosis.

Resources

BOOKS

Foreman, John C., and Torben Johansen. *Textbook of Receptor Pharmacology*. 2nd ed. Boca Raton, FL: CRC Press, 2002.

Page, Clive P., et al. *Integrated Pharmacology*. 3rd ed. St. Louis, MO: Elsevier, 2006.

Preston, John D., John H. O'Neal, and Mary C. Talaga. *Handbook of Clinical Psychopharmacology for Therapists*. 5th ed. Oakland, CA: New Harbinger Publications, 2008.

PERIODICALS

Grillon, Christian, et al. "The Benzodiazepine Alprazolam Dissociates Contextual Fear from Cued Fear in Humans as Assessed by Fear-Potentiated Startle." *Biological Psychiatry* 60, no. 7 (October 1, 2006): 760–66.

Khoromi, Suzan, et al. "Topiramate in Chronic Lumbar Radicular Pain." *Journal of Pain* 6, no. 12 (December 2005): 829–36.

Scaife, J.C., et al. "Sensitivity of Late-Latency Auditory and Somatosensory Evoked Potentials to Threat of Electric Shock and the Sedative Drugs Diazepam and Diphenhydramine in Human Volunteers." *Journal of Psychopharmacology* 20, no. 4 (November 1, 2008): 828–35.

Turner, Claire, Alison D. F. Handford, and Anthony N. Nicholson. "Sedation and Memory: Studies with a Histamine H-1 Receptor Antagonist." *Journal of Psychopharmacology* 20, no. 4 (July 2006): 506–17.

ORGANIZATIONS

American Academy of Family Physicians, 11400 Tomahawk Creek Pky., Leawood, KS, 66211-2672, (913) 906-6000, (800) 274-2237, Fax: (913) 906-6075, contactcenter@-aafp.org, http://www.aafp.org.

American Parkinson Disease Association, Inc, 135 Parkinson Ave., Staten Island, NY, 10305, (718) 981-8001, Fax: (718) 981-4399, apda@apdaparkinson.org, http://www.apdaparkinson.com.

American Psychiatric Association, 1000 Wilson Blvd., Ste. 1825, Arlington, VA, 22209-3901, (703) 907-7300, apa@psych.org, http://www.psych.org.

American Society for Clinical Pharmacology and Therapeutics, 528 North Washington St., Alexandria, VA, 22314, (703) 836-6981, http://www.ascpt.org.

American Society for Pharmacology and Experimental Therapeutics, 9650 Rockville Pike, Bethesda, MD, 20814-3995, (301) 634-7060, Fax: (301) 634-7061, http://www.aspet.org.

Parkinson's Disease Foundation, 1359 Broadway, Ste. 1509, New York, NY, 10018, (212) 923-4700, Fax: (212) 923-4778, info@pdf.org, http://www.pdf.org.

U.S. Food and Drug Administration, 10903 New Hampshire Ave., Silver Spring, MD, 20993-0002, (888) INFO-FDA (463-6332), http://www.fda.gov.

L. Fleming Fallon, Jr, MD, DrPH
Ruth A. Wienclaw, PhD

Disease concept of chemical dependency

Definition

Disease concept of chemical dependency is the concept that a disorder (such as chemical dependency) is like a disease and has a characteristic set of signs, symptoms, and natural history (clinical course, or outcome).

Description

The disease concept has long been accepted by the medical community. The concept proposes that a disease is characterized by a specific set of signs and symptoms and that the disease, if left untreated, will progress to some endpoint or outcome (clinical course). However, controversy arises when the medical community is faced with new abnormal conditions, owing mostly to the new technologies in genetic engineering. This controversy becomes especially apparent when examining psychological disorders.

In the past, psychological disorders were thought in general to be due to both psychological and social abnormalities. Although these psychosocial problems are still of utmost importance, researchers have since discovered that many psychological disorders, such as alcoholism, also have genetic causes. Recent studies have identified a genetic area (locus) where a gene is located that can transmit alcoholism from affected father to son. Mental health professionals also know from clinical experience that alcoholics demonstrate a characteristic set of specific signs and symptoms. Additionally, it is well established that the ultimate clinical course for untreated alcoholism is death. Therefore alcoholism, once thought to be a disorder of those with a weak will, or "party people" can now be characterized as a disease.

There is compelling evidence that other chemical dependencies may also have biological causes. All psychoactive mood-altering drugs (alcohol, **cocaine**, marijuana, heroin, etc.) act in specific sites in the **brain** and on a specific neurotransmitter (a chemical that delivers impulses from one nerve cell to another) called **dopamine**. These mood-altering substances cause dopamine depletion, inducing an abnormality in nerve cells that "hijacks" the cells into chemical dependence. In other words, the substance introduced in the body affects the dopamine in a way that makes the affected individual unable to experience everyday pleasures—the individual instead needs that substance to experience pleasure. Thus the individual's driving force is any drug that can provide some kind of transient happiness (euphoria). In fact, the gene for alcoholism is located in the dopamine molecule. This can further suggest that chemical dependencies may have a medical (biological) cause.

The disease concept of chemical dependency is gaining worldwide acceptance, but does have some critics who argue instead that **addiction** must be understood as a general pattern of behavior, not as a medical problem. Advocates of the disease concept of chemical dependency model maintain that the identification of biological causes or correlations is crucially important for treatment. They argue that if clinicians can understand the intricate details concerning the mechanisms associated with drug effects, then measures to interrupt the effects can be devised. These interventions can be both medical (developing new drugs to chemically block effects of illicit drugs) and psychological.

According to the disease concept model, psychological **intervention** includes a vital educational component that teaches people with chemical dependency the concept of understanding addiction as disease. As a result of this understanding, affected people then view their dependency as a disease, similar to other diseases with a biological cause (heart disease, cancer, high blood pressure), and with a specific set of signs and symptoms and an outcome in the future (clinical course). Proponents of this approach believe that this understanding can help affected people to follow treatment recommendations, and can reduce shame and guilt commonly associated with chemical dependence. Alcoholics Anonymous is a prominent example of an organization that embodies the disease concept of chemical dependency.

Resources

PERIODICALS

Kampman, Kyle M. "New Medications for the Treatment of Cocaine Dependence." *Psychiatry* 2, no. 12, (December 2005) 44–48.

Stanger, Catherine. "Behavioral and Emotional Problems Among Children of Drug Abusers." *Psychiatric Times* 20, no. 2 (February 1, 2003).

WEBSITES

U.S. National Institute on Drug Abuse. "Addition Is a Chronic Disease." http://archives.drugabuse.gov/about/welcome/aboutdrugabuse/chronicdisease (accessed November 14, 2011).

U.S. National Institute on Drug Abuse. "Drugs, Brains, and Behavior—The Science of Addiction." http://www.nida.nih.gov/scienceofaddiction (accessed November 14, 2011).

Laith Farid Gulli, MD

Disorder of written expression

Definition

Disorder of written expression, formerly called developmental expressive writing disorder, is a learning disability in which a person's ability to communicate in writing is substantially below the level normally expected based on the individual's age, intelligence, life experiences, educational background, or physical impairments. This disability affects both the physical reproduction of letters and words and the organization of thoughts and ideas in written compositions.

Demographics

Several studies have estimated that between 3% and 5% of students have disorder of written expression. However, it is difficult to separate this disorder from other **learning disorders**. Deficits in written work may be attributed to reading, language, or attention disorders, limited educational background, or lack of fluency in the language of instruction. Disorder of written expression unassociated with any other learning disability is rare. It commonly occurs in conjunction with **reading disorder** or **mathematics disorder**.

Description

Disorder of written expression is one of the more poorly understood learning disabilities. Learning disabilities that manifest themselves only in written work were first described in the late 1960s. These early studies described three main types of written disorders:

- inability to form letters and numbers correctly, also called dysgraphia
- inability to write words spontaneously or from dictation
- inability to organize words into meaningful thoughts

There are several difficulties in studying disorder of written expression and in implementing a remedial program. Disorder of written expression usually appears in conjunction with other reading or language disabilities, making it hard to separate manifestations of the disability related only to written expression. Delays in attention, visual-motor integration, visual processing, and expressive language may also contribute to writing disorders. Also, there are no standard tests specifically designed to evaluate disorder of written expression.

Causes and symptoms

Causes

The causes of disorder of written expression are unknown. Different manifestations of the disorder may have different causes. For example, people who cannot form letters correctly on the page (dysgraphia) may have delays in hand-eye coordination and difficulties concentrating. People who are unable to write words from memory or dictation appear to have deficits in their visual memory. They cannot remember what the words look like. People who produce legible script but cannot organize their thoughts on paper may have cognitive processing problems. Because disorder of written expression is a little-studied disorder, specific causes have not yet been determined.

Symptoms

Symptoms that suggest disorder of written expression include:

- poor or illegible handwriting
- poorly formed letters or numbers
- excessive spelling errors
- excessive punctuation errors
- excessive grammar errors
- sentences that lack logical cohesion
- paragraphs and stories that are missing elements and that do not make sense or lack logical transitions
- deficient writing skills that significantly impact academic achievement or daily life

These symptoms must be evaluated in light of the person's age, intelligence, educational experience, and cultural or life experience. Written expression must be substantially below the level of samples produced by others of the same age, intelligence, and background. Normally, several of the symptoms are present simultaneously.

Diagnosis

There are no specific tests to diagnose disorder of written expression. This disorder is not normally diagnosed before age eight because of the variability with which children acquire writing skills. It is most commonly diagnosed in the fourth or fifth grade, although it can be noted and diagnosed as soon as the first grade. Requests for testing usually originate with a teacher or parent who notes multiple symptoms of the disorder in a child's writing.

Several standardized tests accurately reflect spelling abilities, but do not assess other writing skills with the same reliability. Tests that might be helpful in diagnosing disorder of written expression include the Diagnostic Evaluation of Writing Skills (DEWS), the Test of Early Written Language (TEWL), and the Test of Adolescent Language.

However, assessment using standardized tests is not enough to make a **diagnosis** of disorder of written expression. In addition, a qualified evaluator should compare multiple samples of the student's written work with the written work normally expected from students of comparable backgrounds. The person being evaluated may also be asked to perform tasks such as writing from dictation or copying written material as part of diagnostic testing.

Treatment

Little is known about how to treat disorder of written expression. Intense writing remediation may help, but no specific method or approach to remediation has proved particularly successful. Since disorder of written expression usually occurs in conjunction with other learning disabilities, treatment is often directed at those better-understood learning problems.

Prognosis

Little is known about the long-term outcome for people with disorder of written expression. However, it appears that those who have this disorder may develop low self-esteem and social problems related to their lack of academic achievement. Later in life they may be more likely to drop out of school and may find employment opportunities that require writing skills to be closed to them.

Prevention

There are no known ways to prevent disorder of written expression.

Resources

BOOKS

American Psychiatric Association. *Diagnostic and Statistical Manual of Mental Disorders*. 4th ed., text rev. Washington, DC: American Psychiatric Publishing, 2000.

Sadock, Benjamin J., and Virginia A. Sadock, eds. *Comprehensive Textbook of Psychiatry*. Vol. 2. 7th ed. Philadelphia: Lippincott Williams and Wilkins, 2000.

OTHER

International Dyslexia Association. "Just the Facts: Dysgraphia." Fact Sheet #82. http://ldanh.org/docs/fact sheets4.27.04/dysgraphia.pdf (accessed October 5, 2011).

WEBSITES

MedlinePlus. "Disorders of Written Expression." U.S. National Library of Medicine. National Institutes of Health. November 14, 2010. http://www.nlm.nih.gov/medlineplus/ency/article/001543.htm (accessed October 5, 2011).

U.S. National Institute for Neurological Disorders and Stroke. "NINDS Dysgraphia Information Page." http://www.ninds.nih.gov/disorders/dysgraphia/dysgraphia.htm (accessed October 5, 2011).

ORGANIZATIONS

American Academy of Child and Adolescent Psychiatry , 3615 Wisconsin Ave. NW, Washington, DC, 20016-3007, (202) 966-7300, Fax: (202) 966-2891, http://aacap.org.

Learning Disabilities Association of America, 4156 Library Rd., Pittsburgh, PA, 15234-1349, (412) 341-1515, http://www.ldanatl.org.

National Center for Learning Disabilities, 381 Park Ave. S, Ste. 1401, New York, NY, 10016, (212) 545-7510, Fax: (212) 545-9665, (888) 575-7373, http://www.ncld.org.

Tish Davidson, AM
Emily Jane Willingham, PhD

Disruptive behavior disorder *see* **Conduct disorder**

Disruptive mood dysregulation disorder

Definition

Disruptive mood dysregulation disorder (DMDD) is a new category of childhood mood disorder proposed for the fifth edition of the ***Diagnostic and Statistical Manual of Mental Disorders*** (*DSM-5*, 2013). The disorder is defined by the *DSM* as a chronically unhappy mood in children over the age of six accompanied by frequent outbursts of rage that are more intense than the temper tantrums seen in toddlers.

Demographics

The demographics of the disorder are unknown, as it is a fairly new **diagnosis** and has not yet undergone field testing. It is possible, however, that some children diagnosed with **juvenile bipolar disorder** actually have DMDD. Prior to the 1990s, **bipolar disorder** (BD) in children was considered an extremely rare condition. Beginning in the late 1990s, a team of researchers at Harvard began to think that a diagnosis of bipolar disorder better accounted for chronic irritability and moodiness in children—many of whom had already been diagnosed with **attention deficit hyperactivity disorder (ADHD)**. The number of children diagnosed with bipolar disorder increased 4,000% between 1994 and 2003, according to a 2007 study published in the *Archives of General Psychiatry*.

As of 2011, approximately one million children in the United States had been diagnosed with bipolar disorder; about two-thirds of these children were boys. This finding was puzzling to some psychiatrists for two reasons: first, the gender ratio of bipolar disorder in adults is closer to 50/50, and second, many people diagnosed with BD as children do not meet the criteria for the diagnosis as adults. The latter was an especially unusual finding, as BD is considered a lifelong disorder. Conversely, most people diagnosed with BD as adults did not experience uncontrolled anger issues as children, prompting questions as to whether or not another disorder might account for the childhood symptoms.

Description

Disruptive mood dysregulation disorder is a new disorder proposed for inclusion in the *DSM-5*, although symptoms of the condition have been recognized since the *DSM-III* was published in 1980. Prior to the 1990s, most children with anger management problems were diagnosed as having **conduct disorder**. The problem was that most treatments, including behavioral therapy, had a low record of success in treating conduct disorder. The Harvard psychiatrists evaluated a group of children diagnosed with **ADHD** with severe anger problems and realized that the symptoms might be better accounted for in a mood disorder rather than an impulse control disorder; this realization led them to label the condition as childhood bipolar disorder. Because bipolar disorder can be treated with medications, specifically atypical antipsychotics, some hypothesized that the diagnosis would be more agreeable to insurance companies, who were more willing to reimburse the cost of medications than of psychotherapies, and to parents, who found some relief in believing that their troubled child had a biologically based disorder. The annual sales of atypical antipsychotics for children rose sharply in the United States, from $402,000 in 2000 to $6.8 million by 2006.

In order to diagnose children with bipolar disorder, the Harvard group had to change one of the criteria for BD in adults to accommodate a different symptom profile in children with anger issues. To meet the diagnosis of BD, an adult must be identified as having episodes of mania (a state of abnormal irritability, elevated mood, or high energy lasting for a week or longer) as well as episodes of **depression** and periods of normal mood. The children who were studied in the early 1990s did not have manic episodes lasting for several days or a month, so the researchers redefined manic episodes in children as very brief and very frequent outbursts of temper or aggressive behavior. This redefinition meant that children who were simply overly excitable while they were going through a difficult period of adjustment (geographical relocation, a new school, or death or divorce in the family) were at risk of being labeled as having bipolar disorder. The diagnosis of childhood BD did not account for situational stressors or developmental differences among children.

Children diagnosed with juvenile bipolar disorder may also face issues later in life due to the **stigma** attached to the diagnosis, especially since it is understood to be a lifelong condition. Labeling a child as bipolar risks causing difficulties for the child later in life, such as when he or she seeks admission to college or applies for a job. Further, the atypical antipsychotics have potentially severe side effects that include rapid weight gain, an increased risk of type 2 diabetes, and a shortened lifespan. In addition, there is some evidence that they have an effect on the development of the nervous system in growing children.

KEY TERMS

Mania—A state in which a person has an abnormally elevated ("high") or irritable mood or energy level that is not caused by a medical illness or drugs of abuse.

Stigma—Any personal attribute that causes a person to be socially shamed, avoided, or discredited. Mental disorders are a common cause of stigma.

DMDD is considered a preliminary disorder, as its acceptance is not yet widespread within the psychiatric community. If the incidence of juvenile bipolar disorder is truly overestimated, the diagnosis of DMDD will be helpful in finding effective treatments, especially if children are unnecessarily taking medication for bipolar disorder. However, DMDD has prompted debate within the psychiatric field.

Causes and symptoms

The causes of DMDD were not known as of 2011. There is evidence, however, that the condition can be differentiated from bipolar disorder in that it does not seem to run in families or have a genetic basis.

The core symptoms of DMDD are temper outbursts consisting of verbal or physical aggression that are out of proportion to the triggering situation or event and inappropriate to the child's developmental level. The child also displays irritable, angry, grumpy, or sad moods in between the angry outbursts.

Diagnosis

There are no laboratory, genetic, or imaging tests that can be used to diagnose DMDD. The diagnosis is made on the basis of the child psychiatrist's clinical judgment. Children with a previous diagnosis of bipolar disorder may be rediagnosed with DMDD; the co-director of the Children's Hospital Boston's mood disorder program cites diagnosing 65% and 80% of children previously diagnosed with bipolar disorder who were brought to them for a second opinion with DMDD.

The proposed *DSM* diagnostic criteria for DMDD are as follows:

- Criterion A: The child displays severe and recurrent temper outbursts in response to stress. Outbursts may take the form of verbal or physical attacks on people, pets, or objects. The outbursts must be considered inappropriate for the situation and for the child's level of development.
- Criterion B: Outbursts occur at least three times a week (on average).
- Criterion C: Between outbursts, the child's mood is persistently grumpy, irritable, or sad, to the extent that it is noticed by others.
- Criterion D: The child exhibits the symptoms of criteria A through C for at least 12 months, and any symptom-free periods must last no longer than 3 months.
- Criterion E: The symptoms occur in at least two environments (e.g., home or school) and are considered extreme in at least one of the environments.
- Criterion F: The child is at least six years old.
- Criterion G: The onset of the symptoms occurs before age 10.
- Criterion H: The child does not meet the criteria for a manic episode.
- Criterion I: The behaviors do not occur in the context of a psychotic disorder, do not better meet the criteria for another diagnosis, and are not due to a general medical or neurological condition. The diagnosis of DMDD may, however, coexist with another disorder, including ADHD, conduct disorder, or oppositional defiant disorder.

The present definition of DMDD has been criticized by some child psychiatrists on the grounds that in essence it turns a single symptom—temper outbursts—into a complete syndrome. As a result, the new disorder overlaps with the definitions of several other childhood disorders and is not clearly differentiated from them. Also, the current diagnostic criteria do not take into consideration the great variability in what are considered appropriate expressions of temper across children, developmental phases, families, and subcultures—what is considered a severe outburst in some families or cultures might be less extreme in others.

Treatment

There was no standard approach to treatment for DMDD as of 2011, because the disorder had only been recently identified. Some psychiatrists have suggested a multidimensional approach to therapy, using medications only sparingly, prescribing **antidepressants** rather than antipsychotics, and focusing on helping the child deal with life's challenges without giving in to explosive temper outbursts.

There was one clinical research study of mood dysregulation in children under way as of mid-2011.

QUESTIONS TO ASK YOUR DOCTOR

- Have you ever treated a child with disruptive mood dysregulation disorder?
- What treatment options are available?
- Should my child see a specialist?

The trial was studying the effectiveness of **risperidone** (Risperdal), an atypical antipsychotic, as a treatment for the disorder.

Prognosis

The prognosis of DMDD was not known as of 2011. While many child psychiatrists expect that children with this disorder will have some problems lasting into adulthood, they will not have bipolar disorder (if DMDD is the true cause of their symptoms). It should be noted, however, that bipolar disorder is a serious condition, and if a child exhibits symptoms of juvenile bipolar disorder, they should not be ignored.

Prevention

Because the causes of DMDD are not yet identified, it is not yet known how to prevent DMDD.

Resources

BOOKS

American Psychiatric Association. *Diagnostic and Statistical Manual*. 4th ed., text rev. Washington, DC: American Psychiatric Association, 2000.

Kaplan, Stuart L. *Your Child Does Not Have Bipolar Disorder: How Bad Science and Good Public Relations Created the Diagnosis*. Santa Barbara, CA: Praeger, 2011.

McDonnell, Mary Ann, and Janet Wozniak. *Is Your Child Bipolar?: The Definitive Resource on How to Identify, Treat, and Thrive with a Bipolar Child*. New York: Bantam, 2008.

Papolos, Demitri, and Janice Papolos. *The Bipolar Child: The Definitive and Reassuring Guide to Childhood's Most Misunderstood Disorder*, 3rd ed. New York: Broadway Books, 2006.

PERIODICALS

Carlson, Gabrielle A. "Who Are the Children With Severe Mood Dysregulation, a.k.a. 'Rages?'" *American Journal of Psychiatry* 164 (August 1, 2007): 1140–42.

Moreno, C., et al. "National Trends in the Outpatient Diagnosis and Treatment of Bipolar Disorder in Youth." *Archives of General Psychiatry* 64 (September 2007): 1032–1039.

Olson, Jeremy. "Bipolar Label Soars Among Kids." *Minneapolis Star-Tribune*, June 23, 2011. http://www.startribune.com/lifestyle/wellness/124136764.html?page=all&prepage=1&c=y#continue (accessed August 11, 2011).

Parens, E., and J. Johnston. "Controversies Concerning the Diagnosis and Treatment of Bipolar Disorder in Children." *Child and Adolescent Psychiatry and Mental Health* 4 (March 10, 2010). http://www.ncbi.nlm.nih.gov/pmc/articles/PMC2846895/?tool=pubmed (accessed August 11, 2011).

Stringaris, A. "Irritability in Children and Adolescents: A Challenge for DSM-5." *European Child and Adolescent Psychiatry* 20 (February 2011): 61–66.

OTHER

American Psychiatric Association, Childhood and Adolescent Disorders Work Group. "Justification for Temper Dysregulation Disorder with Dysphoria." DSM-5 Development. http://www.dsm5.org/Proposed%20Revision%20Attachments/Justification%20for%20Temper%20Dysregulation%20Disorder%20with%20Dysphoria.pdf (accessed July 16, 2011).

WEBSITES

American Psychiatric Association. "D 00 Disruptive Mood Dysregulation Disorder." DSM-5 Development. http://www.dsm5.org/proposedrevisions/pages/proposedrevision.aspx?rid=397 (accessed July 16, 2011).

Child and Adolescent Psychiatry Consulting. "Bipolar Disorder versus Temper Dysregulation Disorder." http://www.drjenna.net/disorders-and-treatments/bipolar-disorder/bipolar-disorder-versus-temper-dysregulation-disorder (accessed July 16, 2011).

Children's Hospital Boston. "Q & A: Bipolar Disorder vs. Temper Dysregulation Disorder with Dysphoria." *Pediatric Views*. http://www.childrenshospital.org/views/aug10/bipolar_disorder_vs_temper_dysregulation_disorder_with_dysphoria.html (accessed July 16, 2011).

Frances, Allen. "DSM5 Temper Dysregulation—Good Intentions, Bad Solution." Psychology Today. http://www.psychologytoday.com/blog/dsm5-in-distress/201004/dsm5-temper-dysregulation-good-intentions-bad-solution (accessed July 15, 2011).

Spiegel, Alix. "Children Labeled 'Bipolar' May Get A New Diagnosis." National Public Radio (NPR). http://www.npr.org/templates/story/story.php?storyId=123544191 (accessed July 16, 2011).

ORGANIZATIONS

American Academy of Child and Adolescent Psychiatry (AACAP), 3615 Wisconsin Avenue, NW, Washington, DC, 20016-3007, (202) 966-7300, Fax: (202) 966-2891, http://www.aacap.org.

American Psychiatric Association, 1000 Wilson Boulevard, Suite 1825, Arlington, VA, 22209-3901, (703) 907-7300, apa@psych.org, http://www.psych.org.

Rebecca J. Frey, PhD

Dissociation and dissociative disorders

Definition

The dissociative disorders are a group of mental disorders that affect consciousness and cause significant interference with a patient's general functioning, including in social relationships and employment.

Demographics

The dissociative disorders vary in their severity and the suddenness of onset. It is difficult to give statistics for their frequency in the United States because they are a relatively new category and are often misdiagnosed. Studies suggest a frequency of pathological dissociation in the general North American population of between 2% and 3.3%. In Europe, reported rates are lower, at 0.3% in the nonclinical population and between 1.8% and 2.9% in student populations. Among psychiatric patients, the frequency is much higher, between 5.4% and 12.7%, and it also is higher in groups with specific psychiatric diagnoses; for example, frequency among women with eating disorders can be as high as 48.6%.

Description

In order to have a clear picture of these disorders, dissociation should first be understood. Dissociation is a mechanism that allows the mind to separate or compartmentalize certain memories or thoughts from normal consciousness. These split-off mental contents are not erased, however, and may resurface spontaneously or be triggered by objects or events in the person's environment.

Dissociation occurs along a spectrum of severity, and experiencing dissociation does not necessarily mean that a person has a dissociative disorder or other mental illness. A mild degree of dissociation occurs with some physical stressors; people who have gone without sleep for a long period of time, have had "laughing gas" for dental surgery, or have been in a minor accident often have brief dissociative experiences. Other examples of mild dissociation include becoming involved in a book or movie so completely that surroundings or the passage of time are not noticed, or driving on the highway and passing several exits without recollection. Dissociation is related to hypnosis in that hypnotic trance also involves a temporarily altered state of consciousness. Most patients with dissociative disorders are highly hypnotizable.

People in other cultures sometimes have dissociative experiences in the course of religious or other group activities (in certain trance states). These occurrences should not be judged against what is considered "normal" in the United States.

The pathological forms of dissociation have been dichotomized into the categories of detachment and compartmentalization. Specific characteristics distinguish each of these, although there can be overlap. Patients who have the compartmentalized type of dissociation do not engage in conscious integration of mental systems and do not or cannot consciously access certain areas of memory or information that would normally be available. This type of dissociation can occur in **conversion disorder** or **dissociative amnesia**.

A person exhibiting the detachment form of a dissociation disorder experiences the altered state of consciousness that is more commonly associated with the concept of dissociation. In such cases, the feelings of **depersonalization** are not merely transient, brief manifestations brought on by causes such as a lack of sleep. People with dissociation disorder may exhibit a flat affect (lack of or reduced presentation of mood or emotion) and may experience the sensation of being out of their own bodies. This type of dissociation is present in **depersonalization disorder**.

Dissociative amnesia

Dissociative **amnesia** is a disorder in which the distinctive feature is the patient's inability to remember important personal information to a degree that cannot be explained by normal forgetfulness. In many cases, it is a reaction to a traumatic accident or witnessing a violent crime. Patients with dissociative amnesia may develop depersonalization or trance states as part of the disorder, but they do not experience a change in identity.

Dissociative fugue

Dissociative fugue is a disorder in which a person temporarily loses his or her sense of personal identity and travels to another location where he or she may assume a new identity. Again, this condition usually follows a major stressor or **trauma**. Apart from an inability to recall their past or personal information, patients with dissociative fugue do not behave strangely or appear disturbed to others. Cases of dissociative fugue are more common in wartime or in communities disrupted by a natural disaster.

Depersonalization disorder

Depersonalization disorder is a disturbance in which the patient's primary symptom is a sense of detachment from the self. Depersonalization as a symptom (not as a disorder) is quite common in college-age populations.

It is often associated with **sleep deprivation** or recreational drug use. It may be accompanied by derealization (where objects in an environment appear altered). Patients sometimes describe depersonalization as feeling "like a robot" or as watching themselves from the outside. Depersonalization disorder may also involve feelings of numbness or loss of emotional affect.

Dissociative identity disorder (DID)

Dissociative identity disorder (DID) (formerly multiple personality disorder) is considered the most severe dissociative disorder and involves all of the major dissociative symptoms. People with this disorder have more than one personality state, and the personality state controlling the person's behavior changes from time to time. Often, a stressor will cause the change in personality state. The various personality states have separate names, temperaments, gestures, and vocabularies. This disorder is often associated with severe physical or **sexual abuse**, especially abuse during childhood. Women are diagnosed with this disorder more often than men.

Dissociative disorder not otherwise specified (DDNOS)

DDNOS is a diagnostic category ascribed to patients with dissociative symptoms that do not meet the full criteria for a specific dissociative disorder.

Risk factors

Risk factors for developing a dissociative disorder include possessing an innate ability to dissociate easily, experiencing repeated episodes of severe physical or sexual abuse in childhood, lacking the support to counteract abusive relative(s), and being influenced by relatives with dissociative symptoms or disorders.

The relationship of dissociative disorders to childhood abuse has led to intense controversy and lawsuits concerning the accuracy of childhood memories. The brain's storage, retrieval, and interpretation of memories are still not fully understood. Controversy also exists regarding how much individuals presenting dissociative disorders have been influenced by books and movies to describe a certain set of symptoms (scripting).

Causes and symptoms

Causes

Moderate or severe forms of dissociation can be caused by such traumatic experiences as childhood abuse, combat, criminal attacks, or involvement in a natural or transportation disaster. Patients with **acute stress disorder**, **post-traumatic stress disorder**, conversion disorder, or **somatization disorder** may develop dissociative symptoms. Recent studies of trauma indicate that the human **brain** stores traumatic memories in a different way than normal memories. Traumatic memories are not processed or integrated into a person's ongoing life in the same fashion as normal memories. Instead, they are dissociated, or split off, and may erupt into consciousness from time to time without warning. The affected person cannot control or "edit" these memories. Over a period of time, these two sets of memories, the normal and the traumatic, may coexist as parallel sets without ever being combined or blended. In extreme cases, different sets of dissociated memories may cause people to develop separate personalities for these memories (dissociative identity disorder).

Symptoms

AMNESIA. Amnesia in a dissociative disorder is marked by gaps in a patient's memory for long periods of time or for traumatic events. Doctors can distinguish this type of amnesia from loss of memory caused by head injuries or drug intoxication, because the amnesia is "spotty" and related to highly charged events and feelings.

DEPERSONALIZATION. Depersonalization is a dissociative symptom in which the patient feels that his or her body is unreal, is changing, or is dissolving. Some patients experience depersonalization as being outside their bodies or watching a movie of themselves.

DEREALIZATION. Derealization is a dissociative symptom in which the external environment is perceived as unreal. The patient may see walls, buildings, or other objects as changing in shape, size, or color. In some cases, the patient may feel that other persons are machines or robots, though the patient is able to acknowledge the unreality of this feeling.

IDENTITY DISTURBANCES. Patients with dissociative fugue, DDNOS, or DID often experience confusion about their identities or even assume new identities. Identity disturbances result from the patient having compartmentalized entire personality traits or characteristics as well as memories. When a stressful or traumatic experience triggers the reemergence of these dissociated parts, the patient may act differently, answer to a different name, or appear confused by his or her surroundings.

Diagnosis

Examination

When a doctor is evaluating a patient with dissociative symptoms, he or she will first rule out any physical conditions that might produce those symptoms. These conditions include epilepsy, head injuries, brain disease, side effects of medications, **substance abuse**, intoxication, AIDS, **dementia** complex, or recent periods of extreme physical stress and sleeplessness. In some cases, the doctor may give the patient an electroencephalogram (EEG) to eliminate epilepsy or other seizure disorders.

Tests

If the patient appears to have no physical conditions, the doctor will then test to rule out psychotic disturbances, including **schizophrenia**. Psychological tests such as the Dissociative Experiences Scale (DES) may also help narrow the **diagnosis**. If the patient has a high score on this test, he or she can be evaluated further with the Dissociative Disorders Interview Schedule (DDIS) or the Structured Clinical Interview for *DSM-IV* Dissociative Disorders (SCID-D). It is also possible for doctors to measure a patient's hypnotizability as part of a diagnostic evaluation.

Treatment

Studies now suggest that treatment of a specific dissociative disorder should be based on whether or not the manifestations are considered the compartmentalized type or the detachment type. Treatment recommendations for the compartmentalized types of disorders include focusing on reactivating and integrating the isolated mental compartments, possibly through hypnosis. To address detachment-based dissociation, therapies may include identifying triggers for the detached state and determining how to stop the triggers and/or stop the detached condition when it is triggered. Standard approaches for these tactics may include **cognitive-behavioral therapy**.

Drugs

Some doctors prescribe tranquilizers or **antidepressants** for the anxiety and/or **depression** that often accompanies dissociative disorders. However, patients with dissociative disorders are at risk for abusing or becoming dependent on medications.

Alternative

Patients with dissociative disorders often require treatment by a therapist with some specialized understanding of dissociation. This background is particularly important if the patient's symptoms include identity problems. Many patients with dissociative disorders are helped by both group and individual treatment.

Hypnosis is frequently recommended as a method of treatment for dissociative disorders, partly because hypnosis is related to the process of dissociation. Hypnosis may help patients recover repressed ideas and memories. Therapists treating patients with DID sometimes use hypnosis in the process of "fusing" the patient's alternate personalities.

KEY TERMS

Amnesia—A general medical term for loss of memory that is not due to ordinary forgetfulness. Amnesia can be caused by head injuries, brain disease, or epilepsy, as well as by dissociation.

Depersonalization—A dissociative symptom in which patients feel that their bodies are unreal, are changing, or are dissolving.

Derealization—A dissociative symptom in which the external environment is perceived as unreal.

Dissociation—A reaction to trauma in which the mind splits off certain aspects of the traumatic event from conscious awareness. Dissociation can affect the patient's memory, sense of reality, and sense of identity.

Fugue—A dissociative experience during which those affected travel away from home, have amnesia regarding their past, and may be confused about their identity but otherwise appear normal.

Hypnosis—The means by which a state of extreme relaxation and suggestibility is induced. Hypnosis is used to treat amnesia and identity disturbances that occur in dissociative disorders.

Multiple personality disorder (MPD)—An older term for dissociative identity disorder (DID).

Trauma—A disastrous or life-threatening event that can cause severe emotional distress, including dissociative symptoms and disorders.

Prognosis

Prognoses for dissociative disorders vary. Recovery from dissociative fugue is usually rapid. Dissociative amnesia may resolve quickly, but can become a chronic disorder in some patients. Depersonalization disorder, DDNOS, and DID are usually chronic conditions. DID often requires five or more years of treatment for recovery.

Prevention

Since the primary cause of dissociative disorders is thought to involve extended periods of humanly inflicted trauma, prevention depends on the elimination of physical and psychological abuse.

Resources

BOOKS

Courtois, Christine A., and Julian D. Ford, eds. *Treating Complex Traumatic Stress Disorders: An Evidence-Based Guide*. New York: The Guilford Press, 2009.

Graham, George. *The Disordered Mind: An Introduction to Philosophy of Mind and Mental Illness*. New York: Routledge, 2010.

North, Carol, and Sean Yutzy. *Goodwin and Guze's Psychiatric Diagnosis*. New York: Oxford University Press, 2010.

Shams, M.D.K. *Human Relation and Personified Relational Disorders*. Raleigh, NC: lulu.com, 2009.

ORGANIZATIONS

American Psychiatric Association, 1000 Wilson Blvd., Ste. 1825, Arlington, VA, 22209-3901, (703) 907-7300, apa@psych.org, http://www.psych.org.

American Psychological Association, 750 1st Street NE, Washington, DC, 20002-4242, (202) 336-5500; TDD/TTY: (202) 336-6123, (800) 374-2721, http://www.apa.org.

Mental Health America, 2000 N Beauregard St., 6th Fl., Alexandria, VA, 22311, (703) 684-7722, (800) 969-6642, Fax: (703) 684-5968, http://www1.nmha.org.

National Alliance on Mental Illness, 3803 N Fairfax Dr., Ste. 100, Arlington, VA, 22203, (703) 524-7600, Fax: (703) 524-9094, http://www.nami.org.

National Institute of Mental Health, 6001 Executive Blvd., Rm. 8184, MSC 9663, Bethesda, MD, 20892-9663, (301) 433-4513; TTY: (301) 443-8431, (866) 615-6464; TTY: (866) 415-8051, Fax: (301) 443-4279, nimhinfo@ nih.gov, http://www.nimh.nih.gov.

Rebecca J. Frey, PhD
Emily Jane Willingham, PhD
Laura Jean Cataldo, RN, EdD

Dissociative amnesia

Definition

Dissociative **amnesia** is classified by the ***Diagnostic and Statistical Manual of Mental Disorders***, fourth edition, text revision (*DSM-IV-TR*), as one of the **dissociative disorders**, which are mental disorders in which the normally well-integrated functions of memory, identity, perception, or consciousness are separated (dissociated). The dissociative disorders are usually associated with **trauma** in the recent or distant past, or with an intense internal conflict that forces the mind to separate incompatible or unacceptable knowledge, information, or feelings. In dissociative amnesia, the continuity of the patient's memory is disrupted. Patients with dissociative amnesia have recurrent episodes in which they forget important personal information or events, usually connected with trauma or severe **stress**. The information that is lost to the patient's memory is usually too extensive to be attributed to ordinary absentmindedness or forgetfulness related to aging. Dissociative amnesia was formerly called psychogenic amnesia.

Amnesia is a symptom of other medical and mental disorders; however, the patterns of amnesia differ depending on the cause of the disorder. Amnesia associated with head trauma is typically both retrograde (the patient has no memory of events shortly before the head injury) and anterograde (the patient has no memory of events after the injury). The amnesia that is associated with seizure disorders is sudden onset. Amnesia in patients with **delirium** or **dementia** occurs in the context of extensive disturbances of the patient's cognition (knowing), speech, perceptions, emotions, and behaviors. Amnesia associated with **substance abuse**, which is sometimes called a blackout, typically affects only short-term memory and is irreversible. In dissociative amnesia, in contrast to these other conditions, the patient's memory loss is almost always anterograde, which means that it is limited to the period following the traumatic event(s). In addition, patients with dissociative amnesia do not have problems learning new information.

Demographics

Dissociative amnesia can appear in patients of any age past infancy. Its true prevalence is unknown. In recent years, there has been an intense controversy among therapists regarding the increase in case reports of dissociative amnesia and the accuracy of the memories recovered. Some maintain that the greater awareness of dissociative symptoms and disorders among psychiatrists has led to the identification of cases that were previously misdiagnosed. Other therapists maintain that dissociative disorders are overdiagnosed in people who are extremely vulnerable to suggestion.

It should be noted that psychiatrists in the United States and Canada have significantly different opinions of dissociative disorder diagnoses. On the whole, Canadian psychiatrists, both French- and English-speaking, have serious reservations about the scientific validity and diagnostic status of dissociative amnesia and dissociative identity disorder. Only 30% of Canadian psychiatrists think that these two dissociative disorders should be included in the *DSM-IV-TR* without reservation; and only 13% think that here is strong scientific support for the validity of these diagnoses.

Description

Patients with dissociative amnesia usually report a gap or series of gaps in their recollection of their life history. The gaps are usually related to episodes of **abuse** or equally severe trauma, although some persons with dissociative amnesia also lose recall of their own **suicide** attempts, episodes of **self-mutilation**, or violent behavior.

Five different patterns of memory loss have been reported in patients with dissociative amnesia:

- Localized. The patient cannot recall events that took place within a limited period of time (usually several hours or one to two days) following a traumatic event. For example, some survivors of the World Trade Center attacks do not remember how they got out of the damaged buildings or what streets they took to get away from the area.
- Selective. The patient can remember some, but not all, of the events that took place during a limited period of time. For example, a veteran of D-Day (June 6, 1944) may recall some details, such as eating a meal on the run or taking prisoners, but not others (seeing a close friend hit or losing a commanding officer).
- Generalized. The person cannot recall anything in his/her entire life. Persons with generalized amnesia are usually found by the police or taken by others to a hospital emergency room.
- Continuous. The amnesia covers the entire period without interruption from a traumatic event in the past to the present.
- Systematized. The amnesia covers only certain categories of information, such as all memories related to a certain location or to a particular person.

Most patients diagnosed with dissociative amnesia have either localized or selective amnesia. Generalized amnesia is extremely rare. Patients with generalized, continuous, or systematized amnesia are usually eventually diagnosed as having a more complex dissociative disorder, such as **dissociative identity disorder**.

Causes and symptoms

Causes

The primary cause of dissociative amnesia is stress associated with traumatic experiences that the patient has either survived or witnessed. These may include such major life stressors as serious financial problems, the death of a parent or spouse, extreme internal conflict, and guilt related to serious crimes or turmoil caused by difficulties with another person.

Susceptibility to hypnosis appears to be a predisposing factor in dissociative amnesia. Thus far, no specific genes have been associated with vulnerability to dissociative amnesia.

Some personality types and character traits seem to be risk factors for dissociative disorders. A group of researchers in the United States has found that persons diagnosed with dissociative disorders have much higher scores for immature psychological defenses than normal subjects.

Symptoms

The central symptom of dissociative amnesia is loss of memory for a period or periods of time in the patient's life. The memory loss may take a variety of different patterns.

Other symptoms that have been reported in patients diagnosed with dissociative amnesia include the following:

- confusion
- emotional distress related to the amnesia, usually in direct proportion to the importance of what has been forgotten or the consequences of forgetting
- mild depression

Some patients diagnosed with dissociative amnesia have problems or behaviors that include disturbed interpersonal relationships, sexual dysfunction, employment problems, aggressive behaviors, self-mutilation, or suicide attempts.

Diagnosis

The diagnosis of dissociative amnesia is usually a diagnosis of exclusion. The doctor will take a detailed medical history, give the patient a physical examination, and order blood and urine tests, as well as an electroencephalogram (EEG) or head x ray to rule out memory loss resulting from seizure disorders, substance abuse (including abuse of **inhalants**), head injuries, or medical conditions, such as **Alzheimer's disease** or delirium associated with fever.

Some conditions, such as age-related memory impairment (AAMI), may be ruled out on the basis of the patient's age. **Malingering** can usually be detected in patients who are faking amnesia because they typically exaggerate and dramatize their symptoms; they have obvious financial, legal, or personal reasons (for example, draft evasion) for pretending loss of memory. In addition, patients with genuine dissociative amnesia usually score high on tests of hypnotizability. The examiner may administer the Hypnotic Induction Profile (HIP) or a similar measure that evaluates whether the patient is easily hypnotized. This enables the examiner to rule out malingering or **factitious disorder**.

There are several standard diagnostic questionnaires that may be given to evaluate the presence of a dissociative disorder. The Dissociative Experiences Scale (DES) is a frequently administered self-report screener for all forms of dissociation. The Structured Clinical Interview for the *DSM-IV-TR* Dissociative Disorders (SCID-D) can be used to make the diagnosis of dissociative amnesia distinct from the other dissociative disorders defined by the *DSM-IV-TR*. The SCID-D is a semi-structured interview, which means that the examiner's questions are open-ended and allow the patient to describe experiences of amnesia in some detail, as distinct from simple "yes" or "no" answers.

Diagnosis of dissociative amnesia in children before the age of puberty is complicated by the fact that inability to recall the first four to five years of one's life is a normal feature of human development. As part of the differential diagnosis, a physician who is evaluating a child in this age group will rule out inattention, **learning disorders**, oppositional behavior, **psychosis**, and seizure disorders or head trauma. To make an accurate diagnosis, several different people (such as teachers, therapists, **social workers**, or the child's primary care physician) may be asked to observe or evaluate the child.

Treatment

Treatment of dissociative amnesia usually requires two distinct periods or phases of **psychotherapy**.

Psychotherapy

Psychotherapy for dissociative amnesia is supportive in its initial phase. It begins with creating an atmosphere of safety in the treatment room. Very often, patients gradually regain their memories when they feel safe with and supported by the therapist. This rapport does not mean that they necessarily recover their memories during therapy sessions; one study of 90 patients with dissociative amnesia found that most of them had their memories return while they were at home alone or with family or close friends. The patients denied that their memories were derived from a therapist's suggestions, and a majority of them were able to find independent evidence or corroboration of their childhood abuse.

If the memories do not return spontaneously, hypnosis or sodium amytal (a drug that induces a semi-hypnotic state) may be used to help recover them.

After the patient has recalled enough of the missing past to acquire a stronger sense of self and continuity in their life history, the second phase of psychotherapy commences. During this phase, the patient deals more directly with the traumatic episode(s), and recovery from its aftereffects. Studies of the treatments for dissociative amnesia in combat veterans of World War I (1914–1918) found that recovery and cognitive integration of dissociated traumatic memories within the patient's overall personality were more effective than treatment methods that focused solely on releasing feelings.

Medications

At present, there are no therapeutic agents that prevent amnestic episodes or that cure dissociative amnesia itself. Patients may, however, be given **antidepressants** or other appropriate medications for treatment of the **depression**, anxiety, **insomnia**, or other symptoms that may accompany dissociative amnesia.

Legal implications

Dissociative amnesia poses a number of complex issues for the legal profession. The disorder has been cited by plaintiffs in cases of recovered memories of abuse leading to lawsuits against the perpetrators of the abuse. Dissociative amnesia has also been cited as a defense in cases of murder of adults as well as in cases of neonatricide (murder of an infant shortly after birth). Part of the problem is the adversarial nature of courtroom procedure in the United States, but it is generally agreed that judges and attorneys need better guidelines regarding dissociative amnesia in defendants and plaintiffs.

Prognosis

The prognosis for recovery from dissociative amnesia is generally good. The majority of patients eventually recover the missing parts of their past, either by spontaneous re-emergence of the memories or through hypnosis and similar techniques. A minority of patients are never able to reconstruct their past; they develop a chronic form of dissociative amnesia. The prognosis for a specific patient depends on a combination of his or her present life circumstances; the presence of other mental disorders; and the severity of stresses or conflicts associated with the amnesia.

Prevention

Strategies for the prevention of **child abuse** might lower the incidence of dissociative amnesia in the general population. There are no effective preventive strategies for dissociative amnesia caused by traumatic experiences in adult life in patients without a history of childhood abuse.

KEY TERMS

Age-associated memory impairment (AAMI)—A condition in which an older person has some memory loss and takes longer to learn new information. AAMI is distinguished from dementia because it is not progressive and does not represent a serious decline from the person's previous level of functioning. Benign senescent forgetfulness is another term for AAMI.

Anterograde amnesia—Amnesia for events that occurred after a physical injury or emotional trauma but before the present moment. Anterograde amnesia typically occurs in dissociative amnesia.

Defense—An unconscious mental process that protects the conscious mind from unacceptable or painful thoughts, impulses, or desires. Examples of defenses include denial, rationalization, projection, and repression.

Delirium—A disturbance of consciousness marked by confusion, difficulty paying attention, delusions, hallucinations, or restlessness. It can be distinguished from dissociative amnesia by its relatively sudden onset and variation in the severity of the symptoms.

Dementia—A group of symptoms (syndrome) associated with a progressive loss of memory and other intellectual functions that is serious enough to interfere with a person's ability to perform the tasks of daily life. Dementia impairs memory, alters personality, leads to deterioration in personal grooming, impairs reasoning ability, and causes disorientation.

Depersonalization—A dissociative symptom in which the patient feels that his or her body is unreal, is changing, or is dissolving.

Derealization—A dissociative symptom in which the external environment is perceived as unreal or dreamlike.

Dissociation—A reaction to trauma in which the mind splits off certain aspects of the traumatic event from conscious awareness. Dissociation can affect the patient's memory, sense of reality, and sense of identity.

Factitious disorder—A type of mental disturbance in which patients intentionally act physically or mentally ill without obvious benefits. It is distinguished from malingering by the absence of an obvious motive, and from conversion disorder by intentional production of symptoms.

Malingering—Knowingly pretending to be physically or mentally ill to avoid some unpleasant duty or responsibility, or for economic benefit.

Retrograde amnesia—Amnesia for events that occurred before a traumatic injury. Retrograde amnesia is not usually found in patients with dissociative amnesia.

Supportive—An approach to psychotherapy that seeks to encourage the patient or offer emotional support to him or her, as distinct from insight-oriented or educational approaches to treatment.

Resources

BOOKS

American Psychiatric Association. *Diagnostic and Statistical Manual of Mental Disorders*. 4th ed., text rev. Washington, DC: American Psychiatric Publishing, 2000.

"Dissociative Amnesia." In *The Merck Manual of Diagnosis and Therapy*, edited by Robert S. Porter and Justin L. Kaplan. 19th ed. Whitehouse Station, NJ: Merck Research Laboratories, 2011.

Ellenberger, Henri. *The Discovery of the Unconscious: The History and Evolution of Dynamic Psychiatry*. New York: Basic Books, 1981.

Herman, Judith. *Trauma and Recovery*. 14th printing. New York: Basic Books, 1997.

Stout, Martha. *The Myth of Sanity: Tales of Multiple Personality in Everyday Life*. New York: Penguin Books, 2002.

PERIODICALS

Brandt, J., and W.G. Van Gorp. "Functional ('psychogenic') Amnesia." *Seminars in Neurology* 26, no. 3 (July 2006): 331–40.

Brown, P., O. Van der Hart, and M. Graafland. "Trauma-Induced Dissociative Amnesia in World War I Combat Soldiers. II. Treatment Dimensions." *Australia and New Zealand Journal of Psychiatry* 33 (1999): 392–98. Available online at http://www.onnovdhart.nl/articles/amnesiaWW1_2.pdf (accessed November 9, 2011).

Carrion, V. G., and H. Steiner. "Trauma and Dissociation in Delinquent Adolescents." *Journal of the American Academy of Child and Adolescent Psychiatry* 39, no. 3 (2000): 353–59.

Chu, J.A., et al. "Memories of Childhood Abuse: Dissociation, Amnesia, and Corroboration." *American Journal of Psychiatry* 156 (1999): 749–55.

Durst, R., A. Teitelbaum, and R. Aronzon. "Amnestic State in a Holocaust Survivor Patient: Psychogenic Versus Neurological Basis." *Israel Journal of Psychiatry and Related Sciences* 36, no. 1 (1999): 47–54.

Lalonde, J. K., et al. "Canadian and American Psychiatrists' Attitudes Toward Dissociative Disorders Diagnoses." *Canadian Journal of Psychiatry* 46, no. 5 (June 2001): 407–12. Available online at http://ww1.cpa-apc.org:8080/Publications/Archives/CJP/2001/June/original.asp (accessed November 9, 2011).

Miller, P.W., et al. "An Unusual Presentation of Inhalant Abuse with Dissociative Amnesia." *Veterinary and Human Toxicology* 44, no. 1 (February 2002): 17–19.

Pope, Harrison G., Jr. "Recovered Memories of Childhood Abuse: The Royal College of Psychiatrists Issues Important Precautions." *British Medical Journal* 316 (February 14, 1998): 713. Available online at http://www.bmj.com/content/316/7130/488.full?sid=5c9caa33-0a45-4fb0-9980-a057abd9e57e (accessed November 9, 2011).

Porter, S., et al. "Memory for Murder. A Psychological Perspective on Dissociative Amnesia in Legal Contexts." *International Journal of Law and Psychiatry* 24 (January–February 2001): 23–42.

Simeon, D., et al. "Personality Factors Associated with Dissociation: Temperament, Defenses, and Cognitive Schemata." *American Journal of Psychiatry* 159 (March 2002): 489–91.

Spinelli, M. G. "A Systematic Investigation of 16 Cases of Neonaticide." *American Journal of Psychiatry* 158 (May 2001): 811–13.

"Symposium: Science and Politics of Recovered Memories." Special issue of *Ethics and Behavior* 8, no. 2 (1998).

Zanarini, M.C., et al. "The Dissociative Experiences of Borderline Patients." *Comprehensive Psychiatry* 41, no. 3 (May–June 2000): 223–27.

WEBSITES

National Alliance on Mental Illness. "Dissociative Disorders." June 2000. http://www.nami.org/Content/ContentGroups/Helpline1/Dissociative_Disorders.htm (accessed October 5, 2011).

ORGANIZATIONS

International Society for the Study of Trauma and Dissociation, 8400 Westpark Dr., 2nd Fl., McLean, VA, 22102, (703) 610-9037, Fax: (703) 610-0234, http://www.isst-d.org.

International Society for Traumatic Stress Studies, 111 Deer Lake Rd., Ste. 100, Deerfield, IL, 60015, (847) 480-9028, Fax: (847) 480-9282, http://www.istss.org.

National Institute of Mental Health, 6001 Executive Blvd., Room 8184, MSC 9663, Bethesda, MD, 20892-9663, (301) 433-4513; TTY: (301) 443-8431, Fax: (301) 443-4279, (866) 615-6464; TTY: (866) 415-8051, nimhinfo@nih.gov, http://www.nimh.nih.gov.

National Organization for Rare Disorders, 55 Kenosia Ave., PO Box 1968, Danbury, CT, 06813-1968, (203) 744-0100, Fax: (203) 798-2291, (800) 999-6673, http://www.rarediseases.org.

Rebecca Frey, PhD
Emily Jane Willingham, PhD

Dissociative fugue

Definition

Dissociative fugue is a rare condition in which a person suddenly, without planning or warning, travels far from home or work and leaves behind a past life. Patients show signs of **amnesia** and have no conscious understanding or knowledge of the reason for the flight. The condition is usually associated with severe **stress** or **trauma**. Because people cannot remember all or part of their past, at some point they become confused about their identity and the situations in which they find themselves. In rare cases, they may take on new identities. The **American Psychiatric Association** (APA) classifies dissociative fugue as one of four **dissociative disorders**, along with **dissociative amnesia**, **dissociative identity disorder**, and **depersonalization disorder**.

Demographics

Dissociative fugue is a rare disorder estimated to affect just 0.2% of the population, nearly all of them adults. More people may experience dissociative fugue during or in the aftermath of serious accidents, wars, natural disasters, or other highly traumatic or stressful events.

Description

The key feature of dissociative fugue is "sudden, unexpected travel away from home or one's customary place of daily activities, with inability to recall some or all of one's past," according to the APA. The travels associated with the condition can last for a few hours or as long as several months. Some individuals have traveled thousands of miles from home while in a state of dissociative fugue. (The word *fugue* stems from the Latin word for flight—*fugere*.) At first, people experiencing the condition may appear completely normal. With time, however, confusion appears. This confusion may result from the realization that they cannot remember the past. Those affected may suddenly realize that they do not belong where they find themselves.

During an episode of dissociative fugue, those affected may take on new identities, complete with a new name. They may even establish new homes and ties to their communities. More often those affected realize something is wrong not long after fleeing—in a matter of hours or days. In such cases, they may phone home for help, or come to the attention of police after becoming distressed at finding themselves unexplainably in unfamiliar surroundings.

Dissociative fugue is distinct from dissociative identity disorder (DID). In cases of DID, which previously was called multiple personality disorder, those affected lose memory of events that take place when one of several distinct identities takes control of them. If the person with dissociative fugue assumes a new identity, it does not coexist with other identities, as is typical of DID. Repeated instances of apparent dissociative fugue are more likely a symptom of DID, not true dissociative fugue.

Causes and symptoms

Causes

Episodes of dissociative fugue are often associated with very stressful events. Traumatic experiences, such as war or natural disasters, seem to increase the incidence of the disorder. Other, more personal types of stress might also lead to the unplanned travel and amnesia characteristic of dissociative fugue. The shocking death of a loved one or seemingly unbearable pressures at work or home, for example, might cause some people to run away for brief periods and blank out their pasts.

Symptoms

People in the midst of dissociative fugue episodes may appear to have no psychiatric symptoms at all or to be only slightly confused. Therefore, for a time, it may be very difficult to spot someone experiencing a fugue. After a while, however, patients show significant signs of confusion or distress because they cannot remember recent events, or they realize a complete sense of identity is missing. This amnesia is a characteristic symptom of the disorder.

Diagnosis

The ***Diagnostic and Statistical Manual of Mental Disorders***, 4th edition, text revision, also known as the *DSM-IV-TR,* lists four criteria for diagnosing dissociative fugue:

- unexplained and unexpected travel from a person's usual place of living and working along with partial or complete amnesia
- uncertainty and confusion about one's identity, or in rare instances, the adoption of a new identity
- the flight and amnesia that characterize the fugue are not related exclusively to DID, nor is it the result of substance abuse or a physical illness
- an episode must result in distress or impairment severe enough to interfere with the ability of the patient to function in social, work, or home settings

Accurate **diagnosis** typically must wait until the fugue is over and the person has sought help or has been brought to the attention of mental health care providers. The diagnosis can then be made using the patient's history and reconstruction of events that occurred before, during, and after the patient's excursion.

KEY TERMS

Amnesia—A general medical term for loss of memory that is not due to ordinary forgetfulness. Amnesia can be caused by head injuries, brain disease, or epilepsy, as well as by dissociation.

Dissociation—A reaction to trauma in which the mind splits off certain aspects of the traumatic event from conscious awareness. Dissociation can affect the patient's memory, sense of reality, and sense of identity.

Treatment

Psychotherapy, sometimes involving hypnosis, is often effective in the treatment of dissociative fugue. With support from therapists, patients are encouraged to remember past events by learning to face and cope with the stressful experiences that precipitated the fugue. Because the cause of the fugue is usually a traumatic event, it is often necessary to treat disturbing feelings and emotions that emerge when the patient finally faces the trauma. The troubling events that drove them to run and forget about their past may, when remembered, result in **grief**, **depression**, fear, anger, remorse, and other psychological states that require therapy.

Prognosis

The prognosis for dissociative fugue is often good. Not many cases last longer than a few months and many people make quick recoveries. In more serious cases, patients may take longer to recover memories of the past.

Resources

BOOKS

Allen, Thomas E., et al. *A Primer on Mental Disorders: A Guide for Educators, Families, and Students*. Lantham, MD: Scarecrow Press, 2001.

American Psychiatric Association. *Diagnostic and Statistical Manual of Mental Disorders*. 4th ed., text rev. Washington, DC: American Psychiatric Publishing, 2000.

"Dissociative Fugue." In *The Merck Manual of Diagnosis and Therapy*, edited by Robert S. Porter and Justin L. Kaplan. 19th ed. Whitehouse Station, NJ: Merck Research Laboratories, 2011.

ORGANIZATIONS

American Psychiatric Association, 1000 Wilson Blvd., Ste. 1825, Arlington, VA, 22209-3901, (703) 907-7300, apa@psych.org, http://www.psych.org.

International Society for the Study of Trauma and Dissociation, 8400 Westpark Drive, Second Floor, McLean, VA, 22102, (703) 610-9037, Fax: (703) 610-0234, http://www.isst-d.org.

National Alliance on Mental Illness, 3803 N Fairfax Drive, Ste. 100, Arlington, VA, 22203, (703) 524-7600, http://www.nami.org.

New York Online Access to Health, http://www.noah-health.org/en/mental/disorders/dissociative.html.

Dean A. Haycock, PhD
Emily Jane Willingham, PhD

Dissociative identity disorder

Definition

Previously known as multiple personality disorder, dissociative identity disorder (DID) is a condition in which those affected have more than one distinct identity or personality state. At least two of these personalities repeatedly assert themselves to control the behavior of the affected person. Each personality state has a distinct name, past, identity, and self-image.

Psychiatrists and psychologists use a handbook called the ***Diagnostic and Statistical Manual of Mental Disorders***, fourth edition, text revision (*DSM-IV-TR*) to diagnose mental disorders. In this handbook, DID is classified as a dissociative disorder. Other mental disorders in this category include **depersonalization disorder**, **dissociative fugue**, and **dissociative amnesia**. The nature of DID and even its existence is debated by psychiatrists and psychologists.

Demographics

Studies in North America and Europe indicate that as many as 5% of patients in psychiatric wards have undiagnosed DID. Partially hospitalized patients and outpatients may have an even higher incidence. For every man diagnosed with DID, eight or nine women are diagnosed. Among children, boys and girls diagnosed with DID are pretty closely matched 1:1. No one is sure why this discrepancy between diagnosed adults and children exists.

Description

"Dissociation" describes a state in which the integrated functioning of a person's identity, including consciousness, memory, and awareness of surroundings, is disrupted or eliminated. Dissociation is a mechanism that allows the mind to separate or compartmentalize certain memories or thoughts from normal consciousness. These memories are not erased, but are buried and may resurface at a later time. Dissociation is related to hypnosis in that hypnotic trance also involves a temporarily altered state of consciousness. In severe, impairing dissociation, individuals experience a lack of awareness of important aspects of their identities.

The phrase "dissociative identity disorder" replaced "multiple personality disorder" because the new name emphasizes the disruption of a person's identity that characterizes the disorder. People with the illness are consciously aware of one aspect of their personality or self while being totally unaware of, or dissociated from, other aspects of it. This is a key feature of the disorder. It requires only two distinct identities or personality states to qualify as DID, but there have been cases in which 100 distinct alternate personalities, or alters, were reported. Fifty percent of patients with DID harbor fewer than 11 identities.

Because the alters alternate in controlling the consciousness and behavior of the individual, patients experience long gaps in memory—gaps that far exceed typical episodes of forgetting that occur in those unaffected by DID.

Despite the presence of distinct personalities, one primary identity exists in many cases. The primary identity uses the name the patient was born with and tends to be quiet, dependent, depressed, and guilt-ridden. The alters have their own names and unique traits. They are distinguished by different temperaments, likes, dislikes, manners of expression, and even physical characteristics such as posture and body language. It is not unusual for patients with DID to have alters of different genders, sexual orientations, ages, or nationalities. It typically takes just seconds for one personality to replace another but the shift can be gradual in rarer instances. In either case, the emergence of one personality, and the retreat of another, is often triggered by a stressful event.

People with DID tend to have other severe disorders as well, such as **depression**, **substance abuse**, **borderline personality disorder**, and eating disorders, among others. The degree of impairment ranges from mild to severe, and complications may include **suicide** attempts, **self-mutilation**, violence, or drug abuse.

Left untreated, DID can last a lifetime. Treatment for the disorder consists primarily of individual **psychotherapy**.

Causes and symptoms

Causes

The severe dissociation that characterizes patients with DID is currently understood to result from a set of causes:

- an innate ability to dissociate easily
- repeated episodes of severe physical or sexual abuse in childhood
- lack of supportive or comforting people to counteract abusive relative(s)
- influence of other relatives with dissociative symptoms or disorders

The primary cause of DID appears to be severe and prolonged **trauma** experienced during childhood. This trauma can be associated with emotional, physical, or **sexual abuse**, or some combination. One theory is that young children, faced with a routine of torture, sexual abuse, or **neglect**, dissociate themselves from their trauma by creating separate identities or personality states. Manufactured alters may suffer while primary identities "escape" the unbearable experiences. Dissociation, which is easy for young children to achieve, becomes a useful defense. This strategy displaces the suffering onto another identity. Over time, children, who on average are around six years old at the time of the appearance of the first alter, may create many more.

There is considerable controversy about the nature, and even the existence, of DID. The causes are disputed, with some experts identifying extensive trauma in childhood as causative, while others maintain that the cause of the disorder is iatrogenic, or introduced by the news media or therapist. In this latter form, mass media or therapists plant the seeds that patients suppressed memories and dissociation severe enough to have created separate personalities. One cause for the skepticism is the alarming increase in reports of the disorder since the 1980s; more cases of DID were reported between 1981 and 1986 than in the previous 200 years combined. In some cases, people reporting DID and recovered memory became involved in lawsuits related to the recovered memories, only to find that the memories were not, in fact, real. Another disorder, false memory syndrome, then becomes the explanation. Thus, an area of contention is the notion of suppressed memories, a crucial component in DID. Many experts in memory research say that it is almost impossible for anyone to remember things that happened before the age of three, the age when some patients with DID supposedly experience abuse, but the brain's storage, retrieval, and interpretation of childhood memories are still not fully understood. The relationship of **dissociative disorders** to childhood abuse has led to intense controversy and lawsuits concerning the accuracy of childhood memories. Because childhood trauma is a factor in the development of DID, some doctors think it may be a variation of **post-traumatic stress disorder** (PTSD). In both DID and PTSD, dissociation is a prominent mechanism.

Symptoms

The major dissociative symptoms experienced by patients with DID are **amnesia**, **depersonalization**, derealization, and identity disturbances.

AMNESIA. Amnesia in patients with DID is marked by gaps in their memory for long periods of their past, and, in some cases, their entire childhood. Most patients with DID have amnesia, or "lose time," for periods when another personality is "out." They may report finding items in their house that they cannot remember having purchased, finding notes written in different handwriting, or other evidence of unexplained activity.

DEPERSONALIZATION. Depersonalization is a dissociative symptom in which patients feel that their bodies are unreal, are changing, or are dissolving. Some patients with DID experience depersonalization as feeling outside of their bodies, or as watching a movie of themselves.

DEREALIZATION. Derealization is a dissociative symptom in which patients perceive the external environment as unreal. Patients may see walls, buildings, or other objects as changing in shape, size, or color. Patients with DID may fail to recognize relatives or close friends.

IDENTITY DISTURBANCES. People with DID usually have a main personality that psychiatrists refer to as the "host." This is generally not the person's original personality but is rather one developed in response to childhood trauma. It is usually this personality that seeks psychiatric help. Patients with DID are often frightened by their dissociative experiences, which can include losing awareness of hours or even days, meeting people who claim to know them by another name, or feeling "out of body."

Psychiatrists refer to the phase of transition between alters as the "switch." After a switch, people with DID assume whole new physical postures, voices, and vocabularies. Specific circumstances or stressful situations may bring out particular identities. Some patients have histories of erratic performance in school or in their jobs caused by the emergence of alternate personalities during examinations or other stressful situations. Each alternate identity takes control one at a time, denying control to the others. Patients vary with regard to their alters' awareness of one another. One alter may not acknowledge the existence of others or it may criticize other alters. At times during therapy, one alter may allow another to take control.

Diagnosis

The *DSM-IV-TR* lists four diagnostic criteria for identifying DID and differentiating it from similar disorders:

- Traumatic stressor: Patients have been exposed to catastrophic events involving actual or threatened death or injury, or a serious physical threat to themselves or others. During exposure to the trauma, their emotional response was marked by intense fear, feelings of helplessness, or horror. In general, stressors caused intentionally by human beings (genocide, rape, torture, abuse, etc.) are experienced as more traumatic than accidents, natural disasters, or "acts of God."
- The demonstration of two or more distinct identities or personality states in an individual. Each separate identity must have its own way of thinking about, perceiving, relating to, and interacting with the environment and self.
- Two of the identities assume control of the patient's behavior, one at a time and repeatedly.
- Extended periods of forgetfulness lasting too long to be considered ordinary forgetfulness.
- Determination that the above symptoms are not due to drugs, alcohol, or other substances and that they cannot be attributed to any other general medical condition. It is also necessary to rule out fantasy play or imaginary friends when considering a diagnosis of DID in children.

Proper **diagnosis** of DID is complicated because some of the symptoms of DID overlap with symptoms of other mental disorders. Misdiagnoses are common and include depression, **schizophrenia**, borderline personality disorder, **somatization disorder**, and **panic disorder**.

Because the extreme dissociative experiences related to this disorder can be frightening, people with the disorder may go to emergency rooms or clinics because they fear they are going insane.

When a doctor is evaluating a patient for DID, the first step is to rule out physical conditions that sometimes produce amnesia, depersonalization, or derealization. These conditions include head injuries, **brain** disease (especially seizure disorders), side effects from medications, substance abuse or intoxication, AIDS **dementia** complex, or recent periods of extreme physical stress and sleeplessness. In some cases, the doctor may give the patient an electroencephalograph (EEG) to exclude epilepsy or other seizure disorders. The physician also must consider whether the patient is **malingering** and/or offering fictitious complaints.

If the patient appears to be physically healthy, the doctor will next rule out psychotic disturbances, including schizophrenia. Many patients with DID are misdiagnosed as having schizophrenia because they may "hear" their alters "talking" inside their heads. Doctors who suspect DID can use a screening test called the Dissociative Experiences Scale (DES). Patients with high scores on this test can be evaluated further with the Dissociative Disorders Interview Schedule (DDIS) or the Structured Clinical Interview for Dissociative Disorders (SCID-D).

Treatment

Treatment of DID may last for five to seven years in adults and usually requires several different treatment methods.

Psychotherapy

Ideally, patients with DID should be treated by a therapist with specialized training in dissociation. This specialized training is important because the patient's personality switches can be confusing or startling. In addition, many patients with DID have hostile or suicidal alter personalities. Most therapists who treat patients with DID have rules or contracts for treatment that include such issues as responsibility for the patient's safety. Psychotherapy for patients with DID typically has several stages: an initial phase for uncovering and "mapping" the patient's alters; a phase of treating the traumatic memories and "fusing" the alters; and a phase of consolidating the patient's newly integrated personality.

Most therapists who treat multiples, or patients with DID, recommend further treatment after personality integration, on the grounds that the patients have not learned the social skills that most people acquire in adolescence and early adult life. In addition, **family therapy** is often recommended to help families understand DID and the changes that occur during personality reintegration.

Many patients with DID are helped by **group therapy** as well as individual treatment, provided that the group is limited to people with dissociative disorders. Patients with DID sometimes have setbacks in mixed therapy groups because other patients are bothered or frightened by their personality switches.

Medications

Some doctors prescribe tranquilizers or **antidepressants** for patients with DID because their alter personalities may have anxiety or mood disorders. However, other therapists who treat patients with DID prefer to keep medications to a minimum because these patients

KEY TERMS

Alter—An alternate or secondary personality in a person with dissociative identity disorder. Each alter has a unique way of looking at and interacting with the world.

Amnesia—A general medical term for loss of memory that is not due to ordinary forgetfulness. Amnesia can be caused by head injuries, brain disease, or epilepsy, as well as by dissociation.

Borderline personality disorder—A severe and usually lifelong mental disorder characterized by violent mood swings and severe difficulties in sustaining interpersonal relationships.

Depersonalization—A dissociative symptom in which patients feel that their bodies are unreal, are changing, or are dissolving.

Derealization—A dissociative symptom in which the external environment is perceived as unreal.

Dissociation—A reaction to trauma in which the mind splits off certain aspects of the traumatic event from conscious awareness. Dissociation can affect a patient's memory, sense of reality, and sense of identity.

Host—The dominant or main alter in a person with DID.

Hypnosis—The means by which a state of extreme relaxation and suggestibility is induced. Hypnosis is used to treat amnesia and identity disturbances that occur in people with dissociative disorders.

Malingering—Knowingly pretending to be physically or mentally ill to avoid some unpleasant duty or responsibility, or for economic benefit.

Multiple personality disorder (MPD)—An older term for dissociative identity disorder (DID).

Panic disorder—An anxiety disorder in which an individual experiences sudden, debilitating attacks of intense fear.

Post-traumatic stress disorder (PTSD)—A disorder caused by an extremely stressful or traumatic event (such as rape, act of war, or natural disaster), in which the trauma victim is haunted by flashbacks. In the flashbacks, the event is reexperienced in the present. Other symptoms include nightmares and feelings of anxiety.

Primary personality—The core personality of a patient with DID.

Schizophrenia—A severe mental illness in which a person has difficulty distinguishing what is real from what is not real. It is often characterized by hallucinations, delusions, language and communication disturbances, and withdrawal from people and social activities.

Shift—The transition of control from one alter to another in a person with DID. Usually shifts occur rapidly, within seconds, but in some cases a more gradual changeover is observed. Also referred to as a switch.

Somatization disorder—A type of mental disorder in which the patient has physical complaints that serve as coping strategies for emotional distress.

Trauma—A disastrous or life-threatening event that can cause severe emotional distress.

can easily become psychologically dependent on drugs. In addition, many patients with DID have at least one alter who abuses drugs or alcohol, substances that are dangerous in combination with most tranquilizers.

Hypnosis

Although not always necessary, hypnosis (or **hypnotherapy**) is a standard method of treatment for patients with DID. Hypnosis may help patients recover repressed ideas and memories. Further, hypnosis can also be used to control problematic behaviors that many patients with DID exhibit, such as self-mutilation, or eating disorders like **bulimia nervosa**. In the later stages of treatment, the therapist may use hypnosis to "fuse" the alters as part of the patient's personality integration process.

Prognosis

Unfortunately, no systematic studies of the long-term outcome of DID currently exist. Some therapists believe that the prognosis for recovery is excellent for children and good for most adults. Although treatment takes several years, it is often ultimately effective. As a general rule, the earlier the patient is diagnosed and properly treated, the better the prognosis. Patients may find they are bothered less by symptoms as they advance into middle age, with some relief beginning to appear in the late 40s. Stress or substance abuse, however, can cause a **relapse** of symptoms at any time.

Prevention

Prevention of DID requires **intervention** in abusive families and treating children with dissociative symptoms as early as possible.

Resources

BOOKS

Acocella, Joan. *Creating Hysteria: Women and Multiple Personality Disorder*. San Francisco, CA: Jossey-Bass Publishers, 1999.

Alderman, Tracy, and Karen Marshall. *Amongst Ourselves, A Self-Help Guide to Living with Dissociative Identity Disorder*. Oakland, CA: New Harbinger Publications, 1998.

American Psychiatric Association. *Diagnostic and Statistical Manual of Mental Disorders*. 4th ed., text rev. Washington, DC: American Psychiatric Publishing, 2000.

Saks, Elyn R., and Stephen H. Behnke. *Jekyll on Trial: Multipersonality Disorder and Criminal Law*. New York: New York University Press, 1997.

PERIODICALS

Gleaves, D. H., M. C. May, and E. Cardena. "An Examination of the Diagnostic Validity of Dissociative Identity Disorder." *Clinical Psychology Review* 21, no. 4 (June 2001): 577–608.

Lalonde, J. K., et al. "Canadian and American Psychiatrists' Attitudes Toward Dissociative Disorders Diagnoses." *Canadian Journal of Psychiatry* 46, no. 5 (June 2001): 407–12.

Spitzer, Carsten, et al. "Recent Developments in the Theory of Dissociation." *World Psychiatry* 5, no. 2 (June 2006): 82–86.

Stickley, T., and R. Nickeas. "Becoming One Person: Living with Dissociative Identity Disorder." *Journal of Psychiatric and Mental Health Nursing* 13, no. 2 (April 2006): 180–87.

WEBSITES

Mayo Clinic. "Dissociative Disorders." http://www.mayoclinic.com/health/dissociative-disorders/DS00574/DSECTION=5 (accessed October 3, 2011).

Merck Manual for Healthcare Professionals. "Dissociative Identity Disorder." The Merck Manuals Online Medical Library. June 2008. http://www.merckmanuals.com/professional/psychiatric_disorders/dissociative_disorders/dissociative_identity_disorder.html#v1026117 (accessed October 5, 2011).

ORGANIZATIONS

American Psychiatric Association, 1000 Wilson Blvd., Ste. 1825, Arlington, VA, 22209-3901, (703) 907-7300, apa@psych.org, http://www.psych.org.

International Society for the Study of Trauma and Dissociation, 8400 Westpark Dr., 2nd Fl., McLean, VA, 22102, (703) 610-9037, Fax: (703) 610-0234, http://www.isst-d.org.

National Alliance on Mental Illness, 3803 N Fairfax Drive, Ste. 100, Arlington, VA, 22203, (703) 524-7600, http://www.nami.org.

Rebecca J. Frey, PhD
Dean A. Haycock, PhD
Emily Jane Willingham, PhD

Disulfiram

Definition

Disulfiram is an aldehyde dehydrogenase inhibitor. It prohibits the activity of aldehyde dehydrogenase, an enzyme found in the liver. In the United States, disulfiram is sold under brand name Antabuse.

Purpose

Disulfiram is used as a conditioning treatment for alcohol dependence. When taken with alcohol, disulfiram causes many unwanted and unpleasant effects, and the fear of these is meant to condition the patient to avoid alcohol.

Description

Two Danish physicians who were investigating disulfiram for its potential benefits to destroy parasitic worms took disulfiram and became sick at a cocktail party. After a series of pharmacological and clinical studies, it was determined that disulfiram interacts with alcohol.

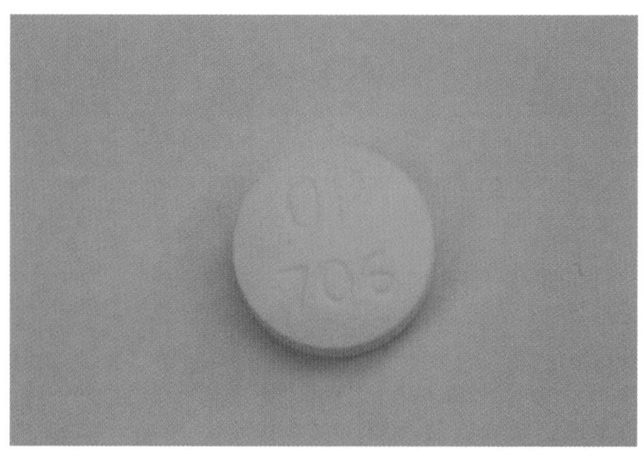

Antabuse (disulfiram), 250 mg. *(© Custom Medical Stock Photo, Inc. Reproduced by permission.)*

Disulfiram by itself is not toxic. If taken with alcohol, however, it alters certain steps in the breakdown of alcohol. When alcohol is ingested, it is converted first to a chemical called acetaldehyde. Acetaldehyde is further broken down into acetate. In order for acetaldehyde to be broken down into acetate, aldehyde dehydrogenase needs to be active. Disulfiram is an aldehyde dehydrogenase inhibitor. Since disulfiram blocks the activity of aldehyde dehydrogenase, acetaldehyde cannot be broken down and the levels of acetaldehyde become five to ten times higher than the normal levels. This causes uncomfortable effects that encourage the person to avoid alcohol.

Disulfiram comes in a 250 mg and 500 mg tablet.

Recommended dosage

Disulfiram therapy should be started only after the patient has abstained from alcohol for at least 12 hours. The initial dose may be as high as 500 mg taken once daily. If the medication is sedating, the dose can be administered in the evening. Ideally, the daily dose should be taken in the morning—the time the resolve not to drink may be strongest. The initial dosing period can last for one to two weeks.

A maintenance dose can range anywhere from 125–500 mg daily with the average dose being 250 mg daily. Disulfiram therapy should continue until full recovery. This may take months to years, depending upon the patient's response and motivation to stop using alcohol. The duration of disulfiram's activity is 14 days after discontinuation, and patients need to avoid alcohol for this period of time.

Precautions

Before beginning therapy, patients should be carefully evaluated for their intellectual capacity to understand the goal of therapy, which can be described as behavioral modification with negative **reinforcement**. Patients with history of **psychosis**, severe myocardial disease, and coronary occlusion should not take disulfiram. People with diabetes taking disulfiram are at an increased risk for complications. Severe liver failure has been associated with the use of disulfiram in patients with or without a prior history of liver problems. People with advanced or severe liver disease should not take disulfiram. Disulfiram should never be given to patients who are in a state of alcohol intoxication or without the patient's knowledge. Those patients with history of **seizures**, hypothyroidism, or nephritis need to use disulfiram with caution and close monitoring.

KEY TERMS

Coronary occlusion—Blockage of the arteries supplying blood to the heart.

Hypothyroidism—Thyroid gland that is abnormally low-functioning. A lowered metabolic rate results.

Jaundice—A yellowing of the skin caused by excess bilirubin in the blood; a liver disorder.

MAO inhibitors—A group of antidepressant drugs that decrease the activity of monoamine oxidase, a neurotransmitter found in the brain that affects mood.

Myocardial disease—Disease of the muscular layer of the heart wall.

Nephritis—Inflammation of the kidney.

Psychosis—Severe state characterized by loss of contact with reality and deterioration in normal social functioning; examples are schizophrenia and paranoia. Psychosis is usually one feature of an overarching disorder, not a disorder in itself. (Plural: psychoses)

Besides avoiding alcohol, patients should also avoid any products containing alcohol. This includes many cold syrups, tonics, and mouthwashes. Patients should not even use topical preparations that contain alcohol such as perfume and aftershave lotion.

Side effects

The most common side effect of disulfiram includes drowsiness and **fatigue**. Many patients experience metallic or garlic-like aftertaste, but most patients develop tolerance to this effect.

In addition, disulfiram is associated with impotence. This is most common in doses of 500 mg daily. Disulfiram can cause blurred vision, skin discoloration, inflammation of the skin, increased heart rate, and mental changes.

During the first three months of therapy, patients should have their liver function evaluated. Patients need to be monitored for the signs of jaundice, nausea, vomiting, abdominal pain, light stools, and dark urine as these may be the signs of liver damage due to disulfiram. The signs of alcohol ingestion include flushing, headache, nausea, vomiting and abdominal pain.

Interactions

Disulfiram can make cisapride, **benzodiazepines**, astemizole, cyclosporine, erythromycin, and cholesterol-lowering drugs called statins more toxic. Disulfiram in combination with isoniazid, **monoamine oxidase inhibitors (MAOIs)** (such as phenelzine and **tranylcypromine**), metronidazole, omeprazole and tricyclic **antidepressants** may cause adverse central nervous system effects.

In addition, disulfiram may raise the concentrations of the medications theophylline and phenytoin in the body. Patients taking warfarin (a blood-thinning drug) are at an increased risk of bleeding. Disulfiram should never be used with tranylcypromine and amprenavir oral solution.

Disulfiram may react even with small amounts of alcohol found in over-the-counter cough and cold preparations and any medication that comes in an elixir form.

Resources

BOOKS

Lacy, Charles F. *Drug Information Handbook with International Trade Names Index*. Hudson, OH: Lexi-Comp, Inc. 2011.

Taylor, David, Carol Paton, and Shitij Kapur. *The Maudsley Prescribing Guidelines Tenth Edition*. London: Informa Healthcare, 2009.

PERIODICALS

Berglund, Mats. "A Better Widget? Three Lessons for Improving Addiction Treatment from a Meta-Analytical Study." *Addiction* 100, no. 6 (June 2005): 742–50.

Boothby, Lisa, A., and Paul L. Doering. "Acamprosate for the Treatment of Alcohol Dependence." *Clinical Therapeutics* 27, no. 6 (June 2005): 695–714.

Buonopane, Alessandra, and Ismene L. Petrakis. "Pharmacotherapy of Alcohol Use Disorders." *Substance Use and Misuse* 40, no. 13–14 (2005): 2001–20, 2043–-48.

Krampe, Henning, et al. "Follow-Up of 180 Alcoholic Patients for Up to 7 Years After Outpatient Treatment: Impact of Alcohol Deterrents on Outcome." *Alcoholism: Clinical and Experimental Research* 30, no. 1 (January 2006): 86–95.

Kulig, Clark C., and Thomas P. Beresford. "Hepatitis C in Alcohol Dependence: Drinking Versus Disulfiram." *Journal of Addictive Diseases* 24, no. 2 (2005): 77–89.

Nava, Felice, et al. "Comparing Treatments of Alcoholism on Craving and Biochemical Measures of Alcohol Consumptions." *Journal of Psychoactive Drugs* 38, no. 3 (September 2006): 211–17.

Petrakis, Ismene L., et al. "Naltrexone and Disulfiram in Patients with Alcohol Dependence and Comorbid Psychiatric Disorders." *Biological Psychiatry* 57, no. 10 (May 15, 2005): 1128–37.

Sofuoglu, Mehmet, and Thomas R. Kosten. "Novel Approaches to the Treatment of Cocaine Addiction." *CNS Drugs* 19, no. 1 (2005): 13–25.

Suh, Jesse J., et al. "The Status of Disulfiram: A Half of a Century Later." *Journal of Clinical Psychopharmacology* 26, no. 3 (June 2006): 290–302.

Ajna Hamidovic, PharmD
Ruth A. Wienclaw, PhD

Divalproex sodium

Definition

Divalproex sodium is an anticonvulsant (anti-seizure) drug. It is also used to treat mania and to help prevent migraine headaches. It is sold under multiple brand names in the United States, including Depacon, Depakene, Depakote, and Depakote Sprinkle.

Purpose

Divalproex sodium is effective in the treatment of epilepsy, particularly for preventing simple, complex (petit mal), absence, mixed, and tonic-clonic (grand mal) **seizures**. Divalproex sodium is also used to treat the manic phase of **bipolar disorder** (also called manic-depressive disorder) in adults, and to prevent migraine headache in adults.

Description

Divalproex sodium is chemically compounded from sodium valproate and **valproic acid** in a 1:1 ratio.

Divalproex sodium is thought to work by increasing the levels of a **brain** neurotransmitter called gamma-aminobutyric acid (GABA). GABA is an inhibitory

Divalproex sodium, 500 mg. *(© Custom Medical Stock Photo, Inc. Reproduced by permission.)*

KEY TERMS

Absence seizures—Also called a petit mal seizure; characterized by abrupt, short-term lack of conscious activity or other abnormal change in behavior.

Epilepsy—A disorder associated with disturbed electrical discharges in the central nervous system that cause seizures.

Seizure—A convulsion, or uncontrolled discharge of nerve cells that may spread to other cells throughout the brain.

Tonic-clonic seizure—A seizure involving the entire body, characterized by unconsciousness, muscle contraction, and rigidity, also called grand mal or generalized seizures.

Trigeminal neuralgia—A disorder of the trigeminal nerve that causes severe facial pain.

neurotransmitter, which means that its presence makes it harder for nerve cells (neurons) in the brain to become activated (fire). It is believed that increasing GABA's inhibitory action on brain neurons accounts for the ability of divalproex sodium to decrease seizures, curb manic behaviors, and decrease the frequency of migraine headaches.

Divalproex sodium was discovered to decrease the likelihood of seizure in 1963. In 1978 the U.S. Food and Drug Administration (FDA) approved it for this use. Other uses for divalproex sodium were researched and approved subsequently, including use against mania (1995) and use to decrease migraine headache frequency. Divalproex sodium's 1995 approval as an anti-mania medication was considered an exciting advance, since it represented the first new drug introduced for this use in 25 years.

Recommended dosage

Divalproex sodium is available in tablets of 125 mg, 250 mg, and 500 mg. Divalproex sodium is also available in 125 mg capsules, in a 500 mg extended release tablet, and in a syrup containing 250 mg active drug per 5 mL.

Divalproex sodium therapy is usually started at 10–15 mg per 2.2 lb. (1 kg) of body weight per day. Dosages are then increased until seizures seem to be well controlled. This effect is usually achieved at averages under 60 mg per kg per day.

To treat mania, divalproex sodium is usually started at a daily dose of about 750 mg.

For migraine prevention, divalproex sodium is started at 250 mg, twice per day. In some patients, this dose will be raised to a total of 1,000 mg per day.

Precautions

Before taking divalproex sodium, patients should read the medication guide. A greater risk of liver damage exists in patients with kidney disease, known liver disease, Addison's disease, blood diseases, children under the age of two, patients with organic brain diseases (such as Alzheimer's, Parkinson's, slow virus infections, Huntington's chorea, or multiple sclerosis), patients with metabolic disorders present at birth, patients with severe seizure disorders and accompanying intellectual disability, and patients who are taking several other anticonvulsant drugs.

Because divalproex sodium can affect a patient's blood by dropping the platelet (a type of blood cell that affects clotting) count and interfering with coagulation (clotting) capability, both platelet count and coagulation parameters should be verified before a patient starts the medication and at intervals throughout its use.

Divalproex sodium is known to cause an increased risk of birth defects when taken during pregnancy. Children born to mothers who took divalproex sodium during their pregnancy tend to score lower on cognitive exams, including IQ tests, than children whose mothers took other anticonvulsants and not divalproex sodium (or related medications) when pregnant. Individuals and their healthcare provider must weigh the potential risks and benefits of using this medication during pregnancy. Women who take this medicine should not breast-feed, since a small amount will pass into the breast milk.

Divalproex sodium causes drowsiness and impairs alertness in some individuals. Patients just beginning to use the medication should avoid driving and using dangerous machinery until they determine how the drug affects them. The sedative effects are increased in the presence of alcohol, so patients should avoid drinking while taking medicines containing divalproex sodium.

Side effects

Some of the more common side effects of divalproex sodium are:

- mild stomach cramps
- change in menstrual cycle
- diarrhea
- loss of hair

- indigestion
- change in appetite
- nausea and vomiting
- trembling in the hands and arms

These side effects usually go away as the patient's body becomes accustomed to the medication.

Another common side effect of this medication is weight gain. Individuals taking divalproex sodium should focus on a balanced, low-fat diet coupled with an increase in physical activity to counter this side effect. Nutrient-rich foods such as fruits, vegetables, and whole grain products should be emphasized in the diet, whereas sweets, fats, and other foods high in carbohydrates but low in nutrients should be limited. Regular physical activity can help limit weight gain caused by this medication.

Less common side effects include:

- severe stomach cramps or continued nausea and vomiting
- changes in mood, behavior, or thinking
- double vision or seeing spots
- severe fatigue
- easy bruising or unusual bleeding
- yellow cast to the skin or the whites of the eyes (jaundice)
- odd eye movements
- increased seizures

Patients who notice these symptoms should check with their doctor to see if their dosage or medication needs to be adjusted.

Rare side effects that should be checked out by a doctor include:

- clumsiness
- difficulty with balance
- constipation
- dizziness
- drowsiness
- headache
- skin rash
- agitation
- restlessness
- irritability

QUESTIONS TO ASK YOUR DOCTOR

- What kind of changes can I expect to see or feel with this medication?
- Does it matter what time of day I take this medication? If so, what is the recommendation?
- Should I take this medication with or without food?
- What are the side effects associated with this medication?
- Will this medication interact or interfere with other medications I am currently taking?
- What symptoms or adverse effects are important enough that I should seek immediate treatment?

Interactions

Divalproex sodium is metabolized (broken down) in the liver. Other drugs that are metabolized in the liver can have too low or too high concentrations in the body when taken with divalproex sodium. Levels of divalproex sodium may be increased when taken with felbamate, isoniazid, salicylates (aspirin-containing medications), clarithromycin, erythromycin, and troleandomycin. Divalproex sodium may increase levels of **carbamazepine**, phenytoin, **lamotrigine**, nimodipine, phenobarbital, and zidovudine. Use with **clonazepam** may cause absence seizures. Cholestyramine and colestipol may reduce the absorption and the blood levels of divalproex sodium.

Resources

BOOKS

Aminoff, Michael J., ed. *Neurology and General Medicine.* 4th ed. New York: Churchill Livingstone, 2007.

Brunton, Laurence, Bruce A. Chabner, and Bjorn Knollman. *Goodman & Gilman's The Pharmacological Basis of Therapeutics.* 12th ed. New York: McGraw-Hill, 2010.

Devinsky, Orrin. *Epilepsy: Patient and Family Guide.* 3rd ed. New York: Demos Medical, 2007.

Diamond, Seymour, and Merle Lea Diamond. *A Patient's Guide to Headache and Migraine.* 2nd ed. Newtown, PA: Handbooks in Health Care, 2009.

Kuzniecky, Ruben, ed. *Epilepsy 101: The Ultimate Guide for Patients and Families.* Leona, NJ: Medicus Press, 2009.

Miklowitz, David Jay. *Bipolar Disorder: A Family-focused Treatment Approach.* 2nd ed. New York: Guilford Press, 2010.

Panayiotopoulos, C.P. *Antiepileptic Drugs, Pharmacopoeia.* New York: Springer, 2010.

Patsalos, Philip N., and Blaise F.D. Bourgeois. *The Epilepsy Prescriber's Guide to Antiepileptic Drugs.* New York: Cambridge University Press, 2010.

Shorvon, Simon. *Handbook of Epilepsy Treatment.* 3rd ed. New York: Wiley-Blackwell, 2010.

Tatum, William O., Peter W. Kaplan, and Pierre Jallon. *Epilepsy A to Z: A Concise Encyclopedia.* 2nd ed. New York: Demos Medical, 2009.

ORGANIZATIONS

American Academy of Neurology, 1080 Montreal Ave., St. Paul, MN, 55116, (651) 695-2717, (800) 879-1960, Fax: (651) 879-2791, memberservices@aan.com, http://www.aan.com.

American Epilepsy Society, 342 N Main St., West Hartford, CT, 06117-2507, (860) 586-7505, Fax: (860) 586-7550, http://www.aesnet.org.

American Neurological Association, 5841 Cedar Lake Rd., Ste. 204, Minneapolis, MN, 55416, (952) 545-6284, ana@llmsi.com, http://www.aneuroa.org.

American Psychiatric Association, 1000 Wilson Blvd., Ste. 1825, Arlington, VA, 22209-3901, (703) 907-7300, apa@psych.org, http://www.psych.org.

American Psychological Association, 750 1st St., NE, Washington, DC, 20002-4242, (202) 336-5500; TDD/TTY: (202) 336-6123, (800) 374-2721, http://www.apa.org.

Epilepsy Foundation, 8301 Professional Pl., Landover, MD, 20785-7223, (800) 332-1000, Fax: (301) 577-2684, http://epilepsyfoundation.org.

National Headache Foundation, 820 N Orleans St., Ste. 217, Chicago, IL, 60610, (312) 274-2650, (888) 643-5552, info@headaches.org, http://www.headaches.org.

National Institutes of Health, 9000 Rockville Pike, Bethesda, MD, 20892, (301) 496-4000; TTY: (301) 402-9612, http://www.nih.gov.

U.S. National Library of Medicine, 8600 Rockville Pike, Bethesda, MD, 20894, (301) 594-5983, (888) 346-3656; TDD: (800) 735-2258, Fax: (301) 402-1384, http://www.nlm.nih.gov.

Rosalyn Carson-Dewitt, MD
Laura Jean Cataldo, RN, EdD

DMDD *see* **Disruptive mood dysregulation disorder**

Dolophine *see* **Methadone**

Domestic abuse *see* **Abuse**

Domestic violence *see* **Abuse**

Donepezil

Definition

Donepezil is a drug approved by the U.S. Food and Drug Administration (FDA) to treat symptoms of **dementia** associated with **Alzheimer's disease**. In the United States, donepezil is sold under the trade name Aricept.

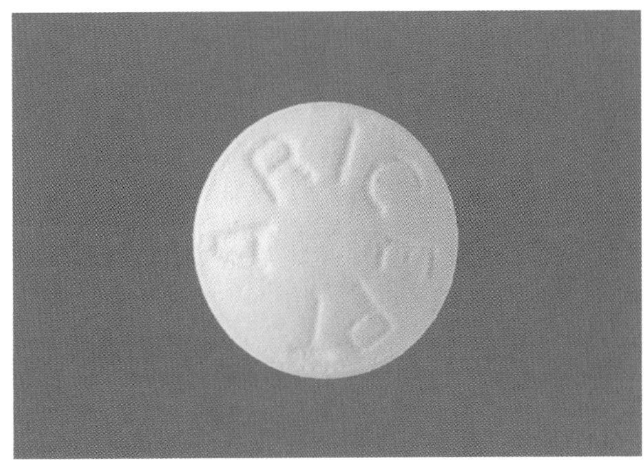

Aricept (donepezil). *(© Custom Medical Stock Photo, Inc. Reproduced by permission.)*

Purpose

Donepezil is used to help treat symptoms in individuals with Alzheimer's disease. The drug may cause small improvements in dementia for a short period of time, but donepezil does not stop the progression of Alzheimer's disease.

Description

Donepezil is in a class of drugs known as cholinesterase inhibitors. Drugs in this class prevent the breakdown of acetylcholine, a neurotransmitter that helps facilitate nerve impulses within the **brain**. In Alzheimer's disease, cells in specific regions of the brain die, meaning they are no longer able to transmit nerve impulses. By sustaining the concentration of acetylcholine in the brain, donepezil and other cholinesterase inhibitors help maintain the transmission of nerve impulses.

Donepezil is available as tablets in two different strengths. It is the only cholinesterase inhibitor approved by the FDA to treat all stages of Alzheimer's disease, from mild to severe.

Recommended dosage

The initial dosage of donepezil is 5 mg taken at bedtime. This dose should be continued for four to six weeks. The dosage may then be increased to 10 mg at bedtime, but there is no clear evidence that the higher dosage is more beneficial. The higher dosage is also likely to cause more side effects.

Precautions

People with certain heart conditions, stomach ulcers, bladder obstruction, asthma, chronic obstructive pulmonary disease, or a history of **seizures** should use

KEY TERMS

Acetylcholine—A naturally occurring chemical in the body that transmits nerve impulses from cell to cell. It causes blood vessels to dilate, lowers blood pressure, and slows the heartbeat. Central nervous system well-being is dependent on a balance among acetylcholine, dopamine, serotonin, and norepinephrine.

Dementia—A group of symptoms (syndrome) associated with a progressive loss of memory and other intellectual functions that is serious enough to interfere with a person's ability to perform the tasks of daily life. Dementia impairs memory, alters personality, leads to deterioration in personal grooming, impairs reasoning ability, and causes disorientation.

Neurotransmitter—A chemical in the brain that transmits messages between neurons, or nerve cells.

donepezil with caution under close physician supervision, as the drug may worsen or aggravate these conditions. Patients taking donepezil should be reassessed periodically to determine whether the drug is providing any benefits. When caregivers feel the drug is no longer beneficial, it may be stopped.

Side effects

More than 5% of people taking donepezil experience difficulty sleeping, dizziness, nausea, diarrhea, muscle cramps, headache, or other pains. Diarrhea, nausea, and vomiting occur more often with the 10 mg dose than the 5 mg dosage. These adverse effects are usually mild, short-lived, and typically subside when the drug is stopped. Other less common side effects include abnormal dreams, **depression**, drowsiness, fainting, loss of appetite, weight loss, frequent urination, arthritis, and easy bruising. Donepezil may slow heart rate, increase acid in the stomach, make urination difficult, cause breathing difficulties, and may increase the risk of seizures in persons with a history of seizure disorder.

Interactions

Research has found that the effects of donepezil on Alzheimer's disease may be enhanced through combination therapy with **memantine** (Namenda). Studies have shown that the use of memantine in combination therapy with donepezil is frequently more effective than the use of donepezil alone in the treatment of moderate to severe Alzheimer's disease. Using memantine and donepezil in combination therapy does not affect the pharmacokinetics of either drug. **Clinical trials** have shown such combination therapy to be both safe and effective, although the safety precautions for both drugs must be considered before combination therapy is undertaken.

Many drugs may alter the effects of donepezil; likewise, donepezil may alter the action of other drugs. Drugs such as dicyclomine, phenytoin, **carbamazepine**, dexamethasone, rifampin, or phenobarbital may lessen the effects of donepezil. Other drugs such as bethanechol, ketoconazole, or quinidine may increase some of the side effects associated with donepezil. When donepezil and nonsteroidal anti-inflammatory drugs such as ibuprofen (Advil) or naproxen (Aleve) are used together, there may be an increased tendency to develop stomach ulcers. Donepezil may increase the side effects associated with use of **fluvoxamine**, an antidepressant. If succinylcholine, a drug commonly used during anesthesia, is used with donepezil, prolonged muscle paralysis may result.

Resources

BOOKS

Ellsworth, Allan J., et al. *Mosby's Medical Drug Reference*. St. Louis, MO: Mosby, 2007.

VandenBos, Gary R. ed. *APA Dictionary of Psychology*. Washington, DC: American Psychological Association, 2006.

Wolters Kluwer Health. *Drug Facts and Comparisons 2012*. 66th ed. St. Louis: Lippincott, Williams & Wilkins, 2011.

PERIODICALS

Asp, Elissa, et al. "Verbal Repetition in Patients with Alzheimer's Disease Who Receive Donepezil." *International Journal of Geriatric Psychiatry* 21, no. 5 (May 2006): 426–31.

Chen, Xiying, et al. "Donepezil Effects on Cerebral Blood Flow in Older Adults with Mild Cognitive Deficits." *Journal of Neuropsychiatry & Clinical Neurosciences* 18, no. 2 (May 2006): 178–85.

Cholongitas, Evangelos, Chrysoula Pipili, and Maria Dasenaki. "Recurrence of Upper Gastrointestinal Bleeding After Donepezil Administration." *Alzheimer Disease and Associated Disorders* 20, no. 4 (October–December 2006): 326.

Cummings, Jeffrey L., Thomas McRae, and Richard Zhang. "Effects of Donepezil on Neuropsychiatric Symptoms in Patients with Dementia and Severe Behavioral Disorders." *American Journal of Geriatric Psychiatry* 14, no. 7 (July 2006): 605–12.

Feldman, Howard H., Frederick A. Schmitt, and Jason T. Olin. "Activities of Daily Living in Moderate-to-Severe Alzheimer Disease: An Analysis of the Treatment Effects of

Memantine in Patients Receiving Stable Donepezil Treatment." *Alzheimer Disease and Associated Disorders* 20, no. 4 (October–December 2006): 263–68.

Hogan, David B. "Donepezil for Severe Alzheimer's Disease." *The Lancet* 367, no. 9516 (April 1, 2006): 1031–32.

Kitabayashi, Yurinosuke, et al. "Donepezil-Induced Nightmares in Mild Cognitive Impairment." *Psychiatry and Clinical Neurosciences* 60, no. 1 (February 2006): 123–24.

Maruyama, Masahiro, et al. "Benefits of Combining Donepezil Plus Traditional Japanese Herbal Medicine on Cognition and Brain Perfusion in Alzheimer's Disease: A 12-Week Observer-Blind, Donepezil Monotherapy Controlled Trial." *Journal of the American Geriatrics Society* Letter to the editor, 54, no. 5 (May 2006): 869–71.

Mazeh, D., et al. "Donepezil for Negative Signs in Elderly Patients with Schizophrenia: An Add-On, Double-Blind, Crossover, Placebo-Controlled Study." *International Psychogeriatrics* 18, no. 3 (September 2006): 429–36.

Ringman, John M., and Jeffrey L. Cummings. "Current and Emerging Pharmacological Treatment Options for Dementia." *Behavioural Neurology* 17, no. 1 (2006): 5–16.

Schredl, M., et al. "The Effect of Donepezil on Sleep in Elderly, Healthy Persons: A Double-Blind Placebo-Controlled Study." *Pharmacopsychiatry* 39, no. 6 (November 2006): 205–208.

Stiles, Melissa M., and Sandra Martin. "Does Treatment with Donepezil Improve Memory for Patients With Mild Cognitive Impairment?" *Journal of Family Practice* 55, no. 5 (May 2006): 435–36. Available online at http://www.jfponline.com/Pages.asp?AID=4104&UID= (accessed November 11, 2011).

Tariot, Pierre N., et al. "Memantine Treatment in Patients with Moderate to Severe Alzheimer Disease Already Receiving Donepezil: A Randomized Controlled Trial." *Journal of the American Medical Association* 291, no. 3 (January 21, 2004): 317–24. Available online at http://jama.ama-assn.org/content/291/3/317.full (accessed November 9, 2011).

Winblad, Bengt, et al. "Donepezil in Patients with Severe Alzheimer's Disease: Double-Blind, Parallel-Group, Placebo-Controlled Study." *The Lancet* 367, no. 9516 (April 1, 2006): 1057–65.

Wong, Shelley. "The Safety of Donepezil in Treating Vascular Dementia." *CNS Spectrums* 11, no. 9 (September 2006): 658–61.

OTHER

Eisai Co., Ltd. "Aricept Prescribing and Patient Information." http://www.aricept.com/assets/pdf/AriceptComboFullPI-November2010.pdf (accessed October 5, 2011).

WEBSITES

Alzheimer's Association. "Medications for Memory Loss." http://www.alz.org/alzheimers_disease_standard_prescriptions.asp (accessed November 14, 2011).

Kelly Karpa, RPh, PhD
Ruth A. Wienclaw, PhD

Dopamine

Definition

Dopamine, identified as a central nervous system agent in 1959, is a neurotransmitter (nerve-signaling molecule) the body makes from the amino acid tyrosine. Dopamine in turn serves as the molecule the body uses to make **adrenaline** and noradrenaline. In addition to operating in nervous system signaling, it also acts as a hormone in an area of the **brain** called the hypothalamus, regulating release of the hormone prolactin, which is involved in parenting behavior and milk production. The body regulates dopamine' activity in the brain in part by using proteins called dopamine transporters, which can take up dopamine and dump it back into a cell, preventing the signaling molecule from exerting its activity. The body also has five types of proteins, called dopamine receptors, responsible for recognizing the dopamine molecule, binding to it, and transmitting its signal to the cell. Dopamine is at the center of the development of a number of psychiatric disorders, including **addiction** and **schizophrenia**, and it also plays a prominent role in the manifestations of Parkinson's disease.

Description

The brain produces dopamine in three primary areas: the substantia nigra, the ventral tegmental area, and the arcuate nucleus. The first two are of particular interest in terms of psychiatric disorders; the arcuate nucleus is associated with dopamine's role as a neurohormone in prolactin regulation.

Disorders associated with dopamine signaling have a biological basis in the brain that appears to be site-specific. The brain has four major dopamine-signaling pathways.

- The mesocortical pathway connects the ventral tegmental area to the cortex, the part of the brain involved in cognition and that may play a role in motivation. This pathway features in hypotheses of dopamine's association with schizophrenia.
- The mesolimbic pathway also begins in the ventral tegmental area, which is linked to the nucleus accumbens, the largest component of the ventral striatum. Much research has associated the nucleus accumbens and the mesolimbic pathway with brain reward processes and addiction and also with different aspects of schizophrenia.
- The nigrostriatal pathway connects the dopamine-producing nigrostriatal area with the striatum and plays a high-profile role in the development of Parkinson's symptoms.

- The tuberoinfundibular pathway involves the hypothalamus and dopamine as a neurohormone.

In terms of neuropsychiatric disorders, dopamine is probably best known as the neurotransmitter underlying the development and persistence of addiction as part of the mesolimbic reward pathway. Experiences people find rewarding, such as food or sex, can become associated with increased dopamine, as can some pathological behaviors, such as compulsive gambling. Some drugs also directly elicit an increase in dopamine, setting off the reward pathway and leading to more use of the drug. Ultimately, some people become addicted to substances or behaviors because of the dopamine release they trigger and the feelings of euphoria or tension relief that can follow the release.

Anatomically, these distinct dopamine-signaling pathways, variously involved in specific pathologies, may overlap with one another. For example, there is some comorbidity among schizophrenia, **depression**, and drug dependence and some anatomical overlap in the dopamine-signaling areas of the brain underlies this.

Dopamine receptors

The dopamine receptors, the five proteins responsible for receiving the dopamine signal for a cell, are divided into two general classes: those that are D1-like, and those that are D2-like. Of the five, the D1A through D1D and D5 receptors are all D1-like, and the D2, D3, and D4 receptors fall into the D2-like category. The distribution of these receptors differs in different dopamine-related areas of the brain. For example, the ventral striatum and limbic cortex of the mesolimbic pathway have more D2-like receptors, and D2 and D4 receptors are more closely associated with people with **substance abuse** problems. The dorsal striatum, involved in dopamine-related disorders such as Parkinson's, has more D2- than D1-like receptors. But in the prefrontal cortex, where dopamine-signaling dysfunction is associated with schizophrenia, the ratio of D1-like receptors to D2-like receptors is higher. The two general classes of receptors have opposite effects at the molecular level, but they act together in complex ways.

Dopamine and schizophrenia

A proposed explanation for the manifestations of schizophrenia is the "dopamine hypothesis of schizophrenia." This hypothesis implicates dopamine-signaling dysfunction along different dopamine pathways in the symptoms associated with schizophrenia. The hypothesis finds its origins in the fact that antipsychotic medications (also called "neuroleptics") exert their effects by blocking or inhibiting D2 receptors. The mesolimbic pathway may be involved, a conclusion based on studies showing a link between dysfunction of this system and the **delusions** and hallucinations of schizophrenia, with an increase in striatal dopamine in association with these occurrences. On the other hand, the mesocortical pathway is also probably involved because of its role in working memory, memorization, and manipulation of spatial information, all of which are affected in schizophrenia. A decrease in dopamine in the prefrontal area, which is linked to the ventral tegmental area in the mesocortical pathway, appears to lead to the cognitive deficits of schizophrenia. In addition, the nigrostriatal pathway may be involved: there is an increase in dopamine transmission from the substantia nigra to the striatum in people with schizophrenia.

Dopamine, the brain reward system, and addiction

The nucleus accumbens (in the ventral striatum and part of the mesolimbic pathway) is the focal point of dopamine's involvement in the brain's reward pathway and addiction. There is an increase in dopamine release in the nucleus accumbens in addiction, and activity in this area is a target of models exploring the mechanisms of behavioral or substance addictions. Human **imaging studies**, which have become quite revelatory in terms of the biological underpinnings of psychiatric disorders, show that endogenous release of dopamine in the striatum is correlated with drug-induced feelings of pleasure. For example, a dose of amphetamine or of alcohol will promote dopamine release in the ventral striatum. Dopamine also is associated with the cravings of addiction and may play a role in the significance an addicted person may assign to cues that others perceive as neutral (known as salience). This system has also been implicated in process or behavioral addiction.

Dopamine and movement and repetitive disorders

Dopamine's role in the extrapyramidal (movement and coordination) symptoms of Parkinson's is seated in a shortage of the neurotransmitter in the nigrostriatal pathway, specifically involving the putamen and caudate nucleus. Tourette syndrome, a condition characterized by onset in childhood, involuntary tics, stereotypic behaviors, and repetitive thoughts and rituals, is also seated in the dorsal striatum. This syndrome can occur as a comorbidity with **obsessive-compulsive disorder** and/or **attention deficit hyperactivity disorder** (ADHD), which some studies also have associated with dopamine-signaling dysfunction.

Dopamine and mood disorders

Changes in dopamine signaling may contribute to symptoms of depression, such as an inability to experience pleasure or loss of motivation. Although low levels of dopamine binding to the D2 receptor are associated with social anxiety, an increase in dopamine can be associated

KEY TERMS

D1, D2, etc.—Dopamine receptor proteins.

Mesolimbic pathway—The "reward pathways" of the brain.

Nucleus accumbens—A part of the brain involved in the mesolimbic reward pathway, which receives dopamine signaling from the ventral tegmental area.

Ventral tegmental area—Produces dopamine and signals to the nucleus accumbens and the rest of the striatum.

with the hypersocial behavior of someone experiencing the manic aspects of **bipolar disorder**.

Drugs related to dopamine/dopamine receptor regulation

Drugs may act at any point along a dopamine-signaling pathway. L-dopa, used in treating Parkinson's, is a dopamine precursor that is synthesized into dopamine in the brain and ameliorates the effects of low dopamine levels in the dorsal striatum. **Monoamine oxidase inhibitors (MAOIs)** block the activity of the enzyme that breaks down dopamine; these may be used as **antidepressants** and can affect dopamine-related pathways. Antipsychotics are divided into two classes, the typical and atypical antipsychotics, and can target different types of dopamine receptors. Atypical antipsychotics, including **clozapine**, may target the D4 receptor more strongly than the D2. Bromocriptine targets D2 and is a partial inhibitor of D1. The recently approved aripiprazole is a partial dopamine agonist (mimic), and **amantadine** is also a dopamine agonist.

Resources

BOOKS

American Psychiatric Association. *Diagnostic and Statistical Manual of Mental Disorders*. 4th ed., text rev. Washington, DC: American Psychiatric Publishing, 2000.

PERIODICALS

Franken, Ingmar H.A., Jan Booij, and Wim van den Brink. "The Role of Dopamine in Human Addiction: From Reward to Motivated Attention." *European Journal of Pharmacology* 526 (2005): 199–206.

Grant, Jon E., Judson A. Brewer, and Marc N. Potenza. "The Neurobiology of Substance and Behavioral Addictions." *CNS Spectrum* 11, no. 12 (December 2006): 924–930.

Greene, James G. "Gene Expression Profiles of Brain Dopamine Neurons and Relevance to Neuropsychiatric Disease." *Journal of Physiology* 575, Pt. 2 (September 1, 2006): 411–416.

Kienast, T., and A. Heinz. "Dopamine and the Diseased Brain." *CNS and Neurological Disorders—Drug Targets* 5, no. 1 (February 2006): 109–131.

Totterdell, Susan. "The Anatomy of Comorbid Neuropsychiatric Disorders Based on Cortico-limbic Synaptic Interactions." *Neurotoxicity Research* 10, no. 2 (October 2006): 65–85.

WEBSITES

MedlinePlus. "Schizophrenia." U.S. National Library of Medicine. National Institutes of Health http://www.nlm.nih.gov/medlineplus/schizophrenia.html (accessed October 5, 2011).

U.S. National Institute of Mental Health. "Schizophrenia." http://www.nimh.nih.gov/healthinformation/schizophreniamenu.cfm (accessed October 5, 2011).

Emily Jane Willingham, PhD

Doral *see* **Quazepam**

Down syndrome

Definition

Down syndrome, or trisomy 21, is a genetic disorder caused by the presence of an extra copy of chromosome 21 or by a portion of chromosome 21 translocated (attached) to another chromosome in one of the affected

Incidence of medical conditions associated with Down syndrome

Disorder	Incidence
Infertility	>99% in men; absence of ovulation in 30% of women
Mental retardation	>95%
Growth retardation	>95%
Alzheimer's disease	Affects up to 75% by age 60
Ophthalmic (eye) disorders	60%
Hearing loss	40%–75%
Congenital heart defects	40%

Rarer complications include epilepsy (5%–10%), gastrointestinal malformations (5%), hypothyroidism (5%), and leukemia (1%).

SOURCE: American Academy of Family Physicians, "Down Syndrome: Prenatal Risk Assessment and Diagnosis."

Report available online at http://www.aafp.org/afp/20000815/825.html. *(Table by PreMediaGlobal. © 2012 Cengage Learning.)*

child's parents. It is not inherited in most cases but is caused by a random genetic abnormality. The disorder is named for John Langdon Haydon Down (1828–1896) a British doctor who pioneered the care and education of children with the syndrome that now bears his name, as well as publishing the first scientific description of it in 1866. The cause of Down syndrome was finally identified in 1959 by Jérôme Lejeune (1926–1994), a French pediatrician and geneticist.

Down syndrome was sometimes referred to in the past as Mongolian idiocy or mongolism because the facial features of some children with the syndrome were thought to resemble those of people from Mongolia. In 1965 the World Health Organization (WHO) stated that *mongolism* should no longer be used as a synonym for Down syndrome, following a request from the organization's Mongolian delegate. Mongolism is presently considered a disrespectful term and should not be used in discussions of the condition, although the word still occasionally appears in print.

Demographics

Down syndrome is the most common human chromosomal abnormality. It occurs in about one in every 733 to 800 live births in the United States, or about 5,400 children per year. The rate is higher among children born to older parents, fathers as well as mothers. The mother's age is a risk factor for Down syndrome, rising from one chance in 1,562 in mothers 24 or younger to one in 19 in mothers over 45. Recent studies indicate that the father's age is also a factor; men 42 years and older are at increased risk of fathering a child with trisomy 21. These babies, however, represent only about a quarter of those conceived with trisomy 21. The condition is linked to so many heart defects and other problems that affect survival before birth that about 75% of fetuses conceived with Down syndrome are miscarried.

Down syndrome occurs with equal frequency in all races and ethnic groups worldwide. Boys are slightly more likely to be affected than girls; the gender ratio is 1.2:1. As of 2011, there were about 400,000 people with Down syndrome living in the United States.

Humans are not the only species affected by the syndrome; comparable conditions have been identified in mice and chimpanzees.

Description

The additional genetic material in Down syndrome results in characteristic physical features and intellectual disability. The average IQ scores of children with the syndrome are between 35 and 70. Characteristic facial features include a head that is smaller than average, upward-slanting eyes with a skin fold in the upper eyelid called an epicanthic fold, and a flattened nose. The hands are short and broad with short fingers, and they often have a single crease across the palm. Another characteristic feature of Down syndrome is hypotonia, which is the medical term for poor muscle tone. Children with Down syndrome often need extensive physical therapy in order to learn to walk and move normally, and are at increased risk of obesity as they grow older. In addition, normal growth is slowed; most of these children never reach full adult height. The average height for adult men with Down syndrome is 5 ft. 1 in. (1.5 m); for women, 4 ft. 9 in. (1.4 m).

Between 40% and 60% of infants with Down syndrome are born with severe heart defects; others have blockages of the esophagus and small intestine. These defects may require surgery shortly after birth. These children are also at increased risk of childhood leukemia.

Adolescents and adults with Down syndrome are more likely than other people to develop health problems that include frequent sinus and ear infections, cataracts, gastrointestinal reflux disease (GERD), hearing problems, sleep apnea, dislocated hips, and hypothyroidism.

Risk factors

There are three known risk factors for having a child with Down syndrome:

- Mother older than 35 years of age and/or father older than 42.
- Having a previous child with Down syndrome. A woman who has borne one child with the syndrome has about a 1% chance of having a second child with the condition.
- Either parent being a carrier of the genetic translocation for Down syndrome.

There are no lifestyle or environmental factors known to cause Down syndrome.

Causes and symptoms

Causes

Down syndrome results from genetic errors during the formation of germ cells (eggs and sperm) or during cell division shortly after the egg is fertilized by the sperm. The most common form of Down syndrome, responsible for about 95% of cases, occurs when an egg or sperm carrying two copies of chromosome 21 is involved in conception. The reason for the extra copy in

KEY TERMS

Chorionic villus sampling (CVS)—A prenatal test that involves taking a small sample of the placenta, the organ that forms inside the uterus during pregnancy and supplies the baby with oxygen and nutrients carried by the blood.

Chromosome—A microscopic thread-like structure found within each cell of the body and consists of a complex of proteins and DNA. Humans have 46 chromosomes arranged into 23 pairs. Changes in either the total number of chromosomes or their shape and size (structure) may lead to physical or mental abnormalities.

Congenital—Present at birth.

Epicanthic fold—A fold in the inner corner of the skin of the upper eyelid, found in about half of children with Down syndrome. The epicanthic fold is found in many people of Mongolian origin and is one of the features that led to earlier writers referring to Down syndrome as mongolism.

Germ cell—A cell involved in reproduction. In humans the germ cells are the sperm (male) and egg (female). Unlike other cells in the body, germ cells contain only half the standard number of chromosomes.

Hypotonia—The medical term for poor muscle tone.

Intellectual disability—Significant impairment in intellectual function and adaptation in society. Usually associated with an intelligence quotient (IQ) below 70.

Karyotype—A standard arrangement of photographic or computer-generated images of chromosome pairs from a cell in ascending numerical order, from largest to smallest.

Mosaic—A term referring to a genetic situation in which a person's cells do not have the exact same composition of chromosomes. In Down syndrome, this may mean that some cells have a normal number (46) of chromosomes while other cells have an abnormal 47 chromosomes.

Nondisjunction—Nonseparation of a chromosome pair during either meiosis or mitosis.

Translocation—The transfer of one part of a chromosome to another chromosome during cell division. A balanced translocation occurs when pieces from two different chromosomes exchange places without loss or gain of any chromosome material. An unbalanced translocation involves the unequal loss or gain of genetic information between two chromosomes.

Trisomy—The condition of having three identical chromosomes, instead of the normal two, in a cell.

Tubal ligation—A surgical procedure in which a woman's fallopian tubes are cut or blocked to prevent an egg from reaching the uterus for fertilization.

the abnormal germ cell is a genetic error called nondisjunction. During the normal process of germ cell formation, the paired chromosomes in the cell divide so that each daughter cell has only one member of the pair. In nondisjunction, one daughter cell gets both members of the chromosome pair and the other cell has none. If a germ cell carrying two copies of chromosome 21 is fertilized by a normal germ cell from the other parent, the child will have three copies of chromosome 21. This genetic error is called a full trisomy 21.

Some children with Down syndrome have some body cells with the extra copy of chromosome 21 and some body cells without the extra copy. This condition is called mosaic trisomy 21. It is thought to result from random errors in cell division during the early stages of fetal development. Mosaic trisomy 21 accounts for about 2% of children with Down syndrome.

About 3% of cases of Down syndrome occur in families with carriers. A part of chromosome 21 may become attached to chromosome 14 either before or at the moment of conception. This type of genetic error is called a balanced translocation because there is no extra material from chromosome 21. A person with this type of translocation looks normal and develops normally; however, he or she has an increased risk of having a child with full trisomy 21.

Symptoms

The extra chromosome 21 affects almost every organ system in the body. Some physical indications of Down syndrome in an infant include:

- an additional skin fold at the inner corner of upper eyelid (epicanthic fold)
- a short neck
- white spots on the iris of the eye known as Brushfield spots
- a round face

- ears that are smaller than normal
- a flattened area at the back of the head
- missing teeth or delayed development of teeth
- protruding tongue and a tendency to breathe through the mouth
- an extra-wide space between the big toe and second toe

Diagnosis

Most babies with Down syndrome are diagnosed at birth on the basis of their physical features. The **diagnosis** can be confirmed by a blood test and karyotype.

Tests

Down syndrome can be screened for and diagnosed before birth. Screening tests are used to estimate the chance that an individual woman will have a baby with Down syndrome. A test called the maternal serum alpha-fetoprotein test (MSAFP) is offered to all pregnant women under the age of 35. If the mother decides to have this test, it is performed between 15 and 22 weeks of pregnancy. The MSAFP screen measures a protein and two hormones that are normally found in maternal blood during pregnancy. A specific pattern of these hormones and protein can indicate an increased risk for having a baby born with Down syndrome. However, this is only a risk-assessment test; MSAFP cannot diagnose Down syndrome directly. Women found to have an increased risk of their babies being affected with Down syndrome are offered amniocentesis. The MSAFP test can detect up to 60% of all babies who will be born with Down syndrome.

Ultrasound screening for Down syndrome is also available. This is generally performed in the mid-trimester of pregnancy. Abnormal growth patterns characteristic of Down syndrome such as growth retardation, heart defects, duodenal atresia, T-E fistula, shorter than normal long-bone lengths, and extra folds of skin along the back of the neck of the developing fetus may all be observed via ultrasonic imaging.

The only way to definitively establish (with about 99% accuracy) the presence or absence of Down syndrome in a developing baby is to test a tissue sample during the pregnancy itself. Testing is usually done either by amniocentesis or chorionic villus sampling (CVS). All women under the age of 35 at high risk for having a baby affected with Down syndrome via an MSAFP screen and all mothers over the age of 35 are offered either CVS or amniocentesis. In CVS, a tiny tube is inserted into the opening of the uterus to retrieve a small sample of the placenta (the organ that attaches the growing baby to the mother via the umbilical cord, and provides oxygen and **nutrition**). In amniocentesis, a small amount of the fluid in which the baby is floating is withdrawn with a long thin needle. CVS may be performed as early as 10 to 12 weeks into a pregnancy. Amniocentesis is generally not performed until at least the fifteenth week. Both CVS and amniocentesis carry small risks of miscarriage. Approximately 1% of women miscarry after undergoing CVS testing, while approximately 0.5% miscarry after undergoing amniocentesis. Both amniocentesis and CVS allow the baby's own karyotype to be determined.

Treatment

Physical issues

There is no cure for Down syndrome. Medical and surgical treatment of children with trisomy 21 is highly individualized. Infants with heart defects or obstructions in the esophagus and digestive tract usually need immediate surgery. Older children require periodic checkups for cataracts, hearing loss, and thyroid problems. Some children need special medications and diuretics for heart problems, and most need to be monitored for frequent infections, particularly ear infections and pneumonia.

ALTERNATIVE. The National Down Syndrome Society (NDSS) notes that various alternative therapies, including pituitary extract, glutamic acid, thyroid hormone, 5-hydroxytryptophan, dimethyl sulfoxide (DMSO), dihydroepiandosterone, sicca cell therapy, vitamin and mineral supplements, and growth hormone have been recommended at various times as treatments for Down syndrome. Sicca cell therapy, also known as dry cell therapy, consists of injections of dried cells taken from fetal or newborn animals under the skin or into the muscle. This treatment has been shown to be dangerous.

The NDSS discourages parents from trying alternative therapies that claim to "normalize" their child's appearance or boost his or her intelligence. There is no harm, however, in using such complementary and alternative approaches as **art therapy**, **music therapy**, pet therapy, or certain types of movement therapy, provided the child enjoys the activity and the therapist is qualified to work with children who have Down syndrome.

Developmental issues

It is not possible to tell at birth whether a baby with Down syndrome will be severely disabled or will have low-normal intelligence. Individualized assessment of the child is critical to providing opportunities for full development. In general, children with mosaic Down syndrome have higher IQ scores than children with full trisomy 21. There are many adults with the syndrome who are able to hold jobs and live independently; some have become successful artists, actors, and singers. In addition, community and family support allows people with Down syndrome to have rich, meaningful relationships.

In general, children with Down syndrome develop on a slower timetable than other children. Some typical developmental milestones for children with Down syndrome are as follows, with the normal milestone in parentheses for purposes of comparison:

- Baby sits up without assistance: 6–30 months (5–9 months).
- Crawls: 8–22 months (6–12 months).
- Stands up: 1–3.25 years (8–17 months).
- Walks without assistance: 1–4 years (9–18 months).
- Says first word: 1–4 years (1–3 years).
- Uses first two-word phrase: 2–7.5 years (15–32 months).
- Smiles at people: 1.5–5 months (1–3 months).
- Eats with fingers: 10–24 months (7–14 months).
- Eats with a spoon: 13–39 months (12–20 months).
- Toilet trained: 2–7 years (16–42 months).
- Dresses self without assistance: 3.5–8.5 years (3.25–5 years).

It is important to keep this distinctive developmental timetable in mind because it affects psychiatric evaluation of mental health issues in children with Down syndrome.

At one time children with Down syndrome were either institutionalized or put in special education programs apart from other children. In the early 2010s, however, the emphasis in treatment is to give these children as many opportunities as possible to go to school with other children in their age group and participate in sports, group activities, and other aspects of social life during the growing years. Some community groups help families deal with the emotional effects of raising a child with Down syndrome. Schools are required to provide services to children with Down syndrome, sometimes in separate special education classrooms, and sometimes in regular classrooms (their presence in regular classrooms is called mainstreaming or inclusion).

Child development specialists recommend that children diagnosed with Down syndrome receive early **intervention**, which is a systematic program of therapy, exercises, and activities mandated by the Individuals with Disabilities Education Act (IDEA) of 2004. Early intervention can begin any time after birth up to age three; the 2004 amendments to IDEA allow states to continue early intervention programs until the child is eligible to enter kindergarten. Each state has its own set of regulations for early intervention. The most common types of early intervention treatments for infants with Down syndrome are physical therapy, speech and language therapy, and occupational therapy.

Mental health issues

In general, children with Down syndrome are at greater risk of developing a mental disorder than other children. Childhood behavioral problems in affected children are similar to those in other children; however, they typically appear at a later age and last longer. For example, the temper tantrums associated with the "terrible twos" in most children may not appear in a child with Down syndrome until age four. To make sure that a child with Down syndrome receives an accurate diagnostic evaluation for behavioral problems or other mental health issues, parents should:

- Make sure that the problem is not caused by or associated with a physical condition or disorder. Because children with Down syndrome can have disorders ranging from visual deficits and hearing loss to digestive disorders and anemia, their mood and behavior are often affected by physical complaints.
- Check to see whether there are stressors at home or in the school that are affecting the child and whether the stress level can be lowered.
- Work with a child psychologist or behavioral pediatrician on a behavior treatment plan based on the ABCs of behavior (Antecedent, Behavior, and Consequence of the behavior).

There were 33 trials of treatments for mental health issues in children with Down syndrome under way as of 2011. Most are trials of social skills therapy, **donepezil**, or vitamin therapy. There are also several trials of new screening and diagnostic measures for mothers at risk of having a child with Down syndrome.

The most common behavioral problems in children with Down syndrome are wandering away from home and oppositional or stubborn behavior. Oppositional behavior is often related to frustration with language and communication difficulties; in many cases this issue can be resolved by finding ways to help the child communicate more effectively, such as by using assistive communication devices.

DEMENTIA. As people with Down syndrome age, they face an increased chance of developing **Alzheimer's disease** (sometimes referred to as **dementia** or senility). Most people have a 12% chance of developing Alzheimer's, but almost all people with Down syndrome will have either Alzheimer's or a similar type of dementia by the age of 50. Alzheimer disease causes the brain to shrink and to break down. The number of brain cells decreases, and abnormal deposits and structural arrangements occur. This process results in a loss of brain functioning and eventual death. A study published by a group of Japanese researchers in 2011 reported that donepezil, a drug given to treat Alzheimer's, is also beneficial to patients with low IQs.

ATTENTION DEFICIT HYPERACTIVITY DISORDER. **Attention deficit hyperactivity disorder (ADHD)** is more common in children with Down syndrome than in the general population, although it usually appears at a later age. One study reported in 2011 that the prevalence of **ADHD** in the sample of children with Down syndrome was 49%. It is important to rule out an anxiety disorder or difficulties with processing language as possible reasons for the child's difficulties with attention. The treatment for ADHD in children with Down syndrome is the same as that for other children.

AUTISM SPECTRUM DISORDERS. As with ADHD, **autism** spectrum disorders manifest in children with Down syndrome at a later age, usually around six to eight years of age. It is estimated that 5% to 7% of children with Down syndrome also have autism spectrum disorders. Treatment is the same as for other children with autism; but it is important for the child to be identified as early as possible so that he or she can receive appropriate services in a timely fashion.

OBSESSIVE-COMPULSIVE DISORDER. Children with Down syndrome are more likely to develop OCD than other children. Symptoms usually develop at a later age than in other children but are often more intense. The obsessive behaviors typically take such forms as rearranging beads, insisting on sitting in the same chair all the time, or playing with belts, shoelaces, or other items of clothing.

DEPRESSION. **Depression** is reported to be more common in children as well as adults with Down syndrome, although it is often underdiagnosed and undertreated. Reasons for the increased risk of depression include the effects of physical disorders, differences in brain structure and function, language difficulties, and greater vulnerability in adult life to the loss of friends and family members. Antidepressant medications, **psychotherapy**, and **electroconvulsive therapy** (ECT) have all been reported to be effective in treating depression in patients with Down syndrome.

SEXUALITY AND FERTILITY. Girls with Down syndrome begin to menstruate on average at age 12-1/2, which is close to the same age as their peers in the general population, although some begin as early as 10 or as late as 14. About 50% of women with Down syndrome are fully capable of having children, although menopause typically begins around age 40. Between 35% and 50% of children born to mothers with Down syndrome are likely to have trisomy 21 or other developmental disabilities.

Boys with Down syndrome reach puberty at about the same age as their peers in the general population. There is limited information about fertility in males with Down syndrome, although there were at least two proven cases of paternity as of 2011. Most researchers believe that adult males with Down syndrome have lower sperm counts than other men. It is not known whether males with Down syndrome are more likely to father children who have the syndrome. Adult males with Down syndrome should always use contraception unless they have decided to start a family.

Given the increased life expectancy of people with Down syndrome and the ability of many to find employment and live in the community, education about human intimacy and sexuality is an important part of their transition to adult life. This education should include information about **sexual abuse**: how to recognize it, how to prevent it, and how to report it.

People with Down syndrome are as susceptible to sexually transmitted diseases as other adolescents and young adults, and need to be taught about the use of condoms and other contraceptives. Young women with Down syndrome can use any method of contraception of their choice without medical risk; however, the chosen method must be appropriate to the individual's ability to use it effectively. With regard to tubal ligation, many states have laws restricting access to this procedure for women with intellectual or developmental disabilities. If tubal ligation is considered, the woman with Down syndrome should be involved in the decision as much as possible.

Prognosis

People with Down syndrome have a shortened life expectancy in addition to a high risk of early Alzheimer's disease; they often show a noticeable loss of mental function by age 30. About 85% of babies born with trisomy 21 survive the first year of life, but only 50% will live to reach age 60. This is a great improvement, however, as the life expectancy of a person with Down syndrome was only 25 years as recently as 1980.

Congenital heart disorders are one reason for the present high mortality rate, as are vulnerability to infections, a high rate of disorders of the digestive tract, and premature aging. Children with Down syndrome are also more likely to develop leukemia than other children. In spite of these risks, the prognosis for a baby born with Down syndrome is better than ever before. Because of

QUESTIONS TO ASK YOUR DOCTOR

- Have you ever treated a child with Down syndrome? An adult?
- What is your opinion of early intervention for children with the syndrome?
- Do you think researchers will ever discover a cure for the syndrome?
- Have you ever referred a couple for genetic counseling regarding their risk of having a baby with the syndrome?

modern medical treatments, including antibiotics to treat infections, and surgery to treat heart defects and duodenal atresia, the life expectancy of people with Down syndrome has greatly increased.

Prevention

There is no known way to prevent Down syndrome, because most cases of the syndrome are caused by a spontaneous mutation. Women can take steps before and during pregnancy to have a healthy pregnancy. Steps include taking a daily multivitamin with folic acid (400 micrograms), not smoking, and not drinking alcohol during pregnancy. Once a couple has had one baby with Down syndrome, they are often concerned about the likelihood of future offspring also being born with the disorder.

When a baby with Down syndrome has the type that results from a translocation, it is possible that one of the two parents is a carrier of a balanced translocation. A carrier has rearranged chromosomal information and can pass it on, but he or she does not have an extra chromosome and is not affected with the disorder. When one parent is a carrier of a translocation, the chance of future offspring having Down syndrome is greatly increased. The specific risk can be assessed by a genetic counselor. Adults who are concerned that they may have a balanced translocation of chromosome 21 can choose to have a karyotype to see whether their chromosomes are in fact abnormal. Pregnant women over 35 should have tests during the first trimester (three-month period) of pregnancy to screen for the syndrome.

Resources

BOOKS

Burack, Jacob A., et al., eds. *Oxford Handbook of Intellectual Disability and Development*, 2nd ed. New York: Oxford University Press, 2011.

Chicoine, Brian, and Dennis McGuire. *Guide to Good Health for Teens and Adults with Down Syndrome*. Bethesda, MD: Woodbine House, 2010.

Goldstein, Sam, and Cecil R. Reynolds, eds. *Handbook of Neurodevelopmental and Genetic Disorders in Children*, 2nd ed. New York: Guilford Press, 2011.

Royston, Angela. *Explaining Down Syndrome*. Mankato, MN: Smart Apple Press, 2010.

Simons, Jo Ann. *The Down Syndrome Transition Handbook: Charting Your Child's Course to Adulthood*. Bethesda, MD: Woodbine House, 2010.

Skallerup, Susan J., ed. *Babies with Down Syndrome: A New Parents' Guide*, 3rd ed. Bethesda, MD: Woodbine House, 2008.

PERIODICALS

Calles, J.L., Jr. "Cognitive-adaptive Disabilities." *Pediatric Clinics of North America* 58 (February 2011): 189–203.

Couzens, D., et al. "Cognitive Development and Down Syndrome: Age-related Change on the Stanford-Binet Test (Fourth Edition)." *American Journal on Intellectual and Developmental Disabilities* 116 (May 2011): 181–204.

Ekstein, S., et al. "Down Syndrome and Attention-Deficit/Hyperactivity Disorder (ADHD)." *Journal of Child Neurology* (May 31, 2011) [e-pub. ahead of print].

Gray, L., et al. "The Continuing Challenge of Diagnosing Autism Spectrum Disorder in Children with Down Syndrome." *Child Care, Health and Development* 37 (July 2011): 459–461.

Kondoh, T., et al. "Donepezil Significantly Improves Abilities in Daily Lives of Female Down Syndrome Patients with Severe Cognitive Impairment: A 24-week Randomized, Double-blind, Placebo-controlled Trial." *International Journal of Psychiatry in Medicine* 41 (January 2011): 71–89.

Landt, J., et al. "Age-related Changes in Plasma Dehydroepiandrosterone Levels in Adults with Down's Syndrome and the Risk of Dementia." *Journal of Neuroendocrinology* 23 (May 2011): 450–455.

Rissman, R.A., and W.C. Mobley. "Implications for Treatment: GABAA Receptors in Aging, Down Syndrome and Alzheimer's Disease." *Journal of Neurochemistry* 117 (May 2011): 613–622.

Urv, T.K., et al. "Psychiatric Symptoms in Adults with Down Syndrome and Alzheimer's Disease." *American Journal on Intellectual and Developmental Disabilities* 115 (July 2010): 265–276.

Walker, J.C., et al. "Depression in Down Syndrome: A Review of the Literature." *Research in Developmental Disabilities* 32 (September-October 2011): 1432–1440.

WEBSITES

Chen, Harold. "Genetics of Down Syndrome." Medscape. November 29, 2011. http://emedicine.medscape.com/article/943216-overview (accessed December 12, 2011).

Mayo Clinic. "Down Syndrome." Medscape. November 29, 2011. http://www.mayoclinic.com/health/down-syndrome/DS00182 (accessed December 12, 2011).

National Human Genome Research Institute (NHGRI). "Learning about Down Syndrome." http://www.genome.gov/19517824 (accessed August 23, 2011).

National Institute of Child Health and Human Development (NICHD). "Down Syndrome." http://www.nichd.nih.gov/health/topics/Down_Syndrome.cfm (accessed August 23, 2011).

Patterson, Bonnie. "Managing Behavior." National Down Syndrome Society (NDSS). http://www.ndss.org/index.php?option=com_ content&view=article&id=69&Itemid=90 (accessed December 15, 2011).

Virginia Commonwealth University Life Sciences. "On Down Syndrome." [9-1/2 minute video about the condition.] http://www.youtube.com/watch?v=bEV kbuooXo4 (accessed August 23, 2011).

ORGANIZATIONS

American Academy of Child and Adolescent Psychiatry (AACAP), 3615 Wisconsin Avenue, N.W., Washington, DC, United States, 20016-3007, (202) 966-7300, Fax: (202) 966-2891, http://www.aacap.org.

American Psychiatric Association (APA), 1000 Wilson Boulevard, Suite 1825, Arlington, VA, United States, 22209-3901, (703) 907-7300, apa@psych.org, http://www.psych.org.

National Down Syndrome Society (NDSS), 666 Broadway, 8th Floor, New York, NY, United States, 10012, Fax: (212) 979-2873, (800) 221-4602, info@ndss.org, http://www.ndss.org/index.php.

National Human Genome Research Institute (NHGRI), Building 31, Room 4B09, 31 Center Drive, MSC 2152, 9000 Rockville Pike, Bethesda, MD, United States, 20892-2152, (301) 402-0911, Fax: (301) 402-2218, http://www.genome.gov.

National Institute of Child Health and Human Development Information Resource Center, PO Box 3006, Rockville, MD, United States, 20847, Fax: (866) 760-5947, (800) 370-2943, NICHDInformationResourceCenter@mail.nih.gov, http://www.nichd.nih.gov.

Rebecca J. Frey, PhD

Doxepin

Definition

Doxepin is a tricyclic antidepressant. It is sold in the United States under the brand name Sinequan and is also available under its generic name.

Purpose

Doxepin is used primarily to treat **depression** and to treat the combination of symptoms of anxiety and depression. Like most **antidepressants**, doxepin has also been used to treat **panic disorder**, **obsessive-compulsive disorder**,**attention deficit hyperactivity disorder** (ADHD), **enuresis** (bed-wetting), eating disorders such as **bulimia nervosa**, **cocaine** dependency, and the depressive phase of bipolar (manic-depressive) disorder. It has also been used to support **smoking cessation** programs.

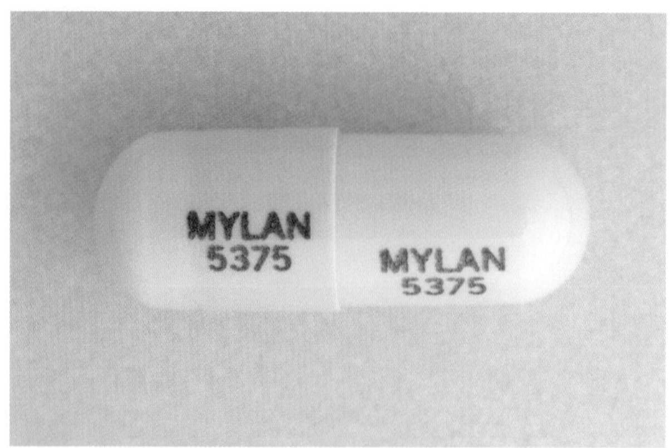

Doxepin. *(© Custom Medical Stock Photo, Inc. Reproduced by permission.)*

Description

Doxepin acts to change the balance of naturally occurring chemicals in the **brain** that regulate the transmission of nerve impulses between cells. Its action primarily increases the concentration of norepinephrine and **serotonin** (both chemicals that stimulate nerve cells) and, to a lesser extent, blocks the action of another brain chemical, acetylcholine. Although not technically a tricyclic antidepressant, doxepin shares most of the properties of these drugs, which include **amitriptyline**, **clomipramine**, **desipramine**, **imipramine**, **nortriptyline**, **protriptyline**, and **trimipramine**. Studies comparing doxepin with these other drugs have shown that doxepin is no more or less effective than other antidepressants of its type. Its choice for treatment is as much a function of physician preference as any other factor.

The therapeutic effects of doxepin, like other antidepressants, appear slowly. Maximum benefit is often not evident for at least two weeks after starting the drug. People taking doxepin should be aware of this and continue taking the drug as directed even if they do not see immediate improvement.

Recommended dosage

As with any antidepressant, doxepin must be carefully adjusted by the physician to produce the desired therapeutic effect. Doxepin is available as 10 mg, 25 mg, 50 mg, 75 mg, 100 mg, and 150 mg oral capsules as well as an oral concentrate solution containing 10 mg of drug in each milliliter of solution.

Therapy is usually started at 30–150 mg per day and gradually increased to 300 mg daily if needed. There is little evidence that doses above 300 mg daily provide any additional benefits. Amounts up to 150 mg may be taken as a single dose at bedtime to decrease daytime sleepiness. Doses of more than 150 mg per day should be divided into two or three doses and taken throughout the day.

In patients over age 60, therapy should be maintained at the low end of the dosing range and increased cautiously and with physician supervision. Patients with organic brain syndrome (psychiatric symptoms of **dementia** often seen in elderly patients) generally require daily doses of only 25–50 mg.

If the oral concentrate of doxepin is used, each dose should be diluted in at least 4 oz (120 mL) of milk, orange, prune, tomato, pineapple, or grapefruit juice just before administration. Doxepin is not compatible with many carbonated beverages and should not be diluted in them.

Precautions

As with other tricyclic antidepressants, doxepin should be used cautiously and with close physician supervision in people, especially the elderly, who have benign prostatic hypertrophy, urinary retention, and glaucoma, especially angle-closure glaucoma (the most severe form). Before starting treatment, people with these conditions should discuss the relative risks and benefits of treatment with their doctors to help determine if doxepin is the right antidepressant for them.

Several antidepressants, including doxepin, have been found to potentially increase the risk of suicidal thoughts and actions in patients younger than 25. All persons taking doxepin, regardless of age, should be monitored for signs of worsening depression or self-harm.

Doxepin may increase heart rate and stress on the heart. It may be dangerous for people with cardiovascular disease, especially those who have recently had a heart attack, to take this drug or other antidepressants in the same pharmacological class. In rare cases where patients with cardiovascular disease must receive doxepin, they should be monitored closely for cardiac rhythm disturbances and signs of cardiac stress or damage. Doxepin may also increase the possibility of having **seizures**. Patients should tell their physician if they have a history of seizures, including seizures brought on by the abuse of drugs or alcohol. These people should use doxepin only with caution and be closely monitored by their physician.

A common problem with antidepressants is sedation (drowsiness, lack of physical and mental alertness). This side effect is especially noticeable early in therapy. In most patients, sedation decreases or disappears entirely with time, but until then patients taking doxepin should not perform activities requiring mental alertness, such as driving or operating machinery.

Doxepin should not be taken by nursing mothers because it is secreted into breast milk and may cause side effects in the nursing infant.

Side effects

Doxepin shares the side effects of tricyclic antidepressants. The most frequent of these are dry mouth, constipation, urinary retention, increased heart rate, sedation, irritability, dizziness, and decreased coordination. As with most side effects associated with tricyclic antidepressants, the intensity is highest at the beginning of therapy and tends to decrease with continued use.

Dry mouth, if severe to the point of causing difficulty speaking or swallowing, may be managed by dosage reduction or temporary discontinuation of the drug. Patients may also chew sugarless gum or suck on sugarless candy in order to increase the flow of saliva. Some artificial saliva products may give temporary relief.

Men with prostate enlargement who take doxepin may be especially likely to have problems with urinary retention. Symptoms include having difficulty starting a urine flow and more difficulty than usual passing urine. In most cases, urinary retention is managed with dose reduction or by switching to another type of antidepressant. In extreme cases, patients may require treatment with bethanechol, a drug that reverses this particular side effect. People who think they may be experiencing any side effects from this or any other medication should tell their physicians.

Interactions

Dangerously high blood pressure has resulted from the combination of antidepressants such as doxepin and members of another class of antidepressants known as **monoamine oxidase inhibitors (MAOIs)**. Because of this, doxepin should never be taken in combination with **MAOIs**. Patient's taking any MAOIs, for example Nardil (**phenelzine** sulfate) or Parnate (**tranylcypromine** sulfate), should stop the MAOI then wait at least 14 days before starting doxepin or any tricyclic antidepressant. The same holds true when discontinuing doxepin and starting an MAOI.

Doxepin may decrease the blood pressure–lowering effects of **clonidine**. Patients who take both drugs should be monitored for loss of blood-pressure control and the dose of clonidine increased as needed.

KEY TERMS

Acetylcholine—A naturally occurring chemical in the body that transmits nerve impulses from cell to cell. Generally, it has opposite effects from dopamine and norepinephrine; it causes blood vessels to dilate, lowers blood pressure, and slows the heartbeat. Central nervous system well-being is dependent on a balance among acetylcholine, dopamine, serotonin, and norepinephrine.

Anticholinergic—Related to the ability of a drug to block the nervous system chemical acetylcholine. When acetylcholine is blocked, patients often experience dry mouth and skin, increased heart rate, blurred vision, and difficulty urinating. In severe cases, blocking acetylcholine may cloud thinking and cause delirium.

Benign prostate hypertrophy—Enlargement of the prostate gland.

Norepinephrine—A neurotransmitter in the brain that acts to constrict blood vessels and raise blood pressure. It works in combination with serotonin.

Organic brain syndrome—A class of disorders characterized by progressive deterioration of mental processes caused by temporary brain dysfunction or permanent brain damage. Symptoms include delusions, dementia, amnesia, and delirium that are not caused by drugs, alcohol, or as a side effect of medication.

Serotonin—A widely distributed neurotransmitter that is found in blood platelets, the lining of the digestive tract, and the brain, and that works in combination with norepinephrine. It causes very powerful contractions of smooth muscle, and is associated with mood, attention, emotions, and sleep. Low levels of serotonin are associated with depression.

The sedative effects of doxepin are increased by other central nervous system depressants such as alcohol, **sedatives**, sleeping medications, antihistamines, or medications used for other mental disorders such as **schizophrenia**. The anticholinergic effects of doxepin are additive with other anticholinergic drugs such as **benztropine**, **biperiden**, **trihexyphenidyl**, and antihistamines.

Resources

BOOKS

American Society of Health-System Pharmacists. *AHFS Drug Information 2008*. Bethesda, MD: American Society of Health-System Pharmacists, 2008.

DeVane, C. Lindsay, Pharm.D. "Drug Therapy for Mood Disorders." In *Fundamentals of Monitoring Psychoactive Drug Therapy*. Baltimore: Williams and Wilkins, 1990.

Jack Raber, PharmD

Draw-a-person test *see* **Figure drawings**

DSM *see* **Diagnostic and Statistical Manual of Mental Disorders**

Dual diagnosis *see* **Co-occurring disorders**

Duloxetine

Definition

Duloxetine is a medication used to treat a variety of nervous system oriented illnesses, including **depression** and neuropathic pain. Neuropathic pain is pain generated by the nervous system, also known as neurogenic pain. Duloxetine belongs to a class of drugs known as selective **serotonin** norepinephrine reuptake inhibitors (SSNRI), which specifically acts on two chemicals called serotonin and norepinephrine. These chemicals are types of neurotransmitter involved in normal **brain** function. These **neurotransmitters** can affect the physiological state of clinical depression as well as neuropathic pain.

Purpose

Duloxetine can be used to treat a broad range of mood and stress-related psychiatric illnesses as well as illnesses involving neuropathic pain. It is mainly used to treat clinical depression, **generalized anxiety disorder** (GAD), and pain associated with diabetic peripheral neuropathy or fibromyalgia. Choice of using duloxetine

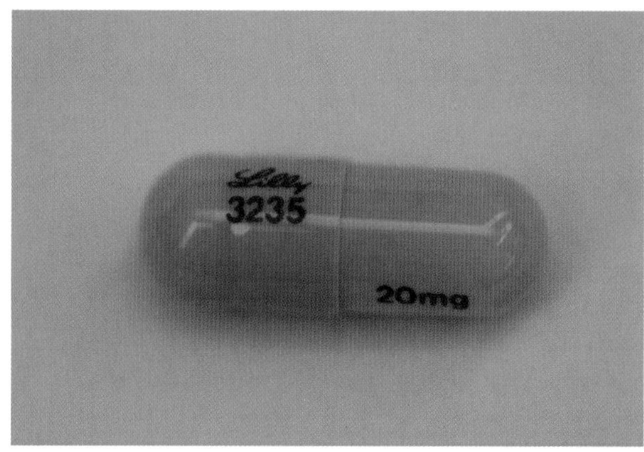

Cymbalta (duloxetine), 20 mg. *(© Custom Medical Stock Photo, Inc. Reproduced by permission.)*

alone or in combination with other drugs depends on the medical disorder and individual health parameters.

Description

Duloxetine has a therapeutic mechanism of action that is focused on the modulation of the natural body chemicals serotonin and norepinephrine. Serotonin and norepinephrine are types of neurotransmitters in the nervous system, chemicals that neurons use to signal one another in complex pathways for normal brain and body functioning. Neurotransmitters like serotonin and norepinephrine bind to chemical receptors on the surface of neurons (brain cells). Once bound to a receptor they affect physiological processes.

The receptors activate a sequence of cellular events known as a chemical cascade or signaling pathway. Neurotransmitter signaling pathways are responsible for many regulatory processes including neuronal signaling that affects mood and pain. During the signaling process, neurotransmitters such as serotonin travel from one neuron to the next. These chemicals need to cross a short space between the end of one neuron and the beginning of the next neuron known as the synapse or synaptic space. Serotonin or norepinephrine is released from the end of neuron one, crosses the synaptic space, and binds to a neurotransmitter-specific receptor on the surface of the next neuron (neuron two). Any extra serotonin or norepinephrine that is left in the synaptic space is taken back up by neuron one in a process known as reuptake. The more neurotransmitter allowed to remain in the synaptic space, the more will eventually be allowed to bind to receptors on neuron two and participate in the signaling process.

Selective serotonin and norepinephrine reuptake inhibitors like duloxetine decrease the reuptake of these neurotransmitters by neuron one, allowing more serotonin or norepinephrine to be present in the synapse and, therefore, more neurotransmitter signaling to occur. It is believed that a decrease in serotonin and norepinephrine signaling contributes to illness such as depression and **anxiety disorders**. Selective serotonin and norepinephrine reuptake inhibitors help by increasing signaling, with little effect on the synaptic levels of other neurotransmitters. An increase in serotonin and norepinephrine in the spinal cord is believed to inhibit the signaling of neurogenic pain pathways, hence their use in controlling pain associated with diabetic neuropathy or fibromyalgia.

Whether a patient is going to benefit from any SSNRI medication may have a genetic component. Individual response to each SSNRI varies greatly, and these drugs tend to require several weeks to take effect. The initial trial of an SSNRI can be difficult because the side effects begin right away while the beneficial effects take up to two weeks to develop. The particular SSNRI that works best for one patient may have no effect on another patient. Also, having no response to one SSNRI does not mean that a patient will not have a good therapeutic response to another SSNRI. Finding which SSNRI is going to work for a patient may require a trial of multiple drugs until an effective agent is found. Generally, an agent is attempted for four to six weeks before concluding it will not have an effect and switching to another agent. If there is an effect but the healthcare provider judges it could be improved, the dose is often increased as the patient is able to tolerate. Duloxetine is often the SSNRI of initial choice, because it is effective and generally well tolerated by many patients.

Recommended dosage

Duloxetine is taken as an oral medication. The dosage used varies depending on the medical condition being treated, individual patient response to the medication regarding its effectiveness, and individual patient response to the medication regarding side effects. Some people naturally require a higher dose of duloxetine in order to achieve the desired effect. Other patients require a lower dose either for effect or because they quickly develop side effects that are not tolerable.

Duloxetine used for **major depressive disorder** and generalized anxiety disorder is usually dosed at 60 mg daily. Duloxetine used for neuropathic pain in diabetic neuropathy or fibromyalgia is dosed similarly. This dose can be taken in one pill or in increments of 30 mg twice daily if a patient tolerates smaller doses better than large ones. Patients may start at a lower 30 mg daily dose for the first week of treatment and gradually work their way up to the dose needed for effect in 10 mg weekly implements or may go directly to a 60 mg daily dose after a week at 30 mg per day. The elderly are usually started at a lower dose, due to their increased sensitivity to these medications and their side effects. The maximum dose that may be used is 120 mg per day, but doses higher than 60 mg per day have rarely been shown to improve symptoms further and may not be tolerable to the patient. Patients are dosed at the lowest possible effective dose to avoid the development of adverse side effects. Slowly increasing the dose over time helps with minimizing side effects, and some side effects become lessened with continued use. Patients are periodically reassessed to determine whether there is need for continued treatment with duloxetine. All SSNRIs, including duloxetine, need to be slowly tapered off if discontinued, to avoid a discontinuation withdrawal syndrome.

Precautions

SSNRIs have many side effects. It usually takes several weeks of medication for the treatment effect to occur, while the undesirable side effects may occur at the onset of treatment. When an SSNRI is prescribed to a patient with a disease like major depression or severe pain, this time lapse in beneficial versus adverse effects may be difficult for patient **compliance** with treatment. The classic description is patients who are already feeling depressed or in pain take an SSNRI, experience side effects and so feel worse, all while being told that they will eventually get better. This situation can be frustrating for patients with depression or severe pain. Fortunately, SSNRIs do help many people and have fewer overall side effects than some older medications used for the same purpose. Great benefit may be gained if a patient is able to get past the first couple weeks of treatment.

It takes some time to determine whether a particular SSNRI such as duloxetine will work for an individual patient. Each SSNRI is tried for four to six weeks to determine whether it is the appropriate agent for a patient. Having one SSNRI fail in treatment for an individual patient does not mean that another SSNRI will not work for that person. Sometimes multiple drugs need to be attempted under physician care before the proper treatment is found for a patient. Duloxetine has a high success rate and is often chosen as the first SSNRI to try for a patient.

When a patient discontinues the use of duloxetine, the dose needs to be tapered down slowly. SSNRIs have little to no abuse potential. However, if an SSNRI is abruptly discontinued without tapering, there may be symptoms of withdrawal known as SSNRI discontinuation syndrome. Withdrawal symptoms of this syndrome may include flu-like symptoms, anxiety, agitation, vivid or bizarre dreams, **insomnia**, nausea, vomiting, diarrhea, sense of imbalance, chills, **fatigue**, dizziness, headache, numbness and tingling of the extremities, and other sensory disturbances. Discontinuation syndrome may be avoided completely if the dose of duloxetine is properly tapered down over time.

SSNRI overdose may result in a condition known as **serotonin syndrome**, also called serotonin toxicity, serotonin poisoning, and serotonin storm. Serotonin overdose may be caused by taking multiple drugs that increase the amount of serotonin signaling in the body. While chemical signaling pathways are a part of normal brain function, over-activation can be dangerous. Drugs that increase serotonin signaling may do so by increasing the amount of serotonin available to bind to and activate receptors or by directly activating serotonin receptors. These drugs can cause serotonin overdose if used at the same time or in time periods too close together. Symptoms of serotonin overdose may range from mild to life-threatening, depending on the individual situation. Symptoms may include high blood pressure, high fever, nausea, diarrhea, headache, sweating, increased heart rate, tremor, muscle twitching, **delirium**, shock, coma, and death.

Duloxetine may be contraindicated or may require caution in use in patients with uncontrolled hypertension, liver function impairment or liver disease, kidney function impairment, seizure disorder, bleeding disorders, glaucoma, dehydration, history of alcohol abuse, and in patients under 25 years of age or the elderly. Kidney and liver function, as well as blood pressure and behavioral changes, may be monitored while taking duloxetine. SSNRIs such as duloxetine are discouraged from use in patients with **bipolar disorder**, as they can induce a state of mania in these individuals. There are selective conditions under which a doctor may prescribe an SSNRI such as duloxetine to a bipolar patient for a short period of time under careful monitoring. Duloxetine is classified as category C for pregnancy, which means either there are no adequate human or animal studies; or that adverse fetal effects were found in animal studies, but there is no available human data. The decision whether or not to use category C drugs in pregnancy is generally based on weighing the critical needs of the mother against the risk to the fetus. Other lower category agents are used whenever possible. The safety of duloxetine use during breast-feeding is unknown and its use is not recommended.

Side effects

SSNRIs are known for having fewer side effects than other types of older antidepressant medications that act on many types of neurotransmitter, which is one reason why they tend to be the drug of choice in treatment of depression. However, as with all medication, SSNRIs such as duloxetine do have side effects. Sensitivity to duloxetine varies among patients, and some patients may find lower doses are more than their body system can tolerate. Common side effects of duloxetine include nausea, headache, dizziness, constipation, sexual dysfunction, diarrhea, sweating, dry mouth, shakiness, tremor, loss of appetite, weight changes, hot flashes, elevated blood pressure, yawning, anxiety, and insomnia. Rare but serious potential side effects include mania, worsened depression and suicidality, **seizures**, serotonin syndrome, discontinuation syndrome, electrolyte imbalances, urinary retention, skin reactions, abnormal bleeding, liver damage, and glaucoma.

Interactions

Patients should make their doctor aware of all medications and supplements they are taking before using duloxetine. Using alcohol while taking duloxetine may create toxic reactions in the body and should be

KEY TERMS

Bipolar disorder—Psychiatric mood disorder characterized by periods of manic behavior that may alternate with periods of depression, also known as manic depressive disorder.

Cytochrome P450 (CYP450)—Enzymes present in the liver that metabolize drugs.

Diabetic peripheral neuropathy—Complication of long–term diabetes involving damage to nerves in the periphery (outside of the brain and spinal cord) that may include symptoms such as numbness and burning pain.

Fibromyalgia—Chronic condition in which patients experience widespread musculoskeletal pain and fatigue; an amplified neuropathic pain pathway may be involved.

Glaucoma—Condition involving increased pressure within the eye that may cause damage and blindness.

Mania—Physiological state of hyperactivity experienced by patients with certain psychiatric illnesses involving inappropriate elevated mood, pressured speech, poor judgment, and sometimes psychotic episodes superimposed on the state of mania.

Monoamine oxidase inhibitors (MAOIs)—Type of antidepressant medication that affects various kinds of neurotransmitters including serotonin.

Neuropathic pain—State of pain also known as neurogenic pain that is caused by neurotransmitter signaling in nervous system pain pathways between either the peripheral nervous system or the spinal cord and the brain.

Neurotransmitter—A chemical messenger that travels through the body and acts in the nervous system. Neurotransmitter signaling is responsible for a wide range of bodily processes and is often the target of medications involving the brain and cardiovascular system.

Neurotransmitter receptor—A physical recipient for chemicals called neurotransmitters. Receptors sit on the surface of cells that make up body tissues, and once bound to the neurotransmitter, they initiate the chemical signaling pathway associated with neurotransmitters.

Selective serotonin norepinephrine reuptake inhibitors (SSNRI)—Drug class that acts to specifically inhibit the reuptake of serotonin and norepinephrine in the neuronal synapse with little effect on other types of neurotransmitters, thereby decreasing side effects associated with broader acting drugs.

Selective serotonin reuptake inhibitors (SSRI)—Drug class that acts to specifically inhibit the reuptake of serotonin only in the neuronal synapse with little effect on other types of neurotransmitters, thereby decreasing side effects associated with broader acting drugs.

Serotonin—A type of neurotransmitter involved in regulation of the blood vessels, brain processes, and disease states such as depression.

Serotonin syndrome—A potentially life threatening drug reaction involving an excess of the neurotransmitter serotonin, usually occurring when too many medications that increase serotonin are taken together such as antimigraine triptans and certain antidepressants.

Synapse—Physical space between neurons that allows the passage of neurotransmitters for chemical signaling pathways.

avoided. Duloxetine is metabolized by a set of liver enzymes known as cytochrome P450 (CYP450). There are many subtypes of CYP450 enzymes and duloxetine interacts with multiple subtypes. Drugs that induce or activate these enzymes may increase the metabolism of duloxetine. This results in lower levels of therapeutic medication, thereby negatively affecting treatment. Drugs that act to inhibit the action of CYP450 may cause undesired increased levels of duloxetine in the body. This could lead to increased side effects or even toxic doses. Likewise duloxetine may affect the metabolism of other drugs, leading to greater or lower doses than therapeutically desired.

SSNRIs such as duloxetine should not be used at the same time as other medications that increase levels of serotonin in the neuronal synapse. Too much serotonin signaling may lead to the medical condition serotonin syndrome, which can be severe and life threatening. **Antidepressants** called **selective serotonin reuptake inhibitors (SSRIs)** are similar to duloxetine, except for lacking effects on the neurotransmitter norepinephrine, and should not be used concurrently due to additive effects. Antidepressants called **monoamine oxidase inhibitors (MAOIs)** increase the amount of serotonin released into the synapse and cannot be used concurrently with duloxetine. Switching drug treatment for an

QUESTIONS TO ASK YOUR DOCTOR

- Can I take the full dose right away or do I need to slowly increase the dose?
- Can I stop taking the medication right away or do I need to slowly decrease the dose?
- When should I eat in reference to taking this medication?
- What time of day should I take this medication?
- How long should I take this medication before I am reassessed?
- Will this medication interact with any of my other prescription medications?
- Are there any over-the-counter medications I should not take with this medicine?
- What are the side effects I should watch for?
- Can I drink alcoholic beverages in the same time frame as taking this medication?

individual patient from an MAOI to duloxetine may require a waiting period of up to two weeks between drugs. Switching from duloxetine to an MAOI may require a waiting period of up to five weeks duration. Another example of a medication that has additive serotonin effects with duloxetine is sumatriptan (Imitrex). Sumatriptan is used to treat migraine headaches and acts directly on serotonin receptors in the brain to activate their serotonin signaling pathway. The combination of an SSNRI increasing the amount of serotonin available to activate serotonin receptor signaling pathways, and sumatriptan directly activating serotonin receptor signaling pathways, may produce undesirable additive effects or overdose. Other drugs that cannot be combined with duloxetine due to risk of serotonin syndrome are the antipsychotics **chlorpromazine** and **fluphenazine**, as well as the herbal supplements yohimbe and **St. John's wort**.

By inhibiting specific subtypes of CYP450, SSNRIs such as duloxetine may dangerously increase the levels of other drugs in the body that would have otherwise been metabolized by the CYP450. Duloxetine may inhibit the metabolism of heart drugs such as **propranolol**, known as **beta blockers**, causing increased toxic levels of propranolol in the blood. Other drugs may cause toxicity when used with duloxetine, either through additive effects or through inhibition of duloxetine metabolism causing toxic levels of duloxetine in the blood. Drugs that may cause toxicity with duloxetine include diuretics (water pills) such as hydrochlorothiazide, diet pills such as sibutramine (Meridia), caffeine, the heart drug amiodarone, certain antibiotics such as ciprofloxacin and linezolid, mood stabilizers such as lithium, antipsychotics such as **haloperidol** and **clozapine**, and certain anti-seizure drugs such as phenytoin. There is increased risk of internal bleeding when duloxetine is used with anticoagulant drugs such as aspirin, warfarin, or large doses of the herbal supplements red clover, **ginkgo biloba**, feverfew, or concentrated green tea. Duloxetine cannot be combined with the antipsychotic medications **pimozide** (Orap) or **thioridazine** (Mellaril) due to dangerous cardiac complications.

Resources

BOOKS

Brunton, Laurence L., et al. *Goodman and Gilman's The Pharmacological Basis of Therapeutics.* 12th ed. New York: McGraw Hill Medical, 2011.

Stargrove, Mitchell Bebel, et al. *Herb, Nutrient, and Drug Interactions: Clinical Implications and Therapeutic Strategies.* St. Louis: Mosby, 2007.

ORGANIZATIONS

American College of Neuropsychopharmacology, 5034-A Thoroughbred Lane, Brentwood, TN, 37027, (615) 324-2360, Fax: (615) 523-1715, acnp@acnp.org, http://www.acnp.org.

American Psychiatric Association, 1000 Wilson Blvd., Ste. 1825, Arlington, VA, 22209-3901, (703) 907-7300, apa@psych.org, http://www.psych.org.

American Society for Clinical Pharmacology and Therapeutics, 528 N Washington St., Alexandria, VA, 22314, (703) 836-6981, info@ascpt.org, http://www.ascpt.org.

Mental Health America, 2000 N Beauregard St., 6th Fl., Alexandria, VA, 22311, (703) 684-7722, (800) 969-6642, Fax: (703) 684-5968, http://www.nmha.org.

Maria Eve Basile, PhD

Dyslexia *see* **Reading disorder**

Dyspareunia

Definition

Dyspareunia is painful sexual intercourse. The same term is used whether the pain results from a medical or a psychosocial problem. Dyspareunia may be diagnosed in men and women, although the **diagnosis** is rare in men;

when it does occur in men, it is almost always caused by a physical problem.

Because of the prevalence of this problem among women in the context of psychosocial associations, only women's experiences are emphasized.

Demographics

About 15% of women may have pain with intercourse at some point in their lives. About 1–2% have true dyspareunia. The incidence is much higher in women who have been raped or otherwise sexually abused. Dyspareunia in men is rare.

Description

Dyspareunia is any pain experienced any time before, during, or following sexual intercourse. The pain may be located in the genitals or within the pelvis. It is not unusual for women to occasionally have pain during intercourse. This is not true dyspareunia.

A woman who has dyspareunia often also has **vaginismus**. Vaginismus is an involuntary tightening of the vaginal muscles in response to penetration. It can make intercourse painful or impossible.

The professional's handbook, the ***Diagnostic and Statistical Manual of Mental Disorders***, fourth edition, text revised (*DSM-IV-TR*), classifies this condition as a sexual dysfunction. There is considerably controversy about whether or not dyspareunia should continue to be classified as it has been in the *DSM-IV*, with some practitioners arguing for its reclassification in the *DSM-5* as a **pain disorder**. The *DSM-5* (to be published in 2013) proposes subsuming dyspareunia into a new disorder: Genito-Pelvic Pain/Penetration Disorder. It also proposes listing dyspareunia in males as a diagnosis not elsewhere specified because of the infrequent use of this diagnosis in males.

Causes and symptoms

Causes

Psychosocial causes of dyspareunia include:

- Prior sexual trauma. Many women who have been raped or sexually abused as children may have dyspareunia. Even when a woman wishes to have sex with someone later, the act of intercourse may trigger memories of the trauma and interfere with her enjoyment of the act. Vaginismus often occurs in such situations.
- Guilt, anxiety, or tension about sex. Any of these can cause tense vaginal muscles and also prevent arousal from occurring. People who were raised with the idea that sex is bad may be more prone to have this problem. Fear of pregnancy may make arousal difficult.
- Prior physical trauma to the vaginal area. Women who have had an accidental injury or surgery in the vaginal area may become sensitive to penetration. Vaginismus is common in these cases.
- Depression or anxiety in general. Either of these can lead to loss of interest in sex. This can be experienced by either sex.
- Problems in a relationship. Dyspareunia may occur when a woman feels her sexual partner is abusive or emotionally distant, she is no longer attracted to her partner, or she fears her partner is no longer attracted to her. Men, too, can lose interest in sex because of prior emotional trauma in a relationship; however, the result is usually impotence, rather than dyspareunia.
- Vasocongestion, which can occur when either partner frequently becomes aroused but does not reach orgasm. Vasocongestion is a pooling of blood in dilated blood vessels. Normally, the pelvic area becomes congested with blood when a person becomes sexually aroused. This congestion goes away quickly after orgasm. If there is no orgasm, the congestion takes much longer to resolve.

Any of these factors may cause painful sex. The affected person may then associate pain with sex and find it even harder to relax and become aroused in the future.

Symptoms

The *DSM-IV* diagnostic criteria for dyspareunia are as follows:

- Recurrent or persistent genital pain associated with sexual intercourse in either a male or a female.
- The disturbance causes marked distress or interpersonal difficulty.
- The disturbance is not caused exclusively by vaginismus or lack of lubrication, is not better accounted for by another Axis I disorder (except another sexual dysfunction), and is not due exclusively to the direct physiological effects of a substance (such as a drug of abuse or a medication) or a general medical condition.

The most common symptom of dyspareunia from psychosocial causes is pain at the vaginal opening as the penis enters the vagina. Entry may be difficult, and the pain may be burning or sharp. The woman may have a sense of being "dry." Pain may continue or ease as thrusting continues.

Vasocongestion can cause an aching pain in the pelvic area that persists for hours after intercourse. Pain with orgasm, or pain deep in the pelvis with thrusting, is more likely to be a sign of a medical problem but can result from lack of arousal and tension.

A person who experiences pain during sex may feel embarrassed or ashamed. Dyspareunia can cause problems in relationships or lead to the affected person's avoiding relationships altogether.

Diagnosis

About 30% to 40% of all women who seek help from a sexual counselor for dyspareunia have a clear physical cause identified as the reason for their pain. Examples of possible physical causes are infections, sexually transmitted diseases (STDs), estrogen deficiencies, and vulvar vestibulitis (severe pain during vaginal penetration).

A full family and sexual history can help pinpoint possible psychosocial causes. A psychological evaluation can determine the cause of the problem. Women who have been raped or abused may also have **post-traumatic stress disorder** (PTSD) or **generalized anxiety disorder**.

There are two types of dyspareunia. Lifelong or primary dyspareunia means that the condition has been present for the entire sexual life of the affected person. This type is usually associated with **sexual abuse**, being raised to believe that sex is bad, fear of sex, or a painful first sexual experience. Acquired or secondary dyspareunia begins after a period of normal sexual function. It often has a medical cause, but it may be a result of some sort of **trauma**, such as rape.

Treatment

Some studies have found that treatments that approach dyspareunia resulting from vulvar vestibulitis syndrome as a pain disorder, rather than as a sexual dysfunction, are quite effective in reducing the symptoms of pain.

Counseling is often helpful to identify and reframe negative feelings about sex. **Couples therapy** can help improve communication between partners and resolve problems that may be a factor in the sexual relationship. Women who have been abused or raped may benefit from counseling techniques designed to help overcome fears and issues caused by traumatic experiences.

Sex therapy may be offered to provide information about the physical aspects of arousal and orgasm. A sex therapist will also offer suggestions for how to improve sexual technique. For example, increasing time for foreplay and allowing the woman to control when and how penetration occurs can help her to relax and become aroused more easily.

Women who also have vaginismus may be given a set of devices they can use at home to dilate the opening of the vagina. Affected women start with a very small device and gradually work up to a penis-sized device, proceeding to a larger size only when they can use the smaller one without pain or fear. This retrains the vaginal muscles and helps the involuntary muscle tightening of vaginismus.

Use of a vaginal lubricant, at least temporarily, may be helpful in some women to reduce anxiety about possible pain.

There are no specific medications that treat dyspareunia. Medications that increase blood flow or relax muscles may be helpful in some cases.

Prognosis

With treatment, the chance of overcoming dyspareunia and having an enjoyable sexual life is good. Treatment can take several months, particularly in the case of survivors of a violent trauma such as rape.

KEY TERMS

Vaginismus—An involuntary tightening of the vaginal muscles that makes sexual intercourse painful, difficult, or impossible.

Vasocongestion—A pooling of blood in dilated blood vessels.

Vulvar vestibulitis syndrome (VVS)—Thought to be the most frequent cause of dyspareunia in premenopausal women. A chronic, persistent clinical syndrome, it is characterized by severe pain on vestibular touch or attempted vaginal entry.

Resources

BOOKS

Hales Robert E., Stuart C. Yudofsky, and John A. Talbott, eds. *The American Psychiatric Press Textbook of Psychiatry*. 3rd ed. Washington, DC: American Psychiatric Press, 1999.

Sadock, Benjamin J., and Virginia A. Sadock, eds. *Comprehensive Textbook of Psychiatry*. Vol. 2. 7th ed. Philadelphia: Lippincott Williams and Wilkins, 2000.

PERIODICALS

Binik, Yitzchak M. "Should Dyspareunia be Retained as a Sexual Dysfunction in DSM-V. A Painful Classification Decision." *Archives of Sexual Behavior* 34, no. 1 (February 2005): 11–21.

Heim, Lori J. "Evaluation and Differential Diagnosis of Dyspareunia." *American Family Physician* 63:8 (April 15, 2001): 1535–44. Available online at http://www.aafp.org/afp/20010415/1535.html (accessed November 9, 2011).

WEBSITES

American Academy of Family Physicians. "Dyspareunia: Painful Sex for Women." *Familydoctor.org*. August 2004. http://familydoctor.org/669.xml (accessed October 5, 2011).

Martirosyan, Armen E. "Dyspareunia (Painful Sexual Intercourse)." Armenian Medical Network. http://www.health.am/diseases/more/dyspareunia_painful_sexual_intercourse (accessed October 5, 2011).

MedlinePlus. "Female Sexual Dysfunction." U.S. National Library of Medicine, National Institutes of Health. March 5, 2007. http://www.nlm.nih.gov/medlineplus/ency/article/003151.htm (accessed October 5, 2011).

Jody Bower, MSW
Emily Jane Willingham, PhD

Dysthymic disorder

Definition

Dysthymic disorder is defined as a mood disorder with chronic (long-term) depressive symptoms that are present most of the day, more days than not, for a period of at least two years.

Demographics

The lifetime prevalence has been estimated to be 4.1% for women and 2.2% for men, with an overall rate of 1.5% of people over age 18 in the U.S. population affected in a given year. This percentage, in actual numbers, is about 3.3 million adults. In adults, dysthymic disorder is more common in women than in men and research suggests that the prevalence in the age group 25 to 64 years is 6% for women. In children, dysthymic disorder can occur equally among both genders. The median age of onset is 31 years.

Description

Everyone experiences feelings of unhappiness and sadness occasionally. When these depressed feelings start to dominate everyday life and cause physical and mental deterioration, the feelings become known as depressive disorders. Depressive disorders can be categorized as **major depressive disorder** or dysthymic disorder. Individuals who have dysthymic disorder have had their depressive symptoms for years—they often cannot pinpoint exactly when they started to feel depressed. People with dysthymic disorder may describe to their doctor feelings of hopelessness, lowered self-esteem, poor concentration, indecisiveness, decreased motivation, sleeping too much or too little, or eating too much or too little. Symptoms are present often and for the whole day and are typically present for at least two years.

Causes and symptoms

Causes

The causes of **depression** are complex and not yet completely understood. Sleep abnormalities, hormones, **neurotransmitters** (chemicals that communicate impulses from one nerve cell to another), upbringing, heredity, and stressors (significant life changes or events that cause **stress**) all have been implicated as causes of depression.

Dysthymic disorder occurs in approximately 25% to 50% of persons who have sleep abnormalities that include reduced rapid eye movement (REM) sleep and impaired sleep continuity. REM sleep is an essential component of the sleep cycle and quality of sleep.

There is some evidence that suggests a correlation with hormonal imbalances of cortisol or thyroid hormones. In many adults, levels of cortisol (a stress hormone) are elevated during acute depressive periods and return to normal when the person is no longer depressed. In children and adolescents, experimental results have been quite inconsistent, although there is some evidence that hypersecretion of cortisol is associated with more severe depressive symptoms and with a higher likelihood of recurrence of depression. A lack of thyroid hormone mimics depression quite well, and thyroid hormone levels are routinely checked in patients with recent-onset depression.

In depression, there appears to be abnormal excess or inhibition of signals that control mood, thoughts, pain, and other sensations. Some studies suggest an imbalance of the neurotransmitter called **serotonin**. It is assumed that the reason **antidepressants** are effective is that they correct these chemical imbalances. For example, the **selective serotonin reuptake inhibitors (SSRIs)**, one class of antidepressant medications that includes **fluoxetine** (Prozac), appears to establish a normal level of serotonin. As the name implies, the drug inhibits the reuptake of the serotonin neurotransmitter from the gaps between nerve cells, thus increasing neurotransmitter action, alleviating depressive symptoms.

A child's upbringing may also be key in the development of dysthymic disorder. For example, it is speculated that if a person is abused and neglected throughout childhood and adolescence, a pattern of low self-esteem and negative thinking may emerge, and, from that, a lifelong pattern of depression may follow.

Heredity seems to play a role in the development of depressive disorders. People with major depression in their immediate family are up to three times more likely to have the disorder themselves. It would seem that biological and **genetic factors** may make certain individuals more prone to depressive disorders, but that environmental circumstances, or stressors, may then trigger the disorder.

Symptoms

The mental health professional's handbook to aid in patient **diagnosis** is the ***Diagnostic and Statistical Manual of Mental Disorders***, fourth edition, text revision (*DSM-IV-TR*). The *DSM-IV-TR* has established a list of criteria that can indicate a diagnosis. These criteria include:

- Depressed mood for most of the day, more days than not.
- When depressed, two (or more) of the following are also present: decreased appetite or overeating, too much or too little sleep, low energy level, low self-esteem, decreased ability to concentrate, difficulty making decisions, and/or feelings of hopelessness.
- During the two years of the disorder, the patient has never been without symptoms listed for more than two months at a time.
- No major depressive episode (a more severe form of depression) has been present during the first two years of the disorder.
- There has never been a manic disorder, and criteria for a less severe depression called cyclothymic disorder has never been established.
- The disorder does not exclusively occur with psychosis, schizophrenia, or delusional illnesses.
- The symptoms of depression cause clinically significant impairment and distress in occupational, social, and general functioning.

Dysthymic disorder can be described as "early onset" (onset before age 21 years), "late onset" (onset is age 21 years or older), and "with atypical features" (features that are not commonly observed).

The *DSM-5* (2013) proposes changing the name of the disorder to chronic depressive disorder and eliminating the exclusion of a major depressive episode from its list of criteria for diagnoses.

Diagnosis

To diagnose a patient with this disorder, the *DSM-IV-TR* criteria must be met, and evaluation of this is accomplished through an extensive psychological interview and evaluation. The affected person seeking the clinician's help usually exhibits symptoms of irritability, feelings of worthlessness and hopelessness, crying spells, decreased sex drive, agitation, and thoughts of death. The clinician must rule out any possible medical conditions that can cause depressed affect. (Affect can be defined as the expression of emotion displayed to others through facial expressions, hand gestures, tone of voice, etc.) The diagnosis cannot be made if depression occurs during an active course of **psychosis**, **delusions**, **schizophrenia**, or **schizoaffective disorder**. If **substance abuse** is determined as the cause of depression, then a diagnosis of substance-induced mood disorder can be established.

Further psychological tests that can be administered to help in the diagnostic process include the **Beck Depression Inventory** and the **Hamilton Depression Scale**.

Treatment

The goals of treatment include remission of symptoms and psychological and social recovery.

Medications

Studies suggest some treatment success with medications such as tricyclic antidepressants (TCAs) or monoaminoxidase inhibitors (**MAOIs**). Medications can be effective in patients who have depression due to sleep abnormalities. Some tricyclic antidepressants include **amitriptyline** (Elavil), **imipramine** (Tofranil), and **nortriptyline** (Aventyl, Pamelor), and some MAOIs include **tranylcypromine** (Parnate) and **phenelzine** (Nardil), although these are not considered first-line use antidepressants. **Selective serotonin reuptake inhibitors** (**SSRIs**) are recommended during initial treatment planning after a definitive diagnosis is well established. The most commonly prescribed SSRIs are fluoxetine (Prozac), **sertraline** (Zoloft), **paroxetine** (Paxil), **fluvoxamine** (Luvox), and **citalopram** (Celexa). Trials are currently ongoing to assess the effects of several other drugs on the symptoms of dysthymic disorder.

Psychological therapies

Clinical reports suggest that **cognitive-behavioral therapy**, interpersonal **psychotherapy**, or **family therapy** can be effective with concurrent antidepressant medication to treat the symptoms of depression. In these therapies, the goal is to help the patient develop healthy problem-solving and coping skills.

Prognosis

Dysthymic disorder often begins in late childhood or adolescence. The disorder follows a chronic (long-term) course. The development of a more major form of clinical depression called major depressive disorder among children with dysthymic disorder is significant. Childhood onset of dysthymic disorder is considered an early indicator for recurrent mood disorder that may even have more severe clinical symptoms in the patient's future. Patients with this disorder usually have impaired emotional, social, and physical functioning.

In general, the clinical course of dysthymic disorder is not promising. Causes of a poorer outcome include not completing treatment, noncompliance with medication intake, and lack of willingness to change behaviors that promote a depressed state. However, patients can do very well with a short course of medications if they have a desire to follow psychotherapy treatment recommendations.

If left untreated, dysthymic disorder can result in significant financial and occupational losses. People with this disorder tend to isolate themselves by restricting daily activities and spending days in bed. Patients often complain of poor health and incur more disability days when compared to the general population. Higher rates of successful outcome occur in people who undergo psychotherapy and treatment with appropriate medications.

Prevention

There is no known prevention for dysthymic disorder. Early **intervention** for children with depression may be effective in arresting the development of more severe problems.

Resources

BOOKS

Goldman, Lee, and Andrew I. Schafer, eds. *Goldman's Cecil Medicine,* 24th ed. Philadelphia: Elsevier, 2011.

Tasman, Allan, et al., eds. *Psychiatry*. 3rd ed. New York: Wiley and Sons, 2008.

PERIODICALS

Brown, C. S. "Depression and Anxiety Disorders." *Obstetrics and Gynecology Clinics of North America* 28, no. 2 (June 2001): 241–68.

Youdim, Moussa B.H., Dale Edmondson, and Keith F. Tipton. "The Therapeutic Potential of Monoamine Oxidase Inhibitors." *Nature Reviews Neuroscience* 7, no. 4 (2006): 295–309.

WEBSITES

U.S. National Institute of Mental Health. "The Invisible Disease: Depression." NIH Publication 01-4591. Updated 2002. http://www.intelihealth.com/IH/ihtIH?t=29391&c=192252&p=~br,IHC|~st,8596|~r,EMIHC277|~b,*|&d=dmtContent (accessed October 5, 2011).

U.S. National Institute of Mental Health. "Dysthymic Disorder Among Adults." http://www.nimh.nih.gov/statistics/1DD_ADULT.shtml (accessed October 5, 2011).

Laith Farid Gulli, MD
Linda Hesson, MA, LLP, CAC
Emily Jane Willingham, PhD

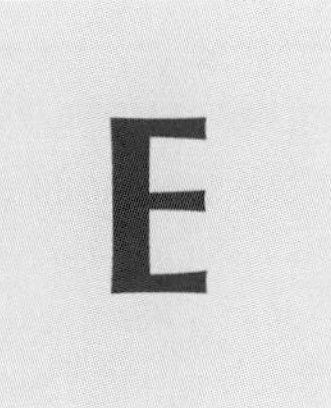

E

Eating disorders *see* **Anorexia nervosa; Binge eating disorder; Bulimia nervosa**

Economic and financial stress

Definition

Economic and financial **stress** is stress caused by a person's money or financial situation and is generally a reaction to the threat or worry of not having enough money to meet basic living needs. This perceived threat, known as a stressor, may result from an unanticipated situation or event that threatens a person's financial stability, or it may be experienced by those who have not yet been able to obtain financial stability.

Demographics

According to the American Psychological Association's *Stress in America* report, in 2010, 76% of Americans cited money as a source of stress. Additional stressors included the general economy (65%), work (70%), and job stability (49%). Women were more likely to stress over money and the economy than men (79% compared to 74% and 68% compared to 61%, respectively). Among different age groups, adults aged 19–64 were more likely to name money as their top source of stress than seniors (65+), who cited the economy.

Description

Economic and financial stress may be arise from a number of circumstances, such as losing a job, moving, going to college, applying for a loan, incurring credit debt, having a child, or buying a house, to name a few. One of the potential factors in developing financial stress is a perceived sense of loss of control, especially when the circumstances surrounding financial stress are unpreventable or unforeseen. A person with a financial "safety net," who can maintain control of his or her life in the event of a layoff or loss of investments, for example, will experience relatively less stress and anxiety from the adverse event. Also, persons who consider their socioeconomic status to be based not only on financial resources but on other factors such as social connections and educational level may feel more optimistic when facing the threat of a financial disruption.

Most approaches to understanding stress emphasize that the cognitive evaluation of an event—that is, how a person thinks about the event—is what leads to the reaction of stress or no stress. After an adverse event, such as the loss of a job, the person evaluates the effects of the event and the amount of resources he or she has to deal with the adversity. If the strength of the resources—financial, social, and psychological—is greater than the strength of the adversity—reduced income—there is less stress. However, if the strength of the adversity is greater than the strength of the resources, there is greater stress. The amount of money a person needs is relative—as a person becomes accustomed to having less, the change in the standard of living starts to feel normal, and what is perceived as normal does not generally cause stress.

Relative deprivation

People tend to compare their circumstances with their peers. If a person perceives him- or herself to have less than friends or neighbors, the person may feel that his or her finances are inadequate. This is known as relative deprivation. Relative deprivation suggests that our evaluation of what is "normal" does not only rest on our own experience but is affected by the experience of others.

Learned helplessness

Another psychological effect of stress is learned helplessness. If rats in a cage receive an electric shock, they will move from the place of the shock to another part of the cage. However, if they receive a shock no matter where in the cage they go, they will lie down and accept the shock. When faced with a stressor, humans look for ways to deal

Percentage of American adults (age 18+) experiencing debt stress, 2009–2011

HOW OFTEN DO YOU WORRY ABOUT THE TOTAL AMOUNT YOU (AND YOUR SPOUSE/PARTNER) OWE IN OVERALL DEBT?

	May/June 2009	November 2009	May 2010	November 2010	June 2011
All/most of the time	19%	23%	21%	20%	20%
All of the time	9%	11%	10%	9%	9%
Most of the time	10%	12%	11%	11%	11%
Some of the time	29%	27%	28%	25%	29%
Hardly ever/not at all	47%	45%	49%	52%	46%
Hardly ever	26%	20%	23%	23%	20%
Not at all	22%	25%	25%	29%	26%
No debt	5%	4%	2%	3%	5%
Don't know	*	*	*	*	*
Refused	*	*	*	*	1%
Total number of persons interviewed	**1,000**	**1,006**	**1,002**	**1,000**	**1,001**

HOW MUCH STRESS DOES THE TOTAL DEBT YOU CARRY CAUSE YOU (AND YOUR SPOUSE/PARTNER)?

	May/June 2009	November 2009	May 2010	November 2010	June 2011
Great deal/quite a bit of stress	17%	22%	20%	18%	16%
Great deal of stress	8%	12%	10%	7%	8%
Quite a bit of stress	9%	11%	10%	11%	8%
Some stress	29%	28%	26%	23%	31%
Not very much/no stress at all	54%	49%	53%	59%	53%
Not very much stress	28%	23%	25%	26%	23%
No stress at all	27%	26%	28%	33%	30%
Don't know	*	*	*	*	*
Refused	-	1%	*	*	1%
Total number of persons interviewed	**941**	**964**	**976**	**973**	**956**

SOURCE: GfK Roper Public Affairs & Corporate Communications, "A Telephone Survey of the American General Population (Ages 18+)," *The AP-GfK Poll*, June 2011.

Report available online at http://surveys.ap.org/data%5CGfK%5CAP-GfK%20Poll_About%20DSI%20072011.pdf. *(Table by PreMediaGlobal.*

with the threat, but if attempts all fail, learned helplessness—often in the form of depression—can develop. Anyone demonstrating the symptoms of agitation, lethargy, and **depression** in response to an aversive financial event may be experiencing economic and financial stress.

Finances and satisfaction with life

Money and financial stability do not necessarily equate with happiness. Satisfaction with life is considered a good resource against stress, although it may not prevent stress completely. A measure of satisfaction with life, as developed by **psychologist** Ed Diener, considers conditions such as having few regrets and achieving major goals. In the United States, for example, income has increased over the years while measures of happiness have remained stable. Since the 1930s, the U.S. government has reported the average per-person income, and since the late 1950s, the National Opinion Research Center has asked participants in a survey study how happy they considered themselves. Although the buying power of individual Americans has steadily increased by nearly three times since 1957, the number of persons describing themselves as "very happy" has remained at close to 30%. If more money led to more happiness, the percentage of people rating themselves as "very happy" should have increased in relation to the increase in disposable income. Happiness is not connected directly with the amount of money one has, and among those who are meeting at least their basic needs (food, shelter), there is no correlation between the amount of income and satisfaction with life.

Risk factors

In general, anyone who misjudges his or her financial security is at risk for economic and financial stress. Those who either do not make financial goals or who strive for unrealistic financial goals are also at risk for economic and financial stress. Further, people who continuously live beyond their means will eventually face the consequences that lead to economic and financial stress.

Causes and symptoms

It is a common perception that an aversive financial event is the cause of the economic and financial stress.

KEY TERMS

"Fight-or-flight" response—A function of the autonomic nervous system that prepares the brain to make an immediate decision to deal with a sudden threat.

Learned helplessness—The tendency to give up on solving a problem when efforts appear to bring no results.

Meditation—Technique of concentration for relaxing the mind and body.

Relative deprivation—The tendency to base one's criteria for normalcy on comparisons with neighbors and relatives.

"Satisfaction with Life"—Term coined by psychologist Ed Diener as a level of satisfaction determined by acceptance of the past, contentment with the present, and optimism for the future.

Socioeconomic status—Perceived status of an individual, family or community based on average income, education level, and social status.

However, the unpleasant event itself is not a stressor—it is the subjective evaluation of the event as a threat that makes it a stressor. As the stock market dips, a multimillionaire might lose more money in one day than most people make in a lifetime. Although unpleasant, this event is not a threat to the multimillionaire, who does not have to change his/her lifestyle or daily pattern.

The physiological effects of stress are the release of hormones usually reserved for reactions to physical danger. When faced with life-threatening situations, the body responds with a "fight-or-flight" reaction—the decision to fight the threat or run away. Natural selection developed "fight or flight" to increase survivability in the face of environmental threats to life. However, modern humans have been shown to react similarly to psychological and social threats. These physiological reactions over time can reduce the efficiency of the immune system. Symptoms of the "fight-or-flight" response include involuntary muscle contractions, increased heart rate, and trouble breathing.

Treatment

Economic and financial stress may be alleviated by finding a solution to the perceived problem. For instance, if the stressor is loss of a job, then searching for a new job may help reduce the stress. If the stressor is credit card debt, cutting up the credit cards to avoid accumulating further debt may help ease anxiety. If the stress persists and begins to interfere with activities of daily life, such as fulfilling familial responsibilities or social zing with friends, the person may wish to see a doctor or therapist to learn about other treatment options.

General treatments for stress

TRADITIONAL. Traditional **psychotherapy** focuses on the patient understanding his or her financial situation clearly. The humanistic approach to counseling encourages individuals to recognize their personal value, which may help counteract any feelings of diminished worth based on financial difficulties. Humanistic counseling often leads participants to more social interactions, which can shift their focus from a financial perspective to deriving pleasure from relationships.

DRUGS. Doctors do not usually prescribe drugs for treatment of commonplace stress brought on by financial difficulties. Some patients may use over-the-counter analgesics but should still discuss this option with their physician. If the stress becomes unmanageable, the doctor might prescribe an antianxiety medication.

ALTERNATIVE. Alternative **stress management** techniques are widely used and are easy for people to do at home. A person might keep a daily record of the onset of stress-related reactions, noting the exact time of the onset, whatever thoughts he or she might had at the onset, and any events that prompted the onset. A therapist can then help the patient evaluate the record and identify any unknown stressors. If the patient recognizes that he or she is putting too much value into these stressors, including financial worries, then the stress reactions may be reduced.

Other alternative therapies include **meditation**, relaxation techniques, massage, **yoga**, **exercise**, **aromatherapy**, and more.

Home remedies

The best thing a person can do to treat financial stress is to organize his or her financial situation. Balancing the household budget is a great first step in regaining control of finances. The person should analyze his or her monthly spending and identify costs that are necessities (e.g., rent, food, bills) and those that are luxuries (dinners out, entertainment). By allotting a portion of income each month to cover all of the necessities, the person is able to see how much is left for luxuries, helping avoid unnecessary spending.

Prevention

Though some circumstances surrounding economic and financial stress are not preventable, such as the state of the national economy or job layoffs, creating and following a budget can help to prevent some financial stress. Saving money, even a little bit at a time, can also help to prevent stress and may help to relieve stress when an unforeseen financial event does arise.

Resources

BOOKS

Durand, V. Mark, and David H. Barlow. *Essentials Of Abnormal Psychology*. Belmont, CA: Wadsworth, Cengage Learning, 2010.

PERIODICALS

Belluck, Pam. "Coping with Financial Stress." *New York Times* (April 8, 2009). http://www.nytimes.com/2009/04/09/health/09stressbox.html (accessed November 3, 2011).

Bruzzese, Anita. "Job, Retirement, Financial Stress Takes Toll on Baby Boomers." *USA Today* (September 9, 2011). http://www.usatoday.com/money/jobcenter/workplace/bruzzese/2011-09-07-tips-to-cope-with-baby-boomers-financial-personal-stresses_n.htm (accessed November 3, 2011).

Wrosch, Carsten, Jutta Heckhausen, and Margie E. Lachman. "Primary and Secondary Control Strategies for Managing Health and Financial Stress Across Adulthood." *Psychology and Aging* 15, no. 3 (2000): 387–99.

OTHER

American Psychological Association. *Stress in America 2010*. Washington, DC: American Psychological Association, 2010. http://www.apa.org/news/press/releases/stress/national-report.pdf (accessed November 3, 2010).

Turner, Jo. "Coping with Financial Stress." University of Florida Extension, Institute of Food and Agricultural Sciences. http://miami-dade.ifas.ufl.edu/old/programs/efnep/publications/Coping-with-Financial-Stress.PDF (accessed November 3, 2011).

WEBSITES

American Psychological Association. "Psychology Topics: Money." http://www.apa.org/topics/money/index.aspx (accessed November 3, 2011).

Cox, Lauren. "Financial Stress: How Bad Can it Get?" ABC News (September 24, 2008). http://abcnews.go.com/Health/story?id=5867963&page=1#.TrMxY3LMqQw (accessed November 3, 2011).

ORGANIZATIONS

American Institute of Stress, 124 Park Avenue, Yonkers, NY, 10703, (914) 963-1200, stress125@optonline.net, http://www.stress.org.

American Psychological Association, 750 1st St. NE, Washington, DC, 20002-4242, (202) 336-5500; TDD/TTY: (202) 336-6123, (800) 374-2721, http://www.apa.org.

National Institute of Mental Health, 6001 Executive Blvd., Rm. 8184, MSC 9663, Bethesda, MD, 20892-9663, (301) 443-4513, (866) 615-6464, nimhinfo@nih.gov, http:// www.nimh.nih.gov.

Ray F. Brogan, PhD

Ecstasy

Definition

Ecstasy is the popular name for the synthetic, psychoactive drug 3,4-methylenedioxymethamphetamine, or MDMA. It is chemically similar to **methamphetamine** and the hallucinogen mescaline. MDMA acts both as a stimulant and psychedelic, producing an energizing effect as well as distortions in time and perception and enhanced enjoyment from tactile experiences. MDMA exerts its primary effects in the **brain** on neurons that use the chemical **serotonin** to communicate with other neurons. The serotonin system plays an important role in regulating mood, aggression, sexual activity, sleep, and sensitivity to pain. Ecstasy has a large number of other street names. These include Adam, B-bombs, bean, Blue Nile, clarity, crystal, decadence, disco biscuit, E, essence, Eve, go, hug drug, Iboga, love drug, morning shot, pollutants, Rolls Royce, Snackies, speed for lovers, sweeties, wheels, X, and XTC.

Demographics

Ecstasy is one of a group of drugs known as club drugs, because the drug is used primarily in dance clubs, at raves, and at dances on college and high school campuses. Use is more common in urban areas. Most users of ecstasy are white teenagers and young adults from middle- and upper-class households. The U.S. Office of National Drug Control Policy reports that, according to the National Survey on Drug Use and Health (NSDUH), in 2010, an estimated 695,000 Americans had used MDMA in the past

Emergency department visits involving ecstasy, 2008

Drugs taken	Number of visits
Ecstasy only	3,968
Ecstasy in combination with other drugs	13,897
One other drug	5,584
Two other drugs	2,682
Three other drugs	2,502
Four or more other drugs	3,129
Total ecstasy-related visits	**17,865**

The drugs most commonly used with ecstasy were marijuana (38.2% of cases), alcohol (38.1%), and cocaine (31.8%).

SOURCE: Substance Abuse and Mental Health Services Administration, Center for Behavioral Health Statistics and Quality, "Emergency Department Visits Involving Ecstasy," *The DAWN Report* (March 24, 2011).

Available online at http://oas.samhsa.gov/2k11/DAWN027/Ecstasy.htm. *(Table by PreMediaGlobal.*

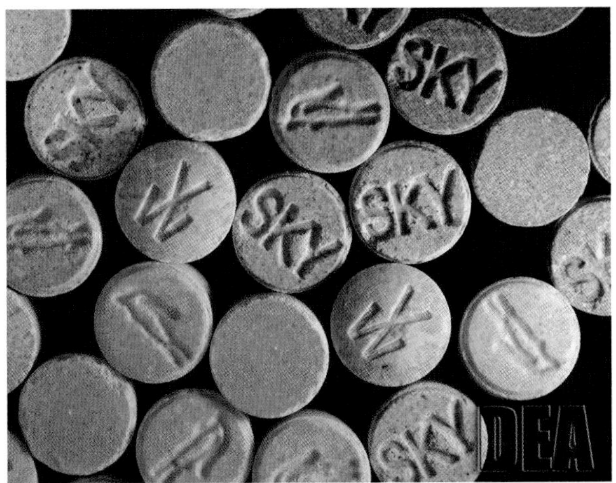

Ecstasy tablets. *(U.S. Drug Enforcement Administration)*

month (considered to be current users of ecstasy), with almost one million Americans using ecstasy for the first time in 2010.

Although the use of ecstasy by teenagers and young adults rose between 1996 and 2002, use appeared to decrease over subsequent years. *Monitoring the Future*, a study conducted every year by the University of Michigan and funded by the National Institute on Drug Abuse (NIDA), surveys middle- and high-school students on their drug use. In 2010, the survey found that 2.4% of eighth graders, 4.7% of tenth graders, and 4.5% of twelfth graders surveyed reported that they had used ecstasy at least once in the past year. In contrast, in 2002, 4.3% of eighth graders, 6.6% of tenth graders, and 10.5% of twelfth graders reported having used ecstasy.

Description

MDMA was first synthesized in 1912 by the German pharmaceutical company Merck. Merck patented the drug in 1914. The U.S. military conducted some studies of MDMA in the 1950s, but the public knew virtually nothing about the drug until the 1970s. In the early 1970s, a few psychotherapists and psychiatrists began to explore the therapeutic uses of MDMA. They believed that they could help people benefit more from treatment if they combined doses of MDMA with **psychotherapy**. The number of clinicians who used MDMA as an adjunct to psychotherapy grew in the next few years.

The name "ecstasy" was coined in the early 1980s, when distributors began to envision a larger market for the drug. Ecstasy became popular as a club drug and was often sold in nightclubs and bars. Because of reports of increases in the recreational use of ecstasy and scientific reports suggesting that the related drug MDA could cause brain damage, the U.S. Drug Enforcement Administration (DEA) banned both ecstasy and 3,4-methylenedioxyamphetamine (MDA) in the mid-1980s. Following the ban on ecstasy, a lawsuit was filed against the DEA by a group of physicians who believed that ecstasy has therapeutic value. Despite the lawsuit, the DEA ban on ecstasy became permanent. As of 2011, ecstasy was classified as a Schedule I drug. Schedule I drugs are considered to have high potential for abuse and no currently accepted medical value. They are not considered safe for use even under medical supervision. It is illegal to use, sell, or manufacture ecstasy in the United States. Ecstasy that is seized by the DEA is manufactured mainly in the Netherlands, Belgium, and Canada, although some is also illegally made in laboratories in the United States.

The recreational use of ecstasy continued to increase despite the DEA ban. Through the late 1980s and 1990s, ecstasy began to be used widely at raves, which are all-night dance parties often held in warehouses and attended by large numbers of young people.

Ecstasy is sometimes described as an "entactogen," because it gives users feelings of peacefulness, acceptance, empathy, euphoria, and closeness to others. Ecstasy is typically synthesized from precursor chemicals such as piperonyl methylketone, piperonal, isosafrole, or safrole. Safrole is an essential oil that is found in the tree *Sassafras albidum*, which grows in the eastern United States, and in the tree *Ocotea pretiosa*, which grows in South America. Safrole is also found in nutmeg, dill, parsley seed, crocus, **saffron**, vanilla beans, and calamus.

Some people use a product called herbal ecstasy. The main constituents of herbal ecstasy are legal herbs that are stimulants such as ephedra, guarana, and caffeine. Other herbs and vitamins may also be included. Herbal ecstasy is sold in tablet form as Cloud 9, Herbal Bliss, Ritual Spirit, Herbal X, GWM, Rave Energy, Ultimate Xphoria, and X. The quantities of ephedrine and caffeine in the tablets can vary widely. Although people who take herbal ecstasy believe it to be a legal, safe alternative to ecstasy, there are reports of numerous adverse effects, including severe reactions such as high blood pressure, **seizures**, heart attacks, strokes, and death.

Method of administration

Most users take ecstasy orally. Users also sometimes inhale or inject it. Although ecstasy is available as a capsule or a powder, it usually is sold in tablet form. The tablets are available in different colors, shapes, and sizes, and are often imprinted with logos such as smiley faces, clover leaves, cartoon characters, or the logos of popular commercial brands, such as those for clothing or automobiles. On average, an ecstasy tablet has about 100 mg of MDMA. However, the MDMA content in tablets can vary a great deal. Pure MDMA salt, which is a white, bitter-tasting substance, is usually not the only ingredient in ecstasy tablets. The MDMA in ecstasy tablets is often blended with other drugs such as caffeine, aspirin, dextromethorphan, ephedrine, methamphetamine, and MDA.

Psychotherapeutic use of ecstasy

Some psychiatrists and psychotherapists still advocate for the therapeutic use of ecstasy. While most of these professionals believe that recreational use of ecstasy is likely to be unsafe, they argue that small doses of unadulterated MDMA can be used effectively as an adjunct to psychotherapy, when used once or twice in a controlled therapeutic setting. They believe that MDMA is beneficial because it can help patients put aside their anxiety and fear and explore psychological issues that would normally be too painful to confront. Although ecstasy-assisted psychotherapy may also be indicated in other situations, it is thought to be particularly helpful in the treatment of **post-traumatic stress disorder** (PTSD) and to help people with terminal illness deal with the fear of dying.

Long-term damage resulting from MDMA use

MDMA causes the release of the **neurotransmitters dopamine** and serotonin and the neurohormone norepinephrine. Research on the long-term effects of MDMA has mainly focused on cognition and behavioral changes related to serotonin levels.

The NIDA reports that studies provide direct evidence that chronic use of MDMA causes brain damage in humans. Using advanced brain imaging techniques, one study found that MDMA harms neurons that release serotonin (serotonin plays an important role in regulating memory and other mental functions). In a related study, researchers found that people who use MDMA heavily have memory problems that persist for at least two weeks after stopping use of the drug. Both studies strongly suggest that the extent of damage is directly related to the amount of MDMA used.

Another study, reported by the *Journal of Neurology Neurosurgery and Psychiatry* on April 6, 2011, supported the hypothesis that long-term users of ecstasy are at risk for brain damage. The study included a total of 17 men; 10 who were in their 20s and were long-term users of ecstasy, and 7 in their 20s who had never used the drug. In a study performed by a group of Dutch researchers, magnetic resonance imaging (MRI) brain scans of the ecstasy users showed an approximate 10% shrinkage in the volume of the hippocampus (a portion of the brain responsible for the functions of learning and memory). The brain scans revealed that the ecstasy users (having taken ecstasy tablets over a six-and-a-half year period) had about 10.5% less hippocampal volume than non-users of ecstasy, as well as a lower (about 4.6% on average) proportion of grey matter in the brain, suggesting that long-term effects of ecstasy may not be limited to the hippocampus. Researchers noted as well that shrinkage of the hippocampus is already known as one finding in older patients who have diseases associated with cognitive impairment, such as **Alzheimer's disease**.

Animal studies indicate that repeated doses of MDMA show long-term decreases in concentrations of serotonin and that ecstasy may cause long-term brain damage from severe damage to brain cells. Brain scans and **psychological assessment** of humans using ecstasy suggest that damage to brain cells may cause memory loss or psychological problems due to destruction of serotonin-producing neurons in the brain. In addition, damage to neurons that regulate dopamine may cause motor disturbances in humans (such as in Parkinson's disease), resulting in tremors, unsteady gait, and paralysis.

Use of MDMA produces cardiovascular effects of increased blood pressure, heart rate, and heart oxygen consumption. People with pre-existing heart disease are at increased risk for cardiovascular catastrophe resulting from MDMA use. Toxicity may rise dramatically when users take multiple doses over brief periods, leading to harmful reactions such as dehydration, hyperthermia, and seizures. Long-term abuse can lead to memory loss.

MDMA tablets often contain other drugs, such as ephedrine, a stimulant, and dextromethorphan, a cough suppressant with PCP-like effects at high doses. These additives increase the harmful effects of MDMA. They also appear to have toxic effects on the brain's serotonin system. In tests of learning and memory, people who use MDMA perform more poorly than people who do not use it. Research with primates shows that MDMA can cause long-lasting brain damage. Exposure to MDMA during the period of pregnancy in which the fetal brain is developing is associated with learning deficits that last into adulthood.

Causes and symptoms

Like other drug use, the decision to use ecstasy results from complex combinations of factors such as genetic predisposition to risk taking, family history, **stress**, and peer pressure.

Ecstasy is absorbed quickly after it is taken orally, and it can be detected in the blood within about 30 minutes. It typically has its effect within 20–60 minutes after it is ingested. The average time for onset of effects is 30 minutes. It has its peak effects about 60–90 minutes after it is ingested. The main effects of ecstasy last about 3–5 hours. Women are more sensitive to ecstasy than men and are more likely to experience an optimal effect of the drug at a lower dose, in proportion to body weight, than men.

Ecstasy mimics the effects of the neurotransmitter serotonin, activating cell receptors in the brain that normally respond to serotonin. Serotonin is involved in many processes in the body, including the regulation of mood, aggression, sexual activity, sleep, sensitivity to pain, and eating. MDMA also causes the release of serotonin, as well as the neurotransmitters norepinephrine and dopamine. The levels of hormones such as cortisol, prolactin, and testosterone increase when ecstasy is used. The level of vasopressin, a hormone that is involved in elevating blood pressure and retaining water in the body, also increases.

Ecstasy users report intensely pleasurable experiences after taking ecstasy. They feel euphoric and are more aware of sensory stimuli. Users often wear fluorescent jewelry or accessories and use mentholated ointments or sprays to enhance the sensory effects they experience. Users of ecstasy usually feel socially uninhibited and close to other people. They find that they have an increased sense of empathy. They also claim to become emotionally open and have exceptionally clear insight into themselves. Time perception may become distorted. Because ecstasy has a stimulant effect, users often feel energetic and can remain awake for long periods. Ecstasy increases sensuality, but it does not directly increase sexual drive or appetite. However, because it decreases inhibitions and makes users more open to others, users sometime engage in sexual activity after taking ecstasy. Men sometimes experience delayed orgasms, although orgasms may be more intense than usual.

Ecstasy users sometimes have undesirable experiences. In one research study, about 25% of users reported having gone through at least one occasion when ecstasy use resulted in unpleasant experiences and body sensations. Short-term adverse reactions that have been reported include dilated pupils, unusual sensitivity to bright light, headache, sweating, increased heart rate, tooth grinding (bruxism), spasms of the jaw muscle (trismus), loss of appetite, nausea, muscle aches, **fatigue**, dizziness, vertigo, thirst, numbness, tingling skin, retention of urine, staggering gait (ataxia), unsteadiness, tics, tremors, restlessness, agitation, **paranoia**, and nystagmus. Research has shown that driving a car under the influence of ecstasy is unsafe.

The scientific literature on the effects of ecstasy is somewhat inconsistent. This is partly because well-controlled studies cannot be carried out on ecstasy use. However, many in the scientific community agree that brain levels of serotonin increase when ecstasy is ingested and that they decrease after an episode of ecstasy use. The depletion of serotonin is thought to cause "midweek blues." This term refers to the lethargy, concentration and memory problems, and depressed mood that many ecstasy users experience for a few days after taking the drug. Other changes that occur for a few days after ecstasy use are increased feelings of aggressiveness, unsociability, irritability, decreased appetite, and poor sleep. Some researchers have reported that chronic, heavy ecstasy use is associated with **sleep disorders**, **depression**, high levels of anxiety, impulsiveness and hostility, and problems with memory and attention. Memory and attention deficits may continue for up to 6 months after drug use is stopped, but symptoms are reported to remit after 6 to 12 months. The extent of cognitive deficits may depend on the number of tablets taken per occasion of use.

Ecstasy causes body temperature to increase. Abnormal increases in body temperature are more likely when the user is in a hot environment, such as on a crowded dance floor. A number of ecstasy-related deaths have been reported that are attributable to drug-induced increases in body temperature. Several users who later died were admitted to hospitals with abnormally high temperatures, ranging from 104°F (40°C) to 109°F (43°C). The immediate cause of death in these users was damage to organs such as the liver and heart. Other deaths have occurred because of water intoxication, which can develop when ecstasy users drink too much water to combat hyperthermia. The increase in vasopressin that accompanies the use of ecstasy makes excessive water intake particularly dangerous. Water intoxication results in decreased levels of sodium in the blood, which can be fatal.

Ecstasy users appear to develop tolerance to the drug with repeated use, needing more of it to achieve the effect they desire. Novice users tend to take one or two tablets per session, whereas highly experienced users may take more than three tablets per session. The use of increased doses may exacerbate the amphetamine-like effects of the drug. Heavy users sometimes binge use, either by taking several tablets simultaneously or by repeatedly taking tablets during a single session that may last up to 48 hours. In such binging sessions, users may go without sleep or food and sometimes consume up to 20 tablets. In some cases, binge users snort powdered ecstasy or inject it. Binging on ecstasy can result in consequences such as

KEY TERMS

Catecholamines—Family of neurotransmitters containing dopamine, norepinephrine and epinephrine, produced and secreted by cells of the adrenal medulla and the brain. Catecholamines have excitatory effects on smooth muscle cells of the vessels that supply blood to the skin and mucous membranes and have inhibitory effects on smooth muscle cells located in the wall of the gut, the bronchial tree of the lungs, and the vessels that supply blood to skeletal muscle. There are two different main types of receptors for these neurotransmitters, called alpha and beta adrenergic receptors. Catecholamines are also known as adrenergic neurotransmitters.

Dopamine—A neurochemical made in the brain that is involved in many brain activities, including movement and emotion.

Neurotransmitter—One of a group of chemicals secreted by a nerve cell (neuron) to carry a chemical message to another nerve cell, often as a way of transmitting a nerve impulse. Examples of neurotransmitters are acetylcholine, dopamine, serotonin, and norepinephrine.

Norepinephrine—A hormone released by nerve cells and the adrenal medulla that causes constriction of blood vessels. Norepinephrine also functions as a neurotransmitter.

Serotonin—5-Hydroxytryptamine; a substance that occurs throughout the body with numerous effects, including neurotransmission. Low serotonin levels are associated with mood disorders, particularly depression and obsessive-compulsive disorder.

loss of appetite, weight loss, days off from work, and depression.

Diagnosis

Diagnosis of ecstasy use is difficult, because the effects tend to wear off after a few hours and because individuals who use ecstasy often use other drugs as well, making the effects difficult to separate.

Treatment

There are no drug treatments for ecstasy use. Behavioral interventions have proved most successful. In **cognitive-behavioral therapy**, users learn to recognize, manage, and avoid situations most likely to lead to illicit drug use, and develop healthy ways to cope with stressful situations. Ecstasy is psychologically addictive in as many as 43% of users, so issues of dependency must be addressed, as must the use of other drugs in conjunction with ecstasy use.

Prognosis

There are scientific and political debates about whether ecstasy causes long-term damage to the human brain. Some researchers and drug enforcement agencies claim that ecstasy is a dangerous drug capable of causing irreversible brain damage, and other researchers suggest that claims of irreversible neurotoxicity in humans are exaggerated and unproven. Because of ethical considerations, ecstasy cannot be given to people who do not use it to study its effects on the brain. However, studies of brain function are sometimes carried out in people who already take ecstasy, using brain-imaging technology. These types of studies are methodologically complex, and results are interpretable in various ways. Therefore, controversy continues about the potential long-term effects of ecstasy on the human brain.

Studies conducted on rats and monkeys have shown that high doses of ecstasy can have long-term negative effects on neurons that contain serotonin. Serotonin levels become depleted in these animals, and serotonin-containing nerves become damaged. The degeneration of neurons is exacerbated when the animals are placed in high-temperature environments. In these types of studies, animals are usually given very high doses of ecstasy, and the drug is usually injected. Some researchers have argued that the results of these animal studies cannot be extrapolated to human users, who use much lower doses and typically ingest the drug orally.

Methodological and ethical problems in ecstasy research

Scientific research on ecstasy use has some limitations. Because ecstasy is classified as a Schedule I drug, researchers cannot easily conduct controlled experimental studies by administering MDMA to people in laboratories. Additionally, people who use ecstasy often use other drugs, such as heroin, **cocaine**, and ketamine, either deliberately or as a result of using contaminated ecstasy. Therefore, it is difficult to determine whether effects observed in users are due to the current or previous use of these other drugs, the use of ecstasy, or the combination of ecstasy with other drugs. Scientists also cannot easily determine whether effects noted in ecstasy users are due to drug use or the personal characteristics of people who choose to use ecstasy recreationally.

Although psychiatrists and psychotherapists used ecstasy in the 1970s as an adjunct to psychotherapy, no controlled **clinical trials** were conducted at the time that could provide evidence for its therapeutic efficacy. After ecstasy became classified as a Schedule I drug, it became difficult for researchers to study its psychotherapeutic uses, because institutional review boards typically do not approve research studies that have the potential for causing harm to humans who participate in them.

Prevention

Social networks and peer pressure play major roles in starting ecstasy use. Peer-led education about the risks of ecstasy is thought to be more effective than adult-led education programs.

Resources

BOOKS

Erickson, Carlton K. *Addiction Essentials: The Go-To Guide for Clinicians and Patients.* New York: Norton, 2011.

Galanter, Marc, and Herbert D. Kleber, eds. *Textbook of Substance Abuse Treatment,* 2nd ed. Washington, DC: American Psychiatric Press, 2008.

Holland, Julie, ed. *Ecstasy: The Complete Guide.* Kindle edition. Rochester, VT: Park Street Press, 2010.

Iversen, Leslie. *Speed, Ecstasy, Ritalin: The Science of Amphetamines.* Oxford: Oxford University Press, 2006.

PERIODICALS

Den Hollander, Bjørnar, et al. "Preliminary Evidence of Hippocampal Damage in Chronic Users of Ecstasy." *Journal of Neurology Neurosurgery and Psychiatry* 28, no. 3 (2011): 1136.

Dumont, G.J.H., and R.J. Verkes. "A Review of Acute Effects of 3,4-Methylenedioxymethamphetamine in Healthy Volunteers." *Journal of Psychopharmacology* 20, no. 2 (2006): 176.

Gahlinger, Paul M. "Club Drugs: MDMA, Gamma-hydroxy-butyrate (GHB), Rohypnol, and Ketamine." *American Family Physician* 69, no. 11 (2004): 2619.

Watkins, Katherine E., et al. "An Update on Adolescent Drug Use: What School Counselors Need to Know." *Professional School Counseling* 10, no. 2 (2006): 131–39.

WEBSITES

"Club Drugs." MedlinePlus. Last updated September 2, 2011. http://www.nlm.nih.gov/medlineplus/clubdrugs.html (accessed October 3, 2011).

"Ecstasy: What We Know and Don't Know About MDMA: A Scientific Review." National Institute on Drug Abuse, July 2001. http://www.drugabuse.gov/Meetings/MDMA/MDMAExSummary.html (accessed October 3, 2011).

Finefrock, Douglas C., Mai Kim Lai, and Karen Tonya Mason. "Club Drugs." eMedicinehealth, October 17, 2005. http://www.emedicinehealth.com/club_drugs/article_em.htm (accessed October 3, 2011).

Hahn, In-Hei. "MDMA Toxicity." Medscape Reference, January 26, 2009. http://emedicine.medscape.com/article/821572-overview (accessed October 3, 2011).

ORGANIZATIONS

American Psychological Association, 750 1st St. NE, Washington, DC, 20002-4242, (202) 336-5500; TDD/TTY: (202) 336-6123, (800) 374-2721, http://www.apa.org.

National Clearinghouse on Alcohol and Drug Information, PO Box 2345, Rockville, MD, 20847, (877) SAMHSA-7; Spanish: (877) 767-8432; TDD: (800) 487-4889, Fax: (240) 221-4292, http://ncadi.samhsa.gov.

National Council on Alcoholism and Drug Dependence, Inc., 244 E 58th St., 4th Fl., New York, NY, 10022, (212) 269-7797, (800) NCA-CALL, Fax: (212) 269-7510, national@mcadd.org, http://www.ncadd.org.

National Institutes of Health, 9000 Rockville Pike, Bethesda, MD, 20892, (301) 496-4000; TTY: (301) 402-9612, http://www.nih.gov.

U.S. National Library of Medicine, 8600 Rockville Pike, Bethesda, MD, 20894, (301) 594-5983, (800) 735-2258, Fax: (301) 402-1384, http://www.nlm.nih.gov.

Barbara S. Sternberg, PhD
Emily Jane Willingham, PhD
Laura Jean Cataldo, RN, EdD

EEG *see* **Electroencephalography**

Effexor *see* **Venlafaxine**

Elavil *see* **Amitriptyline**

Elder abuse

Definition

Elder **abuse** is a general term used to describe harmful acts toward an elderly adult, such as physical abuse, **sexual abuse**, emotional or psychological abuse, financial exploitation, and **neglect**, including self-neglect.

Demographics

Results from the National Elder Abuse Incidence Study, funded in part by the Administration on Aging, suggest that over 500,000 people 60 years of age and older are abused or neglected each year in the United States. It was also found that four times as many incidents of abuse, neglect, or self-neglect are never reported, causing researchers to estimate that as many as two million elderly persons in the United States are abused each year. In 90% of the cases, the abusers were

Types of elder abuse

Type[†]	Description	Examples
Financial exploitation	Illegal or improper use of an older adult's funds, property, or assets	Cashing checks without authorization, forging signatures, misusing or stealing money or possessions
Neglect	Refusal or failure to fulfill any part of a person's obligation or duties to an older adult	Refusing or failing to provide an older adult with such necessities as food, water, clothing, shelter, personal hygiene, medicine, comfort, personal safety, and other essentials
Physical abuse	Use of physical force that may result in bodily injury, physical pain, or impairment	Striking with an object, hitting, pushing, shoving
Psychological abuse±	Infliction of anguish, pain, or distress through verbal or nonverbal acts	Verbal assaults, insults, threats, intimidation, humiliation, and harassment
Sexual abuse	Nonconsensual sexual contact of any kind	Unwanted touching, rape, sodomy, coerced nudity

[†]Federal and state law may define these terms differently.
±Psychological abuse can also be referred to as verbal or emotional abuse.

SOURCE: U.S. Government Accountability Office, *Elder Justice: Stronger Federal Leadership Could Enhance National Response to Elder Abuse*, a report to the chairman, Senate Special Committee on Aging, U.S. Senate, March 2011.

Report available online at http://www.gao.gov/new.items/d11208.pdf. *(Table by PreMediaGlobal. © 2012 Cengage Learning.)*

found to be family members, and most often were the adult children or spouses of those abused. In addition, equal numbers of men and women have been identified as the abusers. However, women, especially those over 80 years of age, tend to be victimized more than men.

Description

Elder abuse can take place anywhere, but the two main settings addressed by law are domestic settings, such as the elder's home or the caregiver's home, and institutional settings, such as a nursing home or group home. In general, there are five basic types of elderly abuse: physical, sexual, emotional or psychological, financial, and neglect. Data from the National Center on Elder Abuse (NCEA) indicate that more than one-half of the cases reported involve some kind of neglect, whereas 1 in 7 cases involve physical abuse. It is considered neglect when a caretaker deprives an elderly person of the necessary care needed in order to avoid physical or mental harm. Sometimes the behavior of an elderly person threatens his or her own health; in those cases, the abuse is called self-neglect. Physical abuse refers to physical force that causes bodily harm to an elderly person, such as slapping, pushing, kicking, pinching, or burning.

Adult Protective Services estimates of elder abuse reports received, investigations, and substantiations (proven cases) in state fiscal year 2009

	Number in state fiscal year 2009	Number of states responding
Reports received[†]	357,000	31
Investigations	292,000	33
Substantiations	95,000	27

[†]States provided data on reports received prior to any screening for eligibility.

SOURCE: U.S. Government Accountability Office, *Elder Justice: Stronger Federal Leadership Could Enhance National Response to Elder Abuse*, a report to the chairman, Senate Special Committee on Aging, U.S. Senate, March 2011.

Report available online at http://www.gao.gov/new.items/d11208.pdf. *(Table by PreMediaGlobal. © 2012 Cengage Learning.)*

About 1 in 8 cases of elderly abuse involve some form of financial exploitation, which is defined as the use of an elderly person's resources without his or her consent. The NCEA defines emotional and psychological abuse of a senior as causing anguish, pain, or distress through verbal or nonverbal acts, such as verbal assaults, insults, intimidation, and humiliation, for example. Isolating elderly persons from their friends and family as well as giving them the silent treatment are two other forms of emotional and psychological abuse. Any kind of non-consensual sexual contact with an elderly person that takes place without his or her consent is considered sexual abuse.

Causes and symptoms

Elder abuse is a complex problem that can be caused by many factors. According to the NCEA, social isolation and mental impairment are two factors of elder abuse. Studies show that people advanced in years, such as in their eighties, with a high level of frailty and dependency, are more likely to be victims of elder abuse than people who are younger and better equipped to stand up for themselves. Because spouses make up a large percentage of elder abusers, at least 40% statistically, some research has been done in the area, which shows that a pattern of domestic violence is associated with many of the cases. The risk of elder abuse appears to be especially high when adult children live with their elderly parents for financial reasons or because they have personal problems, such as drug dependency or mental illness. Some experts have speculated that elderly people living in rural areas with their caretakers may have a higher risk of being abused than city dwellers. The idea behind this theory is that the opportunity exists for the abuse to occur, but there is less likelihood that the abuser will be caught. More research in this very important area is needed in order to illuminate the relationship between these factors.

The NCEA identifies the following as signs of elder abuse:

- Bruises, pressure marks, broken bones, abrasions, and burns may indicate physical abuse or neglect.
- Unexplained withdrawal from normal activities and unusual depression may be indicators of emotional abuse.
- Bruises around the breasts or genital area, as well as unexplained bleeding around the genital area, may be signs of sexual abuse.
- Large withdrawals of money from an elder's bank account, sudden changes in a will, and the sudden disappearance of valuable items may be indications of financial exploitation.
- Bedsores, poor hygiene, unsanitary living conditions, and unattended medical needs may be signs of neglect.
- Failure to take necessary medicines, leaving a burning stove unattended, poor hygiene, confusion, unexplained weight loss, and dehydration may all be signs of self-neglect.

Effects on the abused can be devastating. Victims of elder abuse have the potential to experience extensive and debilitating loss, including financial loss associated with the loss of a home or loss of life savings. In addition, they may suffer loss of health and preventative care, resulting in deleterious mental and physical well-being. Many of these victims suffer loss that is difficult to quantify such as loss of independence, security, and dignity, while feeling **grief**, **depression**, and helplessness.

Victims of nursing home abuse or neglect are especially vulnerable. Nursing homes are regulated by state agencies and are mandated to have staff who are licensed, trained, supervised, and responsible for safe and compassionate treatment of individuals in their care. In the event of any kind of abuse (known or just in question), families may choose to retain an attorney with a background in nursing home and elder abuse issues to assist in determining the possibility of abuse and to help in negotiating appropriate action.

KEY TERMS

Mortality rate—A measure of the number of deaths in a specific population, usually expressed per 1,000 per year.

National Center on Elder Abuse (NCEA)—Association directed by the U.S. Administration on Aging dedicated to the prevention of elder mistreatment; a resource center, assisting at national, state and local levels.

National Committee for the Prevention of Elder Abuse (NCPEA)—Association established in 1988 and dedicated to assuring the safety, security, and dignity of elderly citizens; also serves to provide information and education relating to the prevention of elder abuse.

Diagnosis

The National Committee for the Prevention of Elder Abuse notes that Adult Protective Services (APS) caseworkers are often on the front lines when it comes to elderly abuse. People being abused or those who believe abuse is taking place can turn to their local APS office for help. The APS routinely screens calls, keeps all information confidential, and, if necessary, sends a caseworker out to conduct an investigation. In the event that a **crisis intervention** is needed, the APS caseworker can arrange for any necessary emergency treatment. If it is unclear whether elder abuse has taken place, the APS caseworker can serve as a liaison between the elderly person and other community agencies.

According to the National Committee for the Prevention of Elder Abuse, "professionals in the field of aging are often the first to discover signs of elder abuse." Providing encouragement and advice, they play a critical role in educating others with regard to the needs of the elderly. They provide valuable support to the victims of abuse and also monitor high-risk situations and gather important information that can help confirm that abuse has taken place.

Some people might think that a person who has cognitive impairment might be unable to describe mistreatment; however, that is not the case. In fact, guidelines set by the American Medical Association call for "routine questions about abuse and neglect even among patients with cognitive impairment in order to improve the identification of cases and implement appropriate treatment and referral." Rather than an inability to describe mistreatment, what might stop an elderly person from reporting abuse is a sense of embarrassment or fear of retaliation. To complicate matters, differences exist among cultural groups regarding what defines abuse.

Most states have established laws that define elder abuse and require healthcare providers to report any cases they encounter with penalties attached for failing to do so. Indeed, statistics show that healthcare providers, for example, report almost 25% of the known cases of elder abuse. Therefore, physicians play a very important role in identifying and treating elders who have been abused. Yet only 1 of every 13 cases of elder abuse are estimated to be reported by physicians. There may be several reasons for this pattern. In some cases, the problem may simply go unnoticed, especially if the physician has no obvious reason to suspect any wrongdoing. In other cases, the patient may hide or deny the problem.

In recent years, much media attention has been focused on elderly abuse that takes place in institutional settings. Anyone who believes that a loved one is being abused while in a nursing home or other institutional setting should contact the authorities for assistance immediately.

Treatment

Treatment of elderly persons who have been abused may involve medical care, for treating any injuries; psychotherapy, for treating the emotional trauma; and legal action.

Prognosis

The mortality rate of elderly persons who have been mistreated is higher than the mortality rate of an elderly person who has not experienced abuse. Nonetheless, numerous success stories exist regarding interventions. **Social workers** and healthcare professionals, as well as concerned citizens from a variety of backgrounds, have played a key role in identifying and obtaining treatment for abused elders.

The NCEA and other groups associated with preventing elder abuse work to carry out public awareness activities to increase national awareness and prevention of elder abuse and maintain efforts to secure safe care for elder individuals. Engaging in public awareness campaigns with state, regional, and national organizations is ongoing, including ad campaigns, dissemination of resource materials, and public education on this topic. The NCEA urges individuals, families, organizations, and businesses to join them in preventing elder mistreatment.

Prevention

Planning for the future is one of the best ways to avoid elder abuse. Older persons should consider a variety of retirement options, ones that will encourage safety as well as independence. It is important to stay active in the community. Avoiding isolation minimizes the likelihood that abuse will occur. Individuals ought to seek professional counsel when necessary; it is important for everyone to know their rights and to be advocates on their own behalf.

QUESTIONS TO ASK YOUR DOCTOR

- What are the indications that my loved one may be a victim of elder abuse?
- What examinations are needed for a thorough assessment?
- What measures can be taken to prevent elder abuse?
- How can the quality of life of my loved one be improved?
- Can you recommend an organization that will provide me with additional information about elder abuse?

Resources

BOOKS

Brogden, Mike, and Preeti Nijhar. *Crime, Abuse and the Elderly.* Portland OR: Willan, 2011.

Buchanan, Paul D. *Protecting the Shadow: A Year Inside an Adult Protective Services.* Wellesley, MA: Branden Books, 2011.

Payne, Brian K. *Crime and Elder Abuse,* 3rd ed. Springfield, IL: Charles C. Thomas, 2011.

Pyrek, Kelly M. *Healthcare Crime: Investigating Abuse, Fraud, and Homicide by Caregivers.* Boca Raton, FL: CRC Press, 2011.

WEBSITES

The National Elder Abuse Incidence Study, September 1998. http://www.aoa.gov/AoARoot/AoA_Programs/Elder_Rights/Elder_Abuse/docs/ABuseReport_Full.pdf (accessed October 3, 2011).

"Signs of Nursing Home Abuse." Nursing Home Abuse Center. http://www.nursinghomeabusecenter.org/signs-of-abuse.html (accessed October 3, 2011).

ORGANIZATIONS

American Academy of Family Physicians, 11400 Tomahawk Creek Pkwy., Leawood, KS, 66211-2672, (913) 906-6000, (800) 274-2237, Fax: (913) 906-6075, contactcenter@aafp.org, http://www.aafp.org.

American Medical Association, 515 N State St., Chicago, IL, 60610, (312) 464-5000, (800) 621-8335, http://www.ama-assn.org.

National Alliance on Mental Illness, 3803 N Fairfax Dr., Ste. 100, Arlington, VA, 22203, (703) 524-7600, http://www.nami.org.

National Center on Elder Abuse. Administration on Aging, 1 Massachusetts Ave. NW, Washington, DC, 20001, (202) 619-0724, Fax: (202) 357-3555, asainfo@asa.hhs.gov, http://www.aoa.gov.

National Committee for the Prevention of Elder Abuse, 151 1st Ave., No. 93, New York, NY, 10003, (800) 677-1116, Fax: (212) 420-6026, http://www.preventelderabuse.org.

U.S. National Library of Medicine, 8600 Rockville Pike, Bethesda, MD, 20894, http://www.nlm.nih.gov.

LeeAnn Paradise
Laura Jean Cataldo, RN, EdD

Electroconvulsive therapy

Definition

Electroconvulsive therapy (ECT) is a procedure in which a patient is treated by using controlled low-dose electric currents to induce a seizure. Also known as electroshock therapy, ECT is classified along with **vagus nerve stimulation**, repetitive **transcranial magnetic stimulation**, **magnetic seizure therapy**, and deep **brain** stimulation as a form of brain stimulation therapy.

Purpose

The purpose of ECT is to produce a convulsion that may relieve symptoms associated with such mental illnesses as **major depressive disorder**, treatment-resistant **depression**, **bipolar disorder**, severe mania, acute **psychosis**, and **catatonia**.

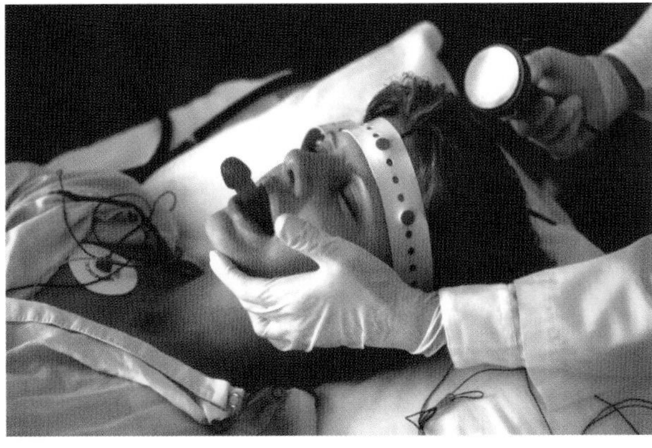

A woman prepares to receive electroconvulsive therapy (ECT), a treatment for depression. ECT works by inducing seizures in the brain; the rubber mouthpiece will keep the patient from biting down on her teeth or her tongue during the procedure. *(© Photo Researchers, Inc.)*

ECT is also used as a treatment of last resort for patients with Parkinson's disease, **Tourette syndrome**, and treatment-resistant **obsessive-compulsive disorder**.

Demographics

The demographics of ECT vary widely around the world: Some countries consider it a safe and effective treatment for severe depression and other mental disorders and have strict guidelines regarding its administration (United States, United Kingdom), whereas other countries either do not permit its use (Slovenia) or severely restrict it (Italy, the Netherlands). One problem has to do with the shortage of anesthesiologists in some countries, resulting in ECT being administered without anesthesia (Japan, India). Other countries permit the administration of ECT without the patient's **informed consent**.

Statistics about the use of ECT in the United States are difficult to obtain because some states require hospitals to report its use and others do not. The **American Psychiatric Association** estimated in the late 1990s that about 100,000 people received ECT each year, with wide variations in different parts of the country. ECT is used more often in private than in public hospitals, and minority patients are underrepresented among those receiving ECT. About 70% of patients receiving ECT in the United States are women, but this figure is usually explained as a result of the fact that more women than men are diagnosed with severe or treatment-resistant depression. The most recent figures from the United Kingdom indicate that 12,000 persons receive ECT each year.

Description

ECT uses low-dose electric currents together with anesthesia, muscle relaxants, and oxygen to produce a mild generalized seizure or convulsion. With repeated administration, usually over a period of weeks, ECT may be effective in relieving symptoms of several mental illnesses.

The American Psychiatric Association's *Practice Guidelines for the Treatment of Psychiatric Disorders* discusses the use of ECT in the treatment of major depressive disorder, bipolar disorder, and **schizophrenia**. It is most closely associated with the treatment of severe depression. Historically, ECT was the treatment of choice for depression when a patient with severe depression or psychotic symptoms was at increased risk of committing **suicide** and had not responded to other treatments. The third edition of the APA practice guide to the treatment of depression, published in November 2010, notes that "Electroconvulsive therapy has the highest rates of response and remission of any form of antidepressant treatment, with 70%–90% of those treated showing improvement.... The proportion of patients with major depressive disorder who respond to ECT is still greater than the proportion who respond to antidepressant medication. In addition, ECT has been associated with significant improvements in health-related quality of life." The guide also notes that patients with catatonia, **neuroleptic malignant syndrome**, and parkinsonism may benefit from the procedure.

According to the APA, the normal course of treatment for patients receiving ECT is 2–3 treatments per week for a total of 6–12 treatments in most cases. The total rarely exceeds 20 treatments. Premature termination of ECT is associated with a worse prognosis.

Although antidepressant medications are effective in many cases, they may take 2–6 weeks to begin to work. In addition, some patients with mania and schizophrenia may not be able to tolerate the side effects of the antipsychotic medications used to treat these disorders. For these individuals, ECT is an option. ECT is also indicated when patients need a treatment that brings about rapid improvement because they are refusing to eat or drink or presenting some other danger to themselves.

ECT is also recommended for certain subgroups of patients diagnosed with depression. Many elderly patients, for example, respond better to ECT than to antidepressant medications. Pregnant women are another subgroup that may benefit from ECT. Because ECT does not harm a fetus as some medications might, pregnant women with severe depression can choose ECT for relief of their depressive symptoms.

As of 2011, other treatments, such as transcranial magnetic stimulation (TMS), were becoming available and replacing ECT in some cases. According to experts at the Mayo Clinic, ECT and TMS have both benefits and drawbacks, and some patients are more likely to benefit from ECT than from TMS.

Origins

ECT was introduced in 1938 by two Italian psychiatrists, Ugo Cerletti (1877–1963) and Lucio Bini (1908–1964). According to Cerletti, the idea of using electroshocks to treat schizophrenia by inducing a convulsion came to him while observing slaughterhouse workers in Rome use electric shocks to anesthetize cattle before cutting their throats. The shocks caused the animals to have epileptic convulsions, which rendered them unable to resist the butchers. Cerletti thought that electroshocks might help schizophrenics, because it was noted in the 1930s that patients with epilepsy rarely developed schizophrenia. After experimenting on animals, Cerletti and his colleague Bini used ECT for the first time on a human patient, a homeless man with schizophrenia, in April 1938. The treatment was successful, and Cerletti and Bini extended the use of ECT to treat patients with depression and bipolar disorder as well as schizophrenia. Some in the medical community were receptive to this approach because physicians were already using a variety of chemicals to produce **seizures** in patients. Unfortunately, many of their patients died or had severe injuries because the strength of the convulsions could not be well controlled.

Cerletti's reasoning about an association between epilepsy and immunity from schizophrenia was incorrect, as was his theory that ECT works by causing the brain to release what he called "vitalizing" chemicals that cure the symptoms of mental illness. He attempted to prove this theory by injecting patients with a liquid suspension that contained particles of electroshocked pigs' brains. Although this treatment apparently helped to relieve the symptoms of some of Cerletti's patients, it never caught on.

In the 1940s and 1950s, the treatment was considered controversial. As ECT became more widely used, many members of the general public and some in the psychiatric profession were opposed to its use. To them it seemed barbaric. ECT joined **psychosurgery** as one of the most intensely distrusted psychiatric and neurological practices. Many people were frightened simply because ECT was called "shock treatment." Many assumed the procedure would be painful; others thought it was a form of electrocution; and still others believed it would cause brain damage. Unfavorable publicity in newspapers, magazines, and movies added to these fears. Indeed, up through the 1960s, doctors and nurses did not usually explain either ECT or other forms of psychiatric treatment to patients and their families. Moreover, many critics had good reasons for opposing the procedure before it was refined. Neither anesthesia nor muscle relaxants were used in the early days of ECT. As a result, patients had violent seizures, and even though they did not remember them, the thought of the procedure itself seemed frightening. Even more unfortunately, this crude early version of ECT was applied sometimes to patients who could never have benefited from ECT under any conditions.

As the procedures used with ECT became more refined, psychiatrists found that ECT could be an effective treatment for schizophrenia, depression, and bipolar disorder. The use of ECT, however, was phased out when antipsychotic and antidepressant drugs were introduced during the 1950s and 1960s. The psychiatric community reintroduced ECT several years later when patients who did not respond to the new drugs stimulated a search by mental health professionals for effective and, if necessary, non-drug treatments. While the new psychotropic medications provided relief for untold thousands of patients who suffered greatly from their illnesses and would otherwise have been condemned to mental hospitals, the drugs unfortunately produced a number of side effects, some irreversible. Another drawback is that some medications do not have a noticeable effect on the patient's mood for 2–6 weeks. During this time, the patient may be at risk for suicide. In addition, there are patients who do not respond to any medications or have severe allergic reactions to them.

ECT in contemporary practice

ECT is performed in both inpatient and outpatient facilities in specially equipped rooms with oxygen, suction, and cardiopulmonary resuscitation equipment readily available to deal with the rare emergency. A team of healthcare professionals, including a **psychiatrist**, an anesthesiologist, a respiratory therapist, and other assistants, is present throughout the entire procedure.

Administration of ECT

ECT is performed while the patient is unconscious. Unconsciousness is induced by a short-acting barbiturate such as methohexital (Brevital Sodium) or another appropriate anesthetic drug. The drug is given intravenously. To prevent patients from harming themselves during the convulsions or seizures induced by ECT, they are given succinylcholine (Anectine) or a similar drug that temporarily paralyzes the muscles. Because the patients' muscles are relaxed, the seizures does not produce any violent contractions of the limbs and torso. Instead, patients lie quietly on the operating table. One of the patient's hands or feet, however, is tied off with a tourniquet before the muscle relaxant is given. The tourniquet prevents the muscles in this limb from being paralyzed like the muscles in other parts of the patient's body. The hand or foot is used to monitor muscle movement induced by the electrical current applied to the brain.

A breathing tube is then inserted into the unconscious patient's airway and a rubber mouthpiece is inserted into the mouth to prevent the person from biting down on teeth or tongue during the electrically induced convulsion. As the current is applied, brain activity is monitored using **electroencephalography**. These brain wave tracings tell the medical team exactly how long the seizure lasts. The contraction of muscles in the arm or leg not affected by the muscle relaxant also provides an indication of the seizure's duration.

The electrodes for ECT may be placed on both sides of the head (bilaterally) or on one side only (unilaterally). Physicians often use bilateral electrode placement during the first week or so of treatments. An electric current is passed through the brain by means of a machine specifically designed for this purpose. The usual dose of electricity is 70–150 volts for 0.1–0.5 seconds. In the first stage of the seizure (tonic phase), the muscles in the body that have not been paralyzed by medication contract for a period of 5–15 seconds. This is followed by the second stage of the seizure (clonic phase) that is characterized by twitching movements, usually visible only in the toes or in a nonparalyzed arm or leg. These are caused by alternating contraction and relaxation of these same muscles. This stage lasts approximately 10–60 seconds. The physician in charge will try to induce a seizure that lasts between 30 seconds and two minutes. If the first application of electricity fails to produce a seizure lasting at least 25 seconds, another attempt is made 60 seconds later. The session is stopped if the patient has no seizures after three attempts. The entire procedure lasts about 30 minutes.

Unilateral placement of the electrodes, usually on the right side of the patient's head because it is on the side opposite the memory and learning areas of the brain, appears to produce fewer side effects. Another method of administration that is gaining favor is the administration of the electric current in several short bursts rather than a single constant high dose. Like unilateral electrode placement, the "brief pulse" approach to ECT produces fewer side effects.

The absence of seizures is most commonly caused either by the patient's physical condition at the time of treatment or by the individual nature of human responses to drugs and other treatment procedures. Just as there are some patients who do not respond to one type of antidepressant medication but do respond to others, some patients do not respond to ECT.

The total number of ECT treatments that will be given depends on such factors as the patient's age, **diagnosis**, the history of illness, family support, and response to therapy. Treatments are normally given every other day at a rate of two to three per week. The ECT treatments are stopped when the patient's psychiatric symptoms show significant signs of improvement. Depending on the patient's condition, this improvement may happen in a few weeks or, rarely, over a six-month period. In most cases, patients with depression require 6–12 ECT sessions. Only rarely is ECT treatment extended beyond six months. In such infrequent cases, treatments are decreased from two to four per week after the first month to one treatment every month or so.

No one knows for certain why ECT is effective. Because the treatment involves passing an electric

KEY TERMS

Catatonia—A syndrome associated with schizophrenia in which the patient may be stupefied and nearly immobile, holding rigid poses for hours and ignoring external stimuli. At the other extreme, the patient may exhibit extreme hyperactivity.

Hippocampus—A structure in the medial temporal lobe of the brain associated with memory consolidation and spatial navigation.

Neurogenesis—The development of new nerve cells in the brain, whether before birth or during adulthood.

Psychosis—A general psychiatric term for a condition in which the patient loses touch with reality. It is marked by such symptoms as hallucinations, delusions, personality changes, and disordered thinking.

Somatization disorder—A disorder in which patients seek medical treatment for a variety of vague physical ailments with no discernible organic cause. It is usually thought to result from the patient's expressing emotional distress through physical complaints.

current through the brain, which is electrically excitable tissue, it is not surprising that ECT has been shown to affect many neurotransmitter systems. **Neurotransmitters** are chemical messengers in the nervous system that carry signals from nerve cell to nerve cell. The neurotransmitters affected by ECT include **dopamine**, norepinephrine, **serotonin**, and gamma-aminobutyric acid (GABA). A newer theory about the effectiveness of ECT is that it stimulates the growth of new nerve cells in the hippocampus, the part of the brain associated with long-term memory formation and consolidation. This process is known as hippocampal neurogenesis.

Benefits

A majority of patients given ECT notice improvements in their symptoms after two or three treatments, although full improvement typically takes longer. Overall, ECT is a safe procedure. There is no convincing evidence of long-term harmful effects from ECT.

Precautions

Precautions include taking a complete medication history and screening patients for heart problems or other disorders that may contraindicate the use of general anesthesia or of ECT itself.

If an ECT-induced seizure lasts too long (more than two minutes) during the procedure, physicians will control it with an intravenous infusion of an anticonvulsant drug, usually **diazepam** (Valium).

Preparation

Patients and their relatives are typically prepared for ECT by viewing a videotape that explains both the procedure and the risks involved. The physician then answers any questions these individuals might have, and the patient is asked to sign an informed consent form. This form gives the doctor and the hospital legal permission to administer the treatment. Informed consent is a requirement for ECT treatment in the United States and the United Kingdom.

After the form has been signed, the doctor performs a complete physical examination and orders a number of tests that can help identify any potential problem. These tests may include a chest x ray, electrocardiogram (EKG), CT scan, urinalysis, spinal x ray, electroencephalogram (EEG), and complete blood count (CBC).

Some medications, such as lithium and a class of **antidepressants** known as **monoamine oxidase inhibitors (MAOIs)**, should be discontinued for some time before ECT administration. Patients are instructed not to eat or drink for at least eight hours prior to the procedure to reduce the possibility of vomiting and choking. During the procedure itself, the members of the healthcare team closely monitor the patient's vital signs, including blood pressure, heart rate, and oxygen content.

Aftercare

The patient is moved to a recovery area after an ECT treatment. Vital signs are recorded every five minutes until the patient is fully awake, which may take 15–30 minutes. The patient may experience some initial confusion, but this feeling usually disappears in a matter of minutes. The patient may complain of headache, muscle pain, or back pain, which can be relieved by aspirin or another mild medication.

Following successful ECT treatments, patients with bipolar disorder may be given maintenance doses of lithium. Similarly, patients with depression may be given antidepressant drugs. These medications are intended to reduce the chance of **relapse** or the recurrence of symptoms. Some studies have estimated that approximately one-third to one-half of patients treated with ECT relapse within 12 months of treatment. After three years, this figure may increase to two-thirds. Follow-up care

QUESTIONS TO ASK YOUR DOCTOR

- What is your opinion of ECT as a treatment for depression? For other mental disorders?
- Have you ever referred a patient to a psychiatrist for ECT? If so, did the patient find ECT beneficial?
- What is the risk of memory loss with ECT?
- In your opinion, why is ECT still controversial?

with medications for bipolar disorder or depression can reduce the relapse rate in the year following ECT treatment from 50% to 20%. Some patients might relapse because they do not respond well to the medications they take after their ECT sessions are completed. In some cases, patients who relapse may have severe forms of depression that are especially difficult to treat by any method.

Risks

Recent advances in medical technology have substantially reduced the complications associated with ECT. According to the NIMH, the most common side effects of contemporary ECT are headache, nausea, pain in the jaw, and mild muscle aches. Because ECT increases heart rate and raises blood pressure, persons at high risk of having complications following ECT include those with a recent heart attack, uncontrolled high blood pressure, brain tumors, and previous spinal injuries.

One of the most common side effects of ECT is memory loss. Patients may be unable to recall events that occurred before and after treatment. Elderly patients, for example, may become increasingly confused and forgetful as the treatments continue. In a minority of individuals, memory loss may last for months. For the majority of patients, however, recent memories return in a few days or weeks. Both unilateral electrode placement and the use of brief pulses of electricity rather than a continual high dose have been found to reduce memory loss.

Research and general acceptance

Research in the effectiveness of ECT and different methods of administering it is ongoing. The procedure has its own specialty journal, the *Journal of ECT*, in its twenty-seventh year of publication as of 2011. In the early 2000s, the **National Institute of Mental Health** (NIMH) supported the formation of the Consortium for Research in ECT (CORE), a group of five medical centers across the United States that conduct studies of the effectiveness of ECT in treating mental disorders and ways to manage its side effects. Between 2004 and 2011, the consortium published ten major papers about the therapy, comparing it to pharmacologic treatment and also investigating different methods of administering ECT.

There were 54 **clinical trials** of ECT under way in 2011 investigating its effectiveness as a treatment for depression, schizophrenia, posttraumatic stress disorder, **somatization disorder**, and bipolar disorder. Some of the trials involved ECT as an adjunctive therapy for patients receiving medications while others were studying its effectiveness in preventing relapse. One study was investigating the comparative benefits of four different ways to administer ECT to depressed patients (right unilateral ECT at high dose; ultra-brief pulse width ECT; bilateral ECT at moderate dose; and traditional pulse width ECT). Three other studies were investigating ketamine as an anesthetic for patients receiving ECT.

Training and certification

While some medical schools in the United States allow third- and fourth-year medical students to learn how to give ECT under supervision, most trainees are residents in psychiatry. Some residency programs in psychiatry now require residents to receive both didactic (classroom) and hands-on training in ECT, and to demonstrate competency in administering ECT before graduating from the program.

Resources

BOOKS

Fink, Max. *Electroconvulsive Therapy: A Guide for Professionals and Their Patients*. New York: Oxford University Press, 2009.

Higgins, Edmund S., and Mark S. George. *Brain Stimulation Therapies for Clinicians*. Washington, DC: American Psychiatric Publishing, 2009.

Mankad, Mehul V., et al. *Clinical Manual of Electroconvulsive Therapy*. Washington, DC: American Psychiatric Publishing, 2010.

Shorter, Edward, and David Healy. *Shock Therapy: A History of Electroconvulsive Treatment in Mental Illness*. New Brunswick, NJ: Rutgers University Press, 2007.

PERIODICALS

Bolwig, T.G. "How Does Electroconvulsive Therapy Work? Theories on Its Mechanism." *Canadian Journal of Psychiatry* 56 (2011): 13–18.

England, M.L., et al. "Catatonia in Psychotic Patients: Clinical Features and Treatment Response." *Journal of Neuropsychiatry and Clinical Neurosciences* 23 (2011): 223–26.

Gahr, M., et al. "Somatization Disorder Treated with Electroconvulsive Therapy." *Journal of ECT* 27 (September 2011): 266–67.

Gosselink, M.J., et al. "Successful Electroconvulsive Therapy in a 95-Year-Old Man with a Cardiac Pacemaker: A Case Report." *American Journal of Geriatric Psychiatry* 19 (2011): 678–79.

Nahas, Z., and B.S. Anderson. "Brain Stimulation Therapies for Mood Disorders: The Continued Necessity of Electroconvulsive Therapy." *Journal of the American Psychiatric Nurses Association* 17 (2011): 214–16.

Petrides, G., et al. "Seizure Threshold in a Large Sample: Implications for Stimulus Dosing Strategies in Bilateral Electroconvulsive Therapy: A Report from CORE." *Journal of ECT* 25 (2009): 232–37.

Rasmussen, K.G. "Some Considerations in Choosing Electroconvulsive Therapy Versus Transcranial Magnetic Stimulation for Depression." *Journal of ECT* 27 (2011): 51–54.

Rasmussen, K.G., et al. "Is Baseline Medication Resistance Associated with Potential for Relapse after Successful Remission of a Depressive Episode with ECT? Data from the Consortium for Research on Electroconvulsive Therapy (CORE)." *Journal of Clinical Psychiatry* 70 (2009): 232–37.

Sienaert, P. "What We Have Learned about Electroconvulsive Therapy and Its Relevance for the Practising Psychiatrist." *Canadian Journal of Psychiatry* 56 (2011): 5–12.

Smith, G.E., et al. "A Randomized Controlled Trial Comparing the Memory Effects of Continuation Electroconvulsive Therapy Versus Continuation Pharmacotherapy: Results from the Consortium for Research in ECT (CORE) Study." *Journal of Clinical Psychiatry* 71 (2010): 185–93.

Tess, A.V., and Smetana, G.W. "Medical Evaluation of Patients Undergoing Electroconvulsive Therapy." *New England Journal of Medicine* 360, no. 14 (April 2, 2009): 1437–1444.

Tominaga, K., et al. "Symptom Predictors of Response to Electroconvulsive Therapy in Older Patients with Treatment-resistant Depression." *International Journal of General Medicine* 4 (2011): 515–19.

OTHER

Mayo Clinic. "Video: Electroconvulsive Therapy (ECT)." http://www.mayoclinic.com/health/electroconvulsive-therapy/MM00606 (accessed September 25, 2011).

WEBSITES

"Brain Stimulation Therapies." National Institute of Mental Health.http://www.nimh.nih.gov/health/topics/brain-stimulation-therapies/brain-stimulation-therapies.shtml (accessed October 14, 2011).

"Electroconvulsive Therapy (ECT)." Mayo Clinic. July 9, 2010. http://www.mayoclinic.com/health/electroconvulsive-therapy/MY00129 (accessed October 14, 2011).

"Practice Guideline for the Treatment of Patients with Major Depressive Disorder." American Psychiatric Association. November 2010. http://www.psychiatryonline.com/pracGuide/pracGuideTopic_7.aspx (accessed October 14, 2011).

ORGANIZATIONS

American Psychiatric Association, 1000 Wilson Blvd., Ste. 1825, Arlington, VA, 22209-3901, (703) 907-7300, apa@psych.org, http://www.psych.org.

National Institute of Mental Health, 6001 Executive Blvd., Rm. 8184, MSC 9663, Bethesda, MD, 20892-9663, (301) 433-4513; TTY: (301) 443-8431, Fax: (301) 443-4279, (866) 615-6464; TTY: (866) 415-8051, nimhinfo@nih.gov, http://www.nimh.nih.gov.

National Institute of Neurological Disorders and Stroke, PO Box 5801, Bethesda, MD, 20824, (301) 496-5751; TTY: (301) 468-5981, (800) 352-9424, http://www.ninds.nih.gov.

Dean A. Haycock, PhD
Ruth A. Wienclaw, PhD
Rebecca J. Frey, PhD

Electroencephalography

Definition

Electroencephalography (EEG), also know as **brain** wave test, is a neurological test that measures and records electrical activity in the brain over time.

Purpose

The EEG is a key tool in the **diagnosis** and management of epilepsy and other seizure disorders. It is also used to assist in the diagnosis of brain damage and diseases such as **stroke**, brain tumors, encephalitis, intellectual disabilities, and **sleep disorders**, and to determine brain status and brain death.

Description

Brain function is associated with electrical activity, which is always accompanied by an electrical field. This field consists of two parts, the electrical field and the magnetic field, and is called an electromagnetic field. The electroencephalogram records electrical field activity through the use of surface electrodes.

Prior to the recording session, a nurse or technologist attaches approximately 16–21 electrodes to a person's scalp using an electrically conductive, washable paste. The electrodes are placed on the head in a standard

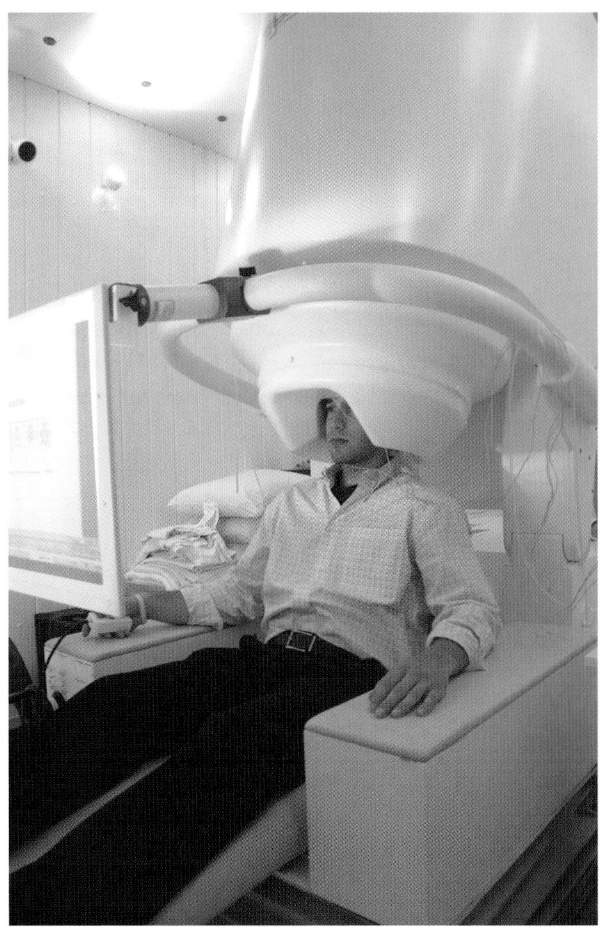

A male patient undergoes magnetoencephalography (MEG). *(U.S. National Institute of Mental Health)*

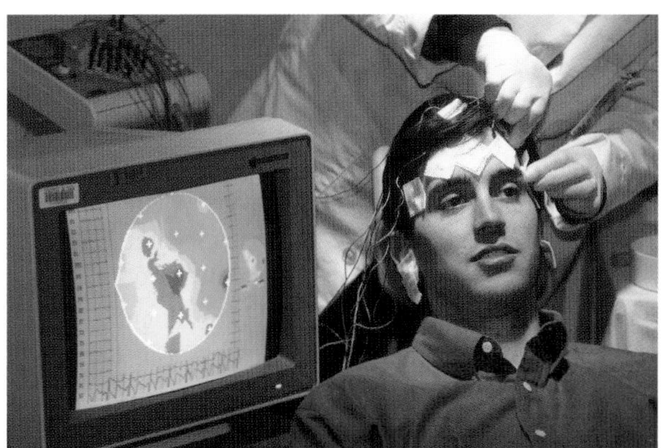

An EEG lab measures the brain waves of a subject. *(© Richard T. Nowitz/Photo Researchers, Inc.)*

pattern based on head circumference measurements. Depending on the purpose for the EEG, implantable, or invasive, electrodes are occasionally used. Implantable electrodes include sphenoidal electrodes, which are fine wires inserted under the zygomatic arch, or cheekbone. Depth electrodes, or subdural strip electrodes, are surgically implanted into the brain and are used to localize a seizure focus in preparation for epilepsy surgery. Once in place, even implantable electrodes do not cause pain. The electrodes are used to measure the electrical activity in various regions of the brain over the course of the test period.

For the test, a person lies on a bed, padded table, or comfortable chair and is asked to relax and remain still while measurements are being taken. An EEG usually takes no more than one hour, although long-term monitoring is often used for diagnosis of seizure disorders. During the test procedure, a person may be asked to breathe slowly or quickly. Visual stimuli such as flashing lights or a patterned board may be used to stimulate certain types of brain activity. Throughout the procedure, the EEG unit makes a continuous graphic record of the person's brain activity, or brain waves, on a long strip of recording paper or computer screen. This graphic record is called an electroencephalogram. If the display is computerized, the test may be called a digital EEG, or dEEG.

The sleep EEG uses the same equipment and procedures as a regular EEG. Persons undergoing a sleep EEG are encouraged to fall asleep completely rather than just relax. They are typically provided a bed and a quiet room conducive to sleep. A sleep EEG lasts up to three hours, or up to eight or nine hours if it is a night's sleep.

In an ambulatory EEG, individuals are hooked up to a portable cassette recorder. They then go about normal activities and take normal rest and sleep for a period of up to 24 hours. During this period, individuals and their family members record any symptoms or abnormal behaviors, which can later be correlated with the EEG to see if they represent **seizures**.

An extension of the EEG technique, called quantitative EEG (qEEG), involves manipulating the EEG signals with a computer using the fast Fourier transform algorithm. The result is then best displayed using a colored gray scale transposed onto a schematic map of the head to form a topographic image. The brain map produced in this technique is a vivid illustration of electrical activity in the brain. This technique also has the ability to compare the similarity of the signals between different electrodes, a measurement known as spectral coherence. Studies have shown the value of this measurement in diagnosis of **Alzheimer's disease** and mild closed-head injuries. The technique can also identify areas of the brain having abnormally slow

KEY TERMS

Encephalitis—Inflammation of the brain.

Epilepsy—A neurological disorder characterized by recurrent seizures with or without a loss of consciousness.

Fast Fourier transform (FFT)—A mathematical process used in EEG analysis to investigate the composition of an EEG signal.

Occipital bone—Bone that forms the back part of the skull.

Sphenoidal electrodes—Fine wire electrodes that are implanted under the cheek bones, used to measure temporal seizures.

Subdural electrodes—Strip electrodes that are placed under dura mater (the outermost, toughest, and most fibrous of the three membranes [meninges] covering the brain and spinal cord). They are used to locate foci of epileptic seizures prior to epilepsy surgery.

Zygomatic arch—Cheekbone. A quadrilateral bone forming the prominence of the cheek. It articulates (touches or moves) with the frontal, sphenoid, maxillary, and temporal bones.

activity when the data are both mapped and compared to known normal values. The result is then known as a statistical or significance probability map (SPM). This allows differentiation between early **dementia** (increased slowing) or otherwise uncomplicated **depression** (no slowing). The quantitative EEG is also known by the acronym BEAM (brain electrical activity mapping).

Magnetoencephalography

Magnetoencephalography, a supplement to EEG, also uses an electroencephalogram to measure the patient's electrical field. Every electrical current generates a magnetic field. The magnetic field is detected by an instrument called a biomagnetometer and recorded as a magnetoencephalograph (MEG). The information provided by the MEG is entirely different from that provided by **computed tomography** (CT), topographic encephalography, or **magnetic resonance imaging** (MRI)—imaging instruments that provide still, structural, and anatomical information. Using MEG, the brain can be observed "in action," rather than just being viewed as a still image. The information recorded by the MEG provides important supplemental information to that recorded by the encephalogram, and when used together, they both provide a much more complete and comprehensive idea of cerebral events.

Magnetoencephalography has been used to map the sensory and motor cortices of the brain, determine the organization of the auditory center of the brain, and study cognitive functions such as speech, memory, attention, and consciousness. This information is critical for neurosurgical planning, such as the removal of brain lesions. Thus, preoperative MEG is valuable in planning the surgical treatment of tumors and malformations. MEG can provide surgeons with real-time computer-generated images of deep-seated lesions that are essential before surgery.

Preparation

An EEG is generally performed as one test in a series of neurological evaluations. Rarely does the EEG form the sole basis for a particular diagnosis.

Full instructions should be given to individuals receiving an EEG when they schedule their test. Typically, individuals taking medications that affect the central nervous system, such as anticonvulsants, stimulants, or **antidepressants**, are told to discontinue their prescription for a short time prior to the test (usually one to two days). However, such requests should be cleared with the treating physician. EEG test candidates may be asked to avoid food and beverages that contain caffeine, a central nervous system stimulant. They may also be asked to arrive for the test with clean hair that is free of styling products to make attachment of the electrodes easier.

Individuals undergoing a sleep EEG may be asked to remain awake the night before their test. They may be given a sedative prior to the test to induce sleep.

Aftercare

If an individual has suspended regular medication for the test, the EEG nurse or technician should advise as to when to begin taking it again.

Risks

The primary risk of EEG is the production of a seizure in a patient with epilepsy. This may result from the temporary discontinuation of anticonvulsant medication or from the provocation of a seizure by an epileptogenic stimulus such as flashing lights or deep breathing. Although the provocation of a seizure may serve to substantiate the diagnosis, all patients with the potential for seizures should be carefully monitored to avoid injury in case a seizure does result.

QUESTIONS TO ASK THE DOCTOR

- Will I experience any side effects after the EEG is performed?
- What preparations are being made to treat an induced seizure?
- Is the supervising physician appropriately certified to interpret an EEG?

Results

In reading and interpreting brain wave patterns, a neurologist or other physician will evaluate the type of brain waves and the symmetry, location, and consistency of brain wave patterns. Brain wave response to certain stimuli presented during the EEG test (such as flashing lights or noise) will also be evaluated.

The rate, height, and length of brain waves vary depending on the part of the brain being studied, and every individual has a unique and characteristic brain-wave pattern. Age and state of consciousness also cause changes in wave patterns. Several wave patterns have been identified:

- Alpha waves—Most of the recorded waves in a normal adult's EEG are the occipital alpha waves, which are best obtained from the back of the head when the subject is awake but resting quietly with eyes closed. These waves, occurring typically in a pattern of 8–13 hertz (cycles per second), are blocked by excitement or by opening the eyes. Abnormal alpha patterns include the presence of alpha rhythms in a newborn, which can signify seizure activity.
- Beta waves—Obtained from the central and frontal parts of the brain, beta waves are closely related to the sensory-motor parts of the brain and are also blocked by opening the eyes. Their frequency is in the range of 13–30 hertz. Marked asymmetry in beta rhythms suggests a structural lesion on the side lacking the beta waves. Beta waves are also commonly measured over skull lesions, such as fractures or burr holes, in activity known as a breach rhythm.
- Delta waves—Delta waves are irregular, slow waves of less than 4 hertz that are normally found in deep sleep and in infants and young children. They indicate an abnormality in an awake adult. Intermittent delta rhythms are also an indication of damage of the relays between the deep gray matter and the cortex of the brain.
- Theta waves—Characterized by rhythmic, slow waves of 4–7 hertz, theta waves usually only occur during sleep. The presence of theta waves in awake adults may indicate an abnormality.

EEG readings of patients with epilepsy or other seizure disorders display bursts, or spikes, of electrical activity. In focal epilepsy, spikes are restricted to one hemisphere of the brain. If spikes are generalized to both hemispheres of the brain, multifocal epilepsy may be present. The EEG can be used to localize the region of the brain where the abnormal electrical activity is occurring. This is most easily accomplished using a recording method, or montage, called an average reference montage. With this type of recording, the signal from each electrode is compared to the average signal from all the electrodes. The negative amplitude (upward movement, by convention) of the spike is observed for the different channels, or inputs, from the various electrodes. The negative deflection will be greatest as recorded by the electrode that is closest in location to the origin of the abnormal activity. The spike will be present but of reduced amplitude as the electrodes move farther away from the site producing the spike. Electrodes distant from the site will not record the spike occurrence.

Diagnostic brain-wave patterns of other disorders vary widely. In general, disease typically increases slow activity, such as theta or delta waves, but decreases fast activity, such as alpha and beta waves. The appearance of excess theta waves (4–8 hertz) may indicate brain injury. Brain-wave patterns in patients with brain disease, intellectual disabilities, and brain injury show overall slowing. A trained medical specialist should interpret EEG results in the context of the patient's medical history and other pertinent medical test results.

Resources

BOOKS

Daube, J.R., and R. Devin. *Clinical Neurophysiology*. 3rd ed. New York: Oxford University Press, 2009.

Ebersole, J.S., and T.A. Pedley. *Current Practice of Clinical Electroencephalography*. 3rd ed. Philadelphia: Lippincott Williams & Wilkins, 2003.

Misulism, Karl E., and T.C. Head. *Essentials of Clinical Neurophysiology*. 3rd ed. London: Butterworth-Heinemann, 2002.

Rowan, A.J., and E. Tolunsky. *Primer of EEG*. London: Elsevier, 2003.

PERIODICALS

Coburn, Kerry L., et al. "The Value of Quantitative Electroencephalography in Clinical Psychiatry: A Report by the Committee on Research of the American Neuropsychiatric Association." *Journal of Neuropsychiatry & Clinical Neurosciences* 18, no. 4 (November 2006): 460–500.

Frith, Chris D. "The Value of Brain Imaging in the Study of Development and Its Disorders." *Journal of Child Psychology and Psychiatry* 47, no. 10 (November 2006): 979–82.

Hurley, Robin A., Ronald Fisher, and Katherine H. Taber. "Windows to the Brain—Sudden Onset Panic: Epileptic Aura or Panic Disorder?" *Journal of Neuropsychiatry & Clinical Neurosciences* 18, no. 4 (November 2006): 436–43.

Knowlton, Robert C., et al. "Magnetic Source Imaging Versus Intracranial Electroencephalogram in Epilepsy Surgery: A Prospective Study." *Annals of Neurology* 59, no. 5 (May 2006): 835–42.

O'Sullivan, S.S., et al. "The Role of the Standard EEG in Clinical Psychiatry." *Human Psychopharmacology: Clinical and Experimental* 21, no. 4 (June 2006): 265–71.

WEBSITES

KidsHealth.org. "EEG (Electroencephalography)." September 2008. http://kidshealth.org/parent/system/medical/eeg.html (accessed October 5, 2011).

ORGANIZATIONS

American Association of Neuromuscular and Electrodiagnostic Medicine, 2621 Superior Drive NW, Rochester, MN, 55901, (507) 288-0100, aanem@aanem.org, http://www.aamnem.org.

American Board of Registration for Electroencephalographic Technologists, 2509 West Iles Ave., Suite 102, Springfield, IL, 62704, (217) 726-7980, Fax: (217) 726-7989, abreteo@att.net, http://www.abret.org.

American Society of Electroneurodiagnostic Technologists, 402 East Bannister Rd., Suite A, Kansas City, MO, 64131-3019, (816) 931-1120, Fax: (816) 931-1145, info@aset.org, http://www.aset.org.

Epilepsy Foundation, 8301 Professional Place, Landover, MD, 20785, (800) 332-1000, Fax: (301) 577-2684, http://www.epilepsyfoundation.org.

L. Fleming Fallon, Jr., MD, DrPH
Laura Jean Cataldo, RN, EdD
Brenda W. Lerner

Enabling behaviors *see* **Addiction**

Encopresis

Definition

Encopresis is an elimination disorder that involves repeatedly having bowel movements in inappropriate places after the age when bowel control is normally expected. Encopresis is also called "soiling" or "fecal incontinence."

Demographics

Encopresis occurs in 1%–3% of children from ages four to seven years and is seen more often in boys than in girls. The frequency of encopresis appears to be independent of social class, and there is no evidence that it runs in families.

Description

By four years of age, most children are toilet trained for bowel movements. After that age, if inappropriate bowel movements occur regularly over a period of several months a child may be diagnosed with encopresis. Encopresis can be intentional or unintentional. Intentional soiling is associated with several psychiatric disorders. Involuntary or unintentional soiling is often the result of constipation.

Causes and symptoms

The only symptom of encopresis is that a person has bowel movements in inappropriate places, such as in clothing or on the floor. This soiling is not caused by taking laxatives or other medications and is not due to a disability or physical defect in the bowel. There are two main types of encopresis, and they have different causes.

Involuntary encopresis

With involuntary encopresis, a person has no control over elimination of feces from the bowel. The feces is semi-soft to almost liquid, and it leaks into clothing without the person making any effort to expel it. Leakage usually occurs during the day when the person is active and ranges from infrequent to almost continuous.

Involuntary soiling usually results from constipation. A hard mass of feces develops in the large intestine and is not completely expelled during a regular bowel movement in the toilet. This mass then stretches the large intestine out of shape, allowing liquid feces behind it to leak out. Up to 95% of encopresis is involuntary.

Although involuntary encopresis, called by the **American Psychiatric Association** (APA) encopresis with constipation and overflow incontinence, is caused by constipation, the constipation may be the result of psychological factors. Experiencing a stressful life event, harsh toilet training, toilet fear, or emotionally disturbing events can cause a child to withhold bowel movements or become constipated. Children separated from their parents during World War II were reported to have shown a high incidence of encopresis, indicating that psychological factors play a role in this disorder.

Voluntary encopresis

A person with voluntary encopresis has control over when and where bowel movements occur and chooses to have them in inappropriate places. Constipation is not a factor, and the feces is usually a normal consistency. Often feces is smeared in an obvious place, although sometimes it is hidden around the house. The APA classifies voluntary encopresis as encopresis without constipation and overflow incontinence.

In young children, voluntary encopresis may represent a power struggle between the child and the caregiver doing the toilet training. In older children, voluntary encopresis is often associated with **oppositional defiant disorder** (ODD), **conduct disorder**, **sexual abuse**, or high levels of psychological stressors.

Diagnosis

To receive an APA **diagnosis** of encopresis, as listed in the ***Diagnostic and Statistical Manual of Mental Disorders*** (*DSM*), a child must have a bowel movement, either intentional or accidental, in an inappropriate place at least once a month for a minimum of three months. In addition, the child must be at least four years old, either chronologically or developmentally, and the soiling cannot be caused by illness, medical conditions (e.g., chronic diarrhea, spina bifida, or anal stenosis), medications or substances, or disabilities. However, it may be caused by constipation.

Treatment

Involuntary encopresis is treated by addressing the cause of the constipation and establishing soft, pain-free stools. This can include:

- increasing the amount of liquids a child drinks
- adding high-fiber foods to the diet
- short-term use of laxatives or stool softeners
- emptying the large intestine by using an enema
- establishing regular bowel habits

Once the constipation is resolved, involuntary encopresis normally stops.

Treatment of voluntary encopresis depends on the cause. When voluntary encopresis results from a power struggle between child and adult, it is treated with **behavior modification**. In addition to taking steps to ensure a soft, pain-free stool, the adult should make toileting a pleasant, pressure-free activity. Some experts suggest transferring the initiative for toileting to the child instead of constantly asking him or her to use the toilet. Others recommend toileting at scheduled times, but without pressure to perform. In either case, success should be praised and failure treated in a matter-of-fact manner. If opposition to using the toilet continues, the family may be referred to a child **psychiatrist** or a pediatric **psychologist**.

KEY TERMS

Feces—Waste products eliminated from the large intestine; excrement.

Incontinence—The inability to control the release of urine or feces.

Laxative—Substance or medication that encourages a bowel movement.

Stools—Feces; bowel movements.

With older children who smear or hide feces, voluntary encopresis is usually a symptom of another more serious disorder. When children are successfully treated for the underlying disorder with psychiatric interventions, behavior modification, and education, the encopresis is often resolved.

Prognosis

Because 80%–95% of encopresis is related to constipation, the success rate in resolving involuntary encopresis is high, although it may take time to establish good bowel habits and eliminate a reoccurrence of constipation. The success rate is also good for younger children in a power struggle with adults over toileting, although the results may be slow. The prognosis for older children with associated behavioral disorders is less promising and depends more on the success of resolving those problems than on direct treatment of the symptoms of encopresis.

Prevention

Power struggles during toilet training that lead to encopresis can be reduced by waiting until the child is developmentally ready and interested in using the toilet. Toilet training undertaken kindly, calmly, and with realistic expectations is most likely to lead to success. Successes should be rewarded and failures accepted. Once toilet training has been established, encopresis can be reduced by developing regular bowel habits and encouraging a healthy, high-fiber diet.

Resources

BOOKS

American Psychiatric Association. *Diagnostic and Statistical Manual of Mental Disorders*. 4th ed., text rev. Washington, DC: American Psychiatric Publishing, 2000.

Sadock, Benjamin J., and Virginia A. Sadock, eds. *Comprehensive Textbook of Psychiatry*. Vol. 2. 7th ed. Philadelphia: Lippincott Williams and Wilkins, 2000.

PERIODICALS

Catto-Smith, Anthony G. "Constipation and Toileting Issues in Children." *Medical Journal of Australia* 182, no. 5 (2005): 242–46. Available online at http://www.mja.com.au/public/issues/182_05_070305/cat10379_fm.html (accessed November 9, 2011).

Coehlo, Deborah Padgett. "Encopresis: A Medical and Family Approach." *Pediatric Nursing* 37, no. 3 (May–June 2011): 107–13.

Friman, Patrick C., Kristi L. Hofstadter, and Kevin M. Jones. "A Biobehavioral Approach to the Treatment of Functional Encopresis in Children." *The Journal of Early and Intensive Behavioral Intervention* 3, no. 3 (Fall 2006): 263–72.

von Gontard, Alexander. "Elimination Disorders: A Critical Comment on DSM-5 Proposals." *European Child & Adolescent Psychiatry* 20, no. 2 (February 2011): 83–88.

OTHER

University of Michigan Health System. "Functional Constipation and Soiling in Children: Guidelines for Clinical Care." September 2008. http://cme.med.umich.edu/pdf/guideline/peds08.pdf (accessed October 5, 2011).

ORGANIZATIONS

American Academy of Child and Adolescent Psychiatry, 3615 Wisconsin Ave. NW, Washington, DC, 20016-3007, (202) 966-7300, Fax: (202) 966-2891, http://aacap.org.

American Psychiatric Association, 1000 Wilson Blvd., Suite 1825, Arlington, VA, 22209-3901, (703) 907-7300, apa@psych.org, http://www.psych.org.

Tish Davidson, AM
Emily Jane Willingham, PhD

Endep *see* **Amitriptyline**

Energy therapies

Definition

Energy therapies is a collective term used to refer to a variety of alternative and complementary treatments based on the use, modification, or manipulation of energy fields. Most energy therapies presuppose or accept the theory that matter and energy are not exclusive opposites, but that matter is simply a denser form of energy that is more easily perceived by the senses. Some energy therapies are associated with systems of traditional Indian or Chinese medicine that are thousands of years old; others draw upon contemporary scientific theories. Energy therapies can be divided for purposes of discussion into two groups—those that utilize energy fields located in, affecting, or emanating from the human body (biofield therapies); and those that use electromagnetic fields in unconventional ways. In addition, there are energy therapies that combine biofield therapy with some aspects of bodywork—Breema, polarity therapy, and qigong are examples of this combined approach.

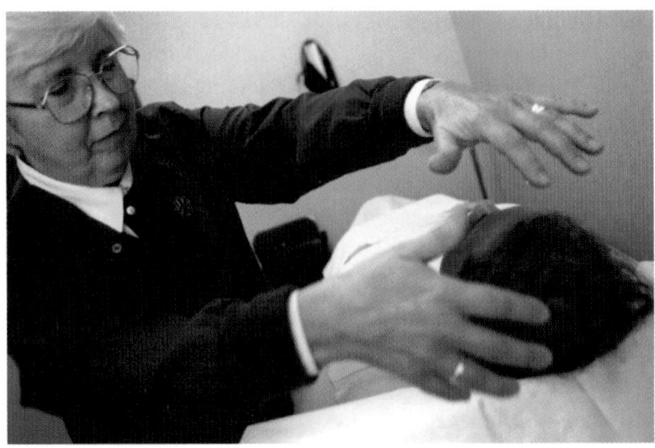

A woman receives healing touch therapy, a type of energy therapy. *(© Susan Tusa/KRT/newscom)*

Purpose

The purpose of energy therapies can be broadly defined as the healing of mental or physical disorders by rebalancing the energy fields in the human body or by drawing upon spiritual energies or forces for such healing. Some energy therapies include internal detoxification or release of trauma-related memories as additional purposes.

Description

Energy therapies vary widely in their understanding of qualifications to be a healer. Some have credentialing or training programs; others do not. Some practitioners of energy therapy believe that all or most people have the capacity to be healers; others regard the ability to use or direct healing energies as a gift or charism that is given only to people who are "chosen" or unusually spiritual.

Although energy therapies are often associated with either Eastern or so-called "New Age" belief systems, most do not expect people in need of healing to give up mainstream Western religious practice or allopathic medical/psychiatric treatments.

Therapeutic touch

Therapeutic touch, or TT, is a form of energy therapy that developed in the United States. It is a noninvasive method of healing derived from an ancient laying-on of hands technique. In TT, practitioners alter the patient's energy field through a transfer of energy from their hands to the patient. Therapeutic touch was developed in 1972 by Dora Kunz, a psychic healer, and Dolores Krieger, a professor of nursing at New York University. The principle behind TT is restoration of balance or harmony to the human energy field, or aura, that is thought to extend several inches to several feet from the body. When illness occurs, it creates a disturbance or blockage in the vital energy field. The TT practitioner uses her/his hands to discern the blockage or disturbance. Although the technique is called "therapeutic touch," there is generally no touching of the client's physical body, only his or her energetic body or field. TT is usually performed on fully clothed patients who are either lying down on a flat surface or sitting up in a chair.

A therapeutic touch session consists of five steps or phases. The first step is a period of **meditation** on the practitioner's part, to become spiritually centered and energized for the task of healing. The second step is assessment or discernment of the energy imbalances in the patient's aura. In this step, the TT practitioner holds his or her hands about 2–3 in. (5–7 cm) above the patient's body and moves them in long, sweeping strokes from the patient's head downward to the feet. The practitioner may feel a sense of warmth, heaviness, tingling, or similar cues, as they are known in TT. The cues are thought to reveal the location of the energy disturbances or imbalances. In the third step, known as the unruffling process, the practitioner removes the energy disturbances with downward sweeping movements. In the fourth step, the practitioner serves as a channel for the transfer of universal energy to the patient. The fifth step consists of smoothing the patient's energy field and restoring a symmetrical pattern of energy flow. After the treatment, the patient rests for 10–15 minutes.

Although therapeutic touch has become a popular alternative or complementary approach in some schools of nursing in the United States and Canada, acceptance by the mainstream medical community varies. Many hospitals permit nurses and staff to perform TT on patients at no extra charge. On the other hand, therapeutic touch became national news in April 1998 when an elementary-school student carried out research for a science project that questioned its claims. Twenty-one TT practitioners with experience ranging from one to 27 years were blindfolded and asked to identify whether the investigator's hand was closer to their right hand or their left. Placement of the investigator's hand was determined by flipping a coin. The TT practitioners were able to identify the correct hand in only 123 (44%) of 280 trials, a figure that could result from random chance alone. Debate about the merits of TT filled the editorial pages of the *Journal of the American Medical Association* for nearly a year after the news reports, and continues to this day.

Qigong

Qigong is a form of Chinese energy therapy that is usually considered a martial art by most Westerners. It is better understood as an ancient Chinese system of postures, exercises, breathing techniques and meditations. Its techniques are designed to improve and enhance the body's *qi*. According to traditional Chinese philosophy and medicine, qi is the fundamental life energy responsible for human health and vitality. Qi travels through the body along channels called meridians. There are 12 main meridians in humans. Each major body organ has qi associated with it, and each organ interacts with particular emotions on the mental level. Qigong techniques are designed to improve the balance and flow of energy throughout the meridians, and to increase the overall quantity and volume of a person's qi.

In the context of energy therapy, qigong is sometimes divided into internal and external qigong. Internal qigong refers to a person's practice of qigong exercises to maintain his or her own health and vitality. Some qigong master teachers are renowned for their skills in external qigong, in which the energy from one person is passed on to another for healing. Chinese hospitals use medical qigong along with herbs, **acupuncture** and other techniques of traditional Chinese medicine. In these hospitals, qigong healers use external qigong and also design specific internal qigong exercises for the patients' health problems.

Reiki

Reiki is a holistic alternative therapy based on Eastern concepts of energy flow and the seven chakras (energy centers) in the human body. Reiki was formulated by a Japanese teacher, Mikao Usui, around 1890, based on Vajrayana (Tibetan) Buddhism, but incorporates meditation techniques, beliefs, and symbols that are considerably older. It is distinctive among energy therapies in its emphasis on self-healing, its spiritual principles, and its accreditation of healers through a system of initiation. Reiki practitioners participate in the healing of emotional and spiritual as well as physical pain through the transmission of universal life energy, called "rei-ki" in Japanese. It is believed that ki flows throughout the universe, but that Reiki connects humans in a more direct way to the universal source. The U.S. Army unveiled a program in 2009 to investigate energy therapies such as Reiki to treat **brain** injuries and **post-traumatic stress disorder** in troops returning home from war. Various other studies are also underway in the United States and Canada, some examining the efficacy of the therapy in coping with pain and anxiety.

Although Reiki involves human touch, it is not massage therapy. The patient lies on a table fully clothed except for shoes while the practitioner places her or his hands over the parts of the body and the chakras in sequence. The hands are held palms downward with the fingers and thumbs extended. If the person is in pain or cannot turn over, the practitioner may touch only the affected part(s). Silence or music appropriate for meditation is considered essential to the treatment. Reiki healers practice daily self-healing, in which they place their hands in traditional positions on their own bodies They may use touch, or distant/non-touch.

Reiki healers are initiated into three levels of practice through attunements, which are ceremonies in which teachers transmit the hand positions and "sacred" symbols. Reiki I healers learn the basic hand positions and can practice direct physical, emotional or mental healing on themselves and others. Reiki II healers are taught the symbols that empower them to do distance or absentee healing. In Reiki III the healer makes a commitment to become a master teacher and do spiritual healing.

Polarity therapy

Polarity therapy, which is sometimes called polarity balancing, is a biofield therapy that resembles Reiki in its emphasis on energy flow, human touch, and the energy centers (chakras) in the human body. Polarity therapy was developed by Dr. Randolph Stone (1890-1981), an American chiropractor and naturopath. It integrates bodywork with diet, yoga-based **exercise**, and self-awareness techniques to release energy blockages in the patient's body, mind, or feelings. Polarity theory divides the body into three horizontal and four vertical zones (right, left, front, and back), each having a positive, negative, or neutral charge. Energy currents in the zones are correlated with five energy centers in the body corresponding to the five elements (ether, air, fire, water, and earth) of Ayurvedic medicine.

Polarity therapy can be done one-on-one or with a group of practitioners working on the patient. The therapist as well as the patient removes shoes. The patient lies fully dressed except for shoes on a massage table or bed, or on the floor. The practitioner takes the patient's history, checks reflexes and touches body parts to determine energy blocks. Polarity therapy uses three levels of touch: no touch (hands held above the body, touching only the energy fields); light touch; and a deep, massaging touch. The therapist balances energy currents in the patient's body by placing his or her "plus" hand on "negative" body parts and vice versa. Polarity therapy involves rocking the patient's body and holding the head as well as more usual massage techniques. It takes about four polarity sessions to treat most conditions, with each session lasting about an hour. After a course of treatment, the polarity practitioner usually suggests drinking plenty of liquids for one to two weeks together with other dietary changes as part of a general internal cleansing or detoxification program. Polarity **yoga** (stretching exercises) is prescribed for the patient's regular workouts at home.

Breema

Breema is a form of body movement energy therapy that combines elements of bodywork, yoga, chiropractic, and New Age philosophy. Breema began in California in 1980. Its founder is Dr. Jon Schreiber, a graduate of Palmer College of Chiropractic. The Breema Health and Wellness Center was opened in Oakland, California, in 1981. The principles of Breema are intended to free people from the conceptual body, defined as "the ideas and images of our body that we carry in our mind." The aim of Breema "is to increase vitality, not to fight sickness, and to create an atmosphere which allows the body to move toward a natural state of balance." A person receiving a Breema treatment works with an instructor or practitioner through a series of individualized exercises on a padded floor. The instructors and practitioners are certified by the Breema Center in Oakland.

Decrystallization is an important part of Breema therapy. According to Breema, decrystallization is a process in which the body is helped to release deeply held, or "crystallized," patterns of chronic discomfort, tension, or emotional pain. As the body releases its crystallizations, its "core energetic patterns" are balanced and realigned. A decrystallization program consists of one or more Breema treatments per week for a year. It includes a set of personalized self-Breema exercises.

Electromagnetic therapies

Electromagnetic therapies cover a variety of treatments that use a source of physical energy outside the body—most often magnets or electromagnetic field stimulation—to treat a range of musculoskeletal disorders. Some forms of magnetic therapy, such as bracelets, gloves, shoe inserts, and similar items containing small magnets meant to be worn near the affected body part, can be self-administered. This form of magnetic therapy has become quite popular among professional athletes and "weekend warriors" to relieve soreness in joints and muscles from over exercise. At present there are two hypothetical explanations of the effectiveness of magnetic therapy. One theory maintains that the magnets stimulate nerve endings in the skin surface to release endorphins, which are pain-relieving chemicals produced by the body in response to **stress** or injury. According to the second hypothesis, the magnets attract certain ions (electrically charged molecules) in the blood, which serves to increase the blood flow in that area of the body. The increased blood flow then relieves the tissue swelling and other side effects of over-exercise that cause pain.

Other forms of electromagnetic therapy require special equipment and cannot be self-administered. These forms of treatment are most commonly used by naturopathic practitioners. One form, called **transcranial magnetic stimulation**, is used in the treatment of **depression**. Another form, called pulsed electromagnetic field stimulation, has been shown to be effective in the treatment of osteoarthritis.

Precautions

In general, persons who are interested in Breema, qigong, or any form of energy therapy that involves vigorous physical exercise or bodywork should seek the advice of a qualified medical practitioner before starting such a program. This precaution is particularly important for persons with chronic heart or lung disease, persons recovering from surgery or acute illness, or persons with arthritis or other disorders that affect the muscles and joints.

Some forms of energy therapy may produce unexpected or startling psychological reactions. For example, a type of psychospiritual energy referred to as Kundalini in Indian yoga sometimes produces experiences of spiritual crisis that may be interpreted by mainstream psychiatrists as symptoms of **schizophrenia** or another psychotic disorder. Practitioners of Reiki healing have reported instances of patients feeling tingling sensations, "spaciness," an "out of body" sensation, sudden warmth, or similar experiences. As a rule, people in treatment for any mental condition or disorder should consult their therapist before beginning any form of energy treatment. This precaution is particularly important for patients diagnosed with post-traumatic stress disorder or a dissociative disorder, and for those who are easily hypnotized. It is also a good idea to find out as much as possible about the background and basic beliefs associated with a specific energy therapy, including the training or credentialing of its practitioners.

KEY TERMS

Aura—An energy field that is thought to emanate from the human body and to be visible to people with special psychic or spiritual powers.

Ayurvedic medicine—The traditional medical system of India. Ayurvedic treatments include diet, exercises, herbal treatments, meditation, massage, breathing techniques, and exposure to sunlight.

Biofield therapies—A subgroup of energy therapies that make use of energy fields (biofields) thought to exist within or emanate from the human body. Biofield therapies include such approaches as Reiki, therapeutic touch, qigong, and polarity balancing.

Bodywork—Any technique involving hands-on massage or manipulation of the body.

Chakra—One of the seven major energy centers in the body, according to traditional Indian yoga.

Endorphins—A group of peptide compounds released by the body in response to stress or traumatic injury. Endorphins react with opiate receptors in the brain to reduce or relieve pain.

Kundalini—In Indian yoga, a vital force or energy at the base of the spine that is activated or released by certain yoga postures or breathing techniques. This release is called the "awakening" of the kundalini. Some Westerners have had kundalini experiences that were diagnosed as psychotic episodes or symptoms of schizophrenia.

Meridians—In traditional Chinese medicine, a network of pathways or channels that convey qi, or vital energy, through the body.

Qi—The traditional Chinese term for vital energy or the life force. The word is also spelled "ki" or "chi" in English translations of Japanese and Chinese medical books.

Preparation

Most forms of energy therapy require little preparation on the patient's part except for the wearing of loose and comfortable clothes. Patients are asked to remove jewelry before a polarity balancing treatment and to remove eyeglasses and shoes prior to Reiki treatment. Qigong should not be practiced on either a full or a completely empty stomach.

Aftercare

Aftercare for therapeutic touch and Reiki usually involves a few moments of quiet rest to maximize the benefits of treatment. Aftercare for polarity therapy includes increased fluid intake for one to two weeks and other dietary adjustments that may be recommended by the practitioner.

Risks

There are no known risks associated with therapeutic touch or polarity balancing. In using Reiki, precautions should be taken with clients diagnosed with schizophrenia, **psychosis**, dissociative disorder, manic/depressive (bipolar) or borderline personality. The risk of physical injury from the exercises involved in Breema or qigong are minimal for patients who have consulted their primary physician beforehand and are working with a qualified instructor.

Mild headache has been reported as a side effect of transcranial magnetic stimulation. No side effects have been associated with self-administered magnetic therapy.

Results

Normal results for energy therapies include increased physical vitality, lowered blood pressure, a sense of calm or relaxation, improved sleep at night, and a strengthened immune system. Some persons report pain relief and speeded-up healing of wounds from magnetic therapy, Reiki, and qigong.

Abnormal results from energy therapies can include physical injury, severe headache, dizziness, depressed mood, or increased anxiety.

Resources

BOOKS

Collinge, William. *Subtle Energy: Awakening to the Unseen Forces in Our Lives.* New York: Warner Books, Inc., 1998.

Krieger, Dolores. *Accepting Your Power to Heal: The Personal Practice of Therapeutic Touch.* New York: Bear and Company, 1993.

Mitchell, Karyn. *Reiki: A Torch in Daylight.* St. Charles, IL: Mind Rivers Publications, 1994.

Pelletier, Kenneth R. "Spirituality and Healing: As Above ... So Below." In *The Best Alternative Medicine.* New York: Touchstone, 2002.

Sovatsky, Stuart. "Kundalini Awakening: Breakdown or Breakthrough?" In *Living Yoga: A Comprehensive Guide for Daily Life,* edited by George Feuerstein and Stephan Bodian. New York: Penguin Books, 1993.

Stein, Diane. *All Women Are Healers: A Comprehensive Guide to Natural Healing.* Freedom, CA: The Crossing Press, 1990.

Stein, Diane. *Essential Reiki: A Complete Guide to an Ancient Healing Art.* Freedom, CA: The Crossing Press, Inc., 1995.

Svoboda, Robert, and Arnie Lade. *Tao and Dharma: Chinese Medicine and Ayurveda.* Twin Lakes, WI: Lotus Press, 1995.

OTHER

U.S. National Center for Complementary and Alternative Medicine. "Major Domains of Complementary and Alternative Medicine, Appendix 1," in *Expanding Horizons of Healthcare: Five-Year Strategic Plan 2001–2005.* http://nccam.nih.gov/about/plans/fiveyear/fiveyear.pdf (accessed October 11, 2011).

ORGANIZATIONS

American Association of Naturopathic Physicians, 4435 Wisconsin Ave., NW Ste. 403, Washington, DC, 20016, (202) 237-8150, Fax: (202) 237-8152, (866) 538-2267, http://www.naturopathic.org.

American Polarity Therapy Association, 122 N. Elm St., Ste. 512, Greensboro, NC, 27401, (336) 574-1121, Fax: (336) 574-1151, aptaoffices@polaritytherapy.org, http://www.polaritytherapy.org.

International Society for the Study of Subtle Energies and Energy Medicine, 2770 Arapahoe Rd., Ste. 132, Lafayette, CO, 80026, (303) 425-4625, Fax: (866) 269-0972, http://www.issseem.org.

National Center for Complementary and Alternative Medicine, NCCAM Clearinghouse, PO Box 7923, Gaithersburg, MD, 20898, (888) 644-6226, Fax: (866) 464-3616, info@nccam.nih.gov, http://www.nccam.nih.gov.

Qigong Human Life Research Foundation, PO Box 5327, Cleveland, OH, 44101,

Therapeutic Touch International Association, PO Box 419, Craryville, NY, 12521, (518) 325-1185, Fax: (509) 693-3537, nhpai@therapeutic-touch.org, http://www.therapeutic-touch.org.

Rebecca J. Frey, PhD

Enuresis

Definition

Enuresis, more commonly called bed-wetting, is an elimination disorder that involves the voluntary or involuntary release of urine into bedding, clothing, or other inappropriate places. In adults, loss of bladder control is often referred to as urinary incontinence rather than enuresis; it is frequently found in patients with late-stage **Alzheimer's disease** or other forms of **dementia**.

Demographics

Enuresis is a problem of the young and is twice as common in boys as in girls. At age five, about 7% of boys and 3% of girls have enuresis. This number declines steadily in older children; by age 18, only about 1% of adolescents experience enuresis. Studies done in several countries suggest that there is no apparent cultural influence on the incidence of enuresis in children. On the other hand, the disorder does appear to run in families; children with one parent who wet the bed as a child are five to seven times more likely to have enuresis than children whose parents did not have the disorder in childhood.

Description

Enuresis is a condition that has been described since 1500 B.C. People with enuresis wet the bed or release urine at other inappropriate times. Release of urine at night (nocturnal enuresis) is much more common than daytime, or diurnal, wetting. Enuresis commonly affects young children and is involuntary. Many cases of enuresis cease as the child matures, although some children need behavioral or physiological treatment in order to remain dry.

There are two main types of enuresis in children. Primary enuresis occurs when a child has never established bladder control. Secondary enuresis occurs when a person has established bladder control for a period of six months, then relapses and begins wetting. To be diagnosed with enuresis, a person must be at least five years old or have reached a developmental age of five years. Below this age, problems with bladder control are considered normal.

Causes and symptoms

Enuresis occurs when a person urinates in inappropriate places or at inappropriate times. The *Diagnostic and Statistical Manual of Mental Disorders (DSM)* does not distinguish between those who wet the bed involuntarily and those who voluntarily release urine. Increasingly, however, research findings suggest that voluntary and involuntary enuresis have different causes.

Enuresis in children

Involuntary enuresis is much more common than voluntary enuresis. Involuntary enuresis may be categorized as either primary or secondary. Primary enuresis occurs when young children lack bladder control from infancy. Most of these children have urine control problems only during sleep; they do not consciously, intentionally, or maliciously wet the bed. Research suggests that children who are nighttime-only bed wetters may have a nervous system that is slow to process the feeling of a full bladder. Consequently, these children do not wake up in time to relieve themselves. In other cases, the child's enuresis may be related to a sleep disorder.

Children with diurnal enuresis wet only during the day. There appear to be two types of daytime wetters. One group seems to have difficulty controlling the urge to urinate. The other group consciously delays urinating until they lose control. Some children have both diurnal and nocturnal enuresis.

Several studies have investigated the association of primary enuresis and psychiatric or behavior problems. The results suggest that primary nocturnal enuresis is not caused by psychological disorders. Bed-wetting runs in families, however, and there is strong evidence of a genetic component to involuntary enuresis.

A small number of children have abnormalities in the anatomical structure of their kidney or bladder that interfere with bladder control, but normally the cause is not the physical structure of the urinary system. A few children appear to have to have a lower-than-normal ability to concentrate urine, due to low levels of antidiuretic hormone (ADH). This hormone helps to regulate fluid balance in the body. Large amounts of dilute urine cause the bladder to overflow at night.

Secondary enuresis occurs when a child has stayed dry day and night for at least six months, then returns to wetting. Secondary enuresis usually occurs at night. Many studies have been done to determine if there is a psychological component to enuresis. Researchers have found that secondary enuresis is more likely to occur after a child has experienced a stressful life event such as the birth of a sibling, divorce or death of a parent, or moving to a new house.

Unlike involuntary enuresis, voluntary enuresis is not common. It is associated with such psychiatric disorders as **oppositional defiant disorder** and is substantially different from ordinary nighttime bed-wetting. Voluntary enuresis is always secondary.

Enuresis in adults

Enuresis or urinary incontinence in elderly adults may be caused by loss of independent control of body functions resulting from dementia, bladder infections, uncontrolled diabetes, side effects of medications, or weakened bladder muscles. Urinary incontinence in adults is managed by treatment of the underlying medical condition, if one is present, or by the use of adult briefs with disposable liners.

Diagnosis

Enuresis is most often diagnosed in children because the parents express concern to the child's doctor. The pediatrician or family physician will give the child a physical examination to rule out medical conditions that may be causing the problem, including structural abnormalities in the child's urinary tract. The doctor may also rule out a sleep disorder as a possible cause. In many cases the pediatrician can reassure the child's parents and give them helpful advice.

According to the **American Psychiatric Association**, making a **diagnosis** of enuresis requires that a child must have reached the chronological or developmental age of five. Inappropriate urination must occur at least twice a week for three months, or the frequency of inappropriate urination must cause significant distress and interfere with the child's school and/or social life. Finally, the behavior cannot be caused exclusively by a medical condition or as a side effect of medication.

Treatment

Treatment for enuresis is not always necessary. About 15% of children who have enuresis outgrow it each year after age six. When treatment is desired, a physician will rule out obvious physical causes of enuresis through a physical examination and medical history. Several different treatment options are then available.

Traditional

BEHAVIOR MODIFICATION. **Behavior modification** is often the treatment of choice for enuresis. It is inexpensive and has a success rate of about 75%. The child's bedding includes a special pad with a sensor that rings a bell when the pad becomes wet. The bell wakes the child, who then gets up and goes to the bathroom to finish emptying his bladder. Over time, the child becomes conditioned to waking up when the bladder feels full.

Once this response is learned, some children continue to wake themselves without help from the alarm, while others are able to sleep all night and remain dry. A less expensive behavioral technique involves setting an alarm clock to wake the child every night after a few hours of sleep, until the child learns to wake up spontaneously. In trials, this method was as effective as the pad-and-alarm system. A newer technique involves an ultrasound monitor worn on the child's pajamas. The monitor can sense bladder size, and sets off an alarm once the bladder reaches a predetermined level of fullness. This technique avoids having to change wet bed pads.

Other behavior modifications that can be used alone or with the pad-and-alarm system include:

- restricting liquids starting several hours before bedtime
- waking the child up in the night to use the bathroom
- teaching urinary retention techniques
- giving the child positive reinforcement for dry nights and being sympathetic and understanding about wet nights

PSYCHOTHERAPY. Primary enuresis does not require **psychotherapy**. Secondary enuresis, however, is often successfully treated with therapy. The goal of the treatment is to resolve the underlying stressful event that has caused a **relapse** into bed-wetting. Unlike children with involuntary enuresis, children who intentionally urinate in inappropriate places often have other serious psychiatric disorders. Voluntary enuresis is usually a symptom of another disorder. Therapy to treat the underlying disorder is essential to resolving the enuresis.

Drugs

There are two main drugs for treating enuresis. **Imipramine**, a tricyclic antidepressant, has been used since the early 1960s. It appears to work in up to 60% of cases, although relapse occurs in about 50% of successful treatments. Desmopressin acetate (DDAVP), which acts as an antidiuretic, has been widely used to treat enuresis since the 1990s. It is available as a nasal spray or tablet and can effective in up to 65% of cases. Relapse rates with DDAVP can be as high as 80%.

Alternative

Some success in treating bed-wetting has been reported using hypnosis. When hypnosis works, the results are seen within four to six sessions. **Acupuncture** and massage have also been used to treat enuresis, with inconclusive results.

Prognosis

Enuresis is a disorder that most children outgrow. The short-term success rate with drug treatments is even higher than with behavioral therapy. Drugs do not, however, eliminate the enuresis. Many children who take drugs to control their bed-wetting relapse when the drugs are stopped.

Prevention

Although enuresis cannot be prevented, one side effect of the disorder is the shame and social embarrassment it causes. Children who wet themselves may avoid sleepovers, camp, and other activities where their bed-wetting will become obvious. Loss of these opportunities can cause a loss of self-esteem, social isolation, and adjustment problems. A kind, low-key approach to enuresis helps to prevent these problems.

KEY TERMS

Bladder—A muscular sac in the lower abdomen that holds urine until it is discharged from the body.

Elimination—The medical term for expelling waste from the body.

Primary enuresis—Bed-wetting in a child who has not yet developed bladder control.

Secondary enuresis—Bed-wetting in a child who has established bladder control but has begun to wet the bed again, usually as the result of emotional stress.

Urinary incontinence—A term that is sometimes used for enuresis in adults. Urinary incontinence is often found in patients with late-stage Alzheimer's disease or other adult-onset dementias.

Urinary system—The kidney, urethra, bladder, and associated organs that process urine and eliminate it from the body.

Resources

BOOKS

American Psychiatric Association. *Diagnostic and Statistical Manual of Mental Disorders*. 4th ed., text rev. Washington, DC: American Psychiatric Publishing, 2000.

Mace, Nancy L., and Peter V. Rabins. *The 36-Hour Day*. 5th ed. Baltimore, MD: Johns Hopkins University Press, 2011.

Maizels, Max, Diane Rosenbaum, and Barbara Keating. *Getting Dry: How to Help Your Child Overcome Bed-wetting*. Boston: Harvard Common Press, 1999.

Sadock, Benjamin J., and Virginia A. Sadock, eds. *Comprehensive Textbook of Psychiatry*. Vol. 2. 7th ed. Philadelphia: Lippincott Williams and Wilkins, 2000.

PERIODICALS

Mikkelsen, Edwin J. "Enuresis and Encopresis: Ten Years of Progress." *Journal of the American Academy of Child and Adolescent Psychiatry* 40, no. 10 (October 2001): 1146–58.

WEBSITES

American Academy of Child & Adolescent Psychiatry (AACAP). "Bedwetting." AACAP Facts For Families Pamphlet, Number 18. Washington, DC: American Academy of Child & Adolescent Psychiatry, December 2011. Available online at http://aacap.org/page.ww?name=Bedwetting§ion=Facts+for+Families (accessed December 10, 2011).

MedlinePlus. "Enuresis." U.S. National Library of Medicine. National Institutes of Health. http://www.nlm.nih.gov/medlineplus/ency/article/001556.htm (accessed October 6, 2011).

National Guideline Clearinghouse. "Nocturnal Enuresis: The Management of Bedwetting in Children and Young People." U.S. Agency for Health Care Research and Quality. 2011. http://www.guideline.gov/content.aspx?id=25680&search=enuresis (accessed October 6, 2011).

National Kidney and Urologic Diseases Information Clearinghouse. "Urinary Incontinence in Children." U.S. National Institute of Diabetes and Digestive and Kidney Diseases. September 2010. http://kidney.niddk.nih.gov/kudiseases/pubs/uichildren/index.aspx (accessed October 6, 2011).

National Kidney Foundation. "Bedwetting." 2001. http://www.kidney.org/patients/bw/index.cfm (accessed October 6 2011).

ORGANIZATIONS

American Academy of Child and Adolescent Psychiatry, 3615 Wisconsin Ave. NW, Washington, DC, 20016-3007, (202) 966-7300, Fax: (202) 966-2891, http://aacap.org.

National Association for Continence, PO Box 1019, Charleston, SC, 29402-1019, (800) 252-3337, http://www.nafc.org.

National Kidney Foundation, 30 East 33rd Street, New York, NY, 10016, (800) 622-9010, http://www.kidney.org.

Tish Davidson, AM
Emily Jane Willingham, PhD

Epigenetics

Definition

Epigenetics refers to the paradigm for explaining mental health, emphasizing how environmental factors affect the expression of genetic predispositions. In psychology, three approaches have evolved defining epigenetics. The first approach stresses that the interaction of genetics and environment is more important than either individual influence. The second approach emphasizes that all human development is shaped by experience while still following a biological blueprint. The third approach emphasizes that any genetic trait can be "switched on" or "switched off" by specific environmental factors. All three approaches are based on the belief that the cause of every mental disorder has a genetic predisposition and an environmental activator.

Description

Across its short history, psychology has sought to explain any mental health phenomenon as the effect of either genetics or experiences. The Freudian model, which was popular in the early twentieth century, emphasized that an adult's personality is determined by early childhood experience. This idea led to the conclusion that all psychological disorders are caused by traumatic disruptions in the healthy development. More advanced research demonstrated that there is a strong genetic influence on personality traits. Also on the genetic side, the medical model of psychopathology suggests that disorders can be solved by finding the right drug to resolve the disorder. The study of genetic influences on development and mental health has appeared to be most suitable for scientific study. Still, many have come to accept that a person's fate or destiny is not determined by genetics or biology.

The interaction approach

The classical debate over whether genetics or environment has more influence has been termed "nature versus nurture" with various theories taking one side or the other. While most practitioners have accepted the influence of both, the evolution of psychological theory has seen the emergence of theories emphasizing either extreme. Contemplating the extremes has led to the conclusion that the two influences interact in such a way that it is difficult to identify the individual influence of either. The term for the genetic predisposition for a trait is the *genotype.* The actual expression of the trait is the *phenotype.* What the genotype goes through to become the phenotype is the interaction with environmental influences, ranging from diet to maternal care.

With advances in genetic studies, identification of those disorders with strong genetic influences started to emerge. However, these studies could not explain why the genetic influence was not absolute. For example, **schizophrenia** has a high genetic influence. If an identical twin has schizophrenia, there is a strong (but not absolute) probability that his or her twin will also become schizophrenic. Since identical twins share the same genetic foundation, if there is a genetic cause to a disorder, the percentage of twins sharing a disorder should be 100%. The genetic influence hypothesis cannot explain why a good proportion of identical twins do not become schizophrenic when their twins develop schizophrenia. Similarly, the experiential influence hypothesis for such disorders as **post-traumatic stress disorder** (PTSD) cannot explain the individual differences in the intensity and endurance of PTSD among victims sharing the same experience.

In 1999, an important study took place over three different research sites illustrating that genetics have been overly emphasized as influences for personality traits, temperament, and psychological disorders. Researchers John C. Crabbe, Douglas Wahlstein, and Bruce C. Dudek assured that each site had the same set of mice with eight different strains. The mice of the same strains were virtually identical. The three sites created the exact same environmental and living conditions. The goal of the study was to standardize methods for testing various genetic traits. However, the surprise findings were that for most of the assessed tasks, there was little genetic influence on results. If genetics had a strong influence, the performance of the genetically similar mice should be the same. This was not found overall, only for a few individual tasks.

The developmental approach

Developmental **psychologist** Erik Erikson was the first theorist to use the term *epigenetics* to describe the process of development. Erikson saw epigenetic influences as biological age-related social skills that emerged to meet the demands of the social environment. Most development theorists see a similar phenomenon in other aspects of development.

An important contribution to healthy development is establishing attachment in infancy. Attachment is established through the primary caregiver—usually the mother—constantly meeting the infant's needs with a goal of the child learning trust. This lesson of trust stays with the child throughout childhood into maturity. Children who have established a secure attachment with their primary caregiver (usually the mother) feel that the world is manageable and that they have a place in it. Establishing attachment can be thwarted by anxiety in the mother or a nervous temperament in the child. Attachment has been studied in mice and rhesus monkeys.

In the animal studies, researchers looked at how upbringing affected temperament. For example, in mice, **stress** reactivity is a genetic trait that affects how the mother takes care of her young. The mice grow up with the tendency to stress based on genetic influence and early experience. However, if the genetically stressed mice are raised by a genetically calm mother, they grow up to tolerate stress and to later be calm mothers themselves. Generations later, the anxious gene was still present, but the mice acted the same as the genetically calm mice. Regardless of the genetic disposition, the early experiences set a pattern for life, which could be passed on to the next generation.

There were similar findings with rhesus monkeys. Grown rhesus monkeys can change temperament patterns depending on community influences, but they will revert back to the inborn pattern if community influences are altered. However, genetically influenced emotions can be changed for life if the baby monkey is raised by a calm mother in the first six months of life.

The lasting effects of highly reactive temperament and early maternal deprivation have also been studied with rhesus monkeys. When rhesus monkeys suffer maternal deprivation in their early years, there is no measurable negative influence on later life. The one key difference is if the rhesus monkey was born with a highly reactive temperament. Those affected have faulty neuroendocrine systems from infancy that interfere with their growth and metabolism. In later life, these monkeys demonstrated abnormal behavioral and emotional reactions.

Among humans, parenting can provide a point of interaction between heredity and environment. In studies, resilient children growing up in a stressful environment appear to be unaffected by negative influences if they had a good attachment with their mothers in the first 12 to 18 months of life. Studies of the genetic influence of schizophrenia found that adopted children with a genetic predisposition for the disorder tend to avoid the disorder if they are adopted into a supportive family. In the cases where the adopted family was dysfunctional, the genetic predisposition was more likely to arise.

It is the hope of epigenetic studies that unwanted traits, temperaments, and disorders can be "treated" by environmental influences. Changing the environment and enhancing parental support in the early years may counter genetic tendencies. Such research expectations have led scientists to accept that although a person may possess a genetic predisposition for a disorder, whether this predisposition is manifested or not may depend on environmental circumstances. Even where there is an extremely negative environmental condition, the effects may be modified by early childhood influences such as resiliency.

The geneticist approach

A more narrow use of the term *epigenetics* comes from geneticists who investigate why the human genome cannot explain all psychological phenomena. This approach relates to the other two but focuses on how specific environmental factors can interfere with the normal expression of a particular gene while not changing the underlying DNA. Since the beginning of the twentieth century, genetic researchers have recognized that gene function could be altered by agents that did not upset the normal sequence of the gene. More recent discoveries of geneticists have long-range implications of enhancing human achievement and more immediate implications of solving mental disorders.

A breakthrough study in genetics was conducted in recent years by Randy Jirtle with a strain of mice known as agouti mice. These mice carried a specific maladaptive gene that gave them a yellow color as they grew. The gene also interfered with the mice's natural inclination to stop eating when full. Some other traits of this gene left the mice vulnerable to diabetes and cancer. The study focused on how to offset the bad conditions of this gene as early in life as possible. The researchers were testing the theoretical assumption that the gene could be "switched off" through changing the diet of the mother before and during the period of conception. The diet was rich in methyl, a biological compound naturally occurring in many foods. The methyl compound is a known agent in gene imprinting. The process of introducing it into the gene is known as DNA methylation.

By feeding the mother this diet, the researchers were able to prevent the agouti gene from expressing itself in the offspring. The important finding was that the gene

KEY TERMS

Attachment—The bond developed between an infant and the primary caregiver within the first 12 to 18 months of life and expected to have lifelong effects.

DNA methylation—The imprinting process of introducing methyl into a gene, suppressing its usual function.

Environmental influence—Any component of the cause of a behavior or condition that is perceived to be developed from experience.

Genetic influence—Any component of the cause of a behavior or condition that is inherited biologically from parents.

Neuroendocrine system—The part of the autonomic nervous system responsible for growth and hormonal regulation.

Paradigm—The commonly accepted foundations among a group of similar theories, usually derived from a philosophy, including assumptions, terminology, measurements and expectations.

Phenylketonuria (PKU)—An enzyme deficiency present at birth that disrupts metabolism and causes brain damage. If left untreated, the disease progresses into intellectual disability.

Post-traumatic stress disorder (PTSD)—A psychological reaction that continues long after a highly stressful event and is characterized by depression, anxiety, flashbacks, and nightmares.

Schizophrenia—A severe mental illness in which a person has difficulty distinguishing what is real from what is not real. It is often characterized by hallucinations, delusions, and withdrawal from people and social activities.

was still present in later generations but still switched off, even with no dietary change in the later parents. Such a finding challenged the long-existing premise that any environmental influence on the expression of genes would not be found in future generations. Any gene whose expression was modified in one generation was presumed to be changed back with every new generation. Many other studies have reached similar conclusions that epigenetic effects can be passed from one generation to the next. However, while the change can happen quickly in one generation, the effects can be reversed in subsequent generations.

The basis for understanding this genetic manipulation lies in the well-researched area of gene imprinting. Scientists have known for a long time that naturally occurring environmental agents can suppress one or both of a gene's alleles. Each gene consists of two alleles that normally work together unless one is damaged or switched off. If one allele is damaged, the healthy one is expressed. Research has shown that, at times, environmental agents might switch off the healthy allele, allowing the damaged one to express itself as a threat to physical or mental health. What imprinting research has yet to show, but strongly implies, is that the healthy allele might be enhanced through epigenetic agents. The work of genetic researchers is to induce imprinting by manipulating genes or their alleles to promote greater mental and physical health.

There are several organizations working to promote epigenetic research at this genetic level. These include the National Institute of Environmental Health Sciences, Johns Hopkins University Center for Epigenetics in Common Human Disease, the European Human Epigenome Project, and the Epigenome Network of Excellence. Most of these include research with an emphasis on mental health, but the emphasis is usually small.

Disorders susceptible to epigenetic research and treatment

Phenylketonuria (PKU) was once a major source of **intellectual disability** in young children. It was first discovered in the middle 1930s, but the appropriate treatment was not developed until the late 1950s. The treatment consists of a diet without a common amino acid known as phenylketone. The crisis of PKU was a clear case of a genetic deficiency rearranged by an environmental **intervention**. Without the special diet, a child who inherited PKU would be intellectually disabled by his or her first birthday. With the special diet, the child can be expected to lead a relatively normal life.

Schizophrenia is an inherited disorder that is still not fully understood. However, accurate tests are being developed to recognize its genetic markers. It is known that there are more instances of schizophrenia in urban than in rural settings and in industrial nations than in nonindustrial nations. Therefore, environmental changes may reduce the chance of schizophrenia expressing itself when the genetic markers are present. Family setting can influence the onset of schizophrenia, with dysfunctional families having a greater occurrence than supportive families among those genetically predisposed. Researchers are working not only to identify the genetic marker but also to investigate its response to methylation or other imprinting manipulations.

Attachment disorders are another area of interest for researchers developing epigenetic therapy. These evolve from a faulty or incomplete attachment between an infant and the mother or primary caregiver. Infants with attachment disorder grow up to display inappropriate emotions, antisocial behaviors, and inconsistent moods. Although the development of attachment appears to be clearly in the "nurture" side, it can be influenced by the infant's inborn temperament. The results can also have an effect on the neuroendocrine and cognitive systems. The occurrence of attachment disorders may be reduced through parenting classes that teach new parents the importance of the behaviors that foster attachment.

Resources

BOOKS

Durand, V. Mark, and David H. Barlow. *Essentials of Abnormal Psychology,* 5th ed. Mason, OH: Wadsworth, Cengage Learning, 2009.

Allis, C. David, Thomas Jenuwein, and Danny Reinberg, eds. *Epigenetics.* Cold Spring Harbor, NY: Cold Spring Harbor Laboratory Press, 2009.

PERIODICALS

Albert, Paul R. "Epigenetics in Mental Illness: Hope or Hype?" *Journal of Psychiatry and Neuroscience* 35, no. 6 (November 2010): 366. http://dx.doi.org/10.1503/jpn.100148 (accessed September 16, 2011).

Cloud, John. "Why Your DNA Isn't Your Destiny." *TIME* 175, no. 2 (January 18, 2010). http://www.time.com/time/magazine/article/0,9171,1952313,00.html (accessed September 16, 2011).

Stahl, Stephen M. "Epigenetic Hypotheses of Schizophrenia." *Psychopharmacology Educational Updates* 6, no. 8 (August 2010).

———. "Essential Psychopharmastahlogy: Fooling Mother Nature: Epigenetics and Novel Treatments for Psychiatric Disorders." *Psychopharmacology Educational Updates* 6, no. 11 (November 2010).

Weinhold, Bob. "Epigenetics: The Science of Change." *Environmental Health Perspective* 114 (March 1, 2006): 160–67. http://dx.doi.org/10.1289/ehp.114-a160 (accessed August 24, 2011).

WEBSITES

Genetic Science Learning Center, University of Utah. "Epigenetics and the Human Brain." http://learn.genetics.utah.edu/content/epigenetics/brain (accessed September 16, 2011).

Marlow, Sally. "Epigenetics in Psychiatric Disorders: A Guide for Beginners." *BioNews* 549 (March 15, 2010). http://www.bionews.org.uk/page_55848.asp (accessed September 16, 2011).

NOVA. "Epigenetics." PBS video (13:02 min.) Aired July 24, 2007. http://www.pbs.org/wgbh/nova/body/epigenetics.html (accessed September 16, 2011).

ORGANIZATIONS

Johns Hopkins University Center for Epigenetics in Common Human Disease, 855 N Wolfe St., Baltimore, MD, 21205, (410) 614-3489, http://www.hopkinsmedicine.org/epigenetics.

National Institute of Environmental Health Sciences, 111 T. W. Alexander Dr., Research Triangle Park, NC, 27709, (919) 541-0049, webcenter@niehs.nih.gov, http://www.niehs.nih.gov.

Ray F. Brogan, PhD

Epilepsy *see* **Seizures**

Epinephrine *see* **Adrenaline**

Erectile dysfunction

Definition

Erectile dysfunction (ED) is the consistent inability to achieve or maintain a penile erection that is sufficient for satisfactory sexual intercourse.

Demographics

It is estimated that 15–30 million American men suffer from some degree of ED. Of these, 10–20 million have severe ED, resulting in the complete inability to attain or maintain a penile erection. However, ED is believed to be underreported, underdiagnosed, and undertreated due to its perceived **stigma**. In a survey of general medical practice, less than 12% of men with ED reported having received treatment. Thus, the actual incidence of ED may be much higher than most estimates.

The incidence of ED increases with age, along with the incidence of chronic disorders and conditions that are commonly associated with ED, including diabetes, hypertension, and cardiovascular disease. It is estimated that 26% of men in their 50s, 40% of men in their 60s, and 77% of men 75 and older have some degree of ED. The number of American men with ED is estimated to increase by nearly 10 million by 2025, and the worldwide incidence is projected to be more than 320 million.

Description

Although most men experience occasional transient impotence, usually associated with **fatigue**, anger, **depression**, or other stressful emotions, erectile dysfunction is the consistent inability to achieve or maintain an erection. The term "impotence" is now rarely used because of its association with weakness and powerlessness.

Penile erection occurs when the penis becomes engorged with blood. The anatomical compartments—the two corpora cavernosa and the corpus spongiosum—can be distended with up to seven times the normal amount of blood. Along with the relaxation of the penile muscles, this distention results in an erection.

The sequence of events resulting in penile erection is complex. Erection is usually initiated by sexual arousal stimuli in the **brain** as a result of visual, auditory, or olfactory sensations or erotic thoughts. Tactile (touch) sensations of the penis, acting through the spinal cord, play a similar role. Sexual arousal results in the release of nitric oxide from specialized cells. Nitric oxide causes the formation of cyclic glutamine monophosphate (cGMP), which is responsible for dilating the blood vessels of the penis and relaxing the penile muscles, enabling increased blood flow and erection. Compression of the dilated blood vessels against the firm outer lining of the penis prevents the blood from escaping and perpetuates the erection. The enzyme called phosphodiesterase-5 (PDE5) causes the breakdown of cGMP and, in association with nerves from the sympathetic nervous system, enables the penis to return to its flaccid relaxed state. Any defect in this complex cascade of events can result in ED.

Sex is an important quality-of-life issue for adults of all ages, and ED usually results in a reduced quality of life. Many affected men experience depression, distress, and relationship difficulties as a result of ED. Despite this fact, men with ED often fail to seek help. Reasons for this failure include:

- patient ignorance of the availability of safe and effective ED therapies
- inadequate information from physicians about the timing of medications, the need for preliminary sexual arousal, and other factors
- marital discord and lack of partner support
- concerns about invasiveness, adverse effects, discomfort, inconvenience, and cost of therapies
- high rates of discontinuation of therapy due to inadequate responses and adverse effects

ED can occur as part of several mental disorders recognized by the mental health professional's manual, the ***Diagnostic and Statistical Manual of Mental Disorders*** (*DSM*). ED is listed as erectile disorder and is classified by the *DSM* as a sexual dysfunction. ED can also be a symptom of other disorders, such as sexual dysfunction due to a general medical condition or substance-induced sexual dysfunction.

Risk factors

ED is frequently associated with vascular conditions such as hypertension and coronary artery heart disease and may even serve as a marker for the detection of cardiovascular disorders. Additionally, ED is associated with depression that is distinct from the reactive depression that it may cause. Lifestyle factors—such as obesity, physical inactivity, cigarette smoking, and excessive intake of alcohol—are also risk factors for ED.

Causes and symptoms

Because of the complicated nature of the human sexual response and the complex physiology of penile erection and relaxation, it is often difficult or impossible to determine the precise cause of ED in individual cases. Normal erectile function requires the coordination of vascular, neurologic, hormonal, and psychological components, and any condition that interferes with one or more of these processes can result in ED. Multiple factors frequently contribute to ED.

Although the incidence of ED increases with age, it is no longer regarded as an inevitable consequence of aging. Likewise, whereas most cases of ED were once considered primarily psychological and/or psychiatric in origin, it is now recognized that organic, nonpsychological factors play a much more significant role, with physical causes underlying at least 80% of cases. However, significant psychological and social factors, such as guilt, depression, anxiety, tension, or marital discord, are often present in addition to one or more of the following physical components:

- Diabetes mellitus is the single most common cause of ED, resulting from a combination of nerve and blood vessel damage. As many as 50% of male diabetics have ED.
- Hardening of the arteries (arteriosclerosis) is the most common vascular (circulation-related) cause of ED. Diseases of the aorta or the arteries supplying the pelvis and penis or damage to arteries from trauma, surgery, or irradiation can cause ED. Surgery involving the prostate gland may affect both arteries and nerves.
- A variety of diseases and factors can influence penile circulation. For example, Peyronie's disease, characterized by fibrous tissue and bending of the penis, limits the expandability of penile tissues and prevents the venous compression that retains blood in the penis. Arteriosclerotic plaque, injury to the inner lining blood vessels from trauma, surgery, or irradiation, or aortic occlusion (blockage in a main artery leading out of the heart) can compromise penile blood flow and prevent erection.
- Neurological causes of ED include diseases of the brain and spinal cord, such as Alzheimer's disease or multiple sclerosis, respectively.
- Hormonal or endocrine causes of ED are uncommon, although deficient testicular function and low circulating levels of the male sex hormone testosterone can result in erectile dysfunction. These are referred to as

KEY TERMS

Arteriosclerosis—A thickening and hardening of the walls of the arteries with loss of elasticity.

Corpora cavernosa—The pair of columns of erectile tissue on either side of the penis that, together with the corpus spongiosum, produce an erection when filled with blood.

Corpus spongiosum—The column of erectile tissue in the penis that contains the urethra.

Dopamine—A chemical in brain tissue that transmits nerve impulses (a neurotransmitter) and helps to regulate movement and emotions.

Hypertension—Abnormally high arterial blood pressure, which if left untreated can lead to heart disease and stroke.

Hypogonadism—Functional incompetence of the male gonads, with impaired production of hormones and sperm cells.

Nitric oxide (NO)—A regulator of various bodily processes, including penile erection.

Phosphodiesterase-5 (PDE5)—An enzyme that is involved in the loss of penile erection.

Prolactin—A hormone produced by the pituitary gland.

Prostate—The walnut-shaped gland that surrounds the urethra at the neck of the bladder in males and supplies fluid for semen.

Testosterone—The primary male sex hormone.

Urethra—The tube in the penis that discharges urine from the bladder to the outside of the body.

hypogonadism and can be due to congenital abnormalities or testicular disease.

- Various classes of medications can cause ED, although not all drugs within a class have the same effect. For example, some antidepressants are associated with ED, whereas the antidepressant trazodone (Desyrel) tends to prolong penile erection. Some high blood pressure medications, central nervous system medications such as methyldopa for Parkinson's disease, sedatives or tranquilizers such as barbiturates, and antianxiety medications such as diazepam (Valium) can also cause ED.
- Tobacco, alcohol, and illicit drugs, including heroin, can cause ED.
- Psychological factor, including stress, fatigue, depression, guilt, low self-esteem, or negative feelings for or by a sexual partner, can precipitate ED. Depressive symptoms or difficulty coping with anger can be particularly detrimental.

Although the primary ED symptom is the inability to attain or maintain an adequate erection for completed sexual activity, patterns of ED vary. Some men are unable to attain any erection. Others cannot maintain an erection adequate for penetration. Some men lose their erection during sexual intercourse. Others experience an erection only upon awakening or during masturbation.

Diagnosis

Diagnosis requires several different processes, including examination and tests.

Examination

Taking thorough medical, psychosocial (both psychological and social), and sexual histories are an essential first step in the diagnosis of ED. A general medical history can indicate the existence of ED-associated conditions such as high blood pressure, diabetes, or arteriosclerosis, as well as medications that may contribute to ED and any history of **substance abuse**. A psychosocial history includes current sexual practices, the existence of stresses or performance anxiety, and any special circumstances under which ED occurs. The sexual partner's participation in the psychosocial history can be beneficial. The sexual history helps distinguish ED from other abnormalities in sexual function, such as ejaculatory and orgasmic disturbances or loss of sexual desire. The patient's sexual history includes:

- the frequency and duration of sexual intercourse
- the degree and quality of penile erections
- nocturnal erections
- the success or failure of penetration
- any sexual dysfunction of the partner, such as painful intercourse (dyspareunia) or vaginal dryness

Self-administered questionnaires can assist in the evaluation of sexual function. The International Index of Erectile Function (IIEF) is the most widely used.

A routine physical examination is conducted with special emphasis on the genitourinary, circulatory, and neurologic systems. The physician may look for evidence of hypogonadism or congenital conditions causing defective testicular function. The genitalia are examined for testicular size and consistency and penile deformities. A rectal examination can evaluate the size and consistency of the prostate gland and certain muscular reflexes. Vital signs such as blood pressure and pulse are measured.

Tests

Blood tests and/or other assessments for high blood cholesterol, hypertension, coronary artery heart disease, and depression may be performed, since ED can be a marker or symptom of such disorders. Blood levels of the hormones testosterone and prolactin may be measured.

Procedures

A self-test is available for ED. Pharmacological testing involves the injection of a small amount of an agent, such as 10 micrograms of alprostadil (prostaglandin E1), that produces an erection in a patient with normal erectile function. Nocturnal studies are used to identify erectile dysfunction due to organic causes. Patients are monitored in a sleep laboratory for nocturnal erections, since men with physiologically normal erectile function have erections during sleep. Duplex Doppler ultrasonography provides information about arterial and venous blood flow.

Treatment

Various treatments are available and often combined for ED. These may include counseling, surgically implanted prostheses, and alternative remedies.

Traditional

Treatment for ED often involves a combination of therapies. Most men with ED benefit from counseling, which may be individual **psychotherapy**, psychosexual counseling, or **couples therapy**.

Various types of vacuum pumps are available for increasing penile blood flow. A constriction ring around the base of the penis traps the blood and maintains the erection.

Various types of penile prostheses can be surgically inserted into the penis to produce erections. In rare cases, surgery may be used to correct a defect that interferes with penile erection.

Drugs

PDE5 inhibitors are the most common drug treatment for ED. These relax the muscles in the penis to increase penile blood flow and produce an erection. This class of drugs includes sildenafil (Viagra), vardenafil (Levitra), and tadalafil (Cialis). Because they can cause a sudden drop in blood pressure, these drugs should not be used by men who take nitroglycerin for heart problems. PDE5 inhibitors also have been associated with an increased risk for a rare condition called nonarteritic ischemic optic neuropathy, which can lead to sudden vision loss.

Intracavernous injection therapy (ICIT) is the injection of penile structures with the drugs alprostadil (Caverject), papaverine (Pavabid), or phentolamine, which promote blood flow. Alprostadil can also be inserted into the urethra to increase blood flow and relax muscles. Alpha-adrenergic blockers target adrenergic receptors in smooth muscles, causing the blood vessels to dilate more easily. Apomorphine is a morphine derivative that targets **dopamine** receptors to facilitate erections. Rarely, hormone treatments are used to treat ED. Finally, in some cases, the adjustment of prescription or over-the-counter medications is required, if these are interfering with erectile function.

Alternative

Some alternative remedies are suggested for treating ED, but results are conflicting, and none have proven to be clinically effective. These include:

- dehydroepiandrosterone (DHEA)
- ginkgo
- ginseng
- L-arginine
- yohimbe
- epimedium (called horny goat weed among other common names)
- zinc
- pomegranate juice, supplements, or seeds
- folic acid and vitamin E in combination with Viagra

Home remedies

A first step in ED treatment is the alteration or elimination of modifiable risk factors or causes, including smoking, obesity, and substance or alcohol abuse. Exercising can also have a beneficial effect on ED.

QUESTIONS TO ASK YOUR DOCTOR

- What might be causing my ED?
- Are there lifestyle changes that I can make that might reduce my ED?
- What treatment options do you recommend and why?
- What is my prognosis?

Prognosis

A better understanding of ED, combined with new, more effective therapies, has markedly improved the prognosis. It is estimated that at least 65% of all ED cases can be treated successfully. The modification of risk factors, such as physical inactivity, smoking, excessive alcohol intake, certain medications, and obesity, improve the prognosis. A 2010 study found that 30% of obese men with ED had improved function following weight loss. However, other risk factors, including aging and conditions such as diabetes or pelvic surgery affecting nerves, negatively impact the prognosis. ED appears to be a strong risk factor for cardiovascular disease, as well as for death from all causes.

Prevention

ED sometimes can be prevented in at-risk patients with medications for high blood pressure and other ED-associated conditions. Various lifestyle changes, including quitting smoking, losing weight, and avoiding alcohol and other substance abuse, can help prevent ED.

Resources

BOOKS

Blum, Ralph, and Mark Scholz. *Invasion of the Prostate Snatchers: No More Unnecessary Biopsies, Radical Treatment or Loss of Sexual Potency.* New York: Other Press, 2010.

Ellsworth, Pamela, and Bob Stanley. *100 Questions & Answers About Erectile Dysfunction,* 2nd ed. Sudbury, MA: Jones & Bartlett, 2008.

McVary, Kevin T. *Contemporary Treatment of Erectile Dysfunction: A Clinical Guide.* Totowa, NJ: Humana, 2010.

Morgentaler, Abraham. *Testosterone for Life: Revitalize Your Vitality, Sex Drive, Muscle Mass & Overall Health.* New York: McGraw-Hill, 2009.

Price, Joan. *Naked at Our Age: Talking Out Loud About Senior Sex.* Berkeley, CA: Seal Press, 2011.

Steidle, Christopher P., Janet Casperson, and John J. Mulcahy. *Sex and the Heart: Erectile Dysfunction's Link to Cardiovascular Disease.* Omaha, NE: Addicus Books, 2009.

Zaslau, Stanley. *Dx/Rx: Sexual Dysfunction in Men and Women.* Sudbury, MA: Jones & Bartlett Learning, 2011.

PERIODICALS

Heidelbaugh, Joel J. "Management of Erectile Dysfunction." *American Family Physician* 81, no. 3 (February 1, 2010): 305–12.

Katz, Alan, and Anne Katz. "Erectile Dysfunction." *Canadian Medical Association Journal* 56 (September 1, 2010): 898–903.

WEBSITES

"Erectile Dysfunction." American Diabetes Association. http://www.diabetes.org/living-with-diabetes/complications/mens-health/sexual-health/erectile-dysfunction.html (accessed July 26, 2011).

"Erectile Dysfunction." MedlinePlus. http://www.nlm.nih.gov/medlineplus/erectiledysfunction.html (accessed July 26, 2011).

"Erectile Dysfunction." National Institute of Digestive and Kidney Diseases. Last modified September 2, 2010. http://kidney.niddk.nih.gov/kudiseases/pubs/ED (accessed July 26, 2011).

"Erection Self-Test." MedlinePlus. http://www.nlm.nih.gov/medlineplus/ency/article/003339.htm (accessed July 26, 2011).

ORGANIZATIONS

American Diabetes Association, 1710 N Beauregard St., Alexandria, VA, 22311, (800) 342-2383, http://www.diabetes.org.

American Urological Association, 1000 Corporate Blvd., Linthicum, MD, 21090, (410) 689-3700, (866) 746-4282, Fax: (410) 689-3800, aua@AUAnet.org, http://www.auanet.org.

National Kidney and Urologic Diseases Information Clearinghouse, 3 Information Way, Bethesda, MD, 20892-3580, (703) 738-4929, (800) 891-5390, Fax: (703) 738-4929, nkudic@info.niddk.nih.gov, http://kidney.niddk.nih.gov.

Ralph Myerson, MD
Stephanie Watson
Margaret Alic, PhD

Escitalopram

Definition

Escitalopram (Lexapro) is a medication that belongs to the drug class called **selective serotonin reuptake inhibitors (SSRIs)**. Selective serotonin reuptake inhibitors are a group of medications used to treat

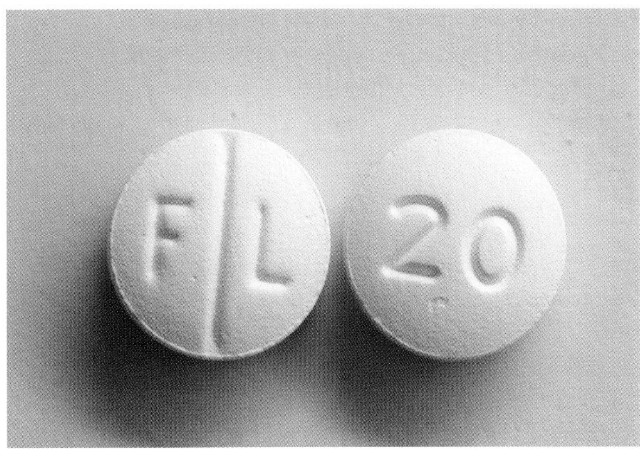

Lexapro (escitalopram), 20 mg. *(© Custom Medical Stock Photo, Inc. Reproduced by permission.)*

clinical **depression**, anxiety, and other psychiatric disorders. They specifically act on a chemical called **serotonin**, a type of **brain** neurotransmitter that is involved in normal brain function and can affect the physiological state of clinical depression.

Purpose

SSRIs such as escitalopram can be used to treat a broad range of mood and **stress** related psychiatric illnesses. They are mainly used to treat clinical depression and **anxiety disorders**, including **generalized anxiety disorder** (GAD), **panic disorder**, post-traumatic stress syndrome (PTSD), **premenstrual syndrome** disorders (PMS), stress related irritable bowel syndrome, **social phobia**, and the eating disorder **bulimia nervosa**. Choice of agent and whether they are used alone or in combination with other drugs depends on the medical disorder and individual health parameters. Escitalopram specifically is most often used for major depression and generalized anxiety disorder.

Description

Selective serotonin reuptake inhibitors like escitalopram have a therapeutic mechanism of action that is focused on the modulation of the natural body chemical serotonin. Serotonin is a type of neurotransmitter in the brain, specifically a chemical that neurons use to signal one another in complex pathways for brain functioning. **Neurotransmitters** like serotonin bind to chemical receptors on the surface of neurons (brain cells). Once bound to a receptor they affect physiological processes. The receptors activate a sequence of cellular events known as a chemical cascade or signaling pathway. Neurotransmitter signaling pathways are responsible for many normal brain functions. During the signaling process, neurotransmitters such as serotonin travel from one neuron to the next. These chemicals need to cross a short space between the end of one neuron and the beginning of the next neuron known as the synapse or synaptic space. Serotonin is released from the end of neuron one, crosses the synaptic space and binds to a specific receptor for serotonin on the surface of the next neuron (neuron two). Any extra serotonin that is left in the synaptic space is taken back up by neuron one in a process known as reuptake. The more serotonin is allowed to remain in the synaptic space, the more will eventually be allowed to bind to receptors on neuron two and participate in the signaling process. SSRIs such as escitalopram decrease the reuptake of serotonin by neuron one, allowing more serotonin to be present in the synapse and, therefore, more serotonin signaling to occur. It is believed that a decrease in serotonin signaling contributes to illness such as depression and anxiety disorders. SSRIs help by increasing serotonin signaling, with little effect on the synaptic levels of other neurotransmitters.

Whether a patient is going to benefit from an SSRI such as escitalopram may have a genetic component. Individual response to each SSRI varies greatly, and these drugs tend to require several weeks to take effect. The initial trial of **SSRIs** such as escitalopram can be difficult because the side effects begin right away while the beneficial effect takes up to two weeks to develop. Generally, escitalopram is attempted for four to six weeks before concluding it will not have an effect and switching to another agent. If there is an effect but the healthcare provider judges it could be improved, the dose is often increased as the patient is able to tolerate.

Recommended dosage

SSRIs such as escitalopram are taken as oral medications. The dosage varies depending on the individual patient response to the medication regarding its effectiveness, and the individual patient response to the medication regarding side effects. Some people naturally require a higher dose of escitalopram in order to achieve the desired effect. Other patients require a lower dose either for effect or because they quickly develop side effects that are not tolerable.

Escitalopram used for **major depressive disorder** or generalized anxiety disorder is dosed at 10–20 mg daily. Patients generally start at the 10 mg dose and gradually work their way up to the dose needed for effect after a week at the 10 mg dose. Children ages 12 to 17 may be given a trial of 10 mg per day of escitalopram under select circumstances with careful medical supervision. The dose may be increased to 20 mg after three weeks at a lower dose in some circumstances. The elderly are usually kept at a lower dose of 10 mg, due to their increased sensitivity to these medications and their side effects. The maximum dose that may be used is 20 mg per day in other adults. However, the maximum dose may be lower for some patients depending on the development of side effects and the individual ability to tolerate them. Slowly increasing the dose helps with minimizing side effects, and some side effects become lessened with continued use. All SSRIs such as escitalopram need to be slowly tapered off if discontinued, to avoid a discontinuation withdrawal syndrome.

Precautions

SSRIs such as escitalopram have many negative side effects. It usually takes several weeks of medication for the treatment effects to occur, while the undesirable side effects may occur at the onset of treatment. When an SSRI such as escitalopram is prescribed for a patient with a disease like major depression, this time lapse in beneficial versus adverse effects may be difficult for patient **compliance** with treatment. The classic description is a patient who is already feeling depressed takes an SSRI then experiences side effects and so feels worse, all while being told that the patient will eventually get better. This situation can be frustrating for patients with depression. Fortunately, SSRIs like escitalopram do help many people and have fewer overall side effects than some older medications used for the same purpose. Great benefit may be gained if a patient is able to get past the first couple weeks of treatment. Escitalopram is generally tried for four to six weeks to determine whether it is the appropriate agent for a patient. It takes some time to determine whether a particular SSRI like escitalopram will eventually be effective for an individual. Having one SSRI fail in treatment for an individual patient does not mean that another SSRI will not work for that person. Sometimes multiple drugs need to be attempted under physician care before the proper treatment is found for a patient.

When a patient discontinues escitalopram, the dose needs to be tapered down slowly. SSRIs have little to no abuse potential. However, if an SSRI is abruptly discontinued without tapering, there may be symptoms of withdrawal known as SSRI discontinuation syndrome. Withdrawal symptoms of this syndrome may include flu-like symptoms, anxiety, agitation, vivid or bizarre dreams, **insomnia**, nausea, vomiting, diarrhea, sense of imbalance, chills, **fatigue**, dizziness, headache, and other sensory disturbances. Discontinuation syndrome may be avoided completely if the dose of escitalopram is properly tapered down over time.

KEY TERMS

Bipolar disorder—Psychiatric mood disorder characterized by periods of manic behavior that may alternate with periods of depression, also known as manic depressive disorder.

Cytochrome P450 (CYP450)—Enzymes present in the liver that metabolize drugs.

Irritable bowel syndrome—Disorder involving dysfunction of the GI tract that may include symptoms of constipation, diarrhea, or both.

Monoamine oxidase inhibitors (MAOIs)—Type of antidepressant medication that affects various kinds of neurotransmitters including serotonin.

Neurotransmitter—A chemical messenger that travels through the body and acts in the nervous system. Neurotransmitter signaling is responsible for a wide range of bodily processes and is often the target of medications involving the brain and cardiovascular system.

Neurotransmitter receptor—A physical recipient for chemicals called neurotransmitters. Receptors sit on the surface of cells that make up body tissues, and once bound to the neurotransmitter, they initiate the chemical signaling pathway associated with neurotransmitters.

Nonsteroidal anti-inflammatory drugs (NSAIDs)—A class of pain relief medications that also decreases inflammation, such as ibuprofen (Advil), naproxen (Aleve), and acetylsalicylic acid (Aspirin).

Post-traumatic stress syndrome (PTSD)—Psychiatric disorder in which the patient experiences persistent disturbing anxiety based symptoms after experiencing a traumatic event.

Priapism—Medical condition in which the penis is painfully engorged with blood over long periods of time, usually due to medication use and may constitute a medical emergency.

Serotonin—A type of neurotransmitter involved in regulation of the blood vessels, brain processes, and disease states such as depression.

Serotonin syndrome—A potentially life-threatening drug reaction involving an excess of the neurotransmitter serotonin, usually occurring when too many medications that increase serotonin are taken together such as antimigraine triptans and certain antidepressants.

Social phobia—Psychiatric disorder involving excessive fear and anxiety due to social situations with other people.

Synapse—Physical space between neurons that allows the passage of neurotransmitters for chemical signaling pathways.

Escitalopram is not approved for use in children younger than 12 years of age. Children and adults up to age 24 are at risk for developing suicidal thoughts and aggressive behavior when taking **antidepressants**, including escitalopram. Persons of any age should be monitored for worsening depression or suicidal behavior when taking antidepressant drugs. If a patient goes from depressed and unmotivated to depressed and highly motivated in the first few weeks of treatment, it may increase the risk of harmful behavior.

If used during pregnancy, SSRIs such as escitalopram cross the placenta and may affect the fetus. SSRI use during the third trimester of pregnancy is associated with some newborn medical problems. Potential effects on the newborn include respiratory problems, gastrointestinal problems, **seizures**, and feeding problems. SSRIs such as escitalopram may also cause a withdrawal syndrome in newborn babies known as neonatal abstinence syndrome. Symptoms of neonatal abstinence syndrome in a newborn include irritability, physical agitation and restlessness, tremors, increased breathing rate, nasal congestion, nausea, vomiting, and diarrhea. Symptoms usually end by two weeks of age and are most commonly caused by maternal use of **fluoxetine** and **paroxetine** SSRIs, less commonly with escitalopram.

Escitalopram overdose may result in a condition known as **serotonin syndrome**, also called serotonin toxicity, serotonin poisoning, and serotonin storm. Serotonin overdose may be caused by taking multiple drugs that increase the amount of serotonin signaling in the body. While chemical signaling pathways are a part of normal brain function, over-activation can be dangerous. Drugs that increase serotonin signaling may do so by increasing the amount of serotonin available to bind to and activate receptors or by directly activating serotonin receptors. These drugs can cause serotonin overdose if used at the same time or in time periods too close together. Symptoms of serotonin overdose may range from mild to life-threatening, depending on the individual situation. Symptoms may include high blood pressure, high fever, nausea, diarrhea, headache, sweating, increased heart rate, tremor, muscle twitching, **delirium**, shock, coma, and death.

Escitalopram and other SSRIs are discouraged from use in patients with **bipolar disorder**, as they can induce a state of mania in these individuals. There are selective conditions under which a doctor may prescribe SSRIs to a bipolar patient for a short period of time under careful monitoring. The risk of gastrointestinal bleeding may be increased when escitalopram is combined with nonsteroidal anti-inflammatory drugs (NSAIDs) such as ibuprofen (Motrin), aspirin (Bayer, Excedrin), and naproxen sodium (Aleve).

Side effects

SSRIs such as escitalopram are known for having fewer side effects than other types of antidepressant medications, which is one reason why they tend to be the drug of choice in treatment of depression. However, as with all medication, escitalopram does have side effects. Common side effects of escitalopram include nausea, headache, dizziness, constipation, sexual dysfunction, diarrhea, sweating, dry mouth, shakiness, loss of appetite, weight loss, rash, and insomnia. Rare but serious potential side effects include mania, worsened depression and suicidality (especially in the pediatric population), pediatric growth suppression in younger age groups, seizures, serotonin syndrome, discontinuation syndrome, electrolyte imbalances, hypoglycemia, abnormal bleeding, priapism, and glaucoma.

Interactions

Patients should make their doctor aware of all medications and supplements they are taking before using SSRIs like escitalopram. Using alcohol while taking escitalopram can create toxic reactions in the body, and alcohol should be avoided while taking this drug. The use of the herb **St. John's wort** or yohimbe while taking escitalopram may also cause toxicity.

Switching drug treatment for an individual patient from an MAOI to an SSRI may require a waiting period of up to two weeks between drugs. Switching from an SSRI to an MAOI may require a waiting period of up to five weeks duration. Another example of a medication that has additive serotonin effects with escitalopram or other SSRIs is sumatriptan (Imitrex). Sumatriptan is a drug used to treat migraine headaches and acts directly on serotonin receptors in the brain to activate their serotonin signaling pathway. The combination of an SSRI increasing the amount of serotonin available to activate serotonin receptor signaling pathways, and sumatriptan directly activating serotonin receptor signaling pathways, may produce undesirable side effects or overdose. Other drugs that cannot be combined with escitalopram due to risk of serotonin syndrome are the antibiotic linezolid and the drug methylene blue used in some blood-related illnesses.

SSRIs such as escitalopram may inhibit metabolic enzymes in the liver known as cytochrome P450s (CYP450). By inhibiting specific subtypes of CYP450, escitalopram may dangerously increase the levels of other drugs in the body that would have otherwise been metabolized by the CYP450. Escitalopram may increase the potency and side effects of the drugs warfarin, digoxin, beta blocker cardiac drugs such as metoprolol, **benzodiazepines** such as **diazepam** (Valium), antipsychotics such as **haloperidol** and **clozapine**, and certain anti-seizure drugs such as phenytoin. Drugs that may cause toxicity with escitalopram include diuretics (water pills), sleep aids like **zolpidem** (Ambien), diet pills such as sibutramine (Meridia), and mood stabilizers such as lithium. Escitalopram cannot be combined with the antipsychotic medications **pimozide** (Orap) or **thioridazine** (Mellaril) due to dangerous cardiac complications. Escitalopram may not be appropriate for use or may require careful monitoring in patients with liver or kidney impairment, electrolyte imbalances, or seizure disorders.

QUESTIONS TO ASK YOUR DOCTOR

- Can I take the full dose right away or do I need to slowly increase the dose?
- Can I stop taking the medication right away or do I need to slowly decrease the dose?
- When should I eat in reference to taking this medication?
- What time of day should I take this medication?
- How long should I take this medication before I am reassessed?
- Will this medication interact with any of my other prescription medications?
- Are there any over-the-counter medications I should not take with this medicine?
- What are the side effects I should watch for?
- Can I drink alcoholic beverages in the same time frame as taking this medication?

Resources

BOOKS

Brunton, Laurence L., et al. *Goodman and Gilman's The Pharmacological Basis of Therapeutics.* 12th ed. New York: McGraw Hill Medical, 2011.

Stargrove, Mitchell Bebel, et al. *Herb, Nutrient, and Drug Interactions: Clinical Implications and Therapeutic Strategies.* St. Louis: Mosby, 2007.

ORGANIZATIONS

American College of Neuropsychopharmacology, 5034-A Thoroughbred Lane, Brentwood, TN, 37027, (615) 324-2360, Fax: (615) 523-1715, acnp@acnp.org, http://www.acnp.org/default.aspx.

American Psychiatric Association, 1000 Wilson Blvd., Ste. 1825, Arlington, VA, 22209-3901, (703) 907-7300, apa@psych.org, http://www.psych.org.

American Society for Clinical Pharmacology and Therapeutics, 528 N Washington St., Alexandria, VA, 22314, (703) 836-6981, info@ascpt.org, http://www.ascpt.org.

Mental Health America, 2000 N Beauregard St., 6th Fl., Alexandria, VA, 22311, (703) 684-7722, (800) 969-6642, Fax: (703) 684-5968, http://www.nmha.org.

Maria Eve Basile, PhD

Eskalith *see* **Lithium carbonate**

Estazolam

Definition

Estazolam is a sedative-hypnotic drug belonging to the class of drugs known as **benzodiazepines**. It is sold in the United States under the names ProSom and Sedarest.

Estazolam, 2 mg. *(© Custom Medical Stock Photo, Inc. Reproduced by permission.)*

Purpose

Estazolam is used as a short-term treatment for **insomnia**. Given at bedtime, estazolam can help patients who have trouble falling asleep, staying asleep, or who have unwanted early morning awakening.

Description

Estazolam belongs to a group of drugs called benzodiazepines. Benzodiazepines are sedative-hypnotic drugs that help to relieve nervousness, tension, and other anxiety symptoms by slowing the central nervous system. To do this, they block the effects of a specific chemical involved in the transmission of nerve impulses in the **brain**, decreasing the excitement level of the nerve cells.

Estazolam, like other benzodiazepines, can be habit-forming and can cause tolerance. Tolerance occurs when a given dosage has less and less effect when the drug is taken over a long time. Therefore, estazolam is recommended only for short-term use.

Estazolam is available in 1 mg and 2 mg tablets, for oral use.

Recommended dosage

Adults are usually prescribed a single 1–2 mg dose of estazolam to be taken at bedtime. The elderly (over age 60) or people with serious health problems require much smaller doses, and are usually started at 0.5 mg at bedtime.

Precautions

Care must be taken when prescribing this medication to anyone with decreased liver or kidney functioning; the elderly; those with a history of **substance abuse**, **depression**, respiratory depression (such as asthma, chronic obstructive pulmonary disease, chronic bronchitis, or other chronic respiratory diseases); narrow-angle glaucoma; or known sleep apnea. People with these health conditions should discuss the risks and benefits of using estazolam with their doctor before starting treatment.

Pregnant women should not use estazolam, because it causes damage to the developing fetus. Because estazolam shows up in breast milk, women who are breast-feeding should not take this drug.

Because estazolam is a nervous system and respiratory depressant, it should not be taken with other such depressants, such as alcohol or other **sedatives**, sleeping pills, or tranquilizers. Furthermore, patients should not drive, operate dangerous machinery, or engage in hazardous activities until the drug's effects have worn off.

Suddenly discontinuing estazolam after several weeks of use may cause uncomfortable symptoms of

KEY TERMS

Benzodiazepines—A group of central nervous system depressants used to relieve anxiety or to induce sleep.

Delusion—A false belief that is resistant to reason or contrary to actual fact.

Depressant—Something that slows down functioning.

Glaucoma—A group of eye diseases characterized by increased pressure within the eye significant enough to damage eye tissue and structures. If untreated, glaucoma results in blindness.

Hallucinations—False sensory perceptions. A person experiencing a hallucination may "hear" sounds or ""see" people or objects that are not really present. Hallucinations can also affect the senses of smell, touch, and taste.

Sleep apnea—Short periods where a person stops breathing during sleep. Breathing restarts spontaneously, however, this condition can lead a lack of oxygen in the body.

withdrawal. Patients should discuss with their doctor how to discontinue estazolam use gradually to avoid such symptoms.

Side effects

The most common side effects of estazolam include sleepiness, slowness of movement, dizziness, and difficulty with coordination.

Less common side effects include anxiety, confusion, depression, memory loss for events occurring after the drug is taken, increased heart rate, and pounding or irregular heartbeat.

Rare side effects include confused thinking, disorientation, **delusions**, irritability, agitation, hallucinations, **seizures**, bizarre and/or aggressive behavior, a drop in blood pressure, weak muscles, skin rash or itching, sores in mouth or throat, fever and chills, difficulty sleeping, odd body and/or eye movements, unusual bruising or easy bleeding, severe **fatigue** or weakness, and yellow eyes or skin (jaundice).

Interactions

Cimetidine (Tagamet), **disulfiram** (Antabuse), and erythromycin (an antibiotic) may increase estazolam's sedative effects.

Rifampin may decrease the effects of estazolam.

Resources

BOOKS

Preston, John D., John H. O'Neal, and Mary C. Talaga. *Handbook of Clinical Psychopharmacology for Therapists*. 5th ed. Oakland, CA: New Harbinger Publications, 2008.

PERIODICALS

Rosenberg, Russell P. "Sleep Maintenance Insomnia: Strengths and Weaknesses of Current Pharmacologic Therapies." *Annals of Clinical Psychiatry* 18, no. 1 (January–March 2006): 49–56.

Rosalyn Carson-DeWitt, MD
Ruth A. Wienclaw, PhD

Etiology of mental illness *see* **Origin of mental illnesses**

Evening primrose oil

Definition

Evening primrose oil is a dietary supplement derived from the seeds of the evening primrose plant, *Oenothera biennis*. Its Latin name is derived from the Greek word for wine, reflecting the folk belief that the plant could relieve the symptoms of a hangover. Other names for the plant are tree primrose and sundrop. Native Americans used the leaves and bark of evening primrose as a sedative and astringent; it was given for stomach and liver complaints as well as disorders of the female reproductive system. More recently, the discovery of antioxidant and other properties of the seed oil has

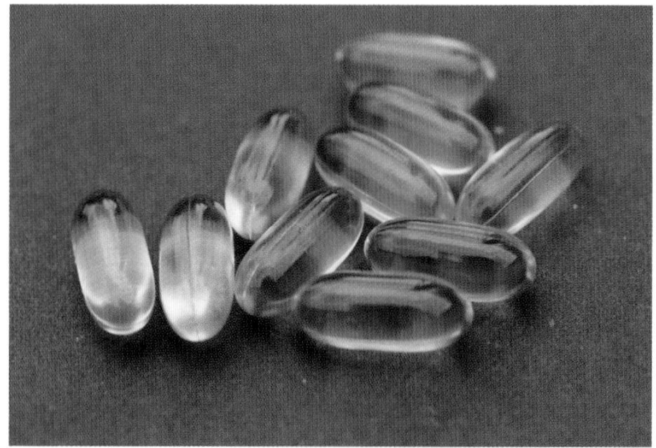

Evening primrose capsules. *(© mitzy/Shutterstock.com)*

focused research on its usefulness in treating a range of diseases and disorders.

Purpose

Evening primrose oil is used by contemporary naturopaths and other alternative practitioners to relieve the discomfort of symptoms associated with PMS, eczema, sunburn, fibrocystic breast disease, arthritis, diabetes, and osteoporosis. However, evening primrose oil has shown little clinical effectiveness in treating most of these conditions, with the best results in treating breast pain and osteoporosis. Some practitioners believe that the supplement can help alleviate symptoms of PMS, **Alzheimer's disease**, and **attention deficit hyperactivity disorder (ADHD)**, but this has not yet been proven in **clinical trials**.

Description

Evening primrose oil is obtained from the seeds of the plant by pressing. The oil can be taken directly as a liquid or in the form of capsules. Evening primrose oil is considered a good source of essential fatty acids (EFAs), predominately Omega 6. EFAs are called essential fatty acids because the human body cannot produce them; they must be obtained from the diet. EFAs maintain the function of cell membranes, regulate pain and inflammation, prevent blood clots, regulate blood pressure and cholesterol levels, and help to produce hormone-like substances known as prostaglandins. Prostaglandins function as inflammation mediators in the short-term regulation of glands and other body organs. It is thought that evening primrose oil relieves symptoms of PMS by preferentially stimulating anti-inflammatory prostaglandins.

Under normal conditions, the body uses an EFA called linoleic acid to produce a compound called gamma linoleic acid, or GLA. Evening primrose oil contains both linoleic acid (74%) and GLA (9%), making it the most familiar and popular source of GLA. The other compounds contained in evening primrose oil are oleic acid (11%) and palmitic acid (6%).

Recommended dosage

Evening primrose oil can be obtained in health food stores in either liquid or capsule form; topical preparations are also available for treating skin conditions. The best quality supplements are organic and cold-pressed, not oxidized by heating. Doses should be stored it in the refrigerator, and standard dosage varies according to the condition being treated.

All parts of the evening primrose plant are safe to eat. The roots can be boiled and eaten like parsnips. The seeds were roasted and used as a coffee substitute when food rationing was in effect during World War II.

KEY TERMS

Antioxidant—Substance that protects the body from damaging reactive oxygen molecules in the body. These reactive oxygen molecules can come from inside the body or from environmental pollution and are thought to play a role in the aging process and the development of degenerative disease.

Astringent—A substance or compound that causes contraction or constriction of soft tissue.

Prostaglandins—A group of unsaturated fatty acids involved in the contraction of smooth muscle, control of inflammation, and many other body processes.

Precautions

Evening primrose oil should not be given to patients with epilepsy, and only after a consultation with a physician should it be given to children.

Side effects

Evening primrose oil has not been reported as having toxic or severe side effects. Some patients, however, have reported nausea, headache, and softening of the stools. Bruising due to damage of the blood platelet function is also possible.

Interactions

Experts in pharmacology advise against using evening primrose oil with phenytoin (Dilantin) or other anticonvulsant medications, as the oil may lower the threshold for **seizures**. No other significant drug interactions have been reported, but persons taking evening primrose oil or any other supplement should alert their physicians to avoid any potential complications.

Resources

BOOKS

Murray, Michael, and Joseph Pizzorno. *Encyclopedia of Natural Medicine*. New York: Three Rivers Press, 1997.

Pelletier, Kenneth R. "Naturopathic Medicine: 'Do No Harm'." In *The Best Alternative Medicine*. New York: Touchstone, 2002.

PERIODICALS

Belch, Jill, and Alexander Hill. "Evening Primrose Oil and Borage Oil in Rheumatologic Conditions." *American Journal of Clinical Nutrition* 71, no. 1 (January 2000): 352S–6S.

Birch, A.E., et al. "Antioxidant Properties of Evening Primrose Seed Extracts." *Journal of Agricultural and Food Chemistry* 49, no. 9 (September 2001): 4502–4507.

Donohue, Maureen. "Evening Primrose Oil May Ease PMS Symptoms." *OB/GYN News* (April 1, 2000).

Dove, D., and P. Johnson. "Oral Evening Primrose Oil: Its Effect on Length of Pregnancy and Selected Intrapartum Outcomes in Low-Risk Nulliparous Women." *Journal of Nurse-Midwifery* 44, no. 3 (May–June 1999): 320–324.

Horowitz, S. "Combining Supplements and Prescription Drugs: What Your Patients Need to Know." *Alternative Complementary Therapy* 6, no. 4 (August 2000): 177–183.

Hudson, Tori. "Evening Primrose Oil." *Townsend Letter for Doctors and Patients* (January 1, 2001): 7.

Miller, Lucinda G. "Herbal Medicinals." *Archives of Internal Medicine* 158 (1998) 2200–11. Available online at http://archinte.ama-assn.org/cgi/content/full/158/20/2200 (accessed November 9, 2011).

Yoon, S., J. Lee, and S. Lee. "The Therapeutic Effect of Evening Primrose Oil in Atopic Dermatitis Patients with Dry Scaly Skin Lesions is Associated with the Normalization of Serum Gamma-Interferon Levels." *Skin Pharmacology and Applied Skin Physiology* 15, no. 1 (January–February 2002) 20–25.

Rebecca J. Frey, PhD

Executive function

Definition

Executive function describes a set of cognitive abilities that control and regulate other abilities and behaviors. Executive functions are necessary for goal-directed behavior. They include the ability to initiate and stop actions, to monitor and change behavior as needed, and to plan future behavior when faced with novel tasks and situations. Executive functions allow individuals to anticipate outcomes and adapt to changing situations. The ability to form concepts and think abstractly are often considered components of executive function.

Description

As the name implies, executive functions are high-level abilities that influence more basic abilities like attention, memory and motor skills. For this reason, they can be difficult to assess directly. Many of the tests used to measure other abilities, particularly those that look at more complex aspects of these abilities, can be used to evaluate executive functions. For example, a person with executive function deficits may perform well on tests of basic attention, such as those that simply ask the individual to look at a computer screen and respond when a particular shape appears, but have trouble with tasks that require divided or alternating attention, such as giving a different response depending on the stimulus presented. Verbal fluency tests that ask people to say a number of words in a certain period of time can also reveal problems with executive function. One commonly used test asks individuals to name as many animals or as many words beginning with a particular letter as they can in one minute. A person with executive function deficits may find the animal naming task simple, but struggle to name words beginning with a particular letter, since this task requires people to organize concepts in a novel way. Executive functions also influence memory abilities by allowing people to employ strategies that can help them remember information. Other tests are designed to assess cognitive function more directly. Such tests may present a fairly simple task but without instructions on how to complete it. Executive functions allow most people to figure out the task demand through trial and error and change strategies as needed.

Executive functions are important for successful adaptation and performance in real-life situations. They allow people to initiate and complete tasks and to persevere in the face of challenges. Because the environment can be unpredictable, executive functions are vital to human ability to recognize the significance of unexpected situations and to quickly make alternative plans when unusual events arise and interfere with normal routines. In this way, executive function contributes to success in work and school and allows people to deal effectively with the stresses of daily life. Executive functions also enable people to inhibit inappropriate behaviors. People with poor executive functions often have problems interacting with other people since they may say or do things that are bizarre or offensive to others. Most people experience impulses to do or say things that could get them in trouble, such as making a sexually explicit comment to a stranger, commenting negatively on someone's appearance, or insulting an authority figure like a boss or police officer; but most people have no trouble suppressing these urges. When executive functions are impaired, however, these urges may not be suppressed. Executive functions are an important component of our ability to fit in socially.

Executive function deficits are associated with a number of psychiatric and developmental disorders,

KEY TERMS

Autism—A developmental disability that appears early in life, in which normal brain development is disrupted and social and communication skills are retarded, sometimes severely.

Cognitive—Pertaining to the mental processes of memory, perception, judgment, and reasoning.

Cortex—Region in the brain where sensation and perception are processed and integrated into thoughts, memories, and abilities; also where actions are planned and initiated.

Dementia—A group of symptoms (syndrome) associated with a progressive loss of memory and other intellectual functions that is serious enough to interfere with a person's ability to perform the tasks of daily life. Dementia impairs memory, alters personality, leads to deterioration in personal grooming, impairs reasoning ability, and causes disorientation.

Executive—Pertaining to supervision, planning, and carrying out duties or actions.

Frontal lobes—A region of the brain that influences higher mental functions often associated with intelligence, such as the ability to foresee the consequences of actions, planning, comprehension, and mood.

Schizophrenia—A severe mental illness in which a person has difficulty distinguishing what is real from what is not real. It is often characterized by hallucinations, delusions, language and communication disturbances, and withdrawal from people and social activities.

Tourette syndrome—Neurological disorder characterized by multiple involuntary movements and uncontrollable vocalizations called tics that come and go over years, usually beginning in childhood and becoming chronic. Sometimes the tics include inappropriate language.

including **obsessive-compulsive disorder**, Tourette syndrome, **depression**, **schizophrenia**, **attention deficit hyperactivity disorder**, and **autism**. Executive function deficits also appear to play a role in antisocial behavior. Chronic heavy users of drugs and alcohol show impairments on tests of executive function. Some of these deficits appear to result from heavy substance use, but there is also evidence suggesting that problems with executive functions may contribute to the development of substance use disorders.

Because executive functions govern so many lower-level abilities, there is some controversy about their physiological basis. Nevertheless, most people who study these abilities agree that the frontal lobes of the **brain** play a major role in executive function. The frontal lobes are the large portions of the brain cortex that lie near the front of the brain. The cortex is the site in the brain where lower level processes like sensation and perception are processed and integrated into thoughts, memories and abilities, and actions are planned and initiated. People with frontal lobe injuries have difficulty with the higher level processing that underlies executive functions. Because of its complexity, the frontal cortex develops more slowly than other parts of the brain, and not surprisingly, many executive functions do not fully develop until adolescence. Some executive functions also appear to decline in old age, and some executive function deficits may be useful in early detection of mild **dementia**.

Resources

BOOKS

Lezak, Muriel Deutsch, et al. *Neuropsychological Assessment.* 3rd ed. New York: Oxford University Press, 2011.

Lichter, David G., and Jeffrey L. Cummings. *Frontal-subcortical Circuits in Psychiatric and Neurological Disorders.* New York: The Guilford Press, 2001.

PERIODICALS

Anderson, Vicki A., et al. "Development of Executive Functions Through Late Childhood and Adolescence in an Australian Sample." *Developmental Neuropsychology* 20, no. 1 (2001): 385–406.

Bryan, Janet, and Mary A. Luszcz. "Measurement of Executive Function: Considerations for Detecting Adult Age Differences." *Journal of Clinical and Experimental Neuropsychology* 22, no. 1 (February 2000): 40–55.

Morgan, Alex B., and Scott O. Lilienfeld. "A Meta-analytic Review of the Relation Between Antisocial Behavior and Neuropsychological Measures of Executive Function." *Clinical Psychology Review* 20, no. 1 (2000): 113–136.

Nathan, Joanna, et al. "The Role of Tests of Frontal Executive Function in the Detection of Mild Dementia." *International Journal of Geriatric Psychiatry* 16, no. 1 (2001): 18–26.

Ready, Rebecca E., Laura Stierman, and Jane S. Paulsen. "Ecological Validity of Neuropsychological and Personality Measures of Executive Functions." *The Clinical Neuropsychologist* 15, no. 3 (2001): 314–323.

Wecker, Nancy S., et al. "Age Effects on Executive Ability." *Neuropsychology* 14, no. 3 (July 2000): 409–414.

ORGANIZATIONS

American Psychological Association, 750 1st Street NE, Washington, DC, 20002-4242, (202) 336-5500; TDD/TTY: (202) 336-6123, (800) 374-2721, http://www.apa.org.

International Neuropsychological Society, 700 Ackerman Rd., Ste. 625, Columbus, OH, 43202, (614) 263-4200, Fax: (614) 263-4366, http://www.the-ins.org.

National Academy of Neuropsychology, 7555 East Hampden Ave., Ste. 525, Denver, CO, 80231, (303) 691-3694, Fax: (303) 691-5983, office@nanonline.org, http://nanonline.org.

Danielle Barry, MS

Exelon *see* **Rivastigmine**

Exercise and mental health

Definition

Exercise directly benefits mental health, in addition to the benefits of exercise-derived improvements in physical health.

Purpose

Exercise helps relieve tension, anxiety, **stress**, anger, and **depression**, and helps enhance a person's general sense of well-being. Exercise and improved physical fitness help build self-confidence, promote positive **body image** and self-esteem, and contribute to a positive outlook. Sports and other physical activities provide an emotional release from anxieties and frustrations. Exercise increases energy levels and mental alertness and improves sleep, all of which contribute to good mental health. Exercising outdoors in the sunlight—so-called "green" activities—can help overcome **seasonal affective disorder** (SAD) or the "winter blues." Many people find exercise to be an enjoyable form of relaxation and an opportunity for socializing. This can be especially important for patients dealing with isolation and loneliness due to a mental health condition.

Over the long term, regular exercise benefits physical health, which contributes to improved mental health. Weight gain is both a common cause and a common result of depression and other mental health problems. Weight gain can also be a side effect of some medications used to treat mental disorders. Exercise can slow or halt weight gain. It can also relieve stress and tension that can otherwise lead to overeating. Aging often has a negative impact on mental health; however, physical activity can help seniors continue to enjoy activities and remain independent—both important contributors to good mental health.

For many people, the effects of exercise on mental health go beyond improving mood and preventing "the blues." Research and clinical experience indicate that exercise can be an effective treatment for more serious mental disorders, including severe depression, **anxiety disorders**, substance dependence, and even **schizophrenia**. Physicians and psychologists commonly prescribe exercise for a range of mental health conditions, in place of or in addition to medications and counseling or **psychotherapy**. Some research suggests that the effects of exercise on mild depression may be longer lasting than the effects of **antidepressants**.

Whereas studies have consistently demonstrated that exercise can benefit mental health, the reverse also appears to be true: the lack of regular exercise is associated with symptoms of depression and anxiety.

Demographics

Approximately 26% of Americans and 20% of Canadians will experience a mental illness at some point in their lives. According to the **National Institute of Mental Health**, more than 4% of Americans have a serious mental illness, including about 6% of females and nearly 8% of young adults between the ages of 18 and 25. Among Americans over age 65, 14% have significant depressive symptoms. Men over age 75 have the highest overall **suicide** rate. Serious mental illness is somewhat more common among Caucasians than among African Americans, Hispanics, and Asian Americans. Mixed-race Americans have the highest rates of serious mental illness.

Regular physical activity is important for the mental health of most people. With the increase in sedentary employment and entertainment via television, video games, and the Internet, activity levels have decreased in recent decades among all age groups. During the same period, the incidence of mental health disorders has risen sharply. Although some of this increase is attributable to greater awareness of mental health issues and improved diagnoses, reduced activity levels may share some of the blame.

Any condition that limits physical activity can have a negative impact on mental health. Physical illnesses and conditions—such as arthritis, cardiovascular disease, **stroke**, cancer, and HIV/AIDS—are often accompanied by depression or other mental problems. Anxiety, fear, or stress can be secondary to such conditions, resulting from concern about the future or restriction of normal activities. Other times, a disease, physical condition, or medication used to treat a condition directly causes depression or other mental problems. For instance, depression is the most common psychiatric **diagnosis** among HIV/AIDS patients, especially women. In addition to causing anxiety and fear, HIV/AIDS and HIV-related medications can contribute directly to depression.

Description

Origins

During the 1970s and 1980s, clinicians began to realize that people who exercised regularly were less likely to experience depression and were less likely to become depressed in the future. A trial conducted in 1999 demonstrated that an aerobic exercise plan was as effective in treating depressed adults as the antidepressant **sertraline** (Zoloft), a drug that earned its manufacturer more than $3 billion annually before its patent expired in 2006. Most subsequent studies have confirmed that regular aerobic exercise can be as effective as medication for treating depression and preventing the recurrence of depressive symptoms.

Effects of exercise

Regular exercise has positive emotional, psychological, and physical effects. Exercise relaxes the mind and body. Physical activity provides a positive means of coping with stress, anxiety, sadness, and depression. It provides a distraction that can break cycles of negative thinking that increase anxiety and depression. In contrast, trying to wait out a depression or attempting to cope with drugs or alcohol often makes symptoms worse. Exercise also can improve self-esteem and self-confidence through a sense of achievement and improved body image and by encouraging social interaction.

Exercise may relieve muscle tension, burn off stress hormones, and increase blood flow to the **brain**. It may lower immune system chemicals that can worsen depression. Exercise also increases body temperature, which may have a calming effect.

Neuroscientists are beginning to understand the ways in which exercise alters brain chemistry. Exercise stimulates the production of endorphins—so-called pleasure hormones that improve mood and relieve stress. It appears that exercise functions in much the same way as antidepressant medications, by regulating the **neurotransmitters serotonin** and norepinephrine. Over a period of several weeks, regular exercise appears to turn on specific genes that increase the levels of galanin in the brain. Galanin is a neurotransmitter that reduces the body's stress response by regulating norepinephrine. This means that new stimuli or negative events—such as a parking ticket or missed appointment—have less effect on emotions.

Exercise also may have a direct effect on nerve cells in the hippocampus—a part of the brain involved in the regulation of mood and responses to antidepressants. In animals, exercise increases the production of brain-derived neurotrophic factor (BDNF), which is necessary for the growth and maintenance of brain cells and can relieve depressive symptoms in humans. Studies in animal models of human depression have found that exercise-induced symptom alleviation depends on the growth of new adult neurons in the brain and may involve the enhanced activity of a nerve growth factor.

Exercise as treatment

Exercise has several advantages as a mental health treatment. It is usually viewed in a positive light, without the **stigma** that is sometimes still associated with medication or psychotherapy. The mood-enhancing effects of exercise are quickly apparent—much faster than the physical benefits of exercise. This immediate effect encourages more exercise. This is particularly important for people who have depression, which is associated with a chronic lack of motivation. Unlike other treatments for mental disorders, exercise provides significant physical health benefits, is inexpensive or free, and is without the side effects that occur with many medications.

Experts generally recommend at least 30 minutes of moderate-intensity aerobic exercise—such as walking—at least five times per week, or 30 minutes of high-intensity aerobic exercise at least three times per week. These are similar to physical fitness recommendations. As little as 30–45 minutes of walking three times per week has been associated with a reduction or alleviation of depressive symptoms. Even small increments of exercise—climbing stairs, walking the dog, or gardening for 10–15 minutes at a time—can have a significant effect. However, more vigorous exercise, such as running or playing a sport, may work faster. Anaerobic exercise, such as weightlifting, may have many of the same mental health benefits as aerobic exercise. Some types of exercise—such as **yoga**, pilates, and tai chi—are geared specifically toward improving mental as well as physical health.

Preparation

Sedentary individuals and those with health problems should always consult their physician before embarking on a new exercise program. Physicians or mental health professionals can prescribe exercise regimens that take into account pain, physical limitations, and mobility issues. It is important to start slowly, gradually increasing exercise intensity and duration as strength and stamina improve.

Regardless of apparent mental health benefits, sticking with an exercise program is a challenge for many people. It is important to choose activities that are both appropriate and enjoyable. Exercise should be

KEY TERMS

Aerobic exercise—Activity that increases the body's requirement for oxygen, thereby increasing respiration and heart rate.

Antidepressant—A drug used to prevent or treat depression.

Anxiety disorder—A group of disorders characterized by anxiety, including panic disorder and post-traumatic stress disorder (PTSD).

Brain-derived neurotrophic factor (BDNF)—A brain protein that helps maintain nerves and promotes the growth of new nerve cells (neurons).

Depression—A mental condition of extreme sadness and loss of interest in life, including problems with appetite, sleep, concentration, and daily functioning; severe depression can lead to suicide attempts.

Eating disorders—Conditions, such as anorexia nervosa and bulimia nervosa, that are characterized by abnormal attitudes toward food, altered appetite control, unhealthy eating habits, and sometimes compulsive exercise; particularly common in young women.

Endorphins—A class of peptides in the brain that are produced during exercise and bind to opiate receptors, resulting in pleasant feelings and pain relief.

Galanin—A neurotransmitter with roles in various physiological processes, including regulation of the stress response.

Hippocampus—A part of the brain that is involved in forming, storing, and processing memory, and in regulating mood.

Hormone—A substance, such as a protein, that is produced in one part of the body and travels through the bloodstream to affect another part of the body.

Neurotransmitter—A chemical—such as norepinephrine or serotonin—that transmits impulses across synapses between nerves.

Norepinephrine—Noradrenaline; a neurotransmitter in the sympathetic nervous system and some parts of the central nervous system, as well as a blood-pressure-raising (vasoconstricting) adrenal hormone.

Pilates—An exercise regimen specifically designed to improve overall physiological and mental functioning.

Schizophrenia—A psychotic disorder characterized by loss of contact with one's environment, deterioration of everyday functioning, and personality disintegration.

Serotonin—A neurotransmitter located primarily in the brain, blood serum, and stomach.

Stroke—A sudden diminishing or loss of consciousness, sensation, or voluntary movement, due to the rupture or obstruction of a blood vessel in the brain.

Tai chi—An ancient Chinese discipline involving controlled movements specifically designed to improve physical and mental well-being.

something to look forward to each day. Goals should be reasonable and achievable, so as not to set oneself up for failure. Some people prefer to exercise at home, out of self-consciousness or financial considerations. Others find that exercising with companions, such as in a gym or group class setting, is more motivating.

Precautions

Although exercise can ease symptoms of anxiety, depression, or another mental disorder, it is not necessarily a substitute for psychotherapy, medication, or other treatment. Appropriate activities and intensity levels should be chosen in consultation with a physician, to avoid the risk of injury.

Compulsive exercise is sometimes a symptom of a mental health disorder, particularly eating disorders such as **anorexia nervosa** or **bulimia nervosa**. People with anorexia may exercise compulsively to lose weight inappropriately. Those with bulimia, which is characterized by episodes of uncontrollable binge eating, may engage in compulsive exercise to prevent weight gain from overeating.

Results

As little as 30 minutes or less of moderate-intensity exercise that raises the heart rate can result in noticeable mood enhancement and anxiety reduction. Many studies have shown that routine exercise can be as effective as medication at relieving depressive symptoms. However, some research suggests that psychological responses to exercise have a genetic component. A large, long-term study of identical twins, published in 2008, found that twins who exercised more had no fewer anxious or depressive symptoms than their identical siblings who

QUESTIONS TO ASK YOUR DOCTOR

- How would I benefit from an exercise program?
- Could exercise replace my antidepressant medication?
- What type of exercise do you recommend?
- How much exercise should I get?

exercised less. It is possible that some types of exercise have more effect on mental health in some people than in others. It is also unclear whether exercise is as effective for treating severe depression as it is for treating mild to moderate depression.

Research and general acceptance

The relationship between mental health and exercise is an area of active research. Studies have extended the mental health benefits of exercise to patients with schizophrenia and schizophrenia-like illnesses, **bipolar disorder**, major depression, and other mental disorders. Exercise has been found to relieve depressive symptoms in adult stroke patients and stroke patients who exercise are much less likely to report depressive symptoms. Studies published in 2010 reported that the amount of exercise by undergraduate students correlated positively with their ratings on mental health scales and that just five minutes of outdoor or "green" activity—walking or gardening—has noticeable mental health benefits, including improved mood and self-esteem. A study published in 2011 found conclusive evidence that tai chi improves mental health in seniors, as well as providing general health benefits and reducing the risk of falls.

A study published in 2010, involving more than 40,000 Norwegians, reported that those who engaged in even small amounts of light, regular exercise were less likely to have depressive symptoms, as long as it was leisure-time exercise rather than physical activity at work. Socializing during exercise was an important beneficial factor. Those who were not active during their free time were almost twice as likely to have depressive symptoms. Exercise intensity did not appear to influence the results.

Schools and hospitals are increasingly using yoga to help children relax and focus and to improve behavior, self-esteem, and academic performance, as well as physical health. Some schools use yoga before statewide tests to help children relax and concentrate. Over the long term, yoga has been found to reduce aggression and improve emotional balance in children. It appears to be particularly helpful for children with special needs, as well as those with eating and mood disorders and **autism**.

Resources

BOOKS

Amen, Daniel G. *Magnificent Mind at Any Age: Natural Ways to Unleash Your Brain's Maximum Potential.* New York: Harmony, 2009.

Carless, David, and Kitrina Douglas. *Sport and Physical Activity for Mental Health.* Ames, IA: Wiley-Blackwell, 2010.

Emmons, Henry. *The Chemistry of Calm: A Powerful, Drug-Free Plan to Quiet Your Fears and Overcome Your Anxiety.* New York: Simon & Schuster, 2010.

Friedman, Peach. *Diary of an Exercise Addict: A Memoir.* Guilford, CT: GPP Life, 2009.

Kemper, Kathi. *Mental Health, Naturally: The Family Guide to Holistic Care for a Healthy Mind and Body.* Elk Grove Village, IL: American Academy of Pediatrics, 2010.

Larsen, Laura. *Fitness and Exercise Sourcebook.* 4th ed. Detroit: Omnigraphics, 2011.

Otto, Michael W., and Jasper A.J. Smits. *Exercise for Mood and Anxiety Disorders: Workbook.* New York: Oxford University Press, 2009.

PERIODICALS

Blue, Laurie. "Is Exercise the Best Drug for Depression?" *Time Health*, June 19, 2010. http://www.time.com/time/health/article/0,8599,1998021,00.html (accessed July 18, 2011).

Dang, Michelle T. "Walking Away the Blues: Exercise for Depression in Older Adults." *Nursing* 40, no. 11 (November 2010): 33.

Demissie, Zewditu, et al., "Physical Activity and Depressive Symptoms Among Pregnant Women: The PIN3 Study." *Women's Mental Health* 14, no. 2 (April 2011): 145–57.

Harvey, William J., et al. "Physical Activity, Leisure, and Health for Persons with Mental Illness." *Palaestra* 25, no. 2 (2010): 36–41.

Lister, Sam. "Lift Your Mood with a Little Leisure-Time Exercise; But Exertion at Work 'Makes No Difference.'" *Times (London)* (November 1, 2010): 17.

Lowry, C.A., S.L. Lightman, and D.J. Nutt. "That Warm Fuzzy Feeling: Brain Serotonergic Neurons and the Regulation of Emotion." *Journal of Psychopharmacology* 23, no. 4 (June 2009): 392–400.

Tyson, Philip, et al. "Physical Activity and Mental Health in a Student Population." *Journal of Mental Health* 19, no. 6 (December 2010): 492–99.

Van Citters, Aricca D., et al. "A Pilot Evaluation of the In SHAPE Individualized Health Promotion Intervention for Adults with Mental Illness." *Community Mental Health Journal* 46, no. 6 (December 2010): 540–52.

WEBSITES

Cassels, Caroline. "Exercise Beneficial for Physical and Mental Health Outcomes in Schizophrenia." Medscape Medical

News. May 12, 2010. http://www.medscape.com/viewarticle/721652 (accessed July 18, 2011).

Mayo Clinic Staff. "Depression and Anxiety: Exercise Eases Symptoms." MayoClinic.com October 23, 2009. http://www.mayoclinic.com/health/depression-and-exercise/MH00043 (accessed July 18, 2011).

National Institute of Mental Health. "Novel Model of Depression from Social Defeat Shows Restorative Power of Exercise." Science Update. April 13, 2010. http://www.nimh.nih.gov/science-news/2010/novel-model-of-depression-from-social-defeat-shows-restorative-power-of-exercise.shtml (accessed July 18, 2011).

National Institute of Mental Health. "Stress-Defeating Effects of Exercise Traced to Emotional Brain Circuit." Science Update. June 9, 2011. http://www.nimh.nih.gov/science-news/2011/stress-defeating-effects-of-exercise-traced-to-emotional-brain-circuit.shtml (accessed July 18, 2011).

Preidt, Robert. "Tai Chi Prevents Falls, Boosts Mental Health in Seniors: Study." *HealthDay*. May 17, 2011. http://www.nlm.nih.gov/medlineplus/news/fullstory_112150.html (accessed July 17, 2011).

ORGANIZATIONS

Mental Health America, 2000 North Beauregard Street, 6th Floor, Alexandria, VA, 22311, (703) 684-7722, Fax: (703) 684-5968, (800) 969-6642, infoctr@mentalhealthamerica.net, http://www.mentalhealthamerica.net.

National Institute on Aging, Building 31, Room 5C27, 31 Center Drive, MSC 2292, Bethesda, MD, 20892, (301) 496-1752, Fax: (301) 496-1072, (800) 222-2225, http://www.nia.nih.gov.

National Institute of Mental Health, Science Writing, Press, and Dissemination Branch, 6001 Executive Boulevard, Room 8184, MSC 9663, Bethesda, MD, 20892-9663, (301) 443-4513, Fax: (301) 443-4279, (866) 615-6464, nimhinfo@nih.gov, http://www.nimh.nih.gov.

Margaret Alic, PhD

Exhibitionism

Definition

Exhibitionism is a mental disorder characterized by a **compulsion** to display one's genitals to an unsuspecting stranger. The term *paraphilia* is derived from two Greek words meaning "outside of" and "friendship-love."

In the United States and Canada, the slang term "flasher" is often used for exhibitionists.

Demographics

The incidence of exhibitionism in the general population is difficult to estimate because persons with this disorder do not usually seek counseling by their own free will. Exhibitionism is one of the three most common sexual offenses in police records (the other two are **voyeurism** and **pedophilia**). It is rarely diagnosed in general mental health clinics, but most professionals believe that it is probably underdiagnosed and under-reported.

In terms of the technical definition of exhibitionism, almost all reported cases involve males. A number of mental health professionals, however, have noted that gender bias may be built into the standard definition. Some women engage in a form of exhibitionism by undressing in front of windows as if they are encouraging someone to watch them. In addition, wearing the low-cut gowns favored by some models and actresses have been described as socially sanctioned exhibitionism.

Although the stereotype of an exhibitionist is a "dirty old man in a raincoat," most males arrested for exhibitionism are in their late teens or early twenties. The disorder appears to have its onset before age 18. Like most **paraphilias**, exhibitionism is rarely found in men over 50 years of age.

In the United States most exhibitionists are Caucasian males. About half of exhibitionists are married.

Description

The ***Diagnostic and Statistical Manual of Mental Disorders***, also known as the *DSM-IV-TR,* classifies exhibitionism under the heading of the paraphilias, a subcategory of sexual and gender identity disorders. The paraphilias are a group of mental disorders marked by **obsession** with unusual sexual practices or with sexual activity involving nonconsenting or inappropriate partners (e.g., children or animals).

Exhibitionism is described in the *DSM-IV-TR,* as the exposure of one's genitals to a stranger, usually with no intention of further sexual activity with the other person. For this reason, the term exhibitionism is sometimes grouped together with voyeurism, (peeping, or watching an unsuspecting person or people, usually strangers, undressing or engaging in sexual activity) as a "hands-off" paraphilia. This contrasts with the "hands-on disorders" that involve physical contact with other persons. Some exhibitionists are aware of a conscious desire to shock or upset their target; while others fantasize that the target will become sexually aroused by their display. In some cases, the exhibitionist masturbates while exposing himself (or while fantasizing that he is exposing himself) to the other person.

Changes proposed for the fifth edition of the *DSM* (*DSM-5*, 2013) include renaming exhibitionism to exhibitionistic disorder.

Causes and symptoms

Causes

Several theories have been proposed regarding the origins of exhibitionism, although none are considered conclusive. They include:

- Biological theories. These generally hold that testosterone, the hormone that influences the sexual drive in both men and women, increases the susceptibility of males to develop deviant sexual behaviors. Some medications used to treat exhibitionists are given to lower the patients' testosterone levels.
- Learning theories. Several studies have shown that emotional abuse in childhood and family dysfunction are both significant risk factors in the development of exhibitionism. A Swedish survey (Sweden is globally recognized for its excellent health data survey system) found that exhibitionism is associated with psychological problems, although whether the problems precipitate the behavior or vice versa was not identified. This same study found no association between exhibitionistic behavior and a history of sexual abuse.
- Psychoanalytical theories. These are based on an unsubstantiated assumption that male gender identity requires the male child's separation from his mother psychologically so that he does not identify with her as a member of the same sex, the way a girl does. It is thought that exhibitionists regard their mothers as rejecting them on the basis of their different genitals. Therefore, they grow up with the desire to force women to accept them by making women look at their genitals.
- Head trauma. There are a small number of documented cases of men becoming exhibitionists following traumatic brain injury (TBI) without previous histories of alcohol abuse or sexual offenses.
- A childhood history of attention deficit hyperactivity disorder (ADHD). The reason for the connection is not yet known, but researchers at Harvard have discovered that patients with multiple paraphilias have a much greater likelihood of having had ADHD as children than patients with only one paraphilia.

Some psychiatrists disagree about whether exhibitionism should be considered a disorder of impulse control or whether it falls within the spectrum of obsessive-compulsive disorders (OCDs). Recent studies suggest that there is an obsessive-compulsive element to these behaviors, and some papers now describe these behaviors in a category of compulsive-impulsive sexual behaviors. Single case studies have suggested some effectiveness of drugs used to treat **bipolar disorder** in treating exhibitionistic behaviors, implying a potential link also to bipolar disorders. People who exhibit pedophilia, which is also characterized as a paraphilia, have abnormalities in **brain imaging studies** that are similar to those observed in imaging studies of people with **obsessive-compulsive disorder**. Disruption of **dopamine** and **serotonin** (both nerve signaling molecules) pathways is implicated in many of these disorders.

Symptoms

One expert in the field of treating paraphilias has suggested classifying the symptoms of exhibitionism according to level of severity, based on criteria from the *DSM-III-R* (1987):

- Mild. The person has recurrent fantasies of exposing himself, but has rarely or never acted on them.
- Moderate. The person has occasionally exposed himself (three targets or fewer) and has difficulty controlling urges to do so.
- Severe. The person has exposed himself to more than three people and has serious problems with control.
- A fourth level of severity, catastrophic, would not be found in exhibitionists without other paraphilias. This level denotes the presence of sadistic fantasies which, if acted upon, would result in severe injury or death to the victim.

Because exhibitionism is a hands-off paraphilia, it rarely rises above the level of moderate severity in the absence of other paraphilias.

Diagnosis

Diagnosis of exhibitionism is complicated by several factors. For example, most persons with the disorder come to therapy because of court orders. Some are motivated by fear of discovery by employers or family members, and a minority of exhibitionists enter therapy because their wife or girlfriend is distressed by the disorder. Emotional attitudes toward the disorder vary; some men maintain that the only problem they have with exhibitionism is society's disapproval of it; others, however, feel intensely guilty and anxious.

A second complication of diagnosing exhibitionism is the high rate of comorbidity among the paraphilias as a group and between the paraphilias as a group and other mental disorders. In other words, a patient in treatment for exhibitionism is highly likely to engage in other forms of deviant sexual behavior and to have **depression** (an anxiety or substance-abuse disorder). In addition, many patients with paraphilias do not cooperate with physicians, who may have considerable difficulty making an accurate diagnosis of other disorders that may also exist.

A diagnosis of exhibitionism follows a somewhat different pattern from the standard procedures for diagnosing most mental disorders. A thorough workup in a clinic for specialized treatment of sexual disorders includes the following components:

- A psychiatric evaluation and mental status examination to diagnose concurrent psychiatric and medical conditions, and to rule out schizophrenia, post-traumatic stress disorder (PTSD), intellectual disabilities, and depression.
- A neurologic examination to rule out head trauma, seizures, or other abnormalities of brain structure and function, followed by a computed tomography (CT) scan or magnetic resonance imaging (MRI), if needed.
- Blood and urine tests for substance abuse and sexually transmitted diseases, including an HIV screen.
- Assessment of sexual behaviors. This includes creation of a sex hormone profile and responses to questionnaires. The questionnaires are intended to measure cognitive distortions regarding rape and other forms of coercion, pedophilia, aggression, and impulsivity.

Treatment

Exhibitionism is usually treated with a combination of **psychotherapy**, medications, and adjunctive treatments.

Psychotherapy

Several different types of psychotherapy have been found helpful in treating exhibitionism:

- Cognitive-behavioral therapy (CBT). This approach is generally regarded as the most effective form of psychotherapy for exhibitionism. Patients are encouraged to recognize the irrational justifications that they offer for their behavior, and to alter other distorted thinking patterns.
- Orgasmic reconditioning. In this technique, the patient is conditioned to replace fantasies of exposing himself with fantasies of more acceptable sexual behavior while masturbating.
- Group therapy. This form of therapy is used to get patients past the denial frequently associated with paraphilias, and as a form of relapse prevention.
- Twelve-step groups for sexual addicts. Exhibitionists who feel guilty and anxious about their behavior are often helped by the social support and emphasis on healthy spirituality found in these groups, as well as by the cognitive restructuring that is built into the twelve steps.
- Couples therapy or family therapy. This approach is particularly helpful for patients who are married and whose marriages and family ties have been strained by their disorder.

Medications

There are several different classes of drugs used to treat the patient with exhibitionism and the other paraphilias. However, one difficulty in evaluating the comparative efficacy of different medications should be noted: ethical limitation. Double-blind placebo-controlled studies of medication treatment of sexually deviant men raises the ethical question of the possibility of **relapse** in the subjects who receive the placebo. Withholding a potentially effective drug in circumstances that might lead to physical or psychological injury to a third party is difficult to justify.

Medications are often the only form of treatment for patients with exhibitionism that can suppress deviant behaviors. The categories of drugs used to treat exhibitionism are as follows:

- Selective serotonin reuptake inhibitors (SSRIs). The SSRIs show promise in treating the paraphilias, as well as depression and other mood disorders. It has been found that decreased levels of serotonin in the brain result in an increased sex drive. The SSRIs are appropriate for patients with mild- or moderate-level paraphilias; these patients include the majority of exhibitionists.
- Hormones, their mimics, and their antagonists. The three classes of medications most often used to treat paraphilias are hormones, particularly the synthetic medroxyprogesterone acetate, or MPA; luteinizing hormone-releasing hormone (LHRH) agonists (mimics), which include such drugs as triptorelin (Trelstar), leuprolide acetate, and goserelin acetate; and antiandrogens, which block the uptake and metabolism of testosterone as well as reducing blood levels of this hormone. In particular, these drugs with antiandrogenic effects (interfering with the action of the body's androgenic hormones) have shown some effectiveness.

Surgery

Surgical castration, which involves removal of the testes, is effective in significantly reducing levels of

KEY TERMS

Castration—Desexing a person or animal by surgical removal of the testes (in males) or ovaries (in females). Castration is sometimes offered as a treatment option to violent rapists and pedophiles who are repeat offenders.

Comorbidity—Association or presence of two or more mental disorders in the same patient. A disorder that is said to have a high degree of comorbidity is likely to occur in patients diagnosed with other disorders that may share or reinforce some of its symptoms.

Denial—A psychological defense mechanism that reduces anxiety by excluding recognition of an addiction or similar problem from the conscious mind.

Double-blind placebo-controlled study—A study in which patients are divided into two groups—those who will receive a medication, and those who will receive a placebo (a pill that looks like the medication but has no active ingredients). Neither the patients nor their physicians know which pill any specific patient is receiving.

Paraphilias—A group of mental disorders that is characterized by recurrent intense sexual urges and sexually arousing fantasies generally involving (1) nonhuman objects, (2) the suffering or humiliation of oneself or one's partner (not merely simulated), or (3) children or other nonconsenting persons.

Placebo—An inactive substance or preparation used as a control in experiments with human subjects to test the effectiveness of a medication.

Recidivism—A tendency to return to a previously treated activity, or repeated relapse into criminal or deviant behavior.

Serotonin—A chemical produced by the brain that functions as a neurotransmitter. Low serotonin levels are associated with the paraphilias as well as with mood disorders. Medications known as selective serotonin reuptake inhibitors (SSRIs) can be used to treat exhibitionism and other paraphilias.

Voyeurism—A paraphilia that involves watching unsuspecting people, usually strangers, undress or engage in sexual activity.

testosterone in blood plasma. This form of treatment for paraphilias, however, is generally reserved for more serious offenders than exhibitionists (violent rapists and pedophiles with a history of repeated offenses, for example).

Other treatment methods

Another treatment method that is often offered to people with exhibition disorder is **social skills training**. It is thought that some men develop paraphilias partially because they do not know how to form healthy relationships, whether sexual or nonsexual, with other people. Although social skills training is not considered a substitute for medications or psychotherapy, it appears to be a useful adjunctive treatment for exhibitionism disorder.

Prognosis

The prognosis for people with exhibition disorder depends on a number of factors, including the age of onset, the reasons for the patient's referral to psychiatric care, degree of cooperation with the therapist, and comorbidity with other paraphilias or other mental disorders. For some patients, exhibitionism is a temporary disorder related to sexual experimentation during their adolescence. For others, however, it is a lifelong problem with potentially serious legal, interpersonal, financial, educational, and occupational consequences. People with exhibition disorder have the highest recidivism rate of all the paraphilias; between 20% and 50% of men arrested for exhibitionism are rearrested within two years.

People with exhibitionism disorder are at risk for lifetime employment problems if they acquire a police record. The Americans with Disabilities Act (ADA), enacted by Congress in 1990 to protect workers against discrimination on grounds of mental impairment or physical disability, does not protect persons with paraphilias. People with exhibitionism disorder were specifically excluded by Congress from the provisions of the ADA, along with voyeurs and persons with other sexual behavior disorders.

Prevention

One important preventive strategy includes the funding of programs for the treatment of paraphilias in adolescents. According to one expert in the field, males in this age group have not been studied and are undertreated, yet it is known that paraphilias are usually established before age 18. Recognition of paraphilias in adolescents and treatment for those at risk would lower the risk of recidivism. A second important preventive approach is early recognition and appropriate treatment of people who have committed **child abuse**.

Resources

BOOKS

American Psychiatric Association. *Diagnostic and Statistical Manual of Mental Disorders*. 4th ed., text rev. Washington, DC: American Psychiatric Publishing, 2000.

Carnes, Patrick. *Out of the Shadows: Understanding Sexual Addiction*. 3rd ed. Center City, MN: Hazelden Publishing, 2001.

"Exhibitionism." In *The Merck Manual of Diagnosis and Therapy*, edited by Robert S. Porter and Justin L. Kaplan. 19th ed. Whitehouse Station, NJ: Merck Research Laboratories, 2011.

Kasl, Charlotte D. *Women, Sex, and Addiction*. New York: Harper and Row, 1990.

PERIODICALS

Abouesh, A., and A. Clayton. "Compulsive Voyeurism and Exhibitionism: A Clinical Response to Paroxetine." *Archives of Sexual Behavior* 28, no. 1 (February 1999): 23–30.

Bradford, John M.W. "The Treatment of Sexual Deviation Using a Pharmacological Approach." *The Journal of Sex Research* 37 (August 1, 2000): 485–92.

Carnes, P., and J.P. Schneider. "Recognition and Management of Addictive Sexual Disorders: Guide for the Primary Care Clinician." *Lippincotts Primary Care Practitioner* 4, no. 3 (May–June 2000): 302–18.

de Silva, W. P. "Sexual Variations." *British Medical Journal* 318 (March 6, 1999): 654. Available online at http://www.bmj.com/content/318/7184/654.full (accessed November 9, 2011).

Kafka, Martin P., and J. Hennen. "Psychostimulant Augmentation During Treatment with Selective Serotonin Reuptake Inhibitors in Men with Paraphilias and Paraphilia-Related Disorders: A Case Series." *Journal of Clinical Psychiatry* 61, no. 9 (September 2000): 664–70.

Langstrom, Niklas, and Michael C. Seto. Exhibitionistic and Voyeuristic Behavior in a Swedish National Population Survey." *Archives of Sexual Behavior* 35, no. 4 (2006): 427–35.

Lee, J.K., et al. "Developmental Risk Factors for Sexual Offending." *Child Abuse and Neglect: The International Journal* 26, no. 1 (January 2002): 73–92.

Marazziti, Donatella, and Bernardo Dell. 'Osso. "Topiramate Plus Citalopram in the Treatment of Compulsive-Impulsive Sexual Behaviors." *Clinical Practice in Epidemiology in Mental Health* 2 (May 2006): 9. Available online at http://www.cpementalhealth.com/content/2/1/9 (accessed November 9, 2011).

Schiffer, Boris, et al. "Structural Brain Abnormalities in the Frontostriatal System and Cerebellum in Pedophilia." *Journal of Psychiatric Research* 41, no. 9 (2007) 753–62.

Schober, Justine M., Peter M. Byrne, and Phyllis J. Kuhn. "Leuprolide Acetate is a Familiar Drug that May Modify Sex-Offender Behavior: The Urologist's Role." *BJU International* 97, no. 4 (April 2006) 684–86.

Simpson, G., A. Blaszczynski, and A. Hodgkinson. "Sex Offending as a Psychosocial Sequela of Traumatic Brain Injury." *Journal of Head Trauma and Rehabilitation* 14, no. 6 (December 1999): 567–80.

Sonnenberg, Stephen P. "Mental Disabilities in the Workplace." *Workforce* 79 (June 2000): 632. Available online at http://findarticles.com/p/articles/mi_m0FXS/is_6_79/ai_63256161 (accessed November 9, 2011).

WEBSITES

Miller, John L. "Paraphilias." @athealth.com. December 30, 2010. Available online at http://www.athealth.com/Consumer/disorders/Paraphilias.html (accessed October 6, 2011).

ORGANIZATIONS

Augustine Fellowship, Sex and Love Addicts Anonymous, PO Box 119, New Town Branch, Boston, MA, 02258, (617) 332-1845.

National Association on Sexual Addiction Problems, 22937 Arlington Ave., Ste. 201, Torrance, CA, 90501, (213) 546-3103.

Rebecca Frey, PhD
Emily Jane Willingham, PhD

Exposure treatment

Definition

Exposure treatment is a technique that is widely used in **cognitive-behavioral therapy** (CBT) to help patients systematically confront a feared stimulus in a live or virtual environment or in the imagination. Through repeated exposure to the stimulus, patients are helped to nullify fears and increase self-efficacy. Exposure treatment is also called exposure therapy.

Purpose

Exposure treatment is used for a variety of **anxiety disorders**, and it has also recently been extended to the treatment of substance-related disorders. Generally, exposure treatment involves presenting patients with anxiety-producing stimulus for a long enough time to decrease the intensity of their emotional reactions. As a result, the feared situation or object no longer makes the patients anxious. Exposure treatment can be carried out in real situations, which is called in vivo exposure, or it can be done through imagination, which is called imaginal exposure. More recently, exposure treatment has been extended to include the use of computer-based virtual environments.

The category of imaginal exposure includes **systematic desensitization**, in which patients imagine certain aspects of the feared object or situation combined with relaxation. Graded or graduated exposure refers to exposing the patients to the feared situation in a gradual manner. Flooding refers to exposing patients to the anxiety-provoking or feared situation all at once and keeping them in it until the anxiety and fear subside. There are several variations in the delivery of exposure treatment: patient-directed exposure instructions or self-exposure; therapist-assisted exposure; group exposure; and exposure with response prevention.

The basic purpose of exposure treatment is to decrease a person's anxious and fearful reactions (emotions, thoughts, or physical sensations) through repeated exposures to anxiety-producing material. This reduction of the patient's anxiety response is known as habituation. A related purpose of exposure treatment is to eliminate the anxious or fearful response altogether so that patients can face the feared situation repeatedly without experiencing anxiety or fear. This elimination of the anxiety response is known as extinction.

Description

Exposure treatment usually begins with making lists or hierarchies of situations that make the patients anxious or fearful. The situations are ranked on a scale of zero (representing the situation producing the least anxiety) to ten (representing the situation of highest anxiety). In addition, patients are usually asked to rate their level of anxiety in each situation on a scale from zero (no anxiety or discomfort) to 100 (extreme anxiety and discomfort). This scale is called the subjective units of distress scale (SUDS). Patients may be asked to provide SUDS ratings at regular intervals (for example every five minutes) during exposure treatment.

Methods of delivering exposure treatment

PATIENT-DIRECTED EXPOSURE. Patient-directed exposure is the simplest variation of exposure treatment. After patients make their hierarchy lists with their therapist, they are instructed to move through the situations on the hierarchy at their own rates. Patients start with the lowest anxiety situation on the list, and keep a journal of their experiences. They continue the patient-directed exposure on a daily basis until their fears and anxieties have decreased. For example, if patients are afraid of leaving the house, the first item on the hierarchy might be to stand outside the front door for a certain period of time. After they are able to perform this action without feeling anxious, they would move to the next item on the hierarchy, which might be walking to the end of the driveway. Treatment would proceed in this way until the patients have completed all the items on the hierarchy. During therapy sessions, the therapist reviews their journal, gives them positive feedback for any progress that they have made, and discusses any obstacles that they encountered during exposures to the feared situation.

THERAPIST-ASSISTED EXPOSURE. In this form of exposure treatment, therapists go with patients to the feared location or situation and provides on-the-spot coaching to help them manage their anxieties. Therapists may challenge their patients to experience the maximum amount of anxiety. In prolonged in vivo exposure, therapists and patients stay in the situation as long as it takes for the anxiety to decrease. For example, they might remain in a crowded shopping mall for four or more hours. The therapists also explore the thoughts of patients during this exposure to confront any irrational ways of thinking.

GROUP EXPOSURE. In group exposure, self-exposure and practice are combined with group education and discussion of experiences during exposure to feared situations. These sessions may last as long as three hours and include 30 minutes of education, time for individual exposure practice, and 45 minutes of discussion. Group sessions may be scheduled on a daily basis for 10–14 days.

Exposure treatment for specific anxiety disorders

AGORAPHOBIA. Many research studies have shown that graded exposure treatment is effective for **agoraphobia**. Long-term studies have shown that improvement can be maintained for as long as seven years. Exposure treatment for agoraphobia is best conducted in vivo, in the actual feared situation, such as entering a packed subway car. Exposure treatment for agoraphobia is likely to be more effective when the patient's spouse or friend is involved, perhaps because of the support a companion can offer the patient during practice sessions.

PANIC DISORDER. Exposure treatment is the central component of cognitive-behavioral treatment for **panic disorder**. Treatment for this disorder involves identifying patients' specific fears within their experiences of panic, such as fears of being sick, of losing control, and of embarrassment. Once these fears are identified, patients are instructed to expose themselves to situations in which the fearful thoughts arise (such as walking away from a safe person or place). The rationale behind this instruction is that enduring the anxiety associated with the situation will accustom patients to the situation itself, so that over time the anxiety will diminish or disappear. In this way, patients discover that the feared consequences do not happen in real life.

In some patients, physical symptoms of panic lead to fears about the experience of panic itself. Fears related to the physical symptoms associated with panic can be targeted for treatment by inducing the bodily sensations that mimic those experienced during panic attacks. This technique is called interoceptive exposure. Patients are asked to induce the feared sensations in a number of ways. For example, patients may spin in a revolving chair to induce dizziness or run up the stairs to induce increased heart rate and shortness of breath. They are then instructed to notice what the symptoms feel like, and allow them to remain without doing anything to control them. With repeated exposure, patients learn that the bodily sensations do not signal harm or danger, and need not be feared. Patients are taught such strategies as muscle relaxation and slow breathing to control anxiety before, during, and after the exposure.

Interoceptive exposure treatment for panic usually begins with practice sessions in a therapist's office. Patients may be instructed to practice at home and then practice in a less "safe" environment, such as their work setting or a nearby park. The next step is the addition of the physical activities that naturally produce the feared symptoms. Situational or in vivo exposure would then be introduced for patients with agoraphobia combined with panic disorder. Patients would be instructed to go back into situations that they have been avoiding, such as elevators or busy railroad terminals. If patients develop symptoms of anxiety, they are instructed to use the techniques for controlling anxiety that were previously learned.

The effectiveness of exposure treatment for decreasing panic attacks and avoidance has been well demonstrated. In research studies, 50–90% of patients experience relief from symptoms.

SPECIFIC PHOBIA AND SOCIAL PHOBIA. Graded exposure is used most often to treat specific or simple phobias. In graded exposure, patients approach the feared object or situation by degrees. For example, those afraid of swimming in the ocean might begin by looking at photographs of the ocean, then watching movies of people swimming, then going to the beach and walking along the water's edge, and then working up to a full swim in the ocean. Graded exposure can be done through patient-directed instruction or therapist-assisted exposure. Research studies indicate that most patients respond quickly to graded exposure treatment, and that the benefits of treatment are well maintained.

Treatment for **social phobia** usually combines exposure treatment with cognitive restructuring. This combination seems to help prevent a recurrence of symptoms. In general, studies of exposure treatment for social phobia have shown that it leads to a reduction of symptoms. Since cognitive restructuring is usually combined with exposure, it is unclear which component is responsible for patients' improvement, but there is some indication that exposure alone may be sufficient.

Exposure treatment can be more difficult to arrange for treating social phobia, however, because patients have less control over social situations, which are unpredictable by their nature and can unexpectedly become more intense and anxiety-provoking. Furthermore, social exchanges usually last only a short time; therefore, they may not provide the length of exposure that patients need.

OBSESSIVE-COMPULSIVE DISORDER. The most common nonmedication treatment for **obsessive-compulsive disorder** (OCD) is exposure to the feared or anxiety-producing situation plus response prevention (preventing the patient from performing a compulsive behavior, such as hand washing after exposure to something thought to be contaminated). This form of treatment also uses a hierarchy, and begins with the easiest situation and gradually moves to more difficult situations. Research has shown that exposure to contamination situations leads to a decrease in fears of contamination, but does not lead to changes in the compulsive behavior. In a similar fashion, the response prevention component leads to a decrease in compulsive behavior, but does not affect the patient's fears of contamination. Since each form of treatment affects different OCD symptoms, a combination of exposure and response prevention is more effective than either modality by itself. Exposure combined with response prevention also appears to be effective for treating children and adolescents with OCD.

Prolonged continuous exposure is better than short, interrupted periods of exposure in treating people with OCD. On average, exposure treatment of people with OCD requires 90-minute sessions, although the frequency of sessions varies. Some studies have shown good results with 15 daily treatments spread over a period of three weeks. This intensive treatment format may be best suited for cases that are more severe and complex, as in patients with **depression** as well as OCD. Patients who are less severely affected and are highly motivated may benefit from sessions once or twice a week. Treatment may include both therapist-assisted exposure and self-exposure as homework between sessions. Imaginal exposure may be useful for addressing fears that are hard to incorporate into in vivo exposure, such as fears of a loved one's death. Patients usually prefer gradual exposure to the most distressing situations in their hierarchy; however, gradual exposure does not appear to be more effective than flooding or immediate exposure to the situation.

POST-TRAUMATIC STRESS DISORDER. Exposure treatment has been used successfully in the therapy of **post-traumatic stress disorder** (PTSD) resulting from such traumatic experiences as combat, sexual assault, and motor vehicle accidents. Research studies have reported encouraging results for exposure treatment in reducing PTSD or PTSD symptoms in children, adolescents, and adults. Intrusive symptoms of PTSD, such as nightmares and flashbacks, may be reduced by having patients relive the emotional aspects of the **trauma** in a safe, therapeutic environment. It may take 10–15 exposure sessions to decrease the negative physical sensations associated with PTSD. These sessions may range from one to two hours in length and may occur once or twice a week. Relaxation techniques are usually included before and after exposure. The exposure may be therapist-assisted or patient-directed.

A recent study showed that imaginal exposure and cognitive treatment are equally effective in reducing symptoms associated with chronic or severe PTSD, but that neither brought about complete improvement. In addition, more patients treated with exposure worsened over the course of treatment than patients treated with cognitive approaches. This finding may have been related to the fact that the patients receiving exposure treatment had less frequent sessions with long periods of time between sessions. Some patients diagnosed with PTSD, however, do not seem to benefit from exposure therapy. They may have difficulty tolerating exposure, or have difficulty imagining, visualizing, or describing their traumatic experiences. The use of cognitive therapy to help the patient focus on thoughts may be a useful adjunctive treatment, or serve as an alternative to exposure treatment.

Many people who have experienced sexual assault or rape meet the criteria for PTSD defined in the ***Diagnostic and Statistical Manual of Mental Disorders***, fourth edition, text revision (*DSM-IV-TR*). They may reexperience the traumatic event, avoid items or places associated with the trauma, and have increased levels of physical arousal. Exposure treatment in these cases involves using either imaginal or in vivo exposure to reduce anxiety and any tendencies to avoid aspects of the situation that produce anxiety (also known as avoidance behavior). Verbal description of the event (imaginal exposure) is critical for recovery, although it usually feels painful and threatening to patients. It is important that the patients' verbal descriptions of the traumatic events, along with their expressions of thoughts and feelings related to it, occur as early in the treatment process as possible, to minimize long-term suffering.

Prolonged exposure is the most effective nonmedical treatment for reducing traumatic memories related to PTSD. It combines flooding with systematic desensitization. The goal is to expose patients using both imaginal and in vivo exposure techniques in order to reduce avoidance behaviors and fears. Prolonged exposure may occur over nine to 12 90-minute sessions. During the imaginal exposure phase of treatment, patients are asked to describe the details of the traumatic experiences repeatedly, in the present tense. Patients use the SUDS scale to monitor levels of fear and anxiety. The in vivo component occurs outside a therapist's office; this component involves having clients expose themselves to cues in the environment that they have been avoiding—for example, the place where the motor vehicle accident or rape occurred. Patients are instructed to stay in the fear-producing situation for at least 45 minutes, or until their anxiety levels have gone down significantly on the SUDS rating scale. Often patients will use a coach or someone who will stay with them at the beginning of in vivo practice. The coach's role gradually decreases over time as the patients experience less anxiety.

Recent innovations in exposure treatment

VIRTUAL REALITY EXPOSURE TREATMENT. Virtual reality is a technique that allows people to participate actively in a computer-generated (or virtual) scenario or environment. The participants have a sense of being present in the virtual environment. Virtual reality uses a device mounted on the participant's head that shows computer graphics and visual displays in real time, and tracks the person's body movements. Some forms of virtual reality also allow participants to hold a second device in their hands that enables them to interact more fully with the virtual environment, such as opening a car door.

Virtual reality has been proposed as a new way of conducting exposure therapy because it can provide a sense of being present in a feared situation. Virtual reality exposure may be useful for treating such phobias as fear of heights, flying, or driving, as well as for treating PTSD. This method appears to have several advantages over standard exposure therapy. First, virtual reality may offer patients a greater sense of control because they can instantly turn the device on and off or change its level of intensity. Second, virtual reality protects patients from harm or social embarrassment during their practice sessions. Third, it can be implemented regardless of the patient's ability to imagine or to remain with prolonged imaginal exposure. These proposed advantages of virtual reality over standard exposure therapy have yet to be tested, however.

Some studies have been conducted using virtual reality in the treatment of patients with fear of heights and fear of flying, and in a sample of Vietnam veterans diagnosed with PTSD. These studies of virtual reality exposure therapy have limitations in terms of study design and small sample size, but their positive results suggest that virtual reality exposure therapy deserves further investigation.

CUE EXPOSURE TREATMENT FOR ALCOHOL DEPENDENCE. Cue exposure is a relatively new approach to treating substance-related disorders. It is designed to re-create real-life situations in safe therapeutic environments that expose patients repeatedly to alcohol-related cues, such as the sight or smell of alcohol. It is thought that this repeated exposure to cues, plus prevention of the usual response (drinking alcohol) will reduce and possibly eliminate urges experienced in reaction to the cues.

People diagnosed with alcohol dependence face a number of alcohol-related cues in their environments, including moods associated with previous drinking patterns; people, places, times, and objects associated with the pleasurable effects of alcohol; and the sight or smell of alcoholic beverages. Exposure to these cues increases the patient's risk of **relapse**, because the cues can interfere with a person's use of coping skills to resist the urge to drink. The purpose of cue exposure is to teach patients coping skills for responding to these urges. It is thought that people who practice coping skills in the presence of cues will find the coping skills strengthened, along with the conviction that they can respond effectively when confronted by similar cues in real-life situations.

There are various approaches to cue exposure. The choice of cues is usually based on treatment philosophy and goals, which may require abstinence from alcohol or permit moderate drinking. In abstinence-only programs, patients may be exposed to actual alcohol cues and/or imagined high-risk situations. This imaginal exposure is useful for dealing with cues and circumstances that cannot be reproduced in treatment settings, such as fights. Patients learn and practice urge-specific coping skills. While patients may learn to cope successfully with one cue (e.g., the smell of alcohol), the urge to drink may reappear in response to another cue, such as seeing a friend with whom they used to go to bars. Patients would then learn how to manage this particular cue. This program may take six to eight individual or group sessions and may occur on an inpatient or outpatient basis. Often patients remain in the treatment setting for several hours after the exposure to ensure that any lasting urges are safely managed with a therapist's help.

More specifically, cue exposure focuses on the aspect of alcohol consumption that produces the strongest urge. Patients would report each change in their level of urgency, using a scale of zero to 10 that resembles the SUDS scale. The urge to drink usually peaks after one to five minutes. When the desire for a drink arises, patients are instructed to focus on the cue to see what happens to their desire. In most cases the urge subsides within 15 minutes, which is often different from what the patients expected. In later sessions, the patients are instructed when the urge peaks to imagine using the coping skills that they recently learned. Patients may also be instructed to imagine being in high-risk situations and using the coping skills. Some examples of these coping skills include telling oneself that the urge will go away, picturing the negative consequences of drinking alcohol, and thinking of the positive consequences of staying sober.

Although there has been little research on cue exposure, available studies show positive outcomes in terms of decreasing the patients' consumption of alcohol. There have been, however, few outcome studies comparing cue exposure treatment to other treatment approaches. It may be hard to separate the benefits of exposure from the benefits of coping skills training. In any event, cue exposure treatment is a promising approach that deserves further study to determine if either component alone is sufficient or if a combination of the two is more effective.

Precautions

Exposure treatment is generally a safe treatment method; however, some patients may find that the level of anxiety that occurs during treatment sessions is higher than they can handle. Some studies of exposure treatment have reported a high dropout rate, perhaps because the method itself produces anxiety. In addition, exposure treatment is not effective for all patients; after treatment, some continue to experience anxiety symptoms.

Results

Progress in exposure therapy is often slow in the beginning, and occasional setbacks are to be expected. As patients gain experience with various anxiety-producing

KEY TERMS

Cognitive restructuring—An approach to psychotherapy that focuses on helping patients examine distorted patterns of perceiving and thinking in order to change their emotional responses to people and situations.

Cue—Any behavior or event in a person's environment that serves to stimulate a particular response. For example, the smell of liquor may be a cue for some people to pour themselves a drink.

Desensitization—The reduction or elimination of an overly intense reaction to a cue by controlled repeated exposures to the cue.

Extinction—The elimination or removal of a person's reaction to a cue as a result of exposure treatment.

Flooding—A type of exposure treatment in which patients are exposed to anxiety-provoking or feared situations all at once and kept in it until the anxiety and fear subside.

Habituation—The reduction of a person's emotional or behavioral reaction to a cue by repeated or prolonged exposure.

Hierarchy—In exposure therapy, a list of feared items or situations, ranked from least fearsome to most fearsome.

In vivo—A Latin phrase that means "in life." In modeling and exposure therapies, it refers to practicing new behaviors in a real setting, as distinct from using imagery or imagined settings.

Interoceptive—Referring to stimuli or sensations that arise inside the body. In interoceptive exposure treatment, patients are asked to exercise or perform other actions that produce feared internal physical sensations.

Modality—The medical term for a method of treatment.

Subjective units of distress (SUDS) scale—A scale used by patients during exposure treatment to rate their levels of fear and anxiety with numbers from zero to 100.

Virtual reality—A realistic simulation of an environment, produced by a computer system using interactive hardware and software.

situations, their rates of progress may increase. While flooding can produce positive results more quickly than graded exposure, it is rarely used because of the high level of discomfort associated with it.

Resources

BOOKS

American Psychiatric Association. *Practice Guidelines for the Treatment of Psychiatric Disorders: Compendium 2006*. Washington, DC: American Psychiatric Publishing, 2006.

Richard, David C. S., and Dean Lauterbach, eds. *Handbook of Exposure Therapies*. San Diego, CA: Academic Press, 2006.

Rosqvist, Johan. *Exposure Treatments for Anxiety Disorders: A Practioner's Guide to Concepts, Methods, and Evidence-Based Practice*. New York: Routledge, 2005.

VandenBos, Gary R. ed. *APA Dictionary of Psychology*. Washington, DC: American Psychological Association, 2006.

PERIODICALS

Bornas, Xavier, Miquel Tortella-Feliu, and Jordi Llabrés. "Do All Treatments Work for Flight Phobia? Computer-Assisted Exposure Versus a Brief Multicomponent Non-exposure Treatment." *Psychotherapy Research* 16, no. 1 (January 2006): 41–50.

Conklin, Cynthia A. "Environments as Cues to Smoke: Implications for Human Extinction-Based Research and Treatment." *Experimental and Clinical Psychopharmacology* 14, no. 1 (February 2006): 12–9.

Cottraux, Jean. "Recent Developments in Research and Treatment for Social Phobia (Social Anxiety Disorder)." *Current Opinion in Psychiatry* 18, no. 1 (January 2005): 51–54.

Massad, Phillip M., and Timothy L. Hulsey. "Exposure Therapy Renewed." *Journal of Psychotherapy Integration* 16, no. 4 (December 2006): 417–-28.

Thewissen, Roy, et al. "Renewal of Cue-Elicited Urge to Smoke: Implications for Cue Exposure Treatment." *Behaviour Research and Therapy* 44, no. 10 (October 2006): 1441–49.

Vansteenwegen, Debora, et al. "Verbal, Behavioural and Physiological Assessment of the Generalization of Exposure-Based Fear Reduction in a Spider-Anxious Population." *Behaviour Research and Therapy* 45, no. 2 (February 2007): 291–300.

Wilhelm, Frank H., et al. "Mechanisms of Virtual Reality Exposure Therapy: The Role of the Behavioral Activation and Behavioral Inhibition Systems." *Applied Psychophysiology and Biofeedback* 30, no. 3 (September 2005): 271–84.

Joneis Thomas, PhD
Ruth A. Wienclaw, PhD

Expressive language disorder

Definition

Expressive language disorder occurs when an individual has problems expressing himself or herself using spoken language.

Demographics

Expressive language disorder is a relatively common childhood disorder. Language delays occur in 10%–15% of children under age three, and in 3%–7% of school-age children. Expressive language disorder is more common in boys than in girls: studies suggest that developmental expressive language disorder occurs two to five times more often in boys. The developmental form of the disorder is far more common than the acquired type.

Description

Expressive language disorder is generally a childhood disorder. There are two types of expressive language disorder: the developmental type and the acquired type. Developmental expressive language disorder does not have a known cause and generally appears at the time a child is learning to talk. Acquired expressive language disorder is caused by damage to the **brain**. It occurs suddenly after events such as **stroke** or traumatic head injury. The acquired type can occur at any age.

Causes and symptoms

Causes

There is no clearly identified cause of developmental expressive language disorder. Research is ongoing to determine which biological or environmental factors may be the cause. Acquired expressive language disorder is caused by damage to the brain. Damage can be sustained during a stroke, or as the result of traumatic head injury, **seizures**, or other medical conditions. The way in which acquired expressive language disorder manifests itself depends on which parts of the brain are injured and how badly they are damaged.

Symptoms

Expressive language disorder is characterized by a child having difficulty with self-expression using speech. The signs and symptoms vary drastically from child to child. The child does not have problems with the pronunciation of words, as occurs in **phonological disorder**. The child does have problems putting sentences together coherently, using proper grammar, recalling the appropriate word to use, or other similar problems. A child with expressive language disorder cannot communicate thoughts, needs, or wants at the same level or with the same complexity as peers and often has a smaller vocabulary compared to peers.

Children with expressive language disorder have the same ability to understand speech as their peers and have the same level of intelligence. A child with this disorder may understand words but be unable to use the same words in sentences. The child may understand complex spoken sentences and be able to carry out intricate instructions, although unable to form complex sentences.

There are many different ways in which expressive language disorder can manifest itself. Some children do not properly use pronouns, or leave out functional words such as “is” or “the.” Other children cannot recall words that they want to use in the sentence and substitute general words such as “thing” or “stuff.” Some children cannot organize their sentences so that the sentences are easy to understand. These children do comprehend the material they are trying to express—they just cannot create the appropriate sentences with which to express their thoughts.

Diagnosis

To diagnose expressive language disorder, children must be performing below their peers at tasks that require communication in the form of speech. This can be hard to determine because it must be shown that an individual understands the material but cannot express that comprehension. Nonverbal tests must be used in addition to tests that require spoken answers. Hearing should also be evaluated because children who do not hear well may have problems putting together sentences in a way that is similar to children with expressive language disorder. In children who are mildly hearing-impaired, the problem can often be resolved by using hearing aids to enhance the child’s hearing. Also, children who speak a language other than the dominant language of their society (e.g., English in the United States) in the home should be tested in that language if possible. The child’s ability to communicate in English may be the problem, not the child’s ability to communicate in general.

The ***Diagnostic and Statistical Manual of Mental Disorders***, fourth edition, text revision (*DSM-IV-TR*), states that there are four general criteria for diagnosing expressive language disorder. The first is that the child communicates using speech at a level that is less developed than expected for his or her intelligence and ability to understand spoken language. The problem with communication using speech must create difficulties for the child in everyday life or in achieving goals. The child must understand what is being said at a level that is age-appropriate, or at a developmental level consistent with the child's age. Otherwise the diagnoses should be **mixed receptive-expressive language disorder**. If the child has intellectual disabilities, poor hearing, or other problems, the difficulties with speech must be greater than is generally associated with disabilities of the child.

Treatment

There are two types of treatment used for expressive language disorder. The first involves the child working one-on-one with a speech therapist on a regular schedule and practicing speech and communication skills. The second type of treatment involves the child's parents and teachers working together to incorporate spoken language that the child needs into everyday activities and play. Both of these treatment can be effective and are often used together.

Prognosis

The developmental form of expressive language disorder generally has a good prognosis. Most children develop normal or nearly normal language skills by high school. In some cases, minor problems with expressive language may never resolve. The acquired type of expressive language disorder has a prognosis that depends on the nature and location of the brain injury. Some people get their language skills back over days or months. For others it takes years, and some people never fully recover expressive language function.

Prevention

There is no known way to prevent developmental expressive language disorder. Because acquired language disorder is caused by damage to the brain, anything that would help to prevent brain damage may help to prevent that type of the disorder. This can include things ranging from lowering cholesterol to preventing stroke to wearing a bicycle helmet to prevent **traumatic brain injury**.

Resources

BOOKS

American Psychiatric Association. *Diagnostic and Statistical Manual of Mental Disorders*. 4th ed., text rev. Washington, DC: American Psychiatric Publishing, 2000.

Sadock, Benjamin J., and Virginia A. Sadock, eds. *Comprehensive Textbook of Psychiatry*. Vol. 2. 7th ed. Philadelphia: Lippincott Williams and Wilkins, 2000.

PERIODICALS

Roberts, Joanne E., Richard M. Rosenfeld, and Susan A. Zeisel. "Otitis Media and Speech and Language: A Meta-Analysis of Prospective Studies." *Pediatrics* 113, no. 3 (March 2004): 238–48.

Stein, Martin T., ed. "Expressive Language Delay in a Toddler." *Journal of Developmental & Behavioral Pediatrics* 22, no. 2 (April 2001): S99–S103.

WEBSITES

MedlinePlus. "Language Disorder—Children." U.S. National Library of Medicine, National Institutes of Health. 2006. http://www.nlm.nih.gov/medlineplus/ency/article/001545.htm (accessed October 6, 2011).

ORGANIZATIONS

American Academy of Pediatrics, 141 Northwest Point Blvd., Elk Grove Village, IL, 60007-1098, (847) 434-4000, Fax: (847) 434-8000, http://www.aap.org.

American Psychological Association, 750 1st Street NE, Washington, DC, 20002-4242, (202) 336-5500; TDD/TTY: (202) 336-6123, (800) 374-2721, http://www.apa.org.

American Speech-Language-Hearing Association, 2200 Research Blvd., Rockville, MD, 20785, (301) 296-5700, http://www.asha.org.

Tish Davidson, AM
Emily Jane Willingham, PhD

Factitious disorder

Definition

Factitious disorder (FD) is an umbrella category that covers a group of mental disturbances in which patients intentionally act physically or mentally ill without obvious benefits. According to one estimate, the unnecessary tests and waste of other medical resources caused by FD cost the United States $40 million per year. The term factitious comes from a Latin word that means artificial or contrived.

The ***Diagnostic and Statistical Manual of Mental Disorders,*** fourth edition, text revision (*DSM-IV-TR*) distinguishes FD from **malingering**, which is defined as pretending illness when the individual has a clear motive—usually for economic benefit or to avoid legal trouble.

FD is sometimes referred to as hospital **addiction**, pathomimia, or polysurgical addiction. Variant names for individuals with FD include hospital vagrants, hospital hoboes, peregrinating patients, problem patients, and professional patients.

Demographics

The demographics of FD vary considerably across the different subtypes. Most individuals with the predominantly psychological subtype of FD are males with a history of hospitalizations beginning in late adolescence; few of these people, however, are older than 45. For nonchronic FD with predominantly physical symptoms, women outnumber men by a 3:1 ratio. Most of these women are between 20 and 40 years of age. Individuals with Munchausen syndrome are mostly middle-aged males who are unmarried and estranged from their families. Mothers involved in MSBP are usually married, educated, middle-class women in their early 20s.

Little is known about the rates of various subcategories of FD in different racial or ethnic groups. The prevalence of FD worldwide is not known. In the United States, some experts think that FD is underdiagnosed because hospital personnel often fail to spot the deceptions that are symptomatic of the disorder. In addition, people with this disorder tend to migrate from one medical facility to another, making tracking difficult. It is also not clear which subtypes of FD are most common. Most observers in developed countries agree, however, that the prevalence of factitious physical symptoms is much higher than the prevalence of factitious psychological symptoms. A large teaching hospital in Toronto reported that 10 of 1,288 patients referred to a consultation service had FD (0.8%). The National Institute for Allergy and Infectious Disease reported that 9.3% of patients referred for fevers of unknown origin had FD. A clinic in Australia found that 1.5% of infants brought in for serious illness by parents were cases of Munchausen syndrome by proxy.

Description

Cases of FD are referenced in the medical literature as early as the second century A.D. by Galen, a famous Roman physician. The term factitious is derived from a book by an English physician named Gavin, published in 1843, entitled *On Feigned and Factitious Diseases*. The modern study of FD, however, began with a 1951 article in *Lancet* by a British **psychiatrist**, Richard Asher, who also coined the term Munchausen's syndrome to describe a chronic subtype of FD. The name Munchausen comes from an eighteenth-century German baron whose stories of his military exploits were published with substantial embellishments. In 1977, the first case of FD with primarily psychological symptoms was reported. FD was recognized as a formal diagnostic category by *DSM-III* in 1980.

DSM-IV-TR defines FD as having three major subtypes: FD with predominantly psychological signs and symptoms; FD with predominantly physical signs and symptoms; and FD with combined psychological and physical signs and symptoms. A fourth syndrome, known as Ganser syndrome, has been classified in the past as a form of FD, although *DSM-IV-TR* groups it with the **dissociative disorders**.

DSM-IV-TR specifies three criteria for FD:

- the patient is intentionally producing or pretending to have physical or psychological symptoms or signs of illness
- the patient's motivation is to assume the role of a sick person
- there are no external motives (as in malingering) that explain the behavior

Psychological FD

FD with predominantly psychological signs and symptoms is listed by *DSM-IV-TR* as the first subcategory of the disorder. It is characterized by the individual feigning psychological symptoms.

Some researchers have suggested adding the following criteria for this subtype of FD.

- The symptoms are inconsistent, changing markedly from day to day and from one hospitalization to the next.
- The changes are influenced by the environment (as when the patient feels observed by others) rather than by the treatment.
- The patient's symptoms are unusual or unbelievable.
- The patient has a large number of symptoms that belong to several different psychiatric disorders.

Physical FD

FD with predominantly physical signs and symptoms is the most familiar to medical personnel. Chronic FD of this type is often referred to as Munchausen's syndrome. The most common ways of pretending illness are: presenting a factitious history (claiming to have had a seizure that never happened); combining a factitious history with external agents that mimic the symptoms of disease (adding blood from a finger prick to a urine sample); or combining a factitious history with maneuvers that produce a genuine medical condition (taking a psychoactive drug to produce psychiatric symptoms). In most cases, these patients sign out of the hospital when they are confronted by staff with proof of their pretending, usually in the form of a laboratory report. Many individuals with Munchausen's syndrome move from hospital to hospital, seeking treatment, and thus are known commonly as "hospital hoboes."

FD with mixed symptoms

FD in this category is characterized by a mix of psychological and physical signs and symptoms.

FD not otherwise specified

FD not otherwise specified is a category that *DSM-IV-TR* included to cover a bizarre subtype in which one person fabricates misleading information about another's health or induces actual symptoms of illness in the other person. First described in 1977 by an American pediatrician, this syndrome is known as Munchausen syndrome by proxy (MSBP) and almost always involves a parent (usually the mother) and child. MSBP is now understood as a form of **child abuse** involving premeditation rather than impulsive acting out. Many pediatricians in the United States believe that MSBP is underdiagnosed.

Ganser syndrome

Ganser syndrome is a rare disorder (with about a 100 documented cases worldwide) that has been variously categorized as a FD or a dissociative disorder. It is named for a German psychiatrist named Sigbert Ganser, who first described it in 1898 from an examination of male prisoners who were thought to be psychotic. Ganser syndrome is used to describe dissociative symptoms and the pretending of **psychosis** that occur in forensic settings.

There are four symptoms regarded as diagnostic of Ganser syndrome:

- *Vorbeireden*: A German word that means "talking beside the point," it refers to a type of approximate answer to an examiner's questions that may appear silly but usually indicates that the patient understands the question. If the examiner asks how many legs a dog has, the patient may answer, "five."
- Clouding of consciousness: The patient is drowsy or inattentive.
- Conversion symptoms: These are physical symptoms produced by unconscious psychological issues rather than diagnosable medical causes. A common conversion symptom is temporary paralysis of an arm or leg.
- Hallucinations.

Virtual FD

Although virtual FD does not appear as a heading in any present diagnostic manual, it is a phenomenon that has appeared with increasing frequency with the rise of Internet usage. The growing use of the personal computer has affected presentations of FD in two important ways. First, computers allow people with sufficient technical skills to access medical records from hospital databases and to cut and paste changes into their own records to falsify their medical histories. Second, computers allow people to enter Internet chat rooms for people with serious illnesses and pretend to be patients with that illness to obtain attention and sympathy. "Munchausen by Internet" can have devastating effects on chat groups, destroying trust when the hoax is exposed.

Causes and symptoms

Causes

The causes of FD, whether physical or psychiatric, are difficult to determine because these patients are often lost to follow-up when they sign out of the hospital. **Magnetic resonance imaging** (MRI) has detected abnormalities in the **brain** structure of some patients with chronic FD, suggesting that there may be biological or **genetic factors** associated with the disorder. Positron-emission tomography (**PET**) scans of patients diagnosed with Ganser syndrome have also revealed brain abnormalities. The results of EEG (**electroencephalography**) studies of these patients are nonspecific.

Several different psychodynamic explanations have been proposed for FD. These include:

- Patients with FD are trying to reenact unresolved childhood issues with parents.
- They have underlying problems with masochism.
- They need to be the center of attention and feel important.
- They need to receive care and nurturance.
- They are bothered by feelings of vulnerability.
- Deceiving a physician allows them to feel superior to an authority figure.

There are several known risk factors for FD, including:

- the presence of other mental or physical disorders in childhood that resulted in considerable medical attention
- a history of significant past relationships with doctors, or of grudges against them
- present diagnosis of borderline, narcissistic, or antisocial personality disorder

Symptoms

SYMPTOMS OF FACTITIOUS DISORDER IN ADULTS OR ADOLESCENTS. Reasons for suspecting FD include:

- The individual's history is vague and inconsistent, or the individual has a long medical record with many admissions at different hospitals in different cities.
- The patient has an unusual knowledge of medical terminology or describes the illness as if reciting a textbook description of it.
- The patient is employed in a medical or hospital-related occupation.
- *Pseudologia fantastica,* a Latin phrase for "uncontrollable lying," is a condition in which the individual provides fantastic descriptions of events that never took place.
- The patient visits emergency rooms at times such as holidays or late Friday afternoons when experienced staff are not usually present and obtaining old medical records is difficult.
- The patient has few visitors even though claiming to be an important person.
- The patient is unusually accepting of surgery or uncomfortable diagnostic procedures.
- The patient's behavior is controlling, attention-seeking, hostile, or disruptive.
- Symptoms are present only when the patient is being watched.
- The patient is abusing substances, particularly prescription painkillers or tranquilizers.
- The course of the "illness" fluctuates, or complications develop with unusual speed.
- The patient has multiple surgical scars, a so-called "gridiron abdomen," or evidence of self-inflicted wounds or injuries.

SYMPTOMS OF MUNCHAUSEN SYNDROME BY PROXY. Factors that suggest a **diagnosis** of MSBP include:

- The patient is a young child; the average age of patients with MSBP is 40 months.
- There is a history of long hospitalizations and frequent emergency room visits.
- Siblings have histories of MSBP, failure to thrive, or death in early childhood from an unexplained illness.
- The mother is employed in a health care profession.
- The mother has been diagnosed with depression or histrionic or borderline personality disorder.
- There is significant dysfunction in the family.

Diagnosis

Diagnosis of FD is usually based on a combination of laboratory findings and the gradual exclusion of other possible diagnoses. In the case of MSBP, the **abuse** is often discovered through covert video surveillance.

The most important differential diagnoses, when FD is suspected, are malingering, **conversion disorder**, or another genuine psychiatric disorder.

Treatment

Medications

Medications have not proved helpful in treating FD by itself, although they may be prescribed for symptoms of anxiety or **depression** if the individual also meets criteria for an anxiety or mood disorder.

Psychotherapy

Knowledge of the comparative effectiveness of different psychotherapeutic approaches is limited by the fact that few people diagnosed with FD remain in long-term treatment. In many cases, however, the factitious disorder improves or resolves if the individual receives appropriate therapy for a comorbid psychiatric disorder. Ganser syndrome usually resolves completely with supportive **psychotherapy**.

One approach that has proven helpful in confronting patients with an examiner's suspicions is a supportive manner that focuses on the individual's emotional distress as the source of the illness rather than on the anger or righteous indignation of hospital staff. Although most individuals with FD refuse psychiatric treatment when it is offered, those who accept it appear to benefit most from supportive rather than insight-oriented therapy.

Family therapy is often beneficial in helping family members understand the individual's behavior and need for attention.

KEY TERMS

Conversion disorder—A type of somatoform disorder in which unconscious psychological conflicts or other factors take the form of physical symptoms that are produced unintentionally. Conversion disorder is part of the differential diagnosis of factitious disorder.

Forensic—Pertaining to courtroom procedure or evidence used in courts of law.

Ganser syndrome—A rare subtype of factitious disorder accompanied by dissociative symptoms. It is most often seen in male patients under severe stress in prison or courtroom settings.

Gridiron abdomen—An abdomen with a network of parallel scars from repeated surgical operations.

Malingering—Knowingly pretending to be physically or mentally ill to avoid some unpleasant duty or responsibility, or for economic benefit.

Masochism—A mental disorder in which people obtain sexual satisfaction through pain or humiliation inflicted by themselves or by another person. The term is sometimes used more generally to refer to a tendency to find pleasure in submissiveness or self-denial.

Legal considerations

In dealing with cases of Munchausen syndrome by proxy, physicians and hospital staff should seek appropriate legal advice. Although covert video surveillance of parents suspected of MSBP is highly effective (between 56% and 92%) in exposing the fraud, it may also be considered grounds for a lawsuit by the parents on argument of entrapment. Hospitals can usually satisfy legal concerns by posting signs stating that they use hidden video monitoring.

All 50 states presently require hospital staff and physicians to notify law enforcement authorities when MSBP is suspected, and to take steps to protect the child. Protection usually includes removing the child from the home, but it should also include an evaluation of the child's sibling(s) and long-term monitoring of the family. Criminal prosecution of one or both parents may also be necessary.

Prognosis

The prognosis of FD varies by subcategory. Males diagnosed with the psychological subtype of FD are generally considered to have the worst prognosis. **Self-mutilation** and **suicide** attempts are common in these individuals. The prognosis for Munchausen's syndrome is also poor; the statistics for recurrent episodes and successful suicides range between 30% and 70%. These individuals do not usually respond to psychotherapy. The prognosis for non-chronic FD in women is variable; some of these patients accept treatment and do quite well. This subcategory of FD, however, often resolves itself after the patient turns 40. MSBP involves considerable risks for the child; 9%–10% of these cases end in the child's death.

Ganser syndrome is the one subtype of FD with a good prognosis. Almost all patients recover within days of the diagnosis, especially if the **stress** that precipitated the syndrome is resolved.

Prevention

FD is not sufficiently well understood to allow for effective preventive strategies—apart from protection of child patients and their siblings in cases of MSBP.

Resources

BOOKS

American Psychiatric Association. *Diagnostic and Statistical Manual of Mental Disorders*. 4th ed., text rev. Washington, DC: American Psychiatric Publishing, 2000.

Eisendrath, Stuart J. "Psychiatric Disorders." *Current Medical Diagnosis & Treatment 2011,* edited by Lawrence M. Tierney, Jr., et al. New York: McGraw-Hill, 2010.

"Psychiatry in Medicine." In *The Merck Manual of Diagnosis and Therapy,* edited by Robert S. Porter and Justin L. Kaplan. 19th ed. Whitehouse Station, NJ: Merck Sharp & Dohme Corp., 2011.

PERIODICALS

Andersen, H.S., D. Sestoft, and T. Lillebaek. "Ganser Syndrome After Solitary Confinement in Prison: A Short Review and a Case Report." *Norwegian Journal of Psychiatry* 55, no. 3 (2001): 199–201.

Feldman, Marc D., and Charles V. Ford. "Liejacking." *Journal of the American Medical Association* 271, no. 2 (May 25, 1994): 1574.

Libow, Judith A. "Child and Adolescent Illness Falsification." *Pediatrics* 105, no. 2 (February 1, 2000): 336–342.

McEwen, Donna R., BSN. "Recognizing Munchausen's Syndrome." *AORN Journal* 67, no. 2 (February 1998): 440–42. Available online at http://findarticles.com/p/articles/mi_m0FSL/is_n2_v67/ai_20651296 (accessed November 9, 2011).

Paulk, David. "Munchausen Syndrome by Proxy." *Clinician Reviews* 11 (August 2001): 783–91.

Russo, Francine. "Cybersickness: Muchausen by internet Breeds a Generation of Fakers." *The Village Voice* June 26, 2001. Available online at http://www.villagevoice.com/2001-06-26/news/cybersickness/1 (accessed November 9, 2011).

Snyder, S.L., M.S. Buchsbaum, and R.C. Krishna. "Unusual Visual Symptoms and Ganser-Like State Due to Cerebral Injury: A Case Study Using (18) F-Deoxyglucose Positron Emission Tomography." *Behavioral Neurology* 11, no. 1 (1998): 51–54.

Stern, Theodore A. "Is Your Patient Faking?" *Medical Economics* 81, no. 23 (December 2004) 60–63.

Szoke, Andrei, and Didier Boillet. "Factitious Disorder with Psychological Signs and Symptoms: Case Reports and Proposals for Improving Diagnosis." *Psychiatry On-Line,* 1999. http://www.priory.com/psych/factitious.htm (accessed November 9, 2011).

Worley, Courtney B., Marc D. Feldman, and James C. Hamilton. "The Case of Factitious Disorder Versus Malingering." *Psychiatric Times* 26, no. 11 (October 30, 2009).

WEBSITES

Cleveland Clinic. "An Overview of Factitious Disorders." November 11, 2008. http://my.clevelandclinic.org/disorders/Factitious_Disorders/hic_An_Overview_of_Factitious_Disorders.aspx (accessed October 6, 2011).

Elwyn, Todd S. "Factitious Disorder." Medscape Reference. 2006. http://emedicine.medscape.com/article/291304-overview (accessed October 6, 2011).

ORGANIZATIONS

American Academy of Child and Adolescent Psychiatry, 3615 Wisconsin Ave. NW, Washington, DC, 20016-3007, (202) 966-7300, Fax: (202) 966-2891, http://aacap.org.

Munchausen by Proxy Survivors Network, PO Box 806177, Saint Clair Shores, MI, 48080, http://www.mbpsnetwork.com.

Rebecca Frey, PhD
Emily Jane Willingham, PhD

False belief of pregnancy *see* **Pseudocyesis**

Familial British dementia *see* **Dementia**

Family education

Definition

Family education or "psychoeducation" is the ongoing process of educating family members about a serious mental illness, or psychological disturbance, in order to improve their coping skills and their ability to help a relative affected by the illness. It may also involve helping family members learn more about how to treat such mental illnesses, along with those physical ailments that may also be present. One of the goals of family education is to help family members and patients better understand and deal with the illness so that the best possible situation can be attained, with a minimum risk of relapses.

Purpose

When someone is diagnosed with a chronic illness, such as diabetes or heart disease, efforts are typically made by his or her doctor not only to educate the individual directly affected by the illness, but to educate and involve his/her family in treatment and care. Historically, this has not been the case with severe mental illnesses such as **schizophrenia**, major **depression** and **anxiety disorders**, **bipolar disorder**, **schizoaffective disorder**, eating disorders, or **personality disorders**.

Historically, most mental health professionals did not educate families about what to expect or how to care for their loved one. In fact, for much of the twentieth century it was believed that mental illness was caused by overly strict or overly permissive parenting styles and, consequently, families were often unfairly blamed for causing these disorders. Mothers were labeled schizophrenogenic, and even well-meaning clinicians tried to keep them and other family members at a distance. Gregory Bateson's "double-bind" theory of the time suggested that contradictory messages and communications by parents were the root cause of the problem. Because of these ideas and the **diagnosis**, the only recourse for most families was to go to public libraries to read and learn as much as they could on their own.

Over the last 25 years, however, advances in genetics, neuroscience, and imaging techniques have provided new evidence that severe mental illnesses are neurobiological in origin. With this scientific knowledge has come greater awareness and understanding that these are "no-fault" **brain** illnesses, and that neither families nor patients should be blamed. Rather, they both should receive the necessary information and support to help them better cope with these complex disorders.

Description

In the United States and elsewhere, the large majority of individuals with severe mental illness live with their families and depend on them for housing, financial assistance, advocacy, and support. For this reason, families require knowledge and skills to actively help their relative benefit from treatment, avoid **relapse**, and achieve recovery. Specifically, family caregivers require information about the illness and its symptoms, including:

- how to better communicate with their family member and professionals the pros and cons of different treatment options, medications and their therapeutic uses and their adverse side effects, signs of relapse, availability of community services and supports
- how to access benefits and entitlements
- how to handle crises or bizarre and troubling behaviors

Because living with an individual with a serious mental disorder can be very stressful, family education must also focus on teaching families about the importance of taking care of themselves.

The National Alliance on Mental Illness (NAMI) is an umbrella organization of more than 1,100 local support and advocacy groups in 50 states. The organization comprises families and individuals affected by serious mental illness who come together for family education, mutual support, and advocacy. Through conferences, **support groups**, and newsletters, family members have opportunities to educate one another and exchange experiences. NAMI has also made great inroads in teaching mental health professionals about the importance of educating family members and involving them in plans for the patient's treatment and rehabilitation. On a more formal level, NAMI has sponsored the Family-to-Family Program, a 12-week free education course that has been attended by over 115,000 family members in more than 42 states. Taught by family volunteers, this is the first peer program in family education in the United States.

Family education is slowly becoming an integral part of treatment, as the practice guidelines for professionals have begun to recommend its use. Families are also utilizing a new generation of books about mental illness—some written by professionals, and others written by, and for, family members. Families are also increasingly using the Internet to learn more about mental disorders.

KEY TERMS

Bipolar disorder—A type of mood disorder characterized by one or more episodes of abnormally high energy levels that may or not be accompanied by depression.

Depression—A psychiatric disorder involving feelings of hopelessness and symptoms of fatigue, sleeplessness, suicidal tendencies, and poor concentration.

Eating disorders—A number of medical conditions characterized by abnormal eating habits that can involve either the lack, or the excessive intake, of food and results in physical and/or emotional stress. Two types of eating disorders include anorexia nervosa and bulimia nervosa.

Mental disorder—A psychiatric disorder of mental faculties.

Schizophrenia—A mental disorder involving degraded thinking and emotions.

Family education for parents of children and adolescents

Because major mental illnesses tend to occur in adolescence or early adulthood, most family interventions focus on parents of adult children. However, any parent of a younger child with an emotional or behavioral disturbance can testify to the extraordinary challenges involved in coordinating care. For this reason, more public and private agencies are beginning to provide training, information, education, and financial assistance to family members of children and adolescents with emotional disturbances. The results of research about family education interventions for parents of children

QUESTIONS TO ASK YOUR DOCTOR

- Will family education help me and my family?
- What should I do if family education does not solve our problems?
- Is there a local organization that can help? A national one?
- Do you recommend any professionals that can help?
- Will my health insurance pay for any of the expenses?
- Do you recommend any books to read? Can I find information on the Internet?

with serious emotional disturbances are just beginning to emerge. Some research suggests that family participation improves service delivery and patient outcomes for this group. In a randomized controlled trial of the training of 200 parents who did or did not receive training, while there were no significant effects on child's mental health status, those family members who were trained showed significant knowledge enhancement and increased effectiveness.

Preparation

To prepare for family education in response to a mental health problem of someone in the family, the first step may be to talk with the family doctor or another trusted health care professional. Many local and national organizations, such as the National Alliance on Mental Illness, the National Family Caregivers Association, the **National Institute of Mental Health**, and Mental Health America, can be of service.

Aftercare

Family education is a process that, once implemented, is continued on a regular basis to provide the best health results for the patient and the best outcome for the caregiver.

Risks

Even with the implementation of family education, the risk of mental relapses is still present. However, with better education, both caregiver and patient should be better equipped to deal with such problems.

Results

Recent research has provided evidence that family education and support leads to improved patient outcomes. For example, **family psychoeducation** provided by mental health professionals has such a compelling research base that it is considered a practice based on the findings of real-life studies of family education and support.

Another type of therapy discussed in the scientific literature has been used in China and India. The family consultation model uses individualized, private consultations between the family and a trained consultant to assist the family on an as-needed basis.

Resources

BOOKS

Lefley, Harriet P. *Family Psychoeducation for Serious Mental Illness*. New York: Oxford University Press, 2009.

Torrey, E. Fuller. *Surviving Schizophrenia: A Manual for Families, Consumers and Providers*. New York: Collins, 2006.

Substance Abuse and Mental Health Services Administration, Center for Mental Health Services. *Family Psychoeducation*. Rockville, MD: U.S. Department of Health and Human Services, 2009.

Walsh, Joseph. *Psychoeducation in Mental Health*. Chicago: Lyceum, 2010.

PERIODICALS

Archie, Suzanne, et.al. "Psychotic Disorders Clinic and First-Episode Psychosis: A Program Evaluation." *Canadian Journal of Psychiatry* 50.1 (January 2005): 46–51.

Dunbar, Sandra B., et.al. "Family Education and Support Interventions in Heart Failure. A Pilot Study." *Nursing Research* 54.3 (May–June 2005): 158–66.

Edelman, Perry, Daniel Kuhn, Bradley R. Fulton, and Gregory A. Kyrouac. "Information and Service Needs of Persons With Alzheimer's Disease and Their Family Caregivers Living in Rural Communities." *American Journal of Alzheimer's Disease and Other Dementias* 21.4 (August–September 2006): 226–33.

Murray-Swank, Aaron B., Alicia Lucksted, Deborah R. Medoff, Ye Yang, Karen Wohlheiter, and Lisa B. Dixon. "Religiosity, Psychosocial Adjustment, and Subjective Burden of Persons Who Care for Those With Mental Illness." *Psychiatric Services* 57.3 (March 2006): 361–65.

WEBSITES

"Basic Facts on Family Psychoeducation." National Alliance of Mental Illness. (August 2003). http://www.nami.org/Template.cfm?Section=About_Treatments_and_Supports&template=/ContentManagement/ContentDisplay.cfm&ContentID=9546 (accessed December 3, 2010).

"Mental Health: A Report of the Surgeon General." U.S. Department of Health and Human Services. http://www.surgeongeneral.gov/library/mentalhealth/home.html (accessed December 3, 2010).

"Schizophrenia." National Institute of Mental Health. (November 29, 2010). http://www.nimh.nih.gov/health/topics/schizophrenia/index.shtml (accessed December 3, 2010).

ORGANIZATIONS

Mental Health America, 2000 N. Beauregard St., 6th Fl., Alexandria, VA, 22311, (703) 684-7722, (800) 969-6642, Fax: (703) 684-5968, http://www1.nmha.org.

National Alliance on Mental Illness, 3803 N Fairfax Dr., Ste. 100, Arlington, VA, 22203, (703) 524-7600, http://www.nami.org.

National Family Caregivers Association, 10400 Connecticut Ave., Ste. 500, Kensington, MD, 20895-3944, (301) 942-6430, (800) 896-3650, Fax: (301) 942-2302, info@thefamilycaregiver.org, http://www.nfcacares.org.

National Institute of Mental Health, 6001 Executive Blvd., Rm. 8184, MSC 9663, Bethesda, MD, 20892-9663, (301) 433-4513; TTY: (301) 443-8431, Fax: (301) 443-4279, (866) 615-6464; TTY: (866) 415-8051, nimhinfo@nih.gov, http://www.nimh.nih.gov.

Irene S. Levine, PhD
Ruth A. Wienclaw, PhD

Family psychoeducation

Definition

Psychoeducation is an educational approach used to help people with severe psychological problems learn to cope with their problems. When family members are included in this education, it is called family psychoeducation. Thus, family psychoeducation is a method for training families under the direction of mental health professionals, so that family members with psychiatric disorders can recover and maintain psychological health. Family psychoeducation has been shown to improve patient outcomes for people with **schizophrenia**, bipolar disorders, **personality disorders**, **depression**, **anxiety disorders**, eating disorders (such as **anorexia nervosa**), and other major mental illnesses.

Purpose

The goal of family psychoeducation is to prevent patients with severe mental illnesses from relapsing, and to promote their re-entry into their home communities, with particular regard for their social and occupational functioning. To achieve this goal, family psychoeducation programs seek to provide families with the information they need about mental illness and give them the coping skills to deal with their family members' psychiatric disorders.

One associated goal of family psychoeducation is to provide support for the patients' families. Families experience many burdens (financial, social, and psychological) in serving as long-term caregivers for their loved ones. Although the primary focus of family psychoeducation groups is improved patient outcomes, one essential intermediate goal is to promote the well-being of the family.

Description

There are several different models of family psychoeducation. Although they include many common elements, these different models are: single- and multiple-family groups; mixed groups that include family members and consumers (patients); groups of varying duration ranging from nine months to more than five years; and groups that focus on patients and families at different phases in the illness. Family psychoeducation programs have been studied extensively and refined by a number of researchers, including Drs. Ian Falloon, Gerald Hogarty, William McFarlane, and Lisa Dixon. For example, the late Dr. Falloon was one of the first psychiatrists to suggest that families should be involved in the treatment of schizophrenia.

The evidence suggests that multiple-family groups, which bring together several patients and their families, lead to better outcomes than single-family psychoeducation groups. The origins of multiple-family **group therapy** go back as far as 1960, when these groups were first assembled to solve ward-management problems in a psychiatric hospital. Lasting a minimum of nine months, the programs provided their participants with information about mental illness, its symptoms and treatment; medication and its side effects; how to communicate with a person with mental illness; and techniques for **crisis intervention** and mutual problem solving.

Dr. Dixon, who is a professor of psychology at the University of Maryland, recently outlined the characteristics of successful family psychoeducation programs.

- The programs consider schizophrenia an illness like any other.
- They are led by mental health professionals.
- They are part of a total treatment plan that includes medication.
- Families are treated as partners rather than patients.
- The programs focus primarily on patient outcomes, and secondarily on family outcomes.
- The programs differ from traditional family therapy in that they do not treat families as part of the problem; they see them as part of the solution.

It is also important that **family education** programs take into account the phase of the patient's illness, the life cycle of both the patient and the family, and the family's cultural context.

Family-to-Family program

The National Alliance on Mental Illness coordinates the Family-to-Family (FTF) Education Program. It is a 12-week course free that is to family caregivers of individuals with severe mental illness. The highly structured, standardized classes are offered in hundreds of communities in the United States, along with several places in Canada, Puerto Rico, and Mexico. Over the years, over 115,000 family members have attended the course. They learn from volunteers who are trained family counselors and, specifically, people who have previously provided (or are currently providing) care to mentally ill family members or loved ones. These instructors provide course materials and instruction to all participants. Some of the topics included within the course include:

- schizophrenia
- major depression
- bipolar disorder (manic depression)
- panic disorder
- obsessive-compulsive disorder
- borderline personality disorder
- brain disorders
- addictive disorders.

Side effects, effective treatment plans, medication strategies, research into **brain** disorders, dealing with mental illness (including problem solving, listening techniques, and communication techniques) are some of the subjects taught during the course. Special attention is given to the emotions and problems that caregivers deal with while caring for mentally ill individuals. The instructors also provide information on advocacy initiatives and local support services. At the end of the course, participants who succeed in all aspects of the course are certified as graduates of the Family-to-Family Education Program.

In 2005, Dixon and colleagues at the University of Maryland were provided a four-year National Alliance on Mental Illness (NAMI) grant to study the effectiveness of the Family-to-Family Education Program. Although ample research has shown that families provide major benefits to adults with serious mental illnesses, little is known about the educational programs and **support groups** that help these family members care for mentally ill relatives. Consequently, Dixon headed a $2.2 million study to determine whether the NAMI Family-to-Family Education Program is effective at providing information and guidance so family members can properly care for mentally ill relatives or loved ones.

Dr. Dixon, the principal investigator on the study, comments on how important it is to provide effective care to mentally ill people and to make sure that caregivers to such people can do the best job possible. Dixon posits that the stresses of mental illness on a family and/or loved one can be so extreme that they put the relationship at risk. As a result of a compromised relationship due to all the difficulties including disrupted family roles and financial strain, the patient's well-being is disrupted.

The study used the Family to Family Education Program that was in operation in five Maryland counties. In all, 318 participants were involved in the study, with about half of them randomly assigned either to immediately enroll in the class or to wait at least three months before another class became available (the control group). All participants (whether they took the class or not) were evaluated (interviewed) before the class started and after it was completed three months later with respect to such topics as (1) problem-focused coping, (2) emotion-focused coping, (3) subjective illness burden, and (4) distress. In other words, the control group had not taken the class at the time of both interviews, but its members were to take the class after the study was completed. The researchers were particularly interested in what benefits accrued from the class that were able to help caregivers provide better care to their mentally ill patients.

The results of the study were published in the journal *Psychiatric Services* under the title "Outcomes of a Randomized Study of a Peer-Taught Family-to-Family Education Program for Mental Illness." The June 2011 article, headed by Dixon, stated that FTF participants had "significantly greater improvement" than the control group in problem-focused coping with respect to empowerment and illness knowledge. The researchers also reported that the FTF participants, but not the members of the control group, had significantly better "emotion-focused coping" when measured by increased acceptances of mental illness of their family members. The FTF participants also had reduced distress and improved "problem-focused coping" when compared with the control group.

However, the researchers found no difference between the two groups with respect to "subjective illness burden." The authors concluded, "This study provides evidence that FTF is effective for enhancing coping and empowerment of families of persons with mental illness, although not for reducing subjective burden. Other benefits for problem solving and reducing distress are suggested but require replication."

Precautions

Precautions should be used when selecting a family psychoeducation program. Make sure that its primary goal is the well-being of the patient, with the secondary goal being the welfare of the family member(s). The program should be conducted by a qualified mental health professional. For the most part, the program is usually offered as part of a comprehensive clinical treatment plan for the mentally ill person. As such, it is incorporated within a medically approved treatment plan. Most family psychoeducation programs last from one to three years, and they are usually conducted based on a specific **diagnosis**.

Preparation

Preparation for family psychoeducation is not necessary. However, it is always wise to learn as much about a subject before delving into it. Therefore, the more knowledge gained in family psychoeducation, the better prepared one will be once involved with its methods.

Aftercare

Family psychoeducation is often a long-term method for treating mental illness. Whether formal treatment is active or not, the use of its techniques within the family setting is necessary and recommended for the continued well-being of the patient (and to avoid relapses) and his or her family members.

Complications

Patients can become overwhelmed with the involvement necessary within family psychoeducation. Consequently, participants and professionals should use caution when treating patients, especially if they are dealing with schizophrenia. It is also wise to realistically describe the situation to all participating members, especially concerning the patient's chances of recovery and the process of treatment. However, it is likely best to minimize any details that may overly **stress** members who are already especially emotional and anxious about the situation. Family psychoeducation experts see information received by the patient in small amounts as much more beneficial than large amounts at any given time.

Results

A large body of evidence supports the use of family psychoeducation as a best practice for young adults with schizophrenia and their families. Because of this compelling evidence, researchers at the University of Maryland, as part of the Schizophrenia Patient Outcomes Research Team (PORT), identified family psychoeducation as an evidence-based practice that should be offered to all families. This and other research studies have shown reduced rates of **relapse** and lower rates of **hospitalization** among patients and families involved in these programs. Other outcomes included increased rates of patient participation in **vocational rehabilitation** programs and employment, decreased costs of care, and improved well-being of family members.

A meta-analysis of 16 individual studies published in 1999 in the *Journal of Mental Health* found that family interventions of fewer than 10 sessions have no effect on the reduction of family burden. Controlled studies in the 2000s continued to support the effectiveness of single- and multiple-family interventions for **bipolar disorder**, major depression, **obsessive-compulsive disorder**, anorexia nervosa, and **borderline personality disorder**. In addition, studies of family psychoeducation have been conducted with a Hispanic population in Los Angeles, California, and outside the United States in China, Norway, and the Netherlands.

Further studies of family psychoeducation were ongoing in the 2010s. For instance, in 2011, a study performed in the Czech Republic was published in the journal *Biomedical Papers.* The article "Psychoeducation for Psychotic Patients" was authored by Drs. Jan Prasko, Kristyna Vrbova, Klara Latalova, and Barbora Mainerova, all of Palacky University in Olomouc, in the Czech Republic. The study looked at psychoeducation

KEY TERMS

Anorexia nervosa—An eating disorder highlighted by a person's denial of a healthy body weight, distortion of their outward appearance, and steadfast refusal to eat much food for a fear that they may gain weight.

Bipolar disorder—A mood disorder characterized by abnormally high energy levels and moodiness, usually without depression.

Depression—A psychiatric disorder involving feelings of hopelessness and symptoms of fatigue, sleeplessness, suicidal tendencies, and poor concentration.

Schizophrenia—A mental disorder involving distorted thinking and emotions.

QUESTIONS TO ASK YOUR DOCTOR

- Do you know how effective family psychoeducation could be for our family?
- Are there any underlying concerns that need to be addressed or corrected before we proceed with family psychoeducation?
- Will our family health insurance cover the training method?
- Will we need family psychoeducation for a short or long time?
- What will happen if it is stopped?

programs given in hospital settings with regard to schizophrenia patients recently discharged from the hospital. They found that the benefits of psychoeducation (those that are provided by the family) continue for up to seven years after leaving the hospital. The authors concluded that the perception of patients is that the program was beneficial and provided better understanding of their lives.

Unfortunately, putting family psychoeducation into effect in clinical settings has not kept pace with research. The Schizophrenia Patient Outcomes Research Team (PORT) study found that only 31% of patients studied reported that their families received information about their illness. One recent strategy to expand these programs includes integrating family psychoeducation into **assertive community treatment** (ACT) programs.

Parental concerns

When children are involved, parents should feel confident that family psychoeducation will better prepare them to respond to all of the problems associated with psychiatric disorders of children.

See also Case management

Resources

BOOKS

Bray, James H., and Mark Stanton, editors. *The Wiley-Blackwell Handbook of Family Psychology.* Chichester, UK: Wiley-Blackwell, 2009.

Gladding, Samuel T. *Family Therapy: History, Theory, and Practice.* Boston: Pearson, 2011.

Hughes, Daniel A. *Attachment Focused Family Therapy Workbook.* New York: W.W. Norton, 2011.

Nichols, Michael P. *The Essentials of Family Therapy.* Boston: Allyn & Bacon, 2011.

Sexton, Thomas L. *Functional Family Therapy in Clinical Practice: An Evidence-Based Treatment Model for Working with Troubled Adolescents.* New York, Routledge, 2011.

Torrey, E. Fuller. *Surviving Schizophrenia: A Manual for Families, Consumers and Providers,* 5th ed. New York: Collins, 2006.

VandenBos, Gary R., editor. *APA Dictionary of Psychology.* Washington, DC: American Psychological Association, 2007.

WEBSITES

Dixon, Lisa B., et al. "Outcomes of a Randomized Study of a Peer-Taught Family-to-Family Education Program for Mental Illness." Psychiatric Services. (June 2011). http://psychservices.psychiatryonline.org/cgi/content/abstract/62/6/591 (accessed August 24, 2011).

"Family to Family Education Program." National Alliance on Mental Illness. http://www.nami.org/template.cfm?Section=Family-to-Family (accessed August 24, 2011).

"Family Psychoeducation vs. Family-to-Family Education Program (FFEP)." National Alliance on Mental Illness. http://www.nami.org/Content/NavigationMenu/Inform_Yourself/About_Mental_Illness/About_Treatments_and_Supports/Family_Psychoeducation.htm (accessed August 24, 2011).

"Lisa B. Dixon M.D." University of Maryland Medical Center. http://medschool.umaryland.edu/facultyresearchprofile/viewprofile.aspx?id=719 (accessed August 24, 2011).

"Pioneer Psychiatrist Brought Families In." New Zealand Herald. (July 22, 2006). http://www.nzherald.co.nz/nz/news/article.cfm?c_id=1&objectid=10392461 (accessed August 24, 2011).

"Schizophrenia." National Alliance on Mental Illness. (February 2007). http://www.nami.org/Template.cfm?Section=By_Illness&template=/ContentManagement/ContentDisplay.cfm&ContentID=7416 (accessed August 24, 2011).

"University of Maryland Gets 4-Year NIMH Grant to Study the Effectiveness of NAMI's Family-to-Family Education Program." National Alliance on Mental Illness. (October 1, 2005). http://www.nami.org/Template.cfm?Section=Family-to-Family&template=/ContentManagement/ContentDisplay.cfm&ContentID=89938 (accessed August 24, 2011).

ORGANIZATIONS

American Psychiatric Association, 1000 Wilson Boulevard, Suite 1825, Arlington, VA, 22209-3901, (703) 907-7300, apa@psych.org, http://www.psych.org

American Psychological Association, 750 First Street, N.E., Washington, DC, 20002, (202) 336-5500, (800) 374-2721, http://www.apa.org

National Alliance on Mental Illness, 3803 North Fairfax Drive, Suite 100, Arlington, VA, 22203, (703) 524-7600, Fax: (703) 524-9094, (800) 950-6264, http://www.nami.org

National Institute of Mental Health, 6001 Executive Boulevard, Room 8184, MSC 9663, Bethesda, MD, 20892-9663, (301) 443-4513, Fax: (301) 443-4279, (866) 615-6464, nimhinfo@nih.gov, http://www.nimh.nih.gov

Irene S. Levine, PhD
Ruth A. Wienclaw, PhD
William A. Atkins, B.B., B.S., M.B.A.

Family therapy

Definition

Family therapy is a form of **psychotherapy** that involves all the members of a nuclear or extended family. It may be conducted by a pair or team of therapists, often a man and a woman in order to treat gender-related issues or to serve as role models for family members. Although some forms of family therapy are based on behavioral or psychodynamic principles, the most widespread form is based on family systems theory. This approach regards the family as a whole, as the unit of treatment, and emphasizes such factors as relationships and communication patterns rather than traits or symptoms in individual members.

Purpose

The purpose of family therapy is to improve relationships between family members and improve behavior patterns of the family as a whole or of subgroups within the family.

Family therapy is often recommended when:

- A family member has schizophrenia or another severe psychosis; the goal in these cases is to help other family members understand the disorder and adjust to the psychological changes that may be occurring in the patient.
- Problems cross generational boundaries, such as when parents share a home with grandparents or children are being raised by grandparents.
- Families deviate from social norms (unmarried parents, gay couples rearing children, etc.). These families may or may not have internal problems, but could be troubled by outside perceptions.
- Family members come from mixed racial, cultural, or religious backgrounds.
- One member is being scapegoated, or their treatment in individual therapy is being undermined.
- The identified patient's problems seem inextricably tied to problems with other family members.
- A blended (i.e., step) family is having adjustment difficulties.

Most family therapists presuppose an average level of intelligence and education on the part of adult members of the family.

Precautions

Some families are not considered suitable candidates for family therapy. They include:

- families in which one, or both, of the parents is psychotic or has been diagnosed with antisocial or paranoid personality disorder
- families whose cultural or religious values are opposed to, or suspicious of, psychotherapy
- families with members who cannot participate in treatment sessions because of physical illness or similar limitations
- families with members who have very rigid personality structures (family members might be at risk for an emotional or psychological crisis)
- families whose members cannot or will not be able to meet regularly for treatment
- families that are unstable or on the verge of breakup

Description

Family therapy tends to be a short-term treatment, usually several months in length, with a focus on resolving specific problems such as eating disorders, difficulties with school, or adjustments to **bereavement** or geographical relocation. It is not normally used for long-term or intensive restructuring of families with severe dysfunctions.

Family therapy is becoming an increasingly common form of treatment as changes in American society are reflected in family structures. It has led to two further developments: couple's therapy, which treats relationship problems between marriage partners or homosexual couples, and the extension of family therapy to religious communities or other groups that resemble families.

In family-therapy sessions, all members of the family and all therapists (if there is more than one) are present at most sessions. The therapists seek to analyze the process of family interaction and communication as a whole and do not take sides with specific members. They may make occasional comments or remarks intended to help family members become more conscious of patterns or structures that had been previously taken for granted. Family therapists who work as a team also model new behaviors for the family through their interactions with each other during sessions.

Family therapy is based on family-systems theory, an approach that considers the family a living organism more than the sum of its individual members. Family therapy uses systems theory to evaluate family members in terms of their position or role within the system. Problems are treated by changing the way the system works rather than trying to "fix" a specific member. Family systems theory is based on several major concepts.

The identified patient

The identified patient (IP) is the family member with the symptom that has brought the family into treatment. The concept of the IP is used by family therapists to keep the family from scapegoating the IP or using him or her as a way of avoiding problems in the rest of the system.

Homeostasis (balance)

The concept of homeostasis presumes that the family system seeks to maintain its customary organization and functioning over time and tends to resist change. The family therapist can use the concept of homeostasis to explain why a certain family symptom has surfaced at a given time, why a specific member has become the IP, and what is likely to happen when the family begins to change.

The extended family field

The extended family field refers to the nuclear family, plus the network of grandparents and other members of the extended family. This concept is used to explain the intergenerational transmission of attitudes, problems, behaviors, and other issues.

Differentiation

Differentiation refers to the ability of each family member to maintain his or her own sense of self while remaining emotionally connected to the family. The capacity to allow members to differentiate is one mark of a healthy family.

Triangular relationships

Family systems theory maintains that emotional relationships in families are usually triangular. Whenever any two persons in the family system have problems with each other, they will "triangle in" a third member as a way of stabilizing their own relationship. The triangles in a family system usually interlock in a way that maintains family homeostasis. Common family triangles include a child and his or her parents; two children and one parent; a parent, a child, and a grandparent; three siblings; or a husband, wife, and an in-law.

Origins

Family therapy is a relatively recent development in psychotherapy. It began shortly after World War II, when doctors treating patients with **schizophrenia** noticed that the patients' families communicated in disturbed ways. The doctors also found that the patients' symptoms rose or fell according to the level of tension between their parents. These observations led to considering a family as an organism or system with its own internal rules, patterns of functioning, and tendency to resist change. The therapists started to treat the families of their patients as whole units rather than focusing on the hospitalized member. They found that in many cases the family member with schizophrenia improved when the "patient" was the entire family system. (This should not be misunderstood to mean that schizophrenia is caused by family problems, although family problems may worsen the condition.) This approach of involving the entire family in the treatment plan and therapy was then applied to families dealing with problems or conditions other than schizophrenia.

Benefits

Results vary, but in good circumstances, the benefits of family therapy include greater insight, increased differentiation of individual family members, improved communication within the family, loosening of previously automatic behavior patterns, and resolution of the problem that led the family to seek treatment.

Preparation

Families are often referred to a specialist in family therapy by a pediatrician or other primary care provider. (Some estimates suggest that as many as 50% of pediatric office visits concern developmental problems in children that are affecting their families.) Physicians may use symptom checklists or psychological screeners to assess a family's need for therapy.

Family therapists may be psychiatrists, clinical psychologists, or other professionals certified by a specialty board in marriage and family therapy. They will usually evaluate a family for treatment by scheduling a series of interviews with members of the immediate family, including young children, and significant or symptomatic members of the extended family. This process allows the therapist(s) to find out how each member of the family sees the problem and provides an initial impression of the

KEY TERMS

Blended family—A family formed by the remarriage of a divorced or widowed parent. It includes a new husband and wife, plus some or all of their children from previous marriages.

Differentiation—The ability to retain one's identity within a family system while maintaining emotional connections with the other members.

Extended family field—A person's family of origin plus grandparents, in-laws, and other relatives.

Family systems theory—An approach to treatment that emphasizes the interdependency of family members rather than focusing on individuals in isolation from the family. This theory underlies the most influential forms of contemporary family therapy.

Genogram—A family tree diagram that represents the names, birth order, sex, and relationships of the members of a family. Therapists use genograms to detect recurrent patterns in the family history and to help the members understand their problems.

Homeostasis—The tendency of a family system to maintain internal stability and resist change.

Identified patient (IP)—The family member whose symptom has emerged or is most obvious.

Nuclear family—The basic family unit, consisting of father, mother, and their biological children.

Scapegoating—The emergence of behavioral problems in one family member, usually the identified patient, who is often punished for problems within the entire family.

Triangling—A process in which two family members diminish the tension between them by drawing in a third member.

family's functioning. Family therapists typically look for the level and types of emotions expressed, patterns of dominance and submission, the roles played by family members, communication styles, and the existence of emotional triangles. They will also note whether these patterns are rigid or relatively flexible.

Preparation also usually includes drawing a genogram—a diagram that depicts significant persons and events in the family's history. Genograms also include annotations about the medical history and major personality traits of each member. Genograms help in uncovering intergenerational patterns of behavior, marriage choices, family alliances and conflicts, the existence of family secrets, and other information that sheds light on the family's present situation.

Risks

There are no major risks involved in receiving family therapy, especially if family members seek therapy with honesty, openness, and a willingness to change. However, some changes that result from the therapy may be seen as risks, such as the possible unsettling of rigid personality defenses in individuals, or the unsettling of couple relationships that had been fragile before the beginning of therapy, for example.

Training and certification

Family therapy can be and is usually provided by clinical **social workers** or licensed therapists known as marriage and family therapists. Many of these therapists have postgraduate degrees and often become credentialed by the American Association for Marriage and Family Therapy (AAMFT).

Resources

BOOKS

Clark, R. Barkley. "Psychosocial Aspects of Pediatrics & Psychiatric Disorders: Psychosocial Assessment of Children & Families." In *Current Pediatric Diagnosis & Treatment,* by William W. Hay Jr., et al. 17th ed. New York: McGraw-Hill Medical, 2004.

Gurman A.S., et al. Family Therapy and Couple Therapy. In *Comprehensive Textbook of Psychiatry,* by B.J. Sadock et al. Philadelphia, PA.: Lippincott Williams & Wilkins, 2009.

ORGANIZATIONS

American Association for Marriage and Family Therapy (AAMFT), 112 South Alfred Street, Alexandria, VA, 22314-3061, (703) 838-9808, Fax: (703) 838-9805, http://www.aamft.org.

Rebecca J. Frey, PhD
Karl Finley

Fanapt *see* **Iloperidone**

Fatigue

Definition

Fatigue may be defined as a subjective state in which one feels tired or exhausted, and in which the capacity for normal work or activity is reduced. There is, however, no commonly accepted definition of fatigue when it is considered in the context of health and illness.

Demographics

Fatigue is a common experience. It is one of the top ten symptoms that people mention when they visit the doctor. Some people, however, are at higher risk for developing fatigue. For example, the risk for women is about 1.5 times the risk for men, and the risk for people who do not exercise is twice that of active people. Some researchers question whether women really are at higher risk: they are more likely than men to go to the doctor with health problems, and men are less likely to admit feeling fatigued. Other risk factors include obesity, smoking, use of alcohol, high stress levels, **depression**, anxiety, and low blood pressure. Having low blood pressure is usually considered desirable in the United States but is regarded as a treatable condition in other countries. Low blood pressure or postural hypotension (sudden lowering of blood pressure caused by standing up) may cause fatigue, dizziness, or fainting.

Description

Fatigue is sometimes described as being primary or secondary. Primary fatigue is a symptom of a disease or mental disorder and may be part of a cluster of such symptoms as pain, fever, or nausea. As the disease or disorder progresses, however, the fatigue may be intensified by the patient's worsening condition, other disease symptoms, or surgical or medical treatment. This subsequent fatigue is called secondary.

A person's experience of fatigue depends on a variety of factors. These factors include culture, personality, the physical environment (light, noise, vibration), availability of social support through networks of family members and friends, the nature of a particular fatiguing disease or disorder, and the type and duration of work or **exercise**. For example, the experience of fatigue associated with disease will be different for someone who is clinically depressed, socially isolated, and out of shape compared to another person who is not depressed, has many friends, and is aerobically fit.

Fatigue is sometimes characterized as normal or abnormal. For example, the feeling of tiredness or even exhaustion after exercising is a normal response and is relieved by resting; many people report that the experience of ordinary tiredness after exercise is pleasant. Moreover, this type of fatigue is called acute because the onset is sudden and the desired activity level returns after resting. On the other hand, there is a kind of fatigue that is not perceived as ordinary and that may develop insidiously over time. This type of fatigue is unpleasant or seriously distressing and is not resolved by rest. Fatigue of this nature is abnormal and referred to as chronic.

Some researchers regard fatigue as a defense mechanism that promotes the effective regulation of energy expenditures. According to this theory, when people feel tired, they take steps to avoid further **stress** (physical or emotional) by resting or by avoiding the stressor. They are then conserving energy. Because chronic fatigue is not normal, however, it is an important symptom of some mental disorders, a variety of physical diseases with known etiologies (causes), and some medical conditions that have no biological markers although they are recognizable syndromes (patterns of symptoms and signs).

Physical sources of fatigue

DISEASE. There are many diseases and disorders in which fatigue is a major symptom. These include cancer, cardiovascular disease, emphysema, multiple sclerosis, rheumatic arthritis, systemic lupus erythematosus, HIV/AIDS, infectious mononucleosis, chronic fatigue syndrome, and fibromyalgia. The reasons for the fatigue, however, vary according to the organ system or body function affected by the disease.

FIBROMYALGIA AND CHRONIC FATIGUE SYNDROME. Fibromyalgia (also known as myofascial syndrome or fibrositis) is a syndrome characterized by pain and achiness in muscles, tendons, and ligaments. There are 18 locations on the body where patients typically feel sore. These locations include areas on the lower back and along the spine, neck, and thighs. A diagnostic criterion for fibromyalgia (FM) is that at least 11 of the 18 sites are painful. In addition to pain, people with FM may experience **sleep disorders**, fatigue, anxiety, and irritable bowel syndrome. Experts have suggested that FM and chronic fatigue syndrome (CFS) are manifestations of the same pain and fatigue syndrome. The care that patients receive for FM or CFS depends in large measure on whether they were referred to a rheumatologist (a doctor who specializes in treating diseases of the joints and muscles), neurologist, or **psychiatrist**.

PAIN. When pain is severe enough, it may disrupt sleep and lead to the development of sleep disorders such as insomnia or hypersomnia. Insomnia is the term for having difficulty falling and/or staying asleep. Hypersomnia refers to excessive sleeping. In general, disrupted sleep is not restorative; people wake up feeling tired, and as a result their pain is worsened and they may become depressed. Furthermore, pain may interfere with movement or lead to too much bed rest, resulting in deconditioning. Sometimes pain leads to social isolation because the person cannot cope with the physical effort involved in maintaining social relationships, or because family members are unsympathetic or resentful of the ill or injured person's reduced capacity for work or participation in family life. All of these factors worsen pain, contributing to further sleep disruption, fatigue, and depression.

SLEEP DISORDERS. There are a variety of sleep disorders that cause fatigue, including insomnia, hypersomnia, sleep apnea, and restless legs syndrome. For example, hypersomnia may be the result of brain abnormalities caused by viral infections. Researchers studying the aftermath of infectious mononucleosis proposed that exposure to viral infections might change brain function with the effect of minimizing restorative sleep; hence, some people developed hypersomnia. Another common disorder is sleep apnea, in which the patient's breathing stops for at least ten seconds, usually more than 20 times per hour. Snoring is common. People may experience choking and then wake up gasping for air; they may develop daytime hypersomnia to compensate. Sleep apnea is associated with aging, weight gain, and depression. It is also a risk factor for stroke and myocardial infarctions. Restless legs syndrome is a condition in which very uncomfortable sensations in the patient's legs cause them to move and wake up from sleep, or keep them from falling asleep. All of these disorders reduce the quality of a person's sleep and are associated with fatigue.

Psychological disorders

While fatigue may be caused by many organic diseases and medical conditions, it is a chief complaint for several mental disorders, including **generalized anxiety disorder** and clinical depression. Moreover, mental disorders may coexist with physical disease. When there is considerable symptom overlap, the differential **diagnosis** of fatigue is especially difficult.

DEPRESSION. In the fourth edition of the ***Diagnostic and Statistical Manual of Mental Disorders*** (*DSM-IV*), the presence of depressed mood or sadness, or loss of pleasure in life, is an important diagnostic criterion for depression. Daily fatigue, lack of energy, **insomnia**, and **hypersomnia** are indicators of a depressed mood. The symptoms of depression overlap with those of CFS; for example, some researchers report that 89% of people with depression are fatigued, as compared to 86–100% of people with CFS. The experience of fatigue, however, seems to be more disabling with CFS than with depression. Another difference between CFS and depression concerns the onset of the disorder. Most patients with CFS experience a sudden or acute onset, whereas depression may develop over a period of weeks or months. Also, while both types of patients experience sleep disorders, CFS patients tend to have difficulty falling asleep, whereas depressed patients tend to wake early in the morning. It is possible for CFS and depression to be comorbidities.

Some researchers believe that there is a link between depression, fatigue, and exposure to too much REM sleep. There are five distinct phases in human sleep. The first two are characterized by light sleep; the second two by a deep restorative sleep called slow-wave sleep; and the last by rapid eye movement or REM sleep. Most dreams occur during REM sleep. Throughout the night, the intervals of REM sleep increase and usually peak around 8:30 A.M. A **sleep deprivation** treatment for depression involves reducing the patient's amount of REM sleep by waking him or her around 6:00 A.M. Researchers think that some fatigue associated with disease may be a form of mild depression and that reducing the amount of REM sleep will reduce fatigue by moderating depression.

GENERALIZED ANXIETY DISORDER. People are diagnosed as having generalized anxiety disorder (GAD) if they experience overwhelming worry or apprehension that persists, usually daily, for at least six months, and if they also experience some of the following symptoms: unusual tiredness, restlessness and irritability, problems with concentration, muscle tension, and disrupted sleep. Stressful life events such as divorce, unemployment, illness, or being the victim of a violent crime are associated with GAD, as is a history of psychiatric problems. Some evidence suggests that women who have been exposed to danger are at risk of developing GAD; women who suffer loss are at risk of developing depression; and women who experience danger and loss are at risk of developing a mix of both GAD and depression.

While the symptoms of CFS and GAD overlap, the disorders have different primary complaints. Patients with CFS complain primarily of tiredness, whereas people with GAD describe being excessively worried. In general, some researchers believe that anxiety contributes to fatigue by disrupting rest and restorative sleep.

STRESS. When someone experiences ongoing pain and stress, organ systems and functional processes eventually break down. These include cardiovascular, digestive, and respiratory systems, as well as the efficient elimination of body wastes. According to the American Psychiatric Association, various chronic diseases are related to stress, including rheumatoid arthritis, cardiac angina, and secondary dysmenorrhea (painful menstruation).

Managing fatigue

The management of fatigue depends in large measure on its causes and the person's experience of it.

KEY TERMS

Biological marker—An indicator or characteristic trait of a disease that facilitates differential diagnosis (the process of distinguishing one disorder from other, similar disorders).

Deconditioning—Loss of physical strength or stamina resulting from bed rest or lack of exercise.

Electrolytes—Substances or elements that dissociate into electrically charged particles (ions) when dissolved in the blood. The electrolytes in human blood include potassium, magnesium, and chloride.

Stress—A physical and psychological response that results from being exposed to a demand or pressure.

Syndrome—A group of symptoms that together characterize a disease or disorder.

For example, if fatigue is acute and normal, the person will recover from feeling tired after exertion by resting. In cases of fatigue associated with influenza or other infectious illnesses, the person will feel energy return as they recover from the illness. When fatigue is chronic and abnormal, however, the doctor will tailor a treatment program to the patient's needs. There are a variety of approaches that include:

- Aerobic exercise. Physical activity increases fitness and counteracts depression.
- Hydration (adding water). Water improves muscle turgor or tension and helps to carry electrolytes.
- Improving sleep patterns. The patient's sleep may be more restful when its timing and duration are controlled.
- Pharmacotherapy (treatment with medications). The patient may be given various medications to treat physical diseases or mental disorders, to control pain, or to manage sleeping patterns.
- Psychotherapy. There are several different treatment approaches that help patients manage stress, understand the motives that govern their behavior, or change maladaptive ideas and negative thinking patterns.
- Physical therapy. This form of treatment helps patients improve or manage functional impairments or disabilities.

In addition to seeking professional help, people can understand and manage fatigue by joining appropriate **self-help groups**, reading informative books, seeking information from clearinghouses on the Internet, and visiting websites maintained by national organizations for various diseases.

Resources

BOOKS

Glaus, A. *Fatigue in Patients with Cancer: Analysis and Assessment*. Thesis published in Recent Results in Cancer Research, 145:I–XI, 1–172. Berlin, Germany: Springer-Verlag, 1998.

Hubbard, John R., and Edward A. Workman, eds. *Handbook of Stress Medicine: An Organ System Approach*. Boca Raton, FL: CRC Press, 1998.

Natelson, Benjamin H. *Facing and Fighting Fatigue: A Practical Approach*. New Haven, CT: Yale University Press, 1998.

Porter, Robert S., and Justin L. Kaplan, eds. *The Merck Manual of Diagnosis and Therapy*. 19th ed. Whitehouse Station, NJ: Merck Research Laboratories, 2011.

Winningham, Maryl L., and Margaret Barton-Burke, eds. *Fatigue in Cancer: A Multidimensional Approach*. Sudbury, MA: Jones and Bartlett Publishers, 2000.

PERIODICALS

Natelson, Benjamin H. "Chronic Fatigue Syndrome." *Journal of the American Medical Association* 285, no. 20 (May 23–30 2001): 2557–59.

WEBSITES

Davis, Caralyn. "What's In a Name: Fibro vs. CFS." Arthritis Foundation. http://forum.psychlinks.ca/fibromyalgia-and-chronic-fatigue/16865-whats-in-a-name-fms-vs-cfs.html (accessed October 7, 2011).

U.S. Centers for Disease Control. "Chronic Fatigue Syndrome." http://www.cdc.gov/cfs (accessed October 7, 2011).

ORGANIZATIONS

National Chronic Fatigue Syndrome and Fibromyalgia Association, PO Box 18426, Kansas City, MO, 64133, (816) 737-1343, http://www.ncfsfa.org.

Tanja Bekhuis, PhD
Emily Jane Willingham, PhD

Feeding disorder of infancy or early childhood

Definition

Feeding Disorder of Infancy or Early Childhood (FDIEC) is characterized by the failure of an infant or young child under six years of age to eat sufficient food and a well-balanced assortment of nutritious foods to order to gain weight and grow normally over a period of one month or more. The disorder can also be characterized by the loss of a significant amount of weight over one month. Feeding disorder is similar to failure to thrive, except that no medical or physiological condition can explain the low food intake or lack of growth.

The ***Diagnostic and Statistical Manual of Mental Disorders***, the guidelines used by medical professionals to diagnose mental disorders, was being updated as of 2012. Proposed changes for the fifth edition include changing the name of feeding disorder of infancy or early childhood to avoidant/restrictive food intake disorder (ARFID). The change encompasses a greater age range than just infancy to early childhood. It will cover individuals who do not eat enough or show little interest in feeding or eating, individuals who accept only a limited diet in relation to sensory features, and individuals whose food refusal is related to aversive experience. The revised version (fifth edition, or *DSM-5*) is scheduled to be available in May 2013.

Demographics

Although minor feeding problems are common in infancy and childhood—parents and caregivers report that 25% to 40% of infants and children have such problems as vomiting, colic, and slow eater or picky eater—true feeding disorder of infancy or early childhood is estimated to occur in 1% to 3% of infants and children. Children separated from their families or living in conditions of poverty or **stress** are at greater risk for contracting the disorder. Mental illness in a parent, or **child abuse** or **neglect**, may also increase the risk of the child developing a feeding disorder. Infants and children with developmental disorders and those born prematurely are also at higher risk of having a feeding disorder.

Description

Infants and children with a feeding disorder fail to grow adequately, or even lose weight with no underlying medical explanation. They do not eat enough energy or nutrients to support growth and do not eat a broad variety of foods from the major groupings of foods. Consequently, they may become irritable or apathetic. Eventually, such children may develop more slowly, physically and mentally. Severe cases of FDIEC that continue into adolescence may cause such children to feel socially isolated. Factors that contribute to development of a feeding disorder include lack of nurturing, failure to read the child's hunger and satiety cues accurately, poverty, or parental mental illness. Successful treatment involves dietary, behavioral, social, and/or psychological **intervention** by a multidisciplinary team of health professionals.

According to the *DSM-5*, an eating or feeding disturbance can be associated with one or more of the following:

- substantial weight loss, failure to gain weight, or halting growth
- extensive deficiency in nutrition
- dependence on external feeding sources
- distinct interference with psychosocial functioning

Causes and symptoms

Causes

Although the cause of feeding disorder of infancy or early childhood is unknown, it can result from many different factors. Some of these factors include poverty; inappropriate parent-child interactions such as failure to read the child's hunger cues or forcing food when the child is not hungry; and lack of proper dietary information. Lack of nurturing and/or parental aggression, anger, or **apathy** can make eating a negative experience for the child, increasing the risk of feeding disorders.

Such disorders are usually diagnosed when the infant or young child is seen by a caregiver or a doctor to be malnourished. After dismissing various medical conditions that could be causing the problem, such as intellectual disability or congenital heart disease, a **diagnosis** of FDIEC is made.

Feeding disorders are more common in infants and children who are born prematurely, had a low birth weight, or who are developmentally delayed. Many medical (or physiological) causes can contribute to eating difficulties, eating aversions, or failure to thrive. These causes include:

- diseases of the central nervous system
- metabolic diseases
- sensory defects
- anatomical abnormalities, such as cleft palate
- muscular disorders, such as cerebral palsy
- heart disease
- gastrointestinal diseases, such as Crohn's disease

To meet criteria for a true feeding disorder of infancy or childhood, these medical conditions must be ruled out.

Symptoms

Because the child or infant with a feeding disorder is not consuming enough energy, vitamins, or minerals to support normal growth, symptoms resemble those seen in malnourished or starving children. The infant or child

KEY TERMS

Cleft palate—A failure of the two sides of the palate within the mouth to meet during fetal development.

Colic—Excessive crying and irritability in babies, which may be caused by numerous problems such as stomach discomfort.

Gastrostomy—A surgical opening into the stomach.

Nasogastric intubation—A process in which a tube is inserted down the throat and into the stomach.

may be irritable, difficult to console, apathetic, withdrawn, and unresponsive. They may have constipation, along with bouts of excessive crying and sleepiness. Children with such disorders may also have tantrums at meals, refuse to eat certain groups of food, or refuse to eat any types of solid or liquid foods.

Children with FDIEC may have physical ailments, such as difficulties accepting or swallowing certain types of foods. They may choke or gag when given food. Such children might also have oral motor and sensory problems. Delays in development, as well as growth, can occur. In general, the younger the child, the greater the risk of developmental delays associated with the feeding disorder.

Laboratory abnormalities may also be associated with the disorder. Blood tests may reveal a low level of protein or hemoglobin in the blood. Hemoglobin is an iron-containing substance in blood that carries oxygen to body cells.

Diagnosis

Between 25% and 35% of children experience minor feeding problems. In infants born prematurely, 40% to 70% experience some type of feeding problem. For a child to be diagnosed with feeding disorder of infancy or early childhood, the disorder must be severe enough to affect growth for a significant period of time. Generally, growth failure is considered to be below the fifth percentile of weight and height.

Diagnosis for feeding disorders begins with an attempt to identify any medical illnesses that might contribute to the problem. The doctor will examine the historical record for height, weight, and head circumference of the child. Medical imaging devices and laboratory studies may be used to complete the examination.

Feeding disorder of infancy of early childhood is diagnosed if all four of the following criteria are present:

- failure to eat adequately over one month or more, with resultant weight loss or failure to gain weight.
- inadequate eating and lack of growth not explained by any general medical or physiological condition, such as gastrointestinal problems, nervous system abnormalities, or anatomical deformations.
- the feeding disorder cannot be better explained by lack of food or by another mental disorder, such as rumination disorder.
- the inadequate eating and weight loss or failure to gain weight occurs before the age of six years.

If feeding behavior or weight gain improves when another person feeds and cares for the child, the existence of a true feeding disorder, rather than some underlying medical condition, is more likely.

Treatment

Successful treatment of feeding disorders requires a multidisciplinary team approach to assess the child's needs and to provide recommendations and education to improve feeding skills, behavior, and nutrient intake. The multidisciplinary team for treatment of feeding disorders in childhood usually includes physicians specializing in problems of the gastrointestinal tract or of the ear, nose, and throat; a dietitian, a **psychologist**, a speech pathologist, and an occupational therapist. Support from **social workers** and physicians in related areas of medicine is also helpful.

An initial evaluation should focus on feeding history, including detailed information on type and timing of food intake, feeding position, meal duration, energy and nutrient intake, and behavioral and parental factors that influence the feeding experience. Actual observation of a feeding session can give valuable insight into the cause of the feeding disorder and appropriate treatments. A medical examination should also be conducted to rule out any potential medical problems or physical causes of the feeding disorder.

After a thorough history is taken and assessment completed, dietary and behavioral therapy is started. The goal of diet therapy is to gradually increase energy and nutrient intake as tolerated by the child to allow for catch-up growth. Depending on the diet history, energy and nutrient content of the diet may be kept lower initially to avoid vomiting and diarrhea. As the infant or child is able to tolerate more food and liquids, energy and nutrient intake is slowly increased over a period of one to two weeks, or more. Eventually, the diet should provide about 50% more than normal nutritional needs of infants

QUESTIONS TO ASK YOUR DOCTOR

- How can we best treat my child's feeding disorder?
- Why did this happen to my child?
- How serious is my child's feeding disorder?
- Could a medical or psychological problem cause my child's feeding disorder?
- How do you diagnose a feeding disorder?

or children of similar age and size. Vitamin and mineral supplements may also be given to correct for any deficiencies unable to be corrected with diet.

Behavioral therapy can help the parent and child overcome conditioned feeding problems and food aversions. Parents must be educated to accurately recognize their child's hunger and satiety cues and to promote a pleasant, positive feeding environment. Changing the texture of foods, the pace and timing of feedings, the position of the body, and even feeding utensils can help the child to overcome aversions to eating. Issues that may contribute to the feeding disorder, such as poverty, abuse, or parental mental illness, must be addressed. Physical and psychosocial problems are also treated to correct any problems that these may be producing within the child.

For extreme cases, a stay in the hospital or other such medical facility may be recommended. In other cases, surgical procedures may be necessary, such as gastrostomy or nasogastric intubation. Gastrostomy is an external surgical opening made into the stomach for such purposes as nutritional support. Nasogastric intubation involves the insertion of a plastic tube through the nose and throat and into the stomach.

Prognosis

If left untreated, infants and children with feeding disorders can have permanent physical, mental, and behavioral damage. However, most children with feeding disorders show significant improvements after treatment, particularly if the child and parent receive intensive nutritional, psychological, and social intervention. Improvement is normally gradual over time. Although it can be fully eliminated with proper treatment, such feeding and eating disorders can lead to permanent and serious mental and physical problems. Such problems can be minimized with early treatment.

Prevention

Providing balanced, age-appropriate foods at regular intervals—for example, three meals and two or three snacks daily for toddlers—can help to establish healthy eating patterns. If a child is allowed to fill up on soft drinks, juice, chips, or other snack prior to meals, appetite for other, more nutritious foods will decrease.

Positive infant and childhood feeding experiences require the child to communicate hunger and satiety effectively, and the parent or caregiver to interpret these signals accurately. This set of events requires a nurturing environment and an attentive, caring adult. Efforts should be made to establish feeding as a positive, pleasant experience. Further, forcing a child to eat or punishing a child for not eating should be avoided.

Resources

BOOKS

American Psychiatric Association. *Diagnostic and Statistical manual of Mental Disorders.* 4th edition, text revised. Washington, DC: American Psychiatric Association, 2000.

Beers, Mark H., et al. *The Merck Manual of Diagnosis and Therapy.* Whitehouse Station, NJ: Merck Research Laboratories, 2006.

Kleinman, Ronald E., editor. *Pediatric Nutrition Handbook.* Elk Grove Village, IL: American Academy of Pediatrics, 2009.

Rakel, Robert E., editor. *Textbook of Family Medicine.* Philadelphia: Saunders/Elsevier, 2007.

Samour, Patricia Queen, and Kathy King, editors. *Pediatric Nutrition.* Sudbury, MA: Jones & Bartlett, 2012.

Sullivan, Peter B., editor. *Feeding and Nutrition in Children with Neurodevelopmental Disability.* London: Mac Keith Press, 2009.

WEBSITES

American Psychiatric Association. "Avoidant/Restrictive Food Intake Disorder." *DSM-5* Development. http://www.dsm5.org/ProposedRevisions/Pages/proposedrevision.aspx?rid=110 (accessed May 23, 2011).

Kennedy Krieger Institute. "Feeding Disorders." http://www.kennedykrieger.org/kki_diag.jsp?pid=1084 (accessed May 23, 2011).

MedlinePlus. "Feeding Disorder of Infancy or Early Childhood." U.S. National Library of Medicine and National Institutes of Health. August 8, 2009. http://www.nlm.nih.gov/medlineplus/ency/article/001540.htm (accessed May 23, 2011).

University of Maryland Medical Center. "Feeding Disorder of Infancy or Early Childhood—Overview." August 2, 2009. http://www.umm.edu/ency/article/001540.htm (accessed May 23, 2011).

ORGANIZATIONS

American Academy of Child and Adolescent Psychiatry, 3615 Wisconsin Avenue, NW, Washington, DC, 20016-3007, (202) 966-7300, Fax: (202) 966-2891, http://www.aacap.org.

American Psychiatric Association, 1000 Wilson Boulevard, Suite 1825, Arlington, VA, 22209-3901, (703) 907-7300, apa@psych.org, http://www.psych.org.

American Psychological Association, 750 First Street, NE, Washington, DC, 20002-4242, (202) 336-5500, (800) 374-2721, http://www.apa.org.

Nancy Gustafson, M.S., R.D., F.A.D.A., E.L.S.
William Atkins, BB, BS, MBA

Female orgasmic disorder

Definition

Female orgasmic disorder (FOD) is the persistent or recurrent inability of a woman to achieve orgasm (climax or sexual release) despite adequate sexual arousal and stimulation. FOD is also known as orgasmic dysfunction or anorgasmia and used to be called inhibited sexual orgasm.

Demographics

The inability to achieve orgasm, discontent with the quality of orgasms, and the ability to achieve orgasm only with a particular type of sexual stimulation are very common sexual complaints among women. It has been suggested that 33%–50% of all women are dissatisfied with the frequencies of their orgasms and that fewer than one third of women consistently experience orgasm with sexual activity. However, FOD applies to the 10%–15% of women have never experienced an orgasm, regardless of the situation or stimulation, and to women who can no longer achieve an orgasm. The occasional failure to reach orgasm or dependence on a particular type of stimulation is not the same as FOD. Women who have never experienced orgasm are more likely to be unmarried, young, and/or sexually inexperienced. FOD has also been associated with menopause and aging, although many women find that their orgasms increase with age.

Description

When a woman becomes sexually excited, the blood vessels in the pelvic region expand, allowing more blood to flow to the genitals—the same process that occurs when men become sexually excited. This effusion is followed by seepage of fluid into the vagina to provide lubrication before and during intercourse. These events are called the lubrication-swelling response.

Body tension and blood flow to the pelvic region continue to build as sexual stimulation increases, either by direct pressure on the clitoris or pressure on the walls of the vagina and cervix. This tension builds as blood flow increases. When tension is released, involuntary, rhythmic contractions of the pelvic floor muscles and possibly the vagina and uterus occur, accompanied by a feeling of intense physical pleasure; this release is called an orgasm. The contractions carry blood away from the genital area and back into general circulation.

The exact physiological mechanisms of the female orgasm are not well understood. Women do not necessarily experience orgasms in the same way, and an individual woman may experience orgasms differently at various times and in different situations. Orgasms vary in intensity, length, and the number of contractions, and, unlike men, women can have multiple orgasms in a short period of time. Some 50%–80% of women experience orgasm only through direct clitoral stimulation. Mature, more sexually experienced women may find it easier to have orgasms than younger or sexually inexperienced women.

Women with FOD still experience sexual arousal and lubrication. However, as body tension builds, they have extreme difficulty or are completely unable to reach climax and release the tension. This can lead to frustration and unfulfilling sexual experiences for both partners, as well as anger, frustration, and other relationship problems. FOD often occurs in conjunction with other **sexual dysfunctions**.

According to the American Psychiatric Association's *Diagnostic and Statistical Manual of Mental Disorders,* the *DSM,* a **diagnosis** of FOD requires that the anorgasmia cannot be solely due to physiological problems nor a symptom of another major mental health disorder. However, FOD can be caused by a combination of physiological and psychological difficulties. To receive a diagnosis of FOD, the condition also must cause personal distress or relationship problems.

FOD is most often a primary or lifelong condition in which women never achieve orgasm with any type of stimulation, including self-stimulation (masturbation), direct stimulation of the clitoris by a partner, or vaginal intercourse. Secondary or acquired FOD affects women who have experienced orgasm at least once in the past, but have lost the ability following an illness or emotional **trauma** or as a side effect of surgery or medication. Acquired FOD is often temporary. Anorgasmia may also be classified as general, meaning that orgasm is never achieved under any circumstances or with any partner, or as situational, meaning that orgasm is only achieved under certain circumstances or with certain types of sexual activity.

Risk factors

Recent studies of twins suggest that genes and heredity play a large role in the development of FOD. A history of sexual or physical **abuse** is also a risk factor for FOD.

Causes and symptoms

FOD is characterized by a woman's inability to achieve orgasm, by extreme difficulty in regularly reaching climax, or by having only unsatisfying orgasms. Some women often come close to orgasm but never reach it. FOD can be caused by psychological factors or by a combination of psychological and physiological factors.

Psychological causes of FOD include:

- feelings of isolation, disconnection, or boredom during sex
- shyness or embarrassment
- performance anxiety or sexual activity that is overly goal-oriented, with excessive pressure to achieve orgasm
- past sexual or physical abuse, rape, incest, or other traumatic sexual experiences
- emotional abuse
- fear of pregnancy
- fear of rejection
- fear of loss of control during orgasm
- self-image problems
- relationship problems
- life stresses, such as financial worries, job loss, or divorce
- guilt or negative feelings toward sex or sexual pleasure—attitudes that are usually learned in childhood or adolescence
- religious or cultural beliefs about sex
- other mental health disorders, such as major depression

Various prescription and over-the-counter medications can cause anorgasmia. These include:

- antidepressants called selective serotonin reuptake inhibitors (SSRIs), such as fluoxetine (Prozac), paroxetine (Paxil), and sertraline (Zoloft)
- antianxiety drugs such as Xanax
- sedatives such as Halcion
- narcotics
- antihistamines
- blood-pressure medications
- chemotherapy drugs

Other physiological causes of FOD include:

- inadequate sexual stimulation and the inability to discuss or explore more stimulating sexual techniques
- lower estrogen levels during and after menopause, which reduce lubrication and require greater stimulation for relaxing and promoting blood flow to the clitoris and vagina
- other normal aging processes
- smoking, alcohol, or other substance abuse
- hormonal disorders and chronic illnesses that affect general health and sexual interest
- damage to the blood vessels of the pelvic region
- conditions that affect or damage pelvic nerves, including pelvic surgery, multiple sclerosis, diabetes, neurological disease, or spinal cord injury
- pelvic floor prolapse—a loosening of the muscles that support internal pelvic organs
- removal of the clitoris (female genital mutilation), a cultural practice in much of Africa and some regions of the Middle East and Asia

Diagnosis

FOD is often self-diagnosed. However, a woman who has never had an orgasm may not realize what is missing in her sexual experience without diagnosis by a physician, women's healthcare specialist, **psychiatrist**, **psychologist**, or sex therapist.

Examination

Diagnosis of FOD includes a complete physical exam and medical, psychological, and sexual histories. The clinician or therapist helps determine whether the problem is primary or acquired and general or situational. FOD sometimes occurs in conjunction with **sexual aversion disorder** and/or **female sexual arousal disorder**, complicating the diagnosis. A diagnosis of FOD requires that:

- Orgasms occur less frequently than would be expected based on the patient's age, sexual experience, and level of sexual stimulation.
- The absence of orgasm results in emotional distress or relationship difficulties.
- The cause is psychological or a combination of psychological and physical factors.
- The absence of orgasm is not a symptom of another psychological disorder, such as depression.

Tests

Blood tests may be performed to measure the levels of estrogen and testosterone.

Treatment

Treatment of FOD requires addressing any underlying physiological causes, psychological factors such as **depression**, and lifestyle factors such as **substance abuse**. Medications may require adjustment. Any associated sexual dysfunctions, such as lack of interest in sex or painful intercourse, must also be addressed. FOD is commonly treated with education, counseling, **cognitive-behavioral therapy**, **psychotherapy**, and/or sex therapy.

Traditional

Psychotherapy or counseling can be effective for treating psychological causes of FOD, especially those causes that are rooted in **sexual abuse**, past sexual or emotional experiences, or cultural taboos. **Couples therapy** may be used to resolve relationship issues that have either caused or resulted from FOD. These processes require time and a joint commitment by couples.

Sex therapists have specialized training for assisting individuals and couples in overcoming sexual dysfunctions. Sex therapy may include:

- directed exercises for increasing stimulation and decreasing inhibitions
- techniques for relaxation, sexual exploration, and direct clitoral stimulation
- encouragement of masturbation, either by self-stimulation or with a vibrator
- Kegel exercises for enhancing sexual response
- communication training and relationship enhancement for couples
- desensitization, or learning to halt responses that are preventing orgasm, particularly in women with severe sexual anxiety

Drugs

Estrogen or a combination of estrogen and progesterone may be used to treat FOD in menopausal women and others with low hormone levels. FOD is sometimes treated with methyltestosterone, a synthetic form of the male sex hormone testosterone, although this practice is controversial and can have various side effects. Testosterone appears to be most effective for women with low testosterone levels resulting from surgical removal of the ovaries.

Alternative

Zestra is a botanical massage oil that warms the clitoris and may increase sexual arousal and orgasm. L-arginine, available in various nutritional supplements and topical applications, may relax the blood vessels and increase blood flow to the genital area, especially the clitoris; however, these assertions have not yet been well studied.

KEY TERMS

Cervix—The neck or narrow lower end of a woman's uterus.

Clitoris—The most sensitive area of the external genitals. Stimulation of the clitoris causes most women to reach orgasm.

Uterus—The hollow muscular sac in which a fetus develops; sometimes called the womb.

Vagina—The part of the female reproductive system that opens to the exterior of the body and into which the penis is inserted during sexual intercourse.

Home remedies

One of the most important factors in overcoming FOD is open and honest communication between partners about sexuality and sexual techniques. Erotic books or videos may help initiate such conversations. Sometimes focusing on clitoral stimulation is all that is needed to overcome FOD. Experimenting with different sexual positions may improve clitoral stimulation. Using a vibrator during sex can also help trigger orgasms.

Many women have found that Kegel exercises which involve the repetitive contraction and relaxation of the pelvic floor muscles, can improve both the frequency and intensity of orgasmic experiences. Repeatedly stopping and starting a urine stream identifies the muscles to be exercised, working up to five sets of ten contractions per day. The longer the contractions are held, the more benefit may result.

Prognosis

FOD can often be successfully treated with a combination of psychotherapy and guided sexual exercises. However, women should not expect to always achieve orgasm in every situation, nor should they expect to always be satisfied with the strength and quality of their climax. Women whose FOD is not due to an identifiable condition or disorder may be more difficult to treat. Couples often need to work through relationship issues that have either resulted from or caused the FOD before they see improvement. Unresolved FOD usually results in a decline in sexual desire and can create resentment and conflict within relationships.

Prevention

Although there is no sure way to prevent FOD, reducing life factors that cause **stress** can be effective. Healthy attitudes toward sex and education about sexual stimulation and responses can help prevent FOD. Seeking counseling or psychotherapy for past trauma or relationship issues can help minimize FOD and other sexual dysfunction problems.

Resources

BOOKS

American Psychiatric Association. *Diagnostic and Statistical Manual of Mental Disorders*. 4th ed., text rev. Washington, DC: American Psychiatric Publishing, 2000.

Komisaruk, Barry. R., et al. *The Orgasm Answer Guide*. Baltimore: Johns Hopkins University Press, 2009.

McCabe, Marita P. "Anorgasmia in Women." In *Systemic Sex Therapy* edited by Katherine M. Hertlein, Gerald R. Weeks, and Nancy Gambescia. New York: Routledge, 2008.

PERIODICALS

Frank, J. E., et al. "Diagnosis and Treatment of Female Sexual Dysfunction." *American Family Physician* 77, no. 5 (March 1, 2008): 635–642. Available online at http://www.aafp.org/afp/2008/0301/p635.html (accessed November 9, 2011).

Graham, Cynthia A. "The *DSM* Diagnostic Criteria for Female Orgasmic Disorder." *Archives of Sexual Behavior* 39, no. 2 (April 2010): 256–270. http://www.dsm5.org/Documents/Sex%20and%20GID%20Lit%20Reviews/SD/GRAHAM.FSAD.DSM.pdf (accessed November 9, 2011).

WEBSITES

Discovery Fit & Health. "Female Orgasmic Disorder: 'I'm Not Able to Climax'." http://health.discovery.com/centers/sex/articles/orgasmic.html (accessed October 7, 2011).

Mayo Clinic. "Anorgasmia." December 23, 2009. http://www.mayoclinic.com/health/anorgasmia/DS01051/METHOD=print (accessed October 7, 2011).

Mayo Clinic. "Female Sexual Dysfunction." April 24, 2010. http://www.mayoclinic.com/health/female-sexual-dysfunction/DS00701 (accessed October 7, 2011).

MedlinePlus. "Orgasmic Dysfunction." U.S. National Library of Medicine, National Institutes of Health. June 5, 2010. http://www.nlm.nih.gov/medlineplus/ency/article/001953.htm (accessed October 7, 2011).

MedlinePlus. "Sexual Problems in Women." U.S. National Library of Medicine, National Institutes of Health. May 2011. http://www.nlm.nih.gov/medlineplus/femalesexualdysfunction.html (accessed October 7, 2011).

ORGANIZATIONS

American Association of Sexuality Educators, Counselors, and Therapists, 1444 I St. NW, Ste. 700, Washington, DC, 20005, (202) 449-1099, Fax: (202) 216-9646, info@aasect.org, http://www.aasect.org.

American College of Obstetricians and Gynecologists, PO Box 96920, Washington, DC, 20090-6920, (202) 638-5577, http://www.acog.org.

U.S. Department of Health and Human Services, Office on Women's Health, 200 Independence Ave., SW, Washington, DC, 20201, (800) 994-9662; TDD: (888) 220-5446, http://www.womenshealth.gov.

Tish Davidson, AM
Emily Jane Willingham, PhD
Margaret Alic, PhD

Female sexual arousal disorder

Definition

Female sexual arousal disorder (FSAD) refers to the persistent or recurrent inability of a woman to achieve or maintain an adequate lubrication-swelling response during sexual activity, despite sexual desire. FSAD stems from both physiological and psychological factors, and it often results in avoidance of sex, painful intercourse, and sexual tension in relationships.

Demographics

FSAD is common in older women due to decreased hormone production after menopause and medical conditions associated with aging. However, because FSAD often occurs in combination with other female **sexual dysfunctions** and can be difficult to distinguish, and because women are often reluctant to seek help for FSAD, it is difficult to determine its incidence. There is also disagreement within the medical community concerning the exact demarcations of the various female sexual dysfunctions. One published review of the medical literature found that 22%–43% of women experience some form of sexual dysfunction. Another study found that about 20% of women have problems with sexual lubrication.

Description

FSAD results from a woman's inability to undergo lubrication and swelling in response to sexual desire and stimulation. This lack of response interferes with sexual desire and satisfying intercourse.

William Masters and Virginia Johnson—the first researchers to extensively examine the physical components of human sexuality—identified four stages of

ALFRED KINSEY (1894–1956)

Alfred Kinsey became a household name in the 1950s with his groundbreaking research on the sexual mores of American women and men. His two major texts, *Sexual Behavior in the Human Male* (1948) and *Sexual Behavior in the Human Female* (1953), opened the way for research into human sexuality.

During the 1940s, Kinsey embarked on a large-scale study of the sexual habits of men and women. Initially, his resources were limited, and he used his own money to hire staff and pay expenses. In 1943, he received a $23,000 grant from the Rockefeller Foundation that enabled him to hire additional employees and expand his efforts. Chief among his staff were colleagues W.B. Pomeroy, Paul Gebhard, and Clyde Martin. The funding legitimized his research, which evolved into the Institute for Sex Research of Indiana University, where Kinsey taught.

Kinsey and his colleagues at the Institute for Sex Research at Indiana University conducted thousands of interviews with men and women about their sexual habits. The 804-page *Sexual Behavior in the Human Male* sold 185,000 copies in its first year and became a *New York Times* bestseller. The work was scientifically based and nonjudgmental, with frank descriptions of biological functions. Although early polls indicated that most Americans were relieved to have an honest and open airing of human sexual practices, there was a tremendous backlash from conservative and religious organizations. *Sexual Behavior in the Human Female* caused an even greater stir. Its more controversial findings included the low incidence of female frigidity, high rates of premarital and extramarital sex, the rapidness of erotic responses, and a detailed discussion of clitoral versus vaginal orgasm. As sales of the book reached 250,000 in the United States alone, Kinsey's methods and motives came under scrutiny. Evangelist Billy Graham stated: "It is impossible to estimate the damage this book will do to the already deteriorating morals of America." The notoriety and resulting conflicts caused Kinsey's research funding to be revoked, and for the remainder of his life he struggled to find support for his work. On August 25, 1956, at the age of 62, Kinsey died of pneumonia and heart complications.

sexual response: excitement, plateau, climax or orgasm, and resolution. More recent models have included emotional aspects of arousal. One model identifies three stages: desire, arousal, and orgasm. FSAD affects the excitement or arousal stage.

The first physiological change in the female body upon becoming aroused or sexually excited is the expansion of the blood vessels in the pelvic region, allowing more blood to flow to the lower abdomen and genitals. Some women experience this as a feeling of fullness in the pelvis, and either consciously or involuntarily contract the muscles in the genital area. The increased blood flow normally results in transudation—the seepage of fluid through the walls of the blood vessels—in this case into the vagina to provide lubrication before and during intercourse. Vaginal lubrication can occur very rapidly, within one minute, and is often very noticeable by the woman and her partner. The increase in blood flow also expands the upper portion of the vagina, the uterus, and the cervix. The lower third of the vagina, the labia, and the area around the clitoris swell and may tingle. The breasts also swell slightly. Together these physiological changes constitute the lubrication-swelling response, designed to facilitate entry of the penis into the vagina.

With FSAD the lubrication-swelling response is either absent or is not maintained through the completion of sexual activity. The lack of arousal and lubrication can result in painful intercourse (**dyspareunia**), emotional distress, and/or relationship problems. FSAD can be lifelong or acquired and generalized or situation-specific.

Causes and symptoms

The major symptom of FSAD is insufficient transudation, often resulting in painful and unsatisfactory intercourse. In addition to vaginal dryness, there is a lack of swelling, tingling, or throbbing in the genital region. Generalized FSAD occurs with different partners and in many different situations, whereas situation-specific FSAD occurs only with certain partners or under particular circumstances. FSAD can be caused by psychological factors or a combination of psychological and physiological factors. Whereas some women have never had a normal lubrication-swelling response, others develop FSAD from physiological changes, such as illness or emotional **trauma**, or as a side effect of surgery, radiation therapy for cancer, or a medication. Physiologically based FSAD can lead to psychological problems that reinforce the disorder.

Arousal disorder that primarily affects the genitals can result from low estrogen or testosterone levels during and after menopause, as well as from vaginal or bladder infections, or changes in the skin around the vulva. Other physiological causes of FSAD include:

- insufficient sexual stimulation
- irritation from contraceptive creams or foams
- smoking, which decreases blood flow throughout the body
- illicit drug use
- lower levels of sex hormones due to breast-feeding
- medical conditions that cause changes in hormone levels, including thyroid disorders, adrenal gland disorders, or removal of the ovaries
- side effects of medications such as antidepressants, antipsychotics, sedatives, high–blood pressure drugs (antihypertensives), or birth control pills or other hormone-containing medications
- reduced blood flow due to damaged blood vessels in the pelvic region, often from an injury or medical conditions such as coronary artery disease, high blood pressure, or diabetes
- damage to nerves in the pelvic area, as from diabetes or multiple sclerosis

Psychological causes of FSAD include:

- fear or anxiety around sex
- chronic mild depression (dysthymia)
- emotional stress
- low self-esteem
- past sexual abuse
- emotional abuse
- bereavement
- self-image problems
- relationship problems
- other mental health disorders, including major depression, posttraumatic stress disorder, or obsessive-compulsive disorder

Diagnosis

Since most women occasionally experience difficulties with sexual arousal, a **diagnosis** of FSAD requires that the lack of lubrication-swelling response is persistent or has occurred intermittently over an extended period and causes emotional distress or relationship difficulties. The ***Diagnostic and Statistical Manual of Mental Disorders*** (*DSM*) requires that FSAD be caused by psychological factors alone or a combination of psychological and physiological factors. Under these criteria, arousal disorder caused by physiological factors alone, such as injury, illness, or menopause, is diagnosed as sexual dysfunction due to a general medical condition. Arousal disorder caused by medication or **substance abuse** alone is diagnosed as substance-induced sexual dysfunction. Arousal difficulties that are symptoms of a major psychological disorder, such as **depression**, or that result from inadequate sexual stimulation are not considered to be FSAD.

Examination

FSAD is usually diagnosed after a woman reports sexual difficulties to her gynecologist, family doctor, psychotherapist, or sex therapist. The physician will take complete medical, psychological, and sexual histories, including a list of medications and details about sexual symptoms. A physical examination, including a gynecological/pelvic exam, will be performed.

Tests

Blood and urine tests may be performed to rule out undiagnosed diabetes or other medical conditions. Hormone levels in the blood may be measured.

Treatment

FSAD treatment requires addressing underlying physiological and psychological causes. When there are physical causes, the root problem or disease is treated. Forms of treatment include therapy, medication, and at-home techniques.

Traditional

Psychotherapy, either as individual or **couples therapy**, addresses emotions, communication, relationship problems, and problem-solving strategies. Sex therapy focuses primarily on the sexual dysfunction. Many couples experiencing sexual dysfunction develop relationship problems and can benefit from traditional psychotherapy even after sexual arousal difficulties are resolved.

The U.S. Food and Drug Administration (FDA) has approved one medical device for treating FSAD. The Eros-Clinical Therapy Device (Eros-CTD) is a small vacuum pump that fits over the clitoral area and exerts a gentle sucking action that stimulates blood flow. In **clinical trials** the device has proved safe and effective for increasing blood flow, sensation, and vaginal lubrication.

Drugs

Sometimes medications, such as the type or timing of an antidepressant, can be adjusted. Poor lubrication related to decreasing hormone levels associated with menopause can often be successfully treated with some forms of hormone replacement therapy (HRT), such as estrogen or testosterone. Nonprescription lubricating gels and hormone creams can supplement a woman's natural lubricant. These are especially useful for pre- and postmenopausal women and for those with occasional arousal difficulties.

Research is focusing on new drugs that increase blood flow to the female genitals, thereby improving lubrication. Some of these drugs are aimed at increasing nitric oxide levels, similar to the drug sildenafil (Viagra) for men.

Alternative

A type of **meditation** called mindfulness, which promotes increased awareness and acceptance, has been found to be helpful in treating FSAD, at least when practiced in the context of **group therapy**.

Home remedies

Home remedies for FSAD include:

- Kegel exercises that increase blood flow to the vulvar and vaginal tissues
- relaxation techniques
- aerobic exercise
- changing the circumstances and settings of sexual activity
- sexual activities other than vaginal intercourse
- exploring sexual techniques that increase stimulation
- experimenting with a vibrator, fantasies, or erotic movies
- couples-focusing exercises to enhance intimacy, lessen anxiety, and increase arousal

Prognosis

Because FSAD has multiple causes, individual response to treatment varies widely. Difficulties with lubrication related to menopause generally have a good prognosis. Stress-related difficulties with arousal typically resolve when the stressor is no longer present. Couples may need to work through relationship issues that have either resulted from or caused the sexual dysfunction before they see an improvement in sexual arousal. This process takes time and a joint commitment to problem solving.

KEY TERMS

Adrenal gland—A small organ located above each kidney that produces hormones related to the sex drive.

Cervix—The neck or narrow lower end of a woman's uterus.

Clitoris—The most sensitive area of the external genitals. Stimulation of the clitoris causes most women to reach orgasm.

Labia—The outside folds of tissue that surround the clitoris and the opening of the urethra in women.

Menopause—A period of decreasing hormonal activity in women, when ovulation stops and conception is no longer possible.

Pelvis—The basin-like cavity in the human body below the abdomen, enclosed by a framework of four bones.

Penis—The external male sex organ.

Thyroid—A gland in the neck that produces the hormone thyroxine, which is responsible for regulating metabolic activity in the body. Supplemental synthetic thyroid hormone is available as pills taken daily when the thyroid fails to produce enough hormone.

Uterus—The hollow muscular sac in which a fetus develops; sometimes called the womb.

Vagina—The part of the female reproductive system that opens to the exterior of the body and into which the penis is inserted during sexual intercourse.

Prevention

There is no sure way to prevent FSAD. Eating a healthy, well-balanced diet, getting enough rest, having regular gynecological checkups, and seeking counseling or psychotherapy when problems begin to appear in a relationship can help minimize sexual arousal problems. Aerobic **exercise** and not smoking also can help prevent FSAD.

Resources

BOOKS

American Psychiatric Association. *Diagnostic and Statistical Manual of Mental Disorders*. 4th ed., text rev. Washington, DC: American Psychiatric Publishing, 2000.

Clinton, Tim, and Laaser, Mark. *The Quick-Reference Guide to Sexuality and Relationship Counseling*. Grand Rapids, MI: Baker Books, 2010.

Rowland, David, and Luca Incrocci. *Handbook of Sexual and Gender Identity Disorders*. Hoboken, NJ: John Wiley & Sons, 2008.

PERIODICALS

Brotto, Lori A., Julia R. Heiman, and Deborah L. Tolman. "Narratives of Desire in Mid-Age Women With and Without Arousal Difficulties." *Journal of Sex Research* 46, no. 5 (September 2009): 387–399.

Graham, Cynthia A. "The *DSM* Diagnostic Criteria for Female Sexual Arousal Disorder." *Archives of Sexual Behavior* 39, no. 2 (April 2010): 240.–55. http://www.dsm5.org/Documents/Sex%20and%20GID%20Lit%20Reviews/SD/GRAHAM.FSAD.DSM.pdf (accessed November 9, 2011).

"Study Explores Possibility of a Female Viagra." *HealthDay*, April 14, 2010.

WEBSITES

Basson, Rosemary. "Overview of Sexual Dysfunction in Women." *The Merck Manual Home Health Handbook for Patients & Caregivers*. November 2008. http://www.merckmanuals.com/home/womens_health_issues/sexual_dysfunction_in_women/overview_of_sexual_dysfunction_in_women.html?qt=female sexual arousal disorder&alt=shl (accessed October 7, 2011).

Family.org. "Sexual Dysfunction in Women." August 2010. http://familydoctor.org/familydoctor/en/diseases-conditions/sexual-dysfunction-women.html (accessed October 7, 2011).

Mayo Clinic staff. "Female Sexual Dysfunction." MayoClinic.com. http://www.mayoclinic.com/health/female-sexual-dysfunction/DS00701 (accessed October 7, 2011).

MedlinePlus. "Sexual Problems Overview." U.S. National Library of Medicine, National Institutes of Health. September 11, 2010. http://www.nlm.nih.gov/medlineplus/ency/article/001951.htm (accessed October 7, 2011).

———. "Sexual Problems in Women." U.S. National Library of Medicine, National Institutes of Health. May 2011. http://www.nlm.nih.gov/medlineplus/femalesexualdysfunction.html (accessed October 7, 2011).

ORGANIZATIONS

American Academy of Family Physicians, 11400 Tomahawk Creek Pkwy., Leawood, KS, 66211-2672, (913) 906-6000, (800) 274-2237, Fax: (913) 906-6075, contactcenter@aafp.org, http://www.aafp.org.

American Association of Sexuality Educators, Counselors, and Therapists, 1444 I Street NW, Suite 700, Washington, DC, 20005, (202) 449-1099, Fax: (202) 216-9646, info@aasect.org, http://www.aasect.org.

American College of Obstetricians and Gynecologists, PO Box 96920, Washington, DC, 20090-6920, (202) 638-5577, http://www.acog.org.

Tish Davidson, AM
Emily Jane Willingham, PhD
Margaret Alic, PhD

Fetal alcohol syndrome

Definition

Fetal alcohol syndrome (FAS) is a pattern of birth defects, learning, and behavioral problems affecting individuals whose mothers drank alcohol during pregnancy. It is the most severe of a range of disorders represented by the term fetal alcohol spectrum disorder (FASD).

Demographics

The occurrence of FAS/FASD is independent of race, ethnicity, or gender of the individual. Individuals from different genetic backgrounds exposed to similar amounts of alcohol during pregnancy may show different symptoms of FAS. The reported rates of FAS vary widely among different populations studied depending on the degree of **alcohol use** within the population and the monitoring methods used. Studies by the Centers for Disease Control (CDC) show that FAS occurs in 0.2 to 1.5 per 1,000 live births in different areas of the United States. FASDs are believed to occur approximately three times as often as FAS.

Description

FAS/FASD is caused by exposure of a developing fetus to alcohol. FASD is used to describe individuals with some, but not all, of the features of FAS. Other terms used to describe specific types of FASD are alcohol-related neurodevelopmental disorder (ARND) and alcohol-related birth defects (ARBD).

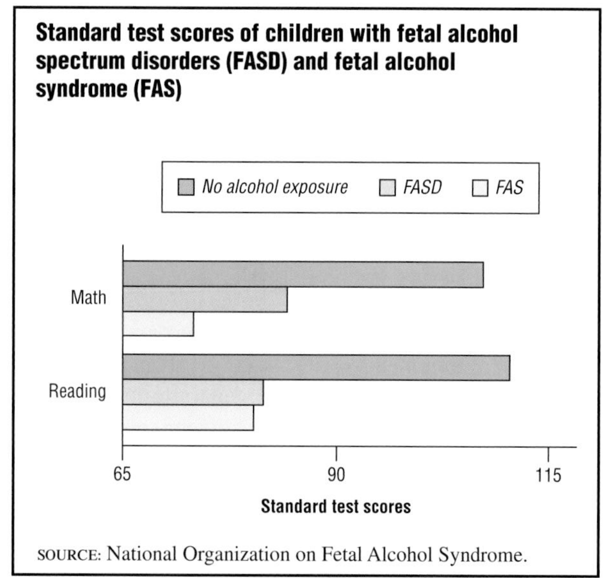

(Graph by PreMediaGlobal. © 2012 Cengage Learning.)

FAS is the most common preventable cause of intellectual disabilities. This condition was first recognized and reported in the medical literature in 1968 in France and in 1973 in the United States. Alcohol is a teratogen, the term used for any drug, chemical, maternal disease, or other environmental exposure that can cause birth defects or functional impairment in a developing fetus. Some features of FAS that may be present at birth include low birth weight, prematurity, and microcephaly. Characteristic facial features may be present at birth or may become more obvious over time. Signs of **brain** damage include delays in development, behavioral abnormalities, and intellectual disabilities, but affected individuals exhibit a wide range of abilities and disabilities.

Fetal alcohol syndrome is one of the conditions being recommended for inclusion in the ***Diagnostic and Statistical Manual of Mental Disorders*** *(DSM-5*, 2013).

FAS is a life-long condition. It is not curable and has serious long-term consequences. Learning, behavioral, and emotional problems are common in adolescents and adults with FAS/FASD.

Risk factors

The only risk factor for a child to develop FAS is the consumption of alcohol by a women who is pregnant. There is no known amount of alcohol use that is safe during pregnancy, nor is there a particular stage of pregnancy during which alcohol use is safe.

Causes and symptoms

Causes

The only cause of FAS is maternal use of alcohol during pregnancy. FAS is not a genetic or inherited disorder. Alcohol drunk by the mother freely crosses the placenta and damages the developing fetus. Alcohol use by the father cannot cause FAS. Not all offspring who are exposed to alcohol during pregnancy have signs or symptoms of FAS; individuals of different genetic backgrounds may be more or less susceptible to the damage that alcohol can cause. The amount of alcohol, stage of development of the fetus, and the pattern of alcohol use create the range of symptoms that encompass FASD.

Symptoms

Classic features of FAS include short stature, low birth weight, poor weight gain, microcephaly, and a characteristic pattern of abnormal facial features. These facial features in infants and children may include small eye openings (measured from inner corner to outer corner), epicanthal folds (folds of tissue at the inner corner of the eye), small or short nose, low or flat nasal bridge, smooth or poorly developed philtrum (the area of the upper lip above the colored part of the lip and below the nose), thin upper lip, and small chin. Some of these features are nonspecific, meaning they can occur in other conditions, or be appropriate for age, racial, or family background.

Other major and minor birth defects that have been reported to occur in conjunction with FAS/FASD include cleft palate, congenital heart defects, strabismus, hearing loss, defects of the spine and joints, alteration of the hand creases, small fingernails, and toenails. Since FAS was first described in infants and children, the **diagnosis** is sometimes more difficult to recognize in older adolescents and adults. Short stature and microcephaly remain common features, but weight may normalize, and the individual may actually become overweight for his/her height. The chin and nose grow proportionately more than the middle part of the face, and dental crowding may become a problem. The small eye openings and the appearance of the upper lip and philtrum may continue to be characteristic. Pubertal changes typically occur at the normal time.

Newborns with FAS may have difficulty nursing due to a poor sucking response, have irregular sleep-wake cycles, decreased or increased muscle tone, **seizures** or tremors. Delays in achieving developmental milestones such as rolling over, crawling, walking, and talking may become apparent in infancy. Behavior and learning difficulties typical in the preschool or early school years include poor attention span, hyperactivity, poor motor skills, and slow language development. **Attention deficit hyperactivity disorder (ADHD)** is often associated with FASD. Learning or intellectual disabilities may be diagnosed during this time.

During middle school and high school years the behavioral difficulties and learning difficulties can be significant. Memory problems, poor judgment, difficulties with daily living skills, difficulties with abstract reasoning skills, and poor social skills are often apparent by this time. It is important to note that animal and human studies have shown that neurologic and behavioral abnormalities can be present without characteristic facial features. These individuals may not be identified as having FAS, but may fulfill criteria for alcohol-related neurodevelopmental disorder (ARND).

FASD continues to affect individuals into adulthood. One study looked atFAS adults and found that about 95% had mental health problems, 82% lacked the ability to live independently, 70% had problems staying employed, 60% had been in trouble with the law, and 50% of men and 70% of women were alcohol or drug abusers.

Another long-term study found that the average IQ of the group of adolescents and adults with FAS in the study was 68 (70 is lower limit of the normal range). However, the range of IQ was quite large, ranging from a low of 20 (severely disabled) to a high of 105 (normal). Academic abilities and social skills were also below normal levels. The average achievement levels for reading, spelling, and arithmetic were fourth grade, third grade, and second grade, respectively. The Vineland Adaptive Behavior Scale was used to measure adaptive functioning in these individuals. The composite score for this group showed functioning at the level of a seven-year-old. Daily living skills were at a level of nine years, and social skills were at the level of a six-year-old.

Diagnosis

In 1996, the Institute of Medicine suggested a five-level system to describe the birth defects, learning problems, and behavioral difficulties in offspring of women who drank alcohol during pregnancy. This system contains criteria including confirmation of maternal alcohol exposure, characteristic facial features, growth problems, learning and behavioral problems, and birth defects known to be associated with prenatal alcohol exposure.

FAS is a clinical diagnosis, meaning that there is no blood, x ray or psychological test that can be performed to confirm the suspected diagnosis. The diagnosis is made based on the history of maternal alcohol use, and detailed physical examination for the characteristic major and minor birth defects and characteristic facial features. It is often helpful to examine siblings and parents of an individual suspected of having FAS, either in person or by photographs, to determine whether findings on the examination might be familial, of if other siblings may also be affected. Sometimes, genetic tests are performed to rule out other conditions that may present with developmental delay or birth defects. Individuals with developmental delay, birth defects, or other unusual features are often referred to a clinical geneticist, developmental pediatrician, or neurologist for evaluation and diagnosis of FAS. Psychoeducational testing to determine IQ and/or the presence of learning disabilities may also be part of the evaluation process.

Treatment

There is no cure for FAS. The disorder is irreversible. Nothing can change the physical features or brain damage associated with maternal alcohol use during the pregnancy. Children should have psychoeducational evaluation to help plan appropriate educational interventions. Common associated diagnoses such **ADHD**, **depression**, or anxiety can be recognized and treated. The disabilities that present during childhood persist into adult life. However, some of the behavioral problems mentioned above may be avoided or lessened by early and correct diagnosis, better understanding of the life-long complications of FAS, and **intervention**. The goal of treatment is to help the individual affected by FAS become as independent and successful in school, employment, and social relationships as possible.

QUESTIONS TO ASK YOUR DOCTOR

- I drank alcohol before I knew I was pregnant. How might this affect my baby?
- How soon can you evaluate the degree to which my baby has been affected by my use of alcohol?
- I am a heavy drinker. Can you refer me to a program to help me control my drinking while I am pregnant?
- My baby was born with FAS. What kind of social services are available to our family?

Prognosis

The prognosis for FAS/FASD depends on the severity of birth defects and the brain damage present at birth. Miscarriage, stillbirth, or death in the first few weeks of life may be outcomes in very severe cases. Generally individuals with FAS have a long list of mental health problems and associated social difficulties: alcohol and drug problems, inappropriate sexual behavior, problems with employment, trouble with the law, inability to live independently, and often confinement in prison, drug or alcohol treatment centers, or psychiatric institutions.

Some of the factors that have been found to reduce the risk of learning and behavioral disabilities in FAS individuals include diagnosis before the age of six years, stable and nurturing home environments, never having experienced personal violence, and referral and eligibility for disability services. Some physical birth defects associated with FAS are treatable with surgery. The long-term data help in understanding the difficulties that individuals with FAS encounter throughout their lifetime and can help families, caregivers, and professionals provide the care, supervision, education and treatment geared toward their special needs.

KEY TERMS

Alcohol—An organic chemical and the active agent in beer, wine, and liquor; chemically known as ethanol.

Alcoholism—Chronic and compulsive use of alcohol that interferes with everyday life.

Binge drinking—The practice of drinking alcoholic beverages to the point of intoxication.

Fetus—The stage of development between embryo and newborn.

Intellectual disability—Characterized by persistently slow learning and below normal intelligence.

Prenatal exposure—Coming in contact with a fetus during pregnancy.

Teratogen—An agent or chemical that causes a birth defect.

Prevention

FAS and FASD are completely preventable by avoiding all use of alcohol while pregnant. Prevention efforts include public education efforts aimed at the entire population, not just women of child bearing age, appropriate treatment for women with high-risk drinking habits, and increased recognition and knowledge about FAS/FASD by professionals, parents, and caregivers.

Resources

BOOKS

Golden, Janet. *Message in a Bottle: The Making of Fetal Alcohol Syndrome*. Cambridge, MA: Harvard University Press, 2005.

Kulp, Jodee, and Liz Kulp. *The Best I Can Be: Living with Fetal Alcohol Syndrome—Effects*. Brooklyn Park, MN: Better Endings New Beginnings, 2006.

Lawryk, Liz. *Finding Perspective: Raising Successful Children Affected by Fetal Alcohol Spectrum Disorders*. Bragg Creek, AB (Canada): OBD Triage Institute, 2005.

Soby, Jeanette M. *Prenatal Exposure to Drugs/Alcohol: Characteristics and Educational Implications of Fetal Alcohol Syndrome and Cocaine/Polydrug Effects*, 2nd ed. Springfield, IL: Charles C Thomas Publishing Ltd, 2006.

PERIODICALS

Franklin, L., et al. "Children With Fetal Alcohol Spectrum Disorders: Problem Behaviors and Sensory Processing." *American Journal of Occupational Therapy* 62, no. 3 (May –June 2008): 265–273.

Green, J. H. "Fetal Alcohol Spectrum Disorders: Understanding the Effects of Prenatal Alcohol Exposure and Supporting Students." *Journal of School Health* 77, no. 3 (March 2007): 103–108.

WEBSITES

Keith Vaux, ed. "Fetal Alcohol Syndrome." Medscape Reference, October 20, 2006. http://emedicine.medscape.com/article/974016-overview (accessed October 7, 2011).

MedlinePlus. "Fetal Alcohol Syndrome." U.S. National library of Medicine, National Institutes of Health. September 5, 2011. http://www.nlm.nih.gov/medlineplus/fetalalcoholsyndrome.html (accessed October 7, 2011).

U.S. Centers for Disease Control and Prevention. "Fetal Alcohol Spectrum Disorders (FASDs)." August 11, 2011. http://www.cdc.gov/ncbddd/fasd/index.html (accessed October 7, 2011).

ORGANIZATIONS

Fetal Alcohol Spectrum Disorders Center for Excellence, 2101 Gaither Rd., Suite 600, Rockville, MD, 20850, (866) 786-7327, fasdcenter@samhsa.hhs.gov, http://www.fascenter.samhsa.gov.

Fetal Alcohol Syndrome (FAS) World Canada, 2448 Hamilton Rd., Bright's Grove, ON, N0N 1C0, (519) 869-8026, http://www.faslink.org.

March of Dimes Foundation, 1275 Mamaroneck Ave., White Plains, NY, 10605, (914) 997-4488, http://www.marchofdimes.com.

National Institute on Alcohol Abuse and Alcoholism, 5635 Fishers Lane, MSC 9304, Bethesda, MD, 20892-9304, http://www.niaaa.nih.gov.

National Organization on Fetal Alcohol Syndrome, 1200 Eton Court NW, 3rd Floor, Washington, DC, 20007, (202) 785-4585, Fax: (202) 466-6456, information@nofas.org, http://www.nofas.org.

Laurie Heron Seaver, M.D.
Tish Davidson, A.M.

Fetishism

Definition

Fetishism is a form of paraphilia, a disorder characterized by recurrent intense sexual urges and sexually arousing fantasies generally involving nonhuman objects, the suffering or humiliation of oneself or one's partner (not merely simulated), or children or other nonconsenting persons. The essential feature of fetishism is recurrent intense sexual urges and sexually arousing fantasies involving specific objects. While any object may become a fetish in the psychological sense, the distinguishing feature is its connection with sex or sexual gratification. A **diagnosis** of fetishism is made only if an individual has acted on these urges, is markedly distressed by them, or if the fetish object is required for gratification.

For some people with a paraphilia such as fetishism, paraphilic fantasies or stimuli may be necessary for erotic arousal and are always included in sexual activity, or the presence of the fetish object may occur only episodically. For example, the fetish object may only be necessary for arousal during periods of **stress**, and at other times the person can function sexually without the fetish or stimuli related to the fetish.

Demographics

How many people have a fetish and the extent the fetish influences their lives and sexual activities are not accurately known. In some rare instances, people with fetishes may enter the legal system as a result of their fetishes, and those cases may be counted or tracked.

Paraphilias such as fetishism are uncommon among females, but some cases have been reported. Females may attach erotic thoughts to specific objects such as items of clothing or pets, but these are uncommon elements in sexual activity. Virtually no information is available on family patterns.

Description

A fetish is a form of paraphilia, and in fetishism, the affected person has created a strong association between an object and sexual pleasure or gratification. A fetish is not simply a pleasant memory—it is a dominant component of most sexual situations. Most fetishes are objects or body parts. Common fetishes involve items of clothing, stuffed animals, or other nonsexual objects. Body fetishes may involve breasts, legs, buttocks, or genitals.

A person with a fetish often spends significant amounts of time thinking about the object of the fetish. Further, the object is intimately related to sexual pleasure or gratification. In the extreme, the presence of the fetish object is required for sexual release and gratification.

Causes and symptoms

Causes

The cause of the association between an object and sexual arousal may be adolescent curiosity or a random association between the object and feelings of sexual pleasure. A random association may be innocent or unappreciated for its sexual content when it initially occurs. For example, a male may enjoy the texture or tactile sensation of female undergarments or stockings. At first, the pleasurable sensation occurs randomly, and then, in time and with experience, the behavior of using female undergarments or stockings as part of sexual activity is reinforced, and the association between the garments and the sexual arousal is made. A person with a fetish may not be able to pinpoint exactly when his or her fetish began. A fetish may be related to activities associated with **sexual abuse**.

Symptoms

Early symptoms for a fetish involve touching the object of desire. The amount of time spent thinking about the fetish object may increase. Over time, the importance of the fetish object expands. In the extreme, it becomes a requirement for achieving sexual pleasure and gratification.

Diagnosis

A diagnosis of a paraphilia involving a fetish is most commonly made by taking a detailed history or by direct observation. According to the ***Diagnostic and Statistical Manual of Mental Disorders*** (the fourth edition, text revision, or *DSM-IV-TR*), the person must have experienced the fantasies or urges centered on a nonliving object or objects for at least six months. In addition, these fantasies, urges, or behaviors must meet the criterion of causing significant distress or impairment in the person's ability to function socially or at work, or in other important environments. Last, the fetish cannot be solely focused on female clothing used in cross-dressing (which falls into the classification of transvestic fetishism) or on sex-aid devices that promote tactile genital stimulation, such as vibrators.

The fifth edition of the *Diagnostic and Statistical Manual of Mental Disorders* (*DSM-5*, 2013) proposes changing the condition fetish to fetishistic disorder.

Treatment

In the earliest stages of behavior therapy, fetishes were narrowly viewed as attractions to inappropriate objects. Aversive stimuli such as shocks were administered to persons undergoing therapy. This approach was not successful. People with fetishes have also been behaviorally treated by orgasmic reorientation, which attempts to help them develop sexual responses to culturally appropriate stimuli that have been otherwise neutral. This therapy has had only limited success.

Most persons who have a fetish never seek treatment from professionals. Many can achieve sexual gratification in culturally appropriate situations. In recent years, American society has developed more tolerance for persons with fetishes than in the past, thus further reducing the already minimal demand for professional treatment.

KEY TERM

Paraphilia—A disorder that is characterized by recurrent intense sexual urges and sexually arousing fantasies generally involving (1) nonhuman objects, (2) the suffering or humiliation of oneself or one's partner (not merely simulated), or (3) children or other nonconsenting persons.

Prognosis

The prognosis for eliminating a fetish is poor because fetishism is generally chronic. Most cases in which treatment has been demanded as a condition of continuing a marriage have not been successful. Most fetishes are relatively harmless in that they usually do not involve other persons or endanger the person with the fetish. Persons with a fetish rarely involve nonconsenting partners.

The personal prognosis for a person with a fetish is good if the fetish and related activities do not impact others or place the person with the fetish in physical danger.

Prevention

Most experts agree that providing gender-appropriate guidance in a culturally appropriate situation will prevent the formation of a fetish. The origin of some fetishes may be random associations between a particular object or situation and sexual gratification. There is no way to predict such an association.

Resources

BOOKS

American Psychiatric Association. *Diagnostic and Statistical Manual of Mental Disorders*. 4th ed., text rev. Washington, DC: American Psychiatric Publishing, 2000.

Gelder, Michael, Paul Harrison, and Philip Cowen. *Shorter Oxford Textbook of Psychiatry*. 5th ed. New York: Oxford University Press, 2006.

Wilson, Josephine F. *Biological Foundations of Human Behavior*. Farmington Hills, MI: Cengage Learning, 2002.

PERIODICALS

Chalkley, A.J., and G.E. Powell. "The Clinical Description of Forty-Eight Cases of Sexual Fetishism." *British Journal of Psychiatry* 142 (1983): 292–95.

FitzGerald, W. A. "Explaining the Variety of Human Sexuality." *Medical Hypotheses* 55, no. 5 (November 2000): 435–39.

Nersessian E. "A Cat as Fetish: a Contribution to the Theory of Fetishism." *International Journal of Psychoanalysis* 79 (1998): 713–25.

Reed, G. S. "The Analyst's Interpretation as Fetish." *Journal of the American Psychoanalytical Association* 45, no. 4 (1997): 1153–81.

Weiss, J. "Bondage Fantasies and Beating Fantasies." *Psychoanalytic Quarterly* 67, no. 4 (October 1998): 626–44.

Wise, T.N., and R.C. Kalyanam. "Amputee Fetishism and Genital Mutilation: Case Report and Literature Review." *Journal of Sexual and Marital Therapy* 26, no. 4 (October–December 2000): 339–44.

ORGANIZATIONS

American Psychiatric Association, 1000 Wilson Blvd., Ste. 1825, Arlington, VA, 22209-3901, (703) 907-7300, apa@psych.org, http://www.psych.org.

American Psychological Association, 750 1st Street NE, Washington, DC, 20002-4242, (202) 336-5500; TDD/TTY: (202) 336-6123, (800) 374-2721, http://www.apa.org.

L. Fleming Fallon, Jr., MD, Dr. P.H.
Emily Jane Willingham, PhD

Figure drawings

Definition

Figure drawings are projective diagnostic techniques in which an individual is instructed to draw a person, an object, or a situation so that cognitive, interpersonal, or psychological functioning can be assessed.

Purpose

A projective test is one in which a test taker responds to or provides ambiguous, abstract, or unstructured stimuli, often in the form of pictures or drawings. While other projective tests, such as the Rorschach Technique and **Thematic Apperception Test**, ask the test taker to interpret existing pictures, figure drawing tests require the test taker to create the pictures themselves. In most cases, figure drawing tests are given to children. This is because it is a simple, manageable task that children can relate to and enjoy.

Some figure drawing tests are primarily measures of cognitive abilities or cognitive development. In these tests, there is a consideration of how well a child draws and the content of a child's drawing. In some tests, the child's self-image is considered through the use of the drawings. In other figure drawing tests, interpersonal relationships are assessed by having the child draw a family or some other situation in which more than one person is present. Some tests are used for the evaluation of **child abuse**. Other tests involve personality interpretation through drawings of objects, such as a tree or a house, as well as people. Finally, some figure drawing tests are used as part of the diagnostic procedure for specific types of psychological or neuropsychological impairment, such as central nervous system dysfunction or intellectual disability.

Precautions

Despite the flexibility in administration and interpretation of figure drawings, these tests require skilled and trained administrators familiar with both the theory behind the tests and the structure of the tests themselves. Interpretations should be made with caution and the limitations of projective tests should be considered. It is generally a good idea to use projective tests as part of an overall test battery. There is little professional support for the use of figure drawing, so the examples that follow should be interpreted with caution.

Description

The Draw-A-Man Test, developed by Goodenough in 1926 was the first formal figure drawing test. It was used to estimate a child's cognitive and intellectual abilities reflected in the drawing's quality. The test was later revised by Harris in 1963 as the Goodenough Harris Drawing Test (GHDT), which included a detailed scoring system and allowed for drawings of men, women, and the self. The scoring system primarily reflected the way in which the child is maturing cognitively. The GHDT is appropriate for children between the ages of 3 and 17, although it has been found to be most useful for children between 3 and 10.

The Draw-A-Person test (DAP) was developed by Machover in 1948 and used figure drawings in a more projective way, focusing on how the drawings reflected the anxieties, impulses, self-esteem, and personality of the test taker. In this test, children are first asked to draw a picture of a person. Then, they are asked to draw a picture of a person of the sex opposite of the first drawing. Sometimes, children are also asked to draw a picture of the self and/or family members. Then, they are asked a series of questions about themselves and the drawings. These questions can be about the mood, the ambitions, and the good and bad qualities of the people in the drawings. The pictures and the questions on the DAP are meant to elicit information about the child's anxieties, impulses, and overall personality. The DAP is the most frequently used figure drawing test today. A scoring system appropriate for adults was developed in 1993 by Mitchel, Trent, and McArthur.

In 1992, Naglieri and his colleagues created a more specific scoring system for figure drawing tests called the Draw-A-Person: Screening Procedure of Emotional Disturbance (DAP:SPED), based on a large standardization sample. This scoring method includes 55 items rated by the test administrator and based on the child's drawings and responses to questions. The DAP:SPED is appropriate for children aged six to 17. It is often used as a screening method for children who may be having difficulties with regard to social adjustment and require further evaluation.

The House-Tree-Person (HTP) test, created by Buck in 1948, provides a measure of a self-perception and attitudes by requiring the test taker to draw a house, a tree, and a person. The picture of the house is supposed to conjure the child's feelings toward his or her family. The picture of the tree is supposed to elicit feelings of strength or weakness. The picture of the person, as with other figure drawing tests, elicits information regarding the child's self-concept. The HTP, though mostly given to children and adolescents, is appropriate for anyone over the age of three.

The Kinetic Family Drawing technique (KFD), developed in 1970 by Burns and Kaufman, requires the test taker to draw a picture of his or her entire family. Children are asked to draw a picture of their family, including themselves, "doing something." This picture is meant to elicit the child's attitudes toward his or her family and the overall family dynamics. The KFD is sometimes interpreted as part of an evaluation of child **abuse**.

The Kinetic School Drawing technique (KSD), developed in 1974 by Prout and Phillips, requires the child to draw a picture of himself or herself, a teacher, and one or more classmates. This picture is meant to elicit the child's attitudes toward people at school and his or her functioning in the school environment.

Results

As with all projective measures, scoring on figure drawing tests is more subjective. Specific scoring systems, such as the DAP:SPED can be used to provide more objective information. Most figure drawing tests have some sort of objective scoring system; however, the instructions given to the child, the questions asked by the test administrator, and the interpretations the administrator makes of the drawings are flexible and this makes it difficult to compare results between children, even on the same measure. Also, many clinicians choose not to rely on the scoring systems and rely entirely on their own intuitive judgments regarding their interpretation of picture content.

KEY TERMS

Projective test—A psychological test in which the test taker responds to or provides ambiguous, abstract, or unstructured stimuli, often in the form of pictures or drawings.

Reliability—The ability of a test to yield consistent, repeatable results.

Standardization—The administration of a test to a sample group of people for the purpose of establishing scoring norms. The DAP:SPED structured scoring system was standardized using a sample of over 2,300 children and adolescents.

Validity—The ability of a test to measure accurately what it claims to measure.

Figure drawings are often interpreted with regard to appropriate cognitive development. Naglieri's DAP: SPED scoring system includes a consideration of what features in a drawing are appropriate for children of various ages. For example, five-year old children are expected to make fairly basic drawings of people, consisting of a head, eyes, nose, mouth, body, arms, and legs. An 11-year-old, on the other hand is expected to have more details in the picture, such as a more defined neck, clothes, and arms in a particular direction.

Sometimes, figure drawings are assessed with regard to self image. Children often projective themselves in the drawings. For example, females with **body image** concerns may reflect these concerns in their drawings. Victims of **sexual abuse** may stress sexual characteristics in their drawings.

Psychological, neuropsychological, or emotional dysfunction can also be considered in figure drawing interpretation. This type of interpretation is often done with figure drawings made by adults. For example, a person who omits or distorts body parts may have emotional impairment. Excessive detail with regard to the sexual nature of the drawing may indicate sexual maladjustment.

Family dynamics are also interpreted through figure drawings. For example, in the Kinetic Family Drawing test, a picture where family members are in separate rooms may indicate isolation or a lack of interaction between family members.

Figure drawings are also interpreted with regard to child abuse. In 1994, Von Hutton developed a scoring system for both the HTP and DAP focusing on indicators of child abuse that may be present in drawings. The drawing of the family in the KFD test may also provide indicators of abuse.

There has been much debate over the overall reliability and validity of figure drawing tests (and projective tests in general). For example, when structured scoring systems are used, the DAP has been found to be a reliable measure, especially for cognitive development in children. However, with regard to specific personality characteristics, self-image issues, or personality dysfunctions, there has been relatively little support for the use of figure drawings.

Resources

BOOKS

Groth-Marnat, Gary. *Handbook of Psychological Assessment*. 5th ed. New York: John Wiley and Sons, 2009.

Kline, Paul. *The Handbook of Psychological Testing*. New York: Routledge, 1999.

Reynolds, Cecil R. *Comprehensive Clinical Psychology, Volume 4: Assessment*. Amsterdam: Elsevier, 1998.

Ali Fahmy, Ph.D.

5-HTP

Definition

5-HTP is the acronym for 5-hydroxytryptophan, also called 5-hydroxy-L-tryptophan. 5-HTP is found primarily in the **brain** and is a by-product of tryptophan, an amino acid found in foods. Tryptophan is an essential amino acid—it cannot be made by the body and must be obtained from food, particularly proteins. In the liver and brain, 5-HTP is converted to an important monoamine neurotransmitter called

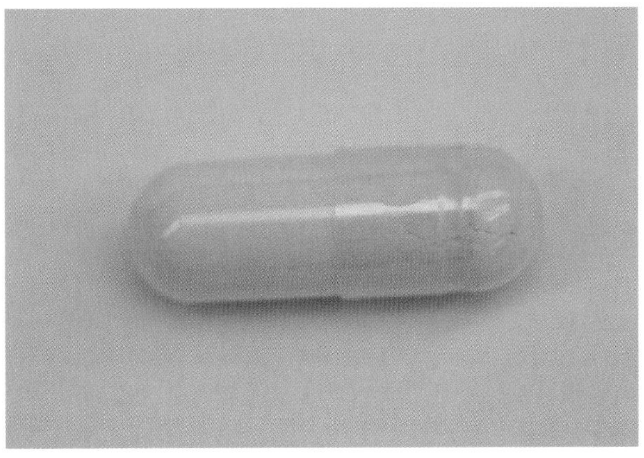

5-HTP supplement. *(© Custom Medical Stock Photo, Inc. Reproduced by permission.)*

serotonin. **Neurotransmitters** are chemical messengers that transmit signals between neurons (nerve cells), coordinating different functions within the body.

Purpose

Because it is converted to serotonin in the body, resulting in higher serotonin levels in the brain, 5-HTP is used to help treat or prevent conditions associated with low levels of serotonin. Serotonin, also called 5-hydroxytryptamine or 5-HT, plays an important role in controlling behavior and moods. It influences many normal brain activities and also regulates the activity of other neurotransmitters. Having adequate levels of serotonin instills a feeling of relaxation, calm, and mild euphoria (extreme happiness). Low levels of serotonin, known as serotonin deficiency syndrome, can lead to **depression**, anxiety, irritability, and **insomnia**.

Other conditions associated with low levels of serotonin include:

- attention deficit hyperactivity disorder (ADHD)
- bulimia
- epilepsy
- fibromyalgia
- headaches
- hyperactivity
- obesity
- obsessive compulsive disorder (OCD)
- panic attacks
- premenstrual syndrome (PMS)
- schizophrenia
- seasonal affective disorder (SAD)

5-HTP is an antioxidant; antioxidants protect the body from damage caused by substances called free radicals (unstable, toxic molecules). In this role, 5-HTP may help slow the aging process and protect the body from illness. Because serotonin is used to make melatonin, taking 5-HTP may help achieve some of the same benefits as melatonin, such as treating jet lag, depression, and insomnia. In treating insomnia, 5-HTP is thought to increase the length of rapid eye movement (REM) sleep, improving overall sleep quality. There is some evidence that 5-HTP can replenish the supply of the pain-relieving molecules called endorphins. Studies have shown that low levels of endorphins are associated with chronic **fatigue** syndrome, fibromyalgia, **stress**, and depression. In addition, 5-HTP affects other neurotransmitters, including norepinephrine and **dopamine**.

Description

In clinical studies, 5-HTP has been proven effective in the treatment of depression and fibromyalgia. Much of the clinical research with 5-HTP focused on the treatment of depression. In 15 separate studies, 5-HTP was tested on a total of 511 patients with different kinds of depression. Over half (56%) of these patients had significant improvement in depression while taking 5-HTP. The compound was found to be as effective as the selective serotonin reuptake inhibitor (SSRI) **fluvoxamine** and the tricyclic **antidepressants** clomipramine and **imipramine**. Many of these studies used relatively high doses ranging from 50–3,250 mg daily.

Three clinical studies found that 5-HTP can significantly improve the pain, anxiety, morning stiffness, and fatigue associated with fibromyalgia. The doses ranged from 300–400 mg daily. In one study, 5-HTP treatment was as effective as a tricyclic antidepressant (**amitriptyline**) and as **monoamine oxidase inhibitors** (MAOI; pargyline or **phenelzine**).

5-HTP may also be useful in treating carbohydrate cravings and binge eating, obesity, insomnia, anxiety, and panic disorders, but further research is needed, as results have been mixed. Three clinical studies found that 5-HTP use led to decreased intake of food and subsequent weight loss in obese patients. The dose used in one study was 900 mg daily, which initially caused nausea in 80% of the patients. In studies done on treating panic disorders, use of 5-HTP instilled patients with a sense of relief.

Although 5-HTP may be a useful alternative to conventional antidepressant drugs, one study indicated that it may be of no value for patients who have failed to respond to traditional drugs. In this study, patients who failed to respond to tricyclic antidepressants were treated with either 5-HTP or a monoamine oxidase inhibitor (MAO–I). Half of the patients improved with the MAOI treatment, while none showed any benefit from 5-HTP treatment.

Recommended dosage

The 5-HTP preparation available commercially is isolated from the seed of an African plant called *Griffonia simplicifolia*. It is available as an enteric coated tablet, which does not break down until it reaches the intestine.

The recommended starting dose for headaches, weight loss, depression, and fibromyalgia is 50 mg three times daily. It can be taken with food, though for weight loss it should be taken 20 minutes before eating. If the supplement is not effective after two weeks, the dose may be increased to 100 mg three times daily, but only with the recommendation of a physician. Insomnia is treated

KEY TERMS

Eosinophilia myalgia syndrome (EMS)—A chronic, painful disease of the immune system that causes joint pain, fatigue, shortness of breath, and swelling of the arms and legs. EMS can be fatal.

Monoamine oxidase inhibitor (MAOI)—An antidepressant drug that prevents the breakdown of monoamine neurotransmitters (such as serotonin) in the gaps between nerve cells. Nardil and Parnate are common MAOI brands.

Neurotransmitter—A chemical messenger that transmits signals between nerve cells.

Selective serotonin reuptake inhibitor (SSRI)—A family of antidepressant drugs that block the reabsorption of serotonin by nerve cells; common brand names include Prozac, Zoloft, and Paxil.

Serotonin syndrome—A syndrome characterized by agitation, confusion, delirium, and perspiration, which is caused by high levels of serotonin in the brain.

Tricyclic antidepressant—A group of antidepressant drugs that all have three rings in their chemical structure. Their mechanism of action is not fully understood, but they appear to extend the duration of action of some neurohormones, including serotonin and norepinephrine. They have also been used to treat some forms of chronic pain. Common brand names are Aventyl, Elavil, Surmontil, and Vivactil.

with 25 mg (which may be increased to 100 mg after a few days) taken 30–45 minutes before bedtime.

Precautions

A very small number of persons taking 5-HTP developed eosinophilia myalgia syndrome (EMS), a potentially fatal condition characterized by blood abnormalities and muscle tenderness and pain. In 1989, a contaminant was found in L-tryptophan that was linked to the development of EMS in some users, and the L-tryptophan supplements were subsequently banned by the U.S. Food and Drug Administration. A similar contaminant (peak X) was found in 5-HTP products produced by six different manufacturers. The 5-HTP contaminant was not at levels high enough to cause illness, so it is not known whether the development of EMS in persons taking 5-HTP is caused by a contaminant or by the drug itself. Excessive doses of 5-HTP may lead to toxic levels of peak X, and until the cause of EMS is determined, 5-HTP is considered unsafe.

Pregnant women should not take 5-HTP because there are no clinical studies on the effects of the supplement on the fetus or newborn. Persons with **Down syndrome** should also not take 5-HTP due to risk of **seizures**; in one study of patients with Down syndrome, 15% of participants suffered seizures after long-term 5-HTP use.

Side effects

Side effects associated with 5-HTP are rare but may include headaches, mild stomachaches, nausea, nasal congestion, and constipation. There are anecdotal reports that taking high doses of 5-HTP causes nightmares or vivid dreams. Side effects may be minimized by starting with a low dose of 5-HTP and taking it with food.

Interactions

5-HTP should not be used with other antidepressant drugs. 5-HTP and antidepressant drugs both work to increase serotonin levels in the brain, and too much serotonin can lead to **serotonin syndrome**, a potentially life threatening condition. Other drugs or supplements that may prove harmful in combination with 5-HTP include carbidopa (Lodosyn), dextromethorphan (Robitussin DM and others), meperidine (Demerol), pentazocine (Talwin), tramadol (Ultram), and **St. John's wort**.

Resources

PERIODICALS

Halford, Jason C.G., et al. "Serotonin (5-HT) Drugs: Effects on Appetite Expression and Use for the Treatment of Obesity." *Current Drug Targets* (March 2005): 201–213.

Keithahn, Christian, and Alexander Lerch. "5-Hydroxytryptophan Is a More Potent in Vitro Hydroxyl Radical Scavenger than Melatonin or Vitamin C." *Journal of Pineal Research* (January 2005): 62–66.

WEBSITES

MedlinePlus. "5-HTP." U.S. National Library of Medicine, National Institutes of Health. http://www.nlm.nih.gov/medlineplus/druginfo/natural/794.html (accessed September 20, 2011).

University of Maryland Medical Center. "5-Hydroxytryptophan (5-HTP)." http://www.umm.edu/altmed/articles/5-htp–000283.htm (accessed September 20, 2011).

University of Michigan Health System. "5-HTP." http://www.uofmhealth.org/health-library/hn-2793000www.uofmhealth.org/health-library/hn-2793000 (accessed September 20, 2011).

Belinda Rowland
Samuel Uretsky, Pharm.D.
David Edward Newton, Ed.D.

Flooding *see* **Exposure treatment**

Fluoxetine

Definition

Fluoxetine is an antidepressant of the type known as **selective serotonin reuptake inhibitors** (SSRI). It is sold in the United States under the brand names Prozac and Sarafem.

Purpose

Fluoxetine is used to treat **depression**, **premenstrual syndrome**, bulimia, and **obsessive-compulsive disorder**.

Description

Serotonin is a neurotransmitter—a **brain** chemical that carries nerve impulses from one nerve cell to another. Researchers think that depression and certain other mental disorders may be caused, in part, because there is not enough serotonin being released and transmitted in the brain. Like the other SSRI **antidepressants**, **fluvoxamine** (Luvox), **sertraline** (Zoloft), and **paroxetine** (Paxil), fluoxetine increases the level of brain serotonin (also known as 5-HT). Increased serotonin levels in the brain may be beneficial in patients with obsessive-compulsive disorder, alcoholism, certain types of headaches, **post-traumatic stress disorder** (PTSD), premenstrual tension and mood swings, and **panic disorder**.

Fluoxetine was the first of the class of antidepressants called **SSRIs** to be approved for use in the United States. In 2000, fluoxetine was approved by the Food and Drug Administration (FDA) for use in treating **premenstrual dysphoric disorder**.

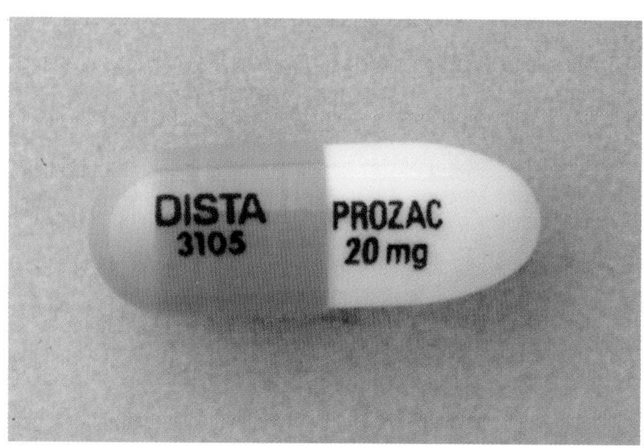

Prozac (fluoxetine hydrochloride). *(© Custom Medical Stock Photo, Inc. Reproduced by permission.)*

The benefits of fluoxetine develop slowly over a period of several weeks. Patients should be aware of this and continue to take the drug as directed, even if they feel no immediate improvement.

Fluoxetine (marketed as Prozac) is available in 10, 20, and 40 mg capsules, 10 mg tablets, and in a liquid solution with 20 mg of active drug per 5 mL. Prozac Weekly capsules are a time-release formula containing 90 mg of active drug. Sarafem is available in 10 and 20 mg capsules.

Recommended dosage

Fluoxetine therapy in adults is started as a single 20 mg dose, initially taken in the morning. Depending on the patient's response after four to six weeks of therapy, this dose can be increased up to a total of 80 mg per day. Doses over 20 mg per day can be given as equally divided morning and afternoon doses.

Precautions

Fluoxetine use should not be stopped abruptly. Patients taking fluoxetine should be monitored closely for **insomnia**, anxiety, mania, significant weight loss, **seizures**, and thoughts of **suicide**. Like other SSRIs, fluoxetine carries a warning regarding use in children and adults up to 24 years of age, who are at an increased risk of developing suicidal thoughts while taking the drug. Caution should also be exercised when prescribing fluoxetine to patients with impaired liver or kidney function, the elderly (over age 60), children, individuals with known manic-depressive disorder or a history of seizures, people with diabetes, and individuals expressing ideas of committing suicide.

Individuals should not take **monoamine oxidase inhibitors (MAOIs)** during fluoxetine therapy and should wait before beginning fluoxetine therapy. If so, they likely will need to wait before taking fluoxetine. Patients should wait at least five weeks after stopping fluoxetine therapy before taking **MAOIs**.

Care should be taken to weigh the risks and benefits of this drug in women who are, or wish to become, pregnant, as well as those who are breastfeeding.

People with diabetes should monitor their blood or urine sugar more carefully, since fluoxetine can affect blood sugar.

Until an individual understands the effects that fluoxetine may have, he or she should avoid driving, operating dangerous machinery, or participating in hazardous activities. Alcohol should not be used while taking fluoxetine.

Side effects

Common side effects include:

- decreased sexual drive
- restlessness
- difficulty sitting still
- skin rash, hives, and itching

Less common side effects include fever and/or chills and pain in joints or muscles.

Rare side effects include:

- pain or enlargement of breasts and/or abnormal milk production in women
- seizures
- fast heart rate
- irregular heartbeats
- red or purple spots on the skin
- low blood sugar and its symptoms (anxiety, chills, cold sweats, confusion, difficulty concentrating, drowsiness, excess hunger, rapid heart rate, headache, shakiness or unsteadiness, severe fatigue)
- low blood sodium and its symptoms (confusion, seizures, drowsiness, dry mouth, severe thirst, decreased energy)
- serotonin syndrome (usually at least three of the following: diarrhea, fever, sweatiness, mood or behavior changes, overactive reflexes, fast heart rate, restlessness, shivering or shaking)
- excitability, agitation, irritability
- pressured talking
- difficulty breathing
- odd body or facial movements

Interactions

Fluoxetine interacts with many other medications. People who may be starting this drug should review the other medications they are taking with their physician and pharmacist for possible interactions. Patients should always inform all of their healthcare providers, including dentists, that they are taking fluoxetine.

When taken with fluoxetine, blood levels of the following drugs may increase:

- benzodiazepines
- beta blockers
- carbamazepine
- dextromethorphan
- haloperidol
- atorvastatin
- lovastatin
- simvastatin
- phenytoin
- tricyclic antidepressants

The following drugs may increase the risk of **serotonin syndrome**: dexfenfluramine, fenfluramine, and tryptophan.

When **buspirone** is taken with fluoxetine, the therapeutic effect of buspirone may be impaired.

Low blood sodium may occur when fluoxetine is taken along with diuretics.

Increased risk of mania and high blood pressure occurs when selegiline is taken along with fluoxetine.

Severe, fatal reactions have occurred when fluoxetine is given along with MAOIs.

KEY TERMS

Diabetes—A disease in which sugar is not metabolized properly. People with diabetes need to monitor their blood or urine sugar carefully if they are taking fluoxetine, because this drug affects blood sugar.

Monoamine oxidase inhibitor (MAOI)—An older class of antidepressants.

Serotonin—A brain chemical that carries nerve impulses from one nerve cell to another.

Resources

BOOKS

Preston, John D., John H. O'Neal, and Mary C. Talaga. *Handbook of Clinical Psychopharmacology for Therapists.* 4th ed. Oakland, CA: New Harbinger, 2004.

PERIODICALS

Anderson, Shawanda W., and Marvin B. Booker. "Cognitive Behavioral Therapy Versus Psychosurgery for Refractory Obsessive-Compulsive Disorder." *Journal of Neuropsychiatry and Clinical Neurosciences* 18, no. 1 (Winter 2006): 129.

Denninger, John W., et al. "Somatic Symptoms in Outpatients with Major Depressive Disorder Treated with Fluoxetine." *Psychosomatics: Journal of Consultation Liaison Psychiatry* 47, no. 4 (July/August 2006): 348–52.

Fava, Maurizio, et al. "Eszopiclone Co-Administered with Fluoxetine in Patients with Insomnia Coexisting with Major Depressive Disorder." *Biological Psychiatry* 59, no. 11 (June 2006): 1052–60.

Hammad, Tarek A., Thomas Laughren, and Judith Racoosin. "Suicidality in Pediatric Patients Treated with Antidepressant Drugs." *Archives of General Psychiatry* 63, no. 3 (March 2006): 332–39.

Kratochvil, Christopher J., et al. "Selecting an Antidepressant for the Treatment of Pediatric Depression." *Journal of the American Academy of Child and Adolescent Psychiatry* 45, no. 3 (March 2006): 371–73.

Lam, Raymond W., et al. "The Can-SAD Study: A Randomized Controlled Trial of the Effectiveness of Light Therapy and Fluoxetine in Patients with Winter Seasonal Affective Disorder." *American Journal of Psychiatry* 163, no. 5 (May 2006): 805–12.

Martenyi, Ferenc, and Victoria Soldatenkova. "Fluoxetine in the Acute Treatment and Relapse Prevention of Combat-Related Post-traumatic Stress Disorder: Analysis of the Veteran Group of a Placebo-Controlled, Randomized Clinical Trial." *European Neuropsychopharmacology* 16, no. 5 (July 2006): 340–49.

McGrath, Patrick J., et al. "Predictors of Relapse in a Prospective Study of Fluoxetine Treatment of Major Depression." *American Journal of Psychiatry* 163, no. 9 (September 2006): 1542–48.

Moreno, Carmen, Ansley M. Roche, and Laurence L. Greenhill. "Pharmacotherapy of Child and Adolescent Depression." *Child and Adolescent Psychiatric Clinics of North America* 15, no. 4 (October 2006): 977–98.

Mowla, Arash, Ahmad Ghanizadeh, and Azadeh Pani. "A Comparison of the Effects of Fluoxetine and Nortriptyline on the Symptoms of Major Depressive Disorder." *Journal of Clinical Psychopharmacology* 26, no. 2 (April 2006): 209–11.

Mulder, Roger T., et al. "Six Months of Treatment for Depression: Outcome and Predictors of the Course of Illness." *American Journal of Psychiatry* 163, no. 1 (January 2006): 95–100.

Nemeroff, Charles B., and Michael E. Thase. "A Double-Blind, Placebo-Controlled Comparison of Venlafaxine and Fluoxetine Treatment in Depressed Outpatients." *Journal of Psychiatric Research* 41, no. 3–4 (April–June 2007): 351–59.

Pinto-Meza, Alejandra, et al. "Gender Differences in Response to Antidepressant Treatment Prescribed in Primary Care. Does Menopause Make a Difference?" *Journal of Affective Disorders* 93, no. 1–3 (July 2006): 53–60.

Pollack, Mark H., et al. "Olanzapine Augmentation of Fluoxetine for Refractory Generalized Anxiety Disorder: A Placebo Controlled Study." *Biological Psychiatry* 59, no. 3 (February 2006): 211–15.

Schreiber, Shaul, and Chaim G. Pick. "From Selective to Highly Selective SSRIs: A Comparison of the Antinociceptive Properties of Fluoxetine, Fluvoxamine, Citalopram, and Escitalopram." *European Neuropsychopharmacology* 16, no. 6 (August 2006): 464–68.

Serrano-Blanco, A., et al. "Effectiveness and Cost-Effectiveness of Antidepressant Treatment in Primary Health Care: A Six-Month Randomised Study Comparing Fluoxetine to Imipramine." *Journal of Affective Disorders* 91, no. 2–3 (Aprril 2006): 153–63.

Taravosh-Lahn, Kereshmeh Christel Bastida, and Yvon Delville. "Differential Responsiveness to Fluoxetine During Puberty." *Behavioral Neuroscience* 120, no. 5 (October 2006): 1084–92.

Taylor, Bonnie P., et al. "Psychomotor Slowing as a Predictor of Fluoxetine Nonresponse in Depressed Outpatients." *American Journal of Psychiatry* 163, no. 1 (January 2006): 73–78.

Tiihonen, Jari, et al. "Antidepressants and the Risk of Suicide, Attempted Suicide, and Overall Mortality in a Nationwide Cohort." *Archives of General Psychiatry* 63, no. 12 (December 2006): 1358–67.

Vasa, Roma A., Anthony R. Carlino, and Daniel S. Pine. "Pharmacotherapy of Depressed Children and Adolescents: Current Issues and Potential Directions." *Biological Psychiatry* 59, no. 11 (June 2006): 1021–28.

ORGANIZATIONS

American Psychiatric Association, 1000 Wilson Blvd., Ste. 1825, Arlington, VA, 22209-3901, (703) 907-7300, apa@psych.org, http://www.psych.org.

National Alliance on Mental Illness, 2107 Wilson Blvd., Ste. 300, Arlington, VA, 22201-3042, Fax: (703) 524-9094, (800) 950-6264, http://www.nami.org.

National Institute of Mental Health, 6001 Executive Blvd., Rm. 8184, MSC 9663, Bethesda, MD, 20892-9663, (301) 433-4513; TTY: (301) 443-8431, Fax: (301) 443-4279, (866) 615-6464; TTY: (866) 415-8051, nimhinfo@nih.gov, http://www.nimh.nih.gov.

Rosalyn Carson-DeWitt, MD
Ruth A. Wienclaw, PhD

Fluphenazine

Definition

Fluphenazine is a phenothiazine antipsychotic sold in the United States under the brand names Permitil and Prolixin. It is also available under its generic name.

Purpose

Fluphenazine is used to treat **schizophrenia** and symptoms of psychotic disorders such as **delusions**, hallucinations, and agitation.

Description

Fluphenazine is one of many drugs in the group called the phenothiazines. Phenothiazines work by inhibiting the actions of the **brain** chemicals **dopamine** and norepinephrine, which are overproduced in individuals with **psychosis**.

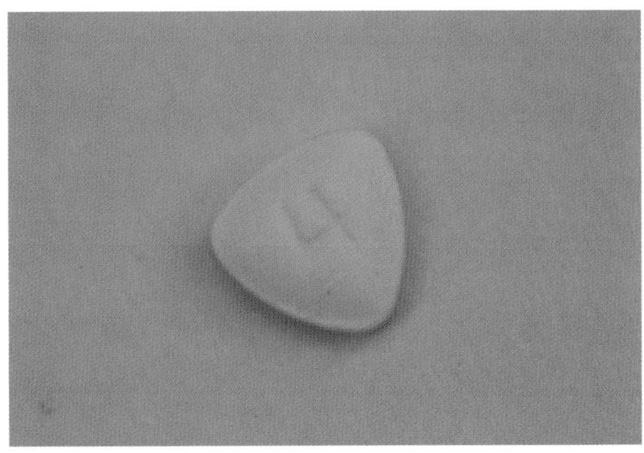

Fluphenazine, 1 mg. *(© Custom Medical Stock Photo, Inc. Reproduced by permission.)*

Fluphenazine is available in 1 mg, 2.5 mg, 5 mg, and 10 mg tablets, a liquid concentrate containing 5 mg/mL, a rapid-onset injectable form containing 2.5 mg/mL, and a long-acting injectable form containing 25 mg/mL.

Recommended dosage

In children over age 16 and in adults, fluphenazine is usually given in oral dosages ranging from 0.5–10 mg daily. The total dosage is usually divided and taken two to four times throughout the day. The dosage is typically reduced at a gradual pace over time to a range between 1 mg and 5 mg. Older adults usually receive lower doses that begin in the range of 1.0–2.5 mg per day. In children under age 16, the usual range is 0.25–3.5 mg per day divided into several doses. Maximum dosage is normally 10 mg per day for this age group.

This drug is also available by injection. In adults, injections into the muscle range from 1.25 to 10 mg per day divided into several doses. A long-acting injectable form can also be administered to patients who have been stabilized on the drug. The dose for the long-acting preparation ranges from 12.5 to 25 mg given every one to four weeks in adults. The dosage for children is lower in all cases.

Precautions

Though fluphenazine treats symptoms similar to those seen in **dementia**, it is not approved by the U.S. Food and Drug Administration (FDA) for this use. Elderly patients taking fluphenazine for dementia-related psychosis are at an increased risk of death.

People with a history of **depression**, lung problems, heart disease, glaucoma, **seizures**, and kidney disease should take fluphenazine only after careful evaluation by their physician. In addition, those undergoing alcohol withdrawal and those who have received **electroconvulsive therapy** should take this drug with great caution and close physician supervision after discussing the risks and benefits with their doctor. Those over age 60 and children under age 12 should take fluphenazine only after a thorough assessment by their physician. Pregnant women should use fluphenazine with great caution.

Fluphenazine may cause drowsiness. People who take this drug should not drive, operate heavy machinery, or perform other hazardous tasks requiring mental alertness until they see how the drug affects them. People taking fluphenazine should avoid significant exposure to sunlight, as the drug may cause people to sunburn more easily. This drug can sometimes change the color of urine to a pinkish or reddish-brown color. Fluphenazine use can make people more susceptible to heat and increase the risk of heatstroke. People taking fluphenazine should get up slowly after being in a reclining position because of potential dizziness.

Side effects

Relatively common side effects that accompany fluphenazine include:

- drowsiness
- dizziness
- rash
- dry mouth
- insomnia
- fatigue
- muscular weakness
- anorexia
- blurred vision
- some loss of muscular control
- amenorrhea (lack of menstruation) in women

Dystonia (difficulty walking or moving) may occur with fluphenazine use. This condition may subside in 24 to 48 hours even when the person continues taking the drug and usually disappears when fluphenazine is discontinued.

Fluphenazine use may lead to the development of symptoms that resemble Parkinson's disease. These symptoms may include a tight or mask-like expression on the face, drooling, tremors, "pill-rolling" motions in the fingers, cogwheel rigidity (abnormal rigidity in muscles characterized by jerky movements when the muscle is passively stretched), and a shuffling gait. Taking anti-Parkinson drugs **benztropine** mesylate or **trihexyphenidyl** hydrochloride along with the fluphenazine usually controls these symptoms.

KEY TERMS

Neuroleptic malignant syndrome—A complicated and potentially fatal condition characterized by muscle rigidity; high fever; alterations in mental status; and cardiac symptoms such as irregular pulse or blood pressure, sweating, tachycardia (fast heartbeat), and arrhythmias (irregular heartbeat).

Phenothiazines—Works by inhibiting the actions of the brain chemicals dopamine and norepinephrine, which are overproduced in individuals with psychosis.

Tardive dyskinesia—A syndrome consisting of involuntary, uncoordinated movements that may appear late in therapy and may not disappear even after the drug is stopped.

Fluphenazine has the potential to produce a serious side effect called **tardive dyskinesia**. This syndrome consists of involuntary, uncoordinated movements that may appear late in therapy and may not disappear even after the drug is stopped. Tardive dyskinesia involves involuntary movements of the tongue, jaw, mouth or face or other groups of skeletal muscles. The incidence of tardive dyskinesia increases with increasing age and with increasing dosage of fluphenazine. Women are at greater risk than men for developing tardive dyskinesia. There is no known effective treatment for tardive dyskinesia, although gradual (but rarely complete) improvement may occur over a long period.

An occasionally reported side effect of fluphenazine is **neuroleptic malignant syndrome**. This is a complicated and potentially fatal condition characterized by muscle rigidity; high fever; alterations in mental status; and cardiac symptoms such as irregular pulse or blood pressure, sweating, tachycardia (fast heartbeat), and arrhythmias (irregular heartbeat). People who think they may be experiencing any side effects from this or any other medication should tell their physician immediately.

Interactions

Barbiturates and the blood pressure drugs known as **beta blockers** can decrease the level of fluphenazine in the blood. Bromocriptine, a drug used for Parkinson's disease, also lowers the level of fluphenazine in the blood. Conversely, antimalarial drugs can increase the level of fluphenazine in the blood.

The combination of fluphenazine with the drugs known as cyclic **antidepressants** lowers the concentrations of both drugs in the blood. Fluphenazine inhibits the blood pressure-lowering effects of the drug called guanadrel. Levodopa, a drug given to patients with Parkinson's disease, is less effective when combined with fluphenazine. The combination of fluphenazine with meperidine can cause very low blood pressure and significant depression of the central nervous system. The use of the muscle relaxant, orphenadrine, can lower the effective levels of fluphenazine in the blood.

Resources

BOOKS

Ananth, Jambur. "Mode of Action of Antipsychotic Agents." *Trends in Schizophrenia Research,* edited by Mary V. Lang, 151–91. Hauppauge, NY: Nova Biomedical Books, 2005.

Consumer Reports Staff. *Consumer Reports Complete Drug Reference.* 2002 ed. Denver: Micromedex Thomson Healthcare, 2001.

Ellsworth, Allan J., et al. *Mosby's Medical Drug Reference.* 2001–2002 ed. St. Louis: Mosby, 2001.

Preston, John D., John H. O'Neal, and Mary C. Talaga. *Handbook of Clinical Psychopharmacology for Therapists.* 6th ed. Oakland, CA: New Harbinger, 2010.

Shanahan, James F., and Christie Naglieri, eds. *Goodman & Gilman's The Pharmacological Basis of Therapeutics.* 12th ed. New York: McGraw-Hill, 2011.

PERIODICALS

Bhagar, Harpriya A., and Alan D. Schmetzer. "The Conventional Long-Acting Antipsychotics." *Annals of the American Psychotherapy Association* 9, no. 1 (Spring 2006): 26–27.

Conley, Robert R., et al. "Risperidone, Quetiapine, and Fluphenazine in the Treatment of Patients with Therapy-Refractory Schizophrenia." *Clinical Neuropharmacology* 28, no. 4 (July/August 2005): 163–68.

Kelly, Deanna L., and Robert R. Conley. "Thyroid Function in Treatment-Resistant Schizophrenia Patients Treated with Quetiapine, Risperidone, or Fluphenazine." *Journal of Clinical Psychiatry* 66, no. 1 (January 2005): 80–84.

———. "A Randomized Double-Blind 12-Week Study of Quetiapine, Risperidone or Fluphenazine on Sexual Functioning in People with Schizophrenia." *Psychoneuroendocrinology* 31, no. 3 (April 2006): 340–46.

Stöllberger, Claudia, Johannes O. Huber, and Josef Finsterer. "Antipsychotic Drugs and QT Prolongation." *International Clinical Psychopharmacology* 20, no. 5 (September 2005): 243–51.

ORGANIZATIONS

American Psychiatric Association, 1000 Wilson Blvd., Ste. 1825, Arlington, VA, 22209-3901, (703) 907-7300, apa@psych.org, http://www.psych.org.

National Alliance on Mental Illness, 2107 Wilson Blvd., Ste. 300, Arlington, VA, 22201-3042, Fax: (703) 524-9094, (800) 950-6264, http://www.nami.org.

National Institute of Mental Health, 6001 Executive Blvd., Rm. 8184, MSC 9663, Bethesda, MD, 20892-9663, (301) 433-4513; TTY: (301) 443-8431, Fax: (301) 443-4279, (866) 615-6464; TTY: (866) 415-8051, nimhinfo@nih.gov, http://www.nimh.nih.gov.

Mark Mitchell, MD
Ruth A. Wienclaw, PhD

Flurazepam

Definition

Flurazepam is a benzodiazepine hypnotic (sleeping medication) that is given by mouth. It is sold in the United States under the brand name of Dalmane, but is also manufactured and sold by several companies under its generic name.

Purpose

Flurazepam is used for the short-term treatment of **insomnia**, a sleep disorder characterized by difficulty in falling or staying asleep.

Description

Flurazepam decreases the time it takes the patient to fall asleep and reduces the number of nighttime awakenings. Flurazepam is a member of a class of drugs called **benzodiazepines**. Such drugs are prescribed to reduce anxiety, relax the skeletal muscles, and induce sleep; other benzodiazepine hypnotics include **temazepam** (Restoril), **triazolam** (Halcion), **quazepam** (Doral), and **estazolam** (ProSom). Benzodiazepines work by enhancing the effects of a naturally occurring chemical in the body called gamma-aminobutyric acid (GABA). GABA is a neurotransmitter, a chemical that helps to conduct nerve impulses across the tiny gaps between nerve cells. GABA works to lower the level of activity in the central nervous system, promoting muscle relaxation, sedation, and sleep. It also plays a role in preventing seizure activity.

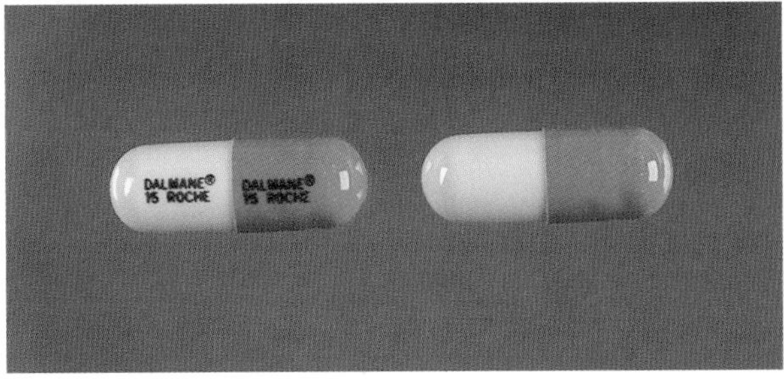

Dalmane (flurazepam), 15 mg. *(U.S. Drug Enforcement Administration)*

Flurazepam is available in 15 mg and 30 mg capsules.

Recommended dosage

The usual dose of flurazepam is 15–30 mg taken by mouth at bedtime. Older or physically weakened patients are usually given the lower dose. Children younger than 15 and women who are pregnant or nursing a baby should not be given flurazepam. In addition, the drug should not be used for longer than four weeks.

Precautions

Because flurazepam is used to help people fall asleep, it should only be taken when the patient is preparing for a full night's sleep (7 to 8 hours). Some patients taking sleep medications have engaged in sleep-related behaviors, including eating, talking, and even driving while asleep, with no recollection of the events. Some of the flurazepam is metabolized (broken down) in the body to form another compound called desalkylflurazepam, which remains in the body for a longer period of time and can cause next-day drowsiness. This kind of hangover effect is most common in people who are taking flurazepam on a daily basis. People who are taking flurazepam may not be able to safely operate machinery or drive a car the next day and should avoid these activities until they learn how the medication affects them.

Patients who take flurazepam for several days or weeks may experience a reaction called rebound insomnia when they stop taking the drug. When a person takes a medication for sleep on a regular basis, the body adjusts to the presence of the drug and tries to counteract the effects of the medication. As a result, when the person stops taking the sleeping medication, the body will take a few nights to return to its normal condition. During this period of readjustment, the person may experience a few sleepless hours each night.

Elderly patients who are taking flurazepam should be monitored for signs of dizziness or loss of coordination. They are at increased risk of falling if they wake up and get out of bed during the night to get a drink of water or use the bathroom.

Side effects

There is a risk of severe allergic reaction upon taking a sleep medication for the first time. Some people experience dizziness, daytime drowsiness, and loss of

KEY TERMS

Benzodiazepines—A group of central nervous system depressants used to relieve anxiety or to induce sleep.

Central nervous system depressant—Any drug that lowers the level of stimulation or excitement in the central nervous system.

Central nervous system stimulant—Any drug that raises the level of activity in the central nervous system.

Gamma-aminobutyric acid (GABA)—A neurotransmitter that helps to lower or reduce the level of excitement in the nerves, leading to muscle relaxation, calmness, sleep, and the prevention of seizures.

Hypnotic—A type of medication that induces sleep.

Metabolism—The group of biochemical processes within the body that release energy in support of life.

Neurotransmitter—A chemical in the brain that transmits messages between neurons, or nerve cells.

Rebound effect—A physical reaction to stopping a medication characterized by the reappearance of the symptom that the medication was given to suppress. For example, people who stop taking flurazepam may experience rebound insomnia.

coordination while they are taking flurazepam. Less common side effects include blurred vision, nausea and vomiting, diarrhea or constipation, nightmares, **depression**, and memory loss or **amnesia**.

Interactions

The effects of flurazepam may be intensified by alcoholic beverages or other central nervous system depressants, such as **sedatives** or antihistamines (allergy medications). These substances should be avoided when taking flurazepam. In addition, flurazepam may interact with antiseizure medications.

Resources

BOOKS

American Society of Health-System Pharmacists. *AHFS Drug Information 2008*. Bethesda, MD: American Society of Health-System Pharmacists, 2008.

Preston, John D., John H. O'Neal, and Mary C. Talaga. *Handbook of Clinical Psychopharmacology for Therapists*. 5th ed. Oakland, CA: New Harbinger Publications, 2008.

PERIODICALS

Blin, Olivier, et al. "A Double-Blind, Placebo- and Flurazepam-Controlled Investigation of the Residual Psychomotor and Cognitive Effects of Modified Release Zolpidem in Young Healthy Volunteers." *Journal of Clinical Psychopharmacology* 26, no. 3 (June 2006): 284–89.

Rosenberg, Russell P. "Sleep Maintenance Insomnia: Strengths and Weaknesses of Current Pharmacologic Therapies." *Annals of Clinical Psychiatry* 18, no. 1 (January–March 2006): 49–56.

Rowlett, James K., et al. "Anti-Conflict Effects of Benzodiazepines in Rhesus Monkeys: Relationship with Therapeutic Doses in Humans and Role of GABA-Sub(A) Receptors." *Psychopharmacology* 184, no. 2 (January 2006): 201–11.

Tamblyn, Robyn, et al. "A 5-Year Prospective Assessment of the Risk Associated with Individual Benzodiazepines and Doses in New Elderly Users." *Journal of the American Geriatrics Society* 53, no. 2 (February 2005): 233–41.

Thomas, Sandra P. "From the Editor—Caution Urged in Prescribing Psychotropic Drugs for Older Patients." *Issues in Mental Health Nursing* 26, no. 4 (May 2005): 357–58.

Jack Raber, Pharm.D.
Ruth A. Wienclaw, PhD

Fluvoxamine

Definition

Fluvoxamine is an antidepressant of the type known as **selective serotonin reuptake inhibitors** (SSRI). It is marketed in the United States under the brand name Luvox.

Purpose

Fluvoxamine is used to treat **obsessive-compulsive disorder** (OCD). It was the first SSRI to be approved by the U. S. Food and Drug Administration (FDA) for treating OCD in children, adolescents, and adults. It may also be prescribed off-label for treating **depression**, but it is not approved by the FDA for this purpose.

Description

Serotonin is a **brain** chemical that carries nerve impulses from one nerve cell to another. Researchers think that depression and certain other mental disorders may be caused, in part, by there not being enough serotonin

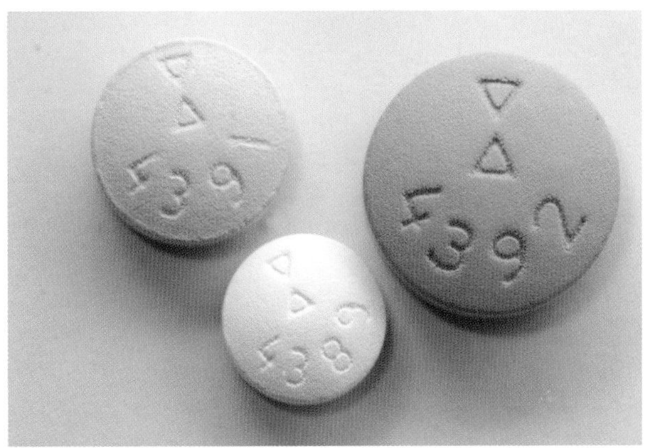

Fluvoxamine, 25, 50, and 100 mg. *(© Custom Medical Stock Photo, Inc. Reproduced by permission.)*

released and transmitted in the brain. Like the other SSRI **antidepressants**, **fluoxetine** (Prozac), **sertraline** (Zoloft), and **paroxetine** (Paxil), fluvoxamine increases the level of brain serotonin (also known as 5-HT). Increased serotonin levels in the brain may be beneficial in patients with OCD, alcoholism, certain types of headaches, **post-traumatic stress disorder** (PTSD), premenstrual tension and mood swings, and **panic disorder**.

Fluvoxamine was approved for use in adults in 1993. In 1997, the FDA approved this medication for the treatment of OCD in children and adolescents.

Fluvoxamine is available in 25, 50 and 100 mg tablets.

Recommended dosage

Fluvoxamine therapy in adults is started as a single 50 mg dose taken at bedtime. Based on the patient's response to the medication, the dosage can be increased by 50 mg every four to seven days, until maximum benefit is achieved. Maximum dosage is 300 mg per day. Dosage over 100 mg per day should be given as equally divided morning and afternoon doses.

Fluvoxamine therapy in children is started as a single 25 mg dose, initially taken at bedtime. Based on the patient's response to the medication, the dosage can be increased by 25 mg every four to seven days, until maximum benefit is achieved. Maximum dosage in children is 200 mg per day. Dosage over 100 mg per day should be given as equally divided morning and afternoon doses.

Precautions

Patients taking fluvoxamine should be monitored closely for the onset of mania, **seizures**, thoughts of **suicide**, and skin problems (including itching, hives, and rashes).

People with impaired liver function, **bipolar disorder** (manic depression), a history of seizures, or individuals contemplating suicide should take fluvoxamine only under close physician supervision.

A group of serious side effects, called **serotonin syndrome**, has resulted from the combination of SSRI drugs such as fluvoxamine and members of another class of antidepressants known as **monoamine oxidase inhibitors (MAOIs)**. Serotonin syndrome usually consists of at least three of the following symptoms:

- diarrhea
- fever
- extreme perspiration
- mood or behavior changes
- overactive reflexes
- fast heart rate
- restlessness
- shivering or shaking

Because of this risk, fluvoxamine should never be taken in combination with **MAOIs**. People taking any MAOI, for example, **phenelzine** sulfate (Nardil) or **tranylcypromine** sulfate (Parnate), should stop the MAOI inhibitor and wait at least 14 days before starting fluvoxamine or any other antidepressant. The same holds true when discontinuing fluvoxamine before starting an MAOI.

Physicians and their patients should weigh the risks and benefits of this drug for women who are or wish to become pregnant, as well as for women who are breastfeeding.

Until patients understand the effects that fluvoxamine may have on them, they should avoid driving, operating dangerous machinery, or participating in hazardous activities.

Like other **SSRIs**, fluvoxamine carries a warning regarding use in children and young people up to 24 years of age, who may be at risk for increased suicidal thoughts and actions during treatment, especially during the first few months. Persons with a personal history or family history of bipolar disorder or who have previously attempted or considered suicide are also at increased risk.

People should not use alcohol while taking fluvoxamine. Fluvoxamine treatment should not be abruptly discontinued.

Side effects

Common side effects of fluvoxamine therapy include decreased sex drive and diminished sexual performance.

Less common side effects of fluvoxamine therapy are changes in mood, behavior, or thinking; difficulty breathing; difficulty urinating; and twitches or uncontrollable movements of the face or body.

Rare side effects include:

- difficulty moving
- blurred vision
- clumsiness or problems with balance
- seizures
- difficulty moving the eyes
- increased uncontrollable movements of the body or face
- changes in the menstrual period
- redness or irritation of the eyes or skin
- peeling, itching, or burning sensation of the skin
- sore throat
- fever, and/or chills
- easy bruising
- nosebleeds
- in women, abnormal milk production

People may also experience symptoms of serotonin syndrome, which usually consists of at least three of the following:

- restlessness
- overexcitement
- irritability
- confusion
- diarrhea
- fever
- overactive reflexes
- difficulty with coordination
- uncontrollable shivering or shaking
- trembling or twitching

Interactions

Fluvoxamine interacts with a long list of other medications. Individuals who are starting this drug should review the other medications they are taking with their physician and pharmacist for possible interactions. Patients should always inform all their healthcare providers, including dentists, that they are taking fluvoxamine.

KEY TERMS

Off-label—The use of a prescription medication to treat conditions outside the indications approved by the Food and Drug Administration (FDA). It is legal for physicians to administer these drugs, but it is not legal for pharmaceutical companies to advertise drugs for off-label uses.

Serotonin—A brain chemical that carries nerve impulses from one nerve cell to another.

Serotonin syndrome—A condition that results from the combination of SSRI drugs such as fluvoxamine and members of another class of antidepressants known as monoamine oxidase inhibitors (MAOIs).

When taken together with fluvoxamine, the effect of the following drugs may be enhanced: **benzodiazepines**, **beta blockers**, **clozapine**, antiseizure drugs phenytoin and **carbamazepine**, tricyclic antidepressants, **pimozide**, and cholesterol-lowering drugs such as atorvastatin, lovastatin, and simvastatin.

The diet pills dexfenfluramine and fenfluramine may increase the incidence of serotonin syndrome when taken with fluvoxamine.

When **buspirone** is given with fluvoxamine, the therapeutic effect of buspirone may be decreased and the risk of seizures increased.

Increased risk of mania and high blood pressure occurs with selegiline.

Severe, fatal reactions mentioned above have occurred when fluvoxamine is given along with MAOIs.

Fluvoxamine given with warfarin (a blood thinner) may increase the possibility of bleeding.

Resources

BOOKS

Preston, John D., John H. O'Neal, and Mary C. Talaga. *Handbook of Clinical Psychopharmacology for Therapists.* 6th ed. Oakland, CA: New Harbinger, 2010.

PERIODICALS

Albers, Lawrence J., et al. "Low-Dose Fluvoxamine as an Adjunct to Reduce Olanzapine Therapeutic Dose Requirements: A Prospective Dose-Adjusted Drug Interaction Strategy." *Journal of Clinical Psychopharmacology* 25, no. 2 (April 2005): 170–74.

Erzegovesi, Stefano, et al. "Low-Dose Risperidone Augmentation of Fluvoxamine Treatment in Obsessive-Compulsive Disorder: A Double-Blind, Placebo-Controlled Study." *European Neuropsychopharmacology* 15, no. 1 (January 2005): 69–74.

Ginsburg, Golda S., Mark A. Riddle, and Mark Davies. "Somatic Symptoms in Children and Adolescents with Anxiety Disorders." *Journal of the American Academy of Child and Adolescent Psychiatry* 45, no. 10 (October 2006): 1179–87.

Husted, David S., et al. "Effect of Comorbid Tics on a Clinically Meaningful Response to 8-Week Open-Label Trial of Fluoxetine in Obsessive-Compulsive Disorder." *Journal of Psychiatric Research* 41, no. 3–4 (April–June 2007): 332–37.

Irons, Jane. "Fluvoxamine in the Treatment of Anxiety Disorders." *Neuropsychiatric Disease and Treatment* 1, no. 4 (2005): 289–99.

Mandelli, Laura, et al. "Improvement of Cognitive Functioning in Mood Disorder Patients with Depressive Symptomatic Recovery During Treatment: An Exploratory Analysis." *Psychiatry and Clinical Neurosciences* 60, no. 5 (October 2006): 598–604.

Morishita, Shigeru, and Seizaburo Arita. "Clinical Characteristics as Predictors of Response to Fluvoxamine, Paroxetine, and Milnacipran in Patients with Depression." *Current Psychiatry Reviews* 1, no. 3 (November 2005): 319–24.

———. "Treatment of Bipolar II Depression with Milnacipran, Fluvoxamine, Paroxetine, or Maprotiline." *International Medical Journal* 12, no. 4 (Dec. 2005): 283–85.

O'Connor, K.P., et al. "Cognitive Behaviour Therapy and Medication in the Treatment of Obsessive-Compulsive Disorder." *Acta Psychiatrica Scandinavica* 113, no. 5 (May 2006): 408–19.

Preskorn, Sheldon H., et al. "The Potential for Clinically Significant Drug-Drug Interactions Involving the CYP 2D6 System: Effects with Fluoxetine and Paroxetine Versus Sertraline." *Journal of Psychiatric Practice* 13, no. 1 (January 2007): 5–12.

Schreiber, Shaul, and Chaim G. Pick. "From Selective to Highly Selective SSRIs: A Comparison of the Antinociceptive Properties of Fluoxetine, Fluvoxamine, Citalopram and Escitalopram." *European Neuropsychopharmacology* 16, no. 6 (August 2006): 464–68.

Van Oppen, Patricia, et al. "Cognitive Therapy and Exposure in Vivo Alone and in Combination With Fluvoxamine in Obsessive-Compulsive Disorder: A 5-Year Follow-Up." *Journal of Clinical Psychiatry* 66, no. 11 (November 2005): 1415–22.

Yoshimura, Reiji, et al. "Successful Treatment for Obsessive-Compulsive Disorder with Addition of Low-Dose Risperidone to Fluvoxamine: Implications for Plasma Levels of Catecholamine Metabolites and Serum Brain-Derived Neurotrophic Factor Levels." *Psychiatry and Clinical Neurosciences* 60, no. 3 (June 2006): 389–93.

ORGANIZATIONS

American Psychiatric Association, 1000 Wilson Blvd., Ste. 1825, Arlington, VA, 22209-3901, (703) 907-7300, apa@psych.org, http://www.psych.org.

National Alliance on Mental Illness, 2107 Wilson Blvd., Ste. 300, Arlington, VA, 22201-3042, Fax: (703) 524-9094, (800) 950-6264, http://www.nami.org.

National Institute of Mental Health, 6001 Executive Blvd., Rm. 8184, MSC 9663, Bethesda, MD, 20892-9663, (301) 433-4513; TTY: (301) 443-8431, Fax: (301) 443-4279, (866) 615-6464; TTY: (866) 415-8051, nimhinfo@nih.gov, http://www.nimh.nih.gov.

Rosalyn Carson-DeWitt, MD
Ruth A. Wienclaw, PhD

Focalin, Focalin XR *see* **Dexmethylphenidate**

Folie á deux *see* **Shared psychotic disorder**

Folstein mini-mental state examination *see* **Mini-mental state examination**

Frontal lobe dementias *see* **Dementia**

Frontotemporal dementia *see* **Pick's disease**

Frotteurism

Definition

Frotteurism is a disorder in which a person derives sexual pleasure or gratification from rubbing, especially the genitals, against another person, usually in a crowd. The person being rubbed is a victim. Frotteurism is a paraphilia, a disorder that is characterized by recurrent intense sexual urges and sexually arousing fantasies generally involving objects, the suffering or humiliation of oneself or one's partner (not merely simulated), or children or other nonconsenting people.

Demographics

Males are much more likely to engage in frotteurism than females. Females are the most common victims of frotteurism. Most acts of frotteurism are performed by people between 15 to 25 years of age. After the age of 25, the acts decline.

Description

The primary focus of frotteurism is touching or rubbing one's genitals against the clothing or body of a nonconsenting person. This behavior most often occurs in situations that allow rapid escape. The frottage (the act of rubbing against the other person) is most commonly practiced in crowded places such as malls, elevators, on busy sidewalks, and on public transportation vehicles.

The most commonly practiced form of frotteurism is rubbing one's genitals against the victim's thighs or buttocks. A common alternative is to rub one's hands over the victim's genitals or breasts.

Most people who engage in frotteurism (sometimes called frotteurs) usually fantasize that they have an exclusive and caring relationship with their victims during the moment of contact. However, once contact is made and broken, the person committing the act realizes that escape is important to avoid prosecution.

Causes and symptoms

Causes

There is no scientific consensus concerning the cause of frotteurism. Most experts attribute the behavior to an initially random or accidental touching of another's genitals that the person finds sexually exciting. Successive repetitions of the act tend to reinforce and perpetuate the behavior.

Symptoms

For the disorder to be clinically diagnosed, the symptoms must meet the diagnostic criteria as listed in the professional's handbook, the ***Diagnostic and Statistical Manual of Mental Disorders.*** These symptoms include:

- experiencing recurrent, intense, or sexually arousing fantasies, sexual urges, or behaviors that involve touching and rubbing against a nonconsenting person
- acting on these sexual urges, or the fantasies or urges cause significant distress to the individual or are disruptive to his everyday functioning

Diagnosis

Most people with frotteurism never seek professional help, but people with the disorder may come into the mental health system as a result of a court order. The **diagnosis** is established in an interview between the person accused of frotteurism and the mental health professional (a **psychiatrist** or a **psychologist**, for example). In the interview, the individual acknowledges that touching others is a preferred or exclusive means of sexual gratification. Because this acknowledgment can bring criminal charges, the disorder is underdiagnosed and its prevalence is largely unknown. In some cases, other people besides the accused may be interviewed, including observers or the victim.

Treatment

For treatment to be successful, the patient must want to modify existing patterns of behavior. This initial step is difficult for most people with this disorder to take.

KEY TERMS

Frottage—The act of touching or rubbing against the body or genitals of a nonconsenting individual.

Paraphilia—A disorder that is characterized by recurrent intense sexual urges and sexually arousing fantasies generally involving (1) nonhuman objects, (2) the suffering or humiliation of oneself or one's partner (not merely simulated), or (3) children or other nonconsenting people.

Behavior therapy is commonly used to try to treat frotteurism. The patient must learn to control the impulse to touch nonconsenting victims. One pharmacological therapy that has been tried with some success in people who engage in frotteurism and other **paraphilias** is leuprolide. The action of this drug ultimately results in suppression of testosterone production, with the effect of reducing sexual urges.

Frotteurism is a criminal act in many jurisdictions. It is usually classified as a misdemeanor. As a result, legal penalties are often minor. It is also not easy to prosecute people who are charged with frotteurism because intent to touch is difficult to prove. In their defense statements, the accused often claim that the contact was accidental.

Prognosis

The prognosis for eliminating frotteurism is poor as most people who engage in the behavior have no desire to change it. Because frotteurism involves nonconsenting partners and is against the law in many jurisdictions, the possibility of embarrassment may deter some individuals.

Prevention

Most experts agree that providing guidance as to behavior that is culturally acceptable will prevent the development of a paraphilia such as frotteurism. The origin of some instances of frotteurism may be a truly accidental contact that becomes associated with sexual gratification. There is no way to predict when such an association will occur.

Resources

BOOKS

American Psychiatric Association. *Diagnostic and Statistical Manual of Mental Disorders*. 4th ed., text rev. Washington, DC: American Psychiatric Publishing, 2000.

Gelder, Michael, Paul Harrison, and Philip Cowen. *Shorter Oxford Textbook of Psychiatry*. 5th ed. New York: Oxford University Press, 2006.

Kohut, John J., and Roland Sweet. *Real Sex: Titillating but True Tales of Bizarre Fetishes, Strange Compulsions, and Just Plain Weird Stuff.* New York: Penguin Group, 2000.

Wilson, Josephine F. *Biological Foundations of Human Behavior*. Farmington Hills, MI: Cengage Learning, 2002.

PERIODICALS

Eiguer, A. "Cynicism: Its Function in the Perversions." *International Journal of Psychoanalysis* 80, no. 4 (1999): 671–84.

Rosler, A., and E. Witztum. "Pharmacotherapy of Paraphilias in the Next Millennium." *Behavioral Sciences & the Law* 18, no. 1 (January/February 2000): 43–56.

Schober, Justine M., Peter M. Byrne, and Phyllis J. Kuhn. "Leuprolide Acetate is a Familiar Drug that May Modify Sex-Offender Behavior: The Urologist's Role." *BJU International* 97, no. 4 (April 2006) 684–86.

Seelig, B.J., and L.S. Rosof. "Normal and Pathological Altruism." *Journal of the American Psychoanalytic Association* 49, no. 3 (2001): 933–59.

ORGANIZATIONS

American Psychiatric Association, 1000 Wilson Blvd., Ste. 1825, Arlington, VA, 22209-3901, (703) 907-7300, apa@psych.org, http://www.psych.org.

American Psychological Association, 750 1st St. NE, Washington, DC, 20002-4242, (202) 336-5500; TDD/TTY: (202) 336-6123, (800) 374-2721, http://www.apa.org.

L.Fleming Fallon, Jr., MD, Dr.P.H.
Emily Jane Willingham, PhD

Fugue *see* **Dissociative fugue**

G

Gabapentin

Definition

Gabapentin is an antiseizure medication. It is sold in the United States under the trade name Neurontin.

Purpose

Gabapentin is used in combination with other antiseizure (anticonvulsant) drugs to manage partial **seizures** with or without generalization in individuals over the age of 12. Gabapentin can also be used to treat partial seizures in children between the ages of 3 and 12. Off-label uses (legal uses not approved by the U.S. Food and Drug Administration [FDA]) include treatment of severe, chronic pain caused by nerve damage, such as occurs in shingles, diabetic neuropathy, multiple sclerosis, or post-herpetic neuralgia. Gabapentin was previously studied in the treatment of **bipolar disorder** but did not show any effectiveness in **clinical trials**.

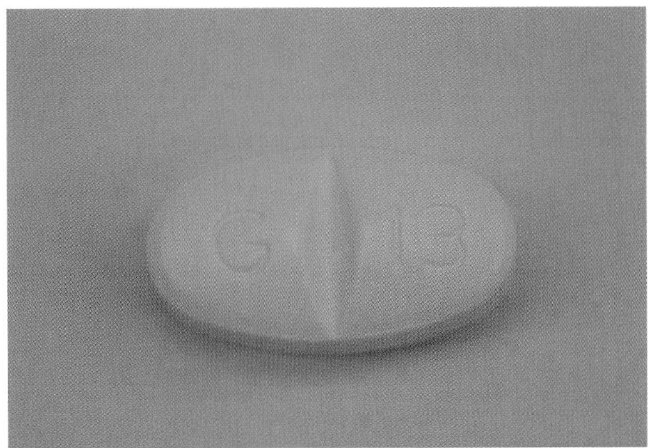

Gabapentin, 800 mg. *(© Custom Medical Stock Photo, Inc. Reproduced by permission.)*

Description

Brain cells normally transmit nerve impulses from one cell to another by secreting chemicals known as **neurotransmitters**. Gabapentin is chemically related to a naturally occurring neurotransmitter called GABA (gamma-amino butyric acid). The actual mechanism of action by which gabapentin acts in the brain to control seizures and treat pain is not known, although it appears to alter the action of nerve cells.

Gabapentin was approved for use in the United States in 1993. A liquid formulation was approved for use in 2000. Use in children ages 3 to 12 was also approved by the FDA in 2000.

Gabapentin is available in 100, 300, and 400 mg capsules; in 600 and 800 mg tablets; and in a liquid solution containing 250 mg per 5 mL.

Recommended dosage

For epilepsy

People over the age of 12 can begin with an initial does of 300 mg three times a day, which can be gradually increased as necessary, usually to no more than 1,800 mg daily. For children ages 3 to 12, the dose is based on body weight, initially 10–15 mg per kilogram per day in three separate doses. The physician may choose to increase this dose as necessary. For a child under the age of 3, the decision about use and dosage will be made by the doctor. For older adults, the maximum daily dose does not usually exceed 600 mg three times a day.

For pain

This dosing involves a gradual increase, with an initial does of 300 mg on the first day, followed by 300 mg twice on the second day, and 300 mg three times on day three. A physician may increase this dose to a maximum daily dose of 1,800 mg.

Precautions

Women who are breast-feeding and people with decreased kidney functioning should discuss the risks and benefits of this drug with their physician. Women who are or wish to become pregnant will also require a careful assessment of the risks and benefits of gabapentin.

Patients should not suddenly discontinue gabapentin, which can result in an increased risk of seizures. If the medication needs to be discontinued, the dosage should be reduced gradually over a week.

Until an individual understands the effects that gabapentin may have, he or she should avoid driving, operating dangerous machinery, or participating in hazardous activities. Alcohol should be avoided while taking gabapentin.

Some patients taking gabapentin have shown changes in their mental health, including the development of suicidal thoughts and behavior. If patients taking gabapentin exhibit any changes in mood or behavior they (or their caregivers) should contact their physician.

Side effects

Multiple side effects often occur when a patient starts taking gabapentin. While these side effects usually go away on their own, if they last or are particularly troublesome, the patient should consult a doctor. More common side effects that occur when first starting to take gabapentin include blurred or double vision; muscle weakness or pain; swollen hands, feet, or legs; trembling or shaking; increased **fatigue** or weakness; unsteadiness; clumsiness; and uncontrollable back-and-forth eye movements or eye rolling. Less common side effects include back pain, constipation, decreased sexual drive, diarrhea, dry mouth and eyes, frequent urination, headache, indigestion, low blood pressure, nausea, ringing in the ears, runny nose, slurred speech, difficulty thinking and sleeping, weight gain, twitching, nausea and/or vomiting, weakness, **depression**, irritability, other mood changes or changes in thinking, and decreased memory. Rare side effects include pain in the lower back or side, difficulty urinating, fever and/or chills, cough, or hoarseness.

Children under age 12 who have the following more common side effects should see a doctor immediately: aggressive behavior, irritability, anxiety, difficulty concentrating and paying attention, crying, depression, mood swings, increased emotionality, hyperactivity, and suspiciousness or distrust.

KEY TERMS

Diabetic neuropathy—A condition in which the nerve endings, particularly in the legs and feet, become less sensitive. Minor injuries, such as blisters or callouses, are not felt and can thus become infected and become more serious problems.

Multiple sclerosis—A disease characterized by patches of hardened tissue in the brain or spinal cord, paralysis, and/or muscle tremors.

Neuralgia—Pain that extends along the course of a nerve.

Neurotransmitter—A chemical in the brain that transmits messages between neurons, or nerve cells.

Interactions

Antacids can decrease gabapentin levels in the blood. They should be taken at least two hours before taking gabapentin.

Resources

BOOKS

Ellsworth, Allan J., et al. *Mosby's Medical Drug Reference.* St. Louis, MO: Mosby, 2007.

PERIODICALS

Vieta, Eduard, et al. "A Double-Blind, Randomized Placebo-Controlled, Prophylaxis Study of Adjunctive Gabapentin for Bipolar Disorder." *Journal of Clinical Psychiatry* 67, no. 3 (March 2006): 473–77.

WEBSITES

MedlinePlus. "Gabapentin." National Library of Medicine, National Institutes of Health. September 22, 2011. http://www.nlm.nih.gov/medlineplus/druginfo/meds/a694007.html (accessed October 7, 2011).

Rosalyn Carson-DeWitt, MD
Emily Jane Willingham, PhD

Galantamine

Definition

Galantamine belongs to a class of drugs called acetylcholinesterase inhibitors. In the United States, galantamine is sold under the brand name Razadyne (formerly Reminyl).

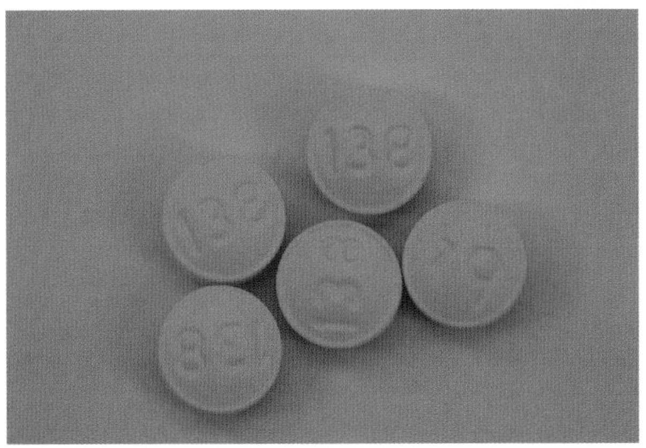

Galantamine, 4 mg. *(© Custom Medical Stock Photo, Inc. Reproduced by permission.)*

Purpose

Galantamine is used to treat the symptoms of **Alzheimer's disease** (AD).

Description

Alzheimer's disease develops when **brain** cells, called neurons, undergo an early death. Though AD cannot be cured, it is thought that the premature death of these neurons may be prevented or slowed if stimulated by a brain chemical called acetylcholine. Acetylcholine is recycled by an enzyme called acetylcholinesterase. Galantamine works by inhibiting this enzyme. The inhibition of acetylcholinesterase increases the concentration of available acetylcholine.

Galantamine has only been studied and is only used, in patients with mild-to-moderate AD according to the Alzheimer's Disease Assessment Scale. It is not used in patients with severe AD.

Galantamine is available in 4 mg, 8 mg, and 12 mg tablets.

Recommended dosage

The recommended initial dose of galantamine in adults is 4 mg twice daily. After a minimum of four weeks of treatment with galantamine, the dosage may be increased to 8 mg twice daily. Further increases to 12 mg twice daily should be initiated only after a minimum of four weeks at the previous dose.

Increased side effects associated with higher doses may prevent the increase in dose in some patients. Patients with moderate liver or kidney problems should not exceed 16 mg of galantamine daily.

KEY TERMS

Acetylcholine—A naturally occurring chemical in the body that transmits nerve impulses from cell to cell. Acetylcholine causes blood vessels to dilate, lowers blood pressure, and slows the heartbeat. Central nervous system well-being is dependent on a balance among the neurotransmitters acetylcholine, dopamine, serotonin, and norepinephrine.

Acetylcholinesterase—The chemical responsible for the breakdown of acetylcholine.

Parkinson's disease—A disease of the nervous system most common in people over age 60, characterized by a shuffling gait, trembling of the fingers and hands, and muscle stiffness.

Precautions

Galantamine should not be used in patients with severe liver or kidney problems. Since there are no well-controlled studies for the use of galantamine in pregnancy, galantamine should only be used if the potential benefits justify the potential risks to the fetus.

Patients who are undergoing anesthesia or bladder or gastrointestinal surgery should take galantamine only after a discussion with their physician. Patients with gastrointestinal problems should be closely monitored if it is decided that they should take galantamine. Galantamine should also be used under close physician supervision in patients who have Parkinson's disease, severe asthma, or chronic obstructive pulmonary disease. Because galantamine may slow down the heart, patients with any heart conditions, and especially patients taking other medications that slow down the heart, should be evaluated before taking galantamine.

Side effects

The most common side effects reported with the use of galantamine are nausea, vomiting, diarrhea, loss of appetite, and abdominal pain. These occur most often during dosage escalation. The average duration of nausea is five to seven days. Side effects tend to be less frequent if the patient is taking a total daily dosage of 16 mg. Eleven percent of patients receiving 24 mg daily lose weight, while 6% of patients receiving 16 mg daily experience weight loss.

Other common side effects include dizziness, headache, tremors, **fatigue**, **depression**, agitation, irritation, and **insomnia**. These side effects have a higher incidence and severity if higher doses are used. If side effects become severe, the dosage should be adjusted downward under physician supervision.

Interactions

There is currently little data regarding potential drug interactions with galantamine. Medications that are known to increase levels of galantamine in the body include cimetidine, erythromycin, ketoconazole, and **paroxetine**.

Resources

PERIODICALS

Ancoli-Israel, Sonia, et al. "Effects of Galantamine Versus Donepezil on Sleep in Patients with Mild to Moderate Alzheimer Disease and Their Caregivers: A Double-Blind, Head-To-Head, Randomized Pilot Study." *Alzheimer Disease & Associated Disorders* 19, no. 4 (October/December 2005): 240–45.

Biederman, Joseph, et al. "A Double-Blind Comparison of Galantamine Hydrogen Bromide and Placebo in Adults with Attention-Deficit/Hyperactivity Disorder: A Pilot Study." *Journal of Clinical Psychopharmacology* 26, no. 2 (April 2006): 163–66.

Brodaty, Henry, et al. "Galantamine Prolonged-Release Formulation in the Treatment of Mild to Moderate Alzheimer's Disease." *Dementia and Geriatric Cognitive Disorders* 20, no. 2–3 (August 2005): 120–32.

Harry, Robin D. J., and Konstantine K. Zakzanis. "A Comparison of Donepezil and Galantamine in the treatment of Cognitive Symptoms of Alzheimer's Disease: A Meta-Analysis." *Human Psychopharmacology: Clinical and Experimental* 20, no. 3 (April 2005): 183–87.

Koontz, Jennifer, and Andrius Baskys. "Effects of Galantamine on Working Memory and Global Functioning in Patients with Mild Cognitive Impairment: A Double-Blind Placebo-Controlled Study." *American Journal of Alzheimer's Disease and Other Dementias* 20, no. 5 (September/October 2005): 295–302.

López-Pousa, S., et al. "Differential Efficacy of Treatment with Acetylcholinesterase Inhibitors in Patients with Mild and Moderate Alzheimer's Disease Over a 6-Month Period." *Dementia and Geriatric Cognitive Disorders* 19, no. 4 (March 2005): 189–95.

Ochoa, Enrique L. M. "Galantamine May Improve Attention and Speech in Schizophrenia." *Human Psychopharmacology: Clinical and Experimental* 21, no. 2 (March 2006): 127–28.

Robinson, Dean M., and Greg L. Plosker. "Galantamine Extended Release in Alzheimer's Disease: Profile Report." *Drugs and Aging* 23, no. 10 (2006): 839–42.

Rockwood, Kenneth, et al. "Attainment of Treatment Goals by People with Alzheimer's Disease Receiving Galantamine: A Randomized Controlled Trial." *Canadian Medical Association Journal* 174, no. 8 (April 11, 2006): 1099–1105.

Schubert, Max H., Keith A. Young, and Paul B. Hicks. "Galantamine Improves Cognition in Schizophrenic Patients Stabilized on Risperidone." *Biological Psychiatry* 60, no. 6 (September 2006): 530–33.

Takeda, A., et al. "A Systematic Review of the Clinical Effectiveness of Donepezil, Rivastigmine and Galantamine on Cognition, Quality of Life and Adverse Events in Alzheimer's Disease." *International Journal of Geriatric Psychiatry* 21, no. 1 (January 2006): 17–28.

WEBSITES

Ortho-McNeil Neurologics, Inc. "Full U.S. Prescribing Information for Razadyne." http://www.razadyneer360.com/full-prescribing-information.html (accessed October 7, 2011).

Ajna Hamidovic, Pharm.D.
Ruth A. Wienclaw, PhD

Gambling disorder

Definition

Gambling disorder (GD), sometimes also called pathological gambling disorder, occurs when a person gambles compulsively to such an extent that the wagering has a severe negative effect on his or her job or career, relationships, mental health, or other important aspects of life. The person may continue to gamble even after they have developed social, economic, interpersonal, or legal problems as a result of the gambling.

The related medical term "ludomania" is defined as a progressive urge to gamble, one that eventually becomes a gambling disorder characterized by frequent, uncontrollable episodes of compulsive gambling. Medical professionals can **diagnosis** clinical pathological

A man plays a slot machine in a casino. *(© Mika/Corbis)*

gambling when the patient meets certain criteria. Such problem gambling is considered an impulse control disorder in medicine.

Demographics

About twice as many males as females in the United States are diagnosed with gambling disorder. Relatively few women, however, are in treatment programs for the disorder, probably because of the greater social **stigma** attached to women who gamble. As a rule, men diagnosed with gambling disorder began gambling as teenagers, whereas women tend to start compulsive gambling at a later age and develop a gambling problem faster than men. In addition, women are developing a gambling disorder at rates that are up to 25% higher than are men. Gambling disorder also tends to be more common in minority groups and in people of a lower socioeconomic status. About 25% of people diagnosed as pathological gamblers had a parent with the disorder. People who smoke tobacco or abuse alcohol are more likely to have GD than people who do not use these substances.

As much as 5% of the general population in the United States may meet criteria for gambling disorder at some point in their lives. In some countries, such as Australia, the number is thought to be as high as 7%.

Description

Gambling disorder is characterized by uncontrollable gambling well beyond the point of a social or recreational activity, such that the gambling has a major disruptive effect on the gambler's life. People who are pathological gamblers may lose their life savings and may even commit crimes (e.g., stealing, embezzling, or forging checks) to get money for their "habit." Relationships and jobs may also be lost as a result of the disorder.

Gambling disorder is sometimes considered as an example of a process, or behavioral, **addiction**, which is as distinct from an addiction to such substances as food, drugs, tobacco, or alcohol. In process addictions, the characteristic "rush" or "high" comes from the series of steps or actions that are involved in the addictive behavior. With gambling, the "high" may be stimulated by the social atmosphere or group setting of the casino, race track, or bingo hall as well as by the excitement of risk-taking. Some gamblers have a "lucky" outfit, item of clothing, or accessory that they wear or take along when gambling; sometimes putting on the outfit or item in question is enough to start the "rush."

People with gambling disorder may engage in many different types of gambling activities. These may include games of chance that are found in casinos, such as slot machines, card games, and roulette. Many of these games are now available on the Internet, the chief difference being that the bettor uses a credit card instead of cash or chips. Other gambling activities may include the state lottery, horse or dog racing, or bingo. The person may place bets on the outcome of an election, baseball or football games, or even the weather on a particular day. Pathological gambling usually develops slowly; people tend to begin with acceptable levels of social or recreational gambling and slowly progress to pathological gambling. In most cases the disorder develops slowly over a period of years; however, there are cases of patients who gambled socially for decades and then began to gamble compulsively under the impact of a major life stressor, such as divorce or being laid off from work.

The **American Psychiatric Association**, through its upcoming *Diagnostic and Statistical Manual of Mental Disorders 5* (*DSM-5*), has proposed to reclassify gambling disorder from the category Impulse-Control Disorders Not Elsewhere Classified to the category Substance-Related Disorders, which will be renamed Addiction and Related Disorders. The revised version (*DSM-5*) of the ***Diagnostic and Statistical Manual of Mental Disorders*** is scheduled to be available in 2013.

Causes and symptoms

Causes

Gambling disorder is considered a **brain** disease similar to other disorders of addiction, like alcohol or drug addiction. The primary mechanism underlying the development and persistence of pathological gambling is the brain's dopamine-based reward system, which is thought to underlie many disorders of addiction or impulse control. The central pathway involved is the mesolimbic pathway of **dopamine** signaling. This pathway exhibits alterations in dopamine levels or signaling in response to some substances; and a similar dopamine response is thought by medical professionals to underlie process addictions, including pathological gambling. The key feature in the brain involved in this process is the nucleus accumbens.

There also are significant psychological factors that may contribute to excessive gambling, often associated with the common comorbidities of pathological gambling, including **depression** and substance use disorder. People who are pathological gamblers may use gambling as an emotional escape from depression; this pattern appears more often in females with the disorder than in males. Some people who are pathological gamblers seek the mood alteration associated with gambling—specifically the excitement and energy that they find in the activity—more than the money involved. In other words, the person with the disorder is reinforced by an emotional "high" rather than by the money itself. Some researchers have found that males diagnosed with gambling disorder were more likely to have been diagnosed with **attention deficit hyperactivity disorder (ADHD)** as children than males in the general population. Other researchers have described compulsive gamblers in general as highly competitive people who are restless and easily bored. People with this disorder exhibit many features in common with those who have substance use disorder, including the urge to engage in the behavior, mounting tension before engaging in the behavior, relief or euphoria during the behavior, a return of the urge, and the presence of external cues that may trigger the behavior.

Other theories about the causes of gambling disorder emphasize cognitive distortions rather than mood problems. Pathological gambling has been associated with dysfunctional thinking patterns; many people with this disorder are highly superstitious or believe that they can control the outcome of events when they are gambling. Many people diagnosed with the disorder also have distorted beliefs about money, tending to see it at the same time as the source of all their problems and the answer to all their problems.

One social change that has been linked with the rise in the number of adults diagnosed with gambling disorder in the United States is the increased availability of legalized gambling. Some studies show that proximity to a casino is associated with increased rates of pathological gambling in a population. However, other studies show the opposite. For instance, a 2008 study in the journal *Psychology of Addictive Behaviors* found that the rates of pathological gambling were not higher near a casino when compared to rates away from such establishments. The study did find, however, that participation and monetary expenditures in gambling establishments were higher the closer in distance individuals were to gambling places.

Symptoms

The symptoms of pathological gambling include preoccupation with gambling activity, often to the extent of interfering with the person's occupational or social functioning. The person often cannot control the gambling behavior, continuing to place bets or go to casinos in spite of attempts to cut back or stop. One common behavior in persons with gambling disorder is "chasing," which refers to betting larger sums of money or taking greater risks in order to undo or make up for previous losses. The person may also lie about his or her gambling or engage in such antisocial behaviors as stealing, credit card fraud, check forgery, embezzling from an employer, or similar dishonest behaviors in order to obtain more money for gambling.

KEY TERMS

Dopamine—A chemical neurotransmitting compound found in the brain that is a precursor of epinephrine.

Functional magnetic resonance imaging—A special type of magnetic resonance imaging (MRI) scan that measures changes in blood flow and blood oxygenation within the body; often abbreviated fMRI.

Histrionic—Relating to being very dramatic or excessive in behavior.

Narcissistic—Relating to a personality disorder in which an individual overestimates his or her own abilities or appearance, such as an extraordinary ability to win at gambling.

Nucleus accumbens—Abbreviated NAcc and also known as accumbens nucleus, is a part of the brain reward system, located in the limbic system, that processes information related to motivation and reward.

Opioid antagonist—A type of receptor antagonist (drug) that acts on opioid receptors.

Pathological—Uncontrollable in nature; relating to disease.

Diagnosis

Pathological gambling disorder is more likely to be diagnosed when the affected person's spouse or family becomes concerned than to be self-reported. **Denial** is common among persons with the disorder. The professional handbook, the *Diagnostic and Statistical Manual of Mental Disorders*, fourth edition, text revision (*DSM-IV-TR*) specifies that the patient must have at least five of the following symptoms to meet criteria for the disorder:

- thinks about gambling all the time
- uses larger and larger amounts of money when gambling
- has tried to stop gambling but failed
- is moody or cranky when trying to stop gambling
- uses gambling as a way to escape problems
- keeps gambling to try to make back money that had previously been lost ("chasing")

- lies about the extent of gambling
- has tried to make money for gambling by engaging in illegal or immoral behavior
- has problems at work or home caused by the gambling
- relies on other people to get him or her out of financial problems caused by the gambling.

Gambling disorder is distinguished from social gambling, in which the person is typically socializing with friends, gambling for a limited period of time, and gambling with a limited sum of money that they can afford to lose. GD is also distinguished from professional gambling, in which participants limit their risks, and discipline their behaviors. Lastly, gambling disorder must be distinguished from a **manic episode**; in most cases, the distinguishing feature of the disorder is that the manic-like behavior disappears after the person leaves the gambling setting, and that other symptoms of a manic episode, such as euphoria, irritability, and sleeplessness, are not present.

Treatment

There are a number of different treatments for gambling disorder. **Psychodynamic psychotherapy** attempts to uncover any underlying psychological factors that trigger the gambling. For people who are gambling to escape, such as those who are depressed, this approach may be very successful. Treating any **substance abuse** problems that may coexist with the pathological gambling can also be helpful. Other types of treatments involve behavioral techniques used to teach relaxation and avoidance of stimuli associated with gambling. **Aversion therapy** appears to be successful in treating pathological gambling disorder in highly motivated patients with some insight into the problem, but is not helpful for patients who are less educated or resistant to behavioral methods of treatment.

Gamblers Anonymous (GA) is a twelve-step program modeled after Alcoholics Anonymous (AA). The gambler's admission that she or he does have a gambling problem, and a willingness to go to meetings are considered the first steps in treating gambling disorder. Looking realistically at what gambling has done to a person's life and a willingness to work hard to stop gambling are also important parts of GA. People involved in this program are expected to attend meetings regularly, make amends for wrongs that their gambling has caused, and find a sponsor (usually of the same gender) to help them through the program. GA also expects people who stop gambling to understand that they probably will never be able to gamble again socially, just as recovering alcoholics cannot drink socially.

Pharmacological treatments for pathological gambling and other process addictions are still being developed and explored. In studies reported thus far, the most effective pharmaceutical treatment has been opioid antagonists, such as **naltrexone** (Depade, ReVia) or nalmefene (Revex), possibly because of their effects on opioid pathways that interact with dopamine signaling pathways in the brain reward system. Treatment may also target co-morbidities of pathological gambling, such as using **selective serotonin reuptake inhibitors (SSRIs)** if mood disorder or **obsessive-compulsive disorder** is present.

Doctors at the University of California at Los Angeles (UCLA), are treating gambling disorders as a brain disease. The amount and severity of gambling disorder in California is increasing annually. Consequently, the state provided $15 million for three years, beginning around 2011, to fund treatment programs for California citizens with a gambling disorder. Dr. Timothy Fong, the codirector of the UCLA Gambling Studies Program, works with the state's Office of Problem Gambling to design, develop, and evaluate treatment programs for gambling disorder. Part of the state funding for gambling disorder is to certify nearly 300 mental health therapists in the treatment of gambling problems.

Prognosis

There are very few statistics on the number of people successfully treated for gambling disorder. It is estimated that one-third of all people with gambling disorder can recover from the disease without treatment. However, that still leaves two-thirds who do not recover. In fact, as many as two out of three people who begin treatment (medication, therapy, or both) for gambling disorder drop out before its completion. Consequently, the negative effects of gambling disorder often leave their lives, and their family, in ruin. It is estimated that $5 billion is spent annually on gambling in the United States. However, during each of those years, people with a gambling disorder are estimated to have accrued tens to hundreds of thousands of dollars in debt.

Besides financial problems, people with gambling disorders suffer from a multitude of mental problems, such as an increased risk of causing domestic violence and **child abuse**. The mental problems are not reserved to the problem gamblers. Children of gamblers with problems are at increased risk from suffering behavioral problems, depression, and substance abuse.

Treatment for any underlying psychological disorders or substance abuse can be very helpful. Sometimes **family therapy** is recommended. Some types of relaxation or behavioral therapy can also be helpful. Gamblers Anonymous can help in many cases, although the program has a high dropout and recurrence rate, and there are few studies that fully analyze the benefits or efficacy of the program. For many people, a combination of more than one of these approaches may be most effective. Even when a person has successfully stopped compulsive gambling, it is unlikely that he or she will ever be able to gamble socially again, or even spend time in places where he or she once gambled.

The Institute for Research on Gambling Disorders announced that five new research projects were awarded in 2010 for the study of gambling disorders. The grants, which totaled $380,466, were awarded by the National Center for Responsible Gaming to researchers at Duke University (North Carolina), Southern Illinois University, the University of Florida, the University of Minnesota, and the University of Missouri.

The research studies were in the grant areas called Exploration Grants, Seed Grants, and Large Grants. The Exploration Grants involve evaluating the risk difference of online gambling versus non-Internet based gambling. A virtual Internet site will be built to simulate online gambling. Subjects will be divided into a pathological gambling group and a control group. Using functional **magnetic resonance imaging** (fMRI) scans, the researchers from the University of Florida will research the neurological activity in the brain when excessive gambling is involved.

Duke University researchers were granted a Seed Grant to test the hypothesis that whether "someone makes a risky or safe choice depends not simply on preferences, but on the strategies they use to acquire and integrate new information." The study will provide further information on the reasons why some people make risky decisions while gambling. Another Seed Grant was awarded to scientists at Southern Illinois University to use fMRI to examine the brain activity of "disordered gamblers" before and after undergoing acceptance and commitment therapy, which is a new therapy being developed to help treat gambling disorders.

Researchers at the University of Missouri were awarded a Large Grant of $172,500 to test whether college students report more or less gambling when they are provided information about their own behaviors while gambling (in what is called "personalized feedback-only intervention"). In addition, University of Minnesota scientists will study the various factors, such as race and gender, which distinguish recreational gamblers and pathological gamblers. They will also study factors that may be responsible for turning recreational gamblers into problem gamblers. This study will use data from the National Epidemiologic Survey on Alcohol and Related Conditions.

QUESTIONS TO ASK YOUR DOCTOR

- Am I addicted to gambling?
- Where can I find more information on gambling disorder?
- I can't afford treatment. Will my medical insurance pay for it?
- Do I have an underlying mental illness that is causing me to have gambling disorder?
- How do I stop gambling?
- What type of medicine do you recommend?
- What type of treatment is best for me?

In addition, a research study performed in Australia has shown that nearly one in five problem gamblers (17%) has attempted **suicide**. Their statistics are based on patients entering the emergency department at the Alfred hospital in Prahran, Victoria, Australia. The report concluded that this rate of suicide among problem gamblers is about 20 times the rate in a normal population without gambling problems. Commenting on the results of the Australian report, state gaming minister Tony Robinson stated that "one of the underlying drivers of problem gambling is a pre-existing mental health condition."

Prevention

Prevention of pathological gambling disorder is very difficult because it is impossible to predict when someone will react to gambling in a way that leads to compulsive gambling. If, however, a person begins to feel that he or she may have a problem, immediate treatment can prevent the development of a disorder that affects all areas of life and may have legal as well as economic consequences. Given the role of proximity to available gambling in the development of the disorder, this factor may be a target in prevention.

Resources

BOOKS

Adamec, Christine. *Pathological Gambling.* New York: Chelsea House, 2011.

Diagnostic and Statistical Manual of Mental Disorders 4th ed., text rev. American Psychiatric Association. Washington D.C.: American Psychiatric Association, 2000.

Haugen, David, and Susan Musser, editors. *Gambling*. Detroit: Greenhaven Press, 2007.

Orford, Jim. *An Unsafe Bet?: The Dangerous Rise of Gambling and the Debate We Should be Having*. Chichester, U.K.: Wiley-Blackwell, 2011

Plante, Thomas G., editor. *Mental Disorders of the New Millennium*. Westport, CT: Praeger, 2006.

Sadock, Benjamin J., Virginia A. Sadock, and Pedro Ruiz, editors. *Kaplan & Sadock' Comprehensive Textbook of Psychiatry*. Philadelphia: Wolters Kluwer Health/Lippincott Williams & Wilkins, 2009.

PERIODICALS

Grant, Jon E., JD, MD, M.P.H., Judson A. Brewer, MD, Ph.D., and Marc N. Potenza, MD, Ph.D. "The Neurobiology of substance and behavioral addictions." *CNS Spectrums* 11 (2006): 924–30.

Hagan, Kate. "Gambling Linked to One in Five Suicidal Patients." *The Age*, (April 21, 2010). http://www.theage.com.au/national/gambling-linked-to-one-in-five-suicidal-patients-20100420-srri.html (accessed May 26, 2011).

Lee, Cynthia. "Doctors Treat Gambling Addiction as Brain Disease." *UCLA Today*, (January 10, 2011). http://www.today.ucla.edu/portal/ut/gambling-addicts-suffer-from-brain-190668.aspx (accessed May 26, 2011).

Lobo, Daniela, S.S., and James L. Kennedy. "The genetics of gambling and behavioral addictions." *CNS Spectrums* 11 (2006): 931–9.

Sevigny S., R. Ladouceur, C. Jacques, and M. Cantinotti. "Links between casino proximity and gambling participation, expenditure, and pathology." *Psychology of Addictive Behaviors* 22, no. 2 (June 2008) 295–301.

WEBSITES

Dryden-Edwards, Roxanne, and William C. Shiel Jr. "Gambling Addiction (Compulsive or Pathological Gambling)." MedicineNet.com. http://www.medicinenet.com/gambling_addiction/article.htm (accessed May 26, 2011).

MedlinePlus. "Pathological Gambling." U.S. Library of Medicine, National Institutes of Health. February 18, 2010. http://www.nlm.nih.gov/medlineplus/ency/article/001520.htm (accessed May 26, 2011).

Reilly, Christine. "NCRG Awarded $380,466 in Research Grants in 2010." Institute on Research for Gambling Disorders. (January 2011). http://www.gamblingdisorders.org/issues-insights/ncrg-awarded-380466-research-grants-2010 (accessed May 26, 2011).

ORGANIZATIONS

Gamblers Anonymous, PO Box 17173, Los Angeles, CA, 90017, (213) 386-8789, Fax: (213) 386-0030, http://www.gamblersanonymous.org.

Institute for Research on Gambling Disorders, 900 Cummings Center, Suite 418-U, Beverly, MA, 01915, (978) 338-6610, Fax: (978) 522-8452, info@gamblingdisorders.org, http://www.gamblingdisorders.org.

National Alliance on Mental Illness, 3803 North Fairfax Drive, Suite 100, Arlington, VA, 22203, (703) 524-7600, Fax: (703) 524-9094, http://www.nami.org.

National Institute of Mental Health, 6001 Executive Boulevard, Room 8184, MSC 9663, Bethesda, MD, 20892-9663, (301) 443-4513, (866) 615-6464, Fax: (301) 443-4279, nimhinfo@nih.gov, http://www.nimh.nih.gov.

Tish Davidson, A.M.
Emily Jane Willingham, Ph.D.
William A. Atkins

Ganser's syndrome

Definition

Ganser's syndrome is a rare disorder in which the individual simulates a psychotic illness or dissociated state. The individual's actions are presumed to be the result of unconscious efforts to escape from an intolerable situation, most typically in psychiatric institutions or prisons. The most common feature of Ganser's syndrome is the giving of approximate answers to questions (e.g., $5 + 3 = 7$).

Description

Although this disorder was previously classified as a **factitious disorder**, the **American Psychiatric Association** has redefined Ganser's syndrome and placed it in the category called "Dissociative Disorder Not Otherwise Specified." Sometimes called "the syndrome of approximate answers," Ganser's syndrome is most often seen in male prisoners. In the past, this was so much the case that early clinicians called the syndrome prison **psychosis**, despite the fact that it is not a true psychosis. (Psychosis is characterized by a radical change in personality and a distorted sense of reality.) The disorder has also been referred to as hysterical pseudodementia, due to the resemblance of responses to those of demented patients. However, data on the prevalence of the syndrome and on links within families have not been gathered and analyzed.

Ganser's syndrome is usually sudden in onset and, like **malingering**, seems to arise in response to an opportunity for personal gain or the avoidance of some responsibility. The patient will offer nearly correct replies when asked questions about facts of common knowledge, such as the number of days in a year, the number of months in a year, subtracting 7 from 100, the product of 4 times 5, etc. To such questions, the patient may respond by stating that there are 360 days in a year, 11 months in a year, 94 for the result of subtracting 7 from 100, and that 21 is the product of 4 times 5. These

KEY TERMS

Factitious disorder—A type of mental disturbance in which patients intentionally act physically or mentally ill without obvious benefits. It is distinguished from malingering by the absence of an obvious motive, and from conversion disorder by intentional production of symptoms.

Malingering—Knowingly pretending to be physically or mentally ill to avoid some unpleasant duty or responsibility, or for economic benefit.

persons appear to have no difficulty in understanding questions asked, but appear to provide incorrect answers deliberately.

This syndrome is seen in conjunction with a preexisting severe personality disorder. However, unless the patient is willing to admit to the manufactured nature of the symptoms, or unless there is conclusive objective evidence contradicting the syndrome, determining whether the patient has a true disorder may be impossible. As with its sudden onset, disappearance of the symptoms can be just as fast. However, symptoms can also appear to worsen if the patient believes someone is watching. When reviewing a case of Ganser's syndrome, the clinician must consider factitious disorder and malingering as alternative diagnoses.

Resources

BOOKS

American Psychiatric Association. *Diagnostic and Statistical Manual of Mental Disorders*. 4th ed., text rev. Washington, DC: American Psychiatric Publishing, 2000.

Enoch, M. David, and Hadrian N. Ball. *Uncommon Psychiatric Syndromes*. New York: Oxford University Press, 2001.

VandenBos, Gary R. ed. *APA Dictionary of Psychology*. Washington, DC: American Psychological Association, 2006.

PERIODICALS

Levenson, James L. "Somatoform Disorders: A Medicolegal Guide." *Journal of Psychosomatic Research* 59, no. 5 (November 2005): 349.

Merckelbach, Harald, et al. "Detecting Malingering of Ganser-Like Symptoms with Tests: A Case Study." *Psychiatry and Clinical Neurosciences* 60, no. 5 (October 2006): 636–38. Available online at http://onlinelibrary.wiley.com/doi/10.1111/j.1440-1819.2006.01571.x/full (accessed November 9, 2011).

Jack H. Booth, PsyD
Ruth A. Wienclaw, PhD

Gender dysphoria *see* **Gender identity disorder**

Gender identity disorder

Definition

Gender identity disorder (GID) as defined by the fourth edition of the ***Diagnostic and Statistical Manual of Mental Disorders*** (*DSM-IV*), is a condition characterized by a persistent feeling of discomfort or inappropriateness concerning one's anatomic sex. The disorder typically begins in childhood with gender identity disconnects and is manifested in adolescence or adulthood by a person dressing in clothing associated with the desired gender (cross-dressing), as opposed to one's birth gender, and exhibiting other behaviors associated with the self-perceived sex identity. In extreme cases, persons with gender identity disorder may seek sexual reassignment surgery (SRS), also known as a "sex-change" operation.

Proposals for the forthcoming fifth edition of *DSM* (*DSM-5*) in 2013 include changing the name of GID to gender dysphoria, eliminating the term "disorder" and dividing the condition into two subgroups on the basis of age. The proposed names for the condition are "Gender dysphoria in children" and "Gender dysphoria in adolescents or adults." The English word *dysphoria* comes from two Greek words meaning "hard" or "difficult" and "to bear" or "to carry," and refers to a chronic or persistent mood of sadness or generalized unease or discomfort. The reader should note that dysphoria is a general term for a condition that can be experienced as a result of **bereavement** or everyday **stress** as well as being a feature of gender issues, **depression**, and some **anxiety disorders**.

The remainder of this entry will discuss the changes in definition and diagnostic criteria proposed for *DSM-5* alongside the present understanding of GID. The major changes proposed for *DSM-5* were based on the desire to remove the **stigma** of mental illness associated with the term "disorder" and to acknowledge the distinction between gender dysphoria related to a disorder of sex development (DSD) and gender dysphoria in a person without a DSD. "Disorder of sexual development" is the preferred term for disorders in which a genetic mutation or hormonal imbalance leads to ambiguous genitalia at birth or other abnormalities of sexual development. The baby's genitalia may appear as normally female, ambiguous, or male but with a very small penis (micropenis). DSDs are sometimes called "intersex conditions."

Demographics

Gender identity disorder/dysphoria is thought to be more prevalent in males than in females. *DSM-IV* estimates that 1 in every 30,000 males and 1 in every 100,000 females in European and North American countries seeks sexual reassignment surgery (SRS). Other researchers note, however, that these figures do not include people who experience a conflict between their biological sex and their perception of themselves as members of the opposite sex but who choose not to seek surgical treatment. Other figures that have been given are 1 in every 10,000 males and 1 in every 30,000 females. Reliable estimates of prevalence for either males or females, however, were not available as of 2011.

Description

Gender identity disorder/dysphoria is a distressing condition to those who have it. It is especially difficult to cope with because it remains unresolved unless and until sexual reassignment surgery has been performed. Most people with this disorder grow up feeling rejected and out of place. **Suicide** attempts and **substance abuse** are common. Most adolescents and adults with the disorder eventually attempt to pass or live as members of the opposite sex.

Gender identity disorder/dysphoria may be as old as humanity. Cultural anthropologists and other scientists have observed a number of cross-gender behaviors in classical and Hindu mythology, Western and Asian classical history, and in many late nineteenth- and early twentieth-century preliterate cultures, including several Native American tribes. This consistent record across cultures and time lends support to the notion that the disorder may be, at least in part, biological in origin. Not all behavioral scientists share this hypothesis, however.

Behavioral experimentation, particularly when a child is young, is considered normal. As they grow, children will often experiment with a variety of gender role behaviors as they learn to make the fine distinctions between masculine and feminine role expectations of the society in which they live. Some young boys occasionally exhibit behaviors that Western culture has traditionally labeled as feminine. Examples of these behaviors include wearing a dress, using cosmetics, or playing with dolls.

In a similar manner, some young girls will occasionally assume masculine roles during play. An example of this behavior includes pretending to be the father when playing house. Some girls temporarily adopt a cluster of masculine behaviors. These youngsters are often designated as tomboys. Most experts agree that such temporary or episodic adopting of behaviors opposite to one's gender is normal and usually constitute learning experiences in the acquisition of normal sex role socialization.

In cases that are considered pathological, however, children deviate from the typical model of exploring masculine and feminine behaviors. Such children develop inflexible, compulsive, persistent, and rigidly stereotyped patterns. On one extreme are boys who become excessively masculine. The opposite extreme is seen in effeminate boys who reject their masculinity and rigidly insist that they are really girls or that they want to become mothers and bear children.

Boys with these traits frequently avoid playing with other boys, dress in female clothing, play predominantly with girls, try out cosmetics and wigs, and display stereotypically feminine gait, arm movements, and body gestures. Although much less common, some girls may similarly reject traditionally feminine roles and mannerisms in favor of masculine characteristics, including a refusal to urinate sitting down. Professional **intervention** is required for both extremes of gender role behavior.

Gender identity disorder/dysphoria is different from transvestitism or **transvestic fetishism**. Transvestic **fetishism** is classified as a paraphilia or type of sexual behavior in which a person derives sexual excitement from behavior that is unusual, extreme, or criminal. Transvestic fetishism refers to deriving sexual excitement from wearing clothing and accessories associated with the opposite sex in one's particular society, as distinguished from wearing such clothing for a theatrical performance or costume party. It is a paraphilia found primarily in males; there were no cases in the English-language medical literature as of 2011 of women becoming sexually excited by wearing men's clothing. Transvestic fetishism is not necessarily associated with gender identity disorder/dysphoria, as most men who engage in transvestic fetishism are content with their assigned sex.

Adults with gender identity disorder sometimes live their lives as members of the opposite sex. They often cross-dress and prefer to be seen in public as a member of the other sex. Some people with the disorder seek gender reassignment surgery.

Persons with gender identity disorder frequently state that they were born the wrong sex. They may describe their sexual organs as being ugly and may refrain from touching their genitalia. People with gender identity disorder may also try to hide their secondary sex characteristics. For instance, males may try to shave off or pluck their body hair. Many men elect to take estrogens in an effort to enlarge their breasts. Females may try to hide their breasts by binding them. There is a growing movement among people who consider themselves transgendered to demand that the condition not be viewed or classified as a disorder but as part of a spectrum of sexual development; the proposed changes in *DSM-5* reflect this demand.

Causes and symptoms

Causes

There was no consensus as of 2011 regarding the causes of gender identity disorder/dysphoria. Various theories have been proposed, such as:

- childhood sexual abuse or traumatic injury to the genitals
- homosexual orientation
- genetic mutations
- variations in brain structure
- variations in brain function
- prenatal exposure to androgens (male sex hormones), the lack of such exposure, or fetal insensitivity to androgens

The sex of a human baby is determined by chromosomes. Males have a Y chromosome and one X chromosome, while females have two X chromosomes. The Y chromosome carries a gene known as the "testis-determining factor." This gene sets off a developmental pathway that is typically male, resulting in testicular development and development of secondary sexual structures that are male, including a penis and scrotum and differentiation in the fetal **brain**. Embryos lacking the testis-determining factor usually develop as females. The newly formed testes are responsible for releasing the hormones that continue the fetus on a male developmental pathway.

These prenatal events provide the biological basis for gender identity disorder. Hormone levels must be appropriate for male development during the appropriate developmental windows for typical male development to occur. In addition, the cellular pathways that recognize the signals the hormones send must also be in place. Changes in hormone levels from the norm or exposure to environmental compounds that behave like hormones in the fetus can alter male development, resulting in a feminized fetus if this alteration ends in inhibition of typical male development.

Disruptions of hormone signaling may arise from a variety of sources, including a disorder in the mother's endocrine system, maternal stress, maternal medications, and some environmental endocrine-active substances.

Postmortem studies conducted on male-to-female transsexuals, non-transsexual men, and non-transsexual women show a significant difference in sex-specific brain structures. Studies have shown that in male-to-female transsexuals, for example, brain structures look like those of nontransgendered women. These studies indicate that one's sense of gender resides in the brain and that it may be biochemically determined. One hypothesis underlying the link between gonadal sex and the sex of the brain is the organization-activation hypothesis. According to this hypothesis, the hormones that organize the body as masculine (result in the formation of a penis rather than a clitoris) also organize the brain as masculine. At puberty, hormones activate the brain for gender-specific sex behavior. In some cases, there may be a disconnect between gonadal development and the brain's sexual development.

In addition to biological factors, such environmental conditions as socialization are thought by some to contribute to gender identity disorder. Social learning theory, for example, proposes that a combination of

KEY TERMS

Cross-dressing—Wearing clothes and other accessories associated with the opposite sex in one's particular society.

Disorder of sex development (DSD)—The term that is increasingly preferred for an atypical pattern of chromosomal, genital, or gonadal development. It is also known as "disorder of sex differentiation."

Dysphoria—A persistent mood of sadness, discomfort, or general unease. The English word comes from two Greek words meaning "difficult" or "hard" and "to bear."

Eunuch—A castrated male, often one castrated at an early age with noticeable hormonal consequences.

Gender dysphoria—Persistent personal discomfort with one's present gender.

Intersex—A term that is sometimes used to refer to having a sexual anatomy that is not standard for either a male or a female. It covers a number of different conditions but is considered a convenient umbrella term for discussing disorders of sex development.

Paraphilia—A type of sexual behavior in which a person derives sexual excitement from behavior that is unusual, extreme, or criminal.

Stigma—Any personal attribute that causes a person to be socially shamed, avoided, or discredited. Mental disorders are a common cause of stigma.

Transvestic fetishism—A condition in which a person is sexually aroused by wearing the clothing of the other sex (as distinct from cross-dressing for a theater role or costume party).

observational learning and different levels and forms of **reinforcement** by parents, family, and friends determine a child's sense of gender, which in turn leads to what society considers appropriate or inappropriate behavior. Recent research, however, suggests that even when people who are transgendered or born with ambiguous genitalia are reared based on their assigned sex, they still retain their perceived sexual identity.

Diagnosis

While a patient with gender issues may begin by consulting a family doctor, referral to a mental health professional is needed to make a formal **diagnosis** of gender identity disorder. In most cases, the professional will be either a **psychiatrist** or a clinical **psychologist**. He or she begins by taking a careful personal history of the patient and obtaining the age of the patient, and determines whether the patient's sexual attraction is to males, females, both, or neither. Laboratory tests are neither available nor required to make a diagnosis of gender identity disorder.

Patients and their families may wish to visit clinics that specialize in assessment of gender identity/dysphoria issues. Two of these facilities are listed under Resources below.

Examination

It is very important not to overlook a physical illness, such as a tumor that might mimic or contribute to a psychological disorder. If there is any question that a physical problem might be the underlying cause of an apparent gender identity disorder, a mental health professional should recommend a complete physical examination by a medical doctor. The patient may be referred to an endocrinologist, a physician who specializes in diagnosing and treating disorders of the glands that produce sex hormones, to determine whether a hormonal imbalance is a factor in the patient's condition.

Tests

Urine and blood samples are taken to rule out previously undiagnosed hormonal disorders. In a few cases, the patient may be given an x ray or other **imaging studies** to rule out abnormalities of, or injuries to, the brain.

DSM-IV criteria for gender identity disorder

Diagnosis of a psychiatric disorder or condition according to *DSM* requires the psychiatrist or psychologist to determine whether the patient meets a set of criteria defined by the manual. The *DSM-IV* criteria requires that:

- The person feels a strong and persistent cross-gender identification.
- The person experiences persistent discomfort with his or her sex or a sense of inappropriateness in the gender role of one's birth sex.
- The disturbance is not concurrent with a physical intersex condition.
- The disturbance causes clinically significant distress or impairment in social, occupational, or other important areas of functioning.

In children with a persistent cross-gender identification, the disturbance is manifested by four (or more) of the following:

- Repeatedly stating a desire to be, or insistence that he or she is, a member of the other sex.
- Strong preference for wearing clothes of the opposite gender. In boys, displaying a preference for cross-dressing or simulating female attire; in girls, insistence on wearing only stereotypically masculine clothing.
- Displaying strong and persistent preferences for cross-sex roles in make-believe play or experiencing persistent fantasies of being a member of the other sex.
- Having an intense desire to participate in the games and pastimes that are stereotypical of the other sex.
- Exhibiting a strong preference for playmates of the other sex.

Among adolescents and adults, the disturbance is manifested by symptoms such as a stated desire to become a member of the other sex, frequent passing as a person of the other sex, a desire to live or be treated as the other sex, or the conviction that he or she has the typical feelings and reactions of the other sex. These characteristics cannot be merely from a desire for any perceived cultural advantages of being the other sex.

Among children that feel a discomfort regarding his or her gender, the disturbance is manifested by any of the following:

- Among boys, asserting that his penis or testes are disgusting or will disappear, asserting that it would be better not to have a penis, or having an aversion toward rough-and-tumble play and rejecting male stereotypical toys, games, and activities.
- Among girls, rejecting the gender-typical practice of urinating in a sitting position, asserting that she has or will grow a penis, or stating that she does not want to grow breasts or menstruate, or having a marked aversion toward normative feminine clothing.

Among adolescents and adults, the disturbance is manifested by symptoms such as preoccupation with getting rid of primary and secondary sex characteristics (e.g., request for hormones, surgery, or other procedures to alter sexual characteristics to simulate the other sex) or a belief that he or she was born the wrong sex.

DSM-5 criteria for gender dysphoria

The proposed criteria for gender dysphoria have been updated several times since the change in name for the condition was suggested, and may change again with the publication of *DSM-5*. The following criteria were posted in May 2011:

IN CHILDREN. There are two subtypes specified of gender dysphoria in children: a) with a disorder of sex development; and b) without a disorder of sex development.

- Criterion A: A marked incongruence between one's experienced/expressed gender and assigned gender, of at least 6 months duration, as manifested by at least 6 of the following indicators, including the first: 1. a strong desire to be of the other gender or an insistence that he or she is the other gender (or some alternative gender different from one's assigned gender); 2. in boys, a strong preference for cross-dressing or simulating female attire; in girls, a strong preference for wearing only typical masculine clothing and a strong resistance to the wearing of typical feminine clothing; 3. a strong preference for cross-gender roles in make-believe or fantasy play; 4. a strong preference for the toys, games, or activities typical of the other gender; 5. a strong preference for playmates of the other gender; 6. in boys, a strong rejection of typically masculine toys, games, and activities and a strong avoidance of rough-and-tumble play; in girls, a strong rejection of typically feminine toys, games, and activities; 7. a strong dislike of one's sexual anatomy; 8. a strong desire for the primary and/or secondary sex characteristics that match one's experienced gender
- Criterion B: the condition is associated with clinically significant distress or impairment in social, occupational, or other important areas of functioning, or with a significantly increased risk of suffering, such as distress or disability.

IN ADOLESCENTS AND ADULTS. As with children, *DSM-5* specifies two subtypes of gender dysphoria in adolescents and adults: with or without a disorder of sex development.

- Criterion A: A marked incongruence between one's experienced/expressed gender and assigned gender, of at least 6 months duration, as manifested by two or more of the following indicators: 1. a marked incongruence between one's experienced/expressed gender and primary and/or secondary sex characteristics (or, in young adolescents, the anticipated secondary sex characteristics); 2. a strong desire to be rid of one's primary and/or secondary sex characteristics because of a marked incongruence with one's experienced/expressed gender (or, in young adolescents, a desire to prevent the development of the anticipated secondary sex characteristics); 3. a strong desire for the primary and/or secondary sex characteristics of the other gender; 4. a strong desire to be of the other gender (or some alternative gender different from one's assigned gender); 5. a strong desire to be treated as the other gender (or some alternative gender different from one's assigned gender); 6. a strong conviction that one has the typical feelings and reactions of the other gender (or some alternative gender different from one's assigned gender).
- Criterion B: same as Criterion B for children.

MALE-TO-EUNUCH GENDER DYSPHORIA. Some researchers have suggested that *DSM-5* add a new category of gender dysphoria known as male-to-eunuch gender dysphoria. This category would include males who do not identify with either their birth sex or with a female gender identity. They seek castration as a way to align their bodies with their brain sex. It was estimated that there were between 7,000 and 10,000 voluntary eunuchs in Canada and the United States in 2011. *DSM-5* had not incorporated male-to-eunuch gender identity disorder in its list of proposed revisions as of 2011; it had, however, listed the condition under the heading of "Conditions Proposed by Outside Sources."

Treatment

Psychotherapy

One common form of treatment for gender identity disorder is **psychotherapy**. The initial aim of treatment is to help individuals function in their biologic sex roles to the greatest degree possible. The World Professional Association for Transgender Health, which has formulated and published its own *Standards of Care* manual for working with transgendered people, does not support psychotherapy designed to convert a transgendered person from their own personal perception of their sex.

Sexual reassignment

Adults who have had severe gender identity disorder for many years sometimes request reassignment of their sex, or sex-change surgery. Before undertaking such surgery, they usually undergo hormone therapy to suppress same-sex characteristics and to accentuate other-sex characteristics. For instance, the female hormone estrogen is given to males to make breasts grow, reduce facial hair, and widen hips. The male hormone testosterone is administered to females to suppress menstruation, deepen the voice, and increase body hair. Following the hormone treatments, preoperative candidates are usually required to live in the cross-gender role for at least a year before surgery is performed. This period is known as "real-life experience" or RLE.

Adults seeking sexual reassignment should be screened for medical conditions that can be worsened by cross-sex hormone therapy. These conditions include heart disease, breast cancer, liver disease, migraine headaches, and blood disorders. There are two goals of hormone therapy in adult transsexuals: reduce the secondary sex characteristics of the patient's biological sex; and supply the individual with the hormones of the desired sex. Adults should also be counseled about the possibility of permanent infertility if they choose to proceed with sex reassignment. In addition, males seeking reassignment as women should be warned that hormone treatment is likely to lower their sex drive, while women seeking reassignment as men are likely to find their sex drive increased by hormone therapy. In terms of cost, hormone therapy costs between $25 and $200 per month.

Transsexuals in any country must also attend to a number of legal concerns, ranging from changing their name and sex on documents ranging from birth certificates (permitted in some states in the United States) and Social Security registration to driver's licenses, bank accounts, passports, voter registration forms, and the like.

Prognosis

If gender identity disorder/dysphoria in a child persists into adolescence, it tends to be chronic in nature. There may be periods of remission. However, adoption of characteristics and activities typical for one's birth sex is unlikely to occur.

Most individuals with gender identity disorder require and appreciate support from several sources. Families, as well as the person with the disorder, need and appreciate both information and support. Local and national **support groups** and informational services exist, and health care providers and mental health professionals can provide referrals.

There is some disagreement regarding the post-treatment satisfaction of people who have undergone sexual reassignment surgery. Early surveys indicated that only 1% regretted their transition; however, other surveys have reported that between 8% and 14% regret their change, and that a few persons have re-transitioned to their original gender. In terms of adjustment after SRS, heterosexual transsexuals have poorer outcomes than homosexual transsexuals; older persons and effeminate homosexuals have poorer outcomes; and male-to-female transsexuals have poorer outcomes than female-to-male. In general, satisfactory results are reported in 87% of male-to-female and 97% of female-to-male SRS patients.

QUESTIONS TO ASK YOUR DOCTOR

- Have you ever treated a patient with gender issues? A patient who has had sexual reassignment hormone therapy or surgery?
- Should I be concerned about a small child's wishes to change his or her sex?
- How can I tell whether my child has a gender identity disorder or is just going through a phase?
- If my child is diagnosed with gender dysphoria, what are the chances that it will resolve by the teen years?
- What is your opinion of sex reassignment surgery?

Prevention

There is no known way to prevent gender identity disorder/dysphoria because there are several possible causes of the condition that are not completely understood.

Resources

BOOKS

American Psychiatric Association. *Diagnostic and Statistical Manual*. 4th ed., text rev. Washington, DC: American Psychiatric Association, 2000.

Balon, Richard, and Robert Taylor Segraves, eds. *Clinical Manual of Sexual Disorders*. Washington, DC: American Psychiatric Publishing, 2009.

Bamberg-Smith, Barbara A. *The Psychology of Sex and Gender*. Boston: Pearson/Allyn and Bacon, 2007.

Bockting, Walter O., and Joshua Goldberg, eds. *Guidelines for Transgender Care*. Binghamton, NY: Haworth Medical Press, 2006.

Einstein, Gillian, ed. *Sex and the Brain*. Cambridge, MA: MIT Press, 2007.

Shrage, Laurie J., ed. *"You've Changed": Sex Reassignment and Personal Identity*. New York: Oxford University Press, 2009.

PERIODICALS

Cohen-Kettenis, P.T., and F. Pfäfflin. "The DSM Diagnostic Criteria for Gender Identity Disorder in Adolescents and Adults." *Archives of Sexual Behavior* 39 (April 2010): 499–513.

Hoshiai, M., et al. "Psychiatric Comorbidity among Patients with Gender Identity Disorder." *Psychiatry and Clinical Neurosciences* 64 (October 2010): 514–519.

Lawrence, A.A. "Proposed Revisions to Gender Identity Disorder Diagnoses in the DSM-5." *Archives of Sexual Behavior* 39 (December 2010): 1253–1260.

Paap, M.C., et al. "Assessing the Utility of Diagnostic Criteria: A Multisite Study on Gender Identity Disorder." *Journal of Sexual Medicine* 8 (January 2011): 180–190.

Roberts, L.F., et al. "A Passion for Castration: Characterizing Men Who Are Fascinated with Castration, But Have Not Been Castrated." *Journal of Sexual Medicine* 5 (July 2008): 1669–1680.

Selvaggi, G., and J. Bellringer. "Gender Reassignment Surgery: An Overview." *Nature Reviews. Urology* 8 (May 2011): 274–282.

WEBSITES

American Psychiatric Association. DSM-5 Development. "Conditions Proposed by Outside Sources." http://www.dsm5.org/PROPOSEDREVISIONS/Pages/ConditionsProposedbyOutsideSources.aspx (accessed May 22, 2011).

American Psychiatric Association. DSM-5 Development. "P 00 Gender Dysphoria in Children." http://www.dsm5.org/ProposedRevisions/Pages/proposedrevision.aspx?rid=192 (accessed May 19, 2011).

American Psychiatric Association. DSM-5 Development. "P 01 Gender Dysphoria in Adolescents or Adults." http://www.dsm5.org/ProposedRevisions/Pages/proposedrevision.aspx?rid=482 (accessed May 19, 2011).

MedlinePlus. "Gender Identity Disorder." http://www.nlm.nih.gov/medlineplus/ency/article/001527.htm (accessed May 19, 2011).

Medscape. "Sexual and Gender Identity Disorders." http://emedicine.medscape.com/article/293890-overview (accessed May 19, 2011).

World Professional Association for Transgender Health (WPATH). "Standards of Care for Gender Identity Disorders." http://www.wpath.org/documents2/socv6.pdf (accessed May 20, 2011).

ORGANIZATIONS

American Association of Sexuality Educators, Counselors, and Therapists (AASECT), 1444 I Street NW, Suite 700, Washington, DC, United States 20005, (202) 449-1099, Fax: (202) 216-9646, info@aasect.org, http://www.aasect.org

Endocrine Society, 8401 Connecticut Ave., Suite 900, Chevy Chase, MD, United States 20815, (301) 941-0200, Fax: (301) 941-0259, (888) 363-6274, http://www.endo-society.org

The Johns Hopkins Hospital, Sexual Behaviors Consultation Unit, 600 North Wolfe Street, Meyer 144, Baltimore, MD, United States 21287, (410) 583-1661, Fax: (410)583-2693, http://www.hopkinsmedicine.org/psychiatry/specialty_areas/sexual_behaviors

University of Minnesota Clinic, Center for Sexual Health, 1300 South 2nd Street, Minneapolis, MN, United States 55454, (612) 624-7821, http://www.fm.umn.edu/phs/clinic/home.html

World Professional Association for Transgender Health (WPATH) [formerly the Harry Benjamin International Gender Dysphoria Association (HBIGDA)], 1300 South Second Street, Suite 180, Minneapolis, MN, United States 55454, [no telephone number given], wpath@wpath.org, http://www.wpath.org

L. Fleming Fallon, Jr., M.D., Dr. P.H.
Rebecca J. Frey, Ph.D.

Gender issues in mental health

Defining gender

In the social sciences, the concept of gender means much more than biological sex. It refers to socially constructed expectations regarding the ways in which people should think and behave, depending on their sexual classification. These stereotypical expectations are commonly referred to as "gender roles." Attitudes toward gender roles are thought to result from complex

Characteristic	Percentage of women		Percentage of men
Classify stress as an 8 or higher on a 10-point scale	28%	vs.	20%
Experienced increasing stress over the last 5 years	49%	vs.	39%
Primary sources of stress	Money (79%) and economy (68%)	vs.	Work (76%)
Preferred forms of stress relief	Reading (57%)	vs.	Listening to music (52%)
Eat as a form of stress relief	31%	vs.	21%
Choose unhealthy foods because of stress	49%	vs.	30%
Experience stress headaches	41%	vs.	30%
Experience upset stomach/indigestion caused by stress	32%	vs.	21%
Do nothing to manage stress	4%	vs.	9%

SOURCE: American Psychological Association.

Differences in causes and effects of stress between men and women. *(Table by PreMediaGlobal. © 2012 Cengage Learning.)*

interactions among societal, cultural, familial, religious, ethnic, and political influences.

Gender affects many aspects of life, including access to resources, methods of coping with **stress**, styles of interacting with others, self-evaluation, spirituality, and expectations of others. These are all factors that can influence mental health either positively or negatively. Psychological gender studies seek to better understand the relationship between gender and mental health in order to reduce risk factors and improve treatment methods.

Traditional gender roles in many Western societies identify masculinity as having power and being in control in emotional situations, in the workplace, and in sexual relationships. Acceptable male behaviors in this traditional construct include competitiveness, independence, assertiveness, ambition, confidence, toughness, anger, and even violence (to varying degrees). Men are expected to avoid characteristics considered feminine, such as emotional expressiveness, vulnerability (weakness, helplessness, insecurity, worry), and intimacy (especially showing affection to other males).

Traditional femininity is defined as being nurturing, supportive, and assigning high priority to one's relationships. Women are expected to be emotionally expressive, dependent, passive, cooperative, warm, and accepting of subordinate status in marriage and employment. Competitiveness, assertiveness, anger, and violence are viewed as unfeminine and are not generally tolerated as acceptable female behavior, although competitiveness is becoming more widely accepted as appropriate for female athletes and political leaders.

Theories of gender

Differences in gender roles have existed throughout history. Evolutionary theorists attribute these differences to the physiological characteristics of men and women that prescribed their best function for survival of the species. In primitive societies, men adopted the roles of hunting and protecting their families because of their physical strength. Women's ability to bear and nurse children led them to adopt the roles of nurturing young, as well as the less physically dependent roles of gathering and preparing food. These gender-dependent labor roles continued into the period of written human history, when people began to live in cities and form the earliest civilized societies.

In the nineteenth century, the industrial movement marked a prominent division of labor into public and private domains. Men began leaving home to work, whereas women worked within the home. Previously, both men and women frequently engaged in comparably respected, productive activities on their homestead. When men began working in the public domain, they acquired money, which was transferable for goods or services. Women's work, on the other hand, was not transferable. Men's relative economic independence contributed to their power and influence, while women were reduced to an image of frailty and emotionality deemed appropriate only for domestic tasks and child rearing.

Sigmund Freud's psychoanalytic theory of human development, which emerged from Freud's late nineteenth-century European setting and medical training, reflected an attitude of male superiority. Freud asserted that as children, boys recognize they are superior to girls when they discover the difference in their genitals, and that girls, on the other hand, equate their lack of a penis with inferiority. According to Freud, this feeling of inferiority causes girls to idolize and desire their fathers, resulting in passivity, masochistic tendencies, jealousy, and vanity, all seen by Freud as feminine characteristics.

Other developmental theorists rejected Freud's notions. Eric Erikson (in 1950) and Lawrence Kohlberg (in 1969) theorized that all humans begin as dependent on caregivers and gradually mature into independent and autonomous beings. Such theories, however, still favored men because independence has historically been considered a masculine trait. By such a standard, men would consistently achieve greater levels of maturity than females.

Nancy Chodorow's object-relations theory (in 1978) favored neither sex. She proposed that children develop according to interactions with their primary caregivers, who tend to be mothers. Mothers, according to her theory, identify with girls to a greater extent, fostering an ability to form rich interpersonal relationships, as well as dependency traits. Mothers push boys toward independence, helping them to adjust to the male-dominated work environment but rendering them unaccustomed to emotional connection. Chodorow's theory suggests both strengths and weaknesses inherent in male and female development, with neither deemed superior.

Around that same time (1974), Sandra Bem advocated for androgyny, or high levels of both masculinity and femininity, as the key to mental health. Bem constructed the Bem Sex Role Inventory (BSRI), a 60-item questionnaire that measures 20 feminine, 20 masculine, and 20 neutral traits. It classifies subjects as masculine, feminine, androgynous, or undifferentiated. Bem maintains that gender roles are primarily cognitive; that is, that people spontaneously sort attitudes and behaviors into masculine and feminine categories according to the models their culture provides. Sex-typed individuals score highly on the dimension corresponding to their gender while rejecting the characteristics of the other gender. Androgynous individuals score high on both masculine and feminine traits, and typically use situational examples to explain their behavior. Bem concluded that androgyny is a particular way of processing information and that individuals who are androgynous are those who do not use sex-role related cognitive frameworks to guide their information processing.

In the 1980s, such psychologists as Carol Gilligan sought to build respect for stereotypically feminine traits. They introduced the notion that women function according to an ethic of care and relatedness that is not inferior to men's, just different. In 1985, Daniel Stern's developmental theory favored traditional femininity, suggesting that humans start out as unconnected to others and gradually form more complex interpersonal connections as they mature.

The process of learning gender roles is known as "socialization." Children learn which behaviors are acceptable or not acceptable for their sex by observing other people. They may also be shamed by caregivers or peers when they violate gender-role expectations. As a result, gender roles usually become an internal guide for behavior early in childhood. Current studies focus on the ways in which extreme notions of masculinity or femininity affect mental health, and the social processes that shape one's concept of maleness or femaleness.

Psychological and behavioral androgyny are less of a problem in North America and Europe because of widespread changes in society, particularly the entrance of women in large numbers into the military, politics, law, medicine, the ministry, and other occupations that were partly or completely closed to them before World War II. Another factor that has influenced social attitudes toward androgyny is androgynous parenting, a trend in childrearing in which a child's mother and father share equally and relatively interchangeably in parenting responsibilities.

In terms of choices made after adolescence, most young people whose career interests or lifestyle preferences fall outside stereotypical gender roles may more easily find welcoming and supportive communities than they might have before the 1960s. There is also some evidence that older adults with androgynous gender roles enjoy better health and satisfaction with their lives than those who adhere to traditional gender roles. On the other hand, people who grow up within families that recently emigrated from countries still marked by rigid gender roles and stereotypes may find the greater acceptance of androgyny in the West disorienting and upsetting.

Gender-role conflict

According to some researchers, the concepts of masculinity and femininity may simply be sets of personality traits that can be exhibited by either sex, and there may be no true gender differences, although this conclusion is controversial. Individuals vary in degree of adherence to gender roles, resulting in large amounts of behavioral variation within the sexes and potentially less variation between them. However, some scholars maintain that there are specific gender-related traits, including gender bias in mental illness.

Although attitudes toward gender roles are now much more flexible, different cultures retain varying degrees of expectations regarding male and female behavior. Individuals may personally disregard gender expectations, but society may disapprove of their behavior and impose external social consequences. On the other hand, individuals may feel internal shame if they experience emotions or desires characteristic of the opposite sex. In some cultures in which a person's social role is emphasized over individualism, the failure to fulfill that role in ways considered traditionally appropriate can lead to feelings of shame as well. Gender-role conflict, or gender-role stress, results when people feel a discrepancy between how they believe they should act based on gender-role expectations learned in childhood, and how they actually think, feel, or behave. If these discrepancies are unresolved, gender-role conflict contributes to poor mental health.

Gender-role complications

A person's attitude toward the roles associated with his or her gender can be complicated by a number of factors, ranging from having a nonstandard sexual anatomy to bisexual or homosexual orientation to unhappiness with one's biological sex (gender dysphoria).

Sexual orientation

Gay men, lesbians, and bisexuals can experience gender-role conflict as well as heterosexual people. Some studies of gay men indicate that effeminate gays are stigmatized inside as well as outside the gay community, and that they have a higher level of mental health problems than gay men who conform more closely to male gender norms. In addition, same-sex partnerships are complicated by the same gender stereotypes that cause stress in male/female relationships. While research does not support the commonplace belief that gay or lesbian couples organize their relationships around traditional gender roles, with one partner being the "butch" (the "man") and the other being the "femme" (the "woman"), such couples are still often troubled by power struggles and domestic violence. In addition to internal conflict about gender roles, bisexuals suffer the additional complication of being distrusted by both homosexual and heterosexual partners; homosexual **support groups** may reject them if they reveal their heterosexual side; heterosexuals may reject them if they reveal their homosexual feelings.

Disorders of sexual development

Disorders of sexual development (DSDs) is an umbrella term for a group of conditions in which a person has a congenital (present at birth) abnormality or atypical combination of features that make it difficult to determine sex. The abnormalities may be chromosomal, genital, or gonadal. It is estimated that about 1%–1.7% of human infants are born with some degree of sexual ambiguity and that between 0.1% and 0.2% are sexually ambiguous enough to require the attention of a medical specialist. Some doctors prefer the term *intersex* to DSD.

In general, parents are more likely to be concerned about a child with ambiguous genitalia than about other intersex conditions that may not be apparent at birth. The most important consideration is to determine the cause of the ambiguous genitalia. The usual tests that are performed include a karyogram to determine the child's karyotype; this diagram of the chromosomes in a cell is usually made from a white blood cell. Other tests include blood and urine samples to evaluate the levels of sex hormones in the blood, and x-ray or ultrasound studies to clarify the structure of the child's internal sex organs.

The nest step is gender assignment. The doctor may suggest the gender, depending on the baby's genetic sex, the anatomy of the internal sex organs, and the possibility of future reproduction. Depending on the cause of the DSD, treatment may include hormone therapy or surgery. The therapy plan should always include psychological counseling for both the child and the parents, particularly because the child may wish to identify with the other sex when he or she is older.

Gender-free childrearing

One recent complication in gender issues related to mental health is whether it is either possible or desirable to raise a child without an assigned gender identity. This question was discussed intensively in the spring of 2011 when a couple in Canada made headlines with their announcement that they were keeping their third child's sex a secret from everyone except their two older children. The baby's name, Storm, was deliberately chosen to be gender-neutral. Child psychologists are divided on whether the parents' decision is likely to create problems for Storm as she or he grows older. The same division among experts surfaced in 2009 when a Swedish couple had a child they named Pop; they told a Swedish newspaper that "the decision [to give the baby a gender-free name] stemmed from a feminist philosophy that gender is a social construction." It will take a number of years to evaluate whether these experiments in gender-free childrearing are successful, and if so, what defines their "success."

Gender dysphoria

"Gender dysphoria" is the proposed name change for **gender identity disorder** (GID) as defined by the fourth edition of the ***Diagnostic and Statistical Manual of Mental Disorders*** (*DSM-IV*). GID is a condition characterized by a persistent feeling of discomfort or inappropriateness concerning one's anatomic sex. The disorder typically begins in childhood with rejection of or discomfort with one's birth gender and is manifested in adolescence or adulthood by a person dressing in clothing associated with the desired gender (cross-dressing) and exhibiting other behaviors associated with the self-perceived sex identity. In extreme cases, persons with gender identity disorder may seek sexual reassignment surgery (SRS), also known as a "sex-change" operation.

Proposals for the forthcoming fifth edition of the *DSM* (*DSM-5*) in 2013 include changing the name of GID to "Gender Dysphoria," thus eliminating the term "disorder," and dividing the condition into two subgroups on the basis of age. The proposed names for the condition are "Gender dysphoria in children" and "Gender dysphoria in adolescents or adults." The English word *dysphoria* comes from two Greek words meaning "hard" or "difficult" and "to bear" or "to carry," and refers to a chronic or persistent mood of sadness or generalized unease or discomfort. Most people with this disorder grow up feeling rejected and out of place. **Suicide** attempts and **substance abuse** are common. Most adolescents and adults with the disorder eventually attempt to "pass" or live as members of the opposite sex.

Women's issues

Typical stressors

Women are often expected to occupy a number of roles at the same time: wife, mother, homemaker, employee, or caregiver to an elderly parent. Meeting the demands of so many roles simultaneously leads to stressful situations in which choices must be prioritized.

Women often must choose whether to pursue or further a career versus whether to devote more time to home and family.

Many women prefer to work outside the home because it gives them a greater sense of life satisfaction. For other women, such as those who run single-parent households, employment is not an optionit is a necessity. Compared with men, women frequently have jobs with less autonomy or creativity, which decreases their level of job satisfaction. Women may also have more difficulty being accepted in the workplace because of hierarchical structures preferring men. Documentation repeatedly shows that women's salaries are lower than those of men in comparable positions; women tend to be paid less even when performing the same jobs as men.

When women do choose or are required to work outside the home, they continue to perform the bulk of household duties as well. Sarah Rosenfield reported that, compared to men, women perform 66% more of the domestic work, sleep a half hour less per night, and perform an extra month of work each year. Needless to say, increased workloads and decreased attention to rest and relaxation are stressful and pose obstacles to women's mental health.

Divorce results in more severe consequences for women who choose or are able to stay home in deference to child rearing. Such women depend on marriage for financial security. Such domestic skills as child care and housecleaning are not highly valued by society and thus are poorly compensated in terms of money. Women who have never been employed and then experience divorce often have few options for securing adequate income.

Although women's ability to form meaningful relationships is a buffer against stress, it can also be a source of stress. Caring about another person can be stressful when that person is not doing well physically or emotionally. Many families take for granted that the female members care for sick children or for elderly parents who are no longer self-sufficient. As a result, many women in their forties or fifties are caught between the needs of their college-age offspring and the needs of dependent parents or in-laws. Interpersonal conflicts resulting from these heavy burdens may cause stress or lower self-esteem; a Canadian study reported in 2011 that women caregivers are still more likely to suffer **depression** or post-traumatic stress than men placed in a caregiver role. Women may also view unsuccessful relationships as representing failure on their part to fulfill such traditional feminine qualities as nurturance, warmth, and empathy.

Additional sources of stress common to women include victimization, assertiveness, and physical unattractiveness. Victimization is a constant concern due to the power differential between men and women. Assertiveness may be stressful for women who have had little experience in competitive situations. Physical unattractiveness may cause some women who adhere to unrealistic standards of feminine beauty to experience shame. Women considered unattractive may also experience discrimination in the workplace or in admission to higher education. In addition, the double standard of aging in contemporary society means that all women will eventually have to cope with the **stigma** of the putative unattractiveness associated with aging.

Typical coping strategies

Studies suggest that women typically react to stress by seeking social support, expressing feelings, or using distraction. These strategies might include praying, worrying, venting, getting advice, or engaging in behaviors that are not related to the problem at all (including such antisocial behaviors as drinking alcohol). Seeking social support and distraction are considered avoidant coping strategies because they do not focus on solving or overcoming a problem, only on alleviating the stress associated with the problem. Research is inconclusive regarding whether men or women are more likely to use problem solving, which is considered an active coping strategy.

Typical patterns of psychopathology

Women are more likely than men to experience internalizing disorders. Primary symptoms of internalizing disorders involve negative inner emotions as opposed to outward negative behavior. Depression (both mild and severe) and anxiety (generalized or free-floating anxiety, phobias, and panic attacks) are internalizing disorders common to women. Symptoms include sadness; a sense of loss, helplessness, or hopelessness; doubt about one's ability to handle problems; high levels of worry or nervousness; poor self-esteem; guilt, self-reproach, and self-blame; decreased energy, motivation, interest in life, or concentration; and problems with sleep or appetite. Women also are more likely than men to have eating disorders, and although incidence of **bipolar disorder** is similar between men and women, women manifest rapid cycling more often and have longer depressive episodes.

Men's issues

Typical stressors

Situations that typically produce stress for men are those that challenge their self-identity and cause them to feel inadequate. If their identity closely matches a

KEY TERMS

Androgyny—The condition of having the characteristics of both a man and a woman, or not being clearly identified as male or female. The English word is a combination of two Greek words meaning "(adult) man" and "woman." Androgyny may refer to a person's physical characteristics, to psychological characteristics, or to behavior.

Bem Sex Role Inventory (BSRI)—A 60-item self-administered test that researchers often use to measure psychological androgyny in test subjects. It was devised in 1971 by Sandra Bem.

Congenital—Present at birth.

Disorder of sex development (DSD)—The term that is increasingly preferred for an atypical pattern of chromosomal, genital, or gonadal development. It is also known as disorder of sex differentiation.

Externalizing disorders—Disorders in which a person acts out inner turmoil or conflict on the external environment. The three major characteristics of externalizing disorders are disruptive, hyperactive, and aggressive behaviors.

Gender dysphoria—Persistent personal discomfort with one's present biological sex.

Genitals—The reproductive organs in either sex, especially the external reproductive organs.

Gonad—The organ that makes gametes (germ cells). The gonads in males are called "testicles" and produce sperm; those in females are called "ovaries" and produce eggs.

Internalizing disorders—Disorders related to issues within the self; depression and the anxiety disorders are two common types of internalizing disorders.

Intersex—A term that is sometimes used to refer to having a sexual anatomy that is not standard for either a male or a female. It covers a number of different conditions but is considered a convenient umbrella term for discussing disorders of sex development.

Karyotype—The number and appearance of a complete set of chromosomes in a species or an individual organism. The arrangement of microphotographs of the chromosomes in a standard photographic format is called a "karyogram."

Socialization—The process through which a person learns his or her roles in society. It includes the society's customs, traditions, and professional roles as well as gender roles.

traditional male role, they will experience stress in situations requiring subordination to women or emotional expressiveness. They will also experience stress if they feel they are not meeting expectations for superior physical strength, intellect, or sexual performance. Research indicates that men who strictly adhere to extreme gender roles are at higher risk for mental disorders. They are also at greater risk of dying from undiagnosed cancer, heart disease, and other physical disorders due to reluctance to consult a doctor when symptoms first appear.

Certain cultures are thought to adhere more strictly to traditional male gender roles. In a study by Jose Abreu and colleagues, Latin American men were identified as adopting the most exaggerated form of masculinity, followed by European Americans, and then African Americans. The Latino image of masculinity is often referred to as *machismo* and includes such qualities as concern for personal honor, virility, physical strength, heavy drinking, toughness, aggression, risk taking, authoritarianism, and self-centeredness. African American males are also thought to have a unique image of masculinity; however, Abreu's study showed that African Americans are more egalitarian in terms of gender roles than European Americans.

Typical coping strategies

Men may respond to stress by putting on a tough image, keeping their feelings inside, releasing stress through such activities as sports, actively attempting to solve the problem, denying the problem, abusing drugs or alcohol, or otherwise attempting to control the problem. As stated previously, research is inconclusive regarding whether males or females use problem-solving strategies more often. This type of coping strategy, however, has more frequently been attributed to males. Problem solving is seen as an active coping strategy, which is more effective than such avoidant strategies as **denial**, abuse of drugs or alcohol, or refusal to talk about problems.

Typical patterns of psychopathology

Men are more likely than women to experience externalizing disorders. Externalizing disorders are characterized by symptoms involving negative outward behavior as opposed to internal negative emotions. Such externalizing disorders as substance abuse (both drugs and alcohol) and antisocial behavior (such as anger, hostility, aggression, violence, or stealing) are common to men. Substance abuse results in such negative physical and social consequences as hallucinations, blackouts, physical dependency, job loss, divorce, arrest, organ and **brain** damage, and financial debt. Antisocial behavior impairs interpersonal relationships and can also result in negative consequences in other areas of life, such as run-ins with the criminal justice system.

Men are not exempt from such internalizing disorders as anxiety and depression. In fact, one study found that high levels of masculinity appear to be related to depression in males. Some researchers feel that men's abuse of substances could be considered the male version of depression. Because male gender roles discourage admitting vulnerability, men may resort to substance abuse as a way of covering their feelings.

Men who adhere to rigid gender roles are also at a disadvantage in interpersonal relationships, especially intimate relationships. They may avoid emotional expressiveness or may behave in domineering and hostile ways. These behaviors increase their risk of social isolation, disconnection from nurturance, and participation in unhealthy relationships.

Mental health

Research indicates that, overall, neither men nor women are at greater risk for developing mental disorders as such. Being male or female may indicate susceptibility to certain types of disorders, however. Neither masculinity nor femininity is uniformly positive; both gender identifications have strengths and weaknesses. For example, femininity appears to be protective against antisocial behaviors and substance abuse but is associated with high levels of avoidant coping strategies and low levels of achievement. Masculinity appears to be protective against depression but is high in antisocial behavior and substance abuse.

Information about gender roles has implications for treatment. Women might not seek treatment because of a lack of such resources as money, transportation, or time away from child-care duties. A treatment center that is sensitive to women's issues should seek to provide these resources in order to facilitate access to treatment. Men, on the other hand, might not seek treatment because it is incongruent with their image of masculinity. Therapists may need to offer men less threatening forms of treatment, such as those that focus on cognitive problem solving rather than on emotions.

The focus of therapy may differ according to one's gender issues. Therapists should recognize the potential for shame and defensiveness when exploring gender norms. Externalizing behaviors may point to underlying hidden shame. For women, the importance placed on various roles in their lives and how closely those roles are tied to their self-identity is relevant. Men may be encouraged to connect to the spiritual aspects of their being and to consider less stringent views of masculinity. Therapists should also consider the associated influences of generation, culture, class, occupation, and educational level when exploring gender-role issues. Men often are entering therapy under duress, as the result of a court order or a spousal ultimatum and may begin the therapeutic process from a perspective of defensiveness. In addition, men's reluctance to discuss their emotions means that less is known about their responses to mental health crises than is known about women's responses. A number of researchers maintain that further study of men's experience of mental distress is needed.

Taking either masculine or feminine qualities to an extreme and to the exclusion of the other appears to be detrimental. A non-traditional gender-role orientation would combine the best of both genders: a social focus (reciprocally supportive relationships and a balance between interests of self and others) and active coping strategies.

Flexibility in using coping strategies is also important. Active, problem-focused coping strategies help to change the situation that is causing the problem. Avoidant or emotion-focused coping strategies manage or reduce emotional distress. Avoidant and emotion-focused strategies may be helpful for the immediate crisis but should be used in combination with more active strategies for complete problem resolution.

QUESTIONS TO ASK YOUR DOCTOR

- Have you ever treated a patient with gender dysphoria?
- Can you recommend a support group for men (or women)?
- Can you recommend any treatments to help me deal with stress?
- Where can I learn more about gender issues?

Resources

BOOKS

American Psychiatric Association. *Diagnostic and Statistical Manual of Mental Disorders*. 4th ed., Text rev. Washington, DC: American Psychiatric Association, 2000.

Balon, Richard, and Robert Taylor Segraves, eds. *Clinical Manual of Sexual Disorders*. Washington, DC: American Psychiatric Publishing, 2009.

Bem, Sandra L. *An Unconventional Family*. New Haven, CT: Yale University Press, 1998.

Denmark, Florence L., and Michele A. Paludi, eds. *Psychology of Women: A Handbook of Issues and Theories*, 2nd ed. Westport, CT: Praeger, 2008.

Firestein, Beth A. *Becoming Visible: Counseling Bisexuals across the Lifespan*. New York: Columbia University Press, 2007.

Gilligan, Carol. *In a Different Voice: Psychological Theory and Women's Development.* Cambridge, MA: Harvard University Press, 1982.

Kimmel, Michael S., and Michael A. Messner. *Men's Lives*, 7th ed. Boston, MA: Pearson Allyn and Bacon, 2007.

Miller, Karen, ed. *Male and Female Roles*. Detroit, MI: Greenhaven Press, 2010.

PERIODICALS

Andermann, L. "Culture and the Social Construction of Gender: Mapping the Intersection with Mental Health." *International Review of Psychiatry* 22 (May 2010): 501–512.

Bianchi, F.T., et al. "Partner Selection among Latino Immigrant Men Who Have Sex with Men." *Archives of Sexual Behavior* 39 (December 2010): 1321–1330.

Brennan, D.J., et al. "Men's Sexual Orientation and Health in Canada." *Canadian Journal of Public Health* 101 (May-June 2010): 255–58.

Gale-Ross, R., et al. "Gender Role, Life Satisfaction, and Wellness: Androgyny in a Southwestern Ontario Sample." *Canadian Journal of Aging* 28 (June 2009): 135–46.

Gannon, K., et al. "Re-constructing Masculinity following Radical Prostatectomy for Prostate Cancer." *Aging Male* 13 (December 2010): 258–264.

Kertzner, R.M., et al. "Social and Psychological Well-being in Lesbians, Gay Men, and Bisexuals: The Effects of Race, Gender, Age, and Sexual Identity." *American Journal of Orthopsychiatry* 79 (October 2009): 500–510.

Lawrence, A.A. "Proposed Revisions to Gender Identity Disorder Diagnoses in the DSM-5." *Archives of Sexual Behavior* 39 (December 2010): 1253–1260.

Loughrey, M. "Just How Male Are Male Nurses?" *Journal of Clinical Nursing* 17 (May 2008): 1327–34.

Peate, I. "The Mental Health of Men and Boys: An Overview." *British Journal of Nursing* 19 (October 28-November 10, 2010): 1231–1235.

Ridge, D., et al. "Understanding How Men Experience, Express and Cope with Mental Distress: Where Next?" *Sociology of Health and Illness* 33 (January 2011): 145–159.

Sánchez, F. J., et al. "Reported Effects of Masculine Ideals on Gay Men." *Psychology of Men and Masculinity* 10 (January 2009): 73–87.

Schneider, M., et al. "Differences on Psychosocial Outcomes between Male and Female Caregivers of Children with Life-limiting Illnesses." *Journal of Pediatric Nursing* 26 (June 2011): 186–199.

WEBSITES

American Association for Marriage and Family Therapy (AAMFT). "Therapeutic Issues for Same-sex Couples: Gender Roles." http://www.aamft.org/imis15/Content/Consumer_Updates/Therapeutic_Issues_for_Same-sex_Couples.aspx (accessed May 29, 2011).

American Psychiatric Association. DSM-5 Development. "P 00 Gender Dysphoria in Children." http://www.dsm5.org/ProposedRevisions/Pages/proposedrevision.aspx?rid=192 (accessed May 19, 2011).

American Psychiatric Association. DSM-5 Development. "P 01 Gender Dysphoria in Adolescents or Adults." http://www.dsm5.org/ProposedRevisions/Pages/proposedrevision.aspx?rid=482 (accessed May 19, 2011).

Domestic Violence in Gay Couples. "Choosing to Abuse: Gender Roles." http://www.psychpage.com/gay/library/gay_lesbian_violence/choosing_gender.html (accessed May 29, 2011).

Medscape. "Sexual and Gender Identity Disorders." http://emedicine.medscape.com/article/293890-overview (accessed May 19, 2011).

San Diego Union-Tribune. "Couple's Gender Secret for Baby Touches Off Debate." http://www.signonsandiego.com/news/2011/may/27/couples-gender-secret-for-baby-touches-off-debate (accessed May 27, 2011).

ORGANIZATIONS

American Association for Marriage and Family Therapy (AAMFT), 112 South Alfred Street, Alexandria, VA, United States 22314-3061, (703) 838-9808, Fax: (703) 838-9805, http://www.aamft.org/iMIS15/AAMFT

American Association of Sexuality Educators, Counselors, and Therapists (AASECT), 1444 I Street NW, Suite 700, Washington, DC, United States 20005, (202) 449-1099, Fax: (202) 216-9646, info@aasect.org, http://www.aasect.org

Society for the Psychological Study of Men and Masculinity (Division 51), American Psychological Association, 750 First St. NE, Washington, DC, United States 20002-4242, (202) 216-7602, Fax: (202) 218-3599, kcooke@apa.org, http://www.apa.org/about/division/div51.aspx

University of Minnesota Clinic, Center for Sexual Health, 1300 South 2nd Street, Minneapolis, MN, United States 55454, (612) 624-7821, http://www.fm.umn.edu/phs/clinic/home.html

Wellesley Centers for Women (WCW), Wellesley College, 106 Central Street, Wellesley, MA, United States 02481-8203, (781) 283-2500, wcw@wellesley.edu, http://www.wcwonline.org

Sandra L. Friedrich, M.A.
Emily Jane Willingham, Ph.D.
Rebecca J. Frey, Ph.D.

Generalized anxiety disorder

Definition

Generalized anxiety disorder (GAD) is a disorder characterized by excessive worry and anxiety concerning a number of events and activities. This anxiety is accompanied by such symptoms as restlessness, **fatigue**, inability to concentrate, muscle tension, or disturbed sleep. Individuals with this disorder experience symptoms on most days for a period of at least six months, and find the symptoms difficult to control.

Demographics

The **National Institute of Mental Health** (NIMH) estimates that approximately 6.8 million Americans have GAD. Further it is estimated that twice as many women as men develop GAD. One study that used the *DSM-III-R* criteria concluded that 5% of the United States population, or one person in every 20, will develop GAD at some point.

Some psychiatrists think that generalized anxiety disorder is overdiagnosed in both adults and children. One reason for this possibility is that diagnostic screening tests used by primary care physicians for mental disorders produce a large number of false positives for GAD. One study of the PRIME-MD, a screening instrument for mental disorders frequently used in primary care practices, found that 7 of 10 patients met the criteria for GAD. In-depth follow-up interviews with the patients, however, revealed that only a third of the GAD diagnoses could be confirmed.

Description

Generalized anxiety disorder is characterized by persistent worry that is excessive and that patients find hard to control. Common worries associated with generalized anxiety disorder include work responsibilities, money, health, safety, car repairs, and household chores. Unlike people with phobias or post-traumatic disorders, people with GAD do not have their worries provoked by specific triggers; they may worry about almost anything having to do with ordinary life. It is not unusual for patients diagnosed with GAD to shift the focus of their anxiety from one issue to another as their daily circumstances change. For example, people with GAD may start worrying about finances when several bills arrive in the mail, and then fret about the state of their health when they notice that one of the bills is for health insurance. Later in the day they may read a newspaper article that moves the focus of the worry to a third concern.

Patients usually recognize that their worry is out of proportion in its duration or intensity to the actual likelihood or impact of the feared situation or event. For example, a husband or wife may worry about an accident happening to a spouse who commutes to work by train, even though the worried partner knows objectively that rail travel is much safer than automobile travel on major highways. The anxiety levels of patients with GAD may rise and fall somewhat over a period of weeks or months but tend to become chronic problems. The disorder typically becomes worse during stressful periods in the patient's life.

The ***Diagnostic and Statistical Manual of Mental Disorders,*** fourth edition, text revision (*DSM-IV-TR*) specifies interference with work, family life, social activities, or other areas of functioning as a criterion for generalized anxiety disorder. This may be accompanied by such physical symptoms as **insomnia**, sore muscles, headaches, and digestive upsets. According to the *DSM-IV-TR,* adult patients must experience three symptoms out of a list of six (restlessness, being easily fatigued, having difficulty concentrating, being irritable, high levels of muscle tension, and sleep disturbances) in order to be diagnosed with the disorder.

Patients diagnosed with GAD have a high rate of concurrent mental disorders, particularly major **depression** disorder, other **anxiety disorders**, or a **substance abuse** disorder. They also frequently have or develop such stress-related physical illnesses and conditions as tension headaches, irritable bowel syndrome (IBS), temporomandibular joint dysfunction (TMJ), bruxism (grinding of the teeth during sleep), and hypertension. In addition, GAD often intensifies the discomfort or complications associated with arthritis, diabetes, and other chronic disorders. Patients with GAD are more likely to seek help from a primary care physician than a **psychiatrist**; they are also more likely than patients with other disorders to make frequent medical appointments, to undergo extensive or repeated diagnostic testing, to describe their health as poor, and to smoke tobacco or abuse other substances. In addition, patients with anxiety disorders have higher rates of mortality from all causes than people who are less anxious.

In many cases, it is difficult for the patient's doctor to determine whether the anxiety preceded the physical condition or followed it; sometimes people develop generalized anxiety disorder after being diagnosed with a chronic organic health problem. In other instances, the wear and tear on the body caused by persistent and recurrent worrying leads to physical diseases and disorders. There is an overall "vicious circle" quality to the relationship between GAD and other disorders, whether mental or organic.

Children diagnosed with GAD have much the same anxiety symptoms as adults. The mother of a six-year-old boy with the disorder told his pediatrician that her son "acted like a little man" rather than a typical first-grader. He would worry about such matters as arriving on time for school field trips, whether the family had enough money for immediate needs, whether his friends would get hurt climbing on the playground jungle gym, whether there was enough gas in the tank of the family car, and similar concerns. The little boy had these worries in spite of the fact that his family was stable and happy and had no serious financial or other problems.

GAD often has an insidious onset that begins relatively early in life, although it can be precipitated by a sudden crisis at any age above six or seven years. The idea that GAD often begins in the childhood years even though the symptoms may not become clearly noticeable until late adolescence or the early adult years is gaining acceptance. About half of all patients diagnosed with the disorder report that their worrying began in childhood or their teenage years. Many will say that they cannot remember a time in their lives when they were not worried about something. This type of persistent anxiety can be regarded as part of a person's temperament, or inborn disposition; it is sometimes called trait anxiety. It is not unusual, however, for people to develop the disorder in their early adult years or even later in reaction to chronic **stress** or anxiety-producing situations. For example, there are instances of people developing GAD after several years of taking care of a relative with **dementia**, living with domestic violence, or living in close contact with a friend or relative with **borderline personality disorder**.

The specific worries of people with GAD may be influenced by their ethnic background or culture. The *DSM-IV-TR* cited an observation that being punctual is a common concern of patients with GAD that reflects the value that Western countries place on using time as efficiently as possible. One study of worry in college students from different ethnic backgrounds found that Caucasian and African American students tended to worry a variable amount about a wider range of concerns, whereas Asian Americans tended to worry more intensely about a smaller number of issues. Another study found that a community sample of older Puerto Ricans with GAD overlapped with a culture-specific syndrome called *ataque de nervios*, which resembles **panic disorder** but has features of other anxiety disorders as well as dissociative symptoms. (People experience dissociative symptoms when their perception of reality is temporarily altered—they may feel as if they were in a trance, or that they were observing activity around them instead of participating.) Further research is needed regarding the relationship between people's ethnic backgrounds and their outward expression of anxiety symptoms.

Causes and symptoms

Causes

The causes of generalized anxiety disorder appear to be a mixture of genetic and environmental factors. It has been known for some years that the disorder runs in families. Twin studies as well as the ongoing mapping of the human genome point to a genetic factor in the development of GAD. The role of the family environment (social **modeling**) in an individual's susceptibility to GAD is uncertain. Social modeling, the process of learning behavioral and emotional response patterns from observing one's parents or other adults, appears to be a more important factor for women than for men.

Another factor in the development of GAD is social expectations related to gender roles. Research findings indicate that women have higher levels of emotional distress and lower quality of life than men. The higher incidence of GAD in women has been linked to the diffuse yet comprehensive expectations of women as caregivers. Many women assume responsibility for the well-being and safety of other family members in addition to holding jobs or completing graduate or professional school. The global character of these responsibilities as well as their unrelenting nature has been described as a mirror image of the persistent but nonspecific anxiety associated with GAD.

Socioeconomic status may also contribute to generalized anxiety. One British study found that GAD is more closely associated with an accumulation of minor stressors than with any demographic factors. People of lower socioeconomic status, however, have fewer resources for dealing with minor stressors and so appear to be at greater risk for generalized anxiety.

An additional factor may be the patient's level of muscle tension. Several studies have found that patients diagnosed with GAD tend to respond to physiological stress in a rigid, stereotyped manner. Their autonomic reactions (reactions in the part of the nervous system that governs involuntary bodily functions) are similar to those of people without GAD, but their muscular tension shows a significant increase. It is not yet known, however, whether this level of muscle tension is a cause or an effect of GAD.

Symptoms

The symptomatology of GAD has changed somewhat over time with redefinitions of the disorder in successive editions of the *DSM*. The first edition of the *DSM* and the *DSM-II* did not make a sharp distinction between generalized anxiety disorder and panic disorder. After specific treatments were developed for panic disorder, GAD was introduced in the *DSM-III* as an anxiety disorder without panic attacks or symptoms of major depression. This definition proved to be unreliable. As a result, the *DSM-IV* constructed its definition of GAD around the psychological symptoms of the disorder (excessive worrying) rather than the physical (muscle tension) or autonomic symptoms of anxiety. The *DSM-IV-TR* continued that emphasis, and no changes or revisions have been suggested for the *DSM-5*.

According to the *DSM-IV-TR,* the symptoms of GAD are:

- excessive anxiety and worry about a number of events or activities occurring more days than not for at least six months
- worry that cannot be controlled
- worry that is associated with several symptoms such as restlessness, fatigue, irritability, or muscle tension
- worry that causes distress or impairment in relationships, at work, or at school

In addition, to meet the diagnostic criteria for GAD, the content or focus of the worry cannot change the **diagnosis** from GAD to another anxiety disorder such as panic disorder, **social phobia**, or **obsessive-compulsive disorder**, and the anxiety cannot be caused by a substance (a drug or a medication).

One categorization of GAD symptoms that some psychiatrists use in addition to the *DSM* framework consists of three symptom clusters:

- symptoms related to high levels of physiological arousal: muscle tension, irritability, fatigue, restlessness, insomnia
- symptoms related to distorted thinking processes: poor concentration, unrealistic assessment of problems, recurrent worrying
- symptoms associated with poor coping strategies: procrastination, avoidance, inadequate problem-solving skills

Diagnosis

Diagnosis of GAD, particularly in primary care settings, is complicated by several factors. One is the high level of comorbidity (co-occurrence) between GAD and other mental or physical disorders. Another is the considerable overlap between anxiety disorders and depression. Some practitioners believe that depression and GAD may not be separate disorders after all, because studies have repeatedly confirmed the existence and common occurrence of a "mixed" anxiety/depression syndrome.

Evaluating patients for generalized anxiety disorder includes the following steps:

- Patient interview. The doctor will ask the patients to describe the anxiety, and will note whether it is acute (lasting hours to weeks) or persistent (lasting from months to years). If the patients describe a recent stressful event, the doctor will evaluate them for "double anxiety," which refers to acute anxiety added to underlying persistent anxiety. The doctor may also give the patients a diagnostic questionnaire to evaluate the presence of anxiety disorders. The Hamilton Anxiety Scale is a commonly used instrument to assess anxiety disorders in general. The Generalized Anxiety Disorder Questionnaire for *DSM-IV* (GAD-Q-IV) is a more recent diagnostic tool, and is specific to GAD.
- Medical evaluation. Nonpsychiatric disorders that are known to cause anxiety (hyperthyroidism, Cushing's disease, mitral valve prolapse, carcinoid syndrome, and pheochromocytoma) must be ruled out, as well as certain medications (steroids, digoxin, thyroxine, theophylline, and selective serotonin reuptake inhibitors) that may also cause anxiety as a side effect. Patients should be asked about their use of herbal preparations as well.
- Substance abuse evaluation. Because anxiety is a common symptom of substance abuse and withdrawal syndrome, doctors will ask about patients' use of caffeine, nicotine, alcohol, and other common substances (including prescription medications) that may be abused.
- Evaluation for other psychiatric disorders. This step is necessary because of the frequent overlap between GAD and depression or between GAD and other anxiety disorders.

In some instances the doctor will consult the patient's family for additional information about the onset of the patient's anxiety symptoms, dietary habits, etc.

Treatment

There are several treatment types that have been found effective in treating people with GAD. Most patients with the disorder are treated with a combination of medications and **psychotherapy**.

Medications

Pharmacologic therapy is usually prescribed for patients whose anxiety is severe enough to interfere with daily functioning. Several different groups of medications have been used to treat generalized anxiety disorder.

These medications include the following:

- Benzodiazepines. This group of tranquilizers does not decrease worry, but lowers anxiety by decreasing muscle tension and hypervigilance. They are often prescribed for patients with double anxiety because they act very quickly. The benzodiazepines, however, have several disadvantages: they are unsuitable for long-term therapy because they can cause dependence, and GAD is a long-term disorder; they cannot be given to patients who abuse alcohol; and they cause short-term memory loss and difficulty in concentration. One British study found that benzodiazepines significantly increased a patient's risk of involvement in a traffic accident.

- Buspirone (BuSpar). Buspirone appears to be as effective as benzodiazepines and antidepressants in controlling anxiety symptoms. It is slower to take effect (about two–three weeks), but has fewer side effects. In addition, it treats the worry associated with GAD rather than the muscle tension.
- Tricyclic antidepressants. Imipramine (Tofranil), nortriptyline (Pamelor), and desipramine (Norpramin) have been given to patients with GAD. They have, however, some problematic side effects: imipramine has been associated with disturbances in heart rhythm, and the other tricyclics often cause drowsiness, dry mouth, constipation, and confusion. They increase the patient's risk of falls and other accidents.
- Selective serotonin reuptake inhibitors (SSRIs). Paroxetine (Paxil), one of the SSRIs, was approved by the U.S. Food and Drug Administration (FDA) in 2001 as a treatment for GAD. Venlafaxine (Effexor) appears to be particularly beneficial to patients with a mixed anxiety/depression syndrome; it is the first drug to be labeled by the FDA as an antidepressant as well as an anxiolytic. Venlafaxine is also effective in treating patients with GAD whose symptoms are primarily somatic (manifesting as physical symptoms or bodily complaints).

Psychotherapy

Some studies have found cognitive therapy to be superior to medications and **psychodynamic psychotherapy** in treating GAD, but other researchers disagree with these findings. As a rule, patients with GAD who have **personality disorders**, who are living with chronic social stress (e.g., caring for a parent with **Alzheimer's disease**), or who do not trust psychotherapeutic approaches require treatment with medications. The greatest benefit of cognitive therapy is its effectiveness in helping patients with the disorder to learn more realistic ways to appraise their problems and to use better problem-solving techniques.

Family therapy is recommended insofar as family members can be helpful in offering patients a different perspective on their problems. They can also help patients practice new approaches to problem solving.

Alternative and complementary therapies

Several alternative and complementary therapies have been found helpful in treating patients with

KEY TERMS

Anxiolytic—A preparation or substance given to relieve anxiety; a tranquilizer.

Ataque de nervios—A culture-specific anxiety syndrome found among some Latin American groups in the United States and in Latin America. It resembles panic disorder in some respects but also includes dissociative symptoms, and frequently occurs in response to stressful events.

Autonomic nervous system—The part of the nervous system that governs the heart, involuntary muscles, and glands.

Double anxiety—Acute anxiety from a recent stressful event combined with underlying persistent anxiety associated with generalized anxiety disorder.

Free-floating—A term used in psychiatry to describe anxiety that is unfocused or lacking an apparent cause or object.

Insidious—Proceeding gradually and inconspicuously but with serious effect.

Social modeling—A process of learning behavioral and emotional response patterns from observing one's parents or other adults. Some researchers think that social modeling plays a part in the development of generalized anxiety disorder in women.

Temperament—A person's natural disposition or inborn combination of mental and emotional traits.

Temporomandibular joint dysfunction—A condition resulting in pain in the head, face, and jaw. Muscle tension or abnormalities of the bones in the area of the hinged joint (the temporomandibular joint) between the lower jaw and the temporal bone are usually the cause.

Trait anxiety—A type of persistent anxiety found in some patients with generalized anxiety disorder. Trait anxiety is regarded as a feature (trait) of a person's temperament.

Twin study—Research studies that use pairs of twins to study the effects of heredity and environment on behavior or other characteristics.

generalized anxiety disorder. These include **hypnotherapy**, **music therapy**, Ayurvedic medicine, **yoga**, religious practice, and guided imagery **meditation**.

Biofeedback and relaxation techniques are also recommended for patients with GAD in order to lower physiologic arousal. In addition, massage therapy, hydrotherapy, shiatsu, and **acupuncture** have been reported to relieve muscle spasms or soreness associated with GAD.

One herbal remedy that has been used in **clinical trials** for treating GAD is **passionflower** (*Passiflora incarnata*). One team of researchers found that passionflower extract was as effective as **oxazepam** (Serax) in relieving anxiety symptoms in a group of 36 outpatients diagnosed with GAD according to *DSM-IV* criteria. In addition, the passionflower extract did not impair the subjects' job performance as frequently or as severely as the oxazepam.

Prognosis

Generalized anxiety disorder is generally regarded as a long-term condition that may become a lifelong problem. Patients frequently find their symptoms resurfacing or getting worse during stressful periods in their lives. It is rare for patients with GAD to recover spontaneously.

Prevention

The best preventive strategy, given the early onset of GAD, is the modeling of realistic assessment of stressful events by parents, and the teaching of effective coping strategies to their children.

Resources

BOOKS

American Psychiatric Association. *Diagnostic and Statistical Manual of Mental Disorders*. 4th ed., text rev. Washington, DC: American Psychiatric Publishing, 2000.

Dugas, Michel J., and Melisa Robichaud. *Cognitive-Behavioral Treatment for Generalized Anxiety Disorder: From Science to Practice*. New York: Brunner-Routledge, 2006.

Heimberg, Richard G., Cynthia L. Turk, and Douglas S. Mennin, eds. *Generalized Anxiety Disorder: Advances in Research and Practice*. New York: The Guilford Press, 2004.

Nutt, David J., Karl Rickels, and Dan J. Stein. *Generalized Anxiety Disorder: Symptomatology, Pathogenesis and Management*. Oxford: Informa Healthcare, 2002.

Pelletier, Kenneth R. "CAM Therapies for Specific Conditions: Anxiety." In *The Best Alternative Medicine*. Part II. New York: Touchstone, 2007.

Rygh, Jayne L., and William C. Sanderson. *Treating Generalized Anxiety Disorder: Evidence-Based Strategies, Tools, and Techniques*. New York: The Guilford Press, 2004.

PERIODICALS

Allgulander, Christer. "Generalized Anxiety Disorder: What Are We Missing?" *European Neuropsychopharmacology* 16, Suppl. 2 (July 2006): S101–S108.

Allgulander, Christer, Ioana Florea, and Anna K. Trap Huusom. "Prevention of Relapse in Generalized Anxiety Disorder by Escitalopram Treatment." *International Journal of Neuropsychopharmacology* 9, no. 5 (October 2006): 495–505.

Angst, Jules, et al. "Varying Temporal Criteria for Generalized Anxiety Disorder: Prevalence and Clinical Characteristics in a Young Age Cohort." *Psychological Medicine* 36, no. 9 (September 2006): 1283–92.

Baldwin, David S., Anna Karina Trap Huusom, and Eli Maehlum. "Escitalopram and Paroxetine in the Treatment of Generalised Anxiety Disorder: Randomised, Placebo-Controlled, Double-Blind Study." *British Journal of Psychiatry* 189, no. 3 (September 2006): 264–72. Available online at http://bjp.rcpsych.org/content/189/3/264.full (accessed November 9, 2011).

Connor, Kathryn M., Victoria Payne, and Jonathan R. T. Davidson. "Kava in Generalized Anxiety Disorder: Three Placebo-Controlled Trials." *International Clinical Psychopharmacology* 21, no. 5 (September 2006): 249–53.

Goldston, David B., et al. "Reading Problems, Psychiatric Disorders, and Functional Impairment from Mid- to Late Adolescence." *Journal of the American Academy of Child & Adolescent Psychiatry* 46, no. 1 (January 2007): 25–32.

Gosselin, Patrick, et al. "Benzodiazepine Discontinuation Among Adults With GAD: A Randomized Trial of Cognitive-Behavioral Therapy." *Journal of Consulting and Clinical Psychology* 74, no. 5 (October 2006): 908–19.

Hoge, Elizabeth A., et al. "Cross-Cultural Differences in Somatic Presentation in Patients with Generalized Anxiety Disorder." *Journal of Nervous & Mental Disease* 194, no. 12 (December 2006): 962–66.

Kim, Tae-Suk, et al. "Comparison of Venlafaxine Extended Release Versus Paroxetine for Treatment of Patients with Generalized Anxiety Disorder." *Psychiatry and Clinical Neurosciences* 60, no. 3 (June 2006): 347–51.

Kopecek, Miloslav, Pavel Mohr, and Tomas Novak. "Sedative Effects of Low-Dose Risperidone in GAD Patients and Risk of Drug Interactions." *Journal of Clinical Psychiatry* 67, no. 8 (August 2006): 1308–1309.

Labrecque, Joane, et al. "Cognitive-Behavioral Therapy for Comorbid Generalized Anxiety Disorder and Panic Disorder With Agoraphobia." *Behavior Modification* 30, no. 4 (July 2006): 383–410.

Lyddon, William J. "Review: Generalized Anxiety Disorder: Advances in Research and Practice." *Journal* of Cognitive Psychotherapy 20, no. 4 (December 2006): 463–64.

Mennin, Douglas S. "Emotion Regulation Therapy: An Integrative Approach to Treatment-Resistant Anxiety Disorders." *Journal of Contemporary Psychotherapy* 36, no. 2 (June 2006): 95–105.

Montgomery, Stuart A., et al. "Efficacy and Safety of Pregabalin in the Treatment of Generalized Anxiety Disorder: A 6-Week, Multicenter, Randomized, Double-Blind, Placebo-Controlled Comparison of Pregabalin and Venlafaxine." *Journal of Clinical Psychiatry* 67, no. 5 (May 2006): 771–82.

Nutt, David, et al. "Generalized Anxiety Disorder: A Comorbid Disease." *European Neuropsychopharmacology* 16, Suppl. 2 (July 2006): S109–S118.

Skopp, Nancy A., et al. "Investigation of Cognitive Behavior Therapy." *American Journal of Geriatric Psychiatry* 14, no. 3 (March 2006): 292.

Weems, Carl F., et al. "Predisaster Trait Anxiety and Negative Affect Predict Posttraumatic Stress in Youths After Hurricane Katrina." *Journal of Consulting and Clinical Psychology* 75, no. 1 (February 2007): 154–59. http://cretscmhd.psych.ucla.edu/nola/Volunteer/EmpiricalStudies/Predisaster%20trait%20anxiety%20and%20negative%20affect%20predict%20posttraumatic%20stress%20in%20youths%20after%20hurricane%20katrina.pdf (accessed November 9, 2011).

WEBSITES

U.S. National Institute of Mental Health. "Anxiety Disorders." http://www.nimh.nih.gov/anxiety/anxiety.cfm (accessed October 8, 2011).

———. "Generalized Anxiety Disorder." October 6, 2011. http://www.nimh.nih.gov/health/topics/generalized-anxiety-disorder-gad/index.shtml (accessed October 8, 2011).

ORGANIZATIONS

American Psychiatric Association, 1000 Wilson Blvd., Suite 1825, Arlington, VA, 22209-3901, (703) 907-7300, apa@psych.org, http://www.psych.org.

Anxiety Disorders Association of America, 8730 Georgia Ave., Suite 600, Silver Spring, MD, 20910, (240) 485-1001, Fax: (240) 485-1035, http://www.adaa.org.

Mental Health America, 2000 North Beauregard Street, 6th Floor, Alexandria, VA, 22311, (703) 684-7722, (800) 969-6642, Fax: (703) 684-5968, http://www1.nmha.org.

National Alliance on Mental Illness, 3803 North Fairfax Drive, Suite 100, Arlington, VA, 22203, (703) 524-7600, Fax: (703) 524-9094, http://www.nami.org.

National Institute of Mental Health, 6001 Executive Blvd., Room 8184, MSC 9663, Bethesda, MD, 20892-9663, (301) 433-4513; TTY: (301) 443-8431, (866) 615-6464; TTY: (866) 415-8051, Fax: (301) 443-4279, nimhinfo@nih.gov, http://www.nimh.nih.gov.

Rebecca J. Frey, PhD
Ruth A. Wienclaw, PhD

Genetic factors and mental disorders

Definition

Genetic factors play an important role in the etiology (causes) of many mental disorders. In 1990, the Human Genome Project began mapping the entire sequence of human DNA. Completed in 2003, the project has had great implications for psychiatric **diagnosis** and treatment.

Description

Genes appear to influence the development of mental disorders in three major ways:

1. They may govern the organic causes of such disorders as Alzheimer's disease (AD) and schizophrenia.
2. They may be responsible for abnormalities in a person's development before or after birth.
3. They may influence a person's susceptibility to anxiety, depression, personality disorders, and substance abuse disorders.

The two most important examples of mental disorders caused by organic changes or abnormalities in the **brain** are late-onset AD and **schizophrenia**. Both disorders are polygenic, which means that their expression is determined by more than one gene.

Disorders with genetic components

SCHIZOPHRENIA. Researchers have known for many years that first-degree biological relatives of patients with schizophrenia have a greater risk of developing the disorder than the general population. The identical twin of a person with schizophrenia has a 40%–50% risk of developing the disorder.

LATE-ONSET AD. Late-onset AD is another polygenic disorder. It has been known since 1993 that a specific form of a gene for apolipoprotein E (apoE4) on human chromosome 19 is a genetic risk factor for late-onset AD. People who inherited the gene from one parent have a 50% chance of developing AD and a 90% chance if they inherited the gene from both parents. They are also likely to develop AD earlier in life. One of the remaining puzzles about this particular gene, however, is that it is not a consistent marker for AD. In other words, some people who have the apoE4 gene do not develop AD, and some who do not have the gene do develop the disorder.

There are two other forms of AD, early-onset AD and familial AD (FAD), which have different patterns of genetic transmission. Early-onset AD is caused by a defect in one of three genes known as APP, presenilin-1, and presenilin-2, found on human chromosomes 21, 14, and 1, respectively. Early-onset AD is also associated with **Down syndrome**, in that persons with trisomy 21 (three forms of human chromosome 21 instead of two) often develop this form of AD. The brains of people with Down syndrome age prematurely, so those who develop early-onset AD are often only in their late 40s or early 50s when the symptoms of the disease first appear. FAD appears to be related to abnormal genes on human chromosomes 21 and 14.

FRAGILE X SYNDROME. Fragile X syndrome is the most common inherited form of **intellectual disability** and should be considered in the differential diagnosis of any child with developmental delays, signs of intellectual disability, or learning difficulties. The syndrome is caused by a large expansion of a cytosine-guanine-guanine (CGG) repeat, which interferes with normal protein transcription from a gene called the FMR1 gene on the X chromosome. Since males have only one X chromosome, they are more severely affected than females who have a normal FMR1 gene on their second X chromosome. In both genders, there is a correlation between the length of the expansion mutation and the severity of the syndrome.

In addition to developmental disorders of childhood, expansion mutations, such as the one found in Fragile X syndrome, may also be involved in other psychiatric disorders. Clinicians had noticed as early as 1910 that some disorders produce a more severe phenotype or occur at earlier and earlier ages in each successive generation of an affected family. This phenomenon is known as anticipation, but its biological basis was not understood until recently. It is now known that triplet repeats that are long enough to cause disorders are unstable and tend to grow longer from generation to generation. Anticipation has been found in some families affected by **bipolar disorder** and schizophrenia, and some researchers think that it may also be present in some forms of **autism**.

POST-TRAUMATIC SYNDROMES. Researchers have found that some persons are more vulnerable than others to developing dissociative and anxiety-related symptoms following a traumatic experience. Vulnerability to **trauma** is affected by such inherited factors as temperament as well as by family or cultural influences; shy or introverted persons are at greater risk for developing **post-traumatic stress disorder** (PTSD) than their extroverted or outgoing peers. In addition, twin studies indicate that certain abnormalities in brain hormone levels and brain structure are inherited, and that these increase a person's susceptibility to developing **acute stress disorder** (ASD) or PTSD following exposure to trauma.

ANXIETY DISORDERS. It has been known for some time that **anxiety disorders** run in families. Recent twin studies as well as the human genome mapping point to a genetic factor in the development of **generalized anxiety disorder** (GAD). Research has also confirmed earlier hypotheses that there is a genetic component to **agoraphobia**, and that it can be separated from susceptibility to **panic disorder** (PD). Panic disorder was found to be associated with two loci, one on human chromosome 1 and the other on chromosome 11q. Researchers have concluded that agoraphobia and PD are common, heritable anxiety disorders that share some but not all of their genetic loci for susceptibility.

Behavioral phenotypes

Although medical professionals are familiar with the physical phenotypes associated with genetic disorders, the notion of behavioral phenotypes is still controversial. A behavioral phenotype is the characteristic set of behaviors found in patients with a genetic disorder. Behavioral phenotypes include patterns of language usage, cognitive development, and social adjustment as well as behavioral problems. It is important for psychiatrists who treat children and adolescents to understand behavioral phenotypes, because they are better able to identify problem behaviors as part of a genetic syndrome and refer children to a geneticist for an accurate diagnosis.

Examples of behavioral phenotypes are those associated with Down, Prader-Willi, and Williams syndromes. Children with Down syndrome have an increased risk of developing early-onset AD. They are usually quiet and good-tempered, but may also be hyperactive and impulsive. Their behavioral phenotype includes delayed language development and moderate to severe intellectual disability.

Children with Prader-Willi syndrome are often quiet in childhood but develop stubborn, aggressive, or impulsive patterns of behavior as they grow older. They are typically obsessed with food, frequently **hoarding** it, stealing it, or stealing money to buy food. The onset of their overeating is often associated with temper tantrums and other behavioral problems. About 50% of children diagnosed with Prader-Willi syndrome meet the criteria for **obsessive-compulsive disorder** (OCD).

Williams syndrome is a genetic disorder that results from a deletion of locus 23 on chromosome 7q11. Children with this syndrome often have an "elf-like" face with short upturned noses and small chins. Their behavioral phenotype includes talkativeness, friendliness, and a willingness to follow strangers. They are also hyperactive and easily distracted from tasks. The personality profile of children with Williams syndrome is so distinctive that many are diagnosed on the basis of behavioral rather than physical characteristics.

BEHAVIORAL TRAITS. There has been considerable controversy in the past decade concerning the mapping of genetic loci associated with specific human behaviors, as distinct from behavioral phenotypes related to developmental disorders. Research into the genetic component of human behavior is currently conducted with an awareness of the social and political implications of any potential results. Given contemporary concerns about the misuse of findings related to biological race or sex, investigators are usually careful to acknowledge the importance of environmental as well as genetic factors.

Genetic epidemiology

Genetic epidemiology is the branch of medicine that investigates the incidence and prevalence of genetic disorders in specific populations. Researchers in this field make use of specific types of studies to assess the relative importance of genetic and environmental factors in families with a history of inherited disorders.

TWIN STUDIES. Twin studies are based on the assumption that twins reared in the same family share a common environment. Monozygotic (identical) twins have all their genes in common, whereas dizygotic (fraternal) twins share only half their genes. If a certain disorder appears more frequently in monozygotic twins of affected persons than in dizygotic twins, one may assume that the difference is due to genetic factors rather than the family environment. Some phenotypes show clear differences between identical and fraternal twins, including schizophrenia, childhood autism, **attention deficit hyperactivity disorder (ADHD)**, unipolar **depression**, manic depressive disorder, and cognitive abilities as measured by IQ tests.

Twin studies have proved to be particularly important in genetic research into autism. Until the early 1970s, autism was thought to develop as a result of negative parental interaction. The first small-scale twin study of children with autism was done in 1977, and its findings showed that there was a significant difference between monozygotic and dizygotic twin pairs with regard to the appearance of the disorder in siblings. More importantly, the study showed that the similarities within monozygotic pairs of twins included a range of social and cognitive disabilities, not just the autism itself. This finding implied that the phenotype of autism was broader than the older diagnostic categories assumed. In the 1970s and 1980s, advances in cytogenetic techniques led to the discovery that autism was associated with several different chromosomal abnormalities, including the defect that produces fragile X syndrome. A much larger British twin study done in 1995 confirmed earlier findings in the United States: a monozygotic twin of a child diagnosed with autism was 12 times more likely to have the disorder than a dizygotic twin (60% versus 5%). Secondly, the British study confirmed the hypothesis that the genetic risk of autism extends to a broader phenotype; over 90% of the monozygotic twin pairs in the British study shared social and intellectual disabilities similar to those found in patients with autism, but less severe. The causes of autism are not yet known, but research continues to support the hypothesis that there is a genetic component.

FAMILY STUDIES. Family studies are important tools for evaluating environmental effects on children with genetic disorders—and also for evaluating the impact of the disorder on the family environment. Family studies have indicated that families may develop problems in response to a child's illness that may also affect the child's prognosis for recovery.

Family factors fall into three categories: shared genetic material, shared environment, and nonshared environment. These three categories are complicated, however, by the fact that genetic as well as environmental factors affect interactions between parents and children. For example, a parent's behavior toward a child diagnosed with depression is partly shaped by the parent's genetic vulnerability to depression.

In general, much of the impact of a family's environment on a child with a mental disorder is due to nonshared rather than shared interactions. A clinical research measurement called expressed emotion (EE), originally developed to study young adults with schizophrenia, is now used to study families with younger children with mental disorders. EE measures three primary aspects of family members' attitudes toward the child with the illness: criticism, hostility, and emotional over-involvement. A growing number of research studies indicate that EE is a good predictor of the outcome of the child's illness; high EE is a marker of a more difficult course of the disorder and a poorer prognosis.

Clinical applications of genetics in psychiatry

Recent advances in genetics have affected the practice of psychiatry in several ways:

- Genetic counseling is recommended when a couple has already produced a child with intellectual disability, dysmorphic (malformed) features, or developmental delays; when either parent is suspected or known to have a genetic disorder; when the mother is

KEY TERMS

Agoraphobia—An intense fear of being trapped in a crowded, open, or public space where it may be hard to escape, combined with the dread of having a panic attack.

Anxiety—Can be experienced as a troubled feeling, a sense of dread, fear of the future, or distress over a possible threat to a person's physical or mental well-being.

Attention deficit hyperactivity disorder (ADHD)—A developmental disorder characterized by distractibility, hyperactivity, impulsive behaviors, and the inability to remain focused on tasks or activities.

Autism—A severe developmental disorder that usually begins before three years of age and affects a child's social as well as intellectual development.

Body dysmorphic disorder—A psychiatric disorder marked by preoccupation with an imagined physical defect.

Chromosome—A microscopic thread–like structure found within each cell of the body and consists of a complex of proteins and DNA. Humans have 46 chromosomes arranged into 23 pairs. Changes in either the total number of chromosomes or their shape and size (structure) may lead to physical or mental abnormalities.

Depression—A mental state characterized by feelings of sadness, despair, and discouragement.

Differential diagnosis—Comparing and contrasting the signs, symptoms, and laboratory findings of two or more diseases to determine which is causing the patient's condition.

Heritability—The effects of differences in genetics (among the population) in producing differences in behavior.

Obsessive-compulsive disorder—An anxiety disorder in which people cannot prevent themselves from dwelling on unwanted thoughts, acting on urges, or performing repetitious rituals, such as washing their hands or checking to make sure they turned off the lights.

Phenotypes—Observable traits or characteristics.

Prader-Willi syndrome—An uncommon genetic disorder that causes a constant feeling of hunger.

Schizophrenia—A major mental illness marked by psychotic symptoms, including hallucinations, delusions, and severe disruptions in thinking.

Seizure—A convulsion, or uncontrolled discharge of nerve cells that may spread to other cells throughout the brain.

Somatoform disorder—A category of psychiatric disorder characterized by physical complaints that appear to be medical in origin but that cannot be explained in terms of a physical disease, the results of substance abuse, or by another mental disorder.

Substance abuse—Illicit, inaccurate, or recreational use of either prescription or illegal drugs. Alcohol can also be abused as a substance but has its own category, alcohol abuse.

over 35; when there is a family history of a genetic disorder, especially if several members are affected; or if the mother has been exposed during pregnancy to drugs or environmental toxins known to cause birth defects. Genetic counselors do not try to control the couple's decision about a present or future pregnancy; rather, they offer information about the disorder, including treatment options as well as the risk of recurrence. They discuss possible reproductive choices available to the couple and help them adjust to caring for a child who is already affected.

- Preliminary studies of patients with schizophrenia indicate that DNA testing of the gene for a specific serotonin receptor can predict the patient's response to antipsychotic drugs. In the near future, researchers hope to devise genetic tests that will measure patients' responsiveness to specific antidepressant and antianxiety medications. Such tests would greatly simplify the present process of trial-and-error prescribing of drugs for psychiatric disorders.
- Nosology is the branch of psychiatry that deals with the classification of mental disorders. Some current diagnostic labels, including autism and attention deficit hyperactivity disorder, may represent groups of related syndromes rather than a single diagnostic entity. In other instances, genetic studies may lead to eventual reclassification of certain disorders. For example, body dysmorphic disorder, previously considered a somatoform disorder, has been proposed to be reclassified as an obsessive-compulsive disorder in the fifth edition of the *Diagnostic and Statistical Manual of Mental Disorders*, the handbook used by medical professionals in diagnosing mental disorders.

Research and advances in genetics and mental disorders

Geneticist Jonathan Sebat, chief of the Beyster Center for Molecular Genomics of Neuropsychiatric Diseases at the University of California, San Diego, has led studies linking variations in the genetic code (the number of gene copies within the genome) to mental illness. He has demonstrated that certain gene copies within the genome are an underlying factor in autism, schizophrenia, and bipolar disorder. Clinicians at the Beyster Center continue work in this field with the hope that research findings will enable the development of diagnostic and screening tests for psychiatric disease. Sebat and his team of clinicians (which include psychiatrists, cellular scientists, disease biologists and molecular scientists), continue to lead the way in research and advances to further understand the role of genetic factors in mental disorders.

The ongoing search for genes related to psychiatric symptoms and disorders is, however, complicated by several factors:

- Psychiatric diagnosis relies on a doctor's human judgment and evaluation of a patient's behavior or appearance to a greater degree than diagnosis in other fields of medicine. For example, there are no blood or urine tests for schizophrenia or a personality disorder. Diagnostic questionnaires for mental disorders are helpful in trimming the list of possible diagnoses but do not have the same degree of precision or objectivity as laboratory findings.
- Mental disorders almost always involve more than one gene. Studies have shown that one mental disorder can be caused by different genes on different chromosomes in different populations. For example, one study in the late 1980s found two genes on two different chromosomes among two populations that caused manic depression. Studies of schizophrenia done in the late 1980s and early 1990s revealed the same finding—different genes on different chromosomes produced schizophrenia in different populations. It now appears that specific mental disorders are related to different sets of genes that vary across family and ethnic groups.
- Genes associated with mental disorders do not always show the same degree of penetrance, which is defined as the frequency with which a gene produces its effects in a specific group of people. Penetrance is expressed as a percentage. For example, a gene for manic depression may have 20% penetrance, which means that 20% of the members of the family being studied are at risk of developing the disorder.
- Genetic factors in mental disorders interact with a person's family and cultural environment. For example, a person who has a gene associated with susceptibility to alcohol abuse may not develop the disorder if he or she grows up in a family that teaches effective ways to cope with stress and responsible attitudes toward drinking.

Ethical concerns

As the number of tests available for determining genetic markers for mental disorders continues to increase, ethical issues are being debated. These concerns include:

- Regulation of genetic testing—some companies have started to market tests for the apoE4 Alzheimer's gene even though the present benefits of such testing are not clear. The U.S. Department of Health and Human Services has established an advisory committee to study the question of government regulation of genetic testing.
- Confidentiality—the fear of losing health insurance is a major barrier to the acceptance of genetic testing in the general population. Many people do not trust hospitals or research laboratories to keep test results confidential.
- Discrimination—some people are concerned that genetic findings could be used to deny college or graduate school admission to persons at risk for certain disorders, or to restrict their access to employment opportunities.

Resources

BOOKS

American Psychiatric Association. *Diagnostic and Statistical Manual of Mental Disorders*. 4th ed., text rev. Washington, DC: American Psychiatric Association, 2000.

Bennett, Robin L. *The Practical Guide to the Genetic Family History*. 2nd ed. New York: Wiley-Blackwell, 2010.

Dodge, Kenneth A., and Michael Rutter, eds. *Gene-Environment Interactions in Developmental Psychopathology*. New York: The Guilford Press, 2011.

Fusar-Poli, Paolo, Stefan J. Borgwardt, and Phillip McGuire, eds. *Vulnerability to Psychosis: From Neurosciences to Psychopathology*. New York: Psychology Press, 2011.

Leigh, Hoyle. *Genes, Memes, Culture, and Mental Illness*. New York: Springer, 2010.

Peay, Holly Landrum, and Jehannine Claire Austin. *How to Talk with Families About Genetics and Psychiatric Illness*. New York: W. W. Norton & Company, 2011.

PERIODICALS

Boomsma, Dorret I., et al. "Longitudinal Stability of the CBCL-Juvenile Bipolar Disorder Phenotype: A Study in Dutch Twins." *Biological Psychiatry* 60, no. 9 (2006): 912–20.

Douthit, Kathryn Z. "The Convergence of Counseling and Psychiatric Genetics: An Essential Role for Counselors." *Journal of Counseling & Development* 84, no. 1 (2006): 16–28.

Durston, Sarah, et al. "Activation in Ventral Prefrontal Cortex Is Sensitive to Genetic Vulnerability for Attention-Deficit Hyperactivity Disorder." *Biological Psychiatry* 60, no. 10 (2006): 1062–70.

Farmer, Anne, Amanda Elkin, and Peter McGuffin. "The Genetics of Bipolar Affective Disorder." *Current Opinion in Psychiatry* 20, no. 1 (2007): 8–12.

Giménez-Llort, L., et al. "Modeling Behavioral and Neuronal Symptoms of Alzheimer's Disease in Mice: A Role for Intraneuronal Amyloid." *Neuroscience & Biobehavioral Reviews* 1, no. 1 (2007): 125–47.

Harris, Julie Aitken, Philip A. Vernon, and Kerry L. Jang. "Rated Personality and Measured Intelligence in Young Twin Children." *Personality and Individual Differences* 42, no. 1 (2007): 75–86.

Hollingworth, P. "Genome-Wide Association Study of Alzheimer's Disease with Psychotic Symptoms." *Molecular Psychiatry* (October 18, 2011) [e-pub ahead of print]. http://dx.doi.org/10.1038/mp.2011.125 (accessed November 4, 2011).

Hurd, Yasmin L. "Perspectives on Current Directions in the Neurobiology of Addiction Disorders Relevant to Genetic Risk Factors." *CNS Spectrums* 11, no. 11 (2006): 855–62.

Nierenberg, Andrew A., et al. "Family History of Mood Disorder and Characteristics of Major Depressive Disorder: A STAR*D (Sequenced Treatment Alternatives to Relieve Depression) Study." *Journal of Psychiatric Research* 41, no. 3–4 (2007): 214–21.

O'Tuathaigh, Colm M. P., et al. "Susceptibility Genes for Schizophrenia: Characterisation of Mutant Mouse Models at the Level of Phenotypic Behaviour." *Neuroscience & Biobehavioral Reviews* 31, no. 1 (2007): 60–78.

Potter, Alexandra S., Paul A. Newhouse, and David J. Bucci. "Central Nicotinic Cholinergic Systems: A Role in the Cognitive Dysfunction in Attention-Deficit/Hyperactivity Disorder?" *Behavioural Brain Research* 175, no. 2 (2006): 201–11.

State, M. W., and P. Levitt. "The Conundrums of Understanding Genetic Risks for Autism Spectrum Disorders." *Nature Neuroscience* (October 30, 2011) [e-pub ahead of print]. http://dx.doi.org/10.1038/nn.2924 (accessed November 4, 2011).

Taylor, Warren D., David C. Steffens, and K. Ranga Krishnan. "Psychiatric Disease in the Twenty-First Century: The Case for Subcortical Ischemic Depression." *Biological Psychiatry* 60, no. 12 (2006): 1299–1303.

WEBSITES

"Genetics Home Reference." U.S. National Library of Medicine, National Institutes of Health. http://ghr.nlm.nih.gov (accessed November 4, 2011).

"Human Genome Project Information." U.S. Department of Energy Office of Science, Office of Biological and Environmental Research. http://www.ornl.gov/sci/techresources/Human_Genome/home.shtml (accessed November 4, 2011).

ORGANIZATIONS

International Society of Psychiatric Genetics (ISPG), 5034-A Thoroughbred Lane, Brentwood, TN, 37027, (202) 336-5500, http://www.apa.org/index.aspx.

National Human Genome Research Institute, Building 31, Room 4B09, 31 Center Drive, MSC 2152, 9000 Rockville Pike, Bethesda, MD, 20892, (301) 402-0911, Fax: (301) 402-2218, http://www.genome.gov.

National Institute of Mental Health, 6001 Executive Blvd., Rm. 8184, MSC 9663, Bethesda, MD, 20892-9663, (301) 433-4513; TTY: (301) 443-8431, Fax: (301) 443-4279, (866) 615-6464; TTY: (866) 415-8051, nimhinfo@nih.gov, http://www.nimh.nih.gov.

Rebecca J. Frey, Ph.D.
Ruth Wineclaw, Ph.D.
Laura Jean Cataldo, RN, Ed.D.

Gen-XENE *see* **Clorazepate**

Geodon *see* **Ziprasidone**

Geriatric Depression Scale

Definition

The Geriatric **Depression** Scale (GDS) is a 30-item self-report assessment designed specifically to identify depression in the elderly. It is generally recommended as a routine part of a comprehensive geriatric assessment. A short version of the GDS containing 15 questions has been developed. The GDS is also available in a number of languages other than English.

Purpose

Depression is widespread among the elderly, affecting one in six patients treated in general medical practice and an even higher percentage of those in hospitals and nursing homes. Older people have the highest **suicide** rate of any group, and many medical problems common to older people may be related to, or intensified by, a depressive disorder. Recognition of the prevalence of depression among older people prompted the development of the geriatric depression scale in 1982-83. Yes/no responses are thought to be more easily used than the graduated responses found on other standard assessment scales such as the **Beck Depression Inventory**, the Hamilton rating scale for depression, or the Zung self-rating depression scale.

While it is not found in the ***Diagnostic and Statistical Manual of Mental Disorders*** (*DSM-IV-TR*)

Geriatric Depression Scale

1. Are you basically satisfied with your life? YES **NO**
2. Have you dropped many of your activities and interests? **YES** NO
3. Do you feel that your life is empty? **YES** NO
4. Do you often get bored? **YES** NO
5. Are you hopeful about the future? YES **NO**
6. Are you bothered by thoughts you can't get out of your head? **YES** NO
7. Are you in good spirits most of the time? YES **NO**
8. Are you afraid that something bad is going to happen to you? **YES** NO
9. Do you feel happy most of the time? YES **NO**
10. Do you often feel helpless? **YES** NO
11. Do you often get restless and fidgety? **YES** NO
12. Do you prefer to stay at home, rather than going out and doing new things? **YES** NO
13. Do you frequently worry about the future? **YES** NO
14. Do you feel you have more problems with memory than most? **YES** NO
15. Do you think it is wonderful to be alive now? YES **NO**
16. Do you often feel downhearted and blue? **YES** NO
17. Do you feel pretty worthless the way you are now? **YES** NO
18. Do you worry a lot about the past? **YES** NO
19. Do you find life very exciting? YES **NO**
20. Is it hard for you to get started on new projects? **YES** NO
21. Do you feel full of energy? YES **NO**
22. Do you feel that your situation is hopeless? **YES** NO
23. Do you think that most people are better off than you are? **YES** NO
24. Do you frequently get upset over little things? **YES** NO
25. Do you frequently feel like crying? **YES** NO
26. Do you have trouble concentrating? **YES** NO
27. Do you enjoy getting up in the morning? YES **NO**
28. Do you prefer to avoid social gatherings? **YES** NO
29. Is it easy for you to make decisions? YES **NO**
30. Is your mind as clear as it used to be? YES **NO**

Scoring is based on one point for each bolded answer.
Normal: 0–9
Mild depression: 10–19
Severe depression: 20–30

SOURCE: Stanford/VA Aging Clinical Research Center (ACRC).

(Table by PreMediaGlobal. © 2012 Cengage Learning.)

produced by the **American Psychiatric Association**, the GDS is widely recommended for clinical use and is included as a routine part of a comprehensive geriatric assessment. It is also increasingly being used in research on depression in the elderly.

Description

The Geriatric Depression Scale is a self-report assessment developed in 1982 by J.A. Yesavitch and colleagues. Depression scales are either interviewer-administered or by means of self-report. A self-report assessment is easier and quicker to administer, though an interviewer-administered test is generally more sensitive and specific—another reason for using more than one tool to obtain an accurate **diagnosis**. The items may be answered yes or no, which is thought to be simpler than scales that use a five-category response set. One point is assigned to each answer and corresponds to a scoring grid. A score of 10 or 11 or lower is the usual threshold to separate depressed from nondepressed patients.

Yesavitch and his coworkers chose 100 statements that they determined were related to seven common characteristics of depression in later life. These included:

- somatic concern
- lowered affect (affect is the outward expression of emotion)
- cognitive impairment
- feelings of discrimination
- impaired motivation
- lack of future orientation
- lack of self-esteem

The best 30 items were selected after administration of the 100 items to 46 depressed and normal elders. Those items were then administered to 20 elders without depression and 51 who were in treatment for depression. The test was 84% sensitive and 95% specific for a depression diagnosis. Repeated studies have demonstrated the value of GDS.

Examples of the questions in the GDS include:

- Are you basically satisfied with your life?
- Have you dropped many of your activities and interests?
- Are you hopeful about the future?
- Do you often get restless and fidgety?
- Do you frequently get upset over little things?
- Do you enjoy getting up in the morning?

A time frame should be specified for administration of the test, for example, "Answer these questions by thinking of how you've felt the past two weeks."

Precautions

The Geriatric diagnosis of clinical depression should not be made on the GDS results alone. Although the test has well-established reliability and validity, responses should be considered in conjunction with other results from a comprehensive diagnostic work-up.

There is some controversy over whether the GDS is reliable for depression screening in individuals with mild or moderate **dementia**. Several studies have shown good agreement with observer ratings of depression, whether or not the patient had dementia. However, persons with dementia may deny symptoms of depression. It also appears that less educated people are more likely to score in the depressed range on the GDS 15-item short form. These caveats notwithstanding, the GDS can be usefully applied in general medical settings in combination with other clinical assessments,

KEY TERMS

Low affect—Severe lack of interest and emotions; emotional numbness.

Somatic concern—Excessive concern about the body, particularly in relation to illness.

observation, and interviews with elder patient and their families.

Both symptom pattern and symptom severity must be considered when trying to identify depression. These dimensions are taken into account in the development of symptom scales and, while clinical judgment takes priority, a scale such as the GDS can help in identifying persons with depression, whether they are making satisfactory progress with treatment, or when they may need further assessment or referral.

Results

A scoring grid accompanies the GDS. One point is given for each respondent's answer that matches those on the grid. For example, the grid response to "Are you basically satisfied with your life?" is "no." If the elderly person responds in the negative one point is scored; if the response is "yes," then no point is scored. For the 30-item assessment, a score of 0–9 is considered normal; 10–19 indicates mild depression, and a score over 20 is suggestive of severe depression. The maximum number of points that can be scored is 30.

Resources

BOOKS

Gallo, Joseph J., et al. *Handbook of Geriatric Assessment*. 4th ed. Burlington, MA: Jones & Bartlett Publishers, 2005.

Sadavoy, Joel, et al., eds. *Comprehensive Review of Geriatric Psychiatry-II*. 3rd ed. New York: W.W. Norton & Company, 2004.

PERIODICALS

Reynolds, Charles F. III, and David J. Kupfer. "Depression and Aging: A Look to the Future." *Psychiatric Services* 50 (September 1999): 1167–1172.

Wancata, J., et al. "The Criterion Validity of the Geriatric Depression Scale: A Systematic Review." *Acta Psychiatrica Scandanavica* 114, no. 6 (December 2006) 398–410.

ORGANIZATIONS

American Association for Geriatric Psychiatry, 7910 Woodmont Ave., Ste. 1050, Bethesda, MD, 20814-3004, (301) 654-7850, Fax: (301) 654-4137, http://www.AAGPonline.org.

Judy Leaver, MA

Gestalt therapy

Definition

Gestalt therapy is a form of **psychotherapy** that helps the client focus on the here and now rather than on the past. Gestalt therapy stresses the development of client self-awareness and personal responsibility.

Purpose

The goal of Gestalt therapy is to raise clients' awareness regarding how they function in their environment; with family, at work or school, and with friends. The focus of therapy is more on what is happening (the moment-to-moment process) than what is being discussed (the content). Awareness is being alert to the most important events in one's life and environment with full sensorimotor, emotional, cognitive, and energy support. Support is defined as anything that makes contact with or withdrawal from the environment possible, including energy, body support, breathing, information, concern for others, and language, for example.

In therapy, clients become aware of what they are doing, how they are doing it, and how they can change themselves, and at the same time, they learn to accept and value themselves. According to this approach, individuals define, develop, and learn about themselves in relationship to others, and they are constantly changing.

Gestalt therapy is "unpredictable" in that the therapist and client follow moment-to-moment experience and neither knows exactly where this will take them. Gestalt therapy is complex and intuitive, but it is based on the following principles:

- Holism. Gestalt therapy takes into account the whole person including thoughts, feelings, behavior, body sensations, and dreams. The focus is on integration, that is, how the many parts of the person fit together, and how the client makes contact (interacts) with the environment.
- Field theory. According to this theory, everything is related, in flux, interrelated, and in process. The therapist focuses on how the client makes contact with the environment (family, work, school, friends, authority figures).
- The figure-formation process describes how individuals organize or manipulate their environment from moment to moment.
- Organismic self-regulation is the creative adjustment the organism (person) makes in relation to the environment. The person's equilibrium with his or her environment is "disturbed" by the emergence of a

client need, sensation, or interest and is related to the figure-formation process in that the need of the person organizes the field. For example, if an individual wants coffee, this coffee need is what comes out of the diffuse background and becomes "figural" (comes to the forefront of the client's environment or field) and when the individual enters a room, the figural will be related to the coffee need. The therapist is interested in what is figural for a person because it may provide insight into the person's need(s).

- The Now. The concept of the here and now is what is being done, thought, and felt at the moment, and not in the past or the future.
- Unfinished business is defined as the unexpressed feelings that are associated with distinct memories and fantasies. These feelings may be resentment, rage, hatred, pain, anxiety, grief, guilt, and/or abandonment that are not fully experienced in awareness and linger on in the background. The feelings are carried into the present life and cause preoccupations, compulsive behaviors, wariness, and other self-defeating behaviors. Unfinished business will persist until the person faces and deals with these denied or alienated feelings.

The current practice of Gestalt therapy includes treatment of a wide range of problems and has been successfully used to address a wide range of "psychosomatic" disorders including migraine, ulcerative colitis, and spastic neck and back. Therapists work with couples and families, and with individuals who have difficulties coping with authority figures. In addition, Gestalt therapy has been used for brief **crisis intervention**, to help persons with post-traumatic stress disorders, alcohol and drug abuse, **depression**, or **anxiety disorders**; with adults in a poverty program; with seriously mentally ill individuals with psychotic disorders; and those with borderline **personality disorders**.

Description

The relationship between the therapist and the client is the most important aspect of psychotherapy in Gestalt therapy. In Gestalt therapy, the interaction between therapist and client is an ever-changing dialogue marked by straightforward caring, warmth, acceptance, and self-responsibility. There are four characteristics of dialogue:

- inclusion, in which the therapist puts him- or herself, as much as is possible, into the experience of the client. The therapist does not judge, analyze, or interpret what he or she observes.
- presence refers to the therapist expressing his or her observations, preferences, feelings, personal experience, and thoughts to the client.
- commitment to dialogue allows a feeling of connection, or contact, between the therapist and the client.
- dialogue is active and can be nonverbal as well as verbal. It can be dancing, song, words, or any modality that expresses and moves the energy between the therapist and the client.

Gestalt therapy holds the view that people are endlessly remaking or discovering themselves; therefore, individuals are always in constant transformation. The therapist's approach is to help clients: increase or deepen their awareness of themselves and their relationships with others, by attending and engaging with the client; to explore the client's experience; and to describe what is perceived. All techniques used within the therapeutic relationship help clients to work through and move beyond painful emotional blocks. This allows the client to explore new behavior, first in the context of the therapeutic relationship and then, as appropriate, in the outside world.

The therapeutic process begins at the first contact between client and therapist. Assessment and screening are usually done as part of the ongoing relationship with the client and not as a separate period of diagnostic testing and history taking. Assessment information is obtained by beginning the therapeutic work and includes the client's willingness and support for work in the Gestalt therapy framework, the match between the client and the therapist, diagnostic and personality information, the decision regarding the frequency of sessions, the need for adjunctive treatment (such as day treatment or **biofeedback** training), and the need for medication and medical consultation.

Gestalt therapists now make use of the traditional diagnostic categories to obtain necessary information to help patients with serious mental illnesses (such as psychotic disorders and borderline disorders) and because of administrative and insurance reimbursement procedures. Despite these changes, it is believed that Gestalt therapy assessment techniques will continue to be varied since Gestalt therapists draw on other therapeutic systems.

In therapy, the Gestalt therapist is active and sessions are lively and characterized by warmth, acceptance, caring, and self-responsibility and promote direct experiencing of a situation or event rather than passively talking about the event. Events recalled from the past are explored and felt in the here and now of the therapy session. Clients receive input from the therapists in many ways: they can see and hear the therapists react; the therapists can tell them how they are seen and what is seen; therapists may share their own feelings and reveal personal information about themselves; and therapists can discuss how client awareness is limited by how the client and therapist interact with or engage each other—that is, make contact.

The Gestalt therapist has a wide range of active interventions (cognitive and behavioral) at his or her disposal and may use any techniques or methods as long as they are (a) aimed toward increasing awareness, (b) arise out of the dialogue and the therapist's perception of what is going on with the client (sensing, feeling, thinking) in the immediate therapy session, and (c) within the parameters of ethical practice.

Exercises and experiments

Many therapeutic interventions called exercises and experiments have been developed to enhance awareness and bring about client change. Exercises are defined as ready-made techniques that are sometimes used to evoke certain emotions (such as the expression of anger) in clients. Experiments, on the other hand, grow out of the immediate interaction (dialogue) between client and therapist. They are spontaneous, one-of-a-kind, and relevant to a particular moment and the particular development of an emerging issue such as the client's reports of a need, dream, fantasy, and body awareness. Experiments are done with full participation and collaboration with clients and are designed to expand clients' awareness and to help them to try out new ways of behaving rather than to achieve a particular result. These experiments may take many forms. According to Gerald Corey, some are: "imagining a threatening future event; setting up a dialogue between a client and some significant person in his and her life; dramatizing the memory of a painful event; reliving a particularly profound early experience in the present; assuming the identity of one's mother or father through role-playing; focusing on gestures, posture, and other nonverbal signs of inner expression; carrying on a dialogue between two conflicting aspects within the person."

While participating in experiments, clients actually experience the feelings associated with their conflicts or issues. Experiments are tailored to each individual client and used in a timely manner; they are to be carried out in a context that offers safety and support while encouraging the client to risk trying out new behavior. The Gestalt therapy focus is on the entire person and all parts—verbal and nonverbal behaviors, emotional feelings—all are attended to.

Gestalt therapists are said to rely on spontaneity, inventiveness, "present-centeredness," and a range of possible therapeutic encounters, interactions that lead to exercises, and experiments are potentially infinite but can be categorized as follows.

USING STATEMENTS AND QUESTIONS TO FOCUS AWARENESS. Many interventions have to do with simply asking what the client is aware of experiencing or asking simple and direct questions as, "What are you feeling?" and "What are you thinking?" The client may be instructed to start a sentence with "Now, I am aware . . ." or asked to repeat a behavior, as in, "Please wring your hands together again." A frequent technique is to follow the client's awareness report with the instruction, "Stay with it!" or "Feel it out!"

CLIENT'S VERBAL BEHAVIOR OR LANGUAGE. Awareness can be enhanced and emphasized through the client's verbal behavior or language since client speech patterns are considered to be an expression of their feelings, thoughts, and attitudes. Some aspects of language that might indicate the clients' avoidance of strong emotions or of self-responsibility are the general pronouns such as "it" and "you." Clients are instructed to substitute, when appropriate, the personal pronoun "I" for these pronouns to assume a sense of responsibility for his or her feelings or thoughts (ownership). Sometimes clients may be asked to change their questions into direct statements in order to assume responsibility for what they say. Other examples of helping clients to be more in control using language are to have them omit qualifiers and disclaimers such as "maybe," "perhaps," or "I guess" from their language patterns. This changes ambivalent and weak statements into more clear and direct statements; to substitute "I won't" for "I can't" because often "can't" gives the feeling of being unable to do something. It may be more accurate to say "I won't" meaning "I choose not to do this for any of various reasons," or use the word, "want" instead of "need" which is considered an indication of urgency and anxiety, and is less accurate. Other changes might be to change "should" and "ought" to "I choose to" or "I want to" increasing the clients' power and control of their lives.

NONVERBAL BEHAVIOR. Awareness can also be enhanced by focusing on nonverbal behavior and may include any technique that makes the clients more aware of their body functioning or helps them to be see how they can use their bodies to support excitement, awareness, and contact. The parts of the body that therapists may attend to include the mouth, jaw, eyes, nose, neck, shoulders, arms, hands, torso, legs, and feet, or the entire body. The therapist, for example, may point out to and explore with the client how he or she is smiling while at the same time expressing anger.

SELF-DIALOGUE. Self-dialogue by clients is an **intervention** used by Gestalt therapists that allows clients to get in touch with feelings that they may be unaware of and, therefore, increase the integration of different parts of clients that do not match or conflicts in clients. Examples of some common conflicts include: "the parent inside versus the child inside," "the responsible one versus the impulsive one," "the puritanical side versus the sexual side," "the good side versus the bad side," "the aggressive self versus the passive self," "the autonomous side versus the resentful side," and "the hard worker versus the goof-off." The client is assisted in accepting and learning to live with his or her polarities and not necessarily getting rid of any one part or trait.

The client is engaged in the self-dialogue by using what is called the empty-chair technique. Using two chairs, the client is asked to take one role (the parent inside, for example) in one chair and then play the other role (the child inside) in the second chair. As the client changes roles and the dialogue continues between both sides of the client he or she moves back and forth between the two chairs. Other examples of situations in which dialogues can be used, according to Corey, include "one part of the body versus the other (one hand versus the other), between a client and another person, or between the self and object such as a building or an accomplishment."

ENACTMENT AND DRAMATIZATION. Enactment increases awareness through the dramatizing of some part of the client's existence by asking him or her to put his or her feelings or thoughts into action, such as instructing the client to "Say it to the person" (when in **group therapy**), or to role-play using the empty chair technique. Exaggeration is a form of enactment in which clients are instructed to exaggerate a feeling, thought, or movement in order to provide more intensity of feelings. Enactment can be therapeutic and give rise to creativity.

GUIDED FANTASY. Guided fantasy (visualization) is a technique some clients are able to use more effectively than using enactment to bring an experience into the here and now. Clients are asked to close their eyes and, with the guidance of the therapist, slowly imagine a scene of the past or future event. More and more details are used to describe the event with all senses and thoughts.

DREAM WORK. Dream work is most important in Gestalt therapy. Working with clients' dreams requires developing a list of all the details of the dream, remembering each person, event, and mood in it and then becoming each of these parts through role-playing and inventing dialogue. Each part of the dream is thought to represent the clients' own contradictory and inconsistent sides. Dialogue between these opposing sides leads clients toward gradual insight into the range of their feelings and important themes in their lives.

AWARENESS OF SELF AND OTHERS. An example of how this technique is used by the Gestalt therapist would be asking the client to "become" another person such as asking the client to be his mother and say what his mother would say if the client came in at 2:00 A.M. This provides more insight for the client rather just asking what the client thinks his mother would say if he came home at 2:00 A.M.

AVOIDANCE BEHAVIORS. Awareness of and the reintegration the client's avoidance behaviors are assisted by the interventions used to increase and enhance awareness of feelings, thoughts, and behaviors.

HOMEWORK. Homework assignments between therapy sessions may include asking clients to write dialogues between parts of themselves or between parts of their bodies, gather information, or do other tasks that are related to and fit with what is going on in the therapy process. Homework may become more difficult as the awareness develops.

Therapy sessions are generally scheduled once a week and individual therapy is often combined with group therapy, marital or **family therapy**, movement therapy, **meditation**, or biofeedback training. Sessions can be scheduled anywhere from once every other week to five times a week and depends on how long the client can go between sessions without loss of continuity or relapsing. Meetings less frequent than once a week are thought to diminish the intensity of the therapy unless the client attends a weekly group with the same therapist. More than twice a week is not usually indicated except with clients who have psychotic disorders, and is contraindicated with those who have a **borderline personality disorder**.

Weekly group therapy may vary from one and one-half hours to three hours in length, with the average length being two hours. A typical group is composed of ten members and usually balanced between males and females. Any age is thought to be appropriate for Gestalt therapy. There are groups for children as well.

Gestalt therapy is considered to have a greater range of styles and modalities than any other therapeutic system, and is practiced in individual therapy, groups, workshops, couples, families, with children, and in agencies such as clinics, family service agencies, hospitals, private practice, growth centers. According to Corey, "The therapeutic style of therapists in each modality vary drastically on many dimensions including degree and type of structure; quantity and quality of techniques used; frequency of sessions, abrasiveness and ease of relating, focus on body, cognitions, feelings; interpersonal contact; knowledge of work within psychodynamic themes; and degree of personal encountering."

Risks

Gestalt therapy is considered to have pioneered the development of many useful and creative innovations in psychotherapy theory and practice. However, there is some concern regarding the abuse of power by the therapist, as well as the high-intensity interaction involved. Therapists who use other techniques can become enchanted with using the techniques of Gestalt therapy without having the appropriate training in Gestalt therapy theory. Gestalt therapists are very active and directive within the therapy session and, therefore, care must be taken that they have characteristics that include sensitivity, timing, inventiveness, empathy, and respect for the client. These characteristics, are dependent on the skill, training, experience, ethics, and judgment of the therapist. In addition, the intensity of the therapy might not be suitable for all patients, and even disruptive for some, despite the competence of the therapist.

Results

Gestalt therapists expect that as a result of their involvement in the Gestalt process clients will: have increased awareness of themselves; assume ownership of their experience rather than making others responsible for what they are thinking, feeling, or doing; develop skills and acquire values that will allow them to satisfy their needs without violating the rights of others; become aware of all their senses (smelling, tasting, touching, hearing, and seeing); accept responsibility for their actions and the resulting consequences; move from expectations for external support toward internal self-support; to be able to ask for and get help from others and be able to give to others.

Resources

BOOKS

Blom, Rinda. *The Handbook of Gestalt Play Therapy: Practical Guidelines for Child Therapists.* London: Jessica Kingsley Publishers, 2006.

Corey, Gerald. "Gestalt Therapy." *Theory and Practice of Counseling and Psychotherapy.* 8th ed. Belmont, CA: Thomson/Brooks/Cole, 2008.

O'Leary, Eleanor. "Breathing and Awareness: The Integrating Mechanisms of Cognitive-Behavioural Gestalt Therapy in Working with Cardiac Patients." In *New Approaches to Integration in Psychotherapy,* edited by Eleanor O'Leary and Mike Murphy. New York: Taylor and Francis, 2006.

VandenBos, Gary R. ed. *APA Dictionary of Psychology.* Washington, DC: American Psychological Association, 2006.

Woldt, Ansel L., and Sarah M. Toman. *Gestalt Therapy: History, Theory, and Practice.* Thousand Oaks, CA: Sage, 2005.

PERIODICALS

Bowman, Deborah, and Tricia A. Leakey. "The Power of Gestalt Therapy in Accessing the Transpersonal: Working with Physical Difference and Disability." *Gestalt Review* 10, no. 1 (2006): 42–59.

Kitzler, Richard. "The Ontology of Action: A Place on Which to Stand for Modern Gestalt Therapy Theory." *International Gestalt Journal* 29, no. 1 (Spring 2006): 43–100.

Wheeler, Gordon. "New Directions in Gestalt Theory and Practice: Psychology and Psychotherapy in the Age of Complexity." In *Co-Creating the Field: Intention and Practice in the Age of Complexity,* edited by Deborah Ullman and Gordon Wheeler. New York: Gestalt Press, June 2009.

Williams, Lynn. "Spirituality and Gestalt: A Gestalt-Transpersonal Perspective." *Gestalt Review* 10, no. 1 (2006): 6–21.

WEBSITES

Miller, Michael Vincent. "Elegiac Reflections on Isadore From." http://www.gestalt.org/from.htm (accessed October 30, 2011).

ORGANIZATIONS

American Psychological Association, 750 1st Street NE, Washington, DC, 20002-4242, (202) 336-5500; TDD/TTY: (202) 336-6123, (800) 374-2721, http://www.apa.org.

Association for the Advancement of Gestalt Therapy, http://www.aagt.org.

Mental Health America, 2000 N. Beauregard Street, 6th Floor, Alexandria, VA, 22311, (703) 684-7722, (800) 969-6642, Fax: (703) 684-5968, http://www1.nmha.org.

National Institute of Mental Health, 6001 Executive Blvd., Room 8184, MSC 9663, Bethesda, MD, 20892-9663, (301) 433-4513; TTY: (301) 443-8431, Fax: (301) 443-4279, (866) 615-6464; TTY: (866) 415-8051, nimhinfo@nih.gov, http://www.nimh.nih.gov.

Janice Van Buren, PhD
Ruth A. Wienclaw, PhD

Ginkgo biloba

Definition

Ginkgo biloba is an herbal dietary supplement made from the leaves of the tree *Ginkgo biloba*. Having been used for thousands of years as a home remedy for various ailments, ginkgo biloba is still used for many medical conditions. Although yet to be medically verified, ginkgo biloba has shown evidence that is also is effective in the treatment of mental illnesses such as **dementia** (including **Alzheimer's disease**), **depression**, and anxiety.

Purpose

Ginkgo biloba, generically called ginkgo and sometimes called *bai guo*, has been used in Traditional

Ginkgo biloba leaves. *(© iStockPhoto.com/Ma Sai)*

Chinese Medicine (TCM) for about 5,000 years to treat memory loss and mood, nerve, circulatory and many other health problems. It often is combined with **ginseng** to boost memory, improve the quality of life, and increase a sense of well-being. The effectiveness of some TCM uses of ginkgo, such as relieving pain caused by clogged arteries in the leg (claudication), treating Alzheimer's disease, and improving blood flow to the **brain** have been evaluated in well-designed studies and are generally accepted by practitioners of conventional medicine. Many other TCM uses of ginkgo biloba are currently being investigated, including those for mental illnesses.

Description

Ginkgo biloba is the last existing member of an ancient family of trees. The fossil record shows that ginkgo trees existed 200 million years ago. *Ginkgo biloba* is native to China, Japan, and Korea. The tree was introduced to North America in the 1700s. Ginkgo trees grow to a height of 65–115 ft (20–35 m). They are extremely resistant to disease and insect damage and can live for several hundred years. Female trees produce bad-smelling fruit-like bodies the size of an apricot that contain seeds. Herbal practitioners sometimes use the seeds in treatment. The much cleaner male ginkgo is a popular tree for urban landscaping.

The fan-shaped leaves of the ginkgo are used for medicinal purposes. About 20 different compounds have been identified in ginkgo leaves, but the medically active ingredients appear to be flavonoids and terpenoids. Flavonoids are antioxidants that help lower the level of free radicals in the body. Terpenoids are thought to protect nerves from damage, reduce inflammation, and decrease blood clotting.

In the United States, *Ginkgo biloba* is cultivated, and the leaves are harvested and dried, then often used to make a standardized extract that contains 24–25% flavonoids and 6% terpenoids. U.S. law does not require the standardization of dietary supplements, so consumers should read all labels carefully. Ginkgo biloba is often sold as capsules and tablets. Dry and liquid ginkgo extract is added to other herbal remedies as well as teas, energy or health bars, and similar products. An injectable form of ginkgo biloba extract that was available in Europe has been withdrawn from the market because of adverse side effects. Most well-designed studies have been done using a total of 80–240 mg of 50:1 standardized extract divided into two or three doses daily and taken by mouth.

Regulation of ginkgo biloba sales

Ginkgo biloba is one of the top-selling herbal remedies in the United States and is even more popular in Europe. Under the 1994 Dietary Supplement Health and Education Act (DSHEA), the U.S. Food and Drug Administration (FDA) regulates the sale of ginkgo biloba as a dietary supplement. At the time the act was passed, legislators felt that supplements did not need to be regulated as rigorously as prescription and over-the-counter drugs used in conventional medicine because many dietary supplements such as ginkgo biloba come from natural sources and have been used for hundreds of years by practitioners of complementary and alternative medicine (CAM).

The DSHEA regulates ginkgo biloba in the same way that food is regulated. Like food manufacturers, manufacturers of herbal products containing ginkgo biloba do not have to prove that they are either safe or effective before they can be sold to the public. This differs from conventional pharmaceutical drugs, which must undergo extensive human testing to prove their safety and effectiveness before they can be marketed. Also unlike conventional drugs, the label for a dietary supplement such as ginkgo biloba does not have to contain any statements about possible side effects. All herbal supplements sold in the United States must show the scientific name of the herb on the label.

Health claims

Ginkgo biloba is one of the most promising traditional herbs investigated by Western medicine. The National Center for Complementary and Alternative Medicine (NCCAM), a government organization within the National Institutes of Health (NIH), is sponsoring **clinical trials** to determine safety and effectiveness of ginkgo biloba as a treatment for more than a dozen diseases and disorders. Individuals interested in participating in a clinical trial at no charge can find a list of open trials at http://www.clinicaltrials.gov.

Some health claims for ginkgo biloba have already been evaluated in large, well-controlled studies that satisfy the proof of safety and effectiveness demanded by conventional medicine. Several mental disorders are included on the effectiveness of ginkgo biloba.

DEMENTIAS AND ALZHEIMER'S DISEASE. There is good evidence that ginkgo biloba can cause short-term improvement in mental function in people with Alzheimer's disease (AD). In a well-designed study, ginkgo biloba was as effective as the prescription drug **donepezil** (Aricept) in slowing the development of dementia in people with mild to moderate Alzheimer's. Ginkgo biloba has also been shown to be effective in improving blood flow to the brain and in treating certain other dementias. The effect of ginkgo biloba on memory in healthy young adults and in people with age-related memory impairment is inconsistent but strong enough to continue to study the effects of the herb in these populations.

However, the National Institutes of Health (NIH) recently funded a comprehensive study—the largest clinical trial on the use of ginkgo biloba for dementia—which ran for eight years. Completed in 2008, 3,069 people aged 75 years and older participated in the study. These people, from four clinical sites, had either normal cognition or mild cognitive impairment. The study was called the "Ginkgo biloba for the Evaluation of Memory (GEM) Study."

These researchers, led by Dr. Steven T. DeKosky of the School of Medicine at the University of Virginia (Charlottesville), found that ginkgo biloba at a dose of 120 mg twice per day was not effective in lowering the incidence rate of dementia nor Alzheimer's disease in these older adults within the United States. The U.S. researchers recommended that further large studies be performed on older adults with respect to the use of ginkgo biloba.

Ginkgo biloba has been shown to be effective with multi-infarct dementia (MID), another type of dementia. Scientific studies have shown that ginkgo biloba was as effective as acetylcholinesterase inhibitor (AChEI) drugs, such as donepezil (Aricept) for the treatment of MID, along with early-stage AD. However, researchers continue to recommend that further studies be performed to compare established drugs with ginkgo biloba.

Age-associated memory impairment (AAMI) is a problem with some older adults, and it is believed to be part of the normal aging process. Most symptoms of AAMI only mildly interfere with daily functions of such individuals. Some researchers contend that AAMI is an early sign of AD or MID. The use of ginkgo biloba has been shown to help with controlling these AAMI symptoms. Some studies show small improvement in memory and other brain function in older adults taking ginkgo biloba. Generally, though, further research is necessary to ensure that such studies are valid.

CEREBRAL INSUFFICIENCY. Cerebral insufficiency is a condition that involves such symptoms as confusion, forgetfulness, **fatigue**, dizziness, depression, anxiety, and decreased physical capabilities. Scientists contend that it is caused by a decreased flow of blood within the brain due to blocked blood vessels. Recent research has shown that ginkgo biloba can help to reduce the severity of such symptoms. However, medical researchers are performing further studies to validate these initial studies.

DEPRESSION AND SEASON AFFECTIVE DISORDER. Some researchers have suggested that ginkgo biloba is useful in treating such mental conditions as depression and **seasonal affective disorder** (SAD), what is sometimes called "winter depression." Some studies of the elderly show minor improvement in the symptoms of depression and SAD with the use of ginkgo biloba. Further studies need to be accomplished to evaluate these health claims.

SCHIZOPHRENIA. Ginkgo biloba has antioxidant properties that have been shown to help in the treatment of **schizophrenia**. Early studies show positive results, although sufficient evidence has yet to be collected to verify this claim.

QUALITY OF LIFE. Ginkgo biloba has been shown to help in providing a better quality of life for people with mental illnesses and other medical conditions. Although ginkgo biloba has helped in such patients, further research is necessary before a clear conclusion can be reached.

Recommended dosage

The recommended dosage of ginkgo biloba is based on research performed on the herbal supplement. Because herbs and supplements, including ginkgo biloba, are neither evaluated nor approved by the U.S. Food and Drug Administration (FDA) concerning their effectiveness, purity, and safety, individual companies may manufacturer them in differing concentrations per product. (As mentioned earlier, the FDA only regulates the sale of ginkgo biloba as a dietary supplement through the DSHEA.) Consequently, these dosages should be used only as basic guidelines. Consult with a trusted medical professional, such as a family doctor or pharmacist, before taking ginkgo biloba.

For adults 18 years or older, 80–240 mg within a 50-to-1 standardized leaf extract have been studied for recommended daily use. Such doses can be taken by mouth two to three times a day. Ginkgo biloba also comes in teabag form, with bags usually containing 30 mg of ginkgo. Concentrated amounts of ginkgo biloba often come in 3–6 mL of 40 mg per mL of leaf extract; with a daily input of three doses. Ginkgo biloba also comes within fortified foods.

For children under the age of 18 years, sufficient medical research has not been performed to make any recommended dosages of ginkgo biloba.

Precautions

Ginkgo biloba seeds contain toxins that can cause vomiting, **seizures**, loss of consciousness, and death, especially in young children. Ginkgo biloba seeds are not safe for anyone, and they should be avoided.

Extracts of the leaf of *Ginkgo biloba* are generally safe and cause few side effects when taken at recommended doses for up to six months. People who are planning to have surgery should stop taking ginkgo biloba at least two days before their operation because of the risk of increased bleeding. The safety of ginkgo biloba in children and pregnant and breastfeeding women is still being studied.

Interactions

Ginkgo biloba is generally well tolerated by most people. However, it has blood-thinning properties and is likely to increase the blood-thinning and anticoagulant effects of medicines such as warfarin (Coumadin), clopidogrel (Plavix), aspirin, and nonsteroidal anti-inflammatory drugs (e.g., Advil, Motrin). Individuals taking these drugs should not begin taking ginkgo biloba without consulting their health care provider. People preparing for dental or surgical procedures should not take ginkgo biloba, and they should get more specific information from the attending physician as to when to temporarily stop taking the herbal supplement.

Ginkgo biloba may also interact with monoamine oxidase inhibitors (MAOIs) used to treat certain kinds of depression and mental illness. Examples of MAOIs include **isocarboxazid** (Marplan), **phenelzine** (Nardil), and **tranylcypromine** (Parnate). Individuals taking MAOIs along with ginkgo biloba may experience increased effects from the drug.

KEY TERMS

Alzheimer's disease—The most common type of dementia that usually occurs late in life and involves confusion, irritability, mood swings, language problems, short-term memory loss, and general decline of the senses.

Dementia—A medical condition that involves the progressive deterioration of intellectual and cognitive function, such as memory.

Diabetes—A medical disorder that involves the production of excessive urine; medically called *diabetes mellitus*; type 1 diabetes (juvenile diabetes) involves failure of body to produce insulin, while type 2 diabetes (adult onset diabetes) involves the body's cells failing to use insulin properly.

Monoamine oxidase—Also called L-monoamine oxidase (MAO), a family of enzymes that catalyze the oxidation of monoamines.

Schizophrenia—A psychiatric disorder with symptoms of self withdrawal, emotional instability, and reality detachment.

Some reports suggest that ginkgo biloba lowers blood sugar levels. Individuals who are taking insulin or other medications that also lower blood sugar, and those with type 2 diabetes, should consult their health care provider before starting to take ginkgo biloba.

Complications

Serious side effects of ginkgo biloba are rare. The most common mild side effects are headache, dizziness, nausea, diarrhea, increased restlessness, and racing heart. Increased bleeding may occur. Allergic reactions to ginkgo are possible but uncommon. In severe rare cases, the skin blisters and sloughs off, a condition called Stevens-Johnson syndrome. People who are allergic to sumac, mango rind, cashews, poison oak, and poison ivy are at slightly higher risk to have an allergic reaction to ginkgo biloba. Ginkgo biloba is not recommended during pregnancy and breastfeeding, due to lack of reliable medical information.

Parental concerns

Parents should be aware that a safe dose of many herbal supplements has not been established for children. Accidental overdose may occur if children are give adult herbal supplements.

QUESTIONS TO ASK YOUR DOCTOR

- Should I try ginkgo biloba?
- What dose would be appropriate for me to take?
- Are there any foods I should avoid?
- Where can I learn reliable information about ginkgo biloba?

Resources

BOOKS

Dasgupta, Amitava, and Catherine A. Hammett-Stabler, editors. *Herbal Supplements: Efficacy, Toxicity, Interactions with Western Drugs, and Effects on Clinical Laboratory Tests.* Hoboken, NJ: Wiley, 2011.

Fragakis, Allison. *The Health Professional's Guide to Popular Dietary Supplements* Chicago: American Dietetic Association, 2007

Hsu, Elisabeth, and Stephen Harris, editors. *Plants, Health and Healing: On the Interface of Ethnobotany and Medical Anthropology.* New York: Berghahn, 2010.

PDR for Herbal Medicines. Montvale, NJ: Thompson, 2007.

Peilin, Sun, editor. *The Treatment of Pain with Chinese Herbs and Acupuncture.* Edinburgh: Elsevier Churchill Livingstone, 2011.

Sutton, Amy L, editor. *Complementary and Alternative Medicine Sourcebook.* Detroit: Omnigraphics, 2010.

Tracy, Timothy S. and Richard L. Kingston, eds. *Herbal Products: Toxicology and Clinical Pharmacology.* Totowa, NJ, Humana Press, 2007.

Wildman, Robert E. C., editor. *Handbook of Nutraceuticals and Functional Foods,* 2nd ed. Boca Raton, FL: CRC/Taylor & Francis, 2007.

PERIODICALS

Akhondzadeh, S. and S. H. Abbasi. "Herbal Medicine in the Treatment of Alzheimer's Disease." *American Journal of Alzheimer's Disease and Other Dementias* 21, no. 2 (Mar-April 2006):113–8.

Dugoua, J. J., et al. "Safety and Efficacy of Ginkgo (Ginkgo biloba) During Pregnancy and Lactation." *Canadian Journal of Clinical Pharmacology* 13, no. 3 (Fall, 2006): e277–84. http://www.cjcp.ca/pdf/CJCP05-037_e277e284F.pdf

Mazza, M., et al., "Ginkgo Biloba and Donepezil: A Comparison in the Treatment of Alzheimer's dementia in a Randomized Placebo-Controlled Double-blind Study." *European Journal of Neurology* 13, no. 9 (September 2006):981–5.

Oh, S. M. and K. H. Chung. "Antiestrogenic Activities of Ginkgo Biloba Extracts." *Steroid Biochemistry and Molecular Biology* 100, nos. 4–5 (August 2006):167–76.

WEBSITES

"Ginkgo." MedlinePlus. October 21, 2011. http://www.nlm.nih.gov/medlineplus/druginfo/natural/333.html (accessed January 13, 2012).

"Ginkgo Biloba." Maryland Medical Center Programs Center for Integrative Medicine. http://www.umm.edu/altmed/articles/ginkgo-biloba-000247.htm (accessed January 13, 2012).

"Ginkgo (Ginkgo Biloba)." Mayo Clinic. April 1, 2011. http://www.mayoclinic.com/health/ginkgo-biloba/NS_patient-ginkgo (accessed July 5, 2011).

"Ginkgo Biloba for the Evaluation of Memory (GEM) Study." National Institutes of Health. March 11, 2011. http://nccam.nih.gov/research/results/gems/qa.htm (accessed July 5, 2011).

"Ginkgo Evaluation of Memory (GEM) Study Fails To Show Benefit in Preventing Dementia in the Elderly." National Center for Complementary and Alternative Medicine. (November 18, 2008). http://nccam.nih.gov/news/2008/111808.htm (accessed July 5, 2011).

ORGANIZATIONS

American Association of Acupuncture and Oriental Medicine, PO Box 162340, Sacramento, CA, 95816, Fax: 1(916) 443-4766, (866) 455-7999, http://www.aaaomonline.org

American Botanical Council, PO Box 14435, Austin, TX, 78723, 1(512) 926-4900, Fax: 1(512) 926-2345, (800) 373-7105, http://abc.herbalgram.org

National Center for Complementary and Alternative Medicine Clearinghouse, PO Box 7923, Gaithersburg, MD, 20898, Fax: 1(866) 464-3616, (888) 644-6226, info@nccam.nih.gov, http://nccam.nih.gov

National Certification Commission for Acupuncture and Oriental Medicine, 76 South Laura St., Suite 1290, Jacksonville, FL, 32202, 1(904) 598-1005, Fax: 1(904) 598-5001, http://www.nccaom.org

Natural Standard, One Davis Square, Somerville, MA, 02144, 1(617) 591-3300, Fax: 1(617) 591-3399, questions@naturalstandard.com, http://naturalstandard.com

Office of Dietary Supplements, Natonal Institutes of Health, 6100 Executive Blvd., Room 3B01, MSC 7517, Bethesda, MD, 20892-7517, 1(301) 435-2920, Fax: 1(301) 480-1845, ods@nih.gov, http://ods.od.nih.gov.

Tish Davidson, A.M.
William Atkins, B.B., B.S., M.B.A.

Ginseng

Definition

Ginseng refers to two closely related herbs of the genus *Panax*. Asian ginseng (*P. ginseng*) and American ginseng (*P. quinquefolius*) have traditionally been used for healing for many centuries. Asian ginseng is also known as Korean

Ginseng root. *(© iStockPhoto.com/Yungshu Chao)*

red ginseng, Chinese ginseng, Japanese ginseng, ginseng radix, ninjin, sang, and ren shen. American ginseng is also known as Canadian ginseng, North American ginseng, Ontario ginseng, Wisconsin ginseng, red berry, sang, and ren shen. Siberian ginseng (*Eleutherococcus senticosus*) is a plant with different properties that belongs to a completely different genus. Ginseng in this entry refers only to Asian and American ginseng of the genus *Panax*.

Purpose

Ginseng has been used for over 2,000 years in Traditional Chinese Medicine (TCM) to boost energy, hasten recovery from illness or injury, reduce **stress**, improve mental and physical performance (including sexual performance) and treat several dozen different infections, gastrointestinal disorders, circulatory problems, and conditions as diverse as burns, cancers, diabetes, migraine headaches, and weight loss. The genus name *Panax* means "heal all," and herbalists consider ginseng to be an almost universal remedy. Most of these traditional uses of ginseng have not yet been substantiated by conventional medicine; however, encouraging results from some well-designed, controlled human studies strongly suggest that ginseng may improve mental performance, especially concerning mental illnesses, and may have other health benefits.

Description

Ginseng is a perennial herb that grows in cool, damp, shady forests. Asian ginseng is native to Northern China, and today it is grown as a cash crop in China, Korea, Japan, and Russia. American ginseng once grew wild from the Appalachian Mountains to Minnesota. Today, it is cultivated mainly in Wisconsin and in the Canadian provinces of Ontario and British Columbia. Most cultivated ginseng from North America is exported to Asia. In both Asia and North America, wild ginseng is threatened with extinction from over-harvesting. In the United States, a government permit is usually required to export wild ginseng. High-quality wild ginseng is very expensive. Illegal harvesting of wild ginseng from public lands is an ongoing law enforcement problem for the U.S. Fish and Wildlife Service.

Ginseng is a slow-growing plant that reaches a height of 12–30 in. (30.5–76.2 cm) and produces red berries. Only the root is used for medicinal purposes. Ginseng is difficult to cultivate. Plants must grow four to six years before the roots can be harvested. Ginseng roots are forked and twisted, looking somewhat like a miniature human body. They are occasionally used fresh but more often are dried and ground or powdered. The root can be soaked to make an extract or tincture. Ground ginseng can be added to tea, and powered ginseng is often placed into capsules. Ginseng extract can be added to products as diverse as chewing gum and soft drinks. In addition, ginseng is sold under dozens of different brand names. It is often found in multi-herb remedies sold under a huge variety of names. The active ingredients of ginseng are thought to be more than 20 compounds called "ginsenosides." Some manufacturers standardize the amount of ginsengosides in their product, while others do not. Standardized products usually contain at least 4 ginsenosides.

Regulation of ginseng sales

In the United States, ginseng is regulated by the Food and Drug Administration (FDA) as a dietary supplement under the 1994 Dietary Supplement Health and Education Act (DSHEA). When the act was passed, legislators felt that these supplements did not need to be regulated as rigorously as prescription and over-the-counter drugs used in conventional medicine, because many dietary supplements such as ginseng come from natural sources and have been used for hundreds of years by practitioners of complementary and alternative medicine (CAM).

The DSHEA regulates ginseng in the same way that food is regulated. Like food manufacturers, manufacturers of herbal products containing ginseng do not have to prove that they are either safe or effective before they can be sold to the public. This differs from conventional pharmaceutical drugs, which must undergo extensive human testing to prove their safety and effectiveness before they can be marketed. Also unlike conventional drugs, the label for a dietary supplement such as ginseng does not have to contain any statements about possible side effects. All herbal supplements sold in the United States must show the scientific name of the herb on the label. Consumers should look for ginseng of the *Panax* variety. Sometimes less-expensive herbs such as Siberian "ginseng" are substituted for true ginseng.

Health claims

Dozens of health claims are made for ginseng, many based on traditional or folk use of the herb. These claims are difficult to substantiate in ways that satisfy conventional medicine, for several reasons, including:

- The amount and strength of ginseng in dietary supplements is not standardized, and a wide range of doses are used in different studies.
- Ginseng is often one of several herbs contained in herbal remedies, making it difficult to tell whether the effects are due to ginseng or another herb.
- Many studies performed on ginseng are poorly designed, so it is impossible to show a direct link between cause and effect, or they are poorly reported, making analysis of the results difficult.
- Many rigorous and well-designed human studies have a small sample size.
- Many studies are sponsored by ginseng growers, manufacturers, or importers who have a financial interest in obtaining positive results.

Despite these drawbacks, there is sufficient scientific evidence that ginseng does provides health benefits. Consequently, the National Center for Complementary and Alternative Medicine (NCCAM), a government organization within the National Institutes of Health (NIH), is sponsoring **clinical trials** to determine safety and effectiveness of ginseng as a treatment for several diseases and disorders, some involving mental conditions. Individuals interested in participating in a clinical trial at no charge can find a list of open trials at http://www.clinicaltrials.gov.

Some health claims for ginseng appear more promising than others. There is good evidence that ginseng can cause short-term improvement in mental performance in both healthy young adults and ill elderly adults. Not enough information is available to determine whether long-term gains also occur, but the results have been promising enough that ginseng is being studied in patients with **Alzheimer's disease** and other dementias. Along with improved mental performance, some studies have shown that ginseng improves the sense of well-being and quality of life. Results of these studies are mixed, with some finding improvements, and others finding no change. The situation is complicated by the fact that different studies define and measure "well-being" and "quality of life" in different ways. In general, people with the worst quality of life report the most improvement.

Many other health claims are made for herbal mixtures that contain ginseng. These claims are extremely difficult to evaluate because of the number of variables, including the strength of the mixture, the effects of the different herbs, and potential interactions among other herbs. Until much more is known about the chemical properties and active ingredients of common medicinal herbs, it will be almost impossible to evaluate these mixtures in a way that satisfies the demands of conventional medicine.

MEMORY. A combination of *Panax* ginseng and ginkgo leaf extract seems to help improve thinking, mathematical skills, and reaction times in middle-age people who are otherwise healthy. Because memory problems could be an early sign of **dementia**, further studies are being pursued to learn more about a potential relationship between ginseng and memory.

ERECTILE DYSFUNCTION. Ginseng has been found to help male impotence, what is often called erectile dysfunction (ED). Taking *Panax* ginseng orally (by mouth) seems to improve sexual function in men with ED. Early studies are being supplemented with further research to validate these initial results.

PREMATURE EJACULATION. Some men have problems during sexual activity that involve **premature ejaculation**. When a *Panax* ginseng-based cream is applied to the skin of the penis, better control of the sexual organism is possible, which helps with premature ejaculation.

Recommended dosage

Always consult with a medical professional before taking ginseng. The recommended dosage should be stated clearly on the package. Use the recommended dosage from the package unless a doctor, pharmacist, or other health care provider states otherwise. If the package does not contain dosage information, do not use it. Different formulations of ginseng are safer than are others. The safest forms are extracts, tinctures, and solids. Always use the same formulation; do not mix forms, because such a practice may cause an accidental overdose. Fluid retention, muscle tension, sleeplessness, or swelling can be signs of an overdose.

According to medical research, when used for **erectile dysfunction**, use approximately 900 mg orally three times daily. For premature ejaculation, a cream containing *Panax* ginseng and other ingredients should be applied to the skin of the penis about one hour before sexual intercourse. Wash the cream off before having intercourse.

Precautions

Ginseng is generally safe and causes few side effects when taken at recommended doses. The generally recommended dose is 100–200 mg of standardized ginseng extract containing 4% ginsenosides once or twice daily. The safety of ginseng in children and pregnant and breastfeeding women has not been studied. Pregnant and breastfeeding women should be aware that some tinctures of ginseng contain high levels of alcohol. Some herbalists recommend that individuals take ginseng for two to three weeks and then take a break of one to two weeks before beginning the herb again.

Independent laboratory analyses have repeatedly found that many products labeled as ginseng contain little or none of the herb. True ginseng is expensive, and unscrupulous manufacturers often substitute low-cost herbs for ginseng. Another problem is that some ginseng products have been found to be contaminated with pesticides, toxins, or other dangerous chemicals that can cause serious side effects. Always purchase ginseng from reputable retailers.

When using ginseng to help with erectile dysfunction, use caution if diabetic. The herb may cause blood sugar levels to decrease. In addition, in a small number of cases, ginseng has been found to cause mania when used together with some **antidepressants**.

Consult with a doctor before considering ginseng if the following conditions are present (or medicines are being taken to treat them): bleeding or blood clotting disorder, high blood pressure, heart disease, or diabetes. In addition, before starting ginseng make sure the doctor is aware of any medicines or herbal supplements being taken, and whether medical conditions, such as plant allergies, are present.

Giving ginseng to infants or children has sometimes lead to serious medical problems and even death from poisoning. It is not known whether ginseng is safe for older children. To be safe, do not give ginseng to any child or adolescent, regardless of age.

Interactions

Ginseng appears to interact with blood-thinning and anti-coagulant medicines such as dalteparin (Fragmin), ticlopidine (Ticlid), cilostazol (Pletal), enoxaparin (Lovenox), heparin, warfarin (Coumadin), clopidogrel (Plavix), aspirin, and nonsteroidal anti-inflammatory drugs (e.g. Advil, Motrin). Individuals taking these drugs should not begin taking ginseng without consulting their health care provider.

Because ginseng lowers blood sugar levels, individuals who are taking insulin or other medications that also lower blood sugar, and those with type 2 diabetes, should be monitored for low blood sugar if they begin taking ginseng. Adjustments in the other medications by the attending physician may be needed.

Ginseng may also interact with **monoamine oxidase inhibitors (MAOIs)** used to treat certain kinds of **depression** and mental illness. Ginseng stimulates the body, as do many of these **MAOIs**. Using them together can use an excessive amount of stimulation, which can lead to restlessness, **insomnia**, anxiousness, and headaches. Examples of MAOIs include **isocarboxazid** (Marplan), **phenelzine** (Nardil) and **tranylcypromine** (Parnate). Individuals taking MAOIs with ginseng may also develop tremors and mania.

Immunosuppressants, those that solve medical problems by reducing the efficiency in which the immune system works, can adversely interact with

KEY TERMS

Alzheimer's disease—The most common type of dementia that usually occurs late in life, involving confusion, irritability, mood swings, language problems, short-term memory loss, and general decline of the senses.

Dementia—A medical condition that involves the progressive deterioration of intellectual and cognitive function, such as memory.

Diabetes—A medical disorder that involves the production of excessive urine; medically called diabetes mellitus; type 1 diabetes (juvenile diabetes) involves failure of the body to produce insulin, while type 2 diabetes (adult onset diabetes) involves the body's cells failing to use insulin properly.

Monoamine oxidase inhibitor—Also called L-monoamine oxidase inhibitor (MAOI), a family of enzymes that catalyze the oxidation of monoamines.

Schizophrenia—A psychiatric disorder with symptoms of self withdrawal, emotional instability, and reality detachment.

ginseng. Ginseng increases the immune system, so taking it with immunosuppressants can cause these medicines to work less effectively. Some immunosuppressant drugs include: azathioprine (Imuran), basiliximab (Simulect), cyclosporine (Neoral), daclizumab (Zenapax), muromonab-CD3 (OKT3), mycophenolate (CellCept), tacrolimus (FK506), sirolimus (Rapamune), prednisone (Deltasone), and corticosteroids (glucocorticoids).

Preliminary evidence suggests that ginseng may interact with certain blood pressure and heart medications, such as digoxin (Lanoxin), a medication used to treat congestive heart failure. The herb may also interfere with the way the liver processes other drugs and herbs. Before beginning to take a supplement containing ginseng, individuals should review their current medications with their health care provider to determine any possible interactions.

Ginseng has been reported to interact with caffeine to cause overstimulation and insomnia in some people. During the day, the two together may cause a person to feel nervous or jittery; it may also cause the heart to beat faster than normal and one's blood pressure to increase. It is not recommended to take coffee, tea, cola, or other drinks or foods containing caffeine together with ginseng. Other stimulant drugs can also cause similar problems. Some of these include diethylpropion (Tenuate), epinephrine, phentermine (Ionamin), and pseudoephedrine (Sudafed).

Other herbs may also adversely react with ginseng. Bitter orange may increase the risk of an irregular heartbeat. Any substance that contains ephedra, such as country mallow, can produce an irregular heartbeat, so using it with ginseng can increase the problem. Herbs that lower blood sugar, such as bitter melon, ginger, goat's rue, fenugreek, kudzu, willow bark, and others, can lower such levels even more when taken with ginseng. Avoid such substances.

Complications

Serious side effects of ginseng are rare. The most common complications are increased restlessness, insomnia, nausea, diarrhea, and rash. Allergic reactions are possible but uncommon. Difficulty breathing; swelling (narrowing) of the throat; or swelling of the lips, tongue, or face may also occur due to a serious allergic reaction. Some of the more serious side effects reported are thought to be the result of contamination with pesticides, heavy metals, or other chemicals rather than side effects caused by ginseng.

High doses of ginseng can increase certain symptoms of **schizophrenia**. Some of the more common symptoms that can be worsened are problems with sleeping at night and feelings of agitation or irritability during the day. Consult with a doctor before taking ginseng if schizophrenia is present.

Contemporary Chinese practitioners recognize a condition known as "ginseng abuse syndrome," caused by taking ginseng incorrectly or excessively. The symptoms of ginseng abuse syndrome include heart palpitations, heaviness in the chest, high blood pressure, dizziness, insomnia, agitation, restlessness, nausea, vomiting, abdominal pain and/or bloating, diarrhea, possible upper digestive tract bleeding, edema, and a red skin rash that is most noticeable on the face. Western herbalists recommend that anyone taking ginseng who develops these symptoms should stop taking the herb at once and contact a licensed practitioner of TCM to determine whether ginseng abuse is the cause of the problem.

QUESTIONS TO ASK YOUR DOCTOR

- Should I try ginseng?
- What dose would be appropriate for me to take?
- Are there any foods I should avoid?
- Where is a reliable place to buy ginseng?
- Where can I find reliable information about ginseng?

Resources

BOOKS

Dasgupta, Amitava, and Catherine A. Hammett-Stabler, editors. *Herbal Supplements: Efficacy, Toxicity, Interactions with Western Drugs, and Effects on Clinical Laboratory Tests.* Hoboken, NJ: Wiley, 2011.

Fragakis, Allison. *The Health Professional's Guide to Popular Dietary Supplements* Chicago: American Dietetic Association, 2007.

Hsu, Elisabeth, and Stephen Harris, editors. *Plants, Health and Healing: On the Interface of Ethnobotany and Medical Anthropology.* New York: Berghahn, 2010.

Johanssen, Kristin. *Ginseng Dreams: The Secret World of America's Most Valuable Plant.* Lexington, KY: University Press of Kentucky, 2006.

PDR for Herbal Medicines. Montvale, NJ: Thompson, 2007.

Peilin, Sun, editor. *The Treatment of Pain with Chinese Herbs and Acupuncture.* Edinburgh: Elsevier Churchill Livingstone, 2011.

Sutton, Amy L, editor. *Complementary and Alternative Medicine Sourcebook.* Detroit: Omnigraphics, 2010.

Taylor, David. *Ginseng, the Divine Root: The Curious History of the Plant That Captivated the World.* Chapel Hill, NC: Algonquin Books of Chapel Hill, 2006.

Tracy, Timothy S. and Richard L. Kingston, eds. *Herbal Products: Toxicology and Clinical Pharmacology.* Totowa, NJ, Humana Press, 2007.

Wildman, Robert E. C., editor. *Handbook of Nutraceuticals and Functional Foods,* 2nd edition. Boca Raton, FL: CRC/ Taylor & Francis, 2007.

WEBSITES

Ginseng. American Cancer Society. (November 28, 2008). http://www.cancer.org/Treatment/TreatmentsandSideEffects/ComplementaryandAlternativeMedicine/HerbsVitaminsandMinerals/ginseng?sitearea=eto (accessed July 6, 2011).

Ginseng. National Center for Complimentary and Alternative Medicine. (April 1, 2011). http://nccam.nih.gov/health/asianginseng (accessed July 6, 2011).

Ginseng, Panax. MedlinePlus. (April 22, 2011). http://www.nlm.nih.gov/medlineplus/druginfo/natural/1000.html (accessed July 5, 2011).

ORGANIZATIONS

American Association of Acupuncture and Oriental Medicine, PO Box 162340, Sacramento, CA, 95816, Fax: 1(916) 443-4766, (866) 455-7999, http://www.aaaomonline.org

American Botanical Council, PO Box 14435, Austin, TX, 78723, 1(512) 926-4900, Fax: 1(512) 926-2345, (800) 373-7105, http://abc.herbalgram.org

National Center for Complementary and Alternative Medicine Clearinghouse, PO Box 7923, Gaithersburg, MD, 20898, Fax: 1(866) 464-3616, (888) 644-6226, info@nccam.nih.gov, http://nccam.nih.gov

National Certification Commission for Acupuncture and Oriental Medicine, 76 South Laura St., Suite 1290, Jacksonville, FL, 32202, 1(904) 598-1005, Fax: 1(904) 598-5001, http://www.nccaom.org

Natural Standard, One Davis Square, Somerville, MA, 02144, 1(617) 591-3300, Fax: 1(617) 591-3399, questions@naturalstandard.com, http://naturalstandard.com

Office of Dietary Supplements, National Institutes of Health, 6100 Executive Blvd., Room 3B01, MSC 7517, Bethesda, MD, 20892-7517, 1(301) 435-2920, Fax: 1(301) 480-1845, ods@nih.gov, http://ods.od.nih.gov.

Tish Davidson, A.M.
William Atkins, B.B., B.S., M.B.A.

Grief

Definition

Grief, which is also known as **bereavement**, is a term used to describe the intense and painful emotions experienced when someone or something a person cares about either dies or is lost. The emotional pain from losing a loved one, whether it is a spouse, child, parent, sibling, friend, or pet, can be the most severe suffering a person must endure. At its most intense, grief can dominate every facet of a person's life, making the carrying out of ordinary responsibilities impossible. Loss and subsequent grief, however, are an inevitable part of life. Painful as it is, grief is a normal response to loss and generally resolves with the passage of time.

KEY TERMS

Anxiety—An overwhelming sense of apprehension and fear; can be experienced as a troubled feeling, a sense of dread, fear of the future, or distress over a possible threat to a person's physical or mental well-being.

Depression—A mental condition characterized by feelings of sadness, despair, and discouragement.

Stressor—A stimulus, or event, that provokes a stress response in an organism. Stressors can be categorized as acute or chronic, and as external or internal to the organism.

Description

Grief is usually characterized by psychological numbness, tearfulness, physical feelings of emptiness in the pit of the stomach, weak knees, shortness of breath, a tendency to sigh deeply, a sense of unreality, and overall emotional distress. Anxiety and longing may alternate with **depression** and despair. **Insomnia** and loss of appetite are common. Initially, people often feel a lack of extreme emotion and may be immune to sensory stimuli; they may find it difficult to accept their loss. Numbness is followed by shock as reality begins to penetrate.

There is generally a disorganization of normal behavior patterns that may make it impossible for a bereaved person to return to work immediately or to take social initiatives. Such acute symptoms usually begin to subside after several months, with emotional balance typically regained within a year. Studies using instruments developed to measure symptoms of grief and bereavement demonstrate wide individual variations in specific symptoms and their intensity. Long after the immediate period of mourning, bereaved persons may continue to feel upset, empty, or tearful. In addition, further losses, additional stressors, or dates of such important anniversaries as a wedding, birthday, or the date of death can reactivate the acute symptoms of grief.

ELISABETH KÜBLER–ROSS (1926–2004)

Swiss-born psychiatrist Elisabeth Kübler–Ross dedicated her career to a topic that had previously been avoided by many physicians and mental health care professionals—the psychological state of the dying. In her counseling of and research on dying patients, Kübler–Ross determined that individuals go through five distinct mental stages when confronted with death, a discovery that has helped other counselors provide more appropriate advice and treatment to grieving clients. Her ideas have been presented to the public in a number of popular texts, including her groundbreaking 1969 work, *On Death and Dying*. She also supported hospice and palliative care, and offered instruction and treatment at the seminars and healing centers she ran for the terminally ill and their caretakers. Her career ended with controversy, but the five stages of grief, also referred to as the Kübler–Ross model, are well known in psychiatric medicine.

Dimensions of grief

Grief and mourning are important life experiences in that they permit a bereaved person to accept the reality of loss and begin to find ways of filling the resultant emptiness. Loss is a significant part of the aging process and can contribute to emotional problems in older people. The impact of loss and resulting grief and mourning is not limited to the death of a loved one. It is also present to a lesser extent in the loss of physical acuity and agility and the loss of social status as a result of retirement and/or growing older.

Unfortunately, people in the United States do not generally receive cultural support for the losses they experience and the need to mourn those losses. Unlike other cultures with specific rituals for grief and mourning, there is often subtle but insistent pressure on Americans—particularly males—to move forward with resumption of regular activities. Onlookers may try to divert the mourner's attention to other topics or discourage crying or talking about the loved one. These responses suggest that grief is not healthy or that it should be minimized or avoided. If the grief is associated with the loss of a pet, the person may be shamed for grieving because "it was just an animal." Women who have had a pregnancy ended by miscarriage also encounter responses that minimize or trivialize the loss of their expected child. Social insensitivity may drive the mourner to grieve in secret or feel guilty because of continued intense feelings of loss.

Stages of grief

Elisabeth Kübler–Ross, a **psychiatrist** who studied death and dying, identified five stages of acceptance in the process of dying. While her work initially referred to the person who is dying, the five stages are also applied to people who are grieving a loss. The stages are sometimes collapsed into three, but the general grieving process includes these components:

- Shock/denial. This stage comprises the initial period after receiving news of the loss. The affected person may say, "There must be a mistake," "This can't be true," or similar expressions of disbelief. People often describe feeling numb or cold in this stage.
- Bargaining. This stage represents an attempt to persuade God or a higher power to change the reality of loss in exchange for improved behavior or some sacrifice on the part of the bereaved person. The mourner may offer, for example, to take better care of their relationship with the loved one if God will bring the loved one back.
- Anger. This emotion may be directed toward the medical establishment, family members, a higher power, or even the person who has died.
- Depression. In this stage, the person's body begins to absorb the reality of the loss. The bereaved person may be unable to eat, sleep, or talk normally with people. They may have episodes of spontaneous crying and such physical symptoms as nausea, headaches, chills, or trembling.
- Acceptance. This is the phase in which the mourner comes to terms with the loss and begins to look ahead once more. Energy returns and the bereaved person is able to reconnect with others, engage in enjoyable activities, and make plans for the future.

There is, however, no "normal" pattern for grief; it is a highly variable experience. People pass through the stages outlined by Kübler–Ross at their own rate, depending on the significance of the loss, previous losses they've experienced, individual resiliency, presence of a support system, and permission to grieve from those around them. Grieving is not a linear process. There is movement back and forth between the stages until acceptance is reached. Occasionally, a person may remain "stuck" in one stage, particularly anger or depression, and may benefit from professional help in order to move on. Remaining in one of the stages indefinitely can create emotional and occupational difficulties.

Bereavement and marriage

Studies show that some widowed people have hallucinations or **delusions** of contact with the lost spouse that may last for years. These hallucinations are more likely to occur in people who were happily married. The most common **hallucination** reported is a sense of the dead spouse's presence. Others report seeing, hearing, or being touched by or spoken to by the spouse.

The interplay of grief and marital quality has led to research findings that contradict earlier widespread beliefs. A 2000 study by Deborah Carr and her colleagues found that anxiety was greater in those who had been highly dependent on their spouses than in those who were less dependent. People who had been in conflicted relationships reported lower levels of yearning for the spouse than those who had enjoyed high levels of marital closeness. Women who had relied on their husbands to do the driving and perform other similar tasks had much higher levels of yearning than men who depended on their wives. This finding contradicts the common belief that grief is more severe if the marriage was conflicted, suggesting a more complex relationship between bereavement and characteristics of the marriage.

Another suggestion of the complex relationship between bereavement and marriage is reflected in studies of sudden and anticipated loss among older widowed people. The sudden death of a spouse was associated with slightly higher levels of yearning among women, but significantly lower yearning among men. Forewarning of the death (extended illness, advancing age) did not affect depression, anger, shock or overall grief 6 or 18 months after the loss. Prolonged forewarning was associated with increased anxiety at 6- and 18-month follow-up interviews after the death.

Grief and mourning may also occur when the loss of a partner occurs through divorce or the end of a dating relationship. Some researchers think that moving to the stage of acceptance is more difficult in such cases because the partner can still be contacted, especially if there are children involved. Seeing a former partner involved in a new relationship can cause the partner mourning the loss to reexperience acute symptoms of grief. Some research evidence suggests that grief related to the breakup of an intimate relationship is more intense for the individual who was left behind than for the person who ended the relationship.

Grieving may be particularly prolonged and intense when certain unexpected losses occur that are outside the ordinary progression of life events. The loss of a parent before a child reaches adulthood or a parent's loss of a child inflict deep emotional wounds for an extended period of time. Similarly, the loss of a loved one to murder, terrorism, or other acts of intentional violence can be harder to bear than death resulting from natural causes or accidents. Death from **suicide** complicates grief by adding possible feelings of shame, blame, or guilt, or unanswered questions as to the deceased's reasons, to the other painful emotions associated with bereavement. The opportunity to fully grieve such significant losses, however, enables survivors to move forward despite the magnitude of their loss.

QUESTIONS TO ASK YOUR DOCTOR

- What counseling options do you recommend for me?
- Can you recommend any support groups for me and my family?

Resources

BOOKS

Burns, Donna M. *When Kids Are Grieving: Addressing Grief and Loss in School.* Thousand Oaks, CA: Corwin Press, 2010.

Coor, C.A., and D.E. Balk, eds. *Handbook of Adolescent Death and Bereavement.*New York: Springer Publishing Co., Inc., 2004.

Harris, Maxine, Ph.D. *The Loss That Is Forever: The Lifelong Impact of the Early Death of a Mother or Father.* New York: Plume, 1996.

James, John W., and Russell Friedman. *The Grief Recovery Handbook,* 20th Anniversary ed. New York, NY: William Morrow Paperbacks, 2009.

Kübler–Ross, Elizabeth, and David Kessler. *Life Lessons.* New York: Scribner. 2001.

Manfred, Erica. *He's History, You're Not: Surviving Divorce After 40.* Guilford, CT: GPP Life, 2009.

Noel, Brook., and Pamela D. Blair. *I Wasn't Ready to Say Goodbye: Surviving, Coping and Healing After the Sudden Death of a Loved One.* Naperville, IL: Sourcebooks, 2008.

Segal, Daniel L., Sara Honn Qualls, and Michael A. Smyer. *Aging and Mental Health.* 2nd ed. New York, NY: Wiley-Blackwell, 2010.

PERIODICALS

Carr, Deborah, et al. "Marital Quality and Psychological Adjustment to Widowhood Among Older Adults." *Journals of Gerontology Series B: Psychological Sciences and Social Sciences* 55, no. 4 (2000): S197–S207.

Carr, Deborah, et al. "Psychological Adjustment to Sudden and Anticipated Spousal Loss Among Older Widowed Persons." *Journals of Gerontology Series B: Psychological Sciences and Social Sciences* 56B, no. 4 (2001): S237-S248. Available online at http://www.cloc.isr.umich.edu/papers/carr2001_jogss.pdf (accessed November 9, 2011).

Zisook, S., et al. "Bereavement, Complicated Grief, and DSM, Part 2: complicated Grief." *Journal of clinical Psychiatry* 71, no. 8 (August 2010): 1097–8 (accessed October 30, 2011).

Zisook, S., R. A. Devaul, and M. A. Click Jr. "Measuring Symptoms of Grief and Bereavement." *American Journal of Psychiatry* 139 (1982): 1590–1593.

ORGANIZATIONS

The Compassionate Friends, PO Box 3696, Oak Brook, IL, 60522, (877) 969-0010, Fax: (630) 990-0246, (630) 990-0010, http://www.compassionatefriends.org.

GROWW (Grief Recovery Online [founded by] Widows and Widowers), 11877 Douglas Rd., #102-PMB101, Alpharetta, GA, 30005, http://www.groww.org.

SHARE Pregnancy and Infant Loss Support, 402 Jackson Street, St. Charles, MO, 63301, (800) 821-6819; (636) 947-6164, Fax: (636) 947-7486, http://www.nationalshare.org.

Widowed Persons Service, 4211 Clyde Park, SW, Unit C, Wyoming, MI, 49509, (616) 538-0101, director@wpsgr.org, http://www.wpsgr.org.

Judy Leaver, MA
Laura Jean Cataldo, RN, Ed.D.

Grief counseling

Definition

Grief counseling refers to a specific form of therapy, or a focus in general counseling with the goal of helping the individual grieve and address personal loss in a healthy manner. Grief counseling is offered individually by psychologists, clergy, counselors or **social workers**, in groups led by professionals, as well as informal **support groups** offered by churches, community groups, or organizations devoted to helping individuals grieve specific losses.

Purpose

The purpose of grief counseling is to help individuals work through the feelings, thoughts, and memories associated with the loss of a loved one. Although grieving can occur for other types of loss as well (such as loss of goals, ideals, and relationships), grief counseling is generally directed toward positive adjustment following loss after the death of a loved one.

Specific tasks of grief counseling include emotional expression about the loss (which can include a wide range of feelings), accepting the loss, adjusting to life after the loss, and coping with the changes within oneself and the world after the loss. Typical feelings experienced by individuals, and addressed in grief counseling, include sadness, anxiety, anger, loneliness, guilt, relief, isolation, confusion, or numbness. Behavioral changes may also be noticed, such as being disorganized, feeling tired, having trouble concentrating, sleep problems, appetite changes, vivid dreams, or daydreaming about the deceased.

Grief counseling helps the individual recognize normal aspects of the grieving or mourning process, cope with the pain associated with the loss, feel supported through the anxiety surrounding life changes that may follow the loss, and develop strategies for seeking support and self-care.

KEY TERMS

Anxiety—Can be experienced as a troubled feeling, a sense of dread, fear of the future, or distress over a possible threat to a person's physical or mental well-being.

Behavioral—Means related to the way a person acts.

Psychological—Refers to mental processes, including thoughts, feelings, and emotions.

Psychologist—A mental health professional who can do psychological testing and provide mental health counseling.

Description

Grief counseling helps the individual work through the feelings associated with the loss of another, accept that loss, determine how life can go on without that person, and consolidate memories in order to be able to move forward. Grief counseling also provides information about the normal grieving process, to help individuals understand that many of the symptoms and changes they are experiencing are a normal, temporary reaction to loss. For some individuals, the primary focus of grief counseling is to help identify ways to express feelings about the loss that the person has been unable to express on his or her own. Individuals who seek grief counseling may be experiencing an emotional numbness, or a residual shock in reaction to the loss, and need assistance to return to a normal life. In those cases, grief counseling will focus on helping the individual get in touch with those feelings and become more active in ones daily routine.

For some people, grieving may initially be so extreme that physical and psychological symptoms may be experienced, while other people appear to experience no symptoms whatsoever. Activities of daily living may feel overwhelming to an individual who has experienced a loss. In these cases, grief counseling may focus on specific coping skills to help the individual resume some normalcy in his or her daily routine. For example, if sleep patterns are disrupted, grief counseling may include consultation with the individual's physician to assist with temporary strategies to increase sleep. If the individual is having trouble getting to work on time, behavioral strategies may be used as an interim measure to help the person return to aspects of normal daily life.

Additional work in grief counseling may involve identifying ways to let go or say good–bye if the individual has not been able to do so successfully. Therapeutic letters may be a helpful mechanism to express thoughts that were not conveyed prior to the death. Dreams are frequently experienced by survivors, and these can be a focus in grief counseling as well. The dreams can often be consoling and as well, a way of consolidating the memories about the deceased.

Precautions

Grieving is a normal life process—an adjustment reaction to a loss. Grief counseling is meant to facilitate that normal process. No specific precautions are warranted. However, there are certain circumstances in which complications to the normal grieving process may occur. These circumstances may involve the loss of a child, or the loss of a loved one due to an accident or homicide, for example.

In these cases of complicated grieving, more extreme responses to the loss may be observed, depending on the individual's capacity for coping, personal resiliency, and support system. For example, if the individual feels isolated, he may be at greater risk for severe depressive symptoms or a **suicide** attempt. Alternatively, if the survivors feel rage or anger over the loss, there may be a risk of harm to others.

Preparation

No specific preparation is required by the participant; however, a need for grief counseling is indicated by prolonged symptoms (such as crying spells, preoccupation with the deceased, lack of motivation, or suicidal thoughts), and the severity of personal distress over the loss. A patient seeking grief counseling would most likely undergo a clinical evaluation by a therapist, before the grief counseling began, so that the therapist could understand the patient's personal history and goals for treatment.

QUESTIONS TO ASK YOUR DOCTOR OR COUNSELOR

- What counseling options do you recommend for me?
- Are there medications to help me with my grief? If so, what are they and should I take a medication?
- What kind of changes can I expect to see with the medication you have prescribed for me?
- What are the side effects associated with the medication you have prescribed for me?
- Can you recommend any counseling or support groups for me and my family?

Aftercare

Aftercare is usually provided through informal support systems, which may include family and friends, as well as support groups.

Risks

A slight risk exists regarding treatment of complicated grief. Such circumstances include chronic, prolonged grieving or unexpected loss (particularly due to a violent accident, suicide, homicide, or the death of a child). These factors complicate the grieving process due to the unexpected, sometimes violent nature of the loss, that feels inconsistent with expectations and desires for loved ones. In these cases, an initial adverse effect may be seen from participation in treatment, due to the increased focus on the loss. This reaction improves over time, as adjustment is facilitated. Two other factors impacting individual adjustment include the type of relationship the individual had with the deceased, and the resiliency of the individual.

Results

Normal results from grief counseling include being able to move on with one's life, recognizing and accepting the physical loss of the individual, and being able to bridge that loss with positive memories of the deceased. Successful coping will be characterized by a return to normal routines, although some symptoms may be experienced periodically throughout the year or on dates of important anniversaries such as a wedding, birthday, or the date of the loss.

Abnormal results would include an unsuccessful outcome of prolonged grief, exhibited by continued preoccupation with the loss of the individual, crying spells, and depressive symptoms being the most likely complications. Some disruption of the daily routine would persist, and there may be extreme emotional responses, that could include no apparent reaction to difficulty containing feelings. Other complications include "unfinished business," or feelings of unresolved issues with the deceased. Sometimes the feelings of unresolved issues can be as simple as wishing they had communicated their love and affection for the person the last time they saw them, or may be as complicated as unresolved feelings about a history of **abuse** by the deceased.

Resources

BOOKS

Burns, Donna M. *When Kids Are Grieving: Addressing Grief and Loss in School.* Thousand Oaks, CA: Corwin Press, 2010.

Coor, C.A., and D.E. Balk, eds. *Handbook of Adolescent Death and Bereavement.*New York, NY: Springer Publishing Co., Inc., 2004.

James, John W., and Russell Friedman. *The Grief Recovery Handbook,* 20th Anniversary ed. New York, NY: Harper Paperbacks, 2009.

Jeffreys, J. Shep. *Helping Grieving People - When Tears Are Not Enough: A Handbook for Care Providers,* 2nd ed. New York, NY: Routledge, 2011.

Kübler–Ross, Elizabeth, and David Kessler. *Life Lessons.* New York: Simon and Schuster and the Elizabeth Kübler–Ross Family Partnership, Ltd. 2001.

Meier, Scott T., and Susan R. Davis. *The Elements of Counseling,* 7th ed. Belmont, CA: Brooks Cole, 2010.

Noel, Brook, and Pamela D. Blair. *I Wasn't Ready to Say Goodbye: Surviving, Coping and Healing After the Sudden Death of a Loved One.* Naperville, IL: Sourcebooks, 2008.

ORGANIZATIONS

The Compassionate Friends, Inc, PO Box 3696, Oak Brook, IL, 60522, http://www.compassionatefriends.org/home.aspx.

GROWW (Grief Recovery Online [founded by] Widows & Widowers), 11877 Douglas Rd., #102-PMB101, Alpharetta, GA, 30005, http://www.groww.org.

SHARE Pregnancy and Infant Loss Support, 402 Jackson Street, St. Charles, MO, 63301, (800) 821-6819, Fax: (636) 947-7486, http://www.nationalshare.org.

SIDS Alliance, 1314 Bedford Ave., Ste. 230, Baltimore, MD, 21208, (800) 221-SIDS, http://www.sidsalliance.org.

Widowed Persons Service, AARP, 601 E. St. NW, Washington, DC, 20049, (202) 434-2260, http://www.aarp.org/relationships/grief-loss/info-2005/newly_widowed.html.

Deanna Pledge, Ph.D.
Laura Jean Cataldo, RN, Ed.D.

Group homes

Definition

Group homes are small, residential facilities located within a community and designed to serve children or adults with chronic disabilities. These homes usually have six or fewer occupants and are staffed 24 hours a day by trained caregivers.

Description

Most group homes are standard, single-family houses, purchased by group home administrators and adapted to meet the needs of the residents. Except for any adaptive features such as wheelchair ramps, group homes are virtually indistinguishable from other homes in the surrounding neighborhood. Group homes may be located in neighborhoods of any socioeconomic status.

Residents of group homes usually have some type of chronic mental disorder that impairs their ability to live independently. Many residents also have physical disabilities such as impairments of vision communication, or ambulation. These individuals require continual assistance to complete daily living and self-care tasks. Some also require supervision due to behavior that may be dangerous to self or others, such as aggression or a tendency to run away.

Although most group homes provide long-term care, some residents eventually acquire the necessary skills to move to more independent living situations. Group homes for children are usually temporary placements, providing care until a foster family can be secured. Others may return to their natural families. Occasionally, halfway homes for people recently released from prison or discharged from a **substance abuse** program may also

A woman with Down syndrome is visited by her sister at a group home. *(© Ellen B. Senisi/Photo Researchers, Inc.)*

be referred to as group homes. These types of group homes are also transitory in nature.

History and mission

The development of group homes occurred in response to the **deinstitutionalization** movement of the 1960s and 1970s. As psychiatric hospitals closed, discharged individuals needed places to live. Group homes were designed to provide care in the least restrictive environment and to integrate individuals with disabilities into the community, reducing **stigma** and improving quality of life. The environment of a group home was intended to simulate typical family life as much as possible.

Since the passage of the **Community Mental Health** Centers Act in 1963, grants have been available to group homes. State and federal funds such as the Medicaid Home and Community-Based Waiver continue to support the majority of group homes. However, some homes operate on donations from private citizens or civic and religious organizations. Most group homes are owned by private rather than governmental organizations, and can be either nonprofit or for-profit organizations. Group homes are considered more cost effective compared to institutional care. Unfortunately, the number of available group homes has not always matched need, resulting in **homelessness** or rehospitalization for some individuals.

One of the goals of group home living is to increase the independence of residents. Group home staff members teach residents daily living and self-care skills, providing as little assistance as possible. Daily living skills include meal preparation, laundry, housecleaning, home maintenance, money management, and appropriate social interactions. Self-care skills include bathing or showering, dressing, toileting, eating, and taking prescribed medications.

Staff also assure that residents receive necessary services from community service providers, including medical care, physical therapy, occupational therapy, vocational training, education, and mental health services. Most group home residents are assigned a case manager from a community mental health center or other government agency who oversees their care. Case managers review group home documentation regarding skills learned and services received, and make recommendations for adjustments in care.

NIMBY

Unfortunately, group homes have received much opposition from communities. NIMBY (acronym for "not in my backyard") describes the common reaction of community residents when they discover that a group home is targeted for their neighborhood. Current research suggests that protests frequently involve concerns over personal security, declining property values, or a generalized threat to the neighborhood's quality. Some researchers believe that prejudiced attitudes such as ignorance, fear, and distrust are the true reasons for protest.

Usually, neighborhood opposition is unsuccessful due to provisions of the Fair Housing Act of 1968. However, such opposition can be detrimental to the goal of integrating residents into the community. The NIMBY principal is also a concern because as deinstitutionalization continues, the need for additional group homes increases. Statistics show that between 1987 and 1999, the use of group homes serving individuals with developmental disabilities and containing six residents or less increased by 240%.

Social service workers are constantly looking for ways to address NIMBY. Some research has suggested that community concerns decrease with time as community members become familiar with group home residents. Studies have shown that opposition can be decreased by providing advanced notice of plans for a group home, as well as adequate information and discussion about expectations.

Factors affecting group home success

Initially, many people were skeptical about the adequacy of group home care compared to psychiatric hospitals or other institutions. Over the past 25 years, many studies have examined the impact of group home care on residents. These studies have consistently shown increases in adaptive behavior, productivity, community integration, and level of independence.

Risks involved in successfully transitioning an individual to a group home include psychological deterioration such as severe cognitive or physical impairments, physical deterioration that includes being nonambulatory, or mortality issues such as being age 70 or older.

Before considering group home placement—especially for those in the high risk category—extensive planning should be conducted. A complete assessment plan of the individual's needs should specify which agency will be responsible for meeting medical needs, particularly in the event of a crisis. The individual's strengths should be incorporated into the plan whenever possible. For example, if a supportive family is an identified strength, the preferred group home should be close in proximity to facilitate family visits.

KEY TERMS

Ambulation—Ability to walk.

Case manager—A professional who designs and monitors implementation of comprehensive care plans (i.e., services addressing medical, financial, housing, psychiatric, vocational, social needs) for individuals seeking mental health or social services.

Community mental health centers—Organizations that manage and deliver a comprehensive range of mental health services, education, and outreach to residents of a given community.

Community Mental Health Centers Act of 1963—Federal legislation providing grants for the operation of community mental health centers and related services.

Deinstitutionalization—The process of moving people out of mental hospitals into treatment programs or halfway houses in local communities. With this movement, the responsibility for care shifted from large (often governmental) agencies to families and community organizations.

Fair Housing Act of 1968—Federal legislation regarding access to housing that prohibits discrimination based on race, color, national origin, sex, religion, disability, or familial status.

Least restrictive environment—Refers to care options that involve the least amount of restraint and the greatest degree of independence possible, while still meeting the individual's needs and maintaining safety.

Medicaid Home and Community Based-Waiver—Legislation regarding the use of Medicaid funds for care services; allows certain federal requirements to be bypassed so that states can use the funds more flexibly for accessing home- and community-based services rather than using hospitals or intermediate-care facilities.

NIMBY phenomenon—Acronym for Not In My Backyard, describing the common opposition displayed by citizens toward the placement of group homes or other social service facilities in their neighborhoods.

Non-ambulatory—Unable to walk.

Other factors that contribute to group home success are a small staff-to-resident ratio, well-trained staff, and a home-like atmosphere. As with any type of organization, some group homes are better run than others. A careful investigation into a home's procedures is recommended. Research suggests that individuals with severe cognitive impairments often experience a period of disorientation, and may need additional support or supervision for the first few months while adjusting to their new surroundings. Preplacement visits and discussion can reduce anxiety for the future resident.

Resources

BOOKS

Robinson, Julia W., and Travis Thompson. "Stigma and Architecture." In *Enabling Environments: Measuring the Impact of Environment on Disability and Rehabilitation,* edited by Edward Steinfeld and G. Scott Danford. New York: Kluwer Academic/Plenum Publishers, 1999.

Udell, Leslie. "Supports in Small Group Home Settings." In *Dementia, Aging, and Intellectual Disabilities: A Handbook,* edited by Matthew P. Janicki and Arthur J. Dalton. Philadelphia: Brunner/Mazel, Inc. (Routledge), 1999.

PERIODICALS

Anderson, Lynda, Robert Prouty, and K. Charlie Lakin. "Parallels in Size of Residential Settings and Use of Medicaid-Financed Programs." *Mental Retardation* 38, no. 5 (2000): 468–471.

Ducharme, Joseph M., Larry Williams, Anne Cummings, Pina Murray, and Terry Spencer. "General Case Quasi-Pyramidal Staff Training to Promote Generalization of Teaching Skills in Supervisory and Direct-Care Staff." *Behavior Modification* 25, no. 2 (April 2001): 233–254.

"The Impact of Deinstitutionalization on the Seriously and Persistently Mentally Ill Elderly: A One-Year Follow-Up." *Abstracts in Social Gerontology* 45, no. 2 (June 2002): 157–301.

Kim, Dong Soo. "Another Look at the NIMBY Phenomenon." *Health & Social Work* 25, no. 2 (May 2000): 146–148.

Piat, Myra. "The NIMBY Phenomenon: Community Residents' Concerns About Housing for Deinstitutionalized People." *Health & Social Work* 25, no. 2 (May 2000): 127–38.

Spreat, Scott, and James W. Conroy. "Community Placement for Persons with Significant Cognitive Challenges: An Outcome Analysis." *Brief Report Number 13 of a Series on the Well Being of People with Developmetnal Disabilities in Oklahoma* February 2000. Available online at http://www.outcomeanalysis.com/DL/pubs/okr13.pdf (accessed November 9, 2011).

Whittaker, James K. "The Future of Residential Group Care." *Child Welfare* 79, no. 1 (January–February 2000): 59–74.

ORGANIZATIONS

The Arc National Headquarters, 1660 L Street, NW, Ste. 301, Washington, DC, 20036, (202) 534-3700, Fax: (202) 534-3731, info@thearc.org, http://www.thearc.org.

Child Welfare League of America, 1726 M Street NW, Ste. 500, Washington, DC, 20036, (202) 688-4200, Fax: (202) 833-1689, http://www.cwla.org.

National Institute of Mental Health, 6001 Executive Blvd., Room 8184, MSC 9663, Bethesda, MD, 20892-9663, (301) 433-4513; TTY: (301) 443-8431, Fax: (301) 443-4279, (866) 615-6464; TTY: (866) 415-8051, nimhinfo@nih.gov, http://www.nimh.nih.gov.

Office of Fair Housing and Equal Opportunity, Department of Housing and Urban Development, 451 Seventh Street, SW, Washington, DC, 20410, http://portal.hud.gov/hudportal/HUD?src=/program_offices/fair_housing_equal_opp.

Sandra L. Friedrich, MA

Group therapy

Definition

Group therapy is a form of psychosocial treatment where a small group of patients meet regularly to talk, interact, and discuss problems with each other and the group leader (therapist).

Purpose

Group therapy attempts to give individuals a safe and comfortable place where they can work out problems and emotional issues. Patients gain insight into their own thoughts and behavior, and offer suggestions and support to others. In addition, patients who have a difficult time with interpersonal relationships can benefit from the social interactions that are a basic part of the group therapy experience.

Precautions

Patients who are suicidal, homicidal, psychotic, or in the midst of a major acute crisis are typically not referred for group therapy until their behavior and emotional state have stabilized. Depending on their level of functioning, cognitively impaired patients (like patients with organic **brain** disease or a **traumatic brain injury**) may also be unsuitable for group therapy **intervention**. Some patients with sociopathic traits are not suitable for most groups.

A group of men attend a substance abuse therapy session. *(© David Grossman/Photo Researchers, Inc.)*

Description

A **psychologist**, **psychiatrist**, social worker, or other healthcare professional typically arranges and conducts group therapy sessions. In some therapy groups, two co-therapists share the responsibility of group leadership. Patients are selected on the basis of what they might gain from group therapy interaction and what they can contribute to the group as a whole.

Therapy groups may be homogeneous or heterogeneous. Homogeneous groups have members with similar diagnostic backgrounds (for example, they may all suffer from **depression**). Heterogeneous groups have a mix of individuals with different emotional issues. The number of group members varies widely, but is typically no more than 12. Groups may be time limited (with a predetermined number of sessions) or indefinite (where the group determines when therapy ends). Membership may be closed or open to new members once sessions begin.

The number of sessions in group therapy depends on the makeup, goals, and setting of the group. For example, a therapy group that is part of a **substance abuse** program to rehabilitate inpatients would be called short-term group therapy. This term is used because, as patients, the group members will only be in the hospital for a relatively short period of time. Long-term therapy groups may meet for six months, a year, or longer. The therapeutic approach used in therapy depends on the focus of the group and the psychological training of the therapist. Some common techniques include psychodynamic, cognitive-behavioral, and **Gestalt therapy**.

In a group therapy session, group members are encouraged to openly and honestly discuss the issues that brought them to therapy. They try to help other group members by offering their own suggestions, insights, and empathy regarding their problems. There are no definite rules for group therapy, only that members participate to the best of their ability. However, most therapy groups do have some basic ground rules that are usually discussed during the first session. Patients are asked not to share what goes on in therapy sessions with anyone outside of the group. This protects the confidentiality of the other members. They may also be asked not to see other group members socially outside of therapy because of the harmful effect it might have on the dynamics of the group.

The therapist's main task is to guide the group in self-discovery. Depending on the goals of the group and the training and style of the therapist, he or she may lead the group interaction or allow the group to take their own direction. Typically, the group leader does some of both, providing direction when the group gets off track while letting them set their own agenda. The therapist may guide the group by simply reinforcing the positive behaviors they engage in. For example, if a group member shows empathy to another member, or offers a constructive suggestion, the therapist will point this out and explain the value of these actions to the group. In almost all group therapy situations, the therapist will attempt to emphasize the common traits among group members so that members can gain a sense of group identity. Group members realize that others share the same issues they do.

The main benefit group therapy may have over individual **psychotherapy** is that some patients behave and react more like themselves in a group setting than they would one-on-one with a therapist. The group therapy patient gains a certain sense of identity and social acceptance from their membership in the group. Suddenly, they are not alone. They are surrounded by others who have the same anxieties and emotional issues that they have. Seeing how others deal with these issues may give them new solutions to their problems. Feedback from group members also offers them a unique insight into their own behavior, and the group provides a safe forum in which to practice new behaviors. Lastly, by helping others in the group work through their problems, group therapy members can gain more self-esteem. Group therapy may also simulate family experiences of patients and will allow family dynamic issues to emerge.

Self-help groups like Alcoholics Anonymous and Weight Watchers fall outside of the psychotherapy realm. These self-help groups do offer many of the same benefits of social support, identity, and belonging that make group therapy effective for many. Self-help group members meet to discuss a common area of concern (like alcoholism, eating disorders, **bereavement**, parenting). Group sessions are not run by a therapist, but by a nonprofessional leader, group member, or the group as a whole. Self-help groups are sometimes used in addition to psychotherapy or regular group therapy.

Preparation

Patients are typically referred for group therapy by a psychologist or psychiatrist. Some patients may need individual therapy first. Before group sessions begin, the therapist leading the session may conduct a short intake interview with the patient to determine if the group is right for the patient. This interview will also allow the therapist to determine if the addition of the patient will benefit the group. The patient may be given some preliminary information on the group before sessions begin. This may include guidelines for success (like being open, listening to others, taking risks), rules of the group (like maintaining confidentiality), and educational information on what group therapy is about.

Aftercare

The end of long-term group therapy may cause feelings of **grief**, loss, abandonment, anger, or rejection in some members. The group therapist will attempt to foster a sense of closure by encouraging members to explore their feelings and use newly acquired coping techniques to deal with them. Working through this termination phase of group therapy is an important part of the treatment process.

Risks

Some very fragile patients may not be able to tolerate aggressive or hostile comments from group members. Patients who have trouble communicating in group situations may be at risk for dropping out of group therapy. If no one comments on their silence or makes an attempt to interact with them, they may begin to feel even more isolated and alone instead of identifying with the group. Therefore, the therapist usually attempts to encourage silent members to participate early on in treatment.

Results

Studies have shown that both group and individual psychotherapy benefit about 85% of the patients that participate in them. Optimally, patients gain a better understanding of themselves, and perhaps a stronger set of interpersonal and coping skills through the group therapy process. Some patients may continue therapy after group therapy ends, either individually or in another group setting.

Resources

BOOKS

Bieling, Peter J., Randi E. McCabe, and Martin M. Antony. *Cognitive-Behavioral Therapy in Groups*. New York: Guilford Press, 2006.

Yalom, Irvin D., and Molyn Leszcz. *Theory and Practice of Group Psychotherapy*. 5th ed. New York: Basic Books, 2005.

ORGANIZATIONS

American Psychiatric Association, 1000 Wilson Blvd., Suite 1825, Arlington, VA, 22209-3901, (703) 907-7300, apa@psych.org, http://www.psych.org.

American Psychological Association, 750 1st Street NE, Washington, DC, 20002-4242, (202) 336-5500; TDD/TTY: (202) 336-6123, (800) 374-2721, http://www.apa.org.

Paula Anne Ford-Martin
brenda w. lerner

Guanfacine

Definition

Guanfacine is a medication that inhibits the neurological signaling chemical norepinephrine. Norepinephrine is a type of neurotransmitter involved in normal **brain** function and has an effect on blood pressure, mood, concentration, and impulse control. Guanfacine helps regulate norepinephrine levels in the body and is used in treating high blood pressure, **attention deficit hyperactivity disorder (ADHD)**, and anxiety.

Purpose

Guanfacine is used to treat some of the symptoms of **ADHD** and anxiety, although it is not one of the main drugs used to treat anxiety. It works by regulating actions of the sympathetic nervous system, resulting in decreased blood pressure, reduced anxiety, improved concentration, and control of impulsive behavior and other stressful emotions present with both anxiety and ADHD.

Description

Guanfacine affects the natural body chemical norepinephrine. Norepinephrine is a type of neurotransmitter in the nervous system, a chemical that neurons use to signal one another in complex pathways for normal brain and body functioning. **Neurotransmitters** bind to chemical receptors on the surface of neurons (brain cells) and blood vessels. Once bound to a receptor they affect physiological processes. Neurotransmitter signaling pathways are responsible for many regulatory processes, including blood pressure and neuronal signaling that affects mood, concentration, and impulse control. Drugs such as guanfacine block

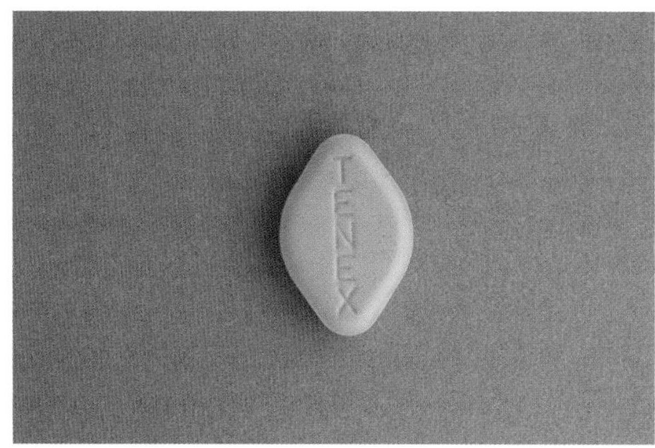

Tenex (guanfacine), 1 mg. *(© Custom Medical Stock Photo, Inc. Reproduced by permission.)*

the receptors for norepinephrine, resulting in more of the chemical left in the brain. This affects areas of the brain involving judgment, response to external stimuli, emotional responses, mental focus, sleep, and impulse control.

Recommended dosage

Guanfacine is given in pill form, and doses are taken at bedtime. The dose chosen depends on the disorder being treated, the patient's age, individual patient response to the medication regarding its effectiveness, and individual patient response to the medication regarding side effects. The dose of guanfacine in adults for treating high blood pressure or anxiety is 1–3 mg taken once per day, as needed to control symptoms. Patients are dosed at the lowest possible effective dose to avoid the development of adverse side effects. Slowly increasing the dose over time helps with minimizing side effects.

Guanfacine used in children for ADHD is dosed based on weight, and the dose is gradually increased over time. For example, children who weigh between 60 and 90 lb (27–40.5 kg) are usually started at a dose of 0.5 mg at bedtime. The dose is increased by 0.5 mg per day per week up to 1.5 mg per day if needed. If higher doses are required for improvement, after two weeks at the 1.5 mg-per-day dosing, the dose is increased to 2 mg per day. Doses are lowered if side effects become intolerable. If guanfacine is discontinued, it is tapered off gradually to avoid nervous system instability.

Precautions

Guanfacine may not be appropriate for use or may require caution in patients with kidney or liver dysfunction, some types of heart disease or recent heart attack, or elderly patients. Kidney and liver function as well as blood pressure may be monitored while taking guanfacine. When a patient discontinues the use of guanfacine, the dose needs to be tapered down slowly. If guanfacine is abruptly discontinued, there may be side effects such as rebound high blood pressure and anxiety. Rare but serious side effects of guanfacine may include sudden loss of consciousness or abnormally low heart rate. Guanfacine is classified as category B for pregnancy. Category B drugs have not been studied in humans during pregnancy, so fetal harm is possible, but it is unlikely. The safety of guanfacine use during breastfeeding is unknown, and so its use is not recommended.

Side effects

Sensitivity to guanfacine varies between patients, and some patients may find lower doses are more than their body system can tolerate. Common side effects of guanfacine are dry mouth, drowsiness, dizziness, constipation, **fatigue**, weakness, headache, and sexual dysfunction. Side effects of abrupt discontinuation of guanfacine include anxiety, restlessness, and increased blood pressure.

KEY TERMS

Neurotransmitter—A chemical messenger that travels through the body and acts in the nervous system. Neurotransmitter signaling is responsible for a wide range of bodily processes and is often the target of medications involving the brain and cardiovascular system.

Neurotransmitter receptor—A physical recipient for chemicals called neurotransmitters. Receptors sit on the surface of cells that make up body tissues, and once bound to the neurotransmitter, they initiate the chemical signaling pathway associated with neurotransmitters.

Norepinephrine—A type of neurotransmitter involved in regulation of concentration, impulse control, judgment, mood, attention span, psychostimulation, and disease states such as ADHD and depression.

Sympathetic nervous system—Part of the nervous system that increases heart rate and blood pressure, sweating, pupil dilation, and mental stress arousal.

Interactions

Patients should make their doctor aware of all medications and supplements they are taking before using guanfacine. Using alcohol while taking guanfacine may create toxic reactions in the body and should be avoided. Drugs that affect the liver, including the antidepressant **mirtazapine**, may affect the metabolism of guanfacine, resulting in too much or too little of the drug in the body. This could lead to increased side effects or even toxic doses. Likewise, guanfacine may affect the metabolism of other drugs, leading to greater or lower doses than therapeutically desired.

Guanfacine should not be used at the same time as **antidepressants** called **monoamine oxidase inhibitors (MAOIs)**. Use of these medications in the same time period may cause a high blood pressure crisis, which can be severe and life-threatening. Switching between drug treatment with an MAOI to guanfacine may require a

QUESTIONS TO ASK YOUR DOCTOR

- Can I take the full dose right away or do I need to slowly increase the dose up to the full amount?
- Can I stop taking the medication right away or do I need to slowly decrease the dose in order to go off the medication?
- Should I eat before taking this medication?
- Will this medication interact with any of my other prescription medications? Over-the-counter drugs? Herbal supplements?
- What side effects indicate that I have taken too much of this medication?
- Can I drink alcoholic beverages when I am taking this medication?

waiting period of up to several weeks between drugs. Other drugs that cannot be combined with guanfacine due to risk of high blood pressure include the antibiotic linezolid. Some medications interact with guanfacine to cause additive adverse effects of abnormally low blood pressure, such as the muscle relaxant tizanidine. Sedative drugs also should not be used with guanfacine due to additive effects. Blood pressure medications such as atenolol have antagonistic, or opposing, effects with guanfacine and should not be used in the same time period. Guanfacine should not be used with the herbal supplement yohimbe, as the combination may decrease the efficacy of guanfacine.

Resources

BOOKS

Brunton, Laurence, et al. *Goodman and Gilman's the Pharmacological Basis of Therapeutics*. 12th ed. New York: McGraw Hill Medical, 2011.

Zorumski, Charles F., and Eugene H. Rubin. *Psychiatry and Clinical Neuroscience: A Primer*. New York: Oxford University Press, 2011.

PERIODICALS

Connor, D. F., et al. "Effects of Guanfacine Extended Release on Oppositional Symptoms in Children Aged 6–12 Years with Attention-Deficit Hyperactivity Disorder and Oppositional Symptoms: A Randomized, Double-Blind, Placebo-Controlled Trial." *CNS Drugs* 24, no. 9 (2010): 755–68.

WEBSITES

PubMed Health. "Guanfacine." U.S. National Library of Medicine. http://www.ncbi.nlm.nih.gov/pubmedhealth/PMH0000057 (accessed November 12, 2011).

ORGANIZATIONS

American College of Neuropsychopharmacology, 5034-A Thoroughbred Lane, Brentwood, TN, 37027, (615) 324-2360, Fax: (615) 523-1715, acnp@acnp.org, http://www.acnp.org/default.aspx.

Children and Adults with Attention Deficit/Hyperactivity Disorder, 8181 Professional Place, Ste. 150, Landover, MD, 20785, (301) 306-7070, (800) 233-4050, Fax: (301) 306-7090, http://www.chadd.org.

Mental Health America, 2000 N Beauregard St., 6th Fl., Alexandria, VA, 22311, (703) 684-7722, (800) 969-6642, Fax: (703) 684-5968, http://www.nmha.org.

U.S. Food and Drug Administration, 10903 New Hampshire Ave., Silver Spring, MD, 20993-0002, (888) INFO-FDA (463-6332), http://www.fda.gov.

Maria Eve Basile, PhD

Guided imagery therapy

Definition

Guided imagery therapy (GIT) is a cognitive-behavioral technique in which a client is guided in imagining a relaxing scene or series of experiences, and then in learning to retrieve such images at a later time. As a traditional mind-body technique, it offers ways to concentrate on an image or images in order to influence physical and emotional states. Guided imagery therapy is based on the connections between the emotional control center in the **brain** and the autonomic nervous system, immune system, and endocrine system. The patient produces such remembered images without actually seeing them with the eyes.

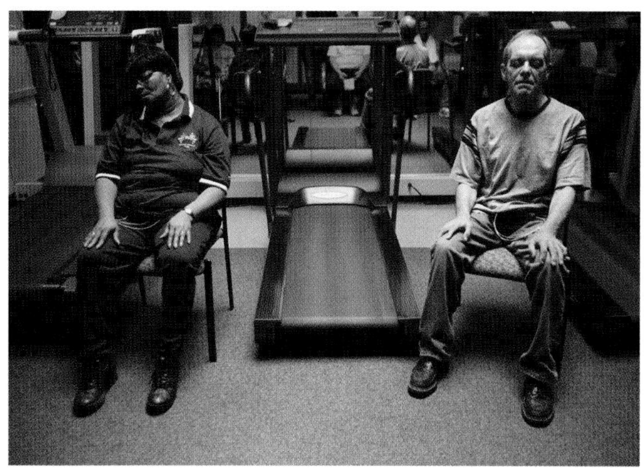

A group of patients in rehabilitation for substance abuse participate in guided imagery therapy. *(© Lisa Dejong/The Plain Dealer/Landov)*

The Academy for Guided Imagery classifies guided imagery therapy into three parts: **stress reduction** and relaxation; active visualization or directed imagery (to improve performance or behavior, or to influence outcomes); and receptive imagery (to provide conscious images to deal with symptoms, illnesses, or other problems).

GIT has been shown to be an effective form of mental-health therapy for such stress-related conditions as **insomnia**, anxiety, migraine headaches, **depression**, breathing rate, and high blood pressure. It is also effective for reducing the symptoms for such non-stress-related conditions as skin rashes (including hives and allergies), irritable bowel syndrome, rheumatoid arthritis, asthma, and Crohn's disease. Guided imagery therapy has also been found to be useful to reduce some side effects of cancer.

Purpose

Numerous clinical observations suggest that an individual visualizing an imagined scene reacts as though it were actually occurring; therefore, "induced" images can have a profound effect on behavior and a marked improvement on mental health. The usefulness of guided imagery techniques has been shown to be effective in helping individuals learn or modify behaviors such as:

- learning to relax
- changing or controlling negative emotions in response to a particular situation, event (e.g., loss of a job), or belief
- preparing for changes they are likely to face in the future (e.g., children leaving home, a parent moving)
- eliminating or reducing undesirable behaviors (e.g., smoking, excessive eating)
- increasing effective pain management
- coping with difficult situations (e.g., an unpleasant boss)
- learning new and desirable behaviors (e.g., assertiveness)
- becoming more motivated (e.g., doing homework between therapy sessions)
- learning from behavior in an earlier situation (e.g., a temper tantrum) in order to feel less shame or guilt
- experimenting with ways to manage stressful or anxiety-producing situations (e.g., giving a presentation in public) by mentally rehearsing the needed behavior(s)

Guided imagery techniques have been applied to—and found to be effective or show promise with—a variety of populations, including individuals with:

- phobias (including agoraphobia, social phobia, and specific phobias)
- mild to moderate depression
- generalized anxiety disorders
- post-traumatic stress disorder
- obsessive-compulsive disorder
- sexual difficulties
- habit disorders
- chronic fatigue syndrome
- children's behavioral disorders
- stuttering
- acute and chronic pain (and other physical disorders)

Guided imagery has also contributed to the achievement of skills and overcoming anxiety in normal life situations that include learning or improving motor skills, test-taking, and public speaking. In addition, visualization and imagery, along with other behavioral techniques, have been applied to the fields of business, industry, child rearing, education, behavioral medicine, and sports.

Demographics

Guided imagery therapy can be conducted on anyone who is willing to participate this form of mental-health therapy and willing to make improvements in psychological problems within their lives. It is not limited by age, race, ethnic background, socioeconomic condition, or other such factors—only on a person' willingness to participate.

Description

Imagery techniques have been combined with a wide range of behavioral and cognitive procedures and treatment methods of some psychotherapeutic approaches, including **behavior modification**, cognitive processing therapy, cognitive-behavior therapy, rational-emotive therapy, multimodal therapy, and **hypnotherapy**. Combinations of treatment methods among these approaches lead to the following general uses of imagery:

- antifuture shock imagery (preparing for a feared future event)
- positive imagery (using pleasant scenes for relaxation training)
- aversive imagery (using an unpleasant image to help eliminate or reduce undesirable behavior)
- associated imagery (using imagery to track unpleasant feelings)
- coping imagery (using images to rehearse to reach a behavioral goal or manage a situation)

- "step-up" technique (exaggerating a feared situation and using imagery to cope with it)

An assessment of the individual's presenting problems is an essential part of treatment, both at the beginning of therapy and throughout the entire process. This is to ensure that the therapist has sufficient understanding of the client's situation and **diagnosis** of the problem(s). The assessment generally covers a variety of areas, such as developmental history (including family, education, employment, and social relationships), past traumatic experiences, specific psychological symptoms, medical and psychiatric treatments, and client goals. Often, clients have several problems, and both the therapist and the client work together on prioritizing specific treatment goals.

Following the assessment, the therapist will present a general rationale for the use of imagery. The therapist might explain that the client will learn techniques in which he or she imagines they or another person are performing a particular behavior. To enhance visualization, it is important to involve all senses in the image. For example, if the client is to be walking down a busy street, he or she is encouraged to imagine hearing sounds from traffic and other people, smell exhaust fumes from buses and aromas from a nearby bakery, and observe body movements and wind in the face. It is stressed to the client that the most critical aspect of imagining is the feeling of actually experiencing the scene—of being in it rather than just seeing oneself in it.

Both the therapist and the client construct a relaxing scene by discussing exactly what the client finds pleasant. It is better if the client chooses all images (positive or negative) and the therapist trains the client to visualize the selected images as vividly as possible.

Once a pleasant scene is decided upon, the client is asked to assume a relaxed position and with closed eyes, if this is comfortable, before being guided in visualization. One common beginning instruction may be: "Imagine you are lying on a warm, sandy beach." The therapist continues to guide the relaxation by saying such phrases as: "Notice the texture of the sand and the color of the sky. Focus on the sounds you hear, and the smells . . . ." The client is asked to practice the image at home between sessions. A tape of the guided imagery in the familiar voice of the therapist can be helpful to some clients in practicing at home.

During visualization, clients are given permission to take control if they need to by changing the image or stopping the activity completely. To help clients maintain control of the image, the therapist may also say to the client, "Take as long as you need to relax," and "Do whatever you need to do in order to feel safe." This empowers clients in using such techniques.

KEY TERMS

Depression—A psychiatric disorder involving feelings of hopelessness and symptoms of fatigue, sleeplessness, suicidal tendencies, and poor concentration.

Generalized anxiety disorder—An anxiety disorder characterized by daily irrational worry that is often also excessive and uncontrolled.

Length of treatment

Treatments using behavioral techniques tend to be relatively brief. However, many factors determine the length of therapy. Generally, treatment takes longer if target behaviors are more numerous and more difficult to specify. Some types of treatments require more sessions than others. For example, techniques using imagery require more sessions than treatments in which the client is exposed to the actual feared situations in real life.

Other factors that determine the length of treatment are the types of presenting disorders, the client's willingness to do homework, how long the client has had the problem, client financial resources, and whether there are supportive family members and friends. The therapist's style and experience may also affect the length of therapy. Clients may be seen several times a week at the start of therapy and then once weekly for several months, and every other month for follow-up for a few more months.

Precautions

The practitioner of guided imagery therapy should use caution when attempting such therapy on someone who is hesitant to use it for personal, religious, spiritual, or other such reasons.

Guided imagery is not used in isolation but as a part of a therapeutic formulation and is appropriate for a range of problems and disorders. It is, however, thought that some techniques—such as imagery used in rational-emotive therapy—can trigger high levels of anxiety in some clients. Therefore, caution should be taken when using these techniques if clients have the following conditions:

- asthma attacks triggered by stress or anxiety
- seizures triggered by stress or anxiety
- cardiac condition or related conditions
- depression with suicidal ideation

- emotional excitability and disturbances
- pregnancy
- severe psychiatric disorders

In these instances, other strategies and techniques that do not trigger high levels of anxiety, such as relaxation exercises or coping imagery, should be considered. When working with clients with these conditions, the therapist should be in consultation with their medical provider.

Preparations

People who perform guided imagery therapy on themselves will be guided with instructions provided by self-help books, CDs, and DVDs. When used under the guidance of a licensed practitioner, no preparations are necessary or advised.

Aftercare

Guided imagery techniques have been taken from behavior therapy and are used by different psychological theories and systems of counseling and **psychotherapy**, including **cognitive-behavioral therapy**. Research has shown these techniques to be effective when applied to specific problems.

Results

Depending on the combination of visualization and imagery techniques used, the therapeutic approach, and client problem(s), it is expected that clients will have positive changes. Specifically, it is normal to have positive changes in specifically defined target behaviors. There should also be a reduction in biases or distortions in thinking, resulting in more effective functioning that, in turn, leads to more positive feelings, behavior, and thinking; and fewer emotional disturbances, more effective coping skills, decreased self-defeating behaviors, and less tension.

Risks

There are no known major risks associated with the technique called guided imagery therapy. Potential risks could occur if it is used to replace traditional therapies, however, but under no circumstances should this be done. Guided imagery therapy always should be used in conjunction with such traditional practices.

Research and general acceptance

Guided imagery therapy is accepted as effective therapy within the realm of **mind-body medicine**. It is well suited to be used with other alternative therapies, such as massage and other such touch therapies and various types of psychotherapy when behavioral improvements are desired.

QUESTIONS TO ASK YOUR DOCTOR

- How likely will guided imagery therapy help me?
- Can you help me find literature to provide more information about the therapy?
- What are some of the best resources on guided imagery therapy?
- How do I find a professional to conduct guided imagery therapy?
- Do you recommend any websites that can help?

Training and certification

The Academy for Guided Imagery (AGI) provides a Professional Certification Training Program in Interactive Guided Imagerysm (IGIsm). According to the AGI, only those individuals certified through the AGI may represent themselves as practicing IGIsm. Licensed psychologists can conduct guided imagery therapy.

Resources

BOOKS

Austad, Carol Shaw. *Counseling and Psychotherapy Today: Theory, Practice, and Research.* Boston: McGraw-Hill Higher Education, 2009.

Feltham, Colin, and Ian E. Horton, editors. *The SAGE Handbook of Counseling and Psychotherapy.* London: Sage, 2006.

Kazantzis, Nikolaos, Mark A. Reinecke, and Arthur Freeman, editors. *Cognitive and Behavioral Theories in Clinical Practice.* New York: Guilford Press, 2010.

WEBSITES

Mayo Clinic staff. "Enhance Healing Through Guided Imagery." MayoClinic.com. January 2, 2008. http://www.mayoclinic.org/news2008-mchi/4403.html (accessed May 23, 2011).

ORGANIZATIONS

Academy for Guided Imagery, 10780 Santa Monica Boulevard, Los Angeles, CA, 90025, (800) 726-2070, Fax: (800) 727-2070, info@acadhi.com, http://acadgi.com.

American Psychiatric Association, 1000 Wilson Boulevard, Suite 1825, Arlington, VA, 22209-3901, (703) 907-7300, apa@psych.org, http://www.psych.org.

American Psychological Association, 750 First Street, NE, Washington, DC, 20002-4242, (202) 336-5500, (800) 374-2721, http://www.apa.org.

Anxiety Disorders Association of America, 8730 Georgia Avenue, Silver Spring, MD, 20910, (240) 485-1001, http://www.adaa.org.

Mental Health America, 2000 North Beauregard Street, Sixth Floor, Alexandria, VA, 22311, (703) 684-7722, (800) 969-6642, Fax: (703) 684-5968, http://www.nmha.org.

National Institute of Mental Health, 6001 Executive Boulevard, Room 8184, MSC 9663, Bethesda, MD, 20892-9663, (301) 443-4513, (866) 615-6464, Fax: (301) 443-4279, http://www.nimh.nih.gov.

Janice Van Buren, PhD
William Atkins

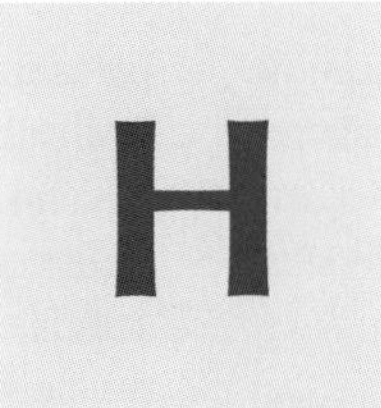

Halcion *see* **Triazolam**

Haldol *see* **Haloperidol**

Hallucination

Definition

A hallucination is a sensory perception without a source in the external world. The English word "hallucination" comes from the Latin verb *hallucinari*, which means "to wander in the mind." Hallucinations can affect any of the senses, although certain diseases or disorders are associated with specific types of hallucinations.

It is important to distinguish between hallucinations and illusions or **delusions**, as the terms are often confused in conversation and popular journalism. A hallucination is a distorted sensory experience that appears to be a perception of something real even though it is *not* caused by an external stimulus. For example, some elderly people who have been recently bereaved may have hallucinations in which they "see" the dead loved one. An illusion, by contrast, is a mistaken or false interpretation of a real sensory experience, as when a traveler in the desert sees what looks like a pool of water, but in fact is a mirage caused by the refraction of light as it passes through layers of air of different densities. The bluish-colored light is a real sensory stimulus, but mistaking it for water is an illusion. A delusion is a false belief that a person maintains in spite of evidence to the contrary and in spite of proof that other members of their culture do not share the belief. For example, some people insist that they have seen flying saucers or unidentified flying objects (UFOs) even though the objects they have filmed or photographed can be shown to be ordinary aircraft, weather balloons, satellites, etc.

Demographics

The demographics of hallucinations vary depending on their cause; however, many researchers think that they are underreported for several reasons:

- Fear of being thought "crazy" or mentally ill.
- Gaps in research. For example, some types of hallucinations are associated with disorders that primarily affect the elderly, who are often underrepresented in health surveys.
- Fear of being reported to law enforcement for illegal drug use.

There is no evidence that hallucinations occur more frequently in some racial or ethnic groups than in others. In addition, gender does not appear to make a difference. The demographics of hallucinations associated with some specific age groups, conditions, or disorders are as follows:

- Children. Hallucinations are rare in children below the age of eight. About 40% of children diagnosed with schizophrenia, however, have visual or auditory hallucinations.
- Eye disorders. About 14% of patients treated in eye clinics for glaucoma or age-related macular degeneration report visual hallucinations.
- Alzheimer's disease (AD). About 40%–50% of patients diagnosed with AD develop hallucinations in the later stages of the disease.
- Drug use. According to the 2010 National Survey on Drug Use and Health, 14.8% of persons living in the United States have used hallucinogens in their lifetime, with LSD being the most popular (9.2%), followed by MDMA, or Ecstasy (6.3%). The highest rate of hallucinogen abuse is found in males between the ages of 18 and 25.
- Normal sleep/wake cycles. Sleep researchers in Great Britain and the United States have reported that 30%–37% of adults experience hypnagogic hallucinations, which occur during the passage from wakefulness

into sleep, while about 10%–12% report hypnopompic hallucinations, which occur as a person awakens. Hallucinations related to ordinary sleeping and waking are not considered an indication of a mental or physical disorder.

- Migraine headaches. About 10% of patients diagnosed with migraine headaches experience visual hallucinations prior to the onset of an acute attack.
- Adult-onset schizophrenia. According to the National Institute of Mental Health (NIMH), about 75% of adults diagnosed with schizophrenia experience hallucinations, most commonly auditory or visual. The auditory hallucinations may be command hallucinations, in which the person hears voices ordering him or her to do something.
- Temporal lobe epilepsy (TLE). About 80% of patients diagnosed with TLE report gustatory and olfactory hallucinations as well as auditory and visual hallucinations.
- Narcolepsy. Frequent hypnagogic hallucinations are considered one of four classic symptoms of narcolepsy and are experienced by 60% of patients diagnosed with the disorder.
- Post-traumatic stress disorder (PTSD). Studies of combat veterans diagnosed with PTSD have found that 50%–65% have experienced auditory hallucinations. Visual, olfactory, and haptic hallucinations have been reported by survivors of rape and childhood sexual abuse.

Description

It would be difficult to describe a "typical" hallucination, as these experiences vary considerably in length of time, quality, and sense or senses affected. Some hallucinations last only a few seconds; however, some people diagnosed with Charles Bonnet syndrome (CBS) have reported visual hallucinations lasting over several days, while people who have taken certain drugs have experienced hallucinations involving colors, sounds, and smells lasting for hours. Albert Hoffman, the Swiss chemist who first synthesized lysergic acid diethylamide (LSD), experienced nine hours of hallucinations after taking a small amount of the drug in 1943. In 1896, the American neurologist S. Weir Mitchell published an account of the six hours of hallucinations that followed his experimental swallowing of peyote buttons.

There is not always a close connection between the cause of a person's hallucinations and the emotional response to them. One study of patients diagnosed with CBS found that 30% of the patients were upset by their hallucinations, while 13% found them amusing or pleasant. The environment in which LSD and other **hallucinogens** are taken may affect an individual's psychological constitution and personal reactions. The writer Peter Matthiessen, for example, noted that his 1960s experiences with LSD "were magic shows, mysterious, enthralling," while his wife ". . . freaked out; that is the drug term, and there is no better. . . . [H]er armor had cracked, and all the night winds of the world went howling through." Indeed, like Mathiessen's wife, and in contrast to those for whom hallucinogens prove amusing, most patients with **narcolepsy**, alcoholic hallucinosis, or post-traumatic disorders find their hallucinations frightening.

Causes

Though there are many known causes of hallucinations, the neurological mechanism behind their origin is not yet known. Researchers have identified some factors in the context of specific disorders, and have proposed various hypotheses to explain hallucinations in others, but there does not appear to be a single causal factor that accounts for hallucinations in all people who experience them.

Sleep deprivation

Research subjects who have undergone **sleep deprivation** experiments typically begin to hallucinate after 72–96 hours without sleep. It is thought that these hallucinations result from the malfunctioning of nerve cells within the prefrontal cortex of the **brain**. This area of the brain is associated with judgment, impulse control, attention, and visual association, and is refreshed during the early stages of sleep. When a person is sleep-deprived, the nerve cells in the prefrontal cortex must work harder than usual without an opportunity to recover. The hallucinations that develop on the third day of wakefulness are thought to be hypnagogic hallucinations that occur during "microsleeps," or short periods of light sleep lasting about one to ten seconds.

Post-traumatic memory formation

Hallucinations in **trauma** survivors are caused by abnormal patterns of memory formation during the traumatic experience. In normal situations, memories are formed from sensory data, organized in a part of the brain known as the hippocampus, and integrated with previous memories in the frontal cortex. People then "make sense" of their memories through the use of language, which helps them to describe their experiences to others and to themselves. In traumatic situations, however, bits and pieces of memory are stored in the amygdala, an almond-shaped structure in the brain that ordinarily attaches emotional significance to memories, without being integrated by the hippocampus and interpreted in the frontal cortex. In addition, the region of the brain that governs speech (Broca's area) often shuts down under extreme **stress**. The result is that memories of the traumatic event remain in the amygdala as a chaotic wordless jumble of physical sensations or sensory images that can re-emerge as hallucinations during stressful situations at later points in the patient's life.

Irritative hallucinations

In 1973, a British researcher named Cogan categorized hallucinations into two major groups that he called "irritative" and "release" hallucinations. Irritative hallucinations result from abnormal electrical discharges in the brain, and are associated with such disorders as migraine headaches and epilepsy. Brain tumors and traumatic damage to the brain are other possible causes of abnormal electrical activity manifesting as visual hallucinations.

Hallucinations have also been reported with a number of infectious diseases that affect the brain, including bacterial meningitis, rabies, herpes virus infections, Lyme disease, HIV infection, toxoplasmosis, Jakob-Creuzfeldt disease, and late-stage syphilis.

Release hallucinations

Release hallucinations are most common in people with impaired eyesight or hearing. They are produced by the spontaneous activity of nerve cells in the visual or auditory cortex of the brain in the absence of actual sensory data from the eyes or ears. These experiences differ from the hallucinations of **schizophrenia** in that those patients experiencing release hallucinations are often able to recognize them as unreal. Release hallucinations are also more elaborate and usually longer in duration than irritative hallucinations. The visual hallucinations of patients with CBS are an example of release hallucinations.

Neurotransmitter imbalances

Neurotransmitters are chemicals produced by the body that carry electrical impulses across the gaps (synapses) between adjoining nerve cells. Some neurotransmitters inhibit the transmission of nerve impulses, while others excite or intensify them. Hallucinations in some conditions or disorders result from imbalances among these various chemicals.

NARCOLEPSY. Narcolepsy is a disorder characterized by uncontrollable brief episodes of sleep, frequent hypnagogic or hypnopompic hallucinations, and sleep paralysis. Between 1999 and 2000, researchers discovered that people with narcolepsy have a much lower than normal number of hypocretin neurons, which are nerve cells in the hypothalamus that secrete a neurotransmitter known as hypocretin. Low levels of this chemical are thought to be responsible for the daytime sleepiness and hallucinations of narcolepsy.

PRESCRIPTION MEDICATIONS. Hallucinations have been reported as side effects of such drugs as ketamine (Ketalar), which is sometimes used as an anesthetic but has also been used illegally to commit date rape; **paroxetine** (Paxil), an SSRI antidepressant; **mirtazapine** (Remeron), a serotonin-specific antidepressant; and **zolpidem** (Ambien), a sleep medication. Ketamine prevents brain cells from taking up glutamate, a neurotransmitter that governs perception of pain and of one's relationship to the environment. Paroxetine alters the balance between the neurotransmitters **serotonin** and acetylcholine.

Hallucinations in patients with **Alzheimer's disease** are thought to be a side effect of treatment with neuroleptics (antipsychotic medications), although they may also result from inadequate blood flow in certain regions of the brain. The antiretroviral drugs used to treat HIV infection may also produce hallucinations in some patients.

HALLUCINOGENS AND DRUGS OF ABUSE. Like the hallucinations caused by prescription drugs, hallucinations caused by drugs of abuse result from disruption of the normal balance of neurotransmitters in the brain. Hallucinations in **cocaine** and amphetamine users, for example, are associated with the overproduction of **dopamine**, a neurotransmitter associated with arousal and motor excitability. LSD appears to produce hallucinations by blocking the action of the neurotransmitters serotonin (particularly serotonin-2) and norepinephrine. Phencyclidine (PCP) acts like ketamine in producing hallucinations by blocking the reception of glutamate.

People who have used LSD sometimes experience flashbacks, which are spontaneous recurrences of the hallucinations and other distorted perceptions caused by the drug. Some doctors refer to this condition as hallucinogen persisting perception disorder, or HPPD.

There are two types of alcohol withdrawal syndromes characterized by hallucinations. Alcoholic hallucinosis typically occurs after abrupt withdrawal from alcohol after a long period of excessive drinking. The patient hears threatening or accusing voices rather than "seeing things," and his or her consciousness is otherwise normal. **Delirium** tremens (DTs), on the other hand, is a

KEY TERMS

Amygdala—An almond-shaped brain structure in the limbic system that is activated in stressful situations to trigger the emotion of fear. Hallucinations related to post-traumatic stress are thought to be caused by the activation of memory traces in the amygdala that have not been integrated and modified by other parts of the brain.

Auditory—Pertaining to the sense of hearing.

Charles Bonnet syndrome (CBS)—A disorder characterized by visual hallucinations following a sudden age-related deterioration in a person's vision, most commonly glaucoma or macular degeneration. CBS is named for a Swiss doctor who first described it in his visually impaired grandfather in 1780.

Command hallucination—A type of auditory hallucination in which the person hears voices ordering him or her to perform a specific act.

Corollary discharge—A mechanism in the brain that allows one to distinguish between self-generated and external stimuli or perceptions.

Delusion—A false belief that a person maintains in spite of obvious proof or evidence to the contrary.

Flashback—A vivid sensory or emotional experience that happens independently of the initial event or experience. Flashbacks resulting from the use of LSD are sometimes referred to as hallucinogen persisting perception disorder, or HPPD.

Gustatory—Pertaining to the sense of taste.

Hallucinogen—A drug or other substance that induces hallucinations.

Haptic—Pertaining to the sense of touch; sometimes called tactile hallucinations.

Hippocampus—A part of the brain that is involved in memory formation and learning. The hippocampus is shaped like a curved ridge and belongs to an organ system called the limbic system.

Hypnagogic—Pertaining to drowsiness; refers to hallucinations that occur as a person falls asleep.

Hypnopompic—Persisting after sleep; refers to hallucinations that occur as a person awakens.

Illusion—A false interpretation of a real sensory image or impression.

Irritative hallucinations—Hallucinations caused by abnormal electrical activity in the brain.

Lysergic acid diethylamide (LSD)—The first synthetic hallucinogen, discovered in 1938.

Neuroleptic—Another name for an antipsychotic medication.

Neurotransmitters—Chemicals that carry nerve impulses from one nerve cell to another.

Olfactory—Pertaining to the sense of smell.

Psychosis—A severe mental disorder characterized by loss of contact with reality. Hallucinations are associated with such psychotic disorders as schizophrenia and brief psychotic disorder.

Release hallucinations—Hallucinations that develop after partial loss of sight or hearing, and represent images or sounds formed from memory traces rather than present sensory input. They are called "release" hallucinations because they would ordinarily be blocked by incoming sensory data.

withdrawal syndrome that begins several days after drinking stops. A patient with the DTs is disoriented, confused, depressed, feverish, and sweating heavily as well as hallucinating, and the hallucinations are usually visual.

MOOD DISORDERS. Visual hallucinations occasionally occur in patients diagnosed with **depression**, particularly the elderly. These hallucinations are thought to result from low levels of the neurotransmitter serotonin. The hallucinations that occur in patients with Parkinson's disease appear to result from a combination of medication side effects, depressed mood, and impaired eyesight.

Schizophrenia

The auditory hallucinations associated with schizophrenia may be the end result of a combination of factors. These hallucinations have sometimes been attributed to unusually high levels of the neurotransmitter dopamine in the patient's brain. Other researchers have noted abnormal patterns of brain activity in patients with schizophrenia. In particular, these patients suffer from dysfunction of a mechanism known as corollary discharge, which allows people to distinguish between stimuli outside the self and internal intentions and thoughts. Electroencephalograms (EEGs) of patients with schizophrenia that were taken while the patients were talking showed that corollary discharges from the frontal cortex of the brain (where thoughts are produced) failed to inform the auditory cortex (where sounds are interpreted) that the talking was self-generated. This failure would lead the patients to interpret internal speech as coming from external sources, thus producing auditory hallucinations. In addition, the brains of patients with schizophrenia appear to suffer tissue loss in certain regions. In early 2004, some German researchers reported a direct correlation between the severity of auditory hallucinations in patients with schizophrenia and the amount of brain tissue that had been lost from the primary auditory cortex.

Diagnosis

The differential **diagnosis** of hallucinations can be complicated, but in most cases taking the patient's medical history will help the doctor narrow the list of possible diagnoses. If the patient has been taken to a hospital emergency room, the doctor may ask those who accompanied the patient for information. The doctor may also need to perform a medical evaluation before a psychiatric assessment of the hallucinations can be made. The medical evaluation may include laboratory tests and **imaging studies** as well as a physical examination, depending on the patient's other symptoms. If it is suspected that the patient is suffering from delirium, **dementia**, or a psychotic disorder, the doctor may assess the patient's mental status by using a standard instrument known as the mini-mental status examination (MMSE) or the Folstein (after the clinician who devised it). The MMSE yields a total score based on the patient's appearance, mood, cognitive skills, thought content, judgment, and speech patterns. A score of 20 or lower usually indicates delirium, dementia, schizophrenia, or severe depression.

Hallucinations in elderly patients may require specialized evaluation because of the possibility of overlapping causes. The American Association for Geriatric Psychiatry lists hallucinations as an indication for consulting a geriatric **psychiatrist**. In addition, elderly patients should be routinely screened for visual or hearing impairments.

Treatment

Hallucinations are treated with regard to the underlying disorder. Depending on the disorder, treatment may involve antipsychotic, anticonvulsant, or antidepressant medications; **psychotherapy**; brain or ear surgery; or therapy for drug dependence. Hallucinations related to normal sleeping and waking are not a cause for concern.

Prognosis

The prognosis of hallucinations depends on the underlying cause or disorder.

Resources

BOOKS

American Psychiatric Association. *Diagnostic and Statistical Manual of Mental Disorders*. 4th ed., text rev. Washington, DC: American Psychiatric Publishing, 2000.

Beers, Mark H. "Behavior Disorders in Dementia." In *The Merck Manual of Geriatrics*, edited by Mark H. Beers and Robert Berkow. Whitehouse Station, NJ: Merck Research Laboratories, 2002.

"Drug Use and Dependence." In *The Merck Manual of Diagnosis and Therapy*, edited by Robert S. Porter and Justin L. Kaplan. 19th ed. Whitehouse Station, NJ: Merck Research Laboratories, 2011.

"Fungi—Infecting and Hallucinating." In *Who Goes First? The Story of Self-Experimentation in Medicine*, by Lawrence K. Altman. Berkeley, CA: University of California Press, 1998.

"Psychiatric Emergencies." In *The Merck Manual of Diagnosis and Therapy,* edited by Robert S. Porter and Justin L. Kaplan. Whitehouse Station, NJ: Merck Research Laboratories, 2011.

"Schizophrenia and Related Disorders." In *The Merck Manual of Diagnosis and Therapy,* edited by Robert S. Porter and Justin L. Kaplan. Whitehouse Station, NJ: Merck Research Laboratories, 2011.

PERIODICALS

Braun, Claude M. J., et al. "Brain Modules of Hallucination: An Analysis of Multiple Patients with Brain Lesions." *Journal of Psychiatry and Neuroscience* 28, no. 6 (November 2003): 432–439.

Ford, J. M., and D. H. Mathalon. "Electrophysiological Evidence of Corollary Discharge Dysfunction in Schizophrenia During Talking and Thinking." *Journal of Psychiatric Research* 38, no. 1 (January 2004): 37–46.

Gaser, C., et al. "Neuroanatomy of 'Hearing Voices': A Frontotemporal Brain Structural Abnormality Associated with Auditory Hallucinations in Schizophrenia." *Cerebral Cortex* 14, no. 1 (January 2004): 91–96.

Gleason, Ondria C. "Delirium." *American Family Physician* 67, no. 5 (March 1, 2003): 1027–1034. http://www.aafp.org/afp/2003/0301/p1027.html (accessed November 9, 2011).

Ohayon, M.M. "Prevalence of Hallucinations and Their Pathological Associations in the General Population." *Psychiatry Research* 97, no. 2–3 (December 27, 2000): 153–164.

Pelak, V.S., and G.T. Liu. "Visual Hallucinations." *Current Treatment Options in Neurology* 6, no. 1 (January 2004): 75–83.

Rovner, Barry R. "The Charles Bonnet Syndrome: Visual Hallucinations Caused by Vision Impairment."

Geriatrics 57, no. 8 (June 2002): 45–46. Available online at http://geriatrics.modernmedicine.com/geriatrics/data/articlestandard/geriatrics/232002/21083/article.pdf (accessed November 9, 2011).

Schneider, L. S., and K. S. Dagerman. "Psychosis of Alzheimer's Disease: Clinical Characteristics and History." *Journal of Psychiatric Research* 38, no. 1 (January 2004): 105–111.

Tsai, M.J., Y.B. Huang, and P. C. Wu. "A Novel Clinical Pattern of Visual Hallucination After Zolpidem Use." *Journal of Toxicology: Clinical Toxicology* 41, no. 6 (June 2003): 869–872.

WEBSITES

Cameron, Scott, and Michael Richards. "Hallucinogens." Medscape Reference. Updated June 23, 2011. http://emedicine.medscape.com/article/293752-overview (accessed October 8, 2011).

Chuang, Linda, and Nancy Forman. "Mental Disorders Secondary to General Medical Conditions." Medscape Reference. http://emedicine.medscape.com/article/294131-overview (accessed October 8, 2011).

U.S. National Institute on Drug Abuse. "Research Report: Hallucinogens and Dissociative Drugs." NIH Publication No. 01-4209. http://www.nida.nih.gov/PDF/RRHalluc.pdf (accessed October 8, 2011).

U.S. National Institute of Mental Health. "Schizophrenia." NIH Publication No. 09-3517. September 22, 2011. http://www.nimh.nih.gov/publicat/schizoph.cfm (accessed October 8, 2011).

ORGANIZATIONS

American Academy of Neurology, 1080 Montreal Ave., St. Paul, MN, 55116, (651) 695-2717, (800) 879-1960, Fax: (651) 879-2791, memberservices@aan.com, http://www.aan.com.

American Association for Geriatric Psychiatry, 7910 Woodmont Ave., Ste. 1050, Bethesda, MD, 20814-3004, (301) 654-7850, Fax: (301) 654-4137, http://www.AAGPonline.org.

American Psychiatric Association, 1000 Wilson Blvd., Ste. 1825, Arlington, VA, 22209-3901, (703) 907-7300, apa@psych.org, http://www.psych.org.

National Institute of Mental Health, 6001 Executive Blvd., Room 8184, MSC 9663, Bethesda, MD, 20892-9663, (301) 433-4513; TTY: (301) 443-8431 Fax: (301) 443-4279, (866) 615-6464; TTY: (866) 415-8051, nimhinfo@nih.gov, http://www.nimh.nih.gov.

National Schizophrenia Foundation, 403 Seymour Ave., Ste. 202, Lansing, MI, 48933, (517) 485-7168, Fax: (517) 485-7180, (800) 482-9534, inquiries@nsfoundation.org, http://www.schizophrenia.com.

National Sleep Foundation, 1010 N Glebe Rd., Ste. 310, Arlington, VA, 22201, (703) 243-1697, nsf@sleepfoundation.org, http://www.sleepfoundation.org.

Rebecca Frey, PhD

Hallucinogens and related disorders

Definition

Hallucinogens are a chemically diverse group of drugs that cause changes in a person's thought processes, perceptions of the physical world, and sense of time passing. They can be found naturally in some plants and can be synthesized in the laboratory. Most hallucinogens are abused as recreational drugs. Hallucinogens are also called psychedelic drugs.

Demographics

Hallucinogen use, excluding MDMA, peaked in the United States in the late 1960s as part of the counterculture movement. It then gradually declined until the early 1990s, when it increased. The 2010 U.S. National Survey on Drug Use and Health reported 1.2 million persons had used hallucinogens in the past month, with 695,000 persons taking MDMA, or ecstasy.

Description

Use of hallucinogens is at least as old as civilization. Many cultures have recorded eating certain plants specifically to induce visions or alter the perception of reality. These hallucinations were often part of a religious

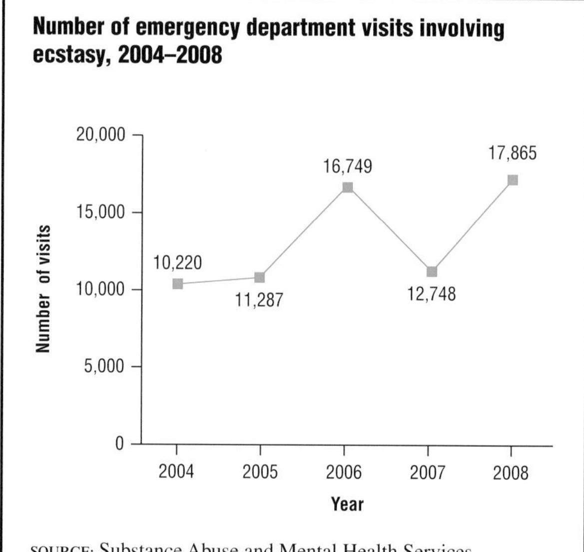

Available online at http://oas.samhsa.gov/2k11/DAWN027/Ecstasy.htm. *(Graph by PreMediaGlobal. © 2012 Cengage Learning.)*

or prophetic experience. Shamans in Siberia were known to eat the hallucinogenic mushroom *Amanita muscaria.* The ancient Greeks and the Vikings also used naturally occurring plant hallucinogens. Peyote, a spineless cactus native to the southwestern United States and Mexico, was used by native peoples, including the Aztecs, to produce visions.

Although several hundred plants are known to contain compounds that cause hallucinations, most hallucinogens are synthesized in illegal laboratories for delivery as street drugs. The best known hallucinogens are lysergic acid diethylamide (LSD), mescaline, psilocybin, and MDMA (**ecstasy**). Phencyclidine (PCP, angel dust) can produce hallucinations, as can **amphetamines** and marijuana, but these drugs are considered dissociative drugs, rather than hallucinogens, and act by a different pathway from classic hallucinogens. Dextromorphan, the main ingredient in many cough medicines, has become popular among some populations because of the PCP-like hallucinations it produces. In addition, new designer drugs that are chemical variants of classic hallucinogens are apt to appear on the street at any time. One drug that only recently was added to Schedule I of the 1970 Controlled Substances Act (the classification for many other "hard" drugs with no known therapeutic value) is 5-methoxy-N, N-diisopropyltryptamine (5-MeO-DIPT), a drug derived from the chemical tryptamine that is more commonly known as "Foxy" or "Foxy Methoxy." A related hallucinogen, dimethyltryptamine, occurs naturally in plants in the Amazon but is now synthesized in labs. This drug, more commonly known as DMT, can be a powerful hallucinogen.

Although the various hallucinogens produce similar physical and psychological effects, they are a diverse group of compounds. However, all hallucinogens appear to affect the **brain** in similar ways. While the mechanism of action of hallucinogens is not completely understood, researchers have shown that these drugs bind with one type of **serotonin** receptor (5-HT_2) in the brain.

Serotonin is a neurotransmitter that facilitates transmission of nerve impulses in the brain and is associated with feelings of well-being, as well as many physiological responses. When a hallucinogenic compound binds with serotonin receptors, serotonin is blocked from those receptor sites, and nerve transmission is altered. There is an increase in free (unbound) serotonin in the brain. The result is a distortion of the senses of sight, sound, and touch, disorientation in time and space, and alterations of mood. In the case of hallucinogen intoxication, however, a person is not normally delirious, unconscious, or dissociated. He or she is aware that these changes in perception are caused by the hallucinogen.

LSD

LSD was first synthesized by Albert Hoffman for a pharmaceutical company in Germany in 1938 while he was searching for a headache remedy. Hoffman discovered the hallucinogenic properties of LSD accidentally in 1943. The drug became popular with the counterculture youth of the mid-1960s when its sense-altering properties were reputed to offer a window into enhanced creativity and self-awareness. LSD also occurs naturally in morning glory seeds.

Pure LSD is a white, odorless, crystalline powder that dissolves easily in water, although contaminants can cause it to range in color from yellow to dark brown. LSD was listed as a Schedule I drug under the Controlled Substance Act of 1970, meaning that it has no medical or legal uses and has a high potential for abuse. LSD is not easy to manufacture in a home laboratory, and some of its ingredients are controlled substances that are difficult to obtain. However, LSD is very potent, and a small amount can produce a large number of doses.

On the street, LSD is sold in several forms. Microdots are tiny pills smaller than a pinhead. Windowpane is liquid LSD applied to thin squares of gelatin. Liquid LSD can also be sprayed on sugar cubes. The most common street form of the drug is liquid LSD sprayed onto blotter paper and dried. The paper, often printed with colorful or psychedelic pictures, is divided into tiny squares, each square being one dose. Liquid LSD can also be sprayed on the back of a postage stamp and licked off. Street names for the drug include "acid," "yellow sunshine," "windowpane," "cid," "doses," "trips," and "boomers."

Mescaline

Mescaline is a naturally occurring plant hallucinogen. Its primary source is the cactus *Lophophora williamsii.* This cactus is native to the southwestern United States and Mexico. The light blue-green plant is spineless and has a crown called a "peyote button." This button contains mescaline and can be eaten or made into a bitter tea. Mescaline is also the active ingredient of at least ten other cacti of the genus *Trichocereus* that are native to parts of South America.

Mescaline was first isolated in 1897 by the German chemist Arthur Heffter and first synthesized in the laboratory in 1919. Some experiments were done with the drug to determine whether it was medically useful, but no medical uses were found. However, peyote is culturally significant. It has been used for centuries as part of religious celebrations and vision quests of Native Americans. The Native American Church, which fuses elements of Christianity with indigenous practices, has long used peyote as part of its religious practices.

In 1970, mescaline was listed as a Schedule I drug under the Controlled Substances Act. However, that same year, the state of Texas legalized peyote for use in Native American religious ceremonies. In 1995, a federal law was passed making peyote legal (but only for this use) in all 50 states.

Psilocybin

Psilocybin is the active ingredient in what are known on the street as "magic mushrooms," "shrooms," "mushies," or "Mexican mushrooms." There are several species of mushrooms that contain psilocybin, including *Psilocybe mexicana, P. muscorumi,* and *Stropharia cubensis*. These mushrooms grow in most moderate, moist climates.

Psilocybin-containing mushrooms are usually cooked and eaten (they have a bitter taste) or dried and boiled to make a tea. Although psilocybin can be made synthetically in the laboratory, there is no street market for synthetic psilocybin, and virtually all the drug comes from cultivated mushrooms. In the United States, it is legal to possess psilocybin-containing mushrooms, but it is illegal to traffic in them, and psilocybin and psilocyn (another psychoactive drug found in small quantities in these mushrooms) are both Schedule I drugs.

MDMA

MDMA, short for 3,4-methylenedioxymethamphetamine, and better known as "ecstasy," "XTC," "E," "X," or "Adam," has become an increasingly popular club drug since the 1980s. The hallucinogenically active portion of the drug is chemically similar to mescaline, while its stimulant portion is similar to **methamphetamine**. MDMA was first synthesized in 1912 by a German pharmaceutical company looking for a new compound that would stop bleeding. The company patented the drug but never did anything with it. A closely related drug, methylenedioxyamphetimine, or MDA, was tested by a pharmaceutical company as an appetite suppressant in the 1950s, but its use was discontinued when it was discovered to have hallucinogenic properties. In the 1960s, MDA was a popular drug of abuse in some large cities such as San Francisco.

During the early 1980s, therapists experimented with MDMA, which was legal at the time, as a way to help patients open up and become more empathetic. Recreational use soon followed, and it was declared an illegal Schedule I drug in 1985. For about a year between 1987 and 1988, the drug was again legal as the result of court challenges, but it permanently joined other Schedule I hallucinogens in March 1988.

MDMA is a popular club drug often associated with all-night raves or dance parties. The drug, sold in tablets, is attractive because it combines stimulant effects that allow ravers to dance for hours with a feeling of empathy, reduced anxiety, reduced inhibitions, and euphoria. Some authorities consider MDA and MDMA to be stimulant-hallucinogens and do not group them with classic hallucinogens such as LSD, but research indicates that MDA and MDMA affect the brain in the same way as classic hallucinogens. The **American Psychiatric Association** considers MDMA to be a drug that can cause hallucinogen-related disorders.

PMMA

PMMA (para-Methoxymethamphetamine) is a hallucinogen with effects similar to MDMA, causing rapid heartbeat, high blood pressure, **seizures**, kidney failure, hyperthermia, hallucinations, and death. The compound in PMMA is often found in MDMA, making the substance even more potent and potentially fatal.

Salvia

Salvia (*Salvia divinorum*) is known by many other names, including "Sally D," "Magic Mint," "Shepherdess Herb," "Ska Maria Pastora," "Diviners Sage," and "Sage of the Seers." Originating in Mexico, the drug is a perennial herb in the mint family. It grows in clusters up to three feet high with green leaves and white and purple flowers. Salvia is a potent psychoactive drug containing a chemical called salvinorin A, causing hallucinations noted to be up to five times more potent than the drug LSD. It is thought to act on opioid receptors of the brain, causing both physical and visual impairment and hallucinogenic effects. It is sold in the form of leaves, seeds, and extract and can be chewed or smoked when used. Salvia is not regulated by the federal government, but many states are creating legislation to ban the cultivation and sale of this plant.

Some hallucinogens (such as Salvia), act on opioid receptors of the brain, which like many narcotics, affect perceived levels of physical pain. As such, their use in the future may be implicated as therapeutic agents in pain control. Research and attention to legislation regarding intent for this use are ongoing.

Jimson weed

Jimson weed (*Datura stramonium*) is an herb producing fragrant flowers with a trumpet–like appearance. It grows as a bush in warm climates, and the seeds and leaves of the plant are poisonous and potentially fatal. Also known as "Devils Trumpet," "Devils Weed," "Moonflower," "Thorn Apple," and "Locoweed," jimson weed induces hallucinations, and users are often unaware of its toxicity. Effects include **delirium**, hallucinations, **amnesia**, and violent behavior; symptoms of overdose include seizure, coma, and respiratory arrest. Ingestion of the plant requires emergency treatment and **hospitalization**, as symptoms may last for up to three days.

Causes and symptoms

Hallucinogens are attractive to recreational drug users for a number of reasons:

- They are minimally addictive and there are no physical withdrawal symptoms upon stopping use.
- They produce few serious or debilitating physical side effects.
- They do not usually produce a delusional state, excessive stupor, or excessive stimulation.
- They are easily and cheaply available.
- They produce a high that gives the illusion of increasing creativity, empathy, or self-awareness.
- Deaths from overdoses are rare.

Despite their perceived harmlessness, strong hallucinogens such as LSD can cause frightening and anxiety-evoking emotional experiences, known as "bad trips." Flashbacks, where the sensations experienced while under the influence of a drug recur uncontrollably without drug use, can occur for months after a single drug use. During hallucinogen intoxication, reality may be so altered that a person may endanger himself by believing he is capable of feats such as flying off buildings. Hallucinogens also may induce or cause a worsening of latent psychiatric disorders such as anxiety, **depression**, and **psychosis**. Hallucinogens can also cause **paranoia**, long-term memory loss, personality changes (especially if there is a latent psychiatric disorder), and psychological drug dependence.

Psychological symptoms

Hallucinogens work primarily on the perception of reality. They usually do not create true hallucinations, which are imagined visions or sounds (voices heard in the head, for example) in the absence of any corresponding reality. Instead, classic hallucinogens alter the perception of something that is physically present. A face may appear to "melt" or colors may become brighter, move, and change shape. Sounds may be "seen," rather than heard.

More than with other drugs, the mental state of the hallucinogen user and the environment in which the drug is taken influence the user's experience. LSD, especially, is known for symptoms that range from mellowness and psychedelic visions ("good trips") to anxiety and panic attacks ("bad trips"). Previous good experiences with a drug do not guarantee continued good experiences. People with a history of psychiatric disorders are more likely to experience harmful reactions, as are those who are given the drug without their knowledge.

Normally, mescaline and psilocybin produce uniformly milder symptoms than LSD. During a single drug experience, the user can experience a range of symptoms. Mood can shift from happy to sad or pleasant to frightening and back again several times. Some symptoms occur primarily with MDMA, as indicated. Psychological symptoms of hallucinogen intoxication include:

- distortion of sight, sound, and touch
- confusion of the senses—sounds are "seen" or vision is "heard"
- disorientation in time and space
- delusions of physical invulnerability (especially with LSD)
- paranoia
- unreliable judgment and increased risk taking
- anxiety attacks
- flashbacks after the drug has been cleared from the body
- blissful calm or mellowness
- reduced inhibitions
- increased empathy (MDMA)
- elation or euphoria
- impaired concentration and motivation
- long-term memory loss
- personality changes, especially if there is a latent psychiatric disorder
- psychological drug dependence

Physical symptoms

Although the primary effects of hallucinogens are on perceptions, some physical effects do occur. Physical symptoms include:

- increased blood pressure
- increased heart rate
- nausea and vomiting (especially with psilocybin and mescaline)
- blurred vision, which can last after the drug has worn off
- poor coordination
- enlarged pupils
- sweating
- diarrhea (plant hallucinogens)
- restlessness
- muscle cramping (especially clenched jaws with MDMA)
- dehydration (MDMA)

KEY TERMS

Anxiety—Can be experienced as a troubled feeling, a sense of dread, fear of the future, or distress over a possible threat to a person's physical or mental well-being.

Depression—A mental state characterized by feelings of sadness, despair, and discouragement.

Ecstasy—Best known of the so-called designer amphetamines, also known as MDMA. It produces both stimulant and hallucinogenic effects.

Hallucinations—To hear, see, or otherwise sense things that are not real.Hallucinations can result from nervous system abnormalities, mental disorders, or the use of certain drugs.

Methamphetamine—The most common illegally produced amphetamine.

Panic attack—A period of intense fear or discomfort with a feeling of doom and a desire to escape. The person may shake, sweat, be short of breath, and experience chest pain.

Serotonin—A widely distributed neurotransmitter that is found in blood platelets, the lining of the digestive tract, and the brain, and that works in combination with norepinephrine. It causes very powerful contractions of smooth muscle, and is associated with mood, attention, emotions, and sleep. Low levels of serotonin are associated with depression. Large amounts of serotonin are released after ingestion of MDMA.

- serious increase in body temperature, leading to seizures (MDMA)

Diagnosis

Although not all experts agree, the **diagnosis** of mental disorders recognizes two hallucinogen-related disorders: hallucinogen dependence and hallucinogen abuse. Hallucinogen dependence is the continued use of hallucinogens even when the substances cause the affected individual significant problems, or when the individual knows of adverse effects (memory impairment while intoxicated, anxiety attacks, flashbacks) but continues to use the substances anyway. "Craving" hallucinogens after not using them for a period of time has been reported. Hallucinogen abuse is repeated use of hallucinogens even after they have caused the user impairment that undermines his or her ability to fulfill obligations at work, school, or home, but the use is usually not as frequent as it is among dependent users. In addition to these two disorders, the American Psychiatric Association recognizes eight hallucinogen-induced disorders. These are:

- hallucinogen intoxication
- hallucinogen persistent perception disorder (flashbacks)
- hallucinogen intoxication delirium
- hallucinogen-induced psychotic disorder with delusions
- hallucinogen-induced psychotic disorder with hallucinations
- hallucinogen-induced mood disorder
- hallucinogen-induced anxiety disorder
- hallucinogen-related disorder not otherwise specified

Hallucinogen dependence and abuse are normally diagnosed from reports by the patient (or person accompanying the patient) of use of a hallucinogenic drug. Active hallucinations and accompanying physical symptoms can confirm the diagnosis but need not be present. Routine drug screening does not detect LSD in the blood or urine, although specialized laboratory methods can detect the drug. Hallucinogen dependence differs from other drug dependence in that there are no withdrawal symptoms when the drug is stopped, and the extent of tolerance (needing a higher and higher dose to achieve the same effect) appears minimal.

The fifth edition of the ***Diagnostic and Statistical Manual of Mental Disorders***, also known as the *DSM-5*, is due for publication in May 2013. This edition may include proposed changes and revisions to some current diagnostic criteria for psychiatric diagnoses, including combining "Hallucinogen Abuse" and "Hallucinogen Dependence" into the single diagnosis of "Hallucinogen Use Disorder."

Hallucinogen intoxication is diagnosed based on psychological changes, perceptual changes, and physical symptoms that are typical of hallucinogen use. These changes must not be caused by a general medical condition, other **substance abuse**, or another mental disorder.

Hallucinogen persisting perception disorder, better known as "flashbacks," occur after hallucinogen use followed by a period of lucidity. Flashbacks may occur weeks or months after the drug was used and may occur after a single use or many uses.

To be diagnosed as a psychiatric disorder, flashbacks must cause significant distress or interfere with daily life activities. They can come on suddenly with no warning or be triggered by specific environments. Flashbacks may include emotional symptoms, seeing colors, geometric forms, or, most commonly, persistence of trails of light across the visual field. They may last for months. Flashbacks are most strongly associated with LSD.

Hallucinogen intoxication delirium is rare unless the hallucinogen is contaminated by another drug or chemical such as strychnine. In hallucinogen intoxication, the patient is still grounded in reality and recognizes that the experiences of altered perception are due to using a hallucinogen. In hallucinogen intoxication delirium, the patient is no longer grounded in reality. Hallucinogen-induced psychotic disorders are similar in that the patient loses touch with reality. Psychotic states can occur immediately after using the drug, or days or months later.

Hallucinogen-induced mood disorder and hallucinogen-induced anxiety disorder are somewhat controversial, as hallucinogen use may uncover latent or pre-existing anxiety or mood disorders rather than being the cause of them. However, it does appear that MDMA use can cause major depression.

Treatment

Acute treatment is aimed at preventing the patient from harming himself or anyone else. Since most people experiencing hallucinogen intoxication remain in touch with reality, "talking down" or offering reassurance and support that emphasizes that the disturbing sensations, anxiety, **panic attack**, or paranoia will pass as the drug wears off is often helpful. Patients are kept in a calm, pleasant, but lighted environment and are encouraged to move around while being helped to remain oriented to reality. Occasionally, drugs such as **lorazepam** are given for anxiety. Complications in treatment occur when the hallucinogen has been contaminated with other street drugs or chemicals. The greatest life-threatening risk is associated with MDMA, in which users may develop dangerously high body temperatures. Reducing the patient's temperature is an essential acute treatment.

Treatment for long-term effects of hallucinogen use involves long-term **psychotherapy** after drug use has stopped. Many people find 12-step programs or group support helpful. In addition, underlying psychiatric disorders must be addressed.

Prognosis

Because hallucinogens are not physically addictive, many people are able to stop using these drugs successfully. However, users may be haunted by chronic problems such as flashbacks or mood and **anxiety disorders** either brought about or worsened by use of hallucinogens. It is difficult to predict who will have long-term complications and who will not.

QUESTIONS TO ASK YOUR DOCTOR

- What risks are associated with hallucinogen use?
- What symptoms are associated with hallucinogen dependence?
- Does having hallucinogen dependence and abuse put me at risk for other health conditions?
- Can you recommend any treatment and support groups for me?

Prevention

Hallucinogen use is difficult to prevent, because these drugs have a false reputation for being nonaddictive and harmless. Drug education and social outlets that provide people with a sense of self-worth are the best ways to prevent hallucinogen and other substance abuse.

Resources

BOOKS

American Psychiatric Association. *Diagnostic and Statistical Manual of Mental Disorders,* 4th ed., Text rev. Washington, DC: American Psychiatric Association, 2000.

American Psychological Association. *Publication Manual of the American Psychological Association,* 6th ed. Washington, DC: American Psychological Association, 2009.

Erickson, Carlton K, Ph.D. *Addiction Essentials: The Go-To Guide for Clinicians and Patients.* New York, NY: W. W. Norton & Company, 2011.

Galanter, Marc, and Herbert D. Kleber, eds. *Textbook of Substance Abuse Treatment,* 2nd ed. Washington, DC: American Psychiatric Press, Inc., 2008.

Holland, Julie, ed. *Ecstasy: The Complete Guide.*Kindle edition. Rochester, Vermont: Park Street Press, 2010.

North, Carol, and Sean Yutzy. *Goodwin and Guze's Psychiatric Diagnosis.* New York, NY: Oxford University Press, 2010.

Sadock, Benjamin J., Virginia Alcott Sadock, and Pedro Ruiz, eds. *Kaplan and Sadock's Comprehensive Textbook of Psychiatry,* 2nd ed. New York, NY: Lippincott Williams & Wilkins, 2009.

WEBSITES

National Institute on Drug Abuse. "NIDA InfoFacts: Hallucinogens—LSD, Peyote, Psilocybin, and PCP." http://drugabuse.gov/infofacts/hallucinogens.html (accessed November 14, 2011).

U.S. Drug Enforcement Administration. "Hallucinogens." http://www.justice.gov/dea/concern/hallucinogens.html (accessed November 14, 2011).

ORGANIZATIONS

American Psychological Association, 750 First Street NE, Washington, DC, 20003, (202) 336-5500, http://www.apa.org/index.aspx.

National Institute on Drug Abuse, 6001 Executive Blvd., Rm. 5213, Bethesda, MD, 20892, (301) 442-1124; Spanish: (240) 221-4007, information@nida.nih.gov, http://www.nida.nih.gov.

The Partnership at Drugfree.org, 352 Park Ave. South, 9th Fl., New York, NY, 10010, (212) 922-1560, http://www.drugfree.org.

Substance Abuse and Mental Health Services Administration, 1 Choke Cherry Rd., Rockville, MD, 20857, (877) SAMHSA-7 (726-4727), (800) TTY: 487-4889, Fax: (240) 221-4292, SAMHSAInfo@samhsa.hhs.gov, http://www.samhsa.gov.

Tish Davidson, A.M.
Emily Jane Willingham, Ph.D.
Laura Jean Cataldo, RN, Ed.D.

Haloperidol

Definition

Haloperidol is a major tranquilizer. It is used to treat psychoses, symptoms of **dementia**, **Tourette syndrome**, and certain serious behavioral disorders in children. In the United States it is sold under the brand name Haldol.

Purpose

Haloperidol is used in the management of symptoms in people requiring long-term antipsychotic therapy. It is also used for controlling tics and inappropriate vocalizations associated with Tourette syndrome in children and adults.

In children, haloperidol is occasionally used to treat severe behavior problems such as combativeness and extreme outbursts that occur without immediate provocation. Occasionally it is used for short-term treatment of children who display excessive motor activity with accompanying difficulty in attention, aggression, impulse control, mood changes, and coping with frustration.

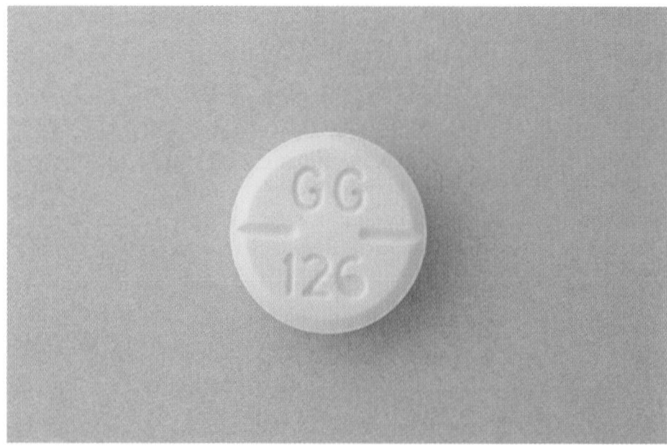

Haloperidol, 10 mg. *(© Custom Medical Stock Photo, Inc. Reproduced by permission.)*

Haloperidol is used only after **psychotherapy** and other medications have been tried and are found to be unsuccessful.

Description

Haloperidol is a major tranquilizer. It is used to control symptoms of psychotic disorders. It can be administered as a pill or by intramuscular injection (a shot).

The precise way in which haloperidol helps control symptoms associated with psychoses or dementia had as of 2011 not been clearly established.

A 2011 study published in *The Lancet* found that haloperidol and two other antipsychotic drugs, **risperidone** and **olanzapine**, better treated the mania associated with **bipolar disorder** than traditional mood stabilizers. The study included 16,000 participants over a 30-year period. Haloperidol treated manic episodes more successfully than ten other drugs, but it was not effective in managing **depression**, a key component of bipolar disorder.

Recommended dosage

For adults, the recommended initial dosage of haloperidol is 0.5–5.0 mg taken two or three times each day. The initial dosage depends on the severity of the symptoms in the person being treated. All people taking haloperidol must be carefully monitored to establish an individualized dosage. Physicians have found a great variability in the amount of haloperidol required to control symptoms.

Children require smaller dosages of haloperidol than do adults. The recommended initial dosage of haloperidol for controlling psychotic symptoms in children is

0.5–2.0 mg taken two or three times each day. The recommended dosage for controlling symptoms of Tourette syndrome and other nonpsychotic disorders is between 0.075 mg and 0.05 mg daily per 2.2 pounds (1 kilogram) of body weight. The total dosage is usually divided into two or three administrations per day. The goal of therapy is to use the smallest amount of haloperidol that will control symptoms. Children under age three should not be given this drug.

Precautions

Haloperidol may cause hypotension (low blood pressure). For this reason people with heart and blood pressure problems should be carefully monitored while taking the drug. Haloperidol carries a risk of causing fatal heart arrhythmias and increases the possibility of having **seizures**. People with a history of seizures or who are taking anticonvulsants (medication to control seizures) should take lower dosages of haloperidol and be closely monitored by a physician until a safe dosage is established. Haloperidol also interferes with the action of the anticoagulant (blood thinning) drug phenindione.

Women who are pregnant, wanting to become pregnant, or are breastfeeding should consult with their doctor before taking haloperidol. Haloperidol may cause extrapyramidal symptoms (EPS) and signs of withdrawal in newborns, especially if the drug was taken during the last trimester of the mother's pregnancy. The primary symptoms of EPS are involuntary movements, such as tremor, contractions, and other motions. Signs of withdrawal include increased agitation, respiratory problems, and trouble feeding. Haloperidol also travels through the breast milk of lactating mothers.

Haloperidol may increase the action of central nervous system depressants such as anesthetics, alcohol, and opiates (some pain killers and sleeping pills). It may also decrease the time required to change from mania to depression among people with bipolar (manic-depressive) disorder.

Like other antipsychotic medications, haloperidol carries a warning regarding use in elderly people with dementia, who suffer from an increased risk of death during treatment with these agents. The drug is not approved by the U.S. Food and Drug Administration (FDA) for use in treating behavior problems related to senile dementia.

Side effects

Haloperidol has the potential to produce a serious side effect called **tardive dyskinesia**. This syndrome consists of involuntary, uncoordinated movements that may not disappear or may only partially improve after the drug is stopped. Tardive dyskinesia involves involuntary movements of the tongue, jaw, mouth, face, or other groups of skeletal muscles. These side effects may appear after people have stopped taking haloperidol. The chance of developing tardive dyskinesia increases with increasing age and dosage of haloperidol. Women are at greater risk than men for developing tardive dyskinesia. There is no known effective treatment for tardive dyskinesia, although gradual (but rarely complete) improvement may occur over a long period.

Haloperidol use may lead to the development of symptoms that resemble Parkinson's disease, but that are not caused by Parkinson's. These symptoms may include a taut or mask-like expression on the face, drooling, tremors, pill-rolling motions in the hands, cogwheel rigidity (abnormal rigidity in muscles characterized by jerky movements when the muscle is passively stretched), and a shuffling gait. Taking the anti-Parkinson's drugs **benztropine** mesylate or **trihexyphenidyl** hydrochloride along with haloperidol helps to control these symptoms. Medication to control parkinsonian symptoms may have to be continued after haloperidol is stopped because the drugs are eliminated at different rates from the body.

Other side effects of haloperidol include:

- anxiety
- restlessness
- agitation
- insomnia
- headache
- euphoria
- drowsiness
- depression
- confusion
- dizziness
- seizures

Unwanted or unexpected effects associated with the use of haloperidol have been reported for virtually all organ systems in the body. Although numerous, such side effects are relatively uncommon.

Interactions

The simultaneous use of haloperidol and lithium, a common treatment for bipolar (manic-depressive) disorder, has been associated with encephalopathic syndrome. People with this syndrome have symptoms

KEY TERMS

Bipolar disorder—A mood disorder marked by alternating episodes of extremely low mood (depression) and exuberant highs (mania), also known as manic-depressive disorder.

Extrapyramidal symptoms (EPS)—A group of side effects associated with antipsychotic medications. EPS includes Parkinson-like symptoms, akathisia (restless leg syndrome), dystonia, and tardive dyskinesia.

of weakness, lethargy, fever, confusion, and high levels of white blood cells.

Haloperidol may increase the effect of central nervous system depressants such as anesthetics, opiates, and alcohol.

Resources

BOOKS

Foreman, John C., and Torben Johansen. *Textbook of Receptor Pharmacology*. 2nd ed. Boca Raton, FL: CRC Press, 2002.

Page, Clive P., and Michael Murphy. *Integrated Pharmacology*. St. Louis: Mosby-Year Book, 2002.

Von Boxtel, Chris J., et al. *Handbook of Clinical Psychopharmacology for Therapists*. 4th ed. Oakland, CA: New Harbinger Publications, 2004.

PERIODICALS

Akhondzadeh, Shahin, et al. "Allopurinol as an Adjunct to Lithium and Haloperidol for Treatment of Patients with Acute Mania: A Double-Blind, Randomized, Placebo-Controlled Trial." *Bipolar Disorders* 8, no. 5, part 1 (October 2006): 485–89.

Aziz, Mohamed, et al. "Remission of Positive and Negative Symptoms in Refractory Schizophrenia with a Combination of Haloperidol and Quetiapine: Two Case Studies." *Journal of Psychiatric Practice* 12, no. 5 (September 2006): 332–36.

Cipriani, Andrea. "Comparative Efficacy and Acceptability of Antimanic Drugs in Acute Mania: A Multiple-treatments Meta-analysis." *The Lancet* (August 17, 2011). Available online at http://www.bioportfolio.com/news/article/772923/articles-Comparative-Efficacy-And-Acceptability-Of-Antimanic-Drugs-In-Acute-Mania.html (accessed August 25, 2011).

Dunn, Michael J., and Simon Killcross. "Clozapine but Not Haloperidol Treatment Reverses Sub-Chronic Phencyclidine-Induced Disruption of Conditional Discrimination Performance." *Behavioural Brain Research* 175, no. 2 (December 2006): 271–77.

Emsley, Robin, Jonathan Rabinowitz, and Rossella Medori. "Remission in Early Psychosis: Rates, Predictors, and Clinical and Functional Outcome Correlates." *Schizophrenia Research* 89, no. 1–3 (January 2007): 129–39.

Green, A.I., et al. "Olanzapine and Haloperidol in First Episode Psychosis: Two-Year Data." *Schizophrenia Research* 86, no. 1–3 (September 2006): 234–43.

Morrens, Manuel, et al. "Psychomotor and Memory Effects of Haloperidol, Olanzapine, and Paroxetine in Healthy Subjects after Short-Term Administration." *Journal of Clinical Psychopharmacology* 27, no. 1 (February 2007): 15–21.

Nasrallah, Henry A., Martin Brecher, and Björn Paulsson. "Placebo-Level Incidence of Extrapyramidal Symptoms (EPS) with Quetiapine in Controlled Studies of Patients with Bipolar Mania." *Bipolar Disorders* 8, no. 5, part 1 (October 2006): 467–74.

Woodward, Neil D., et al. "A Meta-analysis of Cognitive Change with Haloperidol in Clinical Trials of Atypical Antipsychotics: Dose Effects and Comparison to Practice Effects." *Schizophrenia Research* 89, no. 1–3 (January 2007): 211–24.

Zhang, Xiang Yang, et al. "The Effects of Ginkgo Biloba Extract Added to Haloperidol on Peripheral T Cell Subsets in Drug-Free Schizophrenia: A Double-Blind, Placebo-Controlled Trial." *Psychopharmacology* 188, no. 1 (September 2006): 12–17.

ORGANIZATIONS

American Academy of Clinical Toxicology, 6728 Old McLean Village Dr., McLean, VA, 22101, (703) 556-9222, Fax: (703) 556-8729, admin@clintox.org, http://www.clintox.org.

American Academy of Family Physicians, 11400 Tomahawk Creek Pkwy., Leawood, KS, 66211-2672, (913) 906-6000, (800) 274-2237, Fax: (913) 906-6075, contactcenter@aafp.org, http://www.aafp.org.

American Medical Association, 515 N State St., Chicago, IL, 60610, (312) 464-5000, (800) 621-8335, http://www.amaassn.org.

American Psychiatric Association, 1000 Wilson Blvd., Ste. 1825, Arlington, VA, 22209-3901, (703) 907-7300, apa@psych.org, http://www.psych.org.

American Society for Clinical Pharmacology and Therapeutics, 528 N Washington St., Alexandria, VA, 22314, (703) 836-6981, info@ascpt.org, http://www.ascpt.org.

American Society for Pharmacology and Experimental Therapeutics, 9650 Rockville Pike, Bethesda, MD, 20814-3995, (301) 634-7060, http://www.aspet.org.

L. Fleming Fallon, Jr., MD, DrPH
Ruth A. Wienclaw, PhD

Halstead-Reitan Battery

Definition

The Halstead-Reitan Neuropsychological Test Battery (HRNB) is a fixed set of tests used to evaluate **brain** and nervous system functioning in individuals aged 15 years and older. Children's versions are the Halstead Neuropsychological Test Battery for Older Children (ages nine to 14 years) and the Reitan Indiana Neuropsychological Test Battery (ages five to eight years). The set of tests includes those used to measure abstract thoughts, imperception, language, memory, motor dexterity, and sensory-motor integration. The time to complete the HRNB is reported to vary widely among individuals.

Purpose

Neuropsychological functioning refers to the ability of the nervous system and brain to process and interpret information received through the senses. The Halstead-Reitan evaluates a wide range of nervous system and brain functions, including visual, auditory, and tactual input; verbal communication; spatial and sequential perception; the ability to analyze information, form mental concepts, and make judgments; motor output; and attention, concentration, and memory.

The Halstead-Reitan is typically used to evaluate individuals with suspected brain damage, including the extent, location, and nature of the damage. The battery provides useful information regarding the cause of damage (for example, closed head injury, alcohol abuse, **Alzheimer's disease**, **stroke**), which part of the brain is damaged, whether the damage occurred during childhood development, and whether the damage is getting worse, staying the same, or getting better. Information regarding the severity of impairment and areas of personal strengths can be used to develop plans for rehabilitation or care.

Description

Dr. Ward Halstead and Dr. Ralph M. Reitan were the developers of the Halstead-Reitan Battery. Based on studies of patients with neurologic impairments at the University of Chicago, Halstead recognized the need for an evaluation of brain functioning that was more extensive than intelligence testing. He began experimenting with psychological tests that might help identify types and severity of brain damage through observation of a person's behavior in various tasks involving neuropsychological abilities. Initially he chose a set of ten tests; all but three are in the current Halstead-Reitan Battery.

Ralph Reitan, one of Halstead's students, contributed to the battery by researching the tests' ability to identify neurological problems. In a remarkable study, Reitan diagnosed 8,000 patients using only their test results—without meeting the patients or knowing anything about their background. This provided strong support for the battery's effectiveness. Reitan, who is now associated with the Reitan Neuropsychological Laboratory in Tucson, Arizona, adapted the original battery by including additional tests.

The Halstead-Reitan has been researched more than any other neuropsychological test battery. Research continues to support its ability to accurately detect impairment in a large range of neuropsychological functions.

Category Test (CT)

A series of 208 pictures consisting of geometric figures are presented, sorted in groups according to some underlying principle, which the test subject is asked to determine. For each picture, individuals are asked to decide which of four principles they believe is represented and to press a key that corresponds to the number of choice. If they chose correctly, a chime sounds. If they chose incorrectly, a buzzer sounds. The pictures are presented in seven subtests.

The key to this test is that one principle, or common characteristic, underlies each subtest. The numbers 1, 2, 3, and 4 represent the possible principles. If individuals are able to recognize the correct principle in one picture, they will respond correctly for the remaining pictures in that subtest. The next subtest may have the same or a different underlying principle, and individuals must again try to determine that principle using the feedback of the chime and buzzer. The last subtest contains two underlying principles. The test takes approximately one hour to complete, but individuals with severe brain damage may take as long as two hours.

The Category Test is considered the battery's most effective test for detecting brain damage, but does not help determine where the problem is occurring in the brain. The test evaluates abstraction ability, or the ability to draw specific conclusions from general information. Related abilities are solving complex and unique problems, and learning from experience. Children's versions consist of 80 items and five subtests for young children, and 168 items and six subtests for older children.

Scoring involves recording the number of errors. Based on traditional scoring using cutoff values (cutoff scores are scores that indicate the borderline between normal and impaired functioning), scores above 41 are considered indicative of brain impairment for ages 15 to 45 years. For ages 46 years and older, scores above 46 indicate impairment. Reitan has suggested a cutoff of 50 or 51 errors. Recommended cutoffs also vary depending on age and education level.

Tactual Performance Test (TPT)

A form board containing ten cutout shapes, and ten wooden blocks matching those shapes are placed in front of a blindfolded individual. Individuals are then instructed to use only their dominant hand to place the blocks in their appropriate space on the form board. The same procedure is repeated using only the nondominant hand, and then using both hands. Finally, the form board and blocks are removed, followed by the blindfold. From memory, individuals are asked to draw the form board and the shapes in their proper locations. The test usually takes anywhere from 15 to 50 minutes to complete. There is a time limit of 15 minutes for each trial, or each performance segment.

Other names for this test are the Form Board Test and the Seguin-Goddard Formboard. It evaluates sensory ability, memory for shapes and spatial location, motor functions, and the brain's ability to transfer information between its two hemispheres. In addition to simple detection of brain damage, this test also helps determine the side of the brain where damage may have occurred. For children under the age of 15 years, only six shapes are used.

Scoring involves recording the time to complete each of the three blindfolded trials and the total time for all trials combined (time score), the number of shapes recalled (memory score), and the number of shapes drawn in their correct locations (localization score). Generally, the trial for the nondominant hand should be 20% to 30% faster than the trial for the dominant hand, due to the benefit of practice. If the nondominant hand is slower than the dominant hand or more than 30% faster than the dominant hand, brain damage is possible. However, some people without brain damage do not exhibit this typical improvement rate. Injuries of the arms, shoulders, or hands can also affect performance. Scores should be adjusted depending on education level and may vary depending on age.

Trail Making Test (TM)

This test consists of two parts. Part A is a page with 25 numbered circles randomly arranged. Individuals are instructed to draw lines between the circles in increasing sequential order until they reach the circle labeled "End." Part B is a page with circles containing the letters A through L and 13 numbered circles intermixed and randomly arranged. Individuals are instructed to connect the circles by drawing lines alternating between numbers and letters in sequential order, until they reach the circle labeled "End." If individuals make mistakes, the mistakes are quickly brought to their attention, and they continue from the last correct circle. The test takes approximately 5 to 10 minutes to complete.

This test was originally known as Partington's Pathways, or the Divided Attention Test, which was part of the Army Individual Test Battery. The test evaluates information-processing speed, visual-scanning ability, integration of visual and motor functions, letter and number recognition and sequencing, and the ability to maintain two different trains of thought. The test can be administered orally if an individual is incapable of writing. The Color Trails Test, designed for children and individuals of different cultures, uses colors instead of numbers and letters.

Scoring is based on the time it takes to complete each part. Errors naturally increase the total time. Some have argued that the time taken to alert individuals of errors may vary depending on the person giving the test. For adults, scores above 40 seconds for Part A and 91 seconds for Part B have traditionally indicated brain impairment. Current research discourages the use of such traditional cutoffs, preferring ranges depending on age, education, and gender. For example, one study reported that for ages 15 to 19 years, the average time to complete Part A was 25.7 seconds and the time to complete Part B was 49.8 seconds. For ages 80 to 85 years, however, the average time to complete Part A was 60.7 seconds and the time to complete Part B was 152.2 seconds. This demonstrates the importance of considering other variables when scoring.

Finger Tapping Test (FTT)

Individuals place their dominant hand palm down, fingers extended, with the index finger resting on a lever that is attached to a counting device. Individuals are instructed to tap their index finger as quickly as possible for ten seconds, keeping the hand and arm stationary. This trial is repeated five to ten times, until the examiner has collected counts for five consecutive trials that are within five taps of each other. Before starting the test, individuals are given a practice session. They are also given brief rests between each 10-second trial, and one- to two-minute rests after every third trial. This entire procedure is repeated with the nondominant hand. The test takes approximately 10 minutes to complete.

This test is also called the Finger Oscillation Test and the Finger Tapper. The children's version uses an electronic tapper instead of a manual one, which was difficult for children to operate. The test measures motor speed and helps determine particular areas of the brain that may be damaged. Scoring involves using the five accepted trials to calculate an average number of taps per trial for each hand. In general, the dominant hand should perform 10% better than the nondominant hand. Yet this is not always the case, especially with left-handed individuals. Men and younger people tend to perform better than women and older people. Interpretation should also consider education level, intelligence, **fatigue**, general weakness or lack of coordination, **depression**, and injuries to the shoulders, arms, or hands. This test should only be interpreted in combination with other tests in the battery.

Rhythm Test (RT)

Thirty pairs of tape-recorded, nonverbal sounds are presented. For each pair, individuals decide if the two sounds are the same or different, marking "S" or "D" respectively on their answer sheets. The pairs are grouped into three subtests. This test is also called the Seashore Rhythm Test, and is based on the Seashore Tests of Musical Ability. It evaluates auditory attention and concentration, and the ability to discriminate between nonverbal sounds. The test helps detect brain damage, but not the location of damage. Adequate hearing and visual abilities are needed to take this test. Scoring is based on the number of correct items, with higher scores indicating less damage or good recovery. Scores should be interpreted along with information from other tests. Some researchers consider this test unreliable and simplistic. The children's version does not include this test.

Speech Sounds Perception Test (SSPT)

Sixty tape-recorded nonsense syllables containing the sound "ee" (for example, "meer" and "weem") are presented. After each syllable, individuals underline, from a set of four written syllables, the spelling that represents the syllable they heard. This test evaluates auditory attention and concentration and the ability to discriminate between verbal sounds. It provides some information regarding specific areas of brain damage, and may also indicate attention deficits or hearing loss. Scoring and interpretation are similar to that used for the Rhythm Test. The children's version contains fewer syllable choices.

Reitan-Indiana Aphasia Screening Test

Aphasia is the loss of ability to understand or use written or spoken language, due to brain damage or deterioration. In this test, individuals are presented with a variety of questions and tasks that would be easy for someone without impairment. Examples of test items include verbally naming pictures, writing the name of a picture without saying the name aloud, reading printed material of increasing length, repeating words stated by the examiner, simple arithmetic problems, drawing shapes without lifting the pencil, and placing one hand to an area on the opposite side of the body.

This test is a modification of the Halstead-Wepman Aphasia Screening Test. It evaluates language-related difficulties, right/left confusion, and nonverbal tasks. A typical scoring procedure is not used because this is a screening test; its purpose is to detect possible signs of aphasia that may require further evaluation. Subtle language deficits may not be detected.

Reitan-Klove Sensory-Perceptual Examination

This test detects whether individuals are unable to perceive stimulation on one side of the body when both sides are stimulated simultaneously. It has tactile, auditory, and visual components involving the ability to (a) specify whether touch, sound, or visible movement is occurring on the right, left, or both sides of the body; (b) recall numbers assigned to particular fingers (the examiner assigns numbers by touching each finger and stating the number with the individual's eyes closed); (c) identify numbers "written" on fingertips while eyes are closed; and (d) identify the shape of a wooden block placed in one hand by pointing to its shape on a form board with the opposite hand.

Ancillary tests

In addition to the core tests, examiners may choose to administer other tests based on the difficulties that individuals experience. Tests commonly used in combination with the Halstead-Reitan Battery include the Grip Strength Test (or Strength Of Grip Test [SOGT]), the Grooved Pegboard Test, and the Reitan-Klove Lateral Dominance Examination. The SOGT uses a hand dynamometer to measure the strength of both hands, where one hand is considered the dominant hand and the other the nondominant one. The Reitan-Klove Lateral Dominance Examination measures preferences for right versus left in activities involving the arms, eyes, feet, hands, and legs.

Still other tests commonly used with the HRNB are the Wechsler Memory Scale, the California Verbal Learning Test, the Buschke Selective Reminding Test, the Rey Auditory Verbal Memory Test, the Rey Complex Figure Test, the Test of Memory and Learning, the **Wide Range Achievement Test**, the **Minnesota Multiphasic Personality Inventory**, and the Wechsler Adult Intelligence Scale or **Wechsler Intelligence Scales** for Children. Some of these tests expand on these measures of functioning in the latest revision of the battery.

Preparation

Preparation for the Halstead-Reitan Neuropsychological Test Battery is not necessary for participants nor is it recommended by professionals.

Precautions

Because of its complexity, the Halstead-Reitan requires administration by a professional examiner and interpretation by a trained **psychologist**. Test results are affected by the examinee's age, education level, intellectual ability, and—to some extent—gender or ethnicity, which should always be taken into account.

Because the Halstead-Reitan is a fixed battery of tests, some unnecessary information may be gathered or some important information may be missed. Overall, the battery requires five to six hours to complete, involving considerable patience, stamina, and cost. The battery has also been criticized for not including specific tests of memory; rather, memory is evaluated within the context of other tests.

Results

Interpretation of the Halstead-Reitan involves analysis of various factors:

- Overall performance on the battery. The Halstead Impairment Index (HII) and the General Neuropsychological Deficit Scale (GNDS) are commonly used to obtain an overall score, although the latest revision now facilitates calculation of a global deficit score that reflects the number and severity of deficits or impairments and incorporates more test measures than were used in previous versions. This summary score weighs deficits more heavily than strengths, which reduces the chance that better performance on a few components of the test will hide impairments. The HII is calculated by counting the total number of tests in the impaired range, and dividing that number by the total tests administered, resulting in a decimal between zero and one (0.0–0.2: normal functioning; 0.3–0.4: mild impairment; 0.5–0.7: moderate impairment; and 0.8–1.0: severe impairment). The GNDS is calculated by assigning a value between zero and four to 42 variables contained in the tests, then summing those values (0–25: normal functioning; 26–40: mild impairment; 41–67: moderate impairment; and 68 and higher: severe impairment).
- Performance on individual tests. Each test must be interpreted in relation to other tests in the battery. Significant poor performance on one test may be due to various factors. However, if a pattern of poor performance occurs on three or more tests, or if significant discrepancies occur on two or more tests, impairment is likely.
- Indications of lateralization and localization. This refers to the particular region of the brain that is damaged. Performance on sensory and motor tasks provides the necessary clues.

The tests within the HRNB have been shown to be effective at differentiating between the brains of normal individuals and those with brain damage. One combined score, called the Halstead Impairment Index, is used for final analysis of its results.

With the test information, a psychologist can diagnose the type of condition present, predict the course of the impairment (staying the same, getting better, or getting worse), and make recommendations regarding treatment, care, or rehabilitation.

In 2004, a revision in the norms used to make determinations about results on the battery was published. This revision includes corrections based on ethnicity in addition to age, gender, and education. The results can be adjusted to demographic components, including African American or Caucasian ethnicity. Also updated is the global deficit score, which reflects the severity and number of deficits on more test measures than previously assessed. The sample used to determine the norms for this 2004 revision also was larger, including more than 1,000 adults, ages 20 to 85 years, for most test endpoints. The revision also has expanded measures of psychological functioning, including Wechsler scores.

QUESTIONS TO ASK YOUR DOCTOR

- Will the HRNB be able to tell specifically what has caused the brain damage?
- Do you know of a psychologist or other professional trained in administering the HRNB?
- Will health insurance cover the test?

See also Executive function; Luria-Nebraska Inventory; Mini-Mental State Exam; Neuropsychological Status Exam; Neuropsychological testing; Psychological assessment and diagnosis

Resources

BOOKS

Goldstein, Laura H., and Jane E. McNeil, editors. *Clinical Neuropsychology: A Practical Guide to Assessment and Management for Clinicians.* Chichester, UK: Wiley, 2004.

Hersen, Michel, and Alan M. Gross, editors. *Handbook of Clinical Psychology.* Hoboken, NJ: J. Wiley & Sons, 2008.

Horton, Jr., Arthur MacNeill, and Danny Wedding, editors. *The Neuropsychology Handbook.* New York City: Springer Publishing, 2008.

Lezak, Muriel D., et al. *Neuropsychological Assessment.* Oxford: Oxford University Press, 2004.

Poreh, Amir M., editor. *The Quantified Process Approach to Neuropsychological Assessment.* New York City: Taylor & Francis, 2006.

Strauss, Esther, Elisabeth M. S. Sherman, and Otfied Spreen. *A Compendium of Neuropsychological Tests: Administration, Norms, and Commentary.* Oxford: Oxford University Press, 2006.

Uzzell, Barbara P., Marcel O. Pontón, and Alfredo Ardila, editors. *International Handbook of Cross-cultural Neuropsychology.* Mahwah, NJ: Lawrence Erlbaum, 2007.

OTHER

"The Halstead-Reitan Neuropsychological Test Battery for Adults: Theoretical, Methodological and Validational Bases." Ralph M. Reitan and Deborah Wolfson, Reitan Neuropsychological Laboratory. http://www.reitanlabs.com/PDFFiles/halstead-reitan%20battery.pdf (accessed December 6, 2011).

WEBSITES

"Halstead-Reitan Neuropsychological Test Battery." Center for Psychological Studies, Nova Southeastern University. http://www.cps.nova.edu/~cpphelp/HRNTB.html (accessed December 6, 2011).

"Revised Comprehensive Norms for an Expanded Halstead-Reitan Battery: Demographically Adjusted Neuropsychological Norms for African American and Caucasian Adults (HRB)." National Alliance of Mental Illness. http://www4.parinc.com/Products/Product.aspx?ProductID=RCNAAC (accessed December 6, 2011).

ORGANIZATIONS

American Psychiatric Association, 1000 Wilson Boulevard, Suite 1825, Arlington, VA, 22209-3901, (703) 907-7300, apa@psych.org, http://www.psych.org.

American Psychological Association, 750 First St., NE, Washington, DC, 20002, (202) 336-5500, (800) 374-2721, http://www.apa.org.

International Neuropsychological Society, 700 Ackerman Road, Suite 625, Columbus, OH, 43202, (614) 263-4200, Fax: (614) 263-4366, http://www.the-ins.org.

National Institute of Mental Health, 6001 Executive Boulevard, Room 8184, MSC 9663, Bethesda, MD, 20892-9663, (301) 443-4513, (866) 615-6464, Fax: (301) 443-4279, nimhinfo@nih.gov, http://www.nimh.nih.gov.

Sandra L. Friedrich, MA
Emily Jane Willingham, PhD

Hamilton Anxiety Scale

Definition

The Hamilton Anxiety Scale (HAS, HAM-A, or HAMA) is a 14-item test measuring the severity of anxiety symptoms developed by German-born-British **psychologist** Max Hamilton (1912–1988) in 1959. It is also sometimes called the Hamilton Anxiety Rating Scale (HARS). The test is administered in an interview format. It measures the severity of anxiety, including anxious mood, fears, abnormal behavior, **insomnia**, and somatic complaints at the time of the interview. It measures many of the features of **generalized anxiety disorder** (GAD), along with accessing its severity, although the test was developed before the medical term was defined. It takes about 15 to 20 minutes to administer the test.

Purpose

The HAS is used to assess the severity of anxiety symptoms present in children and adults. It is also used as an outcome measure when assessing the impact of antianxiety medications, therapies, and treatments and is a standard measure of anxiety used in evaluations of psychotropic drugs. The HAS can be administered prior to medication being started and then again during follow-up visits, so that medication dosage can be changed in part based on the patient's test score.

The HAS provides measures of overall anxiety, psychic anxiety (mental agitation and psychological distress), and somatic anxiety (physical complaints related to anxiety). Hamilton developed the HAS to be appropriate for adults and children; although it is most often used for younger adults, there has been support for the test's use with older adults as well. Hamilton also developed the widely used **Hamilton Depression Scale** (HDS) to measure symptoms of **depression**.

Hamilton developed the scale by using the statistical technique of factor analysis. With this

Hamilton Anxiety Rating Scale (HAM-A)

Code: 0 = Not present, 1 = Mild, 2 = Moderate, 3 = Severe, 4 = Very severe

1 Anxious mood	0 1 2 3 4
Worries, anticipation of the worst, fearful anticipation, irritability	
2 Tension	0 1 2 3 4
Feelings of tension, fatigability, startle response, moved to tears easily, trembling, feelings of restlessness, inability to relax	
3 Fears	0 1 2 3 4
Of dark, of strangers, of being left alone, of animals, of traffic, of crowds	
4 Insomnia	0 1 2 3 4
Difficulty in falling asleep, broken sleep, unsatisfying sleep and fatigue on waking, dreams, nightmares, night terrors	
5 Intellectual	0 1 2 3 4
Difficulty in concentration, poor memory	
6 Depressed mood	0 1 2 3 4
Loss of interest, lack of pleasure in hobbies, depression, early waking, diurnal swing	
7 Somatic (muscular)	0 1 2 3 4
Pains and aches, twitching, stiffness, myoclonic jerks, grinding of teeth, unsteady voice, increased muscular tone	
8 Somatic (sensory)	0 1 2 3 4
Tinnitus, blurring of vision, hot and cold flushes, feelings of weakness, pricking sensation	
9 Cardiovascular symptoms	0 1 2 3 4
Tachycardia, palpitations, pain in chest, throbbing of vessels, fainting feelings, missing beat	
10 Respiratory symptoms	0 1 2 3 4
Pressure or constriction in chest, choking feelings, sighing, dyspnea	
11 Gastrointestinal symptoms	0 1 2 3 4
Difficulty in swallowing, wind abdominal pain, burning sensations, abdominal fullness, nausea, vomiting, borborygmi, looseness of bowels, loss of weight, constipation	
12 Genitourinary symptoms	0 1 2 3 4
Frequency of micturition, urgency of micturition, amenorrhea, menorrhagia, development of frigidity, premature ejaculation, loss of libido, impotence	
13 Autonomic symptoms	0 1 2 3 4
Dry mouth, flushing, pallor, tendency to sweat, giddiness, tension headache, raising of hair	
14 Behavior at interview	0 1 2 3 4
Fidgeting, restlessness or pacing, tremor of hands, furrowed brow, strained face, sighing or rapid respiration, facial pallor, swallowing, etc.	

(Table by PreMediaGlobal. © 2012 Cengage Learning.)

method, he generated a set of symptoms related to anxiety and further determined which symptoms related to psychic anxiety and which related to somatic anxiety. Its major use is as a pharmacotherapy or **psychotherapy** tool, rather than as one used for **diagnosis** or screening.

Description

The HAS is administered by an interviewer who asks a semi-structured series of questions related to symptoms of anxiety. The interviewer then rates the individuals on a five-point scale for each of the 14 items. Seven of the items specifically address psychic anxiety, and the remaining seven items address somatic anxiety. For example, one item specifically addresses fears related to anxiety, another addresses insomnia and sleeping difficulties related to anxiety, and still another item addresses respiratory symptoms related to anxiety.

The seven items rated by the HAS as being psychic symptoms include:

- anxious mood (worries, anticipates the worst, negative attitude)
- heightened fears (various types of fears including fear of strangers, fear of being alone, fear of the dark)
- depressed mood (insomnia, lack of interest in activities and life in general)
- behavior at interview (pacing, tremors, anxiousness, uneasiness during interview process)
- intellectual (loss of concentration, poor memory)
- feelings of tension (restless, easily emotional, frequent bursts of crying, trembling)
- cardiovascular symptoms (chest pains, feelings of lightheadedness and fainting)

The seven items rated by the HAS as being somatic symptoms include:

- somatic complaints (muscular pain)
- gastrointestinal symptoms (weight loss, vomiting, nausea)
- autonomic symptoms (sweaty, pallor, dry mouth)
- insomnia (difficulties falling asleep and staying asleep, having frequent nightmares when asleep)
- somatic complaints (sensory such as blurred vision, tinnitus)
- respiratory symptoms (chest pressure, feeling of choking, shortness of breath)
- genitourinary symptoms (impotence, urgency to urinate, dysmenorrhea)

KEY TERMS

Dysmenorrhea—Painful menstruation.

Psychic—Relating to the mind rather than the body.

Somatic—Relating to the body, rather than the mind.

Tinnitus—Consistent noise in ear.

Preparation

It is not necessary for the individual to prepare for the test.

Risks

The test has been criticized on the grounds that it does not always discriminate between people with anxiety symptoms and those with depressive symptoms (people with depression also score fairly high on the HAS).

Precautions

Because the HAS is administered and rated by the interviewer, there is some subjectivity when it comes to interpretation and scoring. Interviewer bias can affect the results. For this reason, some people prefer self-report measures where scores are completely based on the interviewee's responses.

Results

For the 14 items, the values on the scale range from zero to four: zero means that there is no anxiety (none present), one indicates mild anxiety, two indicates moderate anxiety, three indicates severe anxiety, and four indicates very severe or grossly disabling anxiety. The total anxiety score ranges from 0 to 56. The seven psychic anxiety items elicit a psychic anxiety score that ranges from 0 to 28. The remaining seven items yield a somatic anxiety score that also ranges from 0 to 28. A total score of 17 or less indicates mild anxiety, 18–24 indicates moderate anxiety, and 25 or higher indicates severe anxiety.

One reason that the HAS is widely used is that reliability studies have shown that it measures anxiety symptoms in a fairly consistent way. The measure's validity has also been supported by research.

While there is a tendency for depressed people to also score high on the HAS, some researchers have suggested that anxiety and depression are so closely linked that people can easily score high on measures of both types of symptoms.

QUESTIONS TO ASK YOUR DOCTOR

- Do I need to find an administrator who is knowledgeable at administering the Hamilton Anxiety Scale?
- Should I take the test over the Internet or the telephone rather than in an interview format?
- Will the HAS tell me what type of medicine I need (if any), and the amount I will need to take?
- Where can I learn more about the HAS?
- Are there other tests that I can take to help verify its conclusion? Do I need such extra tests to re-verify?

The paper and pencil version of this test is in the public domain, meaning that it can easily be found on the Internet for people who are interested in reviewing it. There is also a computer-administered version for use in a computerized, telephone-based interview. This version uses voice recognition to take answers to the respondent's questions. The computerized "interviewer" can even interact in a programmed way with the respondent. A study has indicated that some respondents feel more comfortable answering the questions when they are administered in the telephone format compared to the in-person format.

Resources

BOOKS

Baer, Lee, and Mark A. Blais, eds. *Handbook of Clinical Rating Scales and Assessment in Psychiatry and Mental Health.* New York: Humana Press, 2010.

Boyer, Bret A., and M. Indira Paharia. *Comprehensive Handbook of Clinical Health Psychology.* Hoboken, NJ: John Wiley & Sons, 2008.

Maruish, Mark R., ed. *The Use of Psychological Testing for Treatment Planning and Outcomes Assessment.* Mahwah, NJ: Lawrence Erlbaum Associates, 2004.

Rush Jr., A. John, Michael B. First, and Deborah Blacker, eds. *Handbook of Psychiatric Measures.* Washington, DC: American Psychiatric, 2008.

OTHER

"Hamilton Anxiety Test (HAM-A)." Assessment Psychology Online. http://www.assessmentpsychology.com/HAM-A.pdf (accessed December 6, 2010).

WEBSITES

"Hamilton Anxiety Scale (HAMA)—IVR Version." Healthcare Technology Systems. http://www.healthtechsys.com/ivr/assess/ivrhama.html (accessed December 6, 2010).

Ali Fahmy, PhD
Emily Jane Willingham, PhD

Hamilton Depression Scale

Definition

The Hamilton Depression Scale (HDS, HAMD, or HAM-D) is a multiple-choice questionnaire test measuring the severity, and the change, of depressive symptoms in individuals, often those who have already been diagnosed as having a depressive disorder. HDS was originally developed by German-born-British **psychologist** Max Hamilton (1912–1988) in 1960, and revised in 1967, 1969, and 1980. It is sometimes known as the Hamilton Rating Scale for Depression (HRSD) or the Hamilton Depression Rating Scale (HDRS). The test is composed of questions that relate to symptoms common to **depression** such as anxiety, **insomnia**, mood, agitation, and weight loss. The HDS is considered one of the most common clinician-administered tests used to rate the severity of depression and its symptoms. The test takes from 20 to 30 minutes to administer.

Purpose

The HDS is used to assess the severity of depressive symptoms present in both children and adults. It is often used as an outcome measure of depression in evaluations of antidepressant psychotropic medications and is a standard measure of depression used in research of the effectiveness of depression therapies and treatments. It can be administered prior to medication being started and then again during follow-up visits, so that medication dosage can be changed in part based on the patient's test score. The HDS is often used as the standard against which other measures of depression are validated. There is a computerized version available intended for administration by telephone using a voice-recognition system and a computerized "interviewer."

The HDS was developed as a measure of depressive symptoms that could be used in conjunction with clinical interviews with depressed in-hospital patients. Hamilton also designed the Hamilton Depression Inventory (HDI), a self-report measure for adults consistent with his theoretical formulation of depression in the HDS, and the **Hamilton Anxiety Scale** (HAS), an interviewer-rated test measuring the severity of anxiety symptoms.

Description

Depending on the version used, an interviewer can provide ratings for a test with 17 items ($HDRS_{17}$) or 24 items ($HDRS_{24}$). In addition to the items on the 17-item scale, the 24-item scale addresses daytime-only symptoms, helplessness, hopelessness, worthlessness, obsessional symptoms, and paranoid feelings. A 21-item version ($HDRS_{21}$) has also been used for evaluations. Along with the patient interview answers, other information can be used in formulating ratings, such as information gathered from family, friends, and patient records. Hamilton devised the test as an easy-going interview process by keeping its questions informal and general.

Examples of items for which interviewers must give ratings include overall depression, guilt, **suicide**, insomnia, problems related to work, psychomotor disabilities, agitation, anxiety, gastrointestinal and other physical symptoms, loss of libido, **hypochondriasis**, loss of insight, and loss of weight. For the overall rating of depression, for example, Hamilton believed one should look for feelings of hopelessness and gloominess, pessimism regarding the future, and a tendency to cry. For the rating of suicide, an interviewer should look for suicidal ideas and thoughts, as well as information regarding suicide attempts.

For the 17 item HDRS, the following items are included:

- depressed mood (such feelings as helplessness, hopelessness, sadness, worthlessness)
- feelings of guilt
- suicide
- insomnia: early in the night
- insomnia: middle of the night
- insomnia: early in the morning
- work and activities
- intellectual disabilities (such as slowness of thinking and talking, degraded ability to concentrate, decreased motor activity)
- agitation
- anxiety psychic
- anxiety somatic (physiological concomitants of anxiety)—gastrointestinal (dry mouth, gas, indigestion, diarrhea, cramps, belching), cardiovascular (palpitations, headaches), respiratory (hyperventilation, sighing), urinary frequency, sweating
- somatic symptoms—gastrointestinal
- general somatic symptoms
- genital symptoms (such as loss of libido, menstrual disturbances)
- hypochondriasis
- loss of weight
- insight

Hamilton Depression Rating Scale (HDRS)

1 Depressed mood (*sadness, hopeless, helpless, worthless*)

0 Absent.
1 These feeling states indicated only on questioning.
2 These feeling states spontaneously reported verbally.
3 Communicates feeling states nonverbally (e.g., through facial expression, posture, voice and tendency to weep).
4 Patient reports virtually only these feeling states in his/her spontaneous verbal and nonverbal communication.

2 Feelings of guilt

0 Absent.
1 Self reproach, feels he/she has let people down.
2 Ideas of guilt or rumination over past errors or sinful deeds.
3 Present illness is a punishment. Delusions of guilt.
4 Hears accusatory or denunciatory voices and/or experiences threatening visual hallucinations.

3 Suicide

0 Absent.
1 Feels life is not worth living.
2 Wishes he/she were dead or any thoughts of possible death to self.
3 Ideas or gestures of suicide.
4 Attempts at suicide (any serious attempt rate 4).

4 Insomnia: Early in the night

0 No difficulty falling asleep.
1 Complains of occasional difficulty falling asleep (e.g., more than 1/2 hour).
2 Complains of nightly difficulty falling asleep.

5 Insomnia: Middle of the night

0 No difficulty.
1 Patient complains of being restless and disturbed during the night.
2 Waking during the night—any getting out of bed rates 2 (except for purposes of voiding).

6 Insomnia: Early hours of the morning

0 No difficulty.
1 Waking in early hours of the morning but goes back to sleep.
2 Unable to fall asleep again if he/she gets out of bed.

7 Work and activities

0 No difficulty.
1 Thoughts and feelings of incapacity, fatigue or weakness related to activities, work or hobbies.
2 Loss of interest in activity, hobbies or work—either directly reported by the patient or indirect in listlessness, indecision and vacillation (feels he/she has to push self to work or activities).
3 Decrease in actual time spent in activities or decrease in productivity. Rate 3 if the patient does not spend at least three hours a day in activities (job or hobbies) excluding routine chores.
4 Stopped working because of present illness. Rate 4 if patient engages in no activities except routine chores, or if patient fails to perform routine chores unassisted.

8 Retardation (slowness of thought and speech, impaired ability to concentrate, decreased motor activity)

0 Normal speech and thought.
1 Slight retardation during the interview.
2 Obvious retardation during the interview.
3 Interview difficult.
4 Complete stupor.

9 Agitation

0 None.
1 Fidgetiness.
2 Playing with hands, hair, etc.
3 Moving about, can't sit still.
4 Hand wringing, nail biting, hair-pulling, biting of lips.

10 Anxiety psychic

0 No difficulty.
1 Subjective tension and irritability.
2 Worrying about minor matters.
3 Apprehensive attitude apparent in face or speech.
4 Fears expressed without questioning.

11 Anxiety somatic (physiological concomitants of anxiety) such as: gastrointestinal (dry mouth, wind, indigestion, diarrhea, cramps, belching), cardiovascular (palpitations, headaches), respiratory (hyperventilation, sighing), urinary frequency, sweating

0 Absent.
1 Mild.
2 Moderate.
3 Severe.
4 Incapacitating.

12 Somatic symptoms gastrointestinal

0 None.
1 Loss of appetite but eating without staff encouragement. Heavy feelings in abdomen.
2 Difficulty eating without staff urging. Requests or requires laxatives or medication for bowels or medication for gastrointestinal symptoms.

13 General somatic symptoms

0 None.
1 Heaviness in limbs, back or head. Backaches, headaches, muscle aches. Loss of energy and fatigability.
2 Any clear-cut symptom rates 2.

14 Genital symptoms (symptoms such as loss of libido, menstrual disturbances)

0 Absent.
1 Mild.
2 Severe.

15 Hypochondriasis

0 Not present.
1 Self-absorption (bodily).
2 Preoccupation with health.
3 Frequent complaints, requests for help, etc.
4 Hypochondriacal delusions.

16 Loss of weight (*rate either a or b*)

a) According to the patient:	**b) According to weekly measurements:**
0 No weight loss.	0 Less than 1 lb weight loss in week.
1 Probable weight loss associated with present illness.	1 Greater than 1 lb weight loss in week.
2 Definite (according to patient) weight loss.	2 Greater than 2 lb weight loss in week.
3 Not assessed.	3 Not assessed.

17 Insight

0 Acknowledges being depressed and ill.
1 Acknowledges illness but attributes cause to bad food, climate, overwork, virus, need for rest, etc.
2 Denies being ill at all.

(Table by PreMediaGlobal. © 2012 Cengage Learning.)

For the 17 items, a "cue" is provided with a position of 0 through 2, 0 through 3, or 0 through 4, depending on the individual cue. For instance, for the item called agitation, 0 represents none; 1, fidgetiness; 2, playing with hands, hair; 3, moving about, unable to sit still; and 4, hand wringing, nail biting, hair-pulling, lip biting. The administrator chooses the cue that best represents the state of the person. Scoring varies depending on the number of items present. For the HDRS17, a score from 0 to 7 indicates a normal range, while a score of 20 or higher indicates at least moderate severity for depression.

The HDS has also been translated into numerous languages, including French, German, Italian, Thai, and Turkish. In addition, an Interactive Voice Response version (IVR) is also available, as is a **Seasonal Affective Disorder** version (SIGH-SAD) and a Structured Interview Version (HDS-SIV). Various lengths, besides the three already mentioned, are also available including HDRS-6 (6 items), HDRS-7 (7 items), HDRS-8 (8 items), and HDRS-29 (29 items),

The HDS is sometimes used in parallel with the one or more of the following tests: the **Beck Depression Inventory**, the Inventory of Depressive Symptomatology, the Montgomery-Asberg Depression Rating Scale, the Raskin Depression Rating Scale, the Quick Inventory of Depressive Symptomatology the Wechsler Depression Rating Scale, and the Zung Self-Rating Depression Scale.

Preparation

It is not necessary to prepare for the HDS, nor is any preparation required of medical professionals.

Risks

The test has been criticized on the grounds that it does not adequately identify depression. However, it remains one of the most widely used tests for depression.

Precautions

Some symptoms related to depression, such as self-esteem and self-deprecation, are not explicitly included in the HDS items. Also, because anxiety is specifically asked about on the HDS, it is not always possible to separate symptoms related to anxiety from symptoms related to depression.

Because the HDS is administered and rated by the interviewer, there is some subjectivity when it comes to interpretation and scoring. Interviewer bias can affect the results. For this reason, some people prefer self-report measures where scores are completely based on the interviewee's responses.

Results

In the 17-item version, which is most commonly used, nine of the items are scored on a five-point scale, ranging from zero to four. A score of zero represents an absence of the depressive symptom being measured, a score of one indicates doubt concerning the presence of the symptom, a score of two shows mild to moderate symptoms, a score of three describes moderate to severe symptoms, and a score of four represents the presence of extreme symptoms. The remaining seven items are scored on a three-point scale, from zero to two, with zero representing absence of symptom, one indicating that the symptom is present to a mild or moderate degree, and two showing clear presence of symptoms; while the last item is scored on a two-point scale, with zero representing absence of symptom, one indicating that the symptom is mild, and two showing that it is severe.

For the 17-item version, scores can range from 0 to 54. One formulation suggests that scores between zero and six indicate a person who is typical and lacks morbidity with regard to depression; scores between seven and 17 indicate mild depression; scores between 18 and 24 indicate moderate depression; and scores over 24 indicate severe depression.

There has been evidence to support the reliability and validity of the HDS. The scale correlates highly with other clinician-rated and self-report measures of depression.

KEY TERMS

Depression—A psychiatric disorder involving feelings of hopelessness and symptoms of fatigue, sleeplessness, suicidal tendencies, and poor concentration.

Hypochondriasis—Also called hypochondria, an excessive preoccupation with health, especially with having an impression of having a serious disease without any medical evidence.

Libido—Emotions relating to sex drive.

Psychic—Relating to the mind rather than the body.

Somatic—Relating to the body, rather than the mind.

Resources

BOOKS

Baer, Lee, and Mark A. Blais, editors. *Handbook of Clinical Rating Scales and Assessment in Psychiatry and Mental Health.* New York: Humana Press, 2010.

QUESTIONS TO ASK YOUR DOCTOR

- Do I need to find an administrator who is knowledgeable at administering the Hamilton Depression Scale? If so, do you have recommendations?
- Can I take the test in any other format than with an interviewer?
- Will the HDS tell me what type of medicine I need (if any), and the amount I will need to take?
- Where can I learn more about the HDS?
- Are there other tests that I can take to help verify its conclusion? Do I need such extra tests to re-verify? Which ones do you recommend for me?

Boyer, Bret A., and M. Indira Paharia. *Comprehensive Handbook of Clinical Health Psychology*. Hoboken, NJ: John Wiley & Sons, 2008.

Maruish, Mark R., ed. *The Use of Psychological Testing for Treatment Planning and Outcomes Assessment*. Mahwah, NJ: Lawrence Erlbaum Associates, 2004.

Nezu, Arthur, George F. Ronan, and Elizabeth A. Meadows, eds. *Practitioner's Guide to Empirically Based Measures of Depression*. New York City: Springer Publishing Company, 2006.

Rush Jr., A. John, Michael B. First, and Deborah Blacker, eds. *Handbook of Psychiatric Measures*. Washington, DC: American Psychiatric, 2008.

VandenBos, Gary R., ed. *APA Dictionary of Psychology*. Washington, DC: American Psychological Association, 2007.

OTHER

"Description of the Hamilton Depression Rating Scale (HAMD) and the Montgomery-Asberg Depression Rating Scale (MADRS)." U.S. Food and Drug Administration. http://www.fda.gov/ohrms/dockets/AC/07/briefing/2007-4273b1_04-DescriptionofMADRSHAMDDepressionR(1).pdf (accessed December 7, 2010).

"Hamilton Depression Rating Scale For Depression." UMass Health Net, University of Massachusetts Medical Center. http://healthnet.umassmed.edu/mhealth/HAMD.pdf (accessed December 7, 2010).

"Hamilton Depression Rating Scale (HDRS)." Servier. http://www.servier.com/App_Download/Neurosciences/Echelles/HDRS.pdf (accessed December 7, 2010).

Ali Fahmy, PhD
Emily Jane Willingham, PhD

Hare Psychopathy Checklist

Definition

The Hare Psychopathy Checklist-Revised (PCL-R) is a psychodiagnostic tool used to rate a person's psychopathic or antisocial tendencies. Psychopaths are people who prey ruthlessly on others using charm, deceit, violence or other methods that allow them to get what they want. The symptoms of psychopathy include lack of a conscience or sense of guilt, lack of empathy; egocentricity, pathological lying, repeated violations of social norms, disregard for the law, shallow emotions, and a history of victimizing others. It also predicts the potential risk for repeat criminal offenders and, on the other hand, the probability for rehabilitation.

Purpose

The PCL-R is used for diagnosing psychopathy in individuals for clinical, legal or research purposes. Developed in the early 1990s, the test was originally designed to identify the degree of a person's psychopathic tendencies. Because psychopaths, however, are often repeat offenders who commit sexual assaults or other violent crimes again and again, the PCL-R is now finding use in the courtroom and in institutions as an indicator of the potential risk posed by subjects or prisoners. The results of the examination have been used in forensic settings as a factor in deciding the length and type of prison sentences and the treatment subjects should or should not receive.

Originally designed to assess people accused or convicted of crimes, the PCL-R consists of a 20-item symptom rating scale that allows qualified examiners to compare a subject's degree of psychopathy with that of a prototypical psychopath. It is accepted by many in the field as the best method for determining the presence and extent of psychopathy in a person.

The Hare checklist is still used to diagnose members of the original population for which it was developed—adult males in prisons, criminal psychiatric hospitals, and awaiting psychiatric evaluations or trial in other correctional and detention facilities. Recent experience suggests that the PCL-R may also be used effectively to diagnose sex offenders as well as female and adolescent offenders.

Description

The Psychopathy Checklist (PCL) and the Psychopathy Checklist Revised were both developed by Canadian researcher and criminal **psychologist** Robert D. Hare (1934–), who is a professor emeritus of the University of British Columbia. The PCL-R contains two parts, a semi-structured interview and a review of the subject's file records and history. During the evaluation, the clinician, usually a psychologist or other such professional, scores 20 items that measure central elements of the psychopathic character. The items cover the nature of the subject's interpersonal relationships; his or her affective or emotional involvement; responses to other people and to situations; evidence of social deviance; and lifestyle. The material thus covers two key aspects that help define the psychopath: selfish and unfeeling victimization of other people, and an unstable and antisocial lifestyle.

The twenty traits assessed by the PCL-R score are:

- glib and superficial charm
- grandiose (exaggeratedly high) estimation of self
- need for stimulation
- pathological lying
- cunning and manipulativeness
- lack of remorse or guilt
- shallow affect (superficial emotional responsiveness)
- callousness and lack of empathy
- parasitic lifestyle
- poor behavioral controls
- sexual promiscuity
- early behavior problems
- lack of realistic long-term goals
- impulsivity
- irresponsibility
- failure to accept responsibility for own actions
- many short-term marital relationships
- juvenile delinquency
- revocation of conditional release
- criminal versatility

The interview portion of the evaluation covers the subject's background, including such items as work and educational history, marital and family status, and criminal background. Because psychopaths lie frequently and easily, the information they provide must be confirmed by a review of the documents in the subject's case history.

The PCL-R (1991 edition) is available in many languages, including Bulgarian, Dutch, Finnish, French, German, Korean, Portuguese (Brazilian), and Spanish (Chilean and European). The PCL-R (second edition) is available in Hebrew, Japanese, and Swedish.

KEY TERMS

Psychopath—A person inflicted with psychopathy.

Psychopathy—A serious personality disorder characterized by antisocial, aggressive, and violent behavior and thoughts, along with a lack of empathy for ones actions.

Preparation

Preparation is not desired nor recommended.

Risks

Dr. Hare considers the results of the test to be highly dependent on the skill of a qualified and experienced clinician. Therefore, Hare requires that the test be tightly controlled, with proper licensing. The administrator is required to be registered with the local state or provincial registration body and have experience with forensic populations. Consequently, Hare receives a royalty on each use of the test. However, under such tight conditions, the results of the test are regarded as highly reliable.

Precautions

Diagnosing someone as a psychopath is a very serious step. It has important implications for a person and for his or her associates in family, clinical, and forensic settings. Therefore, the test must be administered by professionals who have been specifically trained in its use and who have a wide-ranging and up-to-date familiarity with studies of psychopathy.

Professionals who administer the diagnostic examination should have advanced degrees (medical doctor [MD], doctor of philosophy [PhD], or doctor of education [DEd] in a medical, behavioral, or social science field); and registered with a reputable organization that oversees psychiatric or psychological testing and diagnostic procedures. Other recommendations include experience working with convicted or accused criminals or several years of some other related on-the-job training. Because the results are used so often in legal cases, those who administer the test should be qualified to serve as expert witnesses in the courtroom. It is also a good idea, if possible, for two experts to independently test a subject with the PCL-R. The final rating would then be determined by averaging their scores.

Many studies conducted in North America and Europe attest to the value of the PCL-R for evaluating a person's degree of psychopathic traits and, in many cases, for predicting the likelihood of future violent behavior. Some critics, however, are more skeptical about its value.

QUESTIONS TO ASK YOUR DOCTOR

- Will the PCL-R be able to accurately identify psychopathy?
- Do you know a trained and qualified professional to administer the PCL-R?
- Should a second test by another administrator be used to verify the result?

Results

When properly completed by a qualified professional, the PCL-R provides a total score that indicates how closely the test subject matches the "perfect" score that a classic or prototypical psychopath would rate. Each of the twenty items is given a score of 0 (does not apply), 1 (applies somewhat), or 2 (completely applies) based on how well it applies to the subject being tested. A prototypical psychopath would receive a maximum score of 40, while someone with a complete absence of psychopathic traits or tendencies would receive a score of zero. A score of 30 or above qualifies a person for a **diagnosis** of psychopathy. People without criminal backgrounds normally score around 5. Many non-psychopathic criminal offenders score around 22.

The PCL-R has a demonstrated record of reliability and validity among researchers and clinicians. In 2007, a legal controversy arose between two researchers and the PCL-R developer when a paper was about to be published by the **American Psychological Association** concerning the PCL-R.

Three years later, *The New York Times* reported that American researcher Jennifer L. Skeem, from the University of California, Irvine, and Scottish researcher David J. Cooke, from Glasgow Caledonian University, stated the "... checklist was increasingly being mistaken for a complete definition of psychopathy—a broader personality construct that includes deceitfulness, impulsivity and recklessness, though not always aggression or illegal acts." Dr. Hare countered that the test emphasizes "problematic, not antisocial or criminal, behavior."

The paper was published in the June 2010 issue of the journal *Psychological Assessment,* along with a rebuttal from Dr. Hare and a return response from Drs. Skeem and Cooke. The PCL-R is considered by the international scientific community to be one of several forensic psychology tests used for the assessment of psychopathy.

See also Antisocial personality disorder; Sexual sadism

Resources

BOOKS

Babiak, Paul, and Robert D. Hare. *Snakes in Suits: When Psychopaths Go to Work.* New York: Collins Business, 2007.

Fitzgerald, Michael. *Young, Violent and Dangerous to Know.* New York: Nova Science, 2010.

Kantor, Martin. *The Psychopathy of Everyday Life: How Antisocial Personality Disorder Affects All of Us.* Westport, CT: Praeger Publishers, 2006.

Simon, Robert I. *Bad Men Do What Good Men Dream: A Forensic Psychiatrist Illuminates the Darker Side of Human Behavior.* Washington, DC: American Psychiatric, 2008.

Stout, Martha. *The Sociopath Next Door: The Ruthless Versus the Rest of Us.* New York: Broadway Books, 2006.

PERIODICALS

Carey, Benedict. "Academic Battle Delays Publication by 3 Years." *New York Times*, June 11, 2010. http://www.nytimes.com/2010/06/12/health/12psych.html?_r=1 (accessed December 7, 2011).

WEBSITES

"Dr. Robert Hare's Page for the Study of Psychopaths." Hare, Robert D. http://www.hare.org (accessed December 7, 2010).

"Is Criminal Behavior a Central Component of Psychopathy? Conceptual Directions for Resolving the Debate." J.L. Skeem and D.J. Cooke, NCBI. http://www.ncbi.nlm.nih.gov/pubmed/20528069 (accessed December 12, 2010).

"PCL—R™: 2nd Ed. Hare Psychopathy Checklist—Revised: 2nd Edition." Multi-Health Systems. http://www.mhs.com/product.aspx?gr=saf&prod=pcl-r2&id=overview (accessed December 7, 2010).

"Psychopathy Scales: PCL-R." Hare.org. http://www.hare.org/scales/pclr.html (accessed December 7, 2010).

Dean Haycock, PhD

HCR-20 *see* **Historical, Clinical, Risk Management-20**

Health maintenance organization *see* **Managed care**

Historical, Clinical, Risk Management-20 (HCR-20)

Definition

The Historical, Clinical, Risk Management-20 (HCR-20) is an assessment tool that helps mental health professionals estimate a person's probability of violence. It is frequently used in such areas as civil psychiatric, forensic psychiatric, and prison institutional and community settings. The HCR-20 is considered a type of a Structured Professional Judgment (SPJ) risk assessment instrument. The current version of the HCR-20 is version 2. As of December 2011, version 3 was considered "near final," but additional information on its publication was not available. The HCR-20 (version 2) is authored by Christopher D. Webster, Kevin S. Douglas, Derek Eaves, and Stephen D. Hart.

Purpose

The HCR-20's results help mental health professionals make structured clinical decisions about the best treatment and management strategies for potentially violent, mentally disordered individuals, including parolees, forensic mental health patients, and others. For example, if an individual is standing trial for a violent offense, a judge might order that assessments (such as the HCR-20, as well as others) be performed. The results of the evaluation could be used to determine the person's future potential for violence, how the court should proceed, and which kind of facility the person might require. As such, the HCR-20 helps to formulate treatment and management strategies that reduce the risk of violent behaviors in such individuals.

Description

The HCR-20 is an assessment tool. It consists of a list of 20 probing questions about the person being evaluated for violence. The clinician gathers qualitative information about the person being assessed, guided by the HCR-20, and the results are used to make treatment decisions.

The HCR-20 provides significantly improved valid predictions over previous testing methods. Earlier testing methods tended to be more subjective, less focused, and based on the loosely supported judgment of test administrators, or on comparing characteristics of the person being tested with base rates of violent behavior in populations with similar characteristics. The HCR-20 extends the methods of earlier tests and supplements them with a review of dynamic variables, such as **stress** and lack of personal support—both factors important to the person's future adjustment. This review adds to the accuracy of the HCR-20 and increases its practicality.

Available in more than a dozen languages, the HCR-20 has been adopted by numerous criminal justice, forensic, and mental health agencies in Europe, Asia, and North America for the purpose of providing risk assessment and management decisions.

The HCR-20 consists of three main areas: historical, clinical, and risk management. It takes its name (HCR-20) from these three scales and the total number of items (20). The HCR-20 domains are coded with a rating of 0 (not present), 1 (possible/less serious), or 3 (definite/serious).

Historical area

To rate historical areas, the test administrator must do an exhaustive review of background documents, interview people who know the person being assessed, and complete the **Hare Psychopathy Checklist**, another useful assessment. The historical (H) area is considered by many to anchor the full assessment. It includes ten domains or scales (H1 through H10):

- previous violence (H1)
- young age at first violent incident (H2)
- relationship instability (H3)
- employment problems (H4)
- substance use problems (H5)
- major mental illness (H6), such as schizophrenia or bipolar disorder
- psychopathy (H7), which can be defined as personality traits that deviate from social norms, such as manipulating and exploiting others for personal gain
- early maladjustment (H8), or exposure to family and social disruptions during childhood that may have led to coping problems (e.g., abuse, divorce)
- personality disorder (H9), such as paranoia
- prior supervision failure (H10), such as failure to respond to clinical supervision or treatment in the past or refusal to take medications or attend therapy sessions (noncompliance)

Clinical area

The rating of the clinical area requires a clinical interview between the person being assessed and the mental health professional. The professional will apply his or her judgment to the patient's responses. The clinical area (C) consists of five domains or scales (C1 through C5):

- lack of insight (C1), or difficulty understanding cause and effect; for example, people with poor insight might not understand why they do what they do and why their actions matter
- negative attitudes (C2)
- active symptoms of major mental illness (C3)
- impulsivity (C4)
- unresponsiveness to treatment (C5)

KEY TERMS

Psychopath—A person inflicted with psychopathy.

Psychopathy—A serious personality disorder characterized by antisocial, aggressive, and violent behavior and thoughts, along with a lack of empathy for one's actions.

Risk management

The third area, risk management (R), includes five domains or scales (R1 through R5) and assesses the following risks:

- [the person's] plans lack feasibility (R1)
- exposure to destabilizers (R2); family or social supports are missing, or alcohol and drugs are available
- lack of personal support (R3)
- noncompliance with remediation attempts (R4); refusal to attend counseling sessions or take medications
- stress (R5)

Preparation

Preparation is not desired nor recommended by medical professionals.

Precautions

When possible, the test administrator should use supplemental test measures and investigate any unique patterns of violence and its triggers in the person's history. The HCR-20 is not meant to be administered just once; the nature of risk assessment requires ongoing reassessment as circumstances change. Final interpretation of HCR-20 results should be in the context of several factors, including the reason for the person's test referral, base rates of violence in populations with similar characteristics, and assessment of future risks in the person's environment.

A professional trained in conducting individual assessments and in the study of violence should administer the HCR-20. The test administrator should have a background in using assessment tests or should consult a mental health professional. The HCR-20 is not intended to be a stand-alone measure, and it does not cover all risk factors.

Results

The HCR-20 does not allow for a definite prediction of violence. Predictions based on the HCR-20 are estimates of the likelihood of violence and should be presented in terms of low, moderate, or high probability of violence. Probability levels should be considered conditional, given short- and long-term time frames, and should be considered in relation to any relevant factors the individual may encounter. These factors include situations and states of being that may dispose a person to violence or help insulate them against it. Consideration of such factors can aid in reporting the type and extent of risk presented by a person and in selecting **intervention** strategies intended to reduce the probability that an individual will demonstrate violence. These strategies when taken as a whole are called a risk management plan.

Ultimately, HCR-20 results are intended to provide information for decision-makers, so that criminal and mental health–related decisions can be based on the best available estimates of risk of violence. Drs. Kevin Douglas and Laura Guy, both from Simon Fraser University, state, "... the HCR-20 is an attempt to merge science and practice by offering an instrument that can be integrated into clinical practice but also is empirically based and testable."

Resources

BOOKS

Webster, Christopher et. al. *HCR-20: Assessing Risk for Violence, Version 2*. Burnaby, British Columbia, Canada: Mental Health, Law, and Policy Institute, Simon Fraser University, 1997.

OTHER

Douglas, Kevin S., and Laura S. Guy. HCR-20 Violence Risk Assessment Scheme: Overview and Annotated Bibliography. January 12, 2006. http://www.cvp.se/publications/downloadables/hcr-20-bibliography-12jan2005.pdf (accessed October 8, 2011).

WEBSITES

Douglas, Kevin S., LLB, PhD. "HCR-20" http://kdouglas.wordpress.com/hcr-20 (accessed October 8, 2011).

Geoffrey G. Grimm, PhD, LPC

Histrionic personality disorder

Definition

Histrionic personality disorder, often abbreviated as HPD, is a type of personality disorder in which affected individuals display enduring patterns of attention-seeking and excessively dramatic behaviors beginning in early adulthood and present across a broad range of situations.

Individuals with HPD are highly emotional, charming, energetic, manipulative, seductive, impulsive, erratic, and demanding.

Mental health professionals use the ***Diagnostic and Statistical Manual of Mental Disorders*** (*DSM*) to diagnose mental disorders. The 2000 edition of this manual (the fourth edition, text revision, also called the *DSM-IV-TR*) classifies HPD as a personality disorder. More specifically, HPD is classified as a Cluster B (dramatic, emotional, or erratic) personality disorder. Cluster B includes the histrionic, antisocial, borderline, and narcissistic **personality disorders**.

Demographics

General United States population

The prevalence of HPD in the general population is estimated to be approximately 2%-3%.

High-risk populations

Individuals who have experienced pervasive **trauma** during childhood have been shown to be at a greater risk for developing HPD as well as for developing other personality disorders.

Cross-cultural issues

HPD may be diagnosed more frequently in Hispanic and Latin American cultures and less frequently in Asian cultures. Further research is needed on the effects of culture on the symptoms of HPD.

Gender issues

Clinicians tend to diagnose HPD more frequently in females; however, when structured assessments are used to diagnose HPD, clinicians report approximately equal prevalence rates for men and women. In considering the prevalence of HPD, it is important to recognize that gender role stereotypes may influence the behavioral display of HPD and that women and men may display HPD symptoms differently.

Diagnosis

The **diagnosis** of HPD is complicated because it may seem like many other disorders, and also because it commonly occurs simultaneously with other personality disorders. The 1994 version of the *DSM* introduced the criterion of suggestibility and the criterion of overestimation of intimacy in relationships to further refine the diagnostic criteria set of HPD, so that it could be more easily recognizable. Prior to assigning a diagnosis of HPD, clinicians need to evaluate whether the traits evident of HPD cause significant distress. (The *DSM-IV-TR* requires that the symptoms cause significant distress in order to be considered a disorder.) The diagnosis of HPD is frequently made on the basis of an individual's history and results from unstructured and semistructured interviews.

Time of onset/symptom duration

Some psychoanalysts propose that the determinants of HPD date back to early childhood. The pattern of craving attention and displaying dramatic behavior for individuals with HPD begins by early adulthood. Symptoms can last a lifetime, but may decrease or change their form with age.

Individual variations in HPD

Some classification systems distinguish between different types of individuals with HPD: patients with appeasing HPD and patients with disingenuous HPD. Individuals with appeasing HPD have personalities with histrionic, dependent, and obsessive-compulsive components. Individuals with disingenuous HPD possess personality traits that are classified as histrionic and antisocial. Studies have shown that relationships exist between somatic behaviors and women with HPD and between antisocial behaviors and men with HPD.

Dual diagnoses

HPD has been associated with alcoholism and with higher rates of **somatization disorder**, **conversion disorder**, and **major depressive disorder**. Personality disorders such as borderline, narcissistic, antisocial, and dependent can occur with HPD.

Differential diagnosis

Differential diagnosis is the process of distinguishing one mental disorder from other similar disorders. For example, at times, it is difficult to distinguish between HPD and **borderline personality disorder**. **Suicide** attempts, identity diffusion, and numerous chaotic relationships occur less frequently, however, with people diagnosed with HPD. Another example of overlap can occur between people with HPD and **dependent personality disorder**. Patients with HPD and dependent personality disorder share high dependency needs, but only dependent personality disorder is linked to high levels of self-attributed dependency needs. Whereas patients with HPD tend to be active and seductive, individuals with dependent personality disorder tend to be subservient in their demeanor.

Psychological measures

Self-report inventories and projective tests can also be used to help clinicians diagnose HPD. The Minnesota

Multiphasic Personality Inventory-2 (MMPI-2) and the Millon Clinical Multiaxial Inventory-III (MCMI-III) are self-report inventories with extensive empirical support. Results of intelligence examinations for individuals with HPD may indicate a lack of perseverance on arithmetic or on tasks that require concentration.

Description

HPD has a unique position among the personality disorders because it is the only one explicitly connected to a patient's physical appearance. Researchers have found that HPD appears primarily in men and women with above-average physical appearances. Some research has suggested that the connection between HPD and physical appearance holds for women rather than for men. Both women and men with HPD express a strong need to be the center of attention. Individuals with HPD exaggerate, throw temper tantrums, and cry if they are not the center of attention. Patients with HPD are naive and gullible and have a low frustration threshold and strong dependency needs.

Cognitive style can be defined as a way in which individuals work with and solve cognitive tasks such as reasoning, learning, thinking, understanding, making decisions, and using memory. The cognitive style of individuals with HPD is superficial and lacks detail. In their interpersonal relationships, individuals with HPD use dramatization with the goal of impressing others. The enduring pattern of their insincere and stormy relationships leads to impairment in social and occupational areas.

Causes and symptoms

Causes

There is a lack of research on the causes of HPD. Even though the causes for the disorder are not definitively known, it is thought that HPD may be caused by biological, developmental, cognitive, and social factors.

NEUROCHEMICAL/PHYSIOLOGICAL CAUSES. Studies show that patients with HPD have highly responsive noradrenergic systems, the mechanisms surrounding the release of a neurotransmitter called norepinephrine. **Neurotransmitters** are chemicals that communicate impulses from one nerve cell to another in the **brain**, and these impulses dictate behavior. The tendency toward an excessively emotional reaction to rejection, common among patients with HPD, may be attributed to a malfunction in a group of neurotransmitters called catecholamines. Norepinephrine belongs to this group of neurotransmitters.

DEVELOPMENTAL CAUSES. Most psychoanalysts agree that a traumatic childhood can contribute to the development of HPD.

Defense mechanisms are sets of systematic, unconscious methods that people develop to cope with conflict and to reduce anxiety. According to Freud, all people use defense mechanisms, but different people use different types of defense mechanisms. Individuals with HPD differ in the severity of the maladaptive defense mechanisms they use. Patients with more severe cases of HPD may use the following defense mechanisms:

- Repression. Repression is the most basic defense mechanism. When patients' thoughts produce anxiety or are unacceptable to them, they use repression to bar the unacceptable thoughts or impulses from consciousness.
- Denial. Patients who use denial may say that a prior problem no longer exists, suggesting that their competence has increased; however, others may note that there is no change in the patients' behaviors.
- Dissociation. When patients with HPD use the defense mechanism of dissociation, they may display two or more personalities. These two or more personalities exist in one individual without integration.

Patients with less severe cases of HPD tend to employ the following defenses:

- Displacement. Displacement occurs when patients shift an affect from one idea to another. For example, a man with HPD may feel angry at work because the boss did not consider him to be the center of attention. The patient may displace his anger onto his wife rather than becoming angry with his boss.
- Rationalization. Rationalization occurs when individuals explain their behaviors so that they appear to be acceptable to others.

BIOSOCIAL LEARNING CAUSES. A biosocial model in psychology asserts that social and biological factors contribute to the development of personality. Biosocial learning models of HPD suggest that individuals may acquire HPD from inconsistent interpersonal **reinforcement** offered by parents. Proponents of biosocial learning models indicate that individuals with HPD have learned to get what they want from others by drawing attention to themselves.

PERSONAL VARIABLES. Researchers have found some connections between the age of individuals with HPD and the behavior displayed by these individuals. The symptoms of HPD are long-lasting; however, histrionic character traits that are exhibited may change with age. For example, research suggests that young adults employ seductiveness more often than older ones. To impress others, older adults with HPD may shift their strategy from sexual seductiveness to a paternal or maternal seductiveness. Some histrionic symptoms such as attention-seeking, however, may become more apparent as individuals with HPD age.

Symptoms

The *DSM-IV-TR* lists eight symptoms that form the diagnostic criteria for HPD:

- Center of attention: Patients with HPD experience discomfort when they are not the center of attention.
- Sexually seductive: Patients with HPD display inappropriate sexually seductive or provocative behaviors toward others.
- Shifting emotions: The expression of emotions of patients with HPD tends to be shallow and to shift rapidly.
- Physical appearance: Individuals with HPD consistently employ physical appearance to gain attention for themselves.
- Speech style: The speech style of patients with HPD lacks detail. Individuals with HPD tend to generalize, and when these individuals speak, they aim to please and impress.
- Dramatic behaviors: Patients with HPD display self-dramatization and exaggerate their emotions.
- Suggestibility: Other individuals or circumstances can easily influence patients with HPD.
- Overestimation of intimacy: Patients with HPD overestimate the level of intimacy in a relationship.

Treatment

Psychodynamic therapy

HPD, like other personality disorders, may require several years of therapy and may affect individuals throughout their lives. Some professionals believe that psychoanalytic therapy is a treatment of choice for people with HPD because it helps patients become aware of their own feelings. Long-term psychodynamic therapy needs to target the underlying conflicts of individuals with HPD and to assist patients in decreasing their emotional reactivity. Therapists work with thematic material related to intimacy and recall. Individuals with HPD may have difficulty recalling because of their tendency to repress material.

Cognitive-behavioral therapy

Cognitive therapy is a treatment directed at reducing the dysfunctional thoughts of individuals with HPD. Such thoughts include themes about not being able to take care of oneself. Cognitive therapy for people with HPD focuses on a shift from global, suggestible thinking to a more methodical, systematic, and structured focus on problems. Cognitive-behavioral training in relaxation for individuals with HPD emphasizes challenging automatic thoughts about inferiority and not being able to handle one's life. **Cognitive-behavioral therapy** teaches individuals with HPD to identify automatic thoughts, to work on impulsive behavior, and to develop better problem-solving skills. Behavioral therapists employ **assertiveness training** to assist individuals with HPD to learn to cope using their own resources. Behavioral therapists use response cost to decrease the excessively dramatic behaviors of these individuals. Response cost is a behavioral technique that involves removing a stimulus from an individual's environment so that the response that directly precedes the removal is weakened. Behavioral therapy for HPD includes techniques such as **modeling** and behavioral rehearsal to teach patients about the effect of their theatrical behavior on others in a work setting.

Group therapy

Group therapy is suggested to assist individuals with HPD to work on interpersonal relationships. Psychodrama techniques or group role-playing can assist individuals with HPD to practice problems at work and to learn to decrease the display of excessively dramatic behaviors. Using role-playing, individuals with HPD can explore interpersonal relationships and outcomes to understand better the process associated with different scenarios. Group therapists need to monitor the group because individuals with HPD tend to take over and dominate others.

Family therapy

To teach assertion rather than avoidance of conflict, family therapists need to direct individuals with HPD to speak directly to other family members. **Family therapy** can support family members to meet their own needs without supporting the histrionic behavior of the individual with HPD who uses dramatic crises to keep the family closely connected. Family therapists employ behavioral contracts to support assertive behaviors rather than temper tantrums.

Medications

Pharmacotherapy is not a treatment of choice for individuals with HPD unless HPD occurs with another disorder. For example, if HPD occurs with **depression**, **antidepressants** may be prescribed. Medication needs to be monitored for abuse.

Alternative therapies

Meditation has been used to assist extroverted patients with HPD to relax and to focus on their own

KEY TERMS

Behavioral contracts—A behavioral contract is a written agreement that defines the behaviors to be performed and the consequences of the specified behaviors.

Biosocial—A biosocial model in psychology asserts that social and biological factors contribute toward the development of personality.

Catecholamine—A group of neurotransmitters synthesized from the amino acid tyrosine and released by the hypothalamic-pituitary-adrenal system in the brain, in response to acute stress. The catecholamines include dopamine, serotonin, norepinephrine, and epinephrine.

Cognitive style—A way in which individuals work with and perform cognitive tasks such as reasoning, learning, thinking, understanding, making decisions, and using memory.

Differential diagnosis—The process of distinguishing one disorder from other similar disorders.

Disingenuous—Insincere, deceitful, dishonest.

Dissociation—A reaction to trauma in which the mind splits off certain aspects of the traumatic event from conscious awareness. Dissociation can affect the patient's memory, sense of reality, and sense of identity.

Etiology—The cause or origin of a disease or disorder. The word is also used to refer to the study of the causes of disease.

Histrionic—Theatrical.

Identity diffusion—A character formation that is scattered or spread around rather than an identity that becomes solidified or consolidated.

Noradrenergic—Acts similarly to norepinephrine or noradrenaline.

Oral phase—The first of Freud's psychosexual stages of development in which satisfaction is focused on the mouth and lips. During this stage sucking and eating are the primary means of gratification.

Personality disorder—A personality disorder is a maladaptive pattern of behavior, affect, and/or cognitive style displayed in a broad range of settings. The pattern deviates from the accepted norms of the individual's culture and can occur over a lifetime.

Response cost—A behavioral technique that involves removing a stimulus from an individual's environment so that the response that directly precedes the removal is weakened. In a token economy system, response cost is a form of punishment involving loss of tokens due to inappropriate behavior, which consequently results in decreased ability to purchase backup reinforcers.

Somatic—Relating to the body or to the physical.

inner feelings. Some therapists employ hypnosis to assist individuals with HPD to relax when they experience a fast heart rate or palpitations during an expression of excessively dramatic, emotional, and excitable behavior.

Prognosis

The personality characteristics of individuals with HPD are long-lasting. Individuals with HPD use medical services frequently, but they usually do not stay in psychotherapeutic treatment long enough to make changes. They tend to set vague goals and to move toward something more exciting. Treatment for HPD can take a minimum of one to three years and tends to take longer than treatment for disorders that are not personality disorders, such as anxiety or mood disorders. Suicidal tendencies are common in people with HPD and should always be taken seriously.

As individuals with HPD age, they display fewer symptoms. Some research suggests that the difference between older and younger individuals may be attributed to the fact that older individuals have less energy.

Research indicates that a relationship exists between poor treatment outcomes and premature termination from treatment for individuals with Cluster B personality disorders. Some researchers suggest that studies that link HPD to continuation in treatment need to consider the connection between overestimates of intimacy and premature termination from therapy.

Prevention

Early diagnosis can assist patients and family members to recognize the pervasive pattern of reactive emotion among individuals with HPD. Educating people, particularly mental health professionals, about the enduring character traits of individuals with HPD may prevent some cases of mild histrionic behavior from developing into full-blown cases of maladaptive HPD.

Further research in prevention needs to investigate the relationship between variables such as age, gender, culture, and ethnicity in people with HPD.

Resources

BOOKS

American Psychiatric Association. *Diagnostic and Statistical Manual of Mental Disorders*. 4th ed., text rev. Washington, DC: American Psychiatric Publishing, 2000.

Bockian, Neil, and Arthur E. Jongsma, Jr. *The Personality Disorders Treatment Planner*. New York: Wiley, 2001.

Bornstein, Robert F., and Iris L. Malka. "Dependent and Histrionic Personality Disorders." In *Oxford Textbook of Psychopathology*, edited by Theodore Millon and Paul H. Blaney. New York: Oxford University Press, 2008.

Widiger, Thomas A., and Robert F. Bornstein. "Histrionic, Narcissistic, and Dependent Personality Disorders." In *Comprehensive Handbook of Psychopathology*, edited by Patricia B. Sutker and Henry E. Adams. 3rd ed. New York: Springer Science, 2004.

PERIODICALS

Bornstein, Robert F. "Histrionic Personality Disorder, Physical Attractiveness, and Social Adjustment." *Journal of Psychopathology and Behavioral Assessment* 21, no. 1 (March 1999): 79–94.

Bornstein, Robert F. "Implicit and Self-Attributed Dependency Needs in Dependent and Histrionic Personality Disorders." *Journal of Personality Assessment* 71, no. 1 (August 1998): 1–14.

Hilsenroth, Mark J., et al. "The Effects of DSM-IV Cluster B Personality Disorder Symptoms on the Termination and Continuation of Psychotherapy." *Psychotherapy* 35, no. 2 (Summer 1998): 163–76.

ORGANIZATIONS

American Psychiatric Association, 1000 Wilson Blvd., Ste. 1825, Arlington, VA, 22209-3901, (703) 907-7300, apa@psych.org, http://www.psych.org.

American Psychological Association, 750 1st Street NE, Washington, DC, 20002-4242, (202) 336-5500; TDD/TTY: (202) 336-6123, (800) 374-2721, http://www.apa.org.

Judy Koenigsberg, PhD
Emily Jane Willingham, PhD

HMO *see* **Managed care**

Hoarding

Definition

Hoarding is a behavior that leads to the accumulation of objects or pets in the household to the point that the items or animals interfere with daily life and prevent the hoarder's living space from being used for its intended purposes. In some cases, the clutter may pose safety or health hazards. The modern English word *hoard* comes from an Old English or Germanic word meaning "to cover" or "to conceal." Compulsive hoarding is also known as "pathological hoarding" or "disposophobia."

Demographics

Psychiatrists estimate that between 2% and 5% of the adult population in the United States and Canada are compulsive hoarders, with about 4,000 cases of animal hoarding involving up to 250,000 reported animals each year in North America. It is possible that the actual rate of hoarding disorder is higher, as researchers only began to study hoarding in the 1980s, which means that relatively little is known about it in comparison to such disorders as **depression** or **panic disorder**. In addition, many hoarders never seek help for their condition because they do not see it as a problem. Researchers think that hoarding is more prevalent among older adults, although it typically begins in late childhood or adolescence and becomes progressively worse as the person grows older. There are relatively few cases of late-onset hoarding.

There is no indication that race or ethnicity is a factor in hoarding. Women typically begin hoarding at earlier ages than men, but men are more likely than women to become hoarders. With regard to content, clothes, books, and newspapers or magazines are the most commonly hoarded items, but almost any imaginable object can be hoarded. Other commonly hoarded objects include empty boxes and deli containers, junk mail, and craft items.

Description

Hoarding behavior is a combination of three factors: inability to discard unnecessary items, accumulation of a large number of possessions, and difficulty organizing living space. The working group of psychiatrists specializing in **obsessive-compulsive disorder** (OCD) and related disorders for the fifth edition of the ***Diagnostic and Statistical Manual of Mental Disorders*** (*DSM-5*) has proposed adding hoarding disorder to the new edition on the grounds that hoarding differs from OCD in several significant respects, and that inclusion of the disorder would draw greater public awareness.

Hoarding is a complex disorder in that each of the three factors may develop in different ways in different people.

Tendency to accumulate many items:

- Many hoarders are also compulsive shoppers, and may purchase multiples of each item rather than only one.

A man prepares to clean out the home of his recently deceased mother, who suffered from hoarding disorder. *(© Sandy Huffaker/Corbis News/Corbis)*

Male hoarders appear to favor such items as hardware, automotive equipment, and electronic gadgets, while women are more likely to purchase jewelry and cosmetics. Both sexes are equally likely to buy clothing, shoes, compact discs, and household items on their shopping sprees.

- About 50% of hoarders report excessive collecting of free items.
- Excessive collecting can also occur without effort, as when the hoarder accumulates boxes or packing material from mail-order purchases.

Difficulty discarding unneeded or useless items:

- Hoarders find it emotionally difficult to throw away, give away, sell, or recycle unused items.
- The most frequent reasons hoarders give for holding on to their possessions are thrift; not wanting to lose the informational content of such items as books, records, magazines; sentimental or emotional attachment to the item; and liking the way the object looks or feels.
- In some cases, the hoarder has tried to clean out the clutter but finds the process so time-consuming that he or she gives up.

Disorganization:

- Many hoarders have difficulty organizing their possessions because they are easily distracted or have problems with information processing (classifying their possessions in order to create and organize storage spaces for them).
- It is not uncommon for hoarders simply to move piles of items from one location to another without effective reorganization.

Researchers who have studied hoarding note that it is different from collecting items of interest to an individual or having some clutter in the home. Collectors usually keep their valued items well organized and often group them in attractive or informative arrangements that others with the same hobby or interest can enjoy. By contrast, hoarders rarely organize their acquisitions. With regard to clutter, having a desk, attic, basement, closet, or other limited part of the house that is cluttered is not by itself evidence of hoarding. It is when the clutter results from excessive acquisition and refusal to discard items, overflows into all living areas, blocks exits, and otherwise interferes with daily activities that it becomes a sign of hoarding.

Hoarding associated with obsessive-compulsive disorder

When hoarding first became a topic of interest to psychiatrists in the 1980s, it was thought to be a subtype of obsessive-compulsive disorder (OCD), an anxiety disorder characterized by intrusive thoughts that produce anxiety (obsessions) accompanied by repetitive behaviors intended to relieve the anxiety (compulsions). Many psychiatrists maintain, however, that most cases of hoarding are not associated with OCD, because the hoarder shows no signs of anxiety and genuinely enjoys his or her possessions. Unlike people with OCD, who recognize that their obsessions and compulsions are abnormal, most hoarders consider their behavior normal and acceptable. The minority of hoarding cases identified with OCD have the following four characteristics:

- Throwing away the item(s) is linked to fear of contamination (from touching the object), fear of catastrophe from discarding the object, or fear of incompleteness (loss of symmetry).
- The hoarder derives no pleasure from the hoarded objects.
- The hoarder has no sentimental attachment to the hoarded items.
- Excessive acquisition is rare in cases of OCD hoarding.

Hoarding in older adults

Hoarding among seniors is increasingly regarded as a serious public health concern as well as a danger to the elderly themselves. First, it is now known that hoarding is more common among older adults than among younger ones; this finding is interesting given the fact that the only other psychiatric disorder that is known to worsen with increasing age is **dementia**. It is not yet known whether hoarding in the elderly is an early indication of dementia or whether dementia follows an earlier history of hoarding.

Hoarding can cause health problems for seniors, given that many suffer from physical as well as cognitive impairments. One study of elderly hoarders found that 45% could not get to their refrigerators because of clutter, 42% could not use their kitchen sink, 42% could not reach their bathtub, 20% could not use their bathroom sink, and 10% could not use their toilet. The space occupied by hoarded items increases the senior's risk of falls, fires, rodent infestation due to unsanitary conditions, and malnutrition resulting from inability to store and prepare food properly. Some seniors on fixed incomes also report **financial stress** from making unnecessary purchases, having to pay for self-storage units, or having to pay housing fines.

Animal hoarding

Animal hoarding was first defined as follows by a research consortium established at Tufts University in 1997:

- The hoarder has more than the typical number of companion animals (cats, dogs, rabbits, hamsters, and birds); however, there are also cases of people hoarding farm animals, wild animals (raccoons, wolves), and exotic animals (snakes, alligators, tigers).
- The hoarder fails to provide even minimal standards of food and water, cleanliness, shelter, and veterinary care. This neglect often results in the animals' illness and death from starvation, spread of infectious disease, and untreated injuries.
- The hoarder is in denial of his or her inability to provide for the animals as well as the effects of that failure on the animals, the house, and other human occupants of the building.
- The hoarder persists in accumulating more animals in spite of failure to care for those already in his or her possession.

Almost any type of animal can be hoarded, although cats appear to be the species most commonly hoarded because they are small, easy to obtain, and easily concealed. Most animal hoarders concentrate on only one species, although there are also many cases of hoarders found with several animal species in their households. It is not known whether there are any psychological factors that influence a hoarder's preference for a particular animal species. Animal hoarders are found among men as well as women, and among medical and veterinary professionals as well as persons with lower levels of education.

Animal hoarding is a type of hoarding behavior that differs from the hoarding of inanimate objects in several important respects. Animal hoarders are usually more disturbed emotionally and have much less insight into their disorder than persons who hoard objects. Their hoarding behavior causes genuine suffering to the animals, many of whom end up being euthanized when the hoarding is discovered, because of advanced infectious disease, malnutrition, or behavior problems caused by the overcrowding. Animal hoarding also presents a considerable public health problem associated with the transmission of zoonoses, a group of infectious viral, bacterial, parasitic, fungal, or prion diseases that can be transmitted from animals to humans or from humans to animals. In addition, animal hoarders are more likely than hoarders of objects to come in contact with the criminal justice system, because most states have stiff legal penalties for animal cruelty; Illinois and Hawaii explicitly mention hoarding as a form of animal cruelty in their relevant legislation.

There is little agreement among psychiatrists as to the best model for explaining animal hoarding. Some consider it an **addiction** similar to a substance addiction, others regard it as a form of OCD, still others think it is best explained as an attachment disorder, and a fourth group regards it as a **delusional disorder** (a disorder in which the person is out of touch with reality).

Risk factors

Risk factors for hoarding disorder include:

- Age. Hoarding seems to begin in late childhood or early adolescence and gets worse during adulthood. School-age children often begin by hoarding such items as broken toys, pens and pencils, old school papers, or old clocks and other small appliances. The disorder becomes more noticeable in adults in their 20s and 30s and a serious problem in those in their 40s and 50s.
- Family history. People who have a family member who is a hoarder are much more likely to become hoarders themselves.
- Traumatic experiences. Such events as death of a loved one (including a pet), divorce, eviction, or losing treasured possessions in a fire or earthquake appear to trigger hoarding in some people.
- Alcohol abuse. About 50% of hoarders have a history of alcoholism.
- Social isolation. This risk factor appears to work in both directions; some people withdraw from human companionship because they are hoarders, whereas others report that they turned to hoarding because they were lonely.

Causes and symptoms

Causes

The causes of hoarding are unclear; however, the disorder is known to run in families, so it is possible that a combination of **genetic factors** and family upbringing contributes to the disorder. A 2007 study published in the *American Journal of Psychiatry* postulated that a region in chromosome 14 might link to the development of compulsive hoarding in families with OCD, but further research is needed.

Another theory maintains that hoarders have different patterns of **brain** activation; namely, that the parts of the brain that control such functions as focusing attention, making decisions, and organizing operate differently in hoarders. One **psychologist** has noted that hoarders pay much more attention to the unusual details of an object (its color, shape, and texture) rather than its use, and that they tend to identify their sense of an object's location visually or spatially (for example, "it's six inches down from the top in the pile of papers on the desk in the back bedroom") rather than by category (for example, "bills to be paid"). Another psychological characteristic that differentiates hoarders of objects from other people is a tendency to humanize their possessions; that is, they attribute human-like qualities to the objects and feel genuine **grief** at the thought of parting with them. Hoarders also form emotional attachments to a wider variety of objects than people who don't hoard.

Symptoms

The symptoms of hoarding include:

- large amounts of clutter in the home or office that make it difficult to move around easily, get work done, or use furniture or appliances
- losing money, bills, or other important items in the clutter
- feeling overwhelmed by the sheer volume of possessions
- being unable to stop taking free items from restaurants or displays
- purchasing multiples of items in order to stock up or because the item is a bargain
- refusing to let repair people into the home
- not inviting friends or family to the home because of embarrassment about the clutter

Diagnosis

There are no laboratory or imaging tests that can diagnose hoarding disorder. The **American Psychiatric Association** (APA) has proposed the following criteria for hoarding disorder to be included in *DSM-5*:

- Criterion A: The person is persistently unable to discard or part with possessions, without regard to the value others place on those items.
- Criterion B: The difficulty arises from strong urges to save items and/or emotional distress at the thought of discarding them.
- Criterion C: The items accumulate to the point that the intended use of the living space or workplace is no longer possible (or the living space is uncluttered only because of the intervention of family members or other third parties).
- Criterion D: The symptoms cause clinically significant distress or impairment in the person's social, occupational, or academic functioning, including maintaining

KEY TERMS

Attachment disorder—A general term used to describe emotional and behavioral problems in children or adults resulting from a failure to form healthy attachments in early childhood to parents or other primary caregivers.

Delusional disorder—A mental illness characterized by the presence of nonbizarre delusions in the absence of other mood or psychotic symptoms. "Nonbizarre" means that the delusion is about a situation that could occur in real life, such as being followed or losing a loved one. In the case of an animal hoarder, the delusion would be that the animals would die or be euthanized if the hoarder did not house them.

Semi-structured interview—A type of psychiatric interview in which the interviewer can ask new questions in the course of the interview, depending on the interviewee's answers to previous questions.

Zoonosis (plural, zoonoses)—Any contagious disease that can be transmitted from nonhuman animals to humans or from humans to nonhuman animals. Zoonoses include viral, bacterial, parasitic, fungal, and prion diseases.

a safe environment for the person and others in the household.

- Criterion E: The hoarding symptoms are not due to a general medical condition (e.g., brain injury, heart disease).
- Criterion F: The hoarding symptoms are not restricted to the symptoms of another mental disorder (e.g., lack of energy in major depression, delusions in schizophrenia, loss of cognitive abilities in dementia)

The proposal also includes two specifiers. The first concerns excessive acquisition; that is, the symptoms "are accompanied by excessive collecting or buying or stealing of items that are not needed or for which there is no available space." The second qualifier concerns the person's degree of insight into their condition, which the **psychiatrist** can rate as "good or fair," "poor," or "absent."

Tests

There are several pencil-and-paper tests that people can take to evaluate whether they have a hoarding disorder. One is the Saving Inventory Revised (SIR), which is a 23-item scale that measures three dimensions of hoarding: excessive acquisition, difficulty discarding, and clutter. Another test is the Hoarding Rating Scale (HRS), which is a five-item semi-structured interview. The URLs for the PDF versions of these two tests are included in the Websites section of the Resources.

Treatment

Treatment of hoarding disorder is a subject of ongoing research. With regard to medications, it was the discovery that hoarders do not respond to the medications usually prescribed for OCD that led researchers to suggest that hoarding is a distinctive disorder rather than a subtype of OCD. While some psychiatrists think that **selective serotonin reuptake inhibitors (SSRIs)** are directly beneficial in treating hoarding, most specialists believe that SSRIs are primarily useful in treating the anxiety or depression associated with hoarding rather than the disorder itself.

Individualized **cognitive-behavioral therapy** (CBT) has been found to be helpful in patients who hoard inanimate objects. The reason for tailoring the specific interventions to each patient is that hoarders vary widely in the types of items they hoard and their reasons for hoarding. CBT for hoarding involves a combination of motivational training (giving the person a reason to stop hoarding), skills training (how to organize possessions and living space), and behavioral experiments (e.g., going shopping without buying anything, or throwing away a specific item) designed to help the person revise their thoughts and feelings about their possessions.

Group therapy is another approach that works well for hoarders. First, it breaks down their social isolation and feelings of shame about the condition of their homes. Second, group therapy helps increase motivation as the group's members swap tips about organization skills, cleaning up clutter, and the like. Third, group therapy lowers the depression and anxiety that many hoarders feel. Internet-based **support groups**, including some for adult sons and daughters of hoarders, are reported to be effective in maintaining the benefits of CBT.

Professional organizers may also be able to help patients with hoarding disorder develop and strengthen organizational skills. Professional organizers can help clients establish systems (e.g., filing) for maintaining organization and teach clients to prioritize activities, which may help persons with hoarding disorder feel more in control of their actions.

Treatment of animal hoarders is much more difficult than therapy for hoarders of objects. As noted above, animal hoarders are usually more seriously disturbed than

QUESTIONS TO ASK YOUR DOCTOR

- Do you have special expertise in helping people with hoarding disorders?
- What are my treatment options?
- What is your opinion of CBT as a treatment for hoarding disorder?
- Will my family be involved in treatment in any way?

other hoarders, and their rate of **relapse** is close to 100% even after receiving fines or prison sentences for animal **abuse**. There was no established effective therapy for animal hoarding as of 2011, although some observers think that placing animal hoarders under extended probation with regular visits from a probation officer would be more effective than a prison term to prevent reoffending.

There were two **clinical trials** that focused solely on hoarding in 2011 (as opposed to including hoarding as a symptom of OCD). One trial was investigating the use of **methylphenidate** ER (Daytrana) as a pharmacological treatment for hoarding, and the other was testing the effectiveness of **cognitive remediation** and **exposure treatment**.

Prognosis

The prognosis of hoarding disorder depends on the person's motivation to change and such other factors as involvement with the legal system. Individualized CBT is reported to be effective in about 70% to 80% of patients. In general, hoarders of animals have a considerably worse prognosis than hoarders of objects.

Prevention

There is no known way to prevent hoarding disorder.

Resources

BOOKS

Antony, Martin M., and Murray B. Stein, eds. *Oxford Handbook of Anxiety and Related Disorders*. New York: Oxford University Press, 2009.

Arluke, Arnold, and Celeste Killeen. *Inside Animal Hoarding: The Case of Barbara Erickson and Her 552 Dogs*. West Lafayette, IN: Purdue University Press, 2009.

Frost, Randy O., and Gail Steketee. *Stuff: Compulsive Hoarding and the Meaning of Things*. Boston, MA: Houghton Mifflin Harcourt, 2010.

Sholl, Jessie. *Dirty Secret: A Daughter Comes Clean about Her Mother's Compulsive Hoarding*. New York: Gallery Books, 2011.

Tolin, David F., Randy O. Frost, and Gail Steketee. *Buried in Treasures: Help for Compulsive Acquiring, Saving, and Hoarding*. New York: Oxford University Press, 2007.

PERIODICALS

Kurutz, Steven. "Children of Hoarders on Leaving the Cluttered Nest." *New York Times*, May 12, 2011. http://www.nytimes.com/2011/05/12/garden/children-of-hoarders-on-leaving-the-cluttered-nest.html?_r=2&hpw=&pagewanted=all (accessed August 3, 2011).

Lambros, Valerie. "Hoarding Disorder Can Have Dangerous Ramifications." *NIH Record*, January 21, 2011. http://nihrecord.od.nih.gov/newsletters/2011/01_21_2011/story1.htm (accessed July 17, 2011).

Mackin, R.S., et al. "Cognitive Functioning in Individuals with Severe Compulsive Hoarding Behaviors and Late Life Depression." *International Journal of Geriatric Psychiatry* 26 (March 2011): 314–321.

Mataix-Cois, D., et al. "Testing the Validity and Acceptability of the Diagnostic Criteria for Hoarding Disorder: a DSM-5 Survey." *Psychological Medicine* 13 (May 2011): 1–10.

Morgan, Kim. "Getting Help to Overcome a Hoarding Disorder." *Houston Chronicle*, March 16, 2010. http://www.chron.com/disp/story.mpl/life/main/6915900.html (accessed July 17, 2011).

Samuels, Jack, et al. "Significant Linkage to Compulsive Hoarding on Chromosome 14 in Families With Obsessive-Compulsive Disorder: Results From the OCD Collaborative Genetics Study." *American Journal of Psychiatry* 164 (March 2007): 493–99. http://dx.doi.org/10.1176/appi.ajp.164.3.493 (accessed September 14, 2011).

Saxena, S. "Pharmacotherapy of Compulsive Hoarding." *Journal of Clinical Psychology* 67 (May 2011): 477–484.

Steketee, G., and D.F. Tolin. "Cognitive-Behavioral Therapy for Hoarding in the Context of Contamination Fears." *Journal of Clinical Psychology* 67 (May 2011): 485–496.

Storch, E.A., et al. "Compulsive Hoarding in Children." *Journal of Clinical Psychology* 67 (May 2011): 507–516.

Timpano, K.R., et al. "The Epidemiology of the Proposed DSM-5 Hoarding Disorder: Exploration of the Acquisition Specifier, Associated Features, and Distress." *Journal of Clinical Psychiatry* 72 (June 2011): 780–786.

Tolin, D.F. and A. Villavicencio. "Inattention, but not OCD, Predicts the Core Features of Hoarding Disorder." *Behaviour Research and Therapy* 49 (February 2011): 120–125.

Wick, J.Y. and G.R. Zanni. "Helping Those with Hoarding Behaviors." *Consultant Pharmacist* 26 (July 2011): 458–467.

OTHER

International OCD Foundation Hoarding Center. "Hoarding Rating Scale (HRS)." http://www.ocfoundation.org/uploadedFiles/Hoarding/Resources/Hoarding%20Rating%20Scale%20with%20interpret.pdf (accessed July 17, 2011).

———. "Saving Inventory Revised (SIR)." http://www.ocfoundation.org/uploadedFiles/Hoarding/Resources/SI-R%28ModifiedFormat%29.pdf (accessed July 17, 2011).

WEBSITES

"About Hoarding." International OCD Foundation Hoarding Center. http://www.ocfoundation.org/hoarding/about.aspx (accessed July 17, 2011).

American Psychiatric Association. "F 02 Hoarding Disorder." DSM-5 Development. http://www.dsm5.org/proposedrevision/pages/proposedrevision.aspx?rid=398 (accessed July 17, 2011).

"Animal Hoarding." American Society for the Prevention of Cruelty to Animals (ASPCA). http://www.aspca.org/aspca-nyc/animal-rescuers/animal-hoarding.aspx (accessed July 17, 2011).

Children of Hoarders: Awareness, Understanding, and Support for COH. http://childrenofhoarders.com/wordpress (accessed July 18, 2011).

"Common Questions about Animal Hoarding." Hoarding of Animals Research Consortium (HARC). http://www.tufts.edu/vet/hoarding/abthoard.htm (accessed July 17, 2011).

Johns Hopkins Health Alerts. "Hoarding: From Cluttered to Clinical." Johns Hopkins Medicine. http://www.johnshopkinshealthalerts.com/alerts/depression_anxiety/hoarding_3826-1.html (accessed July 17, 2011).

Mayo Clinic staff. "Hoarding." MayoClinic.com. http://www.mayoclinic.com/health/hoarding/DS00966 (accessed July 17, 2011).

National Public Radio. "Hoarding: When Too Much 'Stuff' Causes Grief." *Fresh Air from WHYY* [radio program]. http://www.npr.org/templates/story/story.php?storyId=126386317 (accessed September 14, 2011).

Song, Anna, and KATU Web Staff. "Living Landfill: A Portrait of Hoarding Disorder." *KOMO News*, April 28, 2007. http://www.komonews.com/news/local/7224116.html (accessed July 17, 2011).

ORGANIZATIONS

American Psychiatric Association, 1000 Wilson Boulevard, Suite 1825, Arlington, VA, 22209-3901, (703) 907-7300, apa@psych.org, http://www.psych.org.

American Society for the Prevention of Cruelty to Animals (ASPCA), 424 E. 92nd Street, New York, NY, 10128-6804, (212) 876-7700, http://www.aspca.org.

Hoarding of Animals Research Consortium (HARC), c/o Gary Patronek, Animal Rescue League of Boston, 10 Chandler Street, Boston, MA, 02116, (617) 426-9170, Fax: (617) 426-3028, cfapp@tufts.edu, http://www.tufts.edu/vet/hoarding.

International OCD Foundation Hoarding Center, PO Box 961029, Boston, MA, 02196, (617) 973-5801, Fax: (617) 973-5803, info@ocfoundation.org, http://www.ocfoundation.org/hoarding.

Rebecca J. Frey, Ph.D.

Homelessness

Definition

In the United States, definitions of homelessness help determine who can receive shelter and assistance from certain health and social service providers. The Stewart McKinney Homeless Assistance Act of 1987 defines a homeless person as any individual who lacks housing, including an individual whose primary residence during the night is a supervised public or private facility that provides temporary living accommodations, or an individual who is a resident in transitional housing. More specifically, this means that a homeless person is any individual who lacks fixed, regular, and adequate nighttime residence, and an individual who has a primary nighttime residence that is either (i) a supervised temporary living shelter (including transitional housing for the mentally ill), (ii) an institution that provides temporary residence for individuals intended to be institutionalized, or (iii) a place not designed for, or ordinarily used as, a regular sleeping accommodation for human beings.

In addition, the U.S. Department of Housing and Urban Development (HUD) defines chronic homelessness as "an unaccompanied disabled individual who has been continuously homeless for over one year."

Demographics

Methods for estimating the size of the homeless population are evolving and sometimes contested, and are complicated by varying definitions of homelessness. The U.S. Census, while attempting to identify the number of people who are homeless and who use particular types of homeless services, has complex and service-based definitions of homelessness. It also has recognized its limited abilities to define and enumerate the homeless (it is after all a national household survey). In 2000, the Census Bureau defined the Emergency and Transitional Shelter (E&TS) population by surveying people who used a sample of homeless services. They counted homeless people in emergency shelters for adults, runaway youth shelters, shelters for abused women and their children, soup kitchens, and certain outdoor locations. Technically, however, homeless people may reside in "E&TS," in foster care, in jails and prisons, in **group homes**, in worker dorms, non-sheltered in the outdoors, doubled up with families or friends, or temporarily in Census-recognized households. According to the National Coalition for the Homeless, while counting the number of people who use services such as shelters and soup kitchens can yield important information about services, applying these numbers toward estimating numbers of homeless people can result in underestimates of homelessness.

Further complicating the issue of counting homeless people is the fact that in many cases, homelessness is a temporary condition. Because of this fact, some researchers advocate a method of counting all the people who are homeless in a given week or, alternatively, over a given period. However, the numbers of people who find housing and the number of people who newly find themselves homeless fluctuate over time. In contrast, people with mental illness or **substance abuse** problems tend to be chronically without homes—it is difficult for many of these people to find permanent housing. Thus, while these two time-oriented methods of counting homeless can be useful, they, too, have statistical problems—they can overestimate the numbers of homeless people.

According to the 2010 Census, the number of people utilizing emergency shelters and transitional housing was 424,042. However, this figure does not include homeless adults not using such services, sampling error, or some groups outside of the sampled jurisdictions.

Another estimate of homelessness, in a 2007 report by the National Alliance to End Homelessness, estimated that 744,313 people were homeless in 2005. Forty-four percent of those people were unsheltered, and 56% were sheltered. Forty-one percent of the homeless were families.

According to the National Law Center on Homelessness and Poverty, about 3.5 million people (of these about 1.35 million children) are likely to experience homelessness at least once in any given year. This statistic is much higher than the other ones, based on its more relaxed definition of homelessness.

The large variation among these estimates illustrates that, as the National Coalition for the Homeless states, "By its very nature, homelessness is impossible to measure with 100% accuracy."

Description

Homelessness is an acute version of residential instability, which can be compared or contrasted with definitions of poverty. Thus the term "homeless" may also be extended to include people who have nowhere to go and are at imminent risk of losing housing through eviction or institutional discharge. Some definitions of homelessness further specify the duration of time without regular and adequate residence, or the types of temporary living shelter or institutions that are not fixed residences. People who live without alternatives in overcrowded or unhealthy housing conditions may be at risk of homelessness. Worldwide, national, and cultural groups may have variable, and often different, definitions of homelessness, different terms for the condition of being without housing, and different definitions of adequate housing. For all of these reasons, related both to methods of counting and varying definitions, estimating the size of the homeless population is extremely difficult.

The history of homelessness is intertwined with the history of poverty in the United States. Poverty has always been problematic for humanitarian reasons and because it conflicts with the ideal of prosperity for all. Social welfare, based on individualistic ideas of the deserving and undeserving poor, has improved society but not eliminated persistent poverty or homelessness. The 1960s war on poverty was a widely shared value but, in the 1980s, concern about homelessness was confounded by moral evaluations of individual behaviors. While many in the United States have been poor or come from poor families, fewer have experienced homelessness. Therefore, the collective understanding of homelessness in the United States is limited in ways that the understanding of poverty is not.

Homeless adults are poor and have high rates of unmet need for health care. This is in part because poverty is associated with higher risk and rates of illness, particularly mental illnesses including substance abuse. Homeless people experience disproportionate rates and symptoms of mental health disorders, including substance-abuse disorders and dual diagnoses. For these reasons, large portions of federally funded homeless services are medical services, and homeless people are often viewed according to their present or past medical classifications.

Studies researching the incidence, distribution, and control of a disease in a population (known as epidemiological studies) find that between one-third and one-half of homeless people have mental health disorders, and approximately two-thirds have either a mental health or substance-abuse disorder. People with severe mental illness are likewise more likely to become homeless particularly when the disorder is co-morbid (co-occurring) with substance abuse. For this reason, changes in rates of homelessness are often associated with changes in mental health care and **hospitalization** policies.

Mental illnesses compound the vulnerability and needs of homeless adults, as reported by the Surgeon General. Psychiatric disorders exacerbate many types of problems, including housing instability, morbidity (disease), and mortality (death). Psychiatric disorders and lack of stable living conditions complicate general health care for homeless adults.

Causes and consequences

Causes

People with mental illness are at higher risk for becoming homeless due to challenges associated with **deinstitutionalization** and transition planning, and both poverty and disability associated with mental illness.

Social research has studied the causes and consequences of homelessness, surveying homeless people, examining entrances into homelessness, exits from homelessness, and effects of homelessness on health and well-being. Promising explanations for increasing rates of homelessness in the 1980s have included mental disability and illness, lack of social support through jobs and marriage, increased use of drugs and alcohol, and the erosion of low-income housing in urban areas. These explanations mirror the processes of deinstitutionalization in mental health policy, unemployment, **addiction** and abuse, and urban decay. In other words, a direct correlation can be demonstrated between policies and trends, and the rates of homelessness. As deinstitutionalization occurred, for example, the number of mentally ill people without homes increased.

Consequences

Consequences of homelessness include the exacerbation of problems that may have caused homelessness. Homeless people have reduced access to housing, jobs, health care, and basic needs like food and clothing. Isolation and lack of social support are well-documented aspects of homelessness, particularly for homeless people living with mental health or substance abuse disorders. Homeless women and men have been found to have significantly less family support than never-homeless women and men. Disaffiliation from family often limits opportunities for recovery and prevention.

Treatment

Whatever the underlying reason for homelessness (such as poor health, be it mental or physical), two forms of treatment include employment and housing. A person living in a sheltered dwelling is better protected against the myriad causes of homelessness than is a person who is without shelter. People who were previously homeless, but are now living in a home, have a much better chance to recover from the underlying cause(s) of their homelessness.

Treating the underlying causes and eliminating (or managing) them is the first step back to employment and eventually to permanent housing. Private and public projects contribute to the treatment of homelessness, including better education and training of such individuals within the workforce. For instance, case-management programs for the homeless, such as **assertive community treatment** (ACT), can help to ensure that such programs are more effective.

KEY TERMS

Assertive community treatment—An approach to mental health services within a small population that helps individuals manage their mental illness with respect to themselves, family members, work associates, and the community at large.

Epidemiological—The study of the origin, cause, and transmission of diseases.

Mentally ill—A person with a psychiatric disorder of mental faculties.

Psychiatric disorders—Any behavioral or psychological symptoms that impair basic bodily functions and increase one's risk of death and disability.

Prognosis

Homelessness is both a form of poverty and an acute condition of residential instability. Homelessness is compounded by behavioral problems, mental health policy changes, disparities in health and health care, racial inequalities, fluctuations in affordable housing, and lack of social support.

Homelessness in context

Overly individualistic views and explanations of homelessness do not reflect its multiple causes and effects. Like all groups, homeless people are diverse, experiencing and exiting homelessness for a myriad of reasons. Services for homeless adults likewise reflect a variety of needs and experiences. Nonetheless, homelessness remains a national and international concern, particularly in urban areas, for the twenty-first century.

Prevention

Homelessness can be minimized, and in some instances prevented, with the use of effective strategies within homeless service agencies and among individualized efforts. For instance, in 2002, the U.S. Department of Housing and Urban Development (HUD), the Department of Health and Human Services (HHS), and Veterans Affairs (VA) began a combined effort to reduce chronic homelessness in the United States. The grant-funded program provides access by homeless persons to health and social services, along with employment programs. The program guarantees that at least 30% of the grant money goes to providing permanent housing to the homeless.

Homeless service agencies

Services for homeless people can be divided into those providing medical care (including mental health care), those providing housing, and those providing other basic needs. Publicly funded agencies provide the majority of medical care, especially primary and mental health care. Public and private organizations share the responsibilities of providing shelter and housing services, through both large federal programs and smaller need- and faith-based programs. Private agencies deliver most other daily needs to homeless people, through food pantries, soup kitchens, and other charities. Limited data exist on vocational services for homeless adults.

Title VI of the McKinney Homeless Assistance Act of 1987 created the Health Care for the Homeless (HCH) program, authorizing federal funds for primary and mental health care to homeless people. Title VI authorizes several programs to provide an HCH program, a **Community Mental Health** Services block grant program, and two demonstration programs providing mental health and alcohol and drug abuse treatment services to homeless people. HCH funds support providers who offer mental health, **case management**, and health education services, as well as substance-abuse treatment. In 1987, 109 grants were made for homeless health services with $46 million. In 1992, the Act was amended to include homeless and at-risk children, creating a medical home and source of health insurance for young people. In 2010, Congress appropriated $171 million for grants for health care for the homeless. The HCH program is the largest single effort to address the medical needs of the homeless. Each year, the HCH Program serves around 600,000 clients in the United States. To be an HCH service agency requires cultural and linguistic competencies, compassionate community outreach, and providers who reflect the community they serve.

The federal Center for Mental Health Services oversees the Projects for Assistance in Transition from Homelessness (PATH) grant program. The program provides state funds in support services to individuals who are homeless or at risk of becoming homeless, and to those who have serious mental illnesses. These funds amounted to more than $52 million allocated to 463 providers in 2005. States contract with local agencies and nonprofit organizations to provide an array of services, including outreach, support services, a limited set of housing services, and mental health treatment.

QUESTIONS TO ASK YOUR DOCTOR

- What programs are available locally for homelessness?
- Where can medical care be found?
- Where is temporary housing available?
- Is affordable permanent housing available?
- What employment-assistance problems are available?
- What support groups area found in the area?

There are several obstacles or barriers in providing health care to homeless people. First, homeless or persistently poor people may be concerned about their work and sustenance, devaluing their own medical needs. Alienation and **depression** among the homeless can also be an obstacle to providing care. There can be mutual communication problems between providers and patients. Providers may lack cultural understanding that would ease work with homeless clients. Finally, lack of preventive maintenance of medical care by the homeless may result in expensive and extensive needs for care, including hospital care, which may stress the capacities of certain service providers.

How to help the homeless mentally ill

There are many ways that the public can support community and federal efforts to help homeless people living with mental illness. Some strategies include:

- Support collective public and private efforts to build homes, and provide health care for people with unmet medical needs.
- Become educated about the challenges faced by homeless and mentally ill people in American society.
- Stop the practice of equating people in poverty and with illness with their medical conditions, instead of recognizing them as human beings. Succeeding in this step could open doors for recovery of health and housing without demeaning the humanity of people in need.

Recently, the federal government approved the American Recovery and Reinvestment Act of 2009, which allocated $1.5 billion for a Homelessness Prevention and Rapid Re-Housing Program (HPRP), and the Homeless Emergency Assistance and Rapid Transition to Housing (HEARTH) Act, which reauthorizes the HUD Homeless Assistance programs.

Resources

BOOKS

Cloke, Paul, Jon May, and Sarah Johnsen. *Swept Up Lives?* Chichester, West Sussex: Wiley-Blackwell, 2010.

Daly, Gerald. *Homeless.* New York City: Routledge, 2005.

Doak, Melissa J. *Social Welfare: Fighting Poverty and Homelessness.* Detroit: Gale Cengage Living, 2010.

Ellen, Ingrid Gould, and Brendan O'Flaherty, editors. *How to House the Homeless* New York City: Russell Sage Foundation, 2010.

Hartmann, Robert Hartmann, editor. *Homelessness in America.* Westport, CT: Praeger, 2008.

OTHER

"Health Care and Homelessness." National Coalition for the Homeless. May 27, 2009. http://www.nationalhomeless.org/factsheets/Health.pdf (accessed December 12, 2011).

WEBSITES

"Chronic Homelessness." U.S. Department of Housing and Urban Development. July 2009. http://www.hud.gov/offices/cpd/homeless/chronic.cfm (accessed December 12, 2011).

"Homeless Emergency and Rapid Transition to Housing (HEARTH) Act." U.S. Department of Housing and Urban Development. http://www.hudhre.info/hearth (accessed December 12, 2011).

"Homelessness Prevention and Rapid Re-Housing Program." U.S. Department of Housing and Urban Development. http://www.hudhre.info/HPRP (accessed December 12, 2011).

"How Many People Experience Homelessness?" National Coalition for the Homeless. July 2009. http://www.nationalhomeless.org/factsheets/How_Many.html (accessed December 12, 2011).

ORGANIZATIONS

National Alliance on Mental Illness, 3803 North Fairfax Drive, Suite 100, Arlington, VA, 22203, (703) 524-7600, (800) 950-6264, Fax: (703) 524-9094, http://www.nami.org.

National Coalition for the Homeless, 2201 P Street, NW, Washington, DC, 20037, (202) 462-4822, Fax: (202) 462-4823, info@nationalhomeless.org, http://www.nationalhomeless.org.

National Coalition for Homeless Veterans, 333 1/2 Pennsylvania Ave., SE, Washington, DC, 20003-1148, (202) 546-1969, (800) 838-4357, Fax: (202) 546-2063, info@nchv.org, http://www.nchv.org.

National Health Care for the Homeless Council, PO Box 60427, Nashville, TN, 37206-0427, (615) 226-2292, Fax: (615) 226-1656, http://www.nhchc.org.

National Institute of Mental Health, 6001 Executive Boulevard, Room 8184, MSC 9663, Bethesda, MD, 20892-9663, (301) 443-4513, (866) 615-6464, Fax: (301) 443-4279, nimhinfo@nih.gov, http://www.nimh.nih.gov.

Substance Abuse and Mental Health Services Administration, 1 Choke Cherry Road, Rockville, MD, 20857, (877) 726-4727, Fax: (240) 221-4292, http://www.samhsa.gov.

U.S. Department of Housing and Urban Development, 451 7th Street SW, Washington, DC, 20410, (202) 708-1112, http://www.hud.gov.

Michael Polgar, PhD
Stephanie N. Watson

Hospitalization

Definition

Hospitalization, or inpatient care, is the admission to the hospital or other such medical healthcare facility for the treatment of various types of mental illness. For someone with disorders such as **depression** or **bipolar disorder**, a stay in the hospital can help to stabilize the condition for eventually better mental health. However, hospitalization is the most restrictive form of treatment for a psychiatric disorder, addictive disorder, or someone with more than one **diagnosis**. Whether treatment is voluntary or involuntary, the patient relinquishes the freedom to move about and, once admitted, becomes subject to the rules and schedule of a treatment environment.

The use of hospitalization is necessary in cases where individuals are in imminent danger of harming themselves or others or have made **suicide** attempts. Crisis stabilization, **behavior modification**, supervised **substance abuse**, **detoxification**, and medication management are compelling reasons to consider hospitalization. People having hallucinations, **delusions**, thoughts of hurting oneself or others, feelings of exhaustion or depression, or problems with alcohol or substance abuse may need to consider hospitalization. Those people who have not slept or eaten for days due to psychiatric or medical illness, have tried outpatient treatment without an improvement in their lives, or need to make major changes in an existing treatment or medicine are other candidates for hospitalization.

Ideally, hospitalization is at one end of a comprehensive continuum of services for people needing treatment for behavioral problems. It is generally viewed as a last resort after other, less restrictive forms of treatment have failed.

Purpose

For a person to be admitted to a hospital, a medical doctor (in the case of mental health, most often a **psychiatrist**) must "admit" the patient or approve the patient's request to be admitted. Although hospitalization may be considered a drastic treatment **intervention**, it can be essential in keeping people safe, helping monitor and adjust medications, treating medication side effects, supervising alcohol and/or drug detoxification, and stabilizing a patient after an acute psychiatric episode.

Before an individual is hospitalized, an evaluation and a diagnosis must be made by a medical professional. This is required in order for the patient to receive maximum insurance coverage and to receive the most appropriate treatment.

Demographics

Anyone may need the services of a hospital to receive a comprehensive array of medical services to overcome a mental problem. A hospital is an appropriate place to receive those services because a group of trained professionals is associated with all hospitals in the United States. As such, it is a safe and effective way to treat mental illness or other related problems and to learn how to cope with its symptoms. A hospital is also an appropriate place to eliminate stresses that may be contributing to mental problems.

Hospitalization statistics

The U.S. Centers for Disease Control and Prevention (CSC), in its *National Hospital Discharge Survey: 2007 Summary*, states that the number of discharges with mental disorders from hospitals numbered 2.4 million. In addition, the average length of stay within a hospital for inpatient mental-health care was 7.1 days.

The U.S. Department of Health and Human Services (HHS) ranked the principal diagnosis of various mental illnesses according to the number of discharges from hospitals in the United States. In 2009, HHS found that the top five mental illnesses (and the number of hospital discharges) were for: mood disorders (873,176), **schizophrenia** and other psychotic disorders (419,395), alcohol-related disorders (268,093), substance-related disorders (240,837), and **delirium**, **dementia**, and amnestic and other cognitive disorders (133,460).

In 2006, according to the **Substance Abuse and Mental Health Services Administration**, 1,850,000 patients received inpatient treatment in the United States for substance abuse, with 816,000 patients in hospitals, and 934,000 in inpatient treatment centers.

The U.S. government is transferring some mental health patients from federally supported hospitals to outpatient facilities supported by local communities. In a similar move, various states across the United States are doing likewise with their state-sponsored hospitals. Such moves are a response to large financial woes that the federal government and many state governments are currently dealing with because of recessionary conditions in the United States. These community-based treatment facilities have become the focus for treatment of mental health cases in the United States, both at the federal and state levels. Due to overcrowding in many hospitals and the closing of others, private providers are also being contracted to supply services to mental health patients.

Description

Most hospital rooms are similar to basic hotel rooms and are generally large enough for two people. In the case of public hospitals, the rooms may be larger and may contain more beds. Men and women are in separate wings or on separate floors. If a treatment program is housed in a medical hospital, it may cover one or more floors. If one admits oneself into the facility, then one can also sign out within two to seven days (depending on specific state laws) unless the medical staff feels the person has the potential to do harm to one's self or others. If someone else admits the patient, then the patient cannot release himself or herself. In all cases, patients have the right to be explained the treatments planned for them.

Although there is wide variation in the quality of the physical surroundings and the resources available, most inpatient facilities are highly regimented. Patients get up, go to bed, eat, and take medication (if indicated) on a regular schedule. Times are set to awaken in the morning, and eat breakfast, lunch, and dinner. Days are filled with scheduled activities such as individual, family, or **group therapy**, expressive and occupational therapies, psychoeducation, recreation, and, in the case of children or adolescents, several hours of school. Several different doctors on staff and other mental health professionals (e. g., nurses, **social workers**) at the hospital, besides the admitting doctor, may visit to conduct interviews, monitor status, and check on medications.

Most hospital inpatient programs are based on a therapeutic milieu, which means that all the people involved in the patient's care and all the activities are designed to have a therapeutic function for the patient. For example, direct care workers are not simply aides; they are supportive of the patient and provide valuable feedback to the physician, **psychologist**, and social worker about the patient's conduct and progress.

Hospitalization for mental illness may necessitate that the person being admitted to the hospital be confined to a locked section. For the safety of the patient, all personal items, such as jewelry, watches, and cell phones, may be taken away and stored in a secure location. Items that have

Number of certified U.S. psychiatric hospitals and intermediate care facilities for persons with intellectual disabilities (ICF/ID), by state: selected years, 1995–2009

	Psychiatric hospitals				ICF/ID			
	1995	2000	2007	2009	1995	2000	2007	2009
United States	**689**	**515**	**486**	**502**	**7,106**	**6,767**	**6,443**	**6,437**
Alabama	10	9	10	11	8	8	6	5
Alaska	3	2	2	2	6	0	0	0
Arizona	11	8	7	7	12	11	12	12
Arkansas	9	9	9	8	40	40	41	41
California	64	39	31	33	687	1,043	1,151	1,171
Colorado	9	6	7	9	7	3	3	3
Connecticut	10	8	7	6	145	122	118	114
Delaware	3	3	4	4	6	2	2	2
District of Columbia	2	3	3	3	122	130	110	85
Florida	43	26	21	24	110	108	105	102
Georgia	28	15	13	15	12	13	11	9
Hawaii	1	1	1	1	15	22	18	18
Idaho	6	5	5	5	48	66	65	66
Illinois	19	17	14	14	315	317	313	310
Indiana	30	21	20	22	578	574	530	547
Iowa	4	4	4	4	116	127	139	139
Kansas	10	5	4	4	47	42	30	32
Kentucky	13	12	11	11	9	12	9	12
Louisiana	40	17	35	37	454	473	528	548
Maine	4	4	4	4	42	28	20	17
Maryland	14	11	9	9	5	5	4	4
Massachusetts	18	18	16	15	8	7	6	6
Michigan	15	10	10	10	503	2	1	1
Minnesota	6	7	6	7	348	270	218	218
Mississippi	4	2	5	5	12	13	14	14
Missouri	17	15	14	14	26	18	18	18
Montana	2	2	2	2	3	2	1	1
Nebraska	5	4	4	3	4	4	4	3
Nevada	5	4	5	6	14	20	9	9
New Hampshire	3	2	2	2	7	1	1	1
New Jersey	14	16	16	17	10	9	9	8
New Mexico	6	3	2	2	32	43	42	42
New York	35	35	29	28	892	749	581	568
North Carolina	15	11	9	10	320	333	332	332
North Dakota	1	3	3	3	65	66	67	66
Ohio	19	16	16	15	416	461	435	426
Oklahoma	18	12	10	10	37	54	88	84
Oregon	4	4	2	3	2	1	1	1
Pennsylvania	31	26	23	24	252	232	202	200
Rhode Island	3	3	2	2	55	20	5	5
South Carolina	9	7	8	8	174	157	89	89
South Dakota	2	1	1	1	10	4	1	1
Tennessee	16	12	10	11	74	83	83	86
Texas	52	30	34	36	879	915	868	867
Utah	7	4	3	3	14	14	15	15
Vermont	2	2	1	1	6	2	2	1
Virginia	19	17	10	9	20	19	35	39
Washington	4	5	5	5	28	17	14	14
West Virginia	5	4	4	4	63	62	66	67
Wisconsin	17	13	11	11	44	41	19	16
Wyoming	2	2	2	2	4	2	2	2

Data are based on a census of certified facilities.

SOURCE: National Center for Health Statistics, *Health, United States, 2010: With Special Feature on Death and Dying*, Hyattsville, MD: U.S. Department of Health and Human Services, 2011.

Report available online at http://www.cdc.gov/nchs/hus.htm. *(Table by PreMediaGlobal. © 2012 Cengage Learning.)*

KEY TERMS

Bipolar disorder—A disorder characterized by the psychological symptom of extreme mood swings from euphoria mania ("highs") to serious depression ("lows").

Dementia—A progressive deteriorating disease that causes degradation of the intellectual (cognitive) facilities of the brain, such as memory; however, often without problems in other brain functions such as controlling the senses.

Depression—A disorder that presents psychiatric symptoms such as dejection, hopelessness, lack of concentration, sleeplessness, and sometimes suicidal thoughts.

Psychiatrist—A medical doctor trained to treat people with psychiatric disorders.

Psychologist—A professional with an advanced graduate degree (master's or doctorate), trained to study psychological behavior and provide therapeutic services.

Schizophrenia—A disorder relating to psychiatric symptoms relating to emotional instability, self-withdrawal, and inability to comprehend reality.

the potential to harm the patient, such as sharp objects, may also be taken away. In other cases, the person may have more leeway with respect to their ability to move about within the facility and having personal items.

Precautions

In the public mental health system, less-restrictive forms of treatment other than hospitalization are strongly recommended first. In the late 1960s, the patients' rights movement led to reforms governing **involuntary hospitalization**. Today, the criteria for admission, particularly in the case of involuntary hospitalization, are extremely narrow, reflecting a strong reluctance in the United States to infringe on any person's liberty. The unintended consequences of this public policy are often observed in the numbers of people with mental illnesses who are homeless. So long as they are not posing a danger to themselves or others, they are likely to remain outside the traditional treatment system.

Hospitalization has long been negatively characterized in the media, contributing to the **stigma** of seeking inpatient treatment, even when it is voluntary. Scenes from the 1975 movie *One Flew Over the Cuckoo's Nest* have defined the worst in psychiatric hospital treatment. Such conditions cannot exist long in today's more sophisticated mental health, consumer-focused environment. A reputable facility will be accredited by the Joint Commission on Accreditation of Health Care Organizations, or by a similar governing body, which usually assures a minimum level of service. Most hospitals now have a Patient Advocate, usually an attorney who is on-site daily, or accessible by telephone, and whose job is to investigate complaints and protect patients' rights. In addition, a federal law mandates that every state have a Protection and Advocacy Agency to handle complaints of abuse in hospitals. Although the effectiveness of these agencies varies from state to state, they can be helpful in explaining the rights of hospitalized patients. Some states have also implemented ombudsman programs to address patient complaints and to help people negotiate the mental health system.

Treatment facilities may be locked or unlocked. A locked unit will have tighter security to protect patient privacy and to keep patients from running away. In most cases when patients are voluntarily admitted, they may leave treatment at any time, invoking the right to do so against medical advice.

In the past, patients were often not part of their own treatment planning process. The rise of the patients' rights movement has led to more active patient involvement in all phases of treatment. They have the right to refuse certain forms of treatment. Most hospitals now have a clearly posted Patient's Bill of Rights and may also have a patient's council or other body to represent their interests and recommend changes to the inpatient environment.

Confidentiality is paramount in a hospital setting, and medical professionals are bound by laws to safeguard patient confidentiality. Group therapy rules generally stress the importance of keeping members and the content of group sessions confidential.

Preparation

Even voluntary hospitalization can be overwhelming and anxiety-provoking. As a result, hospital staff will closely observe patients when they are first admitted. If the patients were admitted because of a suicide attempt or a violent episode, a "suicide watch" may be set up with more intensive staffing or in a room that can be monitored easily by nursing staff.

As patients adjust to the hospital routine, more privileges and freedom will be made available. For example, patients may earn privileges or rewards like outings with staff, a weekend pass to go home for a visit, or some other positive consequence if they follow hospital rules and engage in therapeutic activities.

QUESTIONS TO ASK YOUR DOCTOR

- What can I expect during the treatment process?
- What can I do if I reject a particular treatment?
- Do I have to tell my family and friends?
- What happens if I do not get better in the hospital?
- Will my insurance pay for all of it? What is covered, and what is not covered? What happens if I do not have health insurance?

An interdisciplinary treatment team made up of a psychiatrist, psychologist, social worker, nurse, direct care worker (sometimes called a "psychiatric technician" or "mental health worker"), and an expressive therapist usually oversees the care of patients while they are in the hospital. Treatment goals are developed by the team with patient input, and with discharge as a major objective.

Aftercare

Optimally, inpatient treatment prepares patients to cope with the realities of life outside the hospital. Emphasis is placed on how patients will behave differently in order to remain healthy and avoid future hospitalizations. During the discharge phase, patients may be scheduled for outpatient therapy and informed about various medications. Patients often experience anxiety at the thought of leaving the hospital, and this apprehension is addressed in therapy sessions as discharge nears.

In the past, a patient might be admitted to a hospital for a minimum of 30 days. Today's rising health care costs and the prevalence of **managed care** have led to dramatically reduced hospital stays. An optimal outcome under these conditions is medication adjustment, monitoring, and the beginning of stabilization. Studies are continuing to be funded to determine whether shortened stays ultimately lead to more frequent hospitalizations later on.

Risks

Many risks are present whenever facing mental illness. Medical professions are trained to assess the risks that individual patients may pose to themselves and others. For the patient, it is best to abide by the rules during hospitalization and expect that a positive result will occur during the stay. Trained medical personnel are on call 24-hours a day, seven days a week, to treat mental patients confined to a hospital setting.

Resources

BOOKS

Desai, Abhilash K., and George T. Grossberg. *Psychiatric Consultation in Long-term Care: A Guide for Health Care Professionals.* Baltimore: Johns Hopkins University Press, 2010.

Harrison, Anthony, and Chris Hart, editors. *Mental Health Care for Nurses: Applying Mental Health Skills in the General Hospital.* Oxford: Blackwell, 2006.

Jarvis, Carolyn. *Physical Examination and Health Assessment.* St. Louis: Elsevier/Saunders, 2012.

Whittington, Richard, and Caroline Logan, editors. *Self-harm and Violence: Towards Best Practice in Managing Risk in Mental Health Services.* Chichester, U.K.: Wiley-Blackwell, 2011.

PERIODICALS

Link, Bruce, Dorothy M. Castille, and Jennifer Stuber. "Stigma and Coercion in the Context of Outpatient Treatment for People with Mental Illnesses." *Social Science and Medicine* 67 (April 30, 2008): 409–19. http://www.psychodyssey.net/wp-content/uploads/2010/11/Stigma-and-coercion-in-the-context-of-outpatient-treatment-for-people-with-mental-illness.pdf (accessed May 24, 2011).

OTHER

"Understanding Hospitalization for Mental Health." Depression and Bipolar Support Alliance. http://www.dbsalliance.org/pdfs/patienthospitalization.pdf (accessed May 23, 2011).

WEBSITES

Centers for Disease Control and Prevention (CDC). "Mental Health." (October 27, 2010). http://www.cdc.gov/nchs/fastats/mental.htm (accessed May 23, 2011).

———. "Mental Health Organizations by State." http://www.cdc.gov/mentalhealth/state_orgs.htm (accessed May 24, 2011).

Mental Health America. "Mental Illness and the Family: Is Hospitalization Necessary." http://www.nmha.org/go/information/get-info/mi-and-the-family/is-hospitalization-necessary (accessed May 23, 2011).

ORGANIZATIONS

American Psychiatric Association, 1000 Wilson Boulevard, Suite 1825, Arlington, VA, 22209-3901, (703) 907-7300, apa@psych.org, http://www.psych.org.

American Psychological Association, 750 First Street, N.E., Washington, DC, 20002-4242, (202) 336-5500, (800) 374-2721, http://www.apa.org.

Anxiety Disorders Association of America, 8730 Georgia Avenue, Silver Spring, MD, 20910, (240) 485-1001, http://www.adaa.org.

Depression and Bipolar Support Alliance, 730 North Franklin Street, Suite 501, Chicago, IL, 60654-7225, (312) 642-7243, (800) 826-3632, http://www.dbsalliance.org.

Mental Health America, 2000 North Beauregard Street, Sixth Floor, Alexandria, VA, 22311, (703) 684-7722, (800) 969-6642, Fax: (703) 684-5968, http://www.nmha.org.

National Institute of Mental Health, 6001 Executive Boulevard, Room 8184, MSC 9663, Bethesda, MD, 20892-9663, (301) 443-4513, (866) 615-6464, Fax: (301) 443-4279, http://www.nimh.nih.gov.

Substance Abuse and Mental Health Services Administration, 1 Choke Cherry Rd., Rockville, MD, 20857, (877) SAMHSA-7, http://www.samhsa.gov/index.aspx.

Judy Leaver, MA
Emily Jane Willingham, Ph.D.
William A. Atkins

House-tree-person test

Definition

The house-tree-person (HTP) test is a projective personality test, a type of examination in which the test taker responds to or provides ambiguous, abstract, or unstructured stimuli (often in the form of pictures or drawings). In the HTP test, which was developed by American clinical **psychologist** John N. Buck (1906–1983), the test taker is asked to separately draw houses, trees, and persons (as well as possible), and these freehand drawings provide a measure of self-perceptions and attitudes for the administrator. The test also reveals areas of concern or conflict within the individual. As with other projective tests, it has flexible and subjective administration and interpretation.

Purpose

The primary purpose of the HTP is to measure aspects of a person's personality (inner self), along with their outlook to his/her environment and what the person thinks is important, all through interpretation of drawings and responses to questions. It is also sometimes intended as part of an assessment of **brain** damage or overall neurological functioning. It is often used with children and those with limited vocabulary because few words are needed to complete the test. The test is also useful for people with limited intelligence or education or with limited or deprived cultural backgrounds, and those that do not speak English, are mute, or are shy and withdrawn. However, the HTP test is difficult for people with motor-derived problems such as people with strokes and muscular or neurological disabilities.

It is also used with children who have been sexually abused. Such children are often hesitant to verbally state their feelings. However, they will indirectly expose their feelings during the completion of the HTP test. The test can be valuable at helping to provide discrete information on the problems hidden within the child and the unconscious aspects of their personality.

The HTP was developed in 1948 by Mr. Buck, and later updated in 1969 by Buck and American psychologist Emanuel F. Hammer. (Hammer had earlier used the test as a way to compare normal people with sex offenders.) Tests requiring human **figure drawings** were already being utilized as projective personality tests. Buck believed that drawings of houses and trees could also provide relevant information about the functioning of an individual's personality.

Description

The HTP was originally developed to measure intelligence from aspects of the Goodenough scale (also called the Draw-A-Man test), which was designed to measure intellectual function. Today, it is similar to the Draw-A-Person (DAP) test, which is an adoption of the Draw-A-Man test. Buck felt that personality characteristics would be described through art; specifically, that unconscious problems would surface through the drawing of objects. It can be given to anyone over the age of three years. Because the HTP test requires test takers to draw pictures, it is often directed toward children and adolescents. It is also often helpful with individuals suspected of having brain damage or other neurological impairment. The test takes an average of 150 minutes (2.5 hours) to complete; it may take less time with normally functioning adults and much more time with neurologically impaired individuals.

A quantitative scoring system was developed by Buck to provide a measure of interpretation to the drawings. Basic levels of intelligence and personality characteristics were provided and classified in groups. After the drawings are completed, the administrator normally asks sixty questions. The drawings are basically used to interpret associations with home and general lifestyle, families (intrafamilial relationships), home life (including children), parents and children, and married adults.

During the first phase of the test, test takers are asked to use a crayon and white paper to draw pictures, respectively, of a house, a tree, and a person. Each drawing is performed on a separate piece of paper and the test taker is asked to draw each as accurately as possible. Upon completion of the drawings, the test taker is asked questions about the drawings. Buck created sixty questions, which can be asked by examiners. Examiners can also create their own questions or ask unscripted follow-up questions. For example, with reference to the house, Buck wrote questions such as, "Is it a happy house?" and "What is the house made of?" Regarding the tree, questions include, "About how old is that tree?" and "Is the tree alive?" Concerning the person, questions include, "Is that person happy?" and "How does that person feel?"

During the second phase of the test, test takers are asked to draw the same pictures on white paper with a pencil. The questions that follow this phase are similar to the ones in the first phase. Some examiners give only one of the two phases, choosing a crayon, a pencil, or some other writing instrument. In some instances a pencil drawing is first drawn, which is later filled in with different colored crayons.

The way the pictures are drawn reflect characteristics of the individual. The administrator sees a depressed person when few details and faint lines are drawn in any image. The characteristics of drawn lines are important: whether they are long or short, bold or slight, straight or crooked, many or few breaks all tell a story. For instance, bold lines are the sign of an outgoing individual. Generally, the house figure reflects the test taker's home life and family relationships, the tree figure reveals the test taker's experiences, and the person figure discerns the relationships between the test taker and people other than his/her family.

Specifically, if the branches of the tree are upward and/or outward, then the individual is said to be one who strives for achievement. A trunk symbolizes inner strength (ego). In another instance, the head of a person drawn in profile with the body forward shows someone who avoids social conflicts. A house with the ground sloping downward and away is likely to be perceived as a person who, for instance, has feelings of isolation and helplessness when in stressful situations. An overly large roof on a house can represent **schizophrenia**. The windows, doors, and other features of the house all help to define the inner person.

Questions asked by the administrator also reveal much about the test taker. When the question is asked, "Is the tree alive?" and the answer is "No," then such an answer may reveal a maladjusted attitude.

One variation of test administration involves asking the individual to draw two separate persons, one of each sex. Another variation is to have test takers put all the drawings on one page. The specific drawing of the house, tree, and person in each drawing provides the administrator with an assessment of different aspects of the test taker (drawer), and how the individual feels about him or herself.

KEY TERMS

Neurological—Referring to neurology, which is the study of the nervous system.

Qualitative—Relating to quality.

Quantitative—Relating to quantities.

Psychodiagnostic—Various methods used to find abnormal or maladjusted behavior in individuals.

Preparation

There is no need to prepare for the HTP test.

Risks

Because the administration of the test is mostly subjective, scoring and interpreting of the HTP is difficult. Biases may be introduced if a trained administrator is not used.

Precautions

Anyone administering the HTP must be properly trained. The test publishers provide a very detailed 350-page administration and scoring manual. In any case, the administrator should be very cautious as to not to make incorrect assumptions or interpretations.

Parental concerns

The test is easy to administer and does not take much time to complete. In addition, children find it fun to draw pictures, so the HTP test is a simple way for parents to learn more about their children, and to find out whether they are having problems. However, the results of the test can be biased based on the administrator. A well-trained administrator is needed to remove or, at least, minimize the chance of biases creeping into the scoring process. Overall, the NTP test is one of the most widely used projective personality tests used. It is popular with professionals because it yields much clinical information about the patient, while being easy and non-threatening to administer. It is often the first of a battery of psychodiagnostic tests used to assess personality in individuals, especially those that are culturally

QUESTIONS TO ASK YOUR DOCTOR

- What other tests should be performed in addition to the HTP test?
- Do you know of a well-trained administrator for the test?
- Should we be concerned with the subjective nature of interpretation and scoring for the test?
- Will health insurance cover the test?

isolated, educationally deprived, developmentally disabled, and/or non-English speaking.

Results

The HTP is scored in both an objective quantitative manner and a subjective qualitative manner. The quantitative scoring scheme involves analyzing the details of drawings to arrive at a general assessment of intelligence, using a scoring method devised by the test creators. Research has shown this assessment of intelligence correlates highly with other **intelligence tests** such as the Wechsler Adult Intelligence Scale (WAIS).

The primary use of the HTP, however, is related to the qualitative scoring scheme in which the test administrator subjectively analyzes the drawings and the responses to questions in a way that assesses the test taker's personality. For example, a very small house might indicate rejection of one's home life. A tree that has a slender trunk but has large expansive branches might indicate a need for satisfaction. A drawing of a person that has a lot of detail in the face might indicate a need to present oneself in an acceptable social light.

Other methods of interpretation focus on the function of various parts in each of the drawings. In the house drawing, the roof might represent one's intellectual side, the walls might represent the test taker's degree of ego strength, and the doors and windows might represent the individual's relation to the outside world. In the tree drawing, the branches might indicate the test taker's relation to the outside world and the trunk might indicate inner strength.

As with other subjectively scored personality tests, there is little support for its reliability and validity. Individual HTP signs do not correspond to single meanings (and can point to various interpretations); only a series of similar signs can point to a specific problem or concern. Therefore, its interpretation is highly subjective, and its conclusion may be entirely inappropriate. However, there is some evidence that the HTP can differentiate people with specific types of brain damage. More specifically, it has been shown to be effective when looking at the brain damage present in schizophrenic patients.

Resources

BOOKS

Boyer, Bret A., and M. Indira Paharia, eds. *Comprehensive Handbook of Clinical Health Psychology.* Hoboken, NJ: John Wiley and Sons, 2008.

Boyle, Gregory J., Gerald Matthews and Donald H. Saklofske, eds. *The SAGE Handbook of Personality Theory and Assessment* Los Angeles: SAGE, 2008.

Groth-Marnat, Gary. *Handbook of Psychological Assessment.* 4th edition. Hoboken, NJ: John Wiley and Sons, 2003.

Hersen, Michel, ed. *Comprehensive Handbook of Psychological Assessment.* Hoboken, NJ: John Wiley and Sons, 2004.

Kellerman, Henry, and Anthony Burry. *Handbook of Psychodiagnostic Testing: Analysis of Personality in the Psychological Report.* New York: Springer, 2007.

Leeming, David A., Kathryn Madden and Stanton Marlan, eds. *Encyclopedia of Psychology and Religion.* New York: Springer, 2010.

PERIODICALS

"Hammer, Emanuel F., PhD." *New York Times*, May 22, 2005. http://query.nytimes.com/gst/fullpage.html?res=9C0DE5D91F30F931A15756C0A9639C8B63 (accessed December 13, 2011).

Rowe, F. B., W. D. Crews, Jr., and F. W. Finger. "John N. Buck (1906–1983): Did He Practically Establish Clinical Psychology in Virginia?" *Journal of Clinical Psychology* 49, no. 3 (1993): 428–34.

OTHER

Fallahi, Carolyn, R. "The House-Tree-Person Test." Department of Psychology, Central Connecticut State University. http://www.psychology.ccsu.edu/fallahic/HTP%20Outline.ppt#256,1,The House-Tree-Person Test (accessed December 13, 2011).

WEBSITES

Deffenbaugh, Anne M. "The House-Tree-Person Test with Kids Who Have Been Sexually Abused." Education Resources Information Center (ERIC). 2003. http://www.eric.ed.gov/ERICWebPortal/search/detailmini.jsp?_nfpb=true&_&ERICExtSearch_SearchValue_0=ED482760&ERICExtSearch_SearchType_0=no&accno=ED482760 (accessed December 13, 2011).

"House-Tree-Person (H-T-P) Projective Drawing Technique." Western Psychological Services. http://portal.wpspublish.

com/portal/page?_pageid=53,70613&_dad=portal&_schema=PORTAL (accessed December 13, 2011).

Ali Fahmy, PhD

Hypericum *see* **St. John's wort**

Hyperkinetic disorder (HKD) *see* **Attention deficit hyperactivity disorder**

Hypersomnia

Definition

Hypersomnia refers to a group of related disorders that involve excessive daytime sleepiness (EDS). The name of the condition comes from two Greek words that mean "more than normal" and "sleep."

Demographics

There is some disagreement among researchers regarding the prevalence of hypersomnia in the general population because of the lack of clear biological markers for the disorder and the lack of precise diagnostic criteria. On the one hand, general surveys of adults in Canada and the United States report rates of EDS in 0.5%–5% of respondents. On the other hand, the National Sleep Foundation (NSF) reports that as many as 40% of adults have some symptoms of hypersomnia from time to time. In a poll taken by the NSF in 2000, 20% of the respondents reported a level of daytime sleepiness sufficient to interfere with work and other activities. Hypersomnia is the single most common symptom among people who seek help from sleep clinics and accounts for 5%–10% of these patients.

Description

The categorization of excessive daytime sleepiness is not completely clear. In 1966, an American physician William Dement, widely considered the founder of sleep medicine as a medical subspecialty, introduced a distinction between **narcolepsy** and a condition of excessive sleepiness that lacks the symptoms of rapid-onset rapid eye movement (REM) sleep, cataplexy, and sleep paralysis. The International Classification of Sleep Disorders has defined this second condition—primary or idiopathic hypersomnia—as "a disorder of presumed central nervous system (CNS) cause that is associated with excessive sleepiness consisting of prolonged sleep episodes of non-rapid eye movement (NREM) sleep." The fourth edition of the ***Diagnostic and Statistical Manual of Mental Disorders*** (*DSM-IV*) defines primary hypersomnia as excessive daytime sleepiness without narcolepsy or the associated features of other sleep disorders. Changes proposed for the fifth edition of *DSM* (*DSM-5*), due for publication in 2013, include renaming the disorder as "Primary Hypersomnia/Narcolepsy without Cataplexy."

In contrast to narcolepsy, which has well-defined characteristic symptoms, primary or idiopathic hypersomnia is less precisely characterized. Some observers distinguish between a form of primary hypersomnia in which the patient has isolated episodes of EDS without abnormal nighttime awakening and a form in which the patient sleeps for an abnormally long period of time at night (longer than nine hours) and suffers from sleep drunkenness on awaking.

A third but rare condition known as **Kleine-Levin syndrome** (KLS), sometimes called Sleeping Beauty syndrome, is also classified as primary hypersomnia of central origin because it is thought to be caused by some type of systemic disorder (possibly an autoimmune disorder) even though its cause was not fully understood as of 2011. KLS is characterized by periods of sleep lasting up to 20 or more hours a day in episodes that last for several weeks. In addition, people with KLS are often irritable, sometimes to the point of violence. They may be sexually uninhibited (hypersexual) and make indiscriminate sexual advances. There may also be some confusion, depressed mood, and memory deficits. People with Kleine-Levin syndrome often eat uncontrollably and rapidly gain weight, unlike people with other forms of hypersomnia. This form of recurrent hypersomnia is very rare. The disorder, which most often starts in adolescence, generally resolves by the early adult years. The male/female ratio in KLS is 4:1.

Hypersomnia associated with certain medical or psychiatric conditions is classified as secondary hypersomnia. Such conditions include:

- sleep disorders, including sleep-related breathing disorders, sleep-related movement disorders, and circadian rhythm sleep disorders
- sleep deprivation
- mood disorders, particularly depression
- drugs of abuse and some classes of prescription medications
- head trauma
- cancer
- stroke
- encephalitis
- some inflammatory conditions

Risk factors

Risk factors for primary hypersomnia include a family history of the disorder and a history of viral illnesses—particularly Guillain-Barré syndrome, viral hepatitis, mononucleosis, and atypical viral pneumonia. With the exception of KLS, sex is not known to be a risk factor for primary hypersomnia. The onset of primary hypersomnia occurs most commonly in adolescents; it is rare for onset of the disorder to occur in adults over 30. There is no indication that race or ethnicity is a risk factor for primary hypersomnia.

Risk factors for secondary hypersomnia include:

- being a shift worker
- history of alcoholism or drug abuse
- history of head injury or multiple sclerosis
- treatment with prescription drugs associated with daytime sleepiness, including antipsychotics, antihistamines, antidepressants, benzodiazepine tranquilizers, antiepileptic drugs, muscle relaxants, barbiturates, and drugs given to treat nausea or diarrhea
- being diagnosed with obstructive sleep apnea or circadian sleep disorder
- obesity

Causes and symptoms

The cause of primary hypersomnia is not yet known, although some researchers think that it may be associated with malfunctions of the norepinephrine system. Norepinephrine is a neurotransmitter released by specialized neurons in the locus coeruleus, a structure located in the brainstem. Norepinephrine plays a role in the ability to pay attention and focus as well as in the fight-or-flight reaction to **stress**. No genetic or environmental causes of primary hypersomnia had been identified as of 2011.

The symptoms of primary hypersomnia typically include long periods of sleep (as long as 12 hours) with daytime naps that are not refreshing followed by sleep drunkenness on awaking. Patients with primary hypersomnia may fall asleep at work or in class, during meals or conversations with others, or even while driving or operating machinery. They are typically difficult to awaken from daytime naps. Other symptoms may include headaches, trouble thinking clearly, general lack of energy, **depression**, anxiety, fainting episodes, automatic behavior, and orthostatic hypotension (sudden drop in blood pressure when standing upright suddenly after being in a sitting or lying position).

KEY TERMS

Automatic behavior—Activity that a person with narcolepsy can carry out while partially awake but is not conscious of at the time and cannot recall afterward.

Cataplexy—A sudden episode of muscle weakness triggered by emotions. The muscle weakness may cause the person's knees to buckle or the head to drop. In severe cases, the patient may become paralyzed for a few seconds to minutes.

Hypersomnolence—Excessive daytime sleepiness in spite of sufficient nighttime sleep.

Hypothalamus—A part of the forebrain that controls heartbeat, body temperature, thirst, hunger, body temperature and pressure, blood sugar levels, and other functions.

Idiopathic—Arising spontaneously or from an unknown or obscure cause.

Obstructive sleep apnea—A disorder caused by obstruction of the upper airway during sleep and characterized by repeated pauses in breathing during sleep despite efforts to breathe.

Rapid eye movement (REM) sleep—The phase of a sleep cycle in which dreaming occurs; it is characterized by rapid eye movements.

Sleep cycle—A period of NREM sleep followed by a shorter phase of REM sleep. Most adults have four to six sleep cycles per night.

Sleep drunkenness—A condition associated with primary hypersomnia in which the person has an abnormally prolonged period of transition from sleep to wakefulness; is disoriented, drowsy, and uncoordinated; and may behave in an excited or violent fashion.

Sleep paralysis—An abnormal episode of sleep in which the patient cannot move for a few minutes, usually occurring on falling asleep or waking up. It is often found in patients with narcolepsy.

Diagnosis

The **diagnosis** of primary hypersomnia involves a process of exclusion. The editors of *DSM-5* have proposed the following five criteria for Primary Hypersomnia/Narcolepsy without Cataplexy:

- The patient's chief complaint is either unexplained hypersomnia and/or hypersomnolence (sleepiness in spite of sufficient sleep at night), for at least 3 months, occurring three or more times per week. The proposed criterion defines hypersomnia as "a prolonged nocturnal sleep episode or daily sleep amounts" greater than 9 hours per day; and hypersomnolence as "excessive daytime sleepiness with recurrent daytime naps or lapses into sleep that occurs daily or almost daily over at least the last 3 months (when the patient is untreated) and daily sleep amounts greater than 6 hours."

- The patient's periods of sleep are either unrefreshing or last so long that the person's social, academic, or occupational functioning is impaired.
- The hypersomnia is not better accounted for by insomnia or by another sleep disorder, and cannot be accounted for by sleep deprivation or inadequate amounts of sleep.
- The hypersomnia does not occur exclusively during the course of another medical or psychiatric disorder but may occur together with such a disorder.
- The hypersomnia is not caused directly by a medication or drug of abuse.

Examination

Careful history-taking during an office examination is useful in ruling out secondary hypersomnia associated with medications, shift work, drug or alcohol abuse, or jet lag related to frequent travel. The patient may be referred to a neurologist to rule out traumatic head injury, **brain** tumors, or such diseases as encephalitis, or to a **psychiatrist** to be evaluated for a mood or anxiety disorder. Obese patients may require evaluation for obstructive sleep apnea.

Tests

Paper-and-pencil tests that can be given during an office examination include the Epworth Sleepiness Scale, or ESS, which was developed in Australia in the early 1990s. A score of 12 or higher on the ESS suggests hypersomnia. Another questionnaire that can be used in the office is the Stanford Sleepiness Scale (SSS).

Patients may be given tests of motor coordination and complex reaction time, particularly if they have reported falling asleep while driving or if they are employed in occupations that involve driving or operating complex machinery (including train conductors, truckers, airline pilots, and taxicab and school bus drivers). Some states require doctors to report patients who fail to comply with treatment for excessive daytime sleepiness.

Patients with hypersomnia are also evaluated in a sleep laboratory with two tests known as the multiple sleep latency test (MSLT) and the maintenance of wakefulness test (MWT). These tests measure the amount of time that it takes for the patient to fall asleep and the person's ability to stay awake for a certain period of time. Falling asleep in less than 10 minutes on the MSLT is considered an indication of hypersomnia. Unlike patients with narcolepsy, however, patients with hypersomnia have normal REM sleep latency and fewer than 2 sleep-onset REM periods during the test. The MSLT can also be used to rule out obstructive sleep apnea.

Laboratory tests include a complete blood cell count, a test of thyroid function, and (in some cases) a drug screen to rule out a substance-induced sleep disorder. The patient may also be given a CT scan to rule out multiple sclerosis or another neurological disorder, or an electroencephalogram (EEG), a test that measures the electrical activity of the brain.

Treatment

Treatment depends on whether the hypersomnia is primary or secondary. Secondary hypersomnia associated with obstructive sleep apnea can be treated with the use of a continuous positive air pressure (CPAP) machine during sleep. Hypersomnia associated with prescription medications can be treated by discontinuing the drug or switching the patient to a similar medication that is less likely to cause drowsiness.

Drugs

Patients with primary hypersomnia can be treated with such stimulant drugs as modafinil, sodium oxybate, amphetamine, **methamphetamine**, **dextroamphetamine**, **methylphenidate**, and selegiline. Other drugs used to treat hypersomnia include **clonidine**, levodopa, bromocriptine, **antidepressants**, and **monoamine oxidase inhibitors**.

Relatively little research has been done on primary hypersomnia, and the American Academy of Sleep Medicine (AASM) has called for further work in this area. There were only two **clinical trials** under way as of 2011 of other drugs for the treatment of primary hypersomnia. One drug was flumazenil (Anexate), a drug developed in the 1980s to reverse the effects of benzodiazepine tranquilizers. The other drug was clarithromycin (Crixan, Clarac), a macrolide antibiotic used to treat tonsillitis, acute sinusitis, and severe pneumonia. Both studies were being conducted at Emory University in Georgia.

Psychotherapy and lifestyle changes

The AASM recommends **cognitive-behavioral therapy** and changing the patient's daily schedule to

QUESTIONS TO ASK YOUR DOCTOR

- What is the difference between narcolepsy and primary hypersomnia?
- How can I tell whether my sleepiness is a response to sleep deprivation or a symptom of hypersomnia?
- What is your opinion of stimulants as a treatment for hypersomnia?
- I have a relative who has been diagnosed with primary hypersomnia. What should I know about the disorder in order to be helpful to him/her?
- Have you ever treated a patient who was diagnosed with primary hypersomnia?
- Do you think there will ever be a cure for the disorder?

allow for daytime naps, because stimulant drugs are not a substitute for sleep. Other recommended lifestyle changes include avoiding late-night work and social activities that interfere with an early bedtime, along with avoidance of alcohol and caffeinated beverages.

Education of patients and their family about the nature of the disorder is vital. It is not unusual for patients with primary hypersomnia to be misjudged by others as lazy or incompetent. Patients generally function better when their friends, family members, and employers or workplace colleagues are helped to understand the disorder and the available treatments for it.

Prognosis

The prognosis of secondary hypersomnia is generally better than that of primary hypersomnia. Although primary hypersomnia is not fatal by itself, it can result in fatal accidents. Primary hypersomnia typically continues indefinitely; it is a lifelong disorder and may cause severe disruption of the patient's education, employment, and social relationships. There are no known cases of spontaneous remission.

Prevention

There is no known way to prevent primary hypersomnia, because the causes of the disorder are not yet understood.

Resources

BOOKS

American Psychiatric Association. *Diagnostic and Statistical Manual of Mental Disorders,* 4th ed., Text rev. Washington, DC: American Psychiatric Association, 2000.

Benca, Ruth M. *Sleep Disorders: The Clinician's Guide to Diagnosis and Management.* Oxford: Oxford University Press, 2011.

Silvestri, Rosalia, ed. *Sleep Disorders in Neurology.* Hauppauge, NY: Nova Science, 2011.

Wilson, Sue, and David Nutt. *Sleep Disorders.* New York: Oxford University Press, 2008.

PERIODICALS

Ali, M., et al. "Idiopathic Hypersomnia: Clinical Features and Response to Treatment." *Journal of Clinical Sleep Medicine* 15 (2009): 562–68.

Bassetti, C.L., et al. "Cerebrospinal Fluid Histamine Levels Are Decreased in Patients with Narcolepsy and Excessive Daytime Sleepiness of Other Origin." *Journal of Sleep Research* 19 (2010): 620–23.

Janácková, S., et al. "Idiopathic Hypersomnia: A Report of Three Adolescent-onset Cases in a Two-generation Family." *Journal of Child Neurology* 26 (2011): 522–25.

Kotagal, S. "Hypersomnia in Children: Interface with Psychiatric Disorders." *Child and Adolescent Psychiatric Clinics of North America* 18 (2009): 967–77.

Lavault, S., et al. "Benefit and Risk of Modafinil in Idiopathic Hypersomnia vs. Narcolepsy with Cataplexy." *Sleep Medicine* 12 (2011): 550–56.

Pizza, F., et al. "Different Sleep Onset Criteria at the Multiple Sleep Latency Test (MSLT): An Additional Marker to Differentiate Central Nervous System (CNS) Hypersomnias." *Journal of Sleep Research* 20 (2011): 250–56.

Quinnell, T.G., and I.E. Smith. "Narcolepsy, Idiopathic Hypersomnolence and Related Conditions." *Clinical Medicine* 11 (2011): 282–86.

Vernet, C., et al. "Subjective Symptoms in Idiopathic Hypersomnia: Beyond Excessive Sleepiness." *Journal of Sleep Research* 19 (2010): 525–34.

WEBSITES

"Extreme Sleepiness." National Sleep Foundation. http://www.sleepfoundation.org/article/sleep-related-problems/idiopathic-hypersomnia-and-sleep (accessed October 14, 2011).

"Hypersomnia Information Page." National Institute of Neurological Disorders and Stroke. Last updated June 23, 2008. http://www.ninds.nih.gov/disorders/hypersomnia/hypersomnia.htm (accessed October 14, 2011).

"M 01 Primary Hypersomnia/Narcolepsy without Cataplexy." American Psychiatric Association. DSM-5 Development. http://www.dsm5.org/ProposedRevision/Pages/proposedrevision.aspx?rid=66 (accessed October 14, 2011).

Pagel, J.F. "Excessive Daytime Sleepiness." *American Family Physician* 79 (2009): 391–96. http://www.aafp.org/afp/2009/0301/p391.html (accessed September 20, 2011).

"Primary Hypersomnia." Medscape. Last updated February 3, 2011. http://emedicine.medscape.com/article/291699-overview (accessed October 14, 2011).

"Sleep and Hypersomnia." WebMD. Last reviewed March 3, 2010. http://www.webmd.com/sleep-disorders/guide/hypersomnia (accessed October 14, 2011).

ORGANIZATIONS

American Academy of Sleep Medicine, 2510 N Frontage Rd., Darien, IL, 60561, (630) 737-9700, Fax: (630) 737-9790, inquiries@assmnet.org, http://www.aasmnet.org.

American Psychiatric Association, 1000 Wilson Blvd., Ste. 1825, Arlington, VA, 22209-3901, (703) 907-7300, apa@psych.org, http://www.psych.org.

National Institute of Mental Health, 6001 Executive Blvd., Rm. 8184, MSC 9663, Bethesda, MD, 20892-9663, (301) 433-4513; TTY: (301) 443-8431, Fax: (301) 443-4279, (866) 615-6464; TTY: (866) 415-8051, nimhinfo@nih.gov, http://www.nimh.nih.gov.

National Institute of Neurological Disorders and Stroke, PO Box 5801, Bethesda, MD, 20824, (301) 496-5751; TTY: (301) 468-5981, (800) 352-9424, http://www.ninds.nih.gov.

Tish Davidson, AM
Emily Jane Willingham, PhD
Rebecca J. Frey, PhD

Hypnotherapy

Definition

Hypnotherapy is the use of hypnosis as part of psychological or psychiatric treatment. Hypnotherapy may be used in short-term **psychotherapy** to help alleviate symptoms or as part of a long-term plan of psychotherapeutic **intervention** for personality change. Hypnotherapy may use any one or a combination of techniques administered by a trained professional who induces a hypnotic state in the patient and then presents therapeutic suggestions.

Purpose

Hypnosis, when used in conjunction with proven therapeutic procedures, can be a highly effective form of treatment for many mental, psychosomatic, and physical disorders. For example, through the use of regressive techniques, an adult patient may mentally travel back to a point in youth that was particularly troublesome, allowing the healing of old emotional wounds. Another patient can be led to understand that emotional pain has been converted to physical pain, and that the pain can be eliminated once the source has been addressed. Hypnotherapy can also be used to help persons with chronic pain to control the pain without use of medications. There are a number of techniques for correcting dysfunctional behaviors such as self-destructive habits, **anxiety disorders**, and even managing side effects of various medical treatments and procedures.

Hypnotherapy has been used to stop self-destructive and addictive habits like smoking. It has also been used to curb overeaters' urge to eat, to stem the disruptive actions of tics, cure **insomnia**, stop bed-wetting, and minimize anxiety. Excessive **stress** can be generated from any number of sources and can be the springboard for anxiety. Some of the more prominent sources of anxiety and stress for which people seek hypnotherapy are: public speaking, test taking, and job stress. Hypnotherapy also works well for other anxiety disorders such as phobias and has proven to be an effective treatment for mild to moderate **depression**. In one study, hypnotherapy was used in conjunction with traditional

MILTON ERICKSON (1901–1980)

Erickson rose to prominence during the 1940s and 1950s as a pioneer in the medical, dental, and psychotherapeutic uses of hypnosis. He was considered the world's leading authority on the subject of hypnotherapy and was instrumental in establishing worldwide recognition and acceptance of hypnosis as a valid and effective therapeutic technique. He was frequently consulted by doctors and scientists, including anthropologist Margaret Mead, and during the 1950s he collaborated with author Aldous Huxley on research on hypnosis and other states of consciousness.

Erickson practiced psychiatry in Massachusetts and Michigan before moving to Arizona in the late 1940s. He was confined to a wheelchair following a bout with polio but continued to conduct teaching seminars from his Phoenix home. Erickson's teaching style was similar to his psychotherapeutic method—distraction by verbal communication and other forms of indirection disrupted the conscious set, providing access to the subject's unconscious mind. His orientation was eclectic, drawing on the widest range of schools of personality theory for the most useful elements of each. Erickson's books on the subject of hypnotherapy are geared toward health professionals and are, according to a *Psychology Today* reviewer, "written in a style ... as original and personal as [Erickson's] technique."

cognitive therapy to assist persons who had severe aversion to needles. The treatment was necessary, because it was essential that each participant receive periodic medical injections. However, the participants would have become noncompliant without the adjunct intervention of hypnotherapy. In another case, involving care for terminally ill cancer patients, it was concluded that hypnotherapy was more effective at enhancing quality of life and relieving anxiety and depressive symptoms, when compared to others who received traditional care.

Precautions

Confusion can occur when one seeks a hypnotherapist as a result of the various titles, certifications, and licenses in the field. Many states do not regulate the title "hypnotist" or "hypnotherapist," so care must be exercised when selecting someone to see. As a rule, it is best to consult a professional in the field of mental health or medicine, although alternative sources for hypnosis are available. Care must also be taken by the therapist to ensure adequate training and sufficient experience for rendering this specialized service. The therapist must be well-grounded in a psychotherapeutic approach before undertaking the use of hypnotherapy. Professionals should not attempt hypnotherapy with any disorder for which they would not use traditional therapeutic approaches. The patient seeking hypnotherapy is reminded that unskilled or amateur hypnotists can cause harm and should not be consulted for the purpose of implementing positive change in an individual's life. The detrimental effects of being subjected to amateur or inadequately trained persons can be severe and long lasting.

Description

In order to understand hypnotherapy, it is necessary to understand the underlying concepts of hypnosis. A brief review of the history of hypnosis, description of hypnosis, and modern techniques follows.

History of hypnosis

It appears that hypnosis, under other names, has been used since the beginning of time. In fact, it has been insinuated that the earliest description of hypnosis may be portrayed in the Old Testament and in the Talmud. There is also evidence of hypnosis in ancient Egypt, some 3,000 years ago. However, the man credited with the development of what has become modern hypnosis is Friedrich Anton Mesmer. An Austrian physician, Friedrich Anton Mesmer one day watched a magician on a street in Paris demonstrate that he could have spectators do his bidding by touching them with magnets. Fascinated by the demonstration, Mesmer believed the magnets had power of their own and from this belief developed his theory of "animal magnetism." He also believed that good health depended on having correct magnetic flow and that the direction of one's magnetic flow could easily be reversed. He further believed that he could direct this magnetic flow into inanimate objects, which could then be used for the good health of others. The term "mesmerism" came to be applied to his mystical workings. He experienced much success in helping the people of Paris as well as visitors who came from other countries, upon hearing of his powers. Later he was completely discredited by a special commission of the French Academy appointed by the king, resulting in Mesmer's departure from France. Two of the more famous members of the French Academy at the time were chairman of the commission Benjamin Franklin, American ambassador to France, and Dr. Guillotine, the inventor of the execution device.

Later, around 1840, a patient in the office of Scottish physician James Braid accidentally entered a state of trance while waiting for an eye examination. Braid, aware of the disfavor of mesmerism and animal magnetism coined the term "hypnosis," and thus began the serious study of this altered state of awareness.

What is hypnosis?

It is far easier to describe what hypnosis is not than to describe what it is. For example, it is not one person controlling the mind of another. The patient is not unconscious and does not lose control of his or her faculties. People will not do things under hypnosis that they would be unwilling to do otherwise. The person being hypnotized is always in control. The hypnotized person decides how deep the trance will be, what suggestions will be accepted, and when to awaken. Therefore, a hypnotized person cannot be forever "lost" if the therapist should fall dead during an induction or while the patient is deep in trance.

Hypnosis is first and foremost a self-accepted journey away from the reality of the moment. Although the trance state is often referred to as if the patient is asleep, nothing could be further from the truth. The patient is fully awake at all times. The hypnotic subject is simply in a heightened, more receptive state of mind. This fact is proven with inductions called open-eye techniques, where the patient keeps his/her eyes open during the hypnotherapy. Full and deep trance is still achievable.

Trance is commonplace. People fall into trances many times without even being aware that it has happened. Examples of this include reaching the destination of a morning commute, but not recalling the passing of familiar landmarks; daydreaming while sitting in a college classroom; or that anxiety-free state achieved just before going to sleep. The difference between these altered states and clinically used hypnotherapy is that a professionally trained person is involved in helping the patient achieve the trance, which can be done in many ways.

A typical hypnotherapy session has the patient seated comfortably with their feet on the floor and palms on their lap. Of course, the patient could choose to lie down if that option is available and if that will meet the patient's expectation of hypnosis. The therapist can even set the stage for a favorable outcome by asking questions like, "Would you prefer to undergo hypnosis in this chair or on the sofa?" Once patients makes the choice, they are in effect agreeing to undergo hypnosis. Depending on the approach used by the therapist, the next events can vary, but generally will involve some form of relaxing the patient. Suggestions will lead the patient to an increasingly relaxed state. The therapist may wish to confirm the depth of trance by performing tests with the patient. For example, the therapist may suggest that when the eyes close that they will become locked and cannot be opened. The therapist then checks for this by having patients try to open their eyes. Following a successful trial showing the patient's inability to open the eyes, the therapist might then further relax them by using deepening techniques. Deepening techniques will vary for each patient and depend largely on whether the patient represents information through auditory, visual, or kinesthetic means. If the patient is more affected by auditory suggestions, the therapist would use comments such as "You hear the gentle patter of rain on the roof;" or, "The sound of the ocean waves allow you to relax more and more." For the visual person, the therapist might use statements such as, "You see the beautiful placid lake, with trees bending slightly with the breeze." Finally, with the kinesthetic person phrases like, "You feel the warm sun and gentle breeze on your skin," could be used. It is important for the therapist to know if the patient has difficulty with the idea of floating or descending because these sensations are sometimes used to enhance the experience for the patient. However, if the patient has a fear of heights or develops a feeling of oppression with the thought of traveling downward and going deeper and deeper, suggestions implying the unwanted or feared phenomenon will not be taken and can thwart the attempt.

Modern techniques

In order for a hypnotherapist to convey positive suggestions for change, the patient must be in a receptive state. The state is called trance and the method of achieving a trance is through induction. Induction techniques are many and varied and involve the therapist offering suggestions that the patient follows. The formerly common "your eyes are getting heavy" suggestion may still exist, but other more reliable and acceptable (to the patient) forms of induction have come to the forefront. The artful hypnotherapist is always aware of the present condition of the patient and uses this information to lead him/her down the path of induction. In its lighter stages, trance can be noted by the relaxation of muscles. At this point, hands can levitate when given the suggestion, and paresthesia, a feeling of numbness, can be induced. In a medium trance, a patient can be led to experience partial or complete **amnesia**, or failure to recall events of the induction after the fact. A deep trance opens the patient to powerful auditory, visual, or kinesthetic experiences. The phenomenon of time distortion is experienced most profoundly at this level. Patients may believe they have been away briefly, and may react with disbelief when told they were away much longer. Although some work can be done in lighter states of trance, the best circumstance for implementing change is when the patient reaches a deep trance state. At this level, the patient is focused inwardly and is more receptive to positive suggestions for change. This is also the point at which the therapist can invoke posthypnotic suggestions, or instructions given to the patient so he/she will perform some act or experience some particular sensation following awakening from the trance. These suggestions, if accepted by the patient, can be formed to make foods or cigarettes taste bad, or to delay impulses, curb hunger, or eliminate pain, for example. However, it should be noted that posthypnotic suggestions given to a person which run counter to the person's value system, or are not something they are likely to do under ordinary circumstances, will not be accepted and therefore not implemented.

Neuro-Linguistic Programming (NLP) is the name given to a series of models and techniques used to enhance the therapist's ability to do hypnotherapy. NLP consists of a number of models, with a series of techniques based on those models. Sensory acuity and physiology is one model whose premise is that a person's thought processes change their physiological state. People recognize such a physiological change when startled. The body receives a great dose of **adrenaline**, the heart beats faster, the scare may be verbalized by shouting, and the startled person may sweat. Sensory acuity (i.e., being attuned to changes occurring in another person) will strengthen communication to a person in ways over and above simple verbal cues, therefore making the therapist more effective. A second model of NLP deals with representational systems. The idea behind this model is that different people represent knowledge in different sensory styles. In other words, an individual's language reveals that person's mode of representation. There are three basic modes of representation: auditory, visual, and kinesthetic. The same information will be expressed differently by each type. For example, the auditory person might say, "That sounds good to me," the visual person might offer, "I see it the same way," and the kinesthetic person would say, "I'm comfortable with it too."

Preparation

Before people subject themselves to hypnotherapy they are advised to learn as much about the process and about the chosen therapist as is necessary to feel comfortable. Rapport and trust are two key factors. Therapists should be open and willing to answer all questions regarding qualifications, expertise, and methods used. A well-qualified professional will not undertake the use of hypnosis without interviewing the patient to ascertain their level of understanding of the process. This is very important for two reasons. First, it allows the patient the opportunity to have questions answered and to develop some rapport with the therapist. Second, it is important for the therapist to know the patient's expectations since meeting these expectations will enhance the likelihood of success.

Aftercare

Depending on the purpose of the hypnotherapy (e.g., **smoking cessation**, weight loss, improvement in public speaking, or addressing some deep emotional turmoil), follow-up may be advisable. When trying to eradicate unwanted habits, it is good practice to revisit the therapist, based upon a date prearranged between the therapist and the patient, to report progress and, if necessary, to obtain secondary hypnotherapy to reinforce progress made.

Risks

One obvious risk to patients is the insufficiently trained therapist. The inadequately trained therapist can cause harm and distort the normally pleasant experience of hypnotherapy. A second risk for patients is the unscrupulous practitioner who may be both inadequately trained and may have some hidden agenda. These rare individuals are capable of causing great harm to the patient and to the profession. As mentioned above, the patient should carefully scrutinize their chosen therapist before submitting themselves to this dynamic form of therapy.

Results

The result of hypnotherapy is overwhelmingly positive and effective. Countless success stories exist attesting to the benefits of this technique. Many people have stopped smoking, lost weight, managed pain, remembered forgotten information, stopped other addictions, or improved their health and well-being through its use.

Abnormal results can occur in instances where amateurs, who know the fundamentals of hypnosis, entice friends to become their experimental subjects. Their lack of full understanding can lead to immediate consequences, which can linger for some time after the event. If, for example, the amateur plants the suggestion that the subject is being bitten by mosquitoes, the subject would naturally scratch where the bites were perceived. When awakened from the trance, if the amateur forgets to remove the suggestion, the subject will continue the behavior. Left unchecked, the behavior could land the subject in a physician's office in an attempt to stop the itching and scratching cycle. If the physician is astute enough to question the genesis of the behavior and hypnosis is used to remove the suggestion, the subjects may experience long-term negative emotional distress and anger once they understand exactly what happened. The lack of full understanding, complete training, and supervised experience on the part of the amateur places the subject at risk.

Resources

BOOKS

Barabasz, Arreed, and John G. Watkins. *Hypnotherapeutic Techniques*. 2nd ed. New York: Routledge, 2004.

Flemons, Douglas. *Of One Mind: The Logic of Hypnosis, the Practice of Therapy*. New York: W. W. Norton, 2002.

Hawkins, Peter J. *Hypnosis and Stress: A Guide for Clinicians*. New York: Wiley, 2006.

Lynn, Steven Jay, and Irving Kirsch. *Essentials of Clinical Hypnosis: An Evidence-Based Approach*. Washington, DC: American Psychological Association, 2006.

Spiegel, Herbert, and David Spiegel. *Trance and Treatment: Clinical Uses of Hypnosis*. 2nd ed. Washington, DC: American Psychiatric Association, 2004.

Yapko, M.D, ed. *Hypnosis and Treating Depression*. New York: Routledge, 2006.

Zarren, Jordan I., and Bruce N. Eimer. *Brief Cognitive Hypnosis: Facilitating the Change of Dysfunctional Behavior*. New York: Springer Publishing, 2002.

PERIODICALS

Bamford, Candy. "A Multifaceted Approach to the Treatment of Phantom Limb Pain Using Hypnosis." *Contemporary Hypnosis* 23, no. 3 (August 2006): 115–26.

Bryant, Richard A., et al. "Hypnotherapy and Cognitive Behaviour Therapy of Acute Stress Disorder: A 3-Year Follow-Up." *Behaviour Research and Therapy* 44, no. 9 (September 2006): 1331–35.

Gay, Marie-Claire. "Effectiveness of Hypnosis in Reducing Mild Essential Hypertension: A One-Year Follow-Up." *International Journal of Clinical and Experimental Hypnosis* 55, no. 1 (January 2007): 67–83.

Kihslinger, Daun, and Marty Sapp. "Hypnosis and Diabetes: Applications for Children, Adolescents, and Adults." *Australian Journal of Clinical Hypnotherapy and Hypnosis* 27, no. 1 (Fall 2006): 19–27.

Kraft, Tom, and David Kraft. "The Place of Hypnosis in Psychiatry: Its Applications in Treating Anxiety Disorders and Sleep Disturbances." *Australian Journal of Clinical and Experimental Hypnosis* 34, no. 2 (November 2006): 187–203.

Mende, Matthias. "The Special Effects of Hypnosis and Hypnotherapy: A Contribution to an Ecological Model of Therapeutic Change." *International Journal of Clinical and Experimental Hypnosis* 54, no. 2 (April 2006): 167–85.

Uccheddu, Ornella Manca, and Antonello Viola. "Descriptive Survey of Therapeutic Alliance in Hypnotherapy." *European Journal of Clinical Hypnosis* 7, no. 1 (2006): 10–25.

ORGANIZATIONS

American Society of Clinical Hypnosis, 140 N. Bloomingdale Rd., Bloomingdale, IL, 60108, (630) 980-4740, Fax: (630) 351-8490, info@asch.net, http://www.asch.net.

Society for Clinical and Experimental Hypnosis, PO Box 252, Southborough, MA, 01772, (508) 598-5553, Fax: (866) 397-1839, info@sceh.us.

Jack H. Booth, PsyD
Ruth A. Wienclaw, PhD

Hypnotics *see* **Sedatives and related disorders**

Hypoactive sexual desire disorder

Definition

Hypoactive sexual desire disorder (HSDD) is defined as the persistent or recurrent extreme aversion to, absence of, and avoidance of all, or almost all, genital sexual contact with a sexual partner. Synonyms for HSDD include sexual aversion, inhibited sexual desire, sexual **apathy**, and sexual anorexia. HSDD is not rare, occurring in both sexes. It is the most common of all female sexual disorders, occurring in at least 20% of women in the United States.

Description

The affected person has a low level of sexual interest and desire that is manifested by a failure to initiate or be responsive to a partner's initiation of sexual activity. HSD becomes a diagnosable disorder when it causes marked distress or interpersonal instability, according to the ***Diagnostic and Statistical Manual of Mental Disorders***, fourth edition, text revision (also known as the *DSM-IV-TR*), the handbook used by mental health professionals to diagnose mental disorders. HSDD may be either situational (solely oriented against one partner), or it may be general, in which case there is a lack of sexual interest in anyone. In the extreme form of HSDD, the patient not only lacks sexual desire, but may also find sex to be repulsive, revolting and distasteful. Phobic or panic responses may be present in extreme cases of HSD. HSDD may be the result of either physical or emotional factors.

Causes and symptoms

Causes

PRIMARY HSD. HSDD may be a primary condition in which the patient has never felt much sexual desire or interest, or it may have occurred secondarily when the patient formerly had sexual desire, but no longer has interest. If lifelong or primary, HSDD may be the consequence of sexual **trauma** such as incest, **sexual abuse**, or rape. In the absence of sexual trauma, there is often a repressive family attitude concerning sex that is sometimes enhanced by rigid religious training. A third possibility is that initial attempts at sexual intercourse resulted in pain or sexual failure. Rarely, HSDD in both males and females may result from insufficient levels of the male sex hormone, testosterone.

ACQUIRED HSD. Acquired, situational HSDD in the adult is commonly associated with boredom in the relationship with the sexual partner. **Depression**, the use of psychoactive or antihypertensive medications, and hormonal deficiencies may contribute to the problem. HSDD may also result from impairment of sexual function, particularly **erectile dysfunction** on the part of the male, or **vaginismus** on the part of the female. Vaginismus is defined as a conditioned voluntary contraction or spasm of the lower vaginal muscles resulting from an unconscious desire to prevent vaginal penetration. An incompatibility in sexual interest between the sexual partners may result in relative HSDD in the less sexually active member. This usually occurs in the presence of a sexually demanding partner.

PAINFUL INTERCOURSE. Painful intercourse (**dyspareunia**) is more common in women than in men, but may be a deterrent to genital sexual activity in both sexes. The causes are usually physical in nature and related to an infection of the prostate gland, urethra, or testes. Occasionally, an allergic reaction to a spermicidal preparation or condom may interfere with sexual intercourse. Painful erections may be a consequence of

Peyronie's disease, which is characterized by fibrotic changes in the shaft of the penis that prevent attainment of a normal erection. In the female, dyspareunia may be caused by vaginismus or local urogenital trauma or inflammatory conditions such as hymenal tears, labial lacerations, urethral bruising, or inflammatory conditions of the labial or vaginal glands.

PRIAPISM. Priapism is the occurrence of any persistent erection of more than four hours duration occurring in the absence of sexual stimulation. It is not associated with sexual excitement and the erection does not subside after ejaculation. Priapism can occur at any age, but clusters of occurrence are common between the ages of five and 10 years and between the ages of 20 and 50. In children, priapism is commonly associated with leukemia and sickle cell disease, or occurs secondary to trauma. The most common cause in adults is the intrapenile injection of agents to correct erectile dysfunction. Priapism may also occur secondary to the use of psychotropic drugs, such as **chlorpromazine** and prazosin. The pain accompanying priapism may be a cause of HSDD.

PROLACTINOMA. A rare but important cause of HSDD is a functioning prolactin-secreting tumor of the pituitary gland, a prolactinoma. Men with this condition typically state that they can achieve an erection, but that they have no interest in sexual relations. In the female, prolactinomas are associated with galactorrhea (lactation in the absence of pregnancy), amenorrhea, symptoms of estrogen deficiency and dyspareunia. Although prolactinomas are benign tumors, they can cause visual disturbances by enlarging and causing pressure on the optic nerves within the confines of the *sella turcica,* the location of the pituitary gland at the base of the **diagnosis** is confirmed by the finding of high levels of circulating prolactin in the blood. Enlargement of the pituitary gland area may be detected by the use of **magnetic resonance imaging** (MRI) or computerized axial tomography (CAT) scanning, also called **computed tomography**.

DELAYED SEXUAL MATURATION. Delayed sexual maturation is a potential cause of HSDD. It is present in boys if there is no testicular enlargement by age 13-and-a-half or if there are more than five years between the initial and complete growth of the genitalia. In girls, delayed sexual maturation is characterized by a lack of breast enlargement by age 13, or by a period greater than five years between the beginning of breast growth and the onset of menstruation. Delayed puberty may be the result of familial constitutional disorders, genetic defects such as Turner's syndrome in females and Klinefelter's syndrome in males, central nervous system disorders such as pituitary conditions that interfere with the secretion of gonadotropic hormones, and chronic illnesses such as diabetes mellitus, chronic renal failure, and cystic fibrosis.

SEXUAL ANHEDONIA. Sexual anhedonia is a rare variant of HSDD seen in the male, in which the patient experiences erection and ejaculation, but no pleasure from orgasm. The cause is attributed to penile anesthesia, due to psychogenic factors occurring in an hysterical or obsessive person. Psychiatric referral is indicated unless there is evidence of spinal cord injury or peripheral neuropathy. Loss of tactile sensation of the penis is unlikely to be organic in cause unless there is associated anesthetic areas in the vicinity of the anus or scrotum.

Symptoms

The HSDD patient complains of a lack of interest in sex even under circumstances that are ordinarily erotic in nature, such as pornography. Sexual activity is infrequent and eventually is absent, often resulting in serious marital discord. HSDD may be selective and focused against a specific sexual partner. When boredom with the usual sexual partner is the cause and frequency of sex with the usual partner decreases, real or fantasized sexual desire toward others may be normal or even increased.

If the cause of HSD falls into a detectable category such as abnormalities of the genitalia, or is due to a related condition such as a prolactinoma, chronic renal disease, diabetes mellitus, genetic disorder, or is familial in nature, the patient will manifest the signs and symptoms of the comorbid (co-occurring) condition. It is important to identify such causes, as their presence will usually dictate appropriate therapy.

Treatment

Currently, there is no approved drug or pharmacological treatment for HSDD and **psychotherapy** has proved to be only minimally effective. A primary goal of therapy is aimed at removal of the underlying cause of HSDD. The choice of medical therapy or behavioral or dynamic psychotherapy depends on the cause. If the cause is related to a medical condition, therapy is directed toward the cure or amelioration of that condition. Examples include cure or amelioration of underlying comorbid conditions such as genitourinary infections, improvement in diabetic control, avoidance of **substance abuse** and of medications that may be potentially responsible.

Therapy should also be directed towards other accompanying sexual disorders such as erectile dysfunction, which may be contributory. In cases where insufficient testosterone is suspected as a possible cause, serum androgen levels should be tested. A testosterone level less than 300 ng/dL in males and less than 10 ng/dL

KEY TERMS

Comorbid—Having another disorder or condition simultaneously.

Dyspareunia—Painful sexual intercourse.

Galactorrhea—Lactation occurring in the absence of pregnancy.

Hypogonadism—Abnormally decreased gonad function with retardation of sexual development.

Priapism—Painful involuntary penile erection persisting in excess of four hours.

Prolactin—A hormone that stimulates milk production and breast development.

Vaginismus—An involuntary tightening of the vaginal muscles that makes sexual intercourse painful, difficult, or impossible.

in females indicates a need for supplemental replacement therapy. If the cause is deemed to be of an interpersonal nature, **couples therapy** may be beneficial, in which case the support and understanding of the sexual partner is essential. Tricyclic **antidepressants** (TCAs) or **monoamine oxidase inhibitors (MAOIs)** may help in the treatment of accompanying depression or panic symptoms.

A recent study has reported that almost a third of nondepressed women with HSDD responded favorably to therapy with sustained release tablets of **bupropion** hydrochloride. The responders noted significant increases in the number of sexual arousals, sexual fantasies, and in the desire to engage in sexual activities. Bupropion hydrochloride (Wellbutrin) is currently approved by the FDA for the treatment of depression. Its favorable action on HSDD may be attributable to its enhancement of certain **neurotransmitters** that affect sexual desire, principally norepinephrine and **dopamine**.

Prognosis

The prognosis for HSDD depends primarily on the underlying cause or causes. In certain medical conditions, the prognosis for development, or recovery of sexual interest, is good. Examples include therapy of hypogonadism with testosterone, or the appropriate treatment of a prolactin-secreting pituitary tumor. On the other hand, in certain genetic defects such as Turner's syndrome and Klinefelter's syndrome, attainment of sexual function is impossible. By far, however, the vast majority of HSDD cases are situational in nature, usually relating to dissatisfaction or loss of interest in the sexual partner. In cases of marital discord, significant assistance may be obtained by counseling given by a health professional trained in the field. Cases of dissatisfaction by both partners often do not respond to such therapy, and frequently culminate in separation, finding a new sexual partner, and divorce.

Prevention

Unfortunately, it is difficult or impossible to predict the occurrence of HSDD in situational cases that comprise the majority of patients. The patience, understanding and support of the sexual partner is essential in those cases of HSDD in which the cause is temporary or transient. Some therapists recommend a period of abstinence from genital sex and have emphasized the value of a period of concentration on non-genital sex in the treatment of HSD.

Resources

BOOKS

Carnes, Patrick, and Joseph Moriarity. *Sexual Anorexia: Overcoming Sexual Self-Hatred.* Center City, MN: Hazelden Press, 1997.

Hawton, Keith. *Sex Therapy: A Practical Guide.* New York: Oxford University Press, 1985.

Lue, Tom F., et al. *Atlas of Clinical Urology: Impotence and Infertility, Volume I.* New York: Current Medicine Group, 1999.

Porter, Robert S., and Justin L. Kaplan, eds. *The Merck Manual of Diagnosis and Therapy.* 19th ed. Whitehouse Station, NJ: Merck Research Laboratories, 2011.

PERIODICALS

Brauer, M. "Attentional and Affective Processing of Sexual Stimuli in Women with Hypoactive Sexual Desire Disorder." *Archives of Sexual Behavior* (September 3, 2011) [e-pub ahead of print]. http://dx.doi.org/10.1007/s10508-011-9820-7 (accessed December 18, 2011).

Fabre, L. F., and L. C. Smith. "The Effect of Major Depression on Sexual Function in Women." *Journal of Sexual Medicine* (August 30, 2011) [e-pub ahead of print]. http://dx.doi.org/10.1111/j.1743-6109.2011.02445.x (accessed December 18, 2011).

Kingsberg, S. "Hypoactive Sexual Desire Disorder: When is Low Sexual Desire a Sexual Dysfunction?" *Journal of Sexual Medicine* 7, no. 8 (2010): 2907–8.

Ralph Myerson, MD

Hypochondriasis

Definition

Hypochondriasis is a mental disorder in which the individual is preoccupied with the thought of having a serious physical disease based on the incorrect or exaggerated interpretation of physical symptoms. This preoccupation continues for at least six months and interferes with the individual's social and occupational functioning even in the face of medical evidence to the contrary. Hypochondriasis is considered a somatoform disorder.

Demographics

According to the *DSM-IV-TR*, hypochondriasis affects 1%–5% of the general population in the United States. The rates of the disorder are higher among clinical outpatients, between 2% and 7%. One recent study suggests that full-blown hypochondriasis is fairly rare, although lesser degrees of worry about illness are more common, affecting as many as 6% of people in a community sample.

Hypochondriasis can appear at any age, although it frequently begins in early adulthood. Men and women appear to equally develop the disorder. The *DSM-IV-TR* notes that people from some cultures may appear to have fears of illness that resemble hypochondriasis, but are in fact influenced by beliefs that are traditional in their culture.

Description

The primary feature of hypochondriasis is excessive fear of having a serious disease. This fear is not relieved when a medical examination finds no evidence of disease. People with hypochondriasis are often able to acknowledge that their fears are unrealistic, but this intellectual realization is not enough to reduce their **diagnosis** of hypochondriasis, preoccupation with fear of disease must cause a great deal of distress or interfere with a person's ability to perform important activities, such as work, school activities, or family and social responsibilities. Hypochondriasis is included in the category of **somatoform disorders** in the ***Diagnostic and Statistical Manual of Mental Disorders*** (*DSM-IV-TR*), which is the reference handbook that clinicians use to guide the diagnosis of mental disorders. Some experts, however, have argued that hypochondriasis shares many features with **obsessive-compulsive disorder** or **panic disorder** and would be more appropriately classified with the **anxiety disorders**.

The fears of a person with hypochondriasis may be focused on the possibility of a single illness, but more often they include a number of possible conditions. The focus of the fears may shift over time as a person notices a new symptom or learns about an unfamiliar disease. The fears appear to develop in response to minor physical abnormalities, like **fatigue**, aching muscles, a mild cough, or a small sore. People with hypochondriasis may also interpret normal sensations as signs of disease. For instance, an occasional change in heart rate or a feeling of dizziness upon standing up will lead a person with hypochondriasis to fears of heart disease or **stroke**. Sometimes hypochondriacal fears develop after the death of a friend or family member, or in response to reading an article or seeing a television program about a disease. Fear of illness can also increase in response to **stress**.

Individuals with hypochondriasis visit physicians frequently; and when told there is nothing physically wrong, they are likely to seek a second opinion since their fears are not soothed. Their apparent distrust of their physicians' opinions can cause tensions in doctor-patient relationships, leading to the patient's further dissatisfaction with health-care providers. Physicians who regularly see a patient with hypochondriasis may become skeptical about any reported symptom, increasing the danger that a real illness may be overlooked. People with hypochondriasis also run the risk of undergoing unnecessary medical tests or receiving unneeded medications. Although they are usually not physically disabled, they may take frequent sick days from work, or annoy friends and family with constant conversation or complaints about illness, reducing their ability to function effectively in some aspects of life.

Causes and symptoms

Causes

The causes behind the development of hypochondriasis are not known, but there are several theories regarding its origin.

AMPLIFICATION OF SENSORY EXPERIENCE. One theory suggests that people with hypochondriasis are highly sensitive to physical sensations. They are more likely than most people to pay close attention to sensations within their bodies (heart rate, minor noises in the digestive tract, the amount or taste of saliva in the mouth, etc.), which magnifies their experience of these feelings. While many people fail to notice minor discomfort as they go about their regular activities, the individual with hypochondriasis pays constant attention to inner sensations and becomes alarmed when these sensations vary in any way. This heightened scrutiny may actually increase the intensity of the sensations, and the intensity of the experience fuels fears that the sensations signal an underlying illness. Once the fears are aroused, preoccupation with the symptom increases, further enhancing the intensity of sensations. The tendency to amplify may be either temporary or chronic; it may also be influenced by situational factors, which helps to explain why hypochondriacal fears are made worse by stress or by events that appear to justify concerns about illness. Some researchers have observed that heightened sensitivity to internal sensations is also a feature of panic disorder, and have suggested that there may be an overlap between the two disorders.

DISTORTED INTERPRETATION OF SYMPTOMS. Another theory points to the centrality of dysfunctional thinking in hypochondriasis. According to this theory, the internal physical sensations of the person with hypochondriasis are not necessarily more intense than those of most people. Instead, people with hypochondriasis are prone to make catastrophic misinterpretations of their physical symptoms. They are pessimistic about the state of their physical health and overestimate their chances of falling ill. Hypochondriasis thus represents a cognitive bias; whereas most people assume they are healthy unless there is clear evidence of disease, the person with hypochondriasis assumes he or she is sick unless given a clean bill of health. Research suggests that people with hypochondriasis make more realistic estimations of their risk of disease than most people, and in fact underestimate their risk of illness. People without hypochondriasis underestimate their risk even more. Some studies indicate that people with hypochondriasis are more likely to have had frequent or serious illnesses as children, which may explain the development of a negative cognitive bias in interpreting physical sensations or symptoms.

Symptoms

The primary symptom of hypochondriasis is preoccupation with fears of serious physical illness or injury. The fears of persons with hypochondriasis have an obsessive quality; they find thoughts about illness intrusive and difficult to dismiss, even when they recognize that their fears are unrealistic. In order to relieve the anxiety that arises from their thoughts, people with hypochondriasis may act on their fears by talking about their symptoms, by seeking information about feared diseases in books or on the Internet, or by "doctor-shopping," going from one specialist to another for consultations. Others may deal with their fears through avoidance, staying away from anything that might remind them of illness or death. Persons with hypochondriasis vary in their insight into their disorder. Some recognize themselves as "hypochondriacs," but have anxiety in spite of their recognition. Others are unable to see that their concerns are unreasonable or exaggerated.

Diagnosis

Hypochondriasis is most likely to be diagnosed when one of the doctors consulted by the patient considers the patient's preoccupation with physical symptoms and concerns excessive or problematic. After giving the patient a thorough physical examination to rule out a general medical condition, the doctor will usually give him or her a psychological test that screens for anxiety or **depression** as well as hypochondriasis. If the results suggest a diagnosis of hypochondriasis, the patient should be referred for **psychotherapy**. It is important to note, however, that patients with hypochondriasis usually resist the notion that their core problem is psychological. A successful referral to psychotherapy is much more likely if the patient's medical practitioner has been able to relate well to the patient and work gradually toward the notion that psychological problems might be related to fears of physical illness.

Specific approaches that have been found useful by primary care doctors in bringing psychological issues to the patient's attention in nonthreatening ways include the following:

- Drawing connections between the patient's current physical symptoms and recent setbacks or upsetting incidents in the patient's life. For example, the patient may come in with health worries within a few days of having a problem in other areas of life, such as their car needing repairs, a quarrel with a family member, an overdue bill, etc.
- Asking the patient to keep a careful diary of his or her symptoms and other occurrences. This diary may be useful in guiding the patient to see patterns in his or her worries about health.
- Scheduling the patient for regular but short appointments. It is also better to see the patient briefly than to prescribe medications in place of an appointment, because many patients with hypochondriasis abuse medications.
- Conducting routine screening tests during a yearly physical for patients with hypochondriasis, while discouraging them from scheduling extra appointments each time they notice a minor physical problem.
- Maintaining a realistic but optimistic tone in conversations with the patient. He or she may wish to talk to the patient about health-related fears and clarify the differences between normal internal body sensations and serious symptoms.

In order to receive a *DSM-IV-TR* diagnosis of hypochondriasis, a person must meet all six of the following criteria:

- The person must be preoccupied with the notion or fear of having a serious disease. This preoccupation is based on misinterpretation of physical symptoms or sensations.

- Appropriate medical evaluation and reassurance that there is no illness present do not eliminate the preoccupation.
- The belief or fear of illness must not be of delusional intensity. Delusional health fears are more likely to be bizarre in nature—for instance, the belief that one's skin emits a foul odor or that food is rotting in one's intestines. The preoccupations must not be limited to a concern about appearance; excessive concerns that focus solely on defects in appearance would receive a diagnosis of body dysmorphic disorder.
- The preoccupation must have lasted for at least six months.
- The person's preoccupation with illness must not simply be part of the presentation of another disorder, including generalized anxiety disorder, obsessive-compulsive disorder, panic disorder, separation anxiety, major depressive episode, or another somatoform disorder.

The *DSM-IV-TR* also differentiates between hypochondriasis with and without poor insight. Poor insight is specified when the patient does not recognize that his or her concerns are excessive or unreasonable.

DSM-5

Proposed changes for the fifth edition of the *DSM* (*DSM-5*, 2013) include changing the diagnosis of hypochondriasis to illness anxiety disorder. Aspects of hypochondriasis are also proposed to be subsumed, along with somatization disorder, undifferentiated somatoform disorder, and pain disorder, into the diagnosis of complex somatic symptom disorder.

Treatment

Traditionally, hypochondriasis has been considered difficult to treat. In the last few years, however, cognitive and behavioral treatments have demonstrated effectiveness in reducing the symptoms of the disorder.

Cognitive therapy

The goal of cognitive therapy for hypochondriasis is to guide patients to the recognition that their chief problem is fear of illness, rather than vulnerability to illness. Patients are asked to monitor worries and to evaluate how realistic and reasonable they are. Therapists encourage patients to consider alternative explanations for the physical signs they normally interpret as disease symptoms. Behavioral experiments are also employed in an effort to change the patient's habitual thoughts. For instance, a patient may be told to focus intently on a specific physical sensation and monitor increases in anxiety. Another behavioral assignment might ask the patient to suppress urges to talk about health-related worries with family members, then observe their anxiety level. Most people with hypochondriasis believe that their anxiety will escalate until they release it by seeking reassurance from others. In fact, anxiety usually crests and subsides in a matter of minutes. Cognitive therapy effectively reduces many symptoms of the disorder, and many improvements persist up to a year after treatment ends.

BEHAVIORAL STRESS MANAGEMENT. One study compared cognitive therapy to behavioral **stress management**. This second form of therapy focuses on the notion that stress contributes to excessive worry about health. Patients were asked to identify stressors in their lives and taught stress management techniques to help them cope with these stressors. The researchers taught the patients relaxation techniques and problem-solving skills, and the patients practiced these techniques in and out of sessions. Although this treatment did not focus directly on hypochondriacal worries, it was helpful in reducing symptoms. At the end of the study, behavioral stress management appeared to be less effective than cognitive therapy in treating hypochondriasis, but a follow-up a year later found that the results of two therapies were comparable.

EXPOSURE AND RESPONSE PREVENTION. This therapy begins by asking patients to make a list of their hypochondriacal behaviors, such as checking body sensations, seeking reassurance from physicians or friends, and avoiding reminders of illness. Behavioral assignments are then developed. Patients who frequently monitor their physical sensations or seek reassurance are asked not to do so, and to allow themselves to experience the anxiety that accompanies suppression of these behaviors. Patients practice exposing themselves to anxiety until it becomes manageable, gradually reducing hypochondriacal behaviors in the process. In a study comparing exposure and response prevention to cognitive therapy, both therapies produced clinically significant results. Although cognitive therapy focuses more on thoughts and exposure therapy more on behaviors, both

KEY TERMS

Comorbid psychopathology—The presence of other mental disorders in a patient together with the disorder that is the immediate focus of therapy.

Somatoform disorders—A group of psychiatric disorders in the *DSM-IV-TR* classification that are characterized by the patient's concern with external physical symptoms or complaints. Hypochondriasis is classified as a somatoform disorder.

appear to be effective in reducing both dysfunctional thoughts and behaviors.

Prognosis

Untreated hypochondriasis tends to be a chronic disorder, although the intensity of the patient's symptoms may vary over time. The *DSM-IV-TR* notes that the following factors are associated with a better prognosis: the symptoms develop quickly, are relatively mild, are associated with an actual medical condition, and are not associated with comorbid psychopathology or benefits derived from being ill.

Prevention

Hypochondriasis may be difficult to prevent in a health-conscious society, in which people are constantly exposed to messages reminding them to seek regular medical screenings for a variety of illnesses, and telling them in detail about the illnesses of celebrities and high-ranking political figures. Trendy new diagnostic techniques like full-body MRIs may encourage people with hypochondriasis to seek unnecessary and expensive medical consultations. Referring patients with suspected hypochondriasis to psychotherapy may also help to reduce their overuse of medical services.

Resources

BOOKS

American Psychiatric Association. *Diagnostic and Statistical Manual of Mental Disorders.* 4th ed., text rev. Washington, DC: American Psychiatric Publishing, 2000.

Asmundson, Gordon J. G., Steven Taylor, and Brian J. Cox, eds. *Health Anxiety: Hypochondriasis and Related Disorders.* New York: John Wiley and Sons, 2002.

Maj, Mario, et al., eds. *Somatoform Disorders,* WPA Series, Evidence and Experience in Psychiatry, Volume 9. New York: John Wiley and Sons, 2005.

VandenBos, Gary R. ed. *APA Dictionary of Psychology.* Washington, DC: American Psychological Association, 2006.

Walker, John R., and Patricia Furer. "Treatment of Hypochondriasis and Psychogenic Movement Disorders: Focus on Cognitive-Behavior Therapy." In *Psychogenic Movement Disorders: Neurology and Neuropsychiatry.* edited by Mark Hallett et al. Philadelphia: Lippincott Williams and Wilkins Publishers, 2005.

PERIODICALS

Abramowitz, Jonathan S. "Hypochondriasis: Conceptualization, Treatment, and Relationship to Obsessive Compulsive Disorder." *Annals of Clinical Psychiatry* 17, no. 4 (October–December 2005): 211–17.

Asmundson, Gordon J. G., Steven Taylor, and Michael J. Coons. "Current Directions in the Treatment of Hypochondriasis." *Journal of Cognitive Psychotherapy* 19, no. 3 (Fall 2005): 285–304.

Avia, M.D., and M. A. Ruiz. "Recommendations for the Treatment of Hypochondriac Patients." *Journal of Contemporary Psychotherapy* 35, no. 3 (October 2005): 301–13.

Bleichhardt, Gaby, Barbara Timmer, and Winfried Rief. "Hypochondriasis Among Patients with Multiple Somatoform Symptoms—Psychopathology and Outcome of a Cognitive-Behavioral Therapy." *Journal of Contemporary Psychotherapy* 35, no. 3 (October 2005): 239–49.

Furer, Patricia, and John R. Walker. "Treatment of Hypochondriasis with Exposure." *Journal of Contemporary Psychotherapy* 35, no. 3 (October 2005): 251–67.

Martínez, M. Pilar, and Cristina Botella. "An Exploratory Study of the Efficacy of a Cognitive-Behavioral Treatment for Hypochondriasis Using Different Measures of Change." *Psychotherapy Research* 15, no. 4 (October 2005): 392–408.

Monopoli, John. "Managing Hypochondriasis in Elderly Clients." *Journal of Contemporary Psychotherapy* 35, no. 3 (October 2005): 285–300.

Noyes, Russell Jr., et al. "Distinguishing Between Hypochondriasis and Somatization Disorder: A Review of the Existing Literature." *Psychotherapy and Psychosomatics* 75, no. 5 (August 2006): 270–81.

Starcevic, Vladan. "Fear of Death in Hypochondriasis: Bodily Threat and Its Treatment Implications." *Journal of Contemporary Psychotherapy* 35, no. 3 (October 2005): 227–37.

Stuart, Scott, and Russell Noyes Jr. "Treating Hypochondriasis with Interpersonal Psychotherapy." *Journal of Contemporary Psychotherapy* 35, no. 3 (Fall 2005): 269–83.

Danielle Barry, MS
Ruth A. Wienclaw, PhD

Hypomania

Definition

A hypomanic episode is a distinct period of time that lasts at least four days during which the individual's mood is consistently elevated, expansive, or irritable and is distinct from his or her usual nondepressed mood. Hypomanic episodes are characteristic of bipolar II disorder as well as features of **cyclothymic disorder**. They may also occur as a transitional phase from euthymia (feeling of well-being often associated with individuals with **bipolar disorder** when they are not having a manic or a depressive episode) to mania in cases of bipolar I disorder.

Demographics

Hypomanic episodes associated with bipolar II disorder have the same demographics as that disorder.

Hypomanic episodes can affect both adults and younger patients. In younger patients and adolescents, hypomania may be associated with such behaviors as school truancy, antisocial behavior, failure in school, or **substance abuse**.

Cultural differences can affect the experience and communication of the symptoms of hypomanic disorder, with different cultures interpreting such symptoms as irritability or inflated self-esteem in various ways. Some cultures and subcultures, for example, value such aspects of hypomania as decreased need for sleep, racing thoughts, or increased goal orientation as positive qualities of a productive individual, and do not regard them negatively.

Description

Hypomanic episodes usually begin suddenly with the symptoms rapidly increasing over the course of a day or two. A hypomanic episode may last anywhere from four days to several months, although some clinicians are beginning to argue that hypomanic episodes may be as short as two days in duration. However, because such research is based on the self-reports of patients (who tend not to be aware of their symptoms at first), there is not widespread agreement about this change in diagnostic criteria.

Causes and symptoms

Hypomania is not a disorder in and of itself. The causes of hypomania vary depending on whether it is a characteristic of bipolar I disorder, bipolar II disorder, or cyclothymic disorder.

During a hypomanic episode, the individual's mood is consistently elevated, expansive, or irritable and distinct from his or her usual nondepressed mood. During this period, the individual must also display at least three of the following symptoms (or four if he or she is only irritable) to be diagnosed as hypomanic:

- inflated sense of self-esteem
- decreased need for sleep
- increased talkativeness or need to talk
- racing thoughts or flight of ideas
- easily distracted
- increased goal-oriented activity
- excessive involvement in pleasurable but high-risk activities (for example, buying sprees, sexual indiscretions, foolish investments)

In hypomania, these symptoms are associated with a clear change from the individual's normal behavior and are readily observable by others. Hypomanic symptoms, however, are not severe enough to noticeably affect the individual's functioning at work or in social situations, nor does their presence require **hospitalization**. To be classified as hypomanic, the individual's symptoms cannot contain psychotic features or be due to the direct physiological effects of a substance (such as drug abuse or medication) or a general medical condition (for example, hyperthyroidism).

Diagnosis

It is important to distinguish hypomania from euthymia in patients who are not used to a nondepressed mood state. In addition, although the two have the same list of diagnostic symptoms, hypomanic episodes are different from manic episodes. Hypomanic symptoms are less severe than manic symptoms and do not cause marked impairment of social or occupational functioning. However, approximately 5% to 15% of individuals experiencing hypomanic episodes will eventually develop a **manic episode**.

Many of the warning signs of a hypomanic episode such as increased goal-oriented behavior can also be normal and appropriate given the situation. Sometimes a patient's good mood is just that. Some of the signs of a normal good mood that could distinguish it from hypomania include:

- ability to enjoy reading for a significant period of time without becoming bored
- ability to listen more than talk in a social setting
- no need to do something risky just to shake things up
- ability to complete tasks without repeatedly being distracted
- experience of appropriate anxiety about demands of life such as responsibilities, deadlines, and financial obligations
- ability to enjoy times of peace and quiet
- ability to sleep well at night for an appropriate period of time
- ability to accept well-meaning, constructive criticism without undue irritation

Treatment

Cognitive-behavioral therapy

Cognitive-behavioral therapy (CBT) is regularly used to help patients test how realistic their thought processes and resultant behaviors are. The goal of such reality testing is to help patients weigh the facts more carefully than they would otherwise do and to seek the insights of others before acting on their beliefs. This approach can help patients be more independent in controlling their lives.

One of the tools used in CBT to assist patients in controlling their impulses during hypomanic episodes is keeping a daily journal of their thoughts. Such daily thought records are a structured method to help patients do a reality check on their thinking and actions. For example, patients can look for situations in which they overestimate their capabilities, rely on luck, underestimate risks, minimize problems, or overvalue immediate gratification.

Patients with hypomanic episodes can also be taught to test the validity of their thoughts and beliefs by consulting trusted others. By talking things through with a trusted and objective person, a patient in a hypomanic episode can be helped to test the reality of his or her thoughts and beliefs.

Another method that can help hypomanic patients test reality is to have them rate the relative risks of the options that they are considering by listing the productive potential and destructive risks of their alternatives. If patients are unable to think of examples of destructive risks for their plans, the therapist or other objective outsider can help by giving them examples and helping them to develop their own list of potential risks. Similarly, lists can be made of the benefit to others versus the cost to oneself or the benefit to oneself versus the cost to others.

Patients can also be helped to more realistically evaluate their thoughts and plans through role playing or playing "devil's advocate." Such techniques can be used to do a hypothetical trial run to see what possible consequences might be incurred if an unreasonable risk is taken.

To help reduce impulsivity and recklessness in hypomanic patients, psychotherapists use various different techniques. One technique is to institute a "wait 48 hours before acting" rule to help the patient avoid spur-of-the-moment reckless actions. It is also sometimes helpful for the patient to try to foresee the possible negative consequences of their proposed actions through imagery by describing the bad things that could happen if they took their proposed course of action. Because hypomanic patients are often overly active, it is sometimes also helpful to have them schedule their activities to help them focus their attention on what is important so that they do not become overextended. Hypomanic patients can also be taught listening skills that can help them focus and break the vicious circle of constant activity and to listen to others. Similarly, patients can be taught anticipatory problem-solving skills that help them recognize the symptoms of a building hypomanic episode and to reduce the stressors that put them at risk. It is also helpful for hypomanic patients to minimize or completely avoid situations that are apt to trigger a hypomanic episode such as daredevil hobbies, exaggerated acts of generosity or intimacy with relative strangers, unsupervised expenditures of large amounts of money, or situations that require the use of a lethal weapon. Hypomanic patients can also be taught to help control or adjust their moods through relaxation techniques and breathing control exercises.

KEY TERMS

Bipolar II disorder—One of a group of mood disorders in which the individual has one or more major depressive episodes and at least one hypomanic episode.

Cognitive-behavioral therapy (CBT)—A form of psychotherapy used to help patients modify their behavior by testing their thought processes.

Cyclothymic disorder—A mood disorder in which hypomanic episodes and depressive episodes both occur over the course of at least two years during which time symptom-free periods last no more than two months.

Euthymia—A feeling of well-being often associated with individuals with bipolar disorder when they are not having a manic or a depressive episode.

Mania—Excitement, overactivity, and inappropriate physical and mental restlessness, often accompanied by impaired judgment.

Psychotic—Behavior characteristic of any of a number of severe mental disorders in which the accuracy of perceptions and thoughts is incorrectly evaluated despite evidence to the contrary, affecting the individual's interaction with external reality.

Role playing—A technique used in psychotherapy in which the patient acts out a situation to test attitudes, relationships, actions, and their potential consequences.

Biological treatments

In addition to CBT approaches in controlling hypomanic episodes, several biologic management strategies may help patients. These include:

- optimizing the dose of mood stabilizer or antimanic medication
- encouraging good sleep practices

- discontinuing antidepressants
- including lorazepam or clonazepam (1–6 mg/day) as clinically indicated
- including mood stabilizers such as lithium, divalproex, or carbamazepine in the treatment regimen as appropriate

In most cases, such biologic treatments can be used on an outpatient basis.

Prevention

There are a number of warning signs of hypomania. If patients can be taught to recognize such early warning signs, they have a better chance of using various techniques to help lessen the possibility of acting out and the negative consequences of inappropriate actions that may be associated with hypomania. Attending to such warning signs also can give patients and their doctors more time to adjust medications or arrange for greater supervision to reduce the potential harm from inappropriate behavior.

Some of the typical early warning signs of an impending hypomanic episode include:

- disruption in sleep patterns (for example, decreased subjective need for sleep)
- decrease in anxiety without cause (such as ignoring a deadline or less concern about owing money)
- high levels of optimism without appropriate sound planning and problem-solving (for example, belief that everything will turn out all right even though nothing has been done to make that a reality)
- increased desire to be with others along with relatively poor listening skills (for example, talking at length to someone who is obviously anxious to leave)
- decreased mental concentration (such as difficulty following through or becoming more disorganized than usual)
- increased libido to the point where it affects other areas of life (for example, dressing more provocatively than usual, or inappropriate talk of or joking about sex)
- increased goal-directed behavior to the point where the individual appears driven

According to CBT, if the patient can be taught to recognize the signs of an impending hypomanic episode early enough, he or she will have the time necessary to put into practice the various techniques already discussed to help avoid the negative consequences of potential risky actions.

Resources

BOOKS

American Psychiatric Association. *Diagnostic and Statistical Manual of Mental Disorders*. 4th ed., text rev. Washington, DC: American Psychiatric Publishing, 2000.

Newman, Cory F., et al. *Bipolar Disorder: A Cognitive Therapy Approach*. Washington, DC: American Psychological Association, 2001.

VandenBos, Gary R. ed. *APA Dictionary of Psychology*. Washington, DC: American Psychological Association, 2006.

Yatham, Lakshmi N., and Mario Maj. *Bipolar Disorder: A Clinicianís Guide to Biological Treatments*. New York: John Wiley and Sons, 2010.

PERIODICALS

Akiskal, Hagop S., and Franco Benazzi. "The DSM-IV and ICD-10 Categories of Recurrent [Major] Depressive and Bipolar II Disorders: Evidence that They Lie on a Dimensional Spectrum." *Journal of Affective Disorders* 92, no. 1 (May 2006): 45–54.

Bauer, Michael, et al. "Self-Reported Data from Patients with Bipolar Disorder: Impact on Minimum Episode Length for Hypomania." *Journal of Affective Disorders* 96, no. 1–2 (November 2006): 101–105.

Benazzi, Franco, and Hagop Akiskal. "The Duration of Hypomania in Bipolar-II Disorder in Private Practice: Methodology and Validation." *Journal of Affective Disorders* 96, no. 3 (2006): 189–96.

Mansell, Warren. "The Hypomanic Attitudes and Positive Predictions Inventory (HAPPI): A Pilot Study to Select Cognitions that Are Elevated in Individuals with Bipolar Disorder Compared to Non-Clinical Controls." *Behavioural and Cognitive Psychotherapy* 34, no. 4 (2006): 1–10.

Utsumi, Takeshi, et al. "Clinical Features of Soft Bipolarity in Major Depressive Inpatients." *Psychiatry and Clinical Neurosciences* 60, no. 5 (October 2006): 611–15.

Ruth A. Wienclaw, PhD

Hypomanic episode *see* **Manic episode**

I

Illusion of doubles *see* **Capgras syndrome**

Illusion of false recognition *see* **Capgras syndrome**

Iloperidone

Definition

Iloperidone (Fanapt) is a medication used in the treatment of **schizophrenia**. Iloperidone belongs to a class of drugs known as atypical antipsychotics, which specifically act on two natural body chemicals, **serotonin** and **dopamine**. These chemicals are types of **neurotransmitters** involved in normal **brain** function and can affect the state of **psychosis** and other symptoms of schizophrenia. Iloperidone acts as a neurotransmitter blocker, inhibiting the effects of serotonin and dopamine at their chemical receptors.

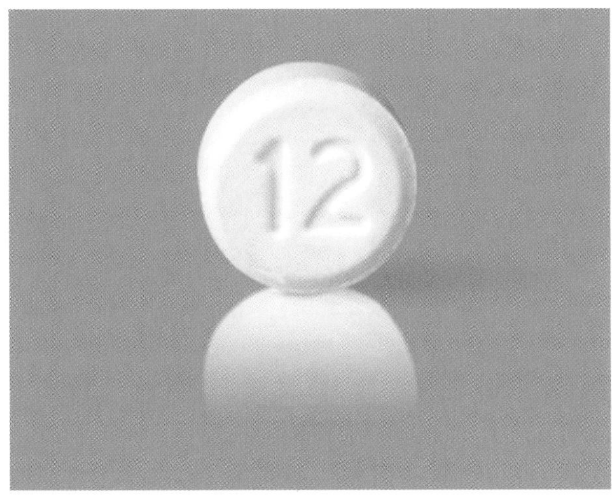

Iloperidone (Fanapt). *(Novartis Pharmaceuticals Corp.)*

Purpose

Iloperidone is an antipsychotic medication. It is in the drug class known as atypical antipsychotics, which have less adverse effects involving **medication-induced movement disorders** than older antipsychotic compounds. The choice of using iloperidone alone or in combination with other drugs in the treatment of schizophrenia depends on the response of the patient to the medication and his or her individual health parameters.

Description

Iloperidone works by inhibiting the absorption of serotonin and norepinephrine in the brain. Since the causes of schizophrenia involve the overactivity of neurotransmitters in some areas of the brain and underactivity in others, antipsychotics such as iloperidone do not completely treat the disorder. The symptoms of schizophrenia known as **positive symptoms**, such as psychosis, are best treated with iloperidone. The cognitive and **negative symptoms** such as withdrawal and difficulty with reasoning are not as well addressed with iloperidone, though the drug has more impact on these types of symptoms than the older and more traditional antipsychotics.

Recommended dosage

Iloperidone is taken as an oral medication. The available doses are 1, 2, 4, 6, 8, 10, and 12 mg pills. The dose is started low and gradually increased to the most effective dose that does not cause intolerable side effects. The first day a patient may take 1 mg twice a day, then 2 mg twice a day on the second day, and then 4 mg per day as needed. The maximum dose is 24 mg per day. If side effects develop or if other drugs are used in combination with iloperidone, the dose may be decreased. Side effects impacting the immune system may make a lower dose or discontinuation of the drug necessary. Some types of severe liver disease may require modification of the dose.

Precautions

Iloperidone is an atypical antipsychotic medication, a class that was developed for the purpose of avoiding some of the side effects often seen with older antipsychotic medications. As a class, these medications cause far fewer movement disorders than older medications, but they still have the potential to cause some disturbing movement-related effects. Patients taking iloperidone must be monitored for the development of movement disorders as well as stiffness, mental status changes, and increased temperature associated with the dangerous **neuroleptic malignant syndrome**. However, iloperidone is less likely to cause these disorders than many other types of antipsychotic medications. Patients taking iloperidone must have their immune system function monitored via periodic blood tests, as the drug can cause dangerous decreases in white blood cells. High blood sugar may also develop, especially in patients at risk for diabetes. Blood sugar is measured before initiating iloperidone dosing, then monitored periodically. Iloperidone carries a risk of low blood pressure and possible temporary loss of consciousness, especially in older or dehydrated patients rising quickly from a lying down position.

Iloperidone and other antipsychotic drugs are associated with an increased risk of death when used in elderly patients with **dementia**. In June 2008, the U.S. Food and Drug Administration (FDA) announced a requirement for manufacturers of iloperidone (and other antipsychotic drugs) to add a warning label to their packaging stating this risk. The reason for the increase was unclear in studies, but most deaths were found to be related to either cardiovascular complications or complications associated with infection. Iloperidone is not approved by the FDA for the treatment of behavior problems in older adults with dementia, and patients in this category (or caregivers of patients in this category) should discuss the risks of taking the drug with their physician.

Iloperidone may not be appropriate for use or may require caution in patients with certain heart abnormalities or disease, liver dysfunction, history of **stroke** or seizure, diabetes, immune dysfunction, patients who are dehydrated, and the elderly. Iloperidone is classified as category C for pregnancy, which means that either there are no adequate human or animal studies or that adverse fetal effects were found in animal studies but there is no available human data. The decision to use category C drugs in pregnancy is generally based on weighing the critical needs of the mother against the risk to the fetus. Other lower category agents are used whenever possible. The safety of iloperidone use during breast-feeding is unknown and so its use is not recommended.

KEY TERMS

Cognitive—Associated with thinking, learning, perception, awareness, and judgment.

Dopamine—A type of neurotransmitter involved in regulation of concentration, impulse control, judgment, mood, attention span, psychostimulation, and disease states such as addiction, and depression.

Insomnia—Disorder involving disturbance of sleep.

Neuroleptic malignant syndrome—Dangerous reaction to antipsychotic medications that involves temperature instability, muscular rigidity, and altered mental status.

Neurotransmitter—A chemical messenger that travels through the body and acts in the nervous system. Neurotransmitter signaling is responsible for a wide range of bodily processes and is often the target of medications involving the brain and cardiovascular system.

Neurotransmitter receptor—A physical recipient for chemicals called neurotransmitters. Receptors sit on the surface of cells that make up body tissues, and once bound to the neurotransmitter, they initiate the chemical signaling pathway associated with neurotransmitters.

Prolactin—Hormone responsible for endocrine function, including lactation.

Psychosis—Loss of contact with reality that may involve false beliefs or hallucinations.

Schizophrenia—Severe psychiatric illness involving the disintegration of thought processes and sometimes including hallucinations.

Serotonin—A type of neurotransmitter involved in regulation of the blood vessels, brain processes, and disease states such as depression.

Side effects

Atypical antipsychotics such as iloperidone are known for having fewer movement related side effects than other types of older antipsychotic medications that act on neurotransmitter receptors in different parts of the brain. This is one reason why as a general class they tend to be the drug of choice in treatment of schizophrenia. However, as with all medication, antipsychotics such as iloperidone do have side effects. Sensitivity to iloperidone varies among patients, and some patients may find

QUESTIONS TO ASK YOUR DOCTOR

- Can I take the full dose right away or do I need to slowly increase the dose up to the full amount?
- Can I stop taking the medication right away or do I need to slowly decrease the dose in order to go off the medication?
- Should I eat before taking this medication?
- Will this medication interact with any of my other prescription medications?
- Are there any over-the-counter medications I should not take with this medicine?
- Will this medicine interact with any of my herbal supplements?
- What side effects indicate that I have taken too much of this medication?
- Can I drink alcoholic beverages when I am taking this medication?

lower doses are more than their body system can tolerate. Common side effects of iloperidone include dizziness, dry mouth, abdominal pain, nausea, diarrhea, weight gain, **fatigue**, increased heart rate, nasal congestion, anxiety, joint pain, sore throat, upper respiratory infections, sexual dysfunction, blurred vision, tremor, rash, and alterations in liver enzymes. Antipsychotics such as iloperidone that act to antagonize dopamine receptors may cause an increase in prolactin, the hormone that causes lactation in women and impotence in men. Low blood pressure or a drop in blood pressure upon standing may result in loss of consciousness. Elderly patients may also be particularly sensitive to sedation, low blood pressure, and other side effects. Rare but serious potential side effects include severe movement disorders, high blood sugar or overt diabetes, stroke, severe difficulty swallowing, dangerous changes in heart rhythm, **seizures**, and changes in blood cells including anemia and decreased immune function. A rare but dangerous possible side effect is neuroleptic malignant syndrome, a reaction involving very high body temperature, altered mental status, and muscular rigidity.

Interactions

Patients should make their doctor aware of all medications and supplements they are taking before using iloperidone. Using alcohol while taking iloperidone may create toxic reactions in the body and should be avoided. Drugs that affect the liver may affect the metabolism of iloperidone, resulting in too much or too little of the drug in the body. This could lead to increased side effects or even toxic doses. Likewise, iloperidone may affect the metabolism of other drugs, leading to greater or lower doses than therapeutically desired.

Many drugs may cause toxicity when used with iloperidone due to additive effects affecting heart rhythm. Drugs that cause these additive effects include the heart medications dronedarone and amiodarone, the chemotherapeutic toremifene, the antibiotics azithromycin and ciprofloxacin, the antifungal fluconazole, the antinausea drug ondansetron, and antipsychotics such as **pimozide**, among many others. The drug bromocriptine used in various neurological and endocrine disorders may cause dangerously low blood pressure when used with iloperidone. Sedative drugs such as codeine and herbal supplements such as calendula, capsicum, kava, and lemon balm may cause additive effects of severe sedation in patients using iloperidone. The herbal supplement Siberian **ginseng** causes antagonizing effects and decreases the effectiveness of iloperidone, as well as exacerbating many psychiatric conditions.

Resources

BOOKS

Brunton, Laurence, et al. *Goodman and Gilman's the Pharmacological Basis of Therapeutics*. 12th ed. New York: McGraw Hill Medical, 2011.

Torrey, E. Fuller. *Surviving Schizophrenia: A Manual for Patients, Family and Providers*. New York: HarperCollins, 2001.

PERIODICALS

Crabtree, B. L., and J. Montgomery. "Iloperidone for the Management of Adults with Schizophrenia." *Clinical Therapeutics* 33, no. 3 (2011): 330–45.

WEBSITES

PubMed Health. "Iloperidone." U.S. National Library of Medicine. http://www.ncbi.nlm.nih.gov/pubmedhealth/PMH0000504 (accessed November 12, 2011).

ORGANIZATIONS

American Society for Clinical Pharmacology and Therapeutics, 528 N Washington St., Alexandria, VA, 22314, (703) 836-6981, info@ascpt.org, http://www.ascpt.org.

National Institute of Mental Health, 6001 Executive Blvd., Rm. 8184, MSC 9663, Bethesda, MD, 20892-9663, (301) 443-4513; TTY: (301) 443-8431, Fax: (301) 443-4279, (866) 615-6464; TTY: (866) 415-8051, nimhinfo@nih.gov, http://www.nimh.nih.gov.

U.S. Food and Drug Administration, 10903 New Hampshire Ave., Silver Spring, MD, 20993-0002, (888) INFO-FDA (463-6332), http://www.fda.gov.

Maria Eve Basile, PhD

Imaginal desensitization *see* **Exposure treatment**

Imaginal exposure *see* **Exposure treatment**

Imaging studies

Definition

Imaging studies are medical tests performed with a variety of techniques that produce pictures of the inside of a patient's body.

Purpose

Imaging studies, also called medical imaging, provide images of parts of the body in order for medical professionals, such as surgeons and family doctors, to diagnose diseases, identify broken bones, and examine the functionality of organs, tissues, and other portions of the body.

Description

Imaging tests are performed using sound waves, radioactive particles, magnetic fields, or x rays that are detected and converted into images after passing through body tissues. Dyes are sometimes used as contrasting agents with x-ray tests so that organs or tissues not seen with conventional x rays can be enhanced. The operating principle of the various techniques is based on the fact that rays and particles interact differently with various types of tissues, especially when abnormalities are present. In this way, the interior of the body can be visualized, and pictures are provided of normal structure and functioning as well as of abnormalities. In the fields pertaining to mental health, including psychology and psychiatry, imaging is often used to help rule out other health problems that could be causing symptoms. Once a **diagnosis** has been established, various imaging techniques may help to confirm the diagnosis and also serve as a way to study the disorder. The imaging techniques may shed new light on the way the disorder affects the **brain**, so that new treatment methods can be implemented. Imaging techniques for psychiatric illnesses are used more in research than in treatment and diagnosis in the clinical setting.

Computed tomography (CT)

Computed tomography (CT), or computed axial tomography (CAT), scans show a cross-section of a part of the body, such as the brain. In this technique, a thin beam of x-ray radiation is used to produce a series of two-dimensional exposures detected at different angles. The exposures are fed into a computer that overlaps them, yielding a single three-dimensional image, such as around a single axis of rotation, analogous to a slice of the organ or body part being scanned. A dye is often injected into the patient to improve contrast and obtain images that are clearer than images obtained solely with x rays. The latest CT equipment allows data to be processed by a computer in various planes, not only in axial (along the axis of the body) or transverse (perpendicular to the body axis) planes.

Around 72 million CT scans were performed in the United States in 2007. Now, in the second decade of the twenty-first century, even more such scans are annually produced in the country and in many parts of the world. The technology's popularity is based on its ability to supplement the use of long-used traditional x rays and diagnosis sonography. CT scans are frequently used to scan the head, lungs, pulmonary arteries, heart, abdomen, pelvis, and extremities. In addition, its popularity is rapidly increasing as CT scans are used more frequently in preventative medicine, such as with people at high risk for colon cancer or heart disease. Further, full-body CT scans are offered at select hospitals and other medical facilities around the United States.

Magnetic resonance imaging (MRI)

Magnetic resonance imaging (MRI) scans also produce cross-sectional images of the body using powerful magnetic fields instead of ionizing radiation. MRI uses a cylinder housing a magnet that will induce the required magnetic field. The patient lies on a platform inside the scanner. The magnetic field aligns nuclei of atoms, such as hydrogen atoms, present in the tissue being scanned in a given direction—what is called magnetization. Following a burst of radio-frequency radiation, the atoms flip back to their original orientation, producing a rotating magnetic field that is detectable by the scanning device. The emitting signals are fed into a computer for conversion into a two-dimensional (2-D) or three-dimensional (3-D) image. When 3-D images are needed, the magnetic field gradients can force nuclei of atoms at various locations to rotate at different speeds. The resulting data allows for 3-D images. Dyes can also be injected into patients to produce clearer images.

Also called nuclear magnetic resonance imaging (NMRI), MRI provides for a clear contrast among the various soft tissues of the body. Consequently, MRI scans are especially useful for such areas of the body as the brain, heart, and muscles. These scans can detect cancer in the body when other types of scans, such as CT scans, cannot.

FUNCTIONAL MAGNETIC RESONANCE IMAGING (FMRI). Functional magnetic resonance imaging (fMRI) scans are a special type of MRI scans. They are used to measure changes in blood flow and blood oxygenation—what are called hemodynamic responses—within the body. Because changes in blood flow and blood oxygenation are related to constantly changing neurological activity in the brain and spinal column, it can be effectively used to detect problems within these highly important regions of the human body.

INTRAOPERATIVE MAGNETIC RESONANCE IMAGING. Intraoperative magnetic resonance imaging (iMRI) scans, another specialized form of MRI scans, are used to view images of the brain while brain surgery is being performed. In other words, intraoperative imaging allows surgeons to see changes taking place within the body, such as the brain, while surgery is progressing. A subset of interventional MRI scanning (MRI scans that generally allow minimally invasive procedures to observe progress being made), iMRI allows surgeons to find the best approach—for example, to remove tumors from the brain without damaging other parts. At the end of the surgery, the iMRI scans also reassure the surgeon that the entire tumor was removed from the brain, and that the surgery was a success. This confirmation prevents the surgical team from having to re-enter the brain a second time, thus making it much more efficient for the medical team and safer for the patient.

Magnetoencephalography

Magnetoencephalography (MEG) is a noninvasive technique that measures magnetic fields produced by neuron activity in the brain. The field measurements provide information about where in the brain the recorded activity is located. MEG is often used in conjunction with other scans, since it produces information about locales (coordinates) that then need to be mapped against an image of the brain.

MEG is primarily used to detect the origin of epileptic **seizures** in the brain. It is also being used to research other disorders, including **schizophrenia**, **dementia**, and **post-traumatic stress disorder**. The advantage of MEG compared to other scans is that it provides information almost instantaneously, offering clinicians a real-time picture of brain activity. It also is very accurate in terms of spatial location. However, MEG is expensive and therefore not as readily available as other types of imaging studies.

Positron emission tomography (PET)

Positron emission tomography (PET) is a noninvasive scanning/imaging technique that utilizes small amounts of radioactive positrons (positively charged particles; also called antielectrons) to visualize body function and metabolism. The **PET** scan uses a special camera and tracer (such as glucose with an added radioactive chemical) to take images of organs and tissues within the body. The camera records the position of the tracer, and the resulting data are then sent to a computer for analysis.

PET scans are especially useful for brain-imaging studies. They are often used to illustrate the differences between brains of people without mental disorders and brains of people with mental disorders. For example, because PET scans can detect brain activity, PET scans of the brains of depressed and nondepressed persons can show researchers where brain activity is decreased in depressed patients. Similar scans have been taken of brains affected by schizophrenia or **Alzheimer's disease**. Such research can help scientists discover new ways to treat these disorders.

Single photon emission computerized tomography (SPECT)

Single photon emission computerized tomography (SPECT) scans are used in research and in diagnosing brain disorders such as Alzheimer's disease and Parkinson's disease. As with PET scans, SPECT scans use gamma-ray-emitting radioisotopes (radioactive isotopes) as a way to produce images of active brain regions. A radioactive tracer is injected into the brain. Because the radioactive tracer does not spread out in the brain, lasts up to one minute, and can be injected at any time, it is especially useful for scanning the brains of epileptic patients because the scan can be taken after an epileptic seizure has passed.

KEY TERMS

Electromagnetic radiation—Radiation including gamma rays, x rays, ultraviolet light, visible light, infrared radiation, microwaves, and radio waves.

Magnetic field—A region around a magnetized body or a current-carrying circuit in which a magnetic force can be detected.

Photon—The smallest amount of electromagnetic radiation that possesses both particle and wave properties.

Positron—The antimatter form of an electron, with the same mass as an electron but with an opposite electrical charge.

SPECT research is ongoing in the early twenty-first century as a way to evaluate patients with various types of seizures, including epileptic seizures, before having surgical procedures. For instance, the Children's Hospital of Pittsburgh, through its Epilepsy Monitoring Unit, regularly performs SPECT scans on children with epilepsy in order to detect changes in blood flow in their brains before epilepsy surgery is performed.

Preparation

The amount of preparation, if any, for the different types of imaging studies is dependent on the type of study being used. Preparation instructions are in place for each type of imaging procedure. Check with the attending medical team or the referring physician before having any scan to determine what type of preparation is necessary. It is important to follow preparatory instructions strictly because failure to do so could result in the session being cancelled or rescheduled.

General guidelines include wearing comfortable clothing, preferably garments that will keep one warm in examination rooms that are usually cool. Avoid wearing jewelry and clothes with metal zippers or other such accessories that could interfere with the operation of the scanning devices. Generally, patients should not eat or have any liquids, except water, for at least four hours before the scheduled scan. Limit the amount of sugar and caffeine for one day before the examination. Drink plenty of water before the scanning session in order to avoid dehydration. These instructions may vary, depending on the type of scan. In addition, most scans require that strenuous physical activity, such as jogging, lifting heavy objects, and bicycling, be avoided for 24 hours before the scan.

Aftercare

A normal schedule and level of activity can be resumed after the scan is complete. One may drink plenty of water or other fluids throughout the rest of the day. Eating a normal amount of food throughout the rest of the day is also recommended.

Risks

When electromagnetic radiation, such as x rays, is used for imaging studies, there is risk from radiation exposure. Exposure to radiation has been linked to cancer, although its exact relationship with respect to imaging studies has yet to be determined. Research is ongoing to determine this link in more detail. Thus, many medical professionals try to reduce the number of scans used on an individual and, when possible, on the duration of each individual scan. Reducing the duration of scans on children is also widely thought to reduce their risks for cancer, although scientific studies have yet to prove such a relationship.

Recently, several scientific studies have suggested a link between cancer and excessive exposure to radiation in such imaging scans. Consequently, under international guidelines set up for anyone using imaging scans, it is assumed that any radiation dose, even a tiny one, poses a health risk to the patient. International consensus states that any radiation exposure through imaging studies provides a very small risk of inducing cancer into the patient.

QUESTIONS TO ASK YOUR DOCTOR

- Will I need to have someone stay with me during the imaging study? Will this person need to drive me home?
- What special precautions should be taken with a child?
- Should I expect any side effects?
- How many scans is it safe to receive in any one year? How far apart should they be spaced?

Results

The images produced during these scans are normally sent to the attending physician. Make an appointment with this medical professional to discuss the results of the scan.

Resources

BOOKS

Armstrong, Peter, Martin L. Wastie, and Andrea G. Rockall. *Diagnostic Imaging.* Chichester, U.K.: Wiley-Blackwell, 2009.

Seeram, Euclid. *Computed Tomography: Physical Principles, Clinical Applications and Quality Control.* St. Louis: Saunders/Elsevier, 2009.

Valk, Peter P., et al., editors. *Positron Emission Tomography: Clinical Practice.* London: Springer, 2006.

Westbrook, Catherine. *Handbook of MRI Techniques.* Chichester, U.K.: Wiley-Blackwell, 2008.

WEBSITES

"Alzheimer's Disease and Dementia." Alzheimer Society of British Columbia. http://www.alzheimerbc.org/Alzheimers-Disease-and-Dementia.aspx (accessed May 25, 2011).

"Intraoperative Magnetic Resonance Imaging (iMRI)." Mayo Clinic. http://www.mayoclinic.org/intraoperative-mri (accessed May 24, 2011).

"Parkinson's Disease." PubMed Health, U.S. National Library of Medicine. (May 6, 2011). http://www.ncbi.nlm.nih.gov/pubmedhealth/PMH0001762 (accessed May 25, 2011).

"Single Photon Emission Computed Tomography (SPECT)." Children's Hospital of Pittsburgh. (October 19, 2010). http://www.chp.edu/CHP/single+photon+emission+computed+tomography+(spect) (accessed May 24, 2011).

ORGANIZATIONS

National Institute of Biomedical Imaging and Bioengineering, 31 Center Dr., 1C14, Bethesda, MD, 20892-8859, (301) 469-8859, http://www.nibib.gov.

Monique Laberge, Ph.D.
William Atkins, BB, BS, MBA

Imipramine

Definition

Imipramine is a tricyclic antidepressant. It is sold under the brand name Tofranil in the United States.

Purpose

Imipramine is used to relieve symptoms of **depression**. It is also used in the treatment of **enuresis** (bed-wetting) in people between the ages of 6 and 25.

Description

Imipramine hydrochloride was the first tricyclic antidepressant to be discovered. Tricyclic **antidepressants** act to change the balance of naturally occurring chemicals in the **brain** that regulate the transmission of nerve impulses between cells. Mental well-being is partially dependent on maintaining a correct balance of these brain chemicals. Imipramine is thought to act primarily by increasing the concentration of norepinephrine and **serotonin** (both chemicals that stimulate nerve cells) and, to a lesser extent, by blocking the action of another brain chemical, acetylcholine. Imipramine shares most of the properties of other tricyclic antidepressants, such as **amitriptyline**, **amoxapine**, **clomipramine**, **desipramine**, **nortriptyline**, **protriptyline**, and **trimipramine**.

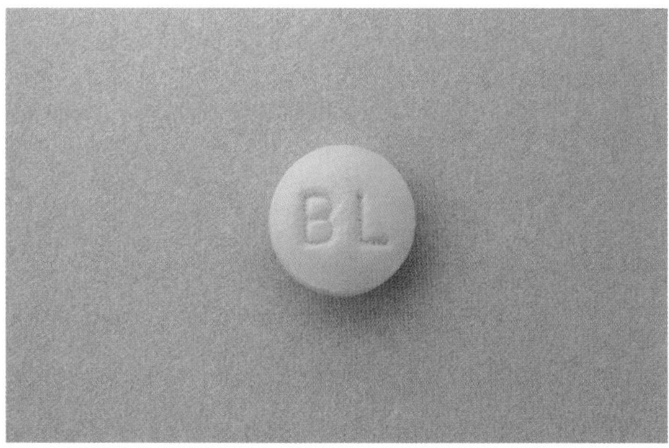

Imipramine, 10 mg. *(© Custom Medical Stock Photo, Inc. Reproduced by permission.)*

The therapeutic effects of imipramine, like other antidepressants, appear slowly. Maximum benefit is often not evident for two to three weeks after starting the drug. People taking imipramine should be aware of this and continue taking the drug as directed even if they do not see immediate improvement.

Recommended dosage

Imipramine is usually started with a total dosage of up to 100 mg per day divided into several smaller doses. This is generally increased to a total of 200 mg per day divided into several doses. Total dosages for patients who are not hospitalized should be no more than 200 mg per day. The recommended maximum dosage for the drug for all patients is 250–300 mg per day. Before dosages greater than 200 mg per day are taken, an electrocardiogram (ECG) should be done. This should be repeated at regular intervals until a steady-state dosage is reached. Lower dosages are recommended for adolescents and older people (over age 60). The lowest dosage that controls symptoms of depression should be used.

Imipramine should be withdrawn gradually, rather than abruptly discontinued. This will help reduce the possibility of a **relapse** into depression.

Precautions

Some studies have shown that children and adults up to age 24 are at an increased risk of developing suicidal thoughts or behaviors when taking antidepressants, including imipramine. Any patient taking imipramine should be closely monitored for signs of worsening depression or other risk factors including panic attacks, difficulty falling asleep, irritability, planning to engage in self-harm or to attempt **suicide**, or abnormal excitement. Any signs that a persons is considering self-harm or suicide warrants an immediate call to the doctor. The risk of suicide may also be increased when imipramine is taken in overdose or combined with alcohol.

Like all tricyclic antidepressants, imipramine should be used cautiously and with close physician supervision in patients, especially the elderly, with benign prostatic hypertrophy, urinary retention, and glaucoma, especially angle-closure glaucoma (the most severe form). Before starting treatment, people with these conditions should discuss the relative risks and benefits of treatment with their doctors to help determine if imipramine is the right antidepressant for them.

A common problem with tricyclic antidepressants is sedation (drowsiness, lack of physical and mental alertness). This side effect is especially noticeable early in therapy. In most patients, sedation decreases or disappears entirely with time, but until then patients taking imipramine should not perform hazardous activities requiring mental alertness or coordination. The sedative effect is increased when imipramine is taken with other central nervous system depressants, such as alcoholic beverages, sleeping medications, other **sedatives**, or antihistamines, and combinations of imipramine with any of these substances should be avoided.

Imipramine may increase heart rate and stress on the heart. It may be dangerous for people with cardiovascular disease, especially those who have recently had a heart attack, to take this drug or other antidepressants in the same pharmacological class. Older people and people with a history of heart disease may develop heart arrhythmias (irregular heartbeat), heart conduction abnormalities, congestive heart failure, heart attack, abnormally rapid heart rates, and strokes. Changes in blood pressure have also been reported.

Manic episodes and the emergence of symptoms of preexisting psychotic states have been reported when imipramine therapy is started.

Patients undergoing surgery should stop taking imipramine at least two weeks before their procedure (if possible), to avoid adverse interactions with the anesthesia.

Side effects

Imipramine shares side effects common to all tricyclic antidepressants. The most frequent of these are dry mouth, constipation, urinary retention, increased heart rate, sedation, irritability, dizziness, and decreased coordination. As with most side effects associated with tricyclic antidepressants, the intensity is highest at the beginning of therapy and tends to decrease with continued use.

Confusion, disorientation, **delusions**, **insomnia**, and anxiety have been reported as side effects in a small percentage of people taking imipramine, as have problems associated with the skin (loss of sensation, numbness and tingling, rashes, spots, itching, and puffiness), **seizures**, ringing in the ears, nausea, vomiting, loss of appetite, diarrhea, and abdominal cramping.

Dry mouth, if severe to the point of causing difficulty speaking or swallowing, may be managed by dosage reduction or temporary discontinuation of the drug. Patients may also chew sugarless gum or suck on sugarless candy in order to increase the flow of saliva. Some artificial saliva products may provide temporary relief.

Interactions

Methylphenidate may increase the effects of imipramine. This is usually avoided by reducing the dosage of imipramine.

Imipramine may increase the depressant action of alcohol. For this reason, people taking imipramine should not drink alcoholic beverages.

Dangerously high blood pressure has resulted from the combination of tricyclic antidepressants, such as imipramine, and members of another class of antidepressants known as **monoamine oxidase inhibitors (MAOIs)**. Patients taking imipramine should not take **MAOIs** (or vice versa). Patients taking any MAOIs, such as Nardil (**phenelzine** sulfate) or Parnate (**tranylcypromine** sulfate), should stop taking the drug and wait at least 14 days before starting treatment with imipramine or any other tricyclic antidepressant. The same holds true when discontinuing imipramine and starting an MAOI.

The sedative effects of imipramine are increased by other central nervous system depressants such as alcohol, sedatives, sleeping medications, or medications used for other mental disorders such as **schizophrenia**. The anticholinergic (drying out) effects of imipramine are additive with other anticholinergic drugs such as **benztropine**, **biperiden**, **trihexyphenidyl**, and antihistamines.

Resources

BOOKS

Adams, Michael, and Norman Holland. *Core Concepts in Pharmacology*. 3rd ed. Upper Saddle River, NJ: 2010.

Foreman, John C., and Torben Johansen. *Textbook of Receptor Pharmacology*. 2nd ed. Boca Raton, FL: CRC Press, 2002.

Page, Clive P., et al. *Integrated Pharmacology*. 3rd ed. St. Louis, MO: Elsevier, 2006.

Von Boxtel, Chris J., Budiono Santoso, and I. Ralph Edwards, eds. *Drug Benefits and Risks: International Textbook of Clinical Pharmacology*. New York: John Wiley and Sons, 2001.

PERIODICALS

Jain A. K., N. S. Thomas, and R. Panchagnula. "Transdermal Drug Delivery of Imipramine Hydrochloride. I. Effect of Terpenes." *Journal of Controlled Release* 79, no. 1–3; (February 19, 2002): 93–101.

Juarez-Olguin, Hugo, et al. "Clinical Evidence of an Interaction Between Imipramine and Acetylsalicylic Acid on Protein Binding in Depressed Patients." *Clinical Neuropharmacology* 25, no. 1 (2002): 32–36.

OTHER

U.S. Food and Drug Administration. "Class Suicidality Labeling Language for Antidepressants." http://www.accessdata.fda.gov/drugsatfda_docs/label/2005/20152s035lbl.pdf (accessed October 9, 2011).

WEBSITES

Daily Med. "Tofranil (imipramine hydrochloride) Injection, Solution (Geigy Pharmaceuticals)." U.S. National Library of Medicine, National Institutes of Health. http://dailymed.nlm.nih.gov/dailymed/drugInfo.cfm?id=2039 (accessed October 9, 2011).

MedlinePlus. "Imipramine." U.S. National Library of Medicine, National Institutes of Health. September 22, 2011. http://www.nlm.nih.gov/medlineplus/druginfo/medmaster/a682389.html (accessed October 9, 2011).

ORGANIZATIONS

American Academy of Clinical Toxicology, 6728 Old McLean Village Drive, McLean, VA, 22101, (703) 556-9222, Fax: (703) 556-8729, admin@clintox.org, http://www.clintox.org.

American Academy of Family Physicians, 11400 Tomahawk Creek Parkway, Leawood, KS, 66211-2672, (913) 906-6000, (800) 274-2237, Fax: (913) 906-6075, contactcenter@aafp.org, http://www.aafp.org.

American Psychiatric Association, 1000 Wilson Blvd., Ste. 1825, Arlington, VA, 22209-3901, (703) 907-7300, apa@psych.org, http://www.psych.org.

American Society for Clinical Pharmacology and Therapeutics, 528 North Washington Street, Alexandria, VA, 22314, (703) 836-6981, http://www.ascpt.org.

American Society for Pharmacology and Experimental Therapeutics, 9650 Rockville Pike, Bethesda, MD, 20814-3995, (301) 634-7060, Fax: (301) 634-7061, http://www.aspet.org.

U.S. Food and Drug Administration, 10903 New Hampshire Ave., Silver Spring, MD, 20993-0002, (888) INFO-FDA (463-6332), http://www.fda.gov.

L. Fleming Fallon, Jr., M.D, Dr. P.H.
Emily Jane Willingham, PhD

Impulse control disorders

Definition

Impulse control disorders are characterized by an individual's inability to resist the impulse to perform an action that is harmful to one's self or others. This condition is a relatively new class of **personality disorders**. Medical researchers surmise that at the root of the problem, the afflicted person desires small, short–term pleasures or gains—often performed impulsively and without the ability to resist such behaviors—over the likelihood of much larger, long–term loses. Some of the most common types of these disorders are **intermittent explosive disorder**, **kleptomania**, **pyromania**, compulsive **gambling disorder**, and **trichotillomania**.

Demographics

Such disorders are found in both genders of the population. They usually begin to appear in children in and around the ages of seven to 15 years of age.

Description

All of these impulse control disorders involve the loss or lack of control in certain specific situations. The hallmark of these disorders is the individual's inability to stop impulses that may cause harm to themselves or others. Affected individuals often feel anxiety or tension in considering these behaviors. This anxiety or tension is relieved or diminished once the action is performed.

Intermittent explosive disorder (IED) is more common among males, and involves repeated and aggressive, violet outbursts that lead to assaults on others or destruction of property. These outbursts, often only ten to twenty minutes in duration, are unprovoked or seem to be out of proportion to the event that precedes them. Afterwards, such people often feel remorse and regret from such actions. The outbursts may happen in several separate incidents over a few hours or days or may occur as one or more every so many weeks or months. Examples of intermittent explosive disorder commonly found in daily life include **road rage** and domestic violence and **abuse**.

Kleptomania is more common among females, and involves the theft of objects that are seemingly worthless. The act of stealing relieves tension and anxiety, and increases personal gratification during the act. Once the act is accomplished, individuals feel relieved of their tensions. In addition, they do not steal for the sense of monetary gain. The actual stealing is not preplanned, and the concept of punishment for the crime does not occur to these individuals, although they are aware that what they are doing is wrong. The people afflicted with kleptomania are often very ashamed of their actions afterwards, but are unable to stop themselves and oftentimes unwilling to seek medical or psychological help.

Pyromania is more common among males, and involves setting fires in order to feel pleasure and relieve tension. It is classified by the deliberate setting of fires more than once. Pyromaniacs do not start fires for the same reasons as do arsonists. They are not looking for revenge, monetary gain, or political reasons, only feelings of relief or gratification. They do not start fires as direct part of criminal behavior or due to hallucinations (such as with drug use). The individual exhibits a fascination and attraction to fire and any objects associated with it. Pyromanics often direct their actions toward fire stations and other buildings associated with fire control and prevention.

Pathological gambling occurs in roughly 1%–3% of the population, and involves excessive (compulsive) gambling despite heavy monetary losses. This disorder typically begins in youth, and affected individuals are often competitive, easily bored, restless, and generous. Their losses actually act as a motivating factor in continuing gambling in order to recoup some of what was lost. Pathological gamblers often use lies, theft, and fraud to continue their compulsive gambling habit. They often gamble more during periods of high **stress** or anxiety in order to counter their feelings. Often they gamble for the excitement and not for the money. However, many of them lose large amounts of money, making them more anxious and, in turn, more likely to place larger and riskier bets.

Trichotillomania, also commonly called hair–pulling disorder, involves the uncontrollable, nearly continuous pulling of hair from one's own scalp, face, or other areas of the body, and is more common in females. It often begins in childhood, and is often associated with major **depression** or **attention deficit hyperactivity disorder** (ADHD). There is an increased sense of tension before pulling the hair that is relieved once it is pulled out. Recurrent pulling out of one's hair may result in noticeable hair loss. It can be a mild problem for some people and in others, quite devastating. For all of them, the disorder is very emotional, especially when large amounts of hair are pulled from visible parts of the body, such as from the head. Affected individuals can undergo significant distress and impaired social, occupational, and functional behavior.

Causes and symptoms

The exact causes of impulse control disorders were not fully understood as of 2011. Individuals who have had serious head injuries, however, can be at a higher risk for developing impulse control disorders, as are those with epilepsy.

Some cases of impulse control disorders appear to be side effects of general medical conditions. Several groups of researchers have noted that some older adults with Parkinson's disease become compulsive gamblers as the disease progresses. It is thought that this gambling behavior is a side effect of dopaminergic drugs, as it does not respond to standard treatments for compulsive gambling but only to changes in the patient's medication. A study performed in 2007, headed by a medical researcher from the U.S. National Institute of Neurological Disorders and **Stroke**, found that pathological gamblers who received **dopamine** agonists developed Parkinson's disease at a younger age than those without the disorder. Those with the disorder also scored lower on an impulsivity scale than did other people.

Another medical condition that is associated with impulse control disorders is carcinoid syndrome. In one group of 20 patients with the syndrome, 75% met *DSM–IV* diagnostic criteria for one or another impulse control disorder. The researchers attribute the connection to the high levels of **serotonin** (a neurotransmitter) produced by carcinoid tumors.

The cause of intermittent explosive disorder may be due to environmental, genetic, or biological factors, but the exact cause is still undetermined.

Numerous symptoms of intermittent explosive disorder are:

- irritability
- rage and anger
- tingling
- increased energy
- tremors and palpitations
- tightness of the chest
- headache or pressure in or about the head

The cause of kleptomania is not known for sure in the medical community. Some researchers have suggested that certain chemicals in the **brain** may be linked to the condition. However, additional research is needed before a determination of the cause of the disorder can be announced.

Some of the symptoms of kleptomania are:

- strong urges to steal even though the items are not needed
- tension and anxiety leading up to the act of stealing
- feelings of pleasure and satisfaction while in the act of the theft
- feelings of guilt, embarrassment, and shame afterwards

Although not known for sure, genetic and environmental factors are considered to be possible causes for pathological gambling. Certain natural occurring chemicals in the brain, such as dopamine, norepinephrine, and serotonin indicate possible associations with the disorder. Sometimes, medications taken (external to the disorder) may bring on the disorder. Serious injuries, such as brain **trauma**, can also contribute to pathological gambling.

Several symptoms of pathological gambling are:

- extreme excitement from taking large gambling bets
- being preoccupied with gambling
- increasing the number and/or amount of gambling bets
- showing more interest in gambling than other personal and professional interests
- lying about gambling
- feelings of remorse and guilt after gambling
- large debts and financial problems; also, some legal difficulties may develop
- problems holding onto job and career, and difficulties coping with family responsibilities

For trichotillomania, mutations in the gene SLITRK1 have been associated with the disorder. Tourette syndrome—a syndrome characterized by unusual movements and sounds—is also linked to the disorder. Problems with natural chemicals in the brain, such as dopamine and serotonin, are suggested as a possible cause of trichotillomania.

Symptoms of trichotillomania include:

- bald or patchy spots on the scalp or other parts of the body
- excessive playing with hair or pulled–out hair, including chewing of hair
- thin or missing eyebrows and eyelashes
- pulling hair across the face, especially the lips

Diagnosis

A **diagnosis** of any of these impulse control disorders can be made only after other medical and psychiatric disorders that may cause the same symptoms have been ruled out. Once this is done a medical professional analyzes the physical and mental problems apparent to the patient.

In addition, many doctors administer questionnaires or similar psychiatric screeners as part of the differential diagnosis. Two instruments that were devised in the early 2000s to specifically target impulsive behavior are the Gambling Urge Scale (GUS) and the Lifetime History of Impulsive Behaviors (LHIB) Interview.

For instance, in a medical diagnosis of pathological gambling, five or more of the following symptoms must be present:

- a preoccupation with gambling
- a need to gamble with more money to achieve the thrill of winning
- repeated attempts to control or stop gambling
- irritability or restlessness due to repeated attempts of control
- gambling as an escape from stress
- lying to cover up gambling
- conducting illegal activities, such as embezzling or fraud, to finance gambling
- losing a job or personal relationship due to gambling
- borrowing money to fund gambling

Treatment

A combination of psychological counseling and medication are the preferred treatments for impulse control disorders. For kleptomania, pyromania, and trichotillomania, **behavior modification** is usually the treatment of choice. Children with trichotillomania are often helped by antidepressant medication. For pathological gambling, treatment usually involves an adaptation of the model set forth by Alcoholics Anonymous. Individuals are counseled with the goal of eventual responding to appropriate social limits. In the case of intermittent explosive disorder, anger management and medication may be used in extreme cases of aggression.

KEY TERMS

Carcinoid syndrome—The pattern of symptoms (often including asthma and diarrhea) associated with carcinoid tumors of the digestive tract or lungs.

Compulsive gambling disorder—An impulse control disorder in which an individual cannot resist gambling despite repeated losses.

Intermittent explosive disorder—A personality disorder in which an individual is prone to intermittent explosive episodes of aggression during which he or she causes bodily harm or destroys property.

Kleptomania—An impulse control disorder characterized by stealing objects that are of little or no value.

Pyromania—An impulse control disorder in which one sets fires.

Trichotillomania—An impulse or compulsion to pull out one's own hair.

Prognosis

These disorders can usually be controlled with medication, although the medication may need to be continued long–term to help prevent further aggressive outbursts. Long–term counseling is usually necessary as well. **Support groups** and meetings may also help these individuals.

The prognosis for intermittent explosive disorder, kleptomania, and pyromania is fair. Little is known about the prognosis for trichotillomania, and studies have shown that the condition can disappear for long periods (months to years) without any psychological counseling. For pathological gambling, the prognosis varies greatly from person to person. While total cure for this condition is unlikely, much like alcoholism, long periods of abstinence or continuous abstinence are possible.

Prevention

There are no known preventive treatments or measures for impulse control disorders.

Resources

BOOKS

Aboujaoude, Elias, and Lorrin M. Koran. *Impulse Control Disorders*. New York: Cambridge University Press, 2010.

Grant, Jon E. *Impulse Control Disorders: A Clinician's Guide to Understanding and Treating Behavioral Addictions*. New York: W. W. Norton, 2008.

Hollander, Eris, and Dan J. Stein, eds. *Clinical Manual of Impulse–Control Disorders*. Arlington, VA: American Psychiatric Publishing, 2005.

WEBSITES

Mayo Clinic. "Compulsive Gambling" January 19, 2011. http://www.mayoclinic.com/health/compulsive–gambling/DS00443 (accessed October 9, 2011).

Mayo Clinic. "Intermittent Explosive Disorder." June 10, 2010. http://www.mayoclinic.com/health/intermittent-explosive-disorder/DS00730 (accessed October 9, 2011).

Mayo Clinic. "Kleptomania." October 5, 2011. http://www.mayoclinic.com/health/kleptomania/DS01034 (accessed October 9, 2011).

Mayo Clinic. "Trichotillomania." January 19, 2011. http://www.mayoclinic.com/health/trichotillomania/DS00895 (accessed October 9, 2011).

ScienceDaily. "Characteristics of Increased Risk For Compulsive Gambling Linked To Parkinson's Disease Medications." February 15, 2007. http://www.sciencedaily.com/releases/2007/02/070212184152.htm (accessed October 9, 2011).

ORGANIZATIONS

American Psychiatric Association, 1000 Wilson Blvd., Suite 1825, Arlington, VA, 22209-3901, (703) 907-7300, apa@psych.org, http://www.psych.org.

Gamblers Anonymous International Service Office, PO Box 17173, Los Angeles, CA, 90017, (626) 960-3500, isomain@gamblersanonymous.org, http://www.gamblersanonymous.org.

National Institute of Mental Health, 6001 Executive Blvd., Room 8184, MSC 9663, Bethesda, MD, 20892-9663, (301) 433-4513; TTY: (301) 443-8431, (866) 615-6464; TTY: (866) 415-8051, Fax: (301) 443-4279, nimhinfo@nih.gov, http://www.nimh.nih.gov.

Trichotillomania Learning Center, Inc, 207 McPherson St., Suite H, Santa Cruz, CA, 95060-5863, (831) 457-1004, Fax: (831) 426-4383, info@trich.org, http://www.trich.org.

Liz Meszaros
Rebecca Frey, PhD

Inderal *see* **Propranolol**

Informed consent

Definition

Informed consent is a legal document in all 50 U. S. states, prepared as an agreement for treatment, non-treatment, or for an invasive procedure that requires physicians to disclose the benefits, risks, and alternatives to the treatment, non-treatment, or procedure. It is the method by which a fully informed, rational patient may be involved in the choices about his or her health. Informed consent applies to mental health practitioners (psychiatrists, psychologists, etc.) in their treatment with their clients in generally the same way as physicians with their patients.

Description

Informed consent stems from the legal and ethical right the patient has to decide what is done to his or her body, and from the mental health provider's ethical duty to ensure that the patient is involved in decisions about his or her own health care. The process of ensuring informed consent for treatment involves five elements. All involve information exchange between doctor and patient and are a part of patient education. First, in words the patient can understand, the therapist must convey three things: (1) the details of a treatment or procedure, (2) its potential benefits and serious risks, and (3) any feasible alternatives. The patient should be presented with information on the most likely outcomes of treatment. Next, the practitioner must evaluate whether or not the person has understood what has been said, must ascertain that the risks have been accepted, and that the patient is giving consent to proceed with the treatment with full knowledge and forethought. Finally, the patient must sign the consent form, which documents in generic format the major points of consideration. The only exception to this is securing informed consent during extreme emergencies. It is critical that the patient receive enough information on which to base his or her informed consent, and that the consent is wholly voluntary and has not been forced in any way.

Anyone suffering from an illness, anticipating surgery, or undergoing treatment for a disease is under a great deal of **stress** and anxiety. It may be natural for a patient to be confused or indecisive. When the attending physician has serious doubts about the patient's understanding of the **intervention** and its risks, the patient may be referred for a psychiatric consultation. This is strictly a precaution to ensure that the patient understands what has been explained; declining to be treated or operated on does not necessarily mean the person is incompetent. It could mean that the person is exercising the right to make his or her own healthcare decisions.

Consent is generally not assumed or considered to be implied except in emergency cases where a patient's life is in danger, no prior wishes have been expressed, and a family member or guardian is not present to give consent. Furthermore, a person must possess the mental faculties to understand and give consent; people who are intellectually disabled, intoxicated, or otherwise impaired may not be legally able to consent to treatment.

According to the "Ethical Principles of Psychologists" and "Code of Conduct" designed by the **American Psychological Association**, informed consent also applies when conducting research involving human subjects prior to their participation. Participants in the study should be informed in understandable language to three main points. First, the participant should be informed about the nature of the research. Secondly, participants should be informed that their participation is completely voluntary and that they are free to withdraw from or not participate in the study at any time. Consent must be made without pressure being put on the participant to engage in the study. Finally, the potential consequences of participating or withdrawing should be presented to the participant. This includes risks, discomfort, and limitations of confidentiality.

With regard to either therapy treatment or research participation, another member of the healthcare/research team may obtain the signed informed consent with the assurance that the provider has satisfied the requirements of informed consent.

The actual informed consent form is to document the process and protect the provider and the hospital. Legally, it is proof of what has been covered and the patient agrees to the procedure, risks, benefits and options. The informed consent process is in place for the protection of the patient. It also serves to ensure that everything is discussed with the patient: all of the options, all of the common risks, the worst case scenario, and other similar situations.

Origins

There is a theory that the practice of acquiring informed consent is rooted in the post–World War II Nuremberg Trials. Following the war crimes tribunal in 1949, as a result of the Karl Brandt case, 10 standards were put forth regarding physician's requirements for experimentation on human subjects. This established a new standard of ethical medical behavior for the post–World War II human rights age, and the concept of voluntary informed consent was established. A number of rules accompanied voluntary informed consent within the realms of research. It could only be requested for experimentation for the gain of society, for the potential acquisition of knowledge of the pathology, and for studies performed that avoided physical and mental suffering to the fullest extent possible.

Benefits

There are advantages to the informed consent process. First, it can be empowering to the patient to understand that he/she plays an important role in their own treatment. They are encouraged to be active participants in the treatment process and know their options well enough to make the best treatment decisions for themselves. This also shifts the responsibility to patients to work with the therapist towards their mental health goals possibly increasing self-confidence and autonomy, and decreasing dependence on the therapist.

Precautions

A crucial component of informed consent is that the person signing it is competent or able to make a rational decision and meaningfully give consent. This situation gets more complicated when working with people who are unable to understand what has been explained or are unable to make a reasonable decision about their health care. According to the "Code of Conduct" for psychologists designed by the American Psychological Association, if this is the case, informed permission from a "legally authorized person" should then be sought, if that is a legal alternative. The ethical guidelines are more stringent than legal guidelines in many states, where the informed consent of the parent or guardian is all that is required, whether or not the professional has attempted to explain the procedure to the client.

Although it is necessary to present the procedure or treatment formally to the patient, there is concern that this process could hurt the therapeutic relationship between the client and therapist. For example, if an informed consent is too detailed, it could frighten a new client who may be hesitant about therapy to begin with. In addition, informing patients about the risks of treatment might scare them into refusing it when the risks of non-treatment are even greater.

There are undoubtedly many issues regarding informed consent. As modern society continues to be litigious, the courts and/or government may take on a more active role in deciding the extent to which patients must be informed of treatments, procedures, and **clinical trials** in which they voluntarily become enrolled. Therefore, healthcare providers must become more educated as to what needs to be conveyed to patients, and to what extent.

Resources

BOOKS

Berg, Jessica W., et al. *Informed Consent: Legal Theory and Clinical Practice.* 2nd ed. New York: Oxford University Press, 2001.

PERIODICALS

Caplan, Arthur L. "Ethical Issues Surrounding Forced, Mandated, or Coerced Treatment." *Journal of Substance Abuse Treatment* 31, no. 2, September 2006: 117–20.

Dunn, Laura B., et al. "Assessing Decisional Capacity for Clinical Research or Treatment: A Review of Instruments." *American Journal of Psychiatry* 163, no. 8, August 2006: 1323–34.

Fallon, April. "Informed Consent in the Practice of Group Psychotherapy." *International Journal of Group Psychotherapy* 56, no. 4 (2006): 431–53.

Jackson, Grace E. "Mental Health Screening in Schools: Essentials of Informed Consent." *Ethical Human Psychology and Psychiatry* 8, no. 3, Fall–Winter 2006: 217–24.

WEBSITES

CRICO/RMF.com "Risk Management Issues: Improved Informed Consent." http://www.rmf.harvard.edu/patient-safety-strategies/informed-consent/index.aspx (accessed October 9, 2011).

National Organization of Circumcision Information Resource Centers. "Informed Consent." January 16, 2010. http://www.nocirc.org/consent (accessed October 9, 2011).

University of Washington. "Informed Consent." April 11, 2008. http://depts.washington.edu/bioethx/topics/consent.html (accessed October 9, 2011).

U.S. National Cancer Institute. "A Guide to Understanding Informed Consent." http://www.cancer.gov/clinicaltrials/patientsafety/informed-consent-guide/page1 (accessed October 31, 2011).

Yale University School of Medicine. "Informed Consent." http://www.yalemedicalgroup.org/stw/Page.asp?PageID=STW027361 (accessed October 31, 2011).

Jenifer P. Marom, Ph.D.

Inhalants and related disorders

Definition

The inhalants are a class of drugs that include a broad range of chemicals found in hundreds of different products. Many inhalants are readily available to the general population. These chemicals include volatile solvents (liquids that vaporize at room temperature) and aerosols (sprays that contain solvents and propellants). Examples include glue, gasoline, paint thinner, hair spray, lighter fluid, spray paint, nail polish remover, correction fluid, rubber cement, felt-tip marker fluids, vegetable sprays, and certain cleaners such as spot removers, computer keyboard cleaner, and carburetor cleaner. The inhalants share a common route of administration—that is, they are all drawn into the body by breathing. They are usually taken either by breathing in the vapors directly from a container (sniffing); by inhaling fumes from substances placed in a bag (bagging); or by inhaling the substance from a cloth soaked in it (huffing). Inhalants take effect very quickly because they get into the bloodstream rapidly via the lungs. The high from inhalants is usually brief, so that users often take inhalants repeatedly over several hours.

A teenager huffs glue. *(© Mark Harvey/Alamy)*

This pattern of use can be dangerous, leading to unconsciousness or even death.

The latest revision of the manual that is used by mental health professionals to diagnose mental disorders is the ***Diagnostic and Statistical Manual of Mental Disorders*** published in 2000 (also known as *DSM-IV-TR*). It lists inhalant dependence and inhalant abuse as substance use disorders. In addition, the inhalant-induced disorder of inhalant intoxication is listed in the substance-related disorders section as well. Inhalant withdrawal is not listed in the *DSM-IV-TR,* because it is not clear that there is a "clinically significant" withdrawal syndrome. In addition, withdrawal is not included as a symptom of inhalant dependence, whereas withdrawal is a symptom of dependence for all other substances.

The fifth edition of the *Diagnostic and Statistical Manual of Mental Disorders,* also known as the *DSM-5,* is due for publication in May 2013. This edition may include proposed changes and revisions to some current diagnostic criteria for psychiatric diagnoses, including combining inhalant abuse and inhalant dependence into a single diagnosis of inhalant use disorder.

Anesthetic gases (such as nitrous oxide, chloroform, or ether) and nitrites (including amyl or butyl nitrite) are not included under inhalant-related disorders in the *DSM-IV-TR,* because they have slightly different intoxication syndromes. Problems with the use of these substances are to be diagnosed under "other substance-related disorders." There is, however, a significant degree of overlap between the symptoms of disorders related to inhalants and these other substances.

Inhalant dependence

Inhalant dependence, or **addiction**, is essentially a syndrome in which a person continues to use inhalants in spite of significant problems caused by, or made worse by, the use of these substances. People who use inhalants heavily may develop tolerance to the drug, which indicates that they are physically dependent on it.

Inhalant abuse

Inhalant abuse is a less serious condition than inhalant dependence; in most cases, it does not involve physical dependence on the drug. Inhalant abuse refers essentially to significant negative consequences from the recurrent use of inhalants.

Inhalant intoxication

When a person uses enough of an inhalant, they will get high from it. The symptoms of intoxication differ slightly, depending on the type of inhalant, the amount used, and other factors. There is, however, a predictable set of symptoms of inhalant intoxication. When too much of the substance is taken, an individual can overdose.

Demographics

Inhalants are some of the few substances more commonly used by younger children rather than older ones. It has been estimated that 10%–20% of youths aged 12–17 have tried inhalants. About 6% of the United States population admits to having tried inhalants prior to fourth grade. The peak time for inhalant use appears to be between the seventh and ninth grades. Inhalants are sometimes referred to as gateway drugs, meaning they are some of the first drugs that people try before moving on to such other substances as alcohol, marijuana, and **cocaine**. Only a small proportion of those who have used inhalants would meet diagnostic criteria for dependence or abuse.

Males generally use inhalants more frequently than females. However, a National Household Survey on Drug Abuse has shown no gender differences in rates of inhalant use in youths between the ages of 12 and 17. Children younger than 12 and adults who use inhalants, however, are more likely to be male.

A Monitoring The Future (MTF) survey reports that African American children consistently show lower rates of inhalant abuse than youth of other ethnic populations, however, individuals from both rural and urban environments abuse inhalants.

According to a 2008 National Survey on Drug Use and Health (NSDUH) study, 729,000 persons aged 12 or older used inhalants for the first time within the past 12 months, 70% of whom were under the age of 18. In a 2009 report, 2.1 million Americans age 12 and older had abused inhalants. In fact, as of 2011, the **Substance Abuse and Mental Health Services Administration** (SAMHSA) viewed inhalant abuse as a multi–generational problem.

Description

Inhalant dependence

Dependence on inhalants involves problems related to the use of inhalants. It is often difficult for a person to stop using the inhalants despite these problems. Individuals dependent on inhalants may use these chemicals several times per week or every day. They may have problems with unemployment or with family relationships, and/or such physical problems as kidney or liver damage caused by the use of inhalants.

Inhalant abuse

People who abuse inhalants typically use them less frequently than those who are dependent on them. Despite less frequent use, however, a person with inhalant abuse suffers negative consequences. For example, the use of inhalants may contribute to poor grades or school truancy.

Inhalant intoxication

Intoxication from inhalants occurs rapidly (usually within five minutes) and lasts for a short period of time (from 5–30 minutes). Inhalants typically have a depressant effect on the central nervous system, similar to the effects of alcohol; and produce feelings of euphoria (feeling good), excitement, dizziness, and slurred speech. In addition, persons intoxicated by inhalants may feel as if they are floating, or may feel a sense of increased power. Severe intoxication from inhalants can cause coma or even death.

Causes and symptoms

Causes

Because inhalants are readily available and inexpensive, they are often used by children (ages 6–16) and the poor. Factors that are associated with inhalant use include poverty, a history of childhood abuse, poor grades, and dropping out of school. The last two factors may simply be results of inhalant use, however, rather than its causes.

The use of inhalants is highly likely to be influenced by peers. Inhalants are often used in group settings. The solitary consumption of inhalants is associated with heavy, prolonged use; it may indicate that the person has a more serious problem with these substances.

Symptoms

INHALANT DEPENDENCE. The *DSM-IV-TR* specifies that three or more of the following symptoms must occur at any time during a 12-month period (and cause significant impairment or distress) in order to meet diagnostic criteria for inhalant dependence:

- Tolerance. The individual either must use increasingly higher amounts of the drug over time in order to achieve the same effect, or finds that the same amount of the drug has much less of an effect over time than before. After using inhalants regularly for a while, people may find that they need to use at least 50% more than the amount they started with in order to get the same effect.
- Loss of control. The person either repeatedly uses a larger quantity of inhalant than planned or uses the inhalant over a longer period of time than planned. For instance, someone may begin using inhalants on school days, after initially limiting their use to weekends.
- Inability to stop using. The person has either unsuccessfully attempted to cut down or stop using the inhalants, or has a persistent desire to stop using. Users may find that despite efforts to stop using inhalants on school days, they cannot stop.
- Time. The affected person spends large amounts of time obtaining inhalants, using them, being under the influence of inhalants, and recovering from their effects. Obtaining the inhalants might not take up much time because they are readily available for little money, but the person may use them repeatedly for hours each day.
- Interference with activities. The affected person either gives up or reduces the amount of time involved in recreational activities, social activities, and/or occupational activities because of the use of inhalants. The person may use inhalants instead of playing sports, spending time with friends, or going to work.
- Harm to self. The person continues to use inhalants in spite of developing either a physical (liver damage or heart problems, for example) or psychological problem (such as depression or memory problems) that is caused by, or made worse by, the use of inhalants.

INHALANT ABUSE. The *DSM-IV-TR* specifies that one or more of the following symptoms must occur at any time during a 12-month period (and cause significant impairment or distress) in order to meet diagnostic criteria for inhalant abuse:

- Interference with role fulfillment. The person's use of inhalants frequently interferes with his or her ability to fulfill obligations at work, home, or school. People may find they are unable to do chores or pay attention in school because they are under the influence of inhalants.
- Danger to self. The person repeatedly uses inhalants in situations in which their influence may be physically hazardous (while driving a car, for example).
- Legal problems. The person has recurrent legal problems related to using inhalants (such as arrests for assaults while under the influence of inhalants).
- Social problems. The person continues to use inhalants despite repeated interpersonal or relationship problems caused by, or made worse by, the use of inhalants. For example, the affected person may get into arguments related to inhalant use.

KEY TERMS

Addiction—A strong physical or psychological dependence on a physical substance.

Inhalant—A substance a person can sniff, or inhale, to get high.

Stupor—A state of sluggishness or impaired consciousness.

Syndrome—A group or pattern of symptoms or signs that occur together.

INHALANT INTOXICATION. The *DSM-IV-TR* specifies that the following symptoms must be present in order to meet diagnostic criteria for inhalant intoxication:

- Use. The person recently intentionally used an inhalant.
- Personality changes. The person experiences significant behavioral or psychological changes during or shortly after use of an inhalant. These changes may include spoiling for a fight, assaultiveness, poor judgment, apathy ("don't care" attitude), or impaired functioning socially or at work or school.
- Inhalant-specific intoxication syndrome. Two or more of the following symptoms occur during or shortly after inhalant use or exposure: dizziness, involuntary side-to-side eye movements (nystagmus), loss of coordination, slurred speech, unsteady gait (difficulty walking), lethargy (fatigue), slowed reflexes, psychomotor retardation (moving slowly), tremor (shaking), generalized muscle weakness, blurred vision or double vision, stupor or coma, and euphoria (a giddy sensation of happiness or well-being).

Diagnosis

People rarely seek treatment on their own for inhalant dependence or abuse. In some cases, the child or adolescent is taken to a doctor by a parent or other relative who is concerned about personality changes, a chemical odor on the child's breath, or other signs of inhalant abuse. The parent may also have discovered empty containers of the inhaled substance in the child's room or elsewhere in the house. In other cases, the child's or adolescent's use of inhalants is diagnosed during a medical interview, when he or she is taken to a hospital emergency room after overdosing on the inhalant or being injured in an accident related to inhalant use. Although inhalants can be detected in blood or urine samples, laboratory tests might not always confirm the **diagnosis**, because the inhalants do not remain in the system very long.

Inhalant dependence

Other substance use disorders are commonly seen among people diagnosed with inhalant dependence. The use of inhalants is usually secondary to the use of other substances; however, only occasionally are inhalants a person's primary drug of choice.

Inhalant abuse

The use of other substances is not uncommon among people who abuse inhalants.

Inhalant intoxication

Intoxication from the use of such other substances as alcohol, **sedatives**, hypnotics (medications to induce sleep), and anxiolytics (tranquilizers) can resemble intoxication caused by inhalants. Furthermore, people under the influence of inhalants may experience hallucinations (typically auditory, visual, or tactile), other perceptual disturbances (such as illusions), or **delusions** (believing they can fly, for example).

Treatment

Inhalant dependence and abuse

Chronic inhalant users are difficult to treat because they often have many serious personal and social problems. They also have difficulty staying away from inhalants; **relapse** rates are high. Treatment usually takes a long time and involves enlisting the support of the person's family, changing the friendship network if the individual uses with others, teaching coping skills, and increasing self-esteem.

Inhalant intoxication

Inhalant intoxication is often treated in a hospital emergency room when the affected person begins to suffer serious psychological (such as hallucinations or delusions) or medical consequences (such as difficulty breathing, headache, nausea, vomiting) from inhalant use. The most serious medical risk from inhalant use is sudden sniffing death. A person using inhalants, especially if they are using the substance repeatedly in a single, prolonged session, may start to have a rapid and irregular heartbeat or severe difficulty breathing, followed by heart failure and death. Sudden sniffing death can occur within minutes. In addition, inhalant use can cause permanent damage to the **brain**, lungs, kidneys, muscles, and heart. The vapors themselves cause damage, but there are also dangerously high levels of copper, **zinc**, and heavy metals in many inhalants.

People who use inhalants may also be treated for injuries sustained while under the influence of inhalants or while using them. For example, individuals intoxicated by inhalants may fall and injure themselves, or they may drive while intoxicated and have an accident. People who use inhalants may also die from, or require treatment for, burns because many inhalants are highly flammable. They may also need emergency treatment for suffocation from inhaling with a plastic bag over the head or for choking on inhaled vomit.

Prognosis

Inhalant dependence and abuse

The course of inhalant abuse and dependence differs somewhat, depending on the affected person's age. Younger children who are dependent on or abuse inhalants use them regularly, especially on weekends and after school. As children get older, they often stop using inhalants. They may stop substance use altogether, or they may move on to other substances. Adults who abuse or are dependent on inhalants may use inhalants regularly for years. They may also frequently "binge" on inhalants (i.e., use them much more frequently for shorter periods of time). This pattern of use can go on for years.

The use of inhalants and subsequent dependence on the substance occurs among people who do not have access to other drugs or are otherwise isolated (such as prison inmates). Also, as with other substance use disorders, people who have greater access to inhalants are more likely to develop dependence on them. This group of people may include workers in industrial settings with ready access to inhalants.

Prevention

Comprehensive prevention programs that involve families, schools, communities, and the media (such as television) can be effective in reducing **substance abuse**. The recurring theme in these programs is to stay away from drugs in the first place. Avoiding drugs altogether is the primary method of ensuring that one does not develop a substance use disorder.

Parents can help prevent the misuse of inhalants by educating their children about the negative effects of inhalant use. Teachers and parents can help prevent inhalant abuse and dependence by recognizing the signs of inhalant use. Signs include chemical odors on the child's breath or clothes, slurred speech, a drunken or disoriented appearance, nausea or lack of appetite, and inattentiveness and lack of coordination.

QUESTIONS TO ASK YOUR DOCTOR

- What risks are associated with abuse of inhalants?
- What symptoms are associated with inhalant dependence?
- Does having inhalant dependence and abuse put me at risk for other health conditions?
- Can you recommend any treatment and support groups for me?

Resources

BOOKS

American Psychiatric Association. *Diagnostic and Statistical Manual of Mental Disorders,* 4th ed., Text rev. Washington, DC: American Psychiatric Association, 2000.

American Psychological Association. *Publication Manual of the American Psychological Association,*6th ed. Washington, DC: American Psychological Association, 2009.

Erickson, Carlton K, Ph.D. *Addiction Essentials: The Go-To Guide for Clinicians and Patients.*New York, NY: W. W. Norton & Company, 2011.

Galanter, Marc, and Herbert D. Kleber, eds. *Textbook of Substance Abuse Treatment,* 2nd ed. Washington, DC: American Psychiatric Press, Inc., 2008.

Sadock, Benjamin J., MD., Virginia Alcott Sadock, MD., and Pedro Ruiz, MD., eds. *Kaplan and Sadock's Comprehensive Textbook of Psychiatry,* 2nd ed. New York, NY: Lippincott Williams & Wilkins, 2009.

ORGANIZATIONS

National Clearinghouse on Alcohol and Drug Information, PO Box 2345, Rockville, MD, 20847, (877) SAMHSA-7; Hablamos español: (877) 767-8432; TDD: (800) 487-4889, Fax: (240) 221-4292, http://ncadi.samhsa.gov.

National Institute on Drug Abuse, 6001 Executive Blvd., Rm. 5213, Bethesda, MD, 20892, (301) 442-1124; Spanish: (240) 221-4007, information@nida.nih.gov, http://www.nida.nih.gov.

The Partnership at Drugfree.org, 352 Park Ave. S, 9th Floor, New York, NY, 10010, (212) 922-1560, Fax: (212) 922-1570, http://www.drugfree.org.

Substance Abuse and Mental Health Services Administration, 1 Choke Cherry Rd., Rockville, MD, 20857, (877) SAMHSA-7 (726-4727), (800) TTY: 487-4889, Fax: (240) 221-4292, SAMHSAInfo@samhsa.hhs.gov, http://www.samhsa.gov.

Jennifer Hahn, Ph.D.
Laura Jean Cataldo, RN, Ed.D.

Inkblot test *see* **Rorschach inkblot test**

Insomnia

Definition

Insomnia is the inability to obtain an adequate amount or quality of sleep. The difficulty may be in falling asleep, remaining asleep, or waking up too early, or a combination of all three. Sleeplessness is a symptom that may be caused by physical or mental conditions or circumstances, including a general medical condition or psychiatric disorder.

Demographics

The U.S. Centers for Disease Control and Prevention estimates that between 50 and 70 million Americans are affected by some type of sleep disorder, and nearly half of the U.S. population reports at least occasional sleeping problems. Accurate data is difficult to gather, as many people misperceive how much sleep they actually get and how many times they normally wake up during the night. It is generally thought, however, that women are more likely than men to suffer from insomnia. As people age, they are also more likely to experience insomnia, as are people who are generally nervous or tense. According to the National Sleep Foundation (NSF), people who are divorced, widowed, or separated are more likely to experience insomnia than married couples, and insomnia is more frequently reported by persons with a lower socioeconomic status.

Anti-insomnia drugs

Brand name (generic name)	Possible side effects
Ambien (zolpidem tartrate)	Daytime drowsiness, dizziness, headache, muscle or joint pain, tremors
Dalmane (flurazepam hydrochloride)	Decreased coordination, irritability, lightheadedness, pain
Doral (quazepam)	Daytime drowsiness, dizziness, dry mouth, headache
Halcion (triazolam)	Chest pain, decreased coordination, memory impairment
Lunesta (eszopiclone)	Daytime drowsiness, decreased libido, heartburn, nausea, pain
ProSom (estazolam)	Dizziness, headache, nausea, sleep inertia (grogginess), weakness
Restoril (temazepam)	Dizziness, fatigue, headache, nausea, sleep inertia
Sonata (zaleplon)	Change in vision, decreased coordination, loss of appetite, numbness or tingling

(Table by PreMediaGlobal. Reproduced by permission of Gale, a part of Cengage Learning.)

Description

Insomnia is classified both by its nightly symptoms and its duration. Sleep-onset insomnia refers to difficulty falling asleep; maintenance insomnia refers to waking frequently during the night or waking early. Insomnia is also classified in relation to the number of sleepless nights. Short-term insomnia, also called transient or acute insomnia, is a common occurrence and usually lasts only a few days. Long-term, or chronic, insomnia lasts more than three to four weeks. Insomnia can also be classified as either primary or secondary. Primary insomnia is a disorder that cannot be attributed to another condition or disorder, whereas secondary insomnia can be traced back to a source. Possible sources of secondary insomnia include a medical condition; the use of medications, alcohol, or other substances; or a mental disorder such as severe **depression**.

Sleep is essential for mental and physical restoration. Chronic insomnia increases the risk for personal injury and error because of the **fatigue** and delayed reflexes experienced due to lack of sleep. Chronic insomnia can also lead to mood disorders such as depression. On average, adults require approximately 7–8 hours of sleep each night, teenagers need about 9 hours per night, and infants need 16 to 18 hours of sleep each day to function properly and maintain health.

Not all disruptions in the normal pattern of sleeping and waking are considered insomnia. Such factors as jet lag, unusually high levels of **stress**, changing work shifts, or other drastic changes in the person's routine can all lead to sleep problems. Unless the problems are ongoing and severe enough that they are causing distress for the person in important areas of life, he or she is not considered to have insomnia.

Stages of sleep

Sleep consists of two separate states that constantly cycle: rapid eye movement (REM), the stage in which most dreaming occurs, and non-REM (NREM). Four stages of sleep take place during NREM: stage I, when the person passes from relaxed wakefulness; stage II, an early stage of light sleep; and stages III and IV, which are increasing degrees of deep sleep. Most stage IV sleep (also called delta sleep) occurs in the first several hours of sleep. A period of REM sleep normally follows a period of NREM sleep.

Causes and symptoms

Causes

Sleeplessness or insomnia can have many causes, including physical conditions (such as sleep apnea), mental conditions (such as depression), shift work schedules with irregular hours, or experiencing a traumatic event. In the days immediately following the terrorist attacks on September 11, 2001, 47% of Americans rated their sleep as "poor" or "fair," according to NSF's "2002 Sleep in America" poll. In comparison, 27% of poll participants rated sleep as poor or fair for most nights of that year.

Transient insomnia is often caused by a temporary situation in a person's life such as an argument with a loved one, a brief medical illness, or jet lag. When the situation is resolved or the precipitating factor disappears, the condition goes away, usually without medical treatment. Side effects of prescription drugs such as asthma medicines, **steroids**, and **antidepressants** may include insomnia, and it may also be a side effect of over-the-counter products such as nasal decongestants or appetite suppressants.

Chronic insomnia usually has different causes, and there may be more than one factor contributing to sleeplessness. Causes of insomnia include:

- a medical condition or its treatment, including sleep apnea, diabetes, arthritis, a heart condition, and asthma
- use of substances such as caffeine, alcohol, and nicotine
- psychiatric conditions such as mood or anxiety disorders
- stress or depression, such as sadness caused by the loss of a loved one or a job
- a change in work shift
- a work schedule with nontraditional hours, such as those worked by medical professionals, truck drivers, the military, and persons employed by 24-hour businesses
- sleep-disordered breathing, such as snoring
- periodic jerky leg movements (*nocturnal myoclonus*) that occur just as the individual is falling asleep
- restless legs syndrome, which involves the urge to move the legs and may also include feelings of tingling or cramping
- repeated nightmares or panic attacks during sleep

Excessive worrying about whether or not a person will be able to fall asleep may also cause insomnia. The concern creates so much anxiety that the individual's bedtime rituals and behavior actually trigger insomnia, a condition called psychophysiological insomnia.

Symptoms

People with insomnia are unable to achieve a good night's sleep and wake up feeling tired. They may have difficulty falling asleep or may be able to fall asleep without a problem but wake up in the early hours of the morning. The person is then either unable to go back to sleep or drifts into a restless, unsatisfying sleep. Insomnia is a common condition in the elderly and persons suffering from depression. Sometimes sleep patterns are reversed and the individual has difficulty staying awake during the day and takes frequent naps, with the sleep at night being fitful and frequently interrupted.

The lack of restful sleep may result in daytime symptoms of **sleep deprivation**, including a lack of concentration, headaches, anxiety, irritability, fatigue, delayed reflexes, and gastrointestinal symptoms. Lack of sleep has also been associated with an increase in appetite, which can lead to weight gain.

Diagnosis

Insomnia is a disorder that is usually self-reported; that is, patients usually bring up the subject of sleep problems with their doctors rather than the doctor suggesting the **diagnosis**. There are no laboratory tests for insomnia, but the doctor may review a patient's health history or order tests to determine if a medical condition is causing the insomnia. The physician may ask if the patient is depressed, in pain, under stress, working irregular schedules, or taking any medications. The physician may also suggest keeping a sleep diary, in which the patient notes details such as the time they went to bed, the time(s) at which they got up during the night, their activities before bed, use of caffeine, etc. If the patient has a bed partner, information can be obtained about whether the patient snores or is restless during sleep. This information, together with a medical history and physical examination, can help confirm the doctor's assessment and uncover specific factors related to the insomnia.

Insomnia is included in the ***Diagnostic and Statistical Manual of Mental Disorders***, fourth edition, text revised (*DSM-IV-TR*), the guidelines used by medical professionals in diagnosing mental disorders. In order to meet the *DSM-IV-TR* criteria for primary insomnia, a person must experience the symptoms for at least a month, and the symptoms must cause them distress or reduce their ability to function successfully. The symptoms cannot be caused by a different sleep disorder or medical condition or be a side effect of medications or **substance abuse**, though insomnia may be comorbid with (occur together with) other psychiatric disorders, including mania, depression, and **anxiety disorders**.

A fifth edition of the *DSM* (*DSM-5*) is expected to publish in 2013. Proposed revisions to the diagnostic criteria for insomnia include adding the requirement that the sleep difficulty must occur at least three nights per week. Patients should also report at least one daytime impairment related to the loss of sleep.

Treatment

Treatments for insomnia include treating any physical or mental conditions contributing to the sleeplessness, as well as exploring changes in lifestyle that may improve the situation (such as changing work schedules). Behavioral and educational therapies, such as **cognitive-behavioral therapy**, are usually tried first, because they do not have side effects and cannot create a chemical dependence the way some sleep medications can. In seeking treatment, patients may wish to consult a sleep clinic or a doctor who specializes in the treatment of **sleep disorders** as well as their family doctor. Treatment using a combination of approaches is usually most effective.

Traditional

Behavioral and lifestyle changes may help patients overcome sleeplessness. Patients should try to go to bed only when sleepy and use the bedroom only for sleep; activities such as reading, watching television, or snacking should take place elsewhere. Maintaining a comfortable bedroom temperature, reducing noise, and eliminating light may also help. If a person is unable to fall asleep, he or she can go into another room and do some quiet activity such as reading and return to bed when sleepy. Setting an alarm and getting up every morning at the same time, no matter how long a person has slept, may help to establish a regular sleep-wake pattern. Naps during the day should be avoided, but if absolutely necessary, a 30-minute nap early in the afternoon may not interfere with sleep at night.

Sleep-restriction therapy is a technique that restricts the time in bed to the actual time spent sleeping. This approach allows a slight sleep debt to build up, increasing the individual's ability to fall asleep and stay asleep. If a patient sleeps five hours a night, the time in bed is limited to 5–5.5 hours. The time in bed is gradually increased in small segments, with the individual rising at the same time each morning; at least 85% of the time in bed must be spent sleeping.

Drugs

A physician may determine that drug therapy is necessary to treat insomnia. Drugs may be prescribed if the patient is undergoing a crisis or if insomnia persists after a patient has made lifestyle changes. However, drug therapy is regarded as a short-term remedy, not a solution.

Conventional medications given for insomnia include **sedatives**, tranquilizers, and **antianxiety drugs**. All require a doctor's prescription and may be habit-forming. Medications may lose effectiveness over time and can reduce alertness during the day. The medications should be taken up to four times daily or as directed for approximately three to four weeks. The dose will vary with the physician, patient, and medication. If insomnia is related to depression, then an antidepressant medication may be helpful.

Drugs prescribed for improving sleep are called hypnotics. Hypnotics include **benzodiazepines** that are prescribed for anxiety and insomnia. Benzodiazepines commonly prescribed for insomnia include **triazolam** (Halcion), **temazepam** (Restoril), **lorazepam** (Ativan), **alprazolam** (Xanax), **flurazepam** (Dalmane), and **oxazepam** (Serax). Other drugs that may be prescribed include **zolpidem** (Ambien), ramelteon (Rozerem), and eszopiclone (Lunesta). In clinical studies, ramelteon has shown no evidence of potential for abuse, dependence, or withdrawal. Both ramelteon and eszopiclone are approved for long-term use by prescription only.

Over-the-counter sleep products include Nytol, Sominex, Unisom Nightime Tablets, and Tylenol PM. While these products are usually not addictive, some experts believe they are not very effective in sustaining stage IV sleep and can affect the quality of sleep, resulting in daytime drowsiness.

Alternative

Alternative treatments may be used in treating both the symptom of insomnia and its underlying causes. Much treatment is centered on herbal remedies, but as the U.S. Food and Drug Administration does not regulate the safety or efficacy of these treatments, consumers should be cautious when using herbal supplements. Persons interested in herbal supplements should consult with their healthcare provider or complementary medicine practitioner before taking any herbal remedies. This is especially important because some remedies such as melatonin interact with other herbals like **valerian** and prescription medicines.

VALERIAN. Valerian is one of the herbs most commonly used to treat insomnia. In **clinical trials**, people who took valerian fell asleep more quickly and experienced improved slumber. Because of the herb's sedative properties, valerian is used to treat both insomnia and anxiety. Valerian is sold commercially in the form of capsules, extracts, and teas. The capsule or extract dosage ranges from 300 to 600 mg; teas may consist of a mixture of herbs with sedative properties, such as valerian, **chamomile**, hops, lemon balm, **passionflower**, or **St. John's wort**. As a sleep aid, it should be taken shortly before bedtime. People who have trouble falling asleep may see results quickly. It could take from two weeks to a month before a person with chronic insomnia experiences improved sleep.

MELATONIN. Melatonin is a natural hormone that is secreted from the brain's pineal gland. The gland regulates a person's biological clock, particularly day and night cycles. Supplement melatonin is available to help promote sleep and regulate sleep cycles. Melatonin is generally used as a jet lag remedy and may also help establish sleep patterns for shift workers. It has also been successful in clinical trials in treating sleep problems in children with **autism** and **intellectual disability** disorders and in persons who are blind. While melatonin may help people fall asleep more quickly, studies indicate limited success when used for treating insomnia. Melatonin is available in pill form; long-term effects of taking it are not known.

MIND AND BODY RELAXATION. Incorporating relaxation techniques into bedtime rituals may help a person go to sleep faster and improve the quality of sleep. Relaxation techniques are safe and may be effective in reducing sleeplessness. Suggestions include learning to substitute pleasant thoughts for unpleasant ones (imagery training) to help reduce worrying, or listening to recordings that combine the sounds of nature with soft relaxing music. **Meditation**, prayer, and breathing exercises may also be effective.

AROMATHERAPY AND HYDROTHERAPY. **Aromatherapy** promotes relaxation through the use of essential oils, the aromatic extracts of plants. Essential oils may be used for a soothing bath; applied to the face, neck, shoulders, and pillow; or diffused in air. Dream pillows, also known as sleep pillows, are pillows with an opening to insert essential oils, so that scents such as chamomile or **lavender** can be smelled while the person attempts to sleep. Hydrotherapy incorporated with aromatherapy consists of a warm bath scented with essential oils, such as rose, lavender, or marjoram. Valerian may also be added to bath water. Taking a warm bath before bed is thought to naturally reduce the body's temperature, which prepares the body for sleep.

LIGHT THERAPY. **Light therapy** may help some patients with insomnia, particularly those affected by repeatedly waking in the morning rather than having difficulty falling asleep at night. During a light therapy session, the patient sits in front of a light box for a specified period of time. The rays of the light box mimic those of the sun, helping to reset the patient's biological clock. Light therapy is traditionally used in treating **seasonal affective disorder**, a depressive condition caused by the loss of sunlight during winter months.

QUESTIONS TO ASK YOUR DOCTOR

- Why can't I sleep through the night?
- What can I do to help fall asleep and prevent waking up during the night?
- Is it okay for me to take sleeping pills?
- Will I be able to enjoy sleep again?

MASSAGE THERAPY. Massage therapy promotes relaxation by relaxing tense muscles throughout the body. It is especially helpful for restless leg syndrome. A massage once a week by a registered massage therapist may help the individual relieve any stress that is causing sleeplessness.

NUTRITION AND DIETARY THERAPIES. Persons with insomnia should avoid alcohol and caffeine products, which may disrupt the sleep-wake cycle. Eating a healthy diet rich in calcium, magnesium, and the B vitamins, or taking nutritional supplements, may also be beneficial in treating insomnia.

Prognosis

Insomnia can be successfully treated in most adults, although any underlying illness will require treatment in order to correct the related insomnia. Sleep apnea, one possible medical cause of insomnia, is a potentially serious disorder related to breathing difficulties and chronic lung conditions that can be fatal if not treated.

Untreated insomnia has potentially serious consequences, including an increased risk of motor vehicle accidents, impaired school or job performance, and a high rate of absenteeism from work. Though insomnia can be treated, patients who have had insomnia once are at an increased risk for recurrent insomnia.

Prevention

Prevention of insomnia centers around the promotion of a healthy lifestyle. A balance of rest, recreation, and **exercise** in combination with **stress management**, regular physical examinations, and a healthy diet can do much to reduce the risk. Walking is also recommended. However, exercise should be done at least three hours before bedtime, to avoid a stimulating effect. Exercise,

KEY TERMS

Mood disorder—A group of mental disorders involving a disturbance of mood, along with either a full or partial excessively happy (manic) or extremely sad (depressive) syndrome not caused by any other physical or mental disorder. Mood refers to a prolonged emotion.

Sleep apnea—A condition in which a person stops breathing while asleep. These periods can last up to a minute or more and can occur many times each hour. In order to start breathing again, the person must become semi-awake. The episodes are not remembered, but the following day the person feels tired and sleepy. If severe, sleep apnea can cause other medical problems.

Sleep disorder—Any condition that interferes with sleep.

relaxation, and **nutrition** should be considered ongoing preventive measures.

Resources

BOOKS

American Psychiatric Association. *Diagnostic and Statistical Manual of Mental Disorders*. 4th ed., text rev. Washington, DC: American Psychiatric Association, 2000.

Currie, Shawn R. "Sleep Dysfunction." *Clinicians's Handbook of Adult Behavioral Assessment*, edited by Michel Hersen. San Diego, CA: Elsevier Academic Press, 2006: 401–30.

Lee-Chiong, Teofilo L., ed. *Sleep: A Comprehensive Handbook*. New York: Wiley-Liss, 2006.

Mayo Clinic Book of Alternative Medicine. New York: Time Inc. Home Entertainment, 2007.

PERIODICALS

Irwin, Michael R., and Cole, Jason C. "Comparative Meta-Analysis of Behavioral Interventions for Insomnia and Their Efficacy in Middle-Aged Adults and in Older Adults 55+ Years of Age." *Health Psychology* 25, no. 1 (2006): 3–14.

Jansson, Markus, and Steven J. Linton. "The Role of Anxiety and Depression in the Development of Insomnia: Cross-Sectional and Prospective Analyses." *Psychology and Health* 21, no. 3 (2006): 383–97.

———. "Psychosocial Work Stressors in the Development and Maintenance of Insomnia: A Prospective Study." *Journal of Occupational Health Psychology* 11, no. 3 (2006): 241–48.

Lack, Leon, Helen Wright, Kristyn Kemp, and Samantha Gibb. "The Treatment of Early-Morning Awakening Insomnia with 2 Evenings of Bright Light." *SLEEP* 28, no. 5 (2005): 616–23.

Lande, R. G., and C. Gragnani. "Nonpharmacologic Approaches to the Management of Insomnia." *Journal of the American Osteopathic Association* 110, no. 12 (2010): 695–701.

Manber, Rachel, and Allison Harvey. "Historical Perspective and Future Directions in Cognitive Behavioral Therapy for Insomnia and Behavioral Sleep Medicine." *Clinical Psychology Review* 25, no. 5 (2005): 535–38.

Smith, Michael T., and Michael L. Perlis. "Who is a Candidate for Cognitive-Behavioral Therapy for Insomnia?" *Health Psychology* 25, no. 1 (2006): 15–19.

WEBSITES

American Psychiatric Association. "Insomnia." DSM5.org. http://www.dsm5.org/ProposedRevision/Pages/proposedrevision.aspx?rid=65 (accessed September 18, 2011).

Johns Hopkins Health Alert. "Q & As on Insomnia." John Hopkins Medicine. http://www.johnshopkinshealthalerts.com/alerts/depression_anxiety/JohnsHopkinsDepressionAnxietyHealthAlert_799-1.html (accessed November 2, 2011).

Johnston, Smith L., III. "Societal and Workplace Consequences of Insomnia, Sleepiness, and Fatigue." Medscape Education (September 29, 2005). http://www.medscape.org/viewarticle/513572_1 (accessed November 2, 2011).

Mayo Clinic staff. "Insomnia." MayoClinic.com. http://www.mayoclinic.com/health/insomnia/DS00187 (accessed November 2, 2011).

National Sleep Foundation. "Diet, Exercise, and Sleep." http://www.sleepfoundation.org/article/sleep-topics/diet-exercise-and-sleep (accessed November 2, 2011).

ORGANIZATIONS

American Academy of Sleep Medicine, 2510 N Frontage Rd., Darien, IL, 60561, (630) 737-9700, Fax: (630) 737-9790, inquiries@assmnet.org, http://www.aasmnet.org.

American Sleep Association, 614 South 8th St., Ste. 282, Philadelphia, PA, 19147, (443) 593-2285, sleep@1sleep.com, http://www.sleepassociation.org.

National Sleep Foundation, 1010 N. Glebe Rd., Suite 310, Arlington, VA, 22201, (703) 243-1697, http://www.sleepfoundation.org.

L. Lee Culvert
Laura Jean Cataldo, RN, EdD
Heidi Splete

Intake evaluation *see* **Psychological assessment and diagnosis**

Intellectual disability

Definition

Intellectual disability or intellectual developmental disorder (IDD), referred to as intellectual disability in the fourth edition of the ***Diagnostic and Statistical Manual***

Persons under age 18 receiving special education or early intervention services in the United States, by selected characteristics, 2010

Selected characteristic	Number of persons receiving special education or early intervention services	Percentage of total persons under age 18†
Total	**5,162,000**	**6.9%**
Gender		
Male	3,465,000	9.1%
Female	1,697,000	4.7%
Age		
Under 12 years	3,177,000	6.3%
12–17 years	1,985,000	8.2%
Race		
White	3,922,000	7.0%
Black or African American	862,000	7.8%
American Indian or Alaska Native	54,000	7.0%
Asian	105,000	3.1%
Native Hawaiian or other Pacific Islander	*19,000	*11.2%
Two or more races	200,000	7.0%

†Total number of persons under age 18 years = 74,625,000.
*Estimates preceded by an asterisk have a relative standard error of greater than 30% and less than or equal to 50% and should be used with caution, as they do not meet standards of reliability or precision.

SOURCE: National Center for Health Statistics, Centers for Disease Control and Prevention, "Summary Health Statistics for the U.S. Population: National Health Interview Survey, 2010," *Vital and Health Statistics* 10, no. 251 (December 2011).

(Table by PreMediaGlobal. © 2012 Cengage Learning.)

of Mental Disorders (*DSM-IV*), is a developmental disability that first appears in children under the age of 18. It is defined as a level of intellectual functioning (as measured by standard **intelligence tests**) that is well below average and results in significant limitations in daily living skills (adaptive functioning). The forthcoming edition of the *Diagnostic and Statistical Manual of Mental Disorders* (*DSM-5*, 2013) proposes to rename intellectual disability as intellectual developmental disorder (IDD) and define it as "a disorder that includes both a current intellectual deficit and a deficit in adaptive functioning with onset during the developmental period."

IDD is therefore not a mental illness in the usual sense but rather a disorder defined in order to identify groups of people who need social support and special educational services to carry out tasks of everyday living. On October 5, 2010, "Rosa's Law" went into effect in the United States. Named for a child with IDD living in Maryland, the law requires federal agencies to remove the terms mentally retarded or mental retardation from official documents and replace them with "individual with an intellectual disability" and "intellectual disability."

Demographics

The prevalence of intellectual disability in North America is a subject of heated debate. It is thought to be between 1% and 3% depending upon the population, methods of assessment, and criteria of assessment that are used. Many people believe that the actual prevalence is probably closer to 1%, and that the 3% figure is based on misleading mortality rates; cases that are diagnosed in early infancy; and the instability of the **diagnosis** across the age span. If the 1% figure is accepted, however, it means that about 3 million people with intellectual disability live in the United States. The three most common causes of intellectual disability, accounting for about 30% of cases, are **Down syndrome**, fragile X syndrome, and **fetal alcohol syndrome**. Males are more likely than females to have an intellectual disability in a 1.5:1 ratio, primarily because of the association with fragile X.

Description

Intellectual developmental disorder begins in childhood or adolescence before the age of 18. In most cases, it persists throughout adult life. A diagnosis of IDD is made if an individual has an intellectual functioning level well below average, as well as significant limitations in two or more adaptive skill areas. Intellectual functioning level is defined by standardized tests that measure the ability to reason in terms of mental age (intelligence quotient or IQ). Intellectual disability is generally defined as an IQ score below 70–75. Adaptive skills is a term that refers to skills needed for daily life. Such skills include the ability to produce and understand language (communication); practical skills needed for activities of daily living (ADLs); use of community resources; health, safety, leisure, self-care, and social skills; self-direction; functional academic skills (reading, writing, and arithmetic); and job-related skills.

In general, children with intellectual and developmental impairments reach such developmental milestones as walking and talking much later than children in the general population. Symptoms of intellectual disability may appear at birth or later in childhood. The child's age at onset depends on the suspected cause of the disability. Some people with a mild intellectual disability might not be diagnosed before entering preschool or kindergarten. These children typically have difficulties with social, communication, and functional academic skills. Children who have a neurological disorder or illness such as encephalitis or meningitis may suddenly show signs of cognitive impairment and adaptive difficulties.

DSM-IV categories

The level of impairment varies in severity. The *Diagnostic and Statistical Manual of Mental Disorders,* fourth edition, text revision (*DSM-IV-TR*), the diagnostic standard for mental health care professionals in the United States, classifies four different degrees of intellectual disability: mild, moderate, severe, and profound. These categories are based on the person's level of functioning. The reader should note, however, that *DSM-5* has proposed changes in the categories of severity of IDD. The *DSM-5* website states as of mid-2011 that "Recommendations for severity criteria for this disorder are forthcoming." The present *DSM-IV* categories of severity are as follows:

- Mild intellectual disability: Approximately 85% of people who fall into the *DSM-IV* categories of intellectual disability are in the mild category. Their IQ scores range from 50 to 70, and they can often learn academic skills up to about the sixth-grade level. They can become fairly self-sufficient and in some cases live independently with community and social support.
- Moderate intellectual disability: About 10% of people with intellectual disability are considered moderately disabled. People in this category have IQ scores ranging from 35 to 55. They can carry out work and self-care tasks with moderate supervision. They typically acquire communication skills in childhood and are able to live and function successfully within the community in such supervised environments as group homes.
- Severe intellectual disability: About 3–4% of people with intellectual disability are classified as severe. People in this category have IQ scores of 20 to 40. They may master very basic self-care skills and some communication skills. Many people with this level of impairment can live in a group home.
- Profound intellectual disability: Only 1–2% of people with intellectual disability are classified as profoundly disabled, meaning that they have IQ scores under 20 to 25. They may be able to develop basic self-care and communication skills with appropriate support and training. Their disability is often caused by an accompanying neurological disorder. People with profound intellectual disability need high levels of structure and supervision.

Reasons for changes in DSM-5

The primary reason given by the authors of *DSM-5* for changing the name of the disorder is greater consistency with international opinion and the position of the American Association on Intellectual and Developmental Disabilities (AAIDD). This organization, formerly known as the American Association on Mental Retardation, or AAMR, has developed a widely accepted diagnostic classification system for intellectual disability. In this system, intellectual disability is defined in terms of the environment and context in which the person functions. The AAIDD offers five assumptions that are necessary for defining the presence of an intellectual disability. First, a mental health practitioner must consider the limitations of functioning in a community environmental context, including the person's age group and culture. Second, cultural and linguistic differences and differences in behavioral, sensory, and other factors should be considered. Third, strengths should be given consideration along with weaknesses. Fourth, the purpose of identifying limitations is to determine what supports the person needs. The fifth assumption is that when the appropriate supports are available, the quality of life and functional ability of a person with an intellectual disability will improve. The AAIDD has pushed for changing the name of the disorder because of the **stigma** associated with the term mental retardation.

Other reasons for the proposed changes in *DSM-5* include the need to exclude inaccurate testing as a factor in evaluating persons for IDD; the use of factor analysis to provide greater accuracy in measuring a person's adaptive functioning; and the need for greater accuracy in measuring a person's overall level of functioning. The basic cutoff point (an IQ of 70 or below) will remain unchanged.

Causes and symptoms

Causes

The cause of IDD cannot be identified in about 40% of cases. The following sections discuss known biological and environmental factors that can cause IDD.

GENETIC FACTORS. Hereditary factors are the most common single cause of IDD and are involved in about 30% of cases. The disorder may be caused by an inherited genetic abnormality, such as fragile X syndrome. Fragile X, a defect in the X chromosome in which a repeated group of letters in the DNA sequence reaches a certain threshold number that results in impairment, is the most common inherited cause of IDD. Such single-gene disorders as phenylketonuria (PKU) and other inborn errors of metabolism may also cause IDD if they are not discovered and treated early, although testing of infants for PKU is required at birth, and problems associated with this disorder can be avoided through dietary measures. Abnormalities in chromosome number can also be the cause of IDD. The presence of an extra chromosome 18 (trisomy 18) or chromosome 21 (trisomy 21 or Down syndrome) will result in some level of intellectual disability. In addition, there may be only a partial extra chromosome as a result of accidents at the cellular level, which sometimes results in milder forms of IDD compared to complete trisomies.

PRENATAL AND PERINATAL ILLNESSES AND ISSUES. Fetal alcohol syndrome (FAS) affects one in 3,000 children in Western countries. It is caused when mothers drink heavily during the first twelve weeks (trimester) of pregnancy. Some studies have shown that even moderate **alcohol use** during pregnancy may cause learning disabilities in children. Drug abuse and cigarette smoking during pregnancy have also been linked to intellectual disability.

Maternal infections and such illnesses as glandular disorders, rubella, toxoplasmosis, and cytomegalovirus (CMV) infection can result in IDD in the child, among many other problems, if the developing fetus is exposed. When the mother has high blood pressure (hypertension) or develops toxemia (also called pregnancy-induced hypertension or preeclampsia) during pregnancy, the flow of oxygen to the fetus may in some cases be reduced, potentially resulting in **brain** damage and IDD.

Birth defects that cause physical deformities of the head, brain, and central nervous system frequently cause IDD. A neural tube defect, for example, is a birth defect in which the neural tube that forms the spinal cord does not close completely. This defect, which occurs with varying levels of severity, may cause children to develop an accumulation of cerebrospinal fluid inside the skull (hydrocephalus). The pressure on the brain resulting from hydrocephalus can lead to changes that cause learning impairment.

CHILDHOOD ILLNESSES AND INJURIES. Hyperthyroidism, whooping cough, chicken pox, measles, and Hib disease (a bacterial infection caused by *Haemophilus influenzae* type B) may cause intellectual disability if they are not treated adequately. An infection of the membrane covering the brain (meningitis) or an inflammation of the brain itself (encephalitis) can cause swelling that in turn may cause brain damage and IDD. **Traumatic brain injury** caused by a blow to the head or by violent shaking of the upper body (shaken baby syndrome) may also cause brain damage and IDD in children.

ENVIRONMENTAL FACTORS. Neglected infants who are not provided with the mental and physical stimulation required for normal development may suffer irreversible learning impairment. Children who live in poverty and/or suffer from malnutrition, unhealthy living conditions, abuse, and improper or inadequate medical care are at higher risk. Exposure to lead or mercury can also cause IDD. Many children have developed **lead poisoning** from eating the flaking lead-based paint often found in older buildings.

KEY TERMS

Activities of daily living (ADLs)—A general term for routine activities of self-care (e.g., brushing teeth, dressing oneself, bathing) and functioning independently (e.g., managing money, preparing meals, cleaning house)

Adaptive functioning—A term used to describe a person's having the intellectual, social, and practical skills needed to live independently.

Cytogenetics—The branch of genetics concerned with the structure and function of the individual cell, particularly its chromosome content.

Stigma—Any personal attribute that causes a person to be socially shamed, avoided, or discredited. Mental disorders are a common cause of stigma.

Symptoms

Low IQ scores and limitations in adaptive skills are the hallmarks of IDD, as is failure to reach normal developmental milestones. Aggression, self-injury, and mood disorders are sometimes associated with the disability. The severity of the symptoms and the age at which they first appear depend on the cause. Children with IDD reach developmental milestones significantly later than expected, if at all. If the disorder is caused by chromosomal or other genetic disorders, it is often apparent from infancy. If IDD is caused by childhood illnesses or injuries, learning and adaptive skills that were once easy may suddenly become difficult or impossible to master.

Diagnosis

Examination

If IDD is suspected, a comprehensive physical examination and medical history should be done immediately to discover any organic cause of symptoms. Such conditions as hyperthyroidism and PKU are treatable if discovered early enough when the progression of IDD can be stopped and, in some cases, partially reversed. If a neurological cause, such as brain injury or epilepsy, is suspected, the child may be referred to a neurologist or neuropsychologist for testing.

A complete medical, family, social, and educational history is compiled from existing medical and school records (if applicable) and from interviews with parents.

Tests

In many cases of mild IDD, the disorder is not identified until the child starts school. Schoolchildren are given intelligence tests to measure their learning abilities and intellectual functioning. Such tests include the Stanford-Binet Intelligence Scale, the **Wechsler Intelligence Scales**, the Wechsler Preschool and Primary Scale of Intelligence, and the **Kaufman Assessment Battery for Children**. For infants, the Bayley Scales of Infant Development may be used to assess motor, language, and problem-solving skills. Interviews with parents or other caregivers are used to assess the child's daily living, muscle control, communication, and social skills. The Woodcock-Johnson Scales of Independent Behavior and the Vineland Adaptive Behavior Scales (VABS) are frequently used to evaluate these skills.

Procedures

Recent advances in cytogenetics and microscopy have made the detection of chromosomal abnormalities after birth much more accurate. To investigate the possibility of a genetic disorder, the doctor will obtain a sample of cells from the child's blood or skin. The cells are cultured in the laboratory and prepared for examination under a microscope by one of several purification, preservation, and staining techniques. Analysis of the chromosomes in the cell must be done by a board-certified specialist in cytogenetics.

In addition, amniocentesis (often called amnio) can be performed on fetal cells found in the amniotic fluid in the early second trimester of pregnancy. A sample of the amniotic fluid that surrounds a fetus in the womb is collected through a pregnant woman's abdomen using a needle and syringe. Tests performed on fetal cells found in the amniotic fluid can reveal the presence of Down syndrome as well as many types of genetic disorders. Amniocentesis is recommended for women who will be older than 35 on their due date.

One alternative to amniocentesis now in general use is chorionic villus sampling (CVS), which can be performed as early as the eighth week of pregnancy. CVS can be riskier and is more expensive. The procedure involves the removal of a small piece of placenta tissue (chorionic villi) from the uterus during early pregnancy to screen the baby for genetic defects.

Treatment

Federal legislation entitles children with intellectual impairments and developmental disabilities to free testing and appropriate, individualized education and skills training within the school system from ages three to 21. For children under the age of three, many states have established early **intervention** programs that assess children, make recommendations, and begin treatment programs. Many day schools are available to help train children with developmental and intellectual impairments in skills such as bathing and feeding themselves. Extracurricular activities and social programs are also important in helping children and adolescents who have developmental and intellectual impairments gain self-esteem. Special interventions (usually some form of behavioral therapy) may be needed for children with IDD who have problems with aggression.

Training in independent living and job skills is often begun in late adolescence or early adulthood. The level of training depends on the degree of impairment. People with mild levels of functional and intellectual impairment can often learn the skills needed to live independently and hold outside jobs. People with a great level of impairment may require supervised community living in **group homes** or other residential settings.

Family therapy can help relatives of people with intellectual disabilities develop coping skills. It can also help parents deal with feelings of guilt or anger. A supportive and warm home environment is essential to help people with intellectual disabilities reach their full potential.

Prognosis

People with mild to moderate intellectual disability are frequently able to achieve some self-sufficiency and to lead happy and fulfilling lives. To reach these goals, they need appropriate and consistent educational, community, social, family, and vocational supports. The outlook is less promising for those with severe to profound disability. Studies have shown that these people have a shortened life expectancy. The diseases that are usually associated with severe IDD may cause a shorter

QUESTIONS TO ASK YOUR DOCTOR

- What options are available for treating intellectual disabilities?
- What tests would you recommend to diagnose the condition?
- What are the differences between intellectual disabilities and learning problems like dyslexia?
- Have you ever evaluated a child for an intellectual disability disorder?

life span. People with Down syndrome will develop the brain changes that characterize **Alzheimer's disease** in later life and may develop the clinical symptoms of this disease as well. One additional complication in assessing the future health status and life expectancy of children with IDD is their unequal access to high-quality health care.

Prevention

Immunization against diseases such as measles and Hib prevents many of the illnesses that can cause IDD. In addition, all children should undergo routine developmental screening as part of their pediatric care. Screening is particularly critical for those children who may be neglected or undernourished or may live in disease-producing conditions. Newborn screening and immediate treatment for PKU and hyperthyroidism can usually catch these disorders early enough to prevent adverse intellectual and developmental effects.

Good prenatal care can also be preventive. Pregnant women should be educated about the risks of alcohol and drug consumption and the need to maintain good **nutrition** during pregnancy. Tests such as an ultrasonography can determine whether a fetus is developing normally.

Resources

BOOKS

American Psychiatric Association. *Diagnostic and Statistical Manual of Mental Disorders.* 4th ed., text rev. Washington, DC: American Psychiatric Press, 2000.

Burack, Jacob A., et al., eds. *The Oxford Handbook of Intellectual Disability and Development*, 2nd ed. New York: Oxford University Press, 2011.

Knight, Samantha J.L., ed. *Genetics of Mental Retardation: An Overview Encompassing Learning Disability and Intellectual Disability.* New York: Karger, 2010.

Schalock, Robert L., James F. Gardner, and Valerie J. Bradley. *Quality of Life for People with Intellectual and Other Developmental Disabilities: Applications across Individuals, Organizations, Communities, and Systems.* Washington, DC: American Association on Intellectual and Developmental Disabilities, 2007.

PERIODICALS

Brosnan, J., and O. Healy. "A Review of Behavioral Interventions for the Treatment of Aggression in Individuals with Developmental Disabilities." *Research in Developmental Disabilities* 32 (March-April 2011): 437–446.

Gray-Stanley, J.A., and N. Muramatsu. "Work Stress, Burnout, and Social and Personal Resources among Direct Care Workers." *Research in Developmental Disabilities* 32 (May-June 2011): 1065–1074.

McLaughlin, M. R. "Speech and Language Delay in Children." *American Family Physician* 83 (May 15, 2011): 1183–1188.

Prince, E., and H. Ring. "Causes of Learning Disability and Epilepsy: A Review." *Current Opinion in Neurology* 24 (April 2011): 154–158.

Schalock, R.L., et al. "Evidence-based Practices in the Field of Intellectual and Developmental Disabilities: An International Consensus Approach."*Evaluation and Program Planning* 34 (August 2011): 273–282.

Schieve, L.A., et al. "Risk for Cognitive Deficit in a Population-based Sample of U.S. Children with Autism Spectrum Disorders: Variation by Perinatal Health Factors." *Disability and Health Journal* 3 (July 2010): 202–212.

Shaffer, L.G., and B.A. Bejjani. "Development of New Postnatal Diagnostic Methods for Chromosome Disorders." *Seminars in Fetal and Neonatal Medicine* 16 (April 2011): 114–118.

Ward, R.L., et al. "Uncovering Health Care Inequalities among Adults with Intellectual and Developmental Disabilities." *Health and Social Work* 35 (November 2010): 280–290.

WEBSITES

American Association on Intellectual and Developmental Disabilities (AAIDD). "Definition of Intellectual Disability." http://www.aaidd.org/content_100.cfm?navID=21 (accessed May 18, 2011).

American Psychiatric Association. *DSM-5* Development. "A 00 Intellectual Developmental Disorder." http://www.dsm5.org/proposedrevision/pages/proposedrevision.aspx?rid=384# (accessed May 18, 2011).

Medscape. "Pediatric Mental Retardation." http://emedicine.medscape.com/article/289117-overview (accessed May 18, 2011).

National Dissemination Center for Children with Disabilities (NICHCY). NICHCY Disability Fact Sheet #8. "Intellectual Disability." http://nichcy.org/disability/specific/intellectual (accessed May 18, 2011).

ORGANIZATIONS

American Association on Intellectual and Developmental Disabilities (AAIDD), 501 3rd St., NW, Ste. 200, Washington, DC, United States 20001, (202) 387-1968, Fax: (202) 387-2193, (800) 424-3688, http://www.aaidd.org

The Arc, 1660 L St. NW, Ste. 301, Washington, DC, United States 20036, (202) 534-3700, Fax: (202) 534-3731, (800) 433-5255, info@thearc.org, http://www.thearc.org

National Dissemination Center for Children with Disabilities (NICHCY) (formerly National Information Center for Children and Youth and Disabilities), 1825 Connecticut Ave. NW, Ste. 700, Washington, DC, United States 20009, (202) 884-8200, Fax: (202) 884-8441, (800) 695-0285, nichcy@aed.org, http://nichcy.org

President's Committee for People with Intellectual Disabilities (AAIDD), Aerospace Center, Ste. 210, 370 L'Enfant Promenade SW, Washington, DC, United States 20447, (202) 619-0634, Fax: (202) 205-9519, (800) 424-3688, http://www.acf.hhs.gov/programs/pcpid.

Paula Anne Ford-Martin, M.S.
Emily Jane Willingham, Ph.D.
Rebecca J. Frey, Ph.D.

Intelligence tests

Definition

Intelligence tests are psychological tests that are designed to measure a variety mental functions, such as reasoning, comprehension, and judgment.

Purpose

The goal of intelligence tests is to obtain an idea of the person's intellectual potential. The tests center around a set of stimuli designed to yield a score based on the test maker's model of what makes up intelligence. Intelligence tests are often given as a part of a battery of tests.

Description

When taking an intelligence test, a person can expect to do a variety of tasks. These tasks may include having to answer questions that are asked verbally, doing mathematical problems, and doing a variety of tasks that require eye hand coordination. Some tasks may be timed and require the person to work as quickly as possible. Typically, most questions and tasks start out easy and progressively get more difficult. It is unusual for anyone to know the answer to all of the questions or be able to complete all of the tasks. If a person is unsure of an answer, guessing is usually allowed.

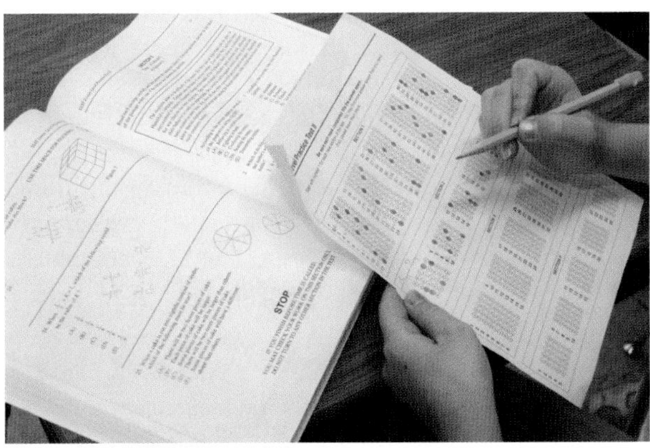

A student checks their work during an SSAT camp. *(© Jen Hulshizer/Star Ledger/Corbis)*

The four most commonly used intelligence tests are:

- Stanford-Binet Intelligence Scales
- Wechsler-Adult Intelligence Scale
- Wechsler Intelligence Scale for Children
- Wechsler Primary & Preschool Scale of Intelligence

In general, intelligence tests measure a wide variety of human behaviors better than any other measure that has been developed. They allow professionals to have a uniform way of comparing a person's performance with that of other people who are similar in age. These tests also provide information on cultural and biological differences among people.

Intelligence tests are excellent predictors of academic achievement and provide an outline of a person's mental strengths and weaknesses. Many times the scores have revealed talents in people that have led to an improvement in their educational opportunities. Teacher, parents, and psychologists are able to devise individual curriculum that matches a person's level of development and expectations.

Some researchers argue that intelligence tests have serious shortcomings. For example, many intelligence tests produce a single intelligence score. This single score is often inadequate in explaining the multidimensional aspects of intelligence. Another problem with a single score is the fact that individuals with similar intelligence test scores can vary greatly in their expression of these talents. It is important to know the person's performance on the various subtests that make up the overall intelligence test score. Knowing the performance on these various scales can influence the understanding of a person's abilities and how these abilities are expressed. For example, two people may have identical scores on intelligence tests, but one person may have obtained the score because of strong verbal skills while the other may have obtained the score because of strong skills in perceiving and organizing various tasks.

Furthermore, intelligence tests only measure a sample of behaviors or situations in which intelligent behavior is revealed. For instance, some intelligence tests do not measure a person's everyday functioning, social knowledge, mechanical skills, and/or creativity. Along with this, the formats of many intelligence tests do not capture the complexity and immediacy of real-life situations. Therefore, intelligence tests have been criticized for their limited ability to predict non-test or nonacademic intellectual abilities. Since intelligence test scores can be influenced by a variety of different experiences and behaviors, they should not be considered a perfect indicator of a person's intellectual potential.

Precautions

There are many different types of intelligence tests and they all do not measure the same abilities. Although the tests often have aspects that are related with each other, we should not expect that scores of one intelligence test measuring a single factor will be similar to scores on another intelligence test measuring a variety of factors. Also, when determining whether or not to use an intelligence test, a person should make sure that the test has been adequately developed and has solid research to show its reliability and validity. Additionally, psychometric testing requires a clinically trained examiner, therefore, the test should only be administered and interpreted by a trained professional.

A central criticism of intelligence tests is that psychologists and educators use these tests to distribute the limited resources of our society. These test results are used to provide rewards such as special classes for gifted students, admission to college, and employment. Those who do not qualify for these resources based on intelligence test scores may feel angry and denied opportunities for success. Unfortunately, intelligence test scores have not only become associated with a person's ability to perform certain tasks, but with self-worth.

Many people are under the false assumption that intelligence tests measure a person's inborn or biological intelligence. Intelligence tests are based on an individual's interaction with the environment and never exclusively measure inborn intelligence. Intelligence tests have been associated with categorizing and stereotyping people. Additionally, knowledge of one's performance on an intelligence test may affect a person's aspirations and motivation to obtain goals. Intelligence tests can be culturally biased against certain minority groups.

Results

The person's raw scores on an intelligence test are typically converted to standard scores. The standard scores allow the examiner to compare the individual's score to other people who have taken the test. Additionally, by converting raw scores to standard scores the examiner has uniform scores and can more easily compare an individual's performance on one test with the individual's performance on another test. Depending on the intelligence test that is used, a variety of scores can be obtained. Most intelligence tests generate an overall intelligence quotient or IQ. As previously noted, it is valuable to know how a person performs on the various tasks that make up the test. This can influence the interpretation of the test and what the IQ means. The average of score for most intelligence tests is 100.

Resources

BOOKS

Kaufman, Alan, S., and Elizabeth O. Lichtenberger. *Assessing Adolescent and Adult Intelligence*. 3rd ed. New York: Wiley, 2005.

Matarazzo, J. D. *Wechsler's Measurement and Appraisal of Adult Intelligence*. 5th ed. New York: Oxford University Press, 1972.

Sattler, Jerome M. "Issues Related to the Measurement and Change of Intelligence." In *Assessment of Children: Cognitive Applications*. 4th ed. San Diego: Jerome M. Sattler, Publisher, Inc., 2001.

Sattler, Jerome M., and Lisa Weyandt. "Specific Learning Disabilities." In *Assessment of Children: Behavioral and Clinical Applications,* by Jerome M. Sattler. 4th ed. San Diego: Jerome M. Sattler, Publisher, Inc., 2002.

Keith Beard, Psy.D.

Intermittent explosive disorder

Definition

Intermittent explosive disorder (IED) is characterized by impulsive acts of aggression, as contrasted with planned violent or aggressive acts. The aggressive episodes may take the form of spells or attacks, with symptoms beginning minutes to hours before the actual acting-out. Other names for IED include rage attacks, anger attacks, and episodic dyscontrol.

Demographics

IED is apparently more common than originally thought. Current research suggests that as many as 16 million Americans may suffer from this disorder. Most studies, however, indicate that it occurs more frequently in males. The most common age of onset is the period from late childhood through the early 20s. The onset of the disorder is frequently abrupt, with no warning period. Close to 82% of patients with IED are often diagnosed with at least one other disorder—particularly **personality disorders**, substance-abuse (especially alcohol abuse) disorders, and neurological disorders.

Description

Intermittent explosive disorder was originally described by the eminent French **psychiatrist** Esquirol as a "partial insanity" related to senseless impulsive acts. Esquirol termed this disorder *monomanies* *instinctives*, or *instinctual monomanias*. These apparently unmotivated acts were thought to result from instinctual or involuntary impulses, or from impulses related to ideological obsessions.

People with intermittent explosive disorder have a problem with controlling their temper. In addition, their violent behavior is out of proportion to the incident or event that triggered the outburst. Impulsive acts of aggression, however, are not unique to intermittent explosive disorder. Impulsive aggression can be present in many psychological and nonpsychological disorders. The diagnosis of intermittent explosive disorder (IED) is essentially a diagnosis of exclusion, meaning that it is given only after other disorders have been ruled out as causes of impulsive aggression.

Patients diagnosed with IED usually feel a sense of arousal or tension before an outburst, and relief of tension after the aggressive act. Patients with IED believe that their aggressive behaviors are justified; however, they feel genuinely upset, regretful, remorseful, bewildered or embarrassed by their impulsive and aggressive behavior.

IED is often grouped with **impulse control disorders**. Recent research, however, suggests an association with **bipolar disorder**, although the exact nature of this association is unclear. Some studies have suggested that some children who have IED are mistakenly diagnosed with bipolar disorder; other studies suggest that IED and Bipolar disorder may lie along the same continuum, may represent different stops along a common trajectory, or may be common comorbid conditions.

Causes and symptoms

Causes

Recent findings suggest that IED may result from abnormalities in the areas of the **brain** that regulate behavioral arousal and inhibition. Research indicates that impulsive aggression is related to abnormal brain mechanisms in a system that inhibits motor (muscular movement) activity, called the *serotoninergic system*. This system is directed by a neurotransmitter called *serotonin* that regulates behavioral inhibition (control of behavior). Some studies have correlated IED with abnormalities on both sides of the front portion of the brain. These localized areas in the front of the brain appear to be involved in information processing and controlling movement, both of which are unbalanced in persons diagnosed with IED. Studies using **positron emission tomography (PET)** scanning have found lower levels of brain glucose (sugar) metabolism in patients who act in impulsively aggressive ways.

Another study based on data from electroencephalograms (EEGs) of 326 children and adolescents treated in a psychiatric clinic found that 46% of the youths who manifested explosive behavior had unusual high-amplitude brain wave forms. The researchers concluded that a significant subgroup of people with IED may be predisposed to explosive behavior by an inborn characteristic of their central nervous system. In sum, there is a substantial amount of convincing evidence that IED has biological causes, at least in some people diagnosed with the disorder.

Other clinicians attribute IED to cognitive distortions. According to cognitive therapists, persons with IED have a set of strongly negative beliefs about other people, often resulting from harsh punishments inflicted by the parents. The child grows up believing that others "have it in for him" and that violence is the best way to restore damaged self-esteem. He or she may also have observed one or both parents, older siblings, or other relatives acting out in explosively violent ways. In short, people who develop IED have learned, usually in their family of origin, to believe that certain acts or attitudes on the part of other people justify aggressive attacks on them.

Although gender roles are not a cause of IED to the same extent as biological and familial factors, some researchers regard them as helping to explain why most people diagnosed with IED are males. According to this theory, men have greater permission from society to act violently and impulsively than women do. They therefore have less reason to control their aggressive impulses. Women who act explosively, on the other hand, would be considered unfeminine as well as unfriendly or dangerous.

Symptoms

IED is characterized by violent behaviors that are impulsive as well as assaultive. One example involved a man who felt insulted by another customer in a neighborhood bar during a conversation that had lasted for several minutes. Instead of finding out whether the other customer intended his remark to be insulting, or answering the insult verbally, the man impulsively punched the other customer in the mouth. Within a few minutes, however, he felt ashamed of his violent act. As this example indicates, the urge to commit the impulsive aggressive act may occur from minutes to hours before acting out and is characterized by the buildup of tension. After the outburst, the IED patient experiences a sense of relief from the tension. While many patients with IED blame someone else for causing their violent outbursts, they also express remorse and guilt for their actions.

Diagnosis

As mentioned, IED is essentially a diagnosis of exclusion. Patients who are eventually diagnosed with IED may come to the attention of a psychiatrist or other mental health professional by several different routes. Some patients with IED, often adult males who have assaulted their wives and are trying to save their marriages, are aware that their outbursts are not normal and seek treatment to control them. Younger males with IED are more likely to be referred for diagnosis and treatment by school authorities or the juvenile justice system, or brought to the doctor by concerned parents.

A psychiatrist who is evaluating a patient for IED would first take a complete medical and psychiatric history. Depending on the contents of the patient's history, the doctor would give the patient a physical examination to rule out head **trauma**, epilepsy, and other general medical conditions that may cause violent behavior. If the patient appears to be intoxicated by a drug of abuse, or suffering symptoms of withdrawal, the doctor may order a toxicology screen of the patient's blood or urine. Specific substances that are known to be associated with violent outbursts include phencyclidine (PCP or angel dust), alcohol, and **cocaine**. The doctor will also give the patient a **mental status examination** and a test to screen for neurological damage. If necessary, a neurologist may be consulted, and **imaging studies** performed of the patient's brain.

If the physical findings and laboratory test results are normal, the doctor may evaluate the patient for personality disorders, usually by administering diagnostic questionnaires. The patient may be given a diagnosis of antisocial or **borderline personality disorder** in addition to a diagnosis of IED.

In some cases, the doctor may need to rule out **malingering**, particularly if the patient has been referred for evaluation by a court order and is trying to evade legal responsibility for his behavior.

Treatment

Some adult patients with IED appear to benefit from cognitive therapy. A team of researchers at the University of Pennsylvania found that cognitive approaches that challenged the patients' negative views of the world and of other people were effective in reducing the intensity as well as the frequency of violent episodes. With regard to gender roles, many of the men reported that they were helped by rethinking manliness in terms of self-control rather than as something to be proved by hitting someone else or damaging property.

Several medications have been used for treating IED. These include **carbamazepine** (Tegretol), an anti-seizure medication; **propranolol** (Inderal), a heart medication that controls blood pressure and irregular heart rhythms; and lithium, a drug used to treat bipolar type II manic-depressive disorder. The success of treatment with lithium and other mood-stabilizing medications is consistent with findings that patients with IED have a high lifetime rate of bipolar disorder.

Prognosis

Little research has been done on patients with IED, although one study did find that such patients have a high lifetime rate of comorbid (co-occurring) bipolar disorder. In some persons IED decreases in severity or resolves completely as the person grows older. In others, the disorder appears to be chronic.

Prevention

As of 2011, preventive strategies included educating young people in parenting skills and teaching children skills related to self-control. Self-control can be practiced like many other skills, and people can improve their present level of self-control with appropriate coaching and practice.

Resources

BOOKS

American Psychiatric Association. *Diagnostic and Statistical Manual of Mental Disorders*. 4th ed., text rev. Washington, DC: American Psychiatric Association, 2000.

Dombrowski, Stefan, Karen L. Gischlar, and Martin Mrazik. *Assessing and Treating Low Incidence/High Severity Psychological Disorders of Childhood*. New York: Springer, 2011.

Grant, Jon E. *Impulse Control Disorders: A Clinician's Guide to Understanding and Treating Behavioral Addictions*. New York: W. W. Norton & Company, 2008.

Stern, Theodore A., Jerrold F. Rosenbaum, Maurizio Fava, Joseph Biederman, and Scott L. Rauch. *Massachusetts General Hospital Comprehensive Clinical Psychiatry*. Philadelphia: Mosby Elsevier, 2008.

PERIODICALS

Ahmed, A. "Latent Structure of Intermittent Explosive Disorder in an Epidemiological Sample." *Journal of Psychiatric Research* 44, no. 10 (2010): 663–72.

Coccaro, E.F. "A Family History Study of Intermittent Explosive Disorder." *Journal of Psychiatric Research* 44, no. 15 (2010): 1101–15.

———. "Intermittent Explosive Disorder: Development of Integrated Research Criteria for Diagnostic and Statistical Manual of Mental Disorders, Fifth Edition." *Comprehensive Psychiatry* 52, no. 2 (2011): 119–25.

WEBSITES

Harvard Medical School. "Treating Intermittent Explosive Disorder." *Harvard Mental Health Letter* (April 2011). http://www.health.harvard.edu/newsletters/Harvard_Mental_Health_Letter/2011/April/treating-intermittent-explosive-disorder (accessed September 7, 2011).

Laith Farid Gulli, M.D.
Bilal Nasser, M.D.

Internet addiction disorder

Definition

Internet **addiction** disorder (IAD) refers to the problematic use of the Internet, including the various aspects of its technology, such as electronic mail (email) and the World Wide Web. It is also known as problematic computer use, pathological computer use, and Internet overuse. The reader should note that Internet addiction disorder is not listed in the mental health professional's handbook, the ***Diagnostic and Statistical Manual of Mental Disorders***, fourth edition, text revision (2000), also called the *DSM*, possibly because the name of the disorder was originally proposed as a satirical spoof by a New York City **psychiatrist** in 1995. Internet addiction has, however, been formally recognized as a disorder by the **American Psychological Association**.

Although some psychiatrists have recommended adding diagnostic criteria for IAD to the forthcoming edition of the *DSM*, known as *DSM-5*, the disorder was not listed among the proposed additions to the manual in mid-2011. Much of the debate focuses on whether IAD is a distinctive disorder or whether it is simply an instance of a new technology being used to support other addictions. For example, there are gambling casinos on the Internet that could reinforce a person's pre-existing gambling addiction. Similarly, someone addicted to shopping could transfer their addiction from the local mall to online stores or such auction sites as eBay. Persons addicted to certain forms of sexual behavior can visit pornography sites on the Internet or use chat rooms as a way to meet others who might be willing to participate in those forms of behavior. The consensus seems to be that most, if not all, persons with IAD fall into established diagnostic categories.

Demographics

In the past, people reported to have an Internet addiction disorder were stereotyped as young, introverted, socially awkward, computer-oriented males. While this stereotype may have been true in the past, the availability of computers and the increased ease of access to the Internet are quickly challenging this notion. As a result, problematic Internet use can be found worldwide in any age group, social class, racial or ethnic group, level of education and income, and gender. One researcher in the Boston area estimates that between 6% and 10% of people who surf the Web suffer from some type of Internet dependency; and the American Academy of Pediatrics (AAP) estimates that between 8% and 12% of American children and adolescents have IAD. One reason for ongoing debate about the demographics of IAD, however, is that the disorder appears to have subtypes (described more fully in the next section) with different subpopulations.

Description

In some respects, addictive use of the Internet resembles other so-called process addictions, in which a person is addicted to an activity or behavior (including gambling, shopping, or certain sexual behaviors) rather than a substance (mood-altering drugs, tobacco, food, etc.). People who develop problems with their Internet use may start off using the Internet on a casual basis and then progress to using the technology in dysfunctional ways.

Some researchers maintain that there are several distinctive types of IAD rather than a single disorder:

- Online gaming. There are reported instances of people falling dead from exhaustion after several days of uninterrupted Internet gaming, although no one knows for certain how often such extreme cases arise.
- Internet pornography. This is a large subgroup; over 60% of people seeking treatment for IAD claim they are involved with online sexual activities that they consider inappropriate. People in this subgroup are more likely than others with IAD to have a substance abuse disorder.
- Online shopping. Most researchers consider online shopping addiction to be an extension of compulsive shopping in brick-and-mortar stores rather than a distinctive disorder, although some consider addiction to online auction sites like eBay to be a separate subtype.
- Email and texting.
- Social media. Social media is a general term for both Web-based and mobile technologies that facilitate

social (rather than business or academic) interaction online. It was estimated that as of 2011, about 22% of all online use in the United States involved social networking sites.

- Blogging. Blogging is a word derived from "weblog," a personal website maintained by an individual or group, with regular additions of commentary, descriptions of events, or personal videos. Most blogs are set up to allow comments from readers, which make a form of social media in many cases.

Many people believe that spending large amounts of time on the Internet is a core feature of the disorder. The amount of time by itself, however, is not as important a factor as the ways in which the person's Internet use is interfering with their daily functioning. Use of the Internet may interfere with social life, school work, or job-related tasks at work. In addition, cases have been reported of persons entering Internet chat rooms for people with serious illnesses or disorders, and pretending to be a patient with that disorder in order to get attention or sympathy. Treatment options often mirror those for other addictions. Although only a limited amount of research has been done on this disorder, the treatments that have been used appear to be effective.

One newer concern about IAD is the growing use of portable or handheld devices that can access the Internet, such as tablet PCs, smartphones, and other devices connected to the Internet via wireless networks. In 2008, mobile access to the Internet exceeded desktop computer-based access for the first time, and the popularity of mobile devices continues to rise. While these devices have much to offer users who need Web access in situations where a desktop computer is unavailable, they also allow others to spend excessive time on the Internet outside their houses or offices.

Risk factors

The most commonly identified risk factors for IAD include age between 12 and 25; pre-existing mood disorders; **diagnosis** of **attention deficit hyperactivity disorder (ADHD)** or **obsessive-compulsive disorder** (OCD); a history of **process addiction**; and a history of drug or alcohol abuse.

Gender is a risk factor for some forms of IAD. Most online gaming and pornography addicts are males, while women are at slightly greater risk for online shopping addiction. There is some evidence that male online shopping addicts are often unrecognized, because they tend to purchase different types of items (e.g., hardware, automotive equipment, and electronic devices or gadgets) from those favored by women (e.g., clothing, jewelry, and cosmetics).

Causes and symptoms

Causes

No one knows what causes a person to be addicted to the Internet, but there are several factors that have been proposed as contributing to Internet addiction. One theory concerns the mood-altering potential of behaviors related to process addictions. Just as a person addicted to shopping may feel a "rush" or pleasurable change in mood from the series of actions related to a spending spree-checking one's credit cards, driving to the mall, going into one's favorite store, etc.-the person with an Internet addiction may feel a similar rush from booting up their computer and going to their favorite websites. In other words, some researchers think that there are chemical changes that occur in the body when someone is engaging in an addictive behavior. Furthermore, from a biological standpoint, there may be a combination of genes that make a person more susceptible to addictive behaviors, just as researchers have located genes that affect a person's susceptibility to alcohol.

In addition to having features of a process addiction, Internet use might be reinforced by pleasurable thoughts and feelings that occur while the person is using the Internet. Although researchers in the field of addiction studies question the concept of an addictive personality as such, it is possible that someone who has one addiction may be prone to become addicted to other substances or activities, including Internet use. People with such other mental disorders or symptoms as **depression**, feelings of isolation, **stress**, or anxiety, may self-medicate by using the Internet in the same way that some people use alcohol or drugs of abuse to self-medicate the symptoms of their mental disorder. Still another theory is that Internet overuse is akin to dissociation in that it allows a person to compartmentalize difficulties in their present life and escape from reality into an online virtual world.

From a social or interpersonal standpoint, there may be familial factors prompting use of the Internet. For example, a person might "surf the Web" to escape family conflict. Another possibility is that social or peer dynamics might prompt excessive Internet use. Some affected persons may lack the social skills that would enable them to meet people in person rather than online. Peer behavior might also encourage Internet use if all of one's friends are using it. **Modeling** may play a role-users can witness and experience how others engage in Internet use and then replicate that behavior. The interactive aspects of the Internet, such as chat rooms, email, and interactive games like Multi-User Dungeons and Dragons (MUDS), seem to be more likely to lead to Internet addiction than purely solitary web surfing.

Symptoms

The most noticeable symptom of Internet addiction is excessive time devoted to Internet use. A person might have difficulty cutting down on his or her online time even when they are threatened with poor grades or loss of a job. There have been cases reported of college students failing courses because they would not take time off from Internet use to attend classes. Other symptoms of addiction may include lack of sleep; **fatigue**; declining grades or poor job performance; **apathy**; and racing thoughts. There may also be a decreased investment in social relationships and activities. A person may lie about how much time was spent online or deny that they have a problem. They may be irritable when offline or angry toward anyone who questions their time on the Internet.

Some pediatricians attribute an increase in depression among adolescents to the widespread popularity of social media. The term Facebook depression has been coined to describe the low self-esteem and mood disorders among some vulnerable adolescents induced by spending hours on Facebook and similar social networking sites. The researchers attribute Facebook depression to the way in which the medium facilitates constant comparisons of the self to other, presumably more popular, peers, and the common practice of posting negative or sarcastic comments on someone else's Facebook page.

Diagnosis

As previously noted, Internet addiction disorder has not yet been added as an official diagnosis to the *DSM*. The following, however, is a set of criteria for Internet addiction that has been proposed by addiction researchers. The criteria are based on the diagnostic standards for pathological gambling.

The patient must meet all of the following criteria:

- Preoccupation with the Internet (thinks about previous online activity or is anticipating the next online session)
- The need to spend longer and longer periods of time online in order to feel satisfied
- Unsuccessful efforts to control, cut back, or stop Internet use.
- Restlessness, moodiness, depression, or irritability when attempting to cut down or stop Internet use.
- Repeatedly staying online longer than originally intended.

The person must meet at least one of the following criteria:

- Jeopardized or risked the loss of a significant relationship, job, educational or career opportunity because of Internet use.
- Lied to family members, a therapist, or others to conceal the extent of involvement with the Internet.
- Uses the Internet as a way of escaping from problems or of relieving an unpleasant mood (such as feelings of helplessness, guilt, anxiety, or depression).

Examination

There are no physical symptoms unique to IAD that can be detected during a standard physical examination.

Tests

There are no laboratory or imaging tests that can detect IAD. A set of self-tests for such specific problems as online pornography, online gaming, online auction addiction, online gambling, and general Internet addiction are available at http://www.netaddiction.com/

KEY TERMS

Blogging—Creating and maintaining an online personal website, in most cases allowing readers to add comments. The term comes from the word weblog, or online diary.

Dissociation—A condition in which a person's thoughts, emotions, sensations, or memories become compartmentalized, usually as a result of a severe emotional trauma.

Facebook depression—A term used to describe an adolescent mood disorder associated with low self-esteem and depressed mood triggered by excessive concern with online social media.

Process addiction—A term used to describe addiction to an activity or behavior rather than a mood-altering chemical. It is also known as behavioral addiction or non-substance-related addiction.

Social media—A general term for both Web-based and mobile technologies that facilitate social (as distinct from commercial or academic) interaction online.

index.php?option=com_content&view=article&id=64&Itemid=88.

Two psychological inventories administered by mental health professionals, the Internet Addiction Test (IAT) and the Internet-Related Problem Scale (IRPS) were still undergoing clinical evaluation as of 2011.

Treatment

Traditional

Since Internet addiction disorder is a relatively new phenomenon, there is little research on the effectiveness of treatment procedures. It may be unrealistic to have a person completely end all Internet use. As our society becomes more and more dependent on computers for business transactions, educational programs, entertainment, and access to information as well as interpersonal communication, it will be difficult for a computer-literate person to avoid using the Internet. Learning how to use the Internet in moderation is often the main objective in therapy, in a way analogous to the way that people with eating disorders need to come to terms with food. Many of the procedures that have been used to treat Internet addiction have been modeled after other addiction treatment programs and **support groups**, particularly twelve-step groups.

Psychological interventions may include such approaches as changing the environment to alter associations that have been made with Internet use, or decrease the **reinforcement** received from excessive Internet use. Psychological interventions such as **cognitive-behavioral therapy** may also help the person identify thoughts and feelings that trigger their use of the Internet. Interpersonal interventions may include such approaches as **social skills training** or coaching in communication skills. Family and couple therapy may be indicated if the user is turning to the Internet to escape from problems in these areas of life. There is also a residential treatment program called ReSTART, which opened in the Pacific Northwest in 2009. The on-site program lasts 45 days and includes intensive individualized assessment as well as individual and **group therapy**.

Relapsing into an addictive behavior is common for anyone dealing with addiction disorders. Recognizing and preparing for **relapse** is often a part of the treatment process. Identifying situations that would trigger excessive Internet use and generating ways to deal with these situations can greatly reduce the possibility of total relapse. One option that works for some people is the installation of individualized content-control software on their computer; the software can be customized to block access to the types of websites that are most problematic for that person.

QUESTIONS TO ASK YOUR DOCTOR

- How can I tell whether I am becoming addicted to Internet use?
- How can I tell whether another family member or friend has IAD?
- Do you consider IAD a distinctive disorder or simply a technological variant of other disorders?
- What treatment would you recommend for someone concerned about excessive Internet use?
- What is your opinion of content-control software as a form of self-treatment?

Drugs

If a person's Internet addiction disorder has a biological dimension, then medication such as an antidepressant or antianxiety drug may help him or her with these aspects of the addiction. There were no medications as of 2011 that specifically targeted IAD. One clinical trial completed in 2008 of **escitalopram** (Lexapro), an SSRI antidepressant, as a treatment for IAD found no difference between subjects who took the drug and those given a placebo. There were no new **clinical trials** for treatments for IAD as of 2011.

Prognosis

Although extensive studies have not yet been done, treatment appears to be effective in maintaining and changing the behavior of people drawn to excessive use of the Internet. If the disorder is left untreated, the person may experience an increased amount of conflict in his or her relationships. Excessive Internet use may jeopardize a person's employment or academic standing. In addition, such physical problems as fatigue, carpal tunnel syndrome, back pain, and eyestrain may develop.

Prevention

If a person knows that he or she has difficulty with other forms of addictive behavior, they should be cautious in exploring the types of applications that are used on the Internet. In addition, it is important for people to engage in social activities outside the Internet. One recommendation for parents of adolescents is to teach them about the proper uses and limitations of Facebook and other social networking sites as well as showing them how to make friends in everyday life. Finally, mental health workers should investigate ways to participate in the implementation of new technology rather than waiting for its aftereffects.

Resources

BOOKS

McQuade, Samuel C., et al., eds. *Internet Addiction and Online Gaming*. New York: Chelsea House, 2011.

Price, Hannah O., ed. *Internet Addiction*. Hauppauge, NY: Nova Science Publishers, 2010.

Young, Kimberley, and Cristiano Nabuco de Abreu, eds. *Internet Addiction: A Handbook and Guide to Evaluation and Treatment*. Hoboken, NJ: John Wiley and Sons, 2010.

PERIODICALS

Bernardi, S., and S. Pallanti. "Internet Addiction: A Descriptive Clinical Study Focusing on Comorbidities and Dissociative Symptoms." *Comprehensive Psychiatry* 50 (November-December 2009): 510-516.

Dell'Osso, B., et al. "Escitalopram in the Treatment of Impulsive-compulsive Internet Usage Disorder: An Open-label Trial Followed by a Double-blind Discontinuation Phase." *Journal of Clinical Psychiatry* 69 (March 2008): 452–456.

Dong, G., et al. "Precursor or Sequela: Pathological Disorders in People with Internet Addiction Disorder." *PLoS One* 6 (February 16, 2011): e14703.

Gentile, D.A., et al. "Pathological Video Game Use among Youths: A Two-year Longitudinal Study." *Pediatrics* 127 (February 2011): e319–e329.

Stieger, S., and C. Burger. "Implicit and Explicit Self-esteem in the Context of Internet Addiction." *Cyberpsychology, Behavior and Social Networking* 13 (December 2010): 681–688.

Waldron, Heather. "Internet Addiction a Real Problem for U.S. Kids." *AAP News* 31 (May 2010): 26,

Widyanto, L., et al. "A Psychometric Comparison of the Internet Addiction Test, the Internet-Related Problem Scale, and Self-diagnosis." *Cyberpsychology, Behavior and Social Networking* 14 (March 2011): 141–149.

WEBSITES

Laurance, Jeremy. "Addicted! Scientists Show How Internet Dependency Alters the Human Brain." *The Independent UK*, January 12, 2012. http://www.independent.co.uk/news/science/addicted-scientists-show-how-internet-dependency-alters-the-human-brain-6288344.html (accessed January 12, 2012).

MSNBC.com. "Docs Warn about Teens and 'Facebook Depression.'" http://www.msnbc.msn.com/id/42298789/ns/health-mental_health (accessed May 10, 2011).

ReSTART. "Behavioral Addictions FAQs." http://www.netaddictionrecovery.com/the-problem/behavioral-addiction-faq.html (accessed May 10, 2011).

ORGANIZATIONS

American Academy of Pediatrics (AAP), 141 Northwest Point Boulevard, Elk Grove Village, IL, United States 60007-1098, (847) 434-4000, Fax: (847) 434-8000, http://www.aap.org/default.htm

American Psychiatric Association, 1000 Wilson Boulevard, Suite 1825, Arlington, VA, United States 22209-3901, (703) 907-7300, apa@psych.org http://www.psych.org

Center for Online Addiction, PO Box 72, Bradford, PA, United States 16701, (814) 451-2405, Fax: (814) 368-9560, http://www.netaddiction.com

ReSTART, 1001 290th Ave. SE, Fall City, WA, United States 98024-7403, (425) 417-1715, (800) 682-6934, restart@netaddictionrecovery.com, http://www.netaddictionrecovery.com

Keith Beard, Psy.D.
Rebecca J. Frey, Ph.D.

Internet-based therapy

Definition

Internet-based therapy is a form of **psychotherapy** conducted over the Internet rather than in face-to-face sessions. Therapeutic sessions may be conducted using instant messaging, chat rooms, or email messages. Internet-based therapy is also called online therapy or e-therapy.

Internet-based therapy is sometimes classified together with telephone therapy and videoconferencing as remote therapy, as all three forms depend on remote communication technologies. A number of online therapy providers, in fact, offer telephone-based therapy as well as email and online live chat therapy.

Purpose

The purpose of Internet-based therapy is to provide psychological help to persons who either cannot get to a physical office for reasons of disability, geographical isolation, or reluctance to be seen visiting a therapist, or who simply prefer electronic to face-to-face communication.

Description

Online therapy can take several different forms, depending on whether the client chooses live online chat/telephone, webcam, or email sessions. One common practice of online therapists is to ask potential clients to complete an online form in which the client provides basic personal information and a description of their problem or reason for seeking counseling. With e-mail sessions, the client fills out the online pre-session form and sends it by a special secure email service, and the therapist replies within one or two business days. Live online chat can begin as soon as the client fills out the pre-session form. For telephone counseling, the client provides the remote therapist with a telephone number and time to call, and the therapist will call at the scheduled time.

Clients are expected to pay in advance, usually via credit card or PayPal. Some online therapists stipulate that all prepaid sessions must be used within six months of purchase.

Online therapy is recommended only for non-emergency mental health services; most online therapy websites state that their services are not appropriate for persons who are suicidal, suffering from **psychosis**, or having an acute psychiatric crisis. In addition, most will not accept patients under age 18.

Benefits

As the Information Age progresses, more and more services are becoming available over the Internet. We can buy not only books online but also electronics, clothes, and even groceries. In the business world, the requirement and expense of traveling to in-person meetings are often negated by the ability to teleconference. College degrees no longer need to be earned in the classroom but can be acquired in the comfort of one's own home at one's own pace. The wait for a technician on a manufacturer's help line is often replaced by the ability to search the company's database on one's own or to engage in online chat with the same technician to whom one once spoke. Even for medical problems, one can often chat with a physician or nurse practitioner by email rather than going to the office; this service is known as telemedicine.

There is little wonder, therefore, that there is a demand for psychological services over the Internet. Chatting with one's therapist online is more private than going to an office and waiting in an open waiting room. For those in rural areas where access to a therapist is exceedingly difficult, the Internet can provide a convenient alternative for getting the help that one needs.

There are pros and cons to both sides of the issue of online versus face-to-face therapy. First, communicating through email, online chat, or instant messages has the same drawbacks of any written-only communication: Such nonverbal cues as tone of voice, facial expression, and body language are missing, making interpretation of the message more problematic than in a face-to-face situation. On the other hand, the relative anonymity of online interactions make such therapeutic relationships more attractive to those who would hesitate to go into a therapist's office for fear of being found out by others, fear of embarrassment, or unwillingness or inability to get to the office. In addition, online therapy tends to be less expensive than in-office therapy, a consideration for many clients.

There are, of course, some things that cannot be done over the Internet. For example, psychologists and psychiatrists use a variety of tools and techniques to diagnose mental disorders so that they can prescribe the appropriate course of treatment. Some of the tools used in **diagnosis** include such psychometric instruments as the **Minnesota Multiphasic Personality Inventory** (MMPI), such projective instruments as the Rorschach test or the **Thematic Apperception Test** (TAT), and diagnostic interviews. The various tests and instruments used in diagnosis should ethically be given only by a credentialed professional in a controlled situation and cannot be given across the Internet where there is no control over who will see the test; how long the client takes to answer the questions; or even whether it was the client or someone else who took the test. In addition, it would be extremely difficult to diagnose a patient's problem without a face-to-face meeting for a diagnostic interview.

Research into the effectiveness of online therapy is only beginning. However, a number of disorders have been successfully treated electronically. For example, Internet-based therapy has been successful in the treatment of **panic disorder**, **social phobia**, child adjustment after **traumatic brain injury**, and complicated **grief**, among others. It is also recommended for treatment of **agoraphobia**, an anxiety disorder in which people are afraid of wide-open spaces, uncontrolled social situations, and crowds; many are unable to leave their homes without suffering a **panic attack**.

KEY TERMS

Agoraphobia—An anxiety disorder characterized by fear of crowds, open spaces, and/or locations or situations that trigger panic attacks.

Remote therapy—A general term for therapy delivered by electronic communication technologies; it includes Internet-based therapy along with telephone therapy and videoconferencing.

Precautions

As with any service provided over the Internet, one must be an informed consumer not only before choosing an e-therapist, but even before deciding to use Internet-based therapy itself. Because Internet-based therapy is an emerging field, there are still many issues to be resolved. Obviously, one must check the professional credentials of a therapist to make sure that he or she is licensed and must determine whether one is choosing a therapist for online or in-office therapy. In addition, it is unclear at this time whether it is legal for a therapist licensed in one state to treat a patient in another state. Choosing a therapist in one's own state makes this issue irrelevant but requires research.

Client/therapist confidentiality is important in any therapeutic relationship. When choosing an online provider of psychological services, one must be certain not only that the therapist subscribes to a professional code of ethics but also that any information, including personal data about the client, is kept confidential and not sold to, or shared with, third parties. Similarly, it is important to check that the website used in online therapy is secure and that conversations, instant messages, and email transmissions between client and therapist are not recorded on the site's secured host computer.

A statement of ethical principles for conducting online therapy is available on the website of the International Society for Mental Health Online (ISMHO). These principles were officially adopted in 2000. It is important to remember that anything sent over the Internet may be subject to being unlawfully sought out by others and that there is an inherent risk to such communication even on secured servers.

Preparation

As noted above, preparation for online counseling requires the client to complete an online form with contact information and a description of the reason for seeking counseling. The client is also asked to choose the preferred method of contact with the therapist (telephone, email, online chat, or webcam) and to pay in advance for one or more sessions. Preparation should also include researching the therapist's company and/or credentials before making contact.

Risks

Potential risks include technical difficulties with Internet or telephone communication and breaches of security by hackers.

QUESTIONS TO ASK YOUR DOCTOR

- What is your opinion of Internet-based therapy? Of other forms of remote therapy?
- Have you ever referred a patient to an online therapist?
- Have any of your patients mentioned consulting an online therapist? If so, what were their experiences?

Research and general acceptance

Internet-based therapy shows promise for helping people who could not or would not otherwise engage in a therapeutic relationship. This potential is beginning to be tested in research. However, much of this research also recommends that Internet-based therapy be used in conjunction with face-to-face sessions. There are still many technical, logistical, and ethical questions to be answered regarding how the Internet best can be used for therapy. Most insurance companies will not provide reimbursement for therapy conducted over the Internet.

As of early 2011, there were 130 **clinical trials** of Internet-based therapy under way. Some are trials of **cognitive-behavioral therapy** or other specific approaches; other trials are comparing online therapy with face-to-face therapy for specific problems or disorders, including **smoking cessation**, **depression**, social anxiety, panic disorder, and grief disorder. Still other trials are evaluating the effectiveness of Internet-based counseling for patients suffering from chronic physical conditions with an emotional dimension, such as cancer, chronic pain syndromes, **brain** injury, or congestive heart failure.

Training and certification

Online therapists are expected to meet the same educational and state licensure requirements as office- or clinic-based therapists. They may be psychiatrists, clinical or counseling psychologists, **social workers**, marriage and family therapists, or psychiatric nurses. Most have doctoral degrees (M.D., Ph.D., or Psy.D.), with the remainder having master's degrees in psychology, social work, or nursing. There is one professional organization specifically for online therapists, the International Society for Mental Health Online (ISMHO), which was formed in 1997.

Resources

BOOKS

Hsiung, Robert C., ed. *E-therapy: Case Studies, Guiding Principles, and the Clinical Potential of the Internet.* New York: Norton, 2002.

Kraus, Ron, ed. *Online Counseling: A Handbook for Mental Health Professionals*, 2nd ed. Amsterdam, The Netherlands: Elsevier, 2011.

Rochlen, Aaron B. *Applying Counseling Theories: An Online Case-based Approach.* Upper Saddle River, NJ: Pearson/ Merrill Prentice Hall, 2007.

PERIODICALS

Bee, P.E., et al. "Psychotherapy Mediated by Remote Communication Technologies: A Meta-analytic Review." *BMC Psychiatry* 8 (July 2008):

Bockling, C.L., et al. "Disrupting the Rhythm of Depression Using Mobile Cognitive Therapy for Recurrent Depression: Randomized Controlled Trial Design and Protocol." *BMC Psychiatry* 14 (January 2011): 12.

Buhrman, M., et al. "Guided Internet-based Cognitive Behavioural Treatment for Chronic Back Pain Reduces Pain Catastrophizing: A Randomized Controlled Trial." *Journal of Rehabilitation Medicine* 43 (May 2011): 500–505.

Carlbring, P., et al. "Individually-tailored, Internet-based Treatment for Anxiety Disorders: A Randomized Controlled Trial." *Behaviour Research and Therapy* 49 (January 2011): 18–24.

Gainsbury, S., and A. Blaszczynski. "A Systematic Review of Internet-based Therapy for the Treatment of Addictions." *Clinical Psychology Review* 31 (April 2011): 490–498.

Hedman, E., et al. "Internet-Based Cognitive Behavior Therapy vs. Cognitive Behavioral Group Therapy for Social Anxiety Disorder: A Randomized Controlled Non-inferiority Trial." *PLoS One* 6 (March 25, 2011): e18001.

Lampe, L.A. "Internet-based Therapy: Too Good to be True?" *Australian and New Zealand Journal of Psychiatry* 45 (April 2011): 342–343.

Warmerdam, L., et al. "Cost-utility and Cost-effectiveness of Internet-based Treatment for Adults with Depressive Symptoms: Randomized Trial."*Journal of Medical Internet Research* 12 (December 19, 2010): e53.

WEBSITES

eTherapistsonline.com. "About Online Counseling." http://www.etherapistsonline.com/therapy/about.htm (accessed May 11, 2011).

International Society for Mental Health Online (ISMHO). "Suggested Principles for the Online Provision of Mental Health Services." https://www.ismho.org/suggestions.asp#principles (accessed May 11, 2011).

ORGANIZATIONS

Find a Therapist, Inc, 6942 E Lomita, Mesa, AZ, United States 85209, (480) 325-8330, Fax: (480) 396-3213, (866) 450-3463, http://www.etherapistsonline.com

International Society for Mental Health Online (ISMHO), [online contact only] https://www.ismho.org/contact.asp, https://www.ismho.org/home.asp

MyTherapyNet, 22425 Ventura Blvd., Suite 350, Woodland Hills, CA, United States 91364, Fax: (800) 931-9956, (800) 931-9956, customerservice@mytherapynet.com, https://www.mytherapynet.com

Ruth A. Wienclaw, Ph.D.
Rebecca J. Frey, Ph.D.

Interpersonal therapy

Definition

Interpersonal therapy (IPT) is a short-term supportive **psychotherapy** that focuses on the connection between interactions between people and the development of a person's psychiatric symptoms.

Purpose

Interpersonal therapy was initially developed to treat adult **depression**. It has since been applied to the treatment of depression in adolescents, the elderly, and people with Human Immunodeficiency Virus (HIV) infection. There is an IPT conjoint (couple) therapy for people whose marital disputes contribute to depressive episodes. IPT has also been modified for the treatment of a number of disorders, including **substance abuse**; bulimia and **anorexia nervosa**; **bipolar disorder**; and dysthymia. Research is underway to determine the efficacy of IPT in the treatment of patients with **panic disorder** or **borderline personality disorder**; depressed caregivers of patients with traumatic **brain** injuries; depressed pregnant women; and people suffering from protracted **bereavement**.

Interpersonal therapy is a descendant of psychodynamic therapy, itself derived from **psychoanalysis**, with its emphasis on the unconscious and childhood experiences. Symptoms and personal difficulties are regarded as arising from deep, unresolved personality or character problems. **Psychodynamic psychotherapy** is a long-term method of treatment, with in-depth exploration of past family relationships as they were perceived during the client's infancy, childhood, and adolescence.

There are seven types of interventions that are commonly used in IPT, many of which reflect the influence of psychodynamic psychotherapy: a focus on clients' emotions; an exploration of clients' resistance to treatment; discussion of patterns in clients' relationships and experiences; taking a detailed past history; an emphasis on clients' current interpersonal experiences;

exploration of the therapist/client relationship; and the identification of clients' wishes and fantasies. IPT is, however, distinctive for its brevity and its treatment focus. IPT emphasizes the ways in which a person's current relationships and social context cause or maintain symptoms rather than exploring the deep-seated sources of the symptoms. Its goals are rapid symptom reduction and improved social adjustment. A frequent byproduct of IPT treatment is more satisfying relationships in the present.

IPT has the following goals in the treatment of depression: to diagnose depression explicitly; to educate the client about depression, its causes, and the various treatments available for it; to identify the interpersonal context of depression as it relates to symptom development; and to develop strategies for the client to follow in coping with the depression. Because interpersonal therapy is a short-term approach, the therapist addresses only one or two problem areas in the client's current functioning. In the early sessions, the therapist and client determine which areas would be most helpful in reducing the client's symptoms. The remaining sessions are then organized toward resolving these agreed-upon problem areas. This time-limited framework distinguishes IPT from therapies that are open-ended in their exploration. The targeted approach of IPT has demonstrated rapid improvement for patients with problems ranging from mild situational depression to severe depression with a recent history of **suicide** attempts.

Interpersonal therapy has been outlined in a manual by Klerman and Weissman, which ensures some standardization in the training of interpersonal therapists and their practice. Because of this standardized training format, IPT is not usually combined with other talk therapies. Treatment with IPT, however, is often combined with drug therapy, particularly when the client suffers from such mood disorders as depression, dysthymia, or bipolar disorder.

Precautions

Training programs in interpersonal therapy are still not widely available, so that many practicing therapists base their work on the manual alone without additional supervision. It is unclear whether reading the manual alone is sufficient to provide an acceptable standard of care.

While interpersonal therapy has been adapted for use with substance abusers, it has not demonstrated its effectiveness with this group of patients. Researchers studying patients addicted to opiates or **cocaine** found little benefit to incorporating IPT into the standard recovery programs. These findings suggest that another treatment method that offers greater structure and direction would be more successful with these patients.

Description

Since the interpersonal therapy model was developed for the treatment of depression and then modified for use with other populations and mental disorders, an understanding of IPT's approach to depression is crucial. Interpersonal therapists focus on the functional role of depression rather than on its etiology or cause; and they look at the ways in which problematic interactions develop when a person becomes depressed. The IPT framework considers clinical depression as having three components: the development of symptoms that arise from biological, genetic and/or psychodynamic processes; social interactions with other people, which are learned over the course of one's life; and personality, made up of the more enduring traits and behaviors that may predispose a person to depressive symptoms. IPT intervenes at the levels of symptom formation and social functioning, and does not attempt to alter aspects of the client's personality.

Subtypes of IPT

Interpersonal therapy offers two possible treatment plans for persons with depressive disorders. The first plan treats the acute episode of depression by eliminating the current depressive symptoms. This approach requires intervening while the person is in the midst of a depression. The acute phase of treatment typically lasts 2–4 months with weekly sessions. Many clients terminate treatment at that point, after their symptoms have subsided. Maintenance treatment (IPT-M) is the second treatment plan and is much less commonly utilized than acute treatment. IPT-M is a longer-term therapy based on the principles of interpersonal therapy but with the aim of preventing or reducing the frequency of further depressive episodes. Some clients choose IPT-M after the acute treatment phase. IPT-M can extend over a period of 2–3 years, with therapy sessions once a month.

Psychoeducation in IPT

Treatment with IPT is based on the premise that depression occurs in a social and interpersonal context that must be understood for improvement to occur. In the first session, the psychiatric history includes a review of the client's current social functioning and current close relationships, their patterns and their mutual expectations. Changes in relationships prior to the onset of symptoms are clarified, such as the death of a loved one, a child leaving home, or worsening marital conflict.

IPT is psychoeducational in nature to some degree. It involves teaching the client about the nature of depression and the ways that it manifests in his or her life and relationships. In the initial sessions, depressive symptoms are reviewed in detail, and the accurate naming of the problem is essential. The therapist then explains depression and its treatment and may explain to the client that he or she has adopted the "sick role." The concept of the "sick role" is derived from the work of a sociologist named Talcott Parsons, and is based on the notion that illness is not merely a condition but a social role that affects the attitudes and behaviors of the client and those around him or her. Over time, the client comes to see that the sick role has increasingly come to govern his or her social interactions.

Identification of problem areas

The techniques of IPT were developed to manage four basic interpersonal problem areas: unresolved **grief**; role transitions; interpersonal role disputes (often marital disputes); and interpersonal deficits (deficiencies). In the early sessions, the interpersonal therapist and the client attempt to determine which of these four problems is most closely associated with the onset of the current depressive episode. Therapy is then organized to help the client deal with the interpersonal difficulties in the primary problem area. The coping strategies that the client is encouraged to discover and employ in daily life are tailored to his or her individual situation.

UNRESOLVED GRIEF. In normal bereavement, a person experiences symptoms such as sadness, disturbed sleep, and difficulty functioning but these usually resolve in 2–4 months. Unresolved grief in depressed people is usually either delayed grief that has been postponed and then experienced long after the loss; or distorted grief, in which there is no felt emotion of sadness but there may be nonemotional symptoms, often physical. If unresolved grief is identified as the primary issue, the goals of treatment are to facilitate the mourning process. Successful therapy will help the client re-establish interests and relationships that can begin to fill the void of what has been lost.

ROLE DISPUTES. Interpersonal role disputes occur when the client and at least one other significant person have differing expectations of their relationship. The IPT therapist focuses on these disputes if they seem stalled or repetitious, or offer little hope of improvement. The treatment goals include helping the client identify the nature of the dispute; decide on a plan of action; and begin to modify unsatisfying patterns, reassess expectations of the relationship, or both. The therapist does not direct the client to one particular resolution of difficulties and should not attempt to preserve unworkable relationships.

ROLE TRANSITIONS. Depression associated with role transitions occurs when a person has difficulty coping with life changes that require new roles. These may be such transitions as retirement, a career change, moving, or leaving home. People who are clinically depressed are most likely to experience role changes as losses rather than opportunities. The loss may be obvious, as when a marriage ends, or more subtle, as the loss of freedom people experience after the birth of a child. Therapy is terminated when a client has given up the old role; expressed the accompanying feelings of guilt, anger, and loss; acquired new skills; and developed a new social network around the new role.

INTERPERSONAL DEFICITS. Interpersonal deficits are the focus of treatment when the client has a history of inadequate or unsupportive interpersonal relationships. The client may never have established lasting or intimate relationships as an adult, and may experience a sense of inadequacy, lack of self-assertion, and guilt about expressing anger. Generally, clients with a history of extreme social isolation come to therapy with more severe emotional disturbances. The goal of treatment is to reduce the client's social isolation. Instead of focusing on current relationships, IPT therapy in this area focuses on the client's past relationships; the present relationship with the therapist; and ways to form new relationships.

IPT in special populations

ELDERLY CLIENTS. In translating the IPT model of depression to work with different populations, the core principles and problem areas remain essentially the same, with some modifications. In working with the elderly, IPT sessions may be shorter to allow for decreased energy levels, and dependency issues may be more prominent. In addition, the therapist may work with an elderly client toward tolerating rather than eliminating long-standing role disputes.

CLIENTS WITH HIV INFECTION. In IPT with HIV-positive clients, particular attention is paid to the clients' unique set of psychosocial stressors: the **stigma** of the disease; the effects of being gay (if applicable); dealing with family members who may isolate themselves; and coping with the medical consequences of the disease.

ADOLESCENTS. In IPT with adolescents, the therapist addresses such common developmental issues as separation from parents; the client's authority in relationship to parents; the development of new interpersonal relationships; first experiences of the death of a relative or friend; peer pressure; and single-parent families. Adolescents are seen weekly for 12 weeks with once-weekly additional phone contact between therapist and client for the first four weeks of treatment. The parents are interviewed in the initial session to get a comprehensive history of the adolescent's symptoms, and to educate the parents as well as the young person about depression and possible treatments, including a discussion of the need for medication. The therapist refrains from giving advice when working with adolescents, and will primarily use supportive listening, while assessing the client for evidence of suicidal thoughts or problems with school attendance. So far, research does not support the efficacy of antidepressant medication in treating adolescents, though most clinicians will give some younger clients a trial of medication if it appears to offer relief.

CLIENTS WITH SUBSTANCE ABUSE DISORDERS. While IPT has not yet demonstrated its efficacy in the field of substance abuse recovery, a version of IPT has been developed for use with substance abusers. The two goals are to help the client stop or cut down on drug use; and to help the client develop better strategies for dealing with the social and interpersonal consequences of drug use. To meet these goals, the client must accept the need to stop; take steps to manage impulsiveness; and recognize the social contexts of drug purchase and use. **Relapse** is viewed as the rule rather than the exception in treating substance abuse disorders, and the therapist avoids treating the client in a punitive or disapproving manner when it occurs. Instead, the therapist reminds the client of the fact that staying away from drugs is the client's decision.

CLIENTS WITH EATING DISORDERS. IPT has been extended to the treatment of eating disorders. The IPT therapist does not focus directly on the symptoms of the disorder, but rather, allows for identification of problem areas that have contributed to the emergence of the disorder over time. IPT appears to be useful in treating clients with bulimia whose symptoms are maintained by interpersonal issues, including social anxiety; sensitivity to conflict and rejection; and difficulty managing negative emotions. IPT is helpful in bringing the problems underlying the bingeing and purging to the surface, such as conflict avoidance; difficulties with role expectations; confusion regarding needs for closeness and distance; and deficiencies in solving social problems. IPT also helps people with bulimia to regulate the emotional states that maintain the bulimic behavior.

Anorexia nervosa also appears to be responsive to treatment with IPT. Research indicates that there is a connection between interpersonal and family dysfunction and the development of anorexia nervosa. Therapists disagree as to whether interpersonal dysfunction causes or is caused by anorexia. IPT has been helpful because it is not concerned with the origin but rather seeks to improve the client's interpersonal functioning and thereby decreasing symptoms. IPT's four categories of grief, interpersonal disputes, interpersonal deficits, and role transitions correspond to the core issues of clients with anorexia. **Social phobia** is another disorder that responds well to IPT therapy.

KEY TERMS

Bereavement—The emotional experience of loss after the death of a friend or relative.

Bingeing—An excessive amount of food consumed in a short period of time. Usually, while a person binge eats, he or she feels disconnected from reality, and feels unable to stop. The bingeing may temporarily relieve depression or anxiety, but after the binge, the person usually feels guilty and depressed.

Dysthymia—Depression of low intensity.

Dysthymic disorder—A mood disorder that is less severe than depression but usually more chronic.

Etiology—The cause or origin of a disease or disorder. The word is also used to refer to the study of the causes of disease.

Psychosocial—A term that refers to the emotional and social aspects of psychological disorders.

Purging—Inappropriate actions taken to prevent weight gain, often after bingeing, including self-induced vomiting or the misuse of laxatives, diuretics, enemas, or other medications.

Remission—In the course of an illness or disorder, a period of time when symptoms are absent.

Role—The set of customary or expected behavior patterns associated with a particular position or function in society. For example, a person's role as mother is associated with one set of expected behaviors, and her role as a worker with a very different set.

Role transition—Life changes that require an alteration in one's social or occupational status or self-image.

Stigma—A mark or characteristic trait of a disease or defect; by extension, a cause for reproach or a stain on one's reputation. Such sexually transmitted diseases as HIV infection carry a severe social stigma.

Supportive—An approach to psychotherapy that seeks to encourage the patient or offer emotional support to him or her, as distinct from insight-oriented or exploratory approaches to treatment.

Aftercare

Interpersonal therapy as a maintenance approach (IPT-M) could be viewed as aftercare for clients suffering from depression. It is designed as a preventive measure by focusing on the period after the acute depression has passed. Typically, once the client is in remission and is symptom-free, he or she takes on more responsibilities and has increased social contact. These changes can lead to increased **stress** and greater vulnerability to another episode of depression. IPT-M enables clients to reduce the stresses associated with remission and thereby lower the risk of recurrence. The goal of maintenance therapy is to keep the client at his or her current level of functioning. Research has shown that for clients with a history of recurrent depression, total prevention is unlikely, but that maintenance therapy may delay a recurrence.

In general, long-term maintenance psychotherapy by itself is not recommended unless there are such reasons as pregnancy or severe side effects that prevent the client from being treated with medication. IPT-M does, however, seem to be particularly helpful with certain groups of patients, either alone or in combination with medication. Women appear to benefit, due to the importance of social environment and social relations in female gender roles; the effects of the menstrual cycle on symptoms; and complications related to victimization by rape, incest, or battering. IPT is also useful for elderly clients who can't take **antidepressants** due to intolerable side effects or such medical conditions as autoimmune disorders, cardiovascular disorders, diabetes, or other general medical conditions.

Results

The expected outcomes of interpersonal therapy are a reduction or the elimination of symptoms and improved interpersonal functioning. There will also be a greater understanding of the presenting symptoms and ways to prevent their recurrence. For example, in the case of depression, a person will have been educated about the nature of depression; what it looks like for him or her; and the interpersonal triggers of a depressive episode. A person will also leave therapy with strategies for minimizing triggers and for resolving future depressive episodes more effectively. While interpersonal therapy focuses on the present, it can also improve the client's future through increased awareness of preventive measures and strengthened coping skills.

Research has shown that IPT requires clients' commitment to therapy prior to starting the treatment. If clients are resistant to an educational approach, the results of IPT are generally poor. It has been found that when people do not accept IPT's methods and approach at the outset; they are unlikely to be convinced over the course of therapy and they receive little benefit from treatment. IPT clients appear to do better in therapy if they have confidence in their therapist; therefore, if the initial fit between therapist and client is not good, therapy will often be unsuccessful. A client should listen to his or her instincts early in treatment, and either seek out another interpersonal therapist or find a therapist who uses a different approach—such as **cognitive-behavioral therapy**, which was also developed specifically for the treatment of depression.

Resources

BOOKS

American Psychiatric Association. *Diagnostic and Statistical Manual of Mental Disorders*. 4th ed., text rev. Washington, DC: American Psychiatric Publishing, 2000.

Klerman, Gerald L., et al. *Interpersonal Psychotherapy of Depression*. New York: Basic Books, Inc., 1984.

Klerman, Gerald L. and Myrna M. Weissman, eds. *New Applications of Interpersonal Psychotherapy*. Washington, DC: American Psychiatric Press, Inc., 1993.

Mufson, Laura, et al. *Interpersonal Psychotherapy for Depressed Adolescents*. 2nd ed. New York: Guilford Press, 2004.

PERIODICALS

Apple, Robin F. "Interpersonal Therapy for Bulimia Nervosa." *Journal of Clinical Psychology* 55, no. 6 (June 1999): 715–725.

Barkham, Michael, and Gillian E. Hardy. "Counselling and Interpersonal Therapies for Depression: Towards Securing an Evidence-base." *British Medical Bulletin* 57, no. 1 (2001): 115–132.

Frank, Ellen, and Michael E. Thase. "Natural History and Preventative (sic) Treatment of Recurrent Mood Disorders." *Annual Reviews Medicine* 50 (1999): 453–468.

House, Allan, D. M. "Brief Psychodynamic Interpersonal Therapy After Deliberate Self-poisoning Reduced Suicidal Ideation and Deliberate Self-harm." *Evidence Based Mental Health* 5, no. 1 (February 2002): 14.

McIntosh, Virginia V., et al. "Interpersonal Psychotherapy for Anorexia Nervosa." *International Journal of Eating Disorders* 27, no. 2 (March 2000): 125–139.

Mufson, Laura, et al. "Efficacy of Interpersonal Psychotherapy for Depressed Adolescents." *Archives of General Psychiatry* 56, no. 6 (June 1999): 573–579. Available online at http://archpsyc.ama-assn.org/cgi/reprint/56/6/573.pdf (accessed November 9, 2011).

Weissman, Myrna M., and John C. Markowitz. "Interpersonal Psychotherapy: Current Status." *Archives of General Psychiatry* 51, no. 8 (August 1994): 599–606.

ORGANIZATIONS

International Society for Interpersonal Psychotherapy, University of Iowa, Department of Psychiatry, 1-293 Medical Education Building, Iowa City, IA, 52242, (391) 353-4230, Fax: (391) 353-3003, scott-stuart@uiowa.edu, http://interpersonalpsychotherapy.org.

Holly Scherstuhl, M.Ed.

Intervention

Definition

A standard dictionary defines intervention as an influencing force or act that occurs in order to modify a given state of affairs. In the context of behavioral health, an intervention may be any outside process that has the effect of modifying an individual's behavior, cognition, or emotional state. For example, a person experiencing **stress** symptoms may find a variety of interventions effective in bringing relief. Deep breathing, vigorous **exercise**, talking with a therapist or counselor, taking an antianxiety medication, or a combination of these activities are all interventions designed to modify the symptoms and potentially the causes of stress-related discomfort.

The term is also used to describe a specific process designed to break through **denial** on the part of persons with serious addictive disorders. Interventions in this sense of the word involve carefully orchestrated confrontations in which friends, family members, and (in many cases) employers confront the person with the negative impact and consequences of his or her **addiction**. The goal of an intervention is to bring the addicted person to acknowledge that he or she suffers from a disorder and agree to treatment. This goal, however, is not always realized.

Description

There is no one-size-fits-all-intervention for behavioral health disorders. Recent research advances and greater understanding of behavioral health problems have provided an expanded range of treatments that promise better outcomes than those available in the past. For people who overcome the barriers of **stigma**, discrimination, and limited access, there is a broad variety of helpful interventions from which to choose. Both personal preference and the severity of discomfort may influence the choice of talk therapy, the use of medications, participation in self-help or **support groups**, or even inpatient treatment. In most cases, a combination of different interventions has proven to be most effective. As a result, many therapists tend to be eclectic in their practice and use a combination of approaches to in order to be as effective as possible with a wide variety of people.

Psychotherapy or talk therapy involves face-to-face meetings with a therapist who may specialize in a certain approach to treatment, and may include:

- Psychoanalysis is the oldest form of talk therapy. It is a long-term form of treatment intended to uncover a person's subconscious motivations and early patterns in order to resolve present issues.
- Behavioral therapy is designed to change thinking patterns and behavior. Exposure therapy is a subtype of behavioral therapy that is useful in treating obsessive-compulsive disorder and post-traumatic stress disorder. The client is deliberately exposed to stimuli that trigger the painful thoughts or feelings under carefully controlled conditions that include support from the therapist. The individual is then taught techniques to avoid performing the compulsive behaviors or to work through the traumatic event.
- Cognitive therapy seeks to identify and correct dysfunctional thinking patterns that lead to troublesome feelings or behavior.
- Family therapy includes discussion and problem-solving sessions that include all members of the family.
- Group therapy takes place in a small group with the guidance of a therapist. The focus is on individual issues; group members assist each other in problem solving.
- Movement, art, and music therapists use these forms of creative expression to help people deal with strong emotions that are less easily handled in a talk therapy format.

Drug therapy involves the use of prescribed medications to treat the symptoms of certain mental or emotional disorders. It is important for patients to be aware of possible side effects of the medications; to inform the doctor of all other medications and alternative remedies that they are taking; and to have their blood, blood pressure, or other vital signs monitored regularly by the prescribing physician.

Electroconvulsive therapy (ECT) is used to treat **depression** and a few other specific conditions that have not responded to other interventions. It involves a controlled series of electric shocks to certain areas of the **brain**. It has been proven effective for some people despite the fact that it continues to be controversial. Patients should be fully aware of the side effects of ECT and assure themselves that the professional has been properly trained to administer ECT.

Psychosocial treatments may include **talk therapy** and medication in combination with social and vocational training to assist people recovering from severe mental illnesses. Psychosocial interventions may also include education about the illness itself, techniques for managing its symptoms, and ways in which friends and family members can help.

Psychoeducation is a word used to describe the process of teaching people about their illness, its treatment, and early warning signs of **relapse**, so that they can seek treatment before the illness worsens.

Psychoeducation may also include learning about coping strategies, problem solving, and preparation of a crisis plan in the event of a relapse or future episode.

Self-help and support groups are another form of intervention that has become increasingly common in recent years. They exist for almost all disorders and are often based on the basic principles and values of the Alcoholics Anonymous movement founded in the 1930s. Although they are not led by professionals, these groups may be therapeutic because members give one another ongoing support and assistance. Group members share frustrations and successes, recommendations about specialists and community resources, and helpful tips about recovery. They also share friendship and hope for themselves, their loved ones, and others in the group. Unqualified acceptance by other people can be a powerful intervention for people recovering from a mental illness or addictive disorder.

A common question about interventions concerns sources of help or further information. Many communities have a local hotline number that provides referrals and resources, or a mental health association that can direct callers to appropriate clinics, agencies, or groups. Helping resources may include the following:

- A community mental health center, usually a part of the state's department of mental health.
- Local mental health organizations.
- Family physicians.
- Clergy or spiritual counselors.
- Family service agencies, including charities and family or social services sponsored by various churches, synagogues, or other religious groups.
- High school or college guidance counselors.
- Marriage and family counselors.
- Child guidance counselors.
- Accredited psychiatric hospitals.
- Hotlines, crisis centers, and emergency rooms.

There are several categories of mental health professionals who have been specially trained to provide a range of interventions to relieve suffering, treat specific symptoms, or improve overall mental health. Competent professionals are licensed or certified by a particular specialty board or state licensing body. Their credentials imply a certain level of education, training, experience, and subscription to a code of ethics. Mental health professionals include:

- Psychiatrists. Medical doctors with specialized training in the diagnosis and treatment of behavioral and emotional illnesses. They are qualified to prescribe medications. They may also specialize in certain fields within psychiatry, such as child/adolescent or geriatric psychiatry.
- Psychologists. Professional counselors with a doctoral degree (PhD or PsyD) and two or more years of supervised work experience. They are trained to make diagnoses, administer and interpret psychological tests, and provide individual, family and group therapy.
- Clinical social workers. Professionals with a master's degree in social work from an accredited graduate program. They are trained to make diagnoses and provide individual, family and group therapy.
- Licensed professional counselors and mental health counselors. Professionals with a master's degree with supervised work experience and are trained to make diagnoses and provide individual, family and group therapy.
- Certified alcohol and drug abuse counselors. Professionals with specialized training in the treatment of alcohol and drug abuse. They are able to diagnose and provide counseling to individuals, families and groups.
- Nurse psychotherapists. Registered nurses (RNs) with specialized training in psychiatric and mental health nursing. They can diagnose disorders and provide counseling to individuals, families and groups.
- Marital and family therapists. Counselors with a master's or doctor's degree with specialized training in marital and family therapy. They are also trained to diagnose and provide individual, family and group counseling.
- Pastoral counselors. Ordained clergy with advanced training and certification in Level II clinical pastoral education as well as the master's degree in theology (M. Div.) required by most American denominations for ordination. In addition to offering psychological counseling to individuals, families and groups, pastoral counselors have been trained to offer spiritual and sacramental ministry to those who request it.

Resources

WEBSITES

Mental Health America. "When a Parent has a Mental Illness: Interventions and Services for Families." http://www.nmha.org/go/information/get-info/strengthening-families/when-a-parent-has-a-mental-illness-interventions-and-services-for-families (accessed November 14, 2011).

ORGANIZATIONS

American Psychological Association, 750 1st St. NE, Washington, DC, 20002-4242, (202) 336-5500; TDD/TTY: (202) 336-6123, (800) 374-2721, http://www.apa.org.

Mental Health America, 2000 N. Beauregard St., 6th Fl., Alexandria, VA, 22311, (703) 684-7722,

(800) 969-6642, Fax: (703) 684-5968, http://www1.nmha.org.

National Alliance on Mental Illness, 3803 N Fairfax Dr., Ste. 100, Arlington, VA, 22203, (703) 524-7600, http://www.nami.org.

National Mental Health Consumers' Self-Help Clearinghouse, 1211 Chestnut St., Ste. 1207, Philadelphia, PA, 19107, (215) 751-1810, Fax: (215) 636-6312, info@mhselfhelp.org, http://www.mhselfhelp.org.

Substance Abuse and Mental Health Services Administration, 1 Choke Cherry Rd., Rockville, MD, 20857, (877) SAMHSA-7 (726-4727); TTY: (800) 487-4889, Fax: (240) 221-4292, SAMHSAInfo@samhsa.hhs.gov, http://www.samhsa.gov.

Judy Leaver, M.A.

Intuniv *see* **Guanfacine**

Invega *see* **Paliperidone**

Involuntary hospitalization

Definition

Involuntary hospitalization is a legal procedure used to require individuals with mental health disorders to receive inpatient treatment without their consent. The legal justifications vary from state to state but are generally based on a determination that a person is imminently dangerous to self or others, is gravely disabled, or needs immediate care and treatment but is unable to request it. Involuntary hospitalization is considered a controversial course of action and is generally a last resort used in dealing with persons who are either unable to use proper judgment or insight in deciding to accept or refuse treatment or who are considered a danger to themselves or others.

Purpose

The historical justification of civil commitment laws in the United States is based on two primary powers and responsibilities of government. First, governments are responsible for protecting each citizen from injury by another. This power of protection is commonly called police powers. The second power, known as *parens patriae* (Latin for "parent of the nation"), is based on the government's responsibility to care for disabled citizens. A person with a significant mental illness may be civilly committed, or involuntarily hospitalized, under either of these powers. It is understood that the purpose of civil commitment is protecting the safety of the public or of the person with mental illness.

As of 2011, 38 states permitted some type of involuntary commitment procedure (outpatient or inpatient civil commitment), while 34 states (all 38 states except Alabama, Pennsylvania, Virginia, and Wyoming) allowed police pickup or emergency hospitalization. Federal law does not specifically address involuntary commitment or hospitalization of U.S. citizens, so state procedures, and the length of involuntary confinement, vary widely. Most require proof of dangerousness, which can be interpreted in ambiguous ways but generally means that danger is imminent or provable. Confinement usually requires a court hearing within 24 to 72 hours after the emergency commitment procedure to assure due process, or that the individual's rights are met.

Beyond safety issues, mental health professionals have thought that proper psychiatric treatment, even when administered against a person's wishes, is preferable to the continued worsening of a serious mental illness. There is some question currently about the effectiveness of forced treatment in the legal and mental health communities. Involuntary treatment is considered by many patients' rights advocates and mental health consumers to be an oxymoron (a figure of speech that appears contradictory), in that it may protect public safety at the expense of rights of the person with a mental illness. Other public interest groups, such as the Treatment Advocacy Center, support involuntary commitment, arguing that the consequences of non-treatment are far more severe.

Description

Involuntary hospitalization is a complex process because of legal requirements that have been put in place to protect citizens from being hospitalized because of a family quarrel or similar interpersonal issue. In the nineteenth century, for example, it was commonplace for husbands who wanted to end a marriage to have wives hospitalized against their will, or for parents to commit "disobedient" children. At present, however, most states require the person who thinks someone else should be hospitalized to call 911 or their local police department. The procedure thereafter varies from state to state, but in many cases, the department will send a patrol team to answer the call. If the person who has made the call is in the same location as the person needing treatment, one officer will usually talk to the caller in one room while another talks to the person in question. The officers may also interview family members, neighbors, bystanders, or others who may know the affected person or have witnessed their behavior. The police officers will compare their evaluations of the situation, and in most jurisdictions, the officers can then make one of three decisions: decide that the person who made the call has misjudged the situation (for example, the other person may be intoxicated); decide that the affected person is mentally ill but not necessarily dangerous; or take the affected person to the nearest hospital emergency room. They may ask the person who called to accompany them to the hospital. In some states, however, the officers themselves must witness the affected person attempting to harm him- or herself or someone else before they can take him or her to the emergency room.

In the emergency room, the **psychiatrist** on duty will evaluate the affected person for dangerousness as well as the presence of mental illness. He or she will interview the police officers and anyone who accompanied them as well as the affected person. If the affected person has been receiving treatment for a mental disorder, the psychiatrist will usually contact the therapist. In some cases, the affected person will need a medical evaluation, including assessment for **substance abuse** or withdrawal, before the doctor can proceed with a psychiatric assessment. The psychiatric assessment will be thorough, and documented as completely as possible; laboratory tests will be ordered if necessary. When the assessment is complete, the doctor is legally required to decide in favor of the least restrictive environment to which the patient can be safely discharged for continued care.

If the doctor decides that the person is dangerous but not mentally ill, he or she may turn the person back over to law enforcement if necessary. If the person has threatened **suicide** but the psychiatrist does not consider the threat to be legitimate, then he or she may allow the patient to leave the emergency room after assessment. A decision to hospitalize a person involuntarily is based on three considerations: loss of emotional control, clear evidence of a psychotic disorder, or evidence of impulsivity with serious thoughts, threats, or plans to harm self or others. Persons with severe disabilities who are unable to care for themselves or make decisions regarding their treatment may also be candidates for involuntary hospitalization. The affected person is often reassessed the next day to confirm any initial findings. Most states stipulate that the affected person is entitled to a hearing before a judge who specializes in **mental health law** within 72 hours of hospitalization; the judge can order the person released if he or she thinks the person is not dangerous.

Precautions

The use of involuntary hospitalization or any other form of forced treatment is highly controversial, with citizen advocacy groups, mental health professionals, and the general public taking different sides on the topic. In addition, legal advocates and the courts take very seriously the denial of a person's liberty. Involuntary hospitalization is one of the most extreme examples of denial of liberty in a democratic society.

Advocates against involuntary hospitalization argue that forced treatment is indicative of a failed treatment system. People with an intensely personal stake in such a decision may see the necessity of forced treatment to prevent harm to the person with an illness or to others. Some advocates believe that if involuntary **intervention** is enforced, only custodial care should be provided. There is great concern that a person who has been civilly committed to a treatment facility will also receive such forced treatment as strong antipsychotic medications or **electroconvulsive therapy** (ECT). The issue of a person's ability to exercise **informed consent** about his or her treatment is also an area of concern. In addition, there may be worry that inpatient treatment will add to the **stigma** of being diagnosed with a mental illness. One research study found that persons who had been hospitalized (voluntarily or involuntarily) for treatment of a mental illness were even more likely to suffer discrimination in the job market than those who had received only outpatient treatment.

On the other hand, there are patients who claim that an incident of involuntary hospitalization in their own treatment history may not only have saved their lives, but also enabled them to receive treatment at a time when they were not capable of making a decision to do so. Family members sometimes consider involuntary hospitalization their only recourse to prevent worsening of a severe and debilitating mental illness, contact with the criminal justice system, or the devastation and dangers of **homelessness**.

Most persons involved in the mental health community believe that an adequately funded, community-based continuum of care and treatment would drastically reduce the number of cases in which involuntary treatment of any kind is necessary. The use of psychiatric **advance directives** may have an effect on the use of involuntary treatment as well. A psychiatric advance directive is a clearly written statement of an individual's psychiatric treatment preferences or instructions, somewhat like a living will for medical conditions. Psychiatric advance directives have not yet been tested in the court system but are widely endorsed throughout the mental health community as an alternative to involuntary treatment.

Controversy

A number of factors in the early 1980s led to a trend toward declining use of involuntary hospitalization for people with significant mental illnesses. The development and effectiveness of a range of new medications meant that treatment in general was more successful. The continued move toward **deinstitutionalization**, or moving people out of hospitals and into community-based treatments, contributed as well. Treating people in hospitals is inherently expensive and was being viewed as less effective, compared to more innovative and less costly forms of treatment in smaller community programs. A continuing concern about civil liberties led to closer court scrutiny, the right to a hearing and legal counsel, and laws establishing a person's rights to the least restrictive form of treatment.

Recently, however, after a number of tragic and highly publicized violent incidents involving people with severe untreated mental illness, there appears to be a trend toward modification of the criteria required for involuntary hospitalization, court-ordered treatment, and outpatient commitment. Those who advocate liberalizing the process would like a person's previous mental health history to be included in the court's consideration and the standard of dangerousness to be broadened.

For instance, the Virginia Tech shootings that occurred on April 16, 2007, on the campus of Virginia Polytechnic Institute and State University at Blacksburg, Virginia, have caused the state to re-evaluate its requirements for imminent danger in order to commit a person. During the incident, Seung-Hui Cho killed 32 people and wounded another 25 before committing suicide. Cho had previously been diagnosed with severe anxiety disorder. The imminent danger was clarified to eliminate much of the ambiguity within its definition as to whether to involuntarily commit a person that could cause serious physical harm to others or to him- or herself. In 2008, the state of Virginia updated its laws so that people with mental problems now have an easier process to go through in order to get help. Improvements were made to the procedures and criteria for involuntary commitment proceedings, emergency custody orders, temporary detention orders, and other such measures within the commitment process.

In 2011, Jared Lee Loughner attempted to assassinate Arizona Congresswoman Gabrielle Giffords, severely wounding Giffords and killing six others. Prior to the shooting, Loughner's mental health was questioned by his college professors and peers, resulting in his being suspended from school after producing disturbing videos and consistently displaying erratic behavior. If he had wanted to return to school, Loughner would have had to undergo a mental health evaluation, which he did not seek; questions remain as to whether or not forcing treatment could have prevented the events that followed. Still, it's important to remember that the cases of Cho and Loughner are extreme examples and cannot be used as representative of all individuals with mental disorders or all individuals placed under involuntary hospitalization.

KEY TERMS

Electroconvulsive therapy—Treatment involving the use of a small electric current through the brain, which produces an electric shock and results in a seizure.

Mental illness—Any psychiatric disorder that causes unusual (atypical) behavior.

Psychotic disorder—Any psychiatric disorder involving the loss of sense of with reality including symptoms such as hallucinations, delusions, and incoherence; types of such disorder include schizophrenia or mania.

Stigma—A mark or characteristic trait of a disease or disorder generally perceived as negative by society (regardless of fact).

Variances in state laws

The enforcement and breadth of involuntary hospitalization vary depending on state law. Arizona has one of the least restrictive laws in the country, dictating that the state government can place anyone in involuntary hospitalization who is determined to be "persistently or acutely disabled." Other states, such as Nevada, have much more restrictive laws. Before the state of Nevada is able to confine anyone against his or her wishes, it has to demonstrate that the person is a threat to him- or herself or to others. Likewise, in Connecticut, a person can be committed when the person has "psychiatric disabilities and is dangerous to himself or herself or others or gravely disabled."

In North Carolina, the state modified its law (HB 243—Mental Health/Law Enforcement Custody, North Carolina Statutory Changes for Involuntary Commitment) on October 1, 2009, for the involuntary commitment of its citizens for mental health treatment. The amended statute now "allows for termination of the proceedings by the interim facility if the patient no longer warrants commitment or has not been placed in a 24-hour facility within 7 days." The improvement to the law was enacted to clarify what should happen when a person is taken to an emergency department for involuntary commitment when that person is deemed a danger to self or others but is unable to be placed into a state institution.

Preparation

People who are concerned about the mental health of a family member, roommate, or friend are advised to gather information about the legal requirements for involuntary hospitalization in their state ahead of time, because it is not easy to think clearly when someone is acting in a bizarre or frightening manner. It is also a good idea to write down the name and telephone number of the affected person's therapist (if they have one) and the names of any medications that the person is taking.

Results

In the middle part of the twentieth century, the goal of involuntary hospitalization emphasized the rights of the individual—it was generally very difficult to commit someone against his or her will. However, in the later part of that century and now in the first quarter of the twenty-first century, many such laws are being modified to expand the legitimate ways that states can commit someone to a mental institution. Balancing individual rights and the safety of the general population is not an easy task, and for this and other reasons, the right to involuntarily commit someone to a mental hospital continues to be the subject of debate.

Resources

BOOKS

Bloch, Sidney, and Stephen A. Green. *Psychiatric Ethics.* Oxford: Oxford University Press, 2009.

Casher, Michael I., and Joshua D. Bess. *Manual of Inpatient Psychiatry.* New York: Cambridge University Press, 2010.

Kallert, Thomas W., Juan E. Mezzich, and John Monahan, eds. *Coercive Treatment in Psychiatry.* Hoboken, NJ: John Wiley & Sons, 2011.

Kemp, Donna R. *Mental Health in America: A Reference Handbook.* Santa Barbara, CA: ABC-CLIO, 2007.

Ovsiew, Fred, and Richard L. Munich, eds. *Principles of Inpatient Psychiatry.* Philadelphia: Lippincott Williams & Wilkins, 2009.

Ryan, Patrick, and Barry J. Coughlan. *Aging and Older Adult Mental Health: Issues and Implications for Practice.* Hove, UK: Routledge, 2011.

Wahl, Otto F. *Telling Is Risky Business: Mental Health Consumers Confront Stigma.* New Brunswick, NJ: Rutgers University Press, 1999.

PERIODICALS

Abramowitz, M. Z., et al. "Attitudes among Medical and Law Students toward Decision-Making in Regard to Involuntary Psychiatric Hospitalization." *International Journal of Law and Psychiatry* 34, no. 5 (2011): 368–73.

Katsakou, C, et al. "Psychiatric Patients' Views on Why Their Involuntary Hospitalisation was Right or Wrong: A Qualitative Study." *Social Psychiatry and Psychiatric Epidemiology* (August 24, 2011) [e-pub ahead of print]. http://dx.doi.org/10.1007/s00127-011-0427-z (accessed November 4, 2011).

O'Donoghue, B. "Perceptions of Involuntary Admission and Risk of Subsequent Readmission at One-Year Follow-Up: The Influence of Insight and Recovery Style." *Journal of Mental Health* (UK) 20, no. 3 (2011): 249–59.

Russell, B. J. "How Research Ethics' Protections can Contribute to Public Policy: The Case of Community Treatment Orders." *International Journal of Law and Psychiatry* 34, no. 5 (2011): 349–53.

OTHER

Lee, Megan. "HB 243—Mental Health/Law Enforcement Custody: North Carolina Statutory Changes for Involuntary Commitment" (October 1, 2009). North Carolina American Society for Healthcare Risk Management. http://www.nc-ashrm.org/pdfs/HB_243.pdf (accessed July 14, 2011).

WEBSITES

Join Together staff. "Laws About Involuntary Commitment for Substance Abuse Vary Widely among States." DrugFree.org. http://www.drugfree.org/join-together/addiction/laws-about-involuntary-commitment-for-substance-abuse-vary-widely-among-states (accessed July 14, 2011).

Longstreth, Andrew. "Before Tucson Rampage, a Powerful Law Went Unused." Reuters Legal (January 13, 2011). http://www.reuters.com/article/2011/01/13/us-usa-shooting-law-idUSTRE70C6JQ20110113 (accessed July 14, 2011).

Virginia Department of Behavioral Health and Development Services. "Mental Health Law Reform." Virginia.gov. http://www.dbhds.virginia.gov/OMH-MHReform.htm (accessed July 14, 2011).

ORGANIZATIONS

Mental Health America, 2000 N Beauregard St., 6th Fl., Alexandria, VA, 22311, (703) 684-7722, (800) 969-6642, Fax: (703) 684-5968, http://www.nmha.org.

National Alliance on Mental Illness, 3803 North Fairfax Dr., Ste. 100, Arlington, VA, 22203, (703) 524-7600, Fax: (703) 524-9094, http://www.nami.org.

National Mental Health Consumers' Self-Help Clearinghouse, 1211 Chestnut St., Ste. 1207, Philadelphia, PA, 19107, (215) 751-1810, Fax: (215) 636-6312, (800) 553-4539, info@mhselfhelp.org, http://mhselfhelp.org.

Treatment Advocacy Center, 200 N. Glebe Rd., Ste. 730, Arlington, VA, 22203, (703) 294-6001, Fax: (703) 294-6010, info@treatmentadvocacycenter.org, http://www.treatmentadvocacycenter.org.

Judy Leaver, MA
William Atkins, BB, BS, MBA

Isocarboxazid

Definition

Isocarboxazid (brand name Marplan) is an older-generation antidepressant drug.

Purpose

It is used to treat symptoms associated with **major depressive disorder**. Major depressive disorder refers to a long-lasting bout of depressed mood that is severe enough to interfere with basic life activities like work, relationships, sleeping, and eating. Feelings of self-worth, interest, motivation, and pleasure are typically absent while worthlessness, emptiness, being overwhelmed, and sadness are often reported.

Isocarboxazid is used for long-term maintenance of major **depression** and may be most useful for patients whose depression has atypical features. Unless effectiveness has already been established for a particular patient, isocarboxazid would not be the first drug of choice. Its use is limited to those patients who do not respond to first-line **antidepressants** and who are amenable to close supervision. Isocarboxazid's status as a drug of last resort (as is the case with other drugs in its class) is due to its potentially dangerous side effects and the dietary restrictions taking it requires.

The safety of isocarboxazid in children has not been established.

Description

Isocarboxazid belongs to the class of antidepressants known as **monoamine oxidase inhibitors (MAOIs)**. The **MAOIs** inhibit the function of an enzyme in the body called monoamine oxidase; that enzyme breaks down monoamine neurotransmitters—namely **serotonin**, **dopamine**, and norepinephrine. Under normal conditions, monoamine oxidase halts the action of these **neurotransmitters**. With MAOIs, the neurotransmitters last longer and accumulate, and their action is enhanced. It is this enhancement of neurotransmitter action that is thought to contribute to isocarboxazid's therapeutic efficacy.

There are two types of monoamine oxidases; they are denoted MAO-A and MAO-B. Isocarboxazid acts on both types, as do other nonselective **monoamine oxidase inhibitors** such as **phenelzine** and tranylcypromine.

Monoamine oxidase inhibitors do not elevate mood in non-depressed people. In depressed patients, they are used when other, first-line antidepressants are ineffective.

KEY TERMS

Antidepressant—A medication taken to alleviate clinical depression.

Dopamine—A chemical messenger in the brain that regulates reward and movement.

Hypertensive crisis—A precipitous rise in high blood pressure that can lead to brain hemorrhage or heart failure.

Major depressive disorder—A clinical psychiatric diagnosis of chronic depressed mood that interferes with normal life activities.

Monoamine oxidase inhibitors (MAOIs)—A class of antidepressant drugs that work by enhancing the neurotransmitters dopamine, norepinephrine, and serotonin in the brain.

Neurotransmitters—Chemical messengers that transmit signals between nerves.

Norepinephrine—A chemical messenger in the brain that regulates arousal and attention.

Serotonin—A chemical messenger in the brain that regulates arousal and mood.

Recommended dosage

Isocarboxazid is taken orally. As is the case with most antidepressant drugs, patients are started at one dose and medication is gradually increased to a so-called maintenance dose to achieve the best outcome. For isocarboxazid, the starting dose is 10 mg, twice a day. Whereas dosage can vary widely in individual patients, a typical progression would be to increase the dose gradually to 15–30 mg twice a day as a maintenance dose. Because of the delayed therapeutic response, at least one to two weeks should pass before increasing the dose.

Precautions

Patients taking isocarboxazid must be warned about food interactions. Foods like aged cheese, beer, and red wine contain tyramine and in concert with MAOIs can result in hypertensive crisis. Other foods high in tyramine (or dopamine itself) are bananas, fava beans, figs, raisins, yogurt, sour cream, soy sauce, pickled herring, caviar, liver, and tenderized meats; these foods should not be consumed when taking isocarboxazid.

Hypertensive crisis can also occur with certain drug interactions. Monoamine oxidase inhibitors should not be taken with asthma drugs, cold and allergy medications, or diet drugs. Patients taking isocarboxazid should inform their doctors and dentists to avoid being administered a contraindicated medication.

Isocarboxazid use may negatively interact with certain health conditions. It should not be used in patients with cardiovascular disease, cerebrovascular disease, or liver disease, and great caution should be used if there is poor kidney function or a history of **seizures**.

Worsening of depression and risk of **suicide** are relevant to isocarboxazid, as they are to all antidepressant drugs. The risk is especially high during the lag time until therapeutic efficacy can be achieved. Close monitoring of patients for the first four weeks of treatment is advised.

Children and adults up to age 24 are at an increased risk of developing suicidal thoughts and behavior when taking antidepressants, including isocarboxazid. Patients of any age taking isocarboxazid should be monitored for signs of worsening depression or changes in behavior.

Side effects

Isocarboxazid, like the other MAOIs, can cause a variety of side effects apart from food interactions. Common side effects include dizziness and fainting associated with low blood pressure when standing up (orthostatic hypotension), sexual dysfunction, anxiety, headache, nausea, sleep disturbances, edema, constipation, and weight gain. Serious but less common side effects include hepatic damage.

Interactions

A patient should not take isocarboxazid at the same time as other antidepressants. Two to five weeks of wash-out time must pass before switching from a non-MAOI antidepressant drug to isocarboxazid.

The following drugs should not be taken with MAOIs: Stimulants like amphetamine, **methylphenidate**, and epinephrine; dopaminergic drugs like levodopa, L-tryptophan, and phenylalanine; over-the-counter cold and allergy medications like pseudoephedrine and dextromethorphan; diet drugs like ephedrine and phenylpropanolamine; and analgesics like meperidine.

Resources

BOOKS

Charney, Dennis S., and Charles B. Nemeroff. *The Peace of Mind Prescription: An Authoritative Guide to Finding the Most Effective Treatment for Anxiety and Depression.* New York: Mariner Books, 2006.

"Depressive Disorders." In *The Merck Manual of Diagnosis and Therapy*, edited by Robert S. Porter and Justin L. Kaplan. 19th ed. Whitehouse Station, NJ: Merck, 2011.

"Major Depressive Disorder: A Quick Reference Guide." In *Quick Reference to the American Psychiatric Association Practice Guidelines for the Treatment of Psychiatric Disorders: Compendium 2006/Edition 1.* Arlington, VA: American Psychiatric Publishing, 2006.

"Monoamine Oxidase Inhibitors." In *AHFS Drug Information* Bethesda, MD: American Society of Health-System Pharmacists, 2012.

Morrison, Andrew L. *The Antidepressant Sourcebook: A User's Guide for Patients and Families.*New York: Doubleday, 1999.

Jill U. Adams

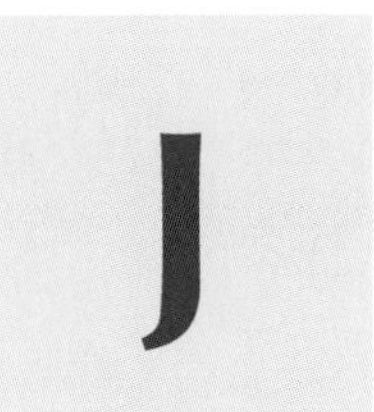

Jet lag *see* **Circadian rhythm sleep disorder**

Journal therapy

Definition

Journal therapy is the purposeful and intentional use of a written record of personal thoughts or feelings to promote growth and psychological healing. It is often used as an adjunct to **psychotherapy** and recovery programs. Healthcare practitioners maintain that written expression fills a very important role in the therapeutic process by providing a mechanism of emotional expression in circumstances in which interpersonal expression is not possible or viable.

Purpose

People have kept journals and diaries to record dreams, memories, and thoughts since ancient times. Emotional expression has also long held a central role in the study and practice of psychology. Throughout history, psychologists have advocated the expression of emotions as essential for good mental and physical health. Since the early 1980s, interest in this topic has resulted in numerous research studies investigating the health benefits of expressive writing.

Description

Journal writing and other forms of writing therapy are based on the premise that the mind and the body are inseparably joined in the healing process. Although there are many methods of conducting journal writing therapy, the therapist often instructs the participant to write about a distressing or traumatic event or thought in one or more sessions.

KEY TERMS

Art therapy—The use of art to assess and treat an individual's development, abilities, personality, interests, concerns, or conflicts.

Psychodynamic—The scientific study of mental or conditional forces developing especially in early childhood and their effect on behavior and mental states.

Although researchers are uncertain about exactly how writing about traumas produces improvements in psychological well-being, some traumatic **stress** researchers believe that ordinary memories are qualitatively different from traumatic memories. Traumatic memories are more emotional and perceptual in nature. The memory is stored as a sensory perception, obsessional thought, or behavioral reenactment. It is associated with persistent, intrusive, and distressing symptoms, including avoidance and intense anxiety that result in observed psychological and biological dysfunction. Thus, one goal in treating traumatic memories is to find a means of processing them.

A narrative that becomes more focused and coherent over a number of writing sessions is often associated with increased improvement, according to several research studies. The memories become deconditioned and restructured into a personal, integrated narrative. Changes in psychological well-being after writing therapy may result from cognitive shifts about the **trauma** either during or after the writing process.

Benefits

Journal writing produces a number of benefits in healthy people. It enhances creativity, helps cope with stress, and provides a written record of memorable life experiences. Likewise, some researchers have found that journal writing has a number of psychological and physical health benefits for people who are ill.

Aside from a reduction in physical symptoms of disease, the psychological benefits include reconciling emotional conflicts, fostering self-awareness, managing behavior, solving problems, reducing anxiety, aiding reality orientation, and increasing self-esteem. Writing therapy has been used as an effective treatment for people with developmental, medical, educational, social, or psychological impairments and is practiced in mental health, rehabilitation, medical, educational, and forensic institutions. Populations of all ages, races, and ethnic backgrounds are served by writing therapy in individual, couple, family, and **group therapy** formats.

The therapeutic use of expressive writing allows individuals to confront topics that may be difficult to address verbally, which alleviates the constraints or inhibitions associated with not talking about the event. The psychological drain of prolonged inhibition is believed to cause or exacerbate stress-related disease processes. Some researchers have found that emotional expression facilitates cognitive processing of traumatic memories, which can help lead to positive emotional and physiological changes. Specifically, written emotional expression is believed to promote integration and understanding of the event(s), thereby reducing the negative emotions associated with the memories.

Precautions

It is advisable that journal therapy be conducted only by a licensed health professional, such as a certified **art therapy** practitioner or trained **psychologist** or **psychiatrist**. While journal writing classes available to the public may perform a variety of useful functions, these classes are not intended to provide psychological therapy. In journal therapy, the participant may, for example, uncover potentially traumatic, repressed, or painful memories. Therefore, a trained health professional may be necessary to supervise the process and treat these symptoms as they arise.

Preparation

In a healthcare setting, the participant often prepares for journal writing by receiving a set of instructions from the therapist. The therapist will explain the length and focus of the writing session or sessions. Other instructions may include directions about how to write, such as in a stream-of-consciousness fashion, without censorship or concern about grammar or style.

Research & general acceptance

Therapeutic writing became an increasingly popular topic in the late twentieth century, not only among trained healthcare professionals, but also among self-improvement speakers without medical training. Seminars, workshops, and Internet sites purportedly offering therapy though expressive writing sprang up around the nation and gained some popular acceptance. Despite the large body of research indicating that writing confers benefits on healthy people, the topic of writing therapy's affects on diseased individuals has not received a great deal of research attention. Although increasingly used by healthcare professionals as an adjunct to various therapeutic approaches, the practice has been criticized by some members of the healthcare community. Many researchers are skeptical of reports that so much measurable improvement in health status can occur in just a few brief writing sessions.

In the United Kingdom, the focus of journal therapy is on descriptive accounts and psychodynamic explanations for subjective improvements in the health status of participants. In the United States, on the other hand, the focus is on formal scientific research aimed at validating the impact of brief, highly standardized writing exercises on physical measures of illness. The research demonstrates that although physical measures of illness may change, the reasons for the change are not always clear.

Journal therapy is not a replacement for medical therapy or other forms of psychotherapy. It is generally accepted as a adjunct therapy that can help relieve stress and allow individuals to communicate feelings and emotions that may be difficult to verbalize.

Training & certification

Although journal therapy is often provided by certified instructors who receive variable amounts of training, journal therapy is best administered by a licensed psychologist (who may also be an art therapist) or psychiatrist.

Educational, professional, and ethical standards for art therapists who conduct writing therapy are regulated

QUESTIONS TO ASK YOUR DOCTOR

- Is journal therapy a good choice for me or my loved one?
- Can you recommend a therapist trained in journal therapy?
- What other mental or physical health treatments might be beneficial to me in addition to journal therapy?

by the American Art Therapy Association. The American Art Therapy Credentials Board (ATCB), an independent organization, grants postgraduate supervised experience. A registered art therapist who successfully completes the written examination administered by the ATCB qualifies as Board Certified (ATR-BC), a credential requiring maintenance through continuing education credits.

Resources

BOOKS

Kapitan, Lynn. *An Introduction to Art Therapy Research.* New York: Routledge, 2010.

Penn, Peggy. *Joined Imaginations: Writing and Language in Therapy.* Chagrin Falls, OH: Taos Institute Publications, 2009.

Wadeson, Harriet. *Art Psychotherapy.* 2nd ed. Hoboken, NJ: John Wiley and Sons, 2010.

PERIODICALS

van Emmerik, Arnold, J.H. Kamphuis, and P.M.G. Emmelkamp. "Treating Acute Stress Disorder and Posttraumatic Stress Disorder with Cognitive Behavioral Therapy or Structured Writing Therapy: A Randomized Controlled Trial." *Psychotherapy and Psychosomatics* (2008) 77, no. 2, 93–100.

ORGANIZATIONS

American Art Therapy Association, 225 North Fairfax Street, Alexandria, VA, 22314, info@arttherapy.org, http://www.americanarttherapyassociation.org.

Art Therapy Credentials Board, 3 Terrace Way, Greensboro, NC, 27403-3660, (336) 482-2856, (877) 213-2822, Fax: (336) 482-2852, atcb@nbcc.org, http://www.atcb.org.

Genevieve Slomski
Tish Davidson, AM

Juvenile bipolar disorder

Definition

Juvenile **bipolar disorder** (also called manic-depressive illness) is a chronic condition characterized by repeated swings in mood between mania (a state of elation and high energy) and **depression**. Early-onset bipolar disorder is manic depression that appears very early in life. Historically it was thought that children could not suffer the mood swings of mania or depression, but recent research has revealed that bipolar disorder (or early temperamental features of it) can occur in very young children and that it is much more common than previously thought. This finding has sparked some controversy and some concern that the disorder is being overdiagnosed. As a result of further investigation into this controversy, a new classification has been suggested, for the fifth edition of the ***Diagnostic and Statistical Manual of Mental Disorders*** (*DSM-5*), due to publish in 2013. The new diagnosis, **disruptive mood dysregulation disorder** (DMDD), will not replace juvenile bipolar disorder but may allow more precise **diagnosis** of that entity and may also allow for improved treatment of children with bipolar disorder and children who have DMDD.

Although children with bipolar disorder have not been well studied, the condition is believed to occur as frequently as it does in adults, and it can affect children more severely, affecting about 1% of all adolescents between ages 14 and 18. Adults typically experience abnormally intense moods for weeks or months at a time, but children can have rapid shifts of mood that commonly cycle many times within the day. This cycling pattern is called ultra-ultra rapid or ultradian cycling, and it is most often associated with low arousal states in the mornings followed by afternoons and evenings of increased energy. Bipolar disorder is often hard to diagnose in children, because its symptoms are difficult to distinguish from those of other mental disorders. If left untreated, bipolar disorder can significantly affect a child's relationships, overall functioning, and school performance. It also can lead to violence, drug and **alcohol use**, and **suicide** attempts.

Demographics

The lifetime prevalence of bipolar disorder is between 1% and 3%. However, considering borderline cases, the rate may be as high as 6%. Some research suggests that as many as 1% of children may have bipolar disorder. Although the condition affects males and females equally, in children under 13 the cases are predominantly male.

Description

Juvenile bipolar disorder is a mental condition characterized by repeated episodes of depression, mania, or both symptoms. The child may experience extreme shifts in mood and behavior. For a child to be diagnosed with bipolar disorder, the condition must be severe enough to disrupt the child's normal functioning.

The fourth edition (revised text) of the ***Diagnostic and Statistical Manual of Mental Disorders*** (*DSM-IV-TR*) identifies three types of bipolar mood episodes (these episodes were defined for adults, not children):

- Manic episodes: an elevated or irritable mood that lasts for a period of at least one week

- Hypomanic episodes: a distinct period of persistently elevated, expansive, or irritable mood that lasts for at least four days
- Mixed episodes: increased energy and agitation, coupled with feelings of sadness and worthlessness

Three major subtypes of bipolar disorder exist—bipolar I disorder (BP-I), bipolar II disorder (BP-II), and bipolar disorder not otherwise specified (BP-NOS). The *DSM-IV-TR* defines these bipolar disorder subtypes as follows:

- BP-I: the occurrence of a manic or mixed episode that lasts for at least one week
- BP-II: alternating depressive and hypomanic episodes
- BP-NOS: cases that do not meet the full criteria for the other two bipolar disorder subtypes but that involve an elevated or irritable mood, plus two or three bipolar symptoms (difficulty concentrating, sleep changes, and so on) that are severe enough to interfere with functioning

Evidence exists that juvenile bipolar disorder is a different and more severe form than adult-onset bipolar disorder. The child may cycle more rapidly from emotional highs (elation) to lows (anger and irritability). Bipolar disorder often can coexist with other emotional and behavioral problems, such as **attention deficit hyperactivity disorder (ADHD)**, **conduct disorder** (CD), **schizophrenia**, and **anxiety disorders**.

Controversy surrounds the increasing incidence of juvenile bipolar disorder diagnoses. There are both clinicians and parents who feel that difficult children are often saddled unnecessarily with this diagnosis, which exposes children to the risks and potential side effects of the serious medications used to treat the disorder.

Causes and symptoms

Bipolar disorder has a strong genetic component. Studies suggest that the children or siblings of bipolar individuals have a four-to-six-fold increased risk of developing the disorder. Environmental factors, such as child maltreatment, also may play a role in the development of the condition.

Symptoms of bipolar disorder can be divided into two categories—manic symptoms and depressive symptoms. Children with bipolar disorder may swing through cycles of these two different types of emotions. Manic symptoms include:

- extreme shifts in mood, from anger to euphoria
- bursts of rage
- irritability
- increased energy
- over-inflated sense of self-esteem, grandiose behavior
- decreased need for sleep, without any apparent drowsiness during the day
- lack of attention, moving quickly from one topic or task to the next
- increased sexuality inappropriate to age
- agitation
- willingness to engage in risky behaviors

Depressive symptoms are at the opposite end of the mood spectrum. They include:

- persistent sadness (this can include unexplained crying episodes, reclusiveness, and increased sensitivity)
- decreased energy
- low self-esteem
- sleepiness and increased desire to sleep
- difficulty concentrating
- lack of interest in school and other activities
- persistent thoughts of death or suicide
- unexplained aches and pains
- alcohol or drug use

Children and adolescents with bipolar disorder may have difficulty regulating between these two types of moods. They may have explosive outbursts of anger lasting anywhere from a few minutes to a few hours, followed by periods of extreme happiness. Whereas adults can take months to cycle between mania and depression, children can cycle within weeks or even days, so they are more often symptomatic.

It is sometimes difficult to distinguish manic symptoms with those of ADHD, because hyperactivity and irritability can be hallmarks of both conditions, and both often occur simultaneously. Research suggests that more than half of children and adolescents with bipolar disorder also have ADHD. To distinguish bipolar disorder from ADHD, doctors look for symptoms that are unique to bipolar disorder, such as elated mood, decreased sleep, and grandiose behavior.

Diagnosis

Children with symptoms of bipolar disorder should see a **psychologist** or **psychiatrist** for evaluation, especially if a first-degree family member has a history of the condition. Evaluation is also important in children who are taking stimulant medications for ADHD and who are experiencing manic symptoms as a result. Children with bipolar disorder should be carefully monitored for associated problems, such as **substance abuse**, developmental delays, and suicide.

Diagnosis of children with bipolar disorder is often challenging because the condition can present with other mental disorders, such as depression, and because symptoms (such as boasting and elation) can be difficult to distinguish from other childhood disorders and normal childhood emotions. Doctors often use *DSM-IV* guidelines to diagnose children with bipolar disorder, but these were developed for adults, and the symptoms can differ.

Assessment should include personal and family histories of depression and mood disorders, and identification of mood changes. Diagnostic interviews and questionnaires, such as the diagnostic interview for children and adolescents-revised (DICA-R), the Diagnostic Interview Schedule for Children (DISC), and the Kiddie Schedule for Affective Disorders and Schizophrenia for School-Age Children (K-SADS), can be useful for diagnosis. Clinical rating scales, such as the Mania Rating Scale, can help doctors initially identify illness severity and later assess the effects of treatment on the child's symptoms.

When diagnosing mania episodes, 2005 treatment guidelines from the Academy of Child and Adolescent Psychiatry (AACAP) suggest that doctors use Frequency, Intensity, Number, and Duration (FIND) as a guide:

- Frequency: symptoms occur most days of the week
- Intensity: symptoms are severe enough to cause extreme disturbance in one area of a child's life or moderate disturbance in two areas
- Number: symptoms occur three to four times per day
- Duration: symptoms last for four hours a day (not necessarily contiguous)

Treatment

Most treatment recommendations for children with bipolar disorder are made based on adult research data, because little research has been done on the safety and efficacy of mood stabilizing medications in children. Doctors typically use two types of drugs to treat children with bipolar disorder: mood stabilizers (lithium, divalproex, **carbamazepine**, valproate) and atypical antipsychotics (**olanzapine**, **quetiapine**, **risperidone**). These drugs have only been approved by the U.S. Food and Drug Administration for bipolar disorder in adults, with the exception of lithium, which has been approved for children age 12 and older.

The AACAP panel recommends that doctors treat their patients with medication for a minimum of four to six weeks and reassess if there is a lack of response. Doctors should carefully monitor their patients who are taking these medications because of the risks of side effects. According to the AACAP practice parameters, doctors should consider effectiveness, phase of illness, tolerability, and patient history of medication response, among other factors, when prescribing these medications. Atypical antipsychotics can cause marked weight gain in some children, which can lead to heart problems and diabetes later in life. They have also been linked to a rare but serious condition called **tardive dyskinesia**, which is characterized by abnormal movements.

Drugs used to treat other mental health conditions, such as **antidepressants** for depression and stimulant medications used to treat ADHD, may lead to manic symptoms. If a child becomes manic while taking antidepressants or stimulants, the child may require treatment for bipolar disorder.

Some children with bipolar disorder may benefit from a combination of medication and **psychotherapy**, including **cognitive-behavioral therapy**, which teaches children how to recognize and cope with the emotions that are leading to their condition.

Prognosis

Children with bipolar disorder will typically require ongoing treatment with medication to prevent a **relapse**, and some will require a lifetime of treatment. Even with medication, bipolar disorder can be chronic, with symptoms persisting for many months or even years. In adolescents, bipolar disorder tends to be more chronic and treatment-resistant than it is in adults. The rate of relapse in young people can be greater than 50%.

Prevention

Although the initial onset of bipolar disorder is not preventable, there are strategies to help avoid a relapse. The family of the bipolar child can learn ways to identify relapse symptoms and how to avoid factors that may trigger relapse (such as substance abuse, **stress**, medication noncompliance, or **sleep deprivation**). Families also may be taught communication skills to improve their interpersonal relationships.

Resources

BOOKS

American Psychiatric Association. *Diagnostic and Statistical Manual of Mental Disorders,* 4th ed., text rev. Washington, DC: American Psychiatric Association, 2000.

Faedda, Gianni L., and Nancy B. Austin. *Parenting a Bipolar Child: What to Do and Why.* Oakland, CA: New Harbinger, 2006.

Lombardo, Gregory T. *Understanding the Mind of Your Bipolar Child: The Complete Guide to the Development, Treatment, and Parenting of Children with Bipolar Disorder.* New York: St. Martin's Press, 2006.

Mash, Eric J., and Russell A. Barkley, eds. *Treatment of Childhood Disorders,* 3rd ed. New York: Guilford Press, 2006.

PERIODICALS

Carlson, G. "The Concept of Bipolar Disorder in Children: A History of the Bipolar Controversy." *Child and Adolescent Psychiatry Clinics of North America* 18 (April 1, 2009): 257–71.

Schapir, L. "Bipolar Disorder and Severe Mood Dysregulation in Children and Adolescents." *Harefuah* 147 (June 1, 2008): 526–31.

Stringaris, A. "Irritability in Children and Adolescents: A Challenge for DSM-5." *European Child and Adolescent Psychiatry* 20 (February 1, 2011): 61–66.

ORGANIZATIONS

Child & Adolescent Bipolar Foundation, 820 Davis St., Ste. 520, Evanston, IL, 60201, (847) 492-8510, info@thebalancedmind.org, http://www.thebalancedmind.org.

Depression and Bipolar Support Alliance, 730 N Franklin St., Ste. 501, Chicago, IL, 60654-7225, (800) 826-3632, http://www.dbsalliance.org.

Mental Health America, 2000 N Beauregard St., 6th Fl., Alexandria, VA, 22311, (800) 969-6642, http://www.nmha.org.

National Alliance on Mental Illness, 2107 Wilson Blvd., Ste. 300, Arlington, VA, 22201-3042, Fax: (703) 524-9094, (800) 950-6264, http://www.nami.org.

National Institute of Mental Health, 6001 Executive Blvd., Rm. 8184, MSC 9663, Bethesda, MD, 20892-9663, (301) 433-4513; TTY: (301) 443-8431, Fax: (301) 443-4279, (866) 615-6464; TTY: (866) 415-8051, nimhinfo@nih.gov, http://www.nimh.nih.gov.

Stephanie N. Watson

Juvenile depression

Definition

A **diagnosis** of **depression** is made when the feelings of sadness are severe enough to disrupt the child's daily life. Significant depression also can interfere with a child's development and can potentially lead to alcohol or drug use or **suicide**. Children who experience depression are more likely to be depressed as adults.

Demographics

Approximately 1% to 2% of children and 5% of adolescents experience symptoms of depression, and 3% to 5% of young people have major depressive disorder. The incidence of depression is lower in young children and rises after puberty. In childhood, the rates of depression are about equal in boys and girls, but in adolescence, girls are more than twice as likely to be depressed as boys, possibly due to hormonal changes that occur during puberty. Additionally, girls tend to have an internal locus of control, which is related to self-blame versus the external locus of control experienced by many adolescent males.

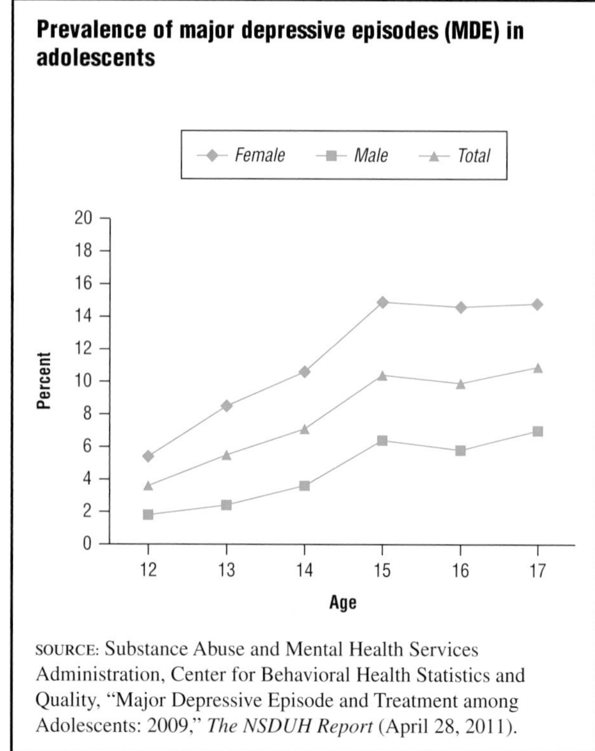

Percentage of adolescents who have experienced an MDE during the past year, by gender. Data available online at http://oas.samhsa.gov/2k11/009/AdolescentDepression.htm. *(Graph by PreMediaGlobal. © 2012 Cengage Learning.)*

One in eight adolescents may suffer from depression; in fact, depression is the most common mental disease in United States for this age group. Studies show that 10–15% of teenagers have already experienced traumatic feelings of depression at some time of their life.

About two-thirds of children with depression have a concurrent mental disorder and thus are at higher risk for developing depression again after receiving treatment. Children with depression have a two- to fourfold increased risk of being depressed as adults. Nearly three-quarters of children and adolescents with depressive disorders do not receive appropriate treatment.

Description

Research has indicated that rates of depression have risen in children and adolescents during the last few decades, although the reason for this rise is unclear. Just as in adults, depression in children can range in severity.

Major depressive disorder is the most severe form of depression. The ***Diagnostic and Statistical Manual***

of Mental Disorders, fourth edition, text revised (*DSM-IV TR*), defines a major depressive episode as five or more symptoms (which can include depressed mood or irritability most of the day, markedly diminished interest in activities, significant weight loss without dieting, **insomnia** or **hypersomnia** nearly every day, agitation, **fatigue**, feelings of worthlessness or guilt, diminished ability to think or concentrate, and recurrent thoughts of death or suicide) within a two-week period.

Dysthymic disorder is a milder, but chronic, form of depression that persists for at least one year in children (episodes last between two and three years). It is characterized by symptoms of depression or irritability, as well as appetite changes, difficulty sleeping, low self-esteem, fatigue, poor concentration, or feelings of hopelessness. Dysthymia can interfere with a child's relationships, schoolwork, and self-esteem.

Causes and symptoms

Although in some cases depression stems from a life event, in other situations it arises without apparent cause.

Causes

Doctors are unsure about the underlying causes of depression, but the problem may arise from neurotransmitter abnormalities in the **brain**. Changes in the prefrontal cortex have been noted in childhood depression, and hormones also seem to play a role.

Depression has both genetic and social components. The condition runs in families, and there is evidence that a child is more likely to develop depression if his or her parent is depressed. Studies have indicated that identical twins, who share the same genes, are about three times more likely to both have major depressive disorder than are fraternal twins, who share fewer of the same genes. It also is possible that growing up with a parent who is depressed makes a child more prone to duplicating the behavior. Negative parenting tactics (such as rejection and lack of nurturing) also can influence the development of depression.

Stressful experiences, such as the death of a loved one, moving to a new city, living in poverty, or suffering sexual or physical **abuse**, can trigger depression, especially in children who are already vulnerable due to inherited factors. Depression can be distinguished from normal sadness during these experiences because its duration is disproportionate to the event.

In some cases, a medical condition, such as cancer, infectious mononucleosis, anemia, thyroid disease, or vitamin deficiency, can trigger depression. Some medications, such as isotretinoin (Accutane), may also lead to depressive symptoms. Depression stemming from illness or medication is referred to as secondary depressive mood disorder.

Symptoms

A child who is experiencing depression may have uncontrollable feelings of sadness. He or she may lose interest in friends, school, and activities. Other symptoms of depression include:

- Feelings of worthlessness or hopelessness
- Crying for no apparent reason
- Change in appetite
- Weight loss or gain
- Disrupted or prolonged sleep
- Lack of energy
- Difficulty concentrating
- Irritable, aggressive, or hostile behaviors
- Aches and pains that have no known medical cause (this is particularly common in children under age seven, who are less able to articulate their emotions)
- Alcohol or drug use
- Suicidal thoughts or actions

Depression often occurs together with other mental disorders, including **anxiety disorders**, **attention deficit hyperactivity disorder**, **substance abuse** disorder, and **oppositional defiant disorder**.

Diagnosis

Diagnosing depression may begin with the child's primary care doctor, who can make a referral to a child **psychiatrist** or **psychologist** if necessary. The doctor will typically start a depression evaluation by interviewing the child and his or her parents. The assessment may include a physical history and examination to rule out any conditions that can cause depression, such as thyroid disorders.

To diagnose depression, doctors sometimes used questionnaires or scales. The **Children's Depression Inventory** (CDI) is commonly used to diagnose children ages 7 to 17 years old. The results of this inventory are represented as a t-score. A t-score of greater than 20 on the long form or greater than 7 on the short form indicates a diagnosis of clinical depression.

Because patients with depression are at greater risk for attempting suicide (major depression increases the suicide risk 12-fold), doctors should assess the child's suicide risk during the initial visit.

QUESTIONS TO ASK YOUR DOCTOR

- What are the indications that my child may suffer from juvenile depression?
- What diagnostic tests are needed for a thorough assessment?
- What treatment options do you recommend for my child?
- What kind of changes can I expect to see with the medications you have prescribed for my child?
- What are the side effects associated with the medications you have prescribed for my child?
- Should we see a specialist? If so, what kind of specialist should I contact?
- Does having depression put my child at risk for other health conditions?
- What tests or evaluation techniques will you perform to see whether treatment has been beneficial for my child?
- What symptoms or adverse effects are important enough that I should seek immediate treatment?
- Can you recommend an organization that will provide me with additional information about juvenile depression?
- Can you recommend any support groups for me and my family?

Treatment

Treatment methods for children with depression include therapy and medication. Therapy may be conducted individually, in groups, or with the child's family. **Cognitive-behavioral therapy** (CBT) is the most thoroughly studied treatment for childhood depression, and research indicates that it is effective for treating mild to moderate depression. CBT involves changing the negative or distorted thoughts that are leading to the depression, and improving the child's coping skills. The therapist can help the child deal with **grief** and more appropriately handle his or her emotions, as well as educate the parents about developing healthier communication strategies and familial relationships. **Interpersonal therapy** (IPT), which is based on the belief that depression is triggered by interpersonal disputes, has also been shown to positively influence depressive symptoms in children and adolescents.

Some newer complementary approaches may be helpful to children with mild depression, including **music therapy**, pet therapy, **dance therapy**, guided imagery, and **yoga**.

In moderate to severe cases of depression, doctors may prescribe antidepressant medications called **selective serotonin reuptake inhibitors (SSRIs)**, such as **fluoxetine** (Sarafem) and **paroxetine** (Paxil). As of 2011, fluoxetine was the only SSRI approved by the U.S. Food and Drug Administration for treating depression in children 8 to 17 years of age. **SSRIs** work by restoring the correct balance of **serotonin** in the brain. However, because **antidepressants** have been linked to an increased risk of suicidal thoughts and behaviors in children and adolescents (the packaging of SSRIs carries a black-box warning regarding this risk), doctors should carefully monitor their young patients for any signs of suicidal tendencies during treatment. Due to their high risk of side effects and lack of effectiveness in a younger population, tricyclic antidepressants such as **imipramine** (Tofranil) are not recommended for children and adolescents.

The recommended treatment duration for children experiencing their first episode of depression is at least six months. Medication should be tapered off over a period of one to two months to prevent symptoms of withdrawal. Subsequent depressive episodes require at least one year of treatment, and children who have had more than three episodes should be treated indefinitely. More severe cases of depression may require a combination of medication and **psychotherapy**. Patients with treatment-resistant depression may require additional medication, such as lithium, as well as extended CBT.

Children or adolescents who are exhibiting suicidal behaviors may be hospitalized until it has been determined that they are no longer a danger to themselves.

Prognosis

Research indicates that starting treatment early can improve the outcomes for children and adolescents with depression. Children usually recover sooner from major depressive episodes than adults. In most cases, children will recover from an initial depressive episode within one to two years, even if they have not been treated in some cases. However, children who have had at least one depressive episode face an increased risk of recurrence during adolescence and adulthood.

Prevention

Although little research exists on the prevention of depression in children, there is some evidence that CBT can prevent the onset of major depression in children

KEY TERMS

Anxiety—Can be experienced as a troubled feeling, a sense of dread, fear of the future, or distress over a possible threat to a person's physical or mental well-being.

Attention deficit hyperactivity disorder (ADHD)—A developmental disorder characterized by distractibility, hyperactivity, impulsive behaviors, and the inability to remain focused on tasks or activities.

Cognitive-behavioral therapy—Psychotherapy technique designed to help people change their attitudes, perceptions, and patterns of thinking.

Insomnia—Waking in the middle of the night and having difficulty returning to sleep, or waking too early in the morning.

Serotonin—A chemical messenger in the brain thought to play a role in mood regulation.

with depressive symptoms and/or anxiety disorders. Family dynamics also can have an impact on the development of depression. A stable, loving, and communicative family can decrease a child's vulnerability to the condition. Parents can help prevent potential problems by identifying depression earlier, when the treatment success odds are greatest. Early identification of depression involves looking for the warning signs, which may be more subtle in children than they are in adults. For example, a depressed child may appear bored, overly tired, withdrawn, or irritable. Children with depression also may experience aches and pains that are not associated with any obvious medical condition.

Resources

BOOKS

American Psychiatric Association. *Diagnostic and Statistical Manual of Mental Disorders.* 4th ed., Text rev. Washington, DC: American Psychiatric Association, 2000.

American Psychological Association. *Publication Manual of the American Psychological Association,* 6th ed. Washington, DC: American Psychological Association, 2009.

Gillberg, Christopher, Richard Harrington, and Hans-Christoph Steinhausen, eds. *A Clinician's Handbook of Child and Adolescent Psychiatry.* Cambridge: Cambridge University Press, 2011.

Jongsma, Arthur E., Jr., L. Mark Peterson, and William P. McInnis. *The Child Psychotherapy Treatment Planner.* 4th ed. Hoboken, NJ: John Wiley & Sons, 2009.

North, Carol, and Sean Yutzy. *Goodwin and Guze's Psychiatric Diagnosis.*New York, NY: Oxford University Press, 2010.

WEBSITES

U.S. National Institute of Mental Health. "Combination Treatment Most Effective in Adolescents with Depression." http://www.nimh.nih.gov/science-news/2004/combination-treatment-most-effective-in-adolescents-with-depression.shtml (accessed November 14, 2011).

ORGANIZATIONS

American Academy of Child and Adolescent Psychiatry, 3615 Wisconsin Ave. NW, Washington, DC, 20016-3007, (202) 966-7300, Fax: (202) 966-2891, http://aacap.org.

American Academy of Pediatrics (AAP), 141 Northwest Point Blvd., Elk Grove Village, IL, 60009-0927, (847) 434-4000, http://www.aap.org.

American Psychological Association, 750 First Street NE, Washington, DC, 20003, (202) 336-5500, http://www.apa.org/index.aspx.

Eunice Kennedy Shriver National Institute of Child Health and Human Development (NICHD), Bldg 31, Room 2A32, MSC 2425, 31 Center Drive, Bethesda, MD, 20892, (800) 370-2943; TTY: (888) 320-6942, Fax: (866) 760-5947, NICHDInformationResourceCenter@mail.nih.gov, http://www.nichd.nih.gov.

Families for Depression Awareness, 395 Totten Pond Road, Ste. 404, Waltham, MA, 02451, (781) 890-0220, Fax: (781) 890-2411, http://www.familyaware.org.

Mental Health America, 2000 N. Beauregard Street, 6th Floor, Alexandria, VA, 22311, (703) 684-7722, (800) 969-6642, Fax: (703) 684-5968, http://www1.nmha.org.

National Alliance on Mental Illness (NAMI), Colonial Place Three, 2107 Wilson Blvd., Suite 300, Arlington, VA, 22201, (703) 524-7600, (800) 950-NAMI (6264), Fax: (703) 524-9094, http://www.nami.org/Hometemplate.cfm.

National Institute of Mental Health (NIMH), 6001 Executive Boulevard, Room 8184, MSC 9663, Bethesda, MD, 20892, (301) 443-4513, (866) 615-6464, Fax: (301) 443-4279, nimhinfo@nih.gov, http://www.nimh.nih.gov/index.shtml.

Stephanie N. Watson
Laura Jean Cataldo, RN, Ed.D.

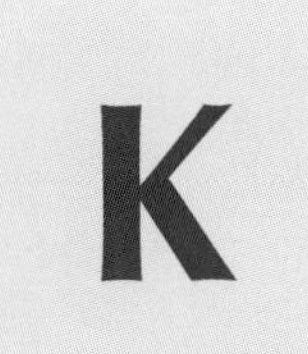

Kaufman Adolescent and Adult Intelligence Test

Definition

The Kaufman Adolescent and Adult Intelligence Test (KAIT) is an individually administered general intelligence test appropriate for adolescents and adults aged 11 to over 85 years. The multi-subtest is considered a battery of neuropsychological, vocational, and clinical tasks, what is called a psychoeducational evaluation. The KAIT requires reasoning and planning abilities, which makes it an interesting and challenging test for anyone to take.

Purpose

The KAIT is intended to measure both fluid and crystallized intelligence. Fluid intelligence refers to abilities such as problem solving and reasoning, and it is generally thought not to be influenced by one's cultural experience or education. Crystallized intelligence refers to acquired knowledge, and it is thought to be influenced by one's cultural experience and education.

The KAIT was developed by American psychologists Alan S. Kaufman (1944–) and Nadeen L. Kaufman (1945–), a husband and wife team, as a method of measuring intelligence assuming broader definitions of fluid and crystallized abilities than assumed by other measures. In addition, they wanted a test based on theories that accounted for developmental changes in intelligence, such as the Cattell-Horn model of fluid/crystallized intelligence. Although the Kaufmans had earlier designed a test for younger children, the **Kaufman Assessment Battery for Children** (K-ABC), they did not consider the KAIT to be an extension of this test. They believed that the developmental and neuropsychological changes specific to adults and adolescents warranted a different testing approach than did the changes relevant to younger children. Thus, a different approach was used when developing the KAIT, although the K-ABC was also based somewhat on the split between fluid and crystallized intelligence.

Theoretically, the KAIT is most influenced by J.L. Horn and Raymond B. Cattell's formulation of the distinction between fluid and crystallized intelligence, sometimes referred to as Gf-Gc theory. Gf refers to general fluid abilities and Gc refers to general crystallized abilities. The KAIT is also influenced by Piaget's theory of cognitive development, specifically the formal operations stage experienced in adolescence. During this stage, adolescents begin to perform complex mental operations and are better able to transform and manipulate information. Another theoretical influence of the KAIT is Luria's theory of planning ability. This theory attempted to explain developmental changes occurring in early adolescence that influence decision making and problem solving.

Description

The KAIT includes two components, a core battery and an expanded battery. The core battery consists of a fluid scale (Fluid IQ, which is short for intelligence quotient), a crystallized scale (Crystallized IQ), composite scale (Composite IQ), and six subtests, and takes about one hour (58 to 73 minutes) to complete. The expanded battery includes the core battery elements as well as four additional subtests and takes about 1.5 hours (83 to 102 minutes) to complete.

The tests for fluid intelligence use paired-associative learning and deductive reasoning. The test taker must use inductive reasoning and deductive reasoning to complete the assignments. The following core battery subtests are related to fluid intelligence (general fluid scale, Gf):

- logical steps, a test of sequential reasoning (visual and oral statements are presented, and the test taker uses logic to solve problems)
- mystery codes, a test measuring induction (test taker must solve a code used to identify a set of pictures, and then uses that code on a new set of pictures)

- rebus learning, a test of long-term memory (a word or concept is learned as provided by a picture representing the word [a rebus], and the test taker reads phrases and sentences composed of these rebuses)

The tests for crystallized intelligence use measures of lexical (word) knowledge and listening abilities. The test taker must synthesize and integrate the provided materials, along with memory, to complete the tasks. The following core battery subtests are related to crystallized intelligence (general crystallized scale, Gc):

- definitions: a test of word knowledge and language development (two sets of word clues are presented, and the test taker provides a word with two different meanings that fits both clues)
- double meanings: a measure of language comprehension (two clues are provided, a word with some letters missing and an oral clue about the meaning of the word, and the test taker responds with the word)
- auditory comprehension: a test of listening ability (test taker listens to a recording or words spoken by the administrator and answers questions about the story)

The expanded battery (measures of delayed recall) also includes:

- memory for block designs, a measure of visual processing related to fluid intelligence (test taker briefly looks at a printed design and builds the design using six cubes and a formboard)
- famous faces, a test of cultural knowledge related to crystallized intelligence (test taker names people of current or historical notoriety based on their picture and verbal clues)
- auditory delayed recall (test taker answers questions about news stories during the administration of auditory comprehension, within crystallized intelligence)
- rebus delayed recall, the two delayed recall subtests provide a general measure of delayed memory (test taker reads phrases and sentences composed of rebuses earlier learned during rebus learning, within fluid intelligence)

There is also an optional supplemental **mental status examination** included in the KAIT battery. The ten items within the mental status measure attention and orientation in time and space. This subtest is only given to examinees with possible mental impairment.

One strength of the KAIT is that most of the subtests are presented in both visual and auditory formats. This gives test takers more variety and allows for measurement of intelligence in different contexts. Also, the test was designed in a way to keep test takers active and engaged.

In contrast to other adult-specific or adolescent-specific **intelligence tests**, the KAIT is appropriate for a wider age range. This allows for more accurate tracking of intelligence changes between adolescence and adulthood.

KEY TERMS

IQ—The acronym for intelligence quotient, or a score derived from one of several standardized tests for intelligence.

Lexical—Relating to individual words that make up a language.

Neuropsychological—Relating to neuropsychology, or the branch of neurology that studies behavior disorders such as memory loss, speech impairment, epilepsy, and others.

Rebus—A puzzle in which syllables of words and names are represented by pictures of objects that sound similar or by letters.

Preparation

Preparation for the Kaufman Adolescent and Adult Intelligence Test is not needed nor necessary.

Precautions

There are very specific rules governing administration of the test that must be adhered to for scoring to be accurate. Thus, administrators must be properly trained to administer the KAIT. Specifically, for all subtests there is a discontinue rule, instructing administrators when to stop administering test items.

The KAIT is not appropriate for children younger than 11 years. A test more appropriate for younger children, such as the K-ABC, should be given instead. The K-ABC is appropriate for children up to the age of 12 years, 6 months, so there is some overlap between the two tests, specifically for children between the ages of 11 and 12 years, 6 months.

Parental concerns

When children take the KAIT, parents should be comforted that it is considered highly reliable and valid, consistently measured, and widely used throughout the professional psychological community for assessment of intelligence.

Results

The KAIT yields several different kinds of scores, including raw scores, scaled scores, and intelligent quotient (IQ) scores. Raw scores and scaled scores are calculated for each subtest (6 for the core battery; 10 for the expanded battery). Raw scores are calculated first, and simply refer to the number of points achieved by the examinee on a particular subtest. Raw scores are converted to scaled scores to ease comparison between subtests and between examinees. The subtest scaled scores are standardized to have a mean of 10 and a standard deviation of 3.

Three IQ scores are obtained: composite intelligence, fluid intelligence, and crystallized intelligence. The IQ scores have a mean of 100 and a standard deviation of 15. The fluid intelligence IQ score is based on the sum of the three fluid intelligence subtests (logical steps, mystery codes, and rebus learning). The crystallized intelligence IQ score is based on the sum of the three crystallized intelligence subtests (definitions, double meanings, and auditory comprehension). The composite intelligence IQ score is based on all six core subtests. The expanded battery subtests are not utilized when computing the three IQ scores.

The KAIS was normalized on a sample of 2,000 people, aged 11 to over 85 years, taken from a representative population within the United States, based on gender, race/ethnic group, and socioeconomic status (of adults or parents, in the case of children). Thirteen age levels composed the group, with at least 125 individuals in each level. Overall, the KAIT has high reliability and validity. Studies have indicated that in relation to other general intelligence tests, the crystallized, fluid, and composite IQ scores are accurately and consistently measured. Data looking at trends related to age show that average subtest and IQ scores are fairly consistent across the age range in which the KAIT is administered.

The KAIT yields IQ scores in a relatively wide range, from much lower than average intelligence to much higher than average intelligence. Because of this, the KAIT is often used as an assessment of individuals with exceptional abilities, such as gifted children.

There have been factor analysis studies comparing the KAIT to the widely used **Wechsler Intelligence Scales** (the Wechsler Intelligence Scale for Children and the Wechsler Adult Intelligence Scale). The KAIT crystallized IQ has been shown to measure abilities similar to those measured by the Wechsler scales' verbal intelligence factor. However, the KAIT Fluid IQ has been shown to measure abilities considerably different from those measured by the Wechsler performance factor, which is thought to be a measure of fluid intelligence.

QUESTIONS TO ASK YOUR DOCTOR

- Do you know of a properly trained administrator for the KAIT?
- Should another test for intelligence be administered in parallel with the KAIT?
- Will my health insurance cover the test?

See also Stanford-Binet intelligence scales

Resources

BOOKS

Boyer, Bret A., and M. Indira Paharia, eds. *Comprehensive Handbook of Clinical Health Psychology*. Hoboken, NJ: John Wiley and Sons, 2008.

Groth-Marnat, Gary. *Handbook of Psychological Assessment*. 4th ed. Hoboken, NJ: John Wiley and Sons, 2003.

Hersen, Michel, ed. *Comprehensive Handbook of Psychological Assessment*. Hoboken, NJ: John Wiley and Sons, 2004.

Kellerman, Henry, and Anthony Burry. *Handbook of Psychodiagnostic Testing: Analysis of Personality in the Psychological Report*. New York: Springer, 2007.

Leeming, David A., Kathryn Madden and Stanton Marlan, eds. *Encyclopedia of Psychology and Religion*. New York: Springer, 2010.

WEBSITES

"Alan S. Kaufman, PhD, and Nadeen L. Kaufman, EdD" [biography]. McGraw-Hill Higher Education. http://www.mhhe.com/mayfieldpub/psychtesting/profiles/karfmann.htm (accessed December 15, 2011).

"Author Bios: Alan S. Kaufman, PhD, and Nadeen L. Kaufman, EdD." Pearson. http://pearsonassessments.com/pai/ca/research/resources/authors/Alan_Nadeen_Kaufman (accessed December 15, 2011).

"Kaufman Adolescent and Adult Intelligence Test (KAIT)." Pearson. http://pearsonassessments.com/HAIWEB/Cultures/en-us/Productdetail.htm?Pid=PAa3650&Mode=summary (accessed December 15, 2011).

"Kaufman Adolescent and Adult Intelligence Test." Nova Southeastern University. http://www.cps.nova.edu/~cpphelp/KAIT.html (accessed December 15, 2011).

Ali Fahmy, Ph.D.

Kaufman Assessment Battery for Children

Definition

The Kaufman Assessment Battery for Children (K-ABC) is a standardized, psychological diagnostic test that assesses cognitive ability (intelligence measured through an intelligence quotient, or IQ) and achievement in children. The original K-ABC was geared to children aged 2 years and 6 months to 12 years and 6 months. The first edition published in 1983 by American psychologists Alan S. Kaufman (1944–) and Nadeen L. Kaufman (1945–) was revised in 2002 (second edition: KABC-II) by the husband-and-wife team to expand its age range (to cover children ages 2.5 to 18 years) and enhance its usefulness. In addition, new subtests were added and existing subtests updated. The KABC-II (referred to as the K-ABC) has a dual theoretical foundation: the Luria neuropsychological model and the Cattell/Horn/Carroll (CHC) model.

Purpose

The K-ABC was developed specifically to evaluate preschoolers, minority groups, and children with learning disabilities and various other disabilities. It is used to provide educational planning and placement, neurological assessment, and research. The assessment is to be administered in a school or clinical setting and is intended for use with English-speaking, bilingual, or nonverbal children. There is also a Spanish edition for use with children whose primary language is Spanish.

Description

Administration of the K-ABC core battery takes between 25 and 55 minutes when the Luria model is administered and between 35 and 70 minutes when the CHC model is used. The Luria model is generally administered for children with "mainstream" cultural and language knowledge and background. The CHC model, which excludes verbal testing, is used for "non-mainstream" children. The older the child, the longer the test generally takes to administer. It is comprised of four global test scores that include:

- sequential processing scales (Gsm), in which the child solves problems involving sequences, such as arranging objects in a series, and completes tasks involving short-term memory, such as recalling numbers or objects in sequence
- simultaneous processing scales (Gv), in which the child solves complex problems involving (1) face recognition, (2) partially complete picture identification, (3) design reproduction with use of rubber triangles, (4) picture selection that completes another picture, (5) picture selection that is similar to another picture, (6) picture location recall, and (7) picture arrangement based on logical order
- achievement scales, in which the child answers questions based on facts learned about famous people and places, mathematics, and story characters
- mental processing composite, a combination of the sequential processing scales and the simultaneous processing scales

There is an additional nonverbal scale that allows applicable subtests to be administered through gestures to hearing impaired, speech/language impaired, or children who do not speak English.

The test consists of 16 subtests—10 mental processing subtests and 6 achievement subtests. Not all subtests are administered to each age group, and only 3 subtests are administered to all age groups. Children ages 2 years, 6 months are given 7 subtests, and the number of subtests given increase with the child's age. For any one child, a maximum of 13 subtests are administered. Children from age 7 years to 12 years, 6 months are given 13 subtests.

The sequential processing scales primarily measure short-term memory and consists of subtests that measure problem-solving skills where the emphasis is on following a sequence or order. The child solves tasks by arranging items in serial or sequential order including reproducing hand taps on a table or recalling numbers that were presented. It also contains a subtest that measures a child's ability to recall objects in the correct order as presented by the examiner.

The simultaneous processing scales examine problem-solving skills that involve several processes at once.

KEY TERMS

IQ—The acronym for intelligence quotient, or a score derived from one of several standardized tests for intelligence.

Neuropsychological—Relating to neuropsychology, or the branch of neurology that studies behavior disorders such as memory loss, speech impairment, epilepsy, and others.

Psychometric—The branch of psychology that deals with the measurement of mental capacities, traits, and processes.

The scales use seven subtests: facial recognition, identification of objects or scenes in a partially completed picture, reproduction of a presented design by using rubber triangles, selecting a picture that completes or is similar to another picture, memory for location of pictures presented on a page, and arrangement of pictures in meaningful order.

The achievement scales measure achievement and focus on applied skills and facts that were learned through the school or home environment. The subtests are expressive vocabulary; ability to name fictional characters, famous persons, and well-known places; mathematical skills; ability to solve riddles; readings and decoding skills; and reading and comprehension skills.

The sequential and simultaneous processing scales are combined to comprise the mental processing composite. This composite measures intelligence on the K-ABC and concentrates on the child's ability to solve unfamiliar problems simultaneously and sequentially. The simultaneous processing scales have a greater impact on the mental processing composite score than do the sequential processing scales. The mental processing composite score is considered the global estimate of a child's level of intellectual functioning.

Preparation

Preparation for the Kaufman Assessment Battery for Children is not needed nor necessary.

Risks

The K-ABC is especially useful in providing information about nonverbal intellectual abilities. However, it has been criticized for not focusing on measures of verbal intelligence in the mental processing composite score, which measures intelligence. Additionally, researchers, who claim the two terms are misleading, have questioned the separation of intelligence and achievement scores. For example, many subtests in the achievement composite are in fact measures of intelligence rather than achievement (knowledge acquired through school and/or home environment). The K-ABC should be used with caution as the primary instrument for identifying the intellectual abilities of children.

Precautions

Administration and interpretation of results (as with all psychometric testing) requires a competent examiner who is trained in psychology and individual intellectual assessment—preferably a **psychologist**.

QUESTIONS TO ASK YOUR DOCTOR

- Do you know of a properly trained administrator for the K-ABC?
- What other test(s) for intelligence could be administered in parallel with the K-ABC? Which ones are best to be taken with the K-ABC?
- Should my child take the Lucia model or the CHC model of the test?
- Where can I learn more about the K-ABC?
- Will my health insurance cover the test?

Results

The K-ABC is a standardized test, which means that a large sample of children in the 2 years, 6 months to 12 years, 6 months age range was administered the examination as a means of developing test norms. Children in the sample were representative of the population of the United States based on age, gender, race or ethnic group, geographic region, community size, parental education, and educational placement (normal versus special classes). From this sample, norms were established.

Based on these norms, the global scales on the K-ABC each have a mean or average score of 100 and a standard deviation of 15. For this test, as with most measures of intelligence, a score of 100 is in the normal or average range. The standard deviation indicates how far above or below the norm a child's score is. For example, a score of 85 is one standard deviation below the norm score of 100.

Test scores provide an estimate of the level at which a child is functioning based on a combination of many different subtests or measures of skills. A trained psychologist is needed to evaluate and interpret the results, determine strengths and weaknesses, and make overall recommendations based on the findings and behavioral observations.

Parental concerns

When children take the K-ABC, parents should be comforted that it is considered highly reliable and valid, consistently measured, and widely used throughout the professional community for assessment of intelligence. However, the K-ABC primarily evaluates nonverbal intelligence, so it is limited with respect to measuring verbal intelligence. In addition, only a trained administrator should interpret the scores of the test.

Professionals advise that the K-ABC should not be used as the primary test, or as the only test, to assess intelligence in children. The K-ABC should be used in parallel with other appropriate intelligence and achievement tests, such as the Wechsler Intelligence Scale for Children.

Resources

BOOKS

Boyer, Bret A., and M. Indira Paharia, eds. *Comprehensive Handbook of Clinical Health Psychology*. Hoboken, NJ: John Wiley and Sons, 2008.

Groth-Marnat, Gary. *Handbook of Psychological Assessment*. 4th ed. Hoboken, NJ: John Wiley and Sons, 2003.

Hersen, Michel, ed. *Comprehensive Handbook of Psychological Assessment*. Hoboken, NJ: John Wiley and Sons, 2004.

Kellerman, Henry, and Anthony Burry. *Handbook of Psychodiagnostic Testing: Analysis of Personality in the Psychological Report*. New York: Springer, 2007.

Leeming, David A., Kathryn Madden and Stanton Marlan, eds. *Encyclopedia of Psychology and Religion*. New York: Springer, 2010.

Sattler, Jerome M. *Assessment of Children: Cognitive Foundations*. San Diego, CA: J.M. Sattler, 2008.

WEBSITES

"Alan S. Kaufman, PhD, and Nadeen L. Kaufman, EdD" [biography]. McGraw-Hill Higher Education. http://www.mhhe.com/mayfieldpub/psychtesting/profiles/karfmann.htm (accessed December 15, 2011).

"Author Bios: lan S. Kaufman, PhD, and Nadeen L. Kaufman, EdD." Pearson. http://pearsonassessments.com/pai/ca/research/resources/authors/Alan_Nadeen_Kaufman (accessed December 15, 2011).

"Kaufman Assessment Battery for Children." Nova Southeastern University. http://www.cps.nova.edu/~cpphelp/KABC.html (accessed December 16, 2011).

"Kaufman Assessment Battery for Children, Second Edition (KABC-II)." Pearson. http://psychcorp.pearsonassessments.com/HAIWEB/Cultures/en-us/Productdetail.htm?Pid=PAa21000&Mode=summary (accessed December 16, 2011).

ORGANIZATIONS

American Psychiatric Association, 1000 Wilson Blvd., Ste. 1825, Arlington, VA, 22209-3901, (703) 907-7300, apa@psych.org, http://www.psych.org.

American Psychological Association, 750 1st St. NE, Washington, DC, 20002-4242, (202) 336-5500; TDD/TTY: (202) 336-6123, (800) 374-2721, http://www.apa.org.

National Association of School Psychologists, 4340 East West Highway, Ste. 402, Bethesda, MD, 20002, (301) 657-0270, (800) 331-5277, Fax: (301) 657-0275, http://www.nasponline.org.

See also Intelligence tests; Luria-Nebraska Neuropsychological Battery

Jenifer P. Marom, Ph.D.

Kaufman Short Neurological Assessment Procedure

Definition

The Kaufman Short Neurological Procedure, often abbreviated as K-SNAP, is a brief test of mental functioning appropriate for adolescents and adults between the ages of 11 and 85 years. It is administered on an individual basis, and measures mental functioning at varying levels of cognitive complexity as well as addressing possible neurological damage.

Purpose

The K-SNAP is intended as a short measure of mental functioning and is sometimes preferable to other longer mental status and intelligence (IQ) examinations. Compared to the **Kaufman Adolescent and Adult Intelligence Test** (KAIT), which is given to people in the same age range and takes over an hour to complete, the K-SNAP takes only 20 to 30 minutes. The K-SNAP provides a measure of general mental status, as well as addressing specific mental abilities. It also allows for assessment of damage to the nervous system.

The K-SNAP was developed by American psychologists Alan S. Kaufman (1944–) and Nadeen L. Kaufman (1945–). Other Kaufman tests include the KAIT and the **Kaufman Assessment Battery for Children** (K-ABC). The Kaufmans based their tests on Horn and Cattell's formulation of the distinction between fluid and crystallized intelligence, sometimes referred to as the Gf-Gc Theory. Gf refers to such general fluid abilities as problem solving and reasoning. Fluid intelligence is thought not to be influenced by a person's cultural experience and education. Gc refers to such general crystallized abilities as acquired knowledge. Crystallized intelligence, unlike fluid intelligence, is thought to be shaped by a person's cultural experience and education.

Because the K-SNAP provides a measure of possible neurological impairment, it is often preferable to other measures of mental status and intelligence. If the doctor suspects that a patient may have a disorder of the nervous system, the doctor can use the K-SNAP as a short initial assessment. Depending on the results of the K-SNAP, the doctor can give more specific tests.

Description

The K-SNAP consists of four subtests administered in the following order of complexity: Mental Status, Gestalt Closure, Number Recall, and Four-Letter Words. Each subtest contains between 10 and 25 items.

The Mental Status subtest assesses the test taker's alertness, attentiveness, and orientation to the environment. In this subtest, the examiner asks the examinee to answer verbal questions. It is the easiest and shortest of the four subtests, containing only 10 items.

The Gestalt Closure subtest provides an assessment of visual closure and simultaneous processing. In this subtest, the examinee is shown partially completed inkblot pictures and is asked to name the objects in the pictures.

The Number Recall subtest assesses sequential processing and short-term auditory memory. In this subtest, the examiner recites series of numbers and the examinee repeats the numbers.

The Four-Letter Words subtest measures the test taker's ability to solve problems and make plans. In this subtest, the examinee is asked to guess a secret word by analyzing a series of four-letter words that provide clues to the answer. It is the most complex of the subtests.

The K-SNAP is a relatively easy test to administer. Except for the Mental Status subtest, the test items are presented on an easel, which is visually appealing to many test takers. Also, because the test is brief and includes a variety of tasks, the test takers often find the test engaging and interesting.

The K-SNAP is considered to be useful in evaluating elderly people, especially with regard to decline in fluid intelligence. The Mental Status subtest can also detect possible age-related impairment in mental functioning.

Compared to other neurological and cognitive assessments, there are smaller than usual differences in K-SNAP performance between African American and Caucasian individuals, especially with regard to fluid intelligence. This cultural neutrality makes the K-SNAP a preferred method for testing African Americans.

Preparation

Preparation for the Kaufman Short Neurological Assessment Procedure is not needed nor necessary.

KEY TERMS

Cognitive—Relating to thoughts and the acquisition of knowledge.

IQ—The acronym for intelligence quotient, or a score derived from one of several standardized tests for intelligence.

Neurological—Relating to neurology, or the branch of medicine dealing with the function and structure of the nervous system, along with its associated diseases and disorders.

Standard deviation—A statistical measure of dispersion; that is, how much a set of values differ from an arithmetic mean.

Risks

One should be careful when using the results of the K-SNAP to assess neurological impairment. It should be used as a supplement to other more extensive and more specific measures of neuropsychological functioning.

Precautions

The K-SNAP is primarily a test of mental and neuropsychological functioning. Although it measures cognitive skills, it should not be used to measure someone's overall intelligence.

Parental concerns

The K-SNAP is suitable for parents and children because it is a short and easy test to take, while still providing a good cognitive evaluation. It is also used as part of a more comprehensive assessment. The K-SNAP is frequently used as the first step in such evaluations, especially within correctional, medical, and psychological facilities.

Results

The K-SNAP was normalized on a representative sample of 2,000 people in the United States. All people were selected to eliminate cultural biases. The procedure yields several scores, including raw scores, scaled scores, a composite score, and an impairment index. Interpretation of the results are based on age-based normative scores or are evaluated from an eight-point impairment index, which is used to determine whether further testing is needed. Raw scores and scaled scores are calculated for each of the four subtests. Raw scores are calculated first; they refer simply to the number of points that the examinee scored on a particular subtest. The raw scores are converted to scaled scores to simplify comparisons between the subtests and between examinees. The subtest scaled scores are standardized to have a mean of 10 and a standard deviation of three.

One composite score is obtained on the K-SNAP. The composite score has a mean of 100 and a standard deviation of 15 and is based on the scores of the four subtests.

The results of the Mental Status subtest are primarily of interest when working with middle-aged or elderly people, as well as people with neurological or cognitive impairments. Most people find the Mental Status subtest very easy, and they get most, if not all, of the items correct.

Some of the interpretation of the K-SNAP involves comparisons of performance on tasks of varying complexity. For example, Gestalt Closure is considered a less complex task than Number Recall. Someone who performs better on the more difficult Number Recall subtest may exhibit some kind of **brain** dysfunction. On the other hand, that person may simply prefer sequential processing tasks.

An impairment index is also calculated and provides an objective measure of cognitive and neurological impairment. The impairment index is based on the following four factors: the K-SNAP composite score; the test taker's performance on the Mental Status subtest; the difference between the scaled scores on the Number Recall and Gestalt Closure subtests; and the difference between the actual composite score and the predicted composite score based on the test taker's level of education. These four factors determine whether a more comprehensive assessment of impairment is necessary. For example, if an examinee has a composite score below 70, a low score on the Mental Status subtest, a large difference in performance in the Number Recall and Gestalt Closure subtests, and a difference of at least 24 points between the predicted and actual composite scores, there may be indications of impairment. One example of such impairment is damage to one hemisphere of the brain.

Overall, the K-SNAP has above-average to good reliability. As a **mental status examination**, it has been shown to have good validity as well. There have been no studies, however, demonstrating the K-SNAP's validity as a measure of neuropsychological impairment. Because the K-SNAP is based on similar theories and on the same standardization sample as other Kaufman tests, such as the KAIT, interpretation across the range of Kaufman tests is easier than comparing results from the K-SNAP to results from tests designed by other persons.

QUESTIONS TO ASK YOUR DOCTOR

- Do you know of a properly trained administrator for the K-SNAP?
- What other test(s) for intelligence could be administered after completing the K-SNAP?
- Should my child take other tests for a better overall assessment of his/her condition?
- Where can I learn more about the K-SNAP?
- Will health insurance cover the test?

Resources

BOOKS

Boyer, Bret A., and M. Indira Paharia, eds. *Comprehensive Handbook of Clinical Health Psychology.* Hoboken, NJ: John Wiley and Sons, 2008.

Groth-Marnat, Gary. *Handbook of Psychological Assessment.* 4th edition. Hoboken, NJ: John Wiley and Sons, 2003.

Hersen, Michel, ed. *Comprehensive Handbook of Psychological Assessment.* Hoboken, NJ: John Wiley and Sons, 2004.

Kellerman, Henry, and Anthony Burry. *Handbook of Psychodiagnostic Testing: Analysis of Personality in the Psychological Report.* New York: Springer, 2007.

Leeming, David A., Kathryn Madden and Stanton Marlan, eds. *Encyclopedia of Psychology and Religion.* New York: Springer, 2010.

Sattler, Jerome M. *Assessment of Children: Cognitive Foundations.* San Diego, CA: J.M. Sattler, 2008.

WEBSITES

"Alan S. Kaufman, PhD, and Nadeen L. Kaufman, EdD." McGraw-Hill Higher Education. http://www.mhhe.com/mayfieldpub/psychtesting/profiles/karfmann.htm (accessed December 15, 2010).

"Alan S. Kaufman, PhD, and Nadeen L. Kaufman, EdD." Pearson. http://pearsonassessments.com/pai/ca/research/resources/authors/Alan_Nadeen_Kaufman (accessed December 15, 2010).

"Kaufman Short Neuropsychological Assessment Procedure (K-SNAP)." Pearson. http://www.pearsonassessments.com/HAIWEB/Cultures/en-us/Productdetail.htm?Pid=paa3560&Mode=summary (accessed December 16, 2010).

ORGANIZATIONS

American Psychiatric Association, 1000 Wilson Blvd., Ste. 1825, Arlington, VA, 22209-3901, (703) 907-7300, apa@psych.org, http://www.psych.org.

American Psychological Association, 750 1st St. NE, Washington, DC, 20002-4242, (202) 336-5500; TDD/TTY: (202) 336-6123, (800) 374-2721, http://www.apa.org.

Ali Fahmy, Ph.D.

Kava kava

Definition

Kava kava is a dioecious shrub native to the Pacific islands. Its botanical name is *Piper methysticum*; it is a member of the Piperaceae, or pepper, family. It is also known as asava pepper or intoxicating pepper. The narcotic drink made from the roots of this shrub is also called kava kava. Kava kava has been widely recommended in recent years as a mild tranquilizer due to its painkilling properties. However, kava kava has been the subject of official safety warnings from the U.S. Food and Drug Administration (FDA) and its counterparts in Canada, France, Germany, Switzerland, and Spain; kava kava is considered "possibly unsafe" by the U.S. National Institutes of Health.

Purpose

The German Commission E, a panel of physicians and pharmacists that reviews the safety and efficacy of herbal preparations, at one time approved the use of kava kava as a nonprescription dietary supplement for the relief of nervous anxiety, **stress**, and restlessness. That approval was withdrawn in the fall of 2001 due to the risks associated with the substance. Kava kava has, however, shown effectiveness in **clinical trials** in treating anxiety and in reducing withdrawal symptoms of patients taking **benzodiazepines**.

In addition to relief of stress and anxiety, kava kava has also been used for **insomnia**, sore or stiff muscles, toothache or sore gums, **attention deficit hyperactivity disorder**, menstrual cramps, uncontrolled epilepsy, and jet lag; however, none of these uses have been proven in clinical trials, either due to unsuccessful results or a lack of evidence.

Kava Kava leaf. *(© bildagentur-online.com/th-foto/Alamy)*

Description

The beverage form of kava kava was traditionally prepared in the Pacific Islands by chewing the roots of the kava plant and spitting them into a bowl. The active compounds, known as kavalactones and kavapyrones, are found primarily in the root of the plant and are activated by human saliva. Contemporary Pacific Islanders prepare kava kava by pounding or grinding the roots and mixing them with coconut milk or water. Modern Western manufacturers use alcohol or acetate in making liquid kava preparations. Kava kava is also available in capsule, tablet, powdered, or crushed forms. Experts in herbal medicine recommended the use of kava preparations standardized to contain 70% kavalactones.

Kavalactones are chemicals that affect the **brain** in the same way as benzodiazepines, such as valium, which are sometimes prescribed for **depression**, anxiety, or **sleep disorders**. Kavalactones also have anesthetic properties that can cause the tongue or gums to feel numb. Kavapyrones are chemicals that have anticonvulsant and muscle relaxant properties.

Origins

Captain James Cook is credited with introducing kava kava to Europeans when he visited the South Pacific in 1773. Previously, the inhabitants of the Pacific Islands used kava kava as a ceremonial beverage. It was consumed at weddings, funerals, and birth rituals, and it was offered to honored guests. Kava kava was also drunk as part of healing rituals. The first commercial products containing kava kava were offered to European consumers around 1860.

Recommended dosage

Kava kava should never be given to children, particularly in view of recent health warnings concerning adults.

The usual dose of kava kava that has been recommended to relieve stress or insomnia in adults is 2–4 g of the plant boiled in water, up to three times daily. Alternately, 60–600 mg of kavalactones in a standardized formula could be taken per day.

Precautions

Kava kava has been linked to several cases of severe liver problems, including hepatitis, cirrhosis, and liver failure. Further studies need to be conducted to investigate whether kava kava was truly the cause of liver complications. Until more is known, the U.S. government considers kava kava to be potentially unsafe and advises against its use. If kava kava is used, it should

KEY TERMS

Dioecious—A category of plants that reproduce sexually but have male and female reproductive organs on different individuals.

Kavalactones—Medically active compounds in kava root that act as local anesthetics in the mouth and as minor tranquilizers.

Kavapyrones—Compounds in kava root that act as muscle relaxants and anticonvulsants.

not be used by pregnant or lactating women, as it might adversely affect the fetus or infant. Because of its effects on the central nervous system, persons should not take kava kava prior to driving or operating heavy machinery, and patients undergoing surgery should stop taking kava kava two weeks prior to their procedure. Kava kava may worsen any existing depression and should not be taken by persons with a history of depression.

Side effects

Before reports of liver damage, most side effects from kava kava concerned relatively minor problems, such as numbness in the mouth, headaches, mild dizziness, or skin rashes. In the nineteenth-century, missionaries to the Pacific Islands noted that people who drank large quantities of kava kava developed yellowish scaly skin. A recent study found the same side effect in test subjects who took 100 times the recommended dose of the plant. Kava kava also appears to produce psychological side effects in some patients. A team of Spanish physicians reported that beverages containing kava kava may cause anxiety, depression, and insomnia. In addition, kava kava may cause tremors severe enough to be mistaken for symptoms of Parkinson's disease.

Interactions

Kava kava has been shown to interact adversely with alcoholic beverages and with several categories of prescription medications. It increases the effect of **barbiturates** and other psychoactive medications; in one case study, a patient who took kava kava together with **alprazolam** (a benzodiazepine used to treat anxiety) went into a coma. It may produce dizziness and other unpleasant side effects if taken together with phenothiazines (used to treat **schizophrenia**). Kava kava has also been reported to reduce the effectiveness of levodopa, a drug used in the treatment of Parkinson's disease. To avoid potential reactions with prescription medications, people should inform their physician if they are taking kava kava or any other supplement.

Resources

BOOKS

Cass, Hyla, and Terrence McNally. *Kava: Nature's Answer to Stress, Anxiety, and Insomnia*. Prima Lifestyles, Inc., 1998.

Schulz, V., R. Hänsel, and V. Tyler. *Rational Phytotherapy: A Physician's Guide to Herbal Medicine*. 5th ed. Transl. by T.C. Telger. New York, NY: Springer, 2011.

PERIODICALS

Almeida, J. C., and E. W. Grimsley. "Coma from the Health Food Store: Interaction Between Kava and Alprazolam." *Annals of Internal Medicine* 125, no. 11 (1996): 940–941.

Ballesteros, S., et al. "Severe Adverse Effect Associated with Kava-Kava." *Journal of Toxicology: Clinical Toxicology* 39 (April 2001): 312.

Beltman, W., et al. "An Overview of Contemporary Herbal Drugs Used in the Netherlands." *Journal of Toxicology: Clinical Toxicology* 38 (March 2000): 174.

"France Is Latest to Pull Kava Kava Products." *Nutraceuticals International* (February 2002).

Humbertson, C. L., J. Akhtar, and E. P. Krenzelok. "Acute Hepatitis Induced by Kava Kava, an Herbal Product Derived from *Piper methysticum*." *Journal of Toxicology: Clinical Toxicology* 39 (August 2001): 549.

Kubetin, Sally Koch. "FDA Investigating Kava Kava." *OBGYN News* 37 (February 1, 2002): 29. Available online at http://findarticles.com/p/articles/mi_m0CYD/is_3_37/ai_82879244 (accessed November 9, 2011).

WEBSITES

MedlinePlus."Kava." U.S. National Library of Medicine, National Institutes of Health. http://www.nlm.nih.gov/medlineplus/druginfo/natural/872.html (accessed November 14, 2011).

U.S. Food and Drug Administration. "Kava (Piper methysticum) Dear Healthcare Professional Letter" MedWatch: The FDA Safety and Adverse Event Reporting Program. December 2001. http://www.fda.gov/Safety/MedWatch/SafetyInformation/SafetyAlertsforHumanMedicalProducts/ucm174452.htm (accessed October 9, 2011).

ORGANIZATIONS

American Botanical Council, 6200 Manor Rd., Austin, TX, 78723, (512) 926-4900, (800) 373-7105, Fax: (512) 926-2345, abc@herbalgram.org, http://www.herbalgram.org.

National Center for Complementary and Alternative Medicine, 9000 Rockville Pike, Bethesda, MD, 20892, (888) 644-6226, http://nccam.nih.gov.

NIH Office of Dietary Supplements, 6100 Executive Blvd., Room 3B01, MSC 7517, Bethesda, MD, 20892-7517, (301) 435-2920, Fax: (301) 480-1845, ods@nih.gov, http://www.odp.od.nih.gov.

Rebecca J. Frey, Ph.D.

Kleine-Levin syndrome

Definition

Kleine-Levin syndrome (also known as KLS) is a rare disorder. The most prevalent characteristic of the syndrome is recurring periods of excessive drowsiness and sleep (up to 20 hours per day) that can last weeks.

Demographics

Kleine-Levine syndrome is more common in adolescent males with a 3:1 ratio to females. Approximately 15% of the reported cases in the United States are people with Jewish origins. Age at onset is usually in the late teens and average age at onset is about 16.9 years, with a range from 4 to 82 years. About 81% of cases start in the preteen and teen years. Although it occurs more often in males, symptoms may be worse or the disease longer lasting in females.

Description

Kleine-Levin Syndrome is listed as a "rare disease" by the Office of Rare Diseases of the National Institutes of Health. KLS was first described in 1862 and is considered extremely rare. In addition to excessive drowsiness, an episode of KLS can also involve hypersexuality and compulsive behaviors, including compulsive eating. It usually first manifests in adolescence and appears to lessen and resolve on its own with age. Although cognitive and behavioral disturbances, including transient confusion and memory deficits, can accompany the disorder, there appear to be no lasting, permanent effects. In addition to other manifestations, KLS can be accompanied by mood disorders and an extreme irritability that translates into violent behaviors in atypical cases.

The average number of episodes of KLS among cases is seven, each lasting a median 10 days about every 3.5 months. The median length of time a person experiences the syndrome is eight years, although this time is longer in women and in people who experience less frequent episodes in their first year following onset.

Causes and symptoms

Causes

Most studies suggest that KLS is related to the hypothalamus, the organ in the **brain** that governs appetite, sleep, and hormone cycles, among other things. Researchers have failed to identify specific causes of KLS, although there are some apparent associations between events preceding the first episode of the disorder and its manifestation. The majority of cases are isolated, meaning that they do not appear to have a heritable basis.

Because many people with KLS experienced a viral illness just prior to their first episode, some experts propose that the causative agent is a type of viral or post-autoimmune encephalitis that affects the hypothalamus. Reported infections included tonsillitis, nonspecific flu-like fever, upper respiratory tract infection, and gastroenteritis. One study revealed that three of four autopsied patients with KLS had signs of inflammatory encephalitis in the hypothalamus.

Despite the suggested involvement of the hypothalamus, no association has been found clinically between a KLS episode and changes in hypothalamic hormones, cerebrospinal fluid, or other neurological signs. Similarly, in spite of symptoms such as hypersexuality, there have been no identified related changes in sex steroid hormones. One clinical association with KLS that has been found in 70% of patients is a nonspecific slowing of background brain activity on electroencephalogram testing. All **magnetic resonance imaging** (MRI) and CAT scan imaging of the brain in KLS cases have been normal.

KLS can occur as the primary disease, with onset in the teen years, or it can occur secondary to another disease or health problem, such as multiple sclerosis or brain **trauma**. Although fewer cases of secondary KLS occur compared to primary KLS, patients with secondary KLS may experience much longer and more frequent episodes.

Symptoms

Symptoms of a Kleine-Levin episode can last weeks or even months. In addition to **hypersomnia** (excessive sleepiness), symptoms can include excessive eating without regard to content or quantity, extreme irritability, disorientation and confusion, low energy or no energy, hypersensitivity to noise, disconnection from reality, and

KEY TERMS

Hypersexuality—A clinically significant level of desire to engage in sexual behaviors.

Hypersomnia—Excessive sleepiness.

Hypothalamus—The hypothalamus is part of the brain that links the nervous and endocrine systems and also governs emotion, sexual activity, body temperature, hunger, thirst, and sleep cycles.

blurred vision. A person experiencing a KLS episode may also report hallucinations. The abnormally uninhibited sex drive associated with some KLS episodes occurs more frequently in males and manifests in ways that can be alarming: those affected may expose themselves and make unwanted sexual advances. The disorder is episodic, and affected people behave normally between episodes. Intervals between episodes can sometimes last years.

Although an episode can come on without much warning, there are sometimes prodromal (pre-occurrence) signs that a KLS event is impending, especially a feeling of sudden, overwhelming tiredness. The excessive drowsiness of a KLS episode precludes normal participation in activities. In spite of the hypersomnia, a person experiencing a KLS episode is still able to wake to eat or void.

There may be some **depression** or **amnesia** after an attack. Depression can accompany KLS and an episode of KLS can occur with a recurring episode of depression. About half of patients report a depressive mood in conjunction with a KLS event.

Diagnosis

According to one source, diagnosing KLS is an difficult process and can result in an average delay of four years before a patient receives the correct **diagnosis**.

Treatment

No definitive treatment for KLS exists, and response to current treatments can be limited. A clinician can try to address the excessive sleepiness using orally administered stimulants (**amphetamines**, **methylphenidate**, modafinil). Because there are crossover characteristics between KLS and other mood disorders, lithium or **carbamazepine** are sometimes prescribed, and lithium appears to have some beneficial effect on **relapse** rates in a little less than half of the cases.

Prognosis

Excluding quality-of-life issues, KLS is a benign disorder that usually improves or resolves with age without permanent effects on intellect or physical function.

Prevention

Because the causes of KLS are undefined, prevention measures have not been identified.

Resources

PERIODICALS

Arnulf, I., et al. "Kleine-Levin Syndrome: A Systematic Review of 186 Cases in the Literature." *Brain* 128, no. 12 (2006): 2763–2776. Available online at http://brain.oxfordjournals.org/content/128/12/2763.full (accessed November 9, 2011).

WEBSITES

National Institute of Neurological Disorders and Stroke. "NINDS Kleine-Levin Syndrome Information Page." U.S. National Institutes of Health. http://www.ninds.nih.gov/disorders/kleine_levin/kleine_levin.htm (accessed November 14, 2011).

ORGANIZATIONS

Kleine-Levin Syndrome Foundation, PO Box 5382, San Jose, CA, 95150-5382, (408) 265-1099, Fax: (408) 269-2131, facts@klsfoundation.org, http://www.klsfoundation.org.

National Institute of Neurological Disorders and Stroke, PO Box 5801, Bethesda, MD, 20824, (301) 496-5751; TTY: (301) 468-5981, (800) 352-9424, http://www.ninds.nih.gov.

National Organization for Rare Disorders, 55 Kenosia Ave., PO Box 1968, Danbury, CT, 06813-1968, (203) 744-0100, Fax: (203) 798-2291, (800) 999-6673, http://www.rarediseases.org.

National Sleep Foundation, 1010 N Glebe Rd., Ste. 310, Arlington, VA, 22201, (703) 243-1697, nsf@sleepfoundation.org, http://www.sleepfoundation.org.

Emily Jane Willingham, Ph.D.

Kleptomania

Definition

Kleptomania is an impulse control disorder characterized by a recurrent failure to resist stealing.

Demographics

Studies suggest that 0.6% of the general population may have this disorder and that it is more common in females. In patients who have histories of **obsessive-compulsive disorder**, some studies suggest a 7% correlation with kleptomania. Other studies have reported a particularly high (65%) correlation of kleptomania in patients with bulimia.

Description

Kleptomania is a complex disorder characterized by repeated, failed attempts to stop stealing. It is often seen in patients who are chemically dependent or who have a coexisting mood, anxiety, or eating disorder. Other coexisting mental disorders may include major **depression**, panic attacks, **social phobia**, **anorexia nervosa**, **bulimia nervosa**, **substance abuse**, and obsessive-compulsive disorder. People with this disorder have an overwhelming urge to steal and get a thrill from doing so. The recurrent act of stealing may be restricted to specific objects and settings, but the affected person may or may not describe these special preferences. People with this disorder usually exhibit guilt after the theft.

Detection of kleptomania, even by close family members, is difficult and the disorder often proceeds undetected. There may be preferred objects and environments where theft occurs. One theory proposes that the thrill of stealing helps to alleviate symptoms in persons who are clinically depressed.

Causes and symptoms

Causes

The cause of kleptomania is unknown, although it may have a genetic component and may be transmitted among first-degree relatives. There also seems to be a strong propensity for kleptomania to coexist with obsessive-compulsive disorder, bulimia nervosa, and clinical depression.

Symptoms

The handbook used by mental health professionals to diagnose mental disorders is the *Diagnostic and Statistical Manual of Mental Disorders.* Published by the **American Psychiatric Association**, the *DSM* contains diagnostic criteria and research findings for mental disorders. It is the primary reference for mental health professionals in the United States. The 2000 edition of this manual (fourth edition, text revision), known as the *DSM-IV-TR,* lists five diagnostic criteria for kleptomania:

- Repeated theft of objects that are unnecessary for either personal use or monetary value.
- Increasing tension immediately before the theft.
- Pleasure or relief upon committing the theft.
- The theft is not motivated by anger or vengeance, and is not caused by a delusion or hallucination.
- The behavior is not better accounted for by a conduct disorder, manic episode, or antisocial personality disorder.

Diagnosis

Diagnosing kleptomania is usually difficult since patients do not seek medical help for this complaint, and it may not be detected by initial psychological assessments. The disorder is often diagnosed when patients seek help for another reason, such as depression, bulimia, or for feeling emotionally unstable (labile) or unhappy in general (dysphoric). Initial psychological evaluations may detect a history of poor parenting, relationship conflicts, or acute stressors—abrupt occurrences that cause **stress**, such as moving from one home to another. The recurrent act of stealing may be restricted to specific objects and settings, but the patient may or may not describe these special preferences.

KEY TERMS

Anorexia nervosa—An eating disorder characterized by an intense fear of weight gain accompanied by a distorted perception of one's own underweight body.

Bulimia nervosa—An eating disorder characterized by binges in which large amounts of food are consumed, followed by forced vomiting.

Cognitive-behavioral therapy—An approach to psychotherapy that emphasizes the correction of distorted thinking patterns and changing one's behaviors accordingly.

Obsessive-compulsive disorder—Disorder in which the affected individual has an obsession (such as a fear of contamination, or thoughts he or she doesn't like to have and can't control) and feels compelled to perform a certain act to neutralize the obsession (such as repeated handwashing).

Panic disorder—An anxiety disorder in which an individual experiences sudden, debilitating attacks of intense fear.

Phobia—Irrational fear of places, things, or situations that lead to avoidance.

Rational emotive therapy—A form of psychotherapy developed by Albert Ellis and other psychotherapists based on the theory that emotional response is based on the subjective interpretation of events, not on the events themselves.

Treatment

Once the disorder is suspected and verified by an extensive psychological interview, therapy is normally directed towards impulse control, as well as any accompanying mental disorder(s). **Relapse prevention** strategies, with a clear understanding of specific triggers, should be stressed. Treatment may include psychotherapies such as **cognitive-behavioral therapy** and **rational emotive therapy**. Recent studies have indicated that **fluoxetine** (Prozac) and **naltrexone** (Revia) may also be helpful.

Prognosis

Not much solid information is known about this disorder. Since it is not usually the presenting problem or chief complaint, it is frequently not even diagnosed. There are some case reports that document treatment success with antidepressant medications, although as with almost all psychological disorders, the outcomes vary.

Prevention

There is little evidence concerning prevention. A healthy upbringing, positive intimate relationships, and management of acutely stressful situations may lower the incidence of kleptomania and coexisting disorders.

Resources

BOOKS

Tasman, Allan, et al., eds. *Psychiatry*. 3rd ed. New York: Wiley and Sons, 2008.

Laith Farid Gulli, M.D.

Klonopin *see* **Clonazepam**

K-SNAP *see* **Kaufman Short Neurological Assessment Procedure**

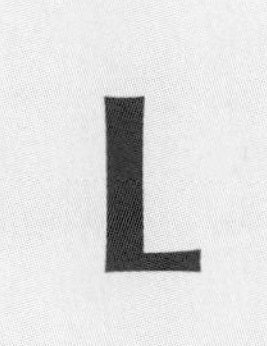

Laboratory tests *see* **Imaging studies**
Lamictal *see* **Lamotrigine**

Lamotrigine

Definition

Lamotrigine is an anticonvulsant drug commonly used to prevent **seizures**. In the United States, lamotrigine is available under the trade name of Lamictal.

Purpose

Lamotrigine is used to prevent seizures in individuals with seizure disorders. It is also used as a mood stabilizer in people with **bipolar disorder**.

Description

The U.S. Food and Drug Administration (FDA) approved Lamotrigine in 1994. This drug appears to suppress the activity of neurons (nerve cells) in the **brain**. By stabilizing neurons, lamotrigine prevents seizure activity and may also stabilize abnormal mood swings.

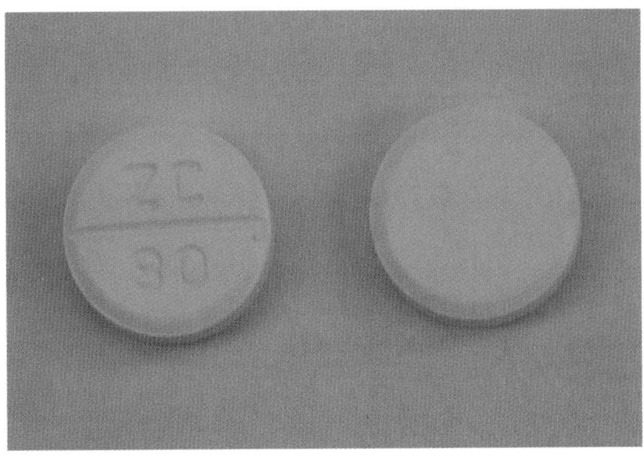

Lamotrigine, 100 mg. *(© Custom Medical Stock Photo, Inc. Reproduced by permission.)*

Lamotrigine is available as both oral and chewable tablets. It is broken down in the liver.

Recommended dosage

The dosage of lamotrigine varies depending upon the age and weight of the patient, other medications that the patient is taking, and whether the patient has heart, liver, or kidney disease. It is common for patients to start with a low dosage of lamotrigine. The dosage is then increased slowly over several weeks to help prevent side effects. The dosage may be adjusted frequently by the prescribing physician.

A common dose for an adult who takes no other medications and has no other diseases is 150–250 mg taken twice daily.

Precautions

A serious and permanently disfiguring rash may occur as a result of lamotrigine. The rash, which is symptom of a systemic reaction to the drug, may be fatal. If a rash occurs, a doctor should be contacted immediately, and the drug should be stopped. People who have experienced any kind of rash while taking lamotrigine should never take the drug again.

Lamotrigine should be used under physician supervision. In persons with heart, kidney, or liver disease, lamotrigine should only be used if the patient and physician determine that the benefits outweigh the risks. The dosage is usually reduced in these individuals. Lamotrigine has also been associated with the risks of developing aseptic meningitis or blood disorders.

Side effects

Side effects that occur in more than 10% of people taking lamotrigine include headache, dizziness, unsteadiness while walking, blurred vision, double vision, nausea, cold-like symptoms such as runny noses or sore throats, and infections.

Although relatively rare, any rash that develops while taking lamotrigine should be evaluated by a healthcare professional, since life-threatening rashes may occur.

Other side effects include confusion, impaired memory, **sleep disorders**, nonspecific pain all over the body, and disruption of menstrual cycles.

Interactions

Some drugs can decrease the levels of lamotrigine in the body. This may make the drug less effective; examples include **carbamazepine**, phenobarbital, primidone, phenytoin, and **valproic acid**. Valproic acid and its close relative, **divalproex sodium**, have also been reported to increase lamotrigine levels in some people, which could increase the side effects of the drug. When lamotrigine and valproic acid or divalproex sodium are used together, there is a greater chance that a serious rash may develop. Very specific dosage guidelines must be followed when these two drugs are used at the same time.

Lamotrigine may increase the levels of carbamazepine in the body, increasing adverse effects associated with carbamazepine.

An increased risk of certain side effects may occur if lamotrigine is used with drugs, such as methotrexate, that inhibit folic acid synthesis.

Resources

BOOKS

Ellsworth, Allan J., et al., eds. *Mosby's Medical Drug Reference.* St. Louis, MO: Mosby, Inc., 1999.

Facts and Comparisons Staff. *Drug Facts and Comparisons.* 6th ed. Saint Louis: Facts and Comparisons; Philadelphia: Lippincott Williams and Wilkins, 2002.

Kelly Karpa, RPh, Ph.D.

Late-life depression

Definition

Late-life depression is **depression** occurring in older individuals. Although often associated with the **stress** and physical problems attendant with advancing age, depression is not a normal part of the aging process.

Demographics

The percentage of Americans 65 years old and older who have clinical depression is significantly greater than for the general population. Whereas approximately 1% of Americans are clinically depressed, nearly 16% of those 65 years of age and older meet the criteria for clinical depression. Similarly, suicide rates for older adults are disproportionately high, particularly for white males.

A **diagnosis** of major depressive disorder is more likely in elderly patients who are also medically ill, older than 70 years of age, and hospitalized or institutionalized. Depression in the elderly is more common when there is a history of depression earlier in life, chronic physical illness, **brain** disease, alcohol abuse, or stressful life events. Elderly women are more likely to become depressed than are elderly men, and single seniors are more likely to become depressed than are those who are married. It has been estimated that as many as 15% of widowed adults will have a serious depression for a year or more after the death of their spouse.

Subsyndromal depression (depression that is clinically significant but does not meet the criteria for major depressive disorder) is more common than major depressive disorder in elderly adults. It is estimated that 15% to 50% of older adults with subsyndromal depression will develop major depressive disorder within two years. Approximately 30% of nursing home residents have subsyndromal depression. As with major depressive disorder, elders with subsyndromal depression tend to be female.

Description

Depression in the aging and the aged is a major public health problem. Many who suffer from late-life depression go undiagnosed. The insidious nature of depression in the elderly is that its symptoms are often obfuscated in the context of the multiple physical problems of many elderly people. As the body ages, it becomes less able to respond to stress and is at increased risk for disease. Disabilities resulting from external factors such as stress, **trauma**, chronic diseases, lifestyle limitations, financial factors, and isolation may accelerate the process, resulting in the symptoms we think of as defining old age. Depression, however, is not a normal part of aging, nor is it inevitable.

The symptoms of late-life depression can be the same as they are for other depressive disorders in younger people, such as **major depressive disorder**, a **bipolar disorder**, or subsyndromal depression. The individual may experience a profound and persistent feeling of sadness or despair or lose interest in things that were once pleasurable (anhedonia). Late-life depression can also exhibit itself in less obvious ways, including sleep disturbance, change in appetite, or disturbed mental functioning. In extreme cases, late-life depression can lead to **suicide**. Depression in late life, however, is treatable.

Late-life depression has a serious association with high rates of suicide. About 16% of all suicides occur in adults over age 65. These statistics suggest that late-life depression is a potentially life-threatening disorder; healthcare providers should maintain a low threshold of suspicion of this disorder in dysthymic older patients, in order to avoid missing the opportunity to intervene effectively.

Causes and symptoms

As opposed to younger individuals, older adults are more likely to have a medical condition in addition to depression. A number of medical conditions have commonly been associated with depression in the elderly. These include:

- coronary artery disease (high blood pressure, history of heart attack, coronary artery bypass surgery, congestive heart failure)
- neurologic disorders (stroke, Alzheimer's disease, Parkinson's disease, Lou Gehrig's disease, multiple sclerosis, Binswanger's disease, senile dementia)
- metabolic disturbances (diabetes, hypoglycemia, hypothyroidism, hyperthyroidism, hyperparathyroidism, Addison's disease)
- cancer (particularly of the pancreas)
- other medical conditions (chronic obstructive pulmonary disease, rheumatoid arthritis, chronic pain, sexual dysfunction, renal dialysis, chronic constipation, viral pneumonia, hepatitis, influenza)

In addition, a number of medications routinely taken by elderly patients may cause depression. These include:

- cardiovascular drugs (clonidine, digitalis, guanethidine, hydralazine, methyldopa, procainamide, propranolol, reserpine, thiazide diuretics)
- chemotherapeutics (6-azauridine, asparaginase, azathioprine, bleomycin, cisplatin, cyclophosphamide, doxorubicin, mithramycin)
- antiparkinsonian drugs (amantadine, bromocriptine, levodopa)
- antipsychotic drugs (fluphenazine, haloperidol)
- sedatives and antianxiety drugs (barbiturates, benzodiazepines, chloral hydrate, ethanol)
- anticonvulsants (carbamazepine, ethosuximide, phenobarbital, phenytoin, primidone)
- anti-inflammatory/anti-infective agents (ampicillin, cycloserine, dapsone, ethambutol, griseofulvin, isoniazid, metoclopramide, metronidazole, nalidixic acid, nitrofurantoin, nonsteroidal anti-inflammatory drugs [NSAIDs], penicillin G procaine, streptomycin, sulfonamides, tetracycline)
- stimulants (amphetamines, caffeine, cocaine, methylphenidate)
- hormones (adrenocorticotropin, anabolic steroids, glucocorticoids, oral contraceptives)
- other medications (choline, cimetidine, disulfiram, lecithin, methysergide, phenylephrine, physostigmine, ranitidine, vinblastine, vincristine)

Because of concurrent medical problems and lowered expectations for functionality, elderly patients with depression are often undiagnosed. In addition, elderly patients often are reluctant to speak about psychological symptoms and consider depression to be a normal response to the aging process. Depressed older people may not report being depressed because they have no hope that anyone will intervene. These factors can make diagnosis difficult.

Depression in older adults does not necessarily present with the same symptoms as in the younger population. Common symptoms in older people that can signify a problem with depression include:

- Unexplained physical complaints—older adults are often reluctant to discuss psychological symptoms, and as a result, symptoms of depression may be expressed in terms of a physical rather than a psychological complaint. For example, depression in older adults is often characterized by physical complaints for which no medical cause can be found, or by physical symptoms that are out of proportion to the underlying medical illness.
- Hopelessness or helplessness—in older adults, it is hopelessness, rather than sadness, that tends to be associated with thoughts of suicide. Statements such as "I wish I were dead already," "I wish I would fall asleep and not wake up," or "what's the use in trying" are cause for immediate concern and should be responded to with psychological assessment rather than platitudes or meaningless assurances that everything is all right. Talk of suicide—even in jest—should always be taken seriously
- Anxiety and worries—older adults often experience general feelings of worry and tension not associated with specific anxiety or panic disorders. Statements of anxiety and worry in older adults often are signs of depression in addition to, or instead of, an anxiety

disorder. Treatment for an anxiety disorder, however, will not treat any underlying depression.

- Memory complaints—depressed older adults may complain about memory loss with or without objective signs of cognitive impairment. Particularly when no demonstrable memory problems can be discerned by simple tests, it is important that the patient also be assessed for depression and treated accordingly.
- Loss of feeling of pleasure (anhedonia)—one common symptom of depression in older adults is the inability to experience pleasure from life and daily events. Expressions of anhedonia might include no longer deriving enjoyment from being with grandchildren; not wanting to read, listen to music, or participate in hobbies once found enjoyable; or feeling estranged from God or no longer being comforted by religion. Although it might seem that being less active and involved in life is a response to illness or decreased abilities associated with aging, research suggests that depression might, in fact, contribute to heart disease, diabetes, and arthritis.
- Slowed movement—"slowing down" is often associated with old age. However, things such as stooped posture, slowed movements, or slowed speech may also be signs of depression. In particular, depression associated with vascular disease is often expressed in such symptoms.
- Irritability—depression in older adults may also be expressed by excessive or easily provoked anger, annoyance, or impatience. Symptoms of irritability include fussiness, whining, or fretfulness even in the face of comforting. When such a pattern is persistent, assessment for depression should be considered.
- Lack of interest in personal care—depressed older adults may believe that they are "not worth the trouble" and fail to follow instructions for taking medications or dietary guidelines as a result. Similarly, depressed older adults may display such symptoms as lack of care about personal appearance—including not getting dressed, bathing, or performing other hygiene activities. Individuals displaying such symptoms should be assessed for depression.
- Other symptoms—sleep disturbance, decreased appetite, weight loss, difficulty concentrating, and fatigue are all common symptoms of late-life depression.

Diagnosis

According to the ***Diagnostic and Statistical Manual of Mental Disorders*** (*DSM-IV-TR*) of the **American Psychiatric Association**, there are nine criteria for major depressive disorder:

- depressed mood
- sleep disturbance
- lack of interest or pleasure in activities
- guilt and feelings of worthlessness
- lack of energy
- loss of concentration and difficult making decisions
- anorexia or weight loss
- psychomotor agitation or delay
- suicidal ideation (thoughts of suicide)

A diagnosis of depression requires at least five of these criteria to be present nearly every day during a two-week period, or a score of 10 or more on the **Beck Depression Inventory** (BDI) or on the **Geriatric Depression Scale**.

Significant depression in older adults does not always meet the criteria for a *DSM-IV-TR* diagnosis of depression. As a result, although depression occurs more frequently in older adults than in the general population, it often goes undiagnosed in seniors. In addition to, or instead of, the classic diagnostic symptoms, older adults may exhibit other symptoms that should be considered when diagnosing depression in older adults.

Screening of an elderly patient for depression should include an electrocardiogram (ECG), urinalysis, general blood chemistry screen, complete blood count, and determination of the levels of thyroid-stimulating hormone, vitamin B12, folate, and medication in the blood.

Treatment

Depression in elderly patients may be treated with medication and/or **psychotherapy** (including **talk therapy** and behavior therapy). Research has shown that a combination of the two treatment options is more effective than the use of medication or therapy alone. Although improvement may be seen as early as two weeks, the full effect of therapy may not be observable for several months. If the patient is having a major depressive episode, recovery may take from 6 to 12 months. This means that therapy for older adults is typically needed for longer periods of time than for the general population.

Medication for depression is generally well tolerated in older adults. Drugs used in treating depression in older adults include **selective serotonin reuptake inhibitors (SSRIs)** (**sertraline**, **fluoxetine**, **paroxetine**, **fluvoxamine**, **citalopram**, **escitalopram**), secondary tricyclic **antidepressants** (**nortriptyline**, **protriptyline**, **desipramine**, **amoxapine**), tertiary tricyclic antidepressants (**amitriptyline**, **imipramine**, **doxepin**, **trimipramine**, **clomipramine**), **monoamine oxidase inhibitors (MAOIs)** (**phenelzine**, **tranylcypromine**), and other antidepressants (**maprotiline**, **bupropion**, **trazodone**, **venlafaxine**, **nefazodone**, **mirtazapine**). As with any medication, the patient should be monitored closely to determine how well he or she is reacting to the medication. If adverse reactions occur, another medication can be tried.

Prognosis

The general prognosis for recovery from depression in older adults is good, although recovery may take longer for older adults than for the general population.

Prevention

Increasingly, it is recognized that although it is imperative to diagnose and treat depression in late life, it is equally important to prevent late-life depression in the first place. Researchers are currently investigating several models of prevention. These focus on individuals at high risk for depression in late life, including those with diseases that often occur with depression.

There are a number of steps that can be taken to help prevent depression. Eating a balanced diet and keeping regular meal times is important, particularly if one has problems with insulin or blood sugar levels. Getting regular **exercise** also helps stave off depression. If one's depression has a seasonal component, taking walks in the morning sunshine or using a light box can also help. Maintaining a regular sleep pattern is also helpful, as is avoiding drugs and alcohol. Those seniors living alone should also make an effort to widen their social support network. Research has found that making friends at a senior center is an excellent way to do this. Steps that can be taken by those who have been diagnosed and are being treated for depression include: continuing to take any antidepressant medications as prescribed until directed to stop by one's physician, and continuing with therapy even after the medications have been stopped.

Researchers are continuing to investigate depression prevention for older adults in the hope that this too-common and undiagnosed disorder can be not only successfully treated, but also prevented in the first place.

Resources

BOOKS

American Psychiatric Association. *Diagnostic and Statistical Manual of Mental Disorders*. 4th ed., text rev. Washington, DC: American Psychiatric Association, 2000.

Baldwin, Robert C., and Jane Garner. "Anxiety and Depression in Women in Old Age." In *Mood and Anxiety Disorders in Women*, edited by David J. Castle, Jayashri Kulkarni, and Kathryn M. Abel. New York: Cambridge University Press, 2006. 242–66.

Ellison, James E., and Sumer K. Verma, eds. *Depression in Later Life: A Multidisciplinary Psychiatric Approach*. London: Informa Healthcare, 2003.

Hinrichsen, Gregory A., and Kathleen F. Clougherty. *Interpersonal Psychotherapy for Depressed Older Adults*. Washington, DC: American Psychological Association, 2006.

Karel, Michele J., Suzann Ogland-Hand, and Margaret Gatz. *Assessing and Treating Late-Life Depression*. New York: Basic Books, 2002.

Roose, Steven P., and Harold A. Sackeim. *Late-Life Depression*. New York: Oxford University Press, 2004.

VandenBos, Gary R., ed. *APA Dictionary of Psychology*. Washington, DC: American Psychological Association, 2007.

PERIODICALS

Aday, Ronald H., Gayle C. Kehoe, and Lori A. Farney. "Impact of Senior Center Friendships on Aging Women Who Live Alone." *Journal of Women and Aging* 18, no. 1 (2006): 57–73.

Akpaffiong, M. J., Mark E. Kunik, and Melanie Wilson-Lawson. "Antidepressant-Associated Side Effects in Older Adult Depressed Patients." *Geriatrics* 63, no. 4 (2008): 18–23.

Beaudreau, Sherry A., and Ruth O'Hara. "The Association of Anxiety and Depressive Symptoms with Cognitive Performance in Community-Dwelling Older Adults." *Psychology and Aging* 24, no. 2 (2009): 507–12.

Braun, Ursula K., Mark E. Kunik, and Catherine Pham. "Recognizing and Managing Depression at End of Life." *Geriatrics* 63, no. 6 (2008): 25–27.

Brenes, G. A., et al. "Treatment of Minor Depression in Older Adults: A Pilot Study Comparing Sertraline and Exercise." *Aging & Mental Health* 11, no. 1 (2007): 61–68.

Carter, Janet, Joanne Rodda, and Zuzana Walker. "Depression in Older Adults." *British Medical Journal* 343, no. 7825 (2011): 683+.

Elderkin-Thompson, et al. "Executive Dysfunction and Memory in Older Patients with Major and Minor Depression." *Archives of Clinical Neuropsychology* 21, no. 7 (2006): 669–76.

Hinton, Ladson, Mark Zweifach, Sabine Oishi, Lingqi Tang, and Jürgen Unützer. "Gender Disparities in the Treatment of Late-Life Depression: Qualitative and Quantitative Findings from the IMPACT Trial." *American Journal of Geriatric Psychiatry* 14, no. 10 (2006): 884–92.

Holley, Caitlin, Stanley A. Murrell, and Benjamin T. Mast. "Psychosocial and Vascular Risk Factors for Depression in the Elderly." *American Journal of Geriatric Psychiatry* 14, no. 1 (2006): 84–90.

Karp, Jordan F., et al. "Preventing Depression in Older Adults." *Clinical Neuropsychiatry: Journal of Treatment Evaluation* 3, no. 1 (2006): 69–80. http://www.clinicalneuropsychiatry.org/pdf/07_Karp.pdf (accessed November 9, 2011).

Schoevers, Robert A., et al. "Prevention of Late-Life Depression in Primary Care: Do We Know Where to Begin?" *American Journal of Psychiatry* 163, no. 9 (2006): 1611–21.

Smit, Filip, Agnieska Ederveen, Pim Cuijpers, Dorly Deeg, Aartjan Beekman. "Opportunities for Cost-effective Prevention of Late-Life Depression: An Epidemiological Approach." *Archives of General Psychiatry* 63, no. 3 (2006): 290–96.

Szanto, Katalin, Benoit H. Mulsant, Patricia R. Houck, Mary Amanda Dew, Alexandre Dombrovski, Bruce G. Pollock, and Charles F. Reynolds III. "Emergence, Persistence, and Resolution of Suicidal Ideation During Treatment of Depression in Old Age." *Journal of Affective Disorders* 98, no. 1–2 (2007): 153–61.

Vaishnavi, Sandeep, and Warren D. Taylor. "Neuroimaging in Late-Life Depression." *International Review of Psychiatry* 18, no. 5 (2006): 443–51.

von Gunten, Armin, Panteleimon Giannakopoulos, and René Duc. "Cognitive and Demographic Determinants of Dementia in Depressed Patients with Subjective Memory Complaints." *European Neurology* 54, no. 3 (2005): 154–58.

Wilby, Frances. "Depression and Social Networks in Community Dwelling Elders: A Descriptive Study." *Journal of Gerontological Social Work* 43, no. 3 (2011): 246–59. http://dx.doi.org/10.1080/01634372.2010.540074 (accessed December 15, 2011).

Yang, Yang. "How Does Functional Disability Affect Depressive Symptoms in Late Life? The Role of Perceived Social Support and Psychological Resources." *Journal of Health and Social Behavior* 47, no. 4 (2006): 355–72.

ORGANIZATIONS

American Association for Geriatric Psychiatry, 7910 Woodmont Ave., Ste. 1050, Bethesda, MD, 20814-3004, (301) 654-7850, Fax: (301) 654-4137, http://www.AAGPonline.org.

American Psychiatric Association, 1000 Wilson Blvd., Ste. 1825, Arlington, VA, 22209-3901, (703) 907-7300, apa@psych.org, http://www.psych.org.

American Psychological Association, 750 1st Street NE, Washington, DC, 20002-4242, (202) 336-5500; TDD/TTY: (202) 336-6123, (800) 374-2721, http://www.apa.org.

Depression and Bipolar Support Alliance, 730 N Franklin Street, Ste. 501, Chicago, IL, 60654-7225, (800) 826-3632, Fax: (312) 642-7243, http://www.dbsalliance.org.

Fuqua Center for Late-Life Depression, Wesley Woods Health Center, 4th Floor, 1841 Clifton Rd. NE, Atlanta, GA, 30329, (404) 728-6948, http://www.fuquacenter.org.

Geriatric Mental Health Foundation, 7910 Woodmont Ave., Ste. 1050, Bethesda, MD, 20814, (301) 654-7850, Fax: (301) 654-4137, web@GMHFonline.org, http://www.gmhfonline.org.

National Alliance on Mental Illness, 3803 N Fairfax Drive, Ste. 100, Arlington, VA, 22203, (703) 524-7600, http://www.nami.org.

Ruth A. Wienclaw, PhD

Lavender

Definition

Lavender is the shrub-like aromatic plant, *Lavandula officinalis,* sometimes called *Lavandula vera* or true lavender.

Purpose

Lavender is a mild sedative and antispasmodic. The essential oil derived from lavender is used in **aromatherapy** to treat anxiety, difficulty sleeping, nervousness, and restlessness. Other preparations of the plant are taken internally to treat sleep disturbances, stomach complaints, loss of appetite, and as a general tonic.

Description

Lavender is a shrubby evergreen bush that grows to about 3 feet (1 m) tall and 4 feet (1.4 m) in diameter. The plant produces aromatic spiky flowers from June to September. An essential oil used for healing and in perfume is extracted from the flowers just before they open.

Lavender is native to the Mediterranean region and is cultivated in temperate regions across the world. There are many species and subspecies. The preferred lavender for medicinal use is *L. officinalis* or true lavender. In Europe lavender has been used as a healing herb for centuries. It was a prominent component of smelling salts popular with women in the late 1800s.

Lavender is used both externally and internally in healing. Externally the essential oil is used in aromatherapy as a relaxant and to improve mood. Aromatherapy can be facilitated through massage, used in the bath, placed in potpourri jars, and burned in specially designed oil burners. Lavender is also used to

Lavender plant. *(© Iurii Konoval/Shutterstock.com)*

treat **fatigue**, restlessness, nervousness, and difficulty sleeping. Pillows stuffed with lavender have been used as a sleep aid in Europe for many years. Lavender oil applied to the forehead and temples is said to ease headache.

Researchers have isolated the active compounds in lavender. The most important of these is an aromatic volatile oil. Lavender also contains small amounts of coumarins, compounds that dilate (open up) the blood vessels and help control spasms. Some modern scientific research supports the claim that lavender is effective as a mild sedative and a calming agent. In one Japanese study, people exposed to the odor of lavender were found to show less mental **stress** and more alertness than those not exposed to the fragrance when evaluated by psychological tests. In a peer-reviewed British study, when the sleeping room was perfumed with lavender, elderly nursing home residents with **insomnia** slept as well as they did when they took sleeping pills and better than they did when they were given neither sleeping pills nor exposed to lavender fragrance.

Other external uses of the essential oil of lavender are as an antiseptic to disinfect wounds. When used on wounds, lavender oil often is combined with other essential oil extracts to enhance its antiseptic and dehydrating properties. Lavender oil added to bathwater is believed to stimulate the circulation.

Taken internally as a tea made from lavender flowers or as a few drops of lavender oil on a sugar cube, this herb is used as a mild sedative and antispasmodic. The German Federal Health Agency's Commission E established to independently review and evaluate scientific literature and case studies pertaining to medicinal plants has approved the use of lavender tea or lavender oil on a sugar cube to treat restlessness and insomnia. Despite conflicting scientific claims, this organization has also endorsed the internal use of lavender for stomach upsets, loss of appetite, and excess gas. Animal research confirms that lavender oil has an antispasmodic effect on smooth muscle of the intestine and uterus. These results have not been confirmed in humans.

Recommended dosage

Lavender tea is made by steeping 1 to 2 teaspoons of flowers per cup of boiling water. One cup of tea can be drunk three times a day. Alternatively, 1 to 4 drops of lavender oil can be placed on a sugar cube and eaten once a day. Externally, a few drops of oil can be added to bath water or rubbed on the temples to treat headache. Like any herbal product, the strength of the active ingredients can vary from batch to batch, making it difficult to determine exact dosages.

Precautions

The use of lavender, either alone or in combination with other herbs, is not regulated by the U.S. Food and Drug Administration. Unlike pharmaceuticals, herbal and dietary supplements are not subjected to rigorous scientific testing to prove their claims of safety and effectiveness. The strength of active ingredients varies from manufacturer to manufacturer, and the label may not accurately reflect the contents.

Particular problems with lavender oil revolve around substitution of oil from species of lavender other than *Lavandula officinalis*, the preferred medicinal lavender. Most often true lavender oil is adulterated with less expensive lavadin oil. Lavadin oil comes from other species of lavender. It has a pleasant lavender odor, but its chemical compositions, and thus its healing actions, are different from true lavender oil. People purchasing lavender oil or tonics containing lavender should be alert to substitutions.

KEY TERM

Antispasmodic—A medication or preparation given to relieve muscle or digestive cramps.

Side effects

When used in the recommended dosage, lavender is not considered harmful. Some people have reported developing contact dermatitis (a rash) when lavender oil is used directly on the skin.

Interactions

There are no studies on interactions of lavender with conventional pharmaceuticals. Traditionally lavender has been used in combination with other herbs such as tea oil and lemon balm without adverse interactions.

Resources

BOOKS

Peirce, Andrea. *The American Pharmaceutical Association Practical Guide to Natural Medicines*. New York: William Morrow and Company, 1999.

Thomson Healthcare. *PDR for Herbal Medicines*. 4th ed. Montvale, NJ: Thomson Reuters, 2007.

Weiner, Michael, and Janet Weiner. *Herbs that Heal:Prescription for Herbal Healing*. Mill Valley, CA: Quantum Books, 1999.

WEBSITES

Brett, Jennifer. "Lavender: Herbal Remedies." Discovery Fit & Health. http://health.howstuffworks.com/wellness/natural-medicine/herbal-remedies/lavender-herbal-remedies.htm (accessed October 22, 2011).

Tish Davidson, A.M.

Lead poisoning

Definition

Lead poisoning occurs when a person swallows, absorbs, or inhales lead in any form. The result can be damaging to the **brain**, nerves, and many other parts of the body. Acute lead poisoning, which is somewhat rare, occurs when a relatively large amount of lead is taken into the body over a short period of time. Chronic lead poisoning—a common problem in children—occurs when small amounts of lead are taken in over a longer period. The U.S. Centers for Disease Control and Prevention (CDC) defines childhood lead poisoning as a whole-blood lead concentration equal to or greater than 10 micrograms/dL.

Description

Lead can damage almost every system in the human body, and it can also cause high blood pressure (hypertension). It is particularly harmful to the developing brain of fetuses and young children. The higher the level of lead in a child's blood, and the longer this elevated level lasts, the greater the chance of ill effects. Over the long term, lead poisoning in a child can lead to learning disabilities, behavioral problems, and **intellectual disability**. At very high levels, lead poisoning can cause **seizures**, coma, and even death. Most deaths are among males (74%), African Americans (67%), adults over the age of 45 (76%), and Southerners (70%).

About one out of every six children in the United States has a high level of lead in the blood, according to the Agency for Toxic Substances and Disease Registry. Many of these children are exposed to lead through peeling paint in older homes. Others are exposed through dust or soil that has been contaminated by old paint or past emissions of leaded gasoline. Since children between the ages of 12–36 months are apt to put things in their mouths, they are more likely than older children to ingest lead. Pregnant women who come into contact with lead can pass it along to the fetus.

More than 80% of American homes built before 1978 have lead-based paint in them, according to the CDC. The older the home, the more likely it is to contain lead paint and have higher concentrations of lead in the paint. Some homes also have lead in the water pipes or plumbing. People may have lead in the paint, dust, or soil around their homes or in their drinking water without knowing it, since lead can't be seen, smelled, or tasted. Because lead doesn't break down naturally, it can continue to cause problems until it is removed.

Lead poisoning and the broad issue of dangerously high levels of lead in common consumer products is an increasing concern. In 2008, the Consumer Product Safety Improvement Act was introduced, which placed new regulations on the levels of lead in consumer products.

Causes and symptoms

Before scientists knew how harmful it could be, lead was widely used in paint, gasoline, water pipes, and many other products. Today house paint is almost lead free, gasoline is unleaded, and household plumbing is no longer made with lead materials. Still, remnants of the old hazards remain. Sources of lead exposure include:

- Lead-based paint. This is the most common source of exposure to large amounts of lead among preschoolers. Children may eat paint chips from older homes that have fallen into disrepair. They may also chew on painted surfaces such as windowsills. In addition, paint may be disturbed during remodeling.
- Dust and soil. These can be contaminated with lead from old paint or past emissions of leaded gasoline. In addition, pollution from operating or abandoned industrial sites and smelters can find its way into the soil, resulting in soil contamination.
- Drinking water. Exposure may come from lead water pipes, found in many homes built before 1930. Even newer copper pipes may have lead solder. Also, some new homes have brass faucets and fittings that can leach lead.
- Jobs and hobbies. A number of activities can expose participants to lead. These include making pottery or stained glass, refinishing furniture, doing home repairs, and using indoor firing ranges. When adults take part in such activities, they may inadvertently expose children to lead residue that is on their clothing or on scrap materials.
- Food. Imported food cans often have lead solder. Lead may also be found in leaded crystal glassware and some imported ceramic or old ceramic dishes (e.g., ceramic dishes from Mexico). A 2003 study of cases of lead poisoning in pregnant women found that 70% of the patients were Hispanics, most of whom had absorbed the lead from their pottery. In addition, food may be contaminated by lead in the water or soil.
- Folk medicines. Certain folk medicines (for example, alarcon, alkohl, azarcon, bali goli, coral, ghasard, greta, liga, pay-loo-ah, and rueda) and traditional cosmetics (kohl, for example) contain large amounts of lead.
- Moonshine whiskey. Lead poisoning from drinking illegally distilled liquor is a cause of death among adults in the southern United States.
- Gunshot wounds. Toxic amounts of lead can be absorbed from bullets or bullet fragments that remain in the body after emergency surgery.

Chronic lead poisoning

New evidence suggests that lead may be harmful to children even at low levels that were once thought to be safe, and the risk of damage rises as blood levels of lead increase. The symptoms of chronic lead poisoning take time to develop. Children can appear healthy despite having high levels of lead in their blood. Over time, though, problems such as the following may arise:

- learning **disabilities**
- hyperactivity
- intellectual disability
- slowed growth
- hearing loss
- headaches

Certain **genetic factors** increase the harmful effects of lead poisoning in susceptible children; however, these factors are not completely understood.

Lead poisoning is also harmful to adults, in whom it can cause high blood pressure, digestive problems, nerve disorders, memory loss, and muscle and joint pain. In addition, it can lead to difficulties during pregnancy, as well as cause reproductive problems in men and women.

More recently, chronic exposure to lead in the environment has been found to speed up the progression of kidney disorders in patients without diabetes.

Acute lead poisoning

Acute lead poisoning, while less common, shows up more quickly and can be fatal. Symptoms such as the following may occur:

- severe abdominal pain
- diarrhea
- nausea and vomiting
- weakness of the limbs
- seizures
- coma

Diagnosis

A high level of lead in the blood can be detected with a simple blood test. In fact, testing is the only way to know for sure if children without symptoms have been exposed to lead, since they can appear healthy even as long-term damage occurs. The CDC recommends testing all children at 12 months of age and, if possible, again at 24 months. Testing should start at 6 months for children at risk for lead poisoning. Based on these test results and a child's risk factors, the doctor will then decide whether further testing is needed and how often. In some states, more frequent testing is required by law.

Children at risk

Children with an increased risk of lead poisoning include those who:

- live in or regularly visit a house built before 1978 in which chipped or peeling paint is present
- live in or regularly visit a house that was built before 1978 where remodeling is planned or underway
- have a brother or sister, housemate, or playmate that has been diagnosed with lead poisoning
- have the habit of eating dirt or have been diagnosed with pica
- live with an adult whose job or hobby involves exposure to lead
- live near an active lead smelter, battery-recycling plant, or other industry that can create lead pollution

Adults at risk

Testing is also important for adults whose job or hobby puts them at risk for lead poisoning. This includes people who take part in the following activities:

- glazed pottery or stained glass making
- furniture refinishing
- home renovation
- target shooting at indoor firing ranges
- battery reclamation
- precious metal refining
- radiator repair
- art restoration

Treatment

The first step in treating lead poisoning is to avoid further contact with lead. For adults, this usually means making changes at work or in hobbies. For children, it means finding and removing sources of lead in the home. In most states, the public health department can help assess the home and identify lead sources.

If the problem is lead paint, a professional with special training should remove it. Removal of lead paint is not a do-it-yourself project. Scraping or sanding lead paint creates large amounts of dust that can poison people in the home. This dust can stay around long after the work is completed. In addition, heating lead paint can release lead into the air. For these reasons, lead paint should only be removed by someone who knows how to do the job safely and has the equipment to clean up thoroughly. Occupants, especially children and pregnant women, should leave the home until the cleanup is finished.

KEY TERMS

Chelation therapy—Treatment with chemicals that bind to a poisonous metal and help the body pass it in urine at a faster rate.

Pica—An abnormal appetite or craving for non-food items, often such substances as chalk, clay, dirt, laundry starch, or charcoal.

Medical professionals should take all necessary steps to remove bullets or bullet fragments from patients with gunshot injuries.

Chelation therapy

If blood levels of lead are high enough, the doctor may also prescribe chelation therapy. This refers to treatment with chemicals that bind to the lead and help the body pass it in urine at a faster rate. There are four chemical agents that may be used for this purpose, either alone or in combination. Edetate calcium disodium (EDTA calcium) and dimercaprol (BAL) are given through an intravenous line or in shots, while succimer (Chemet) and penicillamine (Cuprimine, Depen) are taken by mouth. (Although many doctors prescribe penicillamine for lead poisoning, this use of the drug has not been approved by the U.S. Food and Drug Administration.)

Alternative treatment

Changes in diet are no substitute for medical treatment. However, getting enough calcium, **zinc**, and protein may help reduce the amount of lead the body absorbs. Iron is also important, since people who are deficient in this nutrient absorb more lead. Garlic and thiamine, a B-complex vitamin, have been used to treat lead poisoning in animals. However, their usefulness in humans for this purpose has not been proved. Nutritional, botanical, and homeopathic medicines can be administered once the source is removed to help correct any imbalances brought on by lead toxicity.

Prognosis

If acute lead poisoning reaches the stage of seizures and coma, there is a high risk of death. Even if the person survives, there is a good chance of permanent brain damage. The long-term effects of lower levels of lead can also be permanent and severe. However, if chronic lead poisoning is caught early, these negative effects can be limited by reducing future exposure to lead and getting proper medical treatment.

Prevention

Many cases of lead poisoning can be prevented. These steps can help:

- Keep the areas where children play as clean and dust-free as possible.
- Wash pacifiers and bottles when they fall to the floor, and wash stuffed animals and toys often.
- Make sure children wash their hands before meals and at bedtime.
- Mop floors and wipe windowsills and other chewable surfaces, such as cribs, with a damp cloth or mild soap solution.
- Plant bushes next to an older home with painted exterior walls to keep children at a distance.
- Plant grass or another ground cover in soil that is likely to be contaminated, such as soil around a home built before 1960 or located near a major highway.
- Have household tap water tested to find out if it contains lead.
- Use only water from the cold-water tap for drinking, cooking, and making baby formula, since hot water is likely to contain higher levels of lead.
- If the cold water hasn't been used for six hours or more, run it for several seconds, until it becomes as cold as it will get, before using it for drinking or cooking. The more time water has been sitting in the pipes, the more lead it may contain.
- If you work with lead in your job or hobby, change your clothes before you go home.
- Do not store food in open cans, especially imported cans.
- Do not store or serve food in pottery meant for decorative use.

Resources

BOOKS

Legge, Thomas M. *Lead Poisoning and Lead Absorption: The Symptoms, Pathology and Prevention*. Whitefish, MT: Kessinger Publishing, 2007.

PERIODICALS

Lanphear, Bruce P. "The Conquest of Lead Poisoning: A Pyrrhic Victory." *Environmental Health Perspectives* 115 (October 2007): A484–A485.

Parham, Marti. "Toy Recalls & Lead Poisoning: What Parents Need to Know." *Jet*. (September 24, 2007).

Pekkanen, John. "Poisonous Predator: Lead Is Gone from Gasoline and Paint but Continues to Pose Danger to Kids, Particularly in Older Neighborhoods." *Children's Voice Magazine* 16:4 (July–August 2007): 26(5).

Sharmer, L., K. Northrup-Snyder, and W. Juan. "Newly Recognized Pathways of Exposure to Lead in the Middle-Income Home." *Journal of Environmental Health* 70, no. 3, (October 2007): 15–9.

Sloviter, Vikki. "Lead, Lead, Everywhere, What's A Parent to Do?" *Pediatrics for Parents*. (August 2007).

Warniment, Crista. "Lead Poisoning in Children—What Parents Should Know." *Pediatrics for Parents*. (January 1, 2011).

ORGANIZATIONS

Childhood Lead Poisoning Prevention Branch, Centers for Disease Control and Prevention, 1600 Clifton Rd., Atlanta, GA, 30333, (800) 232-4636; TTY: (888) 232-6348, cdcinfo@cdc.gov, http://www.cdc.gov/nceh/lead.

Consumer Product Safety Commission, 4330 East West Highway, Bethesda, MD, 20814, (301) 504-7923, http://www.cpsc.gov.

National Lead Information Center, 422 South Clinton Ave., Rochester, NY, 14620, (1-800) 424-5323, Fax: (585) 232-3111, http://www.epa.gov.

National Safety Council, 1121 Spring Lake Drive, Itasca, IL, 60143-3201, (630) 285-1121, (800) 621-7615, Fax: (630) 285-1315, customerservice@nsc.org, http://www.nsc.org.

Linda Wasmer Smith
Ken R. Wells

Learning disorders

Definition

Learning disorders (LDs), or learning disabilities, are disorders that cause problems in speaking, listening, reading, writing, or mathematical ability in children and adults of average to above-average intelligence. These difficulties significantly interfere with academic achievement or daily living.

In the United States and Canada, LDs are considered to be neurological disorders and reflect problems with information processing in the **brain**. They are not considered to be automatic indications of low intelligence. The Learning Disabilities Association of America (LDA) states, "Learning disabilities should not be confused with learning problems which are primarily the result of visual, hearing, or motor disabilities; of intellectual disability; of emotional disturbance; or of environmental, cultural or economic disadvantages." In the United Kingdom, by contrast, the term "learning disability" is usually associated with low intelligence as well as with specific difficulties with reading, language use, mathematical calculations, or other aspects of learning.

The forthcoming fifth edition of the ***Diagnostic and Statistical Manual of Mental Disorders***, due for publication in 2013, defines four learning disorders, grouped under the general heading of neurodevelopmental disorders. The four learning disorders to be included in the *DSM-5* are:

- learning disorder
- dyslexia (reading disorder)
- dyscalculia (mathematics disorder)
- disorder of written expression

Demographics

Exact statistics for the number of people in the United States and Canada with LDs are difficult to obtain, as many of these disorders go undiagnosed. The National Center for Learning Disabilities states that 15 million children, adolescents, and adults in the United States have learning disorders, with 2.6 million school children involved in special education programs as of 2011. Other sources estimate that LDs occur in approximately 5% to 10% of the North American population. According to the National Institute of Neurological Disorders and Stroke (NINDS), between 8% and 10% of American youngsters below 18 years of age have some type of learning disability.

Between 50% and 70% of LDs are classified as dyslexia; the remaining 30% to 50% fall under the categories of **disorder of written expression**, dyscalculia, or atypical LD. One estimate for disorder of written expression is 6% of the school-age population in Canada and the United States, with another 6% diagnosed with dyscalculia. The statistics can be confusing, however, because it is possible for someone to have more than one learning disorder; in one study, 56% of children with a **reading disorder** also showed poor mathematics achievement, and 43% of children with a mathematical learning disorder showed poor reading skills.

LDs are more common in males than females by a 2:1 or 4:1 ratio. Children with LDs have an increased risk for emotional-behavioral problems and comorbidity; 50% of the 1.6 million children with **attention deficit hyperactivity disorder (ADHD)** have an LD. Approximately 2% to 8% of elementary school children have dyslexia. Speech disorder occurs in approximately 10% of children younger than eight years of age. ADHD is a comorbid condition that occurs in approximately four million school-aged children; 20% of them are unable to focus their attention on required tasks in school and at home.

Dyslexia rates in the United States do not show any racial or ethnic differences.

U.S. children (ages 3–17) thought to have a learning disability[1], by selected characteristics: 2010

	Number of children interviewed[2]	Number of children with a learning disability	Percent
Total (age adjusted)	**61,655**	**4,838**	**7.9%**
Gender			
Male	31,519	2,917	9.3%
Female	30,137	1,921	6.4%
Age			
3–4 years	8,443	267	3.2%
5–11 years	28,666	2,291	8.0%
12–17 years	24,546	2,280	9.3%
Race			
One race	59,155	4,598	7.8%
White	46,607	3,532	7.6%
Black or African American	9,106	904	10.0%
American Indian or Alaska Native	541	*57	*10.2%
Asian	2,746	95	3.5%
Native Hawaiian or other Pacific Islander	155	†	†
Two or more races	2,500	240	9.3%
Black or African American and white	1,082	142	11.5%
American Indian or Alaska Native and white	425	*40	*10.6%

[1]Based on the question, "Has a representative from a school or a health professional ever told you that [child's name] had a learning disability?"
[2]All numbers in thousands
*Estimates preceded by an asterisk had a relative standard error between 30% and 50% and should be used with caution, as they do not meet standards of reliability or precision.
†Estimates had a relative standard error greater than 50% and were not included.

SOURCE: National Center for Health Statistics, U.S. Centers for Disease Control and Prevention, "Summary Health Statistics for U.S. Children: National Health Interview Survey, 2010," *Vital and Health Statistics* 10, no. 250 (December 2011).

(Table by PreMediaGlobal. © 2012 Cengage Learning.)

Some LDs are more common in North America than in other parts of the world. The incidence of dyscalculia among American children is higher than in Japanese, German, or French children.

Description

A learning disability, or specific developmental disorder, is a disorder that inhibits or interferes with the skills of learning; that is, people's abilities to store, process, or produce information. Under federal law, public schools in the United States consider a child to be learning disabled if his or her level of academic achievement is two or more years below the standard for age and IQ level. The term *learning disorder* was first used in the 1960s to describe learning difficulties in

A learning disorder makes reading and writing a challenge. *(© Will & Deni McIntyre/Science Source/Photo Researchers, Inc.)*

individuals of at least average intelligence whose academic achievement lagged significantly behind their expected potential. It was assumed that some type of central nervous dysfunction was responsible for the discrepancy.

It is important to note that although learning disorders can be classified into subtypes, they are actually a group of disorders with varying characteristics. In addition, there are wide variations in the severity and development of LDs that are unique to each individual diagnosed with a learning disorder. Some experts in the field classify LDs by the specific type of mental processing difficulty that the affected person has rather than whether it appears in reading, writing, or mathematics. Processing difficulties can be identified as affecting input, integration, memory, and output. Any of these processing difficulties could affect a person's ability to read, write, or perform mathematical calculations.

- Input refers to a person's ability to take in information through the senses; for example, to distinguish between similarly shaped letters or similar sounds in spoken language.
- Integration refers to a person's ability to make sense of inputs; that is, to place information obtained through the senses in a logical sequence, organize the information, and make sense of it.
- Memory refers to a person's ability to store information in their short-term, long-term, or working memory so that they can retrieve the information when it is needed.
- Output refers to the person's ability to express what has been integrated and stored, either through language or through motor activity like writing, drawing, or making gestures.

Risk factors

Risk factors for learning disorders include a range of factors that can affect the structure of the brain, its functioning, or both. Some are congenital (present at birth), while others have to do with genetic influences and the family environment. Known risk factors include:

- Fetal alcohol syndrome.
- Prenatal exposure to the mother's cigarette smoking or use of cocaine.
- Family history of learning disorders. LDs are known to run in families. According to the Institute for Behavioral Genetics at the University of Colorado, there is a 36% to 45% heritability of reading disorders in some families.
- History of delayed early language development.
- Being diagnosed with ADHD. Many pediatricians recommend that all children with ADHD should be screened for learning disorders.
- Male sex. Some doctors attribute the higher rate of LDs in boys to abnormally high levels of the male sex hormone testosterone during fetal development, particularly between the sixteenth and twenty-fourth weeks of pregnancy.

Causes and symptoms

The causes of learning disorders are not completely understood. While certain areas of the brain are definitely known to be associated with dyslexia, the structural or functional causes of other learning disorders are still being researched. The Colorado Learning Disabilities Research Center (CLDRC) was conducting five separate research projects as of 2011 involving pairs of identical twins in which at least one twin had either an LD or ADHD. DNA analysis of the twins and their parents was being conducted as well as measurements of the affected twin's response to treatment. The CLDRC researchers were hoping to discover whether there are definite **genetic factors** involved in learning disorders, and whether reading disabilities represent a single syndrome or a group of disorders with several subtypes.

Dyslexia

Modern research techniques have demonstrated that dyslexia is the result of brain deficits in processing sound units and sound-symbol relationships. The cause of dyslexia has been identified as variations in the right temporoparietal-occipital region of the brain, specifically in structures known as the "angular gyrus" and "corpus callosum." The angular gyrus is involved in mathematical as well as language skills, which may explain the connection between dyslexia and dyscalculia. In addition, the left temporo-occipital region, which is active during the automatic perception and processing of visually presented words in skilled readers, is implicated in reading problems. Activity in this region is necessary for rapid perception of word forms.

Genetic studies have identified 8 genetic defects associated with dyslexia as of 2011, with another 20 genetic conditions characterized by normal intelligence combined with reading difficulties in those affected. In addition, the heritability of dyslexia may be higher than 50%, especially in a disorder with a focal deficit in phonologic processing (phonologic dyslexia). Family studies indicate that dyslexia is found in clusters in families and probably reflects an autosomal dominant mode of transmission. Some genetic investigations have identified possible genes for dyslexia located on chromosomes 6 and 15; as of 2011, there were 14 genes identified as candidates.

Most people diagnosed with dyslexia have average or higher intelligence. Persons with dyslexia often have trouble spelling. Affected individuals have difficulty with phonologic processing, which means that they have deficits in identifying and manipulating individual sounds (phonemes) within larger sound units (morphemes and words). The symptoms of dyslexia usually appear before the early school grades. Patients cannot translate a visual stimulus (letters) into a meaningful blend of sounds. Reading is slower and more mechanical, even with treatment. The increased concentration required during reading can impair the person's ability to pay attention. A somewhat less common cause of dyslexia is visualization-comprehension deficits. Persons with visualization-comprehension weakness often exhibit difficulty visualizing what is being read.

Dyscalculia

The cause of dyscalculia is thought to be a nonverbal weakness. There may be deficits visualizing and visually organizing mathematical concepts and manipulations; one recently proposed theory holds that children with dyscalculia are less precise in working with the approximate number system (an intuitive "number sense" of the comparative magnitude and relationships among numbers). Some researchers have identified as many as 16 separate skills required in learning mathematics, including memorizing facts (such as the multiplication tables); recalling those facts; understanding details; mastering procedures that must be carried out in a particular sequence (such as solving a problem in plane geometry); recognizing patterns; and accumulating knowledge over time. Mathematics is a cumulative discipline that requires students to build on what they have learned in lower grades. Some persons diagnosed with dyscalculia may have short-term or working memory deficits that can interfere with processing mathematical calculations. In addition, children who also have dyslexia will have considerable difficulty with the

KEY TERMS

CAPD—Central auditory processing disorder, the inability to differentiate, recognize, or understand sounds; hearing and intelligence are normal.

Comorbidity—The presence of one or more diseases or disorders in addition to a primary disease or disorder.

Dyscalculia—Difficulty in performing mathematical computations. It is also called "mathematical learning disorder."

Dysgraphia—A writing disorder characterized by illegible handwriting.

Dyslexia—Unexpected difficulty learning to read despite adequate intelligence, motivation, and educational opportunities.

Incidence—A measurement of the risk of developing a specific disease or disorder within a given time period in a specific population.

IQ—Intelligence quotient, or a measure of the intelligence of an individual based on the results of a written test.

Morpheme—The smallest meaningful speech sound.

Motivational therapy—An approach to treatment for learning disorders that emphasizes problem-solving skills, the ability to set and attain goals, and ways to counteract negative thinking and poor self-image.

Phoneme—The smallest detectable sound within a spoken word.

Phonics—A system to teach reading by teaching the speech sounds associated with single letters, letter combinations, and syllables.

Response to intervention (RTI)—An approach to diagnosis of learning disorders based on a child's response (or lack of response) to early interventions with learning problems.

word problems that are a staple of mathematics instruction in the middle and upper grades. Last, some children have difficulty with mathematics because they are afraid of the subject. The child's anxiety may be related either to difficulty acquiring specific mathematical skills or to fear of humiliation in class.

The symptoms of dyscalculia vary but are usually apparent during the early grade-school years. Some children may show weakness in one particular area, such as counting, but perform adequately in other areas of mathematics. Patients can exhibit either great difficulty or complete inability (known as "acalculia") to perform mathematical calculations.

Disorder of written expression

The causes of disorder of written expression (DWE) were unknown as of 2011. It is relatively unusual for this disorder to appear by itself without dyslexia, dyscalculia, or both. In some persons, DWE may be due to deficits in visual-motor integration and motor coordination. Most causes of DWE occur because there are deficits in the brain concerning information translation from auditory-oral modality to visual-written modality. DWE is usually diagnosed around the time the child is in second or third grade.

Patients with DWE often exhibit spelling deficits that include problems with punctuation, grammar, and development of written ideas. Writing samples from affected persons are typically brief, simple, and difficult to comprehend because of the large number of errors in grammar and punctuation. Patients with visual-motor deficits write with so much care that they often lose track of ideas and thoughts. If motor coordination is the only cause of the problem, then the person's symptoms may be classified more appropriately as a motor skills disorder, not a DWE. The symptoms of DWE are not usually apparent until the third or fourth grade, when written academic work demands the development of ideas.

Diagnosis

In order to meet the criteria established by the **American Psychiatric Association** (APA) for these various diagnoses, the child's skills in these areas must be significantly below those of his or her peers on standardized tests (taking age, schooling, and level of intelligence into account), and the disorders must significantly interfere with academic achievement and/or daily living. **Diagnosis** can be a complex process, however, because there is no universal agreement concerning the magnitude of discrepancy between test scores. There is no consensus concerning which test scores should be analyzed to obtain a statistical analysis of discrepancy. Tests should be administered to establish that low intelligence alone is not the cause of underachievement.

A newer approach to diagnosis is known as response to intervention or RTI. RTI is a treatment model intended to identify children at risk for an LD at an early point, before they meet the full *DSM* criteria for a learning disorder. It is considered an alternative to the discrepancy model for evaluating children with learning difficulties, which has sometimes been criticized as the "wait-to-fail" model. RTI is characterized by early **intervention**, frequent progress measurement, and increasingly intensive research-based instructional interventions for children who continue to have difficulties in learning. Children who respond to early intervention will not require further interventions. Those who do not respond adequately to regular classroom instruction and a more intensive intervention are considered nonresponders. These students can then be referred for further educational assistance through special education programs. One drawback to RTI, however, is that the early interventions must be competently carried out; otherwise, children may be evaluated as nonresponders to treatment and as having a learning disorder when the real cause is poor instruction. Another criticism of RTI is that it is a covert form of school budget management that functions to limit access to expensive special education services by delaying the diagnosis of children who need them.

Examination

A child thought to have a learning disorder should undergo a complete medical examination to rule out an eye disorder, hearing loss, or other organic cause. If a medical problem is not found, a psychoeducational assessment should be performed by a **psychologist**, **psychiatrist**, neurologist, neuropsychologist, or learning specialist. A complete medical, family, social, and educational history is compiled from existing medical and school records and from interviews with the child and the child's parents and teachers. In the case of children suspected of having DWE, it is important to evaluate the child's posture, handedness, pencil grip, and other traits to rule out possible problems related to slow motor development or other physical disorders affecting the hand and wrist.

Tests

A series of written and verbal tests are given to the child to evaluate his or her cognitive and intellectual functioning. Commonly used tests include the Wechsler

Intelligence Scale for Children (WISC-III), the Woodcock-Johnson Psychoeducational Battery, the Peabody Individual Achievement Test-Revised (PIAT-R), and the California Verbal Learning Test (CVLT). Specific tests used to evaluate disorders of written expression include the Test of Early Written Language, for children between 3 and 11 years of age; the Test of Written Language, for children between 7 and 18 years of age; and the Test of Written Spelling, for children between the ages of 6 and 18 years. Federal legislation mandates that all these tests be given free of charge within the public school system.

Treatment

Treatment for a learning disorder is highly individualized. It depends on the specific disorder, the age of the person at the time of diagnosis, the severity of the disorder, the presence of ADHD or other comorbidity, and the assumed underlying cause. For example, people with central auditory processing disorder (CAPD), a common underlying cause of some learning disorders that is centered on a person's inability to process heard language correctly, may undergo therapy with a speech-language pathologist. Other experts may use different kinds of auditory therapies to improve the person's ability to process heard language.

Once a learning disorder has been diagnosed, an individual education plan (IEP) is developed for the child in question. IEPs are based on psychoeducational test findings. They provide for annual testing to measure a child's progress. Students with learning disorders may receive special instruction within a regular general education class, or they may be taught in a special education or learning center for a portion of the day.

Traditional

The treatment team for a child diagnosed with an LD typically includes school counselors, education specialists, specialists in learning disorders, school psychologists, or clinical psychologists with advanced clinical training in administration and interpretation of psychological tests, or psychometrics. Tests for achievement and intelligence should be administered and interpreted by a clinical psychologist or school psychologist. Only a duly licensed or certified clinical or school psychologist can administer the recommended psychological tests. A full written report of results and interpretation of results is typically prepared and submitted to concerned persons.

DYSLEXIA. Common strategies for the treatment of dyslexia focus first on improving a child's recognition of the sounds of letters and language through phonics training. Later strategies focus on comprehension, retention, and study skills. Treatment for affected persons involves intensive tutoring to develop phonologic processing and fluent word reading with treatment objectives that emphasize comprehension. There are several treatment approaches (the Gillingham-Stillman Approach, the Fernald-Keller Approach, or the Lindamood-Bell Reading Program) that provide intensive phonic practice and phonic associations with sensory integration or mnemonic strategies to remember letter-sound blends and relationships.

It is important for parents of a child diagnosed with dyslexia to understand that the disorder is not related to the visual system but is caused by defects in the development of the language processing areas of the brain. Thus, bifocals, eye muscle exercises, or other forms of visual training will not help children with dyslexia.

DYSCALCULIA. Treatment for dyscalculia can vary widely because the disorder may have a variety of causes and presentations, particularly if the child also has dyslexia or ADHD. The treatment program is typically highly individualized. Flash cards and practice drills can help children to memorize simple mathematical operations such as multiplication tables. Dyscalculia due to visual-organization deficits can be treated with visualization techniques to improve math-related skills. Instruction for students with mathematical disorders also emphasizes such real-world uses of mathematics as balancing a checkbook or comparing prices.

Children with dyscalculia may be helped by motivational therapy and investigation of the role of anxiety or phobia in their difficulties with mathematics. New approaches to treatment for dyscalculia are being researched, because the disorder is not yet understood as well as dyslexia or disorders or written expression. There was one clinical study under way as of 2011 investigating transcranial stimulation as a potential treatment for dyscalculia.

DISORDER OF WRITTEN EXPRESSION. There are several treatment plans for DWE, including: writing in more natural environments, for example, keeping a diary and making lists; writing notes and outlines before writing prose; and talking-to-writing progression, which involves the affected child dictating while another person writes down what is dictated. As this latter treatment progresses, the roles are gradually reversed until the child is able to dictate and write without assistance. Treatment continues with dictation made more quiet and discreet until the child is independently thinking and writing. Treatment interventions for atypical LDs involve objectives to expand on the child's strengths and to provide additional experience and practice in nonverbal weakness areas. Students with disorders of written expression are often encouraged to keep journals and to write on a computer keyboard instead of using a pencil; however, most experts maintain that children with DWE should use computers and other assistive technology to complement handwritten exercises rather than relying on them to eliminate handwriting completely.

Other forms of therapy that benefit children with DWE are coaching in basic study skills; the use of child-friendly templates (outlines) to help children structure and sequence their thoughts and ideas before writing their story or essay; and teaching children to think of writing as a process with five parts based on the word "POWER," which stands for "plan, organize, write, edit, and revise." Motivational therapy, which teaches children problem-solving strategies, goal setting, and modifying or eliminating negative beliefs that interfere with academic achievement, is also helpful to those diagnosed with DWE.

Drugs

There are no medications that can treat or cure learning disorders. Some medications, such as stimulants or **antidepressants**, may be prescribed for children with ADHD, **depression**, or other comorbid disorders. These drugs may be effective in helping the child learn by enhancing his or her ability to pay attention and concentrate in school, or in coping with anxiety or depression associated with the LD.

Alternative

There are no alternative therapies that claim to cure learning disorders; however, nutritional therapy and some forms of **relaxation therapy** may be helpful to children and adults during mainstream treatment. Some older children or adolescents may also benefit from **meditation**, which helps in focusing the mind and learning to shut out distractions.

Prognosis

The prognosis for learning disorders depends in part on early diagnosis. However, learning disabilities do persist across the lifespan. The prognosis is highly individualized; some persons with more than one LD, or with an LD in addition to ADHD, may fail to complete high school; the high-school dropout rate for children with learning disabilities is almost 40%. On the other hand, some people diagnosed with LDs may have a single isolated disability that has little effect on their day-to-day functioning.

Children with learning disabilities that go undiagnosed or are improperly treated might never achieve functional literacy. They often develop serious behavioral problems as a result of their frustration with school; in addition, their learning problems are often stressful for other family members and may strain family relationships. The keys to helping these students reach their fullest potential are early detection and the implementation of an appropriate individualized education plan. The prognosis is good for a large percentage of children with reading disorders that are identified and treated early. Learning disorders continue into adulthood, but with proper educational and vocational training, an individual can complete college and pursue a challenging career. Studies of the occupational choices of adults with dyslexia indicate that they do particularly well in such people-oriented professions and occupations as nursing or sales.

QUESTIONS TO ASK YOUR DOCTOR

- How can I tell whether my child has an LD?
- Some of my relatives have been diagnosed with dyslexia. Does that mean that my child will have a reading disorder, too?
- Why are boys more likely to develop LDs than girls?
- What is your opinion of RTI as an approach to learning disorders?
- What are the chances that a child diagnosed with an LD will have a second LD or ADHD?

Prevention

Some learning disorders are potentially preventable if women of childbearing age avoid alcohol, **cocaine**, and tobacco during pregnancy. However, LDs related to heredity and structural abnormalities of the brain are not preventable.

Resources

BOOKS

Burack, Jacob A., et al., eds. *The Oxford Handbook of Intellectual Disability and Development*, 2nd ed. New York: Oxford University Press, 2011.

Goldstein, Sam, Jack A. Naglieri, and Melissa DeVries, eds. *Learning and Attention Disorders in Adolescence and*

Adulthood: Assessment and Treatment, 2nd ed. Hoboken, NJ: John Wiley and Sons, 2011.

Hoover, John J. *Differentiating Learning Differences from Disabilities: Meeting Diverse Needs through Multi-tiered Response to Intervention*. Upper Saddle River, NJ: Pearson, 2009.

Parks, Peggy J. *Learning Disabilities*. San Diego, CA: ReferencePoint Press, 2010.

Pennington, Bruce Franklin. *Diagnosing Learning Disorders: A Neuropsychological Framework*, 2nd ed. New York: Guilford Press, 2009.

PERIODICALS

Annett, M. "Dyslexia and Handedness: Developmental Phonological and Surface Dyslexias Are Associated with Different Biases for Handedness."*Perceptual and Motor Skills* 112 (April 2011): 417–425.

Butterworth, B., et al. "Dyscalculia: From Brain to Education." *Science* 332 (May 27, 2011): 1049–1053.

Duff, F.J., and P.J. Clarke. "Practitioner Review: Reading Disorders: What Are the Effective Interventions and How Should They Be Implemented and Evaluated?" *Journal of Child Psychology and Psychiatry, and Allied Disciplines* 52 (January 2011): 3–12.

Kupfer, D.J., and D.A. Regier. "Neuroscience, Clinical Evidence, and the Future of Psychiatric Classification in DSM-5." *American Journal of Psychiatry* 168 (July 2011): 672–674.

Mazzocco, M.M., et al. "Impaired Acuity of the Approximate Number System Underlies Mathematical Learning Disability (Dyscalculia)." *Child Development* 82 (July-August 2011): 1224–1237.

Miller, B., and P. McCardle. "Moving Closer to a Public Health Model of Language and Learning Disabilities: The Role of Genetics and the Search for Etiologies." *Behavior Genetics* 41 (January 2011): 1–5.

Miller, C.A. "Auditory Processing Theories of Language Disorders: Past, Present, and Future." *Language, Speech, and Hearing Services in Schools* 42 (July 2011): 309–319.

Poelmans, G., et al. "A Theoretical Molecular Network for Dyslexia: Integrating Available Genetic Findings." *Molecular Psychiatry* 16 (April 2011): 365–82.

Willcutt, E.G., et al. "Understanding the Complex Etiologies of Developmental Disorders: Behavioral and Molecular Genetic Approaches." *Journal of Developmental and Behavioral Pediatrics* 31 (September 2010): 533–544.

WEBSITES

American Psychiatric Association. DSM-5 Development. "Neurodevelopmental Disorders." http://www.dsm5.org/proposedrevision/pages/neurodevelopmentaldisorders.aspx (accessed September 26, 2011).

International Dyslexia Association (IDA). "Frequently Asked Questions about Dyslexia." http://www.interdys.org/FAQ.htm (accessed September 27, 2011).

Learning Disabilities Association of America (LDA). "LD Basics." http://www.ldaamerica.org/aboutld/parents/ld_basics/index.asp (accessed September 27, 2011).

Medscape. "Learning Disorder, Mathematics." http://emedicine.medscape.com/article/915176-overview (accessed September 28, 2011).

Medscape. "Learning Disorder, Written Expression." http://emedicine.medscape.com/article/1835883-overview (accessed September 28, 2011).

Medscape. "Reading Learning Disorder." http://emedicine.medscape.com/article/1835801-overview (accessed September 27, 2011).

National Center for Learning Disabilities (NCLD). "LD Explained." http://www.ncld.org/ld-basics/ld-explained (accessed September 27, 2011).

National Institute of Neurological Disorders and Stroke (NINDS). "Learning Disabilities Information Page." http://www.ninds.nih.gov/disorders/learningdisabilities/learningdisabilities.htm (accessed September 27, 2011).

Nemours. "Learning Disabilities." TeensHealth.org. http://teenshealth.org/teen/diseases_conditions/learning/learn ing_disabilities.html (accessed January 12, 2012).

ORGANIZATIONS

American Psychiatric Association (APA), 1000 Wilson Boulevard, Suite 1825, Arlington, VA, 22209-3901, (703) 907-7300, apa@psych.org, http://www.psych.org.

American Speech-Language-Hearing Association (ASHA), 2200 Research Boulevard, Rockville, MD, 20850-3289, (301) 296-5700, Fax: (301) 296-8580, (800) 638-8255, http://www.asha.org.

Colorado Learning Disabilities Research Center (CLDRC), Institute for Behavioral Genetics, 1480 30th St., Boulder, CO, 80303, (303) 492-7362, Fax: (303) 492-8063, info@ibg.colorado.edu, http://ibgwww.colorado.edu/cldrc.

International Dyslexia Association (IDA), 40 York Rd., 4th Floor, Baltimore, MD, 21204, (410) 296-0232, Fax: (410) 321-5069, http://www.interdys.org ContactUs.htm, http://www.interdys.org.

Learning Disabilities Association of America (LDA), 4156 Library Road, Pittsburgh, PA, 15234–1349, (412) 341-1515, Fax: (412) 344-0224, http://www.ldanatl.org/contact/contact.cfm, http://www.ldanatl.org.

National Center for Learning Disabilities (NCLD), 381 Park Avenue South, Suite 1401, New York, NY, 10016, (212) 545-7510, Fax: (212) 545-9665, (888) 575-7373, ncld@ncld.org, http://www.ncld.org.

National Institute on Deafness and Other Communication Disorders (NIDCD) Information Clearinghouse, 1 Communication Avenue, Bethesda, MD, 20892-3456, Fax: (301) 770-8977, (800) 241-1044, nidcdinfo@ nidcd.nih.gov, http://www.nidcd.nih.gov.

National Institute of Neurological Disorders and Stroke (NINDS), PO Box 5801, Bethesda, MD, 20824, (301) 496-5751, (800) 352-9424, http://www.ninds.nih.gov.

Emily Jane Willingham, Ph.D.
Rebecca J. Frey, Ph.D.

Lexapro *see* **Escitalopram**
Librax *see* **Chlordiazepoxide**
Librium *see* **Chlordiazepoxide**
Lidone *see* **Molindone**

Light therapy

Definition

Light therapy, or phototherapy, is the administration of doses of bright light in order to treat a variety of sleep and mood disorders. It is most commonly used to reregulate the body's internal clock and relieve **depression**.

Purpose

Light therapy is most often prescribed to treat **seasonal affective disorder**, a form of depression resulting from shortened daylight hours in northern latitudes from the late fall to the early spring. It is also occasionally employed to treat such sleep-related disorders as **insomnia** and jet lag. Recently, light therapy has also been found effective in the treatment of nonseasonal forms of depression, including the depressive symptoms of **bipolar disorder**. One study found that bright light reduced depressive symptoms 12%–35% more than a placebo treatment in 9 out of 10 randomized controlled trials.

When used to treat SAD or other forms of depression, light therapy has several advantages over prescription **antidepressants**. Light therapy tends to work faster than medications, alleviating depressive symptoms within 2 to 14 days after beginning light therapy as opposed to an average of 4 to 6 weeks with medication. And unlike antidepressants, which can cause a variety of side effects from nausea to concentration problems, light therapy is extremely well tolerated. Some side effects are possible with light but are generally not serious enough to cause discontinuation of the therapy.

A woman uses a sun lamp to treat seasonal affective disorder. *(© Jochem Wijnands/Picture Contact BV/Alamy)*

There are several other different applications for light therapy, including:

- Full-spectrum/UV light therapy for disorders of the skin. A subtype of light therapy that is often prescribed to treat skin diseases, rashes, and jaundice.
- Cold laser therapy. The treatment involves focusing very low-intensity beams of laser light on the skin and is used in laser acupuncture to treat a myriad of symptoms and illnesses, including pain, stress, and tendinitis.
- Colored light therapy. In colored light therapy, different colored filters are applied over a light source to achieve specific therapeutic effects. The colored light is then focused on the patient, either with a floodlight which covers the patient with the colored light, or with a beam of light that is focused on the area of the illness.
- Back-of-the-knee light therapy. According to a 1998 study published in the journal *Science*, the area behind the human knee known as the popliteal region contains photoreceptors that can help to adjust the body's circadian rhythms. The authors of the study found that they could manipulate circadian rhythms by focusing a bright light on the popliteal region. Further studies are underway to determine the efficacy of this treatment on disorders such as SAD, although there have been cases of treating pain with this method.

Description

Light therapy is generally administered at home. The most commonly used light therapy equipment is a portable lighting device known as a light box. The light box may be a full-spectrum box, in which the lighting element contains all wavelengths of light found in natural light (including UV rays), or it may be a bright light box, in which the lighting element emits non-UV white light. The box may be mounted upright to a wall or slanted down toward a table.

The patient sits in front of the box for a prescribed period of time (anywhere from 15 minutes to several hours). For patients just starting on the therapy, initial sessions are usually only 10–15 minutes in length. Some patients with SAD undergo light therapy sessions two or three times a day, others only once. The time of day and number of times treatment is administered depends on the physical needs and lifestyle of the individual patient. If

KEY TERMS

Dawn simulation—A form of light therapy in which the patient is exposed while asleep to gradually brightening white light over a period of an hour and a half.

Lux—The International System (IS) unit for measuring illumination, equal to one lumen per square meter.

Neurotransmitter—A chemical in the brain that transmits messages between neurons, or nerve cells.

Seasonal affective disorder (SAD)—A mood disorder characterized by depression, weight gain, and sleepiness during the winter months. An estimated 4%–6% of the population of Canada and the northern United States suffers from SAD.

Serotonin—A neurotransmitter that is involved in mood disorders.

light therapy has been prescribed for the treatment of SAD, it typically begins in the fall and continues throughout the winter and possibly into the early spring. Patients with a long-standing history of SAD are usually able to establish a timetable or pattern to their depressive symptoms and can initiate treatment accordingly before symptoms begin.

The light from a slanted light box is designed to focus on the table it sits upon, so patients may look down to read or do other sedentary activities during therapy. Patients using an upright light box must face the light source and should glance toward the box occasionally without staring directly into the light. The light sources in these light boxes typically range from 2,500–10,000 lux (in contrast, average indoor lighting is 300–500 lux; a sunny summer day is about 100,000 lux).

Patients can purchase their own light boxes for a few hundred dollars, or they may be able to rent them from a healthcare provider or healthcare supply company. Renting gives patients the opportunity to have a trial run of the therapy before making the investment in a light box. Recently, several new light box products have become available, in addition to the traditional boxes. Dawn simulators are lighting devices or fixtures that are programmed to turn on gradually, from dim to bright light, to simulate the sunrise. They are sometimes prescribed for individuals who have difficulty getting up in the morning due to SAD symptoms. Another device known as a light visor is designed to give an individual more mobility during treatment. The visor is a lighting apparatus that is worn like a sun visor around the crown of the head. Patients with any history of eye problems should consult their healthcare professional before attempting to use a light visor.

Precautions

Patients with eye problems should see an ophthalmologist regularly both before and during light therapy. Because UV rays are emitted by the light box, patients taking photosensitizing medications should consult with their healthcare provider before beginning treatment. In addition, patients with medical conditions that make them sensitive to UV rays should also be seen by a healthcare professional before starting phototherapy.

Patients beginning light therapy for SAD may need to adjust the length, frequency, and timing of their phototherapy sessions in order to achieve the maximum benefits. Patients should keep their healthcare provider informed of their progress and the status of their depressive symptoms. Occasionally, additional treatment measures for depression (e.g., antidepressants, herbal remedies, **psychotherapy**) may be recommended as an adjunct, or companion, treatment to light therapy.

Preparation

Full-spectrum light boxes do emit UV rays, so patients with sun-sensitive skin should apply sunscreen before sitting in front of the box for an extended period of time.

Risks

Some patients undergoing light therapy treatments report side effects of eyestrain, headaches, insomnia, **fatigue**, sunburn, and dry eyes and nose. Most of these effects can be managed by adjusting the timing and duration of the light therapy sessions. A strong sunblock and eye and nose drops can alleviate the others. Long-term studies have shown no negative effects to eye function of individuals undergoing light therapy treatment.

A small percentage of light therapy patients may experience **hypomania**, a feeling of exaggerated, hyperelevated mood. Again, adjusting the length and frequency of treatment sessions can usually manage this side effect.

Research and general acceptance

Light therapy is widely accepted by both traditional and complementary medicine as an effective treatment for SAD. The exact mechanisms by which the treatment

QUESTIONS TO ASK YOUR DOCTOR

- Can I use phototherapy while I am taking antidepressants?
- Has bright-light phototherapy been proven to be effective in easing symptoms of seasonal affective disorder?
- What is the correct way to use the lights?

works are not known, but the bright light employed in light therapy may help readjust the body's circadian rhythms, or internal clock. Other popular theories are that light triggers the production of **serotonin**, a neurotransmitter believed to be associated with depressive disorders, or that it influences the body's production of melatonin, a hormone related to circadian rhythms. A recent British study suggests that dawn simulation, in which the patient is exposed to white light of gradually increasing brightness (peaking at 250 lux after 90 min), may be even more effective in treating depression than exposure to bright light. Dawn simulation is typically started around 4:30 or 5 A.M., while the patient is still asleep.

Training and certification

Psychiatrists, psychologists, and other mental healthcare professional prescribe light therapy treatment for SAD. There are also Holistic healthcare professionals and light therapists who specialize in this treatment; in some states, these professionals require a license, so individuals should check with their state board of health to ensure their practitioner has the proper credentials.

Resources

BOOKS

Lam, Raymond W., and Edwin M. Tam. *A Clinician's Guide to Using Light Therapy*. Cambridge: Cambridge University Press, 2009.

Rosenthal, N.E. *Winter Blues: Everything You Need to Know to Beat Seasonal Affective Disorder*. New York: Guilford Press, 2006.

PERIODICALS

Even, C., et al. "Efficacy of Light Therapy in Nonseasonal Depression: A Systematic Review." *Journal of Affective Disorders* 108 (May 2008): 11–23.

Lurie, S.J., et al. "Seasonal Affective Disorder." *American Family Physician* 74 (November 1, 2006): 1521–24.

Sit, D., et al. "Light Therapy for Bipolar Disorder: A Case Series in Women." *Bipolar Disorders* 9, no. 8 (2007): 918–27.

ORGANIZATIONS

National Depressive and Manic Depressive Association, 730 Franklin Street, Suite 501, Chicago, IL, 60610, (800) 826-3632, http://www.ndmda.org.

Society for Light Treatment and Biological Rhythms, 824 Howard Ave., New Haven, CT, 60610.sltbrinfo@gmail.com, http://www.sltbr.org.

Paula Ford-Martin
Rebecca J. Frey, PhD
Heidi Splete

Limbic system *see* **Brain**

Lisdexamfetamine

Definition

Lisdexamfetamine (sold under the brand name Vyvanse) is a medication used to treat **attention deficit hyperactivity disorder (ADHD)**. It belongs to the class of drugs known as central nervous system (CNS) stimulants and acts on the neurological signaling chemicals norepinephrine and **dopamine**. Norepinephrine and dopamine are types of neurotransmitter involved in normal **brain** function and have an effect on mood, concentration, and impulse control.

Purpose

Lisdexamfetamine is used to treat some of the symptoms of **ADHD** in both adults and children six years old and older. It is a CNS stimulant that improves memory, concentration, and impulse control, and belongs

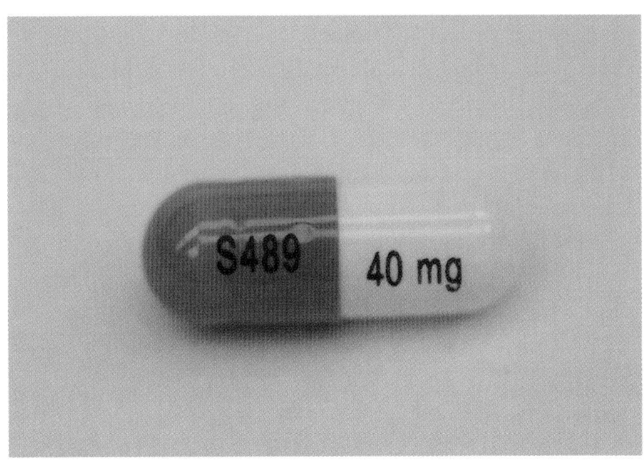

Vyvanse (lisdexamfetamine), 40 mg. *(© Custom Medical Stock Photo, Inc. Reproduced by permission.)*

to the category of drug that remains the mainstay of ADHD therapy. Lisdexamfetamine acts as a prodrug, meaning that the chemical compound present in the swallowed pill is metabolized and altered to another, active drug, once inside the body. Lisdexamfetamine is the inactive prodrug for the active compound **dextroamphetamine**, a compound that acts to treat ADHD. The prodrug compound is used in treatment because this formulation is thought to extend the period of time the drug is effective. The active compound only starts working as the prodrug is metabolized, creating a longer lasting effect. Proper metabolism to the active stimulant requires absorption to the bloodstream from the gastrointestinal (GI) tract and metabolism by the liver. This means no stimulant effect would be gained from injecting the drug directly into the bloodstream, bypassing the GI route that accesses the liver. The required route of administration as well as the delay to metabolism and time of effect also decreases the potential for abuse compared to other types of stimulant medication. The extended effective time mainly removes the need for re-dosing through the school or work day. It is used for patients for whom this is a priority.

Description

After it is taken, lisdexamfetamine is converted to the active compound dextroamphetamine within the body, which has a therapeutic mechanism of action focused on the natural body chemicals norepinephrine and dopamine. Norepinephrine and dopamine are types of neurotransmitter in the nervous system, chemicals that neurons use to signal to one another for normal brain and body functioning. **Neurotransmitters** bind to chemical receptors on the surface of neurons (brain cells). Once bound to a receptor, they affect physiological processes, including mood, concentration, and impulse control. Neurotransmitter reuptake inhibitors such as dextroamphetamine (lisdexamfetamine) decrease the absorption of norepinephrine and dopamine by neuron one, allowing more of the neurotransmitters to be present in the brain. It is believed that a decrease of norepinephrine and dopamine contributes to ADHD. When dextroamphetamine increases the amounts of norepinephrine and dopamine left in the brain, it has an impact on the areas of the brain that involve attention span, judgment, response to external stimuli, memory, motor function, mental focus, and impulse control.

Recommended dosage

Lisdexamfetamine is given as an oral medication in pill form, taken once each morning. It is available in doses that range from 20 to 70 mg. Patients are frequently reassessed for the need for treatment, as drugs for ADHD are avoided unless absolutely necessary. The dose chosen depends on individual patient response to the medication regarding its effectiveness, and individual patient response to the medication regarding side effects. Patients are dosed at the lowest possible effective dose to avoid the development of adverse side effects. Slowly increasing the dose helps with minimizing side effects. The usual dose of lisdexamfetamine in both adults and children six years old and older is 30 mg taken once a day. The dose is increased by 10 or 20 mg increments every week for a maximum of 70 mg a day as needed. Doses are lowered if side effects become intolerable.

Precautions

Lisdexamfetamine reactions vary from patient to patient, with some patients more sensitive to the medication and the development of side effects. Higher doses increase the risk of adverse events, hence the lowest dose possible is used for treatment. Clinicians weigh the potential for benefit with lisdexamfetamine treatment against the potential undesirable outcomes when making treatment decisions.

Lisdexamfetamine has a high potential for abuse and should never be used for longer time periods or at higher doses than prescribed. Patients are often given "drug holidays"—for example, when school is over for the summer—during which they forgo medication to avoid the development of adverse effects. Caution is used in patients with a history of **substance abuse**. Lisdexamfetamine causes a withdrawal syndrome when stopped abruptly and needs to be tapered off.

There is an association between ADHD and **Tourette syndrome**. Patients with Tourette syndrome typically have involuntary movements or vocalizations known as tics. Patients who have Tourette syndrome with ADHD may find that the stimulant medications used to treat ADHD worsen their tics. Caution must be used in treating patients with motor tics, Tourette syndrome, or a family history of the disorder. Lisdexamfetamine may not be appropriate for use in these patients. Rare but serious reactions include severe elevations in blood pressure, heart arrhythmias, heart attack, **stroke**, **seizures**, toxic skin reactions, and sudden death. Some patients develop increased aggressiveness, **psychosis**, mania, or suicidality in the first weeks of use. Children are especially at risk for these behavioral side effects. Patients taking lisdexamfetamine are monitored closely for behavioral changes, especially when starting treatment or after dose changes. Growth retardation may occur with prolonged use.

Lisdexamfetamine may be contraindicated or may require caution in use in patients with high blood pressure, blood vessel disease, heart rhythm abnormalities, heart

KEY TERMS

Bipolar disorder—Psychiatric mood disorder characterized by periods of manic behavior that may alternate with periods of depression, also known as manic depressive disorder.

Dopamine—A type of neurotransmitter involved in regulation of concentration, impulse control, judgment, mood, attention span, psychostimulation, and disease states such as addiction, ADHD, and depression.

Glaucoma—Condition involving increased pressure within the eye that may cause damage and blindness.

Mania—Physiological state of hyperactivity experienced by patients with certain psychiatric illnesses involving inappropriate elevated mood, pressured speech, poor judgment, and sometimes psychotic episodes superimposed on the state of mania.

Monoamine oxidase inhibitors (MAOIs)—Type of antidepressant medication that affects various kinds of neurotransmitters including serotonin.

Neurotransmitter—One of a group of chemicals secreted by a nerve cell (neuron) to carry a chemical message to another nerve cell, often as a way of transmitting a nerve impulse. Examples of neurotransmitters include acetylcholine, dopamine, serotonin, and norepinephrine.

Norepinephrine—A type of neurotransmitter involved in regulation of concentration, impulse control, judgment, mood, attention span, psychostimulation, and disease states such as ADHD and depression.

Prodrug—The inactive form of a drug that is metabolized into an active compound inside the body.

Tic—Involuntary movements (such as twitching or facial grimacing) or vocalizations (such as throat clearing or barking) associated with Tourette syndrome.

Tourette syndrome—An inherited neuropsychiatric disorder characterized by the development of both motor and vocal tics. The tics are preceded by a feeling of tension or urgency in the affected individual until the tic behavior is performed and relieves the perceived feeling of tension.

conditions or structural abnormalities, certain thyroid disorders, liver function impairment or liver disease, kidney function impairment, or glaucoma. Lisdexamfetamine may lower seizure threshold in some patients and may not be appropriate for use in patients with seizure disorder. Cardiac function, heart rate, and blood pressure may be monitored while taking lisdexamfetamine. Lisdexamfetamine is discouraged from use in patients with **bipolar disorder**, as it is more likely to induce a state of mania in these individuals than in those without bipolar disorder. Lisdexamfetamine is classified as category C for pregnancy, which means either there are no adequate human or animal studies; or that adverse fetal effects were found in animal studies, but there is no available human data. The decision whether to use category C drugs in pregnancy is generally based on weighing the critical needs of the mother against the risk to the fetus. Other lower category agents are used whenever possible. There are data that suggest lisdexamfetamine is considered unsafe for use during breastfeeding.

Side effects

Lisdexamfetamine has many side effects in addition to the intended treatment effect. Sensitivity to lisdexamfetamine varies between patients, and some patients may find even lower doses are more than their body system can tolerate. Common reactions include rash, fever, sweating, dizziness, **insomnia**, anxiety, restlessness, mood swings, abdominal pain, nausea and vomiting, decreased appetite, weight loss, changes in blood pressure, tremor, dry mouth, diarrhea, tic exacerbation, shortness of breath, and visual disturbances.

Interactions

Patients should make their doctor aware of all medications and supplements they are taking before using lisdexamfetamine. Using alcohol while taking lisdexamfetamine may create toxic reactions in the body and should be avoided. Patients taking drugs that affect the liver may alter the metabolism of lisdexamfetamine, resulting in too little or too much of the drug in the body. Other drugs may also cause serious effects when used in combination with lisdexamfetamine, such as serious heart rhythm abnormalities, excess nervous system stimulation, or blood pressure changes. Such medica-tions and substances include caffeine, marijuana derivatives, the obesity drug sibutramine, some migraine medications such as ergotamines, and decongestants such as phenylephrine.

QUESTIONS TO ASK YOUR DOCTOR

- Can I take the full dose right away or do I need to slowly increase the dose?
- Can I stop taking the medication right away or do I need to slowly decrease the dose?
- Should I eat when taking this medication?
- What time of day should I take this medication?
- How long should I take this medication before I am reassessed?
- Will this medication interact with any of my other prescription medications? Over-the-counter drugs?
- What are the side effects I should watch for?
- Can I drink alcoholic beverages in the same time frame as taking this medication?

Use of the antipsychotic **pimozide** with lisdexamfetamine increases the risk of motor tics as a side effect of medication. Use of certain other antipsychotics such as **fluphenazine** increase risk of psychosis. Antacids and the glaucoma and diuretic drug acetazolamide decrease the excretion of lisdexamfetamine and its metabolites from the body and may cause toxic levels. Many **antidepressants** interact with lisdexamfetamine, as well. The antidepressant **bupropion** increases the risk of seizures when used with lisdexamfetamine, and **venlafaxine** may cause greater than expected weight loss when used with lisdexamfetamine. A class of antidepressants known as **monoamine oxidase inhibitors (MAOIs)** increase the amount of norepinephrine and dopamine released into the brain and should not be used concurrently with lisdexamfetamine or its metabolites, as the combination may cause overstimulation of the central nervous system and toxicity. A patient switching from an MAOI to lisdexamfetamine will need to stop taking the MAOI for at least two weeks before starting treatment with lisdexamfetamine (and vice versa). Many herbal supplements also interact with lisdexamfetamine and may cause toxicity, including green tea and **ginseng**.

Resources

BOOKS

Brunton, Laurence L., et al. *Goodman and Gilman's The Pharmacological Basis of Therapeutics*. 12th ed. New York: McGraw Hill Medical, 2011.

Stargrove, Mitchell Bebel, et al. *Herb, Nutrient, and Drug Interactions: Clinical Implications and Therapeutic Strategies*. St. Louis: Mosby, 2007.

ORGANIZATIONS

American College of Neuropsychopharmacology, 5034-A Thoroughbred Lane, Brentwood, TN, 37027, (615) 324-2360, Fax: (615) 523-1715, acnp@acnp.org, http://www.acnp.org/default.aspx.

American Psychiatric Association, 1000 Wilson Blvd., Ste. 1825, Arlington, VA, 22209-3901, (703) 907-7300, apa@psych.org, http://www.psych.org.

American Society for Clinical Pharmacology and Therapeutics, 528 N Washington St., Alexandria, VA, 22314, (703) 836-6981, info@ascpt.org, http://www.ascpt.org.

Mental Health America, 2000 N Beauregard St., 6th Fl., Alexandria, VA, 22311, (703) 684-7722, (800) 969-6642, Fax: (703) 684-5968, http://www.nmha.org.

Maria Eve Basile, PhD

Lithium carbonate

Definition

Lithium is a naturally occurring element that is classified as an antimanic drug. It is available in the United States under the brand names Eskalith, Lithonate, Lithane, Lithotabs, and Lithobid. It is also sold under its generic name.

Purpose

Lithium is commonly used to treat mania and bipolar **depression** (manic depression). Less commonly, lithium is used to treat certain mood disorders, such as

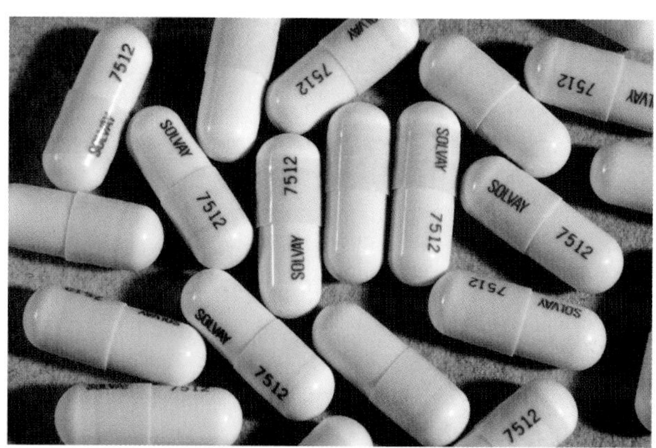

Lithium carbonate. *(© Phil Degginger/Alamy)*

schizoaffective disorder and aggressive behavior and emotional instability in adults and children. Rarely is lithium taken to treat depression in the absence of mania. When this is the case, it is usually taken in addition to other antidepressant medications.

Description

Lithium was first noted as a possible treatment for depression in the 1880s, and in the 1950s it was seen to improve the symptoms of bipolar disease. The way lithium works in the body is unclear, but its therapeutic benefits are probably related to its effects on electrolytes such as sodium, potassium, magnesium, and calcium. Lithium is taken either as lithium carbonate tablets or capsules or as lithium citrate syrup.

The therapeutic effects of lithium may appear slowly. Maximum benefit is often not evident for at least two weeks after starting the drug. People taking lithium should be aware of this and should continue taking the drug as directed even if they do not see immediate changes in mood.

Lithium is available in 300 mg tablets and capsules, 300 mg and 450 mg sustained-release tablets, and a syrup containing approximately 300 mg per teaspoonful.

Recommended dosage

Depending on the patient's medical needs, age, weight, and kidney function, doses of lithium can range from 600 to 2,400 mg per day, although most patients will be stabilized on 600 to 1,200 mg per day. Patients who require large amounts of lithium often benefit from the addition of another antimanic drug, which may allow the dose of lithium to be lowered.

Generally, lithium is taken two or three times daily. However, the entire dose may be taken at once if the physician believes that a single-dose program will increase patient **compliance**. The single-dose schedule is especially helpful for people who are forgetful and may skip doses on a multiple-dose schedule. Additionally, evidence indicates that once-daily doses are associated with fewer side effects.

More than with any other drugs used in the treatment of mental disorders, it is essential to maintain lithium blood levels within a certain narrow range to derive the maximum therapeutic benefit while minimizing serious negative side effects. It is important that patients have their blood levels of lithium measured at regular intervals.

Precautions

Because lithium intoxication may be serious and even life-threatening, blood concentrations of lithium should be measured weekly during the first four weeks of therapy and less often after that.

Patients taking lithium should have their thyroid function monitored and should maintain an adequate sodium (salt) and water balance. Lithium should not be used, or should be used only with very close physician supervision, in patients with kidney impairment, heart disease, and other conditions that affect sodium balance. Dosage reduction or complete discontinuation may be necessary during infection, diarrhea, vomiting, or a prolonged fast. Patients who are pregnant, breast-feeding, over age 60, or taking diuretics ("water" pills) should discuss the risks and benefits of lithium treatment with their doctors before beginning therapy. Lithium should be discontinued 24 hours before a major surgery, but it may be continued normally for minor surgical procedures.

Side effects

Tremor is the most common neurological side effect. Lithium tremor is an irregular, nonrhythmic twitching of the arms and legs that is variable in both intensity and frequency. Lithium-induced tremors occur in approximately half of people taking this medication. The chance of tremors decreases if the dose is reduced. Acute lithium toxicity (poisoning) can result in neurological side effects, ranging from confusion and coordination impairment, to coma, **seizures**, and death. Other neurological side effects associated with lithium therapy include lethargy, memory impairment, difficulty finding words, and loss of creativity.

About 30% to 35% of patients experience excessive thirst and urination, usually due to the inability of the kidneys to retain water and sodium. However, lithium is not known to cause kidney damage.

Lithium inhibits the synthesis of thyroid hormone. About 10% to 20% of patients treated with lithium develop some degree of thyroid insufficiency, but they usually do not require supplementation with thyroid hormone tablets.

Gastrointestinal side effects include loss of appetite, nausea, vomiting, diarrhea, and stomach pain. Weight gain is another common side effect for patients receiving long-term treatment. Changes in saliva flow and enlargement of the salivary glands may occur. An increase in tooth cavities and the need for dental care among patients taking lithium has been reported.

Skin reactions to lithium are common but usually can be managed without discontinuing lithium therapy. Lithium may worsen folliculitis (inflammation of hair follicles), psoriasis, and acne. Thinning of the hair may occur, and, less commonly, hair loss may be experienced. Swollen feet are an uncommon side effect that responds to dose reduction.

Electrocardiographic abnormalities may occur with lithium therapy, but significant cardiovascular effects are uncommon except as the result of deliberate or accidental overdose.

A mild-to-moderate increase in the number of white blood cells is a frequent side effect of lithium use. Conversely, lithium may slow the formation of red blood cells and cause anemia.

Increased risk of fetal cardiovascular disease may be associated with the use of lithium during pregnancy, especially during the first trimester (first three months). For this reason, pregnant women should discontinue lithium use until the second or third trimester and should receive alternative treatments for their mania.

Interactions

Patients taking lithium should always be concerned that other medications they are taking may adversely interact with it; patients should consult their physician or pharmacists about these interactions. The following list represents just some of the medications that lithium may interact with to either (a) increase or decrease the effectiveness of the lithium or (b) increase or decrease the effectiveness of the other drug:

- angiotensin-converting enzyme inhibitors such as captopril, lisinopril, or enalapril
- nonsteroidal anti-inflammatory drugs such as ibuprofen or naprosyn
- diuretics (water pills) such as hydrochlorothiazide, furosemide, or ethacrynic acid
- asthma drugs such as theophylline and aminophylline
- anticonvulsants such as phenytoin and carbamazepine
- calcium channel blockers such as verapamil or diltiazem
- muscle relaxants such as methocarbamol, carisoprodol, and cyclobenzaprine
- metronidazole, a commonly prescribed antibiotic used to treat infections
- antidiabetic therapy
- amiodarone, an antiarrhythmic drug
- antacids containing sodium bicarbonate
- antidepressants

Resources

BOOKS

American Society of Health-System Pharmacists. *AHFS Drug Information 2002*. Bethesda: American Society of Health-System Pharmacists, 2002.

Preston, John D., John H. O'Neal, and Mary C. Talaga. *Handbook of Clinical Psychopharmacology for Therapists*. 4th ed. Oakland, CA: New Harbinger Publications, 2004.

PERIODICALS

Baldessarini, Ross J., Maurizio Pompili, and Leonardo Tondo. "Suicide in Bipolar Disorder: Risks and Management." *CNS Spectrums* 11, no. 6 (June 2006): 465–71.

Baldessarini, Ross J., et al. "Decreased Risk of Suicides and Attempts During Long-Term Lithium Treatment: A Meta-Analytic Review." *Bipolar Disorders* 8, no. 5, part 2 (Oct. 2006): 625–39.

De Fruyt, Jürgen, and Koen Demyttenaere. "Bipolar (Spectrum) Disorder and Mood Stabilization: Standing at the Crossroads?" *Psychotherapy and Psychosomatics* 76, no. 2 (Jan. 2007): 77–88.

El-Mallakh, Rif, et al. "Bipolar II Disorder: Current and Future Treatment Options." *Annals of Clinical Psychiatry* 18, no. 4 (Oct.–Dec). 2006: 259–66.

Eyer, Florian, et al. "Lithium Poisoning: Pharmacokinetics and Clearance During Different Therapeutic Measures." *Journal of Clinical Psychopharmacology* 26, no. 3 (June 2006): 325–30.

Gonzalez-Pinto, Ana, et al. "Suicidal Risk in Bipolar I Disorder Patients and Adherence to Long-Term Lithium Treatment." *Bipolar Disorders* 8, no. 5, part 2 (Oct. 2006): 618–24.

Kellner, Charles H., et al. "Continuation Electroconvulsive Therapy vs Pharmacotherapy for Relapse Prevention in Major Depression." *Archives of General Psychiatry* 63, no. 12 (Dec. 2006): 1337–44.

Livingstone, Callum, and Hagen Rampes. "Lithium: A Review of Its Metabolic Adverse Effects." *Journal of Psychopharmacology* 20, no. 3 (May 2006): 347–55.

McElroy, Susan L., et al. "Antidepressants and Suicidal Behavior in Bipolar Disorder." *Bipolar Disorders* 8, no. 5, part 2 (Oct. 2006): 596–617.

Ozcan, Mehmet Erkan, Geetha Shivakumar, and Trisha Suppes. "Treating Rapid Cycling Bipolar Disorder with Novel Medications." *Current Psychiatry Reviews* 2, no. 3 (Aug. 2006): 361–69.

Patel, Nick C., et al. "Lithium Treatment Effects on Myo-Inositol in Adolescents with Bipolar Depression." *Biological Psychiatry* 60, no. 9 (Nov. 2006): 998–1004.

Singh, Jaskaran B., and Carlos A. Zarate, Jr. "Pharmacological Treatment of Psychiatric Comorbidity in Bipolar Disorder: A Review of Controlled Trials." *Bipolar Disorders* 8, no. 6 (Dec. 2006): 696–709.

Jack H. Raber, Pharm.D.
Ruth A. Wienclaw, PhD

Lithobid *see* **Lithium carbonate**

Lithonate *see* **Lithium carbonate**

Lithotabs *see* **Lithium carbonate**

Living wills *see* **Advance directives**

Lobotomy *see* **Psychosurgery**

Lorazepam

Definition

Lorazepam, a mild tranquilizer in the class of drugs known as **benzodiazepines**, is sold in the United States under the brand names Alzapam, Ativan, or Loraz. It is also available generically.

Purpose

Lorazepam is used for management of anxiety, nausea and vomiting, **insomnia**, and **seizures** (the injectable form). It is also used prior to surgery to produce sedation, sleepiness, drowsiness, relief of anxiety, and a decreased ability to recall the events surrounding the surgery.

Description

Lorazepam is a member of the benzodiazepine family. Benzodiazepines primarily work by enhancing the function of a certain naturally occurring **brain** chemical, gamma-aminobutyric acid (GABA), which is responsible for inhibiting the transmission of nervous impulses in the brain and spinal cord. At the same time, the enhancement of GABA in the brain decreases symptoms associated with anxiety. Lorazepam differs from drugs such as **diazepam** (Valium) and **chlordiazepoxide** (Librium) in that it is shorter-acting and does not accumulate in the body after repeated doses.

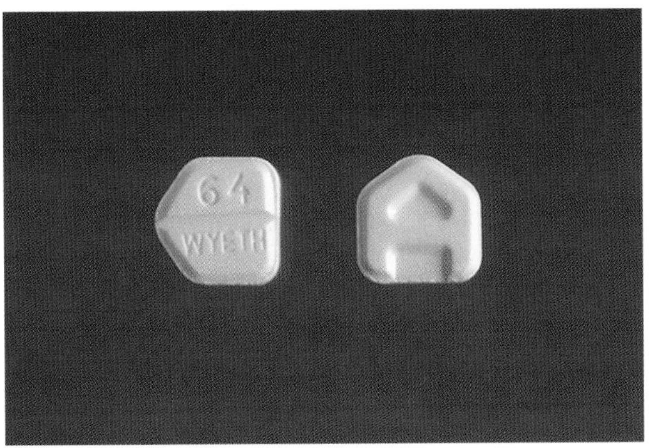

Ativan (lorazepam), 5 mg. *(U.S. Drug Enforcement Administration)*

Lorazepam is available in 0.5 mg, 1 mg, and 2 mg tablets and in an injectable form.

Recommended dosage

Lorazepam is taken several times daily by mouth, or injected, to treat anxiety. Dosage ranges from 1–2 mg taken either every 12 or every eight hours. The maximum daily total dosage for anxiety is 10 mg given in two to three divided doses. For sleep, patients may take from 2 to 4 mg at bedtime. Doses taken before surgery range from 2.5 to 5 mg.

Between 0.5 mg and 1 mg of lorazepam may be taken every six to eight hours to help control treatment-related nausea and vomiting (nausea and vomiting that occur as a side effect of a drug or medical treatment). Two mg of lorazepam are often given half an hour before chemotherapy to help prevent stomach upset. An additional 2 mg may be taken every four hours as needed.

The usual dose to treat seizures is 4 mg given intravenously (through a vein). This dose may be increased to 8 mg in patients who do not respond to the 4 mg dose.

Precautions

Lorazepam, like other drugs of this type, can cause physical and psychological dependence. Patients should not increase the dose or frequency of this drug on their own, nor should they suddenly stop taking this medication. Instead, when stopping the drug, the dosage should gradually be decreased, and then discontinued. If the drug is stopped abruptly, patients may experience agitation, irritability, difficulty sleeping, convulsions, and other withdrawal symptoms.

Patients who are allergic to benzodiazepines should not take lorazepam. Those with narrow-angle glaucoma, pre-existing **depression** of the central nervous system, severe uncontrolled pain, or severe low blood pressure should not take lorazepam. This drug should be used with caution in patients with a history of drug abuse. Children under age 12 should not take lorazepam. Children between the ages of 12 and 18 may take the drug by mouth but not intravenously. Pregnant women and those trying to become pregnant should not take lorazepam. This drug has been associated with damage to the developing fetus when taken during the first three months of pregnancy. Patients taking this drug should not breastfeed. Lorazepam has also been associated with the risk of developing anterograde **amnesia**.

Side effects

Drowsiness and sleepiness are common and expected effects of lorazepam. Patients should not drive,

KEY TERMS

Anterograde amnesia—The inability to form new memories.

Benzodiazepines—A class of drugs that have a hypnotic and sedative action, used mainly as tranquilizers to control symptoms of anxiety.

operate machinery, or perform hazardous activities that require mental alertness until they have a sense of how lorazepam will affect their alertness. Patients over age 50 may experience deeper and longer sedation after taking lorazepam. These effects may subside with continued use or dosage reduction.

The effects of an injection may impair performance and driving ability for 24–48 hours. The impairment may last longer in older patients and those taking other central nervous system depressants, such as some pain medication.

Lorazepam may also make patients feel dizzy, weak, unsteady, or clumsy. Less frequently, they may feel depressed, disoriented, nauseous, or agitated while taking this drug. Other side effects include headache, difficulty sleeping, rash, yellowing eyes, vision changes, and hallucinations. Redness and pain may occur at the injection site.

Patients may experience high or low blood pressure and difficulty in breathing after an injection of lorazepam. Nausea, vomiting, dry mouth, and constipation may also occur. The patient's sex drive may decrease, but this side effect is reversible once the drug is stopped. Patients should alert their physician to confusion, depression, excitation, nightmares, impaired coordination, changes in personality, changes in urinary pattern, chest pain, heart palpitations, or any other side effects.

Interactions

Alcohol and other central nervous system depressants can increase the drowsiness associated with this drug. Some over-the-counter medications depress the central nervous system. The herbal remedies **kava kava** and **valerian** may increase the effects of lorazepam. Patients should check with their doctors before starting any new medications while taking lorazepam. People should not drink alcoholic beverages when taking lorazepam and for 24–48 hours before receiving an injection prior to surgery.

Resources

BOOKS

Lacy, Charles F. *Drug Information Handbook with International Trade Names Index*. Hudson, OH: Lexi-Comp, Inc. 2011.

Preston, John D., John H. O'Neal, and Mary C. Talaga. *Handbook of Clinical Psychopharmacology for Therapists*. 5th ed. Oakland, CA: New Harbinger Publications, 2008.

PERIODICALS

Giersch, Anne, et al. "Impairment of Contrast Sensitivity in Long-Term Lorazepam Users." *Psychopharmacology* 186, no. 4 (July 2006): 594–600.

Hung, Yi-Yung, and Tiao-Lai Huang. "Lorazepam and Diazepam Rapidly Relieve Catatonic Features in Major Depression." *Clinical Neuropharmacology* 29, no. 3 (May–June 2006): 144–47.

Izaute, M., and E. Bacon. "Effects of the Amnesic Drug Lorazepam on Complete and Partial Information Retrieval and Monitoring Accuracy." *Psychopharmacology* 188, no. 4 (November 2006): 472–81.

Kamboj, Sunjeev K., and H. Valerie Curran. "Neutral and Emotional Episodic Memory: Global Impairment After Lorazepam or Scopolamine." *Psychopharmacology* 188, no. 4 (November 2006): 482–88.

Pomara, Nunzio, et al. "Dose-Dependent Retrograde Facilitation of Verbal Memory in Healthy Elderly After Acute Oral Lorazepam Administration." *Psychopharmacology* 185, no. 4 (May 2006): 487–94.

Verster, Joris C., Dieuwke S. Veldhuijzen, and Edmund R. Volkerts. "Is It Safe to Drive a Car When Treated with Anxiolytics? Evidence from On-the-Road Driving Studies During Normal Traffic." *Current Psychiatry Reviews* 1, no. 2 (June 2005): 215–25.

Yacoub, Adee, and Andrew Francis. "Neuroleptic Malignant Syndrome Induced by Atypical Neuroleptics and Responsive to Lorazepam." *Neuropsychiatric Disease and Treatment* 2, no. 2 (February 2006): 235–40.

Debra Wood, RN
Ajna Hamidovic, Pharm.D.
Ruth A. Wienclaw, PhD

Loss *see* **Bereavement; Grief**

Loxapine

Definition

Loxapine is a prescription-only drug used to treat serious mental, nervous, and emotional disorders. Loxapine is sold under the brand name Loxitane in the United States. It is also available in generic form.

Purpose

Loxapine is used to treat a variety of mental disorders including anxiety, mania, **depression**, and psychotic disorders.

KEY TERMS

Extrapyramidal symptoms—A group of side effects associated with antipsychotic medications and characterized by involuntary muscle movements, including contraction and tremor.

Mania—A mood disorder in which a person experiences prolonged elation or irritability characterized by overactivity that can lead to exhaustion and medical emergencies.

Description

Loxapine is in the class of drugs known as *antipsychotic agents.* The exact mode of action of loxapine has not been precisely determined, but this drug has a tranquilizing effect on patients with anxiety, mania, and other psychotic disorders. It is known that loxapine reduces the amount of **dopamine** transmitted within the **brain**. Loxapine is available in 5, 10, 25, and 50 mg tablets.

Recommended dosage

Loxapine is available in oral solution, capsules, tablets, and injectable form. The typical starting dose for adults and children over the age of 16 years is 10 mg given two to four times daily. The maximum range after the initial period is between 60 mg and 100 mg given two to four times daily. After a period of time, the dose is usually lowered to 20–60 mg per day, given in divided doses. Injections are usually given only during the initial phase and are delivered into muscle (IM) in doses ranging from 12.5 mg to 50 mg every four to six hours until a desired level of response is reached. Then, the patient is usually put on the oral (PO) form for maintenance therapy. Guidelines for use in people under the age of 16 have not been established.

Precautions

People taking loxapine should not stop taking this medication suddenly. The dosage should be gradually decreased over time. Loxapine should not be combined with other agents that depress the central nervous system, such as antihistamines, alcohol, tranquilizers, sleeping medications, and seizure medications. Loxapine can cause the skin to become more sensitive to the sun. People taking this drug should use sunscreen with a skin protection factor (SPF) greater than 15.

Loxapine is typically not administered to people who are in a severe drug-induced state or a coma. People with a history of **seizures**, heart disease, prostate enlargement, glaucoma, or chronic obstructive pulmonary disorder should receive loxapine only after careful evaluation. Guidelines for use in children under the age of 16 years have not been established. Loxapine should not be used by women who are pregnant, trying to become pregnant, or breast-feeding. Babies born to mothers who took loxapine during pregnancy may develop extrapyramidal symptoms (EPS) and withdrawal symptoms, including agitation, trouble breathing, and difficulty feeding.

Like other antipsychotic medications, loxapine carries a warning regarding use in elderly people with **dementia**, who suffer from an increased risk of death during treatment. The reason for the increase was unclear in studies, but most deaths were found to be related to either cardiovascular complications or complications associated with infection. Loxapine is not approved by the U.S. Food and Drug Administration for the treatment of behavior problems in older adults with dementia.

Side effects

Rare side effects, which must be reported immediately to a doctor, include seizures, breathing difficulties, irregular heartbeat, significant changes in blood pressure, increased sweating, severe stiffness, extreme weakness, and unusually pale skin. Patients who experience these symptoms should stop using the medication immediately, as these symptoms are considered emergencies. More common, but less serious, side effects include uncontrolled movement of the arms or legs, lip smacking, unusual movements of the tongue, puffing of the cheeks, and uncontrolled chewing movements. These symptoms should also be reported to a doctor immediately.

More common, and even less serious, side effects include difficulty in speaking or swallowing, restlessness, stiffness of arms and legs, trembling, and loss of balance. These symptoms also need to be reported to a doctor. Less common, and not especially significant, side effects include urination problems, muscle spasms, skin rash, and severe constipation. Rare, and not particularly serious, side effects include uncontrolled twisting and movement of the neck, fever, sore throat, unusual bleeding, yellowing of the eyes or skin, and changes in facial expression.

Overdose symptoms include significant drowsiness, severe dizziness, significant breathing difficulties, severe weakness, trembling muscles, and severe uncontrolled movements.

Interactions

Loxapine should not be combined with anticholinergic drugs because of the potential of decreased antipsychotic effects. Loxapine should not be combined with bromocriptine, because the combination can decrease the effectiveness of bromocriptine in patients with pituitary tumors. The combination of loxapine with lithium significantly increases the toxicity of both drugs. Likewise, loxapine and **lorazepam** should not be combined, because the combination of the two has produced very low blood pressure, severe drowsiness, and respiratory depression in rare cases.

Resources

BOOKS

Consumer Reports and American Society of Health-System Pharmacists. *Consumer Reports Complete Drug Reference.* Yonkers, NY: Consumers Reports, 2009.

Ellsworth, Allan J., et al. *Mosby's Medical Drug Reference.* St. Louis, MO: Mosby, 2007.

Preston, John D., John H. O'Neal, and Mary C. Talaga. *Handbook of Clinical Psychopharmacology for Therapists.* 5th ed. Oakland, CA: New Harbinger Publications, 2008.

PERIODICALS

Bourin, Michel, Olivier Lambert, and Bernard Guitton. "Treatment of Acute Mania—From Clinical Trials to Recommendations for Clinical Practice." *Human Psychopharmacology: Clinical and Experimental* 20, no. 1 (January 2005): 15–26.

Janowsky, David S., et al. "Minimally Effective Doses of Conventional Antipsychotic Medications Used to Treat Aggression, Self-Injurious and Destructive Behaviors in Mentally Retarded Adults." *Journal of Clinical Psychopharmacology* 25, no. 1 (February 2005): 19–25.

Reinblatt, Shauna P., et al. "Advanced Pediatric Psychopharmacology: Loxapine Treatment in an Autistic Child with Aggressive Behavior: Therapeutic Challenges." *Journal of Child and Adolescent Psychopharmacology* 16, no. 5 (October 2006): 639–43.

Mark Mitchell, MD
Ruth A. Wienclaw, PhD

Loxitane *see* **Loxapine**

LSD *see* **Hallucinogens and related disorders**

Ludiomil *see* **Maprotiline**

Luria-Nebraska Neuropsychological Battery

Definition

The Luria-Nebraska Neuropsychological Battery, also known as LNNB or Luria-Nebraska Battery, is a standardized test battery used in the screening and evaluation of neuropsychologically impaired individuals.

Purpose

The LNNB was developed in an attempt to combine the qualitative techniques of some neuropsychological tests with the quantitative techniques of other tests. However, the scoring system that most clinicians use is primarily quantitative. The battery measures specific neuropsychological functioning in several areas including motor skills, language abilities, intellectual abilities, nonverbal auditory skills, and visual-spatial skills.

The battery is used by clinicians as a screening tool to determine whether a significant **brain** injury is present or to learn more about known brain injuries. It is also used to determine what the patient is or is not able to do with regard to neuropsychological functioning. For example, the LNNB may be used to determine which intellectual or cognitive tasks a patient may or may not be able to complete. The battery can also be used to arrive at underlying causes of a patient's behavior. More specifically, information regarding the location and nature of the brain injury or dysfunction causing a patient's problems is collected.

The LNNB is also used to help distinguish between brain damage and functional mental disorders such as **schizophrenia**. In addition, within the category of schizophrenia, the battery can be used to help distinguish between patients with normal neuropsychological functioning and those with clear deficits. Besides its specifically clinical use, the battery is sometimes used for legal purposes—the presence or severity of a brain injury may be measured as part of an evaluation used in the court system.

Description

The LNNB is based on the work of Alexander Romanovich Luria (1902–1977), a Soviet neuropsychologist and developmental **psychologist** who performed pioneering theoretical and clinical work with regard to brain function. Luria believed in a primarily qualitative approach to assessment and was opposed to standardization. He did not believe that neuropsychological functioning could be measured quantitatively. Thus, although his name is part of the test itself, his contribution to the LNNB is entirely theoretical. Also, the LNNB is based, in part, on Luria's Neuropsychological Investigation, a measure developed by Danish neuropsychologist Anne-Lise Christensen in 1975. This test included items asked by Luria in his clinical interviews, some of which are used in the LNNB.

The battery, written in 1981 by Charles J. Golden, Arnold D. Purisch, and Thomas A. Hammeke, is designed for people aged 15 years and older and takes between 90 and 150 minutes (1.5 to 2.5 hours) to complete. It has also been shown effective for children 13 and 14 years of age. The battery can be administered in one session or a series of shorter sessions.

Two equivalent forms are available. Form I consists of 269 items and Form II has 279 items. Though both yield similar information, Form II contains improved stimulus cards, which are easier to read than those contained on Form I. In addition, Form II contains an additional scale, the intermediate memory scale, which allows better assessment of memory. Form I is hand scored or computer scored, while Form II is only computer scored. Both contain the following 11 clinical scales:

- reading
- writing
- arithmetic
- visual functions
- memory
- expressive language
- receptive language (speech)
- motor functions
- rhythm
- tactile functions
- intellectual processes

Scores for five summary scales can also be calculated: pathognomonic, right hemisphere, left hemisphere, profile elevation, and impairment. A children's version of the battery, called the Luria-Nebraska Neuropsychological Battery for Children (LNNB-C), appropriate for children aged 8 to 12 years, is also available.

In addition, there are two optional scales, spelling and motor writing. Eight localization scales are also available. These are:

- left frontal
- left sensorimotor
- left parietal-occipital
- left temporal
- right frontal
- right sensorimotor
- right parietal-occipital
- right temporal

Also included are 28 factor scales, which deal with specific sensory and cognitive functions.

KEY TERMS

Frontal—Relating to the forehead (the anterior part of the roof of the brain case).

Neuropsychological—Relating to neuropsychology, or the branch of neurology that studies behavior disorders such as memory loss, speech impairment, epilepsy, and others.

Parietal-occipital—Relating to the parietal and occipital bones or lobes.

Schizophrenia—A mental disorder involving degraded thinking and emotions.

Sensorimotor—Relating to sensory and motor coordination of the nervous system.

Temporal—Relating to the temples.

Preparation

Preparation for the Luria-Nebraska Neuropsychological Battery is not needed nor necessary.

Risks

Risks are inherent in the administration of the LNNB. Because of the length of the test and complexity in interpretation, the examiner (administrator) must be competent and properly trained.

Precautions

Test administration can be difficult or frustrating because many patients undergoing testing have brain damage. The LNNB is portable, so the test can be taken to the patient if he or she is unable to travel to the administration site.

Results

The probability of brain damage is assessed by comparing an individual's score on each of the battery's 11 clinical scales to a critical level appropriate for that person's age and education level. For example, if a person has five to seven scores above the critical level, they most likely have some sign of neurological impairment. Eight or more scores above the critical level indicate a clear history of neurological disorder.

The battery has been criticized by researchers on the grounds that it overestimates the degree of neuropsychological impairment. In other cases, it has failed to detect neuropsychological problems. Also, the intellectual processes scale has not been found to correspond well

QUESTIONS TO ASK YOUR DOCTOR

- Do you know of a properly trained administrator for the LNNB?
- Should another test, or several tests, be administered in parallel with the LNNB?
- Where can I learn more about the test?
- Will health insurance cover the LNNB?

to other measures of intelligence, such as the Wechsler Adult Intelligence Scale (WAIS).

Other research, however, has found it to be a useful measure. It has been found as effective as the **Halstead-Reitan Battery** in distinguishing between individuals with brain damage and individuals without brain damage with psychiatric problems. Part of the inconsistencies in opinion regarding the LNNB may be due to the specific nature of the population being tested by the battery and the difficulties in administration and scoring that some clinicians experience.

American neurologist Arnold D. Purisch reports in a well-researched paper within the journal *NeuroRehabilitation* (2001) about both sides of this issue. Dr. Purisch states, "The major criticisms related to the belief that the qualitative and quantitative approaches could not be fused, that the scales were too heterogeneous to produce meaningful scores, that the battery suffered from significant limitations in sampling of neuropsychological skills, and that it had questionable sensitivity to brain dysfunction." Purisch goes on to state, "These criticisms generally reflected an unawareness of the interpretive process and theory underlying the LNNB, and have been largely negated by a large empirical literature that has evolved over many years."

Resources

BOOKS

Barnovitz, Mary Ann L.C., and Pria Joglekar. *Medical Psychiatry: The Quick Reference.* Philadelphia: Wolters Kluwer Health/Lippincott Williams & Wilkins, 2008.

Golden, Charles J. *Luria-Nebraska Neuropsychological Battery: Adult Form, Screening Test.* Los Angeles: Western Psychological Services, 1987.

Groth-Marnat, Gary. *Handbook of Psychological Assessment.* 4th edition. Hoboken, NJ: John Wiley, 2003.

Gutman, Sharon A., and Alison B. Schonfeld. *Screening Adult Neurologic Populations: A Step-by-Step Instruction Manual.* Bethasda, MD: AOTA Press, 2009.

Hebben, Nancy, and William Milberg. *Essentials of Neuropsychological Assessment.* Hoboken, NJ: John Wiley, 2009.

Hersen, Michel, ed. *Comprehensive Handbook of Psychological Assessment.* Hoboken, NJ: John Wiley, 2004.

Kellerman, Henry, and Anthony Burry. *Handbook of Psychodiagnostic Testing: Analysis of Personality in the Psychological Report.* New York: Springer, 2007.

Leeming, David A., Kathryn Madden, and Stanton Marlan, eds. *Encyclopedia of Psychology and Religion.* New York: Springer, 2010.

Lezak, Muriel D. *Neuropsychological Assessment.* New York: Oxford University Press, 2004.

Riccio, Cynthia A., Jeremy R. Sullivan and Morris J. Cohen. *Neuropsychological Assessment and Intervention for Children and Adolescent Disorders.* Hoboken, NJ: John Wiley, 2010.

WEBSITES

"Luria-Nebraska Neuropsychological Battery (LNNB)." Western Psychological Services. http://portal.wpspublish.com/portal/page?_pageid=53,69305&_dad=portal&_schema=PORTAL (accessed December 17, 2010).

"Misconceptions about the Luria-Nebraska Neuropsychological Battery." NeuroRehabilitation, IOS Press. http://iospress.metapress.com/content/6yyy8w0l4r44674h (accessed December 17, 2010).

ORGANIZATIONS

American Psychiatric Association, 1000 Wilson Blvd., Ste. 1825, Arlington, VA, 22209-3901, (703) 907-7300, apa@psych.org, http://www.psych.org.

American Psychological Association, 750 1st St. NE, Washington, DC, 20002-4242, (202) 336-5500; TDD/TTY: (202) 336-6123, (800) 374-2721, http://www.apa.org.

See also Intelligence tests; Kaufman Assessment Battery for Children; Kaufman Short Neuropsychological Assessment; Neuropsychological testing

Ali Fahmy, Ph.D.

Luvox *see* **Fluvoxamine**